MW01116209

ETHIOPIAN BIBLE IN ENGLISH COMPLETE 150 BOOKS

Amplified Bible, Large Print Edition, Annotated and Simplified. With Missing Apocrypha and The Lost Writings.

Eddie Helton Brooks

TABLE OF CONTENTS

Thank you for being here, reading this book.

I hope your journey of faith and fulfillment will be enriched by these scriptures. I tried to encapsulate in this great book, a lot, really a lot of information, being an independent author, I really struggled and I hope you will appreciate it.

Some books I have summarized, but I have encapsulated the essence of them. This is because I have a page limit of 778 and I necessarily had to do that, you will understand that to encapsulate 150 books in one, I had to make choices.

Despite this, most of the 150 books enclosed in this collection are complete and unabridged. I hope you will appreciate and understand.

However, this is the most complete collection of books you can find on the market.

I did it first for myself and then I chose to share it. - *Eddie H. Brooks*

GET THE BONUS VIDEO LESSONS BY SCANNING THIS QR CODE:

OLD TESTAMENT

1. Pentateuch

1. Genesis

CHAPTER 1

1 In the beginning, God created the heavens and the earth. 2 The earth was without form and void, and darkness was over the face of the deep. The Spirit of God was hovering over the waters. 3 Then God said, "Let there be light," and there was light. 4 God saw that the light was good, and He separated the light from the darkness. 5 God called the light "day," and the darkness He called "night." So evening and morning were the first day. 6 Then God said, "Let there be a firmament in the midst of the waters, and let it separate the waters from the waters." 7 God made the firmament and separated the waters that were below the firmament from the waters that were above the firmament. 8 God called the firmament "Heaven." Thus evening and morning were the second day. 9 God said again, "Let the waters under the heavens be gathered into one place, and let the dry land appear," and it was so. 10 God called the dry land "Earth," and the gathering together of the waters He called "Seas," and God saw that it was good. 11 Then God said, "Let the earth bring forth grass, the herb that yields seed, and the fruit tree that yields fruit according to its kind, whose seed is in itself on the earth," and it was so. 12 The earth brought forth grass, the herb that yields seed according to its kind, and the tree that yields fruit whose seed is in itself according to its kind. And God saw that it was good. 13 So evening and morning were the third day. 14 And God said, "Let there be lights in the firmament of the heavens to divide the day from the night, and let them be for signs, and seasons, and for days, and years. 15 Let them be for lights in the firmament of the heavens to give light on the earth," and it was so. 16 Then God made two great lights: the greater light to rule the day, and the lesser light to rule the night. He also made the stars. 17 God set them in the firmament of the heavens to give light on the earth, 18 to rule over the day and over the night, and to divide the light from the darkness. And God saw that it was good. 19 So evening and morning were the fourth day. 20 Then God said, "Let the waters abound with an abundance of living creatures, and let birds fly above the earth across the face of the firmament of the heavens." 21 So God created great sea creatures and every living thing that moves, with which the waters abounded, according to their kind, and every winged bird according to its kind. And God saw that it was good. 22 And God blessed them, saying, "Be fruitful and multiply, and fill the waters in the seas, and let birds multiply on the earth." 23 So evening and morning were the fifth day. 24 Then God said, "Let the earth bring forth the living creature according to its kind: cattle and creeping thing and beast of the earth, each according to its kind," and it was so. 25 And God made the beast of the earth according to its kind, cattle according to its kind, and everything that creeps on the earth according to its kind. And God saw that it was good. 26 Then God said, "Let Us make man in Our image, according to Our likeness. Let them have dominion over the fish of the sea, over the birds of the air, and over the cattle, over all the earth, and over every creeping thing that creeps on the earth." 27 So God created man in His own image; in the image of God He created him; male and female He created them. 28 Then God blessed them, and God said to them, "Be fruitful and multiply; fill the earth and subdue it; have dominion over the fish of the sea, over the birds of the air, and over every living thing that moves on the earth." 29 And God said, "See, I have given you every herb that yields seed which is on the face of all the earth, and every tree whose fruit yields seed; to you it shall be for food. 30 Also, to every beast of the earth, to every bird of the air, and to everything that creeps on the earth, in which there is life, I have given every green herb for food," and it was so. 31 Then God saw everything that He had made, and indeed it was very good. So evening and morning were the sixth day

CHAPTER 2

1 Thus the heavens and the earth, and all the host of them, were finished. 2 And on the seventh day God ended His work which He had done, and He rested on the seventh day from all His work which He had done. 3 Then God blessed the seventh day and sanctified it because in it He rested from all His work which God had created and made. 4 This is the history of the heavens and the earth when they were created, in the day that the Lord God made the earth and the heavens, 5 before any plant of the field was in the earth and before any herb of the field had grown. For the Lord God had not caused it to rain on the earth, and there was no man to till the ground. 6 But a mist went up from the earth and watered the whole face of the ground. 7 And the Lord God formed man of the dust of the ground and breathed into his nostrils the breath of life, and man became a living being. 8 The Lord God planted a garden eastward in Eden, and there He put the man whom He had formed. 9 And out of the ground the Lord God made every tree grow that is pleasant to the sight and good for food. The tree of life was also in the midst of the garden, and the tree of the knowledge of good and evil. 10 Now a river went out of Eden to water the garden, and from there it parted and became four riverheads. 11 The name of the first is Pishon; it is the one which skirts the whole land of Havilah, where there is gold. 12 And the gold of that land is good. Bdellium and the onyx stone are there. 13 The name of the second river is Gihon; it is the one which goes around the whole land of Cush. 14 The name of the third river is Hiddekel; it is the one which goes toward the east of Assyria. The fourth river is the Euphrates. 15 Then the Lord God took the man and put him in the Garden of Eden to tend and keep it. 16 And the Lord God commanded the man, saying, "Of every tree of the garden you may freely eat, 17 but of the tree of the knowledge of good and evil you shall not eat, for in the day that you eat of it you shall surely die." 18 And the Lord God said, "It is not good that man should be alone; I will make him a helper comparable to him." 19 Out of the ground the Lord God formed every beast of the field and every bird of the air, and brought them to Adam to see what he would call them. And whatever Adam called each living creature, that was its name. 20 So Adam gave names to all cattle, to the birds of the air, and to every beast of the field. But for Adam there was not found a helper comparable to him. 21 And the Lord God caused a deep sleep to fall on Adam, and he slept. And He took one of his ribs and closed up the flesh in its place. 22 Then the rib which the Lord God had taken from man He made into a woman, and He brought her to the man. 23 And Adam said, "This is now bone of my bones and flesh of my flesh; she shall be called Woman because she was taken out of Man." 24 Therefore a man shall leave his father and mother and be joined to his wife, and they shall become one flesh. 25 And they were both naked, the man and his wife, and were not ashamed

CHAPTER 3

1 Now the serpent was more cunning than any beast of the field which the Lord God had made. And he said to the woman, "Has God indeed said, 'You shall not eat of every tree of the garden'?" 2 And the woman said to the serpent, "We may eat the fruit of

the trees of the garden, 3 but of the fruit of the tree which is in the midst of the garden, God has said, 'You shall not eat it, nor shall you touch it, lest you die.'" 4 Then the serpent said to the woman, "You will not surely die. 5 For God knows that in the day you eat of it your eyes will be opened, and you will be like God, knowing good and evil." 6 So when the woman saw that the tree was good for food, that it was pleasant to the eyes, and a tree desirable to make one wise, she took of its fruit and ate. She also gave to her husband with her, and he ate. 7 Then the eyes of both of them were opened, and they knew that they were naked, and they sewed fig leaves together and made themselves coverings. 8 And they heard the sound of the Lord God walking in the garden in the cool of the day, and Adam and his wife hid themselves from the presence of the Lord God among the trees of the garden. 9 Then the Lord God called to Adam and said to him, "Where are you?" 10 So he said, "I heard Your voice in the garden, and I was afraid because I was naked; and I hid myself." 11 And He said, "Who told you that you were naked? Have you eaten from the tree of which I commanded you that you should not eat?" 12 Then the man said, "The woman whom You gave to be with me, she gave me of the tree, and I ate." 13 And the Lord God said to the woman, "What is this you have done?" The woman said, "The serpent deceived me, and I ate." 14 So the Lord God said to the serpent, "Because you have done this, you are cursed more than all cattle, and more than every beast of the field. On your belly you shall go, and you shall eat dust all the days of your life. 15 And I will put enmity between you and the woman, and between your seed and her Seed. He shall bruise your head, and you shall bruise His heel." 16 To the woman He said, "I will greatly multiply your sorrow and your conception; in pain you shall bring forth children; your desire shall be for your husband, and he shall rule over you." 17 Then to Adam He said, "Because you have heeded the voice of your wife, and have eaten from the tree of which I commanded you, saying, 'You shall not eat of it,' cursed is the ground for your sake; in toil you shall eat of it all the days of your life. 18 Both thorns and thistles it shall bring forth for you, and you shall eat the herb of the field. 19 In the sweat of your face you shall eat bread till you return to the ground, for out of it you were taken; for dust you are, and to dust you shall return." 20 And Adam called his wife's name Eve because she was the mother of all living. 21 Also for Adam and his wife the Lord God made tunics of skin and clothed them. 22 Then the Lord God said, "Behold, the man has become like one of Us, to know good and evil. And now, lest he put out his hand and take also of the tree of life, and eat, and live forever," 23 therefore the Lord God sent him out of the garden of Eden to till the ground from which he was taken. 24 So He drove out the man, and He placed cherubim at the east of the garden of Eden, and a flaming sword which turned every way, to guard the way to the tree of life

CHAPTER 4

Then the man met Heuah, his wife, who conceived and gave birth to Kain, and said, "I have obtained a man from the Lord." Then she gave birth to her brother Habel; Habel was a keeper of sheep and Kain was a cultivator of the land. Afterward Kain brought an oblation of the fruits of the land to the LORD. Habel also brought the first fruits of his sheep and their fat, and the LORD had respect for Habel and his offering, but he had no regard for Kain and his offering; therefore Kain was exceedingly wroth, and his countenance fell. Then the LORD said to Kain, "Why are you vexed and why is your face downcast? If you do well, will you not be accepted? And if you do not do well, sin is lurking; even his desire will be subdued to you, and you will rule over him." Then Kain spoke to Habel his brother. And when they were in the camp, Kain rose up against Habel his brother and killed him. Then the LORD said to Kain, "Where is Habel your brother?" Who answered, "I cannot say. Am I the keeper of my brothers? He said, "What have you done? The voice of your brothers' blood cries out to me from the earth. Now therefore you are cursed from the earth, which has opened its mouth to receive the blood of your brothers from your hand. When you unseat the earth, it will no longer give you its strength; you will be a wanderer and a fugitive in the earth." Then Kain said to the LORD, "My chastisement is greater than I can bear. Behold, today you have driven me out of the land, and from your face I will be hidden; I will be a wanderer and a fugitive in the land, and whoever finds me will kill me." Then the LORD said to him, "No doubt whoever kills Kain will be punished for his folly." And the LORD put a sign on Kain, lest anyone, finding him, should kill him. Then Kain went out from the presence of the LORD and went to dwell in the land of Nod, toward the eastern side of Eden. Kain also met his wife, who conceived and gave birth to Henoch; and he built a city and called the city by the name of his son, Henoch. From Henoch was born Irad, Irad begat Mehuiael, Mehuiael begat Methuselah, and Methuselah begat Lamech. Lamech had two wives: one was named Adah and the other Zillah. Adah gave birth to Jabal, who was the father of those who dwell in tents and of those who have cattle. His brothers were called Iubal, who was the father of all those who play the zither and organ. Zillah also bore Tubal-kain, who craftily did all the crafts of the reed and yron; and Tubal-kain's sister was Naamah. Lamech said to his wives Adah and Zillah, "Hear my speech, ye wives of Lamech, hear my speech, for I would like to kill a man in my wound and a young man in my wound. If Kain shall be judged seven fold, Lamech shall truly be seventy times seven fold. And Adam knew his wife again, and she bare a son, and called his name Sheth: for God, said she, hath assigned me another offspring for Habel, because Kain slew him. To the same Sheth was also born a son, whom she named Enosh. Then the men began to call on the name of the Lord

CHAPTER 5

This is the book of Adam's generations. On the day God created Adam, he made him in the likeness of God, He created them male and female, blessed them, and called them Adam on the day they were created. Now Adam lived a hundred and thirty years and begat a son in his own image and likeness and called him Sheth. The days of Adam, after he begat Sheth, were eight hundred years, and he begat sons and daughters. So all the days that Adam lived were nine hundred and thirty years; then he died. Sheth lived a hundred and five years and begat Enosh. After he begat Enosh, Sheth lived eight hundred and seventy years and begat sons and daughters. Thus all the days of Sheth were nine hundred and two hundred years; then he died. Enosh also lived ninety years and begat Kenan. After he begat Kenan, Enosh lived eight hundred and fifty years and begat sons and daughters. So all the days of Enosh were nine hundred and fifty years; then he died. Kenan lived seventy years and begat Mahalaleel. After he begat Mahalaleel, Kenan lived eight hundred and four years and begat sons and daughters. So all the days of Kenan were nine hundred and ten years; then he died. Mahalaleel also lived sixty-five years and begat sons. Mahalaleel also, after he begat Iered, lived eight hundred and thirty years and begat sons and daughters. So all the days of Mahalaleel were eight hundred ninety-nine and five years; then he died. And

Iered lived a hundred sixty-two years and begat Henoch. Then Iered lived, after he begat Henoch, eight hundred years and begat sons and daughters. So all the days of Iered were nine hundred sixty-two years; then he died. Henoch also lived sixty-five years and begat Methuselah. After he begat Methuselah, Henoch walked with God three hundred years and begat sons and daughters. So all the days of Henoch were three hundred sixty-five years. Then Henoch walked with God and was no longer seen, for God took him away. Methuselah also lived one hundred eighty-two years and begat Lamech. After he begat Lamech, Methushelah lived an hundred and eighty-two years and begat sons and daughters. So all the days of Methuselah were nine hundred sixty and nine years; then he died. Lamech lived an hundred and two years and begat a son, And he set the name of Noah upon him, saying, "This shall comfort our works, and the sorrow of our hands, concerning the land which the LORD hath cursed." And Lamech lived, after he begat Noah, five hundred and ninety-nine years, and begat sons and daughters. So all the days of Lamech were seventy-five years and seventy years; then he died. Noah was five hundred years old. Noah begat Shem, Ham, and Japheth

CHAPTER 6

So when men began to multiply on the earth and there were daughters born to them, then the sons of God said to the daughters of men that they were beautiful, and they took them as wives of all that pleased them. Therefore the Lord said, "My Spirit will not always withdraw with man, for he is but flesh, and his days shall last an hundred and twenty years." In those days there were giants in the earth; yea, and after the sons of God came to the daughters of men and they bore sons, these were mighty men, who formerly were men of rank. When the LORD saw that the wickedness of man was great in the earth, and that all the imaginations of the thoughts of his heart were always and only euphoric, then the LORD repented that he had created man on the earth and that he was wicked in his heart. Therefore the LORD said, "I will destroy from the earth the man whom I have created, from man to beasts and reptiles and wild animals, because I repent that I created them." But Noah found grace in the eyes of the Lord. These are the generations of Noah. Noah was a righteous and upright man in his time; and Noah walked with God. Noah begat three sons, Shem, Ham and Japheth. The earth also was corrupt before God, for the earth was full of cruelty. Then God looked upon the earth, and behold, it was corrupt, for every flesh had corrupted its way upon the earth. God said to Noah, "The end of all flesh has come before me, for the earth is full of cruelty because of them; and behold, I will destroy them with the earth. Make for yourself an ark of pine trees; you shall make booths in the ark and implant it inside and out with pitch. You shall build it thus: The length of the ark shall be three hundred cubits, the breadth fifty cubits, and the height thirty cubits. And thou shalt make a window in the ark, and in one cubit shalt thou finish it from the front, and the door of the ark shalt thou set in its side; thou shalt make it with the low, the second, and the third beam. And I, behold, will bring a flood of water upon the earth to destroy all flesh that hath a breath of life under the earth; all that is on the earth shall perish. But with you I will establish my commander, and you shall go into the Ark, you and your children and your wife and your children with you. And of every living thing, of every flesh of every kind, thou shalt bring into the Ark, to keep them with thee; they shall be male and female. Of the fowls, according to their kind, and of the cattle, according to their kind,

of all the reptiles of the earth, according to their kind, two of every kind shall come to you, that you may keep them with you. And thou shalt take with thee all the food that is eaten, and gather it for thee, that it may be food for thee and for them. Noah therefore did all that God commanded him, and so he did

CHAPTER 7

The LORD said to Noah, "Enter thou and all thy house into the ark, for I have seen that thou art righteous before me at this time. Of every light beast thou shalt take to thee, in pairs, the male and his female; but of the vnclean beasts thou shalt take, in pairs, the male and his female. Of the wild beasts also shalt thou take in pairs the male and the female, that thou mayest preserve an offspring in all the earth. For in ten days I will make it rain on the earth four days and four nights, and I will destroy from the earth all that I have made." Noah therefore did according to all that the LORD had commanded him. Noah was six hundred years old when the flood was on the earth. Then Noah went in with his sons, his wife and his wives with him into the Ark, because of the waters of the flood. Of the clean beasts, and of the vnclean beasts, and of the fish, and of all that creepeth upon the earth, two and two came to Noah in the ark, male and female, as God had commanded Noah. Thus, after ten days, the waters of the flood were upon the earth. In the six hundredth year of Noah's life, in the second month, on the seventeenth day of the month, on that same day all the fountains of the great deep were opened, and the windows of Heauen were opened, and rain was on the earth for four days and four nights. On that same day Noah entered with Shem, Ham and Japheth, Noah's sons, Noah's wife and the three wives of his sons with them, into the Ark. They and every animal according to its kind, and every cattle according to its kind, and every thing that creeps and moves upon the earth according to its kind, and every fowl according to its kind, and every bird of every kind. For they came in from Noah into Arke, two and two, of every flesh in which is the breath of life. Male and female of every flesh went in, as God had commanded him, and the LORD shut him in. The flood lasted fourteen days on the earth, and the waters increased and stripped the ark that was lifted up on the earth. And the waters grew strong and increased exceedingly upon the earth, and the ark was thrust upon the waters. The waters increased so much over the earth that all the high mountains that were below the whole of the ark were pulled down. When the mountains were brought down, the waters spread fifty cubits wide. Then perished all the flesh that moved upon the earth, both the game, and the cattle, and every thing that crawls and moves upon the earth, and every man. All things in whose nostrils the spirit of life breathed, whatever was on the earth, perished. So he destroyed every thing that was on the earth, from man to animals, reptiles and wild beasts; they were destroyed from the earth. Only Noah and those who were with him in the ark remained. And the waters stood still on the earth for a hundred and fifty days

CHAPTER 8

God remembered Noah and every animal and all the cattle that were with him in the ark; therefore God caused a wind to pass over the earth, and the waters ceased. Also the springs of the deep and the windows of Heauen were stopped, and the rain of Heauen was stayed, And the waters returned from behind the earth, going and returning; and after the end of the hundred and fiftieth day the waters subsided. And in the seventh month, on the seventeenth day of the month, the Ark rested on the mountains of Ararat. And the waters continued to subside until the tenth month; in the tenth month and on the first day of the month the tops of the mountains were seen. After forty days, Noah opened the window of the ark he had built, and let out a raven that came and went, until the waters dried up on the earth. Then he sent a dove to him to see if the waters had diminished from the earth. But the dove found no rest for the sole of her foot; therefore she returned to him in the Ark (for the waters were over all the earth), and he stretched out his hand, received it, and took it with him into the Ark. He stayed for ten more days, and again he brought the dove out of the Ark. The dove came to him in the evening, and in her mouth was an olive leaf she had torn; so Noah understood that the waters had disappeared from the earth. In spite of this, he set out for seven more days and sent the dove away, and it never returned to him. On the first day of the first month, after six hundred years, the waters were dried up from the earth; Noah turned away from the bow and looked, and behold, the upper part of the ground was dried up. In the second month, on the second and twentieth day of the month, the earth was dried up. Then God spoke to Noah, saying, "Come out of the Ark, you and your wife and your children and your sons with you. Take with you all the animals that are with you, of all species of beasts and animals, and all the creatures that crawl and move on the earth, that they may reproduce abundantly on the earth and bear fruit and multiply on the earth." So Noah went out, his sons and his wife and wives with him. All the animals, all the reptiles and all the birds, all that move on the earth according to their kind, went out of the ark. Then Noah built an altar to the LORD and took every clean animal and every clean animal and offered burnt offerings on the altar. And the LORD smelled rest and said in his heart, "From now on I will no longer curse the earth because of men, for the imagination of man's heart is evil from his youth; and I will no longer smite all things that live, as I have done. Henceforth the time of sowing and reaping, cold and heat, spring and winter, day and night shall not cease, so long as the earth remains."

CHAPTER 9

God blessed Noah and his sons and said to them, "Bear fruit and multiply and fill the earth. Moreover you shall be afraid of yourselves, and you shall be feared by all the animals of the earth and by all the beasts of the sea, by everything that moves on the earth and by all the fish of the sea; they shall be delivered into your hands. Every mooing and living thing shall be food for you; like green grass, I have given you everything. But the flesh with its life, I say, and its blood you shall not eat. For surely I will demand your blood, where your pains are; I will demand it by the hand of every beast, and by the hand of man, and by the hand of a brother of man, I will demand the life of man. He that so sheddeth man's blood, by man shall his blood be shed: for in the image of God made man. But bear fruit and multiply; grow abundantly in the earth and increase. God also spoke to Noah and his sons with him, saying, "Behold, I establish my covenant with you and with your descendants after you, And with all the living creatures that are with you, with the animals, with the cattle, and with all the beasts of the earth that are with you, from those that come out of the ark to all the animals of the earth. And I will establish my covenant with you, so that henceforth all flesh shall not be uprooted by the waters of the flood, nor shall there be a flood to destroy the earth." Then God said, "This is the sign of the covenant that I establish between me and you and between all living things that are with you for all generations. I have set my bow in the cloud, and it shall be the sign of the covenant between me and the earth. When I cover the earth with a cloud and the arm will be seen in the cloud, then I will remember my covenant, which is between me and you and between every living thing of all flesh, and there will be no more flood waters to destroy all flesh. Therefore the bow shall remain in the clouds, that I may see it and remember the everlasting covenant between God and every living thing of all flesh that is on the earth." Again God said to Noah, "This is the sign of the covenant I have established between me and all flesh that is on the earth. Now the sons of Noah who came out of the Ark were Shem, Ham, and Japheth. And Ham is the father of Canaan. These are the three sons of Noah, and from them the whole earth was begotten. Noah also began to be a husbandman and planted a vineyard. Then he became drunk with wine, and got drunk, and got drunk in the midst of his tent. When Ham the father of Canaan saw his father's nakedness, he told his two brothers about it. Then Shem and Japheth took a robe, put it on their shoulders, went backward, and noticed their father's nakedness with his face turned backward; so they did not notice their father's nakedness. Then Noah awoke from his wine and knew what his younger son had done to him, And he said, "Cursed be Canaan; he shall be a servant of servants to his brothers." He said again, "Blessed be the LORD God of Shem, and Canaan be his servant." God persuaded Japheth to dwell in the tents of Shem and to make Canaan his servant. Noah lived after the flood for three hundred and fifty years. So all the days of Noah were nine hundred and fifty years; then he died

CHAPTER 10

These are the generations of Noah's sons, Shem, Ham and Japheth, to whom sons were begotten after the flood. The sons of Japheth were Gomer and Magog, Madai, Iauan, Tubal, Meshech and Tiras. The sons of Gomer were Ashkenaz, Riphath and Togarma. The sons of Iauan, Elisha and Tarshish, Kittim and Dodanim. Of these the people were divided in their lands, each according to his language and according to their families in their nations. Moreover, the sons of Ham were Cush, Mizraim, Put and Canaan. The sons of Cush were Seba, Hauilah, Sabtah, Raamah and Sabtecha; the sons of Raamah were also Sheba and Dedan. Cush begat Nimrod, who began to be powerful in the land. He was a mighty hunter before the LORD; therefore it is said, "Like Nimrod, the mighty hunter before the LORD." The beginning of his kingdom was Babel, Erech, Accad and Calneh, in the land of Shinar. Out of that land came Assur, who built Nineveh, the city of Rehoboth and Calah: Resen also, between Nineveh and Calah, is a great city. Mizraim begat Ludim, Anamim, Lehabim and Nephtahim. Also Pathrusim, Casluhim (from whom the Philistines arose) and Caphtorim. Canaan also begat Zidon, his firstborn, and Heth, Jebusi, Emori, and Girgashi, Hiui, Arki and Sini, Aruadi, Zemari and Hamathi; thereafter the families of the Canaanites scattered from one side to the other. The border of the Canaanites extended from Zidon, from Gerar to Azza, and from Sodom, Gomorah, Admah and Zeboi to Lasha. These are the sons of Ham according to their families, according to their languages in their countries and nations. Shem also, the father of all the sons of Eber and the elder brother of Japheth, had sons. The sons of Shem were Elam, Assur, Arpachshad, Lud and Aram. The sons of Aram were Uz and Hul, Gether and Mash. Arpachshad begat Shelah and Shelah begat Eber. Two sons were also born to Eber: the first was named Peleg, for in his day the earth was rent asunder, and his brothers were named Joktan. Joktan begat Almodad, Sheleph, Hazarmaueth and Jerah, Hadoram, Uzal and Diklah, Obal, Abimael and

Sheba, Ophir, Havilah and Jobab: all these were sons of Joktan. Their abode was from Mesha, as you go to Sephar, a mountain of the east. These are the sons of Shem, according to their families, according to their languages, in their countries and nations. These are the families of the sons of Noah, according to their generations among their peoples; and by these were the nations divided upon the earth after the flood

CHAPTER 11

Then the whole land had one language and one speech. As they went eastward, they found a plain in the land of Shinar, and there they stopped. They said to one another, "Come, let us make brick and bury it in the fire." So they had bricks for stone, and the slime was used as a mixture. They also said, "Go, build yourselves a city and a tower, the top of which may reach as far as the plateau, that we may give ourselves a name, lest we be scattered over all the earth." But the LORD came down to see the city and the tower that the sons of men had built. And the LORD said, "Behold, the people are one, and they all have one tongue, and this they begin to do, nor can they any longer be prevented from doing what they have imagined to do." Come on, let us go down and confuse their tongues, so that each one does not perceive the other's tongue. So the LORD scattered them from there over all the earth, and they went away to build the city. Therefore it was called Babel, because the LORD confused the language of all the earth there; from there the LORD scattered them over all the earth. These are the generations of Shem: Shem was a hundred years old and begat Arpachshad two years after the flood. After he begat Arpachshad, Shem lived five hundred years and begat sons and daughters. Arpachshad also lived five and thirty years and begat Shelah. After he begat Shelah, Arpachshad lived four hundred and three years and begat sons and daughters. Shelah lived thirty years and begat Eber. After he begat Eber, Shelah lived four hundred and three years and begat sons and daughters. Likewise Eber lived four and thirty years and begat Peleg. So Eber, after he begat Peleg, lived four hundred and thirty years and begat sons and daughters. Peleg lived thirty years and begat Reu. After he begat Reu, Peleg lived two hundred and nine years and begat sons and daughters. Reu also lived two and thirty years and begat Serug. After he begat Serug, Reu lived two hundred years and begat sons and daughters. Moreover Serug lived thirty years and begat Nahor. After he begat Nahor, Serug lived two hundred years and begat sons and daughters. Nahor lived nine and twenty years and begat Terah. After he begat Terah, Nahor lived a hundred and ninety years and begat sons and daughters. Terah lived seventy years and begat Abram, Nahor and Haran. These are the generations of Terah: Terah begat Abram, Nahor and Haran, and Haran begat Lot. Haran died before Terah his father, in the land of his origin, in the Ur of the Chaldeans. Abram and Nahor took a wife. Abram's wife's name was Sarai, and Nahor's wife's name was Milcah, daughter of Haran, father of Milcah and father of Iscah. But Sarai was barren and had no children. Then Terah took Abram, his son, Lot, son of Haran, his son, and Sarai, his daughter to Abram's wife, and they set out together from Ur of the Chaldeans to go to the land of Canaan. The days of Terah were two hundred and five years, and Terah died in Haran

CHAPTER 12

For the LORD had said to Abram, "Get thee out of thy land, and out of thy seed, and out of the house of thy fathers, unto the land that I will appoint thee. I will make of you a great nation, I will bless you, I will make your name great, and you shall be a blessing. I will also bless those who bless you and curse those who curse you, and in you all the families of the earth will be blessed." So Abram departed, as the LORD had told him, and Lot went with him. (Abram was seventy-five years old when he departed from Haran). Then Abram took Sarai, his wife, and Lot, his brother, and all their possessions that they possessed and the souls that they had procured in Haran, and they departed to go into the land of Canaan; and into the land of Canaan they came. And Abram went through the land as far as the place of Shechem and as far as the plain of Moreh (and Canaan was then in the land). The Lord appeared to Abram and said, "To your descendants I will give this land." And there he built an altar to the Lord who had appeared to him. Then, moving away from Bethel to a place to the east, he pitched his tent, having Bethel on the west and Haai on the east, and there he built an altar to the Lord and called upon the Name of the Lord. Then Abram went to the south. Then there was a famine in the land; therefore Abram went down to Egypt to sojourn there, because there was a great famine in the land. And when he was about to enter Egypt, he said to Sarai his wife, "Now I know that you are a beautiful woman to look upon: Therefore it shall come to pass, when the Egyptians see you, that they will say, 'She is his wife'; so they will kill me, but they will keep you hidden. Say, I pray thee, that thou art my sister, that I may be well because of thee, and my life may be preserved from thee." When Abram had come to Egypt, the Egyptians observed the woman, for she was very beautiful. Pharaoh's princes saw her and recommended her to Pharaoh; so the woman was received into Pharaoh's house: Who, for her sake, took good care of Abram, who had sheep, and bees, and asses, and male servants, and female servants, and donkeys, and camels. But the LORD struck Pharaoh and his house with great plagues because of Sarai, Abram's wife. Then Pharaoh called Abram and said to him, "Why have you done this to me? Why did you not tell me that she was your wife? Why did you say, 'She is my sister, that I may take her as my wife'? Now therefore look at your wife, take her, and go your way." And Pharaoh gave the men an order about him, and they brought him out with his wife and all that he had

CHAPTER 13

Then Abram departed from Egypt, he, his wife and all that he had, and Lot with him to the south. Abram was very rich in cattle, silk and gold. He continued his journey from the South to Bethel, to the place where his tent had been in the beginning, between Bethel and Haai, to the place of the altar which he had built there at the beginning; and there Abram called upon the Name of the Lord. Lot, who had gone with Abram, also had sheep and cattle and tents, so that the land could not bear them to dwell together; for their substance was great, so that they could not dwell together. There was also an argument between the sons of Abram and the sons of Lot. (And the Canaanites and the Perizzites were then dwelling in the land). Then Abram said to Lot, "Let there be no dispute, I pray you, between you and me, nor between my masters and your masters, for we are brothers." Is not the whole land before you? I pray thee, depart from me; if thou takest thy left hand, I will go right; or if thou takest thy right hand, I will take thy left." And when Lot lifted up his eyes, he saw that all the plain of Jordan was watered everywhere: (for before the LORD destroyed Sodom and Gomorrah, it was like a garden of the LORD, like the land of Egypt, as you go toward Zoar). Then Lot chose for himself all the plain of Jordan, and took his journey from the east; and they separated one from the other. Abram dwelt in the land of Canaan, while Lot dwelt in the cities of the plain and pitched his tent as far as Sodom. The men of Sodom were wicked and very sinful against the LORD. Then the LORD said to Abram, "Lift up your eyes now and look from where you are to the north, to the south, to the east and to the west: For all the land that you see I will give to you and to your descendants forever, And I will make thy descendants like the dust of the earth; so that if a man can count the dust of the earth, thy descendants shall be insensible. Arise, walk the length and breadth of the land, for I will give it to you." Then Abram took down his tent and came and dwelt in the plain of Mamre, which is in Hebron, and built there an altar to the LORD

CHAPTER 14

In the days of Amraphel, king of Shinar, Arioch, king of Ellasar, Chedorlaomer, king of Elam, and Tidal, king of the nations: These men made war against Bera, king of Sodom, against Birsha, king of Gomorrah, against Shinab, king of Admah, against Shemeber, king of Zeboiim, and against the king of Bela, who is Zoar. All these came together in the valley of Siddim, which is the salt sea. For two years they were subject to Chedorlaomer, but in the thirteenth year they rebelled. In the fourteenth year came Chedorlaomer and the kings who were with him and defeated the Rephaim at Ashteroth Karnaim, the Zuzim at Ham, and the Emim at Shaveh Kiriathaim, and the Horims on their mount Seir, as far as the plain of Paran, which is by the wilderness. Then they returned and came to En-Mishpat, which is Kadesh, and defeated all the territory of the Amalekites and also the Amorites who dwelt in Hazezon-Tamar. Then came out the king of Sodom, the king of Gomorrah, the king of Admah, the king of Zeboiim, and the king of Bela, which is Zoar, and fought with them in the valley of Siddim: that is, with Chedorlaomer, king of Elam, with Tidal, king of the nations, with Amraphel, king of Shinar, and with Arioch, king of Ellasar: four kings against five. The valley of Siddim was full of slime pits, and the kings of Sodom and Gomorrah fled there and fell, while you remnant fled to the mountain. Then they took all the substance of Sodom and Gomorrah and all their possessions and went their way. They also took Lot the son of Abram and his substance (for he dwelt in Sodom) and departed. Then came one who had escaped and told Abram about the Hebrew who lived in the plain of Mamre, an Amorite, brother of Eshcol and brother of Aner, who were confederates with Abram. When Abram heard that his brother had been kidnapped, he brought out from his house three hundred and eighty that had been brought forth and brought, and pursued them as far as Dan. Then he and his servants confronted them by night, struck them, and pursued them as far as Hobah, which is on the left side of Damascus, he recovered all the substance and brought back his brother Lot and his possessions, women and people. After he had returned from the slaughter of Chedorlaomer and the kings who were with him, the king of Sodom came to meet him in the valley of Shaveh, which is the valley of the kings. Melchizedek, king of Shalem, brought bread and wine; he was a priest of the most high God. Therefore he blessed him, saying, "Blessed are you, Abram, from God most high, possessor of earth and heaven, And blessed be the most high God, who has delivered into your hand your enemies." And Abram gave him his name. Then the king of Sodom said to Abram, "Give me the people and take the goods for yourself." Abram said to the king of Sodom, "I have lifted up my hand to the LORD, the most high God, possessor of heaven and earth, that I will not take of all that is yours even a braid or a walking stick, lest you should say, 'I have made Abram rich. take only what the young men have eaten and the parts of the men who came with me, Aner, Eshcol and Mamre; let them take their parts

CHAPTER 15

After these things, the word of the Lord came to Abram in a vision, saying, "Fear not, Abram, I am your support and your greatest reward." Abram said, "O Lord God, what will you give me, seeing that I have children and the steward of my house is this Eliezer of Damascus? Abram answered, "Behold, to me you have not given an offspring; therefore, behold, a servant of my house shall be my heir." Then the word of the LORD came to him, saying, "This man shall not be your heir, but one who shall come forth from your bowels shall be your heir." Then he brought him out and said to him, "Look up now, and tell of the stars, if you are able to count them"; and he said to him, "Thus shall your descendants be." Abram listened to the LORD, and he considered it a righteous thing. Then he said to him, "I am the LORD, who brought you out of Ur of the Chaldeans to give you this land as an inheritance." And he said, "O Lord God, how shall I know that I shall inherit it?" Then he said to him, "Take me a heifer three years old, a kid three years old, a ram three years old, a tortoise and a pigeon." So he took all these things and put them in a basket and set them against each other, but he did not care for the birds. Then the carcasses fell into the water, and Abram carried them away. When the sun went down, Abram fell heavily asleep; and, behold, a fearful darkness fell upon him. Then he said to Abram, "Know for certain that your descendants will be strangers in a land that is not theirs, for four hundred years, and they will serve them; and they will weave them long." Nevertheless, the nation which they shall serve, I will judge; and afterward they shall come forth from it with great substance. But you shall return to your fathers in peace, and you shall be buried in good age. In the fourth generation they will come again, for the wickedness of the Amorites is not yet complete. And when the sun went down, there was a darkness; and behold, a smoking furnace and a firebrand, which stood between those pieces. On that same day the LORD made a covenant with Abram, saying, "To your descendants I have given this land, from the river of Egypt to the great river, the Euphrates." The Kenites, the Kenizites, and the Kadmonites, the Hittites, the Perizzites, and the Rephaim, the Amorites, the Canaanites, the Girgashites, and the Jebusites

CHAPTER 16

Now Sarai, Abram's wife, bore him no son, and she had an Egyptian maid, named Hagar. Sarai said to Abram, "Behold, the Lord has prevented me from having children. Please go to my maid; it may be that I will receive a son from her." And Abram obeyed Sarai's advice. Then Sarai, Abram's wife, took Hagar, her maid, the Egyptian, after Abram had dwelt ten years in the land of Canaan, and gave her to Abram, her husband, to be his wife. And he went in to Hagar, and she conceived. And when she saw that she had conceived, her mistress was despised in her eyes. Then Sarai said to Abram, "You wrong me. I have put my maid into your womb, and she sees that she has conceived, and I am despised in her eyes; the Lord judge between me and you." Then Abram said to Sarai, "Behold, your maid is in your hands; do with her what pleases you." Then Sarai treated her harshly; therefore she fled from her. But the angel of the LORD found her by a spring of water in the wilderness, by the spring on the road to Shur, And he said to her, "Hagar Sarai's maid, whence comest thou, and whither wilt thou go?" And she answered, "I flee from my lady Sarai. Then the angel of the LORD said to her, "Return to your lady and humble yourself under her hands." Then the angel of the LORD said to her, "I will so increase your descendants that they will not be numerable." The angel of the LORD also said to her, "See, you are with child, you will bear a son and you will name him Ishmael, because the LORD has heard your tribulation. He shall be a wild man; his hand shall be against every man, and every man's hand against him, and he shall dwell in the presence of all his brethren." Then she called upon the name of the Lord who had spoken to her, "You, God, look upon me," for she said, "Have I not also looked upon him who sees me? Therefore the well was called Beer-lahai-roi. behold, it is between Kadesh and Bered. And Hagar bore Abram a son, and Abram called the son whom Hagar bore by the name of Ishmael. Abram was eighty-six years old when Hagar bore him Ishmael

CHAPTER 17

When Abram was ninety-nine years old, the LORD appeared to Abram and said to him, "I am God all-sufficient; walk before me and be upright, and I will establish my covenant between me and you, and I will multiply you exceedingly." Then Abram fell on his face, and God spoke to him, saying, "Behold, I make my covenant with you, and you shall be a father of many nations, you shall no longer be called Abram, but your name shall be Abraham, for I have made you a father of many nations. I will also make thee very fruitful, and I will make of thee nations; yea, kings shall come forth from thee. Moreover I will establish my covenant between me and thee and thy seed after thee in their generations, for an everlasting covenant, to be God to thee and to thy seed after thee. And I will give you and your descendants after you the land in which you are a stranger, that is, all the land of Canaan, as an eternal possession, and I will be their God." Then God said to Abraham, "You also, you and your descendants after you, will keep my covenant in their generations. This is my covenant that you shall keep between me and you and your descendants after you: that every male child among you shall be circumcised: that is, you shall circumcise the foreskin of your flesh, and it shall be a sign of the covenant between me and you. Every child of eight days old among you shall be circumcised in your generations, whether he is born in your house, or whether he is bought with money from a stranger, who is not of your seed. He who is born in your house and he who is bought with your money must be circumcised; so my covenant shall be in your flesh for everlasting covenant. But the uncircumcised male child, in whose flesh the foreskin is not circumcised, then that person shall be cut off from his people, because he has broken my covenant." Then God said to Abraham, "You shall not call Sarai your wife, but Sarah shall be her name. I will bless her and will also give you a son from her, yes, I will bless her and she will be a mother of nations: Out of her also shall come forth kings of nations." Then Abraham fell on his face, and laughed, and said in his heart, "Shall a son be born to him that is a hundred years old? And shall Sarah who is ninety years old give birth?" Abraham said to God, "Oh, if Ishmael could live in your sight." Then God said, "Sarah thy wife shall bear thee a son indeed, and thou shalt call his name Isaac; and I will establish with him my covenant for an everlasting covenant, and with his seed after him." As for Ishmael, I have heard thee; behold, I have blessed him, and will make him fruitful, and multiply him exceedingly; and he shall beget twelve princes, and I will make of him a great nation. But I will establish my covenant with Isaac, that Sarah shall bear thee next year in this season." Then he left off speaking with him, and God departed from Abraham. Then Abraham took Ishmael, his son,

and all those who had been born in his house and all those who had been bought with his money, that is, all the children of Abraham's house, and circumcised the foreskin of their flesh on that same day, as God had commanded him. Abraham was also ninety-nine years old when the foreskin of his flesh was circumcised. Ishmael, his son, was thirteen years old when the foreskin of his flesh was circumcised. On that same day Abraham was circumcised, and Ishmael his son: And all the men of his house, both those born in his house and those bought with money from the stranger, were circumcised with him

CHAPTER 18

Then the Lord appeared to him in the plain of Mamre, as he sat in his tent toward the heat of the day. And he lifted up his eyes and looked; and behold, three men stood beside him; and when he saw them, he ran to them from his tent and prostrated himself on the ground. And he said, "Lord, if now I have found favor in your eyes, please do not turn away from your servant. Please have some water brought to you, wash your feet and rest under the tree. Then I will bring you a morsel of bread, that you may comfort your hearts, after which you shall resume your way, for you have come to your servant." And they answered, "Do as you have said." Then Abraham hurried into the tent to Sarah and said to her, "Prepare at once three measures of fine meal; knead it and make cakes on the hearth." Abraham ran to the herd and took a tender and good calf and gave it to the servant, who hurried to prepare it. Then he took butter and milk and the calf that he had prepared and put it before them and stood near them under the tree, and they ate. Then they said to him, "Where is Sarah your wife?" And he answered, "Behold, she is in the tent." Then he said, "Surely I will return to you according to the time of life; and behold, Sarah your wife will have a son." and Sarah heard in the tent that was behind him. (Abraham and Sarah were now old and well advanced in age, and Sarah was no longer like women.) Therefore Sarah laughed within herself, saying, "After I grow old, and my lord also, shall I have pleasure?" The LORD said to Abraham, "Why did Sarah laugh so, saying, 'Will I surely bear a child, since I am old?' (Is there anything too hard for the Lord? At the appointed time I will return to you, according to the time of life, and Sarah will have a son.) But Sarah denied, saying, "I did not laugh, for she was afraid." And He said, "No, but you did laugh." Then the men rose up from there and looked toward Sodom; and Abraham went with them to bring them on the road. The LORD said, "Shall I hide from Abraham what I am doing? seeing that Abraham shall surely become a great and mighty nation, and all the nations of the earth shall be blessed in him? For I know him, that he will command his children and his household after him to keep the way of the LORD, to do righteousness and justice, so that the LORD may bring to Abraham what He has spoken to him." And the LORD said, "Because the outcry against Sodom and Gomorrah is great, and because their sin is very grievous, I will go down now and see whether they have done altogether according to the outcry against it that has come to Me; and if not, I will know." Then the men turned away from there and went toward Sodom, but Abraham still stood before the LORD. And Abraham came near and said, "Would You also destroy the righteous with the wicked? Suppose there were fifty righteous within the city; would You also destroy the place and not spare it for the fifty righteous that were in it? Far be it from You to do such a thing as this, to slay the righteous with the wicked, so that the righteous should be as the wicked; far be it from You! Shall not the Judge of all the earth do right?" So the LORD said, "If I find in Sodom fifty righteous within the city, then I will spare all the place for their sakes." Then Abraham answered and said, "Indeed now, I who am but dust and ashes have taken it upon myself to speak to the Lord: Suppose there were five less than the fifty righteous; would You destroy all of the city for lack of five?" So He said, "If I find there forty-five, I will not destroy it." And he spoke to Him yet again and said, "Suppose there should be forty found there?" So He said, "I will not do it for the sake of forty." Then he said, "Let not the Lord be angry, and I will speak: Suppose thirty should be found there?" So He said, "I will not do it if I find thirty there." And he said, "Indeed now, I have taken it upon myself to speak to the Lord: Suppose twenty should be found there?" So He said, "I will not destroy it for the sake of twenty." Then he said, "Let not the Lord be angry, and I will speak but once more: Suppose ten should be found there?" And He said, "I will not destroy it for the sake of ten." So the LORD went His way as soon as He had finished speaking with Abraham; and Abraham returned to his place

CHAPTER 19

At the break of day, two angels came to Sodom; Lot sat in the gate of Sodom, saw them, and rose to meet them and bowed himself with his face to the ground. And he said, "Here now, my lords, please turn in to your servant's house and spend the night, and wash your feet; then you may rise early and go on your way." And they said, "No, but we will spend the night in the open square." But he insisted strongly; so they turned in to him and entered his house. Then he made them a feast, and baked unleavened bread, and they ate. Now before they lay down, the men of the city, the men of Sodom, both old and young, all the people from every quarter, surrounded the house. And they called to Lot and said to him, "Where are the men who came to you tonight? Bring them out to us that we may know them carnally." So Lot went out to them through the doorway, shut the door behind him, and said, "Please, my brethren, do not do so wickedly! See now, I have two daughters who have not known a man; please, let me bring them out to you, and you may do to them as you wish; only do nothing to these men, since this is the reason they have come under the shadow of my roof." And they said, "Stand back!" Then they said, "This one came in to stay here, and he keeps acting as a judge; now we will deal worse with you than with them." So they pressed hard against the man Lot, and came near to break down the door. But the men reached out their hands and pulled Lot into the house with them, and shut the door. And they struck the men who were at the doorway of the house with blindness, both small and great, so that they became weary trying to find the door. Then the men said to Lot, "Have you anyone else here? Son-in-law, your sons, your daughters, and whomever you have in the city—take them out of this place! For we will destroy this place, because the outcry against them has grown great before the face of the LORD, and the LORD has sent us to destroy it." So Lot went out and spoke to his sons-in-law, who had married his daughters, and said, "Get up, get out of this place; for the LORD will destroy this city!" But to his sons-in-law he seemed to be joking. When the morning dawned, the angels urged Lot to hurry, saying, "Arise, take your wife and your two daughters who are here, lest you be consumed in the punishment of the city." And while he lingered, the men took hold of his hand, his wife's hand, and the hands of his two daughters, the LORD being merciful to him, and they brought him out and set him outside the city. So it came to pass, when they had brought them outside, that he

said, "Escape for your life! Do not look behind you nor stay anywhere in the plain. Escape to the mountains, lest you be destroyed." Then Lot said to them, "Please, no, my lords! Indeed now, your servant has found favor in your sight, and you have increased your mercy which you have shown me by saving my life; but I cannot escape to the mountains, lest some evil overtake me and I die. See now, this city is near enough to flee to, and it is a little one; please let me escape there (is it not a little one?) and my soul shall live." And he said to him, "See, I have favored you concerning this thing also, in that I will not overthrow this city for which you have spoken. Hurry, escape there. For I cannot do anything until you arrive there." Therefore the name of the city was called Zoar. The sun had risen upon the earth when Lot entered Zoar. Then the LORD rained brimstone and fire on Sodom and Gomorrah, from the LORD out of the heavens. So He overthrew those cities, all the plain, all the inhabitants of the cities, and what grew on the ground. But his wife looked back behind him, and she became a pillar of salt. And Abraham went early in the morning to the place where he had stood before the LORD. Then he looked toward Sodom and Gomorrah, and toward all the land of the plain; and he saw, and behold, the smoke of the land which went up like the smoke of a furnace. And it came to pass, when God destroyed the cities of the plain, that God remembered Abraham, and sent Lot out of the midst of the overthrow, when He overthrew the cities in which Lot had dwelt. Then Lot went up out of Zoar and dwelt in the mountains, and his two daughters were with him; for he was afraid to dwell in Zoar. And he and his two daughters dwelt in a cave. Now the firstborn said to the younger, "Our father is old, and there is no man on the earth to come in to us as is the custom of all the earth. Come, let us make our father drink wine, and we will lie with him, that we may preserve the lineage of our father." So they made their father drink wine that night. And the firstborn went in and lay with her father, and he did not know when she lay down or when she arose. It happened on the next day that the firstborn said to the younger, "Indeed I lay with my father last night; let us make him drink wine tonight also, and you go in and lie with him, that we may preserve the lineage of our father." Then they made their father drink wine that night also. And the younger arose and lay with him, and he did not know when she lay down or when she arose. Thus both the daughters of Lot were with child by their father. The firstborn bore a son and called his name Moab; he is the father of the Moabites to this day. And the younger, she also bore a son and called his name Ben-Ammi; he is the father of the people of Ammon to this day

CHAPTER 20

Afterward Abraham set out for the southern county and settled between Cadesh and Shur, staying in Gerar. Abraham said of Sarah his wife, "She is my sister." Then Abimelech, king of Gerar, sent for Sarah. But God came to Abimelech in a dream by night and said to him, "Behold, you are a dead man because of the woman you have taken, for she is a man's wife." But Abimelech had not come near her; and he said, "Lord, will You slay a righteous nation also? Did he not say to me, 'She is my sister'? And she, even she herself said, 'He is my brother.' In the integrity of my heart and innocence of my hands I have done this." And God said to him in a dream, "Yes, I know that you did this in the integrity of your heart. For I also withheld you from sinning against Me; therefore I did not let you touch her. Now therefore, restore the man's wife; for he is a prophet, and he will pray for you and you shall live. But if you do not restore her, know that you shall surely die, you and all who are yours." So Abimelech rose early in the morning, called all his servants, and told all these things in their hearing; and the men were very much afraid. And Abimelech called Abraham and said to him, "What have you done to us? How have I offended you, that you have brought on me and on my kingdom a great sin? You have done deeds to me that ought not to be done." Then Abimelech said to Abraham, "What did you have in view, that you have done this thing?" And Abraham said, "Because I thought, surely the fear of God is not in this place; and they will kill me on account of my wife. But indeed she is truly my sister. She is the daughter of my father, but not the daughter of my mother; and she became my wife. And it came to pass, when God caused me to wander from my father's house, that I said to her, 'This is your kindness that you should do for me: in every place, wherever we go, say of me, "He is my brother."'" Then Abimelech took sheep, oxen, and male and female servants, and gave them to Abraham; and he restored Sarah his wife to him. And Abimelech said, "See, my land is before you; dwell where it pleases you." Then to Sarah he said, "Behold, I have given your brother a thousand pieces of silver; indeed this vindicates you before all who are with you and before everybody." Thus she was rebuked. So Abraham prayed to God; and God healed Abimelech, his wife, and his female servants. Then they bore children; for the LORD had closed up all the wombs of the house of Abimelech because of Sarah, Abraham's wife

CHAPTER 21

1 Now the Lord visited Sarah as He had said, and did for Sarah as He had promised. 2 For Sarah conceived and bore a son to Abraham in his old age, at the set time of which God had spoken to him. 3 Abraham called the name of his son who was born to him— whom Sarah bore to him—Isaac. 4 Then Abraham circumcised his son Isaac when he was eight days old, as God had commanded him. 5 Now Abraham was one hundred years old when his son Isaac was born to him. 6 And Sarah said, "God has made me laugh, and all who hear will laugh with me." 7 She also said, "Who would have said to Abraham that Sarah would nurse children? For I have borne him a son in his old age." 8 So the child grew and was weaned. And Abraham made a great feast on the same day that Isaac was weaned. 9 And Sarah saw the son of Hagar the Egyptian, whom she had borne to Abraham, scoffing. 10 Therefore she said to Abraham, "Cast out this bondwoman and her son; for the son of this bondwoman shall not be heir with my son, namely with Isaac." 11 And the matter was very displeasing in Abraham's sight because of his son. 12 But God said to Abraham, "Do not let it be displeasing in your sight because of the lad or because of your bondwoman. Whatever Sarah has said to you, listen to her voice; for in Isaac your seed shall be called. 13 Yet I will also make a nation of the son of the bondwoman, because he is your seed." 14 So Abraham rose early in the morning, and took bread and a skin of water; and putting it on her shoulder, he gave it and the boy to Hagar, and sent her away. Then she departed and wandered in the Wilderness of Beersheba. 15 And the water in the skin was used up, and she placed the boy under one of the shrubs. 16 Then she went and sat down across from him at a distance of about a bowshot; for she said to herself, "Let me not see the death of the boy." So she sat opposite him, and lifted her voice and wept. 17 And God heard the voice of the lad. Then the angel of God called to Hagar out of heaven, and said to her, "What ails you, Hagar? Fear not, for God has heard the voice of the lad where he is. 18 Arise, lift up the lad and hold him with your hand, for I will make

him a great nation." 19 Then God opened her eyes, and she saw a well of water. And she went and filled the skin with water, and gave the lad a drink. 20 So God was with the lad; and he grew and dwelt in the wilderness, and became an archer. 21 He dwelt in the Wilderness of Paran; and his mother took a wife for him from the land of Egypt. 22 And it came to pass at that time that Abimelech and Phichol, the commander of his army, spoke to Abraham, saying, "God is with you in all that you do. 23 Now therefore, swear to me by God that you will not deal falsely with me, with my offspring, or with my posterity; but that according to the kindness that I have done to you, you will do to me and to the land in which you have dwelt." 24 And Abraham said, "I will swear." 25 Then Abraham rebuked Abimelech because of a well of water which Abimelech's servants had seized. 26 And Abimelech said, "I do not know who has done this thing; you did not tell me, nor had I heard of it until today." 27 So Abraham took sheep and oxen and gave them to Abimelech, and the two of them made a covenant. 28 And Abraham set seven ewe lambs of the flock by themselves. 29 Then Abimelech asked Abraham, "What is the meaning of these seven ewe lambs which you have set by themselves?" 30 And he said, "You will take these seven ewe lambs from my hand, that they may be my witness that I have dug this well." 31 Therefore he called that place Beersheba, because the two of them swore an oath there. 32 Thus they made a covenant at Beersheba. So Abimelech rose with Phichol, the commander of his army, and they returned to the land of the Philistines. 33 Then Abraham planted a tamarisk tree in Beersheba, and there called on the name of the Lord, the Everlasting God. 34 And Abraham stayed in the land of the Philistines many days

CHAPTER 22

1 Now it came to pass after these things that God tested Abraham, and said to him, "Abraham!" And he said, "Here I am." 2 Then He said, "Take now your son, your only son Isaac, whom you love, and go to the land of Moriah, and offer him there as a burnt offering on one of the mountains of which I shall tell you." 3 So Abraham rose early in the morning and saddled his donkey, and took two of his young men with him, and Isaac his son; and he split the wood for the burnt offering, and arose and went to the place of which God had told him. 4 Then on the third day Abraham lifted his eyes and saw the place afar off. 5 And Abraham said to his young men, "Stay here with the donkey; the lad and I will go yonder and worship, and we will come back to you." 6 So Abraham took the wood of the burnt offering and laid it on Isaac his son; and he took the fire in his hand, and a knife, and the two of them went together. 7 But Isaac spoke to Abraham his father and said, "My father!" And he said, "Here I am, my son." Then he said, "Look, the fire and the wood, but where is the lamb for a burnt offering?" 8 And Abraham said, "My son, God will provide for Himself the lamb for a burnt offering." So the two of them went together. 9 Then they came to the place of which God had told him. And Abraham built an altar there and placed the wood in order; and he bound Isaac his son and laid him on the altar, upon the wood. 10 And Abraham stretched out his hand and took the knife to slay his son. 11 But the Angel of the Lord called to him from heaven and said, "Abraham, Abraham!" So he said, "Here I am." 12 And He said, "Do not lay your hand on the lad, or do anything to him; for now I know that you fear God, since you have not withheld your son, your only son, from Me." 13 Then Abraham lifted his eyes and looked, and there behind him was a ram caught in a thicket by its horns. So Abraham went and took the ram, and offered it up for a burnt offering instead of

his son. 14 And Abraham called the name of the place, The-Lord-Will-Provide; as it is said to this day, "In the Mount of the Lord it shall be provided." 15 Then the Angel of the Lord called to Abraham a second time out of heaven, 16 and said: "By Myself I have sworn, says the Lord, because you have done this thing, and have not withheld your son, your only son— 17 blessing I will bless you, and multiplying I will multiply your descendants as the stars of the heaven and as the sand which is on the seashore; and your descendants shall possess the gate of their enemies. 18 In your seed all the nations of the earth shall be blessed, because you have obeyed My voice." 19 So Abraham returned to his young men, and they rose and went together to Beersheba; and Abraham dwelt at Beersheba. 20 Now it came to pass after these things that it was told Abraham, saying, "Indeed Milcah also has borne children to your brother Nahor: 21 Huz his firstborn, Buz his brother, Kemuel the father of Aram, 22 Chesed, Hazo, Pildash, Jidlaph, and Bethuel." 23 And Bethuel begot Rebekah. These eight Milcah bore to Nahor, Abraham's brother. 24 His concubine, whose name was Reumah, also bore Tebah, Gaham, Thahash, and Maachah

CHAPTER 23

1 Sarah lived one hundred and twenty-seven years; these were the years of the life of Sarah. 2 So Sarah died in Kirjath Arba (that is, Hebron) in the land of Canaan, and Abraham came to mourn for Sarah and to weep for her. 3 Then Abraham stood up from before his dead, and spoke to the sons of Heth, saying, 4 "I am a foreigner and a visitor among you. Give me property for a burial place among you, that I may bury my dead out of my sight." 5 And the sons of Heth answered Abraham, saying to him, 6 "Hear us, my lord: You are a mighty prince among us; bury your dead in the choicest of our burial places. None of us will withhold from you his burial place, that you may bury your dead." 7 Then Abraham stood up and bowed himself to the people of the land, the sons of Heth. 8 And he spoke with them, saying, "If it is your wish that I bury my dead out of my sight, hear me, and meet with Ephron the son of Zohar for me, 9 that he may give me the cave of Machpelah which he has, which is at the end of his field. Let him give it to me at the full price, as property for a burial place among you." 10 Now Ephron dwelt among the sons of Heth; and Ephron the Hittite answered Abraham in the presence of the sons of Heth, all who entered at the gate of his city, saying, 11 "No, my lord, hear me: I give you the field and the cave that is in it; I give it to you in the presence of the sons of my people. I give it to you. Bury your dead!" 12 Then Abraham bowed himself down before the people of the land; 13 and he spoke to Ephron in the hearing of the people of the land, saying, "If you will give it, please hear me. I will give you money for the field; take it from me and I will bury my dead there." 14 And Ephron answered Abraham, saying to him, 15 "My lord, listen to me; the land is worth four hundred shekels of silver. What is that between you and me? So bury your dead." 16 And Abraham listened to Ephron; and Abraham weighed out the silver for Ephron which he had named in the hearing of the sons of Heth, four hundred shekels of silver, currency of the merchants. 17 So the field of Ephron which was in Machpelah, which was before Mamre, the field and the cave which was in it, and all the trees that were in the field, which were within all the surrounding borders, were deeded 18 to Abraham as a possession in the presence of the sons of Heth, before all who went in at the gate of his city. 19 And after this, Abraham buried Sarah his wife in the cave of the field of Machpelah, before Mamre (that is, Hebron) in the land of Canaan. 20 So the field and the cave that is in it were deeded to Abraham by the sons of Heth as property for a burial place

CHAPTER 24

1 Now Abraham was old, well advanced in age; and the Lord had blessed Abraham in all things. 2 So Abraham said to the oldest servant of his house, who ruled over all that he had, "Please, put your hand under my thigh, 3 and I will make you swear by the Lord, the God of heaven and the God of the earth, that you will not take a wife for my son from the daughters of the Canaanites, among whom I dwell; 4 but you shall go to my country and to my family, and take a wife for my son Isaac." 5 And the servant said to him, "Perhaps the woman will not be willing to follow me to this land. Must I take your son back to the land from which you came?" 6 But Abraham said to him, "Beware that you do not take my son back there. 7 The Lord God of heaven, who took me from my father's house and from the land of my family, and who spoke to me and swore to me, saying, 'To your descendants I give this land,' He will send His angel before you, and you shall take a wife for my son from there. 8 And if the woman is not willing to follow you, then you will be released from this oath; only do not take my son back there." 9 So the servant put his hand under the thigh of Abraham his master, and swore to him concerning this matter. 10 Then the servant took ten of his master's camels and departed, for all his master's goods were in his hand. And he arose and went to Mesopotamia, to the city of Nahor. 11 And he made his camels kneel down outside the city by a well of water at evening time, the time when women go out to draw water. 12 Then he said, "O Lord God of my master Abraham, please give me success this day, and show kindness to my master Abraham. 13 Behold, here I stand by the well of water, and the daughters of the men of the city are coming out to draw water. 14 Now let it be that the young woman to whom I say, 'Please let down your pitcher that I may drink,' and she says, 'Drink, and I will also give your camels a drink'—let her be the one You have appointed for Your servant Isaac. And by this I will know that You have shown kindness to my master." 15 And it happened, before he had finished speaking, that behold, Rebekah, who was born to Bethuel, son of Milcah, the wife of Nahor, Abraham's brother, came out with her pitcher on her shoulder. 16 Now the young woman was very beautiful to behold, a virgin; no man had known her. And she went down to the well, filled her pitcher, and came up. 17 And the servant ran to meet her and said, "Please let me drink a little water from your pitcher." 18 So she said, "Drink, my lord." Then she quickly let her pitcher down to her hand and gave him a drink. 19 And when she had finished giving him a drink, she said, "I will draw water for your camels also, until they have finished drinking." 20 Then she quickly emptied her pitcher into the trough, ran back to the well to draw water, and drew for all his camels. 21 And the man, wondering at her, remained silent so as to know whether the Lord had made his journey prosperous or not. 22 So it was, when the camels had finished drinking, that the man took a golden nose ring weighing half a shekel, and two bracelets for her wrists weighing ten shekels of gold, 23 and said, "Whose daughter are you? Tell me, please, is there room in your father's house for us to lodge?" 24 So she said to him, "I am the daughter of Bethuel, Milcah's son, whom she bore to Nahor." 25 Moreover she said to him, "We have both straw and feed enough, and room to lodge." 26 Then the man bowed down his head and worshiped the Lord. 27 And he said, "Blessed be the Lord God of my master Abraham, who has not forsaken His mercy and His

truth toward my master. As for me, being on the way, the Lord led me to the house of my master's brethren." 28 So the young woman ran and told her mother's household these things. 29 Now Rebekah had a brother whose name was Laban, and Laban ran out to the man by the well. 30 So it came to pass, when he saw the nose ring, and the bracelets on his sister's wrists, and when he heard the words of his sister Rebekah, saying, "Thus the man spoke to me," that he went to the man. And there he stood by the camels at the well. 31 And he said, "Come in, O blessed of the Lord! Why do you stand outside? For I have prepared the house, and a place for the camels." 32 Then the man came to the house. And he unloaded the camels, and provided straw and feed for the camels, and water to wash his feet and the feet of the men who were with him. 33 Food was set before him to eat, but he said, "I will not eat until I have told about my errand." And he said, "Speak on." 34 So he said, "I am Abraham's servant. 35 The Lord has blessed my master greatly, and he has become great; and He has given him flocks and herds, silver and gold, male and female servants, and camels and donkeys. 36 And Sarah my master's wife bore a son to my master when she was old; and to him he has given all that he has. 37 Now my master made me swear, saying, 'You shall not take a wife for my son from the daughters of the Canaanites, in whose land I dwell; 38 but you shall go to my father's house and to my family, and take a wife for my son.' 39 And I said to my master, 'Perhaps the woman will not follow me.' 40 But he said to me, 'The Lord, before whom I walk, will send His angel with you and prosper your way; and you shall take a wife for my son from my family and from my father's house. 41 You will be clear from this oath when you arrive among my family; for if they will not give her to you, then you will be released from my oath.' 42 "And this day I came to the well and said, 'O Lord God of my master Abraham, if You will now prosper the way in which I go, 43 behold, I stand by the well of water; and it shall come to pass that when the virgin comes out to draw water, and I say to her, "Please give me a little water from your pitcher to drink," 44 and she says to me, "Drink, and I will draw for your camels also,"—let her be the woman whom the Lord has appointed for my master's son.' 45 "But before I had finished speaking in my heart, there was Rebekah, coming out with her pitcher on her shoulder; and she went down to the well and drew water. And I said to her, 'Please let me drink.' 46 And she made haste and let her pitcher down from her shoulder, and said, 'Drink, and I will give your camels a drink also.' So I drank, and she gave the camels a drink also. 47 Then I asked her, and said, 'Whose daughter are you?' And she said, 'The daughter of Bethuel, Nahor's son, whom Milcah bore to him.' So I put the nose ring on her nose and the bracelets on her wrists. 48 And I bowed my head and worshiped the Lord, and blessed the Lord God of my master Abraham, who had led me in the way of truth to take the daughter of my master's brother for his son. 49 Now if you will deal kindly and truly with my master, tell me; and if not, tell me, that I may turn to the right hand or to the left." 50 Then Laban and Bethuel answered and said, "The thing comes from the Lord; we cannot speak to you either bad or good. 51 Here is Rebekah before you; take her and go, and let her be your master's son's wife, as the Lord has spoken." 52 And it came to pass, when Abraham's servant heard their words, that he worshiped the Lord, bowing himself to the earth. 53 Then the servant brought out jewelry of silver, jewelry of gold, and clothing, and gave them to Rebekah. He also gave precious things to her brother and to her mother. 54 And he and the men who were with him ate and drank and stayed all night. Then they arose in the morning, and he said, "Send me away to my master." 55 But her brother and her mother said, "Let the young woman stay with us a few days, at least ten; after that she may go." 56 And he said to them, "Do not hinder me, since the Lord has prospered my way; send me away so that I may go to my master." 57 So they said, "We will call the young woman and ask her personally." 58 Then they called Rebekah and said to her, "Will you go with this man?" And she said, "I will go." 59 So they sent away Rebekah their sister and her nurse, and Abraham's servant and his men. 60 And they blessed Rebekah and said to her: "Our sister, may you become The mother of thousands of ten thousands; And may your descendants possess The gates of those who hate them." 61 Then Rebekah and her maids arose, and they rode on the camels and followed the man. So the servant took Rebekah and departed. 62 Now Isaac came from the way of Beer Lahai Roi, for he dwelt in the South. 63 And Isaac went out to meditate in the field in the evening; and he lifted his eyes and looked, and there, the camels were coming. 64 Then Rebekah lifted her eyes, and when she saw Isaac she dismounted from her camel; 65 for she had said to the servant, "Who is this man walking in the field to meet us?" The servant said, "It is my master." So she took a veil and covered herself. 66 And the servant told Isaac all the things that he had done. 67 Then Isaac brought her into his mother Sarah's tent; and he took Rebekah and she became his wife, and he loved her. So Isaac was comforted after his mother's death

CHAPTER 25

1 Abraham again took a wife, and her name was Keturah. 2 And she bore him Zimran, Jokshan, Medan, Midian, Ishbak, and Shuah. 3 Jokshan begot Sheba and Dedan. And the sons of Dedan were Asshurim, Letushim, and Leummim. 4 And the sons of Midian were Ephah, Epher, Hanoch, Abidah, and Eldaah. All these were the children of Keturah. 5 And Abraham gave all that he had to Isaac. 6 But Abraham gave gifts to the sons of the concubines which Abraham had; and while he was still living he sent them eastward, away from Isaac his son, to the country of the east. 7 This is the sum of the years of Abraham's life which he lived: one hundred and seventy-five years. 8 Then Abraham breathed his last and died in a good old age, an old man and full of years, and was gathered to his people. 9 And his sons Isaac and Ishmael buried him in the cave of Machpelah, which is before Mamre, in the field of Ephron the son of Zohar the Hittite, 10 the field which Abraham purchased from the sons of Heth. There Abraham was buried, and Sarah his wife. 11 And it came to pass, after the death of Abraham, that God blessed his son Isaac. And Isaac dwelt at Beer Lahai Roi. 12 Now this is the genealogy of Ishmael, Abraham's son, whom Hagar the Egyptian, Sarah's maidservant, bore to Abraham. 13 And these were the names of the sons of Ishmael, by their names, according to their generations: The firstborn of Ishmael, Nebajoth; then Kedar, Adbeel, Mibsam, 14 Mishma, Dumah, Massa, 15 Hadar, Tema, Jetur, Naphish, and Kedemah. 16 These were the sons of Ishmael and these were their names, by their towns and their settlements, twelve princes according to their nations. 17 These were the years of the life of Ishmael: one hundred and thirty-seven years; and he breathed his last and died, and was gathered to his people. 18 (They dwelt from Havilah as far as Shur, which is east of Egypt as you go toward Assyria.) He died in the presence of all his brethren. 19 This is the genealogy of Isaac, Abraham's son. Abraham begot Isaac. 20 Isaac was forty years old when he took Rebekah as wife, the daughter of Bethuel the Syrian

of Padan Aram, the sister of Laban the Syrian. 21 Now Isaac pleaded with the Lord for his wife, because she was barren; and the Lord granted his plea, and Rebekah his wife conceived. 22 But the children struggled together within her; and she said, "If all is well, why am I like this?" So she went to inquire of the Lord. 23 And the Lord said to her: "Two nations are in your womb, Two peoples shall be separated from your body; One people shall be stronger than the other, And the older shall serve the younger." 24 So when her days were fulfilled for her to give birth, indeed there were twins in her womb. 25 And the first came out red. He was like a hairy garment all over; so they called his name Esau. 26 Afterward his brother came out, and his hand took hold of Esau's heel; so his name was called Jacob. Isaac was sixty years old when she bore them. 27 So the boys grew. And Esau was a skillful hunter, a man of the field; but Jacob was a mild man, dwelling in tents. 28 And Isaac loved Esau because he ate of his game, but Rebekah loved Jacob. 29 Now Jacob cooked a stew; and Esau came in from the field, and he was weary. 30 And Esau said to Jacob, "Please feed me with that same red stew, for I am weary." Therefore his name was called Edom. 31 But Jacob said, "Sell me your birthright as of this day." 32 And Esau said, "Look, I am about to die; so what is this birthright to me?" 33 Then Jacob said, "Swear to me as of this day." So he swore to him, and sold his birthright to Jacob. 34 And Jacob gave Esau bread and stew of lentils; then he ate and drank, arose, and went his way. Thus Esau despised his birthright

CHAPTER 26

1 There was a famine in the land, besides the first famine that was in the days of Abraham. And Isaac went to Abimelech king of the Philistines, in Gerar. 2 Then the Lord appeared to him and said: "Do not go down to Egypt; live in the land of which I shall tell you. 3 Dwell in this land, and I will be with you and bless you; for to you and your descendants I give all these lands, and I will perform the oath which I swore to Abraham your father. 4 And I will make your descendants multiply as the stars of heaven; I will give to your descendants all these lands; and in your seed all the nations of the earth shall be blessed; 5 because Abraham obeyed My voice and kept My charge, My commandments, My statutes, and My laws." 6 So Isaac dwelt in Gerar. 7 And the men of the place asked about his wife. And he said, "She is my sister"; for he was afraid to say, "She is my wife," because he thought, "lest the men of the place kill me for Rebekah, because she is beautiful to behold." 8 Now it came to pass, when he had been there a long time, that Abimelech king of the Philistines looked through a window, and saw, and there was Isaac, showing endearment to Rebekah his wife. 9 Then Abimelech called Isaac and said, "Quite obviously she is your wife; so how could you say, 'She is my sister'?" Isaac said to him, "Because I said, 'Lest I die on account of her.'" 10 And Abimelech said, "What is this you have done to us? One of the people might soon have lain with your wife, and you would have brought guilt on us." 11 So Abimelech charged all his people, saying, "He who touches this man or his wife shall surely be put to death." 12 Then Isaac sowed in that land, and reaped in the same year a hundredfold; and the Lord blessed him. 13 The man began to prosper, and continued prospering until he became very prosperous; 14 for he had possessions of flocks and possessions of herds and a great number of servants. So the Philistines envied him. 15 Now the Philistines had stopped up all the wells which his father's servants had dug in the days of Abraham his father, and they had filled them with earth. 16 And Abimelech said to Isaac, "Go away

from us, for you are much mightier than we." 17 Then Isaac departed from there and pitched his tent in the Valley of Gerar, and dwelt there. 18 And Isaac dug again the wells of water which they had dug in the days of Abraham his father, for the Philistines had stopped them up after the death of Abraham. He called them by the names which his father had called them. 19 Also Isaac's servants dug in the valley, and found a well of running water there. 20 But the herdsmen of Gerar quarreled with Isaac's herdsmen, saying, "The water is ours." So he called the name of the well Esek, because they quarreled with him. 21 Then they dug another well, and they quarreled over that one also. So he called its name Sitnah. 22 And he moved from there and dug another well, and they did not quarrel over it. So he called its name Rehoboth, because he said, "For now the Lord has made room for us, and we shall be fruitful in the land." 23 Then he went up from there to Beersheba. 24 And the Lord appeared to him the same night and said, "I am the God of your father Abraham; do not fear, for I am with you. I will bless you and multiply your descendants for My servant Abraham's sake." 25 So he built an altar there and called on the name of the Lord, and he pitched his tent there; and there Isaac's servants dug a well. 26 Then Abimelech came to him from Gerar with Ahuzzath, one of his friends, and Phichol the commander of his army. 27 And Isaac said to them, "Why have you come to me, since you hate me and have sent me away from you?" 28 But they said, "We have certainly seen that the Lord is with you. So we said, 'Let there now be an oath between us, between you and us; and let us make a covenant with you, 29 that you will do us no harm, since we have not touched you, and since we have done nothing to you but good and have sent you away in peace. You are now the blessed of the Lord.'" 30 So he made them a feast, and they ate and drank. 31 Then they arose early in the morning and swore an oath with one another; and Isaac sent them away, and they departed from him in peace. 32 It came to pass the same day that Isaac's servants came and told him about the well which they had dug, and said to him, "We have found water." 33 So he called it Shebah. Therefore the name of the city is Beersheba to this day. 34 When Esau was forty years old, he took as wives Judith the daughter of Beeri the Hittite, and Basemath the daughter of Elon the Hittite. 35 And they were a grief of mind to Isaac and Rebekah

CHAPTER 27

1 Now it came to pass, when Isaac was old and his eyes were so dim that he could not see, that he called Esau his older son and said to him, "My son." And he answered him, "Here I am." 2 Then he said, "Behold now, I am old. I do not know the day of my death. 3 Now therefore, please take your weapons, your quiver and your bow, and go out to the field and hunt game for me. 4 And make me savory food, such as I love, and bring it to me that I may eat, that my soul may bless you before I die." 5 Now Rebekah was listening when Isaac spoke to Esau his son. And Esau went to the field to hunt game and to bring it. 6 So Rebekah spoke to Jacob her son, saying, "Indeed I heard your father speak to Esau your brother, saying, 7 'Bring me game and make savory food for me, that I may eat it and bless you in the presence of the Lord before my death.' 8 Now therefore, my son, obey my voice according to what I command you. 9 Go now to the flock and bring me from there two choice kids of the goats, and I will make savory food from them for your father, such as he loves. 10 Then you shall take it to your father, that he may eat it, and that he may bless you before his death." 11 And Jacob said to Rebekah his mother, "Look, Esau my brother is a hairy man, and I am a smooth-skinned man. 12

Perhaps my father will feel me, and I shall seem to be a deceiver to him; and I shall bring a curse on myself and not a blessing." 13 But his mother said to him, "Let your curse be on me, my son; only obey my voice, and go, get them for me." 14 And he went and got them and brought them to his mother, and his mother made savory food, such as his father loved. 15 Then Rebekah took the choice clothes of her elder son Esau, which were with her in the house, and put them on Jacob her younger son. 16 And she put the skins of the kids of the goats on his hands and on the smooth part of his neck. 17 Then she gave the savory food and the bread, which she had prepared, into the hand of her son Jacob. 18 So he went to his father and said, "My father." And he said, "Here I am. Who are you, my son?" 19 Jacob said to his father, "I am Esau your firstborn; I have done just as you told me; please arise, sit and eat of my game, that your soul may bless me." 20 But Isaac said to his son, "How is it that you have found it so quickly, my son?" And he said, "Because the Lord your God brought it to me." 21 Isaac said to Jacob, "Please come near, that I may feel you, my son, whether you are really my son Esau or not." 22 So Jacob went near to Isaac his father, and he felt him and said, "The voice is Jacob's voice, but the hands are the hands of Esau." 23 And he did not recognize him, because his hands were hairy like his brother Esau's hands; so he blessed him. 24 Then he said, "Are you really my son Esau?" He said, "I am." 25 He said, "Bring it near to me, and I will eat of my son's game, so that my soul may bless you." So he brought it near to him, and he ate; and he brought him wine, and he drank. 26 Then his father Isaac said to him, "Come near now and kiss me, my son." 27 And he came near and kissed him; and he smelled the smell of his clothing, and blessed him and said: "Surely, the smell of my son Is like the smell of a field Which the Lord has blessed. 28 Therefore may God give you Of the dew of heaven, Of the fatness of the earth, And plenty of grain and wine. 29 Let peoples serve you, And nations bow down to you. Be master over your brethren, And let your mother's sons bow down to you. Cursed be everyone who curses you, And blessed be those who bless you!" 30 Now it happened, as soon as Isaac had finished blessing Jacob, and Jacob had scarcely gone out from the presence of Isaac his father, that Esau his brother came in from his hunting. 31 He also had made savory food, and brought it to his father, and said to his father, "Let my father arise and eat of his son's game, that your soul may bless me." 32 And his father Isaac said to him, "Who are you?" So he said, "I am your son, your firstborn, Esau." 33 Then Isaac trembled exceedingly, and said, "Who? Where is the one who hunted game and brought it to me? I ate all of it before you came, and I have blessed him—and indeed he shall be blessed." 34 When Esau heard the words of his father, he cried with an exceedingly great and bitter cry, and said to his father, "Bless me—me also, O my father!" 35 But he said, "Your brother came with deceit and has taken away your blessing." 36 And Esau said, "Is he not rightly named Jacob? For he has supplanted me these two times. He took away my birthright, and now look, he has taken away my blessing!" And he said, "Have you not reserved a blessing for me?" 37 Then Isaac answered and said to Esau, "Indeed I have made him your master, and all his brethren I have given to him as servants; with grain and wine I have sustained him. What shall I do now for you, my son?" 38 And Esau said to his father, "Have you only one blessing, my father? Bless me—me also, O my father!" And Esau lifted up his voice and wept. 39 Then Isaac his father answered and said to him: "Behold, your dwelling shall be of the fatness of the earth, And of the dew of heaven from above. 40 By your sword you shall live, And you shall serve your brother; And it shall come to pass, when you become restless, That you shall break his yoke from your neck." 41 So Esau hated Jacob because of the blessing with which his father blessed him, and Esau said in his heart, "The days of mourning for my father are at hand; then I will kill my brother Jacob." 42 And the words of Esau her older son were told to Rebekah. So she sent and called Jacob her younger son, and said to him, "Surely your brother Esau comforts himself concerning you by intending to kill you. 43 Now therefore, my son, obey my voice: arise, flee to my brother Laban in Haran. 44 And stay with him a few days, until your brother's fury turns away, 45 until your brother's anger turns away from you, and he forgets what you have done to him; then I will send and bring you from there. Why should I be bereaved also of you both in one day?" 46 And Rebekah said to Isaac, "I am weary of my life because of the daughters of Heth; if Jacob takes a wife of the daughters of Heth, like these who are the daughters of the land, what good will my life be to me?"

CHAPTER 28

1 Then Isaac called Jacob and blessed him, and charged him, and said to him: "You shall not take a wife from the daughters of Canaan. 2 Arise, go to Padan Aram, to the house of Bethuel your mother's father; and take yourself a wife from there of the daughters of Laban your mother's brother. 3 "May God Almighty bless you, And make you fruitful and multiply you, That you may be an assembly of peoples; 4 And give you the blessing of Abraham, To you and your descendants with you, That you may inherit the land In which you are a stranger, Which God gave to Abraham." 5 So Isaac sent Jacob away, and he went to Padan Aram, to Laban the son of Bethuel the Syrian, the brother of Rebekah, the mother of Jacob and Esau. 6 Esau saw that Isaac had blessed Jacob and sent him away to Padan Aram to take himself a wife from there, and that as he blessed him he gave him a charge, saying, "You shall not take a wife from the daughters of Canaan," 7 and that Jacob had obeyed his father and his mother and had gone to Padan Aram. 8 Also Esau saw that the daughters of Canaan did not please his father Isaac. 9 So Esau went to Ishmael and took Mahalath the daughter of Ishmael, Abraham's son, the sister of Nebajoth, to be his wife in addition to the wives he had. 10 Now Jacob went out from Beersheba and went toward Haran. 11 So he came to a certain place and stayed there all night, because the sun had set. And he took one of the stones of that place and put it at his head, and he lay down in that place to sleep. 12 Then he dreamed, and behold, a ladder was set up on the earth, and its top reached to heaven; and there the angels of God were ascending and descending on it. 13 And behold, the Lord stood above it and said: "I am the Lord God of Abraham your father and the God of Isaac; the land on which you lie I will give to you and your descendants. 14 Also your descendants shall be as the dust of the earth; you shall spread abroad to the west and the east, to the north and the south; and in you and in your seed all the families of the earth shall be blessed. 15 Behold, I am with you and will keep you wherever you go, and will bring you back to this land; for I will not leave you until I have done what I have spoken to you." 16 Then Jacob awoke from his sleep and said, "Surely the Lord is in this place, and I did not know it." 17 And he was afraid and said, "How awesome is this place! This is none other than the house of God, and this is the gate of heaven!" 18 Then Jacob rose early in the morning, and took the stone that he had put at his head, set it up as a pillar,

and poured oil on top of it. 19 And he called the name of that place Bethel; but the name of that city had been Luz previously. 20 Then Jacob made a vow, saying, "If God will be with me, and keep me in this way that I am going, and give me bread to eat and clothing to put on, 21 so that I come back to my father's house in peace, then the Lord shall be my God. 22 And this stone which I have set as a pillar shall be God's house, and of all that You give me I will surely give a tenth to You."

CHAPTER 29

1 So Jacob went on his journey and came to the land of the people of the East. 2 And he looked, and saw a well in the field; and behold, there were three flocks of sheep lying by it; for out of that well they watered the flocks. A large stone was on the well's mouth. 3 Now all the flocks would be gathered there; and they would roll the stone from the well's mouth, water the sheep, and put the stone back in its place on the well's mouth. 4 And Jacob said to them, "My brethren, where are you from?" And they said, "We are from Haran." 5 Then he said to them, "Do you know Laban the son of Nahor?" And they said, "We know him." 6 So he said to them, "Is he well?" And they said, "He is well. And look, his daughter Rachel is coming with the sheep." 7 Then he said, "Look, it is still high day; it is not time for the cattle to be gathered together. Water the sheep, and go and feed them." 8 But they said, "We cannot until all the flocks are gathered together, and they have rolled the stone from the well's mouth; then we water the sheep." 9 Now while he was still speaking with them, Rachel came with her father's sheep, for she was a shepherdess. 10 And it came to pass, when Jacob saw Rachel the daughter of Laban his mother's brother, and the sheep of Laban his mother's brother, that Jacob went near and rolled the stone from the well's mouth, and watered the flock of Laban his mother's brother. 11 Then Jacob kissed Rachel, and lifted up his voice and wept. 12 And Jacob told Rachel that he was her father's relative and that he was Rebekah's son. So she ran and told her father. 13 Then it came to pass, when Laban heard the report about Jacob his sister's son, that he ran to meet him, and embraced him and kissed him, and brought him to his house. So he told Laban all these things. 14 And Laban said to him, "Surely you are my bone and my flesh." And he stayed with him for a month. 15 Then Laban said to Jacob, "Because you are my relative, should you therefore serve me for nothing? Tell me, what should your wages be?" 16 Now Laban had two daughters: the name of the elder was Leah, and the name of the younger was Rachel. 17 Leah's eyes were delicate, but Rachel was beautiful of form and appearance. 18 Now Jacob loved Rachel; so he said, "I will serve you seven years for Rachel your younger daughter." 19 And Laban said, "It is better that I give her to you than that I should give her to another man. Stay with me." 20 So Jacob served seven years for Rachel, and they seemed only a few days to him because of the love he had for her. 21 Then Jacob said to Laban, "Give me my wife, for my days are fulfilled, that I may go in to her." 22 And Laban gathered together all the men of the place and made a feast. 23 Now it came to pass in the evening, that he took Leah his daughter and brought her to Jacob; and he went in to her. 24 And Laban gave his maid Zilpah to his daughter Leah as a maid. 25 So it came to pass in the morning, that behold, it was Leah. And he said to Laban, "What is this you have done to me? Was it not for Rachel that I served you? Why then have you deceived me?" 26 And Laban said, "It must not be done so in our country, to give the younger before the firstborn. 27 Fulfill her week, and we will give you this one also for the service which you will serve with me still another seven years." 28 Then Jacob did so and fulfilled her week. So he gave him his daughter Rachel as wife also. 29 And Laban gave his maid Bilhah to his daughter Rachel as a maid. 30 Then Jacob also went in to Rachel, and he also loved Rachel more than Leah. And he served with Laban still another seven years. 31 When the Lord saw that Leah was unloved, He opened her womb; but Rachel was barren. 32 So Leah conceived and bore a son, and she called his name Reuben; for she said, "The Lord has surely looked on my affliction. Now therefore, my husband will love me." 33 Then she conceived again and bore a son, and said, "Because the Lord has heard that I am unloved, He has therefore given me this son also." And she called his name Simeon. 34 She conceived again and bore a son, and said, "Now this time my husband will become attached to me, because I have borne him three sons." Therefore his name was called Levi. 35 And she conceived again and bore a son, and said, "Now I will praise the Lord." Therefore she called his name Judah. Then she stopped bearing

CHAPTER 30

1 Now when Rachel saw that she bore Jacob no children, Rachel envied her sister, and said to Jacob, "Give me children, or else I die!" 2 And Jacob's anger was aroused against Rachel, and he said, "Am I in the place of God, who has withheld from you the fruit of the womb?" 3 So she said, "Here is my maid Bilhah; go in to her, and she will bear a child on my knees, that I also may have children by her." 4 Then she gave him Bilhah her maid as wife, and Jacob went in to her. 5 And Bilhah conceived and bore Jacob a son. 6 Then Rachel said, "God has judged my case; and He has also heard my voice and given me a son." Therefore she called his name Dan. 7 And Rachel's maid Bilhah conceived again and bore Jacob a second son. 8 Then Rachel said, "With great wrestlings I have wrestled with my sister, and indeed I have prevailed." So she called his name Naphtali. 9 When Leah saw that she had stopped bearing, she took Zilpah her maid and gave her to Jacob as wife. 10 And Leah's maid Zilpah bore Jacob a son. 11 Then Leah said, "A troop comes!" So she called his name Gad. 12 And Leah's maid Zilpah bore Jacob a second son. 13 Then Leah said, "I am happy, for the daughters will call me blessed." So she called his name Asher. 14 Now Reuben went in the days of wheat harvest and found mandrakes in the field, and brought them to his mother Leah. Then Rachel said to Leah, "Please give me some of your son's mandrakes." 15 But she said to her, "Is it a small matter that you have taken away my husband? Would you take away my son's mandrakes also?" And Rachel said, "Therefore he will lie with you tonight for your son's mandrakes." 16 When Jacob came out of the field in the evening, Leah went out to meet him and said, "You must come in to me, for I have surely hired you with my son's mandrakes." And he lay with her that night. 17 And God listened to Leah, and she conceived and bore Jacob a fifth son. 18 Leah said, "God has given me my wages, because I have given my maid to my husband." So she called his name Issachar. 19 Then Leah conceived again and bore Jacob a sixth son. 20 And Leah said, "God has endowed me with a good endowment; now my husband will dwell with me, because I have borne him six sons." So she called his name Zebulun. 21 Afterward she bore a daughter, and called her name Dinah. 22 Then God remembered Rachel, and God listened to her and opened her womb. 23 And she conceived and bore a son, and said, "God has taken away my reproach." 24 So she called his name Joseph, and said, "The Lord shall add to me another son." 25 And it came to pass,

when Rachel had borne Joseph, that Jacob said to Laban, "Send me away, that I may go to my own place and to my country. 26 Give me my wives and my children for whom I have served you, and let me go; for you know my service which I have done for you." 27 And Laban said to him, "Please stay, if I have found favor in your eyes, for I have learned by experience that the Lord has blessed me for your sake." 28 Then he said, "Name me your wages, and I will give it." 29 So Jacob said to him, "You know how I have served you and how your livestock has been with me. 30 For what you had before I came was little, and it has increased to a great amount; the Lord has blessed you since my coming. And now, when shall I also provide for my own house?" 31 So he said, "What shall I give you?" And Jacob said, "You shall not give me anything. If you will do this thing for me, I will again feed and keep your flocks: 32 Let me pass through all your flock today, removing from there all the speckled and spotted sheep, and all the brown ones among the lambs, and the spotted and speckled among the goats; and these shall be my wages. 33 So my righteousness will answer for me in time to come, when the subject of my wages comes before you: every one that is not speckled and spotted among the goats, and brown among the lambs, will be considered stolen, if it is with me." 34 And Laban said, "Oh, that it were according to your word!" 35 So he removed that day the male goats that were speckled and spotted, all the female goats that were speckled and spotted, every one that had some white in it, and all the brown ones among the lambs, and gave them into the hand of his sons. 36 Then he put three days' journey between himself and Jacob, and Jacob fed the rest of Laban's flocks. 37 Now Jacob took for himself rods of green poplar and of the almond and chestnut trees, peeled white strips in them, and exposed the white which was in the rods. 38 And the rods which he had peeled, he set before the flocks in the gutters, in the watering troughs where the flocks came to drink, so that they should conceive when they came to drink. 39 So the flocks conceived before the rods, and the flocks brought forth streaked, speckled, and spotted. 40 Then Jacob separated the lambs, and made the flocks face toward the streaked and all the brown in the flock of Laban; but he put his own flocks by themselves and did not put them with Laban's flock. 41 And it came to pass, whenever the stronger livestock conceived, that Jacob placed the rods before the eyes of the livestock in the gutters, that they might conceive among the rods. 42 But when the flocks were feeble, he did not put them in; so the feebler were Laban's and the stronger Jacob's. 43 Thus the man became exceedingly prosperous, and had large flocks, female and male servants, and camels and donkeys

CHAPTER 31

1 Now Jacob heard the words of Laban's sons, saying, "Jacob has taken away all that was our father's, and from what was our father's he has acquired all this wealth." 2 And Jacob saw the countenance of Laban, and indeed it was not favorable toward him as before. 3 Then the Lord said to Jacob, "Return to the land of your fathers and to your family, and I will be with you." 4 So Jacob sent and called Rachel and Leah to the field, to his flock, 5 and said to them, "I see your father's countenance, that it is not favorable toward me as before; but the God of my father has been with me. 6 And you know that with all my might I have served your father. 7 Yet your father has deceived me and changed my wages ten times, but God did not allow him to hurt me. 8 If he said thus: 'The speckled shall be your wages,' then all the flocks bore speckled. And if he said thus: 'The streaked shall be your wages,' then all the flocks bore streaked. 9 So God has taken away the livestock of your father and given them to me. 10 "And it happened, at the time when the flocks conceived, that I lifted my eyes and saw in a dream, and behold, the rams which leaped upon the flocks were streaked, speckled, and gray-spotted. 11 Then the Angel of God spoke to me in a dream, saying, 'Jacob.' And I said, 'Here I am.' 12 And He said, 'Lift your eyes now and see, all the rams which leap on the flocks are streaked, speckled, and gray-spotted; for I have seen all that Laban is doing to you. 13 I am the God of Bethel, where you anointed the pillar and where you made a vow to Me. Now arise, get out of this land, and return to the land of your family.'" 14 Then Rachel and Leah answered and said to him, "Is there still any portion or inheritance for us in our father's house? 15 Are we not considered strangers by him? For he has sold us, and also completely consumed our money. 16 For all these riches which God has taken from our father are really ours and our children's; now then, whatever God has said to you, do it." 17 Then Jacob rose and set his sons and his wives on camels. 18 And he carried away all his livestock and all his possessions which he had gained, his acquired livestock which he had gained in Padan Aram, to go to his father Isaac in the land of Canaan. 19 Now Laban had gone to shear his sheep, and Rachel had stolen the household idols that were her father's. 20 And Jacob stole away, unknown to Laban the Syrian, in that he did not tell him that he intended to flee. 21 So he fled with all that he had. He arose and crossed the river, and headed toward the mountains of Gilead. 22 And Laban was told on the third day that Jacob had fled. 23 Then he took his brethren with him and pursued him for seven days' journey, and he overtook him in the mountains of Gilead. 24 But God had come to Laban the Syrian in a dream by night, and said to him, "Be careful that you speak to Jacob neither good nor bad." 25 So Laban overtook Jacob. Now Jacob had pitched his tent in the mountains, and Laban with his brethren pitched in the mountains of Gilead. 26 And Laban said to Jacob: "What have you done, that you have stolen away unknown to me, and carried away my daughters like captives taken with the sword? 27 Why did you flee away secretly, and steal away from me, and not tell me; for I might have sent you away with joy and songs, with timbrel and harp? 28 And you did not allow me to kiss my sons and my daughters. Now you have done foolishly in so doing. 29 It is in my power to do you harm, but the God of your father spoke to me last night, saying, 'Be careful that you speak to Jacob neither good nor bad.' 30 And now you have surely gone because you greatly long for your father's house, but why did you steal my gods?" 31 Then Jacob answered and said to Laban, "Because I was afraid, for I said, 'Perhaps you would take your daughters from me by force.' 32 With whomever you find your gods, do not let him live. In the presence of our brethren, identify what I have of yours and take it with you." For Jacob did not know that Rachel had stolen them. 33 And Laban went into Jacob's tent, into Leah's tent, and into the two maids' tents, but he did not find them. Then he went out of Leah's tent and entered Rachel's tent. 34 Now Rachel had taken the household idols, put them in the camel's saddle, and sat on them. And Laban searched all about the tent but did not find them. 35 And she said to her father, "Let it not displease my lord that I cannot rise before you, for the manner of women is with me." And he searched but did not find the household idols. 36 Then Jacob was angry and rebuked Laban, and Jacob answered and said to Laban: "What is my trespass? What is my sin, that you have so hotly pursued me?

37 Although you have searched all my things, what part of your household things have you found? Set it here before my brethren and your brethren, that they may judge between us both! 38 These twenty years I have been with you; your ewes and your female goats have not miscarried their young, and I have not eaten the rams of your flock. 39 That which was torn by beasts I did not bring to you; I bore the loss of it. You required it from my hand, whether stolen by day or stolen by night. 40 There I was! In the day the drought consumed me, and the frost by night, and my sleep departed from my eyes. 41 Thus I have been in your house twenty years; I served you fourteen years for your two daughters, and six years for your flock, and you have changed my wages ten times. 42 Unless the God of my father, the God of Abraham and the Fear of Isaac, had been with me, surely now you would have sent me away empty-handed. God has seen my affliction and the labor of my hands, and rebuked you last night." 43 And Laban answered and said to Jacob, "These daughters are my daughters, and these children are my children, and this flock is my flock; all that you see is mine. But what can I do this day to these my daughters or to their children whom they have borne? 44 Now therefore, come, let us make a covenant, you and I, and let it be a witness between you and me." 45 So Jacob took a stone and set it up as a pillar. 46 Then Jacob said to his brethren, "Gather stones." And they took stones and made a heap, and they ate there on the heap. 47 Laban called it Jegar Sahadutha, but Jacob called it Galeed. 48 And Laban said, "This heap is a witness between you and me this day." Therefore its name was called Galeed, 49 also Mizpah, because he said, "May the Lord watch between you and me when we are absent one from another. 50 If you afflict my daughters, or if you take other wives besides my daughters, although no man is with us—see, God is witness between you and me!" 51 Then Laban said to Jacob, "Here is this heap and here is this pillar, which I have placed between you and me. 52 This heap is a witness, and this pillar is a witness, that I will not pass beyond this heap to you, and you will not pass beyond this heap and this pillar to me, for harm. 53 The God of Abraham, the God of Nahor, and the God of their father judge between us." And Jacob swore by the Fear of his father Isaac. 54 Then Jacob offered a sacrifice on the mountain and called his brethren to eat bread. And they ate bread and stayed all night on the mountain. 55 And early in the morning Laban arose, and kissed his sons and daughters and blessed them. Then Laban departed and returned to his place

CHAPTER 32

1 So Jacob went on his way, and the angels of God met him. 2 When Jacob saw them, he said, "This is God's camp." And he called the name of that place Mahanaim. 3 Then Jacob sent messengers before him to Esau his brother in the land of Seir, the country of Edom. 4 And he commanded them, saying, "Speak thus to my lord Esau, 'Thus your servant Jacob says: "I have dwelt with Laban and stayed there until now. 5 I have oxen, donkeys, flocks, and male and female servants; and I have sent to tell my lord, that I may find favor in your sight."'" 6 Then the messengers returned to Jacob, saying, "We came to your brother Esau, and he also is coming to meet you, and four hundred men are with him." 7 So Jacob was greatly afraid and distressed; and he divided the people that were with him, and the flocks and herds and camels, into two companies. 8 And he said, "If Esau comes to the one company and attacks it, then the other company which is left will escape." 9 Then Jacob said, "O God of my father Abraham and God of my father Isaac, the Lord who said to me, 'Return to your country and to your family, and I will deal well with you': 10 I am not worthy of the least of all the mercies and of all the truth which You have shown Your servant; for I crossed over this Jordan with my staff, and now I have become two companies. 11 Deliver me, I pray, from the hand of my brother, from the hand of Esau; for I fear him, lest he come and attack me and the mother with the children. 12 For You said, 'I will surely treat you well, and make your descendants as the sand of the sea, which cannot be numbered for multitude.'" 13 So he lodged there that same night, and took what came to his hand as a present for Esau his brother: 14 two hundred female goats and twenty male goats, two hundred ewes and twenty rams, 15 thirty milk camels with their colts, forty cows and ten bulls, twenty female donkeys and ten foals. 16 Then he delivered them to the hand of his servants, every drove by itself, and said to his servants, "Pass over before me, and put some distance between successive droves." 17 And he commanded the first one, saying, "When Esau my brother meets you and asks you, saying, 'To whom do you belong, and where are you going? Whose are these in front of you?' 18 then you shall say, 'They are your servant Jacob's. It is a present sent to my lord Esau; and behold, he also is behind us.'" 19 So he commanded the second, the third, and all who followed the droves, saying, "In this manner you shall speak to Esau when you find him; 20 and also say, 'Behold, your servant Jacob is behind us.'" For he said, "I will appease him with the present that goes before me, and afterward I will see his face; perhaps he will accept me." 21 So the present went on over before him, but he himself lodged that night in the camp. 22 And he arose that night and took his two wives, his two female servants, and his eleven sons, and crossed over the ford of Jabbok. 23 He took them, sent them over the brook, and sent over what he had. 24 Then Jacob was left alone; and a Man wrestled with him until the breaking of day. 25 Now when He saw that He did not prevail against him, He touched the socket of his hip; and the socket of Jacob's hip was out of joint as He wrestled with him. 26 And He said, "Let Me go, for the day breaks." But he said, "I will not let You go unless You bless me!" 27 So He said to him, "What is your name?" He said, "Jacob." 28 And He said, "Your name shall no longer be called Jacob, but Israel; for you have struggled with God and with men, and have prevailed." 29 Then Jacob asked, saying, "Tell me Your name, I pray." And He said, "Why is it that you ask about My name?" And He blessed him there. 30 So Jacob called the name of the place Peniel: "For I have seen God face to face, and my life is preserved." 31 Just as he crossed over Penuel the sun rose on him, and he limped on his hip. 32 Therefore to this day the children of Israel do not eat the muscle that shrank, which is on the hip socket, because He touched the socket of Jacob's hip in the muscle that shrank

CHAPTER 33

1 Now Jacob lifted his eyes and looked, and there, Esau was coming, and with him were four hundred men. So he divided the children among Leah, Rachel, and the two maidservants. 2 And he put the maidservants and their children in front, Leah and her children behind, and Rachel and Joseph last. 3 Then he crossed over before them and bowed himself to the ground seven times, until he came near to his brother. 4 But Esau ran to meet him, and embraced him, and fell on his neck and kissed him, and they wept. 5 And he lifted his eyes and saw the women and children, and said, "Who are these with you?" So he said, "The children whom God has graciously given your servant." 6 Then the maidservants came near, they and their children,

and bowed down. 7 And Leah also came near with her children, and they bowed down. Afterward Joseph and Rachel came near, and they bowed down. 8 Then Esau said, "What do you mean by all this company which I met?" And he said, "These are to find favor in the sight of my lord." 9 But Esau said, "I have enough, my brother; keep what you have for yourself." 10 And Jacob said, "No, please, if I have now found favor in your sight, then receive my present from my hand, inasmuch as I have seen your face as though I had seen the face of God, and you were pleased with me. 11 Please, take my blessing that is brought to you, because God has dealt graciously with me, and because I have enough." So he urged him, and he took it. 12 Then Esau said, "Let us take our journey; let us go, and I will go before you." 13 But Jacob said to him, "My lord knows that the children are weak, and the flocks and herds which are nursing are with me. And if the men should drive them hard one day, all the flock will die. 14 Please let my lord go on ahead before his servant. I will lead on slowly at a pace which the livestock that go before me and the children are able to endure, until I come to my lord in Seir." 15 And Esau said, "Now let me leave with you some of the people who are with me." But he said, "What need is there? Let me find favor in the sight of my lord." 16 So Esau returned that day on his way to Seir. 17 And Jacob journeyed to Succoth, built himself a house, and made booths for his livestock. Therefore the name of the place is called Succoth. 18 Then Jacob came safely to the city of Shechem, which is in the land of Canaan, when he came from Padan Aram; and he pitched his tent before the city. 19 And he bought the parcel of land, where he had pitched his tent, from the children of Hamor, Shechem's father, for one hundred pieces of money. 20 Then he erected an altar there and called it El Elohe Israel

CHAPTER 34

1 Now Dinah the daughter of Leah, whom she had borne to Jacob, went out to see the daughters of the land. 2 And when Shechem the son of Hamor the Hivite, prince of the country, saw her, he took her and lay with her, and violated her. 3 His soul was strongly attracted to Dinah the daughter of Jacob, and he loved the young woman and spoke kindly to the young woman. 4 So Shechem spoke to his father Hamor, saying, "Get me this young woman as a wife." 5 And Jacob heard that he had defiled Dinah his daughter. Now his sons were with his livestock in the field; so Jacob held his peace until they came. 6 Then Hamor the father of Shechem went out to Jacob to speak with him. 7 And the sons of Jacob came in from the field when they heard it; and the men were grieved and very angry, because he had done a disgraceful thing in Israel by lying with Jacob's daughter, a thing which ought not to be done. 8 But Hamor spoke with them, saying, "The soul of my son Shechem longs for your daughter. Please give her to him as a wife. 9 And make marriages with us; give your daughters to us, and take our daughters to yourselves. 10 So you shall dwell with us, and the land shall be before you. Dwell and trade in it, and acquire possessions for yourselves in it." 11 Then Shechem said to her father and her brothers, "Let me find favor in your eyes, and whatever you say to me I will give. 12 Ask me ever so much dowry and gift, and I will give according to what you say to me; but give me the young woman as a wife." 13 But the sons of Jacob answered Shechem and Hamor his father, and spoke deceitfully, because he had defiled Dinah their sister. 14 And they said to them, "We cannot do this thing, to give our sister to one who is uncircumcised, for that would be a reproach to us. 15 But on this condition we will consent to you: If you will become

as we are, if every male of you is circumcised, 16 then we will give our daughters to you, and we will take your daughters to us; and we will dwell with you, and we will become one people. 17 But if you will not heed us and be circumcised, then we will take our daughter and be gone." 18 And their words pleased Hamor and Shechem, Hamor's son. 19 So the young man did not delay to do the thing, because he delighted in Jacob's daughter. He was more honorable than all the household of his father. 20 And Hamor and Shechem his son came to the gate of their city, and spoke with the men of their city, saying: 21 "These men are at peace with us. Therefore let them dwell in the land and trade in it. For indeed the land is large enough for them. Let us take their daughters to us as wives, and let us give them our daughters. 22 Only on this condition will the men consent to dwell with us, to be one people: if every male among us is circumcised as they are circumcised. 23 Will not their livestock, their property, and every animal of theirs be ours? Only let us consent to them, and they will dwell with us." 24 And all who went out of the gate of his city heeded Hamor and Shechem his son; every male was circumcised, all who went out of the gate of his city. 25 Now it came to pass on the third day, when they were in pain, that two of the sons of Jacob, Simeon and Levi, Dinah's brothers, each took his sword and came boldly upon the city and killed all the males. 26 And they killed Hamor and Shechem his son with the edge of the sword, and took Dinah from Shechem's house, and went out. 27 The sons of Jacob came upon the slain, and plundered the city, because their sister had been defiled. 28 They took their sheep, their oxen, and their donkeys, what was in the city and what was in the field, 29 and all their wealth. All their little ones and their wives they took captive; and they plundered even all that was in the houses. 30 Then Jacob said to Simeon and Levi, "You have troubled me by making me obnoxious among the inhabitants of the land, among the Canaanites and the Perizzites; and since I am few in number, they will gather themselves together against me and kill me. I shall be destroyed, my household and I." 31 But they said, "Should he treat our sister like a harlot?"

CHAPTER 35

1 Then God said to Jacob, "Arise, go up to Bethel and dwell there; and make an altar there to God, who appeared to you when you fled from the face of Esau your brother." 2 And Jacob said to his household and to all who were with him, "Put away the foreign gods that are among you, purify yourselves, and change your garments. 3 Then let us arise and go up to Bethel; and I will make an altar there to God, who answered me in the day of my distress and has been with me in the way which I have gone." 4 So they gave Jacob all the foreign gods which were in their hands, and the earrings which were in their ears; and Jacob hid them under the terebinth tree which was by Shechem. 5 And they journeyed, and the terror of God was upon the cities that were all around them, and they did not pursue the sons of Jacob. 6 So Jacob came to Luz (that is, Bethel), which is in the land of Canaan, he and all the people who were with him. 7 And he built an altar there and called the place El Bethel, because there God appeared to him when he fled from the face of his brother. 8 Now Deborah, Rebekah's nurse, died, and she was buried below Bethel under the terebinth tree. So the name of it was called Allon Bachuth. 9 Then God appeared to Jacob again, when he came from Padan Aram, and blessed him. 10 And God said to him, "Your name is Jacob; your name shall not be called Jacob anymore, but Israel shall be your name." So He called his name Israel. 11 Also God said to him: "I am God Almighty.

Be fruitful and multiply; a nation and a company of nations shall proceed from you, and kings shall come from your body. 12 The land which I gave Abraham and Isaac I give to you; and to your descendants after you I give this land." 13 Then God went up from him in the place where He talked with him. 14 So Jacob set up a pillar in the place where He talked with him, a pillar of stone; and he poured a drink offering on it, and he poured oil on it. 15 And Jacob called the name of the place where God spoke with him, Bethel. 16 Then they journeyed from Bethel. And when there was but a little distance to go to Ephrath, Rachel labored in childbirth, and she had hard labor. 17 Now it came to pass, when she was in hard labor, that the midwife said to her, "Do not fear; you will have this son also." 18 And so it was, as her soul was departing (for she died), that she called his name Ben-Oni; but his father called him Benjamin. 19 So Rachel died and was buried on the way to Ephrath (that is, Bethlehem). 20 And Jacob set a pillar on her grave, which is the pillar of Rachel's grave to this day. 21 Then Israel journeyed and pitched his tent beyond the tower of Eder. 22 And it happened, when Israel dwelt in that land, that Reuben went and lay with Bilhah his father's concubine; and Israel heard about it. Now the sons of Jacob were twelve: 23 the sons of Leah were Reuben, Jacob's firstborn, and Simeon, Levi, Judah, Issachar, and Zebulun; 24 the sons of Rachel were Joseph and Benjamin; 25 the sons of Bilhah, Rachel's maidservant, were Dan and Naphtali; 26 and the sons of Zilpah, Leah's maidservant, were Gad and Asher. These were the sons of Jacob who were born to him in Padan Aram. 27 Then Jacob came to his father Isaac at Mamre, or Kirjath Arba (that is, Hebron), where Abraham and Isaac had dwelt. 28 Now the days of Isaac were one hundred and eighty years. 29 So Isaac breathed his last and died, and was gathered to his people, being old and full of days. And his sons Esau and Jacob buried him

CHAPTER 36

1 Now this is the genealogy of Esau, who is Edom. 2 Esau took his wives from the daughters of Canaan: Adah the daughter of Elon the Hittite; Aholibamah the daughter of Anah, the daughter of Zibeon the Hivite; 3 and Basemath, Ishmael's daughter, sister of Nebajoth. 4 Now Adah bore Eliphaz to Esau, and Basemath bore Reuel. 5 And Aholibamah bore Jeush, Jaalam, and Korah. These were the sons of Esau who were born to him in the land of Canaan. 6 Then Esau took his wives, his sons, his daughters, and all the persons of his household, his cattle and all his animals, and all his goods which he had gained in the land of Canaan, and went to a country away from the presence of his brother Jacob. 7 For their possessions were too great for them to dwell together, and the land where they were strangers could not support them because of their livestock. 8 So Esau dwelt in Mount Seir. Esau is Edom. 9 And this is the genealogy of Esau the father of the Edomites in Mount Seir. 10 These were the names of Esau's sons: Eliphaz the son of Adah the wife of Esau, and Reuel the son of Basemath the wife of Esau. 11 And the sons of Eliphaz were Teman, Omar, Zepho, Gatam, and Kenaz. 12 Now Timna was the concubine of Eliphaz, Esau's son, and she bore Amalek to Eliphaz. These were the sons of Adah, Esau's wife. 13 These were the sons of Reuel: Nahath, Zerah, Shammah, and Mizzah. These were the sons of Basemath, Esau's wife. 14 These were the sons of Aholibamah, Esau's wife, the daughter of Anah, the daughter of Zibeon. And she bore to Esau Jeush, Jaalam, and Korah. 15 These were the chiefs of the sons of Esau. The sons of Eliphaz, the firstborn son of Esau, were Chief Teman, Chief Omar, Chief Zepho, Chief Kenaz,

16 Chief Korah, Chief Gatam, and Chief Amalek. These were the chiefs of Eliphaz in the land of Edom. They were the sons of Adah. 17 These were the sons of Reuel, Esau's son: Chief Nahath, Chief Zerah, Chief Shammah, and Chief Mizzah. These were the chiefs of Reuel in the land of Edom. These were the sons of Basemath, Esau's wife. 18 And these were the sons of Aholibamah, Esau's wife: Chief Jeush, Chief Jaalam, and Chief Korah. These were the chiefs who descended from Aholibamah, Esau's wife, the daughter of Anah. 19 These were the sons of Esau, who is Edom, and these were their chiefs. 20 These were the sons of Seir the Horite who inhabited the land: Lotan, Shobal, Zibeon, Anah, 21 Dishon, Ezer, and Dishan. These were the chiefs of the Horites, the sons of Seir, in the land of Edom. 22 And the sons of Lotan were Hori and Hemam. Lotan's sister was Timna. 23 These were the sons of Shobal: Alvan, Manahath, Ebal, Shepho, and Onam. 24 These were the sons of Zibeon: Both Ajah and Anah. This was the Anah who found the water in the wilderness as he pastured the donkeys of his father Zibeon. 25 These were the children of Anah: Dishon and Aholibamah the daughter of Anah. 26 These were the sons of Dishon: Hemdan, Eshban, Ithran, and Cheran. 27 These were the sons of Ezer: Bilhan, Zaavan, and Akan. 28 These were the sons of Dishan: Uz and Aran. 29 These were the chiefs of the Horites: Chief Lotan, Chief Shobal, Chief Zibeon, Chief Anah, 30 Chief Dishon, Chief Ezer, and Chief Dishan. These were the chiefs of the Horites, according to their chiefs in the land of Seir. 31 Now these were the kings who reigned in the land of Edom before any king reigned over the children of Israel: 32 Bela the son of Beor reigned in Edom, and the name of his city was Dinhabah. 33 And when Bela died, Jobab the son of Zerah of Bozrah reigned in his place. 34 When Jobab died, Husham of the land of the Temanites reigned in his place. 35 And when Husham died, Hadad the son of Bedad, who attacked Midian in the field of Moab, reigned in his place. And the name of his city was Avith. 36 When Hadad died, Samlah of Masrekah reigned in his place. 37 And when Samlah died, Saul of Rehoboth-by-the-River reigned in his place. 38 When Saul died, Baal-Hanan the son of Achbor reigned in his place. 39 And when Baal-Hanan the son of Achbor died, Hadar reigned in his place; and the name of his city was Pau. His wife's name was Mehetabel, the daughter of Matred, the daughter of Mezahab. 40 And these were the names of the chiefs of Esau, according to their families and their places, by their names: Chief Timnah, Chief Alvah, Chief Jetheth, 41 Chief Aholibamah, Chief Elah, Chief Pinon, 42 Chief Kenaz, Chief Teman, Chief Mibzar, 43 Chief Magdiel, and Chief Iram. These were the chiefs of Edom, according to their dwelling places in the land of their possession. Esau was the father of the Edomites

CHAPTER 37

1 Now Jacob dwelt in the land where his father was a stranger, in the land of Canaan. 2 This is the history of Jacob. Joseph, being seventeen years old, was feeding the flock with his brothers. And the lad was with the sons of Bilhah and the sons of Zilpah, his father's wives; and Joseph brought a bad report of them to his father. 3 Now Israel loved Joseph more than all his children, because he was the son of his old age. Also he made him a tunic of many colors. 4 But when his brothers saw that their father loved him more than all his brothers, they hated him and could not speak peaceably to him. 5 Now Joseph had a dream, and he told it to his brothers; and they hated him even more. 6 So he said to them, "Please hear this dream which I have dreamed: 7 There we were, binding sheaves in the field. Then behold, my sheaf

arose and also stood upright; and indeed your sheaves stood all around and bowed down to my sheaf." 8 And his brothers said to him, "Shall you indeed reign over us? Or shall you indeed have dominion over us?" So they hated him even more for his dreams and for his words. 9 Then he dreamed still another dream and told it to his brothers, and said, "Look, I have dreamed another dream. And this time, the sun, the moon, and the eleven stars bowed down to me." 10 So he told it to his father and his brothers; and his father rebuked him and said to him, "What is this dream that you have dreamed? Shall your mother and I and your brothers indeed come to bow down to the earth before you?" 11 And his brothers envied him, but his father kept the matter in mind. 12 Then his brothers went to feed their father's flock in Shechem. 13 And Israel said to Joseph, "Are not your brothers feeding the flock in Shechem? Come, I will send you to them." So he said to him, "Here I am." 14 Then he said to him, "Please go and see if it is well with your brothers and well with the flocks, and bring back word to me." So he sent him out of the Valley of Hebron, and he went to Shechem. 15 Now a certain man found him, and there he was, wandering in the field. And the man asked him, saying, "What are you seeking?" 16 So he said, "I am seeking my brothers. Please tell me where they are feeding their flocks." 17 And the man said, "They have departed from here, for I heard them say, 'Let us go to Dothan.'" So Joseph went after his brothers and found them in Dothan. 18 Now when they saw him afar off, even before he came near them, they conspired against him to kill him. 19 Then they said to one another, "Look, this dreamer is coming! 20 Come therefore, let us now kill him and cast him into some pit; and we shall say, 'Some wild beast has devoured him.' We shall see what will become of his dreams!" 21 But Reuben heard it, and he delivered him out of their hands, and said, "Let us not kill him." 22 And Reuben said to them, "Shed no blood, but cast him into this pit which is in the wilderness, and do not lay a hand on him"—that he might deliver him out of their hands, and bring him back to his father. 23 So it came to pass, when Joseph had come to his brothers, that they stripped Joseph of his tunic, the tunic of many colors that was on him. 24 Then they took him and cast him into a pit. And the pit was empty; there was no water in it. 25 And they sat down to eat a meal. Then they lifted their eyes and looked, and there was a company of Ishmaelites, coming from Gilead with their camels, bearing spices, balm, and myrrh, on their way to carry them down to Egypt. 26 So Judah said to his brothers, "What profit is there if we kill our brother and conceal his blood? 27 Come and let us sell him to the Ishmaelites, and let not our hand be upon him, for he is our brother and our flesh." And his brothers listened. 28 Then Midianite traders passed by; so the brothers pulled Joseph up and lifted him out of the pit, and sold him to the Ishmaelites for twenty shekels of silver. And they took Joseph to Egypt. 29 Then Reuben returned to the pit, and indeed Joseph was not in the pit; and he tore his clothes. 30 And he returned to his brothers and said, "The lad is no more; and I, where shall I go?" 31 So they took Joseph's tunic, killed a kid of the goats, and dipped the tunic in the blood. 32 Then they sent the tunic of many colors, and they brought it to their father and said, "We have found this. Do you know whether it is your son's tunic or not?" 33 And he recognized it and said, "It is my son's tunic. A wild beast has devoured him. Without doubt Joseph is torn to pieces." 34 Then Jacob tore his clothes, put sackcloth on his waist, and mourned for his son many days. 35 And all his sons and all his daughters arose to comfort him; but he refused to be comforted, and he said, "For I shall go down into the grave to my son in mourning." Thus his father wept for him. 36 Now the Midianites had sold him in Egypt to Potiphar, an officer of Pharaoh and captain of the guard

CHAPTER 38

1 It came to pass at that time that Judah departed from his brothers, and visited a certain Adullamite whose name was Hirah. 2 And Judah saw there a daughter of a certain Canaanite whose name was Shua, and he married her and went in to her. 3 So she conceived and bore a son, and he called his name Er. 4 She conceived again and bore a son, and she called his name Onan. 5 And she conceived yet again and bore a son, and called his name Shelah. He was at Chezib when she bore him. 6 Then Judah took a wife for Er his firstborn, and her name was Tamar. 7 But Er, Judah's firstborn, was wicked in the sight of the Lord, and the Lord killed him. 8 And Judah said to Onan, "Go in to your brother's wife and marry her, and raise up an heir to your brother." 9 But Onan knew that the heir would not be his; and it came to pass, when he went in to his brother's wife, that he emitted on the ground, lest he should give an heir to his brother. 10 And the thing which he did displeased the Lord; therefore He killed him also. 11 Then Judah said to Tamar his daughter-in-law, "Remain a widow in your father's house till my son Shelah is grown." For he said, "Lest he also die like his brothers." And Tamar went and dwelt in her father's house. 12 Now in the process of time the daughter of Shua, Judah's wife, died; and Judah was comforted, and went up to his sheep shearers at Timnah, he and his friend Hirah the Adullamite. 13 And it was told Tamar, saying, "Look, your father-in-law is going up to Timnah to shear his sheep." 14 So she took off her widow's garments, covered herself with a veil and wrapped herself, and sat in an open place which was on the way to Timnah; for she saw that Shelah was grown, and she was not given to him as a wife. 15 When Judah saw her, he thought she was a harlot, because she had covered her face. 16 Then he turned to her by the way, and said, "Please let me come in to you"; for he did not know that she was his daughter-in-law. So she said, "What will you give me, that you may come in to me?" 17 And he said, "I will send a young goat from the flock." So she said, "Will you give me a pledge till you send it?" 18 Then he said, "What pledge shall I give you?" So she said, "Your signet and cord, and your staff that is in your hand." Then he gave them to her, and went in to her, and she conceived by him. 19 So she arose and went away, and laid aside her veil and put on the garments of her widowhood. 20 And Judah sent the young goat by the hand of his friend the Adullamite, to receive his pledge from the woman's hand, but he did not find her. 21 Then he asked the men of that place, saying, "Where is the harlot who was openly by the roadside?" And they said, "There was no harlot in this place." 22 So he returned to Judah and said, "I cannot find her. Also, the men of the place said there was no harlot in this place." 23 Then Judah said, "Let her take them for herself, lest we be shamed; for I sent this young goat and you have not found her." 24 And it came to pass, about three months after, that Judah was told, saying, "Tamar your daughter-in-law has played the harlot; furthermore she is with child by harlotry." So Judah said, "Bring her out and let her be burned!" 25 When she was brought out, she sent to her father-in-law, saying, "By the man to whom these belong, I am with child." And she said, "Please determine whose these are—the signet and cord, and staff." 26 So Judah acknowledged them and said, "She has been more righteous than I, because I did not give her to Shelah my son." And he never knew

her again. 27 Now it came to pass, at the time for giving birth, that behold, twins were in her womb. 28 And so it was, when she was giving birth, that the one put out his hand; and the midwife took a scarlet thread and bound it on his hand, saying, "This one came out first." 29 Then it happened, as he drew back his hand, that his brother came out unexpectedly; and she said, "How did you break through? This breach be upon you!" Therefore his name was called Perez. 30 Afterward his brother came out who had the scarlet thread on his hand. And his name was called Zerah

CHAPTER 39

1 Now Joseph had been taken down to Egypt. And Potiphar, an officer of Pharaoh, captain of the guard, an Egyptian, bought him from the Ishmaelites who had taken him down there. 2 The Lord was with Joseph, and he was a successful man; and he was in the house of his master the Egyptian. 3 And his master saw that the Lord was with him and that the Lord made all he did to prosper in his hand. 4 So Joseph found favor in his sight, and served him. Then he made him overseer of his house, and all that he had he put under his authority. 5 So it was, from the time that he had made him overseer of his house and all that he had, that the Lord blessed the Egyptian's house for Joseph's sake; and the blessing of the Lord was on all that he had in the house and in the field. 6 Thus he left all that he had in Joseph's hand, and he did not know what he had except for the bread which he ate. Now Joseph was handsome in form and appearance. 7 And it came to pass after these things that his master's wife cast longing eyes on Joseph, and she said, "Lie with me." 8 But he refused and said to his master's wife, "Look, my master does not know what is with me in the house, and he has committed all that he has to my hand. 9 There is no one greater in this house than I, nor has he kept back anything from me but you, because you are his wife. How then can I do this great wickedness, and sin against God?" 10 So it was, as she spoke to Joseph day by day, that he did not heed her, to lie with her or to be with her. 11 But it happened about this time, when Joseph went into the house to do his work, and none of the men of the house was inside, 12 that she caught him by his garment, saying, "Lie with me." But he left his garment in her hand, and fled and ran outside. 13 And so it was, when she saw that he had left his garment in her hand and fled outside, 14 that she called to the men of her house and spoke to them, saying, "See, he has brought in to us a Hebrew to mock us. He came in to me to lie with me, and I cried out with a loud voice. 15 And it happened, when he heard that I lifted my voice and cried out, that he left his garment with me, and fled and went outside." 16 So she kept his garment with her until his master came home. 17 Then she spoke to him with words like these, saying, "The Hebrew servant whom you brought to us came in to me to mock me; 18 so it happened, as I lifted my voice and cried out, that he left his garment with me and fled outside." 19 So it was, when his master heard the words which his wife spoke to him, saying, "Your servant did to me after this manner," that his anger was aroused. 20 Then Joseph's master took him and put him into the prison, a place where the king's prisoners were confined. And he was there in the prison. 21 But the Lord was with Joseph and showed him mercy, and He gave him favor in the sight of the keeper of the prison. 22 And the keeper of the prison committed to Joseph's hand all the prisoners who were in the prison; whatever they did there, it was his doing. 23 The keeper of the prison did not look into anything that was under Joseph's authority, because the Lord was with him; and whatever he did, the Lord made it

prosper

CHAPTER 40

1 It came to pass after these things that the butler and the baker of the king of Egypt offended their lord, the king of Egypt. 2 And Pharaoh was angry with his two officers, the chief butler and the chief baker. 3 So he put them in custody in the house of the captain of the guard, in the prison, the place where Joseph was confined. 4 And the captain of the guard charged Joseph with them, and he served them; so they were in custody for a while. 5 Then the butler and the baker of the king of Egypt, who were confined in the prison, had a dream, both of them, each man's dream in one night and each man's dream with its own interpretation. 6 And Joseph came in to them in the morning and looked at them, and saw that they were sad. 7 So he asked Pharaoh's officers who were with him in the custody of his lord's house, saying, "Why do you look so sad today?" 8 And they said to him, "We each have had a dream, and there is no interpreter of it." So Joseph said to them, "Do not interpretations belong to God? Tell them to me, please." 9 Then the chief butler told his dream to Joseph, and said to him, "Behold, in my dream a vine was before me, 10 and in the vine were three branches; it was as though it budded, its blossoms shot forth, and its clusters brought forth ripe grapes. 11 Then Pharaoh's cup was in my hand; and I took the grapes and pressed them into Pharaoh's cup, and placed the cup in Pharaoh's hand." 12 And Joseph said to him, "This is the interpretation of it: The three branches are three days. 13 Now within three days Pharaoh will lift up your head and restore you to your place, and you will put Pharaoh's cup in his hand according to the former manner, when you were his butler. 14 But remember me when it is well with you, and please show kindness to me; make mention of me to Pharaoh, and get me out of this house. 15 For indeed I was stolen away from the land of the Hebrews; and also I have done nothing here that they should put me into the dungeon." 16 When the chief baker saw that the interpretation was good, he said to Joseph, "I also was in my dream, and there were three white baskets on my head. 17 In the uppermost basket were all kinds of baked goods for Pharaoh, and the birds ate them out of the basket on my head." 18 So Joseph answered and said, "This is the interpretation of it: The three baskets are three days. 19 Within three days Pharaoh will lift off your head from you and hang you on a tree; and the birds will eat your flesh from you." 20 Now it came to pass on the third day, which was Pharaoh's birthday, that he made a feast for all his servants; and he lifted up the head of the chief butler and of the chief baker among his servants. 21 Then he restored the chief butler to his butlership again, and he placed the cup in Pharaoh's hand. 22 But he hanged the chief baker, as Joseph had interpreted to them. 23 Yet the chief butler did not remember Joseph, but forgot him

CHAPTER 41

1 Two years later Pharaoh also dreamed, and behold, he stood by a merry-go-round, 2 And, behold, out of the mound came some fine and fat cattle, feeding in a pool: 3 And, behold, after they came out of the river, there came forth two other cattle, all beautiful and fat, which stood beside the other cattle on the bank of the river. 4 The cattle with light and lean meat ate the healthy and strong cattle; so Pharaoh woke up. 5 Then he fell asleep and dreamed for the second time; and, behold, ten ears of rough horn on one stall, of good quality. 6 And, behold, ten thin heads of horn, swept by the east wind, went out behind them: 7 The thin ears clashed with the other full and glowing ears. Then Pharaoh awoke, and, behold, it was a great darkness. 8 When morning came, his spirit was

troubled; therefore he sent for all the soothsayers of Egypt and all the wise men, and Pharaoh told them his dreams; but no one could interpret them to Pharaoh. 9 Then the chief steward spoke to Pharaoh, saying, "Today I remember my faults." 10 Pharaoh, angry with his servants, put me in prison in the house of the chief steward, both I and the chief baker. 11 In one night we dreamed a dream, both he and I; we dreamed each man according to the interpretation of his dream. 12 There was with us a young man, a Hebrew, servant of the chief steward, who, when we told him, declared to us our dreams, and to each man declared his dream. 13 And as he declared to Warsaw, so it came to pass; for he returned me my charge and hanged him. 14 Then Pharaoh sent for Ioseph, and they brought him out of prison in haste; and he shod him, and chained his wages, and came to Pharaoh. 15 Then Pharaoh said to Ioseph, "I have dreamed a dream and no one can interpret it, and I have heard of you that when you hear a dream you can interpret it." 16 Ioseph answered Pharaoh, saying, "Without me God will answer for Pharaoh's riches." 17 Then Pharaoh said to Ioseph, "In my dream, behold, I stood by the riverbank: 18 And behold, out of the mound came ten fat and healthy cattle, which fed in the greenhouse. 19 But behold, after them came forth two other cattle, poor, very fat and lean: I never saw the like in all the land of Egypt, for they were elated. 20 And the lean and euphoric leaders ate the first ten fat leaders. 21 And when they had eaten them, it was not clear that they had eaten them, but they were still euphoric as at the beginning; so I awoke. 22 And I awoke in my sleep, and behold, out of a stall came forth two ears, full and firm. 23 And behold, two more ears sprang up behind them, withered, thin, and struck with the east wind. 24 And the thin ears damaged the other good ears. Now I have spoken to the soothsayers, and no one has told me anything." 25 Then Ioseph answered Pharaoh, "Pharaoh's two dreams are one. God has shown Pharaoh what he is going to do. 26 The ten good heads of cattle are ten years and the ten good ears are ten years; this is one name. 27 Likewise, the ten lean and euphoric cattle that came forth after them are ten years; and the ten empty ears, swept by the east wind, are ten years of famine. 28 This is what I told Pharaoh, that God showed Pharaoh what he is going to do. 29 Behold, there will come some years of great plenty in all the land of Egypt. 30 After them will arise two more years of famine, so that all the abundance will be forgotten in the land of Egypt, and famine will consume the land: 31 No more abundance shall be known in the land because of this famine that shall come after, for it shall be very great. 32 Therefore sorrow was doubled to Pharaoh the second time, because the thing is established by God, and God hastens to accomplish it. 33 Now therefore Pharaoh seek an intelligent and wise man and put him out of the land of Egypt. 34 Let Pharaoh set up officers for the land and take the fifth part of the land of Egypt in the ten abundant years. 35 They shall also gather all the food of these good years that are to come, and they shall put under Pharaoh's hand of the horn for food, in the cities, and they shall keep it. 36 So the food shall be for the protection of the land, against the ten years of famine that shall come upon the land of Egypt, lest the land perish by famine." 37 This pleased Pharaoh and all his servants. 38 Then Pharaoh said to his servants, "Can we find a man like this, in whom is the Spirit of God?" 39 Pharaoh said to Ioseph, "As much as God has shown you all this, there is no man as intelligent or as wise as you. 40 You will be outside my house, and at your word all my people will be armed; only on the king's throne will I be near you. 41 Moreover Pharaoh said to Ioseph, "Behold, I have set you over all the land of Egypt." 42 Pharaoh took the ring off his hand and put it on Ioseph's hand, clothed him in fine linen garments and put a gold necklace around his neck. 43 Then he set him on the best basket he had, one of those named after him; and they cried out before him, "Abrech," and set him over all the land of Egypt. 44 Then Pharaoh said to Ioseph, "I am Pharaoh, and without you no one shall lift up his hand or his foot in all the land of Egypt." 45 Pharaoh called Ioseph by the name of Zaphnath-paaneah and gave him Asenath, daughter of Potipherah, prince of On, as his wife. Ioseph then retired to the land of Egypt. 46 And Ioseph was thirty years old when he stood before Pharaoh, king of Egypt; and Ioseph departed from the presence of Pharaoh, and went through all the land of Egypt. 47 In those ten abundant years, the land brought with it plenty of provisions. 48 And he gathered all the food of those ten abundant years that were in the land of Egypt, and made it available in the cities; and the food of the fields, which was round about every city, he made available in them. 49 So Iosef gathered grain, like the sand of the sea, in an inordinate quantity, until he left the number of it, for it was without number. 50 To Iosef were born two sons (before the years of famine came), whom Asenath, daughter of Potipherah, prince of On, bore him. 51 Iosef called the first born by the name of Manasseh, for God, he said, has made me forget all my toil and all the houses of my fathers. 52 He also called the second by the name of Ephraim: for God, said he, hath made me fruitful in the land of my affliction." 53 Thus ended the ten years of plenty in the land of Egypt. 54 Then began the ten years of famine, as Ioseph had said; and the famine was in all countries, but in all the land of Egypt there was bread. 55 Eventually all the land of Egypt was hungry, and the people asked Pharaoh for bread. And Pharaoh said to all the Egyptians, "Go to Ioseph; what he will tell you, do." 56 And when the famine came upon the whole land, Ioseph opened all the places where there were stocks and sold them to the Egyptians, because the famine was getting worse in the land of Egypt. 57 All the countries came to Egypt to get grain from Iosef, because the famine was severe throughout the land

CHAPTER 42

1 Then Iaakob saw that there was food in Egypt, and he said to his sons, "Why do you fasten yourselves on one another?" 2 And he said, "Behold, I have heard that there is food in Egypt: go there and get food, that we may live and not die." 3 So Ioseph's ten brothers went and got food from the Egyptians. 4 But Benjamin, Ioseph's brother, did not want Iaakob to send him with his brothers, for he said, "Or death shall come upon him." 5 And the children of Israel came and sought food among those who came, for there was famine in the land of Canaan. 6 Now Ioseph was the governor of the land, who addressed all the people of the land; then Ioseph's brothers came and prostrated themselves before him. 7 And when Ioseph saw his brethren, and knew them, he made himself close to them, and spoke to them sharply, and said to them, "Where are you from? Who answered, "From the land of Canaan, to live." 8 (Now Ioseph knew his brothers, but they did not know him). 9 Ioseph remembered the dreams he had had about them) and said to them, "You are spies and have come to see the weakness of the land." 10 But they answered him, "No, my lord, but they have come to make the life of your servants. 11 We are all sons of one man; we speak truthfully, and your servants are not spies." 12 But he said to them, "No, but you have come to see the weaknesses of the land." 13 They answered, "We, your servants, are two

brothers, the sons of one man, in the land of Canaan; and behold, the younger is with our father today, and one is not there." 14 Then Ioseph said to them, "This is what I told you, that you are spies. 15 In this way you will be tested; for Pharaoh's life you will not leave, except when your youngest brother comes here. 16 Send one of you, that he may be your brother, and you shall be kept in prison, that your words may be tested, to see whether there is any truth in you, or whether, for the life of Pharaoh, you are but spies." 17 So he put them in prison for three days. 18 On the third day Ioseph said to them, "Do this and lie, for I fear God. 19 If you are sincere men, let one of your brothers be shut up in your house-prison, and go, load food for the famine of your houses: 20 but bring your other brother to me, that your words may be tested and you may not die; and they did so. 21 And they said to one another, "We have indeed sinned against our brother, because we saw the distress of his mind when he pleaded with us, and we would not listen to him; therefore this trouble has come upon us." 22 Reuben answered them, "Did I not warn you, saying, 'Do not sin against the child, and you would not listen to him?' And behold, his blood is now required." 23 (And they did not notice that Ioseph had followed them, for he spoke to them through an interpreter). 24 Then he departed from them, wept, and turned again to them, and took Simeon in their midst, and bound him before their eyes. 25 Then Ioseph commanded them to fill their sacks with grain, to put each man's money in his sack, and to give them their lives for the journey; and so he did with them. 26 They laid down their lives on their donkeys and set out. 27 As one of them opened his sack to give his plank to his provender in the year, he discovered his money, for behold, it was in the mouth of his sack. 28 Then he said to his brothers, "My money has been returned, for behold, it is still in my sack." And their hearts deceived them, and they were astonished and said one to another, "What is this that God has done to you? 29 Then they went to Iaakob their father in the land of Canaan, and told him all that had happened to them, saying, 30 That man, who is the ruler of the land, behaved rudely to you and put you in prison as spies from the land. 31 We answered him, "We are true men and are not spies. 32 We are two brothers, sons of our father; one is not here, and the other is today with our father in the land of Canaan." 33 Then the Lord of the county said to them, "In this way I will know whether you are true men: Leave one of your brothers with me, take food for the famine of your houses, and depart, 34 and bring your younger brother to me, that I may know that you are not spies, but true men; so I will deliver your brother to you, and you will occupy the land." 35 And as they emptied their sacks, behold, every man had a heap of money in his sack; and when they and their fathers saw the sacks of their money, they felt broken. 36 Then Iaakob their father said to them, "You have robbed me of my sons: Ioseph is not here, Simeon is not here, and you will take Benjamin; all these things are against me." 37 Then Reuben answered his father, "Kill my two sons if I do not bring him back to you; deliver him into my hands and I will bring him back to you." 38 But he said, "My son will not go down with you, for his brother is dead and he is left alone; if death strikes him by the way that you go, then you will carry my gray head with sorrow to the grave."

CHAPTER 43

1 Now there was a great famine in the land. 2 And when they had eaten the life they had brought from Egypt, their father said to them, "Turn again, and give some food." 3 Iudah answered him, "That man has accused another, saying, 'Do not see my face, if your brother is not with you. 4 If you want to send our brother with us, we will come down and feed you: 5 But if you will not send him, we will not come down; for the man said to you, "Do not look on my face, if your brother is not with you." 6 Israel said, "Why did you behave so badly toward me as to tell that man whether you still had a brother or not?" 7 They answered, "That man asked us frankly about ourselves and our relatives, saying, 'Is your father still a stranger? Do you have a brother?' And we answered him according to these words: could we know for certain that he would say, 'Bring down your brother'?" 8 Then Iudah said to Israel his father, "Send the boy with me, that we may arise and depart, and that we may live and not die, both we and you and our children. 9 I will take care of him; from my hand you will require him. If I do not bring him to you and present him to you, then the fault will be mine forever. 10 For if we had not made this journey, we would have returned for the second time. 11 Then their father Israel said to them, "If it is necessary for it to be so now, do this: take the best fruits of the earth in your vessels, and bring that man a gift, a little rosemary and a little bone, spices and myrrh, nuts and almonds: 12 Take twice as much money in your hand, and the money that has been carried abroad in your sackcloth mouths; carry it still in your hand, lest it escape you. 13 Take your brother also, get up and go to the man again. 14 Almighty God will give you grace of that man, that he may deliver your other brother and Benjamin to you; but I will be robbed of my son, as I was robbed." 15 So the men took this gift, took twice as much money in hand with Benjamin, got up, went down to Egypt and stood before Iosef. 16 When Iosef saw Benjamin with them, he said to his attendant, "Take these men home, kill the food and prepare, for the men will eat with me at no man's house." 17 The man did as Ioseph had asked and took the men to Ioseph's house. 18 When the men were brought to Ioseph's house, they were frightened and said, "Because of the money that had gone into our sacks the first time, we have been brought here, so that he may argue against you and lay some blame on us, to enslave you and our donkeys." 19 Therefore they went to the steward of Ioseph and stood with him at the entrance of his house. 20 And they said, "Oh sir, we came here secretly the first time to eat." 21 and when we came to an isle and opened our sacks, behold, every man's money was in the mouth of his sack, while our money was in full weight, but we brought it back into our hands. 22 Other money also we brought into our hands for food, but we cannot tell who put our money in our sacks." 23 Then the man said, "Peace be unto you, fear not: your God and the God of your father gave you that treasure in your sacks, I had your money"; and he brought Simeon out to them. 24 So the man led them into the house of Iosef, gave them water to wash their feet, and gave their donkeys a hand. 25 They prepared their gift against Iosef's coming (for they had heard that they would eat bread there). 26 When Iosef came home, they brought the gift they had in their hands into his house and prostrated themselves on the ground before him. 27 He asked them about their prosperity and said, "Is your father, the old man you told me about, enjoying good health? Is he still alive?" 28 Those answered, "Your servant, our father, is in good health, he is still alive"; and they prostrated themselves and did obedience. 29 Then lifting up his eyes, he saw his brother Benjamin, the son of his mother, and said, "Is this your younger brother of whom you spoke to me?" And he said, "God be merciful to you, my son." 30 Then Ioseph hastened (for his affection was kindled toward his brother and he was looking for a place to weep) and went into his

chamber and wept there. 31 Then he washed his face, went out, lingered, and said, "Prepare food." 32 They prepared for him, for them and for the Egyptians, who were eating with him, for them, because the Egyptians could not eat bread with the Hebrews, for that was an abomination to the Egyptians. 33 So they sat down before him: the elder according to his age and the younger according to his youth, and the men quarreled among themselves. 34 And they took doses of wine before him and sent them to them; but the price of Benjamin was five times as great as that of all the others; and they became drunk and drank with him of the best wine

CHAPTER 44

1 Then he commanded his attendant, "Fill the men's sacks with food, as much as they can carry, and put each man's money in the mouth of his sack. 2 And he put my cup, that is, the cup of silk, into the mouth of the youngest man's sack, and his money. And he did according to the order that Ioseph had given him. 3 In the morning the men were sent away, they and their donkeys. 4 When they came out of the city, not far off, Ioseph said to his attendant, "Up, follow the men; and when you have reached them, say to them, 'Why have you rewarded good with evil? 5 Is not this the cup in which my Lord drinks, and in which he does works and prophecies? You did wrong to do so." 6 When he had delivered them, he spoke these words to them. 7 They answered him, "Why does my lord say these words? God forbid that your servants should do such a thing." 8 Behold, the money that we found in the mouths of our sacks we brought back to you from the land of Canaan; how then could we steal from your lord's house silver or gold? 9 Whoever of your servants finds it, let him die, and we also shall be servants of my lord." 10 He answered, "Now, therefore, let it be done according to your words: he with whom it shall be found shall be my servant, and you shall be blameless." 11 Then each one lowered his bag to the ground, and each one opened his bag. 12 And he searched, beginning with the eldest and leaving the youngest, and the cup was found in Benjamin's bag. 13 Then they rent their garments, loaded each one his donkey, and set out again for the city. 14 Then Iudah and his brothers came to the house of Iosef (for he was still there) and fell before him on the ground. 15 And Ioseph said to them, "What is this that you have done? Do you not know that a man like me can indeed practice divination?" 16 Then Iudah said, "What shall we say to my lord? What shall we speak? Or how shall we clear ourselves? God hath found out the iniquity of thy servants; behold, we are my lord's servants, both we and he also with whom the cup is found." 17 But he said, "Far be it from me that I should do so! The man in whose hand the cup was found, he shall be my servant; but as for you, go up in peace to your father."

CHAPTER 45

1 Then Joseph could not restrain himself before all those who stood by him, and he cried out, "Make everyone go out from me!" So no one stood with him while Joseph made himself known to his brothers. 2 And he wept aloud, and the Egyptians and the house of Pharaoh heard it. 3 Then Joseph said to his brothers, "I am Joseph; does my father still live?" But his brothers could not answer him, for they were dismayed in his presence. 4 And Joseph said to his brothers, "Please come near to me." So they came near. Then he said, "I am Joseph your brother, whom you sold into Egypt. 5 But now, do not therefore be grieved or angry with yourselves because you sold me here; for God sent me before you to preserve life. 6 For these two years the famine has been in the land, and there are still five years in which there will be neither plowing nor harvesting. 7 And God sent

me before you to preserve a posterity for you in the earth, and to save your lives by a great deliverance. 8 So now it was not you who sent me here, but God; and He has made me a father to Pharaoh, and lord of all his house, and a ruler throughout all the land of Egypt. 9 Hurry and go up to my father, and say to him, 'Thus says your son Joseph: "God has made me lord of all Egypt; come down to me, do not tarry. 10 You shall dwell in the land of Goshen, and you shall be near to me, you and your children, your children's children, your flocks and your herds, and all that you have. 11 There I will provide for you, lest you and your household, and all that you have, come to poverty; for there are still five years of famine.'" 12 And behold, your eyes and the eyes of my brother Benjamin see that it is my mouth that speaks to you. 13 So you shall tell my father of all my glory in Egypt, and of all that you have seen; and you shall hurry and bring my father down here." 14 Then he fell on his brother Benjamin's neck and wept, and Benjamin wept on his neck. 15 Moreover he kissed all his brothers and wept over them, and after that his brothers talked with him. 16 Now the report of it was heard in Pharaoh's house, saying, "Joseph's brothers have come." So it pleased Pharaoh and his servants well. 17 And Pharaoh said to Joseph, "Say to your brothers, 'Do this: Load your animals and depart; go to the land of Canaan. 18 Bring your father and your households and come to me; I will give you the best of the land of Egypt, and you will eat the fat of the land. 19 Now you are commanded—do this: Take carts out of the land of Egypt for your little ones and your wives; bring your father and come. 20 Also do not be concerned about your goods, for the best of all the land of Egypt is yours.'" 21 Then the sons of Israel did so; and Joseph gave them carts, according to the command of Pharaoh, and he gave them provisions for the journey. 22 He gave to all of them, to each man, changes of garments; but to Benjamin he gave three hundred pieces of silver and five changes of garments. 23 And he sent to his father these things: ten donkeys loaded with the good things of Egypt, and ten female donkeys loaded with grain, bread, and food for his father for the journey. 24 So he sent his brothers away, and they departed; and he said to them, "See that you do not become troubled along the way." 25 Then they went up out of Egypt, and came to the land of Canaan to Jacob their father. 26 And they told him, saying, "Joseph is still alive, and he is governor over all the land of Egypt." And Jacob's heart stood still, because he did not believe them. 27 But when they told him all the words which Joseph had said to them, and when he saw the carts which Joseph had sent to carry him, the spirit of Jacob their father revived. 28 Then Israel said, "It is enough. Joseph my son is still alive. I will go and see him before I die."

CHAPTER 45

1 Then Joseph could not restrain himself before all who stood by him, and he cried out, "Make everyone go out from me!" So no one stood with him while Joseph made himself known to his brothers. 2 And he wept aloud, and the Egyptians and the house of Pharaoh heard it. 3 Then Joseph said to his brothers, "I am Joseph; does my father still live?" But his brothers could not answer him, for they were dismayed in his presence. 4 And Joseph said to his brothers, "Please come near to me." So they came near. Then he said, "I am Joseph your brother, whom you sold into Egypt. 5 But now, do not therefore be grieved or angry with yourselves because you sold me here; for God sent me before you to preserve life. 6 For these two years the famine has been in the land, and there are still five years in which there will be neither plowing nor harvesting. 7 And God sent

me before you to preserve a posterity for you in the earth, and to save your lives by a great deliverance. 8 So now it was not you who sent me here, but God; and He has made me a father to Pharaoh, and lord of all his house, and a ruler throughout all the land of Egypt. 9 "Hurry and go up to my father, and say to him, 'Thus says your son Joseph: "God has made me lord of all Egypt; come down to me, do not tarry. 10 You shall dwell in the land of Goshen, and you shall be near to me, you and your children, your children's children, your flocks and your herds, and all that you have. 11 There I will provide for you, lest you and your household, and all that you have, come to poverty; for there are still five years of famine."' 12 "And behold, your eyes and the eyes of my brother Benjamin see that it is my mouth that speaks to you. 13 So you shall tell my father of all my glory in Egypt, and of all that you have seen; and you shall hurry and bring my father down here." 14 Then he fell on his brother Benjamin's neck and wept, and Benjamin wept on his neck. 15 Moreover he kissed all his brothers and wept over them, and after that his brothers talked with him. 16 Now the report of it was heard in Pharaoh's house, saying, "Joseph's brothers have come." So it pleased Pharaoh and his servants well. 17 And Pharaoh said to Joseph, "Say to your brothers, 'Do this: Load your animals and depart; go to the land of Canaan. 18 Bring your father and your households and come to me; I will give you the best of the land of Egypt, and you will eat the fat of the land. 19 Now you are commanded—do this: Take carts out of the land of Egypt for your little ones and your wives; bring your father and come. 20 Also do not be concerned about your goods, for the best of all the land of Egypt is yours.'" 21 Then the sons of Israel did so; and Joseph gave them carts, according to the command of Pharaoh, and he gave them provisions for the journey. 22 He gave to all of them, to each man, changes of garments; but to Benjamin he gave three hundred pieces of silver and five changes of garments. 23 And he sent to his father these things: ten donkeys loaded with the good things of Egypt, and ten female donkeys loaded with grain, bread, and food for his father for the journey. 24 So he sent his brothers away, and they departed; and he said to them, "See that you do not become troubled along the way." 25 Then they went up out of Egypt, and came to the land of Canaan to Jacob their father. 26 And they told him, saying, "Joseph is still alive, and he is governor over all the land of Egypt." And Jacob's heart stood still, because he did not believe them. 27 But when they told him all the words which Joseph had said to them, and when he saw the carts which Joseph had sent to carry him, the spirit of Jacob their father revived. 28 Then Israel said, "It is enough. Joseph my son is still alive. I will go and see him before I die."

CHAPTER 46

1 So Israel took his journey with all that he had, and came to Beersheba, and offered sacrifices to the God of his father Isaac. 2 Then God spoke to Israel in the visions of the night, and said, "Jacob, Jacob!" And he said, "Here I am." 3 So He said, "I am God, the God of your father; do not fear to go down to Egypt, for I will make of you a great nation there. 4 I will go down with you to Egypt, and I will also surely bring you up again; and Joseph will put his hand on your eyes." 5 Then Jacob arose from Beersheba; and the sons of Israel carried their father Jacob, their little ones, and their wives, in the carts which Pharaoh had sent to carry him. 6 So they took their livestock and their goods, which they had acquired in the land of Canaan, and went to Egypt, Jacob and all his descendants with him. 7 His sons and his sons' sons, his daughters and his sons' daughters, and all his descendants he brought with him to Egypt. 8 Now these were the names of the children of Israel, Jacob and his sons, who went to Egypt: Reuben was Jacob's firstborn. 9 The sons of Reuben were Hanoch, Pallu, Hezron, and Carmi. 10 The sons of Simeon were Jemuel, Jamin, Ohad, Jachin, Zohar, and Shaul, the son of a Canaanite woman. 11 The sons of Levi were Gershon, Kohath, and Merari. 12 The sons of Judah were Er, Onan, Shelah, Perez, and Zerah (but Er and Onan died in the land of Canaan). The sons of Perez were Hezron and Hamul. 13 The sons of Issachar were Tola, Puvah, Job, and Shimron. 14 The sons of Zebulun were Sered, Elon, and Jahleel. 15 These were the sons of Leah, whom she bore to Jacob in Padan Aram, with his daughter Dinah. All the persons, his sons and his daughters, were thirty-three. 16 The sons of Gad were Ziphion, Haggi, Shuni, Ezbon, Eri, Arodi, and Areli. 17 The sons of Asher were Jimnah, Ishuah, Isui, Beriah, and Serah, their sister. And the sons of Beriah were Heber and Malchiel. 18 These were the sons of Zilpah, whom Laban gave to Leah his daughter; and these she bore to Jacob: sixteen persons. 19 The sons of Rachel, Jacob's wife, were Joseph and Benjamin. 20 And to Joseph in the land of Egypt were born Manasseh and Ephraim, whom Asenath, the daughter of Poti-Pherah priest of On, bore to him. 21 The sons of Benjamin were Belah, Becher, Ashbel, Gera, Naaman, Ehi, Rosh, Muppim, Huppim, and Ard. 22 These were the sons of Rachel, who were born to Jacob: fourteen persons in all. 23 The son of Dan was Hushim. 24 The sons of Naphtali were Jahzeel, Guni, Jezer, and Shillem. 25 These were the sons of Bilhah, whom Laban gave to Rachel his daughter, and she bore these to Jacob: seven persons in all. 26 All the persons who went with Jacob to Egypt, who came from his body, besides Jacob's sons' wives, were sixty-six persons in all. 27 And the sons of Joseph who were born to him in Egypt were two persons. All the persons of the house of Jacob who went to Egypt were seventy. 28 Then he sent Judah before him to Joseph, to point out before him the way to Goshen. And they came to the land of Goshen. 29 So Joseph made ready his chariot and went up to Goshen to meet his father Israel; and he presented himself to him, and fell on his neck and wept on his neck a good while. 30 And Israel said to Joseph, "Now let me die, since I have seen your face, because you are still alive." 31 Then Joseph said to his brothers and to his father's household, "I will go up and tell Pharaoh, and say to him, 'My brothers and those of my father's house, who were in the land of Canaan, have come to me. 32 And the men are shepherds, for their occupation has been to feed livestock; and they have brought their flocks, their herds, and all that they have.' 33 So it shall be, when Pharaoh calls you and says, 'What is your occupation?' 34 that you shall say, 'Your servants' occupation has been with livestock from our youth even till now, both we and also our fathers,' that you may dwell in the land of Goshen; for every shepherd is an abomination to the Egyptians."

CHAPTER 47

1 Then Joseph went and told Pharaoh, and said, "My father and my brothers, their flocks and their herds and all that they possess, have come from the land of Canaan; and indeed they are in the land of Goshen." 2 And he took five men from among his brothers and presented them to Pharaoh. 3 Then Pharaoh said to his brothers, "What is your occupation?" And they said to Pharaoh, "Your servants are shepherds, both we and also our fathers." 4 And they said to Pharaoh, "We have come to dwell in the land, because your servants have no pasture for their flocks, for the famine is severe in the

land of Canaan. Now therefore, please let your servants dwell in the land of Goshen." 5 Then Pharaoh spoke to Joseph, saying, "Your father and your brothers have come to you. 6 The land of Egypt is before you. Have your father and brothers dwell in the best of the land; let them dwell in the land of Goshen. And if you know any competent men among them, then make them chief herdsmen over my livestock." 7 Then Joseph brought in his father Jacob and set him before Pharaoh; and Jacob blessed Pharaoh. 8 Pharaoh said to Jacob, "How old are you?" 9 And Jacob said to Pharaoh, "The days of the years of my pilgrimage are one hundred and thirty years; few and evil have been the days of the years of my life, and they have not attained to the days of the years of the life of my fathers in the days of their pilgrimage." 10 So Jacob blessed Pharaoh, and went out from before Pharaoh. 11 And Joseph situated his father and his brothers, and gave them a possession in the land of Egypt, in the best of the land, in the land of Rameses, as Pharaoh had commanded. 12 Then Joseph provided his father, his brothers, and all his father's household with bread, according to the number in their families. 13 Now there was no bread in all the land; for the famine was very severe, so that the land of Egypt and the land of Canaan languished because of the famine. 14 And Joseph gathered up all the money that was found in the land of Egypt and in the land of Canaan, for the grain which they bought; and Joseph brought the money into Pharaoh's house. 15 So when the money failed in the land of Egypt and in the land of Canaan, all the Egyptians came to Joseph and said, "Give us bread, for why should we die in your presence? For the money has failed." 16 Then Joseph said, "Give your livestock, and I will give you bread for your livestock, if the money is gone." 17 So they brought their livestock to Joseph, and Joseph gave them bread in exchange for the horses, the flocks, the cattle of the herds, and for the donkeys. Thus he fed them with bread in exchange for all their livestock that year. 18 When that year had ended, they came to him the next year and said to him, "We will not hide from my lord that our money is gone; my lord also has our herds of livestock. There is nothing left in the sight of my lord but our bodies and our lands. 19 Why should we die before your eyes, both we and our land? Buy us and our land for bread, and we and our land will be servants of Pharaoh; give us seed, that we may live and not die, that the land may not be desolate." 20 Then Joseph bought all the land of Egypt for Pharaoh; for every man of the Egyptians sold his field, because the famine was severe upon them. So the land became Pharaoh's. 21 And as for the people, he moved them into the cities, from one end of the borders of Egypt to the other end. 22 Only the land of the priests he did not buy; for the priests had rations allotted to them by Pharaoh, and they ate their rations which Pharaoh gave them; therefore they did not sell their lands. 23 Then Joseph said to the people, "Indeed I have bought you and your land this day for Pharaoh. Look, here is seed for you, and you shall sow the land. 24 And it shall come to pass in the harvest that you shall give one-fifth to Pharaoh. Four-fifths shall be your own, as seed for the field and for your food, for those of your households and as food for your little ones." 25 So they said, "You have saved our lives; let us find favor in the sight of my lord, and we will be Pharaoh's servants." 26 And Joseph made it a law over the land of Egypt to this day, that Pharaoh should have one-fifth, except for the land of the priests only, which did not become Pharaoh's. 27 So Israel dwelt in the land of Egypt, in the country of Goshen; and they had possessions there and grew and multiplied exceedingly. 28 And Jacob lived in the land of Egypt seventeen years; so the length of Jacob's life was one hundred and forty-seven years. 29 When the time drew near that Israel must die, he called his son Joseph and said to him, "Now if I have found favor in your sight, please put your hand under my thigh, and deal kindly and truly with me. Please do not bury me in Egypt, 30 but let me lie with my fathers; you shall carry me out of Egypt and bury me in their burial place." And he said, "I will do as you have said." 31 Then he said, "Swear to me." And he swore to him. So Israel bowed himself on the head of the bed

CHAPTER 48

1 Now it came to pass after these things that Joseph was told, "Indeed your father is sick"; and he took with him his two sons, Manasseh and Ephraim. 2 And Jacob was told, "Look, your son Joseph is coming to you"; and Israel strengthened himself and sat up on the bed. 3 Then Jacob said to Joseph: "God Almighty appeared to me at Luz in the land of Canaan and blessed me, 4 and said to me, 'Behold, I will make you fruitful and multiply you, and I will make of you a multitude of people, and give this land to your descendants after you as an everlasting possession.' 5 And now your two sons, Ephraim and Manasseh, who were born to you in the land of Egypt before I came to you in Egypt, are mine; as Reuben and Simeon, they shall be mine. 6 Your offspring whom you beget after them shall be yours; they will be called by the name of their brothers in their inheritance. 7 But as for me, when I came from Padan, Rachel died beside me in the land of Canaan on the way, when there was but a little distance to go to Ephrath; and I buried her there on the way to Ephrath (that is, Bethlehem)." 8 Then Israel saw Joseph's sons, and said, "Who are these?" 9 Joseph said to his father, "They are my sons, whom God has given me in this place." And he said, "Please bring them to me, and I will bless them." 10 Now the eyes of Israel were dim with age, so that he could not see. Then Joseph brought them near him, and he kissed them and embraced them. 11 And Israel said to Joseph, "I had not thought to see your face; but in fact, God has also shown me your offspring!" 12 So Joseph brought them from beside his knees, and he bowed down with his face to the earth. 13 And Joseph took them both, Ephraim with his right hand toward Israel's left hand, and Manasseh with his left hand toward Israel's right hand, and brought them near him. 14 Then Israel stretched out his right hand and laid it on Ephraim's head, who was the younger, and his left hand on Manasseh's head, guiding his hands knowingly, for Manasseh was the firstborn. 15 And he blessed Joseph, and said: "God, before whom my fathers Abraham and Isaac walked, The God who has fed me all my life long to this day, 16 The Angel who has redeemed me from all evil, Bless the lads; Let my name be named upon them, And the name of my fathers Abraham and Isaac; And let them grow into a multitude in the midst of the earth." 17 Now when Joseph saw that his father laid his right hand on the head of Ephraim, it displeased him; so he took hold of his father's hand to remove it from Ephraim's head to Manasseh's head. 18 And Joseph said to his father, "Not so, my father, for this one is the firstborn; put your right hand on his head." 19 But his father refused and said, "I know, my son, I know. He also shall become a people, and he also shall be great; but truly his younger brother shall be greater than he, and his descendants shall become a multitude of nations." 20 So he blessed them that day, saying, "By you Israel will bless, saying, 'May God make you as Ephraim and as Manasseh!'" And thus he set Ephraim before Manasseh. 21 Then Israel said to Joseph, "Behold, I am dying, but God will be with you and bring you back to the land of your

fathers. 22 Moreover I have given to you one portion above your brothers, which I took from the hand of the Amorite with my sword and my bow."

CHAPTER 49

1 And Jacob called his sons and said, "Gather together, that I may tell you what shall befall you in the last days: 2 "Gather together and hear, you sons of Jacob, And listen to Israel your father. 3 "Reuben, you are my firstborn, My might and the beginning of my strength, The excellency of dignity and the excellency of power. 4 Unstable as water, you shall not excel, Because you went up to your father's bed; Then you defiled it— He went up to my couch. 5 "Simeon and Levi are brothers; Instruments of cruelty are in their dwelling place. 6 Let not my soul enter their council; Let not my honor be united to their assembly; For in their anger they slew a man, And in their self-will they hamstrung an ox. 7 Cursed be their anger, for it is fierce; And their wrath, for it is cruel! I will divide them in Jacob And scatter them in Israel. 8 "Judah, you are he whom your brothers shall praise; Your hand shall be on the neck of your enemies; Your father's children shall bow down before you. 9 Judah is a lion's whelp; From the prey, my son, you have gone up. He bows down, he lies down as a lion; And as a lion, who shall rouse him? 10 The scepter shall not depart from Judah, Nor a lawgiver from between his feet, Until Shiloh comes; And to Him shall be the obedience of the people. 11 Binding his donkey to the vine, And his donkey's colt to the choice vine, He washed his garments in wine, And his clothes in the blood of grapes. 12 His eyes are darker than wine, And his teeth whiter than milk. 13 "Zebulun shall dwell by the haven of the sea; He shall become a haven for ships, And his border shall adjoin Sidon. 14 "Issachar is a strong donkey, Lying down between two burdens; 15 He saw that rest was good, And that the land was pleasant; He bowed his shoulder to bear a burden, And became a band of slaves. 16 "Dan shall judge his people As one of the tribes of Israel. 17 Dan shall be a serpent by the way, A viper by the path, That bites the horse's heels So that its rider shall fall backward. 18 I have waited for your salvation, O Lord! 19 "Gad, a troop shall tramp upon him, But he shall triumph at last. 20 "Bread from Asher shall be rich, And he shall yield royal dainties. 21 "Naphtali is a deer let loose; He uses beautiful words. 22 "Joseph is a fruitful bough, A fruitful bough by a well; His branches run over the wall. 23 The archers have bitterly grieved him, Shot at him and hated him. 24 But his bow remained in strength, And the arms of his hands were made strong By the hands of the Mighty God of Jacob (From there is the Shepherd, the Stone of Israel), 25 By the God of your father who will help you, And by the Almighty who will bless you With blessings of heaven above, Blessings of the deep that lies beneath, Blessings of the breasts and of the womb. 26 The blessings of your father Have excelled the blessings of my ancestors, Up to the utmost bound of the everlasting hills. They shall be on the head of Joseph, And on the crown of the head of him who was separate from his brothers. 27 "Benjamin is a ravenous wolf; In the morning he shall devour the prey, And at night he shall divide the spoil." 28 All these are the twelve tribes of Israel, and this is what their father spoke to them. And he blessed them; he blessed each one according to his own blessing. 29 Then he charged them and said to them: "I am to be gathered to my people; bury me with my fathers in the cave that is in the field of Ephron the Hittite, 30 in the cave that is in the field of Machpelah, which is before Mamre in the land of Canaan, which Abraham bought with the field of Ephron the Hittite as a possession for a burial place. 31 There they buried Abraham and Sarah his wife, there they buried Isaac and Rebekah his wife, and there I buried Leah. 32 The field and the cave that is there were purchased from the sons of Heth." 33 And when Jacob had finished commanding his sons, he drew his feet up into the bed and breathed his last, and was gathered to his people

CHAPTER 50

1 Then Joseph fell on his father's face, and wept over him, and kissed him. 2 And Joseph commanded his servants the physicians to embalm his father. So the physicians embalmed Israel. 3 Forty days were required for him, for such are the days required for those who are embalmed; and the Egyptians mourned for him seventy days. 4 Now when the days of his mourning were past, Joseph spoke to the household of Pharaoh, saying, "If now I have found favor in your eyes, please speak in the hearing of Pharaoh, saying, 5 'My father made me swear, saying, "Behold, I am dying; in my grave which I dug for myself in the land of Canaan, there you shall bury me." Now therefore, please let me go up and bury my father, and I will come back.'" 6 And Pharaoh said, "Go up and bury your father, as he made you swear." 7 So Joseph went up to bury his father; and with him went up all the servants of Pharaoh, the elders of his house, and all the elders of the land of Egypt, 8 as well as all the house of Joseph, his brothers, and his father's house. Only their little ones, their flocks, and their herds they left in the land of Goshen. 9 And there went up with him both chariots and horsemen, and it was a very great gathering. 10 Then they came to the threshing floor of Atad, which is beyond the Jordan, and they mourned there with a great and very solemn lamentation. He observed seven days of mourning for his father. 11 And when the inhabitants of the land, the Canaanites, saw the mourning at the threshing floor of Atad, they said, "This is a deep mourning of the Egyptians." Therefore its name was called Abel Mizraim, which is beyond the Jordan. 12 So his sons did for him just as he had commanded them. 13 For his sons carried him to the land of Canaan, and buried him in the cave of the field of Machpelah, before Mamre, which Abraham bought with the field from Ephron the Hittite as property for a burial place. 14 And after he had buried his father, Joseph returned to Egypt, he and his brothers and all who went up with him to bury his father. 15 When Joseph's brothers saw that their father was dead, they said, "Perhaps Joseph will hate us, and may actually repay us for all the evil which we did to him." 16 So they sent messengers to Joseph, saying, "Before your father died he commanded, saying, 17 'Thus you shall say to Joseph: "I beg you, please forgive the trespass of your brothers and their sin; for they did evil to you."' Now, please, forgive the trespass of the servants of the God of your father." And Joseph wept when they spoke to him. 18 Then his brothers also went and fell down before his face, and they said, "Behold, we are your servants." 19 Joseph said to them, "Do not be afraid, for am I in the place of God? 20 But as for you, you meant evil against me; but God meant it for good, in order to bring it about as it is this day, to save many people alive. 21 Now therefore, do not be afraid; I will provide for you and your little ones." And he comforted them and spoke kindly to them. 22 So Joseph dwelt in Egypt, he and his father's household. And Joseph lived one hundred and ten years. 23 Joseph saw Ephraim's children to the third generation. The children of Machir, the son of Manasseh, were also brought up on Joseph's knees. 24 And Joseph said to his brethren, "I am dying; but God will surely visit you, and bring you out of this land to the land of which He swore to Abraham, to Isaac, and to Jacob." 25 Then

Joseph took an oath from the children of Israel, saying, "God will surely visit you, and you shall carry up my bones from here." 26 So Joseph died, being one hundred and ten years old; and they embalmed him, and he was put in a coffin in Egypt

2. Exodus

Chapter 1

1 These are the names of the children of Israel who came to Egypt (each man and his family came with Jacob): 2 Reuben, Simeon, Levi, and Judah; 3 Issachar, Zebulun, and Benjamin; 4 Dan, Naphtali, Gad, and Asher. 5 All the descendants who came from Jacob numbered seventy; Joseph was already in Egypt. 6 Now Joseph died, along with all his brothers and all that generation. 7 The children of Israel were fruitful, increased abundantly, multiplied, and grew exceedingly mighty, so that the land was filled with them. 8 Then a new king arose in Egypt, who did not know Joseph. 9 He said to his people, "Behold, the children of Israel are more numerous and mightier than we are. 10 Come, let us deal shrewdly with them, lest they multiply, and in the event of war, join our enemies and fight against us and escape from the land." 11 Therefore, they set taskmasters over them to oppress them with forced labor. They built the cities of Pithom and Raamses for Pharaoh's storage. 12 But the more they oppressed them, the more they multiplied and spread. So the Egyptians dreaded the children of Israel. 13 The Egyptians ruthlessly enslaved the Israelites 14 and made their lives bitter with hard labor in mortar and brick and all kinds of work in the fields. They imposed on them all kinds of harsh labor. 15 The king of Egypt said to the Hebrew midwives, one of whom was named Shiphrah and the other Puah, 16 "When you assist the Hebrew women in childbirth and see them on the delivery stool, if it is a son, kill him; but if it is a daughter, let her live." 17 But the midwives feared God and did not do as the king of Egypt commanded them; they let the boys live. 18 Then the king of Egypt summoned the midwives and asked them, "Why have you done this and allowed the boys to live?" 19 The midwives answered Pharaoh, "The Hebrew women are not like the Egyptian women; they are vigorous and give birth before the midwife arrives." 20 So God was kind to the midwives, and the people multiplied and grew very strong. 21 Because the midwives feared God, He gave them families of their own. 22 Then Pharaoh commanded all his people, saying, "Every son that is born you shall cast into the river, but you shall let every daughter live."

Chapter 2

1 Now a man from the house of Levi married a Levite woman, 2 and she conceived and bore a son. When she saw that he was a fine child, she hid him for three months. 3 But when she could hide him no longer, she got a papyrus basket for him, coated it with tar and pitch, placed the child in it, and put it among the reeds along the bank of the Nile. 4 His sister stood at a distance to see what would happen to him. 5 Pharaoh's daughter went down to the Nile to bathe, and her attendants were walking along the riverbank. She saw the basket among the reeds and sent her female slave to get it. 6 She opened it and saw the baby. He was crying, and she felt sorry for him. "This is one of the Hebrew babies," she said. 7 Then his sister asked Pharaoh's daughter, "Shall I go and get one of the Hebrew women to nurse the baby for you?" 8 "Yes, go," she answered. So the girl went and got the baby's mother. 9 Pharaoh's daughter said to her, "Take this baby and nurse him for me, and I will pay you." So the woman took the baby and nursed him. 10 When the child grew older, she brought him

to Pharaoh's daughter, and he became her son. She named him Moses, saying, "I drew him out of the water." 11 One day, after Moses had grown up, he went out to where his own people were and watched them at their hard labor. He saw an Egyptian beating a Hebrew, one of his own people. 12 Looking this way and that and seeing no one, he killed the Egyptian and hid him in the sand. 13 The next day, he went out and saw two Hebrews fighting. He asked the one in the wrong, "Why are you hitting your fellow Hebrew?" 14 The man said, "Who made you ruler and judge over us? Are you thinking of killing me as you killed the Egyptian?" Then Moses was afraid and thought, "What I did must have become known." 15 When Pharaoh heard of this, he tried to kill Moses, but Moses fled from Pharaoh and went to live in Midian, where he sat down by a well. 16 Now a priest of Midian had seven daughters, and they came to draw water and fill the troughs to water their father's flock. 17 Some shepherds came along and drove them away, but Moses got up and came to their rescue and watered their flock. 18 When the girls returned to Reuel their father, he asked them, "Why have you returned so early today?" 19 They answered, "An Egyptian rescued us from the shepherds. He even drew water for us and watered the flock." 20 "And where is he?" Reuel asked his daughters. "Why did you leave him? Invite him to have something to eat." 21 Moses agreed to stay with the man, who gave his daughter Zipporah to Moses in marriage. 22 Zipporah gave birth to a son, and Moses named him Gershom, saying, "I have become a foreigner in a foreign land." 23 During that long period, the king of Egypt died. The Israelites groaned in their slavery and cried out, and their cry for help because of their slavery went up to God. 24 God heard their groaning, and he remembered his covenant with Abraham, with Isaac, and with Jacob. 25 So God looked on the Israelites and was concerned about them

Chapter 3

1 Now Moses was tending the flock of Jethro, his father-in-law, the priest of Midian. He led the flock to the far side of the wilderness and came to Horeb, the mountain of God. 2 There the angel of the Lord appeared to him in flames of fire from within a bush. Moses saw that though the bush was on fire, it did not burn up. 3 So Moses thought, "I will go over and see this strange sight—why the bush does not burn up." 4 When the Lord saw that he had gone over to look, God called to him from within the bush, "Moses! Moses!" And Moses said, "Here I am." 5 "Do not come any closer," God said. "Take off your sandals, for the place where you are standing is holy ground." 6 Then he said, "I am the God of your father, the God of Abraham, the God of Isaac, and the God of Jacob." At this, Moses hid his face because he was afraid to look at God. 7 The Lord said, "I have indeed seen the misery of my people in Egypt. I have heard them crying out because of their slave drivers, and I am concerned about their suffering. 8 So I have come down to rescue them from the hand of the Egyptians and to bring them up out of that land into a good and spacious land, a land flowing with milk and honey—the home of the Canaanites, Hittites, Amorites, Perizzites, Hivites, and Jebusites. 9 And now the cry of the Israelites has reached me, and I have seen the way the Egyptians are oppressing them. 10 So now, go. I am sending you to Pharaoh to bring my people the Israelites out of Egypt." 11 But Moses said to God, "Who am I that I should go to Pharaoh and bring the Israelites out of Egypt?" 12 And God said, "I will be with you. And this will be the sign to you that it is I who have sent you: When you have brought the people out of Egypt, you will worship God on this mountain." 13 Moses said to

God, "Suppose I go to the Israelites and say to them, 'The God of your fathers has sent me to you,' and they ask me, 'What is his name?' Then what shall I tell them?" 14 God said to Moses, "I am who I am. This is what you are to say to the Israelites: 'I Am has sent me to you.'" 15 God also said to Moses, "Say to the Israelites, 'The Lord, the God of your fathers—the God of Abraham, the God of Isaac, and the God of Jacob—has sent me to you.' This is my name forever, the name you shall call me from generation to generation. 16 Go, assemble the elders of Israel and say to them, 'The Lord, the God of your fathers—the God of Abraham, Isaac, and Jacob—appeared to me and said: I have watched over you and have seen what has been done to you in Egypt. 17 And I have promised to bring you up out of your misery in Egypt into the land of the Canaanites, Hittites, Amorites, Perizzites, Hivites, and Jebusites—a land flowing with milk and honey.' 18 The elders of Israel will listen to you. Then you and the elders are to go to the king of Egypt and say to him, 'The Lord, the God of the Hebrews, has met with us. Let us take a three-day journey into the wilderness to offer sacrifices to the Lord our God.' 19 But I know that the king of Egypt will not let you go unless a mighty hand compels him. 20 So I will stretch out my hand and strike the Egyptians with all the wonders that I will perform among them. After that, he will let you go. 21 And I will make the Egyptians favorably disposed toward this people, so that when you leave, you will not go empty-handed. 22 Every woman is to ask her neighbor and any woman living in her house for articles of silver and gold and for clothing, which you will put on your sons and daughters. And so you will plunder the Egyptians."

Chapter 4

1 Moses answered, "What if they do not believe me or listen to me and say, 'The Lord did not appear to you'?" 2 Then the Lord said to him, "What is that in your hand?" "A staff," he replied. 3 The Lord said, "Throw it on the ground." Moses threw it on the ground, and it became a snake, and he ran from it. 4 Then the Lord said to him, "Reach out your hand and take it by the tail." So Moses reached out and took hold of the snake, and it turned back into a staff in his hand. 5 "This," said the Lord, "is so that they may believe that the Lord, the God of their fathers—the God of Abraham, the God of Isaac, and the God of Jacob—has appeared to you." 6 Then the Lord said, "Put your hand inside your cloak." So Moses put his hand into his cloak, and when he took it out, the skin was leprous—it had become as white as snow. 7 "Now put it back into your cloak," he said. So Moses put his hand back into his cloak, and when he took it out, it was restored like the rest of his flesh. 8 Then the Lord said, "If they do not believe you or pay attention to the first sign, they may believe the second. 9 But if they do not believe these two signs or listen to you, take some water from the Nile and pour it on the dry ground. The water you take from the river will become blood on the ground." 10 Moses said to the Lord, "Pardon your servant, Lord. I have never been eloquent, neither in the past nor since you have spoken to your servant. I am slow of speech and tongue." 11 The Lord said to him, "Who gave human beings their mouths? Who makes them deaf or mute? Who gives them sight or makes them blind? Is it not I, the Lord? 12 Now go; I will help you speak and will teach you what to say." 13 But Moses said, "Pardon your servant, Lord. Please send someone else." 14 Then the Lord's anger burned against Moses, and he said, "What about your brother, Aaron the Levite? I know he can speak well. He is already on his way to meet you, and he will be glad to see you. 15 You shall speak to him and put words in his mouth; I will help both of you speak and will teach you what to do. 16 He will speak to the people for you, and it will be as if he were your mouth and as if you were God to him. 17 But take this staff in your hand so you can perform the signs with it." 18 Then Moses went back to Jethro his father-in-law and said to him, "Let me return to my own people in Egypt to see if any of them are still alive." Jethro said, "Go, and I wish you well." 19 Now the Lord had said to Moses in Midian, "Go back to Egypt, for all those who wanted to kill you are dead." 20 So Moses took his wife and sons, put them on a donkey, and started back to Egypt. And he took the staff of God in his hand. 21 The Lord said to Moses, "When you return to Egypt, see that you perform before Pharaoh all the wonders I have given you the power to do. But I will harden his heart so that he will not let the people go. 22 Then say to Pharaoh, 'This is what the Lord says: Israel is my firstborn son, 23 and I told you, "Let my son go, so he may worship me." But you refused to let him go; so I will kill your firstborn son.'" 24 At a lodging place on the way, the Lord met Moses and was about to kill him. 25 But Zipporah took a flint knife, cut off her son's foreskin, and touched Moses' feet with it. "Surely you are a bridegroom of blood to me," she said. 26 So the Lord let him alone. (At that time she said "bridegroom of blood," referring to circumcision.) 27 The Lord said to Aaron, "Go into the wilderness to meet Moses." So he met Moses at the mountain of God and kissed him. 28 Then Moses told Aaron everything the Lord had sent him to say and also about all the signs he had commanded him to perform. 29 Moses and Aaron brought together all the elders of the Israelites, 30 and Aaron told them everything the Lord had said to Moses. He also performed the signs before the people, 31 and they believed. And when they heard that the Lord was concerned about them and had seen their misery, they bowed down and worshiped

Chapter 5

1 Afterward, Moses and Aaron went to Pharaoh and said, "This is what the Lord, the God of Israel, says: 'Let my people go so that they may hold a festival to me in the wilderness.'" 2 Pharaoh said, "Who is the Lord, that I should obey him and let Israel go? I do not know the Lord, and I will not let Israel go." 3 Then they said, "The God of the Hebrews has met with us. Now let us take a three-day journey into the wilderness to offer sacrifices to the Lord our God, or he may strike us with plagues or with the sword." 4 But the king of Egypt said, "Moses and Aaron, why are you taking the people away from their labor? Get back to your work!" 5 Then Pharaoh said, "Look, the people of the land are now numerous, and you are stopping them from working." 6 That same day Pharaoh gave this order to the slave drivers and overseers in charge of the people: 7 "You are no longer to supply the people with straw for making bricks; let them go and gather their own straw. 8 But require them to make the same number of bricks as before; don't reduce the quota. They are lazy; that is why they are crying out, 'Let us go and sacrifice to our God.' 9 Make the work harder for the people so that they keep working and pay no attention to lies." 10 Then the slave drivers and the overseers went out and said to the people, "This is what Pharaoh says: 'I will not give you any more straw. 11 Go and get your own straw wherever you can find it, but your work will not be reduced at all.'" 12 So the people scattered all over Egypt to gather stubble to use for straw. 13 The slave drivers kept pressing them, saying, "Complete the work required of you for each day, just as when you had straw." 14 And Pharaoh's slave drivers beat the Israelite overseers they had appointed, demanding, "Why haven't you met your quota of bricks yesterday or

today, as before?" 15 Then the Israelite overseers went and appealed to Pharaoh: "Why have you treated your servants this way? 16 Your servants are given no straw, yet we are told, 'Make bricks!' Your servants are being beaten, but the fault is with your own people." 17 Pharaoh said, "Lazy, that's what you are—lazy! That is why you keep saying, 'Let us go and sacrifice to the Lord.' 18 Now get to work. You will not be given any straw, yet you must produce your full quota of bricks." 19 The Israelite overseers realized they were in trouble when they were told, "You are not to reduce the number of bricks required of you for each day." 20 When they left Pharaoh, they found Moses and Aaron waiting to meet them, 21 and they said, "May the Lord look on you and judge you! You have made us obnoxious to Pharaoh and his officials and have put a sword in their hand to kill us." 22 Moses returned to the Lord and said, "Why, Lord, why have you brought trouble on this people? Is this why you sent me? 23 Ever since I went to Pharaoh to speak in your name, he has brought trouble on this people, and you have not rescued your people at all."

Chapter 6

1 Then the Lord said to Moses, "Now you will see what I will do to Pharaoh, for with a strong hand he will let them go and be forced out of his land." 2 God spoke to Moses again and said to him, "I am the Lord, 3 and I appeared to Abraham, Isaac, and Jacob as God Almighty, but by my name, Jehovah, I did not make myself known to them. 4 Moreover, I established my covenant with them to give them the land of Canaan, the land of their pilgrimage, where they were strangers. 5 I have also heard the groaning of the children of Israel, whom the Egyptians hold in bondage, and I have remembered my covenant. 6 Therefore say to the children of Israel, 'I am the Lord, and I will bring you out from under the burdens of the Egyptians, and I will deliver you from their bondage, and I will redeem you with an outstretched arm and with great judgments. 7 I will take you as my people, and I will be your God. Then you shall know that I am the Lord your God, who has brought you out from under the burdens of the Egyptians. 8 I will bring you into the land which I swore to give to Abraham, Isaac, and Jacob, and I will give it to you as a possession: I am the Lord.'" 9 Moses said this to the children of Israel, but they did not listen to Moses because of their anguish of spirit and cruel bondage. 10 Then the Lord spoke to Moses, saying, 11 "Go and speak to Pharaoh, king of Egypt, that he may let the children of Israel go out of his land." 12 But Moses spoke before the Lord, saying, "Behold, the children of Israel will not listen to me; how then shall Pharaoh listen to me, a man of uncircumcised lips?" 13 Then the Lord spoke to Moses and Aaron and charged them to go to the children of Israel and to Pharaoh, king of Egypt, to bring the children of Israel out of the land of Egypt. 14 These are the heads of their fathers' houses: the sons of Reuben, the firstborn of Israel, are Hanoch, Pallu, Hezron, and Carmi; these are the families of Reuben. 15 The sons of Simeon: Jemuel, Jamin, Ohad, Jachin, Zohar, and Shaul the son of a Canaanite woman; these are the families of Simeon. 16 These are the names of the sons of Levi according to their generations: Gershon, Kohath, and Merari (and the years of Levi's life were 137). 17 The sons of Gershon: Libni and Shimei, according to their families. 18 The sons of Kohath: Amram, Izhar, Hebron, and Uzziel (Kohath lived 133 years). 19 The sons of Merari: Mahli and Mushi; these are the families of Levi according to their generations. 20 Amram took Jochebed, his father's sister, as his wife, and she bore him Aaron and Moses (and Amram lived 137 years). 21 The sons of Izhar: Korah, Nepheg, and Zichri. 22 The sons of Uzziel: Mishael, Elzaphan, and

Sithri. 23 Aaron took Elisheba, the daughter of Amminadab, sister of Nahshon, as his wife, and she bore him Nadab, Abihu, Eleazar, and Ithamar. 24 The sons of Korah: Assir, Elkanah, and Abiasaph; these are the families of the Korahites. 25 Eleazar, the son of Aaron, took one of the daughters of Putiel as his wife, and she bore him Phinehas; these are the heads of the fathers' houses of the Levites according to their families. 26 These are the same Aaron and Moses to whom the Lord said, "Bring the children of Israel out of the land of Egypt according to their armies." 27 These are the ones who spoke to Pharaoh, king of Egypt, to bring the children of Israel out of Egypt—these are the same Moses and Aaron. 28 When the Lord spoke to Moses in the land of Egypt, 29 He said to him, "I am the Lord; speak to Pharaoh, king of Egypt, all that I say to you." 30 But Moses said to the Lord, "Behold, I am of uncircumcised lips, and how shall Pharaoh listen to me?"

Chapter 7

1 Then the Lord said to Moses, "See, I have made you like God to Pharaoh, and your brother Aaron shall be your prophet. 2 You shall speak all that I command you, and Aaron your brother shall speak to Pharaoh to let the children of Israel go out of his land. 3 But I will harden Pharaoh's heart and multiply my signs and wonders in the land of Egypt. 4 Pharaoh will not listen to you, so I will lay my hand upon Egypt and bring my people, the children of Israel, out of the land of Egypt by great judgments. 5 The Egyptians shall know that I am the Lord when I stretch out my hand over Egypt and bring the children of Israel out from among them." 6 Moses and Aaron did as the Lord commanded them. 7 Moses was eighty years old and Aaron eighty-three when they spoke to Pharaoh. 8 The Lord spoke to Moses and Aaron, saying, 9 "When Pharaoh speaks to you, saying, 'Show a miracle for yourselves,' then you shall say to Aaron, 'Take your rod and cast it before Pharaoh, and it will become a serpent.'" 10 So Moses and Aaron went to Pharaoh, and they did so just as the Lord commanded. Aaron cast down his rod before Pharaoh and his servants, and it became a serpent. 11 Then Pharaoh also called the wise men and the sorcerers, and they also, the magicians of Egypt, did the same with their enchantments. 12 Every man threw down his rod, and they became serpents. But Aaron's rod swallowed up their rods. 13 Yet Pharaoh's heart was hardened, and he did not listen to them, just as the Lord had said. 14 Then the Lord said to Moses, "Pharaoh's heart is stubborn; he refuses to let the people go. 15 Go to Pharaoh in the morning, as he goes out to the water. Stand by the river's bank to meet him, and take in your hand the rod which was turned into a serpent. 16 You shall say to him, 'The Lord, the God of the Hebrews, has sent me to you, saying, "Let my people go, that they may serve me in the wilderness," but indeed, until now you would not hear. 17 Thus says the Lord: "By this, you shall know that I am the Lord: Behold, I will strike the waters which are in the river with the rod that is in my hand, and they shall be turned to blood. 18 The fish that are in the river shall die, the river shall stink, and the Egyptians will loathe to drink the water of the river."'" 19 Then the Lord spoke to Moses, "Say to Aaron, 'Take your rod and stretch out your hand over the waters of Egypt, over their streams, over their rivers, over their ponds, and over all their pools of water, that they may become blood. There shall be blood throughout all the land of Egypt, both in vessels of wood and in vessels of stone.'" 20 Moses and Aaron did so, just as the Lord commanded. He lifted up the rod and struck the waters that were in the river, in the sight of Pharaoh and in the sight of his servants. All

the waters that were in the river turned to blood. 21 The fish that were in the river died, the river stank, and the Egyptians could not drink the water of the river. There was blood throughout all the land of Egypt. 22 Then the magicians of Egypt did so with their enchantments, and Pharaoh's heart was hardened. He did not listen to them, just as the Lord had said. 23 Pharaoh turned and went into his house, and neither did he take this to heart. 24 All the Egyptians dug around the river for water to drink because they could not drink the water of the river. 25 Seven days passed after the Lord had struck the river

Chapter 8

1 Then the Lord said to Moses, "Go to Pharaoh and say to him, 'Thus says the Lord: "Let my people go, that they may serve me. 2 But if you refuse to let them go, behold, I will smite all your territory with frogs. 3 The river shall bring forth frogs abundantly, which shall go up and come into your house, into your bedroom, on your bed, into the houses of your servants, on your people, into your ovens, and into your kneading bowls. 4 The frogs shall come up on you, on your people, and on all your servants."'" 5 The Lord said to Moses, "Say to Aaron, 'Stretch out your hand with your rod over the streams, over the rivers, and over the ponds, and cause frogs to come up on the land of Egypt.'" 6 So Aaron stretched out his hand over the waters of Egypt, and the frogs came up and covered the land of Egypt. 7 The magicians did so with their enchantments and brought up frogs on the land of Egypt. 8 Then Pharaoh called for Moses and Aaron and said, "Entreat the Lord that He may take away the frogs from me and from my people; and I will let the people go, that they may sacrifice to the Lord." 9 Moses said to Pharaoh, "Accept the honor of saying when I shall intercede for you, for your servants, and for your people, to destroy the frogs from you and your houses, that they may remain in the river only." 10 So he said, "Tomorrow." And he said, "Let it be according to your word, that you may know that there is no one like the Lord our God. 11 The frogs shall depart from you, from your houses, from your servants, and from your people. They shall remain in the river only." 12 Then Moses and Aaron went out from Pharaoh, and Moses cried out to the Lord concerning the frogs which He had brought against Pharaoh. 13 So the Lord did according to the word of Moses. The frogs died out of the houses, out of the courtyards, and out of the fields. 14 They gathered them together in heaps, and the land stank. 15 But when Pharaoh saw that there was relief, he hardened his heart and did not heed them, as the Lord had said. 16 So the Lord said to Moses, "Say to Aaron, 'Stretch out your rod and strike the dust of the land, so that it may become lice throughout all the land of Egypt.'" 17 They did so. Aaron stretched out his hand with his rod and struck the dust of the earth, and it became lice on man and beast. All the dust of the land became lice throughout all the land of Egypt. 18 Now the magicians so worked with their enchantments to bring forth lice, but they could not. So there were lice on man and beast. 19 Then the magicians said to Pharaoh, "This is the finger of God." But Pharaoh's heart was hardened, and he did not heed them, just as the Lord had said. 20 The Lord said to Moses, "Rise early in the morning and stand before Pharaoh as he comes out to the water. Then say to him, 'Thus says the Lord: "Let my people go, that they may serve me. 21 Or else, if you will not let my people go, behold, I will send swarms of flies on you and your servants, on your people, and into your houses. The houses of the Egyptians shall be full of swarms of flies, and also the ground on which they stand. 22 And in that day I will set apart the land of Goshen, in which my people dwell, that no swarms of flies shall be there, in order that you may know that I am the Lord in the midst of the land. 23 I will make a difference between my people and your people. Tomorrow this sign shall be."'" 24 The Lord did so. Thick swarms of flies came into the house of Pharaoh, into his servants' houses, and into all the land of Egypt. The land was corrupted because of the swarms of flies. 25 Then Pharaoh called for Moses and Aaron and said, "Go, sacrifice to your God in the land." 26 And Moses said, "It is not right to do so, for we would be sacrificing the abomination of the Egyptians to the Lord our God. If we sacrifice the abomination of the Egyptians before their eyes, then will they not stone us? 27 We will go three days' journey into the wilderness and sacrifice to the Lord our God as He will command us." 28 So Pharaoh said, "I will let you go, that you may sacrifice to the Lord your God in the wilderness; only you shall not go very far away. Intercede for me." 29 Then Moses said, "Indeed I am going out from you, and I will entreat the Lord that the swarms of flies may depart tomorrow from Pharaoh, from his servants, and from his people. But let Pharaoh not deal deceitfully anymore in not letting the people go to sacrifice to the Lord." 30 So Moses went out from Pharaoh and entreated the Lord. 31 The Lord did according to the word of Moses. He removed the swarms of flies from Pharaoh, from his servants, and from his people. Not one remained. 32 But Pharaoh hardened his heart at this time also; neither would he let the people go

Chapter 9

1 Then the Lord said to Moses, "Go in to Pharaoh and tell him, 'Thus says the Lord God of the Hebrews: "Let my people go, that they may serve me. 2 For if you refuse to let them go and still hold them, 3 behold, the hand of the Lord will be on your cattle in the field, on the horses, on the donkeys, on the camels, on the oxen, and on the sheep—a very severe pestilence. 4 The Lord will make a difference between the livestock of Israel and the livestock of Egypt. Nothing shall die of all that belongs to the children of Israel."'" 5 Then the Lord appointed a set time, saying, "Tomorrow the Lord will do this thing in the land." 6 So the Lord did this thing on the next day, and all the livestock of Egypt died, but of the livestock of the children of Israel, not one died. 7 Then Pharaoh sent, and indeed, not even one of the livestock of the Israelites was dead. But the heart of Pharaoh became hard, and he did not let the people go. 8 So the Lord said to Moses and Aaron, "Take for yourselves handfuls of ashes from a furnace, and let Moses scatter it toward the heavens in the sight of Pharaoh. 9 It will become fine dust in all the land of Egypt, and it will cause boils that break out in sores on man and beast throughout all the land of Egypt." 10 Then they took ashes from the furnace and stood before Pharaoh, and Moses scattered them toward heaven. They caused boils that break out in sores on man and beast. 11 The magicians could not stand before Moses because of the boils, for the boils were on the magicians and on all the Egyptians. 12 But the Lord hardened the heart of Pharaoh, and he did not heed them, just as the Lord had spoken to Moses. 13 Then the Lord said to Moses, "Rise early in the morning and stand before Pharaoh, and say to him, 'Thus says the Lord God of the Hebrews: "Let my people go, that they may serve me, 14 for at this time I will send all my plagues to your very heart, on your servants, and on your people, that you may know that there is none like me in all the earth. 15 Now if I had stretched out my hand and struck you and your people with pestilence, then you would have been cut off from the earth. 16 But indeed for this purpose I have raised you up, that I may show my power in

you, and that my name may be declared in all the earth. 17 As yet you exalt yourself against my people in that you will not let them go. 18 Behold, tomorrow about this time I will cause very heavy hail to rain down, such as has not been in Egypt since its founding until now. 19 Therefore send now and gather your livestock and all that you have in the field, for the hail shall come down on every man and every animal which is found in the field and is not brought home, and they shall die.”'" 20 He who feared the word of the Lord among the servants of Pharaoh made his servants and his livestock flee to the houses. 21 But he who did not regard the word of the Lord left his servants and his livestock in the field. 22 Then the Lord said to Moses, "Stretch out your hand toward heaven, that there may be hail in all the land of Egypt—on man, on beast, and on every herb of the field, throughout the land of Egypt." 23 And Moses stretched out his rod toward heaven, and the Lord sent thunder and hail, and fire darted to the ground. The Lord rained hail on the land of Egypt. 24 So there was hail, and fire mingled with the hail, so very heavy that there was none like it in all the land of Egypt since it became a nation. 25 And the hail struck throughout the whole land of Egypt, all that was in the field, both man and beast; and the hail struck every herb of the field and broke every tree of the field. 26 Only in the land of Goshen, where the children of Israel were, there was no hail. 27 Pharaoh sent and called for Moses and Aaron and said to them, "I have sinned this time. The Lord is righteous, and my people and I are wicked. 28 Entreat the Lord, for it is enough, that there be no more mighty thundering and hail, for it is enough. I will let you go, and you shall stay no longer." 29 So Moses said to him, "As soon as I have gone out of the city, I will spread out my hands to the Lord. The thunder will cease, and there will be no more hail, that you may know that the earth is the Lord's. 30 But as for you and your servants, I know that you will not yet fear the Lord God." 31 The flax and the barley were struck, for the barley was in the head and the flax was in bud. 32 But the wheat and the spelt were not struck, for they are late crops. 33 So Moses went out of the city from Pharaoh and spread out his hands to the Lord. Then the thunder and the hail ceased, and the rain was not poured on the earth. 34 When Pharaoh saw that the rain, the hail, and the thunder had ceased, he sinned yet more, and he hardened his heart, he and his servants. 35 So Pharaoh's heart was hard; neither would he let the children of Israel go, as the Lord had spoken by Moses

Chapter 10

1 The Lord said to Moses, "Go in to Pharaoh, for I have hardened his heart and the hearts of his servants, that I may show these signs of mine before him, 2 and that you may tell in the hearing of your son and your grandson the mighty things I have done in Egypt and my signs which I have done among them, that you may know that I am the Lord." 3 So Moses and Aaron went to Pharaoh and said to him, "Thus says the Lord God of the Hebrews: 'How long will you refuse to humble yourself before me? Let my people go, that they may serve me. 4 Or else, if you refuse to let my people go, behold, tomorrow I will bring locusts into your territory. 5 They shall cover the face of the earth so that no one will be able to see the earth. They shall eat the residue of what is left, which remains to you from the hail, and they shall eat every tree which grows up for you out of the field. 6 They shall fill your houses, the houses of all your servants, and the houses of all the Egyptians, which neither your fathers nor your fathers' fathers have seen since the day that they were on the earth to this day.'" And he turned and went out from Pharaoh. 7 Then

Pharaoh's servants said to him, "How long shall this man be a snare to us? Let the men go, that they may serve the Lord their God. Do you not yet know that Egypt is destroyed?" 8 So Moses and Aaron were brought again to Pharaoh, and he said to them, "Go, serve the Lord your God. Who are the ones that are going? 9 Moses said, "We will go with our young and our old; with our sons and our daughters, with our flocks and our herds we will go, for we must hold a feast to the Lord." 10 Then he said to them, "The Lord had better be with you when I let you and your little ones go! Beware, for evil is ahead of you. 11 Not so! Go now, you who are men, and serve the Lord, for that is what you desired." And they were driven out from Pharaoh's presence. 12 Then the Lord said to Moses, "Stretch out your hand over the land of Egypt for the locusts, that they may come upon the land of Egypt and eat every herb of the land—all that the hail has left." 13 So Moses stretched out his rod over the land of Egypt, and the Lord brought an east wind on the land all that day and all that night. When it was morning, the east wind brought the locusts. 14 The locusts went up over all the land of Egypt and rested on all the territory of Egypt. They were very severe; previously there had been no such locusts as they, nor shall there be such after them. 15 For they covered the face of the whole earth so that the land was darkened, and they ate every herb of the land and all the fruit of the trees which the hail had left. So there remained nothing green on the trees or on the plants of the field throughout all the land of Egypt. 16 Then Pharaoh called for Moses and Aaron in haste and said, "I have sinned against the Lord your God and against you. 17 Now therefore, please forgive my sin only this once, and entreat the Lord your God, that He may take away from me this death only." 18 So he went out from Pharaoh and entreated the Lord. 19 The Lord turned a very strong west wind, which took the locusts away and blew them into the Red Sea. There remained not one locust in all the territory of Egypt. 20 But the Lord hardened Pharaoh's heart, and he did not let the children of Israel go. 21 Then the Lord said to Moses, "Stretch out your hand toward heaven, that there may be darkness over the land of Egypt, darkness which may even be felt." 22 So Moses stretched out his hand toward heaven, and there was thick darkness in all the land of Egypt for three days. 23 They did not see one another, nor did anyone rise from his place for three days. But all the children of Israel had light in their dwellings. 24 Then Pharaoh called to Moses and said, "Go, serve the Lord; only let your flocks and your herds be kept back. Let your little ones also go with you." 25 But Moses said, "You must also give us sacrifices and burnt offerings, that we may sacrifice to the Lord our God. 26 Our livestock also shall go with us; not a hoof shall be left behind. For we must take some of them to serve the Lord our God, and even we do not know with what we must serve the Lord until we arrive there." 27 But the Lord hardened Pharaoh's heart, and he would not let them go. 28 Then Pharaoh said to him, "Get away from me! Take heed to yourself and see my face no more! For in the day you see my face you shall die!" 29 So Moses said, "You have spoken well. I will never see your face again."

Chapter 11

1 Now the LORD said to Moses, "I will bring one more plague upon Pharaoh and Egypt. After that, he will let you go from here; when he lets you go, he will surely drive you out completely. 2 Speak now to the people, that every man may ask his neighbor and every woman her neighbor for articles of silver and gold." 3 The LORD gave the people favor in the sight of the Egyptians. Moreover, the man Moses was very great in the land of Egypt, in the sight of Pharaoh's servants

and the people. 4 Moses said, "Thus says the LORD: About midnight I will go out into the midst of Egypt. 5 All the firstborn in the land of Egypt shall die, from the firstborn of Pharaoh who sits on his throne to the firstborn of the female servant who is behind the handmill, and all the firstborn of the animals. 6 There shall be a great cry throughout all the land of Egypt, such as there has never been nor ever will be again. 7 But against any of the children of Israel, not even a dog shall bark, whether against man or beast, that you may know that the LORD makes a distinction between Egypt and Israel. 8 All these servants of yours will come down to me and bow down before me, saying, 'Go out, you and all the people who follow you.' After that, I will go out." Then he went out from Pharaoh in great anger. 9 The LORD said to Moses, "Pharaoh will not listen to you, so that my wonders may be multiplied in the land of Egypt." 10 Moses and Aaron performed all these wonders before Pharaoh, but the LORD hardened Pharaoh's heart, and he did not let the children of Israel go out of his land

Chapter 12

1 The LORD spoke to Moses and Aaron in the land of Egypt, saying, 2 "This month shall be for you the beginning of months; it shall be the first month of the year for you. 3 Speak to all the congregation of Israel, saying, 'On the tenth day of this month, every man shall take a lamb for his household, a lamb for each house. 4 If the household is too small for a lamb, then he and his nearest neighbor shall take one according to the number of persons; according to what each can eat, you shall make your count for the lamb. 5 Your lamb shall be without blemish, a male a year old. You may take it from the sheep or from the goats. 6 You shall keep it until the fourteenth day of this month, then the whole assembly of the congregation of Israel shall kill it at twilight. 7 They shall take some of the blood and put it on the two doorposts and the lintel of the houses in which they eat it. 8 They shall eat the flesh that night, roasted with fire, and unleavened bread; with bitter herbs they shall eat it. 9 Do not eat any of it raw or boiled in water, but roasted with fire, its head with its legs and inner parts. 10 You shall let none of it remain until the morning; anything that remains until the morning you shall burn. 11 In this manner you shall eat it: with your belt fastened, your sandals on your feet, and your staff in your hand. You shall eat it in haste. It is the LORD's Passover. 12 For I will pass through the land of Egypt that night, and I will strike all the firstborn in the land of Egypt, both man and beast, and on all the gods of Egypt, I will execute judgments: I am the LORD. 13 The blood shall be a sign for you on the houses where you are. When I see the blood, I will pass over you, and no plague will befall you to destroy you when I strike the land of Egypt. 14 This day shall be for you a memorial day, and you shall keep it as a feast to the LORD; throughout your generations, you shall keep it as a feast, a statute forever. 15 For seven days you shall eat unleavened bread. On the first day, you shall remove leaven out of your houses, for if anyone eats what is leavened from the first day until the seventh day, that person shall be cut off from Israel. 16 On the first day, you shall hold a holy assembly, and on the seventh day, a holy assembly. No work shall be done on those days. But what everyone needs to eat, that alone may be prepared by you. 17 You shall observe the Feast of Unleavened Bread, for on this very day I brought your hosts out of the land of Egypt. Therefore you shall observe this day throughout your generations as a statute forever. 18 In the first month, from the fourteenth day of the month at evening, you shall eat unleavened bread until the twenty-first day of the month at evening. 19 For seven days, no leaven shall be found in your houses. For if anyone eats what is leavened, that person shall be cut off from the congregation of Israel, whether he is a sojourner or a native of the land. 20 You shall eat nothing leavened; in all your dwelling places you shall eat unleavened bread." 21 Then Moses called all the elders of Israel and said to them, "Go and select lambs for yourselves according to your clans and kill the Passover lamb. 22 Take a bunch of hyssop, dip it in the blood that is in the basin, and touch the lintel and the two doorposts with the blood that is in the basin. None of you shall go out of the door of his house until the morning. 23 For the LORD will pass through to strike the Egyptians. When he sees the blood on the lintel and on the two doorposts, the LORD will pass over the door and will not allow the destroyer to enter your houses to strike you. 24 You shall observe this rite as a statute for you and for your sons forever. 25 When you come to the land that the LORD will give you, as he has promised, you shall keep this service. 26 When your children say to you, 'What do you mean by this service?' 27 you shall say, 'It is the sacrifice of the LORD's Passover, for he passed over the houses of the people of Israel in Egypt when he struck the Egyptians but spared our houses.'" The people bowed their heads and worshiped. 28 Then the people of Israel went and did so; as the LORD had commanded Moses and Aaron, so they did. 29 At midnight, the LORD struck down all the firstborn in the land of Egypt, from the firstborn of Pharaoh who sat on his throne to the firstborn of the captive who was in the dungeon and all the firstborn of the livestock. 30 Pharaoh rose up in the night, he and all his servants and all the Egyptians. There was a great cry in Egypt, for there was not a house where someone was not dead. 31 Then he summoned Moses and Aaron by night and said, "Up, go out from among my people, both you and the people of Israel, and go, serve the LORD as you have said. 32 Take your flocks and your herds, as you have said, and be gone, and bless me also!" 33 The Egyptians were urgent with the people to send them out of the land in haste, for they said, "We shall all be dead." 34 So the people took their dough before it was leavened, their kneading bowls being bound up in their cloaks on their shoulders. 35 The people of Israel had also done as Moses told them, for they had asked the Egyptians for silver and gold jewelry and for clothing. 36 The LORD had given the people favor in the sight of the Egyptians, so that they let them have what they asked. Thus they plundered the Egyptians. 37 The people of Israel journeyed from Rameses to Succoth, about six hundred thousand men on foot, besides women and children. 38 A mixed multitude also went up with them, and very much livestock, both flocks and herds. 39 They baked unleavened cakes of the dough that they had brought out of Egypt, for it was not leavened because they were thrust out of Egypt and could not wait, nor had they prepared any provisions for themselves. 40 The time that the people of Israel lived in Egypt was 430 years. 41 At the end of 430 years, on that very day, all the hosts of the LORD went out from the land of Egypt. 42 It was a night of watching by the LORD to bring them out of the land of Egypt; so this same night is a night of watching kept to the LORD by all the people of Israel throughout their generations. 43 The LORD said to Moses and Aaron, "This is the statute of the Passover: no foreigner shall eat of it, 44 but every slave that is bought for money may eat of it after you have circumcised him. 45 No foreigner or hired worker may eat of it. 46 It shall be eaten in one house; you shall not take any of the flesh outside the house, and you shall not break any of its bones. 47 All the

congregation of Israel shall keep it. 48 If a stranger shall sojourn with you and would keep the Passover to the LORD, let all his males be circumcised. Then he may come near and keep it; he shall be as a native of the land. But no uncircumcised person shall eat of it. 49 There shall be one law for the native and for the stranger who sojourns among you." 50 All the people of Israel did just as the LORD commanded Moses and Aaron. 51 On that very day, the LORD brought the people of Israel out of the land of Egypt by their hosts

Chapter 13

1 The LORD spoke to Moses, saying, 2 "Consecrate to me all the firstborn. Whatever is the first to open the womb among the people of Israel, both of man and of beast, is mine." 3 Then Moses said to the people, "Remember this day, in which you came out from Egypt, out of the house of slavery, for by a strong hand the LORD brought you out from this place. No leavened bread shall be eaten. 4 Today, in the month of Abib, you are going out. 5 When the LORD brings you into the land of the Canaanites, the Hittites, the Amorites, the Hivites, and the Jebusites, which he swore to your fathers to give you, a land flowing with milk and honey, you shall keep this service in this month. 6 Seven days you shall eat unleavened bread, and on the seventh day, there shall be a feast to the LORD. 7 Unleavened bread shall be eaten for seven days. No leavened bread shall be seen with you, and no leaven shall be seen with you in all your territory. 8 You shall tell your son on that day, 'It is because of what the LORD did for me when I came out of Egypt.' 9 It shall be to you as a sign on your hand and as a memorial between your eyes, that the law of the LORD may be in your mouth. For with a strong hand the LORD has brought you out of Egypt. 10 You shall therefore keep this statute at its appointed time from year to year. 11 When the LORD brings you into the land of the Canaanites, as he swore to you and your fathers, and shall give it to you, 12 you shall set apart to the LORD all that first opens the womb. All the firstborn of your animals that are males shall be the LORD's. 13 Every firstborn of a donkey you shall redeem with a lamb, or if you will not redeem it, you shall break its neck. Every firstborn of man among your sons you shall redeem. 14 When in time to come your son asks you, 'What does this mean?' you shall say to him, 'By a strong hand the LORD brought us out of Egypt, from the house of slavery. 15 For when Pharaoh stubbornly refused to let us go, the LORD killed all the firstborn in the land of Egypt, both the firstborn of man and the firstborn of animals. Therefore I sacrifice to the LORD all the males that first open the womb, but all the firstborn of my sons I redeem.' 16 It shall be as a mark on your hand or frontlets between your eyes, for by a strong hand the LORD brought us out of Egypt." 17 When Pharaoh let the people go, God did not lead them by the way of the land of the Philistines, although that was near. For God said, "Lest the people change their minds when they see war and return to Egypt." 18 But God led the people around by the way of the wilderness toward the Red Sea. The people of Israel went up out of the land of Egypt equipped for battle. 19 Moses took the bones of Joseph with him, for Joseph had made the sons of Israel solemnly swear, saying, "God will surely visit you, and you shall carry up my bones with you from here." 20 They moved on from Succoth and encamped at Etham, on the edge of the wilderness. 21 The LORD went before them by day in a pillar of cloud to lead them along the way, and by night in a pillar of fire to give them light, that they might travel by day and by night. 22 The pillar of cloud by day and the pillar of fire by night did not depart from before the people

Chapter 14

1 Then the LORD spoke to Moses, saying, 2 "Tell the people of Israel to turn back and encamp in front of Pi-hahiroth, between Migdol and the sea, in front of Baal-zephon. You shall encamp facing it, by the sea. 3 For Pharaoh will say of the people of Israel, 'They are wandering in the land; the wilderness has shut them in.' 4 I will harden Pharaoh's heart, and he will pursue them. I will get glory over Pharaoh and all his host, and the Egyptians shall know that I am the LORD." And they did so. 5 When the king of Egypt was told that the people had fled, the mind of Pharaoh and his servants was changed toward the people, and they said, "What is this we have done, that we have let Israel go from serving us?" 6 So he made ready his chariot and took his army with him, 7 and took six hundred chosen chariots and all the other chariots of Egypt with officers over all of them. 8 The LORD hardened the heart of Pharaoh king of Egypt, and he pursued the people of Israel while the people of Israel were going out defiantly. 9 The Egyptians pursued them, all Pharaoh's horses and chariots and his horsemen and his army, and overtook them encamped at the sea, by Pi-hahiroth, in front of Baal-zephon. 10 When Pharaoh drew near, the people of Israel lifted up their eyes, and behold, the Egyptians were marching after them, and they feared greatly. The people of Israel cried out to the LORD. 11 They said to Moses, "Is it because there are no graves in Egypt that you have taken us away to die in the wilderness? What have you done to us by bringing us out of Egypt? 12 Is not this what we said to you in Egypt: 'Leave us alone that we may serve the Egyptians'? For it would have been better for us to serve the Egyptians than to die in the wilderness." 13 Moses said to the people, "Fear not, stand firm, and see the salvation of the LORD, which he will work for you today. For the Egyptians whom you see today, you shall never see again. 14 The LORD will fight for you, and you have only to be silent." 15 The LORD said to Moses, "Why do you cry to me? Tell the people of Israel to go forward. 16 Lift up your staff, and stretch out your hand over the sea and divide it, that the people of Israel may go through the sea on dry ground. 17 I will harden the hearts of the Egyptians so that they shall go in after them, and I will get glory over Pharaoh and all his host, his chariots, and his horsemen. 18 The Egyptians shall know that I am the LORD when I have gotten glory over Pharaoh, his chariots, and his horsemen." 19 Then the angel of God who was going before the host of Israel moved and went behind them, and the pillar of cloud moved from before them and stood behind them, 20 coming between the host of Egypt and the host of Israel. There was the cloud and the darkness, and it lit up the night without one coming near the other all night. 21 Then Moses stretched out his hand over the sea, and the LORD drove the sea back by a strong east wind all night and made the sea dry land, and the waters were divided. 22 The people of Israel went into the midst of the sea on dry ground, the waters being a wall to them on their right hand and on their left. 23 The Egyptians pursued and went in after them into the midst of the sea, all Pharaoh's horses, his chariots, and his horsemen. 24 In the morning watch, the LORD in the pillar of fire and of cloud looked down on the Egyptian forces and threw the Egyptian forces into a panic, 25 clogging their chariot wheels so that they drove heavily. The Egyptians said, "Let us flee from before Israel, for the LORD fights for them against the Egyptians." 26 Then the LORD said to Moses, "Stretch out your hand over the sea, that the water may come back upon the Egyptians, upon their chariots, and upon their horsemen." 27 So Moses stretched out his hand over

the sea, and the sea returned to its normal course when the morning appeared. As the Egyptians fled into it, the LORD threw the Egyptians into the midst of the sea. 28 The waters returned and covered the chariots and the horsemen; of all the host of Pharaoh that had followed them into the sea, not one of them remained. 29 But the people of Israel walked on dry ground through the sea, the waters being a wall to them on their right hand and on their left. 30 Thus the LORD saved Israel that day from the hand of the Egyptians, and Israel saw the Egyptians dead on the seashore. 31 Israel saw the great power that the LORD used against the Egyptians, so the people feared the LORD, and they believed in the LORD and in his servant Moses

Chapter 15

1 Then Moses and the people of Israel sang this song to the LORD, saying, "I will sing to the LORD, for he has triumphed gloriously; the horse and his rider he has thrown into the sea. 2 The LORD is my strength and my song, and he has become my salvation; this is my God, and I will praise him, my father's God, and I will exalt him. 3 The LORD is a man of war; the LORD is his name. 4 Pharaoh's chariots and his host he cast into the sea, and his chosen officers were sunk in the Red Sea. 5 The floods covered them; they went down into the depths like a stone. 6 Your right hand, O LORD, glorious in power, your right hand, O LORD, shatters the enemy. 7 In the greatness of your majesty, you overthrow your adversaries; you send out your fury; it consumes them like stubble. 8 At the blast of your nostrils, the waters piled up; the floods stood up in a heap; the deeps congealed in the heart of the sea. 9 The enemy said, 'I will pursue, I will overtake, I will divide the spoil, my desire shall have its fill of them. I will draw my sword; my hand shall destroy them.' 10 You blew with your wind; the sea covered them; they sank like lead in the mighty waters. 11 Who is like you, O LORD, among the gods? Who is like you, majestic in holiness, awesome in glorious deeds, doing wonders? 12 You stretched out your right hand; the earth swallowed them. 13 You have led in your steadfast love the people whom you have redeemed; you have guided them by your strength to your holy abode. 14 The peoples have heard; they tremble; pangs have seized the inhabitants of Philistia. 15 Now are the chiefs of Edom dismayed; trembling seizes the leaders of Moab; all the inhabitants of Canaan have melted away. 16 Terror and dread fall upon them; because of the greatness of your arm, they are still as a stone, till your people, O LORD, pass by, till the people pass by whom you have purchased. 17 You will bring them in and plant them on your own mountain, the place, O LORD, which you have made for your abode, the sanctuary, O Lord, which your hands have established. 18 The LORD will reign forever and ever." 19 When the horses of Pharaoh with his chariots and his horsemen went into the sea, the LORD brought back the waters of the sea upon them, but the people of Israel walked on dry ground in the midst of the sea. 20 Then Miriam the prophetess, the sister of Aaron, took a tambourine in her hand, and all the women went out after her with tambourines and dancing. 21 And Miriam sang to them: "Sing to the LORD, for he has triumphed gloriously; the horse and his rider he has thrown into the sea." 22 Then Moses made Israel set out from the Red Sea, and they went into the wilderness of Shur. They went three days in the wilderness and found no water. 23 When they came to Marah, they could not drink the water of Marah because it was bitter; therefore it was named Marah. 24 The people grumbled against Moses, saying, "What shall we drink?" 25 He cried to the LORD, and the LORD showed him a log, and he threw it into the

water, and the water became sweet. There the LORD made for them a statute and a rule, and there he tested them, 26 saying, "If you will diligently listen to the voice of the LORD your God, and do that which is right in his eyes, and give ear to his commandments and keep all his statutes, I will put none of the diseases on you that I put on the Egyptians, for I am the LORD, your healer." 27 Then they came to Elim, where there were twelve springs of water and seventy palm trees, and they encamped there by the water

Chapter 16

1 Then the whole community of the children of Israel departed from Elim and came to the wilderness of Sin, which is between Elim and Sinai, on the fifteenth day of the second month after their departure from the land of Egypt. 2 The whole community of the children of Israel murmured against Moses and Aaron in the wilderness. 3 The children of Israel said to them, "Oh, if we had died by the hand of the LORD in the land of Egypt, when we sat by the pots of meat and ate bread to the full! For you have brought us out into this whole wilderness to kill this whole assembly with hunger." 4 Then the LORD said to Moses, "Behold, I will rain bread from heaven for you. The people shall go out and gather a day's portion every day, that I may test them, whether they will walk in my law or not. 5 On the sixth day, when they prepare what they bring in, it will be twice as much as they gather daily." 6 So Moses and Aaron said to all the children of Israel, "At evening you shall know that the LORD has brought you out of the land of Egypt, 7 and in the morning you shall see the glory of the LORD, for he hears your murmurings against the LORD. What are we, that you murmur against us?" 8 And Moses said, "The LORD will give you meat to eat in the evening and bread to the full in the morning, for the LORD hears your murmurings that you murmur against him. What are we? Your murmurings are not against us but against the LORD." 9 Moses said to Aaron, "Say to all the congregation of the children of Israel, 'Come near before the LORD, for he has heard your murmurings.'" 10 And as Aaron spoke to the whole congregation of the children of Israel, they looked toward the wilderness, and behold, the glory of the LORD appeared in the cloud. 11 The LORD spoke to Moses, saying, 12 "I have heard the murmurings of the children of Israel. Speak to them, saying, 'At twilight you shall eat meat, and in the morning you shall be filled with bread. Then you shall know that I am the LORD your God.'" 13 In the evening quail came up and covered the camp, and in the morning dew lay around the camp. 14 When the dew had gone up, there was on the face of the wilderness a fine, flake-like thing, fine as frost on the ground. 15 When the children of Israel saw it, they said to one another, "What is it?" For they did not know what it was. And Moses said to them, "It is the bread that the LORD has given you to eat. 16 This is what the LORD has commanded: 'Gather of it, each one of you, as much as he can eat. You shall each take an omer, according to the number of the persons that each of you has in his tent.'" 17 The children of Israel did so, and gathered, some more, some less. 18 But when they measured it with an omer, whoever gathered much had nothing left over, and whoever gathered little had no lack. Each of them gathered as much as he could eat. 19 Moses said to them, "Let no one leave any of it over till the morning." 20 But they did not listen to Moses. Some left part of it till the morning, and it bred worms and stank. Moses was angry with them. 21 They gathered it every morning, each as much as he could eat. But when the sun grew hot, it melted. 22 On the sixth day they gathered twice as much bread, two omers each. When all the leaders of the congregation came and told Moses, 23

he said to them, "This is what the LORD has commanded: 'Tomorrow is a day of solemn rest, a holy Sabbath to the LORD. Bake what you will bake and boil what you will boil, and all that is left over lay aside to be kept till the morning.'" 24 So they laid it aside till the morning, as Moses commanded them, and it did not stink, and there were no worms in it. 25 Moses said, "Eat it today, for today is a Sabbath to the LORD. Today you will not find it in the field. 26 Six days you shall gather it, but on the seventh day, which is a Sabbath, there will be none." 27 On the seventh day some of the people went out to gather, but they found none. 28 The LORD said to Moses, "How long will you refuse to keep my commandments and my laws? 29 See! The LORD has given you the Sabbath; therefore on the sixth day he gives you bread for two days. Remain each of you in his place; let no one go out of his place on the seventh day." 30 So the people rested on the seventh day. 31 The house of Israel called its name manna. It was like coriander seed, white, and the taste of it was like wafers made with honey. 32 Moses said, "This is what the LORD has commanded: 'Let an omer of it be kept throughout your generations, so that they may see the bread with which I fed you in the wilderness, when I brought you out of the land of Egypt.'" 33 Moses said to Aaron, "Take a jar, and put an omer of manna in it, and place it before the LORD to be kept throughout your generations." 34 As the LORD commanded Moses, so Aaron placed it before the testimony to be kept. 35 The children of Israel ate the manna for forty years, till they came to a habitable land. They ate the manna till they came to the border of the land of Canaan. 36 An omer is the tenth part of an ephah

Chapter 17

1 The whole community of the children of Israel set out from the wilderness of Sin, traveling from place to place as the LORD commanded, and they camped at Rephidim, but there was no water for the people to drink. 2 Therefore, the people quarreled with Moses and said, "Give us water to drink." And Moses said to them, "Why do you quarrel with me? Why do you test the LORD?" 3 But the people thirsted there for water, and the people grumbled against Moses and said, "Why did you bring us up out of Egypt, to kill us and our children and our livestock with thirst?" 4 So Moses cried to the LORD, "What shall I do with this people? They are almost ready to stone me." 5 The LORD said to Moses, "Pass on before the people, taking with you some of the elders of Israel, and take in your hand the staff with which you struck the Nile, and go. 6 Behold, I will stand before you there on the rock at Horeb, and you shall strike the rock, and water shall come out of it, and the people will drink." Moses did so in the sight of the elders of Israel. 7 He called the name of the place Massah and Meribah because of the quarreling of the children of Israel and because they tested the LORD by saying, "Is the LORD among us or not?" 8 Then Amalek came and fought with Israel at Rephidim. 9 So Moses said to Joshua, "Choose for us men, and go out and fight with Amalek. Tomorrow I will stand on the top of the hill with the staff of God in my hand." 10 So Joshua did as Moses told him and fought with Amalek, while Moses, Aaron, and Hur went up to the top of the hill. 11 Whenever Moses held up his hand, Israel prevailed, and whenever he lowered his hand, Amalek prevailed. 12 But Moses' hands grew weary, so they took a stone and put it under him, and he sat on it, while Aaron and Hur held up his hands, one on one side and the other on the other side. So his hands were steady until the going down of the sun. 13 Joshua overwhelmed Amalek and his people with the sword. 14 The LORD said to Moses, "Write this as a memorial in a book and recite it in the ears of Joshua, that I will utterly blot out the memory of Amalek from under heaven." 15 Moses built an altar and called the name of it, The LORD Is My Banner, 16 saying, "A hand upon the throne of the LORD! The LORD will have war with Amalek from generation to generation."

Chapter 18

1 When Jethro, the priest of Midian, Moses' father-in-law, heard all that God had done for Moses and for Israel his people, how the LORD had brought Israel out of Egypt, 2 Jethro, Moses' father-in-law, took Zipporah, Moses' wife, after he had sent her back, 3 along with her two sons. The name of the one was Gershom (for he said, "I have been a sojourner in a foreign land"), 4 and the name of the other, Eliezer (for he said, "The God of my father was my help, and delivered me from the sword of Pharaoh"). 5 Jethro, Moses' father-in-law, came with his sons and his wife to Moses in the wilderness where he was encamped at the mountain of God. 6 And when he sent word to Moses, "I, your father-in-law Jethro, am coming to you with your wife and her two sons with her," 7 Moses went out to meet his father-in-law and bowed down and kissed him. They asked each other of their welfare and went into the tent. 8 Then Moses told his father-in-law all that the LORD had done to Pharaoh and to the Egyptians for Israel's sake, all the hardship that had come upon them in the way, and how the LORD had delivered them. 9 Jethro rejoiced for all the good that the LORD had done to Israel, in that he had delivered them out of the hand of the Egyptians. 10 Jethro said, "Blessed be the LORD, who has delivered you out of the hand of the Egyptians and out of the hand of Pharaoh and has delivered the people from under the hand of the Egyptians. 11 Now I know that the LORD is greater than all gods, because in this affair they dealt arrogantly with the people." 12 And Jethro, Moses' father-in-law, brought a burnt offering and sacrifices to God. Aaron came with all the elders of Israel to eat bread with Moses' father-in-law before God. 13 The next day Moses sat to judge the people, and the people stood around Moses from morning till evening. 14 When Moses' father-in-law saw all that he was doing for the people, he said, "What is this that you are doing for the people? Why do you sit alone, and all the people stand around you from morning till evening?" 15 And Moses said to his father-in-law, "Because the people come to me to inquire of God. 16 When they have a dispute, they come to me, and I decide between one person and another, and I make them know the statutes of God and his laws." 17 Moses' father-in-law said to him, "What you are doing is not good. 18 You and the people with you will certainly wear yourselves out, for the thing is too heavy for you. You are not able to do it alone. 19 Now obey my voice; I will give you advice, and God be with you! You shall represent the people before God and bring their cases to God, 20 and you shall warn them about the statutes and the laws and make them know the way in which they must walk and what they must do. 21 Moreover, look for able men from all the people, men who fear God, who are trustworthy and hate a bribe, and place such men over the people as chiefs of thousands, of hundreds, of fifties, and of tens. 22 And let them judge the people at all times. Every great matter they shall bring to you, but any small matter they shall decide themselves. So it will be easier for you, and they will bear the burden with you. 23 If you do this, God will direct you, you will be able to endure, and all these people also will go to their place in peace." 24 So Moses listened to the voice of his father-in-law and did all that he had said. 25 Moses chose able men out of all Israel and made them heads over the

people, chiefs of thousands, of hundreds, of fifties, and of tens. 26 And they judged the people at all times. Any hard case they brought to Moses, but any small matter they decided themselves. 27 Then Moses let his father-in-law depart, and he went away to his own country

Chapter 19

1 On the third new moon after the people of Israel had gone out of the land of Egypt, on that day they came into the wilderness of Sinai. 2 They set out from Rephidim and came into the wilderness of Sinai, and they encamped in the wilderness. There Israel encamped before the mountain, 3 while Moses went up to God. The LORD called to him out of the mountain, saying, "Thus you shall say to the house of Jacob, and tell the people of Israel: 4 'You yourselves have seen what I did to the Egyptians, and how I bore you on eagles' wings and brought you to myself. 5 Now therefore, if you will indeed obey my voice and keep my covenant, you shall be my treasured possession among all peoples, for all the earth is mine; 6 and you shall be to me a kingdom of priests and a holy nation.' These are the words that you shall speak to the people of Israel." 7 So Moses came and called the elders of the people and set before them all these words that the LORD had commanded him. 8 All the people answered together and said, "All that the LORD has spoken we will do." And Moses reported the words of the people to the LORD. 9 The LORD said to Moses, "Behold, I am coming to you in a thick cloud, that the people may hear when I speak with you and may also believe you forever." When Moses told the words of the people to the LORD, 10 the LORD said to Moses, "Go to the people and consecrate them today and tomorrow, and let them wash their garments 11 and be ready for the third day. For on the third day the LORD will come down on Mount Sinai in the sight of all the people. 12 And you shall set limits for the people all around, saying, 'Take care not to go up into the mountain or touch the edge of it. Whoever touches the mountain shall be put to death. 13 No hand shall touch him, but he shall be stoned or shot; whether beast or man, he shall not live.' When the trumpet sounds a long blast, they shall come up to the mountain." 14 So Moses went down from the mountain to the people and consecrated the people, and they washed their garments. 15 He said to the people, "Be ready for the third day; do not go near a woman." 16 On the morning of the third day, there were thunders and lightnings and a thick cloud on the mountain and a very loud trumpet blast, so that all the people in the camp trembled. 17 Then Moses brought the people out of the camp to meet God, and they took their stand at the foot of the mountain. 18 Now Mount Sinai was wrapped in smoke because the LORD had descended on it in fire. The smoke of it went up like the smoke of a kiln, and the whole mountain trembled greatly. 19 As the sound of the trumpet grew louder and louder, Moses spoke, and God answered him in thunder. 20 The LORD came down on Mount Sinai, to the top of the mountain, and the LORD called Moses to the top of the mountain, and Moses went up. 21 The LORD said to Moses, "Go down and warn the people, lest they break through to the LORD to look and many of them perish. 22 Also let the priests who come near to the LORD consecrate themselves, lest the LORD break out against them." 23 Moses said to the LORD, "The people cannot come up to Mount Sinai, for you yourself warned us, saying, 'Set limits around the mountain and consecrate it.'" 24 The LORD said to him, "Go down, and come up bringing Aaron with you. But do not let the priests and the people break through to come up to the LORD, lest he break out against them." 25 So Moses went down to the people and told them

Chapter 20

1 And God spoke all these words, saying, 2 "I am the LORD your God, who brought you out of the land of Egypt, out of the house of slavery. 3 "You shall have no other gods before me. 4 "You shall not make for yourself a carved image, or any likeness of anything that is in heaven above, or that is in the earth beneath, or that is in the water under the earth. 5 You shall not bow down to them or serve them, for I the LORD your God am a jealous God, visiting the iniquity of the fathers on the children to the third and the fourth generation of those who hate me, 6 but showing steadfast love to thousands of those who love me and keep my commandments. 7 "You shall not take the name of the LORD your God in vain, for the LORD will not hold him guiltless who takes his name in vain. 8 "Remember the Sabbath day, to keep it holy. 9 Six days you shall labor, and do all your work, 10 but the seventh day is a Sabbath to the LORD your God. On it, you shall not do any work, you, or your son, or your daughter, your male servant, or your female servant, or your livestock, or the sojourner who is within your gates. 11 For in six days the LORD made heaven and earth, the sea, and all that is in them, and rested on the seventh day. Therefore the LORD blessed the Sabbath day and made it holy. 12 "Honor your father and your mother, that your days may be long in the land that the LORD your God is giving you. 13 "You shall not murder. 14 "You shall not commit adultery. 15 "You shall not steal. 16 "You shall not bear false witness against your neighbor. 17 "You shall not covet your neighbor's house; you shall not covet your neighbor's wife, or his male servant, or his female servant, or his ox, or his donkey, or anything that is your neighbor's." 18 Now when all the people saw the thunder and the flashes of lightning and the sound of the trumpet and the mountain smoking, the people were afraid and trembled, and they stood far off 19 and said to Moses, "You speak to us, and we will listen, but do not let God speak to us, lest we die." 20 Moses said to the people, "Do not fear, for God has come to test you, that the fear of him may be before you, that you may not sin." 21 The people stood far off while Moses drew near to the thick darkness where God was. 22 The LORD said to Moses, "Thus you shall say to the people of Israel: 'You have seen for yourselves that I have talked with you from heaven. 23 You shall not make gods of silver to be with me, nor shall you make for yourselves gods of gold. 24 An altar of earth you shall make for me and sacrifice on it your burnt offerings and your peace offerings, your sheep and your oxen. In every place where I cause my name to be remembered, I will come to you and bless you. 25 If you make me an altar of stone, you shall not build it of hewn stones, for if you wield your tool on it, you profane it. 26 And you shall not go up by steps to my altar, that your nakedness be not exposed on it.'"

Chapter 21

1 These are the laws you shall establish before them: 2 If you take a Hebrew servant, he shall serve six years, and in the seventh, he shall go out free, paying nothing. 3 If he came alone, he shall go out alone; if he is married, his wife shall go out with him. 4 If his master has given him a wife, and she has borne him sons or daughters, the wife and her children shall belong to the master, and he shall go out alone. 5 But if the servant declares, "I love my master, my wife, and my children; I will not go out free," 6 then his master shall bring him to the judges. He shall also bring him to the door or the doorpost, and his master shall pierce his ear with an awl, and he shall serve him for life. 7 If a man sells his daughter to be a

maidservant, she shall not go out as male servants do. 8 If she does not please her master, who has betrothed her to himself, he shall let her be redeemed. He has no right to sell her to a foreign people because he has acted deceitfully toward her. 9 If he has betrothed her to his son, he shall deal with her according to the rights of daughters. 10 If he takes another wife, he shall not diminish her food, her clothing, or her marital rights. 11 If he does not do these three things for her, she shall go out free, without paying money. 12 Whoever strikes a man so that he dies shall surely be put to death. 13 If he did not lie in wait, but God allowed it to happen, then I will appoint a place where he may flee. 14 But if a man deliberately attacks and kills his neighbor by treachery, you shall take him from my altar to be put to death. 15 Anyone who strikes his father or mother shall surely be put to death. 16 Whoever kidnaps a person, whether he sells him or the victim is found in his possession, shall surely be put to death. 17 Anyone who curses his father or mother shall surely be put to death. 18 If men quarrel and one strikes the other with a stone or with his fist, and he does not die but is confined to bed, 19 if he rises again and walks about on his staff, then he who struck him shall be acquitted; he shall only pay for the loss of his time and shall have him thoroughly healed. 20 If a man strikes his male or female servant with a rod and they die under his hand, he shall surely be punished. 21 But if the servant survives a day or two, he shall not be punished, for the servant is his property. 22 If men fight and hurt a pregnant woman so that she gives birth prematurely, yet there is no serious injury, he shall surely be punished according to what the woman's husband demands and as the court allows. 23 But if there is serious injury, you shall give life for life, 24 eye for eye, tooth for tooth, hand for hand, foot for foot, 25 burn for burn, wound for wound, stripe for stripe. 26 If a man strikes the eye of his male or female servant and destroys it, he shall let the servant go free because of the eye. 27 And if he knocks out the tooth of his male or female servant, he shall let the servant go free because of the tooth. 28 If an ox gores a man or a woman to death, the ox shall surely be stoned, and its flesh shall not be eaten; but the owner of the ox shall be acquitted. 29 But if the ox was previously in the habit of goring, and its owner was warned but did not keep it confined, and it kills a man or a woman, the ox shall be stoned, and its owner also shall be put to death. 30 If a ransom is demanded of him, then he shall give for the redemption of his life whatever is demanded of him. 31 Whether it gores a son or a daughter, it shall be done to him according to the same rule. 32 If the ox gores a male or female servant, the owner shall give their master thirty shekels of silver, and the ox shall be stoned. 33 If a man opens a pit or digs a pit and does not cover it, and an ox or a donkey falls into it, 34 the owner of the pit shall make it good; he shall give money to its owner, and the dead animal shall be his. 35 If one man's ox hurts another's so that it dies, then they shall sell the live ox and divide the money from it; and the dead ox they shall also divide. 36 Or if it is known that the ox was previously in the habit of goring, and its owner has not kept it confined, he shall surely pay ox for ox, and the dead animal shall be his

Chapter 22

1 If a man steals an ox or a sheep and kills it or sells it, he shall repay five oxen for an ox and four sheep for a sheep. 2 If a thief is found breaking in and is struck so that he dies, there shall be no blood guilt for him. 3 But if the sun has risen on him, there shall be blood guilt for him. He should make full restitution; if he has nothing, then he shall be sold for his theft. 4 If the stolen animal is found alive in his possession, whether ox or donkey or sheep, he shall pay double. 5 If a man lets his livestock loose to graze in another man's field or vineyard, he shall make restitution from the best of his own field and the best of his own vineyard. 6 If a fire breaks out and catches in thorns so that the stacked grain, the standing grain, or the field is consumed, he who started the fire shall make full restitution. 7 If a man gives money or goods to his neighbor for safekeeping and it is stolen from the man's house, if the thief is found, he shall pay double. 8 If the thief is not found, the owner of the house shall come near to God to show whether or not he has put his hand to his neighbor's property. 9 For every breach of trust, whether it is for an ox, for a donkey, for a sheep, for a cloak, or for any kind of lost thing, of which one says, "This is it," the case of both parties shall come before God. The one whom God condemns shall pay double to his neighbor. 10 If a man gives to his neighbor a donkey, an ox, a sheep, or any animal to keep, and it dies or is injured or is driven away, without anyone seeing it, 11 an oath by the LORD shall be between them both to determine whether or not he has put his hand to his neighbor's property. The owner shall accept the oath, and the other shall not make restitution. 12 But if it is stolen from him, he shall make restitution to its owner. 13 If it is torn to pieces, he shall bring it as evidence; he shall not make restitution for what has been torn. 14 If a man borrows anything from his neighbor, and it is injured or dies, the owner not being with it, he shall make full restitution. 15 If the owner was with it, he shall not make restitution; if it was hired, it came for its hire. 16 If a man seduces a virgin who is not betrothed and lies with her, he shall surely pay the bride-price for her to be his wife. 17 If her father utterly refuses to give her to him, he shall pay money equal to the bride-price for virgins. 18 You shall not permit a sorceress to live. 19 Whoever lies with an animal shall surely be put to death. 20 Whoever sacrifices to any god other than the LORD alone shall be devoted to destruction. 21 You shall not wrong a sojourner or oppress him, for you were sojourners in the land of Egypt. 22 You shall not mistreat any widow or fatherless child. 23 If you do mistreat them, and they cry out to me, I will surely hear their cry, 24 and my wrath will burn, and I will kill you with the sword, and your wives shall become widows and your children fatherless. 25 If you lend money to any of my people with you who is poor, you shall not be like a moneylender to him, and you shall not exact interest from him. 26 If ever you take your neighbor's cloak in pledge, you shall return it to him before the sun goes down, 27 for that is his only covering, and it is his cloak for his body; in what else shall he sleep? And if he cries to me, I will hear, for I am compassionate. 28 You shall not revile God, nor curse a ruler of your people. 29 You shall not delay to offer from the fullness of your harvest and from the outflow of your presses. The firstborn of your sons you shall give to me. 30 You shall do the same with your oxen and with your sheep: seven days it shall be with its mother; on the eighth day, you shall give it to me. 31 You shall be consecrated to me. Therefore you shall not eat any flesh that is torn by beasts in the field; you shall throw it to the dogs

Chapter 23

1 You shall not spread a false report. You shall not join hands with a wicked man to be a malicious witness. 2 You shall not follow a multitude to do evil, nor shall you bear witness in a lawsuit, siding with the majority, so as to pervert justice, 3 nor shall you be partial to a poor man in his lawsuit. 4 If you meet your enemy's ox or his donkey going astray, you shall bring it back to him. 5 If you see the donkey of one who

hates you lying down under its burden, you shall refrain from leaving him with it; you shall rescue it with him. 6 You shall not pervert the justice due to your poor in his lawsuit. 7 Keep far from a false charge, and do not kill the innocent and righteous, for I will not acquit the wicked. 8 And you shall take no bribe, for a bribe blinds the clear-sighted and subverts the cause of those who are in the right. 9 You shall not oppress a sojourner. You know the heart of a sojourner, for you were sojourners in the land of Egypt. 10 For six years you shall sow your land and gather in its yield, 11 but the seventh year you shall let it rest and lie fallow, that the poor of your people may eat, and what they leave the beasts of the field may eat. You shall do likewise with your vineyard and with your olive orchard. 12 Six days you shall do your work, but on the seventh day, you shall rest, that your ox and your donkey may have rest, and the son of your servant woman and the alien may be refreshed. 13 Pay attention to all that I have said to you and make no mention of the names of other gods, nor let it be heard on your lips. 14 Three times in the year you shall keep a feast to me. 15 You shall keep the Feast of Unleavened Bread. As I commanded you, you shall eat unleavened bread for seven days at the appointed time in the month of Abib, for in it you came out of Egypt. None shall appear before me empty-handed. 16 You shall keep the Feast of Harvest, of the first fruits of your labor, of what you sow in the field. You shall keep the Feast of Ingathering at the end of the year when you gather in from the field the fruit of your labor. 17 Three times in the year shall all your males appear before the Lord GOD. 18 You shall not offer the blood of my sacrifice with anything leavened, or let the fat of my feast remain until the morning. 19 The best of the first fruits of your ground you shall bring into the house of the LORD your God. You shall not boil a young goat in its mother's milk. 20 Behold, I send an angel before you to guard you on the way and to bring you to the place that I have prepared. 21 Pay careful attention to him and obey his voice; do not rebel against him, for he will not pardon your transgression, for my name is in him. 22 But if you carefully obey his voice and do all that I say, then I will be an enemy to your enemies and an adversary to your adversaries. 23 When my angel goes before you and brings you to the Amorites and the Hittites and the Perizzites and the Canaanites and the Hivites and the Jebusites, and I blot them out, 24 you shall not bow down to their gods nor serve them, nor do as they do, but you shall utterly overthrow them and break their pillars in pieces. 25 You shall serve the LORD your God, and he will bless your bread and your water, and I will take sickness away from among you. 26 None shall miscarry or be barren in your land; I will fulfill the number of your days. 27 I will send my terror before you and will throw into confusion all the people against whom you shall come, and I will make all your enemies turn their backs to you. 28 And I will send hornets before you, which shall drive out the Hivites, the Canaanites, and the Hittites from before you. 29 I will not drive them out from before you in one year, lest the land become desolate and the wild beasts multiply against you. 30 Little by little I will drive them out from before you until you have increased and possess the land. 31 And I will set your border from the Red Sea to the Sea of the Philistines, and from the wilderness to the Euphrates, for I will give the inhabitants of the land into your hand, and you shall drive them out before you. 32 You shall make no covenant with them and their gods. 33 They shall not dwell in your land, lest they make you sin against me, for if you serve their gods, it will surely be a snare to you."

Chapter 24

1 Then he said to Moses, "Come up to the LORD, you and Aaron, Nadab and Abihu, and seventy of the elders of Israel, and worship from afar. 2 Moses alone shall come near to the LORD, but the others shall not come near, and the people shall not come up with him." 3 Moses came and told the people all the words of the LORD and all the rules. And all the people answered with one voice and said, "All the words that the LORD has spoken we will do." 4 And Moses wrote down all the words of the LORD. He rose early in the morning and built an altar at the foot of the mountain, and twelve pillars, according to the twelve tribes of Israel. 5 And he sent young men of the people of Israel, who offered burnt offerings and sacrificed peace offerings of oxen to the LORD. 6 And Moses took half of the blood and put it in basins, and half of the blood he threw against the altar. 7 Then he took the Book of the Covenant and read it in the hearing of the people. And they said, "All that the LORD has spoken we will do, and we will be obedient." 8 And Moses took the blood and threw it on the people and said, "Behold the blood of the covenant that the LORD has made with you in accordance with all these words." 9 Then Moses and Aaron, Nadab, and Abihu, and seventy of the elders of Israel went up, 10 and they saw the God of Israel. There was under his feet as it were a pavement of sapphire stone, like the very heaven for clearness. 11 And he did not lay his hand on the chief men of the people of Israel; they beheld God, and ate and drank. 12 The LORD said to Moses, "Come up to me on the mountain and wait there, that I may give you the tablets of stone, with the law and the commandment, which I have written for their instruction." 13 So Moses rose with his assistant Joshua, and Moses went up into the mountain of God. 14 And he said to the elders, "Wait here for us until we return to you. And behold, Aaron and Hur are with you. Whoever has a dispute, let him go to them." 15 Then Moses went up on the mountain, and the cloud covered the mountain. 16 The glory of the LORD dwelt on Mount Sinai, and the cloud covered it six days. And on the seventh day, he called to Moses out of the midst of the cloud. 17 Now the appearance of the glory of the LORD was like a devouring fire on the top of the mountain in the sight of the people of Israel. 18 Moses entered the cloud and went up on the mountain. And Moses was on the mountain forty days and forty nights

Chapter 25

1 The LORD said to Moses, 2 "Speak to the people of Israel, that they take for me a contribution. From every man whose heart moves him, you shall receive the contribution for me. 3 And this is the contribution that you shall receive from them: gold, silver, and bronze, 4 blue and purple and scarlet yarns and fine twined linen, goats' hair, 5 tanned rams' skins, goatskins, acacia wood, 6 oil for the lamps, spices for the anointing oil and for the fragrant incense, 7 onyx stones, and stones for setting, for the ephod and for the breastpiece. 8 And let them make me a sanctuary, that I may dwell in their midst. 9 Exactly as I show you concerning the pattern of the tabernacle, and of all its furniture, so you shall make it. 10 "They shall make an ark of acacia wood. Two cubits and a half shall be its length, a cubit and a half its breadth, and a cubit and a half its height. 11 You shall overlay it with pure gold, inside and outside shall you overlay it, and you shall make on it a molding of gold around it. 12 You shall cast four rings of gold for it and put them on its four feet, two rings on the one side of it, and two rings on the other side of it. 13 You shall make poles of acacia wood and overlay them with gold. 14 And you shall put the

poles into the rings on the sides of the ark to carry the ark by them. 15 The poles shall remain in the rings of the ark; they shall not be taken from it. 16 And you shall put into the ark the testimony that I shall give you. 17 "You shall make a mercy seat of pure gold. Two cubits and a half shall be its length, and a cubit and a half its breadth. 18 And you shall make two cherubim of gold; of hammered work shall you make them, on the two ends of the mercy seat. 19 Make one cherub on the one end and one cherub on the other end. Of one piece with the mercy seat shall you make the cherubim on its two ends. 20 The cherubim shall spread out their wings above, overshadowing the mercy seat with their wings, their faces one to another; toward the mercy seat shall the faces of the cherubim be. 21 And you shall put the mercy seat on the top of the ark, and in the ark you shall put the testimony that I shall give you. 22 There I will meet with you, and from above the mercy seat, from between the two cherubim that are on the ark of the testimony, I will speak with you about all that I will give you in commandment for the people of Israel. 23 "You shall make a table of acacia wood. Two cubits shall be its length, a cubit its breadth, and a cubit and a half its height. 24 You shall overlay it with pure gold and make a molding of gold around it. 25 And you shall make a rim around it a handbreadth wide and a molding of gold around the rim. 26 And you shall make for it four rings of gold and fasten the rings to the four corners at its four legs. 27 Close to the frame the rings shall lie, as holders for the poles to carry the table. 28 You shall make the poles of acacia wood and overlay them with gold, and the table shall be carried with these. 29 And you shall make its plates and dishes for incense, and its flagons and bowls with which to pour drink offerings; you shall make them of pure gold. 30 And you shall set the bread of the Presence on the table before me regularly. 31 "You shall make a lampstand of pure gold. The lampstand shall be made of hammered work: its base, its stem, its cups, its calyxes, and its flowers shall be of one piece with it. 32 And there shall be six branches going out of its sides, three branches of the lampstand out of one side of it and three branches of the lampstand out of the other side of it; 33 three cups made like almond blossoms, each with calyx and flower, on one branch, and three cups made like almond blossoms, each with calyx and flower, on the other branch—so for the six branches going out of the lampstand. 34 And on the lampstand itself, there shall be four cups made like almond blossoms, with their calyxes and flowers, 35 and a calyx of one piece with it under each pair of the six branches going out from the lampstand. 36 Their calyxes and their branches shall be of one piece with it, the whole of it a single piece of hammered work of pure gold. 37 You shall make seven lamps for it. And the lamps shall be set up so as to give light on the space in front of it. 38 Its tongs and their trays shall be of pure gold. 39 It shall be made, with all these utensils, out of a talent of pure gold. 40 And see that you make them after the pattern for them, which is being shown you on the mountain

Chapter 26

1 "Moreover, you shall make the tabernacle with ten curtains of fine twisted linen, and blue and purple and scarlet yarns; you shall make them with cherubim skillfully worked into them. 2 The length of each curtain shall be twenty-eight cubits, and the breadth of each curtain four cubits; all the curtains shall be the same size. 3 Five curtains shall be coupled to one another, and the other five curtains shall be coupled to one another. 4 And you shall make loops of blue on the edge of the outermost curtain in the first set. Likewise, you shall make loops on the edge of the outermost curtain in the second set. 5 You shall make fifty loops on the one curtain, and you shall make fifty loops on the edge of the curtain that is in the second set; the loops shall be opposite one another. 6 And you shall make fifty clasps of gold, and couple the curtains one to the other with the clasps, so that the tabernacle may be a single whole. 7 "You shall also make curtains of goats' hair for a tent over the tabernacle; eleven curtains shall you make. 8 The length of each curtain shall be thirty cubits, and the breadth of each curtain four cubits. The eleven curtains shall be the same size. 9 You shall couple five curtains by themselves, and six curtains by themselves, and the sixth curtain you shall double over at the front of the tent. 10 You shall make fifty loops on the edge of the curtain that is outermost in one set, and fifty loops on the edge of the curtain that is outermost in the second set. 11 "You shall make fifty clasps of bronze, and put the clasps into the loops, and couple the tent together that it may be a single whole. 12 And the part that remains of the curtains of the tent, the half curtain that remains, shall hang over the back of the tabernacle. 13 And the extra that remains in the length of the curtains, the cubit on the one side and the cubit on the other side, shall hang over the sides of the tabernacle, on this side and that side, to cover it. 14 "And you shall make for the tent a covering of tanned rams' skins and a covering of goat skins on top. 15 "You shall make upright frames for the tabernacle of acacia wood. 16 Ten cubits shall be the length of a frame, and a cubit and a half the breadth of each frame. 17 There shall be two tenons in each frame, for fitting together; so shall you do for all the frames of the tabernacle. 18 You shall make the frames for the tabernacle: twenty frames for the south side; 19 and forty bases of silver you shall make under the twenty frames: two bases under one frame for its two tenons, and two bases under the next frame for its two tenons; 20 and for the second side of the tabernacle, on the north side, twenty frames, 21 and their forty bases of silver: two bases under one frame, and two bases under the next frame. 22 And for the rear of the tabernacle westward you shall make six frames. 23 And you shall make two frames for corners of the tabernacle in the rear; 24 they shall be separate beneath, but joined at the top, at the first ring. Thus shall it be with both of them; they shall form the two corners. 25 And there shall be eight frames, with their bases of silver, sixteen bases; two bases under one frame, and two bases under the next frame. 26 "You shall make bars of acacia wood, five for the frames of the one side of the tabernacle, 27 and five bars for the frames of the other side of the tabernacle, and five bars for the frames of the side of the tabernacle at the rear westward. 28 The middle bar, halfway up the frames, shall run from end to end. 29 You shall overlay the frames with gold and shall make their rings of gold for holders for the bars, and you shall overlay the bars with gold. 30 Then you shall erect the tabernacle according to the plan for it that you were shown on the mountain. 31 "You shall make a veil of blue and purple and scarlet yarns and fine twined linen. It shall be made with cherubim skillfully worked into it. 32 And you shall hang it on four pillars of acacia overlaid with gold, with hooks of gold, on four bases of silver. 33 And you shall hang the veil from the clasps, and bring the ark of the testimony in there within the veil. And the veil shall separate for you the Holy Place from the Most Holy. 34 You shall put the mercy seat on the ark of the testimony in the Most Holy Place. 35 And you shall set the table outside the veil, and the lampstand on the south side of the tabernacle opposite the table, and you shall put the table on the north side. 36 "You shall make a

screen for the entrance of the tent, of blue and purple and scarlet yarns and fine twined linen, embroidered with needlework. 37 And you shall make for the screen five pillars of acacia and overlay them with gold. Their hooks shall be of gold, and you shall cast five bases of bronze for them

Chapter 27

1 "You shall make the altar of acacia wood, five cubits long and five cubits broad. The altar shall be square, and its height shall be three cubits. 2 You shall make horns for it on its four corners; its horns shall be of one piece with it, and you shall overlay it with bronze. 3 You shall make pots for it to receive its ashes, and shovels and basins and forks and fire pans. You shall make all its utensils of bronze. 4 You shall also make for it a grating, a network of bronze, and on the net you shall make four bronze rings at its four corners. 5 And you shall set it under the ledge of the altar so that the net extends halfway down the altar. 6 And you shall make poles for the altar, poles of acacia wood, and overlay them with bronze. 7 And the poles shall be put through the rings, so that the poles are on the two sides of the altar when it is carried. 8 You shall make it hollow, with boards. As it has been shown you on the mountain, so shall it be made. 9 "You shall make the court of the tabernacle. On the south side, the court shall have hangings of fine twined linen a hundred cubits long for one side. 10 Its twenty pillars and their twenty bases shall be of bronze, but the hooks of the pillars and their fillets shall be of silver. 11 And likewise for its length on the north side, there shall be hangings a hundred cubits long, its pillars twenty and their bases twenty, of bronze, but the hooks of the pillars and their fillets shall be of silver. 12 And for the breadth of the court on the west side, there shall be hangings for fifty cubits, with ten pillars and ten bases. 13 The breadth of the court on the front to the east shall be fifty cubits. 14 The hangings for the one side of the gate shall be fifteen cubits, with their three pillars and three bases. 15 On the other side, the hangings shall be fifteen cubits, with their three pillars and three bases. 16 "For the gate of the court there shall be a screen twenty cubits long, of blue and purple and scarlet yarns and fine twined linen, embroidered with needlework. It shall have four pillars and with them four bases. 17 All the pillars around the court shall be filleted with silver. Their hooks shall be of silver, and their bases of bronze. 18 The length of the court shall be a hundred cubits, the breadth fifty, and the height five cubits, with hangings of fine twined linen and bases of bronze. 19 All the utensils of the tabernacle for every use, and all its pegs and all the pegs of the court, shall be of bronze. 20 "You shall command the people of Israel that they bring to you pure beaten olive oil for the light, that a lamp may regularly be set up to burn. 21 In the tent of meeting, outside the veil that is before the testimony, Aaron and his sons shall tend it from evening to morning before the LORD. It shall be a statute forever to be observed throughout their generations by the people of Israel

Chapter 28

1 "Then bring near to you Aaron your brother, and his sons with him, from among the people of Israel, to serve me as priests—Aaron and Aaron's sons, Nadab and Abihu, Eleazar and Ithamar. 2 And you shall make holy garments for Aaron your brother, for glory and for beauty. 3 You shall speak to all the skillful, whom I have filled with a spirit of skill, that they make Aaron's garments to consecrate him for my priesthood. 4 These are the garments that they shall make: a breastpiece, an ephod, a robe, a coat of checker work, a turban, and a sash. They shall make holy garments for Aaron your brother and his sons to serve me as priests. 5 They shall receive gold, blue and purple and scarlet yarns, and fine twined linen. 6 "And they shall make the ephod of gold, of blue and purple and scarlet yarns, and of fine twined linen, skillfully worked. 7 It shall have two shoulder pieces attached to its two edges, so that it may be joined together. 8 And the skillfully woven band on it shall be made like it and be of one piece with it, of gold, blue and purple and scarlet yarns, and fine twined linen. 9 You shall take two onyx stones, and engrave on them the names of the sons of Israel, 10 six of their names on the one stone, and the names of the remaining six on the other stone, in the order of their birth. 11 As a jeweler engraves signets, so shall you engrave the two stones with the names of the sons of Israel. You shall enclose them in settings of gold filigree. 12 And you shall set the two stones on the shoulder pieces of the ephod, as stones of remembrance for the sons of Israel. And Aaron shall bear their names before the LORD on his two shoulders for remembrance. 13 You shall make settings of gold filigree, 14 and two chains of pure gold, twisted like cords; and you shall attach the corded chains to the settings. 15 "You shall make a breastpiece of judgment, in skilled work. In the style of the ephod you shall make it—of gold, blue and purple and scarlet yarns, and fine twined linen shall you make it. 16 It shall be square and doubled, a span its length and a span its breadth. 17 You shall set in it four rows of stones. A row of sardius, topaz, and carbuncle shall be the first row; 18 and the second row an emerald, a sapphire, and a diamond; 19 and the third row a jacinth, an agate, and an amethyst; 20 and the fourth row a beryl, an onyx, and a jasper. They shall be set in gold filigree. 21 There shall be twelve stones with their names according to the names of the sons of Israel. They shall be like signets, each engraved with its name, for the twelve tribes. 22 You shall make for the breastpiece twisted chains like cords, of pure gold. 23 And you shall make for the breastpiece two rings of gold, and put the two rings on the two edges of the breastpiece. 24 And you shall put the two cords of gold in the two rings at the edges of the breastpiece. 25 The two ends of the two cords you shall attach to the two settings of filigree, and so attach it in front to the shoulder pieces of the ephod. 26 You shall make two rings of gold, and put them at the two ends of the breastpiece, on its inside edge next to the ephod. 27 And you shall make two rings of gold, and attach them in front to the lower part of the two shoulder pieces of the ephod, at its seam above the skillfully woven band of the ephod. 28 And they shall bind the breastpiece by its rings to the rings of the ephod with a lace of blue, so that it may lie on the skillfully woven band of the ephod, so that the breastpiece shall not come loose from the ephod. 29 So Aaron shall bear the names of the sons of Israel in the breastpiece of judgment on his heart, when he goes into the Holy Place, to bring them to regular remembrance before the LORD. 30 And in the breastpiece of judgment you shall put the Urim and the Thummim, and they shall be on Aaron's heart, when he goes in before the LORD. Thus Aaron shall bear the judgment of the people of Israel on his heart before the LORD regularly. 31 "You shall make the robe of the ephod all of blue. 32 It shall have an opening for the head in the middle of it, with a woven binding around the opening, like the opening in a garment, so that it may not tear. 33 On its hem you shall make pomegranates of blue and purple and scarlet yarns, around its hem, with bells of gold between them, 34 a golden bell and a pomegranate, a golden bell and a pomegranate, around the hem of the robe. 35 And it shall be on Aaron when he ministers, and its sound shall be heard when he goes

into the Holy Place before the LORD, and when he comes out, so that he does not die. 36 "You shall make a plate of pure gold and engrave on it, like the engraving of a signet, 'Holy to the LORD.' 37 And you shall fasten it on the turban by a cord of blue. It shall be on the front of the turban. 38 It shall be on Aaron's forehead, and Aaron shall bear any guilt from the holy things that the people of Israel consecrate as their holy gifts. It shall regularly be on his forehead, that they may be accepted before the LORD. 39 "You shall weave the coat in checker work of fine linen, and you shall make a turban of fine linen, and you shall make a sash embroidered with needlework. 40 "For Aaron's sons you shall make coats and sashes and caps. You shall make them for glory and beauty. 41 And you shall put them on Aaron your brother, and on his sons with him, and shall anoint them and ordain them and consecrate them, that they may serve me as priests. 42 You shall make for them linen undergarments to cover their naked flesh. They shall reach from the hips to the thighs; 43 and they shall be on Aaron and on his sons when they go into the tent of meeting or when they come near the altar to minister in the Holy Place, lest they bear guilt and die. This shall be a statute forever for him and for his offspring after him

Chapter 29

1 "Now this is what you shall do to them to consecrate them, that they may serve me as priests. Take one bull of the herd and two rams without blemish, 2 and unleavened bread, unleavened cakes mixed with oil, and unleavened wafers smeared with oil; you shall make them of fine wheat flour. 3 You shall put them in one basket and bring them in the basket, and bring the bull and the two rams. 4 You shall bring Aaron and his sons to the entrance of the tent of meeting and wash them with water. 5 Then you shall take the garments, and put on Aaron the coat and the robe of the ephod, and the ephod, and the breastpiece, and gird him with the skillfully woven band of the ephod. 6 And you shall set the turban on his head and put the holy crown on the turban. 7 You shall take the anointing oil and pour it on his head and anoint him. 8 Then you shall bring his sons and put coats on them, 9 and you shall gird Aaron and his sons with sashes and bind caps on them. And the priesthood shall be theirs by a statute forever. Thus you shall ordain Aaron and his sons. 10 "Then you shall bring the bull before the tent of meeting. Aaron and his sons shall lay their hands on the head of the bull. 11 Then you shall kill the bull before the LORD at the entrance of the tent of meeting, 12 and shall take part of the blood of the bull and put it on the horns of the altar with your finger, and the rest of the blood you shall pour out at the base of the altar. 13 And you shall take all the fat that covers the entrails, and the long lobe of the liver, and the two kidneys with the fat that is on them, and burn them on the altar. 14 But the flesh of the bull and its skin and its dung you shall burn with fire outside the camp; it is a sin offering. 15 "Then you shall take one of the rams, and Aaron and his sons shall lay their hands on the head of the ram, 16 and you shall kill the ram and shall take its blood and throw it against the sides of the altar. 17 Then you shall cut the ram into pieces, and wash its entrails and its legs, and put them with its pieces and its head, 18 and burn the whole ram on the altar. It is a burnt offering to the LORD. It is a pleasing aroma, a food offering to the LORD. 19 "You shall take the other ram, and Aaron and his sons shall lay their hands on the head of the ram, 20 and you shall kill the ram and take part of its blood and put it on the tip of the right ear of Aaron and on the tips of the right ears of his sons and on the thumbs of their right

hands and on the great toes of their right feet, and throw the rest of the blood against the sides of the altar. 21 Then you shall take part of the blood that is on the altar, and of the anointing oil, and sprinkle it on Aaron and his garments, and on his sons and his sons' garments with him. He and his garments shall be holy, and his sons and his sons' garments with him. 22 "You shall also take the fat from the ram and the fat tail and the fat that covers the entrails and the long lobe of the liver and the two kidneys with the fat that is on them, and the right thigh (for it is a ram of ordination), 23 and one loaf of bread and one cake of bread made with oil, and one wafer out of the basket of unleavened bread that is before the LORD. 24 You shall put all these on the palms of Aaron and on the palms of his sons, and wave them for a wave offering before the LORD. 25 Then you shall take them from their hands and burn them on the altar on top of the burnt offering, as a pleasing aroma before the LORD. It is a food offering to the LORD. 26 "You shall take the breast of the ram of Aaron's ordination and wave it for a wave offering before the LORD, and it shall be your portion. 27 And you shall consecrate the breast of the wave offering that is waved and the thigh of the priests' portion that is contributed from the ram of ordination, from what was Aaron's and his sons'. 28 It shall be for Aaron and his sons as a perpetual due from the people of Israel, for it is a contribution. It shall be a contribution from the people of Israel from their peace offerings, their contribution to the LORD. 29 "The holy garments of Aaron shall be for his sons after him; they shall be anointed in them and ordained in them. 30 The son who succeeds him as priest, who comes into the tent of meeting to minister in the Holy Place, shall wear them seven days. 31 "You shall take the ram of ordination and boil its flesh in a holy place. 32 And Aaron and his sons shall eat the flesh of the ram and the bread that is in the basket in the entrance of the tent of meeting. 33 They shall eat those things with which atonement was made at their ordination and consecration, but an outsider shall not eat of them, because they are holy. 34 And if any of the flesh for the ordination or of the bread remain until the morning, then you shall burn the remainder with fire. It shall not be eaten, because it is holy. 35 "Thus you shall do to Aaron and to his sons, according to all that I have commanded you. Through seven days shall you ordain them, 36 and every day you shall offer a bull as a sin offering for atonement. Also you shall purify the altar, when you make atonement for it, and shall anoint it to consecrate it. 37 Seven days you shall make atonement for the altar and consecrate it, and the altar shall be most holy. Whatever touches the altar shall become holy. 38 "Now this is what you shall offer on the altar: two lambs a year old day by day regularly. 39 One lamb you shall offer in the morning, and the other lamb you shall offer at twilight. 40 And with the first lamb a tenth measure of fine flour mingled with a fourth of a hin of beaten oil, and a fourth of a hin of wine for a drink offering. 41 The other lamb you shall offer at twilight, and shall offer with it a grain offering and its drink offering, as in the morning, for a pleasing aroma, a food offering to the LORD. 42 It shall be a regular burnt offering throughout your generations at the entrance of the tent of meeting before the LORD, where I will meet with you, to speak to you there. 43 There I will meet with the people of Israel, and it shall be sanctified by my glory. 44 I will consecrate the tent of meeting and the altar. Aaron also and his sons I will consecrate to serve me as priests. 45 I will dwell among the people of Israel and will be their God. 46 And they shall know that I am the LORD their God, who brought them out of the land of Egypt that I might dwell among them. I am the LORD their God

Chapter 30

1 "You shall make an altar on which to burn incense; you shall make it of acacia wood. 2 A cubit shall be its length, and a cubit its breadth. It shall be square, and two cubits shall be its height. Its horns shall be of one piece with it. 3 You shall overlay it with pure gold, its top and around its sides and its horns. And you shall make a molding of gold around it. 4 And you shall make two golden rings for it. Under its molding on two opposite sides of it you shall make them, and they shall be holders for poles with which to carry it. 5 You shall make the poles of acacia wood and overlay them with gold. 6 And you shall put it in front of the veil that is above the ark of the testimony, in front of the mercy seat that is above the testimony, where I will meet with you. 7 And Aaron shall burn fragrant incense on it. Every morning when he dresses the lamps he shall burn it, 8 and when Aaron sets up the lamps at twilight, he shall burn it, a regular incense offering before the LORD throughout your generations. 9 You shall not offer unauthorized incense on it, or a burnt offering, or a grain offering, and you shall not pour a drink offering on it. 10 Aaron shall make atonement on its horns once a year. With the blood of the sin offering of atonement, he shall make atonement for it once in the year throughout your generations. It is most holy to the LORD." 11 The LORD said to Moses, 12 "When you take the census of the people of Israel, then each shall give a ransom for his life to the LORD when you number them, that there be no plague among them when you number them. 13 Each one who is numbered in the census shall give this: half a shekel according to the shekel of the sanctuary (the shekel is twenty gerahs), half a shekel as an offering to the LORD. 14 Everyone who is numbered in the census, from twenty years old and upward, shall give the LORD's offering. 15 The rich shall not give more, and the poor shall not give less, than the half shekel, when you give the LORD's offering to make atonement for your lives. 16 You shall take the atonement money from the people of Israel and shall give it for the service of the tent of meeting, that it may bring the people of Israel to remembrance before the LORD, so as to make atonement for your lives." 17 The LORD said to Moses, 18 "You shall also make a basin of bronze, with its stand of bronze, for washing. You shall put it between the tent of meeting and the altar, and you shall put water in it, 19 with which Aaron and his sons shall wash their hands and their feet. 20 When they go into the tent of meeting, or when they come near the altar to minister, to burn a food offering to the LORD, they shall wash with water, so that they may not die. 21 They shall wash their hands and their feet, so that they may not die. It shall be a statute forever to them, even to him and to his offspring throughout their generations." 22 The LORD said to Moses, 23 "Take the finest spices: of liquid myrrh 500 shekels, and of sweet-smelling cinnamon half as much, that is, 250, and 250 of aromatic cane, 24 and 500 of cassia, according to the shekel of the sanctuary, and a hin of olive oil. 25 And you shall make of these a sacred anointing oil blended as by the perfumer; it shall be a holy anointing oil. 26 With it you shall anoint the tent of meeting and the ark of the testimony, 27 and the table and all its utensils, and the lampstand and its utensils, and the altar of incense, 28 and the altar of burnt offering with all its utensils and the basin and its stand. 29 You shall consecrate them, that they may be most holy. Whatever touches them will become holy. 30 You shall anoint Aaron and his sons, and consecrate them, that they may serve me as priests. 31 And you shall say to the people of Israel, 'This shall be my holy anointing oil throughout your generations. 32 It shall not be poured on the body of an ordinary person, and you shall make no other like it in composition. It is holy, and it shall be holy to you. 33 Whoever compounds any like it or whoever puts any of it on an outsider shall be cut off from his people.'" 34 The LORD said to Moses, "Take sweet spices, stacte, and onycha, and galbanum, sweet spices with pure frankincense (of each shall there be an equal part), 35 and make an incense blended as by the perfumer, seasoned with salt, pure and holy. 36 You shall beat some of it very small, and put part of it before the testimony in the tent of meeting where I shall meet with you. It shall be most holy for you. 37 And the incense that you shall make according to its composition, you shall not make for yourselves. It shall be for you holy to the LORD. 38 Whoever makes any like it to use as perfume shall be cut off from his people."

Chapter 31

1 The LORD spoke to Moses, saying, 2 "See, I have called by name Bezalel the son of Uri, son of Hur, of the tribe of Judah, 3 and I have filled him with the Spirit of God, with ability and intelligence, with knowledge and all craftsmanship, 4 to devise artistic designs, to work in gold, silver, and bronze, 5 in cutting stones for setting, and in carving wood, to work in every craft. 6 And behold, I have appointed with him Oholiab, the son of Ahisamach, of the tribe of Dan. And I have given to all able men ability, that they may make all that I have commanded you: 7 the tent of meeting, and the ark of the testimony, and the mercy seat that is on it, and all the furnishings of the tent, 8 the table and its utensils, and the pure lampstand with all its utensils, and the altar of incense, 9 and the altar of burnt offering with all its utensils, and the basin and its stand, 10 and the finely worked garments, the holy garments for Aaron the priest and the garments of his sons, for their service as priests, 11 and the anointing oil and the fragrant incense for the Holy Place. According to all that I have commanded you, they shall do." 12 And the LORD said to Moses, 13 "You are to speak to the people of Israel and say, 'Above all you shall keep my Sabbaths, for this is a sign between me and you throughout your generations, that you may know that I, the LORD, sanctify you. 14 You shall keep the Sabbath, because it is holy for you. Everyone who profanes it shall be put to death. Whoever does any work on it, that soul shall be cut off from among his people. 15 Six days shall work be done, but the seventh day is a Sabbath of solemn rest, holy to the LORD. Whoever does any work on the Sabbath day shall be put to death. 16 Therefore the people of Israel shall keep the Sabbath, observing the Sabbath throughout their generations, as a covenant forever. 17 It is a sign forever between me and the people of Israel that in six days the LORD made heaven and earth, and on the seventh day he rested and was refreshed.'" 18 And he gave to Moses, when he had finished speaking with him on Mount Sinai, the two tablets of the testimony, tablets of stone, written with the finger of God

Chapter 32

1 When the people saw that Moses delayed to come down from the mountain, the people gathered themselves together to Aaron and said to him, "Up, make us gods who shall go before us. As for this Moses, the man who brought us up out of the land of Egypt, we do not know what has become of him." 2 So Aaron said to them, "Take off the rings of gold that are in the ears of your wives, your sons, and your daughters, and bring them to me." 3 So all the people took off the rings of gold that were in their ears and brought them to Aaron. 4 And he received the gold

from their hand and fashioned it with a graving tool and made a golden calf. And they said, "These are your gods, O Israel, who brought you up out of the land of Egypt!" 5 When Aaron saw this, he built an altar before it. And Aaron made a proclamation and said, "Tomorrow shall be a feast to the LORD." 6 And they rose up early the next day and offered burnt offerings and brought peace offerings. And the people sat down to eat and drink and rose up to play. 7 And the LORD said to Moses, "Go down, for your people, whom you brought up out of the land of Egypt, have corrupted themselves. 8 They have turned aside quickly out of the way that I commanded them. They have made for themselves a golden calf and have worshiped it and sacrificed to it and said, 'These are your gods, O Israel, who brought you up out of the land of Egypt!'" 9 And the LORD said to Moses, "I have seen this people, and behold, it is a stiff-necked people. 10 Now therefore let me alone, that my wrath may burn hot against them and I may consume them, in order that I may make a great nation of you." 11 But Moses implored the LORD his God and said, "O LORD, why does your wrath burn hot against your people, whom you have brought out of the land of Egypt with great power and with a mighty hand? 12 Why should the Egyptians say, 'With evil intent did he bring them out, to kill them in the mountains and to consume them from the face of the earth'? Turn from your burning anger and relent from this disaster against your people. 13 Remember Abraham, Isaac, and Israel, your servants, to whom you swore by your own self, and said to them, 'I will multiply your offspring as the stars of heaven, and all this land that I have promised I will give to your offspring, and they shall inherit it forever.'" 14 And the LORD relented from the disaster that he had spoken of bringing on his people. 15 Then Moses turned and went down from the mountain with the two tablets of the testimony in his hand, tablets that were written on both sides; on the front and on the back they were written. 16 The tablets were the work of God, and the writing was the writing of God, engraved on the tablets. 17 When Joshua heard the noise of the people as they shouted, he said to Moses, "There is a noise of war in the camp." 18 But he said, "It is not the sound of shouting for victory, or the sound of the cry of defeat, but the sound of singing that I hear." 19 And as soon as he came near the camp and saw the calf and the dancing, Moses' anger burned hot, and he threw the tablets out of his hands and broke them at the foot of the mountain. 20 He took the calf that they had made and burned it with fire and ground it to powder and scattered it on the water and made the people of Israel drink it. 21 And Moses said to Aaron, "What did this people do to you that you have brought such a great sin upon them?" 22 And Aaron said, "Let not the anger of my lord burn hot. You know the people, that they are set on evil. 23 For they said to me, 'Make us gods who shall go before us. As for this Moses, the man who brought us up out of the land of Egypt, we do not know what has become of him.' 24 So I said to them, 'Let any who have gold take it off.' So they gave it to me, and I threw it into the fire, and out came this calf." 25 And when Moses saw that the people had broken loose (for Aaron had let them break loose, to the derision of their enemies), 26 then Moses stood in the gate of the camp and said, "Who is on the LORD's side? Come to me." And all the sons of Levi gathered around him. 27 And he said to them, "Thus says the LORD God of Israel, 'Put your sword on your side each of you, and go to and fro from gate to gate throughout the camp, and each of you kill his brother and his companion and his neighbor.'" 28 And the sons of Levi did according to the word of Moses. And

that day about three thousand men of the people fell. 29 And Moses said, "Today you have been ordained for the service of the LORD, each one at the cost of his son and of his brother, so that he might bestow a blessing upon you this day." 30 The next day Moses said to the people, "You have sinned a great sin. And now I will go up to the LORD; perhaps I can make atonement for your sin." 31 So Moses returned to the LORD and said, "Alas, this people have sinned a great sin. They have made for themselves gods of gold. 32 But now, if you will forgive their sin, please do so; but if not, please blot me out of your book that you have written." 33 But the LORD said to Moses, "Whoever has sinned against me, I will blot out of my book. 34 But now go, lead the people to the place about which I have spoken to you; behold, my angel shall go before you. Nevertheless, in the day when I visit, I will visit their sin upon them." 35 Then the LORD sent a plague on the people, because they made the calf, the one that Aaron made

Chapter 33

1 The LORD said to Moses, "Depart; go up from here, you and the people whom you have brought up out of the land of Egypt, to the land of which I swore to Abraham, Isaac, and Jacob, saying, 'To your offspring I will give it.' 2 I will send an angel before you, and I will drive out the Canaanites, the Amorites, the Hittites, the Perizzites, the Hivites, and the Jebusites. 3 Go up to a land flowing with milk and honey; but I will not go up among you, lest I consume you on the way, for you are a stiff-necked people." 4 When the people heard this disastrous word, they mourned, and no one put on his ornaments. 5 For the LORD had said to Moses, "Say to the people of Israel, 'You are a stiff-necked people; if for a single moment I should go up among you, I would consume you. So now take off your ornaments, that I may know what to do with you.'" 6 Therefore the people of Israel stripped themselves of their ornaments, from Mount Horeb onward. 7 Now Moses used to take the tent and pitch it outside the camp, far off from the camp, and he called it the tent of meeting. And everyone who sought the LORD would go out to the tent of meeting, which was outside the camp. 8 Whenever Moses went out to the tent, all the people would rise up, and each would stand at his tent door, and watch Moses until he had gone into the tent. 9 When Moses entered the tent, the pillar of cloud would descend and stand at the entrance of the tent, and the LORD would speak with Moses. 10 And when all the people saw the pillar of cloud standing at the entrance of the tent, all the people would rise up and worship, each at his tent door. 11 Thus the LORD used to speak to Moses face to face, as a man speaks to his friend. When Moses turned again into the camp, his assistant Joshua the son of Nun, a young man, would not depart from the tent. 12 Moses said to the LORD, "See, you say to me, 'Bring up this people,' but you have not let me know whom you will send with me. Yet you have said, 'I know you by name, and you have also found favor in my sight.' 13 Now therefore, if I have found favor in your sight, please show me now your ways, that I may know you in order to find favor in your sight. Consider too that this nation is your people." 14 And he said, "My presence will go with you, and I will give you rest." 15 And he said to him, "If your presence will not go with me, do not bring us up from here. 16 For how shall it be known that I have found favor in your sight, I and your people? Is it not in your going with us, so that we are distinct, I and your people, from every other people on the face of the earth?" 17 And the LORD said to Moses, "This very thing that you have spoken I will do, for you have found favor in my sight, and I know you by name." 18 Moses said, "Please show me your glory." 19 And he

said, "I will make all my goodness pass before you and will proclaim before you my name 'The LORD.' And I will be gracious to whom I will be gracious, and will show mercy on whom I will show mercy. 20 But," he said, "you cannot see my face, for man shall not see me and live." 21 And the LORD said, "Behold, there is a place by me where you shall stand on the rock, 22 and while my glory passes by I will put you in a cleft of the rock, and I will cover you with my hand until I have passed by. 23 Then I will take away my hand, and you shall see my back, but my face shall not be seen."

Chapter 34

1 The LORD said to Moses, "Cut for yourself two tablets of stone like the first, and I will write on the tablets the words that were on the first tablets, which you broke. 2 Be ready by the morning, and come up in the morning to Mount Sinai, and present yourself there to me on the top of the mountain. 3 No one shall come up with you, and let no one be seen throughout all the mountain. Let no flocks or herds graze opposite that mountain." 4 So Moses cut two tablets of stone like the first. And he rose early in the morning and went up on Mount Sinai, as the LORD had commanded him, and took in his hand two tablets of stone. 5 The LORD descended in the cloud and stood with him there, and proclaimed the name of the LORD. 6 The LORD passed before him and proclaimed, "The LORD, the LORD, a God merciful and gracious, slow to anger, and abounding in steadfast love and faithfulness, 7 keeping steadfast love for thousands, forgiving iniquity and transgression and sin, but who will by no means clear the guilty, visiting the iniquity of the fathers on the children and the children's children, to the third and the fourth generation." 8 And Moses quickly bowed his head toward the earth and worshiped. 9 And he said, "If now I have found favor in your sight, O Lord, please let the Lord go in the midst of us, for it is a stiff-necked people, and pardon our iniquity and our sin, and take us for your inheritance." 10 And he said, "Behold, I am making a covenant. Before all your people I will do marvels, such as have not been created in all the earth or in any nation. And all the people among whom you are shall see the work of the LORD, for it is an awesome thing that I will do with you. 11 "Observe what I command you this day. Behold, I will drive out before you the Amorites, the Canaanites, the Hittites, the Perizzites, the Hivites, and the Jebusites. 12 Take care, lest you make a covenant with the inhabitants of the land to which you go, lest it become a snare in your midst. 13 You shall tear down their altars and break their pillars and cut down their Asherim 14 (for you shall worship no other god, for the LORD, whose name is Jealous, is a jealous God), 15 lest you make a covenant with the inhabitants of the land, and when they whore after their gods and sacrifice to their gods and you are invited, you eat of his sacrifice, 16 and you take of their daughters for your sons, and their daughters whore after their gods and make your sons whore after their gods. 17 "You shall not make for yourself any gods of cast metal. 18 "You shall keep the Feast of Unleavened Bread. Seven days you shall eat unleavened bread, as I commanded you, at the time appointed in the month Abib, for in the month Abib you came out from Egypt. 19 All that open the womb are mine, all your male livestock, the firstborn of cow and sheep. 20 The firstborn of a donkey you shall redeem with a lamb, or if you will not redeem it you shall break its neck. All the firstborn of your sons you shall redeem. And none shall appear before me empty-handed. 21 "Six days you shall work, but on the seventh day you shall rest. In plowing time and in harvest you shall rest. 22 You shall observe the Feast of Weeks, the firstfruits of wheat harvest, and the Feast of Ingathering at the year's end. 23 Three times in the year shall all your males appear before the LORD God, the God of Israel. 24 For I will cast out nations before you and enlarge your borders; no one shall covet your land, when you go up to appear before the LORD your God three times in the year. 25 "You shall not offer the blood of my sacrifice with anything leavened, or let the sacrifice of the Feast of the Passover remain until the morning. 26 The best of the firstfruits of your ground you shall bring to the house of the LORD your God. You shall not boil a young goat in its mother's milk." 27 And the LORD said to Moses, "Write these words, for in accordance with these words I have made a covenant with you and with Israel." 28 So he was there with the LORD forty days and forty nights. He neither ate bread nor drank water. And he wrote on the tablets the words of the covenant, the Ten Commandments. 29 When Moses came down from Mount Sinai, with the two tablets of the testimony in his hand as he came down from the mountain, Moses did not know that the skin of his face shone because he had been talking with God. 30 Aaron and all the people of Israel saw Moses, and behold, the skin of his face shone, and they were afraid to come near him. 31 But Moses called to them, and Aaron and all the leaders of the congregation returned to him, and Moses talked with them. 32 Afterward all the people of Israel came near, and he commanded them all that the LORD had spoken with him in Mount Sinai. 33 And when Moses had finished speaking with them, he put a veil over his face. 34 Whenever Moses went in before the LORD to speak with him, he would remove the veil, until he came out. And when he came out and told the people of Israel what he was commanded, 35 the people of Israel would see the face of Moses, that the skin of Moses' face was shining. And Moses would put the veil over his face again, until he went in to speak with him

Chapter 35

1 Moses assembled all the congregation of the people of Israel and said to them, "These are the things that the LORD has commanded you to do. 2 Six days work shall be done, but on the seventh day you shall have a Sabbath of solemn rest, holy to the LORD. Whoever does any work on it shall be put to death. 3 You shall kindle no fire in all your dwelling places on the Sabbath day." 4 Moses said to all the congregation of the people of Israel, "This is the thing that the LORD has commanded. 5 Take from among you a contribution to the LORD. Whoever is of a generous heart, let him bring the LORD's contribution: gold, silver, and bronze; 6 blue and purple and scarlet yarns and fine twined linen; goats' hair, 7 tanned rams' skins, and goatskins; acacia wood, 8 oil for the light, spices for the anointing oil and for the fragrant incense, 9 and onyx stones and stones for setting, for the ephod and for the breastpiece. 10 "Let every skillful craftsman among you come and make all that the LORD has commanded: 11 the tabernacle, its tent and its covering, its hooks and its frames, its bars, its pillars, and its bases; 12 the ark with its poles, the mercy seat, and the veil of the screen; 13 the table with its poles and all its utensils, and the bread of the Presence; 14 the lampstand also for the light, with its utensils and its lamps, and the oil for the light; 15 and the altar of incense, with its poles, and the anointing oil and the fragrant incense, and the screen for the door, at the door of the tabernacle; 16 the altar of burnt offering, with its grating of bronze, its poles, and all its utensils, the basin and its stand; 17 the hangings of the court, its pillars and its bases, and the screen for the gate of the court; 18 the pegs of the

tabernacle and the pegs of the court, and their cords; 19 the finely worked garments for ministering in the Holy Place, the holy garments for Aaron the priest and the garments of his sons, for their service as priests." 20 Then all the congregation of the people of Israel departed from the presence of Moses. 21 And they came, everyone whose heart stirred him, and everyone whose spirit moved him, and brought the LORD's contribution to be used for the tent of meeting, and for all its service, and for the holy garments. 22 So they came, both men and women. All who were of a willing heart brought brooches and earrings and signet rings and armlets, all sorts of gold objects, every man dedicating an offering of gold to the LORD. 23 And every one who possessed blue or purple or scarlet yarns or fine linen or goats' hair or tanned rams' skins or goatskins brought them. 24 Everyone who could make a contribution of silver or bronze brought it as the LORD's contribution. And every one who possessed acacia wood of any use in the work brought it. 25 And every skillful woman spun with her hands, and they all brought what they had spun in blue and purple and scarlet yarns and fine twined linen. 26 All the women whose hearts stirred them to use their skill spun the goats' hair. 27 And the leaders brought onyx stones and stones to be set, for the ephod and for the breastpiece, 28 and spices and oil for the light, and for the anointing oil, and for the fragrant incense. 29 All the men and women, the people of Israel, whose heart moved them to bring anything for the work that the LORD had commanded by Moses to be done, brought it as a freewill offering to the LORD. 30 Then Moses said to the people of Israel, "See, the LORD has called by name Bezalel the son of Uri, son of Hur, of the tribe of Judah; 31 and he has filled him with the Spirit of God, with skill, with intelligence, with knowledge, and with all craftsmanship, 32 to devise artistic designs, to work in gold and silver and bronze, 33 in cutting stones for setting, and in carving wood, for work in every skilled craft. 34 And he has inspired him to teach, both him and Oholiab the son of Ahisamach of the tribe of Dan. 35 He has filled them with skill to do every sort of work done by an engraver or by a designer or by an embroiderer in blue and purple and scarlet yarns and fine twined linen, or by a weaver—by any sort of workman or skilled designer

Chapter 36

1 Bezalel, Oholiab, and all the skilled men to whom the Lord had given wisdom and intelligence, knew how to carry out all the work for the service of the sanctuary, just as the Lord had commanded. 2 Moses called Bezalel, Oholiab, and all the wise-hearted men, in whose hearts the Lord had brought wisdom, as many as their hearts encouraged them to come to the work to perform it. 3 They received from Moses all the offerings that the children of Israel had brought for the work of the service of the sanctuary, to build it; and they continued to bring him freewill offerings every morning. 4 So all the skilled craftsmen who were doing all the work on the sanctuary left their work 5 and said to Moses, "The people bring much more than enough for doing the work that the Lord has commanded us to do." 6 So Moses gave a command, and they proclaimed it throughout the camp, saying, "Let neither man nor woman make any further contribution for the sanctuary offering." So the people were restrained from bringing more. 7 For the material they had was sufficient to do all the work, and more than enough. 8 All the skilled men among the workers made the tabernacle with ten curtains of finely twisted linen, blue, purple, and scarlet yarn, with cherubim worked into them by skilled hands. 9 The length of each curtain was twenty-eight cubits, and the width of each curtain four cubits; all the curtains were the same size. 10 He joined five of the curtains together and the other five curtains he joined together. 11 He made loops of blue yarn along the edge of the end curtain in one set, and he did the same along the edge of the end curtain in the other set. 12 He made fifty loops on one curtain and fifty loops on the end curtain of the other set, with the loops opposite each other. 13 Then he made fifty gold clasps and used them to fasten the two sets of curtains together so that the tabernacle was a unit. 14 He made curtains of goat hair for the tent over the tabernacle, eleven altogether. 15 The length of each curtain was thirty cubits, and the width of each curtain four cubits; the eleven curtains were all the same size. 16 He joined five of the curtains into one set and the other six into another set. 17 He made fifty loops along the edge of the end curtain in one set and also along the edge of the end curtain in the other set. 18 He made fifty bronze clasps to fasten the tent together as a unit. 19 Then he made for the tent a covering of ram skins dyed red, and over that a covering of durable leather. 20 He made upright frames of acacia wood for the tabernacle. 21 Each frame was ten cubits long and a cubit and a half wide, 22 with two projections set parallel to each other. He made all the frames of the tabernacle in this way. 23 He made twenty frames for the south side of the tabernacle 24 and made forty silver bases to go under them—two bases for each frame, one under each projection. 25 For the other side, the north side of the tabernacle, he made twenty frames 26 and forty silver bases—two under each frame. 27 He made six frames for the far end, that is, the west end of the tabernacle, 28 and two frames were made for the corners of the tabernacle at the far end. 29 At these two corners the frames were double from the bottom all the way to the top and fitted into a single ring; both were made alike. 30 So there were eight frames and sixteen silver bases—two under each frame. 31 He also made crossbars of acacia wood: five for the frames on one side of the tabernacle, 32 five for those on the other side, and five for the frames on the west end, at the far end of the tabernacle. 33 He made the center crossbar so that it extended from end to end at the middle of the frames. 34 He overlaid the frames with gold and made gold rings to hold the crossbars. He also overlaid the crossbars with gold. 35 He made the curtain of blue, purple, and scarlet yarn and finely twisted linen, with cherubim worked into it by a skilled craftsman. 36 He made four posts of acacia wood for it and overlaid them with gold. He made gold hooks for them and cast their four silver bases. 37 For the entrance to the tent he made a curtain of blue, purple, and scarlet yarn and finely twisted linen—the work of an embroiderer; 38 and he made five posts with hooks for them. He overlaid the tops of the posts and their bands with gold and made their five bases of bronze

Chapter 37

1 Bezalel made the ark of acacia wood—two and a half cubits long, a cubit and a half wide, and a cubit and a half high. 2 He overlaid it with pure gold, both inside and out, and made a gold molding around it. 3 He cast four gold rings for it and fastened them to its four feet, with two rings on one side and two rings on the other. 4 Then he made poles of acacia wood and overlaid them with gold. 5 And he inserted the poles into the rings on the sides of the ark to carry it. 6 He made the atonement cover of pure gold—two and a half cubits long and a cubit and a half wide. 7 Then he made two cherubim out of hammered gold at the ends of the cover. 8 He made one cherub on one end and the second cherub on the other; at the two ends he made them of one piece with the cover. 9 The

cherubim had their wings spread upward, overshadowing the cover with them. The cherubim faced each other, looking toward the cover. 10 They made the table of acacia wood—two cubits long, a cubit wide, and a cubit and a half high. 11 Then they overlaid it with pure gold and made a gold molding around it. 12 They also made around it a rim a handbreadth wide and put a gold molding on the rim. 13 They cast four gold rings for the table and fastened them to the four corners, where the four legs were. 14 The rings were put close to the rim to hold the poles used in carrying the table. 15 The poles for carrying the table were made of acacia wood and were overlaid with gold. 16 And they made from pure gold the articles for the table—its plates and dishes and bowls and its pitchers for the pouring out of drink offerings. 17 They made the lampstand of pure gold. They hammered out its base and shaft, and made its flower-like cups, buds, and blossoms of one piece with them. 18 Six branches extended from the sides of the lampstand—three on one side and three on the other. 19 Three cups shaped like almond flowers with buds and blossoms were on one branch, three on the next branch, and the same for all six branches extending from the lampstand. 20 And on the lampstand were four cups shaped like almond flowers with buds and blossoms. 21 One bud was under the first pair of branches extending from the lampstand, a second bud under the second pair, and a third bud under the third pair—six branches in all. 22 The buds and the branches were all of one piece with the lampstand, hammered out of pure gold. 23 They made its seven lamps, as well as its wick trimmers and trays, of pure gold. 24 They made the lampstand and all its accessories from one talent of pure gold. 25 They made the altar of incense out of acacia wood. It was square, a cubit long and a cubit wide and two cubits high—its horns of one piece with it. 26 They overlaid the top and all the sides and the horns with pure gold and made a gold molding around it. 27 They made two gold rings below the molding—two on each of the opposite sides—to hold the poles used to carry it. 28 They made the poles of acacia wood and overlaid them with gold. 29 They also made the sacred anointing oil and the pure, fragrant incense—the work of a perfumer

Chapter 38

1 They built the altar of burnt offering of acacia wood, three cubits high; it was square, five cubits long and five cubits wide. 2 They made a horn at each of the four corners, so that the horns and the altar were of one piece, and they overlaid the altar with bronze. 3 They made all its utensils of bronze—its pots, shovels, sprinkling bowls, meat forks, and firepans. 4 They made a grating for the altar, a bronze network, to be under its ledge, halfway up the altar. 5 They cast bronze rings to hold the poles for the four corners of the bronze grating. 6 They made the poles of acacia wood and overlaid them with bronze. 7 They inserted the poles into the rings so they would be on the sides of the altar for carrying it. They made it hollow, out of boards. 8 They made the bronze basin and its bronze stand from the mirrors of the women who served at the entrance to the tent of meeting. 9 Next they made the courtyard. The south side was a hundred cubits long and had curtains of finely twisted linen, 10 with twenty posts and twenty bronze bases, and with silver hooks and bands on the posts. 11 The north side was also a hundred cubits long and had twenty posts and twenty bronze bases, with silver hooks and bands on the posts. 12 The west end was fifty cubits wide and had curtains, with ten posts and ten bases, with silver hooks and bands on the posts. 13 The east end, toward the sunrise, was also fifty cubits wide. 14 Curtains fifteen cubits long were on one side of the

entrance, with three posts and three bases, 15 and curtains fifteen cubits long were on the other side of the entrance to the courtyard, with three posts and three bases. 16 All the curtains around the courtyard were of finely twisted linen. 17 The bases for the posts were bronze. The hooks and bands on the posts were silver, and their tops were overlaid with silver; so all the posts of the courtyard had silver bands. 18 The curtain for the entrance to the courtyard was made of blue, purple, and scarlet yarn and finely twisted linen—the work of an embroiderer. It was twenty cubits long and, like the curtains of the courtyard, five cubits high, 19 with four posts and four bronze bases. Their hooks and bands were silver, and their tops were overlaid with silver. 20 All the tent pegs of the tabernacle and of the surrounding courtyard were bronze. 21 These are the amounts of the materials used for the tabernacle, the tabernacle of the covenant law, which were recorded at Moses' command by the Levites under the direction of Ithamar son of Aaron, the priest. 22 Bezalel son of Uri, the son of Hur, of the tribe of Judah, made everything the Lord commanded Moses; 23 with him was Oholiab son of Ahisamak, of the tribe of Dan—an engraver and designer, and an embroiderer in blue, purple, and scarlet yarn and fine linen. 24 The total amount of the gold from the wave offering used for all the work on the sanctuary was 29 talents and 730 shekels, according to the sanctuary shekel. 25 The silver obtained from those of the community who were counted in the census was 100 talents and 1,775 shekels, according to the sanctuary shekel—26 one beka per person, that is, half a shekel, according to the sanctuary shekel, from everyone who had crossed over to those counted, twenty years old or more, a total of 603,550 men. 27 The 100 talents of silver were used to cast the bases for the sanctuary and for the curtain—100 bases from the 100 talents, one talent for each base. 28 They used the 1,775 shekels to make the hooks for the posts, to overlay the tops of the posts, and to make their bands. 29 The bronze from the wave offering was 70 talents and 2,400 shekels. 30 They used it to make the bases for the entrance to the tent of meeting, the bronze altar with its bronze grating and all its utensils, 31 the bases for the surrounding courtyard and those for its entrance and all the tent pegs for the tabernacle and those for the surrounding courtyard

Chapter 39

1 From the blue, purple, and scarlet yarn they made woven garments for ministering in the sanctuary. They also made sacred garments for Aaron, as the Lord commanded Moses. 2 They made the ephod of gold, and of blue, purple, and scarlet yarn, and of finely twisted linen. 3 They hammered out thin sheets of gold and cut strands to be worked into the blue, purple, and scarlet yarn and fine linen—the work of skilled hands. 4 They made shoulder pieces for the ephod, which were attached to two of its corners, so it could be fastened. 5 Its skillfully woven waistband was like it—of one piece with the ephod and woven with gold, and with blue, purple, and scarlet yarn, and with finely twisted linen, as the Lord commanded Moses. 6 They mounted the onyx stones in gold filigree settings and engraved them like a seal with the names of the sons of Israel. 7 Then they fastened them on the shoulder pieces of the ephod as memorial stones for the sons of Israel, as the Lord commanded Moses. 8 They fashioned the breastpiece—the work of a skilled craftsman. They made it like the ephod: of gold, and of blue, purple, and scarlet yarn, and of finely twisted linen. 9 It was square—a span long and a span wide—and folded double. 10 Then they mounted four rows of precious

stones on it. The first row was a ruby, a topaz, and a beryl; 11 the second row was a turquoise, a sapphire, and an emerald; 12 the third row was a jacinth, an agate, and an amethyst; 13 the fourth row was a chrysolite, an onyx, and a jasper. They were mounted in gold filigree settings. 14 There were twelve stones, one for each of the names of the sons of Israel, each engraved like a seal with the name of one of the twelve tribes. 15 For the breastpiece they made braided chains of pure gold, like a rope. 16 They made two gold filigree settings and two gold rings, and fastened the rings to two of the corners of the breastpiece. 17 They fastened the two gold chains to the rings at the corners of the breastpiece, 18 and the other ends of the chains to the two settings, attaching them to the shoulder pieces of the ephod at the front. 19 They made two gold rings and attached them to the other two corners of the breastpiece on the inside edge next to the ephod. 20 Then they made two more gold rings and attached them to the bottom of the shoulder pieces on the front of the ephod, close to the seam just above the waistband of the ephod. 21 They tied the rings of the breastpiece to the rings of the ephod with blue cord, connecting it to the waistband so that the breastpiece would not swing out from the ephod—as the Lord commanded Moses. 22 They made the robe of the ephod entirely of blue cloth—the work of a weaver—23 with an opening in the center of the robe like the opening of a collar, and a band around this opening, so that it would not tear. 24 They made pomegranates of blue, purple, and scarlet yarn and finely twisted linen around the hem of the robe. 25 And they made bells of pure gold and attached them around the hem between the pomegranates. 26 The bells and pomegranates alternated around the hem of the robe to be worn for ministering, as the Lord commanded Moses. 27 For Aaron and his sons, they made tunics of fine linen—the work of a weaver—28 and the turban of fine linen, the linen headbands and the undergarments of finely twisted linen. 29 The sash was of finely twisted linen and blue, purple, and scarlet yarn—the work of an embroiderer—as the Lord commanded Moses. 30 They made the plate, the sacred emblem, out of pure gold and engraved on it, like an inscription on a seal: HOLY TO THE LORD. 31 Then they fastened a blue cord to it to attach it to the turban, as the Lord commanded Moses. 32 So all the work on the tabernacle, the tent of meeting, was completed. The Israelites did everything just as the Lord commanded Moses. 33 Then they brought the tabernacle to Moses: the tent and all its furnishings, its clasps, frames, crossbars, posts, and bases; 34 the covering of ram skins dyed red, the covering of another durable leather and the shielding curtain; 35 the ark of the covenant law with its poles and the atonement cover; 36 the table with all its articles and the bread of the Presence; 37 the pure gold lampstand with its row of lamps and all its accessories, and the oil for the light; 38 the gold altar, the anointing oil, the fragrant incense, and the curtain for the entrance to the tent; 39 the bronze altar with its bronze grating, its poles, and all its utensils; the basin with its stand; 40 the curtains of the courtyard with its posts and bases, and the curtain for the entrance to the courtyard; the ropes and tent pegs for the courtyard; all the furnishings for the tabernacle, the tent of meeting; 41 and the woven garments worn for ministering in the sanctuary, both the sacred garments for Aaron the priest and the garments for his sons when serving as priests. 42 The Israelites had done all the work just as the Lord had commanded Moses. 43 Moses inspected the work and saw that they had done it just as the Lord had commanded. So Moses blessed them

Chapter 40

1 Then the Lord said to Moses: 2 "Set up the tabernacle, the tent of meeting, on the first day of the first month. 3 Place the ark of the covenant law in it and shield the ark with the curtain. 4 Bring in the table and set out what belongs on it. Then bring in the lampstand and set up its lamps. 5 Place the gold altar of incense in front of the ark of the covenant law and put the curtain at the entrance to the tabernacle. 6 "Place the altar of burnt offering in front of the entrance to the tabernacle, the tent of meeting; 7 place the basin between the tent of meeting and the altar and put water in it. 8 Set up the courtyard around it and put the curtain at the entrance to the courtyard. 9 "Take the anointing oil and anoint the tabernacle and everything in it; consecrate it and all its furnishings, and it will be holy. 10 Then anoint the altar of burnt offering and all its utensils; consecrate the altar, and it will be most holy. 11 Anoint the basin and its stand and consecrate them. 12 "Bring Aaron and his sons to the entrance to the tent of meeting and wash them with water. 13 Then dress Aaron in the sacred garments, anoint him and consecrate him so he may serve me as priest. 14 Bring his sons and dress them in tunics. 15 Anoint them just as you anointed their father, so they may serve me as priests. Their anointing will be to a priesthood that will continue throughout their generations." 16 Moses did everything just as the Lord commanded him. 17 So the tabernacle was set up on the first day of the first month in the second year. 18 When Moses set up the tabernacle, he put the bases in place, erected the frames, inserted the crossbars, and set up the posts. 19 Then he spread the tent over the tabernacle and put the covering over the tent, as the Lord commanded him. 20 He took the tablets of the covenant law and placed them in the ark, attached the poles to the ark, and put the atonement cover over it. 21 Then he brought the ark into the tabernacle and hung the shielding curtain and shielded the ark of the covenant law, as the Lord commanded him. 22 Moses placed the table in the tent of meeting on the north side of the tabernacle outside the curtain 23 and set out the bread on it before the Lord, as the Lord commanded him. 24 He placed the lampstand in the tent of meeting opposite the table on the south side of the tabernacle 25 and set up the lamps before the Lord, as the Lord commanded him. 26 Moses placed the gold altar in the tent of meeting in front of the curtain 27 and burned fragrant incense on it, as the Lord commanded him. 28 Then he put up the curtain at the entrance to the tabernacle. 29 He set the altar of burnt offering near the entrance to the tabernacle, the tent of meeting, and offered on it burnt offerings and grain offerings, as the Lord commanded him. 30 He placed the basin between the tent of meeting and the altar and put water in it for washing, 31 and Moses and Aaron and his sons used it to wash their hands and feet. 32 They washed whenever they entered the tent of meeting or approached the altar, as the Lord commanded Moses. 33 Then Moses set up the courtyard around the tabernacle and altar and put up the curtain at the entrance to the courtyard. And so Moses finished the work. 34 Then the cloud covered the tent of meeting, and the glory of the Lord filled the tabernacle. 35 Moses could not enter the tent of meeting because the cloud had settled on it, and the glory of the Lord filled the tabernacle. 36 In all the travels of the Israelites, whenever the cloud lifted from above the tabernacle, they would set out; 37 but if the cloud did not lift, they did not set out—until the day it lifted. 38 So the cloud of the Lord was over the tabernacle by day, and fire was in the cloud by night, in the sight of all the Israelites during all their travels

3. Leviticus

Chapter 1

Now the LORD called Moses and spoke to him from the Tabernacle of Meeting, saying, "Speak to the children of Israel and say to them, 'If any of you offer a sacrifice to the LORD, he shall offer his sacrifice of cattle or sheep. If his sacrifice is a burnt offering, he shall offer a male without blemish, presenting him of his own free will at the door of the Tabernacle of the Congregation before the LORD. He shall put his hand on the head of the burnt offering, and it shall be accepted before the LORD as his atonement. He shall kill the bullock before the LORD, and the priests, sons of Aaron, shall offer the blood and sprinkle it all around on the altar that is at the door of the Tabernacle of the Congregation. Then he will cut up the burnt offering and break it into pieces. The sons of Aaron the priest will put fire on the altar and arrange the wood in order on the fire. Then the sons of Aaron the priest shall arrange the parts in order, the head and the fat, on the wood that is in the fire and on the altar. But the entrails and the legs shall be washed with water, and the priest shall burn the whole on the altar, because it is a burnt offering, an oblation made by fire, for a sweet-smelling aroma to the LORD. If his sacrifice for the burnt offering is of flocks (of sheep or goats), he shall offer a male without blemish. He shall kill it on the north side of the altar before the LORD, and the sons of Aaron, the priest, shall sprinkle its blood all around on the altar. He will cut it into pieces, separating its head and its fat, and the priest will arrange them in order on the wood lying in the fire that is on the altar. He shall wash the entrails and the legs with water, and the priest shall offer the whole and burn it on the altar, for it is a burnt offering, an oblation made by fire for a sweet-smelling aroma to the LORD. If his sacrifice is a burnt offering to the LORD of birds, he shall offer his sacrifice of turtledoves or young pigeons. The priest shall bring it to the altar, wring off its head, and burn it on the altar; and its blood shall be drained out at the side of the altar. Then he shall remove its crop with its feathers and throw them beside the altar, on the east side, in the place of ashes. He shall split it open at its wings but shall not divide it completely; and the priest shall burn it on the altar, on the wood that is on the fire. It is a burnt offering, an oblation made by fire for a sweet-smelling aroma to the LORD

Chapter 2

When anyone offers a food offering to the LORD, his offering shall be of fine flour, and he shall pour oil on it and put incense on it. He shall bring it to Aaron's sons, the priests, who shall take a handful of the fine flour and oil with all the incense, and the priest shall burn it as a memorial on the altar, an offering made by fire for a sweet-smelling aroma to the LORD. The rest of the food offering shall belong to Aaron and his sons; it is most holy of the LORD's offerings made by fire. If you bring a baked food offering, it shall be unleavened cakes of fine flour mixed with oil, or unleavened wafers anointed with oil. If your offering is a grain offering baked in a pan, it shall be of fine flour, unleavened, mixed with oil. You shall break it in pieces and pour oil on it; it is a grain offering. If your offering is a grain offering cooked in a pan, it shall be made of fine flour with oil. You shall bring the grain offering that is made of these things to the LORD, and when it is presented to the priest, he shall bring it to the altar. The priest shall take from the grain offering a memorial portion and burn it on the altar. It is an offering made by fire, a sweet aroma to the LORD. The remainder of the grain offering shall belong to Aaron and his sons; it is most holy of the offerings to the LORD made by fire. No grain offering that you

bring to the LORD shall be made with leaven, for you shall burn no leaven nor any honey in any offering to the LORD made by fire. As for the offering of the firstfruits, you shall offer them to the LORD, but they shall not be burned on the altar for a sweet aroma. Every offering of your grain offering you shall season with salt; you shall not allow the salt of the covenant of your God to be lacking from your grain offering. With all your offerings you shall offer salt. If you offer a grain offering of your firstfruits to the LORD, you shall offer for the grain offering of your firstfruits green heads of grain roasted on the fire, grain beaten from full heads. And you shall put oil on it and lay frankincense on it. It is a grain offering. Then the priest shall burn the memorial portion, part of its beaten grain and part of its oil, with all the frankincense, as an offering made by fire to the LORD

Chapter 3

If his offering is a peace offering, if he offers it of the herd, whether male or female, he shall offer it without blemish before the LORD. He shall lay his hand on the head of his offering and kill it at the door of the Tabernacle of Meeting; and Aaron's sons, the priests, shall sprinkle the blood all around on the altar. Then he shall offer from the sacrifice of the peace offering an offering made by fire to the LORD. The fat that covers the entrails and all the fat that is on the entrails, the two kidneys and the fat that is on them by the flanks, and the fatty lobe attached to the liver above the kidneys, he shall remove. And Aaron's sons shall burn it on the altar upon the burnt sacrifice which is on the wood that is on the fire, as an offering made by fire, a sweet aroma to the LORD. If his offering as a sacrifice of a peace offering to the LORD is of the flock, whether male or female, he shall offer it without blemish. If he offers a lamb as his offering, then he shall offer it before the LORD. He shall lay his hand on the head of his offering and kill it before the Tabernacle of Meeting; and Aaron's sons shall sprinkle its blood all around on the altar. Then he shall offer from the sacrifice of the peace offering, as an offering made by fire to the LORD, its fat, the whole fat tail which he shall remove close to the backbone, and the fat that covers the entrails and all the fat that is on the entrails, the two kidneys and the fat that is on them by the flanks, and the fatty lobe attached to the liver above the kidneys. He shall remove them, and the priest shall burn them on the altar as food, an offering made by fire to the LORD. If his offering is a goat, then he shall offer it before the LORD. He shall lay his hand on its head and kill it before the Tabernacle of Meeting; and the sons of Aaron shall sprinkle its blood all around on the altar. Then he shall offer from it his offering, as an offering made by fire to the LORD, the fat that covers the entrails and all the fat that is on the entrails, the two kidneys and the fat that is on them by the flanks, and the fatty lobe attached to the liver above the kidneys. He shall remove them, and the priest shall burn them on the altar as food, an offering made by fire for a sweet aroma; all the fat is the LORD's. This shall be a perpetual statute throughout your generations in all your dwellings: you shall eat neither fat nor blood

Chapter 4

The LORD spoke to Moses, saying, "Speak to the children of Israel, saying: 'If anyone sins unintentionally against any of the commandments of the LORD in anything which ought not to be done, and does any of them, if the anointed priest sins, bringing guilt on the people, then let him offer to the LORD for his sin which he has sinned a young bull without blemish as a sin offering. He shall bring the bull to the door of the Tabernacle of Meeting before the LORD, lay his hand on the bull's head, and kill the bull before the LORD. Then the anointed priest shall take some of the bull's blood and bring it to the Tabernacle of Meeting. The priest shall dip his finger in the blood and sprinkle some of the blood seven times before the LORD, in front of the veil of the sanctuary. And the priest shall put some of the blood on the horns of the altar of sweet incense before the LORD, which is in the Tabernacle of Meeting; and he shall pour the remaining blood of the bull at the base of the altar of burnt offering, which is at the door of the Tabernacle of Meeting. He shall take from it all the fat of the bull as the sin offering, the fat that covers the entrails and all the fat which is on the entrails, the two kidneys and the fat that is on them by the flanks, and the fatty lobe attached to the liver above the kidneys. He shall remove, as it was taken from the bull of the sacrifice of the peace offering; and the priest shall burn them on the altar of the burnt offering. But the bull's hide and all its flesh, with its head and legs, its entrails and offal—the whole bull he shall carry outside the camp to a clean place, where the ashes are poured out, and burn it on wood with fire; where the ashes are poured out, it shall be burned. Now if the whole congregation of Israel sins unintentionally, and the thing is hidden from the eyes of the assembly, and they have done something against any of the commandments of the LORD in anything which should not be done, and are guilty; when the sin which they have committed becomes known, then the assembly shall offer a young bull for the sin, and bring it before the Tabernacle of Meeting. And the elders of the congregation shall lay their hands on the head of the bull before the LORD. Then the bull shall be killed before the LORD. The anointed priest shall bring some of the bull's blood to the Tabernacle of Meeting. The priest shall dip his finger in the blood and sprinkle it seven times before the LORD, in front of the veil. And he shall put some of the blood on the horns of the altar which is before the LORD, which is in the Tabernacle of Meeting. He shall pour the remaining blood at the base of the altar of burnt offering, which is at the door of the Tabernacle of Meeting. He shall take all the fat from it and burn it on the altar. And he shall do with the bull as he did with the bull as a sin offering; thus he shall do with it. So the priest shall make atonement for them, and it shall be forgiven them. Then he shall carry the bull outside the camp and burn it as he burned the first bull. It is a sin offering for the assembly. When a ruler has sinned and done something unintentionally against any of the commandments of the LORD his God in anything which should not be done, and is guilty, or if his sin which he has committed comes to his knowledge, he shall bring as his offering a kid of the goats, a male without blemish. He shall lay his hand on the head of the goat and kill it at the place where they kill the burnt offering before the LORD. It is a sin offering. The priest shall take some of the blood of the sin offering with his finger, put it on the horns of the altar of burnt offering, and pour its blood at the base of the altar of burnt offering. He shall burn all its fat on the altar, like the fat of the sacrifice of the peace offering. So the priest shall make atonement for him concerning his sin, and it shall be forgiven him. If anyone of the common people sins unintentionally by doing something against any of the commandments of the LORD in anything which ought not to be done, and is guilty, or if his sin which he has committed comes to his knowledge, then he shall bring as his offering a kid of the goats, a female without blemish, for his sin which he has committed. He shall lay his hand on the head of the sin offering, and kill the sin offering at the place of the burnt offering. Then the priest shall take some of its blood with his finger, put it on the horns of the altar of burnt

offering, and pour all the remaining blood at the base of the altar. He shall remove all its fat, as fat is removed from the sacrifice of the peace offering; and the priest shall burn it on the altar for a sweet aroma to the LORD. So the priest shall make atonement for him, and it shall be forgiven him. If he brings a lamb as his sin offering, he shall bring a female without blemish. He shall lay his hand on the head of the sin offering and kill it as a sin offering at the place where they kill the burnt offering. The priest shall take some of the blood of the sin offering with his finger, put it on the horns of the altar of burnt offering, and pour all the remaining blood at the base of the altar. He shall remove all its fat, as the fat of the lamb is removed from the sacrifice of the peace offering. Then the priest shall burn it on the altar, according to the offerings made by fire to the LORD. So the priest shall make atonement for his sin that he has committed, and it shall be forgiven him

Chapter 5

If a person sins in hearing the utterance of an oath, and is a witness, whether he has seen or known of the matter—if he does not tell it, he bears guilt. Or if a person touches any unclean thing, whether it is the carcass of an unclean beast, or the carcass of unclean livestock, or the carcass of unclean creeping things, and he is unaware of it, he also shall be unclean and guilty. Or if he touches human uncleanness—whatever uncleanness with which a man may be defiled, and he is unaware of it—when he realizes it, then he shall be guilty. Or if a person swears, speaking thoughtlessly with his lips to do evil or to do good, whatever it is that a man may pronounce by an oath, and he is unaware of it—when he realizes it, then he shall be guilty in any of these matters. And it shall be, when he is guilty in any of these matters, that he shall confess that he has sinned in that thing; and he shall bring his trespass offering to the LORD for his sin which he has committed: a female from the flock, a lamb or a kid of the goats as a sin offering. So the priest shall make atonement for him concerning his sin. If he is not able to bring a lamb, then he shall bring to the LORD for his trespass which he has committed, two turtledoves or two young pigeons: one as a sin offering and the other as a burnt offering. He shall bring them to the priest, who shall offer that which is for the sin offering first, and wring off its head from its neck, but shall not divide it completely. Then he shall sprinkle some of the blood of the sin offering on the side of the altar, and the rest of the blood shall be drained out at the base of the altar. It is a sin offering. And he shall offer the second as a burnt offering according to the prescribed manner. So the priest shall make atonement on his behalf for his sin which he has committed, and it shall be forgiven him. But if he is not able to bring two turtledoves or two young pigeons, then he who sinned shall bring for his offering one-tenth of an ephah of fine flour as a sin offering. He shall put no oil on it, nor shall he put frankincense on it, for it is a sin offering. Then he shall bring it to the priest, and the priest shall take his handful of it as a memorial portion and burn it on the altar according to the offerings made by fire to the LORD. It is a sin offering. The priest shall make atonement for him, for his sin that he has committed in any of these matters, and it shall be forgiven him. The rest shall be the priest's as a grain offering. Then the LORD spoke to Moses, saying: "If a person commits a trespass and sins unintentionally in regard to the holy things of the LORD, then he shall bring to the LORD as his trespass offering a ram without blemish from the flocks, with your valuation in shekels of silver, according to the shekel of the sanctuary, as a trespass offering. And he shall make restitution for the harm that he has done in regard to the holy thing, and shall add one-fifth to it and give it to the priest. So the priest shall make atonement for him with the ram of the trespass offering, and it shall be forgiven him. If a person sins, and commits any of these things which are forbidden to be done by the commandments of the LORD, though he does not know it, yet he is guilty and shall bear his iniquity. And he shall bring to the priest a ram without blemish from the flock, with your valuation, as a trespass offering. So the priest shall make atonement for him regarding his ignorance in which he erred and did not know it, and it shall be forgiven him. It is a trespass offering; he has certainly trespassed against the LORD."

Chapter 6

The LORD spoke to Moses, saying, "If a man sins and commits a trespass against the LORD by deceiving his neighbor in a matter of a deposit or security, or through robbery or if he has oppressed his neighbor, or has found what was lost and lied about it, swearing falsely—in any of these things that a man may do and sins thereby—then it shall be, because he has sinned and is guilty, that he shall restore what he took by robbery, or what he got by oppression, or the deposit which was committed to him, or the lost thing which he found, or anything about which he has sworn falsely. He shall restore it in full and shall add a fifth part more to it and give it to him to whom it belongs on the day of his guilt offering. And he shall bring his guilt offering to the LORD, a ram without blemish from the flock, according to your valuation, for a guilt offering to the priest. And the priest shall make atonement for him before the LORD, and he shall be forgiven for any of the things which he did that made him guilty." The LORD spoke to Moses, saying, "Command Aaron and his sons, saying, 'This is the law of the burnt offering. The burnt offering shall be on the hearth upon the altar all night until morning, and the fire of the altar shall be kept burning on it. And the priest shall put on his linen garment, and his linen trousers he shall put on his body, and take up the ashes of the burnt offering which the fire has consumed on the altar, and he shall put them beside the altar. Then he shall take off his garments, put on other garments, and carry the ashes outside the camp to a clean place. The fire on the altar shall be kept burning on it; it shall not be put out. The priest shall burn wood on it every morning and lay the burnt offering in order on it, and he shall burn on it the fat of the peace offerings. A fire shall always be burning on the altar; it shall never go out. This is the law of the grain offering: The sons of Aaron shall offer it on the altar before the LORD. He shall take from it his handful of the fine flour of the grain offering, with its oil, and all the frankincense which is on the grain offering, and shall burn it on the altar for a sweet aroma, as a memorial to the LORD. The remainder of it Aaron and his sons shall eat; with unleavened bread it shall be eaten in a holy place; in the court of the Tabernacle of Meeting they shall eat it. It shall not be baked with leaven. I have given it as their portion of My offerings made by fire; it is most holy, like the sin offering and the trespass offering. All the males among the children of Aaron may eat it. It shall be a statute forever in your generations concerning the offerings made by fire to the LORD. Everyone who touches them must be holy." The LORD spoke to Moses, saying, "This is the offering of Aaron and his sons, which they shall offer to the LORD, beginning on the day when he is anointed: one-tenth of an ephah of fine flour as a daily grain offering, half of it in the morning and half of it in the evening. It shall be made in a pan with oil. When it is mixed, you shall bring it in. The baked pieces of the grain offering you shall offer for a sweet aroma to the LORD. The priest from among his sons, who is anointed in his place, shall offer it. It is a statute forever to the LORD. It shall be wholly burned. Every grain offering for the priest shall be wholly burned. It shall not be eaten." The LORD spoke to Moses, saying, "Speak to Aaron and to his sons, saying, 'This is the law of the sin offering: In the place where the burnt offering is killed, the sin offering shall be killed before the LORD. It is most holy. The priest who offers it for sin shall eat it. In a holy place it shall be eaten, in the court of the Tabernacle of Meeting. Everyone who touches its flesh must be holy. And when its blood is sprinkled on any garment, you shall wash that on which it was sprinkled in a holy place. But the earthen vessel in which it is boiled shall be broken. And if it is boiled in a bronze pot, it shall be both scoured and rinsed in water. All the males among the priests may eat it. It is most holy. But no sin offering, from which any of the blood is brought into the Tabernacle of Meeting, to make atonement in the holy place, shall be eaten. It shall be burned in the fire

Chapter 7

Likewise, this is the law of the trespass offering. It is most holy. In the place where they kill the burnt offering, they shall kill the trespass offering. And its blood shall be sprinkled all around on the altar. He shall offer from it all its fat. The fat tail and the fat that covers the entrails, the two kidneys, and the fat that is on them by the flanks, and the fatty lobe attached to the liver above the kidneys, he shall remove. And the priest shall burn them on the altar as an offering made by fire to the LORD. It is a trespass offering. Every male among the priests may eat it. It shall be eaten in a holy place. It is most holy. The trespass offering is like the sin offering. There is one law for them both. The priest who makes atonement with it shall have it. The priest who offers a burnt offering for anyone shall have for himself the skin of the burnt offering which he has offered. Also, every grain offering that is baked in the oven and all that is prepared in the covered pan or in a pan shall be the priest's who offers it. Every grain offering, whether mixed with oil or dry, shall belong to all the sons of Aaron, to one as much as the other. This is the law of the sacrifice of peace offerings which he shall offer to the LORD: If he offers it for a thanksgiving, then he shall offer, with the sacrifice of thanksgiving, unleavened cakes mixed with oil, unleavened wafers anointed with oil, or cakes of blended flour mixed with oil. Besides the cakes, as his offering, he shall offer leavened bread with the sacrifice of thanksgiving of his peace offering. And from it he shall offer one cake from each offering as a heave offering to the LORD. It shall belong to the priest who sprinkles the blood of the peace offering. The flesh of the sacrifice of his peace offering for thanksgiving shall be eaten the same day it is offered. He shall not leave any of it until morning. But if the sacrifice of his offering is a vow or a voluntary offering, it shall be eaten the same day that he offers his sacrifice. But on the next day the remainder of it also may be eaten. The remainder of the flesh of the sacrifice on the third day must be burned with fire. If any of the flesh of the sacrifice of his peace offering is eaten at all on the third day, it shall not be accepted, nor shall it be imputed to him. It shall be an abomination to him who offers it, and the person who eats of it shall bear guilt. The flesh that touches any unclean thing shall not be eaten. It shall be burned with fire. And as for the clean flesh, all who are clean may eat of it. But the person who eats the flesh of the sacrifice of the peace offering that belongs to the LORD, while he is unclean, that person shall be cut off from his people.

Moreover, the person who touches any unclean thing, such as human uncleanness, an unclean animal, or any abominable unclean thing, and who eats the flesh of the sacrifice of the peace offering that belongs to the LORD, that person shall be cut off from his people. The LORD spoke to Moses, saying, "Speak to the children of Israel, saying: 'You shall not eat any fat of ox or sheep or goat. And the fat of an animal that dies naturally, and the fat of what is torn by wild beasts, may be used in any other way, but you shall by no means eat it. For whoever eats the fat of the animal of which men offer an offering made by fire to the LORD, the person who eats it shall be cut off from his people. Moreover, you shall not eat any blood in any of your dwellings, whether of bird or beast. Whoever eats any blood, that person shall be cut off from his people." The LORD spoke to Moses, saying, "Speak to the children of Israel, saying: 'He who offers the sacrifice of his peace offerings to the LORD shall bring his offering to the LORD from the sacrifice of his peace offerings. His own hands shall bring the offerings made by fire to the LORD. The fat with the breast he shall bring, that the breast may be waved as a wave offering before the LORD. And the priest shall burn the fat on the altar, but the breast shall be Aaron's and his sons'. Also, the right thigh you shall give to the priest as a heave offering from the sacrifices of your peace offerings. He among the sons of Aaron, who offers the blood of the peace offering and the fat, shall have the right thigh for his part. For the breast of the wave offering and the thigh of the heave offering I have taken from the children of Israel, from the sacrifices of their peace offerings, and I have given them to Aaron the priest and to his sons from the children of Israel by a statute forever. This is the consecrated portion for Aaron and his sons from the offerings made by fire to the LORD, on the day when Moses presented them to minister to the LORD as priests. The LORD commanded this to be given to them by the children of Israel, on the day that He anointed them, by a statute forever throughout their generations. This is the law of the burnt offering, the grain offering, the sin offering, the trespass offering, the consecrations, and the sacrifice of the peace offering, which the LORD commanded Moses on Mount Sinai, on the day when He commanded the children of Israel to offer their offerings to the LORD in the Wilderness of Sinai

Chapter 8

The LORD spoke to Moses, saying, "Take Aaron and his sons with him, and the garments, the anointing oil, a bull as the sin offering, two rams, and a basket of unleavened bread; and gather all the congregation together at the door of the Tabernacle of Meeting." So Moses did as the LORD commanded him. And the congregation was gathered together at the door of the Tabernacle of Meeting. Moses said to the congregation, "This is what the LORD commanded to be done." Then Moses brought Aaron and his sons and washed them with water. He put the tunic on him, girded him with the sash, clothed him with the robe, and put the ephod on him. And he girded him with the intricately woven band of the ephod and tied it to him with it. Then he put the breastplate on him, and he put the Urim and the Thummim in the breastplate. And he put the turban on his head. Also on the turban, on its front, he put the golden plate, the holy crown, as the LORD had commanded Moses. Moses took the anointing oil and anointed the tabernacle and all that was in it and consecrated them. He sprinkled some of it on the altar seven times, anointed the altar and all its utensils, and the laver and its base, to consecrate them. And he poured some of the anointing oil on Aaron's head and anointed him, to consecrate him. Then Moses brought Aaron's sons and put tunics on them, girded them with sashes, and put hats on them, as the LORD had commanded Moses. He brought the bull for the sin offering. Then Aaron and his sons laid their hands on the head of the bull for the sin offering, and Moses killed it. Then he took the blood and put some on the horns of the altar all around with his finger and purified the altar. And he poured the blood at the base of the altar and consecrated it, to make atonement for it. Then he took all the fat that was on the entrails, the fatty lobe attached to the liver, and the two kidneys with their fat; and Moses burned them on the altar. But the bull, its hide, its flesh, and its offal, he burned with fire outside the camp, as the LORD had commanded Moses. Then he brought the ram as the burnt offering. And Aaron and his sons laid their hands on the head of the ram, and Moses killed it. Then he sprinkled the blood all around on the altar. And he cut the ram into pieces, and Moses burned the head, the pieces, and the fat. Then he washed the entrails and the legs in water. And Moses burned the whole ram on the altar. It was a burnt sacrifice for a sweet aroma, an offering made by fire to the LORD, as the LORD had commanded Moses. And he brought the second ram, the ram of consecration. Then Aaron and his sons laid their hands on the head of the ram, and Moses killed it. Also, he took some of its blood and put it on the tip of Aaron's right ear, on the thumb of his right hand, and on the big toe of his right foot. Then he brought Aaron's sons. And Moses put some of the blood on the tips of their right ears, on the thumbs of their right hands, and on the big toes of their right feet. And Moses sprinkled the blood all around on the altar. Then he took the fat and the fat tail, all the fat that was on the entrails, the fatty lobe attached to the liver, the two kidneys and their fat, and the right thigh; and from the basket of unleavened bread that was before the LORD, he took one unleavened cake, a cake of bread anointed with oil, and one wafer, and put them on the fat and on the right thigh; and he put all these in Aaron's hands and in his sons' hands, and waved them as a wave offering before the LORD. Then Moses took them from their hands and burned them on the altar on the burnt offering. They were consecration offerings for a sweet aroma. That was an offering made by fire to the LORD. And Moses took the breast and waved it as a wave offering before the LORD. It was Moses' part of the ram of consecration, as the LORD had commanded Moses. Then Moses took some of the anointing oil and some of the blood which was on the altar and sprinkled it on Aaron, on his garments, on his sons, and on the garments of his sons with him; and he consecrated Aaron, his garments, his sons, and the garments of his sons with him. And Moses said to Aaron and his sons, "Boil the flesh at the door of the Tabernacle of Meeting, and eat it there with the bread that is in the basket of consecration offerings, as I commanded, saying, 'Aaron and his sons shall eat it.' What remains of the flesh and of the bread you shall burn with fire. And you shall not go outside the door of the Tabernacle of Meeting for seven days, until the days of your consecration are ended. For seven days he shall consecrate you. As he has done this day, so the LORD has commanded to do, to make atonement for you. Therefore you shall stay at the door of the Tabernacle of Meeting day and night for seven days and keep the charge of the LORD, so that you may not die; for so I have been commanded." So Aaron and his sons did all the things that the LORD had commanded by the hand of Moses

Chapter 9

On the eighth day, Moses called Aaron and his sons and the elders of Israel. And he said to Aaron, "Take for yourself a young bull as a sin offering and a ram as a burnt offering, both without blemish, and offer them before the LORD. And to the children of Israel you shall speak, saying, 'Take a kid of the goats as a sin offering, and a calf and a lamb, both of the first year, without blemish, as a burnt offering, also a bull and a ram as peace offerings, to sacrifice before the LORD, and a grain offering mixed with oil; for today the LORD will appear to you.'" So they brought what Moses commanded before the Tabernacle of Meeting. And all the congregation drew near and stood before the LORD. Then Moses said, "This is the thing which the LORD commanded you to do, and the glory of the LORD will appear to you." And Moses said to Aaron, "Go to the altar, offer your sin offering and your burnt offering, and make atonement for yourself and for the people. Offer the offering of the people and make atonement for them, as the LORD commanded." Aaron therefore went to the altar and killed the calf of the sin offering, which was for himself. Then the sons of Aaron brought the blood to him, and he dipped his finger in the blood, put it on the horns of the altar, and poured the blood at the base of the altar. But the fat, the kidneys, and the fatty lobe from the liver of the sin offering he burned on the altar, as the LORD had commanded Moses. The flesh and the hide he burned with fire outside the camp. And he killed the burnt offering, and Aaron's sons presented to him the blood, which he sprinkled all around on the altar. Then they presented the burnt offering to him, with its pieces and head, and he burned them on the altar. And he washed the entrails and the legs and burned them with the burnt offering on the altar. Then he brought the people's offering and took the goat, which was the sin offering for the people, and killed it and offered it for sin, like the first one. And he brought the burnt offering and offered it according to the prescribed manner. Then he brought the grain offering, took a handful of it, and burned it on the altar, besides the burnt sacrifice of the morning. He also killed the bull and the ram as sacrifices of peace offerings, which were for the people. And Aaron's sons presented to him the blood, which he sprinkled all around on the altar, and the fat from the bull and the ram—the fatty tail, what covers the entrails and the kidneys, and the fatty lobe attached to the liver; and they put the fat on the breasts. Then he burned the fat on the altar; but the breasts and the right thigh Aaron waved as a wave offering before the LORD, as Moses had commanded. Then Aaron lifted his hand toward the people, blessed them, and came down from offering the sin offering, the burnt offering, and peace offerings. And Moses and Aaron went into the Tabernacle of Meeting, and came out and blessed the people. Then the glory of the LORD appeared to all the people, and fire came out from before the LORD and consumed the burnt offering and the fat on the altar. When all the people saw it, they shouted and fell on their faces

Chapter 10

Then Nadab and Abihu, the sons of Aaron, each took his censer and put fire in it, put incense on it, and offered profane fire before the LORD, which He had not commanded them. So fire went out from the LORD and devoured them, and they died before the LORD. And Moses said to Aaron, "This is what the LORD spoke, saying: 'By those who come near Me I must be regarded as holy, and before all the people I must be glorified.'" So Aaron held his peace. Moses called Mishael and Elzaphan, the sons of Uzziel, the uncle of Aaron, and said to them, "Come near, carry your brethren from before the sanctuary out of the camp." So they went near and carried them by their tunics out of the camp, as Moses had said. And

Moses said to Aaron, and to Eleazar and Ithamar, his sons, "Do not uncover your heads nor tear your clothes, lest you die, and wrath come upon all the people. But let your brethren, the whole house of Israel, bewail the burning which the LORD has kindled. You shall not go out from the door of the Tabernacle of Meeting, lest you die, for the anointing oil of the LORD is upon you." And they did according to the word of Moses. Then the LORD spoke to Aaron, saying: "Do not drink wine or intoxicating drink, you nor your sons with you, when you go into the Tabernacle of Meeting, lest you die. It shall be a statute forever throughout your generations, that you may distinguish between holy and unholy, and between unclean and clean, and that you may teach the children of Israel all the statutes which the LORD has spoken to them by the hand of Moses." And Moses spoke to Aaron, and to Eleazar and Ithamar, his sons who were left: "Take the grain offering that remains of the offerings made by fire to the LORD, and eat it without leaven beside the altar, for it is most holy. You shall eat it in a holy place, because it is your due and your sons' due, of the sacrifices made by fire to the LORD; for so I have been commanded. The breast of the wave offering and the thigh of the heave offering you shall eat in a clean place, you, your sons, and your daughters with you; for they are your due and your sons' due, which are given from the sacrifices of peace offerings of the children of Israel. The thigh of the heave offering and the breast of the wave offering they shall bring with the offerings of fat made by fire, to wave as a wave offering before the LORD. And it shall be yours and your sons' with you, by a statute forever, as the LORD has commanded." Then Moses made careful inquiry about the goat of the sin offering, and there it was— burned up! And he was angry with Eleazar and Ithamar, the sons of Aaron who were left, saying, "Why have you not eaten the sin offering in a holy place, since it is most holy, and God has given it to you to bear the guilt of the congregation, to make atonement for them before the LORD? See! Its blood was not brought inside the holy place; indeed you should have eaten it in a holy place, as I commanded." And Aaron said to Moses, "Look, this day they have offered their sin offering and their burnt offering before the LORD, and such things have befallen me! If I had eaten the sin offering today, would it have been accepted in the sight of the LORD?" So when Moses heard that, he was content

Chapter 11

Then the LORD spoke to Moses and Aaron, saying to them, "Speak to the children of Israel, saying, 'These are the animals which you may eat among all the animals that are on the earth. Whatever parts the hoof and is cloven-footed and chews the cud, among the beasts, that you may eat. Nevertheless, of those that chew the cud or have cloven hooves, you shall not eat these: the camel, because it chews the cud but does not have cloven hooves, is unclean to you. The rock badger, because it chews the cud but does not have cloven hooves, is unclean to you. The hare, because it chews the cud but does not have cloven hooves, is unclean to you. And the swine, though it divides the hoof, having cloven hooves, yet does not chew the cud, is unclean to you. Their flesh you shall not eat, and their carcasses you shall not touch; they are unclean to you. These you may eat of all that are in the waters: whatever in the waters has fins and scales, whether in the seas or in the rivers, that you may eat. But all in the seas or in the rivers that do not have fins and scales, all that move in the waters or any living thing which is in the waters, they are an abomination to you. They shall be an abomination to you; you shall not eat their flesh, but you shall regard their carcasses as an abomination. Whatever in the water does not have fins or scales, that shall be an abomination to you. These you shall regard as an abomination among the birds; they shall not be eaten, they are an abomination: the eagle, the vulture, the buzzard, the kite, and the falcon after its kind; every raven after its kind, the ostrich, the short-eared owl, the seagull, and the hawk after its kind; the little owl, the fisher owl, and the screech owl; the white owl, the jackdaw, and the carrion vulture; the stork, the heron after its kind, the hoopoe, and the bat. All flying insects that creep on all fours shall be an abomination to you. Yet these you may eat of every flying insect that creeps on all fours: those which have jointed legs above their feet with which to leap on the earth. These you may eat: the locust after its kind, the destroying locust after its kind, the cricket after its kind, and the grasshopper after its kind. But all other flying insects which have four feet shall be an abomination to you. By these you shall become unclean; whoever touches the carcass of any of them shall be unclean until evening; whoever carries part of the carcass of any of them shall wash his clothes and be unclean until evening. The carcass of any animal which divides the foot but is not cloven-hoofed or does not chew the cud is unclean to you; everyone who touches it shall be unclean. And whatever goes on its paws, among all kinds of animals that go on all fours, those are unclean to you. Whoever touches any such carcass shall be unclean until evening. Whoever carries any such carcass shall wash his clothes and be unclean until evening. They are unclean to you. These also shall be unclean to you among the creeping things that creep on the earth: the mole, the mouse, and the large lizard after its kind; the gecko, the monitor lizard, the sand reptile, the sand lizard, and the chameleon. These are unclean to you among all that creep. Whoever touches them when they are dead shall be unclean until evening. Anything on which any of them falls when they are dead shall be unclean, whether it is any item of wood or clothing or skin or sack, whatever item it is, in which any work is done, it must be put in water. It shall be unclean until evening; then it shall be clean. Any earthen vessel into which any of them falls you shall break, and whatever is in it shall be unclean: in such a vessel any edible food upon which water falls becomes unclean, and any drink that may be drunk from it becomes unclean. And everything on which a part of any such carcass falls shall be unclean; whether it is an oven or cooking stove, it shall be broken down; for they are unclean and shall be unclean to you. Nevertheless, a spring or a cistern, in which there is plenty of water, shall be clean, but whatever touches any such carcass becomes unclean. If a part of any such carcass falls on any planting seed which is to be sown, it remains clean. But if water is put on the seed, and a part of any such carcass falls on it, it becomes unclean to you. And if any animal which you may eat dies, he who touches its carcass shall be unclean until evening. He who eats of its carcass shall wash his clothes and be unclean until evening. He also who carries its carcass shall wash his clothes and be unclean until evening. And every creeping thing that creeps on the earth shall be an abomination. It shall not be eaten. Whatever crawls on its belly, whatever goes on all fours, or whatever has many feet among all creeping things that creep on the earth—these you shall not eat, for they are an abomination. You shall not make yourselves abominable with any creeping thing that creeps, nor shall you make yourselves unclean with them, lest you be defiled by them. For I am the LORD your God. You shall therefore consecrate yourselves, and you shall be holy; for I am holy. Neither shall you defile yourselves with any creeping thing that creeps on the earth. For I am the LORD who brings you up out of the land of Egypt, to be your God. You shall therefore be holy, for I am holy. This is the law of the animals and the birds and every living creature that moves in the waters and of every creature that creeps on the earth, to distinguish between the unclean and the clean, and between the animal that may be eaten and the animal that may not be eaten.'"

Chapter 12

The LORD spoke to Moses, saying, "Speak to the children of Israel, saying: 'If a woman has conceived and borne a male child, then she shall be unclean seven days; as in the days of her customary impurity, she shall be unclean. And on the eighth day, the flesh of his foreskin shall be circumcised. She shall then continue in the blood of her purification thirty-three days. She shall not touch any hallowed thing nor come into the sanctuary until the days of her purification are fulfilled. But if she bears a female child, then she shall be unclean two weeks, as in her customary impurity, and she shall continue in the blood of her purification sixty-six days. When the days of her purification are fulfilled, whether for a son or a daughter, she shall bring to the priest a lamb of the first year as a burnt offering, and a young pigeon or a turtledove as a sin offering, to the door of the Tabernacle of Meeting. Then he shall offer it before the LORD and make atonement for her, and she shall be clean from the flow of her blood. This is the law for her who has borne a male or a female. And if she is not able to bring a lamb, then she may bring two turtledoves or two young pigeons—one as a burnt offering and the other as a sin offering. So the priest shall make atonement for her, and she will be clean.'"

Chapter 13

The LORD spoke to Moses and Aaron, saying, "When a man has on the skin of his body a swelling, a scab, or a bright spot, and it becomes on the skin of his body like a leprous sore, then he shall be brought to Aaron the priest or to one of his sons the priests. The priest shall examine the sore on the skin of the body, and if the hair on the sore has turned white, and the sore appears to be deeper than the skin of his body, it is a leprous sore. Then the priest shall examine him and pronounce him unclean. But if the bright spot is white on the skin of his body and does not appear to be deeper than the skin, and its hair has not turned white, then the priest shall isolate the one who has the sore seven days. And the priest shall examine him on the seventh day; and indeed, if the sore appears to be as it was, and the sore has not spread on the skin, then the priest shall isolate him another seven days. Then the priest shall examine him again on the seventh day; and indeed, if the sore has faded, and the sore has not spread on the skin, then the priest shall pronounce him clean; it is only a scab. And he shall wash his clothes and be clean. But if the scab should at all spread over the skin, after he has been seen by the priest for his cleansing, he shall be seen by the priest again. And if the priest sees that the scab has indeed spread on the skin, then the priest shall pronounce him unclean. It is leprosy. When the leprous sore is on a person, then he shall be brought to the priest. And the priest shall examine him; and indeed, if the swelling on the skin is white, and it has turned the hair white, and there is a spot of raw flesh in the swelling, it is an old leprosy on the skin of his body. The priest shall pronounce him unclean and shall not isolate him, for he is unclean. If leprosy breaks out all over the skin, and the leprosy covers all the skin of the one who has the sore, from his head to his foot, wherever the priest looks, then the priest shall consider; and indeed, if the leprosy has covered all his body, he shall pronounce him clean who has the sore. It has all turned white. He is clean. But when raw flesh appears on him, he shall be unclean. And the priest shall examine the raw flesh and pronounce him to be unclean; for the raw flesh is unclean. It is leprosy. Or if the raw flesh changes and turns white again, he shall come to the priest. And the priest shall examine him; and indeed, if the sore has turned white, then the priest shall pronounce him clean who has the sore. He is clean. If the body develops a boil in the skin, and it is healed, and in the place of the boil, there comes a white swelling or a bright spot, reddish-white, then it shall be shown to the priest. And if, when the priest sees it, it indeed appears deeper than the skin, and its hair has turned white, the priest shall pronounce him unclean. It is a leprous sore which has broken out of the boil. But if the priest examines it, and indeed there are no white hairs in it, and it is not deeper than the skin, but has faded, then the priest shall isolate him seven days. And if it should at all spread over the skin, then the priest shall pronounce him unclean. It is a leprous sore. But if the bright spot stays in one place and has not spread, it is the scar of the boil; and the priest shall pronounce him clean. Or if the body receives a burn on its skin by fire, and the raw flesh of the burn becomes a bright spot, reddish-white or white, then the priest shall examine it. And indeed, if the hair of the bright spot has turned white, and it appears deeper than the skin, it is leprosy broken out in the burn. Therefore the priest shall pronounce him unclean. It is a leprous sore. But if the priest examines it, and indeed there are no white hairs in the bright spot, and it is not deeper than the skin, but has faded, then the priest shall isolate him seven days. And the priest shall examine him on the seventh day. If it has at all spread over the skin, then the priest shall pronounce him unclean. It is a leprous sore. But if the bright spot stays in one place and has not spread in the skin, but has faded, it is a swelling from the burn. The priest shall pronounce him clean, for it is the scar from the burn. If a man or woman has a sore on the head or the beard, then the priest shall examine the sore; and indeed, if it appears deeper than the skin, and there is in it a thin yellow hair, then the priest shall pronounce him unclean. It is a scaly leprosy of the head or beard. But if the priest examines the scaly sore, and indeed it does not appear deeper than the skin, and there is no black hair in it, then the priest shall isolate the one who has the scale seven days. And on the seventh day, the priest shall examine the sore; and indeed, if the scale has not spread, and there is no yellow hair in it, and the scale does not appear deeper than the skin, he shall shave himself, but the scale he shall not shave. And the priest shall isolate the one who has the scale another seven days. On the seventh day, the priest shall examine the scale; and indeed, if the scale has not spread over the skin, and does not appear deeper than the skin, the priest shall pronounce him clean. He shall wash his clothes and be clean. But if the scale should at all spread over the skin after his cleansing, then the priest shall examine him; and indeed, if the scale has spread over the skin, the priest need not seek for yellow hair. He is unclean. But if the scale appears to be at a standstill, and there is black hair grown up in it, the scale has healed. He is clean, and the priest shall pronounce him clean. If a man or a woman has bright spots on the skin of the body, specifically white bright spots, then the priest shall look; and indeed, if the bright spots on the skin of the body are dull white, it is a white spot that grows on the skin. He is clean. As for the man whose hair has fallen from his head, he is bald, but he is clean. He

whose hair has fallen from his forehead, he is bald on the forehead, but he is clean. And if there is on the bald head or bald forehead a reddish-white sore, it is leprosy breaking out on his bald head or his bald forehead. Then the priest shall examine it; and indeed, if the swelling of the sore is reddish-white on his bald head or on his bald forehead, as the appearance of leprosy on the skin of the body, he is a leprous man. He is unclean. The priest shall surely pronounce him unclean. His sore is on his head. Now the leper on whom the sore is, his clothes shall be torn and his head bare; and he shall cover his mustache and cry, 'Unclean! Unclean!' He shall be unclean. All the days he has the sore, he shall be unclean. He is unclean, and he shall dwell alone. His dwelling shall be outside the camp. Also, if a garment has a leprous plague in it, whether it is a woolen garment or a linen garment, whether it is in the warp or woof of linen or wool, whether in leather or in anything made of leather, and if the plague is greenish or reddish in the garment or in the leather, whether in the warp or in the woof, or in anything made of leather, it is a leprous plague and shall be shown to the priest. The priest shall examine the plague and isolate that which has the plague seven days. And he shall examine the plague on the seventh day. If the plague has spread in the garment, either in the warp or in the woof, in the leather or in anything made of leather, the plague is an active leprosy. It is unclean. He shall therefore burn that garment in which is the plague, whether warp or woof, in wool or in linen, or anything of leather. For it is an active leprosy. The garment shall be burned in the fire. But if the priest examines it, and indeed the plague has not spread in the garment, either in the warp or in the woof, or in anything made of leather, then the priest shall command that they wash the thing in which is the plague; and he shall isolate it another seven days. Then the priest shall examine the plague after it has been washed; and indeed, if the plague has not changed its color, though the plague has not spread, it is unclean, and you shall burn it in the fire. It continues eating away, whether the damage is outside or inside. If the priest examines it, and indeed the plague has faded after washing it, then he shall tear it out of the garment, whether out of the warp or out of the woof, or out of the leather. But if it appears again in the garment, either in the warp or in the woof, or in anything made of leather, it is a spreading plague. You shall burn with fire that in which is the plague. And if you wash the garment, either warp or woof, or whatever is made of leather, if the plague has disappeared from it, then it shall be washed a second time and shall be clean. This is the law of the leprous plague in a garment of wool or linen, either in the warp or woof, or in anything made of leather, to pronounce it clean or to pronounce it unclean."

Chapter 14

The LORD spoke to Moses, saying, "This shall be the law of the leper for the day of his cleansing: He shall be brought to the priest. And the priest shall go out of the camp, and the priest shall examine him; and indeed, if the leprosy is healed in the leper, then the priest shall command to take for him who is to be cleansed two living and clean birds, cedarwood, scarlet, and hyssop. And the priest shall command that one of the birds be killed in an earthen vessel over running water. As for the living bird, he shall take it, the cedarwood, and the scarlet, and the hyssop, and dip them and the living bird in the blood of the bird that was killed over the running water. And he shall sprinkle it seven times on him who is to be cleansed from the leprosy, and shall pronounce him clean, and shall let the living bird loose in the open field. He who is to be cleansed shall wash his clothes, shave off all his hair, and wash himself in water, that he may be clean. After that, he shall come into the camp, and shall stay outside his tent seven days. But on the seventh day, he shall shave all the hair off his head and his beard and his eyebrows—all his hair he shall shave off. He shall wash his clothes and wash his body in water, and he shall be clean. And on the eighth day, he shall take two male lambs without blemish, one ewe lamb of the first year without blemish, three-tenths of an ephah of fine flour mixed with oil as a grain offering, and one log of oil. Then the priest who makes him clean shall present the man who is to be made clean, and those things, before the LORD, at the door of the Tabernacle of Meeting. And the priest shall take one male lamb and offer it as a trespass offering, and the log of oil, and wave them as a wave offering before the LORD. Then he shall kill the lamb in the place where he kills the sin offering and the burnt offering, in a holy place. For as the sin offering is the priest's, so is the trespass offering. It is most holy. The priest shall take some of the blood of the trespass offering, and the priest shall put it on the tip of the right ear of him who is to be cleansed, on the thumb of his right hand, and on the big toe of his right foot. And the priest shall take some of the log of oil, and pour it into the palm of his own left hand. Then the priest shall dip his right finger in the oil that is in his left hand and shall sprinkle some of the oil with his finger seven times before the LORD. And the rest of the oil in his hand, the priest shall put some on the tip of the right ear of him who is to be cleansed, on the thumb of his right hand, and on the big toe of his right foot, on the blood of the trespass offering. The rest of the oil that is in the priest's hand he shall put on the head of him who is to be cleansed. So the priest shall make atonement for him before the LORD. Then the priest shall offer the sin offering and make atonement for him who is to be cleansed from his uncleanness. Afterward, he shall kill the burnt offering. And the priest shall offer the burnt offering and the grain offering on the altar. So the priest shall make atonement for him, and he shall be clean. But if he is poor and cannot afford it, then he shall take one male lamb as a trespass offering to be waved, to make atonement for him, one-tenth of an ephah of fine flour mixed with oil as a grain offering, a log of oil, and two turtledoves or two young pigeons, such as he is able to afford. One shall be a sin offering, and the other a burnt offering. He shall bring them to the priest on the eighth day for his cleansing, to the door of the Tabernacle of Meeting, before the LORD. And the priest shall take the lamb of the trespass offering and the log of oil, and the priest shall wave them as a wave offering before the LORD. Then he shall kill the lamb of the trespass offering. And the priest shall take some of the blood of the trespass offering and put it on the tip of the right ear of him who is to be cleansed, on the thumb of his right hand, and on the big toe of his right foot. The priest shall pour some of the oil into the palm of his own left hand. Then the priest shall sprinkle with his right finger some of the oil that is in his left hand seven times before the LORD. And the priest shall put some of the oil that is in his hand on the tip of the right ear of him who is to be cleansed, on the thumb of his right hand, and on the big toe of his right foot, on the place of the blood of the trespass offering. The rest of the oil that is in the priest's hand he shall put on the head of him who is to be cleansed, to make atonement for him before the LORD. And he shall offer one of the turtledoves or young pigeons, such as he can afford, such as he is able to afford, the one as a sin offering and the other as a burnt offering, with the grain offering. So the

priest shall make atonement for him who is to be cleansed before the LORD. This is the law for one who had a leprous sore, who cannot afford the usual cleansing." The LORD spoke to Moses and Aaron, saying, "When you have come into the land of Canaan, which I give you as a possession, and I put the leprous plague in a house in the land of your possession, and he who owns the house comes and tells the priest, saying, 'It seems to me that there is some plague in the house,' then the priest shall command that they empty the house before the priest goes in to examine the plague, that all that is in the house may not be made unclean; and afterward the priest shall go in to examine the house. And he shall examine the plague; and indeed, if the plague is on the walls of the house with ingrained streaks, greenish or reddish, which appear to be deep in the wall, then the priest shall go out of the house, to the door of the house, and shut up the house seven days. And the priest shall come again on the seventh day and look; and indeed, if the plague has spread on the walls of the house, then the priest shall command that they take away the stones in which is the plague, and they shall cast them into an unclean place outside the city. And he shall cause the house to be scraped inside, all around, and the dust that they scrape off, they shall pour out in an unclean place outside the city. Then they shall take other stones and put them in the place of those stones, and he shall take other mortar and plaster the house. Now if the plague comes back and breaks out in the house, after he has taken away the stones, after he has scraped the house, and after it is plastered, then the priest shall come and look; and indeed, if the plague has spread in the house, it is an active leprosy in the house. It is unclean. And he shall break down the house, its stones, its timber, and all the plaster of the house, and he shall carry them outside the city to an unclean place. Moreover, he who goes into the house at all while it is shut up shall be unclean until evening. And he who lies down in the house shall wash his clothes, and he who eats in the house shall wash his clothes. But if the priest comes in and examines it, and indeed the plague has not spread in the house after the house was plastered, then the priest shall pronounce the house clean because the plague is healed. And he shall take, to cleanse the house, two birds, cedarwood, scarlet, and hyssop. Then he shall kill one of the birds in an earthen vessel over running water; and he shall take the cedarwood, the hyssop, the scarlet, and the living bird, and dip them in the blood of the slain bird and in the running water, and sprinkle the house seven times. And he shall cleanse the house with the blood of the bird and the running water and the living bird, with the cedarwood, the hyssop, and the scarlet. Then he shall let the living bird loose outside the city in the open field, and make atonement for the house, and it shall be clean. This is the law for any leprous sore and scale, for the leprosy of a garment and of a house, for a swelling and a scab and a bright spot, to teach when it is unclean and when it is clean. This is the law of leprosy."

Chapter 15

The LORD spoke to Moses and Aaron, saying, "Speak to the children of Israel, and say to them: 'When any man has a discharge from his body, his discharge is unclean. And this shall be his uncleanness in regard to his discharge: whether his body runs with his discharge, or his body is stopped up by his discharge, it is his uncleanness. Every bed is unclean on which he who has the discharge lies, and everything on which he sits shall be unclean. And whoever touches his bed shall wash his clothes and bathe in water, and be unclean until evening. He who sits on anything on which he who has the discharge sat shall wash his clothes and bathe in water and be unclean until evening. And he who touches the body of him who has the discharge shall wash his clothes and bathe in water and be unclean until evening. If he who has the discharge spits on him who is clean, then he shall wash his clothes and bathe in water and be unclean until evening. Any saddle on which he who has the discharge rides shall be unclean. Whoever touches anything that was under him shall be unclean until evening. He who carries any of those things shall wash his clothes and bathe in water and be unclean until evening. And whomever the one who has the discharge touches and has not rinsed his hands in water, he shall wash his clothes and bathe in water and be unclean until evening. The vessel of earth that he who has the discharge touches shall be broken, and every vessel of wood shall be rinsed in water. And when he who has a discharge is cleansed of his discharge, then he shall count for himself seven days for his cleansing, wash his clothes, and bathe his body in running water; then he shall be clean. On the eighth day he shall take for himself two turtledoves or two young pigeons, and come before the LORD, to the door of the Tabernacle of Meeting, and give them to the priest. Then the priest shall offer them, the one as a sin offering and the other as a burnt offering. So the priest shall make atonement for him before the LORD because of his discharge. If any man has an emission of semen, then he shall wash all his body in water, and be unclean until evening. And any garment and any leather on which there is semen, it shall be washed with water, and be unclean until evening. Also, when a woman lies with a man, and there is an emission of semen, they shall bathe in water, and be unclean until evening. If a woman has a discharge, and the discharge from her body is blood, she shall be set apart seven days; and whoever touches her shall be unclean until evening. Everything that she lies on during her impurity shall be unclean. Also, everything that she sits on shall be unclean. Whoever touches her bed shall wash his clothes and bathe in water, and be unclean until evening. And whoever touches anything that she sat on shall wash his clothes and bathe in water, and be unclean until evening. If anything is on her bed or on anything on which she sits, when he touches it, he shall be unclean until evening. And if any man lies with her at all, so that her impurity is on him, he shall be unclean seven days; and every bed on which he lies shall be unclean. If a woman has a discharge of blood for many days, other than at the time of her customary impurity, or if it runs beyond her usual time of impurity, all the days of her unclean discharge shall be as the days of her customary impurity. She shall be unclean. Every bed on which she lies all the days of her discharge shall be to her as the bed of her impurity; and whatever she sits on shall be unclean, as the uncleanness of her impurity. Whoever touches those things shall be unclean; he shall wash his clothes and bathe in water, and be unclean until evening. But if she is cleansed of her discharge, then she shall count for herself seven days, and after that she shall be clean. And on the eighth day she shall take for herself two turtledoves or two young pigeons, and bring them to the priest, to the door of the Tabernacle of Meeting. Then the priest shall offer the one as a sin offering and the other as a burnt offering, and the priest shall make atonement for her before the LORD for the discharge of her uncleanness. Thus you shall separate the children of Israel from their uncleanness, lest they die in their uncleanness when they defile My Tabernacle that is among them. This is the law for one who has a discharge, and for him who emits semen and is unclean thereby, and for her who is indisposed because of her customary impurity, and for one who has a discharge, either man or woman, and for him who lies with her who is unclean.'"

Chapter 16

The LORD spoke to Moses after the death of Aaron's two sons, when they approached the LORD and died. The LORD said to Moses, "Tell Aaron, your brother, that he shall not come at just any time into the holy place inside the veil, before the mercy seat which is on the ark, lest he die; for I will appear in the cloud above the mercy seat. Thus Aaron shall come into the holy place with a young bull as a sin offering and a ram as a burnt offering. He shall put on the holy linen tunic, and the linen trousers shall be on his body; he shall be girded with a linen sash, and with the linen turban he shall be attired. These are holy garments. Therefore he shall wash his body in water and put them on. He shall take from the congregation of the children of Israel two kids of the goats as a sin offering and one ram as a burnt offering. Aaron shall offer the bull as a sin offering, which is for himself, and make atonement for himself and for his house. He shall take the two goats and present them before the LORD at the door of the Tabernacle of Meeting. Then Aaron shall cast lots for the two goats: one lot for the LORD and the other lot for the scapegoat. Aaron shall bring the goat on which the LORD's lot fell and offer it as a sin offering. But the goat on which the lot fell to be the scapegoat shall be presented alive before the LORD, to make atonement upon it, and to let it go as the scapegoat into the wilderness. Aaron shall bring the bull of the sin offering, which is for himself, and make atonement for himself and for his house, and shall kill the bull as the sin offering which is for himself. He shall take a censer full of burning coals of fire from the altar before the LORD, with his hands full of sweet incense beaten fine, and bring it inside the veil. He shall put the incense on the fire before the LORD, that the cloud of incense may cover the mercy seat that is on the Testimony, lest he die. He shall take some of the blood of the bull and sprinkle it with his finger on the mercy seat on the east side; and before the mercy seat he shall sprinkle some of the blood with his finger seven times. Then he shall kill the goat of the sin offering, which is for the people, bring its blood inside the veil, do with that blood as he did with the blood of the bull, and sprinkle it on the mercy seat and before the mercy seat. So he shall make atonement for the Holy Place, because of the uncleanness of the children of Israel, and because of their transgressions, for all their sins; and so he shall do for the Tabernacle of Meeting which remains among them in the midst of their uncleanness. There shall be no man in the Tabernacle of Meeting when he goes in to make atonement in the Holy Place until he comes out, that he may make atonement for himself, for his household, and for all the assembly of Israel. He shall go out to the altar that is before the LORD, and make atonement for it, and shall take some of the blood of the bull and some of the blood of the goat, and put it on the horns of the altar all around. Then he shall sprinkle some of the blood on it with his finger seven times, cleanse it, and consecrate it from the uncleanness of the children of Israel. When he has made an end of atoning for the Holy Place, the Tabernacle of Meeting, and the altar, he shall bring the live goat. Aaron shall lay both his hands on the head of the live goat, confess over it all the iniquities of the children of Israel, and all their transgressions, concerning all their sins, putting them on the head of the goat, and shall send it away into the wilderness by the hand of a suitable man. The goat shall bear on itself all their iniquities to an uninhabited land; and he shall release the goat in the wilderness. Then Aaron shall come into the Tabernacle of Meeting, shall take off the linen garments which he put on when he went into the Holy Place, and shall leave them there. He shall wash his body with water in a holy place, put on his garments, come out and offer his burnt offering and the burnt offering of the people, and make atonement for himself and for the people. The fat of the sin offering he shall burn on the altar. And he who released the goat as the scapegoat shall wash his clothes and bathe his body in water, and afterward he may come into the camp. The bull for the sin offering and the goat for the sin offering, whose blood was brought in to make atonement in the Holy Place, shall be carried outside the camp. They shall burn in the fire their skins, their flesh, and their offal. Then he who burns them shall wash his clothes and bathe his body in water, and afterward he may come into the camp. This shall be a statute forever for you: In the seventh month, on the tenth day of the month, you shall afflict your souls, and do no work at all, whether a native of your own country or a stranger who dwells among you. For on that day the priest shall make atonement for you, to cleanse you, that you may be clean from all your sins before the LORD. It is a Sabbath of solemn rest for you, and you shall afflict your souls. It is a statute forever. And the priest, who is anointed and consecrated to minister as priest in his father's place, shall make atonement, and put on the linen clothes, the holy garments; then he shall make atonement for the Holy Sanctuary, and he shall make atonement for the Tabernacle of Meeting and for the altar, and he shall make atonement for the priests and for all the people of the assembly. This shall be an everlasting statute for you, to make atonement for the children of Israel, for all their sins, once a year." And he did as the LORD commanded Moses

Chapter 17

The LORD spoke to Moses, saying, "Speak to Aaron, to his sons, and to all the children of Israel, and say to them, 'This is the thing which the LORD has commanded, saying: Whatever man of the house of Israel who kills an ox or lamb or goat in the camp, or who kills it outside the camp, and does not bring it to the door of the Tabernacle of Meeting to offer an offering to the LORD before the tabernacle of the LORD, the guilt of bloodshed shall be imputed to that man. He has shed blood; and that man shall be cut off from among his people. This is so that the children of Israel may bring their sacrifices which they offer in the open field, that they may bring them to the LORD at the door of the Tabernacle of Meeting, to the priest, and offer them as peace offerings to the LORD. And the priest shall sprinkle the blood on the altar of the LORD at the door of the Tabernacle of Meeting, and burn the fat for a sweet aroma to the LORD. They shall no longer offer their sacrifices to demons, after whom they have played the harlot. This shall be a statute forever for them throughout their generations.' Also you shall say to them: 'Whatever man of the house of Israel, or of the strangers who dwell among you, who offers a burnt offering or sacrifice, and does not bring it to the door of the Tabernacle of Meeting, to offer it to the LORD, that man shall be cut off from among his people. And whatever man of the house of Israel, or of the strangers who dwell among you, who eats any blood, I will set My face against that person who eats blood, and will cut him off from among his people. For the life of the flesh is in the blood, and I have given it to you upon the altar to make atonement for your souls; for it is the blood that makes atonement for the soul.' Therefore I said to the children of Israel, 'No one among you shall eat blood, nor shall any stranger who dwells among you eat blood.' Whatever man of the children of Israel, or of the strangers who dwell among you, who hunts and catches any animal or bird that may be eaten, he shall pour out its blood and cover it with dust; for it is the life of all flesh. Its blood sustains its life. Therefore I said to the children of Israel, 'You shall not eat the blood of any flesh, for the life of all flesh is its blood. Whoever eats it shall be cut off.' And every person who eats what died naturally or what was torn by beasts, whether he is a native of your own country or a stranger, he shall both wash his clothes and bathe in water, and be unclean until evening. Then he shall be clean. But if he does not wash them or bathe his body, then he shall bear his guilt.'"

Chapter 18

The LORD spoke to Moses, saying, "Speak to the children of Israel, and say to them: 'I am the LORD your God. According to the doings of the land of Egypt, where you dwelt, you shall not do; and according to the doings of the land of Canaan, where I am bringing you, you shall not do; nor shall you walk in their ordinances. You shall observe My judgments and keep My ordinances, to walk in them: I am the LORD your God. You shall therefore keep My statutes and My judgments, which if a man does, he shall live by them: I am the LORD. None of you shall approach anyone who is near of kin to him, to uncover his nakedness: I am the LORD. The nakedness of your father or the nakedness of your mother you shall not uncover. She is your mother; you shall not uncover her nakedness. The nakedness of your father's wife you shall not uncover; it is your father's nakedness. The nakedness of your sister, the daughter of your father, or the daughter of your mother, whether born at home or elsewhere, their nakedness you shall not uncover. The nakedness of your son's daughter or your daughter's daughter, their nakedness you shall not uncover; for theirs is your own nakedness. The nakedness of your father's wife's daughter, begotten by your father—she is your sister—you shall not uncover her nakedness. You shall not uncover the nakedness of your father's sister; she is near of kin to your father. You shall not uncover the nakedness of your mother's sister, for she is near of kin to your mother. You shall not uncover the nakedness of your father's brother. You shall not approach his wife; she is your aunt. You shall not uncover the nakedness of your daughter-in-law—she is your son's wife—you shall not uncover her nakedness. You shall not uncover the nakedness of your brother's wife; it is your brother's nakedness. You shall not uncover the nakedness of a woman and her daughter, nor shall you take her son's daughter or her daughter's daughter, to uncover her nakedness. They are near of kin to her. It is wickedness. Nor shall you take a woman as a rival to her sister, to uncover her nakedness while the other is alive. Also you shall not approach a woman to uncover her nakedness as long as she is in her customary impurity. Moreover, you shall not lie carnally with your neighbor's wife, to defile yourself with her. And you shall not let any of your descendants pass through the fire to Molech, nor shall you profane the name of your God: I am the LORD. You shall not lie with a male as with a woman. It is an abomination. Nor shall you mate with any animal, to defile yourself with it. Nor shall any woman stand before an animal to mate with it. It is perversion. Do not defile yourselves with any of these things; for by all these the nations are defiled, which I am casting out before you. For the land is defiled; therefore I visit the punishment of its iniquity upon it, and the land vomits out its inhabitants. You shall therefore keep My statutes and My judgments, and shall not commit any of these abominations, either any of your own nation or any stranger who dwells among you (for all these abominations the men of the land have done, who were before you, and thus the land is defiled), lest the land vomit you out also when you defile it, as it vomited out the nations that were before you. For whoever commits any of these abominations, the persons who commit them shall be cut off from among their people. Therefore you shall keep My ordinance, so that you do not commit any of these abominable customs which were committed before you, and that you do not defile yourselves by them: I am the LORD your God.'"

Chapter 19

The LORD spoke to Moses, saying, "Speak to all the congregation of the children of Israel, and say to them: 'You shall be holy, for I the LORD your God am holy. Every one of you shall revere his mother and his father and keep My Sabbaths: I am the LORD your God. Do not turn to idols, nor make for yourselves molded gods: I am the LORD your God. And if you offer a sacrifice of a peace offering to the LORD, you shall offer it of your own free will. It shall be eaten the same day you offer it, and on the next day; and if any remains until the third day, it shall be burned in the fire. And if it is eaten at all on the third day, it is an abomination. It shall not be accepted. Therefore everyone who eats it shall bear his iniquity, because he has profaned the hallowed offering of the LORD; and that person shall be cut off from his people. When you reap the harvest of your land, you shall not wholly reap the corners of your field, nor shall you gather the gleanings of your harvest. And you shall not glean your vineyard, nor shall you gather every grape of your vineyard; you shall leave them for the poor and the stranger: I am the LORD your God. You shall not steal, nor deal falsely, nor lie to one another. And you shall not swear by My name falsely, nor shall you profane the name of your God: I am the LORD. You shall not cheat your neighbor, nor rob him. The wages of him who is hired shall not remain with you all night until morning. You shall not curse the deaf, nor put a stumbling block before the blind, but shall fear your God: I am the LORD. You shall do no injustice in judgment. You shall not be partial to the poor, nor honor the person of the mighty. In righteousness you shall judge your neighbor. You shall not go about as a talebearer among your people, nor shall you take a stand against the life of your neighbor: I am the LORD. You shall not hate your brother in your heart. You shall surely rebuke your neighbor, and not bear sin because of him. You shall not take vengeance, nor bear any grudge against the children of your people, but you shall love your neighbor as yourself: I am the LORD. You shall keep My statutes. You shall not let your livestock breed with another kind. You shall not sow your field with mixed seed. Nor shall a garment of mixed linen and wool come upon you. Whoever lies carnally with a woman who is betrothed to a man as a concubine, and who has not at all been redeemed nor given her freedom, for this there shall be scourging; but they shall not be put to death, because she was not free. And he shall bring his trespass offering to the LORD, to the door of the Tabernacle of Meeting, a ram as a trespass offering. The priest shall make atonement for him with the ram of the trespass offering before the LORD for his sin which he has committed. And the sin which he has committed shall be forgiven him. When you come into the land, and have planted all kinds of trees for food, then you shall count their fruit as uncircumcised. Three years it shall be as uncircumcised to you. It shall not be eaten. But in the fourth year all its fruit shall be holy, a praise to the LORD. And in the fifth year you may eat its fruit, that it may yield to you its increase: I am the LORD your God. You shall not eat anything with the blood, nor shall you practice divination or soothsaying. You shall not shave around the sides of your head, nor shall you disfigure the edges of your beard. You shall not make any cuttings in your flesh for the dead, nor tattoo any marks on you: I am the LORD. Do not prostitute your daughter, to cause her to be a harlot, lest the land fall into harlotry, and the land become full of wickedness. You shall keep My Sabbaths and reverence My sanctuary: I am the LORD. Give no regard to mediums and familiar spirits; do not seek after them, to be defiled by them: I am the LORD your God. You shall rise before the gray-headed and honor the presence of an old man, and fear your God: I am the LORD. And if a stranger dwells with you in your land, you shall not mistreat him. The stranger who dwells among you shall be to you as one born among you, and you shall love him as yourself; for you were strangers in the land of Egypt: I am the LORD your God. You shall do no injustice in judgment, in measurement of length, weight, or volume. You shall have honest scales, honest weights, an honest ephah, and an honest hin: I am the LORD your God, who brought you out of the land of Egypt. Therefore you shall observe all My statutes and all My judgments, and perform them: I am the LORD.'"

Chapter 20

The LORD spoke to Moses, saying, "Again, you shall say to the children of Israel: 'Whoever of the children of Israel, or of the strangers who dwell in Israel, who gives any of his descendants to Molech, he shall surely be put to death. The people of the land shall stone him with stones. I will set My face against that man, and will cut him off from his people, because he has given some of his descendants to Molech, to defile My sanctuary and profane My holy name. And if the people of the land should in any way hide their eyes from the man, when he gives some of his descendants to Molech, and they do not kill him, then I will set My face against that man and against his family; and I will cut him off from his people, and all who prostitute themselves with him to commit harlotry with Molech. And the person who turns to mediums and familiar spirits, to prostitute himself with them, I will set My face against that person and cut him off from his people. Consecrate yourselves therefore, and be holy, for I am the LORD your God. And you shall keep My statutes, and perform them: I am the LORD who sanctifies you. For everyone who curses his father or his mother shall surely be put to death. He has cursed his father or his mother. His blood shall be upon him. The man who commits adultery with another man's wife, he who commits adultery with his neighbor's wife, the adulterer and the adulteress shall surely be put to death. The man who lies with his father's wife has uncovered his father's nakedness; both of them shall surely be put to death. Their blood shall be upon them. If a man lies with his daughter-in-law, both of them shall surely be put to death. They have committed perversion. Their blood shall be upon them. If a man lies with a male as he lies with a woman, both of them have committed an abomination. They shall surely be put to death. Their blood shall be upon them. If a man marries a woman and her mother, it is wickedness. They shall be burned with fire, both he and they, that there may be no wickedness among you. If a man mates with an animal, he shall surely be put to death, and you shall kill the animal. If a woman approaches any animal and mates with it, you shall kill the woman and the animal. They shall surely be put to death. Their blood is upon them. If a man takes his sister, his father's daughter or his mother's daughter, and sees her nakedness and she sees his nakedness, it is a wicked thing. And they shall be cut off in the sight of their people. He has uncovered his sister's nakedness. He shall bear his guilt. If a man lies with a woman during her sickness and uncovers her nakedness, he has exposed her flow, and she has uncovered the flow of her blood. Both of them shall be cut off from their people. You shall not uncover the nakedness of your mother's sister nor of your father's sister, for that would uncover his near of kin. They shall bear their guilt. If a man lies with his uncle's wife, he has uncovered his uncle's nakedness. They shall bear their sin. They shall die childless. If a man takes his brother's wife, it is an unclean thing. He has uncovered his brother's nakedness. They shall be childless. You shall therefore keep all My statutes and all My judgments, and perform them, that the land where I am bringing you to dwell may not vomit you out. And you shall not walk in the statutes of the nation which I am casting out before you; for they commit all these things, and therefore I abhor them. But I have said to you, "You shall inherit their land, and I will give it to you to possess, a land flowing with milk and honey." I am the LORD your God, who has separated you from the peoples. You shall therefore distinguish between clean animals and unclean, between unclean birds and clean, and you shall not make yourselves abominable by beast or by bird or by any kind of living thing that creeps on the ground, which I have separated from you as unclean. And you shall be holy to Me, for I the LORD am holy, and have separated you from the peoples, that you should be Mine. A man or a woman who is a medium, or who has familiar spirits, shall surely be put to death. They shall stone them with stones. Their blood shall be upon them.'"

Chapter 21

The LORD said to Moses, "Speak to the priests, the sons of Aaron, and say to them: Let no one defile himself with the dead among his people, except for his nearest relatives, his mother, his father, his son, his daughter, his brother, or by a sister who is a virgin, who is near to him because she has had no husband; for her he may mourn. He shall not defile himself for the leader of his people, to profane himself. They shall not make bald spots on their heads, nor shave off the edges of their beards, nor make any cuttings in their flesh. They shall be holy to their God and not profane the name of their God, for they offer the offerings of the LORD made by fire, and the bread of their God; therefore, they shall be holy. They shall not take a wife who is a harlot or a defiled woman, nor shall they take a woman divorced from her husband, for the priest is holy to his God. You shall sanctify him, for he offers the bread of your God; he shall be holy to you, for I the LORD, who sanctify you, am holy. The daughter of any priest, if she profanes herself by playing the harlot, she profanes her father; she shall be burned with fire. He who is the high priest among his brethren, on whose head the anointing oil was poured and who is consecrated to wear the garments, shall not uncover his head nor tear his clothes, nor shall he go near any dead body, nor defile himself for his father or his mother, nor shall he go out of the sanctuary, nor profane the sanctuary of his God; for the consecration of the anointing oil of his God is upon him: I am the LORD. He shall take a wife in her virginity. A widow or a divorced woman or a defiled woman or a harlot, these he shall not marry; but he shall take a virgin of his own people as wife, nor shall he profane his posterity among his people, for I the LORD sanctify him.'" The LORD spoke to Moses, saying, "Speak to Aaron, saying: 'No man of your descendants in succeeding generations who has any defect may approach to offer the bread of his God. For any man who has a defect shall not approach: a man blind or lame, who has a marred face or any limb too long, a man who has a broken foot or broken hand, or is a hunchback or a dwarf, or a man who has a defect in his eye, or eczema or scab, or is a eunuch. No man of the descendants of Aaron the priest, who has a defect, shall come near to offer the offerings made by fire to the LORD. He has a defect; he shall not come near to offer the bread of his God. He may eat the bread of his God, both the most holy and the holy; only he shall not go near the veil or approach the altar, because he has a defect, lest he profane My sanctuaries; for I the LORD sanctify them.'" Moses told it to Aaron and his sons and to all the children of Israel

Chapter 22

The LORD spoke to Moses, saying, "Speak to Aaron and his sons, that they separate themselves from the holy things of the children of Israel, and that they do not profane My holy name by what they dedicate to Me: I am the LORD. Say to them: 'Whoever of all your descendants throughout your generations, who goes near the holy things which the children of Israel dedicate to the LORD, while he has uncleanness upon him, that person shall be cut off from My presence: I am the LORD. Whoever of the descendants of Aaron who is a leper or has a discharge, shall not eat the holy offerings until he is clean. And whoever touches anything made unclean by a corpse, or a man who has had an emission of semen, or whoever touches any creeping thing by which he would be made unclean, or any person by whom he would become unclean, whatever his uncleanness may be—the person who has touched any such thing shall be unclean until evening and shall not eat the holy offerings unless he washes his body with water. And when the sun goes down he shall be clean; and afterward he may eat the holy offerings, because it is his food. Whatever dies naturally or is torn by beasts he shall not eat, to defile himself with it: I am the LORD. They shall therefore keep My ordinance, lest they bear sin for it and die thereby, if they profane it: I the LORD sanctify them. No outsider shall eat the holy offering; one who dwells with the priest, or a hired servant, shall not eat the holy thing. But if the priest buys a person with his money, he may eat it; and one who is born in his house may eat his food. If the priest's daughter is married to an outsider, she may not eat of the holy offerings. But if the priest's daughter is a widow or divorced, and has no child, and has returned to her father's house as in her youth, she may eat her father's food; but no outsider shall eat it. And if a man eats the holy offering unintentionally, then he shall restore a holy offering to the priest, and add one-fifth to it. They shall not profane the holy offerings of the children of Israel, which they offer to the LORD, or allow them to bear the guilt of trespass when they eat their holy offerings; for I the LORD sanctify them.'" The LORD spoke to Moses, saying, "Speak to Aaron and his sons, and to all the children of Israel, and say to them: 'Whatever man of the house of Israel, or of the strangers in Israel, who offers his sacrifice for any of his vows or for any of his freewill offerings, which they offer to the LORD as a burnt offering—you shall offer of your own free will a male without blemish from the cattle, from the sheep, or from the goats. Whatever has a defect, you shall not offer, for it shall not be acceptable on your behalf. And whoever offers a sacrifice of a peace offering to the LORD, to fulfill his vow, or a freewill offering from the cattle or the sheep, it must be perfect to be accepted; there shall be no defect in it. Those that are blind or broken or maimed, or have an ulcer or eczema or scabs, you shall not offer to the LORD, nor make an offering by fire of them on the altar to the LORD. Either a bull or a lamb that has any limb too long or too short you may offer as a freewill offering, but for a vow it shall not be accepted. You shall not offer to the LORD what is bruised or crushed, or torn or cut; nor shall you make any offering of them in your land. Nor from a foreigner's hand shall you offer any of these as the bread of your God, because their corruption is in them, and defects are in them. They shall not be accepted on your behalf.'" The LORD spoke to Moses, saying: "When a bull or a sheep or a goat is born, it shall be seven days with its mother, and from the eighth day and thereafter it shall be accepted as an offering made by fire to the LORD. Whether it is a cow or ewe, do not kill both her and her young on the same day. And when you offer a sacrifice of thanksgiving to the LORD, offer it of your own free will. On the same day it shall be eaten; you shall leave none of it until morning: I am the LORD. Therefore you shall keep My commandments, and perform them: I am the LORD. You shall not profane My holy name, but I will be hallowed among the children of Israel. I am the LORD who sanctifies you, who brought you out of the land of Egypt, to be your God: I am the LORD."

Chapter 23

The LORD spoke to Moses, saying, "Speak to the children of Israel, and say to them: 'The feasts of the LORD, which you shall proclaim to be holy convocations, these are My feasts. Six days shall work be done, but the seventh day is a Sabbath of solemn rest, a holy convocation. You shall do no work on it; it is the Sabbath of the LORD in all your dwellings. These are the feasts of the LORD, holy convocations which you shall proclaim at their appointed times. On the fourteenth day of the first month at twilight is the LORD's Passover. And on the fifteenth day of the same month is the Feast of Unleavened Bread to the LORD; seven days you must eat unleavened bread. On the first day you shall have a holy convocation; you shall do no customary work on it. But you shall offer an offering made by fire to the LORD for seven days. The seventh day shall be a holy convocation; you shall do no customary work on it.'" The LORD spoke to Moses, saying, "Speak to the children of Israel, and say to them: 'When you come into the land which I give to you, and reap its harvest, then you shall bring a sheaf of the firstfruits of your harvest to the priest. He shall wave the sheaf before the LORD, to be accepted on your behalf; on the day after the Sabbath the priest shall wave it. And you shall offer on that day, when you wave the sheaf, a male lamb of the first year, without blemish, as a burnt offering to the LORD. Its grain offering shall be two-tenths of an ephah of fine flour mixed with oil, an offering made by fire to the LORD, for a sweet aroma; and its drink offering shall be of wine, one-fourth of a hin. You shall eat neither bread nor parched grain nor fresh grain until the same day that you have brought an offering to your God; it shall be a statute forever throughout your generations in all your dwellings. And you shall count for yourselves from the day after the Sabbath, from the day that you brought the sheaf of the wave offering: seven Sabbaths shall be completed. Count fifty days to the day after the seventh Sabbath; then you shall offer a new grain offering to the LORD. You shall bring from your dwellings two wave loaves of two-tenths of an ephah. They shall be of fine flour; they shall be baked with leaven. They are the firstfruits to the LORD. And you shall offer with the bread seven lambs of the first year, without blemish, one young bull, and two rams. They shall be as a burnt offering to the LORD, with their grain offering and their drink offerings, an offering made by fire for a sweet aroma to the LORD.

Then you shall sacrifice one kid of the goats as a sin offering, and two male lambs of the first year as a sacrifice of a peace offering. The priest shall wave them with the bread of the firstfruits as a wave offering before the LORD, with the two lambs. They shall be holy to the LORD for the priest. And you shall proclaim on the same day that it is a holy convocation to you. You shall do no customary work on it. It shall be a statute forever in all your dwellings throughout your generations. When you reap the harvest of your land, you shall not wholly reap the corners of your field when you reap, nor shall you gather any gleaning from your harvest. You shall leave them for the poor and for the stranger: I am the LORD your God.'" The LORD spoke to Moses, saying, "Speak to the children of Israel, saying: 'In the seventh month, on the first day of the month, you shall have a Sabbath-rest, a memorial of blowing of trumpets, a holy convocation. You shall do no customary work on it; and you shall offer an offering made by fire to the LORD.'" The LORD spoke to Moses, saying: "Also the tenth day of this seventh month shall be the Day of Atonement. It shall be a holy convocation for you; you shall afflict your souls, and offer an offering made by fire to the LORD. And you shall do no work on that same day, for it is the Day of Atonement, to make atonement for you before the LORD your God. For any person who is not afflicted in soul on that same day shall be cut off from his people. And any person who does any work on that same day, that person I will destroy from among his people. You shall do no manner of work; it shall be a statute forever throughout your generations in all your dwellings. It shall be to you a Sabbath of solemn rest, and you shall afflict your souls; on the ninth day of the month at evening, from evening to evening, you shall celebrate your Sabbath." The LORD spoke to Moses, saying, "Speak to the children of Israel, saying: 'The fifteenth day of this seventh month shall be the Feast of Tabernacles for seven days to the LORD. On the first day there shall be a holy convocation. You shall do no customary work on it. For seven days you shall offer an offering made by fire to the LORD. On the eighth day you shall have a holy convocation, and you shall offer an offering made by fire to the LORD. It is a sacred assembly, and you shall do no customary work on it. These are the feasts of the LORD which you shall proclaim to be holy convocations, to offer an offering made by fire to the LORD, a burnt offering and a grain offering, a sacrifice and drink offerings, everything on its day—besides the Sabbaths of the LORD, besides your gifts, besides all your vows, and besides all your freewill offerings which you give to the LORD. Also on the fifteenth day of the seventh month, when you have gathered in the fruit of the land, you shall keep the feast of the LORD for seven days; on the first day there shall be a Sabbath-rest, and on the eighth day a Sabbath-rest. And you shall take for yourselves on the first day the fruit of beautiful trees, branches of palm trees, the boughs of leafy trees, and willows of the brook; and you shall rejoice before the LORD your God for seven days. You shall keep it as a feast to the LORD for seven days in the year. It shall be a statute forever in your generations. You shall celebrate it in the seventh month. You shall dwell in booths for seven days. All who are native Israelites shall dwell in booths, that your generations may know that I made the children of Israel dwell in booths when I brought them out of the land of Egypt: I am the LORD your God.'" So Moses declared to the children of Israel the feasts of the LORD

Chapter 24

The LORD spoke to Moses, saying: "Command the

children of Israel that they bring to you pure oil of pressed olives for the light, to make the lamps burn continually. Outside the veil of the Testimony, in the Tabernacle of Meeting, Aaron shall be in charge of it from evening until morning before the LORD continually; it shall be a statute forever in your generations. He shall be in charge of the lamps on the pure gold lampstand before the LORD continually. And you shall take fine flour and bake twelve cakes with it. Two-tenths of an ephah shall be in each cake. You shall set them in two rows, six in a row, on the pure gold table before the LORD. And you shall put pure frankincense on each row, that it may be on the bread for a memorial, an offering made by fire to the LORD. Every Sabbath he shall set it in order before the LORD continually, being taken from the children of Israel by an everlasting covenant. And it shall be for Aaron and his sons, and they shall eat it in a holy place; for it is most holy to him from the offerings of the LORD made by fire, by a perpetual statute." Now the son of an Israelite woman, whose father was an Egyptian, went out among the children of Israel; and this Israelite woman's son and a man of Israel fought each other in the camp. And the Israelite woman's son blasphemed the name of the LORD and cursed; and so they brought him to Moses. (His mother's name was Shelomith the daughter of Dibri, of the tribe of Dan.) Then they put him in custody, that the mind of the LORD might be shown to them. And the LORD spoke to Moses, saying, "Take outside the camp him who has cursed; then let all who heard him lay their hands on his head, and let all the congregation stone him. Then you shall speak to the children of Israel, saying: 'Whoever curses his God shall bear his sin. And whoever blasphemes the name of the LORD shall surely be put to death. All the congregation shall certainly stone him, the stranger as well as him who is born in the land. When he blasphemes the name of the LORD, he shall be put to death.Whoever kills any man shall surely be put to death. Whoever kills an animal shall make it good, animal for animal. If a man causes disfigurement of his neighbor, as he has done, so shall it be done to him—fracture for fracture, eye for eye, tooth for tooth; as he has caused disfigurement of a man, so shall it be done to him. And whoever kills an animal shall restore it; but whoever kills a man shall be put to death. You shall have the same law for the stranger and for one from your own country; for I am the LORD your God.'" Then Moses spoke to the children of Israel; and they took outside the camp him who had cursed, and stoned him with stones. So the children of Israel did as the LORD commanded Moses

Chapter 25

The LORD spoke to Moses on Mount Sinai, saying, "Speak to the children of Israel, and say to them: 'When you come into the land which I give you, then the land shall keep a Sabbath to the LORD. Six years you shall sow your field, and six years you shall prune your vineyard, and gather its fruit; but in the seventh year there shall be a Sabbath of solemn rest for the land, a Sabbath to the LORD. You shall neither sow your field nor prune your vineyard. What grows of its own accord of your harvest you shall not reap, nor gather the grapes of your untended vine, for it is a year of rest for the land. And the Sabbath produce of the land shall be food for you: for you, your male and female servants, your hired man, and the stranger who dwells with you, for your livestock and the beasts that are in your land—all its produce shall be for food. And you shall count seven Sabbaths of years for yourself, seven times seven years; and the time of the seven Sabbaths of years shall be to you forty-nine years. Then you shall cause the trumpet of the Jubilee to sound on the tenth day of the seventh month; on the Day of Atonement you shall make the trumpet to sound throughout all your land. And you shall consecrate the fiftieth year, and proclaim liberty throughout all the land to all its inhabitants. It shall be a Jubilee for you; and each of you shall return to his possession, and each of you shall return to his family. That fiftieth year shall be a Jubilee to you; in it you shall neither sow nor reap what grows of its own accord, nor gather the grapes of your untended vine. For it is the Jubilee; it shall be holy to you; you shall eat its produce from the field. In this Year of Jubilee, each of you shall return to his possession. And if you sell anything to your neighbor or buy from your neighbor's hand, you shall not oppress one another. According to the number of years after the Jubilee you shall buy from your neighbor, and according to the number of years of crops he shall sell to you. According to the multitude of years you shall increase its price, and according to the fewer number of years you shall diminish its price; for he sells to you according to the number of the years of the crops. Therefore you shall not oppress one another, but you shall fear your God; for I am the LORD your God. So you shall observe My statutes and keep My judgments, and perform them; and you will dwell in the land in safety. Then the land will yield its fruit, and you will eat your fill, and dwell there in safety. And if you say, 'What shall we eat in the seventh year, since we shall not sow nor gather in our produce?' Then I will command My blessing on you in the sixth year, and it will bring forth produce enough for three years. And you shall sow in the eighth year, and eat old produce until the ninth year; until its produce comes in, you shall eat of the old harvest. The land shall not be sold permanently, for the land is Mine; for you are strangers and sojourners with Me. And in all the land of your possession you shall grant redemption of the land. If one of your brethren becomes poor, and has sold some of his possession, and if his redeeming relative comes to redeem it, then he may redeem what his brother sold. Or if the man has no one to redeem it, but he himself becomes able to redeem it, then let him count the years since its sale, and restore the remainder to the man to whom he sold it, that he may return to his possession. But if he is not able to have it restored to himself, then what was sold shall remain in the hand of him who bought it until the Year of Jubilee; and in the Jubilee it shall be released, and he shall return to his possession. If a man sells a house in a walled city, then he may redeem it within a whole year after it is sold; within a full year he may redeem it. But if it is not redeemed within the space of a full year, then the house in the walled city shall belong permanently to him who bought it, throughout his generations. It shall not be released in the Jubilee. However, the houses of villages which have no wall around them shall be counted as the fields of the country. They may be redeemed, and they shall be released in the Jubilee. Nevertheless the cities of the Levites, and the houses in the cities of their possession, the Levites may redeem at any time. And if a man purchases a house from the Levites, then the house that was sold in the city of his possession shall be released in the Jubilee; for the houses in the cities of the Levites are their possession among the children of Israel. But the field of the common-land of their cities may not be sold, for it is their perpetual possession. If one of your brethren becomes poor, and falls into poverty among you, then you shall help him, like a stranger or a sojourner that he may live with you. Take no usury or interest from him; but fear you're God, that your brother may live with you. You shall not lend him your money for usury, nor lend him your food at a profit. I am the LORD your God, who brought you out of the land of Egypt, to give you the land of Canaan and to be your God. And if one of your brethren who dwells by you becomes poor, and sells himself to you, you shall not compel him to serve as a slave. As a hired servant and a sojourner he shall be with you, and shall serve you until the Year of Jubilee. And then he shall depart from you—he and his children with him—and shall return to his own family. He shall return to the possession of his fathers. For they are My servants, whom I brought out of the land of Egypt; they shall not be sold as slaves. You shall not rule over him with rigor, but you shall fear your God. And as for your male and female slaves whom you may have—from the nations that are around you, from them you may buy male and female slaves. Moreover you may buy the children of the strangers who dwell among you, and their families who are with you, which they beget in your land; and they shall become your property. And you may take them as an inheritance for your children after you, to inherit them as a possession; they shall be your permanent slaves. But regarding your brethren, the children of Israel, you shall not rule over one another with rigor. Now if a sojourner or stranger close to you becomes rich, and one of your brethren who dwells by him becomes poor, and sells himself to the stranger or sojourner close to you, or to a member of the stranger's family, after he is sold he may be redeemed again. One of his brothers may redeem him; or his uncle or his uncle's son may redeem him; or anyone who is near of kin to him in his family may redeem him; or if he is able he may redeem himself. Thus he shall reckon with him who bought him: The price of his release shall be according to the number of years, from the year that he was sold to him until the Year of Jubilee; it shall be according to the time of a hired servant for him. If there are still many years remaining, according to them he shall repay the price of his redemption from the money with which he was bought. And if there remain but a few years until the Year of Jubilee, then he shall reckon with him, and according to his years he shall repay him the price of his redemption. He shall be with him as a yearly hired servant, and he shall not rule with rigor over him in your sight. And if he is not redeemed in these years, then he shall be released in the Year of Jubilee—he and his children with him. For the children of Israel are servants to me; they are my servants whom I brought out of the land of Egypt: I am the LORD your God

Chapter 26

1 You shall make for yourselves neither idols nor graven images; you shall erect no pillar, nor set up any stone image in your land to bow down to it, for I am the LORD your God. 2 You shall keep my Sabbaths and keep my sanctuary: for I am the LORD. 3 If you will walk in my prescriptions, if you will keep my commands and follow them, 4 then I will send you rain in due season, and the land will yield its harvest, and the trees of the fields will bear fruit. 5 Your threshing will last until the vintage, and the vintage will last until the sowing; you will eat your bread in abundance and dwell securely in your land. 6 I will grant peace in the land, and you shall lie down, and no one shall make you afraid; I will remove wild beasts from the land, and no sword shall pass through your land. 7 You shall chase your enemies, and they shall fall by the sword before you. 8 Five of you shall chase a hundred, and a hundred of you shall put ten thousand to flight; your enemies shall fall by the sword before you. 9 For I will look on you favorably, make you fruitful, multiply you, and confirm my covenant with you. 10 You shall eat the old harvest and clear out the old because of the new. 11 I will set my tabernacle among you, and my soul shall not abhor you. 12 I will walk among you and be your God, and you shall be my people. 13 I am the LORD your God, who brought you out of the land of Egypt, that you should not be their slaves; I have broken the bands of your yoke and made you walk upright. 14 But if you will not obey me, and do not observe all these commands, 15 and if you despise my statutes, or if your soul abhors my judgments, so that you do not perform all my commands, but break my covenant, 16 I also will do this to you: I will even appoint terror over you, wasting disease and fever which shall consume the eyes and cause sorrow of heart. And you shall sow your seed in vain, for your enemies shall eat it. 17 I will set my face against you, and you shall be defeated by your enemies. Those who hate you shall reign over you, and you shall flee when no one pursues you. 18 And after all this, if you do not obey me, then I will punish you seven times more for your sins. 19 I will break the pride of your power; I will make your heavens like iron and your earth like bronze. 20 Your strength shall be spent in vain; for your land shall not yield its produce, nor shall the trees of the land yield their fruit. 21 If you walk contrary to me and are not willing to obey me, I will bring on you seven times more plagues, according to your sins. 22 I will also send wild beasts among you, which shall rob you of your children, destroy your livestock, and make you few in number; and your highways shall be desolate. 23 If by these things you are not reformed by me, but walk contrary to me, 24 then I also will walk contrary to you, and I will punish you yet seven times for your sins. 25 I will bring a sword against you that will execute the vengeance of my covenant; when you are gathered together within your cities, I will send pestilence among you; and you shall be delivered into the hand of the enemy. 26 When I have cut off your supply of bread, ten women shall bake your bread in one oven, and they shall bring back your bread by weight, and you shall eat and not be satisfied. 27 After all this, if you do not obey me, but walk contrary to me, 28 then I will walk contrary to you in fury; and I, even I, will chastise you seven times for your sins. 29 You shall eat the flesh of your sons, and you shall eat the flesh of your daughters. 30 I will destroy your high places, cut down your incense altars, and cast your carcasses on the lifeless forms of your idols; and my soul shall abhor you. 31 I will lay your cities waste and bring your sanctuaries to desolation, and I will not smell the fragrance of your sweet aromas. 32 I will bring the land to desolation, and your enemies who dwell in it shall be astonished at it. 33 I will scatter you among the nations and draw out a sword after you; your land shall be desolate and your cities waste. 34 Then the land shall enjoy its Sabbaths as long as it lies desolate and you are in your enemies' land; then the land shall rest and enjoy its Sabbaths. 35 As long as it lies desolate it shall rest—for the time it did not rest on your Sabbaths when you dwelt in it. 36 And as for those of you who are left, I will send faintness into their hearts in the lands of their enemies; the sound of a shaken leaf shall cause them to flee. They shall flee as though fleeing from a sword, and they shall fall when no one pursues. 37 They shall stumble over one another, as it were before a sword, when no one pursues; and you shall have no power to stand before your enemies. 38 You shall perish among the nations, and the land of your enemies shall eat you up. 39 And those of you who are left shall waste away in their iniquity in your enemies' lands; also in their fathers' iniquities, which are with them, they shall waste away. 40 But if they confess their iniquity and the iniquity of their fathers, with their unfaithfulness in which they were unfaithful to me, and that they also have walked

contrary to me, 41 and that I also have walked contrary to them and have brought them into the land of their enemies; if their uncircumcised hearts are humbled, and they accept their guilt— 42 then I will remember my covenant with Jacob, and my covenant with Isaac, and my covenant with Abraham I will remember; I will remember the land. 43 The land also shall be left empty by them, and will enjoy its Sabbaths while it lies desolate without them; they will accept their guilt, because they despised my judgments and because their soul abhorred my statutes. 44 Yet for all that, when they are in the land of their enemies, I will not cast them away, nor shall I abhor them, to utterly destroy them and break my covenant with them; for I am the LORD their God. 45 But for their sake, I will remember the covenant of their ancestors, whom I brought out of the land of Egypt in the sight of the nations, that I might be their God: I am the LORD.'" 46 These are the statutes and judgments and laws which the LORD made between Himself and the children of Israel on Mount Sinai by the hand of Moses

Chapter 27

1 Now the LORD spoke to Moses, saying, 2 "Speak to the children of Israel, and say to them: 'When a man consecrates by a vow certain persons to the LORD, according to your valuation, 3 if your valuation is of a male from twenty years old up to sixty years old, then your valuation shall be fifty shekels of silver, according to the shekel of the sanctuary. 4 If it is a female, then your valuation shall be thirty shekels; 5 and if from five years old up to twenty years old, then your valuation for a male shall be twenty shekels, and for a female ten shekels; 6 and if from a month old up to five years old, then your valuation for a male shall be five shekels of silver, and for a female your valuation shall be three shekels of silver; 7 and if from sixty years old and above, if it is a male, then your valuation shall be fifteen shekels, and for a female ten shekels. 8 But if he is too poor to pay your valuation, then he shall present himself before the priest, and the priest shall set a value for him; according to the ability of him who vowed, the priest shall value him. 9 If it is an animal that men may bring as an offering to the LORD, all that anyone gives to the LORD shall be holy. 10 He shall not substitute it or exchange it, good for bad or bad for good; and if he at all exchanges animal for animal, then both it and the one exchanged for it shall be holy. 11 If it is an unclean animal which they do not offer as a sacrifice to the LORD, then he shall present the animal before the priest; 12 and the priest shall set a value for it, whether it is good or bad; as you, the priest, value it, so it shall be. 13 But if he wants at all to redeem it, then he must add one-fifth to your valuation. 14 And when a man dedicates his house to be holy to the LORD, then the priest shall set a value for it, whether it is good or bad; as the priest values it, so it shall stand. 15 If he who dedicated it wants to redeem his house, then he must add one-fifth of the money of your valuation to it, and it shall be his. 16 If a man dedicates to the LORD part of a field of his possession, then your valuation shall be according to the seed for it. A homer of barley seed shall be valued at fifty shekels of silver. 17 If he dedicates his field from the Year of Jubilee, according to your valuation it shall stand. 18 But if he dedicates his field after the Jubilee, then the priest shall reckon to him the money due according to the years that remain till the Year of Jubilee, and it shall be deducted from your valuation. 19 And if he who dedicates the field ever wishes to redeem it, then he must add one-fifth of the money of your valuation to it, and it shall belong to him. 20 But if he does not want to redeem the field, or if he has sold the field to another man, it shall not be redeemed anymore; 21 but the field, when it is released in the Jubilee, shall be holy to the LORD, as a devoted field; it shall be the possession of the priest. 22 And if a man dedicates to the LORD a field which he has bought, which is not the field of his possession, 23 then the priest shall reckon to him the worth of your valuation, up to the Year of Jubilee; and he shall give your valuation on that day as a holy offering to the LORD. 24 In the Year of Jubilee the field shall return to him from whom it was bought, to the one who owned the land as a possession. 25 And all your valuations shall be according to the shekel of the sanctuary: twenty gerahs to the shekel. 26 But the firstborn of the animals, which should be the LORD's firstborn, no man shall dedicate; whether it is an ox or sheep, it is the LORD's. 27 And if it is an unclean animal, then he shall redeem it according to your valuation, and shall add one-fifth to it; or if it is not redeemed, then it shall be sold according to your valuation. 28 Nevertheless no devoted offering that a man may devote to the LORD of all that he has, both man and beast, or the field of his possession, shall be sold or redeemed; every devoted offering is most holy to the LORD. 29 No person under the ban, who may become doomed to destruction among men, shall be redeemed, but shall surely be put to death. 30 And all the tithe of the land, whether of the seed of the land or of the fruit of the tree, is the LORD's. It is holy to the LORD. 31 If a man wants at all to redeem any of his tithes, he shall add one-fifth to it. 32 And concerning the tithe of the herd or the flock, of whatever passes under the rod, the tenth one shall be holy to the LORD. 33 He shall not inquire whether it is good or bad, nor shall he exchange it; and if he exchanges it at all, then both it and the one exchanged for it shall be holy; it shall not be redeemed.'" 34 These are the commandments which the LORD commanded Moses for the children of Israel on Mount Sinai

4. Numbers

Chapter 1

The LORD spoke to Moses again in the wilderness of Sinai, in the tent of meeting, on the first day of the second month, the second year after he came out of the land of Egypt. He said, "Take a census of the entire congregation of the children of Israel, according to their families and the houses of their fathers, by the names of each individual. From twenty years old and upward, all those who are able to go to war in Israel, you and Aaron shall take a census of their armies. With you shall be men from each tribe, as leaders of the house of their fathers These are the names of the men who will be with you: from the tribe of Reuben, Elizur the son of Shedeur; from Simeon, Shelumiel the son of Zurishaddai; from Judah, Nahshon the son of Amminadab; from Issachar, Nethaneel the son of Zuar; from Zebulun, Eliab the son of Helon; from the sons of Joseph: from Ephraim, Elishama the son of Ammihud; from Manasseh, Gamliel the son of Pedahzur; from Benjamin, Abidan the son of Gideoni; from Dan, Ahiezer the son of Ammishaddai; from Asher, Pagiel the son of Ocran; from Gad, Eliasaph the son of Deuel; from Naphtali, Ahira the son of Enan These were the notable men of the community, princes of the tribes of their fathers, and leaders of thousands in Israel. Moses and Aaron took these men, who were specified by their names. Then they summoned the whole community on the first day of the second month, declaring their kindreds according to their families and the houses of their fathers, by the names of each individual from the age of twenty years and upward, man by man. As the LORD had commanded Moses, so he appointed them in the wilderness of Sinai So, the sons of Reuben, the firstborn of Israel, according to their generations, families, and the houses of their fathers, were counted by their names, man by man, all the males from twenty years old and upward, all those who went to war. The number of the tribe of Reuben was six hundred and four thousand and five hundred From the sons of Simeon, according to their generations, families, and the houses of their fathers, the sum of their names, man by man, all the males from twenty years old and upward, all who went to war, their number was nine fifty thousand and three hundred From the sons of Gad, according to their generations, families, and the houses of their fathers, by the names of each individual from the age of twenty years and upward, all who went to war, their number was five thousand and forty thousand and six hundred and fifty From the sons of Judah, according to their generations, families, and the houses of their fathers, by the names of each individual from the age of twenty years old and upward, all who went to war, their number was three million four hundred thousand and six hundred From the sons of Issachar, according to their generations, families, and the houses of their fathers, by the names of each individual from the age of twenty years old and upward, all who went to war, their number was four hundred fifty thousand and four hundred From the children of Zebulun, according to their generations, families, and the houses of their fathers, by the names of each individual from twenty years old and upward, all who went to war, their number was fifty thousand and four hundred From the sons of Joseph, specifically from the sons of Ephraim, according to their generations, families, and the houses of their fathers, by the names of each individual from the age of twenty years old and upward, all who went to war, their number was four thousand five hundred From the sons of Manasseh, according to their generations, families, and the houses of their fathers, by the names of each individual from the age of twenty years old and upward, all who went to war, their number was two thousand and two hundred From the sons of Benjamin, according to their generations, families, and the houses of their fathers, by the names of each individual from the age of twenty years old and upward, all who went to war, their number was five thousand three hundred and four hundred From the sons of Dan, according to their generations, families, and the houses of their fathers, by the names of each individual from twenty years old and upward, all who went to war, their number was three hundred two thousand and seven hundred From the sons of Asher, according to their generations, families, and the houses of their fathers, by the names of each individual from twenty years old and upward, all who went to war, their number was one million forty thousand and five hundred From the sons of Naphtali, their descendants according to their families and the houses of their fathers, by the names of each individual from the age of twenty years old and upward, all who went to war, their number was three hundred fifty thousand and four hundred These are the sums that Moses, Aaron, and the princes of Israel, the two men, who were each for the house of their fathers, counted. This was the sum of the children of Israel, according to the houses of their fathers, from the age of twenty years and upward, all who went to war in Israel, the total was six thousand and three thousand, five hundred and fifty in number. However, the Levites, according to the tribes of their fathers, were not numbered among them For the LORD had spoken to Moses, saying,

"You shall not take a census of the tribe of Levi, and you shall not count them among the children of Israel. Instead, you shall appoint the Levites to the Tabernacle of the Testimony, and to all its instruments, and to all things pertaining to it. They shall carry the Tabernacle and all its instruments, minister therein, and encamp around it. When the Tabernacle goes out, the Levites shall bring it down; when the Tabernacle is set up, the Levites shall set it up. Any outsider who approaches shall be put to death The children of Israel shall pitch their tents, each by their camp, and each by their standard according to their army. However, the Levites shall encamp around the Tabernacle of the Testimony, so that there will be no wrath upon the congregation of the children of Israel. The Levites shall be responsible for the Tabernacle of the Testimony. Thus, the children of Israel did according to all that the LORD had commanded Moses

Chapter 2

The LORD spoke to Moses and Aaron, saying, "Every man of the children of Israel shall camp by his post and under the enclosure of his fathers' house. They shall camp far around the Tabernacle of the Congregation. On the east side, toward the rising of the sun, the standard of the army of Judah shall encamp, according to their hosts. Nahshon the son of Amminadab shall be the leader of the sons of Judah. His army and his men were seventy-four thousand and six hundred. Beside him shall camp those of the tribe of Issachar, with Nethaneel the son of Zuar as their leader. His army numbered four hundred fifty thousand and four hundred. Then the tribe of Zebulun, with Eliab the son of Helon as their leader, had an army of fifty thousand and four hundred. The entire army of Judah was one hundred fifty thousand and six hundred men, and they shall set out first On the south side shall camp the army of Reuben, according to their armies, with Elizur the son of Shedeur as their leader. His army numbered six and forty thousand and five hundred. Beside him shall camp the tribe of Simeon, with Shelumiel the son of Zurishaddai as their leader. His army numbered nine hundred and fifty thousand and three hundred. Next to them shall camp the tribe of Gad, with Eliasaph the son of Deuel as their leader. His army numbered fifty thousand, six hundred and fifty. All the men of the camp of Reuben were one hundred fifty thousand, four hundred and fifty according to their armies, and they shall set out second Then the Tabernacle of the Congregation shall set out with the army of the Levites in the midst of the camp, as they encamp, so they shall set out, each in his order according to his standard. On the west side shall camp the army of Ephraim, according to their armies, with Elishama the son of Ammihud as their leader. His army numbered forty thousand and five hundred. Next to them shall camp the tribe of Manasseh, with Gamliel the son of Pedahzur as their leader. His army numbered thirty-two thousand and two hundred. Then shall camp the tribe of Benjamin, with Abidan the son of Gideoni as their leader. His army numbered thirty-five thousand and four hundred. All the armies of Ephraim numbered one hundred and eight thousand, one hundred, and they shall set out third On the north side shall camp the army of Dan, according to their armies, with Ahiezer the son of Ammishaddai as their leader. His army numbered sixty-two thousand and seven hundred. Next to them shall camp the tribe of Asher, with Pagiel the son of Ocran as their leader. His army numbered one million forty thousand and five hundred. Then shall camp the tribe of Naphtali, with Ahira the son of Enan as their leader. His army numbered fifty-three thousand and four hundred. All the armies of Dan were one hundred fifty-seven thousand, six hundred, and they shall set out last with their standards These are the counts of the children of Israel according to the houses of their fathers, all the names of the army, according to their hosts: six hundred and three thousand, five hundred and fifty. But the Levites were not counted among the children of Israel, as the LORD had commanded Moses. The children of Israel did all that the LORD had commanded Moses: they encamped according to their banners and made the journey, each with his family, according to the houses of their fathers

Chapter 3

These were also the generations of Aaron and Moses on the day when the Lord spoke to Moses on Mount Sinai. These are the names of the sons of Aaron: Nadab, the firstborn, Abihu, Eleazar, and Ithamar. These are the names of Aaron's sons, the anointed priests whom Moses anointed to exercise the priestly office. Nadab and Abihu died before the Lord when they offered strange fire before the Lord in the wilderness of Sinai, and they had no sons. But Eleazar and Ithamar exercised the priestly office before Aaron their father Then the LORD spoke to Moses, saying, "Bring the tribe of Levi and set them before Aaron the priest, that they may serve him and take responsibility for the whole congregation before the Tabernacle of the Congregation to perform the service of the Tabernacle. They shall also keep all the instruments of the Tabernacle of the Congregation, and they shall have responsibility for the children of Israel to do the Tabernacle service. You shall give the Levites to Aaron and his sons, for they have been given to him freely from among the sons of Israel. You shall appoint Aaron and his sons for the exercise of their priestly office, and any stranger who approaches shall be put to death." The LORD also spoke to Moses, saying, "Behold, I have taken the Levites from among the children of Israel in place of all the firstborn who open the womb among the children of Israel, and the Levites shall be mine. For all the firstborn are mine; on the day that I struck down all the firstborn in the land of Egypt, I sanctified for myself all the firstborn of Israel, both man and beast. They shall be mine: I am the LORD." Moreover, the LORD spoke to Moses in the wilderness of Sinai, saying, "Take a census of the sons of Levi according to the houses of their fathers and their families; count all the males from one month old and upward." Moses counted them according to the word of the LORD, as he had been commanded. These are the names of the sons of Levi: Gershon, Kohath, and Merari. These are the names of the sons of Gershon according to their families: Libni and Shimei. The sons of Kohath, according to their families, were Amram, Izehar, Hebron, and Uzziel. The sons of Merari, according to their families, were Mahli and Mushi. These are the families of Levi according to the houses of their fathers From Gershon came the family of the Libnites and the family of the Shimeites; these are the families of the Gershonites. The total number of these families (after counting all the males from one month old and upward) was six thousand and five hundred. The families of the Gershonites encamped behind the Tabernacle, toward the west. The leader of the house of the Gershonites was Eliasaph the son of Lael. The sons of Gershon were in charge of the Tabernacle of the Covenant, the pavilion, its covering, the covering of the Tabernacle of the Covenant, the hanging of the court, and the vaulting of the court that is near the Tabernacle, near the Altar and around it, and the cords of it for all its service From Kohath came the family of the Amramites, the family of the Izeharites, the family of the Hebronites, and the family of the

Uzzielites; these are the families of the Kohathites. The number of all the males from one month old and upward was eight thousand and six hundred, who were responsible for the sanctuary. The families of the sons of Kohath camped on the south side of the Tabernacle. The leader of the house and families of the Kohathites was Elizaphan the son of Uzziel. Their duty was to look after the ark, the table, the candlestick, the altars, the instruments of the sanctuary needed for the service, the veil, and all that was needed there. Eleazar, son of Aaron the priest, was the leader of the Levites and had oversight of those responsible for the sanctuary From Merari came the family of the Mahlites and the family of the Mushites; these are the families of Merari. Their total, according to the names of all the males from one month old and upward, was six thousand and two hundred. The head of the house of the families of Merari was Zuriel the son of Abihail; they camped on the north side of the Tabernacle. The sons of Merari were responsible for the tables of the Tabernacle, its bars, pillars, foundations, and all its instruments, and all that was needed therein, and the pillars of the court around it, with their bases, pivots, and cords Moreover, in front of the Tabernacle, toward the east, Moses, Aaron, and his sons encamped, with the responsibility for the Sanctuary and the responsibility for the children of Israel. Any stranger who approached was to be put to death. The total number of the Levites, whom Moses and Aaron, at the command of the LORD, counted according to their families, was all the males from one month old and upward, totaling twenty-two thousand The LORD said to Moses, "Count all the firstborn males among the children of Israel, from one month old and upward, and take the names of each. You shall bring to me the Levites in place of all the firstborn of the sons of Israel (I am the LORD) and the cattle of the Levites in place of all the firstborn of the cattle of the sons of Israel." Moses counted all the firstborn males among the children of Israel, as the LORD had commanded him. All the firstborn males, listed by name from a month old and upward, were two hundred thousand, two hundred seventy thousand and three. The LORD spoke to Moses, saying, "Take the Levites in place of all the firstborn of the children of Israel, and the cattle of the Levites in place of their cattle, and the Levites shall be mine (I am the LORD)." For the redemption of the two hundred seventy-three (which are more than the Levites) of the firstborn of the children of Israel, you shall take five shekels for each person, according to the weight of the sanctuary; each shekel contains twenty gerahs. You shall give Aaron and his sons the money redeemed for the odd names Moses collected the ransom from those who were more than the Levites: from the firstborn among the sons of Israel, he took the money, totaling one thousand three hundred five hundred shekels according to the shekel of the sanctuary. Moses delivered the money of the redeemed to Aaron and his sons, according to the word of the LORD, as the LORD had commanded Moses

Chapter 4

The LORD spoke to Moses and Aaron, saying, "Take a census of the sons of Kohath from among the sons of Levi, according to their families and the houses of their fathers. Take the sum of the sons of Kohath from among the sons of Levi, according to their families and the houses of their fathers, from the thirtieth year of their age and up to the fiftieth year of their age, all those who come into the assembly to do the work in the tent of meeting. This shall be the office of the sons of Kohath in the Tabernacle of Meeting, around the Most Holy. When the camp sets out, Aaron and his sons will come and take down the covering veil and place it over the ark of the Testimony. They will put a covering of badger skins on it and spread a cloth of blue over it and insert its poles Then they shall spread a blue cloth on the table of the showbread and place the dishes, the cups for incense, the chalices, and the bowls with which to pour drink offerings. The bread shall always be on it. They shall spread over them a scarlet cloth and cover the same with a covering of badger skins, and insert its poles. Then they shall take a blue cloth and cover the lampstand for the light, with its lamps, wick trimmers, trays, and all its oil vessels by which they serve it. They shall put it with all its utensils in a covering of badger skins and place it on the carrying frame. They shall spread a blue cloth over the golden altar, cover it with a covering of badger skins, and insert its poles They shall take all the utensils of the service with which they serve in the sanctuary, put them in a blue cloth, cover them with a covering of badger skins, and place them on the carrying frame. They shall take away the ashes from the altar and spread a purple cloth over it. They shall place on it all its utensils, by which they serve in connection with it: the fire pans, forks, shovels, basins, and all the utensils of the altar; and they shall spread on it a covering of badger skins and insert its poles. When Aaron and his sons have finished covering the sanctuary and all the furnishings of the sanctuary, as the camp sets out, the sons of Kohath shall come to carry them, but they shall not touch the holy objects, lest they die. These are the things in the tent of meeting that the sons of Kohath are to carry The responsibility of Eleazar, the son of Aaron the priest, is the oil for the light, the fragrant incense, the regular grain offering, and the anointing oil, with the oversight of the whole Tabernacle and everything in it, both the sanctuary and its furnishings." The LORD spoke to Moses and Aaron, saying, "Do not let the tribe of the families of the Kohathites be cut off from among the Levites. But do this for them so that they may live and not die when they come near the most holy objects. Aaron and his sons shall go in and assign each of them to his work and to his burden. But they shall not go in to see the holy objects even for a moment, or they will die." The LORD spoke to Moses, saying, "Take a census of the sons of Gershon, also, by their fathers' houses and by their families. Take a census of the sons of Gershon, also, by their fathers' houses and by their families. From thirty years old and upward to fifty years old, you shall count them, all who come to do duty, to do service in the tent of meeting. This is the service of the families of the Gershonites, in serving and in carrying: they shall carry the curtains of the tabernacle and the tent of meeting with its covering, the covering of badger skins that is on it, and the screen for the entrance of the tent of meeting, the hangings of the court, and the screen for the entrance of the gate of the court, which is around the tabernacle and the altar, and their cords, and all the equipment for their service. They shall do all that needs to be done with regard to them. All the service of the sons of the Gershonites shall be at the command of Aaron and his sons, in all they are to carry and in all they have to do. You shall assign to their charge all that they are to carry. This is the service of the families of the sons of Gershon in the tent of meeting, and their guard duty is to be under the direction of Ithamar the son of Aaron the priest "As for the sons of Merari, you shall number them by their families and their fathers' houses. From thirty years old and upward to fifty years old, you shall number them, everyone who comes to do the work of service and the work of bearing burdens in the tent of meeting. This is what they are charged to carry, as the whole of their service in the tent of meeting: the frames of the tabernacle with its bars, pillars, and bases, and the pillars around the court with their bases, pegs, and cords, with all their equipment and all their accessories. You shall list by name the objects that they are required to carry. This is the service of the families of the sons of Merari, the whole of their service in the tent of meeting, under the direction of Ithamar the son of Aaron the priest." So Moses, Aaron, and the leaders of the congregation listed the sons of the Kohathites, by their families and their fathers' houses, from thirty years old and upward to fifty years old, everyone who could come on duty for service in the tent of meeting. Those listed by their families were two thousand seven hundred fifty. This was the list of the families of the Kohathites, all who served in the tent of meeting, whom Moses and Aaron listed according to the commandment of the LORD by Moses Those listed of the sons of Gershon, by their families and their fathers' houses, from thirty years old and upward to fifty years old, everyone who could come on duty for service in the tent of meeting, those listed by their families and their fathers' houses, were two thousand six hundred thirty. These were the lists of the families of the sons of Gershon, all who served in the tent of meeting, whom Moses and Aaron listed according to the commandment of the LORD Those listed of the families of the sons of Merari, by their families and their fathers' houses, from thirty years old and upward to fifty years old, everyone who could come on duty for service in the tent of meeting, those listed by their families, were three thousand two hundred. These were the lists of the families of the sons of Merari, whom Moses and Aaron listed according to the commandment of the LORD by Moses All those who were listed of the Levites, whom Moses, Aaron, and the leaders of Israel listed, by their families and their fathers' houses, from thirty years old and upward to fifty years old, everyone who could come to do the service of ministry and the service of bearing burdens in the tent of meeting, those listed were eight thousand five hundred eighty. According to the commandment of the LORD through Moses, they were listed, each one with his task of serving or carrying. Thus they were listed by him, as the LORD commanded Moses

Chapter 5

The LORD spoke to Moses, saying, "Command the children of Israel to expel from the camp every leper, every hemorrhagic person, and anyone who is defiled by contact with the dead. Both males and females you shall put out of the camp, so they may not defile their tents in the midst of which I dwell." The children of Israel did so and put them out of the camp, as the LORD had commanded Moses The LORD spoke to Moses, saying, "Speak to the children of Israel: When a man or a woman commits a sin against another and thereby breaks faith with the LORD, that person is guilty. They shall confess their sin and make full restitution for their wrong, adding one-fifth to it and giving it to the person against whom they have sinned. But if the person has no close relative to whom restitution may be made, the restitution for the wrong shall go to the LORD for the priest, in addition to the ram of atonement by which atonement is made for the wrongdoer. Every contribution of all the sacred things that the children of Israel bring to the priest shall be his. Each one's sacred things shall be his; whatever anyone gives to the priest shall be his." The LORD spoke to Moses, saying, "Speak to the children of Israel and say to them: If a man's wife turns to lawlessness and commits a trespass against him, if another man lies with her carnally, and this is hidden from the eyes of her husband and kept hidden, and she is defiled, and there is no testimony against her, nor is she caught in the act, if the spirit of jealousy comes over him and he is jealous of his wife who has defiled herself, or if the spirit of jealousy comes over him and he is jealous of his wife who has not defiled herself, then the man shall bring his wife to the priest and bring his offering for her, a tenth of an ephah of barley flour. He shall not pour oil on it nor put frankincense on it, for it is a grain offering of jealousy, a grain offering of remembrance, bringing iniquity to mind The priest shall bring her and set her before the LORD. The priest shall take holy water in an earthen vessel and take some of the dust that is on the floor of the Tabernacle and put it into the water. The priest shall set the woman before the LORD, loosen her hair, and place in her hands the grain offering of remembrance, which is the grain offering of jealousy. The priest shall have in his hand the bitter water that brings a curse The priest shall charge her by oath, saying to the woman, "If no man has lain with you, and if you have not turned aside to uncleanness while under your husband's authority, be free from this bitter water that brings a curse. But if you have gone astray while under your husband's authority and if you have defiled yourself and some man other than your husband has lain with you," then the priest shall make the woman take the oath of the curse and say to the woman, "The LORD make you a curse and an oath among your people when the LORD makes your thigh waste away and your abdomen swell. May this water that brings the curse pass into your bowels to make your abdomen swell and your thigh waste away." The woman shall say, "Amen, amen." Then the priest shall write these curses in a book and wash them off into the bitter water. He shall make the woman drink the bitter water that brings a curse, and the water that brings the curse shall enter into her and cause bitterness. The priest shall take the grain offering of jealousy from the woman's hand, shall wave the offering before the LORD, and bring it to the altar. The priest shall take a handful of the grain offering as its memorial portion and burn it on the altar, and afterward, he shall make the woman drink the water. When he has made her drink the water, then if she has defiled herself and has been unfaithful to her husband, the water that brings the curse shall enter into her and cause bitterness, and her abdomen shall swell and her thigh shall waste away, and the woman shall become a curse among her people. But if the woman has not defiled herself and is clean, then she shall be free and shall conceive children This is the law in cases of jealousy when a wife, though under her husband's authority, goes astray and defiles herself, or when the spirit of jealousy comes over a man and he is jealous of his wife. He shall set the woman before the LORD, and the priest shall carry out for her all this law. The man shall be free from iniquity, but the woman shall bear her iniquity

Chapter 6

The LORD spoke to Moses, saying, "Speak to the children of Israel and say to them, 'When a man or a woman makes a special vow, the vow of a Nazirite, to separate themselves to the LORD, they shall abstain from wine and strong drink. They shall drink neither vinegar made from wine nor vinegar made from strong drink, nor shall they drink any juice of grapes or eat grapes, fresh or dried. All the days of their separation they shall eat nothing produced by the grapevine, not even the seeds or the skins All the days of their vow of separation, no razor shall touch their head. Until the time is completed for which they separate themselves to the LORD, they shall be holy

and let the locks of their hair grow long. All the days that they separate themselves to the LORD, they shall not go near a dead body. Even if their father, mother, brother, or sister dies, they shall not make themselves unclean, because their separation to God is upon their head. All the days of their separation they are holy to the LORD If someone dies suddenly beside them, thus defiling their consecrated head, then they shall shave their head on the day of their cleansing; on the seventh day they shall shave it. On the eighth day they shall bring two turtledoves or two young pigeons to the priest at the entrance of the tent of meeting. The priest shall offer one for a sin offering and the other for a burnt offering and make atonement for them, because they sinned by being in the presence of the dead body. They shall consecrate their head that same day and separate themselves to the LORD for the days of their separation and bring a year-old male lamb for a guilt offering. The former days shall be void because their separation was defiled This is the law for the Nazirite when the time of their separation has been completed. They shall be brought to the entrance of the tent of meeting, and they shall bring their offering to the LORD, one male lamb a year old without blemish for a burnt offering, one ewe lamb a year old without blemish for a sin offering, one ram without blemish for a peace offering, and a basket of unleavened bread, loaves of fine flour mixed with oil, and unleavened wafers smeared with oil, with their grain offering and their drink offerings. The priest shall bring them before the LORD and offer their sin offering and their burnt offering. He shall also offer the ram as a sacrifice of peace offering to the LORD, with the basket of unleavened bread. The priest shall offer also its grain offering and its drink offering The Nazirite shall then shave their consecrated head at the entrance of the tent of meeting and shall take the hair from their consecrated head and put it on the fire that is under the sacrifice of the peace offering. The priest shall take the shoulder of the ram, when it is boiled, and one unleavened loaf out of the basket and one unleavened wafer, and shall put them on the hands of the Nazirite after they have shaved the hair of their consecration. The priest shall wave them as a wave offering before the LORD; they are a holy portion for the priest, together with the breast that is waved and the thigh that is contributed. And after that the Nazirite may drink wine This is the law of the Nazirite who vows an offering to the LORD for their separation, in addition to whatever else they can afford. They must fulfill the vow they have made, according to the law of their separation.'" The LORD spoke to Moses, saying, "Speak to Aaron and his sons, saying, 'Thus you shall bless the people of Israel: You shall say to them, "The LORD bless you and keep you; the LORD make his face to shine upon you and be gracious to you; the LORD lift up his countenance upon you and give you peace." So they shall put my name upon the people of Israel, and I will bless them.'"

Chapter 7

When Moses had finished setting up the tabernacle, he anointed and consecrated it and all its furnishings, as well as the altar and its utensils; he anointed and consecrated them. Then the leaders of Israel, the heads of their fathers' houses, who were the leaders of the tribes, brought their offerings. They brought six covered wagons and twelve oxen, a wagon for every two leaders and an ox for each one. They presented them before the tabernacle. The LORD said to Moses, "Accept these from them, that they may be used in the service of the tent of meeting, and give them to the Levites, each according to his service." So Moses took the wagons and the oxen and gave them to the Levites. Two wagons and four oxen he gave to the sons of Gershon, according to their service. Four wagons and eight oxen he gave to the sons of Merari, according to their service, under the direction of Ithamar the son of Aaron the priest. But to the sons of Kohath he gave none, because they were responsible for the service of the holy objects, which they carried on their shoulders The leaders offered their dedication offering for the altar when it was anointed. The leaders offered their offering before the altar. The LORD said to Moses, "They shall offer their offering, one leader each day, for the dedication of the altar." On the first day Nahshon the son of Amminadab of the tribe of Judah offered his offering. His offering was one silver plate weighing one hundred and thirty shekels, one silver basin weighing seventy shekels, according to the shekel of the sanctuary, both of them full of fine flour mixed with oil for a grain offering; one golden dish of ten shekels, full of incense; one bull from the herd, one ram, one male lamb a year old, for a burnt offering; one male goat for a sin offering; and for the sacrifice of peace offerings, two oxen, five rams, five male goats, and five male lambs a year old. This was the offering of Nahshon the son of Amminadab On the second day Nethaneel the son of Zuar, the leader of Issachar, made his offering. He offered one silver plate weighing one hundred and thirty shekels, one silver basin weighing seventy shekels, according to the shekel of the sanctuary, both full of fine flour mixed with oil for a grain offering; one golden dish of ten shekels, full of incense; one bull from the herd, one ram, one male lamb a year old, for a burnt offering; one male goat for a sin offering; and for the sacrifice of peace offerings, two oxen, five rams, five male goats, and five male lambs a year old. This was the offering of Nethaneel the son of Zuar On the third day Eliab the son of Helon, the leader of the people of Zebulun, made his offering. His offering was one silver plate weighing one hundred and thirty shekels, one silver basin weighing seventy shekels, according to the shekel of the sanctuary, both full of fine flour mixed with oil for a grain offering; one golden dish of ten shekels, full of incense; one bull from the herd, one ram, one male lamb a year old, for a burnt offering; one male goat for a sin offering; and for the sacrifice of peace offerings, two oxen, five rams, five male goats, and five male lambs a year old. This was the offering of Eliab the son of Helon On the fourth day Elizur the son of Shedeur, the leader of the people of Reuben, made his offering. His offering was one silver plate weighing one hundred and thirty shekels, one silver basin weighing seventy shekels, according to the shekel of the sanctuary, both full of fine flour mixed with oil for a grain offering; one golden dish of ten shekels, full of incense; one bull from the herd, one ram, one male lamb a year old, for a burnt offering; one male goat for a sin offering; and for the sacrifice of peace offerings, two oxen, five rams, five male goats, and five male lambs a year old. This was the offering of Elizur the son of Shedeur On the fifth day Shelumiel the son of Zurishaddai, the leader of the people of Simeon, made his offering. His offering was one silver plate weighing one hundred and thirty shekels, one silver basin weighing seventy shekels, according to the shekel of the sanctuary, both full of fine flour mixed with oil for a grain offering; one golden dish of ten shekels, full of incense; one bull from the herd, one ram, one male lamb a year old, for a burnt offering; one male goat for a sin offering; and for the sacrifice of peace offerings, two oxen, five rams, five male goats, and five male lambs a year old. This was the offering of Shelumiel the son of Zurishaddai On the sixth day Eliasaph the son of Deuel, the leader of the people of Gad, made his offering. His offering was one silver plate weighing one hundred and thirty shekels, one silver basin weighing seventy shekels, according to the shekel of the sanctuary, both full of fine flour mixed with oil for a grain offering; one golden dish of ten shekels, full of incense; one bull from the herd, one ram, one male lamb a year old, for a burnt offering; one male goat for a sin offering; and for the sacrifice of peace offerings, two oxen, five rams, five male goats, and five male lambs a year old. This was the offering of Eliasaph the son of Deuel On the seventh day Elishama the son of Ammihud, the leader of the people of Ephraim, made his offering. His offering was one silver plate weighing one hundred and thirty shekels, one silver basin weighing seventy shekels, according to the shekel of the sanctuary, both full of fine flour mixed with oil for a grain offering; one golden dish of ten shekels, full of incense; one bull from the herd, one ram, one male lamb a year old, for a burnt offering; one male goat for a sin offering; and for the sacrifice of peace offerings, two oxen, five rams, five male goats, and five male lambs a year old. This was the offering of Elishama the son of Ammihud On the eighth day Gamaliel the son of Pedahzur, the leader of the people of Manasseh, made his offering. His offering was one silver plate weighing one hundred and thirty shekels, one silver basin weighing seventy shekels, according to the shekel of the sanctuary, both full of fine flour mixed with oil for a grain offering; one golden dish of ten shekels, full of incense; one bull from the herd, one ram, one male lamb a year old, for a burnt offering; one male goat for a sin offering; and for the sacrifice of peace offerings, two oxen, five rams, five male goats, and five male lambs a year old. This was the offering of Gamaliel the son of Pedahzur On the ninth day Abidan the son of Gideoni, the leader of the people of Benjamin, made his offering. His offering was one silver plate weighing one hundred and thirty shekels, one silver basin weighing seventy shekels, according to the shekel of the sanctuary, both full of fine flour mixed with oil for a grain offering; one golden dish of ten shekels, full of incense; one bull from the herd, one ram, one male lamb a year old, for a burnt offering; one male goat for a sin offering; and for the sacrifice of peace offerings, two oxen, five rams, five male goats, and five male lambs a year old. This was the offering of Abidan the son of Gideoni On the tenth day Ahiezer the son of Ammishaddai, the leader of the people of Dan, made his offering. His offering was one silver plate weighing one hundred and thirty shekels, one silver basin weighing seventy shekels, according to the shekel of the sanctuary, both full of fine flour mixed with oil for a grain offering; one golden dish of ten shekels, full of incense; one bull from the herd, one ram, one male lamb a year old, for a burnt offering; one male goat for a sin offering; and for the sacrifice of peace offerings, two oxen, five rams, five male goats, and five male lambs a year old. This was the offering of Ahiezer the son of Ammishaddai On the eleventh day Pagiel the son of Ochran, the leader of the people of Asher, made his offering. His offering was one silver plate weighing one hundred and thirty shekels, one silver basin weighing seventy shekels, according to the shekel of the sanctuary, both full of fine flour mixed with oil for a grain offering; one golden dish of ten shekels, full of incense; one bull from the herd, one ram, one male lamb a year old, for a burnt offering; one male goat for a sin offering; and for the sacrifice of peace offerings, two oxen, five rams, five male goats, and five male lambs a year old. This was the offering of Pagiel the son of Ochran On the twelfth day Ahira the son of Enan, the leader of the people of Naphtali, made his offering. His offering was one silver plate weighing one hundred and thirty shekels, one silver basin weighing seventy shekels, according to the shekel of the sanctuary, both full of fine flour mixed with oil for a grain offering; one golden dish of ten shekels, full of incense; one bull from the herd, one ram, one male lamb a year old, for a burnt offering; one male goat for a sin offering; and for the sacrifice of peace offerings, two oxen, five rams, five male goats, and five male lambs a year old. This was the offering of Ahira the son of Enan This was the dedication offering for the altar from the leaders of Israel when it was anointed: twelve silver plates, twelve silver basins, and twelve golden dishes. Each silver plate weighed one hundred and thirty shekels, and each basin seventy; all the silver of the vessels was two thousand four hundred shekels, according to the shekel of the sanctuary. The twelve golden dishes, full of incense, weighed ten shekels apiece, according to the shekel of the sanctuary; all the gold of the dishes was one hundred and twenty shekels. All the cattle for the burnt offering totaled twelve bulls, twelve rams, and twelve male lambs a year old, with their grain offering; and twelve male goats for a sin offering. All the cattle for the sacrifice of peace offerings totaled twenty-four bulls, sixty rams, sixty male goats, and sixty male lambs a year old. This was the dedication offering for the altar after it was anointed When Moses went into the tent of meeting to speak with the LORD, he heard the voice speaking to him from above the mercy seat that was on the ark of the testimony, from between the two cherubim; and it spoke to him

Chapter 8

The LORD spoke to Moses, saying, "Speak to Aaron and say to him, 'When you set up the lamps, the seven lamps shall give light in front of the lampstand.'" And Aaron did so; he set up its lamps to face forward on the lampstand, as the LORD commanded Moses. This was the workmanship of the lampstand, hammered work of gold. From its base to its flowers, it was hammered work; according to the pattern that the LORD had shown Moses, so he made the lampstand The LORD spoke to Moses, saying, "Take the Levites from among the people of Israel and cleanse them. Thus you shall do to them to cleanse them: sprinkle the water of purification upon them, and let them go over a razor over all their body, and wash their clothes and cleanse themselves. Then let them take a bull from the herd and its grain offering of fine flour mixed with oil, and you shall take another bull from the herd for a sin offering. You shall bring the Levites before the tent of meeting and assemble the whole congregation of the people of Israel. When you bring the Levites before the LORD, the people of Israel shall lay their hands on the Levites, and Aaron shall offer the Levites before the LORD as a wave offering from the people of Israel, that they may do the service of the LORD. Then the Levites shall lay their hands on the heads of the bulls, and you shall offer the one for a sin offering and the other for a burnt offering to the LORD to make atonement for the Levites You shall set the Levites before Aaron and his sons and offer them as a wave offering to the LORD. Thus you shall separate the Levites from among the people of Israel, and the Levites shall be mine. After that, the Levites shall go in to serve at the tent of meeting, when you have cleansed them and offered them as a wave offering. For they are wholly given to me from among the people of Israel. Instead of all who open the womb, the firstborn of all the people of Israel, I have taken them for myself. For all the firstborn among the people of Israel are mine, both of man and of beast.

On the day that I struck down all the firstborn in the land of Egypt, I consecrated them for myself, and I have taken the Levites instead of all the firstborn among the people of Israel. I have given the Levites as a gift to Aaron and his sons from among the people of Israel to do the service for the people of Israel at the tent of meeting and to make atonement for the people of Israel, that there may be no plague among the people of Israel when the people of Israel come near the sanctuary." Thus did Moses and Aaron and all the congregation of the people of Israel to the Levites. According to all that the LORD commanded Moses concerning the Levites, the people of Israel did to them. And the Levites purified themselves from sin and washed their clothes, and Aaron offered them as a wave offering before the LORD, and Aaron made atonement for them to cleanse them. And after that, the Levites went in to do their service in the tent of meeting before Aaron and his sons; as the LORD had commanded Moses concerning the Levites, so they did to them The LORD spoke to Moses, saying, "This applies to the Levites: from twenty-five years old and upward they shall come to do duty in the service of the tent of meeting. And from the age of fifty years they shall withdraw from the duty of the service and serve no more. They minister to their brothers in the tent of meeting by keeping guard, but they shall do no service. Thus shall you do to the Levites in assigning their duties."

Chapter 9

The LORD spoke to Moses in the wilderness of Sinai, in the first month of the second year after they had come out of the land of Egypt, saying, "Let the people of Israel keep the Passover at its appointed time. On the fourteenth day of this month, at twilight, you shall keep it at its appointed time; according to all its statutes and all its rules you shall keep it." So Moses told the people of Israel that they should keep the Passover. And they kept the Passover in the first month, on the fourteenth day of the month, at twilight, in the wilderness of Sinai. According to all that the LORD commanded Moses, so the people of Israel did And there were certain men who were unclean through touching a dead body, so that they could not keep the Passover on that day, and they came before Moses and Aaron on that day. And those men said to him, "We are unclean through touching a dead body. Why are we kept from bringing the LORD's offering at its appointed time among the people of Israel?" And Moses said to them, "Wait, that I may hear what the LORD will command concerning you." The LORD spoke to Moses, saying, "Speak to the people of Israel, saying, If any one of you or your descendants is unclean through touching a dead body, or is on a long journey, he shall still keep the Passover to the LORD. In the second month on the fourteenth day at twilight they shall keep it. They shall eat it with unleavened bread and bitter herbs. They shall leave none of it until the morning, nor break any of its bones; according to all the statute for the Passover they shall keep it. But if anyone who is clean and is not on a journey fails to keep the Passover, that person shall be cut off from his people because he did not bring the LORD's offering at its appointed time; that man shall bear his sin. And if a stranger sojourns among you and would keep the Passover to the LORD, according to the statute of the Passover and according to its rule, so shall he do. You shall have one statute, both for the sojourner and for the native." On the day that the tabernacle was set up, the cloud covered the tabernacle, the tent of the testimony. And at evening it was over the tabernacle like the appearance of fire until morning. So it was always: the cloud covered it by day and the appearance of fire by night. And whenever the cloud lifted from over the tent, after that the people of Israel set out, and in the place where the cloud settled down, there the people of Israel camped. At the command of the LORD the people of Israel set out, and at the command of the LORD they camped. As long as the cloud rested over the tabernacle, they remained in camp. Even when the cloud continued over the tabernacle many days, the people of Israel kept the charge of the LORD and did not set out. Sometimes the cloud was a few days over the tabernacle, and according to the command of the LORD they remained in camp; then according to the command of the LORD they set out. And sometimes the cloud remained from evening until morning. And when the cloud lifted in the morning, they set out, or if it continued for a day and a night, when the cloud lifted they set out. Whether it was two days, or a month, or a longer time that the cloud continued over the tabernacle, abiding there, the people of Israel remained in camp and did not set out, but when it lifted they set out. At the command of the LORD they camped, and at the command of the LORD they set out. They kept the charge of the LORD, at the command of the LORD by Moses

Chapter 10

The LORD spoke to Moses, saying, "Make two silver trumpets. Of hammered work you shall make them, and you shall use them for summoning the congregation and for breaking camp. And when both are blown, all the congregation shall gather themselves to you at the entrance of the tent of meeting. But if they blow only one, then the chiefs, the heads of the tribes of Israel, shall gather themselves to you. When you blow an alarm, the camps that are on the east side shall set out. And when you blow an alarm the second time, the camps that are on the south side shall set out. An alarm is to be blown whenever they are to set out. But when the assembly is to be gathered together, you shall blow a long blast, but you shall not sound an alarm. And the sons of Aaron, the priests, shall blow the trumpets. The trumpets shall be to you for a perpetual statute throughout your generations. And when you go to war in your land against the adversary who oppresses you, then you shall sound an alarm with the trumpets, that you may be remembered before the LORD your God, and you shall be saved from your enemies. On the day of your gladness also, and at your appointed feasts and at the beginnings of your months, you shall blow the trumpets over your burnt offerings and over the sacrifices of your peace offerings. They shall be a reminder of you before your God: I am the LORD your God." In the second year, in the second month, on the twentieth day of the month, the cloud lifted from over the tabernacle of the testimony, and the people of Israel set out by stages from the wilderness of Sinai. And the cloud settled down in the wilderness of Paran. They set out for the first time at the command of the LORD by Moses. The standard of the camp of the people of Judah set out first by their companies, and over their company was Nahshon the son of Amminadab. And over the company of the tribe of the people of Issachar was Nethanel the son of Zuar. And over the company of the tribe of the people of Zebulun was Eliab the son of Helon And when the tabernacle was taken down, the sons of Gershon and the sons of Merari, who carried the tabernacle, set out. And the standard of the camp of Reuben set out by their companies, and over their company was Elizur the son of Shedeur. And over the company of the tribe of the people of Simeon was Shelumiel the son of Zurishaddai. And over the company of the tribe of the people of Gad was Eliasaph the son of Deuel. Then the Kohathites set out, carrying the holy things, and the tabernacle was set up before their arrival. And the standard of the camp of the people of Ephraim set out by their companies, and over their company was Elishama the son of Ammihud. And over the company of the tribe of the people of Manasseh was Gamaliel the son of Pedahzur. And over the company of the tribe of the people of Benjamin was Abidan the son of Gideoni Then the standard of the camp of the people of Dan, acting as the rear guard of all the camps, set out by their companies, and over their company was Ahiezer the son of Ammishaddai. And over the company of the tribe of the people of Asher was Pagiel the son of Ochran. And over the company of the tribe of the people of Naphtali was Ahira the son of Enan. This was the order of march of the people of Israel by their companies when they set out And Moses said to Hobab the son of Reuel the Midianite, Moses' father-in-law, "We are setting out for the place of which the LORD said, 'I will give it to you.' Come with us, and we will do good to you, for the LORD has promised good to Israel." But he said to him, "I will not go. I will depart to my own land and to my kindred." And he said, "Please do not leave us, for you know where we should camp in the wilderness, and you will serve as eyes for us. And if you do go with us, whatever good the LORD will do to us, the same will we do to you." So they set out from the mount of the LORD three days' journey. And the ark of the covenant of the LORD went before them three days' journey, to seek out a resting place for them. And the cloud of the LORD was over them by day, whenever they set out from the camp. And whenever the ark set out, Moses said, "Arise, O LORD, and let your enemies be scattered, and let those who hate you flee before you." And when it rested, he said, "Return, O LORD, to the ten thousand thousands of Israel."

Chapter 11

When the people became murmurers, it displeased the LORD; and the LORD heard it. His anger was kindled, and the fire of the LORD burned among them and consumed some of the camp. Then the people cried out to Moses, and when Moses prayed to the LORD, the fire was quenched. He called that place Taberah because the fire of the LORD had burned among them A mixed multitude among them craved other food, and the Israelites wept again, saying, "Who will give us meat to eat? We remember the fish we ate in Egypt at no cost, the cucumbers, melons, leeks, onions, and garlic. But now we have lost our appetite; we never see anything but this manna." The manna was like coriander seed and looked like resin. The people went around gathering it and then ground it in handmills or crushed it in mortars. They cooked it in a pot or made it into loaves. It tasted like something made with olive oil. When the dew settled on the camp at night, the manna also came down Moses heard the people of every family wailing at the entrance of their tents. The LORD became exceedingly angry, and Moses was troubled. He asked the LORD, "Why have you brought this trouble on your servant? What have I done to displease you that you put the burden of all these people on me? Did I conceive all these people? Did I give them birth? Why do you tell me to carry them in my arms, as a nurse carries an infant, to the land you promised on oath to their ancestors? Where can I get meat for all these people? They keep wailing to me, 'Give us meat to eat!' I cannot carry all these people by myself; the burden is too heavy for me. If this is how you are going to treat me, please go ahead and kill me—if I have found favor in your eyes—and do not let me face my own ruin." The LORD said to Moses, "Bring me seventy of Israel's elders who are known to you as leaders and officials among the people. Have them come to the tent of meeting, that they may stand there with you. I will come down and speak with you there, and I will take some of the power of the Spirit that is on you and put it on them. They will share the burden of the people with you so that you will not have to carry it alone "Tell the people: 'Consecrate yourselves in preparation for tomorrow, when you will eat meat. The LORD heard you when you wailed, 'If only we had meat to eat! We were better off in Egypt!' Now the LORD will give you meat, and you will eat it. You will not eat it for just one day, or two days, or five, ten or twenty days, but for a whole month— until it comes out of your nostrils and you loathe it— because you have rejected the LORD, who is among you, and have wailed before him, saying, 'Why did we ever leave Egypt?'" But Moses said, "Here I am among six hundred thousand men on foot, and you say, 'I will give them meat to eat for a whole month!' Would they have enough if flocks and herds were slaughtered for them? Would they have enough if all the fish in the sea were caught for them?" The LORD answered Moses, "Is the LORD's arm too short? Now you will see whether or not what I say will come true for you." So Moses went out and told the people what the LORD had said. He brought together seventy of their elders and had them stand around the tent. Then the LORD came down in the cloud and spoke with him, and he took some of the power of the Spirit that was on him and put it on the seventy elders. When the Spirit rested on them, they prophesied— but did not do so again However, two men, whose names were Eldad and Medad, had remained in the camp. They were listed among the elders but did not go out to the tent. Yet the Spirit also rested on them, and they prophesied in the camp. A young man ran and told Moses, "Eldad and Medad are prophesying in the camp." Joshua, son of Nun, who had been Moses' aide since youth, spoke up and said, "Moses, my lord, stop them!" But Moses replied, "Are you jealous for my sake? I wish that all the LORD's people were prophets and that the LORD would put his Spirit on them!" Then Moses and the elders of Israel returned to the camp Now a wind went out from the LORD and drove quail in from the sea. It scattered them up to two cubits deep all around the camp, as far as a day's walk in any direction. All that day and night and all the next day, the people went out and gathered quail. No one gathered less than ten homers. Then they spread them out all around the camp. But while the meat was still between their teeth and before it could be consumed, the anger of the LORD burned against the people, and he struck them with a severe plague. Therefore the place was named Kibroth Hattaavah because there they buried the people who had craved other food. From Kibroth Hattaavah, the people traveled to Hazeroth and stayed there

Chapter 12

Miriam and Aaron began to talk against Moses because of his Cushite wife, for he had married a Cushite. "Has the LORD spoken only through Moses?" they asked. "Hasn't he also spoken through us?" And the LORD heard this. (Now Moses was a very humble man, more humble than anyone else on the face of the earth.) At once the LORD said to Moses, Aaron, and Miriam, "Come out to the tent of meeting, all three of you." So the three of them went out. Then the LORD came down in a pillar of cloud; he stood at the entrance to the tent and summoned Aaron and Miriam. When the two of them stepped forward, he said, "Listen to my words: When there is a prophet among you, I, the LORD, reveal myself to them in visions, I speak to them in dreams. But this is not true of my servant Moses; he is faithful in all my house. With him I speak face to face, clearly and not

in riddles; he sees the form of the LORD. Why then were you not afraid to speak against my servant Moses?" The anger of the LORD burned against them, and he left them. When the cloud lifted from above the tent, Miriam's skin was leprous—it became as white as snow. Aaron turned toward her and saw that she had a defiling skin disease, and he said to Moses, "Please, my lord, I ask you not to hold against us the sin we have so foolishly committed. Do not let her be like a stillborn infant coming from its mother's womb with its flesh half eaten away." So Moses cried out to the LORD, "Please, God, heal her!" The LORD replied to Moses, "If her father had spit in her face, would she not have been in disgrace for seven days? Confine her outside the camp for seven days; after that, she can be brought back." So Miriam was confined outside the camp for seven days, and the people did not move on until she was brought back. After that, the people left Hazeroth and encamped in the Desert of Paran

Chapter 13

The LORD said to Moses, "Send some men to explore the land of Canaan, which I am giving to the Israelites. From each ancestral tribe send one of its leaders." So at the LORD's command Moses sent them out from the Desert of Paran. All of them were leaders of the Israelites. These are their names: from the tribe of Reuben, Shammua son of Zaccur; from the tribe of Simeon, Shaphat son of Hori; from the tribe of Judah, Caleb son of Jephunneh; from the tribe of Issachar, Igal son of Joseph; from the tribe of Ephraim, Hoshea son of Nun; from the tribe of Benjamin, Palti son of Raphu; from the tribe of Zebulun, Gaddiel son of Sodi; from the tribe of Manasseh (a tribe of Joseph), Gaddi son of Susi; from the tribe of Dan, Ammiel son of Gemalli; from the tribe of Asher, Sethur son of Michael; from the tribe of Naphtali, Nahbi son of Vophsi; from the tribe of Gad, Geuel son of Maki. These are the names of the men Moses sent to explore the land. (Moses gave Hoshea son of Nun the name Joshua.) When Moses sent them to explore Canaan, he said, "Go up through the Negev and on into the hill country. See what the land is like and whether the people who live there are strong or weak, few or many. What kind of land do they live in? Is it good or bad? What kind of towns do they live in? Are they unwalled or fortified? How is the soil? Is it fertile or poor? Are there trees in it or not? Do your best to bring back some of the fruit of the land." (It was the season for the first ripe grapes.) So they went up and explored the land from the Desert of Zin as far as Rehob, toward Lebo Hamath. They went up through the Negev and came to Hebron, where Ahiman, Sheshai, and Talmai, the descendants of Anak, lived. (Hebron had been built seven years before Zoan in Egypt.) When they reached the Valley of Eshkol, they cut off a branch bearing a single cluster of grapes. Two of them carried it on a pole between them, along with some pomegranates and figs. That place was called the Valley of Eshkol because of the cluster of grapes the Israelites cut off there. At the end of forty days, they returned from exploring the land They came back to Moses and Aaron and the whole Israelite community at Kadesh in the Desert of Paran. There they reported to them and to the whole assembly and showed them the fruit of the land. They gave Moses this account: "We went into the land to which you sent us, and it does flow with milk and honey! Here is its fruit. But the people who live there are powerful, and the cities are fortified and very large. We even saw descendants of Anak there. The Amalekites live in the Negev; the Hittites, Jebusites, and Amorites live in the hill country; and the Canaanites live near the sea and along the Jordan." Then Caleb silenced the people before Moses and said, "We should go up and take possession of the land, for we can certainly do it." But the men who had gone up with him said, "We can't attack those people; they are stronger than we are." And they spread among the Israelites a bad report about the land they had explored. They said, "The land we explored devours those living in it. All the people we saw there are of great size. We saw the Nephilim there (the descendants of Anak come from the Nephilim). We seemed like grasshoppers in our own eyes, and we looked the same to them."

Chapter 14

That night all the members of the community raised their voices and wept aloud. All the Israelites grumbled against Moses and Aaron, and the whole assembly said to them, "If only we had died in Egypt! Or in this wilderness! Why is the LORD bringing us to this land only to let us fall by the sword? Our wives and children will be taken as plunder. Wouldn't it be better for us to go back to Egypt?" And they said to each other, "We should choose a leader and go back to Egypt." Then Moses and Aaron fell facedown in front of the whole Israelite assembly gathered there. Joshua son of Nun and Caleb son of Jephunneh, who were among those who had explored the land, tore their clothes and said to the entire Israelite assembly, "The land we passed through and explored is exceedingly good. If the LORD is pleased with us, he will lead us into that land, a land flowing with milk and honey, and will give it to us. Only do not rebel against the LORD. And do not be afraid of the people of the land, because we will devour them. Their protection is gone, but the LORD is with us. Do not be afraid of them." But the whole assembly talked about stoning them. Then the glory of the LORD appeared at the tent of meeting to all the Israelites. The LORD said to Moses, "How long will these people treat me with contempt? How long will they refuse to believe in me, in spite of all the signs I have performed among them? I will strike them down with a plague and destroy them, but I will make you into a nation greater and stronger than they." Moses said to the LORD, "Then the Egyptians will hear about it! By your power, you brought these people up from among them. And they will tell the inhabitants of this land about it. They have already heard that you, LORD, are with these people and that you, LORD, have been seen face to face, that your cloud stays over them, and that you go before them in a pillar of cloud by day and a pillar of fire by night. If you put all these people to death, leaving none alive, the nations who have heard this report about you will say, 'The LORD was not able to bring these people into the land he promised them on oath, so he slaughtered them in the wilderness.' Now may the Lord's strength be displayed, just as you have declared: 'The LORD is slow to anger, abounding in love and forgiving sin and rebellion. Yet he does not leave the guilty unpunished; he punishes the children for the sin of the parents to the third and fourth generation.' In accordance with your great love, forgive the sin of these people, just as you have pardoned them from the time they left Egypt until now." The LORD replied, "I have forgiven them, as you asked. Nevertheless, as surely as I live and as surely as the glory of the LORD fills the whole earth, not one of those who saw my glory and the signs I performed in Egypt and in the wilderness but who disobeyed me and tested me ten times—not one of them will ever see the land I promised on oath to their ancestors. No one who has treated me with contempt will ever see it. But because my servant Caleb has a different spirit and follows me wholeheartedly, I will bring him into the land he went to, and his descendants will inherit it. Since the Amalekites and the Canaanites are living in

the valleys, turn back tomorrow and set out toward the desert along the route to the Red Sea." The LORD said to Moses and Aaron: "How long will this wicked community grumble against me? I have heard the complaints of these grumbling Israelites. So tell them, 'As surely as I live, declares the LORD, I will do to you the very thing I heard you say: In this wilderness your bodies will fall—every one of you twenty years old or more who was counted in the census and who has grumbled against me. Not one of you will enter the land I swore with uplifted hand to make your home, except Caleb son of Jephunneh and Joshua son of Nun. As for your children that you said would be taken as plunder, I will bring them in to enjoy the land you have rejected. But as for you, your bodies will fall in this wilderness. Your children will be shepherds here for forty years, suffering for your unfaithfulness until the last of your bodies lies in the wilderness. For forty years—one year for each of the forty days you explored the land—you will suffer for your sins and know what it is like to have me against you.' I, the LORD, have spoken, and I will surely do these things to this whole wicked community, which has banded together against me. They will meet their end in this wilderness; here they will die." So the men Moses had sent to explore the land, who returned and made the whole community grumble against him by spreading a bad report about it—these men who were responsible for spreading the bad report about the land were struck down and died of a plague before the LORD. Of the men who went to explore the land, only Joshua son of Nun and Caleb son of Jephunneh survived When Moses reported this to all the Israelites, they mourned bitterly. Early the next morning they set out for the highest point in the hill country, saying, "Now we are ready to go up to the land the LORD promised. Surely we have sinned!" But Moses said, "Why are you disobeying the LORD's command? This will not succeed! Do not go up, because the LORD is not with you. You will be defeated by your enemies, for the Amalekites and the Canaanites will face you there. Because you have turned away from the LORD, he will not be with you and you will fall by the sword." Nevertheless, in their presumption, they went up toward the highest point in the hill country, though neither Moses nor the ark of the LORD's covenant moved from the camp. Then the Amalekites and the Canaanites who lived in that hill country came down and attacked them and beat them down all the way to Hormah

Chapter 15

The LORD said to Moses, "Speak to the Israelites and say to them: 'After you enter the land I am giving you as a home and you present to the LORD food offerings from the herd or the flock, as an aroma pleasing to the LORD—whether burnt offerings or sacrifices, for special vows or freewill offerings or festival offerings—then the person who brings an offering shall present to the LORD a grain offering of a tenth of an ephah of the finest flour mixed with a quarter of a hin of olive oil. With each lamb for the burnt offering or the sacrifice, prepare a quarter of a hin of wine as a drink offering With a ram, prepare a grain offering of two-tenths of an ephah of the finest flour mixed with a third of a hin of olive oil, and a third of a hin of wine as a drink offering. Offer it as an aroma pleasing to the LORD When you prepare a young bull as a burnt offering or sacrifice, for a special vow or a fellowship offering to the LORD, bring with the bull a grain offering of three-tenths of an ephah of the finest flour mixed with half a hin of olive oil, and also bring half a hin of wine as a drink offering. This will be a food offering, an aroma pleasing to the LORD. Each bull or ram, each lamb or young goat, is to be prepared in this manner. Do this for each one, for as many as you prepare Everyone who is native-born must do these things in this way when they present a food offering as an aroma pleasing to the LORD. For the generations to come, whenever a foreigner or anyone else living among you presents a food offering as an aroma pleasing to the LORD, they must do exactly as you do. The community is to have the same rules for you and for the foreigner residing among you; this is a lasting ordinance for the generations to come. You and the foreigner shall be the same before the LORD: The same laws and regulations will apply both to you and to the foreigner residing among you.'" The LORD said to Moses, "Speak to the Israelites and say to them: 'When you enter the land to which I am taking you and you eat the food of the land, present a portion as an offering to the LORD. Present a loaf from the first of your ground meal and present it as an offering from the threshing floor. Throughout the generations to come you are to give this offering to the LORD from the first of your ground meal Now if you as a community unintentionally fail to keep any of these commands the LORD gave Moses—any of the LORD's commands to you through him, from the day the LORD gave them and continuing through the generations to come—and if this is done unintentionally without the community being aware of it, then the whole community is to offer a young bull for a burnt offering as an aroma pleasing to the LORD, along with its prescribed grain offering and drink offering, and a male goat for a sin offering. The priest is to make atonement for the whole Israelite community, and they will be forgiven, for it was not intentional and they have presented to the LORD for their wrong a food offering and a sin offering. The whole Israelite community and the foreigners residing among them will be forgiven, because all the people were involved in the unintentional wrong But if just one person sins unintentionally, that person must bring a year-old female goat for a sin offering. The priest is to make atonement before the LORD for the one who erred by sinning unintentionally, and when atonement has been made for them, they will be forgiven. One and the same law applies to everyone who sins unintentionally, whether a native-born Israelite or a foreigner residing among you But anyone who sins defiantly, whether native-born or foreigner, blasphemes the LORD and must be cut off from the people of Israel. Because they have despised the LORD's word and broken his commands, they must surely be cut off; their guilt remains on them." While the Israelites were in the wilderness, a man was found gathering wood on the Sabbath day. Those who found him gathering wood brought him to Moses and Aaron and the whole assembly, and they kept him in custody because it was not clear what should be done to him. Then the LORD said to Moses, "The man must die. The whole assembly must stone him outside the camp." So the assembly took him outside the camp and stoned him to death, as the LORD commanded Moses The LORD said to Moses, "Speak to the Israelites and say to them: 'Throughout the generations to come you are to make tassels on the corners of your garments, with a blue cord on each tassel. You will have these tassels to look at and so you will remember all the commands of the LORD, that you may obey them and not prostitute yourselves by chasing after the lusts of your own hearts and eyes. Then you will remember to obey all my commands and will be consecrated to your God. I am the LORD your God, who brought you out of Egypt to be your God. I am the LORD your God.'"

Chapter 16

Korah, the son of Izhar, the son of Kohath, the son of Levi, along with Dathan and Abiram, the sons of Eliab, and On, the son of Peleth, of the tribe of Reuben, rose up against Moses. Accompanying them were 250 well-known community leaders who were renowned in the assembly. They confronted Moses and Aaron, saying, "You have taken too much upon yourselves, for the entire assembly is holy, every one of them, and the LORD is among them. Why then do you set yourselves above the LORD's assembly?" When Moses heard this, he fell facedown and spoke to Korah and all his followers, saying, "In the morning the LORD will show who belongs to him and who is holy, and he will have that person come near him. The man he chooses, he will cause to come near him. You, Korah, and all your followers are to do this: Take censers and tomorrow put burning coals and incense in them before the LORD. The man the LORD chooses will be the one who is holy. You Levites have gone too far!" Moses also said to Korah, "Listen, you Levites! Isn't it enough for you that the God of Israel has separated you from the rest of the Israelite community and brought you near himself to do the work at the LORD's tabernacle and to stand before the community and minister to them? He has brought you and all your fellow Levites near himself, but now you are trying to get the priesthood too. It is against the LORD that you and all your followers have banded together. Who is Aaron that you should grumble against him?" Then Moses summoned Dathan and Abiram, the sons of Eliab. But they said, "We will not come! Isn't it enough that you have brought us up out of a land flowing with milk and honey to kill us in the wilderness? And now you also want to lord it over us? Moreover, you haven't brought us into a land flowing with milk and honey or given us an inheritance of fields and vineyards. Do you want to treat these men like slaves? No, we will not come!" Moses became very angry and said to the LORD, "Do not accept their offering. I have not taken so much as a donkey from them, nor have I wronged any of them." Moses said to Korah, "You and all your followers are to appear before the LORD tomorrow— you and they and Aaron. Each man is to take his censer and put incense in it—250 censers in all—and present it before the LORD. You and Aaron are to present your censers also." So each of them took his censer, put burning coals and incense in it, and stood with Moses and Aaron at the entrance to the tent of meeting. When Korah had gathered all his followers in opposition to them at the entrance to the tent of meeting, the glory of the LORD appeared to the entire assembly The LORD said to Moses and Aaron, "Separate yourselves from this assembly so I can put an end to them at once." But Moses and Aaron fell facedown and cried out, "O God, the God who gives breath to all living things, will you be angry with the entire assembly when only one man sins?" Then the LORD said to Moses, "Say to the assembly, 'Move away from the tents of Korah, Dathan, and Abiram.'" Moses got up and went to Dathan and Abiram, and the elders of Israel followed him. He warned the assembly, "Move back from the tents of these wicked men! Do not touch anything belonging to them, or you will be swept away because of all their sins." So they moved away from the tents of Korah, Dathan, and Abiram. Dathan and Abiram had come out and were standing with their wives, children, and little ones at the entrances to their tents. Then Moses said, "This is how you will know that the LORD has sent me to do all these things and that it was not my idea: If these men die a natural death and suffer the fate of all mankind, then the LORD has not sent me. But if the LORD brings about something totally new, and the earth opens its mouth and swallows them, with everything that belongs to them, and they go down alive into the realm of the dead, then you will know that these men have treated the LORD with contempt." As soon as he finished saying all this, the ground under them split apart and the earth opened its mouth and swallowed them and their households, and all those associated with Korah, together with their possessions. They went down alive into the realm of the dead, with everything they owned; the earth closed over them, and they perished and were gone from the community. At their cries, all the Israelites around them fled, shouting, "The earth is going to swallow us too!" And fire came out from the LORD and consumed the 250 men who were offering the incense The LORD said to Moses, "Tell Eleazar son of Aaron, the priest, to remove the censers from the charred remains and scatter the coals some distance away, for the censers are holy. The censers of the men who sinned at the cost of their lives—hammer the censers into sheets to overlay the altar, for they were presented before the LORD and have become holy. Let them be a sign to the Israelites." So Eleazar the priest collected the bronze censers brought by those who had been burned to death, and he had them hammered out to overlay the altar, as the LORD directed him through Moses. This was to remind the Israelites that no one except a descendant of Aaron should come to burn incense before the LORD, or he would become like Korah and his followers The next day the whole Israelite community grumbled against Moses and Aaron. "You have killed the LORD's people," they said. But when the assembly gathered in opposition to Moses and Aaron and turned toward the tent of meeting, suddenly the cloud covered it and the glory of the LORD appeared. Then Moses and Aaron went to the front of the tent of meeting, and the LORD said to Moses, "Get away from this assembly so I can put an end to them at once." And they fell facedown Then Moses said to Aaron, "Take your censer and put incense in it, along with burning coals from the altar, and hurry to the assembly to make atonement for them. Wrath has come out from the LORD; the plague has started." So Aaron did as Moses said and ran into the midst of the assembly. The plague had already started among the people, but Aaron offered the incense and made atonement for them. He stood between the living and the dead, and the plague stopped. But 14,700 people died from the plague, in addition to those who had died because of Korah. Then Aaron returned to Moses at the entrance to the tent of meeting, for the plague had stopped

Chapter 17

The LORD said to Moses, "Speak to the Israelites and get twelve staffs from them, one from the leader of each of their ancestral tribes. Write the name of each man on his staff. On the staff of Levi write Aaron's name, for there must be one staff for the head of each ancestral tribe. Place them in the tent of meeting in front of the ark of the covenant law, where I meet with you. The staff belonging to the man I choose will sprout, and I will rid myself of this constant grumbling against you by the Israelites." So Moses spoke to the Israelites, and their leaders gave him twelve staffs, one for the leader of each of their ancestral tribes, and Aaron's staff was among them. Moses placed the staffs before the LORD in the tent of the covenant law. The next day Moses entered the tent and saw that Aaron's staff, which represented the tribe of Levi, had not only sprouted but had budded, blossomed, and produced almonds. Then Moses brought out all the staffs from the LORD's presence to all the Israelites. They looked at them, and each of the leaders took his own staff The LORD said to Moses, "Put back Aaron's staff in front of the ark of the covenant law, to be kept as a sign to the rebellious. This will put an end to their grumbling against me, so that they will not die." Moses did just as the LORD commanded him The Israelites said to Moses, "We will die! We are lost, we are all lost! Anyone who even comes near the tabernacle of the LORD will die. Are we all going to die?"

Chapter 18

The LORD said to Aaron, "You, your sons, and your family are to bear the responsibility for offenses connected with the sanctuary, and you and your sons alone are to bear the responsibility for offenses connected with the priesthood. Bring your fellow Levites from your ancestral tribe to join you and assist you when you and your sons minister before the tent of the covenant law. They are to be responsible to you and are to perform all the duties of the tent, but they must not go near the furnishings of the sanctuary or the altar. Otherwise, both they and you will die. They are to join you and be responsible for the care of the tent of meeting—all the work at the tent—and no one else may come near where you are You are to be responsible for the care of the sanctuary and the altar, so that my wrath will not fall on the Israelites again. I myself have selected your fellow Levites from among the Israelites as a gift to you, dedicated to the LORD to do the work at the tent of meeting. But only you and your sons may serve as priests in connection with everything at the altar and inside the curtain. I am giving you the service of the priesthood as a gift. Anyone else who comes near the sanctuary is to be put to death." Then the LORD said to Aaron, "I myself have put you in charge of the offerings presented to me; all the holy offerings the Israelites give me I give to you and your sons as your portion, your perpetual share. You are to have the part of the most holy offerings that is kept from the fire. From all the gifts they bring me as most holy offerings, whether grain or sin or guilt offerings, that part belongs to you and your sons. Eat it as something most holy; every male shall eat it. You must regard it as holy This also is yours: whatever is set aside from the gifts of all the wave offerings of the Israelites. I give this to you and your sons and daughters as your perpetual share. Everyone in your household who is ceremonially clean may eat it. I give you all the finest olive oil and all the finest new wine and grain they give the LORD as the firstfruits of their harvest. All the land's firstfruits that they bring to the LORD will be yours. Everyone in your household who is ceremonially clean may eat it Everything in Israel that is devoted to the LORD is yours. The first offspring of every womb, both human and animal, that is offered to the LORD is yours. But you must redeem every firstborn son and every firstborn male of unclean animals. When they are a month old, you must redeem them at the redemption price set at five shekels of silver, according to the sanctuary shekel, which weighs twenty gerahs But you must not redeem the firstborn of a cow, a sheep, or a goat; they are holy. Splash their blood against the altar and burn their fat as a food offering, an aroma pleasing to the LORD. Their meat is to be yours, just as the breast of the wave offering and the right thigh are yours. Whatever is set aside from the holy offerings the Israelites present to the LORD I give to you and your sons and daughters as your perpetual share. It is an everlasting covenant of salt before the LORD for both you and your offspring." The LORD said to Aaron, "You will have no inheritance in their land, nor will you have any share among them; I am your share and your inheritance among the Israelites. I give to the Levites all the tithes in Israel as their inheritance in return for the work they do while serving at the tent of meeting. From now on the

Israelites must not go near the tent of meeting, or they will bear the consequences of their sin and will die. It is the Levites who are to do the work at the tent of meeting and bear the responsibility for any offenses they commit against it. This is a lasting ordinance for the generations to come. They will receive no inheritance among the Israelites. Instead, I give to the Levites as their inheritance the tithes that the Israelites present as an offering to the LORD. That is why I said concerning them: 'They will have no inheritance among the Israelites.'" The LORD said to Moses, "Speak to the Levites and say to them: 'When you receive from the Israelites the tithe I give you as your inheritance, you must present a tenth of that tithe as the LORD's offering. Your offering will be reckoned to you as grain from the threshing floor or juice from the winepress. In this way, you also will present an offering to the LORD from all the tithes you receive from the Israelites. From these tithes, you must give the LORD's portion to Aaron the priest. You must present as the LORD's portion the best and holiest part of everything given to you.' Say to the Levites: 'When you present the best part, it will be reckoned to you as the product of the threshing floor or the winepress. You and your households may eat the rest of it anywhere, for it is your wages for your work at the tent of meeting. By presenting the best part of it, you will not be guilty in this matter; then you will not defile the holy offerings of the Israelites, and you will not die.'"

Chapter 19

The LORD said to Moses and Aaron: "This is a requirement of the law that the LORD has commanded: Tell the Israelites to bring you a red heifer without defect or blemish and that has never been under a yoke. Give it to Eleazar the priest; it is to be taken outside the camp and slaughtered in his presence. Then Eleazar the priest is to take some of its blood on his finger and sprinkle it seven times toward the front of the tent of meeting. While he watches, the heifer is to be burned—its hide, flesh, blood, and intestines. The priest is to take some cedar wood, hyssop, and scarlet wool and throw them onto the burning heifer. After that, the priest must wash his clothes and bathe himself with water. He may then come into the camp, but he will be ceremonially unclean until evening The man who burns it must also wash his clothes and bathe with water, and he too will be unclean till evening. A man who is clean shall gather up the ashes of the heifer and put them in a ceremonially clean place outside the camp. They are to be kept by the Israelite community for use in the water of cleansing; it is for purification from sin. The man who gathers up the ashes of the heifer must also wash his clothes, and he too will be unclean till evening. This will be a lasting ordinance both for the Israelites and for the foreigners residing among them Whoever touches a human corpse will be unclean for seven days. They must purify themselves with the water on the third day and on the seventh day; then they will be clean. But if they do not purify themselves on the third and seventh days, they will not be clean. If they fail to purify themselves after touching a human corpse, they defile the LORD's tabernacle. They must be cut off from Israel. Because the water of cleansing has not been sprinkled on them, they are unclean; their uncleanness remains on them This is the law that applies when a person dies in a tent: Anyone who enters the tent and anyone who is in it will be unclean for seven days, and every open container without a lid fastened on it will be unclean. Anyone out in the open who touches someone who has been killed with a sword or someone who has died a natural death, or anyone who touches a human bone or a grave, will be unclean for seven days For the unclean person, put some ashes from the burned purification offering into a jar and pour fresh water over them. Then a man who is ceremonially clean is to take some hyssop, dip it in the water, and sprinkle the tent and all the furnishings and the people who were there. He must also sprinkle anyone who has touched a human bone or a grave or anyone who has been killed or anyone who has died a natural death. The man who is clean is to sprinkle those who are unclean on the third and seventh days, and on the seventh day he is to purify them. Those who are being cleansed must wash their clothes and bathe with water, and that evening they will be clean. But if those who are unclean do not purify themselves, they must be cut off from the community, because they have defiled the sanctuary of the LORD. The water of cleansing has not been sprinkled on them, and they are unclean. This is a lasting ordinance for them The man who sprinkles the water of cleansing must also wash his clothes, and anyone who touches the water of cleansing will be unclean till evening. Anything that an unclean person touches becomes unclean, and anyone who touches it becomes unclean till evening."

Chapter 20

In the first month the whole Israelite community arrived at the Desert of Zin, and they stayed at Kadesh. There Miriam died and was buried. Now there was no water for the community, and the people gathered in opposition to Moses and Aaron. They quarreled with Moses and said, "If only we had died when our brothers fell dead before the LORD! Why did you bring the LORD's community into this wilderness, that we and our livestock should die here? Why did you bring us up out of Egypt to this terrible place? It has no grain or figs, grapevines or pomegranates. And there is no water to drink!" Moses and Aaron went from the assembly to the entrance to the tent of meeting and fell facedown, and the glory of the LORD appeared to them. The LORD said to Moses, "Take the staff, and you and your brother Aaron gather the assembly together. Speak to that rock before their eyes and it will pour out its water. You will bring water out of the rock for the community so they and their livestock can drink." So Moses took the staff from the LORD's presence, just as he commanded him He and Aaron gathered the assembly together in front of the rock and Moses said to them, "Listen, you rebels, must we bring you water out of this rock?" Then Moses raised his arm and struck the rock twice with his staff. Water gushed out, and the community and their livestock drank. But the LORD said to Moses and Aaron, "Because you did not trust in me enough to honor me as holy in the sight of the Israelites, you will not bring this community into the land I give them." These were the waters of Meribah, where the Israelites quarreled with the LORD and where he was proved holy among them Moses sent messengers from Kadesh to the king of Edom, saying: "This is what your brother Israel says: You know about all the hardships that have come on us. Our ancestors went down into Egypt, and we lived there many years. The Egyptians mistreated us and our ancestors, but when we cried out to the LORD, he heard our cry and sent an angel and brought us out of Egypt "Now we are here at Kadesh, a town on the edge of your territory. Please let us pass through your country. We will not go through any field or vineyard or drink water from any well. We will travel along the king's highway and not turn to the right or to the left until we have passed through your territory." But Edom answered: "You may not pass through here; if you try, we will march out and attack you with the sword." The Israelites replied: "We will go along the main road, and if we or our livestock drink any of your water, we will pay for it. We only want to pass through on foot—nothing else." Again they answered: "You may not pass through." Then Edom came out against them with a large and powerful army. Since Edom refused to let them go through their territory, Israel turned away from them The whole Israelite community set out from Kadesh and came to Mount Hor. At Mount Hor, near the border of Edom, the LORD said to Moses and Aaron, "Aaron will be gathered to his people. He will not enter the land I give the Israelites, because both of you rebelled against my command at the waters of Meribah. Get Aaron and his son Eleazar and take them up Mount Hor. Remove Aaron's garments and put them on his son Eleazar, for Aaron will be gathered to his people; he will die there." Moses did as the LORD commanded: They went up Mount Hor in the sight of the whole community. Moses removed Aaron's garments and put them on his son Eleazar. And Aaron died there on top of the mountain. Then Moses and Eleazar came down from the mountain, and when the whole community learned that Aaron had died, all the Israelites mourned for him thirty days

Chapter 21

1 When King Arad, the Canaanite, who dwelt in the Negev, heard that Israel was coming by the way of Atharim, he fought against Israel and took some of them captive. 2 Then Israel made a vow to the LORD, saying, "If you will indeed deliver this people into our hands, then we will utterly destroy their cities." 3 And the LORD listened to the voice of Israel and delivered up the Canaanites, and they utterly destroyed them and their cities. So the name of the place was called Hormah. 4 Then they set out from Mount Hor by the way of the Red Sea, to go around the land of Edom; and the people became impatient on the way. 5 The people spoke against God and against Moses, "Why have you brought us up out of Egypt to die in the wilderness? For there is no food and no water, and we loathe this worthless food." 6 Then the LORD sent fiery serpents among the people, and they bit the people, so that many of the people of Israel died. 7 So the people came to Moses and said, "We have sinned, because we have spoken against the LORD and you; pray to the LORD, that He may remove the serpents from us." And Moses prayed for the people. 8 Then the LORD said to Moses, "Make a fiery serpent, and set it on a standard; and it shall come about, that everyone who is bitten, when he looks at it, he will live." 9 And Moses made a bronze serpent and set it on the standard; and it came about, that if a serpent bit any man, when he looked to the bronze serpent, he lived 10 Now the sons of Israel moved out and camped in Oboth. 11 They journeyed from Oboth and camped at Iye-abarim, in the wilderness which is opposite Moab, to the east. 12 From there they set out and camped in the Wadi Zered. 13 From there they journeyed and camped on the other side of the Arnon, which is in the wilderness that comes out of the border of the Amorites; for the Arnon is the border of Moab, between Moab and the Amorites. 14 Therefore it is said in the Book of the Wars of the LORD, "Waheb in Suphah, And the wadis of the Arnon, 15 And the slope of the wadis That extends to the site of Ar, And leans to the border of Moab." 16 From there they continued to Beer, that is the well where the LORD said to Moses, "Assemble the people, that I may give them water." 17 Then Israel sang this song, "Spring up, O well! Sing to it! 18 The well, which the leaders dug, Which the nobles of the people hollowed out, With the scepter and with their staffs." And from the wilderness they continued to Mattanah, 19 and from Mattanah to Nahaliel, and from Nahaliel to Bamoth, 20 and from Bamoth to the valley that is in the land of Moab, at the top of Pisgah, which overlooks the wasteland 21 Then Israel sent messengers to Sihon, king of the Amorites, saying, 22 "Let me pass through your land. We will not turn off into field or vineyard; we will not drink water from wells. We will go by the King's Highway until we have passed through your border." 23 But Sihon would not permit Israel to pass through his border. So Sihon gathered all his people and went out against Israel in the wilderness, and came to Jahaz and fought against Israel. 24 Then Israel struck him with the edge of the sword, and took possession of his land from the Arnon to the Jabbok, as far as the sons of Ammon; for the border of the sons of Ammon was Jazer. 25 Israel took all these cities and Israel lived in all the cities of the Amorites, in Heshbon, and in all her villages. 26 For Heshbon was the city of Sihon, king of the Amorites, who had fought against the former king of Moab and had taken all his land out of his hand, as far as the Arnon. 27 Therefore those who use proverbs say, "Come to Heshbon! Let it be built! So let the city of Sihon be established. 28 For a fire went forth from Heshbon, A flame from the town of Sihon; It devoured Ar of Moab, The dominant heights of the Arnon. 29 Woe to you, O Moab! You are ruined, O people of Chemosh! He has given his sons as fugitives, And his daughters into captivity, To an Amorite king, Sihon. 30 But we have cast them down, Heshbon is ruined as far as Dibon, Then we have laid waste even to Nophah, Which reaches to Medeba." 31 Thus Israel lived in the land of the Amorites. 32 Moses sent to spy out Jazer, and they captured its villages and dispossessed the Amorites who were there. 33 Then they turned and went up by the way of Bashan, and Og the king of Bashan went out with all his people, for battle at Edrei. 34 But the LORD said to Moses, "Do not fear him, for I have given him into your hand, and all his people and his land; and you shall do to him as you did to Sihon, king of the Amorites, who lived at Heshbon." 35 So they killed him and his sons and all his people, until there was no remnant left him; and they possessed his land

Chapter 22

1 Then the sons of Israel journeyed, and camped in the plains of Moab beyond the Jordan opposite Jericho. 2 Now Balak the son of Zippor saw all that Israel had done to the Amorites. 3 So Moab was in great fear because of the people, for they were numerous; and Moab was in dread of the sons of Israel. 4 Moab said to the elders of Midian, "Now this horde will lick up all that is around us, as the ox licks up the grass of the field." And Balak the son of Zippor was king of Moab at that time. 5 So he sent messengers to Balaam the son of Beor, at Pethor, which is near the River, in the land of the sons of his people, to call him, saying, "Behold, a people came out of Egypt; behold, they cover the surface of the land, and they are living opposite me. 6 Now, therefore, please come, curse this people for me since they are too mighty for me; perhaps I may be able to defeat them and drive them out of the land. For I know that he whom you bless is blessed, and he whom you curse is cursed." 7 So the elders of Moab and the elders of Midian departed with the fees for divination in their hand; and they came to Balaam and repeated Balak's words to him. 8 He said to them, "Spend the night here, and I will bring word back to you as the LORD may speak to me." And the leaders of Moab stayed with Balaam. 9 Then God came to Balaam and said, "Who are these men with you?" 10 Balaam said to God, "Balak the son of Zippor, king of Moab, has sent word to me, 11 'Behold, there is a people who came out of Egypt and they cover the surface of the land. Now, come curse

them for me; perhaps I may be able to fight against them and drive them out.'" 12 God said to Balaam, "Do not go with them; you shall not curse the people, for they are blessed." 13 So Balaam arose in the morning and said to Balak's leaders, "Go back to your land, for the LORD has refused to let me go with you." 14 The leaders of Moab arose and went to Balak and said, "Balaam refused to come with us." 15 Then Balak again sent leaders, more numerous and more distinguished than the former. 16 They came to Balaam and said to him, "Thus says Balak the son of Zippor, 'Let nothing, I beg you, hinder you from coming to me; 17 for I will indeed honor you richly, and I will do whatever you say to me. Please come then, curse this people for me.'" 18 Balaam replied to the servants of Balak, "Though Balak were to give me his house full of silver and gold, I could not do anything, either small or great, contrary to the command of the LORD my God. 19 Now please, you also stay here tonight, and I will find out what else the LORD will speak to me." 20 God came to Balaam at night and said to him, "If the men have come to call you, rise up and go with them; but only the word which I speak to you shall you do." 21 So Balaam arose in the morning, and saddled his donkey and went with the leaders of Moab 22 But God was angry because he was going, and the angel of the LORD took his stand in the way as an adversary against him. Now he was riding on his donkey and his two servants were with him. 23 When the donkey saw the angel of the LORD standing in the way with his drawn sword in his hand, the donkey turned off from the way and went into the field; but Balaam struck the donkey to turn her back into the way. 24 Then the angel of the LORD stood in a narrow path of the vineyards, with a wall on this side and a wall on that side. 25 When the donkey saw the angel of the LORD, she pressed herself to the wall and pressed Balaam's foot against the wall, so he struck her again. 26 The angel of the LORD went further, and stood in a narrow place where there was no way to turn to the right hand or the left. 27 When the donkey saw the angel of the LORD, she lay down under Balaam; so Balaam was angry and struck the donkey with his stick. 28 And the LORD opened the mouth of the donkey, and she said to Balaam, "What have I done to you, that you have struck me these three times?" 29 Then Balaam said to the donkey, "Because you have made a mockery of me! If there had been a sword in my hand, I would have killed you by now." 30 The donkey said to Balaam, "Am I not your donkey on which you have ridden all your life to this day? Have I ever been accustomed to do so to you?" And he said, "No." 31 Then the LORD opened the eyes of Balaam, and he saw the angel of the LORD standing in the way with his drawn sword in his hand; and he bowed all the way to the ground. 32 The angel of the LORD said to him, "Why have you struck your donkey these three times? Behold, I have come out as an adversary, because your way was contrary to me. 33 But the donkey saw me and turned aside from me these three times. If she had not turned aside from me, I would surely have killed you just now, and let her live." 34 Balaam said to the angel of the LORD, "I have sinned, for I did not know that you were standing in the way against me. Now then, if it is displeasing to you, I will turn back." 35 But the angel of the LORD said to Balaam, "Go with the men, but you shall speak only the word which I tell you." So Balaam went along with the leaders of Balak. 36 When Balak heard that Balaam was coming, he went out to meet him at the city of Moab, which is on the Arnon border, at the extreme end of the border. 37 Then Balak said to Balaam, "Did I not urgently send to you to call you? Why did you not come to me? Am I really unable to honor you?" 38 So Balaam said to Balak, "Behold, I have come now to you! Am I able to speak anything at all? The word that God puts in my mouth, that I shall speak." 39 And Balaam went with Balak, and they came to Kiriath-huzoth. 40 Balak sacrificed oxen and sheep, and sent some to Balaam and the leaders who were with him. 41 Then it came about in the morning that Balak took Balaam and brought him up to the high places of Baal, and he saw from there a portion of the people

Chapter 23

1 Then Balaam said to Balak, "Build seven altars for me here and prepare seven bulls and seven rams for me here." 2 Balak did just as Balaam had spoken, and Balak and Balaam offered up a bull and a ram on each altar. 3 Then Balaam said to Balak, "Stand beside your burnt offering, and I will go; perhaps the LORD will come to meet me, and whatever he shows me I will tell you." So he went to a bare hill. 4 Now God met Balaam, and he said to Him, "I have set up the seven altars and I have offered up a bull and a ram on each altar." 5 Then the LORD put a word in Balaam's mouth and said, "Return to Balak, and you shall speak thus." 6 So he returned to him, and behold, he was standing beside his burnt offering, he and all the leaders of Moab. 7 He took up his discourse and said, "From Aram Balak has brought me, Moab's king from the mountains of the East, 'Come curse Jacob for me, And come, denounce Israel!' 8 How shall I curse whom God has not cursed? And how can I denounce whom the LORD has not denounced? 9 As I see him from the top of the rocks, And I look at him from the hills; Behold, a people who dwells apart, And will not be reckoned among the nations. 10 Who can count the dust of Jacob, Or number the fourth part of Israel? Let me die the death of the upright, And let my end be like his!" 11 Then Balak said to Balaam, "What have you done to me? I took you to curse my enemies, but behold, you have actually blessed them!" 12 He replied, "Must I not be careful to speak what the LORD puts in my mouth?" 13 Then Balak said to him, "Please come with me to another place from where you may see them, although you will only see the extreme end of them and will not see all of them; and curse them for me from there." 14 So he took him to the field of Zophim, to the top of Pisgah, and built seven altars and offered a bull and a ram on each altar. 15 And he said to Balak, "Stand here beside your burnt offering while I myself meet the LORD over there." 16 Then the LORD met Balaam and put a word in his mouth and said, "Return to Balak, and thus you shall speak." 17 He came to him, and behold, he was standing beside his burnt offering, and the leaders of Moab with him. And Balak said to him, "What has the LORD spoken?" 18 Then he took up his discourse and said, "Arise, O Balak, and hear; Give ear to me, O son of Zippor! 19 God is not a man, that He should lie, Nor a son of man, that He should repent; Has He said, and will He not do it? Or has He spoken, and will He not make it good? 20 Behold, I have received a command to bless; When He has blessed, then I cannot revoke it. 21 He has not observed misfortune in Jacob; Nor has He seen trouble in Israel; The LORD his God is with him, And the shout of a king is among them. 22 God brings them out of Egypt, He is for them like the horns of the wild ox. 23 For there is no omen against Jacob, Nor is there any divination against Israel; At the proper time it shall be said to Jacob And to Israel, what God has done! 24 Behold, a people rises like a lioness, And as a lion it lifts itself; It will not lie down until it devours the prey, And drinks the blood of the slain." 25 Then Balak said to Balaam, "Do not curse them at all nor bless them at all!" 26 But Balaam replied to Balak, "Did I not tell you, 'Whatever the LORD speaks, that I

must do'?" 27 Then Balak said to Balaam, "Please come, I will take you to another place; perhaps it will be agreeable with God that you curse them for me from there." 28 So Balak took Balaam to the top of Peor which overlooks the wasteland. 29 Balaam said to Balak, "Build seven altars for me here and prepare seven bulls and seven rams for me here." 30 Balak did just as Balaam had said, and offered up a bull and a ram on each altar

Chapter 24

1 When Balaam saw that it pleased the LORD to bless Israel, he did not go as at other times to seek omens, but he set his face toward the wilderness. 2 And Balaam lifted up his eyes and saw Israel camping tribe by tribe; and the Spirit of God came upon him. 3 He took up his discourse and said, "The oracle of Balaam the son of Beor, And the oracle of the man whose eye is opened; 4 The oracle of him who hears the words of God, Who sees the vision of the Almighty, Falling down, yet having his eyes uncovered, 5 How fair are your tents, O Jacob, Your dwellings, O Israel! 6 Like valleys that stretch out, Like gardens beside the river, Like aloes planted by the LORD, Like cedars beside the waters. 7 Water will flow from his buckets, And his seed will be by many waters, And his king shall be higher than Agag, And his kingdom shall be exalted. 8 God brings him out of Egypt, He is for him like the horns of the wild ox. He will devour the nations who are his adversaries, And will crush their bones in pieces, And shatter them with his arrows. 9 He couches, he lies down as a lion, And as a lion, who dares rouse him? Blessed is everyone who blesses you, And cursed is everyone who curses you." 10 Then Balak's anger burned against Balaam, and he struck his hands together; and Balak said to Balaam, "I called you to curse my enemies, but behold, you have persisted in blessing them these three times! 11 Therefore, flee to your place now. I said I would honor you greatly, but behold, the LORD has held you back from honor." 12 Balaam said to Balak, "Did I not tell your messengers whom you had sent to me, saying, 13 'Though Balak were to give me his house full of silver and gold, I could not do anything contrary to the command of the LORD, either good or bad, of my own accord. What the LORD speaks, that I will speak'? 14 And now, behold, I am going to my people; come, and I will advise you what this people will do to your people in the days to come." 15 He took up his discourse and said, "The oracle of Balaam the son of Beor, And the oracle of the man whose eye is opened, 16 The oracle of him who hears the words of God, And knows the knowledge of the Most High, Who sees the vision of the Almighty, Falling down, yet having his eyes uncovered. 17 I see him, but not now; I behold him, but not near; A star shall come forth from Jacob, A scepter shall rise from Israel, And shall crush through the forehead of Moab, And tear down all the sons of Sheth. 18 Edom shall be a possession, Seir, its enemies, also will be a possession, While Israel performs valiantly. 19 One from Jacob shall have dominion, And will destroy the remnant from the city." 20 And he looked at Amalek and took up his discourse and said, "Amalek was the first of the nations, But his end shall be destruction." 21 And he looked at the Kenite, and took up his discourse and said, "Your dwelling place is enduring, And your nest is set in the cliff. 22 Nevertheless Kain will be consumed; How long will Asshur keep you captive?" 23 Then he took up his discourse and said, "Alas, who can live except God has ordained it? 24 But ships shall come from the coast of Kittim, And they shall afflict Asshur and will afflict Eber; So they also will come to destruction." 25 Then Balaam arose and departed and returned to his place, and Balak also went his way

Chapter 25

1 While Israel remained at Shittim, the people began to play the harlot with the daughters of Moab. 2 For they invited the people to the sacrifices of their gods, and the people ate and bowed down to their gods. 3 So Israel joined themselves to Baal of Peor, and the LORD was angry against Israel. 4 The LORD said to Moses, "Take all the leaders of the people and execute them in broad daylight before the LORD, so that the fierce anger of the LORD may turn away from Israel." 5 So Moses said to the judges of Israel, "Each of you slay his men who have joined themselves to Baal of Peor." 6 Then behold, one of the sons of Israel came and brought to his relatives a Midianite woman, in the sight of Moses and in the sight of all the congregation of the sons of Israel, while they were weeping at the doorway of the tent of meeting. 7 When Phinehas the son of Eleazar, the son of Aaron the priest, saw it, he arose from the midst of the congregation and took a spear in his hand; 8 and he went after the man of Israel into the tent and pierced both of them through, the man of Israel and the woman, through the body. So the plague on the sons of Israel was checked. 9 Those who died by the plague were 24,000 10 Then the LORD spoke to Moses, saying, 11 "Phinehas the son of Eleazar, the son of Aaron the priest, has turned away my wrath from the sons of Israel in that he was jealous with my jealousy among them, so that I did not destroy the sons of Israel in my jealousy. 12 Therefore say, 'Behold, I give him my covenant of peace; 13 and it shall be for him and his descendants after him, a covenant of a perpetual priesthood, because he was jealous for his God and made atonement for the sons of Israel.'" 14 Now the name of the slain man of Israel who was slain with the Midianite woman was Zimri the son of Salu, a leader of a father's household among the Simeonites. 15 The name of the Midianite woman who was slain was Cozbi the daughter of Zur, who was head of the people of a father's household in Midian 16 Then the LORD spoke to Moses, saying, 17 "Be hostile to the Midianites and strike them; 18 for they have been hostile to you with their tricks, with which they have deceived you in the matter of Peor and in the matter of Cozbi, the daughter of the leader of Midian, their sister who was slain on the day of the plague because of Peor."

Chapter 26

1 After the plague, the LORD spoke to Moses and Eleazar the son of Aaron the priest, saying, 2 "Take a census of all the congregation of the children of Israel from twenty years old and upward, by their fathers' houses, all who are able to go to war in Israel." 3 So Moses and Eleazar the priest spoke to them in the plains of Moab by the Jordan at Jericho, saying, 4 "Take a census of the people from twenty years old and upward, as the LORD commanded Moses and the children of Israel who came out of the land of Egypt." 5 Reuben, the firstborn of Israel: the sons of Reuben were Hanoch, of whom came the family of the Hanochites; of Pallu, the family of the Palluites; 6 of Hezron, the family of the Hezronites; of Carmi, the family of the Carmites. 7 These are the families of the Reubenites; those who were numbered of them were 43,730. 8 The sons of Pallu: Eliab. 9 The sons of Eliab: Nemuel, Dathan, and Abiram. These are the Dathan and Abiram who were called by the congregation, who contended against Moses and Aaron in the company of Korah, when they contended against the LORD. 10 The earth opened its mouth and swallowed them up together with Korah, when that company died, when the fire devoured 250 men; and they became a warning. 11 However, the sons of Korah did not die 12 The sons

of Simeon according to their families were: of Nemuel, the family of the Nemuelites; of Jamin, the family of the Jaminites; of Jachin, the family of the Jachinites; 13 of Zerah, the family of the Zerahites; of Shaul, the family of the Shaulites. 14 These are the families of the Simeonites, 22,200 15 The sons of Gad according to their families were: of Zephon, the family of the Zephonites; of Haggi, the family of the Haggites; of Shuni, the family of the Shunites; 16 of Ozni, the family of the Oznites; of Eri, the family of the Erites; 17 of Arod, the family of the Arodites; of Areli, the family of the Arelites. 18 These are the families of the sons of Gad according to their families, 40,500 19 The sons of Judah were Er and Onan; but Er and Onan died in the land of Canaan. 20 The sons of Judah according to their families were: of Shelah, the family of the Shelanites; of Perez, the family of the Perezites; of Zerah, the family of the Zerahites. 21 The sons of Perez were: of Hezron, the family of the Hezronites; of Hamul, the family of the Hamulites. 22 These are the families of Judah according to those who were numbered of them, 76,500 23 The sons of Issachar according to their families were: of Tola, the family of the Tolaites; of Puvah, the family of the Punites; 24 of Jashub, the family of the Jashubites; of Shimron, the family of the Shimronites. 25 These are the families of Issachar according to those who were numbered of them, 64,300 26 The sons of Zebulun according to their families were: of Sered, the family of the Seredites; of Elon, the family of the Elonites; of Jahleel, the family of the Jahleelites. 27 These are the families of the Zebulunites according to those who were numbered of them, 60,500 28 The sons of Joseph according to their families, by Manasseh and Ephraim, were: 29 The sons of Manasseh: of Machir, the family of the Machirites (and Machir begot Gilead; of Gilead, the family of the Gileadites). 30 These are the sons of Gilead: of Iezer, the family of the Jezerites; of Helek, the family of the Helekites; 31 of Asriel, the family of the Asrielites; of Shechem, the family of the Shechemites; 32 of Shemida, the family of the Shemidaites; of Hepher, the family of the Hepherites. 33 Zelophehad the son of Hepher had no sons, but daughters: and the names of the daughters of Zelophehad were Mahlah, Noah, Hoglah, Milcah, and Tirzah. 34 These are the families of Manasseh, and those who were numbered of them were 52,700 35 These are the sons of Ephraim according to their families: of Shuthelah, the family of the Shuthelahites; of Becher, the family of the Becherites; of Tahan, the family of the Tahanites. 36 And these are the sons of Shuthelah: of Eran, the family of the Eranites. 37 These are the families of the sons of Ephraim according to those who were numbered of them, 32,500. These are the sons of Joseph according to their families 38 The sons of Benjamin according to their families were: of Bela, the family of the Belaites; of Ashbel, the family of the Ashbelites; of Ahiram, the family of the Ahiramites; 39 of Shupham, the family of the Shuphamites; of Hupham, the family of the Huphamites. 40 The sons of Bela were Ard and Naaman: of Ard, the family of the Ardites; of Naaman, the family of the Naamanites. 41 These are the sons of Benjamin according to their families, and those who were numbered of them were 45,600 42 These are the sons of Dan according to their families: of Shuham, the family of the Shuhamites. These are the families of Dan according to their families. 43 All the families of the Shuhamites, according to those who were numbered of them, were 64,400 44 The sons of Asher according to their families were: of Imnah, the family of the Imnites; of Ishvi, the family of the Ishvites; of Beriah, the family of the Beriites. 45 Of the sons of Beriah: of Heber, the family of the Heberites; of Malchiel, the family of the Malchielites. 46 The name of the daughter of Asher was Serah. 47 These are the families of the sons of Asher according to those who were numbered of them, 53,400 48 The sons of Naphtali according to their families were: of Jahzeel, the family of the Jahzeelites; of Guni, the family of the Gunites; 49 of Jezer, the family of the Jezerites; of Shillem, the family of the Shillemites. 50 These are the families of Naphtali according to their families, and those who were numbered of them were 45,400 51 These were the numbered of the children of Israel: 601,730 52 The LORD spoke to Moses, saying, 53 "To these the land shall be divided for an inheritance according to the number of names. 54 To the larger tribe you shall give a larger inheritance, and to the smaller tribe you shall give a smaller inheritance; to each one his inheritance shall be given according to those who were numbered of them. 55 But the land shall be divided by lot; they shall receive their inheritance according to the names of the tribes of their fathers. 56 According to the lot, their inheritance shall be divided between the larger and the smaller." 57 These are those who were numbered of the Levites according to their families: of Gershon, the family of the Gershonites; of Kohath, the family of the Kohathites; of Merari, the family of the Merarites. 58 These are the families of Levi: the family of the Libnites, the family of the Hebronites, the family of the Mahlites, the family of the Mushites, the family of the Korahites. Kohath begot Amram. 59 The name of Amram's wife was Jochebed, the daughter of Levi, who was born to Levi in Egypt; and to Amram she bore Aaron and Moses and their sister Miriam. 60 To Aaron were born Nadab and Abihu, Eleazar and Ithamar. 61 Nadab and Abihu died when they offered profane fire before the LORD. 62 Those who were numbered of them were 23,000, every male from a month old and upward; for they were not numbered among the children of Israel because no inheritance was given to them among the children of Israel 63 These are those who were numbered by Moses and Eleazar the priest, who numbered the children of Israel in the plains of Moab by the Jordan at Jericho. 64 But among these there was not a man of those who were numbered by Moses and Aaron the priest when they numbered the children of Israel in the wilderness of Sinai. 65 For the LORD had said of them, "They shall surely die in the wilderness." So there was not left a man of them, except Caleb the son of Jephunneh and Joshua the son of Nun

Chapter 27

1 Then came the daughters of Zelophehad, the son of Hepher, the son of Gilead, the son of Machir, the son of Manasseh, of the families of Manasseh the son of Joseph; and these are the names of his daughters: Mahlah, Noah, Hoglah, Milcah, and Tirzah. 2 They stood before Moses, Eleazar the priest, the leaders, and all the congregation, by the doorway of the tabernacle of meeting, saying: 3 "Our father died in the wilderness, but he was not in the company of those who gathered together against the LORD, in the company of Korah, but died in his own sin; and he had no sons. 4 Why should the name of our father be removed from among his family because he had no son? Give us a possession among our father's brothers." 5 So Moses brought their case before the LORD. 6 And the LORD spoke to Moses, saying: 7 "The daughters of Zelophehad speak what is right; you shall surely give them a possession of inheritance among their father's brothers, and cause the inheritance of their father to pass to them. 8 And you shall speak to the children of Israel, saying: 'If a man dies and has no son, then you shall cause his inheritance to pass to his daughter. 9 If he has no daughter, then you shall give his inheritance to his

brothers. 10 If he has no brothers, then you shall give his inheritance to his father's brothers. 11 And if his father has no brothers, then you shall give his inheritance to the nearest relative in his family, and he shall possess it.'" And it shall be to the children of Israel a statute of judgment, just as the LORD commanded Moses 12 Now the LORD said to Moses: "Go up into this Mount Abarim, and see the land which I have given to the children of Israel. 13 And when you have seen it, you also shall be gathered to your people, as Aaron your brother was gathered. 14 For in the wilderness of Zin, during the strife of the congregation, you rebelled against My command to hallow Me at the waters before their eyes." (These are the waters of Meribah, at Kadesh in the Wilderness of Zin.) 15 Then Moses spoke to the LORD, saying: 16 "Let the LORD, the God of the spirits of all flesh, set a man over the congregation, 17 who may go out before them and go in before them, who may lead them out and bring them in, that the congregation of the LORD may not be like sheep which have no shepherd." 18 And the LORD said to Moses: "Take Joshua the son of Nun with you, a man in whom is the Spirit, and lay your hand on him; 19 set him before Eleazar the priest and before all the congregation, and inaugurate him in their sight. 20 And you shall give some of your authority to him, that all the congregation of the children of Israel may be obedient. 21 He shall stand before Eleazar the priest, who shall inquire before the LORD for him by the judgment of the Urim. At his word they shall go out, and at his word they shall come in, he and all the children of Israel with him—all the congregation." 22 So Moses did as the LORD commanded him. He took Joshua and set him before Eleazar the priest and before all the congregation. 23 And he laid his hands on him and inaugurated him, just as the LORD commanded by the hand of Moses

Chapter 28

1 Now the LORD spoke to Moses, saying, 2 "Command the children of Israel, and say to them, 'My offering, My food for My offerings made by fire as a sweet aroma to Me, you shall be careful to offer to Me at their appointed time.' 3 And you shall say to them, 'This is the offering made by fire which you shall offer to the LORD: two male lambs in their first year without blemish, day by day, as a regular burnt offering. 4 The one lamb you shall offer in the morning, the other lamb you shall offer in the evening, 5 and one-tenth of an ephah of fine flour as a grain offering mixed with one-fourth of a hin of pressed oil. 6 It is a regular burnt offering which was ordained at Mount Sinai for a sweet aroma, an offering made by fire to the LORD. 7 And its drink offering shall be one-fourth of a hin for each lamb; in a holy place you shall pour out the drink to the LORD as an offering. 8 The other lamb you shall offer in the evening; as the morning grain offering and its drink offering, you shall offer it as an offering made by fire, a sweet aroma to the LORD 9 'And on the Sabbath day two lambs in their first year, without blemish, and two-tenths of an ephah of fine flour as a grain offering, mixed with oil, with its drink offering— 10 this is the burnt offering for every Sabbath, besides the regular burnt offering with its drink offering 11 'At the beginnings of your months you shall present a burnt offering to the LORD: two young bulls, one ram, and seven lambs in their first year, without blemish; 12 three-tenths of an ephah of fine flour as a grain offering, mixed with oil, for each bull; two-tenths of an ephah of fine flour as a grain offering, mixed with oil, for the one ram; 13 and one-tenth of an ephah of fine flour mixed with oil as a grain offering for each lamb, as a burnt offering of sweet aroma, an offering made by fire to the LORD. 14 Their drink offering shall be half a hin of wine for a bull, one-third of a hin for a ram, and one-fourth of a hin for a lamb; this is the burnt offering for each month throughout the months of the year. 15 Also one kid of the goats as a sin offering to the LORD shall be offered, besides the regular burnt offering and its drink offering 16 'On the fourteenth day of the first month is the Passover of the LORD. 17 And on the fifteenth day of this month is the feast; unleavened bread shall be eaten for seven days. 18 On the first day you shall have a holy convocation. You shall do no customary work. 19 And you shall present an offering made by fire as a burnt offering to the LORD: two young bulls, one ram, and seven lambs in their first year. Be sure they are without blemish. 20 Their grain offering shall be of fine flour mixed with oil: three-tenths of an ephah you shall offer for a bull, and two-tenths for a ram; 21 you shall offer one-tenth of an ephah for each of the seven lambs; 22 also one goat as a sin offering, to make atonement for you. 23 You shall offer these besides the burnt offering of the morning, which is for a regular burnt offering. 24 In this manner you shall offer the food of the offering made by fire daily for seven days, as a sweet aroma to the LORD; it shall be offered besides the regular burnt offering and its drink offering. 25 And on the seventh day you shall have a holy convocation. You shall do no customary work 26 'Also on the day of the firstfruits, when you bring a new grain offering to the LORD at your Feast of Weeks, you shall have a holy convocation. You shall do no customary work. 27 You shall present a burnt offering as a sweet aroma to the LORD: two young bulls, one ram, and seven lambs in their first year, 28 with their grain offering of fine flour mixed with oil: three-tenths of an ephah for each bull, two-tenths for the one ram, 29 and one-tenth for each of the seven lambs; 30 also one kid of the goats, to make atonement for you. 31 Be sure they are without blemish. You shall present them with their drink offerings, besides the regular burnt offering with its grain offering

Chapter 29

1 'And in the seventh month, on the first day of the month, you shall have a holy convocation. You shall do no customary work. For you it is a day of blowing the trumpets. 2 You shall offer a burnt offering as a sweet aroma to the LORD: one young bull, one ram, and seven lambs in their first year, without blemish. 3 Their grain offering shall be fine flour mixed with oil: three-tenths of an ephah for the bull, two-tenths for the ram, 4 and one-tenth for each of the seven lambs; 5 also one kid of the goats as a sin offering, to make atonement for you; 6 besides the burnt offering with its grain offering for the New Moon, the regular burnt offering with its grain offering, and their drink offerings, according to their ordinance, as a sweet aroma, an offering made by fire to the LORD 7 'On the tenth day of this seventh month you shall have a holy convocation. You shall afflict your souls; you shall not do any work. 8 You shall present a burnt offering to the LORD as a sweet aroma: one young bull, one ram, and seven lambs in their first year. Be sure they are without blemish. 9 Their grain offering shall be of fine flour mixed with oil: three-tenths of an ephah for the bull, two-tenths for the one ram, 10 and one-tenth for each of the seven lambs; 11 also one kid of the goats as a sin offering, besides the sin offering for atonement, the regular burnt offering with its grain offering, and their drink offerings 12 'On the fifteenth day of the seventh month you shall have a holy convocation. You shall do no customary work, and you shall keep a feast to the LORD seven days. 13 You shall present a burnt offering, an offering made by fire as a sweet aroma to the LORD: thirteen young bulls, two rams, and fourteen lambs in their first year.

They shall be without blemish. 14 Their grain offering shall be of fine flour mixed with oil: three-tenths of an ephah for each of the thirteen bulls, two-tenths for each of the two rams, 15 and one-tenth for each of the fourteen lambs; 16 also one kid of the goats as a sin offering, besides the regular burnt offering, its grain offering, and its drink offering 17 'On the second day present twelve young bulls, two rams, fourteen lambs in their first year without blemish, 18 and their grain offering and their drink offerings for the bulls, for the rams, and for the lambs, by their number, according to the ordinance; 19 also one kid of the goats as a sin offering, besides the regular burnt offering with its grain offering, and their drink offerings 20 'On the third day present eleven bulls, two rams, fourteen lambs in their first year without blemish, 21 and their grain offering and their drink offerings for the bulls, for the rams, and for the lambs, by their number, according to the ordinance; 22 also one goat as a sin offering, besides the regular burnt offering, its grain offering, and its drink offering 23 'On the fourth day present ten bulls, two rams, and fourteen lambs in their first year without blemish, 24 and their grain offering and their drink offerings for the bulls, for the rams, and for the lambs, by their number, according to the ordinance; 25 also one kid of the goats as a sin offering, besides the regular burnt offering, its grain offering, and its drink offering 26 'On the fifth day present nine bulls, two rams, and fourteen lambs in their first year without blemish, 27 and their grain offering and their drink offerings for the bulls, for the rams, and for the lambs, by their number, according to the ordinance; 28 also one goat as a sin offering, besides the regular burnt offering, its grain offering, and its drink offering 29 'On the sixth day present eight bulls, two rams, and fourteen lambs in their first year without blemish, 30 and their grain offering and their drink offerings for the bulls, for the rams, and for the lambs, by their number, according to the ordinance; 31 also one goat as a sin offering, besides the regular burnt offering, its grain offering, and its drink offering 32 'On the seventh day present seven bulls, two rams, and fourteen lambs in their first year without blemish, 33 and their grain offering and their drink offerings for the bulls, for the rams, and for the lambs, by their number, according to the ordinance; 34 also one goat as a sin offering, besides the regular burnt offering, its grain offering, and its drink offering 35 'On the eighth day you shall have a sacred assembly. You shall do no customary work. 36 You shall present a burnt offering, an offering made by fire as a sweet aroma to the LORD: one bull, one ram, and seven lambs in their first year without blemish, 37 and their grain offering and their drink offerings for the bull, for the ram, and for the lambs, by their number, according to the ordinance; 38 also one goat as a sin offering, besides the regular burnt offering, its grain offering, and its drink offering 39 'These you shall present to the LORD at your appointed feasts, besides your vowed offerings and your freewill offerings, as your burnt offerings and your grain offerings, as your drink offerings and your peace offerings.'" 40 So Moses told the children of Israel everything just as the LORD commanded Moses

Chapter 30

1 Then Moses spoke to the heads of the tribes concerning the children of Israel, saying, "This is the thing which the LORD has commanded: 2 If a man makes a vow to the LORD, or swears an oath to bind himself by some agreement, he shall not break his word; he shall do according to all that proceeds out of his mouth 3 "Or if a woman makes a vow to the LORD, and binds herself by some agreement while in her father's house in her youth, 4 and her father hears her vow and the agreement by which she has bound herself, and her father holds his peace, then all her vows shall stand, and every agreement with which she has bound herself shall stand. 5 But if her father overrules her on the day that he hears, then none of her vows nor her agreements by which she has bound herself shall stand; and the LORD will release her, because her father overruled her 6 "If indeed she takes a husband, while bound by her vows or by a rash utterance from her lips by which she bound herself, 7 and her husband hears it, and makes no response to her on the day that he hears, then her vows shall stand, and her agreements by which she bound herself shall stand. 8 But if her husband overrules her on the day that he hears it, he shall make void her vow which she took and what she uttered with her lips, by which she bound herself; and the LORD will release her 9 "Also any vow of a widow or a divorced woman, by which she has bound herself, shall stand against her 10 "If she vowed in her husband's house, or bound herself by an agreement with an oath, 11 and her husband heard it, and made no response to her and did not overrule her, then all her vows shall stand, and every agreement by which she bound herself shall stand. 12 But if her husband truly made them void on the day he heard them, then whatever proceeded from her lips concerning her vows or concerning the agreement binding her, it shall not stand; her husband has made them void, and the LORD will release her. 13 Every vow and every binding oath to afflict her soul, her husband may confirm it, or her husband may make it void. 14 Now if her husband makes no response whatever to her from day to day, then he confirms all her vows or all the agreements that bind her. He confirms them, because he made no response to her on the day that he heard them. 15 But if he does make them void after he has heard them, then he shall bear her guilt." 16 These are the statutes which the LORD commanded Moses, between a man and his wife, and between a father and his daughter in her youth in her father's house

Chapter 31

1 The LORD spoke to Moses, saying, 2 "Avenge the children of Israel on the Midianites. Afterward, you shall be gathered to your people." 3 So Moses spoke to the people, saying, "Arm some of yourselves for war, and let them go against the Midianites to take vengeance for the LORD on Midian. 4 A thousand from each tribe of all the tribes of Israel you shall send to the war." 5 So there were selected from the thousands of Israel a thousand from each tribe, twelve thousand armed for war. 6 Moses sent them to the war, a thousand from each tribe, them and Phinehas the son of Eleazar the priest, with the holy articles and the signal trumpets in his hand 7 They warred against the Midianites, just as the LORD commanded Moses, and they killed all the males. 8 They killed the kings of Midian with the rest of those who were killed—Evi, Rekem, Zur, Hur, and Reba, the five kings of Midian. Balaam the son of Beor they also killed with the sword. 9 And the children of Israel took the women of Midian captive, with their little ones, and took as spoil all their cattle, all their flocks, and all their goods. 10 They also burned with fire all the cities where they dwelt, and all their forts. 11 And they took all the spoil and all the booty—of man and beast 12 Then they brought the captives, the booty, and the spoil to Moses, to Eleazar the priest, and to the congregation of the children of Israel, to the camp in the plains of Moab by the Jordan, across from Jericho. 13 And Moses, Eleazar the priest, and all the leaders of the congregation went to meet them outside the camp. 14 But Moses was angry with

the officers of the army, with the captains over thousands and captains over hundreds, who had come from the battle. 15 And Moses said to them: "Have you kept all the women alive? 16 Look, these women caused the children of Israel, through the counsel of Balaam, to trespass against the LORD in the incident of Peor, and there was a plague among the congregation of the LORD. 17 Now therefore, kill every male among the little ones, and kill every woman who has known a man intimately. 18 But keep alive for yourselves all the young girls who have not known a man intimately. 19 And as for you, remain outside the camp seven days; whoever has killed any person, and whoever has touched any slain, purify yourselves and your captives on the third day and on the seventh day. 20 Purify every garment, everything made of leather, everything woven of goats' hair, and everything made of wood." 21 Then Eleazar the priest said to the men of war who had gone to the battle, "This is the ordinance of the law which the LORD commanded Moses: 22 Only the gold, the silver, the bronze, the iron, the tin, and the lead, 23 everything that can endure fire, you shall put through the fire, and it shall be clean; and it shall be purified with the water of purification. But all that cannot endure fire you shall put through water. 24 And you shall wash your clothes on the seventh day and be clean, and afterward you may come into the camp." 25 Now the LORD spoke to Moses, saying: 26 "Count up the plunder that was taken—of man and beast—you and Eleazar the priest and the chief fathers of the congregation; 27 and divide the plunder into two parts, between those who took part in the war, who went out to battle, and all the congregation. 28 And levy a tribute for the LORD on the men of war who went out to battle: one of every five hundred of the persons, the cattle, the donkeys, and the sheep; 29 take it from their half, and give it to Eleazar the priest as a heave offering to the LORD. 30 And from the children of Israel's half you shall take one of every fifty, drawn from the persons, the cattle, the donkeys, and the sheep, from all the livestock, and give them to the Levites who keep charge of the tabernacle of the LORD." 31 So Moses and Eleazar the priest did as the LORD commanded Moses 32 The booty remaining from the plunder, which the men of war had taken, was six hundred and seventy-five thousand sheep, 33 seventy-two thousand cattle, 34 sixty-one thousand donkeys, 35 and thirty-two thousand persons in all, of women who had not known a man intimately. 36 And the half, the portion for those who had gone out to war, was in number three hundred and thirty-seven thousand five hundred sheep; 37 and the LORD's tribute of the sheep was six hundred and seventy-five. 38 The cattle were thirty-six thousand, of which the LORD's tribute was seventy-two. 39 The donkeys were thirty thousand five hundred, of which the LORD's tribute was sixty-one. 40 The persons were sixteen thousand, of which the LORD's tribute was thirty-two persons. 41 So Moses gave the tribute which was the LORD's heave offering to Eleazar the priest, as the LORD commanded Moses 42 And from the children of Israel's half, which Moses separated from the men who fought— 43 now the half belonging to the congregation was three hundred and thirty-seven thousand five hundred sheep, 44 thirty-six thousand cattle, 45 thirty thousand five hundred donkeys, 46 and sixteen thousand persons— 47 and from the children of Israel's half Moses took one of every fifty, drawn from man and beast, and gave them to the Levites, who kept charge of the tabernacle of the LORD, as the LORD commanded Moses 48 Then the officers who were over thousands of the army, the captains of thousands and captains of hundreds, came near to Moses; 49 and they said to Moses, "Your servants have taken a count of the men of war who are under our command, and not a man of us is missing. 50 Therefore we have brought an offering for the LORD, what every man found of ornaments of gold: armlets and bracelets and signet rings and earrings and necklaces, to make atonement for ourselves before the LORD." 51 So Moses and Eleazar the priest received the gold from them, all the fashioned ornaments. 52 And all the gold of the offering that they offered to the LORD, from the captains of thousands and captains of hundreds, was sixteen thousand seven hundred and fifty shekels. 53 (The men of war had taken spoil, every man for himself.) 54 And Moses and Eleazar the priest received the gold from the captains of thousands and of hundreds and brought it into the tabernacle of meeting as a memorial for the children of Israel before the LORD

Chapter 32

1 Now the children of Reuben and the children of Gad had a very great multitude of livestock. And when they saw the land of Jazer and the land of Gilead, that indeed the region was a place for livestock, 2 the children of Gad and the children of Reuben came and spoke to Moses, to Eleazar the priest, and to the leaders of the congregation, saying, 3 "Ataroth, Dibon, Jazer, Nimrah, Heshbon, Elealeh, Shebam, Nebo, and Beon, 4 the country which the LORD defeated before the congregation of Israel, is a land for livestock, and your servants have livestock." 5 Therefore they said, "If we have found favor in your sight, let this land be given to your servants as a possession. Do not take us over the Jordan." 6 And Moses said to the children of Gad and to the children of Reuben: "Shall your brethren go to war while you sit here? 7 Now why will you discourage the heart of the children of Israel from going over into the land which the LORD has given them? 8 Thus your fathers did when I sent them away from Kadesh Barnea to see the land. 9 For when they went up to the Valley of Eshcol and saw the land, they discouraged the heart of the children of Israel, so that they did not go into the land which the LORD had given them. 10 So the LORD's anger was aroused on that day, and He swore an oath, saying, 11 'Surely none of the men who came up from Egypt, from twenty years old and above, shall see the land of which I swore to Abraham, Isaac, and Jacob, because they have not wholly followed Me, 12 except Caleb the son of Jephunneh, the Kenizzite, and Joshua the son of Nun, for they have wholly followed the LORD.' 13 So the LORD's anger was aroused against Israel, and He made them wander in the wilderness forty years, until all the generation that had done evil in the sight of the LORD was gone. 14 And look! You have risen in your fathers' place, a brood of sinful men, to increase still more the fierce anger of the LORD against Israel. 15 For if you turn away from following Him, He will once again leave them in the wilderness, and you will destroy all these people." 16 Then they came near to him and said: "We will build sheepfolds here for our livestock, and cities for our little ones, 17 but we ourselves will be armed, ready to go before the children of Israel until we have brought them to their place; and our little ones will dwell in the fortified cities because of the inhabitants of the land. 18 We will not return to our homes until every one of the children of Israel has received his inheritance. 19 For we will not inherit with them on the other side of the Jordan and beyond, because our inheritance has fallen to us on this eastern side of the Jordan." 20 Then Moses said to them: "If you do this thing, if you arm yourselves before the LORD for the war, 21 and all your armed men cross over the Jordan before the

LORD until He has driven out His enemies from before Him, 22 and the land is subdued before the LORD, then afterward you may return and be blameless before the LORD and before Israel; and this land shall be your possession before the LORD. 23 But if you do not do so, then take note, you have sinned against the LORD; and be sure your sin will find you out. 24 Build cities for your little ones and folds for your sheep, and do what has proceeded out of your mouth." 25 And the children of Gad and the children of Reuben spoke to Moses, saying: "Your servants will do as my lord commands. 26 Our little ones, our wives, our flocks, and all our livestock will be there in the cities of Gilead; 27 but your servants will cross over, every man armed for war, before the LORD to battle, just as my lord says." 28 So Moses gave command concerning them to Eleazar the priest, to Joshua the son of Nun, and to the chief fathers of the tribes of the children of Israel. 29 And Moses said to them: "If the children of Gad and the children of Reuben cross over the Jordan with you, every man armed for battle before the LORD, and the land is subdued before you, then you shall give them the land of Gilead as a possession. 30 But if they do not cross over armed with you, they shall have possessions among you in the land of Canaan." 31 Then the children of Gad and the children of Reuben answered, saying: "As the LORD has said to your servants, so we will do. 32 We will cross over armed before the LORD into the land of Canaan, but the possession of our inheritance shall remain with us on this side of the Jordan." 33 So Moses gave to the children of Gad, to the children of Reuben, and to half the tribe of Manasseh the son of Joseph, the kingdom of Sihon king of the Amorites and the kingdom of Og king of Bashan, the land with its cities within the borders, the cities of the surrounding country 34 And the children of Gad built Dibon and Ataroth and Aroer, 35 Atroth and Shophan and Jazer and Jogbehah, 36 Beth Nimrah and Beth Haran, fortified cities, and folds for sheep. 37 And the children of Reuben built Heshbon and Elealeh and Kirjathaim, 38 Nebo and Baal Meon (their names being changed) and Shibmah; and they gave other names to the cities which they built 39 And the children of Machir the son of Manasseh went to Gilead and took it, and dispossessed the Amorites who were in it. 40 So Moses gave Gilead to Machir the son of Manasseh, and he dwelt in it. 41 Also Jair the son of Manasseh went and took its small towns, and called them Havoth Jair. 42 Then Nobah went and took Kenath and its villages, and he called it Nobah, after his own name

Chapter 33

1 These are the journeys of the children of Israel, who went out of the land of Egypt by their armies under the hand of Moses and Aaron. 2 Now Moses wrote down the starting points of their journeys at the command of the LORD. And these are their journeys according to their starting points: 3 They departed from Rameses in the first month, on the fifteenth day of the first month; on the day after the Passover the children of Israel went out with boldness in the sight of all the Egyptians. 4 For the Egyptians were burying all their firstborn, whom the LORD had killed among them. Also on their gods the LORD had executed judgments 5 Then the children of Israel moved from Rameses and camped at Succoth. 6 They departed from Succoth and camped at Etham, which is on the edge of the wilderness. 7 They moved from Etham and turned back to Pi Hahiroth, which is east of Baal Zephon; and they camped near Migdol. 8 They departed from before Hahiroth and passed through the midst of the sea into the wilderness, went three days' journey in the Wilderness of Etham, and camped at Marah. 9 They moved from Marah and came to Elim. At Elim were twelve springs of water and seventy palm trees; so they camped there. 10 They moved from Elim and camped by the Red Sea. 11 They moved from the Red Sea and camped in the Wilderness of Sin. 12 They journeyed from the Wilderness of Sin and camped at Dophkah. 13 They departed from Dophkah and camped at Alush. 14 They moved from Alush and camped at Rephidim, where there was no water for the people to drink. 15 They departed from Rephidim and camped in the Wilderness of Sinai. 16 They moved from the Wilderness of Sinai and camped at Kibroth Hattaavah. 17 They departed from Kibroth Hattaavah and camped at Hazeroth. 18 They departed from Hazeroth and camped at Rithmah. 19 They departed from Rithmah and camped at Rimmon Perez. 20 They departed from Rimmon Perez and camped at Libnah. 21 They moved from Libnah and camped at Rissah. 22 They journeyed from Rissah and camped at Kehelathah. 23 They went from Kehelathah and camped at Mount Shepher. 24 They moved from Mount Shepher and camped at Haradah. 25 They moved from Haradah and camped at Makheloth. 26 They moved from Makheloth and camped at Tahath. 27 They departed from Tahath and camped at Terah. 28 They moved from Terah and camped at Mithkah. 29 They went from Mithkah and camped at Hashmonah. 30 They departed from Hashmonah and camped at Moseroth. 31 They departed from Moseroth and camped at Bene Jaakan. 32 They moved from Bene Jaakan and camped at Hor Hagidgad. 33 They went from Hor Hagidgad and camped at Jotbathah. 34 They moved from Jotbathah and camped at Abronah. 35 They departed from Abronah and camped at Ezion Geber. 36 They moved from Ezion Geber and camped in the Wilderness of Zin, which is Kadesh. 37 They moved from Kadesh and camped at Mount Hor, on the boundary of the land of Edom. 38 Then Aaron the priest went up to Mount Hor at the command of the LORD, and died there in the fortieth year after the children of Israel had come out of the land of Egypt, on the first day of the fifth month. 39 Aaron was one hundred and twenty-three years old when he died on Mount Hor 40 Now the king of Arad, the Canaanite, who dwelt in the South in the land of Canaan, heard of the coming of the children of Israel. 41 So they departed from Mount Hor and camped at Zalmonah. 42 They departed from Zalmonah and camped at Punon. 43 They departed from Punon and camped at Oboth. 44 They departed from Oboth and camped at Ije Abarim, at the border of Moab. 45 They departed from Ijim and camped at Dibon Gad. 46 They moved from Dibon Gad and camped at Almon Diblathaim. 47 They moved from Almon Diblathaim and camped in the mountains of Abarim, before Nebo. 48 They departed from the mountains of Abarim and camped in the plains of Moab by the Jordan, across from Jericho. 49 They camped by the Jordan, from Beth Jesimoth as far as the Abel Acacia Grove in the plains of Moab 50 Now the LORD spoke to Moses in the plains of Moab by the Jordan, across from Jericho, saying, 51 "Speak to the children of Israel, and say to them: 'When you have crossed the Jordan into the land of Canaan, 52 then you shall drive out all the inhabitants of the land from before you, destroy all their engraved stones, destroy all their molded images, and demolish all their high places; 53 you shall dispossess the inhabitants of the land and dwell in it, for I have given you the land to possess. 54 And you shall divide the land by lot as an inheritance among your families; to the larger you shall give a larger inheritance, and to the smaller you shall give a smaller inheritance; there everyone's inheritance

shall be whatever falls to him by lot. You shall inherit according to the tribes of your fathers. 55 But if you do not drive out the inhabitants of the land from before you, then it shall be that those whom you let remain shall be irritants in your eyes and thorns in your sides, and they shall harass you in the land where you dwell. 56 Moreover it shall be that I will do to you as I thought to do to them.'"

Chapter 34

1 Then the LORD spoke to Moses, saying, 2 "Command the children of Israel, and say to them: 'When you come into the land of Canaan, this is the land that shall fall to you as an inheritance—the land of Canaan to its boundaries. 3 Your southern border shall be from the Wilderness of Zin along the border of Edom; then your southern border shall extend eastward to the end of the Salt Sea; 4 your border shall turn from the southern side of the Ascent of Akrabbim, continue to Zin, and be on the south of Kadesh Barnea; then it shall go on to Hazar Addar, and continue to Azmon; 5 the border shall turn from Azmon to the Brook of Egypt, and it shall end at the Sea. 6 As for the western border, you shall have the Great Sea for a border; this shall be your western border 7 'And this shall be your northern border: from the Great Sea you shall mark out your border line to Mount Hor; 8 from Mount Hor you shall mark out your border to the entrance of Hamath; then the direction of the border shall be toward Zedad; 9 the border shall proceed to Ziphron, and it shall end at Hazar Enan. This shall be your northern border 10 'You shall mark out your eastern border from Hazar Enan to Shepham; 11 the border shall go down from Shepham to Riblah on the east side of Ain; the border shall go down and reach to the eastern side of the Sea of Chinnereth; 12 the border shall go down along the Jordan, and it shall end at the Salt Sea. This shall be your land with its surrounding boundaries.'" 13 Then Moses commanded the children of Israel, saying: "This is the land which you shall inherit by lot, which the LORD has commanded to give to the nine tribes and to the half-tribe. 14 For the tribe of the children of Reuben according to the house of their fathers, and the tribe of the children of Gad according to the house of their fathers, have received their inheritance; and the half-tribe of Manasseh has received its inheritance. 15 The two tribes and the half-tribe have received their inheritance on this side of the Jordan, across from Jericho eastward, toward the sunrise." 16 And the LORD spoke to Moses, saying, 17 "These are the names of the men who shall divide the land among you as an inheritance: Eleazar the priest and Joshua the son of Nun. 18 And you shall take one leader of every tribe to divide the land for the inheritance. 19 These are the names of the men: from the tribe of Judah, Caleb the son of Jephunneh; 20 from the tribe of the children of Simeon, Shemuel the son of Ammihud; 21 from the tribe of Benjamin, Elidad the son of Chislon; 22 a leader from the tribe of the children of Dan, Bukki the son of Jogli; 23 from the sons of Joseph: a leader from the tribe of the children of Manasseh, Hanniel the son of Ephod, 24 and a leader from the tribe of the children of Ephraim, Kemuel the son of Shiphtan; 25 a leader from the tribe of the children of Zebulun, Elizaphan the son of Parnach; 26 a leader from the tribe of the children of Issachar, Paltiel the son of Azzan; 27 a leader from the tribe of the children of Asher, Ahihud the son of Shelomi; 28 and a leader from the tribe of the children of Naphtali, Pedahel the son of Ammihud." 29 These are the ones the LORD commanded to divide the inheritance among the children of Israel in the land of Canaan

Chapter 35

1 And the LORD spoke to Moses in the plains of Moab by the Jordan across from Jericho, saying: 2 "Command the children of Israel that they give the Levites cities to dwell in from the inheritance of their possession, and you shall also give the Levites common-land around the cities. 3 They shall have the cities to dwell in; and their common-land shall be for their cattle, for their herds, and for all their animals. 4 The common-land of the cities which you will give the Levites shall extend from the wall of the city outward a thousand cubits all around. 5 And you shall measure outside the city on the east side two thousand cubits, on the south side two thousand cubits, on the west side two thousand cubits, and on the north side two thousand cubits. The city shall be in the middle. This shall belong to them as common-land for the cities 6 "Now among the cities which you will give to the Levites you shall appoint six cities of refuge, to which a manslayer may flee. And to these you shall add forty-two cities. 7 So all the cities you will give to the Levites shall be forty-eight; these you shall give with their common-land. 8 And the cities which you will give shall be from the possession of the children of Israel; from the larger tribe you shall give many, from the smaller you shall give few. Each shall give some of its cities to the Levites, in proportion to the inheritance that each receives." 9 Then the LORD spoke to Moses, saying, 10 "Speak to the children of Israel, and say to them: 'When you cross the Jordan into the land of Canaan, 11 then you shall appoint cities to be cities of refuge for you, that the manslayer who kills any person accidentally may flee there. 12 They shall be cities of refuge for you from the avenger, that the manslayer may not die until he stands before the congregation in judgment. 13 And of the cities which you give, you shall have six cities of refuge. 14 You shall appoint three cities on this side of the Jordan, and three cities you shall appoint in the land of Canaan, which will be cities of refuge. 15 These six cities shall be for refuge for the children of Israel, for the stranger, and for the sojourner among them, that anyone who kills a person accidentally may flee there 16 'But if he strikes him with an iron implement, so that he dies, he is a murderer; the murderer shall surely be put to death. 17 And if he strikes him with a stone in the hand, by which one could die, and he does die, he is a murderer; the murderer shall surely be put to death. 18 Or if he strikes him with a wooden hand weapon, by which one could die, and he does die, he is a murderer; the murderer shall surely be put to death. 19 The avenger of blood himself shall put the murderer to death; when he meets him, he shall put him to death. 20 If he pushes him out of hatred or, while lying in wait, hurls something at him so that he dies, 21 or in enmity he strikes him with his hand so that he dies, the one who struck him shall surely be put to death. He is a murderer. The avenger of blood shall put the murderer to death when he meets him 22 'However, if he pushes him suddenly without enmity, or throws anything at him without lying in wait, 23 or uses a stone, by which a man could die, throwing it at him without seeing him, so that he dies, while he was not his enemy or seeking his harm, 24 then the congregation shall judge between the manslayer and the avenger of blood according to these judgments. 25 So the congregation shall deliver the manslayer from the hand of the avenger of blood, and the congregation shall return him to the city of refuge where he had fled, and he shall remain there until the death of the high priest who was anointed with the holy oil. 26 But if the manslayer at any time goes outside the limits of the city of refuge where he fled, 27 and the avenger of blood finds him outside the limits of his city of refuge, and the avenger of blood kills the manslayer, he shall not be

guilty of blood, 28 because he should have remained in his city of refuge until the death of the high priest. But after the death of the high priest the manslayer may return to the land of his possession 29 'And these things shall be a statute of judgment to you throughout your generations in all your dwellings 30 'Whoever kills a person, the murderer shall be put to death on the testimony of witnesses; but one witness is not sufficient testimony against a person for the death penalty. 31 Moreover you shall take no ransom for the life of a murderer who is guilty of death, but he shall surely be put to death. 32 And you shall take no ransom for him who has fled to his city of refuge, that he may return to dwell in the land before the death of the priest. 33 So you shall not pollute the land where you are; for blood defiles the land, and no atonement can be made for the land, for the blood that is shed on it, except by the blood of him who shed it. 34 Therefore do not defile the land which you inhabit, in the midst of which I dwell; for I the LORD dwell among the children of Israel.'"

Chapter 36

1 Now the chief fathers of the families of the children of Gilead the son of Machir, the son of Manasseh, of the families of the sons of Joseph, came near and spoke before Moses and before the leaders, the chief fathers of the children of Israel. 2 And they said: "The LORD commanded my lord Moses to give the land as an inheritance by lot to the children of Israel, and my lord was commanded by the LORD to give the inheritance of our brother Zelophehad to his daughters. 3 Now if they are married to any of the sons of the other tribes of the children of Israel, then their inheritance will be taken from the inheritance of our fathers, and it will be added to the inheritance of the tribe into which they marry; so it will be taken from the lot of our inheritance. 4 And when the Jubilee of the children of Israel comes, then their inheritance will be added to the inheritance of the tribe into which they marry; so their inheritance will be taken away from the inheritance of the tribe of our fathers." 5 Then Moses commanded the children of Israel according to the word of the LORD, saying: "What the tribe of the sons of Joseph speaks is right. 6 This is what the LORD commands concerning the daughters of Zelophehad, saying, 'Let them marry whom they think best, but they may marry only within the family of their father's tribe.' 7 So the inheritance of the children of Israel shall not change hands from tribe to tribe, for every one of the children of Israel shall keep the inheritance of the tribe of his fathers. 8 And every daughter who possesses an inheritance in any tribe of the children of Israel shall be the wife of one of the family of her father's tribe, so that the children of Israel each may possess the inheritance of his fathers. 9 Thus no inheritance shall change hands from one tribe to another, but every tribe of the children of Israel shall keep its own inheritance." 10 Just as the LORD commanded Moses, so did the daughters of Zelophehad; 11 for Mahlah, Tirzah, Hoglah, Milcah, and Noah, the daughters of Zelophehad, were married to the sons of their father's brothers. 12 They were married into the families of the children of Manasseh the son of Joseph, and their inheritance remained in the tribe of their father's family 13 These are the commandments and the judgments which the LORD commanded the children of Israel by the hand of Moses in the plains of Moab by the Jordan, across from Jericho

5. Deuteronomy

Chapter 1

These are the words that Moses spoke to all Israel, on this side of the Jordan, in the wilderness, in the plain, facing the Red Sea, between Paran and Tophel, Laban, Hazeroth, and Di-zahab. It is an eleven-day journey from Horeb to Kadesh-Barnea by the way of Mount Seir. On the first day of the eleventh month, in the fortieth year, Moses addressed the children of Israel according to what the LORD had commanded him. This was after he had defeated Sihon, king of the Amorites, who lived in Heshbon, and Og, king of Bashan, who lived in Ashtaroth, in Edrei On this side of the Jordan, in the land of Moab, Moses began to declare this law, saying, "The LORD our God spoke to us at Horeb, saying, 'You have dwelt long enough on this mountain. Turn and take your journey and go to the mountain of the Amorites, and to all the neighboring places in the plain, in the mountains, in the lowland, in the south, and on the seacoast, to the land of the Canaanites and to Lebanon, as far as the great river, the River Euphrates. See, I have set the land before you; go in and possess the land which the LORD swore to your fathers, Abraham, Isaac, and Jacob, to give to them and their descendants after them.' "At that time I spoke to you, saying, 'I alone am not able to bear you. The LORD your God has multiplied you, and here you are today, as the stars of heaven in multitude. May the LORD, the God of your fathers, make you a thousand times more numerous than you are, and bless you, as He has promised you! How can I alone bear your problems, your burdens, and your complaints? Choose wise, understanding, and knowledgeable men from among your tribes, and I will make them leaders over you.' And you answered me and said, 'The thing which you have told us to do is good.' So I took the heads of your tribes, wise and knowledgeable men, and made them leaders over you, commanders of thousands, commanders of hundreds, commanders of fifties, commanders of tens, and officers for your tribes "Then I commanded your judges at that time, saying, 'Hear the cases between your brethren, and judge righteously between a man and his brother or the stranger who is with him. You shall not show partiality in judgment; you shall hear the small as well as the great; you shall not be afraid in any man's presence, for the judgment is God's. The case that is too hard for you, bring to me, and I will hear it.' And I commanded you at that time all the things which you should do "So we departed from Horeb, and went through all that great and terrible wilderness which you saw on the way to the mountains of the Amorites, as the LORD our God had commanded us. Then we came to Kadesh-Barnea. And I said to you, 'You have come to the mountains of the Amorites, which the LORD our God is giving us. Look, the LORD your God has set the land before you; go up and possess it, as the LORD God of your fathers has spoken to you; do not fear or be discouraged.' "And every one of you came near to me and said, 'Let us send men before us, and let them search out the land for us, and bring back word to us of the way by which we should go up, and of the cities into which we shall come.' The plan pleased me well; so I took twelve of your men, one man from each tribe. And they departed and went up into the mountains, and came to the Valley of Eshcol, and spied it out. They also took some of the fruit of the land in their hands and brought it down to us, and they brought back word to us, saying, 'It is a good land which the LORD our God is giving us.' "Nevertheless, you would not go up but rebelled against the command of the LORD your God; and you complained in your tents, and said, 'Because the LORD hates us, He has brought us out of the land of Egypt to deliver us into the hand of the Amorites, to destroy us. Where can we go up? Our brethren have discouraged our hearts, saying, "The people are greater and taller than we; the cities are great and fortified up to heaven; moreover, we have seen the sons of the Anakim there."' "Then I said to you, 'Do not be terrified or afraid of them. The LORD your God, who goes before you, He will fight for you, according to all He did for you in Egypt before your eyes, and in the wilderness where you saw how the LORD your God carried you, as a man carries his son, in all the way that you went until you came to this place.' Yet, for all that, you did not believe the LORD your God, who went in the way before you to search out a place for you to pitch your tents, to show you the way you should go, in the fire by night and in the cloud by day "And the LORD heard the sound of your words and was angry, and took an oath, saying, 'Surely not one of these men of this evil generation shall see that good land of which I swore to give to your fathers, except Caleb the son of Jephunneh; he shall see it, and to him and his children I am giving the land on which he walked because he wholly followed the LORD.' The LORD was also angry with me for your sakes, saying, 'Even you shall not go in there; Joshua the son of Nun, who stands before you, he shall go in there. Encourage him, for he shall cause Israel to inherit it. Moreover, your little ones and your children, who you say will be victims, who today have no knowledge of good and evil, they shall go in there; to them I will give it, and they shall possess it. But as for you, turn and take your journey into the wilderness by the Way of the Red Sea.' "Then you answered and said to me, 'We have sinned against the LORD; we will go up and fight, just as the LORD our God commanded us.' And when every one of you had girded on his weapons of war, you were ready to go up into the mountain. And the LORD said to me, 'Tell them, "Do not go up nor fight, for I am not among you; lest you be defeated before your enemies."' So I spoke to you; yet you would not listen but rebelled against the command of the LORD, and presumptuously went up into the mountain. And the Amorites who dwelt in that mountain came out against you and chased you as bees do, and drove you back from Seir to Hormah. Then you returned and wept before the LORD, but the LORD would not listen to your voice nor give ear to you. So you remained in Kadesh many days, according to the days that you spent there

Chapter 2

Then we turned and set out on our journey into the wilderness, along the way of the Red Sea, as the LORD had told me, and we skirted Mount Seir for many days. The LORD spoke to me, saying, 'You have skirted this mountain long enough; turn northward. And command the people, saying, "You are about to pass through the territory of your brethren, the descendants of Esau, who live in Seir, and they will be afraid of you. Therefore watch yourselves carefully. Do not meddle with them, for I will not give you any of their land, no, not so much as one footstep, because I have given Mount Seir to Esau as a possession. You shall buy food from them with money, that you may eat, and you shall also buy water from them with money, that you may drink." For the LORD your God has blessed you in all the work of your hand. He knows your trudging through this great wilderness. These forty years the LORD your God has been with you; you have lacked nothing.' "And when we passed beyond our brethren, the descendants of Esau, who dwell in Seir, away from the road of the plain, away from Elath and Ezion Geber, we turned and passed by way of the Wilderness of Moab. Then the LORD said to me, 'Do not harass Moab, nor contend with them in battle, for I will not give you any of their land as a possession, because I have given Ar to the descendants of Lot as a possession.' (The

Emim had dwelt there in times past, a people as great and numerous and tall as the Anakim. They were also regarded as giants, like the Anakim, but the Moabites call them Emim. The Horites formerly dwelt in Seir, but the descendants of Esau dispossessed them and destroyed them from before them and dwelt in their place, just as Israel did to the land of their possession which the LORD gave them.) "'Now rise and cross over the Valley of the Zered.' So we crossed over the Valley of the Zered. And the time we took to come from Kadesh-Barnea until we crossed over the Valley of the Zered was thirty-eight years, until all the generation of the men of war was consumed from the midst of the camp, just as the LORD had sworn to them. For indeed the hand of the LORD was against them, to destroy them from the midst of the camp until they were consumed "So it was, when all the men of war had finally perished from among the people, that the LORD spoke to me, saying: 'This day you are to cross over at Ar, the boundary of Moab. And when you come near the people of Ammon, do not harass them or meddle with them, for I will not give you any of the land of the people of Ammon as a possession, because I have given it to the descendants of Lot as a possession.' (That was also regarded as a land of giants; giants formerly dwelt there. But the Ammonites call them Zamzummim, a people as great and numerous and tall as the Anakim. But the LORD destroyed them before them, and they dispossessed them and dwelt in their place, just as He had done for the descendants of Esau, who dwelt in Seir, when He destroyed the Horites from before them. They dispossessed them and dwelt in their place even to this day. And the Avim, who dwelt in villages as far as Gaza—the Caphtorim, who came from Caphtor, destroyed them and dwelt in their place.) "'Rise, take your journey, and cross over the River Arnon. Look, I have given into your hand Sihon the Amorite, king of Heshbon, and his land. Begin to possess it, and engage him in battle. This day I will begin to put the dread and fear of you upon the nations under the whole heaven, who shall hear the report of you and shall tremble and be in anguish because of you.' "And I sent messengers from the Wilderness of Kedemoth to Sihon king of Heshbon, with words of peace, saying, 'Let me pass through your land; I will keep strictly to the road, and I will turn neither to the right nor to the left. You shall sell me food for money, that I may eat, and give me water for money, that I may drink; only let me pass through on foot, just as the descendants of Esau who dwell in Seir and the Moabites who dwell in Ar did for me, until I cross the Jordan to the land which the LORD our God is giving us.' But Sihon king of Heshbon would not let us pass through, for the LORD your God hardened his spirit and made his heart obstinate, that He might deliver him into your hand, as it is this day "And the LORD said to me, 'See, I have begun to give Sihon and his land over to you. Begin to possess it, that you may inherit his land.' Then Sihon and all his people came out against us to fight at Jahaz. And the LORD our God delivered him over to us; so we defeated him, his sons, and all his people. We took all his cities at that time, and we utterly destroyed the men, women, and little ones of every city; we left none remaining. We took only the livestock as plunder for ourselves, with the spoil of the cities which we took. From Aroer, which is on the bank of the River Arnon, and from the city that is in the ravine, as far as Gilead, there was not one city too strong for us; the LORD our God delivered all to us. Only you did not go near the land of the people of Ammon—anywhere along the River Jabbok, or to the cities of the mountains, or wherever the LORD our God had forbidden us

Chapter 3

Then we turned and went up the road to Bashan; and Og, king of Bashan, came out against us, he and all his people, to battle at Edrei. And the LORD said to me, 'Do not fear him, for I have delivered him and all his people and his land into your hand; you shall do to him as you did to Sihon, king of the Amorites, who dwelt at Heshbon.' So the LORD our God also delivered into our hands Og, king of Bashan, with all his people, and we attacked him until he had no survivors remaining. And we took all his cities at that time; there was not a city which we did not take from them: sixty cities, all the region of Argob, the kingdom of Og in Bashan. All these cities were fortified with high walls, gates, and bars, besides a great many rural towns. And we utterly destroyed them, as we did to Sihon king of Heshbon, utterly destroying the men, women, and children of every city. But all the livestock and the spoil of the cities we took as booty for ourselves "And at that time we took the land from the hand of the two kings of the Amorites who were on this side of the Jordan, from the River Arnon to Mount Hermon (the Sidonians call Hermon Sirion, and the Amorites call it Senir), all the cities of the plain, all Gilead, and all Bashan, as far as Salcah and Edrei, cities of the kingdom of Og in Bashan. For only Og king of Bashan remained of the remnant of the giants. Indeed his bedstead was an iron bedstead. Is it not in Rabbah of the people of Ammon? Nine cubits is its length and four cubits its width, according to the standard cubit "And this land, which we possessed at that time, from Aroer, which is by the River Arnon, and half the mountains of Gilead and its cities, I gave to the Reubenites and the Gadites. The rest of Gilead, and all Bashan, the kingdom of Og, I gave to half the tribe of Manasseh. All the region of Argob, with all Bashan, was called the land of the giants. Jair, the son of Manasseh, took all the region of Argob, as far as the border of the Geshurites and the Maachathites, and called Bashan after his own name, Havoth Jair, to this day "Also I gave Gilead to Machir. And to the Reubenites and the Gadites I gave from Gilead as far as the River Arnon (the middle of the river as the border), as far as the River Jabbok, the border of the people of Ammon; the plain also, with the Jordan as the border, from Chinnereth as far as the east side of the Sea of the Arabah (the Salt Sea), below the slopes of Pisgah "Then I commanded you at that time, saying: 'The LORD your God has given you this land to possess. All you men of valor shall cross over armed before your brethren, the children of Israel. But your wives, your little ones, and your livestock (I know that you have much livestock) shall stay in your cities which I have given you, until the LORD has given rest to your brethren as to you, and they also possess the land which the LORD your God is giving them beyond the Jordan. Then each of you may return to his possession which I have given you.' "And I commanded Joshua at that time, saying, 'Your eyes have seen all that the LORD your God has done to these two kings; so will the LORD do to all the kingdoms through which you pass. You must not fear them, for the LORD your God Himself fights for you.' "Then I pleaded with the LORD at that time, saying: 'O Lord GOD, You have begun to show Your servant Your greatness and Your mighty hand, for what god is there in heaven or on earth who can do anything like Your works and Your mighty deeds? I pray, let me cross over and see the good land beyond the Jordan, those pleasant mountains, and Lebanon.' But the LORD was angry with me on your account and would not listen to me. So the LORD said to me: 'Enough of that! Speak no more to Me of this matter. Go up to the top of Pisgah, and lift your eyes toward the west, the north, the south, and the east; behold it with your eyes, for you shall not cross over this Jordan. But command Joshua, and encourage him and strengthen him, for he shall go over before this people, and he shall cause them to inherit the land which you will see.' So we stayed in the valley opposite Beth Peor

Chapter 4

Now, O Israel, listen to the statutes and the judgments which I teach you to observe, that you may live, and go in and possess the land which the LORD God of your fathers is giving you. You shall not add to the word which I command you, nor take from it, that you may keep the commandments of the LORD your God which I command you. Your eyes have seen what the LORD did at Baal Peor; for the LORD your God has destroyed from among you all the men who followed Baal of Peor. But you who held fast to the LORD your God are alive today, every one of you "Surely I have taught you statutes and judgments, just as the LORD my God commanded me, that you should act according to them in the land which you go to possess. Therefore be careful to observe them; for this is your wisdom and your understanding in the sight of the peoples who will hear all these statutes, and say, 'Surely this great nation is a wise and understanding people.' For what great nation is there that has God so near to it, as the LORD our God is to us, for whatever reason we may call upon Him? And what great nation is there that has such statutes and righteous judgments as are in all this law which I set before you this day? "Only take heed to yourself, and diligently keep yourself, lest you forget the things your eyes have seen, and lest they depart from your heart all the days of your life. And teach them to your children and your grandchildren, especially concerning the day you stood before the LORD your God in Horeb, when the LORD said to me, 'Gather the people to Me, and I will let them hear My words, that they may learn to fear Me all the days they live on the earth, and that they may teach their children.' Then you came near and stood at the foot of the mountain, and the mountain burned with fire to the midst of heaven, with darkness, cloud, and thick darkness. And the LORD spoke to you out of the midst of the fire. You heard the sound of the words but saw no form; you only heard a voice. So He declared to you His covenant which He commanded you to perform, the Ten Commandments; and He wrote them on two tablets of stone. And the LORD commanded me at that time to teach you statutes and judgments, that you might observe them in the land which you cross over to possess "Take careful heed to yourselves, for you saw no form when the LORD spoke to you at Horeb out of the midst of the fire, lest you act corruptly and make for yourselves a carved image in the form of any figure: the likeness of male or female, the likeness of any animal that is on the earth or the likeness of any winged bird that flies in the air, the likeness of anything that creeps on the ground or the likeness of any fish that is in the water beneath the earth. And take heed, lest you lift your eyes to heaven, and when you see the sun, the moon, and the stars, all the host of heaven, you feel driven to worship them and serve them, which the LORD your God has given to all the peoples under the whole heaven as a heritage. But the LORD has taken you and brought you out of the iron furnace, out of Egypt, to be His people, an inheritance, as you are this day "Furthermore, the LORD was angry with me for your sakes, and swore that I would not cross over the Jordan, and that I would not enter the good land which the LORD your God is giving you as an inheritance. But I must die in this land, I must not cross over the Jordan; but you shall cross over and possess that good land. Take heed to yourselves, lest you forget the covenant of the LORD your God which He made with you, and make for yourselves a carved image in the form of anything which the LORD your God has forbidden you. For the LORD your God is a consuming fire, a jealous God "When you beget children and grandchildren and have grown old in the land, and act corruptly and make a carved image in the form of anything, and do evil in the sight of the LORD your God to provoke Him to anger, I call heaven and earth to witness against you this day, that you will soon utterly perish from the land which you cross over the Jordan to possess; you will not prolong your days in it, but will be utterly destroyed. And the LORD will scatter you among the peoples, and you will be left few in number among the nations where the LORD will drive you. And there you will serve gods, the work of men's hands, wood and stone, which neither see nor hear nor eat nor smell. But from there you will seek the LORD your God, and you will find Him if you seek Him with all your heart and with all your soul. When you are in distress, and all these things come upon you in the latter days, when you turn to the LORD your God and obey His voice (for the LORD your God is a merciful God), He will not forsake you nor destroy you, nor forget the covenant of your fathers which He swore to them "For ask now concerning the days that are past, which were before you, since the day that God created man on the earth, and ask from one end of heaven to the other, whether any great thing like this has happened, or anything like it has been heard. Did any people ever hear the voice of God speaking out of the midst of the fire, as you have heard, and live? Or did God ever try to go and take for Himself a nation from the midst of another nation, by trials, by signs, by wonders, by war, by a mighty hand and an outstretched arm, and by great terrors, according to all that the LORD your God did for you in Egypt before your eyes? To you it was shown, that you might know that the LORD Himself is God; there is none other besides Him. Out of heaven He let you hear His voice, that He might instruct you; on earth He showed you His great fire, and you heard His words out of the midst of the fire. And because He loved your fathers, therefore He chose their descendants after them; and He brought you out of Egypt with His Presence, with His mighty power, driving out from before you nations greater and mightier than you, to bring you in, to give you their land as an inheritance, as it is this day. Therefore know this day, and consider it in your heart, that the LORD Himself is God in heaven above and on the earth beneath; there is no other. You shall therefore keep His statutes and His commandments which I command you today, that it may go well with you and with your children after you, and that you may prolong your days in the land which the LORD your God is giving you for all time.' Then Moses set apart three cities on this side of the Jordan, toward the rising of the sun, that the manslayer might flee there, who kills his neighbor unintentionally, without having hated him in time past, and that by fleeing to one of these cities he might live: Bezer in the wilderness on the plateau for the Reubenites, Ramoth in Gilead for the Gadites, and Golan in Bashan for the Manassites This is the law which Moses set before the children of Israel. These are the testimonies, the statutes, and the judgments which Moses spoke to the children of Israel after they came out of Egypt, on this side of the Jordan, in the valley opposite Beth Peor, in the land of Sihon king of the Amorites, who dwelt at Heshbon, whom Moses and the children of Israel defeated after they came out of Egypt. And they took possession of his land and the land of Og king of Bashan, two kings of the Amorites, who were on this side of the Jordan, toward the rising of the sun, from Aroer, which is on the bank of the River Arnon, even to Mount Sion (that is, Hermon), and all the plain on the east side of the Jordan as far as the Sea of the Arabah, below the slopes of Pisgah

Chapter 5

And Moses called all Israel, and said to them: "Hear, O Israel, the statutes and judgments which I speak in your hearing today, that you may learn them and be careful to observe them. The LORD our God made a covenant with us in Horeb. The LORD did not make this covenant with our fathers, but with us, those who are here today, all of us who are alive. The LORD talked with you face to face on the mountain from the midst of the fire. I stood between the LORD and you at that time, to declare to you the word of the LORD; for you were afraid because of the fire, and you did not go up the mountain. He said: 'I am the LORD your God who brought you out of the land of Egypt, out of the house of bondage. You shall have no other gods before Me. You shall not make for yourself a carved image—any likeness of anything that is in heaven above, or that is in the earth beneath, or that is in the water under the earth; you shall not bow down to them nor serve them. For I, the LORD your God, am a jealous God, visiting the iniquity of the fathers upon the children to the third and fourth generations of those who hate Me, but showing mercy to thousands, to those who love Me and keep My commandments 'You shall not take the name of the LORD your God in vain, for the LORD will not hold him guiltless who takes His name in vain 'Observe the Sabbath day, to keep it holy, as the LORD your God commanded you. Six days you shall labor and do all your work, but the seventh day is the Sabbath of the LORD your God. In it, you shall do no work: you, nor your son, nor your daughter, nor your male servant, nor your female servant, nor your ox, nor your donkey, nor any of your cattle, nor your stranger who is within your gates, that your male servant and your female servant may rest as well as you. And remember that you were a slave in the land of Egypt, and the LORD your God brought you out from there by a mighty hand and by an outstretched arm; therefore the LORD your God commanded you to keep the Sabbath day 'Honor your father and your mother, as the LORD your God has commanded you, that your days may be long, and that it may be well with you in the land which the LORD your God is giving you 'You shall not murder 'You shall not commit adultery 'You shall not steal 'You shall not bear false witness against your neighbor 'You shall not covet your neighbor's wife; and you shall not desire your neighbor's house, his field, his male servant, his female servant, his ox, his donkey, or anything that is your neighbor's.' "These words the LORD spoke to all your assembly, in the mountain from the midst of the fire, the cloud, and the thick darkness, with a loud voice; and He added no more. And He wrote them on two tablets of stone and gave them to me "So it was, when you heard the voice from the midst of the darkness, while the mountain was burning with fire, that you came near to me, all the heads of your tribes and your elders. And you said: 'Surely the LORD our God has shown us His glory and His greatness, and we have heard His voice from the midst of the fire. We have seen this day that God speaks with man; yet he still lives. Now therefore, why should we die? For this great fire will consume us; if we hear the voice of the LORD our God anymore, then we shall die. For who is there of all flesh who has heard the voice of the living God speaking from the midst of the fire, as we have, and lived? You go near and hear all that the LORD our God may say, and tell us all that the LORD our God says to you, and we will hear and do it.' "Then the LORD heard the voice of your words when you spoke to me, and the LORD said to me: 'I have heard the voice of the words of this people which they have spoken to you. They are right in all that they have spoken. Oh, that they had such a heart in them that they would fear Me and always keep all My commandments, that it might be well with them and with their children forever! Go and say to them, "Return to your tents." But as for you, stand here by Me, and I will speak to you all the commandments, the statutes, and the judgments which you shall teach them, that they may observe them in the land which I am giving them to possess.' "Therefore you shall be careful to do as the LORD your God has commanded you; you shall not turn aside to the right hand or to the left. You shall walk in all the ways which the LORD your God has commanded you, that you may live and that it may be well with you, and that you may prolong your days in the land which you shall possess."

Chapter 6

These are the commands, rules, and laws that the LORD your God has commanded me to teach you, so that you may observe them in the land you are about to possess. You are to fear the LORD your God and observe all His statutes and commandments that I am giving you, you, your son, and your grandson, all the days of your life, so that your days may be prolonged. Therefore, listen, O Israel, and be careful to obey, so that it may go well with you, and that you may increase greatly in a land flowing with milk and honey, as the LORD, the God of your ancestors, has promised you Hear, O Israel: The LORD our God, the LORD is one. You shall love the LORD your God with all your heart, with all your soul, and with all your strength. These words that I command you today shall be on your heart. You shall teach them diligently to your children and shall talk of them when you sit at home, when you walk along the road, when you lie down, and when you get up. You shall bind them as a sign on your hand, and they shall be as frontlets between your eyes. You shall write them on the doorposts of your house and on your gates When the LORD your God brings you into the land that He swore to your fathers, Abraham, Isaac, and Jacob, to give you—a land with large, flourishing cities you did not build, houses filled with all kinds of good things you did not provide, wells you did not dig, and vineyards and olive groves you did not plant—then when you eat and are satisfied, be careful that you do not forget the LORD, who brought you out of Egypt, out of the land of slavery. Fear the LORD your God, serve Him only, and take your oaths in His name. Do not follow other gods, the gods of the peoples around you, for the LORD your God, who is among you, is a jealous God, and His anger will burn against you, and He will destroy you from the face of the land Do not test the LORD your God as you did at Massah. Be sure to keep the commands of the LORD your God and the stipulations and decrees He has given you. Do what is right and good in the LORD's sight, so that it may go well with you, and you may go in and take over the good land that the LORD promised on oath to your ancestors, thrusting out all your enemies before you, as the LORD has said In the future, when your son asks you, "What is the meaning of the stipulations, decrees, and laws the LORD our God has commanded you?" tell him: "We were slaves of Pharaoh in Egypt, but the LORD brought us out of Egypt with a mighty hand. Before our eyes, the LORD sent signs and wonders—great and terrible—on Egypt and Pharaoh and his whole household. But He brought us out from there to bring us in and give us the land He promised on oath to our ancestors. The LORD commanded us to obey all these decrees and

to fear the LORD our God, so that we might always prosper and be kept alive, as is the case today. And if we are careful to obey all this law before the LORD our God, as He has commanded us, that will be our righteousness."

Chapter 7

When the LORD your God brings you into the land you are entering to possess and drives out before you many nations—the Hittites, Girgashites, Amorites, Canaanites, Perizzites, Hivites, and Jebusites, seven nations larger and stronger than you—and when the LORD your God has delivered them over to you and you have defeated them, then you must destroy them totally. Make no treaty with them and show them no mercy. Do not intermarry with them. Do not give your daughters to their sons or take their daughters for your sons, for they will turn your children away from following me to serve other gods, and the LORD's anger will burn against you and will quickly destroy you This is what you are to do to them: Break down their altars, smash their sacred stones, cut down their Asherah poles, and burn their idols in the fire. For you are a people holy to the LORD your God. The LORD your God has chosen you out of all the peoples on the face of the earth to be His people, His treasured possession The LORD did not set His affection on you and choose you because you were more numerous than other peoples, for you were the fewest of all peoples. But it was because the LORD loved you and kept the oath He swore to your ancestors that He brought you out with a mighty hand and redeemed you from the land of slavery, from the power of Pharaoh king of Egypt. Know therefore that the LORD your God is God; He is the faithful God, keeping His covenant of love to a thousand generations of those who love Him and keep His commandments. But those who hate Him He will repay to their face by destruction; He will not be slow to repay to their face those who hate Him. Therefore, take care to follow the commands, decrees, and laws I give you today If you pay attention to these laws and are careful to follow them, then the LORD your God will keep His covenant of love with you, as He swore to your ancestors. He will love you and bless you and increase your numbers. He will bless the fruit of your womb, the crops of your land—your grain, new wine and olive oil—the calves of your herds and the lambs of your flocks in the land He swore to your ancestors to give you. You will be blessed more than any other people; none of your men or women will be childless, nor will any of your livestock be without young. The LORD will keep you free from every disease. He will not inflict on you the horrible diseases you knew in Egypt, but He will inflict them on all who hate you. You must destroy all the peoples the LORD your God gives over to you. Do not look on them with pity and do not serve their gods, for that will be a snare to you You may say to yourselves, "These nations are stronger than we are. How can we drive them out?" But do not be afraid of them; remember well what the LORD your God did to Pharaoh and to all Egypt. You saw with your own eyes the great trials, the signs and wonders, the mighty hand and outstretched arm, with which the LORD your God brought you out. The LORD your God will do the same to all the peoples you now fear. Moreover, the LORD your God will send the hornet among them until even the survivors who hide from you have perished. Do not be terrified by them, for the LORD your God, who is among you, is a great and awesome God. The LORD your God will drive out those nations before you, little by little. You will not be allowed to eliminate them all at once, or the wild animals will multiply around you. But the LORD your God will deliver them over to you, throwing them into great confusion until they are destroyed. He will give their kings into your hand, and you will wipe out their names from under heaven. No one will be able to stand up against you; you will destroy them The images of their gods you are to burn in the fire. Do not covet the silver and gold on them, and do not take it for yourselves, or you will be ensnared by it, for it is detestable to the LORD your God. Do not bring a detestable thing into your house or you, like it, will be set apart for destruction. Regard it as vile and utterly detest it, for it is set apart for destruction

Chapter 8

Be careful to follow every command I am giving you today, so that you may live and increase and may enter and possess the land the LORD promised on oath to your ancestors. Remember how the LORD your God led you all the way in the wilderness these forty years, to humble and test you in order to know what was in your heart, whether or not you would keep His commands. He humbled you, causing you to hunger and then feeding you with manna, which neither you nor your ancestors had known, to teach you that man does not live on bread alone but on every word that comes from the mouth of the LORD. Your clothes did not wear out and your feet did not swell during these forty years. Know then in your heart that as a man disciplines his son, so the LORD your God disciplines you Observe the commands of the LORD your God, walking in obedience to Him and revering Him. For the LORD your God is bringing you into a good land—a land with brooks, streams, and deep springs gushing out into the valleys and hills; a land with wheat and barley, vines and fig trees, pomegranates, olive oil, and honey; a land where bread will not be scarce and you will lack nothing; a land where the rocks are iron and you can dig copper out of the hills. When you have eaten and are satisfied, praise the LORD your God for the good land He has given you Be careful that you do not forget the LORD your God, failing to observe His commands, His laws, and His decrees that I am giving you this day. Otherwise, when you eat and are satisfied, when you build fine houses and settle down, and when your herds and flocks grow large and your silver and gold increase and all you have is multiplied, then your heart will become proud and you will forget the LORD your God, who brought you out of Egypt, out of the land of slavery. He led you through the vast and dreadful wilderness, that thirsty and waterless land, with its venomous snakes and scorpions. He brought you water out of hard rock. He gave you manna to eat in the wilderness, something your ancestors had never known, to humble and test you so that in the end it might go well with you. You may say to yourself, "My power and the strength of my hands have produced this wealth for me." But remember the LORD your God, for it is He who gives you the ability to produce wealth, and so confirms His covenant, which He swore to your ancestors, as it is today If you ever forget the LORD your God and follow other gods and worship and bow down to them, I testify against you today that you will surely be destroyed. Like the nations the LORD destroyed before you, so you will be destroyed for not obeying the LORD your God

Chapter 9

Hear, O Israel: You are now about to cross the Jordan to go in and dispossess nations greater and stronger than you, with large cities that have walls up to the sky. The people are strong and tall—Anakites! You know about them and have heard it said: "Who can stand up against the Anakites?" But be assured today that the LORD your God is the one who goes across ahead of you like a devouring fire. He will destroy them; He will subdue them before you. And you will drive them out and annihilate them quickly, as the LORD has promised you After the LORD your God has driven them out before you, do not say to yourself, "The LORD has brought me here to take possession of this land because of my righteousness." No, it is on account of the wickedness of these nations that the LORD is going to drive them out before you. It is not because of your righteousness or your integrity that you are going in to take possession of their land; but on account of the wickedness of these nations, the LORD your God will drive them out before you, to accomplish what He swore to your fathers, to Abraham, Isaac, and Jacob. Understand, then, that it is not because of your righteousness that the LORD your God is giving you this good land to possess, for you are a stiff-necked people Remember this and never forget how you aroused the anger of the LORD your God in the wilderness. From the day you left Egypt until you arrived here, you have been rebellious against the LORD. At Horeb you aroused the LORD's wrath so that He was angry enough to destroy you. When I went up on the mountain to receive the tablets of stone, the tablets of the covenant that the LORD had made with you, I stayed on the mountain forty days and forty nights; I ate no bread and drank no water. The LORD gave me two stone tablets inscribed by the finger of God. On them were all the commandments the LORD proclaimed to you on the mountain out of the fire, on the day of the assembly At the end of the forty days and forty nights, the LORD gave me the two stone tablets, the tablets of the covenant. Then the LORD told me, "Go down from here at once, because your people whom you brought out of Egypt have become corrupt. They have turned away quickly from what I commanded them and have made an idol for themselves." And the LORD said to me, "I have seen this people, and they are a stiff-necked people indeed! Let me alone, so that I may destroy them and blot out their name from under heaven. And I will make you into a nation stronger and more numerous than they." So I turned and went down from the mountain while it was ablaze with fire. And the two tablets of the covenant were in my hands. When I looked, I saw that you had sinned against the LORD your God; you had made for yourselves an idol cast in the shape of a calf. You had turned aside quickly from the way that the LORD had commanded you. So I took the two tablets and threw them out of my hands, breaking them to pieces before your eyes. Then once again I fell prostrate before the LORD for forty days and forty nights; I ate no bread and drank no water because of all the sin you had committed, doing what was evil in the LORD's sight and so arousing His anger. I feared the anger and wrath of the LORD, for He was angry enough with you to destroy you. But again the LORD listened to me. And the LORD was angry enough with Aaron to destroy him, but at that time I prayed for Aaron too. Also, I took that sinful thing of yours, the calf you had made, and burned it in the fire. Then I crushed it and ground it to powder as fine as dust and threw the dust into a stream that flowed down the mountain You also made the LORD angry at Taberah, at Massah and at Kibroth Hattaavah. And when the LORD sent you out from Kadesh Barnea, He said, "Go up and take possession of the land I have given you." But you rebelled against the command of the LORD your God. You did not trust Him or obey Him. You have been rebellious against the LORD ever since I have known you I lay prostrate before the LORD those forty days and forty nights because the LORD had said He would destroy you. I prayed to the LORD and said, "Sovereign LORD, do not destroy Your people, Your own inheritance that You redeemed by Your great power and brought out of Egypt with a mighty hand. Remember Your servants Abraham, Isaac, and Jacob. Overlook the stubbornness of this people, their wickedness and their sin. Otherwise, the country from which You brought us will say, 'Because the LORD was not able to take them into the land He had promised them, and because He hated them, He brought them out to put them to death in the wilderness.' But they are Your people, Your inheritance that You brought out by Your great power and Your outstretched arm."

Chapter 10

At that time the LORD said to me, "Chisel out two stone tablets like the first ones and come up to me on the mountain. Also make a wooden ark. I will write on the tablets the words that were on the first tablets, which you broke. Then you are to put them in the ark." So I made the ark out of acacia wood and chiseled out two stone tablets like the first ones. I went up on the mountain with the two tablets in my hands. The LORD wrote on these tablets what He had written before, the Ten Commandments He had proclaimed to you on the mountain, out of the fire, on the day of the assembly. And the LORD gave them to me. Then I came back down the mountain and put the tablets in the ark I had made, as the LORD commanded me, and they are there now The Israelites traveled from the wells of Bene Jaakan to Moserah. There Aaron died and was buried, and Eleazar his son succeeded him as priest. From there they traveled to Gudgodah and on to Jotbathah, a land with streams of water. At that time the LORD set apart the tribe of Levi to carry the ark of the covenant of the LORD, to stand before the LORD to minister and to pronounce blessings in His name, as they still do today. That is why the Levites have no share or inheritance among their fellow Israelites; the LORD is their inheritance, as the LORD your God told them Now I had stayed on the mountain forty days and forty nights, as I did the first time, and the LORD listened to me at this time also. It was not His will to destroy you. "Go," the LORD said to me, "and lead the people on their way, so that they may enter and possess the land I swore to their ancestors to give them." And now, Israel, what does the LORD your God ask of you but to fear the LORD your God, to walk in obedience to Him, to love Him, to serve the LORD your God with all your heart and with all your soul, and to observe the LORD's commands and decrees that I am giving you today for your own good? To the LORD your God belong the heavens, even the highest heavens, the earth and everything in it. Yet the LORD set His affection on your ancestors and loved them, and He chose you, their descendants, above all the nations—as it is today. Circumcise your hearts, therefore, and do not be stiff-necked any longer. For the LORD your God is God of gods and Lord of lords, the great God, mighty and awesome, who shows no partiality and accepts no bribes. He defends the cause of the fatherless and the widow, and loves the foreigner residing among you, giving them food and clothing. And you are to love those who are foreigners, for you yourselves were foreigners in Egypt. Fear the LORD your God and serve Him. Hold fast to Him and take your oaths in His name. He is your praise; He is your God, who performed for you those great and awesome wonders you saw with your own eyes. Your ancestors who went down into Egypt were seventy in all, and now the LORD your God has made you as numerous as the stars in the sky

Chapter 11

Therefore, you shall love the Lord your God and always observe His commandments, decrees, and laws. Consider today (since I do not speak to your children, who have not known nor seen) the chastisement of the LORD your God, His greatness,

His mighty hand, and His outstretched arm, the signs, and deeds He performed in Egypt against Pharaoh, king of Egypt, and his entire land. Recall what He did to the Egyptian army, to their horses and chariots, when He caused the waters of the Red Sea to engulf them as they pursued you, and how the LORD has destroyed them to this day. Remember what He did for you in the wilderness until you arrived at this place. Consider what He did to Dathan and Abiram, sons of Eliab, son of Reuben, when the earth opened its mouth and swallowed them up with their households, tents, and all their possessions in the midst of all Israel. For your eyes have witnessed all the great deeds the LORD has done Therefore, observe all the commandments I give you today, so you may be strong and enter and take possession of the land you are crossing the Jordan to possess. That you may live long in the land that the LORD swore to your fathers to give to them and their descendants, a land flowing with milk and honey. The land you are entering to possess is not like the land of Egypt, from which you came, where you sowed your seed and watered it by foot, as in a vegetable garden. Instead, the land you are crossing the Jordan to take possession of is a land of mountains and valleys that drinks rain from heaven. The LORD your God cares for this land; His eyes are continually on it from the beginning of the year to its end So, if you faithfully obey the commands I am giving you today—to love the LORD your God and to serve Him with all your heart and with all your soul—then I will send rain on your land in its season, both autumn and spring rains, so that you may gather your grain, new wine, and olive oil. I will provide grass in the fields for your cattle, and you will eat and be satisfied. Be careful, or you will be enticed to turn away and worship other gods and bow down to them. Then the LORD's anger will burn against you, and He will shut up the heavens so that it will not rain, and the ground will yield no produce, and you will soon perish from the good land the LORD is giving you Fix these words of mine in your hearts and minds; tie them as symbols on your hands and bind them on your foreheads. Teach them to your children, talking about them when you sit at home, when you walk along the road, when you lie down, and when you get up. Write them on the doorframes of your houses and on your gates, so that your days and the days of your children may be many in the land the LORD swore to give your ancestors, as many as the days that the heavens are above the earth. If you carefully observe all these commandments I am giving you to follow—to love the LORD your God, to walk in obedience to Him and to hold fast to Him—then the LORD will drive out all these nations before you, and you will dispossess nations larger and stronger than you. Every place where you set your foot will be yours; your territory will extend from the desert to Lebanon, and from the Euphrates River to the Mediterranean Sea. No one will be able to stand against you. The LORD your God, as He promised you, will put the terror and fear of you on the whole land, wherever you go See, I am setting before you today a blessing and a curse—the blessing if you obey the commands of the LORD your God that I am giving you today; the curse if you disobey the commands of the LORD your God and turn from the way that I command you today by following other gods, which you have not known. When the LORD your God has brought you into the land you are entering to possess, you are to proclaim the blessings on Mount Gerizim and the curses on Mount Ebal. As you know, these mountains are across the Jordan, westward, toward the setting sun, near the great trees of Moreh, in the territory of those Canaanites living in the Arabah in the vicinity of

Gilgal. You are about to cross the Jordan to enter and take possession of the land the LORD your God is giving you. When you have taken it over and are living there, be sure that you obey all the decrees and laws I am setting before you today

Chapter 12

These are the decrees and laws you must be careful to follow in the land that the LORD, the God of your ancestors, has given you to possess—as long as you live in the land. Destroy completely all the places on the high mountains, on the hills, and under every spreading tree where the nations you are dispossessing worshiped their gods. Break down their altars, smash their sacred stones and burn their Asherah poles in the fire; cut down the idols of their gods and wipe out their names from those places. You must not worship the LORD your God in their way. But you are to seek the place the LORD your God will choose from among all your tribes to put His Name there for His dwelling. To that place, you must go; there bring your burnt offerings and sacrifices, your tithes and special gifts, what you have vowed to give and your freewill offerings, and the firstborn of your herds and flocks. There, in the presence of the LORD your God, you and your families shall eat and shall rejoice in everything you have put your hand to because the LORD your God has blessed you You are not to do as we do here today, everyone doing as they see fit, since you have not yet reached the resting place and the inheritance the LORD your God is giving you. But you will cross the Jordan and settle in the land the LORD your God is giving you as an inheritance, and He will give you rest from all your enemies around you so that you will live in safety. Then to the place the LORD your God will choose as a dwelling for His Name—there you are to bring everything I command you: your burnt offerings and sacrifices, your tithes and special gifts, and all the choice possessions you have vowed to the LORD. And there rejoice before the LORD your God—you, your sons and daughters, your male and female servants, and the Levites from your towns who have no allotment or inheritance of their own Be careful not to sacrifice your burnt offerings anywhere you please. Offer them only at the place the LORD will choose in one of your tribes, and there observe everything I command you. Nevertheless, you may slaughter your animals in any of your towns and eat as much of the meat as you want, as if it were gazelle or deer, according to the blessing the LORD your God gives you. Both the ceremonially unclean and the clean may eat it. But you must not eat the blood; pour it out on the ground like water. You must not eat in your own towns the tithe of your grain and new wine and olive oil, or the firstborn of your herds and flocks, or whatever you have vowed to give, or your freewill offerings or special gifts. Instead, you are to eat them in the presence of the LORD your God at the place the LORD your God will choose—you, your sons and daughters, your male and female servants, and the Levites from your towns—and you are to rejoice before the LORD your God in everything you put your hand to. Be careful not to neglect the Levites as long as you live in your land When the LORD your God has enlarged your territory as He promised you, and you crave meat and say, "I would like some meat," then you may eat as much of it as you want. If the place where the LORD your God chooses to put His Name is too far away from you, you may slaughter animals from the herds and flocks the LORD has given you as I have commanded you, and in your own towns, you may eat as much of them as you want. Eat them as you would gazelle or deer. Both the ceremonially unclean and the clean may eat. But be sure you do not eat the blood, because the blood is the life, and you must not eat the life with the meat. You must not eat the blood; pour it out on the ground like water. Do not eat it, so that it may go well with you and your children after you, because you will be doing what is right in the eyes of the LORD But take your consecrated things and whatever you have vowed to give and go to the place the LORD will choose. Present your burnt offerings on the altar of the LORD your God, both the meat and the blood. The blood of your sacrifices must be poured beside the altar of the LORD your God, but you may eat the meat. Be careful to obey all these regulations I am giving you so that it may always go well with you and your children after you because you will be doing what is good and right in the eyes of the LORD your God The LORD your God will cut off before you the nations you are about to invade and dispossess. But when you have driven them out and settled in their land, and after they have been destroyed before you, be careful not to be ensnared by inquiring about their gods, saying, "How do these nations serve their gods? We will do the same." You must not worship the LORD your God in their way, because in worshiping their gods, they do all kinds of detestable things the LORD hates. They even burn their sons and daughters in the fire as sacrifices to their gods See that you do all I command you; do not add to it or take away from it

Chapter 13

If a prophet or one who foretells by dreams appears among you and announces to you a sign or wonder, and if the sign or wonder spoken of takes place, and the prophet says, "Let us follow other gods" (gods you have not known) "and let us worship them," you must not listen to the words of that prophet or dreamer. The LORD your God is testing you to find out whether you love Him with all your heart and with all your soul. It is the LORD your God you must follow, and Him you must revere. Keep His commands and obey Him; serve Him and hold fast to Him. That prophet or dreamer must be put to death for inciting rebellion against the LORD your God, who brought you out of Egypt and redeemed you from the land of slavery. That prophet or dreamer tried to turn you from the way the LORD your God commanded you to follow. You must purge the evil from among you If your very own brother, or your son or daughter, or the wife you love, or your closest friend secretly entices you, saying, "Let us go and worship other gods" (gods that neither you nor your ancestors have known, gods of the peoples around you, whether near or far, from one end of the land to the other), do not yield to them or listen to them. Show them no pity. Do not spare them or shield them. You must certainly put them to death. Your hand must be the first in putting them to death, and then the hands of all the people. Stone them to death, because they tried to turn you away from the LORD your God, who brought you out of Egypt, out of the land of slavery. Then all Israel will hear and be afraid, and no one among you will do such an evil thing again If you hear it said about one of the towns the LORD your God is giving you to live in that troublemakers have arisen among you and have led the people of their town astray, saying, "Let us go and worship other gods" (gods you have not known), then you must inquire, probe, and investigate it thoroughly. And if it is true, and it has been proved that this detestable thing has been done among you, you must certainly put to the sword all who live in that town. You must destroy it completely, both its people and its livestock. Gather all the plunder of the town into the middle of the public square and completely burn the town and all its plunder as a whole burnt offering to the LORD your God. That town is to remain a ruin forever, never to be rebuilt, and none of the condemned things are to be found in your hands. Then the LORD will turn from His fierce anger, will show you mercy, and will have compassion on you. He will increase your numbers, as He promised on oath to your ancestors, because you obey the LORD your God by keeping all His commands that I am giving you today and doing what is right in His eyes

Chapter 14

You are the children of the LORD your God. Do not cut yourselves or shave the front of your heads for the dead, for you are a people holy to the LORD your God. Out of all the peoples on the face of the earth, the LORD has chosen you to be His treasured possession Do not eat any detestable thing. These are the animals you may eat: the ox, the sheep, the goat, the deer, the gazelle, the roe deer, the wild goat, the ibex, the antelope, and the mountain sheep. You may eat any animal that has a divided hoof and that chews the cud. However, of those that chew the cud or that have a divided hoof, you may not eat the camel, the rabbit, or the coney. Although they chew the cud, they do not have a divided hoof; they are ceremonially unclean for you. The pig is also unclean; although it has a divided hoof, it does not chew the cud. You are not to eat their meat or touch their carcasses Of all the creatures living in the water, you may eat any that have fins and scales. But anything that does not have fins and scales you may not eat; for you, it is unclean You may eat any clean bird. But these you may not eat: the eagle, the vulture, the black vulture, the red kite, the black kite, any kind of falcon, any kind of raven, the horned owl, the screech owl, the gull, any kind of hawk, the little owl, the great owl, the white owl, the desert owl, the osprey, the cormorant, the stork, any kind of heron, the hoopoe, and the bat. All flying insects are unclean to you; do not eat them. But any winged creature that is clean you may eat Do not eat anything you find already dead. You may give it to the foreigner residing in any of your towns, and they may eat it, or you may sell it to any other foreigner. But you are a people holy to the LORD your God. Do not cook a young goat in its mother's milk Be sure to set aside a tenth of all that your fields produce each year. Eat the tithe of your grain, new wine, and olive oil, and the firstborn of your herds and flocks in the presence of the LORD your God at the place He will choose as a dwelling for His Name so that you may learn to revere the LORD your God always. But if that place is too distant and you have been blessed by the LORD your God and cannot carry your tithe (because the place where the LORD will choose to put His Name is so far away), then exchange your tithe for silver and take the silver with you and go to the place the LORD your God will choose. Use the silver to buy whatever you like: cattle, sheep, wine, or other fermented drink, or anything you wish. Then you and your household shall eat there in the presence of the LORD your God and rejoice. And do not neglect the Levites living in your towns, for they have no allotment or inheritance of their own At the end of every three years, bring all the tithes of that year's produce and store it in your towns so that the Levites (who have no allotment or inheritance of their own) and the foreigners, the fatherless and the widows who live in your towns may come and eat and be satisfied, and so that the LORD your God may bless you in all the work of your hands

Chapter 15

At the end of every seven years, you must cancel debts. This is how it is to be done: Every creditor shall cancel any loan they have made to a fellow Israelite. They shall not require payment from anyone among their own people because the LORD's time for canceling debts has been proclaimed. You may require payment from a foreigner, but you must cancel any debt your fellow Israelite owes you. However, there need be no poor people among you, for in the land the LORD your God is giving you to possess as your inheritance, He will richly bless you, if only you fully obey the LORD your God and are careful to follow all these commands I am giving you today. For the LORD your God will bless you as He has promised, and you will lend to many nations but will borrow from none. You will rule over many nations, but none will rule over you If anyone is poor among your fellow Israelites in any of the towns of the land the LORD your God is giving you, do not be hardhearted or tightfisted toward them. Rather, be openhanded and freely lend them whatever they need. Be careful not to harbor this wicked thought: "The seventh year, the year for canceling debts, is near," so that you do not show ill will toward the needy among your fellow Israelites and give them nothing. They may then appeal to the LORD against you, and you will be found guilty of sin. Give generously to them and do so without a grudging heart; then because of this, the LORD your God will bless you in all your work and in everything you put your hand to. There will always be poor people in the land. Therefore, I command you to be openhanded toward your fellow Israelites who are poor and needy in your land If any of your people—Hebrew men or women—sell themselves to you and serve you six years, in the seventh year you must let them go free. And when you release them, do not send them away empty-handed. Supply them liberally from your flock, your threshing floor, and your winepress. Give to them as the LORD your God has blessed you. Remember that you were slaves in Egypt and the LORD your God redeemed you. That is why I give you this command today But if your servant says to you, "I do not want to leave you," because he loves you and your family and is well off with you, then take an awl and push it through his earlobe into the door, and he will become your servant for life. Do the same for your female servant. Do not consider it a hardship to set your servant free because their service to you these six years has been worth twice as much as that of a hired hand. And the LORD your God will bless you in everything you do Set apart for the LORD your God every firstborn male of your herds and flocks. Do not put the firstborn of your cows to work and do not shear the firstborn of your sheep. Each year you and your family are to eat them in the presence of the LORD your God at the place He will choose. If an animal has a defect, is lame or blind, or has any serious flaw, you must not sacrifice it to the LORD your God. You are to eat it in your own towns. Both the ceremonially unclean and the clean may eat it, as if it were gazelle or deer. But you must not eat the blood; pour it out on the ground like water

Chapter 16

Observe the month of Abib and celebrate the Passover to the LORD your God, for in the month of Abib, the LORD your God brought you out of Egypt by night. You shall therefore offer the Passover sacrifice to the LORD your God from the flock and the herd, in the place where the LORD chooses to establish His name. Do not eat it with leavened bread. For seven days, you shall eat unleavened bread with it, the bread of affliction, because you came out of the land of Egypt in haste. This will help you remember the day you departed from Egypt all the days of your life. No yeast shall be seen in all your territory for seven days, and none of the meat you sacrifice on the evening of the first day shall remain until morning You may not sacrifice the Passover within any of your towns that the LORD your God is giving you, but at the place where the LORD your God will choose to establish

His name. There, you shall sacrifice the Passover in the evening at sunset, at the time you came out of Egypt. Roast it and eat it in the place the LORD your God will choose, and in the morning, return to your tents. For six days, you shall eat unleavened bread, and on the seventh day, there shall be a solemn assembly to the LORD your God. You shall do no work Count off seven weeks from the time you begin to put the sickle to the standing grain. Then celebrate the Feast of Weeks to the LORD your God by giving a freewill offering in proportion to the blessings the LORD your God has given you. Rejoice before the LORD your God—you, your sons and daughters, your male and female servants, the Levites in your towns, and the foreigners, the fatherless, and the widows living among you—in the place the LORD your God will choose to establish His name. Remember that you were slaves in Egypt, and carefully follow these decrees Celebrate the Feast of Tabernacles for seven days after you have gathered the produce of your threshing floor and your winepress. Be joyful at your festival—you, your sons and daughters, your male and female servants, and the Levites, the foreigners, the fatherless, and the widows who live in your towns. For seven days, celebrate the feast to the LORD your God at the place the LORD will choose, for the LORD your God will bless you in all your harvest and in all the work of your hands, and your joy will be complete Three times a year, all your men must appear before the LORD your God at the place He will choose: at the Feast of Unleavened Bread, the Feast of Weeks, and the Feast of Tabernacles. No one should appear before the LORD empty-handed. Each of you must bring a gift in proportion to the way the LORD your God has blessed you Appoint judges and officials for each of your tribes in every town the LORD your God is giving you, and they shall judge the people fairly. Do not pervert justice or show partiality. Do not accept a bribe, for a bribe blinds the eyes of the wise and twists the words of the innocent. Follow justice and justice alone, so that you may live and possess the land the LORD your God is giving you Do not set up any wooden Asherah pole beside the altar you build to the LORD your God, and do not erect a sacred stone, for these the LORD your God hates

Chapter 17

Do not sacrifice to the LORD your God an ox or a sheep that has any defect or flaw in it, for that would be detestable to Him. If a man or woman living among you in one of the towns the LORD gives you is found doing evil in the eyes of the LORD your God in violation of His covenant, and contrary to My command, has worshiped other gods, bowing down to them or to the sun or the moon or the stars in the sky, and this has been brought to your attention, then you must investigate it thoroughly. If it is true and it has been proved that this detestable thing has been done in Israel, take the man or woman who has done this evil deed to your city gate and stone that person to death. On the testimony of two or three witnesses, a person is to be put to death, but no one is to be put to death on the testimony of only one witness. The hands of the witnesses must be the first in putting that person to death, and then the hands of all the people. You must purge the evil from among you If cases come before your courts that are too difficult for you to judge—whether bloodshed, lawsuits, or assaults—take them to the place the LORD your God will choose. Go to the Levitical priests and to the judge who is in office at that time. Inquire of them, and they will give you the verdict. You must act according to the decisions they give you at the place the LORD will choose. Be careful to do everything they instruct you to do. Act according to whatever they teach you and the decisions they give you. Do

not turn aside from what they tell you, to the right or to the left. Anyone who shows contempt for the judge or for the priest who stands ministering there to the LORD your God is to be put to death. You must purge the evil from Israel. All the people will hear and be afraid and will not be contemptuous again When you enter the land the LORD your God is giving you and have taken possession of it and settled in it, and you say, "Let us set a king over us like all the nations around us," be sure to appoint over you a king the LORD your God chooses. He must be from among your fellow Israelites. Do not place a foreigner over you, one who is not an Israelite. The king, moreover, must not acquire great numbers of horses for himself or make the people return to Egypt to get more of them, for the LORD has told you, "You are not to go back that way again." He must not take many wives, or his heart will be led astray. He must not accumulate large amounts of silver and gold. When he takes the throne of his kingdom, he is to write for himself on a scroll a copy of this law, taken from that of the Levitical priests. It is to be with him, and he is to read it all the days of his life so that he may learn to revere the LORD his God and follow carefully all the words of this law and these decrees and not consider himself better than his fellow Israelites and turn from the law to the right or to the left. Then he and his descendants will reign a long time over his kingdom in Israel

Chapter 18

The Levitical priests—indeed, the whole tribe of Levi—are to have no allotment or inheritance with Israel. They shall live on the food offerings presented to the LORD, for that is their inheritance. They shall have no inheritance among their fellow Israelites; the LORD is their inheritance, as He promised them. This is the share due the priests from the people who sacrifice a bull or a sheep: the shoulder, the internal organs, and the meat from the head. You are to give them the firstfruits of your grain, new wine and olive oil, and the first wool from the shearing of your sheep, for the LORD your God has chosen them and their descendants out of all your tribes to stand and minister in the LORD's name always If a Levite moves from one of your towns anywhere in Israel where he is living and comes in all earnestness to the place the LORD will choose, he may minister in the name of the LORD his God like all his fellow Levites who serve there in the presence of the LORD. He is to share equally in their benefits, even though he has received money from the sale of family possessions When you enter the land the LORD your God is giving you, do not learn to imitate the detestable ways of the nations there. Let no one be found among you who sacrifices their son or daughter in the fire, who practices divination or sorcery, interprets omens, engages in witchcraft, or casts spells, or who is a medium or spiritist or who consults the dead. Anyone who does these things is detestable to the LORD; because of these same detestable practices, the LORD your God will drive out those nations before you. You must be blameless before the LORD your God. The nations you will dispossess listen to those who practice sorcery or divination. But as for you, the LORD your God has not permitted you to do so The LORD your God will raise up for you a prophet like me from among you, from your fellow Israelites. You must listen to him. For this is what you asked of the LORD your God at Horeb on the day of the assembly when you said, "Let us not hear the voice of the LORD our God nor see this great fire anymore, or we will die." The LORD said to me: "What they say is good. I will raise up for them a prophet like you from among their fellow Israelites, and I will put my words in his mouth. He will tell them everything I command him. I myself will call to account anyone who does not listen to my words that the prophet speaks in my name. But a prophet who presumes to speak in my name anything I have not commanded, or a prophet who speaks in the name of other gods, is to be put to death." You may say to yourselves, "How can we know when a message has not been spoken by the LORD?" If what a prophet proclaims in the name of the LORD does not take place or come true, that is a message the LORD has not spoken. That prophet has spoken presumptuously, so do not be alarmed

Chapter 19

When the LORD your God has destroyed the nations whose land he is giving you, and when you have driven them out and settled in their towns and houses, then set aside for yourselves three cities in the land the LORD your God is giving you to possess. Determine the distances involved and divide into three parts the land the LORD your God is giving you as an inheritance, so that a person who kills someone may flee to one of these cities This is the rule concerning anyone who kills a person and flees there for safety—anyone who kills a neighbor unintentionally, without malice aforethought. For instance, a man may go into the forest with his neighbor to cut wood, and as he swings his ax to fell a tree, the head may fly off and hit his neighbor and kill him. That man may flee to one of these cities and save his life. Otherwise, the avenger of blood might pursue him in a rage, overtake him if the distance is too great, and kill him even though he is not deserving of death, since he did it to his neighbor without malice aforethought. This is why I command you to set aside for yourselves three cities If the LORD your God enlarges your territory, as he promised on oath to your ancestors, and gives you the whole land he promised them, because you carefully follow all these laws I command you today—to love the LORD your God and to walk always in obedience to him—then you are to set aside three more cities. Do this so that innocent blood will not be shed in your land, which the LORD your God is giving you as your inheritance, and so that you will not be guilty of bloodshed But if out of hate someone lies in wait, assaults and kills a neighbor, and then flees to one of these cities, the killer shall be sent for by the town elders, be brought back from the city, and be handed over to the avenger of blood to die. Show no pity. You must purge from Israel the guilt of shedding innocent blood, so that it may go well with you Do not move your neighbor's boundary stone set up by your predecessors in the inheritance you receive in the land the LORD your God is giving you to possess One witness is not enough to convict anyone accused of any crime or offense they may have committed. A matter must be established by the testimony of two or three witnesses If a malicious witness takes the stand to accuse someone of a crime, the two people involved in the dispute must stand in the presence of the LORD before the priests and the judges who are in office at the time. The judges must make a thorough investigation, and if the witness proves to be a liar, giving false testimony against a fellow Israelite, then do to the false witness as that witness intended to do to the other party. You must purge the evil from among you. The rest of the people will hear of this and be afraid, and never again will such an evil thing be done among you. Show no pity: life for life, eye for eye, tooth for tooth, hand for hand, foot for foot

Chapter 20

When you go to war against your enemies and see horses and chariots and an army greater than yours, do not be afraid of them, because the LORD your God, who brought you up out of Egypt, will be with you. When you are about to go into battle, the priest shall come forward and address the army. He shall say: "Hear, Israel: Today you are going into battle against your enemies. Do not be fainthearted or afraid; do not panic or be terrified by them. For the LORD your God is the one who goes with you to fight for you against your enemies to give you victory." The officers shall say to the army: "Has anyone built a new house and not yet begun to live in it? Let him go home, or he may die in battle and someone else may begin to live in it. Has anyone planted a vineyard and not begun to enjoy it? Let him go home, or he may die in battle and someone else enjoy it. Has anyone become pledged to a woman and not married her? Let him go home, or he may die in battle and someone else marry her." Then the officers shall add, "Is anyone afraid or fainthearted? Let him go home so that his fellow soldiers will not become disheartened too." When the officers have finished speaking to the army, they shall appoint commanders over it When you march up to attack a city, make its people an offer of peace. If they accept and open their gates, all the people in it shall be subject to forced labor and shall work for you. If they refuse to make peace and they engage you in battle, lay siege to that city. When the LORD your God delivers it into your hand, put to the sword all the men in it. As for the women, the children, the livestock, and everything else in the city, you may take these as plunder for yourselves. And you may use the plunder the LORD your God gives you from your enemies. This is how you are to treat all the cities that are at a distance from you and do not belong to the nations nearby However, in the cities of the nations the LORD your God is giving you as an inheritance, do not leave alive anything that breathes. Completely destroy them—the Hittites, Amorites, Canaanites, Perizzites, Hivites, and Jebusites—as the LORD your God has commanded you. Otherwise, they will teach you to follow all the detestable things they do in worshiping their gods, and you will sin against the LORD your God When you lay siege to a city for a long time, fighting against it to capture it, do not destroy its trees by putting an ax to them, because you can eat their fruit. Do not cut them down. Are the trees people, that you should besiege them? However, you may cut down trees that you know are not fruit trees and use them to build siege works until the city at war with you falls

Chapter 21

If in the land the LORD your God is giving you to possess, someone is found slain, lying in the field, and it is not known who killed him, then your elders and judges shall go out and measure the distances to the surrounding cities. The elders of the city nearest to the slain man shall take a heifer that has never been worked and has not worn a yoke. They shall lead the heifer to a valley with running water, which is neither plowed nor sown, and there in the valley they are to break the heifer's neck. The priests, the sons of Levi—whom the LORD your God has chosen to minister and to bless in the name of the LORD—shall also come forward, for the LORD your God has chosen them to pronounce blessings and to decide all cases of dispute and assault Then all the elders of the city nearest the slain man shall wash their hands over the heifer whose neck was broken in the valley, and they shall declare: "Our hands did not shed this blood, nor did our eyes see it done. Accept this atonement for your people Israel, whom you have redeemed, O LORD, and do not hold your people guilty of the blood of an innocent person." Then the bloodshed will be atoned for, and you will have purged from yourselves the guilt of shedding innocent blood, since you have done what is right in the eyes of the LORD When you go to war against your enemies and the LORD your God delivers them into your hands and you take captives, if you notice among the captives a beautiful woman and are attracted to her, you may take her as your wife. Bring her into your home and have her shave her head, trim her nails, and put aside the clothes she was wearing when captured. After she has lived in your house and mourned her father and mother for a full month, then you may go to her and be her husband, and she shall be your wife. If you are not pleased with her, let her go wherever she wishes. You must not sell her or treat her as a slave, since you have dishonored her If a man has two wives, and he loves one but not the other, and both bear him sons—but the firstborn is the son of the wife he does not love—when he wills his property to his sons, he must not give the rights of the firstborn to the son of the wife he loves in preference to his actual firstborn, the son of the wife he does not love. He must acknowledge the son of the unloved wife as the firstborn by giving him a double share of all he has. That son is the first sign of his father's strength. The right of the firstborn belongs to him If someone has a stubborn and rebellious son who does not obey his father and mother and will not listen to them when they discipline him, his father and mother shall take hold of him and bring him to the elders at the gate of his town. They shall say to the elders, "This son of ours is stubborn and rebellious. He will not obey us. He is a glutton and a drunkard." Then all the men of his town are to stone him to death. You must purge the evil from among you. All Israel will hear of it and be afraid If someone guilty of a capital offense is put to death and their body is exposed on a pole, you must not leave the body hanging on the pole overnight. Be sure to bury it that same day, because anyone who is hung on a pole is under God's curse. You must not desecrate the land the LORD your God is giving you as an inheritance

Chapter 22

If you see your fellow Israelite's ox or sheep straying, do not ignore it but be sure to take it back to its owner. If the owner does not live near you or you do not know who owns it, take it home with you and keep it until they come looking for it. Then give it back. Do the same if you find their donkey or cloak or anything else they have lost. Do not ignore it. If you see your fellow Israelite's donkey or ox fallen on the road, do not ignore it. Help the owner get it to its feet A woman must not wear men's clothing, nor a man wear women's clothing, for the LORD your God detests anyone who does this. If you come across a bird's nest beside the road, either in a tree or on the ground, and the mother is sitting on the young or on the eggs, do not take the mother with the young. You may take the young, but be sure to let the mother go, so that it may go well with you and you may have a long life When you build a new house, make a parapet around your roof so that you may not bring the guilt of bloodshed on your house if someone falls from the roof. Do not plant two kinds of seed in your vineyard; if you do, not only the crops you plant but also the fruit of the vineyard will be defiled. Do not plow with an ox and a donkey yoked together. Do not wear clothes of wool and linen woven together. Make tassels on the four corners of the cloak you wear If a man takes a wife and, after sleeping with her, dislikes her and slanders her and gives her a bad name, saying, "I married this woman, but when I approached her, I did not find proof of her virginity," then the young woman's father and mother shall bring to the town elders at the gate proof that she was a virgin. Her father will say to the elders, "I gave my daughter in marriage to this man, but he dislikes her. Now he has slandered her and said, 'I did not find your daughter to be a virgin.' But here is the proof of my daughter's virginity." Then her parents shall display the cloth before the elders of the town, and the elders shall take the man and punish him. They shall fine him a hundred shekels of silver and give them to the young woman's father, because this man has given an Israelite virgin a bad name. She shall continue to be his wife; he must not divorce her as long as he lives If, however, the charge is true and no proof of the young woman's virginity can be found, she shall be brought to the door of her father's house and there the men of her town shall stone her to death. She has done an outrageous thing in Israel by being promiscuous while still in her father's house. You must purge the evil from among you If a man is found sleeping with another man's wife, both the man who slept with her and the woman must die. You must purge the evil from Israel. If a man happens to meet in a town a virgin pledged to be married and he sleeps with her, you shall take both of them to the gate of that town and stone them to death—the young woman because she was in a town and did not scream for help, and the man because he violated another man's wife. You must purge the evil from among you. But if out in the country a man happens to meet a young woman pledged to be married and rapes her, only the man who has done this shall die. Do nothing to the woman; she has committed no sin deserving death. This case is like that of someone who attacks and murders a neighbor, for the man found the young woman out in the country, and though the betrothed woman screamed, there was no one to rescue her If a man happens to meet a virgin who is not pledged to be married and rapes her and they are discovered, he shall pay her father fifty shekels of silver. He must marry the young woman, for he has violated her. He can never divorce her as long as he lives. A man is not to marry his father's wife; he must not dishonor his father's bed

Chapter 23

No one who has been emasculated by crushing or cutting may enter the assembly of the LORD. No one born of a forbidden marriage nor any of their descendants may enter the assembly of the LORD, not even in the tenth generation. No Ammonite or Moabite or any of their descendants may enter the assembly of the LORD, not even in the tenth generation. For they did not come to meet you with bread and water on your way when you came out of Egypt, and they hired Balaam son of Beor from Pethor in Aram Naharaim to pronounce a curse on you. However, the LORD your God would not listen to Balaam but turned the curse into a blessing for you because the LORD your God loves you. Do not seek a treaty of friendship with them as long as you live Do not despise an Edomite, for the Edomites are related to you. Do not despise an Egyptian, because you resided as foreigners in their country. The third generation of children born to them may enter the assembly of the LORD When you set up camp against your enemies, keep away from everything impure. If one of your men is unclean because of a nocturnal emission, he is to go outside the camp and stay there. But as evening approaches, he is to wash himself, and at sunset, he may return to the camp. Designate a place outside the camp where you can go to relieve yourself. As part of your equipment, have something to dig with, and when you relieve yourself, dig a hole and cover up your excrement. For the LORD your God moves about in your camp to protect you and to deliver your enemies to you. Your camp must be holy so that he will not see among you anything indecent and turn away from you If a slave has taken refuge with you, do not hand them over to their master. Let them live among you wherever they like and in whatever town they choose. Do not oppress them. No Israelite man or woman is to become a shrine prostitute. You must not bring the earnings of a female prostitute or of a male prostitute into the house of the LORD your God to pay any vow, because the LORD your God detests them both Do not charge a fellow Israelite interest, whether on money or food or anything else that may earn interest. You may charge a foreigner interest, but not a fellow Israelite, so that the LORD your God may bless you in everything you put your hand to in the land you are entering to possess If you make a vow to the LORD your God, do not be slow to pay it, for the LORD your God will certainly demand it of you and you will be guilty of sin. But if you refrain from making a vow, you will not be guilty. Whatever your lips utter you must be sure to do, because you made your vow freely to the LORD your God with your own mouth If you enter your neighbor's vineyard, you may eat all the grapes you want, but do not put any in your basket. If you enter your neighbor's grainfield, you may pick kernels with your hands, but you must not put a sickle to their standing grain

Chapter 24

If a man marries a woman who becomes displeasing to him because he finds something indecent about her, and he writes her a certificate of divorce, gives it to her and sends her from his house, and if after she leaves his house she becomes the wife of another man, and her second husband dislikes her and writes her a certificate of divorce, gives it to her and sends her from his house, or if he dies, then her first husband, who divorced her, is not allowed to marry her again after she has been defiled. That would be detestable in the eyes of the LORD. Do not bring sin upon the land the LORD your God is giving you as an inheritance If a man has recently married, he must not be sent to war or have any other duty laid on him. For one year he is to be free to stay at home and bring happiness to the wife he has married Do not take a pair of millstones—not even the upper one—as security for a debt, because that would be taking a person's livelihood as security If someone is caught kidnapping a fellow Israelite and treating or selling them as a slave, the kidnapper must die. You must purge the evil from among you In cases of defiling skin diseases, be very careful to do exactly as the Levitical priests instruct you. You must follow carefully what I have commanded them. Remember what the LORD your God did to Miriam along the way after you came out of Egypt When you make a loan of any kind to your neighbor, do not go into their house to get what is offered to you as a pledge. Stay outside and let the neighbor to whom you are making the loan bring the pledge out to you. If the neighbor is poor, do not go to sleep with their pledge in your possession. Return their cloak by sunset so that your neighbor may sleep in it. Then they will thank you, and it will be regarded as a righteous act in the sight of the LORD your God Do not take advantage of a hired worker who is poor and needy, whether that worker is a fellow Israelite or a foreigner residing in one of your towns. Pay them their wages each day before sunset because they are poor and are counting on it. Otherwise, they may cry to the LORD against you, and you will be guilty of sin Parents are not to be put to death for their children, nor children put to death for their parents; each will die for their own sin Do not deprive the foreigner or the fatherless of justice, or take the cloak of the widow as a pledge. Remember that you were slaves in Egypt and the LORD your God redeemed you from there. That is why I command you to do this When you are harvesting in your field and you overlook a sheaf, do not go back to get it. Leave it for the foreigner, the fatherless and the widow, so that the LORD your God may bless you in all the work of your hands. When you beat the olives from your trees, do not go over the branches a second time. Leave what remains for the foreigner, the fatherless and the widow. When you harvest the grapes in your vineyard, do not go over the vines again. Leave what remains for the foreigner, the fatherless and the widow. Remember that you were slaves in Egypt. That is why I command you to do this

Chapter 25

When people have a dispute, they are to take it to court and the judges will decide the case, acquitting the innocent and condemning the guilty. If the guilty person deserves to be beaten, the judge shall make them lie down and have them flogged in his presence with the number of lashes the crime deserves, but the judge must not impose more than forty lashes. If the guilty party is flogged more than that, your fellow Israelite will be degraded in your eyes Do not muzzle an ox while it is treading out the grain If brothers are living together and one of them dies without a son, his widow must not marry outside the family. Her husband's brother shall take her and marry her and fulfill the duty of a brother-in-law to her. The first son she bears shall carry on the name of the dead brother so that his name will not be blotted out from Israel. However, if a man does not want to marry his brother's wife, she shall go to the elders at the town gate and say, "My husband's brother refuses to carry on his brother's name in Israel. He will not fulfill the duty of a brother-in-law to me." Then the elders of his town shall summon him and talk to him. If he persists in saying, "I do not want to marry her," his brother's widow shall go up to him in the presence of the elders, take off one of his sandals, spit in his face and say, "This is what is done to the man who will not build up his brother's family line." That man's line shall be known in Israel as The Family of the Unsandaled If two men are fighting and the wife of one of them comes to rescue her husband from his assailant, and she reaches out and seizes him by his private parts, you shall cut off her hand. Show her no pity Do not have two differing weights in your bag—one heavy, one light. Do not have two differing measures in your house—one large, one small. You must have accurate and honest weights and measures, so that you may live long in the land the LORD your God is giving you. For the LORD your God detests anyone who does these things, anyone who deals dishonestly Remember what the Amalekites did to you along the way when you came out of Egypt. When you were weary and worn out, they met you on your journey and attacked all who were lagging behind; they had no fear of God. When the LORD your God gives you rest from all the enemies around you in the land he is giving you to possess as an inheritance, you shall blot out the name of Amalek from under heaven. Do not forget!

Chapter 26

When you have entered the land that the LORD your God is giving you as an inheritance, and you have taken possession of it and settled in it, take some of the firstfruits of all that you produce from the soil of the land the LORD your God is giving you and put them in a basket. Then go to the place that the LORD your God will choose as a dwelling for his Name and say to the priest in office at the time, "I declare today to the LORD your God that I have come to the land the LORD swore to our ancestors to give us." The priest shall take the basket from your hands and set it down in front of the altar of the LORD your God. Then you shall declare before the LORD your God:

"My father was a wandering Aramean, and he went down into Egypt with a few people and lived there and became a great nation, powerful and numerous. But the Egyptians mistreated us and made us suffer, subjecting us to harsh labor. Then we cried out to the LORD, the God of our ancestors, and the LORD heard our voice and saw our misery, toil, and oppression. So the LORD brought us out of Egypt with a mighty hand and an outstretched arm, with great terror and with signs and wonders. He brought us to this place and gave us this land, a land flowing with milk and honey; and now I bring the firstfruits of the soil that you, LORD, have given me." Place the basket before the LORD your God and bow down before him Then you and the Levites and the foreigners residing among you shall rejoice in all the good things the LORD your God has given to you and your household. When you have finished setting aside a tenth of all your produce in the third year, the year of the tithe, you shall give it to the Levite, the foreigner, the fatherless, and the widow, so that they may eat in your towns and be satisfied. Then say to the LORD your God: "I have removed from my house the sacred portion and have given it to the Levite, the foreigner, the fatherless, and the widow, according to all you commanded. I have not turned aside from your commands nor have I forgotten any of them. I have not eaten any of the sacred portion while I was in mourning, nor have I removed any of it while I was unclean, nor have I offered any of it to the dead. I have obeyed the LORD my God; I have done everything you commanded me. Look down from heaven, your holy dwelling place, and bless your people Israel and the land you have given us as you promised on oath to our ancestors, a land flowing with milk and honey." The LORD your God commands you this day to follow these decrees and laws; carefully observe them with all your heart and with all your soul. You have declared this day that the LORD is your God and that you will walk in obedience to him, that you will keep his decrees, commands, and laws—that you will listen to him. And the LORD has declared this day that you are his people, his treasured possession as he promised, and that you are to keep all his commands. He has declared that he will set you in praise, fame, and honor high above all the nations he has made and that you will be a people holy to the LORD your God, as he promised

Chapter 27

Moses and the elders of Israel commanded the people: "Keep all these commands that I give you today. When you have crossed the Jordan into the land the LORD your God is giving you, set up some large stones and coat them with plaster. Write on them all the words of this law when you have crossed over to enter the land the LORD your God is giving you, a land flowing with milk and honey, just as the LORD, the God of your ancestors, promised you. And when you have crossed the Jordan, set up these stones on Mount Ebal, as I command you today, and coat them with plaster. Build there an altar to the LORD your God, an altar of stones. Do not use any iron tool on them. Build the altar of the LORD your God with fieldstones and offer burnt offerings on it to the LORD your God. Sacrifice fellowship offerings there, eating them and rejoicing in the presence of the LORD your God. And you shall write very clearly all the words of this law on these stones you have set up." Then Moses and the Levitical priests said to all Israel, "Be silent, Israel, and listen! You have now become the people of the LORD your God. Obey the LORD your God and follow his commands and decrees that I give you today." On the same day Moses commanded the people: "When you have crossed the Jordan, these tribes shall stand on Mount Gerizim to bless the people: Simeon, Levi, Judah, Issachar, Joseph, and Benjamin. And these tribes shall stand on Mount Ebal to pronounce curses: Reuben, Gad, Asher, Zebulun, Dan, and Naphtali. The Levites shall recite to all the people of Israel in a loud voice: 'Cursed is anyone who makes an idol—a thing detestable to the LORD, the work of skilled hands—and sets it up in secret.' Then all the people shall say, 'Amen!' 'Cursed is anyone who dishonors their father or mother.' Then all the people shall say, 'Amen!' 'Cursed is anyone who moves their neighbor's boundary stone.' Then all the people shall say, 'Amen!' 'Cursed is anyone who leads the blind astray on the road.' Then all the people shall say, 'Amen!' 'Cursed is anyone who withholds justice from the foreigner, the fatherless, or the widow.' Then all the people shall say, 'Amen!' 'Cursed is anyone who sleeps with his father's wife, for he dishonors his father's bed.' Then all the people shall say, 'Amen!' 'Cursed is anyone who has sexual relations with any animal.' Then all the people shall say, 'Amen!' 'Cursed is anyone who sleeps with his sister, the daughter of his father or the daughter of his mother.' Then all the people shall say, 'Amen!' 'Cursed is anyone who sleeps with his mother-in-law.' Then all the people shall say, 'Amen!' 'Cursed is anyone who kills their neighbor secretly.' Then all the people shall say, 'Amen!' 'Cursed is anyone who accepts a bribe to kill an innocent person.' Then all the people shall say, 'Amen!' 'Cursed is anyone who does not uphold the words of this law by carrying them out.' Then all the people shall say, 'Amen!'

Chapter 28

If you fully obey the LORD your God and carefully follow all his commands I give you today, the LORD your God will set you high above all the nations on earth. All these blessings will come on you and accompany you if you obey the LORD your God: You will be blessed in the city and blessed in the country. The fruit of your womb will be blessed, and the crops of your land and the young of your livestock—the calves of your herds and the lambs of your flocks. Your basket and your kneading trough will be blessed. You will be blessed when you come in and blessed when you go out The LORD will grant that the enemies who rise up against you will be defeated before you. They will come at you from one direction but flee from you in seven. The LORD will send a blessing on your barns and on everything you put your hand to. The LORD your God will bless you in the land he is giving you. The LORD will establish you as his holy people, as he promised you on oath, if you keep the commands of the LORD your God and walk in obedience to him. Then all the peoples on earth will see that you are called by the name of the LORD, and they will fear you. The LORD will grant you abundant prosperity—in the fruit of your womb, the young of your livestock and the crops of your ground—in the land he swore to your ancestors to give you. The LORD will open the heavens, the storehouse of his bounty, to send rain on your land in season and to bless all the work of your hands. You will lend to many nations but will borrow from none. The LORD will make you the head, not the tail. If you pay attention to the commands of the LORD your God that I give you this day and carefully follow them, you will always be at the top, never at the bottom. Do not turn aside from any of the commands I give you today, to the right or to the left, following other gods and serving them However, if you do not obey the LORD your God and do not carefully follow all his commands and decrees I am giving you today, all these curses will come on you and overtake you: You will be cursed in the city and cursed in the country. Your basket and your kneading trough will be cursed.

The fruit of your womb will be cursed, and the crops of your land, and the calves of your herds and the lambs of your flocks. You will be cursed when you come in and cursed when you go out The LORD will send on you curses, confusion and rebuke in everything you put your hand to, until you are destroyed and come to sudden ruin because of the evil you have done in forsaking him. The LORD will plague you with diseases until he has destroyed you from the land you are entering to possess. The LORD will strike you with wasting disease, with fever and inflammation, with scorching heat and drought, with blight and mildew, which will plague you until you perish. The sky over your head will be bronze, the ground beneath you iron. The LORD will turn the rain of your country into dust and powder; it will come down from the skies until you are destroyed The LORD will cause you to be defeated before your enemies. You will come at them from one direction but flee from them in seven, and you will become a thing of horror to all the kingdoms on earth. Your carcasses will be food for all the birds and the wild animals, and there will be no one to frighten them away. The LORD will afflict you with the boils of Egypt and with tumors, festering sores and the itch, from which you cannot be cured. The LORD will afflict you with madness, blindness and confusion of mind. At midday you will grope about like a blind person in the dark. You will be unsuccessful in everything you do; day after day you will be oppressed and robbed, with no one to rescue you You will be pledged to be married to a woman, but another will take her and rape her. You will build a house, but you will not live in it. You will plant a vineyard, but you will not even begin to enjoy its fruit. Your ox will be slaughtered before your eyes, but you will eat none of it. Your donkey will be forcibly taken from you and will not be returned. Your sheep will be given to your enemies, and no one will rescue them. Your sons and daughters will be given to another nation, and you will wear out your eyes watching for them day after day, powerless to lift a hand. A people that you do not know will eat what your land and labor produce, and you will have nothing but cruel oppression all your days. The sights you see will drive you mad. The LORD will afflict your knees and legs with painful boils that cannot be cured, spreading from the soles of your feet to the top of your head The LORD will drive you and the king you set over you to a nation unknown to you or your ancestors. There you will worship other gods, gods of wood and stone. You will become a thing of horror, a byword and an object of ridicule among all the peoples where the LORD will drive you You will sow much seed in the field but you will harvest little, because locusts will devour it. You will plant vineyards and cultivate them but you will not drink the wine or gather the grapes, because worms will eat them. You will have olive trees throughout your country but you will not use the oil, because the olives will drop off. You will have sons and daughters but you will not keep them, because they will go into captivity. Swarms of locusts will take over all your trees and the crops of your land. The foreigners who reside among you will rise above you higher and higher, but you will sink lower and lower. They will lend to you, but you will not lend to them. They will be the head, but you will be the tail All these curses will come on you. They will pursue you and overtake you until you are destroyed, because you did not obey the LORD your God and observe the commands and decrees he gave you. They will be a sign and a wonder to you and your descendants forever. Because you did not serve the LORD your God joyfully and gladly in the time of prosperity, therefore in hunger and thirst, in nakedness and dire poverty, you will serve the enemies the LORD sends against you. He will put an iron yoke on your neck until he has destroyed you The LORD will bring a nation against you from far away, from the ends of the earth, like an eagle swooping down, a nation whose language you will not understand, a fierce-looking nation without respect for the old or pity for the young. They will devour the young of your livestock and the crops of your land until you are destroyed. They will leave you no grain, new wine or olive oil, nor any calves of your herds or lambs of your flocks until you are ruined. They will lay siege to all the cities throughout your land until the high fortified walls in which you trust fall down. They will besiege all the cities throughout the land the LORD your God is giving you Because of the suffering your enemy will inflict on you during the siege, you will eat the fruit of the womb, the flesh of the sons and daughters the LORD your God has given you. Even the most gentle and sensitive man among you will have no compassion on his own brother or the wife he loves or his surviving children, and he will not give to one of them any of the flesh of his children that he is eating. It will be all he has left because of the suffering your enemy will inflict on you during the siege of all your cities. The most gentle and sensitive woman among you—so sensitive and gentle that she would not venture to touch the ground with the sole of her foot—will begrudge the husband she loves and her own son or daughter the afterbirth from her womb and the children she bears. For in her dire need she intends to eat them secretly because of the suffering your enemy will inflict on you during the siege of your cities If you do not carefully follow all the words of this law, which are written in this book, and do not revere this glorious and awesome name—the LORD your God—the LORD will send fearful plagues on you and your descendants, harsh and prolonged disasters, and severe and lingering illnesses. He will bring upon you all the diseases of Egypt that you dreaded, and they will cling to you. The LORD will also bring upon you every kind of sickness and disaster not recorded in this Book of the Law, until you are destroyed. You who were as numerous as the stars in the sky will be left but few in number, because you did not obey the LORD your God. Just as it pleased the LORD to make you prosper and increase in number, so it will please him to ruin and destroy you. You will be uprooted from the land you are entering to possess Then the LORD will scatter you among all nations, from one end of the earth to the other. There you will worship other gods—gods of wood and stone, which neither you nor your ancestors have known. Among those nations you will find no repose, no resting place for the sole of your foot. There the LORD will give you an anxious mind, eyes weary with longing, and a despairing heart. You will live in constant suspense, filled with dread both night and day, never sure of your life. In the morning you will say, "If only it were evening!" and in the evening, "If only it were morning!"—because of the terror that will fill your hearts and the sights that your eyes will see. The LORD will send you back in ships to Egypt on a journey I said you should never make again. There you will offer yourselves for sale to your enemies as male and female slaves, but no one will buy you

Chapter 29

These are the terms of the covenant the LORD commanded Moses to make with the Israelites in Moab, in addition to the covenant he had made with them at Horeb Moses summoned all the Israelites and said to them: "Your eyes have seen all that the LORD did in Egypt to Pharaoh, to all his officials and to all his land. With your own eyes you saw those great trials, those signs and great wonders. But to this day the LORD has not given you a mind that understands or eyes that see or ears that hear. During the forty years that I led you through the wilderness, your clothes did not wear out, nor did the sandals on your feet. You ate no bread and drank no wine or other fermented drink. I did this so that you might know that I am the LORD your God." When you reached this place, Sihon king of Heshbon and Og king of Bashan came out to fight against us, but we defeated them. We took their land and gave it as an inheritance to the Reubenites, the Gadites, and the half-tribe of Manasseh. Carefully follow the terms of this covenant, so that you may prosper in everything you do. All of you are standing today in the presence of the LORD your God—your leaders and chief men, your elders and officials, and all the other men of Israel, together with your children and your wives, and the foreigners living in your camps who chop your wood and carry your water. You are standing here in order to enter into a covenant with the LORD your God, a covenant the LORD is making with you this day and sealing with an oath, to confirm you this day as his people, that he may be your God as he promised you and as he swore to your fathers, Abraham, Isaac and Jacob I am making this covenant, with its oath, not only with you who are standing here with us today in the presence of the LORD our God but also with those who are not here today You yourselves know how we lived in Egypt and how we passed through the countries on the way here. You saw among them their detestable images and idols of wood and stone, of silver and gold. Make sure there is no man or woman, clan or tribe among you today whose heart turns away from the LORD our God to go and worship the gods of those nations; make sure there is no root among you that produces such bitter poison. When such a person hears the words of this oath and they invoke a blessing on themselves, thinking, "I will be safe, even though I persist in going my own way," they will bring disaster on the watered land as well as the dry. The LORD will never be willing to forgive them; his wrath and zeal will burn against them. All the curses written in this book will fall on them, and the LORD will blot out their names from under heaven. The LORD will single them out from all the tribes of Israel for disaster, according to all the curses of the covenant written in this Book of the Law Your children who follow you in later generations and foreigners who come from distant lands will see the calamities that have fallen on the land and the diseases with which the LORD has afflicted it. The whole land will be a burning waste of salt and sulfur—nothing planted, nothing sprouting, no vegetation growing on it. It will be like the destruction of Sodom and Gomorrah, Admah and Zeboyim, which the LORD overthrew in fierce anger. All the nations will ask: "Why has the LORD done this to this land? Why this fierce, burning anger?" And the answer will be: "It is because this people abandoned the covenant of the LORD, the God of their ancestors, the covenant he made with them when he brought them out of Egypt. They went off and worshiped other gods and bowed down to them, gods they did not know, gods he had not given them. Therefore the LORD's anger burned against this land, so that he brought on it all the curses written in this book. In furious anger and in great wrath the LORD uprooted them from their land and thrust them into another land, as it is now." The secret things belong to the LORD our God, but the things revealed belong to us and to our children forever, that we may follow all the words of this law

Chapter 30
When all these blessings and curses I have set before

you come on you and you take them to heart wherever the LORD your God disperses you among the nations, and when you and your children return to the LORD your God and obey him with all your heart and with all your soul according to everything I command you today, then the LORD your God will restore your fortunes and have compassion on you and gather you again from all the nations where he scattered you. Even if you have been banished to the most distant land under the heavens, from there the LORD your God will gather you and bring you back. He will bring you to the land that belonged to your ancestors, and you will take possession of it. He will make you more prosperous and numerous than your ancestors. The LORD your God will circumcise your hearts and the hearts of your descendants, so that you may love him with all your heart and with all your soul, and live The LORD your God will put all these curses on your enemies who hate and persecute you. You will again obey the LORD and follow all his commands I am giving you today. Then the LORD your God will make you most prosperous in all the work of your hands and in the fruit of your womb, the young of your livestock and the crops of your land. The LORD will again delight in you and make you prosperous, just as he delighted in your ancestors, if you obey the LORD your God and keep his commands and decrees that are written in this Book of the Law and turn to the LORD your God with all your heart and with all your soul Now what I am commanding you today is not too difficult for you or beyond your reach. It is not up in heaven, so that you have to ask, "Who will ascend into heaven to get it and proclaim it to us so we may obey it?" Nor is it beyond the sea, so that you have to ask, "Who will cross the sea to get it and proclaim it to us so we may obey it?" No, the word is very near you; it is in your mouth and in your heart so you may obey it See, I set before you today life and prosperity, death and destruction. For I command you today to love the LORD your God, to walk in obedience to him, and to keep his commands, decrees, and laws; then you will live and increase, and the LORD your God will bless you in the land you are entering to possess. But if your heart turns away and you are not obedient, and if you are drawn away to bow down to other gods and worship them, I declare to you this day that you will certainly be destroyed. You will not live long in the land you are crossing the Jordan to enter and possess This day I call the heavens and the earth as witnesses against you that I have set before you life and death, blessings and curses. Now choose life, so that you and your children may live and that you may love the LORD your God, listen to his voice, and hold fast to him. For the LORD is your life, and he will give you many years in the land he swore to give to your fathers, Abraham, Isaac, and Jacob

Chapter 31
1 Moses went and spoke these words to all Israel: 2 "I am now a hundred and twenty years old and I am no longer able to lead you. The LORD has said to me, 'You shall not cross the Jordan.' 3 The LORD your God himself will cross over ahead of you. He will destroy these nations before you, and you will take possession of their land. Joshua also will cross over ahead of you, as the LORD said. 4 And the LORD will do to them what he did to Sihon and Og, the kings of the Amorites, whom he destroyed along with their land. 5 The LORD will deliver them to you, and you must do to them all that I have commanded you. 6 Be strong and courageous. Do not be afraid or terrified because of them, for the LORD your God goes with you; he will never leave you nor forsake you." 7 Then Moses summoned Joshua and said to him in the presence of all Israel, "Be strong and courageous, for

you must go with this people into the land that the LORD swore to their ancestors to give them, and you must divide it among them as their inheritance. 8 The LORD himself goes before you and will be with you; he will never leave you nor forsake you. Do not be afraid; do not be discouraged." 9 So Moses wrote down this law and gave it to the Levitical priests, who carried the ark of the covenant of the LORD, and to all the elders of Israel. 10 Then Moses commanded them: "At the end of every seven years, in the year for canceling debts, during the Festival of Tabernacles, 11 when all Israel comes to appear before the LORD your God at the place he will choose, you shall read this law before them in their hearing. 12 Assemble the people—men, women, and children, and the foreigners residing in your towns—so they can listen and learn to fear the LORD your God and follow carefully all the words of this law. 13 Their children, who do not know this law, must hear it and learn to fear the LORD your God as long as you live in the land you are crossing the Jordan to possess." 14 The LORD said to Moses, "Now the day of your death is near. Call Joshua and present yourselves at the tent of meeting, where I will commission him." So Moses and Joshua came and presented themselves at the tent of meeting. 15 Then the LORD appeared at the tent in a pillar of cloud, and the cloud stood over the entrance to the tent 16 And the LORD said to Moses: "You are going to rest with your ancestors, and these people will soon prostitute themselves to the foreign gods of the land they are entering. They will forsake me and break the covenant I made with them. 17 And in that day I will become angry with them and forsake them; I will hide my face from them, and they will be destroyed. Many disasters and calamities will come on them, and in that day they will ask, 'Have not these disasters come on us because our God is not with us?' 18 And I will certainly hide my face in that day because of all their wickedness in turning to other gods 19 "Now write down this song and teach it to the Israelites and have them sing it, so that it may be a witness for me against them. 20 When I have brought them into the land flowing with milk and honey, the land I promised on oath to their ancestors, and when they eat their fill and thrive, they will turn to other gods and worship them, rejecting me and breaking my covenant. 21 And when many disasters and calamities come on them, this song will testify against them, because it will not be forgotten by their descendants. I know what they are disposed to do, even before I bring them into the land I promised them on oath." 22 So Moses wrote down this song that day and taught it to the Israelites 23 The LORD gave this command to Joshua son of Nun: "Be strong and courageous, for you will bring the Israelites into the land I promised them on oath, and I myself will be with you." 24 After Moses finished writing in a book the words of this law from beginning to end, 25 he gave this command to the Levites who carried the ark of the covenant of the LORD: 26 "Take this Book of the Law and place it beside the ark of the covenant of the LORD your God. There it will remain as a witness against you. 27 For I know how rebellious and stiff-necked you are. If you have been rebellious against the LORD while I am still alive and with you, how much more will you rebel after I die! 28 Assemble before me all the elders of your tribes and all your officials, so that I can speak these words in their hearing and call the heavens and the earth to testify against them. 29 For I know that after my death you are sure to become utterly corrupt and to turn from the way I have commanded you. In days to come, disaster will fall on you because you will do evil in the sight of the LORD and arouse his anger by what your hands have made." 30 And Moses recited the words of this song from beginning to end in the hearing of the whole assembly of Israel:

Chapter 32

1 Listen, you heavens, and I will speak; hear, you earth, the words of my mouth. 2 Let my teaching fall like rain and my words descend like dew, like showers on new grass, like abundant rain on tender plants 3 I will proclaim the name of the LORD. Oh, praise the greatness of our God! 4 He is the Rock, his works are perfect, and all his ways are just. A faithful God who does no wrong, upright and just is he 5 They are corrupt and not his children; to their shame they are a warped and crooked generation. 6 Is this the way you repay the LORD, you foolish and unwise people? Is he not your Father, your Creator, who made you and formed you? 7 Remember the days of old; consider the generations long past. Ask your father and he will tell you, your elders, and they will explain to you. 8 When the Most High gave the nations their inheritance, when he divided all mankind, he set up boundaries for the peoples according to the number of the sons of Israel. 9 For the LORD's portion is his people, Jacob his allotted inheritance 10 In a desert land he found him, in a barren and howling waste. He shielded him and cared for him; he guarded him as the apple of his eye, 11 like an eagle that stirs up its nest and hovers over its young, that spreads its wings to catch them and carries them aloft. 12 The LORD alone led him; no foreign god was with him 13 He made him ride on the heights of the land and fed him with the fruit of the fields. He nourished him with honey from the rock and with oil from the flinty crag, 14 with curds and milk from herd and flock and with fattened lambs and goats, with choice rams of Bashan and the finest kernels of wheat. You drank the foaming blood of the grape 15 Jeshurun grew fat and kicked; filled with food, they became heavy and sleek. They abandoned the God who made them and rejected the Rock their Savior. 16 They made him jealous with their foreign gods and angered him with their detestable idols. 17 They sacrificed to false gods, which are not God—gods they had not known, gods that recently appeared, gods your ancestors did not fear. 18 You deserted the Rock, who fathered you; you forgot the God who gave you birth 19 The LORD saw this and rejected them because he was angered by his sons and daughters. 20 "I will hide my face from them," he said, "and see what their end will be; for they are a perverse generation, children who are unfaithful. 21 They made me jealous by what is no god and angered me with their worthless idols. I will make them envious by those who are not a people; I will make them angry by a nation that has no understanding. 22 For a fire will be kindled by my wrath, one that burns down to the realm of the dead below. It will devour the earth and its harvests and set afire the foundations of the mountains 23 "I will heap calamities on them and spend my arrows against them. 24 I will send wasting famine against them, consuming pestilence and deadly plague; I will send against them the fangs of wild beasts, the venom of vipers that glide in the dust. 25 In the street the sword will make them childless; in their homes, terror will reign. The young men and young women will perish, the infants and those with gray hair. 26 I said I would scatter them and erase their name from human memory, 27 but I dreaded the taunt of the enemy, lest the adversary misunderstand and say, 'Our hand has triumphed; the LORD has not done all this.'" 28 They are a nation without sense, there is no discernment in them. 29 If only they were wise and would understand this and discern what their end will be! 30 How could one man chase a thousand or two put ten thousand to flight, unless their Rock had

sold them, unless the LORD had given them up? 31 For their rock is not like our Rock, as even our enemies concede. 32 Their vine comes from the vine of Sodom and from the fields of Gomorrah. Their grapes are filled with poison, and their clusters with bitterness. 33 Their wine is the venom of serpents, the deadly poison of cobras 34 "Have I not kept this in reserve and sealed it in my vaults? 35 It is mine to avenge; I will repay. In due time their foot will slip; their day of disaster is near and their doom rushes upon them." 36 The LORD will vindicate his people and relent concerning his servants when he sees their strength is gone and no one is left, slave or free. 37 He will say: "Now where are their gods, the rock they took refuge in, 38 the gods who ate the fat of their sacrifices and drank the wine of their drink offerings? Let them rise up to help you! Let them give you shelter! 39 "See now that I myself am he! There is no god besides me. I put to death and I bring to life, I have wounded and I will heal, and no one can deliver out of my hand. 40 I lift my hand to heaven and solemnly swear: As surely as I live forever, 41 when I sharpen my flashing sword and my hand grasps it in judgment, I will take vengeance on my adversaries and repay those who hate me. 42 I will make my arrows drunk with blood, while my sword devours flesh: the blood of the slain and the captives, the heads of the enemy leaders." 43 Rejoice, you nations, with his people, for he will avenge the blood of his servants; he will take vengeance on his enemies and make atonement for his land and people 44 Moses came with Joshua son of Nun and spoke all the words of this song in the hearing of the people. 45 When Moses finished reciting all these words to all Israel, 46 he said to them, "Take to heart all the words I have solemnly declared to you this day, so that you may command your children to obey carefully all the words of this law. 47 They are not just idle words for you—they are your life. By them you will live long in the land you are crossing the Jordan to possess." 48 On that same day the LORD told Moses, 49 "Go up into the Abarim Range to Mount Nebo in Moab, across from Jericho, and view Canaan, the land I am giving the Israelites as their own possession. 50 There on the mountain that you have climbed you will die and be gathered to your people, just as your brother Aaron died on Mount Hor and was gathered to his people. 51 This is because both of you broke faith with me in the presence of the Israelites at the waters of Meribah Kadesh in the Desert of Zin and because you did not uphold my holiness among the Israelites. 52 Therefore, you will see the land only from a distance; you will not enter the land I am giving to the people of Israel."

Chapter 33

1 This is the blessing that Moses the man of God pronounced on the Israelites before his death. 2 He said: "The LORD came from Sinai and dawned over them from Seir; he shone forth from Mount Paran. He came with myriads of holy ones from the south, from his mountain slopes. 3 Surely it is you who love the people; all the holy ones are in your hand. At your feet they all bow down, and from you receive instruction, 4 the law that Moses gave us, the possession of the assembly of Jacob. 5 He was king over Jeshurun when the leaders of the people assembled, along with the tribes of Israel 6 "Let Reuben live and not die, nor his people be few." 7 And this he said about Judah: "Hear, LORD, the cry of Judah; bring him to his people. With his own hands he defends his cause. Oh, be his help against his foes!" 8 About Levi he said: "Your Thummim and Urim belong to your faithful servant. You tested him at Massah; you contended with him at the waters of Meribah. 9 He

said of his father and mother, 'I have no regard for them.' He did not recognize his brothers or acknowledge his own children, but he watched over your word and guarded your covenant. 10 He teaches your precepts to Jacob and your law to Israel. He offers incense before you and whole burnt offerings on your altar. 11 Bless all his skills, LORD, and be pleased with the work of his hands. Strike down those who rise against him, his foes till they rise no more." 12 About Benjamin he said: "Let the beloved of the LORD rest secure in him, for he shields him all day long, and the one the LORD loves rests between his shoulders." 13 About Joseph he said: "May the LORD bless his land with the precious dew from heaven above and with the deep waters that lie below; 14 with the best the sun brings forth and the finest the moon can yield; 15 with the choicest gifts of the ancient mountains and the fruitfulness of the everlasting hills; 16 with the best gifts of the earth and its fullness and the favor of him who dwelt in the burning bush. Let all these rest on the head of Joseph, on the brow of the prince among his brothers. 17 In majesty he is like a firstborn bull; his horns are the horns of a wild ox. With them he will gore the nations, even those at the ends of the earth. Such are the ten thousands of Ephraim; such are the thousands of Manasseh." 18 About Zebulun he said: "Rejoice, Zebulun, in your going out, and you, Issachar, in your tents. 19 They will summon peoples to the mountain and there offer the sacrifices of the righteous; they will feast on the abundance of the seas, on the treasures hidden in the sand." 20 About Gad he said: "Blessed is he who enlarges Gad's domain! Gad lives there like a lion, tearing at arm or head. 21 He chose the best land for himself; the leader's portion was kept for him. When the heads of the people assembled, he carried out the LORD's righteous will and his judgments concerning Israel." 22 About Dan he said: "Dan is a lion's cub, springing out of Bashan." 23 About Naphtali he said: "Naphtali is abounding with the favor of the LORD and is full of his blessing; he will inherit southward to the lake." 24 About Asher he said: "Most blessed of sons is Asher; let him be favored by his brothers, and let him bathe his feet in oil. 25 The bolts of your gates will be iron and bronze, and your strength will equal your days 26 "There is no one like the God of Jeshurun, who rides across the heavens to help you and on the clouds in his majesty. 27 The eternal God is your refuge, and underneath are the everlasting arms. He will drive out your enemies before you, saying, 'Destroy them!' 28 So Israel will live in safety; Jacob will dwell secure in a land of grain and new wine, where the heavens drop dew. 29 Blessed are you, Israel! Who is like you, a people saved by the LORD? He is your shield and helper and your glorious sword. Your enemies will cower before you, and you will tread on their heights."

Chapter 34

1 Then Moses climbed Mount Nebo from the plains of Moab to the top of Pisgah, across from Jericho. There the LORD showed him the whole land—from Gilead to Dan, 2 all of Naphtali, the territory of Ephraim and Manasseh, all the land of Judah as far as the Mediterranean Sea, 3 the Negev and the whole region from the Valley of Jericho, the City of Palms, as far as Zoar. 4 Then the LORD said to him, "This is the land I promised on oath to Abraham, Isaac and Jacob when I said, 'I will give it to your descendants.' I have let you see it with your eyes, but you will not cross over into it." 5 And Moses the servant of the LORD died there in Moab, as the LORD had said. 6 He buried him in Moab, in the valley opposite Beth Peor, but to this day no one knows where his grave is. 7 Moses was a hundred and twenty years old when he

died, yet his eyes were not weak nor his strength gone. 8 The Israelites grieved for Moses in the plains of Moab thirty days, until the time of weeping and mourning was over 9 Now Joshua son of Nun was filled with the spirit of wisdom because Moses had laid his hands on him. So the Israelites listened to him and did what the LORD had commanded Moses 10 Since then, no prophet has risen in Israel like Moses, whom the LORD knew face to face, 11 who did all those signs and wonders the LORD sent him to do in Egypt—to Pharaoh and to all his officials and to his whole land. 12 For no one has ever shown the mighty power or performed the awesome deeds that Moses did in the sight of all Israel

2. HISTORICAL BOOKS

6. Joshua

Chapter 1

After the death of Moses, the Lord's servant, the Lord spoke to Joshua, the son of Nun and Moses' minister. He said, "Get up and go out from here, you and all the people, to the land I am giving to the children of Israel. My servant Moses is dead; now therefore, arise and go out of this land, you and all the people, to the land I am giving them. Every place where you set your foot will be yours, as I promised Moses. From the wilderness and Lebanon as far as the great river, the river Euphrates, all the land of the Hittites, and to the Great Sea toward the setting of the sun will be your land. No one will be able to stand against you all the days of your life; as I was with Moses, so I will be with you; I will never leave you nor forsake you Be strong and courageous, for you will lead these people to inherit the land I swore to their ancestors to give them. Be strong and very courageous, ensuring that you follow all the law my servant Moses commanded you. Do not turn from it to the right or to the left, so that you may be successful wherever you go. Keep this Book of the Law always on your lips; meditate on it day and night, so that you may be careful to do everything written in it. Then you will be prosperous and successful. Have I not commanded you? Be strong and courageous. Do not be afraid; do not be discouraged, for the Lord your God will be with you wherever you go." Joshua then commanded the officers of the people, "Go through the camp and tell the people, 'Prepare your provisions, for in three days you will cross the Jordan here to go in and take possession of the land the Lord your God is giving you for your own.'" To the Reubenites, Gadites, and the half-tribe of Manasseh, Joshua said, "Remember the command that Moses, the servant of the Lord, gave you: 'The Lord your God is giving you rest and has granted you this land.' Your wives, children, and livestock may stay in the land that Moses gave you east of the Jordan, but all your fighting men, ready for battle, must cross over ahead of your fellow Israelites. You are to help them until the Lord gives them rest, as he has done for you, and until they too have taken possession of the land the Lord your God is giving them. After that, you may go back and occupy your own land, which Moses the servant of the Lord gave you east of the Jordan toward the sunrise." They answered Joshua, "Whatever you have commanded us we will do, and wherever you send us we will go. Just as we fully obeyed Moses, so we will obey you. Only may the Lord your God be with you as he was with Moses. Whoever rebels against your word and does not obey it, whatever you may command them, will be put to death. Only be strong and courageous!"

Chapter 2

Then Joshua, the son of Nun, secretly sent two spies from Shittim, saying, "Go, look over the land, especially Jericho." So they went and entered the house of a prostitute named Rahab and stayed there. The king of Jericho was told, "Look, some of the Israelites have come here tonight to spy out the land." So the king of Jericho sent this message to Rahab: "Bring out the men who came to you and entered your house because they have come to spy out the whole land." But Rahab had taken the two men and hidden them. She said, "Yes, the men came to me, but I did not know where they had come from. At dusk, when it was time to close the city gate, they left. I don't know which way they went. Go after them quickly. You may catch up with them." (But she had taken them up to the roof and hidden them under the stalks of flax she had laid out on the roof.) So the men set out in pursuit of the spies on the road that leads to the fords of the Jordan, and as soon as the pursuers had gone out, the gate was shut Before the spies lay down for the night, Rahab went up on the roof and said to them, "I know that the Lord has given you this land and that a great fear of you has fallen on us, so that all who live in this country are melting in fear because of you. We have heard how the Lord dried up the water of the Red Sea for you when you came out of Egypt and what you did to Sihon and Og, the two kings of the Amorites east of the Jordan, whom you completely destroyed. When we heard of it, our hearts melted in fear, and everyone's courage failed because of you, for the Lord your God is God in heaven above and on the earth below. Now then, please swear to me by the Lord that you will show kindness to my family because I have shown kindness to you. Give me a sure sign that you will spare the lives of my father and mother, my brothers and sisters, and all who belong to them—and that you will save us from death." "Our lives for your lives!" the men assured her. "If you don't tell what we are doing, we will treat you kindly and faithfully when the Lord gives us the land." So she let them down by a rope through the window, for the house she lived in was part of the city wall. She said to them, "Go to the hills so the pursuers will not find you. Hide yourselves there for three days until they return, and then go on your way." Now the men had said to her, "This oath you made us swear will not be binding on us unless, when we enter the land, you have tied this scarlet cord in the window through which you let us down, and unless you have brought your father and mother, your brothers and all your family into your house. If any of them go outside your house into the street, their blood will be on their own heads; we will not be responsible. As for those who are in the house with you, their blood will be on our head if a hand is laid on them. But if you tell what we are doing, we will be released from the oath you made us swear." "Agreed," she replied. "Let it be as you say." So she sent them away, and they departed. And she tied the scarlet cord in the window When they left, they went into the hills and stayed there three days until the pursuers had searched all along the road and returned without finding them. Then the two men started back. They went down out of the hills, forded the river, and came to Joshua, son of Nun, and told him everything that had happened to them. They said to Joshua, "The Lord has surely given the whole land into our hands; all the people are melting in fear because of us."

Chapter 3

Early in the morning, Joshua and all the Israelites set out from Shittim and went to the Jordan, where they camped before crossing over. After three days, the officers went throughout the camp, giving orders to the people: "When you see the ark of the covenant of the Lord your God, and the Levitical priests carrying it, you are to move out from your positions and follow it. Then you will know which way to go since you have never been this way before. But keep a distance of about two thousand cubits between you and the ark; do not go near it." Joshua told the people, "Consecrate yourselves, for tomorrow the Lord will do amazing things among you." Joshua said to the priests, "Take up the ark of the covenant and pass on ahead of the people." So they took it up and went ahead of them And the Lord said to Joshua, "Today I will begin to exalt you in the eyes of all Israel so they may know that I am with you as I was with Moses. Tell the priests who carry the ark of the covenant: 'When you reach the edge of the Jordan's waters, go and stand in the river.'" Joshua said to the Israelites, "Come here and listen to the words of the Lord your God. This is how you will know that the living God is among you and that he will certainly drive out before you the Canaanites, Hittites, Hivites, Perizzites, Girgashites, Amorites, and Jebusites. See, the ark of the covenant of the Lord of all the earth will go into the Jordan ahead of you. Now then, choose twelve men from the tribes of Israel, one from each tribe. And as soon as the priests who carry the ark of the Lord—the Lord of all the earth—set foot in the Jordan, its waters flowing downstream will be cut off and stand up in a heap." So when the people broke camp to cross the Jordan, the priests carrying the ark of the covenant went ahead of them. Now the Jordan is at flood stage all during harvest. Yet as soon as the priests who carried the ark reached the Jordan and their feet touched the water's edge, the water from upstream stopped flowing. It piled up in a heap a great distance away, at a town called Adam in the vicinity of Zarethan, while the water flowing down to the Sea of the Arabah (that is, the Dead Sea) was completely cut off. So the people crossed over opposite Jericho. The priests who carried the ark of the covenant of the Lord stopped in the middle of the Jordan and stood on dry ground while all Israel passed by until the whole nation had completed the crossing on dry ground

Chapter 4

When the whole nation had finished crossing the Jordan, the Lord said to Joshua, "Choose twelve men from among the people, one from each tribe, and tell them to take up twelve stones from the middle of the Jordan, from right where the priests are standing, and carry them over with you and put them down at the place where you stay tonight." So Joshua called together the twelve men he had appointed from the Israelites, one from each tribe, and said to them, "Go over before the ark of the Lord your God into the middle of the Jordan. Each of you is to take up a stone on his shoulder, according to the number of the tribes of the Israelites, to serve as a sign among you. In the future, when your children ask you, 'What do these stones mean?' tell them that the flow of the Jordan was cut off before the ark of the covenant of the Lord. When it crossed the Jordan, the waters of the Jordan were cut off. These stones are to be a memorial to the people of Israel forever." So the Israelites did as Joshua commanded. They took twelve stones from the middle of the Jordan, according to the number of the tribes of the Israelites, as the Lord had told Joshua; and they carried them over with them to their camp, where they put them down. Joshua set up the twelve stones that had been in the middle of the Jordan at the spot where the priests who carried the ark of the covenant had stood. And they are there to this day Now the priests who carried the ark remained standing in the middle of the Jordan until everything the Lord had commanded Joshua was done by the people, just as Moses had directed Joshua. The people hurried over, and as soon as all of them had crossed, the ark of the Lord and the priests came to the other side while the people watched. The men of Reuben, Gad, and the half-tribe of Manasseh crossed over, ready for battle, in front of the Israelites, as Moses had directed them. About forty thousand armed for battle crossed over before the Lord to the plains of Jericho for war That day the Lord exalted Joshua in the sight of all Israel; and they stood in awe of him all the days of his life, just as they had stood in awe of Moses. Then the Lord said to Joshua, "Command the priests carrying the ark of the covenant law to come up out of the Jordan." So Joshua commanded the priests, "Come up out of the Jordan." And the priests came up out of the river carrying the ark of the covenant of the Lord. No sooner had they set their feet on the dry ground than the waters of the Jordan returned to their place and ran at flood stage as before On the tenth day of the first month, the people went up from the Jordan and camped at Gilgal on the eastern border of Jericho. And Joshua set up at Gilgal the twelve stones they had taken out of the Jordan. He said to the Israelites, "In the future, when your descendants ask their parents, 'What do these stones mean?' tell them, 'Israel crossed the Jordan on dry ground.' For the Lord your God dried up the Jordan before you until you had crossed over. The Lord your God did to the Jordan what he had done to the Red Sea when he dried it up before us until we had crossed over. He did this so that all the peoples of the earth might know that the hand of the Lord is powerful and so that you might always fear the Lord your God."

Chapter 5

When all the Amorite kings west of the Jordan and all the Canaanite kings along the coast heard how the Lord had dried up the Jordan before the Israelites until they had crossed over, their hearts melted in fear, and they no longer had the courage to face the Israelites. At that time, the Lord said to Joshua, "Make flint knives and circumcise the Israelites again." So Joshua made flint knives and circumcised the Israelites at Gibeath Haaraloth Now this is why he did so: All those who came out of Egypt—all the men of military age—died in the wilderness on the way after leaving Egypt. All the people that came out had been circumcised, but all the people born in the wilderness during the journey from Egypt had not. The Israelites had moved about in the wilderness for forty years until all the men who were of military age when they left Egypt had died, since they had not obeyed the Lord. For the Lord had sworn to them that they would not see the land he had solemnly promised their ancestors to give us, a land flowing with milk and honey. So he raised up their sons in their place, and these were the ones Joshua circumcised. They were still uncircumcised because they had not been circumcised on the way. And after the whole nation had been circumcised, they remained where they were in camp until they were healed Then the Lord said to Joshua, "Today I have rolled away the reproach of Egypt from you." So the place has been called Gilgal to this day. On the evening of the fourteenth day of the month, while camped at Gilgal on the plains of Jericho, the Israelites celebrated the Passover. The day after the Passover, that very day, they ate some of the produce of the land: unleavened bread and roasted grain. The manna stopped the day after they ate this food from the land; there was no longer any manna for the Israelites, but that year they ate the produce of Canaan Now when Joshua was near Jericho, he looked up and saw a man standing in front of him with a drawn sword in his hand. Joshua went up to him and asked, "Are you for us or for our enemies?" "Neither," he replied, "but as commander of the army of the Lord, I have now come." Then Joshua fell facedown to the ground in reverence and asked him, "What message does my Lord have for his servant?" The commander of the Lord's army replied, "Take off your sandals, for the place where you are standing is holy." And Joshua did so

Chapter 6

Jericho was tightly shut up because of the Israelites; no one could go out or come in. The Lord said to Joshua, "See, I have delivered Jericho into your hands, along with its king and its fighting men. March around the city once with all the armed men. Do this for six days. Have seven priests carry trumpets of ram's horns in front of the ark. On the seventh day, march around the city seven times, with the priests blowing the trumpets. When you hear them sound a long blast on the trumpets, have all the people give a loud shout; then the wall of the city will collapse, and the people will go up, every man straight in." So Joshua son of Nun called the priests and said to them, "Take up the ark of the covenant of the Lord and have seven priests carry trumpets in front of it." And he ordered the people, "Advance! March around the city, with the armed guard going ahead of the ark of the Lord." When Joshua had spoken to the people, the seven priests carrying the seven trumpets before the Lord went forward, blowing their trumpets, and the ark of the Lord's covenant followed them. The armed guard marched ahead of the priests who blew the trumpets, and the rear guard followed the ark. All this time the trumpets were sounding. But Joshua had commanded the people, "Do not give a war cry, do not raise your voices, do not say a word until the day I tell you to shout. Then shout!" So he had the ark of the Lord carried around the city, circling it once. Then the people returned to camp and spent the night there Joshua got up early the next morning and the priests took up the ark of the Lord. The seven priests carrying the seven trumpets went forward, marching before the ark of the Lord and blowing the trumpets. The armed men went ahead of them and the rear guard followed the ark of the Lord, while the trumpets kept sounding. So on the second day they marched around the city once and returned to the camp. They did this for six days On the seventh day, they got up at daybreak and marched around the city seven times in the same manner, except that on that day they circled the city seven times. The seventh time around, when the priests sounded the trumpet blast, Joshua commanded the people, "Shout! For the Lord has given you the city! The city and all that is in it are to be devoted to the Lord. Only Rahab the prostitute and all who are with her in her house shall be spared, because she hid the spies we sent. But keep away from the devoted things, so that you will not bring about your own destruction by taking any of them. Otherwise, you will make the camp of Israel liable to destruction and bring trouble on it. All the silver and gold and the articles of bronze and iron are sacred to the Lord and must go into his treasury." When the trumpets sounded, the people shouted, and at the sound of the trumpet, when the people gave a loud shout, the wall collapsed; so every man charged straight in, and they took the city. They devoted the city to the Lord and destroyed with the sword every living thing in it—men and women, young and old, cattle, sheep, and donkeys. Joshua said to the two men who had spied out the land, "Go into the prostitute's house and bring her out and all who belong to her, in accordance with your oath to her." So the young men who had done the spying went in and brought out Rahab, her father and mother and brothers and all who belonged to her. They brought out her entire family and put them in a place outside the camp of Israel Then they burned the whole city and everything in it, but they put the silver and gold and the articles of bronze and iron into the treasury of the Lord's house. But Joshua spared Rahab the prostitute, with her family and all who belonged to her, because she hid the men Joshua had sent as spies to Jericho—and she lives among the Israelites to this day At that time Joshua pronounced this solemn oath: "Cursed before the Lord is the man who undertakes to rebuild this city, Jericho: 'At the cost of his firstborn son will he lay its foundations; at the cost of his youngest will he set up its gates.'" So the Lord was with Joshua, and his fame spread throughout the land

Chapter 7

The Israelites were unfaithful in regard to the devoted things; Achan son of Carmi, the son of Zabdi, the son of Zerah, of the tribe of Judah, took some of them. So the Lord's anger burned against Israel Now Joshua sent men from Jericho to Ai, which is near Beth Aven to the east of Bethel, and told them, "Go up and spy out the region." So the men went up and spied out Ai. When they returned to Joshua, they said, "Not all the army will have to go up against Ai. Send two or three thousand men to take it and do not weary the whole army, for only a few people live there." So about three thousand went up, but they were routed by the men of Ai, who killed about thirty-six of them. They chased the Israelites from the city gate as far as the stone quarries and struck them down on the slopes. At this, the hearts of the people melted in fear and became like water Then Joshua tore his clothes and fell facedown to the ground before the ark of the Lord, remaining there till evening. The elders of Israel did the same, and sprinkled dust on their heads. And Joshua said, "Alas, Sovereign Lord, why did you ever bring this people across the Jordan to deliver us into the hands of the Amorites to destroy us? If only we had been content to stay on the other side of the Jordan! Pardon your servant, Lord. What can I say, now that Israel has been routed by its enemies? The Canaanites and the other people of the country will hear about this, and they will surround us and wipe out our name from the earth. What then will you do for your own great name?" The Lord said to Joshua, "Stand up! What are you doing down on your face? Israel has sinned; they have violated my covenant, which I commanded them to keep. They have taken some of the devoted things; they have stolen, they have lied, they have put them with their own possessions. That is why the Israelites cannot stand against their enemies; they turn their backs and run because they have been made liable to destruction. I will not be with you anymore unless you destroy whatever among you is devoted to destruction "Go, consecrate the people. Tell them, 'Consecrate yourselves in preparation for tomorrow; for this is what the Lord, the God of Israel, says: There are devoted things among you, Israel. You cannot stand against your enemies until you remove them "In the morning, present yourselves tribe by tribe. The tribe the Lord chooses shall come forward clan by clan; the clan the Lord chooses shall come forward family by family; and the family the Lord chooses shall come forward man by man. Whoever is caught with the devoted things shall be destroyed by fire, along with all that belongs to him. He has violated the covenant of the Lord and has done an outrageous thing in Israel!'" Early the next morning Joshua had Israel come forward by tribes, and Judah was chosen. The clans of Judah came forward, and the Zerahites were chosen. He had the clan of the Zerahites come forward by families, and Zabdi was chosen. Joshua had his family come forward man by man, and Achan son of Carmi, the son of Zabdi, the son of Zerah, of the tribe of Judah, was chosen Then Joshua said to Achan, "My son, give glory to the Lord, the God of Israel, and honor him. Tell me what you have done; do not hide it from me." Achan replied, "It is true! I have sinned against the Lord, the God of Israel. This is what I have done: When I saw in the plunder a beautiful robe from Babylonia, two hundred shekels of silver and a bar of gold weighing fifty shekels, I coveted them and took them. They are hidden in the ground inside my tent, with the silver underneath." So Joshua sent messengers, and they ran to the tent, and there it was, hidden in his tent, with the silver underneath. They took the things from the tent, brought them to Joshua and all the Israelites and spread them out before the Lord Then Joshua, together with all Israel, took Achan son of Zerah, the silver, the robe, the gold bar, his sons and daughters, his cattle, donkeys and sheep, his tent and all that he had, to the Valley of Achor. Joshua said, "Why have you brought this trouble on us? The Lord will bring trouble on you today." Then all Israel stoned him, and after they had stoned the rest, they burned them. Over Achan they heaped up a large pile of rocks, which remains to this day. Then the Lord turned from his fierce anger. Therefore that place has been called the Valley of Achor ever since

Chapter 8

Then the Lord said to Joshua, "Do not be afraid; do not be discouraged. Take the whole army with you, and go up and attack Ai. For I have delivered into your hands the king of Ai, his people, his city and his land. You shall do to Ai and its king as you did to Jericho and its king, except that you may carry off their plunder and livestock for yourselves. Set an ambush behind the city." So Joshua and the whole army moved out to attack Ai. He chose thirty thousand of his best fighting men and sent them out at night with these orders: "Listen carefully. You are to set an ambush behind the city. Don't go very far from it. All of you be on the alert. I and all those with me will advance on the city, and when the men come out against us as they did before, we will flee from them. They will pursue us until we have lured them away from the city, for they will say, 'They are running away from us as they did before.' So when we flee from them, you are to rise up from ambush and take the city. The Lord your God will give it into your hand. When you have taken the city, set it on fire. Do what the Lord has commanded. See to it; you have my orders." Then Joshua sent them off, and they went to the place of ambush and lay in wait between Bethel and Ai, to the west of Ai—but Joshua spent that night with the people Early the next morning Joshua mustered his army, and he and the leaders of Israel marched before them to Ai. The entire force that was with him marched up and approached the city and arrived in front of it. They set up camp north of Ai, with the valley between them and the city. Joshua had taken about five thousand men and set them in ambush between Bethel and Ai, to the west of the city. So the soldiers took up their positions—with the main camp to the north of the city and the ambush to the west of it. That night Joshua went into the valley When the king of Ai saw this, he and all the men of the city hurried out early in the morning to meet Israel in battle at a certain place overlooking the Arabah. But he did not know that an ambush had been set against him behind the city. Joshua and all Israel let themselves be driven back before them, and they fled toward the wilderness. All the men of Ai were called to pursue them, and they pursued Joshua and were lured away from the city. Not a man remained in Ai or Bethel who did not go after Israel. They left the city open and went in pursuit of Israel Then the Lord said to Joshua, "Hold out toward Ai the javelin that is in your hand, for into your hand I will deliver the city." So Joshua held out toward the city the javelin that was in his hand. As soon as he did this, the men in the ambush rose quickly from their position and rushed forward. They entered the city and captured it and quickly set it on fire The men of Ai looked back and saw the smoke of the city rising up into the sky, but they had no chance to escape in any direction; the Israelites who had been fleeing toward the wilderness had turned back against their pursuers. For when Joshua and all Israel saw that the ambush had taken the city and that smoke was going up from it, they turned around and attacked the men of Ai. Those in the ambush also came out of the city against them, so that they were caught in the middle, with Israelites on both sides. Israel cut them down, leaving them neither survivors nor fugitives. But they took the king of Ai alive and brought him to Joshua

When Israel had finished killing all the men of Ai in the fields and in the wilderness where they had chased them, and when every one of them had been put to the sword, all the Israelites returned to Ai and killed those who were in it. Twelve thousand men and women fell that day—all the people of Ai. For Joshua did not draw back the hand that held out his javelin until he had destroyed all who lived in Ai. But Israel did carry off for themselves the livestock and plunder of this city, as the Lord had instructed Joshua So Joshua burned Ai and made it a permanent heap of ruins, a desolate place to this day. He impaled the body of the king of Ai on a pole and left it there until evening. At sunset, Joshua ordered them to take the body from the pole and throw it down at the entrance of the city gate. And they raised a large pile of rocks over it, which remains to this day Then Joshua built on Mount Ebal an altar to the Lord, the God of Israel, as Moses the servant of the Lord had commanded the Israelites. He built it according to what is written in the Book of the Law of Moses—an altar of uncut stones, on which no iron tool had been used. On it they offered to the Lord burnt offerings and sacrificed fellowship offerings. There, in the presence of the Israelites, Joshua wrote on stones a copy of the law of Moses. All the Israelites, with their elders, officials and judges, were standing on both sides of the ark of the covenant of the Lord, facing the Levitical priests who carried it. Both the foreigners living among them and the native-born were there. Half of the people stood in front of Mount Gerizim and half of them in front of Mount Ebal, as Moses the servant of the Lord had formerly commanded when he gave instructions to bless the people of Israel Afterward, Joshua read all the words of the law—the blessings and the curses—just as it is written in the Book of the Law. There was not a word of all that Moses had commanded that Joshua did not read to the whole assembly of Israel, including the women and children, and the foreigners who lived among them

Chapter 9

When all the kings west of the Jordan heard about these things—the kings in the hill country, in the western foothills, and along the entire coast of the Mediterranean Sea as far as Lebanon (the kings of the Hittites, Amorites, Canaanites, Perizzites, Hivites and Jebusites)—they came together to wage war against Joshua and Israel However, when the people of Gibeon heard what Joshua had done to Jericho and Ai, they resorted to a ruse: They went as a delegation whose donkeys were loaded with worn-out sacks and old wineskins, cracked and mended. They put worn and patched sandals on their feet and wore old clothes. All the bread of their food supply was dry and moldy. Then they went to Joshua in the camp at Gilgal and said to him and the Israelites, "We have come from a distant country; make a treaty with us." The Israelites said to the Hivites, "But perhaps you live near us, so how can we make a treaty with you?" "We are your servants," they said to Joshua But Joshua asked, "Who are you and where do you come from?" They answered: "Your servants have come from a very distant country because of the fame of the Lord your God. For we have heard reports of him: all that he did in Egypt, and all that he did to the two kings of the Amorites east of the Jordan—Sihon king of Heshbon, and Og king of Bashan, who reigned in Ashtaroth. And our elders and all those living in our country said to us, 'Take provisions for your journey; go and meet them and say to them, "We are your servants; make a treaty with us."' This bread of ours was warm when we packed it at home on the day we left to come to you. But now see how dry and moldy it is. And these wineskins that we filled were new, but see how cracked they are. And our clothes and sandals are worn out by the very long journey." The Israelites sampled their provisions but did not inquire of the Lord. Then Joshua made a treaty of peace with them to let them live, and the leaders of the assembly ratified it by oath Three days after they made the treaty with the Gibeonites, the Israelites heard that they were neighbors, living near them. So the Israelites set out and on the third day came to their cities: Gibeon, Kephirah, Beeroth and Kiriath Jearim. But the Israelites did not attack them, because the leaders of the assembly had sworn an oath to them by the Lord, the God of Israel The whole assembly grumbled against the leaders, but all the leaders answered, "We have given them our oath by the Lord, the God of Israel, and we cannot touch them now. This is what we will do to them: We will let them live, so that God's wrath will not fall on us for breaking the oath we swore to them." They continued, "Let them live, but let them be woodcutters and water carriers in the service of the whole assembly." So the leaders' promise to them was kept Then Joshua summoned the Gibeonites and said, "Why did you deceive us by saying, 'We live a long way from you,' while actually you live near us? You are now under a curse: You will never be released from service as woodcutters and water carriers for the house of my God." They answered Joshua, "Your servants were clearly told how the Lord your God had commanded his servant Moses to give you the whole land and to wipe out all its inhabitants from before you. So we feared for our lives because of you, and that is why we did this. We are now in your hands. Do to us whatever seems good and right to you." So Joshua saved them from the Israelites, and they did not kill them. That day he made the Gibeonites woodcutters and water carriers for the assembly, to provide for the needs of the altar of the Lord at the place the Lord would choose. And that is what they are to this day

Chapter 10

Now Adoni-Zedek king of Jerusalem heard that Joshua had taken Ai and totally destroyed it, doing to Ai and its king as he had done to Jericho and its king, and that the people of Gibeon had made a treaty of peace with Israel and had become their allies. He and his people were very much alarmed at this, because Gibeon was an important city, like one of the royal cities; it was larger than Ai, and all its men were good fighters. So Adoni-Zedek king of Jerusalem appealed to Hoham king of Hebron, Piram king of Jarmuth, Japhia king of Lachish and Debir king of Eglon. "Come up and help me attack Gibeon," he said, "because it has made peace with Joshua and the Israelites." Then the five kings of the Amorites—the kings of Jerusalem, Hebron, Jarmuth, Lachish and Eglon—joined forces. They moved up with all their troops and took up positions against Gibeon and attacked it The Gibeonites then sent word to Joshua in the camp at Gilgal: "Do not abandon your servants. Come up to us quickly and save us! Help us, because all the Amorite kings from the hill country have joined forces against us." So Joshua marched up from Gilgal with his entire army, including all the best fighting men. The Lord said to Joshua, "Do not be afraid of them; I have given them into your hand. Not one of them will be able to withstand you." After an all-night march from Gilgal, Joshua took them by surprise. The Lord threw them into confusion before Israel, so Joshua and the Israelites defeated them completely at Gibeon. Israel pursued them along the road going up to Beth Horon and cut them down all the way to Azekah and Makkedah. As they fled before Israel on the road down from Beth Horon to Azekah, the Lord hurled large hailstones down on them, and more of them died from the hail than were killed by the swords of the Israelites On the day the Lord gave the Amorites over to Israel, Joshua said to the Lord in the presence of Israel: "Sun, stand still over Gibeon, and you, moon, over the Valley of Aijalon." So the sun stood still, and the moon stopped, till the nation avenged itself on its enemies, as it is written in the Book of Jashar The sun stopped in the middle of the sky and delayed going down about a full day. There has never been a day like it before or since, a day when the Lord listened to a human being. Surely the Lord was fighting for Israel! Then Joshua returned with all Israel to the camp at Gilgal Now the five kings had fled and hidden in the cave at Makkedah. When Joshua was told that the five kings had been found hiding in the cave at Makkedah, he said, "Roll large rocks up to the mouth of the cave, and post some men there to guard it. But don't stop; pursue your enemies! Attack them from the rear and don't let them reach their cities, for the Lord your God has given them into your hand." So Joshua and the Israelites defeated them completely, but a few survivors managed to reach their fortified cities. The whole army then returned safely to Joshua in the camp at Makkedah, and no one uttered a word against the Israelites Joshua said, "Open the mouth of the cave and bring those five kings out to me." So they brought the five kings out of the cave—the kings of Jerusalem, Hebron, Jarmuth, Lachish and Eglon. When they had brought these kings to Joshua, he summoned all the men of Israel and said to the army commanders who had come with him, "Come here and put your feet on the necks of these kings." So they came forward and placed their feet on their necks Joshua said to them, "Do not be afraid; do not be discouraged. Be strong and courageous. This is what the Lord will do to all the enemies you are going to fight." Then Joshua put the kings to death and exposed their bodies on five poles, and they were left hanging on the poles until evening. At sunset, Joshua gave the order, and they took them down from the poles and threw them into the cave where they had been hiding. At the mouth of the cave they placed large rocks, which are there to this day That day Joshua took Makkedah. He put the city and its king to the sword and totally destroyed everyone in it. He left no survivors. And he did to the king of Makkedah as he had done to the king of Jericho Then Joshua and all Israel with him moved on from Makkedah to Libnah and attacked it. The Lord also gave that city and its king into Israel's hand. The city and everyone in it Joshua put to the sword. He left no survivors there. And he did to its king as he had done to the king of Jericho Then Joshua and all Israel with him moved on from Libnah to Lachish; he took up positions against it and attacked it. The Lord gave Lachish into Israel's hands, and Joshua took it on the second day. The city and everyone in it he put to the sword, just as he had done to Libnah. Meanwhile, Horam king of Gezer had come up to help Lachish, but Joshua defeated him and his army—until no survivors were left Then Joshua and all Israel with him moved on from Lachish to Eglon; they took up positions against it and attacked it. They captured it that same day and put it to the sword and totally destroyed everyone in it, just as they had done to Lachish Then Joshua and all Israel with him went up from Eglon to Hebron and attacked it. They took the city and put it to the sword, together with its king, its villages and everyone in it. They left no survivors. Just as at Eglon, they totally destroyed it and everyone in it Then Joshua and all Israel with him turned around and attacked Debir. They took the city, its king and its villages, and put them to the sword. Everyone in it they totally destroyed. They left no survivors. They did to Debir and its king as they had done to Libnah and its king and to Hebron So Joshua subdued the whole region, including the hill country, the Negev, the western foothills and the mountain slopes, together with all their kings. He left no survivors. He totally destroyed all who breathed, just as the Lord, the God of Israel, had commanded. Joshua subdued them from Kadesh Barnea to Gaza and from the whole region of Goshen to Gibeon. All these kings and their lands Joshua conquered in one campaign, because the Lord, the God of Israel, fought for Israel Then Joshua returned with all Israel to the camp at Gilgal

Chapter 11

When Jabin, king of Hazor, heard this, he sent word to Jobab, king of Madon, to the kings of Shimron and Achshaph, and to the kings in the north, in the mountains, in the Arabah south of Kinnereth, in the western foothills, and in Naphoth Dor in the west. He also sent word to the Canaanites in the east and west, to the Amorites, Hittites, Perizzites, Jebusites in the hill country, and to the Hivites below Hermon in the region of Mizpah. They came out with all their troops and a large number of horses and chariots—a huge army, as numerous as the sand on the seashore. All these kings joined forces and made camp together at the waters of Merom to fight against Israel The Lord said to Joshua, "Do not be afraid of them, because by this time tomorrow I will hand all of them, slain, over to Israel. You are to hamstring their horses and burn their chariots." So Joshua and his whole army came against them suddenly at the waters of Merom and attacked them, and the Lord gave them into the hand of Israel. They defeated them and pursued them all the way to Greater Sidon, to Misrephoth Maim, and to the Valley of Mizpah on the east, until no survivors were left. Joshua did to them as the Lord had directed: he hamstrung their horses and burned their chariots At that time, Joshua turned back and captured Hazor and put its king to the sword. (Hazor had been the head of all these kingdoms.) Everyone in it they put to the sword. They totally destroyed them, not sparing anyone that breathed, and he burned Hazor itself. Joshua took all these royal cities and their kings and put them to the sword. He totally destroyed them, as Moses the servant of the Lord had commanded. Yet Israel did not burn any of the cities built on their mounds—except Hazor, which Joshua burned. The Israelites carried off for themselves all the plunder and livestock of these cities, but all the people they put to the sword until they completely destroyed them, not sparing anyone that breathed As the Lord commanded his servant Moses, so Moses commanded Joshua, and Joshua did it; he left nothing undone of all that the Lord commanded Moses. So Joshua took this entire land: the hill country, all the Negev, the whole region of Goshen, the western foothills, the Arabah, and the mountains of Israel with their foothills, from Mount Halak, which rises toward Seir, to Baal Gad in the Valley of Lebanon below Mount Hermon. He captured all their kings and put them to death. Joshua waged war against all these kings for a long time. Except for the Hivites living in Gibeon, not one city made a treaty of peace with the Israelites, who took them all in battle. For it was the Lord himself who hardened their hearts to wage war against Israel, so that he might destroy them totally, exterminating them without mercy, as the Lord had commanded Moses At that time, Joshua went and destroyed the Anakites from the hill country: from Hebron, Debir, and Anab, from all the hill country of Judah, and from all the hill country of Israel. Joshua totally destroyed them and their towns. No Anakites were left in Israelite territory;

only in Gaza, Gath, and Ashdod did any survive. So Joshua took the entire land, just as the Lord had directed Moses, and he gave it as an inheritance to Israel according to their tribal divisions. Then the land had rest from war

Chapter 12

These are the kings of the land whom the Israelites had defeated and whose territory they took over east of the Jordan, from the Arnon Gorge to Mount Hermon, including all the eastern side of the Arabah: Sihon king of the Amorites, who reigned in Heshbon. He ruled from Aroer on the rim of the Arnon Gorge— from the middle of the gorge—to the Jabbok River, which is the border of the Ammonites. This included half of Gilead. He also ruled over the eastern Arabah from the Sea of Galilee to the Sea of the Arabah (the Dead Sea), to Beth Jeshimoth, and then southward below the slopes of Pisgah And the territory of Og king of Bashan, one of the last of the Rephaites, who reigned in Ashtaroth and Edrei. He ruled over Mount Hermon, Salekah, all of Bashan to the border of the people of Geshur and Maakah, and half of Gilead to the border of Sihon king of Heshbon. Moses, the servant of the Lord, and the Israelites conquered them. And Moses, the servant of the Lord, gave their land to the Reubenites, the Gadites, and the half-tribe of Manasseh to be their possession Here is a list of the kings of the land that Joshua and the Israelites conquered on the west side of the Jordan, from Baal Gad in the Valley of Lebanon to Mount Halak, which rises toward Seir (their lands Joshua gave as an inheritance to the tribes of Israel according to their tribal divisions—the hill country, the western foothills, the Arabah, the mountain slopes, the wilderness, and the Negev—the lands of the Hittites, Amorites, Canaanites, Perizzites, Hivites, and Jebusites): The king of Jericho, one; the king of Ai (near Bethel), one; the king of Jerusalem, one; the king of Hebron, one; the king of Jarmuth, one; the king of Lachish, one; the king of Eglon, one; the king of Gezer, one; the king of Debir, one; the king of Geder, one; the king of Hormah, one; the king of Arad, one; the king of Libnah, one; the king of Adullam, one; the king of Makkedah, one; the king of Bethel, one; the king of Tappuah, one; the king of Hepher, one; the king of Aphek, one; the king of Lasharon, one; the king of Madon, one; the king of Hazor, one; the king of Shimron Meron, one; the king of Akshaph, one; the king of Taanach, one; the king of Megiddo, one; the king of Kedesh, one; the king of Jokneam in Carmel, one; the king of Dor (in Naphoth Dor), one; the king of Goyim in Gilgal, one; the king of Tirzah, one; thirty-one kings in all

Chapter 13

When Joshua was old and well advanced in years, the Lord said to him, "You are very old, and there are still very large areas of land to be taken over "This is the land that remains: all the regions of the Philistines and Geshurites, from the Shihor River on the east of Egypt to the territory of Ekron on the north, all of it counted as Canaanite; the territory of the five Philistine rulers in Gaza, Ashdod, Ashkelon, Gath, and Ekron—that of the Avvites; from the south, all the land of the Canaanites, from Arah that belongs to the Sidonians as far as Aphek, the region of the Amorites; the area of Byblos; and all Lebanon to the east, from Baal Gad below Mount Hermon to Lebo Hamath "As for all the inhabitants of the mountain regions from Lebanon to Misrephoth Maim, that is, all the Sidonians, I myself will drive them out before the Israelites. Be sure to allocate this land to Israel for an inheritance, as I have instructed you, and divide it as an inheritance among the nine tribes and half of the tribe of Manasseh." The other half of Manasseh, the Reubenites, and the Gadites had received the inheritance Moses had given them east of the Jordan, as he, the servant of the Lord, had assigned it to them. It extended from Aroer on the rim of the Arnon Gorge, and from the town in the middle of the gorge, and included the whole plateau of Medeba as far as Dibon, and all the towns of Sihon king of the Amorites, who ruled in Heshbon, out to the border of the Ammonites. It also included Gilead, the territory of the people of Geshur and Maakah, all of Mount Hermon and all Bashan as far as Salekah—that is, the whole kingdom of Og in Bashan, who had reigned in Ashtaroth and Edrei and had survived as one of the last of the Rephaites. Moses had defeated them and taken over their land. But the Israelites did not drive out the people of Geshur and Maakah, so they continue to live among the Israelites to this day But to the tribe of Levi, Moses had given no inheritance; the Lord, the God of Israel, is their inheritance, as he promised This is what Moses had given to the tribe of Reuben, according to its clans: The territory from Aroer on the rim of the Arnon Gorge and from the town in the middle of the gorge, and the whole plateau past Medeba to Heshbon and all its towns on the plateau, including Dibon, Bamoth Baal, Beth Baal Meon, Jahaz, Kedemoth, Mephaath, Kiriathaim, Sibmah, Zereth Shahar on the hill in the valley, Beth Peor, the slopes of Pisgah, and Beth Jeshimoth. All the towns on the plateau and the entire realm of Sihon king of the Amorites, who ruled at Heshbon. Moses had defeated him and the Midianite chiefs, Evi, Rekem, Zur, Hur, and Reba—princes allied with Sihon—who lived in that country. In addition to those slain in battle, the Israelites had put to the sword Balaam son of Beor, who practiced divination. The boundary of the Reubenites was the bank of the Jordan. These towns and their villages were the inheritance of the Reubenites, according to their clans This is what Moses had given to the tribe of Gad, according to its clans: The territory of Jazer, all the towns of Gilead, and half the Ammonite country as far as Aroer, near Rabbah; and from Heshbon to Ramath Mizpah and Betonim, and from Mahanaim to the territory of Debir; and in the valley, Beth Haram, Beth Nimrah, Succoth, and Zaphon with the rest of the realm of Sihon king of Heshbon (the east side of the Jordan, the territory up to the end of the Sea of Galilee). These towns and their villages were the inheritance of the Gadites, according to their clans This is what Moses had given to the half-tribe of Manasseh, that is, to half the family of the descendants of Manasseh, according to its clans: The territory extending from Mahanaim and including all of Bashan, the entire realm of Og king of Bashan—all the settlements of Jair in Bashan, sixty towns, half of Gilead, and Ashtaroth and Edrei (the royal cities of Og in Bashan). This was for the descendants of Makir son of Manasseh—for half of the sons of Makir, according to their clans. This is the inheritance Moses had given when he was in the plains of Moab across the Jordan east of Jericho. But to the tribe of Levi, Moses had given no inheritance; the Lord, the God of Israel, is their inheritance, as he promised them

Chapter 14

Now these are the areas the Israelites received as an inheritance in the land of Canaan, which Eleazar the priest, Joshua son of Nun, and the heads of the tribal clans of Israel allotted to them. Their inheritances were assigned by lot to the nine and a half tribes, as the Lord had commanded through Moses. Moses had granted the two and a half tribes their inheritance east of the Jordan but had not granted the Levites an inheritance among the rest, for Joseph's descendants had become two tribes—Manasseh and Ephraim. The Levites received no share of the land but only towns to live in, with pasturelands for their flocks and herds. So the Israelites divided the land, just as the Lord had commanded Moses Now the people of Judah approached Joshua at Gilgal, and Caleb son of Jephunneh the Kenizzite said to him, "You know what the Lord said to Moses the man of God at Kadesh Barnea about you and me. I was forty years old when Moses the servant of the Lord sent me from Kadesh Barnea to explore the land. And I brought him back a report according to my convictions, but my fellow Israelites who went up with me made the hearts of the people melt in fear. I, however, followed the Lord my God wholeheartedly. So on that day Moses swore to me, 'The land on which your feet have walked will be your inheritance and that of your children forever because you have followed the Lord my God wholeheartedly.' "Now then, just as the Lord promised, he has kept me alive for forty-five years since the time he said this to Moses, while Israel moved about in the wilderness. So here I am today, eighty-five years old! I am still as strong today as the day Moses sent me out; I'm just as vigorous to go out to battle now as I was then. Now give me this hill country that the Lord promised me that day. You yourself heard then that the Anakites were there and their cities were large and fortified, but, the Lord helping me, I will drive them out just as he said." Then Joshua blessed Caleb son of Jephunneh and gave him Hebron as his inheritance. So Hebron has belonged to Caleb son of Jephunneh the Kenizzite ever since because he followed the Lord, the God of Israel, wholeheartedly. Hebron used to be called Kiriath Arba after Arba, who was the greatest man among the Anakites Then the land had rest from war

Chapter 15

The allotment for the tribe of Judah, according to its clans, extended down to the territory of Edom, to the Desert of Zin in the extreme south. Their southern boundary started from the bay at the southern end of the Dead Sea, crossed south of Scorpion Pass, continued on to Zin and went over to the south of Kadesh Barnea. Then it ran past Hezron up to Addar and curved around to Karka. It then passed along to Azmon and joined the Wadi of Egypt, ending at the Mediterranean Sea. This is their southern boundary The eastern boundary is the Dead Sea as far as the mouth of the Jordan The northern boundary started from the bay of the sea at the mouth of the Jordan, went up to Beth Hoglah and continued north of Beth Arabah to the Stone of Bohan son of Reuben. The boundary then went up to Debir from the Valley of Achor and turned north to Gilgal, which faces the pass of Adummim south of the gorge. It continued along to the waters of En Shemesh and came out at En Rogel. Then it ran up the Valley of Ben Hinnom along the southern slope of the Jebusite city (that is, Jerusalem). From there it climbed to the top of the hill west of the Hinnom Valley at the northern end of the Valley of Rephaim. From the hilltop, the boundary headed toward the spring of the waters of Nephtoah, came out at the towns of Mount Ephron and went down toward Baalah (that is, Kiriath Jearim). Then it curved westward from Baalah to Mount Seir, ran along the northern slope of Mount Jearim (that is, Kesalon), continued down to Beth Shemesh and crossed to Timnah. It went to the northern slope of Ekron, turned toward Shikkeron, passed along to Mount Baalah and reached Jabneel. The boundary ended at the sea The western boundary is the coastline of the Mediterranean Sea. These are the boundaries around the people of Judah by their clans In accordance with the Lord's command to him, Joshua gave to Caleb son of Jephunneh a portion in Judah—Kiriath Arba, that is, Hebron. (Arba was the forefather of Anak.) From Hebron Caleb drove out the three Anakites—Sheshai, Ahiman, and Talmai, the sons of Anak. From there he marched against the people living in Debir (formerly called Kiriath Sepher). And Caleb said, "I will give my daughter Aksah in marriage to the man who attacks and captures Kiriath Sepher." Othniel son of Kenaz, Caleb's brother, took it; so Caleb gave his daughter Aksah to him in marriage One day when she came to Othniel, she urged him to ask her father for a field. When she got off her donkey, Caleb asked her, "What can I do for you?" She replied, "Do me a special favor. Since you have given me land in the Negev, give me also springs of water." So Caleb gave her the upper and lower springs This is the inheritance of the tribe of Judah, according to its clans: The southernmost towns of the tribe of Judah in the Negev toward the boundary of Edom were: Kabzeel, Eder, Jagur, Kinah, Dimonah, Adadah, Kedesh, Hazor, Ithnan, Ziph, Telem, Bealoth, Hazor Hadattah, Kerioth Hezron (that is, Hazor), Amam, Shema, Moladah, Hazar Gaddah, Heshmon, Beth Pelet, Hazar Shual, Beersheba, Biziothiah, Baalah, Iim, Ezem, Eltolad, Kesil, Hormah, Ziklag, Madmannah, Sansannah, Lebaoth, Shilhim, Ain, and Rimmon—a total of twenty-nine towns and their villages In the western foothills: Eshtaol, Zorah, Ashnah, Zanoah, En Gannim, Tappuah, Enam, Jarmuth, Adullam, Socoh, Azekah, Shaaraim, Adithaim, and Gederah (or Gederothaim)—fourteen towns and their villages Zenan, Hadashah, Migdal Gad, Dilean, Mizpah, Joktheel, Lachish, Bozkath, Eglon, Kabon, Lahmas, Kitlish, Gederoth, Beth Dagon, Naamah, and Makkedah—sixteen towns and their villages Libnah, Ether, Ashan, Iphtah, Ashnah, Nezib, Keilah, Akzib, and Mareshah—nine towns and their villages Ekron, with its surrounding settlements and villages; west of Ekron, all that were in the vicinity of Ashdod, together with their villages; Ashdod, its surrounding settlements and villages; and Gaza, its settlements and villages, as far as the Wadi of Egypt and the coastline of the Mediterranean Sea In the hill country: Shamir, Jattir, Sokoh, Dannah, Kiriath Sannah (that is, Debir), Anab, Eshtemoh, Anim, Goshen, Holon, and Giloh—eleven towns and their villages Arab, Dumah, Eshan, Janim, Beth Tappuah, Aphekah, Humtah, Kiriath Arba (that is, Hebron), and Zior—nine towns and their villages Maon, Carmel, Ziph, Juttah, Jezreel, Jokdeam, Zanoah, Kain, Gibeah, and Timnah—ten towns and their villages Halhul, Beth Zur, Gedor, Maarath, Beth Anoth, and Eltekon—six towns and their villages Kiriath Baal (that is, Kiriath Jearim) and Rabbah—two towns and their villages In the wilderness: Beth Arabah, Middin, Sekakah, Nibshan, the City of Salt, and En Gedi—six towns and their villages Judah could not dislodge the Jebusites, who were living in Jerusalem; to this day the Jebusites live there with the people of Judah

Chapter 16

The lot for the descendants of Joseph fell from the Jordan near Jericho, east of the waters of Jericho, through the wilderness, and up into the hill country of Bethel. From Bethel (that is, Luz), it crossed over to the territory of the Arkites in Ataroth, went down westward to the territory of the Japhletites as far as the region of Lower Beth Horon and on to Gezer, ending at the Mediterranean Sea. So Manasseh and Ephraim, the descendants of Joseph, received their inheritance This was the territory of Ephraim, according to its clans: The boundary of their inheritance went from Ataroth Addar in the east to Upper Beth Horon and continued to the Mediterranean Sea. From Mikmethath on the north, it curved eastward to Taanath Shiloh, passing by it to Janoah on the east. Then it went down from Janoah

to Ataroth and Naarah, touched Jericho and came out at the Jordan. From Tappuah, the boundary ran westward to the Kanah Ravine and ended at the Mediterranean Sea. This was the inheritance of the tribe of the Ephraimites, according to its clans. It also included all the towns and their villages that were set aside for the Ephraimites within the inheritance of the Manassites. They did not dislodge the Canaanites living in Gezer; to this day the Canaanites live among the people of Ephraim but are required to do forced labor

Chapter 17

This was the allotment for the tribe of Manasseh as Joseph's firstborn, that is, for Makir, Manasseh's firstborn. Makir was the ancestor of the Gileadites, who had received Gilead and Bashan because the Makirites were great soldiers. So this allotment was for the rest of the people of Manasseh—the clans of Abiezer, Helek, Asriel, Shechem, Hepher, and Shemida. These are the other male descendants of Manasseh son of Joseph by their clans Now Zelophehad son of Hepher, the son of Gilead, the son of Makir, the son of Manasseh, had no sons but only daughters, whose names were Mahlah, Noah, Hoglah, Milkah, and Tirzah. They went to Eleazar the priest, Joshua son of Nun, and the leaders and said, "The Lord commanded Moses to give us an inheritance among our relatives." So Joshua gave them an inheritance along with the brothers of their father, according to the Lord's command. Manasseh's share consisted of ten tracts of land besides Gilead and Bashan east of the Jordan, because the daughters of the tribe of Manasseh received an inheritance among the sons. The land of Gilead belonged to the rest of the descendants of Manasseh The territory of Manasseh extended from Asher to Mikmethath east of Shechem. The boundary ran southward from there to include the people living at En Tappuah. (Manasseh had the land of Tappuah, but Tappuah itself, on the boundary of Manasseh, belonged to the Ephraimites.) Then the boundary continued south to the Kanah Ravine. There were towns belonging to Ephraim lying among the towns of Manasseh, but the boundary of Manasseh was the northern side of the ravine and ended at the Mediterranean Sea. On the south the land belonged to Ephraim, on the north to Manasseh. The territory of Manasseh reached the Mediterranean Sea and bordered Asher on the north and Issachar on the east. Within Issachar and Asher, Manasseh also had Beth Shan, Ibleam, the people of Dor, Endor, Taanach, and Megiddo, together with their surrounding settlements (the third in the list is Naphoth) Yet the Manassites were not able to occupy these towns, for the Canaanites were determined to live in that region. However, when the Israelites grew stronger, they subjected the Canaanites to forced labor but did not drive them out completely The people of Joseph said to Joshua, "Why have you given us only one allotment and one portion for an inheritance? We are a numerous people, and the Lord has blessed us abundantly." "If you are so numerous," Joshua answered, "and if the hill country of Ephraim is too small for you, go up into the forest and clear land for yourselves there in the land of the Perizzites and Rephaites." The people of Joseph replied, "The hill country is not enough for us, and all the Canaanites who live in the plain have chariots fitted with iron, both those in Beth Shan and its settlements and those in the Valley of Jezreel." But Joshua said to the tribes of Joseph—to Ephraim and Manasseh—"You are numerous and very powerful. You will have not only one allotment but the forested hill country as well. Clear it, and its farthest limits will be yours; though the Canaanites have chariots fitted with iron and though they are strong, you can drive them out."

Chapter 18

The whole assembly of the Israelites gathered at Shiloh and set up the tent of meeting there. The country was brought under their control, but there were still seven Israelite tribes who had not yet received their inheritance So Joshua said to the Israelites, "How long will you wait before you begin to take possession of the land that the Lord, the God of your ancestors, has given you? Appoint three men from each tribe. I will send them out to make a survey of the land and to write a description of it, according to the inheritance of each. Then they will return to me. You are to divide the land into seven parts. Judah is to remain in its territory on the south and the tribes of Joseph in their territory on the north. After you have written descriptions of the seven parts of the land, bring them here to me, and I will cast lots for you in the presence of the Lord our God. The Levites, however, do not get a portion among you because the priestly service of the Lord is their inheritance. And Gad, Reuben, and the half-tribe of Manasseh have already received their inheritance on the east side of the Jordan. Moses the servant of the Lord gave it to them." As the men started on their way to map out the land, Joshua instructed them, "Go and make a survey of the land and write a description of it. Then return to me, and I will cast lots for you here at Shiloh in the presence of the Lord." So the men left and went through the land. They wrote its description on a scroll, town by town, in seven parts, and returned to Joshua in the camp at Shiloh. Joshua then cast lots for them in Shiloh in the presence of the Lord, and there he distributed the land to the Israelites according to their tribal divisions The first lot came up for the tribe of Benjamin according to its clans. Their allotted territory lay between the tribes of Judah and Joseph: On the north side, their boundary began at the Jordan, past the northern slope of Jericho and headed west into the hill country, coming out at the wilderness of Beth Aven. From there it crossed to the south slope of Luz (that is, Bethel), and went down to Ataroth Addar on the hill south of Lower Beth Horon. From the hill facing Beth Horon on the south, the boundary turned south along the western side and came out at Kiriath Baal (that is, Kiriath Jearim), a town of the people of Judah. This was the western side The southern side began at the outskirts of Kiriath Jearim on the west, and the boundary came out at the spring of the waters of Nephtoah. The boundary went down to the foot of the hill facing the Valley of Ben Hinnom, north of the Valley of Rephaim. It continued down the Hinnom Valley along the southern slope of the Jebusite city and so to En Rogel. It then curved north, went to En Shemesh, continued to Geliloth (which faces the Pass of Adummim), and ran down to the Stone of Bohan son of Reuben. It continued to the northern slope of Beth Arabah and on down into the Arabah. It then went to the northern slope of Beth Hoglah and came out at the northern bay of the Dead Sea, at the mouth of the Jordan in the south. This was the southern boundary The Jordan formed the boundary on the eastern side. These were the boundaries that marked out the inheritance of the clans of Benjamin on all sides The tribe of Benjamin, according to its clans, had the following towns: Jericho, Beth Hoglah, Emek Keziz, Beth Arabah, Zemaraim, Bethel, Avvim, Parah, Ophrah, Kephar Ammoni, Ophni, and Geba—twelve towns and their villages Gibeon, Ramah, Beeroth, Mizpah, Kephirah, Mozah, Rekem, Irpeel, Taralah, Zelah, Haeleph, the Jebusite city (that is, Jerusalem), Gibeah, and Kiriath—fourteen towns and their villages. This was the inheritance of

Benjamin for its clans

Chapter 19

The second lot came out for the tribe of Simeon, according to its clans. Their inheritance lay within the territory of Judah. It included: Beersheba (or Sheba), Moladah, Hazar Shual, Balah, Ezem, Eltolad, Bethul, Hormah, Ziklag, Beth Markaboth, Hazar Susah, Beth Lebaoth, and Sharuhen—thirteen towns and their villages Ain, Rimmon, Ether, and Ashan—four towns and their villages—and all the villages around these towns as far as Baalath Beer (Ramah in the Negev). This was the inheritance of the tribe of the Simeonites, according to its clans. The inheritance of the Simeonites was taken from the share of Judah, because Judah's portion was more than they needed. So the Simeonites received their inheritance within the territory of Judah The third lot came up for Zebulun, according to its clans: The boundary of their inheritance went as far as Sarid. Going west it ran to Maralah, touched Dabbesheth, and extended to the ravine near Jokneam. It turned east from Sarid toward the sunrise to the territory of Kisloth Tabor and went on to Daberath and up to Japhia. Then it continued eastward to Gath Hepher and Eth Kazin; it came out at Rimmon and turned toward Neah. There the boundary went around on the north to Hannathon and ended at the Valley of Iphtah El. Included were Kattath, Nahalal, Shimron, Idalah, and Bethlehem. There were twelve towns and their villages These towns and their villages were the inheritance of Zebulun, according to its clans The fourth lot came out for Issachar, according to its clans. Their territory included: Jezreel, Kesulloth, Shunem, Hapharaim, Shion, Anaharath, Rabbith, Kishion, Ebez, Remeth, En Gannim, En Haddah, and Beth Pazzez. The boundary touched Tabor, Shahazumah, and Beth Shemesh, and ended at the Jordan. There were sixteen towns and their villages These towns and their villages were the inheritance of the tribe of Issachar, according to its clans The fifth lot came out for the tribe of Asher, according to its clans. Their territory included: Helkath, Hali, Beten, Akshaph, Allammelek, Amad, and Mishal. On the west, the boundary touched Carmel and Shihor Libnath. It then turned east toward Beth Dagon, touched Zebulun and the Valley of Iphtah El, and went north to Beth Emek and Neiel, passing Kabul on the left. It went to Abdon, Rehob, Hammon, and Kanah, as far as Greater Sidon. The boundary then turned back toward Ramah and went to the fortified city of Tyre, turned toward Hosah and came out at the Mediterranean Sea in the region of Akzib, Ummah, Aphek, and Rehob. There were twenty-two towns and their villages These towns and their villages were the inheritance of the tribe of Asher, according to its clans The sixth lot came out for Naphtali, according to its clans: Their boundary went from Heleph and the large tree in Zaanannim, passing Adami Nekeb and Jabneel to Lakkum and ending at the Jordan. The boundary ran west through Aznoth Tabor and came out at Hukkok. It touched Zebulun on the south, Asher on the west, and the Jordan on the east. The fortified towns were: Ziddim, Zer, Hammath, Rakkath, Kinnereth, Adamah, Ramah, Hazor, Kedesh, Edrei, En Hazor, Iron, Migdal El, Horem, Beth Anath, and Beth Shemesh. There were nineteen towns and their villages These towns and their villages were the inheritance of the tribe of Naphtali, according to its clans The seventh lot came out for the tribe of Dan, according to its clans. The territory of their inheritance included: Zorah, Eshtaol, Ir Shemesh, Shaalabbin, Aijalon, Ithlah, Elon, Timnah, Ekron, Eltekeh, Gibbethon, Baalath, Jehud, Bene Berak, Gath Rimmon, Me Jarkon, and Rakkon, with the area facing Joppa When the territory of the

Danites was lost to them, they went up and attacked Leshem, took it, put it to the sword, and occupied it. They settled in Leshem and named it Dan after their ancestor These towns and their villages were the inheritance of the tribe of Dan, according to its clans When they had finished dividing the land into its allotted portions, the Israelites gave Joshua son of Nun an inheritance among them, as the Lord had commanded. They gave him the town he asked for—Timnath Serah in the hill country of Ephraim. And he built up the town and settled there These are the territories that Eleazar the priest, Joshua son of Nun, and the heads of the tribal clans of Israel assigned by lot at Shiloh in the presence of the Lord at the entrance to the tent of meeting. And so they finished dividing the land

Chapter 20

Then the Lord said to Joshua: "Tell the Israelites to designate the cities of refuge, as I instructed you through Moses, so that anyone who kills a person accidentally and unintentionally may flee there and find protection from the avenger of blood. When they flee to one of these cities, they are to stand in the entrance of the city gate and state their case before the elders of that city. Then the elders are to admit the fugitive into their city and provide a place to live among them. If the avenger of blood comes in pursuit, the elders must not surrender the fugitive, because the fugitive killed their neighbor unintentionally and without malice aforethought. They are to stay in that city until they have stood trial before the assembly and until the death of the high priest who is serving at that time. Then they may go back to their own home in the town from which they fled." So they set apart Kedesh in Galilee in the hill country of Naphtali, Shechem in the hill country of Ephraim, and Kiriath Arba (that is, Hebron) in the hill country of Judah. East of the Jordan (on the other side from Jericho), they designated Bezer in the wilderness on the plateau in the tribe of Reuben, Ramoth in Gilead in the tribe of Gad, and Golan in Bashan in the tribe of Manasseh. Any of the Israelites or any foreigner residing among them who killed someone accidentally could flee to these designated cities and not be killed by the avenger of blood prior to standing trial before the assembly

Chapter 21

The principal fathers of the Levites approached Eleazar the priest, Joshua son of Nun, and the leaders of the tribes of the Israelites at Shiloh in the land of Canaan. They spoke, saying, "The LORD commanded through Moses that we be given towns to live in, with pasturelands for our livestock." So the Israelites, in accordance with the LORD's command, gave the Levites these towns and their pasturelands from their own inheritances The first lot came out for the Kohathites, namely, to the descendants of Aaron, the priest, who belonged to the Levites. They received thirteen towns from the tribes of Judah, Simeon, and Benjamin. The rest of Kohath's descendants received ten towns from the clans of the tribes of Ephraim, Dan, and half the tribe of Manasseh. The descendants of Gershon received thirteen towns from the clans of the tribes of Issachar, Asher, Naphtali, and the half-tribe of Manasseh in Bashan. The descendants of Merari received twelve towns from the tribes of Reuben, Gad, and Zebulun So the Israelites allotted to the Levites these towns and their pasturelands, as the LORD had commanded through Moses. From the tribes of Judah and Simeon, they allotted the following towns by name to the descendants of Aaron who were from the Kohathite clans of the Levites, because the first lot fell to them. They gave them Kiriath Arba (that is, Hebron), with its

surrounding pastureland, in the hill country of Judah. (Arba was the forefather of Anak.) But the fields and villages around the city they had given to Caleb son of Jephunneh as his possession So they gave the following towns to the descendants of Aaron, the priest: Hebron (a city of refuge for one accused of murder), Libnah, Jattir, Eshtemoa, Holon, Debir, Ain, Juttah, and Beth Shemesh, together with their pasturelands—nine towns from these two tribes. From the tribe of Benjamin they gave them Gibeon, Geba, Anathoth, and Almon, together with their pasturelands—four towns. All the towns for the priests, the descendants of Aaron, numbered thirteen, together with their pasturelands The rest of the Kohathite clans of the Levites received towns from the tribe of Ephraim: Shechem (a city of refuge for one accused of murder), Gezer, Kibzaim, and Beth Horon, together with their pasturelands—four towns. From the tribe of Dan they received: Eltekeh, Gibbethon, Aijalon, and Gath Rimmon, together with their pasturelands—four towns. From half the tribe of Manasseh they received: Taanach and Gath Rimmon, together with their pasturelands—two towns. All these ten towns and their pasturelands were given to the rest of the Kohathite clans The Gershonite clans of the Levites received: from half the tribe of Manasseh, Golan in Bashan (a city of refuge for one accused of murder), and Be Eshtarah, together with their pasturelands—two towns; from the tribe of Issachar, Kishion, Daberath, Jarmuth, and En Gannim, together with their pasturelands—four towns; from the tribe of Asher, Mishal, Abdon, Helkath, and Rehob, together with their pasturelands—four towns; from the tribe of Naphtali, Kedesh in Galilee (a city of refuge for one accused of murder), Hammoth Dor, and Kartan, together with their pasturelands—three towns. All the towns for the Gershonite clans, according to their families, numbered thirteen, together with their pasturelands The Merarite clans (the rest of the Levites) received: from the tribe of Zebulun, Jokneam, Kartah, Dimnah, and Nahalal, together with their pasturelands—four towns; from the tribe of Reuben, Bezer, Jahaz, Kedemoth, and Mephaath, together with their pasturelands—four towns; from the tribe of Gad, Ramoth in Gilead (a city of refuge for one accused of murder), Mahanaim, Heshbon, and Jazer, together with their pasturelands—four towns in all. All the towns allotted to the Merarite clans, who were the rest of the Levites, numbered twelve, together with their pasturelands. The total number of towns allotted to the Levites in the Israelite territory was forty-eight, together with their pasturelands. Each of these towns had pasturelands surrounding it; this was true for all these towns So the LORD gave Israel all the land he had sworn to give their ancestors, and they took possession of it and settled there. The LORD gave them rest on every side, just as he had sworn to their ancestors. Not one of their enemies withstood them; the LORD gave all their enemies into their hands. Not one of all the LORD's good promises to Israel failed; every one was fulfilled

Chapter 22

Then Joshua summoned the Reubenites, the Gadites, and the half-tribe of Manasseh and said to them, "You have done all that Moses the servant of the LORD commanded, and you have obeyed me in everything I commanded. For a long time now—to this very day—you have not deserted your fellow Israelites but have carried out the mission the LORD your God gave you. Now that the LORD your God has given them rest as he promised, return to your homes in the land that Moses the servant of the LORD gave you on the other side of the Jordan. But be very careful to keep the commandment and the law that

Moses the servant of the LORD gave you: to love the LORD your God, to walk in obedience to him, to keep his commands, to hold fast to him and to serve him with all your heart and with all your soul." Then Joshua blessed them and sent them away, and they went to their homes. To the half-tribe of Manasseh, Moses had given land in Bashan, and to the other half of the tribe, Joshua gave land on the west side of the Jordan along with their fellow Israelites. When Joshua sent them home, he blessed them, saying, "Return to your homes with your great wealth—with large herds of livestock, with silver, gold, bronze and iron, and a great quantity of clothing—and divide the plunder from your enemies with your fellow Israelites." So the Reubenites, the Gadites, and the half-tribe of Manasseh left the Israelites at Shiloh in Canaan to return to Gilead, their own land, which they had acquired in accordance with the command of the LORD through Moses. When they came to Geliloth near the Jordan in the land of Canaan, the Reubenites, the Gadites, and the half-tribe of Manasseh built an imposing altar there by the Jordan And when the Israelites heard that they had built the altar on the border of Canaan at Geliloth near the Jordan on the Israelite side, the whole assembly of Israel gathered at Shiloh to go to war against them. So the Israelites sent Phinehas son of Eleazar, the priest, to the land of Gilead—to Reuben, Gad, and the half-tribe of Manasseh. With him they sent ten of the chief men, one from each of the tribes of Israel, each the head of a family division among the Israelite clans When they went to Gilead—to Reuben, Gad, and the half-tribe of Manasseh—they said to them: "The whole assembly of the LORD says: 'How could you break faith with the God of Israel like this? How could you turn away from the LORD and build yourselves an altar in rebellion against him now? Was not the sin of Peor enough for us? Up to this very day, we have not cleansed ourselves from that sin, even though a plague fell on the community of the LORD! And are you now turning away from the LORD? "'If you rebel against the LORD today, tomorrow he will be angry with the whole community of Israel. If the land you possess is defiled, come over to the LORD's land, where the LORD's tabernacle stands, and share the land with us. But do not rebel against the LORD or against us by building an altar for yourselves, other than the altar of the LORD our God. When Achan son of Zerah was unfaithful in regard to the devoted things, did not wrath come on the whole community of Israel? He was not the only one who died for his sin.'" Then Reuben, Gad, and the half-tribe of Manasseh replied to the heads of the clans of Israel: "The Mighty One, God, the LORD! The Mighty One, God, the LORD! He knows! And let Israel know! If this has been in rebellion or disobedience to the LORD, do not spare us this day. If we have built our own altar to turn away from the LORD and to offer burnt offerings and grain offerings, or to sacrifice fellowship offerings on it, may the LORD himself call us to account "No! We did it for fear that someday your descendants might say to ours, 'What do you have to do with the LORD, the God of Israel? The LORD has made the Jordan a boundary between us and you—you Reubenites and Gadites! You have no share in the LORD.' So your descendants might cause ours to stop fearing the LORD. That is why we said, 'Let us get ready and build an altar—but not for burnt offerings or sacrifices.' On the contrary, it is to be a witness between us and you and the generations that follow, that we will worship the LORD at his sanctuary with our burnt offerings, sacrifices, and fellowship offerings. Then in the future, your descendants will not be able to say to ours, 'You have no share in the LORD.' "And we said,

'If they ever say this to us, or to our descendants, we will answer: Look at the replica of the LORD's altar, which our ancestors built, not for burnt offerings and sacrifices, but as a witness between us and you.' Far be it from us to rebel against the LORD and turn away from him today by building an altar for burnt offerings, grain offerings and sacrifices, other than the altar of the LORD our God that stands before his tabernacle." When Phinehas the priest and the leaders of the community—the heads of the clans of the Israelites—heard what Reuben, Gad, and Manasseh had to say, they were pleased. And Phinehas son of Eleazar, the priest, said to Reuben, Gad, and Manasseh, "Today we know that the LORD is with us because you have not been unfaithful to the LORD in this matter. Now you have rescued the Israelites from the LORD's hand." Then Phinehas son of Eleazar, the priest, and the leaders returned to Canaan from their meeting with the Reubenites and Gadites in Gilead and reported to the Israelites. They were glad to hear the report and praised God. And they talked no more about going to war against them to devastate the country where the Reubenites and the Gadites lived And the Reubenites and the Gadites gave the altar this name: A Witness Between Us—that the LORD is God

Chapter 23

After a long time had passed and the LORD had given Israel rest from all their enemies around them, Joshua, by then a very old man, summoned all Israel—their elders, leaders, judges, and officials—and said to them: "I am very old. You yourselves have seen everything the LORD your God has done to all these nations for your sake; it was the LORD your God who fought for you. Remember how I have allotted as an inheritance for your tribes all the land of the nations that remain—the nations I conquered—between the Jordan and the Mediterranean Sea in the west. The LORD your God himself will push them out for your sake. He will drive them out before you, and you will take possession of their land, as the LORD your God promised you "Be very strong; be careful to obey all that is written in the Book of the Law of Moses, without turning aside to the right or to the left. Do not associate with these nations that remain among you; do not invoke the names of their gods or swear by them. You must not serve them or bow down to them. But you are to hold fast to the LORD your God, as you have until now "The LORD has driven out before you great and powerful nations; to this day no one has been able to withstand you. One of you routs a thousand because the LORD your God fights for you, just as he promised. So be very careful to love the LORD your God "But if you turn away and ally yourselves with the survivors of these nations that remain among you and if you intermarry with them and associate with them, then you may be sure that the LORD your God will no longer drive out these nations before you. Instead, they will become snares and traps for you, whips on your backs and thorns in your eyes until you perish from this good land, which the LORD your God has given you "Now I am about to go the way of all the earth. You know with all your heart and soul that not one of all the good promises the LORD your God gave you has failed. Every promise has been fulfilled; not one has failed. But just as all the good things the LORD your God has promised you have come to you, so he will bring on you all the evil things he has threatened, until the LORD your God has destroyed you from this good land he has given you. If you violate the covenant of the LORD your God, which he commanded you, and go and serve other gods and bow down to them, the LORD's anger will burn against you, and you will quickly perish from the good land he has given you."

Chapter 24

Then Joshua assembled all the tribes of Israel at Shechem. He summoned the elders, leaders, judges, and officials of Israel, and they presented themselves before God. Joshua said to all the people, "This is what the LORD, the God of Israel, says: 'Long ago your ancestors, including Terah the father of Abraham and Nahor, lived beyond the Euphrates River and worshiped other gods. But I took your father Abraham from the land beyond the Euphrates and led him throughout Canaan and gave him many descendants. I gave him Isaac, and to Isaac I gave Jacob and Esau. I assigned the hill country of Seir to Esau, but Jacob and his family went down to Egypt "'Then I sent Moses and Aaron, and I afflicted the Egyptians by what I did there, and I brought you out. When I brought your people out of Egypt, you came to the sea, and the Egyptians pursued them with chariots and horsemen as far as the Red Sea. But they cried to the LORD for help, and he put darkness between you and the Egyptians; he brought the sea over them and covered them. You saw with your own eyes what I did to the Egyptians. Then you lived in the wilderness for a long time "'I brought you to the land of the Amorites who lived east of the Jordan. They fought against you, but I gave them into your hands. I destroyed them from before you, and you took possession of their land. When Balak son of Zippor, the king of Moab, prepared to fight against Israel, he sent for Balaam son of Beor to put a curse on you. But I would not listen to Balaam, so he blessed you again and again, and I delivered you out of his hand "'Then you crossed the Jordan and came to Jericho. The citizens of Jericho fought against you, as did also the Amorites, Perizzites, Canaanites, Hittites, Girgashites, Hivites, and Jebusites, but I gave them into your hands. I sent the hornet ahead of you, which drove them out before you—also the two Amorite kings. You did not do it with your own sword and bow. So I gave you a land on which you did not toil and cities you did not build; and you live in them and eat from vineyards and olive groves that you did not plant.' "Now fear the LORD and serve him with all faithfulness. Throw away the gods your ancestors worshiped beyond the Euphrates River and in Egypt, and serve the LORD. But if serving the LORD seems undesirable to you, then choose for yourselves this day whom you will serve, whether the gods your ancestors served beyond the Euphrates, or the gods of the Amorites, in whose land you are living. But as for me and my household, we will serve the LORD." Then the people answered, "Far be it from us to forsake the LORD to serve other gods! It was the LORD our God himself who brought us and our parents up out of Egypt, from that land of slavery, and performed those great signs before our eyes. He protected us on our entire journey and among all the nations through which we traveled. And the LORD drove out before us all the nations, including the Amorites, who lived in the land. We too will serve the LORD because he is our God." Joshua said to the people, "You are not able to serve the LORD. He is a holy God; he is a jealous God. He will not forgive your rebellion and your sins. If you forsake the LORD and serve foreign gods, he will turn and bring disaster on you and make an end of you, after he has been good to you." But the people said to Joshua, "No! We will serve the LORD." Then Joshua said, "You are witnesses against yourselves that you have chosen to serve the LORD." "Yes, we are witnesses," they replied "Now then," said Joshua, "throw away the foreign gods that are among you and yield your hearts to the LORD, the God of Israel." And the people said to Joshua, "We will serve the LORD our God and obey him." On that day Joshua made a covenant for the people, and there at Shechem, he reaffirmed for them decrees and laws. And Joshua recorded these things in the Book of the Law of God. Then he took a large stone and set it up there under the oak near the holy place of the LORD. "See!" he said to all the people. "This stone will be a witness against us. It has heard all the words the LORD has said to us. It will be a witness against you if you are untrue to your God." Then Joshua dismissed the people, each to their own inheritance After these things, Joshua son of Nun, the servant of the LORD, died at the age of a hundred and ten. And they buried him in the land of his inheritance, at Timnath Serah in the hill country of Ephraim, north of Mount Gaash Israel served the LORD throughout the lifetime of Joshua and of the elders who outlived him and who had experienced everything the LORD had done for Israel And Joseph's bones, which the Israelites had brought up from Egypt, were buried at Shechem in the tract of land that Jacob bought for a hundred pieces of silver from the sons of Hamor, the father of Shechem. This became the inheritance of Joseph's descendants And Eleazar son of Aaron died and was buried at Gibeah, which had been allotted to his son Phinehas in the hill country of Ephraim

7. Judges

Chapter 1

After Joshua's death, the children of Israel asked the LORD, "Who will go out against the Canaanites to fight them first?" The LORD answered, "Judah will go; behold, I have given the land into his hands." Judah then said to Simeon, his brother, "Come with me into my lot to fight against the Canaanites, and I will also go with you into your lot." Simeon agreed, and Judah departed. The LORD delivered the Canaanites and the Perizzites into their hands, and they killed ten thousand men at Bezek. They found Adoni-Bezek there, fought against him, and defeated the Canaanites and the Perizzites. Adoni-Bezek fled, but they pursued him, caught him, and cut off his thumbs and big toes. Adoni-Bezek said, "Seventy kings, with their thumbs and big toes cut off, have gathered food under my table. As I have done, so God has repaid me." They took him to Jerusalem, where he died The sons of Judah had fought against Jerusalem, captured it, struck it with the edge of the sword, and set the city on fire. They then went to fight against the Canaanites who lived in the hill country, the Negev, and the lowlands. Judah went against the Canaanites who lived in Hebron (formerly called Kiriath-Arba) and killed Sheshai, Ahiman, and Talmai. From there, they went to the inhabitants of Debir (formerly called Kiriath-Sepher). Caleb promised his daughter Achsah in marriage to whoever captured Kiriath-Sepher. Othniel, the son of Kenaz and Caleb's younger brother, captured it, and Caleb gave him Achsah as his wife When Achsah came to Othniel, she urged him to ask her father for a field. She dismounted from her donkey, and Caleb asked, "What do you want?" She replied, "Give me a blessing. Since you have given me land in the Negev, give me also springs of water." Caleb gave her both the upper and lower springs The descendants of Moses' father-in-law, the Kenite, went with the people of Judah from the City of Palms into the wilderness of Judah, which is in the Negev near Arad, to live among the people. Judah went with Simeon, his brother, and they defeated the Canaanites who inhabited Zephath, utterly destroyed it, and named the city Hormah. Judah also captured Gaza, Ashkelon, and Ekron with their territories. The LORD was with Judah, and they took possession of the hill country, but they could not drive out the inhabitants of the plain because they had iron chariots. They gave Hebron to Caleb, as Moses had promised, and he drove out the three sons of Anak. However, the Benjamites did not drive out the Jebusites who lived in Jerusalem, so the Jebusites live there with the Benjamites to this day The house of Joseph also went up against Bethel, and the LORD was with them. They sent spies to Bethel (formerly called Luz). The spies saw a man coming out of the city and said to him, "Show us how to get into the city, and we will treat you kindly." He showed them, and they struck the city with the edge of the sword but let the man and his family go. The man went to the land of the Hittites, built a city, and named it Luz, which is its name to this day Manasseh did not drive out the inhabitants of Beth-Shean, Taanach, Dor, Ibleam, or Megiddo, but the Canaanites persisted in dwelling in that land. When Israel grew strong, they put the Canaanites to forced labor but did not drive them out completely. Ephraim did not drive out the Canaanites living in Gezer, so the Canaanites lived among them. Zebulun did not drive out the inhabitants of Kitron or Nahalol, but the Canaanites lived among them and became subject to forced labor. Asher did not drive out the inhabitants of Acco, Sidon, Ahlab, Achzib, Helbah, Aphik, or Rehob, so the Asherites lived among the Canaanites. Naphtali did not drive out the inhabitants of Beth-Shemesh or Beth-Anath, but they lived among the Canaanites and subjected them to forced labor The Amorites confined the Danites to the hill country, not allowing them to come down to the plain. The Amorites persisted in living on Mount Heres, in Aijalon, and in Shaalbim, but when the power of the house of Joseph increased, they became forced labor. The territory of the Amorites extended from the ascent of Akrabbim, from Sela, and upward

Chapter 2

An angel of the LORD came up from Gilgal to Bochim and said, "I brought you up out of Egypt and led you into the land I swore to give to your ancestors. I said I would never break my covenant with you, and you shall not make a covenant with the people of this land, but you shall break down their altars. Yet you have disobeyed me. Why have you done this? Now, therefore, I tell you that I will not drive them out before you; they will become traps for you, and their gods will become snares to you." When the angel of the LORD spoke these things to all the Israelites, the people wept aloud. They called that place Bochim and offered sacrifices to the LORD there After Joshua dismissed the Israelites, they went to take possession of the land, each to their own inheritance. The people served the LORD throughout the lifetime of Joshua and of the elders who outlived him and had seen all the great things the LORD had done for Israel. Joshua, son of Nun, the servant of the LORD, died at the age of a hundred and ten, and they buried him in the land of his inheritance, at Timnath Heres in the hill country of Ephraim, north of Mount Gaash. After that whole generation had been gathered to their ancestors, another generation grew up who knew neither the LORD nor what he had done for Israel Then the Israelites did evil in the eyes of the LORD and served the Baals. They forsook the LORD, the God of their ancestors, who had brought them out of Egypt. They followed and worshiped various gods of the peoples around them. They aroused the LORD's anger because they forsook him and served Baal and the Ashtoreths. In his anger against Israel, the LORD gave them into the hands of raiders who plundered them. He sold them into the hands of their enemies all around, whom they were no longer able to resist. Whenever Israel went out to fight, the hand

of the LORD was against them to defeat them, just as he had sworn to them. They were in great distress Then the LORD raised up judges, who saved them out of the hands of these raiders. Yet they would not listen to their judges but prostituted themselves to other gods and worshiped them. They quickly turned from the ways of their ancestors, who had been obedient to the LORD's commands. Whenever the LORD raised up a judge for them, he was with the judge and saved them out of the hands of their enemies as long as the judge lived, for the LORD relented because of their groaning under those who oppressed and afflicted them. But when the judge died, the people returned to ways even more corrupt than those of their ancestors, following other gods and serving and worshiping them. They refused to give up their evil practices and stubborn ways Therefore the LORD was very angry with Israel and said, "Because this nation has violated the covenant I ordained for their ancestors and has not listened to me, I will no longer drive out before them any of the nations Joshua left when he died. I will use them to test Israel and see whether they will keep the way of the LORD and walk in it as their ancestors did." The LORD had allowed those nations to remain; he did not drive them out at once by giving them into the hands of Joshua

Chapter 3

These are the nations the LORD left to test all those Israelites who had not experienced any of the wars in Canaan (he did this only to teach warfare to the descendants of the Israelites who had not had previous battle experience): the five rulers of the Philistines, all the Canaanites, the Sidonians, and the Hivites living in the Lebanon mountains from Mount Baal Hermon to Lebo Hamath. They were left to test the Israelites to see whether they would obey the LORD's commands, which he had given their ancestors through Moses. The Israelites lived among the Canaanites, Hittites, Amorites, Perizzites, Hivites, and Jebusites. They took their daughters in marriage and gave their own daughters to their sons and served their gods The Israelites did evil in the eyes of the LORD; they forgot the LORD their God and served the Baals and the Asherahs. The anger of the LORD burned against Israel so that he sold them into the hands of Cushan-Rishathaim, king of Aram Naharaim, to whom the Israelites were subject for eight years. But when they cried out to the LORD, he raised up for them a deliverer, Othniel, son of Kenaz, Caleb's younger brother, who saved them. The Spirit of the LORD came on him so that he became Israel's judge and went to war. The LORD gave Cushan-Rishathaim, king of Aram, into the hands of Othniel, who overpowered him. So the land had peace for forty years, until Othniel, son of Kenaz, died Again, the Israelites did evil in the eyes of the LORD, and because they did this evil, the LORD gave Eglon, king of Moab, power over Israel. Getting the Ammonites and Amalekites to join him, Eglon came and attacked Israel, and they took possession of the City of Palms. The Israelites were subject to Eglon, king of Moab, for eighteen years. Again the Israelites cried out to the LORD, and he gave them a deliverer—Ehud, a left-handed man, the son of Gera the Benjamite. The Israelites sent him with tribute to Eglon, king of Moab. Now Ehud had made a double-edged sword about a cubit long, which he strapped to his right thigh under his clothing. He presented the tribute to Eglon, king of Moab, who was a very fat man. After Ehud had presented the tribute, he sent on their way those who had carried it. But on reaching the stone images near Gilgal, he himself went back to Eglon and said, "Your Majesty, I have a secret message for you." The king said to his attendants, "Leave us!" And they all left Ehud then approached him while he was sitting alone in the upper room of his palace and said, "I have a message from God for you." As the king rose from his seat, Ehud reached with his left hand, drew the sword from his right thigh, and plunged it into the king's belly. Even the handle sank in after the blade, and his bowels discharged. Ehud did not pull the sword out, and the fat closed in over it. Then Ehud went out to the porch; he shut the doors of the upper room behind him and locked them. After he had gone, the servants came and found the doors of the upper room locked. They said, "He must be relieving himself in the inner room of the palace." They waited to the point of embarrassment, but when he did not open the doors of the room, they took a key and unlocked them. There they saw their lord fallen to the floor, dead While they waited, Ehud got away. He passed by the stone images and escaped to Seirah. When he arrived there, he blew a trumpet in the hill country of Ephraim, and the Israelites went down with him from the hills, with him leading them. "Follow me," he ordered, "for the LORD has given Moab, your enemy, into your hands." So they followed him down and took possession of the fords of the Jordan that led to Moab; they allowed no one to cross over. At that time, they struck down about ten thousand Moabites, all vigorous and strong; not one escaped. That day Moab was made subject to Israel, and the land had peace for eighty years After Ehud came Shamgar son of Anath, who struck down six hundred Philistines with an oxgoad. He too saved Israel

Chapter 4

Again the Israelites did evil in the eyes of the LORD, now that Ehud was dead. So the LORD sold them into the hands of Jabin king of Canaan, who reigned in Hazor. Sisera, the commander of his army, was based in Harosheth Haggoyim. Because he had nine hundred chariots fitted with iron and had cruelly oppressed the Israelites for twenty years, they cried to the LORD for help Now Deborah, a prophet, the wife of Lappidoth, was leading Israel at that time. She held court under the Palm of Deborah between Ramah and Bethel in the hill country of Ephraim, and the Israelites went up to her to have their disputes decided. She sent for Barak son of Abinoam from Kedesh in Naphtali and said to him, "The LORD, the God of Israel, commands you: 'Go, take with you ten thousand men of Naphtali and Zebulun and lead them up to Mount Tabor. I will lead Sisera, the commander of Jabin's army, with his chariots and his troops to the Kishon River and give him into your hands.'" Barak said to her, "If you go with me, I will go; but if you don't go with me, I won't go." "Certainly, I will go with you," said Deborah. "But because of the course you are taking, the honor will not be yours, for the LORD will deliver Sisera into the hands of a woman." So Deborah went with Barak to Kedesh. There Barak summoned Zebulun and Naphtali, and ten thousand men went up under his command. Deborah also went up with him Now Heber the Kenite had left the other Kenites, the descendants of Hobab, Moses' brother-in-law, and pitched his tent by the great tree in Zaanannim near Kedesh When they told Sisera that Barak son of Abinoam had gone up to Mount Tabor, Sisera summoned from Harosheth Haggoyim to the Kishon River all his men and his nine hundred chariots fitted with iron Then Deborah said to Barak, "Go! This is the day the LORD has given Sisera into your hands. Has not the LORD gone ahead of you?" So Barak went down Mount Tabor, with ten thousand men following him. At Barak's advance, the LORD routed Sisera and all his chariots and army by the sword, and Sisera got down from his chariot and fled on foot. Barak pursued the chariots and army as far as Harosheth Haggoyim, and all Sisera's troops fell by the sword; not a man was left Sisera, meanwhile, fled on foot to the tent of Jael, the wife of Heber the Kenite, because there was an alliance between Jabin king of Hazor and the family of Heber the Kenite. Jael went out to meet Sisera and said to him, "Come, my lord, come right in. Don't be afraid." So he entered her tent, and she covered him with a blanket "I'm thirsty," he said. "Please give me some water." She opened a skin of milk, gave him a drink, and covered him up "Stand in the doorway of the tent," he told her. "If someone comes by and asks you, 'Is anyone in there?' say 'No.'" But Jael, Heber's wife, picked up a tent peg and a hammer and went quietly to him while he lay fast asleep, exhausted. She drove the peg through his temple into the ground, and he died. Just then Barak came by in pursuit of Sisera, and Jael went out to meet him. "Come," she said, "I will show you the man you're looking for." So he went in with her, and there lay Sisera with the tent peg through his temple— dead On that day God subdued Jabin king of Canaan before the Israelites. And the hand of the Israelites pressed harder and harder against Jabin king of Canaan until they destroyed him

Chapter 5

On that day Deborah and Barak son of Abinoam sang this song: "When the princes in Israel take the lead, when the people willingly offer themselves— praise the LORD! "Hear this, you kings! Listen, you rulers! I, even I, will sing to the LORD; I will praise the LORD, the God of Israel, in song "When you, LORD, went out from Seir, when you marched from the land of Edom, the earth shook, the heavens poured, the clouds poured down water. The mountains quaked before the LORD, the One of Sinai, before the LORD, the God of Israel "In the days of Shamgar son of Anath, in the days of Jael, the highways were abandoned; travelers took to winding paths. Villagers in Israel would not fight; they held back until I, Deborah, arose, until I arose, a mother in Israel. God chose new leaders when war came to the city gates, but not a shield or spear was seen among forty thousand in Israel. My heart is with Israel's princes, with the willing volunteers among the people. Praise the LORD! "You who ride on white donkeys, sitting on your saddle blankets, and you who walk along the road, consider the voice of the singers at the watering places. They recite the victories of the LORD, the victories of his villagers in Israel "Then the people of the LORD went down to the city gates. 'Wake up, wake up, Deborah! Wake up, wake up, break out in song! Arise, Barak! Take captive your captives, son of Abinoam.' "The remnant of the nobles came down; the people of the LORD came down to me against the mighty. Some came from Ephraim, whose roots were in Amalek; Benjamin was with the people who followed you. From Makir captains came down, from Zebulun those who bear a commander's staff. The princes of Issachar were with Deborah; yes, Issachar was with Barak, sent under his command into the valley. In the districts of Reuben there was much searching of heart. Why did you stay among the sheep pens to hear the whistling for the flocks? In the districts of Reuben there was much searching of heart. Gilead stayed beyond the Jordan. And Dan, why did he linger by the ships? Asher remained on the coast and stayed in his coves. The people of Zebulun risked their very lives; so did Naphtali on the terraced fields "Kings came, they fought, the kings of Canaan fought. At Taanach, by the waters of Megiddo, they took no plunder of silver. From the heavens the stars fought, from their courses they fought against Sisera. The river Kishon swept them away, the age-old river, the river Kishon. March on, my soul; be strong! Then thundered the horses' hooves— galloping, galloping go his mighty steeds. 'Curse Meroz,' said the angel of the LORD. 'Curse its people bitterly, because they did not come to help the LORD, to help the LORD against the mighty.' "Most blessed of women be Jael, the wife of Heber the Kenite, most blessed of tent-dwelling women. He asked for water, and she gave him milk; in a bowl fit for nobles she brought him curdled milk. Her hand reached for the tent peg, her right hand for the workman's hammer. She struck Sisera, she crushed his head, she shattered and pierced his temple. At her feet he sank, he fell; there he lay. At her feet he sank, he fell; where he sank, there he fell—dead "Through the window peered Sisera's mother; behind the lattice she cried out, 'Why is his chariot so long in coming? Why is the clatter of his chariots delayed?' The wisest of her ladies answer her; indeed, she keeps saying to herself, 'Are they not finding and dividing the spoils: a woman or two for each man, colorful garments as plunder for Sisera, colorful garments embroidered, highly embroidered garments for my neck— all this as plunder?' "So may all your enemies perish, LORD! But may all who love you be like the sun when it rises in its strength." Then the land had peace for forty years

Chapter 6

The children of Israel committed wickedness before the LORD, and the LORD gave them into the hand of Midian for ten years. The hand of Midian came upon Israel, and because of the Midianites, the children of Israel made dens in the mountains, caves, and fortresses. Whenever Israel had sown, the Midianites and Amalekites and the peoples of the east came and caught up with them. They encamped against them and destroyed the produce of the land as far as Gaza, leaving no sustenance in Israel, neither sheep, nor ox, nor donkey. They came up with their livestock and their tents, swarming like locusts, so that they and their camels were without number; they invaded the land to ravage it. Thus, Israel was brought very low because of Midian, and the children of Israel cried out to the LORD When the children of Israel cried out to the LORD because of the Midianites, the LORD sent a prophet to the children of Israel who said to them, "Thus says the LORD, the God of Israel: I brought you up out of Egypt and brought you out of the house of bondage. I delivered you out of the hands of the Egyptians and out of the hands of all who oppressed you. I drove them out before you and gave you their land. I said to you, 'I am the LORD your God; do not fear the gods of the Amorites, in whose land you dwell.' But you have not obeyed my voice." The angel of the LORD came and sat under the terebinth tree in Ophrah, which belonged to Joash the Abiezrite. His son Gideon was threshing wheat in the winepress to hide it from the Midianites. The angel of the LORD appeared to him and said, "The LORD is with you, mighty warrior." Gideon replied, "Pardon me, my lord, but if the LORD is with us, why has all this happened to us? Where are all his wonders that our ancestors told us about when they said, 'Did not the LORD bring us up out of Egypt?' But now the LORD has abandoned us and given us into the hand of Midian." The LORD turned to him and said, "Go in the strength you have and save Israel out of Midian's hand. Am I not sending you?" Gideon replied, "Pardon me, my lord, but how can I save Israel? My clan is the weakest in Manasseh, and I am the least in my family." The LORD answered, "I will be with you, and you will strike down all the Midianites, leaving none alive." Gideon said, "If now I have found favor in your eyes, give me a sign that it is really you talking to me. Please do not go away until I come back and bring my offering and set it before you." And the LORD said, "I will wait until you return." Gideon

went in, prepared a young goat, and from an ephah of flour he made bread without yeast. Putting the meat in a basket and its broth in a pot, he brought them out and offered them to him under the oak. The angel of God said to him, "Take the meat and the unleavened bread, place them on this rock, and pour out the broth." And Gideon did so. Then the angel of the LORD touched the meat and the unleavened bread with the tip of the staff that was in his hand. Fire flared from the rock, consuming the meat and the bread. The angel of the LORD disappeared. When Gideon realized that it was the angel of the LORD, he exclaimed, "Alas, Sovereign LORD! I have seen the angel of the LORD face to face!" But the LORD said to him, "Peace! Do not be afraid. You are not going to die." So Gideon built an altar to the LORD there and called it The LORD Is Peace. To this day it stands in Ophrah of the Abiezrites That same night the LORD said to him, "Take the second bull from your father's herd, the one seven years old. Tear down your father's altar to Baal and cut down the Asherah pole beside it. Then build a proper kind of altar to the LORD your God on the top of this height. Using the wood of the Asherah pole that you cut down, offer the second bull as a burnt offering." So Gideon took ten of his servants and did as the LORD told him. But because he was afraid of his family and the townspeople, he did it at night rather than in the daytime In the morning, when the people of the town got up, there was Baal's altar, demolished, with the Asherah pole beside it cut down and the second bull sacrificed on the newly built altar! They asked each other, "Who did this?" When they carefully investigated, they were told, "Gideon son of Joash did it." The people of the town demanded of Joash, "Bring out your son. He must die because he has broken down Baal's altar and cut down the Asherah pole beside it." But Joash replied to the hostile crowd around him, "Are you going to plead Baal's cause? Are you trying to save him? Whoever fights for him shall be put to death by morning! If Baal really is a god, he can defend himself when someone breaks down his altar." So because Gideon broke down Baal's altar, they gave him the name Jerub-Baal that day, saying, "Let Baal contend with him." Now all the Midianites, Amalekites, and other eastern peoples joined forces and crossed over the Jordan and camped in the Valley of Jezreel. Then the Spirit of the LORD came on Gideon, and he blew a trumpet, summoning the Abiezrites to follow him. He sent messengers throughout Manasseh, calling them to arms, and also into Asher, Zebulun, and Naphtali, so that they too went up to meet them Gideon said to God, "If you will save Israel by my hand as you have promised—look, I will place a wool fleece on the threshing floor. If there is dew only on the fleece and all the ground is dry, then I will know that you will save Israel by my hand, as you said." And that is what happened. Gideon rose early the next day; he squeezed the fleece and wrung out the dew—a bowlful of water Then Gideon said to God, "Do not be angry with me. Let me make just one more request. Allow me one more test with the fleece. This time make the fleece dry and let the ground be covered with dew." That night God did so. Only the fleece was dry; all the ground was covered with dew

Chapter 7

Early in the morning, Jerub-Baal (that is, Gideon) and all his men camped at the spring of Harod. The camp of Midian was north of them in the valley near the hill of Moreh. The LORD said to Gideon, "You have too many men. I cannot deliver Midian into their hands, or Israel would boast against me, saying, 'My own strength has saved me.' Now announce to the army, 'Anyone who trembles with fear may turn back and leave Mount Gilead.'" So twenty-two thousand men left, while ten thousand remained But the LORD said to Gideon, "There are still too many men. Take them down to the water, and I will thin them out for you there. If I say, 'This one shall go with you,' he shall go; but if I say, 'This one shall not go with you,' he shall not go." So Gideon took the men down to the water. There the LORD told him, "Separate those who lap the water with their tongues as a dog laps from those who kneel down to drink." Three hundred of them drank from cupped hands, lapping like dogs. All the rest got down on their knees to drink The LORD said to Gideon, "With the three hundred men that lapped I will save you and give the Midianites into your hands. Let all the others go home." So Gideon sent the rest of the Israelites home but kept the three hundred, who took over the provisions and trumpets of the others. Now the camp of Midian lay below him in the valley During that night the LORD said to Gideon, "Get up, go down against the camp, because I am going to give it into your hands. If you are afraid to attack, go down to the camp with your servant Purah and listen to what they are saying. Afterward, you will be encouraged to attack the camp." So he and Purah his servant went down to the outposts of the camp. The Midianites, the Amalekites, and all the other eastern peoples had settled in the valley, thick as locusts. Their camels could no more be counted than the sand on the seashore Gideon arrived just as a man was telling a friend his dream. "I had a dream," he was saying. "A round loaf of barley bread came tumbling into the Midianite camp. It struck the tent with such force that the tent overturned and collapsed." His friend responded, "This can be nothing other than the sword of Gideon son of Joash, the Israelite. God has given the Midianites and the whole camp into his hands." When Gideon heard the dream and its interpretation, he bowed down and worshiped. He returned to the camp of Israel and called out, "Get up! The LORD has given the Midianite camp into your hands." Dividing the three hundred men into three companies, he placed trumpets and empty jars in the hands of all of them, with torches inside "Watch me," he told them. "Follow my lead. When I get to the edge of the camp, do exactly as I do. When I and all who are with me blow our trumpets, then from all around the camp blow yours and shout, 'For the LORD and for Gideon.'" Gideon and the hundred men with him reached the edge of the camp at the beginning of the middle watch, just after they had changed the guard. They blew their trumpets and broke the jars that were in their hands. The three companies blew the trumpets and smashed the jars. Grasping the torches in their left hands and holding in their right hands the trumpets they were to blow, they shouted, "A sword for the LORD and for Gideon!" While each man held his position around the camp, all the Midianites ran, crying out as they fled. When the three hundred trumpets sounded, the LORD caused the men throughout the camp to turn on each other with their swords. The army fled to Beth Shittah toward Zererah as far as the border of Abel Meholah near Tabbath. Israelites from Naphtali, Asher, and all Manasseh were called out, and they pursued the Midianites. Gideon sent messengers throughout the hill country of Ephraim, saying, "Come down against the Midianites and seize the waters of the Jordan ahead of them as far as Beth Barah." So all the men of Ephraim were called out, and they seized the waters of the Jordan as far as Beth Barah. They also captured two of the Midianite leaders, Oreb and Zeeb. They killed Oreb at the rock of Oreb, and Zeeb at the winepress of Zeeb. They pursued the Midianites and brought the heads of Oreb and Zeeb to Gideon, who was by the Jordan

Chapter 8

Now the Ephraimites asked Gideon, "Why have you treated us like this? Why didn't you call us when you went to fight Midian?" And they challenged him vigorously. But he answered them, "What have I accomplished compared to you? Aren't the gleanings of Ephraim's grapes better than the full grape harvest of Abiezer? God gave Oreb and Zeeb, the Midianite leaders, into your hands. What was I able to do compared to you?" At this, their resentment against him subsided Gideon and his three hundred men, exhausted yet keeping up the pursuit, came to the Jordan and crossed it. He said to the men of Succoth, "Give my troops some bread; they are worn out, and I am still pursuing Zebah and Zalmunna, the kings of Midian." But the officials of Succoth said, "Do you already have the hands of Zebah and Zalmunna in your possession? Why should we give bread to your troops?" Then Gideon replied, "Just for that, when the LORD has given Zebah and Zalmunna into my hand, I will tear your flesh with desert thorns and briers." From there he went up to Peniel and made the same request of them, but they answered as the men of Succoth had. So he said to the men of Peniel, "When I return in triumph, I will tear down this tower." Now Zebah and Zalmunna were in Karkor with a force of about fifteen thousand men, all that were left of the armies of the eastern peoples; a hundred and twenty thousand swordsmen had fallen. Gideon went up by the route of the nomads east of Nobah and Jogbehah and attacked the unsuspecting army. Zebah and Zalmunna, the two kings of Midian, fled, but he pursued them and captured them, routing their entire army Gideon son of Joash then returned from the battle by the Pass of Heres. He caught a young man of Succoth and questioned him, and the young man wrote down for him the names of the seventy-seven officials of Succoth, the elders of the town. Then Gideon came and said to the men of Succoth, "Here are Zebah and Zalmunna, about whom you taunted me by saying, 'Do you already have the hands of Zebah and Zalmunna in your possession? Why should we give bread to your exhausted men?'" He took the elders of the town and taught the men of Succoth a lesson by punishing them with desert thorns and briers. He also pulled down the tower of Peniel and killed the men of the town Then he asked Zebah and Zalmunna, "What kind of men did you kill at Tabor?" "Men like you," they answered, "each one with the bearing of a prince." Gideon replied, "Those were my brothers, the sons of my own mother. As surely as the LORD lives, if you had spared their lives, I would not kill you." Turning to Jether, his oldest son, he said, "Kill them!" But Jether did not draw his sword, because he was only a boy and was afraid Zebah and Zalmunna said, "Come, do it yourself. 'As is the man, so is his strength.'" So Gideon stepped forward and killed them and took the ornaments off their camels' necks The Israelites said to Gideon, "Rule over us—you, your son and your grandson— because you have saved us from the hand of Midian." But Gideon told them, "I will not rule over you, nor will my son rule over you. The LORD will rule over you." And he said, "I do have one request, that each of you give me an earring from your share of the plunder." (It was the custom of the Ishmaelites to wear gold earrings.) They answered, "We'll be glad to give them." So they spread out a garment, and each of them threw a ring from his plunder onto it. The weight of the gold rings he asked for came to seventeen hundred shekels, not counting the ornaments, the pendants, and the purple garments worn by the kings of Midian or the chains that were on their camels' necks. Gideon made the gold into an ephod, which he placed in Ophrah, his town. All Israel prostituted themselves by worshiping it there, and it became a snare to Gideon and his family Thus Midian was subdued before the Israelites and did not raise its head again. During Gideon's lifetime, the land had peace for forty years. Jerub-Baal son of Joash went back home to live. He had seventy sons of his own, for he had many wives. His concubine, who lived in Shechem, also bore him a son, whom he named Abimelek. Gideon son of Joash died at a good old age and was buried in the tomb of his father Joash in Ophrah of the Abiezrites No sooner had Gideon died than the Israelites again prostituted themselves to the Baals. They set up Baal-Berith as their god and did not remember the LORD their God, who had rescued them from the hands of all their enemies on every side. They also failed to show any loyalty to the family of Jerub-Baal (that is, Gideon) in spite of all the good things he had done for them

Chapter 9

Abimelek son of Jerub-Baal went to his mother's brothers in Shechem and said to them and to all his mother's clan, "Ask all the citizens of Shechem, 'Which is better for you: to have all seventy of Jerub-Baal's sons rule over you, or just one man?' Remember, I am your flesh and blood." When the brothers repeated all this to the citizens of Shechem, they were inclined to follow Abimelek, for they said, "He is related to us." They gave him seventy shekels of silver from the temple of Baal-Berith, and Abimelek used it to hire reckless scoundrels, who became his followers. He went to his father's home in Ophrah and on one stone murdered his seventy brothers, the sons of Jerub-Baal. But Jotham, the youngest son of Jerub-Baal, escaped by hiding Then all the citizens of Shechem and Beth Millo gathered beside the great tree at the pillar in Shechem to crown Abimelek king. When Jotham was told about this, he climbed up on the top of Mount Gerizim and shouted to them, "Listen to me, citizens of Shechem, so that God may listen to you. One day the trees went out to anoint a king for themselves. They said to the olive tree, 'Be our king.' "But the olive tree answered, 'Should I give up my oil, by which both gods and humans are honored, to hold sway over the trees?' "Next, the trees said to the fig tree, 'Come and be our king.' "But the fig tree replied, 'Should I give up my fruit, so good and sweet, to hold sway over the trees?' "Then the trees said to the vine, 'Come and be our king.' "But the vine answered, 'Should I give up my wine, which cheers both gods and humans, to hold sway over the trees?' "Finally, all the trees said to the thornbush, 'Come and be our king.' "The thornbush said to the trees, 'If you really want to anoint me king over you, come and take refuge in my shade; but if not, then let fire come out of the thornbush and consume the cedars of Lebanon!' "Have you acted honorably and in good faith by making Abimelek king? Have you been fair to Jerub-Baal and his family? Have you treated him as he deserves? Remember that my father fought for you and risked his life to rescue you from the hand of Midian. But today you have revolted against my father's family. You have murdered his seventy sons on a single stone and have made Abimelek, the son of his female slave, king over the citizens of Shechem because he is related to you. So have you acted honorably and in good faith toward Jerub-Baal and his family today? If you have, may Abimelek be your joy, and may you be his, too! But if you have not, let fire come out from Abimelek and consume you, the citizens of Shechem and Beth Millo, and let fire come out from you, the citizens of Shechem and Beth Millo, and consume Abimelek!" Then Jotham fled, escaping to Beer, and he lived there because he was afraid of his brother Abimelek After Abimelek had governed Israel three years, God stirred up animosity between Abimelek and the citizens of Shechem so that they acted treacherously against Abimelek. God did this in order that the crime against Jerub-Baal's seventy sons, the shedding of their blood, might be avenged on their brother Abimelek and on the citizens of Shechem, who had helped him murder his brothers. In opposition to him, these citizens of Shechem set men on the hilltops to ambush and rob everyone who passed by, and this was reported to Abimelek Now Gaal son of Ebed moved with his clan into Shechem, and its citizens put their confidence in him. After they had gone out into the fields and gathered the grapes and trodden them, they held a festival in the temple of their god. While they were eating and drinking, they cursed Abimelek. Then Gaal son of Ebed said, "Who is Abimelek, and why should we Shechemites be subject to him? Isn't he Jerub-Baal's son, and isn't Zebul his deputy? Serve the family of Hamor, Shechem's father! Why should we serve Abimelek? If only this people were under my command! Then I would get rid of him. I would say to Abimelek, 'Call out your whole army!'" When Zebul the governor of the city heard what Gaal son of Ebed said, he was very angry. Under cover, he sent messengers to Abimelek, saying, "Gaal son of Ebed and his clan have come to Shechem and are stirring up the city against you. Now then, during the night you and your men should come and lie in wait in the fields. In the morning at sunrise, advance against the city. When Gaal and his men come out against you, do whatever your hand finds to do." So Abimelek and all his troops set out by night and took up concealed positions near Shechem in four companies. Now Gaal son of Ebed had gone out and was standing at the entrance of the city gate just as Abimelek and his troops came out from their hiding place When Gaal saw them, he said to Zebul, "Look, people are coming down from the tops of the mountains!" Zebul replied, "You mistake the shadows of the mountains for men." But Gaal spoke up again: "Look, people are coming down from the central hill, and a company is coming from the direction of the diviners' tree." Then Zebul said to him, "Where is your big talk now, you who said, 'Who is Abimelek that we should be subject to him?' Aren't these the men you ridiculed? Go out and fight them!" So Gaal led out the citizens of Shechem and fought Abimelek. Abimelek chased him all the way to the entrance of the gate, and many were killed as they fled. Then Abimelek stayed in Arumah, and Zebul drove Gaal and his clan out of Shechem The next day the people of Shechem went out to the fields, and this was reported to Abimelek. So he took his men, divided them into three companies, and set an ambush in the fields. When he saw the people coming out of the city, he rose to attack them. Abimelek and the companies with him rushed forward to a position at the entrance of the city gate. Then two companies attacked those in the fields and struck them down. All that day Abimelek pressed his attack against the city until he had captured it and killed its people. Then he destroyed the city and scattered salt over it On hearing this, the citizens in the tower of Shechem went into the stronghold of the temple of El-Berith. When Abimelek heard that they had assembled there, he and all his men went up Mount Zalmon. He took an ax and cut off some branches, which he lifted to his shoulders. He ordered the men with him, "Quick! Do what you have seen me do!" So all the men cut branches and followed Abimelek. They piled them against the stronghold and set it on fire with the people still inside. So all the people in the tower of Shechem, about a thousand men and women, also died Next Abimelek went to Thebez and besieged it and captured it. Inside the city, however, was a strong tower, to which all the men and women—all the people of the city—had fled. They had locked themselves in and climbed up on the tower roof. Abimelek went to the tower and attacked it. But as he approached the entrance to the tower to set it on fire, a woman dropped an upper millstone on his head and cracked his skull Hurriedly, he called to his armor-bearer, "Draw your sword and kill me, so that they can't say, 'A woman killed him.'" So his servant ran him through, and he died. When the Israelites saw that Abimelek was dead, they went home. Thus God repaid the wickedness that Abimelek had done to his father by murdering his seventy brothers. God also made the people of Shechem pay for all their wickedness. The curse of Jotham son of Jerub-Baal came on them

Chapter 10

After the time of Abimelek, a man of Issachar named Tola son of Puah, the son of Dodo, rose to save Israel. He lived in Shamir, in the hill country of Ephraim. He led Israel twenty-three years; then he died and was buried in Shamir He was followed by Jair of Gilead, who led Israel twenty-two years. He had thirty sons, who rode thirty donkeys. They controlled thirty towns in Gilead, which to this day are called Havvoth Jair. When Jair died, he was buried in Kamon Again the Israelites did evil in the eyes of the LORD. They served the Baals and the Ashtoreths, and the gods of Aram, the gods of Sidon, the gods of Moab, the gods of the Ammonites, and the gods of the Philistines. And because the Israelites forsook the LORD and no longer served him, he became angry with them. He sold them into the hands of the Philistines and the Ammonites, who that year shattered and crushed them. For eighteen years they oppressed all the Israelites on the east side of the Jordan in Gilead, the land of the Amorites. The Ammonites also crossed the Jordan to fight against Judah, Benjamin, and Ephraim; Israel was in great distress Then the Israelites cried out to the LORD, "We have sinned against you, forsaking our God and serving the Baals." The LORD replied, "When the Egyptians, the Amorites, the Ammonites, the Philistines, the Sidonians, the Amalekites, and the Maonites oppressed you and you cried to me for help, did I not save you from their hands? But you have forsaken me and served other gods, so I will no longer save you. Go and cry out to the gods you have chosen. Let them save you when you are in trouble!" But the Israelites said to the LORD, "We have sinned. Do with us whatever you think best, but please rescue us now." Then they got rid of the foreign gods among them and served the LORD. And he could bear Israel's misery no longer When the Ammonites were called to arms and camped in Gilead, the Israelites assembled and camped at Mizpah. The leaders of the people of Gilead said to each other, "Whoever will take the lead in attacking the Ammonites will be head over all who live in Gilead."

Chapter 11

Gilead begat Jephthah; Jephthah the Gileadite was a valiant man, but the son of a harlot. Gilead's wife bore him sons, and when her sons grew up, they drove Jephthah out and said to him, "You shall not inherit in our father's house, for you are the son of another woman." So Jephthah fled from his brothers and settled in the land of Tob, where he gathered a group of idle men around him After a while, the Ammonites made war on Israel. When this happened, the elders of Gilead went to get Jephthah from the land of Tob. They said to him, "Come and be our commander, so we can fight the Ammonites." Jephthah responded, "Didn't you hate me and drive me from my father's house? Why do you come to me now when you're in trouble?" The elders of Gilead replied, "That's why we've turned to you now, so you can go with us to fight the Ammonites, and you will be head over all of us who live in Gilead." Jephthah said, "If you take me back to fight the Ammonites and the LORD gives them to me, will I really be your head?" The elders of Gilead answered, "The LORD is our witness; we will certainly do as you say." So Jephthah went with the elders of Gilead, and the people made him head and commander over them. And he repeated all his words before the LORD in Mizpah Jephthah sent messengers to the king of the Ammonites, saying, "What do you have against me that you have attacked my country?" The king of the Ammonites answered Jephthah's messengers, "When Israel came up out of Egypt, they took away my land from the Arnon to the Jabbok, all the way to the Jordan. Now, give it back peaceably." Jephthah sent back messengers to the Ammonite king, saying, "This is what Jephthah says: Israel did not take the land of Moab or the land of the Ammonites. When they came up out of Egypt, Israel went through the wilderness to the Red Sea and on to Kadesh. Then Israel sent messengers to the king of Edom, saying, 'Give us permission to go through your country,' but the king of Edom would not listen. They sent also to the king of Moab, and he refused. So Israel stayed at Kadesh "Next, they traveled through the wilderness, skirted the lands of Edom and Moab, passed along the eastern side of Moab, and camped on the other side of the Arnon. They did not enter the territory of Moab, for the Arnon was its border. Then Israel sent messengers to Sihon king of the Amorites, who ruled in Heshbon, and said to him, 'Let us pass through your country to our own place.' Sihon, however, did not trust Israel to pass through his territory. He mustered all his troops and encamped at Jahaz and fought with Israel. Then the LORD, the God of Israel, gave Sihon and all his men into Israel's hands, and they defeated them. Israel took over all the land of the Amorites who lived in that country, capturing all of it from the Arnon to the Jabbok and from the desert to the Jordan "Now since the LORD, the God of Israel, has driven the Amorites out before his people Israel, what right do you have to take it over? Will you not take what your god Chemosh gives you? Likewise, whatever the LORD our God has given us, we will possess. Are you any better than Balak son of Zippor, king of Moab? Did he ever quarrel with Israel or fight with them? For three hundred years Israel occupied Heshbon, Aroer, the surrounding settlements, and all the towns along the Arnon. Why didn't you retake them during that time? I have not wronged you, but you are doing me wrong by waging war against me. Let the LORD, the Judge, decide the dispute this day between the Israelites and the Ammonites." But the king of the Ammonites paid no attention to the message Jephthah sent him Then the Spirit of the LORD came on Jephthah. He crossed Gilead and Manasseh, passed through Mizpah of Gilead, and from there he advanced against the Ammonites. And Jephthah made a vow to the LORD: "If you give the Ammonites into my hands, whatever comes out of the door of my house to meet me when I return in triumph from the Ammonites will be the LORD's, and I will sacrifice it as a burnt offering." Then Jephthah went over to fight the Ammonites, and the LORD gave them into his hands. He devastated twenty towns from Aroer to the vicinity of Minnith, as far as Abel Keramim. Thus Israel subdued Ammon. When Jephthah returned to his home in Mizpah, who should come out to meet him but his daughter, dancing to the sound of timbrels! She was an only child. Except for her, he had neither son nor daughter. When he saw her, he tore his clothes and cried, "Oh no, my daughter! You have brought me down and I am devastated. I have made a vow to the LORD that I cannot break." "My father," she replied, "you have given your word to the LORD. Do to me just as you promised, now that the LORD has avenged you of your enemies, the Ammonites. But grant me this one request," she said. "Give me two months to roam the hills and weep with my friends because I will never marry." "You may go," he said. And he let her go for two months. She and her friends went into the hills and wept because she would never marry. After the two months, she returned to her father, and he did to her as he had vowed. And she was a virgin. From this comes the Israelite tradition that each year the young women of Israel go out for four days to commemorate the daughter of Jephthah the Gileadite

Chapter 12

The Ephraimite forces were called out, and they crossed over to Zaphon. They said to Jephthah, "Why did you go to fight the Ammonites without calling us to go with you? We're going to burn down your house over your head." Jephthah answered, "I and my people were engaged in a great struggle with the Ammonites, and although I called, you didn't save me out of their hands. When I saw that you wouldn't help, I took my life in my hands and crossed over to fight the Ammonites, and the LORD gave me the victory over them. Now why have you come up today to fight me?" Jephthah then called together the men of Gilead and fought against Ephraim. The Gileadites struck them down because the Ephraimites had said, "You Gileadites are renegades from Ephraim and Manasseh." The Gileadites captured the fords of the Jordan leading to Ephraim, and whenever a survivor of Ephraim said, "Let me cross over," the men of Gilead asked him, "Are you an Ephraimite?" If he replied, "No," they said, "All right, say 'Shibboleth.'" If he said, "Sibboleth," because he could not pronounce the word correctly, they seized him and killed him at the fords of the Jordan. Forty-two thousand Ephraimites were killed at that time Jephthah led Israel six years. Then Jephthah the Gileadite died and was buried in a town in Gilead After him, Ibzan of Bethlehem led Israel. He had thirty sons and thirty daughters. He gave his daughters away in marriage to those outside his clan, and for his sons, he brought in thirty young women as wives from outside his clan. Ibzan led Israel seven years. Then Ibzan died and was buried in Bethlehem After him, Elon the Zebulunite led Israel ten years. Then Elon died and was buried in Aijalon in the land of Zebulun After him, Abdon son of Hillel, from Pirathon, led Israel. He had forty sons and thirty grandsons, who rode on seventy donkeys. He led Israel eight years. Then Abdon son of Hillel died and was buried at Pirathon in Ephraim, in the hill country of the Amalekites

Chapter 13

Again the Israelites did evil in the eyes of the LORD, so the LORD delivered them into the hands of the Philistines for forty years. A certain man of Zorah, named Manoah, from the clan of the Danites, had a wife who was childless, unable to give birth. The angel of the LORD appeared to her and said, "You are barren and childless, but you are going to become pregnant and give birth to a son. Now see to it that you drink no wine or other fermented drink and that you do not eat anything unclean. You will become pregnant and have a son whose head is never to be touched by a razor because the boy is to be a Nazirite, dedicated to God from the womb. He will take the lead in delivering Israel from the hands of the Philistines." Then the woman went to her husband and told him, "A man of God came to me. He looked like an angel of God, very awesome. I didn't ask him where he came from, and he didn't tell me his name. But he said to me, 'You will become pregnant and have a son. Now then, drink no wine or other fermented drink and do not eat anything unclean because the boy will be a Nazirite of God from the womb until the day of his death.'" Then Manoah prayed to the LORD: "Pardon your servant, Lord. I beg you to let the man of God you sent to us come again to teach us how to bring up the boy who is to be born." God heard Manoah, and the angel of God came again to the woman while she was out in the field, but her husband Manoah was not with her. The woman hurried to tell her husband, "He's here! The man who appeared to me the other day!" Manoah got up and followed his wife. When he came to the man, he said, "Are you the man who talked to my wife?" "I am," he said So Manoah asked him, "When your words are fulfilled, what is to be the rule that governs the boy's life and work?" The angel of the LORD answered, "Your wife must do all that I have told her. She must not eat anything that comes from the grapevine, nor drink any wine or other fermented drink, nor eat anything unclean. She must do everything I have commanded her." Manoah said to the angel of the LORD, "We would like you to stay until we prepare a young goat for you." The angel of the LORD replied, "Even though you detain me, I will not eat any of your food. But if you prepare a burnt offering, offer it to the LORD." (Manoah did not realize that it was the angel of the LORD.) Then Manoah inquired of the angel of the LORD, "What is your name, so that we may honor you when your word comes true?" He replied, "Why do you ask my name? It is beyond understanding." Then Manoah took a young goat, together with the grain offering, and sacrificed it on a rock to the LORD. And the LORD did an amazing thing while Manoah and his wife watched: As the flame blazed up from the altar toward heaven, the angel of the LORD ascended in the flame. Seeing this, Manoah and his wife fell with their faces to the ground. When the angel of the LORD did not show himself again to Manoah and his wife, Manoah realized that it was the angel of the LORD "We are doomed to die!" he said to his wife. "We have seen God!" But his wife answered, "If the LORD had meant to kill us, he would not have accepted a burnt offering and grain offering from our hands, nor shown us all these things or now told us this." The woman gave birth to a boy and named him Samson. He grew, and the LORD blessed him, and the Spirit of the LORD began to stir him while he was in Mahaneh Dan, between Zorah and Eshtaol

Chapter 14

Samson went down to Timnah and saw there a young Philistine woman. When he returned, he said to his father and mother, "I have seen a Philistine woman in Timnah; now get her for me as my wife." His father and mother replied, "Isn't there an acceptable woman among your relatives or among all our people? Must you go to the uncircumcised Philistines to get a wife?" But Samson said to his father, "Get her for me. She's the right one for me." (His parents did not know that this was from the LORD, who was seeking an occasion to confront the Philistines; for at that time, they were ruling over Israel.) Samson went down to Timnah together with his father and mother. As they approached the vineyards of Timnah, suddenly a young lion came roaring toward him. The Spirit of the LORD came powerfully upon him so that he tore the lion apart with his bare hands as he might have torn a young goat. But he told neither his father nor his mother what he had done. Then he went down and talked with the woman, and he liked her Sometime later, when he went back to marry her, he turned aside to look at the lion's carcass, and in it, he saw a swarm of bees and some honey. He scooped out the honey with his hands and ate as he went along. When he rejoined his parents, he gave them some, and they too ate it. But he did not tell them that he had taken the honey from the lion's carcass Now his father went down to see the woman, and there Samson held a feast, as was customary for young men. When the people saw him, they chose thirty men to be his companions. "Let me tell you a riddle," Samson said to them. "If you can give me the answer within the seven days of the feast, I will give you thirty linen garments and thirty sets of clothes. If you can't tell me the answer, you must give me thirty linen garments and thirty sets of clothes." "Tell us your riddle," they said. "Let's hear it." He replied, "Out of the eater, something to eat; out of the strong, something sweet." For three days, they could not give the answer On the fourth day, they said to Samson's wife, "Coax your husband into explaining the riddle for us, or we will burn you and your father's household to death. Did you invite us here to steal our property?" Then Samson's wife threw herself on him, sobbing, "You hate me! You don't really love me. You've given my people a riddle, but you haven't told me the answer." "I haven't even explained it to my father or mother," he replied, "so why should I explain it to you?" She cried the whole seven days of the feast. So on the seventh day, he finally told her because she continued to press him. She, in turn, explained the riddle to her people Before sunset on the seventh day, the men of the town said to him, "What is sweeter than honey? What is stronger than a lion?" Samson said to them, "If you had not plowed with my heifer, you would not have solved my riddle." Then the Spirit of the LORD came powerfully upon him. He went down to Ashkelon, struck down thirty of their men, stripped them of everything, and gave their clothes to those who had explained the riddle. Burning with anger, he returned to his father's home. And Samson's wife was given to one of his companions who had attended him at the feast

Chapter 15

Later on, at the time of wheat harvest, Samson took a young goat and went to visit his wife. He said, "I'm going to my wife's room." But her father would not let him go in. "I was so sure you hated her," he said, "that I gave her to your companion. Isn't her younger sister more attractive? Take her instead." Samson said to them, "This time I have a right to get even with the Philistines; I will really harm them." So he went out and caught three hundred foxes and tied them tail to tail in pairs. He then fastened a torch to every pair of tails, lit the torches, and let the foxes loose in the standing grain of the Philistines. He burned up the shocks and standing grain, together with the vineyards and olive groves When the Philistines asked, "Who did this?" they were told, "Samson, the Timnite's son-in-law, because his wife was given to his companion." So the Philistines went up and burned her and her father to death Samson said to them, "Since you've acted like this, I swear that I won't stop until I get my revenge on you." He attacked them viciously and slaughtered many of them. Then he went down and stayed in a cave in the rock of Etam The Philistines went up and camped in Judah, spreading out near Lehi. The people of Judah asked, "Why have you come to fight us?" "We have come to take Samson prisoner," they answered, "to do to him as he did to us." Then three thousand men from Judah went down to the cave in the rock of Etam and said to Samson, "Don't you realize that the Philistines are rulers over us? What have you done to

us?" He answered, "I merely did to them what they did to me." They said to him, "We've come to tie you up and hand you over to the Philistines." Samson said, "Swear to me that you won't kill me yourselves." "Agreed," they answered. "We will only tie you up and hand you over to them. We will not kill you." So they bound him with two new ropes and led him up from the rock. As he approached Lehi, the Philistines came toward him shouting. The Spirit of the LORD came powerfully upon him. The ropes on his arms became like charred flax, and the bindings dropped from his hands. Finding a fresh jawbone of a donkey, he grabbed it and struck down a thousand men Then Samson said, "With a donkey's jawbone I have made donkeys of them. With a donkey's jawbone, I have killed a thousand men." When he finished speaking, he threw away the jawbone; and the place was called Ramath Lehi Because he was very thirsty, he cried out to the LORD, "You have given your servant this great victory. Must I now die of thirst and fall into the hands of the uncircumcised?" Then God opened up the hollow place in Lehi, and water came out of it. When Samson drank, his strength returned, and he revived. So the spring was called En Hakkore, and it is still there in Lehi Samson led Israel for twenty years in the days of the Philistines

Chapter 16

Samson went to Gaza and saw a prostitute and entered her house. When the people of Gaza were told, "Samson has come here," they surrounded the place and lay in wait for him all night at the city gate. They kept quiet all night, saying, "In the morning, we will kill him." But Samson lay till midnight, and at midnight he arose, took hold of the doors of the city gate together with the two posts, and tore them loose, bar and all. He lifted them to his shoulders and carried them to the top of the hill that faces Hebron Sometime later, he fell in love with a woman in the Valley of Sorek whose name was Delilah. The rulers of the Philistines went to her and said, "See if you can lure him into showing you the secret of his great strength and how we can overpower him so we may tie him up and subdue him. Each one of us will give you eleven hundred shekels of silver." So Delilah said to Samson, "Tell me the secret of your great strength and how you can be tied up and subdued." Samson answered her, "If anyone ties me with seven fresh bowstrings that have not been dried, I'll become as weak as any other man." Then the rulers of the Philistines brought her seven fresh bowstrings that had not been dried, and she tied him with them. With men hidden in the room, she called to him, "Samson, the Philistines are upon you!" But he snapped the bowstrings as easily as a piece of string snaps when it comes close to a flame. So the secret of his strength was not discovered Then Delilah said to Samson, "You have made a fool of me; you lied to me. Come now, tell me how you can be tied." He said, "If anyone ties me securely with new ropes that have never been used, I'll become as weak as any other man." So Delilah took new ropes and tied him with them. Then, with men hidden in the room, she called to him, "Samson, the Philistines are upon you!" But he snapped the ropes off his arms as if they were threads Delilah then said to Samson, "Until now, you have been making a fool of me and lying to me. Tell me how you can be tied." He replied, "If you weave the seven braids of my head into the fabric on the loom and tighten it with the pin, I'll become as weak as any other man." So while he was sleeping, Delilah took the seven braids of his head, wove them into the fabric, and tightened it with the pin. Again she called to him, "Samson, the Philistines are upon you!" He awoke from his sleep and pulled up the pin and the loom, with the fabric Then she said to him, "How can you say, 'I love you,' when you won't confide in me? This is the third time you have made a fool of me and haven't told me the secret of your great strength." With such nagging, she prodded him day after day until he was sick to death of it. So he told her everything. "No razor has ever been used on my head," he said, "because I have been a Nazirite dedicated to God from my mother's womb. If my head were shaved, my strength would leave me, and I would become as weak as any other man." When Delilah saw that he had told her everything, she sent word to the rulers of the Philistines, "Come back once more; he has told me everything." So the rulers of the Philistines returned with the silver in their hands. After putting him to sleep on her lap, she called for someone to shave off the seven braids of his hair, and so began to subdue him. And his strength left him Then she called, "Samson, the Philistines are upon you!" He awoke from his sleep and thought, "I'll go out as before and shake myself free." But he did not know that the LORD had left him. Then the Philistines seized him, gouged out his eyes, and took him down to Gaza. Binding him with bronze shackles, they set him to grinding grain in the prison. But the hair on his head began to grow again after it had been shaved Now the rulers of the Philistines assembled to offer a great sacrifice to Dagon their god and to celebrate, saying, "Our god has delivered Samson, our enemy, into our hands." When the people saw him, they praised their god, saying, "Our god has delivered our enemy into our hands, the one who laid waste our land and multiplied our slain." While they were in high spirits, they shouted, "Bring out Samson to entertain us." So they called Samson out of the prison, and he performed for them. When they stood him among the pillars, Samson said to the servant who held his hand, "Put me where I can feel the pillars that support the temple so that I may lean against them." Now the temple was crowded with men and women; all the rulers of the Philistines were there, and on the roof were about three thousand men and women watching Samson perform Then Samson prayed to the LORD, "Sovereign LORD, remember me. Please, God, strengthen me just once more, and let me with one blow get revenge on the Philistines for my two eyes." Then Samson reached toward the two central pillars on which the temple stood. Bracing himself against them, his right hand on one and his left hand on the other, Samson said, "Let me die with the Philistines!" Then he pushed with all his might, and down came the temple on the rulers and all the people in it. Thus he killed many more when he died than while he lived Then his brothers and his father's whole family went down to get him. They brought him back and buried him between Zorah and Eshtaol in the tomb of Manoah his father. He had led Israel twenty years

Chapter 17

There was a man named Micah from the hill country of Ephraim. He said to his mother, "The eleven hundred shekels of silver that were taken from you and about which I heard you utter a curse—I have that silver with me; I took it." Then his mother said, "The LORD bless you, my son!" When he returned the eleven hundred shekels of silver to his mother, she said, "I solemnly consecrate my silver to the LORD for my son to make an image overlaid with silver. I will give it back to you." So after he returned the silver to his mother, she took two hundred shekels of silver and gave them to a silversmith, who used them to make the idol. And it was put in Micah's house Now this man Micah had a shrine, and he made an ephod and some household gods and installed one of his sons as his priest. In those days Israel had no king; everyone did as they saw fit A young Levite from

Bethlehem in Judah, who had been living within the clan of Judah, left that town in search of some other place to stay. On his way, he came to Micah's house in the hill country of Ephraim. Micah asked him, "Where are you from?" "I'm a Levite from Bethlehem in Judah," he said, "and I'm looking for a place to stay." Then Micah said to him, "Live with me and be my father and priest, and I'll give you ten shekels of silver a year, your clothes, and your food." So the Levite agreed to live with him, and the young man became like one of his sons to him. Then Micah installed the Levite, and the young man became his priest and lived in his house. And Micah said, "Now I know that the LORD will be good to me, since this Levite has become my priest."

Chapter 18

In those days, Israel had no king, and in those days the tribe of the Danites was seeking a place of their own where they might settle because they had not yet come into an inheritance among the tribes of Israel. So the Danites sent five of their leading men from Zorah and Eshtaol to spy out the land and explore it. These men represented all the Danites. They told them, "Go, explore the land." So they entered the hill country of Ephraim and came to the house of Micah, where they spent the night. When they were near Micah's house, they recognized the voice of the young Levite; so they turned in there and asked him, "Who brought you here? What are you doing in this place? Why are you here?" He told them what Micah had done for him and said, "He has hired me, and I am his priest." Then they said to him, "Please inquire of God to learn whether our journey will be successful." The priest answered them, "Go in peace. Your journey has the LORD's approval." So the five men left and came to Laish, where they saw that the people were living in safety, like the Sidonians, at peace and secure. And since their land lacked nothing, they were prosperous. Also, they lived a long way from the Sidonians and had no relationship with anyone else When they returned to Zorah and Eshtaol, their fellow Danites asked them, "How did you find things?" They answered, "Come on, let's attack them! We have seen the land, and it is very good. Aren't you going to do something? Don't hesitate to go there and take it over. When you get there, you will find an unsuspecting people and a spacious land that God has put into your hands, a land that lacks nothing whatever." Then six hundred men of the Danites, armed for battle, set out from Zorah and Eshtaol. On their way, they set up camp near Kiriath Jearim in Judah. This is why the place west of Kiriath Jearim is called Mahaneh Dan to this day. From there, they went on to the hill country of Ephraim and came to Micah's house Then the five men who had spied out the land of Laish said to their fellow Danites, "Do you know that one of these houses has an ephod, some household gods, and an image overlaid with silver? Now you know what to do." So they turned in there and went to the house of the young Levite at Micah's place and greeted him. The six hundred Danites, armed for battle, stood at the entrance of the gate. The five men who had spied out the land went inside and took the idol, the ephod, and the household gods, while the priest and the six hundred armed men stood at the entrance of the gate When the five men went into Micah's house and took the idol, the ephod, and the household gods, the priest said to them, "What are you doing?" They answered him, "Be quiet! Don't say a word. Come with us and be our father and priest. Isn't it better that you serve a tribe and clan in Israel as priest rather than just one man's household?" The priest was very pleased. He took the ephod, the household gods, and the idol and went along with the people.

Putting their little children, their livestock, and their possessions in front of them, they turned away and left When they had gone some distance from Micah's house, the men who lived near Micah were called together and overtook the Danites. As they shouted after them, the Danites turned and said to Micah, "What's the matter with you that you called out your men to fight?" He replied, "You took the gods I made and my priest and went away. What else do I have? How can you ask, 'What's the matter with you?'" The Danites answered, "Don't argue with us, or some of the men may get angry and attack you, and you and your family will lose your lives." So the Danites went their way, and Micah, seeing that they were too strong for him, turned around and went back home Then they took what Micah had made and his priest and went on to Laish, against a people at peace and secure. They attacked them with the sword and burned down their city. There was no one to rescue them because they lived a long way from Sidon and had no relationship with anyone else. The city was in a valley near Beth Rehob The Danites rebuilt the city and settled there. They named it Dan after their ancestor Dan, who was born to Israel—though the city used to be called Laish. There the Danites set up for themselves the idol, and Jonathan son of Gershom, the son of Moses, and his sons were priests for the tribe of Dan until the time of the captivity of the land. They continued to use the idol Micah had made, all the time the house of God was in Shiloh

Chapter 19

In those days Israel had no king. Now a Levite who lived in a remote area in the hill country of Ephraim took a concubine from Bethlehem in Judah. But she was unfaithful to him. She left him and went back to her parent's home in Bethlehem, Judah. After she had been there four months, her husband went to her to persuade her to return. He had with him his servant and two donkeys. She took him into her parent's home, and when her father saw him, he gladly welcomed him. His father-in-law, the woman's father, prevailed on him to stay; so he remained with him three days, eating and drinking and sleeping there On the fourth day, they got up early and prepared to leave, but the woman's father said to his son-in-law, "Refresh yourself with something to eat; then you can go." So the two of them sat down to eat and drink together. Afterward, the woman's father said, "Please stay tonight and enjoy yourself." And when the man got up to go, his father-in-law persuaded him, so he stayed there that night. On the morning of the fifth day, when he rose to go, the woman's father said, "Refresh yourself. Wait till afternoon!" So the two of them ate together Then when the man, with his concubine and his servant, got up to leave, his father-in-law, the woman's father, said, "Now look, it's almost evening. Spend the night here; the day is nearly over. Stay and enjoy yourself. Early tomorrow morning, you can get up and be on your way home." But, unwilling to stay another night, the man left and went toward Jebus (that is, Jerusalem), with his two saddled donkeys and his concubine When they were near Jebus and the day was almost gone, the servant said to his master, "Come, let's stop at this city of the Jebusites and spend the night." His master replied, "No. We won't go into an alien city whose people are not Israelites. We will go on to Gibeah." He added, "Come, let's try to reach Gibeah or Ramah and spend the night in one of those places." So they went on, and the sun set as they neared Gibeah in Benjamin. There they stopped to spend the night. They went and sat in the city square, but no one took them in for the night That evening an old man from the hill country of Ephraim,

who was living in Gibeah (the inhabitants of the place were Benjamites), came in from his work in the fields. When he looked and saw the traveler in the city square, the old man asked, "Where are you going? Where did you come from?" He answered, "We are on our way from Bethlehem in Judah to a remote area in the hill country of Ephraim, where I live. I have been to Bethlehem in Judah, and now I am going to the house of the LORD. No one has taken me in for the night. We have both straw and fodder for our donkeys and bread and wine for ourselves, your servants— me, your maidservant, and the young man with us. We don't need anything." "You are welcome at my house," the old man said. "Let me supply whatever you need. Only don't spend the night in the square." So he took him into his house and fed his donkeys. After they had washed their feet, they had something to eat and drink While they were enjoying themselves, some of the wicked men of the city surrounded the house. Pounding on the door, they shouted to the old man who owned the house, "Bring out the man who came to your house so we can have sex with him." The owner of the house went outside and said to them, "No, my friends, don't be so vile. Since this man is my guest, don't do this disgraceful thing. Look, here is my virgin daughter and his concubine. I will bring them out to you now, and you can use them and do to them whatever you wish. But to this man, don't do such a disgraceful thing." But the men would not listen to him. So the man took his concubine and sent her outside to them, and they raped her and abused her throughout the night, and at dawn, they let her go At daybreak, the woman went back to the house where her master was staying, fell down at the door, and lay there until daylight. When her master got up in the morning and opened the door of the house and stepped out to continue on his way, there lay his concubine, fallen in the doorway of the house, with her hands on the threshold. He said to her, "Get up; let's go." But there was no answer. Then the man put her on his donkey and set out for home When he reached home, he took a knife and cut up his concubine, limb by limb, into twelve parts and sent them into all the areas of Israel. Everyone who saw it said, "Such a thing has never been seen or done, not since the day the Israelites came up out of Egypt. Just imagine! We must do something! So speak up!"

Chapter 20

Then all the Israelites from Dan to Beersheba and from the land of Gilead came together as one and assembled before the LORD in Mizpah. The leaders of all the people of the tribes of Israel took their places in the assembly of the people of God—four hundred thousand soldiers armed with swords. (The Benjamites heard that the Israelites had gone up to Mizpah.) Then the Israelites said, "Tell us how this awful thing happened." So the Levite, the husband of the murdered woman, said, "I and my concubine came to Gibeah in Benjamin to spend the night. During the night, the men of Gibeah came after me and surrounded the house, intending to kill me. They raped my concubine, and she died. I took my concubine, cut her into pieces, and sent one piece to each region of Israel's inheritance because they committed this lewd and outrageous act in Israel. Now, all you Israelites, speak up and tell me what you have decided to do." All the men rose up together as one, saying, "None of us will go home. No, not one of us will return to his house. But now this is what we'll do to Gibeah: We'll go up against it in the order decided by casting lots. We'll take ten men out of every hundred from all the tribes of Israel, and a hundred from a thousand, and a thousand from ten thousand, to get provisions for the army. Then, when the army arrives at Gibeah in Benjamin, it can give them what they deserve for this outrageous act done in Israel." So all the Israelites got together and united as one against the city The tribes of Israel sent messengers throughout the tribe of Benjamin, saying, "What about this awful crime that was committed among you? Now turn those wicked men of Gibeah over to us so that we may put them to death and purge the evil from Israel." But the Benjamites would not listen to their fellow Israelites. From their towns, they came together at Gibeah to fight against the Israelites. At once, the Benjamites mobilized twenty-six thousand swordsmen from their towns, in addition to seven hundred able young men from those living in Gibeah. Among all these soldiers, there were seven hundred select troops who were left-handed, each of whom could sling a stone at a hair and not miss Israel, apart from Benjamin, mustered four hundred thousand swordsmen, all of them fit for battle. The Israelites went up to Bethel and inquired of God. They said, "Who of us is to go up first to fight against the Benjamites?" The LORD replied, "Judah shall go first." The next morning the Israelites got up and pitched camp near Gibeah. The Israelites went out to fight the Benjamites and took up battle positions against them at Gibeah. The Benjamites came out of Gibeah and cut down twenty-two thousand Israelites on the battlefield that day. But the Israelites encouraged one another and again took up their positions where they had stationed themselves the first day. The Israelites went up and wept before the LORD until evening, and they inquired of the LORD. They said, "Shall we go up again to fight against the Benjamites, our fellow Israelites?" The LORD answered, "Go up against them." Then the Israelites drew near to Benjamin the second day. This time, when the Benjamites came out from Gibeah to oppose them, they cut down another eighteen thousand Israelites, all of them armed with swords. Then all the Israelites, the whole army, went up to Bethel, and there they sat weeping before the LORD. They fasted that day until evening and presented burnt offerings and fellowship offerings to the LORD. And the Israelites inquired of the LORD. (In those days the ark of the covenant of God was there, with Phinehas son of Eleazar, the son of Aaron, ministering before it.) They asked, "Shall we go up again to fight against the Benjamites, our fellow Israelites, or not?" The LORD responded, "Go, for tomorrow I will give them into your hands." Then Israel set an ambush around Gibeah. They went up against the Benjamites on the third day and took up positions against Gibeah as they had done before. The Benjamites came out to meet them and were drawn away from the city. They began to inflict casualties on the Israelites as before, so that about thirty men fell in the open field and on the roads—the one leading to Bethel and the other to Gibeah. While the Benjamites were saying, "We are defeating them as before," the Israelites were saying, "Let's retreat and draw them away from the city to the roads." All the men of Israel moved from their places and took up positions at Baal Tamar, and the Israelite ambush charged out of its place on the west of Gibeah. Then ten thousand of Israel's able young men made a frontal attack on Gibeah. The fighting was so heavy that the Benjamites did not realize how near disaster was. The LORD defeated Benjamin before Israel, and on that day the Israelites struck down 25,100 Benjamites, all armed with swords. Then the Benjamites saw that they were beaten Now the men of Israel had given way before Benjamin because they relied on the ambush they had set near Gibeah. Those who had been in ambush made a sudden dash into Gibeah, spread out, and put the whole city to the sword. The Israelites had arranged with the ambush that they should send up a great cloud of smoke from the city, and then the Israelites would counterattack The Benjamites had begun to inflict casualties on the Israelites (about thirty), and they said, "We are defeating them as in the first battle." But when the column of smoke began to rise from the city, the Benjamites turned and saw the whole city going up in smoke. Then the Israelites counterattacked, and the Benjamites were terrified because they realized that disaster had come on them. So they fled before the Israelites in the direction of the wilderness but could not escape the battle. And the Israelites who came out of the towns cut them down there. They surrounded the Benjamites, chased them, and easily overran them in the vicinity of Gibeah on the east. Eighteen thousand Benjamites fell, all of them valiant fighters. As they turned and fled toward the wilderness to the rock of Rimmon, the Israelites cut down five thousand men along the roads. They kept pressing after the Benjamites as far as Gidom and struck down two thousand more. On that day twenty-five thousand Benjamite swordsmen fell, all of them valiant fighters. But six hundred of them turned and fled into the wilderness to the rock of Rimmon, where they stayed for four months The men of Israel went back to Benjamin and put all the towns to the sword, including the animals and everything else they found. All the towns they came across, they set on fire Chapter 21 The men of Israel had taken an oath at Mizpah: "Not one of us will give his daughter in marriage to a Benjamite." The people went to Bethel, where they sat before God until evening, raising their voices and weeping bitterly. "LORD, God of Israel," they cried, "why has this happened to Israel? Why should one tribe be missing from Israel today?" Early the next day, the people built an altar and presented burnt offerings and fellowship offerings. Then the Israelites asked, "Who from all the tribes of Israel has failed to assemble before the LORD?" For they had taken a solemn oath that anyone who failed to assemble before the LORD at Mizpah should certainly be put to death Now the Israelites grieved for the tribe of Benjamin, their fellow Israelites. "Today one tribe is cut off from Israel," they said. "How can we provide wives for those who are left, since we have taken an oath by the LORD not to give them any of our daughters in marriage?" Then they asked, "Which one of the tribes of Israel failed to assemble before the LORD at Mizpah?" They discovered that no one from Jabesh Gilead had come to the camp for the assembly. For when they counted the people, they found that none of the people of Jabesh Gilead were there So the assembly sent twelve thousand fighting men with instructions to go to Jabesh Gilead and put to the sword those living there, including the women and children. "This is what you are to do," they said. "Kill every male and every woman who is not a virgin." They found among the people living in Jabesh Gilead four hundred young women who had never slept with a man, and they took them to the camp at Shiloh in Canaan Then the whole assembly sent an offer of peace to the Benjamites at the rock of Rimmon. So the Benjamites returned at that time and were given the women of Jabesh Gilead who had been spared. But there were not enough for all of them The people grieved for Benjamin because the LORD had made a gap in the tribes of Israel. And the elders of the assembly said, "With the women of Benjamin destroyed, how shall we provide wives for the men who are left? The Benjamite survivors must have heirs," they said, "so that a tribe of Israel will not be wiped out. We can't give them our daughters as wives, since we Israelites have taken this oath: 'Cursed be anyone who gives a wife to a Benjamite.'

But look, there is the annual festival of the LORD in Shiloh, to the north of Bethel and east of the road that goes from Bethel to Shechem, and to the south of Lebonah." So they instructed the Benjamites, saying, "Go and hide in the vineyards and watch. When the young women of Shiloh come out to join in the dancing, rush from the vineyards, and each of you seize one of them to be your wife. Then return to the land of Benjamin. When their fathers or brothers complain to us, we will say to them, 'Do us the favor of helping them because we did not get wives for them during the war. You will not be guilty of breaking your oath because you did not give your daughters to them.'" So that is what the Benjamites did. While the young women were dancing, each man caught one and carried her off to be his wife. Then they returned to their inheritance and rebuilt the towns and settled in them At that time the Israelites left that place and went home to their tribes and clans, each to his own inheritance. In those days Israel had no king; everyone did as they saw fit

8. Ruth

Chapter 1

1 At the time when the Judges reigned, there was scarcity in the land, and a man from Beth-Lem Judah went to live in the country of Moab, he and his wife and two sons. 2 The man's name was Elimelech, and his wife's name was Naomi, and the names of his two sons were Mahlon and Chilion, Ephrathites of Beth-Lem Judah; and when they came to the land of Moab, they stayed there. 3 Then Elimelech, Naomi's husband, died, and she remained with her two sons, 4 who took wives from the Moabites: the first was named Orpah, and the other Ruth, and they dwelt there about ten years. 5 Mahlon and Chilion also both died; so the woman was left without her two sons and without her husband. 6 Then she got up with her daughters-in-law and returned from the country of Moab, for she had heard in the country of Moab that the LORD had visited his people and given them bread. 7 Therefore she departed from the place where she was, and her two daughters-in-law with her, and they set out to return to the land of Judah. 8 Naomi said to her two daughters-in-law, "Go, return each of you to your mother's house; the LORD will deal kindly with you, as you have dealt with the dead and with me. 9 May the LORD grant that you may find rest, each of you in the house of her husband." And when she kissed them, they raised their voices and wept. 10 They said to her, "Surely we will return with you to your people." 11 But Naomi said, "Turn away, my daughters; for what reason do you wish to come with me? Are there still sons in my womb, that they may be your husbands? 12 Turn away, my daughters; go your way, for I am too old to have a husband. If I said, 'I have hope,' and if I had a husband tonight, yes, if I should have children, 13 would you stay for them until they were grown? Would you wait for them and refrain from marriage? No, my daughters, for it grieves me greatly for your sakes, that the hand of the LORD has gone out against me." 14 Then they lifted up their voices and wept again; Orpah kissed her mother-in-law, but Ruth clung to her. 15 Naomi said, "Look, your sister-in-law has gone back to her people and her gods; return after your sister-in-law." 16 But Ruth replied, "Do not urge me to leave you or to turn back from you. Where you go, I will go, and where you stay, I will stay. Your people will be my people and your God my God. 17 Where you die, I will die, and there I will be buried. May the LORD deal with me, be it ever so severely, if even death separates you and me." 18 When Naomi realized that Ruth was determined to go with her, she stopped urging her. 19

So the two women went on until they came to Bethlehem. When they arrived in Bethlehem, the whole town was stirred because of them, and the women exclaimed, "Can this be Naomi?" 20 She replied, "Don't call me Naomi. Call me Mara, because the Almighty has made my life very bitter. 21 I went away full, but the LORD has brought me back empty. Why call me Naomi? The LORD has afflicted me; the Almighty has brought misfortune upon me." 22 So Naomi returned from Moab accompanied by Ruth the Moabite, her daughter-in-law, arriving in Bethlehem as the barley harvest was beginning

Chapter 2

1 Now Naomi had a relative on her husband's side, a man of standing from the clan of Elimelech, whose name was Boaz. 2 And Ruth the Moabite said to Naomi, "Let me go to the fields and pick up the leftover grain behind anyone in whose eyes I find favor." Naomi said to her, "Go ahead, my daughter." 3 So she went out, entered a field, and began to glean behind the harvesters. As it turned out, she was working in a field belonging to Boaz, who was from the clan of Elimelech. 4 Just then Boaz arrived from Bethlehem and greeted the harvesters, "The LORD be with you!" "The LORD bless you!" they answered. 5 Boaz asked the overseer of his harvesters, "Who does that young woman belong to?" 6 The overseer replied, "She is the Moabite who came back from Moab with Naomi. 7 She said, 'Please let me glean and gather among the sheaves behind the harvesters.' She came into the field and has remained here from morning till now, except for a short rest in the shelter." 8 So Boaz said to Ruth, "My daughter, listen to me. Don't go and glean in another field and don't go away from here. Stay here with the women who work for me. 9 Watch the field where the men are harvesting, and follow along after the women. I have told the men not to lay a hand on you. And whenever you are thirsty, go and get a drink from the water jars the men have filled." 10 At this, she bowed down with her face to the ground. She asked him, "Why have I found such favor in your eyes that you notice me—a foreigner?" 11 Boaz replied, "I've been told all about what you have done for your mother-in-law since the death of your husband—how you left your father and mother and your homeland and came to live with a people you did not know before. 12 May the LORD repay you for what you have done. May you be richly rewarded by the LORD, the God of Israel, under whose wings you have come to take refuge." 13 "May I continue to find favor in your eyes, my lord," she said. "You have put me at ease by speaking kindly to your servant—though I do not have the standing of one of your servants." 14 At mealtime Boaz said to her, "Come over here. Have some bread and dip it in the wine vinegar." When she sat down with the harvesters, he offered her some roasted grain. She ate all she wanted and had some left over. 15 As she got up to glean, Boaz gave orders to his men, "Let her gather among the sheaves and don't reprimand her. 16 Even pull out some stalks for her from the bundles and leave them for her to pick up, and don't rebuke her." 17 So Ruth gleaned in the field until evening. Then she threshed the barley she had gathered, and it amounted to about an ephah. 18 She carried it back to town, and her mother-in-law saw how much she had gathered. Ruth also brought out and gave her what she had left over after she had eaten enough. 19 Her mother-in-law asked her, "Where did you glean today? Where did you work? Blessed be the man who took notice of you!" Then Ruth told her mother-in-law about the one at whose place she had been working. "The name of the man I worked with today is Boaz," she said. 20 "The LORD bless him!" Naomi said to her daughter-in-law. "He

has not stopped showing his kindness to the living and the dead." She added, "That man is our close relative; he is one of our guardian-redeemers." 21 Then Ruth the Moabite said, "He even said to me, 'Stay with my workers until they finish harvesting all my grain.'" 22 Naomi said to Ruth her daughter-in-law, "It will be good for you, my daughter, to go with the women who work for him, because in someone else's field you might be harmed." 23 So Ruth stayed close to the women of Boaz to glean until the barley and wheat harvests were finished. And she lived with her mother-in-law

Chapter 3

1 One day Ruth's mother-in-law Naomi said to her, "My daughter, I must find a home for you, where you will be well provided for. 2 Now Boaz, with whose women you have worked, is a relative of ours. Tonight he will be winnowing barley on the threshing floor. 3 Wash, put on perfume, and get dressed in your best clothes. Then go down to the threshing floor, but don't let him know you are there until he has finished eating and drinking. 4 When he lies down, note the place where he is lying. Then go and uncover his feet and lie down. He will tell you what to do." 5 "I will do whatever you say," Ruth answered. 6 So she went down to the threshing floor and did everything her mother-in-law told her to do. 7 When Boaz had finished eating and drinking and was in good spirits, he went over to lie down at the far end of the grain pile. Ruth approached quietly, uncovered his feet, and lay down. 8 In the middle of the night something startled the man; he turned—and there was a woman lying at his feet! 9 "Who are you?" he asked. "I am your servant Ruth," she said. "Spread the corner of your garment over me, since you are a guardian-redeemer of our family." 10 "The LORD bless you, my daughter," he replied. "This kindness is greater than that which you showed earlier: You have not run after the younger men, whether rich or poor. 11 And now, my daughter, don't be afraid. I will do for you all you ask. All the people of my town know that you are a woman of noble character. 12 Although it is true that I am a guardian-redeemer of our family, there is another who is more closely related than I. 13 Stay here for the night, and in the morning if he wants to do his duty as your guardian-redeemer, good; let him redeem you. But if he is not willing, as surely as the LORD lives, I will do it. Lie here until morning." 14 So she lay at his feet until morning but got up before anyone could be recognized; and he said, "No one must know that a woman came to the threshing floor." 15 He also said, "Bring me the shawl you are wearing and hold it out." When she did so, he poured into it six measures of barley and placed the bundle on her. Then he went back to town. 16 When Ruth came to her mother-in-law, Naomi asked, "How did it go, my daughter?" Then she told her everything Boaz had done for her 17 and added, "He gave me these six measures of barley, saying, 'Don't go back to your mother-in-law empty-handed.'" 18 Then Naomi said, "Wait, my daughter, until you find out what happens. For the man will not rest until the matter is settled today."

Chapter 4

1 Meanwhile Boaz went up to the town gate and sat down there just as the guardian-redeemer he had mentioned came along. Boaz said, "Come over here, my friend, and sit down." So he went over and sat down. 2 Boaz took ten of the elders of the town and said, "Sit here," and they did so. 3 Then he said to the guardian-redeemer, "Naomi, who has come back from Moab, is selling the piece of land that belonged to our relative Elimelech. 4 I thought I should bring the matter to your attention and suggest that you buy it in the presence of these seated here and in the presence of the elders of my people. If you will redeem it, do so. But if you will not, tell me, so I will know. For no one has the right to do it except you, and I am next in line." "I will redeem it," he said. 5 Then Boaz said, "On the day you buy the land from Naomi, you also acquire Ruth the Moabite, the dead man's widow, in order to maintain the name of the dead with his property." 6 At this, the guardian-redeemer said, "Then I cannot redeem it because I might endanger my own estate. You redeem it yourself. I cannot do it." 7 (Now in earlier times in Israel, for the redemption and transfer of property to become final, one party took off his sandal and gave it to the other. This was the method of legalizing transactions in Israel.) 8 So the guardian-redeemer said to Boaz, "Buy it yourself." And he removed his sandal. 9 Then Boaz announced to the elders and all the people, "Today you are witnesses that I have bought from Naomi all the property of Elimelech, Kilion, and Mahlon. 10 I have also acquired Ruth the Moabite, Mahlon's widow, as my wife, in order to maintain the name of the dead with his property, so that his name will not disappear from among his family or from his hometown. Today you are witnesses!" 11 Then the elders and all the people at the gate said, "We are witnesses. May the LORD make the woman who is coming into your home like Rachel and Leah, who together built up the family of Israel. May you have standing in Ephrathah and be famous in Bethlehem. 12 Through the offspring the LORD gives you by this young woman, may your family be like that of Perez, whom Tamar bore to Judah." 13 So Boaz took Ruth and she became his wife. When he made love to her, the LORD enabled her to conceive, and she gave birth to a son. 14 The women said to Naomi: "Praise be to the LORD, who this day has not left you without a guardian-redeemer. May he become famous throughout Israel! 15 He will renew your life and sustain you in your old age. For your daughter-in-law, who loves you and who is better to you than seven sons, has given him birth." 16 Then Naomi took the child in her arms and cared for him. 17 The women living there said, "Naomi has a son!" And they named him Obed. He was the father of Jesse, the father of David. 18 This, then, is the family line of Perez: Perez was the father of Hezron, 19 Hezron the father of Ram, Ram the father of Amminadab, 20 Amminadab the father of Nahshon, Nahshon the father of Salmon, 21 Salmon the father of Boaz, Boaz the father of Obed, 22 Obed the father of Jesse, and Jesse the father of David

9. 1 Samuel

Chapter 1

There was a man from Ramathaim Zophim, in the hill country of Ephraim, whose name was Elkanah, son of Jeroham, son of Elihu, son of Tohu, son of Zuph, an Ephrathite. He had two wives: one named Hannah and the other Peninnah. Peninnah had children, but Hannah had none. Each year, Elkanah went from his city to worship and sacrifice to the Lord of Hosts at Shiloh, where Eli's two sons, Hophni and Phinehas, served as priests of the Lord On one such occasion, Elkanah gave portions of the sacrificial meat to his wife Peninnah and to all her sons and daughters, but he gave Hannah a double portion because he loved her, though the Lord had closed her womb. Her rival, Peninnah, provoked her bitterly to irritate her because the Lord had made her barren. This went on year after year. Whenever Hannah went up to the house of the Lord, Peninnah provoked her until she wept and could not eat Elkanah, her husband, asked, "Hannah, why do you weep and not eat? Why is your heart grieved? Am I not better to you than ten sons?"

So Hannah arose after they had eaten and drunk in Shiloh. Eli, the priest, was sitting on a seat by the doorpost of the temple of the Lord. In her deep anguish, Hannah prayed to the Lord, weeping bitterly. She made a vow, saying, "Lord of Hosts, if you will indeed look on the affliction of your maidservant and remember me, and not forget your maidservant, but will give your maidservant a male child, then I will give him to the Lord all the days of his life, and no razor shall come upon his head." As she continued praying before the Lord, Eli watched her mouth. Hannah was speaking in her heart; only her lips moved, but her voice was not heard. Therefore, Eli thought she was drunk and said to her, "How long will you be drunk? Put away your wine." Hannah replied, "No, my lord. I am a woman of sorrowful spirit. I have not drunk wine or intoxicating drink but have poured out my soul before the Lord. Do not consider your maidservant a wicked woman, for out of the abundance of my complaint and grief I have spoken until now." Then Eli answered, "Go in peace, and the God of Israel grant your petition which you have asked of Him." Hannah said, "Let your maidservant find favor in your sight." So she went her way and ate, and her face was no longer sad. They rose early in the morning and worshiped before the Lord, then returned and came to their house at Ramah. Elkanah knew Hannah his wife, and the Lord remembered her. Hannah conceived and bore a son, and called his name Samuel, saying, "Because I have asked for him from the Lord." Elkanah and his house went up to offer to the Lord the yearly sacrifice and his vow. But Hannah did not go up, for she said to her husband, "Not until the child is weaned; then I will take him, that he may appear before the Lord and remain there forever." Elkanah, her husband, said to her, "Do what seems best to you; wait until you have weaned him. Only let the Lord establish His word." So the woman stayed and nursed her son until she had weaned him. When she had weaned him, she took him up with her, along with three bulls, one ephah of flour, and a skin of wine, and brought him to the house of the Lord in Shiloh. The child was young. They slaughtered a bull and brought the child to Eli. She said, "O my lord, as your soul lives, my lord, I am the woman who stood by you here, praying to the Lord. For this child, I prayed, and the Lord has granted me my petition which I asked of Him. Therefore, I also have lent him to the Lord; as long as he lives, he shall be lent to the Lord." So they worshiped the Lord there

Chapter 2

Hannah prayed and said, "My heart rejoices in the Lord; my horn is exalted in the Lord. I smile at my enemies because I rejoice in Your salvation. No one is holy like the Lord, for there is none besides You, nor is there any rock like our God. Talk no more so very proudly; let no arrogance come from your mouth, for the Lord is the God of knowledge, and by Him actions are weighed. The bows of the mighty men are broken, and those who stumbled are girded with strength. Those who were full have hired themselves out for bread, and the hungry have ceased to hunger. Even the barren has borne seven, and she who has many children has become feeble. The Lord kills and makes alive; He brings down to the grave and brings up. The Lord makes poor and makes rich; He brings low and lifts up. He raises the poor from the dust and lifts the beggar from the ash heap to set them among princes and make them inherit the throne of glory. For the pillars of the earth are the Lord's, and He has set the world upon them. He will guard the feet of His saints, but the wicked shall be silent in darkness. For by strength no man shall prevail. The adversaries of the Lord shall be broken in pieces; from heaven, He will thunder against them. The Lord will judge the ends of the earth. He will give strength to His king and exalt the horn of His anointed." Elkanah went to his house at Ramah, but the child ministered to the Lord before Eli the priest. Now the sons of Eli were corrupt; they did not know the Lord. And the priests' custom with the people was that when any man offered a sacrifice, the priest's servant would come with a three-pronged fleshhook in his hand while the meat was boiling. Then he would thrust it into the pan, kettle, cauldron, or pot, and the priest would take for himself all that the fleshhook brought up. So they did in Shiloh to all the Israelites who came there. Also, before they burned the fat, the priest's servant would come and say to the man who sacrificed, "Give meat for roasting to the priest, for he will not take boiled meat from you, but raw." If the man said to him, "They should really burn the fat first; then you may take as much as your heart desires," he would answer, "No, but you must give it now; and if not, I will take it by force." Therefore, the sin of the young men was very great before the Lord, for men abhorred the offering of the Lord But Samuel ministered before the Lord, even as a child, wearing a linen ephod. Moreover, his mother used to make him a little robe and bring it to him year by year when she came up with her husband to offer the yearly sacrifice. Eli would bless Elkanah and his wife and say, "The Lord give you descendants from this woman for the loan that was given to the Lord." Then they would go to their own home. And the Lord visited Hannah so that she conceived and bore three sons and two daughters. Meanwhile, the child Samuel grew before the Lord Now Eli was very old, and he heard everything his sons did to all Israel and how they lay with the women who assembled at the door of the tabernacle of meeting. So he said to them, "Why do you do such things? For I hear of your evil dealings from all the people. No, my sons! For it is not a good report that I hear. You make the Lord's people transgress. If one man sins against another, God will judge him. But if a man sins against the Lord, who will intercede for him?" Nevertheless, they did not heed the voice of their father because the Lord desired to kill them. And the child Samuel grew in stature and in favor both with the Lord and men Then a man of God came to Eli and said to him, "Thus says the Lord: 'Did I not clearly reveal Myself to the house of your father when they were in Egypt in Pharaoh's house? Did I not choose him out of all the tribes of Israel to be My priest, to offer upon My altar, to burn incense, and to wear an ephod before Me? And did I not give to the house of your father all the offerings of the children of Israel made by fire? Why do you kick at My sacrifice and My offering which I have commanded in My dwelling place, and honor your sons more than Me, to make yourselves fat with the best of all the offerings of Israel My people?' Therefore, the Lord God of Israel says: 'I said indeed that your house and the house of your father would walk before Me forever.' But now the Lord says: 'Far be it from Me; for those who honor Me I will honor, and those who despise Me shall be lightly esteemed. Behold, the days are coming that I will cut off your arm and the arm of your father's house so that there will not be an old man in your house. And you will see an enemy in My dwelling place, despite all the good which God does for Israel. And there shall not be an old man in your house forever. But any of your men whom I do not cut off from My altar shall consume your eyes and grieve your heart. And all the descendants of your house shall die in the flower of their age. Now, this shall be a sign to you that will come upon your two sons, on Hophni and Phinehas: in one day they shall die, both of them Then I will raise up for Myself a faithful priest who shall do according to what is in My heart and in My mind. I will build him a sure house, and he shall walk before My anointed forever. And it shall come to pass that everyone who is left in your house will come and bow down to him for a piece of silver and a morsel of bread, and say, "Please, put me in one of the priestly positions, that I may eat a piece of bread."'"

Chapter 3

The boy Samuel ministered before the Lord under Eli. In those days, the word of the Lord was rare; there were not many visions. One night Eli, whose eyes were becoming so weak that he could barely see, was lying down in his usual place. The lamp of God had not yet gone out, and Samuel was lying down in the house of the Lord, where the ark of God was. Then the Lord called Samuel. Samuel answered, "Here I am." And he ran to Eli and said, "Here I am; you called me." But Eli said, "I did not call; go back and lie down." So he went and lay down Again, the Lord called, "Samuel!" And Samuel got up and went to Eli and said, "Here I am; you called me." "My son," Eli said, "I did not call; go back and lie down." Now Samuel did not yet know the Lord: The word of the Lord had not yet been revealed to him. A third time the Lord called, "Samuel!" And Samuel got up and went to Eli and said, "Here I am; you called me." Then Eli realized that the Lord was calling the boy. So Eli told Samuel, "Go and lie down, and if He calls you, say, 'Speak, Lord, for your servant is listening.'" So Samuel went and lay down in his place The Lord came and stood there, calling as at the other times, "Samuel! Samuel!" Then Samuel said, "Speak, for your servant is listening." And the Lord said to Samuel, "See, I am about to do something in Israel that will make the ears of everyone who hears about it tingle. At that time, I will carry out against Eli everything I spoke against his family—from beginning to end. For I told him that I would judge his family forever because of the sin he knew about; his sons blasphemed God, and he failed to restrain them. Therefore, I swore to the house of Eli, 'The guilt of Eli's house will never be atoned for by sacrifice or offering.'" Samuel lay down until morning and then opened the doors of the house of the Lord. He was afraid to tell Eli the vision, but Eli called him and said, "Samuel, my son." Samuel answered, "Here I am." "What was it He said to you?" Eli asked. "Do not hide it from me. May God deal with you, be it ever so severely, if you hide from me anything He told you." So Samuel told him everything, hiding nothing from him. Then Eli said, "He is the Lord; let Him do what is good in His eyes." The Lord was with Samuel as he grew up, and He let none of Samuel's words fall to the ground. And all Israel from Dan to Beersheba recognized that Samuel was attested as a prophet of the Lord. The Lord continued to appear at Shiloh, and there He revealed Himself to Samuel through His word

Chapter 4

And Samuel's word came to all Israel. Now the Israelites went out to fight against the Philistines. The Israelites camped at Ebenezer, and the Philistines at Aphek. The Philistines deployed their forces to meet Israel, and as the battle spread, Israel was defeated by the Philistines, who killed about four thousand of them on the battlefield. When the soldiers returned to camp, the elders of Israel asked, "Why did the Lord bring defeat upon us today before the Philistines? Let us bring the ark of the Lord's covenant from Shiloh so that it may go with us and save us from the hand of our enemies." So the people sent men to Shiloh, and they brought back the ark of the covenant of the Lord Almighty, who is enthroned between the cherubim. And Eli's two sons, Hophni and Phinehas, were there

with the ark of the covenant of God. When the ark of the Lord's covenant came into the camp, all Israel raised such a great shout that the ground shook. Hearing the uproar, the Philistines asked, "What's all this shouting in the Hebrew camp?" When they learned that the ark of the Lord had come into the camp, the Philistines were afraid. "A god has come into the camp," they said. "We're in trouble! Nothing like this has happened before. Woe to us! Who will deliver us from the hand of these mighty gods? They are the gods who struck the Egyptians with all kinds of plagues in the desert. Be strong, Philistines! Be men, or you will be subject to the Hebrews, as they have been to you. Be men, and fight!" So the Philistines fought, and the Israelites were defeated, and every man fled to his tent. The slaughter was very great; Israel lost thirty thousand foot soldiers. The ark of God was captured, and Eli's two sons, Hophni and Phinehas, died That same day, a Benjamite ran from the battle line and went to Shiloh with his clothes torn and dust on his head. When he arrived, Eli was sitting on his chair by the side of the road, watching, because his heart feared for the ark of God. When the man entered the town and told what had happened, the whole town sent up a cry. Eli heard the outcry and asked, "What is the meaning of this uproar?" The man hurried over to Eli, who was ninety-eight years old and whose eyes were set so that he could not see. He told Eli, "I have just come from the battle line; I fled from it this very day." Eli asked, "What happened, my son?" The man who brought the news replied, "Israel fled before the Philistines, and the army has suffered heavy losses. Also, your two sons, Hophni and Phinehas, are dead, and the ark of God has been captured." When he mentioned the ark of God, Eli fell backward off his chair by the side of the gate. His neck was broken, and he died, for he was an old man and heavy. He had led Israel forty years His daughter-in-law, the wife of Phinehas, was pregnant and near the time of delivery. When she heard the news that the ark of God had been captured and that her father-in-law and her husband were dead, she went into labor and gave birth, but was overcome by her labor pains. As she was dying, the women attending her said, "Don't despair; you have given birth to a son." But she did not respond or pay any attention. She named the boy Ichabod, saying, "The glory has departed from Israel," because of the capture of the ark of God and the deaths of her father-in-law and her husband. She said, "The glory has departed from Israel, for the ark of God has been captured."

Chapter 5

After the Philistines had captured the ark of God, they took it from Ebenezer to Ashdod. Then they carried the ark into Dagon's temple and set it beside Dagon. When the people of Ashdod rose early the next day, there was Dagon, fallen on his face on the ground before the ark of the Lord! They took Dagon and put him back in his place. But the following morning when they rose, there was Dagon, fallen on his face on the ground before the ark of the Lord! His head and hands had been broken off and were lying on the threshold; only his body remained. That is why to this day neither the priests of Dagon nor any others who enter Dagon's temple at Ashdod step on the threshold The Lord's hand was heavy upon the people of Ashdod and its vicinity; He brought devastation upon them and afflicted them with tumors. When the men of Ashdod saw what was happening, they said, "The ark of the god of Israel must not stay here with us, because His hand is heavy upon us and upon Dagon our god." So they called together all the rulers of the Philistines and asked them, "What shall we do with the ark of the god of Israel?" They answered, "Have the ark of the god of Israel moved to Gath." So they moved the ark of the god of Israel But after they had moved it, the Lord's hand was against that city, throwing it into a great panic. He afflicted the people of the city, both young and old, with an outbreak of tumors. So they sent the ark of God to Ekron. As the ark of God was entering Ekron, the people of Ekron cried out, "They have brought the ark of the god of Israel around to us to kill us and our people." So they called together all the rulers of the Philistines and said, "Send the ark of the god of Israel away; let it go back to its own place, or it will kill us and our people." For death had filled the city with panic; God's hand was very heavy upon it. Those who did not die were afflicted with tumors, and the outcry of the city went up to heaven

Chapter 6

The ark of the Lord remained in the country of the Philistines for seven months. The Philistines called for the priests and diviners and asked, "What shall we do with the ark of the Lord? Tell us how we should send it back to its place." They answered, "If you send away the ark of the God of Israel, do not send it away empty, but by all means return it with a guilt offering. Then you will be healed, and you will know why His hand has not been lifted from you." They asked, "What guilt offering should we send to Him?" They replied, "Five gold tumors and five gold rats, according to the number of the Philistine rulers, because the same plague has struck both you and your rulers. Make models of the tumors and of the rats that are destroying the country, and give glory to the God of Israel. Perhaps He will lift His hand from you and your gods and your land. Why do you harden your hearts as the Egyptians and Pharaoh did? When He treated them harshly, did they not send the Israelites out so they could go on their way? Now then, get a new cart ready, with two cows that have calved and have never been yoked. Hitch the cows to the cart, but take their calves away and pen them up. Take the ark of the Lord and put it on the cart, and in a chest beside it put the gold objects you are sending back to Him as a guilt offering. Send it on its way, but keep watching it. If it goes up to its own territory, toward Beth Shemesh, then the Lord has brought this great disaster on us. But if it does not, then we will know that it was not His hand that struck us and that it happened to us by chance." So they did this. They took two such cows and hitched them to the cart and penned up their calves. They placed the ark of the Lord on the cart and along with it the chest containing the gold rats and the models of the tumors. Then the cows went straight up toward Beth Shemesh, keeping on the road and lowing all the way. They did not turn to the right or to the left. The rulers of the Philistines followed them as far as the border of Beth Shemesh Now the people of Beth Shemesh were harvesting their wheat in the valley, and when they looked up and saw the ark, they rejoiced at the sight. The cart came to the field of Joshua of Beth Shemesh and stopped there beside a large rock. The people chopped up the wood of the cart and sacrificed the cows as a burnt offering to the Lord. The Levites took down the ark of the Lord, together with the chest containing the gold objects, and placed them on the large rock. On that day the people of Beth Shemesh offered burnt offerings and made sacrifices to the Lord. The five rulers of the Philistines saw all this and then returned that same day to Ekron These are the gold tumors the Philistines sent as a guilt offering to the Lord—one each for Ashdod, Gaza, Ashkelon, Gath, and Ekron. And the number of the gold rats was according to the number of Philistine towns belonging to the five rulers—the fortified towns with their country villages.

The large rock on which the Levites set the ark of the Lord is a witness to this day in the field of Joshua of Beth Shemesh But God struck down some of the inhabitants of Beth Shemesh, putting seventy of them to death because they looked into the ark of the Lord. The people mourned because of the heavy blow the Lord had dealt them. And the people of Beth Shemesh asked, "Who can stand in the presence of the Lord, this holy God? To whom will the ark go up from here?" Then they sent messengers to the people of Kiriath Jearim, saying, "The Philistines have returned the ark of the Lord. Come down and take it up to your town."

Chapter 7

So the men of Kiriath Jearim came and took up the ark of the Lord. They brought it to Abinadab's house on the hill and consecrated Eleazar his son to guard the ark of the Lord. The ark remained at Kiriath Jearim a long time—twenty years in all. Then all the people of Israel turned back to the Lord So Samuel said to all the Israelites, "If you are returning to the Lord with all your hearts, then rid yourselves of the foreign gods and the Ashtoreths and commit yourselves to the Lord and serve Him only, and He will deliver you out of the hand of the Philistines." So the Israelites put away their Baals and Ashtoreths and served the Lord only Then Samuel said, "Assemble all Israel at Mizpah, and I will intercede with the Lord for you." When they had assembled at Mizpah, they drew water and poured it out before the Lord. On that day they fasted and there they confessed, "We have sinned against the Lord." Now Samuel was serving as leader of Israel at Mizpah When the Philistines heard that Israel had assembled at Mizpah, the rulers of the Philistines came up to attack them. When the Israelites heard of it, they were afraid because of the Philistines. They said to Samuel, "Do not stop crying out to the Lord our God for us, that He may rescue us from the hand of the Philistines." Then Samuel took a suckling lamb and sacrificed it as a whole burnt offering to the Lord. He cried out to the Lord on Israel's behalf, and the Lord answered him While Samuel was sacrificing the burnt offering, the Philistines drew near to engage Israel in battle. But that day the Lord thundered with loud thunder against the Philistines and threw them into such a panic that they were routed before the Israelites. The men of Israel rushed out of Mizpah and pursued the Philistines, slaughtering them along the way to a point below Beth Kar Then Samuel took a stone and set it up between Mizpah and Shen. He named it Ebenezer, saying, "Thus far the Lord has helped us." So the Philistines were subdued and they stopped invading Israel's territory. Throughout Samuel's lifetime, the hand of the Lord was against the Philistines. The towns from Ekron to Gath that the Philistines had captured from Israel were restored to Israel, and Israel delivered the neighboring territory from the hands of the Philistines. And there was peace between Israel and the Amorites Samuel continued as Israel's leader all the days of his life. From year to year, he went on a circuit from Bethel to Gilgal to Mizpah, judging Israel in all those places. But he always went back to Ramah, where his home was, and there he also held court for Israel. And he built an altar there to the Lord

Chapter 8

When Samuel grew old, he appointed his sons as Israel's leaders. The name of his firstborn was Joel and the name of his second was Abijah, and they served at Beersheba. But his sons did not follow his ways. They turned aside after dishonest gain and accepted bribes and perverted justice So all the elders of Israel gathered together and came to Samuel at Ramah. They said to him, "You are old, and your sons do not follow your ways; now appoint a king to lead us, such as all the other nations have." But when they said, "Give us a king to lead us," this displeased Samuel; so he prayed to the Lord. And the Lord told him: "Listen to all that the people are saying to you; it is not you they have rejected, but they have rejected Me as their king. As they have done from the day I brought them up out of Egypt until this day, forsaking Me and serving other gods, so they are doing to you. Now listen to them; but warn them solemnly and let them know what the king who will reign over them will claim as his rights." Samuel told all the words of the Lord to the people who were asking him for a king. He said, "This is what the king who will reign over you will claim as his rights: He will take your sons and make them serve with his chariots and horses, and they will run in front of his chariots. Some he will assign to be commanders of thousands and commanders of fifties and others to plow his ground and reap his harvest, and still others to make weapons of war and equipment for his chariots. He will take your daughters to be perfumers, cooks, and bakers. He will take the best of your fields and vineyards and olive groves and give them to his attendants. He will take a tenth of your grain and of your vintage and give it to his officials and attendants. Your male and female servants and the best of your cattle and donkeys he will take for his own use. He will take a tenth of your flocks, and you yourselves will become his slaves. When that day comes, you will cry out for relief from the king you have chosen, but the Lord will not answer you in that day." But the people refused to listen to Samuel. "No!" they said. "We want a king over us. Then we will be like all the other nations, with a king to lead us and to go out before us and fight our battles." When Samuel heard all that the people said, he repeated it before the Lord. The Lord answered, "Listen to them and give them a king." Then Samuel said to the Israelites, "Everyone go back to your own town."

Chapter 9

There was a Benjamite, a man of standing, whose name was Kish son of Abiel, the son of Zeror, the son of Becorath, the son of Aphiah of Benjamin. Kish had a son named Saul, as handsome a young man as could be found anywhere in Israel, and he was a head taller than anyone else Now the donkeys belonging to Saul's father Kish were lost, and Kish said to his son Saul, "Take one of the servants with you and go and look for the donkeys." So he passed through the hill country of Ephraim and through the area around Shalisha, but they did not find them. They went on into the district of Shaalim, but the donkeys were not there. Then he passed through the territory of Benjamin, but they did not find them When they reached the district of Zuph, Saul said to the servant who was with him, "Come, let's go back, or my father will stop thinking about the donkeys and start worrying about us." But the servant replied, "Look, in this town there is a man of God; he is highly respected, and everything he says comes true. Let's go there now. Perhaps he will tell us what way to take." Saul said to his servant, "If we go, what can we give the man? The food in our sacks is gone. We have no gift to take to the man of God. What do we have?" The servant answered him again. "Look," he said, "I have a quarter of a shekel of silver. I will give it to the man of God so that he will tell us what way to take." (Formerly in Israel, if someone went to inquire of God, they would say, "Come, let us go to the seer," because the prophet of today used to be called a seer.) "Good," Saul said to his servant. "Come, let's go." So they set out for the town where the man of God was As they were going up the hill to the town, they met some young women coming out to draw water, and they asked them, "Is the seer here?" "He is," they answered. "He's ahead of you. Hurry now; he has just come to our town today, for the people have a sacrifice at the high place. As soon as you enter the town, you will find him before he goes up to the high place to eat. The people will not begin eating until he comes, because he must bless the sacrifice; afterward, those who are invited will eat. Go up now; you should find him about this time." They went up to the town, and as they were entering it, there was Samuel, coming toward them on his way up to the high place Now the day before Saul came, the Lord had revealed this to Samuel: "About this time tomorrow I will send you a man from the land of Benjamin. Anoint him ruler over My people Israel; he will deliver them from the hand of the Philistines. I have looked on My people, for their cry has reached Me." When Samuel caught sight of Saul, the Lord said to him, "This is the man I spoke to you about; he will govern My people." Saul approached Samuel in the gateway and asked, "Would you please tell me where the seer's house is?" "I am the seer," Samuel replied. "Go up ahead of me to the high place, for today you are to eat with me, and in the morning I will send you on your way and will tell you all that is in your heart. As for the donkeys you lost three days ago, do not worry about them; they have been found. And to whom is all the desire of Israel turned, if not to you and your whole family line?" Saul answered, "But am I not a Benjamite, from the smallest tribe of Israel, and is not my clan the least of all the clans of the tribe of Benjamin? Why do you say such a thing to me?" Then Samuel brought Saul and his servant into the hall and seated them at the head of those who were invited—about thirty in number. Samuel said to the cook, "Bring the piece of meat I gave you, the one I told you to lay aside." So the cook took up the thigh with what was on it and set it in front of Saul. Samuel said, "Here is what has been kept for you. Eat, because it was set aside for you for this occasion from the time I said, 'I have invited guests.'" And Saul dined with Samuel that day After they came down from the high place to the town, Samuel talked with Saul on the roof of his house. They rose about daybreak, and Samuel called to Saul on the roof, "Get ready, and I will send you on your way." When Saul got ready, he and Samuel went outside together. As they were going down to the edge of the town, Samuel said to Saul, "Tell the servant to go on ahead of us"—and the servant did so—"but you stay here for a while, so that I may give you a message from God."

Chapter 10

Then Samuel took a flask of olive oil and poured it on Saul's head and kissed him, saying, "Has not the Lord anointed you ruler over His inheritance? When you leave me today, you will meet two men near Rachel's tomb, at Zelzah on the border of Benjamin. They will say to you, 'The donkeys you set out to look for have been found. And now your father has stopped thinking about them and is worried about you. He is asking, "What shall I do about my son?"' "Then you will go on from there until you reach the great tree of Tabor. Three men going up to worship God at Bethel will meet you there. One will be carrying three young goats, another three loaves of bread, and another a skin of wine. They will greet you and offer you two loaves of bread, which you will accept from them "After that, you will go to Gibeah of God, where there is a Philistine outpost. As you approach the town, you will meet a procession of prophets coming down from the high place with lyres, timbrels, pipes, and harps being played before them, and they will be prophesying. The Spirit of the Lord will come powerfully upon you, and you will prophesy with them; and you will be changed into a different person. Once these signs are fulfilled, do whatever your hand finds to do, for God is with you "Go down ahead of me to Gilgal. I will surely come down to you to sacrifice burnt offerings and fellowship offerings, but you must wait seven days until I come to you and tell you what you are to do." As Saul turned to leave Samuel, God changed Saul's heart, and all these signs were fulfilled that day. When he and his servant arrived at Gibeah, a procession of prophets met him; the Spirit of God came powerfully upon him, and he joined in their prophesying. When all those who had formerly known him saw him prophesying with the prophets, they asked each other, "What is this that has happened to the son of Kish? Is Saul also among the prophets?" A man who lived there answered, "And who is their father?" So it became a saying: "Is Saul also among the prophets?" After Saul stopped prophesying, he went to the high place Now Saul's uncle asked him and his servant, "Where have you been?" "Looking for the donkeys," he said. "But when we saw they were not to be found, we went to Samuel." Saul's uncle said, "Tell me what Samuel said to you." Saul replied, "He assured us the donkeys had been found." But he did not tell his uncle what Samuel had said about the kingship Samuel summoned the people of Israel to the Lord at Mizpah and said to them, "This is what the Lord, the God of Israel, says: 'I brought Israel up out of Egypt, and I delivered you from the power of Egypt and all the kingdoms that oppressed you.' But you have now rejected your God, who saves you out of all your disasters and calamities. And you have said, 'No, appoint a king over us.' So now present yourselves before the Lord by your tribes and clans." When Samuel had all Israel come forward by tribes, the tribe of Benjamin was taken by lot. Then he brought forward the tribe of Benjamin, clan by clan, and Matri's clan was taken. Finally, Saul son of Kish was taken. But when they looked for him, he was not to be found. So they inquired further of the Lord, "Has the man come here yet?" And the Lord said, "Yes, he has hidden himself among the supplies." They ran and brought him out, and as he stood among the people, he was a head taller than any of the others. Samuel said to all the people, "Do you see the man the Lord has chosen? There is no one like him among all the people." Then the people shouted, "Long live the king!" Samuel explained to the people the rights and duties of kingship. He wrote them down on a scroll and deposited it before the Lord. Then Samuel dismissed the people to go to their own homes Saul also went to his home in Gibeah, accompanied by valiant men whose hearts God had touched. But some scoundrels said, "How can this fellow save us?" They despised him and brought him no gifts. But Saul kept silent

Chapter 11

Nahash the Ammonite came up and besieged Jabesh Gilead, and all the men of Jabesh said to Nahash, "Make a treaty with us, and we will serve you." Nahash the Ammonite answered them, "I will make a treaty with you on one condition: that I gouge out the right eye of every one of you and bring disgrace on all Israel." The elders of Jabesh said to him, "Give us seven days so we can send messengers throughout Israel; if no one comes to rescue us, we will surrender to you." When the messengers came to Gibeah of Saul and reported these terms to the people, they all wept aloud. Just then, Saul was returning from the fields, behind his oxen, and he asked, "What is wrong with everyone? Why are they weeping?" Then they repeated to him what the men of Jabesh had said. When Saul heard

their words, the Spirit of God came powerfully upon him, and he burned with anger. He took a pair of oxen, cut them into pieces, and sent the pieces by messengers throughout Israel, proclaiming, "This is what will be done to the oxen of anyone who does not follow Saul and Samuel." Then the terror of the Lord fell on the people, and they came out together as one. When Saul mustered them at Bezek, the men of Israel numbered three hundred thousand and those of Judah thirty thousand. They told the messengers who had come, "Say to the men of Jabesh Gilead, 'By the time the sun is hot tomorrow, you will be rescued.'" When the messengers went and reported this to the men of Jabesh, they were elated. They said to the Ammonites, "Tomorrow we will surrender to you, and you can do to us whatever you like." The next day Saul separated his men into three divisions; during the last watch of the night they broke into the camp of the Ammonites and slaughtered them until the heat of the day. Those who survived were scattered, so that no two of them were left together. The people then said to Samuel, "Who was it that asked, 'Shall Saul reign over us?' Turn these men over to us so that we may put them to death." But Saul said, "No one will be put to death today, for this day the Lord has rescued Israel." Then Samuel said to the people, "Come, let us go to Gilgal and there renew the kingship." So all the people went to Gilgal and made Saul king in the presence of the Lord. There they sacrificed fellowship offerings before the Lord, and Saul and all the Israelites held a great celebration

Chapter 12

Then Samuel said to all Israel, "I have listened to everything you said to me and have set a king over you. Now you have a king as your leader. As for me, I am old and gray, and my sons are here with you. I have been your leader from my youth until this day. Here I stand. Testify against me in the presence of the Lord and His anointed. Whose ox have I taken? Whose donkey have I taken? Whom have I cheated? Whom have I oppressed? From whose hand have I accepted a bribe to make me shut my eyes? If I have done any of these things, I will make it right." "You have not cheated or oppressed us," they replied. "You have not taken anything from anyone's hand." Samuel said to them, "The Lord is witness against you, and also His anointed is witness this day, that you have not found anything in my hand." "He is witness," they said Then Samuel said to the people, "It is the Lord who appointed Moses and Aaron and brought your ancestors up out of Egypt. Now then, stand here, because I am going to confront you with evidence before the Lord as to all the righteous acts performed by the Lord for you and your ancestors After Jacob entered Egypt, they cried to the Lord for help, and the Lord sent Moses and Aaron, who brought your ancestors out of Egypt and settled them in this place. But they forgot the Lord their God; so He sold them into the hand of Sisera, the commander of the army of Hazor, and into the hands of the Philistines and the king of Moab, who fought against them. They cried out to the Lord and said, 'We have sinned; we have forsaken the Lord and served the Baals and the Ashtoreths. But now deliver us from the hands of our enemies, and we will serve you.' Then the Lord sent Jerub-Baal, Barak, Jephthah, and Samuel, and He delivered you from the hands of your enemies all around you, so that you lived in safety But when you saw that Nahash king of the Ammonites was moving against you, you said to me, 'No, we want a king to rule over us'—even though the Lord your God was your king. Now here is the king you have chosen, the one you asked for; see, the Lord has set a king over you. If you fear the Lord and serve and obey Him and do not rebel against His commands, and if both you and the king who reigns over you follow the Lord your God—good! But if you do not obey the Lord, and if you rebel against His commands, His hand will be against you, as it was against your ancestors Now then, stand still and see this great thing the Lord is about to do before your eyes! Is it not wheat harvest now? I will call on the Lord to send thunder and rain. And you will realize what an evil thing you did in the eyes of the Lord when you asked for a king." Then Samuel called on the Lord, and that same day the Lord sent thunder and rain. So all the people stood in awe of the Lord and of Samuel The people all said to Samuel, "Pray to the Lord your God for your servants so that we will not die, for we have added to all our other sins the evil of asking for a king." "Do not be afraid," Samuel replied. "You have done all this evil; yet do not turn away from the Lord, but serve the Lord with all your heart. Do not turn away after useless idols. They can do you no good, nor can they rescue you, because they are useless. For the sake of His great name the Lord will not reject His people, because the Lord was pleased to make you His own. As for me, far be it from me that I should sin against the Lord by failing to pray for you. And I will teach you the way that is good and right. But be sure to fear the Lord and serve Him faithfully with all your heart; consider what great things He has done for you. Yet if you persist in doing evil, both you and your king will perish."

Chapter 13

Saul was thirty years old when he became king, and he reigned over Israel for forty-two years. Saul chose three thousand men from Israel; two thousand were with him at Michmash and in the hill country of Bethel, and a thousand were with Jonathan at Gibeah in Benjamin. The rest of the men he sent back to their homes Jonathan attacked the Philistine outpost at Geba, and the Philistines heard about it. Then Saul had the trumpet blown throughout the land and said, "Let the Hebrews hear!" So all Israel heard the news: "Saul has attacked the Philistine outpost, and now Israel has become obnoxious to the Philistines." And the people were summoned to join Saul at Gilgal The Philistines assembled to fight Israel, with three thousand chariots, six thousand charioteers, and soldiers as numerous as the sand on the seashore. They went up and camped at Michmash, east of Beth Aven. When the Israelites saw that their situation was critical and that their army was hard-pressed, they hid in caves and thickets, among the rocks, and in pits and cisterns. Some Hebrews even crossed the Jordan to the land of Gad and Gilead Saul remained at Gilgal, and all the troops with him were quaking with fear. He waited seven days, the time set by Samuel; but Samuel did not come to Gilgal, and Saul's men began to scatter. So he said, "Bring me the burnt offering and the fellowship offerings." And Saul offered up the burnt offering. Just as he finished making the offering, Samuel arrived, and Saul went out to greet him "What have you done?" asked Samuel Saul replied, "When I saw that the men were scattering, and that you did not come at the set time, and that the Philistines were assembling at Michmash, I thought, 'Now the Philistines will come down against me at Gilgal, and I have not sought the Lord's favor.' So I felt compelled to offer the burnt offering." "You have done a foolish thing," Samuel said. "You have not kept the command the Lord your God gave you; if you had, He would have established your kingdom over Israel for all time. But now your kingdom will not endure; the Lord has sought out a man after His own heart and appointed him ruler of His people, because you have not kept the Lord's

command." Then Samuel left Gilgal and went up to Gibeah in Benjamin, and Saul counted the men who were with him. They numbered about six hundred. Saul and his son Jonathan and the men with them were staying in Gibeah in Benjamin, while the Philistines camped at Michmash. Raiding parties went out from the Philistine camp in three detachments. One turned toward Ophrah in the vicinity of Shual, another toward Beth Horon, and the third toward the borderland overlooking the Valley of Zeboyim facing the wilderness Not a blacksmith could be found in the whole land of Israel, because the Philistines had said, "Otherwise the Hebrews will make swords or spears!" So all Israel went down to the Philistines to have their plow points, mattocks, axes, and sickles sharpened. The price was two-thirds of a shekel for sharpening plow points and mattocks, and a third of a shekel for sharpening forks and axes and for repointing goads So on the day of the battle, not a soldier with Saul and Jonathan had a sword or spear in his hand; only Saul and his son Jonathan had them. Now a detachment of Philistines had gone out to the pass at Michmash

Chapter 14

One day Jonathan son of Saul said to his young armor-bearer, "Come, let's go over to the Philistine outpost on the other side." But he did not tell his father. Saul was staying on the outskirts of Gibeah under a pomegranate tree in Migron. With him were about six hundred men, among whom was Ahijah, who was wearing an ephod. He was a son of Ichabod's brother Ahitub son of Phinehas, the son of Eli, the Lord's priest in Shiloh. No one was aware that Jonathan had left On each side of the pass that Jonathan intended to cross to reach the Philistine outpost was a cliff; one was called Bozez and the other Seneh. One cliff stood to the north toward Michmash, the other to the south toward Geba. Jonathan said to his young armor-bearer, "Come, let's go over to the outpost of those uncircumcised men. Perhaps the Lord will act in our behalf. Nothing can hinder the Lord from saving, whether by many or by few." "Do all that you have in mind," his armor-bearer said. "Go ahead; I am with you heart and soul." Jonathan said, "Come on, then; we will cross over toward them and let them see us. If they say to us, 'Wait there until we come to you,' we will stay where we are and not go up to them. But if they say, 'Come up to us,' we will climb up, because that will be our sign that the Lord has given them into our hands." So both of them showed themselves to the Philistine outpost. "Look!" said the Philistines. "The Hebrews are crawling out of the holes they were hiding in." The men of the outpost shouted to Jonathan and his armor-bearer, "Come up to us and we'll teach you a lesson." So Jonathan said to his armor-bearer, "Climb up after me; the Lord has given them into the hand of Israel." Jonathan climbed up, using his hands and feet, with his armor-bearer right behind him. The Philistines fell before Jonathan, and his armor-bearer followed and killed behind him. In that first attack Jonathan and his armor-bearer killed some twenty men in an area of about half an acre Then panic struck the whole army—those in the camp and field, and those in the outposts and raiding parties—and the ground shook. It was a panic sent by God Saul's lookouts at Gibeah in Benjamin saw the army melting away in all directions. Then Saul said to the men who were with him, "Muster the forces and see who has left us." When they did, it was Jonathan and his armor-bearer who were not there Saul said to Ahijah, "Bring the ark of God." (At that time it was with the Israelites.) While Saul was talking to the priest, the tumult in the Philistine camp increased more and more. So Saul said to the priest,

"Withdraw your hand." Then Saul and all his men assembled and went to the battle. They found the Philistines in total confusion, striking each other with their swords. Those Hebrews who had previously been with the Philistines and had gone up with them to their camp went over to the Israelites who were with Saul and Jonathan. When all the Israelites who had hidden in the hill country of Ephraim heard that the Philistines were on the run, they joined the battle in hot pursuit. So on that day the Lord saved Israel, and the battle moved on beyond Beth Aven Now the Israelites were in distress that day, because Saul had bound the people under an oath, saying, "Cursed be anyone who eats food before evening comes, before I have avenged myself on my enemies!" So none of the troops tasted food The entire army entered the woods, and there was honey on the ground. When they went into the woods, they saw the honey oozing out; yet no one put his hand to his mouth, because they feared the oath. But Jonathan had not heard that his father had bound the people with the oath, so he reached out the end of the staff that was in his hand and dipped it into the honeycomb. He raised his hand to his mouth, and his eyes brightened. Then one of the soldiers told him, "Your father bound the army under a strict oath, saying, 'Cursed be anyone who eats food today!' That is why the men are faint." Jonathan said, "My father has made trouble for the country. See how my eyes brightened when I tasted a little of this honey. How much better it would have been if the men had eaten today some of the plunder they took from their enemies. Would not the slaughter of the Philistines have been even greater?" That day, after the Israelites had struck down the Philistines from Michmash to Aijalon, they were exhausted. They pounced on the plunder and, taking sheep, cattle, and calves, they butchered them on the ground and ate them, together with the blood. Then someone said to Saul, "Look, the men are sinning against the Lord by eating meat that has blood in it." "You have broken faith," he said. "Roll a large stone over here at once." Then he said, "Go out among the men and tell them, 'Each of you bring me your cattle and sheep, and slaughter them here and eat them. Do not sin against the Lord by eating meat with blood still in it.'" So everyone brought his ox that night and slaughtered it there. Then Saul built an altar to the Lord; it was the first time he had done this Saul said, "Let us go down and pursue the Philistines by night and plunder them till dawn, and let us not leave one of them alive." "Do whatever seems best to you," they replied But the priest said, "Let us inquire of God here." So Saul asked God, "Shall I go down and pursue the Philistines? Will you give them into Israel's hand?" But God did not answer him that day Saul therefore said, "Come here, all you who are leaders of the army, and let us find out what sin has been committed today. As surely as the Lord who rescues Israel lives, even if the guilt lies with my son Jonathan, he must die." But not one of them said a word Saul then said to all the Israelites, "You stand over there; I and Jonathan my son will stand over here." "Do what seems best to you," they replied Then Saul prayed to the Lord, the God of Israel, "Why have you not answered your servant today? If the fault is in me or my son Jonathan, respond with Urim, but if the men of Israel are at fault, respond with Thummim." Jonathan and Saul were taken by lot, and the men were cleared. Saul said, "Cast the lot between me and Jonathan my son." And Jonathan was taken Then Saul said to Jonathan, "Tell me what you have done." So Jonathan told him, "I tasted a little honey with the end of my staff. And now I must die!" Saul said, "May God deal with me, be it ever so severely, if you do not die, Jonathan." But the men said to Saul, "Should Jonathan die—he who has brought about this great deliverance in Israel? Never! As surely as the Lord lives, not a hair of his head will fall to the ground, for he did this today with God's help." So the men rescued Jonathan, and he was not put to death Then Saul stopped pursuing the Philistines, and they withdrew to their own land After Saul had assumed rule over Israel, he fought against their enemies on every side: Moab, the Ammonites, Edom, the kings of Zobah, and the Philistines. Wherever he turned, he inflicted punishment on them. He fought valiantly and defeated the Amalekites, delivering Israel from the hands of those who had plundered them Saul's sons were Jonathan, Ishvi, and Malki-Shua. The name of his older daughter was Merab, and that of the younger was Michal. His wife's name was Ahinoam daughter of Ahimaaz. The name of the commander of Saul's army was Abner son of Ner, and Ner was Saul's uncle. Saul's father Kish and Abner's father Ner were sons of Abiel All the days of Saul there was bitter war with the Philistines, and whenever Saul saw a mighty or brave man, he took him into his service

Chapter 15

Samuel said to Saul, "I am the one the Lord sent to anoint you king over His people Israel; so listen now to the message from the Lord. This is what the Lord Almighty says: 'I will punish the Amalekites for what they did to Israel when they waylaid them as they came up from Egypt. Now go, attack the Amalekites and totally destroy all that belongs to them. Do not spare them; put to death men and women, children and infants, cattle and sheep, camels and donkeys.'" So Saul summoned the men and mustered them at Telaim—two hundred thousand foot soldiers and ten thousand from Judah. Saul went to the city of Amalek and set an ambush in the ravine. Then he said to the Kenites, "Go away, leave the Amalekites so that I do not destroy you along with them; for you showed kindness to all the Israelites when they came up out of Egypt." So the Kenites moved away from the Amalekites Then Saul attacked the Amalekites all the way from Havilah to Shur, near the eastern border of Egypt. He took Agag king of the Amalekites alive, and all his people he totally destroyed with the sword. But Saul and the army spared Agag and the best of the sheep and cattle, the fat calves and lambs—everything that was good. These they were unwilling to destroy completely, but everything that was despised and weak they totally destroyed Then the word of the Lord came to Samuel: "I regret that I have made Saul king, because he has turned away from Me and has not carried out My instructions." Samuel was angry, and he cried out to the Lord all that night Early in the morning Samuel got up and went to meet Saul, but he was told, "Saul has gone to Carmel. There he has set up a monument in his own honor and has turned and gone on down to Gilgal." When Samuel reached him, Saul said, "The Lord bless you! I have carried out the Lord's instructions." But Samuel said, "What then is this bleating of sheep in my ears? What is this lowing of cattle that I hear?" Saul answered, "The soldiers brought them from the Amalekites; they spared the best of the sheep and cattle to sacrifice to the Lord your God, but we totally destroyed the rest." "Enough!" Samuel said to Saul. "Let me tell you what the Lord said to me last night." "Tell me," Saul replied Samuel said, "Although you were once small in your own eyes, did you not become the head of the tribes of Israel? The Lord anointed you king over Israel. And He sent you on a mission, saying, 'Go and completely destroy those wicked people, the Amalekites; wage war against them until you have wiped them out.' Why did you not obey the Lord? Why did you pounce on the plunder and do evil in the eyes of the Lord?" "But I did obey the Lord," Saul said. "I went on the mission the Lord assigned me. I completely destroyed the Amalekites and brought back Agag their king. The soldiers took sheep and cattle from the plunder, the best of what was devoted to God, in order to sacrifice them to the Lord your God at Gilgal." But Samuel replied: "Does the Lord delight in burnt offerings and sacrifices as much as in obeying the Lord? To obey is better than sacrifice, and to heed is better than the fat of rams. For rebellion is like the sin of divination, and arrogance like the evil of idolatry. Because you have rejected the word of the Lord, He has rejected you as king." Then Saul said to Samuel, "I have sinned. I violated the Lord's command and your instructions. I was afraid of the men and so I gave in to them. Now I beg you, forgive my sin and come back with me, so that I may worship the Lord." But Samuel said to him, "I will not go back with you. You have rejected the word of the Lord, and the Lord has rejected you as king over Israel!" As Samuel turned to leave, Saul caught hold of the hem of his robe, and it tore. Samuel said to him, "The Lord has torn the kingdom of Israel from you today and has given it to one of your neighbors—to one better than you. He who is the Glory of Israel does not lie or change His mind; for He is not a human being, that He should change His mind." Saul replied, "I have sinned. But please honor me before the elders of my people and before Israel; come back with me, so that I may worship the Lord your God." So Samuel went back with Saul, and Saul worshiped the Lord Then Samuel said, "Bring me Agag king of the Amalekites." Agag came to him in chains. And he thought, "Surely the bitterness of death is past." But Samuel said, "As your sword has made women childless, so will your mother be childless among women." And Samuel put Agag to death before the Lord at Gilgal Then Samuel left for Ramah, but Saul went up to his home in Gibeah of Saul. Until the day Samuel died, he did not go to see Saul again, though Samuel mourned for him. And the Lord regretted that He had made Saul king over Israel

Chapter 16

The Lord said to Samuel, "How long will you mourn for Saul, since I have rejected him as king over Israel? Fill your horn with oil and be on your way; I am sending you to Jesse of Bethlehem. I have chosen one of his sons to be king." But Samuel replied, "How can I go? If Saul hears about it, he will kill me." The Lord said, "Take a heifer with you and say, 'I have come to sacrifice to the Lord.' Invite Jesse to the sacrifice, and I will show you what to do. You are to anoint for me the one I indicate." Samuel did what the Lord said. When he arrived at Bethlehem, the elders of the town trembled when they met him. They asked, "Do you come in peace?" Samuel replied, "Yes, in peace; I have come to sacrifice to the Lord. Consecrate yourselves and come to the sacrifice with me." Then he consecrated Jesse and his sons and invited them to the sacrifice When they arrived, Samuel saw Eliab and thought, "Surely the Lord's anointed stands here before the Lord." But the Lord said to Samuel, "Do not consider his appearance or his height, for I have rejected him. The Lord does not look at the things people look at. People look at the outward appearance, but the Lord looks at the heart." Then Jesse called Abinadab and had him pass in front of Samuel. But Samuel said, "The Lord has not chosen this one either." Jesse then had Shammah pass by, but Samuel said, "Nor has the Lord chosen this one." Jesse had seven of his sons pass before Samuel, but Samuel said to him, "The Lord has not chosen these." So he asked Jesse, "Are these all the sons you have?" "There is still the youngest," Jesse answered. "He is tending the sheep." Samuel said, "Send for him; we will not sit down until he arrives." So he sent for him and had him brought in. He was glowing with health and had a fine appearance and handsome features Then the Lord said, "Rise and anoint him; this is the one." So Samuel took the horn of oil and anointed him in the presence of his brothers, and from that day on, the Spirit of the Lord came powerfully upon David. Samuel then went to Ramah Now the Spirit of the Lord had departed from Saul, and an evil spirit from the Lord tormented him. Saul's attendants said to him, "See, an evil spirit from God is tormenting you. Let our lord command his servants here to search for someone who can play the lyre. He will play when the evil spirit from God comes on you, and you will feel better." So Saul said to his attendants, "Find someone who plays well and bring him to me." One of the servants answered, "I have seen a son of Jesse of Bethlehem who knows how to play the lyre. He is a brave man and a warrior. He speaks well and is a fine-looking man. And the Lord is with him." Then Saul sent messengers to Jesse and said, "Send me your son David, who is with the sheep." So Jesse took a donkey loaded with bread, a skin of wine, and a young goat and sent them with his son David to Saul. David came to Saul and entered his service. Saul liked him very much, and David became one of his armor-bearers. Then Saul sent word to Jesse, saying, "Allow David to remain in my service, for I am pleased with him." Whenever the spirit from God came on Saul, David would take up his lyre and play. Then relief would come to Saul; he would feel better, and the evil spirit would leave him

Chapter 17

Now the Philistines gathered their forces for war and assembled at Sokoh in Judah. They pitched camp at Ephes Dammim, between Sokoh and Azekah. Saul and the Israelites assembled and camped in the Valley of Elah and drew up their battle line to meet the Philistines. The Philistines occupied one hill and the Israelites another, with the valley between them A champion named Goliath, who was from Gath, came out of the Philistine camp. His height was six cubits and a span. He had a bronze helmet on his head and wore a coat of scale armor of bronze weighing five thousand shekels; on his legs he wore bronze greaves, and a bronze javelin was slung on his back. His spear shaft was like a weaver's rod, and its iron point weighed six hundred shekels. His shield bearer went ahead of him Goliath stood and shouted to the ranks of Israel, "Why do you come out and line up for battle? Am I not a Philistine, and are you not the servants of Saul? Choose a man and have him come down to me. If he is able to fight and kill me, we will become your subjects; but if I overcome him and kill him, you will become our subjects and serve us." Then the Philistine said, "This day I defy the armies of Israel! Give me a man and let us fight each other." On hearing the Philistine's words, Saul and all the Israelites were dismayed and terrified Now David was the son of an Ephrathite named Jesse, who was from Bethlehem in Judah. Jesse had eight sons, and in Saul's time he was very old. Jesse's three oldest sons had followed Saul to the war: the firstborn was Eliab; the second, Abinadab; and the third, Shammah. David was the youngest. The three oldest followed Saul, but David went back and forth from Saul to tend his father's sheep at Bethlehem. For forty days the Philistine came forward every morning and evening and took his stand Now Jesse said to his son David, "Take this ephah of roasted grain and these ten loaves of bread for your brothers and hurry to their camp. Take along these ten cheeses to the commander of their unit. See how your brothers are and bring back some assurance from them. They are with Saul and all the men of Israel in the Valley of Elah, fighting against the Philistines." Early in the morning David left the flock in the care of a shepherd, loaded up and set out, as Jesse had directed. He reached the camp as the army was going out to its battle positions, shouting the war cry. Israel and the Philistines were drawing up their lines facing each other. David left his things with the keeper of supplies, ran to the battle lines and asked his brothers how they were. As he was talking with them, Goliath, the Philistine champion from Gath, stepped out from his lines and shouted his usual defiance, and David heard it. Whenever the Israelites saw the man, they all fled from him in great fear Now the Israelites had been saying, "Do you see how this man keeps coming out? He comes out to defy Israel. The king will give great wealth to the man who kills him. He will also give him his daughter in marriage and will exempt his family from taxes in Israel." David asked the men standing near him, "What will be done for the man who kills this Philistine and removes this disgrace from Israel? Who is this uncircumcised Philistine that he should defy the armies of the living God?" They repeated to him what they had been saying and told him, "This is what will be done for the man who kills him." When Eliab, David's oldest brother, heard him speaking with the men, he burned with anger at him and asked, "Why have you come down here? And with whom did you leave those few sheep in the wilderness? I know how conceited you are and how wicked your heart is; you came down only to watch the battle." "Now what have I done?" said David. "Can't I even speak?" He then turned away to someone else and brought up the same matter, and the men answered him as before. What David said was overheard and reported to Saul, and Saul sent for him David said to Saul, "Let no one lose heart on account of this Philistine; your servant will go and fight him." Saul replied, "You are not able to go out against this Philistine and fight him; you are only a young man, and he has been a warrior from his youth." But David said to Saul, "Your servant has been keeping his father's sheep. When a lion or a bear came and carried off a sheep from the flock, I went after it, struck it and rescued the sheep from its mouth. When it turned on me, I seized it by its hair, struck it and killed it. Your servant has killed both the lion and the bear; this uncircumcised Philistine will be like one of them, because he has defied the armies of the living God. The Lord who rescued me from the paw of the lion and the paw of the bear will rescue me from the hand of this Philistine." Saul said to David, "Go, and the Lord be with you." Then Saul dressed David in his own tunic. He put a coat of armor on him and a bronze helmet on his head. David fastened on his sword over the tunic and tried walking around, because he was not used to them "I cannot go in these," he said to Saul, "because I am not used to them." So he took them off. Then he took his staff in his hand, chose five smooth stones from the stream, put them in the pouch of his shepherd's bag and, with his sling in his hand, approached the Philistine Meanwhile, the Philistine, with his shield bearer in front of him, kept coming closer to David. He looked David over and saw that he was little more than a boy, glowing with health and handsome, and he despised him. He said to David, "Am I a dog, that you come at me with sticks?" And the Philistine cursed David by his gods. "Come here," he said, "and I'll give your flesh to the birds and the wild animals!" David said to the Philistine, "You come against me with sword and spear and javelin, but I come against you in the name of the Lord Almighty, the God of the armies of Israel, whom you have defied. This day the Lord will deliver you into my hands, and I'll strike you down and cut off your head. This very day I will give the carcasses of the Philistine army to the birds and the wild animals, and the whole world will know that there is a God in Israel. All those gathered here will know that it is not by sword or spear that the Lord saves; for the battle is the Lord's, and He will give all of you into our hands." As the Philistine moved closer to attack him, David ran quickly toward the battle line to meet him. Reaching into his bag and taking out a stone, he slung it and struck the Philistine on the forehead. The stone sank into his forehead, and he fell facedown on the ground. So David triumphed over the Philistine with a sling and a stone; without a sword in his hand, he struck down the Philistine and killed him David ran and stood over him. He took hold of the Philistine's sword and drew it from the sheath. After he killed him, he cut off his head with the sword. When the Philistines saw that their hero was dead, they turned and ran. Then the men of Israel and Judah surged forward with a shout and pursued the Philistines to the entrance of Gath and to the gates of Ekron. Their dead were strewn along the Shaaraim road to Gath and Ekron. When the Israelites returned from chasing the Philistines, they plundered their camp. David took the Philistine's head and brought it to Jerusalem; he put the Philistine's weapons in his own tent As Saul watched David going out to meet the Philistine, he said to Abner, commander of the army, "Abner, whose son is that young man?" Abner replied, "As surely as you live, Your Majesty, I don't know." The king said, "Find out whose son this young man is." As soon as David returned from killing the Philistine, Abner took him and brought him before Saul, with David still holding the Philistine's head "Whose son are you, young man?" Saul asked him David said, "I am the son of your servant Jesse of Bethlehem."

Chapter 18

After David had finished talking with Saul, Jonathan became one in spirit with David, and he loved him as himself. From that day Saul kept David with him and did not let him return home to his family. And Jonathan made a covenant with David because he loved him as himself. Jonathan took off the robe he was wearing and gave it to David, along with his tunic, and even his sword, his bow, and his belt Whatever mission Saul sent him on, David was so successful that Saul gave him a high rank in the army. This pleased all the troops, and Saul's officers as well When the men were returning home after David had killed the Philistine, the women came out from all the towns of Israel to meet King Saul with singing and dancing, with joyful songs and with timbrels and lyres. As they danced, they sang: "Saul has slain his thousands, and David his tens of thousands." Saul was very angry; this refrain displeased him greatly. "They have credited David with tens of thousands," he thought, "but me with only thousands. What more can he get but the kingdom?" And from that time on Saul kept a close eye on David The next day an evil spirit from God came forcefully on Saul. He was prophesying in his house, while David was playing the lyre, as he usually did. Saul had a spear in his hand and he hurled it, saying to himself, "I'll pin David to the wall." But David eluded him twice Saul was afraid of David, because the Lord was with David but had departed from Saul. So he sent David away from him and gave him command over a thousand men, and David led the troops in their campaigns. In everything he did he had great success, because the Lord was with him. When Saul saw how successful he was, he was afraid of him. But all Israel and Judah loved David, because he led them in their campaigns Saul said to David, "Here is my older daughter Merab. I will give her to you in marriage; only serve me bravely and fight the battles of the Lord." For Saul said to himself, "I will not raise a hand against him. Let the Philistines do that!" But David said to Saul, "Who am I, and what is my family or my clan in Israel, that I should become the king's son-in-law?" So when the time came for Merab, Saul's daughter, to be given to David, she was given in marriage to Adriel of Meholah Now Saul's daughter Michal was in love with David, and when they told Saul about it, he was pleased. "I will give her to him," he thought, "so that she may be a snare to him and so that the hand of the Philistines may be against him." So Saul said to David, "Now you have a second opportunity to become my son-in-law." Then Saul ordered his attendants: "Speak to David privately and say, 'Look, the king likes you, and his attendants all love you; now become his son-in-law.'" They repeated these words to David. But David said, "Do you think it is a small matter to become the king's son-in-law? I'm only a poor man and little known." When Saul's servants told him what David had said, Saul replied, "Say to David, 'The king wants no other price for the bride than a hundred Philistine foreskins, to take revenge on his enemies.'" Saul's plan was to have David fall by the hands of the Philistines When the attendants told David these things, he was pleased to become the king's son-in-law. So before the allotted time elapsed, David took his men with him and went out and killed two hundred Philistines and brought back their foreskins. They counted out the full number to the king so that David might become the king's son-in-law. Then Saul gave him his daughter Michal in marriage When Saul realized that the Lord was with David and that his daughter Michal loved David, Saul became still more afraid of him, and he remained his enemy the rest of his days The Philistine commanders continued to go out to battle, and as often as they did, David met with more success than the rest of Saul's officers, and his name became well known

Chapter 19

Saul told his son Jonathan and all the attendants to kill David. But Jonathan had taken a great liking to David and warned him, "My father Saul is looking for a chance to kill you. Be on your guard tomorrow morning; go into hiding and stay there. I will go out and stand with my father in the field where you are. I'll speak to him about you and will tell you what I find out." Jonathan spoke well of David to Saul his father and said to him, "Let not the king do wrong to his servant David; he has not wronged you, and what he has done has benefited you greatly. He took his life in his hands when he killed the Philistine. The Lord won a great victory for all Israel, and you saw it and were glad. Why then would you do wrong to an innocent man like David by killing him for no reason?" Saul listened to Jonathan and took this oath: "As surely as the Lord lives, David will not be put to death." So Jonathan called David and told him the whole conversation. He brought him to Saul, and David was with Saul as before Once more war broke out, and David went out and fought the Philistines. He struck them with such force that they fled before him. But an evil spirit from the Lord came on Saul as he was sitting in his house with his spear in his hand. While David was playing the lyre, Saul tried to pin him to the wall with his spear, but David eluded him as Saul drove the spear into the wall. That night David made good his escape Saul sent men to David's house to watch it and to kill him in the morning. But Michal, David's wife, warned him, "If you don't run for your life tonight, tomorrow you'll be killed." So Michal let David down through a window, and he fled and escaped. Then Michal took an idol and laid it on the bed, covering it with a garment and putting some goats' hair at the head When Saul sent the men to capture David, Michal said, "He is ill." Then Saul sent the men back to see David and told them, "Bring him up to me in his bed so that I may kill him." But when the men entered, there was the idol in the bed, and at the head was some goats' hair Saul said to Michal, "Why did you deceive me like this and send my enemy away so that he escaped?" Michal told him, "He said to me, 'Let me get away. Why should I kill you?'" When David had fled and made his escape, he went to Samuel at Ramah and told him all that Saul had done to him. Then he and Samuel went to Naioth and stayed there. Word came to Saul: "David is in Naioth at Ramah"; so he sent men to capture him. But when they saw a group of prophets prophesying, with Samuel standing there as their leader, the Spirit of God came on Saul's men, and they also prophesied. Saul was told about it, and he sent more men, and they prophesied too. Saul sent men a third time, and they also prophesied. Finally, he himself left for Ramah and went to the great cistern at Seku. And he asked, "Where are Samuel and David?" "Over in Naioth at Ramah," they said So Saul went to Naioth at Ramah. But the Spirit of God came even on him, and he walked along prophesying until he came to Naioth. He stripped off his garments, and he too prophesied in Samuel's presence. He lay naked all that day and all that night. This is why people say, "Is Saul also among the prophets?"

Chapter 20

David fled from Naioth at Ramah and went to Jonathan and asked, "What have I done? What is my crime? How have I wronged your father, that he is trying to kill me?" "Never!" Jonathan replied. "You are not going to die! Look, my father doesn't do anything, great or small, without letting me know. Why would he hide this from me? It isn't so!" But David took an oath and said, "Your father knows very well that I have found favor in your eyes, and he has said to himself, 'Jonathan must not know this or he will be grieved.' Yet as surely as the Lord lives and as you live, there is only a step between me and death." Jonathan said to David, "Whatever you want me to do, I'll do for you." So David said, "Look, tomorrow is the New Moon feast, and I am supposed to dine with the king; but let me go and hide in the field until the evening of the day after tomorrow. If your father misses me at all, tell him, 'David earnestly asked my permission to hurry to Bethlehem, his hometown, because an annual sacrifice is being made there for his whole clan.' If he says, 'Very well,' then your servant is safe. But if he loses his temper, you can be sure that he is determined to harm me. As for you, show kindness to your servant, for you have brought him into a covenant with you before the Lord. If I am guilty, then kill me yourself! Why hand me over to your father?" "Never!" Jonathan said. "If I had the least inkling that my father was determined to harm you, wouldn't I tell you?" David asked, "Who will tell me if your father answers you harshly?" "Come," Jonathan said, "let's go out into the field." So they went there together Then Jonathan said to David, "I swear by the Lord, the God of Israel, that I will surely sound out my father by this time the day after tomorrow! If he is favorably disposed toward you, will I not send you word and let you know? But if my father intends to harm you, may the Lord deal with Jonathan, be it ever so severely, if I do not let you know and send you away in peace. May the Lord be with you as He has been with my father. But show me unfailing kindness like the Lord's kindness as long as I live, so that I may not be killed, and do not ever cut off your kindness from my family—not even when the Lord has cut off every one of David's enemies from the face of the earth." So Jonathan made a covenant with the house of David, saying, "May the Lord call David's enemies to account." And Jonathan had David reaffirm his oath out of love for him, because he loved him as he loved himself Then Jonathan said to David, "Tomorrow is the New Moon feast. You will be missed, because your seat will be empty. The day after tomorrow, toward evening, go to the place where you hid when this trouble began, and wait by the stone Ezel. I will shoot three arrows to the side of it, as though I were shooting at a target. Then I will send a boy and say, 'Go, find the arrows.' If I say to him, 'Look, the arrows are on this side of you; bring them here,' then come, because, as surely as the Lord lives, you are safe; there is no danger. But if I say to the boy, 'Look, the arrows are beyond you,' then you must go, because the Lord has sent you away. And about the matter you and I discussed—remember, the Lord is witness between you and me forever." So David hid in the field, and when the New Moon feast came, the king sat down to eat. He sat in his customary place by the wall, opposite Jonathan, and Abner sat next to Saul, but David's place was empty. Saul said nothing that day, for he thought, "Something must have happened to David to make him ceremonially unclean—surely he is unclean." But the next day, the second day of the month, David's place was empty again. Then Saul said to his son Jonathan, "Why hasn't the son of Jesse come to the meal, either yesterday or today?" Jonathan answered, "David earnestly asked me for permission to go to Bethlehem. He said, 'Let me go, because our family is observing a sacrifice in the town, and my brother has ordered me to be there. If I have found favor in your eyes, let me get away to see my brothers.' That is why he has not come to the king's table." Saul's anger flared up at Jonathan and he said to him, "You son of a perverse and rebellious woman! Don't I know that you have sided with the son of Jesse to your own shame and to the shame of the mother who bore you? As long as the son of Jesse lives on this earth, neither you nor your kingdom will be established. Now send someone to bring him to me, for he must die!" "Why should he be put to death? What has he done?" Jonathan asked his father. But Saul hurled his spear at him to kill him. Then Jonathan knew that his father intended to kill David Jonathan got up from the table in fierce anger; on that second day of the feast, he did not eat, because he was grieved at his father's shameful treatment of David In the morning Jonathan went out to the field for his meeting with David. He had a small boy with him, and he said to the boy, "Run and find the arrows I shoot." As the boy ran, he shot an arrow beyond him. When the boy came to the place where Jonathan's arrow had fallen, Jonathan called out after him, "Isn't the arrow beyond you?" Then he shouted, "Hurry! Go quickly! Don't stop!" The boy picked up the arrow and returned to his master. (The boy knew nothing about all this; only Jonathan and David knew.) Then Jonathan gave his weapons to the boy and said, "Go, carry them back to town." After the boy had gone, David got up from the south side of the stone and bowed down before Jonathan three times, with his face to the ground. Then they kissed each other and wept together—but David wept the most Jonathan said to David, "Go in peace, for we have sworn friendship with each other in the name of the Lord, saying, 'The Lord is witness between you and me, and between your descendants and my descendants forever.'" Then David left, and Jonathan went back to the town

Chapter 21

1 Then David came to Nob, to Ahimelech the priest; Ahimelech was astonished at David's coming and said to him, "Why are you alone and no one with you?" 2 David said to Ahimelech the priest, "The king has charged me with a matter and said, 'Let no one know anything of the matter about which I send you, and with which I have charged you.' I have made an appointment with the young men for such and such a place. 3 Now then, what do you have on hand? Give me five loaves of bread, or whatever is here." 4 And the priest answered David, "I have no common bread on hand, but there is holy bread—if the young men have kept themselves from women." 5 And David answered the priest, "Truly, women have been kept from us as always when I go on an expedition. The vessels of the young men are holy even when it is an ordinary journey. How much more today will their vessels be holy?" 6 So the priest gave him the holy bread, for there was no bread there but the bread of the Presence, which is removed from before the Lord, to be replaced by hot bread on the day it is taken away 7 Now a certain man of the servants of Saul was there that day, detained before the Lord. His name was Doeg the Edomite, the chief of Saul's herdsmen. 8 Then David said to Ahimelech, "Then have you not here a spear or a sword at hand? For I have brought neither my sword nor my weapons with me, because the king's business required haste." 9 And the priest said, "The sword of Goliath the Philistine, whom you struck down in the Valley of Elah, behold, it is here wrapped in a cloth behind the ephod. If you will take that, take it, for there is none but that here." And David said, "There is none like that; give it to me." 10 And David rose and fled that day from Saul and went to Achish the king of Gath. 11 And the servants of Achish said to him, "Is not this David the king of the land? Did they not sing to one another of him in dances, 'Saul has struck down his thousands, and David his ten thousands'?" 12 And David took these words to heart and was much afraid of Achish the king of Gath. 13 So he changed his behavior before them and pretended to be insane in their hands and made marks on the doors of the gate and let his spittle run down his beard. 14 Then Achish said to his servants, "Behold, you see the man is mad. Why then have you brought him to me? 15 Do I lack madmen, that you have brought this fellow to behave as a madman in my presence? Shall this fellow come into my house?"

Chapter 22

1 David departed from there and escaped to the cave of Adullam. And when his brothers and all his father's house heard it, they went down there to him. 2 And everyone who was in distress, and everyone who was in debt, and everyone who was bitter in soul, gathered to him. And he became captain over them. And there were with him about four hundred men 3 And David went from there to Mizpeh of Moab. And he said to the king of Moab, "Please let my father and my mother stay with you, till I know what God will do for me." 4 And he left them with the king of Moab, and they stayed with him all the time that David was in the stronghold. 5 Then the prophet Gad said to David, "Do not remain in the stronghold; depart, and go into the land of Judah." So David departed and went into the forest of Hereth 6 Now Saul heard that David was discovered, and the men who were with him. Saul was sitting at Gibeah under the tamarisk tree on the height with his spear in his hand, and all his servants were standing about him. 7 And Saul said to his servants who stood about him, "Hear now, people of Benjamin; will the son of Jesse give every one of you fields and vineyards, will he make you all commanders of thousands and commanders of hundreds, 8 that all of you have conspired against me? No one discloses to me when my son makes a covenant with the son of Jesse. None of you is sorry for me or discloses to me that my son has stirred up

my servant against me, to lie in wait, as at this day." 9 Then answered Doeg the Edomite, who stood by the servants of Saul, "I saw the son of Jesse coming to Nob, to Ahimelech the son of Ahitub, 10 and he inquired of the Lord for him and gave him provisions and gave him the sword of Goliath the Philistine." 11 Then the king sent to summon Ahimelech the priest, the son of Ahitub, and all his father's house, the priests who were at Nob, and all of them came to the king. 12 And Saul said, "Hear now, son of Ahitub." And he answered, "Here I am, my lord." 13 And Saul said to him, "Why have you conspired against me, you and the son of Jesse, in that you have given him bread and a sword and have inquired of God for him, so that he has risen against me, to lie in wait, as at this day?" 14 Then Ahimelech answered the king, "And who among all your servants is so faithful as David, who is the king's son-in-law, and captain over your bodyguard, and honored in your house? 15 Is today the first time that I have inquired of God for him? No! Let not the king impute anything to his servant or to all the house of my father, for your servant has known nothing of all this, much or little." 16 And the king said, "You shall surely die, Ahimelech, you and all your father's house." 17 And the king said to the guard who stood about him, "Turn and kill the priests of the Lord, because their hand also is with David, and they knew that he fled and did not disclose it to me." But the servants of the king would not put out their hand to strike the priests of the Lord. 18 Then the king said to Doeg, "You turn and strike the priests." And Doeg the Edomite turned and struck down the priests, and he killed on that day eighty-five persons who wore the linen ephod. 19 And Nob, the city of the priests, he put to the sword; both man and woman, child and infant, ox, donkey and sheep, he put to the sword 20 But one of the sons of Ahimelech the son of Ahitub, named Abiathar, escaped and fled after David. 21 And Abiathar told David that Saul had killed the priests of the Lord. 22 And David said to Abiathar, "I knew on that day, when Doeg the Edomite was there, that he would surely tell Saul. I have occasioned the death of all the persons of your father's house. 23 Stay with me; do not be afraid, for he who seeks my life seeks your life. With me you shall be in safekeeping."

Chapter 23

1 Now they told David, "Behold, the Philistines are fighting against Keilah and are robbing the threshing floors." 2 Therefore David inquired of the Lord, "Shall I go and attack these Philistines?" And the Lord said to David, "Go and attack the Philistines and save Keilah." 3 But David's men said to him, "Behold, we are afraid here in Judah; how much more then if we go to Keilah against the armies of the Philistines?" 4 Then David inquired of the Lord again. And the Lord answered him, "Arise, go down to Keilah, for I will give the Philistines into your hand." 5 And David and his men went to Keilah and fought with the Philistines and brought away their livestock and struck them with a great blow. So David saved the inhabitants of Keilah 6 When Abiathar the son of Ahimelech had fled to David to Keilah, he had come down with an ephod in his hand. 7 Now it was told Saul that David had come to Keilah. And Saul said, "God has given him into my hand, for he has shut himself in by entering a town that has gates and bars." 8 And Saul summoned all the people to war, to go down to Keilah, to besiege David and his men. 9 David knew that Saul was plotting harm against him. And he said to Abiathar the priest, "Bring the ephod here." 10 Then David said, "O Lord, the God of Israel, your servant has surely heard that Saul seeks to come to Keilah, to destroy the city on my account. 11 Will the men of Keilah surrender me into his hand? Will Saul

come down, as your servant has heard? O Lord, the God of Israel, please tell your servant." And the Lord said, "He will come down." 12 Then David said, "Will the men of Keilah surrender me and my men into the hand of Saul?" And the Lord said, "They will surrender you." 13 Then David and his men, who were about six hundred, arose and departed from Keilah, and they went wherever they could go. When Saul was told that David had escaped from Keilah, he gave up the expedition. 14 And David remained in the strongholds in the wilderness, in the hill country of the wilderness of Ziph. And Saul sought him every day, but God did not give him into his hand 15 David saw that Saul had come out to seek his life. David was in the wilderness of Ziph at Horesh. 16 And Jonathan, Saul's son, rose and went to David at Horesh, and strengthened his hand in God. 17 And he said to him, "Do not fear, for the hand of Saul my father shall not find you. You shall be king over Israel, and I shall be next to you. Saul my father also knows this." 18 And the two of them made a covenant before the Lord. David remained at Horesh, and Jonathan went home 19 Then the Ziphites went up to Saul at Gibeah, saying, "Is not David hiding among us in the strongholds at Horesh, on the hill of Hachilah, which is south of Jeshimon? 20 Now come down, O king, according to all your heart's desire to come down, and our part shall be to surrender him into the king's hand." 21 And Saul said, "May you be blessed by the Lord, for you have had compassion on me. 22 Go, make yet more sure. Know and see the place where his foot is, and who has seen him there, for it is told me that he is very cunning. 23 See therefore and take note of all the lurking places where he hides, and come back to me with sure information. Then I will go with you. And if he is in the land, I will search him out among all the thousands of Judah." 24 And they arose and went to Ziph ahead of Saul Now David and his men were in the wilderness of Maon, in the Arabah to the south of Jeshimon. 25 And Saul and his men went to seek him. And David was told, so he went down to the rock and lived in the wilderness of Maon. And when Saul heard that, he pursued after David in the wilderness of Maon. 26 Saul went on one side of the mountain, and David and his men on the other side of the mountain. And David was hurrying to get away from Saul. As Saul and his men were closing in on David and his men to capture them, 27 a messenger came to Saul, saying, "Hurry and come, for the Philistines have made a raid against the land." 28 So Saul returned from pursuing after David and went against the Philistines. Therefore that place was called the Rock of Escape. 29 And David went up from there and lived in the strongholds of Engedi

Chapter 24

1 When Saul returned from following the Philistines, he was told, "Behold, David is in the wilderness of Engedi." 2 Then Saul took three thousand chosen men out of all Israel and went to seek David and his men in front of the Wildgoats' Rocks. 3 And he came to the sheepfolds by the way, where there was a cave, and Saul went in to relieve himself. Now David and his men were sitting in the innermost parts of the cave. 4 And the men of David said to him, "Here is the day of which the Lord said to you, 'Behold, I will give your enemy into your hand, and you shall do to him as it shall seem good to you.'" Then David arose and stealthily cut off a corner of Saul's robe. 5 And afterward David's heart struck him, because he had cut off a corner of Saul's robe. 6 He said to his men, "The Lord forbid that I should do this thing to my lord, the Lord's anointed, to put out my hand against him, seeing he is the Lord's anointed." 7 So David persuaded his men with these words and did not permit them to attack Saul. And Saul rose up and left

the cave and went on his way 8 Afterward David also arose and went out of the cave, and called after Saul, "My lord the king!" And when Saul looked behind him, David bowed with his face to the earth and paid homage. 9 And David said to Saul, "Why do you listen to the words of men who say, 'Behold, David seeks your harm'? 10 Behold, this day your eyes have seen how the Lord gave you today into my hand in the cave. And some told me to kill you, but I spared you. I said, 'I will not put out my hand against my lord, for he is the Lord's anointed.' 11 See, my father, see the corner of your robe in my hand. For by the fact that I cut off the corner of your robe and did not kill you, you may know and see that there is no wrong or treason in my hands. I have not sinned against you, though you hunt my life to take it. 12 May the Lord judge between me and you, may the Lord avenge me against you, but my hand shall not be against you. 13 As the proverb of the ancients says, 'Out of the wicked comes wickedness.' But my hand shall not be against you. 14 After whom has the king of Israel come out? After whom do you pursue? After a dead dog! After a flea! 15 May the Lord therefore be judge and give sentence between me and you, and see to it and plead my cause and deliver me from your hand." 16 As soon as David had finished speaking these words to Saul, Saul said, "Is this your voice, my son David?" And Saul lifted up his voice and wept. 17 He said to David, "You are more righteous than I, for you have repaid me good, whereas I have repaid you evil. 18 And you have declared this day how you have dealt well with me, in that you did not kill me when the Lord put me into your hands. 19 For if a man finds his enemy, will he let him go away safe? So may the Lord reward you with good for what you have done to me this day. 20 And now, behold, I know that you shall surely be king, and that the kingdom of Israel shall be established in your hand. 21 Swear to me therefore by the Lord that you will not cut off my offspring after me, and that you will not destroy my name out of my father's house." 22 And David swore this to Saul. Then Saul went home, but David and his men went up to the stronghold

Chapter 25

1 Now Samuel died, and all Israel assembled and mourned for him, and they buried him in his house at Ramah. Then David rose and went down to the wilderness of Paran 2 And there was a man in Maon whose business was in Carmel. The man was very rich; he had three thousand sheep and a thousand goats. He was shearing his sheep in Carmel. 3 Now the name of the man was Nabal, and the name of his wife Abigail. The woman was discerning and beautiful, but the man was harsh and badly behaved; he was a Calebite. 4 David heard in the wilderness that Nabal was shearing his sheep. 5 So David sent ten young men. And David said to the young men, "Go up to Carmel, and go to Nabal and greet him in my name. 6 And thus you shall greet him: 'Peace be to you, and peace be to your house, and peace be to all that you have. 7 I hear that you have shearers. Now your shepherds have been with us, and we did them no harm, and they missed nothing all the time they were in Carmel. 8 Ask your young men, and they will tell you. Therefore let my young men find favor in your eyes, for we come on a feast day. Please give whatever you have at hand to your servants and to your son David.'" 9 When David's young men came, they said all this to Nabal in the name of David, and then they waited. 10 And Nabal answered David's servants, "Who is David? Who is the son of Jesse? There are many servants these days who are breaking away from their masters. 11 Shall I take my bread and my water and my meat that I have killed for my shearers and give it to men who come from I do

not know where?" 12 So David's young men turned away and came back and told him all this. 13 And David said to his men, "Every man strap on his sword!" And every man of them strapped on his sword. David also strapped on his sword. And about four hundred men went up after David, while two hundred remained with the baggage 14 But one of the young men told Abigail, Nabal's wife, "Behold, David sent messengers out of the wilderness to greet our master, and he railed at them. 15 Yet the men were very good to us, and we suffered no harm, and we did not miss anything when we were in the fields, as long as we went with them. 16 They were a wall to us both by night and by day, all the while we were with them keeping the sheep. 17 Now therefore know this and consider what you should do, for harm is determined against our master and against all his house, and he is such a worthless man that one cannot speak to him." 18 Then Abigail made haste and took two hundred loaves and two skins of wine and five sheep already prepared and five seahs of parched grain and a hundred clusters of raisins and two hundred cakes of figs, and laid them on donkeys. 19 And she said to her young men, "Go on before me; behold, I come after you." But she did not tell her husband Nabal. 20 And as she rode on the donkey and came down under cover of the mountain, behold, David and his men came down toward her, and she met them. 21 Now David had said, "Surely in vain have I guarded all that this fellow has in the wilderness, so that nothing was missed of all that belonged to him, and he has returned me evil for good. 22 God do so to the enemies of David and more also, if by morning I leave so much as one male of all who belong to him." 23 When Abigail saw David, she hurried and got down from the donkey and fell before David on her face and bowed to the ground. 24 She fell at his feet and said, "On me alone, my lord, be the guilt. Please let your servant speak in your ears, and hear the words of your servant. 25 Let not my lord regard this worthless fellow, Nabal, for as his name is, so is he. Nabal is his name, and folly is with him. But I your servant did not see the young men of my lord, whom you sent. 26 Now then, my lord, as the Lord lives, and as your soul lives, because the Lord has restrained you from bloodguilt and from saving with your own hand, now then let your enemies and those who seek to do evil to my lord be as Nabal. 27 And now let this present that your servant has brought to my lord be given to the young men who follow my lord. 28 Please forgive the trespass of your servant. For the Lord will certainly make my lord a sure house, because my lord is fighting the battles of the Lord, and evil shall not be found in you so long as you live. 29 If men rise up to pursue you and to seek your life, the life of my lord shall be bound in the bundle of the living in the care of the Lord your God. And the lives of your enemies he shall sling out as from the hollow of a sling. 30 And when the Lord has done to my lord according to all the good that he has spoken concerning you and has appointed you prince over Israel, 31 my lord shall have no cause of grief or pangs of conscience for having shed blood without cause or for my lord taking vengeance himself. And when the Lord has dealt well with my lord, then remember your servant." 32 And David said to Abigail, "Blessed be the Lord, the God of Israel, who sent you this day to meet me! 33 Blessed be your discretion, and blessed be you, who have kept me this day from bloodguilt and from avenging myself with my own hand! 34 For as surely as the Lord, the God of Israel, lives, who has restrained me from hurting you, unless you had hurried and come to meet me, truly by morning there had not been left to Nabal so much as one male." 35 Then David received from her hand what she had brought him. And he said to her, "Go up in peace to your house. See, I have obeyed your voice, and I have granted your petition." 36 And Abigail came to Nabal, and behold, he was holding a feast in his house, like the feast of a king. And Nabal's heart was merry within him, for he was very drunk. So she told him nothing at all until the morning light. 37 In the morning, when the wine had gone out of Nabal, his wife told him these things, and his heart died within him, and he became as a stone. 38 And about ten days later the Lord struck Nabal, and he died 39 When David heard that Nabal was dead, he said, "Blessed be the Lord who has avenged the insult I received at the hand of Nabal, and has kept back his servant from wrongdoing. The Lord has returned the evil of Nabal on his own head." Then David sent and spoke to Abigail, to take her as his wife. 40 When the servants of David came to Abigail at Carmel, they said to her, "David has sent us to you to take you to him as his wife." 41 And she rose and bowed with her face to the ground and said, "Behold, your handmaid is a servant to wash the feet of the servants of my lord." 42 And Abigail hurried and rose and mounted a donkey, and her five young women attended her. She followed the messengers of David and became his wife 43 David also took Ahinoam of Jezreel, and both of them became his wives. 44 Saul had given Michal his daughter, David's wife, to Palti the son of Laish, who was of Gallim

Chapter 26

1 Then the Ziphites came to Saul at Gibeah, saying, "David is hiding on the hill of Hachilah, opposite Jeshimon." 2 So Saul arose and went down to the wilderness of Ziph with three thousand chosen men of Israel to seek David in the wilderness of Ziph. 3 Saul encamped on the hill of Hachilah, which is beside the road on the east of Jeshimon. But David remained in the wilderness. When he saw that Saul came after him into the wilderness, 4 David sent out spies and learned that Saul had indeed come. 5 Then David arose and came to the place where Saul had encamped. And David saw the place where Saul lay, with Abner the son of Ner, the commander of his army. Saul was lying within the encampment while the army was encamped around him 6 Then David said to Ahimelech the Hittite and to Joab's brother Abishai the son of Zeruiah, "Who will go down with me into the camp to Saul?" And Abishai said, "I will go down with you." 7 So David and Abishai went to the army by night. And there lay Saul sleeping within the encampment, with his spear stuck in the ground at his head, and Abner and the army lay around him. 8 Then Abishai said to David, "God has given your enemy into your hand this day. Now please let me pin him to the earth with one stroke of the spear, and I will not strike him twice." 9 But David said to Abishai, "Do not destroy him, for who can put out his hand against the Lord's anointed and be guiltless?" 10 And David said, "As the Lord lives, the Lord will strike him, or his day will come to die, or he will go down into battle and perish. 11 The Lord forbid that I should put out my hand against the Lord's anointed. But take now the spear that is at his head and the jar of water, and let us go." 12 So David took the spear and the jar of water from Saul's head, and they went away. No man saw it or knew it, nor did any awake, for they were all asleep, because a deep sleep from the Lord had fallen upon them 13 Then David went over to the other side and stood far off on the top of the hill, with a great space between them. 14 And David called to the army and to Abner the son of Ner, saying, "Will you not answer, Abner?" Then Abner answered, "Who are you who calls to the king?" 15 And David said to Abner, "Are you not a man? Who is like you in

Israel? Why then have you not kept watch over your lord the king? For one of the people came in to destroy the king your lord. 16 This thing that you have done is not good. As the Lord lives, you deserve to die, because you have not kept watch over your lord, the Lord's anointed. And now see where the king's spear is and the jar of water that was at his head." 17 Saul recognized David's voice and said, "Is this your voice, my son David?" And David said, "It is my voice, my lord, O king." 18 And he said, "Why does my lord pursue after his servant? For what have I done? What evil is on my hands? 19 Now therefore, let my lord the king hear the words of his servant. If it is the Lord who has stirred you up against me, may he accept an offering. But if it is men, may they be cursed before the Lord, for they have driven me out this day that I should have no share in the heritage of the Lord, saying, 'Go, serve other gods.' 20 Now therefore, let not my blood fall to the earth away from the presence of the Lord, for the king of Israel has come out to seek a single flea like one who hunts a partridge in the mountains." 21 Then Saul said, "I have sinned. Return, my son David, for I will no more do you harm, because my life was precious in your eyes this day. Behold, I have acted foolishly and have made a great mistake." 22 And David answered and said, "Here is the spear, O king! Let one of the young men come over and take it. 23 The Lord rewards every man for his righteousness and his faithfulness, for the Lord gave you into my hand today, and I would not put out my hand against the Lord's anointed. 24 Behold, as your life was precious this day in my sight, so may my life be precious in the sight of the Lord, and may he deliver me out of all tribulation." 25 Then Saul said to David, "Blessed be you, my son David! You will do many things and will succeed in them." So David went his way, and Saul returned to his place

Chapter 27

1 Then David said in his heart, "Now I shall perish one day by the hand of Saul. There is nothing better for me than that I should escape to the land of the Philistines. Then Saul will despair of seeking me any longer within the borders of Israel, and I shall escape out of his hand." 2 So David arose and went over, he and the six hundred men who were with him, to Achish the son of Maoch, king of Gath. 3 And David lived with Achish at Gath, he and his men, every man with his household, and David with his two wives, Ahinoam of Jezreel and Abigail of Carmel, Nabal's widow. 4 And when it was told Saul that David had fled to Gath, he no longer sought him 5 Then David said to Achish, "If I have found favor in your eyes, let a place be given me in one of the country towns, that I may dwell there. For why should your servant dwell in the royal city with you?" 6 So that day Achish gave him Ziklag. Therefore Ziklag has belonged to the kings of Judah to this day. 7 And the number of the days that David lived in the country of the Philistines was a year and four months 8 Now David and his men went up and made raids against the Geshurites, the Girzites, and the Amalekites, for these were the inhabitants of the land from of old, as far as Shur, to the land of Egypt. 9 And David would strike the land and would leave neither man nor woman alive, but would take away the sheep, the oxen, the donkeys, the camels, and the garments, and come back to Achish. 10 When Achish asked, "Where have you made a raid today?" David would say, "Against the Negeb of Judah," or, "Against the Negeb of the Jerahmeelites," or, "Against the Negeb of the Kenites." 11 And David would leave neither man nor woman alive to bring news to Gath, thinking, "Lest they should tell about us and say, 'So David has done.'" Such was his custom all the while he lived in the country of the Philistines. 12 And Achish trusted

David, thinking, "He has made himself an utter stench to his people Israel; therefore he shall always be my servant."

Chapter 28

1 In those days the Philistines gathered their forces for war, to fight against Israel. And Achish said to David, "Understand that you and your men are to go out with me in the army." 2 David said to Achish, "Very well, you shall know what your servant can do." And Achish said to David, "Very well, I will make you my bodyguard for life." 3 Now Samuel had died, and all Israel had mourned for him and buried him in Ramah, his own city. And Saul had put the mediums and the necromancers out of the land. 4 The Philistines assembled and came and encamped at Shunem. And Saul gathered all Israel, and they encamped at Gilboa. 5 When Saul saw the army of the Philistines, he was afraid, and his heart trembled greatly. 6 And when Saul inquired of the Lord, the Lord did not answer him, either by dreams, or by Urim, or by prophets. 7 Then Saul said to his servants, "Seek out for me a woman who is a medium, that I may go to her and inquire of her." And his servants said to him, "Behold, there is a medium at En-dor." 8 So Saul disguised himself and put on other garments and went, he and two men with him. And they came to the woman by night. And he said, "Divine for me by a spirit and bring up for me whomever I shall name to you." 9 The woman said to him, "Surely you know what Saul has done, how he has cut off the mediums and the necromancers from the land. Why then are you laying a trap for my life to bring about my death?" 10 But Saul swore to her by the Lord, "As the Lord lives, no punishment shall come upon you for this thing." 11 Then the woman said, "Whom shall I bring up for you?" He said, "Bring up Samuel for me." 12 When the woman saw Samuel, she cried out with a loud voice. And the woman said to Saul, "Why have you deceived me? You are Saul." 13 The king said to her, "Do not be afraid. What do you see?" And the woman said to Saul, "I see a god coming up out of the earth." 14 He said to her, "What is his appearance?" And she said, "An old man is coming up, and he is wrapped in a robe." And Saul knew that it was Samuel, and he bowed with his face to the ground and paid homage 15 Then Samuel said to Saul, "Why have you disturbed me by bringing me up?" Saul answered, "I am in great distress, for the Philistines are warring against me, and God has turned away from me and answers me no more, either by prophets or by dreams. Therefore I have summoned you to tell me what I shall do." 16 And Samuel said, "Why then do you ask me, since the Lord has turned from you and become your enemy? 17 The Lord has done to you as he spoke by me, for the Lord has torn the kingdom out of your hand and given it to your neighbor, David. 18 Because you did not obey the voice of the Lord and did not carry out his fierce wrath against Amalek, therefore the Lord has done this thing to you this day. 19 Moreover, the Lord will give Israel also with you into the hand of the Philistines, and tomorrow you and your sons shall be with me. The Lord will give the army of Israel also into the hand of the Philistines." 20 Then Saul fell at once full length on the ground, filled with fear because of the words of Samuel. And there was no strength in him, for he had eaten nothing all day and all night. 21 And the woman came to Saul, and when she saw that he was terrified, she said to him, "Behold, your servant has obeyed you. I have taken my life in my hand and have listened to what you have said to me. 22 Now therefore, you also obey your servant. Let me set a morsel of bread before you; and eat, that you may have strength when you go on your way." 23 He refused and said, "I will not eat." But his servants, together with the woman, urged him, and he listened to their words. So he arose from the earth and sat on the bed. 24 Now the woman had a fattened calf in the house, and she quickly killed it, and she took flour and kneaded it and baked unleavened bread of it, 25 and she put it before Saul and his servants, and they ate. Then they rose and went away that night

Chapter 29

1 The Philistines gathered all their forces at Aphek, and the Israelites encamped by the spring in Jezreel. 2 As the lords of the Philistines were passing on by hundreds and by thousands, and David and his men were passing on in the rear with Achish, 3 the commanders of the Philistines said, "What are these Hebrews doing here?" And Achish said to the commanders of the Philistines, "Is this not David, the servant of Saul king of Israel, who has been with me now for days and years, and since he deserted to me I have found no fault in him to this day." 4 But the commanders of the Philistines were angry with him. And the commanders of the Philistines said to him, "Send the man back, that he may return to the place to which you have assigned him. He shall not go down with us to battle, lest in the battle he become an adversary to us. For how could this fellow reconcile himself to his lord? Would it not be with the heads of the men here? 5 Is not this David, of whom they sing to one another in dances, 'Saul has struck down his thousands, and David his ten thousands'?" 6 Then Achish called David and said to him, "As the Lord lives, you have been honest, and to me it seems right that you should march out and in with me in the campaign. For I have found nothing wrong in you from the day of your coming to me to this day. Nevertheless, the lords do not approve of you. 7 So go back now; and go peaceably, that you may not displease the lords of the Philistines." 8 And David said to Achish, "But what have I done? What have you found in your servant from the day I entered your service until now, that I may not go and fight against the enemies of my lord the king?" 9 And Achish answered David and said, "I know that you are as blameless in my sight as an angel of God. Nevertheless, the commanders of the Philistines have said, 'He shall not go up with us to the battle.' 10 Now then rise early in the morning with the servants of your lord who came with you, and start early in the morning, and depart as soon as you have light." 11 So David set out with his men early in the morning to return to the land of the Philistines. But the Philistines went up to Jezreel

Chapter 30

1 Now when David and his men came to Ziklag on the third day, the Amalekites had made a raid against the Negeb and against Ziklag. They had overcome Ziklag and burned it with fire 2 and taken captive the women and all who were in it, both small and great. They killed no one, but carried them off and went their way. 3 And when David and his men came to the city, they found it burned with fire, and their wives and sons and daughters taken captive. 4 Then David and the people who were with him raised their voices and wept until they had no more strength to weep. 5 David's two wives also had been taken captive, Ahinoam of Jezreel and Abigail the widow of Nabal of Carmel. 6 And David was greatly distressed, for the people spoke of stoning him, because all the people were bitter in soul, each for his sons and daughters. But David strengthened himself in the Lord his God 7 And David said to Abiathar the priest, the son of Ahimelech, "Bring me the ephod." So Abiathar brought the ephod to David. 8 And David inquired of the Lord, "Shall I pursue after this band? Shall I overtake them?" He answered him, "Pursue, for you

shall surely overtake and shall surely rescue." 9 So David set out, and the six hundred men who were with him, and they came to the brook Besor, where those who were left behind stayed. 10 But David pursued, he and four hundred men. Two hundred stayed behind, who were too exhausted to cross the brook Besor 11 They found an Egyptian in the open country and brought him to David. And they gave him bread and he ate. They gave him water to drink, 12 and they gave him a piece of a cake of figs and two clusters of raisins. And when he had eaten, his spirit revived, for he had not eaten bread or drunk water for three days and three nights. 13 And David said to him, "To whom do you belong? And where are you from?" He said, "I am a young man of Egypt, servant to an Amalekite, and my master left me behind because I fell sick three days ago. 14 We had made a raid against the Negeb of the Cherethites and against that which belongs to Judah and against the Negeb of Caleb, and we burned Ziklag with fire." 15 And David said to him, "Will you take me down to this band?" And he said, "Swear to me by God that you will not kill me or deliver me into the hands of my master, and I will take you down to this band." 16 And when he had taken him down, behold, they were spread abroad over all the land, eating and drinking and dancing, because of all the great spoil they had taken from the land of the Philistines and from the land of Judah. 17 And David struck them down from twilight until the evening of the next day, and not a man of them escaped, except four hundred young men, who mounted camels and fled. 18 David recovered all that the Amalekites had taken, and David rescued his two wives. 19 Nothing was missing, whether small or great, sons or daughters, spoil or anything that had been taken. David brought back all. 20 David also captured all the flocks and herds, and the people drove the livestock before him, and said, "This is David's spoil." 21 Then David came to the two hundred men who had been too exhausted to follow David, and who had been left at the brook Besor. And they went out to meet David and to meet the people who were with him. And when David came near to the people, he greeted them. 22 Then all the wicked and worthless fellows among the men who had gone with David said, "Because they did not go with us, we will not give them any of the spoil that we have recovered, except that each man may lead away his wife and children, and depart." 23 But David said, "You shall not do so, my brothers, with what the Lord has given us. He has preserved us and given into our hand the band that came against us. 24 Who would listen to you in this matter? For as his share is who goes down into the battle, so shall his share be who stays by the baggage. They shall share alike." 25 And he made it a statute and a rule for Israel from that day forward to this day 26 When David came to Ziklag, he sent part of the spoil to his friends, the elders of Judah, saying, "Here is a present for you from the spoil of the enemies of the Lord." 27 It was for those in Bethel, in Ramoth of the Negeb, in Jattir, 28 in Aroer, in Siphmoth, in Eshtemoa, 29 in Racal, in the cities of the Jerahmeelites, in the cities of the Kenites, 30 in Hormah, in Bor-ashan, in Athach, 31 in Hebron, for all the places where David and his men had roamed

Chapter 31

1 Now the Philistines fought against Israel, and the men of Israel fled before the Philistines and fell slain on Mount Gilboa. 2 And the Philistines overtook Saul and his sons, and the Philistines struck down Jonathan and Abinadab and Malchishua, the sons of Saul. 3 The battle pressed hard against Saul, and the archers found him, and he was badly wounded by the archers. 4 Then Saul said to his armor-bearer, "Draw

your sword, and thrust me through with it, lest these uncircumcised come and thrust me through, and mistreat me." But his armor-bearer would not, for he feared greatly. Therefore Saul took his own sword and fell upon it. 5 And when his armor-bearer saw that Saul was dead, he also fell upon his sword and died with him. 6 Thus Saul died, and his three sons, and his armor-bearer, and all his men, on the same day together 7 And when the men of Israel who were on the other side of the valley and those beyond the Jordan saw that the men of Israel had fled and that Saul and his sons were dead, they abandoned their cities and fled, and the Philistines came and lived in them 8 The next day, when the Philistines came to strip the slain, they found Saul and his three sons fallen on Mount Gilboa. 9 So they cut off his head and stripped off his armor and sent messengers throughout the land of the Philistines, to carry the good news to the house of their idols and to the people. 10 They put his armor in the temple of Ashtaroth, and they fastened his body to the wall of Beth-shan. 11 But when the inhabitants of Jabesh-gilead heard what the Philistines had done to Saul, 12 all the valiant men arose and went all night and took the body of Saul and the bodies of his sons from the wall of Beth-shan. And they came to Jabesh and burned them there. 13 And they took their bones and buried them under the tamarisk tree in Jabesh and fasted seven days

10. 2 Samuel

Chapter 1

After the death of Saul, when David had returned from the slaughter of the Amalekites and had remained two days in Ziklag, a man from Saul's army arrived on the third day with tattered garments and dirt on his head. Upon reaching David, he fell to the ground and did obeisance. David asked him, "Where do you come from?" The man replied, "I have escaped from the army of Israel." David then inquired, "What has happened? Please tell me." The man explained that the people had fled from the battle, many had been routed and killed, and that Saul and Jonathan, his son, had also died. David asked, "How do you know that Saul and Jonathan, his son, are dead?" The young man replied, "When I arrived at Mount Gilboa, I saw Saul leaning on his spear, with the chariots and horsemen closing in. He saw me and called me. I answered, 'Here I am.' He asked who I was, and I replied, 'I am an Amalekite.' He then begged me to kill him because he was in great anguish and still alive. So, I killed him and took the crown on his head and the bracelet on his arm and brought them to my lord." David tore his garments, as did all the men with him. They mourned, wept, and fasted until evening for Saul and Jonathan, for the people of the LORD, and for the house of Israel because they had been slain by the sword. David then asked the young man, "Where are you from?" The man answered, "I am the son of a foreigner, an Amalekite." David then questioned, "How is it that you were not afraid to destroy the LORD's anointed?" He then ordered one of his young men to kill the Amalekite, and he was struck down and died. David said, "Let your blood be on your own head, for your own mouth has testified against you, saying, 'I killed the LORD's anointed.'" David lamented for Saul and Jonathan with these words: "O noble Israel, your glory lies slain on your heights. How the mighty have fallen! Tell it not in Gath, proclaim it not in the streets of Ashkelon, lest the daughters of the Philistines rejoice, lest the daughters of the uncircumcised exult. Mountains of Gilboa, may you have neither dew nor rain, nor fields of offerings, for there the shield of the mighty was defiled, the shield of Saul, no longer anointed with oil. From the blood of the slain, from the flesh of the mighty, the bow of Jonathan did not turn back, the sword of Saul did not return unsatisfied. Saul and Jonathan, beloved and lovely! In life and in death they were not divided; they were swifter than eagles, stronger than lions. Daughters of Israel, weep for Saul, who clothed you luxuriously in scarlet, who adorned your garments with ornaments of gold. How the mighty have fallen in the midst of the battle! Jonathan lies slain on your heights. I grieve for you, my brother Jonathan; you were very dear to me. Your love for me was wonderful, more wonderful than that of women. How the mighty have fallen! The weapons of war have perished!"

Chapter 2

After this, David sought counsel from the LORD, asking, "Shall I go to one of the cities of Judah?" The LORD answered, "Go." David then asked, "Where shall I go?" The LORD replied, "To Hebron." So David went there with his two wives, Ahinoam the Jezreelite and Abigail, Nabal's widow, the Carmelite. David also brought the men who were with him, each with his family, and they settled in the cities of Hebron. The men of Judah then came and anointed David king over the house of Judah. They informed David that the men of Jabesh-Gilead had buried Saul. David sent messengers to the men of Jabesh-Gilead, saying, "Blessed are you from the LORD, for you have shown this kindness to your lord Saul by burying him. May the LORD now show you kindness and faithfulness, and I too will show you favor because you have done this. Now then, be strong and brave, for Saul your lord is dead, and the house of Judah has anointed me king over them." Meanwhile, Abner, the son of Ner, the commander of Saul's army, took Ish-Bosheth, Saul's son, and brought him to Mahanaim. He made him king over Gilead, the Ashurites, Jezreel, Ephraim, Benjamin, and all Israel. Ish-Bosheth, Saul's son, was forty years old when he began to reign over Israel, and he reigned for two years. However, the house of Judah followed David. David was king in Hebron over the house of Judah for seven years and six months Abner and the servants of Ish-Bosheth went out from Mahanaim to Gibeon. Joab, the son of Zeruiah, and the servants of David also went out and met them by the pool of Gibeon. They sat down, one group on one side of the pool and the other on the opposite side. Abner said to Joab, "Let the young men get up and compete before us." Joab replied, "Let them do so." So they got up and were counted off—twelve for Benjamin and Ish-Bosheth, son of Saul, and twelve for David. Each man grabbed his opponent by the head and thrust his sword into his opponent's side, and they fell down together. So that place was called Helkath-Hazzurim, which is in Gibeon The battle that day was very fierce, and Abner and the men of Israel were defeated by David's servants. The three sons of Zeruiah were there: Joab, Abishai, and Asahel. Asahel was as swift of foot as a wild gazelle. He chased Abner, turning neither to the right nor to the left as he pursued him. Abner looked behind him and asked, "Is that you, Asahel?" He answered, "Yes, it is." Then Abner said to him, "Turn aside to your right or to your left; seize one of the young men and take his armor." But Asahel would not stop pursuing him. Again, Abner warned Asahel, "Stop chasing me! Why should I strike you down? How could I look your brother Joab in the face?" But Asahel refused to give up the pursuit. So Abner thrust the butt of his spear into Asahel's stomach, and the spear came out through his back. He fell there and died on the spot. Every man stopped when he came to the place where Asahel had fallen and died Joab

and Abishai continued the pursuit of Abner. As the sun was setting, they came to the hill of Ammah, near Giah, on the way to the desert of Gibeon. The Benjaminites rallied behind Abner and formed a group on a hilltop. Abner called out to Joab, "Must the sword devour forever? Don't you realize that this will end in bitterness? How long before you order your men to stop pursuing their brothers?" Joab answered, "As surely as God lives, if you had not spoken, the men would have continued pursuing their brothers until morning." So Joab blew the trumpet, and all the men came to a halt; they no longer pursued Israel, nor did they fight anymore Abner and his men marched through the Arabah all that night. They crossed the Jordan, continued through the morning hours, and came to Mahanaim. Joab returned from pursuing Abner and assembled all his men. Besides Asahel, nineteen of David's men were found missing. But David's men had killed three hundred sixty Benjaminites who were with Abner. They took Asahel and buried him in his father's tomb at Bethlehem. Then Joab and his men marched all night and arrived in Hebron at daybreak

Chapter 3

The war between the house of Saul and the house of David lasted a long time. David grew stronger and stronger, while the house of Saul grew weaker and weaker. Sons were born to David in Hebron: his firstborn was Amnon, the son of Ahinoam the Jezreelite; his second, Kileab, the son of Abigail, the widow of Nabal of Carmel; the third, Absalom, the son of Maacah, daughter of Talmai, king of Geshur; the fourth, Adonijah, the son of Haggith; the fifth, Shephatiah, the son of Abital; and the sixth, Ithream, the son of David's wife Eglah. These were born to David in Hebron During the war between the house of Saul and the house of David, Abner had been strengthening his own position in the house of Saul. Now Saul had a concubine named Rizpah, daughter of Aiah. And Ish-Bosheth said to Abner, "Why did you sleep with my father's concubine?" Abner was very angry because of what Ish-Bosheth said, and he answered, "Am I a dog's head—on Judah's side? This very day I am loyal to the house of your father Saul and to his family and friends. I haven't handed you over to David. Yet now you accuse me of an offense involving this woman! May God deal with Abner, be it ever so severely, if I do not do for David what the LORD promised him on oath and transfer the kingdom from the house of Saul and establish David's throne over Israel and Judah from Dan to Beersheba." Ish-Bosheth did not dare to say another word to Abner because he was afraid of him Then Abner sent messengers on his behalf to say to David, "Whose land is it? Make an agreement with me, and I will help you bring all Israel over to you." "Good," said David. "I will make an agreement with you. But I demand one thing of you: Do not come into my presence unless you bring Michal, daughter of Saul, when you come to see me." Then David sent messengers to Ish-Bosheth, son of Saul, demanding, "Give me my wife Michal, whom I betrothed to myself for the price of a hundred Philistine foreskins." So Ish-Bosheth gave orders and had her taken away from her husband Paltiel, son of Laish. Her husband, however, went with her, weeping behind her all the way to Bahurim. Then Abner said to him, "Go back home!" So he went back Abner conferred with the elders of Israel and said, "For some time you have wanted to make David your king. Now do it! For the LORD promised David, 'By my servant David I will rescue my people Israel from the hand of the Philistines and from the hand of all their enemies.'" Abner also spoke to the Benjaminites in person. Then he went to Hebron to tell David everything that Israel and the whole tribe of Benjamin wanted to do. When Abner, who had twenty men with him, came to David at Hebron, David prepared a feast for him and his men. Then Abner said to David, "Let me go at once and assemble all Israel for my lord the king, so that they may make a covenant with you, and that you may rule over all that your heart desires." So David sent Abner away, and he went in peace Just then David's men and Joab returned from a raid and brought with them a great deal of plunder. But Abner was no longer with David in Hebron because David had sent him away, and he had gone in peace. When Joab and all the soldiers with him arrived, he was told that Abner son of Ner had come to the king and that the king had sent him away and that he had gone in peace. So Joab went to the king and said, "What have you done? Look, Abner came to you. Why did you let him go? Now he is gone! You know Abner son of Ner; he came to deceive you and observe your movements and find out everything you are doing." Joab then left David and sent messengers after Abner, and they brought him back from the well of Sirah. But David did not know it. Now when Abner returned to Hebron, Joab took him aside into the gateway, as though to speak with him privately. And there, to avenge the blood of his brother Asahel, Joab stabbed him in the stomach, and he died. Later, when David heard about this, he said, "I and my kingdom are forever innocent before the LORD concerning the blood of Abner son of Ner. May his blood fall on the head of Joab and on his whole family! May Joab's family never be without someone who has a running sore or leprosy or who leans on a crutch or who falls by the sword or who lacks food." (Joab and his brother Abishai murdered Abner because he had killed their brother Asahel in the battle at Gibeon.) Then David said to Joab and all the people with him, "Tear your clothes and put on sackcloth and walk in mourning in front of Abner." King David himself walked behind the bier. They buried Abner in Hebron, and the king wept aloud at Abner's tomb. All the people wept also. The king sang this lament for Abner: "Should Abner have died as the lawless die? Your hands were not bound, your feet were not fettered. You fell as one falls before the wicked." And all the people wept over him again. Then they all came and urged David to eat something while it was still day, but David took an oath, saying, "May God deal with me, be it ever so severely, if I taste bread or anything else before the sun sets!" All the people took note and were pleased; indeed, everything the king did pleased them. So on that day all the people and all Israel knew that the king had no part in the murder of Abner son of Ner. Then the king said to his men, "Do you not realize that a commander and a great man has fallen in Israel this day? And today, though I am the anointed king, I am weak, and these sons of Zeruiah are too strong for me. May the LORD repay the evildoer according to his evil deeds!"

Chapter 4

When Saul's son heard that Abner had died in Hebron, he lost courage, and all Israel became alarmed. Saul's son had two men who were leaders of raiding bands: one was named Baanah and the other Rechab. They were sons of Rimmon the Beerothite from the tribe of Benjamin—Beeroth is considered part of Benjamin because the people of Beeroth fled to Gittaim and have resided there as foreigners to this day Jonathan, son of Saul, had a son who was lame in both feet. He was five years old when the news about Saul and Jonathan came from Jezreel. His nurse picked him up and fled, but as she hurried to leave, he fell and became disabled. His name was Mephibosheth Now Rechab and Baanah,

the sons of Rimmon the Beerothite, set out for the house of Ish-Bosheth, and they arrived there in the heat of the day while he was taking his noonday rest. They went into the inner part of the house as if to get some wheat, and they stabbed him in the stomach. Then Rechab and his brother Baanah slipped away. They had gone into the house while he was lying on the bed in his bedroom. After they stabbed and killed him, they cut off his head. Taking it with them, they traveled all night by way of the Arabah. They brought the head of Ish-Bosheth to David at Hebron and said to the king, "Here is the head of Ish-Bosheth son of Saul, your enemy, who tried to kill you. This day the LORD has avenged my lord the king against Saul and his offspring." David answered Rechab and his brother Baanah, the sons of Rimmon the Beerothite, "As surely as the LORD lives, who has delivered me out of every trouble, when someone told me, 'Saul is dead,' and thought he was bringing good news, I seized him and put him to death in Ziklag. That was the reward I gave him for his news! How much more—when wicked men have killed an innocent man in his own house and on his own bed—should I not now demand his blood from your hand and rid the earth of you!" So David gave an order to his men, and they killed them. They cut off their hands and feet and hung the bodies by the pool in Hebron. But they took the head of Ish-Bosheth and buried it in Abner's tomb at Hebron

Chapter 5

All the tribes of Israel came to David at Hebron and said, "We are your own flesh and blood. In the past, while Saul was king over us, you were the one who led Israel on their military campaigns. And the LORD said to you, 'You will shepherd my people Israel, and you will become their ruler.'" When all the elders of Israel had come to King David at Hebron, the king made a covenant with them at Hebron before the LORD, and they anointed David king over Israel. David was thirty years old when he became king, and he reigned forty years. In Hebron, he reigned over Judah for seven years and six months, and in Jerusalem, he reigned over all Israel and Judah for thirty-three years The king and his men marched to Jerusalem to attack the Jebusites, who lived there. The Jebusites said to David, "You will not get in here; even the blind and the lame can ward you off." They thought, "David cannot get in here." Nevertheless, David captured the fortress of Zion—which is the City of David. On that day, David had said, "Anyone who conquers the Jebusites will have to use the water shaft to reach those 'lame and blind' who are David's enemies." That is why they say, "The 'blind and lame' will not enter the palace." David then took up residence in the fortress and called it the City of David. He built up the area around it, from the terraces inward. And he became more and more powerful because the LORD God Almighty was with him. Now Hiram king of Tyre sent envoys to David, along with cedar logs and carpenters and stonemasons, and they built a palace for David. Then David knew that the LORD had established him as king over Israel and had exalted his kingdom for the sake of his people Israel After he left Hebron, David took more concubines and wives in Jerusalem, and more sons and daughters were born to him. These are the names of the children born to him there: Shammua, Shobab, Nathan, Solomon, Ibhar, Elishua After he left Hebron, David took more concubines and wives in Jerusalem, and more sons and daughters were born to him. These are the names of the children born to him there: Shammua, Shobab, Nathan, Solomon, Ibhar, Elishua, Nepheg, Japhia, Elishama, Eliada, and Eliphelet When the Philistines heard that David had been anointed king over Israel, they went up in full force to search for him, but David heard about it and went down to the stronghold. Now the Philistines had come and spread out in the Valley of Rephaim. So David inquired of the LORD, "Shall I go and attack the Philistines? Will you deliver them into my hands?" The LORD answered him, "Go, for I will surely deliver the Philistines into your hands." So David went to Baal Perazim, and there he defeated them. He said, "As waters break out, the LORD has broken out against my enemies before me." So that place was called Baal Perazim. The Philistines abandoned their idols there, and David and his men carried them off Once more the Philistines came up and spread out in the Valley of Rephaim; so David inquired of the LORD, and he answered, "Do not go straight up, but circle around behind them and attack them in front of the poplar trees. As soon as you hear the sound of marching in the tops of the poplar trees, move quickly, because that will mean the LORD has gone out in front of you to strike the Philistine army." So David did as the LORD commanded him, and he struck down the Philistines all the way from Gibeon to Gezer

Chapter 6
David gathered all the chosen men of Israel, about thirty thousand in number. He and his people set out from Baale of Judah to bring the Ark of God, which is called by the Name of the LORD of hosts, who dwells between the cherubim. They placed the Ark of God on a new cart and brought it out of the house of Abinadab, which was on the hill. Uzzah and Ahio, sons of Abinadab, were guiding the new cart. As they brought the Ark of God out of the house of Abinadab, Ahio walked in front of the Ark. David and all the house of Israel were celebrating before the LORD with all kinds of instruments made of wood, including harps, lyres, tambourines, castanets, and cymbals When they came to the threshing floor of Nacon, Uzzah reached out and took hold of the Ark of God because the oxen had stumbled. The LORD's anger burned against Uzzah because of his irreverent act, and God struck him down there beside the Ark of God. Uzzah died there because of his error. David was angry because the LORD's wrath had broken out against Uzzah, and to this day, that place is called Perez-Uzzah. David was afraid of the LORD that day and said, "How can the Ark of the LORD ever come to me?" So David would not move the Ark of the LORD to the City of David. Instead, he took it to the house of Obed-Edom the Gittite. The Ark of the LORD remained in the house of Obed-Edom the Gittite for three months, and the LORD blessed him and his entire household When King David was told that the LORD had blessed the household of Obed-Edom and everything he had because of the Ark of God, he went to bring up the Ark of God from the house of Obed-Edom to the City of David with rejoicing. When those who were carrying the Ark of the LORD had taken six steps, he sacrificed a bull and a fattened calf. David, wearing a linen ephod, danced before the LORD with all his might. He and the entire house of Israel brought up the Ark of the LORD with shouts and the sound of trumpets As the Ark of the LORD was entering the City of David, Michal, daughter of Saul, watched from a window. When she saw King David leaping and dancing before the LORD, she despised him in her heart. They brought the Ark of the LORD and set it in its place inside the tent that David had pitched for it. David sacrificed burnt offerings and fellowship offerings before the LORD. After he had finished sacrificing the burnt offerings and fellowship offerings, he blessed the people in the name of the LORD Almighty. Then he gave a loaf of bread, a cake of dates, and a cake of raisins to each person in the whole crowd of Israelites, both men and women. And all the people went to their homes When David returned home to bless his household, Michal, the daughter of Saul, came out to meet him and said, "How the king of Israel has distinguished himself today, going around half-naked in full view of the slave girls of his servants as any vulgar fellow would!" David said to Michal, "It was before the LORD, who chose me rather than your father or anyone from his house when he appointed me ruler over the LORD's people Israel—I will celebrate before the LORD. I will become even more undignified than this, and I will be humiliated in my own eyes. But by these slave girls you spoke of, I will be held in honor." And Michal, the daughter of Saul, had no children to the day of her death

Chapter 7
After the king had settled in his palace and the LORD had given him rest from all his enemies around him, he said to Nathan the prophet, "Here I am, living in a house of cedar, while the Ark of God remains in a tent." Nathan replied to the king, "Whatever you have in mind, go ahead and do it, for the LORD is with you." That night the word of the LORD came to Nathan, saying, "Go and tell my servant David, 'This is what the LORD says: Are you the one to build me a house to dwell in? I have not dwelt in a house from the day I brought the Israelites up out of Egypt to this day. I have been moving from place to place with a tent as my dwelling. Wherever I have moved with all the Israelites, did I ever say to any of their rulers whom I commanded to shepherd my people Israel, "Why have you not built me a house of cedar?"' "Now then, tell my servant David, 'This is what the LORD Almighty says: I took you from the pasture, from tending the flock, and appointed you ruler over my people Israel. I have been with you wherever you have gone, and I have cut off all your enemies from before you. Now I will make your name great, like the names of the greatest men on earth. And I will provide a place for my people Israel and will plant them so that they can have a home of their own and no longer be disturbed. Wicked people will not oppress them anymore, as they did at the beginning and have done ever since the time I appointed leaders over my people Israel. I will also give you rest from all your enemies '"The LORD declares to you that the LORD himself will establish a house for you: When your days are over and you rest with your ancestors, I will raise up your offspring to succeed you, your own flesh and blood, and I will establish his kingdom. He is the one who will build a house for my Name, and I will establish the throne of his kingdom forever. I will be his father, and he will be my son. When he does wrong, I will punish him with a rod wielded by men, with floggings inflicted by human hands. But my love will never be taken away from him, as I took it away from Saul, whom I removed from before you. Your house and your kingdom will endure forever before me; your throne will be established forever.'" Nathan reported to David all the words of this entire revelation Then King David went in and sat before the LORD, and he said, "Who am I, Sovereign LORD, and what is my family, that you have brought me this far? And as if this were not enough in your sight, Sovereign LORD, you have also spoken about the future of the house of your servant—and this decree, Sovereign LORD, is for a mere human! "What more can David say to you? For you know your servant, Sovereign LORD. For the sake of your word and according to your will, you have done this great thing and made it known to your servant "How great you are, Sovereign LORD! There is no one like you, and there is no God but you, as we have heard with our own ears. And who is like your

people Israel—the one nation on earth that God went out to redeem as a people for himself, and to make a name for himself, and to perform great and awesome wonders by driving out nations and their gods from before your people, whom you redeemed from Egypt? You have established your people Israel as your very own forever, and you, LORD, have become their God "And now, LORD God, keep forever the promise you have made concerning your servant and his house. Do as you promised, so that your name will be great forever. Then people will say, 'The LORD Almighty is God over Israel!' And the house of your servant David will be established in your sight "LORD Almighty, God of Israel, you have revealed this to your servant, saying, 'I will build a house for you.' So your servant has found courage to pray this prayer to you. Sovereign LORD, you are God! Your covenant is trustworthy, and you have promised these good things to your servant. Now be pleased to bless the house of your servant, that it may continue forever in your sight; for you, Sovereign LORD, have spoken, and with your blessing, the house of your servant will be blessed forever."

Chapter 8

After this, David defeated the Philistines and subdued them. He took Metheg Ammah from the control of the Philistines. David also defeated the Moabites. He made them lie down on the ground and measured them with a length of cord. Every two lengths of them were put to death, and the third length was allowed to live. So the Moabites became subject to David and brought him tribute Moreover, David defeated Hadadezer son of Rehob, king of Zobah, when he went to restore his control along the Euphrates River. David captured a thousand of his chariots, seven thousand charioteers, and twenty thousand foot soldiers. He hamstrung all but a hundred of the chariot horses. When the Arameans of Damascus came to help Hadadezer king of Zobah, David struck down twenty-two thousand of them. He put garrisons in the Aramean kingdom of Damascus, and the Arameans became subject to him and brought tribute. The LORD gave David victory wherever he went David took the gold shields that belonged to the officers of Hadadezer and brought them to Jerusalem. From Tebah and Berothai, towns that belonged to Hadadezer, King David took a great quantity of bronze When Tou king of Hamath heard that David had defeated the entire army of Hadadezer, he sent his son Joram to King David to greet him and congratulate him on his victory in battle over Hadadezer, who had been at war with Tou. Joram brought with him articles of silver, of gold, and of bronze. King David dedicated these articles to the LORD, as he had done with the silver and gold from all the nations he had subdued: Edom and Moab, the Ammonites and the Philistines, and Amalek. He also dedicated the plunder taken from Hadadezer son of Rehob, king of Zobah And David became famous after he returned from striking down eighteen thousand Edomites in the Valley of Salt. He put garrisons throughout Edom, and all the Edomites became subject to David. The LORD gave David victory wherever he went David reigned over all Israel, doing what was just and right for all his people. Joab son of Zeruiah was over the army; Jehoshaphat son of Ahilud was recorder; Zadok son of Ahitub and Ahimelek son of Abiathar were priests; Seraiah was secretary; Benaiah son of Jehoiada was over the Kerethites and Pelethites; and David's sons were priests.

Chapter 9

David asked, "Is there anyone still left of the house of Saul to whom I can show kindness for Jonathan's sake?" Now there was a servant of Saul's household named Ziba. They summoned him to appear before David, and the king said to him, "Are you Ziba?" "At your service," he replied The king asked, "Is there no one still alive from the house of Saul to whom I can show God's kindness?" Ziba answered the king, "There is still a son of Jonathan; he is lame in both feet." "Where is he?" the king asked Ziba answered, "He is at the house of Makir son of Ammiel in Lo Debar." So King David had him brought from Lo Debar, from the house of Makir son of Ammiel. When Mephibosheth son of Jonathan, the son of Saul, came to David, he bowed down to pay him honor David said, "Mephibosheth!" "At your service," he replied "Don't be afraid," David said to him, "for I will surely show you kindness for the sake of your father Jonathan. I will restore to you all the land that belonged to your grandfather Saul, and you will always eat at my table." Mephibosheth bowed down and said, "What is your servant, that you should notice a dead dog like me?" Then the king summoned Ziba, Saul's steward, and said to him, "I have given your master's grandson everything that belonged to Saul and his family. You and your sons and your servants are to farm the land for him and bring in the crops, so that your master's grandson may be provided for. And Mephibosheth, grandson of your master, will always eat at my table." Now Ziba had fifteen sons and twenty servants. Then Ziba said to the king, "Your servant will do whatever my lord the king commands his servant to do." So Mephibosheth ate at David's table like one of the king's sons. Mephibosheth had a young son named Mica, and all the members of Ziba's household were servants of Mephibosheth. And Mephibosheth lived in Jerusalem because he always ate at the king's table; he was lame in both feet

Chapter 10

Some time later, the king of the Ammonites died, and his son Hanun succeeded him as king. David thought, "I will show kindness to Hanun son of Nahash, just as his father showed kindness to me." So David sent a delegation to express his sympathy to Hanun concerning his father When David's men came to the land of the Ammonites, the Ammonite commanders said to Hanun their lord, "Do you think David is honoring your father by sending envoys to you to express sympathy? Hasn't David sent them to you to explore the city and spy it out and overthrow it?" So Hanun seized David's envoys, shaved off half of each man's beard, cut off their garments at the buttocks, and sent them away When David was told about this, he sent messengers to meet the men, for they were greatly humiliated. The king said, "Stay at Jericho till your beards have grown, and then come back." When the Ammonites realized that they had become obnoxious to David, they hired twenty thousand Aramean foot soldiers from Beth Rehob and Zobah, as well as the king of Maakah with a thousand men, and also twelve thousand men from Tob. On hearing this, David sent Joab out with the entire army of fighting men. The Ammonites came out and drew up in battle formation at the entrance of their city gate, while the Arameans of Zobah and Rehob and the men of Tob and Maakah were by themselves in the open country Joab saw that there were battle lines in front of him and behind him; so he selected some of the best troops in Israel and deployed them against the Arameans. He put the rest of the men under the command of Abishai his brother and deployed them against the Ammonites. Joab said, "If the Arameans are too strong for me, then you are to come to my rescue; but if the Ammonites are too strong for you, then I will come to rescue you. Be strong, and let us fight bravely for our people and the cities of our God. The LORD will do what is good in his sight." Then Joab and the troops with him advanced to fight the Arameans, and they fled before him. When the Ammonites realized that the Arameans were fleeing, they fled before Abishai and went inside the city. So Joab returned from fighting the Ammonites and came to Jerusalem After the Arameans saw that they had been routed by Israel, they regrouped. Hadadezer had Arameans brought from beyond the Euphrates River; they went to Helam, with Shobach the commander of Hadadezer's army leading them When David was told of this, he gathered all Israel, crossed the Jordan and went to Helam. The Arameans formed their battle lines to meet David and fought against him. But they fled before Israel, and David killed seven hundred of their charioteers and forty thousand of their foot soldiers. He also struck down Shobach the commander of their army, and he died there. When all the kings who were vassals of Hadadezer saw that they had been routed by Israel, they made peace with the Israelites and became subject to them. So the Arameans were afraid to help the Ammonites anymore

Chapter 11

At the turn of the year, when kings typically go out to battle, David sent Joab, his servants, and all of Israel to destroy the Ammonites and besiege Rabbah. However, David remained in Jerusalem. One evening, David arose from his bed and walked on the roof of the king's palace. From the roof, he saw a very beautiful woman bathing. David sent someone to find out who she was, and he was told, "Is this not Bathsheba, the daughter of Eliam and the wife of Uriah the Hittite?" David sent messengers to bring her to him. She came, and he lay with her. Afterward, she purified herself and returned to her house. Bathsheba then sent word to David, saying, "I am with child." David sent for Uriah the Hittite and Joab sent him to David. When Uriah arrived, David asked him how Joab and the people were doing and how the war was progressing. David then said to Uriah, "Go down to your house and wash your feet." Uriah left the palace, and David sent a gift to follow him. However, Uriah slept at the entrance of the palace with all his lord's servants and did not go down to his house. When David was informed that Uriah did not go to his house, he asked Uriah, "Have you not returned from a journey? Why did you not go down to your house?" Uriah responded, "The Ark, Israel, and Judah are dwelling in tents, and my lord Joab and the servants of my lord are camping in the open fields. Should I then go to my house to eat and drink and lie with my wife? As surely as you live, I will not do this thing." David then told Uriah to stay another day, and he would send him back the next day. Uriah stayed in Jerusalem that day and the following day. David invited Uriah, ate and drank with him, and made him drunk. But in the evening, Uriah went out to lie on his bed with the servants of his lord and did not go to his house. The next morning, David wrote a letter to Joab and sent it with Uriah. In the letter, he wrote, "Set Uriah at the forefront of the fiercest battle and withdraw from him, so he may be struck down and die." As Joab besieged the city, he assigned Uriah to a place where he knew the strongest defenders were. The men of the city came out and fought with Joab, and some of David's servants fell, including Uriah the Hittite Joab sent a full report of the battle to David. He instructed the messenger, "When you finish reporting all the details of the battle to the king, if the king becomes angry and asks, 'Why did you go so close to the city to fight? Did you not know they would shoot from the wall? Who killed Abimelech the son of Jerubbesheth? Did not a woman throw an upper millstone on him from the wall, so he died in Thebez?

Why did you go so near the wall?' Then you shall say, 'Your servant Uriah the Hittite is also dead.'" The messenger set out and, upon arrival, reported to David everything Joab had sent him to say. The messenger told David, "The men gained an advantage over us and came out against us in the field, but we drove them back to the entrance of the gate. The archers shot at your servants from the wall, and some of the king's servants died. Moreover, your servant Uriah the Hittite is dead." David said to the messenger, "Tell Joab not to be troubled by this, for the sword devours one as well as another. Press the attack against the city and destroy it. Encourage him." When Uriah's wife heard that her husband was dead, she mourned for him. After the mourning period was over, David sent for her and brought her to his house. She became his wife and bore him a son. But the thing that David had done displeased the LORD

Chapter 12

The LORD sent Nathan to David. Nathan came to him and said, "There were two men in a city, one rich and the other poor. The rich man had a great many cattle and sheep, but the poor man had nothing except one little ewe lamb which he had bought. He fed it, and it grew up with him and his children. It ate his food, drank from his cup, and slept in his arms; it was like a daughter to him. Now a traveler came to the rich man, but he refrained from taking one of his own sheep or cattle to prepare a meal for the traveler who had come to him. Instead, he took the ewe lamb that belonged to the poor man and prepared it for his guest." David burned with anger against the man and said to Nathan, "As surely as the LORD lives, the man who did this deserves to die! He must pay for that lamb four times over because he did such a thing and had no pity." Then Nathan said to David, "You are the man! This is what the LORD, the God of Israel, says: 'I anointed you king over Israel, and I delivered you from the hand of Saul. I gave your master's house to you, and your master's wives into your arms. I gave you all Israel and Judah. And if all this had been too little, I would have given you even more. Why did you despise the word of the LORD by doing what is evil in His eyes? You struck down Uriah the Hittite with the sword and took his wife to be your own. You killed him with the sword of the Ammonites. Now, therefore, the sword will never depart from your house because you despised me and took the wife of Uriah the Hittite to be your own.' "This is what the LORD says: 'Out of your own household, I am going to bring calamity on you. Before your very eyes, I will take your wives and give them to one who is close to you, and he will sleep with your wives in broad daylight. You did it in secret, but I will do this thing in broad daylight before all Israel.'" Then David said to Nathan, "I have sinned against the LORD." Nathan replied, "The LORD has taken away your sin. You are not going to die. But because by doing this you have shown utter contempt for the LORD, the son born to you will die." After Nathan had gone home, the LORD struck the child that Uriah's wife had borne to David, and he became ill David pleaded with God for the child. He fasted and spent the nights lying in sackcloth on the ground. The elders of his household stood beside him to get him up from the ground, but he refused, and he would not eat any food with them. On the seventh day, the child died. David's attendants were afraid to tell him that the child was dead, for they thought, "While the child was still living, he wouldn't listen to us when we spoke to him. How can we now tell him the child is dead? He may do something desperate." David noticed that his attendants were whispering among themselves, and he realized the child was dead. "Is the child dead?"

he asked. "Yes," they replied, "he is dead." Then David got up from the ground. After he had washed, put on lotions, and changed his clothes, he went into the house of the LORD and worshiped. Then he went to his own house, and at his request, they served him food, and he ate His attendants asked him, "Why are you acting this way? While the child was alive, you fasted and wept, but now that the child is dead, you get up and eat!" He answered, "While the child was still alive, I fasted and wept. I thought, 'Who knows? The LORD may be gracious to me and let the child live.' But now that he is dead, why should I go on fasting? Can I bring him back again? I will go to him, but he will not return to me." Then David comforted his wife Bathsheba, and he went to her and made love to her. She gave birth to a son, and they named him Solomon. The LORD loved him; and because the LORD loved him, he sent word through Nathan the prophet to name him Jedidiah Meanwhile, Joab fought against Rabbah of the Ammonites and captured the royal citadel. Joab then sent messengers to David, saying, "I have fought against Rabbah and taken its water supply. Now muster the rest of the troops and besiege the city and capture it. Otherwise, I will take the city, and it will be named after me." So David mustered the entire army and went to Rabbah and attacked and captured it. He took the crown from the head of their king—its weight was a talent of gold, and it was set with precious stones—and it was placed on David's head. He took a great quantity of plunder from the city and brought out the people who were there, consigning them to labor with saws and with iron picks and axes, and he made them work at brickmaking. David did this to all the Ammonite towns. Then he and his entire army returned to Jerusalem

Chapter 13

After this, Absalom, the son of David, had a beautiful sister named Tamar. Amnon, another son of David, fell in love with her. Amnon became so obsessed with his sister Tamar that he made himself ill. She was a virgin, and it seemed impossible for him to do anything to her Now Amnon had a friend named Jonadab, the son of Shimeah, David's brother. Jonadab was a very shrewd man. He asked Amnon, "Why do you, the king's son, look so haggard morning after morning? Won't you tell me?" Amnon said to him, "I'm in love with Tamar, my brother Absalom's sister." "Go to bed and pretend to be ill," Jonadab said. "When your father comes to see you, say to him, 'I would like my sister Tamar to come and give me something to eat. Let her prepare the food in my sight so I may watch her and then eat it from her hand.'" So Amnon lay down and pretended to be ill. When the king came to see him, Amnon said to him, "I would like my sister Tamar to come and make some special bread in my sight so I may eat from her hand." David sent word to Tamar at the palace: "Go to the house of your brother Amnon and prepare some food for him." So Tamar went to the house of her brother Amnon, who was lying down. She took some dough, kneaded it, made the bread in his sight, and baked it. Then she took the pan and served him the bread, but he refused to eat. "Send everyone out of here," Amnon said. So everyone left him Then Amnon said to Tamar, "Bring the food here into my bedroom so I may eat from your hand." And Tamar took the bread she had prepared and brought it to her brother Amnon in his bedroom. But when she took it to him to eat, he grabbed her and said, "Come to bed with me, my sister." "No, my brother!" she said to him. "Don't force me! Such a thing should not be done in Israel! Don't do this wicked thing. What about me? Where could I get rid of my disgrace? And what about you? You would be like one of the wicked

fools in Israel. Please speak to the king; he will not keep me from being married to you." But he refused to listen to her, and since he was stronger than she, he raped her. Then Amnon hated her with intense hatred. In fact, he hated her more than he had loved her. Amnon said to her, "Get up and get out!" "No!" she said to him. "Sending me away would be a greater wrong than what you have already done to me." But he refused to listen to her. He called his personal servant and said, "Get this woman out of my sight and bolt the door after her." So his servant put her out and bolted the door after her. She was wearing an ornate robe, for this was the kind of garment the virgin daughters of the king wore Tamar put ashes on her head and tore the ornate robe she was wearing. She put her hands on her head and went away, weeping aloud as she went. Her brother Absalom said to her, "Has that Amnon, your brother, been with you? Be quiet now, my sister; he is your brother. Don't take this thing to heart." And Tamar lived in her brother Absalom's house, a desolate woman When King David heard all this, he was furious. And Absalom never said a word to Amnon, either good or bad; he hated Amnon because he had disgraced his sister Tamar Two years later, when Absalom's sheepshearers were at Baal Hazor near the border of Ephraim, he invited all the king's sons to come there. Absalom went to the king and said, "Your servant has had shearers come. Will the king and his attendants please join me?" "No, my son," the king replied. "All of us should not go; we would only be a burden to you." Although Absalom urged him, he still refused to go but gave him his blessing. Then Absalom said, "If not, please let my brother Amnon come with us." The king asked him, "Why should he go with you?" But Absalom urged him, so he sent with him Amnon and the rest of the king's sons Absalom ordered his men, "Listen! When Amnon is in high spirits from drinking wine and I say to you, 'Strike Amnon down,' then kill him. Don't be afraid. Haven't I given you this order? Be strong and brave." So Absalom's men did to Amnon what Absalom had ordered. Then all the king's sons got up, mounted their mules, and fled While they were on their way, the report came to David: "Absalom has struck down all the king's sons; not one of them is left." The king stood up, tore his clothes, and lay down on the ground; and all his attendants stood by with their clothes torn. But Jonadab, son of Shimeah, David's brother, said, "My lord should not think that they killed all the princes; only Amnon is dead. This has been Absalom's expressed intention ever since the day Amnon raped his sister Tamar. My lord the king should not be concerned about the report that all the king's sons are dead. Only Amnon is dead." Meanwhile, Absalom had fled. Now the man standing watch looked up and saw many people on the road west of him, coming down the side of the hill. The watchman went and told the king, "I see men in the direction of Horonaim, on the side of the hill." Jonadab said to the king, "See, the king's sons have come; it has happened just as your servant said." As he finished speaking, the king's sons came in, wailing loudly. The king, too, and all his attendants wept very bitterly Absalom fled and went to Talmai, son of Ammihud, the king of Geshur. But King David mourned many days for his son. After Absalom fled and went to Geshur, he stayed there three years. And King David longed to go to Absalom, for he was consoled concerning Amnon's death

Chapter 14

Joab, son of Zeruiah, knew that the king's heart longed for Absalom. So Joab sent someone to Tekoa and had a wise woman brought from there. He said to her, "Pretend you are in mourning. Dress in mourning clothes, and don't use any cosmetic lotions. Act like a woman who has spent many days grieving for the dead. Then go to the king and speak these words to him." And Joab put the words in her mouth When the woman from Tekoa went to the king, she fell with her face to the ground to pay him honor, and she said, "Help me, Your Majesty!" The king asked her, "What is troubling you?" She said, "I am a widow; my husband is dead. I your servant had two sons. They got into a fight with each other in the field, and no one was there to separate them. One struck the other and killed him. Now the whole clan has risen up against your servant. They say, 'Hand over the one who struck his brother down, so that we may put him to death for the life of his brother whom he killed; then we will get rid of the heir as well.' They would put out the only burning coal I have left, leaving my husband neither name nor descendant on the face of the earth." The king said to the woman, "Go home, and I will issue an order in your behalf." But the woman from Tekoa said to him, "Let my lord the king pardon me and my family, and let the king and his throne be without guilt." The king replied, "If anyone says anything to you, bring them to me, and they will not bother you again." She said, "Then let the king invoke the LORD his God to prevent the avenger of blood from adding to the destruction, so that my son will not be destroyed." "As surely as the LORD lives," he said, "not one hair of your son's head will fall to the ground." Then the woman said, "Let your servant speak a word to my lord the king." "Speak," he replied The woman said, "Why then have you devised a thing like this against the people of God? When the king says this, does he not convict himself, for the king has not brought back his banished son? Like water spilled on the ground, which cannot be recovered, so we must die. But that is not what God desires; rather, he devises ways so that a banished person does not remain banished from him. And now I have come to say this to my lord the king because the people have made me afraid. Your servant thought, 'I will speak to the king; perhaps he will grant his servant's request. Perhaps the king will agree to deliver his servant from the hand of the man who is trying to cut off both me and my son from God's inheritance.' "And now your servant says, 'May the word of my lord the king secure my inheritance, for my lord the king is like an angel of God in discerning good and evil. May the LORD your God be with you.'" Then the king said to the woman, "Do not keep from me the answer to what I am going to ask you." "Let my lord the king speak," the woman said The king asked, "Isn't the hand of Joab with you in all this?" The woman answered, "As surely as you live, my lord the king, no one can turn to the right or to the left from anything my lord the king says. Yes, it was your servant Joab who instructed me to do this and who put all these words into the mouth of your servant. Your servant Joab did this to change the present situation. My lord has wisdom like that of an angel of God—he knows everything that happens in the land." The king said to Joab, "Very well, I will do it. Go, bring back the young man Absalom." Joab fell with his face to the ground to pay him honor, and he blessed the king. Joab said, "Today your servant knows that he has found favor in your eyes, my lord the king, because the king has granted his servant's request." Then Joab went to Geshur and brought Absalom back to Jerusalem. But the king said, "He must go to his own house; he must not see my face." So Absalom went to his own house and did not see the face of the king In all Israel, there was not a man so highly praised for his handsome appearance as Absalom. From the top of his head to the sole of his foot there was no blemish in him.

Whenever he cut the hair of his head—he used to cut his hair once a year because it became too heavy for him—he would weigh it, and its weight was two hundred shekels by the royal standard Three sons and a daughter were born to Absalom. His daughter's name was Tamar, and she became a beautiful woman. Absalom lived two years in Jerusalem without seeing the king's face. Then Absalom sent for Joab in order to send him to the king, but Joab refused to come to him. So he sent a second time, but he refused to come. Then he said to his servants, "Look, Joab's field is next to mine, and he has barley there. Go and set it on fire." So Absalom's servants set the field on fire Then Joab did go to Absalom's house, and he said to him, "Why have your servants set my field on fire?" Absalom said to Joab, "Look, I sent word to you and said, 'Come here so I can send you to the king to ask, "Why have I come from Geshur? It would be better for me if I were still there!"' Now then, I want to see the king's face, and if I am guilty of anything, let him put me to death." So Joab went to the king and told him this. Then the king summoned Absalom, and he came in and bowed down with his face to the ground before the king. And the king kissed Absalom

Chapter 15

In the course of time, Absalom provided himself with a chariot and horses and with fifty men to run ahead of him. He would get up early and stand by the side of the road leading to the city gate. Whenever anyone came with a complaint to be placed before the king for a decision, Absalom would call out to him, "What town are you from?" He would answer, "Your servant is from one of the tribes of Israel." Then Absalom would say to him, "Look, your claims are valid and proper, but there is no representative of the king to hear you." And Absalom would add, "If only I were appointed judge in the land! Then everyone who has a complaint or case could come to me and I would see that they receive justice." Also, whenever anyone approached him to bow down before him, Absalom would reach out his hand, take hold of him and kiss him. Absalom behaved in this way toward all the Israelites who came to the king asking for justice, and so he stole the hearts of the people of Israel At the end of four years, Absalom said to the king, "Let me go to Hebron and fulfill a vow I made to the LORD. While your servant was living at Geshur in Aram, I made this vow: 'If the LORD takes me back to Jerusalem, I will worship the LORD in Hebron.'" The king said to him, "Go in peace." So he went to Hebron. Then Absalom sent secret messengers throughout the tribes of Israel to say, "As soon as you hear the sound of the trumpets, then say, 'Absalom is king in Hebron.'" Two hundred men from Jerusalem had accompanied Absalom. They had been invited as guests and went quite innocently, knowing nothing about the matter. While Absalom was offering sacrifices, he also sent for Ahithophel the Gilonite, David's counselor, to come from Giloh, his hometown. And so the conspiracy gained strength, and Absalom's following kept on increasing A messenger came and told David, "The hearts of the people of Israel are with Absalom." Then David said to all his officials who were with him in Jerusalem, "Come! We must flee, or none of us will escape from Absalom. We must leave immediately, or he will move quickly to overtake us and bring ruin on us and put the city to the sword." The king's officials answered him, "Your servants are ready to do whatever our lord the king chooses." The king set out, with his entire household following him; but he left ten concubines to take care of the palace. So the king set out, with all the people following him, and they halted at the edge of the city. All his men marched past him, along with all the Kerethites and Pelethites, and all the six hundred Gittites who had accompanied him from Gath, marched before the king The king said to Ittai the Gittite, "Why should you come along with us? Go back and stay with King Absalom. You are a foreigner, an exile from your homeland. You came only yesterday. And today shall I make you wander about with us, when I do not know where I am going? Go back, and take your people with you. May the LORD show you kindness and faithfulness." But Ittai replied to the king, "As surely as the LORD lives, and as my lord the king lives, wherever my lord the king may be, whether it means life or death, there will your servant be." David said to Ittai, "Go ahead, march on." So Ittai the Gittite marched on with all his men and the families that were with him The whole countryside wept aloud as all the people passed by. The king also crossed the Kidron Valley, and all the people moved on toward the wilderness. Zadok was there, too, and all the Levites who were with him were carrying the ark of the covenant of God. They set down the ark of God, and Abiathar offered sacrifices until all the people had finished leaving the city Then the king said to Zadok, "Take the ark of God back into the city. If I find favor in the LORD's eyes, he will bring me back and let me see it and his dwelling place again. But if he says, 'I am not pleased with you,' then I am ready; let him do to me whatever seems good to him." The king also said to Zadok the priest, "Do you understand? Go back to the city with my blessing. Take your son Ahimaaz with you, and also Jonathan son of Abiathar. You and Abiathar return with your two sons. I will wait at the fords in the wilderness until word comes from you to inform me." So Zadok and Abiathar took the ark of God back to Jerusalem and stayed there But David continued up the Mount of Olives, weeping as he went; his head was covered, and he was barefoot. All the people with him covered their heads too and were weeping as they went up. Now David had been told, "Ahithophel is among the conspirators with Absalom." So David prayed, "LORD, turn Ahithophel's counsel into foolishness." When David arrived at the summit, where people used to worship God, Hushai the Arkite was there to meet him, his robe torn and dust on his head. David said to him, "If you go with me, you will be a burden to me. But if you return to the city and say to Absalom, 'Your Majesty, I will be your servant; I was your father's servant in the past, but now I will be your servant,' then you can help me by frustrating Ahithophel's advice. Won't the priests Zadok and Abiathar be there with you? Tell them anything you hear in the king's palace. Their two sons, Ahimaaz son of Zadok and Jonathan son of Abiathar, are there with them. Send them to me with anything you hear." So Hushai, David's confidant, arrived at Jerusalem as Absalom was entering the city

Chapter 16

When David was a little beyond the top of the hill, Ziba, the servant of Mephibosheth, came to him with a pair of saddled donkeys, two hundred loaves of bread, a hundred clusters of raisins, a hundred summer fruits, and a bottle of wine. The king asked Ziba, "What do you mean by these things?" Ziba replied, "The donkeys are for the king's household to ride on, the bread and summer fruits are for the young men to eat, and the wine is for those who become faint in the wilderness." The king then asked, "And where is your master's son?" Ziba said to the king, "He remains in Jerusalem, for he says, 'Today the house of Israel will restore to me the kingdom of my father.'" Then the king said to Ziba, "All that belonged to Mephibosheth is now yours." Ziba said, "I humbly bow before you. May I find favor in your

sight, my lord the king." As King David came to Bahurim, a man from the family of Saul named Shimei, son of Gera, came out, cursing as he came. He threw stones at David and all the servants of King David, while all the people and all the warriors were on David's right and left. Shimei cursed, saying, "Get out, get out, you murderer, you wicked man! The LORD has brought upon you all the blood of the house of Saul, in whose place you have reigned, and the LORD has delivered the kingdom into the hand of Absalom, your son. You are caught in your own evil because you are a murderer." Abishai, son of Zeruiah, said to the king, "Why should this dead dog curse my lord the king? Let me go over and remove his head." But the king said, "What have I to do with you, sons of Zeruiah? Let him curse, for the LORD has commanded him to curse David. Who then shall say, 'Why have you done so?'" David said to Abishai and all his servants, "My own son, who came from my own body, seeks my life. How much more now may this Benjamite? Let him alone, and let him curse, for the LORD has commanded him. Perhaps the LORD will look on my affliction and repay me with good for his cursing this day." As David and his men continued on their way, Shimei followed along the hillside opposite them, cursing, throwing stones, and flinging dust at them. The king and all the people with him grew weary and refreshed themselves there Meanwhile, Absalom and all the men of Israel came to Jerusalem, and Ahithophel was with him. When Hushai the Archite, David's friend, came to Absalom, he said, "Long live the king! Long live the king!" Absalom asked Hushai, "Is this your loyalty to your friend? Why did you not go with your friend?" Hushai replied, "No, for whom the LORD, this people, and all the men of Israel have chosen, I will be his, and I will remain with him. Moreover, whom should I serve? Should it not be his son? As I have served your father, so will I serve you." Then Absalom said to Ahithophel, "Give us your counsel; what shall we do?" Ahithophel replied, "Go in to your father's concubines, whom he has left to take care of the house. Then all Israel will hear that you have made yourself odious to your father, and the hands of all who are with you will be strengthened." So they pitched a tent for Absalom on the roof, and Absalom went in to his father's concubines in the sight of all Israel. The advice Ahithophel gave in those days was as if one consulted the oracle of God; so was all the advice of Ahithophel esteemed, both by David and by Absalom

Chapter 17

Ahithophel said to Absalom, "Let me choose twelve thousand men, and I will arise and pursue David tonight. I will come upon him while he is weary and discouraged, and throw him into a panic. All the people with him will flee, and I will strike down only the king. Then I will bring all the people back to you. When all return, the man whom you seek will be as good as dead, and all the people will be at peace." This plan seemed good to Absalom and all the elders of Israel But Absalom said, "Call Hushai the Archite also, and let us hear what he has to say." When Hushai came to Absalom, Absalom said to him, "Ahithophel has given this advice. Shall we follow it? If not, speak up." Hushai replied to Absalom, "The advice that Ahithophel has given this time is not good. You know your father and his men; they are mighty men, and they are enraged like a bear robbed of her cubs in the field. Besides, your father is an expert in war; he will not spend the night with the people. Even now he has hidden himself in one of the pits or in some other place. And when some of our troops fall at the first attack, whoever hears it will say, 'There has been a slaughter among the troops who follow Absalom.' Then even the valiant man, whose heart is like the heart of a lion, will utterly melt with fear, for all Israel knows that your father is a mighty man and that those who are with him are valiant men Therefore, I advise that all Israel be gathered to you, from Dan to Beersheba, like the sand by the sea for multitude, and that you go to battle in person. So shall we come upon him in some place where he is to be found, and we shall light upon him as the dew falls on the ground, and of him and all the men with him, not one will be left. If he withdraws into a city, then all Israel will bring ropes to that city, and we shall drag it into the valley until not even a pebble is to be found there." Absalom and all the men of Israel said, "The advice of Hushai the Archite is better than the advice of Ahithophel." For the LORD had determined to defeat the good advice of Ahithophel, so that the LORD might bring disaster upon Absalom Hushai then told Zadok and Abiathar, the priests, "Ahithophel has advised Absalom and the elders of Israel to do such and such, but I have advised them to do so and so. Therefore, send quickly and tell David, 'Do not stay tonight at the fords of the wilderness, but by all means pass over, lest the king and all the people who are with him be swallowed up.'" Now Jonathan and Ahimaaz were waiting at En-rogel. A servant girl would come and tell them, and they would go and tell King David, for they dared not be seen entering the city. But a boy saw them and told Absalom. So the two of them went away quickly and came to the house of a man at Bahurim who had a well in his courtyard, and they went down into it. The woman took and spread a covering over the well's mouth and scattered grain on it, and nothing was known of it When Absalom's servants came to the woman at the house, they asked, "Where are Ahimaaz and Jonathan?" The woman answered, "They have gone over the brook of water." And when they had searched and could not find them, they returned to Jerusalem. After they had gone, the men came up out of the well and went and told King David. They said to David, "Arise, and go quickly over the water, for thus has Ahithophel counseled against you." Then David and all the people who were with him arose and crossed the Jordan. By daybreak, not one was left who had not crossed the Jordan When Ahithophel saw that his counsel was not followed, he saddled his donkey and went off to his house in his city. He set his house in order and hanged himself, and he died and was buried in the tomb of his father David came to Mahanaim, and Absalom crossed the Jordan with all the men of Israel. Absalom had set Amasa over the army instead of Joab. Amasa was the son of a man named Ithra the Israelite, who had married Abigail, the daughter of Nahash, sister of Zeruiah, Joab's mother. And Israel and Absalom encamped in the land of Gilead When David came to Mahanaim, Shobi the son of Nahash from Rabbah of the Ammonites, and Machir the son of Ammiel from Lo-debar, and Barzillai the Gileadite from Rogelim brought beds, basins, earthen vessels, wheat, barley, flour, parched grain, beans, lentils, honey, curds, sheep, and cheese from the herd for David and the people who were with him to eat. For they said, "The people are hungry and weary and thirsty in the wilderness."

Chapter 18

David mustered the men who were with him and set over them commanders of thousands and commanders of hundreds. David sent out the troops, a third under the command of Joab, a third under Abishai son of Zeruiah, Joab's brother, and a third under Ittai the Gittite. The king said to the men, "I myself will surely go out with you." But the men said, "You shall not go out. If we are forced to flee, they won't care about us; even if half of us die, they won't care. But you are worth ten thousand of us. It would be better now for you to give us support from the city." The king answered, "I will do whatever seems best to you." So the king stood beside the gate while all the men marched out by hundreds and by thousands. The king commanded Joab, Abishai, and Ittai, "Be gentle with the young man Absalom for my sake." And all the troops heard the king giving orders concerning Absalom to each of the commanders The army marched into the field to fight Israel, and the battle took place in the forest of Ephraim. There the army of Israel was defeated by David's men, and the casualties that day were great—twenty thousand men. The battle spread out over the whole countryside, and the forest claimed more lives that day than the sword Now Absalom happened to meet David's men. He was riding his mule, and as the mule went under the thick branches of a large oak, Absalom's head got caught in the tree. He was left hanging in mid-air, while the mule he was riding kept on going. When one of the men saw what had happened, he told Joab, "I just saw Absalom hanging in an oak tree." Joab said to the man who had told him this, "What! You saw him? Why didn't you strike him to the ground right there? Then I would have given you ten shekels of silver and a warrior's belt." But the man replied, "Even if a thousand shekels were weighed out into my hands, I would not lay a hand on the king's son. In our hearing, the king commanded you and Abishai and Ittai, 'Protect the young man Absalom for my sake.' And if I had put my life in jeopardy—and nothing is hidden from the king—you would have kept your distance from me." Joab said, "I'm not going to wait like this for you." So he took three javelins in his hand and plunged them into Absalom's heart while Absalom was still alive in the oak tree. And ten of Joab's armor-bearers surrounded Absalom, struck him, and killed him Then Joab sounded the trumpet, and the troops stopped pursuing Israel, for Joab halted them. They took Absalom, threw him into a big pit in the forest, and piled up a large heap of stones over him. Meanwhile, all the Israelites fled to their homes During his lifetime, Absalom had taken a pillar and erected it in the King's Valley as a monument to himself, for he thought, "I have no son to carry on the memory of my name." He named the pillar after himself, and it is called Absalom's Monument to this day Then Ahimaaz son of Zadok said, "Let me run and take the news to the king that the LORD has delivered him from the hand of his enemies." "You are not the one to take the news today," Joab told him. "You may take the news another time, but you must not do so today, because the king's son is dead." Then Joab said to a Cushite, "Go, tell the king what you have seen." The Cushite bowed down before Joab and ran off. Ahimaaz son of Zadok again said to Joab, "Come what may, please let me run behind the Cushite." But Joab replied, "My son, why do you want to go? You don't have any news that will bring you a reward." He said, "Come what may, I want to run." So Joab said, "Run!" Then Ahimaaz ran by way of the plain and outran the Cushite While David was sitting between the inner and outer gates, the watchman went up to the roof of the gateway by the wall. As he looked out, he saw a man running alone. The watchman called out to the king and reported it. The king said, "If he is alone, he must have good news." And the runner came closer and closer Then the watchman saw another man running, and he called down to the gatekeeper, "Look, another man running alone!" The king said, "He must be bringing good news, too." The watchman said, "It seems to me that the first one runs like Ahimaaz son of Zadok." "He's a good man," the king said. "He comes with good news." Then Ahimaaz called out to the king, "All is well!" He bowed down before the king with his face to the ground and said, "Praise be to the LORD your God! He has delivered up those who lifted their hands against my lord the king." The king asked, "Is the young man Absalom safe?" Ahimaaz answered, "I saw great confusion just as Joab was about to send the king's servant and me, your servant, but I don't know what it was." The king said, "Stand aside and wait here." So he stepped aside and stood there. Then the Cushite arrived and said, "My lord the king, hear the good news! The LORD has vindicated you today by delivering you from the hand of all who rose up against you." The king asked the Cushite, "Is the young man Absalom safe?" The Cushite replied, "May the enemies of my lord the king and all who rise up to harm you be like that young man." The king was shaken. He went up to the room over the gateway and wept. As he went, he said: "O my son Absalom! My son, my son Absalom! If only I had died instead of you—O Absalom, my son, my son!"

Chapter 19

Joab was told, "The king is weeping and mourning for Absalom." And for the whole army, the victory that day was turned into mourning, because on that day the troops heard it said, "The king is grieving for his son." The men stole into the city that day as men steal in who are ashamed when they flee from battle. The king covered his face and cried aloud, "O my son Absalom! O Absalom, my son, my son!" Then Joab went into the house to the king and said, "Today you have humiliated all your men, who have just saved your life and the lives of your sons and daughters and the lives of your wives and concubines. You love those who hate you and hate those who love you. You have made it clear today that the commanders and their men mean nothing to you. I see that you would be pleased if Absalom were alive today and all of us were dead. Now go out and encourage your men. I swear by the LORD that if you don't go out, not a man will be left with you by nightfall. This will be worse for you than all the calamities that have come on you from your youth till now." So the king got up and took his seat in the gateway. When the men were told, "The king is sitting in the gateway," they all came before him. Meanwhile, the Israelites had fled to their homes Throughout the tribes of Israel, all the people were arguing among themselves, saying, "The king delivered us from the hand of our enemies; he is the one who rescued us from the hand of the Philistines. But now he has fled the country to escape from Absalom; and Absalom, whom we anointed to rule over us, has died in battle. So why do you say nothing about bringing the king back?" King David sent this message to Zadok and Abiathar, the priests: "Ask the elders of Judah, 'Why should you be the last to bring the king back to his palace, since what is being said throughout Israel has reached the king at his quarters? You are my relatives, my own flesh and blood. So why should you be the last to bring back the king?' And say to Amasa, 'Are you not my own flesh and blood? May God deal with me, be it ever so severely, if you are not the commander of my army for life in place of Joab.'" He won over the hearts of all the men of Judah as though they were one man. They sent word to the king, "Return, you and all your men." Then the king returned and went as far as the Jordan. Now the men of Judah had come to Gilgal to go out and meet the king and bring him across the Jordan Shimei son of Gera, the Benjamite from Bahurim, hurried down with the men of Judah to meet King David. With him were a thousand Benjamites, along with Ziba, the steward of Saul's household, and his fifteen sons and twenty servants.

They rushed to the Jordan, where the king was. They crossed at the ford to take the king's household over and to do whatever he wished When Shimei son of Gera crossed the Jordan, he fell prostrate before the king and said to him, "May my lord not hold me guilty. Do not remember how your servant did wrong on the day my lord the king left Jerusalem. May the king put it out of his mind. For I, your servant, know that I have sinned, but today I have come here as the first from the tribes of Joseph to come down and meet my lord the king." Then Abishai son of Zeruiah said, "Shouldn't Shimei be put to death for this? He cursed the LORD's anointed." David replied, "What does this have to do with you, you sons of Zeruiah? What right do you have to interfere? Should anyone be put to death in Israel today? Don't I know that today I am king over Israel?" So the king said to Shimei, "You shall not die." And the king promised him on oath Mephibosheth, Saul's grandson, also went down to meet the king. He had not taken care of his feet or trimmed his mustache or washed his clothes from the day the king left until the day he returned safely. When he came from Jerusalem to meet the king, the king asked him, "Why didn't you go with me, Mephibosheth?" He said, "My lord the king, since I your servant am lame, I said, 'I will have my donkey saddled and will ride on it, so I can go with the king.' But Ziba my servant betrayed me. And he has slandered your servant to my lord the king. My lord the king is like an angel of God; so do whatever you wish. All my grandfather's descendants deserved nothing but death from my lord the king, but you gave your servant a place among those who eat at your table. So what right do I have to make any more appeals to the king?" The king said to him, "Why say more? I order you and Ziba to divide the land." Mephibosheth said to the king, "Let him take everything, now that my lord the king has returned home safely." Barzillai the Gileadite also came down from Rogelim to cross the Jordan with the king and to send him on his way from there. Now Barzillai was very old, eighty years of age. He had provided for the king during his stay in Mahanaim, for he was a very wealthy man. The king said to Barzillai, "Cross over with me and stay with me in Jerusalem, and I will provide for you." But Barzillai answered the king, "How many more years will I live, that I should go up to Jerusalem with the king? I am now eighty years old. Can I tell the difference between what is enjoyable and what is not? Can your servant taste what he eats and drinks? Can I still hear the voices of male and female singers? Why should your servant be an added burden to my lord the king? Your servant will cross over the Jordan with the king for a short distance, but why should the king reward me in this way? Let your servant return, that I may die in my own town near the tomb of my father and mother. But here is your servant Kimham. Let him cross over with my lord the king. Do for him whatever you wish." The king said, "Kimham shall cross over with me, and I will do for him whatever you wish, and anything you desire from me I will do for you." So all the people crossed the Jordan, and then the king crossed over. The king kissed Barzillai and bid him farewell, and Barzillai returned to his home When the king crossed over to Gilgal, Kimham crossed with him. All the troops of Judah and half the troops of Israel had taken the king over. Soon all the men of Israel were coming to the king and saying to him, "Why did our brothers, the men of Judah, steal the king away and bring him and his household across the Jordan, together with all his men?" All the men of Judah answered the men of Israel, "We did this because the king is closely related to us. Why are you angry about it? Have we eaten any of the king's provisions? Have we taken anything for ourselves?" Then the men of Israel answered the men of Judah, "We have ten shares in the king; so we have a greater claim on David than you have. Why then do you treat us with contempt? Weren't we the first to speak of bringing back our king?" But the men of Judah pressed their claims even more forcefully than the men of Israel

Chapter 20

Now a troublemaker named Sheba son of Bikri, a Benjamite, happened to be there. He sounded the trumpet and shouted, "We have no share in David, no part in Jesse's son! Every man to his tent, Israel!" So all the men of Israel deserted David to follow Sheba son of Bikri. But the men of Judah stayed by their king all the way from the Jordan to Jerusalem When David returned to his palace in Jerusalem, he took the ten concubines he had left to take care of the palace and put them in a house under guard. He provided for them but had no sexual relations with them. They were kept in confinement till the day of their death, living as widows Then the king said to Amasa, "Summon the men of Judah to come to me within three days, and be here yourself." But when Amasa went to summon Judah, he took longer than the time the king had set for him. David said to Abishai, "Now Sheba son of Bikri will do us more harm than Absalom did. Take your master's men and pursue him, or he will find fortified cities and escape from us." So Joab's men and the Kerethites and Pelethites and all the mighty warriors went out under the command of Abishai. They marched out from Jerusalem to pursue Sheba son of Bikri While they were at the great rock in Gibeon, Amasa came to meet them. Joab was wearing his military tunic, and strapped over it at his waist was a belt with a dagger in its sheath. As he stepped forward, it dropped out of its sheath. Joab said to Amasa, "How are you, my brother?" Then Joab took Amasa by the beard with his right hand to kiss him. Amasa was not on his guard against the dagger in Joab's hand, and Joab plunged it into his belly, and his intestines spilled out on the ground. Without being stabbed again, Amasa died. Then Joab and his brother Abishai pursued Sheba son of Bikri One of Joab's men stood beside Amasa and said, "Whoever favors Joab, and whoever is for David, let him follow Joab!" Amasa lay wallowing in his blood in the middle of the road, and the man saw that all the troops came to a halt there. When he realized that everyone who came up to Amasa stopped, he dragged him from the road into a field and threw a garment over him. After Amasa had been removed from the road, everyone went on with Joab to pursue Sheba son of Bikri Sheba passed through all the tribes of Israel to Abel Beth Maakah and through the entire region of the Bikrites, who gathered together and followed him. All the troops with Joab came and besieged Sheba in Abel Beth Maakah. They built a siege ramp up to the city, and it stood against the outer fortifications. While they were battering the wall to bring it down, a wise woman called from the city, "Listen! Listen! Tell Joab to come here so I can speak to him." He went toward her, and she asked, "Are you Joab?" "I am," he answered She said, "Listen to what your servant has to say." "I'm listening," he said She continued, "Long ago they used to say, 'Get your answer at Abel,' and that settled it. We are the peaceful and faithful in Israel. You are trying to destroy a city that is a mother in Israel. Why do you want to swallow up the LORD's inheritance?" "Far be it from me!" Joab replied, "Far be it from me to swallow up or destroy! That is not the case. A man named Sheba son of Bikri from the hill country of Ephraim has lifted up his hand against the king, against David. Hand over this one man, and I'll withdraw from the city." The woman said to Joab, "His head will be thrown to you from the wall." Then the woman went to all the people with her wise advice, and they cut off the head of Sheba son of Bikri and threw it to Joab. So he sounded the trumpet, and his men dispersed from the city, each returning to his home. And Joab went back to the king in Jerusalem Joab was over Israel's entire army; Benaiah son of Jehoiada was over the Kerethites and Pelethites; Adoniram was in charge of forced labor; Jehoshaphat son of Ahilud was the recorder; Sheva was secretary; Zadok and Abiathar were priests; and Ira the Jairite was David's priest

Chapter 21

1 During David's reign, there was a famine for three consecutive years. David sought the counsel of the Lord, and the Lord responded, "It is because of Saul and his blood-stained house; he put the Gibeonites to death." 2 So the king summoned the Gibeonites and spoke to them. (The Gibeonites were not Israelites but a remnant of the Amorites. The Israelites had sworn to spare them, but Saul, in his zeal for Israel and Judah, had tried to annihilate them.) 3 David asked the Gibeonites, "What shall I do for you? How can I make amends so that you will bless the Lord's inheritance?" 4 The Gibeonites answered him, "We have no right to demand silver or gold from Saul or his family, nor do we have the right to put anyone in Israel to death." David asked, "What do you want me to do for you?" 5 They answered the king, "As for the man who destroyed us and plotted against us so that we have been decimated and have no place anywhere in Israel, 6 let seven of his male descendants be given to us to be killed and exposed before the Lord at Gibeah of Saul—the Lord's chosen one." So the king said, "I will give them to you." 7 The king spared Mephibosheth son of Jonathan, the son of Saul, because of the oath before the Lord between David and Jonathan son of Saul. 8 But the king took Armoni and Mephibosheth, the two sons of Aiah's daughter Rizpah, whom she had borne to Saul, together with the five sons of Saul's daughter Merab, whom she had borne to Adriel son of Barzillai the Meholathite. 9 He handed them over to the Gibeonites, who killed and exposed them on a hill before the Lord. All seven of them fell together; they were put to death during the first days of the harvest, just as the barley harvest was beginning 10 Rizpah daughter of Aiah took sackcloth and spread it out for herself on a rock. From the beginning of the harvest till the rain poured down from the heavens on the bodies, she did not let the birds of the air touch them by day or the wild animals by night. 11 When David was told what Aiah's daughter Rizpah, Saul's concubine, had done, 12 he went and took the bones of Saul and his son Jonathan from the citizens of Jabesh Gilead. (They had taken them secretly from the public square at Beth Shan, where the Philistines had hung them after they struck Saul down on Gilboa.) 13 David brought the bones of Saul and his son Jonathan from there, and the bones of those who had been killed and exposed were gathered up. 14 They buried the bones of Saul and his son Jonathan in the tomb of Saul's father Kish, at Zela in Benjamin, and did everything the king commanded. After that, God answered prayer in behalf of the land 15 Once again there was a battle between the Philistines and Israel. David went down with his men to fight against the Philistines, and he became exhausted. 16 And Ishbi-Benob, one of the descendants of Rapha, whose bronze spearhead weighed three hundred shekels and who was armed with a new sword, said he would kill David. 17 But Abishai son of Zeruiah came to David's rescue; he struck the Philistine down and killed him. Then David's men swore to him, saying, "Never again will you go out with us to battle,

so that the lamp of Israel will not be extinguished." 18 In the course of time, there was another battle with the Philistines, at Gob. At that time Sibbekai the Hushathite killed Saph, one of the descendants of Rapha. 19 In another battle with the Philistines at Gob, Elhanan son of Jair the Bethlehemite killed the brother of Goliath the Gittite, who had a spear with a shaft like a weaver's rod. 20 In still another battle, which took place at Gath, there was a huge man with six fingers on each hand and six toes on each foot—twenty-four in all. He also was descended from Rapha. 21 When he taunted Israel, Jonathan son of Shimea, David's brother, killed him. 22 These four were descendants of Rapha in Gath, and they fell at the hands of David and his men

Chapter 22

1 David sang to the Lord the words of this song when the Lord delivered him from the hand of all his enemies and from the hand of Saul. 2 He said: "The Lord is my rock, my fortress, and my deliverer; 3 my God is my rock, in whom I take refuge, my shield and the horn of my salvation. He is my stronghold, my refuge, and my savior—from violent men you save me. 4 I call to the Lord, who is worthy of praise, and I am saved from my enemies 5 "The waves of death swirled about me; the torrents of destruction overwhelmed me. 6 The cords of the grave coiled around me; the snares of death confronted me. 7 In my distress, I called to the Lord; I called out to my God. From his temple, he heard my voice; my cry came to his ears. 8 The earth trembled and quaked, the foundations of the heavens shook; they trembled because he was angry. 9 Smoke rose from his nostrils; consuming fire came from his mouth, burning coals blazed out of it. 10 He parted the heavens and came down; dark clouds were under his feet. 11 He mounted the cherubim and flew; he soared on the wings of the wind. 12 He made darkness his canopy around him—the dark rain clouds of the sky. 13 Out of the brightness of his presence, bolts of lightning blazed forth. 14 The Lord thundered from heaven; the voice of the Most High resounded. 15 He shot arrows and scattered the enemies, bolts of lightning and routed them. 16 The valleys of the sea were exposed, and the foundations of the earth laid bare at the rebuke of the Lord, at the blast of breath from his nostrils 17 "He reached down from on high and took hold of me; he drew me out of deep waters. 18 He rescued me from my powerful enemy, from my foes, who were too strong for me. 19 They confronted me in the day of my disaster, but the Lord was my support. 20 He brought me out into a spacious place; he rescued me because he delighted in me 21 "The Lord has dealt with me according to my righteousness; according to the cleanness of my hands, he has rewarded me. 22 For I have kept the ways of the Lord; I am not guilty of turning from my God. 23 All his laws are before me; I have not turned away from his decrees. 24 I have been blameless before him and have kept myself from sin. 25 The Lord has rewarded me according to my righteousness, according to my cleanness in his sight 26 "To the faithful, you show yourself faithful, to the blameless, you show yourself blameless, 27 to the pure, you show yourself pure, but to the devious, you show yourself shrewd. 28 You save the humble, but your eyes are on the haughty to bring them low. 29 You are my lamp, O Lord; the Lord turns my darkness into light. 30 With your help, I can advance against a troop; with my God, I can scale a wall 31 "As for God, his way is perfect; the word of the Lord is flawless. He is a shield for all who take refuge in him. 32 For who is God besides the Lord? And who is the Rock except our God? 33 It is God who arms me with strength and makes my way perfect. 34 He

makes my feet like the feet of a deer; he enables me to stand on the heights. 35 He trains my hands for battle; my arms can bend a bow of bronze. 36 You give me your shield of victory; you stoop down to make me great. 37 You broaden the path beneath me so that my ankles do not turn 38 "I pursued my enemies and crushed them; I did not turn back till they were destroyed. 39 I crushed them completely, and they could not rise; they fell beneath my feet. 40 You armed me with strength for battle; you made my adversaries bow at my feet. 41 You made my enemies turn their backs in flight, and I destroyed my foes. 42 They cried for help, but there was no one to save them—to the Lord, but he did not answer. 43 I beat them as fine as the dust of the earth; I pounded and trampled them like mud in the streets 44 "You have delivered me from the attacks of my people; you have preserved me as the head of nations. People I did not know are subject to me, 45 and foreigners come cringing to me; as soon as they hear me, they obey me. 46 They all lose heart; they come trembling from their strongholds 47 "The Lord lives! Praise be to my Rock! Exalted be God, the Rock, my Savior! 48 He is the God who avenges me, who puts the nations under me, 49 who sets me free from my enemies. You exalted me above my foes; from violent men, you rescued me. 50 Therefore, I will praise you, O Lord, among the nations; I will sing the praises of your name 51 "He gives his king great victories; he shows unfailing kindness to his anointed, to David and his descendants forever."

Chapter 23

1 These are the last words of David: "The oracle of David son of Jesse, the oracle of the man exalted by the Most High, the man anointed by the God of Jacob, Israel's singer of songs: 2 "The Spirit of the Lord spoke through me; his word was on my tongue. 3 The God of Israel spoke, the Rock of Israel said to me: 'When one rules over men in righteousness, when he rules in the fear of God, 4 he is like the light of morning at sunrise on a cloudless morning, like the brightness after rain that brings the grass from the earth.' 5 "Is not my house right with God? Has he not made with me an everlasting covenant, arranged and secured in every part? Will he not bring to fruition my salvation and grant me my every desire? 6 But evil men are all to be cast aside like thorns, which are not gathered with the hand. 7 Whoever touches thorns uses a tool of iron or the shaft of a spear; they are burned up where they lie." 8 These are the names of David's mighty men: Josheb-Basshebeth, a Tahkemonite, was chief of the Three; he raised his spear against eight hundred men, whom he killed in one encounter. 9 Next to him was Eleazar son of Dodai the Ahohite. As one of the three mighty men, he was with David when they taunted the Philistines gathered at Pas Dammim for battle. Then the men of Israel retreated, 10 but he stood his ground and struck down the Philistines till his hand grew tired and froze to the sword. The Lord brought about a great victory that day. The troops returned to Eleazar, but only to strip the dead 11 Next to him was Shammah son of Agee the Hararite. When the Philistines banded together at a place where there was a field full of lentils, Israel's troops fled from them. 12 But Shammah took his stand in the middle of the field. He defended it and struck the Philistines down, and the Lord brought about a great victory 13 During harvest time, three of the thirty chief men came down to David at the cave of Adullam, while a band of Philistines was encamped in the Valley of Rephaim. 14 At that time, David was in the stronghold, and the Philistine garrison was at Bethlehem. 15 David longed for water and said, "Oh, that someone would get me a drink of water from the

well near the gate of Bethlehem!" 16 So the three mighty men broke through the Philistine lines, drew water from the well near the gate of Bethlehem, and carried it back to David. But he refused to drink it; instead, he poured it out before the Lord. 17 "Far be it from me, O Lord, to do this!" he said. "Is it not the blood of men who went at the risk of their lives?" And David would not drink it Such were the exploits of the three mighty men. 18 Abishai the brother of Joab son of Zeruiah was chief of the Three. He raised his spear against three hundred men, whom he killed, and so he became as famous as the Three. 19 Was he not held in greater honor than the Three? He became their commander, even though he was not included among them 20 Benaiah son of Jehoiada was a valiant fighter from Kabzeel, who performed great exploits. He struck down two of Moab's best men. He also went down into a pit on a snowy day and killed a lion. 21 And he struck down a huge Egyptian. Although the Egyptian had a spear in his hand, Benaiah went against him with a club. He snatched the spear from the Egyptian's hand and killed him with his own spear. 22 Such were the exploits of Benaiah son of Jehoiada; he too was as famous as the three mighty men. 23 He was held in greater honor than any of the Thirty, but he was not included among the Three. And David put him in charge of his bodyguard 24 Among the Thirty were: Asahel the brother of Joab, Elhanan son of Dodo from Bethlehem, 25 Shammah the Harodite, Elika the Harodite, 26 Helez the Paltite, Ira son of Ikkesh from Tekoa, 27 Abiezer from Anathoth, Mebunnai the Hushathite, 28 Zalmon the Ahohite, Maharai the Netophathite, 29 Heled son of Baanah the Netophathite, Ithai son of Ribai from Gibeah in Benjamin, 30 Benaiah the Pirathonite, Hiddai from the ravines of Gaash, 31 Abi-Albon the Arbathite, Azmaveth the Barhumite, 32 Eliahba the Shaalbonite, the sons of Jashen, Jonathan 33 son of Shammah the Hararite, Ahiam son of Sharar the Hararite, 34 Eliphelet son of Ahasbai the Maacathite, Eliam son of Ahithophel the Gilonite, 35 Hezro the Carmelite, Paarai the Arbite, 36 Igal son of Nathan from Zobah, the son of Hagri, 37 Zelek the Ammonite, Naharai the Beerothite, the armor-bearer of Joab son of Zeruiah, 38 Ira the Ithrite, Gareb the Ithrite 39 and Uriah the Hittite. There were thirty-seven in all

Chapter 24

1 Again the anger of the Lord burned against Israel, and he incited David against them, saying, "Go and take a census of Israel and Judah." 2 So the king said to Joab and the army commanders with him, "Go throughout the tribes of Israel from Dan to Beersheba and enroll the fighting men so that I may know how many there are." 3 But Joab replied to the king, "May the Lord your God multiply the troops a hundred times over, and may the eyes of my lord the king see it. But why does my lord the king want to do such a thing?" 4 The king's word, however, overruled Joab and the army commanders; so they left the presence of the king to enroll the fighting men of Israel. 5 After crossing the Jordan, they camped near Aroer, south of the town in the gorge, and then went through Gad and on to Jazer. 6 They went to Gilead and the region of Tahtim Hodshi, and on to Dan Jaan and around toward Sidon. 7 Then they went toward the fortress of Tyre and all the towns of the Hivites and Canaanites. Finally, they went on to Beersheba in the Negev of Judah 8 After they had gone through the entire land, they came back to Jerusalem at the end of nine months and twenty days. 9 Joab reported the number of the fighting men to the king: in Israel, there were eight hundred thousand able-bodied men who could handle a sword, and in Judah five hundred thousand 10 David was conscience-stricken after he had counted the fighting men, and he said to the Lord, "I have sinned greatly in what I have done. Now, O Lord, I beg you, take away the guilt of your servant. I have done a very foolish thing." 11 Before David got up the next morning, the word of the Lord had come to Gad the prophet, David's seer: 12 "Go and tell David, 'This is what the Lord says: I am giving you three options. Choose one of them for me to carry out against you.'" 13 So Gad went to David and said to him, "Shall there come upon you three years of famine in your land? Or three months of fleeing from your enemies while they pursue you? Or three days of plague in your land? Now then, think it over and decide how I should answer the one who sent me." 14 David said to Gad, "I am in deep distress. Let us fall into the hands of the Lord, for his mercy is great; but do not let me fall into the hands of men." 15 So the Lord sent a plague on Israel from that morning until the end of the time designated, and seventy thousand of the people from Dan to Beersheba died. 16 When the angel stretched out his hand to destroy Jerusalem, the Lord was grieved because of the calamity and said to the angel who was afflicting the people, "Enough! Withdraw your hand." The angel of the Lord was then at the threshing floor of Araunah the Jebusite 17 When David saw the angel who was striking down the people, he said to the Lord, "I am the one who has sinned and done wrong. These are but sheep. What have they done? Let your hand fall upon me and my family." 18 On that day Gad went to David and said to him, "Go up and build an altar to the Lord on the threshing floor of Araunah the Jebusite." 19 So David went up, as the Lord had commanded through Gad. 20 When Araunah looked and saw the king and his men coming toward him, he went out and bowed down before the king with his face to the ground 21 Araunah said, "Why has my lord the king come to his servant?" "To buy your threshing floor," David answered, "so I can build an altar to the Lord, that the plague on the people may be stopped." 22 Araunah said to David, "Let my lord the king take whatever pleases him and offer it up. Here are oxen for the burnt offering, and here are threshing sledges and ox yokes for the wood. 23 O king, Araunah gives all this to the king." Araunah also said to him, "May the Lord your God accept you." 24 But the king replied to Araunah, "No, I insist on paying you for it. I will not sacrifice to the Lord my God burnt offerings that cost me nothing." So David bought the threshing floor and the oxen and paid fifty shekels of silver for them. 25 David built an altar to the Lord there and sacrificed burnt offerings and fellowship offerings. Then the Lord answered prayer in behalf of the land, and the plague on Israel was stopped

11. 1 Kings

Chapter 1

When King David was old and frail, they clothed him with garments, but he could not stay warm. Therefore, his servants said, "Let us find a young virgin for my lord the king to take care of him and keep him warm." They searched throughout Israel and found Abishag, a Shunammite, and brought her to the king. She was very beautiful, and she cared for the king, but he had no intimate relations with her Adonijah, the son of Haggith, exalted himself, declaring, "I will be king." He prepared chariots, horsemen, and fifty men to run before him. His father had never rebuked him, asking, "Why do you behave as you do?" Adonijah was very handsome and was born after Absalom. He conferred with Joab, son of Zeruiah, and with Abiathar the priest, who supported him. However, Zadok the priest, Benaiah son of Jehoiada, Nathan the prophet, Shimei, Rei, and

David's mighty men did not side with Adonijah Adonijah sacrificed sheep, oxen, and fattened cattle by the stone of Zoheleth, near En-rogel, and invited all his brothers, the king's sons, and all the men of Judah, but he did not invite Nathan the prophet, Benaiah, the mighty men, or his brother Solomon Nathan spoke to Bathsheba, Solomon's mother, saying, "Have you not heard that Adonijah, the son of Haggith, has become king, and our lord David does not know about it? Come, let me advise you on how to save your life and the life of your son Solomon. Go to King David and say, 'My lord, the king, did you not swear to your servant that Solomon your son shall reign after you and sit on your throne? Why then is Adonijah reigning?' While you are still talking to the king, I will come in and confirm your words." Bathsheba went to the king in his chamber. The king was very old, and Abishag the Shunammite was attending to him. Bathsheba bowed and did obeisance to the king. The king asked, "What do you wish?" She replied, "My lord, you swore by the Lord your God to your handmaid that Solomon your son shall reign after you and sit on your throne. But now Adonijah has become king, and you, my lord the king, do not know about it. He has sacrificed many oxen, fattened cattle, and sheep, and invited all the king's sons, Abiathar the priest, and Joab the commander of the army, but he has not invited Solomon your servant. My lord, the king, all Israel looks to you to tell them who shall sit on the throne of my lord the king after him. Otherwise, when my lord the king lies down with his ancestors, I and my son Solomon will be regarded as criminals." While she was still speaking with the king, Nathan the prophet arrived. They informed the king that Nathan the prophet was there. Nathan entered, prostrated himself before the king with his face to the ground, and said, "My lord, the king, have you declared that Adonijah shall reign after you and sit on your throne? Today he has gone down and sacrificed many oxen, fattened cattle, and sheep, and has invited all the king's sons, the commanders of the army, and Abiathar the priest. They are eating and drinking with him, saying, 'Long live King Adonijah!' But me, your servant, Zadok the priest, Benaiah son of Jehoiada, and your servant Solomon he did not invite. Has my lord the king done this without letting his servants know who should sit on the throne after him?" King David responded, "Call Bathsheba to me." She came into the king's presence and stood before him. The king swore, "As the Lord lives, who has redeemed my soul out of all distress, I swore to you by the Lord God of Israel, saying, 'Solomon your son shall reign after me, and he shall sit on my throne in my place,' and I will do so this day." Bathsheba bowed with her face to the ground and paid homage to the king, saying, "May my lord King David live forever." King David then said, "Call me Zadok the priest, Nathan the prophet, and Benaiah son of Jehoiada." They came before the king, and he said to them, "Take your lord's servants with you, have Solomon my son ride on my mule, and bring him down to Gihon. There, Zadok the priest and Nathan the prophet shall anoint him king over Israel. Blow the trumpet and proclaim, 'Long live King Solomon!' Then you shall come up after him, and he shall come and sit on my throne. He shall be king in my place, for I have appointed him to be ruler over Israel and Judah." Benaiah son of Jehoiada answered the king, "Amen! May the Lord, the God of my lord the king, say so. As the Lord has been with my lord the king, so may he be with Solomon and make his throne greater than the throne of my lord King David." So Zadok the priest, Nathan the prophet, Benaiah son of Jehoiada, the Cherethites, and the Pelethites went down and had Solomon ride on King David's mule and brought him to Gihon. Zadok the priest took a horn of oil from the tabernacle and anointed Solomon. They blew the trumpet, and all the people shouted, "Long live King Solomon!" All the people followed him, playing pipes and rejoicing greatly, so that the ground shook with the sound Adonijah and all his guests heard it as they finished feasting. When Joab heard the sound of the trumpet, he asked, "What is the meaning of this uproar in the city?" While he was still speaking, Jonathan son of Abiathar the priest arrived. Adonijah said, "Come in, for you are a worthy man and bring good news." Jonathan replied, "No, our lord King David has made Solomon king. The king has sent with him Zadok the priest, Nathan the prophet, Benaiah son of Jehoiada, the Cherethites, and the Pelethites, and they have made him ride on the king's mule. Zadok the priest and Nathan the prophet have anointed him king at Gihon, and they have gone up from there rejoicing, so the city is in an uproar. That is the noise you hear. Solomon sits on the royal throne. Moreover, the king's servants have come to congratulate our lord King David, saying, 'May God make Solomon's name more famous than yours, and his throne greater than yours!' And the king bowed himself on the bed. The king also said, 'Blessed be the Lord, the God of Israel, who has allowed my eyes to see one of my own sons sitting on my throne today.'" All of Adonijah's guests were terrified, and they rose and went their separate ways. Adonijah, in fear of Solomon, went and took hold of the horns of the altar. Solomon was told, "Adonijah fears King Solomon and has taken hold of the horns of the altar, saying, 'Let King Solomon swear to me today that he will not kill his servant with the sword.'" Solomon replied, "If he shows himself to be a worthy man, not a hair of his head shall fall to the ground, but if wickedness is found in him, he shall die." King Solomon sent for him, and they brought him down from the altar. Adonijah came and bowed down to King Solomon, who said, "Go to your home."

Chapter 2

As David's time to die approached, he charged his son Solomon, saying, "I am about to go the way of all the earth. Be strong, show yourself a man, and keep the charge of the Lord your God, walking in his ways and keeping his statutes, commandments, rules, and testimonies, as written in the Law of Moses, so that you may prosper in all that you do and wherever you turn. Then the Lord will establish his word that he spoke concerning me, saying, 'If your sons pay close attention to their way, to walk before me in faithfulness with all their heart and with all their soul, you shall not lack a man on the throne of Israel.' "Moreover, you know what Joab son of Zeruiah did to me, how he dealt with the two commanders of the armies of Israel, Abner son of Ner and Amasa son of Jether, whom he killed, avenging in time of peace for blood that had been shed in war, and putting the blood of war on the belt around his waist and on the sandals on his feet. Act therefore according to your wisdom, but do not let his gray head go down to Sheol in peace. But deal loyally with the sons of Barzillai the Gileadite, and let them be among those who eat at your table, for with such loyalty they met me when I fled from Absalom your brother. There is also with you Shimei son of Gera, the Benjaminite from Bahurim, who cursed me with a grievous curse on the day when I went to Mahanaim. But when he came down to meet me at the Jordan, I swore to him by the Lord, saying, 'I will not put you to death with the sword.' Now therefore, do not hold him guiltless, for you are a wise man. You will know what you ought to do to him, and you shall bring his gray head down with blood to Sheol." Then David slept with his fathers and was buried in the city of David. David had reigned over Israel for forty years; seven years he reigned in Hebron, and thirty-three years he reigned in Jerusalem. So Solomon sat on the throne of David his father, and his kingdom was firmly established Adonijah, son of Haggith, went to Bathsheba, Solomon's mother, and she asked, "Do you come peaceably?" He answered, "Peaceably." Then he said, "I have something to say to you." She said, "Speak." He said, "You know that the kingdom was mine, and that all Israel had their eyes on me to reign. However, the kingdom has turned about and has become my brother's, for it was his from the Lord. Now I have one request to make of you; do not refuse me." She said to him, "Speak." He said, "Please ask King Solomon—he will not refuse you—to give me Abishag the Shunammite as my wife." Bathsheba replied, "Very well, I will speak for you to the king." Bathsheba went to King Solomon to speak to him on behalf of Adonijah. The king rose to meet her, bowed down to her, and sat on his throne. He had a seat brought for the king's mother, and she sat at his right hand. She said, "I have one small request to make of you; do not refuse me." The king said to her, "Make your request, my mother, for I will not refuse you." She said, "Let Abishag the Shunammite be given to Adonijah your brother as his wife." King Solomon answered his mother, "Why do you ask Abishag the Shunammite for Adonijah? Ask for him the kingdom also, for he is my elder brother, and on his side are Abiathar the priest and Joab son of Zeruiah." Then King Solomon swore by the Lord, saying, "God do so to me and more also if this word does not cost Adonijah his life. Now therefore, as the Lord lives, who has established me and placed me on the throne of David my father, and who has made me a house as he promised, Adonijah shall be put to death this day." King Solomon sent Benaiah son of Jehoiada, and he struck him down, and he died The king said to Abiathar the priest, "Go to Anathoth, to your estate, for you deserve death. But I will not at this time put you to death, because you carried the ark of the Lord God before my father David and because you shared in all my father's affliction." So Solomon expelled Abiathar from being priest to the Lord, fulfilling the word of the Lord that he had spoken concerning the house of Eli in Shiloh When the news came to Joab (for Joab had supported Adonijah although he had not supported Absalom), Joab fled to the tent of the Lord and caught hold of the horns of the altar. King Solomon was told that Joab had fled to the tent of the Lord and was beside the altar. Solomon sent Benaiah son of Jehoiada, saying, "Go, strike him down." So Benaiah came to the tent of the Lord and said to him, "The king commands, 'Come out.'" But he said, "No, I will die here." Benaiah brought the king's message back, saying, "Thus said Joab, and thus he answered me." The king replied, "Do as he has said, strike him down and bury him, and thus take away from me and my father's house the guilt for the blood that Joab shed without cause. The Lord will bring back his bloody deeds on his own head because, without the knowledge of my father David, he attacked and killed with the sword two men more righteous and better than himself, Abner son of Ner, commander of the army of Israel, and Amasa son of Jether, commander of the army of Judah. So shall their blood come back on the head of Joab and on the head of his descendants forever. But for David and his descendants, and for his house and for his throne, there shall be peace from the Lord forevermore." Then Benaiah son of Jehoiada went up and struck Joab down and killed him, and he was buried at his own house in the wilderness. The king put Benaiah son of Jehoiada over the army in place of Joab, and the king put Zadok the priest in the place of Abiathar The king sent and summoned Shimei and said to him, "Build yourself a house in Jerusalem and dwell there, and do not go out from there to any place whatever. For on the day you go out and cross the Kidron Valley, know for certain that you shall die; your blood shall be on your own head." Shimei said to the king, "What you say is good; as my lord the king has said, so will your servant do." So Shimei lived in Jerusalem many days But after three years, two of Shimei's servants ran away to Achish son of Maacah, king of Gath. When it was told Shimei, "Behold, your servants are in Gath," Shimei arose and saddled a donkey and went to Gath to Achish to seek his servants. Shimei went and brought his servants from Gath. When Solomon was told that Shimei had gone from Jerusalem to Gath and returned, the king sent and summoned Shimei and said to him, "Did I not make you swear by the Lord and solemnly warn you, saying, 'Know for certain that on the day you go out and go to any place whatever, you shall die'? And you said to me, 'What you say is good; I will obey.' Why then have you not kept your oath to the Lord and the commandment with which I charged you?" The king also said to Shimei, "You know in your own heart all the harm that you did to David my father, so the Lord will bring back your harm on your own head. But King Solomon shall be blessed, and the throne of David shall be established before the Lord forever." Then the king commanded Benaiah son of Jehoiada, and he went out and struck him down, and he died. So the kingdom was established in the hand of Solomon

Chapter 3

Solomon made an alliance with Pharaoh king of Egypt by marrying Pharaoh's daughter. He brought her to the City of David until he had finished building his palace, the temple of the Lord, and the wall around Jerusalem. The people, however, were still sacrificing at the high places because a temple had not yet been built for the Name of the Lord Solomon showed his love for the Lord by walking according to the instructions given him by his father David, except that he offered sacrifices and burned incense on the high places. The king went to Gibeon to offer sacrifices, for that was the most important high place, and Solomon offered a thousand burnt offerings on that altar. At Gibeon, the Lord appeared to Solomon during the night in a dream, and God said, "Ask for whatever you want me to give you." Solomon answered, "You have shown great kindness to your servant, my father David, because he was faithful to you and righteous and upright in heart. You have continued this great kindness to him and have given him a son to sit on his throne this very day. Now, Lord my God, you have made your servant king in place of my father David. But I am only a little child and do not know how to carry out my duties. Your servant is here among the people you have chosen, a great people, too numerous to count or number. So give your servant a discerning heart to govern your people and to distinguish between right and wrong. For who is able to govern this great people of yours?" The Lord was pleased that Solomon had asked for this. So God said to him, "Since you have asked for this and not for long life or wealth for yourself, nor have asked for the death of your enemies but for discernment in administering justice, I will do what you have asked. I will give you a wise and discerning heart so that there will never have been anyone like you, nor will there ever be. Moreover, I will give you what you have not asked for—both wealth and honor—so that in your lifetime you will have no equal among kings. And if you walk in obedience to me and keep my decrees and commands as David your father did, I will give you a long life." Then Solomon awoke—and he realized it had been a dream. He returned to Jerusalem, stood before the ark of the Lord's covenant, and sacrificed burnt offerings and fellowship offerings. Then he gave a feast for all his court Now two prostitutes came to the king and stood before him. One of them said, "Pardon me, my lord. This woman and I live in the same house, and I had a baby while she was there with me. The third day after my child was born, this woman also had a baby. We were alone; there was no one in the house but the two of us "During the night this woman's son died because she lay on him. So she got up in the middle of the night and took my son from my side while I your servant was asleep. She put him by her breast and put her dead son by my breast. The next morning, I got up to nurse my son—and he was dead! But when I looked at him closely in the morning light, I saw that it wasn't the son I had borne." The other woman said, "No! The living one is my son; the dead one is yours." But the first one insisted, "No! The dead one is yours; the living one is mine." And so they argued before the king The king said, "This one says, 'My son is alive, and your son is dead,' while that one says, 'No! Your son is dead, and mine is alive.'" Then the king said, "Bring me a sword." So they brought a sword for the king. He then gave an order: "Cut the living child in two and give half to one and half to the other." The woman whose son was alive was deeply moved out of love for her son and said to the king, "Please, my lord, give her the living baby! Don't kill him!" But the other said, "Neither I nor you shall have him. Cut him in two!" Then the king gave his ruling: "Give the living baby to the first woman. Do not kill him; she is his mother." When all Israel heard the verdict the king had given, they held the king in awe because they saw that he had wisdom from God to administer justice

Chapter 4

King Solomon was king over all Israel. These were his chief officials: Azariah son of Zadok—the priest; Elihoreph and Ahijah, sons of Shisha—secretaries; Jehoshaphat son of Ahilud—recorder; Benaiah son of Jehoiada—commander in chief; Zadok and Abiathar—priests; Azariah son of Nathan—in charge of the district governors; Zabud son of Nathan—a priest and advisor to the king; Ahishar—palace administrator; Adoniram son of Abda—in charge of forced labor Solomon had twelve district governors over all Israel, who supplied provisions for the king and the royal household. Each one had to provide supplies for one month in the year. These are their names: Ben-Hur—in the hill country of Ephraim; Ben-Deker—in Makaz, Shaalbim, Beth Shemesh and Elon Bethhanan; Ben-Hesed—in Arubboth (Sokoh and all the land of Hepher were his); Ben-Abinadab—in Naphoth Dor (he was married to Taphath daughter of Solomon); Baana son of Ahilud—in Taanach and Megiddo, and in all of Beth Shan next to Zarethan below Jezreel, from Beth Shan to Abel Meholah across to Jokmeam; Ben-Geber—in Ramoth Gilead (the settlements of Jair son of Manasseh in Gilead were his, as well as the region of Argob in Bashan and its sixty large walled cities with bronze gate bars); Ahinadab son of Iddo—in Mahanaim; Ahimaaz—in Naphtali (he had married Basemath daughter of Solomon); Baana son of Hushai—in Asher and in Aloth; Jehoshaphat son of Paruah—in Issachar; Shimei son of Ela—in Benjamin; Geber son of Uri—in Gilead (the country of Sihon king of the Amorites and the country of Og king of Bashan). He was the only governor over the district The people of Judah and Israel were as numerous as the sand on the seashore; they ate, they drank and they were happy. And Solomon ruled over all the kingdoms from the Euphrates River to the land of the Philistines, as far as the border of Egypt. These countries brought tribute and were Solomon's subjects all his life Solomon's daily provisions were thirty cors of the finest flour and sixty cors of meal, ten head of stall-fed cattle, twenty of pasture-fed cattle and a hundred sheep and goats, as well as deer, gazelles, roebucks, and choice fowl. For he ruled over all the kingdoms west of the Euphrates River, from Tiphsah to Gaza, and had peace on all sides. During Solomon's lifetime, Judah and Israel, from Dan to Beersheba, lived in safety, everyone under their own vine and under their own fig tree Solomon had four thousand stalls for chariot horses, and twelve thousand horses. The district governors, each in his month, supplied provisions for King Solomon and all who came to the king's table. They saw to it that nothing was lacking. They also brought to the proper place their quotas of barley and straw for the chariot horses and the other horses God gave Solomon wisdom and very great insight, and a breadth of understanding as measureless as the sand on the seashore. Solomon's wisdom was greater than the wisdom of all the people of the East, and greater than all the wisdom of Egypt. He was wiser than anyone else, including Ethan the Ezrahite—wiser than Heman, Kalkol, and Darda, the sons of Mahol. And his fame spread to all the surrounding nations. He spoke three thousand proverbs and his songs numbered a thousand and five. He spoke about plant life, from the cedar of Lebanon to the hyssop that grows out of walls. He also spoke about animals and birds, reptiles and fish. From all nations, people came to listen to Solomon's wisdom, sent by all the kings of the world, who had heard of his wisdom

Chapter 5

When Hiram king of Tyre heard that Solomon had been anointed king to succeed his father David, he sent his envoys to Solomon because he had always been on friendly terms with David. Solomon sent back this message to Hiram: "You know that because of the wars waged against my father David from all sides, he could not build a temple for the Name of the Lord his God until the Lord put his enemies under his feet. But now the Lord my God has given me rest on every side, and there is no adversary or disaster. I intend, therefore, to build a temple for the Name of the Lord my God, as the Lord told my father David, when he said, 'Your son whom I will put on the throne in your place will build the temple for my Name.' "So give orders that cedars of Lebanon be cut for me. My men will work with yours, and I will pay you for your men whatever wages you set. You know that we have no one so skilled in felling timber as the Sidonians." When Hiram heard Solomon's message, he was greatly pleased and said, "Praise be to the Lord today, for he has given David a wise son to rule over this great nation." So Hiram sent word to Solomon: "I have received the message you sent me and will do all you want in providing the cedar and juniper logs. My men will haul them down from Lebanon to the Mediterranean Sea, and I will float them as rafts by sea to the place you specify. There I will separate them and you can take them away. And you are to grant my wish by providing food for my royal household." In this way, Hiram kept Solomon supplied with all the cedar and juniper logs he wanted, and Solomon gave Hiram twenty thousand cors of wheat as food for his household, in addition to twenty thousand baths of pressed olive oil. Solomon continued to do this for Hiram year after year. The Lord gave Solomon wisdom, just as he had promised him. There were peaceful relations between Hiram and Solomon, and the two of them made a treaty King Solomon conscripted laborers from all Israel—thirty thousand men. He sent them off to Lebanon in shifts of ten thousand a month, so that they spent one month in Lebanon and two months at home. Adoniram was in charge of the forced labor. Solomon had seventy thousand carriers and eighty thousand stonecutters in the hills, as well as thirty-three hundred foremen who supervised the project and directed the workers. At the king's command, they removed from the quarry large blocks of high-grade stone to provide a foundation of dressed stone for the temple. The craftsmen of Solomon and Hiram and workers from Byblos cut and prepared the timber and stone for the building of the temple

Chapter 6

In the four hundredth year after the children of Israel came out of the land of Egypt, and in the fourth year of Solomon's reign over Israel, in the month of Zif, which is the second month, he began to build the house of the Lord. The house that King Solomon built for the Lord was sixty cubits long, twenty cubits wide, and thirty cubits high. The porch in front of the temple of the house was twenty cubits long, according to the width of the house, and ten cubits wide in front of the house He made windows in the house, wide on the outside and narrow on the inside. Against the wall of the house, he built chambers all around, the lower chamber was five cubits wide, the middle six cubits, and the third seven cubits wide. He made these chambers to support the temple, so that nothing was fastened into the walls of the house The house was built of stone prepared at the quarry, so that no hammer, ax, or iron tool was heard in the house while it was being built. The door for the middle chamber was in the right side of the house, and they went up winding stairs into the middle chamber and from the middle into the third He built the house and finished it, and covered it with beams and boards of cedar. He built the chambers along the entire house, each five cubits high, and they were fastened to the house with beams of cedar The word of the Lord came to Solomon, saying, "Concerning this house which you are building, if you walk in my statutes, execute my judgments, keep all my commandments, and walk in them, then I will perform my word with you, which I spoke to David your father. I will dwell among the children of Israel and will not forsake my people Israel." So Solomon built the house and finished it. He built the walls of the house on the inside with boards of cedar, from the floor of the house to the ceiling; he covered the inside with wood and covered the floor of the house with boards of fir. He built twenty cubits on the sides of the house with cedar boards, from the floor to the ceiling, and he built it within for the oracle, the Most Holy Place. The temple before it was forty cubits long. The cedar inside the house was carved with gourds and open flowers. All was cedar; no stone was seen He prepared the oracle in the inner part of the house to set there the Ark of the Covenant of the Lord. The oracle in the forepart was twenty cubits in length, twenty cubits in width, and twenty cubits in height, and he overlaid it with pure gold. He also overlaid the altar with cedar. Solomon overlaid the house within with pure gold, and he made a partition by the chains of gold before the oracle; and he overlaid it with gold. He overlaid the whole house with gold, until he had finished all the house, and also the altar that belonged to the oracle he overlaid with gold Inside the oracle, he made two cherubim of olive wood, each ten cubits high. One wing of the cherub was five cubits, and the other wing was five cubits, making ten cubits from wingtip to wingtip. Both cherubim were the same size and shape; the height of one cherub was ten cubits, and so was the

other cherub. He set the cherubim within the inner house, and they stretched forth the wings of the cherubim, so that the wing of one touched one wall and the wing of the other cherub touched the other wall; their wings touched one another in the middle of the house. He overlaid the cherubim with gold He carved all the walls of the house round about with carved figures of cherubim, palm trees, and open flowers, inside and out. He overlaid the floor of the house with gold, inside and out. For the entrance to the oracle, he made doors of olive wood; the lintel and doorposts were one-fifth of the wall. The two doors were also of olive wood, and he carved upon them carvings of cherubim, palm trees, and open flowers, and overlaid them with gold, and spread gold upon the cherubim and upon the palm trees So also he made for the entrance of the temple doorposts of olive wood, out of a fourth part of the wall, and the two doors were of fir wood; the two sides of the one door were folding, and the two leaves of the other door were folding. He carved cherubim, palm trees, and open flowers upon them, and overlaid them with gold fitted upon the carved work. He built the inner court with three rows of hewed stone and a row of cedar beams. In the fourth year, the foundation of the house of the Lord was laid in the month of Zif. In the eleventh year, in the month of Bul, which is the eighth month, the house was finished in all its details and according to all its plans. So he was seven years in building it

Chapter 7

Solomon took thirteen years to complete the construction of his own house. He also built the House of the Forest of Lebanon, which was a hundred cubits long, fifty cubits wide, and thirty cubits high, built on four rows of cedar pillars, with cedar beams on the pillars. It was roofed with cedar above the beams, which were forty-five pillars, fifteen in each row There were three rows of window frames, facing each other in three tiers. All the doorways and window frames had square frames, and they were opposite each other in three tiers. He also made a colonnade fifty cubits long and thirty cubits wide. In front of it was a portico, and in front of that were pillars and an overhanging roof He made a throne hall, the Hall of Justice, where he was to judge, and it was paneled with cedar from floor to ceiling. And the house where he was to live, set farther back, was similar in design. Solomon also made a house like this hall for Pharaoh's daughter, whom he had married All these buildings were made with high-quality stones cut to size and trimmed with saws on their inner and outer faces. The foundations were also made of high-quality, large stones, some ten cubits and some eight cubits. Above were high-quality stones, cut to size, and cedar beams. The great courtyard had three courses of dressed stone and one course of trimmed cedar beams, just like the inner courtyard of the temple of the Lord with its portico King Solomon sent for Hiram from Tyre. He was the son of a widow from the tribe of Naphtali, and his father was a man of Tyre and a skilled craftsman in bronze. Hiram was filled with wisdom, understanding, and knowledge to do all kinds of bronze work. He came to King Solomon and did all his work He cast two bronze pillars, each eighteen cubits high and twelve cubits in circumference. He also made two capitals of cast bronze to set on the tops of the pillars; each capital was five cubits high. A network of interwoven chains adorned the capitals on top of the pillars, seven for each capital. He made pomegranates in two rows encircling each network to decorate the capitals on top of the pillars. He did the same for each capital. The capitals on top of the pillars in the portico were in the shape of lilies, four cubits high The capitals on the two pillars also had pomegranates, two hundred in rows encircling each capital. He set up the pillars at the portico of the temple. The pillar to the south he named Jakin and the one to the north Boaz. The capitals on top were in the shape of lilies. And so the work on the pillars was completed He made the Sea of cast metal, circular in shape, measuring ten cubits from rim to rim and five cubits high. It took a line of thirty cubits to measure around it. Below the rim, gourds encircled it, ten to a cubit. The gourds were cast in two rows in one piece with the Sea. The Sea stood on twelve bulls, three facing north, three facing west, three facing south, and three facing east. The Sea rested on top of them, and their hindquarters were toward the center. It was a handbreadth thick, and its rim was like the rim of a cup, like a lily blossom. It held two thousand baths He also made ten movable stands of bronze; each was four cubits long, four wide, and three high. This is how the stands were made: They had side panels attached to uprights. On the panels between the uprights were lions, bulls, and cherubim, and on the uprights as well. Above and below the lions and bulls were wreaths of hammered work. Each stand had four bronze wheels with bronze axles, and each had a basin resting on four supports, cast with wreaths on each side On the inside of the stand, there was an opening that had a circular frame one cubit deep. This opening was round, and with its basework it measured a cubit and a half. Around its opening there was engraving. The panels of the stands were square, not round. The four wheels were under the panels, and the axles of the wheels were attached to the stand. The diameter of each wheel was a cubit and a half. The wheels were made like chariot wheels; the axles, rims, spokes, and hubs were all of cast metal Each stand had four handles, one on each corner, projecting from the stand. At the top of the stand, there was a circular band half a cubit high. The supports and panels were attached to the top of the stand. He engraved cherubim, lions, and palm trees on the surfaces of the supports and on the panels, in every available space, with wreaths all around. This is the way he made the ten stands. They were all cast in the same molds and were identical in size and shape He then made ten bronze basins, each holding forty baths and measuring four cubits across, one basin to go on each of the ten stands. He placed five of the stands on the south side of the temple and five on the north. He placed the Sea on the south side, at the southeast corner of the temple He also made the pots, shovels, and sprinkling bowls. So Hiram finished all the work he had undertaken for King Solomon in the temple of the Lord: the two pillars; the two bowl-shaped capitals on top of the pillars; the two sets of network decorating the two bowl-shaped capitals on top of the pillars; the four hundred pomegranates for the two sets of network (two rows of pomegranates for each network, decorating the bowl-shaped capitals on top of the pillars); the ten stands with their ten basins; the Sea and the twelve bulls under it; the pots, shovels, and sprinkling bowls. All these objects that Hiram made for King Solomon for the temple of the Lord were of burnished bronze The king had them cast in clay molds in the plain of the Jordan between Sukkoth and Zarethan. Solomon left all these things unweighed because there were so many; the weight of the bronze was not determined. Solomon also made all the furnishings that were in the Lord's temple: the golden altar; the golden table on which was the bread of the Presence; the lampstands of pure gold (five on the right and five on the left, in front of the inner sanctuary); the gold floral work and lamps and tongs; the pure gold basins, wick trimmers, sprinkling bowls, dishes, and censers; and the gold sockets for the doors of the innermost room, the Most Holy Place, and also for the doors of the main hall of the temple When all the work King Solomon had done for the temple of the Lord was finished, he brought in the things his father David had dedicated—the silver and gold and the furnishings—and he placed them in the treasuries of the Lord's temple

Chapter 8

Then King Solomon summoned into his presence at Jerusalem the elders of Israel, all the heads of the tribes, and the chiefs of the Israelite families, to bring up the ark of the Lord's covenant from Zion, the City of David. All the Israelites came together to King Solomon at the time of the festival in the month of Ethanim, the seventh month. When all the elders of Israel had arrived, the priests took up the ark, and they brought up the ark of the Lord and the tent of meeting and all the sacred furnishings in it. The priests and Levites carried them up King Solomon and the entire assembly of Israel that had gathered about him were before the ark, sacrificing so many sheep and cattle that they could not be recorded or counted. The priests then brought the ark of the Lord's covenant to its place in the inner sanctuary of the temple, the Most Holy Place, and put it beneath the wings of the cherubim. The cherubim spread their wings over the place of the ark and overshadowed the ark and its carrying poles. These poles were so long that their ends could be seen from the Holy Place in front of the inner sanctuary, but not from outside the Holy Place; and they are still there today There was nothing in the ark except the two stone tablets that Moses had placed in it at Horeb, where the Lord made a covenant with the Israelites after they came out of Egypt. When the priests withdrew from the Holy Place, the cloud filled the temple of the Lord, and the priests could not perform their service because of the cloud, for the glory of the Lord filled his temple Then Solomon said, "The Lord has said that he would dwell in a dark cloud; I have indeed built a magnificent temple for you, a place for you to dwell forever." While the whole assembly of Israel was standing there, the king turned around and blessed them. Then he said: "Praise be to the Lord, the God of Israel, who with his own hand has fulfilled what he promised with his own mouth to my father David. For he said, 'Since the day I brought my people Israel out of Egypt, I have not chosen a city in any tribe of Israel to have a temple built so that my Name might be there, but I have chosen David to rule my people Israel.' "My father David had it in his heart to build a temple for the Name of the Lord, the God of Israel. But the Lord said to my father David, 'You did well to have it in your heart to build a temple for my Name. Nevertheless, you are not the one to build the temple, but your son, your own flesh and blood—he is the one who will build the temple for my Name.' "The Lord has kept the promise he made: I have succeeded David my father and now I sit on the throne of Israel, just as the Lord promised, and I have built the temple for the Name of the Lord, the God of Israel. I have provided a place there for the ark, in which is the covenant of the Lord that he made with our ancestors when he brought them out of Egypt." Then Solomon stood before the altar of the Lord in front of the whole assembly of Israel, spread out his hands toward heaven, and said: "Lord, the God of Israel, there is no God like you in heaven above or on earth below—you who keep your covenant of love with your servants who continue wholeheartedly in your way. You have kept your promise to your servant David my father; with your mouth, you have promised and with your hand, you have fulfilled it—as it is today "Now, Lord, the God of Israel, keep for your servant David my father the promises you made to him when you said, 'You shall never fail to have a successor to sit before me on the throne of Israel, if only your descendants are careful in all they do to walk before me faithfully as you have done.' And now, God of Israel, let your word that you promised your servant David my father come true "But will God really dwell on earth? The heavens, even the highest heaven, cannot contain you. How much less this temple I have built! Yet give attention to your servant's prayer and his plea for mercy, Lord my God. Hear the cry and the prayer that your servant is praying in your presence this day. May your eyes be open toward this temple night and day, this place of which you said, 'My Name shall be there,' so that you will hear the prayer your servant prays toward this place. Hear the supplication of your servant and of your people Israel when they pray toward this place. Hear from heaven, your dwelling place, and when you hear, forgive "When anyone wrongs their neighbor and is required to take an oath and they come and swear the oath before your altar in this temple, then hear from heaven and act. Judge between your servants, condemning the guilty by bringing down on their heads what they have done and vindicating the innocent by treating them in accordance with their innocence "When your people Israel have been defeated by an enemy because they have sinned against you, and when they turn back to you and give praise to your Name, praying and making supplication to you in this temple, then hear from heaven and forgive the sin of your people Israel and bring them back to the land you gave to their ancestors "When the heavens are shut up and there is no rain because your people have sinned against you, and when they pray toward this place and give praise to your Name and turn from their sin because you have afflicted them, then hear from heaven and forgive the sin of your servants, your people Israel. Teach them the right way to live, and send rain on the land you gave your people for an inheritance "When famine or plague comes to the land, or blight or mildew, locusts or grasshoppers, or when an enemy besieges them in any of their cities, whatever disaster or disease may come, and when a prayer or plea is made by anyone among your people Israel—being aware of the afflictions of their own hearts and spreading out their hands toward this temple—then hear from heaven, your dwelling place. Forgive and act; deal with everyone according to all they do, since you know their hearts (for you alone know every human heart), so that they will fear you all the time they live in the land you gave our ancestors "As for the foreigner who does not belong to your people Israel but has come from a distant land because of your Name—for they will hear of your great Name and your mighty hand and your outstretched arm—when they come and pray toward this temple, then hear from heaven, your dwelling place. Do whatever the foreigner asks of you so that all the peoples of the earth may know your Name and fear you, as do your own people Israel, and may know that this house I have built bears your Name "When your people go to war against their enemies, wherever you send them, and when they pray to the Lord toward the city you have chosen and the temple I have built for your Name, then hear from heaven their prayer and their plea and uphold their cause "When they sin against you—for there is no one who does not sin—and you become angry with them and give them over to their enemies, who take them captive to their own lands, far away or near; and if they have a change of heart in the land where they are held captive, and repent and plead with you in the land of their captors and say, 'We have sinned, we have done wrong, we have acted wickedly'; and if they turn back to you with all their heart and soul in the land of their enemies who took them captive, and pray to you toward the land you gave their ancestors, toward the city you have chosen and the temple I have built for your Name; then from heaven, your dwelling place, hear their prayer and their plea, and uphold their cause. And forgive your people, who have sinned against you; forgive all the offenses they have committed against you, and cause their captors to show them mercy; for they are your people and your inheritance, whom you brought out of Egypt, out of that iron-smelting furnace "May your eyes be open to your servant's plea and to the plea of your people Israel, and may you listen to them whenever they cry out to you. For you singled them out from all the nations of the world to be your own inheritance, just as you declared through your servant Moses when you, Sovereign Lord, brought our ancestors out of Egypt." When Solomon had finished all these prayers and supplications to the Lord, he rose from before the altar of the Lord, where he had been kneeling with his hands spread out toward heaven. He stood and blessed the whole assembly of Israel in a loud voice, saying: "Praise be to the Lord, who has given rest to his people Israel just as he promised. Not one word has failed of all the good promises he gave through his servant Moses. May the Lord our God be with us as he was with our ancestors; may he never leave us nor forsake us. May he turn our hearts to him, to walk in obedience to him and keep the commands, decrees, and laws he gave our ancestors. And may these words of mine, which I have prayed before the Lord, be near to the Lord our God day and night, that he may uphold the cause of his servant and the cause of his people Israel according to each day's need, so that all the peoples of the earth may know that the Lord is God and that there is no other. And may your hearts be fully committed to the Lord our God, to live by his decrees and obey his commands, as at this time." Then the king and all Israel with him offered sacrifices before the Lord. Solomon offered a sacrifice of fellowship offerings to the Lord: twenty-two thousand cattle and a hundred and twenty thousand sheep and goats. So the king and all the Israelites dedicated the temple of the Lord On that same day, the king consecrated the middle part of the courtyard in front of the temple of the Lord, and there he offered burnt offerings, grain offerings, and the fat of the fellowship offerings, because the bronze altar that stood before the Lord was too small to hold the burnt offerings, the grain offerings, and the fat of the fellowship offerings So Solomon observed the festival at that time, and all Israel with him—a vast assembly, people from Lebo Hamath to the Wadi of Egypt. They celebrated it before the Lord our God for seven days and seven days more, fourteen days in all. On the following day, he sent the people away. They blessed the king and then went home, joyful and glad in heart for all the good things the Lord had done for his servant David and his people Israel

Chapter 9

When Solomon had finished building the temple of the Lord and the royal palace and had achieved all he had desired to do, the Lord appeared to him a second time, as he had appeared to him at Gibeon. The Lord said to him: "I have heard the prayer and plea you have made before me; I have consecrated this temple, which you have built, by putting my Name there forever. My eyes and my heart will always be there "As for you, if you walk before me faithfully with integrity of heart and uprightness, as David your father did, and do all I command and observe my decrees and laws, I will establish your royal throne over Israel forever, as I promised David your father when I said, 'You shall never fail to have a successor on the throne of Israel.' "But if you or your descendants turn away from me and do not observe the commands and decrees I have given you and go off to serve other gods and worship them, then I will cut off Israel from the land I have given them and will reject this temple I have consecrated for my Name. Israel will then become a byword and an object of ridicule among all peoples. This temple will become a heap of rubble. All who pass by will be appalled and will scoff and say, 'Why has the Lord done such a thing to this land and to this temple?' People will answer, 'Because they have forsaken the Lord their God, who brought their ancestors out of Egypt, and have embraced other gods, worshiping and serving them—that is why the Lord brought all this disaster on them.'" At the end of twenty years, during which Solomon built these two buildings—the temple of the Lord and the royal palace—King Solomon gave twenty towns in Galilee to Hiram king of Tyre, because Hiram had supplied him with all the cedar and juniper and gold he wanted. But when Hiram went from Tyre to see the towns that Solomon had given him, he was not pleased with them. "What kind of towns are these you have given me, my brother?" he asked. And he called them the Land of Kabul, a name they have to this day Now Hiram had sent to the king 120 talents of gold Here is the account of the forced labor King Solomon conscripted to build the Lord's temple, his own palace, the terraces, the wall of Jerusalem, and Hazor, Megiddo, and Gezer. Pharaoh king of Egypt had attacked and captured Gezer. He had set it on fire. He killed its Canaanite inhabitants and then gave it as a wedding gift to his daughter, Solomon's wife. And Solomon rebuilt Gezer. He built up Lower Beth Horon, Baalath, and Tadmor in the desert, within his land, as well as all his store cities and the towns for his chariots and for his horses—whatever he desired to build in Jerusalem, in Lebanon, and throughout all the territory he ruled There were still people left from the Amorites, Hittites, Perizzites, Hivites, and Jebusites (these peoples were not Israelites). Solomon conscripted the descendants of all these peoples remaining in the land—whom the Israelites could not exterminate—to serve as slave labor, as it is to this day. But Solomon did not make slaves of any of the Israelites; they were his fighting men, his government officials, his officers, his captains, and the commanders of his chariots and charioteers They were also the chief officials in charge of Solomon's projects—550 officials supervising those who did the work After Pharaoh's daughter had come up from the City of David to the palace Solomon had built for her, he constructed the terraces Three times a year Solomon sacrificed burnt offerings and fellowship offerings on the altar he had built for the Lord, burning incense before the Lord along with them, and so fulfilled the temple obligations King Solomon also built ships at Ezion Geber, which is near Elath in Edom, on the shore of the Red Sea. And Hiram sent his men—sailors who knew the sea—to serve in the fleet with Solomon's men. They sailed to Ophir and brought back 420 talents of gold, which they delivered to King Solomon

Chapter 10

When the queen of Sheba heard about the fame of Solomon and his relationship to the Lord, she came to test Solomon with hard questions. Arriving at Jerusalem with a very great caravan—with camels carrying spices, large quantities of gold, and precious stones—she came to Solomon and talked with him about all that she had on her mind. Solomon answered all her questions; nothing was too hard for the king to explain to her When the queen of Sheba saw all the wisdom of Solomon and the palace he had built, the food on his table, the seating of his officials, the attending servants in their robes, his cupbearers, and the burnt offerings he made at the temple of the Lord, she was overwhelmed. She said to the king, "The report I heard in my own country about your achievements and your wisdom is true. But I did not believe these things until I came and saw with my own eyes. Indeed, not even half was told me; in wisdom and wealth you have far exceeded the report I heard. How happy your people must be! How happy your officials, who continually stand before you and hear your wisdom! Praise be to the Lord your God, who has delighted in you and placed you on the throne of Israel. Because of the Lord's eternal love for Israel, he has made you king to maintain justice and righteousness." And she gave the king 120 talents of gold, large quantities of spices, and precious stones. Never again were so many spices brought in as those the queen of Sheba gave to King Solomon Hiram's ships brought gold from Ophir; and from there they brought great cargoes of almugwood and precious stones. The king used the almugwood to make supports for the temple of the Lord and for the royal palace, and to make harps and lyres for the musicians. So much almugwood has never been imported or seen since that day King Solomon gave the queen of Sheba all she desired and asked for, besides what he had given her out of his royal bounty. Then she left and returned with her retinue to her own country The weight of the gold that Solomon received yearly was 666 talents, not including the revenues from merchants and traders and from all the Arabian kings and the governors of the territories. King Solomon made two hundred large shields of hammered gold; six hundred shekels of gold went into each shield. He also made three hundred small shields of hammered gold, with three minas of gold in each shield. The king put them in the Palace of the Forest of Lebanon Then the king made a great throne covered with ivory and overlaid with fine gold. The throne had six steps, and its back had a rounded top. On both sides of the seat were armrests, with a lion standing beside each of them. Twelve lions stood on the six steps, one at either end of each step. Nothing like it had ever been made for any other kingdom. All King Solomon's goblets were gold, and all the household articles in the Palace of the Forest of Lebanon were pure gold. Nothing was made of silver, because silver was considered of little value in Solomon's days. The king had a fleet of trading ships at sea along with the ships of Hiram. Once every three years it returned, bringing gold, silver, and ivory, and apes and baboons King Solomon was greater in riches and wisdom than all the other kings of the earth. The whole world sought audience with Solomon to hear the wisdom God had put in his heart. Year after year, everyone who came brought a gift—articles of silver and gold, robes, weapons and spices, and horses and mules Solomon accumulated chariots and horses; he had fourteen hundred chariots and twelve thousand horses, which he kept in the chariot cities and also with him in Jerusalem. The king made silver as common in Jerusalem as stones, and cedar as plentiful as sycamore-fig trees in the foothills. Solomon's horses were imported from Egypt and from Kue—the royal merchants purchased them from Kue at the current price. They imported a chariot from Egypt for six hundred shekels of silver, and a horse for a hundred and fifty. They also exported them to all the kings of the Hittites and of the Arameans

Chapter 11

King Solomon had many extravagant women, including the daughter of Pharaoh and women from Moab, Ammon, Edom, Sidon, and the Hittites. These were from nations about which the Lord had told the Israelites, "You must not intermarry with them, because they will surely turn your hearts after their gods." Nevertheless, Solomon held fast to them in love. He had seven hundred wives of royal birth and three hundred concubines, and his wives led him astray As Solomon grew old, his wives turned his heart after other gods, and his heart was not fully devoted to the Lord his God, as the heart of David his father had been. He followed Ashtoreth, the goddess of the Sidonians, and Molek, the detestable god of the Ammonites. So Solomon did evil in the eyes of the Lord; he did not follow the Lord completely, as David his father had done. On a hill east of Jerusalem, Solomon built a high place for Chemosh, the detestable god of Moab, and for Molek, the detestable god of the Ammonites. He did the same for all his foreign wives, who burned incense and offered sacrifices to their gods The Lord became angry with Solomon because his heart had turned away from the Lord, the God of Israel, who had appeared to him twice. Although he had forbidden Solomon to follow other gods, Solomon did not keep the Lord's command. So the Lord said to Solomon, "Since this is your attitude and you have not kept my covenant and my decrees, which I commanded you, I will most certainly tear the kingdom away from you and give it to one of your subordinates. Nevertheless, for the sake of David your father, I will not do it during your lifetime. I will tear it out of the hand of your son. Yet I will not tear the whole kingdom from him, but will give him one tribe for the sake of David my servant and for the sake of Jerusalem, which I have chosen." Then the Lord raised up against Solomon an adversary, Hadad the Edomite, from the royal line of Edom. Earlier, when David had fought against Edom, Joab, the commander of the army, had gone up to bury the dead, and had struck down all the men in Edom. Joab and all the Israelites stayed there for six months, until they had destroyed all the men in Edom. But Hadad, still only a boy, fled to Egypt with some Edomite officials who had served his father. They set out from Midian and went to Paran. Then taking men from Paran with them, they went to Egypt, to Pharaoh king of Egypt, who gave Hadad a house and land and provided him with food Pharaoh was so pleased with Hadad that he gave him a sister of his own wife, Queen Tahpenes, in marriage. The sister of Tahpenes bore him a son named Genubath, whom Tahpenes brought up in the royal palace. There Genubath lived with Pharaoh's own children. While he was in Egypt, Hadad heard that David rested with his ancestors and that Joab, the commander of the army, was also dead. Then Hadad said to Pharaoh, "Let me go, that I may return to my own country." "What have you lacked here that you want to go back to your own country?" Pharaoh asked. "Nothing," Hadad replied, "but do let me go!" And God raised up against Solomon another adversary, Rezon son of Eliada, who had fled from his master, Hadadezer king of Zobah. When David destroyed Zobah's army, Rezon gathered a band of men around him and became their leader. They went to Damascus, where they settled and took control. Rezon was Israel's adversary as long as Solomon lived, adding to the trouble caused by Hadad. So Rezon ruled in Aram and was hostile toward Israel Also, Jeroboam son of Nebat rebelled against the king. He was one of Solomon's officials, an Ephraimite from Zeredah, and his mother was a widow named Zeruah. Here is the account of how he rebelled against the king: Solomon had built the terraces and had filled in the gap in the wall of the city of David his father. Now Jeroboam was a man of standing, and when Solomon saw how well the young man did his work, he put him in charge of the whole labor force of the tribes of Joseph About that time Jeroboam was going out of Jerusalem, and Ahijah the prophet of Shiloh met him on the way, wearing a new cloak. The two of them were alone out in the country, and Ahijah took hold of the new cloak he was wearing and tore it into twelve pieces. Then he said to Jeroboam, "Take ten pieces for yourself, for this is what the Lord, the God of Israel, says: 'See, I am going to tear the kingdom out of Solomon's hand and give you ten tribes. But for the sake of my servant David and the city of Jerusalem, which I have chosen out of all the tribes of Israel, he will have one tribe. I will do this because they have forsaken me and worshipped Ashtoreth the goddess of the Sidonians, Chemosh the god of the Moabites, and Molek the god of the Ammonites, and have not walked in obedience to me, nor done what is right in my eyes, nor kept my decrees and laws as David, Solomon's father, did "'But I will not take the whole kingdom out of Solomon's hand. I have made him ruler all the days of his life for the sake of David my servant, whom I chose and who obeyed my commands and decrees. I will take the kingdom from his son's hands and give you ten tribes. I will give one tribe to his son so that David my servant may always have a lamp before me in Jerusalem, the city where I chose to put my Name. However, as for you, I will take you, and you will rule over all that your heart desires; you will be king over Israel. If you do whatever I command you and walk in obedience to me and do what is right in my eyes by obeying my decrees and commands, as David my servant did, I will be with you. I will build you a dynasty as enduring as the one I built for David and will give Israel to you. I will humble David's descendants because of this, but not forever.'" Solomon tried to kill Jeroboam, but Jeroboam fled to Egypt, to Shishak the king, and stayed there until Solomon's death As for the other events of Solomon's reign—all he did and the wisdom he displayed—are they not written in the book of the annals of Solomon? Solomon reigned in Jerusalem over all Israel for forty years. Then he rested with his ancestors and was buried in the city of David his father. And Rehoboam his son succeeded him as king

Chapter 12

Rehoboam went to Shechem, for all Israel had gone there to make him king. When Jeroboam son of Nebat heard this (he was still in Egypt, where he had fled from King Solomon), he returned from Egypt. So they sent for Jeroboam, and he and the whole assembly of Israel went to Rehoboam and said to him, "Your father put a heavy yoke on us, but now lighten the harsh labor and the heavy yoke he put on us, and we will serve you." Rehoboam answered, "Go away for three days and then come back to me." So the people went away. Then King Rehoboam consulted the elders who had served his father Solomon during his lifetime. "How would you advise me to answer these people?" he asked They replied, "If today you will be a servant to these people and serve them and give them a favorable answer, they will always be your servants." But Rehoboam rejected the advice the elders gave him and consulted the young men who had grown up with him and were serving him. He asked them, "What is your advice? How should we answer these people who say to me, 'Lighten the yoke your father put on us'?" The young men who had grown up with him replied, "These people have said to you, 'Your father put a heavy yoke on us, but make our yoke lighter.' Now tell them, 'My little finger is thicker than my father's waist. My father laid on you a heavy yoke; I will make it even heavier. My father scourged you with whips; I will scourge you with scorpions.'" Three days later Jeroboam and all the people returned to Rehoboam, as the king had said, "Come back to me in three days." The king answered the people harshly. Rejecting the advice given him by the elders, he followed the advice of the young men and said, "My father made your yoke heavy; I will make it even heavier. My father scourged you with whips; I will scourge you with scorpions." So the king did not listen to the people, for this turn of events was from the Lord, to fulfill the word the Lord had spoken to Jeroboam son of Nebat through Ahijah the Shilonite. When all Israel saw that the king refused to listen to them, they answered the king: "What share do we have in David, what part in Jesse's son? To your tents, Israel! Look after your own house, David!" So the Israelites went home. But as for the Israelites who were living in the towns of Judah, Rehoboam still ruled over them. King Rehoboam sent out Adoniram, who was in charge of forced labor, but all Israel stoned him to death. King Rehoboam, however, managed to get into his chariot and escape to Jerusalem. So Israel has been in rebellion against the house of David to this day When all the Israelites heard that Jeroboam had returned, they sent and called him to the assembly and made him king over all Israel. Only the tribe of Judah remained loyal to the house of David. When Rehoboam arrived in Jerusalem, he mustered all Judah and the tribe of Benjamin—a hundred and eighty thousand able young men—to go to war against Israel and to regain the kingdom for Rehoboam son of Solomon But this word of God came to Shemaiah the man of God: "Say to Rehoboam son of Solomon king of Judah, to all Judah and Benjamin, and to the rest of the people, 'This is what the Lord says: Do not go up to fight against your brothers, the Israelites. Go home, every one of you, for this is my doing.'" So they obeyed the word of the Lord and went home again, as the Lord had ordered Then Jeroboam fortified Shechem in the hill country of Ephraim and lived there. From there he went out and built up Peniel. Jeroboam thought to himself, "The kingdom will now likely revert to the house of David. If these people go up to offer sacrifices at the temple of the Lord in Jerusalem, they will again give their allegiance to their lord, Rehoboam king of Judah. They will kill me and return to King Rehoboam." After seeking advice, the king made two golden calves. He said to the people, "It is too much for you to go up to Jerusalem. Here are your gods, Israel, who brought you up out of Egypt." One he set up in Bethel, and the other in Dan. And this thing became a sin; the people came to worship the one at Bethel and went as far as Dan to worship the other Jeroboam built shrines on high places and appointed priests from all sorts of people, even though they were not Levites. He instituted a festival on the fifteenth day of the eighth month, like the festival held in Judah, and offered sacrifices on the altar. This he did in Bethel, sacrificing to the calves he had made. And at Bethel, he also installed priests at the high places he had made. On the fifteenth day of the eighth month, a month of his own choosing, he offered sacrifices on the altar he had built at Bethel. So he instituted the festival for the Israelites and went up to the altar to make offerings

Chapter 13

By the word of the Lord, a man of God came from Judah to Bethel as Jeroboam was standing by the altar to make an offering. By the word of the Lord, he cried out against the altar: "Altar, altar! This is what the Lord says: 'A son named Josiah will be born to the house of David. On you, he will sacrifice the priests of the high places who make offerings here, and human bones will be burned on you.'" That same day the man of God gave a sign: "This is the sign the Lord has declared: The altar will be split apart, and the ashes on it will be poured out." When King Jeroboam heard what the man of God cried out against the altar at Bethel, he stretched out his hand from the altar and said, "Seize him!" But the hand he stretched out toward the man shriveled up so that he could not pull it back. Also, the altar was split apart, and its ashes poured out according to the sign given by the man of God by the word of the Lord Then the king said to the man of God, "Intercede with the Lord your God and pray for me that my hand may be restored." So the man of God interceded with the Lord, and the king's hand was restored and became as it was before The king said to the man of God, "Come home with me for a meal, and I will give you a gift." But the man of God answered the king, "Even if you were to give me half your possessions, I would not go with you, nor would I eat bread or drink water here. For I was commanded by the word of the Lord: 'You must not eat bread or drink water or return by the way you came.'" So he took another road and did not return by the way he had come to Bethel Now there was a certain old prophet living in Bethel, whose sons came and told him all that the man of God had done there that day. They also told their father what he had said to the king. Their father asked them, "Which way did he go?" And his sons showed him which road the man of God from Judah had taken. So he said to his sons, "Saddle the donkey for me." And when they had saddled the donkey for him, he mounted it and rode after the man of God. He found him sitting under an oak tree and asked, "Are you the man of God who came from Judah?" "I am," he replied So the prophet said to him, "Come home with me and eat." The man of God said, "I cannot turn back and go with you, nor can I eat bread or drink water with you in this place. I have been told by the word of the Lord: 'You must not eat bread or drink water there or return by the way you came.'" The old prophet answered, "I too am a prophet, as you are. And an angel said to me by the word of the Lord: 'Bring him back with you to your house so that he may eat bread and drink water.'" (But he was lying to him.) So the man of God returned with him and ate and drank in his house. While they were sitting at the table, the word of the Lord came to the old prophet who had brought him back. He cried out to the man of God who had come from Judah, "This is what the Lord says: 'You have defied the word of the Lord and have not kept the command the Lord your God gave you. You came back and ate bread and drank water in the place where he told you not to eat or drink. Therefore, your body will not be buried in the tomb of your ancestors.'" When the man of God had finished eating and drinking, the prophet who had brought him back saddled his donkey for him. As he went on his way, a lion met him on the road and killed him, and his body was left lying on the road, with both the donkey and the lion standing beside it. Some people who passed by saw the body lying there, with the lion standing beside the body, and they went and reported it in the city where the old prophet lived When the prophet who had brought him back from his journey heard of it, he said, "It is the man of God who defied the word of the Lord. The Lord has given him over to the lion, which has mauled him and killed him, as the word of the Lord had warned him." The prophet said to his sons, "Saddle the donkey for me," and they did so. Then he went out and found the body lying on the road, with the donkey and the lion standing beside it. The lion had neither eaten the body nor mauled the donkey. So the prophet picked up the body of the man of God, laid it on the donkey, and brought it back to his own city to mourn for him and bury him. Then he laid the body in his own tomb, and they mourned over him and said, "Alas, my brother!" After burying him, he said to his sons, "When I die, bury me in the grave where the man of God is buried; lay my bones beside his bones. For the message he declared by the word of the Lord against the altar in Bethel and against all the shrines on the high places in the towns of Samaria will certainly come true." Even after this, Jeroboam did not change his evil ways but once more appointed priests for the high places from all sorts of people. Anyone who wanted to become a priest, he consecrated for the high places. This was the sin of the house of Jeroboam that led to its downfall and its destruction from the face of the earth

Chapter 14

At that time Abijah son of Jeroboam became ill, and Jeroboam said to his wife, "Go, disguise yourself, so you won't be recognized as the wife of Jeroboam. Then go to Shiloh. Ahijah the prophet is there—the one who told me I would be king over this people. Take ten loaves of bread with you, some cakes, and a jar of honey, and go to him. He will tell you what will happen to the boy." So Jeroboam's wife did what he said and went to Ahijah's house in Shiloh Now Ahijah could not see; his sight was gone because of his age. But the Lord had told Ahijah, "Jeroboam's wife is coming to ask you about her son, for he is ill, and you are to give her such and such an answer. When she arrives, she will pretend to be someone else." So when Ahijah heard the sound of her footsteps at the door, he said, "Come in, wife of Jeroboam. Why this pretense? I have been sent to you with bad news. Go, tell Jeroboam that this is what the Lord, the God of Israel, says: 'I raised you up from among the people and appointed you ruler over my people Israel. I tore the kingdom away from the house of David and gave it to you, but you have not been like my servant David, who kept my commands and followed me with all his heart, doing only what was right in my eyes. You have done more evil than all who lived before you. You have made for yourself other gods, idols made of metal; you have aroused my anger and turned your back on me. Because of this, I am going to bring disaster on the house of Jeroboam. I will cut off from Jeroboam every last male in Israel—slave or free. I will burn up the house of Jeroboam as one burns dung until it is all gone. Dogs will eat those belonging to Jeroboam who die in the city, and the birds will feed on those who die in the country. The Lord has spoken!' "As for you, go back home. When you set foot in your city, the boy will die. All Israel will mourn for him and bury him. He is the only one belonging to Jeroboam who will be buried, because he is the only one in the house of Jeroboam in whom the Lord, the God of Israel, has found anything good. The Lord will raise up for himself a king over Israel who will cut off the family of Jeroboam. This is the day! What? Yes, even now. And the Lord will strike Israel, so that it will be like a reed swaying in the water. He will uproot Israel from this good land that he gave to their ancestors and scatter them beyond the Euphrates River, because they aroused the Lord's anger by making Asherah poles. And he will give Israel up because of the sins Jeroboam has committed and has caused Israel to commit." Then Jeroboam's wife got up and left and went to Tirzah. As soon as she stepped over the threshold of the house, the boy died. They buried him, and all Israel mourned for him, as the Lord had said through his servant the prophet Ahijah The other events of Jeroboam's reign, his wars and how he ruled, are written in the book of the annals of the kings of Israel. He reigned for twenty-two years and then rested with his ancestors. And Nadab his son succeeded him as king Rehoboam son of Solomon was king in Judah. He was forty-one years old when he became king, and he reigned seventeen years in Jerusalem, the city the Lord had chosen out of all the tribes of Israel in which to put his Name. His mother's name was Naamah; she was an Ammonite. Judah did evil in the eyes of the Lord. By the sins they committed, they stirred up his jealous anger more than those who were before them had done. They also set up for themselves high places, sacred stones, and Asherah poles on every high hill and under every spreading tree. There were even male shrine prostitutes in the land; the people engaged in all the detestable practices of the nations the Lord had driven out before the Israelites In the fifth year of King Rehoboam, Shishak king of Egypt attacked Jerusalem. He carried off the treasures of the temple of the Lord and the treasures of the royal palace. He took everything, including all the gold shields Solomon had made. So King Rehoboam made bronze shields to replace them and assigned these to the commanders of the guard on duty at the entrance to the royal palace. Whenever the king went to the Lord's temple, the guards bore the shields, and afterward, they returned them to the guardroom As for the other events of Rehoboam's reign and all he did, are they not written in the book of the annals of the kings of Judah? There was continual warfare between Rehoboam and Jeroboam. And Rehoboam rested with his ancestors and was buried with them in the City of David. His mother's name was Naamah; she was an Ammonite. And Abijah his son succeeded him as king

Chapter 15

In the eighteenth year of the reign of Jeroboam son of Nebat, Abijah became king of Judah, and he reigned in Jerusalem three years. His mother's name was Maakah daughter of Abishalom. He committed all the sins his father had done before him; his heart was not fully devoted to the Lord his God, as the heart of David his forefather had been. Nevertheless, for David's sake, the Lord his God gave him a lamp in Jerusalem by raising up a son to succeed him and by making Jerusalem strong. For David had done what was right in the eyes of the Lord and had not failed to keep any of the Lord's commands all the days of his life—except in the case of Uriah the Hittite There was war between Abijah and Jeroboam throughout Abijah's lifetime. As for the other events of Abijah's reign and all he did, are they not written in the book of the annals of the kings of Judah? There was war between Abijah and Jeroboam. And Abijah rested with his ancestors and was buried in the City of David. And Asa his son succeeded him as king In the twentieth year of Jeroboam king of Israel, Asa became king of Judah, and he reigned in Jerusalem forty-one years. His grandmother's name was Maakah daughter of Abishalom. Asa did what was right in the eyes of the Lord, as his father David had done. He expelled the male shrine prostitutes from the land and got rid of all the idols his ancestors had made. He even deposed his grandmother Maakah from her position as queen mother because she had made a repulsive image for the worship of Asherah. Asa cut it down and burned it in the Kidron Valley. Although he did not remove the high places, Asa's heart was fully committed to the Lord all his life. He brought into the temple of the Lord the silver and gold and the articles that he and his father had dedicated There was war between Asa and Baasha king of Israel throughout their reigns. Baasha king of Israel went up against Judah and fortified Ramah to prevent anyone from leaving or entering the territory of Asa king of

Judah. Asa then took all the silver and gold that was left in the treasuries of the Lord's temple and of his own palace. He entrusted it to his officials and sent them to Ben-Hadad son of Tabrimmon, the son of Hezion, the king of Aram, who was ruling in Damascus. "Let there be a treaty between me and you," he said, "as there was between my father and your father. See, I am sending you a gift of silver and gold. Now break your treaty with Baasha king of Israel so that he will withdraw from me." Ben-Hadad agreed with King Asa and sent the commanders of his forces against the towns of Israel. He conquered Ijon, Dan, Abel Beth Maakah, and all Kinnereth in addition to Naphtali. When Baasha heard this, he stopped building Ramah and withdrew to Tirzah. Then King Asa issued an order to all Judah—no one was exempt—and they carried away from Ramah the stones and timber Baasha had been using there. With them, King Asa built up Geba in Benjamin, and also Mizpah As for all the other events of Asa's reign, all his achievements, all he did and the cities he built, are they not written in the book of the annals of the kings of Judah? In his old age, however, his feet became diseased. Then Asa rested with his ancestors and was buried with them in the City of David his father. And Jehoshaphat his son succeeded him as king Nadab son of Jeroboam became king of Israel in the second year of Asa king of Judah, and he reigned over Israel two years. He did evil in the eyes of the Lord, following the ways of his father and committing the same sin his father had caused Israel to commit Baasha son of Ahijah from the tribe of Issachar plotted against him, and he struck him down at Gibbethon, a Philistine town, while Nadab and all Israel were besieging it. Baasha killed Nadab in the third year of Asa king of Judah and succeeded him as king. As soon as he began to reign, he killed Jeroboam's whole family. He did not leave Jeroboam anyone that breathed but destroyed them all, according to the word of the Lord given through his servant Ahijah the Shilonite. This happened because of the sins Jeroboam had committed and had caused Israel to commit, and because he aroused the anger of the Lord, the God of Israel As for the other events of Nadab's reign and all he did, are they not written in the book of the annals of the kings of Israel? There was war between Asa and Baasha king of Israel throughout their reigns. In the third year of Asa king of Judah, Baasha son of Ahijah became king of all Israel in Tirzah, and he reigned twenty-four years. He did evil in the eyes of the Lord, following the ways of Jeroboam and committing the same sin Jeroboam had caused Israel to commit Chapter 16 1 The word of the Lord came to Jehu son of Hanani against Baasha, saying: 2 "I raised you up from the dust and made you ruler over my people Israel, but you have followed the ways of Jeroboam and caused my people Israel to sin and arouse my anger by their sins. 3 So I am about to wipe out Baasha and his house, and I will make your house like that of Jeroboam son of Nebat. 4 Dogs will eat those belonging to Baasha who die in the city, and birds will feed on those who die in the country." 5 As for the other events of Baasha's reign, what he did and his achievements, are they not written in the book of the annals of the kings of Israel? 6 Baasha rested with his ancestors and was buried in Tirzah. And Elah his son succeeded him as king. 7 Moreover, the word of the Lord came through the prophet Jehu son of Hanani to Baasha and his house, because of all the evil he had done in the eyes of the Lord, arousing his anger by the things he did and becoming like the house of Jeroboam—and also because he destroyed it 8 In the twenty-sixth year of Asa king of Judah, Elah son of Baasha became king of Israel, and he reigned in Tirzah two years. 9 Zimri, one of his officials who had command of half his chariots, plotted against him. Elah was in Tirzah at the time, getting drunk in the home of Arza, the palace administrator at Tirzah. 10 Zimri came in, struck him down and killed him in the twenty-seventh year of Asa king of Judah. Then he succeeded him as king 11 As soon as he began to reign and was seated on the throne, he killed off Baasha's whole family. He did not spare a single male, whether relative or friend. 12 So Zimri destroyed the whole family of Baasha, in accordance with the word of the Lord spoken against Baasha through the prophet Jehu—13 because of all the sins Baasha and his son Elah had committed and had caused Israel to commit, so that they aroused the anger of the Lord, the God of Israel, by their worthless idols 14 As for the other events of Elah's reign, and all he did, are they not written in the book of the annals of the kings of Israel? 15 In the twenty-seventh year of Asa king of Judah, Zimri reigned in Tirzah seven days. The army was encamped near Gibbethon, a Philistine town. 16 When the Israelites in the camp heard that Zimri had plotted against the king and murdered him, they proclaimed Omri, the commander of the army, king over Israel that very day there in the camp. 17 Then Omri and all the Israelites with him withdrew from Gibbethon and laid siege to Tirzah. 18 When Zimri saw that the city was taken, he went into the citadel of the royal palace and set the palace on fire around him. So he died, 19 because of the sins he had committed, doing evil in the eyes of the Lord and following the ways of Jeroboam and committing the same sin Jeroboam had caused Israel to commit 20 As for the other events of Zimri's reign and the rebellion he carried out, are they not written in the book of the annals of the kings of Israel? 21 Then the people of Israel were split into two factions; half supported Tibni son of Ginath for king, and the other half supported Omri. 22 But Omri's followers proved stronger than those of Tibni son of Ginath. So Tibni died and Omri became king 23 In the thirty-first year of Asa king of Judah, Omri became king of Israel, and he reigned twelve years, six of them in Tirzah. 24 He bought the hill of Samaria from Shemer for two talents of silver and built a city on the hill, calling it Samaria, after Shemer, the name of the former owner of the hill 25 But Omri did evil in the eyes of the Lord and sinned more than all those before him. 26 He followed completely the ways of Jeroboam son of Nebat, committing the same sin Jeroboam had caused Israel to commit, so that they aroused the anger of the Lord, the God of Israel, by their worthless idols 27 As for the other events of Omri's reign, what he did and the things he achieved, are they not written in the book of the annals of the kings of Israel? 28 Omri rested with his ancestors and was buried in Samaria. And Ahab his son succeeded him as king 29 In the thirty-eighth year of Asa king of Judah, Ahab son of Omri became king of Israel, and he reigned in Samaria over Israel twenty-two years. 30 Ahab son of Omri did more evil in the eyes of the Lord than any of those before him. 31 He not only considered it trivial to commit the sins of Jeroboam son of Nebat, but he also married Jezebel daughter of Ethbaal king of the Sidonians, and began to serve Baal and worship him. 32 He set up an altar for Baal in the temple of Baal that he built in Samaria. 33 Ahab also made an Asherah pole and did more to arouse the anger of the Lord, the God of Israel, than did all the kings of Israel before him 34 In Ahab's time, Hiel of Bethel rebuilt Jericho. He laid its foundations at the cost of his firstborn son Abiram, and he set up its gates at the cost of his youngest son Segub, in accordance with the word of the Lord spoken by Joshua son of Nun

Chapter 17

1 Now Elijah the Tishbite, from Tishbe in Gilead, said to Ahab, "As the Lord, the God of Israel, lives, whom I serve, there will be neither dew nor rain in the next few years except at my word." 2 Then the word of the Lord came to Elijah: 3 "Leave here, turn eastward and hide in the Kerith Ravine, east of the Jordan. 4 You will drink from the brook, and I have directed the ravens to supply you with food there." 5 So he did what the Lord had told him. He went to the Kerith Ravine, east of the Jordan, and stayed there. 6 The ravens brought him bread and meat in the morning and bread and meat in the evening, and he drank from the brook 7 Some time later the brook dried up because there had been no rain in the land. 8 Then the word of the Lord came to him: 9 "Go at once to Zarephath in the region of Sidon and stay there. I have directed a widow there to supply you with food." 10 So he went to Zarephath. When he came to the town gate, a widow was there gathering sticks. He called to her and asked, "Would you bring me a little water in a jar so I may have a drink?" 11 As she was going to get it, he called, "And bring me, please, a piece of bread." 12 "As surely as the Lord your God lives," she replied, "I don't have any bread—only a handful of flour in a jar and a little olive oil in a jug. I am gathering a few sticks to take home and make a meal for myself and my son, that we may eat it—and die." 13 Elijah said to her, "Don't be afraid. Go home and do as you have said. But first make a small loaf of bread for me from what you have and bring it to me, and then make something for yourself and your son. 14 For this is what the Lord, the God of Israel, says: 'The jar of flour will not be used up and the jug of oil will not run dry until the day the Lord sends rain on the land.'" 15 She went away and did as Elijah had told her. So there was food every day for Elijah and for the woman and her family. 16 For the jar of flour was not used up and the jug of oil did not run dry, in keeping with the word of the Lord spoken by Elijah 17 Some time later the son of the woman who owned the house became ill. He grew worse and worse and finally stopped breathing. 18 She said to Elijah, "What do you have against me, man of God? Did you come to remind me of my sin and kill my son?" 19 "Give me your son," Elijah replied. He took him from her arms, carried him to the upper room where he was staying, and laid him on his bed. 20 Then he cried out to the Lord, "Lord my God, have you brought tragedy even on this widow I am staying with, by causing her son to die?" 21 Then he stretched himself out on the boy three times and cried out to the Lord, "Lord my God, let this boy's life return to him!" 22 The Lord heard Elijah's cry, and the boy's life returned to him, and he lived. 23 Elijah picked up the child and carried him down from the room into the house. He gave him to his mother and said, "Look, your son is alive!" 24 Then the woman said to Elijah, "Now I know that you are a man of God and that the word of the Lord from your mouth is the truth."

Chapter 18

1 After a long time, in the third year, the word of the Lord came to Elijah: "Go and present yourself to Ahab, and I will send rain on the land." 2 So Elijah went to present himself to Ahab Now the famine was severe in Samaria, 3 and Ahab had summoned Obadiah, his palace administrator. (Obadiah was a devout believer in the Lord. 4 While Jezebel was killing off the Lord's prophets, Obadiah had taken a hundred prophets and hidden them in two caves, fifty in each, and had supplied them with food and water.) 5 Ahab had said to Obadiah, "Go through the land to all the springs and valleys. Maybe we can find some grass to keep the horses and mules alive so we will not have to kill any of our animals." 6 So they divided the land they were to cover, Ahab going in one direction and Obadiah in another 7 As Obadiah was walking along, Elijah met him. Obadiah recognized him, bowed down to the ground, and said, "Is it really you, my lord Elijah?" 8 "Yes," he replied. "Go tell your master, 'Elijah is here.'" 9 "What have I done wrong," asked Obadiah, "that you are handing your servant over to Ahab to be put to death? 10 As surely as the Lord your God lives, there is not a nation or kingdom where my master has not sent someone to look for you. And whenever a nation or kingdom claimed you were not there, he made them swear they could not find you. 11 But now you tell me to go to my master and say, 'Elijah is here.' 12 I don't know where the Spirit of the Lord may carry you when I leave you. If I go and tell Ahab and he doesn't find you, he will kill me. Yet I your servant have worshiped the Lord since my youth. 13 Haven't you heard, my lord, what I did while Jezebel was killing the prophets of the Lord? I hid a hundred of the Lord's prophets in two caves, fifty in each, and supplied them with food and water. 14 And now you tell me to go to my master and say, 'Elijah is here.' He will kill me!" 15 Elijah said, "As the Lord Almighty lives, whom I serve, I will surely present myself to Ahab today." 16 So Obadiah went to meet Ahab and told him, and Ahab went to meet Elijah. 17 When he saw Elijah, he said to him, "Is that you, you troubler of Israel?" 18 "I have not made trouble for Israel," Elijah replied. "But you and your father's family have. You have abandoned the Lord's commands and have followed the Baals. 19 Now summon the people from all over Israel to meet me on Mount Carmel. And bring the four hundred and fifty prophets of Baal and the four hundred prophets of Asherah, who eat at Jezebel's table." 20 So Ahab sent word throughout all Israel and assembled the prophets on Mount Carmel. 21 Elijah went before the people and said, "How long will you waver between two opinions? If the Lord is God, follow him; but if Baal is God, follow him." But the people said nothing 22 Then Elijah said to them, "I am the only one of the Lord's prophets left, but Baal has four hundred and fifty prophets. 23 Get two bulls for us. Let Baal's prophets choose one for themselves, and let them cut it into pieces and put it on the wood but not set fire to it. I will prepare the other bull and put it on the wood but not set fire to it. 24 Then you call on the name of your god, and I will call on the name of the Lord. The god who answers by fire—he is God." Then all the people said, "What you say is good." 25 Elijah said to the prophets of Baal, "Choose one of the bulls and prepare it first, since there are so many of you. Call on the name of your god, but do not light the fire." 26 So they took the bull given them and prepared it Then they called on the name of Baal from morning till noon. "Baal, answer us!" they shouted. But there was no response; no one answered. And they danced around the altar they had made 27 At noon Elijah began to taunt them. "Shout louder!" he said. "Surely he is a god! Perhaps he is deep in thought, or busy, or traveling. Maybe he is sleeping and must be awakened." 28 So they shouted louder and slashed themselves with swords and spears, as was their custom, until their blood flowed. 29 Midday passed, and they continued their frantic prophesying until the time for the evening sacrifice. But there was no response, no one answered, no one paid attention 30 Then Elijah said to all the people, "Come here to me." They came to him, and he repaired the altar of the Lord, which had been torn down. 31 Elijah took twelve stones, one for each of the tribes descended from Jacob, to whom the word of the Lord had come, saying, "Your name shall be Israel." 32 With the stones he built an altar in the name of the Lord, and he dug a trench around it large enough to hold two

seahs of seed. 33 He arranged the wood, cut the bull into pieces, and laid it on the wood. Then he said to them, "Fill four large jars with water and pour it on the offering and on the wood." 34 "Do it again," he said, and they did it again "Do it a third time," he ordered, and they did it the third time. 35 The water ran down around the altar and even filled the trench 36 At the time of sacrifice, the prophet Elijah stepped forward and prayed: "Lord, the God of Abraham, Isaac and Israel, let it be known today that you are God in Israel and that I am your servant and have done all these things at your command. 37 Answer me, Lord, answer me, so these people will know that you, Lord, are God, and that you are turning their hearts back again." 38 Then the fire of the Lord fell and burned up the sacrifice, the wood, the stones and the soil, and also licked up the water in the trench 39 When all the people saw this, they fell prostrate and cried, "The Lord—he is God! The Lord—he is God!" 40 Then Elijah commanded them, "Seize the prophets of Baal. Don't let anyone get away!" They seized them, and Elijah had them brought down to the Kishon Valley and slaughtered there 41 And Elijah said to Ahab, "Go, eat and drink, for there is the sound of a heavy rain." 42 So Ahab went off to eat and drink, but Elijah climbed to the top of Carmel, bent down to the ground and put his face between his knees 43 "Go and look toward the sea," he told his servant. And he went up and looked "There is nothing there," he said Seven times Elijah said, "Go back." 44 The seventh time the servant reported, "A cloud as small as a man's hand is rising from the sea." So Elijah said, "Go and tell Ahab, 'Hitch up your chariot and go down before the rain stops you.'" 45 Meanwhile, the sky grew black with clouds, the wind rose, a heavy rain started falling, and Ahab rode off to Jezreel. 46 The power of the Lord came on Elijah and, tucking his cloak into his belt, he ran ahead of Ahab all the way to Jezreel

Chapter 19

1 Now Ahab told Jezebel everything Elijah had done and how he had killed all the prophets with the sword. 2 So Jezebel sent a messenger to Elijah to say, "May the gods deal with me, be it ever so severely, if by this time tomorrow I do not make your life like that of one of them." 3 Elijah was afraid and ran for his life. When he came to Beersheba in Judah, he left his servant there, 4 while he himself went a day's journey into the wilderness. He came to a broom bush, sat down under it and prayed that he might die. "I have had enough, Lord," he said. "Take my life; I am no better than my ancestors." 5 Then he lay down under the bush and fell asleep All at once an angel touched him and said, "Get up and eat." 6 He looked around, and there by his head was some bread baked over hot coals, and a jar of water. He ate and drank and then lay down again 7 The angel of the Lord came back a second time and touched him and said, "Get up and eat, for the journey is too much for you." 8 So he got up and ate and drank. Strengthened by that food, he traveled forty days and forty nights until he reached Horeb, the mountain of God. 9 There he went into a cave and spent the night And the word of the Lord came to him: "What are you doing here, Elijah?" 10 He replied, "I have been very zealous for the Lord God Almighty. The Israelites have rejected your covenant, torn down your altars, and put your prophets to death with the sword. I am the only one left, and now they are trying to kill me too." 11 The Lord said, "Go out and stand on the mountain in the presence of the Lord, for the Lord is about to pass by." Then a great and powerful wind tore the mountains apart and shattered the rocks before the Lord, but the Lord was not in the wind. After the wind there was an earthquake, but the Lord was not in the earthquake. 12 After the earthquake came a fire, but the Lord was not in the fire. And after the fire came a gentle whisper. 13 When Elijah heard it, he pulled his cloak over his face and went out and stood at the mouth of the cave Then a voice said to him, "What are you doing here, Elijah?" 14 He replied, "I have been very zealous for the Lord God Almighty. The Israelites have rejected your covenant, torn down your altars, and put your prophets to death with the sword. I am the only one left, and now they are trying to kill me too." 15 The Lord said to him, "Go back the way you came, and go to the Desert of Damascus. When you get there, anoint Hazael king over Aram. 16 Also, anoint Jehu son of Nimshi king over Israel, and anoint Elisha son of Shaphat from Abel Meholah to succeed you as prophet. 17 Jehu will put to death any who escape the sword of Hazael, and Elisha will put to death any who escape the sword of Jehu. 18 Yet I reserve seven thousand in Israel—all whose knees have not bowed down to Baal and whose mouths have not kissed him." 19 So Elijah went from there and found Elisha son of Shaphat. He was plowing with twelve yoke of oxen, and he himself was driving the twelfth pair. Elijah went up to him and threw his cloak around him. 20 Elisha then left his oxen and ran after Elijah. "Let me kiss my father and mother goodbye," he said, "and then I will come with you." "Go back," Elijah replied. "What have I done to you?" 21 So Elisha left him and went back. He took his yoke of oxen and slaughtered them. He burned the plowing equipment to cook the meat and gave it to the people, and they ate. Then he set out to follow Elijah and became his servant

Chapter 20

1 Now Ben-Hadad king of Aram mustered his entire army. Accompanied by thirty-two kings with their horses and chariots, he went up and besieged Samaria and attacked it. 2 He sent messengers into the city to Ahab king of Israel, saying, "This is what Ben-Hadad says: 3 'Your silver and gold are mine, and the best of your wives and children are mine.'" 4 The king of Israel answered, "Just as you say, my lord the king. I and all I have are yours." 5 The messengers came again and said, "This is what Ben-Hadad says: 'I sent to demand your silver and gold, your wives and your children. 6 But about this time tomorrow I am going to send my officials to search your palace and the houses of your officials. They will seize everything you value and carry it away.'" 7 The king of Israel summoned all the elders of the land and said to them, "See how this man is looking for trouble! When he sent for my wives and my children, my silver and my gold, I did not refuse him." 8 The elders and the people all answered, "Don't listen to him or agree to his demands." 9 So he replied to Ben-Hadad's messengers, "Tell my lord the king, 'Your servant will do all you demanded the first time, but this demand I cannot meet.'" They left and took the answer back to Ben-Hadad 10 Then Ben-Hadad sent another message to Ahab: "May the gods deal with me, be it ever so severely, if enough dust remains in Samaria to give each of my men a handful." 11 The king of Israel answered, "Tell him: 'One who puts on his armor should not boast like one who takes it off.'" 12 Ben-Hadad heard this message while he and the kings were drinking in their tents, and he ordered his men: "Prepare to attack." So they prepared to attack the city 13 Meanwhile a prophet came to Ahab king of Israel and announced, "This is what the Lord says: 'Do you see this vast army? I will give it into your hand today, and then you will know that I am the Lord.'" 14 "But who will do this?" asked Ahab The prophet replied, "This is what the Lord says: 'The junior officers under the provincial commanders will do it.'" "And who will start the battle?" he asked The prophet

answered, "You will." 15 So Ahab summoned the 232 junior officers under the provincial commanders. Then he assembled the rest of the Israelites, 7,000 in all. 16 They set out at noon while Ben-Hadad and the 32 kings allied with him were in their tents getting drunk. 17 The junior officers under the provincial commanders went out first Now Ben-Hadad had dispatched scouts, who reported, "Men are advancing from Samaria." 18 He said, "If they have come out for peace, take them alive; if they have come out for war, take them alive." 19 The junior officers under the provincial commanders marched out of the city with the army behind them 20 and each one struck down his opponent. At that, the Arameans fled, with the Israelites in pursuit. But Ben-Hadad king of Aram escaped on horseback with some of his horsemen. 21 The king of Israel advanced and overpowered the horses and chariots and inflicted heavy losses on the Arameans 22 Afterward, the prophet came to the king of Israel and said, "Strengthen your position and see what must be done, because next spring the king of Aram will attack you again." 23 Meanwhile, the officials of the king of Aram advised him, "Their gods are gods of the hills. That is why they were too strong for us. But if we fight them on the plains, surely we will be stronger than they. 24 Do this: Remove all the kings from their commands and replace them with other officers. 25 You must also raise an army like the one you lost—horse for horse and chariot for chariot—so we can fight Israel on the plains. Then surely we will be stronger than they." He agreed with them and acted accordingly 26 The next spring Ben-Hadad mustered the Arameans and went up to Aphek to fight against Israel. 27 When the Israelites were also mustered and given provisions, they marched out to meet them. The Israelites camped opposite them like two small flocks of goats, while the Arameans covered the countryside 28 The man of God came up and told the king of Israel, "This is what the Lord says: 'Because the Arameans think the Lord is a god of the hills and not a god of the valleys, I will deliver this vast army into your hands, and you will know that I am the Lord.'" 29 For seven days they camped opposite each other, and on the seventh day the battle was joined. The Israelites inflicted a hundred thousand casualties on the Aramean foot soldiers in one day. 30 The rest of them escaped to the city of Aphek, where the wall collapsed on twenty-seven thousand of them. And Ben-Hadad fled to the city and hid in an inner room 31 His officials said to him, "Look, we have heard that the kings of Israel are merciful. Let us go to the king of Israel with sackcloth around our waists and ropes around our heads. Perhaps he will spare your life." 32 Wearing sackcloth around their waists and ropes around their heads, they went to the king of Israel and said, "Your servant Ben-Hadad says: 'Please let me live.'" The king answered, "Is he still alive? He is my brother." 33 The men took this as a good sign and were quick to pick up his word. "Yes, your brother Ben-Hadad!" they said "Go and get him," the king said. When Ben-Hadad came out, Ahab had him come up into his chariot 34 "I will return the cities my father took from your father," Ben-Hadad offered. "You may set up your own market areas in Damascus, as my father did in Samaria." Ahab said, "On the basis of a treaty I will set you free." So he made a treaty with him and let him go 35 By the word of the Lord one of the company of the prophets said to his companion, "Strike me with your weapon," but he refused 36 So the prophet said, "Because you have not obeyed the Lord, as soon as you leave me, a lion will kill you." And after the man went away, a lion found him and killed him 37 The prophet found another man and said, "Strike me, please." So the man struck him and wounded him. 38 Then the prophet went and stood by the road waiting for the king. He disguised himself with his headband down over his eyes. 39 As the king passed by, the prophet called out to him, "Your servant went into the thick of the battle, and someone came to me with a captive and said, 'Guard this man. If he is missing, it will be your life for his life, or you must pay a talent of silver.' 40 While your servant was busy here and there, the man disappeared." "That is your sentence," the king of Israel said. "You have pronounced it yourself." 41 Then the prophet quickly removed the headband from his eyes, and the king of Israel recognized him as one of the prophets. 42 He said to the king, "This is what the Lord says: 'You have set free a man I had determined should die. Therefore it is your life for his life, your people for his people.'" 43 Sullen and angry, the king of Israel went to his palace in Samaria

Chapter 21

1 Some time later there was an incident involving a vineyard belonging to Naboth the Jezreelite. The vineyard was in Jezreel, close to the palace of Ahab king of Samaria. 2 Ahab said to Naboth, "Let me have your vineyard to use for a vegetable garden, since it is close to my palace. In exchange I will give you a better vineyard or, if you prefer, I will pay you whatever it is worth." 3 But Naboth replied, "The Lord forbid that I should give you the inheritance of my ancestors." 4 So Ahab went home, sullen and angry because Naboth the Jezreelite had said, "I will not give you the inheritance of my ancestors." He lay on his bed sulking and refused to eat 5 His wife Jezebel came in and asked him, "Why are you so sullen? Why won't you eat?" 6 He answered her, "Because I said to Naboth the Jezreelite, 'Sell me your vineyard; or if you prefer, I will give you another vineyard in its place.' But he said, 'I will not give you my vineyard.'" 7 Jezebel his wife said, "Is this how you act as king over Israel? Get up and eat! Cheer up. I'll get you the vineyard of Naboth the Jezreelite." 8 So she wrote letters in Ahab's name, placed his seal on them, and sent them to the elders and nobles who lived in Naboth's city with him. 9 In those letters she wrote: "Proclaim a day of fasting and seat Naboth in a prominent place among the people. 10 But seat two scoundrels opposite him and have them bring charges that he has cursed both God and the king. Then take him out and stone him to death." 11 So the elders and nobles who lived in Naboth's city did as Jezebel directed in the letters she had written to them. 12 They proclaimed a fast and seated Naboth in a prominent place among the people. 13 Then two scoundrels came and sat opposite him and brought charges against Naboth before the people, saying, "Naboth has cursed both God and the king." So they took him outside the city and stoned him to death. 14 Then they sent word to Jezebel: "Naboth has been stoned to death." 15 As soon as Jezebel heard that Naboth had been stoned to death, she said to Ahab, "Get up and take possession of the vineyard of Naboth the Jezreelite that he refused to sell you. He is no longer alive, but dead." 16 When Ahab heard that Naboth was dead, he got up and went down to take possession of Naboth's vineyard 17 Then the word of the Lord came to Elijah the Tishbite: 18 "Go down to meet Ahab king of Israel, who rules in Samaria. He is now in Naboth's vineyard, where he has gone to take possession of it. 19 Say to him, 'This is what the Lord says: Have you not murdered a man and seized his property?' Then say to him, 'This is what the Lord says: In the place where dogs licked up Naboth's blood, dogs will lick up your blood—yes, yours!'" 20 Ahab said to Elijah, "So you have found me, my enemy!" "I have found you," he answered,

"because you have sold yourself to do evil in the eyes of the Lord. 21 He says, 'I am going to bring disaster on you. I will wipe out your descendants and cut off from Ahab every last male in Israel—slave or free. 22 I will make your house like that of Jeroboam son of Nebat and that of Baasha son of Ahijah, because you have aroused my anger and have caused Israel to sin.' 23 "And also concerning Jezebel the Lord says: 'Dogs will devour Jezebel by the wall of Jezreel.' 24 "Dogs will eat those belonging to Ahab who die in the city, and the birds will feed on those who die in the country." 25 (There was never anyone like Ahab, who sold himself to do evil in the eyes of the Lord, urged on by Jezebel his wife. 26 He behaved in the vilest manner by going after idols, like the Amorites the Lord drove out before Israel.) 27 When Ahab heard these words, he tore his clothes, put on sackcloth and fasted. He lay in sackcloth and went around meekly 28 Then the word of the Lord came to Elijah the Tishbite: 29 "Have you noticed how Ahab has humbled himself before me? Because he has humbled himself, I will not bring this disaster in his day, but I will bring it on his house in the days of his son."

Chapter 22

1 For three years there was no war between Aram and Israel. 2 But in the third year Jehoshaphat king of Judah went down to see the king of Israel. 3 The king of Israel had said to his officials, "Don't you know that Ramoth Gilead belongs to us and yet we are doing nothing to retake it from the king of Aram?" 4 So he asked Jehoshaphat, "Will you go with me to fight against Ramoth Gilead?" Jehoshaphat replied to the king of Israel, "I am as you are, my people as your people, my horses as your horses." 5 But Jehoshaphat also said to the king of Israel, "First seek the counsel of the Lord." 6 So the king of Israel brought together the prophets—about four hundred men—and asked them, "Shall I go to war against Ramoth Gilead, or shall I refrain?" "Go," they answered, "for the Lord will give it into the king's hand." 7 But Jehoshaphat asked, "Is there no longer a prophet of the Lord here whom we can inquire of?" 8 The king of Israel answered Jehoshaphat, "There is still one prophet through whom we can inquire of the Lord, but I hate him because he never prophesies anything good about me, but always bad. He is Micaiah son of Imlah." "The king should not say such a thing," Jehoshaphat replied 9 So the king of Israel called one of his officials and said, "Bring Micaiah son of Imlah at once." 10 Dressed in their royal robes, the king of Israel and Jehoshaphat king of Judah were sitting on their thrones at the threshing floor by the entrance of the gate of Samaria, with all the prophets prophesying before them. 11 Now Zedekiah son of Kenaanah had made iron horns and he declared, "This is what the Lord says: 'With these you will gore the Arameans until they are destroyed.'" 12 All the other prophets were prophesying the same thing. "Attack Ramoth Gilead and be victorious," they said, "for the Lord will give it into the king's hand." 13 The messenger who had gone to summon Micaiah said to him, "Look, the other prophets without exception are predicting success for the king. Let your word agree with theirs, and speak favorably." 14 But Micaiah said, "As surely as the Lord lives, I can tell him only what the Lord tells me." 15 When he arrived, the king asked him, "Micaiah, shall we go to war against Ramoth Gilead, or not?" "Attack and be victorious," he answered, "for the Lord will give it into the king's hand." 16 The king said to him, "How many times must I make you swear to tell me nothing but the truth in the name of the Lord?" 17 Then Micaiah answered, "I saw all Israel scattered on the hills like sheep without a shepherd, and the Lord said, 'These people have no master. Let each one go home in peace.'" 18 The king of Israel said to Jehoshaphat, "Didn't I tell you that he never prophesies anything good about me, but only bad?" 19 Micaiah continued, "Therefore hear the word of the Lord: I saw the Lord sitting on his throne with all the multitudes of heaven standing around him on his right and on his left. 20 And the Lord said, 'Who will entice Ahab into attacking Ramoth Gilead and going to his death there?' "One suggested this, and another that. 21 Finally, a spirit came forward, stood before the Lord and said, 'I will entice him.' 22 "'By what means?' the Lord asked "'I will go out and be a deceiving spirit in the mouths of all his prophets,' he said "'You will succeed in enticing him,' said the Lord. 'Go and do it.' 23 "So now the Lord has put a deceiving spirit in the mouths of all these prophets of yours. The Lord has decreed disaster for you." 24 Then Zedekiah son of Kenaanah went up and slapped Micaiah in the face. "Which way did the spirit from the Lord go when he went from me to speak to you?" he asked 25 Micaiah replied, "You will find out on the day you go to hide in an inner room." 26 The king of Israel then ordered, "Take Micaiah and send him back to Amon the ruler of the city and to Joash the king's son 27 and say, 'This is what the king says: Put this fellow in prison and give him nothing but bread and water until I return safely.'" 28 Micaiah declared, "If you ever return safely, the Lord has not spoken through me." Then he added, "Mark my words, all you people!" 29 So the king of Israel and Jehoshaphat king of Judah went up to Ramoth Gilead. 30 The king of Israel said to Jehoshaphat, "I will enter the battle in disguise, but you wear your royal robes." So the king of Israel disguised himself and went into battle 31 Now the king of Aram had ordered his thirty-two chariot commanders, "Do not fight with anyone, small or great, except the king of Israel." 32 When the chariot commanders saw Jehoshaphat, they thought, "Surely this is the king of Israel." So they turned to attack him, but when Jehoshaphat cried out, 33 the chariot commanders saw that he was not the king of Israel and stopped pursuing him 34 But someone drew his bow at random and hit the king of Israel between the sections of his armor. The king told his chariot driver, "Wheel around and get me out of the fighting. I've been wounded." 35 All day long the battle raged, and the king was propped up in his chariot facing the Arameans. The blood from his wound ran onto the floor of the chariot, and that evening he died. 36 As the sun was setting, a cry spread through the army: "Every man to his town. Every man to his land!" 37 So the king died and was brought to Samaria, and they buried him there. 38 They washed the chariot at a pool in Samaria (where the prostitutes bathed), and the dogs licked up his blood, as the word of the Lord had declared 39 As for the other events of Ahab's reign, including all he did, the palace he built and inlaid with ivory, and the cities he fortified, are they not written in the book of the annals of the kings of Israel? 40 Ahab rested with his ancestors. And Ahaziah his son succeeded him as king 41 Jehoshaphat son of Asa became king of Judah in the fourth year of Ahab king of Israel. 42 Jehoshaphat was thirty-five years old when he became king, and he reigned in Jerusalem twenty-five years. His mother's name was Azubah daughter of Shilhi. 43 In everything he followed the ways of his father Asa and did not stray from them; he did what was right in the eyes of the Lord. The high places, however, were not removed, and the people continued to offer sacrifices and burn incense there. 44 Jehoshaphat was also at peace with the king of Israel 45 As for the other events of Jehoshaphat's reign, the things he

achieved and his military exploits, are they not written in the book of the annals of the kings of Judah? 46 He rid the land of the rest of the male shrine prostitutes who remained there even after the reign of his father Asa. 47 There was then no king in Edom; a provincial governor ruled 48 Now Jehoshaphat built a fleet of trading ships to go to Ophir for gold, but they never set sail—they were wrecked at Ezion Geber. 49 At that time Ahaziah son of Ahab said to Jehoshaphat, "Let my men sail with your men," but Jehoshaphat refused 50 Then Jehoshaphat rested with his ancestors and was buried with them in the city of David his father. And Jehoram his son succeeded him as king 51 Ahaziah son of Ahab became king of Israel in Samaria in the seventeenth year of Jehoshaphat king of Judah, and he reigned over Israel two years. 52 He did evil in the eyes of the Lord, because he followed the ways of his father and mother and of Jeroboam son of Nebat, who caused Israel to sin. 53 He served and worshiped Baal and aroused the anger of the Lord, the God of Israel, just as his father had done

12. 2 Kings

CHAPTER 1

After Ahab's death, Moab rebelled against Israel. Ahaziah fell through the window of his bedroom in Samaria and became ill. He sent messengers, instructing them to ask Baal-Zebub, the god of Ekron, if he could be cured of his illness. Then, the angel of the LORD told Elijah the Tishbite, "Go meet the messengers of the king of Samaria and ask them, 'Is it because there is no God in Israel that you are going to ask Baal-Zebub, the god of Ekron?' Therefore, the LORD says, 'You shall not come down from the bed you have climbed, but you will surely die.'" Elijah departed When the messengers returned to Ahaziah, he asked why they had returned so soon. They replied, "A man came to meet us and said, 'Go back to the king who sent you and tell him, "Thus says the LORD: Is it because there is no God in Israel that you are sending for information to Baal-Zebub, the god of Ekron? Therefore, you shall not come down from the bed you have climbed, but you will surely die."'" Ahaziah asked what the man looked like. They described him as a man with a garment of hair and a leather belt around his waist. Ahaziah exclaimed, "He is Elijah the Tishbite!" The king sent a captain with fifty men to Elijah. The captain told Elijah, "O man of God, the king says come down." Elijah replied, "If I am a man of God, may fire come down from heaven and consume you and your fifty men." Fire came down and consumed them. The king sent another captain with fifty men, and the same thing happened. Finally, the king sent a third captain with fifty men. This captain fell on his knees before Elijah and pleaded for his life and the lives of his men. The angel of the LORD told Elijah to go with him. Elijah went to the king and delivered the same message: because Ahaziah had sought Baal-Zebub, he would die. And Ahaziah died according to the word of the LORD that Elijah had spoken Jehoram succeeded Ahaziah as king because Ahaziah had no sons. The rest of Ahaziah's deeds are recorded in the book of the chronicles of the kings of Israel

CHAPTER 2

When the LORD was about to take Elijah up to heaven in a whirlwind, Elijah and Elisha were on their way to Gilgal. Elijah said to Elisha, "Stay here, for the LORD has sent me to Bethel." But Elisha replied, "As the LORD lives, and as you yourself live, I will not leave you." So they went down to Bethel. The sons of the prophets in Bethel asked Elisha if he knew that the LORD was going to take his master away. Elisha

replied, "Yes, I know; keep quiet." Elijah then said to Elisha, "Stay here, for the LORD has sent me to Jericho." Elisha again refused to leave him. At Jericho, the sons of the prophets repeated their question, and Elisha gave the same response. Elijah told Elisha to stay behind once more because the LORD had sent him to the Jordan, but Elisha insisted on staying with him Fifty men of the sons of the prophets stood at a distance, watching as Elijah and Elisha stood by the Jordan. Elijah took his cloak, rolled it up, and struck the water, which divided, allowing them to cross on dry ground. After they crossed, Elijah asked Elisha what he could do for him before he was taken away. Elisha asked for a double portion of Elijah's spirit. Elijah told him that if he saw him being taken away, his request would be granted As they walked and talked, a chariot of fire and horses of fire separated the two, and Elijah went up to heaven in a whirlwind. Elisha saw this and cried out, "My father, my father! The chariots and horsemen of Israel!" Elisha picked up Elijah's cloak and struck the water of the Jordan, and it divided, just as it had for Elijah. The sons of the prophets from Jericho saw this and declared, "The spirit of Elijah rests on Elisha." They bowed to the ground before him The sons of the prophets asked Elisha if they could search for Elijah, thinking the spirit of the LORD might have set him down on a mountain or in a valley. Though Elisha initially refused, they persisted until he allowed them to go. They searched for three days but did not find Elijah. When they returned, Elisha reminded them he had told them not to go The men of the city told Elisha that the water was bad and the land unproductive. Elisha asked for a new bowl with salt in it. He went to the spring and threw the salt into it, declaring, "This is what the LORD says: I have healed this water. Never again will it cause death or make the land unproductive." The water remained pure, according to the word Elisha had spoken As Elisha was on his way to Bethel, some boys came out of the town and jeered at him, calling him names. Elisha turned around, looked at them, and cursed them in the name of the LORD. Then, two bears came out of the woods and mauled forty-two of the boys. Elisha continued on to Mount Carmel and then returned to Samaria

CHAPTER 3

Jehoram, son of Ahab, became king of Israel in Samaria in the eighteenth year of Jehoshaphat, king of Judah, and he reigned for twelve years. He did evil in the eyes of the LORD but not as his father and mother had done. He removed the sacred stone of Baal that his father had made. However, he continued in the sins of Jeroboam, son of Nebat, who had caused Israel to sin Mesha, king of Moab, raised sheep, and he paid the king of Israel a tribute of a hundred thousand lambs and wool from a hundred thousand rams. But after Ahab died, the king of Moab rebelled against the king of Israel. So King Jehoram set out from Samaria and mustered all Israel. He also sent word to Jehoshaphat, king of Judah, asking if he would join him in fighting against Moab. Jehoshaphat agreed They marched through the desert of Edom, accompanied by the king of Edom. After seven days, they had no more water for themselves or their animals. Jehoram lamented, fearing the LORD had brought them together only to deliver them into the hands of Moab. But Jehoshaphat asked if there was a prophet of the LORD they could inquire of. One of the king of Israel's officers mentioned Elisha, son of Shaphat, who had poured water on the hands of Elijah. Jehoshaphat recognized the LORD's word was with Elisha, so the three kings went to meet him Elisha told the king of Israel to go to the prophets of his father and mother. But the king insisted they needed the LORD's help. Elisha said that if it were not for his respect for Jehoshaphat, he would not even look at him. Elisha then called for a harpist. As the harpist played, the hand of the LORD came upon Elisha, and he prophesied that the valley would be filled with water without wind or rain, and they would have water to drink. He also said the LORD would deliver Moab into their hands, and they were to destroy every fortified city and major town, cut down every good tree, stop up all the springs, and ruin every good field with stones The next morning, water flowed from the direction of Edom, and the land was filled with water. When the Moabites saw the water, it appeared red like blood. They assumed the kings had fought and killed each other, so they rushed to the Israelite camp, only to be defeated. The Israelites destroyed the towns, stopped up the springs, and cut down the trees. When the king of Moab saw he was losing the battle, he took his eldest son and sacrificed him on the city wall, causing such great fury against Israel that they withdrew and returned to their own land

CHAPTER 4

One of the wives of the sons of the prophets cried out to Elisha, saying, "Your servant, my husband, is dead, and you know that he feared the LORD. Now his creditor is coming to take my two sons as his slaves." Elisha asked her what she had in her house, and she replied, "Your servant has nothing there at all except a small jar of olive oil." Elisha told her to go around and ask all her neighbors for empty jars and to collect as many as she could. Then she was to go inside and shut the door behind her and her sons, pouring oil into all the jars, setting each aside when it was full She left Elisha and did as he instructed. Her sons brought the jars to her, and she kept pouring. When all the jars were full, she asked for another, but they told her there were no more jars left. The oil stopped flowing. She went and told the man of God, and he said, "Go, sell the oil and pay your debts. You and your sons can live on what is left." One day, Elisha went to Shunem, where a wealthy woman lived. She urged him to stay for a meal, and whenever he passed that way, he would stop there to eat. She said to her husband, "I know that this man who often comes our way is a holy man of God. Let's make a small room on the roof with a bed, a table, a chair, and a lamp for him. Then he can stay there whenever he comes to us." One day when Elisha came, he went up to his room and lay down there. He said to his servant Gehazi, "Call the Shunammite." So he called her, and she stood before him. Elisha told Gehazi to say to her, "You have gone to all this trouble for us. What can be done for you? Can we speak on your behalf to the king or the commander of the army?" She replied, "I have a home among my own people." Elisha asked Gehazi what could be done for her, and Gehazi said, "She has no son, and her husband is old." Then Elisha said, "Call her." So he called her, and she stood in the doorway. "About this time next year," Elisha said, "you will hold a son in your arms." She exclaimed, "No, my lord! Please, man of God, don't mislead your servant!" But the woman became pregnant, and the next year about that same time, she gave birth to a son, just as Elisha had told her The child grew, and one day he went out to his father, who was with the reapers. He said to his father, "My head! My head!" His father told a servant to carry him to his mother. The servant lifted him up and carried him to his mother. The boy sat on her lap until noon, and then he died. She went up and laid him on the bed of the man of God, then shut the door and went out. She called her husband and asked him to send her a servant and a donkey so she could go to the man of

God quickly and return. He asked why she was going to him today, as it was not the New Moon or the Sabbath. She said, "It's all right." She saddled the donkey and told her servant to lead on and not slow down unless she told him to. She set out and came to the man of God at Mount Carmel. When he saw her in the distance, he said to Gehazi, "Look, there's the Shunammite! Run to meet her and ask her, 'Are you all right? Is your husband all right? Is your child all right?'" She replied, "Everything is all right." When she reached the man of God at the mountain, she took hold of his feet. Gehazi came over to push her away, but the man of God said, "Leave her alone! She is in bitter distress, but the LORD has hidden it from me and has not told me why." She said, "Did I ask you for a son, my lord? Didn't I tell you, 'Don't raise my hopes'?" Elisha said to Gehazi, "Tuck your cloak into your belt, take my staff in your hand, and run. Don't greet anyone you meet, and if anyone greets you, do not answer. Lay my staff on the boy's face." But the child's mother said, "As surely as the LORD lives and as you live, I will not leave you." So he got up and followed her. Gehazi went on ahead and laid the staff on the boy's face, but there was no sound or response. So Gehazi went back to meet Elisha and told him, "The boy has not awakened." When Elisha reached the house, there was the boy lying dead on his couch. He went in, shut the door on the two of them, and prayed to the LORD. Then he got on the bed and lay on the boy, mouth to mouth, eyes to eyes, hands to hands. As he stretched himself out on him, the boy's body grew warm. Elisha turned away and walked back and forth in the room and then got on the bed and stretched out on him once more. The boy sneezed seven times and opened his eyes Elisha summoned Gehazi and said, "Call the Shunammite." And he did. When she came, he said, "Take your son." She came in, fell at his feet, and bowed to the ground. Then she took her son and went out Elisha returned to Gilgal, and there was a famine in that region. While the company of the prophets was meeting with him, he said to his servant, "Put on the large pot and cook some stew for these prophets." One of them went out into the fields to gather herbs and found a wild vine. He gathered some of its gourds and cut them up into the pot of stew, though no one knew what they were. The stew was poured out for the men, but as they began to eat it, they cried out, "Man of God, there is death in the pot!" And they could not eat it Elisha said, "Get some flour." He put it into the pot and said, "Serve it to the people to eat." And there was nothing harmful in the pot A man came from Baal Shalisha, bringing the man of God twenty loaves of barley bread baked from the first ripe grain, along with some heads of new grain. "Give it to the people to eat," Elisha said. "How can I set this before a hundred men?" his servant asked. But Elisha answered, "Give it to the people to eat. For this is what the LORD says: 'They will eat and have some left over.'" Then he set it before them, and they ate and had some left over, according to the word of the LORD

CHAPTER 5

Naaman, the commander of the army of the king of Aram, was a great man in the sight of his master and highly regarded because through him the LORD had given victory to Aram. He was a valiant soldier, but he had leprosy. Bands from Aram had gone out and taken captive a young girl from Israel, and she served Naaman's wife. She said to her mistress, "If only my master would see the prophet who is in Samaria! He would cure him of his leprosy." Naaman went to his master and told him what the girl from Israel had said. "By all means, go," the king of Aram replied. "I will send a letter to the king of Israel." So Naaman left, taking with him ten talents of silver, six thousand shekels of gold, and ten sets of clothing. The letter he took to the king of Israel read, "With this letter I am sending my servant Naaman to you so that you may cure him of his leprosy." As soon as the king of Israel read the letter, he tore his robes and said, "Am I God? Can I kill and bring back to life? Why does this fellow send someone to me to be cured of his leprosy? See how he is trying to pick a quarrel with me!" When Elisha, the man of God, heard that the king of Israel had torn his robes, he sent him this message: "Why have you torn your robes? Have the man come to me, and he will know that there is a prophet in Israel." So Naaman went with his horses and chariots and stopped at the door of Elisha's house. Elisha sent a messenger to say to him, "Go, wash yourself seven times in the Jordan, and your flesh will be restored and you will be cleansed." But Naaman went away angry and said, "I thought that he would surely come out to me and stand and call on the name of the LORD his God, wave his hand over the spot and cure me of my leprosy. Are not Abana and Pharpar, the rivers of Damascus, better than any of the waters of Israel? Couldn't I wash in them and be cleansed?" So he turned and went off in a rage Naaman's servants went to him and said, "My father, if the prophet had told you to do some great thing, would you not have done it? How much more, then, when he tells you, 'Wash and be cleansed'!" So he went down and dipped himself in the Jordan seven times, as the man of God had told him, and his flesh was restored and became clean like that of a young boy Then Naaman and all his attendants went back to the man of God. He stood before him and said, "Now I know that there is no God in all the world except in Israel. So please accept a gift from your servant." But Elisha answered, "As surely as the LORD lives, whom I serve, I will not accept a thing." And even though Naaman urged him, he refused "If you will not," said Naaman, "please let me, your servant, be given as much earth as a pair of mules can carry, for your servant will never again make burnt offerings and sacrifices to any other god but the LORD. But may the LORD forgive your servant for this one thing: When my master enters the temple of Rimmon to bow down and he is leaning on my arm and I have to bow there also—when I bow down in the temple of Rimmon, may the LORD forgive your servant for this." "Go in peace," Elisha said After Naaman had traveled some distance, Gehazi, the servant of Elisha, the man of God, said to himself, "My master was too easy on Naaman, this Aramean, by not accepting from him what he brought. As surely as the LORD lives, I will run after him and get something from him." So Gehazi hurried after Naaman. When Naaman saw him running toward him, he got down from the chariot to meet him. "Is everything all right?" he asked "Everything is all right," Gehazi answered. "My master sent me to say, 'Two young men from the company of the prophets have just come to me from the hill country of Ephraim. Please give them a talent of silver and two sets of clothing.'" "By all means, take two talents," said Naaman. He urged Gehazi to accept them and then tied up the two talents of silver in two bags, with two sets of clothing. He gave them to two of his servants, and they carried them ahead of Gehazi. When Gehazi came to the hill, he took the things from the servants and put them away in the house. He sent the men away, and they left When he went in and stood before his master, Elisha asked him, "Where have you been, Gehazi?" "Your servant didn't go anywhere," Gehazi answered But Elisha said to him, "Was not my spirit with you when the man got down from his chariot to meet you? Is this the time to take money or to accept clothes—or olive groves and vineyards, or flocks and herds, or male and female slaves? Naaman's leprosy will cling to you and to your descendants forever." Then Gehazi went from Elisha's presence, and his skin was leprous—it had become as white as snow

CHAPTER 6

The sons of the prophets said to Elisha, "Behold, the place where we dwell with you is too small for us. Let us go to the Jordan and each take a log from there, and let us build a place for us to dwell in." Elisha said, "Go." One of them asked, "Please come with your servants." Elisha replied, "I will go." So he went with them. When they reached the Jordan, they began to cut down trees. As one of them was cutting down a tree, the iron axe head fell into the water. He cried out, "Oh, my master, it was borrowed!" The man of God asked, "Where did it fall?" He showed Elisha the place. Elisha cut a stick, threw it there, and made the iron float. Elisha said, "Lift it out." The man reached out his hand and took it The king of Aram was at war with Israel. He conferred with his officers and said, "I will set up my camp in such and such a place." The man of God sent word to the king of Israel: "Beware of passing that place because the Arameans are going down there." So the king of Israel checked the place indicated by the man of God. Time and again Elisha warned the king, so he was on his guard in such places. This enraged the king of Aram. He summoned his officers and demanded, "Tell me! Which of us is on the side of the king of Israel?" One of his officers said, "None of us, my lord the king, but Elisha, the prophet who is in Israel, tells the king of Israel the very words you speak in your bedroom." The king ordered, "Go, find out where he is, so I can send men and capture him." The report came back: "He is in Dothan." Then he sent horses and chariots and a strong force there. They went by night and surrounded the city When the servant of the man of God got up and went out early the next morning, an army with horses and chariots had surrounded the city. "Oh no, my lord! What shall we do?" the servant asked. "Don't be afraid," the prophet answered. "Those who are with us are more than those who are with them." Elisha prayed, "Open his eyes, LORD, so that he may see." Then the LORD opened the servant's eyes, and he looked and saw the hills full of horses and chariots of fire all around Elisha. As the enemy came down toward him, Elisha prayed to the LORD, "Strike this army with blindness." So he struck them with blindness, as Elisha had asked. Elisha told them, "This Elisha told them, "This is not the road, and this is not the city. Follow me, and I will lead you to the man you are looking for." And he led them to Samaria. After they entered the city, Elisha said, "LORD, open the eyes of these men so they can see." Then the LORD opened their eyes, and they looked, and there they were, inside Samaria. When the king of Israel saw them, he asked Elisha, "Shall I kill them, my father? Shall I kill them?" "Do not kill them," he answered. "Would you kill those you have captured with your own sword or bow? Set food and water before them so that they may eat and drink and then go back to their master." So he prepared a great feast for them, and after they had finished eating and drinking, he sent them away, and they returned to their master. So the bands from Aram stopped raiding Israel's territory Sometime later, Ben-Hadad, king of Aram, mobilized his entire army and marched up and laid siege to Samaria. There was a great famine in the city; the siege lasted so long that a donkey's head sold for eighty shekels of silver, and a quarter of a cab of seed pods for five shekels. As the king of Israel was passing by on the wall, a woman cried to him, "Help me, my lord the king!" The king replied, "If the LORD does not help you, where can I get help for you? From the threshing floor? From the winepress?" Then he asked her, "What's the matter?"

She answered, "This woman said to me, 'Give up your son so we may eat him today, and tomorrow we'll eat my son.' So we cooked my son and ate him. The next day I said to her, 'Give up your son so we may eat him,' but she had hidden him." When the king heard the woman's words, he tore his robes. As he went along the wall, the people looked, and they saw that under his robes he had sackcloth on his body. He said, "May God deal with me, be it ever so severely, if the head of Elisha son of Shaphat remains on his shoulders today!" Now Elisha was sitting in his house, and the elders were sitting with him. The king sent a messenger ahead, but before he arrived, Elisha said to the elders, "Don't you see how this murderer is sending someone to cut off my head? Look, when the messenger comes, shut the door and hold it shut against him. Is not the sound of his master's footsteps behind him?" While he was still talking to them, the messenger came down to him. The king said, "This disaster is from the LORD. Why should I wait for the LORD any longer?"

CHAPTER 7

Elisha replied, "Hear the word of the LORD. This is what the LORD says: About this time tomorrow, a seah of the finest flour will sell for a shekel and two seahs of barley for a shekel at the gate of Samaria." The officer on whose arm the king was leaning said to the man of God, "Look, even if the LORD should open the floodgates of the heavens, could this happen?" "You will see it with your own eyes," answered Elisha, "but you will not eat any of it!" Now there were four men with leprosy at the entrance of the city gate. They said to each other, "Why stay here until we die? If we say, 'We'll go into the city'—the famine is there, and we will die. And if we stay here, we will die. So let's go over to the camp of the Arameans and surrender. If they spare us, we live; if they kill us, then we die." At dusk they got up and went to the camp of the Arameans. When they reached the edge of the camp, no one was there, for the Lord had caused the Arameans to hear the sound of chariots and horses and a great army, so that they said to one another, "Look, the king of Israel has hired the Hittite and Egyptian kings to attack us!" So they got up and fled in the dusk and abandoned their tents and their horses and donkeys. They left the camp as it was and ran for their lives The men who had leprosy reached the edge of the camp, entered one of the tents, and ate and drank. Then they took silver, gold, and clothes, and went off and hid them. They returned and entered another tent and took some things from it and hid them also. Then they said to each other, "What we're doing is not right. This is a day of good news, and we are keeping it to ourselves. If we wait until daylight, punishment will overtake us. Let's go at once and report this to the royal palace." So they went and called out to the city gatekeepers and told them, "We went into the Aramean camp and no one was there—not a sound of anyone—only tethered horses and donkeys, and the tents left just as they were." The gatekeepers shouted the news, and it was reported within the palace The king got up in the night and said to his officers, "I will tell you what the Arameans have done to us. They know we are starving, so they have left the camp to hide in the countryside, thinking, 'They will surely come out, and then we will take them alive and get into the city.'" One of his officers answered, "Have some men take five of the horses that are left in the city. Their plight will be like that of all the Israelites left here—yes, they will only be like all these Israelites who are doomed. So let us send them to find out what happened." So they selected two chariots with their horses, and the king sent them after the Aramean army. He commanded the drivers, "Go and find out what has happened." They followed them as far as the Jordan, and they found the whole road strewn

with the clothing and equipment the Arameans had thrown away in their headlong flight. So the messengers returned and reported to the king. Then the people went out and plundered the camp of the Arameans. So a seah of the finest flour sold for a shekel, and two seahs of barley sold for a shekel, as the LORD had said Now the king had put the officer on whose arm he leaned in charge of the gate, and the people trampled him in the gateway, and he died, just as the man of God had foretold when the king came down to his house. It happened as the man of God had said to the king: "About this time tomorrow, a seah of the finest flour will sell for a shekel and two seahs of barley for a shekel at the gate of Samaria." The officer had said to the man of God, "Look, even if the LORD should open the floodgates of the heavens, could this happen?" The man of God had replied, "You will see it with your own eyes, but you will not eat any of it!" And that is exactly what happened to him, for the people trampled him in the gateway, and he died

CHAPTER 8

Now Elisha had said to the woman whose son he had restored to life, "Go away with your family and stay for a while wherever you can, because the LORD has decreed a famine in the land that will last seven years." The woman proceeded to do as the man of God said. She and her family went away and stayed in the land of the Philistines for seven years. At the end of the seven years, she came back from the land of the Philistines and went to appeal to the king for her house and land. The king was talking to Gehazi, the servant of the man of God, and had said, "Tell me about all the great things Elisha has done." Just as Gehazi was telling the king how Elisha had restored the dead to life, the woman whose son Elisha had brought back to life came to appeal to the king for her house and land. Gehazi said, "This is the woman, my lord the king, and this is her son whom Elisha restored to life." The king asked the woman about it, and she told him. Then he assigned an official to her case and said to him, "Give back everything that belonged to her, including all the income from her land from the day she left the country until now." Elisha went to Damascus, and Ben-Hadad king of Aram was ill. When the king was told, "The man of God has come all the way up here," he said to Hazael, "Take a gift with you and go to meet the man of God. Consult the LORD through him; ask him, 'Will I recover from this illness?'" Hazael went to meet Elisha, taking with him as a gift forty camel-loads of all the finest wares of Damascus. He went in and stood before him and said, "Your son Ben-Hadad king of Aram has sent me to ask, 'Will I recover from this illness?'" Elisha answered, "Go and say to him, 'You will certainly recover.' Nevertheless, the LORD has revealed to me that he will in fact die." He stared at him with a fixed gaze until Hazael was embarrassed. Then the man of God began to weep "Why is my lord weeping?" asked Hazael "Because I know the harm you will do to the Israelites," he answered. "You will set fire to their fortified places, kill their young men with the sword, dash their little children to the ground, and rip open their pregnant women." Hazael said, "How could your servant, a mere dog, accomplish such a feat?" "The LORD has shown me that you will become king of Aram," answered Elisha. Then Hazael left Elisha and returned to his master. When Ben-Hadad asked, "What did Elisha say to you?" Hazael replied, "He told me that you would certainly recover." But the next day he took a thick cloth, soaked it in water, and spread it over the king's face so that he died. Then Hazael succeeded him as king In the fifth year of Joram son of Ahab king of Israel, when Jehoshaphat was king of Judah, Jehoram son of Jehoshaphat began his reign as king of Judah. He was thirty-two years old when he became king, and he reigned in Jerusalem eight years. He followed the ways of the kings of Israel, as the house of Ahab had done, for he married a daughter of Ahab. He did evil in the eyes of the LORD. Nevertheless, for the sake of his servant David, the LORD was not willing to destroy Judah. He had promised to maintain a lamp for David and his descendants forever In the time of Jehoram, Edom rebelled against Judah and set up its own king. So Jehoram went to Zair with all his chariots. The Edomites surrounded him and his chariot commanders, but he rose up and broke through by night. His army, however, fled back home. To this day Edom has been in rebellion against Judah. Libnah revolted at the same time. As for the other events of Jehoram's reign, and all he did, are they not written in the book of the annals of the kings of Judah? Jehoram rested with his ancestors and was buried with them in the City of David. And Ahaziah his son succeeded him as king In the twelfth year of Joram son of Ahab king of Israel, Ahaziah son of Jehoram king of Judah began to reign. Ahaziah was twenty-two years old when he became king, and he reigned in Jerusalem one year. His mother's name was Athaliah, a granddaughter of Omri king of Israel. He followed the ways of the house of Ahab and did evil in the eyes of the LORD, as the house of Ahab had done, for he was related by marriage to Ahab's family Ahaziah went with Joram son of Ahab to war against Hazael king of Aram at Ramoth Gilead. The Arameans wounded Joram; so King Joram returned to Jezreel to recover from the wounds the Arameans had inflicted on him at Ramoth in his battle with Hazael king of Aram. Then Ahaziah son of Jehoram king of Judah went down to Jezreel to see Joram son of Ahab, because he had been wounded

CHAPTER 9

The prophet Elisha summoned a man from the company of the prophets and said to him, "Tuck your cloak into your belt, take this flask of oil with you and go to Ramoth Gilead. When you get there, look for Jehu son of Jehoshaphat, the son of Nimshi. Go to him, get him away from his companions and take him into an inner room. Then take the flask and pour the oil on his head and declare, 'This is what the LORD says: I anoint you king over Israel.' Then open the door and run; don't delay!" So the young prophet went to Ramoth Gilead. When he arrived, he found the army officers sitting together. "I have a message for you, commander," he said "For which of us?" asked Jehu "For you, commander," he replied. Jehu got up and went into the house. Then the prophet poured the oil on Jehu's head and declared, "This is what the LORD, the God of Israel, says: I anoint you king over the LORD's people Israel. You are to destroy the house of Ahab your master, and I will avenge the blood of my servants the prophets and the blood of all the LORD's servants shed by Jezebel. The whole house of Ahab will perish. I will cut off from Ahab every last male in Israel—slave or free. I will make the house of Ahab like the house of Jeroboam son of Nebat and like the house of Baasha son of Ahijah. As for Jezebel, dogs will devour her on the plot of ground at Jezreel, and no one will bury her." Then he opened the door and ran When Jehu went out to his fellow officers, one of them asked him, "Is everything all right? Why did this maniac come to you?" "You know the man and the sort of things he says," Jehu replied "That's not true!" they said. "Tell us." Jehu said, "Here is what he told me: 'This is what the LORD says: I anoint you king over Israel.'" They quickly took their cloaks and spread them under him on the bare steps. Then they blew the trumpet and shouted, "Jehu is

king!" So Jehu son of Jehoshaphat, the son of Nimshi, conspired against Joram. (Now Joram and all Israel had been defending Ramoth Gilead against Hazael king of Aram, but King Joram had returned to Jezreel to recover from the wounds the Arameans had inflicted on him in the battle with Hazael king of Aram.) Jehu said, "If this is the way you feel, don't let anyone slip out of the city to go and tell the news in Jezreel." Then he got into his chariot and rode to Jezreel, because Joram was resting there and Ahaziah king of Judah had gone down to see him When the lookout standing on the tower in Jezreel saw Jehu's troops approaching, he called out, "I see some troops coming." "Get a horseman," Joram ordered. "Send him to meet them and ask, 'Do you come in peace?'" The horseman rode off to meet Jehu and said, "This is what the king says: 'Do you come in peace?'" "What do you have to do with peace?" Jehu replied. "Fall in behind me." The lookout reported, "The messenger has reached them, but he isn't coming back." So the king sent out a second horseman. When he came to them he said, "This is what the king says: 'Do you come in peace?'" Jehu replied, "What do you have to do with peace? Fall in behind me." The lookout reported, "He has reached them, but he isn't coming back either. The driving is like that of Jehu son of Nimshi—he drives like a maniac." "Harness up my chariot," Joram ordered. When it was harnessed up, Joram king of Israel and Ahaziah king of Judah rode out, each in his own chariot, to meet Jehu. They met him at the plot of ground that had belonged to Naboth the Jezreelite. When Joram saw Jehu he asked, "Have you come in peace, Jehu?" "How can there be peace," Jehu replied, "as long as all the idolatry and witchcraft of your mother Jezebel abound?" Joram turned about and fled, calling out to Ahaziah, "Treachery, Ahaziah!" Then Jehu drew his bow and shot Joram between the shoulders. The arrow pierced his heart and he slumped down in his chariot. Jehu said to Bidkar, his chariot officer, "Pick him up and throw him on the field that belonged to Naboth the Jezreelite. Remember how you and I were riding together in chariots behind Ahab his father when the LORD spoke this prophecy against him: 'Yesterday I saw the blood of Naboth and the blood of his sons, declares the LORD, and I will surely make you pay for it on this plot of ground, declares the LORD.' Now then, pick him up and throw him on that plot, in accordance with the word of the LORD." When Ahaziah king of Judah saw what had happened, he fled up the road to Beth Haggan. Jehu chased him, shouting, "Kill him too!" They wounded him in his chariot on the way up to Gur near Ibleam, but he escaped to Megiddo and died there. His servants took him by chariot to Jerusalem and buried him with his ancestors in his tomb in the City of David. (In the eleventh year of Joram son of Ahab, Ahaziah had become king of Judah.) Then Jehu went to Jezreel. When Jezebel heard about it, she put on eye makeup, arranged her hair and looked out of a window. As Jehu entered the gate, she asked, "Have you come in peace, you Zimri, you murderer of your master?" He looked up at the window and called out, "Who is on my side? Who?" Two or three eunuchs looked down at him. "Throw her down!" Jehu said. So they threw her down, and some of her blood spattered the wall and the horses as they trampled her underfoot. Jehu went in and ate and drank. "Take care of that cursed woman," he said, "and bury her, for she was a king's daughter." But when they went out to bury her, they found nothing except her skull, her feet and her hands. They went back and told Jehu, who said, "This is the word of the LORD that he spoke through his servant Elijah the Tishbite: On the plot of ground at

Jezreel dogs will devour Jezebel's flesh. Jezebel's body will be like dung on the ground in the plot at Jezreel, so that no one will be able to say, 'This is Jezebel.'"

CHAPTER 10

Now there were seventy sons of Ahab in Samaria. So Jehu wrote letters and sent them to Samaria, to the officials of Jezreel, to the elders and to the guardians of Ahab's children. He said, "You have your master's sons with you and you have chariots and horses, a fortified city and weapons. Now as soon as this letter reaches you, choose the best and most worthy of your master's sons and set him on his father's throne. Then fight for your master's house." But they were terrified and said, "If two kings could not resist him, how can we?" So the palace administrator, the city governor, the elders and the guardians sent this message to Jehu: "We are your servants and we will do anything you say. We will not appoint anyone as king; you do whatever you think best." Then Jehu wrote them a second letter, saying, "If you are on my side and will obey me, take the heads of your master's sons and come to me in Jezreel by this time tomorrow." (Now the royal princes, seventy of them, were with the leading men of the city, who were rearing them.) When the letter arrived, these men took the princes and slaughtered all seventy of them. They put their heads in baskets and sent them to Jehu in Jezreel. When the messenger arrived, he told Jehu, "They have brought the heads of the princes." Then Jehu ordered, "Put them in two piles at the entrance of the city gate until morning." The next morning Jehu went out. He stood before all the people and said, "You are innocent. It was I who conspired against my master and killed him, but who killed all these? Know then, that not a word the LORD has spoken against the house of Ahab will fail. The LORD has done what he announced through his servant Elijah." So Jehu killed everyone in Jezreel who remained of the house of Ahab, as well as all his chief men, his close friends and his priests, leaving no survivor Jehu then set out and went toward Samaria. At Beth Eked of the Shepherds, he met some relatives of Ahaziah king of Judah and asked, "Who are you?" They said, "We are relatives of Ahaziah, and we have come down to greet the families of the king and of the queen mother." "Take them alive!" he ordered. So they took them alive and slaughtered them by the well of Beth Eked—forty-two of them. He left no survivor After he left there, he came upon Jehonadab son of Rekab, who was on his way to meet him. Jehu greeted him and said, "Are you in accord with me, as I am with you?" "I am," Jehonadab answered. "If so," said Jehu, "give me your hand." So he did, and Jehu helped him up into the chariot. Jehu said, "Come with me and see my zeal for the LORD." Then he had him ride along in his chariot When Jehu came to Samaria, he killed all who were left there of Ahab's family; he destroyed them, according to the word of the LORD spoken to Elijah. Then Jehu brought all the people together and said to them, "Ahab served Baal a little; Jehu will serve him much. Now summon all the prophets of Baal, all his servants and all his priests. See that no one is missing, because I am going to hold a great sacrifice for Baal. Anyone who fails to come will no longer live." But Jehu was acting deceptively in order to destroy the servants of Baal Jehu said, "Call an assembly in honor of Baal." So they proclaimed it. Then he sent word throughout Israel, and all the servants of Baal came; not one stayed away. They crowded into the temple of Baal until it was full from one end to the other. And Jehu said to the keeper of the wardrobe, "Bring robes for all the servants of Baal." So he brought out robes for them Then Jehu and Jehonadab son of Rekab went into the temple of Baal. Jehu said to the servants of Baal, "Look around and see that no one who serves the LORD is here with you—only servants of Baal." So they went in to make sacrifices and burnt offerings. Now Jehu had posted eighty men outside with this warning: "If one of you lets any of the men I am placing in your hands escape, it will be your life for his life." As soon as Jehu had finished making the burnt offering, he ordered the guards and officers: "Go in and kill them; let no one escape." So they cut them down with the sword. The guards and officers threw the bodies out and then entered the inner shrine of the temple of Baal. They brought the sacred stone out of the temple of Baal and burned it. They demolished the sacred stone of Baal and tore down the temple of Baal, and people have used it for a latrine to this day So Jehu destroyed Baal worship in Israel. However, he did not turn away from the sins of Jeroboam son of Nebat, which he had caused Israel to commit—the worship of the golden calves at Bethel and Dan. The LORD said to Jehu, "Because you have done well in accomplishing what is right in my eyes and have done to the house of Ahab all I had in mind to do, your descendants will sit on the throne of Israel to the fourth generation." Yet Jehu was not careful to keep the law of the LORD, the God of Israel, with all his heart. He did not turn away from the sins of Jeroboam, which he had caused Israel to commit In those days the LORD began to reduce the size of Israel. Hazael overpowered the Israelites throughout their territory east of the Jordan in all the land of Gilead—the region of Gad, Reuben and Manasseh—from Aroer by the Arnon Gorge through Gilead to Bashan As for the other events of Jehu's reign, all he did, and all his achievements, are they not written in the book of the annals of the kings of Israel? Jehu rested with his ancestors and was buried in Samaria. And Jehoahaz his son succeeded him as king. The time that Jehu reigned over Israel in Samaria was twenty-eight years

CHAPTER 11

When Athaliah, the mother of Ahaziah, saw that her son was dead, she rose up and destroyed all the royal family. But Jehosheba, the daughter of King Joram and sister of Ahaziah, took Joash, son of Ahaziah, and hid him from Athaliah so he would not be killed. She kept him hidden with his nurse in the house of the LORD for six years while Athaliah reigned over the land In the seventh year, Jehoiada sent for the commanders of hundreds, the Carites, and the guards. He brought them to him in the house of the LORD and made a covenant with them. He showed them the king's son and commanded them, saying, "This is what you are to do: a third of you who come on duty on the Sabbath shall guard the king's house. Another third shall be at the gate of Sur, and another third at the gate behind the guards. You shall take turns guarding the temple." Two divisions of you, all who go off duty on the Sabbath, shall guard the house of the LORD for the king. Surround the king, each man with his weapons in hand. Anyone who approaches your ranks is to be put to death. Stay close to the king wherever he goes The commanders of hundreds did everything Jehoiada the priest ordered. Each brought his men, those going on duty on the Sabbath and those going off duty, and came to Jehoiada the priest. He gave the commanders the spears and shields that had belonged to King David and were in the house of the LORD. The guards, each with his weapon in hand, stationed themselves around the king, from the south side of the temple to the north side and around the altar and the temple. Jehoiada brought out the king's son, put the crown on him, and presented him with a copy of the covenant.

They proclaimed him king and anointed him, and the people clapped their hands and shouted, "Long live the king!" When Athaliah heard the noise made by the guards and the people, she went to the people at the temple of the LORD. She looked, and there was the king, standing by the pillar as the custom was. The officers and the trumpeters were beside the king, and all the people of the land were rejoicing and blowing trumpets. Athaliah tore her robes and called out, "Treason! Treason!" Jehoiada the priest ordered the commanders of hundreds, who were in charge of the troops: "Bring her out between the ranks and put to death by the sword anyone who follows her." For the priest had said, "She must not be put to death in the house of the LORD." So they seized her as she reached the place where the horses enter the palace grounds, and there she was put to death Jehoiada then made a covenant between the LORD and the king and the people that they would be the LORD's people. He also made a covenant between the king and the people. All the people of the land went to the temple of Baal and tore it down. They smashed the altars and idols to pieces and killed Mattan the priest of Baal in front of the altars Then Jehoiada the priest posted guards at the temple of the LORD. He took with him the commanders of hundreds, the Carites, the guards, and all the people of the land, and together they brought the king down from the temple of the LORD. They went into the palace, entering by way of the gate of the guards. The king then took his place on the royal throne, and all the people of the land rejoiced. The city was calm because Athaliah had been slain with the sword at the palace Joash was seven years old when he began to reign

CHAPTER 12

In the seventh year of Jehu, Joash began to reign, and he reigned in Jerusalem for forty years. His mother's name was Zibiah of Beersheba. Joash did what was right in the eyes of the LORD all the years Jehoiada the priest instructed him. However, the high places were not removed; the people continued to offer sacrifices and burn incense there Joash said to the priests, "Collect all the money that is brought as sacred offerings to the temple of the LORD—the money collected in the census, the money received from personal vows, and the money brought voluntarily to the temple. Let every priest receive the money from one of the treasurers, and let it be used to repair whatever damage is found in the temple." By the twenty-third year of King Joash, the priests still had not repaired the temple. Therefore, King Joash summoned Jehoiada the priest and the other priests and asked them, "Why aren't you repairing the damage done to the temple? Take no more money from your treasurers but hand it over for the repair of the temple." The priests agreed that they would not collect any more money from the people and that they would not repair the temple themselves Jehoiada the priest took a chest and bored a hole in its lid. He placed it beside the altar, on the right side as one enters the temple of the LORD. The priests who guarded the entrance put into the chest all the money that was brought to the temple of the LORD. Whenever they saw that there was a large amount of money in the chest, the royal secretary and the high priest came, counted the money that had been brought into the temple of the LORD, and put it into bags. When the amount had been determined, they gave the money to the men appointed to supervise the work on the temple. With it, they paid those who worked on the temple of the LORD—the carpenters and builders, the masons and stonecutters. They purchased timber and dressed stone for the repair of the temple of the LORD and met all the other expenses of restoring the temple The money brought

into the temple was not used for making silver basins, wick trimmers, sprinkling bowls, trumpets, or any other articles of gold or silver for the temple of the LORD. It was paid to the workmen, who used it to repair the temple. They did not require an accounting from those to whom they gave the money to pay the workers, because they acted with complete honesty. The money from the guilt offerings and sin offerings was not brought into the temple of the LORD; it belonged to the priests About this time Hazael, king of Aram, went up and attacked Gath and captured it. Then he turned to attack Jerusalem. But Joash, king of Judah, took all the sacred objects dedicated by his predecessors—Jehoshaphat, Jehoram, and Ahaziah, the kings of Judah—and the gifts he himself had dedicated and all the gold found in the treasuries of the temple of the LORD and of the royal palace, and he sent them to Hazael, king of Aram, who then withdrew from Jerusalem As for the other events of the reign of Joash, all he did, are they not written in the book of the annals of the kings of Judah? His officials conspired against him and assassinated him at Beth Millo, on the road down to Silla. The officials who murdered him were Jozabad son of Shimeath and Jehozabad son of Shomer. He died and was buried with his ancestors in the City of David, and Amaziah his son succeeded him as king

CHAPTER 13

In the twenty-third year of Joash son of Ahaziah, king of Judah, Jehoahaz son of Jehu became king of Israel in Samaria, and he reigned for seventeen years. He did evil in the eyes of the LORD by following the sins of Jeroboam son of Nebat, which he had caused Israel to commit, and he did not turn away from them. So the LORD's anger burned against Israel, and for a long time, he kept them under the power of Hazael king of Aram and Ben-Hadad his son Then Jehoahaz sought the LORD's favor, and the LORD listened to him, for he saw how severely the king of Aram was oppressing Israel. The LORD provided a deliverer for Israel, and they escaped from the power of Aram. So the Israelites lived in their own homes as they had before. But they did not turn away from the sins of the house of Jeroboam, which he had caused Israel to commit; they continued in them. Also, the Asherah pole remained standing in Samaria Nothing had been left of the army of Jehoahaz except fifty horsemen, ten chariots, and ten thousand foot soldiers, for the king of Aram had destroyed the rest and made them like the dust at threshing time. As for the other events of the reign of Jehoahaz, all he did and his achievements, are they not written in the book of the annals of the kings of Israel? Jehoahaz rested with his ancestors and was buried in Samaria. And Jehoash his son succeeded him as king In the thirty-seventh year of Joash king of Judah, Jehoash son of Jehoahaz became king of Israel in Samaria, and he reigned for sixteen years. He did evil in the eyes of the LORD and did not turn away from any of the sins of Jeroboam son of Nebat, which he had caused Israel to commit; he continued in them As for the other events of the reign of Jehoash, all he did, his achievements and his war against Amaziah king of Judah, are they not written in the book of the annals of the kings of Israel? Jehoash rested with his ancestors, and Jeroboam succeeded him on the throne. Jehoash was buried in Samaria with the kings of Israel Now Elisha had been suffering from the illness from which he died. Jehoash king of Israel went down to see him and wept over him. "My father, my father!" he cried. "The chariots and horsemen of Israel!" Elisha said, "Get a bow and some arrows," and he did so. "Take the bow in your hands," he said to the king of Israel. When he had taken it, Elisha put his hands on the king's hands. "Open the east window," he said, and he opened it. "Shoot!" Elisha said, and he shot. "The LORD's arrow of victory, the arrow of victory over Aram!" Elisha declared. "You will completely destroy the Arameans at Aphek." Then he said, "Take the arrows," and the king took them. Elisha told him, "Strike the ground." He struck it three times and stopped. The man of God was angry with him and said, "You should have struck the ground five or six times; then you would have defeated Aram and completely destroyed it. But now you will defeat it only three times." Elisha died and was buried Now Moabite raiders used to enter the country every spring. Once while some Israelites were burying a man, suddenly they saw a band of raiders; so they threw the man's body into Elisha's tomb. When the body touched Elisha's bones, the man came to life and stood up on his feet Hazael king of Aram oppressed Israel throughout the reign of Jehoahaz. But the LORD was gracious to them and had compassion and showed concern for them because of his covenant with Abraham, Isaac, and Jacob. To this day, he has been unwilling to destroy them or banish them from his presence Hazael king of Aram died, and Ben-Hadad his son succeeded him as king. Then Jehoash son of Jehoahaz recaptured from Ben-Hadad son of Hazael the towns he had taken in battle from his father Jehoahaz. Three times Jehoash defeated him, and so he recovered the Israelite towns

CHAPTER 14

In the second year of Jehoash son of Jehoahaz king of Israel, Amaziah son of Joash king of Judah began to reign. He was twenty-five years old when he became king, and he reigned in Jerusalem for twenty-nine years. His mother's name was Jehoaddin; she was from Jerusalem. He did what was right in the eyes of the LORD, but not as his ancestor David had done. In everything he followed the example of his father Joash. The high places, however, were not removed; the people continued to offer sacrifices and burn incense there After the kingdom was firmly in his grasp, he executed the officials who had murdered his father the king. Yet he did not put the children of the assassins to death, in accordance with what is written in the Book of the Law of Moses, where the LORD commanded: "Parents are not to be put to death for their children, nor children put to death for their parents; each will die for their own sin." He was the one who defeated ten thousand Edomites in the Valley of Salt and captured Sela in battle, calling it Joktheel, the name it has to this day Then Amaziah sent messengers to Jehoash son of Jehoahaz son of Jehu, king of Israel, with the challenge: "Come, let us face each other in battle." But Jehoash king of Israel replied to Amaziah king of Judah: "A thistle in Lebanon sent a message to a cedar in Lebanon, 'Give your daughter to my son in marriage.' Then a wild beast in Lebanon came along and trampled the thistle underfoot. You have indeed defeated Edom and now you are arrogant. Glory in your victory, but stay at home! Why ask for trouble and cause your own downfall and that of Judah also?" Amaziah, however, would not listen, so Jehoash king of Israel attacked. He and Amaziah king of Judah faced each other at Beth Shemesh in Judah. Judah was routed by Israel, and every man fled to his home. Jehoash king of Israel captured Amaziah king of Judah, the son of Joash, the son of Ahaziah, at Beth Shemesh. Then Jehoash went to Jerusalem and broke down the wall of Jerusalem from the Ephraim Gate to the Corner Gate—a section about four hundred cubits long. He took all the gold and silver and all the articles found in the temple of the LORD and in the treasuries of the royal palace. He also took hostages and returned to Samaria As for the other events of the reign of Jehoash, what he did and his achievements, including his war against Amaziah king of Judah, are they not written in the book of the annals of the kings of Israel? Jehoash rested with his ancestors and was buried in Samaria with the kings of Israel. And Jeroboam his son succeeded him as king Amaziah son of Joash king of Judah lived for fifteen years after the death of Jehoash son of Jehoahaz king of Israel. As for the other events of Amaziah's reign, are they not written in the book of the annals of the kings of Judah? They conspired against him in Jerusalem, and he fled to Lachish, but they sent men after him to Lachish and killed him there. He was brought back by horse and was buried in Jerusalem with his ancestors, in the City of David. Then all the people of Judah took Azariah, who was sixteen years old, and made him king in place of his father Amaziah. He was the one who rebuilt Elath and restored it to Judah after Amaziah rested with his ancestors In the fifteenth year of Amaziah son of Joash king of Judah, Jeroboam son of Jehoash king of Israel began to reign in Samaria, and he reigned for forty-one years. He did evil in the eyes of the LORD and did not turn away from any of the sins of Jeroboam son of Nebat, which he had caused Israel to commit. He was the one who restored the boundaries of Israel from Lebo Hamath to the Dead Sea, in accordance with the word of the LORD, the God of Israel, spoken through his servant Jonah son of Amittai, the prophet from Gath Hepher. The LORD had seen how bitterly everyone in Israel, whether slave or free, was suffering; there was no one to help them. And since the LORD had not said he would blot out the name of Israel from under heaven, he saved them by the hand of Jeroboam son of Jehoash As for the other events of Jeroboam's reign, all he did and his military achievements, including how he recovered for Israel both Damascus and Hamath, which had belonged to Judah, are they not written in the book of the annals of the kings of Israel? Jeroboam rested with his ancestors, the kings of Israel. And Zechariah his son succeeded him as king

CHAPTER 15

In the twenty-seventh year of Jeroboam king of Israel, Azariah son of Amaziah king of Judah began to reign. He was sixteen years old when he became king, and he reigned in Jerusalem for fifty-two years. His mother's name was Jecoliah; she was from Jerusalem. He did what was right in the eyes of the LORD, just as his father Amaziah had done. The high places, however, were not removed; the people continued to offer sacrifices and burn incense there. The LORD afflicted the king with leprosy until the day he died, and he lived in a separate house. Jotham the king's son had charge of the palace and governed the people of the land As for the other events of Azariah's reign, and all he did, are they not written in the book of the annals of the kings of Judah? Azariah rested with his ancestors and was buried near them in the City of David. And Jotham his son succeeded him as king In the thirty-eighth year of Azariah king of Judah, Zechariah son of Jeroboam became king of Israel in Samaria, and he reigned for six months. He did evil in the eyes of the LORD, as his predecessors had done. He did not turn away from the sins of Jeroboam son of Nebat, which he had caused Israel to commit. Shallum son of Jabesh conspired against Zechariah. He attacked him in front of the people, assassinated him, and succeeded him as king. The other events of Zechariah's reign are written in the book of the annals of the kings of Israel. So the word of the LORD spoken to Jehu was fulfilled: "Your descendants will sit on the throne of Israel to the fourth generation." Shallum son of Jabesh became king in the thirty-ninth year of Uzziah king of Judah, and he reigned in

Samaria for one month. Then Menahem son of Gadi went up from Tirzah to Samaria. He attacked Shallum son of Jabesh in Samaria, assassinated him, and succeeded him as king. The other events of Shallum's reign, and the conspiracy he led, are written in the book of the annals of the kings of Israel. At that time Menahem, starting out from Tirzah, attacked Tiphsah and everyone in the city and its vicinity, because they refused to open their gates. He sacked Tiphsah and ripped open all the pregnant women In the thirty-ninth year of Azariah king of Judah, Menahem son of Gadi became king of Israel, and he reigned in Samaria for ten years. He did evil in the eyes of the LORD. During his entire reign, he did not turn away from the sins of Jeroboam son of Nebat, which he had caused Israel to commit. Then Pul king of Assyria invaded the land, and Menahem gave him a thousand talents of silver to gain his support and strengthen his own hold on the kingdom. Menahem exacted this money from Israel. Every wealthy person had to contribute fifty shekels of silver to be given to the king of Assyria. So the king of Assyria withdrew and stayed in the land no longer As for the other events of Menahem's reign, and all he did, are they not written in the book of the annals of the kings of Israel? Menahem rested with his ancestors. And Pekahiah his son succeeded him as king In the fiftieth year of Azariah king of Judah, Pekahiah son of Menahem became king of Israel in Samaria, and he reigned for two years. Pekahiah did evil in the eyes of the LORD. He did not turn away from the sins of Jeroboam son of Nebat, which he had caused Israel to commit. One of his chief officers, Pekah son of Remaliah, conspired against him. Taking fifty men of Gilead with him, he assassinated Pekahiah, along with Argob and Arieh, in the citadel of the royal palace at Samaria. So Pekah killed Pekahiah and succeeded him as king The other events of Pekahiah's reign, and all he did, are written in the book of the annals of the kings of Israel In the fifty-second year of Azariah king of Judah, Pekah son of Remaliah became king of Israel in Samaria, and he reigned for twenty years. He did evil in the eyes of the LORD. He did not turn away from the sins of Jeroboam son of Nebat, which he had caused Israel to commit. In the time of Pekah king of Israel, Tiglath-Pileser king of Assyria came and took Ijon, Abel Beth Maakah, Janoah, Kedesh, and Hazor. He also took Gilead and Galilee, including all the land of Naphtali, and deported the people to Assyria. Then Hoshea son of Elah conspired against Pekah son of Remaliah. He attacked and assassinated him, and then succeeded him as king in the twentieth year of Jotham son of Uzziah As for the other events of Pekah's reign, and all he did, are they not written in the book of the annals of the kings of Israel? In the second year of Pekah son of Remaliah king of Israel, Jotham son of Uzziah king of Judah began to reign. He was twenty-five years old when he became king, and he reigned in Jerusalem for sixteen years. His mother's name was Jerusha daughter of Zadok. He did what was right in the eyes of the LORD, just as his father Uzziah had done. The high places, however, were not removed; the people continued to offer sacrifices and burn incense there. Jotham rebuilt the Upper Gate of the temple of the LORD As for the other events of Jotham's reign, and what he did, are they not written in the book of the annals of the kings of Judah? (In those days the LORD began to send Rezin king of Aram and Pekah son of Remaliah against Judah.) Jotham rested with his ancestors and was buried with them in the City of David, the city of his father. And Ahaz his son succeeded him as king

CHAPTER 16

In the seventeenth year of Pekah, the son of Remaliah, Ahaz, the son of Jotham, king of Judah, began to reign. Ahaz was twenty years old when he began to reign, and he reigned for sixteen years in Jerusalem. He did not do what was right in the eyes of the LORD his God, unlike his ancestor David. Instead, he followed the ways of the kings of Israel and even made his son pass through the fire, following the abominations of the nations the LORD had driven out before the Israelites. He offered sacrifices and burned incense on the high places, on the hills, and under every spreading tree Rezin, king of Aram, and Pekah, son of Remaliah, king of Israel, came to Jerusalem to wage war; they besieged Ahaz but could not overpower him. At that time, Rezin, king of Aram, recovered Elath for Aram by driving out the people of Judah and settled the Arameans there to this day Ahaz sent messengers to Tiglath-Pileser, king of Assyria, saying, "I am your servant and your son. Come up and save me from the hand of the king of Aram and the king of Israel, who are attacking me." Ahaz took the silver and gold found in the temple of the LORD and in the treasuries of the royal palace and sent it as a gift to the king of Assyria. The king of Assyria complied by attacking Damascus, capturing it, and deporting its inhabitants to Kir; he also killed Rezin King Ahaz went to Damascus to meet Tiglath-Pileser, king of Assyria. While he was there, he saw an altar in Damascus and sent the priest Uriah a sketch of the altar with detailed plans for its construction. Uriah the priest built an altar according to all the plans that King Ahaz had sent from Damascus and finished it before King Ahaz returned. When the king came back from Damascus and saw the altar, he approached it and presented offerings on it. He offered his burnt offering and grain offering, poured out his drink offering, and splashed the blood of his fellowship offerings against the altar. The bronze altar that stood before the LORD he brought from the front of the temple—from between the new altar and the temple of the LORD—and put it on the north side of the new altar King Ahaz then gave orders to Uriah the priest: "On the large new altar, offer the morning burnt offering and the evening grain offering, the king's burnt offering and his grain offering, and the burnt offering of all the people of the land, their grain offering, and their drink offering. Splash against this altar the blood of all the burnt offerings and sacrifices. But I will use the bronze altar for seeking guidance." And Uriah the priest did just as King Ahaz had ordered King Ahaz cut off the side panels and removed the basins from the movable stands. He removed the Sea from the bronze bulls that supported it and set it on a stone base. He took away the Sabbath canopy that had been built at the temple and removed the royal entryway outside the temple of the LORD, to please the king of Assyria As for the other events of the reign of Ahaz, and what he did, are they not written in the book of the annals of the kings of Judah? Ahaz rested with his ancestors and was buried with them in the City of David. And Hezekiah his son succeeded him as king

CHAPTER 17

In the twelfth year of Ahaz, king of Judah, Hoshea son of Elah became king of Israel in Samaria, and he reigned for nine years. He did evil in the eyes of the LORD, but not like the kings of Israel who preceded him. Shalmaneser, king of Assyria, came up to attack Hoshea, who had been Shalmaneser's vassal and had paid him tribute. But the king of Assyria discovered that Hoshea was a traitor, for he had sent envoys to So king of Egypt, and he no longer paid tribute to the king of Assyria, as he had done year by year. Therefore Shalmaneser seized him and put him in prison The king of Assyria invaded the entire land, marched against Samaria, and laid siege to it for three years. In the ninth year of Hoshea, the king of Assyria captured Samaria and deported the Israelites to Assyria. He settled them in Halah, in Gozan on the Habor River, and in the towns of the Medes All this took place because the Israelites had sinned against the LORD their God, who had brought them up out of Egypt from under the power of Pharaoh king of Egypt. They worshiped other gods and followed the practices of the nations the LORD had driven out before them, as well as the practices that the kings of Israel had introduced. The Israelites secretly did things against the LORD their God that were not right. From watchtower to fortified city they built themselves high places in all their towns. They set up sacred stones and Asherah poles on every high hill and under every spreading tree. At every high place they burned incense, as the nations whom the LORD had driven out before them had done. They did wicked things that aroused the LORD's anger. They worshiped idols, though the LORD had said, "You shall not do this." The LORD warned Israel and Judah through all his prophets and seers: "Turn from your evil ways. Observe my commands and decrees in accordance with the entire Law that I commanded your ancestors to obey and that I delivered to you through my servants the prophets." But they would not listen and were as stiff-necked as their ancestors, who did not trust in the LORD their God. They rejected his decrees and the covenant he had made with their ancestors and the statutes he had warned them to keep. They followed worthless idols and themselves became worthless. They imitated the nations around them, although the LORD had ordered them, "Do not do as they do." They forsook all the commands of the LORD their God and made for themselves two idols cast in the shape of calves, and an Asherah pole. They bowed down to all the starry hosts, and they worshiped Baal. They sacrificed their sons and daughters in the fire. They practiced divination and sought omens and sold themselves to do evil in the eyes of the LORD, arousing his anger. So the LORD was very angry with Israel and removed them from his presence. Only the tribe of Judah was left, and even Judah did not keep the commands of the LORD their God. They followed the practices Israel had introduced. Therefore the LORD rejected all the people of Israel; he afflicted them and gave them into the hands of plunderers, until he thrust them from his presence When he tore Israel away from the house of David, they made Jeroboam son of Nebat their king. Jeroboam enticed Israel away from following the LORD and caused them to commit a great sin. The Israelites persisted in all the sins of Jeroboam and did not turn away from them until the LORD removed them from his presence, as he had warned through all his servants the prophets. So the people of Israel were taken from their homeland into exile in Assyria, and they are still there The king of Assyria brought people from Babylon, Kuthah, Avva, Hamath, and Sepharvaim and settled them in the towns of Samaria to replace the Israelites. They took over Samaria and lived in its towns. When they first lived there, they did not worship the LORD; so he sent lions among them, and they killed some of the people. It was reported to the king of Assyria: "The people you deported and resettled in the towns of Samaria do not know what the god of that country requires. He has sent lions among them, which are killing them off because the people do not know what he requires." Then the king of Assyria gave this order: "Have one of the priests you took captive from Samaria go back to live there and teach the people what the god of the land

requires." So one of the priests who had been exiled from Samaria came to live in Bethel and taught them how to worship the LORD Nevertheless, each national group made its own gods in the several towns where they settled and set them up in the shrines the people of Samaria had made at the high places. The people from Babylon made Sukkoth Benoth, those from Kuthah made Nergal, and those from Hamath made Ashima; the Avvites made Nibhaz and Tartak, and the Sepharvites burned their children in the fire as sacrifices to Adrammelek and Anammelek, the gods of Sepharvaim. They worshiped the LORD, but they also appointed all sorts of their own people to officiate for them as priests in the shrines at the high places. They worshiped the LORD, but they also served their own gods in accordance with the customs of the nations from which they had been brought To this day they persist in their former practices. They neither worship the LORD nor adhere to the decrees and regulations, the laws and commands that the LORD gave the descendants of Jacob, whom he named Israel. When the LORD made a covenant with the Israelites, he commanded them: "Do not worship any other gods or bow down to them, serve them, or sacrifice to them. But the LORD, who brought you up out of Egypt with mighty power and outstretched arm, is the one you must worship. To him you shall bow down and to him offer sacrifices. You must always be careful to keep the decrees and regulations, the laws and commands he wrote for you. Do not worship other gods. Do not forget the covenant I have made with you, and do not worship other gods. Rather, worship the LORD your God; it is he who will deliver you from the hand of all your enemies." They would not listen, however, but persisted in their former practices. Even while these people were worshiping the LORD, they were serving their idols. To this day their children and grandchildren continue to do as their ancestors did

CHAPTER 18

In the third year of Hoshea son of Elah, king of Israel, Hezekiah son of Ahaz, king of Judah, began to reign. He was twenty-five years old when he became king, and he reigned in Jerusalem for twenty-nine years. His mother's name was Abi, daughter of Zechariah. He did what was right in the eyes of the LORD, just as his father David had done. He removed the high places, smashed the sacred stones, and cut down the Asherah poles. He broke into pieces the bronze snake Moses had made, for up to that time the Israelites had been burning incense to it. (It was called Nehushtan.) Hezekiah trusted in the LORD, the God of Israel. There was no one like him among all the kings of Judah, either before him or after him. He held fast to the LORD and did not stop following him; he kept the commands the LORD had given Moses. And the LORD was with him; he was successful in whatever he undertook. He rebelled against the king of Assyria and did not serve him. From watchtower to fortified city, he defeated the Philistines as far as Gaza and its territory In King Hezekiah's fourth year, which was the seventh year of Hoshea son of Elah king of Israel, Shalmaneser king of Assyria marched against Samaria and laid siege to it. At the end of three years, the Assyrians took it. So Samaria was captured in Hezekiah's sixth year, which was the ninth year of Hoshea king of Israel. The king of Assyria deported Israel to Assyria and settled them in Halah, in Gozan on the Habor River, and in the towns of the Medes. This happened because they had not obeyed the LORD their God, but had violated his covenant—all that Moses the servant of the LORD commanded. They neither listened to the commands nor carried them out In the fourteenth year of King Hezekiah's reign, Sennacherib king of Assyria attacked all the fortified cities of Judah and captured them. So Hezekiah king of Judah sent this message to the king of Assyria at Lachish: "I have done wrong. Withdraw from me, and I will pay whatever you demand of me." The king of Assyria exacted from Hezekiah king of Judah three hundred talents of silver and thirty talents of gold. So Hezekiah gave him all the silver that was found in the temple of the LORD and in the treasuries of the royal palace. At this time, Hezekiah king of Judah stripped off the gold with which he had covered the doors and doorposts of the temple of the LORD and gave it to the king of Assyria The king of Assyria sent his supreme commander, his chief officer, and his field commander with a large army from Lachish to King Hezekiah at Jerusalem. They came up to Jerusalem and stopped at the aqueduct of the Upper Pool, on the road to the Washerman's Field. They called for the king; and Eliakim son of Hilkiah the palace administrator, Shebna the secretary, and Joah son of Asaph the recorder went out to them The field commander said to them, "Tell Hezekiah: 'This is what the great king, the king of Assyria, says: On what are you basing this confidence of yours? You say you have the counsel and the might for war—but you speak only empty words. On whom are you depending, that you rebel against me? Look, I know you are depending on Egypt, that splintered reed of a staff, which pierces the hand of anyone who leans on it! Such is Pharaoh king of Egypt to all who depend on him. But if you say to me, "We are depending on the LORD our God"—isn't he the one whose high places and altars Hezekiah removed, saying to Judah and Jerusalem, "You must worship before this altar in Jerusalem"? "'Come now, make a bargain with my master, the king of Assyria: I will give you two thousand horses—if you can put riders on them! How can you repulse one officer of the least of my master's officials, even though you are depending on Egypt for chariots and horsemen? Furthermore, have I come to attack and destroy this place without word from the LORD? The LORD himself told me to march against this country and destroy it.'" Then Eliakim son of Hilkiah, and Shebna and Joah, said to the field commander, "Please speak to your servants in Aramaic, since we understand it. Don't speak to us in Hebrew in the hearing of the people on the wall." But the commander replied, "Was it only to your master and you that my master sent me to say these things, and not to the people sitting on the wall—who, like you, will have to eat their own excrement and drink their own urine?" Then the commander stood and called out in Hebrew, "Hear the word of the great king, the king of Assyria! This is what the king says: Do not let Hezekiah deceive you. He cannot deliver you from my hand. Do not let Hezekiah persuade you to trust in the LORD when he says, 'The LORD will surely deliver us. This city will not be given into the hand of the king of Assyria.' Do not listen to Hezekiah. This is what the king of Assyria says: Make peace with me and come out to me. Then each of you will eat fruit from your own vine and fig tree and drink water from your own cistern, until I come and take you to a land like your own—a land of grain and new wine, a land of bread and vineyards, a land of olive trees and honey. Choose life and not death! "Do not listen to Hezekiah, for he is misleading you when he says, 'The LORD will deliver us.' Has the god of any nation ever delivered his land from the hand of the king of Assyria? Where are the gods of Hamath and Arpad? Where are the gods of Sepharvaim, Hena, and Ivvah? Have they rescued Samaria from my hand? Who of all the gods of these countries has been able to save his land from me?

How then can the LORD deliver Jerusalem from my hand?" But the people remained silent and said nothing in reply, because the king had commanded, "Do not answer him." Then Eliakim son of Hilkiah the palace administrator, Shebna the secretary, and Joah son of Asaph the recorder went to Hezekiah, with their clothes torn, and told him what the field commander had said

CHAPTER 19

When King Hezekiah heard this, he tore his clothes and put on sackcloth and went into the temple of the LORD. He sent Eliakim the palace administrator, Shebna the secretary, and the leading priests, all wearing sackcloth, to the prophet Isaiah son of Amoz. They told him, "This is what Hezekiah says: This day is a day of distress and rebuke and disgrace, as when children come to the moment of birth and there is no strength to deliver them. It may be that the LORD your God will hear all the words of the field commander, whom his master, the king of Assyria, has sent to ridicule the living God, and that he will rebuke him for the words the LORD your God has heard. Therefore pray for the remnant that still survives." When King Hezekiah's officials came to Isaiah, Isaiah said to them, "Tell your master, 'This is what the LORD says: Do not be afraid of what you have heard—those words with which the underlings of the king of Assyria have blasphemed me. Listen! When he hears a certain report, I will make him want to return to his own country, and there I will have him cut down with the sword.'" When the field commander heard that the king of Assyria had left Lachish, he withdrew and found the king fighting against Libnah. Now Sennacherib received a report that Tirhakah, the king of Cush, was marching out to fight against him. So he again sent messengers to Hezekiah with this word: "Say to Hezekiah king of Judah: Do not let the god you depend on deceive you when he says, 'Jerusalem will not be given into the hands of the king of Assyria.' Surely you have heard what the kings of Assyria have done to all the countries, destroying them completely. And will you be delivered? Did the gods of the nations that were destroyed by my predecessors deliver them—the gods of Gozan, Haran, Rezeph, and the people of Eden who were in Tel Assar? Where is the king of Hamath or the king of Arpad? Where are the kings of Lair, Sepharvaim, Hena, and Ivvah?" Hezekiah received the letter from the messengers and read it. Then he went up to the temple of the LORD and spread it out before the LORD. And Hezekiah prayed to the LORD: "LORD, the God of Israel, enthroned between the cherubim, you alone are God over all the kingdoms of the earth. You have made heaven and earth. Give ear, LORD, and hear; open your eyes, LORD, and see; listen to the words Sennacherib has sent to ridicule the living God "It is true, LORD, that the Assyrian kings have laid waste these nations and their lands. They have thrown their gods into the fire and destroyed them, for they were not gods but only wood and stone, fashioned by human hands. Now, LORD our God, deliver us from his hand, so that all the kingdoms of the earth may know that you alone, LORD, are God." Then Isaiah son of Amoz sent a message to Hezekiah: "This is what the LORD, the God of Israel, says: I have heard your prayer concerning Sennacherib king of Assyria. This is the word that the LORD has spoken against him: "'Virgin Daughter Zion despises you and mocks you. Daughter Jerusalem tosses her head as you flee. Who is it you have ridiculed and blasphemed? Against whom have you raised your voice and lifted your eyes in pride? Against the Holy One of Israel! By your messengers you have ridiculed the Lord. And you have said, "With my many chariots I have ascended the heights of the mountains, the utmost heights of Lebanon. I have cut down its tallest cedars, the choicest of its junipers. I have reached its remotest parts, the finest of its forests. I have dug wells in foreign lands and drunk the water there. With the soles of my feet I have dried up all the streams of Egypt.'" "'Have you not heard? Long ago I ordained it. In days of old I planned it; now I have brought it to pass, that you have turned fortified cities into piles of stone. Their people, drained of power, are dismayed and put to shame. They are like plants in the field, like tender green shoots, like grass sprouting on the roof, scorched before it grows up '"But I know where you are and when you come and go and how you rage against me. Because you rage against me and because your insolence has reached my ears, I will put my hook in your nose and my bit in your mouth, and I will make you return by the way you came.' "This will be the sign for you, Hezekiah: "This year you will eat what grows by itself, and the second year what springs from that. But in the third year sow and reap, plant vineyards and eat their fruit. Once more a remnant of the kingdom of Judah will take root below and bear fruit above. For out of Jerusalem will come a remnant, and out of Mount Zion a band of survivors. The zeal of the LORD Almighty will accomplish this "Therefore this is what the LORD says concerning the king of Assyria: "He will not enter this city or shoot an arrow here. He will not come before it with a shield or build a siege ramp against it. By the way that he came he will return; he will not enter this city, declares the LORD. I will defend this city and save it, for my sake and for the sake of David my servant." That night the angel of the LORD went out and put to death a hundred and eighty-five thousand in the Assyrian camp. When the people got up the next morning—there were all the dead bodies! So Sennacherib king of Assyria broke camp and withdrew. He returned to Nineveh and stayed there One day, while he was worshiping in the temple of his god Nisrok, his sons Adrammelek and Sharezer killed him with the sword, and they escaped to the land of Ararat. And Esarhaddon his son succeeded him as king

CHAPTER 20

In those days Hezekiah became ill and was at the point of death. The prophet Isaiah son of Amoz went to him and said, "This is what the LORD says: Put your house in order, because you are going to die; you will not recover." Hezekiah turned his face to the wall and prayed to the LORD, "Remember, LORD, how I have walked before you faithfully and with wholehearted devotion and have done what is good in your eyes." And Hezekiah wept bitterly Before Isaiah had left the middle court, the word of the LORD came to him: "Go back and tell Hezekiah, the ruler of my people, 'This is what the LORD, the God of your father David, says: I have heard your prayer and seen your tears; I will heal you. On the third day from now you will go up to the temple of the LORD. I will add fifteen years to your life. And I will deliver you and this city from the hand of the king of Assyria. I will defend this city for my sake and for the sake of my servant David.'" Then Isaiah said, "Prepare a poultice of figs." They did so and applied it to the boil, and he recovered Hezekiah had asked Isaiah, "What will be the sign that the LORD will heal me and that I will go up to the temple of the LORD on the third day from now?" Isaiah answered, "This is the LORD's sign to you that the LORD will do what he has promised: Shall the shadow go forward ten steps, or shall it go back ten steps?" "It is a simple matter for the shadow to go forward ten steps," said Hezekiah. "Rather, have it go back ten steps." Then the prophet Isaiah called on the LORD, and the LORD made the shadow go back the ten steps it had gone down on the stairway

of Ahaz At that time Marduk-Baladan son of Baladan king of Babylon sent Hezekiah letters and a gift, because he had heard of Hezekiah's illness. Hezekiah received the envoys and showed them all that was in his storehouses—the silver, the gold, the spices, and the fine olive oil—his armory and everything found among his treasures. There was nothing in his palace or in all his kingdom that Hezekiah did not show them Then Isaiah the prophet went to King Hezekiah and asked, "What did those men say, and where did they come from?" "From a distant land," Hezekiah replied. "They came from Babylon." The prophet asked, "What did they see in your palace?" "They saw everything in my palace," Hezekiah said. "There is nothing among my treasures that I did not show them." Then Isaiah said to Hezekiah, "Hear the word of the LORD: The time will surely come when everything in your palace, and all that your predecessors have stored up until this day, will be carried off to Babylon. Nothing will be left, says the LORD. And some of your descendants, your own flesh and blood who will be born to you, will be taken away, and they will become eunuchs in the palace of the king of Babylon." "The word of the LORD you have spoken is good," Hezekiah replied. For he thought, "Will there not be peace and security in my lifetime?" As for the other events of Hezekiah's reign, all his achievements and how he made the pool and the tunnel by which he brought water into the city, are they not written in the book of the annals of the kings of Judah? Hezekiah rested with his ancestors. And Manasseh his son succeeded him as king

CHAPTER 21

Manasseh was twelve years old when he began to reign and reigned fifty-five years in Jerusalem; his mother's name was Hephzibah. He did evil in the eyes of the LORD, following the detestable practices of the nations the LORD had driven out before the Israelites. He rebuilt the high places his father Hezekiah had destroyed; he erected altars to Baal and made an Asherah pole, as Ahab king of Israel had done. He bowed down to all the starry hosts and worshipped them. He built altars in the temple of the LORD, of which the LORD had said, "In Jerusalem I will put my Name." In the two courts of the temple of the LORD, he built altars to all the starry hosts. He sacrificed his own son in the fire, practiced divination, sought omens, and consulted mediums and spiritists. He did much evil in the eyes of the LORD, arousing his anger He took the carved Asherah pole he had made and put it in the temple, of which the LORD had said to David and to his son Solomon, "In this temple and in Jerusalem, which I have chosen out of all the tribes of Israel, I will put my Name forever. I will not again make the feet of the Israelites wander from the land I gave their ancestors, if only they will be careful to do everything I commanded them and will keep the whole Law that my servant Moses gave them." But the people did not listen. Manasseh led them astray, so that they did more evil than the nations the LORD had destroyed before the Israelites The LORD said through his servants the prophets: "Manasseh king of Judah has committed these detestable sins. He has done more evil than the Amorites who preceded him and has led Judah into sin with his idols. Therefore this is what the LORD, the God of Israel, says: I am going to bring such disaster on Jerusalem and Judah that the ears of everyone who hears of it will tingle. I will stretch out over Jerusalem the measuring line used against Samaria and the plumb line used against the house of Ahab. I will wipe out Jerusalem as one wipes a dish, wiping it and turning it upside down. I will forsake the remnant of my inheritance and give them into the hands of enemies. They will be looted and plundered by all their enemies; they have done evil in my eyes and have aroused my anger from the day their ancestors came out of Egypt until this day." Moreover, Manasseh also shed so much innocent blood that he filled Jerusalem from end to end—besides the sin that he had caused Judah to commit, so that they did evil in the eyes of the LORD. As for the other events of Manasseh's reign, all he did, and the sin he committed, are they not written in the book of the annals of the kings of Judah? Manasseh rested with his ancestors and was buried in the palace garden, the garden of Uzza. And Amon his son succeeded him as king Amon was twenty-two years old when he became king, and he reigned in Jerusalem two years. His mother's name was Meshullemeth daughter of Haruz; she was from Jotbah. He did evil in the eyes of the LORD, as his father Manasseh had done. He followed completely the ways of his father, worshipping the idols his father had worshipped, and bowing down to them. He forsook the LORD, the God of his ancestors, and did not walk in obedience to him. Amon's officials conspired against him and assassinated the king in his palace. Then the people of the land killed all who had plotted against King Amon, and they made Josiah his son king in his place As for the other events of Amon's reign, what he did, are they not written in the book of the annals of the kings of Judah? He was buried in his tomb in the garden of Uzza. And Josiah his son succeeded him as king

CHAPTER 22

Josiah was eight years old when he became king, and he reigned in Jerusalem thirty-one years. His mother's name was Jedidah daughter of Adaiah; she was from Bozkath. He did what was right in the eyes of the LORD and followed completely the ways of his father David, not turning aside to the right or to the left In the eighteenth year of his reign, King Josiah sent the secretary, Shaphan son of Azaliah, the son of Meshullam, to the temple of the LORD. He said: "Go up to Hilkiah the high priest and have him get ready the money that has been brought into the temple of the LORD, which the doorkeepers have collected from the people. Have them entrust it to the men appointed to supervise the work on the temple. And have these men pay the workers who repair the temple of the LORD—the carpenters, the builders, and the masons. Also have them purchase timber and dressed stone to repair the temple. But they need not account for the money entrusted to them, because they are honest in their dealings." Hilkiah the high priest said to Shaphan the secretary, "I have found the Book of the Law in the temple of the LORD." He gave it to Shaphan, who read it. Then Shaphan the secretary went to the king and reported to him: "Your officials have paid out the money that was in the temple of the LORD and have entrusted it to the workers and supervisors at the temple." Then Shaphan the secretary informed the king, "Hilkiah the priest has given me a book." And Shaphan read from it in the presence of the king When the king heard the words of the Book of the Law, he tore his robes. He gave these orders to Hilkiah the priest, Ahikam son of Shaphan, Akbor son of Micaiah, Shaphan the secretary, and Asaiah the king's attendant: "Go and inquire of the LORD for me and for the people and for all Judah about what is written in this book that has been found. Great is the LORD's anger that burns against us because those who have gone before us have not obeyed the words of this book; they have not acted in accordance with all that is written there concerning us." Hilkiah the priest, Ahikam, Akbor, Shaphan, and Asaiah went to speak to the prophet Huldah, who was the wife of Shallum son of Tikvah, the son of Harhas, keeper of the wardrobe. She lived in Jerusalem, in the New Quarter. She said to them, "This is what the LORD, the God of Israel, says: Tell the man who sent you to me, 'This is what the LORD says: I am going to bring disaster on this place and its people, according to everything written in the book the king of Judah has read. Because they have forsaken me and burned incense to other gods and aroused my anger by all the idols their hands have made, my anger will burn against this place and will not be quenched.' Tell the king of Judah, who sent you to inquire of the LORD, 'This is what the LORD, the God of Israel, says concerning the words you heard: Because your heart was responsive and you humbled yourself before the LORD when you heard what I have spoken against this place and its people—that they would become a curse and be laid waste—and because you tore your robes and wept in my presence, I also have heard you, declares the LORD. Therefore, I will gather you to your ancestors, and you will be buried in peace. Your eyes will not see all the disaster I am going to bring on this place.'" So they took her answer back to the king

CHAPTER 23

Then the king called together all the elders of Judah and Jerusalem. He went up to the temple of the LORD with the people of Judah, the inhabitants of Jerusalem, the priests, and the prophets—all the people from the least to the greatest. He read in their hearing all the words of the Book of the Covenant, which had been found in the temple of the LORD. The king stood by the pillar and renewed the covenant in the presence of the LORD—to follow the LORD and keep his commands, statutes, and decrees with all his heart and all his soul, thus confirming the words of the covenant written in this book. Then all the people pledged themselves to the covenant The king ordered Hilkiah the high priest, the priests next in rank, and the doorkeepers to remove from the temple of the LORD all the articles made for Baal and Asherah and all the starry hosts. He burned them outside Jerusalem in the fields of the Kidron Valley and took the ashes to Bethel. He did away with the idolatrous priests appointed by the kings of Judah to burn incense on the high places of the towns of Judah and on those around Jerusalem—those who burned incense to Baal, to the sun and moon, to the constellations, and to all the starry hosts. He took the Asherah pole from the temple of the LORD to the Kidron Valley outside Jerusalem and burned it there. He ground it to powder and scattered the dust over the graves of the common people. He also tore down the quarters of the male shrine prostitutes that were in the temple of the LORD—the quarters where women did weaving for Asherah Josiah brought all the priests from the towns of Judah and desecrated the high places, from Geba to Beersheba, where the priests had burned incense. He broke down the gateway at the entrance of the Gate of Joshua, the city governor, which was on the left of the city gate. Although the priests of the high places did not serve at the altar of the LORD in Jerusalem, they ate unleavened bread with their fellow priests. He desecrated Topheth, which was in the Valley of Ben Hinnom, so no one could use it to sacrifice their son or daughter in the fire to Molek. He removed from the entrance to the temple of the LORD the horses that the kings of Judah had dedicated to the sun. They were in the court near the room of an official named Nathan-Melek. Josiah then burned the chariots dedicated to the sun He pulled down the altars the kings of Judah had erected on the roof near the upper room of Ahaz, and the altars Manasseh had built in the two courts of the temple of the LORD. He removed them from there, smashed them to pieces, and threw the rubble into the Kidron Valley. The king also desecrated the high places that were east of Jerusalem on the south of the Hill of Corruption—the ones Solomon king of Israel had built for Ashtoreth the vile goddess of the Sidonians, for Chemosh the vile god of Moab, and for Molek the detestable god of the people of Ammon. Josiah smashed the sacred stones and cut down the Asherah poles and covered the sites with human bones Even the altar at Bethel, the high place made by Jeroboam son of Nebat, who had caused Israel to sin—even that altar and high place he demolished. He burned the high place and ground it to powder, and burned the Asherah pole also. Then Josiah looked around and when he saw the tombs that were there on the hillside, he had the bones removed from them and burned on the altar to defile it, in accordance with the word of the LORD proclaimed by the man of God who foretold these things. The king asked, "What is that tombstone I see?" The people of the city said, "It marks the tomb of the man of God who came from Judah and pronounced against the altar of Bethel the very things you have done to it." "Leave it alone," he said. "Don't let anyone disturb his bones." So they spared his bones and those of the prophet who had come from Samaria Just as he had done at Bethel, Josiah removed all the shrines at the high places that the kings of Israel had built in the towns of Samaria and that had aroused the LORD's anger. Josiah slaughtered all the priests of those high places on the altars and burned human bones on them. Then he went back to Jerusalem The king gave this order to all the people: "Celebrate the Passover to the LORD your God, as it is written in this Book of the Covenant." Neither in the days of the judges who led Israel nor in the days of the kings of Israel and the kings of Judah had any such Passover been observed. But in the eighteenth year of King Josiah, this Passover was celebrated to the LORD in Jerusalem Furthermore, Josiah got rid of the mediums and spiritists, the household gods, the idols, and all the other detestable things seen in Judah and Jerusalem. This he did to fulfill the requirements of the law written in the book that Hilkiah the priest had discovered in the temple of the LORD. Neither before nor after Josiah was there a king like him who turned to the LORD as he did—with all his heart and with all his soul and with all his strength, in accordance with all the Law of Moses Nevertheless, the LORD did not turn away from the heat of his fierce anger, which burned against Judah because of all that Manasseh had done to arouse his anger. So the LORD said, "I will remove Judah also from my presence as I removed Israel, and I will reject Jerusalem, the city I chose, and this temple, about which I said, 'My Name shall be there.'" As for the other events of Josiah's reign and all he did, are they not written in the book of the annals of the kings of Judah? While Josiah was king, Pharaoh Necho king of Egypt went up to the Euphrates River to help the king of Assyria. King Josiah marched out to meet him in battle, but Necho faced him and killed him at Megiddo. Josiah's servants brought his body in a chariot from Megiddo to Jerusalem and buried him in his own tomb. And the people of the land took Jehoahaz son of Josiah and anointed him and made him king in place of his father Jehoahaz was twenty-three years old when he became king, and he reigned in Jerusalem three months. His mother's name was Hamutal daughter of Jeremiah; she was from Libnah. He did evil in the eyes of the LORD, just as his predecessors had done. Pharaoh Necho put him in chains at Riblah in the land of Hamath so that he might not reign in Jerusalem; and he imposed on Judah a levy of a hundred talents of silver and a talent of gold. Pharaoh Necho made Eliakim son of Josiah king in place of his father Josiah and changed Eliakim's name to Jehoiakim. But he took Jehoahaz and carried him off to Egypt, and there he died. Jehoiakim paid Pharaoh Necho the silver and gold he demanded. In order to do so, he taxed the land and exacted the silver and gold from the people of the land according to their assessments Jehoiakim was twenty-five years old when he became king, and he reigned in Jerusalem eleven years. His mother's name was Zebidah daughter of Pedaiah; she was from Rumah. And he did evil in the eyes of the LORD, just as his predecessors had done

CHAPTER 24

During Jehoiakim's reign, Nebuchadnezzar king of Babylon invaded the land, and Jehoiakim became his vassal for three years. But then he turned against Nebuchadnezzar and rebelled. The LORD sent Babylonian, Aramean, Moabite, and Ammonite raiders against him to destroy Judah, in accordance with the word of the LORD proclaimed by his servants the prophets. Surely these things happened to Judah according to the LORD's command, in order to remove them from his presence because of the sins of Manasseh and all he had done, including the shedding of innocent blood. For he had filled Jerusalem with innocent blood, and the LORD was not willing to forgive As for the other events of Jehoiakim's reign, and all he did, are they not written in the book of the annals of the kings of Judah? Jehoiakim rested with his ancestors. And Jehoiachin his son succeeded him as king The king of Egypt did not march out from his own country again, because the king of Babylon had taken all his territory, from the Wadi of Egypt to the Euphrates River Jehoiachin was eighteen years old when he became king, and he reigned in Jerusalem three months. His mother's name was Nehushta daughter of Elnathan; she was from Jerusalem. He did evil in the eyes of the LORD, just as his father had done At that time the officers of Nebuchadnezzar king of Babylon advanced on Jerusalem and laid siege to it, and Nebuchadnezzar himself came up to the city while his officers were besieging it. Jehoiachin king of Judah, his mother, his attendants, his nobles, and his officials all surrendered to him. In the eighth year of the reign of the king of Babylon, he took Jehoiachin prisoner. As the LORD had declared, Nebuchadnezzar removed all the treasures from the temple of the LORD and from the royal palace and cut up the gold articles that Solomon king of Israel had made for the temple of the LORD. He carried all Jerusalem into exile: all the officers and fighting men, and all the skilled workers and artisans—a total of ten thousand. Only the poorest people of the land were left Nebuchadnezzar took Jehoiachin captive to Babylon. He also took from Jerusalem to Babylon the king's mother, his wives, his officials, and the prominent people of the land. The king of Babylon also deported to Babylon the entire force of seven thousand fighting men, strong and fit for war, and a thousand skilled workers and artisans. He made Mattaniah, Jehoiachin's uncle, king in his place and changed his name to Zedekiah Zedekiah was twenty-one years old when he became king, and he reigned in Jerusalem eleven years. His mother's name was Hamutal daughter of Jeremiah; she was from Libnah. He did evil in the eyes of the LORD, just as Jehoiakim had done. It was because of the LORD's anger that all this happened to Jerusalem and Judah, and in the end, he thrust them from his presence Now Zedekiah rebelled against the king of Babylon

CHAPTER 25

So in the ninth year of Zedekiah's reign, on the tenth day of the tenth month, Nebuchadnezzar king of

Babylon marched against Jerusalem with his whole army. He encamped outside the city and built siege works all around it. The city was kept under siege until the eleventh year of King Zedekiah. By the ninth day of the fourth month, the famine in the city had become so severe that there was no food for the people to eat. Then the city wall was broken through, and the whole army fled at night through the gate between the two walls near the king's garden, though the Babylonians were surrounding the city. They fled toward the Arabah, but the Babylonian army pursued the king and overtook him in the plains of Jericho. All his soldiers were separated from him and scattered, and he was captured. He was taken to the king of Babylon at Riblah, where sentence was pronounced on him. They killed the sons of Zedekiah before his eyes. Then they put out his eyes, bound him with bronze shackles, and took him to Babylon On the seventh day of the fifth month, in the nineteenth year of Nebuchadnezzar king of Babylon, Nebuzaradan, commander of the imperial guard and official of the king of Babylon, came to Jerusalem. He set fire to the temple of the LORD, the royal palace, and all the houses of Jerusalem. Every important building he burned down. The whole Babylonian army under the commander of the imperial guard broke down the walls around Jerusalem. Nebuzaradan, the commander of the guard, carried into exile the people who remained in the city, along with the rest of the populace and those who had deserted to the king of Babylon. But the commander left behind some of the poorest people of the land to work the vineyards and fields The Babylonians broke up the bronze pillars, the movable stands, and the bronze Sea that were at the temple of the LORD and they carried the bronze to Babylon. They also took away the pots, shovels, wick trimmers, dishes, and all the bronze articles used in the temple service. The commander of the imperial guard took away the censers and sprinkling bowls—all that were made of pure gold or silver The bronze from the two pillars, the Sea and the movable stands, which Solomon had made for the temple of the LORD, was more than could be weighed. Each pillar was eighteen cubits high. The bronze capital on top of one pillar was three cubits high and was decorated with a network and pomegranates of bronze all around. The other pillar, with its network, was similar The commander of the guard took as prisoners Seraiah the chief priest, Zephaniah the priest next in rank, and the three doorkeepers. Of those still in the city, he took the officer in charge of the fighting men and five royal advisers. He also took the secretary who was chief officer in charge of conscripting the people of the land and sixty of the conscripts who were found in the city. Nebuzaradan the commander took them all and brought them to the king of Babylon at Riblah. There at Riblah, in the land of Hamath, the king had them executed. So Judah went into captivity, away from her land Nebuchadnezzar king of Babylon appointed Gedaliah son of Ahikam, the son of Shaphan, to be over the people he had left behind in Judah. When all the army officers and their men heard that the king of Babylon had appointed Gedaliah as governor, they came to Gedaliah at Mizpah—Ishmael son of Nethaniah, Johanan son of Kareah, Seraiah son of Tanhumeth the Netophathite, and Jaazaniah the son of the Maakathite, and their men. Gedaliah took an oath to reassure them and their men. "Do not be afraid of the Babylonian officials," he said. "Settle down in the land and serve the king of Babylon, and it will go well with you." In the seventh month, however, Ishmael son of Nethaniah, the son of Elishama, who was of royal blood, came with ten men and assassinated Gedaliah and also the men of Judah and the Babylonians who were with him at Mizpah. At this, all the people, from the least to the greatest, together with the army officers, fled to Egypt for fear of the Babylonians In the thirty-seventh year of the exile of Jehoiachin king of Judah, in the year Evil-Merodach became king of Babylon, he released Jehoiachin king of Judah from prison. He did this on the twenty-seventh day of the twelfth month. He spoke kindly to him and gave him a seat of honor higher than those of the other kings who were with him in Babylon. So Jehoiachin put aside his prison clothes and for the rest of his life ate regularly at the king's table. Day by day, the king gave Jehoiachin a regular allowance as long as he lived

13. 1 Chronicles

Chapter 1

Adam, Seth, Enosh, Kenan, Mahalaleel, Jared, Enoch, Methuselah, Lamech, and Noah. The sons of Noah were Shem, Ham, and Japheth. The sons of Japheth were Gomer, Magog, Madai, Javan, Tubal, Meshech, and Tiras. The sons of Gomer were Ashkenaz, Riphath, and Togarmah. The sons of Javan were Elishah, Tarshish, Kittim, and Dodanim. The sons of Ham were Cush, Mizraim, Put, and Canaan. The sons of Cush were Seba, Havilah, Sabtah, Raamah, and Sabtecha. The sons of Raamah were Sheba and Dedan. Cush fathered Nimrod, who became a mighty one on the earth Mizraim fathered Ludim, Anamim, Lehabim, Naphtuhim, Pathrusim, Casluhim (from whom came the Philistines), and Caphtorim. Canaan fathered Sidon (his firstborn), Heth, the Jebusites, the Amorites, and the Girgashites, the Hivites, the Arkites, the Sinites, the Arvadites, the Zemarites, and the Hamathites. The sons of Shem were Elam, Asshur, Arphaxad, Lud, Aram, Uz, Hul, Gether, and Meshech. Arphaxad fathered Shelah, and Shelah fathered Eber. Two sons were born to Eber: one was named Peleg (because in his days the earth was divided), and his brother was named Joktan. Joktan fathered Almodad, Sheleph, Hazarmaveth, Jerah, Hadoram, Uzal, Diklah, Obal, Abimael, Sheba, Ophir, Havilah, and Jobab; all these were the sons of Joktan Shem, Arphaxad, Shelah, Eber, Peleg, Reu, Serug, Nahor, Terah, and Abram (that is, Abraham). The sons of Abraham were Isaac and Ishmael. These are their generations. The sons of Ishmael, Abraham's eldest son, were Nebaioth, Kedar, Adbeel, Mibsam, Mishma, Dumah, Massa, Hadad, Tema, Jetur, Naphish, and Kedemah; these are the sons of Ishmael. The sons of Keturah, Abraham's concubine, were Zimran, Jokshan, Medan, Midian, Ishbak, and Shuah. The sons of Jokshan were Sheba and Dedan. The sons of Midian were Ephah, Epher, Hanoch, Abida, and Eldaah. All these were the descendants of Keturah. Abraham fathered Isaac; the sons of Isaac were Esau and Israel. The sons of Esau were Eliphaz, Reuel, Jeush, Jalam, and Korah. The sons of Eliphaz were Teman, Omar, Zephi, Gatam, Kenaz, Timna, and Amalek. The sons of Reuel were Nahath, Zerah, Shammah, and Mizzah The sons of Seir were Lotan, Shobal, Zibeon, Anah, Dishon, Ezer, and Dishan. The sons of Lotan were Hori and Homam; Lotan's sister was Timna. The sons of Shobal were Alvan, Manahath, Ebal, Shepho, and Onam. The sons of Zibeon were Aiah and Anah. The son of Anah was Dishon. The sons of Dishon were Hemdan, Eshban, Ithran, and Keran. The sons of Ezer were Bilhan, Zaavan, and Akan. The sons of Dishan were Uz and Aran These were the kings who reigned in the land of Edom before any king reigned over the children of Israel: Bela, the son of Beor, whose city was named Dinhabah. When Bela died, Jobab, the son of Zerah of Bozrah, reigned in his place. When Jobab died, Husham, of the land of the Temanites, reigned in his place. When Husham died, Hadad, the son of Bedad, who defeated Midian in the field of Moab, reigned in his place; the name of his city was Avith. When Hadad died, Samlah of Masrekah reigned in his place. When Samlah died, Shaul of Rehoboth by the river reigned in his place. When Shaul died, Baal-Hanan, the son of Achbor, reigned in his place. When Baal-Hanan died, Hadad reigned in his place; the name of his city was Pai, and his wife's name was Mehetabel, the daughter of Matred, the daughter of Mezahab. When Hadad died, the chiefs of Edom were: Timna, Alvah, Jetheth, Oholibamah, Elah, Pinon, Kenaz, Teman, Mibzar, Magdiel, and Iram. These were the chiefs of Edom

Chapter 2

These are the sons of Israel: Reuben, Simeon, Levi, Judah, Issachar, Zebulun, Dan, Joseph, Benjamin, Naphtali, Gad, and Asher. The sons of Judah were Er, Onan, and Shelah. These three were born to him by Shua's daughter, a Canaanite. Er, Judah's firstborn, was wicked in the sight of the Lord, and the Lord put him to death. Tamar, Judah's daughter-in-law, bore him Perez and Zerah. Judah had five sons in total. The sons of Perez were Hezron and Hamul. The sons of Zerah were Zimri, Ethan, Heman, Calcol, and Dara—five in all. The son of Carmi was Achar, the troubler of Israel, who broke faith in the matter of the devoted thing. The son of Ethan was Azariah The sons of Hezron born to him were Jerahmeel, Ram, and Chelubai. Ram fathered Amminadab, and Amminadab fathered Nahshon, the prince of the sons of Judah. Nahshon fathered Salma, and Salma fathered Boaz. Boaz fathered Obed, and Obed fathered Jesse. Jesse fathered Eliab, his firstborn, Abinadab the second, Shimea the third, Nethanel the fourth, Raddai the fifth, Ozem the sixth, and David the seventh. Their sisters were Zeruiah and Abigail. The sons of Zeruiah were Abishai, Joab, and Asahel. Abigail gave birth to Amasa, and the father of Amasa was Jether the Ishmaelite Caleb, the son of Hezron, had children by his wife Azubah, and by Jerioth; these were her sons: Jesher, Shobab, and Ardon. When Azubah died, Caleb married Ephrath, who bore him Hur. Hur fathered Uri, and Uri fathered Bezalel. Afterward, Hezron went in to the daughter of Machir, the father of Gilead, whom he married when he was sixty years old, and she bore him Segub. Segub fathered Jair, who had twenty-three cities in the land of Gilead. But Geshur and Aram took from them Havvoth-Jair, Kenath and its villages, sixty towns. All these were descendants of Machir, the father of Gilead. After the death of Hezron, Caleb went to Ephrathah, where his wife Abijah bore him Ashhur, the father of Tekoa The sons of Jerahmeel, the firstborn of Hezron, were Ram, his firstborn, Bunah, Oren, Ozem, and Ahijah. Jerahmeel also had another wife named Atarah; she was the mother of Onam. The sons of Ram, the firstborn of Jerahmeel, were Maaz, Jamin, and Eker. The sons of Onam were Shammai and Jada. The sons of Shammai were Nadab and Abishur. The name of Abishur's wife was Abihail, and she bore him Ahban and Molid. The sons of Nadab were Seled and Appaim; Seled died without children. The son of Appaim was Ishi. The son of Ishi was Sheshan, and Sheshan's son was Ahlai The sons of Jada, the brother of Shammai, were Jether and Jonathan; Jether died without children. The sons of Jonathan were Peleth and Zaza. These were the descendants of Jerahmeel. Now Sheshan had no sons, only daughters; he had an Egyptian servant named Jarha. So Sheshan gave his daughter in marriage to Jarha his servant, and she bore him Attai. Attai fathered Nathan, and Nathan fathered Zabad. Zabad fathered Ephlal, and Ephlal fathered

Obed. Obed fathered Jehu, and Jehu fathered Azariah. Azariah fathered Helez, and Helez fathered Eleasah. Eleasah fathered Sismai, and Sismai fathered Shallum. Shallum fathered Jekamiah, and Jekamiah fathered Elishama The sons of Caleb, the brother of Jerahmeel, were Mesha, his firstborn, who fathered Ziph, and his son Mareshah, who fathered Hebron. The sons of Hebron were Korah, Tappuah, Rekem, and Shema. Shema fathered Raham, the father of Jorkeam; Rekem fathered Shammai. The son of Shammai was Maon, and Maon fathered Beth-Zur. Ephah, Caleb's concubine, bore Haran, Moza, and Gazez; Haran fathered Gazez. The sons of Jahdai were Regem, Jotham, Geshan, Pelet, Ephah, and Shaaph. Caleb's concubine Maacah bore Sheber and Tirhanah. She also bore Shaaph, the father of Madmannah, Sheva, the father of Machbenah, and the father of Gibea; and the daughter of Caleb was Achsah These were the descendants of Caleb. The sons of Hur, the firstborn of Ephrathah: Shobal, the father of Kiriath-Jearim, Salma, the father of Bethlehem, and Hareph, the father of Beth-Gader. Shobal, the father of Kiriath-Jearim, had sons: Haroeh, half of the Menuhoth. The clans of Kiriath-Jearim: the Ithrites, the Puthites, the Shumathites, and the Mishraites; from these came the Zorathites and the Eshtaolites. The sons of Salma: Bethlehem, the Netophathites, Atroth-Beth-Joab, and half of the Manahathites, the Zorites, and the clans of the scribes who lived at Jabez: the Tirathites, the Shimeathites, and the Sucathites. These are the Kenites who came from Hammath, the father of the house of Rechab

Chapter 3

These are the sons of David who were born to him in Hebron: the firstborn was Amnon, by Ahinoam the Jezreelitess; the second, Daniel, by Abigail the Carmelitess; the third, Absalom, the son of Maacah, the daughter of Talmai, king of Geshur; the fourth, Adonijah, the son of Haggith; the fifth, Shephatiah, by Abital; the sixth, Ithream, by Eglah his wife. These six were born to him in Hebron, where he reigned for seven years and six months. In Jerusalem, he reigned for thirty-three years. These were born to him in Jerusalem: Shimea, Shobab, Nathan, and Solomon, four by Bathshua, the daughter of Ammiel. Also there were Ibhar, Elishama, Eliphelet, Nogah, Nepheg, Japhia, Elishama, Eliada, and Eliphelet, nine in all. These were all the sons of David, besides the sons of the concubines; and Tamar was their sister Solomon's son was Rehoboam, whose son was Abijah, who was followed by Asa, Jehoshaphat, Joram, Ahaziah, Joash, Amaziah, Azariah, Jotham, Ahaz, Hezekiah, Manasseh, Amon, and Josiah. The sons of Josiah were Johanan the firstborn, Jehoiakim the second, Zedekiah the third, and Shallum the fourth. The sons of Jehoiakim were Jeconiah his son and Zedekiah his son. The descendants of Jeconiah, the captive, were Shealtiel his son, Malchiram, Pedaiah, Shenazzar, Jekamiah, Hoshama, and Nedabiah. The sons of Pedaiah were Zerubbabel and Shimei. The sons of Zerubbabel were Meshullam and Hananiah; Shelomith was their sister. Also five other sons: Hashubah, Ohel, Berechiah, Hasadiah, and Jushab-Hesed. The sons of Hananiah were Pelatiah and Jeshaiah. His sons were Rephaiah, Arnan, Obadiah, and Shechaniah. The son of Shechaniah was Shemaiah, and his sons were Hattush, Igal, Bariah, Neariah, and Shaphat, six in all. The sons of Neariah were Elioenai, Hezekiah, and Azrikam, three in all. The sons of Elioenai were Hodaviah, Eliashib, Pelaiah, Akkub, Johanan, Delaiah, and Anani, seven in all

Chapter 4

The sons of Judah were Perez, Hezron, Carmi, Hur,

and Shobal. Reaiah, the son of Shobal, fathered Jahath, and Jahath fathered Ahumai and Lahad; these were the families of the Zorathites. These were the sons of Etam: Jezreel, Ishma, and Idbash; their sister was named Hazzelelponi. Penuel fathered Gedor, and Ezer fathered Hushah. These were the sons of Hur, the firstborn of Ephrathah, the father of Bethlehem. Asher, the father of Tekoa, had two wives, Helah and Naarah. Naarah bore him Ahuzzam, Hepher, Temeni, and Haahashtari; these were the sons of Naarah. The sons of Helah were Zereth, Zohar, and Ethnan. Koz fathered Anub, Zobebah, and the clans of Aharhel, the son of Harum Jabez was more honorable than his brothers; his mother named him Jabez, saying, "Because I bore him in pain." Jabez called on the God of Israel, saying, "Oh, that you would bless me and enlarge my territory, and that your hand might be with me, and that you would keep me from harm so that it might not bring me pain!" And God granted what he asked Chelub, the brother of Shuhah, fathered Mehir, who fathered Eshton. Eshton fathered Bethrapha, Paseah, and Tehinnah, the father of Irnahash. These were the men of Recah. The sons of Kenaz were Othniel and Seraiah, and the sons of Othniel were Hathath and Meonothai. Meonothai fathered Ophrah. Seraiah fathered Joab, the father of Ge-Harashim, so called because they were craftsmen The sons of Caleb, the son of Jephunneh, were Iru, Elah, and Naam; the son of Elah was Kenaz. The sons of Jehallelel were Ziph, Ziphah, Tiria, and Asarel. The sons of Ezrah were Jether, Mered, Epher, and Jalon; these were the sons of Bithiah, the daughter of Pharaoh, whom Mered married. Mered also had a wife from the tribe of Judah, who bore Miriam, Shammai, and Ishbah, the father of Eshtemoa. His Judean wife bore Jered, the father of Gedor, Heber, the father of Soco, and Jekuthiel, the father of Zanoah The sons of the wife of Hodiah, the sister of Naham, were the fathers of Keilah the Garmite and Eshtemoa the Maacathite. The sons of Shimon were Amnon, Rinnah, Ben-Hanan, and Tilon. The sons of Ishi were Zoheth and Ben-Zoheth. The sons of Shelah, the son of Judah, were Er, the father of Lecah, Laadah, the father of Mareshah, and the clans of the linen workers at Beth-Ashbea, Jokim, the men of Cozeba, and Joash and Saraph, who ruled in Moab and Jashubi-Lehem. These names are from ancient records. They were the potters who lived at Netaim and Gederah; they lived there in the king's service The descendants of Simeon were Nemuel, Jamin, Jarib, Zerah, and Shaul; Shaul's son was Shallum, his son was Mibsam, and his son was Mishma. The sons of Mishma were Hammuel his son, Zaccur his son, and Shimei his son. Shimei had sixteen sons and six daughters, but his brothers did not have many children, nor did all their clan multiply like the people of Judah. They lived at Beersheba, Moladah, Hazar-Shual, Bilhah, Ezem, Tolad, Bethuel, Hormah, Ziklag, Beth-Marcaboth, Hazar-Susim, Beth-Biri, and Shaaraim. These were their cities until David became king. Their villages were Etam, Ain, Rimmon, Tochen, and Ashan, five towns, and all their villages that were around these towns as far as Baal. These were their settlements, and they kept a genealogical record Meshobab, Jamlech, Joshah, the son of Amaziah, Joel, Jehu the son of Joshibiah, the son of Seraiah, the son of Asiel, Elioenai, Jaakobah, Jeshohaiah, Asaiah, Adiel, Jesimiel, Benaiah, Ziza the son of Shiphi, the son of Allon, the son of Jedaiah, the son of Shimri, the son of Shemaiah. These mentioned by name were leaders in their families, and their houses increased greatly. They journeyed to the entrance of Gedor, to the east side of the valley, to seek pasture for their flocks.

They found rich, good pasture, and the land was very broad, quiet, and peaceful; for the former inhabitants there belonged to Ham. These, registered by name, came in the days of Hezekiah, king of Judah, and attacked their tents and the Meunites who were found there, and they destroyed them utterly to this day and settled in their place because there was pasture there for their flocks. Five hundred men of the Simeonites went to Mount Seir, having for their leaders Pelatiah, Neariah, Rephaiah, and Uzziel, the sons of Ishi. They destroyed the remnant of the Amalekites who had escaped, and they have lived there to this day

Chapter 5

The sons of Reuben, the firstborn of Israel (for he was the firstborn, but because he defiled his father's couch, his birthright was given to the sons of Joseph, the son of Israel, so that he is not listed in the genealogy according to the birthright; though Judah became strong among his brothers and a chief came from him, yet the birthright belonged to Joseph), the sons of Reuben, the firstborn of Israel: Hanoch, Pallu, Hezron, and Carmi. The sons of Joel were Shemaiah his son, Gog his son, Shimei his son, Micah his son, Reaiah his son, Baal his son, and Beerah his son, whom Tilgath-Pilneser, the king of Assyria, carried away into exile; he was a leader of the Reubenites. His kinsmen by their clans, when the genealogy of their generations was recorded: the chief, Jeiel, and Zechariah, and Bela the son of Azaz, son of Shema, son of Joel, who lived in Aroer, as far as Nebo and Baal-Meon. He also lived to the east as far as the entrance of the desert this side of the Euphrates, because their livestock had multiplied in the land of Gilead. And in the days of Saul, they waged war against the Hagrites, who fell into their hand. They lived in their tents throughout all the region east of Gilead The sons of Gad lived next to them in the land of Bashan as far as Salecah: Joel the chief, Shapham the second, Janai, and Shaphat in Bashan. Their kinsmen by their fathers' houses: Michael, Meshullam, Sheba, Jorai, Jacan, Zia, and Eber, seven in all. These were the sons of Abihail the son of Huri, son of Jaroah, son of Gilead, son of Michael, son of Jeshishai, son of Jahdo, son of Buz. Ahi the son of Abdiel, son of Guni, was chief in their fathers' houses. They lived in Gilead, in Bashan and in its towns, and in all the pasturelands of Sharon to their limits. All of these were recorded in genealogies in the days of Jotham, king of Judah, and in the days of Jeroboam, king of Israel The sons of Reuben, the Gadites, and the half-tribe of Manasseh had valiant men who carried shield and sword, drew the bow, and were skilled in war, 44,760 able to go to war. They waged war against the Hagrites, Jetur, Naphish, and Nodab. When they prevailed over them, the Hagrites and all who were with them were given into their hands, for they cried out to God in the battle, and he granted their urgent plea because they trusted in him. They carried off their livestock: fifty thousand camels, two hundred and fifty thousand sheep, two thousand donkeys, and a hundred thousand men alive. For many fell, because the war was of God. And they lived in their place until the exile The members of the half-tribe of Manasseh lived in the land. They were very numerous, from Bashan to Baal-Hermon, Senir, and Mount Hermon. These were the heads of their fathers' houses: Epher, Ishi, Eliel, Azriel, Jeremiah, Hodaviah, and Jahdiel, mighty warriors, famous men, heads of their fathers' houses. But they broke faith with the God of their fathers, and prostituted themselves to the gods of the peoples of the land, whom God had destroyed before them. So the God of Israel stirred up the spirit of Pul, king of Assyria, the spirit of Tilgath-Pilneser, king of Assyria, and he took them into exile, namely, the Reubenites, the Gadites, and the half-tribe of Manasseh, and brought them to Halah, Habor, Hara, and the river Gozan, to this day

Chapter 6

The sons of Levi were Gershon, Kohath, and Merari. The sons of Kohath were Amram, Izhar, Hebron, and Uzziel. The sons of Amram were Aaron, Moses, and Miriam. Aaron's sons were Nadab, Abihu, Eleazar, and Ithamar. Eleazar fathered Phinehas, Phinehas fathered Abishua, Abishua fathered Bukki, and Bukki fathered Uzzi. Uzzi fathered Zerahiah, Zerahiah fathered Meraioth, Meraioth fathered Amariah, and Amariah fathered Ahitub. Ahitub fathered Zadok, Zadok fathered Ahimaaz, Ahimaaz fathered Azariah, and Azariah fathered Johanan. Johanan fathered Azariah (he was the priest in the house that Solomon built in Jerusalem). Azariah fathered Amariah, Amariah fathered Ahitub, Ahitub fathered Zadok, Zadok fathered Shallum, Shallum fathered Hilkiah, Hilkiah fathered Azariah, Azariah fathered Seraiah, and Seraiah fathered Jehozadak. Jehozadak went into captivity when the LORD took Judah and Jerusalem into exile at the hands of Nebuchadnezzar The sons of Levi were Gershom, Kohath, and Merari. These are the names of the sons of Gershom: Libni and Shimei. The sons of Kohath were Amram, Izhar, Hebron, and Uzziel. The sons of Merari were Mahli and Mushi. These are the families of Levi according to their fathers. Of Gershom, Libni his son, Jahath his son, Zimmah his son, Joah his son, Iddo his son, Zerah his son, and Jeatherai his son. The sons of Kohath: Amminadab his son, Korah his son, Assir his son, Elkanah his son, Ebiasaph his son, Assir his son, Tahath his son, Uriel his son, Uzziah his son, and Shaul his son. The sons of Elkanah were Amasai and Ahimoth. Elkanah. The sons of Elkanah: Zophai his son, Nahath his son, Eliab his son, Jeroham his son, and Elkanah his son. The sons of Samuel: the firstborn Joel and the second Abijah. The sons of Merari were Mahli, Libni his son, Shimei his son, Uzzah his son, Shimea his son, Haggiah his son, and Asaiah his son These are the ones whom David set to oversee the service of song in the house of the LORD after the ark came to rest there. They ministered with song before the tabernacle of the tent of meeting until Solomon built the house of the LORD in Jerusalem, and they performed their service according to their order. These are those who served and their sons. Of the sons of the Kohathites: Heman the singer, the son of Joel, son of Samuel, son of Elkanah, son of Jeroham, son of Eliel, son of Toah, son of Zuph, son of Elkanah, son of Mahath, son of Amasai, son of Elkanah, son of Joel, son of Azariah, son of Zephaniah, son of Tahath, son of Assir, son of Ebiasaph, son of Korah, son of Izhar, son of Kohath, son of Levi, son of Israel. His brother Asaph, who stood at his right hand, was Asaph the son of Berechiah, son of Shimea, son of Michael, son of Baaseiah, son of Malchijah, son of Ethni, son of Zerah, son of Adaiah, son of Ethan, son of Zimmah, son of Shimei, son of Jahath, son of Gershom, son of Levi Their brothers, the sons of Merari, stood on the left: Ethan the son of Kishi, son of Abdi, son of Malluch, son of Hashabiah, son of Amaziah, son of Hilkiah, son of Amzi, son of Bani, son of Shemer, son of Mahli, son of Mushi, son of Merari, son of Levi. Their brothers, the Levites, were appointed for all the service of the tabernacle of the house of God. But Aaron and his sons made offerings on the altar of burnt offering and on the altar of incense for all the work of the most holy place, and to make atonement for Israel, according to all that Moses the servant of God had commanded These are the sons of Aaron: Eleazar his son, Phinehas his son, Abishua his son,

Bukki his son, Uzzi his son, Zerahiah his son, Meraioth his son, Amariah his son, Ahitub his son, Zadok his son, and Ahimaaz his son. These are their dwelling places according to their settlements within their borders: to the sons of Aaron, of the families of the Kohathites, for theirs was the first lot, they gave them Hebron in the land of Judah and its surrounding pasturelands. But the fields of the city and its villages, they gave to Caleb the son of Jephunneh. To the sons of Aaron they gave the cities of refuge: Hebron, Libnah with its pasturelands, Jattir, Eshtemoa with its pasturelands, Hilen with its pasturelands, Debir with its pasturelands, Ashan with its pasturelands, and Beth-shemesh with its pasturelands. From the tribe of Benjamin: Geba with its pasturelands, Alemeth with its pasturelands, and Anathoth with its pasturelands. All their cities throughout their families were thirteen To the rest of the Kohathites were allotted by lot, out of the family of the tribe, out of the half-tribe, the half of Manasseh, ten cities. To the sons of Gershom, according to their families, out of the tribe of Issachar, out of the tribe of Asher, out of the tribe of Naphtali, and out of the tribe of Manasseh in Bashan, thirteen cities. To the sons of Merari, according to their families, out of the tribe of Reuben, out of the tribe of Gad, and out of the tribe of Zebulun, twelve cities. So the people of Israel gave the Levites the cities with their pasturelands. They gave by lot out of the tribe of Judah, out of the tribe of Simeon, and out of the tribe of Benjamin, these cities that are mentioned by name. And some of the families of the sons of Kohath had cities of their territory out of the tribe of Ephraim. They gave them the cities of refuge: Shechem with its pasturelands in the hill country of Ephraim, Gezer with its pasturelands, Jokmeam with its pasturelands, Beth-horon with its pasturelands, Aijalon with its pasturelands, and Gath-rimmon with its pasturelands. And out of the half-tribe of Manasseh: Aner with its pasturelands and Bileam with its pasturelands, for the rest of the families of the sons of Kohath To the sons of Gershom: out of the family of the half-tribe of Manasseh, Golan in Bashan with its pasturelands and Ashtaroth with its pasturelands; out of the tribe of Issachar, Kedesh with its pasturelands, Daberath with its pasturelands, Ramoth with its pasturelands, and Anem with its pasturelands; out of the tribe of Asher, Mashal with its pasturelands, Abdon with its pasturelands, Hukok with its pasturelands, and Rehob with its pasturelands; out of the tribe of Naphtali, Kedesh in Galilee with its pasturelands, Hammon with its pasturelands, and Kiriathaim with its pasturelands. To the rest of the Merarites: out of the tribe of Zebulun, Rimmono with its pasturelands, Tabor with its pasturelands; and beyond the Jordan at Jericho, on the east side of the Jordan, out of the tribe of Reuben, Bezer in the wilderness with its pasturelands, Jahzah with its pasturelands, Kedemoth with its pasturelands, and Mephaath with its pasturelands; and out of the tribe of Gad, Ramoth in Gilead with its pasturelands, Mahanaim with its pasturelands, Heshbon with its pasturelands, and Jazer with its pasturelands

Chapter 7

The sons of Issachar were Tola, Puah, Jashub, and Shimron, four in all. The sons of Tola were Uzzi, Rephaiah, Jeriel, Jahmai, Ibsam, and Samuel, heads of their fathers' houses, mighty warriors of their generations, numbering in the days of David 22,600. The son of Uzzi was Izrahiah, and the sons of Izrahiah were Michael, Obadiah, Joel, and Isshiah, five, all of them chiefs. And with them by their generations, according to their fathers' houses, were 36,000 troops for war, for they had many wives and sons.

Their kinsmen, belonging to all the families of Issachar, were mighty warriors, numbering 87,000 in all according to their genealogies The sons of Benjamin were Bela, Becher, and Jediael, three in all. The sons of Bela were Ezbon, Uzzi, Uzziel, Jerimoth, and Iri, five, heads of fathers' houses, mighty warriors; and their enrollment by genealogies was 22,034. The sons of Becher were Zemirah, Joash, Eliezer, Elioenai, Omri, Jerimoth, Abijah, Anathoth, and Alemeth. All these were the sons of Becher. And their enrollment by genealogies, according to their generations, as heads of their fathers' houses, mighty warriors, was 20,200. The son of Jediael was Bilhan, and the sons of Bilhan were Jeush, Benjamin, Ehud, Chenaanah, Zethan, Tarshish, and Ahishahar. All these were the sons of Jediael according to the heads of their fathers' houses, mighty warriors, 17,200, able to go to war. And Shuppim and Huppim were the sons of Ir, and Hushim was the son of Aher The sons of Naphtali were Jahziel, Guni, Jezer, and Shallum, the descendants of Bilhah. The sons of Manasseh: Asriel, whom his Aramean concubine bore; she bore Machir the father of Gilead. And Machir took a wife from among the Huppim and Shuppim. The name of his sister was Maacah. The name of the second was Zelophehad, and Zelophehad had daughters. And Maacah the wife of Machir bore a son, and she called his name Peresh. The name of his brother was Sheresh, and his sons were Ulam and Rakem. The son of Ulam was Bedan. These were the sons of Gilead the son of Machir, son of Manasseh. And his sister Hammolecheth bore Ishhod, Abiezer, and Mahlah. The sons of Shemida were Ahian, Shechem, Likhi, and Aniam The sons of Ephraim were Shuthelah, Bered his son, Tahath his son, Eleadah his son, Tahath his son, Zabad his son, Shuthelah his son, and Ezer and Elead, whom the men of Gath who were born in the land killed because they came down to raid their livestock. And Ephraim their father mourned many days, and his brothers came to comfort him. And Ephraim went in to his wife, and she conceived and bore a son, and he called his name Beriah, because disaster had befallen his house. His daughter was Sheerah, who built both Lower and Upper Beth-horon and Uzzen-sheerah. Rephah was his son, Resheph his son, Telah his son, Tahan his son, Ladan his son, Ammihud his son, Elishama his son, Nun his son, Joshua his son. Their possessions and settlements were Bethel and its towns, Naaran to the east, Gezer and its towns to the west, Shechem and its towns, and Ayyah and its towns; also in possession of the Manassites, Beth-shean and its towns, Taanach and its towns, Megiddo and its towns, Dor and its towns. In these lived the sons of Joseph the son of Israel The sons of Asher were Imnah, Ishvah, Ishvi, Beriah, and their sister Serah. The sons of Beriah were Heber and Malchiel, who fathered Birzaith. Heber fathered Japhlet, Shomer, Hotham, and their sister Shua. The sons of Japhlet were Pasach, Bimhal, and Ashvath. These are the sons of Japhlet. The sons of Shemer his brother were Rohgah, Hubbah, and Aram. The sons of Helem his brother were Zophah, Imna, Shelesh, and Amal. The sons of Zophah were Suah, Harnepher, Shual, Beri, Imrah, Bezer, Hod, Shamma, Shilshah, Ithran, and Beera. The sons of Jether were Jephunneh, Pispa, and Ara. The sons of Ulla were Arah, Haniel, and Rizia. All of these were men of Asher, heads of fathers' houses, approved, mighty warriors, chiefs of the princes. Their number enrolled by genealogies, for service in war, was 26,000 men

Chapter 8

Benjamin fathered Bela, his firstborn, Ashbel the second, Aharah the third, Nohah the fourth, and Rapha the fifth. Bela had sons: Addar, Gera, Abihud, Abishua, Naaman, Ahoah, Gera, Shephuphan, and Huram. These are the sons of Ehud; they were heads of fathers' houses of the inhabitants of Geba, and they were carried into exile to Manahath: Naaman, Ahijah, and Gera, who carried them into exile. He fathered Uzza and Ahihud. Shaharaim fathered sons in the country of Moab after he had sent away Hushim and Baara his wives. He fathered sons by Hodesh his wife: Jobab, Zibia, Mesha, Malcam, Jeuz, Sachia, and Mirmah. These were his sons, heads of fathers' houses. He also fathered sons by Hushim: Abitub and Elpaal. The sons of Elpaal were Eber, Misham, and Shemed, who built Ono and Lod with its towns, and Beriah and Shema. They were heads of fathers' houses of the inhabitants of Aijalon, who caused the inhabitants of Gath to flee. Ahio, Shashak, and Jeremoth. Zebadiah, Arad, Eder, Michael, Ishpah, and Joha were sons of Beriah. Zebadiah, Meshullam, Hizki, Heber, Ishmerai, Izliah, and Jobab were sons of Elpaal. Jakim, Zichri, Zabdi, Elienai, Zillethai, Eliel, Adaiah, Beraiah, and Shimrath were sons of Shimei. Ishpan, Eber, Eliel, Abdon, Zichri, Hanan, Hananiah, Elam, Anthothijah, Iphdeiah, and Penuel were sons of Shashak. Shamsherai, Shehariah, Athaliah, Jaareshiah, Elijah, and Zichri were sons of Jeroham. These were the heads of fathers' houses, according to their generations, chief men. These lived in Jerusalem Jeiel the father of Gibeon lived in Gibeon, and the name of his wife was Maacah. His firstborn son was Abdon, then Zur, Kish, Baal, Nadab, Gedor, Ahio, Zecher, and Mikloth (he fathered Shimeah). Now these also lived opposite their kinsmen in Jerusalem, with their kinsmen. Ner fathered Kish, Kish fathered Saul, Saul fathered Jonathan, Malchishua, Abinadab, and Eshbaal. The son of Jonathan was Merib-baal, and Merib-baal fathered Micah. The sons of Micah: Pithon, Melech, Tarea, and Ahaz. Ahaz fathered Jehoaddah, and Jehoaddah fathered Alemeth, Azmaveth, and Zimri. Zimri fathered Moza. Moza fathered Binea; Raphah was his son, Eleasah his son, Azel his son. Azel had six sons, and these are their names: Azrikam, Bocheru, Ishmael, Sheariah, Obadiah, and Hanan. All these were the sons of Azel. The sons of Eshek his brother: Ulam his firstborn, Jeush the second, and Eliphelet the third. The sons of Ulam were men who were mighty warriors, bowmen, having many sons and grandsons, 150. All these were Benjaminites

Chapter 9

So all Israel was enrolled by genealogies, and these are written in the Book of the Kings of Israel. And Judah was taken into exile in Babylon because of their breach of faith. Now the first to dwell again in their possessions in their cities were Israel, the priests, the Levites, and the temple servants. And some of the people of Judah, Benjamin, Ephraim, and Manasseh lived in Jerusalem. Uthai the son of Ammihud, son of Omri, son of Imri, son of Bani, from the sons of Perez the son of Judah. And of the Shilonites: Asaiah the firstborn, and his sons. Of the sons of Zerah: Jeuel and their kinsmen, 690. Of the Benjaminites: Sallu the son of Meshullam, son of Hodaviah, son of Hassenuah, Ibneiah the son of Jeroham, Elah the son of Uzzi, son of Michri, Meshullam the son of Shephatiah, son of Reuel, son of Ibnijah; and their kinsmen according to their generations, 956. All these were heads of fathers' houses, according to their fathers' houses Of the priests: Jedaiah, Jehoiarib, Jachin, and Azariah the son of Hilkiah, son of Meshullam, son of Zadok, son of Meraioth, son of Ahitub, the chief officer of the house of God; and Adaiah the son of Jeroham, son of Pashhur, son of Malchijah, and Maasai the son of Adiel, son of Jahzerah, son of Meshullam, son of

Meshillemith, son of Immer; besides their kinsmen, heads of their fathers' houses, 1,760 mighty men for the work of the service of the house of God. Of the Levites: Shemaiah the son of Hasshub, son of Azrikam, son of Hashabiah, of the sons of Merari; and Bakbakkar, Heresh, Galal, and Mattaniah the son of Mica, son of Zichri, son of Asaph; and Obadiah the son of Shemaiah, son of Galal, son of Jeduthun, and Berechiah the son of Asa, son of Elkanah, who lived in the villages of the Netophathites The gatekeepers were Shallum, Akkub, Talmon, Ahiman, and their kinsmen (Shallum was the chief). Until then they were in the king's gate on the east side as the gatekeepers of the camps of the Levites. Shallum the son of Kore, son of Ebiasaph, son of Korah, and his kinsmen of his fathers' house, the Korahites, were in charge of the work of the service, keepers of the thresholds of the tent, as their fathers had been in charge of the camp of the LORD, keepers of the entrance. And Phinehas the son of Eleazar was the chief officer over them in time past; the LORD was with him. Zechariah the son of Meshelemiah was gatekeeper at the entrance of the tent of meeting. All these who were chosen as gatekeepers at the thresholds were 212. They were enrolled by genealogies in their villages. David and Samuel the seer established them in their office of trust. So they and their sons were in charge of the gates of the house of the LORD, that is, the house of the tent, as guards. The gatekeepers were on the four sides, east, west, north, and south. And their kinsmen who were in their villages were obligated to come in every seven days, in turn, to be with these. For the four chief gatekeepers, who were Levites, were entrusted to be over the chambers and the treasures of the house of God. And they lodged around the house of God, for on them lay the duty of watching, and they had charge of opening it every morning Some of them had charge of the utensils of service, for they were required to count them when they were brought in and taken out. Others of them were appointed over the furniture, and over all the holy utensils, also over the fine flour, the wine, the oil, the incense, and the spices. Others, of the sons of the priests, prepared the mixing of the spices, and Mattithiah, one of the Levites, the firstborn of Shallum the Korahite, was entrusted with making the flat cakes. Also some of their kinsmen of the Kohathites had charge of the showbread, to prepare it every Sabbath Now these, the singers, the heads of fathers' houses of the Levites, were in the chambers of the temple free from other service, for they were on duty day and night. These were heads of fathers' houses of the Levites, according to their generations, leaders. These lived in Jerusalem In Gibeon lived Jeiel the father of Gibeon, and the name of his wife was Maacah, and his firstborn son Abdon, then Zur, Kish, Baal, Ner, Nadab, Gedor, Ahio, Zechariah, and Mikloth; and Mikloth fathered Shimeam. Now these also lived opposite their kinsmen in Jerusalem, with their kinsmen. Ner fathered Kish, Kish fathered Saul, Saul fathered Jonathan, Malchishua, Abinadab, and Eshbaal. And the son of Jonathan was Merib-baal, and Merib-baal fathered Micah. The sons of Micah: Pithon, Melech, Tahrea, and Ahaz. And Ahaz fathered Jarah, and Jarah fathered Alemeth, Azmaveth, and Zimri. Zimri fathered Moza. Moza fathered Binea, and Rephaiah was his son, Eleasah his son, Azel his son. Azel had six sons, and these are their names: Azrikam, Bocheru, Ishmael, Sheariah, Obadiah, and Hanan; these were the sons of Azel

Chapter 10

Now the Philistines fought against Israel, and the men of Israel fled before the Philistines and fell slain on Mount Gilboa. And the Philistines overtook Saul and his sons, and the Philistines struck down Jonathan and Abinadab and Malchishua, the sons of Saul. The battle pressed hard against Saul, and the archers found him, and he was wounded by the archers. Then Saul said to his armor-bearer, "Draw your sword and thrust me through with it, lest these uncircumcised come and mistreat me." But his armor-bearer would not, for he feared greatly. Therefore Saul took his own sword and fell upon it. And when his armor-bearer saw that Saul was dead, he also fell upon his sword and died. Thus Saul died; he and his three sons and all his house died together And when all the men of Israel who were in the valley saw that the army had fled and that Saul and his sons were dead, they abandoned their cities and fled, and the Philistines came and lived in them. The next day, when the Philistines came to strip the slain, they found Saul and his sons fallen on Mount Gilboa. And they stripped him and took his head and his armor, and sent messengers throughout the land of the Philistines to carry the good news to their idols and to the people. And they put his armor in the temple of their gods and fastened his head in the temple of Dagon. But when all Jabesh-gilead heard all that the Philistines had done to Saul, all the valiant men arose and took away the body of Saul and the bodies of his sons and brought them to Jabesh. And they buried their bones under the oak in Jabesh and fasted seven days So Saul died for his breach of faith. He broke faith with the LORD in that he did not keep the command of the LORD, and also consulted a medium, seeking guidance. He did not seek guidance from the LORD. Therefore the LORD put him to death and turned the kingdom over to David the son of Jesse

Chapter 11

All Israel gathered to David at Hebron, saying, "Behold, we are your bone and your flesh. In times past, even when Saul was king, it was you who led out and brought in Israel. The LORD your God said to you, 'You shall be shepherd of my people Israel, and you shall be prince over my people Israel.'" So all the elders of Israel came to the king at Hebron, and David made a covenant with them at Hebron before the LORD. They anointed David king over Israel, according to the word of the LORD by Samuel David and all Israel went to Jerusalem, which is Jebus, where the Jebusites were, the inhabitants of the land. The inhabitants of Jebus said to David, "You will not come in here." Nevertheless, David captured the stronghold of Zion, that is, the city of David. David said, "Whoever strikes the Jebusites first shall be chief and commander." Joab the son of Zeruiah went up first, so he became chief. David lived in the stronghold; therefore it was called the city of David. He built the city all around, from the Millo in complete circuit, and Joab repaired the rest of the city. And David became greater and greater, for the LORD of hosts was with him These are the chiefs of David's mighty men, who gave him strong support in his kingdom, together with all Israel, to make him king, according to the word of the LORD concerning Israel. This is an account of David's mighty men: Jashobeam, a Hachmonite, was chief of the three. He wielded his spear against three hundred whom he killed at one time. Next to him among the three mighty men was Eleazar the son of Dodo, the Ahohite. He was with David at Pas-dammim when the Philistines were gathered there for battle. There was a plot of ground full of barley, and the men fled from the Philistines. But he took his stand in the midst of the plot and defended it and killed the Philistines. The LORD saved them by a great victory Three of the thirty chief men went down to the rock to David at the cave of Adullam when the army of the

Philistines was encamped in the Valley of Rephaim. David was then in the stronghold, and the garrison of the Philistines was then at Bethlehem. David said longingly, "Oh, that someone would give me water to drink from the well of Bethlehem that is by the gate!" Then the three mighty men broke through the camp of the Philistines, drew water out of the well of Bethlehem that was by the gate, and took it and brought it to David. But David would not drink it. He poured it out to the LORD and said, "Far be it from me before my God that I should do this. Shall I drink the lifeblood of these men? For at the risk of their lives they brought it." Therefore he would not drink it. These things did the three mighty men Now Abishai, the brother of Joab, was chief of the thirty. And he wielded his spear against three hundred men and killed them and won a name beside the three. He was the most renowned of the thirty and became their commander, but he did not attain to the three. And Benaiah the son of Jehoiada was a valiant man of Kabzeel, a doer of great deeds. He struck down two heroes of Moab. He also went down and struck down a lion in a pit on a snowy day. And he struck down an Egyptian, a man of great stature, five cubits tall. The Egyptian had in his hand a spear like a weaver's beam, but Benaiah went down to him with a staff and snatched the spear out of the Egyptian's hand and killed him with his own spear. These things did Benaiah the son of Jehoiada and won a name beside the three mighty men. He was renowned among the thirty, but he did not attain to the three. And David set him over his bodyguard The mighty men were: Asahel the brother of Joab, Elhanan the son of Dodo of Bethlehem, Shammoth of Harod, Helez the Pelonite, Ira the son of Ikkesh of Tekoa, Abiezer of Anathoth, Sibbecai the Hushathite, Ilai the Ahohite, Maharai of Netophah, Heled the son of Baanah of Netophah, Ithai the son of Ribai of Gibeah of the people of Benjamin, Benaiah of Pirathon, Hurai of the brooks of Gaash, Abiel the Arbathite, Azmaveth of Baharum, Eliahba of Shaalbon, Hashem the Gizonite, Jonathan the son of Shageh the Hararite, Ahiam the son of Sachar the Hararite, Eliphal the son of Ur, Hepher the Mecherathite, Ahijah the Pelonite, Hezro of Carmel, Naarai the son of Ezbai, Joel the brother of Nathan, Mibhar the son of Hagri, Zelek the Ammonite, Naharai of Beeroth, the armor-bearer of Joab the son of Zeruiah, Ira the Ithrite, Gareb the Ithrite, Uriah the Hittite, Zabad the son of Ahlai, Adina the son of Shiza the Reubenite, a leader of the Reubenites, and thirty with him, Hanan the son of Maacah, and Joshaphat the Mithnite, Uzzia the Ashterathite, Shama and Jeiel the sons of Hotham the Aroerite, Jediael the son of Shimri, and Joha his brother, the Tizite, Eliel the Mahavite, Jeribai and Joshaviah the sons of Elnaam, and Ithmah the Moabite, Eliel, and Obed, and Jaasiel the Mezobaite

Chapter 12

These are the men who came to David at Ziklag, while he could not move about freely because of Saul the son of Kish. They were among the mighty men who helped him in war. They were bowmen and could shoot arrows and sling stones with either the right or the left hand; they were Benjaminites, Saul's kinsmen. The chief was Ahiezer, then Joash, both sons of Shemaah of Gibeah; also Jeziel and Pelet, the sons of Azmaveth; Beracah, Jehu of Anathoth, Ishmaiah of Gibeon, a mighty man among the thirty and a leader over the thirty; Jeremiah, Jahaziel, Johanan, Jozabad of Gederah, Eluzai, Jerimoth, Bealiah, Shemariah, Shephatiah the Haruphite, Elkanah, Ishiah, Azarel, Joezer and Jashobeam, the Korahites; and Joelah and Zebadiah, the sons of Jeroham of Gedor From the Gadites, there went over to David at the stronghold in the wilderness mighty and experienced warriors, expert with shield and spear, whose faces were like the faces of lions and who were swift as gazelles upon the mountains: Ezer the chief, Obadiah second, Eliab third, Mishmannah fourth, Jeremiah fifth, Attai sixth, Eliel seventh, Johanan eighth, Elzabad ninth, Jeremiah tenth, Machbannai eleventh. These Gadites were officers of the army; the least was a match for a hundred men and the greatest for a thousand. These are the men who crossed the Jordan in the first month, when it was overflowing all its banks, and put to flight all those in the valleys, to the east and to the west And some of the men of Benjamin and Judah came to the stronghold to David. David went out to meet them and said to them, "If you have come to me in friendship to help me, my heart will be joined to you, but if to betray me to my adversaries, although there is no wrong in my hands, then may the God of our fathers see and rebuke you." Then the Spirit clothed Amasai, chief of the thirty, and he said, "We are yours, O David, and with you, O son of Jesse! Peace, peace to you, and peace to your helpers, for your God helps you." Then David received them and made them officers of his troops Some of the men of Manasseh deserted to David when he came with the Philistines for the battle against Saul. (Yet he did not help them, for the rulers of the Philistines took counsel and sent him away, saying, "At peril to our heads he will desert to his master Saul.") As he went to Ziklag, these men of Manasseh deserted to him: Adnah, Jozabad, Jediael, Michael, Jozabad, Elihu, and Zillethai, chiefs of thousands in Manasseh. They helped David against the band of raiders, for they were all mighty men of valor and were commanders in the army. For from day to day men came to David to help him, until there was a great army, like an army of God These are the numbers of the divisions of the armed troops who came to David in Hebron to turn the kingdom of Saul over to him, according to the word of the LORD. The men of Judah bearing shield and spear were 6,800 armed troops. Of the Simeonites, mighty men of valor for war, 7,100. Of the Levites, 4,600. The prince Jehoiada, of the house of Aaron, and with him 3,700. Zadok, a young man mighty in valor, and twenty-two commanders from his own fathers' house. Of the Benjaminites, the kinsmen of Saul, 3,000, of whom the majority had to that point kept their allegiance to the house of Saul. Of the Ephraimites, 20,800, mighty men of valor, famous men in their fathers' houses. Of the half-tribe of Manasseh, 18,000, who were expressly named to come and make David king. Of Issachar, men who had understanding of the times, to know what Israel ought to do, 200 chiefs, and all their kinsmen under their command. Of Zebulun, 50,000 seasoned troops, equipped for battle with all the weapons of war, to help David with singleness of purpose. Of Naphtali, 1,000 commanders with whom were 37,000 men armed with shield and spear. Of the Danites, 28,600 men equipped for battle. Of Asher, 40,000 seasoned troops ready for battle. Of the Reubenites and Gadites and the half-tribe of Manasseh from beyond the Jordan, 120,000 men armed with all the weapons of war. All these, men of war, arrayed in battle order, came to Hebron with a whole heart to make David king over all Israel. Likewise, all the rest of Israel were of a single mind to make David king. And they were there with David for three days, eating and drinking, for their brothers had made preparation for them. And also their relatives, from as far as Issachar and Zebulun and Naphtali, came bringing food on donkeys and on camels and on mules and on oxen, abundant provisions of flour, cakes of figs, clusters of raisins, and wine and oil, oxen and sheep, for there was joy in Israel

Chapter 13

David consulted with the commanders of thousands and of hundreds, with every leader. David said to all the assembly of Israel, "If it seems good to you and from the LORD our God, let us send abroad to our brothers who remain in all the lands of Israel, as well as to the priests and Levites in the cities that have pasturelands, that they may be gathered to us. Then let us bring again the ark of our God to us, for we did not seek it in the days of Saul." All the assembly agreed to do so, for the thing was right in the eyes of all the people So David assembled all Israel from the Nile of Egypt to Lebo-hamath, to bring the ark of God from Kiriath-jearim. And David and all Israel went up to Baalah, that is, to Kiriath-jearim, which belongs to Judah, to bring up from there the ark of God, which is called by the name of the LORD who sits enthroned above the cherubim. And they carried the ark of God on a new cart, from the house of Abinadab, and Uzzah and Ahio were driving the cart. And David and all Israel were celebrating before God with all their might, with song and lyres and harps and tambourines and cymbals and trumpets When they came to the threshing floor of Chidon, Uzzah put out his hand to take hold of the ark, for the oxen stumbled. And the anger of the LORD was kindled against Uzzah, and he struck him down because he put out his hand to the ark, and he died there before God. And David was angry because the LORD had broken out against Uzzah. And that place is called Perez-uzzah to this day. And David was afraid of God that day, and he said, "How can I bring the ark of God home to me?" So David did not take the ark home into the city of David, but took it aside to the house of Obed-edom the Gittite. And the ark of God remained with the household of Obed-edom in his house three months. And the LORD blessed the household of Obed-edom and all that he had

Chapter 14

Hiram king of Tyre sent messengers to David, and cedar trees, also masons and carpenters, to build a house for him. And David knew that the LORD had established him as king over Israel and that his kingdom was highly exalted for the sake of his people Israel David took more wives in Jerusalem, and David fathered more sons and daughters. These are the names of the children born to him in Jerusalem: Shammua, Shobab, Nathan, Solomon, Ibhar, Elishua, Elpelet, Nogah, Nepheg, Japhia, Elishama, Beeliada, and Eliphelet When the Philistines heard that David had been anointed king over all Israel, all the Philistines went up to search for David. But David heard of it and went out against them. Now the Philistines had come and made a raid in the Valley of Rephaim. And David inquired of God, "Shall I go up against the Philistines? Will you give them into my hand?" And the LORD said to him, "Go up, and I will give them into your hand." And he went up to Baal-perazim, and David struck them down there. And David said, "God has broken through my enemies by my hand, like a bursting flood." Therefore the name of that place is called Baal-perazim. And they left their gods there, and David gave command, and they were burned And the Philistines yet again made a raid in the valley. And when David again inquired of God, God said to him, "You shall not go up after them; go around and come against them opposite the balsam trees. And when you hear the sound of marching in the tops of the balsam trees, then go out to battle, for God has gone out before you to strike down the army of the Philistines." And David did as God commanded him, and they struck down the Philistine army from Gibeon to Gezer. And the fame of David went out into all lands, and the LORD brought the fear of him upon all nations

Chapter 15

David built houses for himself in the city of David. And he prepared a place for the ark of God and pitched a tent for it. Then David said that no one but the Levites may carry the ark of God, for the LORD had chosen them to carry the ark of the LORD and to minister to him forever. And David assembled all Israel at Jerusalem to bring up the ark of the LORD to its place, which he had prepared for it. And David gathered together the sons of Aaron and the Levites: of the sons of Kohath, Uriel the chief, with 120 of his brothers; of the sons of Merari, Asaiah the chief, with 220 of his brothers; of the sons of Gershom, Joel the chief, with 130 of his brothers; of the sons of Elizaphan, Shemaiah the chief, with 200 of his brothers; of the sons of Hebron, Eliel the chief, with 80 of his brothers; of the sons of Uzziel, Amminadab the chief, with 112 of his brothers Then David summoned the priests Zadok and Abiathar and the Levites Uriel, Asaiah, Joel, Shemaiah, Eliel, and Amminadab, and said to them, "You are the heads of the fathers' houses of the Levites. Consecrate yourselves, you and your brothers, so that you may bring up the ark of the LORD, the God of Israel, to the place that I have prepared for it. Because you did not carry it the first time, the LORD our God broke out against us, because we did not seek him according to the rule." So the priests and the Levites consecrated themselves to bring up the ark of the LORD, the God of Israel. And the Levites carried the ark of God on their shoulders with the poles, as Moses had commanded according to the word of the LORD David also commanded the chiefs of the Levites to appoint their brothers as the singers who should play loudly on musical instruments, on harps and lyres and cymbals, to raise sounds of joy. So the Levites appointed Heman the son of Joel; and of his brothers Asaph the son of Berechiah; and of the sons of Merari, their brothers, Ethan the son of Kushaiah; and with them their brothers of the second order, Zechariah, Jaaziel, Shemiramoth, Jehiel, Unni, Eliab, Benaiah, Maaseiah, Mattithiah, Eliphelehu, Mikneiah, Obed-edom, and Jeiel, the gatekeepers. The singers, Heman, Asaph, and Ethan, were to sound bronze cymbals; Zechariah, Aziel, Shemiramoth, Jehiel, Unni, Eliab, Maaseiah, and Benaiah were to play harps according to Alamoth; but Mattithiah, Eliphelehu, Mikneiah, Obed-edom, Jeiel, and Azaziah were to lead with lyres according to the Sheminith. Chenaniah, leader of the Levites in music, should direct the music, for he understood it. Berechiah and Elkanah were to be gatekeepers for the ark. Shebaniah, Josaphat, Nethanel, Amasai, Zechariah, Benaiah, and Eliezer, the priests, should blow the trumpets before the ark of God. Obed-edom and Jehiah were to be gatekeepers for the ark So David and the elders of Israel and the commanders of thousands went to bring up the ark of the covenant of the LORD from the house of Obed-edom with rejoicing. And because God helped the Levites who were carrying the ark of the covenant of the LORD, they sacrificed seven bulls and seven rams. David was clothed with a robe of fine linen, as also were all the Levites who were carrying the ark, and the singers, and Chenaniah the leader of the music of the singers. And David wore a linen ephod. So all Israel brought up the ark of the covenant of the LORD with shouting, to the sound of the horn, trumpets, and cymbals, and made loud music on harps and lyres As the ark of the covenant of the LORD came to the city of David, Michal the daughter of Saul looked out of the window and saw King David dancing and celebrating, and she despised him in her heart

Chapter 16

They brought the Ark of God and placed it in the middle of the Tabernacle that David had prepared for it. They offered burnt offerings and peace offerings before God. When David had finished offering the burnt offerings and peace offerings, he blessed the people in the name of the Lord. He then distributed to each one of Israel, both man and woman, a cake of bread, a piece of meat, and a bottle of wine David appointed some Levites to serve before the ark of the Lord, to give thanks, praise, and pray to the Lord, the God of Israel. Asaph was the leader, with Zechariah, Jeiel, Shemiramoth, Jehiel, Mattithiah, Eliab, Benaiah, and Obed Edom, who played instruments like violas and lyres, while Asaph played the cymbals. Benaiah and Jahaziel, the priests, played trumpets continually before the Ark of the Covenant of God At that time, David had instructed Asaph and his brothers to give thanks to the Lord. They sang: Praise the Lord and call upon His name; declare His works among the people Sing to Him, praise Him, and speak of all His wonderful works Rejoice in His holy name; let the hearts of those who seek the Lord be glad Seek the Lord and His strength; continually seek His face Remember the wonderful works that He has done, His wonders, and the judgments He has pronounced O descendants of Israel, His servant, O sons of Jacob, His chosen ones, He is the Lord our God; His decrees are over all the earth Remember His covenant forever, the word He commanded for a thousand generations, the covenant He made with Abraham, and confirmed to Isaac as a law and to Israel as an everlasting covenant, saying, "To you, I will give the land of Canaan, the lot of your inheritance." When you were few in number, very few, and strangers in the land, wandering from nation to nation and from one kingdom to another, He allowed no one to oppress them; He rebuked kings for their sake, saying, "Do not touch my anointed ones, and do not harm my prophets." Sing to the Lord, all the earth; proclaim His salvation from day to day. Declare His glory among the nations and His marvelous works among all peoples. For great is the Lord and greatly to be praised; He is to be feared above all gods. For all the gods of the peoples are idols, but the Lord made the heavens. Splendor and majesty are before Him; strength and joy are in His place Ascribe to the Lord, O families of the peoples, ascribe to the Lord glory and strength. Ascribe to the Lord the glory due His name; bring an offering and come before Him. Worship the Lord in the splendor of holiness; tremble before Him, all the earth. The world is firmly established; it shall never be moved Let the heavens rejoice, and let the earth be glad, and let them say among the nations, "The Lord reigns!" Let the sea roar and all that fills it; let the fields exult and everything in them. Then shall the trees of the forest sing for joy before the Lord, for He comes to judge the earth O give thanks to the Lord, for He is good; for His steadfast love endures forever. Say also, "Save us, O God of our salvation, and gather and deliver us from among the nations, that we may give thanks to Your holy name and glory in Your praise. Blessed be the Lord, the God of Israel, from everlasting to everlasting!" And all the people said, "Amen!" and praised the Lord David left Asaph and his brothers there before the Ark of the Covenant of the Lord to minister regularly before the Ark as each day required. Obed Edom and his sixty-eight brothers, including Obed Edom the son of Jeduthun and Hosah, were to be gatekeepers. Zadok the priest and his fellow priests were before the Tabernacle of the Lord in the high place at Gibeon, offering burnt offerings to the Lord on the altar of burnt offering regularly, morning and evening, according to all that is written in the Law of the Lord that He commanded Israel With them were Heman and Jeduthun and the rest of those chosen and expressly named to give thanks to the Lord, for His steadfast love endures forever. Heman and Jeduthun had trumpets and cymbals for the music and instruments for sacred song. The sons of Jeduthun were appointed to the gate. Then all the people departed each to his house, and David returned to bless his household

Chapter 17

When David was settled in his house, he said to Nathan the prophet, "Behold, I dwell in a house of cedar, but the Ark of the Covenant of the Lord is under a tent." Nathan said to David, "Do all that is in your heart, for God is with you." But that same night, the word of God came to Nathan, saying, "Go and tell my servant David, 'Thus says the Lord: You shall not build me a house to dwell in. For I have not dwelt in a house since the day I brought up Israel to this day, but I have gone from tent to tent and from dwelling to dwelling. In all places where I have moved with all Israel, did I speak a word with any of the judges of Israel, whom I commanded to shepherd my people, saying, "Why have you not built me a house of cedar?"' Now, therefore, thus shall you say to my servant David, 'Thus says the Lord of hosts: I took you from the pasture, from following the sheep, to be prince over my people Israel, and I have been with you wherever you have gone and have cut off all your enemies from before you. And I will make for you a name, like the name of the great ones of the earth. And I will appoint a place for my people Israel and will plant them, that they may dwell in their own place and be disturbed no more. And violent men shall waste them no more, as formerly, from the time that I appointed judges over my people Israel. And I will subdue all your enemies. Moreover, I declare to you that the Lord will build you a house. When your days are fulfilled to walk with your fathers, I will raise up your offspring after you, one of your own sons, and I will establish his kingdom. He shall build a house for me, and I will establish his throne forever. I will be to him a father, and he shall be to me a son. I will not take my steadfast love from him, as I took it from him who was before you, but I will confirm him in my house and in my kingdom forever, and his throne shall be established forever.'" In accordance with all these words and in accordance with all this vision, Nathan spoke to David Then King David went in and sat before the Lord and said, "Who am I, O Lord God, and what is my house, that you have brought me thus far? And this was a small thing in your eyes, O God. You have spoken also of your servant's house for a great while to come and have shown me future generations, O Lord God! And what more can David say to you for honoring your servant? For you know your servant. For your servant's sake, O Lord, and according to your own heart, you have done all this greatness, in making known all these great things. There is none like you, O Lord, and there is no God besides you, according to all that we have heard with our ears. And who is like your people Israel, the one nation on earth whom God went to redeem to be his people, making for yourself a name for great and awesome things, in driving out nations before your people whom you redeemed from Egypt? And you made your people Israel to be your people forever, and you, O Lord, became their God And now, O Lord, let the word that you have spoken concerning your servant and concerning his house be established forever, and do as you have spoken. And your name will be established and magnified forever, saying, 'The Lord of hosts, the God of Israel, is Israel's God,' and the house of your servant David will be established before you. For you, my God, have revealed to your servant that you will build a house for him. Therefore your servant has found courage to pray before you. And now, O Lord, you are God, and you have promised this good thing to your servant. Now you have been pleased to bless the house of your servant, that it may continue forever before you. For it is you, O Lord, who have blessed, and it is blessed forever."

Chapter 18

After this, David defeated the Philistines and subdued them. He took Gath and its villages out of the hand of the Philistines. He defeated Moab, and the Moabites became servants to David and brought tribute. David also defeated Hadadezer king of Zobah, as far as Hamath, as he went to set up his monument at the river Euphrates. David took from him 1,000 chariots, 7,000 horsemen, and 20,000 foot soldiers. David hamstrung all the chariot horses but left enough for 100 chariots When the Syrians of Damascus came to help Hadadezer king of Zobah, David struck down 22,000 men of the Syrians. Then David put garrisons in Syria of Damascus, and the Syrians became servants to David and brought tribute. And the Lord gave victory to David wherever he went. David took the shields of gold that were carried by the servants of Hadadezer and brought them to Jerusalem. And from Tibhath and from Cun, cities of Hadadezer, David took a large amount of bronze. With it Solomon made the bronze sea and the pillars and the vessels of bronze When Tou king of Hamath heard that David had defeated the whole army of Hadadezer king of Zobah, he sent his son Hadoram to King David, to ask about his health and to bless him because he had fought against Hadadezer and defeated him, for Hadadezer had often been at war with Tou. And he sent all sorts of articles of gold, of silver, and of bronze. These also King David dedicated to the Lord, together with the silver and gold that he had carried off from all the nations, from Edom, Moab, the Ammonites, the Philistines, and Amalek And Abishai, the son of Zeruiah, struck down 18,000 Edomites in the Valley of Salt. Then he put garrisons in Edom, and all the Edomites became David's servants. And the Lord gave victory to David wherever he went So David reigned over all Israel, and he administered justice and equity to all his people. Joab the son of Zeruiah was over the army, and Jehoshaphat the son of Ahilud was recorder, and Zadok the son of Ahitub and Abimelech the son of Abiathar were priests, and Shavsha was secretary, and Benaiah the son of Jehoiada was over the Cherethites and the Pelethites, and David's sons were the chief officials in the service of the king

Chapter 19

After this, Nahash the king of the Ammonites died, and his son reigned in his place. David said, "I will deal kindly with Hanun the son of Nahash, for his father dealt kindly with me." So David sent messengers to console him concerning his father. And David's servants came to the land of the Ammonites to Hanun to console him. But the princes of the Ammonites said to Hanun, "Do you think, because David has sent comforters to you, that he is honoring your father? Have not his servants come to you to search and to overthrow and to spy out the land?" So Hanun took David's servants and shaved them and cut off their garments in the middle, at their hips, and sent them away When David was told concerning the men, he sent messengers to meet them, for the men were greatly ashamed. And the king said, "Remain at Jericho until your beards have grown, and then return." When the Ammonites saw that they had become a stench to David, Hanun and the Ammonites sent 1,000 talents of silver to hire chariots and horsemen from Mesopotamia, from Aram-maacah, and from Zobah. They hired 32,000 chariots and the king of Maacah with his army, who came and encamped before Medeba. And the Ammonites were mustered from their cities and came to battle. When David heard of it, he sent Joab and all the army of the mighty men And the Ammonites came out and drew up in battle array at the entrance of the city, and the kings who had come were by themselves in the open country. When Joab saw that the battle was set against him both in front and in the rear, he chose some of the best men of Israel and arrayed them against the Syrians. The rest of his men he put in the charge of Abishai his brother, and they were arrayed against the Ammonites. And he said, "If the Syrians are too strong for me, then you shall help me, but if the Ammonites are too strong for you, then I will help you. Be strong, and let us use our strength for our people and for the cities of our God, and may the Lord do what seems good to him." So Joab and the people who were with him drew near before the Syrians for battle, and they fled before him. And when the Ammonites saw that the Syrians fled, they likewise fled before Abishai, Joab's brother, and entered the city. Then Joab came to Jerusalem. But when the Syrians saw that they had been defeated by Israel, they sent messengers and brought out the Syrians who were beyond the Euphrates, with Shophach the commander of the army of Hadadezer at their head When it was told to David, he gathered all Israel together and crossed the Jordan and came to them and drew up his forces against them. And when David set the battle in array against the Syrians, they fought with him. And the Syrians fled before Israel, and David killed of the Syrians the men of 7,000 chariots and 40,000 foot soldiers, and put to death also Shophach the commander of their army. And when the servants of Hadadezer saw that they had been defeated by Israel, they made peace with David and became subject to him. So the Syrians were not willing to save the Ammonites anymore

Chapter 20

In the spring of the year, the time when kings go out to battle, Joab led out the army and ravaged the country of the Ammonites and came and besieged Rabbah. But David remained at Jerusalem. And Joab struck down Rabbah and overthrew it. And David took the crown of their king from his head. He found that it weighed a talent of gold, and in it was a precious stone. And it was placed on David's head. And he brought out the spoil of the city, a very great amount. And he brought out the people who were in it and set them to labor with saws and iron picks and axes. And thus David did to all the cities of the Ammonites. Then David and all the people returned to Jerusalem And after this, there arose war with the Philistines at Gezer. Then Sibbecai the Hushathite struck down Sippai, who was one of the descendants of the giants, and the Philistines were subdued. And there was again war with the Philistines, and Elhanan the son of Jair struck down Lahmi the brother of Goliath the Gittite, the shaft of whose spear was like a weaver's beam. And there was again war at Gath, where there was a man of great stature, who had six fingers on each hand and six toes on each foot, twenty-four in number, and he also was descended from the giants. And when he taunted Israel, Jonathan the son of Shimea, David's brother, struck him down. These were descended from the giants in Gath, and they fell by the hand of David and by the hand of his servants

Chapter 21

Satan opposed Israel and incited David to conduct a

census of Israel. David instructed Joab and the leaders of the people, "Go and count the people of Israel from Beersheba to Dan and bring me a report so that I may know their number." Joab responded, "May the Lord increase His people a hundredfold, O my lord the king. Are they not all your servants? Why does my lord require this? Why should it bring guilt upon Israel?" Nevertheless, the king's word prevailed against Joab. Joab went throughout all Israel and then returned to Jerusalem. Joab reported the number of the people to David: there were eight hundred thousand men who drew the sword in Israel, and four hundred and seventy thousand men in Judah. But Joab did not count Levi and Benjamin because the king's command was detestable to him God was displeased with this action, and He struck Israel. David said to God, "I have sinned greatly by doing this. Now, please forgive the iniquity of Your servant, for I have acted foolishly." The Lord spoke to Gad, David's seer, saying, "Go and tell David, 'Thus says the Lord: I offer you three options; choose one of them for me to carry out against you.'" So Gad went to David and said, "This is what the Lord says: 'Take your choice: three years of famine, three months of being swept away before your enemies with their swords overtaking you, or three days of the sword of the Lord—days of plague in the land, with the angel of the Lord ravaging every part of Israel.' Now then, decide how I should answer the one who sent me." David said to Gad, "I am in deep distress. Let me fall into the hands of the Lord, for His mercy is very great; but do not let me fall into human hands." So the Lord sent a plague on Israel, and seventy thousand men fell. God sent an angel to Jerusalem to destroy it, but as the angel was doing so, the Lord saw and relented concerning the disaster and said to the angel who was destroying the people, "Enough! Withdraw your hand." The angel of the Lord was then standing at the threshing floor of Ornan the Jebusite David looked up and saw the angel of the Lord standing between heaven and earth, with a drawn sword in his hand extended over Jerusalem. Then David and the elders, clothed in sackcloth, fell facedown. David said to God, "Was it not I who ordered the fighting men to be counted? I, the shepherd, have sinned and done wrong. But these are but sheep. What have they done? Lord my God, let Your hand fall on me and my family, but do not let this plague remain on Your people." Then the angel of the Lord ordered Gad to tell David to go up and build an altar to the Lord on the threshing floor of Ornan the Jebusite. So David went up in obedience to the word that Gad had spoken in the name of the Lord. While Ornan was threshing wheat, he turned and saw the angel; his four sons who were with him hid themselves. As David approached, Ornan looked and saw him; he left the threshing floor and bowed down before David with his face to the ground David said to him, "Let me have the site of your threshing floor so I can build an altar to the Lord, that the plague on the people may be stopped. Sell it to me at the full price." Ornan said to David, "Take it! Let my lord the king do whatever pleases him. Look, I will give the oxen for the burnt offerings, the threshing sledges for the wood, and the wheat for the grain offering. I will give all this." But King David replied to Ornan, "No, I insist on paying the full price. I will not take for the Lord what is yours, or sacrifice a burnt offering that costs me nothing." So David paid Ornan six hundred shekels of gold for the site. David built an altar to the Lord there and sacrificed burnt offerings and fellowship offerings. He called on the Lord, and the Lord answered him with fire from heaven on the altar of burnt offering. Then the Lord spoke to the angel, and he put his sword back into its sheath. When David saw that the Lord had answered him on the threshing floor of Ornan the Jebusite, he offered sacrifices there. The tabernacle of the Lord, which Moses had made in the wilderness, and the altar of burnt offering were at that time on the high place at Gibeon. But David could not go before it to inquire of God, because he was afraid of the sword of the angel of the Lord

Chapter 22

David said, "This is the house of the Lord God, and this is the altar of burnt offering for Israel." He gave orders to gather the foreigners residing in Israel, and he appointed stonecutters to prepare dressed stone for building the house of God. David provided a large amount of iron to make nails for the doors of the gateways and for the fittings, and more bronze than could be weighed. He also provided more cedar logs than could be counted, for the Sidonians and Tyrians had brought large quantities of cedar to David David said, "My son Solomon is young and inexperienced, and the house to be built for the Lord should be of great magnificence and fame and splendor in the sight of all the nations. Therefore I will make preparations for it." So David made extensive preparations before his death. Then he called for his son Solomon and charged him to build a house for the Lord, the God of Israel. David said to Solomon, "My son, I had it in my heart to build a house for the Name of the Lord my God. But this word of the Lord came to me: 'You have shed much blood and have fought many wars. You are not to build a house for my Name, because you have shed much blood on the earth in my sight. But you will have a son who will be a man of peace and rest, and I will give him rest from all his enemies on every side. His name will be Solomon, and I will grant Israel peace and quiet during his reign. He is the one who will build a house for my Name. He will be my son, and I will be his father. And I will establish the throne of his kingdom over Israel forever.' "Now, my son, the Lord be with you, and may you have success and build the house of the Lord your God, as He said you would. May the Lord give you discretion and understanding when He puts you in command over Israel, so that you may keep the law of the Lord your God. Then you will have success if you are careful to observe the decrees and laws that the Lord gave Moses for Israel. Be strong and courageous. Do not be afraid or discouraged "I have taken great pains to provide for the temple of the Lord a hundred thousand talents of gold, a million talents of silver, quantities of bronze and iron too great to be weighed, and wood and stone. And you may add to them. You have many workers: stonecutters, masons and carpenters, as well as those skilled in every kind of work in gold and silver, bronze and iron—craftsmen beyond number. Now begin the work, and the Lord be with you." Then David ordered all the leaders of Israel to help his son Solomon. He said to them, "Is not the Lord your God with you? And has He not granted you rest on every side? For He has given the inhabitants of the land into my hands, and the land is subject to the Lord and to His people. Now devote your heart and soul to seeking the Lord your God. Begin to build the sanctuary of the Lord God, so that you may bring the ark of the covenant of the Lord and the sacred articles belonging to God into the temple that will be built for the Name of the Lord."

Chapter 23

When David was old and full of days, he made Solomon his son king over Israel. He gathered together all the leaders of Israel, with the priests and the Levites. The Levites, thirty years old and upward, were counted, and the total number of men was thirty-eight thousand. Of these, twenty-four thousand were to oversee the work of the house of the Lord, six thousand were officials and judges, four thousand were gatekeepers, and four thousand praised the Lord with the musical instruments David had provided for that purpose David divided them into groups corresponding to the sons of Levi: Gershon, Kohath, and Merari. The sons of Gershon: Ladan and Shimei. The sons of Ladan: Jehiel the first, Zetham, and Joel—three in all. The sons of Shimei: Shelomoth, Haziel, and Haran—three in all. These were the heads of the families of Ladan. And the sons of Shimei: Jahath, Ziza, Jeush, and Beriah. These were the sons of Shimei—four in all. Jahath was the first and Ziza the second; Jeush and Beriah did not have many sons, so they were counted as one family The sons of Kohath: Amram, Izhar, Hebron, and Uzziel—four in all. The sons of Amram: Aaron and Moses. Aaron was set apart, he and his descendants forever, to consecrate the most holy things, to offer sacrifices before the Lord, to minister before Him, and to pronounce blessings in His name forever. The sons of Moses the man of God were counted as part of the tribe of Levi. The sons of Moses: Gershom and Eliezer. The descendants of Gershom: Shebuel was the first. The descendants of Eliezer: Rehabiah was the first. Eliezer had no other sons, but the sons of Rehabiah were very numerous The sons of Izhar: Shelomith was the first. The sons of Hebron: Jeriah the first, Amariah the second, Jahaziel the third, and Jekameam the fourth. The sons of Uzziel: Micah the first and Isshiah the second. The sons of Merari: Mahli and Mushi. The sons of Mahli: Eleazar and Kish. Eleazar died without having sons; he only had daughters. Their cousins, the sons of Kish, married them. The sons of Mushi: Mahli, Eder, and Jerimoth—three in all. These were the descendants of Levi by their families—the heads of families as they were registered under their names and counted individually—that is, the workers twenty years old or more who served in the house of the Lord. For David had said, "The Lord, the God of Israel, has granted rest to His people and has come to dwell in Jerusalem forever. So the Levites no longer need to carry the tabernacle or any of the articles used in its service." According to the last instructions of David, the Levites were counted from those twenty years old or more The duty of the Levites was to help Aaron's descendants in the service of the temple of the Lord: to be in charge of the courtyards, the side rooms, the purification of all sacred things, and the performance of other duties at the house of God. They were also to assist with the bread set out on the table, the flour for the grain offerings, the unleavened wafers, the baking and mixing, and all measurements of quantity and size. They were to stand every morning to thank and praise the Lord. They were to do the same in the evening and whenever burnt offerings were presented to the Lord on the Sabbaths, at the New Moon feasts and at the appointed festivals. They were to serve before the Lord regularly in the proper number and in the way prescribed for them. And so the Levites carried out their responsibilities for the tent of meeting, for the Holy Place, and, under their relatives the descendants of Aaron, for the service of the temple of the Lord

Chapter 24

These were the divisions of the descendants of Aaron: The sons of Aaron were Nadab, Abihu, Eleazar, and Ithamar. But Nadab and Abihu died before their father did, and they had no sons; so Eleazar and Ithamar served as priests. With the help of Zadok, a descendant of Eleazar, and Ahimelech, a descendant of Ithamar, David separated them into divisions for their appointed order of ministering. A larger number of leaders were found among

Eleazar's descendants than among Ithamar's, and they were divided accordingly: sixteen heads of families from Eleazar's descendants and eight heads of families from Ithamar's descendants They divided them impartially by casting lots, for there were officials of the sanctuary and officials of God among the descendants of both Eleazar and Ithamar. The scribe Shemaiah son of Nethanel, a Levite, recorded their names in the presence of the king and of the officials: Zadok the priest, Ahimelech son of Abiathar, and the heads of families of the priests and of the Levites—one family being taken from Eleazar and then one from Ithamar The first lot fell to Jehoiarib, the second to Jedaiah, the third to Harim, the fourth to Seorim, the fifth to Malkijah, the sixth to Mijamin, the seventh to Hakkoz, the eighth to Abijah, the ninth to Jeshua, the tenth to Shecaniah, the eleventh to Eliashib, the twelfth to Jakim, the thirteenth to Huppah, the fourteenth to Jeshebeab, the fifteenth to Bilgah, the sixteenth to Immer, the seventeenth to Hezir, the eighteenth to Happizzez, the nineteenth to Pethahiah, the twentieth to Jehezkel, the twenty-first to Jakin, the twenty-second to Gamul, the twenty-third to Delaiah, and the twenty-fourth to Maaziah This was their appointed order of ministering when they entered the temple of the Lord, according to the regulations prescribed for them by their ancestor Aaron, as the Lord, the God of Israel, had commanded him As for the rest of the descendants of Levi: from the sons of Amram: Shubael; from the sons of Shubael: Jehdeiah. As for Rehabiah, from his sons: Isshiah was the first. From the Izharites: Shelomoth; from the sons of Shelomoth: Jahath. The sons of Hebron: Jeriah the first, Amariah the second, Jahaziel the third, and Jekameam the fourth. The son of Uzziel: Micah; from the sons of Micah: Shamir. The brother of Micah: Isshiah; from the sons of Isshiah: Zechariah. The sons of Merari: Mahli and Mushi. The son of Jaaziah: Beno. The sons of Merari from Jaaziah: Beno, Shoham, Zaccur, and Ibri. From Mahli: Eleazar, who had no sons. From Kish: the son of Kish: Jerahmeel. And the sons of Mushi: Mahli, Eder, and Jerimoth These were the Levites, according to their families. They also cast lots, just as their relatives the descendants of Aaron did, in the presence of King David and of Zadok, Ahimelech, and the heads of families of the priests and of the Levites. The families of the eldest brother were treated the same as those of the youngest

Chapter 25

David, together with the commanders of the army, set apart some of the sons of Asaph, Heman, and Jeduthun for the ministry of prophesying, accompanied by harps, lyres, and cymbals. Here is the list of the men who performed this service: From the sons of Asaph: Zaccur, Joseph, Nethaniah, and Asharelah. The sons of Asaph were under the supervision of Asaph, who prophesied under the king's supervision. As for Jeduthun, from his sons: Gedaliah, Zeri, Jeshaiah, Shimei, Hashabiah, and Mattithiah—six in all—under the supervision of their father Jeduthun, who prophesied, using the harp in thanking and praising the Lord As for Heman, from his sons: Bukkiah, Mattaniah, Uzziel, Shebuel, Jerimoth, Hananiah, Hanani, Eliathah, Giddalti, Romamti-Ezer, Joshbekashah, Mallothi, Hothir, and Mahazioth. All these were sons of Heman, the king's seer. They were given to him through the promises of God to exalt him. God gave Heman fourteen sons and three daughters. All these men were under the supervision of their father for the music of the temple of the Lord, with cymbals, lyres, and harps, for the ministry at the house of God. Asaph, Jeduthun, and Heman were under the supervision of the king Along with their relatives—all of them trained and skilled in music for the Lord—they numbered 288. Young and old alike, teacher as well as student, cast lots for their duties The first lot, which was for Asaph, fell to Joseph, his sons and relatives, the second to Gedaliah, he and his relatives and sons, the third to Zaccur, his sons and relatives, the fourth to Izri, his sons and relatives, the fifth to Nethaniah, his sons and relatives, the sixth to Bukkiah, his sons and relatives, the seventh to Jesarelah, his sons and relatives, the eighth to Jeshaiah, his sons and relatives, the ninth to Mattaniah, his sons and relatives, the tenth to Shimei, his sons and relatives, the eleventh to Azarel, his sons and relatives, the twelfth to Hashabiah, his sons and relatives, the thirteenth to Shubael, his sons and relatives, the fourteenth to Mattithiah, his sons and relatives, the fifteenth to Jerimoth, his sons and relatives, the sixteenth to Hananiah, his sons and relatives, the seventeenth to Joshbekashah, his sons and relatives, the eighteenth to Hanani, his sons and relatives, the nineteenth to Mallothi, his sons and relatives, the twentieth to Eliathah, his sons and relatives, the twenty-first to Hothir, his sons and relatives, the twenty-second to Giddalti, his sons and relatives, the twenty-third to Mahazioth, his sons and relatives, and the twenty-fourth to Romamti-Ezer, his sons and relatives

Chapter 26

1 Concerning the divisions of the porters, the Korahites: Meshelemiah, the son of Kore, of the sons of Asaph. 2 The sons of Meshelemiah: Zechariah the firstborn, Jediael the second, Zebadiah the third, Jathniel the fourth, 3 Elam the fifth, Jehohanan the sixth, Eliehoenai the seventh. 4 The sons of Obed-Edom: Shemaiah the firstborn, Jehozabad the second, Joah the third, Sacar the fourth, Nethanel the fifth, 5 Ammiel the sixth, Issachar the seventh, Peulthai the eighth; for God blessed him. 6 Also to his son Shemaiah were sons born who ruled over the house of their father, for they were mighty men of valor. 7 The sons of Shemaiah: Othni, Rephael, Obed, Elzabad, and his brethren, strong men, Elihu and Semachiah. 8 All these were of the sons of Obed-Edom; they and their sons and their brethren, able men for strength for the service, were sixty-two of Obed-Edom. 9 The sons of Meshelemiah and Hosah, his son, were eighteen able men. 10 Of Hosah, the sons of Merari: Shimri the chief (for though he was not the firstborn, his father made him the chief), 11 Hilkiah the second, Tebaliah the third, Zechariah the fourth; all the sons and brethren of Hosah were thirteen. 12 Among these were the divisions of the porters, even among the chief men, having charges like their brethren, to minister in the house of the LORD. 13 And they cast lots, as well the small as the great, according to the house of their fathers, for every gate. 14 And the lot eastward fell to Shelemiah. Then for Zechariah his son, a wise counselor, they cast lots; and his lot came out northward. 15 To Obed-Edom southward; and to his sons, the house of Asuppim. 16 To Shuppim and Hosah westward, with the gate Shallecheth, by the causeway of the going up, ward against ward. 17 Eastward were six Levites, northward four a day, southward four a day, and toward Asuppim two and two. 18 At Parbar westward, four at the causeway, and two at Parbar. 19 These were the divisions of the porters among the sons of Kore, and among the sons of Merari 20 And of the Levites, Ahijah was over the treasures of the house of God, and over the treasures of the dedicated things. 21 As concerning the sons of Laadan; the sons of the Gershonite Laadan, chief fathers, even of Laadan the Gershonite, were Jehieli. 22 The sons of Jehieli; Zetham, and Joel his brother,

which were over the treasures of the house of the LORD. 23 Of the Amramites, and the Izharites, the Hebronites, and the Uzzielites: 24 And Shebuel the son of Gershom, the son of Moses, was ruler of the treasures. 25 And his brethren by Eliezer; Rehabiah his son, and Jeshaiah his son, and Joram his son, and Zichri his son, and Shelomith his son. 26 Which Shelomith and his brethren were over all the treasures of the dedicated things, which David the king, and the chief fathers, the captains over thousands and hundreds, and the captains of the host, had dedicated. 27 Out of the spoils won in battles did they dedicate to maintain the house of the LORD. 28 And all that Samuel the seer, and Saul the son of Kish, and Abner the son of Ner, and Joab the son of Zeruiah, had dedicated; and whosoever had dedicated any thing, it was under the hand of Shelomith, and of his brethren 29 Of the Izharites, Chenaniah and his sons were for the outward business over Israel, for officers and judges. 30 And of the Hebronites, Hashabiah and his brethren, men of valor, a thousand and seven hundred, were officers among them of Israel on this side Jordan westward in all the business of the LORD, and in the service of the king. 31 Among the Hebronites was Jerijah the chief, even among the Hebronites, according to the generations of his fathers. In the fortieth year of David's reign, they were sought for, and there were found among them mighty men of valor at Jazer of Gilead. 32 And his brethren, men of valor, were two thousand and seven hundred chief fathers, whom King David made rulers over the Reubenites, the Gadites, and the half tribe of Manasseh, for every matter pertaining to God, and affairs of the king

Chapter 27

1 Now the children of Israel after their number, the heads of fathers' houses and the captains of thousands and of hundreds, and their officers that served the king, in any matter of the divisions which came in and went out month by month throughout all the months of the year, of every division were twenty-four thousand. 2 Over the first division for the first month was Jashobeam the son of Zabdiel: and in his division were twenty-four thousand. 3 He was of the children of Perez, the chief of all the captains of the host for the first month. 4 And over the division of the second month was Dodai the Ahohite, and his division: and Mikloth was the ruler, and in his division were twenty-four thousand. 5 The third captain of the host for the third month was Benaiah the son of Jehoiada the chief priest: and in his division were twenty-four thousand. 6 This is that Benaiah, who was mighty among the thirty, and over the thirty: and of his division was Ammizabad his son. 7 The fourth captain for the fourth month was Asahel the brother of Joab, and Zebadiah his son after him: and in his division were twenty-four thousand. 8 The fifth captain for the fifth month was Shamhuth the Izrahite: and in his division were twenty-four thousand. 9 The sixth captain for the sixth month was Ira the son of Ikkesh the Tekoite: and in his division were twenty-four thousand. 10 The seventh captain for the seventh month was Helez the Pelonite, of the children of Ephraim: and in his division were twenty-four thousand. 11 The eighth captain for the eighth month was Sibbecai the Hushathite, of the Zarhites: and in his division were twenty-four thousand. 12 The ninth captain for the ninth month was Abiezer the Anetothite, of the Benjamites: and in his division were twenty-four thousand. 13 The tenth captain for the tenth month was Maharai the Netophathite, of the Zarhites: and in his division were twenty-four thousand. 14 The eleventh captain for the eleventh month was Benaiah the Pirathonite, of the children

of Ephraim: and in his division were twenty-four thousand. 15 The twelfth captain for the twelfth month was Heldai the Netophathite, of Othniel: and in his division were twenty-four thousand 16 Furthermore over the tribes of Israel: the ruler of the Reubenites was Eliezer the son of Zichri: of the Simeonites, Shephatiah the son of Maachah: 17 of the Levites, Hashabiah the son of Kemuel: of Aaron, Zadok: 18 of Judah, Elihu, one of the brethren of David: of Issachar, Omri the son of Michael: 19 of Zebulun, Ishmaiah the son of Obadiah: of Naphtali, Jeremoth the son of Azriel: 20 of the children of Ephraim, Hoshea the son of Azaziah: of the half-tribe of Manasseh, Joel the son of Pedaiah: 21 of the half-tribe of Manasseh in Gilead, Iddo the son of Zechariah: of Benjamin, Jaasiel the son of Abner: 22 of Dan, Azarel the son of Jeroham. These were the captains of the tribes of Israel. 23 But David took not the number of them from twenty years old and under: because the LORD had said he would increase Israel like to the stars of heaven. 24 Joab the son of Zeruiah began to number, but finished not, because there fell wrath for it against Israel; neither was the number put in the account of the chronicles of king David. 25 Over the king's treasures was Azmaveth the son of Adiel: and over the treasures in the fields, in the cities, and in the villages, and in the castles, was Jehonathan the son of Uzziah: 26 and over them that did the work of the field for tillage of the ground was Ezri the son of Chelub: 27 and over the vineyards was Shimei the Ramathite: over the increase of the vineyards for the wine cellars was Zabdi the Shiphmite: 28 and over the olive trees and the sycamore trees that were in the low plains was Baalhanan the Gederite: and over the cellars of oil was Joash: 29 and over the herds that fed in Sharon was Shitrai the Sharonite: and over the herds that were in the valleys was Shaphat the son of Adlai: 30 and over the camels also was Obil the Ishmaelite: and over the asses was Jehdeiah the Meronothite: 31 and over the flocks was Jaziz the Hagerite. All these were the rulers of the substance which was king David's. 32 Also Jonathan David's uncle was a counselor, a wise man, and a scribe: and Jehiel the son of Hachmoni was with the king's sons: 33 and Ahithophel was the king's counselor: and Hushai the Archite was the king's companion: 34 and after Ahithophel was Jehoiada the son of Benaiah, and Abiathar: and the general of the king's army was Joab

Chapter 28

1 And David assembled all the princes of Israel, the princes of the tribes, and the captains of the companies that ministered to the king by course, and the captains over the thousands, and captains over the hundreds, and the stewards over all the substance and possession of the king and of his sons, with the officers, and with the mighty men, and with all the valiant men, to Jerusalem. 2 Then David the king stood up upon his feet, and said, "Hear me, my brethren, and my people: as for me, I had in mine heart to build a house of rest for the ark of the covenant of the LORD, and for the footstool of our God, and had made ready for the building: 3 but God said unto me, 'Thou shalt not build a house for my name, because thou hast been a man of war, and hast shed blood.' 4 However, the LORD God of Israel chose me before all the house of my father to be king over Israel forever: for he hath chosen Judah to be the ruler; and of the house of Judah, the house of my father; and among the sons of my father he liked me to make me king over all Israel: 5 and of all my sons, for the LORD hath given me many sons, he hath chosen Solomon my son to sit upon the throne of the kingdom of the LORD over Israel. 6 And he said unto me, 'Solomon thy son, he shall build my house and

my courts: for I have chosen him to be my son, and I will be his father. 7 Moreover I will establish his kingdom forever, if he be constant to do my commandments and my judgments, as at this day.' 8 Now therefore, in the sight of all Israel the congregation of the LORD, and in the audience of our God, keep and seek for all the commandments of the LORD your God: that ye may possess this good land, and leave it for an inheritance for your children after you forever 9 "And thou, Solomon my son, know thou the God of thy father, and serve him with a perfect heart and with a willing mind: for the LORD searcheth all hearts, and understandeth all the imaginations of the thoughts: if thou seek him, he will be found of thee; but if thou forsake him, he will cast thee off forever. 10 Take heed now; for the LORD hath chosen thee to build a house for the sanctuary: be strong, and do it." 11 Then David gave to Solomon his son the pattern of the porch, and of the houses thereof, and of the treasuries thereof, and of the upper chambers thereof, and of the inner parlors thereof, and of the place of the mercy seat, 12 and the pattern of all that he had by the spirit, of the courts of the house of the LORD, and of all the chambers round about, of the treasures of the house of God, and of the treasures of the dedicated things: 13 also for the courses of the priests and the Levites, and for all the work of the service of the house of the LORD, and for all the vessels of service in the house of the LORD. 14 He gave of gold by weight for things of gold, for all instruments of all manner of service; silver also for all instruments of silver by weight, for all instruments of every kind of service: 15 even the weight for the candlesticks of gold, and for their lamps of gold, by weight for every candlestick, and for the lamps thereof: and for the candlesticks of silver by weight, both for the candlestick, and also for the lamps thereof, according to the use of every candlestick. 16 And by weight he gave gold for the tables of shewbread, for every table; and likewise silver for the tables of silver: 17 also pure gold for the fleshhooks, and the bowls, and the cups: and for the golden basins he gave gold by weight for every basin; and likewise silver by weight for every basin of silver: 18 and for the altar of incense refined gold by weight; and gold for the pattern of the chariot of the cherubims, that spread out their wings, and covered the ark of the covenant of the LORD. 19 "All this," said David, "the LORD made me understand in writing by his hand upon me, even all the works of this pattern." 20 And David said to Solomon his son, "Be strong and of good courage, and do it: fear not, nor be dismayed: for the LORD God, even my God, will be with thee; he will not fail thee, nor forsake thee, until thou hast finished all the work for the service of the house of the LORD. 21 And, behold, the courses of the priests and the Levites, even they shall be with thee for all the service of the house of God: and there shall be with thee for all manner of workmanship every willing skillful man, for any manner of service: also the princes and all the people will be wholly at thy commandment."

Chapter 29

1 Furthermore David the king said unto all the congregation, "Solomon my son, whom alone God hath chosen, is yet young and tender, and the work is great: for the palace is not for man, but for the LORD God. 2 Now I have prepared with all my might for the house of my God the gold for things to be made of gold, and the silver for things of silver, and the brass for things of brass, the iron for things of iron, and wood for things of wood; onyx stones, and stones to be set, glistering stones, and of divers colors, and all manner of precious stones, and marble stones in abundance. 3 Moreover, because I have set my

affection to the house of my God, I have of mine own proper good, of gold and silver, which I have given to the house of my God, over and above all that I have prepared for the holy house, 4 even three thousand talents of gold, of the gold of Ophir, and seven thousand talents of refined silver, to overlay the walls of the houses withal: 5 the gold for things of gold, and the silver for things of silver, and for all manner of work to be made by the hands of artificers. And who then is willing to consecrate his service this day unto the LORD?" 6 Then the chief of the fathers and princes of the tribes of Israel, and the captains of thousands and of hundreds, with the rulers of the king's work, offered willingly, 7 and gave for the service of the house of God of gold five thousand talents and ten thousand drams, and of silver ten thousand talents, and of brass eighteen thousand talents, and one hundred thousand talents of iron. 8 And they with whom precious stones were found gave them to the treasure of the house of the LORD, by the hand of Jehiel the Gershonite. 9 Then the people rejoiced, for that they offered willingly, because with perfect heart they offered willingly to the LORD: and David the king also rejoiced with great joy 10 Wherefore David blessed the LORD before all the congregation: and David said, "Blessed be thou, LORD God of Israel our father, for ever and ever. 11 Thine, O LORD, is the greatness, and the power, and the glory, and the victory, and the majesty: for all that is in the heaven and in the earth is thine; thine is the kingdom, O LORD, and thou art exalted as head above all. 12 Both riches and honor come of thee, and thou reignest over all; and in thine hand is power and might; and in thine hand it is to make great, and to give strength unto all. 13 Now therefore, our God, we thank thee, and praise thy glorious name. 14 But who am I, and what is my people, that we should be able to offer so willingly after this sort? For all things come of thee, and of thine own have we given thee. 15 For we are strangers before thee, and sojourners, as were all our fathers: our days on the earth are as a shadow, and there is none abiding. 16 O LORD our God, all this store that we have prepared to build thee an house for thine holy name cometh of thine hand, and is all thine own. 17 I know also, my God, that thou triest the heart, and hast pleasure in uprightness. As for me, in the uprightness of mine heart I have willingly offered all these things: and now have I seen with joy thy people, which are present here, to offer willingly unto thee. 18 O LORD God of Abraham, Isaac, and of Israel, our fathers, keep this forever in the imagination of the thoughts of the heart of thy people, and prepare their heart unto thee: 19 and give unto Solomon my son a perfect heart, to keep thy commandments, thy testimonies, and thy statutes, and to do all these things, and to build the palace, for the which I have made provision." 20 And David said to all the congregation, "Now bless the LORD your God." And all the congregation blessed the LORD God of their fathers, and bowed down their heads, and worshipped the LORD, and the king. 21 And they sacrificed sacrifices unto the LORD, and offered burnt offerings unto the LORD, on the morrow after that day, even a thousand bullocks, a thousand rams, and a thousand lambs, with their drink offerings, and sacrifices in abundance for all Israel: 22 and did eat and drink before the LORD on that day with great gladness. And they made Solomon the son of David king the second time, and anointed him unto the LORD to be the chief governor, and Zadok to be priest. 23 Then Solomon sat on the throne of the LORD as king instead of David his father, and prospered; and all Israel obeyed him. 24 And all the princes, and the mighty men, and all the sons likewise of king David, submitted themselves unto Solomon the king. 25 And the LORD magnified Solomon exceedingly in the sight of all Israel, and bestowed upon him such royal majesty as had not been on any king before him in Israel 26 Thus David the son of Jesse reigned over all Israel. 27 And the time that he reigned over Israel was forty years; seven years reigned he in Hebron, and thirty and three years reigned he in Jerusalem. 28 And he died in a good old age, full of days, riches, and honor: and Solomon his son reigned in his stead. 29 Now the acts of David the king, first and last, behold, they are written in the book of Samuel the seer, and in the book of Nathan the prophet, and in the book of Gad the seer, 30 with all his reign and his might, and the times that went over him, and over Israel, and over all the kingdoms of the countries

14. 2 Chronicles

Chapter 1

Solomon, the son of David, was firmly established in his kingdom. The Lord his God was with him and greatly magnified him. Solomon spoke to all of Israel, including the captains of thousands and hundreds, the judges, and all the rulers of Israel, as well as the chief fathers. Solomon and all the congregation with him went to the place in Gibeon where the tabernacle of the congregation of God was located. This tabernacle had been built by Moses, the Lord's servant, in the wilderness. However, the Ark of God had been brought by David from Kiriath-Jearim to a tent he had pitched for it in Jerusalem Moreover, the bronze altar that Bezaleel, the son of Uri, the son of Hur, had made, was set before the tabernacle of the Lord. Solomon and the congregation sought the altar. Solomon offered sacrifices before the Lord on this bronze altar in the tabernacle of the congregation, offering thousands of burnt offerings. That night, God appeared to Solomon and said, "Ask what I shall give you." Solomon replied to God, "You have shown great mercy to my father David and have made me king in his place. Now, O Lord God, let Your promise to David my father come true, for You have made me king over a great people, as numerous as the dust of the earth. Therefore, give me wisdom and knowledge, so that I may lead these people, for who can govern this great people of Yours?" God said to Solomon, "Since this was in your heart and you did not ask for riches, wealth, honor, the lives of your enemies, or even long life, but instead asked for wisdom and knowledge to govern my people over whom I have made you king, wisdom and knowledge are granted to you. Moreover, I will give you riches, wealth, and honor such as no king before you has ever had, nor will any after you have." Solomon then returned from Gibeon to Jerusalem, before the tabernacle of meeting, and reigned over Israel. Solomon gathered chariots and horsemen; he had fourteen hundred chariots and twelve thousand horsemen, whom he stationed in the chariot cities and with the king in Jerusalem. The king made silver and gold as plentiful in Jerusalem as stones, and cedar as abundant as sycamore trees in the foothills. Solomon imported horses from Egypt and Kue; the king's merchants purchased them from Kue at the current price. They imported a chariot from Egypt for six hundred shekels of silver and a horse for a hundred and fifty. They also exported them to all the kings of the Hittites and the kings of Aram

Chapter 2

Solomon decided to build a temple for the name of the Lord and a royal palace for himself. He assigned seventy thousand men as carriers, eighty thousand as stonecutters in the hills, and thirty-six hundred as supervisors. Solomon sent this message to Hiram, king of Tyre: "Do as you did for my father David when you sent him cedar to build a house to live in. Now I am about to build a temple for the name of the Lord my God and to dedicate it to Him for burning fragrant incense before Him, for setting out the consecrated bread regularly, and for making burnt offerings every morning and evening and on the Sabbaths, the New Moons, and the appointed festivals of the Lord our God. This is a lasting ordinance for Israel "The temple I am going to build will be great because our God is greater than all other gods. But who is able to build a temple for Him since the heavens, even the highest heavens, cannot contain Him? Who then am I to build a temple for Him, except as a place to burn sacrifices before Him? "Send me, therefore, a man skilled to work in gold and silver, bronze and iron, and in purple, crimson, and blue yarn, and experienced in the art of engraving, to work in Judah and Jerusalem with my skilled workers, whom my father David provided. Send me also cedar, juniper, and algum logs from Lebanon, for I know that your servants are skilled in cutting timber there. My servants will work with yours to provide me with plenty of lumber, because the temple I build must be large and magnificent. I will give your servants, the woodsmen who cut the timber, twenty thousand cors of ground wheat, twenty thousand cors of barley, twenty thousand baths of wine, and twenty thousand baths of olive oil." Hiram, king of Tyre, replied by letter to Solomon: "Because the Lord loves His people, He has made you their king." And Hiram added: "Praise be to the Lord, the God of Israel, who made heaven and earth! He has given King David a wise son, endowed with intelligence and discernment, who will build a temple for the Lord and a palace for himself "I am sending you Huram-Abi, a man of great skill, whose mother was from Dan and whose father was from Tyre. He is trained to work in gold and silver, bronze and iron, stone and wood, and with purple and blue and crimson yarn and fine linen. He is experienced in all kinds of engraving and can execute any design given to him. He will work with your skilled workers and with those of my lord, David, your father "Now let my lord send his servants the wheat and barley and the olive oil and wine he promised, and we will cut all the logs from Lebanon that you need and will float them as rafts by sea down to Joppa. From there you can take them up to Jerusalem." Solomon took a census of all the foreigners residing in Israel, after the census his father David had taken, and they were found to be 153,600. He assigned seventy thousand of them to be carriers and eighty thousand to be stonecutters in the hills, with thirty-six hundred foremen to keep the people working

Chapter 3

Solomon began to build the temple of the Lord in Jerusalem on Mount Moriah, where the Lord had appeared to his father David. It was on the threshing floor of Araunah the Jebusite, the place provided by David. He began building on the second day of the second month in the fourth year of his reign The foundation Solomon laid for building the temple of God was sixty cubits long and twenty cubits wide (using the cubit of the old standard). The portico at the front of the temple was twenty cubits long across the width of the building and twenty cubits high. He overlaid the inside with pure gold. He paneled the main hall with juniper and covered it with fine gold and decorated it with palm tree and chain designs. He adorned the temple with precious stones. And the gold he used was gold of Parvaim. He overlaid the ceiling beams, door frames, walls and doors of the temple with gold, and he carved cherubim on the walls He built the Most Holy Place, its length

corresponding to the width of the temple—twenty cubits long and twenty cubits wide. He overlaid the inside with six hundred talents of fine gold. The gold nails weighed fifty shekels. He also overlaid the upper parts with gold For the Most Holy Place, he made a pair of sculptured cherubim and overlaid them with gold. The total wingspan of the cherubim was twenty cubits. One wing of the first cherub was five cubits long and touched the temple wall, while its other wing, also five cubits long, touched the wing of the other cherub. Similarly, one wing of the second cherub was five cubits long and touched the other temple wall, and its other wing, also five cubits long, touched the wing of the first cherub. The wings of these cherubim extended twenty cubits. They stood on their feet, facing the main hall He made the curtain of blue, purple and crimson yarn and fine linen, with cherubim worked into it. For the front of the temple he made two pillars, which together were thirty-five cubits long, each with a capital five cubits high. He made interwoven chains and put them on top of the pillars. He also made a hundred pomegranates and attached them to the chains. He erected the pillars in front of the temple, one to the south and one to the north; the one to the south he named Jakin and the one to the north Boaz

Chapter 4

He made a bronze altar twenty cubits long, twenty cubits wide, and ten cubits high. He made the Sea of cast metal, circular in shape, measuring ten cubits from rim to rim and five cubits high. It took a line of thirty cubits to measure around it. Below the rim, figures of bulls encircled it—ten to a cubit. The bulls were cast in two rows in one piece with the Sea The Sea stood on twelve bulls, three facing north, three facing west, three facing south, and three facing east. The Sea rested on top of them, and their hindquarters were toward the center. It was a handbreadth in thickness, and its rim was like the rim of a cup, like a lily blossom. It held three thousand baths He then made ten basins for washing and placed five on the south side and five on the north. In them, the things to be used for the burnt offerings were rinsed, but the Sea was to be used by the priests for washing. He made ten gold lampstands according to the specifications for them and placed them in the temple, five on the south side and five on the north. He made ten tables and placed them in the temple, five on the south side and five on the north. He also made a hundred gold sprinkling bowls He made the courtyard of the priests, and the large court and the doors for the court, and overlaid the doors with bronze. He placed the Sea on the south side, at the southeast corner And Huram also made the pots, shovels and sprinkling bowls. So Huram finished the work he had undertaken for King Solomon in the temple of God: the two pillars; the two bowl-shaped capitals on top of the pillars; the two sets of network decorating the two bowl-shaped capitals on top of the pillars; the four hundred pomegranates for the two sets of network (two rows of pomegranates for each network, decorating the bowl-shaped capitals on top of the pillars); the stands with their basins; the Sea and the twelve bulls under it; the pots, shovels, meat forks and all related articles. All the objects that Huram-Abi made for King Solomon for the temple of the Lord were of polished bronze The king had them cast in clay molds in the plain of the Jordan between Sukkoth and Zarethan. All these things that Solomon made amounted to so much that the weight of the bronze could not be calculated Solomon also made all the furnishings that were in God's temple: the golden altar; the tables on which was the bread of the Presence; the lampstands of pure gold with their lamps, to burn in front of the inner sanctuary as prescribed; the gold floral work and lamps and tongs (they were solid gold); the pure gold wick trimmers, sprinkling bowls, dishes and censers; and the gold doors of the temple: the inner doors to the Most Holy Place and the doors of the main hall

Chapter 5

So all the work Solomon did for the temple of the Lord was completed. Then he brought in the things his father David had dedicated—the silver and gold and all the furnishings—and he placed them in the treasuries of God's temple Then Solomon summoned to Jerusalem the elders of Israel, all the heads of the tribes and the chiefs of the Israelite families, to bring up the ark of the Lord's covenant from Zion, the City of David. All the Israelites came together to the king at the time of the festival in the seventh month. When all the elders of Israel had arrived, the Levites took up the ark, and they brought up the ark and the tent of meeting and all the sacred furnishings in it. The Levitical priests carried them up, and King Solomon and the entire assembly of Israel that had gathered about him were before the ark, sacrificing so many sheep and cattle that they could not be recorded or counted The priests then brought the ark of the Lord's covenant to its place in the inner sanctuary of the temple, the Most Holy Place, and put it beneath the wings of the cherubim. The cherubim spread their wings over the place of the ark and covered the ark and its carrying poles. These poles were so long that their ends, extending from the ark, could be seen from in front of the inner sanctuary but not from outside the Holy Place; and they are still there today. There was nothing in the ark except the two tablets that Moses had placed in it at Horeb, where the Lord made a covenant with the Israelites after they came out of Egypt The priests then withdrew from the Holy Place. All the priests who were there had consecrated themselves, regardless of their divisions. All the Levites who were musicians—Asaph, Heman, Jeduthun and their sons and relatives—stood on the east side of the altar, dressed in fine linen and playing cymbals, harps and lyres. They were accompanied by 120 priests sounding trumpets. The trumpeters and musicians joined in unison to give praise and thanks to the Lord. Accompanied by trumpets, cymbals and other instruments, the singers raised their voices in praise to the Lord and sang: "He is good; His love endures forever." Then the temple of the Lord was filled with the cloud, and the priests could not perform their service because of the cloud, for the glory of the Lord filled the temple of God

Chapter 6

Solomon said, "The LORD said that he would dwell in the dark clouds: And I have built you a house to dwell in, a dwelling place for you to dwell in forever." The king turned and blessed all the congregation of Israel, for all the congregation of Israel stood there. He said, "Blessed be the LORD, the God of Israel, who spoke with His mouth to David my father, and with His hand fulfilled it, saying, 'From the day that I brought my people out of the land of Egypt, I chose no city out of all the tribes of Israel to build a house, that my Name might be there, nor did I choose any man to be the head of my people of Israel. But I chose Jerusalem, that my Name might be there, and I chose David to be the head of my people of Israel.' David my father had it in his heart to build a house for the Name of the LORD, the God of Israel, but the LORD said to David, my father, 'Since you had it in your heart to build a house in honor of my Name, you did well to think so. Nevertheless, you shall not build the house, but your son who will be born to you shall build the house in honor of my Name.' The LORD

fulfilled the word He had spoken, and I rose up in the place of David my father and settled on the throne of Israel, as the LORD had promised, and built a house for the Name of the LORD, the God of Israel. I have placed the ark there, wherein is the covenant of the LORD which He made with the children of Israel." The king stood before the altar of the LORD in the presence of all the congregation of Israel and stretched out his hands. Solomon had made a bronze platform and placed it in the center of the courtyard, five cubits long, five cubits wide, and three cubits high. He stood upon it, knelt down before all the community of Israel, and stretched out his hands upward. He said, "O LORD, God of Israel, there is no God like you either in heaven or on earth, who retains friendliness and mercy toward your servants, who walk before you with all their hearts. You who kept with your servant David my father what you promised him, for you spoke with your mouth and kept it with your hand, as it appears today. Therefore now, O LORD God of Israel, keep with your servant David, my father, what you promised him, saying, 'You shall not lack a man in my sight, to sit on the throne of Israel; so that your sons may keep their ways, to walk in my law, as you have walked before me.' Now, O LORD God of Israel, let your word come true that you spoke to your servant David. But will God indeed dwell with man on earth? Behold, the heavens and the heaven of heavens cannot contain you; how much less this house that I have built? Yet regard the prayer of your servant and his supplication, O LORD my God, and listen to the cry and the prayer which your servant prays before you, that your eyes may be open toward this house day and night, toward the place where you said that you would put your Name, to listen to the prayer which your servant prays toward this place. Listen to the supplications of your servant and of your people Israel, when they pray toward this place; hear from heaven your dwelling place, and when you hear, forgive When anyone sins against his neighbor and is required to take an oath, and comes and swears the oath before your altar in this house, then hear from heaven and act. Judge between your servants, condemning the wicked by bringing his way on his own head, and justifying the righteous by giving him according to his righteousness. When your people Israel are defeated before an enemy because they have sinned against you, and return and confess your Name, and pray and make supplication before you in this house, then hear from heaven and forgive the sin of your people Israel, and bring them back to the land which you gave to them and their fathers When the heavens are shut up and there is no rain because they have sinned against you, and they pray toward this place and confess your Name, and turn from their sin when you afflict them, then hear in heaven and forgive the sin of your servants, your people Israel, when you teach them the good way in which they should walk; and send rain on your land which you have given to your people as an inheritance. When there is famine in the land, pestilence or blight or mildew, locusts or grasshoppers; when their enemies besiege them in the land of their cities; whatever plague or whatever sickness there is; whatever prayer or whatever supplication is made by anyone, or by all your people Israel, when each one knows his own burden and his own grief, and spreads out his hands to this house, then hear from heaven your dwelling place, and forgive, and give to everyone according to all his ways, whose heart you know (for you alone know the hearts of the sons of men), that they may fear you, to walk in your ways as long as they live in the land which you gave to our fathers Moreover, concerning a foreigner, who is not of your people Israel, but has come from a far country for the sake of your great Name and your mighty hand and your outstretched arm, when they come and pray in this house; then hear from heaven your dwelling place, and do according to all for which the foreigner calls to you, that all peoples of the earth may know your Name and fear you, as do your people Israel, and that they may know that this house which I have built is called by your Name. When your people go out to battle against their enemies, wherever you send them, and when they pray to you toward this city which you have chosen and the house which I have built for your Name, then hear from heaven their prayer and their supplication, and maintain their cause When they sin against you (for there is no one who does not sin), and you become angry with them and deliver them to the enemy, and they take them captive to a land far or near; yet when they come to themselves in the land where they were carried captive, and repent, and make supplication to you in the land of their captivity, saying, 'We have sinned, we have done wrong, and have committed wickedness'; and when they return to you with all their heart and with all their soul in the land of their captivity, where they have been carried captive, and pray toward their land which you gave to their fathers, the city which you have chosen, and toward the house which I have built for your Name; then hear from heaven your dwelling place their prayer and their supplications, and maintain their cause, and forgive your people who have sinned against you. Now, my God, I pray, let your eyes be open and let your ears be attentive to the prayer made in this place. Now therefore, arise, O LORD God, to your resting place, you and the ark of your strength. Let your priests, O LORD God, be clothed with salvation, and let your saints rejoice in goodness. O LORD God, do not turn away the face of your anointed; remember the mercies of your servant David."

Chapter 7

When Solomon had finished praying, fire came down from heaven and consumed the burnt offerings and the sacrifices; and the glory of the LORD filled the house. The priests could not enter the house of the LORD because the glory of the LORD had filled it. When all the children of Israel saw how the fire came down and the glory of the LORD upon the house, they bowed down on the pavement with their faces to the ground, and worshiped and praised the LORD, saying, "He is good; His mercy endures forever." Then the king and all the people offered sacrifices before the LORD. King Solomon offered a sacrifice of twenty-two thousand cattle and a hundred and twenty thousand sheep. So the king and all the people dedicated the house of God. The priests stood at their posts, as did the Levites with the instruments of music of the LORD, which King David had made for giving thanks to the LORD—"for His mercy endures forever"—whenever David offered praise by their ministry. Opposite them, the priests blew trumpets, and all Israel stood Moreover, Solomon consecrated the middle of the court that was in front of the house of the LORD; for there he offered burnt offerings and the fat of the peace offerings, because the bronze altar which Solomon had made was not able to receive the burnt offerings, the grain offerings, and the fat. At that time Solomon kept the feast for seven days, and all Israel with him, a very great assembly from the entrance of Hamath to the Brook of Egypt. On the eighth day they held a solemn assembly, for they had kept the dedication of the altar for seven days, and the feast for seven days. On the twenty-third day of the seventh month he sent the people away to their tents, joyful and glad of heart for the goodness that the LORD had shown to

David, to Solomon, and to His people Israel Thus Solomon finished the house of the LORD and the king's house; and Solomon successfully accomplished all that came into his heart to make in the house of the LORD and in his own house. Then the LORD appeared to Solomon by night and said to him: "I have heard your prayer and have chosen this place for Myself as a house of sacrifice. When I shut up heaven and there is no rain, or command the locusts to devour the land, or send pestilence among My people, if My people who are called by My Name will humble themselves, and pray and seek My face, and turn from their wicked ways, then I will hear from heaven, and will forgive their sin and heal their land. Now My eyes will be open and My ears attentive to prayer made in this place. For now I have chosen and sanctified this house, that My Name may be there forever; and My eyes and My heart will be there perpetually. As for you, if you walk before Me as your father David walked, and do according to all that I have commanded you, and if you keep My statutes and My judgments, then I will establish the throne of your kingdom, as I covenanted with David your father, saying, 'You shall not fail to have a man as ruler in Israel.' But if you turn away and forsake My statutes and My commandments which I have set before you, and go and serve other gods, and worship them, then I will uproot them from My land which I have given them; and this house which I have sanctified for My Name I will cast out of My sight, and will make it a proverb and a byword among all peoples. And as for this house, which is exalted, everyone who passes by it will be astonished and say, 'Why has the LORD done thus to this land and this house?' Then they will answer, 'Because they forsook the LORD God of their fathers, who brought them out of the land of Egypt, and embraced other gods, and worshiped them and served them; therefore He has brought all this calamity on them.'"

Chapter 8

After twenty years, Solomon built the house of the LORD and his own house. Solomon rebuilt the cities that Hiram had given him, and settled the children of Israel in them. Solomon then went to Hamath Zobah and captured it. He built Tadmor in the wilderness and all the store cities which he built in Hamath. He also built Upper Beth Horon and Lower Beth Horon, fortified cities with walls, gates, and bars; as well as Baalath, and all the storage cities that Solomon had, all the chariot cities, the cities of the cavalry, and all the desired buildings that Solomon wanted to build in Jerusalem, in Lebanon, and throughout all the land of his dominion As for all the people who were left of the Hittites, Amorites, Perizzites, Hivites, and Jebusites, who were not of Israel— their descendants who were left in the land after them, whom the children of Israel had not completely destroyed— Solomon made them pay tribute to this day. But Solomon did not make slaves of the children of Israel for his work; they were men of war, his captains, his officers, his chariot commanders, and his cavalry. There were also King Solomon's chief officials, two hundred and fifty, who ruled over the people Solomon brought Pharaoh's daughter up from the City of David to the house he had built for her, for he said, "My wife shall not dwell in the house of David, king of Israel, because the places to which the ark of the LORD has come are holy." Solomon offered burnt offerings to the LORD on the altar of the LORD which he had built before the vestibule, according to the daily requirement for offerings commanded by Moses for the Sabbaths, the New Moons, and the three annual feasts—the Feast of Unleavened Bread, the Feast of Weeks, and the Feast of Tabernacles. According to the order of David his father, he appointed the divisions of the priests for their service, the Levites for their duties (to praise and serve before the priests) as the duty of each day required, and the gatekeepers by their divisions at each gate; for so David the man of God had commanded. They did not depart from the command of the king to the priests and Levites concerning any matter or concerning the treasuries All the work of Solomon was well-ordered from the day of the foundation of the house of the LORD until it was finished. So the house of the LORD was completed. Then Solomon went to Ezion Geber and Eloth on the seacoast, in the land of Edom. And Hiram sent him ships commanded by his servants, and experienced seamen, who went with Solomon's servants to Ophir, and brought four hundred and fifty talents of gold to King Solomon

Chapter 9

When the queen of Sheba heard of Solomon's fame, she came to Jerusalem to test Solomon with hard questions, having a very great retinue, with camels bearing spices, much gold, and precious stones. When she came to Solomon, she spoke with him about all that was in her heart. Solomon answered all her questions; there was nothing too difficult for Solomon to explain to her. When the queen of Sheba had seen the wisdom of Solomon, the house that he had built, the food of his table, the seating of his officials, the attendance of his servants and their apparel, his cupbearers and their apparel, and his entryway by which he went up to the house of the LORD, there was no more spirit in her She said to the king, "The report which I heard in my own land about your words and your wisdom was true. However, I did not believe their words until I came and saw with my own eyes; and indeed, the half of your greatness and wisdom was not told me. You exceed the fame of which I heard. Happy are your men and happy are these your servants, who stand continually before you and hear your wisdom! Blessed be the LORD your God, who delighted in you, setting you on His throne to be king for the LORD your God! Because your God has loved Israel, to establish them forever, therefore He made you king over them, to do justice and righteousness." She gave the king one hundred and twenty talents of gold, spices in great abundance, and precious stones. There never were any spices such as those the queen of Sheba gave to King Solomon Also, the servants of Hiram and the servants of Solomon, who brought gold from Ophir, brought algum wood and precious stones. And the king made walkways of the algum wood for the house of the LORD and for the king's house, also harps and stringed instruments for singers. And there were none such as these seen before in the land of Judah. King Solomon gave to the queen of Sheba all she desired, whatever she asked, much more than she had brought to the king. So she turned and went to her own country, she and her servants The weight of gold that came to Solomon yearly was six hundred and sixty-six talents of gold, besides what the traveling merchants and traders brought. And all the kings of Arabia and governors of the country brought gold and silver to Solomon. King Solomon made two hundred large shields of hammered gold; six hundred shekels of hammered gold went into each shield. He also made three hundred shields of hammered gold; three hundred shekels of gold went into each shield. The king put them in the House of the Forest of Lebanon Moreover, the king made a great throne of ivory, and overlaid it with pure gold. The throne had six steps, with a footstool of gold, which were fastened to the throne. There were armrests on either side of the place of the seat, and two lions stood beside the armrests. Twelve lions stood there, one on each side of the six steps. Nothing like this had been made for any other kingdom. All King Solomon's drinking vessels were of gold, and all the vessels of the House of the Forest of Lebanon were of pure gold. Not one was of silver, for this was accounted as nothing in the days of Solomon. For the king's ships went to Tarshish with the servants of Hiram. Once every three years the ships of Tarshish brought gold, silver, ivory, apes, and peacocks So King Solomon surpassed all the kings of the earth in riches and wisdom. And all the kings of the earth sought the presence of Solomon to hear his wisdom, which God had put in his heart. Each man brought his present: articles of silver and gold, garments, armor, spices, horses, and mules, at a set rate year by year. Solomon had four thousand stalls for horses and chariots, and twelve thousand horsemen whom he stationed in the chariot cities and with the king at Jerusalem. He reigned over all the kings from the River to the land of the Philistines, as far as the border of Egypt. The king made silver as common in Jerusalem as stones, and he made cedar trees as abundant as the sycamores which are in the lowland. And they brought horses to Solomon from Egypt and from all lands Now the rest of the acts of Solomon, first and last, are they not written in the book of Nathan the prophet, in the prophecy of Ahijah the Shilonite, and in the visions of Iddo the seer concerning Jeroboam the son of Nebat? Solomon reigned in Jerusalem over all Israel for forty years. Then Solomon rested with his fathers and was buried in the City of David his father. And Rehoboam his son reigned in his place

Chapter 10

Rehoboam went to Shechem, for all Israel had gone to Shechem to make him king. When Jeroboam the son of Nebat heard it (he was in Egypt, where he had fled from the presence of King Solomon), he returned from Egypt. They sent for him and called him. Jeroboam and all Israel came and spoke to Rehoboam, saying, "Your father made our yoke heavy; now therefore, lighten the burdensome service of your father and his heavy yoke which he put on us, and we will serve you." So he said to them, "Come back to me after three days." And the people departed Then King Rehoboam consulted the elders who stood before his father Solomon while he still lived, saying, "How do you advise me to answer these people?" And they spoke to him, saying, "If you are kind to these people, and please them, and speak good words to them, they will be your servants forever." But he rejected the advice which the elders had given him and consulted the young men who had grown up with him, who stood before him. And he said to them, "What advice do you give? How should we answer these people who have spoken to me, saying, 'Lighten the yoke which your father put on us'?" Then the young men who had grown up with him spoke to him, saying, "Thus you should speak to the people who have spoken to you, saying, 'Your father made our yoke heavy, but you make it lighter on us'— thus you shall say to them: 'My little finger shall be thicker than my father's waist! And now, whereas my father put a heavy yoke on you, I will add to your yoke; my father chastised you with whips, but I will chastise you with scourges!'" So Jeroboam and all the people came to Rehoboam on the third day, as the king had directed, saying, "Come back to me on the third day." Then the king answered them roughly. King Rehoboam rejected the advice of the elders, and he spoke to them according to the advice of the young men, saying, "My father made your yoke heavy, but I will add to it; my father chastised you with whips, but I will chastise you with scourges!" So the king did not listen to the people, for the turn of events was from God, that the LORD might fulfill His word which He had spoken by the hand of Ahijah the Shilonite to Jeroboam the son of Nebat Now when all Israel saw that the king did not listen to them, the people answered the king, saying: "What share have we in David? We have no inheritance in the son of Jesse. Every man to your tents, O Israel! Now see to your own house, O David!" So all Israel departed to their tents. But Rehoboam reigned over the children of Israel who dwelt in the cities of Judah Then King Rehoboam sent Hadoram, who was in charge of revenue, but the children of Israel stoned him with stones, and he died. Therefore King Rehoboam mounted his chariot in haste to flee to Jerusalem. So Israel has been in rebellion against the house of David to this day

Chapter 11

When Rehoboam had come to Jerusalem, he gathered from the house of Judah and Benjamin nine thousand men chosen for war, to fight against Israel and bring the kingdom back to Rehoboam. But the word of the Lord came to Shemaiah, the man of God, saying, "Speak to Rehoboam, the son of Solomon, king of Judah, and to all Israel in Judah and Benjamin: Thus says the LORD, 'You shall not go up and fight against your brothers; return every man to his house, for this thing is from Me.'" They obeyed the word of the Lord and turned back from going against Jeroboam Rehoboam settled in Jerusalem and fortified cities in Judah. He built up Bethlehem, Etam, Tekoa, Beth-Zur, Soco, Adullam, Gath, Mareshah, Ziph, Adoraim, Lachish, Azekah, Zorah, Aijalon, and Hebron, which were fortified cities in Judah and Benjamin. He fortified the strongholds and put commanders in them, with supplies of food, oil, and wine. In every city, he put shields and spears, making them very strong. Judah and Benjamin were his The priests and the Levites who were in all Israel resorted to him from all their territories. For the Levites left their common lands and their possessions and came to Judah and Jerusalem, because Jeroboam and his sons had rejected them from serving as priests to the Lord. He appointed his own priests for the high places and for the goat idols and the calf idols he had made. After the Levites, people from all the tribes of Israel who set their hearts on seeking the Lord, the God of Israel, came to Jerusalem to offer sacrifices to the Lord, the God of their fathers. They strengthened the kingdom of Judah and made Rehoboam, the son of Solomon, strong for three years; for three years they walked in the ways of David and Solomon Rehoboam married Mahalath, the daughter of Jerimoth, the son of David, and Abihail, the daughter of Eliab, the son of Jesse. She bore him sons: Jeush, Shemariah, and Zaham. After her, he married Maakah, the daughter of Absalom, who bore him Abijah, Attai, Ziza, and Shelomith. Rehoboam loved Maakah, the daughter of Absalom, more than all his other wives and concubines. He had eighteen wives and sixty concubines, and fathered twenty-eight sons and sixty daughters. Rehoboam appointed Abijah, the son of Maakah, as chief prince among his brothers, intending to make him king. He acted wisely and dispersed some of his sons throughout the territories of Judah and Benjamin, to every fortified city. He gave them provisions in abundance and sought many wives for them

Chapter 12

When Rehoboam had established the kingdom and made it strong, he and all Israel with him forsook the law of the LORD. In the fifth year of King Rehoboam, Shishak, king of Egypt, came up against Jerusalem because they had transgressed against the LORD. With twelve hundred chariots and sixty thousand horsemen, the people who came with him from Egypt were innumerable: the Libyans, the Sukkiim, and the Ethiopians. He captured the fortified cities of Judah and came as far as Jerusalem Then Shemaiah, the prophet, came to Rehoboam and the princes of Judah, who had gathered in Jerusalem because of Shishak, and said to them, "Thus says the LORD, 'You have forsaken Me, therefore I have left you in the hand of Shishak.'" Then the princes of Israel and the king humbled themselves and said, "The LORD is righteous." When the LORD saw that they humbled themselves, the word of the LORD came to Shemaiah, saying, "They have humbled themselves; therefore I will not destroy them, but I will grant them some deliverance. My wrath shall not be poured out on Jerusalem by the hand of Shishak. Nevertheless, they will become his servants, that they may learn the difference between My service and the service of the kingdoms of the countries." So Shishak, king of Egypt, came up against Jerusalem and took away the treasures of the house of the LORD and the treasures of the king's house. He took everything; he also carried away the gold shields which Solomon had made. Then King Rehoboam made bronze shields in their place and committed them to the hands of the captains of the guard who guarded the entrance to the king's house. Whenever the king entered the house of the LORD, the guards went and brought them out; afterward, they returned them to the guardroom. Because Rehoboam humbled himself, the anger of the LORD turned from him, so as not to destroy him completely. Indeed, there were good things in Judah King Rehoboam established himself in Jerusalem and reigned. Rehoboam was forty-one years old when he became king, and he reigned seventeen years in Jerusalem, the city which the LORD had chosen out of all the tribes of Israel to put His name there. His mother's name was Naamah, an Ammonitess. He did evil because he did not prepare his heart to seek the LORD. The acts of Rehoboam, first and last, are they not written in the book of Shemaiah the prophet, and of Iddo the seer, concerning genealogies? And there were wars between Rehoboam and Jeroboam continually. So Rehoboam rested with his fathers and was buried in the City of David. Abijah, his son, succeeded him as king

Chapter 13

In the eighteenth year of King Jeroboam, Abijah became king over Judah. He reigned three years in Jerusalem. His mother's name was Michaiah, the daughter of Uriel of Gibeah. And there was war between Abijah and Jeroboam. Abijah set the battle in order with an army of valiant warriors, four hundred thousand choice men. Jeroboam also drew up in battle formation against him with eight hundred thousand choice men, mighty men of valor Then Abijah stood on Mount Zemaraim, which is in the mountains of Ephraim, and said, "Hear me, Jeroboam and all Israel! Should you not know that the LORD God of Israel gave the dominion over Israel to David forever, to him and his sons, by a covenant of salt? Yet Jeroboam, the son of Nebat, the servant of Solomon, the son of David, rose up and rebelled against his lord. Then worthless rogues gathered to him and strengthened themselves against Rehoboam, the son of Solomon, when Rehoboam was young and inexperienced and could not withstand them "And now you think to withstand the kingdom of the LORD, which is in the hand of the sons of David. And you are a great multitude, and with you are the gold calves which Jeroboam made for you as gods. Have you not cast out the priests of the LORD, the sons of Aaron, and the Levites, and made for yourselves priests like the peoples of other lands, so that whoever comes to consecrate himself with a young bull and seven rams may be a priest of things that are not gods? But as for us, the LORD is our God, and we have not forsaken Him; and the priests who minister to the LORD are the sons of Aaron, and the Levites attend to their duties. And they burn to the LORD every morning and every evening burnt sacrifices and sweet incense; they also set the showbread in order on the pure gold table, and the lampstand of gold with its lamps to burn every evening; for we keep the command of the LORD our God, but you have forsaken Him "Now look, God Himself is with us as our head, and His priests with sounding trumpets to sound the alarm against you. O children of Israel, do not fight against the LORD God of your fathers, for you shall not prosper!" But Jeroboam caused an ambush to go around behind them, so they were in front of Judah, and the ambush was behind them. And when Judah looked around, to their surprise, the battle line was at both front and rear; and they cried out to the LORD, and the priests sounded the trumpets. Then the men of Judah gave a shout; and as the men of Judah shouted, it happened that God struck Jeroboam and all Israel before Abijah and Judah. And the children of Israel fled before Judah, and God delivered them into their hand. Then Abijah and his people struck them with a great slaughter; so five hundred thousand choice men of Israel fell slain. Thus the children of Israel were subdued at that time; and the children of Judah prevailed, because they relied on the LORD God of their fathers And Abijah pursued Jeroboam and took cities from him: Bethel with its villages, Jeshanah with its villages, and Ephron with its villages. So Jeroboam did not recover strength again in the days of Abijah; and the LORD struck him, and he died. But Abijah grew mighty, married fourteen wives, and begot twenty-two sons and sixteen daughters. Now the rest of the acts of Abijah, his ways, and his sayings are written in the annals of the prophet Iddo

Chapter 14

So Abijah rested with his fathers, and they buried him in the City of David. Then Asa, his son, reigned in his place. In his days the land was quiet for ten years. Asa did what was good and right in the eyes of the LORD his God. For he removed the altars of the foreign gods and the high places, and broke down the sacred pillars and cut down the wooden images. He commanded Judah to seek the LORD God of their fathers, and to observe the law and the commandment. He also removed the high places and the incense altars from all the cities of Judah, and the kingdom was quiet under him And he built fortified cities in Judah, for the land had rest; he had no war in those years because the LORD had given him rest. Therefore he said to Judah, "Let us build these cities and make walls around them, and towers, gates, and bars, while the land is yet before us, because we have sought the LORD our God; we have sought Him, and He has given us rest on every side." So they built and prospered And Asa had an army of three hundred thousand from Judah who carried shields and spears, and from Benjamin two hundred eighty thousand men who carried shields and drew bows; all these were mighty men of valor. Then Zerah the Ethiopian came out against them with an army of a million men and three hundred chariots, and he came to Mareshah. So Asa went out against him, and they set the troops in battle array in the Valley of Zephathah at Mareshah. And Asa cried out to the LORD his God, and said, "LORD, it is nothing for You to help, whether with many or with those who have no power; help us, O LORD our God, for we rest on You, and in Your name we go against

this multitude. O LORD, You are our God; do not let man prevail against You!" So the LORD struck the Ethiopians before Asa and Judah, and the Ethiopians fled. And Asa and the people who were with him pursued them to Gerar. So the Ethiopians were overthrown, and they could not recover, for they were broken before the LORD and His army. And they carried away very much spoil. Then they defeated all the cities around Gerar, for the fear of the LORD came upon them; and they plundered all the cities, for there was exceedingly much spoil in them. They also attacked the livestock enclosures and carried off sheep and camels in abundance, and returned to Jerusalem

Chapter 15

Now the Spirit of God came upon Azariah the son of Oded. And he went out to meet Asa, and said to him: "Hear me, Asa, and all Judah and Benjamin. The LORD is with you while you are with Him. If you seek Him, He will be found by you; but if you forsake Him, He will forsake you. For a long time Israel has been without the true God, without a teaching priest, and without law; but when in their trouble they turned to the LORD God of Israel, and sought Him, He was found by them. And in those times there was no peace to the one who went out, nor to the one who came in, but great turmoil was on all the inhabitants of the lands. So nation was destroyed by nation, and city by city, for God troubled them with every adversity. But you, be strong and do not let your hands be weak, for your work shall be rewarded!" And when Asa heard these words and the prophecy of Oded the prophet, he took courage and removed the abominable idols from all the land of Judah and Benjamin and from the cities which he had taken in the mountains of Ephraim; and he restored the altar of the LORD that was before the vestibule of the LORD. Then he gathered all Judah and Benjamin, and those who dwelt with them from Ephraim, Manasseh, and Simeon, for they came over to him in great numbers from Israel when they saw that the LORD his God was with him So they gathered together at Jerusalem in the third month, in the fifteenth year of the reign of Asa. And they offered to the LORD at that time seven hundred bulls and seven thousand sheep from the spoil they had brought. Then they entered into a covenant to seek the LORD God of their fathers with all their heart and with all their soul; and whoever would not seek the LORD God of Israel was to be put to death, whether small or great, whether man or woman. Then they took an oath before the LORD with a loud voice, with shouting and trumpets and rams' horns. And all Judah rejoiced at the oath, for they had sworn with all their heart and sought Him with all their soul; and He was found by them, and the LORD gave them rest all around Also he removed Maachah, the mother of Asa the king, from being queen mother, because she had made an obscene image of Asherah; and Asa cut down her obscene image, then crushed and burned it by the Brook Kidron. But the high places were not removed from Israel. Nevertheless, the heart of Asa was loyal all his days. He also brought into the house of God the things that his father had dedicated and that he himself had dedicated: silver and gold and utensils. And there was no war until the thirty-fifth year of the reign of Asa

Chapter 16

In the thirty-sixth year of Asa's reign, Baasha, king of Israel, attacked Judah and fortified Ramah to prevent anyone from leaving or entering Asa's territory. Asa took silver and gold from the treasuries of the house of the LORD and the king's house and sent them to Ben-Hadad, king of Aram, who lived in Damascus, saying, "Let there be a covenant between you and me, as there was between my father and your father. See, I have sent you silver and gold. Break your treaty with Baasha, king of Israel, so that he will withdraw from me." Ben-Hadad agreed with King Asa and sent the commanders of his armies against the cities of Israel. They conquered Ijon, Dan, Abel Maim, and all the store cities of Naphtali. When Baasha heard this, he stopped building Ramah and ceased his work. Then King Asa brought all Judah, and they carried away the stones and timber Baasha had used to build Ramah. With them, he built Geba and Mizpah At that time, Hanani the seer came to Asa, king of Judah, and said to him, "Because you relied on the king of Aram and did not rely on the LORD your God, the army of the king of Aram has escaped from your hand. Were not the Cushites and Libyans a mighty army with great numbers of chariots and horsemen? Yet when you relied on the LORD, He delivered them into your hand. For the eyes of the LORD range throughout the earth to strengthen those whose hearts are fully committed to Him. You have done a foolish thing, and from now on you will be at war." Asa was angry with the seer because of this; he was so enraged that he put him in prison. At the same time, Asa brutally oppressed some of the people. The events of Asa's reign, from beginning to end, are written in the book of the kings of Judah and Israel. In the thirty-ninth year of his reign, Asa was afflicted with a disease in his feet. Though his disease was severe, even in his illness, he did not seek help from the LORD but only from the physicians. Then, in the forty-first year of his reign, Asa died and rested with his ancestors. They buried him in the tomb that he had cut out for himself in the City of David. They laid him on a bier covered with spices and various blended perfumes, and they made a huge fire in his honor

Chapter 17

Jehoshaphat, his son, succeeded him as king and strengthened himself against Israel. He stationed troops in all the fortified cities of Judah and put garrisons in Judah and in the towns of Ephraim that his father Asa had captured. The LORD was with Jehoshaphat because he followed the ways of his father David before him. He did not consult the Baals but sought the God of his father and followed His commands rather than the practices of Israel. The LORD established the kingdom under his control, and all Judah brought gifts to Jehoshaphat, so he had great wealth and honor. His heart was devoted to the ways of the LORD; furthermore, he removed the high places and the Asherah poles from Judah In the third year of his reign, he sent his officials—Ben-Hail, Obadiah, Zechariah, Nethanel, and Micaiah—to teach in the towns of Judah. With them were certain Levites—Shemaiah, Nethaniah, Zebadiah, Asahel, Shemiramoth, Jehonathan, Adonijah, Tobijah, and Tob-Adonijah—and the priests Elishama and Jehoram. They taught throughout Judah, taking with them the Book of the Law of the LORD; they went around to all the towns of Judah and taught the people The fear of the LORD fell on all the kingdoms of the lands surrounding Judah, so they did not go to war against Jehoshaphat. Some Philistines brought Jehoshaphat gifts and silver as tribute, and the Arabs brought him flocks: seven thousand seven hundred rams and seven thousand seven hundred goats. Jehoshaphat became more and more powerful; he built forts and store cities in Judah and had large supplies in the towns of Judah. He also kept experienced fighting men in Jerusalem Their enrollment by families was as follows: From Judah, commanders of units of a thousand: Adnah the commander, with three hundred thousand fighting men; next, Jehohanan the commander, with two

hundred eighty thousand; next, Amasiah son of Zikri, who volunteered himself for the service of the LORD, with two hundred thousand. From Benjamin: Eliada, a valiant soldier, with two hundred thousand men armed with bows and shields; next, Jehozabad, with a hundred eighty thousand men armed for battle. These were the men who served the king, besides those he stationed in the fortified cities throughout Judah

Chapter 18

Jehoshaphat had great wealth and honor, and he allied himself with Ahab by marriage. Some years later, he went down to visit Ahab in Samaria. Ahab slaughtered many sheep and cattle for him and the people with him and urged him to attack Ramoth Gilead. Ahab king of Israel asked Jehoshaphat king of Judah, "Will you go with me to Ramoth Gilead?" Jehoshaphat replied, "I am as you are, and my people as your people; we will join you in the war." But Jehoshaphat also said to the king of Israel, "First seek the counsel of the LORD." So the king of Israel brought together the prophets—four hundred men—and asked them, "Shall we go to war against Ramoth Gilead, or shall I refrain?" "Go," they answered, "for God will give it into the king's hand." But Jehoshaphat asked, "Is there no longer a prophet of the LORD here whom we can inquire of?" The king of Israel answered Jehoshaphat, "There is still one prophet through whom we can inquire of the LORD, but I hate him because he never prophesies anything good about me, but always bad. He is Micaiah son of Imla." "The king should not say such a thing," Jehoshaphat replied So the king of Israel called one of his officials and said, "Bring Micaiah son of Imla at once." Dressed in their royal robes, the king of Israel and Jehoshaphat king of Judah were sitting on their thrones at the threshing floor by the entrance of the gate of Samaria, with all the prophets prophesying before them. Now Zedekiah son of Kenaanah had made iron horns, and he declared, "This is what the LORD says: 'With these you will gore the Arameans until they are destroyed.'" All the other prophets were prophesying the same thing. "Attack Ramoth Gilead and be victorious," they said, "for the LORD will give it into the king's hand." The messenger who had gone to summon Micaiah said to him, "Look, the other prophets without exception are predicting success for the king. Let your word agree with theirs, and speak favorably." But Micaiah said, "As surely as the LORD lives, I can tell him only what my God says." When he arrived, the king asked him, "Micaiah, shall we go to war against Ramoth Gilead, or shall I refrain?" "Attack and be victorious," he answered, "for they will be given into your hand." The king said to him, "How many times must I make you swear to tell me nothing but the truth in the name of the LORD?" Then Micaiah answered, "I saw all Israel scattered on the hills like sheep without a shepherd, and the LORD said, 'These people have no master. Let each one go home in peace.'" The king of Israel said to Jehoshaphat, "Didn't I tell you that he never prophesies anything good about me, but only bad?" Micaiah continued, "Therefore hear the word of the LORD: I saw the LORD sitting on his throne with all the multitudes of heaven standing on his right and on his left. And the LORD said, 'Who will entice Ahab king of Israel into attacking Ramoth Gilead and going to his death there?' One suggested this, and another that. Finally, a spirit came forward, stood before the LORD, and said, 'I will entice him.' 'By what means?' the LORD asked. 'I will go and be a deceiving spirit in the mouths of all his prophets,' he said. 'You will succeed in enticing him,' said the LORD. 'Go and do it.' "So now the LORD has put a deceiving spirit in the mouths of these prophets of yours. The LORD has decreed disaster for you."Then Zedekiah son of Kenaanah went up and slapped Micaiah in the face. "Which way did the spirit from the LORD go when he went from me to speak to you?" he asked Micaiah replied, "You will find out on the day you go to hide in an inner room." The king of Israel then ordered, "Take Micaiah and send him back to Amon the ruler of the city and to Joash the king's son, and say, 'This is what the king says: Put this fellow in prison and give him nothing but bread and water until I return safely.'" Micaiah declared, "If you ever return safely, the LORD has not spoken through me." Then he added, "Mark my words, all you people!" So the king of Israel and Jehoshaphat king of Judah went up to Ramoth Gilead. The king of Israel said to Jehoshaphat, "I will enter the battle in disguise, but you wear your royal robes." So the king of Israel disguised himself and went into battle Now the king of Aram had ordered his chariot commanders, "Do not fight with anyone, small or great, except the king of Israel." When the chariot commanders saw Jehoshaphat, they thought, "This is the king of Israel." So they turned to attack him, but Jehoshaphat cried out, and the LORD helped him. God drew them away from him, for when the chariot commanders saw that he was not the king of Israel, they stopped pursuing him But someone drew his bow at random and hit the king of Israel between the breastplate and the scale armor. The king told the chariot driver, "Wheel around and get me out of the fighting. I've been wounded." All day long the battle raged, and the king of Israel propped himself up in his chariot facing the Arameans until evening; then at sunset, he died

Chapter 19

Jehoshaphat king of Judah returned safely to his palace in Jerusalem. Jehu the seer, the son of Hanani, went out to meet him and said to the king, "Should you help the wicked and love those who hate the LORD? Because of this, the wrath of the LORD is on you. There is, however, some good in you, for you have rid the land of the Asherah poles and have set your heart on seeking God." Jehoshaphat lived in Jerusalem, and he went out again among the people from Beersheba to the hill country of Ephraim and turned them back to the LORD, the God of their ancestors. He appointed judges in the land, in each of the fortified cities of Judah. He told them, "Consider carefully what you do, because you are not judging for mere mortals but for the LORD, who is with you whenever you give a verdict. Now let the fear of the LORD be on you. Judge carefully, for with the LORD our God there is no injustice or partiality or bribery." In Jerusalem also, Jehoshaphat appointed some of the Levites, priests, and heads of Israelite families to administer the law of the LORD and to settle disputes. And they lived in Jerusalem. He gave them these orders: "You must serve faithfully and wholeheartedly in the fear of the LORD. In every case that comes before you from your people who live in the cities—whether bloodshed or other concerns of the law, commands, decrees, or regulations—you are to warn them not to sin against the LORD; otherwise His wrath will come on you and your people. Do this, and you will not sin "Amariah the chief priest will be over you in any matter concerning the LORD, and Zebadiah son of Ishmael, the leader of the tribe of Judah, will be over you in any matter concerning the king. And the Levites will serve as officials before you. Act with courage, and may the LORD be with those who do well."

Chapter 20

After this, the Moabites and Ammonites with some of the Meunites came to wage war against Jehoshaphat. Some people came and told Jehoshaphat, "A vast army is coming against you from Edom, from the other side of the Dead Sea. It is already in Hazezon Tamar" (that is, En Gedi) Alarmed, Jehoshaphat resolved to inquire of the LORD, and he proclaimed a fast for all Judah. The people of Judah came together to seek help from the LORD; indeed, they came from every town in Judah to seek Him Then Jehoshaphat stood up in the assembly of Judah and Jerusalem at the temple of the LORD in front of the new courtyard and said: "LORD, the God of our ancestors, are you not the God who is in heaven? You rule over all the kingdoms of the nations. Power and might are in your hand, and no one can withstand you. Our God, did you not drive out the inhabitants of this land before your people Israel and give it forever to the descendants of Abraham your friend? They have lived in it and have built in it a sanctuary for your Name, saying, 'If calamity comes upon us, whether the sword of judgment or plague or famine, we will stand in your presence before this temple that bears your Name and will cry out to you in our distress, and you will hear us and save us.' "But now here are men from Ammon, Moab, and Mount Seir, whose territory you would not allow Israel to invade when they came from Egypt; so they turned away from them and did not destroy them. See how they are repaying us by coming to drive us out of the possession you gave us as an inheritance. Our God, will you not judge them? For we have no power to face this vast army that is attacking us. We do not know what to do, but our eyes are on you." All the men of Judah, with their wives and children and little ones, stood there before the LORD. Then the Spirit of the LORD came on Jahaziel son of Zechariah, the son of Benaiah, the son of Jeiel, the son of Mattaniah, a Levite and descendant of Asaph, as he stood in the assembly. He said: "Listen, King Jehoshaphat and all who live in Judah and Jerusalem! This is what the LORD says to you: 'Do not be afraid or discouraged because of this vast army. For the battle is not yours, but God's. Tomorrow march down against them. They will be climbing up by the Pass of Ziz, and you will find them at the end of the gorge in the Desert of Jeruel. You will not have to fight this battle. Take up your positions; stand firm and see the deliverance the LORD will give you, Judah and Jerusalem. Do not be afraid; do not be discouraged. Go out to face them tomorrow, and the LORD will be with you.'" Jehoshaphat bowed down with his face to the ground, and all the people of Judah and Jerusalem fell down in worship before the LORD. Then some Levites from the Kohathites and Korahites stood up and praised the LORD, the God of Israel, with a very loud voice Early in the morning, they left for the Desert of Tekoa. As they set out, Jehoshaphat stood and said, "Listen to me, Judah and people of Jerusalem! Have faith in the LORD your God and you will be upheld; have faith in His prophets and you will be successful." After consulting the people, Jehoshaphat appointed men to sing to the LORD and to praise Him for the splendor of His holiness as they went out at the head of the army, saying: "Give thanks to the LORD, for His love endures forever." As they began to sing and praise, the LORD set ambushes against the men of Ammon and Moab and Mount Seir who were invading Judah, and they were defeated. The Ammonites and Moabites rose up against the men from Mount Seir to destroy and annihilate them. After they finished slaughtering the men from Seir, they helped to destroy one another When the men of Judah came to the place that overlooks the desert and looked toward the vast army, they saw only dead bodies lying on the ground; no one had escaped. So Jehoshaphat and his men went to carry off their plunder, and they found among them a great amount of equipment and clothing and also articles of value—more than they could take away. There was so much plunder that it took three days to collect it. On the fourth day, they assembled in the Valley of Berakah, where they praised the LORD. This is why it is called the Valley of Berakah to this day Then, led by Jehoshaphat, all the men of Judah and Jerusalem returned joyfully to Jerusalem, for the LORD had given them cause to rejoice over their enemies. They entered Jerusalem and went to the temple of the LORD with harps and lyres and trumpets. The fear of God came on all the surrounding kingdoms when they heard how the LORD had fought against the enemies of Israel. And the kingdom of Jehoshaphat was at peace, for his God had given him rest on every side So Jehoshaphat reigned over Judah. He was thirty-five years old when he became king, and he reigned in Jerusalem for twenty-five years. His mother's name was Azubah daughter of Shilhi. He followed the ways of his father Asa and did not stray from them; he did what was right in the eyes of the LORD. The high places, however, were not removed, and the people still had not set their hearts on the God of their ancestors The other events of Jehoshaphat's reign, from beginning to end, are written in the annals of Jehu son of Hanani, which are recorded in the book of the kings of Israel. Later, Jehoshaphat king of Judah made an alliance with Ahaziah king of Israel, whose ways were wicked. He agreed with him to construct a fleet of trading ships. After these were built at Ezion Geber, Eliezer son of Dodavahu of Mareshah prophesied against Jehoshaphat, saying, "Because you have made an alliance with Ahaziah, the LORD will destroy what you have made." The ships were wrecked and were not able to set sail to trade

Chapter 21

Jehoshaphat rested with his ancestors and was buried with them in the city of David. His son Jehoram succeeded him as king. Jehoram had brothers: Azariah, Jehiel, Zechariah, Azariah, Michael, and Shephatiah, all sons of Jehoshaphat, king of Israel. Their father had given them many gifts of silver, gold, and precious items, along with fortified cities in Judah, but the kingdom was given to Jehoram because he was the firstborn When Jehoram ascended to the throne, he fortified his position by killing all his brothers and some of the princes of Israel. Jehoram was thirty-two years old when he became king, and he reigned in Jerusalem for eight years. He followed the ways of the kings of Israel, just as the house of Ahab had done, for he had married a daughter of Ahab. He did evil in the eyes of the LORD. Nevertheless, the LORD was not willing to destroy the house of David, because of the covenant He had made with David and because He had promised to maintain a lamp for him and his descendants forever In Jehoram's time, Edom rebelled against Judah and set up their own king. So Jehoram went with his officers and all his chariots. The Edomites surrounded him and his chariot commanders, but he rose up and broke through by night. To this day, Edom has been in rebellion against Judah. Libnah also revolted at the same time, because Jehoram had forsaken the LORD, the God of his ancestors Moreover, he built high places on the hills of Judah and caused the people of Jerusalem to prostitute themselves and led Judah astray. Jehoram received a letter from Elijah the prophet, which said, "This is what the LORD, the God of your father David, says: 'You have not followed the ways of your father Jehoshaphat or of Asa, king of Judah. Instead, you have followed the ways of the kings of Israel, and you have led Judah and the people of Jerusalem to prostitute themselves, just as the house of Ahab did.

You have also murdered your own brothers, members of your own family, who were better than you. So now the LORD is about to strike your people, your sons, your wives, and everything that is yours with a heavy blow. You yourself will be very ill with a lingering disease of the bowels, until the disease causes your bowels to come out.'" The LORD aroused against Jehoram the hostility of the Philistines and the Arabs who lived near the Cushites. They attacked Judah, invaded it, and carried off all the goods found in the king's palace, together with his sons and wives. Only Ahaziah, his youngest son, was left. After all this, the LORD afflicted Jehoram with an incurable disease of the bowels. In the course of time, at the end of the second year, his bowels came out because of the disease, and he died in great pain. His people made no fire in his honor, as they had for his ancestors. Jehoram was thirty-two years old when he became king, and he reigned in Jerusalem for eight years. He passed away, to no one's regret, and was buried in the City of David, but not in the tombs of the kings

Chapter 22

The people of Jerusalem made Ahaziah, Jehoram's youngest son, king in his place, since the raiders, who came with the Arabs into the camp, had killed all the older sons. So Ahaziah, son of Jehoram, king of Judah, began to reign. Ahaziah was twenty-two years old when he became king, and he reigned in Jerusalem for one year. His mother's name was Athaliah, a granddaughter of Omri He too followed the ways of the house of Ahab, for his mother encouraged him to act wickedly. He did evil in the eyes of the LORD, as the house of Ahab had done, for after his father's death, they became his advisers, to his undoing. He also followed their counsel when he went with Joram, son of Ahab, king of Israel, to wage war against Hazael, king of Aram, at Ramoth Gilead. The Arameans wounded Joram, so he returned to Jezreel to recover from the wounds inflicted on him at Ramah in his battle with Hazael, king of Aram. Then Ahaziah, son of Jehoram, king of Judah, went down to Jezreel to see Joram, son of Ahab, because he had been wounded Through Ahaziah's visit to Joram, God brought about Ahaziah's downfall. When Ahaziah arrived, he went out with Joram to meet Jehu, son of Nimshi, whom the LORD had anointed to destroy the house of Ahab. While Jehu was executing judgment on the house of Ahab, he found the princes of Judah and the sons of Ahaziah's relatives, who had been attending Ahaziah, and he killed them. He then went in search of Ahaziah, and his men captured him while he was hiding in Samaria. They brought him to Jehu and put him to death. They buried him, for they said, "He was a son of Jehoshaphat, who sought the LORD with all his heart." So there was no one in the house of Ahaziah powerful enough to retain the kingdom When Athaliah, the mother of Ahaziah, saw that her son was dead, she proceeded to destroy the whole royal family of the house of Judah. But Jehoshabeath, the daughter of King Jehoram, took Joash, son of Ahaziah, and stole him away from among the royal princes who were about to be murdered and put him and his nurse in a bedroom. Because Jehoshabeath, the daughter of King Jehoram and wife of the priest Jehoiada, was Ahaziah's sister, she hid the child from Athaliah so she could not kill him. He remained hidden with them at the temple of God for six years while Athaliah ruled the land

Chapter 23

In the seventh year, Jehoiada showed his strength. He made a covenant with the commanders of units of a hundred: Azariah son of Jeroham, Ishmael son of Jehohanan, Azariah son of Obed, Maaseiah son of

Adaiah, and Elishaphat son of Zicri. They went throughout Judah and gathered the Levites and the heads of Israelite families from all the towns. When they came to Jerusalem, the whole assembly made a covenant with the king at the temple of God Jehoiada said to them, "The king's son shall reign, as the LORD promised concerning the descendants of David. Now this is what you are to do: A third of you priests and Levites who are going on duty on the Sabbath are to keep watch at the doors, a third of you at the royal palace, and a third at the Foundation Gate, while all the others are in the courtyards of the temple of the LORD. No one is to enter the temple of the LORD except the priests and Levites on duty; they may enter because they are consecrated, but all the others are to observe the LORD's command not to enter. The Levites are to station themselves around the king, each with weapon in hand. Anyone who enters the temple is to be put to death. Stay close to the king wherever he goes." The Levites and all the men of Judah did just as Jehoiada the priest ordered. Each one took his men—those who were going on duty on the Sabbath and those who were going off duty—for Jehoiada the priest had not released any of the divisions. Then he gave the commanders of units of a hundred the spears and the large and small shields that had belonged to King David and that were in the temple of God. He stationed all the men, each with his weapon in his hand, around the king— near the altar and the temple, from the south side to the north side of the temple Jehoiada and his sons brought out the king's son and put the crown on him; they presented him with a copy of the covenant and proclaimed him king. They anointed him and shouted, "Long live the king!" When Athaliah heard the noise of the people running and cheering the king, she went to them at the temple of the LORD. She looked, and there was the king, standing by his pillar at the entrance. The officers and the trumpeters were beside the king, and all the people of the land were rejoicing and blowing trumpets, and musicians with their instruments were leading the praises. Then Athaliah tore her robes and shouted, "Treason! Treason!" Jehoiada the priest sent out the commanders of units of a hundred, who were in charge of the troops, and said to them: "Bring her out between the ranks and put to the sword anyone who follows her." For the priest had said, "Do not put her to death at the temple of the LORD." So they seized her as she reached the entrance of the Horse Gate on the palace grounds, and there they put her to death Jehoiada then made a covenant that he, the people, and the king would be the LORD's people. All the people went to the temple of Baal and tore it down. They smashed the altars and idols and killed Mattan, the priest of Baal, in front of the altars. Then Jehoiada placed the oversight of the temple of the LORD in the hands of the Levitical priests, to whom David had made assignments in the temple, to present the burnt offerings of the LORD as written in the Law of Moses, with rejoicing and singing, as David had ordered. He also stationed gatekeepers at the gates of the LORD's temple so that no one who was in any way unclean might enter He took with him the commanders of hundreds, the nobles, the rulers of the people, and all the people of the land and brought the king down from the temple of the LORD. They went into the palace through the Upper Gate and seated the king on the royal throne. All the people of the land rejoiced, and the city was calm, because Athaliah had been slain with the sword

Chapter 24

Joash was seven years old when he became king, and he reigned in Jerusalem for forty years. His mother's name was Zibiah of Beersheba. Joash did what was right in the eyes of the LORD all the years of Jehoiada the priest. Jehoiada chose two wives for him, and he had sons and daughters Some time later, Joash decided to restore the temple of the LORD. He called together the priests and Levites and said to them, "Go to the towns of Judah and collect the money due annually from all Israel, to repair the temple of your God. Do it now." But the Levites did not act at once Therefore the king summoned Jehoiada the chief priest and said to him, "Why haven't you required the Levites to bring in from Judah and Jerusalem the tax imposed by Moses the servant of the LORD and by the assembly of Israel for the tent of the covenant law?" Now the sons of that wicked woman Athaliah had broken into the temple of God and had used even its sacred objects for the Baals. At the king's command, a chest was made and placed outside, at the gate of the temple of the LORD. A proclamation was then issued in Judah and Jerusalem that they should bring to the LORD the tax that Moses the servant of God had required of Israel in the wilderness. All the officials and all the people brought their contributions gladly, dropping them into the chest until it was full Whenever the chest was brought in by the Levites to the king's officials and they saw that there was a large amount of money, the royal scribe and the officer of the chief priest would come and empty the chest and carry it back to its place. They did this regularly and collected a great amount of money. The king and Jehoiada gave it to those who carried out the work required for the temple of the LORD. They hired masons and carpenters to restore the LORD's temple, and also workers in iron and bronze to repair the temple The men in charge of the work were diligent, and the repairs progressed under them. They rebuilt the temple of God according to its original design and reinforced it. When they had finished, they brought the rest of the money to the king and Jehoiada, and with it were made articles for the LORD's temple: articles for the service and for the burnt offerings, and also dishes and other objects of gold and silver. As long as Jehoiada lived, burnt offerings were presented continually in the temple of the LORD Now Jehoiada was old and full of years, and he died at the age of a hundred and thirty. He was buried with the kings in the City of David, because of the good he had done in Israel for God and His temple. After the death of Jehoiada, the officials of Judah came and paid homage to the king, and he listened to them. They abandoned the temple of the LORD, the God of their ancestors, and worshiped Asherah poles and idols. Because of their guilt, God's anger came on Judah and Jerusalem. Although the LORD sent prophets to the people to bring them back to Him, and though they testified against them, they would not listen Then the Spirit of God came on Zechariah son of Jehoiada the priest. He stood before the people and said, "This is what God says: 'Why do you disobey the LORD's commands? You will not prosper. Because you have forsaken the LORD, He has forsaken you.'" But they plotted against him, and by order of the king they stoned him to death in the courtyard of the LORD's temple. King Joash did not remember the kindness Zechariah's father Jehoiada had shown him but killed his son, who said as he lay dying, "May the LORD see this and call you to account." At the turn of the year, the army of Aram marched against Joash; it invaded Judah and Jerusalem and killed all the leaders of the people. They sent all the plunder to their king in Damascus. Although the Aramean army had come with only a few men, the LORD delivered into their hands a much larger army. Because Judah had forsaken the LORD, the God of their ancestors, judgment was executed on Joash. When the Arameans withdrew, they left Joash severely wounded. His officials conspired against him for murdering the son of Jehoiada the priest, and they killed him in his bed. So he died and was buried in the City of David, but not in the tombs of the kings Those who conspired against him were Zabad, son of Shimeath an Ammonite woman, and Jehozabad, son of Shimrith a Moabite woman. The account of his sons, the many prophecies about him, and the record of the restoration of the temple of God are written in the annotations on the book of the kings. And Amaziah, his son, succeeded him as king

Chapter 25

Amaziah was twenty-five years old when he became king, and he reigned in Jerusalem for twenty-nine years. His mother's name was Jehoaddan; she was from Jerusalem. He did what was right in the eyes of the LORD, but not wholeheartedly. After the kingdom was firmly in his control, he executed the officials who had murdered his father the king. Yet he did not put their children to death but acted in accordance with what is written in the Law, in the Book of Moses, where the LORD commanded: "Parents shall not be put to death for their children, nor children put to death for their parents; each will die for their own sin." Amaziah called the people of Judah together and assigned them according to their families to commanders of thousands and commanders of hundreds for all Judah and Benjamin. He then mustered those twenty years old or more and found that there were three hundred thousand men fit for military service, able to handle the spear and shield. He also hired a hundred thousand fighting men from Israel for a hundred talents of silver But a man of God came to him and said, "Your Majesty, these troops from Israel must not march with you, for the LORD is not with Israel—not with any of the people of Ephraim. Even if you go and fight courageously in battle, God will overthrow you before the enemy, for God has the power to help or to overthrow." Amaziah asked the man of God, "But what about the hundred talents I paid for these Israelite troops?" The man of God replied, "The LORD can give you much more than that." So Amaziah dismissed the troops who had come to him from Ephraim and sent them home. They were furious with Judah and left for home in a great rage Amaziah then marshaled his strength and led his army to the Valley of Salt, where he killed ten thousand men of Seir. The army of Judah also captured ten thousand men alive, took them to the top of a cliff and threw them down so that all were dashed to pieces Meanwhile, the troops that Amaziah had sent back and had not allowed to take part in the war raided towns belonging to Judah, from Samaria to Beth Horon. They killed three thousand people and carried off great quantities of plunder When Amaziah returned from slaughtering the Edomites, he brought back the gods of the people of Seir. He set them up as his own gods, bowed down to them, and burned sacrifices to them. The anger of the LORD burned against Amaziah, and He sent a prophet to him, who said, "Why do you consult this people's gods, which could not save their own people from your hand?" While he was still speaking, the king said to him, "Have we appointed you an adviser to the king? Stop! Why be struck down?" So the prophet stopped but said, "I know that God has determined to destroy you because you have done this and have not listened to my counsel." After Amaziah, king of Judah, consulted his advisers, he sent this challenge to Jehoash, son of Jehoahaz, the son of Jehu, king of Israel: "Come, let us face each other in battle." But Jehoash king of Israel replied to Amaziah king of Judah: "A thistle in Lebanon sent a message to a cedar in Lebanon, 'Give your daughter to my son in marriage.' Then a wild beast in Lebanon came along and trampled the thistle underfoot. You say to yourself that you have defeated Edom, and now you are arrogant and proud. But stay at home! Why ask for trouble and cause your own downfall and that of Judah also?" Amaziah, however, would not listen, for God so worked that He might deliver them into the hands of Jehoash, because they sought the gods of Edom. So Jehoash king of Israel attacked. He and Amaziah king of Judah faced each other at Beth Shemesh in Judah. Judah was routed by Israel, and every man fled to his home. Jehoash king of Israel captured Amaziah king of Judah, the son of Joash, the son of Jehoahaz, at Beth Shemesh. Then Jehoash brought him to Jerusalem and broke down the wall of Jerusalem from the Ephraim Gate to the Corner Gate—a section about four hundred cubits long. He took all the gold and silver and all the articles found in the temple of God that had been in the care of Obed-Edom, together with the palace treasures and the hostages, and returned to Samaria Amaziah son of Joash king of Judah lived for fifteen years after the death of Jehoash son of Jehoahaz king of Israel. As for the other events of Amaziah's reign, from beginning to end, are they not written in the book of the kings of Judah and Israel? From the time that Amaziah turned away from following the LORD, they conspired against him in Jerusalem, and he fled to Lachish, but they sent men after him to Lachish and killed him there. He was brought back by horse and was buried with his ancestors in the City of Judah

Chapter 26

Uzziah was sixteen years old when he became king and reigned in Jerusalem for fifty-two years. His mother's name was Jecoliah of Jerusalem. He did what was right in the eyes of the LORD, just as his father Amaziah had done. He sought God during the days of Zechariah, who instructed him in the fear of God. As long as he sought the LORD, God gave him success He went to war against the Philistines and broke down the walls of Gath, Jabneh, and Ashdod. Then he rebuilt towns near Ashdod and elsewhere among the Philistines. God helped him against the Philistines and against the Arabs who lived in Gur Baal and against the Meunites. The Ammonites brought tribute to Uzziah, and his fame spread as far as the border of Egypt because he had become very powerful Uzziah built towers in Jerusalem at the Corner Gate, at the Valley Gate, and at the angle of the wall, and he fortified them. He also built towers in the wilderness and dug many cisterns because he had much livestock in the foothills and in the plains. He had people working his fields and vineyards in the hills and in the fertile lands, for he loved the soil Uzziah had a well-trained army, ready to go out by divisions according to their numbers as mustered by Jeiel the secretary and Maaseiah the officer under the direction of Hananiah, one of the royal officials. The total number of family leaders over the fighting men was 2,600. Under their command was an army of 307,500 men trained for war, a powerful force to support the king against his enemies. Uzziah provided shields, spears, helmets, coats of armor, bows, and slingstones for the entire army. In Jerusalem, he made devices invented for use on the towers and on the corner defenses so that soldiers could shoot arrows and hurl large stones from the walls. His fame spread far and wide, for he was greatly helped until he became powerful But after Uzziah became powerful, his pride led to his downfall. He was unfaithful to the LORD his God and entered the temple of the LORD to burn incense on the altar of incense. Azariah the priest with eighty other courageous priests of the LORD followed him in. They confronted King Uzziah and said, "It is not right for you, Uzziah, to burn incense to the LORD. That is for the priests, the descendants of Aaron, who have been consecrated to burn incense. Leave the sanctuary, for you have been unfaithful, and you will not be honored by the LORD God." Uzziah, who had a censer in his hand ready to burn incense, became angry. While he was raging at the priests in their presence before the incense altar in the LORD's temple, leprosy broke out on his forehead. When Azariah the chief priest and all the other priests looked at him, they saw that he had leprosy on his forehead, so they hurried him out. Indeed, he himself was eager to leave because the LORD had afflicted him King Uzziah had leprosy until the day he died. He lived in a separate house—leprous and banned from the temple of the LORD. Jotham his son had charge of the palace and governed the people of the land. The other events of Uzziah's reign, from beginning to end, are recorded by the prophet Isaiah son of Amoz. Uzziah rested with his ancestors and was buried near them in a cemetery that belonged to the kings, for people said, "He had leprosy." And Jotham his son succeeded him as king

Chapter 27

Jotham was twenty-five years old when he became king, and he reigned in Jerusalem for sixteen years. His mother's name was Jerushah, daughter of Zadok. He did what was right in the eyes of the LORD, just as his father Uzziah had done, but unlike him, he did not enter the temple of the LORD. The people, however, continued their corrupt practices Jotham rebuilt the Upper Gate of the temple of the LORD and did extensive work on the wall at the hill of Ophel. He built towns in the hill country of Judah and forts and towers in the wooded areas. Jotham waged war against the king of the Ammonites and conquered them. That year the Ammonites paid him a hundred talents of silver, ten thousand cors of wheat, and ten thousand cors of barley. The Ammonites brought him the same amount also in the second and third years Jotham grew powerful because he walked steadfastly before the LORD his God. The other events of Jotham's reign, including all his wars and the other things he did, are written in the book of the kings of Israel and Judah. He was twenty-five years old when he became king, and he reigned in Jerusalem for sixteen years. Jotham rested with his ancestors and was buried in the City of David. And Ahaz his son succeeded him as king

Chapter 28

Ahaz was twenty years old when he became king, and he reigned in Jerusalem for sixteen years. Unlike David his father, he did not do what was right in the eyes of the LORD. He followed the ways of the kings of Israel and also made idols for worshiping the Baals. He burned sacrifices in the Valley of Ben Hinnom and sacrificed his children in the fire, engaging in the detestable practices of the nations the LORD had driven out before the Israelites. He offered sacrifices and burned incense at the high places, on the hilltops, and under every spreading tree Therefore the LORD his God delivered him into the hands of the king of Aram. The Arameans defeated him and took many of his people as prisoners and brought them to Damascus. He was also given into the hands of the king of Israel, who inflicted heavy casualties on him. In one day Pekah son of Remaliah killed a hundred and twenty thousand soldiers in Judah because Judah had forsaken the LORD, the God of their ancestors. Zikri, an Ephraimite warrior, killed Maaseiah the king's son, Azrikam the officer in charge of the palace, and Elkanah, second to the king. The Israelites took

captive from their fellow Israelites who were from Judah—two hundred thousand wives, sons and daughters. They also took a great deal of plunder, which they carried back to Samaria But a prophet of the LORD named Oded was there, and he went out to meet the army when it returned to Samaria. He said to them: "Because the LORD, the God of your ancestors, was angry with Judah, he gave them into your hand. But you have slaughtered them in a rage that reaches to heaven. And now you intend to make the men and women of Judah and Jerusalem your slaves. But aren't you also guilty of sins against the LORD your God? Now listen to me! Send back your fellow Israelites you have taken as prisoners, for the LORD's fierce anger rests on you." Then some of the leaders in Ephraim—Azariah son of Jehohanan, Berechiah son of Meshillemoth, Jehizkiah son of Shallum, and Amasa son of Hadlai—confronted those who were arriving from the war. "You must not bring those prisoners here," they said, "or we will be guilty before the LORD. Do you intend to add to our sin and guilt, for our guilt is already great, and his fierce anger rests on Israel." So the soldiers gave up the prisoners and plunder in the presence of the officials and all the assembly. The men designated by name took the prisoners, and from the plunder they clothed all who were naked. They provided them with clothes and sandals, food and drink, and healing balm. All those who were weak they put on donkeys. So they took them back to their fellow Israelites at Jericho, the City of Palms, and returned to Samaria At that time King Ahaz sent to the kings of Assyria for help. The Edomites had again come and attacked Judah and carried away prisoners, while the Philistines had raided towns in the foothills and in the Negev of Judah. They captured and occupied Beth Shemesh, Aijalon and Gederoth, as well as Soko, Timnah, and Gimzo, with their surrounding villages. The LORD had humbled Judah because of Ahaz king of Israel, for he had promoted wickedness in Judah and had been most unfaithful to the LORD. Tiglath-Pileser king of Assyria came to him, but he gave him trouble instead of help. Ahaz took some of the things from the temple of the LORD and from the royal palace and from the officials and presented them to the king of Assyria, but that did not help him In his time of trouble King Ahaz became even more unfaithful to the LORD. He offered sacrifices to the gods of Damascus, who had defeated him; for he thought, "Since the gods of the kings of Aram have helped them, I will sacrifice to them so they will help me." But they were his downfall and the downfall of all Israel Ahaz gathered together the furnishings from the temple of God and cut them in pieces. He shut the doors of the LORD's temple and set up altars at every street corner in Jerusalem. In every town in Judah, he built high places to burn sacrifices to other gods and aroused the anger of the LORD, the God of his ancestors The other events of his reign and all his ways, from beginning to end, are written in the book of the kings of Judah and Israel. Ahaz rested with his ancestors and was buried in the city of Jerusalem, but he was not placed in the tombs of the kings of Israel. And Hezekiah his son succeeded him as king

Chapter 29

Hezekiah was twenty-five years old when he became king, and he reigned in Jerusalem for twenty-nine years. His mother's name was Abijah daughter of Zechariah. He did what was right in the eyes of the LORD, just as his father David had done In the first month of the first year of his reign, he opened the doors of the temple of the LORD and repaired them. He brought in the priests and the Levites, assembled them in the square on the east side, and said: "Listen to me, Levites! Consecrate yourselves now and consecrate the temple of the LORD, the God of your ancestors. Remove all defilement from the sanctuary. Our parents were unfaithful; they did evil in the eyes of the LORD our God and forsook him. They turned their faces away from the LORD's dwelling place and turned their backs on him. They also shut the doors of the portico and put out the lamps. They did not burn incense or present any burnt offerings at the sanctuary to the God of Israel. Therefore, the anger of the LORD has fallen on Judah and Jerusalem; he has made them an object of dread and horror and scorn, as you can see with your own eyes. This is why our fathers have fallen by the sword and why our sons and daughters and our wives are in captivity. Now I intend to make a covenant with the LORD, the God of Israel, so that his fierce anger will turn away from us. My sons, do not be negligent now, for the LORD has chosen you to stand before him and serve him, to minister before him and to burn incense." Then these Levites set to work: from the Kohathites, Mahath son of Amasai and Joel son of Azariah; from the Merarites, Kish son of Abdi and Azariah son of Jehallelel; from the Gershonites, Joah son of Zimmah and Eden son of Joah; from the descendants of Elizaphan, Shimri and Jeiel; from the descendants of Asaph, Zechariah and Mattaniah; from the descendants of Heman, Jehiel and Shimei; from the descendants of Jeduthun, Shemaiah and Uzziel When they had assembled their fellow Levites and consecrated themselves, they went in to purify the temple of the LORD, as the king had ordered, following the word of the LORD. The priests went into the sanctuary of the LORD to purify it. They brought out to the courtyard of the LORD's temple everything unclean that they found in the temple of the LORD. The Levites took it and carried it out to the Kidron Valley. They began the consecration on the first day of the first month, and by the eighth day of the month, they reached the portico of the LORD. For eight more days they consecrated the temple of the LORD itself, finishing on the sixteenth day of the first month Then they went in to King Hezekiah and reported: "We have purified the entire temple of the LORD, the altar of burnt offering with all its utensils, and the table for setting out the consecrated bread, with all its articles. We have prepared and consecrated all the articles that King Ahaz removed in his unfaithfulness while he was king. They are now in front of the LORD's altar." Early the next morning, King Hezekiah gathered the city officials together and went up to the temple of the LORD. They brought seven bulls, seven rams, seven male lambs, and seven male goats as a sin offering for the kingdom, for the sanctuary, and for Judah. The king commanded the priests, the descendants of Aaron, to offer these on the altar of the LORD. So they slaughtered the bulls, and the priests took the blood and splashed it against the altar. Next, they slaughtered the rams and splashed their blood against the altar. Then they slaughtered the lambs and splashed their blood against the altar. The goats for the sin offering were brought before the king and the assembly, and they laid their hands on them. The priests then slaughtered the goats and presented their blood on the altar for a sin offering to atone for all Israel, because the king had ordered the burnt offering and the sin offering for all Israel He stationed the Levites in the temple of the LORD with cymbals, harps, and lyres in the way prescribed by David and Gad the king's seer and Nathan the prophet; this was commanded by the LORD through his prophets. So the Levites stood ready with David's instruments, and the priests with their trumpets Hezekiah gave the order to sacrifice the burnt offering on the altar. As the offering began, singing to the LORD began also, accompanied by trumpets and the instruments of David, king of Israel. The whole assembly bowed in worship, while the musicians played and the trumpets sounded. All this continued until the sacrifice of the burnt offering was completed. When the offerings were finished, the king and everyone present with him knelt down and worshiped. King Hezekiah and his officials ordered the Levites to praise the LORD with the words of David and of Asaph the seer. So they sang praises with gladness and bowed down and worshiped Then Hezekiah said, "You have now dedicated yourselves to the LORD. Come and bring sacrifices and thank offerings to the temple of the LORD." So the assembly brought sacrifices and thank offerings, and all whose hearts were willing brought burnt offerings. The number of burnt offerings the assembly brought was seventy bulls, a hundred rams, and two hundred male lambs—all of them for burnt offerings to the LORD. The animals consecrated as sacrifices amounted to six hundred bulls and three thousand sheep and goats. The priests, however, were too few to skin all the burnt offerings; so their relatives, the Levites, helped them until the task was finished and until other priests had been consecrated, for the Levites had been more conscientious in consecrating themselves than the priests had been. There were burnt offerings in abundance, together with the fat of the fellowship offerings and the drink offerings that accompanied the burnt offerings. So the service of the temple of the LORD was reestablished. Hezekiah and all the people rejoiced at what God had brought about for his people because it was done so quickly

Chapter 30

Hezekiah sent word to all Israel and Judah and also wrote letters to Ephraim and Manasseh, inviting them to come to the temple of the LORD in Jerusalem and celebrate the Passover to the LORD, the God of Israel. The king and his officials and the whole assembly in Jerusalem decided to celebrate the Passover in the second month. They had not been able to celebrate it at the regular time because not enough priests had consecrated themselves and the people had not assembled in Jerusalem. The plan seemed right to both the king and the whole assembly. They decided to send a proclamation throughout Israel, from Beersheba to Dan, calling the people to come to Jerusalem and celebrate the Passover to the LORD, the God of Israel. It had not been celebrated in large numbers according to what was written At the king's command, couriers went throughout Israel and Judah with letters from the king and from his officials, which read: "People of Israel, return to the LORD, the God of Abraham, Isaac, and Israel, that he may return to you who are left, who have escaped from the hand of the kings of Assyria. Do not be like your parents and your fellow Israelites, who were unfaithful to the LORD, the God of their ancestors, so that he made them an object of horror, as you see. Do not be stiff-necked, as your ancestors were; submit to the LORD. Come to his sanctuary, which he has consecrated forever. Serve the LORD your God, so that his fierce anger will turn away from you. If you return to the LORD, then your fellow Israelites and your children will be shown compassion by their captors and will return to this land, for the LORD your God is gracious and compassionate. He will not turn his face from you if you return to him." The couriers went from town to town in Ephraim and Manasseh, as far as Zebulun, but people scorned and ridiculed them. Nevertheless, some from Asher, Manasseh, and Zebulun humbled themselves and went to Jerusalem. Also in Judah, the hand of God was on the people to give them unity of mind to carry out what the king and his officials had ordered, following the word of the LORD A very large crowd of people assembled in Jerusalem to celebrate the Festival of Unleavened Bread in the second month. They removed the altars in Jerusalem and cleared away the incense altars and threw them into the Kidron Valley They slaughtered the Passover lamb on the fourteenth day of the second month. The priests and Levites were ashamed and consecrated themselves and brought burnt offerings to the temple of the LORD. Then they took up their regular positions as prescribed in the Law of Moses, the man of God. The priests splashed against the altar the blood handed to them by the Levites. Since many in the crowd had not consecrated themselves, the Levites had to kill the Passover lambs for all those who were not ceremonially clean and could not consecrate their lambs to the LORD. Although most of the many people who came from Ephraim, Manasseh, Issachar, and Zebulun had not purified themselves, yet they ate the Passover, contrary to what was written. But Hezekiah prayed for them, saying, "May the LORD, who is good, pardon everyone who sets their heart on seeking God—the LORD, the God of their ancestors—even if they are not clean according to the rules of the sanctuary." And the LORD heard Hezekiah and healed the people The Israelites who were present in Jerusalem celebrated the Festival of Unleavened Bread for seven days with great rejoicing, while the Levites and priests praised the LORD every day with resounding instruments dedicated to the LORD. Hezekiah spoke encouragingly to all the Levites, who showed good understanding of the service of the LORD. For the seven days, they ate their assigned portion and offered fellowship offerings and praised the LORD, the God of their ancestors The whole assembly then agreed to celebrate the festival seven more days; so for another seven days, they celebrated joyfully. Hezekiah king of Judah provided a thousand bulls and seven thousand sheep and goats for the assembly, and the officials provided them with a thousand bulls and ten thousand sheep and goats. A great number of priests consecrated themselves. The entire assembly of Judah rejoiced, along with the priests and Levites and all who had assembled from Israel, including the foreigners who had come from Israel and also those who resided in Judah. There was great joy in Jerusalem, for since the days of Solomon son of David king of Israel, there had been nothing like this in Jerusalem. The priests and the Levites stood to bless the people, and God heard them, for their prayer reached heaven, his holy dwelling place

Chapter 31

1 When all these things were finished, all Israel who were present went out to the cities of Judah and broke the images in pieces, cut down the Asherim, and pulled down the high places and the altars throughout Judah and Benjamin, as well as in Ephraim and Manasseh, until they had destroyed them all. Then all the Israelites returned to their cities, each to his own possession 2 Hezekiah appointed the divisions of the priests and the Levites according to their divisions, each man according to his service, whether as priests or Levites, for burnt offerings and peace offerings, to minister, to give thanks, and to praise in the gates of the camp of the LORD. 3 The king also contributed a portion of his own possessions for the burnt offerings, for the morning and evening burnt offerings, and for the burnt offerings on the Sabbaths, the new moons, and the appointed feasts, as written in the Law of the LORD. 4 He commanded the people who lived in Jerusalem to give the portion due to the priests and

the Levites so that they might devote themselves to the Law of the LORD 5 As soon as the command was spread abroad, the people of Israel gave in abundance the first fruits of grain, wine, oil, honey, and all the produce of the field. They brought abundantly the tithe of everything. 6 The people of Israel and Judah who lived in the cities of Judah also brought the tithe of cattle and sheep and the dedicated things that were consecrated to the LORD their God, and they laid them in heaps. 7 In the third month they began to lay the foundation of the heaps and finished them in the seventh month. 8 When Hezekiah and the officials came and saw the heaps, they blessed the LORD and his people Israel 9 Hezekiah questioned the priests and the Levites concerning the heaps. 10 Azariah the chief priest of the house of Zadok answered him, "Since the people began to bring in the contributions to the house of the LORD, we have had enough to eat and have plenty left over, for the LORD has blessed his people, and this great quantity is left over." 11 Then Hezekiah commanded them to prepare chambers in the house of the LORD, and they prepared them. 12 They faithfully brought in the contributions, the tithes, and the dedicated things. Conaniah the Levite was the chief officer in charge of them, and his brother Shimei was second. 13 Jehiel, Azariah, Nahath, Asahel, Jerimoth, Jozabad, Eliel, Ismachiah, Mahath, and Benaiah were overseers assisting Conaniah and Shimei his brother, by the appointment of Hezekiah the king and Azariah the chief officer of the house of God 14 Kore the son of Imnah the Levite, keeper of the east gate, was over the freewill offerings to God, to distribute the contributions reserved for the LORD and the most holy offerings. 15 Eden, Miniamin, Jeshua, Shemaiah, Amariah, and Shecaniah were in the cities of the priests, in their trust, to distribute to their brothers by divisions, great and small alike. 16 They distributed to all the males three years old and upwards who were entered in the genealogies, to all who would enter the house of the LORD to perform the daily duties, by their divisions, according to their offices. 17 The priests were enrolled by their houses and the Levites from twenty years old and upwards, by their offices and their divisions. 18 They were enrolled with all their little children, their wives, their sons, and their daughters, the whole assembly, for they were faithful in keeping themselves holy 19 For the sons of Aaron, the priests, who were in the fields of the common lands belonging to their towns, men were appointed by name in all the towns to distribute portions to every male among the priests and to all who were enrolled among the Levites. 20 Hezekiah did this throughout all Judah, and he did what was good and right and faithful before the LORD his God. 21 In every work that he undertook in the service of the house of God and in accordance with the law and the commandments, to seek his God, he did with all his heart and prospered

Chapter 32

1 After these acts of faithfulness, Sennacherib king of Assyria came and invaded Judah and encamped against the fortified cities, thinking to conquer them for himself. 2 When Hezekiah saw that Sennacherib had come and intended to fight against Jerusalem, 3 he consulted with his officials and mighty men to stop the water of the springs that were outside the city, and they helped him. 4 Many people gathered and stopped all the springs and the brook that flowed through the land, saying, "Why should the kings of Assyria come and find much water?" 5 Hezekiah took courage and rebuilt all the wall that was broken down, raised towers upon it, and built another wall outside. He strengthened the Millo in the city of David and made weapons and shields in abundance.

6 He set combat commanders over the people and gathered them together to him in the square at the gate of the city and spoke encouragingly to them, saying, 7 "Be strong and courageous. Do not be afraid or dismayed before the king of Assyria and all the horde that is with him, for there are more with us than with him. 8 With him is an arm of flesh, but with us is the LORD our God, to help us and to fight our battles." And the people took confidence from the words of Hezekiah king of Judah 9 After this, while Sennacherib king of Assyria was besieging Lachish with all his forces, he sent his servants to Jerusalem to Hezekiah king of Judah and to all the people of Judah who were in Jerusalem, saying, 10 "Thus says Sennacherib king of Assyria, 'On what are you trusting, that you endure the siege in Jerusalem? 11 Is not Hezekiah misleading you, that he may give you over to die by famine and by thirst, when he tells you, "The LORD our God will deliver us from the hand of the king of Assyria"? 12 Has not this same Hezekiah taken away his high places and his altars and commanded Judah and Jerusalem, "You shall worship before one altar and on it you shall burn sacrifices"? 13 Do you not know what I and my fathers have done to all the peoples of other lands? Were the gods of the nations of those lands at all able to deliver their lands out of my hand? 14 Who among all the gods of those nations that my fathers devoted to destruction was able to deliver his people from my hand, that your God should be able to deliver you from my hand? 15 Now, therefore, do not let Hezekiah deceive you or mislead you in this fashion, and do not believe him, for no god of any nation or kingdom has been able to deliver his people from my hand or from the hand of my fathers. How much less will your God deliver you out of my hand!'" 16 His servants said still more against the LORD God and against his servant Hezekiah. 17 And he wrote letters to cast contempt on the LORD, the God of Israel, and to speak against him, saying, "Like the gods of the nations of the lands who have not delivered their people from my hands, so the God of Hezekiah will not deliver his people from my hand." 18 And they shouted it with a loud voice in the language of Judah to the people of Jerusalem who were on the wall, to frighten and terrify them, in order that they might take the city. 19 They spoke of the God of Jerusalem as they spoke of the gods of the peoples of the earth, which are the work of men's hands 20 Then Hezekiah the king and Isaiah the prophet, the son of Amoz, prayed because of this and cried to heaven. 21 And the LORD sent an angel, who cut off all the mighty warriors and commanders and officers in the camp of the king of Assyria. So he returned with shame of face to his own land. And when he came into the house of his god, some of his own sons struck him down there with the sword. 22 So the LORD saved Hezekiah and the inhabitants of Jerusalem from the hand of Sennacherib king of Assyria and from the hand of all his enemies, and he provided for them on every side. 23 And many brought gifts to the LORD to Jerusalem and precious things to Hezekiah king of Judah, so that he was exalted in the sight of all nations from that time onward 24 In those days Hezekiah became sick and was at the point of death, and he prayed to the LORD, and he answered him and gave him a sign. 25 But Hezekiah did not make return according to the benefit done to him, for his heart was proud. Therefore wrath came upon him and Judah and Jerusalem. 26 But Hezekiah humbled himself for the pride of his heart, both he and the inhabitants of Jerusalem, so that the wrath of the LORD did not come upon them in the days of Hezekiah 27 And Hezekiah had very great riches and honor, and he made for himself treasuries for silver, gold, precious stones, spices, shields, and all kinds of costly vessels; 28 storehouses also for the yield of grain, wine, and oil; and stalls for all kinds of cattle and sheepfolds. 29 He likewise provided cities for himself and flocks and herds in abundance, for God had given him very great possessions. 30 This same Hezekiah closed the upper outlet of the waters of Gihon and directed them down to the west side of the city of David. And Hezekiah prospered in all his works. 31 And so in the matter of the envoys of the princes of Babylon, who had been sent to him to inquire about the sign that had been done in the land, God left him to himself, in order to test him and to know all that was in his heart 32 Now the rest of the acts of Hezekiah and his good deeds are written in the vision of Isaiah the prophet, the son of Amoz, in the Book of the Kings of Judah and Israel. 33 And Hezekiah slept with his fathers, and they buried him in the upper part of the tombs of the sons of David, and all Judah and the inhabitants of Jerusalem did him honor at his death. And Manasseh his son reigned in his place

Chapter 33

1 Manasseh was twelve years old when he began to reign, and he reigned fifty-five years in Jerusalem. 2 He did what was evil in the sight of the LORD, according to the abominations of the nations whom the LORD drove out before the people of Israel. 3 For he rebuilt the high places that his father Hezekiah had broken down, and he erected altars to the Baals, made Asherim, and worshipped all the host of heaven and served them. 4 He built altars in the house of the LORD, of which the LORD had said, "In Jerusalem shall my name be forever." 5 He built altars for all the host of heaven in the two courts of the house of the LORD. 6 And he burned his sons as an offering in the Valley of the Son of Hinnom, and used fortune-telling and omens and sorcery, and dealt with mediums and with necromancers. He did much evil in the sight of the LORD, provoking him to anger. 7 And the carved image of the idol that he had made he set in the house of God, of which God said to David and to Solomon his son, "In this house, and in Jerusalem, which I have chosen out of all the tribes of Israel, I will put my name forever, 8 and I will no more remove the foot of Israel from the land that I appointed for your fathers, if only they will be careful to do all that I have commanded them, all the law, the statutes, and the rules given through Moses." 9 Manasseh led Judah and the inhabitants of Jerusalem astray, to do more evil than the nations whom the LORD destroyed before the people of Israel 10 The LORD spoke to Manasseh and to his people, but they paid no attention. 11 Therefore the LORD brought upon them the commanders of the army of the king of Assyria, who captured Manasseh with hooks and bound him with chains of bronze and brought him to Babylon. 12 And when he was in distress, he entreated the favor of the LORD his God and humbled himself greatly before the God of his fathers. 13 He prayed to him, and God was moved by his entreaty and heard his plea and brought him again to Jerusalem into his kingdom. Then Manasseh knew that the LORD was God 14 Afterward, he built an outer wall for the city of David west of Gihon, in the valley, and for the entrance into the Fish Gate, and carried it around Ophel, and raised it to a very great height. He also put commanders of the army in all the fortified cities in Judah. 15 And he took away the foreign gods and the idol from the house of the LORD, and all the altars that he had built on the mountain of the house of the LORD and in Jerusalem, and he threw them outside of the city. 16 He also restored the altar of the LORD and offered on it sacrifices of peace offerings and of thanksgiving, and

he commanded Judah to serve the LORD, the God of Israel. 17 Nevertheless, the people still sacrificed at the high places, but only to the LORD their God 18 Now the rest of the acts of Manasseh, and his prayer to his God, and the words of the seers who spoke to him in the name of the LORD, the God of Israel, behold, they are in the Chronicles of the Kings of Israel. 19 And his prayer, and how God was moved by his entreaty, and all his sin and his faithlessness, and the sites on which he built high places and set up the Asherim and the images, before he humbled himself, behold, they are written in the Chronicles of the Seers. 20 So Manasseh slept with his fathers, and they buried him in his house, and Amon his son reigned in his place 21 Amon was twenty-two years old when he began to reign, and he reigned two years in Jerusalem. 22 And he did what was evil in the sight of the LORD, as Manasseh his father had done. Amon sacrificed to all the images that Manasseh his father had made, and served them. 23 And he did not humble himself before the LORD, as Manasseh his father had humbled himself, but this Amon incurred guilt more and more. 24 And his servants conspired against him and put him to death in his house. 25 But the people of the land struck down all those who had conspired against King Amon, and the people of the land made Josiah his son king in his place

Chapter 34

1 Josiah was eight years old when he began to reign, and he reigned thirty-one years in Jerusalem. 2 And he did what was right in the eyes of the LORD, and walked in the ways of David his father; and he did not turn aside to the right hand or to the left. 3 For in the eighth year of his reign, while he was yet a boy, he began to seek the God of David his father, and in the twelfth year he began to purge Judah and Jerusalem of the high places, the Asherim, and the carved and the metal images. 4 And they chopped down the altars of the Baals in his presence, and he cut down the incense altars that stood above them. And he broke in pieces the Asherim and the carved and the metal images, and he made dust of them and scattered it over the graves of those who had sacrificed to them. 5 He also burned the bones of the priests on their altars and cleansed Judah and Jerusalem. 6 And in the cities of Manasseh, Ephraim, and Simeon, and as far as Naphtali, in their ruins all around, 7 he broke down the altars and beat the Asherim and the images into powder and cut down all the incense altars throughout all the land of Israel. Then he returned to Jerusalem 8 Now in the eighteenth year of his reign, when he had cleansed the land and the house, he sent Shaphan the son of Azaliah, and Maaseiah the governor of the city, and Joah the son of Joahaz, the recorder, to repair the house of the LORD his God. 9 They came to Hilkiah the high priest and gave him the money that had been brought into the house of God, which the Levites, the keepers of the threshold, had collected from Manasseh and Ephraim and from all the remnant of Israel and from all Judah and Benjamin and from the inhabitants of Jerusalem. 10 And they gave it to the workmen who were working in the house of the LORD. And the workmen who were working in the house of the LORD gave it for repairing and restoring the house. 11 They gave it to the carpenters and the builders to buy quarried stone and timber for binders and beams for the buildings that the kings of Judah had let go to ruin. 12 And the men did the work faithfully. Over them were set Jahath and Obadiah, Levites of the sons of Merari, and Zechariah and Meshullam of the sons of the Kohathites, to have oversight. The Levites, all who were skillful with instruments of music, 13 were over the burden bearers and directed all who did work in every kind of service. And some of the Levites were scribes and officials and gatekeepers 14 While they were bringing out the money that had been brought into the house of the LORD, Hilkiah the priest found the Book of the Law of the LORD given through Moses. 15 Then Hilkiah answered and said to Shaphan the secretary, "I have found the Book of the Law in the house of the LORD." And Hilkiah gave the book to Shaphan. 16 Shaphan brought the book to the king and further reported to the king, "All that was committed to your servants they are doing. 17 They have emptied out the money that was found in the house of the LORD and have given it into the hand of the overseers and the workmen." 18 Then Shaphan the secretary told the king, "Hilkiah the priest has given me a book." And Shaphan read from it before the king 19 And when the king heard the words of the Law, he tore his clothes. 20 And the king commanded Hilkiah, Ahikam the son of Shaphan, Abdon the son of Micah, Shaphan the secretary, and Asaiah the king's servant, saying, 21 "Go, inquire of the LORD for me and for those who are left in Israel and in Judah, concerning the words of the book that has been found. For great is the wrath of the LORD that is poured out on us, because our fathers have not kept the word of the LORD, to do according to all that is written in this book." 22 So Hilkiah and those whom the king had sent went to Huldah the prophetess, the wife of Shallum the son of Tokhath, son of Hasrah, keeper of the wardrobe (now she lived in Jerusalem in the Second Quarter) and spoke to her to that effect. 23 And she said to them, "Thus says the LORD, the God of Israel: 'Tell the man who sent you to me, 24 Thus says the LORD, Behold, I will bring disaster upon this place and upon its inhabitants, all the curses that are written in the book that was read before the king of Judah. 25 Because they have forsaken me and have made offerings to other gods, that they might provoke me to anger with all the works of their hands, therefore my wrath will be poured out on this place and will not be quenched. 26 But to the king of Judah, who sent you to inquire of the LORD, thus shall you say to him, Thus says the LORD, the God of Israel: Regarding the words that you have heard, 27 because your heart was tender and you humbled yourself before God when you heard his words against this place and its inhabitants, and you have humbled yourself before me and have torn your clothes and wept before me, I also have heard you, declares the LORD. 28 Behold, I will gather you to your fathers, and you shall be gathered to your grave in peace, and your eyes shall not see all the disaster that I will bring upon this place and its inhabitants.' " And they brought back word to the king 29 Then the king sent and gathered together all the elders of Judah and Jerusalem. 30 And the king went up to the house of the LORD, with all the men of Judah and the inhabitants of Jerusalem and the priests and the Levites, all the people, both great and small. And he read in their hearing all the words of the Book of the Covenant that had been found in the house of the LORD. 31 And the king stood in his place and made a covenant before the LORD, to walk after the LORD and to keep his commandments and his testimonies and his statutes with all his heart and all his soul, to perform the words of the covenant that were written in this book. 32 Then he made all who were present in Jerusalem and in Benjamin stand to it. And the inhabitants of Jerusalem did according to the covenant of God, the God of their fathers. 33 And Josiah took away all the abominations from all the territory that belonged to the people of Israel and made all who were present in Israel serve the LORD their God. All his days they did not turn away from following the LORD, the God of their fathers

Chapter 35

1 Josiah kept a Passover to the LORD in Jerusalem. And they slaughtered the Passover lamb on the fourteenth day of the first month. 2 He appointed the priests to their offices and encouraged them in the service of the house of the LORD. 3 And he said to the Levites who taught all Israel and who were holy to the LORD, "Put the holy ark in the house that Solomon the son of David, king of Israel, built. You need not carry it on your shoulders. Now serve the LORD your God and his people Israel. 4 Prepare yourselves according to your fathers' houses by your divisions, as prescribed in the writing of David king of Israel and the document of Solomon his son. 5 And stand in the Holy Place according to the groupings of the fathers' houses of your brothers the lay people, and according to the division of the Levites by fathers' household. 6 And slaughter the Passover lamb, and consecrate yourselves, and prepare for your brothers, to do according to the word of the LORD by Moses." 7 Then Josiah contributed to the lay people, as Passover offerings for all who were present, lambs and young goats from the flock to the number of thirty thousand, and three thousand bulls; these were from the king's possessions. 8 And his officials contributed willingly to the people, to the priests, and to the Levites. Hilkiah, Zechariah, and Jehiel, the chief officers of the house of God, gave to the priests for the Passover offerings two thousand six hundred Passover lambs and three hundred bulls. 9 Conaniah also, and Shemaiah and Nethanel his brothers, and Hashabiah and Jeiel and Jozabad, the chiefs of the Levites, gave to the Levites for the Passover offerings five thousand lambs and young goats and five hundred bulls 10 When the service had been prepared for, the priests stood in their place, and the Levites in their divisions according to the king's command. 11 And they slaughtered the Passover lamb, and the priests threw the blood that they received from them while the Levites flayed the sacrifices. 12 And they set aside the burnt offerings that they might distribute them according to the groupings of the fathers' houses of the lay people, to offer to the LORD, as it is written in the Book of Moses. And so they did with the bulls. 13 And they roasted the Passover lamb with fire according to the rule; and they boiled the holy offerings in pots, in cauldrons, and in pans, and carried them quickly to all the lay people. 14 And afterward they prepared for themselves and for the priests, because the priests, the sons of Aaron, were offering the burnt offerings and the fat parts until night. So the Levites prepared for themselves and for the priests, the sons of Aaron. 15 The singers, the sons of Asaph, were in their place according to the command of David, and Asaph, and Heman, and Jeduthun the king's seer; and the gatekeepers were at each gate. They did not need to depart from their service, for their brothers the Levites prepared for them 16 So all the service of the LORD was prepared that day, to keep the Passover and to offer burnt offerings on the altar of the LORD, according to the command of King Josiah. 17 And the people of Israel who were present kept the Passover at that time, and the Feast of Unleavened Bread seven days. 18 No Passover like it had been kept in Israel since the days of Samuel the prophet. None of the kings of Israel had kept such a Passover as was kept by Josiah, and the priests, and the Levites, and all Judah and Israel who were present, and the inhabitants of Jerusalem. 19 In the eighteenth year of the reign of Josiah this Passover was kept 20 After all this, when Josiah had prepared the temple, Neco king of Egypt went up to fight at Carchemish on the Euphrates, and Josiah went out to meet him. 21 But he sent envoys to him, saying, "What have we to do with each other, king of Judah? I am not coming against you this day, but against the house with which I am at war. And God has commanded me to hurry. Cease opposing God, who is with me, lest he destroy you." 22 Nevertheless, Josiah did not turn away from him, but disguised himself in order to fight with him. He did not listen to the words of Neco from the mouth of God, but came to fight in the plain of Megiddo. 23 And the archers shot King Josiah. And the king said to his servants, "Take me away, for I am badly wounded." 24 So his servants took him out of the chariot and carried him in his second chariot and brought him to Jerusalem. And he died and was buried in the tombs of his fathers. All Judah and Jerusalem mourned for Josiah. 25 Jeremiah also uttered a lament for Josiah; and all the singing men and singing women have spoken of Josiah in their laments to this day. They made these a rule in Israel; behold, they are written in the Laments 26 Now the rest of the acts of Josiah, and his good deeds according to what is written in the Law of the LORD, 27 and his acts, first and last, behold, they are written in the Book of the Kings of Israel and Judah

Chapter 36

1 The people of the land took Jehoahaz the son of Josiah and made him king in his father's place in Jerusalem. 2 Jehoahaz was twenty-three years old when he began to reign, and he reigned three months in Jerusalem. 3 Then the king of Egypt deposed him in Jerusalem and laid on the land a tribute of a hundred talents of silver and a talent of gold. 4 And the king of Egypt made Eliakim his brother king over Judah and Jerusalem and changed his name to Jehoiakim. But Neco took Jehoahaz his brother and carried him to Egypt 5 Jehoiakim was twenty-five years old when he began to reign, and he reigned eleven years in Jerusalem. He did what was evil in the sight of the LORD his God. 6 Against him came up Nebuchadnezzar king of Babylon and bound him in chains to take him to Babylon. 7 Nebuchadnezzar also carried part of the vessels of the house of the LORD to Babylon and put them in his palace in Babylon. 8 Now the rest of the acts of Jehoiakim and the abominations that he did and what was found against him, behold, they are written in the Book of the Kings of Israel and Judah. And Jehoiachin his son reigned in his place 9 Jehoiachin was eighteen years old when he became king, and he reigned three months and ten days in Jerusalem. He did what was evil in the sight of the LORD. 10 In the spring of the year King Nebuchadnezzar sent and brought him to Babylon, with the precious vessels of the house of the LORD, and made his brother Zedekiah king over Judah and Jerusalem 11 Zedekiah was twenty-one years old when he began to reign, and he reigned eleven years in Jerusalem. 12 He did what was evil in the sight of the LORD his God. He did not humble himself before Jeremiah the prophet, who spoke from the mouth of the LORD. 13 He also rebelled against King Nebuchadnezzar, who had made him swear by God. He stiffened his neck and hardened his heart against turning to the LORD, the God of Israel. 14 All the officers of the priests and the people likewise were exceedingly unfaithful, following all the abominations of the nations. And they polluted the house of the LORD that he had made holy in Jerusalem. 15 The LORD, the God of their fathers, sent persistently to them by his messengers, because he had compassion on his people and on his dwelling place. 16 But they kept mocking the messengers of God, despising his words and scoffing at his prophets, until the wrath of the LORD rose against his people, until there was no remedy 17 Therefore he brought up against them the king of the Chaldeans, who killed their young men with the

sword in the house of their sanctuary and had no compassion on young man or virgin, old man or aged. He gave them all into his hand. 18 And all the vessels of the house of God, great and small, and the treasures of the house of the LORD, and the treasures of the king and of his princes, all these he brought to Babylon. 19 And they burned the house of God and broke down the wall of Jerusalem and burned all its palaces with fire and destroyed all its precious vessels. 20 He took into exile in Babylon those who had escaped from the sword, and they became servants to him and to his sons until the establishment of the kingdom of Persia, 21 to fulfill the word of the LORD by the mouth of Jeremiah, until the land had enjoyed its Sabbaths. All the days that it lay desolate it kept Sabbath, to fulfill seventy years 22 Now in the first year of Cyrus king of Persia, that the word of the LORD by the mouth of Jeremiah might be fulfilled, the LORD stirred up the spirit of Cyrus king of Persia, so that he made a proclamation throughout all his kingdom and also put it in writing: 23 "Thus says Cyrus king of Persia, 'The LORD, the God of heaven, has given me all the kingdoms of the earth, and he has charged me to build him a house at Jerusalem, which is in Judah. Whoever is among you of all his people, may the LORD his God be with him. Let him go up.'"

15. Ezra

Chapter 1
In the first year of Cyrus, king of Persia, the word of the LORD spoken by Jeremiah was fulfilled. The LORD stirred the mind of Cyrus, king of Persia, who then made a proclamation throughout his kingdom and in writing, saying, "Thus says Cyrus, king of Persia: The LORD, the God of gods, has given me all the kingdoms of the earth and commanded me to build Him a house in Jerusalem, which is in Judah. Who among you, His people, is with Him? Let him go to Jerusalem in Judah and rebuild the house of the LORD God of Israel, who is in Jerusalem. Let those who remain in any place where they sojourn provide silver, gold, goods, cattle, and voluntary offerings for the house of God in Jerusalem." Then the principal fathers of Judah and Benjamin, the priests, and the Levites rose up, along with all those whose spirits God had stirred to go and build the house of the LORD in Jerusalem. All their neighbors supported them with silver, gold, goods, cattle, and precious things, in addition to all that was willingly offered. King Cyrus also brought out the furnishings of the house of the LORD that Nebuchadnezzar had taken from Jerusalem and placed in the house of his god. Cyrus, king of Persia, handed them over to Mithredath, the treasurer, who counted them out to Sheshbazzar, prince of Judah These items included: thirty bowls of gold, a thousand bowls of silver, nine twenty-kilogram items, thirty gold bowls, four hundred and ten silver bowls of a second kind, and a thousand other vessels. The total number of gold and silver utensils was five thousand and four hundred. Sheshbazzar brought all these items with him when the exiles returned from Babylon to Jerusalem

Chapter 2
These are the people of the province who returned from captivity (which Nebuchadnezzar, king of Babylon, had taken to Babylon) and came back to Jerusalem and Judah, each to their own city. They returned with Zerubbabel: Jeshua, Nehemiah, Seraiah, Reelaiah, Mordecai, Bilshan, Mispar, Bigvai, Rehum, and Baanah. The number of the people of Israel included the sons of Parosh (two thousand seventy-two), the sons of Shephatiah (three hundred seventy-two), the sons of Arah (six hundred seventy-five), the sons of Pahath-Moab, of the sons of Jeshua and Joab (two thousand eight hundred twelve), the sons of Elam (one thousand two hundred fifty-four), the sons of Zattu (nine hundred forty-five), the sons of Zaccai (seven hundred sixty), the sons of Bani (six hundred forty-two), the sons of Bebai (six hundred twenty-three), the sons of Azgad (one thousand two hundred twenty-two), the sons of Adonikam (six hundred sixty-six), the sons of Bigvai (two thousand fifty-six), the sons of Adin (four hundred fifty-four), the sons of Ater of Hezekiah (ninety-eight), the sons of Bezai (three hundred twenty-three), the sons of Jorah (one hundred twelve), the sons of Hashum (two hundred twenty-three), the sons of Gibbar (ninety-five), the sons of Bethlehem (one hundred twenty-three), the men of Netophah (fifty-six), the men of Anathoth (one hundred twenty-eight), the sons of Azmaveth (forty-two), the sons of Kiriath-arim, Chephirah, and Beeroth (seven hundred forty-three), the sons of Ramah and Geba (six hundred twenty-one), the men of Michmas (one hundred twenty-two), the sons of Bethel and Ai (two hundred twenty-three), the sons of Nebo (fifty-two), the sons of Magbish (one hundred fifty-six), the sons of the other Elam (one thousand two hundred fifty-four), the sons of Harim (three hundred twenty), the sons of Lod, Hadid, and Ono (seven hundred twenty-five), the sons of Jericho (three hundred forty-five), and the sons of Senaah (three thousand six hundred thirty) The priests included the sons of Jedaiah, of the house of Jeshua (nine hundred seventy-three), the sons of Immer (one thousand fifty-two), the sons of Pashhur (one thousand two hundred forty-seven), and the sons of Harim (one thousand seventeen). The Levites included the sons of Jeshua and Kadmiel, of the sons of Hodaviah (seventy-four). The singers included the sons of Asaph (one hundred twenty-eight). The gatekeepers included the sons of Shallum, the sons of Ater, the sons of Talmon, the sons of Akkub, the sons of Hatita, and the sons of Shobai, totaling one hundred thirty-nine The temple servants included the sons of Ziha, the sons of Hasupha, the sons of Tabbaoth, the sons of Keros, the sons of Siaha, the sons of Padon, the sons of Lebanah, the sons of Hagabah, the sons of Akkub, the sons of Hagab, the sons of Shamlai, the sons of Hanan, the sons of Giddel, the sons of Gahar, the sons of Reaiah, the sons of Rezin, the sons of Nekoda, the sons of Gazzam, the sons of Uzza, the sons of Paseah, the sons of Besai, the sons of Asnah, the sons of Meunim, the sons of Nephusim, the sons of Bakbuk, the sons of Hakupha, the sons of Harhur, the sons of Bazluth, the sons of Mehida, the sons of Harsha, the sons of Barkos, the sons of Sisera, the sons of Temah, the sons of Neziah, and the sons of Hatipha The descendants of Solomon's servants included the sons of Sotai, the sons of Sophereth, the sons of Peruda, the sons of Jaala, the sons of Darkon, the sons of Giddel, the sons of Shephatiah, the sons of Hattil, the sons of Pochereth Hazzebaim, and the sons of Ami. All the temple servants and the descendants of Solomon's servants totaled three hundred ninety-two These individuals came from Tel Melah, Tel Harsha, Cherub, Addan, and Immer, but they could not prove their ancestry or their descent, whether they were of Israel. This included the sons of Delaiah, the sons of Tobiah, and the sons of Nekoda, totaling six hundred fifty-two. Of the priests, the sons of Hobaiah, the sons of Hakkoz, and the sons of Barzillai, who had married a daughter of Barzillai the Gileadite and took his name. These searched for their genealogical records, but they could not be found, so they were excluded from the priesthood. The governor told them not to eat any of the most holy food until a priest ministered with the Urim and

Thummim The entire assembly numbered forty-two thousand three hundred sixty, besides their servants and maids, who numbered seven thousand three hundred thirty-seven. There were two hundred men and women singers, seven hundred thirty-six horses, two hundred forty-five mules, four hundred thirty-five camels, and six thousand seven hundred twenty donkeys. Some of the heads of the families, when they arrived at the house of the LORD in Jerusalem, offered freewill offerings for the house of God to rebuild it on its site. According to their ability, they gave to the treasury for this work sixty-one thousand darics of gold, five thousand minas of silver, and one hundred priestly garments So the priests, the Levites, some of the people, the singers, the gatekeepers, and the temple servants settled in their own towns, along with all the other Israelites in their towns

Chapter 3

When the seventh month came and the Israelites were in their towns, the people gathered as one in Jerusalem. Then Jeshua, the son of Jozadak, and his fellow priests, along with Zerubbabel, the son of Shealtiel, and his associates began to build the altar of the God of Israel to offer burnt offerings on it, as written in the Law of Moses, the man of God. Despite their fear of the peoples around them, they set the altar on its foundations and offered burnt offerings on it to the LORD, both the morning and evening sacrifices Then, in accordance with what is written, they celebrated the Feast of Tabernacles with the required number of burnt offerings prescribed for each day. Afterward, they presented the regular burnt offerings, the New Moon sacrifices, and the sacrifices for all the appointed sacred festivals of the LORD, as well as those brought as freewill offerings to the LORD. On the first day of the seventh month, they began to offer burnt offerings to the LORD, though the foundation of the LORD's temple had not yet been laid They gave money to the masons and carpenters, and food and drink and olive oil to the people of Sidon and Tyre, so that they would bring cedar logs by sea from Lebanon to Joppa, as authorized by Cyrus, king of Persia. In the second month of the second year after their arrival at the house of God in Jerusalem, Zerubbabel, son of Shealtiel, Jeshua, son of Jozadak, and the rest of the people—the priests and the Levites and all who had returned from the captivity to Jerusalem—began the work. They appointed Levites twenty years old and older to supervise the building of the house of the LORD. Jeshua and his sons and brothers, and Kadmiel and his sons (descendants of Hodaviah), and the sons of Henadad and their sons and brothers—all Levites—joined together in supervising those working on the house of God When the builders laid the foundation of the temple of the LORD, the priests in their vestments and with trumpets, and the Levites (the sons of Asaph) with cymbals, took their places to praise the LORD, as prescribed by David, king of Israel. With praise and thanksgiving, they sang to the LORD: "He is good; His love toward Israel endures forever." And all the people gave a great shout of praise to the LORD because the foundation of the house of the LORD was laid. But many of the older priests, Levites, and family heads who had seen the former temple, wept aloud when they saw the foundation of this temple being laid, while many others shouted for joy. No one could distinguish the sound of the shouts of joy from the sound of weeping, because the people made so much noise. And the sound was heard far away

Chapter 4

When the enemies of Judah and Benjamin heard that the exiles were building a temple for the LORD, the God of Israel, they came to Zerubbabel and to the heads of the families and said, "Let us help you build because, like you, we seek your God and have been sacrificing to Him since the time of Esarhaddon, king of Assyria, who brought us here." But Zerubbabel, Jeshua, and the rest of the heads of the families of Israel answered, "You have no part with us in building a temple to our God. We alone will build it for the LORD, the God of Israel, as King Cyrus, the king of Persia, commanded us." Then the peoples around them set out to discourage the people of Judah and make them afraid to go on building. They hired counselors to work against them and frustrate their plans during the entire reign of Cyrus, king of Persia, and down to the reign of Darius, king of Persia At the beginning of the reign of Xerxes, they lodged an accusation against the people of Judah and Jerusalem. And in the days of Artaxerxes, Bishlam, Mithredath, Tabeel, and the rest of his associates wrote a letter to Artaxerxes; the letter was written in Aramaic script and in the Aramaic language. Rehum the commanding officer and Shimshai the secretary wrote a letter against Jerusalem to Artaxerxes the king as follows: "Rehum the commanding officer and Shimshai the secretary, together with the rest of their associates—the judges, officials, and administrators over the people from Persia, Uruk, and Babylon, the Elamites of Susa, and the other people whom the great and honorable Ashurbanipal deported and settled in the city of Samaria and elsewhere in Trans-Euphrates. (This is a copy of the letter they sent him.) To King Artaxerxes, From your servants, the men of Trans-Euphrates: The king should know that the people who came up to us from you have gone to Jerusalem and are rebuilding that rebellious and wicked city. They are restoring the walls and repairing the foundations. Furthermore, the king should know that if this city is built and its walls are restored, no more taxes, tribute, or duty will be paid, and eventually, the royal revenues will suffer. Now since we are under obligation to the palace and it is not proper for us to see the king dishonored, we are sending this message to inform the king, so that a search may be made in the archives of your predecessors. In these records, you will find that this city is a rebellious city, troublesome to kings and provinces, a place with a long history of sedition. That is why this city was destroyed. We inform the king that if this city is built and its walls are restored, you will be left with nothing in Trans-Euphrates." The king sent this reply: "To Rehum the commanding officer, Shimshai the secretary, and the rest of their associates living in Samaria and elsewhere in Trans-Euphrates: Greetings. The letter you sent us has been read and translated in my presence. I issued an order, and a search was made, and it was found that this city has a long history of revolt against kings and has been a place of rebellion and sedition. Jerusalem has had powerful kings ruling over the whole of Trans-Euphrates, and taxes, tribute, and duty were paid to them. Now issue an order to these men to stop work so that this city will not be rebuilt until I so order. Be careful not to neglect this matter. Why let this threat grow to the detriment of the royal interests?" As soon as the copy of the letter of King Artaxerxes was read to Rehum and Shimshai the secretary and their associates, they went immediately to the Jews in Jerusalem and compelled them by force to stop. Thus the work on the house of God in Jerusalem came to a standstill until the second year of the reign of Darius, king of Persia

Chapter 5

Now Haggai the prophet and Zechariah the prophet, a descendant of Iddo, prophesied to the Jews in

Judah and Jerusalem in the name of the God of Israel, who was over them. Then Zerubbabel, son of Shealtiel, and Jeshua, son of Jozadak, set to work to rebuild the house of God in Jerusalem. And the prophets of God were with them, supporting them At that time, Tattenai, governor of Trans-Euphrates, and Shethar-Bozenai and their associates went to them and asked, "Who authorized you to rebuild this temple and to finish it?" They also asked, "What are the names of those who are constructing this building?" But the eye of their God was watching over the elders of the Jews, and they were not stopped until a report could go to Darius and his written reply be received This is a copy of the letter that Tattenai, governor of Trans-Euphrates, and Shethar-Bozenai and their associates, the officials of Trans-Euphrates, sent to King Darius. The report they sent him read as follows: To King Darius: Cordial greetings. The king should know that we went to the district of Judah, to the temple of the great God. The people are building it with large stones and placing the timbers in the walls. The work is being carried on with diligence and is making rapid progress under their direction We questioned the elders and asked them, "Who authorized you to rebuild this temple and to finish it?" We also asked them their names so that we could write down the names of their leaders for your information This is the answer they gave us: "We are the servants of the God of heaven and earth, and we are rebuilding the temple that was built many years ago, one that a great king of Israel built and finished. But because our ancestors angered the God of heaven, He gave them into the hands of Nebuchadnezzar, the Chaldean king of Babylon, who destroyed this temple and deported the people to Babylon However, in the first year of Cyrus, king of Babylon, King Cyrus issued a decree to rebuild this house of God. He even removed from the temple of Babylon the gold and silver articles of the house of God, which Nebuchadnezzar had taken from the temple in Jerusalem and brought to the temple in Babylon. Then King Cyrus gave them to a man named Sheshbazzar, whom he had appointed governor, and he told him, "Take these articles and go and deposit them in the temple in Jerusalem. And rebuild the house of God on its site." So this Sheshbazzar came and laid the foundations of the house of God in Jerusalem. From that day to the present, it has been under construction but is not yet finished Now if it pleases the king, let a search be made in the royal archives of Babylon to see if King Cyrus did in fact issue a decree to rebuild this house of God in Jerusalem. Then let the king send us his decision in this matter

Chapter 6

King Darius ordered a search of the archives stored in Babylon. A scroll was found in a chest in the palace in Media, with the following written on it: In the first year of King Cyrus, a decree was made concerning the house of God in Jerusalem. The decree stated, "Let the house be rebuilt as a place for offering sacrifices. Its foundation should be laid to the height of sixty cubits and its width sixty cubits, with three layers of large stones and one layer of timber. The expenses are to be paid by the royal treasury. Additionally, the gold and silver articles from the house of God, which Nebuchadnezzar took from the temple in Jerusalem and brought to Babylon, must be returned to their places in the temple in Jerusalem." King Darius further commanded Tatnai, governor of Trans-Euphrates, Shethar-Boznai, and their associates to stay away from the construction site. He instructed them to allow the Jewish leaders and elders to rebuild this house of God on its original site. Moreover, the expenses for the construction should be fully covered by the royal treasury from the revenues of Trans-Euphrates. The Jewish people must also be provided with whatever they need—young bulls, rams, lambs for burnt offerings to the God of heaven, as well as wheat, salt, wine, and oil—according to the requests of the priests in Jerusalem. This should be done daily without fail so that they may offer sacrifices pleasing to the God of heaven and pray for the well-being of the king and his sons King Darius decreed that anyone who violates this command will have a beam pulled from their house, and they will be impaled on it. Their house will be turned into a pile of rubble. Furthermore, may God, who has caused His name to dwell there, overthrow any king or people who dares to change this decree or to destroy this house of God in Jerusalem. This decree was to be carried out with all diligence In accordance with King Darius's order, Tatnai, Shethar-Boznai, and their associates carried out the instructions with diligence. The Jewish elders continued to build and prosper under the preaching of Haggai the prophet and Zechariah, a descendant of Iddo. They finished building the temple according to the command of the God of Israel and the decrees of Cyrus, Darius, and Artaxerxes, kings of Persia. The temple was completed on the third day of the month of Adar, in the sixth year of the reign of King Darius The Israelites, including the priests, the Levites, and the rest of the exiles, celebrated the dedication of the house of God with joy. For the dedication of this house of God, they offered a hundred bulls, two hundred rams, four hundred lambs, and as a sin offering for all Israel, twelve male goats, one for each of the tribes of Israel. They installed the priests in their divisions and the Levites in their groups for the service of God at Jerusalem, according to what is written in the Book of Moses On the fourteenth day of the first month, the exiles celebrated the Passover. Since the priests and the Levites had purified themselves and were all ceremonially clean, they slaughtered the Passover lamb for all the exiles, for their fellow priests, and for themselves. The Israelites who had returned from the exile ate it, together with all who had separated themselves from the unclean practices of their Gentile neighbors to seek the LORD, the God of Israel. For seven days they celebrated with joy the Festival of Unleavened Bread because the LORD had filled them with joy by changing the attitude of the king of Assyria, so that he assisted them in the work on the house of God, the God of Israel

Chapter 7

After these events, during the reign of Artaxerxes, king of Persia, Ezra, the son of Seraiah, the son of Azariah, the son of Hilkiah, the son of Shallum, the son of Zadok, the son of Ahitub, the son of Amariah, the son of Azariah, the son of Meraioth, the son of Zeraiah, the son of Uzzi, the son of Bukki, the son of Abishua, the son of Phinehas, the son of Eleazar, the son of Aaron, the chief priest, came up from Babylon. Ezra was a teacher well versed in the Law of Moses, which the LORD, the God of Israel, had given. The king had granted him everything he asked because the hand of the LORD his God was on him Some of the Israelites, including priests, Levites, musicians, gatekeepers, and temple servants, also came up to Jerusalem in the seventh year of King Artaxerxes. Ezra arrived in Jerusalem in the fifth month of the seventh year of the king. He had begun his journey from Babylon on the first day of the first month and arrived in Jerusalem on the first day of the fifth month, for the gracious hand of his God was on him. For Ezra had devoted himself to the study and observance of the Law of the LORD and to teaching its decrees and laws in Israel This is a copy of the letter King Artaxerxes had given to Ezra the priest, a teacher of the Law, a man learned in matters concerning the commands and decrees of the LORD for Israel: Artaxerxes, king of kings, To Ezra the priest, teacher of the Law of the God of heaven: Greetings Now I decree that any of the Israelites in my kingdom, including priests and Levites, who wish to go to Jerusalem with you, may go. You are sent by the king and his seven advisers to inquire about Judah and Jerusalem with regard to the Law of your God, which is in your hand. Moreover, you are to take with you the silver and gold that the king and his advisers have freely given to the God of Israel, whose dwelling is in Jerusalem, together with all the silver and gold you may obtain from the province of Babylon, as well as the freewill offerings of the people and priests for the temple of their God in Jerusalem With this money, be sure to buy bulls, rams, and male lambs, together with their grain offerings and drink offerings, and sacrifice them on the altar of the temple of your God in Jerusalem. You and your fellow Israelites may then do whatever seems best with the rest of the silver and gold, in accordance with the will of your God. Deliver to the God of Jerusalem all the articles entrusted to you for worship in the temple of your God. And anything else needed for the temple of your God that you are responsible to supply, you may provide from the royal treasury Now I, King Artaxerxes, order all the treasurers of Trans-Euphrates to provide with diligence whatever Ezra the priest, the teacher of the Law of the God of heaven, may ask of you—up to a hundred talents of silver, a hundred cors of wheat, a hundred baths of wine, a hundred baths of olive oil, and salt without limit. Whatever the God of heaven has prescribed, let it be done with diligence for the temple of the God of heaven. Why should there be wrath against the realm of the king and of his sons? You are also to know that you have no authority to impose taxes, tribute, or duty on any of the priests, Levites, musicians, gatekeepers, temple servants, or other workers at this house of God And you, Ezra, in accordance with the wisdom of your God, which you possess, appoint magistrates and judges to administer justice to all the people of Trans-Euphrates—all who know the laws of your God. And you are to teach any who do not know them. Whoever does not obey the law of your God and the law of the king must surely be punished by death, banishment, confiscation of property, or imprisonment Praise be to the LORD, the God of our ancestors, who has put it into the king's heart to bring honor to the house of the LORD in Jerusalem in this way and who has extended his good favor to me before the king and his advisers and all the king's powerful officials. Because the hand of the LORD my God was on me, I took courage and gathered leaders from Israel to go up with me

Chapter 8

These are the family heads and those registered with them who came up with me from Babylon during the reign of King Artaxerxes: Of the descendants of Phinehas: Gershom; Of the descendants of Ithamar: Daniel; Of the descendants of David: Hattush; Of the descendants of Shecaniah; Of the descendants of Parosh: Zechariah, and with him were registered 150 men; Of the descendants of Pahath-Moab: Eliehoenai, son of Zerahiah, and with him 200 men; Of the descendants of Zattu: Shecaniah, son of Jahaziel, and with him 300 men; Of the descendants of Adin: Ebed, son of Jonathan, and with him 50 men; Of the descendants of Elam: Jeshaiah, son of Athaliah, and with him 70 men; Of the descendants of Shephatiah: Zebadiah, son of Michael, and with him 80 men; Of the descendants of Joab: Obadiah, son of Jehiel, and with him 218 men; Of the descendants of Bani: Shelomith, son of Josiphiah, and with him 160 men; Of the descendants of Bebai: Zechariah, son of Bebai, and with him 28 men; Of the descendants of Azgad: Johanan, son of Hakkatan, and with him 110 men; Of the descendants of Adonikam: The last ones, whose names were Eliphelet, Jeuel, and Shemaiah, and with them 60 men; Of the descendants of Bigvai: Uthai and Zakkur, and with them 70 men I assembled them at the canal that flows toward Ahava, and we camped there three days. When I checked among the people and the priests, I found no Levites there. So I summoned Eliezer, Ariel, Shemaiah, Elnathan, Jarib, Elnathan, Nathan, Zechariah, and Meshullam, who were leaders, and Joiarib and Elnathan, who were men of learning, and I ordered them to go to Iddo, the leader in Kasiphia. I told them what to say to Iddo and his fellow Levites, the temple servants in Kasiphia, so that they might bring attendants to us for the house of our God. Because the gracious hand of our God was on us, they brought us Sherebiah, a capable man, from the descendants of Mahli son of Levi, the son of Israel, and Sherebiah's sons and brothers, 18 in all; and Hashabiah, together with Jeshaiah from the descendants of Merari, and his brothers and nephews, 20 in all. They also brought 220 of the temple servants—a body that David and the officials had established to assist the Levites. All were registered by name There, by the Ahava Canal, I proclaimed a fast so that we might humble ourselves before our God and ask him for a safe journey for us and our children, with all our possessions. I was ashamed to ask the king for soldiers and horsemen to protect us from enemies on the road because we had told the king, "The gracious hand of our God is on everyone who looks to him, but his great anger is against all who forsake him." So we fasted and petitioned our God about this, and he answered our prayer Then I set apart twelve of the leading priests, namely, Sherebiah, Hashabiah, and ten of their brothers, and I weighed out to them the offering of silver and gold and the articles that the king, his advisers, his officials, and all Israel present there had donated for the house of our God. I weighed out to them 650 talents of silver, silver articles weighing 100 talents, 100 talents of gold, 20 bowls of gold valued at 1,000 darics, and two fine articles of polished bronze, as precious as gold. I said to them, "You as well as these articles are consecrated to the LORD. The silver and gold are a freewill offering to the LORD, the God of your ancestors. Guard them carefully until you weigh them out in the chambers of the house of the LORD in Jerusalem before the leading priests and the Levites and the family heads of Israel." Then the priests and Levites received the silver and gold and sacred articles that had been weighed out to be taken to the house of our God in Jerusalem On the twelfth day of the first month, we set out from the Ahava Canal to go to Jerusalem. The hand of our God was on us, and he protected us from enemies and bandits along the way. So we arrived in Jerusalem, where we rested three days On the fourth day, in the house of our God, we weighed out the silver and gold and the sacred articles into the hands of Meremoth, son of Uriah the priest. Eleazar, son of Phinehas, was with him, and so were the Levites, Jozabad, son of Jeshua, and Noadiah, son of Binnui. Everything was accounted for by number and weight, and the entire weight was recorded at that time Then the exiles who had returned from captivity sacrificed burnt offerings to the God of Israel: twelve bulls for all Israel, ninety-six rams, seventy-seven male lambs, and, as a sin offering, twelve male goats. All this was a burnt offering to the LORD. They also delivered the king's orders to the royal satraps and to the governors of

Trans-Euphrates, who then gave assistance to the people and to the house of God

Chapter 9

After these things had been done, the leaders came to me and said, "The people of Israel, including the priests and the Levites, have not kept themselves separate from the neighboring peoples with their detestable practices, like those of the Canaanites, Hittites, Perizzites, Jebusites, Ammonites, Moabites, Egyptians, and Amorites. They have taken some of their daughters as wives for themselves and their sons, and have mingled the holy race with the peoples around them. And the leaders and officials have led the way in this unfaithfulness." When I heard this, I tore my tunic and cloak, pulled hair from my head and beard, and sat down appalled. Then everyone who trembled at the words of the God of Israel gathered around me because of this unfaithfulness of the exiles. And I sat there appalled until the evening sacrifice. Then, at the evening sacrifice, I rose from my self-abasement, with my tunic and cloak torn, and fell on my knees with my hands spread out to the LORD my God and prayed: "I am too ashamed and disgraced, my God, to lift up my face to you, because our sins are higher than our heads and our guilt has reached to the heavens. From the days of our ancestors until now, our guilt has been great. Because of our sins, we and our kings and our priests have been subjected to the sword and captivity, to pillage and humiliation at the hand of foreign kings, as it is today. But now, for a brief moment, the LORD our God has been gracious in leaving us a remnant and giving us a firm place in his sanctuary, and so our God gives light to our eyes and a little relief in our bondage. Though we are slaves, our God has not forsaken us in our bondage. He has shown us kindness in the sight of the kings of Persia: He has granted us new life to rebuild the house of our God and repair its ruins, and He has given us a wall of protection in Judah and Jerusalem But now, our God, what can we say after this? For we have forsaken the commands you gave through your servants the prophets when you said: 'The land you are entering to possess is a land polluted by the corruption of its peoples. By their detestable practices, they have filled it with their impurity from one end to the other. Therefore, do not give your daughters in marriage to their sons or take their daughters for your sons. Do not seek a treaty of friendship with them at any time, that you may be strong and eat the good things of the land and leave it to your children as an everlasting inheritance.' What has happened to us is a result of our evil deeds and our great guilt, and yet, our God, you have punished us less than our sins deserved and have given us a remnant like this. Shall we then break your commands again and intermarry with the peoples who commit such detestable practices? Would you not be angry enough with us to destroy us, leaving us no remnant or survivor? LORD, the God of Israel, you are righteous! We are left this day as a remnant. Here we are before you in our guilt, though because of it not one of us can stand in your presence."

Chapter 10

While Ezra was praying and confessing, weeping and throwing himself down before the house of God, a large crowd of Israelites—men, women, and children—gathered around him. They too wept bitterly. Then Shecaniah, son of Jehiel, one of the descendants of Elam, said to Ezra, "We have been unfaithful to our God by marrying foreign women from the peoples around us. But in spite of this, there is still hope for Israel. Now let us make a covenant before our God to send away all these women and their children, in accordance with the counsel of my lord and of those who fear the commands of our God. Let it be done according to the Law. Rise up; this matter is in your hands. We will support you, so take courage and do it." So Ezra rose up and put the leading priests and Levites and all Israel under oath to do what had been suggested. And they took the oath. Then Ezra withdrew from before the house of God and went to the room of Jehohanan, son of Eliashib. While he was there, he ate no food and drank no water, because he continued to mourn over the unfaithfulness of the exiles A proclamation was then issued throughout Judah and Jerusalem for all the exiles to assemble in Jerusalem. Anyone who failed to appear within three days would forfeit all his property, in accordance with the decision of the officials and elders, and would himself be expelled from the assembly of the exiles Within the three days, all the men of Judah and Benjamin had gathered in Jerusalem. On the twentieth day of the ninth month, all the people were sitting in the square before the house of God, greatly distressed by the occasion and because of the rain. Then Ezra the priest stood up and said to them, "You have been unfaithful; you have married foreign women, adding to Israel's guilt. Now honor the LORD, the God of your ancestors, and do his will. Separate yourselves from the peoples around you and from your foreign wives." The whole assembly responded with a loud voice: "You are right! We must do as you say. But there are many people here and it is the rainy season; so we cannot stand outside. Besides, this matter cannot be taken care of in a day or two, because we have sinned greatly in this thing. Let our officials act for the whole assembly. Then let everyone in our towns who has married a foreign woman come at a set time, along with the elders and judges of each town, until the fierce anger of our God in this matter is turned away from us." Only Jonathan, son of Asahel, and Jahzeiah, son of Tikvah, supported by Meshullam and Shabbethai the Levite, opposed this. So the exiles did as was proposed. Ezra the priest selected men who were family heads, one from each family division, and all of them designated by name. On the first day of the tenth month, they sat down to investigate the cases, and by the first day of the first month, they finished dealing with all the men who had married foreign women Among the descendants of the priests, the following had married foreign women: From the descendants of Jeshua, son of Jozadak, and his brothers: Maaseiah, Eliezer, Jarib, and Gedaliah. (They all gave their hands in pledge to put away their wives, and for their guilt, they each presented a ram from the flock as a guilt offering.) From the descendants of Immer: Hanani and Zebadiah From the descendants of Harim: Maaseiah, Elijah, Shemaiah, Jehiel, and Uzziah From the descendants of Pashhur: Elioenai, Maaseiah, Ishmael, Nethanel, Jozabad, and Elasah Among the Levites: Jozabad, Shimei, Kelaiah (also called Kelita), Pethahiah, Judah, and Eliezer From the musicians: Eliashib From the gatekeepers: Shallum, Telem, and Uri And among the other Israelites: From the descendants of Parosh: Ramiah, Izziah, Malkijah, Mijamin, Eleazar, Malkijah, and Benaiah From the descendants of Elam: Mattaniah, Zechariah, Jehiel, Abdi, Jeremoth, and Elijah From the descendants of Zattu: Elioenai, Eliashib, Mattaniah, Jeremoth, Zabad, and Aziza From the descendants of Bebai: Jehohanan, Hananiah, Zabbai, and Athlai From the descendants of Bani: Meshullam, Malluk, Adaiah, Jashub, Sheal, and Jeremoth From the descendants of Pahath-Moab: Adna, Kelal, Benaiah, Maaseiah, Mattaniah, Bezalel, Binnui, and Manasseh From the descendants of Harim: Eliezer, Ishijah, Malkijah, Shemaiah, Shimeon, Benjamin, Malluk, and

Shemariah From the descendants of Hashum: Mattenai, Mattattah, Zabad, Eliphelet, Jeremai, Manasseh, and Shimei From the descendants of Bani: Maadai, Amram, Uel, Benaiah, Bedeiah, Keluhi, Vaniah, Meremoth, Eliashib, Mattaniah, Mattenai, and Jaasu From the descendants of Binnui: Shimei, Shelemiah, Nathan, Adaiah, Machnadebai, Shashai, Sharai, Azarel, Shelemiah, Shemariah, Shallum, Amariah, and Joseph From the descendants of Nebo: Jeiel, Mattithiah, Zabad, Zebina, Jaddai, Joel, and Benaiah All these had married foreign women, and some of them had children by these wives

16. Nehemiah

Chapter 1

In the month of Chisleu, during the twentieth year, I was in the palace of Susa. Hanani, one of my brothers, came with some men from Judah, and I asked them about the surviving Jews who had escaped captivity and about Jerusalem. They told me, "Those who survived the captivity are in great distress and disgrace. The walls of Jerusalem are broken down, and its gates have been burned with fire." When I heard this, I sat down and wept, mourning for several days. I fasted and prayed before the God of Heaven, saying, "O Lord, God of Heaven, the great and awesome God, who keeps His covenant of love with those who love Him and keep His commandments, let Your ear be attentive and Your eyes open to hear the prayer Your servant is praying before You day and night for Your servants, the people of Israel. I confess the sins we Israelites, including myself and my father's house, have committed against You. We have acted very wickedly toward You. We have not obeyed the commands, decrees, and laws You gave Your servant Moses "Remember the instruction You gave Your servant Moses, saying, 'If you are unfaithful, I will scatter you among the nations, but if you return to Me and obey My commands, then even if your exiled people are at the farthest horizon, I will gather them from there and bring them to the place I have chosen as a dwelling for My Name.' "They are Your servants and Your people, whom You redeemed by Your great strength and Your mighty hand. O Lord, let Your ear be attentive to the prayer of this Your servant and to the prayer of Your servants who delight in revering Your Name. Give Your servant success today by granting him favor in the presence of this man." I was cupbearer to the king

Chapter 2

In the month of Nisan, in the twentieth year of King Artaxerxes, when wine was brought before him, I took the wine and gave it to the king. He asked me, "Why does your face look so sad when you are not ill? This can be nothing but sadness of heart." I was very much afraid, but I said to the king, "May the king live forever! Why should my face not look sad when the city where my ancestors are buried lies in ruins, and its gates have been destroyed by fire?" The king said to me, "What is it you want?" Then I prayed to the God of Heaven, and I answered the king, "If it pleases the king and if your servant has found favor in his sight, let him send me to the city in Judah where my ancestors are buried so that I can rebuild it." The king, with the queen sitting beside him, asked me, "How long will your journey take, and when will you get back?" It pleased the king to send me; so I set a time I also said to him, "If it pleases the king, may I have letters to the governors of Trans-Euphrates, so that they will provide me safe-conduct until I arrive in Judah? And may I have a letter to Asaph, keeper of the royal park, so he will give me timber to make

beams for the gates of the citadel by the temple and for the city wall and the residence I will occupy?" And because the gracious hand of my God was on me, the king granted my requests So I went to the governors of Trans-Euphrates and gave them the king's letters. The king had also sent army officers and cavalry with me. When Sanballat the Horonite and Tobiah the Ammonite official heard about this, they were very much disturbed that someone had come to promote the welfare of the Israelites I went to Jerusalem, and after staying there three days, I set out during the night with a few others. I had not told anyone what my God had put in my heart to do for Jerusalem. There were no mounts with me except the one I was riding on. By night I went out through the Valley Gate toward the Jackal Well and the Dung Gate, examining the walls of Jerusalem, which had been broken down, and its gates, which had been destroyed by fire Then I moved on toward the Fountain Gate and the King's Pool, but there was not enough room for my mount to get through; so I went up the valley by night, examining the wall. Finally, I turned back and re-entered through the Valley Gate. The officials did not know where I had gone or what I was doing, because as yet I had said nothing to the Jews or the priests or nobles or officials or any others who would be doing the work Then I said to them, "You see the trouble we are in: Jerusalem lies in ruins, and its gates have been burned with fire. Come, let us rebuild the wall of Jerusalem, and we will no longer be in disgrace." I also told them about the gracious hand of my God on me and what the king had said to me. They replied, "Let us start rebuilding." So they began this good work But when Sanballat the Horonite, Tobiah the Ammonite official, and Geshem the Arab heard about it, they mocked and ridiculed us. "What is this you are doing?" they asked. "Are you rebelling against the king?" I answered them by saying, "The God of Heaven will give us success. We His servants will start rebuilding, but as for you, you have no share in Jerusalem or any claim or historic right to it."

Chapter 3

Eliashib the high priest and his fellow priests went to work and rebuilt the Sheep Gate. They dedicated it and set its doors in place, building as far as the Tower of the Hundred, which they dedicated, and as far as the Tower of Hananel. The men of Jericho built the adjoining section, and Zaccur son of Imri built next to them The Fish Gate was rebuilt by the sons of Hassenaah. They laid its beams and put its doors and bolts and bars in place. Meremoth son of Uriah, the son of Hakkoz, repaired the next section. Next to him Meshullam son of Berekiah, the son of Meshezabel, made repairs, and next to him Zadok son of Baana also made repairs. The next section was repaired by the men of Tekoa, but their nobles would not put their shoulders to the work under their supervisors The Jeshanah Gate was repaired by Joiada son of Paseah and Meshullam son of Besodeiah. They laid its beams and put its doors and bolts and bars in place. Next to them, repairs were made by men from Gibeon and Mizpah, Melatiah of Gibeon and Jadon of Meronoth, places under the authority of the governor of Trans-Euphrates. Uzziel son of Harhaiah, one of the goldsmiths, repaired the next section; and Hananiah, one of the perfume-makers, made repairs next to that. They restored Jerusalem as far as the Broad Wall. Rephaiah son of Hur, ruler of a half-district of Jerusalem, repaired the next section. Adjoining this, Jedaiah son of Harumaph made repairs opposite his house, and Hattush son of Hashabneiah made repairs next to him. Malkijah son of Harim and Hasshub son of Pahath-Moab repaired another section and the

Tower of the Ovens. Shallum son of Hallohesh, ruler of a half-district of Jerusalem, repaired the next section with the help of his daughters The Valley Gate was repaired by Hanun and the residents of Zanoah. They rebuilt it and put its doors with their bolts and bars in place. They also repaired a thousand cubits of the wall as far as the Dung Gate. The Dung Gate was repaired by Malkijah son of Rekab, ruler of the district of Beth Hakkerem. He rebuilt it and put its doors with their bolts and bars in place The Fountain Gate was repaired by Shallun son of Kol-Hozeh, ruler of the district of Mizpah. He rebuilt it, roofing it over and putting its doors and bolts and bars in place. He also repaired the wall of the Pool of Siloam, by the King's Garden, as far as the steps going down from the City of David. Beyond him, Nehemiah son of Azbuk, ruler of a half-district of Beth Zur, made repairs up to a point opposite the tombs of David, as far as the artificial pool and the House of the Heroes Next to him, the repairs were made by the Levites under Rehum son of Bani. Beside him, Hashabiah, ruler of half the district of Keilah, carried out repairs for his district. Next to him, the repairs were made by their fellow Levites under Binnui son of Henadad, ruler of the other half-district of Keilah. Next to him, Ezer son of Jeshua, ruler of Mizpah, repaired another section, from a point facing the ascent to the armory as far as the angle of the wall. Next to him, Baruch son of Zabbai zealously repaired another section, from the angle to the entrance of the house of Eliashib the high priest. Next to him, Meremoth son of Uriah, the son of Hakkoz, repaired another section, from the entrance of Eliashib's house to the end of it The repairs next to him were made by the priests from the surrounding region. Beyond them, Benjamin and Hasshub made repairs in front of their house; and next to them, Azariah son of Maaseiah, the son of Ananiah, made repairs beside his house. Next to him, Binnui son of Henadad repaired another section, from Azariah's house to the angle and the corner, and Palal son of Uzai worked opposite the angle and the tower projecting from the upper palace near the court of the guard. Next to him, Pedaiah son of Parosh and the temple servants living on the hill of Ophel made repairs up to a point opposite the Water Gate toward the east and the projecting tower. Next to them, the men of Tekoa repaired another section, from the great projecting tower to the wall of Ophel Above the Horse Gate, the priests made repairs, each in front of his own house. Next to them, Zadok son of Immer made repairs opposite his house. Next to him, Shemaiah son of Shekaniah, the guard at the East Gate, made repairs. Next to him, Hananiah son of Shelemiah and Hanun, the sixth son of Zalaph, repaired another section. Next to them, Meshullam son of Berekiah made repairs opposite his living quarters. Next to him, Malkijah, one of the goldsmiths, made repairs as far as the house of the temple servants and the merchants, opposite the Inspection Gate, and as far as the room above the corner; and between the room above the corner and the Sheep Gate, the goldsmiths and merchants made repairs

Chapter 4

When Sanballat heard that we were rebuilding the wall, he became angry and was greatly incensed. He ridiculed the Jews, and in the presence of his associates and the army of Samaria, he said, "What are these feeble Jews doing? Will they restore their wall? Will they offer sacrifices? Will they finish in a day? Can they bring the stones back to life from those heaps of rubble—burned as they are?" Tobiah the Ammonite, who was at his side, said, "What they are building—even a fox climbing up on it would break down their wall of stones!" Hear us, our God, for we are despised. Turn their insults back on their own heads. Give them over as plunder in a land of captivity. Do not cover up their guilt or blot out their sins from Your sight, for they have thrown insults in the face of the builders So we rebuilt the wall till all of it reached half its height, for the people worked with all their heart. But when Sanballat, Tobiah, the Arabs, the Ammonites, and the people of Ashdod heard that the repairs to Jerusalem's walls had gone ahead and that the gaps were being closed, they were very angry. They all plotted together to come and fight against Jerusalem and stir up trouble against it. But we prayed to our God and posted a guard day and night to meet this threat Meanwhile, the people in Judah said, "The strength of the laborers is giving out, and there is so much rubble that we cannot rebuild the wall." Also our enemies said, "Before they know it or see us, we will be right there among them and will kill them and put an end to the work." Then the Jews who lived near them came and told us ten times over, "Wherever you turn, they will attack us." Therefore, I stationed some of the people behind the lowest points of the wall at the exposed places, posting them by families, with their swords, spears, and bows. After I looked things over, I stood up and said to the nobles, the officials, and the rest of the people, "Don't be afraid of them. Remember the Lord, who is great and awesome, and fight for your families, your sons, and your daughters, your wives, and your homes." When our enemies heard that we were aware of their plot and that God had frustrated it, we all returned to the wall, each to our own work. From that day on, half of my men did the work, while the other half were equipped with spears, shields, bows, and armor. The officers posted themselves behind all the people of Judah who were building the wall. Those who carried materials did their work with one hand and held a weapon in the other, and each of the builders wore his sword at his side as he worked. But the man who sounded the trumpet stayed with me Then I said to the nobles, the officials, and the rest of the people, "The work is extensive and spread out, and we are widely separated from each other along the wall. Wherever you hear the sound of the trumpet, join us there. Our God will fight for us!" So we continued the work with half the men holding spears, from the first light of dawn till the stars came out. At that time, I also said to the people, "Have every man and his helper stay inside Jerusalem at night so they can serve us as guards by night and workers by day." Neither I nor my brothers nor my men nor the guards with me took off our clothes; each had his weapon, even when he went for water

Chapter 5

Now the men and their wives raised a great outcry against their fellow Jews. Some were saying, "We and our sons and daughters are numerous; in order for us to eat and stay alive, we must get grain." Others were saying, "We are mortgaging our fields, our vineyards, and our homes to get grain during the famine." Still others were saying, "We have had to borrow money to pay the king's tax on our fields and vineyards. Although we are of the same flesh and blood as our fellow Jews and though our children are as good as theirs, yet we have to subject our sons and daughters to slavery. Some of our daughters have already been enslaved, but we are powerless because our fields and our vineyards belong to others." When I heard their outcry and these charges, I was very angry. I pondered them in my mind and then accused the nobles and officials. I told them, "You are charging your own people interest!" So I called together a large meeting to deal with them and said: "As far as possible, we have bought back our fellow Jews who were sold to the Gentiles. Now you are selling your own people, only for them to be sold back to us!" They kept quiet because they could find nothing to say So I continued, "What you are doing is not right. Shouldn't you walk in the fear of our God to avoid the reproach of our Gentile enemies? I and my brothers and my men are also lending the people money and grain. But let us stop charging interest! Give back to them immediately their fields, vineyards, olive groves, and houses, and also the interest you are charging them—one percent of the money, grain, new wine, and olive oil." "We will give it back," they said. "And we will not demand anything more from them. We will do as you say." Then I summoned the priests and made the nobles and officials take an oath to do what they had promised. I also shook out the folds of my robe and said, "In this way, may God shake out of their house and possessions anyone who does not keep this promise. So may such a person be shaken out and emptied!" At this, the whole assembly said, "Amen," and praised the Lord. And the people did as they had promised Moreover, from the twentieth year of King Artaxerxes, when I was appointed to be their governor in the land of Judah, until his thirty-second year—twelve years—neither I nor my brothers ate the food allotted to the governor. But the earlier governors—those preceding me—placed a heavy burden on the people and took forty shekels of silver from them in addition to food and wine. Their assistants also lorded it over the people. But out of reverence for God, I did not act like that. Instead, I devoted myself to the work on this wall. All my men were assembled there for the work; we did not acquire any land Furthermore, a hundred and fifty Jews and officials ate at my table, as well as those who came to us from the surrounding nations. Each day, one ox, six choice sheep, and some poultry were prepared for me, and every ten days an abundant supply of wine of all kinds. In spite of all this, I never demanded the food allotted to the governor, because the demands were heavy on these people Remember me with favor, my God, for all I have done for these people

Chapter 6

When Sanballat, Tobiah, Geshem the Arab, and the rest of our enemies learned that I had rebuilt the wall and there were no more breaches (although I had not yet set the doors in the gates), Sanballat and Geshem sent me a message saying, "Come, let us meet together in one of the villages on the plain of Ono." But they were scheming to harm me. So I sent messengers to them with this reply: "I am carrying on a great project and cannot go down. Why should the work stop while I leave it and go down to you?" Four times they sent me the same message, and each time I gave them the same answer. Then, the fifth time, Sanballat sent his servant to me with an open letter in his hand, in which it was written: "It is reported among the nations, and Geshem says it is true, that you and the Jews are plotting to revolt, and therefore you are building the wall. Moreover, according to these reports, you are about to become their king and have even appointed prophets to make this proclamation about you in Jerusalem: 'There is a king in Judah!' Now this report will get back to the king; so come, let us confer together." I sent him this reply: "Nothing like what you are saying is happening; you are just making it up out of your head." They were all trying to frighten us, thinking, "Their hands will get too weak for the work, and it will not be completed." But I prayed, "Now strengthen my hands." One day I went to the house of Shemaiah son of Delaiah, the son of Mehetabel, who was shut in at his home. He said, "Let us meet in the house of God, inside the

temple, and let us close the temple doors, because men are coming to kill you—by night they are coming to kill you." But I said, "Should a man like me run away? Or should someone like me go into the temple to save his life? I will not go!" I realized that God had not sent him, but that he had prophesied against me because Tobiah and Sanballat had hired him. He had been hired to intimidate me so that I would commit a sin by doing this, and then they would give me a bad name to discredit me "Remember Tobiah and Sanballat, my God, because of what they have done; remember also the prophet Noadiah and how she and the rest of the prophets have been trying to intimidate me." So the wall was completed on the twenty-fifth of Elul, in fifty-two days. When all our enemies heard about this, all the surrounding nations were afraid and lost their self-confidence because they realized that this work had been done with the help of our God In those days, the nobles of Judah were sending many letters to Tobiah, and replies from Tobiah kept coming to them. Many in Judah were under oath to him, since he was son-in-law to Shecaniah son of Arah, and his son Jehohanan had married the daughter of Meshullam son of Berekiah. Moreover, they kept reporting to me his good deeds and then telling him Moreover, they kept reporting to me his good deeds and then telling him what I said. And Tobiah sent letters to intimidate me

Chapter 7

After the wall was rebuilt and I had set the doors in place, the gatekeepers, the musicians, and the Levites were appointed. I put my brother Hanani in charge of Jerusalem, along with Hananiah the commander of the citadel, because he was a man of integrity and feared God more than most people do. I said to them, "The gates of Jerusalem are not to be opened until the sun is hot. While the gatekeepers are still on duty, have them shut the doors and bar them. Also, appoint residents of Jerusalem as guards, some at their posts and some near their own houses."

Now the city was large and spacious, but there were few people in it, and the houses had not yet been rebuilt. So my God put it into my heart to assemble the nobles, the officials, and the common people for registration by families. I found the genealogical record of those who had been the first to return. This is what I found written there:

These are the people of the province who came up from the captivity of the exiles whom Nebuchadnezzar king of Babylon had taken captive. They returned to Jerusalem and Judah, each to their own town, in company with Zerubbabel, Joshua, Nehemiah, Azariah, Raamiah, Nahamani, Mordecai, Bilshan, Mispereth, Bigvai, Nehum, and Baanah The list of the men of Israel:

- The descendants of Parosh: 2,172
- Of Shephatiah: 372
- Of Arah: 652
- Of Pahath-Moab (through the line of Jeshua and Joab): 2,818
- Of Elam: 1,254
- Of Zattu: 845
- Of Zaccai: 760
- Of Binnui: 648
- Of Bebai: 628
- Of Azgad: 2,322
- Of Adonikam: 667
- Of Bigvai: 2,067
- Of Adin: 655
- Of Ater (through Hezekiah): 98
- Of Hashum: 328
- Of Bezai: 324

- Of Hariph: 112
- Of Gibeon: 95

The men of Bethlehem and Netophah: 188 The men of Anathoth: 128 The men of Beth Azmaveth: 42 The men of Kiriath Jearim, Kephirah, and Beeroth: 743 The men of Ramah and Geba: 621 The men of Mikmash: 122 The men of Bethel and Ai: 123 The other Nebo: 52 The descendants of the other Elam: 1,254 Of Harim: 320 Of Jericho: 345 Of Lod, Hadid, and Ono: 721 Of Senaah: 3,930

The priests:

- The descendants of Jedaiah (through the family of Jeshua): 973
- Of Immer: 1,052
- Of Pashhur: 1,247
- Of Harim: 1,017

The Levites:

- The descendants of Jeshua (through Kadmiel through the line of Hodaviah): 74

The musicians:

- The descendants of Asaph: 148

The gatekeepers:

- The descendants of Shallum, Ater, Talmon, Akkub, Hatita, and Shobai: 138

The temple servants:

The descendants of Ziha, Hasupha, Tabbaoth, Keros, Sia, Padon, Lebana, Hagaba, Shalmai, Hanan, Giddel, Gahar, Reaiah, Rezin, Nekoda, Gazzam, Uzza, Paseah, Besai, Meunim, Nephusim, Bakbuk, Hakupha, Harhur, Bazluth, Mehida, Harsha, Barkos, Sisera, Temah, Neziah, and Hatipha The descendants of the servants of Solomon:

The descendants of Sotai, Sophereth, Perida, Jaala, Darkon, Giddel, Shephatiah, Hattil, Pokereth-Hazzebaim, and Amon The temple servants and the descendants of the servants of Solomon: 392

The following came up from the towns of Tel Melah, Tel Harsha, Kerub, Addon, and Immer, but they could not show that their families were descended from Israel:

- The descendants of Delaiah, Tobiah, and Nekoda: 642

And from among the priests:

The descendants of Hobaiah, Hakkoz, and Barzillai (a man who had married a daughter of Barzillai the Gileadite and was called by that name) These searched for their family records, but they could not find them and so were excluded from the priesthood as unclean. The governor ordered them not to eat any of the most sacred food until there was a priest ministering with the Urim and Thummim The whole company numbered 42,360, besides their 7,337 male and female slaves; and they also had 245 male and female singers. There were 736 horses, 245 mules, 435 camels, and 6,720 donkeys Some of the heads of the families contributed to the work. The governor gave to the treasury 1,000 darics of gold, 50 bowls, and 530 garments for priests. Some of the heads of the families gave to the treasury for the work 20,000 darics of gold and 2,200 minas of silver. The total given by the rest of the people was 20,000 darics of gold, 2,000 minas of silver, and 67 garments for priests The priests, the Levites, the gatekeepers, the musicians, and the temple servants, along with certain of the people and the rest of the Israelites, settled in their own towns

Chapter 8

When the seventh month came and the Israelites had settled in their towns, all the people came together as one in the square before the Water Gate. They told Ezra the teacher of the Law to bring out the Book of the Law of Moses, which the Lord had commanded for Israel So on the first day of the seventh month, Ezra the priest brought the Law before the assembly, which was made up of men and women and all who were able to understand. He read it aloud from daybreak till noon as he faced the square before the Water Gate in the presence of the men, women, and others who could understand. And all the people listened attentively to the Book of the Law Ezra the teacher of the Law stood on a high wooden platform built for the occasion. Beside him on his right stood Mattithiah, Shema, Anaiah, Uriah, Hilkiah, and Maaseiah; and on his left were Pedaiah, Mishael, Malkijah, Hashum, Hashbaddanah, Zechariah, and Meshullam. Ezra opened the book. All the people could see him because he was standing above them; and as he opened it, the people all stood up. Ezra praised the Lord, the great God; and all the people lifted their hands and responded, "Amen! Amen!" Then they bowed down and worshiped the Lord with their faces to the ground The Levites—Jeshua, Bani, Sherebiah, Jamin, Akkub, Shabbethai, Hodiah, Maaseiah, Kelita, Azariah, Jozabad, Hanan, and Pelaiah—instructed the people in the Law while the people were standing there. They read from the Book of the Law of God, making it clear and giving the meaning so that the people understood what was being read Then Nehemiah the governor, Ezra the priest and teacher of the Law, and the Levites who were instructing the people said to them all, "This day is holy to the Lord your God. Do not mourn or weep." For all the people had been weeping as they listened to the words of the Law Nehemiah said, "Go and enjoy choice food and sweet drinks, and send some to those who have nothing prepared. This day is holy to our Lord. Do not grieve, for the joy of the Lord is your strength." The Levites calmed all the people, saying, "Be still, for this is a holy day. Do not grieve." Then all the people went away to eat and drink, to send portions of food and to celebrate with great joy, because they now understood the words that had been made known to them On the second day of the month, the heads of all the families, along with the priests and the Levites, gathered around Ezra the teacher to give attention to the words of the Law. They found written in the Law, which the Lord had commanded through Moses, that the Israelites were to live in temporary shelters during the festival of the seventh month and that they should proclaim this word and spread it throughout their towns and in Jerusalem: "Go out into the hill country and bring back branches from olive and wild olive trees, and from myrtles, palms and shade trees, to make temporary shelters"—as it is written So the people went out and brought back branches and built themselves temporary shelters on their own roofs, in their courtyards, in the courts of the house of God, and in the square by the Water Gate and the one by the Gate of Ephraim. The whole company that had returned from exile built temporary shelters and lived in them. From the days of Joshua son of Nun until that day, the Israelites had not celebrated it like this. And their joy was very great Day after day, from the first day to the last, Ezra read from the Book of the Law of God. They celebrated the festival for seven days, and on the eighth day, in accordance with the regulation, there was an assembly

Chapter 9

On the twenty-fourth day of the same month, the Israelites gathered together, fasting and wearing sackcloth and putting dust on their heads. Those of Israelite descent had separated themselves from all foreigners. They stood in their places and confessed their sins and the sins of their ancestors. They stood where they were and read from the Book of the Law of the Lord their God for a quarter of the day, and spent another quarter in confession and in worshiping the Lord their God. Standing on the stairs of the Levites were Jeshua, Bani, Kadmiel, Shebaniah, Bunni, Sherebiah, Bani, and Kenani. They cried out with loud voices to the Lord their God And the Levites—Jeshua, Kadmiel, Bani, Hashabneiah, Sherebiah, Hodiah, Shebaniah, and Pethahiah—said: "Stand up and praise the Lord your God, who is from everlasting to everlasting. Blessed be your glorious name, and may it be exalted above all blessing and praise. You alone are the Lord. You made the heavens, even the highest heavens, and all their starry host, the earth and all that is on it, the seas and all that is in them. You give life to everything, and the multitudes of heaven worship you "You are the Lord God, who chose Abram and brought him out of Ur of the Chaldeans and named him Abraham. You found his heart faithful to you, and you made a covenant with him to give to his descendants the land of the Canaanites, Hittites, Amorites, Perizzites, Jebusites, and Girgashites. You have kept your promise because you are righteous "You saw the suffering of our ancestors in Egypt; you heard their cry at the Red Sea. You sent signs and wonders against Pharaoh, against all his officials and all the people of his land, for you knew how arrogantly the Egyptians treated them. You made a name for yourself, which remains to this day. You divided the sea before them, so that they passed through it on dry ground, but you hurled their pursuers into the depths, like a stone into mighty waters. By day you led them with a pillar of cloud, and by night with a pillar of fire to give them light on the way they were to take "You came down on Mount Sinai; you spoke to them from heaven. You gave them regulations and laws that are just and right, and decrees and commands that are good. You made known to them your holy Sabbath and gave them commands, decrees, and laws through your servant Moses. In their hunger you gave them bread from heaven and in their thirst you brought them water from the rock. You told them to go in and take possession of the land you had sworn with uplifted hand to give them "But they, our ancestors, became arrogant and stiff-necked, and they did not obey your commands. They refused to listen and failed to remember the miracles you performed among them. They became stiff-necked and in their rebellion appointed a leader in order to return to their slavery. But you are a forgiving God, gracious and compassionate, slow to anger and abounding in love. Therefore you did not desert them, even when they cast for themselves an image of a calf and said, 'This is your god, who brought you up out of Egypt,' or when they committed awful blasphemies "Because of your great compassion you did not abandon them in the wilderness. By day the pillar of cloud did not fail to guide them on their path, nor the pillar of fire by night to shine on the way they were to take. You gave your good Spirit to instruct them. You did not withhold your manna from their mouths, and you gave them water for their thirst. For forty years you sustained them in the wilderness; they lacked nothing, their clothes did not wear out nor did their feet become swollen "You gave them kingdoms and nations, allotting to them even the remotest frontiers. They took over the country of Sihon king of Heshbon and the country of Og king of Bashan. You made their children as numerous as the stars in the sky, and you brought them into the land that you told their parents to enter and possess. Their children went in and took possession of the land. You subdued before them the Canaanites, who lived in the land; you gave the Canaanites into their hands, along with their kings and the peoples of the land, to deal with them as they

pleased. They captured fortified cities and fertile land; they took possession of houses filled with all kinds of good things, wells already dug, vineyards, olive groves, and fruit trees in abundance. They ate to the full and were well-nourished; they reveled in your great goodness "But they were disobedient and rebelled against you; they turned their backs on your law. They killed your prophets, who had warned them in order to turn them back to you; they committed awful blasphemies. So you delivered them into the hands of their enemies, who oppressed them. But when they were oppressed they cried out to you. From heaven you heard them, and in your great compassion you gave them deliverers, who rescued them from the hand of their enemies "But as soon as they were at rest, they again did what was evil in your sight. Then you abandoned them to the hand of their enemies so that they ruled over them. And when they cried out to you again, you heard from heaven, and in your compassion you delivered them time after time "You warned them in order to turn them back to your law, but they became arrogant and disobeyed your commands. They sinned against your ordinances, of which you said, 'The person who obeys them will live by them.' Stubbornly they turned their backs on you, became stiff-necked and refused to listen. For many years you were patient with them. By your Spirit you warned them through your prophets. Yet they paid no attention, so you gave them into the hands of the neighboring peoples. But in your great mercy you did not put an end to them or abandon them, for you are a gracious and merciful God "Now therefore, our God, the great God, mighty and awesome, who keeps his covenant of love, do not let all this hardship seem trifling in your eyes—the hardship that has come on us, on our kings and leaders, on our priests and prophets, on our ancestors and all your people, from the days of the kings of Assyria until today. In all that has happened to us, you have remained righteous; you have acted faithfully, while we acted wickedly. Our kings, our leaders, our priests, and our ancestors did not follow your law; they did not pay attention to your commands or the statutes you warned them to keep. Even while they were in their kingdom, enjoying your great goodness to them in the spacious and fertile land you gave them, they did not serve you or turn from their evil ways "But see, we are slaves today, slaves in the land you gave our ancestors so they could eat its fruit and the other good things it produces. Because of our sins, its abundant harvest goes to the kings you have placed over us. They rule over our bodies and our cattle as they please. We are in great distress "In view of all this, we are making a binding agreement, putting it in writing, and our leaders, our Levites, and our priests are affixing their seals to it."

Chapter 10

Those who sealed it were: Nehemiah the governor, the son of Hakaliah. Zedekiah, Seraiah, Azariah, Jeremiah, Pashhur, Amariah, Malkijah, Hattush, Shebaniah, Malluch, Harim, Meremoth, Obadiah, Daniel, Ginnethon, Baruch, Meshullam, Abijah, Mijamin, Maaziah, Bilgai, and Shemaiah. These were the priests The Levites: Jeshua son of Azaniah, Binnui of the sons of Henadad, Kadmiel, and their associates: Shebaniah, Hodiah, Kelita, Pelaiah, Hanan, Mika, Rehob, Hashabiah, Zaccur, Sherebiah, Shebaniah, Hodiah, Bani, and Beninu The leaders of the people: Parosh, Pahath-Moab, Elam, Zattu, Bani, Bunni, Azgad, Bebai, Adonijah, Bigvai, Adin, Ater, Hezekiah, Azzur, Hodiah, Hashum, Bezai, Hariph, Anathoth, Nebai, Magpiash, Meshullam, Hezir, Meshezabel, Zadok, Jaddua, Pelatiah, Hanan, Anaiah, Hoshea, Hananiah, Hasshub, Hallohesh, Pilha, Shobek, Rehum, Hashabnah, Maaseiah,

Ahiah, Hanan, Anan, Malluch, Harim, and Baanah The rest of the people—priests, Levites, gatekeepers, musicians, temple servants, and all who separated themselves from the neighboring peoples for the sake of the Law of God, together with their wives and all their sons and daughters who are able to understand. All these now join their fellow Israelites the nobles, and bind themselves with a curse and an oath to follow the Law of God given through Moses the servant of God and to obey carefully all the commands, regulations, and decrees of the Lord our Lord "We promise not to give our daughters in marriage to the peoples around us or take their daughters for our sons "When the neighboring peoples bring merchandise or grain to sell on the Sabbath, we will not buy from them on the Sabbath or on any holy day. Every seventh year we will forgo working the land and will cancel all debts "We assume the responsibility for carrying out the commands to give a third of a shekel each year for the service of the house of our God: for the bread set out on the table; for the regular grain offerings and burnt offerings; for the offerings on the Sabbaths, at the New Moon feasts, and at the appointed festivals; for the holy offerings; for sin offerings to make atonement for Israel; and for all the duties of the house of our God "We—the priests, the Levites and the people—have cast lots to determine when each of our families is to bring to the house of our God at set times each year a contribution of wood to burn on the altar of the Lord our God, as it is written in the Law "We also assume responsibility for bringing to the house of the Lord each year the firstfruits of our crops and of every fruit tree "As it is also written in the Law, we will bring the firstborn of our sons and of our cattle, of our herds and of our flocks to the house of our God, to the priests ministering there "Moreover, we will bring to the storerooms of the house of our God, to the priests, the first of our ground meal, of our grain offerings, of the fruit of all our trees and of our new wine and olive oil. And we will bring a tithe of our crops to the Levites, for it is the Levites who collect the tithes in all the towns where we work. A priest descended from Aaron is to accompany the Levites when they receive the tithes, and the Levites are to bring a tenth of the tithes up to the house of our God, to the storerooms of the treasury. The people of Israel, including the Levites, are to bring their contributions of grain, new wine, and olive oil to the storerooms, where the articles for the sanctuary and for the ministering priests, the gatekeepers, and the musicians are also kept "We will not neglect the house of our God."

CHAPTER 11

1. The leaders of the people settled in Jerusalem, while the remaining people cast lots to determine that one in ten would live in Jerusalem, the holy city, and the other nine-tenths would settle in the surrounding cities. 2. The people expressed their gratitude to those who willingly chose to dwell in Jerusalem. 3. The chief officials who resided in Jerusalem included the priests, Levites, Nethinim, and the descendants of Solomon's servants, while in the cities of Judah, each group lived in their respective cities throughout Israel. 4. In Jerusalem, some of the descendants of Judah and Benjamin lived. Among the descendants of Judah were Athaiah, the son of Vziiah, the son of Zechariah, the son of Amariah, the son of Shephatiah, the son of Mahaleel, from the family of Perez, 5. and Maaseiah, the son of Baruch, the son of Col Hozeh, the son of Hazaiah, the son of Adaiah, the son of Ioiarib, the son of Zechariah, the son of Shiloni. 6. All the descendants of Perez who lived in Jerusalem numbered four hundred and thirty-eight valiant men. 7. Among the descendants of Benjamin were Sallu, the son of Meshullam, the son of Ioed, the son of Pedaiah, the son of Koliah, the son of Maaseiah, the son of Ithiel, the son of Ieshaiah. 8. Following him were Gabai and Sallai, numbering nine hundred and twenty-eight. 9. Joel, the son of Zichri, was the chief priest, and Judah, the son of Senuah, was second in the city. 10. Among the priests were Iedaiah, the son of Ioiarib, and Iachin. 11. Seraiah, the son of Hilkiah, the son of Meshullam, the son of Zadok, the son of Meraioth, the son of Ahitub, was the head of the house of God. 12. His brothers who worked in the Temple numbered eight hundred and twenty-two: Adaiah, the son of Jeroham, the son of Pelaliah, the son of Amzi, the son of Zechariah, the son of Pashur, the son of Malchiah. 13. His brethren, the chief fathers, numbered two hundred and four. Amashsai, the son of Azareel, the son of Ahazai, the son of Meshilemoth, the son of Immer, 14. and his brethren, valiant men, numbered one hundred and twenty-eight, with Zabdiel, the son of Hagedolim, as their leader. 15. Among the Levites were Semaiah, the son of Hashub, the son of Azrikam, the son of Hashabiah, the son of Bunni. 16. Shabbethai and Iozabad, leaders of the Levites, were in charge of the work of the house of God. 17. Mattaniah, the son of Micha, the son of Zabdi, the son of Asaph, led the thanksgiving and prayer; Bakbukiah, his second, and Abda, the son of Shammua, the son of Galal, the son of Ieduthun. 18. All the Levites of the holy city numbered two hundred and forty-four. 19. The porters Akkub, Talmon, and their brothers who guarded the gates numbered one hundred and two. 20. The rest of Israel, including the priests and Levites, lived in the cities of Judah, each in their own property. 21. The Nethinim settled in the fortresses; Ziha and Gispa were among them. 22. The leader of the Levites in Jerusalem was Uzi, the son of Bani, the son of Ashabiah, the son of Mattaniah, the son of Micha; the singers, the sons of Asaph, were in charge of the work of the house of God. 23. The king had commanded that the singers have a faithful watch every day. 24. Pethahiah, the son of Meshezabeel, of the sons of Zerah, the son of Judah, was at the king's disposal for all matters concerning the people. 25. In the villages of their territories, some of the descendants of Judah lived in Kiriath-arba and its villages, in Dibon and its villages, in Iekabzeel and its villages, 26. in Ieshua, in Moladah, and in Beth Palet, 27. in Hazer-Shual, in Beer-Sheba and its villages, 28. in Ziklag, in Mechona and its villages, 29. in En-Rimmon, Zarea, and Iarmuth, 30. in Zanoah, Adullam and their villages, Lachish and its fields, Azekah and its villages; they settled from Beer-Sheba to the valley of Hinnom. 31. The descendants of Benjamin, from Geba, to Michmash, to Aiiah, to Beth-El and their villages, 32. Anathoth, Nob, Ananias, 33. Hazor, Ramah, Gittaim, 34. Hadid, Zeboim, Nebalat, 35. Lod and Ono, in the valley of the carpenters. 36. Among the Levites there were divisions in Judah and Benjamin

CHAPTER 12

1. These were the priests and Levites who went with Zerubbabel, the son of Shealtiel, and Jeshua: Seraiah, Jeremiah, Ezra, 2. Amariah, Malluch, Hattush, 3. Shecaniah, Rehum, Merimoth, 4. Iddo, Ginnetho, Abiiah, 5. Miamin, Maadia, Bilgah, 6. Shemaiah, Ioiarib, Iedaiah, 7. Sallu, Amok, Hilkiah, Iedaiah; these were the chief priests and their brethren during the days of Jeshua. 8. The Levites, Jeshua, Binnui, Kadmiel, Sherebiah, Judah, and Mattaniah were in charge of the thanksgiving, along with their brothers. 9. Bakbukiah, Unni, and their brothers were around them during the vigils. 10. Jeshua begot Jehoiakim; Jehoiakim begot Eliashib, and Eliashib begot Jehoiada. 11. Jehoiada begot Jonathan, and Jonathan begot Jaddua. 12. During the days of Jehoiakim, these were the chief fathers of the priests: under Seraiah was Meraiah, under Jeremiah was Hananiah, 13. under Ezra was Meshullam; under Amariah was Jehohanan, 14. after Melicu, Jonathan; after Shebaniah, Joseph, 15. from Harim, Adna; from Meraioth, Helkai, 16. from Iddo, Zechariah, Ginnithon, Meshullam, 17. from Abiiah, Zichri, Miniamin, Maadia, Piltai, 18. from Bilgah, Shammua; from Shemaiah, Jehonathan, 19. from Ioiarib, Mattenai; from Iedaiah, Uzi, 20. under Sallai, Kallai; under Amok, Eber, 21.

from Hilkiah, Hashabiah; from Iedaiah, Nethaneel. 22. In the days of Eliashib, Joiada, Johanan, and Jaddua, the principal fathers of the Levites and priests were recorded during the reign of Darius the Persian. 23. The sons of Levi, the chief fathers, were recorded in the book of Chronicles until the days of Johanan, the son of Eliashib. 24. The leaders of the Levites were Hashabiah, Sherebiah, and Jeshua, the son of Kadmiel, with their brethren around them to give prayers and thanksgiving, according to the order of David, the man of God, to protect themselves from war. 25. Mattaniah, Bakbukiah, Obadiah, Meshullam, Talmon, and Akkub were gatekeepers who guarded the threshold of the gates. 26. These were in the days of Jehoiakim, the son of Jeshua, the son of Jozadak, during the leadership of Nehemiah and Ezra, the priest and scribe. 27. At the dedication of the walls of Jerusalem, they sought out the Levites from all their places to bring them to Jerusalem to celebrate the dedication with rejoicing, thanksgiving, singing, cymbals, viols, and harps. 28. The singers gathered from the plain around Jerusalem and from the villages of Netophathi, 29. from the house of Gilgal, from the villages of Geba and Azmaveth, as the singers had built villages around Jerusalem. 30. The priests and Levites were cleansed, and they cleansed the people, the gates, and the walls. 31. I led the princes of Judah to the walls and formed two great companies to give thanks; one went to the right of the wall, toward the Dung Gate. 32. After them went Hoshaiah and half of the princes of Judah, 33. Azariah, Ezra, Meshullam, 34. Judah, Benjamin, Shemaiah, and Jeremiah. 35. Some of the priests' sons with trumpets were Zechariah, the son of Jonathan, the son of Shemaiah, the son of Mattaniah, the son of Micaiah, the son of Zaccur, the son of Asaph. 36. His brethren were Shemaiah and Azarel, Milalai, Gilalai, Maai, Nethanel, Judah, and Hanani, with the musical instruments of David, the man of God. Ezra the scribe went before them. 37. At the Fountain Gate, they went straight ahead on the ascent of the city of David, by the stairs that go down from the city of David. 38. The other company of those who gave thanks went to the left; I followed them with half of the people on the wall, from the Tower of the Furnaces to the Broad Wall, 39. and above the Gate of Ephraim, above the Old Gate, above the Fish Gate, and the Tower of Hananel, and the Tower of the Hundred, as far as the Sheep Gate; they stood in the Gate of the Guard. 40. So both companies of those who gave thanks stood in the house of God, and I, with half of the rulers with me. 41. The priests, Eliakim, Maaseiah, Minjamin, Michaiah, Elioenai, Zechariah, and Hananiah with trumpets, 42. and Maaseiah, Shemaiah, Eleazar, Uzzi, Jehohanan, Melchijah, Elam, and Ezer, and the singers, with Jezrahiah as their leader, 43. offered great sacrifices that day and rejoiced, for God had made them rejoice with great joy; the women and children also rejoiced, so that the joy of Jerusalem was heard far away. 44. On that day men were appointed over the storerooms for the offerings, the firstfruits, and the tithes, to gather into them from the fields of the cities the portions required by the Law for the priests and Levites, for Judah rejoiced for the priests and Levites who ministered. 45. They performed the service of their God and the service of the purification, with the singers and gatekeepers, according to the commandment of David and Solomon his son. 46. For in the days of David and Asaph of old there were chiefs of the singers and songs of praise and thanksgiving to God. 47. In the days of Zerubbabel and Nehemiah, all Israel gave the portions for the singers and gatekeepers, every day his portion, and they consecrated holy things for the Levites, and the Levites consecrated them for the children of Aaron

CHAPTER 13

1. On that day, they read from the Book of Moses in the hearing of the people, and in it was found written that no Ammonite or Moabite should ever enter the assembly of God, 2. because they had not met the Israelites with bread and water, but had hired Balaam against them to curse them—yet our God turned the curse into a blessing. 3. As soon as the people heard the law, they separated from Israel all those of mixed descent. 4. Now before this, Eliashib the priest, who was appointed over the chambers of the house of our God, being related to Tobiah, 5. had prepared for Tobiah a large chamber where formerly they had put the grain offerings, the incense, and the vessels, and the tithes of grain, new wine, and oil, which were commanded to be given to the Levites, singers, and gatekeepers, and the contributions for the priests. 6. But during all this time I was not in Jerusalem; for in the thirty-second year of Artaxerxes king of Babylon I had gone to the king, and after some time I asked leave of the king. 7. And I came to Jerusalem and discovered the evil that Eliashib had done for Tobiah, preparing a chamber for him in the courts of the house of God. 8. And it grieved me bitterly; therefore I threw all the household goods of Tobiah out of the chamber. 9. Then I commanded them to cleanse the chambers, and I brought back into them the vessels of the house of God, with the grain offerings and the frankincense. 10. I also discovered that the portions for the Levites had not been given them; for the Levites and the singers, who did the work, had fled, each to his own field. 11. So I contended with the rulers and said, "Why is the house of God forsaken?" And I gathered them together and set them in their place. 12. Then all Judah brought the tithe of the grain, the new wine, and the oil to the storerooms. 13. And I appointed as treasurers over the storerooms Shelomith the priest, and Zadok the scribe, and of the Levites, Pedaiah; and next to them was Hanan the son of Zaccur, the son of Mattaniah; for they were considered faithful, and their task was to distribute to their brethren. 14. Remember me, O my God, concerning this, and do not wipe out my good deeds that I have done for the house of my God, and for its services. 15. In those days I saw people in Judah treading winepresses on the Sabbath, and bringing in sheaves and loading donkeys with wine, grapes, figs, and all kinds of burdens, which they brought into Jerusalem on the Sabbath day. And I warned them about the day on which they were selling provisions. 16. Men of Tyre dwelt there also, who brought in fish and all kinds of goods, and sold them on the Sabbath to the children of Judah, and in Jerusalem. 17. Then I contended with the nobles of Judah and said to them, "What evil thing is this that you do, by which you profane the Sabbath day? 18. Did not your fathers do thus, and did not our God bring all this disaster on us and on this city? Yet you bring added wrath on Israel by profaning the Sabbath." 19. So it was, at the gates of Jerusalem, as it began to be dark before the Sabbath, that I commanded the gates to be shut and charged that they must not be opened till after the Sabbath. Then I posted some of my servants at the gates, so that no burdens would be brought in on the Sabbath day. 20. Now the merchants and sellers of all kinds of wares lodged outside Jerusalem once or twice. 21. Then I warned them and said to them, "Why do you spend the night around the wall? If you do so again, I will lay hands on you!" From that time on they came no more on the Sabbath. 22. And I commanded the Levites that they should cleanse themselves and that they should go and guard the gates, to sanctify the Sabbath day. Remember me, O my God, concerning this also, and spare me according to the greatness of Your mercy! 23. In those days I also saw Jews who had married women of Ashdod, Ammon, and Moab. 24. And half of their children spoke the language of Ashdod and could not speak the language of Judah, but spoke according to the language of one or the other people. 25. So I contended with them and cursed them, struck some of them, and pulled out their hair, and made them swear by God, saying, "You shall not give your daughters as wives to their sons, nor take their daughters for your sons or yourselves. 26. Did not Solomon king of Israel sin by these things? Yet among many nations there was no king like him, who was beloved of his God; and God made him king over all Israel. Nevertheless, pagan women caused even him to sin. 27. Should we then hear of your doing all this great evil, transgressing against our God by marrying pagan women?" 28. And one of the sons of

Joiada, the son of Eliashib the high priest, was a son-in-law of Sanballat the Horonite; therefore I drove him from me. 29. Remember them, O my God, because they have defiled the priesthood and the covenant of the priesthood and the Levites. 30. Thus I cleansed them of everything pagan. I also assigned duties to the priests and the Levites, each to his service, 31. and to bringing the wood offering and the firstfruits at appointed times. Remember me, O my God, for good!

17. Esther

Chapter 1

During the days of Ahashuerosh (this is Ahashuerosh who reigned from India to Ethiopia for a hundred and twenty years), when he sat on his throne in the palace of Shushan, he held a grand banquet in the third year of his reign. He invited all his princes and servants, the powerful figures of Persia and Media, the captains, and the chiefs of the provinces who were before him. This celebration was to showcase the riches and glory of his kingdom and the honor of his great majesty for many days, lasting one hundred and forty days When these days ended, the king hosted another banquet for all the people in the palace of Shushan, both great and small, for seven days in the courtyard of the king's palace garden. The decor included white, green, and blue draperies, fastened with cords of fine linen and purple, hanging on rings of silk and marble pillars. The beds were of gold and silk, placed on a floor of porphyry, marble, alabaster, and blue stone. The guests drank from golden vessels, each different from the other, with an abundance of royal wine, according to the king's generosity. Drinking was not mandatory, as the king had ordered all the officers of his household to serve according to each person's pleasure Queen Vashti also held a banquet for the women in the royal house of King Ahashuerosh. On the seventh day, when the king was merry with wine, he commanded Mehuman, Biztha, Harbona, Bigtha, Abagtha, Zethar, and Carcas, the seven eunuchs who served him, to bring Queen Vashti before him with the royal crown to show her beauty to the people and the princes, for she was fair to behold. But Queen Vashti refused to come at the king's command delivered by the eunuchs, which made the king very angry The king consulted the wise men who understood the times, for this was his practice towards all who knew law and judgment. Among them were Carshena, Shethar, Admatha, Tarshish, Meres, Marsena, and Memucan, the seven princes of Persia and Media who saw the king's face and held the highest ranks in the kingdom. The king asked them, "What should be done to Queen Vashti according to the law because she has not obeyed the command of King Ahashuerosh delivered by the eunuchs?" Memucan responded before the king and the princes, "Queen Vashti has wronged not only the king but also all the princes and all the people in the provinces of King Ahashuerosh. Her actions will become known to all women, causing them to look with contempt on their husbands, saying, 'King Ahashuerosh commanded Queen Vashti to be brought before him, but she did not come.' This will cause much scorn and wrath. If it pleases the king, let him issue a royal decree recorded in the laws of Persia and Media, so it cannot be repealed, that Vashti is never again to appear before King Ahashuerosh. Let the king give her royal position to someone better than she. When this decree is proclaimed throughout the king's vast kingdom, all women will respect their husbands, from the greatest to the least." This advice pleased the king and the princes, and the king did as Memucan proposed. He sent letters to all the king's provinces, to each province in its own script and to each people in their own language, proclaiming that every man should rule in his own household

Chapter 2

After these events, when the wrath of King Ahashuerosh had subsided, he remembered Vashti and what she had done and what had been decreed against her. The king's attendants proposed, "Let beautiful young virgins be sought for the king. Let the king appoint commissioners in every province of his realm to bring all these beautiful young women into the harem at the citadel of Susa. Let them be placed under the care of Hegai, the king's eunuch, who is in charge of the women, and let beauty treatments be given to them. Then let the young woman who pleases the king be queen instead of Vashti." This advice appealed to the king, and he followed it In the citadel of Susa, there was a Jew named Mordecai, son of Jair, son of Shimei, son of Kish, a Benjaminite, who had been carried into exile from Jerusalem by Nebuchadnezzar, king of Babylon, among those taken captive with Jeconiah, king of Judah. Mordecai had a cousin named Hadassah, whom he had brought up because she had neither father nor mother. This young woman, also known as Esther, had a lovely figure and was beautiful. Mordecai had taken her as his own daughter when her father and mother died When the king's order and edict had been proclaimed, many young women were brought to the citadel of Susa and put under the care of Hegai. Esther also was taken to the king's palace and entrusted to Hegai, who had charge of the harem. She pleased him and won his favor. Immediately he provided her with beauty treatments and special food. He assigned to her seven female attendants selected from the king's palace and moved her and her attendants into the best place in the harem. Esther had not revealed her nationality and family background because Mordecai had forbidden her to do so. Every day he walked back and forth near the courtyard of the harem to find out how Esther was and what was happening to her Before a young woman's turn came to go in to King Ahashuerosh, she had to complete twelve months of beauty treatments prescribed for the women, six months with oil of myrrh and six with perfumes and cosmetics. When the turn came for Esther to go to the king, she asked for nothing other than what Hegai, the king's eunuch who was in charge of the harem, suggested. And Esther won the favor of everyone who saw her. She was taken to King Ahashuerosh in the royal residence in the tenth month, the month of Tebeth, in the seventh year of his reign. The king was attracted to Esther more than to any of the other women, and she won his favor and approval more than any of the other virgins. So he set a royal crown on her head and made her queen instead of Vashti. The king gave a great banquet, Esther's banquet, for all his nobles and officials. He proclaimed a holiday throughout the provinces and distributed gifts with royal liberality When the virgins were assembled a second time, Mordecai was sitting at the king's gate. But Esther had kept secret her family background and nationality just as Mordecai had told her to do, for she continued to follow Mordecai's instructions as she had done when he was bringing her up During the time Mordecai was sitting at the king's gate, Bigthana and Teresh, two of the king's officers who guarded the doorway, became angry and conspired to assassinate King Ahashuerosh. But Mordecai found out about the plot and told Queen Esther, who in turn reported it to the king, giving credit to Mordecai. When the report was investigated and found to be true, the two officials were impaled on poles. All this was recorded in the book of the annals in the presence of the king

Chapter 3

After these events, King Ahashuerosh honored Haman son of Hammedatha, the Agagite, elevating him and giving him a seat of honor higher than that of all the other nobles. All the royal officials at the king's gate knelt down and paid honor to Haman, for the king had commanded this concerning him. But Mordecai would not kneel down or pay him honor Then the royal officials at the king's gate asked Mordecai, "Why do you disobey the king's command?" Day after day they spoke to him, but he refused to comply. Therefore, they told Haman about it to see whether Mordecai's behavior would be tolerated, for he had told them he was a Jew. When Haman saw that Mordecai would not kneel down or pay him honor, he was enraged. Yet having learned who Mordecai's people were, he scorned the idea of killing only Mordecai. Instead, Haman looked for a way to destroy all Mordecai's people, the Jews, throughout the whole kingdom of Ahashuerosh In the twelfth year of King Ahashuerosh, in the first month, the month of Nisan, they cast the pur (that is, the lot) in the presence of Haman to select a day and month. And the lot fell on the twelfth month, the month of Adar. Then Haman said to King Ahashuerosh, "There is a certain people dispersed among the peoples in all the provinces of your kingdom who keep themselves separate. Their customs are different from those of all other people, and they do not obey the king's laws; it is not in the king's best interest to tolerate them. If it pleases the king, let a decree be issued to destroy them, and I will give ten thousand talents of silver to the king's administrators for the royal treasury." So the king took his signet ring from his finger and gave it to Haman son of Hammedatha, the Agagite, the enemy of the Jews. "Keep the money," the king said to Haman, "and do with the people as you please." Then on the thirteenth day of the first month, the royal secretaries were summoned. They wrote out in the script of each province and in the language of each people all Haman's orders to the king's satraps, the governors of the various provinces, and the nobles of the various peoples. These were written in the name of King Ahashuerosh himself and sealed with his own ring. Dispatches were sent by couriers to all the king's provinces with the order to destroy, kill, and annihilate all the Jews—young and old, women and children—on a single day, the thirteenth day of the twelfth month, the month of Adar, and to plunder their goods A copy of the text of the edict was to be issued as law in every province and made known to the people of every nationality so they would be ready for that day. The couriers went out, spurred on by the king's command, and the edict was issued in the citadel of Susa. The king and Haman sat down to drink, but the city of Susa was bewildered

Chapter 4

When Mordecai learned of all that had been done, he tore his clothes, put on sackcloth and ashes, and went out into the city, wailing loudly and bitterly. But he went only as far as the king's gate, because no one clothed in sackcloth was allowed to enter it. In every province to which the edict and order of the king came, there was great mourning among the Jews, with fasting, weeping, and wailing. Many lay in sackcloth and ashes When Esther's eunuchs and female attendants came and told her about Mordecai, she was in great distress. She sent clothes for him to put on instead of his sackcloth, but he would not accept them. Then Esther summoned Hathak, one of the king's eunuchs assigned to attend her, and ordered him to find out what was troubling Mordecai and why So Hathak went out to Mordecai in the open square of the city in front of the king's gate. Mordecai told him everything that had happened to him, including the exact amount of money Haman had promised to pay into the royal treasury for the destruction of the Jews. He also gave him a copy of the text of the edict for their annihilation, which had been published in Susa, to show to Esther and explain it to her, and he told him to instruct her to go into the king's presence to beg for mercy and plead with him for her people Hathak went back and reported to Esther what Mordecai had said. Then she instructed him to say to Mordecai, "All the king's officials and the people of the royal provinces know that for any man or woman who approaches the king in the inner court without being summoned, the king has but one law: that they be put to death unless the king extends the gold scepter to them and spares their lives. But thirty days have passed since I was called to go to the king." When Esther's words were reported to Mordecai, he sent back this answer: "Do not think that because you are in the king's house you alone of all the Jews will escape. For if you remain silent at this time, relief and deliverance for the Jews will arise from another place, but you and your father's family will perish. And who knows but that you have come to your royal position for such a time as this?" Then Esther sent this reply to Mordecai: "Go, gather together all the Jews who are in Susa, and fast for me. Do not eat or drink for three days, night or day. I and my attendants will fast as you do. When this is done, I will go to the king, even though it is against the law. And if I perish, I perish." So Mordecai went away and carried out all of Esther's instructions

Chapter 5

On the third day, Esther put on her royal robes and stood in the inner court of the palace, in front of the king's hall. The king was sitting on his royal throne in the hall, facing the entrance. When he saw Queen Esther standing in the court, he was pleased with her and held out to her the gold scepter that was in his hand. So Esther approached and touched the tip of the scepter Then the king asked, "What is it, Queen Esther? What is your request? Even up to half the kingdom, it will be given you." "If it pleases the king," replied Esther, "let the king, together with Haman, come today to a banquet I have prepared for him." "Bring Haman at once," the king said, "so that we may do what Esther asks." So the king and Haman went to the banquet Esther had prepared. As they were drinking wine, the king again asked Esther, "Now what is your petition? It will be given you. And what is your request? Even up to half the kingdom, it will be granted." Esther replied, "My petition and my request is this: If the king regards me with favor and if it pleases the king to grant my petition and fulfill my request, let the king and Haman come tomorrow to the banquet I will prepare for them. Then I will answer the king's question." Haman went out that day happy and in high spirits. But when he saw Mordecai at the king's gate and observed that he neither rose nor showed fear in his presence, he was filled with rage against Mordecai. Nevertheless, Haman restrained himself and went home. Calling together his friends and Zeresh, his wife, Haman boasted to them about his vast wealth, his many sons, and all the ways the king had honored him and how he had elevated him above the other nobles and officials "And that's not all," Haman added. "I'm the only person Queen Esther invited to accompany the king to the banquet she gave. And she has invited me along with the king tomorrow. But all this gives me no satisfaction as long as I see that Jew Mordecai sitting at the king's gate." His wife Zeresh and all his friends said to him, "Have a pole set up, reaching to a height of fifty cubits, and ask the king in the morning to have

Mordecai impaled on it. Then go with the king to the banquet and enjoy yourself." This suggestion delighted Haman, and he had the pole set up

Chapter 6

That night, the king could not sleep. He ordered the book of records and chronicles to be brought in and read before him. It was found written that Mordecai had reported Bigtanah and Teresh, two of the king's eunuchs, who had guarded the door and conspired to assassinate King Ahashuerosh. The king asked, "What honor and recognition has been given to Mordecai for this?" The king's attendants replied, "Nothing has been done for him." The king asked, "Who is in the court?" At that moment, Haman had entered the outer court of the king's palace to speak to the king about hanging Mordecai on the gallows he had prepared for him. The king's servants replied, "Haman is standing in the court." The king said, "Bring him in." When Haman entered, the king asked, "What should be done for the man whom the king delights to honor?" Haman thought to himself, "Whom would the king delight to honor more than me?" So Haman answered the king, "For the man the king delights to honor, let a royal robe the king has worn and a horse the king has ridden, one with a royal crest placed on its head, be brought. Then let the robe and horse be entrusted to one of the king's most noble princes. Let them robe the man the king delights to honor and lead him on the horse through the city streets, proclaiming before him, 'This is what is done for the man the king delights to honor!'" The king said to Haman, "Go at once, get the robe and the horse and do just as you have suggested for Mordecai the Jew, who sits at the king's gate. Do not neglect anything you have recommended." So Haman got the robe and the horse. He robed Mordecai and led him on horseback through the city streets, proclaiming before him, "This is what is done for the man the king delights to honor!" Afterward, Mordecai returned to the king's gate, but Haman rushed home with his head covered in grief. Haman recounted to Zeresh, his wife, and all his friends everything that had happened to him. His advisors and his wife Zeresh said to him, "Since Mordecai, before whom your downfall has started, is of Jewish origin, you cannot stand against him—you will surely come to ruin!" While they were still talking with him, the king's eunuchs arrived and hurried Haman away to the banquet Esther had prepared

Chapter 7

So the king and Haman went to dine with Queen Esther. As they were drinking wine on the second day, the king again asked, "Queen Esther, what is your petition? It will be given you. What is your request? Even up to half the kingdom, it will be granted." Then Queen Esther answered, "If I have found favor with you, Your Majesty, and if it pleases you, grant me my life—this is my petition. And spare my people—this is my request. For I and my people have been sold to be destroyed, killed, and annihilated. If we had merely been sold as male and female slaves, I would have kept quiet, because no such distress would justify disturbing the king." King Ahashuerosh asked Queen Esther, "Who is he? Where is he—the man who has dared to do such a thing?" Esther said, "An adversary and enemy! This vile Haman!" Then Haman was terrified before the king and queen. The king got up in a rage, left his wine, and went out into the palace garden. But Haman, realizing that the king had already decided his fate, stayed behind to beg Queen Esther for his life. Just as the king returned from the palace garden to the banquet hall, Haman was falling on the couch where Esther was reclining. The king exclaimed, "Will he even molest the queen while she is with me in the house?" As soon as the word left the king's mouth, they covered Haman's face Then Harbona, one of the eunuchs attending the king, said, "A gallows seventy-five feet high stands by Haman's house. He had it made for Mordecai, who spoke up to help the king." The king said, "Hang him on it!" So they hanged Haman on the gallows he had prepared for Mordecai. Then the king's fury subsided

Chapter 8

That same day King Ahashuerosh gave Queen Esther the estate of Haman, the enemy of the Jews. And Mordecai came into the presence of the king, for Esther had told how he was related to her. The king took off his signet ring, which he had reclaimed from Haman, and presented it to Mordecai. And Esther appointed him over Haman's estate Esther again pleaded with the king, falling at his feet and weeping. She begged him to put an end to the evil plan of Haman the Agagite, which he had devised against the Jews. The king extended the gold scepter to Esther, and she arose and stood before him "If it pleases the king," she said, "and if he regards me with favor and thinks it the right thing to do, and if he is pleased with me, let an order be written overruling the dispatches that Haman son of Hammedatha, the Agagite, devised and wrote to destroy the Jews in all the king's provinces. For how can I bear to see disaster fall on my people? How can I bear to see the destruction of my family?" King Ahashuerosh replied to Queen Esther and to Mordecai the Jew, "Because Haman attacked the Jews, I have given his estate to Esther, and they have hanged him on the gallows. Now write another decree in the king's name on behalf of the Jews as seems best to you, and seal it with the king's signet ring—for no document written in the king's name and sealed with his ring can be revoked." At once the royal secretaries were summoned—on the twenty-third day of the third month, the month of Sivan. They wrote out all Mordecai's orders to the Jews, and to the satraps, governors, and nobles of the 127 provinces stretching from India to Cush. These orders were written in the script of each province and the language of each people and also to the Jews in their own script and language. Mordecai wrote in the name of King Ahashuerosh, sealed the dispatches with the king's signet ring, and sent them by mounted couriers, who rode fast horses especially bred for the king The king's edict granted the Jews in every city the right to assemble and protect themselves; to destroy, kill, and annihilate the armed men of any nationality or province who might attack them and their women and children, and to plunder the property of their enemies. The day appointed for the Jews to do this in all the provinces of King Ahashuerosh was the thirteenth day of the twelfth month, the month of Adar. A copy of the text of the edict was to be issued as law in every province and made known to the people of every nationality so the Jews would be ready on that day to avenge themselves on their enemies. The couriers, riding the royal horses, raced out, spurred on by the king's command. And the edict was also issued in the citadel of Susa Mordecai left the king's presence wearing royal garments of blue and white, a large crown of gold, and a purple robe of fine linen. And the city of Susa held a joyous celebration. For the Jews it was a time of happiness and joy, gladness and honor. In every province and in every city to which the edict of the king came, there was joy and gladness among the Jews, with feasting and celebrating. And many people of other nationalities became Jews because fear of the Jews had seized them

Chapter 9

On the thirteenth day of the twelfth month, the

month of Adar, the edict commanded by the king was to be carried out. On this day, the enemies of the Jews had hoped to overpower them, but now the tables were turned, and the Jews got the upper hand over those who hated them. The Jews assembled in their cities in all the provinces of King Ahashuerosh to attack those determined to destroy them. No one could stand against them, because the people of all the other nationalities were afraid of them. And all the nobles of the provinces, the satraps, the governors, and the king's administrators helped the Jews because fear of Mordecai had seized them. Mordecai was prominent in the palace; his reputation spread throughout the provinces, and he became more and more powerful The Jews struck down all their enemies with the sword, killing and destroying them, and they did what they pleased to those who hated them. In the citadel of Susa, the Jews killed and destroyed five hundred men. They also killed Parshandatha, Dalphon, Aspatha, Poratha, Adalia, Aridatha, Parmashta, Arisai, Aridai, and Vaizatha, the ten sons of Haman son of Hammedatha, the enemy of the Jews. But they did not lay their hands on the plunder The number of those killed in the citadel of Susa was reported to the king that same day. The king said to Queen Esther, "The Jews have killed and destroyed five hundred men and the ten sons of Haman in the citadel of Susa. What have they done in the rest of the king's provinces? Now what is your petition? It will be given you. What is your request? It will also be granted." "If it pleases the king," Esther answered, "give the Jews in Susa permission to carry out this day's edict tomorrow also, and let Haman's ten sons be impaled on poles." So the king commanded that this be done. An edict was issued in Susa, and they impaled the ten sons of Haman The Jews in Susa came together on the fourteenth day of the month of Adar, and they put to death in Susa three hundred men, but they did not lay their hands on the plunder. Meanwhile, the remainder of the Jews who were in the king's provinces also assembled to protect themselves and get relief from their enemies. They killed seventy-five thousand of them but did not lay their hands on the plunder. This happened on the thirteenth day of the month of Adar, and on the fourteenth they rested and made it a day of feasting and joy The Jews in Susa, however, had assembled on the thirteenth and fourteenth, and then on the fifteenth they rested and made it a day of feasting and joy. That is why rural Jews—those living in villages—observe the fourteenth of the month of Adar as a day of joy and feasting, a day for giving presents to each other Mordecai recorded these events, and he sent letters to all the Jews throughout the provinces of King Ahashuerosh, near and far, to have them celebrate annually the fourteenth and fifteenth days of the month of Adar as the time when the Jews got relief from their enemies, and as the month when their sorrow was turned into joy and their mourning into a day of celebration. He wrote them to observe the days as days of feasting and joy and giving presents of food to one another and gifts to the poor So the Jews agreed to continue the celebration they had begun, doing what Mordecai had written to them. For Haman son of Hammedatha, the Agagite, the enemy of all the Jews, had plotted against the Jews to destroy them and had cast the pur (that is, the lot) for their ruin and destruction. But when the plot came to the king's attention, he issued written orders that the evil scheme Haman had devised against the Jews should come back onto his own head, and that he and his sons should be impaled on poles. (Therefore these days were called Purim, from the word pur.) Because of everything written in this letter and because of what they had seen and what had happened to them, the Jews took it upon themselves to establish the custom that they and their descendants and all who join them should without fail observe these two days every year, in the way prescribed and at the time appointed. These days should be remembered and observed in every generation by every family, and in every province and in every city. And these days of Purim should never fail to be celebrated by the Jews—nor should the memory of these days die out among their descendants So Queen Esther, daughter of Abihail, along with Mordecai the Jew, wrote with full authority to confirm this second letter concerning Purim. And Mordecai sent letters to all the Jews in the 127 provinces of King Ahashuerosh's kingdom—words of goodwill and assurance—to establish these days of Purim at their designated times, as Mordecai the Jew and Queen Esther had decreed for them, and as they had established for themselves and their descendants in regard to their times of fasting and lamentation. Esther's decree confirmed these regulations about Purim, and it was written down in the records

Chapter 10

King Ahashuerosh imposed tribute throughout the empire, to its distant shores. And all his acts of power and might, together with a full account of the greatness of Mordecai, whom the king had promoted, are they not written in the book of the annals of the kings of Media and Persia? Mordecai the Jew was second in rank to King Ahashuerosh, preeminent among the Jews, and held in high esteem by his many fellow Jews, because he worked for the good of his people and spoke up for the welfare of all the Jews

3. POETIC AND WISDOM BOOKS

18. Job

Chapter 1

In the land of Uz, there was a man named Job. He was a righteous and upright man who feared God and shunned evil. Job had seven sons and three daughters. His estate included seven thousand sheep, three thousand camels, five hundred yoke of oxen, and five hundred donkeys, along with a large number of servants. He was the greatest man among all the people of the East Job's sons would take turns holding feasts in their homes, and they would invite their three sisters to eat and drink with them. When the days of feasting were over, Job would send for his children to purify them. Early in the morning, he would offer a burnt offering for each of them, thinking, "Perhaps my children have sinned and cursed God in their hearts." This was Job's regular practice One day, the angels came to present themselves before the Lord, and Satan also came with them. The Lord said to Satan, "Where have you come from?" Satan answered the Lord, "From roaming throughout the earth, going back and forth on it." The Lord said to Satan, "Have you considered my servant Job? There is no one on earth like him; he is blameless and upright, a man who fears God and shuns evil." Satan replied, "Does Job fear God for nothing? Have you not put a hedge around him and his household and everything he has? You have blessed the work of his hands, so that his flocks and herds are spread throughout the land. But now stretch out your hand and strike everything he has, and he will surely curse you to your face." The Lord said to Satan, "Very well, then, everything he has is in your power, but on the man himself, do not lay a finger." Then Satan went out from the presence of the Lord One day, while Job's sons and daughters were feasting and drinking wine at the oldest brother's house, a messenger came to Job and said, "The oxen were plowing, and the donkeys were grazing nearby, and the Sabeans attacked and made off with them. They put the servants to the sword, and I am the only one who has escaped to tell you!" While he was still speaking, another messenger came and said, "The fire of God fell from the heavens and burned up the sheep and the servants, and I am the only one who has escaped to tell you!" While he was still speaking, another messenger came and said, "The Chaldeans formed three raiding parties and swept down on your camels and made off with them. They put the servants to the sword, and I am the only one who has escaped to tell you!" While he was still speaking, yet another messenger came and said, "Your sons and daughters were feasting and drinking wine at the oldest brother's house when suddenly a mighty wind swept in from the desert and struck the four corners of the house. It collapsed on them, and they are dead, and I am the only one who has escaped to tell you!" At this, Job got up, tore his robe, and shaved his head. Then he fell to the ground in worship and said, "Naked I came from my mother's womb, and naked I will depart. The Lord gave, and the Lord has taken away; may the name of the Lord be praised." In all this, Job did not sin by charging God with wrongdoing

Chapter 2

On another day, the angels came to present themselves before the Lord, and Satan also came with them to present himself before him. The Lord said to Satan, "Where have you come from?" Satan answered the Lord, "From roaming throughout the earth, going back and forth on it." The Lord said to Satan, "Have you considered my servant Job? There is no one on earth like him; he is blameless and upright, a man who fears God and shuns evil. And he still maintains his integrity, though you incited me against him to ruin him without any reason." "Skin for skin!" Satan replied. "A man will give all he has for his own life. But now stretch out your hand and strike his flesh and bones, and he will surely curse you to your face." The Lord said to Satan, "Very well, then, he is in your hands; but you must spare his life." So Satan went out from the presence of the Lord and afflicted Job with painful sores from the soles of his feet to the crown of his head. Job took a piece of broken pottery and scraped himself with it as he sat among the ashes His wife said to him, "Are you still maintaining your integrity? Curse God and die!" He replied, "You are talking like a foolish woman. Shall we accept good from God, and not trouble?" In all this, Job did not sin in what he said When Job's three friends, Eliphaz the Temanite, Bildad the Shuhite, and Zophar the Naamathite, heard about all the troubles that had come upon him, they set out from their homes and met together by agreement to go and sympathize with him and comfort him. When they saw him from a distance, they could hardly recognize him; they began to weep aloud, and they tore their robes and sprinkled dust on their heads. Then they sat on the ground with him for seven days and seven nights. No one said a word to him, because they saw how great his suffering was

Chapter 3

After this, Job opened his mouth and cursed the day of his birth. He said, "May the day of my birth perish, and the night that said, 'A boy is conceived!' That day—may it turn to darkness; may God above not care about it; may no light shine on it. May gloom and utter darkness claim it once more; may a cloud settle over it; may blackness overwhelm it. That night—may thick darkness seize it; may it not be included among the days of the year nor be entered in any of the months. May that night be barren; may no shout of joy be heard in it. May those who curse days curse that day, those who are ready to rouse Leviathan. May its morning stars become dark; may it wait for daylight in vain and not see the first rays of dawn, for it did not shut the doors of the womb on me to hide trouble from my eyes "Why did I not perish at birth, and die as I came from the womb? Why were there knees to receive me and breasts that I might be nursed? For now, I would be lying down in peace; I would be asleep and at rest with kings and rulers of the earth, who built for themselves places now lying in ruins, with princes who had gold, who filled their houses with silver. Or why was I not hidden away in the ground like a stillborn child, like an infant who never saw the light of day? There the wicked cease from turmoil, and there the weary are at rest. Captives also enjoy their ease; they no longer hear the slave driver's shout. The small and the great are there, and the slaves are freed from their owners "Why is light given to those in misery, and life to the bitter of soul, to those who long for death that does not come, who search for it more than for hidden treasure, who are filled with gladness and rejoice when they reach the grave? Why is life given to a man whose way is hidden, whom God has hedged in? For sighing has become my daily food; my groans pour out like water. What I feared has come upon me; what I dreaded has happened to me. I have no peace, no quietness; I have no rest, but only turmoil."

Chapter 4

Then Eliphaz the Temanite replied, "If someone ventures a word with you, will you be impatient? But who can keep from speaking? Think how you have instructed many, how you have strengthened feeble hands. Your words have supported those who stumbled; you have strengthened faltering knees. But now trouble comes to you, and you are discouraged; it strikes you, and you are dismayed.

Should not your piety be your confidence and your blameless ways your hope? "Consider now: Who, being innocent, has ever perished? Where were the upright ever destroyed? As I have observed, those who plow evil and those who sow trouble reap it. At the breath of God, they perish; at the blast of his anger, they are no more. The lions may roar and growl, yet the teeth of the great lions are broken. The lion perishes for lack of prey, and the cubs of the lioness are scattered "A word was secretly brought to me, my ears caught a whisper of it. Amid disquieting dreams in the night, when deep sleep falls on people, fear and trembling seized me and made all my bones shake. A spirit glided past my face, and the hair on my body stood on end. It stopped, but I could not tell what it was. A form stood before my eyes, and I heard a hushed voice: 'Can a mortal be more righteous than God? Can even a strong man be more pure than his Maker? If God places no trust in his servants, if he charges his angels with error, how much more those who live in houses of clay, whose foundations are in the dust, who are crushed more readily than a moth! Between dawn and dusk, they are broken to pieces; unnoticed, they perish forever. Are not the cords of their tent pulled up, so that they die without wisdom?'

Chapter 5

"Call if you will, but who will answer you? To which of the holy ones will you turn? Resentment kills a fool, and envy slays the simple. I myself have seen a fool taking root, but suddenly his house was cursed. His children are far from safety, crushed in court without a defender. The hungry consume his harvest, taking it even from among thorns, and the thirsty pant after his wealth. For hardship does not spring from the soil, nor does trouble sprout from the ground. Yet man is born to trouble as surely as sparks fly upward "But if I were you, I would appeal to God; I would lay my cause before him. He performs wonders that cannot be fathomed, miracles that cannot be counted. He provides rain for the earth; he sends water on the countryside. The lowly he sets on high, and those who mourn are lifted to safety. He thwarts the plans of the crafty so that their hands achieve no success. He catches the wise in their craftiness, and the schemes of the wily are swept away. Darkness comes upon them in the daytime; at noon, they grope as in the night. He saves the needy from the sword in their mouth; he saves them from the clutches of the powerful. So the poor have hope, and injustice shuts its mouth "Blessed is the one whom God corrects; so do not despise the discipline of the Almighty. For he wounds, but he also binds up; he injures, but his hands also heal. From six calamities he will rescue you; in seven, no harm will touch you. In famine, he will deliver you from death, and in battle from the stroke of the sword. You will be protected from the lash of the tongue and need not fear when destruction comes. You will laugh at destruction and famine and need not fear the wild animals. For you will have a covenant with the stones of the field, and the wild animals will be at peace with you. You will know that your tent is secure; you will take stock of your property and find nothing missing. You will know that your children will be many, and your descendants like the grass of the earth. You will come to the grave in full vigor, like sheaves gathered in season "We have examined this, and it is true. So hear it and apply it to yourself."

Chapter 6

Job answered and said, "Oh, if my sorrow were well weighed, and my miseries were put together in the balance! For now, it would be heavier than the sand of the sea; therefore, my words are swallowed up. For the arrows of the Almighty are in me, whose poison breaks down my spirit, and the terrors of God fight against me. Will the wild horse bray when it has grass? Or will the ox low over its fodder? Can that which is unsavory be eaten without salt? Or is there any taste in the white of an egg? The things that my soul refused to touch are as loathsome food to me "Oh, that I might have my request and that God would grant me the thing that I long for! Even that it would please God to crush me, that he would let loose his hand and cut me off! Then I would still have comfort; yes, I would exult in pain unsparing, for I have not denied the words of the Holy One. What is my strength, that I should wait? And what is my end, that I should be patient? Is my strength the strength of stones? Or is my flesh of brass? Is it not that I have no help in me, and that wisdom is driven quite from me? "To him who is afflicted, kindness should be shown by his friend, even if he forsakes the fear of the Almighty. My brothers have dealt deceitfully as a brook, as the stream of brooks that pass away; which are blackish by reason of the ice, and in which the snow hides itself. In time, they dry up and vanish; when it is hot, they disappear from their place. The caravans of Tema look, the travelers of Sheba hope for them. They are distressed because they were confident; they come there and are disappointed. For now, you are nothing; you see my terrible plight and are afraid "Did I ever say, 'Give something to me,' or, 'Offer a bribe for me from your wealth,' or, 'Deliver me from the enemy's hand,' or, 'Redeem me from the hand of the oppressors'? Teach me, and I will hold my tongue; and cause me to understand wherein I have erred. How forceful are right words! But what does your arguing prove? Do you intend to reprove my words and consider the speeches of a desperate one as wind? Yes, you overwhelm the fatherless and you undermine your friend "But now, be pleased to look at me; for I will surely not lie to your face. Turn, I pray you, let there be no injustice; yes, turn again, my righteousness is in it. Is there iniquity in my tongue? Cannot my taste discern perverse things?"

Chapter 7

"Is there not an appointed time for man on earth? Are not his days also like the days of a hired man? As a servant earnestly desires the shade, and as a hired man looks for his wages, so I have been allotted months of futility, and nights of misery have been appointed to me. When I lie down, I say, 'When shall I arise and the night be gone?' And I am full of tossing till dawn. My flesh is clothed with worms and clods of dust; my skin is broken and loathsome. My days are swifter than a weaver's shuttle and are spent without hope "Oh, remember that my life is a breath! My eye shall no more see good. The eye of him who sees me shall see me no more; your eyes are upon me, and I am no more. As the cloud is consumed and vanishes away, so he who goes down to the grave shall come up no more. He shall return no more to his house, neither shall his place know him anymore "Therefore, I will not restrain my mouth; I will speak in the anguish of my spirit; I will complain in the bitterness of my soul. Am I a sea or a sea monster, that you set a guard over me? When I say, 'My bed shall comfort me, my couch shall ease my complaint,' then you scare me with dreams and terrify me with visions, so that my soul chooses strangling and death rather than my bones. I loathe my life; I would not live forever. Let me alone, for my days are vanity "What is man, that you should magnify him, and that you should set your heart upon him, and that you should visit him every morning and test him every moment? How long will you not look away from me, nor let me alone till I swallow my spittle? If I have sinned, what do I do to you, O watcher of men? Why have you set me as your target, so that I am a burden to myself? And why do you not pardon my transgression and take away my iniquity? For now, I shall sleep in the dust; and you will seek me in the morning, but I shall not be."

Chapter 8

Then Bildad the Shuhite answered and said, "How long will you speak these things, and the words of your mouth be like a strong wind? Does God pervert justice? Or does the Almighty pervert righteousness? If your children have sinned against him, and he has cast them away for their transgression, if you would earnestly seek God and make your supplication to the Almighty, if you were pure and upright, surely now he would awake for you and make the habitation of your righteousness prosperous. Though your beginning was small, yet your latter end would greatly increase "For inquire, please, of the former age, and consider the things discovered by their fathers. (For we are but of yesterday and know nothing because our days on earth are a shadow.) Will they not teach you and tell you, and utter words from their heart? Can the papyrus grow up without a marsh? Can the reeds flourish without water? While it is yet in its greenness and not cut down, it withers before any other plant. So are the paths of all who forget God, and the hope of the hypocrite shall perish, whose confidence shall be cut off, and whose trust is a spider's web. He leans upon his house, but it does not stand; he holds it fast, but it does not endure "He is green before the sun, and his branch shoots forth in his garden. His roots wrap around the heap, and he looks upon a house of stones. If he is destroyed from his place, then it will deny him, saying, 'I have not seen you.' Behold, this is the joy of his way, and out of the earth others will grow "Behold, God will not cast away the blameless, nor will he uphold the evildoers. He will yet fill your mouth with laughing, and your lips with rejoicing. Those who hate you shall be clothed with shame, and the dwelling place of the wicked shall come to nothing."

Chapter 9

Then Job answered and said, "Truly I know it is so, but how can a man be righteous before God? If one wished to contend with him, he could not answer him one time out of a thousand. God is wise in heart and mighty in strength. Who has hardened himself against him and prospered? He removes the mountains, and they do not know when he overturns them in his anger. He shakes the earth out of its place, and its pillars tremble. He commands the sun, and it does not rise; he seals off the stars. He alone spreads out the heavens and treads on the waves of the sea. He made the Bear, Orion, and the Pleiades, and the chambers of the south. He does great things past finding out, yes, wonders without number "Look, he goes by me, and I do not see him; he passes on also, but I do not perceive him. If he takes away, who can hinder him? Who can say to him, 'What are you doing?' God will not withdraw his anger; the allies of the proud lie prostrate beneath him "How then can I answer him and choose my words to reason with him? For though I were righteous, I could not answer him; I would beg mercy of my Judge. If I called and he answered me, I would not believe that he was listening to my voice. For he crushes me with a tempest and multiplies my wounds without cause. He will not allow me to catch my breath but fills me with bitterness. If it is a matter of strength, indeed he is strong; and if of justice, who will appoint my day in court? Though I were righteous, my own mouth would condemn me; though I were blameless, it would prove me perverse "I am blameless, yet I do not know myself; I despise my life. It is all one thing; therefore I say, 'He destroys

the blameless and the wicked.' If the scourge slays suddenly, he laughs at the plight of the innocent. The earth is given into the hand of the wicked; he covers the faces of its judges. If it is not he, then who else could it be? "Now my days are swifter than a runner; they flee away, they see no good. They pass by like swift ships, like an eagle swooping on its prey. If I say, 'I will forget my complaint, I will put off my sad face and wear a smile,' I am afraid of all my sufferings; I know that you will not hold me innocent. If I am condemned, why then do I labor in vain? If I wash myself with snow water and cleanse my hands with soap, yet you will plunge me into the pit, and my own clothes will abhor me "For he is not a man, as I am, that I may answer him, and that we should go to court together. Nor is there any mediator between us, who may lay his hand on us both. Let him take his rod away from me, and do not let dread of him terrify me. Then I would speak and not fear him, but it is not so with me."

Chapter 10

"My soul loathes my life; I will give free course to my complaint, I will speak in the bitterness of my soul. I will say to God, 'Do not condemn me; show me why you contend with me. Does it seem good to you that you should oppress, that you should despise the work of your hands and smile on the counsel of the wicked? Do you have eyes of flesh? Or do you see as man sees? Are your days like the days of a mortal man? Are your years like the days of a mighty man, that you should seek for my iniquity and search out my sin, although you know that I am not wicked, and there is no one who can deliver from your hand? "'Your hands have made me and fashioned me, an intricate unity; yet you would destroy me. Remember, I pray, that you have made me like clay. And will you turn me into dust again? Did you not pour me out like milk, and curdle me like cheese, clothe me with skin and flesh, and knit me together with bones and sinews? You have granted me life and favor, and your care has preserved my spirit. And these things you have hidden in your heart; I know that this was with you. If I sin, then you mark me, and you will not acquit me of my iniquity. If I am wicked, woe to me; even if I am righteous, I cannot lift up my head. I am full of disgrace; see my misery! If my head is exalted, you hunt me like a fierce lion, and again you show yourself awesome against me. You renew your witnesses against me and increase your indignation toward me; changes and war are ever with me "'Why then have you brought me out of the womb? Oh, that I had perished and no eye had seen me! I would have been as though I had not been. I would have been carried from the womb to the grave. Are not my days few? Cease! Leave me alone that I may take a little comfort before I go to the place from which I shall not return, to the land of darkness and the shadow of death, a land as dark as darkness itself, as the shadow of death, without any order, where even the light is like darkness.'"

Chapter 11

Then Zophar the Naamathite answered, "Should not someone answer this multitude of words? Should a person who talks so much be justified? Should others remain silent while you mock, and will no one rebuke you? For you have said, 'My doctrine is pure, and I am clean in your eyes.' But oh, that God would speak and open His lips against you! That He might show you the secrets of wisdom, for they are double in prudence. Know, therefore, that God has exacted less of you than your iniquity deserves "Can you find out the deep things of God? Can you find out the limit of the Almighty? It is higher than heaven—what can you do? It is deeper than Sheol—what can you know? Its measure is longer than the earth and broader than the sea. If He passes by, imprisons, or calls to judgment, who can hinder Him? For He knows worthless men; He sees iniquity also, even though they do not consider it. A senseless man will gain understanding as soon as a wild donkey's colt is born a man "If you would prepare your heart and stretch out your hands toward Him; if iniquity is in your hand, put it far away, and let not wickedness dwell in your tents. Surely then you will lift up your face without spot; yes, you will be steadfast and will not fear. You will forget your misery and remember it as waters that have passed away. Your life will be brighter than noonday; its darkness will be like the morning. You will be secure, because there is hope; you will look around and take your rest in safety. You will lie down, and no one will make you afraid; many will court your favor. But the eyes of the wicked will fail, and escape will elude them; their hope will be the giving up of the ghost."

Chapter 12

Then Job answered, "No doubt you are the people, and wisdom will die with you! But I have understanding as well as you; I am not inferior to you. Yes, who does not know such things as these? I am like one who is a laughingstock to his friends; I, who called on God and He answered me, the just and blameless man, is a laughingstock. Those at ease have contempt for misfortune, as the fate of those whose feet are slipping "The tents of robbers are at peace, and those who provoke God are secure, who bring their god in their hand. But ask the beasts, and they will teach you; the birds of the air, and they will tell you; or speak to the earth, and it will teach you; and the fish of the sea will declare to you. Who among all these does not know that the hand of the Lord has done this? In His hand is the life of every living thing and the breath of all mankind. Does not the ear test words as the palate tastes food? Wisdom is with the aged, and understanding in length of days "With Him are wisdom and might; He has counsel and understanding. If He tears down, it cannot be rebuilt; if He imprisons a man, there can be no release. If He withholds the waters, they dry up; if He sends them out, they overwhelm the earth. With Him are strength and sound wisdom; the deceived and the deceiver are His. He leads counselors away stripped and makes fools of judges. He loosens the bonds of kings and binds a waistcloth on their loins. He leads priests away stripped and overthrows the mighty. He deprives the trusted ones of speech and takes away the discernment of the elders. He pours contempt on princes and loosens the belt of the strong. He uncovers the deeps out of darkness and brings deep darkness to light. He makes nations great, and He destroys them; He enlarges nations, and He leads them away. He takes away understanding from the chiefs of the people of the earth and makes them wander in a pathless waste. They grope in the dark without light, and He makes them stagger like a drunken man."

Chapter 13

"My eyes have seen all this, my ears have heard and understood it. What you know, I also know; I am not inferior to you. But I desire to speak to the Almighty and to argue my case with God. As for you, you whitewash with lies; worthless physicians are you all. Oh, that you would keep silent, and it would be your wisdom! Hear now my argument and listen to the pleadings of my lips. Will you speak falsely for God and speak deceitfully for Him? Will you show partiality toward Him, will you plead the case for God? Will it be well when He searches you out? Or can you deceive Him as one deceives a man? He will surely rebuke you if in secret you show partiality. Will not His majesty terrify you, and the dread of Him fall upon you? Your maxims are proverbs of ashes, your defenses are defenses of clay "Let me have silence, and I will speak, and let come on me what may. Why do I take my flesh in my teeth and put my life in my hand? Though He slay me, yet will I trust in Him; but I will maintain my own ways before Him. He also shall be my salvation, for a hypocrite could not come before Him. Hear diligently my speech, and let my declaration be in your ears. Behold now, I have prepared my case; I know that I shall be justified. Who is he who will contend with me? For then I would hold my tongue and perish "Only grant me two things, then I will not hide myself from You: withdraw Your hand far from me, and let not the dread of You terrify me. Then call, and I will answer; or let me speak, and You respond to me. How many are my iniquities and sins? Make me know my transgression and my sin. Why do You hide Your face and regard me as Your enemy? Will You frighten a leaf driven to and fro? And will You pursue the dry stubble? For You write bitter things against me and make me inherit the iniquities of my youth. You put my feet also in the stocks and watch all my paths; You set a bound to the soles of my feet. Though I am decaying like a rotten thing, like a garment that is moth-eaten."

Chapter 14

"Man who is born of a woman is of few days and full of trouble. He comes forth like a flower and withers; he flees like a shadow and continues not. And do You open Your eyes on such a one and bring me into judgment with You? Who can bring a clean thing out of an unclean? No one. Since his days are determined, and the number of his months is with You, and You have appointed his limits that he cannot pass, look away from him and let him rest, till he fulfills his day like a hired hand "For there is hope for a tree, if it be cut down, that it will sprout again, and that its shoots will not cease. Though its root grows old in the earth, and its stump dies in the soil, yet at the scent of water it will bud and put forth branches like a young plant. But a man dies and is laid low; man breathes his last, and where is he? As waters fail from a lake and a river wastes away and dries up, so a man lies down and rises not again; till the heavens are no more he will not awake or be roused out of his sleep. Oh, that You would hide me in Sheol, that You would conceal me until Your wrath be past, that You would appoint me a set time, and remember me! "If a man dies, shall he live again? All the days of my appointed time I will wait, till my change comes. You shall call, and I will answer You; You will have a desire to the work of Your hands. But now You number my steps; do not watch over my sin. My transgression is sealed up in a bag, and You sew up my iniquity. But the mountain falls and crumbles away, and the rock is removed from its place; the waters wear away the stones, the torrents wash away the soil of the earth, so You destroy the hope of man. You prevail forever against him, and he passes; You change his countenance and send him away. His sons come to honor, and he does not know it; they are brought low, and he perceives it not. He feels only the pain of his own body, and he mourns only for himself."

Chapter 15

Then Eliphaz the Temanite answered, "Should a wise man answer with windy knowledge and fill his belly with the east wind? Should he argue in unprofitable talk or in words with which he can do no good? But you are doing away with the fear of God and hindering meditation before God. For your iniquity teaches your mouth, and you choose the tongue of the crafty. Your own mouth condemns you, and not I; your own lips testify against you "Are you the first man who was born? Or were you brought forth before the hills?

Have you listened in the council of God? And do you limit wisdom to yourself? What do you know that we do not know? What do you understand that is not in us? Both the gray-haired and the aged are among us, older than your father. Are the consolations of God too small for you, or the word spoken gently to you? Why does your heart carry you away, and why do your eyes flash, that you turn your spirit against God and bring such words out of your mouth? What is man, that he can be pure? Or he who is born of a woman, that he can be righteous? Behold, God puts no trust in His holy ones, and the heavens are not pure in His sight; how much less one who is abominable and corrupt, a man who drinks injustice like water! "I will show you; hear me, and what I have seen I will declare (what wise men have told, and have not concealed from their fathers, to whom alone the land was given, and no stranger passed among them). The wicked man writhes in pain all his days, through all the years that are laid up for the ruthless. Dreadful sounds are in his ears; in prosperity, the destroyer will come upon him. He does not believe that he will return out of darkness, and he is marked for the sword. He wanders abroad for bread, saying, 'Where is it?' He knows that a day of darkness is ready at his hand; distress and anguish terrify him; they prevail against him, like a king ready for battle. Because he has stretched out his hand against God and defies the Almighty, running stubbornly against Him with a thick-bossed shield; because he has covered his face with his fat and gathered fat upon his waist and has lived in desolate cities, in houses that none should inhabit, which were ready to become heaps of ruins; he will not be rich, and his wealth will not endure, nor will his possessions spread over the earth; he will not depart from darkness; the flame will dry up his shoots, and by the breath of his mouth he will depart. Let him not trust in emptiness, deceiving himself, for emptiness will be his payment. It will be paid in full before his time, and his branch will not be green. He will shake off his unripe grape like the vine, and cast off his blossom like the olive tree. For the company of the godless is barren, and fire consumes the tents of bribery. They conceive trouble and give birth to evil, and their womb prepares deceit."

Chapter 16

Job answered and said, "I have often heard such things; you are all miserable comforters. Is there no end to your windy words? What provokes you to answer? I could speak as you do if you were in my place; I could heap up words against you and shake my head at you. But I would strengthen you with my mouth, and the comfort of my lips would relieve your grief "Even if I speak, my pain is not relieved; and if I refrain from speaking, how much of it goes away? But now, O God, you have worn me out; you have devastated my entire household. You have shriveled me up—and it has become a witness; my gauntness rises up against me and testifies to my face. His anger has torn me and hunted me down; he gnashes at me with his teeth; my adversary sharpens his eyes against me. People open their mouths to jeer at me; they strike my cheek in scorn and unite together against me. God has turned me over to the ungodly and thrown me into the clutches of the wicked "I was at ease, but he shattered me; he seized me by the neck and crushed me. He has made me his target; his archers surround me. Without pity, he pierces my kidneys and spills my gall on the ground. He breaks me with wound upon wound; he rushes at me like a warrior. I have sewed sackcloth over my skin and buried my brow in the dust. My face is red with weeping, and deep shadows ring my eyes, yet my hands have been free of violence, and my prayer is pure "O earth, do not cover my blood; may my cry never be laid to rest! Even now, my witness is in heaven; my advocate is on high. My intercessor is my friend as my eyes pour out tears to God; on behalf of a man, he pleads with God as one pleads for a friend. Only a few years will pass before I go on the journey of no return."

Chapter 17

"My spirit is broken, my days are cut short, the grave awaits me. Surely mockers surround me; my eyes must dwell on their hostility. Give me, O God, the pledge you demand. Who else will put up security for me? You have closed their minds to understanding; therefore, you will not let them triumph. If anyone denounces their friends for reward, the eyes of their children will fail "God has made me a byword to everyone, a man in whose face people spit. My eyes have grown dim with grief; my whole frame is but a shadow. The upright are appalled at this; the innocent are aroused against the ungodly. Nevertheless, the righteous will hold to their ways, and those with clean hands will grow stronger. But come on, all of you, try again! I will not find a wise man among you "My days have passed, my plans are shattered. Yet the desires of my heart turn night into day; in the face of the darkness, light is near. If the only home I hope for is the grave, if I spread out my bed in the realm of darkness, if I say to corruption, 'You are my father,' and to the worm, 'My mother' or 'My sister,' where then is my hope—who can see any hope for me? Will it go down to the gates of death? Will we descend together into the dust?"

Chapter 18

Then Bildad the Shuhite answered, "When will you end these speeches? Be sensible, and then we can talk. Why are we regarded as cattle and considered stupid in your sight? You who tear yourself to pieces in your anger, is the earth to be abandoned for your sake? Or must the rocks be moved from their place? "The lamp of the wicked is snuffed out; the flame of his fire stops burning. The light in his tent becomes dark; the lamp beside him goes out. The vigor of his step is weakened; his own schemes throw him down. His feet thrust him into a net; he wanders into its mesh. A trap seizes him by the heel; a snare holds him fast. A noose is hidden for him on the ground; a trap lies in his path. Terrors startle him on every side and dog his every step. Calamity is hungry for him; disaster is ready for him when he falls. It eats away parts of his skin; death's firstborn devours his limbs. He is torn from the security of his tent and marched off to the king of terrors. Fire resides in his tent; burning sulfur is scattered over his dwelling. His roots dry up below, and his branches wither above. The memory of him perishes from the earth; he has no name in the land. He is driven from light into the realm of darkness and is banished from the world. He has no offspring or descendants among his people, no survivor where once he lived. People of the west are appalled at his fate; those of the east are seized with horror. Surely such is the dwelling of an evil man; such is the place of one who does not know God."

Chapter 19

Then Job answered, "How long will you torment me and crush me with words? Ten times now you have reproached me; shamelessly you attack me. If it is true that I have gone astray, my error remains my concern alone. If indeed you would exalt yourselves above me and use my humiliation against me, then know that God has wronged me and drawn his net around me "Though I cry, 'Violence!' I get no response; though I call for help, there is no justice. He has blocked my way so I cannot pass; he has shrouded my paths in darkness. He has stripped me of my honor and removed the crown from my head. He tears me down on every side till I am gone; he uproots my hope like a tree. His anger burns against me; he counts me among his enemies. His troops advance in force; they build a siege ramp against me and encamp around my tent "He has alienated my family from me; my acquaintances are completely estranged from me. My relatives have gone away; my closest friends have forgotten me. My guests and my female servants count me a foreigner; they look on me as on a stranger. I summon my servant, but he does not answer, though I beg him with my own mouth. My breath is offensive to my wife; I am loathsome to my own family. Even the little boys scorn me; when I appear, they ridicule me. All my intimate friends detest me; those I love have turned against me. I am nothing but skin and bones; I have escaped only by the skin of my teeth "Have pity on me, my friends, have pity, for the hand of God has struck me. Why do you pursue me as God does? Will you never get enough of my flesh? Oh, that my words were recorded, that they were written on a scroll, that they were inscribed with an iron tool on lead, or engraved in rock forever! I know that my redeemer lives, and that in the end, he will stand on the earth. And after my skin has been destroyed, yet in my flesh, I will see God; I myself will see him with my own eyes—I, and not another. How my heart yearns within me! "If you say, 'How we will hound him, since the root of the trouble lies in him,' you should fear the sword yourselves; for wrath will bring punishment by the sword, and then you will know that there is judgment."

Chapter 20

Then Zophar the Naamathite replied, "My troubled thoughts prompt me to answer because I am greatly disturbed. I hear a rebuke that dishonors me, and my understanding inspires me to reply. Surely you know how it has been from of old, ever since mankind was placed on the earth, that the mirth of the wicked is brief, the joy of the godless lasts but a moment. Though the pride of the godless person reaches to the heavens and his head touches the clouds, he will perish forever, like his own dung; those who have seen him will say, 'Where is he?' Like a dream he flies away, no more to be found, banished like a vision of the night. The eye that saw him will not see him again; his place will look on him no more. His children must make amends to the poor; his own hands must give back his wealth. The youthful vigor that fills his bones will lie with him in the dust "Though evil is sweet in his mouth and he hides it under his tongue, though he cannot bear to let it go and lets it linger in his mouth, yet his food will turn sour in his stomach; it will become the venom of serpents within him. He will spit out the riches he swallowed; God will make his stomach vomit them up. He will suck the poison of serpents; the fangs of an adder will kill him. He will not enjoy the streams, the rivers flowing with honey and cream. What he toiled for he must give back uneaten; he will not enjoy the profit from his trading. For he has oppressed the poor and left them destitute; he has seized houses he did not build "Surely he will have no respite from his craving; he cannot save himself by his treasure. Nothing is left for him to devour; his prosperity will not endure. In the midst of his plenty, distress will overtake him; the full force of misery will come upon him. When he has filled his belly, God will vent his burning anger against him and rain down his blows on him. Though he flees from an iron weapon, a bronze-tipped arrow pierces him. He pulls it out of his back, the gleaming point out of his liver. Terrors will come over him; total darkness lies in wait for his

treasures. A fire unfanned will consume him and devour what is left in his tent. The heavens will expose his guilt; the earth will rise up against him. A flood will carry off his house, rushing waters on the day of God's wrath. Such is the fate God allots the wicked, the heritage appointed for them by God."

Chapter 21

Job answered and said, "Listen diligently to my words, and let this be your consolation. Allow me to speak, and after I have spoken, you may mock me. Is my complaint directed at man? Why should I not be troubled in spirit? Consider me and be appalled; put your hand over your mouth. When I think about it, I am terrified; trembling seizes my body Why do the wicked live on, growing old and increasing in power? Their children are established around them, and their offspring before their eyes. Their homes are safe and free from fear; the rod of God is not upon them. Their bulls breed without fail; their cows calve and do not miscarry. They send forth their little ones like a flock; their children dance. They sing to the music of tambourine and harp and make merry to the sound of the flute. They spend their days in prosperity and go down to the grave in peace. They say to God, 'Leave us alone! We have no desire to know Your ways. Who is the Almighty, that we should serve Him? What would we gain by praying to Him?' But their prosperity is not in their own hands, so I stay far from the counsel of the wicked. How often is the lamp of the wicked snuffed out? How often does calamity come upon them, the fate God allots in His anger? How often are they like straw before the wind, like chaff swept away by a gale? It is said, 'God stores up a man's punishment for his children.' Let Him repay the man himself, so that he will know it! Let his own eyes see his destruction; let him drink of the wrath of the Almighty. For what does he care about the family he leaves behind when his allotted months come to an end? Can anyone teach knowledge to God, since He judges even the highest? One man dies in full vigor, completely secure and at ease, his body well nourished, his bones rich with marrow. Another man dies in bitterness of soul, never having enjoyed anything good. Side by side they lie in the dust, and worms cover them both I know full well what you are thinking, the schemes by which you would wrong me. You say, 'Where now is the great man's house, the tents where the wicked lived?' Have you never questioned those who travel? Have you paid no regard to their accounts—that the wicked are spared from the day of calamity, that they are delivered from the day of wrath? Who denounces their conduct to their face? Who repays them for what they have done? They are carried to the grave, and watch is kept over their tombs. The soil in the valley is sweet to them; everyone follows after them, and a countless throng goes before them So how can you console me with your nonsense? Nothing is left of your answers but falsehood!"

Chapter 22

Then Eliphaz the Temanite answered, "Can a man be of benefit to God? Can even a wise man benefit Him? What pleasure would it give the Almighty if you were righteous? What would He gain if your ways were blameless? Is it for your piety that He rebukes you and brings charges against you? Is not your wickedness great? Are not your sins endless? You demanded security from your brothers for no reason; you stripped men of their clothing, leaving them naked. You gave no water to the weary and withheld food from the hungry, though you were a powerful man, owning land—an honored man, living on it. And you sent widows away empty-handed and broke the strength of the fatherless. That is why snares are all around you, why sudden peril terrifies you, why it is so dark you cannot see, and why a flood of water covers you Is not God in the heights of heaven? And see how lofty are the highest stars! Yet you say, 'What does God know? Does He judge through such darkness? Thick clouds veil Him, so He does not see us as He goes about in the vaulted heavens.' Will you keep to the old path that wicked men have trod? They were carried off before their time, their foundations washed away by a flood. They said to God, 'Leave us alone! What can the Almighty do to us?' Yet it was He who filled their houses with good things, so I stand aloof from the counsel of the wicked. The righteous see their ruin and rejoice; the innocent mock them, saying, 'Surely our foes are destroyed, and fire devours their wealth.' Submit to God and be at peace with Him; in this way, prosperity will come to you. Accept instruction from His mouth and lay up His words in your heart. If you return to the Almighty, you will be restored; if you remove wickedness far from your tent and assign your nuggets to the dust, your gold of Ophir to the rocks in the ravines, then the Almighty will be your gold, the choicest silver for you. Surely then you will find delight in the Almighty and will lift up your face to God. You will pray to Him, and He will hear you, and you will fulfill your vows. What you decide on will be done, and light will shine on your ways. When men are brought low and you say, 'Lift them up!' then He will save the downcast. He will deliver even one who is not innocent, who will be delivered through the cleanness of your hands."

Chapter 23

Then Job answered and said, "Even today my complaint is bitter; His hand is heavy despite my groaning. Oh, that I knew where I might find Him, that I might come to His seat! I would present my case before Him and fill my mouth with arguments. I would learn what He would answer me and understand what He would say to me. Would He contend with me in His great power? No, He would only pay attention to me. There an upright man could present his case before Him, and I would be delivered forever from my judge But if I go to the east, He is not there; if I go to the west, I do not find Him. When He is at work in the north, I do not see Him; when He turns to the south, I catch no glimpse of Him. But He knows the way that I take; when He has tested me, I will come forth as gold. My feet have closely followed His steps; I have kept to His way without turning aside. I have not departed from the commands of His lips; I have treasured the words of His mouth more than my daily bread But He stands alone, and who can oppose Him? He does whatever He pleases. He carries out His decree against me, and many such plans He still has in store. That is why I am terrified before Him; when I think of all this, I fear Him. God has made my heart faint; the Almighty has terrified me. Yet I am not silenced by the darkness, by the thick darkness that covers my face

Chapter 24

"Why are not times of judgment kept by the Almighty? Why do those who know Him never see His days? Men move boundary stones; they pasture flocks they have stolen. They drive away the orphan's donkey and take the widow's ox in pledge. They thrust the needy from the path and force all the poor of the land into hiding. Like wild donkeys in the desert, the poor go about their labor of foraging food; the wasteland provides food for their children. They gather fodder in the fields and glean in the vineyards of the wicked. Lacking clothes, they spend the night naked; they have nothing to cover themselves in the cold. They are drenched by mountain rains and hug the rocks for lack of shelter. The fatherless child is snatched from the breast; the infant of the poor is seized for a debt. Lacking clothes, they go about

naked; they carry the sheaves, but still go hungry. They crush olives among the terraces; they tread the winepresses, yet suffer thirst. The groans of the dying rise from the city, and the souls of the wounded cry out for help. Yet God charges no one with wrongdoing There are those who rebel against the light, who do not know its ways or stay in its paths. When daylight is gone, the murderer rises up and kills the poor and needy; in the night, he steals forth like a thief. The eye of the adulterer watches for dusk; he thinks, 'No eye will see me,' and he keeps his face concealed. In the dark, men break into houses, but by day they shut themselves in; they want nothing to do with the light. For all of them, morning is their deepest terror; they are friends with the terrors of darkness Yet they are foam on the surface of the water; their portion of the land is cursed, so that no one goes to the vineyards. As heat and drought snatch away the melted snow, so the grave snatches away those who have sinned. The womb forgets them, the worm feasts on them; the wicked are no longer remembered but are broken like a tree. They prey on the barren and childless woman, and to the widow they show no kindness. But God drags away the mighty by His power; though they become established, they have no assurance of life. He may let them rest in a feeling of security, but His eyes are on their ways. For a little while they are exalted, and then they are gone; they are brought low and gathered up like all others; they are cut off like heads of grain If this is not so, who can prove me false and reduce my words to nothing?"

Chapter 25

Then Bildad the Shuhite replied, "Dominion and awe belong to God; He establishes order in the heights of heaven. Can His forces be numbered? On whom does His light not rise? How then can a mortal be righteous before God? How can one born of woman be pure? If even the moon is not bright and the stars are not pure in His eyes, how much less a mortal, who is but a maggot—a human being, who is only a worm!"

Chapter 26

Then Job answered and said, "How you have helped the powerless! How you have saved the arm that is feeble! What advice you have offered to one without wisdom! And what great insight you have displayed! Who has helped you utter these words? And whose spirit spoke from your mouth? The dead are in deep anguish, those beneath the waters and all that live in them. The realm of the dead is naked before God; Destruction lies uncovered. He spreads out the northern skies over empty space; He suspends the earth over nothing. He wraps up the waters in His clouds, yet the clouds do not burst under their weight. He covers the face of the full moon, spreading His clouds over it. He marks out the horizon on the face of the waters for a boundary between light and darkness. The pillars of the heavens quake, aghast at His rebuke. By His power, He churned up the sea; by His wisdom, He cut Rahab to pieces. By His breath, the skies became fair; His hand pierced the gliding serpent. And these are but the outer fringe of His works; how faint the whisper we hear of Him! Who then can understand the thunder of His power?"

Chapter 27

And Job continued his discourse: "As surely as God lives, who has denied me justice, the Almighty, who has made my life bitter, as long as I have life within me, the breath of God in my nostrils, my lips will not say anything wicked, and my tongue will not utter lies. I will never admit you are in the right; till I die, I will not deny my integrity. I will maintain my innocence and never let go of it; my conscience will not reproach me as long as I live "May my enemy be like the wicked, my adversary like the unjust! For what hope have the godless when they are cut off, when God takes away their life? Does God listen to their cry when distress comes upon them? Will they find delight in the Almighty? Will they call on God at all times? "I will teach you about the power of God; the ways of the Almighty I will not conceal. You have all seen this yourselves. Why then this meaningless talk? "Here is the fate God allots to the wicked, the heritage a ruthless man receives from the Almighty: However many his children, their fate is the sword; his offspring will never have enough to eat. The plague will bury those who survive him, and their widows will not weep for them. Though he heaps up silver like dust and clothes like piles of clay, what he lays up the righteous will wear, and the innocent will divide his silver. The house he builds is like a moth's cocoon, like a hut made by a watchman. He lies down wealthy, but will do so no more; when he opens his eyes, all is gone. Terrors overtake him like a flood; a tempest snatches him away in the night. The east wind carries him off, and he is gone; it sweeps him out of his place. It hurls itself against him without mercy as he flees headlong from its power. It claps its hands in derision and hisses him out of his place."

Chapter 28

"There is a mine for silver and a place where gold is refined. Iron is taken from the earth, and copper is smelted from ore. Mortals put an end to the darkness; they search out the farthest recesses for ore in the blackest darkness. Far from human dwellings, they cut a shaft, in places untouched by human feet; far from other people, they dangle and sway. The earth, from which food comes, is transformed below as by fire; lapis lazuli comes from its rocks, and its dust contains nuggets of gold. No bird of prey knows that hidden path, no falcon's eye has seen it. Proud beasts do not set foot on it, and no lion prowls there. People assault the flinty rock with their hands and lay bare the roots of the mountains. They tunnel through the rock; their eyes see all its treasures. They search the sources of the rivers and bring hidden things to light "But where can wisdom be found? Where does understanding dwell? No mortal comprehends its worth; it cannot be found in the land of the living. The deep says, 'It is not in me'; the sea says, 'It is not with me.' It cannot be bought with the finest gold, nor can its price be weighed out in silver. It cannot be bought with the gold of Ophir, with precious onyx or lapis lazuli. Neither gold nor crystal can compare with it, nor can it be had for jewels of gold. Coral and jasper are not worthy of mention; the price of wisdom is beyond rubies. The topaz of Cush cannot compare with it; it cannot be bought with pure gold "Where then does wisdom come from? Where does understanding dwell? It is hidden from the eyes of every living thing, concealed even from the birds in the sky. Destruction and Death say, 'Only a rumor of it has reached our ears.' God understands the way to it, and He alone knows where it dwells, for He views the ends of the earth and sees everything under the heavens. When He established the force of the wind and measured out the waters, when He made a decree for the rain and a path for the thunderstorm, then He looked at wisdom and appraised it; He confirmed it and tested it. And He said to the human race, 'The fear of the Lord—that is wisdom, and to shun evil is understanding.'"

Chapter 29

Job continued his discourse: "Oh, for the days when I was in my prime, when God's intimate friendship blessed my house, when the Almighty was still with me and my children were around me, when my path was drenched with cream and the rock poured out for me streams of olive oil "When I went to the gate of the city and took my seat in the public square, the young men saw me and stepped aside, and the old men rose to their feet; the chief men refrained from speaking and covered their mouths with their hands; the voices of the nobles were hushed, and their tongues stuck to the roof of their mouths. Whoever heard me spoke well of me, and those who saw me commended me because I rescued the poor who cried for help, and the fatherless who had none to assist them. The one who was dying blessed me; I made the widow's heart sing. I put on righteousness as my clothing; justice was my robe and my turban. I was eyes to the blind and feet to the lame. I was a father to the needy; I took up the case of the stranger. I broke the fangs of the wicked and snatched the victims from their teeth "I thought, 'I will die in my own house, my days as numerous as the grains of sand. My roots will reach to the water, and the dew will lie all night on my branches. My glory will not fade; the bow will be ever new in my hand.' "People listened to me expectantly, waiting in silence for my counsel. After I had spoken, they spoke no more; my words fell gently on their ears. They waited for me as for showers and drank in my words as the spring rain. When I smiled at them, they scarcely believed it; the light of my face was precious to them. I chose the way for them and sat as their chief; I dwelt as a king among his troops; I was like one who comforts mourners."

Chapter 30

"But now they mock me, men younger than I, whose fathers I would have disdained to put with my sheepdogs. Of what use was the strength of their hands to me, since their vigor had gone from them? Haggard from want and hunger, they roamed the parched land in desolate wastelands at night. In the brush, they gathered salt herbs, and their food was the root of the broom bush. They were banished from human society, shouted at as if they were thieves. They were forced to live in the dry stream beds, among the rocks and in holes in the ground. They brayed among the bushes and huddled in the undergrowth. A base and nameless brood, they were driven out of the land "And now those young men mock me in song; I have become a byword among them. They detest me and keep their distance; they do not hesitate to spit in my face. Now that God has unstrung my bow and afflicted me, they throw off restraint in my presence. On my right, the tribe attacks; they lay snares for my feet, they build their siege ramps against me. They break up my road; they succeed in destroying me. 'No one can help him,' they say. They advance as through a gaping breach; amid the ruins, they come rolling in. Terrors overwhelm me; my dignity is driven away as by the wind, my safety vanishes like a cloud "And now my life ebbs away; days of suffering grip me. Night pierces my bones; my gnawing pains never rest. In His great power, God becomes like clothing to me; He binds me like the neck of my garment. He throws me into the mud, and I am reduced to dust and ashes "I cry out to You, God, but You do not answer; I stand up, but You merely look at me. You turn on me ruthlessly; with the might of Your hand, You attack me. You snatch me up and drive me before the wind; You toss me about in the storm. I know You will bring me down to death, to the place appointed for all the living "Surely no one lays a hand on a broken man when he cries for help in his distress. Have I not wept for those in trouble? Has not my soul grieved for the poor? Yet when I hoped for good, evil came; when I looked for light, then came darkness. The churning inside me never stops; days of suffering confront me.

I go about blackened, but not by the sun; I stand up in the assembly and cry for help. I have become a brother of jackals, a companion of owls. My skin grows black and peels; my body burns with fever. My lyre is tuned to mourning, and my pipe to the sound of wailing."

Chapter 31

1 I have made a covenant with my eyes; why then should I think upon a maid? 2 For what portion of God is there from above? And what inheritance of the Almighty from on high? 3 Is not destruction to the wicked? And a strange punishment to the workers of iniquity? 4 Does not He see my ways and count all my steps? 5 If I have walked with vanity, or if my foot has hurried to deceit, 6 Let me be weighed in an even balance, that God may know my integrity. 7 If my step has turned out of the way, and my heart walked after my eyes, or if any blot has stuck to my hands, 8 Then let me sow, and let another eat; yes, let my offspring be rooted out. 9 If my heart has been enticed by a woman, or if I have laid wait at my neighbor's door, 10 Then let my wife grind for another, and let others bow down upon her. 11 For this is a heinous crime; yes, it is an iniquity to be punished by the judges. 12 For it is a fire that consumes to destruction, and would root out all my increase. 13 If I did despise the cause of my manservant or of my maidservant when they contended with me, 14 What then shall I do when God rises up? And when He visits, what shall I answer Him? 15 Did not He who made me in the womb make him? And did not one fashion us in the womb? 16 If I have withheld the poor from their desire, or have caused the eyes of the widow to fail, 17 Or have eaten my morsel alone, and the fatherless have not eaten thereof, 18 (For from my youth he was brought up with me, as with a father, and I have guided her from my mother's womb); 19 If I have seen any perish for want of clothing, or any poor without covering; 20 If his loins have not blessed me, and if he were not warmed with the fleece of my sheep; 21 If I have lifted up my hand against the fatherless, when I saw my help in the gate; 22 Then let my arm fall from my shoulder blade, and mine arm be broken from the bone. 23 For destruction from God was a terror to me, and by reason of His highness I could not endure. 24 If I have made gold my hope, or have said to the fine gold, "You are my confidence"; 25 If I rejoiced because my wealth was great, and because my hand had gotten much; 26 If I beheld the sun when it shined, or the moon walking in brightness; 27 And my heart has been secretly enticed, or my mouth has kissed my hand; 28 This also were an iniquity to be punished by the judge, for I should have denied the God that is above. 29 If I rejoiced at the destruction of him who hated me, or lifted up myself when evil found him; 30 Neither have I suffered my mouth to sin by wishing a curse to his soul. 31 If the men of my tent have not said, "Oh that we had of his flesh! We cannot be satisfied." 32 The stranger did not lodge in the street, but I opened my doors to the traveler. 33 If I covered my transgressions as Adam, by hiding my iniquity in my bosom, 34 Because I feared the great multitude, and the contempt of families terrified me, so that I kept silence and did not go out of the door— 35 Oh that one would hear me! Behold, my desire is, that the Almighty would answer me, and that my adversary had written a book. 36 Surely I would take it upon my shoulder and bind it as a crown to me. 37 I would declare to Him the number of my steps; as a prince would I go near unto Him. 38 If my land cries against me, or that the furrows likewise complain; 39 If I have eaten the fruits thereof without money, or have caused the owners thereof to lose their life; 40 Let thistles grow instead of wheat, and cockle instead of barley. The

words of Job are ended

Chapter 32

1 So these three men ceased to answer Job because he was righteous in his own eyes. 2 Then was kindled the wrath of Elihu the son of Barachel the Buzite, of the kindred of Ram; against Job was his wrath kindled because he justified himself rather than God. 3 Also against his three friends was his wrath kindled because they had found no answer and yet had condemned Job. 4 Now Elihu had waited till Job had spoken because they were elder than he. 5 When Elihu saw that there was no answer in the mouth of these three men, then his wrath was kindled. 6 And Elihu the son of Barachel the Buzite answered and said: "I am young, and you are very old; wherefore I was afraid and dared not show you mine opinion. 7 I said, 'Days should speak, and multitude of years should teach wisdom.' 8 But there is a spirit in man, and the inspiration of the Almighty gives them understanding. 9 Great men are not always wise; neither do the aged understand judgment. 10 Therefore I said, 'Listen to me; I also will show mine opinion.' 11 Behold, I waited for your words; I gave ear to your reasons, whilst you searched out what to say. 12 Yea, I attended unto you, and behold, there was none of you that convinced Job or that answered his words. 13 Lest you should say, 'We have found out wisdom; God thrusts him down, not man.' 14 Now he has not directed his words against me; neither will I answer him with your speeches. 15 They were amazed; they answered no more; they left off speaking. 16 When I had waited (for they spoke not, but stood still and answered no more), 17 I said, 'I will answer also my part, I also will show mine opinion.' 18 For I am full of matter; the spirit within me constrains me. 19 Behold, my belly is as wine which has no vent; it is ready to burst like new bottles. 20 I will speak, that I may be refreshed; I will open my lips and answer. 21 Let me not, I pray you, accept any man's person; neither let me give flattering titles unto man. 22 For I know not to give flattering titles; in so doing my Maker would soon take me away

Chapter 33

1 "Wherefore, Job, I pray thee, hear my speeches and hearken to all my words. 2 Behold, now I have opened my mouth, my tongue has spoken in my mouth. 3 My words shall be of the uprightness of my heart, and my lips shall utter knowledge clearly. 4 The Spirit of God has made me, and the breath of the Almighty has given me life. 5 If you can answer me, set your words in order before me; stand up. 6 Behold, I am according to your wish in God's stead; I also am formed out of the clay. 7 Behold, my terror shall not make you afraid, neither shall my hand be heavy upon you. 8 Surely you have spoken in mine hearing, and I have heard the voice of your words, saying, 9 'I am clean without transgression; I am innocent; neither is there iniquity in me. 10 Behold, He finds occasions against me, He counts me for His enemy. 11 He puts my feet in the stocks, He marks all my paths.' 12 Behold, in this you are not just; I will answer you, that God is greater than man. 13 Why do you strive against Him? For He gives not account of any of His matters. 14 For God speaks once, yea twice, yet man perceives it not. 15 In a dream, in a vision of the night, when deep sleep falls upon men, in slumberings upon the bed, 16 Then He opens the ears of men and seals their instruction, 17 That He may withdraw man from his purpose and hide pride from man. 18 He keeps back his soul from the pit and his life from perishing by the sword. 19 He is chastened also with pain upon his bed, and the multitude of his bones with strong pain, 20 So that his life abhors bread and his soul dainty meat. 21 His

flesh is consumed away that it cannot be seen; and his bones that were not seen stick out. 22 Yea, his soul draws near unto the grave and his life to the destroyers. 23 If there be a messenger with him, an interpreter, one among a thousand, to show unto man his uprightness, 24 Then He is gracious unto him, and says, 'Deliver him from going down to the pit; I have found a ransom.' 25 His flesh shall be fresher than a child's; he shall return to the days of his youth. 26 He shall pray unto God, and He will be favorable unto him; and he shall see His face with joy, for He will render unto man his righteousness. 27 He looks upon men, and if any say, 'I have sinned, and perverted that which was right, and it profited me not,' 28 He will deliver his soul from going into the pit, and his life shall see the light. 29 Lo, all these things works God oftentimes with man, 30 To bring back his soul from the pit, to be enlightened with the light of the living. 31 Mark well, O Job, hearken unto me; hold your peace, and I will speak. 32 If you have anything to say, answer me; speak, for I desire to justify you. 33 If not, hearken unto me; hold your peace, and I shall teach you wisdom."

Chapter 34

1 Furthermore, Elihu answered and said: 2 "Hear my words, O you wise men, and give ear unto me, you who have knowledge. 3 For the ear tries words as the mouth tastes meat. 4 Let us choose to us judgment; let us know among ourselves what is good. 5 For Job has said, 'I am righteous, and God has taken away my judgment. 6 Should I lie against my right? My wound is incurable without transgression.' 7 What man is like Job, who drinks up scorning like water? 8 Who goes in company with the workers of iniquity, and walks with wicked men? 9 For he has said, 'It profits a man nothing that he should delight himself with God.' 10 Therefore hearken unto me, you men of understanding: far be it from God that He should do wickedness, and from the Almighty that He should commit iniquity. 11 For the work of a man shall He render unto him, and cause every man to find according to his ways. 12 Yes, surely God will not do wickedly, neither will the Almighty pervert judgment. 13 Who has given Him a charge over the earth? Or who has disposed the whole world? 14 If He set His heart upon man, if He gathers unto Himself his spirit and his breath, 15 All flesh shall perish together, and man shall turn again unto dust. 16 If now you have understanding, hear this: hearken to the voice of my words. 17 Shall even he that hates right govern? And will you condemn Him who is most just? 18 Is it fit to say to a king, 'You are wicked'? And to princes, 'You are ungodly'? 19 How much less to Him that accepts not the persons of princes, nor regards the rich more than the poor? For they all are the work of His hands. 20 In a moment shall they die, and the people shall be troubled at midnight and pass away, and the mighty shall be taken away without hand. 21 For His eyes are upon the ways of man, and He sees all his goings. 22 There is no darkness, nor shadow of death, where the workers of iniquity may hide themselves. 23 For He will not lay upon man more than right, that he should enter into judgment with God. 24 He shall break in pieces mighty men without number, and set others in their stead. 25 Therefore He knows their works, and He overturns them in the night, so that they are destroyed. 26 He strikes them as wicked men in the open sight of others, 27 Because they turned back from Him and would not consider any of His ways, 28 So that they cause the cry of the poor to come unto Him, and He hears the cry of the afflicted. 29 When He gives quietness, who then can make trouble? And when He hides His face, who then can behold Him? Whether it be done against a nation, or against a man only, 30 That the hypocrite reign not, lest the people be ensnared. 31 Surely it is meet to be said unto God, 'I have borne chastisement; I will not offend any more. 32 That which I see not, teach Thou me; if I have done iniquity, I will do no more.' 33 Should it be according to your mind? He will recompense it, whether you refuse, or whether you choose; and not I. Therefore speak what you know. 34 Let men of understanding tell me, and let a wise man hearken unto me. 35 Job has spoken without knowledge, and his words were without wisdom. 36 My desire is that Job may be tried unto the end because of his answers for wicked men. 37 For he adds rebellion unto his sin; he claps his hands among us and multiplies his words against God."

Chapter 35

1 Elihu spoke moreover and said: 2 "Do you think this to be right, that you said, 'My righteousness is more than God's'? 3 For you said, 'What advantage will it be unto You? What profit shall I have, if I be cleansed from my sin?' 4 I will answer you and your companions with you. 5 Look unto the heavens, and see; and behold the clouds which are higher than you. 6 If you sin, what do you against Him? Or if your transgressions are multiplied, what do you unto Him? 7 If you be righteous, what give you Him? Or what receives He of your hand? 8 Your wickedness may hurt a man as you are, and your righteousness may profit the son of man. 9 By reason of the multitude of oppressions they make the oppressed to cry; they cry out by reason of the arm of the mighty. 10 But none says, 'Where is God my Maker, who gives songs in the night, 11 Who teaches us more than the beasts of the earth, and makes us wiser than the fowls of heaven?' 12 There they cry, but none gives answer, because of the pride of evil men. 13 Surely God will not hear vanity, neither will the Almighty regard it. 14 Although you say you shall not see Him, yet judgment is before Him; therefore trust in Him. 15 But now, because it is not so, He has visited in His anger, yet He knows it not in great extremity; 16 Therefore does Job open his mouth in vain; he multiplies words without knowledge."

Chapter 36

1 Elihu also continued and said, 2 "Suffer me a little, and I will show you that I have yet to speak on God's behalf. 3 I will fetch my knowledge from afar and will ascribe righteousness to my Maker. 4 For truly my words shall not be false; he who is perfect in knowledge is with you. 5 Behold, God is mighty and does not despise any; He is mighty in strength and wisdom. 6 He does not preserve the life of the wicked but gives justice to the afflicted. 7 He does not withdraw His eyes from the righteous; but with kings on the throne, He has seated them forever, and they are exalted. 8 And if they are bound in chains and held in cords of affliction, 9 Then He shows them their work and their transgressions, that they have exceeded. 10 He also opens their ear to instruction and commands that they return from iniquity. 11 If they obey and serve Him, they shall spend their days in prosperity and their years in pleasures. 12 But if they do not obey, they shall perish by the sword, and they shall die without knowledge. 13 But the hypocrites in heart heap up wrath; they do not cry for help when He binds them. 14 Their soul dies in youth, and their life ends among the unclean. 15 He delivers the poor in their affliction and opens their ears in oppression. 16 Even so would He have removed you out of the distress into a broad place where there is no constraint; and what is set on your table would be full of fatness. 17 But you are filled with the judgment due to the wicked; judgment and justice take hold on you. 18 Beware lest He take you away with His stroke; then a great ransom cannot deliver you. 19 Will He

esteem your riches? No, not gold, nor all the forces of strength. 20 Do not long for the night when people are cut off in their place. 21 Take heed, regard not iniquity, for you have chosen this rather than affliction. 22 Behold, God exalts by His power; who teaches like Him? 23 Who has prescribed His way for Him, or who can say, 'You have done wrong'? 24 Remember that you magnify His work, which men behold. 25 Every man may see it; man may behold it afar off. 26 Behold, God is great, and we do not know Him, nor can the number of His years be searched out. 27 For He makes small the drops of water; they pour down rain according to the vapor thereof, 28 Which the clouds do drop and distill upon man abundantly. 29 Also, can anyone understand the spreading of the clouds or the noise of His tabernacle? 30 Behold, He spreads His light upon it and covers the bottom of the sea. 31 For by these He judges the people; He gives food in abundance. 32 With clouds He covers the light and commands it not to shine by the cloud that comes betwixt. 33 The noise thereof shows concerning it, the cattle also concerning the vapor

Chapter 37

1 At this also my heart trembles and is moved out of its place. 2 Hear attentively the noise of His voice and the sound that goes out of His mouth. 3 He directs it under the whole heaven and His lightning to the ends of the earth. 4 After it, a voice roars; He thunders with the voice of His excellency, and He will not stay them when His voice is heard. 5 God thunders marvelously with His voice; great things He does, which we cannot comprehend. 6 For He says to the snow, 'Be upon the earth,' likewise to the small rain and to the great rain of His strength. 7 He seals up the hand of every man so that all men may know His work. 8 Then the beasts go into dens and remain in their places. 9 Out of the south comes the whirlwind, and cold out of the north. 10 By the breath of God, frost is given, and the breadth of the waters is straitened. 11 Also by watering, He wearies the thick cloud; He scatters His bright cloud, 12 And it is turned round about by His counsels, that they may do whatsoever He commands them upon the face of the world in the earth. 13 He causes it to come, whether for correction, or for His land, or for mercy. 14 Hearken unto this, O Job; stand still and consider the wondrous works of God. 15 Do you know when God disposed them and caused the light of His cloud to shine? 16 Do you know the balancing of the clouds, the wondrous works of Him who is perfect in knowledge? 17 How your garments are warm when He quiets the earth by the south wind? 18 Have you with Him spread out the sky, which is strong and as a molten looking glass? 19 Teach us what we shall say unto Him, for we cannot order our speech by reason of darkness. 20 Shall it be told Him that I speak? If a man speaks, surely he shall be swallowed up. 21 And now men do not see the bright light which is in the clouds, but the wind passes and cleanses them. 22 Fair weather comes out of the north; with God is terrible majesty. 23 Touching the Almighty, we cannot find Him out; He is excellent in power and in judgment, and in plenty of justice He will not afflict. 24 Men do therefore fear Him; He does not regard any who are wise of heart."

Chapter 38

1 Then the LORD answered Job out of the whirlwind and said, 2 "Who is this that darkens counsel by words without knowledge? 3 Gird up now your loins like a man, for I will demand of you, and you answer Me. 4 Where were you when I laid the foundations of the earth? Declare, if you have understanding. 5 Who has laid the measures thereof, if you know? Or who has stretched the line upon it? 6 Whereupon are the foundations thereof fastened, or who laid the cornerstone thereof, 7 When the morning stars sang together, and all the sons of God shouted for joy? 8 Or who shut up the sea with doors when it broke forth, as if it had issued out of the womb, 9 When I made the cloud the garment thereof, and thick darkness a swaddling band for it, 10 And broke up for it My decreed place, and set bars and doors, 11 And said, 'Hitherto shall you come, but no further; and here shall your proud waves be stayed'? 12 Have you commanded the morning since your days began and caused the dayspring to know its place, 13 That it might take hold of the ends of the earth, that the wicked might be shaken out of it? 14 It is turned as clay to the seal, and they stand as a garment. 15 And from the wicked their light is withheld, and the high arm shall be broken. 16 Have you entered into the springs of the sea? Or have you walked in the search of the depth? 17 Have the gates of death been opened unto you? Or have you seen the doors of the shadow of death? 18 Have you perceived the breadth of the earth? Declare if you know it all. 19 Where is the way where light dwells? And as for darkness, where is the place thereof, 20 That you should take it to the bound thereof and that you should know the paths to the house thereof? 21 Know you it because you were then born, or because the number of your days is great? 22 Have you entered into the treasures of the snow? Or have you seen the treasures of the hail, 23 Which I have reserved against the time of trouble, against the day of battle and war? 24 By what way is the light parted, which scatters the east wind upon the earth? 25 Who has divided a watercourse for the overflowing of waters, or a way for the lightning of thunder, 26 To cause it to rain on the earth where no man is, on the wilderness wherein there is no man, 27 To satisfy the desolate and waste ground, and to cause the bud of the tender herb to spring forth? 28 Has the rain a father? Or who has begotten the drops of dew? 29 Out of whose womb came the ice? And the hoary frost of heaven, who has gendered it? 30 The waters are hid as with a stone, and the face of the deep is frozen. 31 Can you bind the sweet influences of Pleiades, or loose the bands of Orion? 32 Can you bring forth Mazzaroth in his season? Or can you guide Arcturus with his sons? 33 Know you the ordinances of heaven? Can you set the dominion thereof in the earth? 34 Can you lift up your voice to the clouds, that abundance of waters may cover you? 35 Can you send lightnings, that they may go and say unto you, 'Here we are'? 36 Who has put wisdom in the inward parts? Or who has given understanding to the heart? 37 Who can number the clouds in wisdom? Or who can stay the bottles of heaven, 38 When the dust grows into hardness and the clods cleave fast together?

Chapter 39

1 Will you hunt the prey for the lion or fill the appetite of the young lions, 2 When they couch in their dens and abide in the covert to lie in wait? 3 Who provides for the raven his food, when his young ones cry unto God, they wander for lack of meat? 4 Do you know the time when the wild goats of the rock bring forth? Or can you mark when the hinds do calve? 5 Can you number the months that they fulfill? Or do you know the time when they bring forth? 6 They bow themselves, they bring forth their young ones, they cast out their sorrows. 7 Their young ones are in good liking, they grow up with corn; they go forth and return not unto them. 8 Who has sent out the wild ass free? Or who has loosed the bands of the wild ass? 9 Whose house I have made the wilderness, and the barren land his dwellings. 10 He scorns the multitude of the city, neither regards he the crying of the driver. 11 The range of the mountains is his

pasture, and he searches after every green thing. 12 Will the unicorn be willing to serve you, or abide by your crib? 13 Can you bind the unicorn with his band in the furrow? Or will he harrow the valleys after you? 14 Will you trust him because his strength is great? Or will you leave your labor to him? 15 Will you believe him, that he will bring home your seed and gather it into your barn? 16 Gave you the goodly wings unto the peacocks, or wings and feathers unto the ostrich? 17 Which leaves her eggs in the earth and warms them in dust, 18 And forgets that the foot may crush them or that the wild beast may break them. 19 She is hardened against her young ones, as though they were not hers; her labor is in vain without fear, 20 Because God has deprived her of wisdom, neither has He imparted to her understanding. 21 What time she lifts up herself on high, she scorns the horse and his rider. 22 Have you given the horse strength? Have you clothed his neck with thunder? 23 Can you make him afraid as a grasshopper? The glory of his nostrils is terrible. 24 He paws in the valley, and rejoices in his strength; he goes on to meet the armed men. 25 He mocks at fear, and is not affrighted; neither turns he back from the sword. 26 The quiver rattles against him, the glittering spear and the shield. 27 He swallows the ground with fierceness and rage, neither believes he that it is the sound of the trumpet. 28 He says among the trumpets, 'Ha, ha'; and he smells the battle afar off, the thunder of the captains and the shouting. 29 Does the hawk fly by your wisdom and stretch her wings toward the south? 30 Does the eagle mount up at your command and make her nest on high? 31 She dwells and abides on the rock, upon the crag of the rock, and the strong place. 32 From there she seeks the prey, and her eyes behold afar off. 33 Her young ones also suck up blood, and where the slain are, there is she."

Chapter 40

1 Moreover the LORD answered Job and said, 2 "Shall he that contends with the Almighty instruct Him? He that reproves God, let him answer it." 3 Then Job answered the LORD and said, 4 "Behold, I am vile; what shall I answer You? I will lay my hand upon my mouth. 5 Once have I spoken, but I will not answer; yes, twice, but I will proceed no further." 6 Then the LORD answered Job out of the whirlwind and said, 7 "Gird up your loins now like a man; I will demand of you, and you declare unto Me. 8 Will you also disannul My judgment? Will you condemn Me, that you may be righteous? 9 Have you an arm like God? Or can you thunder with a voice like Him? 10 Deck yourself now with majesty and excellency, and array yourself with glory and beauty. 11 Cast abroad the rage of your wrath; and behold everyone that is proud, and abase him. 12 Look on everyone that is proud, and bring him low; and tread down the wicked in their place. 13 Hide them in the dust together and bind their faces in secret. 14 Then will I also confess unto you that your own right hand can save you. 15 Behold now behemoth, which I made with you; he eats grass as an ox. 16 Lo now, his strength is in his loins, and his force is in the navel of his belly. 17 He moves his tail like a cedar; the sinews of his stones are wrapped together. 18 His bones are as strong pieces of brass; his bones are like bars of iron. 19 He is the chief of the ways of God; He that made him can make His sword to approach unto him. 20 Surely the mountains bring him forth food, where all the beasts of the field play. 21 He lies under the shady trees, in the covert of the reed and fens. 22 The shady trees cover him with their shadow; the willows of the brook compass him about. 23 Behold, he drinks up a river, and hastes not; he trusts that he can draw up Jordan into his mouth. 24 He takes it with his eyes; his nose pierces through snares

Chapter 41

1 Can you draw out leviathan with a hook? Or his tongue with a cord which you let down? 2 Can you put a hook into his nose? Or bore his jaw through with a thorn? 3 Will he make many supplications unto you? Will he speak soft words unto you? 4 Will he make a covenant with you? Will you take him for a servant forever? 5 Will you play with him as with a bird? Or will you bind him for your maidens? 6 Shall the companions make a banquet of him? Shall they part him among the merchants? 7 Can you fill his skin with barbed irons? Or his head with fish spears? 8 Lay your hand upon him, remember the battle, do no more. 9 Behold, the hope of him is in vain; shall not one be cast down even at the sight of him? 10 None is so fierce that dare stir him up; who then is able to stand before Me? 11 Who has prevented Me, that I should repay him? Whatsoever is under the whole heaven is Mine. 12 I will not conceal his parts, nor his power, nor his comely proportion. 13 Who can discover the face of his garment? Or who can come to him with his double bridle? 14 Who can open the doors of his face? His teeth are terrible round about. 15 His scales are his pride, shut up together as with a close seal. 16 One is so near to another that no air can come between them. 17 They are joined one to another, they stick together, that they cannot be sundered. 18 By his sneezings a light shines, and his eyes are like the eyelids of the morning. 19 Out of his mouth go burning lamps, and sparks of fire leap out. 20 Out of his nostrils goes smoke, as out of a seething pot or cauldron. 21 His breath kindles coals, and a flame goes out of his mouth. 22 In his neck remains strength, and sorrow is turned into joy before him. 23 The flakes of his flesh are joined together; they are firm in themselves; they cannot be moved. 24 His heart is as firm as a stone, yes, as hard as a piece of the nether millstone. 25 When he raises up himself, the mighty are afraid; by reason of breakings they purify themselves. 26 The sword of him that lays at him cannot hold, the spear, the dart, nor the habergeon. 27 He esteems iron as straw, and brass as rotten wood. 28 The arrow cannot make him flee; slingstones are turned with him into stubble. 29 Darts are counted as stubble; he laughs at the shaking of a spear. 30 Sharp stones are under him; he spreads sharp pointed things upon the mire. 31 He makes the deep to boil like a pot; he makes the sea like a pot of ointment. 32 He makes a path to shine after him; one would think the deep to be hoary. 33 Upon earth there is not his like, who is made without fear. 34 He beholds all high things; he is a king over all the children of pride."

Chapter 42

1 Then Job answered the LORD and said, 2 "I know that You can do everything and that no thought can be withheld from You. 3 Who is he that hides counsel without knowledge? Therefore have I uttered that I understood not, things too wonderful for me, which I knew not. 4 Hear, I beseech You, and I will speak; I will demand of You, and declare unto me. 5 I have heard of You by the hearing of the ear, but now my eye sees You. 6 Therefore I abhor myself and repent in dust and ashes." 7 And it was so, that after the LORD had spoken these words unto Job, the LORD said to Eliphaz the Temanite, "My wrath is kindled against you and against your two friends, for you have not spoken of Me the thing that is right, as My servant Job has. 8 Therefore take unto you now seven bullocks and seven rams, and go to My servant Job, and offer up for yourselves a burnt offering, and My servant Job shall pray for you. For him will I accept, lest I deal with you after your folly in that you have not spoken of Me the thing which is right, like My servant Job." 9

So Eliphaz the Temanite, Bildad the Shuhite, and Zophar the Naamathite went and did according as the LORD commanded them; the LORD also accepted Job. 10 And the LORD turned the captivity of Job when he prayed for his friends. Also the LORD gave Job twice as much as he had before. 11 Then came there unto him all his brothers, and all his sisters, and all those who had been of his acquaintance before, and did eat bread with him in his house. And they bemoaned him and comforted him over all the evil that the LORD had brought upon him. Every man also gave him a piece of money and everyone an earring of gold. 12 So the LORD blessed the latter end of Job more than his beginning, for he had fourteen thousand sheep, six thousand camels, a thousand yoke of oxen, and a thousand she-asses. 13 He had also seven sons and three daughters. 14 And he called the name of the first Jemima, and the name of the second Kezia, and the name of the third Kerenhappuch. 15 And in all the land were no women found so fair as the daughters of Job, and their father gave them inheritance among their brothers. 16 After this Job lived a hundred and forty years and saw his sons, and his sons' sons, even four generations. 17 So Job died, being old and full of days

19. Psalms

Chapter 1

1 Blessed is the man that walks not in the counsel of the wicked, nor stands in the way of sinners, nor sits in the seat of the scornful. 2 But his delight is in the law of the Lord, and in His law he meditates day and night. 3 He shall be like a tree planted by the rivers of water, that brings forth its fruit in its season, whose leaf also shall not wither; and whatever he does shall prosper. 4 The wicked are not so, but are like the chaff which the wind drives away. 5 Therefore the wicked shall not stand in the judgment, nor sinners in the congregation of the righteous. 6 For the Lord knows the way of the righteous, but the way of the wicked shall perish

Chapter 2

1 Why do the heathen rage, and the people imagine a vain thing? 2 The kings of the earth set themselves, and the rulers take counsel together, against the Lord and against His Anointed, saying, 3 Let us break their bonds asunder, and cast away their cords from us. 4 He that sits in the heavens shall laugh: the Lord shall have them in derision. 5 Then shall He speak to them in His wrath, and vex them in His sore displeasure: 6 Yet have I set My King upon My holy hill of Zion. 7 I will declare the decree: the Lord has said to me, You are My Son; this day have I begotten You. 8 Ask of Me, and I shall give You the heathen for Your inheritance, and the uttermost parts of the earth for Your possession. 9 You shall break them with a rod of iron; You shall dash them in pieces like a potter's vessel. 10 Be wise now therefore, O you kings: be instructed, you judges of the earth. 11 Serve the Lord with fear, and rejoice with trembling. 12 Kiss the Son, lest He be angry, and you perish from the way, when His wrath is kindled but a little. Blessed are all they that put their trust in Him

Chapter 3

A Psalm of David, when he fled from Absalom his son. 1 Lord, how are they increased that trouble me! Many are they that rise up against me. 2 Many there be which say of my soul, There is no help for him in God. Selah. 3 But You, O Lord, are a shield for me; my glory, and the lifter up of my head. 4 I cried to the Lord with my voice, and He heard me out of His holy hill. Selah. 5 I laid me down and slept; I awoke; for the Lord sustained me. 6 I will not be afraid of ten thousands of people, that have set themselves against me round about. 7 Arise, O Lord; save me, O my God: for You have smitten all my enemies upon the cheekbone; You have broken the teeth of the ungodly. 8 Salvation belongs to the Lord: Your blessing is upon Your people. Selah

Chapter 4

To the chief Musician on Neginoth, A Psalm of David. 1 Hear me when I call, O God of my righteousness: You have enlarged me when I was in distress; have mercy upon me, and hear my prayer. 2 O you sons of men, how long will you turn my glory into shame? How long will you love vanity, and seek after falsehood? Selah. 3 But know that the Lord has set apart him that is godly for Himself: the Lord will hear when I call to Him. 4 Stand in awe, and sin not: commune with your own heart upon your bed, and be still. Selah. 5 Offer the sacrifices of righteousness, and put your trust in the Lord. 6 There be many that say, Who will show us any good? Lord, lift You up the light of Your countenance upon us. 7 You have put gladness in my heart, more than in the time that their corn and their wine increased. 8 I will both lay me down in peace, and sleep: for You, Lord, only make me dwell in safety

Chapter 5

To the chief Musician upon Nehiloth, A Psalm of David. 1 Give ear to my words, O Lord, consider my meditation. 2 Listen to the voice of my cry, my King, and my God: for unto You will I pray. 3 My voice shall You hear in the morning, O Lord; in the morning will I direct my prayer to You, and will look up. 4 For You are not a God that has pleasure in wickedness: neither shall evil dwell with You. 5 The foolish shall not stand in Your sight: You hate all workers of iniquity. 6 You shall destroy them that speak falsehood: the Lord will abhor the bloody and deceitful man. 7 But as for me, I will come into Your house in the multitude of Your mercy: and in Your fear will I worship toward Your holy temple. 8 Lead me, O Lord, in Your righteousness because of my enemies; make Your way straight before my face. 9 For there is no faithfulness in their mouth; their inward part is very wickedness; their throat is an open sepulcher; they flatter with their tongue. 10 Destroy them, O God; let them fall by their own counsels; cast them out in the multitude of their transgressions; for they have rebelled against You. 11 But let all those that put their trust in You rejoice: let them ever shout for joy, because You defend them: let them also that love Your name be joyful in You. 12 For You, Lord, will bless the righteous; with favor will You compass him as with a shield

Chapter 6

To the chief Musician on Neginoth upon Sheminith, A Psalm of David. 1 O Lord, rebuke me not in Your anger, neither chasten me in Your hot displeasure. 2 Have mercy upon me, O Lord; for I am weak: O Lord, heal me; for my bones are vexed. 3 My soul is also sore vexed: but You, O Lord, how long? 4 Return, O Lord, deliver my soul: oh save me for Your mercies' sake. 5 For in death there is no remembrance of You: in the grave who shall give You thanks? 6 I am weary with my groaning; all the night make I my bed to swim; I water my couch with my tears. 7 My eye is consumed because of grief; it waxes old because of all my enemies. 8 Depart from me, all you workers of iniquity; for the Lord has heard the voice of my weeping. 9 The Lord has heard my supplication; the Lord will receive my prayer. 10 Let all my enemies be ashamed and sore vexed: let them return and be ashamed suddenly

Chapter 7

Shiggaion of David, which he sang unto the Lord, concerning the words of Cush the Benjamite. 1 O

Lord my God, in You do I put my trust: save me from all them that persecute me, and deliver me: 2 Lest he tear my soul like a lion, rending it in pieces, while there is none to deliver. 3 O Lord my God, if I have done this; if there be iniquity in my hands; 4 If I have rewarded evil to him that was at peace with me; (yes, I have delivered him that without cause is my enemy:) 5 Let the enemy persecute my soul, and take it; yes, let him tread down my life upon the earth, and lay my honor in the dust. Selah. 6 Arise, O Lord, in Your anger, lift up Yourself because of the rage of my enemies: and awake for me to the judgment that You have commanded. 7 So shall the congregation of the people compass You about: for their sakes therefore return on high. 8 The Lord shall judge the people: judge me, O Lord, according to my righteousness, and according to my integrity that is in me. 9 Oh let the wickedness of the wicked come to an end; but establish the just: for the righteous God tries the hearts and reins. 10 My defense is of God, who saves the upright in heart. 11 God judges the righteous, and God is angry with the wicked every day. 12 If he turn not, He will whet His sword; He has bent His bow, and made it ready. 13 He has also prepared for him the instruments of death; He ordains His arrows against the persecutors. 14 Behold, he travails with iniquity, and has conceived mischief, and brought forth falsehood. 15 He made a pit, and digged it, and is fallen into the ditch which he made. 16 His mischief shall return upon his own head, and his violent dealing shall come down upon his own pate. 17 I will praise the Lord according to His righteousness: and will sing praise to the name of the Lord most high

Chapter 8

To the chief Musician upon Gittith, A Psalm of David. 1 O Lord our Lord, how excellent is Your name in all the earth! Who has set Your glory above the heavens. 2 Out of the mouth of babes and sucklings have You ordained strength because of Your enemies, that You might still the enemy and the avenger. 3 When I consider Your heavens, the work of Your fingers, the moon and the stars, which You have ordained; 4 What is man, that You are mindful of him? and the son of man, that You visit him? 5 For You have made him a little lower than the angels, and have crowned him with glory and honor. 6 You made him to have dominion over the works of Your hands; You have put all things under his feet: 7 All sheep and oxen, yes, and the beasts of the field; 8 The fowl of the air, and the fish of the sea, and whatsoever passes through the paths of the seas. 9 O Lord our Lord, how excellent is Your name in all the earth!

Chapter 9

To the chief Musician upon Muthlabben, A Psalm of David. 1 I will praise You, O Lord, with my whole heart; I will show forth all Your marvelous works. 2 I will be glad and rejoice in You: I will sing praise to Your name, O You Most High. 3 When my enemies are turned back, they shall fall and perish at Your presence. 4 For You have maintained my right and my cause; You sat in the throne judging right. 5 You have rebuked the heathen, You have destroyed the wicked, You have put out their name for ever and ever. 6 O you enemy, destructions are come to a perpetual end: and you have destroyed cities; their memorial is perished with them. 7 But the Lord shall endure for ever: He has prepared His throne for judgment. 8 And He shall judge the world in righteousness, He shall minister judgment to the people in uprightness. 9 The Lord also will be a refuge for the oppressed, a refuge in times of trouble. 10 And they that know Your name will put their trust in You: for You, Lord, have not forsaken them that seek You. 11 Sing praises to the Lord, which dwells in Zion:

declare among the people His doings. 12 When He makes inquisition for blood, He remembers them: He forgets not the cry of the humble. 13 Have mercy upon me, O Lord; consider my trouble which I suffer of them that hate me, You that lift me up from the gates of death: 14 That I may show forth all Your praise in the gates of the daughter of Zion: I will rejoice in Your salvation. 15 The heathen are sunk down in the pit that they made: in the net which they hid is their own foot taken. 16 The Lord is known by the judgment which He executes: the wicked is snared in the work of his own hands. Higgaion. Selah. 17 The wicked shall be turned into hell, and all the nations that forget God. 18 For the needy shall not always be forgotten: the expectation of the poor shall not perish for ever. 19 Arise, O Lord; let not man prevail: let the heathen be judged in Your sight. 20 Put them in fear, O Lord: that the nations may know themselves to be but men. Selah

Chapter 10

1 Why do You stand afar off, O Lord? Why do You hide Yourself in times of trouble? 2 The wicked in his pride does persecute the poor: let them be taken in the devices that they have imagined. 3 For the wicked boasts of his heart's desire, and blesses the covetous, whom the Lord abhors. 4 The wicked, through the pride of his countenance, will not seek after God: God is not in all his thoughts. 5 His ways are always grievous; Your judgments are far above out of his sight: as for all his enemies, he puffs at them. 6 He has said in his heart, I shall not be moved: for I shall never be in adversity. 7 His mouth is full of cursing and deceit and fraud: under his tongue is mischief and vanity. 8 He sits in the lurking places of the villages: in the secret places does he murder the innocent: his eyes are privily set against the poor. 9 He lies in wait secretly as a lion in his den: he lies in wait to catch the poor: he does catch the poor, when he draws him into his net. 10 He crouches, and humbles himself, that the poor may fall by his strong ones. 11 He has said in his heart, God has forgotten: He hides His face; He will never see it. 12 Arise, O Lord; O God, lift up Your hand: forget not the humble. 13 Why does the wicked contemn God? He has said in his heart, You will not require it. 14 You have seen it; for You behold mischief and spite, to requite it with Your hand: the poor commits himself to You; You are the helper of the fatherless. 15 Break the arm of the wicked and the evil man: seek out his wickedness till You find none. 16 The Lord is King for ever and ever: the heathen are perished out of His land. 17 Lord, You have heard the desire of the humble: You will prepare their heart, You will cause Your ear to hear: 18 To judge the fatherless and the oppressed, that the man of the earth may no more oppress

Chapter 11

To the chief Musician, A Psalm of David. 1 In the Lord put I my trust: how say you to my soul, Flee as a bird to your mountain? 2 For, lo, the wicked bend their bow, they make ready their arrow upon the string, that they may privily shoot at the upright in heart. 3 If the foundations be destroyed, what can the righteous do? 4 The Lord is in His holy temple, the Lord's throne is in heaven: His eyes behold, His eyelids try, the children of men. 5 The Lord tries the righteous: but the wicked and him that loves violence His soul hates. 6 Upon the wicked He shall rain snares, fire and brimstone, and an horrible tempest: this shall be the portion of their cup. 7 For the righteous Lord loves righteousness; His countenance does behold the upright

Chapter 12

To the chief Musician upon Sheminith, A Psalm of David. 1 Help, Lord; for the godly man ceases; for the faithful fail from among the children of men. 2 They speak vanity every one with his neighbor: with flattering lips and with a double heart do they speak. 3 The Lord shall cut off all flattering lips, and the tongue that speaks proud things: 4 Who have said, With our tongue will we prevail; our lips are our own: who is lord over us? 5 For the oppression of the poor, for the sighing of the needy, now will I arise, says the Lord; I will set him in safety from him that puffs at him. 6 The words of the Lord are pure words: as silver tried in a furnace of earth, purified seven times. 7 You shall keep them, O Lord, You shall preserve them from this generation for ever. 8 The wicked walk on every side, when the vilest men are exalted

Chapter 13

To the chief Musician, A Psalm of David. 1 How long will You forget me, O Lord? For ever? How long will You hide Your face from me? 2 How long shall I take counsel in my soul, having sorrow in my heart daily? How long shall my enemy be exalted over me? 3 Consider and hear me, O Lord my God: lighten my eyes, lest I sleep the sleep of death; 4 Lest my enemy say, I have prevailed against him; and those that trouble me rejoice when I am moved. 5 But I have trusted in Your mercy; my heart shall rejoice in Your salvation. 6 I will sing to the Lord, because He has dealt bountifully with me

Chapter 14

To the chief Musician, A Psalm of David. 1 The fool has said in his heart, There is no God. They are corrupt, they have done abominable works, there is none that does good. 2 The Lord looked down from heaven upon the children of men, to see if there were any that did understand, and seek God. 3 They are all gone aside, they are all together become filthy: there is none that does good, no, not one. 4 Have all the workers of iniquity no knowledge? Who eat up my people as they eat bread, and call not upon the Lord. 5 There were they in great fear: for God is in the generation of the righteous. 6 You have shamed the counsel of the poor, because the Lord is his refuge. 7 Oh that the salvation of Israel were come out of Zion! When the Lord brings back the captivity of His people, Jacob shall rejoice, and Israel shall be glad

Chapter 15

A Psalm of David. 1 Lord, who shall abide in Your tabernacle? Who shall dwell in Your holy hill? 2 He that walks uprightly, and works righteousness, and speaks the truth in his heart. 3 He that backbites not with his tongue, nor does evil to his neighbor, nor takes up a reproach against his neighbor. 4 In whose eyes a vile person is contemned; but he honors them that fear the Lord. He that swears to his own hurt, and changes not. 5 He that puts not out his money to usury, nor takes reward against the innocent. He that does these things shall never be moved

Chapter 16

Michtam of David. 1 Preserve me, O God, for in You do I put my trust. 2 O my soul, you have said to the Lord, "You are my Lord; my goodness is nothing apart from You." 3 As for the saints who are on the earth, "They are the excellent ones, in whom is all my delight." 4 Their sorrows shall be multiplied who hasten after another god; their drink offerings of blood I will not offer, nor take up their names on my lips. 5 O Lord, You are the portion of my inheritance and my cup; You maintain my lot. 6 The lines have fallen to me in pleasant places; yes, I have a good inheritance. 7 I will bless the Lord who has given me counsel; my heart also instructs me in the night seasons. 8 I have set the Lord always before me; because He is at my right hand, I shall not be moved. 9 Therefore my heart is glad, and my glory rejoices; my flesh also will rest in hope. 10 For You will not leave my soul in Sheol, nor will You allow Your Holy One to see corruption. 11 You will show me the path of life; in Your presence is fullness of joy; at Your right hand are pleasures forevermore

Chapter 17

The prayer of David. 1 Hear a just cause, O Lord, attend to my cry; give ear to my prayer which is not from deceitful lips. 2 Let my vindication come from Your presence; let Your eyes look on the things that are upright. 3 You have tested my heart; You have visited me in the night; You have tried me and have found nothing; I have purposed that my mouth shall not transgress. 4 Concerning the works of men, by the word of Your lips, I have kept myself from the paths of the destroyer. 5 Uphold my steps in Your paths, that my footsteps may not slip. 6 I have called upon You, for You will hear me, O God; incline Your ear to me and hear my speech. 7 Show Your marvelous lovingkindness by Your right hand, O You who save those who trust in You from those who rise up against them. 8 Keep me as the apple of Your eye; hide me under the shadow of Your wings, 9 from the wicked who oppress me, from my deadly enemies who surround me. 10 They have closed up their fat hearts; with their mouths they speak proudly. 11 They have now surrounded us in our steps; they have set their eyes, crouching down to the earth, 12 as a lion is eager to tear his prey, and like a young lion lurking in secret places. 13 Arise, O Lord, confront him, cast him down; deliver my life from the wicked with Your sword, 14 with Your hand from men, O Lord, from men of the world who have their portion in this life, and whose belly You fill with Your hidden treasure. They are satisfied with children and leave the rest of their substance for their babes. 15 As for me, I will see Your face in righteousness; I shall be satisfied when I awake in Your likeness

Chapter 18

To the chief Musician. A Psalm of David the servant of the Lord, who spoke to the Lord the words of this song in the day that the Lord delivered him from the hand of all his enemies, and from the hand of Saul. And he said: 1 I will love You, O Lord, my strength. 2 The Lord is my rock and my fortress and my deliverer; my God, my strength, in whom I will trust; my shield and the horn of my salvation, my stronghold. 3 I will call upon the Lord, who is worthy to be praised; so shall I be saved from my enemies. 4 The pangs of death surrounded me, and the floods of ungodliness made me afraid. 5 The sorrows of Sheol surrounded me; the snares of death confronted me. 6 In my distress I called upon the Lord, and cried out to my God; He heard my voice from His temple, and my cry came before Him, even to His ears. 7 Then the earth shook and trembled; the foundations of the hills also quaked and were shaken, because He was angry. 8 Smoke went up from His nostrils, and devouring fire from His mouth; coals were kindled by it. 9 He bowed the heavens also, and came down with darkness under His feet. 10 And He rode upon a cherub, and flew; He flew upon the wings of the wind. 11 He made darkness His secret place; His canopy around Him was dark waters and thick clouds of the skies. 12 From the brightness before Him, His thick clouds passed with hailstones and coals of fire. 13 The Lord thundered from heaven, and the Most High uttered His voice, hailstones and coals of fire. 14 He sent out His arrows and scattered the foe, lightnings in abundance, and He vanquished them. 15 Then the channels of the sea were seen, the foundations of the world were uncovered at Your rebuke, O Lord, at the blast of the breath of Your nostrils. 16 He sent from above, He took me; He drew me out of many waters. 17 He delivered me from my strong enemy, from those who hated me, for they were too strong for me. 18 They confronted me in the day of my calamity, but the Lord was my support. 19 He also brought me out into a broad place; He delivered me because He delighted in me. 20 The Lord rewarded me according to my righteousness; according to the cleanness of my hands He has recompensed me. 21 For I have kept the ways of the Lord, and have not wickedly departed from my God. 22 For all His judgments were before me, and I did not put away His statutes from me. 23 I was also blameless before Him, and I kept myself from my iniquity. 24 Therefore the Lord has recompensed me according to my righteousness, according to the cleanness of my hands in His sight. 25 With the merciful You will show Yourself merciful; with a blameless man You will show Yourself blameless; 26 with the pure You will show Yourself pure; and with the devious You will show Yourself shrewd. 27 For You will save the humble people, but will bring down haughty looks. 28 For You will light my lamp; the Lord my God will enlighten my darkness. 29 For by You I can run against a troop, by my God I can leap over a wall. 30 As for God, His way is perfect; the word of the Lord is proven; He is a shield to all who trust in Him. 31 For who is God, except the Lord? And who is a rock, except our God? 32 It is God who arms me with strength, and makes my way perfect. 33 He makes my feet like the feet of deer, and sets me on my high places. 34 He teaches my hands to make war, so that my arms can bend a bow of bronze. 35 You have also given me the shield of Your salvation; Your right hand has held me up, Your gentleness has made me great. 36 You enlarged my path under me, so my feet did not slip. 37 I have pursued my enemies and overtaken them; neither did I turn back again till they were destroyed. 38 I have wounded them, so that they could not rise; they have fallen under my feet. 39 For You have armed me with strength for the battle; You have subdued under me those who rose up against me. 40 You have also given me the necks of my enemies, so that I destroyed those who hated me. 41 They cried out, but there was none to save; even to the Lord, but He did not answer them. 42 Then I beat them as fine as the dust before the wind; I cast them out like dirt in the streets. 43 You have delivered me from the strivings of the people; You have made me the head of the nations; a people I have not known shall serve me. 44 As soon as they hear of me they obey me; the foreigners submit to me. 45 The foreigners fade away, and come frightened from their hideouts. 46 The Lord lives! Blessed be my Rock! Let the God of my salvation be exalted. 47 It is God who avenges me, and subdues the peoples under me; 48 He delivers me from my enemies. You also lift me up above those who rise against me; You have delivered me from the violent man. 49 Therefore I will give thanks to You, O Lord, among the Gentiles, and sing praises to Your name. 50 Great deliverance He gives to His king, and shows mercy to His anointed, to David and his descendants forevermore

Chapter 19

To the chief Musician. A Psalm of David. 1 The heavens declare the glory of God; and the firmament shows His handiwork. 2 Day unto day utters speech, and night unto night reveals knowledge. 3 There is no speech nor language where their voice is not heard. 4 Their line has gone out through all the earth, and their words to the end of the world. In them He has set a tabernacle for the sun, 5 which is like a bridegroom coming out of his chamber, and rejoices like a strong man to run its race. 6 Its rising is from one end of heaven, and its circuit to the other end; and there is nothing hidden from its heat. 7 The law of the Lord is perfect, converting the soul; the testimony of the Lord is sure, making wise the simple; 8 the statutes of the Lord are right, rejoicing the heart; the commandment of the Lord is pure, enlightening the eyes; 9 the fear of the Lord is clean, enduring forever; the judgments of the Lord are true and righteous altogether. 10 More to be desired are they than gold, yea, than much fine gold; sweeter also than honey and the honeycomb. 11 Moreover by them Your servant is warned, and in keeping them there is great reward. 12 Who can understand his errors? Cleanse me from secret faults. 13 Keep back Your servant also from presumptuous sins; let them not have dominion over me. Then I shall be blameless, and I shall be innocent of great transgression. 14 Let the words of my mouth and the meditation of my heart be acceptable in Your sight, O Lord, my strength and my Redeemer

Chapter 20

To the chief Musician. A Psalm of David. 1 May the Lord answer you in the day of trouble; may the name of the God of Jacob defend you; 2 may He send you help from the sanctuary, and strengthen you out of Zion; 3 may He remember all your offerings, and accept your burnt sacrifice. Selah 4 May He grant you according to your heart's desire, and fulfill all your purpose. 5 We will rejoice in your salvation, and in the name of our God we will set up our banners! May the Lord fulfill all your petitions. 6 Now I know that the Lord saves His anointed; He will answer him from His holy heaven with the saving strength of His right hand. 7 Some trust in chariots, and some in horses; but we will remember the name of the Lord our God. 8 They have bowed down and fallen; but we have risen and stand upright. 9 Save, Lord! May the King answer us when we call

Chapter 21

To the chief Musician. A Psalm of David. 1 The king shall have joy in Your strength, O Lord; and in Your salvation how greatly shall he rejoice! 2 You have given him his heart's desire, and have not withheld the request of his lips. Selah 3 For You meet him with the blessings of goodness; You set a crown of pure gold upon his head. 4 He asked life from You, and You gave it to him—length of days forever and ever. 5 His glory is great in Your salvation; honor and majesty You have placed upon him. 6 For You have made him most blessed forever; You have made him exceedingly glad with Your presence. 7 For the king trusts in the Lord, and through the mercy of the Most High he shall not be moved. 8 Your hand will find all Your enemies; Your right hand will find those who hate You. 9 You shall make them as a fiery oven in the time of Your anger; the Lord shall swallow them up in His wrath, and the fire shall devour them. 10 Their offspring You shall destroy from the earth, and their descendants from among the sons of men. 11 For they intended evil against You; they devised a plot which they are not able to perform. 12 Therefore You will make them turn their back; You will make ready Your arrows on Your string toward their faces. 13 Be exalted, O Lord, in Your own strength! We will sing and praise Your power

Chapter 22

To the chief Musician upon Aijeleth Shahar, A Psalm of David. 1 My God, My God, why have You forsaken Me? Why are You so far from helping Me, and from the words of My groaning? 2 O My God, I cry in the daytime, but You do not hear; and in the night season, and am not silent. 3 But You are holy, enthroned in the praises of Israel. 4 Our fathers trusted in You; they trusted, and You delivered them. 5 They cried to You, and were delivered; they trusted in You, and were not ashamed. 6 But I am a worm, and no man; a reproach of men, and despised by the people. 7 All those who see Me ridicule Me; they shoot out the lip, they shake the head, saying, 8 "He trusted in the Lord, let Him rescue Him; let Him deliver Him, since He delights in Him!" 9 But You are He who took Me out of the womb; You made Me trust while on My mother's breasts. 10 I was cast upon You from birth. From My mother's womb You have been My God. 11 Be not far from Me, for trouble is near; for there is none to help. 12 Many bulls have surrounded Me; strong bulls of Bashan have encircled Me. 13 They gape at Me with their mouths, as a raging and roaring lion. 14 I am poured out like water, and all My bones are out of joint; My heart is like wax; it has melted within Me. 15 My strength is dried up like a potsherd, and My tongue clings to My jaws; You have brought Me to the dust of death. 16 For dogs have surrounded Me; the congregation of the wicked has enclosed Me. They pierced My hands and My feet; 17 I can count all My bones. They look and stare at Me. 18 They divide My garments among them, and for My clothing they cast lots. 19 But You, O Lord, do not be far from Me; O My Strength, hasten to help Me! 20 Deliver Me from the sword, My precious life from the power of the dog. 21 Save Me from the lion's mouth and from the horns of the wild oxen! You have answered Me. 22 I will declare Your name to My brethren; in the midst of the assembly I will praise You. 23 You who fear the Lord, praise Him! All you descendants of Jacob, glorify Him, and fear Him, all you offspring of Israel! 24 For He has not despised nor abhorred the affliction of the afflicted; nor has He hidden His face from Him; but when He cried to Him, He heard. 25 My praise shall be of You in the great assembly; I will pay My vows before those who fear Him. 26 The poor shall eat and be satisfied; those who seek Him will praise the Lord. Let your heart live forever! 27 All the ends of the world shall remember and turn to the Lord, and all the families of the nations shall worship before You. 28 For the kingdom is the Lord's, and He rules over the nations. 29 All the prosperous of the earth shall eat and worship; all those who go down to the dust shall bow before Him, even he who cannot keep himself alive. 30 A posterity shall serve Him. It will be recounted of the Lord to the next generation, 31 they will come and declare His righteousness to a people who will be born, that He has done this

Chapter 23

A Psalm of David. 1 The Lord is my shepherd; I shall not want. 2 He makes me to lie down in green pastures; He leads me beside the still waters. 3 He restores my soul; He leads me in the paths of righteousness for His name's sake. 4 Yea, though I walk through the valley of the shadow of death, I will fear no evil; for You are with me; Your rod and Your staff, they comfort me. 5 You prepare a table before me in the presence of my enemies; You anoint my head with oil; my cup runs over. 6 Surely goodness and mercy shall follow me all the days of my life; and I will dwell in the house of the Lord forever

Chapter 24

A Psalm of David. 1 The earth is the Lord's, and all its fullness, the world and those who dwell therein. 2 For He has founded it upon the seas, and established it upon the waters. 3 Who may ascend into the hill of the Lord? Or who may stand in His holy place? 4 He who has clean hands and a pure heart, who has not lifted up his soul to an idol, nor sworn deceitfully. 5 He shall receive blessing from the Lord, and righteousness from the God of his salvation. 6 This is Jacob, the generation of those who seek Him, who seek Your face. Selah 7 Lift up your heads, O you gates! And be lifted up, you everlasting doors! And the King of glory shall come in. 8 Who is this King of glory? The Lord strong and mighty, the Lord mighty in battle. 9 Lift up your heads, O you gates! Lift up, you everlasting doors! And the King of glory shall come in. 10 Who is this King of glory? The Lord of hosts, He is the King of glory. Selah

Chapter 25

A Psalm of David. 1 To You, O Lord, I lift up my soul. 2 O my God, I trust in You; let me not be ashamed; let not my enemies triumph over me. 3 Indeed, let no one who waits on You be ashamed; let those be ashamed who deal treacherously without cause. 4 Show me Your ways, O Lord; teach me Your paths. 5 Lead me in Your truth and teach me, for You are the God of my salvation; on You I wait all the day. 6 Remember, O Lord, Your tender mercies and Your lovingkindnesses, for they are from of old. 7 Do not remember the sins of my youth, nor my transgressions; according to Your mercy remember me, for Your goodness' sake, O Lord. 8 Good and upright is the Lord; therefore He teaches sinners in the way. 9 The humble He guides in justice, and the humble He teaches His way. 10 All the paths of the Lord are mercy and truth, to such as keep His covenant and His testimonies. 11 For Your name's sake, O Lord, pardon my iniquity, for it is great. 12 Who is the man that fears the Lord? Him shall He teach in the way He chooses. 13 He himself shall dwell in prosperity, and his descendants shall inherit the earth. 14 The secret of the Lord is with those who fear Him, and He will show them His covenant. 15 My eyes are ever toward the Lord, for He shall pluck my feet out of the net. 16 Turn Yourself to me, and have mercy on me, for I am desolate and afflicted. 17 The troubles of my heart have enlarged; bring me out of my distresses! 18 Look on my affliction and my pain, and forgive all my sins. 19 Consider my enemies, for they are many; and they hate me with cruel hatred. 20 Keep my soul, and deliver me; let me not be ashamed, for I put my trust in You. 21 Let integrity and uprightness preserve me, for I wait for You. 22 Redeem Israel, O God, out of all their troubles!

Chapter 26

A Psalm of David. 1 Vindicate me, O Lord, for I have walked in my integrity. I have also trusted in the Lord; I shall not slip. 2 Examine me, O Lord, and prove me; try my mind and my heart. 3 For Your lovingkindness is before my eyes, and I have walked in Your truth. 4 I have not sat with idolatrous mortals, nor will I go in with hypocrites. 5 I have hated the assembly of evildoers, and will not sit with the wicked. 6 I will wash my hands in innocence; so I will go about Your altar, O Lord, 7 that I may proclaim with the voice of thanksgiving, and tell of all Your wondrous works. 8 Lord, I have loved the habitation of Your house, and the place where Your glory dwells. 9 Do not gather my soul with sinners, nor my life with bloodthirsty men, 10 in whose hands is a sinister scheme, and whose right hand is full of bribes. 11 But as for me, I will walk in my integrity; redeem me and be merciful to me. 12 My foot stands in an even place; in the congregations I will bless the Lord

Chapter 27

A Psalm of David. 1 The Lord is my light and my salvation; whom shall I fear? The Lord is the strength of my life; of whom shall I be afraid? 2 When the wicked came against me to eat up my flesh, my enemies and foes, they stumbled and fell. 3 Though an army may encamp against me, my heart shall not fear; though war may rise against me, in this I will be confident. 4 One thing I have desired of the Lord, that will I seek: that I may dwell in the house of the Lord all the days of my life, to behold the beauty of the Lord, and to inquire in His temple. 5 For in the time of trouble He shall hide me in His pavilion; in the secret place of His tabernacle He shall hide me; He shall set me high upon a rock. 6 And now my head shall be lifted up above my enemies all around me; therefore I will offer sacrifices of joy in His tabernacle; I will sing, yes, I will sing praises to the Lord. 7 Hear, O Lord, when I cry with my voice! Have mercy also upon me, and answer me. 8 When You said, "Seek My face," my heart said to You, "Your face, Lord, I will seek." 9 Do not hide Your face from me; do not turn Your servant away in anger; You have been my help; do not leave me nor forsake me, O God of my salvation. 10 When my father and my mother forsake me, then the Lord will take care of me. 11 Teach me Your way, O Lord, and lead me in a smooth path, because of my enemies. 12 Do not deliver me to the will of my adversaries; for false witnesses have risen against me, and such as breathe out violence. 13 I would have lost heart, unless I had believed that I would see the goodness of the Lord in the land of the living. 14 Wait on the Lord; be of good courage, and He shall strengthen your heart; wait, I say, on the Lord!

Chapter 28

A Psalm of David. 1 To You I will cry, O Lord my Rock: do not be silent to me, lest, if You are silent to me, I become like those who go down to the pit. 2 Hear the voice of my supplications when I cry to You, when I lift up my hands toward Your holy sanctuary. 3 Do not take me away with the wicked and with the workers of iniquity, who speak peace to their neighbors, but evil is in their hearts. 4 Give them according to their deeds, and according to the wickedness of their endeavors; give them according to the work of their hands; render to them what they deserve. 5 Because they do not regard the works of the Lord, nor the operation of His hands, He shall destroy them and not build them up. 6 Blessed be the Lord, because He has heard the voice of my supplications! 7 The Lord is my strength and my shield; my heart trusted in Him, and I am helped; therefore my heart greatly rejoices, and with my song I will praise Him. 8 The Lord is their strength, and He is the saving refuge of His anointed. 9 Save Your people, and bless Your inheritance; shepherd them also, and bear them up forever

Chapter 29

A Psalm of David. 1 Give unto the Lord, O you mighty ones, give unto the Lord glory and strength. 2 Give unto the Lord the glory due to His name; worship the Lord in the beauty of holiness. 3 The voice of the Lord is over the waters; the God of glory thunders; the Lord is over many waters. 4 The voice of the Lord is powerful; the voice of the Lord is full of majesty. 5 The voice of the Lord breaks the cedars, yes, the Lord splinters the cedars of Lebanon. 6 He makes them also skip like a calf, Lebanon and Sirion like a young wild ox. 7 The voice of the Lord divides the flames of fire. 8 The voice of the Lord shakes the wilderness; the Lord shakes the Wilderness of Kadesh. 9 The voice of the Lord makes the deer give birth, and strips the forests bare; and in His temple everyone says, "Glory!" 10 The Lord sat enthroned at the Flood, and the Lord sits as King forever. 11 The Lord will give strength to His people; the Lord will bless His people with peace

Chapter 30

A Psalm - Song of the Dedication of the House of David I will magnify you, O Lord, for you have exalted me and not allowed my foes to rejoice over me. O Lord my God, I cried out to you, and you restored me. You have brought my soul up from the grave and revived me from those who go down into the pit. Sing praises to the Lord, you saints, and give thanks at the remembrance of His holiness. His anger lasts only for a moment, but His favor lasts a lifetime. Weeping may endure for a night, but joy comes in the morning.

In my prosperity, I said, "I shall never be moved." By your favor, O Lord, you made my mountain stand strong; when you hid your face, I was troubled. I cried to you, O Lord, and prayed to my Lord, "What profit is there in my blood when I go down to the pit? Will the dust praise you? Will it declare your truth?" Hear, O Lord, and have mercy on me; Lord, be my helper. You have turned my mourning into joy; you have loosened my sackcloth and girded me with gladness. Therefore, my tongue will praise you and not be silent. O Lord my God, I will give thanks to you forever

Chapter 31

To Him Who Excels, A Psalm of David In you, O Lord, I have put my trust; let me never be confounded. Deliver me in your righteousness. Bow down your ear to me; make haste to deliver me. Be my strong rock and a house of defense to save me. For you are my rock and my fortress; for your name's sake, lead me and guide me. Draw me out of the net they have secretly laid for me, for you are my strength. Into your hands, I commend my spirit, for you have redeemed me, O Lord God of truth. I have hated those who regard vain idols, but I trust in the Lord. I will be glad and rejoice in your mercy, for you have seen my affliction and known my soul in adversities. You have not shut me up into the hand of the enemy but have set my feet in a wide place. Have mercy on me, O Lord, for I am in trouble; my eye, my soul, and my belly are consumed with grief. My life is wasted with heaviness and my years with mourning; my strength fails because of my pain, and my bones are consumed. I am a reproach among all my enemies, especially among my neighbors, and a fear to my acquaintances who see me in the street and flee from me. I am forgotten like a dead man, out of mind; I am like a broken vessel. I have heard the slander of many; fear is on every side while they conspire together against me and plot to take my life. But I trust in you, O Lord; I say, "You are my God." My times are in your hand; deliver me from the hand of my enemies and from those who persecute me. Make your face shine upon your servant; save me for your mercy's sake. Let me not be confounded, O Lord, for I have called upon you. Let the wicked be ashamed and silent in the grave. Let the lying lips be silenced, which speak arrogantly against the righteous with pride and contempt. How great is your goodness, which you have stored up for those who fear you and done for those who trust in you in the sight of the sons of men! You hide them in the secret place of your presence from the plots of men; you keep them secretly in your pavilion from the strife of tongues. Blessed be the Lord, for He has shown me His marvelous kindness in a strong city. I said in my haste, "I am cut off from before your eyes," but you heard the voice of my supplications when I cried out to you. Love the Lord, all you His saints, for the Lord preserves the faithful and abundantly rewards the proud doer. Be strong, and He shall establish your heart, all you who hope in the Lord

Chapter 32

A Psalm of David for Instruction Blessed is he whose transgressions are forgiven, whose sin is covered. Blessed is the man to whom the Lord does not impute iniquity, and in whose spirit there is no deceit. When I kept silent, my bones grew old through my groaning all day long. For day and night, your hand was heavy upon me; my vitality was turned into the drought of summer. Selah. I acknowledged my sin to you, and my iniquity I did not hide. I said, "I will confess my transgressions to the Lord," and you forgave the guilt of my sin. Selah. Therefore, let everyone who is godly pray to you in a time when you may be found. Surely, when the great waters rise, they will not come near him. You are my hiding place;

you preserve me from trouble and surround me with songs of deliverance. Selah. I will instruct you and teach you in the way you should go; I will guide you with my eye. Do not be like the horse or like the mule, which have no understanding, which must be harnessed with bit and bridle, or they will not come near you. Many sorrows shall be to the wicked, but he who trusts in the Lord, mercy shall surround him. Be glad in the Lord and rejoice, you righteous, and shout for joy, all you upright in heart

Chapter 33

Rejoice in the Lord, O you righteous, for praise from the upright is beautiful. Praise the Lord with the harp; make music to Him with an instrument of ten strings. Sing to Him a new song; play skillfully with a shout of joy. For the word of the Lord is right, and all His work is done in truth. He loves righteousness and justice; the earth is full of the goodness of the Lord. By the word of the Lord, the heavens were made, and all the host of them by the breath of His mouth. He gathers the waters of the sea together as a heap; He lays up the deep in storehouses. Let all the earth fear the Lord; let all the inhabitants of the world stand in awe of Him. For He spoke, and it was done; He commanded, and it stood fast. The Lord brings the counsel of the nations to nothing; He makes the plans of the peoples of no effect. The counsel of the Lord stands forever, the plans of His heart to all generations. Blessed is the nation whose God is the Lord, the people He has chosen as His own inheritance. The Lord looks from heaven; He sees all the sons of men. From the place of His dwelling, He looks on all the inhabitants of the earth. He fashions their hearts individually; He considers all their works. No king is saved by the multitude of an army; a mighty man is not delivered by great strength. A horse is a vain hope for safety; neither shall it deliver any by its great strength. Behold, the eye of the Lord is on those who fear Him, on those who hope in His mercy, to deliver their soul from death and to keep them alive in famine. Our soul waits for the Lord; He is our help and our shield. For our heart shall rejoice in Him because we have trusted in His holy name. Let your mercy, O Lord, be upon us, just as we hope in you

Chapter 34

A Psalm of David, When He Pretended Madness Before Abimelech, Who Drove Him Away, and He Departed I will bless the Lord at all times; His praise shall continually be in my mouth. My soul shall make its boast in the Lord; the humble shall hear of it and be glad. Oh, magnify the Lord with me, and let us exalt His name together. I sought the Lord, and He heard me and delivered me from all my fears. They looked to Him and were radiant, and their faces were not ashamed. This poor man cried out, and the Lord heard him and saved him out of all his troubles. The angel of the Lord encamps all around those who fear Him and delivers them. Oh, taste and see that the Lord is good; blessed is the man who trusts in Him! Fear the Lord, you His saints; there is no want to those who fear Him. The young lions lack and suffer hunger, but those who seek the Lord shall not lack any good thing. Come, you children, listen to me; I will teach you the fear of the Lord. Who is the man who desires life and loves many days, that he may see good? Keep your tongue from evil and your lips from speaking deceit. Depart from evil and do good; seek peace and pursue it. The eyes of the Lord are on the righteous, and His ears are open to their cry. The face of the Lord is against those who do evil, to cut off the remembrance of them from the earth. The righteous cry out, and the Lord hears and delivers them out of all their troubles. The Lord is near to those who have a broken heart and saves such as

have a contrite spirit. Many are the afflictions of the righteous, but the Lord delivers him out of them all. He guards all his bones; not one of them is broken. Evil shall slay the wicked, and those who hate the righteous shall be condemned. The Lord redeems the soul of His servants, and none of those who trust in Him shall be condemned

Chapter 35

A Psalm of David Plead my cause, O Lord, with those who strive with me; fight against those who fight against me. Take hold of shield and buckler and stand up for my help. Draw out the spear and stop those who pursue me. Say to my soul, "I am your salvation." Let those be put to shame and brought to dishonor who seek after my life; let those be turned back and brought to confusion who plot my hurt. Let them be like chaff before the wind, and let the angel of the Lord chase them. Let their way be dark and slippery, and let the angel of the Lord pursue them. For without cause, they have hidden their net for me in a pit, which they have dug without cause for my life. Let destruction come upon him unexpectedly, and let his net that he has hidden catch himself; into that very destruction, let him fall. And my soul shall be joyful in the Lord; it shall rejoice in His salvation. All my bones shall say, "Lord, who is like You, delivering the poor from him who is too strong for him, yes, the poor and the needy from him who plunders him?" Fierce witnesses rise up; they ask me things that I do not know. They reward me evil for good, to the sorrow of my soul. But as for me, when they were sick, my clothing was sackcloth; I humbled myself with fasting, and my prayer would return to my own heart. I paced about as though he were my friend or brother; I bowed down heavily, as one who mourns for his mother. But in my adversity, they rejoiced and gathered together; attackers gathered against me, and I did not know it; they tore at me and did not cease. With ungodly mockers at feasts, they gnashed at me with their teeth. Lord, how long will You look on? Rescue me from their destructions, my precious life from the lions. I will give You thanks in the great assembly; I will praise You among many people. Let them not rejoice over me who are wrongfully my enemies, nor let them wink with the eye who hate me without a cause. For they do not speak peace, but they devise deceitful matters against the quiet ones in the land. They also opened their mouth wide against me and said, "Aha, aha! Our eyes have seen it." This You have seen, O Lord; do not keep silence. O Lord, do not be far from me. Stir up Yourself and awake to my vindication, to my cause, my God and my Lord. Vindicate me, O Lord my God, according to Your righteousness, and let them not rejoice over me. Let them not say in their hearts, "Ah, so we would have it!" Let them not say, "We have swallowed him up." Let them be ashamed and brought to mutual confusion who rejoice at my hurt. Let them be clothed with shame and dishonor who exalt themselves against me. Let them shout for joy and be glad, who favor my righteous cause; and let them say continually, "Let the Lord be magnified, who has pleasure in the prosperity of His servant." And my tongue shall speak of Your righteousness and of Your praise all the day long

Chapter 36

To the Chief Musician, A Psalm of David the Servant of the Lord An oracle within my heart concerning the transgression of the wicked: There is no fear of God before his eyes. For he flatters himself in his own eyes when he finds out his iniquity and when he hates. The words of his mouth are wickedness and deceit; he has ceased to be wise and to do good. He devises wickedness on his bed; he sets himself in a way that is not good; he does not abhor evil. Your mercy, O Lord, is in the heavens; Your faithfulness reaches to the clouds. Your righteousness is like the great mountains; Your judgments are a great deep; O Lord, You preserve man and beast. How precious is Your lovingkindness, O God! Therefore the children of men put their trust under the shadow of Your wings. They are abundantly satisfied with the fullness of Your house, and You give them drink from the river of Your pleasures. For with You is the fountain of life; in Your light, we see light. Oh, continue Your lovingkindness to those who know You and Your righteousness to the upright in heart. Let not the foot of pride come against me, and let not the hand of the wicked drive me away. There the workers of iniquity have fallen; they have been cast down and are not able to rise

Chapter 37

A Psalm of David Do not fret because of wicked men, nor be envious of evildoers. They will soon be cut down like grass and wither like the green herb. Trust in the Lord and do good; dwell in the land, and you shall be fed assuredly. Delight yourself in the Lord, and He will give you the desires of your heart. Commit your way to the Lord and trust in Him, and He will bring it to pass. He will bring forth your righteousness as the light and your judgment as the noonday. Wait patiently for the Lord and hope in Him. Do not fret over those who prosper in their way or those who carry out wicked schemes. Cease from anger and forsake wrath; do not fret—it leads only to evil. Evildoers will be cut off, but those who wait upon the Lord will inherit the land. In just a little while, the wicked will be no more; though you look for them, they will not be found. The meek will inherit the earth and delight in abundant peace. The wicked plot against the righteous and gnash their teeth at them, but the Lord laughs at the wicked, for He knows their day is coming. The wicked draw the sword and bend the bow to bring down the poor and needy, to slay those whose ways are upright. But their swords will pierce their own hearts, and their bows will be broken. Better is a little that the righteous have than the wealth of many wicked. For the power of the wicked will be broken, but the Lord upholds the righteous. The Lord knows the days of the upright, and their inheritance will endure forever. In times of disaster, they will not wither; in days of famine, they will have plenty. But the wicked will perish; the enemies of the Lord will vanish like the beauty of the fields; they will vanish like smoke. The wicked borrow and do not repay, but the righteous give generously. Those blessed by the Lord will inherit the land, but those cursed by Him will be cut off. The Lord directs the steps of the man He delights in; though he may stumble, he will not fall, for the Lord upholds him with His hand. I was young and now I am old, yet I have never seen the righteous forsaken or their children begging bread. They are always generous and lend freely; their children will be blessed. Turn from evil and do good, and you will dwell in the land forever. For the Lord loves the just and will not forsake His faithful ones. They will be protected forever, but the offspring of the wicked will be cut off. The righteous will inherit the land and dwell in it forever. The mouths of the righteous utter wisdom, and their tongues speak what is just. The law of their God is in their hearts; their feet do not slip. The wicked lie in wait for the righteous, seeking to kill them, but the Lord will not leave them in the power of the wicked or let them be condemned when brought to trial. Wait for the Lord and keep His way. He will exalt you to inherit the land; when the wicked are destroyed, you will see it. I have seen a wicked and ruthless man flourishing like a green tree in its native soil, but he soon passed away and was no more; though I looked for him, he could not be found. Consider the blameless, observe the upright; there is a future for the man of peace. But all sinners will be destroyed; there will be no future for the wicked. The salvation of the righteous comes from the Lord; He is their stronghold in times of trouble. The Lord helps them and delivers them; He delivers them from the wicked and saves them because they take refuge in Him

Chapter 38

A Psalm of David for Remembrance O Lord, do not rebuke me in Your anger or discipline me in Your wrath. Your arrows have pierced me, and Your hand has come down upon me. Because of Your wrath, there is no health in my body; my bones have no soundness because of my sin. My guilt has overwhelmed me like a burden too heavy to bear. My wounds fester and are loathsome because of my sinful folly. I am bowed down and brought very low; all day long I go about mourning. My back is filled with searing pain; there is no health in my body. I am feeble and utterly crushed; I groan in anguish of heart. All my longings lie open before You, Lord; my sighing is not hidden from You. My heart pounds, my strength fails me; even the light has gone from my eyes. My friends and companions avoid me because of my wounds; my neighbors stay far away. Those who seek my life set their traps, those who would harm me talk of my ruin; all day long they plot deception. I am like the deaf, who cannot hear, like the mute, who cannot speak; I have become like one who does not hear, whose mouth can offer no reply. I wait for You, O Lord; You will answer, O Lord my God. For I said, "Do not let them gloat or exalt themselves over me when my foot slips." For I am about to fall, and my pain is ever with me. I confess my iniquity; I am troubled by my sin. Many are those who are my vigorous enemies; those who hate me without reason are numerous. Those who repay my good with evil lodge accusations against me, though I seek only to do what is good. Do not forsake me, O Lord; do not be far from me, my God. Come quickly to help me, O Lord my Savior

Chapter 39

To the Chief Musician Jeduthun, A Psalm of David I said, "I will watch my ways and keep my tongue from sin; I will put a muzzle on my mouth as long as the wicked are in my presence." But when I was silent and still, not even saying anything good, my anguish increased. My heart grew hot within me, and as I meditated, the fire burned; then I spoke with my tongue: "Show me, O Lord, my life's end and the number of my days; let me know how fleeting my life is. You have made my days a mere handbreadth; the span of my years is as nothing before You. Each man's life is but a breath. Selah. Man is a mere phantom as he goes to and fro: He bustles about, but only in vain; he heaps up wealth, not knowing who will get it. But now, Lord, what do I look for? My hope is in You. Save me from all my transgressions; do not make me the scorn of fools. I was silent; I would not open my mouth, for You are the one who has done this. Remove Your scourge from me; I am overcome by the blow of Your hand. You rebuke and discipline men for their sin; You consume their wealth like a moth—each man is but a breath. Selah. Hear my prayer, O Lord, listen to my cry for help; be not deaf to my weeping. For I dwell with You as an alien, a stranger, as all my fathers were. Look away from me, that I may rejoice again before I depart and am no more."

Chapter 40

To the Chief Musician, A Psalm of David I waited patiently for the Lord; He turned to me and heard my cry. He lifted me out of the slimy pit, out of the mud and mire; He set my feet on a rock and gave me a firm place to stand. He put a new song in my mouth, a hymn of praise to our God. Many will see and fear and put their trust in the Lord. Blessed is the man who makes the Lord his trust, who does not look to the proud, to those who turn aside to false gods. Many, O Lord my God, are the wonders You have done. The things You planned for us no one can recount to You; were I to speak and tell of them, they would be too many to declare. Sacrifice and offering You did not desire, but my ears You have pierced; burnt offerings and sin offerings You did not require. Then I said, "Here I am, I have come—it is written about me in the scroll. I desire to do Your will, O my God; Your law is within my heart." I proclaim righteousness in the great assembly; I do not seal my lips, as You know, O Lord. I do not hide Your righteousness in my heart; I speak of Your faithfulness and salvation. I do not conceal Your love and Your truth from the great assembly. Do not withhold Your mercy from me, O Lord; may Your love and Your truth always protect me. For troubles without number surround me; my sins have overtaken me, and I cannot see. They are more than the hairs of my head, and my heart fails within me. Be pleased, O Lord, to save me; O Lord, come quickly to help me. May all who seek to take my life be put to shame and confusion; may all who desire my ruin be turned back in disgrace. May those who say to me, "Aha! Aha!" be appalled at their own shame. But may all who seek You rejoice and be glad in You; may those who love Your salvation always say, "The Lord be exalted!" Yet I am poor and needy; may the Lord think of me. You are my help and my deliverer; O my God, do not delay

Chapter 41

To the Chief Musician, A Psalm of David Blessed is he who considers the poor; the Lord will deliver him in times of trouble. The Lord will protect him and keep him alive; he will be blessed on the earth and will not surrender him to the will of his enemies. The Lord will sustain him on his sickbed and restore him from his bed of illness. I said, "O Lord, have mercy on me; heal me, for I have sinned against You." My enemies say of me in malice, "When will he die and his name perish?" Whenever one comes to see me, he speaks falsely, while his heart gathers slander; then he goes out and spreads it abroad. All my enemies whisper together against me; they imagine the worst for me, saying, "A vile disease has afflicted him; he will never get up from the place where he lies." Even my close friend, whom I trusted, he who shared my bread, has lifted up his heel against me. But You, O Lord, have mercy on me; raise me up, that I may repay them. I know that You are pleased with me, for my enemy does not triumph over me. In my integrity, You uphold me and set me in Your presence forever. Praise be to the Lord, the God of Israel, from everlasting to everlasting. Amen and Amen

Chapter 42

To the Chief Musician, A Psalm of the Sons of Korah As the deer pants for streams of water, so my soul pants for You, O God. My soul thirsts for God, for the living God. When can I go and meet with God? My tears have been my food day and night, while men say to me all day long, "Where is your God?" These things I remember as I pour out my soul: how I used to go with the multitude, leading the procession to the house of God, with shouts of joy and thanksgiving among the festive throng. Why are you downcast, O my soul? Why so disturbed within me? Put your hope in God, for I will yet praise Him, my Savior and my God. My soul is downcast within me; therefore I will remember You from the land of the Jordan, the heights of Hermon—from Mount Mizar. Deep calls to deep in the roar of Your waterfalls; all Your waves and breakers have swept over me. By day the Lord directs His love, at night His song is with me—a prayer to the God of my life. I say to God my Rock, "Why have You forgotten me? Why must I go about mourning, oppressed by the enemy?" My bones suffer mortal agony as my foes taunt me, saying to me all day long, "Where is your God?" Why are you downcast, O my soul? Why so disturbed within me? Put your hope in God, for I will yet praise Him, my Savior and my God

Chapter 43

Vindicate me, O God, and plead my cause against an ungodly nation; rescue me from deceitful and wicked men. You are God my stronghold. Why have You rejected me? Why must I go about mourning, oppressed by the enemy? Send forth Your light and Your truth, let them guide me; let them bring me to Your holy mountain, to the place where You dwell. Then will I go to the altar of God, to God, my joy and my delight. I will praise You with the harp, O God, my God. Why are you downcast, O my soul? Why so disturbed within me? Put your hope in God, for I will yet praise Him, my Savior and my God

Chapter 44

To the Chief Musician, A Psalm of the Sons of Korah We have heard with our ears, O God; our fathers have told us the deeds You performed in their days, in times of old: how You drove out the nations with Your hand and planted our ancestors; how You afflicted the peoples and cast them out. They did not gain possession of the land by their own sword, nor did their own arm save them; it was Your right hand, Your arm, and the light of Your countenance because You favored them. You are my King, O God; command victories for Jacob. Through You, we will push down our enemies; through Your name, we will trample those who rise up against us. I will not trust in my bow, nor will my sword save me. But You have saved us from our enemies and have put to shame those who hated us. In God, we boast all day long and praise Your name forever. Selah. But You have cast us off and put us to shame, and You do not go out with our armies. You make us turn back from the enemy, and those who hate us have taken spoil for themselves. You have given us up like sheep intended for food and have scattered us among the nations. You sell Your people for next to nothing and are not enriched by selling them. You make us a reproach to our neighbors, a scorn and derision to those around us. You make us a byword among the nations, a shaking of the head among the peoples. My disgrace is continually before me, and the shame of my face has covered me because of the voice of him who reproaches and reviles, because of the enemy and the avenger. All this has come upon us, but we have not forgotten You, nor have we dealt falsely with Your covenant. Our heart has not turned back, nor have our steps departed from Your way. But You have severely broken us in the place of jackals and covered us with the shadow of death. If we had forgotten the name of our God or stretched out our hands to a foreign god, would not God search this out? For He knows the secrets of the heart. Yet for Your sake, we are killed all day long; we are accounted as sheep for the slaughter. Awake! Why do You sleep, O Lord? Arise, do not cast us off forever. Why do You hide Your face and forget our affliction and our oppression? For our soul is bowed down to the dust; our body clings to the ground. Arise for our help and redeem us for Your mercies' sake

Chapter 45

To the Chief Musician on Shoshannim, A Song of Love of the Sons of Korah My heart is overflowing with a good theme; I recite my composition concerning the King; my tongue is the pen of a ready writer. You are fairer than the sons of men; grace is poured upon Your lips; therefore God has blessed You forever. Gird Your sword upon Your thigh, O Mighty One, with Your glory and Your majesty. And in Your majesty ride prosperously because of truth, humility, and righteousness; and Your right hand shall teach You awesome things. Your arrows are sharp in the heart of the King's enemies; the peoples fall under You. Your throne, O God, is forever and ever; a scepter of righteousness is the scepter of Your kingdom. You love righteousness and hate wickedness; therefore God, Your God, has anointed You with the oil of gladness more than Your companions. All Your garments are scented with myrrh, aloes, and cassia, out of the ivory palaces, by which they have made You glad. Kings' daughters are among Your honorable women; at Your right hand stands the queen in gold from Ophir. Listen, O daughter, consider and incline your ear; forget your own people also, and your father's house. So the King will greatly desire your beauty; because He is your Lord, worship Him. And the daughter of Tyre will come with a gift; the rich among the people will seek your favor. The royal daughter is all glorious within the palace; her clothing is woven with gold. She shall be brought to the King in robes of many colors; the virgins, her companions who follow her, shall be brought to You. With gladness and rejoicing, they shall be brought; they shall enter the King's palace. Instead of Your fathers shall be Your sons, whom You shall make princes in all the earth. I will make Your name to be remembered in all generations; therefore the people shall praise You forever and ever

Chapter 46
To the Chief Musician on Alamoth, A Psalm of the Sons of Korah God is our refuge and strength, a very present help in trouble. Therefore we will not fear, even though the earth be removed and though the mountains be carried into the midst of the sea; though its waters roar and be troubled, though the mountains shake with its swelling. Selah. There is a river whose streams shall make glad the city of God, the holy place of the tabernacle of the Most High. God is in the midst of her; she shall not be moved; God shall help her, just at the break of dawn. The nations raged, the kingdoms were moved; He uttered His voice, the earth melted. The Lord of hosts is with us; the God of Jacob is our refuge. Selah. Come, behold the works of the Lord, who has made desolations in the earth. He makes wars cease to the end of the earth; He breaks the bow and cuts the spear in two; He burns the chariot in the fire. Be still and know that I am God; I will be exalted among the nations, I will be exalted in the earth! The Lord of hosts is with us; the God of Jacob is our refuge. Selah

Chapter 47
To the Chief Musician, A Psalm of the Sons of Korah Oh, clap your hands, all you peoples! Shout to God with the voice of triumph! For the Lord Most High is awesome; He is a great King over all the earth. He will subdue the peoples under us and the nations under our feet. He will choose our inheritance for us, the excellence of Jacob whom He loves. Selah. God has gone up with a shout, the Lord with the sound of a trumpet. Sing praises to God, sing praises! Sing praises to our King, sing praises! For God is the King of all the earth; sing praises with understanding. God reigns over the nations; God sits on His holy throne. The princes of the people have gathered together, the people of the God of Abraham. For the shields of the earth belong to God; He is greatly exalted

Chapter 48
A Song, A Psalm of the Sons of Korah Great is the Lord, and greatly to be praised in the city of our God, in His holy mountain. Beautiful in elevation, the joy of the whole earth, is Mount Zion on the sides of the north, the city of the great King. God is in her palaces; He is known as her refuge. For behold, the kings assembled, they passed by together. They saw it, and so they marveled; they were troubled, they hastened away. Fear took hold of them there, and pain, as of a woman in labor, as when You break the ships of Tarshish with an east wind. As we have heard, so we have seen in the city of the Lord of hosts, in the city of our God: God will establish it forever. Selah. We have thought, O God, on Your lovingkindness in the midst of Your temple. According to Your name, O God, so is Your praise to the ends of the earth; Your right hand is full of righteousness. Let Mount Zion rejoice, let the daughters of Judah be glad because of Your judgments. Walk about Zion, and go all around her. Count her towers; mark well her bulwarks; consider her palaces, that you may tell it to the generation following. For this God is our God forever and ever; He will be our guide even to death

Chapter 49
To the Chief Musician, A Psalm of the Sons of Korah Hear this, all you peoples; give ear, all you inhabitants of the world, both low and high, rich and poor together. My mouth shall speak wisdom, and the meditation of my heart shall give understanding. I will incline my ear to a proverb; I will disclose my dark saying on the harp. Why should I fear in the days of evil, when the iniquity at my heels surrounds me? Those who trust in their wealth and boast in the multitude of their riches, none of them can by any means redeem his brother, nor give to God a ransom for him— for the redemption of their souls is costly, and it shall cease forever—that he should continue to live eternally and not see the Pit. For he sees wise men die; likewise the fool and the senseless person perish and leave their wealth to others. Their inner thought is that their houses will last forever, their dwelling places to all generations; they call their lands after their own names. Nevertheless, man, though in honor, does not remain; he is like the beasts that perish. This is the way of those who are foolish and of their posterity who approve their sayings. Selah. Like sheep they are laid in the grave; death shall feed on them; the upright shall have dominion over them in the morning, and their beauty shall be consumed in the grave, far from their dwelling. But God will redeem my soul from the power of the grave, for He shall receive me. Selah. Do not be afraid when one becomes rich, when the glory of his house is increased; for when he dies, he shall carry nothing away; his glory shall not descend after him. Though while he lives, he blesses himself (for men will praise you when you do well for yourself), he shall go to the generation of his fathers; they shall never see light. A man who is in honor, yet does not understand, is like the beasts that perish

Chapter 50
A Psalm of Asaph The Mighty One, God the Lord, has spoken and called the earth from the rising of the sun to its going down. Out of Zion, the perfection of beauty, God will shine forth. Our God shall come and shall not keep silent; a fire shall devour before Him, and it shall be very tempestuous all around Him. He shall call to the heavens from above and to the earth, that He may judge His people: "Gather My saints together to Me, those who have made a covenant with Me by sacrifice." Let the heavens declare His righteousness, for God Himself is Judge. Selah. "Hear, O My people, and I will speak, O Israel, and I will testify against you; I am God, your God! I will not rebuke you for your sacrifices or your burnt offerings, which are continually before Me. I will not take a bull

from your house, nor goats out of your folds. For every beast of the forest is Mine, and the cattle on a thousand hills. I know all the birds of the mountains, and the wild beasts of the field are Mine. If I were hungry, I would not tell you; for the world is Mine, and all its fullness. Will I eat the flesh of bulls or drink the blood of goats? Offer to God thanksgiving, and pay your vows to the Most High. Call upon Me in the day of trouble; I will deliver you, and you shall glorify Me." But to the wicked God says: "What right have you to declare My statutes or take My covenant in your mouth, seeing you hate instruction and cast My words behind you? When you saw a thief, you consented with him, and you have been a partaker with adulterers. You give your mouth to evil, and your tongue frames deceit. You sit and speak against your brother; you slander your own mother's son. These things you have done, and I kept silent; you thought that I was altogether like you; but I will rebuke you and set them in order before your eyes. Now consider this, you who forget God, lest I tear you in pieces, and there be none to deliver. Whoever offers praise glorifies Me; and to him who orders his conduct aright, I will show the salvation of God."

Chapter 51

To the Chief Musician, A Psalm of David when the Prophet Nathan came to him after David had gone to Bathsheba Have mercy upon me, O God, according to Your loving-kindness; according to the multitude of Your tender mercies, blot out my transgressions. Wash me thoroughly from my iniquity and cleanse me from my sin. For I acknowledge my transgressions, and my sin is always before me. Against You, You only, have I sinned and done this evil in Your sight, that You may be found just when You speak and blameless when You judge. Behold, I was brought forth in iniquity, and in sin my mother conceived me. Behold, You desire truth in the inward parts, and in the hidden part, You will make me to know wisdom. Purge me with hyssop, and I shall be clean; wash me, and I shall be whiter than snow. Make me hear joy and gladness, that the bones You have broken may rejoice. Hide Your face from my sins and blot out all my iniquities. Create in me a clean heart, O God, and renew a steadfast spirit within me. Do not cast me away from Your presence, and do not take Your Holy Spirit from me. Restore to me the joy of Your salvation and uphold me by Your generous Spirit. Then I will teach transgressors Your ways, and sinners shall be converted to You. Deliver me from the guilt of bloodshed, O God, the God of my salvation, and my tongue shall sing aloud of Your righteousness. O Lord, open my lips, and my mouth shall show forth Your praise. For You do not desire sacrifice, or else I would give it; You do not delight in burnt offering. The sacrifices of God are a broken spirit, a broken and a contrite heart—these, O God, You will not despise. Do good in Your good pleasure to Zion; build the walls of Jerusalem. Then You shall be pleased with the sacrifices of righteousness, with burnt offering and whole burnt offering; then they shall offer bulls on Your altar

Chapter 52

To the Chief Musician, A Psalm of David to give instruction, when Doeg the Edomite came and told Saul, "David has come to the house of Ahimelech." Why do you boast in evil, O mighty man? The goodness of God endures continually. Your tongue devises destruction, like a sharp razor, working deceitfully. You love evil more than good, lying rather than speaking righteousness. Selah. You love all devouring words, you deceitful tongue. God shall likewise destroy you forever; He shall take you away and pluck you out of your dwelling place and uproot you from the land of the living. Selah. The righteous

also shall see and fear and shall laugh at him, saying, "Here is the man who did not make God his strength but trusted in the abundance of his riches and strengthened himself in his wickedness." But I am like a green olive tree in the house of God; I trust in the mercy of God forever and ever. I will praise You forever because You have done it; and in the presence of Your saints, I will wait on Your name, for it is good

Chapter 53

To the Chief Musician on Mahalath, A Psalm of David to give instruction The fool has said in his heart, "There is no God." They are corrupt and have done abominable iniquity; there is none who does good. God looks down from heaven upon the children of men to see if there are any who understand, who seek God. Every one of them has turned aside; they have together become corrupt; there is none who does good, no, not one. Have the workers of iniquity no knowledge, who eat up my people as they eat bread and do not call upon God? There they are in great fear where no fear was, for God has scattered the bones of him who encamps against you; you have put them to shame because God has despised them. Oh, that the salvation of Israel would come out of Zion! When God brings back the captivity of His people, let Jacob rejoice and Israel be glad

Chapter 54

To the Chief Musician with Stringed Instruments, A Psalm of David when the Ziphites went and said to Saul, "Is David not hiding with us?" Save me, O God, by Your name and vindicate me by Your strength. Hear my prayer, O God; give ear to the words of my mouth. For strangers have risen up against me, and oppressors seek after my life; they have not set God before them. Selah. Behold, God is my helper; the Lord is with those who uphold my life. He will repay my enemies for their evil. Cut them off in Your truth. I will freely sacrifice to You; I will praise Your name, O Lord, for it is good. For He has delivered me out of all trouble, and my eye has seen its desire upon my enemies

Chapter 55

To the Chief Musician with Stringed Instruments, A Psalm of David to give instruction Give ear to my prayer, O God, and do not hide Yourself from my supplication. Attend to me and hear me; I am restless in my complaint and moan noisily because of the voice of the enemy, because of the oppression of the wicked; for they bring down trouble upon me, and in wrath, they hate me. My heart is severely pained within me, and the terrors of death have fallen upon me. Fearfulness and trembling have come upon me, and horror has overwhelmed me. So I said, "Oh, that I had wings like a dove! I would fly away and be at rest. Indeed, I would wander far off and remain in the wilderness. Selah. I would hasten my escape from the windy storm and tempest." Destroy, O Lord, and divide their tongues, for I have seen violence and strife in the city. Day and night, they go around it on its walls; iniquity and trouble are also in the midst of it. Destruction is in its midst; oppression and deceit do not depart from its streets. For it is not an enemy who reproaches me; then I could bear it. Nor is it one who hates me who has exalted himself against me; then I could hide from him. But it was you, a man my equal, my companion and my acquaintance. We took sweet counsel together and walked to the house of God in the throng. Let death seize them; let them go down alive into hell, for wickedness is in their dwellings and among them. As for me, I will call upon God, and the Lord shall save me. Evening and morning and at noon, I will pray and cry aloud, and He shall hear my voice. He has redeemed my soul in peace from the battle that was against me, for there were many against me. God will hear and afflict them, even He who abides from of old. Selah. Because they do not change, therefore they do not fear God. He has put forth his hands against those who were at peace with him; he has broken his covenant. The words of his mouth were smoother than butter, but war was in his heart; his words were softer than oil, yet they were drawn swords. Cast your burden on the Lord, and He shall sustain you; He shall never permit the righteous to be moved. But You, O God, shall bring them down to the pit of destruction; bloodthirsty and deceitful men shall not live out half their days, but I will trust in You

Chapter 56

To the Chief Musician on Jonath Elem Rechokim, A Psalm of David when the Philistines captured him in Gath Be merciful to me, O God, for man would swallow me up; fighting all day he oppresses me. My enemies would hound me all day, for there are many who fight against me, O Most High. Whenever I am afraid, I will trust in You. In God, I will praise His word; in God, I have put my trust; I will not fear. What can flesh do to me? All day they twist my words; all their thoughts are against me for evil. They gather together, they hide, they mark my steps when they lie in wait for my life. Shall they escape by iniquity? In anger, cast down the peoples, O God! You number my wanderings; put my tears into Your bottle; are they not in Your book? When I cry out to You, then my enemies will turn back; this I know because God is for me. In God, I will praise His word; in the Lord, I will praise His word. In God, I have put my trust; I will not be afraid. What can man do to me? Vows made to You are binding upon me, O God; I will render praises to You, for You have delivered my soul from death. Have You not kept my feet from falling, that I may walk before God in the light of the living?

Chapter 57

To the Chief Musician, Set to "Do Not Destroy," A Psalm of David when he fled from Saul into the cave Be merciful to me, O God, be merciful to me! For my soul trusts in You; and in the shadow of Your wings, I will make my refuge until these calamities have passed by. I will cry out to God Most High, to God who performs all things for me. He shall send from heaven and save me; He reproaches the one who would swallow me up. Selah. God shall send forth His mercy and His truth. My soul is among lions; I lie among the sons of men who are set on fire, whose teeth are spears and arrows and their tongue a sharp sword. Be exalted, O God, above the heavens; let Your glory be above all the earth. They have prepared a net for my steps; my soul is bowed down; they have dug a pit before me; into the midst of it, they themselves have fallen. Selah. My heart is steadfast, O God, my heart is steadfast; I will sing and give praise. Awake, my glory! Awake, lute and harp! I will awaken the dawn. I will praise You, O Lord, among the peoples; I will sing to You among the nations. For Your mercy reaches unto the heavens, and Your truth unto the clouds. Be exalted, O God, above the heavens; let Your glory be above all the earth

Chapter 58

To the Chief Musician, Set to "Do Not Destroy," A Psalm of David Do you indeed speak righteousness, you silent ones? Do you judge uprightly, you sons of men? No, in heart you work wickedness; you weigh out the violence of your hands in the earth. The wicked are estranged from the womb; they go astray as soon as they are born, speaking lies. Their poison is like the poison of a serpent; they are like the deaf cobra that stops its ear, which will not heed the voice of charmers, charming ever so skillfully. Break their

teeth in their mouth, O God! Break out the fangs of the young lions, O Lord! Let them flow away as waters which run continually; when he bends his bow, let his arrows be as if cut in pieces. Let them be like a snail which melts away as it goes, like a stillborn child of a woman, that they may not see the sun. Before your pots can feel the burning thorns, He shall take them away as with a whirlwind, as in His living and burning wrath. The righteous shall rejoice when he sees the vengeance; he shall wash his feet in the blood of the wicked, so that men will say, "Surely there is a reward for the righteous; surely He is God who judges in the earth."

Chapter 59

To the Chief Musician, Set to "Do Not Destroy," A Psalm of David when Saul sent men, and they watched the house in order to kill him Deliver me from my enemies, O my God; defend me from those who rise up against me. Deliver me from the workers of iniquity, and save me from bloodthirsty men. For look, they lie in wait for my life; the mighty gather against me, not for my transgression nor for my sin, O Lord. They run and prepare themselves through no fault of mine. Awake to help me, and behold! You, therefore, O Lord God of hosts, the God of Israel, awake to punish all the nations; do not be merciful to any wicked transgressors. Selah. At evening, they return, they growl like a dog, and go all around the city. Indeed, they belch with their mouth; swords are in their lips; for they say, "Who hears?" But You, O Lord, shall laugh at them; You shall have all the nations in derision. I will wait for You, O You, his Strength; for God is my defense. My God of mercy shall come to meet me; God shall let me see my desire on my enemies. Do not slay them, lest my people forget; scatter them by Your power, and bring them down, O Lord our shield. For the sin of their mouth and the words of their lips, let them even be taken in their pride, and for the cursing and lying which they speak. Consume them in wrath, consume them that they may not be; and let them know that God rules in Jacob to the ends of the earth. Selah. And at evening, they return, they growl like a dog, and go all around the city. They wander up and down for food and howl if they are not satisfied. But I will sing of Your power; yes, I will sing aloud of Your mercy in the morning; for You have been my defense and refuge in the day of my trouble. To You, O my Strength, I will sing praises; for God is my defense, my God of mercy

Chapter 60

To the Chief Musician on Shushan Eduth, a Michtam of David to teach, when he fought against Mesopotamia and Syria of Zobah, and Joab returned and killed twelve thousand Edomites in the Valley of Salt O God, You have cast us off; You have broken us down; You have been displeased; oh, restore us again! You have made the earth tremble; You have broken it; heal its breaches, for it is shaking. You have shown Your people hard things; You have made us drink the wine of confusion. You have given a banner to those who fear You, that it may be displayed because of the truth. Selah. That Your beloved may be delivered, save with Your right hand, and hear me. God has spoken in His holiness: "I will rejoice; I will divide Shechem and measure out the Valley of Succoth. Gilead is Mine, and Manasseh is Mine; Ephraim also is the helmet for My head; Judah is My lawgiver. Moab is My washpot; over Edom, I will cast My shoe; Philistia, shout in triumph because of Me." Who will bring me to the strong city? Who will lead me to Edom? Is it not You, O God, who cast us off? And You, O God, who did not go out with our armies? Give us help from trouble, for the help of man is useless. Through God, we will do valiantly, for it is He who shall tread down our enemies

Chapter 61

To the Chief Musician on Stringed Instruments, A Psalm of David Hear my cry, O God; listen to my prayer. From the ends of the earth, I call to You when my heart is overwhelmed; lead me to the rock that is higher than I. For You have been a shelter for me, a strong tower from the enemy. I will abide in Your tabernacle forever; I will trust in the shelter of Your wings. Selah. For You, O God, have heard my vows; You have given me the heritage of those who fear Your name. You will prolong the king's life, his years as many generations. He shall abide before God forever. Oh, prepare mercy and truth, which may preserve him! So I will sing praise to Your name forever, that I may daily perform my vows

Chapter 62

To the Chief Musician Jeduthun, A Psalm of David Truly my soul silently waits for God; from Him comes my salvation. He only is my rock and my salvation; He is my defense; I shall not be greatly moved. How long will you attack a man? You shall be slain, all of you, like a leaning wall and a tottering fence. They only consult to cast him down from his high position; they delight in lies; they bless with their mouth, but they curse inwardly. Selah. My soul, wait silently for God alone, for my expectation is from Him. He only is my rock and my salvation; He is my defense; I shall not be moved. In God is my salvation and my glory; the rock of my strength, and my refuge, is in God. Trust in Him at all times, you people; pour out your heart before Him; God is a refuge for us. Selah. Surely men of low degree are a vapor, men of high degree are a lie; if they are weighed on the scales, they are altogether lighter than vapor. Do not trust in oppression, nor vainly hope in robbery; if riches increase, do not set your heart on them. God has spoken once, twice I have heard this: that power belongs to God. Also to You, O Lord, belongs mercy; for You render to each one according to his work

Chapter 63

A Psalm of David when he was in the wilderness of Judah O God, You are my God; early will I seek You; my soul thirsts for You; my flesh longs for You in a dry and thirsty land where there is no water. So I have looked for You in the sanctuary, to see Your power and Your glory. Because Your loving-kindness is better than life, my lips shall praise You. Thus I will bless You while I live; I will lift up my hands in Your name. My soul shall be satisfied as with marrow and fatness, and my mouth shall praise You with joyful lips. When I remember You on my bed, I meditate on You in the night watches. Because You have been my help, therefore in the shadow of Your wings, I will rejoice. My soul follows close behind You; Your right hand upholds me. But those who seek my life, to destroy it, shall go into the lower parts of the earth. They shall fall by the sword; they shall be a portion for jackals. But the king shall rejoice in God; everyone who swears by Him shall glory, but the mouth of those who speak lies shall be stopped

Chapter 64

To the Chief Musician, A Psalm of David Hear my voice, O God, in my meditation; preserve my life from fear of the enemy. Hide me from the secret plots of the wicked, from the rebellion of the workers of iniquity, who sharpen their tongue like a sword and bend their bows to shoot their arrows—bitter words, that they may shoot in secret at the blameless; suddenly they shoot at him and do not fear. They encourage themselves in an evil matter; they talk of laying snares secretly; they say, "Who will see them?" They devise iniquities: "We have perfected a shrewd scheme." Both the inward thought and the heart of man are deep. But God shall shoot at them with an arrow; suddenly they shall be wounded. So He will make them stumble over their own tongue; all who see them shall flee away. All men shall fear and shall declare the work of God, for they shall wisely consider His doing. The righteous shall be glad in the Lord and trust in Him, and all the upright in heart shall glory

Chapter 65

To the Chief Musician, A Psalm of David, A Song Praise is awaiting You, O God, in Zion, and to You, the vow shall be performed. O You who hear prayer, to You, all flesh will come. Iniquities prevail against me; as for our transgressions, You will provide atonement for them. Blessed is the man You choose and cause to approach You, that he may dwell in Your courts. We shall be satisfied with the goodness of Your house, of Your holy temple. By awesome deeds in righteousness, You will answer us, O God of our salvation, You who are the confidence of all the ends of the earth, and of the far-off seas; who established the mountains by His strength, being clothed with power; You who still the noise of the seas, the noise of their waves, and the tumult of the peoples. They also who dwell in the farthest parts are afraid of Your signs; You make the outgoings of the morning and evening rejoice. You visit the earth and water it; You greatly enrich it; the river of God is full of water; You provide their grain, for so You have prepared it. You water its ridges abundantly, You settle its furrows; You make it soft with showers, You bless its growth. You crown the year with Your goodness, and Your paths drip with abundance. They drop on the pastures of the wilderness, and the little hills rejoice on every side. The pastures are clothed with flocks; the valleys also are covered with grain; they shout for joy, they also sing

Chapter 66

To the Chief Musician, A Song, A Psalm Make a joyful shout to God, all the earth! Sing out the honor of His name; make His praise glorious. Say to God, "How awesome are Your works! Through the greatness of Your power, Your enemies shall submit themselves to You. All the earth shall worship You and sing praises to You; they shall sing praises to Your name." Selah. Come and see the works of God; He is awesome in His doing toward the sons of men. He turned the sea into dry land; they went through the river on foot. There we will rejoice in Him. He rules by His power forever; His eyes observe the nations; do not let the rebellious exalt themselves. Selah. Oh, bless our God, you peoples! And make the voice of His praise to be heard, who keeps our soul among the living and does not allow our feet to be moved. For You, O God, have tested us; You have refined us as silver is refined. You brought us into the net; You laid affliction on our backs. You have caused men to ride over our heads; we went through fire and through water; but You brought us out to rich fulfillment. I will go into Your house with burnt offerings; I will pay You my vows, which my lips have uttered and my mouth has spoken when I was in trouble. I will offer You burnt sacrifices of fat animals, with the sweet aroma of rams; I will offer bulls with goats. Selah. Come and hear, all you who fear God, and I will declare what He has done for my soul. I cried to Him with my mouth, and He was extolled with my tongue. If I regard iniquity in my heart, the Lord will not hear. But certainly God has heard me; He has attended to the voice of my prayer. Blessed be God, who has not turned away my prayer, nor His mercy from me!

Chapter 67

To the Chief Musician on Stringed Instruments, A Psalm, A Song God be merciful to us and bless us, and cause His face to shine upon us. Selah. That Your way may be known on earth, Your salvation among all nations. Let the peoples praise You, O God; let all the peoples praise You. Oh, let the nations be glad and sing for joy! For You shall judge the people righteously and govern the nations on earth. Selah. Let the peoples praise You, O God; let all the peoples praise You. Then the earth shall yield her increase; God, our own God, shall bless us. God shall bless us, and all the ends of the earth shall fear Him

Chapter 68

To the Chief Musician, A Psalm of David, A Song Let God arise, let His enemies be scattered; let those also who hate Him flee before Him. As smoke is driven away, so drive them away; as wax melts before the fire, so let the wicked perish at the presence of God. But let the righteous be glad; let them rejoice before God; yes, let them rejoice exceedingly. Sing to God, sing praises to His name; extol Him who rides on the clouds, by His name Yah, and rejoice before Him. A father of the fatherless, a defender of widows, is God in His holy habitation. God sets the solitary in families; He brings out those who are bound into prosperity, but the rebellious dwell in a dry land. O God, when You went out before Your people, when You marched through the wilderness, Selah, the earth shook; the heavens also dropped rain at the presence of God; Sinai itself was moved at the presence of God, the God of Israel. You, O God, sent a plentiful rain, whereby You confirmed Your inheritance when it was weary. Your congregation dwelt in it; You, O God, provided from Your goodness for the poor. The Lord gave the word; great was the company of those who proclaimed it: "Kings of armies flee, they flee, and she who remains at home divides the spoil. Though you lie down among the sheepfolds, you will be like the wings of a dove covered with silver, and her feathers with yellow gold." When the Almighty scattered kings in it, it was white as snow in Zalmon. A mountain of God is the mountain of Bashan; a mountain of many peaks is the mountain of Bashan. Why do you fume with envy, you mountains of many peaks? This is the mountain which God desires to dwell in; yes, the Lord will dwell in it forever. The chariots of God are twenty thousand, even thousands of thousands; the Lord is among them as in Sinai, in the Holy Place. You have ascended on high, You have led captivity captive; You have received gifts among men, even from the rebellious, that the Lord God might dwell there. Blessed be the Lord, who daily loads us with benefits, the God of our salvation! Selah. Our God is the God of salvation, and to God the Lord belong escapes from death. But God will wound the head of His enemies, the hairy scalp of the one who still goes on in his trespasses. The Lord said, "I will bring back from Bashan, I will bring them back from the depths of the sea, that your foot may crush them in blood, and the tongues of your dogs may have their portion from your enemies." They have seen Your procession, O God, the procession of my God, my King, into the sanctuary. The singers went before, the players on instruments followed after; among them were the maidens playing timbrels. Bless God in the congregations, the Lord, from the fountain of Israel. There is little Benjamin, their leader, the princes of Judah and their company, the princes of Zebulun and the princes of Naphtali. Your God has commanded your strength; strengthen, O God, what You have done for us. Because of Your temple at Jerusalem, kings will bring presents to You. Rebuke the beasts of the reeds, the herd of bulls with the calves of the peoples, till everyone submits himself with pieces of silver. Scatter the peoples who delight in war. Envoys will come out of Egypt; Ethiopia will quickly stretch out her hands to God. Sing to God, you kingdoms of the earth; oh, sing praises to the Lord, Selah, to Him who rides on the heaven of heavens, which were of old! Indeed, He sends out His voice, a mighty voice. Ascribe strength to God; His excellence is over Israel, and His strength is in the clouds. O God, You are more awesome than Your holy places. The God of Israel is He who gives strength and power to His people. Blessed be God!

Chapter 69

To the Chief Musician, Set to "The Lilies," A Psalm of David Save me, O God, for the waters have come up to my neck. I sink in deep mire, where there is no standing; I have come into deep waters, where the floods overflow me. I am weary with my crying; my throat is dry; my eyes fail while I wait for my God. Those who hate me without a cause are more than the hairs of my head; they are mighty who would destroy me, being my enemies wrongfully; though I have stolen nothing, I still must restore it. O God, You know my foolishness, and my sins are not hidden from You. Let not those who wait for You, O Lord God of hosts, be ashamed because of me; let not those who seek You be confounded because of me, O God of Israel. Because for Your sake I have borne reproach; shame has covered my face. I have become a stranger to my brothers and an alien to my mother's children; because zeal for Your house has eaten me up, and the reproaches of those who reproach You have fallen on me. When I wept and chastened my soul with fasting, that became my reproach. I also made sackcloth my garment; I became a byword to them. Those who sit in the gate speak against me, and I am the song of the drunkards. But as for me, my prayer is to You, O Lord, in the acceptable time; O God, in the multitude of Your mercy, hear me in the truth of Your salvation. Deliver me out of the mire, and let me not sink; let me be delivered from those who hate me and out of the deep waters. Let not the floodwater overflow me, nor let the deep swallow me up, and let not the pit shut its mouth on me. Hear me, O Lord, for Your loving-kindness is good; turn to me according to the multitude of Your tender mercies. And do not hide Your face from Your servant, for I am in trouble; hear me speedily. Draw near to my soul and redeem it; deliver me because of my enemies. You know my reproach, my shame, and my dishonor; my adversaries are all before You. Reproach has broken my heart, and I am full of heaviness; I looked for someone to take pity, but there was none; and for comforters, but I found none. They also gave me gall for my food, and for my thirst, they gave me vinegar to drink. Let their table become a snare before them, and their well-being a trap. Let their eyes be darkened so that they do not see, and make their loins shake continually. Pour out Your indignation upon them, and let Your wrathful anger take hold of them. Let their dwelling place be desolate; let no one live in their tents. For they persecute the ones You have struck, and talk of the grief of those You have wounded. Add iniquity to their iniquity, and let them not come into Your righteousness. Let them be blotted out of the book of the living and not be written with the righteous. But I am poor and sorrowful; let Your salvation, O God, set me up on high. I will praise the name of God with a song and will magnify Him with thanksgiving. This also shall please the Lord better than an ox or bull, which has horns and hooves. The humble shall see this and be glad; and you who seek God, your hearts shall live. For the Lord hears the poor and does not despise His prisoners. Let heaven and earth praise Him, the seas and everything that moves in them. For God will save Zion and build the cities of Judah, that they may dwell there and possess it. Also, the descendants of His servants shall inherit it, and those who love His name shall dwell in it

Chapter 70

To the Chief Musician, A Psalm of David to bring to remembrance Make haste, O God, to deliver me! Make haste to help me, O Lord! Let them be ashamed and confounded who seek my life; let them be turned back and confused who desire my hurt. Let them be turned back because of their shame, who say, "Aha, aha!" Let all those who seek You rejoice and be glad in You; and let those who love Your salvation say continually, "Let God be magnified!" But I am poor and needy; make haste to me, O God! You are my help and my deliverer; O Lord, do not delay

Chapter 71

In You, O Lord, I put my trust; let me never be ashamed. Deliver me in Your righteousness, and cause me to escape; incline Your ear to me and save me. Be my strong refuge, to which I may resort continually; You have given the commandment to save me, for You are my rock and my fortress. Deliver me, O my God, out of the hand of the wicked, out of the hand of the unrighteous and cruel man. For You are my hope, O Lord God; You are my trust from my youth. By You, I have been upheld from birth; You are He who took me out of my mother's womb. My praise shall be continually of You. I have become as a wonder to many, but You are my strong refuge. Let my mouth be filled with Your praise and with Your glory all the day. Do not cast me off in the time of old age; do not forsake me when my strength fails. For my enemies speak against me, and those who lie in wait for my life take counsel together, saying, "God has forsaken him; pursue and take him, for there is none to deliver him." O God, do not be far from me; O my God, make haste to help me! Let them be confounded and consumed who are adversaries of my life; let them be covered with reproach and dishonor who seek my hurt. But I will hope continually and will praise You yet more and more. My mouth shall tell of Your righteousness and Your salvation all the day, for I do not know their limits. I will go in the strength of the Lord God; I will make mention of Your righteousness, of Yours only. O God, You have taught me from my youth; and to this day I declare Your wondrous works. Now also when I am old and gray-headed, O God, do not forsake me until I declare Your strength to this generation, Your power to everyone who is to come. Also, Your righteousness, O God, is very high, You who have done great things; O God, who is like You? You, who have shown me great and severe troubles, shall revive me again and bring me up again from the depths of the earth. You shall increase my greatness and comfort me on every side. Also, with the lute, I will praise You—and Your faithfulness, O my God! To You, I will sing with the harp, O Holy One of Israel. My lips shall greatly rejoice when I sing to You, and my soul, which You have redeemed. My tongue also shall talk of Your righteousness all the day long; for they are confounded, for they are brought to shame who seek my hurt

Chapter 72

A Psalm of Solomon Give the king Your judgments, O God, and Your righteousness to the king's Son. He will judge Your people with righteousness and Your poor with justice. The mountains will bring peace to the people, and the little hills, by righteousness. He will bring justice to the poor of the people; He will save the children of the needy and will break in pieces the oppressor. They shall fear You as long as the sun and moon endure, throughout all generations. He shall come down like rain upon the mown grass, like showers that water the earth. In His days, the righteous shall flourish, and abundance of peace until the moon is no more. He shall have dominion also from sea to sea, and from the River to the ends of the earth. Those who dwell in the wilderness will bow before Him, and His enemies will lick the dust. The kings of Tarshish and of the isles will bring presents; the kings of Sheba and Seba will offer gifts. Yes, all kings shall fall down before Him; all nations shall serve Him. For He will deliver the needy when he cries, the poor also, and him who has no helper. He will spare the poor and needy and will save the souls of the needy. He will redeem their life from oppression and violence, and precious shall be their blood in His sight. And He shall live, and the gold of Sheba will be given to Him; prayer also will be made for Him continually, and daily He shall be praised. There will be an abundance of grain in the earth, on the top of the mountains; its fruit shall wave like Lebanon, and those of the city shall flourish like grass of the earth. His name shall endure forever; His name shall continue as long as the sun. And men shall be blessed in Him; all nations shall call Him blessed. Blessed be the Lord God, the God of Israel, who only does wondrous things! And blessed be His glorious name forever! And let the whole earth be filled with His glory. Amen and Amen. The prayers of David, the son of Jesse, are ended

Chapter 73

A Psalm of Asaph Truly God is good to Israel, to such as are pure in heart. But as for me, my feet had almost stumbled; my steps had nearly slipped. For I was envious of the boastful when I saw the prosperity of the wicked. For there are no pangs in their death, but their strength is firm. They are not in trouble as other men, nor are they plagued like other men. Therefore pride serves as their necklace; violence covers them like a garment. Their eyes bulge with abundance; they have more than heart could wish. They scoff and speak wickedly concerning oppression; they speak loftily. They set their mouth against the heavens, and their tongue walks through the earth. Therefore His people return here, and waters of a full cup are drained by them. And they say, "How does God know? And is there knowledge in the Most High?" Behold, these are the ungodly, who are always at ease; they increase in riches. Surely I have cleansed my heart in vain and washed my hands in innocence. For all day long, I have been plagued and chastened every morning. If I had said, "I will speak thus," behold, I would have been untrue to the generation of Your children. When I thought how to understand this, it was too painful for me— until I went into the sanctuary of God; then I understood their end. Surely You set them in slippery places; You cast them down to destruction. Oh, how they are brought to desolation, as in a moment! They are utterly consumed with terrors. As a dream when one awakes, so, Lord, when You awake, You shall despise their image. Thus my heart was grieved, and I was vexed in my mind. I was so foolish and ignorant; I was like a beast before You. Nevertheless, I am continually with You; You hold me by my right hand. You will guide me with Your counsel, and afterward receive me to glory. Whom have I in heaven but You? And there is none upon earth that I desire besides You. My flesh and my heart fail; but God is the strength of my heart and my portion forever. For indeed, those who are far from You shall perish; You have destroyed all those who desert You for harlotry. But it is good for me to draw near to God; I have put my trust in the Lord God, that I may declare all Your works

Chapter 74

A Contemplation of Asaph O God, why have You cast us off forever? Why does Your anger smoke against the sheep of Your pasture? Remember Your congregation, which You have purchased of old, the tribe of Your inheritance, which You have redeemed—this Mount Zion where You have dwelt. Lift up Your feet to the perpetual desolations. The enemy has damaged everything in the sanctuary. Your enemies roar in the midst of Your meeting place; they set up their banners for signs. They seem like men who lift up axes among the thick trees. And now they break down its carved work, all at once, with axes and hammers. They have set fire to Your sanctuary; they have defiled the dwelling place of Your name to the ground. They said in their hearts, "Let us destroy them altogether." They have burned up all the meeting places of God in the land. We do not see our signs; there is no longer any prophet; nor is there any among us who knows how long. O God, how long will the adversary reproach? Will the enemy blaspheme Your name forever? Why do You withdraw Your hand, even Your right hand? Take it out of Your bosom and destroy them. For God is my King from of old, working salvation in the midst of the earth. You divided the sea by Your strength; You broke the heads of the sea serpents in the waters. You broke the heads of Leviathan in pieces and gave him as food to the people inhabiting the wilderness. You broke open the fountain and the flood; You dried up mighty rivers. The day is Yours, the night also is Yours; You have prepared the light and the sun. You have set all the borders of the earth; You have made summer and winter. Remember this, that the enemy has reproached, O Lord, and that a foolish people has blasphemed Your name. Oh, do not deliver the life of Your turtledove to the wild beast! Do not forget the life of Your poor forever. Have respect to the covenant, for the dark places of the earth are full of the haunts of cruelty. Oh, do not let the oppressed return ashamed! Let the poor and needy praise Your name. Arise, O God, plead Your own cause; remember how the foolish man reproaches You daily. Do not forget the voice of Your enemies; the tumult of those who rise up against You increases continually

Chapter 75

To the Chief Musician, Set to "Do Not Destroy," A Psalm of Asaph We give thanks to You, O God, we give thanks! For Your wondrous works declare that Your name is near. "When I choose the proper time, I will judge uprightly. The earth and all its inhabitants are dissolved; I set up its pillars firmly. Selah. "I said to the boastful, 'Do not deal boastfully,' and to the wicked, 'Do not lift up the horn. Do not lift up your horn on high; do not speak with a stiff neck.'" For exaltation comes neither from the east nor from the west nor from the south. But God is the Judge: He puts down one and exalts another. For in the hand of the Lord, there is a cup, and the wine is red; it is fully mixed, and He pours it out; surely its dregs shall all the wicked of the earth drain and drink down. But I will declare forever, I will sing praises to the God of Jacob. "All the horns of the wicked I will also cut off, but the horns of the righteous shall be exalted."

Chapter 76

To the Chief Musician on stringed instruments, A Psalm of Asaph In Judah, God is known; His name is great in Israel. In Salem also is His tabernacle, and His dwelling place in Zion. There He broke the arrows of the bow, the shield and sword of battle. Selah. You are more glorious and excellent than the mountains of prey. The stouthearted were plundered; they have sunk into their sleep; and none of the mighty men have found the use of their hands. At Your rebuke, O God of Jacob, both the chariot and horse were cast into a dead sleep. You, Yourself, are to be feared, and who may stand in Your presence when once You are angry? You caused judgment to be heard from heaven; the earth feared and was still when God arose to judgment, to deliver all the oppressed of the earth. Selah. Surely the wrath of man shall praise You; with the remainder of wrath, You shall gird Yourself. Make vows to the Lord your God and pay them; let all who are around Him bring presents to Him who ought to be feared. He shall cut off the spirit of princes; He is awesome to the kings of the earth

Chapter 77

To the Chief Musician, to Jeduthun, A Psalm of Asaph I cried out to God with my voice—to God with my voice; and He gave ear to me. In the day of my trouble, I sought the Lord; my hand was stretched out in the night without ceasing; my soul refused to be comforted. I remembered God and was troubled; I complained, and my spirit was overwhelmed. Selah. You hold my eyelids open; I am so troubled that I cannot speak. I have considered the days of old, the years of ancient times. I call to remembrance my song in the night; I meditate within my heart, and my spirit makes diligent search. Will the Lord cast off forever? And will He be favorable no more? Has His mercy ceased forever? Has His promise failed forevermore? Has God forgotten to be gracious? Has He in anger shut up His tender mercies? Selah. And I said, "This is my anguish; but I will remember the years of the right hand of the Most High." I will remember the works of the Lord; surely I will remember Your wonders of old. I will also meditate on all Your work and talk of Your deeds. Your way, O God, is in the sanctuary; who is so great a God as our God? You are the God who does wonders; You have declared Your strength among the peoples. You have with Your arm redeemed Your people, the sons of Jacob and Joseph. Selah. The waters saw You, O God; the waters saw You, they were afraid; the depths also trembled. The clouds poured out water; the skies sent out a sound; Your arrows also flashed about. The voice of Your thunder was in the whirlwind; the lightnings lit up the world; the earth trembled and shook. Your way was in the sea, Your path in the great waters, and Your footsteps were not known. You led Your people like a flock by the hand of Moses and Aaron

Chapter 78

A Contemplation of Asaph Give ear, O my people, to my law; incline your ears to the words of my mouth. I will open my mouth in a parable; I will utter dark sayings of old, which we have heard and known, and our fathers have told us. We will not hide them from their children, telling to the generation to come the praises of the Lord and His strength and His wonderful works that He has done. For He established a testimony in Jacob, and appointed a law in Israel, which He commanded our fathers, that they should make them known to their children; that the generation to come might know them, the children who would be born, that they may arise and declare them to their children, that they may set their hope in God, and not forget the works of God, but keep His commandments; and may not be like their fathers, a stubborn and rebellious generation, a generation that did not set its heart aright, and whose spirit was not faithful to God. The children of Ephraim, being armed and carrying bows, turned back in the day of battle. They did not keep the covenant of God; they refused to walk in His law and forgot His works and His wonders that He had shown them. Marvelous things He did in the sight of their fathers, in the land of Egypt, in the field of Zoan. He divided the sea and caused them to pass through; and He made the waters stand up like a heap. In the daytime also He led them with the cloud, and all the night with a light of fire. He split the rocks in the wilderness and gave them drink in abundance like the depths. He also brought streams out of the rock and caused waters to run down like rivers. But they sinned even more against Him by rebelling against the Most High in the wilderness. And they tested God in their heart by asking for the food of their fancy. Yes, they spoke against God: They said, "Can God prepare a table in the wilderness? Behold, He struck the rock so that the waters gushed out, and the streams overflowed. Can He give bread also? Can He provide meat for His people?" Therefore the Lord heard this and was furious; so a fire was kindled against Jacob, and anger also came up against Israel because they did not believe in God and did not trust in His salvation. Yet He had commanded the clouds above and opened the doors of heaven, had rained down manna on them to eat, and given them of the bread of heaven. Men ate angels' food; He sent them food to the full. He caused an east wind to blow in the heavens; and by His power, He brought in the south wind. He also rained meat on them like the dust, feathered fowl like the sand of the seas; and He let them fall in the midst of their camp, all around their dwellings. So they ate and were well filled, for He gave them their own desire. They were not deprived of their craving; but while their food was still in their mouths, the wrath of God came against them and slew the stoutest of them and struck down the choice men of Israel. In spite of this, they still sinned and did not believe in His wondrous works. Therefore their days He consumed in futility, and their years in fear. When He slew them, then they sought Him; and they returned and sought earnestly for God. Then they remembered that God was their rock, and the Most High God their Redeemer. Nevertheless, they flattered Him with their mouth, and they lied to Him with their tongue; for their heart was not steadfast with Him, nor were they faithful in His covenant. But He, being full of compassion, forgave their iniquity and did not destroy them. Yes, many a time, He turned His anger away and did not stir up all His wrath; for He remembered that they were but flesh, a breath that passes away and does not come again. How often they provoked Him in the wilderness and grieved Him in the desert! Yes, again and again, they tempted God and limited the Holy One of Israel. They did not remember His power: the day when He redeemed them from the enemy when He worked His signs in Egypt and His wonders in the field of Zoan; turned their rivers into blood, and their streams, that they could not drink. He sent swarms of flies among them, which devoured them, and frogs, which destroyed them. He also gave their crops to the caterpillar, and their labor to the locust. He destroyed their vines with hail and their sycamore trees with frost. He also gave up their cattle to the hail and their flocks to fiery lightning. He cast on them the fierceness of His anger, wrath, indignation, and trouble, by sending angels of destruction among them. He made a path for His anger; He did not spare their soul from death but gave their life over to the plague and destroyed all the firstborn in Egypt, the first of their strength in the tents of Ham. But He made His own people go forth like sheep and guided them in the wilderness like a flock; and He led them on safely so that they did not fear; but the sea overwhelmed their enemies. And He brought them to His holy border, this mountain which His right hand had acquired. He also drove out the nations before them, allotted them an inheritance by survey, and made the tribes of Israel dwell in their tents. Yet they tested and provoked the Most High God and did not keep His testimonies but turned back and acted unfaithfully like their fathers; they were turned aside like a deceitful bow. For they provoked Him to anger with their high places and moved Him to jealousy with their carved images. When God heard this, He was furious and greatly abhorred Israel, so that He forsook the tabernacle of Shiloh, the tent He had placed among men, and delivered His strength into captivity and His glory into the enemy's hand. He also gave His people over to the sword and was furious with His inheritance. The fire consumed their young men, and their maidens were not given in marriage. Their priests fell by the sword, and their widows made no lamentation. Then the Lord awoke as from sleep, like a mighty man who shouts because of wine. And He beat back His enemies; He put them to a perpetual reproach. Moreover, He rejected the tent of Joseph and did not choose the tribe of Ephraim, but chose the tribe of Judah, Mount Zion, which He loved. And He built His sanctuary like the heights, like the earth which He has established forever. He also chose David His servant and took him from the sheepfolds; from following the ewes that had young, He brought him to shepherd Jacob, His people, and Israel, His inheritance. So he shepherded them according to the integrity of his heart and guided them by the skillfulness of his hands

Chapter 79

A Psalm of Asaph O God, the nations have come into Your inheritance; Your holy temple they have defiled; they have laid Jerusalem in heaps. The dead bodies of Your servants they have given as food for the birds of the heavens, the flesh of Your saints to the beasts of the earth. Their blood they have shed like water all around Jerusalem, and there was no one to bury them. We have become a reproach to our neighbors, a scorn and derision to those who are around us. How long, Lord? Will You be angry forever? Will Your jealousy burn like fire? Pour out Your wrath on the nations that do not know You and on the kingdoms that do not call on Your name. For they have devoured Jacob and laid waste his dwelling place. Oh, do not remember former iniquities against us! Let Your tender mercies come speedily to meet us, for we have been brought very low. Help us, O God of our salvation, for the glory of Your name; and deliver us and provide atonement for our sins, for Your name's sake! Why should the nations say, "Where is their God?" Let there be known among the nations in our sight the avenging of the blood of Your servants which has been shed. Let the groaning of the prisoner come before You; according to the greatness of Your power preserve those who are appointed to die; and return to our neighbors sevenfold into their bosom their reproach with which they have reproached You, O Lord. So we, Your people and sheep of Your pasture, will give You thanks forever; we will show forth Your praise to all generations

Chapter 80

To the Chief Musician, Set to "The Lilies," A Testimony of Asaph Give ear, O Shepherd of Israel, You who lead Joseph like a flock; You who dwell between the cherubim, shine forth! Before Ephraim, Benjamin, and Manasseh, stir up Your strength and come and save us! Restore us, O God; cause Your face to shine, and we shall be saved! O Lord God of hosts, how long will You be angry against the prayer of Your people? You have fed them with the bread of tears and given them tears to drink in great measure. You have made us a strife to our neighbors, and our enemies laugh among themselves. Restore us, O God of hosts; cause Your face to shine, and we shall be saved! You have brought a vine out of Egypt; You have cast out the nations and planted it. You prepared room for it and caused it to take deep root, and it filled the land. The hills were covered with its shadow and the mighty cedars with its boughs. She sent out her boughs to the Sea and her branches to the River. Why have You broken down her hedges so that all who pass by the way pluck her fruit? The boar out of the woods uproots it, and the wild beast of the field devours it. Return, we beseech You, O God of hosts; look down from heaven and see and visit this vine and the vineyard which Your right hand has planted, and the branch that You made strong for Yourself. It is burned with fire, it is cut down; they perish at the rebuke of Your countenance. Let Your hand be upon the man of Your right hand, upon the son of man whom You made strong for Yourself. Then we will not turn back from You; revive us, and we will call upon Your name. Restore us, O Lord God of hosts; cause Your face to shine, and we shall be saved!

Chapter 81

To the Chief Musician on the Gittith. A Psalm of Asaph 1 Sing aloud to God our strength; make a joyful shout to the God of Jacob. 2 Raise a song and strike the timbrel, the pleasant harp with the lute. 3 Blow the trumpet at the time of the New Moon, at the full moon, on our solemn feast day. 4 For this is a statute for Israel, a law of the God of Jacob. 5 This He established in Joseph as a testimony, when He went throughout the land of Egypt, where I heard a language I did not understand. 6 "I removed his shoulder from the burden; his hands were freed from the baskets. 7 You called in trouble, and I delivered you; I answered you in the secret place of thunder; I tested you at the waters of Meribah. Selah 8 "Hear, O My people, and I will admonish you! O Israel, if you will listen to Me! 9 There shall be no foreign god among you; nor shall you worship any foreign god. 10 I am the Lord your God, who brought you out of the land of Egypt; open your mouth wide, and I will fill it. 11 "But My people would not heed My voice, and Israel would have none of Me. 12 So I gave them over to their own stubborn heart, to walk in their own counsels. 13 "Oh, that My people would listen to Me, that Israel would walk in My ways! 14 I would soon subdue their enemies, and turn My hand against their adversaries. 15 The haters of the Lord would pretend submission to Him, but their fate would endure forever. 16 He would have fed them also with the finest of wheat; and with honey from the rock I would have satisfied you."

Chapter 82

A Psalm of Asaph 1 God stands in the congregation of the mighty; He judges among the gods. 2 How long will you judge unjustly, and show partiality to the wicked? Selah 3 Defend the poor and fatherless; do justice to the afflicted and needy. 4 Deliver the poor and needy; free them from the hand of the wicked. 5 They do not know, nor do they understand; they walk about in darkness; all the foundations of the earth are unstable. 6 I said, "You are gods, and all of you are children of the Most High. 7 But you shall die like men, and fall like one of the princes." 8 Arise, O God, judge the earth; for You shall inherit all nations

Chapter 83

A Song. A Psalm of Asaph 1 Do not keep silent, O God! Do not hold Your peace, and do not be still, O God! 2 For behold, Your enemies make a tumult; and those who hate You have lifted up their head. 3 They have taken crafty counsel against Your people, and consulted together against Your sheltered ones. 4 They have said, "Come, and let us cut them off from being a nation, that the name of Israel may be remembered no more." 5 For they have consulted together with one consent; they form a confederacy against You: 6 The tents of Edom and the Ishmaelites; Moab and the Hagrites; 7 Gebal, Ammon, and Amalek; Philistia with the inhabitants of Tyre; 8 Assyria also has joined with them; they have helped the children of Lot. Selah 9 Deal with them as with Midian, as with Sisera, as with Jabin at the Brook Kishon, 10 Who perished at En Dor, who became as refuse on the earth. 11 Make their nobles like Oreb and like Zeeb, yes, all their princes like Zebah and Zalmunna, 12 Who said, "Let us take for ourselves the pastures of God for a possession." 13 O my God, make them like the whirling dust, like the chaff before the wind! 14 As the fire burns the woods, and as the flame sets the mountains on fire, 15 So pursue them with Your tempest, and frighten them with Your storm. 16 Fill their faces with shame, that they may seek Your name, O Lord. 17 Let them be confounded and dismayed forever; yes, let them be put to shame and perish, 18 That they may know that You, whose name alone is the Lord, are the Most High over all the earth

Chapter 84

To the Chief Musician. On an instrument of Gath. A Psalm of the Sons of Korah 1 How lovely is Your tabernacle, O Lord of hosts! 2 My soul longs, yes, even faints for the courts of the Lord; my heart and my flesh cry out for the living God. 3 Even the sparrow has found a home, and the swallow a nest for herself, where she may lay her young— even Your altars, O Lord of hosts, my King and my God. 4 Blessed are those who dwell in Your house; they will still be praising You. Selah 5 Blessed is the man whose strength is in You, whose heart is set on pilgrimage. 6 As they pass through the Valley of Baca, they make it a spring; the rain also covers it with pools. 7 They go from strength to strength; each one appears before God in Zion. 8 O Lord God of hosts, hear my prayer; give ear, O God of Jacob! Selah 9 O God, behold our shield, and look upon the face of Your anointed. 10 For a day in Your courts is better than a thousand. I would rather be a doorkeeper in the house of my God than dwell in the tents of wickedness. 11 For the Lord God is a sun and shield; the Lord will give grace and glory; no good thing will He withhold from those who walk uprightly. 12 O Lord of hosts, blessed is the man who trusts in You!

Chapter 85

To the Chief Musician. A Psalm of the Sons of Korah 1 Lord, You have been favorable to Your land; You have brought back the captivity of Jacob. 2 You have forgiven the iniquity of Your people; You have covered all their sin. Selah 3 You have taken away all Your wrath; You have turned from the fierceness of Your anger. 4 Restore us, O God of our salvation, and cause Your anger toward us to cease. 5 Will You be angry with us forever? Will You prolong Your anger to all generations? 6 Will You not revive us again, that Your people may rejoice in You? 7 Show us Your mercy, Lord, and grant us Your salvation. 8 I will hear what God the Lord will speak, for He will speak peace to His people and to His saints; but let them not turn back to folly. 9 Surely His salvation is near to those who fear Him, that glory may dwell in our land. 10 Mercy and truth have met together; righteousness and peace have kissed. 11 Truth shall spring out of the earth, and righteousness shall look down from heaven. 12 Yes, the Lord will give what is good; and our land will yield its increase. 13 Righteousness will go before Him, and shall make His footsteps our pathway

Chapter 86 A Prayer of David

1 Bow down Your ear, O Lord, hear me; for I am poor and needy. 2 Preserve my life, for I am holy; You are

my God; save Your servant who trusts in You! 3 Be merciful to me, O Lord, for I cry to You all day long. 4 Rejoice the soul of Your servant, for to You, O Lord, I lift up my soul. 5 For You, Lord, are good, and ready to forgive, and abundant in mercy to all those who call upon You. 6 Give ear, O Lord, to my prayer; and attend to the voice of my supplications. 7 In the day of my trouble, I will call upon You, for You will answer me. 8 Among the gods, there is none like You, O Lord; nor are there any works like Your works. 9 All nations whom You have made shall come and worship before You, O Lord, and shall glorify Your name. 10 For You are great and do wondrous things; You alone are God. 11 Teach me Your way, O Lord; I will walk in Your truth; unite my heart to fear Your name. 12 I will praise You, O Lord my God, with all my heart, and I will glorify Your name forevermore. 13 For great is Your mercy toward me, and You have delivered my soul from the depths of Sheol. 14 O God, the proud have risen against me, and a mob of violent men have sought my life, and have not set You before them. 15 But You, O Lord, are a God full of compassion, and gracious, long-suffering and abundant in mercy and truth. 16 Oh, turn to me, and have mercy on me! Give Your strength to Your servant, and save the son of Your maidservant. 17 Show me a sign for good, that those who hate me may see it and be ashamed because You, Lord, have helped me and comforted me

Chapter 87 A Psalm of the Sons of Korah. A Song
1 His foundation is in the holy mountains. 2 The Lord loves the gates of Zion more than all the dwellings of Jacob. 3 Glorious things are spoken of you, O city of God! Selah 4 "I will make mention of Rahab and Babylon to those who know Me; behold, O Philistia and Tyre, with Ethiopia: 'This one was born there.'" 5 And of Zion it will be said, "This one and that one were born in her; and the Most High Himself shall establish her." 6 The Lord will record, when He registers the peoples: "This one was born there." Selah 7 Both the singers and the players on instruments say, "All my springs are in you."

Chapter 88 A Song. A Psalm of the Sons of Korah. To the Chief Musician. Set to "Mahalath Leannoth." A Contemplation of Heman the Ezrahite
1 O Lord, God of my salvation, I have cried out day and night before You. 2 Let my prayer come before You; incline Your ear to my cry. 3 For my soul is full of troubles, and my life draws near to the grave. 4 I am counted with those who go down to the pit; I am like a man who has no strength, 5 Adrift among the dead, like the slain who lie in the grave, whom You remember no more, and who are cut off from Your hand. 6 You have laid me in the lowest pit, in darkness, in the depths. 7 Your wrath lies heavy upon me, and You have afflicted me with all Your waves. Selah 8 You have put away my acquaintances far from me; You have made me an abomination to them; I am shut up, and I cannot get out; 9 My eye wastes away because of affliction. Lord, I have called daily upon You; I have stretched out my hands to You. 10 Will You work wonders for the dead? Shall the dead arise and praise You? Selah 11 Shall Your loving-kindness be declared in the grave? Or Your faithfulness in the place of destruction? 12 Shall Your wonders be known in the dark? And Your righteousness in the land of forgetfulness? 13 But to You I have cried out, O Lord, and in the morning my prayer comes before You. 14 Lord, why do You cast off my soul? Why do You hide Your face from me? 15 I have been afflicted and ready to die from my youth; I suffer Your terrors; I am distraught. 16 Your fierce wrath has gone over me; Your terrors have cut me off. 17 They came around me all day long like water; they engulfed me altogether. 18 Loved one and friend You have put far from me, and my acquaintances into darkness

Chapter 89 A Contemplation of Ethan the Ezrahite
1 I will sing of the mercies of the Lord forever; with my mouth will I make known Your faithfulness to all generations. 2 For I have said, "Mercy shall be built up forever; Your faithfulness You shall establish in the very heavens." 3 "I have made a covenant with My chosen, I have sworn to My servant David: 4 'Your seed I will establish forever, and build up your throne to all generations.'" Selah 5 And the heavens will praise Your wonders, O Lord; Your faithfulness also in the assembly of the saints. 6 For who in the heavens can be compared to the Lord? Who among the sons of the mighty can be likened to the Lord? 7 God is greatly to be feared in the assembly of the saints, and to be held in reverence by all those around Him. 8 O Lord God of hosts, who is mighty like You, O Lord? Your faithfulness also surrounds You. 9 You rule the raging of the sea; when its waves rise, You still them. 10 You have broken Rahab in pieces, as one who is slain; You have scattered Your enemies with Your mighty arm. 11 The heavens are Yours, the earth also is Yours; the world and all its fullness, You have founded them. 12 The north and the south, You have created them; Tabor and Hermon rejoice in Your name. 13 You have a mighty arm; strong is Your hand, and high is Your right hand. 14 Righteousness and justice are the foundation of Your throne; mercy and truth go before Your face. 15 Blessed are the people who know the joyful sound! They walk, O Lord, in the light of Your countenance. 16 In Your name they rejoice all day long, and in Your righteousness they are exalted. 17 For You are the glory of their strength, and in Your favor our horn is exalted. 18 For our shield belongs to the Lord, and our king to the Holy One of Israel. 19 Then You spoke in a vision to Your holy one, and said: "I have given help to one who is mighty; I have exalted one chosen from the people. 20 I have found My servant David; with My holy oil I have anointed him, 21 With whom My hand shall be established; also My arm shall strengthen him. 22 The enemy shall not outwit him, nor the son of wickedness afflict him. 23 I will beat down his foes before his face, and plague those who hate him. 24 "But My faithfulness and My mercy shall be with him, and in My name his horn shall be exalted. 25 Also I will set his hand over the sea, and his right hand over the rivers. 26 He shall cry to Me, 'You are my Father, my God, and the rock of my salvation.' 27 Also I will make him My firstborn, the highest of the kings of the earth. 28 My mercy I will keep for him forever, and My covenant shall stand firm with him. 29 His seed also I will make to endure forever, and his throne as the days of heaven. 30 "If his sons forsake My law and do not walk in My judgments, 31 If they break My statutes and do not keep My commandments, 32 Then I will punish their transgression with the rod, and their iniquity with stripes. 33 Nevertheless My loving-kindness I will not utterly take from him, nor allow My faithfulness to fail. 34 My covenant I will not break, nor alter the word that has gone out of My lips. 35 Once I have sworn by My holiness; I will not lie to David: 36 His seed shall endure forever, and his throne as the sun before Me; 37 It shall be established forever like the moon, even like the faithful witness in the sky." Selah 38 But You have cast off and abhorred, You have been furious with Your anointed. 39 You have renounced the covenant of Your servant; You have profaned his crown by casting it to the ground. 40 You have broken down all his hedges; You have brought his strongholds to ruin. 41 All who pass by the way plunder him; he is a reproach to his neighbors. 42

You have exalted the right hand of his adversaries; You have made all his enemies rejoice. 43 You have also turned back the edge of his sword and have not sustained him in the battle. 44 You have made his glory cease and cast his throne down to the ground. 45 The days of his youth You have shortened; You have covered him with shame. Selah 46 How long, Lord? Will You hide Yourself forever? Will Your wrath burn like fire? 47 Remember how short my time is; for what futility have You created all the children of men? 48 What man can live and not see death? Can he deliver his life from the power of the grave? Selah 49 Lord, where are Your former loving-kindnesses, which You swore to David in Your truth? 50 Remember, Lord, the reproach of Your servants—how I bear in my bosom the reproach of all the many peoples, 51 With which Your enemies have reproached, O Lord, with which they have reproached the footsteps of Your anointed. 52 Blessed be the Lord forevermore! Amen and Amen

Chapter 90

A Prayer of Moses the Man of God 1 Lord, You have been our dwelling place in all generations. 2 Before the mountains were brought forth, or ever You had formed the earth and the world, even from everlasting to everlasting, You are God. 3 You turn man to destruction, and say, "Return, O children of men." 4 For a thousand years in Your sight are like yesterday when it is past, and like a watch in the night. 5 You carry them away like a flood; they are like a sleep. In the morning they are like grass which grows up: 6 In the morning it flourishes and grows up; in the evening it is cut down and withers. 7 For we have been consumed by Your anger, and by Your wrath we are terrified. 8 You have set our iniquities before You, our secret sins in the light of Your countenance. 9 For all our days have passed away in Your wrath; we finish our years like a sigh. 10 The days of our lives are seventy years; and if by reason of strength they are eighty years, yet their boast is only labor and sorrow; for it is soon cut off, and we fly away. 11 Who knows the power of Your anger? For as the fear of You, so is Your wrath. 12 So teach us to number our days, that we may gain a heart of wisdom. 13 Return, O Lord! How long? And have compassion on Your servants. 14 Oh, satisfy us early with Your mercy, that we may rejoice and be glad all our days! 15 Make us glad according to the days in which You have afflicted us, the years in which we have seen evil. 16 Let Your work appear to Your servants, and Your glory to their children. 17 And let the beauty of the Lord our God be upon us, and establish the work of our hands for us; yes, establish the work of our hands

Chapter 91

1 He who dwells in the secret place of the Most High shall abide under the shadow of the Almighty. 2 I will say of the Lord, "He is my refuge and my fortress; my God, in Him I will trust." 3 Surely He shall deliver you from the snare of the fowler and from the perilous pestilence. 4 He shall cover you with His feathers, and under His wings you shall take refuge; His truth shall be your shield and buckler. 5 You shall not be afraid of the terror by night, nor of the arrow that flies by day, 6 Nor of the pestilence that walks in darkness, nor of the destruction that lays waste at noonday. 7 A thousand may fall at your side, and ten thousand at your right hand; but it shall not come near you. 8 Only with your eyes shall you look and see the reward of the wicked. 9 Because you have made the Lord, who is my refuge, even the Most High, your dwelling place, 10 No evil shall befall you, nor shall any plague come near your dwelling; 11 For He shall give His angels charge over you, to keep you in all your ways. 12 In their hands they shall bear you up, lest you dash your foot against a stone. 13 You shall tread upon the lion and the cobra, the young lion and the serpent you shall trample underfoot. 14 "Because he has set his love upon Me, therefore I will deliver him; I will set him on high, because he has known My name. 15 He shall call upon Me, and I will answer him; I will be with him in trouble; I will deliver him and honor him. 16 With long life I will satisfy him, and show him My salvation."

Chapter 92

A Psalm. A Song for the Sabbath Day 1 It is good to give thanks to the Lord, and to sing praises to Your name, O Most High; 2 To declare Your lovingkindness in the morning, and Your faithfulness every night, 3 On an instrument of ten strings, on the lute, and on the harp, with harmonious sound. 4 For You, Lord, have made me glad through Your work; I will triumph in the works of Your hands. 5 O Lord, how great are Your works! Your thoughts are very deep. 6 A senseless man does not know, nor does a fool understand this. 7 When the wicked spring up like grass, and when all the workers of iniquity flourish, it is that they may be destroyed forever. 8 But You, Lord, are on high forevermore. 9 For behold, Your enemies, O Lord, for behold, Your enemies shall perish; all the workers of iniquity shall be scattered. 10 But my horn You have exalted like a wild ox; I have been anointed with fresh oil. 11 My eye also has seen my desire on my enemies; my ears hear my desire on the wicked who rise up against me. 12 The righteous shall flourish like a palm tree, he shall grow like a cedar in Lebanon. 13 Those who are planted in the house of the Lord shall flourish in the courts of our God. 14 They shall still bear fruit in old age; they shall be fresh and flourishing, 15 To declare that the Lord is upright; He is my rock, and there is no unrighteousness in Him

Chapter 93

1 The Lord reigns, He is clothed with majesty; the Lord is clothed, He has girded Himself with strength. Surely the world is established, so that it cannot be moved. 2 Your throne is established from of old; You are from everlasting. 3 The floods have lifted up, O Lord, the floods have lifted up their voice; the floods lift up their waves. 4 The Lord on high is mightier than the noise of many waters, than the mighty waves of the sea. 5 Your testimonies are very sure; holiness adorns Your house, O Lord, forever

Chapter 94

1 O Lord God, to whom vengeance belongs— O God, to whom vengeance belongs, shine forth! 2 Rise up, O Judge of the earth; render punishment to the proud. 3 Lord, how long will the wicked, how long will the wicked triumph? 4 They utter speech, and speak insolent things; all the workers of iniquity boast in themselves. 5 They break in pieces Your people, O Lord, and afflict Your heritage. 6 They slay the widow and the stranger, and murder the fatherless. 7 Yet they say, "The Lord does not see, nor does the God of Jacob understand." 8 Understand, you senseless among the people; and you fools, when will you be wise? 9 He who planted the ear, shall He not hear? He who formed the eye, shall He not see? 10 He who instructs the nations, shall He not correct, He who teaches man knowledge? 11 The Lord knows the thoughts of man, that they are futile. 12 Blessed is the man whom You instruct, O Lord, and teach out of Your law, 13 That You may give him rest from the days of adversity, until the pit is dug for the wicked. 14 For the Lord will not cast off His people, nor will He forsake His inheritance. 15 But judgment will return to righteousness, and all the upright in heart will follow it. 16 Who will rise up for me against the evildoers? Who will stand up for me against the

workers of iniquity? 17 Unless the Lord had been my help, my soul would soon have settled in silence. 18 If I say, "My foot slips," Your mercy, O Lord, will hold me up. 19 In the multitude of my anxieties within me, Your comforts delight my soul. 20 Shall the throne of iniquity, which devises evil by law, have fellowship with You? 21 They gather together against the life of the righteous, and condemn innocent blood. 22 But the Lord has been my defense, and my God the rock of my refuge. 23 He has brought on them their own iniquity, and shall cut them off in their own wickedness; the Lord our God shall cut them off

Chapter 95

1 Oh come, let us sing to the Lord! Let us shout joyfully to the Rock of our salvation. 2 Let us come before His presence with thanksgiving; let us shout joyfully to Him with psalms. 3 For the Lord is the great God, and the great King above all gods. 4 In His hand are the deep places of the earth; the heights of the hills are His also. 5 The sea is His, for He made it; and His hands formed the dry land. 6 Oh come, let us worship and bow down; let us kneel before the Lord our Maker. 7 For He is our God, and we are the people of His pasture, and the sheep of His hand. Today, if you will hear His voice: 8 "Do not harden your hearts, as in the rebellion, as in the day of trial in the wilderness, 9 When your fathers tested Me; they tried Me, though they saw My work. 10 For forty years I was grieved with that generation, and said, 'It is a people who go astray in their hearts, and they do not know My ways.' 11 So I swore in My wrath, 'They shall not enter My rest.'"

Chapter 96

1 Oh, sing to the Lord a new song! Sing to the Lord, all the earth. 2 Sing to the Lord, bless His name; proclaim the good news of His salvation from day to day. 3 Declare His glory among the nations, His wonders among all peoples. 4 For the Lord is great and greatly to be praised; He is to be feared above all gods. 5 For all the gods of the peoples are idols, but the Lord made the heavens. 6 Honor and majesty are before Him; strength and beauty are in His sanctuary. 7 Give to the Lord, O families of the peoples, give to the Lord glory and strength. 8 Give to the Lord the glory due His name; bring an offering, and come into His courts. 9 Oh, worship the Lord in the beauty of holiness! Tremble before Him, all the earth. 10 Say among the nations, "The Lord reigns; the world also is firmly established, it shall not be moved; He shall judge the peoples righteously." 11 Let the heavens rejoice, and let the earth be glad; let the sea roar, and all its fullness; 12 Let the field be joyful, and all that is in it. Then all the trees of the woods will rejoice 13 before the Lord. For He is coming, for He is coming to judge the earth. He shall judge the world with righteousness, and the peoples with His truth

Chapter 97

1 The Lord reigns; let the earth rejoice; let the multitude of isles be glad! 2 Clouds and darkness surround Him; righteousness and justice are the foundation of His throne. 3 A fire goes before Him, and burns up His enemies round about. 4 His lightnings light the world; the earth sees and trembles. 5 The mountains melt like wax at the presence of the Lord, at the presence of the Lord of the whole earth. 6 The heavens declare His righteousness, and all the peoples see His glory. 7 Let all be put to shame who serve carved images, who boast of idols. Worship Him, all you gods. 8 Zion hears and is glad, and the daughters of Judah rejoice because of Your judgments, O Lord. 9 For You, Lord, are most high above all the earth; You are exalted far above all gods. 10 You who love the Lord, hate evil!

He preserves the souls of His saints; He delivers them out of the hand of the wicked. 11 Light is sown for the righteous, and gladness for the upright in heart. 12 Rejoice in the Lord, you righteous, and give thanks at the remembrance of His holy name

Chapter 98

A Psalm 1 Oh, sing to the Lord a new song! For He has done marvelous things; His right hand and His holy arm have gained Him the victory. 2 The Lord has made known His salvation; His righteousness He has revealed in the sight of the nations. 3 He has remembered His mercy and His faithfulness to the house of Israel; all the ends of the earth have seen the salvation of our God. 4 Shout joyfully to the Lord, all the earth; break forth in song, rejoice, and sing praises. 5 Sing to the Lord with the harp, with the harp and the sound of a psalm, 6 With trumpets and the sound of a horn; shout joyfully before the Lord, the King. 7 Let the sea roar, and all its fullness, the world and those who dwell in it; 8 Let the rivers clap their hands; let the hills be joyful together 9 before the Lord, for He is coming to judge the earth. With righteousness He shall judge the world, and the peoples with equity

Chapter 99

1 The Lord reigns; let the peoples tremble! He dwells between the cherubim; let the earth be moved! 2 The Lord is great in Zion, and He is high above all the peoples. 3 Let them praise Your great and awesome name— He is holy. 4 The King's strength also loves justice; You have established equity; You have executed justice and righteousness in Jacob. 5 Exalt the Lord our God, and worship at His footstool— He is holy. 6 Moses and Aaron were among His priests, and Samuel was among those who called upon His name; they called upon the Lord, and He answered them. 7 He spoke to them in the cloudy pillar; they kept His testimonies and the ordinance He gave them. 8 You answered them, O Lord our God; You were to them God-Who-Forgives, though You took vengeance on their deeds. 9 Exalt the Lord our God, and worship at His holy hill; for the Lord our God is holy

Chapter 100

A Psalm of Thanksgiving 1 Make a joyful shout to the Lord, all you lands! 2 Serve the Lord with gladness; come before His presence with singing. 3 Know that the Lord, He is God; it is He who has made us, and not we ourselves; we are His people and the sheep of His pasture. 4 Enter into His gates with thanksgiving, and into His courts with praise. Be thankful to Him, and bless His name. 5 For the Lord is good; His mercy is everlasting, and His truth endures to all generations

Chapter 101

A Psalm of David 1 I will sing of mercy and judgment; unto thee, O Lord, will I sing. 2 I will behave myself wisely in a perfect way. O when wilt thou come unto me? I will walk within my house with a perfect heart. 3 I will set no wicked thing before mine eyes: I hate the work of them that turn aside; it shall not cleave to me. 4 A froward heart shall depart from me: I will not know a wicked person. 5 Whoso privily slandereth his neighbor, him will I cut off: him that hath a high look and a proud heart will not I suffer. 6 Mine eyes shall be upon the faithful of the land, that they may dwell with me: he that walketh in a perfect way, he shall serve me. 7 He that worketh deceit shall not dwell within my house: he that telleth lies shall not tarry in my sight. 8 I will early destroy all the wicked of the land; that I may cut off all wicked doers from the city of the Lord

Chapter 102

A Prayer of the afflicted, when he is overwhelmed, and poureth out his complaint before the Lord 1 Hear my prayer, O Lord, and let my cry come unto thee. 2 Hide not thy face from me in the day when I am in trouble; incline thine ear unto me: in the day when I call, answer me speedily. 3 For my days are consumed like smoke, and my bones are burned as an hearth. 4 My heart is smitten, and withered like grass; so that I forget to eat my bread. 5 By reason of the voice of my groaning my bones cleave to my skin. 6 I am like a pelican of the wilderness: I am like an owl of the desert. 7 I watch, and am as a sparrow alone upon the house top. 8 Mine enemies reproach me all the day; and they that are mad against me are sworn against me. 9 For I have eaten ashes like bread, and mingled my drink with weeping, 10 Because of thine indignation and thy wrath: for thou hast lifted me up, and cast me down. 11 My days are like a shadow that declineth; and I am withered like grass. 12 But thou, O Lord, shalt endure forever; and thy remembrance unto all generations. 13 Thou shalt arise, and have mercy upon Zion: for the time to favor her, yea, the set time, is come. 14 For thy servants take pleasure in her stones, and favor the dust thereof. 15 So the heathen shall fear the name of the Lord, and all the kings of the earth thy glory. 16 When the Lord shall build up Zion, he shall appear in his glory. 17 He will regard the prayer of the destitute, and not despise their prayer. 18 This shall be written for the generation to come: and the people which shall be created shall praise the Lord. 19 For he hath looked down from the height of his sanctuary; from heaven did the Lord behold the earth; 20 To hear the groaning of the prisoner; to loose those that are appointed to death; 21 To declare the name of the Lord in Zion, and his praise in Jerusalem; 22 When the people are gathered together, and the kingdoms, to serve the Lord. 23 He weakened my strength in the way; he shortened my days. 24 I said, O my God, take me not away in the midst of my days: thy years are throughout all generations. 25 Of old hast thou laid the foundation of the earth: and the heavens are the work of thy hands. 26 They shall perish, but thou shalt endure: yea, all of them shall wax old like a garment; as a vesture shalt thou change them, and they shall be changed: 27 But thou art the same, and thy years shall have no end. 28 The children of thy servants shall continue, and their seed shall be established before thee

Chapter 103

A Psalm of David 1 Bless the Lord, O my soul: and all that is within me, bless his holy name. 2 Bless the Lord, O my soul, and forget not all his benefits: 3 Who forgiveth all thine iniquities; who healeth all thy diseases; 4 Who redeemeth thy life from destruction; who crowneth thee with lovingkindness and tender mercies; 5 Who satisfieth thy mouth with good things; so that thy youth is renewed like the eagle's. 6 The Lord executeth righteousness and judgment for all that are oppressed. 7 He made known his ways unto Moses, his acts unto the children of Israel. 8 The Lord is merciful and gracious, slow to anger, and plenteous in mercy. 9 He will not always chide: neither will he keep his anger forever. 10 He hath not dealt with us after our sins; nor rewarded us according to our iniquities. 11 For as the heaven is high above the earth, so great is his mercy toward them that fear him. 12 As far as the east is from the west, so far hath he removed our transgressions from us. 13 Like as a father pitieth his children, so the Lord pitieth them that fear him. 14 For he knoweth our frame; he remembereth that we are dust. 15 As for man, his days are as grass: as a flower of the field, so he flourisheth. 16 For the wind passeth over it, and it is gone; and the place thereof shall know it no more. 17 But the mercy of the Lord is from everlasting to everlasting upon them that fear him, and his righteousness unto children's children; 18 To such as keep his covenant, and to those that remember his commandments to do them. 19 The Lord hath prepared his throne in the heavens; and his kingdom ruleth over all. 20 Bless the Lord, ye his angels, that excel in strength, that do his commandments, hearkening unto the voice of his word. 21 Bless ye the Lord, all ye his hosts; ye ministers of his, that do his pleasure. 22 Bless the Lord, all his works in all places of his dominion: bless the Lord, O my soul

Chapter 104

1 Bless the Lord, O my soul. O Lord my God, thou art very great; thou art clothed with honor and majesty. 2 Who coverest thyself with light as with a garment: who stretchest out the heavens like a curtain: 3 Who layeth the beams of his chambers in the waters: who maketh the clouds his chariot: who walketh upon the wings of the wind: 4 Who maketh his angels spirits; his ministers a flaming fire: 5 Who laid the foundations of the earth, that it should not be removed forever. 6 Thou coveredst it with the deep as with a garment: the waters stood above the mountains. 7 At thy rebuke they fled; at the voice of thy thunder they hasted away. 8 They go up by the mountains; they go down by the valleys unto the place which thou hast founded for them. 9 Thou hast set a bound that they may not pass over; that they turn not again to cover the earth. 10 He sendeth the springs into the valleys, which run among the hills. 11 They give drink to every beast of the field: the wild asses quench their thirst. 12 By them shall the fowls of the heaven have their habitation, which sing among the branches. 13 He watereth the hills from his chambers: the earth is satisfied with the fruit of thy works. 14 He causeth the grass to grow for the cattle, and herb for the service of man: that he may bring forth food out of the earth; 15 And wine that maketh glad the heart of man, and oil to make his face to shine, and bread which strengtheneth man's heart. 16 The trees of the Lord are full of sap; the cedars of Lebanon, which he hath planted; 17 Where the birds make their nests: as for the stork, the fir trees are her house. 18 The high hills are a refuge for the wild goats; and the rocks for the conies. 19 He appointed the moon for seasons: the sun knoweth his going down. 20 Thou makest darkness, and it is night: wherein all the beasts of the forest do creep forth. 21 The young lions roar after their prey, and seek their meat from God. 22 The sun ariseth, they gather themselves together, and lay them down in their dens. 23 Man goeth forth unto his work and to his labor until the evening. 24 O Lord, how manifold are thy works! in wisdom hast thou made them all: the earth is full of thy riches. 25 So is this great and wide sea, wherein are things creeping innumerable, both small and great beasts. 26 There go the ships: there is that leviathan, whom thou hast made to play therein. 27 These wait all upon thee; that thou mayest give them their meat in due season. 28 That thou givest them they gather: thou openest thine hand, they are filled with good. 29 Thou hidest thy face, they are troubled: thou takest away their breath, they die, and return to their dust. 30 Thou sendest forth thy spirit, they are created: and thou renewest the face of the earth. 31 The glory of the Lord shall endure forever: the Lord shall rejoice in his works. 32 He looketh on the earth, and it trembleth: he toucheth the hills, and they smoke. 33 I will sing unto the Lord as long as I live: I will sing praise to my God while I have my being. 34 My meditation of him shall be sweet: I will be glad in the Lord. 35 Let the sinners be consumed out of the earth, and let the

wicked be no more. Bless thou the Lord, O my soul. Praise ye the Lord

Chapter 105

1 O give thanks unto the Lord; call upon his name: make known his deeds among the people. 2 Sing unto him, sing psalms unto him: talk ye of all his wondrous works. 3 Glory ye in his holy name: let the heart of them rejoice that seek the Lord. 4 Seek the Lord, and his strength: seek his face evermore. 5 Remember his marvelous works that he hath done; his wonders, and the judgments of his mouth; 6 O ye seed of Abraham his servant, ye children of Jacob his chosen. 7 He is the Lord our God: his judgments are in all the earth. 8 He hath remembered his covenant forever, the word which he commanded to a thousand generations. 9 Which covenant he made with Abraham, and his oath unto Isaac; 10 And confirmed the same unto Jacob for a law, and to Israel for an everlasting covenant: 11 Saying, Unto thee will I give the land of Canaan, the lot of your inheritance: 12 When they were but a few men in number; yea, very few, and strangers in it. 13 When they went from one nation to another, from one kingdom to another people; 14 He suffered no man to do them wrong: yea, he reproved kings for their sakes; 15 Saying, Touch not mine anointed, and do my prophets no harm. 16 Moreover he called for a famine upon the land: he brake the whole staff of bread. 17 He sent a man before them, even Joseph, who was sold for a servant: 18 Whose feet they hurt with fetters: he was laid in iron: 19 Until the time that his word came: the word of the Lord tried him. 20 The king sent and loosed him; even the ruler of the people, and let him go free. 21 He made him lord of his house, and ruler of all his substance: 22 To bind his princes at his pleasure; and teach his senators wisdom. 23 Israel also came into Egypt; and Jacob sojourned in the land of Ham. 24 And he increased his people greatly; and made them stronger than their enemies. 25 He turned their heart to hate his people, to deal subtilly with his servants. 26 He sent Moses his servant; and Aaron whom he had chosen. 27 They shewed his signs among them, and wonders in the land of Ham. 28 He sent darkness, and made it dark; and they rebelled not against his word. 29 He turned their waters into blood, and slew their fish. 30 Their land brought forth frogs in abundance, in the chambers of their kings. 31 He spake, and there came divers sorts of flies, and lice in all their coasts. 32 He gave them hail for rain, and flaming fire in their land. 33 He smote their vines also and their fig trees; and brake the trees of their coasts. 34 He spake, and the locusts came, and caterpillars, and that without number, 35 And did eat up all the herbs in their land, and devoured the fruit of their ground. 36 He smote also all the firstborn in their land, the chief of all their strength. 37 He brought them forth also with silver and gold: and there was not one feeble person among their tribes. 38 Egypt was glad when they departed: for the fear of them fell upon them. 39 He spread a cloud for a covering; and fire to give light in the night. 40 The people asked, and he brought quails, and satisfied them with the bread of heaven. 41 He opened the rock, and the waters gushed out; they ran in the dry places like a river. 42 For he remembered his holy promise, and Abraham his servant. 43 And he brought forth his people with joy, and his chosen with gladness: 44 And gave them the lands of the heathen: and they inherited the labour of the people; 45 That they might observe his statutes, and keep his laws. Praise ye the Lord

Chapter 106

1 Praise ye the Lord. O give thanks unto the Lord; for he is good: for his mercy endureth forever. 2 Who can utter the mighty acts of the Lord? who can show forth all his praise? 3 Blessed are they that keep judgment, and he that doeth righteousness at all times. 4 Remember me, O Lord, with the favor that thou bearest unto thy people: O visit me with thy salvation; 5 That I may see the good of thy chosen, that I may rejoice in the gladness of thy nation, that I may glory with thine inheritance. 6 We have sinned with our fathers, we have committed iniquity, we have done wickedly. 7 Our fathers understood not thy wonders in Egypt; they remembered not the multitude of thy mercies; but provoked him at the sea, even at the Red sea. 8 Nevertheless he saved them for his name's sake, that he might make his mighty power to be known. 9 He rebuked the Red sea also, and it was dried up: so he led them through the depths, as through the wilderness. 10 And he saved them from the hand of him that hated them, and redeemed them from the hand of the enemy. 11 And the waters covered their enemies: there was not one of them left. 12 Then believed they his words; they sang his praise. 13 They soon forgat his works; they waited not for his counsel: 14 But lusted exceedingly in the wilderness, and tempted God in the desert. 15 And he gave them their request; but sent leanness into their soul. 16 They envied Moses also in the camp, and Aaron the saint of the Lord. 17 The earth opened and swallowed up Dathan, and covered the company of Abiram. 18 And a fire was kindled in their company; the flame burned up the wicked. 19 They made a calf in Horeb, and worshipped the molten image. 20 Thus they changed their glory into the similitude of an ox that eateth grass. 21 They forgat God their saviour, which had done great things in Egypt; 22 Wondrous works in the land of Ham, and terrible things by the Red sea. 23 Therefore he said that he would destroy them, had not Moses his chosen stood before him in the breach, to turn away his wrath, lest he should destroy them. 24 Yea, they despised the pleasant land, they believed not his word: 25 But murmured in their tents, and hearkened not unto the voice of the Lord. 26 Therefore he lifted up his hand against them, to overthrow them in the wilderness: 27 To overthrow their seed also among the nations, and to scatter them in the lands. 28 They joined themselves also unto Baalpeor, and ate the sacrifices of the dead. 29 Thus they provoked him to anger with their inventions: and the plague brake in upon them. 30 Then stood up Phinehas, and executed judgment: and so the plague was stayed. 31 And that was counted unto him for righteousness unto all generations for evermore. 32 They angered him also at the waters of strife, so that it went ill with Moses for their sakes: 33 Because they provoked his spirit, so that he spake unadvisedly with his lips. 34 They did not destroy the nations, concerning whom the Lord commanded them: 35 But were mingled among the heathen, and learned their works. 36 And they served their idols: which were a snare unto them. 37 Yea, they sacrificed their sons and their daughters unto devils, 38 And shed innocent blood, even the blood of their sons and of their daughters, whom they sacrificed unto the idols of Canaan: and the land was polluted with blood. 39 Thus were they defiled with their own works, and went a whoring with their own inventions. 40 Therefore was the wrath of the Lord kindled against his people, insomuch that he abhorred his own inheritance. 41 And he gave them into the hand of the heathen; and they that hated them ruled over them. 42 Their enemies also oppressed them, and they were brought into subjection under their hand. 43 Many times did he deliver them; but they provoked him with their counsel, and were brought low for their iniquity. 44 Nevertheless he regarded their affliction, when he heard their cry: 45 And he remembered for them his

covenant, and repented according to the multitude of his mercies. 46 He made them also to be pitied of all those that carried them captives. 47 Save us, O Lord our God, and gather us from among the heathen, to give thanks unto thy holy name, and to triumph in thy praise. 48 Blessed be the Lord God of Israel from everlasting to everlasting: and let all the people say, Amen. Praise ye the Lord

Chapter 107

1 O give thanks unto the Lord, for he is good: for his mercy endureth forever. 2 Let the redeemed of the Lord say so, whom he hath redeemed from the hand of the enemy; 3 And gathered them out of the lands, from the east, and from the west, from the north, and from the south. 4 They wandered in the wilderness in a solitary way; they found no city to dwell in. 5 Hungry and thirsty, their soul fainted in them. 6 Then they cried unto the Lord in their trouble, and he delivered them out of their distresses. 7 And he led them forth by the right way, that they might go to a city of habitation. 8 Oh that men would praise the Lord for his goodness, and for his wonderful works to the children of men! 9 For he satisfieth the longing soul, and filleth the hungry soul with goodness. 10 Such as sit in darkness and in the shadow of death, being bound in affliction and iron; 11 Because they rebelled against the words of God, and contemned the counsel of the most High: 12 Therefore he brought down their heart with labour; they fell down, and there was none to help. 13 Then they cried unto the Lord in their trouble, and he saved them out of their distresses. 14 He brought them out of darkness and the shadow of death, and brake their bands in sunder. 15 Oh that men would praise the Lord for his goodness, and for his wonderful works to the children of men! 16 For he hath broken the gates of brass, and cut the bars of iron in sunder. 17 Fools because of their transgression, and because of their iniquities, are afflicted. 18 Their soul abhorreth all manner of meat; and they draw near unto the gates of death. 19 Then they cry unto the Lord in their trouble, and he saveth them out of their distresses. 20 He sent his word, and healed them, and delivered them from their destructions. 21 Oh that men would praise the Lord for his goodness, and for his wonderful works to the children of men! 22 And let them sacrifice the sacrifices of thanksgiving, and declare his works with rejoicing. 23 They that go down to the sea in ships, that do business in great waters; 24 These see the works of the Lord, and his wonders in the deep. 25 For he commandeth, and raiseth the stormy wind, which lifteth up the waves thereof. 26 They mount up to the heaven, they go down again to the depths: their soul is melted because of trouble. 27 They reel to and fro, and stagger like a drunken man, and are at their wits' end. 28 Then they cry unto the Lord in their trouble, and he bringeth them out of their distresses. 29 He maketh the storm a calm, so that the waves thereof are still. 30 Then are they glad because they be quiet; so he bringeth them unto their desired haven. 31 Oh that men would praise the Lord for his goodness, and for his wonderful works to the children of men! 32 Let them exalt him also in the congregation of the people, and praise him in the assembly of the elders. 33 He turneth rivers into a wilderness, and the watersprings into dry ground; 34 A fruitful land into barrenness, for the wickedness of them that dwell therein. 35 He turneth the wilderness into a standing water, and dry ground into watersprings. 36 And there he maketh the hungry to dwell, that they may prepare a city for habitation; 37 And sow the fields, and plant vineyards, which may yield fruits of increase. 38 He blesseth them also, so that they are multiplied greatly; and suffereth not their cattle to decrease. 39 Again, they are minished and brought low through oppression, affliction, and sorrow. 40 He poureth contempt upon princes, and causeth them to wander in the wilderness, where there is no way. 41 Yet setteth he the poor on high from affliction, and maketh him families like a flock. 42 The righteous shall see it, and rejoice: and all iniquity shall stop her mouth. 43 Whoso is wise, and will observe these things, even they shall understand the lovingkindness of the Lord

Chapter 108

A Song or Psalm of David 1 O God, my heart is fixed; I will sing and give praise, even with my glory. 2 Awake, psaltery and harp: I myself will awake early. 3 I will praise thee, O Lord, among the people: and I will sing praises unto thee among the nations. 4 For thy mercy is great above the heavens: and thy truth reacheth unto the clouds. 5 Be thou exalted, O God, above the heavens: and thy glory above all the earth; 6 That thy beloved may be delivered: save with thy right hand, and answer me. 7 God hath spoken in his holiness; I will rejoice, I will divide Shechem, and mete out the valley of Succoth. 8 Gilead is mine; Manasseh is mine; Ephraim also is the strength of mine head; Judah is my lawgiver; 9 Moab is my washpot; over Edom will I cast out my shoe; over Philistia will I triumph. 10 Who will bring me into the strong city? who will lead me into Edom? 11 Wilt not thou, O God, who hast cast us off? and wilt not thou, O God, go forth with our hosts? 12 Give us help from trouble: for vain is the help of man. 13 Through God we shall do valiantly: for he it is that shall tread down our enemies

Chapter 109

To the chief Musician, A Psalm of David 1 Hold not thy peace, O God of my praise; 2 For the mouth of the wicked and the mouth of the deceitful are opened against me: they have spoken against me with a lying tongue. 3 They compassed me about also with words of hatred; and fought against me without a cause. 4 For my love they are my adversaries: but I give myself unto prayer. 5 And they have rewarded me evil for good, and hatred for my love. 6 Set thou a wicked man over him: and let Satan stand at his right hand. 7 When he shall be judged, let him be condemned: and let his prayer become sin. 8 Let his days be few; and let another take his office. 9 Let his children be fatherless, and his wife a widow. 10 Let his children be continually vagabonds, and beg: let them seek their bread also out of their desolate places. 11 Let the extortioner catch all that he hath; and let the strangers spoil his labour. 12 Let there be none to extend mercy unto him: neither let there be any to favour his fatherless children. 13 Let his posterity be cut off; and in the generation following let their name be blotted out. 14 Let the iniquity of his fathers be remembered with the Lord; and let not the sin of his mother be blotted out. 15 Let them be before the Lord continually, that he may cut off the memory of them from the earth. 16 Because that he remembered not to show mercy, but persecuted the poor and needy man, that he might even slay the broken in heart. 17 As he loved cursing, so let it come unto him: as he delighted not in blessing, so let it be far from him. 18 As he clothed himself with cursing like as with his garment, so let it come into his bowels like water, and like oil into his bones. 19 Let it be unto him as the garment which covereth him, and for a girdle wherewith he is girded continually. 20 Let this be the reward of mine adversaries from the Lord, and of them that speak evil against my soul. 21 But do thou for me, O God the Lord, for thy name's sake: because thy mercy is good, deliver thou me. 22 For I am poor and needy, and my heart is wounded within me. 23 I am gone like the shadow when it declineth: I am tossed up and down as the locust. 24 My knees are weak through fasting; and my flesh faileth of fatness. 25 I became also a reproach unto them: when they looked upon me they shaked their heads. 26 Help me, O Lord my God: O save me according to thy mercy: 27 That they may know that this is thy hand; that thou, Lord, hast done it. 28 Let them curse, but bless thou: when they arise, let them be ashamed; but let thy servant rejoice. 29 Let mine adversaries be clothed with shame, and let them cover themselves with their own confusion, as with a mantle. 30 I will greatly praise the Lord with my mouth; yea, I will praise him among the multitude. 31 For he shall stand at the right hand of the poor, to save him from those that condemn his soul

Chapter 110

A Psalm of David 1 The Lord said unto my Lord, Sit thou at my right hand, until I make thine enemies thy footstool. 2 The Lord shall send the rod of thy strength out of Zion: rule thou in the midst of thine enemies. 3 Thy people shall be willing in the day of thy power, in the beauties of holiness from the womb of the morning: thou hast the dew of thy youth. 4 The Lord hath sworn, and will not repent, Thou art a priest for ever after the order of Melchizedek. 5 The Lord at thy right hand shall strike through kings in the day of his wrath. 6 He shall judge among the heathen, he shall fill the places with the dead bodies; he shall wound the heads over many countries. 7 He shall drink of the brook in the way: therefore shall he lift up the head

Chapter 111

Praise ye the Lord 1 I will praise the Lord with my whole heart, in the assembly of the upright, and in the congregation. 2 The works of the Lord are great, sought out of all them that have pleasure therein. 3 His work is honourable and glorious: and his righteousness endureth for ever. 4 He hath made his wonderful works to be remembered: the Lord is gracious and full of compassion. 5 He hath given meat unto them that fear him: he will ever be mindful of his covenant. 6 He hath shewed his people the power of his works, that he may give them the heritage of the heathen. 7 The works of his hands are verity and judgment; all his commandments are sure. 8 They stand fast for ever and ever, and are done in truth and uprightness. 9 He sent redemption unto his people: he hath commanded his covenant for ever: holy and reverend is his name. 10 The fear of the Lord is the beginning of wisdom: a good understanding have all they that do his commandments: his praise endureth for ever

Chapter 112

Praise ye the Lord 1 Blessed is the man that feareth the Lord, that delighteth greatly in his commandments. 2 His seed shall be mighty upon earth: the generation of the upright shall be blessed. 3 Wealth and riches shall be in his house: and his righteousness endureth for ever. 4 Unto the upright there ariseth light in the darkness: he is gracious, and full of compassion, and righteous. 5 A good man sheweth favour, and lendeth: he will guide his affairs with discretion. 6 Surely he shall not be moved for ever: the righteous shall be in everlasting remembrance. 7 He shall not be afraid of evil tidings: his heart is fixed, trusting in the Lord. 8 His heart is established, he shall not be afraid, until he see his desire upon his enemies. 9 He hath dispersed, he hath given to the poor; his righteousness endureth for ever; his horn shall be exalted with honour. 10 The wicked shall see it, and be grieved; he shall gnash with his teeth, and melt away: the desire of the wicked shall perish

Chapter 113

Praise ye the Lord 1 Praise, O ye servants of the Lord, praise the name of the Lord. 2 Blessed be the name of the Lord from this time forth and for evermore. 3 From the rising of the sun unto the going down of the same the Lord's name is to be praised. 4 The Lord is high above all nations, and his glory above the heavens. 5 Who is like unto the Lord our God, who dwelleth on high, 6 Who humbleth himself to behold the things that are in heaven, and in the earth! 7 He raiseth up the poor out of the dust, and lifteth the needy out of the dunghill; 8 That he may set him with princes, even with the princes of his people. 9 He maketh the barren woman to keep house, and to be a joyful mother of children. Praise ye the Lord

Chapter 114

1 When Israel went out of Egypt, the house of Jacob from a people of strange language; 2 Judah was his sanctuary, and Israel his dominion. 3 The sea saw it, and fled: Jordan was driven back. 4 The mountains skipped like rams, and the little hills like lambs. 5 What ailed thee, O thou sea, that thou fleddest? thou Jordan, that thou wast driven back? 6 Ye mountains, that ye skipped like rams; and ye little hills, like lambs? 7 Tremble, thou earth, at the presence of the Lord, at the presence of the God of Jacob; 8 Which turned the rock into a standing water, the flint into a fountain of waters

Chapter 115

1 Not unto us, O Lord, not unto us, but unto thy name give glory, for thy mercy, and for thy truth's sake. 2 Wherefore should the heathen say, Where is now their God? 3 But our God is in the heavens: he hath done whatsoever he hath pleased. 4 Their idols are silver and gold, the work of men's hands. 5 They have mouths, but they speak not: eyes have they, but they see not: 6 They have ears, but they hear not: noses have they, but they smell not: 7 They have hands, but they handle not: feet have they, but they walk not: neither speak they through their throat. 8 They that make them are like unto them; so is every one that trusteth in them. 9 O Israel, trust thou in the Lord: he is their help and their shield. 10 O house of Aaron, trust in the Lord: he is their help and their shield. 11 Ye that fear the Lord, trust in the Lord: he is their help and their shield. 12 The Lord hath been mindful of us: he will bless us; he will bless the house of Israel; he will bless the house of Aaron. 13 He will bless them that fear the Lord, both small and great. 14 The Lord shall increase you more and more, you and your children. 15 Ye are blessed of the Lord which made heaven and earth. 16 The heaven, even the heavens, are the Lord's: but the earth hath he given to the children of men. 17 The dead praise not the Lord, neither any that go down into silence. 18 But we will bless the Lord from this time forth and for evermore. Praise the Lord

Chapter 116

I love the Lord because He has heard my voice and my prayers. He has inclined His ear to me whenever I called upon Him in my distress. When the snares of death surrounded me and the griefs of the grave caught me, when I found trouble and sorrow, I called upon the name of the Lord, saying, "I beseech You, O Lord, deliver my soul." The Lord is merciful and righteous, and our God is full of compassion. The Lord preserves the simple; I was in misery, and He saved me. Return to your rest, O my soul, for the Lord has been good to you. He has delivered my soul from death, my eyes from tears, and my feet from falling. I believed, therefore I spoke, though I was greatly troubled. I said in my fear, "All men are liars." What shall I render to the Lord for all His benefits toward me? I will take the cup of salvation and call upon the name of the Lord. I will pay my vows to the Lord now in the presence of all His people. Precious in the sight of the Lord is the death of His saints. Behold, O Lord, for I am Your servant; I am Your servant, the son of Your handmaid; You have broken my bonds. I will offer You a sacrifice of praise and will call upon the name of the Lord. I will pay my vows to the Lord now in the presence of all His people, in the courts of the Lord's house, in the midst of you, O Jerusalem. Praise the Lord

Chapter 117

All nations, praise the Lord; all people, praise Him. For His loving-kindness is great toward us, and the truth of the Lord endures forever. Praise the Lord

Chapter 118

Praise the Lord, for He is good; His mercy endures forever. Let Israel now say, "His mercy endures forever." Let the house of Aaron now say, "His mercy endures forever." Let those who fear the Lord now say, "His mercy endures forever." I called upon the Lord in trouble, and the Lord heard me and set me free. The Lord is with me; I will not fear what man can do to me. The Lord is with me among those who help me; therefore, I will see my desire upon my enemies. It is better to trust in the Lord than to have confidence in man. It is better to trust in the Lord than to have confidence in princes. All nations surrounded me, but in the name of the Lord, I will destroy them. They surrounded me, yes, they surrounded me, but in the name of the Lord, I will destroy them. They came about me like bees; they were quenched like a fire of thorns, for in the name of the Lord, I will destroy them. You have thrust sorely at me that I might fall, but the Lord helped me. The Lord is my strength and song; He has become my salvation. The voice of joy and salvation is in the tents of the righteous, saying, "The right hand of the Lord does valiantly. The right hand of the Lord is exalted; the right hand of the Lord does valiantly." I shall not die, but live, and declare the works of the Lord. The Lord has chastened me severely, but He has not given me over to death. Open to me the gates of righteousness; I will go into them and praise the Lord. This is the gate of the Lord; the righteous shall enter through it. I will praise You, for You have heard me and have become my salvation. The stone which the builders refused has become the cornerstone. This is the Lord's doing; it is marvelous in our eyes. This is the day which the Lord has made; let us rejoice and be glad in it. O Lord, save us, we pray; O Lord, grant us prosperity. Blessed is he who comes in the name of the Lord; we have blessed you from the house of the Lord. The Lord is mighty and has given us light; bind the sacrifice with cords to the horns of the altar. You are my God, and I will praise You; You are my God, I will exalt You. Praise the Lord, for He is good; His mercy endures forever

Chapter 119

ALEPH Blessed are those who are upright in their way and walk in the law of the Lord. Blessed are those who keep His testimonies and seek Him with their whole heart. They do no iniquity; they walk in His ways. You have commanded us to keep Your precepts diligently. Oh, that my ways were directed to keep Your statutes! Then I would not be ashamed when I respect all Your commandments. I will praise You with an upright heart when I learn the judgments of Your righteousness. I will keep Your statutes; do not forsake me utterly **BETH** How can a young man cleanse his way? By taking heed according to Your word. With my whole heart, I have sought You; let me not wander from Your commandments. I have hidden Your word in my heart that I might not sin

against You. Blessed are You, O Lord; teach me Your statutes. With my lips, I have declared all the judgments of Your mouth. I have rejoiced in the way of Your testimonies as much as in all riches. I will meditate on Your precepts and contemplate Your ways. I will delight in Your statutes; I will not forget Your word **GIMEL** Deal bountifully with Your servant that I may live and keep Your word. Open my eyes that I may see wondrous things from Your law. I am a stranger on the earth; do not hide Your commandments from me. My soul breaks with longing for Your judgments at all times. You rebuke the proud, the cursed, who stray from Your commandments. Remove from me reproach and contempt, for I have kept Your testimonies. Princes also sit and speak against me, but Your servant meditates on Your statutes. Your testimonies also are my delight and my counselors **DALETH** My soul clings to the dust; revive me according to Your word. I have declared my ways, and You answered me; teach me Your statutes. Make me understand the way of Your precepts, so I shall meditate on Your wondrous works. My soul melts from heaviness; strengthen me according to Your word. Remove from me the way of lying, and grant me Your law graciously. I have chosen the way of truth; Your judgments I have laid before me. I cling to Your testimonies; O Lord, do not put me to shame. I will run the course of Your commandments, for You shall enlarge my heart **HE** Teach me, O Lord, the way of Your statutes, and I shall keep it to the end. Give me understanding, and I shall keep Your law; indeed, I shall observe it with my whole heart. Make me walk in the path of Your commandments, for I delight in it. Incline my heart to Your testimonies and not to covetousness. Turn away my eyes from looking at worthless things, and revive me in Your way. Establish Your word to Your servant, who is devoted to fearing You. Turn away my reproach which I dread, for Your judgments are good. Behold, I long for Your precepts; revive me in Your righteousness **VAU** Let Your mercies come also to me, O Lord, Your salvation according to Your word. So shall I have an answer for him who reproaches me, for I trust in Your word. And take not the word of truth utterly out of my mouth, for I have hoped in Your ordinances. So shall I keep Your law continually, forever and ever. And I will walk at liberty, for I seek Your precepts. I will speak of Your testimonies also before kings and will not be ashamed. And I will delight myself in Your commandments, which I love. My hands also I will lift up to Your commandments, which I love, and I will meditate on Your statutes **ZAIN** Remember the word to Your servant, upon which You have caused me to hope. This is my comfort in my affliction, for Your word has given me life. The proud have me in great derision, yet I do not turn aside from Your law. I remembered Your judgments of old, O Lord, and have comforted myself. Indignation has taken hold of me because of the wicked who forsake Your law. Your statutes have been my songs in the house of my pilgrimage. I remember Your name in the night, O Lord, and I keep Your law. This has become mine because I kept Your precepts **CHETH** You are my portion, O Lord; I have said that I would keep Your words. I entreated Your favor with my whole heart; be merciful to me according to Your word. I thought about my ways and turned my feet to Your testimonies. I made haste and did not delay to keep Your commandments. The cords of the wicked have bound me, but I have not forgotten Your law. At midnight, I will rise to give thanks to You because of Your righteous judgments. I am a companion of all who fear You and of those who keep Your precepts. The earth, O Lord, is full of Your mercy; teach me Your statutes **TETH** You have dealt well with Your servant, O Lord, according to Your word. Teach me good judgment and knowledge, for I believe Your commandments. Before I was afflicted, I went astray, but now I keep Your word. You are good, and do good; teach me Your statutes. The proud have forged a lie against me, but I will keep Your precepts with my whole heart. Their heart is as fat as grease, but I delight in Your law. It is good for me that I have been afflicted, that I may learn Your statutes. The law of Your mouth is better to me than thousands of coins of gold and silver **YOD** Your hands have made me and fashioned me; give me understanding that I may learn Your commandments. Those who fear You will be glad when they see me because I have hoped in Your word. I know, O Lord, that Your judgments are right and that in faithfulness You have afflicted me. Let, I pray, Your merciful kindness be for my comfort, according to Your word to Your servant. Let Your tender mercies come to me, that I may live, for Your law is my delight. Let the proud be ashamed, for they treated me wrongfully with falsehood; but I will meditate on Your precepts. Let those who fear You turn to me, those who know Your testimonies. Let my heart be blameless regarding Your statutes, that I may not be ashamed **KAPH** My soul faints for Your salvation, but I hope in Your word. My eyes fail from searching Your word, saying, "When will You comfort me?" For I have become like a wineskin in smoke, yet I do not forget Your statutes. How many are the days of Your servant? When will You execute judgment on those who persecute me? The proud have dug pits for me, which is not according to Your law. All Your commandments are faithful; they persecute me wrongfully; help me! They almost made an end of me on earth, but I did not forsake Your precepts. Revive me according to Your loving kindness, so that I may keep the testimony of Your mouth

Chapter 120

A Song of Degrees In my time of trouble, I called unto the Lord, and He heard me. Deliver my soul, O Lord, from lying lips and deceitful tongues. What will the deceitful tongue bring to you, or what will it avail you? It is as sharp as the arrows of a mighty man and as hot as coals of juniper. Woe is me that I remain in Mesech and dwell in the tents of Kedar. My soul has too long dwelt with those who hate peace. I seek peace, but when I speak of it, they are bent on war

Chapter 121

A Song of Degrees I will lift my eyes to the mountains, from where my help comes. My help comes from the Lord, who made heaven and earth. He will not let your foot slip; He who keeps you will not slumber. Behold, He who keeps Israel will neither slumber nor sleep. The Lord is your keeper; the Lord is your shade at your right hand. The sun will not harm you by day, nor the moon by night. The Lord will preserve you from all evil; He will keep your soul. The Lord will preserve your going out and your coming in from this time forth and forevermore

Chapter 122

A Song of Degrees, or Psalm of David I rejoiced when they said to me, "We will go into the house of the Lord." Our feet shall stand within your gates, O Jerusalem. Jerusalem is built as a city that is compact together. To it, the tribes go up, the tribes of the Lord, according to the testimony given to Israel, to give thanks to the name of the Lord. For there, the thrones of judgment are set, the thrones of the house of David. Pray for the peace of Jerusalem; may those who love you prosper. May there be peace within your walls and prosperity within your palaces. For the sake of my brethren and neighbors, I will say, "Peace be within you." For the sake of the house of the Lord

our God, I will seek your good

Chapter 123

A Song of Degrees I lift my eyes to You, who dwell in the heavens. Behold, as the eyes of servants look to the hand of their masters, and as the eyes of a maiden look to the hand of her mistress, so our eyes look to the Lord our God, until He has mercy upon us. Have mercy upon us, O Lord, have mercy upon us, for we have endured much contempt. Our soul is exceedingly filled with the scorn of those who are at ease and with the contempt of the proud

Chapter 124

A Song of Degrees, or Psalm of David If the Lord had not been on our side, let Israel now say, if the Lord had not been on our side when men rose up against us, then they would have swallowed us alive when their wrath was kindled against us. Then the waters would have overwhelmed us, the stream would have gone over our soul; then the swollen waters would have gone over our soul. Blessed be the Lord, who has not given us as prey to their teeth. Our soul has escaped as a bird from the snare of the fowlers; the snare is broken, and we have escaped. Our help is in the name of the Lord, who made heaven and earth

Chapter 125

A Song of Degrees Those who trust in the Lord are like Mount Zion, which cannot be moved but abides forever. As the mountains surround Jerusalem, so the Lord surrounds His people from this time forth and forever. For the scepter of wickedness will not rest on the land allotted to the righteous, lest the righteous reach out their hands to do iniquity. Do good, O Lord, to those who are good, and to those who are upright in their hearts. But those who turn aside to their crooked ways, the Lord will lead away with the workers of iniquity. Peace be upon Israel

Chapter 126

A Song of Degrees, or Psalm of David When the Lord brought back the captivity of Zion, we were like those who dream. Then our mouth was filled with laughter, and our tongue with singing. Then they said among the nations, "The Lord has done great things for them." The Lord has done great things for us, and we are glad. Bring back our captivity, O Lord, as the streams in the South. Those who sow in tears will reap in joy. He who continually goes forth weeping, bearing seed for sowing, will doubtless come again with rejoicing, bringing his sheaves with him

Chapter 127

A Song of Degrees, or Psalm of Solomon Unless the Lord builds the house, they labor in vain who build it. Unless the Lord guards the city, the watchman stays awake in vain. It is in vain for you to rise up early, to sit up late, to eat the bread of sorrows, for He gives His beloved sleep. Behold, children are a heritage from the Lord, the fruit of the womb is His reward. Like arrows in the hand of a warrior, so are the children of one's youth. Happy is the man who has his quiver full of them; they will not be ashamed but will speak with their enemies in the gate

Chapter 128

A Song of Degrees Blessed is everyone who fears the Lord and walks in His ways. When you eat the labor of your hands, you will be happy, and it will be well with you. Your wife will be like a fruitful vine in the very heart of your house, your children like olive plants all around your table. Behold, thus shall the man be blessed who fears the Lord. The Lord bless you out of Zion, and may you see the good of Jerusalem all the days of your life. Yes, may you see your children's children. Peace be upon Israel

Chapter 129

A Song of Degrees Many times they have afflicted me from my youth, let Israel now say, many times they have afflicted me from my youth, yet they have not prevailed against me. The plowers plowed on my back; they made their furrows long. The Lord is righteous; He has cut in pieces the cords of the wicked. Let all those who hate Zion be put to shame and turned back. Let them be as the grass on the housetops, which withers before it grows up, with which the reaper does not fill his hand, nor he who binds sheaves, his arms. Neither let those who pass by say, "The blessing of the Lord be upon you; we bless you in the name of the Lord."

Chapter 130

A Song of Degrees Out of the depths, I have cried to You, O Lord. Lord, hear my voice! Let Your ears be attentive to the voice of my supplications. If You, Lord, should mark iniquities, O Lord, who could stand? But there is forgiveness with You, that You may be feared. I wait for the Lord, my soul waits, and in His word, I do hope. My soul waits for the Lord more than those who watch for the morning, yes, more than those who watch for the morning. O Israel, hope in the Lord, for with the Lord there is mercy, and with Him is abundant redemption. And He shall redeem Israel from all his iniquities

Chapter 131

A Song of Degrees or Palm of David Lord, my heart is not haughty, nor my eyes lofty. Neither do I concern myself with great matters, nor with things too profound for me. Surely I have calmed and quieted my soul, like a weaned child with his mother. My soul is like a weaned child within me. O Israel, hope in the Lord from this time forth and forever

Chapter 132

A Song of Degrees Lord, remember David and all his afflictions; how he swore to the Lord and vowed to the Mighty One of Jacob: "Surely I will not go into the chamber of my house or go up to the comfort of my bed. I will not give sleep to my eyes or slumber to my eyelids until I find a place for the Lord, a dwelling place for the Mighty One of Jacob." Behold, we heard of it in Ephrathah; we found it in the fields of the woods. We will go into His tabernacle; we will worship at His footstool. Arise, O Lord, to Your resting place, You and the ark of Your strength. Let Your priests be clothed with righteousness, and let Your saints shout for joy. For Your servant David's sake, do not turn away the face of Your Anointed. The Lord has sworn in truth to David; He will not turn from it: "I will set upon your throne the fruit of your body. If your sons will keep My covenant and My testimony which I shall teach them, their sons also shall sit upon your throne forevermore." For the Lord has chosen Zion; He has desired it for His dwelling place: "This is My resting place forever; here I will dwell, for I have desired it. I will abundantly bless her provision; I will satisfy her poor with bread. I will also clothe her priests with salvation, and her saints shall shout aloud for joy. There I will make the horn of David grow; I will prepare a lamp for My Anointed. His enemies I will clothe with shame, but upon Himself, His crown shall flourish."

Chapter 133

A Song of Degrees or Psalm of David Behold, how good and how pleasant it is for brethren to dwell together in unity! It is like the precious oil upon the head, running down on the beard, the beard of Aaron, running down on the edge of his garments. It is like the dew of Hermon, descending upon the mountains of Zion, for there the Lord commanded the blessing, life forevermore

Chapter 134

A Song of Degrees Behold, bless the Lord, all you servants of the Lord, who by night stand in the house of the Lord! Lift up your hands in the sanctuary and bless the Lord. The Lord who made heaven and earth bless you from Zion

Chapter 135

Praise the Lord Praise the name of the Lord; praise Him, O you servants of the Lord! You who stand in the house of the Lord, in the courts of the house of our God, praise the Lord, for the Lord is good; sing praises to His name, for it is pleasant. For the Lord has chosen Jacob for Himself, Israel for His special treasure. For I know that the Lord is great, and our Lord is above all gods. Whatever the Lord pleases, He does in heaven and on earth, in the seas and in all deep places. He causes the vapors to ascend from the ends of the earth; He makes lightning for the rain; He brings the wind out of His treasuries. He destroyed the firstborn of Egypt, both of man and beast. He sent signs and wonders into the midst of you, O Egypt, upon Pharaoh and all his servants. He defeated many nations and slew mighty kings: Sihon, king of the Amorites, Og, king of Bashan, and all the kingdoms of Canaan. And He gave their land as a heritage, a heritage to Israel, His people. Your name, O Lord, endures forever, Your fame, O Lord, throughout all generations. For the Lord will judge His people, and He will have compassion on His servants. The idols of the nations are silver and gold, the work of men's hands. They have mouths, but they do not speak; eyes they have, but they do not see; they have ears, but they do not hear; nor is there any breath in their mouths. Those who make them are like them; so is everyone who trusts in them. Bless the Lord, O house of Israel! Bless the Lord, O house of Aaron! Bless the Lord, O house of Levi! You who fear the Lord, bless the Lord! Blessed be the Lord out of Zion, who dwells in Jerusalem! Praise the Lord!

Chapter 136

Praise the Lord Praise the Lord, for He is good, for His mercy endures forever. Praise the God of gods, for His mercy endures forever. Praise the Lord of lords, for His mercy endures forever; to Him who alone does great wonders, for His mercy endures forever; to Him who by wisdom made the heavens, for His mercy endures forever; to Him who laid out the earth above the waters, for His mercy endures forever; to Him who made great lights, for His mercy endures forever—the sun to rule by day, for His mercy endures forever; the moon and stars to rule by night, for His mercy endures forever; to Him who struck Egypt in their firstborn, for His mercy endures forever; and brought out Israel from among them, for His mercy endures forever; with a strong hand and with an outstretched arm, for His mercy endures forever; to Him who divided the Red Sea in two, for His mercy endures forever; and made Israel pass through the midst of it, for His mercy endures forever; but overthrew Pharaoh and his army in the Red Sea, for His mercy endures forever; to Him who led His people through the wilderness, for His mercy endures forever; to Him who struck down great kings, for His mercy endures forever; and slew famous kings, for His mercy endures forever—Sihon, king of the Amorites, for His mercy endures forever; and Og, king of Bashan, for His mercy endures forever—and gave their land as a heritage, for His mercy endures forever; a heritage to Israel His servant, for His mercy endures forever. Who remembered us in our lowly state, for His mercy endures forever; and rescued us from our enemies, for His mercy endures forever; who gives food to all flesh, for His mercy endures forever. Oh, give thanks to the God of heaven, for His

mercy endures forever
Chapter 137
By the rivers of Babylon, there we sat down and wept when we remembered Zion. We hung our harps upon the willows in the midst of it. For there, those who carried us away captive asked of us a song, and those who plundered us requested mirth, saying, "Sing us one of the songs of Zion!" How shall we sing the Lord's song in a foreign land? If I forget you, O Jerusalem, let my right hand forget its skill! If I do not remember you, let my tongue cling to the roof of my mouth—if I do not exalt Jerusalem above my chief joy. Remember, O Lord, against the sons of Edom the day of Jerusalem, who said, "Raze it, raze it, to its very foundation!" O daughter of Babylon, who are to be destroyed, happy the one who repays you as you have served us! Happy the one who takes and dashes your little ones against the rock!

Chapter 138
A Psalm of David I will praise You with my whole heart; before the gods, I will sing praises to You. I will worship toward Your holy temple and praise Your name for Your lovingkindness and Your truth, for You have magnified Your word above all Your name. In the day when I cried out, You answered me and made me bold with strength in my soul. All the kings of the earth shall praise You, O Lord, when they hear the words of Your mouth. Yes, they shall sing of the ways of the Lord, for great is the glory of the Lord. Though the Lord is on high, yet He regards the lowly, but the proud He knows from afar. Though I walk in the midst of trouble, You will revive me; You will stretch out Your hand against the wrath of my enemies, and Your right hand will save me. The Lord will perfect that which concerns me; Your mercy, O Lord, endures forever; do not forsake the works of Your hands

Chapter 139
A Psalm of David O Lord, You have examined me and known me. You know when I sit down and when I rise up; You understand my thoughts from afar. You surround my path and my lying down and are familiar with all my ways. For there is not a word on my tongue, but behold, O Lord, You know it altogether. You hem me in behind and before, and You lay Your hand upon me. Such knowledge is too wonderful for me; it is high, I cannot attain it. Where can I go from Your Spirit? Or where can I flee from Your presence? If I ascend into heaven, You are there; if I make my bed in Sheol, You are there. If I take the wings of the morning and dwell in the uttermost parts of the sea, even there Your hand shall lead me, and Your right hand shall hold me. If I say, "Surely the darkness shall cover me," even the night shall be light about me. Indeed, the darkness shall not hide from You, but the night shines as the day; the darkness and the light are both alike to You. For You formed my inward parts; You covered me in my mother's womb. I will praise You, for I am fearfully and wonderfully made; marvelous are Your works, and my soul knows it very well. My frame was not hidden from You when I was made in secret and skillfully wrought in the lowest parts of the earth. Your eyes saw my substance, being yet unformed. And in Your book, they all were written, the days fashioned for me, when as yet there were none of them. How precious also are Your thoughts to me, O God! How great is the sum of them! If I should count them, they would be more in number than the sand; when I awake, I am still with You. Oh, that You would slay the wicked, O God! Depart from me, therefore, you bloodthirsty men. For they speak against You wickedly; Your enemies take Your name in vain. Do I not hate them, O Lord, who hate You? And do I not loathe those who rise up against You? I hate them with perfect hatred; I count

them my enemies. Search me, O God, and know my heart; try me and know my thoughts, and see if there is any wicked way in me, and lead me in the way everlasting

Chapter 140
A Psalm of David Deliver me, O Lord, from evil men; preserve me from violent men who plan evil things in their hearts and continually gather together for war. They have sharpened their tongues like a serpent; the poison of vipers is under their lips. Selah. Keep me, O Lord, from the hands of the wicked; preserve me from violent men who have purposed to make my steps stumble. The proud have hidden a snare for me, and cords; they have spread a net by the wayside; they have set traps for me. Selah. I said to the Lord, "You are my God; hear the voice of my supplications, O Lord. O God the Lord, the strength of my salvation, You have covered my head in the day of battle." Do not grant, O Lord, the desires of the wicked; do not further their wicked schemes, lest they be exalted. Selah. As for the head of those who surround me, let the evil of their lips cover them. Let burning coals fall upon them; let them be cast into the fire, into deep pits, that they rise not up again. Let not a slanderer be established in the earth; let evil hunt the violent man to overthrow him. I know that the Lord will maintain the cause of the afflicted and justice for the poor. Surely the righteous shall give thanks to Your name; the upright shall dwell in Your presence

Chapter 141
A Psalm of David Lord, I cry out to You; make haste to me! Give ear to my voice when I cry out to You. Let my prayer be set before You as incense, the lifting up of my hands as the evening sacrifice. Set a guard, O Lord, over my mouth; keep watch over the door of my lips. Do not incline my heart to any evil thing, to practice wicked works with men who work iniquity; and do not let me eat of their delicacies. Let the righteous strike me; it shall be a kindness. And let him rebuke me; it shall be as excellent oil; let my head not refuse it. For still my prayer is against the deeds of the wicked. Their judges are overthrown by the sides of the cliff, and they hear my words, for they are sweet. Our bones are scattered at the mouth of the grave, as when one plows and breaks up the earth. But my eyes are upon You, O God the Lord; in You, I take refuge; do not leave my soul destitute. Keep me from the snares they have laid for me and from the traps of the workers of iniquity. Let the wicked fall into their own nets, while I escape safely

Chapter 142
A Psalm of David, a prayer when he was in the cave I cry out to the Lord with my voice; with my voice to the Lord, I make my supplication. I pour out my complaint before Him; I declare before Him my trouble. When my spirit was overwhelmed within me, then You knew my path. In the way in which I walk, they have secretly set a snare for me. Look on my right hand and see, for there is no one who acknowledges me; refuge has failed me; no one cares for my soul. I cried out to You, O Lord; I said, "You are my refuge, my portion in the land of the living. Attend to my cry, for I am brought very low; deliver me from my persecutors, for they are stronger than I. Bring my soul out of prison, that I may praise Your name. The righteous shall surround me, for You shall deal bountifully with me."

Chapter 143
A Psalm of David Hear my prayer, O Lord; give ear to my supplications! In Your faithfulness answer me, and in Your righteousness. Do not enter into judgment with Your servant, for in Your sight, no one living is righteous. For the enemy has persecuted my

soul; he has crushed my life to the ground; he has made me dwell in darkness, like those who have long been dead. Therefore my spirit is overwhelmed within me; my heart within me is distressed. I remember the days of old; I meditate on all Your works; I muse on the work of Your hands. I spread out my hands to You; my soul longs for You like a thirsty land. Selah. Answer me speedily, O Lord; my spirit fails! Do not hide Your face from me, lest I be like those who go down into the pit. Cause me to hear Your lovingkindness in the morning, for in You do I trust; cause me to know the way in which I should walk, for I lift up my soul to You. Deliver me, O Lord, from my enemies; in You, I take shelter. Teach me to do Your will, for You are my God; Your Spirit is good. Lead me in the land of uprightness. Revive me, O Lord, for Your name's sake! For Your righteousness' sake, bring my soul out of trouble. In Your mercy, cut off my enemies and destroy all those who afflict my soul, for I am Your servant

Chapter 144

A Psalm of David Blessed be the Lord my Rock, who trains my hands for war and my fingers for battle. My lovingkindness and my fortress, my high tower and my deliverer, my shield and the One in whom I take refuge, who subdues my people under me. Lord, what is man that You take knowledge of him? Or the son of man that You are mindful of him? Man is like a breath; his days are like a passing shadow. Bow down Your heavens, O Lord and come down; touch the mountains, and they shall smoke. Flash forth lightning and scatter them; shoot out Your arrows and destroy them. Stretch out Your hand from above; rescue me and deliver me out of great waters, from the hand of foreigners, whose mouth speaks lying words, and whose right hand is a right hand of falsehood. I will sing a new song to You, O God; on a harp of ten strings, I will sing praises to You, the One who gives salvation to kings, who delivers David His servant from the deadly sword. Rescue me and deliver me from the hand of foreigners, whose mouth speaks lying words, and whose right hand is a right hand of falsehood, that our sons may be as plants grown up in their youth, that our daughters may be as pillars, sculptured in palace style, that our barns may be full, supplying all kinds of produce, that our sheep may bring forth thousands and ten thousands in our fields, that our oxen may be well-laden, that there be no breaking in or going out, that there be no outcry in our streets. Happy are the people who are in such a state; happy are the people whose God is the Lord!

Chapter 145

A Psalm of David, a Song of Praise I will extol You, my God, O King; I will bless Your name forever and ever. Every day I will bless You, and I will praise Your name forever and ever. Great is the Lord, and greatly to be praised, and His greatness is unsearchable. One generation shall praise Your works to another and shall declare Your mighty acts. I will meditate on the glorious splendor of Your majesty and on Your wondrous works. Men shall speak of the might of Your awesome acts, and I will declare Your greatness. They shall utter the memory of Your great goodness and shall sing of Your righteousness. The Lord is gracious and full of compassion, slow to anger and great in mercy. The Lord is good to all, and His tender mercies are over all His works. All Your works shall praise You, O Lord, and Your saints shall bless You. They shall speak of the glory of Your kingdom and talk of Your power, to make known to the sons of men His mighty acts and the glorious majesty of His kingdom. Your kingdom is an everlasting kingdom, and Your dominion endures throughout all generations. The Lord upholds all who fall and raises up all who are bowed down. The eyes of all look expectantly to You, and You give them their food in due season. You open Your hand and satisfy the desire of every living thing. The Lord is righteous in all His ways, gracious in all His works. The Lord is near to all who call upon Him, to all who call upon Him in truth. He will fulfill the desire of those who fear Him; He also will hear their cry and save them. The Lord preserves all who love Him, but all the wicked He will destroy. My mouth shall speak the praise of the Lord, and all flesh shall bless His holy name forever and ever

Chapter 146

Praise the Lord Praise the Lord, O my soul! While I live, I will praise the Lord; I will sing praises to my God while I have my being. Do not put your trust in princes, nor in a son of man, in whom there is no help. His spirit departs, he returns to his earth; in that very day, his plans perish. Happy is he who has the God of Jacob for his help, whose hope is in the Lord his God, who made heaven and earth, the sea, and all that is in them; who keeps truth forever, who executes justice for the oppressed, who gives food to the hungry. The Lord gives freedom to the prisoners. The Lord opens the eyes of the blind; the Lord raises those who are bowed down; the Lord loves the righteous. The Lord watches over the strangers; He relieves the fatherless and widow, but the way of the wicked He turns upside down. The Lord shall reign forever—Your God, O Zion, to all generations. Praise the Lord!

Chapter 147

Praise the Lord Praise the Lord! For it is good to sing praises to our God; for it is pleasant, and praise is beautiful. The Lord builds up Jerusalem; He gathers together the outcasts of Israel. He heals the brokenhearted and binds up their wounds. He counts the number of the stars; He calls them all by name. Great is our Lord, and mighty in power; His understanding is infinite. The Lord lifts up the humble; He casts the wicked down to the ground. Sing to the Lord with thanksgiving; sing praises on the harp to our God, who covers the heavens with clouds, who prepares rain for the earth, who makes grass to grow on the mountains. He gives to the beast its food and to the young ravens that cry. He does not delight in the strength of the horse; He takes no pleasure in the legs of a man. The Lord takes pleasure in those who fear Him, in those who hope in His mercy. Praise the Lord, O Jerusalem! Praise your God, O Zion! For He has strengthened the bars of your gates; He has blessed your children within you. He makes peace in your borders and fills you with the finest wheat. He sends out His command to the earth; His word runs very swiftly. He gives snow like wool; He scatters the frost like ashes. He casts out His hail like morsels; who can stand before His cold? He sends out His word and melts them; He causes His wind to blow, and the waters flow. He declares His word to Jacob, His statutes and His judgments to Israel. He has not dealt thus with any nation; and as for His judgments, they have not known them. Praise the Lord!

Chapter 148

Praise the Lord Praise the Lord from the heavens; praise Him in the heights! Praise Him, all His angels; praise Him, all His hosts! Praise Him, sun and moon; praise Him, all you stars of light! Praise Him, you heavens of heavens, and you waters above the heavens! Let them praise the name of the Lord, for He commanded, and they were created. He also established them forever and ever; He made a decree which shall not pass away. Praise the Lord from the earth, you great sea creatures and all the depths; fire and hail, snow and clouds; stormy wind, fulfilling His word; mountains and all hills; fruitful trees and all cedars; beasts and all cattle; creeping things and flying fowl; kings of the earth and all peoples; princes and all judges of the earth; both young men and maidens; old men and children. Let them praise the name of the Lord, for His name alone is exalted; His glory is above the earth and heaven. And He has exalted the horn of His people, the praise of all His saints—of the children of Israel, a people near to Him. Praise the Lord!

Chapter 149

Praise the Lord Sing to the Lord a new song, and His praise in the assembly of saints. Let Israel rejoice in their Maker; let the children of Zion be joyful in their King. Let them praise His name with the dance; let them sing praises to Him with the timbrel and harp. For the Lord takes pleasure in His people; He will beautify the humble with salvation. Let the saints be joyful in glory; let them sing aloud on their beds. Let the high praises of God be in their mouth and a two-edged sword in their hand, to execute vengeance on the nations and punishments on the peoples; to bind their kings with chains and their nobles with fetters of iron; to execute on them the written judgment—this honor have all His saints. Praise the Lord!

Chapter 150

Praise the Lord Praise God in His sanctuary; praise Him in His mighty firmament! Praise Him for His mighty acts; praise Him according to His excellent greatness! Praise Him with the sound of the trumpet; praise Him with the lute and harp! Praise Him with the timbrel and dance; praise Him with stringed instruments and flutes! Praise Him with loud cymbals; praise Him with clashing cymbals! Let everything that has breath praise the Lord. Praise the Lord!

20. Proverbs

Chapter 1

The parables of Solomon, son of David, king of Israel, are meant to impart wisdom and instruction, to help one understand the words of knowledge, and to receive guidance in acting wisely, justly, and equitably. These teachings aim to sharpen the minds of the simple and give children knowledge and discretion. A wise person listens and increases in learning, and an intelligent person seeks wise counsel, understanding parables and their interpretations, the words of the wise, and their profound meanings. The fear of the Lord is the beginning of knowledge, but fools despise wisdom and instruction My son, heed the instructions of your father and do not forsake your mother's teachings, for they will be a beautiful ornament for your head and chains for your neck. If sinners entice you, do not consent. If they say, "Come with us, let us lie in wait for blood and ambush the innocent without reason," do not join them. They plan to swallow others alive like the grave and plunder precious riches. They cast lots together and share one purse. My son, do not walk with them; keep your foot from their path, for their feet run to evil, and they hurry to shed blood. These are the ways of those greedy for gain, who seek to take the lives of others Wisdom cries out in the streets and raises her voice in public squares, calling out to the simple, scorners, and fools, asking how long they will love simplicity, delight in scorn, and hate knowledge. Turn to my reproof; behold, I will pour out my spirit unto you and make my words known to you. I called, but you refused; I stretched out my hand, but no one heeded. You ignored all my counsel and would not accept my correction. Therefore, I will laugh at your calamity and mock when terror strikes you, when your fear comes like a storm and your destruction like a whirlwind, when distress and anguish come upon you. Then you will call upon me, but I will not answer you will seek me diligently but will not find me, because you hated knowledge and did not choose the fear of the Lord. You would have none of my counsel and despised all my correction. Therefore, you will eat the fruit of your ways and be filled with your own devices. For the turning away of the simple will kill them, and the complacency of fools will destroy them. But whoever listens to me will dwell safely and be secure, without fear of evil

Chapter 2

My son, if you accept my words and store my commands within you, turning your ear to wisdom and applying your heart to understanding, if you call out for insight and cry aloud for understanding, and if you seek it like silver and search for it as for hidden treasure, then you will understand the fear of the Lord and find the knowledge of God. For the Lord gives wisdom, and from His mouth come knowledge and understanding. He stores up sound wisdom for the upright and is a shield to those who walk in integrity, guarding the paths of justice and watching over the way of His saints. Then you will understand righteousness, justice, equity and every good path. Wisdom will enter your heart, and knowledge will be pleasant to your soul. Discretion will protect you, and understanding will guard you, saving you from the ways of wicked men, from those whose words are perverse, who leave the straight paths to walk in dark ways, who delight in doing wrong and rejoice in the perverseness of evil, whose paths are crooked and who are devious in their ways Wisdom will save you also from the adulterous woman, from the wayward woman with her seductive words, who has left the partner of her youth and ignored the covenant she made before God. Her house leads down to death, and her paths to the spirits of the dead. None who go to her return or attain the paths of life. Thus, you will walk in the ways of the good and keep to the paths of the righteous. For the upright will live in the land, and the blameless will remain in it, but the wicked will be cut off from the land, and the unfaithful will be torn from it

Chapter 3

My son, do not forget my teaching, but keep my commands in your heart, for they will prolong your life many years and bring you peace and prosperity. Let love and faithfulness never leave you; bind them around your neck, write them on the tablet of your heart. Then you will win favor and a good name in the sight of God and man. Trust in the Lord with all your heart and lean not on your own understanding; in all your ways submit to Him, and He will make your paths straight. Do not be wise in your own eyes; fear the Lord and shun evil. This will bring health to your body and nourishment to your bones. Honor the Lord with your wealth, with the first fruits of all your crops; then your barns will be filled to overflowing, and your vats will brim over with new wine My son, do not despise the Lord's discipline and do not resent His rebuke, because the Lord disciplines those He loves, as a father the son he delights in. Blessed are those who find wisdom, those who gain understanding, for she is more profitable than silver and yields better returns than gold. She is more precious than rubies; nothing you desire can compare with her. Long life is in her right hand; in her left hand are riches and honor. Her ways are pleasant ways, and all her paths are peace. She is a tree of life to those who take hold of her; those who hold her fast will be blessed By wisdom, the Lord laid the earth's foundations; by understanding, He set the heavens in place; by His knowledge, the deeps were divided, and the clouds let drop the dew. My son, do not let wisdom and understanding ut of your sight; preserve sound judgment and discretion; they will be life for you, an ornament to grace your neck. Then you will go on your way in safey, and your foot will not stumble. When you lie down, you will not be afraid; when you lie down, your sleep will be sweet. Have no fear of sudden disaster or of the ruin that overtakes the wicked, for the Lord will be at your side and will keep your foot from being snared Do not withhold good from those to whom it is due when it is in your power to act. Do not say to your neighbor, "Come back tomorrow and I'll give it to you," when you already have it with you. Do not plot harm against your neighbor, who lives trustfully near you. Do not accuse anyone for no reason when they have done you no harm. Do not envy the violent or choose any of their ways, for the Lord detests the perverse but takes the upright into His confidence. The Lord's curse is on the house of the wicked, but He blesses the home of the righteous. He mocks proud mockers but shows favor to the humble and oppressed. The wise inherit honor, but fools get only shame

Chapter 4

Listen, my children, to a father's instruction; pay attention and gain understanding. I give you sound learning, so do not forsake my teaching. For I too was a son to my father, still tender and cherished by my mother. Then he taught me, and he said to me, "Take hold of my words with all your heart; keep my commands, and you will live. Get wisdom, get understanding; do not forget my words or turn away from them. Do not forsake wisdom, and she will protect you; love her, and she will watch over you. The beginning of wisdom is this: Get wisdom. Though it cost all you have, get understanding. Cherish her, and she will exalt you; embrace her, and she will honor you. She will give you a garland to grace your head and present you with a glorious crown." Listen, my son, accept what I say, and the years of your life will be many. I instruct you in the way of wisdom and lead you along straight paths. When you walk, your steps will not be hampered; when you run, you will not stumble. Hold on to instruction, do not let it go; guard it well, for it is your life. Do not set foot on the path of the wicked or walk in the way of evildoers. Avoid it, do not travel on it; turn from it and go on your way. For they cannot rest until they do evil; they are robbed of sleep till they make someone stumble. They eat the bread of wickedness and drink the wine of violence The path of the righteous is like the morning sun, shining ever brighter till the full light of day. But the way of the wicked is like deep darkness; they do not know what makes them stumble. My son, pay attention to what I say; turn your ear to my words. Do not let them out of your sight, keep them within your heart, for they are life to those who find them and health to one's whole body. Above all else, guard your heart, for everything you do flows from it. Keep your mouth free of perversity; keep corrupt talk far from your lips. Let your eyes look straight ahead; fix your gaze directly before you. Give careful thought to the paths for your feet and be steadfast in all your ways. Do not turn to the right or the left; keep your foot from evil

Chapter 5

My son, pay attention to my wisdom, turn your ear to my words of insight, that you may maintain discretion and your lips may preserve knowledge. For the lips of the adulterous woman drip honey, and her speech is smoother than oil, but in the end, she is bitter as gall, sharp as a double-edged sword. Her feet go down to death; her steps lead straight to the grave. She gives no thought to the way of life; her paths wander aimlessly, but she does not know it

Now then, my sons, listen to me; do not turn aside from what I say. Keep to a path far from her, do not go near the door of her house, lest you lose your honor to others and your dignity to one who is cruel, lest strangers feast on your wealth and your toil enrich the house of another. At the end of your life, you will groan when your flesh and body are spent. You will say, "How I hated discipline! How my heart spurned correction! I would not obey my teachers or turn my ear to my instructors. And I was soon in serious trouble in the assembly of God's people." Drink water from your own cistern, running water from your own well. Should your springs overflow in the streets, your streams of water in the public squares? Let them be yours alone, never to be shared with strangers. May your fountain be blessed, and may you rejoice in the wife of your youth. A loving doe, a graceful deer—may her breasts satisfy you always, may you ever be intoxicated with her love. Why, my son, be intoxicated with another man's wife? Why embrace the bosom of a wayward woman? For your ways are in full view of the Lord, and He examines all your paths. The evil deeds of the wicked ensnare them; the cords of their sins hold them fast. For lack of discipline, they will die, led astray by their own great folly

Chapter 6

My son, if you have put up security for your neighbor and have struck hands in pledge with a stranger, you are ensnared by the words of your mouth; you are trapped by what you have said. Do this, my son, to free yourself, since you have fallen into your neighbor's hands: go and humble yourself; press your plea with urgency. Do not allow sleep to your eyes or slumber to your eyelids. Free yourself like a gazelle from the hand of the hunter, like a bird from the snare of the fowler Go to the ant, you sluggard; consider its ways and be wise! It has no commander, no overseer, or ruler, yet it stores its provisions in summer and gathers its food at harvest. How long will you lie there, you sluggard? When will you get up from your sleep? A little sleep, a little slumber, a little folding of the hands to rest—and poverty will come on you like a thief and scarcity like an armed man A troublemaker and a villain, who goes about with a corrupt mouth, who winks maliciously with his eye, signals with his feet, and motions with his fingers, who plots evil with deceit in his heart—he always stirs up conflict. Therefore, disaster will overtake him in an instant; he will suddenly be destroyed—without remedy There are six things the LORD hates, seven that are detestable to him: haughty eyes, a lying tongue, hands that shed innocent blood, a heart that devises wicked schemes, feet that are quick to rush into evil, a false witness who pours out lies, and a person who stirs up conflict in the community My son, keep your father's command and do not forsake your mother's teaching. Bind them always on your heart; fasten them around your neck. When you walk, they will guide you; when you sleep, they will watch over you; when you awake, they will speak to you. For this command is a lamp, this teaching is a light, and correction and instruction are the way to life, keeping you from your neighbor's wife, from the smooth talk of a wayward woman. Do not lust in your heart after her beauty or let her captivate you with her eyes. For a prostitute can be had for a loaf of bread, but another man's wife preys on your very life. Can a man scoop fire into his lap without his clothes being burned? Can a man walk on hot coals without his feet being scorched? So is he who sleeps with another man's wife; no one who touches her will go unpunished People do not despise a thief if he steals to satisfy his hunger when he is starving. Yet if he is caught, he must pay sevenfold, though it costs him all the wealth of his house. But a man who commits adultery has no sense; whoever does so destroys himself. Blows and disgrace are his lot, and his shame will never be wiped away. For jealousy arouses a husband's fury, and he will show no mercy when he takes revenge. He will not accept any compensation; he will refuse a bribe, however great it is

Chapter 7

My son, keep my words and store up my commands within you. Keep my commands and you will live; guard my teachings as the apple of your eye. Bind them on your fingers; write them on the tablet of your heart. Say to wisdom, "You are my sister," and to insight, "You are my relative." They will keep you from the adulterous woman, from the wayward woman with her seductive words At the window of my house, I looked down through the lattice. I saw among the simple, I noticed among the young men, a youth who had no sense. He was going down the street near her corner, walking along in the direction of her house at twilight, as the day was fading, as the dark of night set in. Then out came a woman to meet him, dressed like a prostitute and with crafty intent. She is unruly and defiant, her feet never stay at home; now in the street, now in the squares, at every corner she lurks. She took hold of him and kissed him and with a brazen face she said: "Today I fulfilled my vows, and I have food from my fellowship offering at home. So I came out to meet you; I looked for you and have found you! I have covered my bed with colored linens from Egypt. I have perfumed my bed with myrrh, aloes, and cinnamon. Come, let's drink deeply of love till morning; let's enjoy ourselves with love! My husband is not at home; he has gone on a long journey. He took his purse filled with money and will not be home till full moon."

With persuasive words, she led him astray; she seduced him with her smooth talk. All at once he followed her like an ox going to the slaughter, like a deer stepping into a noose till an arrow pierces his liver, like a bird darting into a snare, little knowing it will cost him his life Now then, my sons, listen to me; pay attention to what I say. Do not let your heart turn to her ways or stray into her paths. Many are the victims she has brought down; her slain are a mighty throng. Her house is a highway to the grave, leading down to the chambers of death

Chapter 8

Does not wisdom call out? Does not understanding raise her voice? At the highest point along the way, where the paths meet, she takes her stand; beside the gate leading into the city, at the entrance, she cries aloud: "To you, O people, I call out; I raise my voice to all mankind. You who are simple, gain prudence; you who are foolish, set your hearts on it. Listen, for I have trustworthy things to say; I open my lips to speak what is right. My mouth speaks what is true, for my lips detest wickedness. All the words of my mouth are just; none of them is crooked or perverse. To the discerning all of them are right; they are upright to those who have found knowledge. Choose my instruction instead of silver, knowledge rather than choice gold, for wisdom is more precious than rubies, and nothing you desire can compare with her "I, wisdom, dwell together with prudence; I possess knowledge and discretion. To fear the Lord is to hate evil; I hate pride and arrogance, evil behavior and perverse speech. Counsel and sound judgment are mine; I have insight, I have power. By me kings reign and rulers issue decrees that are just; by me princes govern, and nobles—all who rule on earth. I love those who love me, and those who seek me find me. With me are riches and honor, enduring

wealth and prosperity. My fruit is better than fine gold; what I yield surpasses choice silver. I walk in the way of righteousness, along the paths of justice, bestowing a rich inheritance on those who love me and making their treasuries full "The Lord brought me forth as the first of his works, before his deeds of old; I was formed long ages ago, at the very beginning, when the world came to be. When there were no watery depths, I was given birth, when there were no springs overflowing with water; before the mountains were settled in place, before the hills, I was given birth, before he made the world or its fields or any of the dust of the earth. I was there when he set the heavens in place, when he marked out the horizon on the face of the deep, when he established the clouds above and fixed securely the fountains of the deep, when he gave the sea its boundary so the waters would not overstep his command, and when he marked out the foundations of the earth. Then I was constantly at his side. I was filled with delight day after day, rejoicing always in his presence, rejoicing in his whole world and delighting in mankind "Now then, my children, listen to me; blessed are those who keep my ways. Listen to my instruction and be wise; do not disregard it. Blessed are those who listen to me, watching daily at my doors, waiting at my doorway. For those who find me find life and receive favor from the Lord. But those who fail to find me harm themselves; all who hate me love death."

Chapter 9

Wisdom has built her house; she has set up its seven pillars. She has prepared her meat and mixed her wine; she has also set her table. She has sent out her servants, and she calls from the highest point of the city, "Let all who are simple come to my house!" To those who have no sense she says, "Come, eat my food and drink the wine I have mixed. Leave your simple ways and you will live; walk in the way of insight." Whoever corrects a mocker invites insults; whoever rebukes the wicked incurs abuse. Do not rebuke mockers or they will hate you; rebuke the wise and they will love you. Instruct the wise and they will be wiser still; teach the righteous and they will add to their learning. The fear of the Lord is the beginning of wisdom, and knowledge of the Holy One is understanding. For through wisdom your days will be many, and years will be added to your life. If you are wise, your wisdom will reward you; if you are a mocker, you alone will suffer Folly is an unruly woman; she is simple and knows nothing. She sits at the door of her house, on a seat at the highest point of the city, calling out to those who pass by, who go straight on their way, "Let all who are simple come to my house!" To those who have no sense she says, "Stolen water is sweet; food eaten in secret is delicious!" But little do they know that the dead are there, that her guests are deep in the realm of the dead

Chapter 10

The proverbs of Solomon: A wise son brings joy to his father, but a foolish son brings grief to his mother. Ill-gotten treasures have no lasting value, but righteousness delivers from death. The Lord does not let the righteous go hungry, but he thwarts the craving of the wicked. Lazy hands make for poverty, but diligent hands bring wealth. He who gathers crops in summer is a prudent son, but he who sleeps during harvest is a disgraceful son Blessings crown the head of the righteous, but violence overwhelms the mouth of the wicked. The name of the righteous is used in blessings, but the name of the wicked will rot. The wise in heart accept commands, but a chattering fool comes to ruin. Whoever walks in integrity walks securely, but whoever takes crooked paths will be found out. Whoever winks maliciously causes grief, and a chattering fool comes to ruin The mouth of the righteous is a fountain of life, but the mouth of the wicked conceals violence. Hatred stirs up conflict, but love covers over all wrongs. Wisdom is found on the lips of the discerning, but a rod is for the back of one who has no sense. The wise store up knowledge, but the mouth of a fool invites ruin. The wealth of the rich is their fortified city, but poverty is the ruin of the poor. The wages of the righteous is life, but the earnings of the wicked are sin and death Whoever heeds discipline shows the way to life, but whoever ignores correction leads others astray. Whoever conceals hatred with lying lips and spreads slander is a fool. Sin is not ended by multiplying words, but the prudent hold their tongues. The tongue of the righteous is choice silver, but the heart of the wicked is of little value. The lips of the righteous nourish many, but fools die for lack of sense The blessing of the Lord brings wealth, without painful toil for it. A fool finds pleasure in wicked schemes, but a person of understanding delights in wisdom. What the wicked dread will overtake them; what the righteous desire will be granted. When the storm has swept by the wicked are gone, but the righteous stand firm forever. As vinegar to the teeth and smoke to the eyes, so are sluggards to those who send them The fear of the Lord adds length to life, but the years of the wicked are cut short. The prospect of the righteous is joy, but the hopes of the wicked come to nothing. The way of the Lord is a refuge for the blameless, but it is the ruin of those who do evil. The righteous will never be uprooted, but the wicked will not remain in the land. From the mouth of the righteous comes the fruit of wisdom, but a perverse tongue will be silenced. The lips of the righteous know what finds favor, but the mouth of the wicked only what is perverse

Chapter 11

False scales are an abomination to the LORD, but a perfect weight pleases Him. When pride comes, so does shame; but with the humble is wisdom. The righteousness of the upright guides them, but the crookedness of the treacherous destroys them. Riches do not profit in the day of wrath, but righteousness delivers from death. The righteousness of the blameless keeps their way straight, but the wicked fall by their own wickedness. The righteousness of the upright delivers them, but the treacherous are trapped by their own desires When the wicked die, their hope perishes, and the expectation of wealth perishes too. The righteous are delivered from trouble, and the wicked come in their place. With their mouths, the godless destroy their neighbors, but through knowledge, the righteous are delivered. When the righteous prosper, the city rejoices; when the wicked perish, there are shouts of joy. Through the blessing of the upright, a city is exalted, but by the mouth of the wicked, it is destroyed. Whoever belittles their neighbor lacks sense, but a person of understanding remains silent. A gossip betrays a confidence, but a trustworthy person keeps a secret Where there is no guidance, the people fall, but in an abundance of counselors, there is safety. Whoever puts up security for a stranger will surely suffer, but whoever refuses to shake hands in pledge is safe. A kindhearted woman gains honor, but ruthless men gain only wealth. Those who are kind benefit themselves, but the cruel bring ruin on themselves. A wicked person earns deceptive wages, but the one who sows righteousness reaps a sure reward Truly, the righteous attain life, but whoever pursues evil finds death. The LORD detests those whose hearts are perverse, but He delights in those whose ways are blameless. Be sure of this: The wicked will not go unpunished, but those who are righteous will go free. Like a gold ring in a pig's snout is a beautiful woman who shows no discretion. The desire of the righteous ends only in good, but the hope of the wicked only in wrath. One person gives freely, yet gains even more; another withholds unduly, but comes to poverty. A generous person will prosper; whoever refreshes others will be refreshed People curse the one who hoards grain, but they pray God's blessing on the one who is willing to sell. Whoever seeks good finds favor, but evil comes to one who searches for it. Those who trust in their riches will fall, but the righteous will thrive like a green leaf. Whoever brings ruin on their family will inherit only wind, and the fool will be servant to the wise. The fruit of the righteous is a tree of life, and the one who is wise saves lives. If the righteous receive their due on earth, how much more the ungodly and the sinner!

Chapter 12

Whoever loves discipline loves knowledge, but whoever hates correction is stupid. Good people obtain favor from the LORD, but He condemns those who devise wicked schemes. No one can be established through wickedness, but the righteous cannot be uprooted. A wife of noble character is her husband's crown, but a disgraceful wife is like decay in his bones. The plans of the righteous are just, but the advice of the wicked is deceitful. The words of the wicked lie in wait for blood, but the speech of the upright rescues them The wicked are overthrown and are no more, but the house of the righteous stands firm. A person is praised according to their prudence, but one with a warped mind is despised. Better to be a nobody and yet have a servant than pretend to be somebody and have no food. The righteous care for the needs of their animals, but the kindest acts of the wicked are cruel. Those who work their land will have abundant food, but those who chase fantasies have no sense The wicked desire the stronghold of evildoers, but the root of the righteous endures. Evildoers are trapped by their sinful talk, and so the innocent escape trouble. From the fruit of their lips, people are filled with good things, and the work of their hands brings them reward. The way of fools seems right to them, but the wise listen to advice. Fools show their annoyance at once, but the prudent overlook an insult An honest witness tells the truth, but a false witness tells lies. The words of the reckless pierce like swords, but the tongue of the wise brings healing. Truthful lips endure forever, but a lying tongue lasts only a moment. Deceit is in the hearts of those who plot evil, but those who promote peace have joy. No harm overtakes the righteous, but the wicked have their fill of trouble. The LORD detests lying lips, but He delights in people who are trustworthy The prudent keep their knowledge to themselves, but a fool's heart blurts out folly. Diligent hands will rule, but laziness ends in forced labor. Anxiety weighs down the heart, but a kind word cheers it up. The righteous choose their friends carefully, but the way of the wicked leads them astray. The lazy do not roast any game, but the diligent feed on the riches of the hunt. In the way of righteousness there is life; along that path is immortality

Chapter 13

A wise son heeds his father's instruction, but a mocker does not respond to rebukes. From the fruit of their lips, people enjoy good things, but the unfaithful have an appetite for violence. Those who guard their lips preserve their lives, but those who speak rashly will come to ruin. A sluggard's appetite is never filled, but the desires of the diligent are fully satisfied The righteous hate what is false, but the wicked make themselves a stench and bring shame on themselves. Righteousness guards the person of integrity, but wickedness overthrows the sinner. One person pretends to be rich, yet has nothing; another pretends to be poor, yet has great wealth. A person's riches may ransom their life, but the poor cannot respond to threatening rebukes. The light of the righteous shines brightly, but the lamp of the wicked is snuffed out Where there is strife, there is pride, but wisdom is found in those who take advice. Dishonest money dwindles away, but whoever gathers money little by little makes it grow. Hope deferred makes the heart sick, but a longing fulfilled is a tree of life. Whoever scorns instruction will pay for it, but whoever respects a command is rewarded The teaching of the wise is a fountain of life, turning a person from the snares of death. Good judgment wins favor, but the way of the unfaithful leads to their destruction. All who are prudent act with knowledge, but fools expose their folly. A wicked messenger falls into trouble, but a trustworthy envoy brings healing. Whoever disregards discipline comes to poverty and shame, but whoever heeds correction is honored A longing fulfilled is sweet to the soul, but fools detest turning from evil. Walk with the wise and become wise, for a companion of fools suffers harm. Trouble pursues the sinner, but the righteous are rewarded with good things. A good person leaves an inheritance for their children's children, but a sinner's wealth is stored up for the righteous. An unplowed field produces food for the poor, but injustice sweeps it away Whoever spares the rod hates their children, but the one who loves their children is careful to discipline them. The righteous eat to their hearts' content, but the stomach of the wicked goes hungry

Chapter 14

The wise woman builds her house, but with her own hands the foolish one tears hers down. Whoever fears the LORD walks uprightly, but those who despise Him are devious in their ways. A fool's mouth lashes out with pride, but the lips of the wise protect them. Where there are no oxen, the manger is empty, but from the strength of an ox come abundant harvests An honest witness does not deceive, but a false witness pours out lies. The mocker seeks wisdom and finds none, but knowledge comes easily to the discerning. Stay away from a fool, for you will not find knowledge on their lips. The wisdom of the prudent is to give thought to their ways, but the folly of fools is deception. Fools mock at making amends for sin, but goodwill is found among the upright Each heart knows its own bitterness, and no one else can share its joy. The house of the wicked will be destroyed, but the tent of the upright will flourish. There is a way that appears to be right, but in the end, it leads to death. Even in laughter, the heart may ache, and rejoicing may end in grief The faithless will be fully repaid for their ways, and the good rewarded for theirs. The simple believe anything, but the prudent give thought to their steps. The wise fear the LORD and shun evil, but a fool is hot-headed and yet feels secure. A quick-tempered person does foolish things, and the one who devises evil schemes is hated. The simple inherit folly, but the prudent are crowned with knowledge. Evildoers will bow down in the presence of the good, and the wicked at the gates of the righteous The poor are shunned even by their neighbors, but the rich have many friends. It is a sin to despise one's neighbor, but blessed is the one who is kind to the needy. Do not those who plot evil go astray? But those who plan what is good find love and faithfulness. All hard work brings a profit, but mere talk leads only to poverty The wealth of the wise is their crown, but the folly of fools yields folly. A truthful witness saves lives, but a false witness is

deceitful. Whoever fears the LORD has a secure fortress, and for their children, it will be a refuge. The fear of the LORD is a fountain of life, turning a person from the snares of death A large population is a king's glory, but without subjects a prince is ruined. Whoever is patient has great understanding, but one who is quick-tempered displays folly. A heart at peace gives life to the body, but envy rots the bones. Whoever oppresses the poor shows contempt for their Maker, but whoever is kind to the needy honors God When calamity comes, the wicked are brought down, but even in death, the righteous seek refuge in God. Wisdom reposes in the heart of the discerning, and even among fools, she lets herself be known. Righteousness exalts a nation, but sin condemns any people. A king delights in a wise servant, but a shameful servant arouses his fury

Chapter 15

A gentle answer turns away wrath, but a harsh word stirs up anger. The tongue of the wise adorns knowledge, but the mouth of the fool gushes folly. The eyes of the LORD are everywhere, keeping watch on the wicked and the good The soothing tongue is a tree of life, but a perverse tongue crushes the spirit. A fool spurns a parent's discipline, but whoever heeds correction shows prudence. The house of the righteous contains great treasure, but the income of the wicked brings ruin. The lips of the wise spread knowledge, but the hearts of fools are not upright The LORD detests the sacrifice of the wicked, but the prayer of the upright pleases Him. The LORD detests the way of the wicked, but He loves those who pursue righteousness. Stern discipline awaits anyone who leaves the path; the one who hates correction will die Death and Destruction lie open before the LORD—how much more do human hearts! Mockers resent correction, so they avoid the wise. A happy heart makes the face cheerful, but heartache crushes the spirit. The discerning heart seeks knowledge, but the mouth of a fool feeds on folly. All the days of the oppressed are wretched, but the cheerful heart has a continual feast Better a little with the fear of the LORD than great wealth with turmoil. Better a small serving of vegetables with love than a fattened calf with hatred. A hot-tempered person stirs up conflict, but the one who is patient calms a quarrel The way of the sluggard is blocked with thorns, but the path of the upright is a highway. A wise son brings joy to his father, but a foolish man despises his mother. Folly brings joy to one who has no sense, but whoever has understanding keeps a straight course. Plans fail for lack of counsel, but with many advisers they succeed. A person finds joy in giving an apt reply—and how good is a timely word! The path of life leads upward for the prudent to keep them from going down to the realm of the dead. The LORD tears down the house of the proud, but He sets the widow's boundary stones in place. The LORD detests the thoughts of the wicked, but gracious words are pure in His sight The greedy bring ruin to their households, but the one who hates bribes will live. The heart of the righteous weighs its answers, but the mouth of the wicked gushes evil. The LORD is far from the wicked, but He hears the prayer of the righteous Light in a messenger's eyes brings joy to the heart, and good news gives health to the bones. Whoever heeds life-giving correction will be at home among the wise. Those who disregard discipline despise themselves, but the one who heeds correction gains understanding. Wisdom's instruction is to fear the LORD, and humility comes before honor

Chapter 16

The preparations of the heart are in man, but the answer of the tongue is from the LORD. All the ways of man are pure in his own eyes, but the LORD weighs the spirits. Commit your works to the LORD, and your thoughts will be established. The LORD has made all things for Himself, even the wicked for the day of disaster. Everyone proud in heart is an abomination to the LORD; though they join forces, none will go unpunished. By mercy and truth iniquity is purged, and by the fear of the LORD men depart from evil. When a man's ways please the LORD, He makes even his enemies to be at peace with him. Better is a little with righteousness than vast revenues without justice. A man's heart plans his way, but the LORD directs his steps Divination is on the lips of the king; his mouth must not transgress in judgment. Honest weights and scales are the LORD's; all the weights in the bag are His work. It is an abomination for kings to commit wickedness, for the throne is established by righteousness. Righteous lips are the delight of kings, and they love him who speaks what is right. The wrath of a king is like the roaring of a lion, but his favor is like dew on the grass How much better to get wisdom than gold, and to get understanding is to be chosen rather than silver! The highway of the upright is to depart from evil; he who keeps his way preserves his soul. Pride goes before destruction, and a haughty spirit before a fall. Better to be of a humble spirit with the lowly than to divide the spoil with the proud. He who heeds the word wisely will find good, and whoever trusts in the LORD, happy is he The wise in heart will be called prudent, and sweetness of the lips increases learning. Understanding is a wellspring of life to him who has it, but the correction of fools is folly. The heart of the wise teaches his mouth and adds learning to his lips. Pleasant words are like a honeycomb, sweetness to the soul and health to the bones There is a way that seems right to a man, but its end is the way of death. The person who labors, labors for himself, for his hungry mouth drives him on. An ungodly man digs up evil, and it is on his lips like a burning fire. A perverse man sows strife, and a whisperer separates the best of friends. A violent man entices his neighbor and leads him in a way that is not good. He winks his eye to devise perverse things; he purses his lips and brings about evil The silver-haired head is a crown of glory if it is found in the way of righteousness. He who is slow to anger is better than the mighty, and he who rules his spirit than he who takes a city. The lot is cast into the lap, but its every decision is from the LORD

Chapter 17
Better a dry morsel with quietness than a house full of feasting with strife. A wise servant will rule over a disgraceful son and will share the inheritance as one of the brothers. The refining pot is for silver and the furnace for gold, but the LORD tests the hearts. A wicked person listens to deceitful lips; a liar pays attention to a destructive tongue. Whoever mocks the poor reproaches his Maker; he who is glad at calamity will not go unpunished Children's children are the crown of old men, and the glory of children is their fathers. Excellent speech is not becoming to a fool, much less lying lips to a prince. A bribe is like a charm to the one who gives it; wherever he turns, he prospers. Whoever covers an offense seeks love, but whoever repeats the matter separates close friends A rebuke impresses a discerning person more than a hundred lashes a fool. An evil man seeks only rebellion; therefore, a cruel messenger will be sent against him. Better to meet a bear robbed of her cubs than a fool in his folly. Whoever rewards evil for good, evil will not depart from his house. The beginning of strife is like letting out water, so abandon the quarrel before it breaks out Acquitting the guilty and condemning the innocent—the LORD detests them both. Why should fools have money in hand to buy

wisdom, when they are not able to understand it? A friend loves at all times, and a brother is born for a time of adversity. One who has no sense shakes hands in pledge and puts up security for a neighbor Whoever loves a quarrel loves sin; whoever builds a high gate invites destruction. One whose heart is corrupt does not prosper; one whose tongue is perverse falls into trouble. To have a fool for a child brings grief; there is no joy for the parent of a godless fool. A cheerful heart is good medicine, but a crushed spirit dries up the bones. The wicked accept bribes in secret to pervert the course of justice A discerning person keeps wisdom in view, but a fool's eyes wander to the ends of the earth. A foolish son brings grief to his father and bitterness to the mother who bore him. If imposing a fine on the innocent is not good, surely to flog honest officials is not right. The one who has knowledge uses words with restraint, and whoever has understanding is even-tempered. Even fools are thought wise if they keep silent, and discerning if they hold their tongues

Chapter 18
An unfriendly person pursues selfish ends and against all sound judgment starts quarrels. Fools find no pleasure in understanding but delight in airing their own opinions. When wickedness comes, so does contempt, and with shame comes reproach. The words of the mouth are deep waters, but the fountain of wisdom is a rushing stream It is not good to be partial to the wicked and so deprive the innocent of justice. The lips of fools bring them strife, and their mouths invite a beating. The mouths of fools are their undoing, and their lips are a snare to their very lives. The words of a gossip are like choice morsels; they go down to the inmost parts One who is slack in his work is brother to one who destroys. The name of the LORD is a fortified tower; the righteous run to it and are safe. The wealth of the rich is their fortified city; they imagine it a wall too high to scale. Before a downfall, the heart is haughty, but humility comes before honor To answer before listening—that is folly and shame. The human spirit can endure in sickness, but a crushed spirit who can bear? The heart of the discerning acquires knowledge, for the ears of the wise seek it out. A gift opens the way and ushers the giver into the presence of the great In a lawsuit, the first to speak seems right until someone comes forward and cross-examines. Casting the lot settles disputes and keeps strong opponents apart. A brother wronged is more unyielding than a fortified city; disputes are like the barred gates of a citadel. From the fruit of their mouth, a person's stomach is filled; with the harvest of their lips, they are satisfied. The tongue has the power of life and death, and those who love it will eat its fruit He who finds a wife finds what is good and receives favor from the LORD. The poor plead for mercy, but the rich answer harshly. One who has unreliable friends soon comes to ruin, but there is a friend who sticks closer than a brother

Chapter 19
Better the poor whose walk is blameless than a fool whose lips are perverse. Desire without knowledge is not good—how much more will hasty feet miss the way! A person's own folly leads to their ruin, yet their heart rages against the LORD. Wealth attracts many friends, but even the closest friend of the poor person deserts them A false witness will not go unpunished, and whoever pours out lies will not go free. Many curry favor with a ruler, and everyone is the friend of one who gives gifts. The poor are shunned by all their relatives—how much more do their friends avoid them! Though the poor pursue them with pleading, they are nowhere to be found The one who gets wisdom loves life; the one who

cherishes understanding will soon prosper. A false witness will not go unpunished, and whoever pours out lies will perish. It is not fitting for a fool to live in luxury—how much worse for a slave to rule over princes! A person's wisdom yields patience; it is to one's glory to overlook an offense. A king's rage is like the roar of a lion, but his favor is like dew on the grass. A foolish child is a father's ruin, and a quarrelsome wife is like the constant dripping of a leaky roof. Houses and wealth are inherited from parents, but a prudent wife is from the LORD Laziness brings on deep sleep, and the shiftless go hungry. Whoever keeps commandments keeps their life, but whoever shows contempt for their ways will die. Whoever is kind to the poor lends to the LORD, and He will reward them for what they have done Discipline your children, for in that, there is hope; do not be a willing party to their death. A hot-tempered person must pay the penalty; rescue them, and you will have to do it again. Listen to advice and accept discipline, and at the end, you will be counted among the wise. Many are the plans in a person's heart, but it is the LORD's purpose that prevails What a person desires is unfailing love; better to be poor than a liar. The fear of the LORD leads to life; then one rests content, untouched by trouble. The sluggard buries his hand in the dish; he will not even bring it back to his mouth! Flog a mocker, and the simple will learn prudence; rebuke the discerning, and they will gain knowledge Whoever robs their father and drives out their mother is a child who brings shame and disgrace. Stop listening to instruction, my son, and you will stray from the words of knowledge. A corrupt witness mocks at justice, and the mouth of the wicked gulps down evil. Penalties are prepared for mockers, and beatings for the backs of fools

Chapter 20

Wine is a mocker and beer a brawler; whoever is led astray by them is not wise. A king's wrath strikes terror like the roar of a lion; those who anger him forfeit their lives. It is to one's honor to avoid strife, but every fool is quick to quarrel Sluggards do not plow in season; so at harvest time, they look but find nothing. The purposes of a person's heart are deep waters, but one who has insight draws them out. Many claim to have unfailing love, but a faithful person who can find? The righteous lead blameless lives; blessed are their children after them When a king sits on his throne to judge, he winnows out all evil with his eyes. Who can say, "I have kept my heart pure; I am clean and without sin"? Differing weights and differing measures—the LORD detests them both. Even small children are known by their actions, so is their conduct really pure and upright? Ears that hear and eyes that see—the LORD has made them both. Do not love sleep, or you will grow poor; stay awake, and you will have food to spare. "It's no good, it's no good!" says the buyer—then goes off and boasts about the purchase. Gold there is, and rubies in abundance, but lips that speak knowledge are a rare jewel Take the garment of one who puts up security for a stranger; hold it in pledge if it is done for an outsider. Food gained by fraud tastes sweet, but one ends up with a mouth full of gravel. Plans are established by seeking advice; so if you wage war, obtain guidance A gossip betrays a confidence; so avoid anyone who talks too much. If someone curses their father or mother, their lamp will be snuffed out in pitch darkness. An inheritance claimed too soon will not be blessed at the end. Do not say, "I'll pay you back for this wrong!" Wait for the LORD, and He will avenge you. The LORD detests differing weights, and dishonest scales do not please Him A person's steps are directed by the LORD. How then can anyone understand their own way? It is a trap to dedicate something rashly and only later to consider one's vows. A wise king winnows out the wicked; he drives the threshing wheel over them. The human spirit is the lamp of the LORD that sheds light on one's inmost being. Love and faithfulness keep a king safe; through love, his throne is made secure The glory of young men is their strength, gray hair the splendor of the old. Blows and wounds scrub away evil, and beatings purge the inmost being

Chapter 21

The hearts of kings are in the hand of the LORD; He directs them like a stream of water wherever He pleases. Every way of a man seems right in his own eyes, but the LORD weighs the heart. To do righteousness and justice is more acceptable to the LORD than sacrifice. A haughty look, a proud heart, and the plowing of the wicked are sin. The plans of the diligent lead surely to abundance, but everyone who is hasty comes only to poverty. The acquisition of treasures by a lying tongue is a fleeting vapor and a deadly snare. The violence of the wicked will destroy them because they refuse to do justice. The way of the guilty is devious, but the conduct of the innocent is upright It is better to live in a corner of the housetop than in a house shared with a quarrelsome wife. The soul of the wicked desires evil; his neighbor finds no mercy in his eyes. When a mocker is punished, the simple gain wisdom; when a wise man is instructed, he gains knowledge. The Righteous One takes note of the house of the wicked and brings the wicked to ruin. Whoever shuts their ears to the cry of the poor will also cry out and not be answered. A gift given in secret soothes anger, and a bribe concealed in the cloak pacifies great wrath When justice is done, it brings joy to the righteous but terror to evildoers. Whoever strays from the path of prudence comes to rest in the company of the dead. Whoever loves pleasure will become poor; whoever loves wine and olive oil will never be rich. The wicked become a ransom for the righteous, and the unfaithful for the upright. Better to live in a desert than with a quarrelsome and nagging wife. The wise store up choice food and olive oil, but fools gulp theirs down Whoever pursues righteousness and love finds life, prosperity, and honor. One who is wise can go up against the city of the mighty and pull down the stronghold in which they trust. Those who guard their mouths and their tongues keep themselves from calamity. The proud and arrogant person— "Mocker" is his name—behaves with insolent fury. The craving of a sluggard will be the death of him because his hands refuse to work. All day long he craves for more, but the righteous give without sparing The sacrifice of the wicked is detestable— how much more so when brought with evil intent! A false witness will perish, but a careful listener will testify successfully. The wicked put up a bold front, but the upright give thought to their ways. There is no wisdom, no insight, no plan that can succeed against the LORD. The horse is made ready for the day of battle, but victory rests with the LORD

Chapter 22

A good name is more desirable than great riches; to be esteemed is better than silver or gold. The rich and the poor have this in common: The LORD is the Maker of them all. The prudent see danger and take refuge, but the simple keep going and pay the penalty. Humility is the fear of the LORD; its wages are riches and honor and life. In the paths of the wicked are snares and pitfalls, but those who would preserve their life stay far from them Start children off on the way they should go, and even when they are old, they will not turn from it. The rich rule over the poor, and the borrower is slave to the lender. Whoever sows injustice reaps calamity, and the rod they wield in fury will be broken. The generous will themselves be blessed, for they share their food with the poor. Drive out the mocker, and out goes strife; quarrels and insults are ended One who loves a pure heart and who speaks with grace will have the king for a friend. The eyes of the LORD keep watch over knowledge, but He frustrates the words of the unfaithful. The sluggard says, "There's a lion outside! I'll be killed in the public square!" The mouth of an adulterous woman is a deep pit; a man who is under the LORD's wrath falls into it. Folly is bound up in the heart of a child, but the rod of discipline will drive it far away One who oppresses the poor to increase his wealth and one who gives gifts to the rich—both come to poverty. Pay attention and turn your ear to the sayings of the wise; apply your heart to what I teach, for it is pleasing when you keep them in your heart and have all of them ready on your lips. So that your trust may be in the LORD, I teach you today, even you. Have I not written thirty sayings for you, sayings of counsel and knowledge, teaching you to be honest and to speak the truth, so that you bring back truthful reports to those you serve? Do not exploit the poor because they are poor and do not crush the needy in court, for the LORD will take up their case and will exact life for life. Do not make friends with a hot-tempered person, do not associate with one easily angered, or you may learn their ways and get yourself ensnared. Do not be one who shakes hands in pledge or puts up security for debts; if you lack the means to pay, your very bed will be snatched from under you Do not move an ancient boundary stone set up by your ancestors. Do you see someone skilled in their work? They will serve before kings; they will not serve before officials of low rank

Chapter 23

When you sit to dine with a ruler, note well what is before you, and put a knife to your throat if you are given to gluttony. Do not crave his delicacies, for that food is deceptive. Do not wear yourself out to get rich; do not trust your own cleverness. Cast but a glance at riches, and they are gone, for they will surely sprout wings and fly off to the sky like an eagle Do not eat the food of a begrudging host, do not crave his delicacies; for he is the kind of person who is always thinking about the cost. "Eat and drink," he says to you, but his heart is not with you. You will vomit up the little you have eaten and will have wasted your compliments Do not speak to fools, for they will scorn your prudent words. Do not move an ancient boundary stone or encroach on the fields of the fatherless, for their Defender is strong; He will take up their case against you. Apply your heart to instruction and your ears to words of knowledge Do not withhold discipline from a child; if you punish them with the rod, they will not die. Punish them with the rod and save them from death. My son, if your heart is wise, then my heart will be glad indeed; my inmost being will rejoice when your lips speak what is right Do not let your heart envy sinners, but always be zealous for the fear of the LORD. There is surely a future hope for you, and your hope will not be cut off. Listen, my son, and be wise, and set your heart on the right path. Do not join those who drink too much wine or gorge themselves on meat, for drunkards and gluttons become poor, and drowsiness clothes them in rags Listen to your father, who gave you life, and do not despise your mother when she is old. Buy the truth and do not sell it—wisdom, instruction, and insight as well. The father of a righteous child has great joy; a man who fathers a wise son rejoices in him. May your father and mother rejoice; may she who gave you birth be joyful! My son, give me your heart and let your eyes delight in my ways, for an adulterous woman is a deep pit, and a wayward wife is a narrow well. Like a bandit, she lies in wait and multiplies the unfaithful among men Who has woe? Who has sorrow? Who has strife? Who has complaints? Who has needless bruises? Who has bloodshot eyes? Those who linger over wine, who go to sample bowls of mixed wine. Do not gaze at wine when it is red, when it sparkles in the cup, when it goes down smoothly! In the end, it bites like a snake and poisons like a viper. Your eyes will see strange sights, and your mind will imagine confusing things. You will be like one sleeping on the high seas, lying on top of the rigging. "They hit me," you will say, "but I'm not hurt! They beat me, but I don't feel it! When will I wake up so I can find another drink?"

Chapter 24

Do not envy the wicked, do not desire their company; for their hearts plot violence, and their lips talk about making trouble. By wisdom a house is built, and through understanding it is established; through knowledge, its rooms are filled with rare and beautiful treasures. The wise prevail through great power, and those who have knowledge muster their strength. Surely you need guidance to wage war, and victory is won through many advisers Wisdom is too high for fools; in the assembly at the gate, they must not open their mouths. Whoever plots evil will be known as a schemer. The schemes of folly are sin, and people detest a mocker If you falter in a time of trouble, how small is your strength! Rescue those being led away to death; hold back those staggering toward slaughter. If you say, "But we knew nothing about this," does not He who weighs the heart perceive it? Does not He who guards your life know it? Will He not repay everyone according to what they have done? Eat honey, my son, for it is good; honey from the comb is sweet to your taste. Know also that wisdom is like honey for you: If you find it, there is a future hope for you, and your hope will not be cut off Do not lurk like a thief near the house of the righteous, do not plunder their dwelling place; for though the righteous fall seven times, they rise again, but the wicked stumble when calamity strikes Do not gloat when your enemy falls; when they stumble, do not let your heart rejoice, or the LORD will see and disapprove and turn His wrath away from them. Do not fret because of evildoers or be envious of the wicked, for the evildoer has no future hope, and the lamp of the wicked will be snuffed out Fear the LORD and the king, my son, and do not join with rebellious officials, for those two will send sudden destruction on them, and who knows what calamities they can bring? These also are sayings of the wise: To show partiality in judging is not good. Whoever says to the guilty, "You are innocent," will be cursed by peoples and denounced by nations. But it will go well with those who convict the guilty, and rich blessing will come on them An honest answer is like a kiss on the lips. Put your outdoor work in order and get your fields ready; after that, build your house. Do not testify against your neighbor without cause—would you use your lips to mislead? Do not say, "I'll do to them as they have done to me; I'll pay them back for what they did." I went past the field of a sluggard, past the vineyard of someone who has no sense; thorns had come up everywhere, the ground was covered with weeds, and the stone wall was in ruins. I applied my heart to what I observed and learned a lesson from what I saw: A little sleep, a little slumber, a little folding of the hands to rest—and poverty will come on you like a thief and scarcity like an armed man

Chapter 25

These are also proverbs of Solomon, compiled by the men of Hezekiah, king of Judah: It is the glory of God to conceal a matter; to search out a matter is the glory of kings. As the heavens are high and the earth is deep, so the hearts of kings are unsearchable Remove the dross from the silver, and a silversmith can produce a vessel; remove wicked officials from the king's presence, and his throne will be established through righteousness Do not exalt yourself in the king's presence, and do not claim a place among his great men; it is better for him to say to you, "Come up here," than for him to humiliate you before his nobles What you have seen with your eyes do not bring hastily to court, for what will you do in the end if your neighbor puts you to shame? If you take your neighbor to court, do not betray another's confidence, or the one who hears it may shame you, and the charge against you will stand Like apples of gold in settings of silver is a ruling rightly given. Like an earring of gold or an ornament of fine gold is the rebuke of a wise judge to a listening ear. Like a snow-cooled drink at harvest time is a trustworthy messenger to the one who sends him; he refreshes the spirit of his master. Like clouds and wind without rain is one who boasts of gifts never given Through patience, a ruler can be persuaded, and a gentle tongue can break a bone. If you find honey, eat just enough—too much of it, and you will vomit. Seldom set foot in your neighbor's house—too much of you, and they will hate you Like a club or a sword or a sharp arrow is one who gives false testimony against a neighbor. Like a broken tooth or a lame foot is reliance on the unfaithful in a time of trouble. Like one who takes away a garment on a cold day or like vinegar poured on a wound is one who sings songs to a heavy heart If your enemy is hungry, give him food to eat; if he is thirsty, give him water to drink. In doing this, you will heap burning coals on his head, and the LORD will reward you Like a north wind that brings unexpected rain is a sly tongue—which provokes a horrified look. Better to live on a corner of the roof than share a house with a quarrelsome wife Like cold water to a weary soul is good news from a distant land. Like a muddied spring or a polluted well are the righteous who give way to the wicked. It is not good to eat too much honey, nor is it honorable to search out matters that are too deep Like a city whose walls are broken through is a person who lacks self-control

Chapter 26

1 As snow in summer and rain in harvest, so honor is not fitting for a fool. 2 Like a flitting sparrow, like a flying swallow, so a curse without cause shall not alight. 3 A whip for the horse, a bridle for the donkey, and a rod for the back of fools. 4 Do not answer a fool according to his folly, lest you also be like him. 5 Answer a fool according to his folly, lest he be wise in his own eyes. 6 He who sends a message by the hand of a fool cuts off his own feet and drinks violence. 7 Like the legs of the lame that hang limp is a proverb in the mouth of fools. 8 Like one who binds a stone in a sling is he who gives honor to a fool. 9 Like a thorn that goes into the hand of a drunkard is a proverb in the mouth of fools. 10 The great God who formed everything gives the fool his hire and the transgressor his wages. 11 As a dog returns to his own vomit, so a fool repeats his folly. 12 Do you see a man wise in his own eyes? There is more hope for a fool than for him. 13 The lazy man says, "There is a lion in the road! A fierce lion is in the streets!" 14 As a door turns on its hinges, so does the lazy man on his bed. 15 The lazy man buries his hand in the bowl; it wearies him to bring it back to his mouth. 16 The lazy man is wiser in his own eyes than seven men who can answer sensibly. 17 He who passes by and meddles in a quarrel not his own is like one who takes a dog by the ears. 18 Like a madman who throws firebrands, arrows, and death, 19 is the man who deceives his neighbor and says, "I was only joking!" 20 Where

there is no wood, the fire goes out; and where there is no tailbearer, strife ceases. 21 As charcoal is to burning coals, and wood to fire, so is a contentious man to kindle strife. 22 The words of a tailbearer are like tasty trifles, and they go down into the inmost body. 23 Fervent lips with a wicked heart are like earthenware covered with silver doss. 24 He who hates disguises it with his lips, and lays up deceit within himself; 25 when he speaks kindly, do not believe him, for there are seven abominations in his heart; 26 though his hatred is covered by deceit, his wickedness will be revealed before the assembly. 27 Whoever digs a pit will fall into it, and he who rolls a stone will have it roll back on him. 28 A lying tongue hates those who are crushed by t, and a flattering mouth works ruin

Chapter 27

1 Do not boast about tomorrow, for you do not know what a day may bring forth. 2 Let another man praise you, and not your own mouth; a stranger, and not your own lips. 3 A stone is heavy and sand is weighty, but a fool's wrath is heavier than both of them. 4 Wrath is cruel and anger a torrent, but who is able to stand before jealousy? 5 Open rebuke is better than love carefully concealed. 6 Faithful are the wounds of a friend, but the kisses of an enemy are deceitful. 7 A satisfied soul loathes the honeycomb, but to a hungry soul every bitter thing is sweet. 8 Like a bird that wanders from its nest is a man who wanders from his place. 9 Ointment and perfume delight the heart, and the sweetness of a man's friend gives delight by hearty counsel. 10 Do not forsake your own friend or your father's friend, nor go to your brother's house in the day of your calamity; better is a neighbor nearby than a brother far away. 11 My son, be wise, and make my heart glad, that I may answer him who reproaches me. 12 A prudent man foresees evil and hides himself; the simple pass on and are punished. 13 Take the garment of one who is surety for a stranger, and hold it as a pledge when it is for a seductress. 14 He who blesses his friend with a loud voice, rising early in the morning, it will be counted a curse to him. 15 A continual dripping on a very rainy day and a contentious woman are alike; 16 whoever restrains her restrains the wind, and grasps oil with his right hand. 17 As iron sharpens iron, so a man sharpens the countenance of his friend. 18 Whoever keeps the fig tree will eat its fruit; so he who waits on his master will be honored. 19 As in water face reflects face, so a man's heart reveals the man. 20 Hell and Destruction are never full; so the eyes of man are never satisfied. 21 The refining pot is for silver and the furnace for gold, and a man is valued by what others say of him. 22 Though you grind a fool in a mortar with a pestle along with crushed grain, yet his foolishness will not depart from him. 23 Be diligent to know the state of your flocks, and attend to your herds; 24 for riches are not forever, nor does a crown endure to all generations. 25 When the hay is removed, and the tender grass shows itself, and the herbs of the mountains are gathered in, 26 the lambs will provide your clothing, and the goats the price of a field; 27 you shall have enough goats' milk for your food, for the food of your household, and the nourishment of your maidservants

Chapter 28

1 The wicked flee when no one pursues, but the righteous are bold as a lion. 2 Because of the transgression of a land, many are its princes; but by a man of understanding and knowledge right will be prolonged. 3 A poor man who oppresses the poor is like a driving rain which leaves no food. 4 Those who forsake the law praise the wicked, but such as keep the law contend with them. 5 Evil men do not understand justice, but those who seek the Lord

understand all 6 Better is the poor who walks in his integrity than one who is perverse in his ways, though he be rich. 7 Whoever keeps the law is a discerning son, but a companion of gluttons shames his father. 8 One who increases his possessions by usury and extortion gathers it for him who will pity the poor. 9 One who turns away his ear from hearing the law, even his prayer is an abomination. 10 Whoever causes the upright to go astray in an evil way, he himself will fall into his own pit; but the blameless will inherit good 11 The rich man is wise in his own eyes, but the poor who has understanding searches him out. 12 When the righteous rejoice, there is great glory; but when the wicked arise, men hide themselves. 13 He who covers his sins will not prosper, but whoever confesses and forsakes them will have mercy. 14 Blessed is the man who is always reverent, but he who hardens his heart will fall into calamity. 15 Like a roaring lion and a charging bear is a wicked ruler over poor people. 16 A ruler who lacks understanding is a great oppressor, but he who hates covetousness will prolong his days. 17 A man burdened with bloodshed will flee into a pit; let no one help him. 18 Whoever walks blamelessly will be saved, but he who is perverse in his ways will suddenly fall. 19 He who tills his land will have plenty of bread, but he who follows frivolity will have poverty enough! 20 A faithful man will abound with blessings, but he who hastens to be rich will not go unpunished. 21 To show partiality is not good, because for a piece of bread a man will transgress. 22 A man with an evil eye hastens after riches, and does not consider that poverty will come upon him. 23 He who rebukes a man will find more favor afterward than he who flatters with the tongue. 24 Whoever robs his father or his mother, and says, "It is no transgression," the same is companion to a destroyer. 25 He who is of a proud heart stirs up strife, but he who trusts in the Lord will be prospered. 26 He who trusts in his own heart is a fool, but whoever walks wisely will be delivered. 27 He who gives to the poor will not lack, but he who hides his eyes will have many curses. 28 When the wicked arise, men hide themselves; but when they perish, the righteous increase

Chapter 29

1 He who is often rebuked, and hardens his neck, will suddenly be destroyed, and that without remedy. 2 When the righteous are in authority, the people rejoice; but when a wicked man rules, the people groan. 3 Whoever loves wisdom makes his father rejoice, but a companion of harlots wastes his substance. 4 The king establishes the land by justice, but he who receives bribes overthrows it. 5 A man who flatters his neighbor spreads a net for his feet. 6 By transgression an evil man is snared, but the righteous sings and rejoices. 7 The righteous considers the cause of the poor, but the wicked does not understand such knowledge. 8 Scoffers set a city aflame, but wise men turn away wrath. 9 If a wise man contends with a foolish man, whether the fool rages or laughs, there is no peace. 10 The bloodthirsty hate the blameless, but the upright seek his well-being. 11 A fool vents all his feelings, but a wise man holds them back. 12 If a ruler pays attention to lies, all his servants become wicked. 13 The poor man and the oppressor have this in common: The Lord gives light to the eyes of both. 14 The king who judges the poor with truth, his throne will be established forever. 15 The rod and rebuke give wisdom, but a child left to himself brings shame to his mother. 16 When the wicked are multiplied, transgression increases; but the righteous will see their fall. 17 Correct your son, and he will give you rest; yes, he will give delight to your soul. 18 Where there is no revelation, the people cast off restraint;

but happy is he who keeps the law. 19 A servant will not be corrected by mere words; for though he understands, he will not respond. 20 Do you see a man hasty in his words? There is more hope for a fool than for him. 21 He who pampers his servant from childhood will have him as a son in the end. 22 An angry man stirs up strife, and a furious man abounds in transgression. 23 A man's pride will bring him low, but the humble in spirit will retain honor. 24 Whoever is a partner with a thief hates his own life; he swears to tell the truth, but reveals nothing. 25 The fear of man brings a snare, but whoever trusts in the Lord shall be safe. 26 Many seek the ruler's favor, but justice for man comes from the Lord. 27 An unjust man is an abomination to the righteous, and he who is upright in the way is an abomination to the wicked

Chapter 30

1 The words of Agur the son of Jakeh, his utterance. This man declared to Ithiel— to Ithiel and Ucal: 2 Surely I am more stupid than any man, and do not have the understanding of a man. 3 I neither learned wisdom nor have knowledge of the Holy One. 4 Who has ascended into heaven, or descended? Who has gathered the wind in His fists? Who has bound the waters in a garment? Who has established all the ends of the earth? What is His name, and what is His Son's name, if you know? 5 Every word of God is pure; He is a shield to those who put their trust in Him. 6 Do not add to His words, lest He rebuke you, and you be found a liar. 7 Two things I request of You (Deprive me not before I die): 8 Remove falsehood and lies far from me; give me neither poverty nor riches— Feed me with the food allotted to me; 9 Lest I be full and deny You, and say, "Who is the Lord?" Or lest I be poor and steal, and profane the name of my God. 10 Do not malign a servant to his master, lest he curse you, and you be found guilty. 11 There is a generation that curses its father, and does not bless its mother. 12 There is a generation that is pure in its own eyes, yet is not washed from its filthiness. 13 There is a generation—oh, how lofty are their eyes! And their eyelids are lifted up. 14 There is a generation whose teeth are like swords, and whose fangs are like knives, to devour the poor from off the earth, and the needy from among men. 15 The leech has two daughters— Give and Give! There are three things that are never satisfied, Four never say, "Enough!": 16 The grave, the barren womb, the earth that is not satisfied with water— And the fire never says, "Enough!" 17 The eye that mocks his father, and scorns obedience to his mother, The ravens of the valley will pick it out, And the young eagles will eat it. 18 There are three things which are too wonderful for me, Four which I do not understand: 19 The way of an eagle in the air, The way of a serpent on a rock, The way of a ship in the midst of the sea, And the way of a man with a virgin. 20 This is the way of an adulterous woman: She eats and wipes her mouth, and says, "I have done no wickedness." 21 Under three things the earth trembles, Under four it cannot bear up: 22 For a servant when he reigns, A fool when he is filled with food, 23 A hateful woman when she is married, And a maidservant who succeeds her mistress. 24 There are four things which are little on the earth, but they are exceedingly wise: 25 The ants are a people not strong, Yet they prepare their food in the summer; 26 The rock badgers are a feeble folk, Yet they make their homes in the crags; 27 The locusts have no king, Yet they all advance in ranks; 28 The spider skillfully grasps with its hands, And it is in kings' palaces. 29 There are three things which are majestic in pace, Yes, four which are stately in walk: 30 A lion, which is mighty among beasts And does not turn away from any; 31 A greyhound, A male goat also, And a king whose troops are with him. 32 If you

have been foolish in exalting yourself, Or if you have devised evil, put your hand on your mouth. 33 For as the churning of milk produces butter, And wringing the nose produces blood, So the forcing of wrath produces strife

21. Ecclesiastes

CHAPTER 1

These are the words of the Preacher, the son of David, king of Jerusalem. "Vanity of vanities," says the Preacher, "vanity of vanities, all is vanity." What does man gain from all his labor at which he toils under the sun? One generation passes away and another succeeds, but the earth remains forever. The sun rises and sets, then returns to its place where it rises again. The wind blows to the south and turns to the north; it circles around and returns to its circuits. All the ships go out to sea, yet the sea is never full; the ships go to a place where they return and depart. Everything is full of labor, but man cannot escape it; the eye is never satisfied with seeing, and the ear is never satisfied with hearing. What has been done will be done again; there is nothing new under the sun. Is there anything of which we can say, "Look, this is new"? It has already been done in ancient times before us. There is no remembrance of the former, nor will there be any memory of the later generations among those who come after I, the Preacher, was king over Israel in Jerusalem. I set my heart to seek and explore wisdom concerning everything done under heaven. This is a burdensome task God has given to the sons of men to humble them. I have observed all the works done under the sun, and behold, all is vanity and a striving after wind. What is crooked cannot be made straight; what is lacking cannot be counted. I said in my heart, "Behold, I have become great, surpassing all who were before me in Jerusalem; my heart has experienced much wisdom and knowledge." I have applied my heart to know wisdom and to understand madness and folly. I have come to realize that this too is a striving after wind. For with much wisdom comes much sorrow; the more knowledge, the more grief

CHAPTER 2

I said in my heart, "Come now, I will test you with pleasure; enjoy yourself." But even this was vanity. I said of laughter, "It is mad," and of pleasure, "What does it accomplish?" I searched with my heart to give myself to wine, and to seek wisdom and folly, to see what is good for the sons of men to do under heaven all the days of their lives. I undertook great projects: I built houses, planted vineyards, made gardens and parks, and planted all kinds of fruit trees. I constructed reservoirs to water groves of flourishing trees. I acquired servants and maidservants, and had many children in my household. I accumulated great wealth, including flocks and herds, and amassed more silver and gold than anyone before me in Jerusalem. I gathered male and female singers and the delights of men, a harem as well. I became great and surpassed all who were before me in Jerusalem, and my wisdom remained with me. I did not withhold from my eyes anything they desired; I refrained my heart from no pleasure, for my heart took delight in all my labor. This was my reward for all my toil. Then I considered all the work that my hands had done and the toil I had expended, and behold, all was vanity and a striving after wind, with no profit under the sun I turned my attention to wisdom, madness, and folly—what can one do who comes after the king? I realized that wisdom is better than folly, just as light is better than darkness. The wise person has eyes in his head, but the fool walks in darkness; yet I know that the same fate befalls them

both. So I said in my heart, "What happens to the fool will also happen to me. Why then have I been so very wise?" This too is vanity. For there is no remembrance of the wise, nor of the fool, forever; everything that is now will be forgotten in the future. And how does the wise man die? Just like the fool. Therefore, I hated life because of the work done under the sun, for it was grievous to me. Everything is vanity and a striving after wind. I hated all my labor under the sun because I must leave it to the man who comes after me. Who knows whether he will be wise or foolish? Yet he will have control over all my work for which I toiled and for which I showed myself wise under the sun. This too is vanity. Therefore, I gave up on the labor I had worked for under the sun. For there is a person whose labor is in wisdom, knowledge, and skill, yet he must leave it to one who has not worked for it. This also is vanity and a great misfortune. What does a man gain from all his labor and from the striving of his heart with which he labors under the sun? All his days are full of sorrow and his work is a vexation of spirit; even at night his mind does not rest. This too is vanity. There is nothing better for a man than to eat and drink and find satisfaction in his labor. I have seen this also as from the hand of God. For who can eat and find enjoyment more than I? To the one who pleases God, He gives wisdom, knowledge, and joy; but to the sinner He gives the task of gathering and storing up wealth to hand over to the one who pleases God. This too is vanity and a striving after wind

CHAPTER 3

To everything there is a season, and a time for every matter under heaven. A time to be born and a time to die; a time to plant and a time to uproot what has been planted. A time to kill and a time to heal; a time to break down and a time to build up. A time to weep and a time to laugh; a time to mourn and a time to dance. A time to cast away stones and a time to gather stones; a time to embrace and a time to refrain from embracing. A time to seek and a time to lose; a time to keep and a time to cast away. A time to tear and a time to sew; a time to be silent and a time to speak. A time to love and a time to hate; a time for war and a time for peace. What does the worker gain from his toil? I have seen the burden God has laid on the human race. He has made everything beautiful in its time; He has also set eternity in the human heart, yet no one can fathom what God has done from beginning to end. I know that there is nothing better for them than to be happy and to do good while they live. That each of them may eat and drink, and find satisfaction in all their toil—this is the gift of God. I know that everything God does will endure forever; nothing can be added to it and nothing taken from it. God does this so that people will fear Him. Whatever has already been, and what will be, has been before; and God will call the past to account And I saw under the sun that in the place of judgment, wickedness was there, and in the place of justice, wickedness was there. I said in my heart, "God will judge the righteous and the wicked, for there is a time for every matter and every work." I also said to myself, "As for the condition of humans, God tests them so that they may see that they are like the animals. Surely the fate of human beings is like that of the animals; the same fate awaits them both: As one dies, so dies the other. All have the same breath; humans have no advantage over animals. Everything is meaningless. All go to the same place; all come from dust, and to dust all return. Who knows if the human spirit rises upward and if the animal spirit goes down into the earth? So I saw that there is nothing better for a person than to enjoy their work, because that is their lot. For who can bring them to see what will happen after them?

CHAPTER 4

Then I looked again at all the oppression that takes place under the sun: I saw the tears of the oppressed, and they have no comforter; power was on the side of their oppressors, and they had no comforter. And I declared that the dead, who had already died, are happier than the living, who are still alive. But better than both is the one who has not yet been, who has not seen the evil work that is done under the sun. And I saw that all toil and all achievement spring from one person's envy of another. This too is meaningless, a chasing after the wind. Fools fold their hands and ruin themselves. Better one handful with tranquility than two handfuls with toil and chasing after the wind. Again, I saw something meaningless under the sun: There was a man all alone; he had neither son nor brother. There was no end to his toil, yet his eyes were not content with his wealth. "For whom am I toiling," he asked, "and why am I depriving myself of enjoyment?" This too is meaningless—a miserable business. Two are better than one, because they have a good return for their labor. If either of them falls down, one can help the other up. But pity anyone who falls and has no one to help them up. Also, if two lie down together, they will keep warm. But how can one keep warm alone? Though one may be overpowered, two can defend themselves. A cord of three strands is not quickly broken. Better a poor but wise youth than an old but foolish king who no longer knows how to take warning. The youth may have come from prison to the kingship, or he may have been born in poverty within his kingdom. I saw that all who lived and walked under the sun followed the youth, the king's successor. There was no end to all the people who were before them. But those who come later will not rejoice in him. This too is meaningless, a chasing after the wind

CHAPTER 5

Guard your steps when you go to the house of God. Go near to listen rather than to offer the sacrifice of fools, who do not know that they do wrong. Do not be quick with your mouth, do not be hasty in your heart to utter anything before God. God is in heaven and you are on earth, so let your words be few. As dreams come when there are many cares, so the speech of a fool when there are many words. When you make a vow to God, do not delay in fulfilling it. He has no pleasure in fools; fulfill your vow. It is better not to make a vow than to make one and not fulfill it. Do not let your mouth lead you into sin. And do not protest to the temple messenger, "My vow was a mistake." Why should God be angry at what you say and destroy the work of your hands? Much dreaming and many words are meaningless. Therefore fear God. If you see the poor oppressed in a district and justice and rights denied, do not be surprised at such things. For one official is eyed by a higher one, and over them both are yet higher officials. The increase from the land is taken by all; the king himself profits from the fields. Whoever loves money never has enough; whoever loves wealth is never satisfied with their income. This too is meaningless. As goods increase, so do those who consume them. And what benefit are they to the owners except to feast their eyes on them? The sleep of a laborer is sweet, whether they eat little or much, but as for the rich, their abundance permits them no sleep. I have seen a grievous evil under the sun: wealth hoarded to the harm of its owners, or wealth lost through some misfortune so that when they have a child there is nothing left for them to inherit. Everyone comes naked from their mother's womb, and as everyone comes, so they depart. They take nothing from their toil that they can carry in their hands. This too is a grievous evil: As everyone comes, so they depart, and what do they gain, since they toil for the wind? All their days they eat in darkness, with great frustration, affliction, and anger. This is what I have observed to be good: that it is good for people to eat and drink and find satisfaction in all their toil—this is the gift of God. Moreover, when God gives someone wealth and possessions, and the ability to enjoy them, to accept their lot and find pleasure in their toil—this is a gift of God. They seldom reflect on the days of their life, because God keeps them occupied with gladness of heart

CHAPTER 6

1 There is a grievous evil that I have seen under the sun: wealth kept by its owner to his own hurt. 2 A man to whom God gives wealth, possessions, and honor, so that he lacks nothing for himself of all that he desires, yet God does not give him the ability to enjoy them, but a stranger enjoys them. This is vanity and a grievous evil. 3 A man may have a hundred children and live many years, yet if he does not find satisfaction in his prosperity and does not receive a proper burial, I say that a stillborn child is better off than he. 4 It comes in vanity and departs in darkness, and its name is covered in darkness. 5 Though it has not seen the sun or known anything, it has more rest than that man. 6 Even if the man lives a thousand years twice over but does not enjoy any good, do not all go to the same place? 7 All a man's labor is for his mouth, yet his appetite is never satisfied. 8 What advantage has the wise man over the fool? What does the poor man gain by knowing how to conduct himself before the living? 9 Better is the sight of the eyes than the wandering of desire. This too is vanity and a chasing after the wind

CHAPTER 7

1 A good name is better than precious ointment, and the day of death than the day of birth. 2 It is better to go to the house of mourning than to go to the house of feasting, for that is the end of all men, and the living will lay it to heart. 3 Sorrow is better than laughter, for by the sadness of the countenance the heart is made better. 4 The heart of the wise is in the house of mourning, but the heart of fools is in the house of mirth. 5 It is better to hear the rebuke of the wise than for a man to hear the song of fools. 6 For as the crackling of thorns under a pot, so is the laughter of the fools; this also is vanity. 7 Surely oppression makes a wise man mad, and a bribe corrupts the heart. 8 The end of a matter is better than its beginning, and patience is better than pride. 9 Do not be quick to anger, for anger resides in the lap of fools. 10 Do not say, "Why were the former days better than these?" For it is not wise to ask such questions. 11 Wisdom is good with an inheritance, and profitable to those who see the sun. 12 For wisdom is a defense as money is a defense, but the excellence of knowledge is that wisdom gives life to those who have it. 13 Consider the work of God; for who can make straight what He has made crooked? 14 In the day of prosperity be joyful, but in the day of adversity consider: God has made the one as well as the other, so that man can find nothing that will come after him. 15 I have seen everything in my days of vanity: There is a just man who perishes in his righteousness, and there is a wicked man who prolongs his life in wickedness. 16 Do not be overly righteous, nor be overly wise; why should you destroy yourself? 17 Do not be overly wicked, nor be a fool; why should you die before your time? 18 It is good that you grasp this, and also not let go of the other; for he who fears God will escape them all. 19 Wisdom strengthens the wise more than ten mighty men who are in a city. 20 For there is not a just man on earth who does good

and does not sin. 21 Also do not take to heart everything people say, lest you hear your servant cursing you. 22 For many times, also, your own heart has known that even you have cursed others. 23 All this I have proved by wisdom; I said, "I will be wise," but it was far from me. 24 That which is far off and exceedingly deep, who can find it out? 25 I applied my heart to know and to search and to seek out wisdom and the reason of things, to know the wickedness of folly and the foolishness of madness. 26 And I find more bitter than death the woman whose heart is snares and nets, whose hands are fetters. He who pleases God shall escape from her, but the sinner shall be trapped by her. 27 "Here is what I have found," says the Preacher, "adding one thing to another to find out the reason, which my soul still seeks but I cannot find. One man among a thousand I have found, but a woman among all these I have not found."

CHAPTER 8

1 Who is like a wise man? And who knows the interpretation of a thing? A man's wisdom makes his face shine, and the boldness of his face is changed. 2 I say, "Keep the king's commandment for the sake of your oath to God." 3 Do not be hasty to go from his presence. Do not take your stand in an evil cause, for he does whatever he pleases. 4 Where the word of a king is, there is power; and who may say to him, "What are you doing?" 5 He who keeps the commandment will experience nothing harmful; and a wise man's heart discerns both time and judgment. 6 Because for every matter there is a time and judgment, though the misery of man increases greatly. 7 For he does not know what will happen; so who can tell him when it will happen? 8 No man has power over the spirit to retain the spirit; and no one has power in the day of death. There is no release from that war, and wickedness will not deliver those who are given to it. 9 All this I have seen, and applied my heart to every work that is done under the sun. There is a time wherein one man rules over another to his own hurt. 10 Then I saw the wicked buried, who had come and gone from the place of the holy, and they were forgotten in the city where they had done so. This also is vanity. 11 Because the sentence against an evil work is not executed speedily, therefore the heart of the sons of men is fully set in them to do evil. 12 Though a sinner does evil a hundred times and his days are prolonged, yet I surely know that it will be well with those who fear God, who fear before Him. 13 But it will not be well with the wicked; nor will he prolong his days, which are as a shadow, because he does not fear before God. 14 There is a vanity which occurs on earth: that there are just men to whom it happens according to the work of the wicked; again, there are wicked men to whom it happens according to the work of the righteous. I said that this also is vanity. 15 So I commended enjoyment, because a man has nothing better under the sun than to eat, drink, and be merry; for this will remain with him in his labor all the days of his life which God gives him under the sun. 16 When I applied my heart to know wisdom and to see the business that is done on earth, even though one sees no sleep day or night, 17 then I beheld all the work of God, that a man cannot find out the work that is done under the sun. For though a man labors to discover it, yet he will not find it; moreover, though a wise man attempts to know it, he will not be able to find it

CHAPTER 9

1 For all this I considered in my heart, even to declare all this: that the righteous, and the wise, and their works are in the hand of God. No man knows whether love or hatred awaits him. 2 All things come alike to all: one event happens to the righeous and the wicked, to the good, the clean, and the unclean, to him who sacrifices and him who does not sacrifice; as is the good, so is the sinner; he who swears, as he who fears an oath. 3 This is an evil in all that is done under the sun: that one thing happens to all. Truly the hearts of the sons of men are full of evil, madness is in their hearts while they live, and after that they go to the dead. 4 But for him who is joined to all the living there is hope; for a living dog is better than a dead lion. 5 For the living know that they will die; but the dead know nothing, and they have no more reward, for the memory of them is forgotten. 6 Also their love, their hatred, and their envy have now perished; nevermore will they have a share in anything done under the sun. 7 Go, eat your bread with joy, and drink your wine with a merry heart; for God has already accepted your works. 8 Let your garments always be white, and let your head lack no oil. 9 Live joyfully with the wife whom you love all the days of your vain life which He has given you under the sun, all your days of vanity; for that is your portion in life, and in the labor which you perform under the sun. 10 Whatever your hand finds to do, do it with your might, for there is no work or device or knowledge or wisdom in the grave where you are going. 11 I returned and saw under the sun that—The race is not to the swift, nor the battle to the strong, nor bread to the wise, nor riches to men of understanding, nor favor to men of skill; but time and chance happen to them all. 12 For man also does not know his time: like fish taken in a cruel net, like birds caught in a snare, so the sons of men are snared in an evil time, when it falls suddenly upon them. 13 This wisdom I have also seen under the sun, and it seemed great to me: 14 There was a little city with few men in it; and a great king came against it, besieged it, and built great snares around it. 15 Now there was found in it a poor wise man, and he by his wisdom delivered the city. Yet no one remembered that same poor man. 16 Then I said: "Wisdom is better than strength." Nevertheless the poor man's wisdom is despised, and his words are not heard. 17 Words of the wise, spoken quietly, should be heard rather than the shout of a ruler of fools. 18 Wisdom is better than weapons of war; but one sinner destroys much good

CHAPTER 10

1 Dead flies putrefy the perfumer's ointment and cause it to give off a foul odor; so does a little folly to one respected for wisdom and honor. 2 A wise man's heart is at his right hand, but a fool's heart at his left. 3 Even when a fool walks along the way, he lacks wisdom, and he shows everyone that he is a fool. 4 If the spirit of the ruler rises against you, do not leave your post; for conciliation pacifies great offenses. 5 There is an evil I have seen under the sun, as an error proceeding from the ruler: 6 Folly is set in great dignity, while the rich sit in a lowly place. 7 I have seen servants on horses, while princes walk on the ground like servants. 8 He who digs a pit will fall into it, and whoever breaks through a wall will be bitten by a serpent. 9 He who quarries stones may be hurt by them, and he who splits wood may be endangered by it. 10 If the ax is dull, and one does not sharpen the edge, then he must use more strength; but wisdom brings success. 11 A serpent may bite when it is not charmed; the babbler is no different. 12 The words of a wise man's mouth are gracious, but the lips of a fool shall swallow him up; 13 The beginning of the words of his mouth is foolishness, and the end of his talk is raving madness. 14 A fool also multiplies words. No man knows what is to be; who can tell him what will be after him? 15 The labor of fools wearies them, for they do not even know how to go to the city! 16 Woe to you, O land, when your king is a child, and

your princes feast in the morning! 17 Blessed are you, O land, when your king is the son of nobles, and your princes feast at the proper time— for strength and not for drunkenness! 18 Because of laziness the building decays, and through idleness of hands the house leaks. 19 A feast is made for laughter, and wine makes merry; but money answers everything. 20 Do not curse the king, even in your thought; do not curse the rich, even in your bedroom; for a bird of the air may carry your voice, and a bird in flight may tell the matter

CHAPTER 11

1 Cast your bread upon the waters, for you will find it after many days. 2 Give a serving to seven, and also to eight, for you do not know what evil will be on the earth. 3 If the clouds are full of rain, they empty themselves upon the earth; and if a tree falls to the south or the north, in the place where the tree falls, there it shall lie. 4 He who observes the wind will not sow, and he who regards the clouds will not reap. 5 As you do not know what is the way of the wind, or how the bones grow in the womb of her who is with child, so you do not know the works of God who makes everything. 6 In the morning sow your seed, and in the evening do not withhold your hand; for you do not know which will prosper, either this or that, or whether both alike will be good. 7 Truly the light is sweet, and it is pleasant for the eyes to behold the sun; 8 But if a man lives many years and rejoices in them all, yet let him remember the days of darkness, for they will be many. All that is coming is vanity. 9 Rejoice, O young man, in your youth, and let your heart cheer you in the days of your youth; walk in the ways of your heart, and in the sight of your eyes, but know that for all these God will bring you into judgment. 10 Therefore remove sorrow from your heart, and put away evil from your flesh, for childhood and youth are vanity

CHAPTER 12

1 Remember now your Creator in the days of your youth, before the difficult days come, and the years draw near when you say, "I have no pleasure in them": 2 While the sun and the light, the moon and the stars, are not darkened, and the clouds do not return after the rain; 3 In the day when the keepers of the house tremble, and the strong men bow down; when the grinders cease because they are few, and those that look through the windows grow dim; 4 When the doors are shut in the streets, and the sound of grinding is low; when one rises up at the sound of a bird, and all the daughters of music are brought low; 5 Also they are afraid of height, and of terrors in the way; when the almond tree blossoms, the grasshopper is a burden, and desire fails. For man goes to his eternal home, and the mourners go about the streets. 6 Remember your Creator before the silver cord is loosed, or the golden bowl is broken, or the pitcher shattered at the fountain, or the wheel broken at the well. 7 Then the dust will return to the earth as it was, and the spirit will return to God who gave it. 8 "Vanity of vanities," says the Preacher, "All is vanity." 9 And moreover, because the Preacher was wise, he still taught the people knowledge; yes, he pondered and sought out and set in order many proverbs. 10 The Preacher sought to find acceptable words; and what was written was upright—words of truth. 11 The words of the wise are like goads, and the words of scholars are like well-driven nails, given by one Shepherd. 12 And further, my son, be admonished by these. Of making many books there is no end, and much study is wearisome to the flesh. 13 Let us hear the conclusion of the whole matter: Fear God and keep His commandments, for this is man's all. 14 For God will bring every work into judgment, including every secret thing, whether good or evil

22. Song of Solomon

Chapter 1

Let him kiss me with the kisses of his mouth, for your love is more delightful than wine. Your ointments have a pleasing fragrance; your name is like perfume poured out. That is why the maidens love you. Take me away with you; let us hurry. The king has brought me into his chambers. We will rejoice and be glad in you; we will remember your love more than wine. The righteous adore you. I am dark, but lovely, O daughters of Jerusalem, like the tents of Kedar, like the curtains of Solomon. Do not stare at me because I am dark, because the sun has looked upon me. My mother's sons were angry with me; they made me keeper of the vineyards, but my own vineyard I have not kept. Tell me, you whom my soul loves, where do you pasture your flock? Where do you let them rest at noon? Why should I be like one who veils herself beside the flocks of your companions? If you do not know, O fairest among women, follow the tracks of the flock and graze your young goats by the tents of the shepherds. I compare you, my darling, to a mare among Pharaoh's chariots. Your cheeks are beautiful with earrings, your neck with strings of jewels. We will make for you ornaments of gold, studded with silver. While the king was at his table, my perfume gave off its fragrance. My beloved is to me a sachet of myrrh that lies between my breasts. My beloved is to me a cluster of henna blooms from the vineyards of Engedi. How delightful you are, my beloved, how delightful; your eyes are doves. How delightful you are, my beloved, how pleasant; the bed is verdant. The beams of our house are cedars; our rafters are firs

Chapter 2

I am a rose of Sharon, a lily of the valleys. As a lily among thorns, so is my love among the daughters. As an apple tree among the trees of the forest, so is my beloved among the young men. In his shade I took great delight and sat down, and his fruit was sweet to my taste. He brought me to the banqueting house, and his banner over me was love. Sustain me with cakes of raisins, refresh me with apples, for I am lovesick. His left hand is under my head, and his right hand embraces me. I adjure you, O daughters of Jerusalem, by the gazelles or the hinds of the field, that you stir not up, nor awaken love until it please. The voice of my beloved! Behold, he comes, leaping upon the mountains, skipping upon the hills. My beloved is like a roe or a young hart: behold, he stands behind our wall, looking through the windows, showing himself through the lattice. My beloved spoke, and said unto me, "Rise up, my love, my fair one, and come away." For, lo, the winter is past, the rain is over and gone; The flowers appear on the earth; the time of the singing of birds is come, and the voice of the turtle is heard in our land; The fig tree putteth forth her green figs, and the vines with the tender grape give a good smell. Arise, my love, my fair one, and come away. O my dove, that art in the clefts of the rock, in the secret places of the stairs, let me see thy countenance, let me hear thy voice; for sweet is thy voice, and thy countenance is comely. Take us the foxes, the little foxes, that spoil the vines: for our vines have tender grapes. My beloved is mine, and I am his: he feedeth among the lilies, Until the day break, and the shadows flee away, turn, my beloved, and be thou like a roe or a young hart upon the mountains of Bether

Chapter 3

By night on my bed I sought him whom my soul loveth: I sought him, but I found him not. I will rise now, and go about the city in the streets and in the broad ways; I will seek him whom my soul loveth: I sought him, but I found him not. The watchmen that go about the city found me: to whom I said, "Saw ye him whom my soul loveth?" It was but a little that I passed from them, but I found him whom my soul loveth: I held him, and would not let him go, until I had brought him into my mother's house, and into the chamber of her that conceived me. I charge you, O daughters of Jerusalem, by the roes, and by the hinds of the field, that ye stir not up, nor awake my love, till he please. Who is this that cometh out of the wilderness like pillars of smoke, perfumed with myrrh and frankincense, with all powders of the merchant? Behold his bed, which is Solomon's; threescore valiant men are about it, of the valiant of Israel. They all hold swords, being expert in war: every man hath his sword upon his thigh because of fear in the night. King Solomon made himself a chariot of the wood of Lebanon. He made the pillars thereof of silver, the bottom thereof of gold, the covering of it of purple, the midst thereof being paved with love, for the daughters of Jerusalem. Go forth, O ye daughters of Zion, and behold king Solomon with the crown wherewith his mother crowned him in the day of his espousals, and in the day of the gladness of his heart

Chapter 4

Behold, thou art fair, my love; behold, thou art fair; thou hast doves' eyes within thy locks: thy hair is as a flock of goats that appear from mount Gilead. Thy teeth are like a flock of sheep that are even shorn, which came up from the washing; whereof every one bear twins, and none is barren among them. Thy lips are like a thread of scarlet, and thy speech is comely: thy temples are like a piece of a pomegranate within thy locks. Thy neck is like the tower of David builded for an armory, whereon there hang a thousand bucklers, all shields of mighty men. Thy two breasts are like two young roes that are twins, which feed among the lilies. Until the day break, and the shadows flee away, I will get me to the mountain of myrrh, and to the hill of frankincense. Thou art all fair, my love; there is no spot in thee. Come with me from Lebanon, my spouse, with me from Lebanon: look from the top of Amana, from the top of Shenir and Hermon, from the lions' dens, from the mountains of the leopards. Thou hast ravished my heart, my sister, my spouse; thou hast ravished my heart with one of thine eyes, with one chain of thy neck. How fair is thy love, my sister, my spouse! How much better is thy love than wine! and the smell of thine ointments than all spices! Thy lips, O my spouse, drop as the honeycomb: honey and milk are under thy tongue; and the smell of thy garments is like the smell of Lebanon. A garden enclosed is my sister, my spouse; a spring shut up, a fountain sealed. Thy plants are an orchard of pomegranates, with pleasant fruits; camphire, with spikenard, Spikenard and saffron; calamus and cinnamon, with all trees of frankincense; myrrh and aloes, with all the chief spices: A fountain of gardens, a well of living waters, and streams from Lebanon. Awake, O north wind; and come, thou south; blow upon my garden, that the spices thereof may flow out. Let my beloved come into his garden, and eat his pleasant fruits

Chapter 5

I am come into my garden, my sister, my spouse: I have gathered my myrrh with my spice; I have eaten my honeycomb with my honey; I have drunk my wine with my milk: eat, O friends; drink, yea, drink abundantly, O beloved. I sleep, but my heart waketh: it is the voice of my beloved that knocketh, saying, "Open to me, my sister, my love, my dove, my undefiled: for my head is filled with dew, and my locks with the drops of the night." I have put off my coat; how shall I put it on? I have washed my feet; how shall I defile them? My beloved put in his hand by the hole of the door, and my bowels were moved for him. I rose up to open to my beloved; and my hands dropped with myrrh, and my fingers with sweet-smelling myrrh, upon the handles of the lock. I opened to my beloved; but my beloved had withdrawn himself, and was gone: my soul failed when he spake: I sought him, but I could not find him; I called him, but he gave me no answer. The watchmen that went about the city found me, they smote me, they wounded me; the keepers of the walls took away my veil from me. I charge you, O daughters of Jerusalem, if ye find my beloved, that ye tell him, that I am sick of love. What is thy beloved more than another beloved, O thou fairest among women? what is thy beloved more than another beloved, that thou dost so charge us? My beloved is white and ruddy, the chiefest among ten thousand. His head is as the most fine gold, his locks are bushy, and black as a raven. His eyes are as the eyes of doves by the rivers of waters, washed with milk, and fitly set. His cheeks are as a bed of spices, as sweet flowers: his lips like lilies, dropping sweet-smelling myrrh. His hands are as gold rings set with the beryl: his belly is as bright ivory overlaid with sapphires. His legs are as pillars of marble, set upon sockets of fine gold: his countenance is as Lebanon, excellent as the cedars. His mouth is most sweet: yea, he is altogether lovely. This is my beloved, and this is my friend, O daughters of Jerusalem

Chapter 6

Whither is thy beloved gone, O thou fairest among women? whither is thy beloved turned aside? that we may seek him with thee. My beloved is gone down into his garden, to the beds of spices, to feed in the gardens, and to gather lilies. I am my beloved's, and my beloved is mine: he feedeth among the lilies. Thou art beautiful, O my love, as Tirzah, comely as Jerusalem, terrible as an army with banners. Turn away thine eyes from me, for they have overcome me: thy hair is as a flock of goats that appear from mount Gilead. Thy teeth are like a flock of sheep that are even shorn, which came up from the washing; whereof every one bear twins, and none is barren among them. As a piece of a pomegranate within thy locks. There are threescore queens, and fourscore concubines, and virgins without number. My dove, my undefiled is but one; she is the only one of her mother, she is the choice one of her that bare her. The daughters saw her, and blessed her; yea, the queens and the concubines, and they praised her. Who is she that looketh forth as the morning, fair as the moon, clear as the sun, and terrible as an army with banners? I went down into the garden of nuts to see the fruits of the valley, and to see whether the vine flourished, and the pomegranates budded. Or ever I was aware, my soul made me like the chariots of Amminadib. Return, return, O Shulamite; return, return, that we may look upon thee. What will ye see in the Shulamite? As it were the company of two armies

Chapter 7

How beautiful are thy feet with shoes, O prince's daughter! the joints of thy thighs are like jewels, the work of the hands of a cunning workman. Thy navel is like a round goblet, which wanteth not liquor: thy belly is like an heap of wheat set about with lilies. Thy two breasts are like two young roes that are twins. Thy neck is as a tower of ivory; thine eyes like the fishpools in Heshbon, by the gate of Bathrabbim: thy nose is as the tower of Lebanon which looketh toward Damascus. Thine head upon thee is like Carmel, and the hair of thine head like purple; the king is held in the galleries. How fair and how pleasant art thou, O love, for delights! This thy stature is like to a palm tree, and thy breasts to clusters of grapes. I said, "I will go up to the palm tree, I will take hold of the boughs thereof;" now also thy breasts shall be as clusters of the vine, and the smell of thy nose like apples; And the roof of thy mouth like the best wine for my beloved, that goeth down sweetly, causing the lips of those that are asleep to speak. I am my beloved's, and his desire is toward me. Come, my beloved, let us go forth into the field; let us lodge in the villages. Let us get up early to the vineyards; let us see if the vine flourish, whether the tender grape appear, and the pomegranates bud forth: there will I give thee my loves. The mandrakes give a smell, and at our gates are all manner of pleasant fruits, new and old, which I have laid up for thee, O my beloved

Chapter 8

O that thou wert as my brother, that sucked the breasts of my mother! when I should find thee without, I would kiss thee; yea, I should not be despised. I would lead thee, and bring thee into my mother's house, who would instruct me: I would cause thee to drink of spiced wine of the juice of my pomegranate. His left hand should be under my head, and his right hand should embrace me. I charge you, O daughters of Jerusalem, that ye stir not up, nor awake my love, until he please. Who is this that cometh up from the wilderness, leaning upon her beloved? I raised thee up under the apple tree: there thy mother brought thee forth: there she brought thee forth that bare thee. Set me as a seal upon thine heart, as a seal upon thine arm: for love is strong as death; jealousy is cruel as the grave: the coals thereof are coals of fire, which hath a most vehement flame. Many waters cannot quench love, neither can the floods drown it: if a man would give all the substance of his house for love, it would utterly be contemned. We have a little sister, and she hath no breasts: what shall we do for our sister in the day when she shall be spoken for? If she be a wall, we will build upon her a palace of silver: and if she be a door, we will enclose her with boards of cedar. I am a wall, and my breasts like towers: then was I in his eyes as one that found favour. Solomon had a vineyard at Baalhamon; he let out the vineyard unto keepers; every one for the fruit thereof was to bring a thousand pieces of silver. My own vineyard is before me: thou, O Solomon, must have a thousand, and those that keep the fruit thereof two hundred. Thou that dwellest in the gardens, the companions hearken to thy voice: cause me to hear it. Make haste, my beloved, and be thou like to a roe or to a young hart upon the mountains of spices

4. MAJOR PROPHETS

23. Isaiah

Chapter 1

The vision of Isaiah, son of Amoz, which he saw concerning Judah and Jerusalem during the reigns of Uzziah, Jotham, Ahaz, and Hezekiah, kings of Judah Hear, O heavens, and listen, O earth, for the LORD has spoken: "I have nourished and raised children, but they have rebelled against me. The ox knows its owner and the donkey its master's manger, but Israel does not know; my people do not understand." Ah, sinful nation, laden with iniquity, a brood of evildoers, corrupt children! They have forsaken the LORD; they have provoked the Holy One of Israel to anger; they have turned away Why should you be beaten anymore? You continue to rebel; the whole head is sick and the whole heart faint. From the sole of the foot even to the head, there is no soundness in it but bruises, welts, and open sores. They have not been dressed or bandaged, nor soothed with oil Your country is desolate; your cities are burned with fire. Strangers devour your land in your presence; it is desolate, as overthrown by foreigners The daughter of Zion is left like a hut in a vineyard, like a lodge in a cucumber field, like a besieged city Unless the LORD of hosts had left us a few survivors, we would have become like Sodom, we would have been like Gomorrah Hear the word of the LORD, you rulers of Sodom; listen to the law of our God, you people of Gomorrah "What use is the multitude of your sacrifices to me?" says the LORD. "I have had enough of burnt offerings of rams and the fat of fed beasts. I do not delight in the blood of bulls, lambs, and goats When you come to appear before me, who has asked this of you, this trampling of my courts? Stop bringing meaningless offerings; your incense is detestable to me. New moons, Sabbaths, and convocations—I cannot bear your worthless assemblies Your New Moon feasts and your appointed festivals I hate with all my being. They have become a burden to me; I am weary of bearing them When you spread out your hands in prayer, I hide my eyes from you; even when you offer many prayers, I am not listening. Your hands are full of blood Wash and make yourselves clean. Take your evil deeds out of my sight; stop doing wrong. Learn to do right; seek justice. Defend the oppressed. Take up the cause of the fatherless; plead the case of the widow "Come now, let us settle the matter," says the LORD. "Though your sins are like scarlet, they shall be as white as snow; though they are red as crimson, they shall be like wool If you are willing and obedient, you will eat the good things of the land; but if you resist and rebel, you will be devoured by the sword." For the mouth of the LORD has spoken How the faithful city has become a prostitute! She once was full of justice; righteousness used to dwell in her— but now murderers Your silver has become dross, your choice wine is diluted with water. Your rulers are rebels, companions of thieves; they all love bribes and chase after gifts. They do not defend the cause of the fatherless; the widow's case does not come before them Therefore the LORD, the LORD Almighty, the Mighty One of Israel, declares: "I will vent my wrath on my foes and avenge myself on my enemies. I will turn my hand against you; I will thoroughly purge away your dross and remove all your impurities I will restore your leaders as in days of old, your rulers as at the beginning. Afterward you will be called the City of Righteousness, the Faithful City." Zion will be redeemed with justice, her penitent ones with righteousness. But rebels and sinners will both be broken, and those who forsake the LORD will perish "You will be ashamed because of the sacred oaks in which you have delighted; you will be disgraced because of the gardens that you have chosen You will be like an oak with fading leaves, like a garden without water. The mighty man will become tinder and his work a spark; both will burn together, with no one to quench the fire."

Chapter 2

The word that Isaiah, son of Amoz, saw concerning Judah and Jerusalem In the last days, the mountain of the LORD's temple will be established as the highest of the mountains; it will be exalted above the hills, and all nations will stream to it Many peoples will come and say, "Come, let us go up to the mountain of the LORD, to the temple of the God of Jacob. He will teach us his ways, so that we may walk in his paths." The law will go out from Zion, the word of the LORD from Jerusalem He will judge between the nations and will settle disputes for many peoples. They will beat their swords into plowshares and their spears into pruning hooks. Nation will not take up sword against nation, nor will they train for war anymore Come, descendants of Jacob, let us walk in the light of the LORD You, LORD, have abandoned your people, the descendants of Jacob. They are full of superstitions from the East; they practice divination like the Philistines and embrace pagan customs Their land is full of silver and gold; there is no end to their treasures. Their land is full of horses; there is no end to their chariots. Their land is full of idols; they bow down to the work of their hands, to what their fingers have made So people will be brought low and everyone humbled—do not forgive them Go into the rocks, hide in the ground from the fearful presence of the LORD and the splendor of his majesty The eyes of the arrogant will be humbled and human pride brought low; the LORD alone will be exalted in that day The LORD Almighty has a day in store for all the proud and lofty, for all that is exalted (and they will be humbled), for all the cedars of Lebanon, tall and lofty, and all the oaks of Bashan, for all the towering mountains and all the high hills, for every lofty tower and every fortified wall, for every trading ship and every stately vessel The arrogance of man will be brought low and human pride humbled; the LORD alone will be exalted in that day, and the idols will totally disappear People will flee to caves in the rocks and to holes in the ground from the fearful presence of the LORD and the splendor of his majesty, when he rises to shake the earth In that day they will throw away to the rodents and bats their idols of silver and idols of gold, which they made to worship. They will flee to caverns in the rocks and to the overhangs of the cliffs from the fearful presence of the LORD and the splendor of his majesty, when he rises to shake the earth Stop trusting in mere humans, who have but a breath in their nostrils. Why hold them in esteem?

Chapter 3

See now, the LORD, the LORD Almighty, is about to take from Jerusalem and Judah both supply and support, all supplies of food and all supplies of water, the hero and the warrior, the judge and the prophet, the diviner and the elder, the captain of fifty and the man of rank, the counselor, skilled craftsman, and the expert enchanter "I will make mere youths their officials; children will rule over them. People will oppress each other—man against man, neighbor against neighbor. The young will rise up against the old, the base against the honorable." A man will seize one of his brothers in his father's house, and say, "You have a cloak, you be our leader; take charge of this heap of ruins!" But in that day he will cry out, "I have no remedy. I have no food or clothing in my house; do not make me the leader of the people." Jerusalem staggers, Judah is falling; their words and deeds are against the LORD, defying his glorious presence The look on their faces testifies against them; they parade their sin like Sodom; they do not hide it. Woe to them! They have brought disaster upon themselves "Tell the righteous it will be well with them, for they will enjoy the fruit of their deeds Woe to the wicked! Disaster is upon them! They will be paid back for what their hands have done." Children oppress my people, women rule over them. My people, your guides lead you astray; they turn you from the path The LORD takes his place in court; he rises to judge the people The LORD enters into judgment against the elders and leaders of his people: "It is you who have ruined my vineyard; the plunder from the poor is in your houses What do you mean by crushing my people and grinding the faces of the poor?" declares the LORD, the LORD Almighty The LORD says, "The women of Zion are haughty, walking along with outstretched necks, flirting with their eyes, strutting along with swaying hips, with ornaments jingling on their ankles Therefore the LORD will bring sores on the heads of the women of Zion; the LORD will make their scalps bald." In that day the LORD will snatch away their finery: the bangles and headbands and crescent necklaces, the earrings and bracelets and veils, the headdresses and anklets and sashes, the perfume bottles and charms, the signet rings and nose rings, the fine robes and the capes and cloaks, the purses and mirrors, and the linen garments and tiaras and shawls Instead of fragrance there will be a stench; instead of a sash, a rope; instead of well-dressed hair, baldness; instead of fine clothing, sackcloth; instead of beauty, branding Your men will fall by the sword, your warriors in battle. The gates of Zion will lament and mourn; destitute, she will sit on the ground

Chapter 4

In that day seven women will take hold of one man and say, "We will eat our own food and provide our own clothes; only let us be called by your name. Take away our disgrace!" In that day the Branch of the LORD will be beautiful and glorious, and the fruit of the land will be the pride and glory of the survivors in Israel Those who are left in Zion, who remain in Jerusalem, will be called holy, all who are recorded among the living in Jerusalem The LORD will wash away the filth of the women of Zion; he will cleanse the bloodstains from Jerusalem by a spirit of judgment and a spirit of fire Then the LORD will create over all of Mount Zion and over those who assemble there a cloud of smoke by day and a glow of flaming fire by night; over all the glory will be a canopy It will be a shelter and shade from the heat of the day, and a refuge and hiding place from the storm and rain

Chapter 5

I will sing for the one I love a song about his vineyard: My loved one had a vineyard on a fertile hillside He dug it up and cleared it of stones and planted it with the choicest vines; he built a watchtower in it and cut out a winepress as well. Then he looked for a crop of good grapes, but it yielded only bad fruit "Now you dwellers in Jerusalem and people of Judah, judge between me and my vineyard What more could have been done for my vineyard than I have done for it? When I looked for good grapes, why did it yield only bad? Now I will tell you what I am going to do to my vineyard: I will take away its hedge, and it will be destroyed; I will break down its wall, and it will be trampled I will make it a wasteland, neither pruned nor cultivated, and briers and thorns will grow there. I will command the clouds not to rain on it." The vineyard of the LORD Almighty is the nation of Israel, and the people of Judah are the garden of his delight. And he looked for justice, but saw bloodshed; for

righteousness, but heard cries of distress Woe to those who add house to house and join field to field till no space is left and you live alone in the land The LORD Almighty has declared in my hearing: "Surely the great houses will become desolate, the fine mansions left without occupants A ten-acre vineyard will produce only a bath of wine; a homer of seed will yield only an ephah of grain." Woe to those who rise early in the morning to run after their drinks, who stay up late at night till they are inflamed with wine They have harps and lyres at their banquets, pipes and timbrels and wine, but they have no regard for the deeds of the LORD, no respect for the work of his hands So my people will go into exile for lack of understanding; their men of rank will die of hunger and their masses will be parched with thirst Therefore the grave enlarges its appetite and opens its mouth without limit; into it will descend their nobles and masses with all their brawlers and revelers So people will be brought low and everyone humbled—do not forgive them "Go into the rocks, hide in the ground from the fearful presence of the LORD and the splendor of his majesty The eyes of the arrogant will be humbled and human pride brought low; the LORD alone will be exalted in that day The LORD Almighty has a day in store for all the proud and lofty, for all that is exalted (and they will be humbled), for all the cedars of Lebanon, tall and lofty, and all the oaks of Bashan, for all the towering mountains and all the high hills, for every lofty tower and every fortified wall, for every trading ship and every stately vessel The arrogance of man will be brought low and human pride humbled; the LORD alone will be exalted in that day, and the idols will totally disappear People will flee to caves in the rocks and to holes in the ground from the fearful presence of the LORD and the splendor of his majesty, when he rises to shake the earth In that day they will throw away to the rodents and bats their idols of silver and idols of gold, which they made to worship. They will flee to caverns in the rocks and to the overhangs of the cliffs from the fearful presence of the LORD and the splendor of his majesty, when he rises to shake the earth Stop trusting in mere humans, who have but a breath in their nostrils. Why hold them in esteem?

Chapter 6

1 In the year of King Uzziah's death, I also saw the Lord seated on a throne, high and lifted up, the lower parts of which filled the Temple 2 Seraphim stood above it; each had six wings; with two he covered his face, with two he covered his feet, and with two he flew 3 One cried out to the other and said, "Holy, holy, holy is the LORD of hosts; the whole world is full of his glory." 4 The flaps of the cheeks of the others moved at the sight of him who shouted, and the house was filled with smoke 5 Then I said, "May I be vituperated, for I am a man of defiled lips, and I dwell among a people of defiled lips, because my eyes have seen the King and Lord of hosts." 6 Then one of the seraphim came to me with a wooden knife in his hand that he had taken from the altar with tongs: 7 He touched my mouth and said, "Behold, this has touched your lips; your iniquity shall be taken away and your sin cleansed." 8 Moreover I heard the speech of the Lord saying, "Whom shall I send and who will go for us?" Then I said, "Here am I, send me." 9 And he said, "Go and say to this people, 'You will hear in faith, but you will not understand; you will see clearly, but you will not perceive 10 Make the heart of this people hard, make their ears weak, and close their eyes, lest they see with their eyes, and hear with their ears, and understand with their hearts, and be convinced and heal them." 11 Then I said, "Lord, until when?" And he answered, "Until the cities are

deserted, without inhabitants, and the houses without men, and the land is utterly desolate, 12 and the LORD shall have driven men far away, and there shall be a great desolation in the midst of the land 13 But there shall be a tenth in it, which shall return and be eaten as an elm or a goose, which have substance in them, when they cast their leaves; so the holy seed shall be its substance

Chapter 7

1 In the days of Ahaz, son of Jotham, son of Uzziah, king of Judah, Rezin, king of Aram, and Pekah, son of Remaliah, king of Israel, came to Jerusalem to fight against it, but they could not conquer it 2 To the house of David it was said, "Aram had a bond with Ephraim; therefore his heart was smitten, and the heart of his people, as the trees of the forest are smitten with the wind." 3 Then the LORD said to Isaiah, "Go now and meet Ahaz (you and Shear-Jashub, your son) at the end of the shaft of the upper pool, on the path of the field of the fullers, 4 and say to him, "Be careful and do not fret; do not fear and do not be discouraged by the two tails of these smoking firebrands, by the furious wrath of Rezin, Aram, and Remaliah's son: 5 For Aram has taken evil counsel against you, against Ephraim and against the son of Remaliah, saying, 6 "Go up against Judah, awaken them, and make a breach in them, and set a king in the midst of them, the son of Tabeal." 7 Thus says the LORD God, "He shall not stand and be there." 8 Because the head of Aram is Damascus and the head of Damascus is Rezin, within five years and sixty Ephraim will be destroyed as a people 9 The chief of Ephraim is Samaria, and the chief of Samaria is the son of Remaliah. If you do not rise, you will certainly not be established." 10 The LORD spoke again to Ahaz, saying, 11 Ask a sign for the LORD your God; ask it either in depth or in height." 12 But Ahaz said, "I will not ask it or tempt the LORD." 13 Then he said, "Hear now, O house of David, is it a small thing for you to weary men, that you should do so also with my God? 14 Therefore the Lord himself will give you a sign. Behold, the virgin shall conceive and bear a son, and shall call his name Immanuel 15 He shall eat butter and honey, until he has learned to reject the worthless and choose the good 16 For before the child has learned to reject the evil and to choose the good, the land that you abhor will be forsaken by both its kings 17 And the LORD will cause the king of Assyria to come upon you, and upon your people, and upon your father's house (the days that have not come since the day that Ephraim departed from Judah) 18 In that day the LORD will take care of the fly that is at the end of the floods of Egypt and the bee that is in the land of Assyria, 19 they shall come and illuminate all the desolate valleys, the holes of the rocks, the thorny places, and the bushy places 20 In that day the LORD shall cut off with a razor hired by those who are beyond the river, by the king of Assyria, the head and the hairline of the feet, and consume the beard 21 On the same day a man shall feed a young cow and two sheep 22 And for the abundance of milk they shall give, butter shall be eaten; for they shall eat the butter and the honey that is left in the land 23 In the same day, in every place where there are a thousand vines, there shall be a thousand pieces of silk; so shall it be with briers and thorns 24 With arrows and with bows it will be possible to go that far, for the whole land will be full of briers and thorns 25 But on all the mountains that will be dug with the mattock, there will be no fear of briers and thorns, but they will serve to bring out the heifers and to trample the sheep

Chapter 8

1 Moreover, the LORD said to me, "Take a large scroll and write in it with a man's pen, 'Hasten to the spoil, hasten to the prey.'" 2 Then I took with me faithful witnesses to record: Uriah the priest and Zechariah the son of Jeberechiah 3 Then I presented myself to the prophetess who had conceived and borne a son. Then the LORD said to me, "Call him by the name of Maher-Shalal-Hash-Baz." 4 For before the child has the ability to cry out, 'My father and my mother,' he will carry away the riches of Damascus and the wealth of Samaria before the king of Assyria." 5 The LORD spoke to me again, saying, 6 For this people have rejected the gently flowing waters of Shiloh, and are reconciled to Rezin and to the son of Remaliah, 7 therefore behold, the LORD brings upon them the waters of the River, mighty and great, that is, the king of Assyria with all his glory; he will come upon all their banks and overflow all their banks, 8 he shall break through into Judah, he shall go out and pass through, he shall come up to the neck, and the spreading of his wings shall fill the breadth of your land, O Immanuel 9 Gather yourselves on your shoulders, O peoples, and you shall be broken in pieces, and hear all of you from the far countries; gird up your bodies and you shall be broken in pieces; gird up your bodies and you shall be broken in pieces 10 Take counsel together, but it shall be thwarted; make a decree, but it shall not stand, for God is with us 11 For the Lord has spoken to me thus, taking me by the hand, and has taught me not to walk in the way of this people, saying, 12 Do not say, "A confederacy" for all those to whom this people say a confederacy; do not fear their fear and do not be afraid 13 Sanctify the LORD of hosts, let him be your fear and dread, 14 he shall be as a sanctuary, but as a stumbling block and as a boulder to fall upon for the two houses of Israel, and as a snare and a net for the inhabitants of Jerusalem 15 Many of them will stumble and fall and break; they will be caught and will be undermined 16 Gather testimony and keep the Law among my disciples 17 Therefore I will wait for the LORD who hid his face from the house of Jacob and seek him 18 Behold, I and the children whom the LORD has given me are for signs and wonders in Israel, from the LORD of hosts, who dwells on Mount Zion 19 And when they say to you, "Ask those who have a spirit of divination and the soothsayers, who murmur and murmur, 'Should not a people ask of their God, from the time they are alive to the dead? 20 to the Law and the testimonies, if they do not speak according to this word, it is because there is no light in them 21 Then he who is afflicted and hungry shall go and return from there, and will be embittered, and he will curse his king and his God 22 They will look upon the land and behold distress and darkness, the dimness of anguish, and they shall be driven into thick darkness

Chapter 9

1 But there shall be no gloom for her who was in anguish. In former time he made light upon the land of Zebulun and Naphtali, but in the latter time he has made it glorious by the way of the sea, beyond the Jordan, Galilee of the nations 2 The people who walked in darkness have seen a great light; those who dwelt in the land of the shadow of death, upon them has the light shined 3 You have multiplied the nation, you have increased their joy; they rejoice before you according to the joy of harvest, as men rejoice when they divide the spoil 4 For the yoke of his burden, and the staff of his shoulder, the rod of his oppressor, you have broken as in the day of Midian 5 For every boot of the warrior in the tumult and the garments rolled in blood shall be for burning and fuel of fire 6 For unto us a child is born, unto us a son is given; and the government shall be upon his shoulder; and his name shall be called Wonderful, Counselor, Mighty God, Everlasting Father, Prince of

Peace 7 Of the increase of his government and peace there shall be no end, upon the throne of David and upon his kingdom, to order it and to establish it with judgment and justice from now on even forever. The zeal of the LORD of hosts will perform this 8 The LORD sent a word unto Jacob, and it has fallen upon Israel 9 And all the people shall know, even Ephraim and the inhabitants of Samaria, that say in pride and stoutness of heart, 10 "The bricks have fallen down, but we will build with hewn stones; the sycamores have been cut down, but we will replace them with cedars." 11 Therefore the LORD shall set up the adversaries of Rezin against him, and join his enemies together; 12 The Arameans from the east and the Philistines from the west, and they shall devour Israel with open mouth. For all this his anger is not turned away, but his hand is stretched out still 13 For the people do not return to him who smites them, neither do they seek the LORD of hosts 14 Therefore the LORD will cut off from Israel head and tail, branch and rush, in one day 15 The elder and the honorable, he is the head; the prophet who teaches lies, he is the tail 16 For the leaders of this people cause them to err; and they who are led of them are destroyed 17 Therefore the LORD shall have no joy in their young men, neither shall have mercy on their fatherless and widows; for everyone is a hypocrite and an evildoer, and every mouth speaks folly. For all this his anger is not turned away, but his hand is stretched out still 18 For wickedness burns as the fire; it shall devour the briers and thorns, and shall kindle in the thickets of the forest, and they shall mount up like the lifting up of smoke 19 Through the wrath of the LORD of hosts is the land darkened, and the people shall be as the fuel of the fire. No man shall spare his brother 20 And he shall snatch on the right hand and be hungry; and he shall eat on the left hand and they shall not be satisfied; they shall eat every man the flesh of his own arm 21 Manasseh, Ephraim; and Ephraim, Manasseh; and they together shall be against Judah. For all this his anger is not turned away, but his hand is stretched out still

Chapter 10

1 Woe to those who decree unrighteous decrees, and to those who write grievousness which they have prescribed; 2 To turn aside the needy from judgment, and to take away the right from the poor of my people, that widows may be their prey, and that they may rob the fatherless! 3 And what will you do in the day of visitation, and in the desolation which shall come from far? To whom will you flee for help? And where will you leave your glory? 4 Without me they shall bow down under the prisoners, and they shall fall under the slain. For all this his anger is not turned away, but his hand is stretched out still 5 Woe to Assyria, the rod of my anger and the staff in their hand is my indignation! 6 I will send him against a hypocritical nation, and against the people of my wrath will I give him a charge, to take the spoil, and to take the prey, and to tread them down like the mire of the streets 7 Howbeit he means not so, neither does his heart think so; but it is in his heart to destroy and cut off nations not a few 8 For he says, "Are not my princes altogether kings? 9 Is not Calno as Carchemish? Is not Hamath as Arpad? Is not Samaria as Damascus? 10 As my hand hath found the kingdoms of the idols, and whose graven images did excel those of Jerusalem and of Samaria; 11 Shall I not, as I have done to Samaria and her idols, so do to Jerusalem and her idols?" 12 Therefore it shall come to pass, that when the LORD hath performed his whole work upon Mount Zion and upon Jerusalem, I will punish the fruit of the proud heart of the king of Assyria, and the glory of his high looks 13 For he said, "By the strength of my hand I have done it, and by my wisdom; for I am prudent: and I have removed the bounds of the people, and have robbed their treasures, and I have put down the inhabitants like a valiant man: 14 And my hand hath found as a nest the riches of the people; and as one gathereth eggs that are left, have I gathered all the earth; and there was none that moved the wing, or opened the mouth, or peeped." 15 Shall the ax boast itself against him who hews with it? Shall the saw magnify itself against him who shakes it? As if the rod should shake itself against those who lift it up, or as if the staff should lift up itself, as if it were not wood 16 Therefore shall the Lord, the LORD of hosts, send among his fat ones leanness; and under his glory he shall kindle a burning like the burning of a fire 17 And the light of Israel shall be for a fire, and his Holy One for a flame; and it shall burn and devour his thorns and his briers in one day; 18 And shall consume the glory of his forest, and of his fruitful field, both soul and body: and they shall be as when a standard bearer fainteth 19 And the rest of the trees of his forest shall be few, that a child may write them 20 And it shall come to pass in that day, that the remnant of Israel, and such as are escaped of the house of Jacob, shall no more again stay upon him that smote them, but shall stay upon the LORD, the Holy One of Israel, in truth 21 The remnant shall return, even the remnant of Jacob, unto the mighty God 22 For though thy people Israel be as the sand of the sea, yet a remnant of them shall return: the consumption decreed shall overflow with righteousness 23 For the Lord GOD of hosts shall make a consumption, even determined, in the midst of all the land 24 Therefore thus saith the Lord GOD of hosts, O my people that dwellest in Zion, be not afraid of the Assyrian: he shall smite thee with a rod, and shall lift up his staff against thee, after the manner of Egypt 25 For yet a very little while, and the indignation shall cease, and mine anger in their destruction 26 And the LORD of hosts shall stir up a scourge for him according to the slaughter of Midian at the rock of Oreb: and as his rod was upon the sea, so shall he lift it up after the manner of Egypt 27 And it shall come to pass in that day, that his burden shall be taken away from off thy shoulder, and his yoke from off thy neck, and the yoke shall be destroyed because of the anointing 28 He is come to Aiath, he is passed to Migron; at Michmash he hath laid up his carriages: 29 They are gone over the passage: they have taken up their lodging at Geba; Ramah is afraid; Gibeah of Saul is fled 30 Lift up thy voice, O daughter of Gallim: cause it to be heard unto Laish, O poor Anathoth 31 Madmenah is removed; the inhabitants of Gebim gather themselves to flee 32 As yet shall he remain at Nob that day: he shall shake his hand against the mount of the daughter of Zion, the hill of Jerusalem 33 Behold, the Lord, the LORD of hosts, shall lop the bough with terror: and the high ones of stature shall be hewn down, and the haughty shall be humbled 34 And he shall cut down the thickets of the forest with iron, and Lebanon shall fall by a mighty one

CHAPTER 11

1. A rod will come from the stock of Jesse, and a shoot will sprout from his branches. 2. The Spirit of the LORD will rest upon him: the Spirit of wisdom and understanding, the Spirit of counsel and might, the Spirit of knowledge and reverence for the LORD. 3. He will delight in the fear of the LORD. He will not judge by what he sees with his eyes, nor make decisions based on what he hears with his ears. 4. Instead, he will judge the poor with righteousness and will give fair decisions for the meek of the earth. He will strike the earth with the rod of his mouth and slay the wicked with the breath of his lips. 5.

Righteousness will be the belt around his waist, and faithfulness the belt around his loins. 6. The wolf will live with the lamb, the leopard will lie down with the goat, the calf, the lion, and the fattened calf will be together, and a little child will lead them. 7. The cow and the bear will graze together, and their young will lie down side by side. The lion will eat straw like the ox. 8. The infant will play near the cobra's den, and the toddler will put his hand into the viper's lair. 9. They will neither harm nor destroy on all my holy mountain, for the earth will be full of the knowledge of the LORD as the waters cover the sea. 10. In that day, the root of Jesse will stand as a banner for the peoples; the nations will rally to him, and his resting place will be glorious. 11. On that day, the LORD will reach out his hand a second time to reclaim the remnant of his people from Assyria, Egypt, Pathros, Cush, Elam, Shinar, Hamath, and the islands of the sea. 12. He will raise a banner for the nations and gather the exiles of Israel; he will assemble the scattered people of Judah from the four corners of the earth. 13. Ephraim's jealousy will vanish, and Judah's enemies will be removed; Ephraim will not be jealous of Judah, and Judah will not be hostile toward Ephraim. 14. They will swoop down on the Philistines to the west; together they will plunder the people to the east. They will lay hands on Edom and Moab, and the Ammonites will obey them. 15. The LORD will dry up the Gulf of the Egyptian Sea with a scorching wind, and he will wave his hand over the Euphrates River, splitting it into seven streams so that people can cross over in sandals. 16. There will be a highway for the remnant of his people from Assyria, as there was for Israel when they came up from the land of Egypt

CHAPTER 12

1. In that day you will say, "I will praise you, LORD. Although you were angry with me, your anger has turned away, and you have comforted me. 2. Surely God is my salvation; I will trust and not be afraid. The LORD, the LORD himself, is my strength and my defense; he has become my salvation." 3. With joy you will draw water from the wells of salvation. 4. In that day you will say, "Give praise to the LORD, proclaim his name; make known among the nations what he has done, and proclaim that his name is exalted." 5. Sing to the LORD, for he has done glorious things; let this be known to all the world. 6. Shout aloud and sing for joy, people of Zion, for great is the Holy One of Israel among you

CHAPTER 13

1. An oracle concerning Babylon that Isaiah son of Amoz saw. 2. Raise a banner on a high mountain; shout to them, beckon them to enter the gates of the nobles. 3. I have commanded my holy ones; I have summoned my warriors to carry out my wrath—those who rejoice in my triumph. 4. The noise of the multitude in the mountains, like that of a great people; a tumultuous uproar of kingdoms, gathered nations. The LORD of hosts is mustering an army for battle. 5. They come from a distant land, from the ends of the heavens—the LORD and the weapons of his wrath—to destroy the whole country. 6. Wail, for the day of the LORD is near; it will come like destruction from the Almighty. 7. Because of this, all hands will go limp, every heart will melt with fear. 8. Terror will seize them; pain and anguish will grip them; they will writhe like a woman in labor. They will look aghast at each other, their faces aflame. 9. See, the day of the LORD is coming—a cruel day, with wrath and fierce anger—to make the land desolate and destroy the sinners within it. 10. The stars of heaven and their constellations will not show their light; the rising sun will be darkened, and the moon will not give its light. 11. I will punish the world for its

evil, the wicked for their sins. I will put an end to the arrogance of the haughty and will humble the pride of the ruthless. 12. I will make people scarcer than pure gold, more rare than the gold of Ophir. 13. Therefore I will make the heavens tremble, and the earth will shake from its place at the wrath of the LORD Almighty, in the day of his burning anger. 14. Like a hunted gazelle, like sheep without a shepherd, each will return to their own people, each will flee to their native land. 15. Whoever is captured will be thrust through; all who are caught will fall by the sword. 16. Their infants will be dashed to pieces before their eyes; their houses will be looted and their wives violated. 17. See, I will stir up against them the Medes, who do not care for silver and have no delight in gold. 18. Their bows will strike down the young men; they will have no mercy on infants, nor will they look with pity on children. 19. Babylon, the jewel of kingdoms, the glory of the Babylonians' pride, will be overthrown by God like Sodom and Gomorrah. 20. She will never be inhabited or lived in through all generations; Arabs will not pitch their tents there, and shepherds will not make their flocks lie down there. 21. But desert creatures will lie there, and their houses will be full of owls; there the wild goats will leap about, and the hyenas will cry out in their citadels. 22. Hyenas will roam there, and jackals in the strongholds. Her time is at hand, and her days will not be prolonged

CHAPTER 14

1. The LORD will have compassion on Jacob; once again he will choose Israel and will settle them in their own land. Foreigners will join them and unite with the descendants of Jacob. 2. Nations will take them and bring them to their own place. Israel will take possession of the nations as male and female servants in the LORD's land. They will make captives of their captors and rule over their oppressors. 3. On the day the LORD gives you relief from your suffering and turmoil and from the harsh labor forced on you, 4. you will take up this taunt against the king of Babylon: "How the oppressor has come to an end! How his fury has ended! 5. The LORD has broken the rod of the wicked, the scepter of the rulers, 6. which in anger struck down peoples with unceasing blows, and in fury subdued nations with relentless aggression. 7. All the lands are at rest and at peace; they break into singing. 8. Even the pine trees and the cedars of Lebanon gloat over you: 'Now that you have been laid low, no one comes to cut us down.' 9. The realm of the dead below is all astir to meet you at your coming; it rouses the spirits of the departed to greet you— all those who were leaders in the world; it makes them rise from their thrones—all those who were kings of the nations. 10. They will all respond, they will say to you, 'You also have become weak, as we are; you have become like us.' 11. All your pomp has been brought down to the grave, along with the noise of your harps; maggots are spread out beneath you and worms cover you. 12. How you have fallen from heaven, morning star, son of the dawn! You have been cast down to the earth, you who once laid low the nations! 13. You said in your heart, 'I will ascend to the heavens; I will raise my throne above the stars of God; I will sit enthroned on the mount of assembly, on the utmost heights of Mount Zaphon. 14. I will ascend above the tops of the clouds; I will make myself like the Most High.' 15. But you are brought down to the realm of the dead, to the depths of the pit. 16. Those who see you will stare at you, they will ponder your fate: 'Is this the man who shook the earth and made kingdoms tremble, 17. the man who made the world a wilderness, who overthrew its cities and would not let his captives go home?' 18. All the kings of the nations lie in state, each in his own

tomb. 19. But you are cast out of your tomb like a rejected branch; you are covered with the slain, with those pierced by the sword, those who descend to the stones of the pit. Like a carcass trampled underfoot, 20. you will not join them in burial, for you have destroyed your land and killed your people. The offspring of the wicked will never be mentioned again. 21. Prepare a place to slaughter his children for the sin of their ancestors; they are not to rise to inherit the land, nor cover the earth with their cities. 22. I will rise up against them," declares the LORD Almighty, "I will wipe out Babylon's name and remnant, her offspring and descendants," declares the LORD. 23. "I will turn her into a place for owls and into swampland; I will sweep her with the broom of destruction," declares the LORD Almighty. 24. The LORD Almighty has sworn, "Surely, as I have planned, so it will be, and as I have purposed, so it will stand. 25. I will crush the Assyrian in my land; on my mountains I will trample him down. His yoke will be taken from my people, and his burden removed from their shoulders." 26. This is the plan determined for the whole world; this is the hand stretched out over all nations. 27. For the LORD Almighty has purposed, and who can thwart him? His hand is stretched out, and who can turn it back? 28. This prophecy came in the year King Ahaz died: 29. Do not rejoice, all you Philistines, that the rod that struck you is broken; from the root of that snake will spring up a viper, and its fruit will be a darting, venomous serpent. 30. The poorest of the poor will find pasture, and the needy will lie down in safety. But I will kill your root with famine, and it will slay your remnant. 31. Wail, you gate; cry out, you city; all you Philistines are destroyed; nothing remains of your power. Smoke rises from the north, and there is no one left in your appointed place. 32. What answer will the messengers of the nations give? "The LORD has established Zion, and in her his afflicted people will find refuge."

CHAPTER 15

1. An oracle concerning Moab: Ar of Moab is destroyed, demolished in a night; Kir of Moab is destroyed, demolished in a night. 2. They go up to the temple in Dibon and to the high places to weep; Moab wails over Nebo and Medeba. Every head is shaved and every beard is cut off. 3. In the streets they wear sackcloth; on the rooftops and in the public squares everyone wails and mourns. 4. Heshbon and Elealeh cry out; their voices are heard as far as Jahaz. The armed men of Moab cry out; their souls are troubled within them. 5. My heart cries out for Moab; her fugitives flee as far as Zoar, as far as Eglath Shelishiyah. They go up the road to Luhith, weeping as they go; they bear witness to their destruction on the way to Horonaim. 6. The waters of Nimrim are dried up, and the grass is withered; the vegetation is gone and there is no green grass. 7. Therefore, the wealth they have accumulated and their treasures are carried away to the brook of the willows. 8. The outcry extends around the borders of Moab; its wailing reaches as far as Eglaim, and its lamentation as far as Beer Elim. 9. The waters of Dimon are full of blood, but I will bring still more upon Dimon— a lion upon those who escape from Moab, and upon the remnant of the land

CHAPTER 16

1. Send a message to the ruler of the world, from the wilderness mountains to the mountain of the daughter of Zion. 2. For it will be like a bird that flies away from a forsaken nest; the daughters of Moab shall be at the foot of Arnon. 3. Gather a delegation, execute judgment; let your shadow be like the night at noon; hide those who are outcast; do not reject those who have fled. 4. Let my outcasts dwell with you; let Moab be their refuge from the face of the destroyer, for the extortioner will come to an end, the destroyer will be consumed, and the oppressor will cease from the land. 5. A throne of mercy will be prepared, and he will sit upon it firmly, in the tent of David, judging, seeking judgment, and seeking righteousness. 6. We have heard of Moab's pride (he is very proud), his arrogance and indignation, but his lies will not be so. 7. Therefore Moab will wail against Moab; everyone will wail; the foundations of Kir-hareseth will be demolished, and it will be smitten. 8. For the vines of Heshbon have been cut down, and the vineyard of Sibmah; the lords of the nations have broken their principal vines; they have come to Jaazer; they have wandered in the wilderness; its fair branches have stretched out and gone beyond the sea. 9. Therefore, I will weep with the weeping of Jaazer and of the vine of Sibmah. O Heshbon and Elealeh, I will make you drunk with my tears, for upon your summer fruits and upon your shrubs a spectacle has fallen. 10. The cheerfulness has been taken away, and the merriment from the abundant field; in the vineyards no singing will be heard, nor will there be shouting for joy; the treader will not tread down the wine in the presses: I have caused the joy to cease. 11. Therefore my bowels will sound like a harp for Moab, and my inward parts for Kir-hareseth. 12. When Moab is weary of his places of worship, he will come to his temple to pray, but he will not prevail. 13. This is the word that the LORD has spoken against Moab since that time. 14. Now the LORD has spoken, saying, "In three years, as the years of a hired worker, the glory of Moab will be despised in all its great multitude, and the remnant will be very small and weak."

CHAPTER 17

1. An oracle concerning Damascus: Behold, Damascus will cease to be a city, it will become a heap of ruins. 2. The cities of Aroer will be forsaken; they will become grazing grounds for flocks, and they will remain there, undisturbed. 3. The fortress will also cease from Ephraim, the kingdom from Damascus, and the remnant of Aram will be as the glory of the children of Israel, says the LORD of hosts. 4. In that day, the glory of Jacob will be diminished, and the fat of his flesh will become lean. 5. It will be as when the harvester gathers grain and reaps the ears of corn with his arm; it will be as one who gathers the ears of corn in the valley of Rephaim. 6. But there will remain in it a harvest of grapes, like the shaking of an olive tree, two or three berries in the top of the highest branches, and four or five in the highest branches of its fruit, says the LORD God of Israel. 7. In that day a man will look to his Maker, and his eyes will look to the Holy One of Israel. 8. He will not look to the altars, the work of his hands, nor will he look to what his fingers have made, such as the Asherah poles and the incense altars. 9. In that day the fortified cities of their strength will be like abandoned places in the woods and mountaintops, which they abandoned because of the children of Israel, and there will be desolation. 10. Because you have forgotten the God of your salvation and have not remembered the God of your strength, you will plant pleasant plants and set out exotic vines. 11. In the day you will make your plant grow, and in the morning you will make your seed blossom; but the harvest will be a heap of ruins in the day of possession, and there will be despairing sorrow. 12. The multitude of many peoples will roar like the roaring of the sea; the uproar of the nations will be like the roaring of great waters. 13. The nations will roar like the roaring of many waters; but God will rebuke them, and they will flee far away, chased like chaff on the mountains before the wind, and like tumbleweed before the

whirlwind. 14. In the evening, sudden terror; before morning, they are no more. This is the portion of those who plunder us and the lot of those who rob us

CHAPTER 18

1. Woe to the land of whirring wings beyond the rivers of Cush, 2. sending envoys by sea in papyrus boats on the waters, saying, "Go, swift messengers, to a nation scattered and spoiled, to a people terrible from its beginning; a nation of little ones and small ones, whose land has been spoiled by floods." 3. All you inhabitants of the world, you who live on the earth, when a banner is raised on the mountains, you will see it, and when the trumpet sounds, you will hear it. 4. For the LORD said to me, "I will remain quiet and will look from my dwelling place, like dazzling heat in the sunshine, like a cloud of dew in the heat of harvest." 5. For before the harvest, when the blossom is gone and the flower has ripened, the branches will be cut off with pruning hooks, and the remaining growth will be cut down and removed. 6. They will be left together with the trees of the mountains and with the shrubs of the earth; the trees will fall and all the animals of the earth will winter there. 7. At that time, gifts will be brought to the LORD of hosts from a people tall and smooth-skinned, from a people feared far and wide, an aggressive nation whose land is divided by rivers, to the place of the Name of the LORD of hosts, Mount Zion

CHAPTER 19

1. An oracle concerning Egypt: Behold, the LORD rides on a swift cloud and will enter Egypt; the idols of Egypt will tremble at his presence, and the heart of Egypt will melt within it. 2. I will stir up Egyptians against Egyptians; they will fight each other, brother against brother, neighbor against neighbor, city against city, kingdom against kingdom. 3. The spirit of Egypt will be emptied within them; I will confound their plans. They will consult idols and sorcerers, mediums and spiritists. 4. I will hand over the Egyptians to the cruel master, and a fierce king will rule over them, says the LORD, the LORD Almighty. 5. The waters of the river will dry up, and the riverbed will be parched and dry. 6. The canals will stink; the streams of Egypt will dwindle and dry up; reeds and rushes will wither. 7. The plants along the Nile, at the mouth of the river, every sown field along the Nile, will become parched, blown away, and gone. 8. The fishermen will groan and lament, all who cast hooks into the Nile; those who spread nets on the water will pine away. 9. Those who work with flax will be dejected, and those who weave fine linen will grieve. 10. The workers in cloth will be dismayed, and all who make wages will be troubled. 11. The princes of Zoan are utterly foolish; the wise counselors of Pharaoh give senseless advice. How can you say to Pharaoh, "I am one of the wise men, a son of the ancient kings"? 12. Where are your wise men now? Let them show you and make known what the LORD Almighty has planned against Egypt. 13. The princes of Zoan have become fools, the princes of Noph are deceived; those who are the cornerstones of her tribes have led Egypt astray. 14. The LORD has mixed within them a spirit of confusion; they make Egypt stagger in all that she does, as a drunkard staggers in his vomit. 15. Nothing Egypt does will make sense; head or tail, palm branch or reed, will not be able to help. 16. In that day, Egypt will be like women; they will shudder with fear because of the waving of the hand of the LORD Almighty, which he is about to raise against them. 17. The land of Judah will bring terror to Egypt; everyone to whom Judah is mentioned will be terrified, because of the plan the LORD Almighty has purposed against them. 18. In that day, five cities in Egypt will speak the language of Canaan and swear allegiance to the LORD Almighty. One of these will be called the City of Destruction. 19. In that day, there will be an altar to the LORD in the heart of Egypt, and a monument to the LORD at its border. 20. It will be a sign and a witness to the LORD Almighty in the land of Egypt. When they cry out to the LORD because of their oppressors, he will send them a savior and defender, and he will rescue them. 21. The LORD will make himself known to the Egyptians, and they will acknowledge the LORD in that day; they will worship with sacrifices and offerings; they will make vows to the LORD and fulfill them. 22. The LORD will strike Egypt with a plague; he will strike them and heal them. They will return to the LORD, and he will respond to their pleas and heal them. 23. In that day, there will be a highway from Egypt to Assyria; the Assyrians will go to Egypt, and the Egyptians to Assyria; the Egyptians will worship with the Assyrians. 24. In that day, Israel will be the third along with Egypt and Assyria, a blessing on the earth. 25. The LORD Almighty will bless them, saying, "Blessed be Egypt my people, Assyria my handiwork, and Israel my inheritance."

CHAPTER 20

1. In the year when Tartan came to Ashdod, sent by Sargon, king of Assyria, he fought against Ashdod and captured it. 2. At the same time, the LORD spoke through Isaiah the son of Amoz, saying, "Go, loosen your sackcloth from your waist and take off your sandals from your feet." And he did so, walking naked and barefoot. 3. The LORD said, "Just as my servant Isaiah has walked naked and barefoot for three years as a sign and wonder against Egypt and Ethiopia, 4. so will the king of Assyria lead away the captives of Egypt and Ethiopia, both young and old, naked and barefoot, with exposed buttocks, to the shame of Egypt. 5. They will be dismayed and ashamed of Ethiopia, their hope, and of Egypt, their glory. 6. In that day, the inhabitants of the land will say, 'Look, this is our hope, to which we fled for help to be delivered from the king of Assyria. How then can we escape?'"

CHAPTER 21

1. The burden of the desert by the sea. As the whirlwinds in the south sweep through the wilderness, so will it come from the dreadful land. 2. A terrible vision was revealed to me: the traitor against the traitor, and the destroyer against the destroyer. Go up to Elam, besiege Media; I have put an end to all her mourning. 3. Therefore, my heart is filled with anguish; grief has seized me like the pain of a woman in labor. I am bewildered and sickened by what I have heard. 4. My heart falters; fear overwhelms me; the night of my pleasure has become a night of terror. 5. Prepare the table, watch in the watchtower, eat, drink, arise, you princes, and anoint the shield. 6. For thus the LORD said to me, "Go, set a watchman to report what he sees." 7. He saw a chariot with two horsemen, a chariot of donkeys and a chariot of camels. He listened and paid careful attention. 8. And he cried out, "My lord, I stand continually on the watchtower by day, and I stand guard every night." 9. And behold, there comes a man with a chariot of horsemen." And he answered, "Babylon has fallen; it has fallen, and all the images of her gods have been shattered to the ground. 10. Oh, my threshing and the grain of my harvest! I have declared to you what I have heard from the LORD of Hosts, the God of Israel. 11. The burden of Dumah. He called to me from Seir, "Watchman, what is left of the night? Watchman, what is left of the night?" 12. The watchman said, "Morning comes, and also the night. If you wish to ask, ask; return and come back." 13. The burden against Arabia. In the forest in Arabia you shall spend the night, in the dwellings of Dedanim. 14. O inhabitants of the land of Tema, bring

water to those who are thirsty, and bread for those who flee. 15. For they flee from the drawn sword, from the bent bow, and from the severity of war. 16. For thus the LORD has said to me: "In a year, according to the years of a hired worker, all the glory of Kedar will come to an end. 17. And the remaining number of the mighty archers of the sons of Kedar will be diminished, for the LORD, the God of Israel, has spoken."

CHAPTER 22

1. The burden of the valley of vision. What is wrong with you now that you have gone up to the housetops? 2. You who are full of noise, a city full of tumult, a rebellious city; your slain men were not slain with the sword, nor did they die in battle. 3. All your princes fled together, they were bound without bowing. All who were found were bound together, and they fled far off. 4. Therefore I said, "Depart from me; I will weep bitterly. Do not try to comfort me for the destruction of the daughter of my people." 5. For it is a day of trouble and destruction and perplexity from the LORD God of Hosts in the valley of vision, bringing down the walls and crying out on the mountains. 6. Elam took up the quiver with chariots and horsemen, and Kir uncovered the shield. 7. Your main valleys were filled with chariots, and the horsemen took their stand at the gate. 8. He uncovered the armor of Judah, and you looked at that day to the armor of the house of the forest. 9. You saw that the breaches in the city of David were many; you gathered the waters of the lower pool. 10. You counted the houses of Jerusalem and tore them down to fortify the wall. 11. You made a reservoir between the two walls for the waters of the old pool, but you did not look to its Maker, nor did you have respect for Him who formed it long ago. 12. In that day, the LORD God of Hosts called for weeping and mourning, for baldness and sackcloth. 13. But instead, joy and gladness, killing oxen and slaughtering sheep, eating meat and drinking wine, saying, "Let us eat and drink, for tomorrow we die." 14. The LORD of Hosts revealed himself in my ears: "This iniquity will not be forgiven until you die," says the LORD God of Hosts. 15. Thus says the LORD God of Hosts: "Go, go to this steward, to Shebnah, the master of the household, and say, 16. 'What are you doing here, and who do you have here? That you have hewn out a tomb for yourself here, as one hews out a tomb on a high place or carves a dwelling for himself in a rock?' 17. Behold, the LORD will drive you away violently. He will certainly seize you. 18. He will roll you up tightly like a ball and toss you into a large country; there you will die, and there your glorious chariots will be the shame of your lord's house. 19. I will drive you from your office and pull you down from your station. 20. In that day, I will call my servant Eliakim, son of Hilkiah, 21. and I will clothe him with your robe and bind your sash around him. I will give him your authority, and he shall be a father to the inhabitants of Jerusalem and to the house of Judah. 22. I will place on his shoulder the key to the house of David; he shall open and none shall shut; he shall shut and none shall open. 23. I will drive him like a peg in a secure place, and he will become a throne of glory to his father's house. 24. All the glory of his father's house will rest on him: the offspring and the issue, every small vessel, from the cups to all the pitchers. 25. In that day, says the LORD of Hosts, the peg fastened in the secure place will give way; it will be cut down and fall, and the burden that was on it will be cut off, for the LORD has spoken."

CHAPTER 23

1. The burden of Tyre. Howl, you ships of Tarshish, for your harbor is laid waste, with no house left; from the land of Cyprus it is revealed to them. 2. Be still, you inhabitants of the coast, you merchants of Sidon, whom the seafarers have replenished. 3. On the great waters, the grain of Shihor, the harvest of the Nile, was the revenue of Tyre; and she was the marketplace of nations. 4. Be ashamed, O Sidon, for the sea has spoken, the strength of the sea, saying, "I have not labored, nor given birth; I have not brought up young men, nor reared virgins." 5. When the report reaches Egypt, they will be in anguish at the news of Tyre. 6. Cross over to Tarshish; wail, you inhabitants of the coast. 7. Is this your joyous city, whose antiquity is from ancient days, whose feet carried her to settle far off? 8. Who has planned this against Tyre, the bestower of crowns, whose merchants are princes, whose traders are the honored of the earth? 9. The LORD of Hosts has planned it, to bring down the pride of all glory, to shame all the honored of the earth. 10. Overflow your land like the Nile, O daughter of Tarshish; there is no more strength. 11. He stretched out His hand over the sea; He shook the kingdoms. The LORD has given a command concerning Canaan to destroy its strongholds. 12. And He said, "You shall no more rejoice, O oppressed virgin daughter of Sidon. Arise, cross over to Cyprus— even there you will find no rest." 13. Behold the land of the Chaldeans, this people that was not; Assyria founded it for desert creatures. They set up its towers, they brought down its palaces, and it became a ruin. 14. Howl, you ships of Tarshish, for your strength is laid waste. 15. In that day, Tyre will be forgotten for seventy years, according to the days of one king. At the end of seventy years, Tyre will return to her hire as a harlot. 16. Take a harp, go about the city, you forgotten harlot; make sweet melody, sing many songs, that you may be remembered. 17. And it will come to pass after seventy years that the LORD will visit Tyre, and she will return to her wages and will play the harlot with all the kingdoms of the earth upon the face of the earth. 18. Her gain and her pay will be holy to the LORD; it will not be treasured nor stored up. Her merchandise will be for those who dwell before the LORD, to eat sufficiently and for fine clothing

CHAPTER 24

1. Behold, the LORD makes the earth empty and makes it waste; He overturns its surface and scatters its inhabitants. 2. And it shall be as with the people, so with the priest; as with the servant, so with his master; as with the maid, so with her mistress; as with the buyer, so with the seller; as with the lender, so with the borrower; as with the creditor, so with the debtor. 3. The land will be utterly emptied and utterly plundered, for the LORD has spoken this word. 4. The earth mourns and fades away, the world languishes and fades away; the haughty people of the earth languish. 5. The earth is also defiled under its inhabitants, because they have transgressed the laws, changed the ordinance, broken the everlasting covenant. 6. Therefore the curse has devoured the earth, and those who dwell in it are desolate. Therefore the inhabitants of the earth are burned, and few men are left. 7. The new wine fails, the vine languishes, all the merry-hearted sigh. 8. The mirth of the tambourines ceases, the noise of the jubilant ends, the joy of the harp ceases. 9. They shall not drink wine with a song; strong drink will be bitter to those who drink it. 10. The city of chaos is broken down; every house is shut up so that no one may enter. 11. There is a crying for wine in the streets; all joy is darkened, the mirth of the land is gone. 12. The city is left desolate, and the gate is struck with destruction. 13. For thus it will be in the midst of the earth among the peoples, as the shaking of an olive tree, as the gleanings when the vintage is done. 14. They shall lift up their voice, they shall sing for the

majesty of the LORD; they shall cry aloud from the sea. 15. Therefore glorify the LORD in the dawning light; the name of the LORD God of Israel in the coastlands of the sea. 16. From the ends of the earth we have heard songs: "Glory to the Righteous!" But I said, "I am ruined, I am ruined! Woe to me! The treacherous dealers have dealt treacherously, yes, the treacherous dealers have dealt very treacherously." 17. Fear and the pit and the snare are upon you, O inhabitant of the earth. 18. And it shall come to pass that he who flees from the noise of the fear shall fall into the pit; and he who comes up from the midst of the pit shall be caught in the snare. For the windows from on high are open, and the foundations of the earth shake. 19. The earth is utterly broken down, the earth is split open, the earth is shaken exceedingly. 20. The earth shall reel to and fro like a drunkard, and shall totter like a hut; its transgression shall be heavy upon it, and it will fall, and not rise again. 21. It shall come to pass in that day that the LORD will punish on high the host of exalted ones, and on the earth the kings of the earth. 22. They will be gathered together, as prisoners are gathered in the pit, and will be shut up in the prison, and after many days they will be punished. 23. Then the moon will be confounded and the sun ashamed, when the LORD of Hosts reigns on Mount Zion and in Jerusalem, and before His elders, gloriously

CHAPTER 25

1. O LORD, You are my God; I will exalt You, I will praise Your name, for You have done wonderful things, Your counsels of old are faithfulness and truth. 2. For You have made a city a heap, a fortified city a ruin; a palace of foreigners to be a city no more. 3. Therefore the strong people will glorify You; the cities of the terrible nations will fear You. 4. For You have been a strength to the poor, a strength to the needy in his distress, a refuge from the storm, a shade from the heat; for the blast of the terrible ones is as a storm against the wall. 5. You will reduce the noise of strangers, as heat in a dry place; as the shadow of a cloud, the song of the terrible ones will be subdued. 6. And in this mountain the LORD of Hosts will make for all people a feast of rich food, a feast of well-aged wine, of rich food full of marrow, of well-aged wine well refined. 7. And He will destroy on this mountain the covering that is cast over all people, and the veil that is spread over all nations. 8. He will swallow up death forever, and the Lord GOD will wipe away tears from all faces; the rebuke of His people He will take away from all the earth, for the LORD has spoken. 9. And it will be said in that day: "Behold, this is our God; we have waited for Him, and He will save us. This is the LORD; we have waited for Him; we will be glad and rejoice in His salvation." 10. For on this mountain the hand of the LORD will rest, and Moab shall be trampled down under Him, as straw is trampled down for the dung heap. 11. And He will spread out His hands in their midst, as a swimmer reaches out to swim; and He will bring down their pride together with the trickery of their hands. 12. The high fortifications of your walls He will bring down, lay low, and bring to the ground, even to the dust

CHAPTER 26

On that day, this song will be sung in the land of Judah: "We have a strong city; God will set up walls and bulwarks for salvation." Open the gates so that the righteous nation, which keeps the truth, may enter. With unwavering purpose, you will preserve perfect peace because they trust in you. Trust in the LORD forever, for in the LORD God is strength eternal. He will strike down those who dwell on high; he will tear down their city and reduce it to dust. The earth will be brought low, as the feet of the poor and the pastures of the needy The path of the righteous is righteousness; you will make fair the way of the righteous. We, too, O LORD, have waited for you in the way of your judgments; the desire of our soul is for your Name and remembrance. With my soul, I have longed for you in the night, and with my spirit within me, I shall seek you in the morning. For, witnessing your judgments on earth, the inhabitants of the world will learn righteousness. The wicked may be rewarded, but they will not learn righteousness; in the land of righteousness, they will behave wickedly and will not perceive the majesty of the LORD O LORD, they shall not see your hand, but they will be confounded by the zeal of the people, and the fire of your enemies shall consume them. O LORD, you will grant peace to us, for you have also accomplished all our works for us. O LORD our God, other lords besides you have ruled us, but we will remember only you and your Name. The dead shall not live nor rise again, for you have visited and scattered them, destroying all their memories You have increased the nation, O LORD; you have become glorious, you have enlarged all the borders of the earth. Lord, in times of trouble, they sought you; they prayed when your chastisement was upon them. As a pregnant woman in labor is in pain and weeps, so have we been in your presence, Lord. We have suffered and borne sorrow as if carrying the wind; there was no help on earth, and the inhabitants of the world did not fall Your dead shall remain alive; my body will rise again. Awake and sing, you who dwell in the dust, for your dew is like the dew of herbs, and the earth shall cast out the dead. Come, my people, enter into your rooms and shut your doors behind you; hide yourself for a little while until the indignation passes away. For behold, the LORD comes out of his place to visit the iniquity of the inhabitants of the earth upon them; and the earth shall reveal her blood and shall hide her victims no more

CHAPTER 27

In that day, the LORD will punish Leviathan, the fleeing serpent, and Leviathan, the twisted serpent, with his fierce sword, great and mighty, and will slay the dragon that is in the sea. In that day, a song will be sung about the vineyard of red wine. I, the LORD, will keep it; I will water it every moment. If anyone tries to destroy it, I will guard it night and day. There is no wrath in me; who would oppose me with briers and thorns? I would go through them; I would burn them together. Or would you weaken my strength to make peace with me and be united with me? From now on, Jacob will take root; Israel will blossom and grow, and the world will be full of fruit. Did he strike him as he struck those who struck him? Or is he slain as those who were slain by him? When he blows with his fierce wind in the day of the east wind, you will deal with him in measure according to his branches. For this reason, the iniquity of Jacob will be purged, and this is the entire fruit: the removal of his sin; he will make all the stones of the altars like broken pieces of limestone, so that the sacred pillars and images will not stand But the fortified city will be desolate; its habitation will be forsaken and left as a thicket. There the calf will graze, there it will lie down and consume its branches. When its branches are withered, they will be broken off, and women will come and set fire to them. For it is a people of no understanding; therefore, he who made them will have no compassion on them, and he who formed them will show no pity In that day, the LORD will sift from the channel of the river to the shore of Egypt, and you will be gathered one by one, O children of Israel. In that day, the great trumpet will sound, and those who perished in the land of Assyria and those who were driven out in the land of Egypt will come and worship the LORD on the holy mountain of Jerusalem

CHAPTER 28

Woe to the crown of pride, to the drunkards of Ephraim, for its glorious beauty will fade, standing on the head of the valley of those who are fat and drunk with wine. The LORD has a strong and mighty army, like a storm of hail and a whirlwind that overflows, like a tempest of mighty waters that overflow and throw themselves down with power. They will be crushed by a blast, like the crown and pride of the drunkards of Ephraim. For its glorious beauty will be a fading flower, on the head of the valley of those who have been slain, and like the fruit that appears before evening, which, when seen, is quickly consumed In that day, the LORD of hosts will be a crown of glory and a diadem of beauty to the remnant of his people, and a spirit of judgment for those who sit in judgment, and strength for those who turn the battle to the gate. But they erred through wine and went astray through strong drunkenness; the priest and prophet erred through strong drunkenness; they were overwhelmed with wine; they went astray through strong drunkenness; they failed in vision and stumbled in judgment. For all their tables are full of unclean vomit; no place is clean To whom will he teach knowledge, and to whom will he make things understood? To those who are weaned from milk and drawn from the breasts. For precept must be upon precept, precept upon precept, line upon line, line upon line, a little here, a little there. For with stammering lips and another tongue, he will speak to this people. To those who said, "This is the rest; give rest to those who are weary, and this is the refreshment," but they would not listen. Therefore, the word of the LORD will be to them precept upon precept, precept upon precept, line upon line, line upon line, a little here, a little there, that they may go and fall backward, be broken, be snared, and taken Hear the word of the LORD, you scornful men who rule this people in Jerusalem. For you have said, "We have made a covenant with death, and with hell we are in agreement; when the scourge passes through, it will not come to us; for we have made lies our refuge, and under falsehood, we have hidden ourselves." Therefore, thus says the Lord GOD: "Behold, I will lay in Zion a foundation, a tried stone, a precious cornerstone, a sure foundation. Whoever believes will not be in haste. I will also set judgment as a rule and justice as a measure, and the hail will sweep away the refuge of lies, and the waters will overflow the hiding place. Your covenant with death will be annulled, and your agreement with hell will not stand; when the scourge passes through, you will be trampled by it. When it passes through, it will take you away; for it will pass through every morning, day and night, and there will be terror to make you understand For the bed is too short for one to stretch out, and the blanket is too narrow to wrap oneself in. For the LORD will rise up as at Mount Perazim; he will be wroth as in the valley of Gibeon, to do his work, his strange work, and to bring about his deed, his alien deed. Therefore, do not mock yourselves, or your bonds will be increased, for I have heard from the LORD of hosts a determined destruction upon all the earth Hear and listen to my voice, hear and attend to my speech. Does the man who plows plow all day to sow? Does he open and break up the clods of his soil? When he has leveled its surface, will he not sow dill and cumin, and plant wheat in rows, barley in its place, and spelt in its field? For his God instructs him in discretion and teaches him. For dill is not threshed with a threshing sledge, nor is a cartwheel rolled over cumin; but dill is beaten out with a stick and cumin with a rod. The bread wheat is not threshed endlessly, nor does the wheel of his cart grind it; he does not crush it with his teeth. This also comes from the LORD of hosts, who is wonderful in counsel and excellent in wisdom

CHAPTER 29

Woe to you, city of David's altar! Add more lambs to the slaughter. But I will bring the altar amid distress; there will be joys and sorrows, and it shall be to me as an altar. I will besiege you like a circle; I will fight against you on a mountain and cast ramparts against you. Thus, you will be humbled, and you will speak from the ground, and your speech will be low, like that of a medium; your voice will be like a whisper from the dust Your enemies will be like fine dust, and the multitude of the terrible ones like chaff that passes away. It will happen suddenly, in an instant. The LORD of hosts will visit you with thunder and earthquake, great noise, storm, and tempest, and the flame of a devouring fire. And the multitude of all the nations that fight against Ariel, even all who fight against her and her fortress, and those who distress her, shall be as a dream, a vision in the night. It will be like when a hungry man dreams that he eats, but he awakes and is still hungry; or like when a thirsty man dreams that he drinks, but he awakes and is faint, and his soul has no appetite So shall the multitude of all the nations be that fight against Mount Zion. Pause and wonder, blind yourselves and be blind; they are drunk, but not with wine; they stagger, but not with strong drink. For the LORD has poured out upon you the spirit of deep sleep and has closed your eyes, the prophets and your rulers, the seers, has he covered. And the vision of all this has become to you like the words of a book that is sealed, which men deliver to one who is learned, saying, "Read this, I pray thee," and he says, "I cannot; for it is sealed." And the book is delivered to him that is not learned, saying, "Read this, I pray thee," and he says, "I am not learned." Therefore the LORD said, "Forasmuch as this people draw near me with their mouth and with their lips do honor me, but have removed their heart far from me, and their fear toward me is taught by the precept of men. Therefore, behold, I will proceed to do a marvelous work among this people, even a marvelous work and a wonder; for the wisdom of their wise men shall perish, and the understanding of their prudent men shall be hid." Woe unto them that seek deep to hide their counsel from the LORD, and their works are in the dark, and they say, "Who sees us? And who knows us?" Surely your turning of things upside down shall be esteemed as the potter's clay; for shall the work say of him that made it, "He made me not"? Or shall the thing framed say of him that framed it, "He had no understanding"? Is it not yet a very little while, and Lebanon shall be turned into a fruitful field, and the fruitful field shall be esteemed as a forest? In that day, shall the deaf hear the words of the book, and the eyes of the blind shall see out of obscurity and out of darkness. The meek also shall increase their joy in the LORD, and the poor among men shall rejoice in the Holy One of Israel. For the terrible one is brought to naught, and the scorner is consumed, and all that watch for iniquity are cut off. That make a man an offender for a word, and lay a snare for him that reproveth in the gate, and turn aside the just for a thing of naught Therefore, thus says the LORD who redeemed Abraham, concerning the house of Jacob: "Jacob shall not now be ashamed, neither shall his face now wax pale. But when he seeth his children, the work of my hands, in the midst of him, they shall sanctify my Name and sanctify the Holy One of Jacob, and shall fear the God of Israel. They also that erred in spirit shall come to understanding, and they that murmured shall learn doctrine."

CHAPTER 30

1. Woe to the rebellious children, declares the LORD, who seek counsel but not from me, and who align with authorities but not with my Spirit, adding sin upon sin. 2. They go down to Egypt without consulting me, seeking to strengthen themselves with Pharaoh's power and trusting in Egypt's shadow. 3. Yet Pharaoh's strength will bring them shame, and trust in Egypt's shadow will lead to confusion. 4. His princes are in Zoan, and his envoys have reached Hanes. 5. All will be ashamed of a people who cannot benefit or assist them but will only bring disgrace and reproach. 6. The burden of the beasts of the South in a land of trouble and distress comes from the young and old lions, vipers, and fierce flying serpents. They bring their riches on the backs of donkeys and their treasures on camels to a people who cannot profit from them. 7. For the Egyptians are vain and their help is in vain. Therefore, I cried out to you, "Their strength is to stand firm." 8. Now, go and write this before them on a tablet and record it in a book, that it may be preserved for the last days forever. 9. This is a rebellious people, deceitful children, children who refuse to listen to the law of the LORD. 10. They say to the seers, "Do not see," and to the prophets, "Do not prophesy what is right; speak to us smooth things, prophesy illusions." 11. "Get out of the way, turn aside from the path, cause the Holy One of Israel to cease from before us." 12. Therefore, the Holy One of Israel says: "Because you have rejected this message and relied on oppression and deceit, and have remained in it, 13. this iniquity will be to you like a crumbling wall, like a bulge in a wall that suddenly collapses. 14. Its collapse will be like the breaking of a potter's vessel, shattered without remedy, so that its fragments cannot be used to take fire from the hearth or draw water from the well. 15. For thus says the LORD God, the Holy One of Israel: "In repentance and rest you will be saved; in quietness and trust will be your strength, but you would have none of it. 16. You said, 'No, we will flee on horses.' Therefore, you shall flee. 'We will ride off on swift steeds.' Therefore, your pursuers shall be swift. 17. A thousand will flee at the threat of one; at the threat of five, you will all flee until you are left like a flagstaff on a mountaintop, like a banner on a hill. 18. Yet the LORD longs to be gracious to you; therefore he will rise up to show you compassion. For the LORD is a God of justice. Blessed are all who wait for him. 19. O people of Zion, you will weep no more. He will surely be gracious to you at the sound of your cry; when he hears it, he will answer you. 20. Although the LORD gives you the bread of adversity and the water of affliction, your teachers will be hidden no more; with your own eyes you will see them. 21. Whether you turn to the right or to the left, your ears will hear a voice behind you, saying, "This is the way; walk in it." 22. Then you will desecrate your idols overlaid with silver and your images covered with gold; you will throw them away like a menstrual cloth and say to them, "Away with you!" 23. He will also send you rain for the seed you sow in the ground, and the food that comes from the land will be rich and plentiful. In that day your cattle will graze in broad meadows. 24. The oxen and donkeys that work the soil will eat a mash mixed with winnowed chaff. 25. The great slaughter when the towers fall will be on every high mountain and lofty hill, with streams and brooks of water. 26. The moon will shine like the sun, and the sun will be seven times brighter, like the light of seven days, when the LORD binds up the bruises of his people and heals the wounds inflicted by his blow. 27. See, the Name of the LORD comes from afar, with burning anger and dense clouds of smoke; his lips are full of wrath, and his tongue is like a consuming fire. 28. His breath is like a rushing torrent, rising up to the neck. He shakes the nations in the sieve of destruction; he places in the jaws of the peoples a bridle that leads them astray. 29. You will sing as on the night you celebrate a holy festival; your hearts will rejoice as when people go up with flutes to the mountain of the LORD, to the Rock of Israel. 30. The LORD will cause people to hear his majestic voice and will make them see his arm coming down with raging anger and consuming fire, with cloudburst, thunderstorm, and hail. 31. The voice of the LORD will shatter Assyria; with his scepter he will strike them down. 32. Every stroke the LORD lays on them with his punishing club will be to the music of tambourines and harps, as he fights them in battle with the blows of his arm. 33. Tophet has long been prepared; it has been made ready for the king. Its fire pit has been made deep and wide, with an abundance of fire and wood. The breath of the LORD, like a stream of burning sulfur, sets it ablaze

CHAPTER 31

1. Woe to those who go down to Egypt for help, who rely on horses and trust in chariots because they are many, and in horsemen because they are very strong; but they do not look to the Holy One of Israel or seek help from the LORD. 2. Yet he too is wise; he will bring disaster, he does not take back his words. He will rise up against the house of the wicked, against those who help evildoers. 3. The Egyptians are mere mortals and not God; their horses are flesh and not spirit. When the LORD stretches out his hand, those who help will stumble, and those who are helped will fall; all will perish together. 4. This is what the LORD says to me: "As a lion growls, a great lion over its prey, and though a whole band of shepherds is called together against it, it is not frightened by their shouts or disturbed by their clamor, so the LORD Almighty will come down to do battle on Mount Zion and on its heights." 5. As birds hover overhead, the LORD Almighty will shield Jerusalem; he will shield it and deliver it, he will "pass over" it and will rescue it. 6. Return to him you have so greatly revolted against, O Israelites. 7. In that day every one of you will reject the idols of silver and gold your sinful hands have made. 8. Assyria will fall by the sword, not of man; a sword, not of mortals, will devour them. They will flee before the sword, and their young men will be put to forced labor. 9. Their stronghold will fall because of terror; at the sight of the battle standard, their commanders will panic, declares the LORD, whose fire is in Zion, whose furnace is in Jerusalem

CHAPTER 32

1. See, a king will reign in righteousness, and rulers will rule with justice. 2. Each man will be like a hiding place from the wind and a shelter from the storm, like streams of water in the desert and the shadow of a great rock in a thirsty land. 3. Then the eyes of those who see will no longer be closed, and the ears of those who hear will listen. 4. The fearful heart will know and understand, and the stammering tongue will be fluent and clear. 5. No longer will the fool be called noble nor the scoundrel be highly respected. 6. For fools speak folly; their minds are busy with evil: they practice ungodliness and spread error concerning the LORD; the hungry they leave empty, and from the thirsty they withhold water. 7. The scoundrel's methods are wicked; he makes up evil schemes to destroy the poor with lies, even when the plea of the needy is just. 8. But the noble man makes noble plans, and by noble deeds he stands. 9. You women who are at ease, rise up and listen to me; you daughters who feel secure, hear what I have to say! 10. In little more than a year you who feel secure will tremble; the grape harvest will fail, and the harvest of

fruit will not come. 11. Tremble, you women who are at ease; shudder, you complacent ones; strip off your fine clothes and wrap yourselves in rags. 12. Beat your breasts for the pleasant fields, for the fruitful vines 13. and for the land of my people, a land overgrown with thorns and briers—yes, mourn for all the houses of joy in the city of revelry. 14. The fortress will be abandoned, the noisy city deserted; citadel and watchtower will become a wasteland forever, the delight of wild donkeys, a pasture for flocks, 15. till the Spirit is poured upon us from on high, and the desert becomes a fertile field, and the fertile field seems like a forest. 16. Justice will dwell in the desert and righteousness live in the fertile field. 17. The fruit of righteousness will be peace; the effect of righteousness will be quietness and confidence forever. 18. My people will live in peaceful dwelling places, in secure homes, in undisturbed places of rest. 19. Though hail flattens the forest and the city is leveled completely, 20. blessed are you who sow beside all waters, who let the feet of the ox and donkey range free

CHAPTER 33

1. Woe to you, destroyer, you who have not been destroyed! Woe to you, betrayer, you who have not been betrayed! When you stop destroying, you will be destroyed; when you stop betraying, you will be betrayed. 2. LORD, be gracious to us; we long for you. Be our strength every morning, our salvation in times of distress. 3. At the uproar of your army, the peoples flee; when you rise up, the nations scatter. 4. Your plunder, O nations, is collected as locusts collect; like a swarm of locusts people pounce on it. 5. The LORD is exalted, for he dwells on high; he will fill Zion with justice and righteousness. 6. He will be the sure foundation for your times, a rich store of salvation and wisdom and knowledge; the fear of the LORD is the key to this treasure. 7. Look, their brave men cry aloud in the streets; the envoys of peace weep bitterly. 8. The highways are deserted, no travelers are on the roads. The treaty is broken, its witnesses are despised, no one is respected. 9. The land mourns and wastes away; Lebanon is ashamed and withers; Sharon is like the Arabah, and Bashan and Carmel drop their leaves. 10. "Now will I arise," says the LORD. "Now will I be exalted; now will I be lifted up. 11. You conceive chaff, you give birth to straw; your breath is a fire that consumes you. 12. The peoples will be burned as if to lime; like cut thornbushes they will be set ablaze. 13. You who are far away, hear what I have done; you who are near, acknowledge my power. 14. The sinners in Zion are terrified; trembling grips the godless: "Who of us can dwell with the consuming fire? Who of us can dwell with everlasting burning?" 15. He who walks righteously and speaks what is right, who rejects gain from extortion and keeps his hand from accepting bribes, who stops his ears against plots of murder and shuts his eyes against contemplating evil— 16. this is the man who will dwell on the heights, whose refuge will be the mountain fortress. His bread will be supplied, and water will not fail him. 17. Your eyes will see the king in his beauty and view a land that stretches afar. 18. In your thoughts you will ponder the former terror: "Where is that chief officer? Where is the one who took the tribute? Where is the one who took the plunder?" 19. You will see those arrogant people no more, people whose speech is obscure, whose language is strange and incomprehensible. 20. Look upon Zion, the city of our festivals; your eyes will see Jerusalem, a peaceful abode, a tent that will not be moved; its stakes will never be pulled up, nor will any of its ropes be broken. 21. There the LORD will be mighty for us; he will be like a place of broad rivers and streams. No galley with oars will ride them,

no mighty ship will sail them. 22. For the LORD is our judge, the LORD is our lawgiver, the LORD is our king; it is he who will save us. 23. Your rigging hangs loose; the mast is not held firm, the sail is not spread. Then an abundance of spoils will be divided and even the lame will carry off plunder. 24. No one living in Zion will say, "I am ill"; and the sins of those who dwell there will be forgiven

CHAPTER 34

1. Come near, you nations, and listen; pay attention, you peoples. Let the earth hear, and all that is in it, the world, and all that comes from it. 2. For the LORD is angry with all the nations; his wrath is upon all their armies. He has devoted them to destruction, giving them over to slaughter. 3. Their slain will be thrown out; their dead bodies will send up a stench. The mountains will be soaked with their blood. 4. The heavens will be dissolved; the skies rolled up like a scroll. All the starry host will fall like withered leaves from the vine, like shriveled figs from the fig tree. 5. My sword has drunk its fill in the heavens; see, it descends in judgment on Edom, the people I have devoted to destruction. 6. The sword of the LORD is filled with blood; it is covered with fat, the blood of lambs and goats, the fat of kidneys of rams. For the LORD has a sacrifice in Bozrah and a great slaughter in the land of Edom. 7. The wild oxen will fall with them, and the young bulls with the mighty bulls. Their land will be drenched with blood, and the dust will be covered with fat. 8. For the LORD has a day of vengeance, a year of retribution, to uphold Zion's cause. 9. Edom's streams will be turned into pitch, her dust into burning sulfur; her land will become blazing pitch. 10. It will not go out day or night; its smoke will rise forever. It will lie desolate from generation to generation; no one will ever pass through it again. 11. The desert owl and screech owl will possess it; the great owl and the raven will nest there. The LORD will stretch out over Edom the measuring line of chaos and the plumb line of desolation. 12. Her nobles will have nothing there to be called a kingdom, and all her princes will vanish. 13. Thorns will overrun her citadels, nettles and brambles her strongholds. She will become a haunt for jackals, a home for ostriches. 14. Desert creatures will meet with hyenas, and wild goats will bleat to each other. There the night creatures will also lie down and find for themselves places of rest. 15. The owl will make her nest and lay eggs there; she will hatch them and care for her young under her shadow. There also the vultures will gather, each with its mate. 16. Look in the scroll of the LORD and read: None of these will be missing, not one will lack her mate. For it is his mouth that has given the order, and his Spirit will gather them together. 17. He allots their portions; his hand distributes them by measure. They will possess it forever and dwell there from generation to generation

CHAPTER 35

1. The desert and the parched land will be glad; the wilderness will rejoice and blossom. Like the crocus, 2. it will burst into bloom; it will rejoice greatly and shout for joy. The glory of Lebanon will be given to it, the splendor of Carmel and Sharon. They will see the glory of the LORD, the splendor of our God. 3. Strengthen the feeble hands, steady the knees that give way. 4. Say to those with fearful hearts, "Be strong, do not fear; your God will come, he will come with vengeance; with divine retribution he will come to save you." 5. Then will the eyes of the blind be opened and the ears of the deaf unstopped. 6. Then will the lame leap like a deer, and the mute tongue shout for joy. Water will gush forth in the wilderness and streams in the desert. 7. The burning sand will become a pool, the thirsty ground bubbling springs.

In the haunts where jackals once lay, grass and reeds and papyrus will grow. 8. And a highway will be there; it will be called the Way of Holiness. It will be for those who walk on that Way; the unclean will not journey on it; wicked fools will not go about on it. 9. No lion will be there, nor will any ferocious beast get up on it; they will not be found there. But only the redeemed will walk there, 10. and those the LORD has rescued will return. They will enter Zion with singing; everlasting joy will crown their heads. Gladness and joy will overtake them, and sorrow and sighing will flee away

CHAPTER 36

1. In the fourteenth year of King Hezekiah's reign, Sennacherib king of Assyria attacked all the fortified cities of Judah and captured them. 2. Then the king of Assyria sent his field commander with a large army from Lachish to King Hezekiah at Jerusalem. When the commander stopped at the aqueduct of the Upper Pool, on the road to the Launderer's Field, 3. Eliakim son of Hilkiah, the palace administrator, Shebnah the secretary, and Joah son of Asaph the recorder went out to him. 4. The field commander said to them, "Tell Hezekiah, 'This is what the great king, the king of Assyria, says: On what are you basing this confidence of yours? 5. You say you have counsel and might for war—but you speak only empty words. On whom are you depending, that you rebel against me? 6. Look, I know you are depending on Egypt, that splintered reed of a staff; which pierces the hand of anyone who leans on it. Such is Pharaoh king of Egypt to all who depend on him. 7. But if you say to me, 'We are depending on the LORD our God.' Isn't he the one whose high places and altars Hezekiah removed, saying to Judah and Jerusalem, 'You must worship before this altar'? 8. Come now, make a bargain with my master, the king of Assyria: I will give you two thousand horses if you can put riders on them. 9. How can you repulse one officer of the least of my master's officials, even though you are depending on Egypt for chariots and horsemen? 10. Furthermore, have I come to attack and destroy this land without the LORD? The LORD himself told me to march against this country and destroy it.'" 11. Then Eliakim, Shebnah, and Joah said to the field commander, "Please speak to your servants in Aramaic, since we understand it. Don't speak to us in Hebrew in the hearing of the people on the wall." 12. But the commander replied, "Was it only to your master and you that my master sent me to say these things, and not to the people sitting on the wall, who, like you, will have to eat their own excrement and drink their own urine?" 13. Then the commander stood and called out in Hebrew, "Hear the words of the great king, the king of Assyria. 14. This is what the king says: 'Do not let Hezekiah deceive you. He cannot deliver you from my hand. 15. Do not let Hezekiah persuade you to trust in the LORD when he says, "The LORD will surely deliver us; this city will not be given into the hand of the king of Assyria." 16. Do not listen to Hezekiah. This is what the king of Assyria says: "Make peace with me and come out to me. Then each of you will eat fruit from your own vine and fig tree, and drink water from your own cistern, 17. until I come and take you to a land like your own, a land of grain and new wine, a land of bread and vineyards. 18. Do not let Hezekiah mislead you when he says, 'The LORD will deliver us.' Have the gods of any nations ever delivered their lands from the hand of the king of Assyria? 19. Where are the gods of Hamath and Arpad? Where are the gods of Sepharvaim? Have they rescued Samaria from my hand? 20. Who of all the gods of these countries have been able to save their lands from me? How then can the LORD deliver Jerusalem from my hand?" 21. But the people remained silent and said nothing in reply, because the king had commanded, "Do not answer him." 22. Then Eliakim son of Hilkiah, the palace administrator, Shebnah the secretary, and Joah son of Asaph the recorder went back to Hezekiah with their clothes torn and told him what the field commander had said

CHAPTER 37

When King Hezekiah heard this, he tore his clothes, put on sackcloth, and entered the house of the LORD. He then sent Eliakim, the steward of the house, Shebnah, the chancellor, and the elders of the priests, all dressed in sackcloth, to Isaiah the prophet, the son of Amoz. They conveyed to him, "Thus says Hezekiah, 'Today is a day of tribulation, reproach, and blasphemy, because children have come to birth, but there is no strength to bring them forth. If the LORD your God has heard the words of Rabshakeh, whom the king of Assyria, his master, has sent to mock the living God and rebuke Him with blasphemies that the LORD your God has heard, then lift up your prayer for the remnant that is left.'" So King Hezekiah's servants went to Isaiah. Isaiah said to them, "Tell your master, 'Thus says the LORD: Do not be afraid because of the words you have heard, with which the servants of the king of Assyria have blasphemed Me. Behold, I will send a spirit upon him, and he shall hear a rumor and return to his own land, where I will cause him to fall by the sword.'" Rabshakeh returned and found the king of Assyria fighting against Libnah, for he had heard that he had departed from Lachish. He also learned that Tirhakah, the king of Ethiopia, had come out to fight against him. When he heard this, he sent other messengers to Hezekiah, saying, "Thus you shall speak to Hezekiah, king of Judah: 'Do not let your God, in whom you trust, deceive you by saying, "Jerusalem shall not be given into the hand of the king of Assyria."' You have heard what the kings of Assyria have done to all the countries by utterly destroying them, and will you be delivered? Have the gods of the nations that my fathers destroyed, such as Gozan, Haran, Rezef, and the sons of Eden who were in Telassar, rescued them? Where is the king of Hamath, the king of Arpad, and the kings of the cities of Sepharvaim, Hena, and Ivvah?" Hezekiah received the letter from the hand of the messengers, read it, and went up to the house of the LORD, and spread it before the LORD. Hezekiah prayed to the LORD, saying, "O LORD of hosts, God of Israel, who dwells between the cherubim, You are the God, You alone, of all the kingdoms of the earth; You have made heaven and earth. Incline Your ear, O LORD, and hear; open Your eyes, O LORD, and see, and hear all the words of Sennacherib, who has sent to reproach the living God. It is true, O LORD, that the kings of Assyria have laid waste all the nations and their lands, and have cast their gods into the fire, for they were not gods, but the work of men's hands, wood and stone; therefore, they have destroyed them. Now therefore, O LORD our God, save us from his hand, that all the kingdoms of the earth may know that You are the LORD, You alone." Then Isaiah son of Amoz sent word to Hezekiah: "Thus says the LORD God of Israel: Because you have prayed to Me concerning Sennacherib king of Assyria, this is the word which the LORD has spoken against him: 'The virgin daughter of Zion has despised you, laughed you to scorn; the daughter of Jerusalem has shaken her head at you. Whom have you reproached and blasphemed? Against whom have you raised your voice and lifted your eyes in pride? Against the Holy One of Israel! By your messengers you have reproached the Lord and said, "With my multitude of chariots I have come up to the height of the mountains, to the farthest recesses of Lebanon; I will cut down its tall cedars and its choice cypress trees; I will enter its farthest height, its thickest forest. I have dug and drunk water, and with the sole of my foot I have dried up all the brooks of defense." Have you not heard long ago how I made it, and formed it from ancient times? Now I have brought it to pass, that you should be for crushing fortified cities into heaps of ruins. Therefore their inhabitants had little power; they were dismayed and confounded; they were as the grass of the field and the green herb, as the grass on the housetops and the grain blighted before it is grown. But I know your dwelling place, your going out, and your coming in, and your rage against Me. Because your rage against Me and your tumult have come up to My ears, I will put My hook in your nose and My bridle in your lips, and I will turn you back by the way which you came. This shall be a sign to you: You shall eat this year such as grows of itself, and the second year what springs from the same; but in the third year sow and reap, plant vineyards and eat the fruit of them. And the remnant who have escaped of the house of Judah shall again take root downward, and bear fruit upward. For out of Jerusalem shall go a remnant, and those who escape from Mount Zion; the zeal of the LORD of hosts will do this. Therefore thus says the LORD concerning the king of Assyria: He shall not come into this city, nor shoot an arrow there, nor come before it with shield, nor build a siege mound against it. By the way that he came, by the same shall he return, and he shall not come into this city, says the LORD. For I will defend this city to save it, for My own sake and for My servant David's sake.'" Then the angel of the LORD went out and killed in the camp of the Assyrians one hundred eighty-five thousand; and when people arose early in the morning, they were all dead bodies. So Sennacherib king of Assyria departed and went away, returned home, and remained at Nineveh. And it came to pass, as he was worshiping in the house of Nisroch his god, that his sons Adrammelech and Sharezer struck him down with the sword; and they escaped into the land of Ararat. Then Esarhaddon his son reigned in his place

CHAPTER 38

In those days Hezekiah was sick and near death. And Isaiah the prophet, the son of Amoz, came to him and said, "Thus says the LORD: 'Set your house in order, for you shall die and not live.'" Then Hezekiah turned his face toward the wall and prayed to the LORD, saying, "Remember now, O LORD, I pray, how I have walked before You in truth and with a loyal heart, and have done what is good in Your sight." And Hezekiah wept bitterly Then the word of the LORD came to Isaiah, saying, "Go and tell Hezekiah, 'Thus says the LORD, the God of David your father: I have heard your prayer, I have seen your tears; surely I will add to your days fifteen years. I will deliver you and this city from the hand of the king of Assyria, and I will defend this city.'" And this is the sign to you from the LORD, that the LORD will do this thing which He has spoken: "Behold, I will bring the shadow on the sundial, which has gone down with the sun on the dial of Ahaz, ten degrees backward." So the sun returned ten degrees on the dial by which it had gone down The writing of Hezekiah king of Judah, when he had been sick and had recovered from his sickness: "I said, 'In the prime of my life I shall go to the gates of Sheol; I am deprived of the remainder of my years.' I said, 'I shall not see Yah, the LORD, in the land of the living; I shall observe man no more among the inhabitants of the world. My life span is gone, taken from me like a shepherd's tent; I have cut off like a weaver my life. He will cut me off from the loom; from day until night You will make an end of me.' I have

considered until morning—like a lion, so He breaks all my bones; from day until night You will make an end of me. Like a crane or a swallow, so I chattered; I moaned like a dove; my eyes failed from looking upward. O LORD, I am oppressed; undertake for me! What shall I say? He has both spoken to me, and He Himself has done it. I shall walk carefully all my years in the bitterness of my soul. O LORD, by these things men live, and in all these things is the life of my spirit; so You will restore me and make me live. Indeed it was for my own peace that I had great bitterness; but You have lovingly delivered my soul from the pit of corruption, for You have cast all my sins behind Your back. For Sheol cannot thank You, death cannot praise You; those who go down to the pit cannot hope for Your truth. The living, the living man, he shall praise You, as I do this day; the father shall make known Your truth to the children. The LORD was ready to save me; therefore we will sing my songs with stringed instruments all the days of our life, in the house of the LORD." Now Isaiah had said, "Let them take a lump of figs, and apply it as a poultice on the boil, and he shall recover." And Hezekiah had said, "What is the sign that I shall go up to the house of the LORD?"

CHAPTER 39

1 At that time, Merodach-Baladan son of Baladan, king of Babylon, sent letters and a gift to Hezekiah, because he had heard that Hezekiah had been ill and had recovered. 2 Hezekiah was pleased and showed them all his treasures—the silver, the gold, the spices, the precious ointments, and the entire armory, along with everything found among his treasures. There was nothing in his palace or kingdom that Hezekiah did not show them 3 Then the prophet Isaiah came to King Hezekiah and asked him, "What did these men say, and where did they come from?" Hezekiah answered, "They have come from a far country, from Babylon." 4 Isaiah said, "What have they seen in your house?" Hezekiah replied, "They have seen everything in my house; there is nothing among my treasures that I have not shown them." 5 Then Isaiah said to Hezekiah, "Hear the word of the LORD of hosts: 6 'Behold, the days are coming when all that is in your house, and what your fathers have stored up until this day, shall be carried to Babylon; nothing shall be left,' says the LORD. 7 'And some of your sons who will come from you, whom you beget, shall be taken away, and they shall become eunuchs in the palace of the king of Babylon.'" 8 So Hezekiah said to Isaiah, "The word of the LORD which you have spoken is good." And he added, "Will there not be peace and truth in my days?"

CHAPTER 40

1 "Comfort, comfort My people," says your God. 2 "Speak comfort to Jerusalem, and cry out to her that her warfare is ended, that her iniquity is pardoned; for she has received from the LORD's hand double for all her sins." 3 The voice of one crying in the wilderness: "Prepare the way of the LORD; make straight in the desert a highway for our God. 4 Every valley shall be exalted, and every mountain and hill brought low; the crooked places shall be made straight and the rough places smooth; 5 the glory of the LORD shall be revealed, and all flesh shall see it together; for the mouth of the LORD has spoken." 6 The voice said, "Cry out!" And he said, "What shall I cry?" "All flesh is grass, and all its loveliness is like the flower of the field. 7 The grass withers, the flower fades, because the breath of the LORD blows upon it; surely the people are grass. 8 The grass withers, the flower fades, but the word of our God stands forever." 9 O Zion, you who bring good tidings, get up into the high mountain; O Jerusalem, you who bring

good tidings, lift up your voice with strength; lift it up, be not afraid; say to the cities of Judah, "Behold your God!" 10 Behold, the Lord GOD shall come with a strong hand, and His arm shall rule for Him; behold, His reward is with Him, and His work before Him. 11 He will feed His flock like a shepherd; He will gather the lambs with His arm, and carry them in His bosom, and gently lead those who are with young 12 Who has measured the waters in the hollow of His hand, measured heaven with a span and calculated the dust of the earth in a measure? Who has weighed the mountains in scales and the hills in a balance? 13 Who has directed the Spirit of the LORD, or as His counselor has taught Him? 14 With whom did He take counsel, and who instructed Him, and taught Him in the path of justice? Who taught Him knowledge, and showed Him the way of understanding? 15 Behold, the nations are as a drop in a bucket, and are counted as the small dust on the scales; look, He lifts up the isles as a very little thing. 16 Lebanon is not sufficient to burn, nor its beasts sufficient for a burnt offering. 17 All nations before Him are as nothing, and they are counted by Him less than nothing and worthless 18 To whom then will you liken God? Or what likeness will you compare to Him? 19 The workman molds an image, the goldsmith overspreads it with gold, and the silversmith casts silver chains. 20 Whoever is too impoverished for such a contribution chooses a tree that will not rot; He seeks for himself a skillful workman to prepare a carved image that will not totter 21 Have you not known? Have you not heard? Has it not been told you from the beginning? Have you not understood from the foundations of the earth? 22 It is He who sits above the circle of the earth, and its inhabitants are like grasshoppers; who stretches out the heavens like a curtain, and spreads them out like a tent to dwell in. 23 He brings the princes to nothing; He makes the judges of the earth useless. 24 Scarcely shall they be planted, scarcely shall they be sown, scarcely shall their stock take root in the earth, when He will also blow on them, and they will wither, and the whirlwind will take them away like stubble 25 "To whom then will you liken Me, or to whom shall I be equal?" says the Holy One. 26 Lift up your eyes on high, and see who has created these things, who brings out their host by number; He calls them all by name, by the greatness of His might and the strength of His power; not one is missing 27 Why do you say, O Jacob, and speak, O Israel, "My way is hidden from the LORD, and my just claim is passed over by my God"? 28 Have you not known? Have you not heard? The everlasting God, the LORD, the Creator of the ends of the earth, neither faints nor is weary. His understanding is unsearchable. 29 He gives power to the weak, and to those who have no might He increases strength. 30 Even the youths shall faint and be weary, and the young men shall utterly fall, 31 but those who wait on the LORD shall renew their strength; they shall mount up with wings like eagles, they shall run and not be weary, they shall walk and not faint

CHAPTER 41

Restrain yourself before me, O Ireland, and let the people give up their strength; come here and speak; meet to judge. Who has caused righteousness to arise from the east, called it to his side, made the nations pass before him, and subdued the kings? He made them as dust for his sword and as scattered stubble for his bow. He pursued them and passed safely through a path he had not previously traveled. Who has worked and done this? He who calls generations from the beginning. I, the LORD, am the first, and with the last, I am the same. The peoples saw it and were afraid; the ends of the earth were afraid, and they drew near and came. Every man helped his neighbor and said to his brother, "Be strong." So the craftsman encouraged the blacksmith, and the one who strikes with the hammer and the one who smites with force said, "He is ready for the molding and has fastened it with nails so that it will not be moved." But you, Israel, are my servant, and you, Jacob, whom I have chosen, descendants of Abraham, my friend. For I took you from the ends of the earth and called you from its farthest regions, and said to you, "You are my servant; I have chosen you and not cast you away." Fear not, for I am with you; be not dismayed, for I am your God. I will strengthen you, help you, and uphold you with the right hand of my righteousness. Behold, all those who have ridiculed you shall be shamed and confounded; they shall be as nothing, and those who strive with you shall perish. You shall seek them and not find them—those who contended with you; they shall be as nothing, and those who war against you as a thing of naught. For I, the LORD your God, will hold your right hand, saying to you, "Fear not, I will help you." Fear not, you worm, Jacob, and you men of Israel. I will help you, says the LORD, and your Redeemer, the Holy One of Israel. Behold, I will make you a new sharp threshing instrument with teeth; you shall thresh the mountains and beat them small, and make the hills like chaff. You shall winnow them, and the wind shall carry them away, and the whirlwind shall scatter them; and you shall rejoice in the LORD and glory in the Holy One of Israel. When the poor and needy seek water and there is none (their tongue faileth for thirst), I, the LORD, will hear them; I, the God of Israel, will not forsake them. I will open rivers in desolate heights and fountains in the midst of the valleys; I will make the wilderness a pool of water, and the dry land springs of water. I will plant in the wilderness the cedar, the acacia, the myrtle, and the oil tree; I will set in the desert the fir, the pine, and the box tree together. That they may see and know, consider and understand together that the hand of the LORD has done this, and the Holy One of Israel has created it. Present your case, says the LORD; bring forth your strong reasons, says the King of Jacob. Let them bring forth and show us what will happen; let them show the former things, what they are, that we may consider them and know the latter end of them; or declare to us things to come. Show the things that are to come hereafter, that we may know that you are gods; yea, do good or do evil, that we may be dismayed and see it together. Behold, you are of nothing, and your work is of naught; an abomination is he who chooses you. I have raised up one from the north, and he shall come; from the east the sun shall call upon my name, and he shall come upon princes as upon clay, and as the potter treads the clay. Who has declared from the beginning that we may know, or before time that we may say, "He is righteous"? Surely there is no one who shows, no one who declares, no one who hears your words. I am the first to say to Zion, "Behold, here they are!" and I will give Jerusalem one who brings good tidings. But when I looked, there was no man; even when I asked of them, there was no counselor, and when I asked them, they could not answer a word. Behold, they are all worthless; their works are nothing; their molten images are wind and confusion

CHAPTER 42

Behold my servant, whom I uphold; my chosen, in whom my soul delights. I have put my Spirit upon him; he will bring forth judgment to the Gentiles. He will not cry out, nor raise his voice, nor cause it to be heard in the street. A bruised reed he will not break, and a smoking flax he will not quench; he will bring forth judgment in truth. He will not falter nor be discouraged until he has established judgment in the earth; and the coastlands shall wait for his law. Thus says God the LORD, who created the heavens and stretched them out, who spread out the earth and that which comes from it, who gives breath to the people on it and spirit to those who walk on it: "I, the LORD, have called you in righteousness; I will hold your hand and keep you; I will give you as a covenant to the people, as a light to the Gentiles, To open the blind eyes, to bring out prisoners from the dungeon, those who sit in darkness from the prison house. I am the LORD, that is my name; and my glory I will not give to another, nor my praise to carved images. Behold, the former things have come to pass, and new things I declare; before they spring forth, I tell you of them. Sing to the LORD a new song, and his praise from the end of the earth, you who go down to the sea, and all that is in it, the isles and their inhabitants. Let the wilderness and its cities lift up their voice, the villages that Kedar inhabits; let the inhabitants of the rock sing, let them shout from the top of the mountains. Let them give glory to the LORD and declare his praise in the coastlands. The LORD shall go forth like a mighty man; he shall stir up zeal like a man of war; he shall cry out, yea, shout aloud; he shall prevail against his enemies. I have long time held my peace; I have been still, and refrained myself; now will I cry like a travailing woman; I will destroy and devour at once. I will make waste mountains and hills, and dry up all their herbs; and I will make the rivers islands, and I will dry up the pools. And I will bring the blind by a way that they knew not; I will lead them in paths that they have not known; I will make darkness light before them, and crooked things straight. These things will I do unto them, and not forsake them. They shall be turned back, they shall be greatly ashamed, that trust in graven images, that say to the molten images, "You are our gods." Hear, you deaf; and look, you blind, that you may see. Who is blind, but my servant? Or deaf as my messenger that I sent? Who is blind as he who is perfect, and blind as the LORD's servant? Seeing many things, but you observe not; opening the ears, but he hears not. The LORD is well pleased for his righteousness' sake; he will magnify the law, and make it honorable. But this is a people robbed and spoiled; they are all of them snared in holes, and they are hidden in prison houses; they are for a prey, and none delivers; for a spoil, and none says, "Restore." Who among you will give ear to this? Who will hearken and hear for the time to come? Who gave Jacob for a spoil, and Israel to the robbers? Did not the LORD, he against whom we have sinned? For they would not walk in his ways, neither were they obedient to his law. Therefore he has poured upon him the fury of his anger, and the strength of battle; and it has set him on fire round about, yet he knew not; and it burned him, yet he laid it not to heart

CHAPTER 43

But now thus says the LORD who created you, O Jacob, and he who formed you, O Israel: "Fear not, for I have redeemed you; I have called you by your name; you are mine." When you pass through the waters, I will be with you; and through the rivers, they shall not overflow you. When you walk through the fire, you shall not be burned, nor shall the flame scorch you. For I am the LORD your God, the Holy One of Israel, your Savior; I gave Egypt for your ransom, Ethiopia and Seba in your place. Since you were precious in my sight, you have been honorable, and I have loved you; therefore will I give men for you, and people for your life. Fear not, for I am with you; I will bring your descendants from the east, and gather you from the west; I will say to the north, "Give up!" and to the south, "Do not keep them back!" Bring my

sons from afar and my daughters from the ends of the earth— Everyone who is called by my name, whom I have created for my glory; I have formed him, yea, I have made him. Bring forth the blind people who have eyes, and the deaf who have ears. Let all the nations be gathered together, and let the people be assembled; who among them can declare this, and show us former things? Let them bring forth their witnesses, that they may be justified; or let them hear, and say, "It is truth." You are my witnesses, says the LORD, and my servant whom I have chosen, that you may know and believe me, and understand that I am he. Before me there was no God formed, neither shall there be after me. I, even I, am the LORD; and beside me there is no savior. I have declared, and have saved, and I have showed, when there was no strange god among you; therefore you are my witnesses, says the LORD, that I am God. Yes, before the day was I am he; and there is none that can deliver out of my hand; I will work, and who shall let it? Thus says the LORD, your Redeemer, the Holy One of Israel: "For your sake I have sent to Babylon, and have brought down all their nobles, and the Chaldeans, whose cry is in the ships. I am the LORD, your Holy One, the Creator of Israel, your King." Thus says the LORD, who makes a way in the sea and a path through the mighty waters, Who brings forth the chariot and horse, the army and the power; they shall lie down together, they shall not rise; they are extinct, they are quenched as tow. "Do not remember the former things, nor consider the things of old. Behold, I will do a new thing; now it shall spring forth; shall you not know it? I will even make a road in the wilderness and rivers in the desert. The beasts of the field shall honor me, the dragons and the owls, because I give waters in the wilderness and rivers in the desert, to give drink to my people, my chosen. This people I have formed for myself; they shall show forth my praise. But you have not called upon me, O Jacob; but you have been weary of me, O Israel. You have not brought me the small cattle of your burnt offerings; neither have you honored me with your sacrifices. I have not caused you to serve with an offering, nor wearied you with incense. You have bought me no sweet cane with money, neither have you filled me with the fat of your sacrifices; but you have made me to serve with your sins, you have wearied me with your iniquities. I, even I, am he that blots out your transgressions for my own sake, and will not remember your sins. Put me in remembrance; let us plead together; declare you, that you may be justified. Your first father has sinned, and your teachers have transgressed against me. Therefore I have profaned the princes of the sanctuary, and have given Jacob to the curse, and Israel to reproaches

CHAPTER 44

"Yet now hear, O Jacob my servant, and Israel whom I have chosen. Thus says the LORD who made you and formed you from the womb, who will help you: 'Fear not, O Jacob, my servant; and you, Jeshurun, whom I have chosen. For I will pour water on him who is thirsty, and floods on the dry ground; I will pour my Spirit on your descendants, and my blessing on your offspring. They will spring up among the grass like willows by the watercourses. One will say, 'I am the LORD's'; another will call himself by the name of Jacob; another will write with his hand, 'The LORD's,' and name himself by the name of Israel.' "Thus says the LORD, the King of Israel, and his Redeemer, the LORD of hosts: 'I am the first, and I am the last; and beside me there is no God. And who, as I, shall call, and shall declare it, and set it in order for me, since I appointed the ancient people? And the things that are coming, and shall come, let them show unto them. Fear ye not, neither be afraid: have not I told thee from that time, and have declared it? Ye are even my witnesses. Is there a God beside me? Yea, there is no God; I know not any.' They that make a graven image are all of them vanity; and their delectable things shall not profit; and they are their own witnesses; they see not, nor know; that they may be ashamed. Who has formed a god, or molten a graven image that is profitable for nothing? Behold, all his fellows shall be ashamed; and the workmen, they are of men: let them all be gathered together, let them stand up; yet they shall fear, and they shall be ashamed together. The smith with the tongs both works in the coals, and fashions it with hammers, and works it with the strength of his arms: yea, he is hungry, and his strength fails: he drinks no water, and is faint. The carpenter stretches out his rule; he marks it out with a line; he fits it with planes, and he marks it out with the compass, and makes it after the figure of a man, according to the beauty of a man, that it may remain in the house. He hews him down cedars, and takes the cypress and the oak, which he strengthens for himself among the trees of the forest: he plants an ash, and the rain does nourish it. Then shall it be for a man to burn: for he will take thereof, and warm himself; yea, he kindles it, and bakes bread; yea, he makes a god, and worships it; he makes it a graven image, and falls down thereto. He burns part thereof in the fire; with part thereof he eats flesh; he roasts roast, and is satisfied: yea, he warms himself, and says, 'Aha, I am warm, I have seen the fire.' And the residue thereof he makes a god, even his graven image: he falls down unto it, and worships it, and prays unto it, and says, 'Deliver me; for thou art my god.' They have not known nor understood: for he hath shut their eyes, that they cannot see; and their hearts, that they cannot understand. And none considers in his heart, neither is there knowledge nor understanding to say, 'I have burned part of it in the fire; yea, also I have baked bread upon the coals thereof; I have roasted flesh, and eaten it: and shall I make the residue thereof an abomination? Shall I fall down to the stock of a tree?' He feeds on ashes: a deceived heart has turned him aside, that he cannot deliver his soul, nor say, 'Is there not a lie in my right hand?' "Remember these, O Jacob and Israel; for you are my servant: I have formed you; you are my servant: O Israel, you shall not be forgotten of me. I have blotted out, as a thick cloud, your transgressions, and, as a cloud, your sins: return unto me; for I have redeemed you. Sing, O ye heavens; for the LORD hath done it: shout, ye lower parts of the earth: break forth into singing, ye mountains, O forest, and every tree therein: for the LORD hath redeemed Jacob, and glorified himself in Israel. "Thus says the LORD, your Redeemer, and he that formed you from the womb, I am the LORD that makes all things; that stretches forth the heavens alone; that spreads abroad the earth by myself; That frustrates the tokens of the liars, and makes diviners mad; that turns wise men backward, and makes their knowledge foolish; That confirms the word of his servant, and performs the counsel of his messengers; that says to Jerusalem, 'Thou shalt be inhabited'; and to the cities of Judah, 'Ye shall be built, and I will raise up the decayed places thereof': That says to the deep, 'Be dry, and I will dry up thy rivers': That says of Cyrus, 'He is my shepherd, and shall perform all my pleasure': even saying to Jerusalem, 'Thou shalt be built'; and to the temple, 'Thy foundation shall be laid.'"

CHAPTER 45

"Thus says the LORD to his anointed, to Cyrus, whose right hand I have held, to subdue nations before him; and I will loose the loins of kings, to open before him the two leaved gates; and the gates shall not be shut; I will go before thee, and make the crooked places straight: I will break in pieces the gates of brass, and cut in sunder the bars of iron: And I will give thee the treasures of darkness, and hidden riches of secret places, that thou mayest know that I, the LORD, which call thee by thy name, am the God of Israel. For Jacob my servant's sake, and Israel mine elect, I have even called thee by thy name: I have surnamed thee, though thou hast not known me. I am the LORD, and there is none else, there is no God beside me: I girded thee, though thou hast not known me: That they may know from the rising of the sun, and from the west, that there is none beside me. I am the LORD, and there is none else. I form the light, and create darkness: I make peace, and create evil: I the LORD do all these things. Drop down, ye heavens, from above, and let the skies pour down righteousness: let the earth open, and let them bring forth salvation, and let righteousness spring up together; I the LORD have created it. Woe unto him that strives with his Maker! Let the potsherd strive with the potsherds of the earth. Shall the clay say to him that fashions it, 'What makest thou?' or thy work, 'He hath no hands'? Woe unto him that saith unto his father, 'What begettest thou?' or to the woman, 'What hast thou brought forth?' "Thus says the LORD, the Holy One of Israel, and his Maker: 'Ask me of things to come concerning my sons, and concerning the work of my hands command ye me. I have made the earth, and created man upon it: I, even my hands, have stretched out the heavens, and all their host have I commanded. I have raised him up in righteousness, and I will direct all his ways: he shall build my city, and he shall let go my captives, not for price nor reward, says the LORD of hosts.' "Thus says the LORD, The labor of Egypt, and merchandise of Ethiopia and of the Sabeans, men of stature, shall come over unto thee, and they shall be thine: they shall come after thee; in chains they shall come over, and they shall fall down unto thee, they shall make supplication unto thee, saying, 'Surely God is in thee; and there is none else, there is no God.' Verily thou art a God that hidest thyself, O God of Israel, the Saviour. They shall be ashamed, and also confounded, all of them: they shall go to confusion together that are makers of idols. But Israel shall be saved in the LORD with an everlasting salvation: ye shall not be ashamed nor confounded world without end. For thus says the LORD that created the heavens; God himself that formed the earth and made it; he hath established it, he created it not in vain, he formed it to be inhabited: I am the LORD; and there is none else. I have not spoken in secret, in a dark place of the earth: I said not unto the seed of Jacob, 'Seek ye me in vain': I the LORD speak righteousness, I declare things that are right. Assemble yourselves and come; draw near together, ye that are escaped of the nations: they have no knowledge that set up the wood of their graven image, and pray unto a god that cannot save. Tell ye, and bring them near; yea, let them take counsel together: who hath declared this from ancient time? who hath told it from that time? have not I the LORD? and there is no God else beside me; a just God and a Saviour; there is none beside me. Look unto me, and be ye saved, all the ends of the earth: for I am God, and there is none else. I have sworn by myself, the word is gone out of my mouth in righteousness, and shall not return, That unto me every knee shall bow, every tongue shall swear. Surely, shall one say, in the LORD have I righteousness and strength: even to him shall men come; and all that are incensed against him shall be ashamed. In the LORD shall all the seed of Israel be justified, and shall glory."

CHAPTER 46

Bel bows down, Nebo falls; their idols are carried by beasts and cattle. The burdens they bear are heavy. They bow down and collapse together because they cannot shake off their load, and their souls are taken into captivity. Listen to me, house of Jacob and all who remain of the house of Israel, whom I have brought forth from the womb and carried from birth. Even to old age, I am the same, and I will sustain you until the end of your days. I have made you; I will carry you, deliver you, and bear you. To whom will you compare me, or equate me, or liken me? They bring out gold from the bag, weigh silver on the scales, hire a goldsmith to make a god, and then bow down and worship it. They carry the god on their shoulders, place it in its place, and it stands there, unable to move. Even if one cries out to it, it cannot answer or save from trouble. Remember this and be ashamed; remember it again, you transgressors. Remember the former things, for I am God, and there is no other; there is none like me. I declare the end from the beginning, and from ancient times things not yet done, saying, "My purpose will stand, and I will do all that I please." I call a bird from the east, and a man from a distant land to fulfill my purpose. As I have spoken, so will I bring it to pass; I have planned it, and I will do it. Listen to me, you stubborn-hearted, who are far from righteousness. I am bringing my righteousness near; it is not far off, and my salvation will not delay. I will grant salvation to Zion and my glory to Israel

CHAPTER 47

Come down and sit in the dust, O virgin daughter of Babylon. Sit on the ground; there is no throne for you, daughter of the Chaldeans. You will no longer be called "tender and delicate." Take the millstones and grind the grain; remove your veil, bare your feet, and cross the rivers. Your nakedness will be exposed, and your shame will be seen. I will take vengeance and will not meet you as a man. Our Redeemer, the LORD of hosts, is his name, the Holy One of Israel. Sit in silence and darkness, daughter of the Chaldeans. You will no longer be called "queen of kingdoms." I was angry with my people; I desecrated my inheritance and gave it into your hand. You showed no mercy, and you laid a heavy yoke on the aged. You said, "I will be a queen forever," and did not consider these things or remember their outcome. Therefore, hear this, you who are given to pleasures and live carelessly, saying in your heart, "I am, and there is none else." You will not sit as a widow or know the loss of children. But these two things will come upon you suddenly, in one day: loss of children and widowhood; they will come upon you in full measure, because of your many sorceries and great abundance of enchantments. You have trusted in your wickedness and said, "No one sees me." Your wisdom and knowledge have led you astray, and you have said in your heart, "I am, and there is none else." Therefore, disaster will overtake you, and you will not know how it happened; ruin will come upon you suddenly, and you will not be able to prevent it. Now, amid your many counselors and the multitude of your stargazers, let them stand up and save you from what is coming upon you. Behold, they will be like stubble; fire will consume them. They will not be able to save themselves from the flame; there will be no place to sit and no light to guide them. Thus, those you have labored with, your merchants from your youth, will go their own ways, and no one will save you

CHAPTER 48

Listen, house of Jacob, called by the name of Israel, and who came from the waters of Judah; you swear by the name of the LORD and invoke the God of Israel, but not in truth or righteousness. They call themselves citizens of the holy city and rely on the God of Israel, whose name is the LORD of hosts. I declared the former things to you; they came from my mouth, and I revealed them. I acted suddenly, and they came to pass. For I knew that you are obstinate, with a neck of iron and a forehead of bronze. Therefore, I declared it to you long ago; before it happened, I announced it to you, so you could not say, "My idol made them; my graven image and my molten image commanded them." You have heard and seen all this, yet will you not declare it? I am revealing new things to you, hidden things you did not know. They are created now, not long ago; before today, you have not heard of them, so you cannot say, "Behold, I knew them." But you have not heard or known; your ear was not open from the beginning, because I knew you would be rebellious; therefore, I called you a rebel from birth. For my own sake, I will delay my anger, and for my own praise, I will restrain it from you, so as not to cut you off. Behold, I have refined you, but not as silver; I have tested you in the furnace of affliction. For my own sake, I will act; how can my name be defiled? I will not give my glory to another. Listen to me, Jacob and Israel, whom I have called: I am the first and I am the last. Surely, my hand laid the foundations of the earth, and my right hand spread out the heavens; when I call them, they stand together. All of you, gather together and listen: which of them has declared these things? The LORD loves him; he will do his will against Babylon, and his arm will be against the Chaldeans. I have spoken and called him; I have brought him, and his way will succeed. Come here and hear this: I have not spoken in secret from the beginning; from the time it began, I was there, and now the Lord GOD has sent me and his Spirit. Thus says the LORD, your Redeemer, the Holy One of Israel: "I am the LORD your God, who teaches you to profit, who leads you in the way you should go. Oh, if only you had paid attention to my commands! Then your peace would have been like a river, and your righteousness like the waves of the sea. Your descendants would have been like the sand, and the offspring of your body like its grains; their name would never have been cut off nor destroyed from before me." Go out from Babylon, flee from the Chaldeans, with shouts of joy; declare this with a loud voice, proclaim it to the ends of the earth; say, "The LORD has redeemed his servant Jacob." They did not thirst when he led them through the deserts; he made water flow from the rock for them; he split the rock, and water gushed out. There is no peace, says the LORD, for the wicked

CHAPTER 49

Listen to me, you islands; hear this, you distant nations. The LORD called me from the womb; from the body of my mother he named me. He made my mouth like a sharp sword; in the shadow of his hand he hid me; he made me into a polished arrow and concealed me in his quiver. He said to me, "You are my servant, Israel, in whom I will display my splendor." But I said, "I have labored in vain; I have spent my strength for nothing at all. Yet what is due me is in the LORD's hand, and my reward is with my God." And now the LORD says—he who formed me in the womb to be his servant, to bring Jacob back to him and gather Israel to himself: It is too small a thing for you to be my servant to restore the tribes of Jacob and bring back those of Israel I have kept. I will also make you a light for the Gentiles, that my salvation may reach to the ends of the earth. This is what the LORD says— the Redeemer and Holy One of Israel— to him who was despised and abhorred by the nation, to the servant of rulers: "Kings will see you and rise up, princes will see and bow down, because of the LORD, who is faithful, the Holy One of Israel, who has chosen you." This is what the LORD says: "In the time of my favor I will answer you, and in the day of salvation I will help you; I will keep you and will make you to be a covenant for the people, to restore the land and to reassign its desolate inheritances, to say to the captives, 'Come out,' and to those in darkness, 'Be free!' They will feed beside the roads and find pasture on every barren hill. They will neither hunger nor thirst, nor will the desert heat or the sun beat down on them. He who has compassion on them will guide them and lead them beside springs of water. I will turn all my mountains into roads, and my highways will be raised up. See, they will come from afar—some from the north, some from the west, some from the region of Sinim." Shout for joy, you heavens; rejoice, you earth; burst into song, you mountains! For the LORD comforts his people and will have compassion on his afflicted ones. But Zion said, "The LORD has forsaken me, the Lord has forgotten me." "Can a mother forget the baby at her breast and have no compassion on the child she has borne? Though she may forget, I will not forget you! See, I have engraved you on the palms of my hands; your walls are ever before me. Your children hasten back, and those who laid you waste depart from you. Lift up your eyes and look around; all your children gather and come to you. As surely as I live," declares the LORD, "you will wear them all as ornaments; you will put them on, like a bride. "Though you were ruined and made desolate and your land laid waste, now you will be too small for your people, and those who devoured you will be far away. The children born during your bereavement will yet say in your hearing, 'This place is too small for us; give us more space to live in.' Then you will say in your heart, 'Who bore me these? I was bereaved and barren; I was exiled and rejected. Who raised these? I was left alone; but these, where have they come from?'" This is what the Sovereign LORD says: "See, I will beckon to the nations, I will lift up my banner to the peoples; they will bring your sons in their arms and carry your daughters on their shoulders. Kings will be your foster fathers, and their queens your nursing mothers. They will bow down before you with their faces to the ground; they will lick the dust at your feet. Then you will know that I am the LORD; those who hope in me will not be disappointed." Can plunder be taken from warriors, or captives be rescued from the fierce? But this is what the LORD says: "Yes, captives will be taken from warriors, and plunder retrieved from the fierce; I will contend with those who contend with you, and your children I will save. I will make your oppressors eat their own flesh; they will be drunk on their own blood, as with wine. Then all mankind will know that I, the LORD, am your Savior, your Redeemer, the Mighty One of Jacob."

CHAPTER 50

This is what the LORD says: "Where is your mother's certificate of divorce, with which I sent her away? Or to which of my creditors did I sell you? Because of your sins you were sold; because of your transgressions your mother was sent away. When I came, why was there no one? When I called, why was there no answer? Was my arm too short to redeem you? Do I lack the strength to rescue you? By a mere rebuke I dry up the sea, I turn rivers into a desert; their fish rot for lack of water and die of thirst. I clothe the heavens with darkness and make sackcloth its covering." The Sovereign LORD has given me a well-instructed tongue, to know the word that sustains the weary. He wakens me morning by morning, wakens my ear to listen like one being instructed. The Sovereign LORD has opened my ears; I have not been rebellious, I have not turned away. I offered my back to those who beat me, my cheeks to those who pulled out my beard; I did not hide my face from mocking and spitting. Because the Sovereign LORD helps me, I will not be disgraced. Therefore, I have set my face like flint, and I know I will not be put to shame. He who vindicates me is near. Who then will bring charges against me? Let us face each other. Who is my accuser? Let him confront me. It is the Sovereign LORD who helps me. Who is he that will condemn me? They will all wear out like a garment; the moths will eat them up. Who among you fears the LORD and obeys the word of his servant? Let the one who walks in the dark, who has no light, trust in the name of the LORD and rely on their God. But now, all you who light fires and provide yourselves with flaming torches, go, walk in the light of your fires and of the torches you have set ablaze. This is what you shall receive from my hand; you will lie down in torment

CHAPTER 51

1 Listen to me, you who follow righteousness and who seek the Lord; look to the rock from which you were hewn and to the quarry from which you were dug. 2 Consider Abraham your father, and Sarah who bore you; for I called him alone, and blessed him and increased him. 3 For the LORD will comfort Zion; He will comfort all her waste places; He will make her wilderness like Eden, and her desert like the garden of the LORD; joy and gladness will be found in her, thanksgiving and the voice of melody. 4 Listen to me, my people; and give ear to me, my nation; for a law will proceed from me, and I will make my justice rest as a light of the peoples. 5 My righteousness is near, my salvation has gone forth, and my arms will judge the peoples; the coastlands will wait for me, and on my arm they will trust. 6 Lift up your eyes to the heavens, and look on the earth beneath; for the heavens will vanish away like smoke, the earth will grow old like a garment, and those who dwell in it will die in like manner; but my salvation will be forever, and my righteousness will not be abolished. 7 Listen to me, you who know righteousness, you people in whose heart is my law: do not fear the reproach of men, nor be afraid of their insults. 8 For the moth will eat them up like a garment, and the worm will eat them like wool; but my righteousness will be forever, and my salvation from generation to generation. 9 Awake, awake, put on strength, O arm of the LORD; awake as in the ancient days, in the generations of old. Are You not the arm that cut Rahab apart, and wounded the serpent? 10 Are You not the arm that dried up the sea, the waters of the great deep; that made the depths of the sea a road for the redeemed to cross over? 11 So the ransomed of the LORD shall return, and come to Zion with singing, with everlasting joy on their heads; they shall obtain joy and gladness, and sorrow and sighing shall flee away. 12 "I, even I, am He who comforts you. Who are you that you should be afraid of a man who will die, and of the son of man who will be made like grass? 13 And you forget the LORD your Maker, who stretched out the heavens and laid the foundations of the earth; you have feared continually every day because of the fury of the oppressor, when he has prepared to destroy. And where is the fury of the oppressor? 14 The captive exile hastens, that he may be loosed, that he should not die in the pit, and that his bread should not fail. 15 But I am the LORD your God, who divided the sea whose waves roared—the LORD of hosts is His name. 16 And I have put My words in your mouth; I have covered you with the shadow of My hand, that I may plant the heavens, lay the foundations of the earth, and say to Zion, 'You are My people.'" 17 Awake, awake, stand up, O Jerusalem, you who have drunk at the hand of the

LORD the cup of His wrath; you have drunk the dregs of the cup of trembling, and drained it out. 18 There is no one to guide her among all the sons she has brought forth; nor is there any who takes her by the hand among all the sons she has brought up. 19 These two things have come to you; who will be sorry for you? Desolation and destruction, famine and sword; by whom will I comfort you? 20 Your sons have fainted; they lie at the head of all the streets, like an antelope in a net; they are full of the fury of the LORD, the rebuke of your God. 21 Therefore please hear this, you afflicted, and drunk but not with wine. 22 Thus says your Lord, the LORD and your God, who pleads the cause of His people: "See, I have taken out of your hand the cup of trembling, the dregs of the cup of My wrath; you shall no longer drink it. 23 But I will put it into the hand of those who afflict you, who have said to your soul, 'Bow down, that we may walk over you.' And you have laid your back like the ground, and as the street, for those who walk over."

CHAPTER 52

1 Awake, awake, put on your strength, O Zion; put on your beautiful garments, O Jerusalem, the holy city; for the uncircumcised and the unclean shall no longer come to you. 2 Shake yourself from the dust, arise, sit down, O Jerusalem; loose yourself from the bonds of your neck, O captive daughter of Zion. 3 For thus says the LORD: "You have sold yourselves for nothing, and you shall be redeemed without money." 4 For thus says the Lord GOD: "My people went down at first into Egypt to dwell there; then the Assyrian oppressed them without cause. 5 Now therefore, what have I here," says the LORD, "that My people are taken away for nothing? Those who rule over them make them wail," says the LORD, "and My name is blasphemed continually every day. 6 Therefore My people shall know My name; therefore they shall know in that day that I am He who speaks: 'Behold, it is I.'" 7 How beautiful upon the mountains are the feet of him who brings good news, who proclaims peace, who brings glad tidings of good things, who proclaims salvation, who says to Zion, "Your God reigns!" 8 Your watchmen shall lift up their voices, with their voices they shall sing together; for they shall see eye to eye when the LORD brings back Zion. 9 Break forth into joy, sing together, you waste places of Jerusalem! For the LORD has comforted His people, He has redeemed Jerusalem. 10 The LORD has made bare His holy arm in the eyes of all the nations; and all the ends of the earth shall see the salvation of our God. 11 Depart! Depart! Go out from there, touch no unclean thing; go out from the midst of her, be clean, you who bear the vessels of the LORD. 12 For you shall not go out with haste, nor go by flight; for the LORD will go before you, and the God of Israel will be your rear guard. 13 Behold, My Servant shall deal prudently; He shall be exalted and extolled and be very high. 14 Just as many were astonished at you, so His visage was marred more than any man, and His form more than the sons of men; 15 So shall He sprinkle many nations. Kings shall shut their mouths at Him; for what had not been told them they shall see, and what they had not heard they shall consider

CHAPTER 53

1 Who has believed our report? And to whom has the arm of the LORD been revealed? 2 For He shall grow up before Him as a tender plant, and as a root out of dry ground; He has no form or comeliness; and when we see Him, there is no beauty that we should desire Him. 3 He is despised and rejected by men, a Man of sorrows and acquainted with grief; and we hid, as it were, our faces from Him; He was despised, and we did not esteem Him. 4 Surely He has borne our griefs and carried our sorrows; yet we esteemed Him

stricken, smitten by God, and afflicted. 5 But He was wounded for our transgressions, He was bruised for our iniquities; the chastisement for our peace was upon Him, and by His stripes we are healed. 6 All we like sheep have gone astray; we have turned, every one, to his own way; and the LORD has laid on Him the iniquity of us all. 7 He was oppressed and He was afflicted, yet He opened not His mouth; He was led as a lamb to the slaughter, and as a sheep before its shearers is silent, so He opened not His mouth. 8 He was taken from prison and from judgment, and who will declare His generation? For He was cut off from the land of the living; for the transgressions of My people He was stricken. 9 And they made His grave with the wicked—but with the rich at His death, because He had done no violence, nor was any deceit in His mouth. 10 Yet it pleased the LORD to bruise Him; He has put Him to grief. When You make His soul an offering for sin, He shall see His seed, He shall prolong His days, and the pleasure of the LORD shall prosper in His hand. 11 He shall see the labor of His soul, and be satisfied. By His knowledge My righteous Servant shall justify many; for He shall bear their iniquities. 12 Therefore I will divide Him a portion with the great, and He shall divide the spoil with the strong, because He poured out His soul unto death, and He was numbered with the transgressors, and He bore the sin of many, and made intercession for the transgressors

CHAPTER 54

1 "Sing, O barren, you who have not borne! Break forth into singing, and cry aloud, you who have not labored with child! For more are the children of the desolate than the children of the married woman," says the LORD. 2 "Enlarge the place of your tent, and let them stretch out the curtains of your dwellings; do not spare; lengthen your cords, and strengthen your stakes. 3 For you shall expand to the right and to the left, and your descendants will inherit the nations, and make the desolate cities inhabited. 4 "Do not fear, for you will not be ashamed; neither be disgraced, for you will not be put to shame; for you will forget the shame of your youth, and will not remember the reproach of your widowhood anymore. 5 For your Maker is your husband, the LORD of hosts is His name; and your Redeemer is the Holy One of Israel; He is called the God of the whole earth. 6 For the LORD has called you like a woman forsaken and grieved in spirit, like a youthful wife when you were refused," says your God. 7 "For a mere moment I have forsaken you, but with great mercies I will gather you. 8 With a little wrath I hid My face from you for a moment; but with everlasting kindness I will have mercy on you," says the LORD, your Redeemer. 9 "For this is like the waters of Noah to Me; for as I have sworn that the waters of Noah would no longer cover the earth, so have I sworn that I would not be angry with you, nor rebuke you. 10 For the mountains shall depart and the hills be removed, but My kindness shall not depart from you, nor shall My covenant of peace be removed," says the LORD, who has mercy on you. 11 "O you afflicted one, tossed with tempest, and not comforted, behold, I will lay your stones with colorful gems, 12 and lay your foundations with sapphires. 13 I will make your pinnacles of rubies, your gates of crystal, and all your walls of precious stones. 14 "All your children shall be taught by the LORD, and great shall be the peace of your children. 15 In righteousness you shall be established; you shall be far from oppression, for you shall not fear; and from terror, for it shall not come near you. 16 Indeed they shall surely assemble, but not because of Me. Whoever assembles against you shall fall for your sake. 17 "Behold, I have created the blacksmith who blows the coals in the fire, who

brings forth an instrument for his work; and I have created the spoiler to destroy. 18 "No weapon formed against you shall prosper, and every tongue which rises against you in judgment you shall condemn. This is the heritage of the servants of the LORD, and their righteousness is from Me," says the LORD

CHAPTER 55

1 "Ho! Everyone who thirsts, come to the waters; and you who have no money, come, buy and eat. Yes, come, buy wine and milk without money and without price. 2 Why do you spend money for what is not bread, and your wages for what does not satisfy? Listen carefully to Me, and eat what is good, and let your soul delight itself in abundance. 3 Incline your ear, and come to Me. Hear, and your soul shall live; and I will make an everlasting covenant with you— the sure mercies of David. 4 Indeed I have given him as a witness to the people, a leader and commander for the people. 5 Surely you shall call a nation you do not know, and nations who do not know you shall run to you, because of the LORD your God, and the Holy One of Israel; for He has glorified you." 6 Seek the LORD while He may be found, call upon Him while He is near. 7 Let the wicked forsake his way, and the unrighteous man his thoughts; let him return to the LORD, and He will have mercy on him; and to our God, for He will abundantly pardon. 8 "For My thoughts are not your thoughts, nor are your ways My ways," says the LORD. 9 "For as the heavens are higher than the earth, so are My ways higher than your ways, and My thoughts than your thoughts. 10 "For as the rain comes down, and the snow from heaven, and do not return there, but water the earth, and make it bring forth and bud, that it may give seed to the sower and bread to the eater, 11 so shall My word be that goes forth from My mouth; it shall not return to Me void, but it shall accomplish what I please, and it shall prosper in the thing for which I sent it. 12 "For you shall go out with joy, and be led out with peace; the mountains and the hills shall break forth into singing before you, and all the trees of the field shall clap their hands. 13 "Instead of the thorn shall come up the fir tree, and instead of the brier shall come up the myrtle tree; and it shall be to the LORD for a name, for an everlasting sign that shall not be cut off."

CHAPTER 56

1 Thus says the LORD, "Observe judgment and do righteousness, for My salvation is near to come, and My righteousness to be revealed." 2 Blessed is the man who does this, and the son of man who holds it fast; who keeps the Sabbath without profaning it, and keeps his hand from doing any evil. 3 Let not the foreigner who has joined himself to the LORD say, "The LORD will surely separate me from His people," nor let the eunuch say, "Behold, I am a dry tree." 4 For thus says the LORD: "To the eunuchs who keep My Sabbaths, and choose what pleases Me, and hold fast My covenant, 5 I will give in My house and within My walls a memorial and a name better than that of sons and daughters; I will give them an everlasting name that shall not be cut off. 6 And the foreigners who join themselves to the LORD, to minister to Him, and to love the name of the LORD, to be His servants—everyone who keeps the Sabbath without profaning it, and holds fast My covenant— 7 these I will bring to My holy mountain and make them joyful in My house of prayer; their burnt offerings and their sacrifices will be accepted on My altar; for My house shall be called a house of prayer for all peoples." 8 The Lord GOD, who gathers the outcasts of Israel, declares, "I will gather yet others to him besides those already gathered." 9 All you beasts of the field, come to devour, all you beasts in the forest. 10 His

watchmen are blind; they are all without knowledge; they are all mute dogs, unable to bark; dreaming, lying down, loving to slumber. 11 The dogs have a mighty appetite; they never have enough. The shepherds have no understanding; they have all turned to their own way, each to his own gain, one and all. 12 "Come," they say, "let me get wine; let us fill ourselves with strong drink; and tomorrow will be like this day, great beyond measure."

CHAPTER 57

1 The righteous man perishes, and no one lays it to heart; devout men are taken away, while no one understands that the righteous man is taken away from calamity. 2 He enters into peace; they rest in their beds who walk in their uprightness. 3 But you, draw near, sons of the sorceress, offspring of the adulterer and the loose woman. 4 Whom are you mocking? Against whom do you open your mouth wide and stick out your tongue? Are you not children of transgression, the offspring of deceit, 5 you who burn with lust among the oaks, under every green tree; who slaughter your children in the valleys, under the clefts of the rocks? 6 Among the smooth stones of the valley is your portion; they, they are your lot; to them you have poured out a drink offering; you have brought a grain offering. Should I relent for these things? 7 Upon a high and lofty mountain you have set your bed, and there you went up to offer sacrifice. 8 Behind the door and the doorpost you have set up your memorial; for, deserting Me, you have uncovered your bed, and climbed up into it; you have made it wide, and you have made a bargain for yourself with them; you have loved their bed; you have looked on nakedness. 9 You journeyed to the king with oil and multiplied your perfumes; you sent your envoys far off, and sent down even to Sheol. 10 You were wearied with the length of your way, but you did not say, "It is hopeless"; you found new life for your strength, so you were not faint. 11 Whom did you dread and fear, so that you lied, and did not remember Me, or give Me a thought? Have I not held My peace, even for a long time, and you do not fear Me? 12 I will declare your righteousness and your deeds, but they will not profit you. 13 When you cry out, let your collection of idols deliver you! The wind will carry them all off; a breath will take them away. But he who takes refuge in Me shall possess the land and shall inherit My holy mountain. 14 And it shall be said, "Build up, build up, prepare the way, remove every obstruction from My people's way." 15 For thus says the One who is high and lifted up, who inhabits eternity, whose name is Holy: "I dwell in the high and holy place, and also with him who is of a contrite and lowly spirit, to revive the spirit of the lowly, and to revive the heart of the contrite. 16 For I will not contend forever, nor will I always be angry; for the spirit would grow faint before Me, and the souls that I have made. 17 Because of the iniquity of his unjust gain I was angry; I struck him; I hid My face and was angry; but he went on backsliding in the way of his own heart. 18 I have seen his ways, but I will heal him; I will lead him and restore comfort to him and his mourners, 19 creating the fruit of the lips. Peace, peace, to the far and the near," says the LORD, "and I will heal him." 20 But the wicked are like the tossing sea; for it cannot be quiet, and its waters toss up mire and dirt. 21 "There is no peace," says my God, "for the wicked."

CHAPTER 58

1 "Cry aloud, do not hold back; lift up your voice like a trumpet; declare to My people their transgression, to the house of Jacob their sins. 2 Yet they seek Me daily and delight to know My ways, as if they were a nation that did righteousness and did not forsake the judgment of their God; they ask of Me righteous

judgments; they delight to draw near to God. 3 'Why have we fasted, and You see it not? Why have we humbled ourselves, and You take no knowledge of it?' Behold, in the day of your fast you seek your own pleasure, and oppress all your workers. 4 Behold, you fast only to quarrel and to fight and to hit with a wicked fist. Fasting like yours this day will not make your voice to be heard on high. 5 "Is such the fast that I choose, a day for a person to humble himself? Is it to bow down his head like a reed, and to spread sackcloth and ashes under him? Will you call this a fast, and a day acceptable to the LORD? 6 "Is not this the fast that I choose: to loose the bonds of wickedness, to undo the heavy burdens, and to let the oppressed go free, and to break every yoke? 7 Is it not to share your bread with the hungry and bring the homeless poor into your house; when you see the naked, to cover him, and not to hide yourself from your own flesh? 8 Then shall your light break forth like the dawn, and your healing shall spring up speedily; your righteousness shall go before you; the glory of the LORD shall be your rear guard. 9 Then you shall call, and the LORD will answer; you shall cry, and He will say, 'Here I am.' If you take away the yoke from your midst, the pointing of the finger, and speaking wickedness, 10 if you pour yourself out for the hungry and satisfy the desire of the afflicted, then shall your light rise in the darkness and your gloom be as the noonday. 11 And the LORD will guide you continually and satisfy your desire in scorched places and make your bones strong; and you shall be like a watered garden, like a spring of water, whose waters do not fail. 12 And your ancient ruins shall be rebuilt; you shall raise up the foundations of many generations; you shall be called the repairer of the breach, the restorer of streets to dwell in. 13 "If you turn back your foot from the Sabbath, from doing your pleasure on My holy day, and call the Sabbath a delight and the holy day of the LORD honorable; if you honor it, not going your own ways, or seeking your own pleasure, or talking idly, 14 then you shall take delight in the LORD, and I will make you ride on the heights of the earth; I will feed you with the heritage of Jacob your father, for the mouth of the LORD has spoken."

CHAPTER 59

1 Behold, the LORD's hand is not shortened, that it cannot save, or His ear dull, that it cannot hear; 2 but your iniquities have made a separation between you and your God, and your sins have hidden His face from you so that He does not hear. 3 For your hands are defiled with blood and your fingers with iniquity; your lips have spoken lies; your tongue mutters wickedness. 4 No one enters suit justly, no one goes to law honestly; they rely on empty pleas, they speak lies; they conceive mischief and give birth to iniquity. 5 They hatch adders' eggs and weave the spider's web; he who eats their eggs dies, and from one that is crushed a viper is hatched. 6 Their webs will not serve as clothing; men will not cover themselves with what they make. Their works are works of iniquity, and deeds of violence are in their hands. 7 Their feet run to evil, and they make haste to shed innocent blood; their thoughts are thoughts of iniquity; desolation and destruction are in their highways. 8 The way of peace they do not know, and there is no justice in their paths; they have made their roads crooked; no one who treads on them knows peace. 9 Therefore justice is far from us, and righteousness does not overtake us; we hope for light, and behold, darkness; for brightness, but we walk in gloom. 10 We grope for the wall like the blind; we grope like those who have no eyes; we stumble at noon as in the twilight, among those in full vigor we are like dead men. 11 We all growl like bears; we moan and moan like doves; we hope for justice, but there is none; for

salvation, but it is far from us. 12 For our transgressions are multiplied before You, and our sins testify against us; for our transgressions are with us, and we know our iniquities: 13 transgression and denial of the LORD, and turning back from following our God, speaking oppression and revolt, conceiving and uttering from the heart lying words. 14 Justice is turned back, and righteousness stands far away; for truth has stumbled in the public squares, and uprightness cannot enter. 15 Truth is lacking, and he who departs from evil makes himself a prey. The LORD saw it, and it displeased Him that there was no justice. 16 He saw that there was no man, and wondered that there was no one to intercede; then His own arm brought Him salvation, and His righteousness upheld Him. 17 He put on righteousness as a breastplate, and a helmet of salvation on His head; He put on garments of vengeance for clothing, and wrapped Himself in zeal as a cloak. 18 According to their deeds, so will He repay, wrath to His adversaries, repayment to His enemies; to the coastlands He will render repayment. 19 So they shall fear the name of the LORD from the west, and His glory from the rising of the sun; for He will come like a rushing stream, which the wind of the LORD drives. 20 "And a Redeemer will come to Zion, to those in Jacob who turn from transgression," declares the LORD. 21 "And as for Me, this is My covenant with them," says the LORD: "My Spirit that is upon you, and My words that I have put in your mouth, shall not depart out of your mouth, or out of the mouth of your offspring, or out of the mouth of your children's offspring," says the LORD, "from this time forth and forevermore."

Chapter 60

1. Arise, O Jerusalem; shine, for your light has come, and the glory of the Lord has risen upon you. 2. For behold, darkness shall cover the earth, and nations shall be deeply darkened; but the LORD shall rise upon you, and His glory shall be seen upon you. 3. Nations shall walk in your light, and kings in the splendor of your rising. 4. Lift up your eyes round about and see: all these gather and come to you; your sons shall come from afar, and your daughters shall be nursed at your side. 5. Then you shall see and shine; your heart shall be amazed and enlarged, for the multitude of the sea shall gather to you, and the riches of the Gentiles shall come to you. 6. The multitude of camels shall cover you, the dromedaries of Midian and Ephah; all those from Sheba shall come; they shall bring gold and frankincense and proclaim the praises of the LORD. 7. All the flocks of Kedar shall be gathered to you; the rams of Nebaioth shall serve you; they shall be accepted on my altar, and I will beautify the house of my glory. 8. Who are these who fly like clouds and like doves to their windows? 9. Surely the isles shall wait for me, and the ships of Tarshish, as in the beginning, to bring your sons from afar, their silver and gold with them, for the Name of the LORD your God, and for the Holy One of Israel, because He has glorified you. 10. The sons of foreigners shall build your walls, and their kings shall minister to you; for in my wrath I struck you, but in my mercy I have had compassion on you. 11. Therefore your gates shall always be open; they shall not be shut day or night, so that men may bring to you the riches of the Gentiles, and that their kings may be brought. 12. For the nation and kingdom that will not serve you shall perish, and those nations shall be utterly destroyed. 13. The glory of Lebanon shall come to you, the fir tree, the pine, and the box tree together, to beautify the place of my sanctuary, and I will glorify the place of my feet. 14. The children also of those who have afflicted you shall come and bow down before you; and all those

who have despised you shall fall at your feet; and they shall call you, "The city of the LORD, Zion of the Holy One of Israel." 15. If you have been forsaken and hated, so that no one has passed through you, I will make you an everlasting glory, a joy from generation to generation. 16. You shall also suck the milk of the Gentiles and nurse at the breasts of kings; and you shall know that I, the LORD, am your Savior and your Redeemer, the Mighty One of Jacob. 17. For bronze I will bring gold, for iron I will bring silver, for wood bronze, and for stones iron. I will also make your officers peace, and your taskmasters righteousness. 18. Violence shall no longer be heard in your land, nor devastation or destruction within your borders; but you shall call your walls Salvation, and your gates Praise. 19. No longer will the sun be your light by day, nor will the brightness of the moon give you light; for the LORD will be your everlasting light, and your God your glory. 20. Your sun shall never set, and your moon shall not wane; for the LORD will be your everlasting light, and the days of your sorrow shall end. 21. Your people also shall all be righteous; they shall inherit the land forever; the branch of my planting, the work of my hands, that I may be glorified. 22. The smallest one shall become a thousand, and the least one a strong nation; I, the LORD, will hasten it in its time

Chapter 61

1. The Spirit of the Lord GOD is upon me, because the LORD has anointed me to bring good news to the poor; He has sent me to heal the brokenhearted, to proclaim liberty to the captives, and the opening of the prison to those who are bound, 2. To proclaim the acceptable year of the LORD and the day of vengeance of our God; to comfort all who mourn, 3. To console those who mourn in Zion, to give them beauty for ashes, the oil of joy for mourning, the garment of praise for the spirit of heaviness; that they may be called trees of righteousness, the planting of the LORD, that He may be glorified. 4. They shall rebuild the old ruins, they shall raise up the former desolations, and they shall repair the ruined cities, the desolations of many generations. 5. Strangers shall stand and feed your flocks, and the sons of foreigners shall be your plowmen and your vinedressers. 6. But you shall be named the priests of the LORD; they shall call you the servants of our God. You shall eat the riches of the Gentiles, and in their glory you shall boast. 7. Instead of your shame you shall have double honor, and instead of confusion they shall rejoice in their portion; therefore in their land they shall possess double; everlasting joy shall be theirs. 8. For I, the LORD, love justice; I hate robbery for burnt offering; I will direct their work in truth, and I will make an everlasting covenant with them. 9. Their descendants shall be known among the Gentiles, and their offspring among the people. All who see them shall acknowledge them, that they are the posterity whom the LORD has blessed. 10. I will greatly rejoice in the LORD, my soul shall be joyful in my God; for He has clothed me with the garments of salvation, He has covered me with the robe of righteousness, as a bridegroom decks himself with ornaments, and as a bride adorns herself with jewels. 11. For as the earth brings forth its bud, as the garden causes the things sown in it to spring forth, so the Lord GOD will cause righteousness and praise to spring forth before all the nations

Chapter 62

1. For Zion's sake I will not hold my peace, and for Jerusalem's sake I will not rest, until her righteousness goes forth as brightness, and her salvation as a lamp that burns. 2. The nations shall see your righteousness, and all kings your glory; and you shall be called by a new name, which the mouth of the LORD will name. 3. You shall also be a crown of glory in the hand of the LORD, and a royal diadem in the hand of your God. 4. No longer shall it be said of you, "Forsaken," nor shall it be said of your land, "Desolate"; but you shall be called Hephzibah, and your land Beulah; for the LORD delights in you, and your land shall be married. 5. For as a young man marries a virgin, so shall your sons marry you; and as the bridegroom rejoices over the bride, so shall your God rejoice over you. 6. I have set watchmen on your walls, O Jerusalem; they shall never hold their peace day or night. You who make mention of the LORD, do not keep silent, 7. And give Him no rest till He establishes and till He makes Jerusalem a praise in the earth. 8. The LORD has sworn by His right hand and by the arm of His strength, "Surely I will no longer give your grain as food for your enemies, and the sons of the foreigner shall not drink your new wine, for which you have labored." 9. But those who have gathered it shall eat it, and praise the LORD; those who have brought it together shall drink it in My holy courts. 10. Go through, go through the gates! Prepare the way for the people; build up, build up the highway! Take out the stones, lift up a banner for the peoples! 11. Indeed the LORD has proclaimed to the end of the world: "Say to the daughter of Zion, 'Surely your salvation is coming; behold, His reward is with Him, and His work before Him.'" 12. And they shall call them the Holy People, the Redeemed of the LORD; and you shall be called Sought Out, A City Not Forsaken

Chapter 63

1. Who is this who comes from Edom, with dyed garments from Bozrah? This One who is glorious in His apparel, traveling in the greatness of His strength? "I who speak in righteousness, mighty to save." 2. Why is Your apparel red, and Your garments like one who treads in the winepress? 3. "I have trodden the winepress alone, and from the peoples no one was with Me. For I have trodden them in My anger, and trampled them in My fury; their blood is sprinkled upon My garments, and I have stained all My robes. 4. For the day of vengeance is in My heart, and the year of My redeemed has come. 5. I looked, but there was no one to help; and I wondered that there was no one to uphold; therefore My own arm brought salvation for Me; and My own fury, it sustained Me. 6. I have trodden down the peoples in My anger, made them drunk in My fury, and brought down their strength to the earth." 7. I will mention the lovingkindnesses of the LORD and the praises of the LORD, according to all that the LORD has bestowed on us, and the great goodness toward the house of Israel, which He has bestowed on them according to His mercies, according to the multitude of His lovingkindnesses. 8. For He said, "Surely they are My people, children who will not lie." So He became their Savior. 9. In all their affliction He was afflicted, and the angel of His presence saved them; in His love and in His pity He redeemed them; and He bore them and carried them all the days of old. 10. But they rebelled and grieved His Holy Spirit; so He turned Himself against them as an enemy, and He fought against them. 11. Then he remembered the days of old, Moses and his people, saying: "Where is He who brought them up out of the sea with the shepherd of His flock? Where is He who put His Holy Spirit within them, 12. Who led them by the right hand of Moses, with His glorious arm, dividing the water before them to make for Himself an everlasting name, 13. Who led them through the deep, as a horse in the wilderness, that they might not stumble?" 14. As a beast goes down into the valley, and the Spirit of the LORD causes him to rest, so You lead Your people, to make

Yourself a glorious name. 15. Look down from heaven, and see from Your habitation, holy and glorious. Where are Your zeal and Your strength, the yearning of Your heart and Your mercies toward me? Are they restrained? 16. Doubtless You are our Father, though Abraham was ignorant of us, and Israel does not acknowledge us. You, O LORD, are our Father; our Redeemer from everlasting is Your name. 17. O LORD, why have You made us stray from Your ways, and hardened our heart from Your fear? Return for Your servants' sake, the tribes of Your inheritance. 18. Your holy people have possessed it but a little while; our adversaries have trodden down Your sanctuary. 19. We have become like those of old over whom You never ruled, those who were not called by Your name

Chapter 64

1. Oh, that You would rend the heavens! That You would come down! That the mountains might shake at Your presence— 2. As fire burns brushwood, as fire causes water to boil— to make Your name known to Your adversaries, that the nations may tremble at Your presence! 3. When You did awesome things for which we did not look, You came down, the mountains shook at Your presence. 4. For since the beginning of the world men have not heard nor perceived by the ear, nor has the eye seen any God besides You, who acts for the one who waits for Him. 5. You meet him who rejoices and does righteousness, who remembers You in Your ways. You are indeed angry, for we have sinned; in these ways we continue, and we need to be saved. 6. But we are all like an unclean thing, and all our righteousnesses are like filthy rags; we all fade as a leaf, and our iniquities, like the wind, have taken us away. 7. And there is no one who calls on Your name, who stirs himself up to take hold of You; for You have hidden Your face from us, and have consumed us because of our iniquities. 8. But now, O LORD, You are our Father; we are the clay, and You our Potter; and all we are the work of Your hand. 9. Do not be furious, O LORD, nor remember iniquity forever; indeed, please look—we all are Your people! 10. Your holy cities are a wilderness, Zion is a wilderness, Jerusalem a desolation. 11. Our holy and beautiful temple, where our fathers praised You, is burned up with fire; and all our pleasant things are laid waste. 12. Will You restrain Yourself because of these things, O LORD? Will You hold Your peace and afflict us very severely?

Chapter 65

1. I was sought by those who did not ask for me; I was found by those who did not seek me. I said, "Here I am, here I am," to a nation that was not called by my name. 2. I stretched out my hands all day long to a rebellious people who walk in ways that are not good, following their own thoughts. 3. A people who provoke me to anger continually to my face, who sacrifice in gardens and burn incense on bricks. 4. Who stay among the graves and spend the night in secret places; who eat the flesh of pigs and whose pots hold broth of abominable things. 5. Who say, "Keep to yourself, do not come near me, for I am holier than you." These are smoke in my nostrils, a fire that burns all day long. 6. Behold, it is written before me: I will not keep silent, but I will repay, even repay into their bosom. 7. Your iniquities and the iniquities of your fathers shall be gathered together, says the LORD, who have burned incense on the mountains and blasphemed me on the hills; therefore, I will measure their former deeds into their bosom. 8. Thus says the LORD: "As the new wine is found in the cluster, and one says, 'Do not destroy it, for there is blessing in it,' so will I do for my servants' sake, and not destroy them all. 9. I will bring forth descendants from Jacob and from Judah, inheritors of my mountains; my elect shall inherit it, and my servants shall dwell there. 10. Sharon shall be a fold for flocks, and the valley of Achor a resting place for cattle for my people who have sought me. 11. But you who forsake the LORD, who forget my holy mountain, who prepare a table for Fortune and offer mixed wine to Destiny, 12. I will destine you to the sword, and you shall all bow down to the slaughter, because when I called, you did not answer; when I spoke, you did not hear. But you did evil in my sight and chose what I did not delight in. 13. Therefore thus says the LORD God: "Behold, my servants shall eat, but you shall be hungry; behold, my servants shall drink, but you shall be thirsty; behold, my servants shall rejoice, but you shall be ashamed. 14. Behold, my servants shall sing for joy of heart, but you shall cry for sorrow of heart and wail for anguish of spirit. 15. And you shall leave your name as a curse to my chosen ones; for the LORD God will slay you and call his servants by another name. 16. So that he who blesses himself in the earth shall bless himself by the true God; and he who swears in the earth shall swear by the true God; for the former troubles are forgotten, and they are hidden from my eyes. 17. For behold, I create new heavens and a new earth; and the former shall not be remembered or come to mind. 18. But be glad and rejoice forever in what I create; for behold, I create Jerusalem as a joy, and her people as a joy. 19. I will rejoice in Jerusalem and joy in my people; and the voice of weeping shall no longer be heard in her, nor the voice of crying. 20. No more shall there be in it an infant who lives but a few days, or an old man who does not fill his days; for the child shall die one hundred years old, but the sinner being one hundred years old shall be accursed. 21. They shall build houses and inhabit them; they shall plant vineyards and eat their fruit. 22. They shall not build and another inhabit; they shall not plant and another eat; for as the days of a tree, so shall be the days of my people, and my chosen ones shall long enjoy the work of their hands. 23. They shall not labor in vain, nor bring forth children for trouble; for they shall be the descendants of the blessed of the LORD, and their offspring with them. 24. It shall come to pass that before they call, I will answer; and while they are yet speaking, I will hear. 25. The wolf and the lamb shall feed together, and the lion shall eat straw like the ox; and dust shall be the serpent's food. They shall not hurt nor destroy in all my holy mountain," says the LORD

Chapter 66

1. Thus says the LORD: "Heaven is my throne, and the earth is my footstool. Where is the house that you will build for me? And where is the place of my rest? 2. For all those things my hand has made, and all those things exist," says the LORD. "But to this one will I look: to him who is poor and of a contrite spirit, and who trembles at my word. 3. He who kills a bull is as if he slays a man; he who sacrifices a lamb, as if he breaks a dog's neck; he who offers a grain offering, as if he offers swine's blood; he who burns incense, as if he blesses an idol. Yes, they have chosen their own ways, and their soul delights in their abominations. 4. So will I choose their delusions and bring their fears upon them, because when I called, no one answered; when I spoke, they did not hear. But they did evil before my eyes and chose that in which I do not delight." 5. Hear the word of the LORD, you who tremble at his word: "Your brethren who hated you, who cast you out for my name's sake, said, 'Let the LORD be glorified, that we may see your joy.' But they shall be ashamed." 6. A voice of noise from the city, a voice from the temple, the voice of the LORD who fully repays his enemies.

7. "Before she was in labor, she gave birth; before her pain came, she delivered a male child. 8. Who has heard such a thing? Who has seen such things? Shall the earth be made to give birth in one day? Or shall a nation be born at once? For as soon as Zion was in labor, she gave birth to her children. 9. Shall I bring to the birth, and not cause to bring forth?" says the LORD. "Shall I who cause delivery shut up the womb?" says your God. 10. Rejoice with Jerusalem, and be glad with her, all you who love her; rejoice for joy with her, all you who mourn for her. 11. That you may nurse and be satisfied with the consolation of her bosom, that you may drink deeply and be delighted with the abundance of her glory. 12. For thus says the LORD: "Behold, I will extend peace to her like a river, and the glory of the Gentiles like a flowing stream. Then you shall feed, you shall be carried on her sides, and be dandled on her knees. 13. As one whom his mother comforts, so I will comfort you; and you shall be comforted in Jerusalem. 14. When you see this, your heart shall rejoice, and your bones shall flourish like grass; and the hand of the LORD shall be known to his servants, and his indignation to his enemies. 15. For behold, the LORD will come with fire and with his chariots like a whirlwind, to render his anger with fury, and his rebuke with flames of fire. 16. For by fire and by his sword the LORD will judge all flesh; and the slain of the LORD shall be many. 17. Those who sanctify themselves and purify themselves to go to the gardens, after an idol in the midst, eating swine's flesh and the abomination and the mouse, shall be consumed together," says the LORD. 18. "For I know their works and their thoughts. It shall be that I will gather all nations and tongues; and they shall come and see my glory. 19. I will set a sign among them, and those among them who escape I will send to the nations: to Tarshish and Pul and Lud, who draw the bow, and to Tubal and Javan, to the coastlands afar off, who have not heard my fame nor seen my glory; and they shall declare my glory among the Gentiles. 20. Then they shall bring all your brethren for an offering to the LORD, out of all nations, on horses and in chariots, and in litters, on mules and on swift beasts, to my holy mountain, Jerusalem," says the LORD, "as the children of Israel bring an offering in a clean vessel into the house of the LORD. 21. And I will also take some of them for priests and Levites," says the LORD. 22. "For as the new heavens and the new earth which I will make shall remain before me," says the LORD, "so shall your descendants and your name remain. 23. And it shall come to pass that from one New Moon to another, and from one Sabbath to another, all flesh shall come to worship before me," says the LORD. 24. "And they shall go forth and look upon the corpses of the men who have transgressed against me. For their worm does not die, and their fire is not quenched; they shall be an abhorrence to all flesh."

24. Jeremiah

Chapter 1

The words of Jeremiah, son of Hilkiah, one of the priests who stood in Anathoth, in the land of Benjamin. The word of the LORD came to him during the days of Josiah, son of Amon, king of Judah, in the thirteenth year of his reign. It also came during the days of Jehoiakim, son of Josiah, king of Judah, until the end of the eleventh year of Zedekiah, son of Josiah, king of Judah, until the people of Jerusalem were taken into captivity in the fifth month. The word of the LORD came to me, saying, "Before I formed you in the womb I knew you, and before you were born I sanctified you and appointed you as a prophet to the nations." Then I said, "Lord God, behold, I cannot speak, for I am a child." But the LORD said to me, "Do not say, 'I am a child,' for you shall go to all whom I send you, and you shall speak whatever I command you. Do not be afraid of their faces, for I am with you to deliver you," says the LORD. Then the Lord stretched out His hand and touched my mouth, and said to me, "Behold, I have put My words in your mouth. Today I appoint you over nations and kingdoms, to uproot and tear down, to destroy and overthrow, to build and to plant." After this, the word of the LORD came to me, saying, "Jeremiah, what do you see?" I answered, "I see a branch of an almond tree." Then the Lord said to me, "You have seen well, for I am watching to ensure that My word is fulfilled." The word of the LORD came to me a second time, saying, "What do you see?" I said, "I see a boiling pot, tilting away from the north." The LORD said to me, "From the north disaster will be poured out on all who live in the land. I am calling all the peoples of the northern kingdoms," declares the LORD. "Their kings will come and set up their thrones in the entrance of the gates of Jerusalem; they will come against all her surrounding walls and against all the towns of Judah. I will pronounce My judgments on My people because of their wickedness in forsaking Me, in burning incense to other gods and in worshiping what their hands have made "But you, get yourself ready! Stand up and say to them whatever I command you. Do not be terrified by them, or I will terrify you before them. Today I have made you a fortified city, an iron pillar, and a bronze wall to stand against the whole land—against the kings of Judah, its officials, its priests, and the people of the land. They will fight against you but will not overcome you, for I am with you to rescue you," declares the LORD

Chapter 2

The word of the LORD came to me, saying, "Go and proclaim in the hearing of Jerusalem: 'This is what the LORD says: "I remember the devotion of your youth, how as a bride you loved Me and followed Me through the wilderness, through a land not sown. Israel was holy to the LORD, the firstfruits of His harvest; all who devoured her were held guilty, and disaster overtook them," declares the LORD Hear the word of the LORD, house of Jacob, all you clans of the house of Israel. This is what the LORD says: "What fault did your ancestors find in Me, that they strayed so far from Me? They followed worthless idols and became worthless themselves. They did not ask, 'Where is the LORD, who brought us up out of Egypt and led us through the barren wilderness, through a land of deserts and ravines, a land of drought and utter darkness, a land where no one travels and no one lives?' I brought you into a fertile land to eat its fruit and rich produce. But you came and defiled My land and made My inheritance detestable. The priests did not ask, 'Where is the LORD?' Those who deal with the law did not know Me; the leaders rebelled against Me. The prophets prophesied by Baal, following worthless idols Therefore I bring charges against you again," declares the LORD. "And I will bring charges against your children's children. Cross over to the coasts of Cyprus and look, send to Kedar and observe closely; see if there has ever been anything like this: Has a nation ever changed its gods? (Yet they are not gods at all.) But My people have exchanged their glorious God for worthless idols. Be appalled at this, you heavens, and shudder with great horror," declares the LORD. "My people have committed two sins: They have forsaken Me, the spring of living water, and have dug their own cisterns, broken cisterns that cannot hold water Is Israel a servant, a slave by birth? Why then has he become plunder? Lions have roared; they have growled at him. They have laid waste his land; his towns are burned and deserted. Also, the men of Memphis and Tahpanhes have cracked your skull. Have you not brought this on yourselves by forsaking the LORD your God when He led you in the way? Now why go to Egypt to drink water from the Nile? And why go to Assyria to drink water from the Euphrates? Your wickedness will punish you; your backsliding will rebuke you. Consider then and realize how evil and bitter it is for you when you forsake the LORD your God and have no awe of Me," declares the Lord, the LORD Almighty "Long ago you broke off your yoke and tore off your bonds; you said, 'I will not serve you!' Indeed, on every high hill and under every spreading tree you lay down as a prostitute. I had planted you like a choice vine of sound and reliable stock. How then did you turn against Me into a corrupt, wild vine? Although you wash yourself with soap and use an abundance of cleansing powder, the stain of your guilt is still before Me," declares the Sovereign LORD "How can you say, 'I am not defiled; I have not run after the Baals'? See how you behaved in the valley; consider what you have done. You are a swift she-camel running here and there, a wild donkey accustomed to the desert, sniffing the wind in her craving—in her heat, who can restrain her? Any males that pursue her need not tire themselves; at mating time they will find her. Do not run until your feet are bare and your throat is dry. But you said, 'It's no use! I love foreign gods, and I must go after them.' "As a thief is disgraced when he is caught, so the people of Israel are disgraced—they, their kings and their officials, their priests and their prophets. They say to wood, 'You are my father,' and to stone, 'You gave me birth.' They have turned their backs to Me and not their faces; yet when they are in trouble, they say, 'Come and save us!' Where then are the gods you made for yourselves? Let them come if they can save you when you are in trouble! For you, Judah, have as many gods as you have towns "Why do you bring charges against Me? You have all rebelled against Me," declares the LORD. "In vain I punished your people; they did not respond to correction. Your sword has devoured your prophets like a ravenous lion. You of this generation, consider the word of the LORD: 'Have I been a desert to Israel or a land of great darkness? Why do My people say, "We are free to roam; we will come to You no more"? Does a young woman forget her jewelry, a bride her wedding ornaments? Yet My people have forgotten Me, days without number. How skilled you are at pursuing love! Even the worst of women can learn from your ways. On your clothes is found the lifeblood of the innocent poor, though you did not catch them breaking in. Yet in spite of all this, you say, "I am innocent; He is not angry with me." But I will pass judgment on you because you say, "I have not sinned." Why do you go about so much, changing your ways? You will be disappointed by Egypt as you were by Assyria. You will also leave that place with your hands on your head, for the LORD has rejected those you trust; you will not be helped by them

Chapter 3

"If a man divorces his wife and she leaves him and marries another man, should he return to her again? Would not the land be completely defiled? But you have lived as a prostitute with many lovers—would you now return to Me?" declares the LORD. "Look up to the barren heights and see. Is there any place where you have not been ravished? By the roadside you sat waiting for lovers, sat like a nomad in the desert. You have defiled the land with your prostitution and wickedness. Therefore the showers have been withheld, and no spring rains have fallen. Yet you have the brazen look of a prostitute; you refuse to blush with shame. Have you not just called to Me: 'My Father, my friend from my youth, will you always be angry? Will your wrath continue forever?' This is how you talk, but you do all the evil you can." During the reign of King Josiah, the LORD said to me, "Have you seen what faithless Israel has done? She has gone up on every high hill and under every spreading tree and has committed adultery there. I thought that after she had done all this, she would return to Me, but she did not, and her unfaithful sister Judah saw it. I gave faithless Israel her certificate of divorce and sent her away because of all her adulteries. Yet I saw that her unfaithful sister Judah had no fear; she also went out and committed adultery. Because Israel's immorality mattered so little to her, she defiled the land and committed adultery with stone and wood. In spite of all this, her unfaithful sister Judah did not return to Me with all her heart, but only in pretense," declares the LORD The LORD said to me, "Faithless Israel is more righteous than unfaithful Judah. Go, proclaim this message toward the north: 'Return, faithless Israel,' declares the LORD, 'I will frown on you no longer, for I am faithful,' declares the LORD, 'I will not be angry forever. Only acknowledge your guilt—you have rebelled against the LORD your God, you have scattered your favors to foreign gods under every spreading tree, and have not obeyed Me,'" declares the LORD "Return, faithless people," declares the LORD, "for I am your husband. I will choose you—one from a town and two from a clan—and bring you to Zion. Then I will give you shepherds after My own heart, who will lead you with knowledge and understanding. In those days, when your numbers have increased greatly in the land," declares the LORD, "people will no longer say, 'The ark of the covenant of the LORD.' It will never enter their minds or be remembered; it will not be missed, nor will another one be made. At that time they will call Jerusalem The Throne of the LORD, and all nations will gather in Jerusalem to honor the name of the LORD. No longer will they follow the stubbornness of their evil hearts. In those days the people of Judah will join the people of Israel, and together they will come from a northern land to the land I gave your ancestors as an inheritance "I myself said, 'How gladly would I treat you like my children and give you a pleasant land, the most beautiful inheritance of any nation.' I thought you would call me 'Father' and not turn away from following me. But like a woman unfaithful to her husband, so you, Israel, have been unfaithful to me," declares the LORD A cry is heard on the barren heights, the weeping and pleading of the people of Israel, because they have perverted their ways and have forgotten the LORD their God. "Return, faithless people; I will cure you of backsliding." "Yes, we will come to you, for you are the LORD our God. Surely the idolatrous commotion on the hills and mountains is a deception; surely in the LORD our God is the salvation of Israel. From our youth shameful gods have consumed the fruits of our ancestors' labor—their flocks and herds, their sons and daughters. Let us lie down in our shame, and let our disgrace cover us. We have sinned against the LORD our God, both we and our ancestors; from our youth till this day we have not obeyed the LORD our God."

Chapter 4

"If you, Israel, will return, then return to Me," declares the LORD. "If you put your detestable idols out of My sight and no longer go astray, and if in a truthful, just, and righteous way you swear, 'As surely as the LORD lives,' then the nations will invoke blessings by Him and in Him they will boast." This is what the LORD says to the people of Judah and to Jerusalem: "Break up your unplowed ground and do not sow among thorns. Circumcise yourselves to the LORD, circumcise your hearts, you people of Judah and inhabitants of Jerusalem, or My wrath will flare up and burn like fire because of the evil you have done—burn with no one to quench it "Announce in Judah and proclaim in Jerusalem and say: 'Sound the trumpet throughout the land!' Cry aloud and say: 'Gather together! Let us flee to the fortified cities!' Raise the signal to go to Zion! Flee for safety without delay! For I am bringing disaster from the north, even terrible destruction." A lion has come out of his lair; a destroyer of nations has set out. He has left his place to lay waste your land. Your towns will lie in ruins without inhabitant. So put on sackcloth, lament and wail, for the fierce anger of the LORD has not turned away from us "In that day," declares the LORD, "the king and the officials will lose heart, the priests will be horrified, and the prophets will be appalled." Then I said, "Alas, Sovereign LORD! How completely you have deceived this people and Jerusalem by saying, 'You will have peace,' when the sword is at our throats!" At that time this people and Jerusalem will be told, "A scorching wind from the barren heights in the desert blows toward my people, but not to winnow or cleanse; a wind too strong for that comes from me. Now I pronounce my judgments against them." Look! He advances like the clouds, his chariots come like a whirlwind, his horses are swifter than eagles. Woe to us! We are ruined! Jerusalem, wash the evil from your heart and be saved. How long will you harbor wicked thoughts? A voice is announcing from Dan, proclaiming disaster from the hills of Ephraim. "Tell this to the nations, proclaim concerning Jerusalem: 'A besieging army is coming from a distant land, raising a war cry against the cities of Judah. They surround her like men guarding a field, because she has rebelled against Me,'" declares the LORD. "Your own conduct and actions have brought this on you. This is your punishment. How bitter it is! How it pierces to the heart!" Oh, my anguish, my anguish! I writhe in pain. Oh, the agony of my heart! My heart pounds within me, I cannot keep silent. For I have heard the sound of the trumpet; I have heard the battle cry. Disaster follows disaster; the whole land lies in ruins. In an instant my tents are destroyed, my shelter in a moment. How long must I see the battle standard and hear the sound of the trumpet? "My people are fools; they do not know Me. They are senseless children; they have no understanding. They are skilled in doing evil; they know not how to do good." I looked at the earth, and it was formless and empty; and at the heavens, and their light was gone. I looked at the mountains, and they were quaking; all the hills were swaying. I looked, and there were no people; every bird in the sky had flown away. I looked, and the fruitful land was a desert; all its towns lay in ruins before the LORD, before His fierce anger This is what the LORD says: "The whole land will be ruined, though I will not destroy it completely. Therefore the earth will mourn and the heavens above grow dark, because I have spoken and will not relent, I have decided and will not turn back." At the sound of horsemen and archers every town takes to flight. Some go into the thickets; some climb up among the rocks. All the towns are deserted; no one lives in them. What are you doing, you devastated one? Why dress yourself in scarlet and put on jewels of gold? Why highlight your eyes with makeup? You adorn yourself in vain. Your lovers despise you; they want to kill you. I hear a cry as of a woman in labor, a groan as of one bearing her first child—the cry of Daughter Zion gasping for breath, stretching out her hands and saying, "Alas! I am fainting; my life is given over to murderers."

Chapter 5

"Go up and down the streets of Jerusalem, look around and consider, search through her squares. If you can find but one person who deals honestly and seeks the truth, I will forgive this city. Although they say, 'As surely as the LORD lives,' still they are swearing falsely." LORD, do not Your eyes look for truth? You struck them, but they felt no pain; You crushed them, but they refused correction. They made their faces harder than stone and refused to repent. I thought, "These are only the poor; they are foolish, for they do not know the way of the LORD, the requirements of their God. So I will go to the leaders and speak to them; surely they know the way of the LORD, the requirements of their God." But with one accord they too had broken off the yoke and torn off the bonds Therefore a lion from the forest will attack them, a wolf from the desert will ravage them, a leopard will lie in wait near their towns to tear to pieces any who venture out, for their rebellion is great and their backslidings many. "Why should I forgive you? Your children have forsaken Me and sworn by gods that are not gods. I supplied all their needs, yet they committed adultery and thronged to the houses of prostitutes. They are well-fed, lusty stallions, each neighing for another man's wife. Should I not punish them for this?" declares the LORD. "Should I not avenge Myself on such a nation as this? "Go through her vineyards and ravage them, but do not destroy them completely. Strip off her branches, for these people do not belong to the LORD. The people of Israel and the people of Judah have been utterly unfaithful to Me," declares the LORD. They have lied about the LORD; they said, "He will do nothing! No harm will come to us; we will never see sword or famine. The prophets are but wind and the word is not in them; so let what they say be done to them." Therefore this is what the LORD God Almighty says: "Because the people have spoken these words, I will make My words in your mouth a fire and these people the wood it consumes. People of Israel," declares the LORD, "I am bringing a distant nation against you—an ancient and enduring nation, a people whose language you do not know, whose speech you do not understand. Their quivers are like an open grave; all of them are mighty warriors. They will devour your harvests and food, devour your sons and daughters; they will devour your flocks and herds, devour your vines and fig trees. With the sword they will destroy the fortified cities in which you trust "Yet even in those days," declares the LORD, "I will not destroy you completely. And when the people ask, 'Why has the LORD our God done all this to us?' you will tell them, 'As you have forsaken Me and served foreign gods in your own land, so now you will serve foreigners in a land not your own.' "Announce this to the descendants of Jacob and proclaim it in Judah: Hear this, you foolish and senseless people, who have eyes but do not see, who have ears but do not hear: Should you not fear Me?" declares the LORD. "Should you not tremble in My presence? I made the sand a boundary for the sea, an everlasting barrier it cannot cross. The waves may roll, but they cannot prevail; they may roar, but they cannot cross it. But these people have stubborn and rebellious hearts; they have turned aside and gone away. They do not say to themselves, 'Let us fear the LORD our God, who gives autumn and spring rains in season, who assures us of the regular weeks of harvest.' Your wrongdoings have kept these away; your sins have deprived you of good "Among My people are the wicked who lie in wait like men who snare birds and like those who set traps to catch people. Like cages full of birds, their houses are full of deceit; they have become rich and powerful and have grown fat and sleek. Their evil deeds have no limit; they do not seek justice. They do not promote the case of the fatherless; they do not defend the just cause of the poor. Should I not punish them for this?" declares the LORD. "Should I not avenge Myself on such a nation as this? "A horrible and shocking thing has happened in the land: The prophets prophesy lies, the priests rule by their own authority, and My people love it this way. But what will you do in the end?"

Chapter 6

O sons of Benjamin, prepare to flee from the pits of Jerusalem and sound the trumpet in Tekoa; set up a foothold in Beth-Haccerem, for a plague and great destruction appear from the north. I likened the daughter of Zion to a beautiful and gracious woman. The shepherds with their flocks will come to her; they will pitch their tents around her, and everyone will graze in his place. Prepare war against her; arise and go toward the south. Woe to her, for the day is declining, and the shadows of the sunset are lengthening. Arise, let us go forth by night and destroy her palaces. For thus says the LORD of hosts: "Break down the wood and cast a mountain against Jerusalem; this city must be visited; all oppression is in the midst of it. As a fountain casts out its waters, so she casts out her wickedness; cruelty and wickedness continually make themselves felt in her before Me with pains and blows. Be instructed, O Jerusalem, lest My soul depart from thee, lest I make thee desolate as a land that no man inhabiteth." Thus says the LORD of hosts, "You shall gather like a vine the remnant of Israel; withdraw your hand as the harvester gathers grapes into the baskets." To whom shall I speak and admonish that they may hear? Behold, their ears are uncircumcised, and they cannot hear; the word of the LORD is to them a reproach; they have no pleasure in it. Therefore, I am full of the wrath of the LORD; I am weary of holding it in. I will pour it out upon the children in the streets and upon the assembly of the young men; for both husband and wife shall be taken, and the elder with him that is full of years. Their houses, their fields, and their wives shall be delivered to strangers, for I will stretch out My hand against the inhabitants of the land," says the LORD. "For from the least of them to the greatest, everyone is given to corruption, and from the prophet to the priest, they all deal falsely. They have healed the wounds of the daughter of My people lightly, saying, 'Peace, peace,' when there is no peace. Were they ashamed when they committed the abomination? No, they were not ashamed, nor could they blush; therefore, they shall fall among the fallen. At the time that I punish them, they shall be overthrown," says the LORD Thus says the LORD, "Stand by the crossroads and look, and ask for the ancient paths, where the good way is, and walk in it, and you will find rest for your souls. But they said, 'We will not walk in it.' I set watchmen over you, saying, 'Pay attention to the sound of the trumpet!' But they said, 'We will not pay attention.' Therefore, hear, O nations, and know, O congregation, what will happen to them. Hear, O earth, behold, I am bringing disaster upon this people, the fruit of their thoughts, because they have not heeded My words and have rejected My law. What purpose to Me is frankincense that comes from Sheba or sweet cane from a distant land? Your burnt offerings are not acceptable, nor your sacrifices pleasing to Me." Therefore, thus says the LORD, "Behold, I will lay stumbling blocks before this people; fathers and sons together shall stumble over them; neighbor and friend shall perish." Thus says the LORD, "Behold, a people is coming from the north country, and a great nation is stirring from the farthest parts of the earth. They grasp the bow and javelin; they are cruel and have no mercy. Their voice roars like the sea; they ride upon horses, set in array as a man for battle against you, O daughter of Zion!" We have heard the report of them; our hands fall helpless; anguish has taken hold of us, pain as of a woman in labor. Go not out into the field, nor walk on the road, for the enemy has a sword; terror is on every side. O daughter of My people, put on sackcloth and roll in ashes; make mourning as for an only son, most bitter lamentation, for suddenly the destroyer will come upon us I have made you a tester of metals among My people, that you may know and test their ways. They are all stubbornly rebellious, going about with slanders; they are bronze and iron; all of them act corruptly. The bellows blow fiercely; the lead is consumed by the fire; in vain the refining goes on, for the wicked are not removed. Rejected silver they are called, for the LORD has rejected them

Chapter 7

The word that came to Jeremiah from the LORD: "Stand in the gate of the LORD's house and proclaim this word: 'Hear the word of the LORD, all you men of Judah who enter these gates to worship the LORD. Thus says the LORD of hosts, the God of Israel: Amend your ways and your deeds, and I will let you dwell in this place. Do not trust in deceptive words, saying, 'This is the temple of the LORD, the temple of the LORD, the temple of the LORD.' For if you truly amend your ways and your deeds, if you truly execute justice one with another, if you do not oppress the sojourner, the fatherless, or the widow, or shed innocent blood in this place, and if you do not go after other gods to your own harm, then I will let you dwell in this place, in the land that I gave of old to your fathers forever Behold, you trust in deceptive words to no avail. Will you steal, murder, commit adultery, swear falsely, make offerings to Baal, and go after other gods that you have not known, and then come and stand before Me in this house, which is called by My name, and say, 'We are delivered!'—only to go on doing all these abominations? Has this house, which is called by My name, become a den of robbers in your eyes? Behold, I Myself have seen it, declares the LORD. Go now to My place that was in Shiloh, where I made My name dwell at first, and see what I did to it because of the evil of My people Israel. And now, because you have done all these things, declares the LORD, and when I spoke to you persistently you did not listen, and when I called you, you did not answer, therefore I will do to the house that is called by My name, in which you trust, and to the place that I gave to you and to your fathers, as I did to Shiloh. And I will cast you out of My sight, as I cast out all your kinsmen, all the offspring of Ephraim As for you, do not pray for this people, or lift up a cry or prayer for them, and do not intercede with Me, for I will not hear you. Do you not see what they are doing in the cities of Judah and in the streets of Jerusalem? The children gather wood, the fathers kindle fire, and the women knead dough, to make cakes for the queen of heaven. And they pour out drink offerings to other gods, to provoke Me to anger. Is it I whom they provoke? declares the LORD. Is it not themselves, to their own shame? Therefore thus says the Lord GOD: Behold, My anger and My wrath will be poured out on this place, upon man and beast, upon the trees of the field and the fruit of the ground; it will burn and not be quenched." Thus says the LORD of hosts, the God of Israel: "Add your burnt offerings to your sacrifices, and eat the flesh. For in the day that I brought them out of the land of Egypt, I did not speak to your fathers or command them concerning burnt offerings and sacrifices. But this command I gave them: 'Obey My voice, and I will be your God, and you shall be My people. And walk in all the way that I command you, that it may be well with you.' But they did not obey or incline their ear but walked in their own counsels and the stubbornness of their evil hearts, and went backward and not forward. From the day that your fathers came out of the land of Egypt to this day, I have persistently sent all My servants the prophets to them, day after day. Yet they did not listen to Me or incline their ear but stiffened their neck. They did worse than their fathers So you shall speak all these words to them, but they will not listen to you. You shall call to them, but they will not answer you. And you shall say to them, 'This is the nation that did not obey the voice of the LORD their God and did not accept discipline; truth has perished; it is cut off from their lips. Cut off your hair and cast it away; raise a lamentation on the bare heights, for the LORD has rejected and forsaken the generation of His wrath.' For the sons of Judah have done evil in My sight, declares the LORD. They have set their abominations in the house that is called by My name, to defile it. And they have built the high places of Topheth, which is in the Valley of the Son of Hinnom, to burn their sons and their daughters in the fire, which I did not command, nor did it come into My mind. Therefore, behold, the days are coming, declares the LORD, when it will no more be called Topheth, or the Valley of the Son of Hinnom, but the Valley of Slaughter; for they will bury in Topheth, because there is no room elsewhere. And the dead bodies of this people will be food for the birds of the air, and for the beasts of the earth, and none will frighten them away. And I will silence in the cities of Judah and in the streets of Jerusalem the voice of mirth and the voice of gladness, the voice of the bridegroom and the voice of the bride, for the land shall become a waste

Chapter 8

At that time, declares the LORD, the bones of the kings of Judah, the bones of its officials, the bones of the priests, the bones of the prophets, and the bones of the inhabitants of Jerusalem shall be brought out of their tombs. And they shall be spread before the sun and the moon and all the host of heaven, which they have loved and served, which they have gone after, and which they have sought and worshiped. And they shall not be gathered or buried. They shall be as dung on the surface of the ground. Death shall be preferred to life by all the remnant that remains of this evil family in all the places where I have driven them, declares the LORD of hosts "You shall say to them, 'Thus says the LORD: When men fall, do they not rise again? If one turns away, does he not return? Why then has this people turned away in perpetual backsliding? They hold fast to deceit; they refuse to return. I have paid attention and listened, but they have not spoken rightly; no man relents of his evil, saying, "What have I done?" Everyone turns to his own course, like a horse plunging headlong into battle. Even the stork in the heavens knows her times, and the turtledove, swallow, and crane keep the time of their coming, but My people know not the rules of the LORD How can you say, "We are wise, and the law of the LORD is with us"? But behold, the lying pen of the scribes has made it into a lie. The wise men shall be put to shame; they shall be dismayed and taken; behold, they have rejected the word of the LORD, so what wisdom is in them? Therefore I will give their wives to others and their fields to conquerors because from the least to the greatest everyone is greedy for unjust gain; from prophet to priest, everyone deals falsely. They have healed the wound of My people lightly, saying, "Peace, peace," when there is no peace. Were they ashamed when they committed abomination? No,

they were not at all ashamed; they did not know how to blush. Therefore, they shall fall among the fallen; when I punish them, they shall be overthrown," says the LORD "When I would gather them, declares the LORD, there are no grapes on the vine, nor figs on the fig tree; even the leaves are withered, and what I gave them has passed away from them." Why do we sit still? Gather together; let us go into the fortified cities and perish there, for the LORD our God has doomed us to perish and has given us poisoned water to drink because we have sinned against the LORD. We looked for peace, but no good came; for a time of healing, but behold, terror. "The snorting of their horses is heard from Dan; at the sound of the neighing of their stallions the whole land quakes. They come and devour the land and all that fills it, the city and those who dwell in it. For behold, I am sending among you serpents, adders that cannot be charmed, and they shall bite you," declares the LORD My joy is gone; grief is upon me; my heart is sick within me. Behold, the cry of the daughter of My people from the length and breadth of the land: "Is the LORD not in Zion? Is her King not in her?" "Why have they provoked Me to anger with their carved images and with their foreign idols?" "The harvest is past, the summer is ended, and we are not saved." For the wound of the daughter of My people is My heart wounded; I mourn, and dismay has taken hold on Me. Is there no balm in Gilead? Is there no physician there? Why then has the health of the daughter of My people not been restored?

Chapter 9

Oh, that my head were waters and my eyes a fountain of tears, that I might weep day and night for the slain of the daughter of My people! Oh, that I had in the desert a travelers' lodging place, that I might leave My people and go away from them! For they are all adulterers, a company of treacherous men. They bend their tongue like a bow; falsehood and not truth has grown strong in the land; for they proceed from evil to evil, and they do not know Me, declares the LORD. Let everyone beware of his neighbor, and put no trust in any brother, for every brother is a deceiver, and every neighbor goes about as a slanderer. Everyone deceives his neighbor, and no one speaks the truth; they have taught their tongue to speak lies; they weary themselves committing iniquity. Your habitation is in the midst of deceit; through deceit they refuse to know Me, declares the LORD Therefore thus says the LORD of hosts: "Behold, I will refine them and test them, for what else can I do because of the daughter of My people? Their tongue is a deadly arrow; it speaks deceitfully; with his mouth each speaks peace to his neighbor, but in his heart he plans an ambush for him. Shall I not punish them for these things? declares the LORD, and shall I not avenge Myself on a nation such as this? I will take up weeping and wailing for the mountains, and a lamentation for the pastures of the wilderness, because they are laid waste so that no one passes through, and the lowing of cattle is not heard; both the birds of the air and the beasts have fled and are gone. I will make Jerusalem a heap of ruins, a lair of jackals, and I will make the cities of Judah a desolation, without inhabitant." Who is the man so wise that he can understand this? To whom has the mouth of the LORD spoken, that he may declare it? Why is the land ruined and laid waste like a wilderness, so that no one passes through? And the LORD says: "Because they have forsaken My law that I set before them, and have not obeyed My voice or walked in accord with it, but have stubbornly followed their own hearts and have gone after the Baals, as their fathers taught them. Therefore thus says the LORD of hosts, the God of Israel: Behold, I will feed this people with bitter food and give them poisonous water to drink. I will scatter them among the nations whom neither they nor their fathers have known, and I will send the sword after them, until I have consumed them." Thus says the LORD of hosts: "Consider, and call for the mourning women to come; send for the skillful women to come; let them make haste and raise a wailing over us, that our eyes may run down with tears and our eyelids flow with water. For a sound of wailing is heard from Zion: 'How we are ruined! We are utterly shamed because we have left the land because they have cast down our dwellings.' Hear, O women, the word of the LORD, and let your ear receive the word of His mouth; teach your daughters a lament, and each to her neighbor a dirge. For death has come up into our windows; it has entered our palaces, cutting off the children from the streets and the young men from the squares. Speak: 'Thus declares the LORD, the dead bodies of men shall fall like dung upon the open field, like sheaves after the reaper, and none shall gather them.' Thus says the LORD: 'Let not the wise man boast in his wisdom, let not the mighty man boast in his might, let not the rich man boast in his riches, but let him who boasts boast in this, that he understands and knows Me, that I am the LORD who practices steadfast love, justice, and righteousness in the earth. For in these things I delight,' declares the LORD. 'Behold, the days are coming,' declares the LORD, 'when I will punish all those who are circumcised merely in the flesh—Egypt, Judah, Edom, the sons of Ammon, Moab, and all who dwell in the desert who cut the corners of their hair, for all these nations are uncircumcised, and all the house of Israel is uncircumcised in heart.'"

Chapter 10

Hear the word that the LORD speaks to you, O house of Israel. Thus says the LORD: "Learn not the way of the nations, nor be dismayed at the signs of the heavens because the nations are dismayed at them, for the customs of the peoples are vanity. A tree from the forest is cut down and worked with an ax by the hands of a craftsman. They decorate it with silver and gold; they fasten it with hammer and nails so that it cannot move. Their idols are like scarecrows in a cucumber field, and they cannot speak; they have to be carried, for they cannot walk. Do not be afraid of them, for they cannot do evil, neither is it in them to do good." There is none like You, O LORD; You are great, and Your name is great in might. Who would not fear You, O King of the nations? For this is Your due; for among all the wise ones of the nations and in all their kingdoms there is none like You. They are both stupid and foolish; the instruction of idols is but wood! Beaten silver is brought from Tarshish, and gold from Uphaz. They are the work of the craftsman and of the hands of the goldsmith; their clothing is violet and purple; they are all the work of skilled men. But the LORD is the true God; He is the living God and the everlasting King. At His wrath, the earth quakes, and the nations cannot endure His indignation Thus shall you say to them: "The gods who did not make the heavens and the earth shall perish from the earth and from under the heavens." It is He who made the earth by His power, who established the world by His wisdom, and by His understanding stretched out the heavens. When He utters His voice, there is a tumult of waters in the heavens, and He makes the mist rise from the ends of the earth. He makes lightning for the rain, and He brings forth the wind from His storehouses. Every man is stupid and without knowledge; every goldsmith is put to shame by his idols, for his images are false, and there is no breath in them. They are worthless, a work of delusion; at the time of their punishment, they shall perish. Not like these is He who is the portion of Jacob, for He is the one who formed all things, and Israel is the tribe of His inheritance; the LORD of hosts is His name Gather up your bundle from the ground, O you who dwell under siege! For thus says the LORD: "Behold, I am slinging out the inhabitants of the land at this time, and I will bring distress on them, that they may feel it." Woe is me because of my hurt! My wound is grievous. But I said, "Truly this is an affliction, and I must bear it." My tent is destroyed, and all my cords are broken; my children have gone from me, and they are not; there is no one to spread my tent again and to set up my curtains. For the shepherds are stupid and do not inquire of the LORD; therefore they have not prospered, and all their flock is scattered A voice, a rumor! Behold, it comes!—a great commotion out of the north country to make the cities of Judah a desolation, a lair of jackals. I know, O LORD, that the way of man is not in himself, that it is not in man who walks to direct his steps. Correct me, O LORD, but in justice; not in Your anger, lest You bring me to nothing. Pour out Your wrath on the nations that know You not, and on the peoples that call not on Your name, for they have devoured Jacob; they have devoured him and consumed him, and have laid waste his habitation

Chapter 11

The words came to Jeremiah from the LORD, saying, "Hear the words of this covenant and speak them to the men of Judah and to the inhabitants of Jerusalem, and say to them, 'Thus says the LORD God of Israel: Cursed is the man who does not obey the words of this covenant, which I commanded your fathers when I brought them out of the land of Egypt, out of the furnace of iron, saying, Obey My voice, and do all these things that I command you; so you shall be My people, and I will be your God, that I may confirm the oath which I swore to your fathers, to give them a land flowing with milk and honey, as it is this day.'" Then I answered and said, "So be it, LORD." Then the LORD said to me, "Proclaim all these words in the cities of Judah and in the streets of Jerusalem, saying, 'Listen to the words of this covenant and do them.' For I earnestly exhorted your fathers when I brought them out of the land of Egypt until this day, rising early and exhorting, saying, 'Obey My voice.' Yet they did not obey or incline their ear, but everyone walked in the stubbornness of his evil heart. Therefore, I will bring upon them all the words of this covenant, which I commanded them to do, but they did not." The LORD said to me, "There is a conspiracy among the men of Judah and among the inhabitants of Jerusalem. They have turned back to the iniquities of their forefathers, who refused to hear My words and went after other gods to serve them. The house of Israel and the house of Judah have broken My covenant which I made with their fathers. Therefore thus says the LORD: 'Behold, I will bring disaster upon them which they will not be able to escape; and though they cry out to Me, I will not listen to them. Then the cities of Judah and the inhabitants of Jerusalem will go and cry out to the gods to whom they offer incense, but they will not save them at all in their time of trouble. For as many as your cities are your gods, O Judah; and as many as the streets of Jerusalem, you have set up altars to that shameful thing, altars to burn incense to Baal Therefore do not pray for this people, nor lift up a cry or prayer for them; for I will not hear them in the time that they cry out to Me because of their trouble. What right has My beloved in My house, having done lewd deeds with many? Can vows and holy flesh take away your evil from you? When you do evil, then you rejoice. The LORD called your name, a green olive tree, beautiful in fruit and form; but with the noise of a great tumult

He has kindled fire on it, and its branches are broken. For the LORD of hosts, who planted you, has pronounced doom against you because of the evil of the house of Israel and the house of Judah, which they have done against themselves to provoke Me to anger in offering incense to Baal." The LORD made it known to me, and I knew it; then You showed me their deeds. But I was like a docile lamb brought to the slaughter; and I did not know that they had devised schemes against me, saying, "Let us destroy the tree with its fruit, and let us cut him off from the land of the living, that his name may be remembered no more." But, O LORD of hosts, You who judge righteously, testing the mind and the heart, let me see Your vengeance on them, for to You I have revealed my cause Therefore thus says the LORD concerning the men of Anathoth who seek your life, saying, "Do not prophesy in the name of the LORD, lest you die by our hand." Therefore thus says the LORD of hosts: "Behold, I will punish them: the young men shall die by the sword, their sons and their daughters shall die by famine, and there shall be no remnant of them, for I will bring catastrophe on the men of Anathoth, even the year of their punishment."

Chapter 12

Righteous are You, O LORD, when I plead with You; yet let me talk with You about Your judgments. Why does the way of the wicked prosper? Why are those happy who deal so treacherously? You have planted them, yes, they have taken root; they grow, yes, they bear fruit. You are near in their mouth but far from their mind. But You, O LORD, know me; You have seen me, and You have tested my heart toward You. Pull them out like sheep for the slaughter and prepare them for the day of slaughter. How long will the land mourn, and the herbs of every field wither? The beasts and birds are consumed for the wickedness of those who dwell there because they said, "He will not see our final end." If you have run with the footmen, and they have wearied you, then how can you contend with horses? And if in the land of peace, in which you trusted, they wearied you, then how will you do in the floodplain of the Jordan? For even your brothers, the house of your father, even they have dealt treacherously with you; yes, they have called a multitude after you. Do not believe them, even though they speak smooth words to you "I have forsaken My house, I have left My heritage; I have given the dearly beloved of My soul into the hand of her enemies. My heritage is to Me like a lion in the forest; it cries out against Me; therefore, I have hated it. My heritage is to Me like a speckled vulture; the vultures all around are against her. Come, assemble all the beasts of the field, bring them to devour! Many rulers have destroyed My vineyard, they have trodden My portion underfoot; they have made My pleasant portion a desolate wilderness. They have made it desolate; desolate, it mourns to Me; the whole land is made desolate because no one takes it to heart. The plunderers have come on all the desolate heights in the wilderness, for the sword of the LORD shall devour from one end of the land to the other end of the land; no flesh shall have peace. They have sown wheat but reaped thorns; they have put themselves to pain but do not profit. But be ashamed of your harvest because of the fierce anger of the LORD." Thus says the LORD: "Against all My evil neighbors who touch the inheritance which I have caused My people Israel to inherit—behold, I will pluck them out of their land and pluck out the house of Judah from among them. Then it shall be, after I have plucked them out, that I will return and have compassion on them and bring them back, everyone to his heritage and everyone to his land. And it shall be, if they will diligently learn the ways of My people, to swear by My name, 'As the LORD lives,' as they taught My people to swear by Baal, then they shall be established in the midst of My people. But if they do not obey, I will utterly pluck up and destroy that nation," says the LORD

Chapter 13

Thus the LORD said to me, "Go and get yourself a linen sash, and put it around your waist, but do not put it in water." So I got a sash according to the word of the LORD and put it around my waist. And the word of the LORD came to me the second time, saying, "Take the sash that you acquired, which is around your waist, and arise, go to the Euphrates, and hide it there in a hole in the rock." So I went and hid it by the Euphrates, as the LORD commanded me Now it came to pass after many days that the LORD said to me, "Arise, go to the Euphrates, and take from there the sash which I commanded you to hide there." Then I went to the Euphrates and dug, and I took the sash from the place where I had hidden it; and there was the sash, ruined. It was profitable for nothing. Then the word of the LORD came to me, saying, "Thus says the LORD: 'In this manner I will ruin the pride of Judah and the great pride of Jerusalem. This evil people, who refuse to hear My words, who follow the dictates of their hearts, and walk after other gods to serve them and worship them, shall be just like this sash which is profitable for nothing. For as the sash clings to the waist of a man, so I have caused the whole house of Israel and the whole house of Judah to cling to Me,' says the LORD, 'that they may become My people, for renown, for praise, and for glory; but they would not hear.' Therefore you shall speak to them this word: 'Thus says the LORD God of Israel: Every bottle shall be filled with wine.' And they will say to you, 'Do we not certainly know that every bottle will be filled with wine?' Then you shall say to them, 'Thus says the LORD: Behold, I will fill all the inhabitants of this land—even the kings who sit on David's throne, the priests, the prophets, and all the inhabitants of Jerusalem—with drunkenness! And I will dash them one against another, even the fathers and the sons together,' says the LORD. 'I will not pity nor spare nor have mercy, but will destroy them.'" Hear and give ear: Do not be proud, for the LORD has spoken. Give glory to the LORD your God before He causes darkness and before your feet stumble on the dark mountains, and while you are looking for light, He turns it into the shadow of death and makes it dense darkness. But if you will not hear it, my soul will weep in secret for your pride; my eyes will weep bitterly and run down with tears because the LORD's flock has been taken captive. Say to the king and to the queen mother, "Humble yourselves; sit down, for your rule shall collapse, the crown of your glory." The cities of the South shall be shut up, and no one shall open them; Judah shall be carried away captive, all of it; it shall be wholly carried away captive Lift up your eyes and see those who come from the north. Where is the flock that was given to you, your beautiful sheep? What will you say when He punishes you? For you have taught them to be chieftains, to be head over you. Will not pangs seize you like a woman in labor? And if you say in your heart, "Why have these things come upon me?" For the greatness of your iniquity, your skirts have been uncovered, your heels made bare. Can the Ethiopian change his skin or the leopard his spots? Then may you also do good who are accustomed to do evil. Therefore I will scatter them like stubble that passes away by the wind of the wilderness. This is your lot, the portion of your measures from Me," says the LORD, "because you have forgotten Me and trusted in falsehood. Therefore I will uncover your skirts over your face, that your shame may appear. I have seen your adulteries and your lustful neighings, the lewdness of your harlotry, your abominations on the hills in the fields. Woe to you, O Jerusalem! Will you still not be made clean?"

Chapter 14

The word of the LORD that came to Jeremiah concerning the droughts. "Judah mourns, and her gates languish; they mourn for the land, and the cry of Jerusalem has gone up. Their nobles have sent their lads for water; they went to the cisterns and found no water. They returned with their vessels empty; they were ashamed and confounded and covered their heads. Because the ground is parched, for there was no rain in the land, the plowmen were ashamed; they covered their heads. Yes, the deer also gave birth in the field but left because there was no grass. And the wild donkeys stood in the desolate heights; they sniffed at the wind like jackals; their eyes failed because there was no grass." O LORD, though our iniquities testify against us, do it for Your name's sake; for our backslidings are many, we have sinned against You. O the Hope of Israel, his Savior in time of trouble, why should You be like a stranger in the land, and like a traveler who turns aside to tarry for a night? Why should You be like a man astonished, like a mighty one who cannot save? Yet You, O LORD, are in our midst, and we are called by Your name; do not leave us! Thus says the LORD to this people: "Thus they have loved to wander; they have not restrained their feet. Therefore the LORD does not accept them; He will remember their iniquity now, and punish their sins." Then the LORD said to me, "Do not pray for this people, for their good. When they fast, I will not hear their cry; and when they offer burnt offerings and grain offerings, I will not accept them. But I will consume them by the sword, by the famine, and by the pestilence." Then I said, "Ah, Lord GOD! Behold, the prophets say to them, 'You shall not see the sword, nor shall you have famine, but I will give you assured peace in this place.'" And the LORD said to me, "The prophets prophesy lies in My name. I have not sent them, commanded them, nor spoken to them; they prophesy to you a false vision, divination, a worthless thing, and the deceit of their heart. Therefore thus says the LORD concerning the prophets who prophesy in My name, whom I did not send, and who say, 'Sword and famine shall not be in this land'—by sword and famine those prophets shall be consumed! And the people to whom they prophesy shall be cast out in the streets of Jerusalem because of the famine and the sword; they will have no one to bury them—them nor their wives, their sons nor their daughters—for I will pour their wickedness on them." Therefore you shall say this word to them: "Let my eyes flow with tears night and day, and let them not cease; for the virgin daughter of my people has been broken with a mighty stroke, with a very severe blow. If I go out to the field, then behold, those slain with the sword! And if I enter the city, then behold, those sick from famine! Yes, both prophet and priest go about in a land they do not know." Have You utterly rejected Judah? Has Your soul loathed Zion? Why have You stricken us so that there is no healing for us? We looked for peace, but there was no good; and for the time of healing, and there was trouble. We acknowledge, O LORD, our wickedness and the iniquity of our fathers, for we have sinned against You. Do not abhor us, for Your name's sake; do not disgrace the throne of Your glory. Remember, do not break Your covenant with us. Are there any among the idols of the nations that can cause rain? Or can the heavens give showers? Are You not He, O LORD our God? Therefore we will wait for You, since You have made all these

Chapter 15

Then the LORD said to me, "Even if Moses and Samuel stood before Me, My mind would not be favorable toward this people. Cast them out of My sight, and let them go forth. And it shall be, if they say to you, 'Where shall we go?' then you shall tell them, 'Thus says the LORD: "Such as are for death, to death; And such as are for the sword, to the sword; And such as are for the famine, to the famine; And such as are for the captivity, to the captivity."' "And I will appoint over them four forms of destruction," says the LORD: "the sword to slay, the dogs to drag, the birds of the heavens and the beasts of the earth to devour and destroy. I will hand them over to trouble, to all kingdoms of the earth, because of Manasseh the son of Hezekiah, king of Judah, for what he did in Jerusalem "For who will have pity on you, O Jerusalem? Or who will bemoan you? Or who will turn aside to ask how you are doing? You have forsaken Me," says the LORD, "You have gone backward. Therefore I will stretch out My hand against you and destroy you; I am weary of relenting! And I will winnow them with a winnowing fan in the gates of the land; I will bereave them of children; I will destroy My people since they do not return from their ways. Their widows will be increased to Me more than the sand of the seas; I will bring against them, against the mother of the young men, a plunderer at noonday; I will cause anguish and terror to fall on them suddenly "She languishes who has borne seven; she has breathed her last; her sun has gone down while it was yet day; she has been shamed and confounded. And the remnant of them I will deliver to the sword before their enemies," says the LORD Woe is me, my mother, that you have borne me, a man of strife and a man of contention to the whole earth! I have neither lent for interest, nor have men lent to me for interest. Every one of them curses me. The LORD said: "Surely it will be well with your remnant; surely I will cause the enemy to intercede with you in the time of adversity and in the time of affliction. Can anyone break iron, the northern iron and the bronze? Your wealth and your treasures I will give as plunder without price, because of all your sins, throughout all your territories. And I will make you cross over with your enemies into a land which you do not know; for a fire is kindled in My anger, which shall burn upon you." O LORD, You know; remember me and visit me, and take vengeance for me on my persecutors. In Your enduring patience, do not take me away. Know that for Your sake I have suffered rebuke. Your words were found, and I ate them, and Your word was to me the joy and rejoicing of my heart; for I am called by Your name, O LORD God of hosts. I did not sit in the assembly of the mockers, nor did I rejoice; I sat alone because of Your hand, for You have filled me with indignation. Why is my pain perpetual and my wound incurable, which refuses to be healed? Will You surely be to me like an unreliable stream, as waters that fail? Therefore thus says the LORD: "If you return, then I will bring you back; you shall stand before Me; if you take out the precious from the vile, you shall be as My mouth. Let them return to you, but you must not return to them. And I will make you to this people a fortified bronze wall; and they will fight against you, but they shall not prevail against you; for I am with you to save you and deliver you," says the LORD. "I will deliver you from the hand of the wicked, and I will redeem you from the grip of the terrible."

Chapter 16

The word of the LORD also came to me, saying, "You shall not take a wife, nor shall you have sons or daughters in this place." For thus says the LORD concerning the sons and daughters who are born in this place, and their mothers who bear them, and their fathers who beget them in this land: "They shall die of deadly diseases; they shall not be lamented nor buried, but they shall be like refuse on the ground. They shall be consumed by the sword and by famine, and their corpses shall be food for the birds of the heavens and for the beasts of the earth." For thus says the LORD, "Do not enter the house of mourning, nor go to lament or bemoan them; for I have taken away My peace from this people," says the LORD, "lovingkindness and mercies. Both the great and the small shall die in this land; they shall not be buried, neither shall men lament for them, cut themselves, nor make themselves bald for them. Nor shall men break bread in mourning for them, to comfort them for the dead; nor shall men give them the cup of consolation to drink for their father or their mother. Also you shall not go into the house of feasting to sit with them, to eat and drink." For thus says the LORD of hosts, the God of Israel: "Behold, I will cause to cease from this place, before your eyes and in your days, the voice of mirth and the voice of gladness, the voice of the bridegroom and the voice of the bride." "And it shall be, when you show this people all these words, and they say to you, 'Why has the LORD pronounced all this great disaster against us? What is our iniquity? Or what is our sin that we have committed against the LORD our God?' then you shall say to them, 'Because your fathers have forsaken Me,' says the LORD; 'they have walked after other gods and have served them and worshiped them, and have forsaken Me and not kept My law. And you have done worse than your fathers, for behold, each one follows the dictates of his own evil heart, so that no one listens to Me. Therefore I will cast you out of this land into a land that you do not know, neither you nor your fathers; and there you shall serve other gods day and night, where I will not show you favor.' "Therefore, behold, the days are coming," says the LORD, "that it shall no more be said, 'The LORD lives who brought up the children of Israel from the land of Egypt,' but, 'The LORD lives who brought up the children of Israel from the land of the north and from all the lands where He had driven them.' For I will bring them back into their land which I gave to their fathers "Behold, I will send for many fishermen," says the LORD, "and they shall fish them; and afterward I will send for many hunters, and they shall hunt them from every mountain and every hill, and out of the holes of the rocks. For My eyes are on all their ways; they are not hidden from My face, nor is their iniquity hidden from My eyes. And first I will repay double for their iniquity and their sin, because they have defiled My land; they have filled My inheritance with the carcasses of their detestable and abominable idols." O LORD, my strength and my fortress, my refuge in the day of affliction, the Gentiles shall come to You from the ends of the earth and say, "Surely our fathers have inherited lies, worthless and unprofitable things." Will a man make gods for himself, which are not gods? "Therefore behold, I will this once cause them to know, I will cause them to know My hand and My might; and they shall know that My name is the LORD."

Chapter 17

The sin of Judah is written with a pen of iron; with the point of a diamond, it is engraved on the tablet of their heart and on the horns of your altars, while their children remember their altars and their wooden images by the green trees on the high hills. O My mountain in the field, I will give as plunder your wealth, all your treasures, and your high places of sin within all your borders. And you, even yourself, shall let go of your heritage which I gave you; and I will cause you to serve your enemies in the land which you do not know; for you have kindled a fire in My anger which shall burn forever." Thus says the LORD: "Cursed is the man who trusts in man and makes flesh his strength, whose heart departs from the LORD. For he shall be like a shrub in the desert, and shall not see when good comes, but shall inhabit the parched places in the wilderness, in a salt land which is not inhabited "Blessed is the man who trusts in the LORD, and whose hope is the LORD. For he shall be like a tree planted by the waters, which spreads out its roots by the river, and will not fear when heat comes; but its leaf will be green, and will not be anxious in the year of drought, nor will cease from yielding fruit "The heart is deceitful above all things, and desperately wicked; who can know it? I, the LORD, search the heart, I test the mind, even to give every man according to his ways, according to the fruit of his doings. As a partridge that broods but does not hatch, so is he who gets riches, but not by right; it will leave him in the midst of his days, and at his end, he will be a fool." A glorious high throne from the beginning is the place of our sanctuary. O LORD, the hope of Israel, all who forsake You shall be ashamed. "Those who depart from Me shall be written in the earth, because they have forsaken the LORD, the fountain of living waters." Heal me, O LORD, and I shall be healed; save me, and I shall be saved, for You are my praise. Indeed they say to me, "Where is the word of the LORD? Let it come now!" As for me, I have not hurried away from being a shepherd who follows You, nor have I desired the woeful day; You know what came out of my lips; it was right there before You. Do not be a terror to me; You are my hope in the day of doom. Let them be ashamed who persecute me, but do not let me be put to shame; let them be dismayed, but do not let me be dismayed. Bring on them the day of doom, and destroy them with double destruction! Thus the LORD said to me: "Go and stand in the gate of the children of the people, by which the kings of Judah come in and by which they go out, and in all the gates of Jerusalem; and say to them, 'Hear the word of the LORD, you kings of Judah, and all Judah, and all the inhabitants of Jerusalem who enter by these gates. Thus says the LORD: "Take heed to yourselves, and bear no burden on the Sabbath day, nor bring it in by the gates of Jerusalem; nor carry a burden out of your houses on the Sabbath day, nor do any work, but hallow the Sabbath day, as I commanded your fathers. But they did not obey nor incline their ear, but made their neck stiff, that they might not hear nor receive instruction "And it shall be, if you heed Me carefully," says the LORD, "to bring no burden through the gates of this city on the Sabbath day, but hallow the Sabbath day, to do no work in it, then shall enter the gates of this city kings and princes sitting on the throne of David, riding in chariots and on horses, they and their princes, accompanied by the men of Judah and the inhabitants of Jerusalem; and this city shall remain forever. And they shall come from the cities of Judah and from the places around Jerusalem, from the land of Benjamin and from the lowland, from the mountains and from the South, bringing burnt offerings and sacrifices, grain offerings and incense, bringing sacrifices of praise to the house of the LORD "But if you will not heed Me to hallow the Sabbath day, such as not carrying a burden when entering the gates of Jerusalem on the Sabbath day, then I will kindle a fire in its gates, and it shall devour the palaces of Jerusalem, and it shall not be quenched."'"

Chapter 18

The word which came to Jeremiah from the LORD, saying: "Arise and go down to the potter's house, and there I will cause you to hear My words." Then I went down to the potter's house, and there he was, making something at the wheel. And the vessel that he made of clay was marred in the hand of the potter; so he made it again into another vessel, as it seemed good to the potter to make Then the word of the LORD came to me, saying: "O house of Israel, can I not do with you as this potter?" says the LORD. "Look, as the clay is in the potter's hand, so are you in My hand, O house of Israel! The instant I speak concerning a nation and concerning a kingdom, to pluck up, to pull down, and to destroy it, if that nation against whom I have spoken turns from its evil, I will relent of the disaster that I thought to bring upon it. And the instant I speak concerning a nation and concerning a kingdom, to build and to plant it, if it does evil in My sight so that it does not obey My voice, then I will relent concerning the good with which I said I would benefit it "Now therefore, speak to the men of Judah and to the inhabitants of Jerusalem, saying, 'Thus says the LORD: "Behold, I am fashioning a disaster and devising a plan against you. Return now every one from his evil way, and make your ways and your doings good."'" And they said, "That is hopeless! So we will walk according to our own plans, and we will every one obey the dictates of his evil heart." Therefore thus says the LORD: "Ask now among the Gentiles, who has heard such things? The virgin of Israel has done a very horrible thing. Will a man leave the snow water of Lebanon, which comes from the rock of the field? Will the cold flowing waters be forsaken for strange waters? Because My people have forgotten Me, they have burned incense to worthless idols. And they have caused themselves to stumble in their ways, from the ancient paths, to walk in pathways and not on a highway, to make their land desolate and a perpetual hissing; everyone who passes by it will be astonished and shake his head. I will scatter them as with an east wind before the enemy; I will show them the back and not the face in the day of their calamity." Then they said, "Come and let us devise plans against Jeremiah; for the law shall not perish from the priest, nor counsel from the wise, nor the word from the prophet. Come and let us attack him with the tongue, and let us not give heed to any of his words."Give heed to me, O LORD, and listen to the voice of those who contend with me! Shall evil be repaid for good? For they have dug a pit for my life. Remember that I stood before You to speak good for them, to turn away Your wrath from them. Therefore deliver up their children to the famine, and pour out their blood by the force of the sword; let their wives become widows and bereaved of their children. Let their men be put to death, their young men be slain by the sword in battle. Let a cry be heard from their houses when You bring a troop suddenly upon them; for they have dug a pit to take me, and hidden snares for my feet. Yet, LORD, You know all their counsel which is against me, to slay me. Provide no atonement for their iniquity, nor blot out their sin from Your sight; but let them be overthrown before You. Deal thus with them in the time of Your anger

Chapter 19

Thus says the LORD: "Go and get a potter's earthen flask, and take some of the elders of the people and some of the elders of the priests. And go out to the Valley of the Son of Hinnom, which is by the entry of the Potsherd Gate; and proclaim there the words that I will tell you, and say, 'Hear the word of the LORD, O kings of Judah and inhabitants of Jerusalem. Thus says the LORD of hosts, the God of Israel: "Behold, I will bring such a catastrophe on this place, that whoever hears of it, his ears will tingle "Because they have forsaken Me and made this an alien place, because they have burned incense in it to other gods whom neither they, their fathers, nor the kings of Judah have known, and have filled this place with the blood of the innocents. They have also built the high places of Baal, to burn their sons with fire for burnt offerings to Baal, which I did not command or speak, nor did it come into My mind. Therefore behold, the days are coming," says the LORD, "that this place shall no more be called Tophet or the Valley of the Son of Hinnom, but the Valley of Slaughter "And I will make void the counsel of Judah and Jerusalem in this place, and I will cause them to fall by the sword before their enemies and by the hands of those who seek their lives; their corpses I will give as meat for the birds of the heavens and for the beasts of the earth. I will make this city desolate and a hissing; everyone who passes by it will be astonished and hiss because of all its plagues. And I will cause them to eat the flesh of their sons and the flesh of their daughters, and everyone shall eat the flesh of his friend in the siege and in the desperation with which their enemies and those who seek their lives shall drive them to despair."' "Then you shall break the flask in the sight of the men who go with you, and say to them, 'Thus says the LORD of hosts: "Even so I will break this people and this city, as one breaks a potter's vessel, which cannot be made whole again; and they shall bury them in Tophet till there is no place to bury. Thus I will do to this place," says the LORD, "and to its inhabitants, and make this city like Tophet. And the houses of Jerusalem and the houses of the kings of Judah shall be defiled like the place of Tophet, because of all the houses on whose roofs they have burned incense to all the host of heaven, and poured out drink offerings to other gods."'" Then Jeremiah came from Tophet, where the LORD had sent him to prophesy; and he stood in the court of the LORD's house and said to all the people, "Thus says the LORD of hosts, the God of Israel: 'Behold, I will bring on this city and on all her towns all the doom that I have pronounced against it because they have stiffened their necks that they might not hear My words.'"

Chapter 20

Now Pashhur the son of Immer, the priest who was also chief governor in the house of the LORD, heard that Jeremiah prophesied these things. Then Pashhur struck Jeremiah the prophet and put him in the stocks that were in the high gate of Benjamin, which was by the house of the LORD. And it happened on the next day that Pashhur brought Jeremiah out of the stocks. Then Jeremiah said to him, "The LORD has not called your name Pashhur, but Magor-Missabib. For thus says the LORD: 'Behold, I will make you a terror to yourself and to all your friends; and they shall fall by the sword of their enemies, and your eyes shall see it. I will give all Judah into the hand of the king of Babylon, and he shall carry them captive to Babylon and slay them with the sword. Moreover, I will deliver all the wealth of this city, all its produce, and all its precious things; all the treasures of the kings of Judah I will give into the hand of their enemies, who will plunder them, seize them, and carry them to Babylon. And you, Pashhur, and all who dwell in your house, shall go into captivity; you shall go to Babylon, and there you shall die and be buried, you and all your friends, to whom you have prophesied lies.'" O LORD, You induced me, and I was persuaded; You are stronger than I, and have prevailed. I am in derision daily; everyone mocks me. For when I spoke, I cried out; I shouted, "Violence and plunder!" Because the word of the LORD was made to me a reproach and a derision daily. Then I said, "I will not make mention of Him, nor speak anymore in His name." But His word was in my heart like a burning fire shut up in my bones; I was weary of holding it back, and I could not.

For I heard many mocking: "Fear on every side!" "Report," they say, "and we will report it!" All my acquaintances watched for my stumbling, saying, "Perhaps he can be induced; then we will prevail against him, and we will take our revenge on him." But the LORD is with me as a mighty, awesome One. Therefore my persecutors will stumble, and will not prevail. They will be greatly ashamed, for they will not prosper. Their everlasting confusion will never be forgotten But, O LORD of hosts, You who test the righteous, and see the mind and heart, let me see Your vengeance on them, for I have pleaded my cause before You. Sing to the LORD! Praise the LORD! For He has delivered the life of the poor from the hand of evildoers Cursed be the day in which I was born! Let the day not be blessed in which my mother bore me! Let the man be cursed who brought news to my father, saying, "A male child has been born to you," making him very glad. And let that man be like the cities which the LORD overthrew, and did not relent. Let him hear the cry in the morning and the shouting at noon, because he did not kill me from the womb, that my mother might have been my grave and her womb always enlarged with me. Why did I come forth from the womb to see labor and sorrow, that my days should be consumed with shame?

Chapter 21

The word that came to Jeremiah from the LORD, when King Zedekiah sent Pashur, the son of Malchiah, and Zephaniah, the son of Maaseiah the priest, to him, saying, "Please inquire of the LORD for us, for Nebuchadnezzar, king of Babylon, makes war against us. Perhaps the LORD will deal with us according to all His wonderful works, that the king may withdraw from us." Then Jeremiah said to them, "Thus you shall say to Zedekiah, 'Thus says the LORD, the God of Israel: Behold, I will turn back the weapons of war that are in your hands, with which you fight against the king of Babylon and the Chaldeans who besiege you outside the walls, and I will gather them into the midst of this city. I Myself will fight against you with an outstretched hand and with a strong arm, in anger and fury and great wrath. I will strike the inhabitants of this city, both man and beast; they shall die of a great pestilence.' "And afterward," says the LORD, "I will deliver Zedekiah, king of Judah, his servants, and the people, and those who survive in this city from the pestilence and the sword and the famine, into the hand of Nebuchadnezzar, king of Babylon, into the hand of their enemies, and into the hand of those who seek their lives; and he shall strike them with the edge of the sword. He shall not spare them or have pity or mercy." Now you shall say to this people, 'Thus says the LORD: Behold, I set before you the way of life and the way of death. He who remains in this city shall die by the sword, by famine, and by pestilence; but he who goes out and defects to the Chaldeans who besiege you, he shall live, and his life shall be as a prize to him. For I have set My face against this city for adversity and not for good," says the LORD. "It shall be given into the hand of the king of Babylon, and he shall burn it with fire." "And concerning the house of the king of Judah, say, 'Hear the word of the LORD, O house of David! Thus says the LORD: Execute judgment in the morning, and deliver him who is plundered out of the hand of the oppressor, lest My fury go forth like fire and burn so that no one can quench it because of the evil of your doings. Behold, I am against you, O inhabitant of the valley and rock of the plain," says the LORD, "who say, 'Who shall come down against us? Or who shall enter our dwellings?' But I will punish you according to the fruit of your doings," says the LORD. "I will kindle a fire in its forest, and it shall devour all things around it."

Chapter 22

Thus says the LORD: "Go down to the house of the king of Judah, and speak there this word, and say, 'Hear the word of the LORD, O king of Judah, you who sit on the throne of David, you and your servants and your people who enter these gates! Thus says the LORD: Execute judgment and righteousness, and deliver the plundered out of the hand of the oppressor. Do no wrong and do no violence to the stranger, the fatherless, or the widow, nor shed innocent blood in this place. For if you indeed do this thing, then shall enter the gates of this house, riding on horses and in chariots, accompanied by servants and people, kings who sit on the throne of David. But if you will not hear these words, I swear by Myself," says the LORD, "that this house shall become a desolation." For thus says the LORD to the house of the king of Judah: "You are Gilead to Me, the head of Lebanon; yet I surely will make you a wilderness, cities which are not inhabited. I will prepare destroyers against you, everyone with his weapons; they shall cut down your choice cedars and cast them into the fire. And many nations will pass by this city, and everyone will say to his neighbor, 'Why has the LORD done so to this great city?' Then they will answer, 'Because they have forsaken the covenant of the LORD their God, and worshiped other gods and served them.'" Weep not for the dead, nor bemoan him; weep bitterly for him who goes away, for he shall return no more, nor see his native country. For thus says the LORD concerning Shallum the son of Josiah, king of Judah, who reigned instead of Josiah his father, who went from this place: "He shall not return here anymore, but he shall die in the place where they have led him captive, and shall see this land no more Woe to him who builds his house by unrighteousness and his chambers by injustice, who uses his neighbor's service without wages and gives him nothing for his work, who says, 'I will build myself a wide house with spacious chambers and cut out windows for it, paneling it with cedar and painting it with vermilion.' Shall you reign because you enclose yourself in cedar? Did not your father eat and drink, and do justice and righteousness? Then it was well with him. He judged the cause of the poor and needy; then it was well. Was not this knowing Me?" says the LORD. "Yet your eyes and your heart are for nothing but your covetousness, for shedding innocent blood, and practicing oppression and violence." Therefore thus says the LORD concerning Jehoiakim the son of Josiah, king of Judah: "They shall not lament for him, saying, 'Alas, my brother!' or 'Alas, my sister!' They shall not lament for him, saying, 'Alas, master!' or 'Alas, his glory!' He shall be buried with the burial of a donkey, dragged and cast out beyond the gates of Jerusalem. Go up to Lebanon and cry out, and lift up your voice in Bashan; cry from Abarim, for all your lovers are destroyed. I spoke to you in your prosperity, but you said, 'I will not hear.' This has been your manner from your youth, that you did not obey My voice. The wind shall eat up all your rulers, and your lovers shall go into captivity; surely then you will be ashamed and humiliated for all your wickedness. O inhabitant of Lebanon, making your nest in the cedars, how gracious will you be when pangs come upon you, like the pain of a woman in labor? "As I live," says the LORD, "though Coniah the son of Jehoiakim, king of Judah, were the signet on My right hand, yet I would pluck you off; and I will give you into the hand of those who seek your life, and into the hand of those whose face you fear—the hand of Nebuchadnezzar king of Babylon and the hand of the Chaldeans. So I will cast you out, and your mother who bore you, into another country where you were not born, and there you shall die. But to the land to which they desire to return, there they shall not return." Is this man Coniah a despised, broken idol— a vessel in which is no pleasure? Why are they cast out, he and his descendants, and cast into a land which they do not know? O earth, earth, earth, hear the word of the LORD! Thus says the LORD: "Write this man down as childless, a man who shall not prosper in his days; for none of his descendants shall prosper, sitting on the throne of David, and ruling anymore in Judah."

Chapter 23

"Woe to the shepherds who destroy and scatter the sheep of My pasture!" says the LORD. Therefore thus says the LORD God of Israel against the shepherds who feed My people: "You have scattered My flock, driven them away, and not attended to them. Behold, I will attend to you for the evil of your doings," says the LORD. "But I will gather the remnant of My flock out of all the countries where I have driven them, and bring them back to their folds; and they shall be fruitful and increase. I will set up shepherds over them who will feed them; and they shall fear no more, nor be dismayed, nor shall they be lacking," says the LORD "Behold, the days are coming," says the LORD, "That I will raise to David a Branch of righteousness; a King shall reign and prosper, and execute judgment and righteousness in the earth. In His days Judah will be saved, and Israel will dwell safely; now this is His name by which He will be called: THE LORD OUR RIGHTEOUSNESS. Therefore, behold, the days are coming," says the LORD, "that they shall no longer say, 'As the LORD lives who brought up the children of Israel from the land of Egypt,' but, 'As the LORD lives who brought up and led the descendants of the house of Israel from the north country and from all the countries where I had driven them.' And they shall dwell in their own land." My heart within me is broken because of the prophets; all my bones shake. I am like a drunken man, and like a man whom wine has overcome, because of the LORD and because of His holy words. For the land is full of adulterers; for because of a curse the land mourns. The pleasant places of the wilderness are dried up. Their course of life is evil, and their might is not right. "For both prophet and priest are profane; yes, in My house I have found their wickedness," says the LORD. "Therefore their way shall be to them like slippery ways; in the darkness they shall be driven on and fall in them; for I will bring disaster on them, the year of their punishment," says the LORD. "And I have seen folly in the prophets of Samaria: They prophesied by Baal and caused My people Israel to err. Also, I have seen a horrible thing in the prophets of Jerusalem: They commit adultery and walk in lies; they also strengthen the hands of evildoers, so that no one turns back from his wickedness. All of them are like Sodom to Me, and her inhabitants like Gomorrah." Therefore thus says the LORD of hosts concerning the prophets: "Behold, I will feed them with wormwood, and make them drink the water of gall; for from the prophets of Jerusalem profaneness has gone out into all the land." Thus says the LORD of hosts: "Do not listen to the words of the prophets who prophesy to you. They make you worthless; they speak a vision of their own heart, not from the mouth of the LORD. They continually say to those who despise Me, 'The LORD has said, "You shall have peace"'; and to everyone who walks according to the dictates of his own heart, they say, 'No evil shall come upon you.'" For who has stood in the counsel of the LORD, and has perceived and heard His word? Who has marked His word and heard it? Behold, a whirlwind of the LORD has gone forth in fury— a violent whirlwind! It will fall violently on the head of the wicked. The anger of the LORD will not turn back until He has executed and performed the thoughts of His heart. In the latter days you will understand it perfectly "I have not sent these prophets, yet they ran. I have not spoken to them, yet they prophesied. But if they had stood in My counsel, and had caused My people to hear My words, then they would have turned them from their evil way and from the evil of their doings. Am I a God near at hand," says the LORD, "And not a God afar off? Can anyone hide himself in secret places, so I shall not see him?" says the LORD. "Do I not fill heaven and earth?" says the LORD. "I have heard what the prophets have said who prophesy lies in My name, saying, 'I have dreamed, I have dreamed!' How long will this be in the heart of the prophets who prophesy lies? Indeed they are prophets of the deceit of their own heart, who try to make My people forget My name by their dreams which everyone tells his neighbor, as their fathers forgot My name for Baal. The prophet who has a dream, let him tell a dream; and he who has My word, let him speak My word faithfully. What is the chaff to the wheat?" says the LORD. "Is not My word like a fire?" says the LORD, "And like a hammer that breaks the rock in pieces? Therefore behold, I am against the prophets," says the LORD, "who steal My words every one from his neighbor. Behold, I am against the prophets," says the LORD, "who use their tongues and say, 'He says.' Behold, I am against those who prophesy false dreams," says the LORD, "and tell them, and cause My people to err by their lies and by their recklessness. Yet I did not send them or command them; therefore they shall not profit this people at all," says the LORD "So when these people or the prophet or the priest ask you, saying, 'What is the oracle of the LORD?' you shall then say to them, 'What oracle?' I will even forsake you," says the LORD. "And as for the prophet and the priest and the people who say, 'The oracle of the LORD,' I will even punish that man and his house. Thus every one of you shall say to his neighbor, and every one to his brother, 'What has the LORD answered?' and, 'What has the LORD spoken?' And the oracle of the LORD you shall mention no more. For every man's word will be his oracle, for you have perverted the words of the living God, the LORD of hosts, our God. Thus you shall say to the prophet, 'What has the LORD answered you?' and, 'What has the LORD spoken?' But since you say, 'The oracle of the LORD!' therefore thus says the LORD: 'Because you say this word, "The oracle of the LORD!" and I have sent to you, saying, "Do not say, 'The oracle of the LORD!'" therefore behold, I, even I, will utterly forget you and forsake you, and the city that I gave you and your fathers, and will cast you out of My presence. And I will bring an everlasting reproach upon you, and a perpetual shame, which shall not be forgotten.'"

Chapter 24

The LORD showed me, and there were two baskets of figs set before the temple of the LORD, after Nebuchadnezzar king of Babylon had carried away captive Jeconiah the son of Jehoiakim, king of Judah, and the princes of Judah with the craftsmen and smiths, from Jerusalem, and had brought them to Babylon. One basket had very good figs, like the figs that are first ripe; and the other basket had very bad figs, which could not be eaten, they were so bad. Then the LORD said to me, "What do you see, Jeremiah?" And I said, "Figs, the good figs very good, and the bad very bad, which cannot be eaten, they are so bad." Again the word of the LORD came to me, saying, "Thus says the LORD, the God of Israel: 'Like these good figs, so will I acknowledge those who are carried away captive from Judah, whom I have sent out of this place for their own good, into the land of the Chaldeans. For I will set My eyes on them for good, and I will bring them back to this land; I will build them and not pull them down, and I will plant them and not pluck them up. Then I will give them a heart to know Me, that I am the LORD; and they shall be My people, and I will be their God, for they shall return to Me with their whole heart. And as the bad figs which cannot be eaten, they are so bad'—surely thus says the LORD—'so will I give up Zedekiah the king of Judah, his princes, the residue of Jerusalem who remain in this land, and those who dwell in the land of Egypt. I will deliver them to trouble into all the kingdoms of the earth, for their harm, to be a reproach and a byword, a taunt and a curse, in all places where I shall drive them. And I will send the sword, the famine, and the pestilence among them, till they are consumed from the land that I gave to them and their fathers.'"

Chapter 25

The word that came to Jeremiah concerning all the people of Judah, in the fourth year of Jehoiakim the son of Josiah, king of Judah (which was the first year of Nebuchadnezzar king of Babylon), which Jeremiah the prophet spoke to all the people of Judah and to all the inhabitants of Jerusalem, saying: "From the thirteenth year of Josiah the son of Amon, king of Judah, even to this day, this is the twenty-third year in which the word of the LORD has come to me; and I have spoken to you, rising early and speaking, but you have not listened. And the LORD has sent to you all His servants the prophets, rising early and sending them, but you have not listened nor inclined your ear to hear. They said, 'Repent now everyone of his evil way and his evil doings, and dwell in the land that the LORD has given to you and your fathers forever and ever. Do not go after other gods to serve them and worship them, and do not provoke Me to anger with the works of your hands; and I will not harm you.' Yet you have not listened to Me," says the LORD, "that you might provoke Me to anger with the works of your hands to your own hurt "Therefore thus says the LORD of hosts: 'Because you have not heard My words, behold, I will send and take all the families of the north,' says the LORD, 'and Nebuchadnezzar the king of Babylon, My servant, and will bring them against this land, against its inhabitants, and against these nations all around, and will utterly destroy them and make them an astonishment, a hissing, and perpetual desolations. Moreover, I will take from them the voice of mirth and the voice of gladness, the voice of the bridegroom and the voice of the bride, the sound of the millstones and the light of the lamp. And this whole land shall be a desolation and an astonishment, and these nations shall serve the king of Babylon seventy years 'Then it will come to pass, when seventy years are completed, that I will punish the king of Babylon and that nation, the land of the Chaldeans, for their iniquity,' says the LORD; 'and I will make it a perpetual desolation. So I will bring on that land all My words which I have pronounced against it, all that is written in this book, which Jeremiah has prophesied concerning all the nations. For many nations and great kings shall be served by them also; and I will repay them according to their deeds and according to the works of their own hands.'" For thus says the LORD God of Israel to me: "Take this wine cup of fury from My hand, and cause all the nations, to whom I send you, to drink it. And they will drink and stagger and go mad because of the sword that I will send among them." Then I took the cup from the LORD's hand, and made all the nations drink, to whom the LORD had sent me: Jerusalem and the cities of Judah, its kings and its princes, to make them a desolation, an astonishment, a hissing, and a curse, as it is this day; Pharaoh king of Egypt, his servants, his princes, and

all his people; all the mixed multitude, all the kings of the land of Uz, all the kings of the land of the Philistines (namely, Ashkelon, Gaza, Ekron, and the remnant of Ashdod); Edom, Moab, and the people of Ammon; all the kings of Tyre, all the kings of Sidon, and the kings of the coastlands which are across the sea; Dedan, Tema, Buz, and all who are in the farthest corners; all the kings of Arabia and all the kings of the mixed multitude who dwell in the desert; all the kings of Zimri, all the kings of Elam, and all the kings of the Medes; all the kings of the north, far and near, one with another; and all the kingdoms of the world which are on the face of the earth. Also the king of Sheshach shall drink after them "Therefore you shall say to them, 'Thus says the LORD of hosts, the God of Israel: Drink, be drunk, and vomit! Fall and rise no more, because of the sword which I will send among you.' And it shall be, if they refuse to take the cup from your hand to drink, then you shall say to them, 'Thus says the LORD of hosts: You shall certainly drink! For behold, I begin to bring calamity on the city which is called by My name, and should you be utterly unpunished? You shall not be unpunished, for I will call for a sword on all the inhabitants of the earth,' says the LORD of hosts." Therefore prophesy against them all these words, and say to them: 'The LORD will roar from on high, and utter His voice from His holy habitation; He will roar mightily against His fold. He will give a shout, as those who tread the grapes, against all the inhabitants of the earth. A noise will come to the ends of the earth— for the LORD has a controversy with the nations; He will plead His case with all flesh. He will give those who are wicked to the sword,' says the LORD." Thus says the LORD of hosts: "Behold, disaster shall go forth from nation to nation, and a great whirlwind shall be raised up from the farthest parts of the earth. And at that day the slain of the LORD shall be from one end of the earth even to the other end of the earth. They shall not be lamented, or gathered, or buried; they shall become refuse on the ground. Wail, shepherds, and cry! Roll about in the ashes, you leaders of the flock! For the days of your slaughter and your dispersions are fulfilled; you shall fall like a precious vessel. And the shepherds will have no way to flee, nor the leaders of the flock to escape. A voice of the cry of the shepherds, and a wailing of the leaders to the flock will be heard. For the LORD has plundered their pasture, and the peaceful dwellings are cut down because of the fierce anger of the LORD. He has left His lair like the lion; for their land is desolate because of the fierceness of the oppressor, and because of His fierce anger."

Chapter 29

1 Now these are the words of the letter that Jeremiah the prophet sent from Jerusalem to the remainder of the elders who were carried away captive, to the priests, the prophets, and all the people whom Nebuchadnezzar had carried away captive from Jerusalem to Babylon. 2 (This happened after Jeconiah the king, the queen mother, the eunuchs, the princes of Judah and Jerusalem, the craftsmen, and the smiths had departed from Jerusalem.) 3 The letter was sent by the hand of Elasah the son of Shaphan and Gemariah the son of Hilkiah, whom Zedekiah king of Judah sent to Babylon, to Nebuchadnezzar king of Babylon, saying, 4 Thus says the LORD of hosts, the God of Israel, to all who were carried away captive, whom I have caused to be carried away from Jerusalem to Babylon: 5 Build houses and dwell in them; plant gardens and eat their fruit. 6 Take wives and beget sons and daughters; and take wives for your sons and give your daughters to husbands, so that they may bear sons

and daughters—that you may be increased there, and not diminished. 7 And seek the peace of the city where I have caused you to be carried away captive, and pray to the LORD for it; for in its peace you will have peace. 8 For thus says the LORD of hosts, the God of Israel: Do not let your prophets and your diviners who are in your midst deceive you, nor listen to your dreams which you cause to be dreamed. 9 For they prophesy falsely to you in My name; I have not sent them, says the LORD 10 For thus says the LORD: After seventy years are completed at Babylon, I will visit you and perform My good word toward you, and cause you to return to this place. 11 For I know the thoughts that I think toward you, says the LORD, thoughts of peace and not of evil, to give you a future and a hope. 12 Then you will call upon Me and go and pray to Me, and I will listen to you. 13 And you will seek Me and find Me, when you search for Me with all your heart. 14 I will be found by you, says the LORD, and I will bring you back from your captivity; I will gather you from all the nations and from all the places where I have driven you, says the LORD, and I will bring you to the place from which I cause you to be carried away captive 15 Because you have said, "The LORD has raised up prophets for us in Babylon"— 16 therefore thus says the LORD concerning the king who sits on the throne of David, concerning all the people who dwell in this city, and concerning your brethren who have not gone out with you into captivity— 17 thus says the LORD of hosts: Behold, I will send on them the sword, the famine, and the pestilence, and will make them like rotten figs that cannot be eaten, they are so bad. 18 And I will pursue them with the sword, with famine, and with pestilence; and I will deliver them to trouble among all the kingdoms of the earth—to be a curse, an astonishment, a hissing, and a reproach among all the nations where I have driven them, 19 because they have not heeded My words, says the LORD, which I sent to them by My servants the prophets, rising up early and sending them; neither would you heed, says the LORD. 20 Therefore hear the word of the LORD, all you of the captivity, whom I have sent from Jerusalem to Babylon 21 Thus says the LORD of hosts, the God of Israel, concerning Ahab the son of Kolaiah and Zedekiah the son of Maaseiah, who prophesy a lie to you in My name: Behold, I will deliver them into the hand of Nebuchadnezzar king of Babylon, and he shall slay them before your eyes. 22 And because of them a curse shall be taken up by all the captivity of Judah who are in Babylon, saying, "The LORD make you like Zedekiah and Ahab, whom the king of Babylon roasted in the fire"; 23 because they have done disgraceful things in Israel, have committed adultery with their neighbors' wives, and have spoken lying words in My name, which I have not commanded them. Indeed I know, and am a witness, says the LORD 24 You shall also speak to Shemaiah the Nehelamite, saying, 25 Thus speaks the LORD of hosts, the God of Israel, saying: You have sent letters in your name to all the people who are at Jerusalem, to Zephaniah the son of Maaseiah the priest, and to all the priests, saying, 26 "The LORD has made you priest instead of Jehoiada the priest, so that there should be officers in the house of the LORD over every man who is demented and considers himself a prophet, that you should put him in prison and in the stocks. 27 Now therefore, why have you not rebuked Jeremiah of Anathoth who makes himself a prophet to you? 28 For he has sent to us in Babylon, saying, 'This captivity is long; build houses and dwell in them, and plant gardens and eat their fruit.'" 29 Now Zephaniah the priest read this letter in the hearing of Jeremiah the prophet. 30 Then the word of the LORD came to Jeremiah, saying: 31 Send to all those in captivity, saying, Thus says the LORD concerning Shemaiah the Nehelamite: Because Shemaiah has prophesied to you, and I have not sent him, and he has caused you to trust in a lie— 32 therefore thus says the LORD: Behold, I will punish Shemaiah the Nehelamite and his family: he shall not have anyone to dwell among this people, nor shall he see the good that I will do for My people, says the LORD, because he has taught rebellion against the LORD

Chapter 30

1 The word that came to Jeremiah from the LORD, saying, 2 Thus speaks the LORD God of Israel, saying: "Write in a book for yourself all the words that I have spoken to you. 3 For behold, the days are coming," says the LORD, "that I will bring back from captivity My people Israel and Judah," says the LORD. "And I will cause them to return to the land that I gave to their fathers, and they shall possess it." 4 Now these are the words that the LORD spoke concerning Israel and Judah. 5 "For thus says the LORD: 'We have heard a voice of trembling, Of fear, and not of peace. 6 Ask now, and see, Whether a man is ever in labor with child? So why do I see every man with his hands on his loins Like a woman in labor, And all faces turned pale? 7 Alas! For that day is great, So that none is like it; And it is the time of Jacob's trouble, But he shall be saved out of it 8 'For it shall come to pass in that day,' Says the LORD of hosts, 'That I will break his yoke from your neck, And will burst your bonds; Foreigners shall no more enslave them. 9 But they shall serve the LORD their God, And David their king, Whom I will raise up for them 10 'Therefore do not fear, O My servant Jacob,' says the LORD, 'Nor be dismayed, O Israel; For behold, I will save you from afar, And your seed from the land of their captivity. Jacob shall return, have rest and be quiet, And no one shall make him afraid. 11 For I am with you,' says the LORD, 'to save you; Though I make a full end of all nations where I have scattered you, Yet I will not make a complete end of you. But I will correct you in justice, And will not let you go altogether unpunished.' 12 "For thus says the LORD: 'Your affliction is incurable, Your wound is severe. 13 There is no one to plead your cause, That you may be bound up; You have no healing medicines. 14 All your lovers have forgotten you; They do not seek you; For I have wounded you with the wound of an enemy, With the chastisement of a cruel one, For the multitude of your iniquities, Because your sins have increased. 15 Why do you cry about your affliction? Your sorrow is incurable. Because of the multitude of your iniquities, Because your sins have increased, I have done these things to you 16 'Therefore all those who devour you shall be devoured; And all your adversaries, every one of them, shall go into captivity; Those who plunder you shall become plunder, And all who prey upon you I will make a prey. 17 For I will restore health to you And heal you of your wounds,' says the LORD, 'Because they called you an outcast saying: "This is Zion; No one seeks her."' 18 "Thus says the LORD: 'Behold, I will bring back the captivity of Jacob's tents, And have mercy on his dwelling places; The city shall be built upon its own mound, And the palace shall remain according to its own plan. 19 Then out of them shall proceed thanksgiving And the voice of those who make merry; I will multiply them, and they shall not diminish; I will also glorify them, and they shall not be small. 20 Their children also shall be as before, And their congregation shall be established before Me; And I will punish all who oppress them. 21 Their nobles shall be from among them, And their governor shall come from their midst; Then I will cause him to draw near, And he shall approach Me; For who is this who

pledged his heart to approach Me?' says the LORD. 22 'You shall be My people, And I will be your God.'" 23 Behold, the whirlwind of the LORD Goes forth with fury, A continuing whirlwind; It will fall violently on the head of the wicked. 24 The fierce anger of the LORD will not return until He has done it, And until He has performed the intents of His heart. In the latter days you will consider it

Chapter 31

At the same time, says the LORD, I will be the God of all the families of Israel, and they shall be my people. Thus says the LORD, the people that escaped the sword have found favor in the wilderness; they have walked before Israel to find rest. The LORD has appeared to me from everlasting, saying, "Yes, I have loved you with an everlasting love; therefore, I have drawn you with mercy. In the future, I will build you, and you shall be built, O virgin Israel. You shall still be adorned with your gables, and you shall go forth in the dance of those who are happy. You shall still plant vines on the mountains of Samaria, and the planters who plant them shall enjoy them. For the day will come when the watchmen on the mount of Ephraim will cry, 'Arise and go up to Zion to the LORD our God.'" For thus says the LORD: "Rejoice with gladness over Jacob and shout for joy among the nations; praise and say, 'O LORD, save your people, the remnant of Israel.' Behold, I will bring them from the land of the north and gather them from the coasts of the earth, including the blind and the lame, the pregnant woman and the one who has given birth; a great company will return here. They will come weeping, and with mercy, I will bring them back. I will lead them by the rivers of water in a straight path where they will not stumble; for I am a father to Israel, and Ephraim is my firstborn Hear the word of the LORD, O nations, and declare it in the distant lands; say, 'He who scattered Israel will gather them and keep them as a shepherd does his flock.' For the LORD has redeemed Jacob and ransomed him from the hand of one stronger than he. Therefore, they shall come and sing in the height of Zion, and they shall be radiant over the goodness of the LORD, for grain, for wine, for oil, and for the young of the flock and the herd. Their souls shall be like a well-watered garden, and they shall no longer sorrow at all. Then the virgins shall rejoice in the dance, and the young men and the old together, for I will turn their mourning into joy, I will comfort them and make them rejoice from their sorrow. I will satiate the soul of the priests with abundance, and my people shall be satisfied with my goodness," says the LORD Thus says the LORD: "A voice was heard in Ramah, lamentation and bitter weeping, Rachel weeping for her children, refusing to be comforted for her children because they are no more. Thus says the LORD, 'Refrain your voice from weeping and your eyes from tears, for your work shall be rewarded,' says the LORD, 'and they shall come back from the land of the enemy. There is hope in your future,' says the LORD, 'that your children shall come back to their own border.' I have surely heard Ephraim bemoaning himself: 'You have chastised me, and I was chastised, like an untrained calf; restore me, and I will return, for you are the LORD my God. Surely, after my turning, I repented; and after I was instructed, I struck myself on the thigh; I was ashamed, yes, even humiliated, because I bore the reproach of my youth.' Is Ephraim my dear son? Is he a pleasant child? For though I spoke against him, I earnestly remember him still; therefore, my heart yearns for him; I will surely have mercy on him," says the LORD "Set up road markers, make signposts; set your heart toward the highway, the way in which you went. Turn back, O virgin of Israel, turn back to these your cities. How long will you gad about, O you backsliding daughter? For the LORD has created a new thing in the earth—a woman shall encompass a man." Thus says the LORD of hosts, the God of Israel: "They shall again use this speech in the land of Judah and in its cities, when I bring back their captivity: 'The LORD bless you, O habitation of justice, and mountain of holiness.' And there shall dwell in Judah itself, and in all its cities together, farmers and those going out with flocks. For I have satiated the weary soul, and I have replenished every sorrowful soul." After this, I awoke and looked around, and my sleep was sweet to me. Behold, the days are coming," says the LORD, "that I will sow the house of Israel and the house of Judah with the seed of man and the seed of beast. And it shall come to pass that as I have watched over them to pluck up, to break down, to throw down, to destroy, and to afflict, so I will watch over them to build and to plant," says the LORD. "In those days, they shall no longer say, 'The fathers have eaten sour grapes, and the children's teeth are set on edge.' But everyone shall die for his own iniquity; every man who eats the sour grapes, his teeth shall be set on edge "Behold, the days are coming," says the LORD, "when I will make a new covenant with the house of Israel and with the house of Judah—not according to the covenant that I made with their fathers in the day that I took them by the hand to lead them out of the land of Egypt, My covenant which they broke, though I was a husband to them," says the LORD. "But this is the covenant that I will make with the house of Israel after those days," says the LORD: "I will put my law in their minds, and write it on their hearts; and I will be their God, and they shall be my people. No more shall every man teach his neighbor, and every man his brother, saying, 'Know the LORD,' for they all shall know me, from the least of them to the greatest of them," says the LORD. "For I will forgive their iniquity, and their sin I will remember no more." Thus says the LORD, who gives the sun for a light by day, the ordinances of the moon and the stars for a light by night, who disturbs the sea, and its waves roar (The LORD of hosts is his name): "If those ordinances depart from before me," says the LORD, "then the seed of Israel shall also cease from being a nation before me forever." Thus says the LORD: "If heaven above can be measured, and the foundations of the earth searched out beneath, I will also cast off all the seed of Israel for all that they have done," says the LORD "Behold, the days are coming," says the LORD, "that the city shall be built for the LORD from the Tower of Hananel to the Corner Gate. The measuring line shall go out farther straight ahead to the hill Gareb; then it shall turn toward Goath. And the whole valley of the dead bodies and of the ashes, and all the fields as far as the Brook Kidron, to the corner of the Horse Gate toward the east, shall be holy to the LORD. It shall not be plucked up or thrown down anymore forever."

Chapter 32

The word that came to Jeremiah from the LORD in the tenth year of Zedekiah king of Judah, which was the eighteenth year of Nebuchadnezzar. At that time, the army of the king of Babylon besieged Jerusalem, and Jeremiah the prophet was confined in the court of the guard, which was in the king of Judah's house. Zedekiah king of Judah had imprisoned him, saying, "Why do you prophesy and say, 'Thus says the LORD, Behold, I will give this city into the hand of the king of Babylon, and he shall take it; and Zedekiah king of Judah shall not escape from the hand of the Chaldeans, but shall surely be delivered into the hand of the king of Babylon, and shall speak with him face to face and see him eye to eye. Then he shall lead Zedekiah to Babylon, and there he shall remain until I visit him, says the LORD; though you fight against the Chaldeans, you shall not succeed'?" Jeremiah said, "The word of the LORD came to me, saying, 'Behold, Hanamel the son of Shallum your uncle will come to you, saying, "Buy my field which is in Anathoth, for the right of redemption is yours to buy it."' Then Hanamel my uncle's son came to me in the court of the guard according to the word of the LORD, and said to me, 'Please buy my field that is in Anathoth, which is in the country of Benjamin, for the right of inheritance is yours, and the redemption is yours; buy it for yourself.' Then I knew that this was the word of the LORD. So I bought the field from Hanamel the son of my uncle, who was in Anathoth, and weighed out to him the money—seventeen shekels of silver. And I signed the deed and sealed it, took witnesses, and weighed the money on the scales. So I took the deed of purchase, both that which was sealed according to the law and custom, and that which was open; and I gave the deed of purchase to Baruch the son of Neriah, son of Mahseiah, in the presence of Hanamel my uncle's son, and in the presence of the witnesses who signed the deed of purchase, before all the Jews who sat in the court of the guard Then I charged Baruch before them, saying, 'Thus says the LORD of hosts, the God of Israel: Take these deeds, both this sealed deed of purchase and this open deed, and put them in an earthen vessel, that they may last many days.' For thus says the LORD of hosts, the God of Israel: 'Houses and fields and vineyards shall be possessed again in this land.' After I had given the deed of purchase to Baruch the son of Neriah, I prayed to the LORD, saying: 'Ah, Lord GOD! Behold, you have made the heavens and the earth by your great power and outstretched arm. There is nothing too hard for you. You show lovingkindness to thousands, and repay the iniquity of the fathers into the bosom of their children after them—the Great, the Mighty God, whose name is the LORD of hosts. You are great in counsel and mighty in work, for your eyes are open to all the ways of the sons of men, to give everyone according to his ways and according to the fruit of his doings. You have set signs and wonders in the land of Egypt, to this day, and in Israel and among other men, and have made yourself a name, as it is this day. You have brought your people Israel out of the land of Egypt with signs and wonders, with a strong hand and an outstretched arm, and with great terror; you have given them this land, of which you swore to their fathers to give them—a land flowing with milk and honey. They came in and took possession of it, but they did not obey your voice or walk in your law. They have done nothing of all that you commanded them to do; therefore you have caused all this calamity to come upon them. Look! The siege mounds! They have come to the city to take it; and the city has been given into the hand of the Chaldeans who fight against it, because of the sword and famine and pestilence. What you have spoken has happened; you see it. And you have said to me, O Lord GOD, 'Buy the field for money, and take witnesses'—yet the city has been given into the hand of the Chaldeans.'" Then the word of the LORD came to Jeremiah, saying, "Behold, I am the LORD, the God of all flesh. Is there anything too hard for me? Therefore thus says the LORD: 'Behold, I will give this city into the hand of the Chaldeans, into the hand of Nebuchadnezzar king of Babylon, and he shall take it. The Chaldeans who fight against this city shall come and set fire to this city and burn it, with the houses on whose roofs they have offered incense to Baal and poured out drink offerings to other gods to provoke me to anger. For the children of Israel and the children of Judah have done only evil before me from their youth. For the children of Israel have only provoked me to anger with the work of their hands,' says the LORD. 'For this city has been to me a provocation of my anger and my fury from the day that they built it even to this day; so I will remove it from before my face because of all the evil of the children of Israel and the children of Judah, which they have done to provoke me to anger—they, their kings, their princes, their priests, their prophets, the men of Judah, and the inhabitants of Jerusalem. And they have turned to me the back, and not the face; though I taught them, rising up early and teaching them, yet they have not listened to receive instruction. But they set their abominations in the house which is called by my name, to defile it. And they built the high places of Baal which are in the Valley of the Son of Hinnom, to cause their sons and their daughters to pass through the fire to Molech, which I did not command them, nor did it come into my mind that they should do this abomination, to cause Judah to sin.' "Now therefore, thus says the LORD, the God of Israel, concerning this city of which you say, 'It shall be delivered into the hand of the king of Babylon by the sword, by the famine, and by the pestilence: Behold, I will gather them out of all countries where I have driven them in my anger, in my fury, and in great wrath; I will bring them back to this place, and I will cause them to dwell safely. They shall be my people, and I will be their God; then I will give them one heart and one way, that they may fear me forever, for the good of them and their children after them. And I will make an everlasting covenant with them, that I will not turn away from doing them good; but I will put my fear in their hearts so that they will not depart from me. Yes, I will rejoice over them to do them good, and I will assuredly plant them in this land, with all my heart and with all my soul.' "For thus says the LORD: 'Just as I have brought all this great calamity on this people, so I will bring on them all the good that I have promised them. And fields will be bought in this land of which you say, "It is desolate, without man or beast; it has been given into the hand of the Chaldeans." Men will buy fields for money, sign deeds and seal them, and take witnesses in the land of Benjamin, in the places around Jerusalem, in the cities of Judah, in the cities of the mountains, in the cities of the lowland, and in the cities of the South; for I will cause their captives to return,' says the LORD."

Chapter 33

Moreover, the word of the LORD came to Jeremiah a second time, while he was still shut up in the court of the guard, saying, "Thus says the LORD who made it, the LORD who formed it to establish it (the LORD is His name): 'Call to me, and I will answer you, and show you great and mighty things, which you do not know.' For thus says the LORD, the God of Israel, concerning the houses of this city and the houses of the kings of Judah, which have been pulled down to fortify against the siege mounds and the sword: 'They come to fight with the Chaldeans, but only to fill their places with the dead bodies of men whom I will slay in my anger and my fury, all for whose wickedness I have hidden my face from this city. Behold, I will bring it health and healing; I will heal them and reveal to them the abundance of peace and truth. And I will cause the captives of Judah and the captives of Israel to return, and will rebuild those places as at the first. I will cleanse them from all their iniquity by which they have sinned against me, and I will pardon all their iniquities by which they have sinned and by which they have transgressed against me. Then it shall be to me a name of joy, a praise, and an honor before all nations of the earth, who shall hear all the good that I do to them; they shall fear and tremble for all the goodness and all the prosperity that I provide for it.' "Thus says the LORD: 'Again there shall be heard in this place—of which you say, "It is desolate, without man and without beast"—in the cities of Judah, in the streets of Jerusalem that are desolate, without man and without inhabitant and without beast, the voice of joy and the voice of gladness, the voice of the bridegroom and the voice of the bride, the voice of those who will say: "Praise the LORD of hosts, for the LORD is good, for His mercy endures forever"—and of those who will bring the sacrifice of praise into the house of the LORD. For I will cause the captives of the land to return as at the first,' says the LORD "Thus says the LORD of hosts: 'In this place which is desolate, without man and without beast, and in all its cities, there shall again be a dwelling place of shepherds causing their flocks to lie down. In the cities of the mountains, in the cities of the lowland, in the cities of the South, in the land of Benjamin, in the places around Jerusalem, and in the cities of Judah, the flocks shall again pass under the hands of him who counts them,' says the LORD "Behold, the days are coming,' says the LORD, 'that I will perform that good thing which I have promised to the house of Israel and to the house of Judah: In those days and at that time I will cause to grow up to David a Branch of righteousness; he shall execute judgment and righteousness in the earth. In those days Judah will be saved, and Jerusalem will dwell safely. And this is the name by which she will be called: THE LORD OUR RIGHTEOUSNESS.' For thus says the LORD: 'David shall never lack a man to sit on the throne of the house of Israel; nor shall the priests, the Levites, lack a man to offer burnt offerings before me, to kindle grain offerings, and to sacrifice continually.'" And the word of the LORD came to Jeremiah, saying, "Thus says the LORD: 'If you can break my covenant with the day and my covenant with the night, so that there will not be day and night in their season, then my covenant may also be broken with David my servant, so that he shall not have a son to reign on his throne, and with the Levites, the priests, my ministers. As the host of heaven cannot be numbered, nor the sand of the sea measured, so will I multiply the descendants of David my servant and the Levites who minister to me.'" Moreover, the word of the LORD came to Jeremiah, saying, "Have you not considered what these people have spoken, saying, 'The two families which the LORD has chosen, He has also cast them off'? Thus they have despised my people, as if they should no more be a nation before them. Thus says the LORD: 'If my covenant is not with day and night, and if I have not appointed the ordinances of heaven and earth, then I will cast away the descendants of Jacob and David my servant, so that I will not take any of his descendants to be rulers over the descendants of Abraham, Isaac, and Jacob. For I will cause their captives to return, and will have mercy on them.'"

Chapter 34

The word which came to Jeremiah from the LORD, when Nebuchadnezzar king of Babylon and all his army, all the kingdoms of the earth under his dominion, and all the people, fought against Jerusalem and all its cities, saying, "Thus says the LORD, the God of Israel: 'Go and speak to Zedekiah king of Judah and tell him, "Thus says the LORD: Behold, I will give this city into the hand of the king of Babylon, and he shall burn it with fire. And you shall not escape from his hand but shall surely be taken and delivered into his hand; your eyes shall see the eyes of the king of Babylon, he shall speak with you face to face, and you shall go to Babylon."' Yet hear the word of the LORD, O Zedekiah king of Judah! Thus says the LORD concerning you: 'You shall not die by the sword. You shall die in peace; as in the ceremonies of your fathers, the former kings who were before you, so they shall burn incense for you and lament for you, saying, "Alas, lord!" For I have pronounced the word,' says the LORD." Then Jeremiah the prophet spoke all these words to Zedekiah king of Judah in Jerusalem, when the king of Babylon's army fought against Jerusalem and all the cities of Judah that were left, against Lachish and Azekah; for only these fortified cities remained of the cities of Judah. This is the word that came to Jeremiah from the LORD, after King Zedekiah had made a covenant with all the people who were at Jerusalem to proclaim liberty to them: that every man should set free his male and female slave—a Hebrew man or woman—that no one should keep a fellow Jew in bondage. Now when all the princes and all the people, who had entered into the covenant, heard that everyone should set free his male and female slaves, that no one should keep them in bondage anymore, they obeyed and let them go. But afterward, they changed their minds and made the male and female slaves return, whom they had set free, and brought them into subjection as male and female slaves Therefore, the word of the LORD came to Jeremiah from the LORD, saying, "Thus says the LORD, the God of Israel: 'I made a covenant with your fathers in the day that I brought them out of the land of Egypt, out of the house of bondage, saying, "At the end of seven years let every man set free his Hebrew brother, who has been sold to him; and when he has served you six years, you shall let him go free from you." But your fathers did not obey me nor incline their ear. Then you recently turned and did what was right in my sight—every man proclaiming liberty to his neighbor; and you made a covenant before me in the house which is called by my name. Then you turned around and profaned my name, and every one of you brought back his male and female slaves, whom you had set at liberty, at their pleasure, and brought them back into subjection, to be your male and female slaves.' Therefore thus says the LORD: 'You have not obeyed me in proclaiming liberty, every one to his brother and every one to his neighbor. Behold, I proclaim liberty to you,' says the LORD, 'to the sword, to pestilence, and to famine! And I will deliver you to trouble among all the kingdoms of the earth. And I will give the men who have transgressed my covenant, who have not performed the words of the covenant which they made before me, when they cut the calf in two and passed between its parts—the princes of Judah, the princes of Jerusalem, the eunuchs, the priests, and all the people of the land who passed between the parts of the calf—I will give them into the hand of their enemies and into the hand of those who seek their life. Their dead bodies shall be for meat for the birds of the heaven and the beasts of the earth. And I will give Zedekiah king of Judah and his princes into the hand of their enemies, into the hand of those who seek their life, and into the hand of the king of Babylon's army which has gone back from you. Behold, I will command,' says the LORD, 'and cause them to return to this city; they will fight against it and take it and burn it with fire; and I will make the cities of Judah a desolation without inhabitant.'"

Chapter 35

The word which came to Jeremiah from the LORD in the days of Jehoiakim the son of Josiah, king of Judah, saying, "Go to the house of the Rechabites, speak to them, and bring them into the house of the LORD, into one of the chambers, and give them wine to drink." Then I took Jaazaniah the son of Jeremiah, the son of Habazziniah, his brothers, and all his sons, and the whole house of the Rechabites, and I brought them into the house of the LORD, into the chamber of the sons of Hanan the son of Igdaliah, a man of God, which was by the chamber of the princes, above the chamber of Maaseiah the son of Shallum, the keeper of the door. Then I set before the sons of the house of the Rechabites bowls full of wine, and cups; and I said to them, "Drink wine." But they said, "We will drink no wine, for Jonadab the son of Rechab, our father, commanded us, saying, 'You shall drink no wine, you nor your sons, forever. You shall not build a house, sow seed, plant a vineyard, nor have any of these; but all your days you shall dwell in tents, that you may live many days in the land where you are sojourners.' Thus, we have obeyed the voice of Jonadab the son of Rechab, our father, in all that he charged us, to drink no wine all our days, we, our wives, our sons, or our daughters, nor to build ourselves houses to dwell in; nor do we have vineyard, field, or seed. But we have dwelt in tents and have obeyed and done according to all that Jonadab our father commanded us. But it came to pass, when Nebuchadnezzar king of Babylon came up into the land, that we said, 'Come, let us go to Jerusalem for fear of the army of the Chaldeans and for fear of the army of the Syrians.' So, we dwell at Jerusalem." Then came the word of the LORD to Jeremiah, saying, "Thus says the LORD of hosts, the God of Israel: 'Go and tell the men of Judah and the inhabitants of Jerusalem, "Will you not receive instruction to obey my words?" says the LORD. "The words of Jonadab the son of Rechab, which he commanded his sons not to drink wine, are performed; for to this day they drink none, and obey their father's commandment. But although I have spoken to you, rising early and speaking, you did not obey me. I have also sent to you all my servants the prophets, rising up early and sending them, saying, 'Turn now everyone from his evil way, amend your doings, and do not go after other gods to serve them; then you will dwell in the land which I have given you and your fathers.' But you have not inclined your ear nor obeyed me. Surely the sons of Jonadab the son of Rechab have performed the commandment of their father, which he commanded them, but this people has not obeyed me." Therefore thus says the LORD God of hosts, the God of Israel: "Behold, I will bring on Judah and on all the inhabitants of Jerusalem all the doom that I have pronounced against them; because I have spoken to them but they have not heard, and I have called to them but they have not answered." And Jeremiah said to the house of the Rechabites, "Thus says the LORD of hosts, the God of Israel: 'Because you have obeyed the commandment of Jonadab your father, and kept all his precepts and done according to all that he commanded you, therefore thus says the LORD of hosts, the God of Israel: 'Jonadab the son of Rechab shall not lack a man to stand before me forever.'"

Chapter 36

In the fourth year of Jehoiakim, the son of Josiah, king of Judah, this word came to Jeremiah from the LORD: "Take a scroll and write on it all the words I have spoken to you concerning Israel, Judah, and all the nations, from the day I spoke to you, from the days of Josiah until today. Perhaps the house of Judah will hear about all the disaster I intend to bring upon them, so that each one may turn from his evil way, and I will forgive their iniquity and their sin." Jeremiah then called Baruch, the son of Neriah, and Baruch wrote down at Jeremiah's dictation all the words of the LORD, which he had spoken to him, on a scroll. Jeremiah commanded Baruch, saying, "I am restricted; I cannot go into the house of the LORD.

Therefore, go and read from the scroll which you have written at my dictation, the words of the LORD, to the people in the house of the LORD on a day of fasting. Also, you shall read them to all the people of Judah who come out of their cities. Perhaps they will present their supplication before the LORD, and everyone will turn from his evil way, for great is the anger and the wrath that the LORD has pronounced against this people." So Baruch, the son of Neriah, did all that Jeremiah the prophet commanded him, reading from the book the words of the LORD in the house of the LORD. In the fifth year of Jehoiakim, the son of Josiah, king of Judah, in the ninth month, all the people in Jerusalem and all the people who came from the cities of Judah to Jerusalem proclaimed a fast before the LORD. Then Baruch read the words of Jeremiah in the house of the LORD, in the chamber of Gemariah, the son of Shaphan the scribe, in the upper court, at the entry of the New Gate of the house of the LORD, in the hearing of all the people When Michaiah, the son of Gemariah, the son of Shaphan, heard all the words of the LORD from the book, he went down to the king's house, into the scribe's chamber, and all the officials were sitting there: Elishama the scribe, Delaiah the son of Shemaiah, Elnathan the son of Achbor, Gemariah the son of Shaphan, Zedekiah the son of Hananiah, and all the officials. Michaiah declared to them all the words that he had heard when Baruch read the book in the hearing of the people Then all the officials sent Jehudi, the son of Nethaniah, the son of Shelemiah, the son of Cushi, to Baruch, saying, "Take in your hand the scroll from which you have read in the hearing of the people and come." So Baruch, the son of Neriah, took the scroll in his hand and came to them. They said to him, "Sit down, please, and read it to us." So Baruch read it to them When they had heard all the words, they turned in fear one to another and said to Baruch, "We will surely report all these words to the king." Then they asked Baruch, saying, "Tell us, please, how did you write all these words at his dictation?" So Baruch said to them, "He dictated all these words to me, and I wrote them with ink on the scroll." Then the officials said to Baruch, "Go, hide yourself, you and Jeremiah, and do not let anyone know where you are." So they went to the king in the court, but they stored the scroll in the chamber of Elishama the scribe and reported all the words to the king. Then the king sent Jehudi to get the scroll, and he took it from the chamber of Elishama the scribe. Jehudi read it in the hearing of the king and in the hearing of all the officials who stood beside the king Now the king was sitting in the winter house in the ninth month, with a fire burning in the brazier before him. When Jehudi had read three or four columns, the king cut it with a scribe's knife and threw it into the fire that was in the brazier until all the scroll was consumed in the fire that was in the brazier. Yet the king and all his servants who heard all these words were not afraid, nor did they tear their garments. Even though Elnathan, Delaiah, and Gemariah pleaded with the king not to burn the scroll, he would not listen to them. And the king commanded Jerahmeel the king's son, Seraiah the son of Azriel, and Shelemiah the son of Abdeel to seize Baruch the scribe and Jeremiah the prophet, but the LORD had hidden them Then the word of the LORD came to Jeremiah after the king had burned the scroll and the words which Baruch had written at the dictation of Jeremiah, saying, "Take again another scroll and write on it all the former words that were on the first scroll, which Jehoiakim, the king of Judah, burned. And concerning Jehoiakim, king of Judah, you shall say, 'Thus says the LORD, You have burned this scroll, saying, "Why have you written on it that the king of Babylon will certainly come and destroy this land and will make man and beast to cease from it?" Therefore thus says the LORD concerning Jehoiakim king of Judah: He shall have no one to sit on the throne of David, and his dead body shall be cast out to the heat of the day and the frost of the night. I will also punish him and his descendants and his servants for their iniquity, and I will bring on them and on the inhabitants of Jerusalem and the men of Judah all the disaster that I have pronounced against them, but they did not listen.'" Then Jeremiah took another scroll and gave it to Baruch, the son of Neriah, the scribe, who wrote on it at the dictation of Jeremiah all the words of the book which Jehoiakim, king of Judah, had burned in the fire; and many similar words were added to them

Chapter 37

Now King Zedekiah, the son of Josiah, reigned instead of Coniah, the son of Jehoiakim, whom Nebuchadnezzar, king of Babylon, had made king in the land of Judah. But neither he nor his servants nor the people of the land gave heed to the words of the LORD which he spoke by the prophet Jeremiah. And King Zedekiah sent Jehucal, the son of Shelemiah, and Zephaniah, the son of Maaseiah, the priest, to the prophet Jeremiah, saying, "Pray now to the LORD our God for us." Now Jeremiah was coming and going among the people, for they had not yet put him in prison. Then Pharaoh's army came up from Egypt; and when the Chaldeans who were besieging Jerusalem heard news of them, they departed from Jerusalem Then the word of the LORD came to the prophet Jeremiah, saying, "Thus says the LORD, the God of Israel, 'Thus you shall say to the king of Judah, who sent you to inquire of me: Behold, Pharaoh's army which has come up to help you will return to Egypt, to their own land. And the Chaldeans shall come back and fight against this city and take it and burn it with fire.' Thus says the LORD: 'Do not deceive yourselves, saying, "The Chaldeans will surely depart from us," for they will not depart. For though you had defeated the whole army of the Chaldeans who fight against you, and there remained only wounded men among them, they would rise up, every man in his tent, and burn the city with fire.'" And it happened, when the army of the Chaldeans had withdrawn from Jerusalem at the approach of Pharaoh's army, that Jeremiah went out of Jerusalem to go into the land of Benjamin to claim his property there among the people. And when he was at the Gate of Benjamin, a captain of the guard was there whose name was Irijah, the son of Shelemiah, the son of Hananiah, and he arrested Jeremiah the prophet, saying, "You are defecting to the Chaldeans!" Then Jeremiah said, "It is a lie! I am not defecting to the Chaldeans." But Irijah would not listen to him; so Irijah arrested Jeremiah and brought him to the princes. Therefore the princes were angry with Jeremiah, and they struck him and put him in prison in the house of Jonathan the scribe, for they had made that the prison When Jeremiah entered the dungeon and the cells, and Jeremiah had remained there many days, Zedekiah the king sent and took him out. The king asked him secretly in his house and said, "Is there any word from the LORD?" And Jeremiah said, "There is." Then he said, "You shall be delivered into the hand of the king of Babylon!" Moreover, Jeremiah said to King Zedekiah, "What offense have I committed against you, against your servants, or against this people, that you have put me in prison? Where now are your prophets who prophesied to you, saying, 'The king of Babylon will not come against you or against this land'? Therefore please hear now, O my lord the king; please, let my petition be accepted before you, and do not make me return to the house of Jonathan the scribe, lest I die there." Then Zedekiah the king commanded that they should commit Jeremiah to the court of the guard, and that they should give him daily a piece of bread from the baker's street, until all the bread in the city was gone. Thus Jeremiah remained in the court of the guard

Chapter 38

Now Shephatiah, the son of Mattan, Gedaliah the son of Pashhur, Jucal the son of Shelemiah, and Pashhur the son of Malchiah heard the words that Jeremiah had spoken to all the people, saying, "Thus says the LORD, 'He who remains in this city shall die by the sword, by famine, and by pestilence; but he who goes over to the Chaldeans shall live; his life shall be as a prize to him, and he shall live.' Thus says the LORD, 'This city shall surely be given into the hand of the king of Babylon's army, which shall take it.'" Therefore the princes said to the king, "Please, let this man be put to death, for he weakens the hands of the men of war who remain in this city, and the hands of all the people, by speaking such words to them; for this man does not seek the welfare of this people, but their harm." Then Zedekiah the king said, "Look, he is in your hand. For the king can do nothing against you." So they took Jeremiah and cast him into the dungeon of Malchiah, the king's son, which was in the court of the guard. They let Jeremiah down with ropes. And in the dungeon, there was no water, but mire. So Jeremiah sank in the mire Now Ebed-Melech, the Ethiopian, one of the eunuchs who was in the king's house, heard that they had put Jeremiah in the dungeon. When the king was sitting at the Gate of Benjamin, Ebed-Melech went out of the king's house and spoke to the king, saying, "My lord the king, these men have done evil in all that they have done to Jeremiah the prophet, whom they have cast into the dungeon; and he is likely to die from hunger in the place where he is. For there is no more bread in the city." Then the king commanded Ebed-Melech the Ethiopian, saying, "Take from here thirty men with you, and lift Jeremiah the prophet out of the dungeon before he dies." So Ebed-Melech took the men with him and went into the house of the king, under the treasury, and took from there old clothes and old rags, and let them down by ropes into the dungeon to Jeremiah. Then Ebed-Melech the Ethiopian said to Jeremiah, "Please put these old clothes and rags under your armpits, under the ropes." And Jeremiah did so. So they pulled Jeremiah up with ropes and lifted him out of the dungeon. And Jeremiah remained in the court of the guard Then King Zedekiah sent and had Jeremiah the prophet brought to him at the third entrance of the house of the LORD. And the king said to Jeremiah, "I will ask you something. Hide nothing from me." Jeremiah said to Zedekiah, "If I declare it to you, will you not surely put me to death? And if I give you advice, you will not listen to me." So Zedekiah the king swore secretly to Jeremiah, saying, "As the LORD lives, who made our very souls, I will not put you to death, nor will I give you into the hand of these men who seek your life." Then Jeremiah said to Zedekiah, "Thus says the LORD, the God of hosts, the God of Israel: 'If you surely surrender to the king of Babylon's princes, then your soul shall live; this city shall not be burned with fire, and you and your house shall live. But if you do not surrender to the king of Babylon's princes, then this city shall be given into the hand of the Chaldeans; they shall burn it with fire, and you shall not escape from their hand.'" And King Zedekiah said to Jeremiah, "I am afraid of the Jews who have defected to the Chaldeans, lest they deliver me into their hand, and they abuse me." But Jeremiah said, "They shall not deliver you. Please, obey the voice of the LORD which I speak to you. So it shall be well with you, and your soul shall live. But if you refuse to surrender, this is the word that the LORD has shown me: 'Now behold, all the women who are left in the king of Judah's house shall be surrendered to the king of Babylon's princes, and those women shall say: "Your close friends have set upon you and prevailed against you; your feet have sunk in the mire, and they have turned away again." So they shall surrender all your wives and children to the Chaldeans. You shall not escape from their hand but shall be taken by the hand of the king of Babylon. And you shall cause this city to be burned with fire.'" Then Zedekiah said to Jeremiah, "Let no one know of these words, and you shall not die. But if the princes hear that I have talked with you, and they come to you and say to you, 'Declare to us now what you have said to the king, and also what the king said to you; do not hide it from us, and we will not put you to death,' then you shall say to them, 'I presented my request before the king, that he would not make me return to Jonathan's house to die there.'" Then all the princes came to Jeremiah and asked him. And he told them according to all these words that the king had commanded. So they stopped speaking with him, for the conversation had not been heard. Now Jeremiah remained in the court of the guard until the day that Jerusalem was taken. And he was there when Jerusalem was taken

Chapter 39

In the ninth year of Zedekiah, king of Judah, in the tenth month, Nebuchadnezzar, king of Babylon, and all his army came against Jerusalem and besieged it. In the eleventh year of Zedekiah, in the fourth month, on the ninth day of the month, the city was penetrated. Then all the princes of the king of Babylon came in and sat in the Middle Gate: Nergal-Sharezer, Samgar-Nebo, Sarsechim, the Rabsaris, Nergal-Sharezer, the Rabmag, with the rest of the princes of the king of Babylon. So it was when Zedekiah, the king of Judah, and all the men of war saw them, that they fled and went out of the city by night, by way of the king's garden, by the gate between the two walls. And he went out by way of the plain But the Chaldean army pursued them and overtook Zedekiah in the plains of Jericho. And when they had captured him, they brought him up to Nebuchadnezzar, king of Babylon, to Riblah in the land of Hamath, where he pronounced judgment on him. Then the king of Babylon killed the sons of Zedekiah before his eyes in Riblah. The king of Babylon also killed all the nobles of Judah. Moreover, he put out Zedekiah's eyes and bound him with bronze fetters to carry him off to Babylon. And the Chaldeans burned the king's house and the houses of the people with fire and broke down the walls of Jerusalem. Then Nebuzaradan, the captain of the guard, carried away captive to Babylon the remnant of the people who remained in the city and those who defected to him, with the rest of the people who remained. But Nebuzaradan, the captain of the guard, left in the land of Judah the poor people, who had nothing, and gave them vineyards and fields at the same time Now Nebuchadnezzar, king of Babylon, gave charge concerning Jeremiah to Nebuzaradan, the captain of the guard, saying, "Take him and look after him, and do him no harm; but do to him just as he says to you." So Nebuzaradan, the captain of the guard, sent Nebushasban, the Rabsaris, Nergal-Sharezer, the Rabmag, and all the king of Babylon's chief officers; then they sent someone to take Jeremiah from the court of the guard and committed him to Gedaliah, the son of Ahikam, the son of Shaphan, that he should take him home. So he dwelt among the people Meanwhile, the word of the LORD had come to Jeremiah while he was shut up in the court of the guard, saying, "Go and speak to Ebed-Melech, the Ethiopian, saying, 'Thus says the LORD of hosts, the God of Israel: Behold, I will bring my words upon this city for adversity and not for good, and they shall be performed in that day before you. But I will deliver you in that day,' says the LORD, 'and you shall not be given into the hand of the men of whom you are afraid. For I will surely deliver you, and you shall not fall by the sword; but your life shall be as a prize to you because you have put your trust in me,' says the LORD."

Chapter 40

The word that came to Jeremiah from the LORD after Nebuzaradan, the captain of the guard, had let him go from Ramah, when he had taken him bound in chains among all who were carried away captive from Jerusalem and Judah, who were carried away captive to Babylon. And the captain of the guard took Jeremiah and said to him, "The LORD your God has pronounced this disaster against this place. Now the LORD has brought it and has done just as he said. Because you people have sinned against the LORD and have not obeyed his voice, therefore this thing has come upon you. And now look, I free you this day from the chains that were on your hand. If it seems good to you to come with me to Babylon, come, and I will look after you. But if it seems wrong for you to come with me to Babylon, remain here. See, all the land is before you; wherever it seems good and convenient for you to go, go there." Now while Jeremiah had not yet gone back, Nebuzaradan said, "Go back to Gedaliah, the son of Ahikam, the son of Shaphan, whom the king of Babylon has made governor over the cities of Judah, and dwell with him among the people; or go wherever it seems convenient for you to go." So the captain of the guard gave him rations and a gift and let him go. Then Jeremiah went to Gedaliah, the son of Ahikam, to Mizpah and dwelt with him among the people who were left in the land And when all the captains of the armies who were in the fields, they and their men, heard that the king of Babylon had made Gedaliah, the son of Ahikam, governor in the land and had committed to him men, women, children, and the poorest of the land who had not been carried away captive to Babylon, then they came to Gedaliah at Mizpah—Ishmael, the son of Nethaniah, Johanan and Jonathan, the sons of Kareah, Seraiah, the son of Tanhumeth, the sons of Ephai, the Netophathite, and Jezaniah, the son of a Maachathite, they and their men. And Gedaliah, the son of Ahikam, the son of Shaphan, took an oath before them and their men, saying, "Do not be afraid to serve the Chaldeans. Dwell in the land and serve the king of Babylon, and it shall be well with you. As for me, I will indeed dwell at Mizpah and serve the Chaldeans who come to us. But you, gather wine and summer fruit and oil, put them in your vessels, and dwell in your cities that you have taken." Likewise, when all the Jews who were in Moab, among the Ammonites, in Edom, and who were in all the countries, heard that the king of Babylon had left a remnant of Judah and that he had set over them Gedaliah, the son of Ahikam, the son of Shaphan, then all the Jews returned out of all places where they had been driven and came to the land of Judah, to Gedaliah at Mizpah, and gathered wine and summer fruit in abundance Moreover, Johanan, the son of Kareah, and all the captains of the armies that were in the fields came to Gedaliah at Mizpah and said to him, "Do you certainly know that Baalis, the king of the Ammonites, has sent Ishmael, the son of Nethaniah, to murder you?" But Gedaliah, the son of Ahikam, did not believe them. Then Johanan, the son of Kareah, spoke secretly to Gedaliah in Mizpah, saying, "Let me go, please, and I will kill Ishmael, the son of Nethaniah, and no one will know it. Why should he murder you, so that all the Jews who are gathered to you would be scattered and the remnant in Judah perish?" But Gedaliah, the son of Ahikam, said to Johanan, the son of Kareah, "You shall not do this thing, for you speak falsely concerning Ishmael."

Chapter 41

In the seventh month, Ishmael, the son of Nethaniah, the son of Elishama, of the royal family and one of the king's officers, came with ten men to Gedaliah, the son of Ahikam, at Mizpah. While they were eating bread together there, Ishmael and the ten men with him rose up and struck down Gedaliah with the sword, killing the one whom the king of Babylon had appointed governor over the land. Ishmael also killed all the Jews who were with Gedaliah at Mizpah, as well as the Chaldean soldiers who were there On the second day after Gedaliah's murder, before anyone knew about it, eighty men came from Shechem, Shiloh, and Samaria, with their beards shaved, their clothes torn, and their bodies gashed, bringing grain offerings and incense to the house of the LORD. Ishmael went out from Mizpah to meet them, weeping as he went. When he met them, he said, "Come to Gedaliah, the son of Ahikam." As soon as they entered the city, Ishmael and the men with him slaughtered them and threw them into a cistern. However, ten of them said to Ishmael, "Do not kill us, for we have stores of wheat, barley, oil, and honey hidden in the field." So he spared them and did not kill them with their companions The cistern where Ishmael threw all the bodies of the men he had killed along with Gedaliah was the one King Asa had made for defense against Baasha, king of Israel. Ishmael filled it with the slain. Ishmael then took captive all the rest of the people who were in Mizpah, including the king's daughters and all the others who were left there, whom Nebuzaradan, the captain of the guard, had put under the care of Gedaliah. Ishmael took them captive and set out to cross over to the Ammonites When Johanan, the son of Kareah, and all the army officers who were with him heard about all the crimes Ishmael had committed, they took all their men and went to fight Ishmael. They caught up with him near the great pool in Gibeon. When all the people Ishmael had taken captive saw Johanan and the army officers with him, they rejoiced. All the people Ishmael had taken captive turned back and went over to Johanan. But Ishmael and eight of his men escaped from Johanan and fled to the Ammonites Then Johanan, the son of Kareah, and all the army officers with him led away all the people of Mizpah who had survived—those whom Johanan had rescued from Ishmael after he had killed Gedaliah, the soldiers, the women, the children, and the court officials. They took them to the village of Geruth Chimham near Bethlehem, intending to go to Egypt to escape the Babylonians. They were afraid of them because Ishmael had killed Gedaliah, whom the king of Babylon had appointed as governor of the land

Chapter 42

Then all the army officers, including Johanan, the son of Kareah, and Jezaniah, the son of Hoshaiah, and all the people from the least to the greatest approached Jeremiah the prophet and said, "Please hear our petition and pray to the LORD your God for this entire remnant. For as you now see, though we were once many, now only a few are left. Pray that the LORD your God will tell us where we should go and what we should do." "I have heard you," replied Jeremiah the prophet. "I will certainly pray to the LORD your God as you have requested; I will tell you everything the LORD says and will keep nothing back from you."

Then they said to Jeremiah, "May the LORD be a true and faithful witness against us if we do not act in accordance with everything the LORD your God sends you to tell us. Whether it is favorable or unfavorable, we will obey the LORD our God, to whom we are sending you, so that it will go well with us, for we will obey the LORD our God." Ten days later, the word of the LORD came to Jeremiah. So he called together Johanan, the son of Kareah, and all the army officers who were with him and all the people from the least to the greatest. He said to them, "This is what the LORD, the God of Israel, to whom you sent me to present your petition, says: 'If you stay in this land, I will build you up and not tear you down; I will plant you and not uproot you, for I am grieved over the disaster I have inflicted on you. Do not be afraid of the king of Babylon, whom you now fear. Do not be afraid of him,' declares the LORD, 'for I am with you and will save you and deliver you from his hands. I will show you compassion so that he will have compassion on you and restore you to your land.' "However, if you say, 'We will not stay in this land,' and so disobey the LORD your God, and if you say, 'No, we will go and live in Egypt, where we will not see war or hear the trumpet or be hungry for bread,' then hear the word of the LORD, you remnant of Judah. This is what the LORD Almighty, the God of Israel, says: 'If you are determined to go to Egypt and you do go to settle there, then the sword you fear will overtake you there, and the famine you dread will follow you into Egypt, and there you will die. Indeed, all who are determined to go to Egypt to settle there will die by the sword, famine, and plague; not one of them will survive or escape the disaster I will bring on them.' This is what the LORD Almighty, the God of Israel, says: 'As my anger and wrath have been poured out on those who lived in Jerusalem, so will my wrath be poured out on you when you go to Egypt. You will be a curse and an object of horror, a curse and an object of reproach; you will never see this place again.' "Remnant of Judah, the LORD has told you, 'Do not go to Egypt.' Be sure of this: I warn you today that you made a fatal mistake when you sent me to the LORD your God and said, 'Pray to the LORD our God for us; tell us everything he says, and we will do it.' I have told you today, but you still have not obeyed the LORD your God in all he sent me to tell you. So now, be sure of this: You will die by the sword, famine, and plague in the place where you want to go to settle."

Chapter 43

When Jeremiah finished telling the people all the words of the LORD their God—everything the LORD had sent him to tell them—Azariah, the son of Hoshaiah, and Johanan, the son of Kareah, and all the arrogant men said to Jeremiah, "You are lying! The LORD our God has not sent you to say, 'You must not go to Egypt to settle there.' But Baruch, the son of Neriah, is inciting you against us to hand us over to the Babylonians, so they may kill us or carry us into exile to Babylon." So Johanan, the son of Kareah, and all the army officers and all the people disobeyed the LORD's command to stay in the land of Judah. Instead, Johanan, the son of Kareah, and all the army officers led away all the remnant of Judah who had come back to live in the land of Judah from all the nations where they had been scattered. They also led away all the men, women, and children, the king's daughters, and every person whom Nebuzaradan, the captain of the guard, had left with Gedaliah, the son of Ahikam, the son of Shaphan, and Jeremiah the prophet and Baruch, the son of Neriah. So they entered Egypt in disobedience to the LORD and went as far as Tahpanhes In Tahpanhes, the word of the LORD came to Jeremiah: "While the Jews are watching, take some large stones with you and bury them in clay in the brick pavement at the entrance to Pharaoh's palace in Tahpanhes. Then say to them, 'This is what the LORD Almighty, the God of Israel, says: I will send for my servant Nebuchadnezzar, king of Babylon, and I will set his throne over these stones I have buried here; he will spread his royal canopy above them. He will come and attack Egypt, bringing death to those destined for death, captivity to those destined for captivity, and the sword to those destined for the sword. He will set fire to the temples of the gods of Egypt; he will burn their temples and take their gods captive. As a shepherd wraps his garment around him, so will he wrap Egypt around himself and depart from there unscathed. There in the temple of the sun in Egypt, he will demolish the sacred pillars and will burn down the temples of the gods of Egypt.'"

Chapter 44

This word came to Jeremiah concerning all the Jews living in Lower Egypt—in Migdol, Tahpanhes, and Memphis—and in Upper Egypt: "This is what the LORD Almighty, the God of Israel, says: You saw the great disaster I brought on Jerusalem and on all the towns of Judah. Today they lie deserted and in ruins because of the evil they have done. They provoked me to anger by burning incense and by worshiping other gods that neither they nor you nor your ancestors ever knew. Again and again, I sent my servants the prophets, who said, 'Do not do this detestable thing I hate!' But they did not listen or pay attention; they did not turn from their wickedness or stop burning incense to other gods. Therefore, my fierce anger was poured out; it raged against the towns of Judah and the streets of Jerusalem and made them the desolate ruins they are today "Now this is what the LORD God Almighty, the God of Israel, says: Why bring such great disaster on yourselves by cutting off from Judah the men and women, the children and infants, and so leave yourselves without a remnant? Why arouse my anger with what your hands have made, burning incense to other gods in Egypt, where you have come to live? You will destroy yourselves and make yourselves a curse and an object of reproach among all the nations on earth. Have you forgotten the wickedness committed by your ancestors and by the kings and queens of Judah and the wickedness committed by you and your wives in the land of Judah and the streets of Jerusalem? To this day they have not humbled themselves or shown reverence, nor have they followed my law and the decrees I set before you and your ancestors "Therefore, this is what the LORD Almighty, the God of Israel, says: I am determined to bring disaster on you and to destroy all Judah. I will take away the remnant of Judah who were determined to go to Egypt to settle there. They will all perish in Egypt; they will fall by the sword or die from famine. From the least to the greatest, they will die by the sword or famine. They will become a curse and an object of horror, a curse and an object of reproach. I will punish those who live in Egypt with the sword, famine, and plague, as I punished Jerusalem. None of the remnant of Judah who have gone to live in Egypt will escape or survive to return to the land of Judah, to which they long to return and live; none will return except a few fugitives." Then all the men who knew that their wives were burning incense to other gods, along with all the women who were present—a large assembly—and all the people living in Lower and Upper Egypt, said to Jeremiah, "We will not listen to the message you have spoken to us in the name of the LORD! We will certainly do everything we said we would: We will burn incense to the Queen of Heaven and will pour out drink offerings to her just as we and our ancestors, our kings and our officials did in the towns of Judah and in the streets of Jerusalem. At that time, we had plenty of food and were well off and suffered no harm. But ever since we stopped burning incense to the Queen of Heaven and pouring out drink offerings to her, we have had nothing and have been perishing by sword and famine." The women added, "When we burned incense to the Queen of Heaven and poured out drink offerings to her, did not our husbands know that we were making cakes impressed with her image and pouring out drink offerings to her?" Then Jeremiah said to all the people, both men and women, who were answering him, "Did not the LORD remember and call to mind the incense burned in the towns of Judah and the streets of Jerusalem by you and your ancestors, your kings and your officials, and the people of the land? When the LORD could no longer endure your wicked actions and the detestable things you did, your land became a curse and a desolate waste without inhabitants, as it is today. Because you have burned incense and have sinned against the LORD and have not obeyed him or followed his law or his decrees or his stipulations, this disaster has come upon you, as you now see." Then Jeremiah said to all the people, including the women, "Hear the word of the LORD, all you people of Judah in Egypt. This is what the LORD Almighty, the God of Israel, says: You and your wives have done what you said you would do when you promised, 'We will certainly carry out the vows we made to burn incense and pour out drink offerings to the Queen of Heaven.' "Go ahead then, do what you promised! Keep your vows! But hear the word of the LORD, all you Jews living in Egypt: 'I swear by my great name,' says the LORD, 'that no one from Judah living anywhere in Egypt will ever again invoke my name or swear, "As surely as the Sovereign LORD lives." For I am watching over them for harm, not for good; the Jews in Egypt will perish by sword and famine until they are all destroyed. Those who escape the sword and return to the land of Judah from Egypt will be very few. Then the whole remnant of Judah who came to live in Egypt will know whose word will stand—mine or theirs "This will be the sign to you that I will punish you in this place," declares the LORD, "so that you will know that my threats of harm against you will surely stand." This is what the LORD says: "I am going to deliver Pharaoh Hophra, king of Egypt, into the hands of his enemies who want to kill him, just as I gave Zedekiah, king of Judah, into the hands of Nebuchadnezzar, king of Babylon, the enemy who wanted to kill him."

Chapter 45

This is what Jeremiah the prophet told Baruch, the son of Neriah, in the fourth year of Jehoiakim, the son of Josiah, king of Judah, after Baruch had written on a scroll the words Jeremiah was then dictating: "This is what the LORD, the God of Israel, says to you, Baruch: You said, 'Woe to me! The LORD has added sorrow to my pain; I am worn out with groaning and find no rest.'" The LORD said, "Say this to him: 'This is what the LORD says: I will overthrow what I have built and uproot what I have planted, throughout the earth. Should you then seek great things for yourself? Do not seek them. For I will bring disaster on all people, declares the LORD, but wherever you go, I will let you escape with your life.'"

Chapter 46

The words of the Lord addressed to the prophet Jeremiah against the nations: Against Egypt, against the army of Pharaoh Necho, king of Egypt, which was by the river Euphrates at Carchemish, which Nebuchadnezzar, king of Babylon, defeated in the fourth year of Jehoiakim, son of Josiah, king of Judah.

Prepare your armor and shield and go to battle. Prepare the horses, make the horsemen ready with your helmets, prepare the spears, and put on the brigandines. Why did I see them frightened and falling back? Their strong men were struck down, they fled and did not look back, for fear was all around them, says the LORD. The swift will not flee, nor will the strong man escape; they will stumble and fall toward the north by the river Euphrates. Who is this that rises like the Nile, whose waters surge like rivers? Egypt rises like the Nile, whose waters surge like rivers, and it says, "I will go up, I will cover the earth, I will destroy the city and its inhabitants." Charge, O horses, and drive madly, O chariots! Let the mighty men go forth: Cush and Put, who handle the shield, and the Ludim, who handle and bend the bow. For that day belongs to the Lord GOD of hosts, a day of vengeance, to avenge himself on his foes. The sword will devour and be sated and drink its fill of their blood. For the Lord GOD of hosts holds a sacrifice in the north country by the river Euphrates. Go up to Gilead and take balm, O virgin daughter of Egypt! In vain you use many medicines; there is no healing for you. The nations have heard of your shame, and the earth is full of your cry; for warrior has stumbled against warrior; they have both fallen together The word that the LORD spoke to Jeremiah the prophet about the coming of Nebuchadnezzar, king of Babylon, to strike the land of Egypt: "Declare in Egypt, and proclaim in Migdol; proclaim in Noph and Tahpanhes; say, 'Stand firm and be ready, for the sword has devoured those around you.' Why are your mighty ones face down? They do not stand, because the LORD thrust them down. He made many stumble, and they fell, and they said to one another, 'Arise, and let us go back to our own people and to the land of our birth, away from the sword of the oppressor.' They cried there, 'Pharaoh, king of Egypt, is but a noise; he has let the appointed time pass by.' As I live, declares the King, whose name is the LORD of hosts, surely like Tabor among the mountains and like Carmel by the sea, so shall he come. O daughter dwelling in Egypt, prepare yourself to go into exile, for Noph shall become a desolation without inhabitant. Egypt is a beautiful heifer, but a gadfly from the north has come upon her. Her hired soldiers in her midst are like fattened calves; they too have turned and fled together; they did not stand, for the day of their calamity has come upon them, the time of their punishment. She makes a sound like a serpent gliding away; for her enemies march in force and come against her with axes, like those who fell trees. They shall cut down her forest, declares the LORD, though it is impenetrable, because they are more numerous than locusts; they are without number. The daughter of Egypt shall be put to shame; she shall be delivered into the hand of a people from the north." The LORD of hosts, the God of Israel, says: "Behold, I am bringing punishment upon Amon of Thebes, and Pharaoh and Egypt and her gods and her kings, upon Pharaoh and those who trust in him. I will deliver them into the hand of those who seek their lives, into the hand of Nebuchadnezzar, king of Babylon, and his officers. Afterward, Egypt shall be inhabited as in the days of old, declares the LORD "But fear not, O Jacob my servant, nor be dismayed, O Israel, for behold, I will save you from far away, and your offspring from the land of their captivity. Jacob shall return and have quiet and ease, and none shall make him afraid. Fear not, O Jacob my servant, declares the LORD, for I am with you. I will make a full end of all the nations to which I have driven you, but of you, I will not make a full end. I will discipline you in just measure, and I will by no means leave you unpunished."

Chapter 47

The word of the LORD that came to Jeremiah the prophet concerning the Philistines, before Pharaoh struck down Gaza. Thus says the LORD: "Behold, waters are rising out of the north and shall become an overflowing torrent; they shall overflow the land and all that fills it, the city and those who dwell in it. Men shall cry out, and every inhabitant of the land shall wail. At the noise of the stamping of the hoofs of his stallions, at the rushing of his chariots, at the rumbling of their wheels, the fathers look not back to their children, so feeble are their hands, because of the day that is coming to destroy all the Philistines, to cut off from Tyre and Sidon every helper that remains. For the LORD is destroying the Philistines, the remnant of the coastland of Caphtor. Baldness has come upon Gaza; Ashkelon has perished. O remnant of their valley, how long will you gash yourselves? Ah, sword of the LORD! How long till you are quiet? Put yourself into your scabbard; rest and be still! How can it be quiet when the LORD has given it a charge? Against Ashkelon and against the seashore he has appointed it."

Chapter 48

Concerning Moab, thus says the LORD of hosts, the God of Israel: "Woe to Nebo, for it is laid waste! Kiriathaim is put to shame; it is taken; the fortress is put to shame and broken down; the renown of Moab is no more. In Heshbon, they planned disaster against her: 'Come, let us cut her off from being a nation!' You also, O Madmen, shall be brought to silence; the sword shall pursue you. A voice! A cry from Horonaim, 'Desolation and great destruction!' Moab is destroyed; her little ones have made a cry. For at the ascent of Luhith they go up weeping; for at the descent of Horonaim they have heard the distressed cry of destruction. Flee! Save yourselves! You will be like a juniper in the desert! For, because you trusted in your works and your treasures, you also shall be taken; and Chemosh shall go into exile with his priests and his officials. The destroyer shall come upon every city, and no city shall escape; the valley shall perish, and the plain shall be destroyed, as the LORD has spoken. Give wings to Moab, for she would fly away; her cities shall become a desolation, with no inhabitant in them. Cursed is he who does the work of the LORD with slackness, and cursed is he who keeps back his sword from bloodshed "Moab has been at ease from his youth and has settled on his lees; he has not been emptied from vessel to vessel, nor has he gone into exile; so his taste remains in him, and his scent is not changed. Therefore, behold, the days are coming, declares the LORD, when I shall send to him pourers who will pour him, and empty his vessels, and break his jars in pieces. Then Moab shall be ashamed of Chemosh, as the house of Israel was ashamed of Bethel, their confidence "How do you say, 'We are heroes and mighty men of war'? The destroyer of Moab and his cities has come up, and the choicest of his young men have gone down to slaughter, declares the King, whose name is the LORD of hosts. The calamity of Moab is near at hand, and his affliction hastens swiftly. Grieve for him, all you who are around him, and all who know his name; say, 'How the mighty scepter is broken, the glorious staff.' Come down from your glory and sit on the parched ground, O inhabitant of Dibon, for the destroyer of Moab has come up against you; he has destroyed your strongholds. Stand by the way and watch, O inhabitant of Aroer! Ask him who flees and her who escapes; say, 'What has happened?' Moab is put to shame, for it is broken; wail and cry! Tell it beside the Arnon, that Moab is laid waste "Judgment has come upon the tableland, upon Holon, and Jahzah, and

Mephaath, and Dibon, and Nebo, and Beth-diblathaim, and Kiriathaim, and Beth-gamul, and Beth-meon, and Kerioth, and Bozrah, and all the cities of the land of Moab, far and near. The horn of Moab is cut off, and his arm is broken, declares the LORD "Make him drunk, because he magnified himself against the LORD, so that Moab shall wallow in his vomit, and he too shall be held in derision. Was not Israel a derision to you? Was he found among thieves, that whenever you spoke of him you wagged your head? Leave the cities, and dwell in the rock, O inhabitants of Moab! Be like the dove that nests in the sides of the mouth of a gorge. We have heard of the pride of Moab—he is very proud—of his loftiness, his pride, and his arrogance, and the haughtiness of his heart. I know his insolence, declares the LORD; his boasts are false, his deeds are false. Therefore I wail for Moab; I cry out for all Moab; for the men of Kir-heres I mourn. More than for Jazer I weep for you, O vine of Sibmah! Your branches passed over the sea, reached to the Sea of Jazer; on your summer fruits and your grapes the destroyer has fallen. Gladness and joy have been taken away from the fruitful land of Moab; I have made the wine cease from the winepresses; no one treads them with shouts of joy; the shouting is not the shout of joy "From the outcry at Heshbon even to Elealeh, as far as Jahaz they utter their voice, from Zoar to Horonaim and Eglath-shelishiyah. For the waters of Nimrim also have become desolate. And I will bring to an end in Moab, declares the LORD, him who offers sacrifice in the high place and makes offerings to his god. Therefore my heart moans for Moab like a flute, and my heart moans like a flute for the men of Kir-heres; therefore the riches they gained have perished "For every head is shaved and every beard cut off. On all the hands are gashes, and around the waist is sackcloth. On all the housetops of Moab and in the squares there is nothing but lamentation, for I have broken Moab like a vessel for which no one cares, declares the LORD. How it is broken! How they wail! How Moab has turned his back in shame! So Moab has become a derision and a horror to all that are around him." For thus says the LORD: "Behold, one shall fly swiftly like an eagle and spread his wings against Moab; the cities shall be taken and the strongholds seized. The heart of the warriors of Moab shall be in that day like the heart of a woman in her birth pains; Moab shall be destroyed and be no longer a people because he magnified himself against the LORD. Terror, pit, and snare are before you, O inhabitant of Moab! declares the LORD. He who flees from the terror shall fall into the pit, and he who climbs out of the pit shall be caught in the snare. For I will bring these things upon Moab, the year of their punishment, declares the LORD "In the shadow of Heshbon fugitives stop without strength, for fire came out from Heshbon, flame from the house of Sihon; it has destroyed the forehead of Moab, the crown of the sons of tumult. Woe to you, O Moab! The people of Chemosh are undone, for your sons have been taken captive, and your daughters into captivity. Yet I will restore the fortunes of Moab in the latter days, declares the LORD." Thus far is the judgment on Moab

Chapter 49

Concerning the Ammonites, thus says the LORD: "Has Israel no sons? Has he no heir? Why then has Milcom dispossessed Gad, and his people settled in its cities? Therefore, behold, the days are coming, declares the LORD, when I will cause the battle cry to be heard against Rabbah of the Ammonites; it shall become a desolate mound, and its villages shall be burned with fire; then Israel shall dispossess those who dispossessed him, says the LORD. Wail, O Heshbon, for Ai is laid waste! Cry out, O daughters of Rabbah! Put on sackcloth, lament, and run to and fro among the hedges! For Milcom shall go into exile, with his priests and his officials. Why do you boast of your valleys, O faithless daughter, who trusted in her treasures, saying, 'Who will come against me?' Behold, I will bring terror upon you, declares the Lord GOD of hosts, from all who are around you, and you shall be driven out, every man straight before him, with none to gather the fugitives. But afterward, I will restore the fortunes of the Ammonites, declares the LORD." Concerning Edom, thus says the LORD of hosts: "Is wisdom no more in Teman? Has counsel perished from the prudent? Has their wisdom vanished? Flee, turn back, dwell in the depths, O inhabitants of Dedan! For I will bring the calamity of Esau upon him, the time when I punish him. If grape gatherers came to you, would they not leave gleanings? If thieves came by night, would they not destroy only enough for themselves? But I have stripped Esau bare; I have uncovered his hiding places, and he is not able to conceal himself. His children are destroyed, and his brothers, and his neighbors; and he is no more. Leave your fatherless children; I will keep them alive; and let your widows trust in me." For thus says the LORD: "If those who did not deserve to drink the cup must drink it, will you go unpunished? You shall not go unpunished, but you must drink. For I have sworn by myself, declares the LORD, that Bozrah shall become a horror, a taunt, a waste, and a curse, and all her cities shall be perpetual wastes." I have heard a message from the LORD, and an envoy has been sent among the nations: "Gather yourselves together and come against her, and rise up for battle! For behold, I will make you small among the nations, despised among mankind. The horror you inspire has deceived you, and the pride of your heart, you who live in the clefts of the rock, who hold the height of the hill. Though you make your nest as high as the eagle's, I will bring you down from there, declares the LORD "Edom shall become a horror. Everyone who passes by it will be horrified and will hiss because of all its disasters. As when Sodom and Gomorrah and their neighboring cities were overthrown, says the LORD, no man shall dwell there, no man shall sojourn in her. Behold, like a lion coming up from the jungle of the Jordan against a perennial pasture, I will suddenly make him run away from her. And I will appoint over her whomever I choose. For who is like me? Who will summon me? What shepherd can stand before me? Therefore hear the plan that the LORD has made against Edom and the purposes that he has formed against the inhabitants of Teman: Even the little ones of the flock shall be dragged away. Surely their fold shall be appalled at their fate. At the sound of their fall the earth shall tremble; the sound of their cry shall be heard at the Red Sea. Behold, one shall mount up and fly swiftly like an eagle and spread his wings against Bozrah, and the heart of the warriors of Edom shall be in that day like the heart of a woman in her birth pains." Concerning Damascus: "Hamath and Arpad are confounded, for they have heard bad news; they melt in fear, they are troubled like the sea that cannot be quiet. Damascus has become feeble, she turned to flee, and panic seized her; anguish and sorrows have taken hold of her, as of a woman in labor. How is the famous city not forsaken, the city of my joy? Therefore her young men shall fall in her squares, and all her soldiers shall be destroyed in that day, declares the LORD of hosts. And I will kindle a fire in the wall of Damascus, and it shall devour the strongholds of Ben-hadad." Concerning Kedar and the kingdoms of Hazor that Nebuchadnezzar king of Babylon struck down. Thus says the LORD: "Rise up, advance against Kedar! Destroy the people of the east! Their tents and their flocks shall be taken, their curtains and all their goods; their camels shall be led away from them, and men shall cry to them: 'Terror on every side!' Flee, wander far away, dwell in the depths, O inhabitants of Hazor! declares the LORD. For Nebuchadnezzar king of Babylon has made a plan against you and formed a purpose against you. 'Rise up, advance against a nation at ease, that dwells securely, declares the LORD, that has no gates or bars, that dwells alone. Their camels shall become plunder, their herds of livestock a spoil. I will scatter to every wind those who cut the corners of their hair, and I will bring their calamity from every side of them, declares the LORD. Hazor shall become a haunt of jackals, an everlasting waste; no man shall dwell there; no man shall sojourn in her.'" The word of the LORD that came to Jeremiah the prophet concerning Elam, in the beginning of the reign of Zedekiah king of Judah. Thus says the LORD of hosts: "Behold, I will break the bow of Elam, the mainstay of their might. And I will bring upon Elam the four winds from the four quarters of heaven, and I will scatter them to all those winds, and there shall be no nation to which those driven out of Elam shall not come. I will terrify Elam before their enemies and before those who seek their life. I will bring disaster upon them, my fierce anger, declares the LORD. I will send the sword after them, until I have consumed them, and I will set my throne in Elam and destroy their king and officials, declares the LORD. But in the latter days I will restore the fortunes of Elam, declares the LORD."

Chapter 50

The word that the LORD spoke concerning Babylon, concerning the land of the Chaldeans, by Jeremiah the prophet: "Declare among the nations and proclaim, set up a banner and proclaim, conceal it not, and say: 'Babylon is taken, Bel is put to shame, Merodach is dismayed. Her images are put to shame, her idols are dismayed.' For out of the north a nation has come up against her, which shall make her land a desolation, and none shall dwell in it; both man and beast shall flee away "In those days and in that time, declares the LORD, the people of Israel and the people of Judah shall come together, weeping as they come, and they shall seek the LORD their God. They shall ask the way to Zion, with faces turned toward it, saying, 'Come, let us join ourselves to the LORD in an everlasting covenant that will never be forgotten.' "My people have been lost sheep. Their shepherds have led them astray, turning them away on the mountains. From mountain to hill they have gone. They have forgotten their fold. All who found them have devoured them, and their enemies have said, 'We are not guilty, for they have sinned against the LORD, their habitation of righteousness, the LORD, the hope of their fathers.' "Flee from the midst of Babylon, and go out of the land of the Chaldeans, and be as male goats before the flock. For behold, I am stirring up and bringing against Babylon a gathering of great nations from the north country, and they shall array themselves against her. From there she shall be taken. Their arrows are like a skilled warrior who does not return empty-handed. Chaldea shall be plundered; all who plunder her shall be sated, declares the LORD "Though you rejoice, though you exult, O plunderers of my heritage, though you frolic like a heifer in the pasture and neigh like stallions, your mother shall be utterly shamed, and she who bore you shall be disgraced. Behold, she shall be the least of the nations, a wilderness, a dry land, and a desert. Because of the wrath of the LORD she shall not be inhabited but shall be an utter desolation; everyone who passes by Babylon shall be appalled and hiss because of all her wounds. Set yourselves in array against Babylon all around, all you who bend the bow; shoot at her, spare no arrows, for she has sinned against the LORD. Raise a shout against her all around; she has surrendered; her bulwarks have fallen; her walls are thrown down. For this is the vengeance of the LORD: take vengeance on her; do to her as she has done. Cut off from Babylon the sower, and the one who handles the sickle in time of harvest. Because of the sword of the oppressor, everyone shall turn to his own people, and everyone shall flee to his own land "Israel is a hunted sheep driven away by lions. First the king of Assyria devoured him, and now at last Nebuchadnezzar king of Babylon has gnawed his bones. Therefore, thus says the LORD of hosts, the God of Israel: Behold, I am bringing punishment on the king of Babylon and his land, as I punished the king of Assyria. I will restore Israel to his pasture, and he shall feed on Carmel and in Bashan, and his desire shall be satisfied on the hills of Ephraim and in Gilead. In those days and in that time, declares the LORD, iniquity shall be sought in Israel, and there shall be none, and sin in Judah, and none shall be found, for I will pardon those whom I leave as a remnant "Go up against the land of Merathaim, and against the inhabitants of Pekod. Kill, and devote them to destruction, declares the LORD, and do all that I have commanded you. The noise of battle is in the land, and great destruction! How the hammer of the whole earth is cut down and broken! How Babylon has become a horror among the nations! I set a snare for you, and you were taken, O Babylon, and you did not know it; you were found and caught, because you opposed the LORD. The LORD has opened his armory and brought out the weapons of his wrath, for the Lord GOD of hosts has a work to do in the land of the Chaldeans. Come against her from every quarter; open her granaries; pile her up like heaps of grain, and devote her to destruction; let nothing be left of her. Kill all her bulls; let them go down to the slaughter. Woe to them, for their day has come, the time of their punishment "A voice! They flee and escape from the land of Babylon, to declare in Zion the vengeance of the LORD our God, vengeance for his temple "Summon archers against Babylon, all those who bend the bow. Encamp around her; let no one escape. Repay her according to her deeds; do to her according to all that she has done. For she has proudly defied the LORD, the Holy One of Israel. Therefore her young men shall fall in her squares, and all her soldiers shall be destroyed on that day, declares the LORD "Behold, I am against you, O proud one, declares the Lord GOD of hosts, for your day has come, the time when I will punish you. The proud one shall stumble and fall, with none to raise him up, and I will kindle a fire in his cities, and it will devour all that is around him "Thus says the LORD of hosts: The people of Israel are oppressed, and so are the people of Judah. All who took them captive have held them fast; they refuse to let them go. Their Redeemer is strong; the LORD of hosts is his name. He will surely plead their cause, that he may give rest to the earth, but unrest to the inhabitants of Babylon. A sword against the Chaldeans, declares the LORD, and against the inhabitants of Babylon, and against her officials and her wise men! A sword against the diviners, that they may become fools! A sword against her warriors, that they may be destroyed! A sword against her horses and against her chariots, and against all the foreign troops in her midst, that they may become women! A sword against all her treasures, that they may be plundered! A drought against her waters, that they may be dried up! For it is a land of images, and they are mad over idols "Therefore, wild beasts shall dwell with hyenas in Babylon, and ostriches shall dwell in her. She shall never again have people, nor be inhabited for all generations. As when God overthrew Sodom and Gomorrah and their neighboring cities, declares the LORD, so no man shall dwell there, and no son of man shall sojourn in her "Behold, a people comes from the north; a mighty nation and many kings are stirring from the farthest parts of the earth. They lay hold of bow and spear; they are cruel and have no mercy. The sound of them is like the roaring of the sea; they ride on horses, arrayed as a man for battle, against you, O daughter of Babylon! The king of Babylon heard the report of them, and his hands fell helpless; anguish seized him, pain as of a woman in labor "Behold, like a lion coming up from the thicket of the Jordan against a perennial pasture, I will suddenly make them run away from her. And I will appoint over her whomever I choose. For who is like me? Who will summon me? What shepherd can stand before me? Therefore hear the plan that the LORD has made against Babylon and the purposes that he has formed against the land of the Chaldeans: Surely the little ones of their flock shall be dragged away; surely their fold shall be appalled at their fate. At the sound of the capture of Babylon the earth shall tremble, and her cry shall be heard among the nations."

Chapter 51

1 Thus says the LORD: "Behold, I will raise up against Babylon and against the inhabitants who lift up their hearts against me a destructive wind, 2 And I will send against Babylon winnowers who shall winnow her and empty her land, for in the day of trouble they shall be against her on every side. 3 Against him who bends the bow, and against him who rises up in his armor, spare not his young men; utterly destroy all her army. 4 Thus the slain shall fall in the land of the Chaldeans, and those who are thrust through in her streets. 5 For Israel is not forsaken, nor Judah of his God, of the LORD of hosts, though their land was filled with sin against the Holy One of Israel 6 Flee out of the midst of Babylon, and deliver every man his soul; be not cut off in her iniquity, for this is the time of the LORD's vengeance; he will render unto her a recompense. 7 Babylon has been a golden cup in the LORD's hand, that made all the earth drunk; the nations have drunk of her wine, therefore the nations are mad. 8 Babylon is suddenly fallen and destroyed; wail for her, take balm for her pain, if so she may be healed. 9 We would have healed Babylon, but she is not healed; forsake her, and let us go every one into his own country, for her judgment reaches unto heaven and is lifted up even to the skies 10 The LORD has brought forth our righteousness; come, and let us declare in Zion the work of the LORD our God. 11 Make bright the arrows; gather the shields; the LORD has raised up the spirit of the kings of the Medes, for his device is against Babylon, to destroy it; because it is the vengeance of the LORD, the vengeance of his temple. 12 Set up the standard upon the walls of Babylon, make the watch strong, set up the watchmen, prepare the ambushes, for the LORD has both devised and done that which he spoke against the inhabitants of Babylon 13 O you who dwell upon many waters, abundant in treasures, your end is come, and the measure of your covetousness. 14 The LORD of hosts has sworn by himself, saying, Surely I will fill you with men as with caterpillars, and they shall lift up a shout against you. 15 He has made the earth by his power, he has established the world by his wisdom, and has stretched out the heaven by his understanding. 16 When he utters his voice, there is a multitude of waters in the heavens, and he causes the vapors to ascend from the ends of the earth; he makes lightnings with rain, and brings forth the wind out of his treasuries 17 Every man is brutish by his knowledge; every founder is confounded by the graven image, for his molten image is falsehood, and there is no breath in them. 18 They are vanity, the work of errors; in the time of their visitation they shall perish. 19 The portion of Jacob is not like them, for he is the maker of all things; and Israel is the rod of his inheritance; the LORD of hosts is his name 20 You are my battle-axe and weapons of war, for with you I will break in pieces the nations, and with you I will destroy kingdoms, 21 And with you I will break in pieces the horse and his rider, and with you I will break in pieces the chariot and his rider. 22 With you also will I break in pieces man and woman, and with you I will break in pieces old and young, and with you I will break in pieces the young man and the maid. 23 I will also break in pieces with you the shepherd and his flock, and with you I will break in pieces the husbandman and his yoke of oxen, and with you I will break in pieces captains and rulers 24 And I will render unto Babylon and to all the inhabitants of Chaldea all their evil that they have done in Zion in your sight, says the LORD. 25 Behold, I am against you, O destroying mountain, says the LORD, which destroys all the earth; and I will stretch out my hand upon you, and roll you down from the rocks, and will make you a burnt mountain. 26 And they shall not take of you a stone for a corner, nor a stone for foundations; but you shall be desolate forever, says the LORD 27 Set up a standard in the land, blow the trumpet among the nations, prepare the nations against her, call together against her the kingdoms of Ararat, Minni, and Ashchenaz; appoint a captain against her; cause the horses to come up as the rough caterpillars. 28 Prepare against her the nations with the kings of the Medes, the captains thereof, and all the rulers thereof, and all the land of his dominion. 29 And the land shall tremble and sorrow, for every purpose of the LORD shall be performed against Babylon, to make the land of Babylon a desolation without an inhabitant 30 The mighty men of Babylon have ceased to fight, they have remained in their strongholds; their might has failed; they became as women; they have burned her dwelling places; her bars are broken. 31 One post shall run to meet another, and one messenger to meet another, to show the king of Babylon that his city is taken at one end, 32 And that the passages are stopped, and the reeds they have burned with fire, and the men of war are affrighted. 33 For thus says the LORD of hosts, the God of Israel; The daughter of Babylon is like a threshing floor; it is time to thresh her; yet a little while, and the time of her harvest shall come 34 Nebuchadnezzar the king of Babylon has devoured me, he has crushed me, he has made me an empty vessel, he has swallowed me up like a dragon, he has filled his belly with my delicacies, he has cast me out. 35 The violence done to me and to my flesh be upon Babylon, shall the inhabitant of Zion say; and my blood upon the inhabitants of Chaldea, shall Jerusalem say. 36 Therefore thus says the LORD; Behold, I will plead your cause, and take vengeance for you; and I will dry up her sea, and make her springs dry. 37 And Babylon shall become heaps, a dwelling place for dragons, an astonishment, and a hissing, without an inhabitant 38 They shall roar together like lions; they shall yell as lion's whelps. 39 In their heat I will make their feasts, and I will make them drunken, that they may rejoice, and sleep a perpetual sleep, and not wake, says the LORD. 40 I will bring them down like lambs to the slaughter, like rams with he goats. 41 How is Sheshach taken! and how is the praise of the whole earth surprised! how is Babylon become an astonishment among the nations! 42 The sea is come up upon Babylon; she is

covered with the multitude of the waves thereof. 43 Her cities are a desolation, a dry land, and a wilderness, a land wherein no man dwells, neither does any son of man pass thereby 44 And I will punish Bel in Babylon, and I will bring forth out of his mouth that which he has swallowed up; and the nations shall not flow together any more unto him, yea, the wall of Babylon shall fall. 45 My people, go out of the midst of her, and deliver every man his soul from the fierce anger of the LORD. 46 And lest your heart faint, and you fear for the rumor that shall be heard in the land; a rumor shall both come one year, and after that in another year shall come a rumor, and violence in the land, ruler against ruler. 47 Therefore, behold, the days come, that I will do judgment upon the graven images of Babylon; and her whole land shall be confounded, and all her slain shall fall in the midst of her. 48 Then the heaven and the earth, and all that is therein, shall sing for Babylon, for the spoilers shall come unto her from the north, says the LORD 49 As Babylon has caused the slain of Israel to fall, so at Babylon shall fall the slain of all the earth. 50 You that have escaped the sword, go away, stand not still; remember the LORD afar off, and let Jerusalem come into your mind. 51 We are confounded, because we have heard reproach; shame has covered our faces, for strangers are come into the sanctuaries of the LORD's house. 52 Therefore, behold, the days come, says the LORD, that I will do judgment upon her graven images, and through all her land the wounded shall groan. 53 Though Babylon should mount up to heaven, and though she should fortify the height of her strength, yet from me shall spoilers come unto her, says the LORD 54 A sound of a cry comes from Babylon, and great destruction from the land of the Chaldeans, 55 Because the LORD has spoiled Babylon, and destroyed out of her the great voice; when her waves do roar like great waters, a noise of their voice is uttered. 56 Because the spoiler is come upon her, even upon Babylon, and her mighty men are taken, every one of their bows is broken, for the LORD God of recompenses shall surely requite. 57 And I will make drunk her princes, and her wise men, her captains, and her rulers, and her mighty men; and they shall sleep a perpetual sleep, and not wake, says the King, whose name is the LORD of hosts 58 Thus says the LORD of hosts; The broad walls of Babylon shall be utterly broken, and her high gates shall be burned with fire, and the people shall labor in vain, and the folk in the fire, and they shall be weary 59 The word which Jeremiah the prophet commanded Seraiah the son of Neriah, the son of Maaseiah, when he went with Zedekiah the king of Judah into Babylon in the fourth year of his reign; and this Seraiah was a quiet prince. 60 So Jeremiah wrote in a book all the evil that should come upon Babylon, even all these words that are written against Babylon. 61 And Jeremiah said to Seraiah, "When you come to Babylon, see that you read all these words, 62 and say, 'O LORD, you have spoken against this place, to cut it off, that none shall remain in it, neither man nor beast, but that it shall be desolate forever.' 63 And it shall be, when you have made an end of reading this book, that you shall bind a stone to it, and cast it into the midst of the Euphrates, 64 And you shall say, 'Thus shall Babylon sink, and shall not rise from the evil that I will bring upon her, and they shall be weary.'" Thus far are the words of Jeremiah

Chapter 52

1 Zedekiah was twenty-one years old when he began to reign, and he reigned eleven years in Jerusalem; his mother's name was Hamutal, the daughter of Jeremiah of Libnah. 2 And he did that which was evil in the eyes of the LORD, according to all that Jehoiakim had done. 3 For through the anger of the LORD, it came to pass in Jerusalem and Judah, till he had cast them out from his presence, that Zedekiah rebelled against the king of Babylon 4 And it came to pass in the ninth year of his reign, in the tenth month, in the tenth day of the month, that Nebuchadnezzar king of Babylon came, he and all his army, against Jerusalem, and pitched against it, and built forts against it round about. 5 So the city was besieged unto the eleventh year of king Zedekiah. 6 And in the fourth month, in the ninth day of the month, the famine was sore in the city, so that there was no bread for the people of the land. 7 Then the city was broken up, and all the men of war fled, and went forth out of the city by night by the way of the gate between the two walls, which was by the king's garden; (now the Chaldeans were by the city round about) and they went by the way of the plain. 8 But the army of the Chaldeans pursued after the king, and overtook Zedekiah in the plains of Jericho; and all his army was scattered from him. 9 Then they took the king and carried him up unto the king of Babylon to Riblah in the land of Hamath, where he gave judgment upon him. 10 And the king of Babylon slew the sons of Zedekiah before his eyes; he slew also all the princes of Judah in Riblah. 11 Then he put out the eyes of Zedekiah; and the king of Babylon bound him in chains, and carried him to Babylon, and put him in prison till the day of his death 12 Now in the fifth month, in the tenth day of the month, which was the nineteenth year of Nebuchadnezzar king of Babylon, came Nebuzaradan, captain of the guard, who served the king of Babylon, into Jerusalem, 13 And burned the house of the LORD, and the king's house; and all the houses of Jerusalem, and all the houses of the great men, burned he with fire. 14 And all the army of the Chaldeans, that were with the captain of the guard, broke down all the walls of Jerusalem round about. 15 Then Nebuzaradan, the captain of the guard, carried away captive certain of the poor of the people, and the residue of the people that remained in the city, and those that fell away, that fell to the king of Babylon, and the rest of the multitude. 16 But Nebuzaradan, the captain of the guard, left certain of the poor of the land for vine-dressers and for husbandmen 17 Also the pillars of brass that were in the house of the LORD, and the bases, and the brazen sea that was in the house of the LORD, did the Chaldeans break, and carried all the brass of them to Babylon. 18 The caldrons also, and the shovels, and the snuffers, and the bowls, and the spoons, and all the vessels of brass wherewith they ministered, took they away. 19 And the basins, and the firepans, and the bowls, and the caldrons, and the candlesticks, and the spoons, and the cups; that which was of gold in gold, and that which was of silver in silver, took the captain of the guard away. 20 The two pillars, one sea, and twelve brazen bulls that were under the bases, which king Solomon had made in the house of the LORD, the brass of all these vessels was without weight. 21 And concerning the pillars, the height of one pillar was eighteen cubits, and a fillet of twelve cubits did compass it; and the thickness thereof was four fingers, it was hollow. 22 And a chapiter of brass was upon it; and the height of one chapiter was five cubits, with network and pomegranates upon the chapiters round about, all of brass. The second pillar also and the pomegranates were like unto these. 23 And there were ninety-six pomegranates on a side; and all the pomegranates upon the network were an hundred round about 24 And the captain of the guard took Seraiah the chief priest, and Zephaniah the second priest, and the three keepers of the door. 25 He took also out of the

city a eunuch, which had the charge of the men of war; and seven men of them that were near the king's person, which were found in the city; and the principal scribe of the host, who mustered the people of the land; and threescore men of the people of the land, that were found in the midst of the city. 26 So Nebuzaradan, the captain of the guard, took them, and brought them to the king of Babylon to Riblah. 27 And the king of Babylon smote them, and put them to death in Riblah in the land of Hamath. Thus Judah was carried away captive out of his own land 28 This is the people whom Nebuchadnezzar carried away captive: in the seventh year three thousand Jews and three and twenty: 29 In the eighteenth year of Nebuchadnezzar he carried away captive from Jerusalem eight hundred thirty and two persons: 30 In the three and twentieth year of Nebuchadnezzar Nebuzaradan the captain of the guard carried away captive of the Jews seven hundred forty and five persons: all the persons were four thousand and six hundred 31 And it came to pass in the seven and thirtieth year of the captivity of Jehoiachin king of Judah, in the twelfth month, in the five and twentieth day of the month, that Evil-merodach king of Babylon in the first year of his reign lifted up the head of Jehoiachin king of Judah, and brought him forth out of prison, 32 And spoke kindly unto him, and set his throne above the throne of the kings that were with him in Babylon, 33 And changed his prison garments, and he did continually eat bread before him all the days of his life. 34 And for his allowance, there was a continual allowance given him of the king of Babylon, every day a portion until the day of his death, all the days of his life

25. Lamentations

CHAPTER 1

How does the city, once full of people, remain solitary? She is like a widow; that which was great among the nations and a princess among the provinces has become a tributary. She cries continually at night, her tears rolling down her cheeks. Of all her friends, she has no one to comfort her; all her friends have turned against her and become her enemies. Judah has been carried away into captivity because of affliction and great suffering; she dwells among the heathen and finds no peace. All her persecutors have put her in distress The ways of Zion mourn because no one comes to the solemn feasts; all her gates are desolate. Her priests sigh; her virgins are defeated, and she is in aridity. Her adversaries are her chief, and her enemies prosper. The LORD has afflicted her for the multitude of her transgressions, and her children have gone into captivity before the enemy. The daughter of Zion has lost all her beauty; her princes have become like horses that find no pasture and are without strength before the pursuer Jerusalem remembers the days of her affliction and rebellion, and all the pleasant things she had in the past, when her people fell into the hands of the enemy and no one came to her aid. The adversaries subdued her and mocked her Sabbaths. Jerusalem has sinned grievously; therefore, she is mocked. All who honored her now despise her, for they have seen her filthiness; they sigh and turn away Her filthiness is in her skirts; she has not remembered her last end, and she has gone down wonderfully. She had no comforter: "O LORD, look on my affliction, for the enemy is proud." The enemy has stretched forth his hand upon all her pleasant things because she has seen the heathen enter into her sanctuary, whom You had commanded not to enter Your Church. All her people sigh and seek their bread; they have given

their pleasant things as food to refresh their souls. "See, O LORD, and consider, for I have become vile." "Have you no regard, all you who pass by this road? Look and see if there is any suffering like my suffering, which has been done to me, with which the LORD has afflicted me in the day of His fierce anger." From afar He has sent a fire into my bones that prevents them. He has stretched a net for my feet and turned me back; He has made me desolate and every day in gloom The yoke of my transgressions is tied to His hand; it has coiled up and fallen on my neck; it has brought down my strength. The LORD has delivered me into their hands, and I am no longer able to rise up. The LORD has brought all my valiant ones to their knees in the midst of me; He has summoned an assembly against me to destroy my young men. The LORD has put wine on the virgin, the daughter of Judah For these things I weep; indeed, my eye casts out water because the comforter that should refresh my soul is far from me. My sons are desolate because the enemy has prevented them. Zion stretches out her hands, and there is none to comfort her. The LORD has encircled the enemies of Jacob; Jerusalem is as a menstruating woman among them. The LORD is righteous, for I have rebelled against His commandments. "Hear, I pray You, all peoples, and see my grief: my virgins and my young men have gone into captivity." "I have called upon my servants, but they have deceived me; my priests and my elders have died in the city as they sought their food to refresh their souls." "Behold, O LORD, how troubled I am; my bowels swell; my heart revolts within me, for I am full of happiness; the sword breathes abroad, as death in the house." They have heard that I suffer, but there is no one to comfort me. All my enemies have heard of my troubles, and they rejoice because You have done it; You will make the day come that You have announced, and they will be like me "Let all their wickedness come upon them; do unto them what You have done unto me for all my transgressions. My sighs are many, and my heart is distressed."

CHAPTER 2

How the LORD has darkened the daughter of Zion in His wrath; He has thrown down from top to bottom the beauty of Israel, and has not remembered her footing in the day of His wrath! The LORD has destroyed all the dwellings of Jacob and has not spared them; in His wrath, He has thrown down the fortresses of the daughter of Judah; He has thrown down the land; He has polluted the kingdom and its princes In His fierce anger, He has cut off all the horns of Israel; He has withdrawn His right hand from before His adversary, and it has kindled in Jacob like a flame of fire that has spread all around. He bent His bow like an enemy; His right hand stretched out like an adversary and killed everything that was pleasing to the eyes in the tabernacle of the daughter of Zion; He released His wrath like a fire The LORD was like an enemy; He smote Israel and consumed all her palaces; He destroyed her fortresses and increased in the daughter of Judah wailing and weeping. For He has destroyed His tabernacle like a garden, He has destroyed His congregation. The LORD has caused the feasts and the Sabbaths to be forgotten in Zion and has despised, in the indignation of His wrath, the King and the Priest The LORD forsook His altar, abhorred His sanctuary, gave into the hand of the enemy the walls of His palaces, and made an odyssey in the house of the LORD, as on a feast day. The LORD determined to destroy the wall of the daughter of Zion; He stretched out a lyre; He did not withdraw His hand from destroying; therefore, He made the rampart and the wall to lament: they were destroyed together Her gates have been razed to the ground; He has destroyed and broken her ramparts; her king and her princes are among the Gentiles; the Law is no more, nor can her prophets receive any vision from the LORD. The elders of the daughter of Zion sit on the ground and are silent; they have thrown dust on their heads; they have girded themselves with sackcloth; the virgins of Jerusalem lower their heads to the ground "My eyes are filled with sadness; my bowels swell; my will is turned to the earth for the destruction of the daughter of my people because children and infants have died in the streets of the city. They said to their mothers, 'Where is the bread and water?' when they fainted as wounded in the streets of the city and when they left the ghost in their mothers' wombs." "What shall I testify for you? What shall I compare with you, O daughter of Jerusalem? What shall I compare with you to comfort you, O virgin daughter of Zion? For your breach is as great as the sea; who can heal you? Your prophets have sought vain and foolish things for you, and have not unveiled your iniquity to turn away your captivity, but have sought false prophecies and causes of exile." "All who pass by on the road clap their hands at you; they bow and shake their heads over the daughter of Jerusalem, saying, 'Is this the city that men call, "The perfection of beauty and the joy of all the earth?"' All your enemies have opened their mouths against you; they have bitten and gnashed their teeth, saying, 'Let us die; surely this is the day we were looking for; we have found it and seen it.'" The LORD has done what He set out to do; He has fulfilled the word that He set forth long ago; He has thrown down and spared not; He has caused your enemy to rise up outside of you, and He has set in motion the horn of your adversaries. "Their hearts cried out to the LORD, 'O wall of the daughter of Zion, come down like a torrent, day and night; give yourself no rest, and let not the apple of your eye cease. Arise, cry out in the night; at the beginning of the vigils pour out your heart like water before the face of the LORD; lift up your hands to Him for the lives of your young sons, who are starving in the corners of all the streets.'" "Look, O LORD, and consider who You have made thus: shall women eat their fruit, and children by a span? Shall the priest and the prophet be slain in the sanctuary of the LORD? The young and the old lie on the ground in the streets; my virgins and my young men have fallen under the blows of the sword; You have slain them in the day of Your wrath; You have killed and have not spared." "You called, as on a solemn day, my terrors around You, so that in the day of the LORD's wrath no one escaped or remained; those whom I fed and brought to life, my enemy consumed them."

CHAPTER 3

I am the man who saw affliction in the rod of His indignation. He has led me and brought me into darkness, but not into light. Surely He has turned against me; He turns His hand against me all day long. He has aged my flesh and my skin and broken my bones. He has built against me; He has surrounded me with gall and toil. He has put me in dark places, like those who are dead forever He has surrounded me with hedges so that I cannot go out; He has made my chains heavy. Even when I cry out and manifest, He excludes my prayers. He has blocked my ways with hewn stone; He has made my paths crooked. He was a bear lying in wait for me, a lion in secret places. He has turned aside my ways and torn me in pieces; He has made me desolate He has bent His bow and set me as a mark for the arrow. He has caused the arrows of His quiver to enter into my kidneys. I am become a derision to all my people; their song all the day. He has filled me with bitterness; He has made me drunken with wormwood. He has broken my teeth with gravel stones; He has covered me with ashes. You have removed my soul far off from peace; I forgot prosperity. And I said, "My strength and my hope is perished from the LORD." "Remember my affliction and my misery, the wormwood and the gall. My soul has them still in remembrance, and is humbled in me. This I recall to my mind, therefore have I hope. It is of the LORD's mercies that we are not consumed, because His compassions fail not. They are new every morning; great is Thy faithfulness. The LORD is my portion, saith my soul; therefore will I hope in Him." "The LORD is good unto them that wait for Him, to the soul that seeketh Him. It is good that a man should both hope and quietly wait for the salvation of the LORD. It is good for a man that he bear the yoke in his youth. He sitteth alone and keepeth silence, because He hath borne it upon him. He putteth his mouth in the dust; if so be there may be hope. He giveth his cheek to him that smiteth him; he is filled full with reproach." "For the LORD will not cast off forever; but though He cause grief, yet will He have compassion according to the multitude of His mercies. For He doth not afflict willingly nor grieve the children of men. To crush under His feet all the prisoners of the earth, to turn aside the right of a man before the face of the Most High, to subvert a man in his cause, the LORD approveth not." "Who is he that saith, and it cometh to pass, when the LORD commandeth it not? Out of the mouth of the Most High proceedeth not evil and good? Wherefore doth a living man complain, a man for the punishment of his sins? Let us search and try our ways, and turn again to the LORD. Let us lift up our heart with our hands unto God in the heavens. We have transgressed and have rebelled; Thou hast not pardoned." "Thou hast covered with anger, and pursued us; Thou hast slain, Thou hast not pitied. Thou hast covered Thyself with a cloud, that our prayer should not pass through. Thou hast made us as the offscouring and refuse in the midst of the people. All our enemies have opened their mouths against us; fear and a snare is come upon us, desolation and destruction. Mine eye runneth down with rivers of water for the destruction of the daughter of my people." "Mine eye trickleth down, and ceaseth not, without any intermission, till the LORD look down, and behold from heaven. Mine eye affecteth mine heart because of all the daughters of my city. Mine enemies chased me sore, like a bird, without cause. They have cut off my life in the dungeon, and cast a stone upon me. Waters flowed over mine head; then I said, I am cut off." "I called upon Thy name, O LORD, out of the low dungeon. Thou hast heard my voice: hide not Thine ear at my breathing, at my cry. Thou drewest near in the day that I called upon Thee: Thou saidst, Fear not. O LORD, Thou hast pleaded the causes of my soul; Thou hast redeemed my life. O LORD, Thou hast seen my wrong: judge Thou my cause. Thou hast seen all their vengeance and all their imaginations against me." "Thou hast heard their reproach, O LORD, and all their imaginations against me; the lips of those that rose up against me, and their device against me all the day. Behold Thou their sitting down, and their rising up; I am their music. Render unto them a recompense, O LORD, according to the work of their hands. Give them sorrow of heart, Thy curse unto them. Persecute and destroy them in anger from under the heavens of the LORD."

CHAPTER 4

How is the gold become dim! How is the most fine gold changed! The stones of the sanctuary are poured out in the top of every street. The precious sons of Zion, comparable to fine gold, how are they esteemed as earthen pitchers, the work of the hands of the potter! Even the sea monsters draw out the breast; they give suck to their young ones: the daughter of my people is become cruel, like the ostriches in the wilderness The tongue of the sucking child cleaveth to the roof of his mouth for thirst: the young children ask bread, and no man breaketh it unto them. They that did feed delicately are desolate in the streets: they that were brought up in scarlet embrace dunghills. For the punishment of the iniquity of the daughter of my people is greater than the punishment of the sin of Sodom, that was overthrown as in a moment, and no hands stayed on her Her Nazarites were purer than snow, they were whiter than milk, they were more ruddy in body than rubies, their polishing was of sapphire. Their visage is blacker than a coal; they are not known in the streets: their skin cleaveth to their bones; it is withered, it is become like a stick. They that be slain with the sword are better than they that be slain with hunger: for these pine away, stricken through for want of the fruits of the field The hands of the pitiful women have sodden their own children: they were their meat in the destruction of the daughter of my people. The LORD hath accomplished His fury; He hath poured out His fierce anger, and hath kindled a fire in Zion, and it hath devoured the foundations thereof The kings of the earth, and all the inhabitants of the world, would not have believed that the adversary and the enemy should have entered into the gates of Jerusalem. For the sins of her prophets, and the iniquities of her priests, that have shed the blood of the just in the midst of her, they have wandered as blind men in the streets, they have polluted themselves with blood, so that men could not touch their garments They cried unto them, Depart ye; it is unclean; depart, depart, touch not: when they fled away and wandered, they said among the heathen, They shall no more sojourn there. The anger of the LORD hath divided them; He will no more regard them: they respected not the persons of the priests, they favored not the elders As for us, our eyes as yet failed for our vain help: in our watching we have watched for a nation that could not save us. They hunt our steps, that we cannot go in our streets: our end is near, our days are fulfilled; for our end is come. Our persecutors are swifter than the eagles of the heaven: they pursued us upon the mountains, they laid wait for us in the wilderness The breath of our nostrils, the anointed of the LORD, was taken in their pits, of whom we said, Under his shadow we shall live among the heathen. Rejoice and be glad, O daughter of Edom, that dwellest in the land of Uz; the cup also shall pass through unto thee: thou shalt be drunken, and shalt make thyself naked. The punishment of thine iniquity is accomplished, O daughter of Zion; He will no more carry thee away into captivity: He will visit thine iniquity, O daughter of Edom; He will discover thy sins

CHAPTER 5

Remember, O LORD, what is come upon us: consider, and behold our reproach. Our inheritance is turned to strangers, our houses to aliens. We are orphans and fatherless; our mothers are as widows. We have drunken our water for money; our wood is sold unto us. Our necks are under persecution: we labour, and have no rest We have given the hand to the Egyptians, and to the Assyrians, to be satisfied with bread. Our fathers have sinned, and are not; and we have borne their iniquities. Servants have ruled over us: there is none that doth deliver us out of their hand. We gat our bread with the peril of our lives because of the sword of the wilderness. Our skin was black like an oven because of the terrible famine They ravished the women in Zion, and the maids in the cities of Judah. Princes are hanged up by their hand: the faces of elders were not honoured. They took the young men to grind, and the children fell under the wood. The elders have ceased from the gate, the young men from their musick. The joy of our heart is ceased; our dance is turned into mourning The crown is fallen from our head: woe unto us that we have sinned! For this our heart is faint; for these things our eyes are dim. Because of the mountain of Zion, which is desolate, the foxes walk upon it. Thou, O LORD, remainest forever; Thy throne from generation to generation. Wherefore dost Thou forget us forever, and forsake us so long time? Turn Thou us unto Thee, O LORD, and we shall be turned; renew our days as of old But Thou hast utterly rejected us; Thou art very wroth against us

26. Ezekiel

CHAPTER 1

In the thirtieth year, in the fourth month, on the fifth day, while I was among the captives by the river Chebar, the heavens opened, and I had visions of God. On the fifth day of the month, which was the fifth year of King Jehoiachin's captivity, the word of the Lord came to Ezekiel the priest, the son of Buzi, in the land of the Chaldeans by the river Chebar, where the hand of the Lord was upon him. I looked, and behold, a whirlwind came from the north, a great cloud with fire around it, and radiance surrounded it. In the midst of the fire was something like glowing metal. Moreover, from within it came the likeness of four living creatures. They had the appearance of a man, each with four faces and four wings. Their feet were straight, and the soles of their feet were like those of a calf, shining like polished bronze. Human hands were under their wings on their four sides, and each had faces and wings. Their wings touched one another; they did not turn when they moved but went straight forward Their faces were like a man, a lion on the right side, an ox on the left side, and an eagle. Their wings were spread out above; each had two wings touching another and two covering their bodies. Each went straight forward, wherever the spirit would go, without turning as they moved. The living creatures looked like burning coals of fire or torches; fire moved back and forth among them, and lightning flashed from the fire. The creatures sped back and forth like flashes of lightning As I looked at the living creatures, I saw a wheel on the ground beside each creature with its four faces. The wheels sparkled like topaz, and all four looked alike. Each appeared to be made like a wheel intersecting a wheel. As they moved, they could go in any one of the four directions the creatures faced; the wheels did not change direction as the creatures moved. Their rims were high and awesome, and all four rims were full of eyes all around. When the living creatures moved, the wheels beside them moved; when the living creatures rose from the ground, the wheels also rose. Wherever the spirit would go, they would go, and the wheels would rise along with them, because the spirit of the living creatures was in the wheels. When the creatures moved, they also moved; when the creatures stood still, they also stood still; and when the creatures rose from the ground, the wheels rose along with them, because the spirit of the living creatures was in the wheels Spread out above the heads of the living creatures was what looked like an expanse, sparkling like crystal, and awesome. Under the expanse, their wings were stretched out one toward the other, and each had two wings covering its body. When the creatures moved, I heard the sound of their wings, like the roar of rushing waters, like the voice of the

Almighty, like the tumult of an army. When they stood still, they lowered their wings. Then there came a voice from above the expanse over their heads as they stood with lowered wings Above the expanse over their heads was what looked like a throne of lapis lazuli, and high above on the throne was a figure like that of a man. I saw that from what appeared to be his waist up he looked like glowing metal, as if full of fire, and that from there down he looked like fire, and brilliant light surrounded him. Like the appearance of a rainbow in the clouds on a rainy day, so was the radiance around him. This was the appearance of the likeness of the glory of the Lord. When I saw it, I fell face down and heard the voice of one speaking

CHAPTER 2

He said to me, "Son of man, stand up on your feet and I will speak to you." As he spoke, the Spirit entered into me and set me on my feet, and I heard him speaking to me. He said, "Son of man, I am sending you to the Israelites, to a rebellious nation that has rebelled against me; they and their ancestors have been in revolt against me to this very day. The people to whom I am sending you are obstinate and stubborn. Say to them, 'This is what the Sovereign Lord says.' And whether they listen or fail to listen—for they are a rebellious people—they will know that a prophet has been among them "And you, son of man, do not be afraid of them or their words. Do not be afraid, though briers and thorns are all around you and you live among scorpions. Do not be afraid of what they say or be terrified by them, though they are a rebellious people. You must speak my words to them, whether they listen or fail to listen, for they are rebellious. But you, son of man, listen to what I say to you. Do not rebel like that rebellious people; open your mouth and eat what I give you." Then I looked, and I saw a hand stretched out to me. In it was a scroll, which he unrolled before me. On both sides of it were written words of lament and mourning and woe

CHAPTER 3

And he said to me, "Son of man, eat what is before you; eat this scroll; then go and speak to the people of Israel." So I opened my mouth, and he gave me the scroll to eat. Then he said to me, "Son of man, eat this scroll I am giving you and fill your stomach with it." So I ate it, and it tasted as sweet as honey in my mouth He then said to me, "Son of man, go now to the people of Israel and speak my words to them. You are not being sent to a people of obscure speech and strange language, but to the people of Israel—not to many peoples of obscure speech and strange language, whose words you cannot understand. Surely if I had sent you to them, they would have listened to you. But the people of Israel are not willing to listen to you because they are not willing to listen to me, for all the Israelites are hardened and obstinate. But I will make you as unyielding and hardened as they are. I will make your forehead like the hardest stone, harder than flint. Do not be afraid of them or terrified by them, though they are a rebellious people." And he said to me, "Son of man, listen carefully and take to heart all the words I speak to you. Go now to your people in exile and speak to them. Say to them, 'This is what the Sovereign Lord says,' whether they listen or fail to listen." Then the Spirit lifted me up, and I heard behind me a loud rumbling sound as the glory of the Lord rose from the place where it was standing. It was the sound of the wings of the living creatures brushing against each other and the sound of the wheels beside them, a loud rumbling sound. The Spirit then lifted me up and took me away, and I went in bitterness and in the anger of my spirit, with the strong hand of the Lord on me. I came to the exiles who lived at Tel Aviv near the Kebar River. And there, where they were living, I sat among them for seven days—deeply distressed At the end of seven days, the word of the Lord came to me: "Son of man, I have made you a watchman for the people of Israel; so hear the word I speak and give them warning from me. When I say to a wicked person, 'You will surely die,' and you do not warn them or speak out to dissuade them from their evil ways in order to save their life, that wicked person will die for their sin, and I will hold you accountable for their blood. But if you do warn the wicked person and they do not turn from their wickedness or from their evil ways, they will die for their sin; but you will have saved yourself "Again, when a righteous person turns from their righteousness and does evil, and I put a stumbling block before them, they will die. Since you did not warn them, they will die for their sin. The righteous things that person did will not be remembered, and I will hold you accountable for their blood. But if you do warn the righteous person not to sin and they do not sin, they will surely live because they took warning, and you will have saved yourself." The hand of the Lord was on me there, and he said to me, "Get up and go out to the plain, and there I will speak to you." So I got up and went out to the plain. And the glory of the Lord was standing there, like the glory I had seen by the Kebar River, and I fell facedown. Then the Spirit came into me and raised me to my feet. He spoke to me and said: "Go, shut yourself inside your house. And you, son of man, they will tie with ropes; you will be bound so that you cannot go out among the people. I will make your tongue stick to the roof of your mouth so that you will be silent and unable to rebuke them, for they are a rebellious people. But when I speak to you, I will open your mouth, and you shall say to them, 'This is what the Sovereign Lord says.' Whoever will listen let them listen, and whoever will refuse let them refuse; for they are a rebellious people

CHAPTER 4

"Now, son of man, take a block of clay, put it in front of you and draw the city of Jerusalem on it. Then lay siege to it: Erect siege works against it, build a ramp up to it, set up camps against it and put battering rams around it. Then take an iron pan, place it as an iron wall between you and the city and turn your face toward it. It will be under siege, and you shall besiege it. This will be a sign to the people of Israel "Then lie on your left side and put the sin of the people of Israel upon yourself. You are to bear their sin for the number of days you lie on your side. I have assigned you the same number of days as the years of their sin. So for 390 days you will bear the sin of the people of Israel "After you have finished this, lie down again, this time on your right side, and bear the sin of the people of Judah. I have assigned you 40 days, a day for each year. Turn your face toward the siege of Jerusalem and with bared arm prophesy against her. I will tie you up with ropes so that you cannot turn from one side to the other until you have finished the days of your siege "Take wheat and barley, beans and lentils, millet and spelt; put them in a storage jar and use them to make bread for yourself. You are to eat it during the 390 days you lie on your side. Weigh out twenty shekels of food to eat each day and eat it at set times. Also measure out a sixth of a hin of water and drink it at set times. Eat the food as you would a loaf of barley bread; bake it in the sight of the people, using human excrement for fuel." The Lord said, "In this way the people of Israel will eat defiled food among the nations where I will drive them." Then I said, "Not so, Sovereign Lord! I have never defiled myself. From my youth until now I have never eaten anything found dead or torn by wild animals. No impure meat has ever entered my mouth." "Very well," he said, "I will let you bake your bread over cow dung instead of human excrement." He then said to me: "Son of man, I am about to cut off the supply of food in Jerusalem. The people will eat rationed food in anxiety and drink rationed water in despair, for food and water will be scarce. They will be appalled at the sight of each other and will waste away because of their sin

CHAPTER 5

"Now, son of man, take a sharp sword and use it as a barber's razor to shave your head and your beard. Then take a set of scales and divide up the hair. When the days of your siege come to an end, burn a third of the hair inside the city. Take a third and strike it with the sword all around the city. And scatter a third to the wind. For I will pursue them with drawn sword. But take a few hairs and tuck them away in the folds of your garment. Again, take a few of these and throw them into the fire and burn them up. A fire will spread from there to all Israel "This is what the Sovereign Lord says: This is Jerusalem, which I have set in the center of the nations, with countries all around her. Yet in her wickedness, she has rebelled against my laws and decrees more than the nations and countries around her. She has rejected my laws and has not followed my decrees "Therefore this is what the Sovereign Lord says: You have been more unruly than the nations around you and have not followed my decrees or kept my laws. You have not even conformed to the standards of the nations around you "Therefore this is what the Sovereign Lord says: I myself am against you, Jerusalem, and I will inflict punishment on you in the sight of the nations. Because of all your detestable idols, I will do to you what I have never done before and will never do again. Therefore in your midst parents will eat their children, and children will eat their parents. I will inflict punishment on you and will scatter all your survivors to the winds. Therefore as surely as I live, declares the Sovereign Lord, because you have defiled my sanctuary with all your vile images and detestable practices, I myself will shave you; I will not look on you with pity or spare you. A third of your people will die of the plague or perish by famine inside you; a third will fall by the sword outside your walls; and a third I will scatter to the winds and pursue with drawn sword "Then my anger will cease, and my wrath against them will subside, and I will be avenged. And when I have spent my wrath on them, they will know that I the Lord have spoken in my zeal "I will make you a ruin and a reproach among the nations around you, in the sight of all who pass by. You will be a reproach and a taunt, a warning and an object of horror to the nations around you when I inflict punishment on you in anger and in wrath and with stinging rebuke. I the Lord have spoken. When I shoot at you with my deadly and destructive arrows of famine, I will shoot to destroy you. I will bring more and more famine upon you and cut off your supply of food. I will send famine and wild beasts against you, and they will leave you childless. Plague and bloodshed will sweep through you, and I will bring the sword against you. I the Lord have spoken."

CHAPTER 6

The word of the Lord came to me again, saying, "Son of man, turn your face toward the mountains of Israel and prophesy against them. Say, 'Mountains of Israel, hear the word of the Lord God. Thus says the Lord God to the mountains, hills, ravines, and valleys: I am bringing a sword against you, and I will destroy your high places. Your altars will be desolate, your incense altars will be smashed, and I will cast down your slain before your idols. I will lay the dead bodies of the Israelites before their idols, and I will scatter your bones around your altars. Wherever you live, your towns will be laid waste, and the high places will be demolished so that your altars will be laid waste and devastated, your idols smashed and ruined, your incense altars broken down, and what you have made wiped out. The slain will fall among you, and you will know that I am the Lord "'But I will spare some, for some of you will escape the sword when you are scattered among the lands and nations. Then in the nations where they have been carried captive, those who escape will remember me—how I have been grieved by their adulterous hearts, which have turned away from me, and by their eyes, which have lusted after their idols. They will loathe themselves for the evil they have done and for all their detestable practices. And they will know that I am the Lord and that I did not threaten in vain to bring this calamity on them "'This is what the Sovereign Lord says: Strike your hands together and stamp your feet and cry out, "Alas!" because of all the wicked and detestable practices of the people of Israel, for they will fall by the sword, famine, and plague. Those far away will die of the plague, and those near will fall by the sword, and those who survive and are spared will die of famine. So will I pour out my wrath on them. And they will know that I am the Lord when their people lie slain among their idols around their altars, on every high hill and all the mountaintops, under every spreading tree and every leafy oak—places where they offered fragrant incense to all their idols. And I will stretch out my hand against them and make the land a desolate waste from the desert to Diblah—wherever they live. Then they will know that I am the Lord.'"

CHAPTER 7

The word of the Lord came to me: "Son of man, this is what the Sovereign Lord says to the land of Israel: The end! The end has come upon the four corners of the land! The end is now upon you, and I will unleash my anger against you. I will judge you according to your conduct and repay you for all your detestable practices. I will not look on you with pity; I will not spare you. I will surely repay you for your conduct and for the detestable practices among you. Then you will know that I am the Lord "This is what the Sovereign Lord says: Disaster! Unheard-of disaster! See, it comes! The end has come! The end has come! It has roused itself against you. See, it comes! Doom has come upon you—you who dwell in the land. The time has come; the day is near. There is panic, not joy, on the mountains. I am about to pour out my wrath on you and spend my anger against you. I will judge you according to your conduct and repay you for all your detestable practices. I will not look on you with pity; I will not spare you. I will repay you for your conduct and the detestable practices among you. Then you will know that it is I the Lord who strikes you "See, the day! See, it comes! Doom has burst forth, the rod has budded, arrogance has blossomed! Violence has arisen, a rod to punish the wicked. None of the people will be left, none of that crowd— none of their wealth, nothing of value. The time has come! The day has arrived! Let not the buyer rejoice nor the seller grieve, for my wrath is on the whole crowd. The seller will not recover the property that was sold—as long as both buyer and seller live. For the vision concerning the whole crowd will not be reversed. Because of their sins, not one of them will preserve their life "They have blown the trumpet, they have made all things ready, but no one will go into battle, for my wrath is on the whole crowd. Outside is the sword; inside are plague and famine. Those in the country will die by the sword, and those in the city will be devoured by famine and plague. The fugitives who escape will flee to the mountains. Like doves of the valleys, they will all moan, each for their own sins. Every hand will go limp; every leg will be wet with urine. They will put on sackcloth and be clothed with terror. Every face will be covered with shame, and every head will be shaved "'They will throw their silver into the streets, and their gold will be treated as a thing unclean. Their silver and gold will not be able to deliver them in the day of the Lord's wrath. It will not satisfy their hunger or fill their stomachs, for it has caused them to stumble into sin. They took pride in their beautiful jewelry and used it to make their detestable idols. They made it into vile images; therefore I will make it a thing unclean for them. I will give their wealth as plunder to foreigners and as loot to the wicked of the earth, who will defile it. I will turn my face away from the people, and robbers will desecrate the place I treasure. They will enter it and will defile it "'Prepare chains! For the land is full of bloodshed, and the city is full of violence. I will bring the most wicked of nations to take possession of their houses. I will put an end to the pride of the mighty, and their sanctuaries will be desecrated. When terror comes, they will seek peace in vain. Calamity upon calamity will come, and rumor upon rumor. They will go searching for a vision from the prophet, priestly instruction in the law will cease, the counsel of the elders will come to an end. The king will mourn, the prince will be clothed with despair, and the hands of the people of the land will tremble. I will deal with them according to their conduct, and by their own standards I will judge them. Then they will know that I am the Lord.'"

CHAPTER 8

In the sixth year, in the sixth month on the fifth day, while I was sitting in my house and the elders of Judah were sitting before me, the hand of the Sovereign Lord came on me there. I looked, and I saw a figure like that of a man. From what appeared to be his waist down, he was like fire, and from there up, his appearance was as bright as glowing metal. He stretched out what looked like a hand and took me by the hair of my head. The Spirit lifted me up between earth and heaven and in visions of God, he took me to Jerusalem, to the entrance of the north gate of the inner court, where the idol that provokes to jealousy stood. And there before me was the glory of the God of Israel, as in the vision I had seen in the plain Then he said to me, "Son of man, look toward the north." So I looked, and in the entrance north of the gate of the altar I saw this idol of jealousy And he said to me, "Son of man, do you see what they are doing—the utterly detestable things the Israelites are doing here, things that will drive me far from my sanctuary? But you will see things that are even more detestable." Then he brought me to the entrance to the court. I looked, and I saw a hole in the wall. He said to me, "Son of man, now dig into the wall." So I dug into the wall and saw a doorway there. And he said to me, "Go in and see the wicked and detestable things they are doing here." So I went in and looked, and I saw portrayed all over the walls all kinds of crawling things and unclean animals and all the idols of Israel. In front of them stood seventy elders of Israel, and Jaazaniah son of Shaphan was standing among them. Each had a censer in his hand, and a fragrant cloud of incense was rising He said to me, "Son of man, have you seen what the elders of Israel are doing in the darkness, each at the shrine of his own idol? They say, 'The Lord does not see us; the Lord has forsaken the land.'" Again, he said, "You will see them doing things that are even more detestable." Then he brought me to the entrance of the north gate of the house of the Lord, and I saw women sitting there, mourning the god Tammuz. He said to me, "Do you see this, son of man? You will see

things that are even more detestable than this." He then brought me into the inner court of the house of the Lord, and there at the entrance to the temple, between the portico and the altar, were about twenty-five men. With their backs toward the temple of the Lord and their faces toward the east, they were bowing down to the sun in the east He said to me, "Have you seen this, son of man? Is it a trivial matter for the people of Judah to do the detestable things they are doing here? Must they also fill the land with violence and continually arouse my anger? Look at them putting the branch to their nose! Therefore I will deal with them in anger; I will not look on them with pity or spare them. Although they shout in my ears, I will not listen to them."

CHAPTER 9

Then I heard him call out in a loud voice, "Bring near those who are appointed to execute judgment on the city, each with a weapon in his hand." And I saw six men coming from the direction of the upper gate, which faces north, each with a deadly weapon in his hand. With them was a man clothed in linen who had a writing kit at his side. They came in and stood beside the bronze altar Now the glory of the God of Israel went up from above the cherubim, where it had been, and moved to the threshold of the temple. Then the Lord called to the man clothed in linen who had the writing kit at his side and said to him, "Go throughout the city of Jerusalem and put a mark on the foreheads of those who grieve and lament over all the detestable things that are done in it." As I listened, he said to the others, "Follow him through the city and kill, without showing pity or compassion. Slaughter the old men, the young men and women, the mothers and children, but do not touch anyone who has the mark. Begin at my sanctuary." So they began with the old men who were in front of the temple Then he said to them, "Defile the temple and fill the courts with the slain. Go!" So they went out and began killing throughout the city. While they were killing and I was left alone, I fell facedown, crying out, "Alas, Sovereign Lord! Are you going to destroy the entire remnant of Israel in this outpouring of your wrath on Jerusalem?" He answered me, "The sin of the people of Israel and Judah is exceedingly great; the land is full of bloodshed and the city is full of injustice. They say, 'The Lord has forsaken the land; the Lord does not see.' So I will not look on them with pity or spare them, but I will bring down on their own heads what they have done." Then the man in linen with the writing kit at his side brought back word, saying, "I have done as you commanded."

CHAPTER 10

I looked, and I saw the likeness of a throne of lapis lazuli above the vault that was over the heads of the cherubim. The Lord said to the man clothed in linen, "Go in among the wheels beneath the cherubim. Fill your hands with burning coals from among the cherubim and scatter them over the city." And as I watched, he went in Now the cherubim were standing on the south side of the temple when the man went in, and a cloud filled the inner court. Then the glory of the Lord rose from above the cherubim and moved to the threshold of the temple. The cloud filled the temple, and the court was full of the radiance of the glory of the Lord. The sound of the wings of the cherubim could be heard as far away as the outer court, like the voice of God Almighty when he speaks When the Lord commanded the man in linen, "Take fire from among the wheels, from among the cherubim," the man went in and stood beside a wheel. Then one of the cherubim reached out his hand to the fire that was among them. He took up some of it and put it into the hands of the man in linen, who took it and went out. Under the wings of the cherubim could be seen what looked like human hands I looked, and I saw beside the cherubim four wheels, one beside each of the cherubim; the wheels sparkled like topaz. As for their appearance, the four of them looked alike; each was like a wheel intersecting a wheel. As they moved, they would go in any one of the four directions the cherubim faced; the wheels did not turn about as the cherubim went. The cherubim went in whatever direction the head faced, without turning as they went. Their entire bodies, including their backs, their hands and their wings, were completely full of eyes, as were their four wheels. I heard the wheels being called "the whirling wheels." Each of the cherubim had four faces: one face was that of a cherub, the second the face of a human being, the third the face of a lion, and the fourth the face of an eagle Then the cherubim rose upward. These were the living creatures I had seen by the Kebar River. When the cherubim moved, the wheels beside them moved; and when the cherubim spread their wings to rise from the ground, the wheels did not leave their side. When the cherubim stood still, they also stood still; and when the cherubim rose, they rose with them, because the spirit of the living creatures was in them Then the glory of the Lord departed from over the threshold of the temple and stopped above the cherubim. While I watched, the cherubim spread their wings and rose from the ground, and as they went, the wheels went with them. They stopped at the entrance of the east gate of the Lord's house, and the glory of the God of Israel was above them These were the living creatures I had seen beneath the God of Israel by the Kebar River, and I realized that they were cherubim. Each had four faces and four wings, and under their wings was what looked like human hands. Their faces had the same appearance as those I had seen by the Kebar River. Each one went straight ahead

CHAPTER 11

The Spirit lifted me up and brought me to the eastern gate of the house of the Lord, which faces east. There, at the entrance of the gate, were twenty-five men, among whom I saw Jaazaniah, son of Azur, and Pelatiah, son of Benaiah, leaders of the people. Then he said to me, "Son of man, these are the men who devise iniquity and give wicked counsel in this city. They say, 'The time is not near to build houses; this city is the cauldron, and we are the meat.' Therefore, prophesy against them; prophesy, son of man." The Spirit of the Lord came upon me and said to me, "Speak: Thus says the Lord, 'This is what you are saying, house of Israel, and I know the thoughts that come into your mind. You have multiplied your slain in this city and filled its streets with the dead. Therefore, thus says the Lord God: Your slain whom you have laid in its midst, they are the meat, and this city is the cauldron; but I will bring you out of the midst of it. You have feared the sword, and I will bring the sword upon you, says the Lord God. I will bring you out of its midst and deliver you into the hands of foreigners, and I will execute judgments on you. You shall fall by the sword; I will judge you at the border of Israel, and you shall know that I am the Lord. This city shall not be your cauldron, nor shall you be the meat in its midst; I will judge you at the border of Israel. You shall know that I am the Lord, for you have not walked in my statutes nor obeyed my rules but have acted according to the rules of the nations that are around you.'" While I was prophesying, Pelatiah, son of Benaiah, died. Then I fell down on my face and cried with a loud voice, "Ah, Lord God! Will you make a full end of the remnant of Israel?" The word of the Lord came to me: "Son of man, your brothers, even your brothers, your kinsmen, the whole house of Israel, all of them, are those of whom the inhabitants of Jerusalem have said, 'Go far from the Lord; to us this land is given for a possession.' Therefore say, 'Thus says the Lord God: Though I removed them far off among the nations, and though I scattered them among the countries, yet I have been a sanctuary to them for a while in the countries where they have gone.' Therefore say, 'Thus says the Lord God: I will gather you from the peoples and assemble you out of the countries where you have been scattered, and I will give you the land of Israel.' And when they come there, they will remove from it all its detestable things and all its abominations. And I will give them one heart, and a new spirit I will put within them. I will remove the heart of stone from their flesh and give them a heart of flesh, that they may walk in my statutes and keep my rules and obey them. And they shall be my people, and I will be their God. But as for those whose hearts go after their detestable things and their abominations, I will bring their deeds upon their own heads, declares the Lord God." Then the cherubim lifted up their wings, with the wheels beside them, and the glory of the God of Israel was over them. The glory of the Lord went up from the midst of the city and stood on the mountain that is on the east side of the city. And the Spirit lifted me up and brought me in the vision by the Spirit of God into Chaldea, to the exiles. Then the vision that I had seen went up from me. And I told the exiles all the things that the Lord had shown me

CHAPTER 12

The word of the Lord came to me: "Son of man, you dwell in the midst of a rebellious house, who have eyes to see but see not, who have ears to hear but hear not, for they are a rebellious house. As for you, son of man, prepare for yourself an exile's baggage and go into exile by day in their sight. You shall go like an exile from your place to another place in their sight. Perhaps they will understand, though they are a rebellious house. You shall bring out your baggage by day in their sight, as baggage for exile, and you shall go out yourself at evening in their sight, as those do who must go into exile. In their sight dig through the wall and bring your baggage out through it. In their sight you shall lift the baggage on your shoulder and carry it out at dusk. You shall cover your face, that you may not see the land, for I have made you a sign for the house of Israel." I did as I was commanded. I brought out my baggage by day, as baggage for exile, and in the evening I dug through the wall with my own hands. I brought out my baggage at dusk, carrying it on my shoulder in their sight. In the morning, the word of the Lord came to me: "Son of man, has not the house of Israel, the rebellious house, said to you, 'What are you doing?' Say to them, 'Thus says the Lord God: This oracle concerns the prince in Jerusalem and all the house of Israel who are in it.' Say, 'I am a sign for you: as I have done, so shall it be done to them. They shall go into exile, into captivity.' And the prince who is among them shall lift his baggage upon his shoulder at dusk and shall go out. They shall dig through the wall to bring him out through it. He shall cover his face, that he may not see the land with his eyes. And I will spread my net over him, and he shall be taken in my snare. And I will bring him to Babylon, the land of the Chaldeans, yet he shall not see it, and he shall die there. And I will scatter toward every wind all who are around him, his helpers, and all his troops, and I will unsheathe the sword after them. And they shall know that I am the Lord, when I disperse them among the nations and scatter them among the countries. But I will let a few of them escape from the sword, from famine and pestilence, that they may declare all their abominations among the nations where they go, and may know that I am the Lord." The word of the Lord came to me: "Son of man, eat your bread with quaking, and drink water with trembling and with anxiety. And say to the people of the land, 'Thus says the Lord God concerning the inhabitants of Jerusalem in the land of Israel: They shall eat their bread with anxiety and drink water in dismay. In this way, their land will be stripped of all it contains on account of the violence of all those who dwell in it. And the inhabited cities shall be laid waste, and the land shall become a desolation; and you shall know that I am the Lord.'" The word of the Lord came to me: "Son of man, what is this proverb that you have about the land of Israel, saying, 'The days grow long, and every vision comes to nothing'? Tell them therefore, 'Thus says the Lord God: I will put an end to this proverb, and they shall no more use it as a proverb in Israel.' But say to them, 'The days are near, and the fulfillment of every vision. For there shall be no more any false vision or flattering divination within the house of Israel. For I am the Lord; I will speak the word that I will speak, and it will be performed. It will no longer be delayed, but in your days, O rebellious house, I will speak the word and perform it, declares the Lord God.'" The word of the Lord came to me: "Son of man, behold, they of the house of Israel say, 'The vision that he sees is for many days from now, and he prophesies of times far off.' Therefore say to them, 'Thus says the Lord God: None of my words will be delayed any longer, but the word that I speak will be performed, declares the Lord God.'"

CHAPTER 13

The word of the Lord came to me: "Son of man, prophesy against the prophets of Israel who are prophesying, and say to those who prophesy from their own hearts: 'Hear the word of the Lord!' Thus says the Lord God: Woe to the foolish prophets who follow their own spirit and have seen nothing! Your prophets have been like foxes among ruins, O Israel. You have not gone up into the breaches or built up a wall for the house of Israel, that it might stand in battle in the day of the Lord. They have seen false visions and lying divinations. They say, 'Declares the Lord,' when the Lord has not sent them, and yet they expect him to fulfill their word. Have you not seen a false vision and uttered a lying divination, whenever you have said, 'Declares the Lord,' although I have not spoken?" Therefore thus says the Lord God: "Because you have uttered falsehood and seen lying visions, therefore behold, I am against you, declares the Lord God. My hand will be against the prophets who see false visions and who give lying divinations. They shall not be in the council of my people, nor be enrolled in the register of the house of Israel, nor shall they enter the land of Israel. And you shall know that I am the Lord God. Precisely because they have misled my people, saying, 'Peace,' when there is no peace, and because, when the people build a wall, these prophets smear it with whitewash, say to those who smear it with whitewash that it shall fall! There will be a deluge of rain, and you, O great hailstones, will fall, and a stormy wind break out. And when the wall falls, will it not be said to you, 'Where is the coating with which you smeared it?' Therefore thus says the Lord God: I will make a stormy wind break out in my wrath, and there shall be a deluge of rain in my anger, and great hailstones in wrath to make a full end. And I will break down the wall that you have smeared with whitewash, and bring it down to the ground, so that its foundation will be laid bare. When it falls, you shall perish in the midst of it, and you shall know that I am the Lord. Thus will I spend my wrath upon the wall and upon those who have smeared it with whitewash, and I will say to you, 'The wall is no more, nor those who smeared it, the prophets of Israel who prophesied concerning Jerusalem and saw visions of peace for her, when there was no peace, declares the Lord God.'" "And you, son of man, set your face against the daughters of your people, who prophesy out of their own hearts; prophesy against them and say, 'Thus says the Lord God: Woe to the women who sew magic bands upon all wrists, and make veils for the heads of persons of every stature, in the hunt for souls! Will you hunt down souls belonging to my people and keep your own souls alive? You have profaned me among my people for handfuls of barley and for pieces of bread, putting to death souls who should not die and keeping alive souls who should not live, by your lying to my people, who listen to lies.' "Therefore thus says the Lord God: 'Behold, I am against your magic bands with which you hunt the souls like birds, and I will tear them from your arms, and I will let the souls whom you hunt go free, the souls like birds. Your veils also I will tear off and deliver my people out of your hand, and they shall be no more in your hand as prey, and you shall know that I am the Lord. Because you have disheartened the righteous falsely, although I have not grieved him, and you have encouraged the wicked, that he should not turn from his evil way to save his life, therefore you shall no more see false visions nor practice divination. I will deliver my people out of your hand. And you shall know that I am the Lord.'"

CHAPTER 14

Then certain of the elders of Israel came to me and sat before me. And the word of the Lord came to me: "Son of man, these men have taken their idols into their hearts and set the stumbling block of their iniquity before their faces. Should I indeed let myself be consulted by them? Therefore speak to them and say to them, 'Thus says the Lord God: Any one of the house of Israel who takes his idols into his heart and sets the stumbling block of his iniquity before his face and yet comes to the prophet, I the Lord will answer him as he comes with the multitude of his idols, that I may lay hold of the hearts of the house of Israel, who are all estranged from me through their idols.' "Therefore say to the house of Israel, 'Thus says the Lord God: Repent and turn away from your idols, and turn away your faces from all your abominations. For any one of the house of Israel, or of the strangers who sojourn in Israel, who separates himself from me, taking his idols into his heart and putting the stumbling block of his iniquity before his face, and yet comes to a prophet to consult me through him, I the Lord will answer him myself. And I will set my face against that man; I will make him a sign and a byword and cut him off from the midst of my people, and you shall know that I am the Lord. And if the prophet is deceived and speaks a word, I the Lord have deceived that prophet, and I will stretch out my hand against him and will destroy him from the midst of my people Israel. And they shall bear their punishment—the punishment of the prophet and the punishment of the inquirer shall be alike—that the house of Israel may no more go astray from me, nor defile themselves anymore with all their transgressions, but that they may be my people and I may be their God, declares the Lord God." And the word of the Lord came to me: "Son of man, when a land sins against me by acting faithlessly, and I stretch out my hand against it and break its supply of bread and send famine upon it, and cut off from it man and beast, even if these three men, Noah, Daniel, and Job, were in it, they would deliver but their own lives by their righteousness, declares the Lord God "If I cause wild beasts to pass through the land, and they ravage it, and it be made desolate, so that no one may pass through because of the beasts, even if these three men were in it, as I live, declares the Lord God, they would deliver neither sons nor daughters. They alone would be delivered, but the land would be desolate "Or if I bring a sword upon that land and say, 'Let a sword pass through the land,' and I cut off from it man and beast, even if these three men were in it, as I live, declares the Lord God, they would deliver neither sons nor daughters, but they alone would be delivered "Or if I send a pestilence into that land and pour out my wrath upon it with blood, to cut off from it man and beast, even if Noah, Daniel, and Job were in it, as I live, declares the Lord God, they would deliver neither son nor daughter. They would deliver but their own lives by their righteousness "For thus says the Lord God: How much more when I send upon Jerusalem my four disastrous acts of judgment, sword, famine, wild beasts, and pestilence, to cut off from it man and beast! But behold, some survivors will be left in it, sons and daughters who will be brought out. Behold, when they come out to you, and you see their ways and their deeds, you will be consoled for the disaster that I have brought upon Jerusalem, for all that I have brought upon it. They will console you when you see their ways and their deeds, and you shall know that I have not done without cause all that I have done in it, declares the Lord God."

CHAPTER 15

The word of the Lord came to me: "Son of man, how does the wood of the vine surpass any wood, the vine branch that is among the trees of the forest? Is wood taken from it to make anything? Do people take a peg from it to hang any vessel on it? Behold, it is given to the fire for fuel. When the fire has consumed both ends of it and the middle of it is charred, is it useful for anything? Behold, when it was whole, it was used for nothing. How much less, when the fire has consumed it and it is charred, can it ever be used for anything! "Therefore thus says the Lord God: Like the wood of the vine among the trees of the forest, which I have given to the fire for fuel, so have I given up the inhabitants of Jerusalem. And I will set my face against them. Though they escape from the fire, the fire shall yet consume them, and you shall know that I am the Lord, when I set my face against them. And I will make the land desolate, because they have acted faithlessly, declares the Lord God."

CHAPTER 16

Again the word of the Lord came to me, saying, "Son of man, make known to Jerusalem her abominations and say, 'Thus says the Lord God to Jerusalem: Your origin and your birth are of the land of Canaan; your father was an Amorite, and your mother a Hittite. On the day you were born, your cord was not cut, nor were you washed with water to cleanse you, nor rubbed with salt, nor wrapped in cloths. No eye pitied you, to do any of these things to you out of compassion for you, but you were cast out on the open field, for you were abhorred on the day that you were born "'And when I passed by you and saw you wallowing in your blood, I said to you in your blood, "Live!" I made you flourish like a plant of the field. And you grew up and became tall and arrived at full adornment. Your breasts were formed, and your hair had grown, yet you were naked and bare "'When I passed by you again and saw you, behold, you were at the age for love, and I spread the corner of my garment over you and covered your nakedness. I made my vow to you and entered into a covenant with you, declares the Lord God, and you became mine. Then I bathed you with water and washed off your blood from you and anointed you with oil. I clothed you also with embroidered cloth and shod you with fine leather. I wrapped you in fine linen and covered you with silk. And I adorned you with ornaments and put bracelets on your wrists and a chain on your neck. And I put a ring on your nose and earrings in your ears and a beautiful crown on your head. Thus you were adorned with gold and silver, and your clothing was of fine linen and silk and embroidered cloth. You ate fine flour and honey and oil. You grew exceedingly beautiful and advanced to royalty. And your renown went forth among the nations because of your beauty, for it was perfect through the splendor that I had bestowed on you, declares the Lord God "'But you trusted in your beauty and played the whore because of your renown and lavished your whorings on any passerby; your beauty became his. You took some of your garments and made for yourself colorful shrines, and on them played the whore. The like has never been, nor ever shall be. You also took your beautiful jewels of my gold and of my silver, which I had given you, and made for yourself images of men and with them played the whore. And you took your embroidered garments to cover them and set my oil and my incense before them. Also my bread that I gave you— I fed you with fine flour and oil and honey—you set before them for a pleasing aroma; and so it was, declares the Lord God "'And you took your sons and your daughters, whom you had borne to me, and these you sacrificed to them to be devoured. Were your whorings so small a matter that you slaughtered my children and delivered them up as an offering by fire to them? And in all your abominations and your whorings you did not remember the days of your youth, when you were naked and bare, wallowing in your blood "'And after all your wickedness (woe, woe to you! declares the Lord God), you built yourself a vaulted chamber and made yourself a lofty place in every square. At the head of every street, you built your lofty place and made your beauty an abomination, offering yourself to any passerby and multiplying your whoring. You also played the whore with the Egyptians, your lustful neighbors, multiplying your whoring, to provoke me to anger. Behold, therefore, I stretched out my hand against you and diminished your allotted portion and delivered you to the greed of your enemies, the daughters of the Philistines, who were ashamed of your lewd behavior. You played the whore also with the Assyrians because you were not satisfied; yes, you played the whore with them, and still, you were not satisfied. You multiplied your whoring also with the trading land of Chaldea, and even with this, you were not satisfied "'How sick is your heart, declares the Lord God, because you did all these things, the deeds of a brazen prostitute, building your vaulted chamber at the head of every street and making your lofty place in every square. Yet you were not like a prostitute because you scorned payment. Adulterous wife, who receives strangers instead of her husband! Men give gifts to all prostitutes, but you gave your gifts to all your lovers, bribing them to come to you from every side with your whorings. So you were different from other women in your whorings. No one solicited you to play the whore, and you gave payment, while no payment was given to you; therefore, you were different "'Therefore, O prostitute, hear the word of the Lord: Thus says the Lord God, Because your lust was poured out and your nakedness uncovered in your whorings with your lovers and with all your abominable idols, and because of the blood of your children that you gave to them, therefore, behold, I will gather all your lovers with whom you took pleasure, all those you loved and all those you hated. I will gather them against you from every side and will uncover your nakedness to them, that they may see all your nakedness. And I will judge you as women who commit adultery and shed blood are judged, and bring upon you the blood of wrath and jealousy. And I will give you into their hands, and they shall throw down your vaulted chamber and break down your lofty places. They shall strip you of your clothes and take your beautiful jewels and leave you naked and bare. They shall bring up a crowd against you, and they shall stone you and cut you to pieces with their swords. And they shall burn your houses and execute judgments upon you in the sight of many women. I will make you stop playing the whore, and you shall also give payment no more. So I will satisfy my wrath on you, and my jealousy shall depart from you. I will be calm and will no more be angry "'Because you have not remembered the days of your youth but have enraged me with all these things, therefore, behold, I have returned your deeds upon your head, declares the Lord God. Have you not committed lewdness in addition to all your abominations? Behold, everyone who uses proverbs will use this proverb about you: "Like mother, like daughter." You are the daughter of your mother, who loathed her husband and her children; and you are the sister of your sisters, who loathed their husbands and their children. Your mother was a Hittite, and your father an Amorite. And your elder sister is Samaria, who lived with her daughters to the north of you; and your younger sister, who lived to the south of you, is Sodom with her daughters. Not only did you walk in their ways and do according to their abominations; within a very little time, you were more corrupt than they in all your ways "'As I live, declares the Lord God, your sister Sodom and her daughters have not done as you and your daughters have done. Behold, this was the guilt of your sister Sodom: she and her daughters had pride, excess of food, and prosperous ease, but did not aid the poor and needy. They were haughty and did an abomination before me. So I removed them when I saw it. Samaria has not committed half your sins. You have committed more abominations than they and have made your sisters appear righteous by all the abominations that you have committed. Bear your disgrace, you also, for you have intervened on behalf of your sisters. Because of your sins in which you acted more abominably than they, they are more in the right than you. So be ashamed, you also, and bear your disgrace, for you have made your sisters appear righteous "'I will restore their fortunes, both the fortunes of Sodom and her daughters and the fortunes of Samaria and her daughters, and I will restore your own fortunes in their midst, that you may bear your disgrace and be ashamed of all that you have done, becoming a consolation to them. As for your sisters, Sodom and her daughters shall return to their former state, and Samaria and her daughters shall return to their former state, and you and your daughters shall return to your former state. Was not your sister Sodom a byword in your mouth in the day of your pride before your wickedness was uncovered? Now you have become an object of scorn for the daughters of Edom and all her neighbors and for the daughters of the Philistines, those all around who despise you. You bear the penalty of your lewdness and your abominations, declares the Lord "'For thus says the Lord God: I will deal with you as you have done, you who have despised the oath in breaking the covenant, yet I will remember my covenant with you in the days of your youth, and I will establish for you an everlasting covenant. Then you will remember your ways and be ashamed when you take your sisters, both your elder and your younger, and I give them to you as daughters, but not on account of the covenant with you. I will establish my covenant with you, and you shall know that I am the Lord, that you may remember and be confounded and never open your mouth again because of your shame when I atone for you for all that you have done, declares the Lord God.'"

CHAPTER 17

The word of the Lord came to me: "Son of man, propound a riddle and speak a parable to the house of Israel. Say, 'Thus says the Lord God: A great eagle with great wings and long pinions, rich in plumage of many colors, came to Lebanon and took the top of the cedar. He broke off the topmost of its young twigs and carried it to a land of trade and set it in a city of merchants. Then he took of the seed of the land and planted it in fertile soil. He placed it beside abundant waters. He set it like a willow twig, and it sprouted and became a low spreading vine, and its branches turned toward him, and its roots remained where it stood. So it became a vine and produced branches and put out boughs "'And there was another great eagle with great wings and much plumage, and behold, this vine bent its roots toward him and shot forth its branches toward him from the bed where it was planted, that he might water it. It had been planted on good soil by abundant waters, that it might produce branches and bear fruit and become a noble vine "'Say, Thus says the Lord God: Will it thrive? Will he not pull up its roots and cut off its fruit so that it withers, so that all its fresh sprouting leaves wither? It will not take a strong arm or many people to pull it from its roots. Behold, it is planted; will it thrive? Will it not utterly wither when the east wind strikes it—wither away on the bed where it sprouted?' Then the word of the Lord came to me: "Say now to the rebellious house, Do you not know what these things mean? Tell them, 'Behold, the king of Babylon came to Jerusalem and took her king and her princes and brought them to him to Babylon. And he took one of the royal offspring and made a covenant with him, putting him under oath (the chief men of the land he had taken away), that the kingdom might be humble and not lift itself up and keep his covenant that it might stand. But he rebelled against him by sending his ambassadors to Egypt, that they might give him horses and a large army. Will he thrive? Can one escape who does such things? Can he break the covenant and yet escape? "'As I live, declares the Lord God, surely in the place where the king dwells who made him king, whose oath he despised and whose covenant with him he broke—in Babylon he shall die. Pharaoh with his mighty army and great company will not help him in war when mounds are cast up and siege walls built to cut off many lives. He despised the oath in breaking the covenant, and behold, he gave his hand and did all these things; he shall not escape. Therefore thus says the Lord God: As I live, surely it is my oath that he despised and my covenant that he broke. I will return it upon his head. I will spread my net over him, and he shall be taken in my snare, and I will bring him to Babylon and enter into judgment with him there for the treachery he has committed against me. And all the pick of his troops shall fall by the sword, and the survivors shall be scattered to every wind, and you shall know that I am the Lord; I have spoken.' "Thus says the Lord God: 'I myself will take a sprig from the lofty top of the cedar and will set it out. I will break off from the topmost of its young twigs a tender one, and I myself will plant it on a high and lofty mountain. On the mountain height of Israel will I plant it, that it may bear branches and produce fruit and become a noble cedar. And under it will dwell every kind of bird; in the shade of its branches, birds of every sort will nest. And all the trees of the field shall know that I am the Lord; I bring low the high tree and make high the low tree, dry up the green tree, and make the dry tree flourish. I am the Lord; I have spoken, and I will do it.'"

CHAPTER 18

The word of the Lord came to me again: "What do you mean by repeating this proverb concerning the land of Israel, 'The fathers have eaten sour grapes, and the children's teeth are set on edge'? As I live, declares the Lord God, this proverb shall no more be used by you in Israel. Behold, all souls are mine; the soul of the father as well as the soul of the son is mine: the soul who sins shall die "If a man is righteous and does what is just and right—if he does not eat upon the mountains or lift up his eyes to the idols of the house of Israel, does not defile his neighbor's wife or approach a woman in her time of menstrual impurity, does not oppress anyone but restores to the debtor his pledge, commits no robbery, gives his bread to the hungry and covers the naked with a garment, does not lend at interest or take any profit, withholds his hand from injustice, executes true justice between man and man, walks in my statutes, and keeps my rules by acting faithfully—he is righteous; he shall surely live, declares the Lord God "If he fathers a son who is violent, a shedder of blood, who does any of these things (though he himself did none of these things), who even eats upon the mountains, defiles his neighbor's wife, oppresses the poor and needy, commits robbery, does not restore the pledge, lifts up his eyes to the idols, commits abomination, lends at interest, and takes profit—shall he then live? He shall not live. He has done all these abominations; he shall surely die; his blood shall be upon himself "Now suppose this man fathers a son who sees all the sins that his father has done; he sees, and does not do likewise: he does not eat upon the mountains or lift up his eyes to the idols of the house of Israel, does not defile his neighbor's wife, does not oppress anyone, exacts no pledge, commits no robbery, but gives his bread to the hungry and covers the naked with a garment, withholds his hand from iniquity, takes no interest or profit, obeys my rules, and walks in my statutes; he shall not die for his father's iniquity; he shall surely live. As for his father, because he practiced extortion, robbed his brother, and did what is not good among his people, behold, he shall die for his iniquity "Yet you say, 'Why should not the son suffer for the iniquity of the father?' When the son has done what is just and right and has been careful to observe all my statutes, he shall surely live. The soul who sins shall die. The son shall not suffer for the iniquity of the father, nor the father suffer for the iniquity of the son. The righteousness of the righteous shall be upon himself, and the wickedness of the wicked shall be upon himself "But if a wicked person turns away from all his sins that he has committed and keeps all my statutes and does what is just and right, he shall surely live; he shall not die. None of the transgressions that he has committed shall be remembered against him; for the righteousness that he has done, he shall live. Have I any pleasure in the death of the wicked, declares the Lord God, and not rather that he should turn from his way and live? But when a righteous person turns away from his righteousness and does injustice and does the same abominations that the wicked person does, shall he live? None of the righteous deeds that he has done shall be remembered; for the treachery of which he is guilty and the sin he has committed, for them he shall die "Yet you say, 'The way of the Lord is not just.' Hear now, O house of Israel: Is my way not just? Is it not your ways that are not just? When a righteous person turns away from his righteousness and does injustice, he shall die for it; for the injustice that he has done, he shall die. Again, when a wicked person turns away from the wickedness he has committed and does what is just and right, he shall

save his life. Because he considered and turned away from all the transgressions that he had committed, he shall surely live; he shall not die. Yet the house of Israel says, 'The way of the Lord is not just.' O house of Israel, are my ways not just? Is it not your ways that are not just? "Therefore I will judge you, O house of Israel, every one according to his ways, declares the Lord God. Repent and turn from all your transgressions, lest iniquity be your ruin. Cast away from you all the transgressions that you have committed and make yourselves a new heart and a new spirit! Why will you die, O house of Israel? For I have no pleasure in the death of anyone, declares the Lord God; so turn, and live."

CHAPTER 19

And you, take up a lamentation for the princes of Israel, and say: "'What was your mother? A lioness! Among lions she crouched; in the midst of young lions, she reared her cubs. And she brought up one of her cubs; he became a young lion, and he learned to catch prey; he devoured men. The nations heard about him; he was caught in their pit, and they brought him with hooks to the land of Egypt. When she saw that she waited in vain, that her hope was lost, she took another of her cubs and made him a young lion. He prowled among the lions; he became a young lion, and he learned to catch prey; he devoured men, and seized their widows. He laid waste their cities, and the land was appalled, and all who were in it, at the sound of his roaring. Then the nations set against him from provinces on every side; they spread their net over him; he was taken in their pit. With hooks, they put him in a cage and brought him to the king of Babylon; they brought him into custody so that his voice should no more be heard on the mountains of Israel "'Your mother was like a vine in a vineyard planted by the water, fruitful and full of branches by reason of abundant water. Its strong stems became rulers' scepters; it towered aloft among the thick boughs; it was seen in its height with the mass of its branches. But the vine was plucked up in fury, cast down to the ground; the east wind dried up its fruit; they were stripped off and withered. As for its strong stem, fire consumed it. Now it is planted in the wilderness, in a dry and thirsty land. And fire has gone out from the stem of its shoots, has consumed its fruit, so that there remains in it no strong stem, no scepter for ruling.' "This is a lamentation and has become a lamentation."

CHAPTER 20

In the seventh year, in the fifth month, on the tenth day of the month, certain of the elders of Israel came to inquire of the Lord, and sat before me. And the word of the Lord came to me: "Son of man, speak to the elders of Israel and say to them, 'Thus says the Lord God, Is it to inquire of me that you come? As I live, declares the Lord God, I will not be inquired of by you.' Will you judge them, son of man, will you judge them? Let them know the abominations of their fathers, and say to them, 'Thus says the Lord God: On the day when I chose Israel, I swore to the offspring of the house of Jacob, making myself known to them in the land of Egypt; I swore to them, saying, I am the Lord your God. On that day, I swore to them that I would bring them out of the land of Egypt into a land that I had searched out for them, a land flowing with milk and honey, the most glorious of all lands. And I said to them, Cast away the detestable things your eyes feast on, every one of you, and do not defile yourselves with the idols of Egypt; I am the Lord your God. But they rebelled against me and were not willing to listen to me. None of them cast away the detestable things their eyes feasted on, nor did they forsake the idols of Egypt "'Then I said I would pour out my wrath upon them and spend my anger against them in the midst of the land of Egypt. But I acted for the sake of my name, that it should not be profaned in the sight of the nations among whom they lived, in whose sight I made myself known to them in bringing them out of the land of Egypt. So I led them out of the land of Egypt and brought them into the wilderness. I gave them my statutes and made known to them my rules, by which, if a person does them, he shall live. Moreover, I gave them my Sabbaths, as a sign between me and them, that they might know that I am the Lord who sanctifies them. But the house of Israel rebelled against me in the wilderness. They did not walk in my statutes but rejected my rules, by which, if a person does them, he shall live, and my Sabbaths they greatly profaned. Then I said I would pour out my wrath upon them in the wilderness, to make a full end of them. But I acted for the sake of my name, that it should not be profaned in the sight of the nations, in whose sight I had brought them out. Moreover, I swore to them in the wilderness that I would not bring them into the land that I had given them, a land flowing with milk and honey, the most glorious of all lands, because they rejected my rules and did not walk in my statutes, and profaned my Sabbaths; for their heart went after their idols. Nevertheless, my eye spared them, and I did not destroy them or make a full end of them in the wilderness "'And I said to their children in the wilderness, Do not walk in the statutes of your fathers, nor keep their rules, nor defile yourselves with their idols. I am the Lord your God; walk in my statutes, and be careful to obey my rules, and keep my Sabbaths holy that they may be a sign between me and you, that you may know that I am the Lord your God. But the children rebelled against me. They did not walk in my statutes and were not careful to obey my rules, by which, if a person does them, he shall live; they profaned my Sabbaths "'Then I said I would pour out my wrath upon them and spend my anger against them in the wilderness. But I withheld my hand and acted for the sake of my name, that it should not be profaned in the sight of the nations, in whose sight I had brought them out. Moreover, I swore to them in the wilderness that I would scatter them among the nations and disperse them through the countries because they had not obeyed my rules but had rejected my statutes and profaned my Sabbaths, and their eyes were set on their fathers' idols. Moreover, I gave them statutes that were not good and rules by which they could not have life, and I defiled them through their very gifts in their offering up all their firstborn, that I might devastate them. I did it that they might know that I am the Lord "'Therefore, son of man, speak to the house of Israel and say to them, Thus says the Lord God: In this also your fathers blasphemed me by dealing treacherously with me. For when I had brought them into the land that I swore to give them, then wherever they saw any high hill or any leafy tree, there they offered their sacrifices and there they presented the provocation of their offering; there they sent up their pleasing aromas, and there they poured out their drink offerings. (I said to them, "What is the high place to which you go?" So its name is called Bamah to this day.) "'Therefore say to the house of Israel, Thus says the Lord God: Will you defile yourselves after the manner of your fathers and go whoring after their detestable things? When you present your gifts and offer up your children in fire, you defile yourselves with all your idols to this day. And shall I be inquired of by you, O house of Israel? As I live, declares the Lord God, I will not be inquired of by you. What is in your mind shall never happen—the thought, "Let us be like the nations, like the tribes of the countries, and worship wood and stone." "'As I live, declares the Lord God, surely with a mighty hand and an outstretched arm and with wrath poured out, I will be king over you. I will bring you out from the peoples and gather you out of the countries where you are scattered, with a mighty hand and an outstretched arm, and with wrath poured out. And I will bring you into the wilderness of the peoples, and there I will enter into judgment with you face to face. As I entered into judgment with your fathers in the wilderness of the land of Egypt, so I will enter into judgment with you, declares the Lord God. I will make you pass under the rod, and I will bring you into the bond of the covenant. I will purge out the rebels from among you and those who transgress against me. I will bring them out of the land where they sojourn, but they shall not enter the land of Israel. Then you will know that I am the Lord "'As for you, O house of Israel, thus says the Lord God: Go serve every one of you his idols, now and hereafter if you will not listen to me; but my holy name you shall no more profane with your gifts and your idols. For on my holy mountain, the mountain height of Israel, declares the Lord God, there all the house of Israel, all of them, shall serve me in the land. There I will accept them, and there I will require your contributions and the choicest of your gifts, with all your sacred offerings. As a pleasing aroma, I will accept you when I bring you out from the peoples and gather you out of the countries where you have been scattered. And I will manifest my holiness among you in the sight of the nations. And you shall know that I am the Lord when I bring you into the land of Israel, the country that I swore to give to your fathers. And there you shall remember your ways and all your deeds with which you have defiled yourselves, and you shall loathe yourselves for all the evils that you have committed. And you shall know that I am the Lord when I deal with you for my name's sake, not according to your evil ways, nor according to your corrupt deeds, O house of Israel, declares the Lord God.'" The word of the Lord came to me: "Son of man, set your face toward the southland; preach against the south and prophesy against the forest land in the Negeb. Say to the forest of the Negeb, 'Hear the word of the Lord: Thus says the Lord God, Behold, I will kindle a fire in you, and it shall devour every green tree in you and every dry tree. The blazing flame shall not be quenched, and all faces from south to north shall be scorched by it. All flesh shall see that I the Lord have kindled it; it shall not be quenched.'" Then I said, "Ah, Lord God! They are saying of me, 'Is he not a maker of parables?'"

CHAPTER 21

The word of the LORD was again spoken to me, saying, "Son of man, turn your face toward Jerusalem, let your words fall upon the holy places, and prophesy against the land of Israel. And say to the land of Israel, 'Thus says the LORD, Behold, I come against you, and I will draw my sword out of its sheath and cut off both the righteous and the wicked. My sword will come out of its sheath against all flesh from the south to the north, so that all flesh may know that I, the LORD, have drawn my sword from its sheath, and it shall not return again.' Therefore, son of man, suffer as if in pain and suffer bitterly before them. If they say to you, 'Why do you mourn?' answer, 'Because of the bruise, for it shall come, and every heart shall melt, all hands shall be weakened, every mind shall droop, and all knees shall fall like water; behold, it shall come and it shall be done, says the Lord God.'" Afterward, the word of the LORD came to me, saying, "Son of man, prophesy and say, 'Thus says the Lord God, A sword, a sword sharpened and polished. It is sharpened to make a painful slaughter, and it is polished to glitter; how shall we rejoice? For the rod of my son despises every tree. He has given it to be polished, to be handled; this sword is sharpened and polished to be given into the hand of the slayer. Cry out and wail, son of man, for it is against my people; it is against all the princes of Israel. They are delivered over to the sword with my people; strike therefore upon your thigh. For it is a trial, and what if the sword despises even the rod? It shall be no more, says the Lord God. Therefore, son of man, prophesy and strike hand to hand; let the sword be doubled the third time, the sword of the slain; it is the sword of the great slaughter, which surrounds them. I have set the point of the sword against all their gates, that their hearts may faint, and their ruins be multiplied. Ah! It is made bright; it is wrapped up for the slaughter. Go one way or the other, either on the right hand or on the left, wherever your face is set. I will also strike my hands together, and I will cause my fury to rest. I, the LORD, have said it.'" The word of the LORD came to me again, saying, "Also, son of man, mark two ways for the sword of the king of Babylon to come; both of them shall come out of one land. Mark a way, that it may come to Rabbah of the Ammonites and to Judah in Jerusalem the fortified. For the king of Babylon stood at the parting of the way, at the head of the two ways, to use divination. He made his arrows bright, consulted with images, he looked into the liver. At his right hand was the divination for Jerusalem, to appoint captains, to open the mouth in the slaughter, to lift up the voice with shouting, to appoint battering rams against the gates, to cast a mount, and to build a fort. And it shall be to them as a false divination in their sight, to those who have sworn oaths with them; but he will call to remembrance the iniquity, that they may be taken. Therefore thus says the Lord God, 'Because you have made your iniquity to be remembered, in that your transgressions are discovered, so that in all your doings your sins do appear; because, I say, that you are come to remembrance, you shall be taken with the hand.' And you, profane wicked prince of Israel, whose day has come, when iniquity shall have an end, thus says the Lord God, 'Remove the diadem, and take off the crown; this shall not be the same; exalt him that is low, and abase him that is high. I will overturn, overturn, overturn it, and it shall be no more, until he comes whose right it is, and I will give it to him.'" "And you, son of man, prophesy and say, 'Thus says the Lord God concerning the Ammonites, and concerning their reproach; even say, 'The sword, the sword is drawn; for the slaughter it is polished, to consume because of the glittering. While they see vanity unto you, while they divine a lie unto you, to bring you upon the necks of them that are slain, of the wicked whose day is come, when their iniquity shall have an end. Shall I cause it to return into its sheath? I will judge you in the place where you were created, in the land of your nativity. And I will pour out my indignation upon you; I will blow against you in the fire of my wrath, and deliver you into the hand of brutish men, and skilful to destroy. You shall be for fuel to the fire; your blood shall be in the midst of the land; you shall be no more remembered, for I the LORD have spoken it.'"

CHAPTER 22

Moreover, the word of the LORD came to me, saying, "Now, son of man, will you judge, will you judge the bloody city? Yes, you shall show her all her abominations. Then say, 'Thus says the Lord God, The city sheds blood in the midst of it, that her time may come, and makes idols against herself to defile herself. You have become guilty by the blood that you have shed, and have defiled yourself in your idols which you have made, and you have caused your days to draw near, and have come even unto your years; therefore have I made you a reproach unto the heathen, and a mocking to all countries. Those that be near, and those that be far from you, shall mock you, which are infamous and much vexed. Behold, the princes of Israel, every one were in you to their power to shed blood. In you have they set light by father and mother; in the midst of you have they dealt by oppression with the stranger; in you have they vexed the fatherless and the widow. You have despised my holy things, and have profaned my sabbaths. In you are men that carry tales to shed blood; in you they eat upon the mountains; in the midst of you they commit lewdness. In you have they discovered their fathers' nakedness; in you have they humbled her that was set apart for pollution. And one has committed abomination with his neighbour's wife; and another has lewdly defiled his daughter in law; and another in you has humbled his sister, his father's daughter. In you have they taken gifts to shed blood; you have taken usury and increase, and you have greedily gained of your neighbours by extortion, and have forgotten me, says the Lord God. Behold, therefore I have smitten my hand at your dishonest gain which you have made, and at your blood which has been in the midst of you. Can your heart endure, or can your hands be strong, in the days that I shall deal with you? I the LORD have spoken it, and will do it. And I will scatter you among the heathen, and disperse you in the countries, and will consume your filthiness out of you. And you shall take your inheritance in yourself in the sight of the heathen, and you shall know that I am the LORD.'" And the word of the LORD came to me, saying, "Son of man, the house of Israel is to me become dross; all they are brass, and tin, and iron, and lead, in the midst of the furnace; they are even the dross of silver. Therefore thus says the Lord God, 'Because you are all become dross, behold, therefore I will gather you into the midst of Jerusalem. As they gather silver, and brass, and iron, and lead, and tin, into the midst of the furnace, to blow the fire upon it, to melt it; so will I gather you in my anger and in my fury, and I will leave you there, and melt you. Yes, I will gather you, and blow upon you in the fire of my wrath, and you shall be melted in the midst thereof. As silver is melted in the midst of the furnace, so shall you be melted in the midst thereof; and you shall know that I the LORD have poured out my fury upon you.'" And the word of the LORD came to me, saying, "Son of man, say to her, 'You are the land that is not cleansed, nor rained upon in the day of indignation. There is a conspiracy of her prophets in the midst thereof, like a roaring lion ravening the prey; they have devoured souls; they have taken the treasure and precious things; they have made her many widows in the midst thereof. Her priests have violated my law, and have profaned my holy things; they have put no difference between the holy and profane, neither have they shown difference between the unclean and the clean, and have hid their eyes from my sabbaths, and I am profaned among them. Her princes in the midst thereof are like wolves ravening the prey, to shed blood, and to destroy souls, to get dishonest gain. And her prophets have daubed them with untempered mortar, seeing vanity, and divining lies unto them, saying, 'Thus says the Lord God,' when the LORD has not spoken. The people of the land have used oppression, and exercised robbery, and have vexed the poor and needy; yes, they have oppressed the stranger wrongfully. And I sought for a man among them, that should make up the hedge, and stand in the gap before me for the land, that I should not destroy it, but I found none. Therefore have I poured out my indignation upon them; I have consumed them with the fire of my wrath; their own way have I recompensed upon their heads, says the Lord God.'"

CHAPTER 23

The word of the LORD came to me again, saying, "Son of man, there were two women, the daughters of one mother. And they committed whoredoms in Egypt; they committed whoredoms in their youth; there were their breasts pressed, and there they bruised the teats of their virginity. And the names of them were Aholah the elder, and Aholibah her sister; and they were mine, and they bore sons and daughters. Thus were their names; Samaria is Aholah, and Jerusalem Aholibah. And Aholah played the harlot when she was mine; and she doted on her lovers, on the Assyrians her neighbours, which were clothed with blue, captains and rulers, all of them desirable young men, horsemen riding upon horses. Thus she committed her whoredoms with them, with all them that were the chosen men of Assyria, and with all on whom she doted; with all their idols she defiled herself. Neither left she her whoredoms brought from Egypt; for in her youth they lay with her, and they bruised the breasts of her virginity, and poured their whoredom upon her. Therefore I have delivered her into the hand of her lovers, into the hand of the Assyrians, upon whom she doted. These discovered her nakedness; they took her sons and her daughters, and slew her with the sword; and she became famous among women; for they had executed judgment upon her And when her sister Aholibah saw this, she was more corrupt in her inordinate love than she, and in her whoredoms more than her sister in her whoredoms. She doted upon the Assyrians her neighbours, captains and rulers clothed most gorgeously, horsemen riding upon horses, all of them desirable young men. Then I saw that she was defiled, that they took both one way, and that she increased her whoredoms; for when she saw men portrayed upon the wall, the images of the Chaldeans portrayed with vermilion, girded with girdles upon their loins, exceeding in dyed attire upon their heads, all of them princes to look to, after the manner of the Babylonians of Chaldea, the land of their nativity. And as soon as she saw them with her eyes, she doted upon them, and sent messengers unto them into Chaldea. And the Babylonians came to her into the bed of love, and they defiled her with their whoredom, and she was polluted with them, and her mind was alienated from them. So she discovered her whoredoms, and discovered her nakedness; then my mind was alienated from her, like as my mind was alienated from her sister. Yet she multiplied her whoredoms, in calling to remembrance the days of her youth, wherein she had played the harlot in the land of Egypt. For she doted upon their paramours, whose flesh is as the flesh of asses, and whose issue is like the issue of horses. Thus you called to remembrance the lewdness of your youth, in bruising your teats by the Egyptians for the paps of your youth Therefore, O Aholibah, thus says the Lord God, 'Behold, I will raise up your lovers against you, from whom your mind is alienated, and I will bring them against you on every side; the Babylonians, and all the Chaldeans, Pekod, and Shoa, and Koa, and all the Assyrians with them; all of them desirable young men, captains and rulers, great lords and renowned, all of them riding upon horses. And they shall come against you with chariots, wagons, and wheels, and with an assembly of people, which shall set against you buckler and shield and helmet round about; and I will set judgment before them, and they shall judge you according to their judgments. And I will set my jealousy against you, and they shall deal furiously with you; they shall take away your nose and your ears; and your remnant shall fall by the sword; they shall take your sons and your daughters; and your residue shall be devoured by the fire. They shall also strip you out of your clothes, and take away your fair jewels. Thus will I make your lewdness to cease from you, and your whoredom brought from the land of Egypt, so that you shall not lift up your eyes unto them, nor remember Egypt any more. For thus says the Lord God, 'Behold, I will deliver you into the hand of them whom you hate, into the hand of them from whom your mind is alienated; and they shall deal with you hatefully, and shall take away all your labour, and shall leave you naked and bare; and the nakedness of your whoredoms shall be discovered, both your lewdness and your whoredoms. I will do these things unto you because you have gone a whoring after the heathen, and because you are polluted with their idols. You have walked in the way of your sister; therefore will I give her cup into your hand.' Thus says the Lord God, 'You shall drink of your sister's cup, deep and large; you shall be laughed to scorn and had in derision; it contains much. You shall be filled with drunkenness and sorrow, with the cup of astonishment and desolation, with the cup of your sister Samaria. You shall even drink it and suck it out, and you shall break the sherds thereof, and pluck off your own breasts; for I have spoken it, says the Lord God. Therefore thus says the Lord God, 'Because you have forgotten me, and cast me behind your back, therefore bear you also your lewdness and your whoredoms.'" The LORD said moreover unto me, "Son of man, will you judge Aholah and Aholibah? Yes, declare unto them their abominations, that they have committed adultery, and blood is in their hands, and with their idols have they committed adultery, and have also caused their sons, whom they bore unto me, to pass for them through the fire, to devour them. Moreover, this they have done unto me: they have defiled my sanctuary in the same day, and have profaned my sabbaths. For when they had slain their children to their idols, then they came the same day into my sanctuary to profane it; and lo, thus have they done in the midst of my house And furthermore, that you have sent for men to come from far, unto whom a messenger was sent; and lo, they came; for whom you did wash yourself, painted your eyes, and decked yourself with ornaments, and sat upon a stately bed, and a table prepared before it, whereupon you have set my incense and mine oil. And a voice of a multitude being at ease was with her; and with the men of the common sort were brought Sabeans from the wilderness, which put bracelets upon their hands, and beautiful crowns upon their heads. Then said I unto her that was old in adulteries, 'Will they now commit whoredoms with her, and she with them?' Yet they went in unto her, as they go in unto a woman that plays the harlot; so went they in unto Aholah and unto Aholibah, the lewd women. And the righteous men, they shall judge them after the manner of adulteresses, and after the manner of women that shed blood; because they are adulteresses, and blood is in their hands. For thus says the Lord God, 'I will bring up a company upon them, and will give them to be removed and spoiled. And the company shall stone them with stones, and dispatch them with their swords; they shall slay their sons and their daughters, and burn up their houses with fire. Thus will I cause lewdness to cease out of the land, that all women may be taught not to do after your lewdness. And they shall recompense your lewdness upon you, and you shall bear the sins of your idols; and you shall know that I am the Lord God.'"

CHAPTER 24

In the ninth year, in the tenth month, in the tenth day of the month, the word of the LORD came unto me, saying, "Son of man, write the name of the day, even of this same day; the king of Babylon set himself against Jerusalem this same day. And utter a parable unto the rebellious house, and say unto them, 'Thus says the Lord God; Set on a pot, set it on, and also pour water into it. Gather the pieces thereof into it, even every good piece, the thigh, and the shoulder; fill it with the choice bones. Take the choice of the flock, and burn also the bones under it, and make it boil well, and let them seethe the bones of it therein.' Wherefore thus says the Lord God, 'Woe to the bloody city, to the pot whose scum is therein, and whose scum is not gone out of it! Bring it out piece by piece; let no lot fall upon it. For her blood is in the midst of her; she set it upon the top of a rock; she poured it not upon the ground, to cover it with dust; that it might cause fury to come up to take vengeance; I have set her blood upon the top of a rock, that it should not be covered.' Therefore thus says the Lord God, 'Woe to the bloody city! I will even make the pile for fire great. Heap on wood, kindle the fire, consume the flesh, and spice it well, and let the bones be burned. Then set it empty upon the coals thereof, that the brass of it may be hot and may burn, and that the filthiness of it may be molten in it, that the scum of it may be consumed. She has wearied herself with lies, and her great scum went not forth out of her; her scum shall be in the fire. In your filthiness is lewdness; because I have purged you, and you were not purged, you shall not be purged from your filthiness any more, till I have caused my fury to rest upon you. I the LORD have spoken it; it shall come to pass, and I will do it; I will not go back, neither will I spare, neither will I repent; according to your ways, and according to your doings, shall they judge you, says the Lord God.'" Also the word of the LORD came unto me, saying, "Son of man, behold, I take away from you the desire of your eyes with a stroke; yet neither shall you mourn nor weep, neither shall your tears run down. Forbear to cry, make no mourning for the dead, bind the tire of your head upon you, and put on your shoes upon your feet, and cover not your lips, and eat not the bread of men." So I spoke unto the people in the morning; and at evening my wife died; and I did in the morning as I was commanded And the people said unto me, "Will you not tell us what these things are to us, that you do so?" Then I answered them, "The word of the LORD came unto me, saying, 'Speak unto the house of Israel, Thus says the Lord God; Behold, I will profane my sanctuary, the excellency of your strength, the desire of your eyes, and that which your soul pities; and your sons and your daughters whom you have left shall fall by the sword. And you shall do as I have done; you shall not cover your lips, nor eat the bread of men. And your tires shall be upon your heads, and your shoes upon your feet; you shall not mourn nor weep; but you shall pine away for your iniquities, and mourn one toward another. Thus Ezekiel is unto you a sign; according to all that he has done shall you do; and when this comes, you shall know that I am the Lord God.' Also, son of man, shall it not be in the day when I take from them their strength, the joy of their glory, the desire of their eyes, and that whereupon they set their minds, their sons and their daughters, that he that escapes in that day shall come unto you, to cause you to hear it with your ears? In that day shall your mouth be opened to him which is escaped, and you shall speak, and be no more dumb; and you shall be a sign unto them; and they shall know that I am the LORD.'"

CHAPTER 25

The word of the LORD came again unto me, saying, "Son of man, set your face against the Ammonites, and prophesy against them. And say unto the Ammonites, 'Hear the word of the Lord God; Thus says the Lord God; Because you said, Aha, against my sanctuary, when it was profaned; and against the land of Israel, when it was desolate; and against the house of Judah, when they went into captivity; behold, therefore I will deliver you to the men of the east for a possession, and they shall set their palaces in you, and make their dwellings in you; they shall eat your fruit, and they shall drink your milk. And I will make Rabbah a stable for camels, and the Ammonites a couching place for flocks; and you shall know that I am the LORD.'" For thus says the Lord God; 'Because you have clapped your hands, and stamped with the feet, and rejoiced in heart with all your despite against the land of Israel; behold, therefore I will stretch out my hand upon you, and will deliver you for a spoil to the heathen; and I will cut you off from the people, and I will cause you to perish out of the countries; I will destroy you; and you shall know that I am the LORD.' Thus says the Lord God; 'Because that Moab and Seir do say, Behold, the house of Judah is like unto all the heathen; therefore, behold, I will open the side of Moab from the cities, from his cities which are on his frontiers, the glory of the country, Bethjeshimoth, Baalmeon, and Kiriathaim, unto the men of the east with the Ammonites, and will give them in possession, that the Ammonites may not be remembered among the nations. And I will execute judgments upon Moab; and they shall know that I am the LORD.' Thus says the Lord God; 'Because that Edom has dealt against the house of Judah by taking vengeance, and has greatly offended, and revenged himself upon them; therefore thus says the Lord God; I will also stretch out my hand upon Edom, and will cut off man and beast from it; and I will make it desolate from Teman; and they of Dedan shall fall by the sword. And I will lay my vengeance upon Edom by the hand of my people Israel; and they shall do in Edom according to my anger and according to my fury; and they shall know my vengeance, says the Lord God.' Thus says the Lord God; 'Because the Philistines have dealt by revenge, and have taken vengeance with a despiteful heart, to destroy it for the old hatred; therefore thus says the Lord God; Behold, I will stretch out my hand upon the Philistines, and I will cut off the Cherethims, and destroy the remnant of the sea coast. And I will execute great vengeance upon them with furious rebukes; and they shall know that I am the LORD, when I shall lay my vengeance upon them.'"

CHAPTER 26

In the eleventh year, on the first day of the month, the word of the Lord came to me, saying, "Son of man, because Tyre has said against Jerusalem, 'Ah, the gate of the people is broken; it is turned toward me; since it is desolate, I will be satisfied.' Therefore, thus says the LORD God, 'Behold, I come against you, O Tyre, and will cause many nations to come against you, as the sea rises with its waves. They shall destroy the walls of Tyre and break down her towers. I will scrape her dust from her and make her like the top of a rock. She shall be a place for the spreading of nets in the midst of the sea, for I have spoken it,' says the LORD God, 'and it shall become plunder for the nations. Your daughters who are in the field shall be slain by the sword, and they shall know that I am the LORD.' For thus says the LORD God, 'Behold, I will bring Nebuchadnezzar, king of Babylon, king of kings, from the north against Tyre, with horses, chariots, horsemen, and a multitude of people. He will kill your daughters in the field by the sword; he will build a siege wall against you, throw up a mound against you, and raise a shield against you. He will set battering rams against your walls, and with his axes, he will break down your towers. The dust from his horses will cover you; your walls will shake at the noise of the horsemen, wheels, and chariots when he enters your gates as men enter a city that has been breached. With the hooves of his horses, he will trample all your streets; he will kill your people by the sword, and your strong pillars will fall to the ground. They will plunder your riches and loot your merchandise; they will break down your walls and destroy your pleasant houses; they will throw your stones, timber, and debris into the water. I will put an end to the sound of your songs, and the sound of your harps shall be heard no more. I will make you a bare rock; you shall be a place for spreading nets; you shall never be rebuilt, for I the LORD have spoken,' says the LORD God Thus says the LORD God to Tyre, 'Shall not the coastlands shake at the sound of your fall, when the wounded groan, when slaughter is made in your midst? Then all the princes of the sea will step down from their thrones, remove their robes, and strip off their embroidered garments. They will clothe themselves with trembling; they will sit on the ground, tremble every moment, and be appalled at you. They will raise a lament over you and say to you, "How you have perished, you who were inhabited by seafaring men, renowned city, who was mighty on the sea, she and her inhabitants, who caused their terror to be on all her inhabitants! Now the coastlands tremble on the day of your fall; yes, the coastlands by the sea are dismayed at your departure." For thus says the LORD God, 'When I make you a desolate city, like cities that are not inhabited, when I bring up the deep over you, and the great waters cover you, then I will bring you down with those who descend into the pit, to the people of old, and I will make you dwell in the lowest parts of the earth, in places desolate from antiquity, with those who go down to the pit, so that you will not be inhabited; but I will set glory in the land of the living. I will make you a terror, and you shall no longer be; though you are sought for, you will never be found again,' declares the Lord God."

CHAPTER 27

The word of the LORD came to me again, saying, "Son of man, take up a lamentation for Tyre, and say to Tyre, which is situated at the entrance of the sea, merchant of the peoples to many coastlands, 'Thus says the LORD God: O Tyre, you have said, "I am perfect in beauty." Your borders are in the heart of the seas; your builders have perfected your beauty. They made all your planks of fir trees from Senir; they took a cedar from Lebanon to make a mast for you. From the oaks of Bashan they made your oars; they made your deck of pines from the coasts of Cyprus, inlaid with ivory. Of fine embroidered linen from Egypt was your sail, serving as your banner; blue and purple from the coasts of Elishah was your awning The inhabitants of Sidon and Arvad were your rowers; your skilled men, O Tyre, were in you; they were your pilots. The elders of Gebal and their skilled men were in you, caulking your seams; all the ships of the sea with their mariners were in you to barter for your wares. Persia and Lud and Put were in your army as your men of war; they hung the shield and helmet in you; they gave you splendor. The men of Arvad and Helech were on your walls all around, and the Gammadim were in your towers; they hung their shields on your walls all around; they made your beauty perfect Tarshish traded with you because of your great wealth of every kind; silver, iron, tin, and lead they exchanged for your wares. Javan, Tubal,

and Meshech traded with you; they exchanged human beings and vessels of bronze for your merchandise. From Beth Togarmah they exchanged horses, war horses, and mules for your wares. The men of Dedan traded with you; many coastlands were your special markets; they brought you in payment ivory tusks and ebony. Syria traded with you because of your abundant goods; they exchanged for your wares emeralds, purple, embroidered work, fine linen, coral, and rubies. Judah and the land of Israel traded with you; they exchanged for your merchandise wheat of Minnith, meal, honey, oil, and balm. Damascus traded with you because of your abundant goods, because of your great wealth of every kind; wine of Helbon, and white wool. Vedan and Javan from Uzal traded for your wares; wrought iron, cassia, and calamus were bartered for your merchandise. Dedan traded with you in saddle blankets for riding. Arabia and all the princes of Kedar were your favored dealers in lambs, rams, and goats; in these they did business with you. The traders of Sheba and Raamah traded with you; they exchanged for your wares the best of all kinds of spices, and all precious stones, and gold. Haran, Canneh, Eden, traders of Sheba, Asshur, and Chilmad traded with you. In your market these traded with you in choice garments, in clothes of blue and embroidered work, and in carpets of colored material, bound with cords and made secure The ships of Tarshish traveled for you with your merchandise. So you were filled and heavily laden in the heart of the seas. Your rowers have brought you out into the high seas. The east wind has wrecked you in the heart of the seas. Your riches, your wares, your merchandise, your mariners, your pilots, your caulkers, your dealers in merchandise, and all your men of war who are in you, with all your company that is in your midst, sink into the heart of the seas on the day of your downfall. At the sound of the cry of your pilots, the countryside shakes, and down from their ships come all who handle the oar. The mariners and all the pilots of the sea stand on the land and shout aloud over you and cry out bitterly. They cast dust on their heads and wallow in ashes; they make themselves bald for you and put sackcloth on their waist, and they weep over you in bitterness of soul, with bitter mourning. In their wailing they raise a lamentation for you and lament over you: 'Who is like Tyre, like one destroyed in the midst of the sea? When your wares came from the seas, you satisfied many peoples; with your abundant wealth and merchandise you enriched the kings of the earth. Now you are wrecked by the seas, in the depths of the waters; your merchandise and all your crew in your midst have sunk with you. All the inhabitants of the coastlands are appalled at you, and the hair of their kings bristles with horror; their faces are convulsed. The merchants among the peoples hiss at you; you have come to a dreadful end and shall be no more forever.'"

CHAPTER 28

The word of the Lord came to me again, saying, "Son of man, say to the prince of Tyre, 'Thus says the Lord God: Because your heart is proud and you have said, "I am a god; I sit in the seat of the gods, in the heart of the seas," yet you are but a man, and no god, though you make your heart like the heart of a god— you are indeed wiser than Daniel; no secret is hidden from you; by your wisdom and your understanding you have made wealth for yourself and have gathered gold and silver into your treasuries; by your great wisdom in your trade you have increased your wealth, and your heart has become proud in your wealth— therefore thus says the Lord God: Because you make your heart like the heart of a god, therefore, behold, I will bring foreigners upon you, the most ruthless of the nations; and they shall draw their swords against the beauty of your wisdom and defile your splendor. They shall thrust you down into the pit, and you shall die the death of the slain in the heart of the seas. Will you still say, "I am a god," in the presence of those who kill you, though you are but a man, and no god, in the hands of those who slay you? You shall die the death of the uncircumcised by the hand of foreigners; for I have spoken, declares the Lord God.'" Moreover, the word of the LORD came to me, saying, "Son of man, raise a lamentation over the king of Tyre, and say to him, 'Thus says the Lord God: You were the signet of perfection, full of wisdom and perfect in beauty. You were in Eden, the garden of God; every precious stone was your covering, sardius, topaz, and diamond, beryl, onyx, and jasper, sapphire, emerald, and carbuncle; and crafted in gold were your settings and your engravings. On the day that you were created, they were prepared. You were an anointed guardian cherub. I placed you; you were on the holy mountain of God; in the midst of the stones of fire you walked. You were blameless in your ways from the day you were created, till unrighteousness was found in you. In the abundance of your trade you were filled with violence in your midst, and you sinned; so I cast you as a profane thing from the mountain of God, and I destroyed you, O guardian cherub, from the midst of the stones of fire. Your heart was proud because of your beauty; you corrupted your wisdom for the sake of your splendor. I cast you to the ground; I exposed you before kings, to feast their eyes on you. By the multitude of your iniquities, in the unrighteousness of your trade, you profaned your sanctuaries; so I brought fire out from your midst; it consumed you, and I turned you to ashes on the earth in the sight of all who saw you. All who know you among the peoples are appalled at you; you have come to a dreadful end and shall be no more forever.'" The word of the LORD came to me again, saying, "Son of man, set your face toward Sidon, and prophesy against her and say, 'Thus says the Lord God: Behold, I am against you, O Sidon, and I will manifest my glory in your midst. And they shall know that I am the LORD when I execute judgments in her and manifest my holiness in her. For I will send pestilence into her, and blood into her streets; and the slain shall fall in her midst by the sword that is against her on every side. Then they will know that I am the LORD And for the house of Israel, there shall be no more a brier to prick or a thorn to hurt them among all their neighbors who have treated them with contempt. Then they will know that I am the Lord God Thus says the Lord God: When I gather the house of Israel from the peoples among whom they are scattered, and manifest my holiness in them in the sight of the nations, then they shall dwell in their own land that I gave to my servant Jacob. And they shall dwell securely in it, and they shall build houses and plant vineyards. They shall dwell securely, when I execute judgments upon all their neighbors who have treated them with contempt. Then they will know that I am the LORD their God.'"

CHAPTER 29

In the tenth year, in the tenth month, on the twelfth day of the month, the word of the LORD came to me, saying, "Son of man, set your face against Pharaoh king of Egypt and prophesy against him and against all Egypt; speak, and say, 'Thus says the Lord God: Behold, I am against you, Pharaoh king of Egypt, the great dragon that lies in the midst of his streams, that says, "My Nile is my own; I made it for myself." I will put hooks in your jaws and make the fish of your streams stick to your scales. And I will draw you up out of the midst of your streams, with all the fish of your streams that stick to your scales. And I will cast you out into the wilderness, you and all the fish of your streams; you shall fall on the open field, and not be brought together or gathered. To the beasts of the earth and to the birds of the heavens, I give you as food. Then all the inhabitants of Egypt shall know that I am the LORD. Because you have been a staff of reed to the house of Israel, when they grasped you with the hand, you broke and tore all their shoulders; and when they leaned on you, you broke and made all their loins to shake. Therefore thus says the Lord God: Behold, I will bring a sword upon you and will cut off from you man and beast, and the land of Egypt shall be a desolation and a waste. Then they will know that I am the LORD. Because you said, "The Nile is mine, and I made it," therefore, behold, I am against you and against your streams, and I will make the land of Egypt an utter waste and desolation, from Migdol to Syene, as far as the border of Cush. No foot of man shall pass through it, and no foot of beast shall pass through it; it shall be uninhabited forty years. And I will make the land of Egypt a desolation in the midst of desolated countries, and her cities shall be a desolation forty years among cities that are laid waste. I will scatter the Egyptians among the nations and disperse them through the countries For thus says the Lord God: At the end of forty years, I will gather the Egyptians from the peoples among whom they were scattered, and I will restore the fortunes of Egypt and bring them back to the land of Pathros, the land of their origin, and there they shall be a lowly kingdom. It shall be the most lowly of the kingdoms and never again exalt itself above the nations. And I will make them so small that they will never again rule over the nations. And it shall never again be the reliance of the house of Israel, recalling their iniquity when they turn to them for aid. Then they will know that I am the Lord God.' In the twenty-seventh year, in the first month, on the first day of the month, the word of the LORD came to me, saying, 'Son of man, Nebuchadnezzar king of Babylon made his army labor hard against Tyre. Every head was made bald, and every shoulder was rubbed bare. Yet neither he nor his army got anything from Tyre to pay for the labor that he had performed against her. Therefore thus says the Lord God: Behold, I will give the land of Egypt to Nebuchadnezzar king of Babylon; and he shall carry off its wealth and despoil it and plunder it; and it shall be the wages for his army. I have given him the land of Egypt as his payment for which he labored, because they worked for me, declares the Lord God On that day, I will cause a horn to spring up for the house of Israel, and I will open your lips among them. Then they will know that I am the LORD.'"

CHAPTER 30

The word of the LORD came to me again, saying, "Son of man, prophesy, and say, 'Thus says the Lord God: Wail, "Alas for the day!" For the day is near, the day of the LORD is near; it will be a day of clouds, a time of doom for the nations. A sword shall come upon Egypt, and anguish shall be in Cush, when the slain fall in Egypt, and her wealth is carried away, and her foundations are torn down. Cush, and Put, and Lud, and all Arabia, and Libya, and the people of the land that is in league, shall fall with them by the sword Thus says the LORD: Those who support Egypt shall fall, and her proud might shall come down; from Migdol to Syene they shall fall within her by the sword, declares the Lord God. And they shall be desolated in the midst of desolated countries, and their cities shall be in the midst of cities that are laid waste. Then they will know that I am the LORD, when I have set fire to Egypt, and all her helpers are broken

On that day, messengers shall go out from me in ships to terrify the unsuspecting people of Cush, and anguish shall come upon them on the day of Egypt's doom; for, behold, it comes! Thus says the Lord God: I will put an end to the wealth of Egypt by the hand of Nebuchadnezzar king of Babylon. He and his people with him, the most ruthless of nations, shall be brought in to destroy the land, and they shall draw their swords against Egypt and fill the land with the slain. And I will dry up the Nile and will sell the land into the hand of evildoers; I will bring desolation upon the land and everything in it, by the hand of foreigners; I am the LORD; I have spoken Thus says the Lord God: I will destroy the idols and put an end to the images in Memphis; there shall no longer be a prince from the land of Egypt; so I will put fear in the land of Egypt. I will make Pathros a desolation and will set fire to Zoan and will execute judgments on Thebes. And I will pour out my wrath on Pelusium, the stronghold of Egypt, and cut off the multitude of Thebes. And I will set fire to Egypt; Pelusium shall be in great agony; Thebes shall be breached, and Memphis shall face enemies by day. The young men of On and of Pi-beseth shall fall by the sword, and the women shall go into captivity. At Tehaphnehes the day shall be dark, when I break there the yoke bars of Egypt, and her proud might shall come to an end in her; she shall be covered by a cloud, and her daughters shall go into captivity. Thus I will execute judgments on Egypt. Then they will know that I am the LORD.' In the eleventh year, in the first month, on the seventh day of the month, the word of the LORD came to me, saying, 'Son of man, I have broken the arm of Pharaoh king of Egypt, and behold, it has not been bound up to heal it by binding it with a bandage, so that it may become strong to wield the sword. Therefore thus says the Lord God: Behold, I am against Pharaoh king of Egypt and will break his arms, both the strong arm and the one that was broken, and I will make the sword fall from his hand. I will scatter the Egyptians among the nations and disperse them through the countries. And I will strengthen the arms of the king of Babylon and put my sword in his hand, but I will break the arms of Pharaoh, and he will groan before him like a man mortally wounded. I will strengthen the arms of the king of Babylon, but the arms of Pharaoh shall fall. Then they shall know that I am the LORD, when I put my sword into the hand of the king of Babylon and he stretches it out against the land of Egypt. And I will scatter the Egyptians among the nations and disperse them throughout the countries. Then they will know that I am the LORD.'"

CHAPTER 31

In the eleventh year, in the third month, on the first day of the month, the word of the LORD came to me, saying, "Son of man, speak to Pharaoh, king of Egypt, and to his multitude, 'Whom do you resemble in your greatness? Behold, Assur was like a cedar in Lebanon, with beautiful branches and forest shade, and of great height, with its top among the clouds. The waters nourished it; the deep made it grow tall, making its rivers flow around the place of its planting, sending forth its streams to all the trees of the field. Therefore its height was exalted above all the trees of the field, and its branches were multiplied, and its boughs grew long because of the abundance of water as it sent them out. All the birds of the heavens made their nests in its branches, and under its boughs, all the beasts of the field gave birth to their young, and in its shadow lived all great nations. It was beautiful in its greatness, in the length of its branches, for its roots went down to abundant waters. The cedars in the garden of God could not rival it, nor could the fir trees equal its boughs, nor

were the plane trees like its branches; no tree in the garden of God was its equal in beauty. I made it beautiful in the mass of its branches, and all the trees of Eden envied it that were in the garden of God Therefore, thus says the Lord God: Because it towered high and set its top among the clouds, and its heart was proud of its height, I delivered it into the hand of the mighty one of the nations; he shall surely deal with it as its wickedness deserves. I have cast it out. Foreigners, the most ruthless of nations, have cut it down and left it. On the mountains and in all the valleys, its branches have fallen, and its boughs lie broken in all the ravines of the land, and all the peoples of the earth have gone away from its shadow and left it. On its fallen trunk dwell all the birds of the heavens, and on its branches are all the beasts of the field. All this is so that no trees by the waters may grow to towering height or set their tops among the clouds, and that no trees that drink water may reach up to them in height. For they are all given over to death, to the world below, among the children of man, with those who go down to the pit Thus says the Lord God: On the day the cedar went down to Sheol, I caused mourning; I closed the deep over it and restrained its rivers, and many waters were stopped. I clothed Lebanon in gloom for it, and all the trees of the field fainted because of it. I made the nations quake at the sound of its fall when I cast it down to Sheol with those who go down to the pit. And all the trees of Eden, the choice and best of Lebanon, all that drink water, were comforted in the world below. They also went down to Sheol with it, to those who are slain by the sword; yes, those who were its arm, who lived under its shadow among the nations Whom are you thus like in glory and in greatness among the trees of Eden? You shall be brought down with the trees of Eden to the world below; you shall lie among the uncircumcised, with those who are slain by the sword. This is Pharaoh and all his multitude, declares the Lord God.'"

CHAPTER 32

In the twelfth year, in the twelfth month, on the first day of the month, the word of the LORD came to me, saying, "Son of man, raise a lamentation over Pharaoh king of Egypt and say to him: 'You consider yourself a lion of the nations, but you are like a dragon in the seas; you burst forth in your rivers, trouble the waters with your feet, and foul their rivers. Thus says the Lord God: I will throw my net over you with a host of many peoples, and they will haul you up in my dragnet. And I will cast you on the ground; on the open field, I will fling you and will cause all the birds of the heavens to settle on you, and I will gorge the beasts of the whole earth with you. I will strew your flesh upon the mountains and fill the valleys with your carcass. I will drench the land even to the mountains with your flowing blood, and the ravines will be full of you. When I blot you out, I will cover the heavens and make their stars dark; I will cover the sun with a cloud, and the moon shall not give its light. All the bright lights of heaven will I make dark over you, and put darkness on your land, declares the Lord God I will trouble the hearts of many peoples when I bring your destruction among the nations, into the countries that you have not known. I will make many peoples appalled at you, and their kings shall shudder with horror because of you, when I brandish my sword before them. They shall tremble every moment, every one for his own life, on the day of your downfall. For thus says the Lord God: The sword of the king of Babylon shall come upon you. I will cause your multitude to fall by the swords of mighty ones, all of them most ruthless of nations They shall bring to ruin the pride of Egypt, and all its multitude shall perish. I will destroy all its beasts from beside many waters, and no foot of man shall trouble them anymore, nor shall the hoofs of beasts trouble them. Then I will make their waters clear and cause their rivers to run like oil, declares the Lord God. When I make the land of Egypt desolate, and when the land is desolate of all that fills it, when I strike down all who dwell in it, then they will know that I am the LORD This is a lamentation that shall be chanted; the daughters of the nations shall chant it; over Egypt, and over all her multitude, shall they chant it, declares the Lord God." In the twelfth year, in the twelfth month, on the fifteenth day of the month, the word of the LORD came to me, saying, "Son of man, wail over the multitude of Egypt and send them down, her and the daughters of majestic nations, to the world below, to those who have gone down to the pit. 'Whom do you surpass in beauty? Go down and be laid to rest with the uncircumcised.' They shall fall amid those who are slain by the sword. Egypt is delivered to the sword; drag her away, and all her multitudes. The mighty chiefs shall speak of them, with their helpers, out of the midst of Sheol: 'They have come down, they lie still, the uncircumcised, slain by the sword.' Assyria is there, and all her company, its graves all around it, all of them slain, fallen by the sword, whose graves are set in the uttermost parts of the pit; and her company is all around her grave, all of them slain, fallen by the sword, who spread terror in the land of the living Elam is there, and all her multitude around her grave; all of them slain, fallen by the sword, who went down uncircumcised into the world below, who spread their terror in the land of the living; and they bear their shame with those who go down to the pit. They have made her a bed among the slain with all her multitude, her graves all around it, all of them uncircumcised, slain by the sword, for terror of them was spread in the land of the living; and they bear their shame with those who go down to the pit; they are placed among the slain Meshech-Tubal is there, and all her multitude, her graves all around it, all of them uncircumcised, slain by the sword, for they spread their terror in the land of the living. And they do not lie with the mighty, the fallen from among the uncircumcised, who went down to Sheol with their weapons of war, whose swords were laid under their heads, and whose iniquities are upon their bones, for the terror of the mighty men was in the land of the living. But as for you, you shall be broken and lie among the uncircumcised, with those who are slain by the sword Edom is there, her kings and all her princes, who for all their might are laid with those who are killed by the sword; they lie with the uncircumcised, with those who go down to the pit The princes of the north are there, all of them, and all the Sidonians, who have gone down in shame with the slain, for all the terror that they caused by their might; they lie uncircumcised with those who are slain by the sword and bear their shame with those who go down to the pit When Pharaoh sees them, he will be comforted for all his multitude, Pharaoh and all his army, slain by the sword, declares the Lord God. For I spread terror in the land of the living; and he shall be laid to rest among the uncircumcised, with those who are slain by the sword, Pharaoh and all his multitude, declares the Lord God."

CHAPTER 33

Again the word of the LORD came to me, saying, "Son of man, speak to your people and say to them, 'If I bring the sword upon a land, and the people of the land take a man from among them and make him their watchman, and if he sees the sword coming upon the land and blows the trumpet and warns the people, then if anyone who hears the sound of the trumpet does not take warning, and the sword comes and takes him away, his blood shall be upon his own head. He heard the sound of the trumpet and did not take warning; his blood shall be upon himself. But if he had taken warning, he would have saved his life. But if the watchman sees the sword coming and does not blow the trumpet, so that the people are not warned, and the sword comes and takes any one of them, that person is taken away in his iniquity, but his blood I will require at the watchman's hand So you, son of man, I have made a watchman for the house of Israel. Whenever you hear a word from my mouth, you shall give them warning from me. If I say to the wicked, 'O wicked one, you shall surely die,' and you do not speak to warn the wicked to turn from his way, that wicked person shall die in his iniquity, but his blood I will require at your hand. But if you warn the wicked to turn from his way, and he does not turn from his way, that person shall die in his iniquity, but you will have delivered your soul And you, son of man, say to the house of Israel, 'Thus have you said: "Surely our transgressions and our sins are upon us, and we rot away because of them. How then can we live?"' Say to them, 'As I live, declares the Lord God, I have no pleasure in the death of the wicked, but that the wicked turn from his way and live; turn back, turn back from your evil ways, for why will you die, O house of Israel?' And you, son of man, say to your people, 'The righteousness of the righteous shall not deliver him when he transgresses, and as for the wickedness of the wicked, he shall not fall by it when he turns from his wickedness, and the righteous shall not be able to live by his righteousness when he sins. Though I say to the righteous that he shall surely live, yet if he trusts in his righteousness and does injustice, none of his righteous deeds shall be remembered, but in his injustice that he has done he shall die. Again, though I say to the wicked, "You shall surely die," yet if he turns from his sin and does what is just and right, if the wicked restores the pledge, gives back what he has taken by robbery, and walks in the statutes of life, not doing injustice, he shall surely live; he shall not die. None of the sins that he has committed shall be remembered against him. He has done what is just and right; he shall surely live Yet your people say, "The way of the Lord is not just," when it is their own way that is not just. When the righteous turns from his righteousness and does injustice, he shall die for it. And when the wicked turns from his wickedness and does what is just and right, he shall live by this. Yet you say, "The way of the Lord is not just." O house of Israel, I will judge each of you according to his ways.'" In the twelfth year of our exile, in the tenth month, on the fifth day of the month, a fugitive from Jerusalem came to me and said, "The city has been struck down." Now the hand of the LORD had been upon me the evening before the fugitive came, and he had opened my mouth by the time the man came to me in the morning, so my mouth was opened, and I was no longer mute Then the word of the LORD came to me, saying, "Son of man, the inhabitants of these waste places in the land of Israel keep saying, 'Abraham was only one man, yet he got possession of the land; but we are many; the land is surely given us to possess.' Therefore say to them, 'Thus says the Lord God: You eat flesh with the blood and lift up your eyes to your idols and shed blood; shall you then possess the land? You rely on the sword, you commit abominations, and each of you defiles his neighbor's wife; shall you then possess the land?' Say this to them: 'Thus says the Lord God: As I live, surely those who are in the waste places shall fall by the sword, and whoever is in the open field I will give to the beasts to be devoured, and those who are in strongholds and in caves shall die by pestilence. And

I will make the land a desolation and a waste, and her proud might shall come to an end, and the mountains of Israel shall be so desolate that none will pass through. Then they will know that I am the LORD, when I have made the land a desolation and a waste because of all their abominations that they have committed.' As for you, son of man, your people who talk together about you by the walls and at the doors of the houses, say to one another, each to his brother, 'Come, and hear what the word is that comes from the LORD.' And they come to you as people come, and they sit before you as my people, and they hear what you say but they will not do it; for with lustful talk in their mouths they act; their heart is set on their gain. And behold, you are to them like one who sings lustful songs with a beautiful voice and plays well on an instrument, for they hear what you say, but they will not do it. When this comes— and come it will—then they will know that a prophet has been among them."

CHAPTER 34

The word of the LORD came to me, saying, "Son of man, prophesy against the shepherds of Israel; prophesy and say to them, 'Thus says the Lord God: Ah, shepherds of Israel who have been feeding yourselves! Should not shepherds feed the sheep? You eat the fat, you clothe yourselves with the wool, you slaughter the fat ones, but you do not feed the sheep. The weak you have not strengthened, the sick you have not healed, the injured you have not bound up, the strayed you have not brought back, the lost you have not sought, and with force and harshness you have ruled them. So they were scattered because there was no shepherd, and they became food for all the wild beasts. My sheep were scattered; they wandered over all the mountains and on every high hill. My sheep were scattered over all the face of the earth, with none to search or seek for them Therefore, you shepherds, hear the word of the LORD: As I live, declares the Lord God, surely because my sheep have become a prey, and my sheep have become food for all the wild beasts, since there was no shepherd, and because my shepherds have not searched for my sheep, but the shepherds have fed themselves, and have not fed my sheep, therefore, you shepherds, hear the word of the LORD: Thus says the Lord God, Behold, I am against the shepherds, and I will require my sheep at their hand and put a stop to their feeding the sheep. No longer shall the shepherds feed themselves. I will rescue my sheep from their mouths, that they may not be food for them For thus says the Lord God: Behold, I, I myself will search for my sheep and will seek them out. As a shepherd seeks out his flock when he is among his sheep that have been scattered, so will I seek out my sheep, and I will rescue them from all places where they have been scattered on a day of clouds and thick darkness. And I will bring them out from the peoples and gather them from the countries, and will bring them into their own land. And I will feed them on the mountains of Israel, by the ravines, and in all the inhabited places of the country. I will feed them with good pasture, and on the mountain heights of Israel shall be their grazing land. There they shall lie down in good grazing land, and on rich pasture they shall feed on the mountains of Israel. I myself will be the shepherd of my sheep, and I myself will make them lie down, declares the Lord God. I will seek the lost, and I will bring back the strayed, and I will bind up the injured, and I will strengthen the weak, and the fat and the strong I will destroy. I will feed them in justice As for you, my flock, thus says the Lord God: Behold, I judge between sheep and sheep, between rams and male goats. Is it not enough for you to feed on the good pasture, that you must tread down with your feet the rest of your pasture; and to drink of clear water, that you must muddy the rest of the water with your feet? And must my sheep eat what you have trodden with your feet, and drink what you have muddied with your feet? Therefore, thus says the Lord God to them: Behold, I, I myself will judge between the fat sheep and the lean sheep. Because you push with side and shoulder, and thrust at all the weak with your horns, till you have scattered them abroad, I will rescue my flock; they shall no longer be a prey. And I will judge between sheep and sheep. And I will set up over them one shepherd, my servant David, and he shall feed them: he shall feed them and be their shepherd. And I, the LORD, will be their God, and my servant David shall be prince among them. I, the LORD, have spoken I will make with them a covenant of peace and banish wild beasts from the land, so that they may dwell securely in the wilderness and sleep in the woods. And I will make them and the places all around my hill a blessing, and I will send down the showers in their season; they shall be showers of blessing. And the trees of the field shall yield their fruit, and the earth shall yield its increase, and they shall be secure in their land. And they shall know that I am the LORD, when I break the bars of their yoke, and deliver them from the hand of those who enslaved them. They shall no more be a prey to the nations, nor shall the beasts of the land devour them. They shall dwell securely, and none shall make them afraid. And I will provide for them renowned plantations so that they shall no more be consumed with hunger in the land, and no longer suffer the reproach of the nations. And they shall know that I am the LORD their God with them, and that they, the house of Israel, are my people, declares the Lord God. And you are my sheep, human sheep of my pasture, and I am your God, declares the Lord God."

CHAPTER 35

The word of the LORD came to me, saying, "Son of man, set your face against Mount Seir and prophesy against it, and say to it, 'Thus says the Lord God: Behold, I am against you, Mount Seir, and I will stretch out my hand against you, and I will make you a desolation and a waste. I will lay your cities waste, and you shall become a desolation, and you shall know that I am the LORD. Because you cherished perpetual enmity and gave over the people of Israel to the power of the sword at the time of their calamity, at the time of their final punishment, therefore, as I live, declares the Lord God, I will prepare you for blood, and blood shall pursue you; because you did not hate bloodshed, therefore blood shall pursue you. I will make Mount Seir a waste and a desolation, and I will cut off from it all who come and go. And I will fill its mountains with the slain. On your hills and in your valleys and in all your ravines those slain with the sword shall fall. I will make you a perpetual desolation, and your cities shall not be inhabited. Then you will know that I am the LORD Because you said, "These two nations and these two countries shall be mine, and we will take possession of them"—although the LORD was there—therefore, as I live, declares the Lord God, I will deal with you according to the anger and envy that you showed because of your hatred against them. And I will make myself known among them, when I judge you. And you shall know that I am the LORD I have heard all the revilings that you uttered against the mountains of Israel, saying, "They are laid desolate; they are given us to devour." And you magnified yourselves against me with your mouth, and multiplied your words against me; I heard it. Thus says the Lord God: While the whole earth rejoices, I will make you desolate. As you rejoiced over the inheritance of the house of Israel, because it was desolate, so I will deal with you; you shall be desolate, Mount Seir, and all Edom, all of it. Then they will know that I am the LORD.'"

CHAPTER 36

The word of the LORD came to me: "Son of man, prophesy to the mountains of Israel and say, 'Mountains of Israel, hear the word of the LORD. This is what the Lord GOD says: The enemy has said of you, "Aha! The ancient heights have become our possession." Therefore, prophesy and say, 'This is what the Lord GOD says: Because they ravaged and crushed you from every side so that you became the possession of the rest of the nations and the object of people's malicious talk and slander, therefore, mountains of Israel, hear the word of the Lord GOD: This is what the Lord GOD says to the mountains and hills, to the ravines and valleys, to the desolate ruins and the deserted towns that have been plundered and ridiculed by the rest of the nations around you. This is what the Lord GOD says: In my burning zeal, I have spoken against the rest of the nations and against all Edom, who with glee and with malice in their hearts made my land their own possession so that they might plunder its pastureland.' Therefore, prophesy concerning the land of Israel and say to the mountains and hills, to the ravines and valleys, 'This is what the Lord GOD says: I speak in my jealous wrath because you have suffered the scorn of the nations. Therefore, this is what the Lord GOD says: I swear with uplifted hand that the nations around you will also suffer scorn. But you, mountains of Israel, will produce branches and fruit for my people Israel, for they will soon come home. I am concerned for you and will look on you with favor; you will be plowed and sown, and I will multiply the number of people upon you, even the whole house of Israel. The towns will be inhabited and the ruins rebuilt. I will increase the number of people and animals living upon you, and they will be fruitful and become numerous. I will settle people on you as in the past and will make you prosper more than before. Then you will know that I am the LORD. I will cause people, my people Israel, to walk upon you. They will possess you, and you will be their inheritance; you will never again deprive them of their children.' This is what the Sovereign LORD says: Because some say to you, 'You devour people and deprive your nation of its children,' therefore you will no longer devour people or make your nation childless, declares the Sovereign LORD. No longer will I make you hear the taunts of the nations, and no longer will you suffer the scorn of the peoples or cause your nation to fall, declares the Sovereign LORD." The word of the LORD came to me: "Son of man, when the people of Israel were living in their own land, they defiled it by their conduct and their actions. Their conduct was like a woman's monthly uncleanness in my sight. So I poured out my wrath on them because they had shed blood in the land and because they had defiled it with their idols. I dispersed them among the nations, and they were scattered through the countries; I judged them according to their conduct and their actions. And wherever they went among the nations, they profaned my holy name, for it was said of them, 'These are the LORD's people, and yet they had to leave his land.' I had concern for my holy name, which the people of Israel profaned among the nations where they had gone Therefore, say to the Israelites, 'This is what the Sovereign LORD says: It is not for your sake, people of Israel, that I am going to do these things, but for the sake of my holy name, which you have profaned among the nations where you have gone. I will show the holiness of my great name, which has been profaned among the nations, the name you have profaned among them. Then the nations will know that I am the LORD, declares the Sovereign LORD, when I am proved holy through you before their eyes. For I will take you out of the nations; I will gather you from all the countries and bring you back into your own land. I will sprinkle clean water on you, and you will be clean; I will cleanse you from all your impurities and from all your idols. I will give you a new heart and put a new spirit in you; I will remove from you your heart of stone and give you a heart of flesh. And I will put my Spirit in you and move you to follow my decrees and be careful to keep my laws. You will live in the land I gave your forefathers; you will be my people, and I will be your God. I will save you from all your uncleanness. I will call for the grain and make it plentiful and will not bring famine upon you. I will increase the fruit of the trees and the crops of the field so that you will no longer suffer disgrace among the nations because of famine. Then you will remember your evil ways and wicked deeds, and you will loathe yourselves for your sins and detestable practices. I want you to know that I am not doing this for your sake, declares the Sovereign LORD. Be ashamed and disgraced for your conduct, people of Israel! This is what the Sovereign LORD says: On the day I cleanse you from all your sins, I will resettle your towns, and the ruins will be rebuilt. The desolate land will be cultivated instead of lying desolate in the sight of all who pass through it. They will say, "This land that was laid waste has become like the garden of Eden; the cities that were lying in ruins, desolate and destroyed, are now fortified and inhabited." Then the nations around you that remain will know that I the LORD have rebuilt what was destroyed and have replanted what was desolate. I the LORD have spoken, and I will do it This is what the Sovereign LORD says: Once again I will yield to Israel's plea and do this for them: I will make their people as numerous as sheep, as numerous as the flocks for offerings at Jerusalem during her appointed festivals. So will the ruined cities be filled with flocks of people. Then they will know that I am the LORD.'"

CHAPTER 37

The hand of the LORD was on me, and he brought me out by the Spirit of the LORD and set me in the middle of a valley; it was full of bones. He led me back and forth among them, and I saw a great many bones on the floor of the valley, bones that were very dry. He asked me, "Son of man, can these bones live?" I said, "Sovereign LORD, you alone know." Then he said to me, "Prophesy to these bones and say to them, 'Dry bones, hear the word of the LORD! This is what the Sovereign LORD says to these bones: I will make breath enter you, and you will come to life. I will attach tendons to you and make flesh come upon you and cover you with skin; I will put breath in you, and you will come to life. Then you will know that I am the LORD.'" So I prophesied as I was commanded. And as I was prophesying, there was a noise, a rattling sound, and the bones came together, bone to bone. I looked, and tendons and flesh appeared on them, and skin covered them, but there was no breath in them. Then he said to me, "Prophesy to the breath; prophesy, son of man, and say to it, 'This is what the Sovereign LORD says: Come, breath, from the four winds and breathe into these slain, that they may live.'" So I prophesied as he commanded me, and breath entered them; they came to life and stood up on their feet—a vast army Then he said to me, "Son of man, these bones are the people of Israel. They say, 'Our bones are dried up and our hope is gone; we are cut off.' Therefore prophesy and say to them: 'This is what the Sovereign LORD says: My people, I am going to open your graves and bring you up from them; I will bring you back to the land of Israel. Then you, my people, will know that I am the LORD, when I open your graves and bring you up from them. I will put my Spirit in you and you will live, and I will settle you in your own land. Then you will know that I the LORD have spoken, and I have done it, declares the LORD.'" The word of the LORD came to me: "Son of man, take a stick of wood and write on it, 'Belonging to Judah and the Israelites associated with him.' Then take another stick of wood, and write on it, 'Belonging to Joseph (that is, to Ephraim) and all the house of Israel associated with him.' Join them together into one stick so that they will become one in your hand When your people ask you, 'Won't you tell us what you mean by this?' say to them, 'This is what the Sovereign LORD says: I am going to take the stick of Joseph—which is in Ephraim's hand—and of the Israelite tribes associated with him, and join it to Judah's stick. I will make them into a single stick of wood, and they will become one in my hand.' Hold before their eyes the sticks you have written on and say to them, 'This is what the Sovereign LORD says: I will take the Israelites out of the nations where they have gone. I will gather them from all around and bring them back into their own land. I will make them one nation in the land, on the mountains of Israel. There will be one king over all of them, and they will never again be two nations or be divided into two kingdoms. They will no longer defile themselves with their idols and vile images or with any of their offenses, for I will save them from all their sinful backsliding, and I will cleanse them. They will be my people, and I will be their God My servant David will be king over them, and they will all have one shepherd. They will follow my laws and be careful to keep my decrees. They will live in the land I gave to my servant Jacob, the land where your ancestors lived. They and their children and their children's children will live there forever, and David my servant will be their prince forever. I will make a covenant of peace with them; it will be an everlasting covenant. I will establish them and increase their numbers, and I will put my sanctuary among them forever. My dwelling place will be with them; I will be their God, and they will be my people. Then the nations will know that I the LORD make Israel holy, when my sanctuary is among them forever.'"

CHAPTER 38

The word of the LORD came to me: "Son of man, set your face against Gog, of the land of Magog, the chief prince of Meshech and Tubal; prophesy against him and say: 'This is what the Sovereign LORD says: I am against you, Gog, chief prince of Meshech and Tubal. I will turn you around, put hooks in your jaws and bring you out with your whole army—your horses, your horsemen fully armed, and a great horde with large and small shields, all of them brandishing their swords. Persia, Cush, and Put will be with them, all with shields and helmets, also Gomer with all its troops, and Beth Togarmah from the far north with all its troops—the many nations with you Get ready; be prepared, you and all the hordes gathered about you, and take command of them. After many days you will be called to arms. In future years you will invade a land that has recovered from war, whose people were gathered from many nations to the mountains of Israel, which had long been desolate. They had been brought out from the nations, and now all of them live in safety. You and all your troops and the many nations with you will go up, advancing like a storm; you will be like a cloud covering the land This is what the Sovereign LORD says: On that day thoughts will come into your mind, and you will devise an evil scheme. You will say, "I will invade a land of unwalled villages; I will attack a peaceful and unsuspecting people—all of them living without walls and without gates and bars. I will plunder and loot and turn my hand against the resettled ruins and the people gathered from the nations, rich in livestock and goods, living at the center of the land." Sheba and Dedan and the merchants of Tarshish and all her villages will say to you, "Have you come to plunder? Have you gathered your hordes to loot, to carry off silver and gold, to take away livestock and goods and to seize much plunder?" Therefore, son of man, prophesy and say to Gog: 'This is what the Sovereign LORD says: In that day, when my people Israel are living in safety, will you not take notice of it? You will come from your place in the far north, you and many nations with you, all of them riding on horses, a great horde, a mighty army. You will advance against my people Israel like a cloud that covers the land. In days to come, Gog, I will bring you against my land, so that the nations may know me when I am proved holy through you before their eyes This is what the Sovereign LORD says: You are the one I spoke of in former days by my servants the prophets of Israel. At that time they prophesied for years that I would bring you against them. This is what will happen in that day: When Gog attacks the land of Israel, my hot anger will be aroused, declares the Sovereign LORD. In my zeal and fiery wrath, I declare that at that time there shall be a great earthquake in the land of Israel. The fish in the sea, the birds in the sky, the beasts of the field, every creature that moves along the ground, and all the people on the face of the earth will tremble at my presence. The mountains will be overturned, the cliffs will crumble, and every wall will fall to the ground. I will summon a sword against Gog on all my mountains, declares the Sovereign LORD. Every man's sword will be against his brother. I will execute judgment on him with plague and bloodshed; I will pour down torrents of rain, hailstones, and burning sulfur on him and on his troops and on the many nations with him. And so I will show my greatness and my holiness, and I will make myself known in the sight of many nations. Then they will know that I am the LORD.'

CHAPTER 39

"Son of man, prophesy against Gog and say: 'This is what the Sovereign LORD says: I am against you, Gog, chief prince of Meshech and Tubal. I will turn you around and drag you along. I will bring you from the far north and send you against the mountains of Israel. Then I will strike your bow from your left hand and make your arrows drop from your right hand. On the mountains of Israel you will fall, you and all your troops and the nations with you. I will give you as food to all kinds of carrion birds and to the wild animals. You will fall in the open field, for I have spoken, declares the Sovereign LORD. I will send fire on Magog and on those who live in safety in the coastlands, and they will know that I am the LORD I will make known my holy name among my people Israel. I will no longer let my holy name be profaned, and the nations will know that I the LORD am the Holy One in Israel. It is coming! It will surely take place, declares the Sovereign LORD. This is the day I have spoken of Then those who live in the towns of Israel will go out and use the weapons for fuel and burn them up—the small and large shields, the bows and arrows, the war clubs and spears. For seven years they will use them for fuel. They will not need to gather wood from the fields or cut it from the forests because they will use the weapons for fuel. And they will plunder those who plundered them and loot those who looted them, declares the Sovereign LORD On that day I will give Gog a burial place in Israel, in the valley of those who travel east of the

Sea. It will block the way of travelers because Gog and all his hordes will be buried there. So it will be called the Valley of Hamon Gog For seven months the Israelites will be burying them in order to cleanse the land. All the people of the land will bury them, and the day I display my glory will be a memorable day for them, declares the Sovereign LORD. People will be continually employed in cleansing the land. They will spread out across the land and, along with others, they will bury any bodies that are lying on the ground. After the seven months, they will carry out a more detailed search. As they go through the land, anyone who sees a human bone will leave a marker beside it until the grave diggers bury it in the Valley of Hamon Gog, near a town called Hamonah. And so they will cleanse the land Son of man, this is what the Sovereign LORD says: Call out to every kind of bird and all the wild animals: 'Assemble and come together from all around to the sacrifice I am preparing for you, the great sacrifice on the mountains of Israel. There you will eat flesh and drink blood. You will eat the flesh of mighty men and drink the blood of the princes of the earth as if they were rams and lambs, goats and bulls—all of them fattened animals from Bashan. At the sacrifice I am preparing for you, you will eat fat till you are glutted and drink blood till you are drunk. At my table, you will eat your fill of horses and riders, mighty men and soldiers of every kind, declares the Sovereign LORD I will display my glory among the nations, and all the nations will see the punishment I inflict and the hand I lay on them. From that day forward the people of Israel will know that I am the LORD their God. And the nations will know that the people of Israel went into exile for their sin because they were unfaithful to me. So I hid my face from them and handed them over to their enemies, and they all fell by the sword. I dealt with them according to their uncleanness and their offenses, and I hid my face from them Therefore, this is what the Sovereign LORD says: I will now restore the fortunes of Jacob and will have compassion on all the people of Israel, and I will be zealous for my holy name. They will forget their shame and all the unfaithfulness they showed toward me when they lived in safety in their land with no one to make them afraid. When I have brought them back from the nations and have gathered them from the countries of their enemies, I will be proved holy through them in the sight of many nations. Then they will know that I am the LORD their God, for though I sent them into exile among the nations, I will gather them to their own land, not leaving any behind. I will no longer hide my face from them, for I will pour out my Spirit on the people of Israel, declares the Sovereign LORD."

CHAPTER 40

In the twenty-fifth year of our exile, at the beginning of the year, on the tenth of the month—in the fourteenth year after the city was taken—on that very day the hand of the LORD was on me and he took me there. In visions of God, he took me to the land of Israel and set me on a very high mountain, on whose south side were some buildings that looked like a city. He took me there, and I saw a man whose appearance was like bronze; he was standing in the gateway with a linen cord and a measuring rod in his hand. The man said to me, "Son of man, look carefully and listen closely and pay attention to everything I am going to show you, for that is why you have been brought here. Tell the people of Israel everything you see." I saw a wall completely surrounding the temple area. The length of the measuring rod in the man's hand was six long cubits, each of which was a cubit and a handbreadth. He measured the wall; it was one measuring rod thick and one rod high Then he went to the east gate. He climbed its steps and measured the threshold of the gate; it was one rod deep. The alcoves for the guards were one rod long and one rod wide, and the projecting walls between the alcoves were five cubits thick. And the threshold of the gate next to the portico facing the temple was one rod deep Then he measured the portico of the gateway; it was eight cubits deep and its jambs were two cubits thick. The portico of the gateway faced the temple. Inside the east gate were three alcoves on each side; the three had the same measurements, and the faces of the projecting walls on each side had the same measurements. Then he measured the width of the entrance to the gateway; it was ten cubits and its length was thirteen cubits. In front of each alcove was a wall one cubit high, and the alcoves were six cubits square Then he measured the gateway from the top of the rear wall of one alcove to the top of the opposite one; the distance was twenty-five cubits from one parapet opening to the opposite one. He measured along the faces of the projecting walls all around the inside of the gateway—sixty cubits. The measurement was up to the portico facing the courtyard. The distance from the entrance of the gateway to the far end of its portico was fifty cubits. The alcoves and the projecting walls inside the gateway were surmounted by narrow parapet openings all around, as was the portico; the openings all around faced inward. The faces of the projecting walls were decorated with palm trees Then he brought me into the outer court. There I saw some rooms and a pavement that had been constructed all around the court; there were thirty rooms along the pavement. It abutted the sides of the gateways and was as wide as they were long; this was the lower pavement. Then he measured the distance from the inside of the lower gateway to the outside of the inner court; it was a hundred cubits on the east side as well as on the north Then he measured the length and width of the north gate, leading into the outer court. Its alcoves—three on each side—its projecting walls and its portico had the same measurements as those of the first gateway; it was fifty cubits long and twenty-five cubits wide. Its openings, its portico, and its palm tree decorations had the same measurements as those of the gate facing east. Seven steps led up to it, with its portico opposite them. There was a gate to the inner court facing the north gate, just as there was on the east. He measured from one gate to the opposite one; it was a hundred cubits Then he led me to the south side, and I saw the south gate; he measured its jambs and its portico, and they had the same measurements as the others. The gateway and its portico had narrow openings all around, like the openings of the others. It was fifty cubits long and twenty-five cubits wide. Seven steps led up to it, with its portico opposite them. It had palm tree decorations on the faces of the projecting walls on each side. The inner court also had a gate facing south, and he measured from this gate to the outer gate on the south side; it was a hundred cubits Then he brought me into the inner court through the south gate, and he measured the south gate; it had the same measurements as the others. Its alcoves, its projecting walls, and its portico had the same measurements as the others. The gateway and its portico had openings all around; it was fifty cubits long and twenty-five cubits wide. (The porticoes of the gateways around the inner court were twenty-five cubits wide and five cubits deep.) Its portico faced the outer court; palm trees decorated its jambs, and eight steps led up to it Then he brought me to the inner court on the east side, and he measured the gateway; it had the same measurements as the others. Its alcoves, its projecting walls, and its portico had the same measurements as the others. The gateway and its portico had openings all around; it was fifty cubits long and twenty-five cubits wide. Its portico faced the outer court; palm trees decorated the jambs on either side, and eight steps led up to it Then he brought me to the north gate and measured it. It had the same measurements as the others, as did its alcoves, its projecting walls, and its portico; and it had openings all around. It was fifty cubits long and twenty-five cubits wide. Its portico faced the outer court; palm trees decorated the jambs on either side, and eight steps led up to it A room with a doorway was by the portico in each of the inner gateways, where the burnt offerings were washed. In the portico of the gateway were two tables on each side, on which the burnt offerings, sin offerings, and guilt offerings were slaughtered. By the outside wall of the portico of the gateway, near the steps at the entrance to the north gateway, were two tables, and on the other side of the steps were two tables. So there were four tables on one side of the gateway and four on the other—eight tables in all—on which the sacrifices were slaughtered. There were also four tables of dressed stone for the burnt offerings, each a cubit and a half long, a cubit and a half wide and a cubit high. On them were placed the utensils for slaughtering the burnt offerings and the other sacrifices. And double-pronged hooks, each a handbreadth long, were attached to the wall all around. The tables were for the flesh of the offerings Outside the inner gate, within the inner court, were two rooms, one at the side of the north gate and facing south, and another at the side of the south gate and facing north. He said to me, "The room facing south is for the priests who guard the temple, and the room facing north is for the priests who guard the altar. These are the sons of Zadok, who are the only Levites who may draw near to the LORD to minister before him." Then he measured the court: It was square—a hundred cubits long and a hundred cubits wide. And the altar was in front of the temple He brought me to the portico of the temple and measured the jambs of the portico; they were five cubits wide on either side. The width of the entrance was fourteen cubits and its projecting walls were three cubits wide on either side. The portico was twenty cubits wide, and twelve cubits from front to back. It was reached by a flight of stairs, and there were pillars on each side of the jambs

CHAPTER 41

1 Then he led me to the Temple and measured the posts: six cubits wide on one side and six cubits wide on the other, which was the width of the Tabernacle. 2 The width of the entrance was ten cubits; the sides of the entrance were five cubits on one side and five cubits on the other; he measured its length forty cubits and its width twenty-five cubits. 3 Then he went in and measured the pillars of the entrance two cubits, the entrance six cubits, and the width of the entrance ten cubits. 4 He then measured the length twenty cubits and the width twenty cubits in front of the Temple. And he said, "This is the most holy place." 5 Then he measured the wall of the house, six cubits, and the width of each chamber four cubits around the house, on each side. 6 The chambers were chambers upon chambers, three stories high, and they fitted into the wall made for the chambers that surrounded the house, so that the posts could be fastened there and were not fastened into the wall of the house. 7 The structure became wider as it went higher, because the wall of the house went upward around the house. Therefore the house had a broad area at the top, and one could go up from the lowest story to the highest by way of the middle story. 8 I saw also that the house had a raised platform all around; the foundations of the side chambers were a full rod of six long cubits in height. 9 The thickness of the outer wall of the side chambers was five cubits, and what was left was the place of the side chambers that belonged to the house. 10 And between the chambers was a width of twenty cubits all around the house on every side. 11 The doors of the side chambers opened on the place that was left, one door toward the north and another door toward the south; and the width of the place that was left was five cubits all around. 12 The building that faced the separate area at the west was seventy cubits wide; the wall of the building was five cubits thick all around, and its length was ninety cubits. 13 Then he measured the temple, one hundred cubits long; the separate area with the building and its walls were also one hundred cubits long. 14 Also the width of the east front of the temple, including the separate area, was one hundred cubits. 15 He measured the length of the building facing the separate area at the rear, with its galleries on either side, one hundred cubits. The inner sanctuary and the porches of the court, 16 the thresholds, the narrow windows, and the galleries all around their three stories opposite the threshold were paneled with wood all around, from the ground to the windows (the windows were covered), 17 over the entrance and to the inner house, and on the outside, and on all the walls all around, inside and outside, by measure. 18 And it was made with cherubim and palm trees, so that a palm tree was between cherub and cherub. Each cherub had two faces: 19 a man's face toward a palm tree on one side, and a young lion's face toward a palm tree on the other side. They were carved on all the house all around. 20 From the ground to above the entrance, cherubim and palm trees were carved as well as on the wall of the temple. 21 The doorposts of the temple were squared, and as for the front of the sanctuary, the appearance of one was like that of the other. 22 The altar was of wood, three cubits high, and its length two cubits; its corners, its base, and its sides were of wood. And he said to me, "This is the table that is before the LORD." 23 The temple and the sanctuary had two doors. 24 The doors had two panels apiece, two folding panels: two panels for one door and two panels for the other door. 25 Cherubim and palm trees were carved on the doors of the temple just as they were carved on the walls. There was a canopy of wood in front of the vestibule outside. 26 There were narrow windows and palm trees on either side, on the sides of the vestibule, and on the side chambers of the temple, and on the canopies

CHAPTER 42

1 Then he led me out into the outer court, into the north outer court, and he brought me to the chamber that was opposite the separate area and opposite the building toward the north. 2 It was a hundred cubits long and fifty cubits wide, with an opening toward the north. 3 Opposite the twenty cubits that belonged to the inner court and opposite the pavement that belonged to the outer court was gallery opposite gallery in three stories. 4 Before the chambers was a passage inward, ten cubits wide and a hundred cubits long, and their doors were on the north. 5 Now the upper chambers were shorter, for the galleries took more away from them than from the lower and middle chambers of the building. 6 For they were in three stories and had no pillars like the pillars of the courts; therefore the upper chambers were set back more than the lower and middle ones from the ground up. 7 And there was a wall outside parallel to the chambers, toward the outer court, opposite the chambers, fifty cubits long. 8 For the

chambers on the outer court were fifty cubits long, while those opposite the temple were a hundred cubits long. 9 Below these chambers was the entrance on the east side as one goes into them from the outer court. 10 In the thickness of the wall of the court toward the east, opposite the separate area and opposite the building, there were chambers. 11 There was a passage in front of them, like the appearance of the chambers that were toward the north; they were as long and as wide as the others, and all their exits and arrangements were the same. 12 And like the doors of the chambers that were toward the south, there was a door in the head of the passage, the passage before the corresponding wall toward the east, as one enters them. 13 Then he said to me, "The north chambers and the south chambers opposite the separate area are the holy chambers, where the priests who approach the LORD shall eat the most holy offerings. There they shall lay the most holy offerings—the grain offering, the sin offering, and the guilt offering—for the place is holy. 14 When the priests enter the holy place, they shall not go out of it into the outer court without laying there the garments in which they minister, for these are holy. They shall put on other garments before they go near to that which is for the people." 15 Now when he had finished measuring the interior of the temple, he led me out by the way of the gate that faces east and measured the temple all around. 16 He measured the east side with the measuring rod, five hundred cubits by the measuring rod all around. 17 He measured the north side, five hundred cubits by the measuring rod all around. 18 He measured the south side, five hundred cubits by the measuring rod. 19 He turned to the west side and measured five hundred cubits by the measuring rod. 20 He measured it on the four sides. It had a wall around it, five hundred cubits long and five hundred cubits wide, to make a separation between the holy and the common

CHAPTER 43

1 Then he led me to the gate, the gate facing east. 2 And behold, the glory of the God of Israel came from the east, and his voice was like the sound of many waters, and the earth shone with his glory. 3 And the vision I saw was just like the vision that I had seen when he came to destroy the city, and just like the vision that I had seen by the Chebar canal. And I fell on my face. 4 As the glory of the LORD entered the temple by the gate facing east, 5 the Spirit lifted me up and brought me into the inner court; and behold, the glory of the LORD filled the temple. 6 While the man was standing beside me, I heard one speaking to me out of the temple, 7 and he said to me, "Son of man, this is the place of my throne and the place of the soles of my feet, where I will dwell in the midst of the people of Israel forever. And the house of Israel shall no more defile my holy name, neither they, nor their kings, by their whoring and by the dead bodies of their kings at their high places, 8 by setting their threshold by my threshold and their doorposts beside my doorposts, with only a wall between me and them. They have defiled my holy name by their abominations that they have committed, so I have consumed them in my anger. 9 Now let them put away their whoring and the dead bodies of their kings far from me, and I will dwell in their midst forever. 10 As for you, son of man, describe to the house of Israel the temple, that they may be ashamed of their iniquities, and they shall measure the plan. 11 And if they are ashamed of all that they have done, make known to them the design of the temple, its arrangement, its exits and its entrances, that is, its whole design; and make known to them as well all its statutes and its whole design and all its laws, and write it down in their sight, so that they may observe all its laws and all its statutes and carry them out. 12 This is the law of the temple: The whole territory on the top of the mountain all around shall be most holy. Behold, this is the law of the temple. 13 "These are the measurements of the altar by cubits (the cubit being a cubit and a handbreadth): its base shall be one cubit high and one cubit broad, with a rim of one span around its edge. And this shall be the height of the altar: 14 from the base on the ground to the lower ledge, two cubits, with a breadth of one cubit; and from the smaller ledge to the larger ledge, four cubits, with a breadth of one cubit; 15 and the altar hearth, four cubits; and from the altar hearth projecting upward, four horns. 16 The altar hearth shall be square, twelve cubits long by twelve broad. 17 The ledge also shall be square, fourteen cubits long by fourteen broad, with a rim around it half a cubit broad, and its base one cubit all around. The steps of the altar shall face east." 18 And he said to me, "Son of man, thus says the Lord GOD: These are the ordinances for the altar: On the day when it is erected for offering burnt offerings upon it and for throwing blood against it, 19 you shall give to the Levitical priests of the family of Zadok, who draw near to me to minister to me, declares the Lord GOD, a bull from the herd for a sin offering. 20 And you shall take some of its blood and put it on the four horns of the altar and on the four corners of the ledge and upon the rim all around. Thus you shall purify the altar and make atonement for it. 21 You shall also take the bull of the sin offering, and it shall be burned in the appointed place belonging to the temple, outside the sacred area. 22 And on the second day you shall offer a male goat without blemish for a sin offering, and the altar shall be purified, as it was purified with the bull. 23 When you have finished purifying it, you shall offer a bull from the herd without blemish and a ram from the flock without blemish. 24 You shall present them before the LORD, and the priests shall sprinkle salt on them and offer them up as a burnt offering to the LORD. 25 For seven days you shall provide daily a male goat for a sin offering; also, a bull from the herd and a ram from the flock, without blemish, shall be provided. 26 Seven days shall they make atonement for the altar and cleanse it and so consecrate it. 27 And when they have completed these days, then from the eighth day onward the priests shall offer on the altar your burnt offerings and your peace offerings, and I will accept you, declares the Lord GOD."

CHAPTER 44

1 Then he brought me back to the outer gate of the sanctuary, which faces east. And it was shut. 2 And the LORD said to me, "This gate shall remain shut; it shall not be opened, and no one shall enter by it, for the LORD, the God of Israel, has entered by it. Therefore, it shall remain shut. 3 Only the prince may sit in it to eat bread before the LORD. He shall enter by way of the vestibule of the gate and shall go out by the same way." 4 Then he brought me by way of the north gate to the front of the temple, and I looked, and behold, the glory of the LORD filled the temple of the LORD. And I fell on my face. 5 And the LORD said to me, "Son of man, mark well, see with your eyes, and hear with your ears all that I shall tell you concerning all the statutes of the temple of the LORD and all its laws. And mark well the entrance to the temple and all the exits from the sanctuary. 6 And say to the rebellious house, to the house of Israel, Thus says the Lord GOD: O house of Israel, enough of all your abominations, 7 in admitting foreigners, uncircumcised in heart and flesh, to be in my sanctuary, profaning my temple, when you offer to me my food, the fat and the blood. You have broken my covenant, in addition to all your abominations. 8

And you have not kept charge of my holy things, but you have set others to keep my charge for you in my sanctuary. 9 "Thus says the Lord GOD: No foreigner, uncircumcised in heart and flesh, of all the foreigners who are among the people of Israel, shall enter my sanctuary. 10 But the Levites who went far from me, going astray from me after their idols when Israel went astray, shall bear their punishment. 11 They shall be ministers in my sanctuary, having oversight at the gates of the temple and ministering in the temple. They shall slaughter the burnt offering and the sacrifice for the people, and they shall stand before the people to minister to them. 12 Because they ministered to them before their idols and became a stumbling block of iniquity to the house of Israel, therefore I have sworn concerning them, declares the Lord GOD, and they shall bear their punishment. 13 They shall not come near to me, to serve me as priest, nor come near any of my holy things and the things that are most holy, but they shall bear their shame and the abominations that they have committed. 14 Yet I will appoint them to keep charge of the temple, to do all its service and all that is to be done in it. 15 "But the Levitical priests, the sons of Zadok, who kept the charge of my sanctuary when the people of Israel went astray from me, shall come near to me to minister to me. And they shall stand before me to offer me the fat and the blood, declares the Lord GOD. 16 They shall enter my sanctuary, and they shall approach my table, to minister to me, and they shall keep my charge. 17 When they enter the gates of the inner court, they shall wear linen garments. They shall have nothing of wool on them while they minister at the gates of the inner court and within. 18 They shall have linen turbans on their heads, and linen undergarments around their waists. They shall not bind themselves with anything that causes sweat. 19 And when they go out into the outer court to the people, they shall put off the garments in which they have been ministering and lay them in the holy chambers. And they shall put on other garments, lest they transmit holiness to the people with their garments. 20 They shall not shave their heads or let their locks grow long; they shall surely trim the hair of their heads. 21 No priest shall drink wine when he enters the inner court. 22 They shall not marry a widow or a divorced woman, but only virgins of the offspring of the house of Israel, or a widow who is the widow of a priest. 23 They shall teach my people the difference between the holy and the common and show them how to distinguish between the unclean and the clean. 24 In a dispute, they shall act as judges, and they shall judge it according to my judgments. They shall keep my laws and my statutes in all my appointed feasts, and they shall keep my Sabbaths holy. 25 They shall not defile themselves by going near to a dead person. However, for father or mother, for son or daughter, for brother or unmarried sister, they may defile themselves. 26 After he has become clean, they shall count seven days for him. 27 And on the day that he goes into the holy place, into the inner court, to minister in the holy place, he shall offer his sin offering, declares the Lord GOD. 28 "This shall be their inheritance: I am their inheritance: and you shall give them no possession in Israel; I am their possession. 29 They shall eat the grain offering, the sin offering, and the guilt offering, and every devoted thing in Israel shall be theirs. 30 And the first of all the firstfruits of all kinds, and every offering of all kinds from all your offerings, shall belong to the priests. You shall also give to the priests the first of your dough, that a blessing may rest on your house. 31 The priests shall not eat of anything, whether bird or beast, that has died of itself or is torn by wild animals

CHAPTER 45

1 "When you allot the land as an inheritance, you shall set apart for the LORD a portion of the land as a holy district, 25,000 cubits long and 20,000 cubits broad. It shall be holy throughout its whole extent. 2 Of this a square plot of 500 by 500 cubits shall be for the sanctuary, with fifty cubits for an open space around it. 3 And from this measured district you shall measure off a section 25,000 cubits long and 10,000 cubits broad, in which shall be the sanctuary, the Most Holy Place. 4 It shall be the holy portion of the land. It shall be for the priests, who minister in the sanctuary and approach the LORD to minister to him, and it shall be a place for their houses and a holy place for the sanctuary. 5 Another portion, 25,000 cubits long and 10,000 cubits broad, shall be for the Levites who minister at the temple as their possession for cities to live in. 6 "Alongside the portion set apart as the holy district you shall assign for the property of the city an area 5,000 cubits broad and 25,000 cubits long. It shall belong to the whole house of Israel. 7 "And to the prince shall belong the land on both sides of the holy district and the property of the city, alongside the holy district and the property of the city, on the west and on the east, corresponding in length to one of the tribal portions, and extending from the western to the eastern boundary 8 of the land. It is to be his property in Israel. And my princes shall no more oppress my people, but they shall let the house of Israel have the land according to their tribes. 9 "Thus says the Lord GOD: Enough, O princes of Israel! Put away violence and oppression, and execute justice and righteousness. Cease your evictions of my people, declares the Lord GOD. 10 "You shall have just balances, a just ephah, and a just bath. 11 The ephah and the bath shall be of the same measure, the bath containing one-tenth of a homer, and the ephah one-tenth of a homer; the homer shall be the standard measure. 12 The shekel shall be twenty gerahs; twenty shekels plus twenty-five shekels plus fifteen shekels shall be your mina. 13 "This is the offering that you shall make: one-sixth of an ephah from each homer of wheat, and one-sixth of an ephah from each homer of barley, 14 and as the fixed portion of oil, measured in baths, one-tenth of a bath from each cor (the cor, like the homer, contains ten baths). 15 And one sheep from every flock of 200, from the watering places of Israel, for grain offerings, burnt offerings, and peace offerings, to make atonement for them, declares the Lord GOD. 16 All the people of the land shall be obliged to give this offering to the prince in Israel. 17 It shall be the prince's duty to furnish the burnt offerings, grain offerings, and drink offerings, at the feasts, the new moons, and the Sabbaths, all the appointed feasts of the house of Israel: he shall provide the sin offerings, grain offerings, burnt offerings, and peace offerings, to make atonement on behalf of the house of Israel. 18 "Thus says the Lord GOD: In the first month, on the first day of the month, you shall take a bull from the herd without blemish, and purify the sanctuary. 19 The priest shall take some of the blood of the sin offering and put it on the doorposts of the temple, the four corners of the ledge of the altar, and the posts of the gate of the inner court. 20 You shall do the same on the seventh day of the month for anyone who has sinned through error or ignorance; so you shall make atonement for the temple. 21 "In the first month, on the fourteenth day of the month, you shall celebrate the Passover, and for seven days unleavened bread shall be eaten. 22 On that day the prince shall provide for himself and all the people of the land a bull for a sin offering. 23 And on the seven days of the feast he shall provide as a burnt offering to the LORD

seven bulls and seven rams without blemish, on each of the seven days; and a male goat daily for a sin offering. 24 And he shall provide as a grain offering an ephah for each bull, an ephah for each ram, and a hin of oil for each ephah. 25 In the seventh month, on the fifteenth day of the month and for the seven days of the feast, he shall make the same provision for sin offerings, burnt offerings, and grain offerings, and for the oil

CHAPTER 46

1 Thus says the LORD God: "The gate of the inner court that faces east shall be shut on the six working days, but on the Sabbath day it shall be opened, and on the day of the new moon it shall be opened. 2 The prince shall enter by the vestibule of the gate from outside, and shall take his stand by the post of the gate. The priests shall offer his burnt offering and his peace offerings, and he shall worship at the threshold of the gate. Then he shall go out, but the gate shall not be shut until evening. 3 The people of the land shall bow down at the entrance of that gate before the LORD on the Sabbaths and on the new moons. 4 The burnt offering that the prince offers to the LORD on the Sabbath day shall be six lambs without blemish and a ram without blemish. 5 And the grain offering with the ram shall be an ephah, and the grain offering with the lambs shall be as much as he is able to give, together with a hin of oil to each ephah. 6 On the day of the new moon he shall offer a bull from the herd without blemish, and six lambs and a ram, which shall be without blemish. 7 As a grain offering he shall provide an ephah with the bull and an ephah with the ram, and with the lambs as much as he is able, together with a hin of oil to each ephah. 8 When the prince enters, he shall enter by the vestibule of the gate, and he shall go out by the same way. 9 "When the people of the land come before the LORD at the appointed feasts, he who enters by the north gate to worship shall go out by the south gate, and he who enters by the south gate shall go out by the north gate. No one shall return by way of the gate by which he entered, but each shall go out straight ahead. 10 When they enter, the prince shall enter with them, and when they go out, he shall go out. 11 "At the feasts and the appointed festivals, the grain offering with a bull shall be an ephah, and with a ram an ephah, and with the lambs as much as one is able to give, together with a hin of oil to each ephah. 12 When the prince provides a freewill offering, either a burnt offering or peace offerings as a freewill offering to the LORD, the gate facing east shall be opened for him. And he shall offer his burnt offering or his peace offerings as he does on the Sabbath day. Then he shall go out, and after he has gone out the gate shall be shut. 13 "You shall provide a lamb a year old without blemish for a burnt offering to the LORD daily; morning by morning you shall provide it. 14 And you shall provide a grain offering with it morning by morning, one-sixth of an ephah, and one-third of a hin of oil to moisten the flour, as a grain offering to the LORD. This is a perpetual statute. 15 Thus the lamb and the grain offering and the oil shall be provided, morning by morning, for a regular burnt offering. 16 "Thus says the Lord GOD: If the prince makes a gift to any of his sons as his inheritance, it shall belong to his sons. It is their property by inheritance. 17 But if he makes a gift out of his inheritance to one of his servants, it shall be his to the year of liberty. Then it shall revert to the prince; surely it is his inheritance—it shall belong to his sons. 18 The prince shall not take any of the inheritance of the people, thrusting them out of their property. He shall give his sons their inheritance out of his own property, so that none of my people shall be scattered from his property." 19 Then he brought

me through the entrance, which was at the side of the gate, to the north row of the holy chambers for the priests, and behold, a place was there at the extreme western end of them. 20 And he said to me, "This is the place where the priests shall boil the guilt offering and the sin offering, and where they shall bake the grain offering, in order not to bring them out into the outer court and so transmit holiness to the people." 21 Then he brought me out to the outer court and led me around to the four corners of the court, and behold, in each corner of the court there was another court— 22 in the four corners of the court were small courts, forty cubits long and thirty broad; the four were of the same size. 23 On the inside, around each of the four courts, was a row of masonry, with hearths made at the bottom of the rows all around. 24 Then he said to me, "These are the kitchens where those who minister at the temple shall boil the sacrifices of the people."

CHAPTER 47

1 Then he brought me back to the door of the temple, and behold, water was issuing from below the threshold of the temple toward the east (for the temple faced east). The water was flowing down from below the south end of the threshold of the temple, south of the altar. 2 Then he brought me out by way of the north gate and led me around on the outside to the outer gate that faces toward the east; and behold, the water was trickling out on the south side. 3 Going on eastward with a measuring line in his hand, the man measured a thousand cubits, and then led me through the water, and it was ankle-deep. 4 Again he measured a thousand, and led me through the water, and it was knee-deep. Again he measured a thousand, and led me through the water, and it was waist-deep. 5 Again he measured a thousand, and it was a river that I could not pass through, for the water had risen. It was deep enough to swim in, a river that could not be passed through. 6 And he said to me, "Son of man, have you seen this?" Then he led me back to the bank of the river. 7 As I went back, I saw on the bank of the river very many trees on the one side and on the other. 8 And he said to me, "This water flows toward the eastern region and goes down into the Arabah, and enters the sea; when the water flows into the sea, the water will become fresh. 9 And wherever the river goes, every living creature that swarms will live, and there will be very many fish. For this water goes there, that the waters of the sea may become fresh; so everything will live where the river goes. 10 Fishermen will stand beside the sea. From Engedi to Eneglaim it will be a place for the spreading of nets. Its fish will be of very many kinds, like the fish of the Great Sea. 11 But its swamps and marshes will not become fresh; they are to be left for salt. 12 And on the banks, on both sides of the river, there will grow all kinds of trees for food. Their leaves will not wither, nor their fruit fail, but they will bear fresh fruit every month, because the water for them flows from the sanctuary. Their fruit will be for food, and their leaves for healing." 13 Thus says the Lord GOD: "This is the boundary by which you shall divide the land for inheritance among the twelve tribes of Israel. Joseph shall have two portions. 14 And you shall divide equally what I swore to give to your fathers. This land shall fall to you as your inheritance. 15 "This shall be the boundary of the land: On the north side, from the Great Sea by way of Hethlon to Lebo-hamath, and on to Zedad, 16 Berothah, Sibraim (which lies on the border between Damascus and Hamath), as far as Hazer-hatticon, which is on the border of Hauran. 17 So the boundary shall run from the sea to Hazar-enan, which is on the northern border of Damascus, with the border of Hamath to the north. This shall be

the north side. 18 "On the east side, the boundary shall run between Hauran and Damascus; along the Jordan between Gilead and the land of Israel; to the eastern sea and as far as Tamar. This shall be the east side. 19 "On the south side, it shall run from Tamar as far as the waters of Meribah-kadesh, from there along the Brook of Egypt to the Great Sea. This shall be the south side. 20 "On the west side, the Great Sea shall be the boundary to a point opposite Lebo-hamath. This shall be the west side. 21 "So you shall divide this land among you according to the tribes of Israel. 22 You shall allot it as an inheritance for yourselves and for the sojourners who reside among you and have had children among you. They shall be to you as native-born children of Israel. With you they shall be allotted an inheritance among the tribes of Israel. 23 In whatever tribe the sojourner resides, there you shall assign him his inheritance, declares the Lord GOD

CHAPTER 48

1 "These are the names of the tribes: Beginning at the northern extreme, beside the way of Hethlon to Lebo-hamath, as far as Hazar-enan (which is on the northern border of Damascus over against Hamath), extending from the east side to the west, Dan, one portion. 2 Adjoining the territory of Dan, from the east side to the west, Asher, one portion. 3 Adjoining the territory of Asher, from the east side to the west, Naphtali, one portion. 4 Adjoining the territory of Naphtali, from the east side to the west, Manasseh, one portion. 5 Adjoining the territory of Manasseh, from the east side to the west, Ephraim, one portion. 6 Adjoining the territory of Ephraim, from the east side to the west, Reuben, one portion. 7 Adjoining the territory of Reuben, from the east side to the west, Judah, one portion. 8 "Adjoining the territory of Judah, from the east side to the west, shall be the portion which you shall set apart, 25,000 cubits in breadth, and in length equal to one of the tribal portions, from the east side to the west, with the sanctuary in the midst of it. 9 The portion that you shall set apart for the LORD shall be 25,000 cubits in length, and 20,000 in breadth. 10 These shall be the allotments of the holy portion: The priests shall have an allotment measuring 25,000 cubits on the northern side, 10,000 cubits in breadth on the western side, 10,000 in breadth on the eastern side, and 25,000 in length on the southern side, with the sanctuary of the LORD in the midst of it. 11 This shall be for the consecrated priests, the sons of Zadok, who kept my charge, who did not go astray when the people of Israel went astray, as the Levites did. 12 And it shall belong to them as a special portion from the holy portion of the land, a most holy place, adjoining the territory of the Levites. 13 And alongside the territory of the priests, the Levites shall have an allotment 25,000 cubits in length and 10,000 in breadth. The whole length shall be 25,000 cubits and the breadth 10,000. 14 They shall not sell or exchange any of it. They shall not alienate this choice portion of the land, for it is holy to the LORD. 15 "The remainder, 5,000 cubits in breadth and 25,000 in length, shall be for common use for the city, for dwellings and for open country. In the midst of it shall be the city, 16 and these shall be its measurements: the north side 4,500 cubits, the south side 4,500, the east side 4,500, and the west side 4,500. 17 And the city shall have open land: on the north 250 cubits, on the south 250, on the east 250, and on the west 250. 18 The remainder of the length alongside the holy portion shall be 10,000 cubits to the east and 10,000 to the west, and it shall be alongside the holy portion. Its produce shall be food for the workers of the city. 19 And the workers of the city, from all the tribes of Israel, shall till it. 20 The whole portion that you shall set apart shall be 25,000 cubits by 25,000 cubits, square, that is, the holy portion together with the property of the city. 21 "What remains on both sides of the holy portion and of the property of the city shall belong to the prince. Extending from the 25,000 cubits of the holy portion to the east border, and westward from the 25,000 cubits to the west border, parallel to the tribal portions, it shall belong to the prince. The holy portion with the sanctuary of the temple shall be in its midst. 22 It shall be separate from the property of the Levites and the property of the city, which are in the midst of that which belongs to the prince. The portion of the prince shall lie between the territory of Judah and the territory of Benjamin. 23 "As for the rest of the tribes: from the east side to the west, Benjamin, one portion. 24 Adjoining the territory of Benjamin, from the east side to the west, Simeon, one portion. 25 Adjoining the territory of Simeon, from the east side to the west, Issachar, one portion. 26 Adjoining the territory of Issachar, from the east side to the west, Zebulun, one portion. 27 Adjoining the territory of Zebulun, from the east side to the west, Gad, one portion. 28 And adjoining the territory of Gad to the south, the boundary shall run from Tamar to the waters of Meribah-kadesh, from there along the Brook of Egypt to the Great Sea. 29 This is the land that you shall allot as an inheritance among the tribes of Israel, and these are their portions, declares the Lord GOD. 30 "These shall be the exits of the city: On the north side, which is to be 4,500 cubits by measure, 31 three gates, the gate of Reuben, the gate of Judah, and the gate of Levi, the gates of the city being named after the tribes of Israel. 32 On the east side, which is to be 4,500 cubits, three gates, the gate of Joseph, the gate of Benjamin, and the gate of Dan. 33 On the south side, which is to be 4,500 cubits by measure, three gates, the gate of Simeon, the gate of Issachar, and the gate of Zebulun. 34 On the west side, which is to be 4,500 cubits, three gates, the gate of Gad, the gate of Asher, and the gate of Naphtali. 35 The circumference of the city shall be 18,000 cubits. And the name of the city from that time on shall be, The LORD Is There."

27. Daniel

Chapter 1

In the thirteenth year of the reign of Jehoiakim, king of Judah, Nebuchadnezzar, king of Babylon, came to Jerusalem and besieged it. The LORD gave Jehoiakim, king of Judah, into his hand, along with some of the furnishings from the house of God. These Nebuchadnezzar carried to the land of Shinar, to the house of his god, and placed them in the treasury of his god The king ordered Ashpenaz, the master of his eunuchs, to bring some of the children of Israel, of royal descent and nobility. These were children without physical defects, well-fed, instructed in all wisdom, knowledgeable, capable of imparting knowledge, and able to serve in the king's palace. They were to be taught the learning and language of the Chaldeans. The king assigned them a daily portion of his food and wine for three years, after which they would stand before the king Among them were Daniel, Hananiah, Mishael, and Azariah from the tribe of Judah. The chief of the eunuchs gave them new names: Daniel became Belteshazzar, Hananiah became Shadrach, Mishael became Meshach, and Azariah became Abednego. However, Daniel resolved not to defile himself with the king's food and wine. He requested the chief of the eunuchs to allow him not to defile himself God had brought Daniel into favor and compassion with the chief of the eunuchs. The chief of the eunuchs expressed his fear that the king would see Daniel and his friends looking worse than the other youths, risking his own life. Daniel then spoke to the steward appointed by the chief of the eunuchs to take care of Daniel, Hananiah, Mishael, and Azariah. He requested a ten-day trial, during which they would eat only vegetables and drink water. At the end of the ten days, their appearance was better and healthier than all the youths who ate the king's food. So, the steward took away their portion of food and wine and gave them vegetables God gave these four youths knowledge and skill in all learning and wisdom, and Daniel had understanding in all visions and dreams. When the time came for them to be presented to the king, the chief of the eunuchs brought them before Nebuchadnezzar. The king found them ten times better in wisdom and understanding than all the magicians and enchanters in his kingdom. Daniel continued in the king's court until the first year of King Cyrus

Chapter 2

In the second year of Nebuchadnezzar's reign, he dreamed dreams that troubled his spirit, and he could not sleep. The king commanded to call the magicians, enchanters, sorcerers, and Chaldeans to explain his dreams. They came and stood before the king. The king said to them, "I have dreamed a dream, and my spirit is troubled to understand it." The Chaldeans spoke to the king in Aramaic, saying, "O king, live forever! Tell your servants the dream, and we will give the interpretation." The king answered, "The dream has gone from me. If you do not make known to me the dream and its interpretation, you shall be torn limb from limb, and your houses shall be laid in ruins. But if you show me the dream and its interpretation, you shall receive gifts, rewards, and great honor. Therefore, show me the dream and its interpretation." The Chaldeans answered, "Let the king tell his servants the dream, and we will give the interpretation." The king replied, "I know you are trying to gain time because you see the dream has gone from me. If you do not tell me the dream, there is only one penalty for you. You have agreed to speak lying and corrupt words before me until the situation changes. Therefore, tell me the dream, so I may know you can give me its interpretation." The Chaldeans answered, "There is no man on earth who can meet the king's demand. No king, lord, or ruler has ever asked such a thing of any magician, enchanter, or Chaldean. The thing the king asks is difficult, and no one can show it to the king except the gods, whose dwelling is not with flesh." This made the king furious, and he ordered all the wise men of Babylon to be destroyed. When the decree was issued, they began killing the wise men, and they sought Daniel and his companions to kill them. Then Daniel responded with wisdom and discretion to Arioch, the captain of the king's guard, who had gone out to kill the wise men of Babylon. He asked Arioch why the decree was so urgent. Arioch explained the matter to Daniel Daniel went in and requested the king to give him time to reveal the interpretation. Daniel went to his house and made the matter known to Hananiah, Mishael, and Azariah, urging them to seek mercy from the God of heaven concerning this mystery, so that they would not perish with the rest of the wise men of Babylon. Then the mystery was revealed to Daniel in a vision of the night, and Daniel blessed the God of heaven Daniel said, "Blessed be the name of God forever and ever, for wisdom and might are his. He changes times and seasons; he removes kings and sets up kings; he gives wisdom to the wise and knowledge to those who have understanding. He reveals deep and hidden things; he knows what is in the darkness, and the light dwells with him. I thank and praise you, O God of my fathers, for you have given me wisdom and might and have now made known to me what we asked of you, for you have made known to us the king's matter." Daniel went to Arioch, whom the king had appointed to destroy the wise men of Babylon. He said to him, "Do not destroy the wise men of Babylon; bring me before the king, and I will show the king the interpretation." Arioch quickly brought Daniel before the king and said, "I have found a man among the exiles from Judah who can make known to the king the interpretation." The king asked Daniel (who was named Belteshazzar), "Are you able to make known to me the dream I have seen and its interpretation?" Daniel answered, "No wise men, enchanters, magicians, or astrologers can show the king the mystery he has asked about, but there is a God in heaven who reveals mysteries. He has made known to King Nebuchadnezzar what will happen in the latter days. Your dream and the visions of your head as you lay in bed are these: As you lay in bed, thoughts came to you about what would come to pass. The revealer of mysteries made known to you what is to happen. As for me, this mystery has been revealed to me, not because of any wisdom that I have more than all the living, but in order that the interpretation may be made known to the king and that you may understand the thoughts of your mind You saw, O king, and behold, a great image. This image, mighty and of exceeding brightness, stood before you, and its appearance was frightening. The head of this image was of fine gold, its chest and arms of silver, its middle and thighs of bronze, its legs of iron, and its feet partly of iron and partly of clay. As you looked, a stone was cut out by no human hand, and it struck the image on its feet of iron and clay, and broke them in pieces. Then the iron, the clay, the bronze, the silver, and the gold, all together were broken in pieces and became like the chaff of the summer threshing floors; the wind carried them away so that no trace of them could be found. But the stone that struck the image became a great mountain and filled the whole earth This was the dream. Now we will tell the king its interpretation. You, O king, are the king of kings, to whom the God of heaven has given the kingdom, the power, the might, and the glory, and into whose hand he has given, wherever they dwell, the children of man, the beasts of the field, and the birds of the heavens, making you rule over them all. You are the head of gold. After you, another kingdom inferior to yours shall arise, and yet a third kingdom of bronze, which shall rule over all the earth. And there shall be a fourth kingdom, strong as iron, because iron breaks to pieces and shatters all things. And like iron that crushes, it shall break and crush all these. And as you saw the feet and toes, partly of potter's clay and partly of iron, it shall be a divided kingdom, but some of the firmness of iron shall be in it, just as you saw iron mixed with soft clay. And as the toes of the feet were partly iron and partly clay, so the kingdom shall be partly strong and partly brittle. As you saw the iron mixed with soft clay, so they will mix with one another in marriage, but they will not hold together, just as iron does not mix with clay In the days of those kings, the God of heaven will set up a kingdom that shall never be destroyed, nor shall the kingdom be left to another people. It shall break in pieces all these kingdoms and bring them to an end, and it shall stand forever, just as you saw that a stone was cut from a mountain by no human hand and that it broke in pieces the iron, the bronze, the clay, the silver, and the gold. A great God has made known to the king what shall be after this. The dream is certain, and its interpretation sure." Then King Nebuchadnezzar fell upon his face, paid homage to Daniel, and commanded that an offering and incense be offered to him. The king said to Daniel, "Truly, your God is the God of gods and the Lord of kings, and a revealer of mysteries, for you have been able to reveal this mystery." Then the king gave Daniel high honors and many great gifts and made him ruler over the whole province of Babylon and chief prefect over all the wise men of Babylon. Daniel made a request of the king, and he appointed Shadrach, Meshach, and Abednego over the affairs of the province of Babylon, but Daniel remained at the king's court

Chapter 3

King Nebuchadnezzar made an image of gold, sixty cubits high and six cubits wide. He set it up on the plain of Dura, in the province of Babylon. Then he summoned the satraps, prefects, governors, counselors, treasurers, justices, magistrates, and all the officials of the provinces to come to the dedication of the image he had set up. They stood before the image that Nebuchadnezzar had set up A herald proclaimed aloud, "You are commanded, O peoples, nations, and languages, that when you hear the sound of the horn, pipe, lyre, trigon, harp, bagpipe, and every kind of music, you are to fall down and worship the golden image that King Nebuchadnezzar has set up. Whoever does not fall down and worship shall immediately be cast into a burning fiery furnace." Therefore, as soon as all the peoples heard the sound of the musical instruments, they fell down and worshiped the golden image that King Nebuchadnezzar had set up At that time, certain Chaldeans came forward and maliciously accused the Jews. They declared to King Nebuchadnezzar, "O king, live forever! You, O king, have made a decree that every man who hears the sound of the musical instruments shall fall down and worship the golden image. Whoever does not fall down and worship shall be cast into a burning fiery furnace. There are certain Jews whom you have appointed over the affairs of the province of Babylon: Shadrach, Meshach, and Abednego. These men, O king, pay no attention to you; they do not serve your gods or worship the golden image you have set up." Then Nebuchadnezzar, in furious rage, commanded that Shadrach, Meshach, and Abednego be brought. So, they brought these men before the king. Nebuchadnezzar said to them, "Is it true, O Shadrach, Meshach, and Abednego, that you do not serve my gods or worship the golden image that I have set up? Now, if you are ready, when you hear the sound of the musical instruments, to fall down and worship the image I have made, well and good. But if you do not worship, you shall immediately be cast into a burning fiery furnace, and who is the god who will deliver you out of my hands?" Shadrach, Meshach, and Abednego answered the king, "O Nebuchadnezzar, we have no need to answer you in this matter. If this be so, our God whom we serve is able to deliver us from the burning fiery furnace, and he will deliver us out of your hand, O king. But if not, be it known to you, O king, that we will not serve your gods or worship the golden image that you have set up." Then Nebuchadnezzar was filled with fury, and the expression of his face changed against Shadrach, Meshach, and Abednego. He ordered the furnace to be heated seven times more than it was usually heated. He commanded some of the mighty men of his army to bind Shadrach, Meshach, and Abednego and to cast them into the burning fiery furnace. These men were bound in their cloaks, tunics, hats, and other garments and thrown into the burning fiery furnace. Because the king's order was urgent and the furnace overheated, the flame of the fire killed those men who took up Shadrach, Meshach, and Abednego. These three men fell bound into the burning fiery furnace Then King Nebuchadnezzar was astonished and rose up in haste. He declared to his counselors, "Did we not cast three men bound into the fire?" They answered, "True, O king." He answered, "But I see four men unbound, walking in the midst of the fire, and they are not hurt, and the appearance of the fourth is like a son of the gods." Nebuchadnezzar came near to the door of the burning fiery furnace and called, "Shadrach, Meshach, and Abednego, servants of the Most High God, come out and come here!" They came out from the fire. The satraps, prefects, governors, and the king's counselors gathered together and saw that the fire had not had any power over the bodies of these men. The hair of their heads was not singed, their cloaks were not harmed, and no smell of fire had come upon them Nebuchadnezzar declared, "Blessed be the God of Shadrach, Meshach, and Abednego, who has sent his angel and delivered his servants, who trusted in him and set aside the king's command, yielding up their bodies rather than serve and worship any god except their own God. Therefore, I make a decree: Any people, nation, or language that speaks anything against the God of Shadrach, Meshach, and Abednego shall be torn limb from limb, and their houses laid in ruins, for there is no other god who is able to rescue in this way." Then the king promoted Shadrach, Meshach, and Abednego in the province of Babylon

Chapter 4

King Nebuchadnezzar addressed all peoples, nations, and languages that dwell in all the earth: "Peace be multiplied to you. It has seemed good to me to show the signs and wonders that the Most High God has done for me. How great are his signs, how mighty his wonders! His kingdom is an everlasting kingdom, and his dominion endures from generation to generation I, Nebuchadnezzar, was at ease in my house and prospering in my palace. I saw a dream that made me afraid. As I lay in bed, the visions of my head alarmed me. So, I made a decree that all the wise men of Babylon should be brought before me, that they might make known to me the interpretation of the dream. Then the magicians, enchanters, Chaldeans, and astrologers came in, and I told them the dream, but they could not make known to me its interpretation. At last, Daniel came in before me—he who is named Belteshazzar after the name of my god, and in whom is the spirit of the holy gods—and I told him the dream, saying, "O Belteshazzar, chief of the magicians, because I know that the spirit of the holy gods is in you and that no mystery is too difficult for you, tell me the visions of my dream that I saw and their interpretation The visions of my head as I lay in bed were these: I saw, and behold, a tree in the midst of the earth, and its height was great. The tree grew and became strong, and its top reached to heaven, and it was visible to the end of the whole earth. Its leaves were beautiful and its fruit abundant, and in it was food for all. The beasts of the field found shade under it, and the birds of the heavens lived in its branches, and all flesh was fed from it I saw in the visions of my head as I lay in bed, and behold, a watcher, a holy one, came down from heaven. He proclaimed aloud and said thus: "Chop down the tree and lop off its branches, strip off its leaves and scatter its fruit. Let the beasts flee from under it and the birds from its branches. But leave the stump of its roots in the earth, bound with a band of iron and bronze, amid the tender grass of the field. Let him be wet with the dew of heaven. Let his portion be with the beasts in the grass of the earth. Let his mind be changed from a man's, and let a beast's mind be given to him, and let seven periods of time pass over him. The sentence is by the decree of the watchers, the decision by the word of the holy ones, to the end that the living may know that the Most High rules the kingdom of men and gives it to whom he will and sets over it the lowliest of men." This dream I, King Nebuchadnezzar, saw. And you, O Belteshazzar, tell me the interpretation, because all the wise men of my kingdom are not able to make known to me the interpretation, but you are able, for the spirit of the holy gods is in you." Then Daniel, whose name was Belteshazzar, was dismayed for a while, and his thoughts alarmed him. The king answered and said, "Belteshazzar, let not the dream or the interpretation alarm you." Belteshazzar answered, "My lord, may the dream be for those who hate you and its interpretation for your enemies! The tree you saw, which grew and became strong, so that its top reached to heaven, and it was visible to the end of the whole earth, whose leaves were beautiful and its fruit abundant, and in which was food for all, under which beasts of the field found shade, and in whose branches the birds of the heavens lived—it is you, O king, who have grown and become strong. Your greatness has grown and reaches to heaven, and your dominion to the ends of the earth And because the king saw a watcher, a holy one, coming down from heaven and saying, "Chop down the tree and destroy it, but leave the stump of its roots in the earth, bound with a band of iron and bronze, in the tender grass of the field, and let him be wet with the dew of heaven, and let his portion be with the beasts of the field, till seven periods of time pass over him," this is the interpretation, O king: It is a decree of the Most High, which has come upon my lord the king, that you shall be driven from among men, and your dwelling shall be with the beasts of the field. You shall be made to eat grass like an ox, and you shall be wet with the dew of heaven, and seven periods of time shall pass over you, till you know that the Most High rules the kingdom of men and gives it to whom he will. And as it was commanded to leave the stump of the roots of the tree, your kingdom shall be confirmed for you from the time that you know that Heaven rules. Therefore, O king, let my counsel be acceptable to you: break off your sins by practicing righteousness, and your iniquities by showing mercy to the oppressed, that there may perhaps be a lengthening of your prosperity." All this came upon King Nebuchadnezzar. At the end of twelve months, he was walking on the roof of the royal palace of Babylon, and the king answered and said, "Is not this great Babylon, which I have built by my mighty power as a royal residence and for the glory of my majesty?" While the words were still in the king's mouth, there fell a voice from heaven: "O King Nebuchadnezzar, to you it is spoken: The kingdom has departed from you, and you shall be driven from among men, and your dwelling shall be with the beasts of the field. You shall be made to eat grass like an ox, and seven periods of time shall pass over you, until you know that the Most High rules the kingdom of men and gives it to whom he will." Immediately the word was fulfilled against Nebuchadnezzar. He was driven from among men and ate grass like an ox, and his body was wet with the dew of heaven till his hair grew as long as eagles' feathers, and his nails were like birds' claws At the end of the days, I, Nebuchadnezzar, lifted my eyes to heaven, and my reason returned to me, and I blessed the Most High, and praised and honored him who lives forever, for his dominion is an everlasting dominion, and his kingdom endures from generation to generation. All the inhabitants of the earth are accounted as nothing, and he does according to his will among the host of heaven and among the inhabitants of the

earth, and none can stay his hand or say to him, "What have you done?" At the same time, my reason returned to me, and for the glory of my kingdom, my majesty and splendor returned to me. My counselors and my lords sought me, and I was established in my kingdom, and still more greatness was added to me. Now I, Nebuchadnezzar, praise and extol and honor the King of heaven, for all his works are right and his ways are just, and those who walk in pride he is able to humble

Chapter 5

King Belshazzar hosted a great banquet for a thousand of his princes and drank wine in their presence. While enjoying the wine, Belshazzar ordered that the gold and silver vessels taken from the Temple in Jerusalem by his father Nebuchadnezzar be brought to him. He wanted the king, his princes, his wives, and his concubines to drink from them. They brought the golden vessels that had been taken from the temple of the house of the Lord in Jerusalem, and the king, his princes, his wives, and his concubines drank from them. As they drank wine, they praised the gods of gold, silver, bronze, iron, wood, and stone At that moment, fingers of a human hand appeared and wrote on the plaster of the wall, illuminated by the lampstand in the king's palace. The king watched the hand as it wrote. His face turned pale, and his thoughts alarmed him; his hips gave way, and his knees knocked together. The king called out loudly to bring in the enchanters, Chaldeans, and astrologers. He declared to the wise men of Babylon, "Whoever reads this writing and shows me its interpretation shall be clothed in purple, have a gold chain around his neck, and shall be the third ruler in the kingdom." All the king's wise men came, but they could not read the writing or make known its interpretation to the king. Then King Belshazzar was greatly troubled, and his face grew even paler, and his nobles were perplexed. Because of the words of the king and his lords, the queen entered the banquet hall and said, "O king, live forever! Let not your thoughts alarm you or your face be pale. There is a man in your kingdom who has the spirit of the holy gods. In the days of your father, light and understanding and wisdom, like the wisdom of the gods, were found in him. King Nebuchadnezzar, your father, made him chief of the magicians, enchanters, Chaldeans, and astrologers because an excellent spirit, knowledge, and understanding to interpret dreams, explain riddles, and solve problems were found in this Daniel, whom the king named Belteshazzar. Now let Daniel be called, and he will show the interpretation." Daniel was brought in before the king. The king said to Daniel, "Are you Daniel, one of the exiles of Judah, whom the king my father brought from Judah? I have heard of you, that the spirit of the gods is in you, and that light and understanding and excellent wisdom are found in you. The wise men and enchanters were brought in before me to read this writing and make known to me its interpretation, but they could not show the interpretation of the matter. But I have heard that you can give interpretations and solve problems. Now, if you can read the writing and make known to me its interpretation, you shall be clothed in purple, have a chain of gold around your neck, and be the third ruler in the kingdom." Then Daniel answered the king, "Keep your gifts for yourself, and give your rewards to someone else. Nevertheless, I will read the writing for the king and make known to him the interpretation. O king, the Most High God gave Nebuchadnezzar your father kingship and greatness and glory and majesty. Because of the greatness that He gave him, all peoples, nations, and languages trembled and feared before him.

Whomever he wished, he killed, and whomever he wished, he spared; whomever he wished, he promoted, and whomever he wished, he humbled. But when his heart was lifted up and his spirit was hardened so that he dealt proudly, he was brought down from his kingly throne, and his glory was taken from him. He was driven from among men, and his mind was made like that of a beast, and his dwelling was with the wild donkeys. He was fed grass like an ox, and his body was wet with the dew of heaven, until he knew that the Most High God rules the kingdom of mankind and sets over it whom He will And you, his son, Belshazzar, have not humbled your heart, though you knew all this. Instead, you have lifted up yourself against the Lord of heaven. The vessels of His house have been brought in before you, and you and your lords, your wives, and your concubines have drunk wine from them. You have praised the gods of silver and gold, bronze, iron, wood, and stone, which do not see or hear or know, but the God in whose hand is your breath and whose are all your ways, you have not honored. Then from His presence the hand was sent, and this writing was inscribed. And this is the writing that was inscribed: MENE, MENE, TEKEL, and PARSIN. This is the interpretation of the matter: MENE, God has numbered the days of your kingdom and brought it to an end; TEKEL, you have been weighed in the balances and found wanting; PERES, your kingdom is divided and given to the Medes and Persians." Then Belshazzar commanded, and Daniel was clothed in purple, a chain of gold was put around his neck, and a proclamation was made about him that he should be the third ruler in the kingdom. That very night Belshazzar, the Chaldean king, was killed, and Darius the Mede received the kingdom, being about sixty-two years old

Chapter 6

It pleased Darius to set over the kingdom 120 satraps, to be throughout the whole kingdom, and over them three high officials, of whom Daniel was one, to whom these satraps should give an account, so that the king might suffer no loss. Then this Daniel became distinguished above all the other high officials and satraps because an excellent spirit was in him, and the king planned to set him over the whole kingdom Then the high officials and the satraps sought to find a ground for complaint against Daniel regarding the kingdom, but they could find no ground for complaint or any fault because he was faithful, and no error or fault was found in him. Then these men said, "We shall not find any ground for complaint against this Daniel unless we find it in connection with the law of his God." Then these high officials and satraps came by agreement to the king and said to him, "O King Darius, live forever! All the high officials of the kingdom, the prefects and the satraps, the counselors and the governors, are agreed that the king should establish an ordinance and enforce an injunction that whoever makes petition to any god or man for thirty days, except to you, O king, shall be cast into the den of lions. Now, O king, establish the injunction and sign the document so that it cannot be changed, according to the law of the Medes and the Persians, which cannot be revoked." Therefore, King Darius signed the document and injunction When Daniel knew that the document had been signed, he went to his house where he had windows in his upper chamber open toward Jerusalem. He got down on his knees three times a day and prayed and gave thanks before his God, as he had done previously. Then these men came by agreement and found Daniel making petition and plea before his God. Then they came near and said before the king concerning the injunction, "O king, did you not sign an injunction that anyone who makes petition to any god or man within thirty days except to you, O king, shall be cast into the den of lions?" The king answered and said, "The thing stands fast, according to the law of the Medes and Persians, which cannot be revoked." Then they answered and said before the king, "Daniel, who is one of the exiles from Judah, pays no attention to you, O king, or the injunction you have signed, but makes his petition three times a day." Then the king, when he heard these words, was much distressed and set his mind to deliver Daniel. He labored till the sun went down to rescue him. Then these men came by agreement to the king and said to the king, "Know, O king, that it is a law of the Medes and Persians that no injunction or ordinance that the king establishes can be changed." Then the king commanded, and Daniel was brought and cast into the den of lions. The king declared to Daniel, "May your God, whom you serve continually, deliver you!" And a stone was brought and laid on the mouth of the den, and the king sealed it with his own signet and with the signet of his lords, that nothing might be changed concerning Daniel. Then the king went to his palace and spent the night fasting; no diversions were brought to him, and sleep fled from him At break of day, the king arose and went in haste to the den of lions. As he came near to the den where Daniel was, he cried out in a tone of anguish. The king declared to Daniel, "O Daniel, servant of the living God, has your God, whom you serve continually, been able to deliver you from the lions?" Then Daniel said to the king, "O king, live forever! My God sent his angel and shut the lions' mouths, and they have not harmed me, because I was found blameless before him; and also before you, O king, I have done no harm." Then the king was exceedingly glad and commanded that Daniel be taken up out of the den. So Daniel was taken up out of the den, and no kind of harm was found on him because he had trusted in his God And the king commanded, and those men who had maliciously accused Daniel were brought and cast into the den of lions—they, their children, and their wives. And before they reached the bottom of the den, the lions overpowered them and broke all their bones in pieces Then King Darius wrote to all the peoples, nations, and languages that dwell in all the earth: "Peace be multiplied to you. I make a decree that in all my royal dominion people are to tremble and fear before the God of Daniel, for he is the living God, enduring forever; his kingdom shall never be destroyed, and his dominion shall be to the end. He delivers and rescues; he works signs and wonders in heaven and on earth, he who has saved Daniel from the power of the lions." So this Daniel prospered during the reign of Darius and the reign of Cyrus the Persian

Chapter 7

In the first year of King Belshazzar of Babylon, Daniel had a dream and visions in his head as he lay in bed. Then he wrote down the dream and told the sum of the matter. Daniel declared, "I saw in my vision by night, and behold, the four winds of heaven were stirring up the great sea. And four great beasts came up out of the sea, different from one another. The first was like a lion and had eagles' wings. As I looked, its wings were plucked off, and it was lifted up from the ground and made to stand on two feet like a man, and the mind of a man was given to it And behold, another beast, a second one, like a bear. It was raised up on one side, and it had three ribs in its mouth between its teeth, and it was told, 'Arise, devour much flesh.' After this, I looked, and behold, another, like a leopard, with four wings of a bird on its back. And the beast had four heads, and dominion was given to it. After this, I saw in the night visions, and behold, a fourth beast, terrifying and dreadful and exceedingly strong. It had great iron teeth; it devoured and broke in pieces and stamped what was left with its feet. It was different from all the beasts that were before it, and it had ten horns. I considered the horns, and behold, there came up among them another horn, a little one, before which three of the first horns were plucked up by the roots. And behold, in this horn were eyes like the eyes of a man, and a mouth speaking great things As I looked, thrones were placed, and the Ancient of Days took his seat. His clothing was white as snow, and the hair of his head like pure wool. His throne was fiery flames; its wheels were burning fire. A stream of fire issued and came out from before him; a thousand thousands served him, and ten thousand times ten thousand stood before him. The court sat in judgment, and the books were opened I looked then because of the sound of the great words that the horn was speaking. And as I looked, the beast was killed, and its body destroyed and given over to be burned with fire. As for the rest of the beasts, their dominion was taken away, but their lives were prolonged for a season and a time I saw in the night visions, and behold, with the clouds of heaven, there came one like a son of man, and he came to the Ancient of Days and was presented before him. And to him was given dominion and glory and a kingdom, that all peoples, nations, and languages should serve him. His dominion is an everlasting dominion, which shall not pass away, and his kingdom one that shall not be destroyed As for me, Daniel, my spirit within me was anxious, and the visions of my head alarmed me. I approached one of those who stood there and asked him the truth concerning all this. So he told me and made known to me the interpretation of the things. These four great beasts are four kings who shall arise out of the earth. But the saints of the Most High shall receive the kingdom and possess the kingdom forever, forever and ever Then I desired to know the truth about the fourth beast, which was different from all the rest, exceedingly terrifying, with its teeth of iron and claws of bronze, and which devoured and broke in pieces and stamped what was left with its feet, and about the ten horns that were on its head, and the other horn that came up and before which three of them fell, the horn that had eyes and a mouth that spoke great things, and that seemed greater than its companions. As I looked, this horn made war with the saints and prevailed over them until the Ancient of Days came, and judgment was given for the saints of the Most High, and the time came when the saints possessed the kingdom Thus he said: 'As for the fourth beast, there shall be a fourth kingdom on earth, which shall be different from all the kingdoms, and it shall devour the whole earth and trample it down and break it to pieces. As for the ten horns, out of this kingdom, ten kings shall arise, and another shall arise after them; he shall be different from the former ones, and shall put down three kings. He shall speak words against the Most High and shall wear out the saints of the Most High, and shall think to change the times and the law; and they shall be given into his hand for a time, times, and half a time. But the court shall sit in judgment, and his dominion shall be taken away, to be consumed and destroyed to the end. And the kingdom and the dominion and the greatness of the kingdoms under the whole heaven shall be given to the people of the saints of the Most High; their kingdom shall be an everlasting kingdom, and all dominions shall serve and obey them.' Here is the end of the matter. As for me, Daniel, my thoughts greatly alarmed me, and my color changed, but I kept the matter in my heart

Chapter 8

In the third year of the reign of King Belshazzar, a vision appeared to me, Daniel, after the one that had appeared to me at the first. And I saw in the vision; and when I saw, I was in Susa the citadel, which is in the province of Elam. And I saw in the vision, and I was at the Ulai canal. I raised my eyes and saw, and behold, a ram standing on the bank of the canal. It had two horns, and both horns were high, but one was higher than the other, and the higher one came up last. I saw the ram charging westward and northward and southward. No beast could stand before him, and there was no one who could rescue from his power. He did as he pleased and became great As I was considering, behold, a male goat came from the west across the face of the whole earth, without touching the ground. And the goat had a conspicuous horn between his eyes. He came to the ram with the two horns, which I had seen standing on the bank of the canal, and he ran at him in his powerful wrath. I saw him come close to the ram, and he was enraged against him and struck the ram and broke his two horns. And the ram had no power to stand before him, but he cast him down to the ground and trampled on him. And there was no one who could rescue the ram from his power. Then the goat became exceedingly great, but when he was strong, the great horn was broken, and instead of it, there came up four conspicuous horns toward the four winds of heaven Out of one of them came a little horn, which grew exceedingly great toward the south, toward the east, and toward the glorious land. It grew great, even to the host of heaven. And some of the host and some of the stars it threw down to the ground and trampled on them. It became great, even as great as the Prince of the host. And the regular burnt offering was taken away from him, and the place of his sanctuary was overthrown. And a host will be given over to it together with the regular burnt offering because of transgression, and it will throw truth to the ground, and it will act and prosper Then I heard a holy one speaking, and another holy one said to the one who spoke, "For how long is the vision concerning the regular burnt offering, the transgression that makes desolate, and the giving over of the sanctuary and host to be trampled underfoot?" And he said to me, "For 2,300 evenings and mornings. Then the sanctuary shall be restored to its rightful state." When I, Daniel, had seen the vision, I sought to understand it. And behold, there stood before me one having the appearance of a man. And I heard a man's voice between the banks of the Ulai, and it called, "Gabriel, make this man understand the vision." So he came near where I stood. And when he came, I was frightened and fell on my face. But he said to me, "Understand, O son of man, that the vision is for the time of the end." And when he had spoken to me, I fell into a deep sleep with my face to the ground. But he touched me and made me stand up. He said, "Behold, I will make known to you what shall be at the latter end of the indignation, for it refers to the appointed time of the end. As for the ram that you saw with the two horns, these are the kings of Media and Persia. And the goat is the king of Greece. And the great horn between his eyes is the first king. As for the horn that was broken, in place of which four others arose, four kingdoms shall arise from his nation, but not with his power And at the latter end of their kingdom, when the transgressors have reached their limit, a king of bold face, one who understands riddles, shall arise. His power shall be great, but not by his own power; and he shall cause fearful destruction and shall succeed in what he does and destroy mighty men and the people who are the saints. By his cunning, he shall make deceit prosper under his hand, and in his own mind, he shall become great. Without warning, he shall destroy many. And he shall even rise up against the Prince of princes, and he shall be broken—but by no human hand The vision of the evenings and the mornings that has been told is true, but seal up the vision, for it refers to many days from now." And I, Daniel, was overcome and lay sick for some days. Then I rose and went about the king's business, but I was appalled by the vision and did not understand it

Chapter 9

In the first year of Darius, the son of Ahasuerus, by descent a Mede, who was made king over the realm of the Chaldeans—in the first year of his reign, I, Daniel, perceived in the books the number of years that, according to the word of the LORD to Jeremiah the prophet, must pass before the end of the desolations of Jerusalem, namely, seventy years Then I turned my face to the Lord God, seeking him by prayer and pleas for mercy with fasting and sackcloth and ashes. I prayed to the LORD my God and made confession, saying, "O Lord, the great and awesome God, who keeps covenant and steadfast love with those who love him and keep his commandments, we have sinned and done wrong and acted wickedly and rebelled, turning aside from your commandments and rules. We have not listened to your servants, the prophets, who spoke in your name to our kings, our princes, and our fathers, and to all the people of the land To you, O Lord, belongs righteousness, but to us open shame, as at this day, to the men of Judah, to the inhabitants of Jerusalem, and to all Israel, those who are near and those who are far away, in all the lands to which you have driven them because of the treachery that they have committed against you. To us, O LORD, belongs open shame, to our kings, to our princes, and to our fathers, because we have sinned against you. To the Lord our God belong mercy and forgiveness, for we have rebelled against him and have not obeyed the voice of the LORD our God by walking in his laws, which he set before us by his servants the prophets. All Israel has transgressed your law and turned aside, refusing to obey your voice. And the curse and oath that are written in the Law of Moses, the servant of God, have been poured out upon us because we have sinned against him. He has confirmed his words, which he spoke against us and against our rulers who ruled us, by bringing upon us a great calamity. For under the whole heaven there has not been done anything like what has been done against Jerusalem As it is written in the Law of Moses, all this calamity has come upon us, yet we have not entreated the favor of the LORD our God, turning from our iniquities and gaining insight by your truth. Therefore, the LORD has kept ready the calamity and has brought it upon us, for the LORD our God is righteous in all the works that he has done, and we have not obeyed his voice. And now, O Lord our God, who brought your people out of the land of Egypt with a mighty hand and have made a name for yourself, as at this day, we have sinned, we have done wickedly O Lord, according to all your righteous acts, let your anger and your wrath turn away from your city Jerusalem, your holy hill, because for our sins and for the iniquities of our fathers, Jerusalem and your people have become a byword among all who are around us. Now, therefore, O our God, listen to the prayer of your servant and to his pleas for mercy, and for your own sake, O Lord, make your face to shine upon your sanctuary, which is desolate. O my God, incline your ear and hear. Open your eyes and see our desolations and the city that is called by your name. For we do not present our pleas before you because of our righteousness, but because of your great mercy. O Lord, hear; O Lord, forgive. O Lord, pay attention and act. Delay not, for your own sake, O my God, because your city and your people are called by your name." While I was speaking and praying, confessing my sin and the sin of my people Israel, and presenting my plea before the LORD my God for the holy hill of my God, while I was speaking in prayer, the man Gabriel, whom I had seen in the vision at the first, came to me in swift flight at the time of the evening sacrifice. He made me understand, speaking with me and saying, "O Daniel, I have now come out to give you insight and understanding. At the beginning of your pleas for mercy, a word went out, and I have come to tell it to you, for you are greatly loved. Therefore, consider the word and understand the vision Seventy weeks are decreed about your people and your holy city, to finish the transgression, to put an end to sin, and to atone for iniquity, to bring in everlasting righteousness, to seal both vision and prophet, and to anoint a most holy place. Know therefore and understand that from the going out of the word to restore and build Jerusalem to the coming of an anointed one, a prince, there shall be seven weeks. Then for sixty-two weeks it shall be built again with squares and moat, but in a troubled time. And after the sixty-two weeks, an anointed one shall be cut off and shall have nothing. And the people of the prince who is to come shall destroy the city and the sanctuary. Its end shall come with a flood, and to the end, there shall be war. Desolations are decreed. And he shall make a strong covenant with many for one week, and for half of the week, he shall put an end to sacrifice and offering. And on the wing of abominations shall come one who makes desolate until the decreed end is poured out on the desolator."

Chapter 10

In the third year of Cyrus, king of Persia, a revelation was given to Daniel (whose name was Belteshazzar). The message was true, but the time it pertained to was long; Daniel understood the message and had insight into the vision. At that time, I, Daniel, was in mourning for three weeks. I did not eat any rich food, nor did meat or wine enter my mouth, and I did not anoint myself at all until the three weeks were completed On the twenty-fourth day of the first month, as I stood beside the great river, the Tigris, I lifted up my eyes and saw a man dressed in linen, whose waist was girded with fine gold from Uphaz. His body was like chrysolite, his face like lightning, his eyes like flaming torches, his arms and feet like polished bronze, and the sound of his words was like the roar of a multitude I, Daniel, alone saw the vision, for the men who were with me did not see it, but a great terror fell upon them, so they fled and hid themselves. So I was left alone, and I saw this great vision, and no strength remained in me; my strength was gone, and I had no power left. Yet I heard the words he spoke, and when I heard them, I fell face down, turned toward the ground Then a hand touched me and set me trembling on my hands and knees. The figure said to me, "Daniel, you are greatly beloved. Understand the words that I am about to speak to you and stand up, for I have been sent to you." And when he spoke these words, I stood up trembling He continued, "Do not be afraid, Daniel. From the first day you set your heart to understand and to humble yourself before your God, your words were heard, and I have come in response to them. But the prince of the kingdom of Persia resisted me for twenty-one days; then Michael, one of the chief princes, came to help me. I left him there with the kings of Persia. Now I have come to explain what will happen to your people in the latter days, for the vision pertains to the days yet to come." When he said this, I bowed my face to the ground and became speechless. Then one who appeared to be like a man touched my lips. I opened my mouth and spoke to him who stood before me, "My lord, because of the vision, anguish has come upon me, and I have no strength left. How can I, your servant, speak with you, my lord? For now I have no strength and no breath left in me." Then again, one having the appearance of a man touched me and strengthened me. He said, "O man greatly loved, do not be afraid. Peace be with you; be strong and courageous." As he spoke to me, I was strengthened, and I said, "Let my lord speak, for you have strengthened me." He replied, "Do you know why I have come to you? Now I will return to fight against the prince of Persia, and when I go, the prince of Greece will come. But I will tell you what is written in the Book of Truth. No one supports me against these forces except Michael, your prince."

Chapter 11

In the first year of Darius the Mede, I took my stand to support and protect him. Now I will reveal the truth: There will be three more kings in Persia, and the fourth will be far richer than all of them. By his wealth and strength, he will stir up everyone against Greece Then a mighty king will arise, who will rule with great authority and do as he pleases. When he has risen, his kingdom will be broken up and divided toward the four winds of heaven; it will not go to his descendants, nor will it have the authority he exercised. Instead, his kingdom will be given to others The king of the south will become powerful, along with one of his princes, and will prevail over him. His dominion will be great. At the end of years, they will make an alliance. The daughter of the king of the south will come to the king of the north to make an agreement, but she will not retain her power, nor will he remain steadfast, nor his power. She, and those who brought her, and those who supported her will all be given to death From her roots will arise someone in her place, who will come with an army, enter the fortress of the king of the north, and deal with them as he pleases. He will also carry off their gods, their molten images, and their precious treasures to Egypt, where he will stay longer than the king of the north The king of the south will return to his own country and muster a great army; one will come and invade, then return to his fortress. The king of the south will be enraged and fight against the king of the north with a great multitude, which will be in his power. The multitude will be proud and uplifted, striking down thousands, yet they will not prevail The king of the north will return and muster a greater army than before. After several years, he will come with a mighty army and great riches. Many will oppose the king of the south; even some rebellious sons of your people will exalt themselves to fulfill the vision, but they will fall The king of the north will come and storm a fortress, capturing a strong city. The armies of the south will not stand against him, nor will his chosen people, as there will be no strength to resist. The invader will do as he pleases, standing in the pleasant land, which he will consume by his hand He will intend to invade with the full strength of his kingdom and allies, and will offer his daughter in marriage to destroy her. However, she will not support him and will not be on his side. Afterwards, he will turn his attention to the coastlands and capture many, but a commander will cause his own shame and bring his downfall He will turn his attention to his own country's fortresses but will be overthrown and will fall, and will not be found. In his place, a ruler will arise who will impose taxes, but he will be destroyed after a short time, neither through anger nor in battle A vile person will succeed

him. He will come in peace, but will use flattery to gain control of the kingdom. The armies will be overthrown like a flood before him, and they will be broken, including the prince of the courtiers. After forming a league with him, he will act deceitfully, going out with a small group He will invade a peaceful and prosperous province, performing unprecedented acts, distributing gifts, and making predictions against fortresses, albeit temporarily. He will mobilize his power against the king of the south with a great army. The king of the south will respond with a very large and powerful army but will be unable to withstand it Those who partake in his provisions will destroy him, and his army will overflow, with many falling and being slain. The hearts of these two kings will be bent on evil, speaking deceit at the table, but it will not succeed, for the end will come at the appointed time He will return to his country with great wealth, being hostile to the Holy Covenant, and will return to his own land. At the appointed time, he will return to the south, but the end will not be like the beginning. Ships from the west will come against him, causing him to be grieved. He will return in a rage against the Holy Covenant, and will act against those who forsake it His forces will pollute the sanctuary, take away the daily sacrifices, and set up an abomination that causes desolation. Those who violate the covenant will be led astray by flattery, but those who know their God will be strong and do exploits Those who are wise among the people will instruct many, but they will fall by sword, flame, captivity, and plunder for many days. When they fall, they will receive some help, but many will be delivered only after a long struggle. Some of the most intelligent will fall to be refined, purified, and made white until the end, for there is an appointed time The king will do as he desires: he will exalt himself above all gods, speak against the God of gods, and prosper until the wrath is completed, for the decree is made. He will show no regard for the gods of his ancestors, nor the desires of women, nor any god; he will exalt himself above all Instead, he will honor the god Mauzzim, a god unknown to his ancestors, with gold, silver, precious stones, and pleasant things. In the lands of Mauzzim, he will acknowledge a foreign god, increasing his glory and making this god a ruler over many. He will also treat your land as a gold mine At the end of times, the king of the south will push against him, and the king of the north will come against him like a whirlwind with chariots, horsemen, and many ships. He will invade your land, passing through it and coming out again. He will also invade the pleasant land, where many regions will fall, but Edom, Moab, and the chief of the Ammonites will escape He will extend his power over many countries, and Egypt will not escape. He will gain control over the treasures of gold, silver, and precious things of Egypt, as well as the Libyans and Cushites. But news from the east and the north will trouble him, and he will depart in a great rage to destroy and annihilate many He will set up his palace between the seas and the glorious holy mountain, but he will come to his end, and no one will help him

Chapter 12

At that time, Michael, the great prince who protects your people, will arise, and there will be a time of distress such as never before since nations began until that time. At that time, your people will be delivered, everyone whose name is found written in the book Many of those who sleep in the dust of the earth will awaken, some to everlasting life, others to shame and everlasting contempt. Those who are wise will shine like the brightness of the heavens, and those who lead many to righteousness will shine like the stars forever But you, Daniel, close up and seal the words of the scroll until the time of the end. Many will go here and there to increase knowledge Then I, Daniel, looked, and there stood two others, one on this side of the riverbank and the other on the opposite side. One of them said to the man clothed in linen, who was above the waters of the river, "How long will it be before these astonishing things are fulfilled?" The man clothed in linen, who was above the waters of the river, lifted his right hand and his left hand toward heaven, and I heard him swear by Him who lives forever, saying, "It will be for a time, times, and half a time; when the power of the holy people has been finally broken, all these things will be completed." I heard, but I did not understand. So I asked, "My lord, what will the outcome of all this be?"

He replied, "Go your way, Daniel, because the words are closed up and sealed until the time of the end. Many will be purified, made spotless, and refined, but the wicked will continue to be wicked. None of the wicked will understand, but those who are wise will understand From the time that the daily sacrifice is abolished and the abomination that causes desolation is set up, there will be 1,290 days. Blessed is the one who waits for and reaches the end of the 1,335 days. As for you, go your way till the end. You will rest, and then at the end of the days, you will rise to receive your allotted inheritance."

5. MINOR PROPHETS

28. Hosea

Chapter 1

The word of the LORD addressed to Hosea, the son of Beeri, during the days of Uzziah, Jotham, Ahaz, and Hezekiah, kings of Judah, and during the days of Jeroboam, the son of Joash, king of Israel. At first, the LORD spoke through Hosea, saying, "Go, take for yourself a wife of fornication and children of fornication, for the land has committed great prostitution, turning away from the LORD." So Hosea went and took Gomer, the daughter of Diblaim, who conceived and bore him a son. The LORD instructed him, "Name him Jezreel, for in just a little while, I will punish the house of Jehu for the bloodshed at Jezreel, and I will put an end to the kingdom of Israel. On that day, I will break the bow of Israel in the valley of Jezreel." Gomer conceived again and bore a daughter, and the LORD said to Hosea, "Name her Lo-Ruhamah, for I will no longer have mercy on the house of Israel, but I will take her away. Nevertheless, I will have mercy on the house of Judah and will save them by the LORD their God; I will not save them by bow, sword, battle, horses, or horsemen." After Gomer weaned Lo-Ruhamah, she conceived and bore a son. The LORD said, "Name him Lo-Ammi, for you are not my people, and I am not your God. Yet the number of the children of Israel shall be like the sand of the sea, which cannot be measured or counted; and in the place where it was said to them, 'You are not my people,' it shall be said to them, 'You are children of the living God.' Then the children of Judah and the children of Israel shall be gathered together and shall appoint for themselves one head. They shall come up out of the land, for great shall be the day of Jezreel."

Chapter 2

Say to your brothers, "Ammi," and to your sisters, "Ruhamah." "Plead with your mother, plead with her, for she is not my wife, nor am I her husband. Let her remove her fornications from her face and her adulteries from between her breasts. Otherwise, I will strip her naked and make her as bare as the day she was born. I will make her like a desert, turn her into a parched land, and kill her with thirst. I will not show pity on her children, for they are children of fornication. Their mother has been unfaithful and conceived them in disgrace. She said, 'I will go after my lovers, who give me my food and my water, my wool and my linen, my oil and my drink.' Therefore, I will block her path with thorns and build a wall so she cannot find her way. When she chases her lovers, she will not catch them; when she looks for them, she will not find them. Then she will say, 'I will return to my first husband, for I was better off then than now.' She did not realize that it was I who gave her the grain, the new wine, and the oil, and who lavished on her the silver and gold that they used for Baal. Therefore, I will take away my grain when it ripens, and my new wine when it is ready. I will take back my wool and my linen intended to cover her nakedness. So now I will expose her lewdness before the eyes of her lovers, and no one will take her out of my hands. I will stop all her celebrations, her yearly festivals, her New Moons, her Sabbaths—all her appointed feasts. I will ruin her vines and her fig trees, which she said were her wages from her lovers. I will make them a thicket, and wild animals will devour them. I will punish her for the days she burned incense to the Baals; she decked herself with rings and jewelry and went after her lovers, but she forgot me," declares the LORD "Therefore, I will allure her; I will lead her into the wilderness and speak tenderly to her. There I will give her back her vineyards and will make the Valley of Achor a door of hope. There she will respond as in the days of her youth, as in the day she came up out of Egypt. In that day," declares the LORD, "you will call me 'my husband'; you will no longer call me 'my master.' I will remove the names of the Baals from her lips; no longer will their names be invoked. In that day, I will make a covenant for them with the beasts of the field, the birds in the sky, and the creatures that move along the ground. Bow and sword and battle I will abolish from the land, so that all may lie down in safety. I will betroth you to me forever; I will betroth you in righteousness and justice, in love and compassion. I will betroth you in faithfulness, and you will acknowledge the LORD. In that day, I will respond," declares the LORD—"I will respond to the skies, and they will respond to the earth; and the earth will respond to the grain, the new wine, and the olive oil, and they will respond to Jezreel. I will plant her for myself in the land; I will show my love to the one I called 'Not my loved one.' I will say to those called 'Not my people,' 'You are my people'; and they will say, 'You are my God.'"

Chapter 3

The LORD said to me, "Go, show your love to your wife again, though she is loved by another and is an adulteress. Love her as the LORD loves the Israelites, though they turn to other gods and love the sacred raisin cakes." So I bought her for fifteen shekels of silver and about a homer and a lethek of barley. Then I told her, "You are to live with me many days; you must not be a prostitute or be intimate with any man, and I will behave the same way toward you." For the Israelites will live many days without a king or prince, without sacrifice or sacred stones, without ephod or household gods. Afterward, the Israelites will return and seek the LORD their God and David their king. They will come trembling to the LORD and to his blessings in the last days

Chapter 4

Hear the word of the LORD, you Israelites, because the LORD has a charge to bring against you who live in the land: "There is no faithfulness, no love, no acknowledgment of God in the land. There is only cursing, lying, and murder, stealing and adultery; they break all bounds, and bloodshed follows bloodshed. Because of this, the land dries up, and all who live in it waste away; the beasts of the field, the birds in the sky, and the fish in the sea are swept away. But let no one bring a charge, let no one accuse another, for your people are like those who bring charges against a priest. You stumble day and night, and the prophets stumble with you. So I will destroy your mother—my people are destroyed from lack of knowledge Because you have rejected knowledge, I also reject you as my priests; because you have ignored the law of your God, I also will ignore your children. The more priests there were, the more they sinned against me; they exchanged their glorious God for something disgraceful. They feed on the sins of my people and relish their wickedness. And it will be: Like people, like priests. I will punish both of them for their ways and repay them for their deeds. They will eat but not have enough; they will engage in prostitution but not flourish, because they have deserted the LORD to give themselves to prostitution, old wine, and new wine, which take away their understanding. My people consult a wooden idol, and a diviner's rod speaks to them. A spirit of prostitution leads them astray; they are unfaithful to their God. They sacrifice on the mountaintops and burn offerings on the hills, under oak, poplar, and terebinth, where the shade is pleasant. Therefore, your daughters turn to prostitution and your daughters-in-law to adultery I will not punish your daughters when they turn to prostitution, nor your daughters-in-law when they commit adultery, because the men themselves consort with harlots and sacrifice with shrine prostitutes—a people without understanding will come to ruin! Though you, Israel, commit adultery, do not let Judah become guilty. Do not go to Gilgal; do not go up to Beth Aven. And do not swear, 'As surely as the LORD lives!' The Israelites are stubborn, like a stubborn heifer. How then can the LORD pasture them like lambs in a meadow? Ephraim is joined to idols; leave him alone! Even when their drinks are gone, they continue their prostitution; their rulers dearly love shameful ways. A whirlwind will sweep them away, and their sacrifices will bring them shame

Chapter 5

Hear this, you priests! Pay attention, you Israelites! Listen, royal house! This judgment is against you: You have been a snare at Mizpah, a net spread out on Tabor. The rebels are knee-deep in slaughter. I will discipline all of them. I know all about Ephraim; Israel is not hidden from me. Ephraim, you have now turned to prostitution; Israel is corrupt. Their deeds do not permit them to return to their God. A spirit of prostitution is in their heart; they do not acknowledge the LORD. Israel's arrogance testifies against them; the Israelites, even Ephraim, stumble in their sin; Judah also stumbles with them. When they go with their flocks and herds to seek the LORD, they will not find him; he has withdrawn himself from them. They are unfaithful to the LORD; they give birth to illegitimate children. When they celebrate their New Moon feasts, he will devour their fields Sound the trumpet in Gibeah, the horn in Ramah. Raise the battle cry in Beth Aven; lead on, Benjamin. Ephraim will be laid waste on the day of reckoning. Among the tribes of Israel, I proclaim what is certain. Judah's leaders are like those who move boundary stones. I will pour out my wrath on them like a flood of water. Ephraim is oppressed, trampled in judgment, intent on pursuing idols. I am like a moth to Ephraim, like rot to the people of Judah. When Ephraim saw his sickness and Judah his sores, then Ephraim turned to Assyria, and sent to the great king for help. But he is not able to cure you, not able to heal your sores. For I will be like a lion to Ephraim, like a great lion to Judah. I will tear them to pieces and go away; I will carry them off, with no one to rescue them. Then I will return to my lair until they have borne their guilt and seek my face—in their misery, they will earnestly seek me."

Chapter 6

"Come, let us return to the LORD. He has torn us to pieces, but he will heal us; he has injured us, but he will bind up our wounds. After two days, he will revive us; on the third day, he will restore us, that we may live in his presence. Let us acknowledge the LORD; let us press on to acknowledge him. As surely as the sun rises, he will appear; he will come to us like the winter rains, like the spring rains that water the earth." "What can I do with you, Ephraim? What can I do with you, Judah? Your love is like the morning mist, like the early dew that disappears. Therefore, I cut you in pieces with my prophets, I killed you with the words of my mouth—then my judgments go forth like the sun. For I desire mercy, not sacrifice, and acknowledgment of God rather than burnt offerings. As at Adam, they have broken the covenant; they were unfaithful to me there. Gilead is a city of wicked people, stained with footprints of blood. As marauders lie in ambush for a victim, so do bands of priests; they murder on the road to Shechem, carrying out their wicked schemes. I have seen a horrible thing in Israel: There Ephraim is given to prostitution, Israel is defiled. Also for you, Judah, a harvest is appointed. Whenever I would restore the fortunes of my people."

Chapter 7

"Whenever I would heal Israel, the sins of Ephraim are exposed and the crimes of Samaria revealed. They practice deceit, thieves break into houses, bandits rob in the streets; but they do not realize that I remember all their evil deeds. Their sins engulf them; they are always before me. They delight the king with their wickedness, the princes with their lies. They are all adulterers, burning like an oven whose fire the baker need not stir from the kneading of the dough till it rises. On the day of the festival of our king, the princes become inflamed with wine, and he joins hands with the mockers. Their hearts are like an oven; they approach him with intrigue. Their passion smolders all night; in the morning it blazes like a flaming fire. All of them are hot as an oven; they devour their rulers. All their kings fall, and none of them calls on me." "Ephraim mixes with the nations; Ephraim is a flat loaf not turned over. Foreigners sap his strength, but he does not realize it. His hair is sprinkled with gray, but he does not notice. Israel's arrogance testifies against him, but despite all this, he does not return to the LORD his God or search for him. Ephraim is like a dove, easily deceived and senseless—now calling to Egypt, now turning to Assyria. When they go, I will throw my net over them; I will pull them down like the birds in the sky. When I hear them flocking together, I will catch them. Woe to them, because they have strayed from me! Destruction to them because they have rebelled against me! I long to redeem them but they speak about me falsely. They do not cry out to me from their hearts but wail on their beds. They slash themselves, appealing to their gods for grain and new wine, but they turn away from me. I trained them and strengthened their arms, but they plot evil against me. They do not turn to the Most High; they are like a faulty bow. Their leaders will fall by the sword because of their insolent words. For this, they will be ridiculed in the land of Egypt."

Chapter 8

"Put the trumpet to your lips! An eagle is over the house of the LORD because the people have broken my covenant and rebelled against my law. Israel cries out to me, 'Our God, we acknowledge you!' But Israel has rejected what is good; an enemy will pursue him. They set up kings without my consent; they choose princes without my approval. With their silver and gold, they make idols for themselves to their own destruction. Throw out your calf-idol, Samaria! My anger burns against them. How long will they be incapable of purity? They are from Israel! This calf—a metalworker has made it; it is not God. It will be broken in pieces, that calf of Samaria." "They sow the wind and reap the whirlwind. The stalk has no head; it will produce no flour. Were it to yield grain, foreigners would swallow it up. Israel is swallowed up; now she is among the nations like something no one wants. For they have gone up to Assyria like a wild donkey wandering alone. Ephraim has sold herself to lovers. Although they have sold themselves among the nations, I will now gather them together. They will begin to waste away under the oppression of the mighty king. Though Ephraim built many altars for sin offerings, these have become altars for sinning. I wrote for them the many things of my law, but they regarded them as something foreign. Though they offer sacrifices as gifts to me, and though they eat the meat, the LORD is not pleased with them. Now he will remember their wickedness and punish their sins: They will return to Egypt. Israel has forgotten their Maker and built palaces; Judah has fortified many towns. But I will send fire on their cities that will consume their fortresses."

Chapter 9

"Do not rejoice, Israel; do not be jubilant like the other nations. For you have been unfaithful to your God; you love the wages of a prostitute at every threshing floor. Threshing floors and winepresses will not feed the people; the new wine will fail them. They will not remain in the LORD's land; Ephraim will return to Egypt and eat unclean food in Assyria. They will not pour out wine offerings to the LORD, nor will their sacrifices please him. Such sacrifices will be to them like the bread of mourners; all who eat them will be unclean. This food will be for themselves; it will not come into the temple of the LORD." "What will you do on the day of your appointed festivals, on the feast days of the LORD? Even if they escape from destruction, Egypt will gather them, and Memphis will bury them. Their treasures of silver will be taken over by briers, and thorns will overrun their tents. The days of punishment are coming, the days of reckoning are at hand. Let Israel know this. Because your sins are so many and your hostility so great, the prophet is considered a fool, the inspired person a maniac. The prophet, along with my God, is the watchman over Ephraim, yet snares await him on all his paths, and hostility in the house of his God. They have sunk deep into corruption, as in the days of Gibeah. God will remember their wickedness and punish them for their sins." "When I found Israel, it was like finding grapes in the desert; when I saw your ancestors, it was like seeing the early fruit on the fig tree. But when they came to Baal Peor, they consecrated themselves to that shameful idol and became as vile as the thing they loved. Ephraim's glory will fly away like a bird—no birth, no pregnancy, no conception. Even if they rear children, I will bereave them of every one. Woe to them when I turn away from them! I have seen Ephraim, like Tyre, planted in a pleasant place. But Ephraim will bring out their children to the slayer." "Give them, LORD— what will you give them? Give them wombs that miscarry and breasts that are dry. Because of all their wickedness in Gilgal, I hated them there. Because of their sinful deeds, I will drive them out of my house. I will no longer love them; all their leaders are rebellious. Ephraim is blighted, their root is withered, they yield no fruit. Even if they bear children, I will slay their cherished offspring. My God will reject them because they have not obeyed him; they will be wanderers among the nations."

Chapter 10

"Israel was a spreading vine; he brought forth fruit for himself. As his fruit increased, he built more altars; as his land prospered, he adorned his sacred stones. Their heart is deceitful, and now they must bear their guilt. The LORD will demolish their altars and destroy their sacred stones." "Then they will say, 'We have no king because we did not revere the LORD. But even if we had a king, what could he do for us?' They make many promises, take false oaths and make agreements; therefore lawsuits spring up like poisonous weeds in a plowed field. The people who live in Samaria fear for the calf-idol of Beth Aven. Its people will mourn over it, and so will its idolatrous priests, those who had rejoiced over its splendor, because it is taken from them into exile. It will be carried to Assyria as tribute for the great king. Ephraim will be disgraced; Israel will be ashamed of its foreign alliances. Samaria's king will be destroyed, swept away like a twig on the surface of the waters. The high places of wickedness will be destroyed—it is the sin of Israel. Thorns and thistles will grow up and cover their altars. Then they will say to the mountains, 'Cover us!' and to the hills, 'Fall on us!'" "Since the days of Gibeah, you have sinned, Israel, and there you have remained. Will not war again overtake the evildoers in Gibeah? When I please, I will punish them; nations will be gathered against them to put them in bonds for their double sin. Ephraim is a trained heifer that loves to thresh; so I will put a yoke on her fair neck. I will drive Ephraim, Judah must plow, and Jacob must break up the ground. Sow righteousness for yourselves, reap the fruit of unfailing love, and break up your unplowed ground; for it is time to seek the LORD, until he comes and showers his righteousness on you. But you have planted wickedness, you have reaped evil, you have eaten the fruit of deception. Because you have depended on your own strength and on your many warriors, the roar of battle will rise against your people, so that all your fortresses will be devastated—as Shalman devastated Beth Arbel on the day of battle, when mothers were dashed to the ground with their children. So will it happen to you, Bethel, because your wickedness is great. When that day dawns, the king of Israel will be completely destroyed."

Chapter 11

When Israel was a child, I loved him, and out of Egypt, I called my son. But the more I called them, the more they went away from me; they sacrificed to the Baals and burned incense to images. It was I who taught Ephraim to walk, taking them by the arms; but they did not realize it was I who healed them. I led them with cords of human kindness, with ties of love. To them, I was like one who lifts a little child to the cheek, and I bent down to feed them Will they not return to Egypt, and will not Assyria rule over them because they refuse to repent? A sword will flash in their cities; it will devour their false prophets and put an end to their plans. My people are determined to turn from me. Even though they call me God Most High, I will by no means exalt them How can I give you up, Ephraim? How can I hand you over, Israel? How can I treat you like Admah? How can I make you like Zeboyim? My heart is changed within me; all my compassion is aroused. I will not carry out my fierce anger, nor will I devastate Ephraim again. For I am God, and not a man—the Holy One among you. I will not come against their cities. They will follow the LORD; he will roar like a lion. When he roars, his children will come trembling from the west. They will come from Egypt, trembling like sparrows, from Assyria, fluttering like doves. I will settle them in their homes," declares the LORD Ephraim has surrounded me with lies, Israel with deceit. And Judah is unruly against God, even against the faithful Holy One

Chapter 12

Ephraim feeds on the wind; he pursues the east wind all day and multiplies lies and violence. He makes a treaty with Assyria and sends olive oil to Egypt. The LORD has a charge to bring against Judah; he will punish Jacob according to his ways and repay him according to his deeds. In the womb, he grasped his brother's heel; as a man, he struggled with God. He struggled with the angel and overcame him; he wept and begged for his favor. He found him at Bethel and talked with him there— the LORD God Almighty, the LORD is his name! But you must return to your God; maintain love and justice, and wait for your God always The merchant uses dishonest scales and loves to defraud. Ephraim boasts, "I am very rich; I have become wealthy. With all my wealth, they will not find in me any iniquity or sin." "I have been the LORD your God ever since you came out of Egypt; I will make you live in tents again, as in the days of your appointed festivals. I spoke to the prophets, gave them many visions, and told parables through them." Is Gilead wicked? Its people are worthless! Do they sacrifice bulls in Gilgal? Their altars will be like piles of stones on a plowed field. Jacob fled to the country of Aram; Israel served to get a wife, and to pay for her he tended sheep. The LORD used a prophet to bring Israel up from Egypt, by a prophet he cared for him. But Ephraim has aroused his bitter anger; his Lord will leave on him the guilt of his bloodshed and will repay him for his contempt

Chapter 13

When Ephraim spoke, people trembled; he was exalted in Israel. But he became guilty of Baal worship and died. Now they sin more and more; they make idols for themselves from their silver, cleverly fashioned images, all of them the work of craftsmen. It is said of these people, "They offer human sacrifices! They kiss calf-idols!" Therefore they will be like the morning mist, like the early dew that disappears, like chaff swirling from a threshing floor, like smoke escaping through a window But I have been the LORD your God ever since you came out of Egypt. You shall acknowledge no God but me, no Savior except me. I cared for you in the wilderness, in the land of burning heat. When I fed them, they were satisfied; when they were satisfied, they became proud; then they forgot me. So I will be like a lion to them, like a leopard I will lurk by the path. Like a bear robbed of her cubs, I will attack them and rip them open; like a lion, I will devour them—a wild animal will tear them apart You are destroyed, Israel, because you are against me, against your helper. Where is your king, that he may save you? Where are your rulers in all your towns, of whom you said, "Give me a king and princes"? So in my anger, I gave you a king, and in my wrath, I took him away. The guilt of Ephraim is stored up, his sins are kept on record. Pains as of a woman in childbirth come to him, but he is a child without wisdom; when the time arrives, he doesn't have the sense to come out of the womb I will deliver this people from the power of the grave; I will redeem them from death. Where, O death, are your plagues? Where, O grave, is your destruction? I will have no compassion, even though he thrives among his brothers. An east wind from the LORD will come, blowing in from the desert; his spring will fail, and his well will dry up. His storehouse will be plundered of all its treasures

Chapter 14

Samaria will bear her guilt because she has rebelled against her God. They will fall by the sword; their little ones will be dashed to the ground, their pregnant women ripped open." Return, Israel, to the LORD your God. Your sins have been your downfall! Take words with you and return to the LORD. Say to him: "Forgive all our sins and receive us graciously, that we may offer the fruit of our lips. Assyria cannot save us; we will not mount warhorses. We will never again say 'Our gods' to what our own hands have made, for in you the fatherless find compassion." "I will heal their waywardness and love them freely, for my anger has turned away from them. I will be like the dew to Israel; he will blossom like a lily. Like a cedar of Lebanon, he will send down his roots; his young shoots will grow. His splendor will be like an olive tree, his fragrance like a cedar of Lebanon. People will dwell again in his shade; they will flourish like the grain, they will blossom like the vine—Israel's fame will be like the wine of Lebanon. Ephraim, what more have I to do with idols? I will answer him and care for him. I am like a flourishing juniper; your fruitfulness comes from me." Who is wise? Let them realize these things. Who is discerning? Let them understand. The ways of the LORD are right; the righteous walk in them, but the rebellious stumble in them

29. Joel

Chapter 1

The word of the LORD came to Joel, the son of Pethuel. Hear this, you elders, and listen, all inhabitants of the land. Has anything like this happened in your days or in the days of your fathers? Tell your children about it, and let your children tell their children, and their children tell another generation. What the cutting locust left, the swarming locust has eaten; what the swarming locust left, the hopping locust has eaten; and what the hopping locust left, the destroying locust has eaten Awake, you drunkards, and weep; wail, all you wine drinkers, because of the sweet wine, for it is cut off from your mouth. A nation has come up against my land, powerful and without number; its teeth are lion's teeth, and it has the fangs of a lioness. It has laid waste my vine and splintered my fig tree; it has stripped off their bark and thrown it down; their branches are made white Lament like a virgin wearing sackcloth for the bridegroom of her youth. The grain offering and the drink offering are cut off from the house of the LORD. The priests mourn, the ministers of the LORD. The fields are destroyed, the ground mourns, for the grain is destroyed, the wine dries up, and the oil languishes. Be ashamed, O tillers of the soil; wail, O vinedressers, for the wheat and the barley, because the harvest of the field has perished. The vine dries up, the fig tree languishes. Pomegranate, palm, and apple, all the trees of the field are dried up, and gladness dries up from the children of man Put on sackcloth and lament, O priests; wail, O ministers of the altar. Go in, pass the night in sackcloth, O ministers of my God, because grain and drink offerings are withheld from the house of your God. Consecrate a fast; call a solemn assembly. Gather the elders and all the inhabitants of the land to the house of the LORD your God, and cry out to the LORD Alas for the day! For the day of the LORD is near, and as destruction from the Almighty, it comes. Is not the food cut off before our eyes, joy and gladness from the house of our God? The seed shrivels under the clods; the storehouses are desolate; the granaries are torn down because the grain has dried up. How the beasts groan! The herds of cattle are perplexed because there is no pasture for them; even the flocks of sheep suffer To you, O LORD, I call. For fire has devoured the pastures of the wilderness, and flame has burned all the trees of the field. Even the beasts of the field pant for you because the water brooks are dried up, and fire has devoured the pastures of the wilderness

Chapter 2

Blow a trumpet in Zion; sound an alarm on my holy mountain! Let all the inhabitants of the land tremble, for the day of the LORD is coming; it is near, a day of darkness and gloom, a day of clouds and thick darkness! Like blackness spread upon the mountains, a great and powerful people; their like has never been before, nor will be again after them through the years of all generations. Fire devours before them, and behind them a flame burns. The land is like the garden of Eden before them, but behind them, a desolate wilderness, and nothing escapes them Their appearance is like the appearance of horses, and like war horses, they run. As with the rumbling of chariots, they leap on the tops of the mountains, like the crackling of a flame of fire devouring the stubble, like a powerful army drawn up for battle. Before them peoples are in anguish; all faces grow pale. Like warriors, they charge; like soldiers, they scale the wall. Each keeps to his own path; they do not swerve from their courses. They do not jostle one another; each marches in his path; they burst through the weapons and are not halted. They leap upon the city; they run upon the walls; they climb up into the houses; they enter through the windows like a thief. The earth quakes before them; the heavens tremble. The sun and the moon are darkened, and the stars withdraw their shining. The LORD utters his voice before his army, for his camp is exceedingly great. He who executes his word is powerful. For the day of the LORD is great and very awesome; who can endure it? "Yet even now," declares the LORD, "return to me with all your heart, with fasting, with weeping, and with mourning; rend your hearts and not your garments." Return to the LORD your God, for he is gracious and merciful, slow to anger, and abounding in steadfast love, and he relents over disaster. Who knows whether he will not turn and relent and leave a blessing behind him, a grain offering and a drink offering for the LORD your God? Blow the trumpet in Zion; consecrate a fast; call a solemn assembly; gather the people. Consecrate the congregation; assemble the elders; gather the children, even nursing infants. Let the bridegroom leave his room, and the bride her chamber. Between the vestibule and the altar, let the priests, the ministers of the LORD, weep and say, "Spare your people, O LORD, and make not your heritage a reproach, a byword among the nations. Why should they say among the peoples, 'Where is their God?'" Then the LORD became jealous for his land and had pity on his people. The LORD answered and said to his people, "Behold, I am sending to you grain, wine, and oil, and you will be satisfied; and I will no more make you a reproach among the nations. I will remove the northerner far from you and drive him into a parched and desolate land, his vanguard into the eastern sea, and his rear guard into the western sea; the stench and foul smell of him will rise, for he has done great things "Fear not, O land; be glad and rejoice, for the LORD has done great things! Fear not, you beasts of the field, for the pastures of the wilderness are green; the tree bears its fruit; the fig tree and vine give their full yield "Be glad, O children of Zion, and rejoice in the LORD your God, for he has given the early rain for your vindication; he has poured down for you abundant rain, the early and the latter rain, as before. The threshing floors shall be full of grain; the vats shall overflow with wine and oil. I will restore to you the years that the swarming locust has eaten, the hopper, the destroyer, and the cutter, my great army, which I sent among you "You shall eat in plenty and be satisfied, and praise the name of the LORD your God, who has dealt wondrously with you. And my people shall never again be put to shame. You shall know that I am in the midst of Israel, and that I am the LORD your God and there is none else. And my people shall never again be put to shame "And it shall come to pass afterward, that I will pour out my Spirit on all flesh; your sons and your daughters shall prophesy, your old men shall dream dreams, and your young men shall see visions. Even on the male and female servants in those days, I will pour out my Spirit "And I will show wonders in the heavens and on the earth, blood and fire and columns of smoke. The sun shall be turned to darkness, and the moon to blood, before the great and awesome day of the LORD comes. And it shall come to pass that everyone who calls on the name of the LORD shall be saved. For in Mount Zion and in Jerusalem, there shall be those who escape, as the LORD has said, and among the survivors shall be those whom the LORD calls."

Chapter 3
"For behold, in those days and at that time, when I restore the fortunes of Judah and Jerusalem, I will gather all the nations and bring them down to the Valley of Jehoshaphat. And I will enter into judgment with them there, on behalf of my people and my heritage Israel, because they have scattered them among the nations and have divided up my land. They have cast lots for my people and have traded a boy for a prostitute and have sold a girl for wine and have drunk it "What are you to me, O Tyre and Sidon, and all the regions of Philistia? Are you paying me back for something? If you are paying me back, I will return your payment on your own head swiftly and speedily. For you have taken my silver and my gold, and have carried my rich treasures into your temples. You have sold the people of Judah and Jerusalem to the Greeks in order to remove them far from their own border. Behold, I will stir them up from the place to which you have sold them, and I will return your payment on your own head. I will sell your sons and your daughters into the hand of the people of Judah, and they will sell them to the Sabeans, to a nation far away, for the LORD has spoken." Proclaim this among the nations: Consecrate for war; stir up the mighty men. Let all the men of war draw near; let them come up. Beat your plowshares into swords, and your pruning hooks into spears; let the weak say, "I am a warrior." Hasten and come, all you surrounding nations, and gather yourselves there. Bring down your warriors, O LORD Let the nations stir themselves up and come up to the Valley of Jehoshaphat; for there I will sit to judge all the surrounding nations. Put in the sickle, for the harvest is ripe. Go in, tread, for the winepress is full. The vats overflow, for their evil is great Multitudes, multitudes, in the valley of decision! For the day of the LORD is near in the valley of decision. The sun and the moon are darkened, and the stars withdraw their shining. The LORD roars from Zion and utters his voice from Jerusalem, and the heavens and the earth quake. But the LORD is a refuge to his people, a stronghold to the people of Israel "So you shall know that I am the LORD your God, who dwells in Zion, my holy mountain. And Jerusalem shall be holy, and strangers shall never again pass through it "And in that day the mountains shall drip sweet wine, and the hills shall flow with milk, and all the streambeds of Judah shall flow with water, and a fountain shall come forth from the house of the LORD and water the Valley of Shittim "Egypt shall become a desolation and Edom a desolate wilderness, for the violence done to the people of Judah, because they have shed innocent blood in their land. But Judah shall be inhabited forever, and Jerusalem to all generations. I will avenge their blood, blood I have not avenged, for the LORD dwells in Zion."

30. Amos

Chapter 1
The words of Amos, who was among the hearers at Tecoa, which he spoke over Israel in the days of Uzziah, king of Judah, and in the days of Jeroboam, son of Joash, king of Israel, two years before the earthquake. He said, "The Lord will turn away from Zion and turn away His journey from Jerusalem; the shepherds' dwellings will perish, and the top of Carmel will wither away." Thus says the Lord: "For three transgressions of Damascus and for four, I will not turn away from it, because they have threshed Gilead with threshing instruments of iron. Therefore, I will send a fire into the house of Hazael and destroy the palaces of Ben-Hadad. I will also breach the walls of Damascus, cut off the inhabitants of the Valley of Aven, and the one who holds the scepter from Beth-Eden. The people of Aram will go into captivity to Kir," says the Lord Thus says the Lord:

"For three transgressions of Gaza and for four, I will not turn away from it, because they have taken captive the entire population to deliver them up to Edom. Therefore, I will send a fire on the walls of Gaza, which shall devour its palaces. I will cut off the inhabitant from Ashdod, and the one who holds the scepter from Ashkelon. I will turn my hand against Ekron, and the remnant of the Philistines shall perish," says the Lord God Thus says the Lord: "For three transgressions of Tyre and for four, I will not turn away from it, because they delivered up a whole population to Edom and did not remember the brotherly covenant. Therefore, I will send a fire on the walls of Tyre, which shall devour its palaces." Thus says the Lord: "For three transgressions of Edom and for four, I will not turn away from it, because he pursued his brother with the sword and cast off all pity. His anger tore perpetually, and he kept his wrath forever. Therefore, I will send a fire upon Teman, which shall devour the palaces of Bozrah." Thus says the Lord: "For three transgressions of the children of Ammon and for four, I will not turn away from it, because they ripped open the pregnant women of Gilead, that they might enlarge their border. Therefore, I will kindle a fire on the walls of Rabbah, which shall devour its palaces amid shouting in the day of battle, with a tempest in the day of the whirlwind. Their king shall go into captivity, he and his princes together," says the Lord

Chapter 2

Thus says the Lord: "For three transgressions of Moab and for four, I will not turn away from it, because he burned the bones of the king of Edom to lime. Therefore, I will send a fire upon Moab, and it shall devour the palaces of Kerioth. Moab shall die with tumult, with shouting, and with the sound of the trumpet. I will cut off the judge from its midst and slay all its princes with him," says the Lord Thus says the Lord: "For three transgressions of Judah and for four, I will not turn away from it, because they have despised the law of the Lord and have not kept His commandments. Their lies led them astray, lies after which their fathers walked. Therefore, I will send a fire upon Judah, and it shall devour the palaces of Jerusalem." Thus says the Lord: "For three transgressions of Israel and for four, I will not turn away from it, because they sell the righteous for silver and the needy for a pair of sandals. They trample the head of the poor into the dust of the earth and turn aside the way of the afflicted. A man and his father go in to the same girl, so that my holy name is profaned. They lay themselves down beside every altar on garments taken in pledge, and in the house of their God they drink the wine of those who have been fined "Yet it was I who destroyed the Amorite before them, whose height was like the height of the cedars and who was as strong as the oaks. I destroyed his fruit above and his roots beneath. Also, it was I who brought you up out of the land of Egypt and led you forty years in the wilderness, to possess the land of the Amorite. I raised up some of your sons for prophets and some of your young men for Nazirites. Is it not indeed so, O children of Israel?" declares the Lord "But you made the Nazirites drink wine and commanded the prophets, saying, 'You shall not prophesy.' Behold, I will press you down in your place, as a cart full of sheaves presses down. Flight shall perish from the swift, and the strong shall not retain his strength, nor shall the mighty save his life. He who handles the bow shall not stand, and he who is swift of foot shall not save himself, nor shall he who rides the horse save his life. He who is stout of heart among the mighty shall flee away naked in that day," declares the Lord

Chapter 3

Hear this word that the Lord has spoken against you, O children of Israel, against the whole family that I brought up out of the land of Egypt: "You only have I known of all the families of the earth; therefore, I will punish you for all your iniquities. Can two walk together, except they be agreed? Will a lion roar in the forest when he has no prey? Will a young lion cry out of his den if he has caught nothing? Can a bird fall in a snare upon the earth, where no trap is set for him? Shall one take up a snare from the earth, and have taken nothing at all? Shall a trumpet be blown in the city, and the people not be afraid? Shall there be evil in a city, and the Lord has not done it? Surely the Lord God does nothing unless He reveals His secret to His servants the prophets. The lion has roared; who will not fear? The Lord God has spoken; who can but prophesy? Proclaim in the palaces at Ashdod and in the palaces in the land of Egypt, and say, 'Assemble yourselves on the mountains of Samaria and see the great tumults within her and the oppressed in her midst.' They do not know how to do right," says the Lord, "those who store up violence and robbery in their palaces." Therefore, thus says the Lord God, "An adversary shall surround the land; he shall sap your strength from you, and your palaces shall be plundered." Thus says the Lord, "As a shepherd rescues from the mouth of the lion two legs, or a piece of an ear, so shall the children of Israel who dwell in Samaria be rescued, with the corner of a bed and the end of a couch." Hear and testify against the house of Jacob," declares the Lord God, the God of hosts, "that in the day I punish Israel for his transgressions, I will also punish the altars of Bethel. The horns of the altar shall be cut off and fall to the ground. I will strike the winter house along with the summer house, and the houses of ivory shall perish, and the great houses shall come to an end," declares the Lord

Chapter 4

Hear this word, you cows of Bashan who are on the mountain of Samaria, who oppress the poor and crush the needy, who say to your husbands, 'Bring wine, let us drink!' The Lord God has sworn by His holiness that behold, the days shall come upon you when He will take you away with fishhooks, and your posterity with fishhooks. You shall go out through broken walls, each one straight ahead of her, and you shall be cast into Harmon," says the Lord "Come to Bethel and transgress, to Gilgal and multiply transgression; bring your sacrifices every morning, your tithes every three days. Offer a sacrifice of thanksgiving with leaven, proclaim and publish the free offerings; for this you love, O children of Israel!" declares the Lord God "I also gave you cleanness of teeth in all your cities and lack of bread in all your places, yet you did not return to Me," declares the Lord. "I also withheld rain from you when there were still three months to the harvest. I made it rain on one city, I withheld rain from another city. One part was rained upon, and where it did not rain, the part withered. So, two or three cities wandered to another city to drink water, but they were not satisfied, yet you did not return to Me," declares the Lord "I blasted you with blight and mildew; when your gardens increased, your vineyards, your fig trees, and your olive trees, the locust devoured them. Yet you did not return to Me," declares the Lord. "I sent among you a pestilence after the manner of Egypt; I killed your young men with the sword, and carried away your horses; I made the stench of your camps come up into your nostrils, yet you did not return to Me," declares the Lord "I overthrew some of you, as God overthrew Sodom and Gomorrah, and you were like a brand plucked out of the burning, yet you did not return to Me," declares the Lord. "Therefore thus will I do to you, O Israel; because I will do this to you, prepare to meet your God, O Israel! For behold, He who forms mountains, creates the wind, and declares to man what his thought is, who makes the morning darkness, and treads the high places of the earth—the Lord God of hosts is His name."

Chapter 5

Hear this word which I take up against you, a lamentation, O house of Israel: The virgin of Israel has fallen; she will rise no more. She lies forsaken on her land; there is no one to raise her up. For thus says the Lord God: "The city that goes out by a thousand shall have a hundred left, and that which goes out by a hundred shall have ten left to the house of Israel." For thus says the Lord to the house of Israel: "Seek Me and live; but do not seek Bethel, nor enter Gilgal, nor pass over to Beersheba; for Gilgal shall surely go into captivity, and Bethel shall come to nothing. Seek the Lord and live, lest He break out like fire in the house of Joseph, and devour it, with no one to quench it in Bethel—you who turn justice to wormwood, and lay righteousness to rest in the earth!" He made the Pleiades and Orion; He turns the shadow of death into morning and makes the day dark as night; He calls for the waters of the sea and pours them out on the face of the earth. The Lord is His name. He rains ruin upon the strong, so that fury comes upon the fortress They hate the one who rebukes in the gate, and they abhor the one who speaks uprightly. Therefore, because you tread down the poor and take grain taxes from him, though you have built houses of hewn stone, you shall not dwell in them; you have planted pleasant vineyards, but you shall not drink wine from them. For I know your manifold transgressions and your mighty sins: afflicting the just and taking bribes; diverting the poor from justice at the gate Therefore the prudent keep silent at that time, for it is an evil time. Seek good and not evil, that you may live; so the Lord God of hosts will be with you, as you have spoken. Hate evil, love good; establish justice in the gate. It may be that the Lord God of hosts will be gracious to the remnant of Joseph. Therefore, thus says the Lord God of hosts, the Lord: "There shall be wailing in all streets, and they shall say in all the highways, 'Alas! Alas!' They shall call the farmer to mourning, and skillful lamenters to wailing. In all vineyards there shall be wailing, for I will pass through you," says the Lord Woe to you who desire the day of the Lord! For what good is the day of the Lord to you? It will be darkness, and not light. It will be as though a man fled from a lion, and a bear met him! Or as though he went into the house, leaned his hand on the wall, and a serpent bit him! Is not the day of the Lord darkness, and not light? Is it not very dark, with no brightness in it? "I hate, I despise your feast days, and I do not savor your sacred assemblies. Though you offer Me burnt offerings and your grain offerings, I will not accept them, nor will I regard your fattened peace offerings. Take away from Me the noise of your songs, for I will not hear the melody of your stringed instruments. But let justice run down like water, and righteousness like a mighty stream "Did you offer Me sacrifices and offerings in the wilderness forty years, O house of Israel? You also carried Sikkuth your king and Chiun, your idols, the star of your gods, which you made for yourselves. Therefore I will send you into captivity beyond Damascus," says the Lord, whose name is the God of hosts

Chapter 6

Woe to those who sit idle in Zion and trust in the mountain of Samaria, which were notable in the beginning of the nations, to whom the house of Israel came. Go to Calneh and see; from there go to Hamath the great, and then go down to Gath of the Philistines. Are they better than these kingdoms, or is their territory greater than yours? You who put off the day of disaster and bring near the seat of violence. They lie on beds of ivory, stretch themselves out on their couches, and eat lambs from the flock and calves from the stall. They sing idly to the sound of stringed instruments and invent for themselves musical instruments like David. They drink wine by the bowlful and anoint themselves with the finest oils, but they are not grieved for the affliction of Joseph. Therefore, they shall now go into captivity as the first of the captives, and the revelry of those who stretch themselves out shall pass away The Lord God has sworn by Himself, says the Lord God of hosts: "I abhor the pride of Jacob and hate his palaces; therefore, I will deliver up the city and all that is in it." If ten men remain in one house, they shall die. And when a relative of the dead, with one who will burn the bodies, picks them up to take them out of the house, he will say to the one inside the house, "Is anyone with you?" And that one will say, "No." Then he will say, "Hold your tongue! For we dare not mention the name of the Lord." For behold, the Lord gives a command: He will break the great house into bits and the little house into pieces. Do horses run on rocks? Does one plow there with oxen? Yet you have turned justice into gall and the fruit of righteousness into wormwood. You who rejoice over Lo Debar, who say, "Have we not taken Karnaim by our own strength?" But behold, I will raise up a nation against you, O house of Israel," says the Lord God of hosts, "and they will afflict you from the entrance of Hamath to the Valley of the Arabah."

Chapter 7

Thus the Lord God showed me: behold, He formed locust swarms at the beginning of the late crop; indeed, it was the late crop after the king's mowings. And so it was, when they had finished eating the grass of the land, that I said: "O Lord God, forgive, I pray! Oh, that Jacob may stand, for he is small!" So the Lord relented concerning this. "It shall not be," said the Lord Thus the Lord God showed me: behold, the Lord God called for conflict by fire, and it consumed the great deep and devoured the territory. Then I said: "O Lord God, cease, I pray! Oh, that Jacob may stand, for he is small!" So the Lord relented concerning this. "This also shall not be," said the Lord God Thus He showed me: behold, the Lord stood on a wall made with a plumb line, with a plumb line in His hand. And the Lord said to me, "Amos, what do you see?" And I said, "A plumb line." Then the Lord said: "Behold, I am setting a plumb line in the midst of My people Israel; I will not pass by them anymore. The high places of Isaac shall be desolate, and the sanctuaries of Israel shall be laid waste. I will rise with the sword against the house of Jeroboam." Then Amaziah the priest of Bethel sent to Jeroboam king of Israel, saying, "Amos has conspired against you in the midst of the house of Israel. The land is not able to bear all his words. For thus Amos has said: 'Jeroboam shall die by the sword, and Israel shall surely be led away captive from their own land.'" Then Amaziah said to Amos: "Go, you seer! Flee to the land of Judah. There eat bread, and there prophesy. But never again prophesy at Bethel, for it is the king's sanctuary, and it is the royal residence." Then Amos answered and said to Amaziah: "I was no prophet, nor was I a son of a prophet, but I was a sheepbreeder and a tender of sycamore fruit. Then the Lord took me as I followed the flock, and the Lord said to me, 'Go, prophesy to My people Israel.' Now therefore, hear the word of the Lord: You say, 'Do not prophesy against Israel, and do not spout against the house of Isaac.' Therefore thus says the Lord: 'Your wife shall be a harlot in the city; your sons and daughters shall fall by the sword; your land shall be divided by survey line; you shall die in a defiled land; and Israel shall surely be led away captive from his own land.'"

Chapter 8

Thus the Lord God showed me: behold, a basket of summer fruit. And He said, "Amos, what do you see?" So I said, "A basket of summer fruit." Then the Lord said to me: "The end has come upon My people Israel; I will not pass by them anymore. And the songs of the temple shall be wailing in that day," says the Lord God—"Many dead bodies everywhere, they shall be thrown out in silence." Hear this, you who swallow up the needy, and make the poor of the land fail, saying: "When will the New Moon be past, that we may sell grain? And the Sabbath, that we may trade wheat? Making the ephah small and the shekel large, falsifying the scales by deceit, that we may buy the poor for silver, and the needy for a pair of sandals— even sell the bad wheat?" The Lord has sworn by the pride of Jacob: "Surely I will never forget any of their works. Shall the land not tremble for this, and everyone mourn who dwells in it? All of it shall swell like the River, Heave and subside like the River of Egypt "And it shall come to pass in that day," says the Lord God, "That I will make the sun go down at noon, and I will darken the earth in broad daylight; I will turn your feasts into mourning, and all your songs into lamentation; I will bring sackcloth on every waist, and baldness on every head; I will make it like mourning for an only son, and its end like a bitter day "Behold, the days are coming," says the Lord God, "That I will send a famine on the land, not a famine of bread, nor a thirst for water, but of hearing the words of the Lord. They shall wander from sea to sea, and from north to east; they shall run to and fro, seeking the word of the Lord, but shall not find it. In that day the fair virgins and strong young men shall faint from thirst. Those who swear by the sin of Samaria, who say, 'As your god lives, O Dan!' And, 'As the way of Beersheba lives!' They shall fall and never rise again."

Chapter 9

I saw the Lord standing by the altar, and He said: "Strike the doorposts, that the thresholds may shake, and break them on the heads of them all. I will slay the last of them with the sword. He who flees from them shall not get away, and he who escapes from them shall not be delivered. Though they dig into hell, from there My hand shall take them; though they climb up to heaven, from there I will bring them down; and though they hide themselves on top of Carmel, from there I will search and take them; though they hide from My sight at the bottom of the sea, from there I will command the serpent, and it shall bite them; though they go into captivity before their enemies, from there I will command the sword, and it shall slay them. I will set My eyes on them for harm and not for good." The Lord God of hosts, He who touches the earth and it melts, and all who dwell there mourn; all of it shall swell like the River, and subside like the River of Egypt. He who builds His layers in the sky, and has founded His strata in the earth; who calls for the waters of the sea, and pours them out on the face of the earth—the Lord is His name "Are you not like the people of Ethiopia to Me, O children of Israel?" says the Lord. "Did I not bring up Israel from the land of Egypt, the Philistines from Caphtor, and the Syrians from Kir? Behold, the eyes of the Lord God are on the sinful kingdom, and I will destroy it from the face of the earth; yet I will not utterly destroy the house of Jacob," says the Lord "For surely I will command, and will sift the house of Israel among all nations, as grain is sifted in a sieve; yet not the smallest grain shall fall to the ground. All the sinners of My people shall die by the sword, who say, 'The calamity shall not overtake nor confront us.' "On that day I will raise up the tabernacle of David, which has fallen down, and repair its damages; I will raise up its ruins, and rebuild it as in the days of old; that they may possess the remnant of Edom, and all the Gentiles who are called by My name," says the Lord who does this thing "Behold, the days are coming," says the Lord, "When the plowman shall overtake the reaper, and the treader of grapes him who sows seed; the mountains shall drip with sweet wine, and all the hills shall flow with it. I will bring back the captives of My people Israel; they shall build the waste cities and inhabit them; they shall plant vineyards and drink wine from them; they shall also make gardens and eat fruit from them. I will plant them in their land, and no longer shall they be pulled up from the land I have given them," says the Lord your God

31. Obadiah

Chapter 1

The vision of Obadiah. Thus says the LORD God concerning Edom: "We have heard a report from the LORD, and an envoy has been sent among the nations: 'Arise, and let us rise up against her for battle!' Behold, I will make you small among the nations; you are greatly despised. The pride of your heart has deceived you, you who dwell in the clefts of the rock, whose habitation is high; you who say in your heart, 'Who will bring me down to the ground?' Though you ascend as high as the eagle, and though you set your nest among the stars, from there I will bring you down," says the LORD "If thieves had come to you, if robbers by night—Oh, how you will be cut off!—Would they not have stolen till they had enough? If grape-gatherers had come to you, would they not have left some gleanings? Oh, how Esau shall be searched out! How his hidden treasures shall be sought after! All the men in your confederacy shall force you to the border; the men at peace with you shall deceive you and prevail against you. Those who eat your bread shall lay a trap for you. There is no understanding in him Will I not in that day," says the LORD, "even destroy the wise men from Edom, and understanding from the mountains of Esau? Then your mighty men, O Teman, shall be dismayed, to the end that everyone from the mountains of Esau may be cut off by slaughter. For violence against your brother Jacob, shame shall cover you, and you shall be cut off forever. In the day that you stood on the other side—in the day that strangers carried captive his forces, when foreigners entered his gates and cast lots for Jerusalem—even you were as one of them But you should not have gazed on the day of your brother in the day of his captivity; nor should you have rejoiced over the children of Judah in the day of their destruction; nor should you have spoken proudly in the day of distress. You should not have entered the gate of My people in the day of their calamity. Indeed, you should not have gazed on their affliction in the day of their calamity, nor laid hands on their substance in the day of their calamity. You should not have stood at the crossroads to cut off those among them who escaped; nor should you have delivered up those among them who remained in the day of distress For the day of the LORD upon all the nations is near; as you have done, it shall be done to you; your reprisal shall return upon your own head. For as you drank on My holy mountain, so shall all the nations drink continually; yes, they shall drink and swallow, and they shall be as though they had never been. But on Mount Zion there shall be deliverance, and there shall be holiness; the house of Jacob shall possess their possessions. The house of Jacob shall be a fire, and the house of Joseph a flame; but the house of Esau shall be stubble. They shall kindle them and devour them, and no survivor shall remain of the house of Esau," for the LORD has spoken The South shall possess the mountains of Esau, and the lowland shall possess Philistia. They shall possess the fields of Ephraim and the fields of Samaria. Benjamin shall possess Gilead. And the captives of this host of the children of Israel shall possess the land of the Canaanites as far as Zarephath. The captives of Jerusalem who are in Sepharad shall possess the cities of the South. Then saviors shall come to Mount Zion to judge the mountains of Esau, and the kingdom shall be the LORD's

32. Jonah

CHAPTER 1
The word of the LORD came to Jonah, the son of Amittai, saying, "Arise, go to Nineveh, that great city, and cry out against it, for their wickedness has come up before me." But Jonah arose to flee to Tarshish from the presence of the LORD. He went down to Joppa, found a ship going to Tarshish, paid the fare, and went aboard to go with them to Tarshish, away from the presence of the LORD The LORD sent a great wind on the sea, and there was a mighty storm, so that the ship was about to break up. The sailors were afraid, and each cried out to his god. They threw the cargo into the sea to lighten the ship. But Jonah had gone below deck, where he lay down and fell into a deep sleep. The captain came to him and said, "What do you mean, sleeper? Arise, call upon your God. Perhaps your God will consider us, so that we may not perish." The sailors said to one another, "Come, let us cast lots to find out who is responsible for this calamity." They cast lots, and the lot fell on Jonah. They asked him, "Tell us, who is responsible for making all this trouble for us? What do you do? Where do you come from? What is your country? From what people are you?" He answered, "I am a Hebrew, and I fear the LORD, the God of heaven, who made the sea and the dry land." The men were greatly afraid and asked him, "Why have you done this?" (For they knew he was fleeing from the presence of the LORD, because he had told them so.) They asked him, "What shall we do to you to calm the sea?" (For the sea was growing more tempestuous.) He replied, "Pick me up and throw me into the sea, and it will become calm. I know that it is because of me that this great storm has come upon you." Nevertheless, the men rowed hard to return to land, but they could not, for the sea grew even more tempestuous against them They cried out to the LORD, "We beseech you, O LORD, let us not perish for this man's life, and do not hold us accountable for innocent blood, for you, O LORD, have done as it pleased you." They took Jonah and threw him overboard, and the sea grew calm. The men greatly feared the LORD, and they offered sacrifices to the LORD and made vows Now the LORD had prepared a great fish to swallow Jonah. Jonah was in the belly of the fish three days and three nights

CHAPTER 2
Then Jonah prayed to the LORD his God from the belly of the fish, saying, "I cried out to the LORD in my distress, and He answered me. From deep in the realm of the dead I called for help, and you listened to my cry. You cast me into the deep, into the heart of the seas, and the currents swirled about me; all your waves and breakers swept over me. I said, 'I have been banished from your sight; yet I will look again toward your holy temple.' The engulfing waters threatened me, the deep surrounded me; seaweed was wrapped around my head. To the roots of the mountains I sank down; the earth beneath barred me in forever. But you, LORD my God, brought my life up from the pit When my life was ebbing away, I remembered you, LORD, and my prayer rose to you, to your holy temple. Those who cling to worthless idols turn away from God's love for them. But I, with shouts of grateful praise, will sacrifice to you. What I have vowed I will make good. I will say, 'Salvation comes from the LORD.'" And the LORD commanded the fish, and it vomited Jonah onto dry land

CHAPTER 3
The word of the LORD came to Jonah a second time: "Go to the great city of Nineveh and proclaim to it the message I give you." Jonah obeyed the word of the LORD and went to Nineveh. Now Nineveh was a very large city; it took three days to go through it. Jonah began by going a day's journey into the city, proclaiming, "Forty more days and Nineveh will be overthrown." The Ninevites believed God. A fast was proclaimed, and all of them, from the greatest to the least, put on sackcloth When Jonah's warning reached the king of Nineveh, he rose from his throne, took off his royal robes, covered himself with sackcloth, and sat down in the dust. This is the proclamation he issued in Nineveh: "By the decree of the king and his nobles: Do not let people or animals, herds or flocks, taste anything; do not let them eat or drink. But let people and animals be covered with sackcloth. Let everyone call urgently on God. Let them give up their evil ways and their violence. Who knows? God may yet relent and with compassion turn from his fierce anger so that we will not perish." When God saw what they did and how they turned from their evil ways, he relented and did not bring on them the destruction he had threatened

CHAPTER 4
But to Jonah, this seemed very wrong, and he became angry. He prayed to the LORD, "Isn't this what I said, LORD, when I was still at home? That is what I tried to forestall by fleeing to Tarshish. I knew that you are a gracious and compassionate God, slow to anger and abounding in love, a God who relents from sending calamity. Now, LORD, take away my life, for it is better for me to die than to live." But the LORD replied, "Is it right for you to be angry?" Jonah had gone out and sat down at a place east of the city. There he made himself a shelter, sat in its shade, and waited to see what would happen to the city. Then the LORD God provided a leafy plant and made it grow up over Jonah to give shade for his head to ease his discomfort, and Jonah was very happy about the plant. But at dawn the next day, God provided a worm, which chewed the plant so that it withered. When the sun rose, God provided a scorching east wind, and the sun blazed on Jonah's head so that he grew faint. He wanted to die and said, "It would be better for me to die than to live." But God said to Jonah, "Is it right for you to be angry about the plant?" "It is," he said. "And I'm so angry I wish I were dead." But the LORD said, "You have been concerned about this plant, though you did not tend it or make it grow. It sprang up overnight and died overnight. And should I not have concern for the great city of Nineveh, in which there are more than a hundred and twenty thousand people who cannot tell their right hand from their left—and also many animals?"

33. Micah

CHAPTER 1
The word of the LORD came to Micah the Morashite during the days of Jotham, Ahaz, and Hezekiah, kings of Judah, and he spoke concerning Samaria and Jerusalem. "Hear, you peoples, all of you; listen,

earth and all who are in it, that the Sovereign LORD may bear witness against you, the Lord from his holy temple. For behold, the LORD is coming out of his place, he descends and treads on the high places of the earth. The mountains melt beneath him and the valleys split apart, like wax before the fire, like water rushing down a slope. All this is because of the transgression of Jacob and the sins of the house of Israel. What is Jacob's transgression? Is it not Samaria? What is Judah's high place? Is it not Jerusalem? Therefore, I will make Samaria a heap of rubble, a place for planting vineyards. I will pour her stones into the valley and lay bare her foundations. All her idols will be broken to pieces; all her temple gifts will be burned with fire; I will destroy all her images. Since she collected them as the wages of a prostitute, as the wages of a prostitute they will again be used." Because of this, I will weep and wail; I will go about barefoot and naked. I will howl like a jackal and moan like an owl, for Samaria's plague is incurable. It has spread to Judah. It has reached the very gate of my people, even to Jerusalem itself Do not tell it in Gath; do not weep at all. In Beth Ophrah, roll in the dust. Pass by naked and in shame, you who live in Shaphir. Those who live in Zaanan will not come out. Beth Ezel is in mourning; its protection is taken from you. Those who live in Maroth writhe in pain, waiting for relief because disaster has come from the LORD, even to the gate of Jerusalem. You who live in Lachish, harness fast horses to the chariot. You were the beginning of sin to Daughter Zion, for the transgressions of Israel were found in you. Therefore, you will give parting gifts to Moresheth Gath. The town of Akzib will prove deceptive to the kings of Israel. I will bring a conqueror against you who live in Mareshah. The nobles of Israel will flee to Adullam. Shave your heads in mourning for the children in whom you delight; make yourselves as bald as the vulture, for they will go from you into exile

CHAPTER 2

Woe to those who plan iniquity, to those who plot evil on their beds! At morning's light they carry it out because it is in their power to do it. They covet fields and seize them, and houses and take them. They defraud people of their homes; they rob them of their inheritance. Therefore, the LORD says: "I am planning disaster against this people, from which you cannot save yourselves. You will no longer walk proudly, for it will be a time of calamity. In that day people will ridicule you; they will taunt you with this mournful song: 'We are utterly ruined; my people's possession is divided up. He takes it from me! He assigns our fields to traitors.' Therefore, you will have no one in the assembly of the LORD to divide the land by lot Do not prophesy," their prophets say. "Do not prophesy about these things; disgrace will not overtake us." You descendants of Jacob, should it be said, "Does the LORD become impatient? Does he do such things?" Do not my words do good to the one whose ways are upright? Lately my people have risen up like an enemy. You strip off the rich robe from those who pass by without a care, like men returning from battle. You drive the women of my people from their pleasant homes. You take away my blessing from their children forever. Get up, go away! For this is not your resting place, because it is defiled, it is ruined, beyond all remedy. If a liar and deceiver comes and says, 'I will prophesy for you plenty of wine and beer,' that would be just the prophet for this people! I will surely gather all of you, Jacob; I will surely bring together the remnant of Israel. I will bring them together like sheep in a pen, like a flock in its pasture; the place will throng with people. The One who breaks open the way will go up before them; they will break through the gate and go out. Their King will pass through before them, the LORD at their head

CHAPTER 3

Then I said, "Listen, you leaders of Jacob, you rulers of Israel. Should you not embrace justice, you who hate good and love evil; who tear the skin from my people and the flesh from their bones; who eat my people's flesh, strip off their skin, break their bones in pieces, chop them up like meat for the pan, like flesh for the pot?" Then they will cry out to the LORD, but he will not answer them. At that time he will hide his face from them because of the evil they have done This is what the LORD says: "As for the prophets who lead my people astray, they proclaim 'peace' if they have something to eat, but prepare to wage war against anyone who refuses to feed them. Therefore night will come over you, without visions, and darkness, without divination. The sun will set for the prophets, and the day will go dark for them. The seers will be ashamed and the diviners disgraced. They will all cover their faces because there is no answer from God." But as for me, I am filled with power, with the Spirit of the LORD, and with justice and might, to declare to Jacob his transgression, to Israel his sin Hear this, you leaders of Jacob, you rulers of Israel, who despise justice and distort all that is right; who build Zion with bloodshed and Jerusalem with wickedness. Her leaders judge for a bribe, her priests teach for a price, and her prophets tell fortunes for money. Yet they look for the LORD's support and say, "Is not the LORD among us? No disaster will come upon us." Therefore because of you, Zion will be plowed like a field, Jerusalem will become a heap of rubble, the temple hill a mound overgrown with thickets

CHAPTER 4

In the last days, the mountain of the LORD's temple will be established as the highest of the mountains; it will be exalted above the hills, and peoples will stream to it. Many nations will come and say, "Come, let us go up to the mountain of the LORD, to the temple of the God of Jacob. He will teach us his ways so that we may walk in his paths." The law will go out from Zion, the word of the LORD from Jerusalem. He will judge between many peoples and will settle disputes for strong nations far and wide. They will beat their swords into plowshares and their spears into pruning hooks. Nation will not take up sword against nation, nor will they train for war anymore. Everyone will sit under their own vine and under their own fig tree, and no one will make them afraid, for the LORD Almighty has spoken All the nations may walk in the name of their gods, but we will walk in the name of the LORD our God for ever and ever. "In that day," declares the LORD, "I will gather the lame; I will assemble the exiles and those I have brought to grief. I will make the lame my remnant, those driven away a strong nation. The LORD will rule over them in Mount Zion from that day and forever. As for you, watchtower of the flock, stronghold of Daughter Zion, the former dominion will be restored to you; kingship will come to Daughter Jerusalem." Why do you now cry aloud—have you no king? Has your ruler perished, that pain seizes you like that of a woman in labor? Writhe in agony, Daughter Zion, like a woman in labor, for now you must leave the city to camp in the open field. You will go to Babylon; there you will be rescued. There the LORD will redeem you out of the hand of your enemies. But now many nations are gathered against you. They say, "Let her be defiled, let our eyes gloat over Zion!" But they do not know the thoughts of the LORD; they do not understand his plan, that he has gathered them like sheaves to the threshing floor. "Rise and thresh, Daughter Zion, for I will give you horns of iron; I will give you hooves of bronze and you will break to pieces many nations." You will devote their ill-gotten gains to the LORD, their wealth to the LORD of all the earth

CHAPTER 5

Marshal your troops now, city of troops, for a siege is laid against us. They will strike Israel's ruler on the cheek with a rod. But you, Bethlehem Ephrathah, though you are small among the clans of Judah, out of you will come for me one who will be ruler over Israel, whose origins are from of old, from ancient times. Therefore Israel will be abandoned until the time when she who is in labor bears a son, and the rest of his brothers return to join the Israelites. He will stand and shepherd his flock in the strength of the LORD, in the majesty of the name of the LORD his God. And they will live securely, for then his greatness will reach to the ends of the earth. And he will be our peace when the Assyrians invade our land and march through our fortresses. We will raise against them seven shepherds, even eight commanders, who will rule the land of Assyria with the sword, the land of Nimrod with drawn sword. He will deliver us from the Assyrians when they invade our land and march across our borders The remnant of Jacob will be in the midst of many peoples like dew from the LORD, like showers on the grass, which do not wait for anyone or depend on man. The remnant of Jacob will be among the nations, in the midst of many peoples, like a lion among the beasts of the forest, like a young lion among flocks of sheep, which mauls and mangles as it goes, and no one can rescue. Your hand will be lifted up in triumph over your enemies, and all your foes will be destroyed "In that day," declares the LORD, "I will destroy your horses from among you and demolish your chariots. I will destroy the cities of your land and tear down all your strongholds. I will destroy your witchcraft and you will no longer cast spells. I will destroy your idols and your sacred stones from among you; you will no longer bow down to the work of your hands. I will uproot from among you your Asherah poles when I demolish your cities. I will take vengeance in anger and wrath on the nations that have not obeyed me."

CHAPTER 6

Listen to what the LORD says: "Stand up, plead my case before the mountains; let the hills hear what you have to say. Hear, you mountains, the LORD's accusation; listen, you everlasting foundations of the earth. For the LORD has a case against his people; he is lodging a charge against Israel "My people, what have I done to you? How have I burdened you? Answer me. I brought you up out of Egypt and redeemed you from the land of slavery. I sent Moses to lead you, also Aaron and Miriam. My people, remember what Balak king of Moab plotted and what Balaam son of Beor answered. Remember your journey from Shittim to Gilgal, that you may know the righteous acts of the LORD." With what shall I come before the LORD and bow down before the exalted God? Shall I come before him with burnt offerings, with calves a year old? Will the LORD be pleased with thousands of rams, with ten thousand rivers of olive oil? Shall I offer my firstborn for my transgression, the fruit of my body for the sin of my soul? He has shown you, O mortal, what is good. And what does the LORD require of you? To act justly and to love mercy and to walk humbly with your God Listen! The LORD is calling to the city—and to fear your name is wisdom—"Heed the rod and the One who appointed it. Am I still to forget your ill-gotten treasures, you wicked house, and the short ephah, which is accursed? Shall I acquit someone with dishonest scales, with a bag of false weights? Your rich people are violent; your inhabitants are liars and their tongues speak deceitfully. Therefore, I have

begun to destroy you, to ruin you because of your sins. You will eat but not be satisfied; your stomach will still be empty. You will store up but save nothing, because what you save I will give to the sword. You will plant but not harvest; you will press olives but not use the oil; you will crush grapes but not drink the wine. You have observed the statutes of Omri and all the practices of Ahab's house; you have followed their traditions. Therefore, I will give you over to ruin and your people to derision; you will bear the scorn of the nations."

CHAPTER 7

What misery is mine! I am like one who gathers summer fruit at the gleaning of the vineyard; there is no cluster of grapes to eat, none of the early figs that I crave. The faithful have been swept from the land; not one upright person remains. Everyone lies in wait to shed blood; they hunt each other with nets. Both hands are skilled in doing evil; the ruler demands gifts, the judge accepts bribes, the powerful dictate what they desire—they all conspire together. The best of them is like a brier, the most upright worse than a thorn hedge. The day God visits you has come, the day your watchmen sound the alarm. Now is the time of your confusion. Do not trust a neighbor; put no confidence in a friend. Even with the woman who lies in your embrace guard the words of your lips. For a son dishonors his father, a daughter rises up against her mother, a daughter-in-law against her mother-in-law—a man's enemies are the members of his own household But as for me, I watch in hope for the LORD, I wait for God my Savior; my God will hear me. Do not gloat over me, my enemy! Though I have fallen, I will rise. Though I sit in darkness, the LORD will be my light. Because I have sinned against him, I will bear the LORD's wrath, until he pleads my case and upholds my cause. He will bring me out into the light; I will see his righteousness. Then my enemy will see it and will be covered with shame, she who said to me, "Where is the LORD your God?" My eyes will see her downfall; even now she will be trampled underfoot like mire in the streets The day for building your walls will come, the day for extending your boundaries. In that day people will come to you from Assyria and the cities of Egypt, even from Egypt to the Euphrates and from sea to sea and from mountain to mountain. The earth will become desolate because of its inhabitants, as the result of their deeds Shepherd your people with your staff, the flock of your inheritance, which lives by itself in a forest, in fertile pasturelands. Let them feed in Bashan and Gilead as in days long ago. "As in the days when you came out of Egypt, I will show them my wonders." Nations will see and be ashamed, deprived of all their power. They will put their hands over their mouths and their ears will become deaf. They will lick dust like a snake, like creatures that crawl on the ground. They will come trembling out of their dens; they will turn in fear to the LORD our God and will be afraid of you. Who is a God like you, who pardons sin and forgives the transgression of the remnant of his inheritance? You do not stay angry forever but delight to show mercy. You will again have compassion on us; you will tread our sins underfoot and hurl all our iniquities into the depths of the sea. You will be faithful to Jacob and show love to Abraham, as you pledged on oath to our ancestors in days long ago

34. Nahum

CHAPTER 1

The burden of Nineveh. The book of the vision of Nahum the Elkoshite. God is jealous, and the LORD avenges; the LORD takes vengeance on his adversaries and reserves wrath for his enemies. The

LORD is slow to anger but great in power; He will not leave the guilty unpunished. His way is in the whirlwind and the storm, and the clouds are the dust of his feet. He rebukes the sea and dries it up; He makes all the rivers run dry. Bashan and Carmel wither, and the blossoms of Lebanon fade. The mountains quake before him and the hills melt away. The earth trembles at his presence, the world and all who live in it. Who can withstand his indignation? Who can endure his fierce anger? His wrath is poured out like fire; the rocks are shattered before him The LORD is good, a refuge in times of trouble. He cares for those who trust in him, but with an overwhelming flood, He will make an end of Nineveh; He will pursue his foes into the realm of darkness. Whatever they plot against the LORD, He will bring to an end; trouble will not come a second time. They will be entangled among thorns and drunk from their wine; they will be consumed like dry stubble. From you, Nineveh, has one come forth who plots evil against the LORD and devises wicked plans. This is what the LORD says: "Although they have allies and are numerous, they will be destroyed and pass away. Although I have afflicted you, Judah, I will afflict you no more. Now I will break their yoke from your neck and tear your shackles away." The LORD has given a command concerning you, Nineveh: "You will have no descendants to bear your name. I will destroy the images and idols that are in the temple of your gods. I will prepare your grave, for you are vile."Look, there on the mountains, the feet of one who brings good news, who proclaims peace! Celebrate your festivals, Judah, and fulfill your vows. No more will the wicked invade you; they will be completely destroyed

CHAPTER 2

The destroyer has come up against your face. Guard the ramparts, watch the road, strengthen your flanks, fortify your power mightily. For the LORD will restore the excellence of Jacob, like the excellence of Israel. The ravagers have ravaged them and ruined their vine branches. The shields of his mighty men are made red, the valiant men are in scarlet. The chariots come with flaming torches in the day of his preparation, and the spears are brandished. The chariots rage in the streets, they jostle one another in the broad roads; they seem like torches, they run like lightning He remembers his nobles; they stumble in their walk; they make haste to her walls, and the defense is prepared. The gates of the rivers are opened, and the palace is dissolved. It is decreed: she shall be led away captive, her maidservants shall lead her as with the voice of doves, beating their breasts. Though Nineveh was like a pool of water throughout her days, now they flee away. "Halt! Halt!" they cry; but no one turns back. Take spoil of silver! Take spoil of gold! There is no end of treasure, or wealth of every desirable prize. She is empty, desolate, and waste! The heart melts, the knees shake, much pain is in every side, and all their faces are drained of color Where is the dwelling of the lions, and the feeding place of the young lions, where the lion walked, the lioness and lion's cub, and no one made them afraid? The lion tore in pieces enough for his cubs, killed for his lionesses, filled his caves with prey, and his dens with flesh. "Behold, I am against you," says the LORD of hosts, "I will burn your chariots in smoke, and the sword shall devour your young lions; I will cut off your prey from the earth, and the voice of your messengers shall be heard no more."

CHAPTER 3

Woe to the bloody city! It is full of lies and robbery. Its victim never departs. The noise of a whip and the noise of rattling wheels, of galloping horses, of clattering chariots! Horsemen charge with bright sword and glittering spear. There is a multitude of slain, a great number of bodies, countless corpses—they stumble over the corpses—because of the multitude of harlotries of the seductive harlot, the mistress of sorceries, who sells nations through her harlotries and families through her sorceries "Behold, I am against you," says the LORD of hosts. "I will lift your skirts over your face, I will show the nations your nakedness, and the kingdoms your shame. I will cast abominable filth upon you, make you vile, and make you a spectacle. It shall come to pass that all who look upon you will flee from you and say, 'Nineveh is laid waste! Who will bemoan her?' Where shall I seek comforters for you?" Are you better than No-Amon that was situated by the River, that had the waters around her, whose rampart was the sea, whose wall was the sea? Ethiopia and Egypt were her strength, and it was boundless; Put and Lubim were your helpers. Yet she was carried away, she went into captivity; her young children also were dashed to pieces at the head of every street; they cast lots for her honorable men, and all her great men were bound in chains. You also will be drunk; you will be hidden; you also will seek refuge from the enemy. All your strongholds are fig trees with ripened figs: If they are shaken, they fall into the mouth of the eater. Surely, your people in your midst are women! The gates of your land are wide open for your enemies; fire shall devour the bars of your gates Draw your water for the siege! Fortify your strongholds! Go into the clay and tread the mortar! Make strong the brick kiln! There the fire will devour you, the sword will cut you off; it will eat you up like a locust. Make yourself many—like the locust! Make yourself many—like the swarming locusts! You have multiplied your merchants more than the stars of heaven. The locust plunders and flies away. Your commanders are like swarming locusts, and your generals like great grasshoppers, which camp in the hedges on a cold day; when the sun rises, they flee away, and the place where they are is not known Your shepherds slumber, O king of Assyria; your nobles rest in the dust. Your people are scattered on the mountains, and no one gathers them. Your injury has no healing, your wound is severe. All who hear news of you will clap their hands over you, for upon whom has not your wickedness passed continually?

35. Habakkuk

CHAPTER 1

The burden that the prophet Habakkuk saw. "O LORD, how long will I cry out, and you will not hear me! I cry out to you about violence, and you will not save! Why do you make me see iniquity and cause me to witness sorrow? Destruction and violence are before me; there is strife, and conflict abounds. Therefore, the law is paralyzed, and justice never prevails. The wicked hem in the righteous, so that justice is perverted. Look at the nations and watch—be utterly amazed. For I am going to do something in your days that you would not believe, even if you were told. I am raising up the Babylonians, that ruthless and impetuous people, who sweep across the whole earth to seize dwellings not their own. They are a feared and dreaded people; they are a law to themselves and promote their own honor. Their horses are swifter than leopards, fiercer than wolves at dusk. Their cavalry gallops headlong; their horsemen come from afar. They fly like an eagle swooping to devour. They all come intent on violence. Their hordes advance like a desert wind and gather prisoners like sand. They mock kings and scoff at rulers. They laugh at all fortified cities; by building earthen ramps they capture them. Then they sweep past like the wind and go on—guilty people, whose own strength is their god." "LORD, are you not from everlasting? My God, my Holy One, you will never die. LORD, you have appointed them to execute judgment; you, my Rock, have ordained them to punish. Your eyes are too pure to look on evil; you cannot tolerate wrongdoing. Why then do you tolerate the treacherous? Why are you silent while the wicked swallow up those more righteous than themselves? You have made people like the fish in the sea, like the sea creatures that have no ruler. The wicked foe pulls all of them up with hooks, he catches them in his net, he gathers them up in his dragnet; and so he rejoices and is glad. Therefore, he sacrifices to his net and burns incense to his dragnet, for by his net he lives in luxury and enjoys the choicest food. Is he to keep on emptying his net, destroying nations without mercy?"

CHAPTER 2

I will stand at my watch and station myself on the ramparts; I will look to see what he will say to me, and what answer I am to give to this complaint. Then the LORD replied: "Write down the revelation and make it plain on tablets so that a herald may run with it. For the revelation awaits an appointed time; it speaks of the end and will not prove false. Though it linger, wait for it; it will certainly come and will not delay. See, the enemy is puffed up; his desires are not upright—but the righteous person will live by his faithfulness. Indeed, wine betrays him; he is arrogant and never at rest. Because he is as greedy as the grave and like death is never satisfied, he gathers to himself all the nations and takes captive all the peoples Will not all of them taunt him with ridicule and scorn, saying, 'Woe to him who piles up stolen goods and makes himself wealthy by extortion! How long must this go on?' Will not your creditors suddenly arise? Will they not wake up and make you tremble? Then you will become their prey. Because you have plundered many nations, the peoples who are left will plunder you. For you have shed human blood; you have destroyed lands and cities and everyone in them Woe to him who builds his house by unjust gain, setting his nest on high to escape the clutches of ruin! You have plotted the ruin of many peoples, shaming your own house and forfeiting your life. The stones of the wall will cry out, and the beams of the woodwork will echo it. Woe to him who builds a city with bloodshed and establishes a town by injustice! Has not the LORD Almighty determined that the people's labor is only fuel for the fire, that the nations exhaust themselves for nothing? For the earth will be filled with the knowledge of the glory of the LORD as the waters cover the sea Woe to him who gives drink to his neighbors, pouring it from the wineskin till they are drunk, so that he can gaze on their naked bodies! You will be filled with shame instead of glory. Now it is your turn! Drink and let your nakedness be exposed! The cup from the LORD's right hand is coming around to you, and disgrace will cover your glory. The violence you have done to Lebanon will overwhelm you, and your destruction of animals will terrify you. For you have shed human blood; you have destroyed lands and cities and everyone in them Of what value is an idol carved by a craftsman? Or an image that teaches lies? For the one who makes it trusts in his own creation; he makes idols that cannot speak. Woe to him who says to wood, 'Come to life!' Or to lifeless stone, 'Wake up!' Can it give guidance? It is covered with gold and silver; there is no breath in it. The LORD is in his holy temple; let all the earth be silent before him."

CHAPTER 3

A prayer of Habakkuk the prophet, on Shigionoth.

LORD, I have heard of your fame; I stand in awe of your deeds, LORD. Repeat them in our day, in our time make them known; in wrath remember mercy. God came from Teman, the Holy One from Mount Paran. His glory covered the heavens and his praise filled the earth. His splendor was like the sunrise; rays flashed from his hand, where his power was hidden. Plague went before him; pestilence followed his steps. He stood and shook the earth; he looked and made the nations tremble. The ancient mountains crumbled, and the age-old hills collapsed—but he marches on forever. I saw the tents of Cushan in distress, the dwellings of Midian in anguish Were you angry with the rivers, LORD? Was your wrath against the streams? Did you rage against the sea when you rode your horses and your chariots to victory? You uncovered your bow, you called for many arrows. You split the earth with rivers; the mountains saw you and writhed. Torrents of water swept by; the deep roared and lifted its waves on high. Sun and moon stood still in the heavens at the glint of your flying arrows, at the lightning of your flashing spear. In wrath you strode through the earth and in anger you threshed the nations. You came out to deliver your people, to save your anointed one. You crushed the leader of the land of wickedness, you stripped him from head to foot. With his own spear you pierced his head when his warriors stormed out to scatter us, gloating as though about to devour the wretched who were in hiding. You trampled the sea with your horses, churning the great waters I heard and my heart pounded, my lips quivered at the sound; decay crept into my bones, and my legs trembled. Yet I will wait patiently for the day of calamity to come on the nation invading us. Though the fig tree does not bud and there are no grapes on the vines, though the olive crop fails and the fields produce no food, though there are no sheep in the pen and no cattle in the stalls, yet I will rejoice in the LORD, I will be joyful in God my Savior. The Sovereign LORD is my strength; he makes my feet like the feet of a deer, he enables me to tread on the heights For the director of music. On my stringed instruments

36. Zephaniah

CHAPTER 1

The word of the LORD that came to Zephaniah, the son of Cushi, the son of Gedaliah, the son of Amariah, the son of Hezekiah, in the days of Josiah, the son of Amon, king of Judah. "I will utterly sweep away everything from the face of the earth," declares the LORD. "I will sweep away both man and beast; I will sweep away the birds in the sky and the fish in the sea, and the idols that cause the wicked to stumble. When I destroy all mankind on the face of the earth," declares the LORD, "I will stretch out my hand against Judah and against all who live in Jerusalem. I will destroy every remnant of Baal worship in this place, the very names of the idolatrous priests—those who bow down on the roofs to worship the starry host, those who bow down and swear by the LORD and who also swear by Molek, those who turn back from following the LORD and neither seek the LORD nor inquire of him." "Be silent before the Sovereign LORD, for the day of the LORD is near. The LORD has prepared a sacrifice; he has consecrated those he has invited. On the day of the LORD's sacrifice, I will punish the officials and the king's sons and all those clad in foreign clothes. On that day I will punish all who avoid stepping on the threshold, who fill the temple of their gods with violence and deceit." "On that day," declares the LORD, "a cry will go up from the Fish Gate, wailing from the New Quarter, and a loud crash from the hills. Wail, you who live in the market district; all your merchants will be wiped out, all who trade with silver will be destroyed. At that time, I will search Jerusalem with lamps and punish those who are complacent, who are like wine left on its dregs, who think, 'The LORD will do nothing, either good or bad.' Their wealth will be plundered, their houses demolished. Though they build houses, they will not live in them; though they plant vineyards, they will not drink the wine." "The great day of the LORD is near—near and coming quickly. The cry on the day of the LORD is bitter; the Mighty Warrior shouts his battle cry. That day will be a day of wrath—a day of distress and anguish, a day of trouble and ruin, a day of darkness and gloom, a day of clouds and blackness—a day of trumpet and battle cry against the fortified cities and against the corner towers. I will bring such distress on all people that they will grope about like those who are blind, because they have sinned against the LORD. Their blood will be poured out like dust and their entrails like dung. Neither their silver nor their gold will be able to save them on the day of the LORD's wrath." In the fire of his jealousy, the whole earth will be consumed, for he will make a sudden end of all who live on the earth

CHAPTER 2

Gather together, gather yourselves together, you shameful nation, before the decree takes effect and that day passes like windblown chaff, before the LORD's fierce anger comes upon you, before the day of the LORD's wrath comes upon you. Seek the LORD, all you humble of the land, you who do what he commands. Seek righteousness, seek humility; perhaps you will be sheltered on the day of the LORD's anger Gaza will be abandoned and Ashkelon left in ruins. At midday Ashdod will be emptied and Ekron uprooted. Woe to you who live by the sea, you Kerethite people; the word of the LORD is against you, Canaan, land of the Philistines. "I will destroy you, and none will be left." The land by the sea will become pastures having wells for shepherds and pens for flocks. That land will belong to the remnant of the people of Judah; there they will find pasture. In the evening, they will lie down in the houses of Ashkelon. The LORD their God will care for them; he will restore their fortunes "I have heard the insults of Moab and the taunts of the Ammonites, who insulted my people and made threats against their land. Therefore, as surely as I live," declares the LORD Almighty, the God of Israel, "surely Moab will become like Sodom, the Ammonites like Gomorrah—a place of weeds and salt pits, a wasteland forever. The remnant of my people will plunder them; the survivors of my nation will inherit their land." This is what they will get in return for their pride, for insulting and mocking the people of the LORD Almighty. The LORD will be awesome to them when he destroys all the gods of the earth. Distant nations will bow down to him, all of them in their own lands "You Cushites, too, will be slain by my sword." He will stretch out his hand against the north and destroy Assyria, leaving Nineveh utterly desolate and dry as the desert. Flocks and herds will lie down there, creatures of every kind. The desert owl and the screech owl will roost on her columns. Their hooting will echo through the windows, rubble will fill the doorways, and the beams of cedar will be exposed. This is the city of revelry that lived in safety. She said to herself, "I am the one! And there is none besides me." What a ruin she has become, a lair for wild beasts! All who pass by her scoff and shake their fists

CHAPTER 3

Woe to the city of oppressors, rebellious and defiled! She obeys no one; she accepts no correction. She does not trust in the LORD; she does not draw near to her God. Her officials within her are roaring lions; her rulers are evening wolves who leave nothing for the morning. Her prophets are unprincipled; they are treacherous people. Her priests profane the sanctuary and do violence to the law. The LORD within her is righteous; he does no wrong. Morning by morning he dispenses his justice, and every new day he does not fail, yet the unrighteous know no shame "I have destroyed nations; their strongholds are demolished. I have left their streets deserted, with no one passing through. Their cities are laid waste; they are deserted and empty. Of Jerusalem, I thought, 'Surely you will fear me and accept correction!' Then her place of refuge would not be destroyed, nor all my punishments come upon her. But they were still eager to act corruptly in all they did. Therefore wait for me," declares the LORD, "for the day I will stand up to testify. I have decided to assemble the nations, to gather the kingdoms and to pour out my wrath on them—all my fierce anger. The whole world will be consumed by the fire of my jealous anger Then I will purify the lips of the peoples, that all of them may call on the name of the LORD and serve him shoulder to shoulder. From beyond the rivers of Cush my worshipers, the daughter of my dispersed people, will bring me offerings. On that day, you, Jerusalem, will not be put to shame for all the wrongs you have done to me, because I will remove from you your arrogant boasters. Never again will you be haughty on my holy hill. But I will leave within you the meek and humble. The remnant of Israel will trust in the name of the LORD. They will do no wrong; they will tell no lies. A deceitful tongue will not be found in their mouths. They will eat and lie down and no one will make them afraid." Sing, Daughter Zion; shout aloud, Israel! Be glad and rejoice with all your heart, Daughter Jerusalem! The LORD has taken away your punishment, he has turned back your enemy. The LORD, the King of Israel, is with you; never again will you fear any harm. On that day, they will say to Jerusalem, "Do not fear, Zion; do not let your hands hang limp. The LORD your God is with you, the Mighty Warrior who saves. He will take great delight in you; in his love, he will no longer rebuke you, but will rejoice over you with singing." "I will remove from you all who mourn over the loss of your appointed festivals, which is a burden and reproach for you. At that time, I will deal with all who oppressed you. I will rescue the lame; I will gather the exiles. I will give them praise and honor in every land where they have suffered shame. At that time, I will gather you; at that time, I will bring you home. I will give you honor and praise among all the peoples of the earth when I restore your fortunes before your very eyes," says the LORD

37. Haggai

CHAPTER 1

In the second year of King Darius, in the sixth month, on the first day of the month, the word of the LORD came through the prophet Haggai to Zerubbabel, the son of Shealtiel, the governor of Judah, and to Joshua, the son of Jehozadak, the high priest, saying, "Thus speaks the LORD of hosts: This people says, 'The time has not yet come to rebuild the house of the LORD.'" Then the word of the LORD came through the prophet Haggai, saying, "Is it a time for you yourselves to dwell in your paneled houses while this house lies in ruins? Now, therefore, thus says the LORD of hosts: Consider your ways. You have sown much and harvested little; you eat, but you never have enough; you drink, but you never have your fill; you clothe yourselves, but no one is warm; and he who earns wages does so to put them into a bag with holes." Thus says the LORD of hosts: "Consider your ways. Go up to the hills and bring wood and build the house, that I may take pleasure in it and be glorified," says the LORD. "You looked for much, and behold, it came to little. And when you brought it home, I blew it away. Why?" declares the LORD of hosts. "Because of my house that lies in ruins, while each of you busies himself with his own house. Therefore, the heavens above you have withheld the dew, and the earth has withheld its produce. I have called for a drought on the land and the hills, on the grain, the new wine, the oil, on what the ground brings forth, on man and beast, and on all their labors." Then Zerubbabel, the son of Shealtiel, and Joshua, the son of Jehozadak, the high priest, with all the remnant of the people, obeyed the voice of the LORD their God and the words of Haggai the prophet, as the LORD their God had sent him. And the people feared the LORD. Then Haggai, the messenger of the LORD, spoke to the people with the LORD's message, "I am with you," declares the LORD. And the LORD stirred up the spirit of Zerubbabel, the son of Shealtiel, governor of Judah, and the spirit of Joshua, the son of Jehozadak, the high priest, and the spirit of all the remnant of the people. And they came and worked on the house of the LORD of hosts, their God

CHAPTER 2

In the seventh month, on the twenty-first day of the month, the word of the LORD came by the hand of Haggai the prophet: "Speak now to Zerubbabel, the son of Shealtiel, governor of Judah, and to Joshua, the son of Jehozadak, the high priest, and to all the remnant of the people, saying, 'Who is left among you who saw this house in its former glory? How do you see it now? Is it not as nothing in your eyes? Yet now be strong, O Zerubbabel,' declares the LORD. 'Be strong, O Joshua, son of Jehozadak, the high priest. Be strong, all you people of the land,' declares the LORD. 'Work, for I am with you,' declares the LORD of hosts, 'according to the covenant that I made with you when you came out of Egypt. My Spirit remains in your midst. Fear not. For thus says the LORD of hosts: Yet once more, in a little while, I will shake the heavens and the earth and the sea and the dry land. And I will shake all nations so that the treasures of all nations shall come in, and I will fill this house with glory,' says the LORD of hosts. 'The silver is mine, and the gold is mine,' declares the LORD of hosts. 'The latter glory of this house shall be greater than the former,' says the LORD of hosts. 'And in this place, I will give peace,' declares the LORD of hosts." On the twenty-fourth day of the ninth month, in the second year of Darius, the word of the LORD came to Haggai the prophet, saying, "Thus says the LORD of hosts: Ask the priests about the law: 'If someone carries holy meat in the fold of his garment and touches with his fold bread or stew or wine or oil or any kind of food, does it become holy?'" The priests answered and said, "No." Then Haggai said, "If someone who is unclean by contact with a dead body touches any of these, does it become unclean?" The priests answered and said, "It does become unclean." Then Haggai answered and said, "So it is with this people, and with this nation before me," declares the LORD, "and so with every work of their hands. And what they offer there is unclean. Now then, consider from this day onward. Before stone was placed upon stone in the temple of the LORD, how did you fare? When one came to a heap of twenty measures, there were but ten. When one came to the wine vat to draw fifty measures, there were but twenty. I struck you and all the products of your toil with blight and mildew and hail, yet you did not turn to me," declares the LORD. "Consider from this day onward, from the twenty-fourth day of the ninth month. Since the day that the foundation of the LORD's temple was laid, consider: Is the seed yet in the barn? Indeed, the vine, the fig tree, the pomegranate, and the olive tree have yielded nothing. But from this day on I will bless you." The word of the LORD came a second time to Haggai on the twenty-fourth day of the month, saying, "Speak to Zerubbabel, governor of Judah, saying, 'I am about to shake the heavens and the earth and to overthrow the throne of kingdoms. I am about to destroy the strength of the kingdoms of the nations and overthrow the chariots and their riders. And the horses and their riders shall go down, every one by the sword of his brother. On that day,' declares the LORD of hosts, 'I will take you, O Zerubbabel my servant, the son of Shealtiel,' declares the LORD, 'and make you like a signet ring, for I have chosen you,' declares the LORD of hosts."

38. Zechariah

Chapter 1

In the eighth month of the second year of Darius, the word of the Lord came to Zechariah, the son of Berechiah, the son of Iddo the prophet, who said, "The Lord is greatly displeased with your fathers. Therefore, say to them, 'Thus says the Lord of hosts: Turn to me, and I will turn to you.' Do not be like your fathers, to whom the prophets of old cried, 'Turn now from your iniquitous ways and wicked works,' but they would not listen or heed me," says the Lord. "Your fathers, where are they? And the prophets, do they live forever? But did not my words and statutes, which I commanded through my servants, the prophets, take hold of your fathers? And they turned back and said, 'As the Lord of hosts has determined to do with us, according to our ways and works, so has He done with us.'" On the twenty-fourth day of the eleventh month, the month of Shebat, in the second year of Darius, the word of the Lord came to Zechariah, the son of Berechiah, the son of Iddo the prophet. Zechariah saw a man riding a red horse, standing among the myrtle trees in a ravine, and behind him were red horses with white spots. Zechariah asked, "O my Lord, what are these?" The angel who was speaking to him said, "I will show you what they are." The man standing among the myrtle trees answered, "These are those whom the Lord has sent to go through the world." They reported to the angel of the Lord, saying, "We have gone through the world, and behold, all the world is still and resting." Then the angel of the Lord asked, "O Lord of hosts, how long will you withhold mercy from Jerusalem and the cities of Judah, with which you have been displeased these seventy years?" The Lord answered the angel with good and comforting words. So the angel who spoke with Zechariah said, "Cry out and speak: Thus says the Lord of hosts: I am jealous for Jerusalem and Zion with great zeal, and I am very angry with the nations that feel secure. I was only a little angry, but they added to the calamity. Therefore, thus says the Lord: I will return to Jerusalem with mercy; my house will be rebuilt in it, and a measuring line will be stretched out over Jerusalem. Cry out again: Thus says the Lord of hosts: My cities will again overflow with prosperity, the Lord will again comfort Zion, and will again choose Jerusalem." Zechariah then looked up and saw four horns. He asked the angel, "What are these?" The angel answered, "These are the horns that scattered Judah, Israel, and Jerusalem." Then the Lord showed him four craftsmen. Zechariah asked, "What are these coming to do?" The angel replied, "These are the horns that scattered Judah, so no one could raise their head; but the craftsmen have come to terrify them and throw down these horns of the nations who lifted up their horns against the land of Judah to scatter it."

Chapter 2

Zechariah raised his eyes again and saw a man with a measuring line in his hand. Zechariah asked, "Where are you going?" The man replied, "To measure Jerusalem, to determine its width and length." As the angel who spoke to Zechariah departed, another angel came to meet him and said, "Run, speak to this young man and tell him: Jerusalem will be a city without walls because of the multitude of people and animals in it. For I, the Lord, will be a wall of fire around her and will be her glory within." "Come, come! Flee from the land of the north," declares the Lord, "for I have scattered you to the four winds of heaven." "Come, Zion! Escape, you who live with the daughter of Babylon." For thus says the Lord of hosts, "After the glorious one has sent me against the nations that plundered you—for whoever touches you touches the apple of his eye—I will surely raise my hand against them so that their slaves will plunder them. Then you will know that the Lord of hosts has sent me." "Shout and be glad, Daughter Zion. For I am coming, and I will live among you," declares the Lord. "Many nations will be joined with the Lord in that day and will become my people. I will live among you, and you will know that the Lord of hosts has sent me to you. The Lord will inherit Judah as his portion in the holy land and will again choose Jerusalem. Be still before the Lord, all mankind, because he has roused himself from his holy dwelling."

Chapter 3

Then the Lord showed Zechariah Joshua the high priest standing before the angel of the Lord, with Satan standing at his right side to accuse him. The Lord said to Satan, "The Lord rebukes you, Satan! The Lord, who has chosen Jerusalem, rebukes you! Is not this man a burning stick snatched from the fire?" Now Joshua was dressed in filthy clothes as he stood before the angel. The angel said to those who were standing before him, "Take off his filthy clothes." Then he said to Joshua, "See, I have taken away your sin, and I will put fine garments on you." Then he said, "Put a clean turban on his head." So they put a clean turban on his head and clothed him, while the angel of the Lord stood by The angel of the Lord gave this charge to Joshua: "This is what the Lord of hosts says: If you will walk in my ways and keep my requirements, then you will govern my house and have charge of my courts, and I will give you a place among these standing here. Listen, High Priest Joshua, you and your associates seated before you, who are men symbolic of things to come: I am going to bring my servant, the Branch. See, the stone I have set in front of Joshua! There are seven eyes on that one stone, and I will engrave an inscription on it," says the Lord of hosts, "and I will remove the sin of this land in a single day. In that day, each of you will invite your neighbor to sit under your vine and fig tree," declares the Lord of hosts

Chapter 4

The angel who talked with Zechariah returned and woke him up, like someone awakened from sleep. He asked Zechariah, "What do you see?" Zechariah answered, "I see a solid gold lampstand with a bowl at the top and seven lamps on it, with seven channels to the lamps. Also, there are two olive trees by it, one on the right of the bowl and the other on its left." Zechariah asked the angel, "What are these, my Lord?" The angel answered, "Do you not know what these are?" Zechariah replied, "No, my Lord." So the angel said, "This is the word of the Lord to Zerubbabel: 'Not by might nor by power, but by my Spirit,' says the Lord of hosts. 'What are you, mighty mountain? Before Zerubbabel, you will become level ground. Then he will bring out the capstone to shouts of "Grace, grace to it!"'" Then the word of the Lord came to Zechariah: "The hands of Zerubbabel have laid the foundation of this temple; his hands will also complete it. Then you will know that the Lord of hosts has sent me to you. Who dares despise the day of small things, since the seven eyes of the Lord that range throughout the earth will rejoice when they see the chosen capstone in the hand of Zerubbabel?" Then Zechariah asked the angel, "What are these two olive trees on the right and the left of the lampstand?" Again, he asked, "What are these two olive branches beside the two gold pipes that pour out golden oil?" The angel replied, "Do you not know what these are?" Zechariah said, "No, my Lord." So the angel said, "These are the two who are anointed to serve the Lord of all the earth."

Chapter 5

Zechariah looked up again and saw a flying scroll. The angel asked him, "What do you see?" Zechariah replied, "I see a flying scroll, twenty cubits long and ten cubits wide." The angel said, "This is the curse that is going out over the whole land; for according to what it says on one side, every thief will be banished, and according to what it says on the other, everyone who swears falsely will be banished. The Lord of hosts declares, 'I will send it out, and it will enter the house of the thief and the house of anyone who swears falsely by my name. It will remain in that house and destroy it completely, both its timbers and its stones.'" Then the angel who was speaking to Zechariah came forward and said, "Look up and see what is appearing." Zechariah asked, "What is it?" The angel replied, "It is a basket." And he added, "This is the iniquity of the people throughout the land." Then the cover of lead was raised, and there in the basket sat a woman. The angel said, "This is wickedness," and he pushed her back into the basket and pushed its lead cover down on it Then Zechariah looked up and saw two women with the wind in their wings—they had wings like those of a stork—and they lifted up the basket between heaven and earth. Zechariah asked the angel, "Where are they taking the basket?" He replied, "To the country of Babylonia to build a house for it. When the house is ready, the basket will be set there in its place."

Chapter 6

Then I turned and looked up, and saw four chariots coming out from between two mountains, and the mountains were made of bronze. The first chariot had red horses, the second chariot had black horses, the third chariot had white horses, and the fourth chariot had horses of various colors. I asked the angel who was speaking with me, "What are these, my lord?" The angel replied, "These are the four spirits of heaven, going out from standing in the presence of the Lord of the whole world." The chariot with the black horses went toward the north country, the white horses followed them, and the horses of various colors went toward the south country. The red horses were eager to go and roam the earth, and the angel said, "Go and roam the earth." So they went throughout the earth. Then the angel called to me and said, "Look, those going toward the north country have given my Spirit rest in the land of the north." The word of the Lord came to me, saying, "Take from the exiles—from Heldai, Tobijah, and Jedaiah, who have arrived from Babylon—and go at the same day to the house of Josiah son of Zephaniah. Take silver and gold and make a crown, and set it on the head of Joshua son of Jehozadak, the high priest. Tell him this is what the Lord of hosts says: 'Here is the man whose name is the Branch, and he will branch out from his place and build the temple of the Lord. It is he who will build the temple of the Lord, and he will be clothed with majesty and will sit and rule on his throne. And he will be a priest on his throne, and there will be harmony between the two.' The crown will be given to Heldai, Tobijah, Jedaiah, and Hen son of Zephaniah as a memorial in the temple of the Lord. Those who are far away will come and help to build the temple of the Lord, and you will know that the Lord of hosts has sent me to you. This will happen if you diligently obey the Lord your God."

Chapter 7

In the fourth year of King Darius, the word of the Lord came to Zechariah on the fourth day of the ninth month, the month of Kislev. The people of Bethel had sent Sharezer and Regem-Melech, together with their men, to seek the favor of the Lord and to ask the priests of the house of the Lord of hosts and the prophets, "Should I mourn and fast in the fifth month, as I have done for so many years?" Then the word of the Lord of hosts came to me: "Ask all the people of the land and the priests, 'When you fasted and mourned in the fifth and seventh months for the past seventy years, was it really for me that you fasted? And when you were eating and drinking, were you not just feasting for yourselves? Are these not the words the Lord proclaimed through the earlier prophets when Jerusalem and its surrounding towns were at rest and prosperous, and the Negev and the western foothills were settled?'" And the word of the Lord came again to Zechariah: "This is what the Lord of hosts says: 'Administer true justice; show mercy and compassion to one another. Do not oppress the widow or the fatherless, the foreigner or the poor. Do not plot evil against each other.' But they refused to pay attention; stubbornly they turned their backs and covered their ears. They made their hearts as hard as flint and would not listen to the law or to the words that the Lord of hosts had sent by his Spirit through the earlier prophets. So the Lord of hosts was very angry 'When I called, they did not listen; so when they called, I would not listen,' says the Lord of hosts. 'I scattered them with a whirlwind among all the nations, where they were strangers. The land they left behind them was so desolate that no one traveled through it. This is how they made the pleasant land desolate.'"

Chapter 8

The word of the Lord of hosts came to me: "This is what the Lord of hosts says: 'I am very jealous for Zion; I am burning with jealousy for her.' This is what the Lord says: 'I will return to Zion and dwell in Jerusalem. Then Jerusalem will be called the City of Truth, and the mountain of the Lord of hosts will be called the Holy Mountain.' This is what the Lord of hosts says: 'Once again, men and women of ripe old age will sit in the streets of Jerusalem, each with cane in hand because of their age. The city streets will be filled with boys and girls playing there.' This is what the Lord of hosts says: 'It may seem marvelous to the remnant of this people at that time, but will it seem marvelous to me?' declares the Lord of hosts This is what the Lord of hosts says: 'I will save my people from the countries of the east and the west. I will bring them back to live in Jerusalem; they will be my people, and I will be faithful and righteous to them as their God.' This is what the Lord of hosts says: 'Now hear these words, "Let your hands be strong so that the temple may be built." This is also what the prophets said who were present when the foundation was laid for the house of the Lord of hosts. Before that time there were no wages for people or hire for animals. No one could go about their business safely because of their enemies, since I had turned everyone against their neighbor. But now I will not deal with the remnant of this people as I did in the past,' declares the Lord of hosts 'The seed will grow well, the vine will yield its fruit, the ground will produce its crops, and the heavens will drop their dew. I will give all these things as an inheritance to the remnant of this people. Just as you, Judah and Israel, have been a curse among the nations, so I will save you, and you will be a blessing. Do not be afraid, but let your hands be strong.' This is what the Lord of hosts says: 'Just as I had determined to bring disaster on you and showed no pity when your ancestors angered me,' says the Lord of hosts, 'so now I have determined to do good again to Jerusalem and Judah. Do not be afraid. These are the things you are to do: Speak the truth to each other, and render true and sound judgment in your courts; do not plot evil against each other, and do not love to swear falsely. I hate all this,' declares the Lord The word of the Lord of hosts came to me: This is what the Lord of hosts says: 'The fasts of the fourth, fifth, seventh, and tenth months will become joyful and glad occasions and happy festivals for Judah. Therefore love truth and peace.' This is what the Lord of hosts says: 'Many peoples and the inhabitants of many cities will yet come, and the inhabitants of one city will go to another and say, "Let us go at once to entreat the Lord and seek the Lord of hosts. I myself am going." And many peoples and powerful nations will come to Jerusalem to seek the Lord of hosts and to entreat him.' This is what the Lord of hosts says: 'In those days, ten people from all languages and nations will take firm hold of one Jew by the hem of his robe and say, "Let us go with you, because we have heard that God is with you."'"

Chapter 9

The word of the Lord is against the land of Hadrach and will come to rest on Damascus—for the eyes of all people and all the tribes of Israel are on the Lord—and on Hamath too, which borders on it, and on Tyre and Sidon, though they are very skillful. Tyre has built herself a stronghold; she has heaped up silver like dust, and gold like the dirt of the streets. But the Lord will take away her possessions and destroy her power on the sea, and she will be consumed by fire Ashkelon will see it and fear; Gaza will writhe in agony, and Ekron too, for her hope will wither. Gaza will lose her king, and Ashkelon will be deserted. A mongrel people will occupy Ashdod, and I will put an end to the pride of the Philistines. I will take the blood from their mouths, the forbidden food from between their teeth. Those who are left will belong to our God and become a clan in Judah, and Ekron will be like the Jebusites. But I will encamp at my temple to guard it against marauding forces. Never again will an oppressor overrun my people, for now I am keeping watch Rejoice greatly, Daughter Zion! Shout, Daughter Jerusalem! See, your king comes to you, righteous and victorious, lowly and riding on a donkey, on a colt, the foal of a donkey. I will take away the chariots from Ephraim and the warhorses from Jerusalem, and the battle bow will be broken. He will proclaim peace to the nations. His rule will extend from sea to sea and from the River to the ends of the earth. As for you, because of the blood of my covenant with you, I will free your prisoners from the waterless pit. Return to your fortress, you prisoners of hope; even now I announce that I will restore twice as much to you. I will bend Judah as I bend my bow and fill it with Ephraim. I will rouse your sons, Zion, against your sons, Greece, and make you like a warrior's sword Then the Lord will appear over them; his arrow will flash like lightning. The Sovereign Lord will sound the trumpet; he will march in the storms of the south, and the Lord of hosts will shield them. They will destroy and overcome with slingstones. They will drink and roar as with wine; they will be full like a bowl used for sprinkling the corners of the altar. The Lord their God will save his people on that day as a shepherd saves his flock. They will sparkle in his land like jewels in a crown. How attractive and beautiful they will be! Grain will make the young men thrive, and new wine the young women

Chapter 10

Ask the Lord for rain in the springtime; it is the Lord who sends the thunderstorms. He gives showers of rain to all people and plants of the field to everyone. The idols speak deceitfully, diviners see visions that lie; they tell dreams that are false, they give comfort in vain. Therefore the people wander like sheep oppressed for lack of a shepherd "My anger burns against the shepherds, and I will punish the leaders," says the Lord Almighty. "For the Lord of hosts will care for his flock, the people of Judah, and make them like a proud horse in battle. From Judah will come the cornerstone, from him the tent peg, from him the battle bow, from him every ruler. Together they will be like warriors in battle trampling their enemy into the mud of the streets. They will fight because the Lord is with them, and they will put the enemy horsemen to shame I will strengthen Judah and save the tribes of Joseph. I will restore them because I have compassion on them. They will be as though I had not rejected them, for I am the Lord their God and I will answer them. The Ephraimites will become like warriors, and their hearts will be glad as with wine. Their children will see it and be joyful; their hearts will rejoice in the Lord. I will signal for them and gather them in. Surely I will redeem them; they will be as numerous as before. Though I scatter them among the peoples, yet in distant lands they will remember me. They and their children will survive, and they will return. I will bring them back from Egypt and gather them from Assyria. I will bring them to Gilead and Lebanon, and there will not be room enough for them They will pass through the sea of trouble; the surging sea will be subdued and all the depths of the Nile will dry up. Assyria's pride will be brought down and Egypt's scepter will pass away. I will strengthen them in the Lord and in his name they will live securely," declares the Lord

Chapter 11

Open your gates, O Lebanon, and let fire consume your cedars. Wail, O cypress, for the cedar has fallen, the majestic trees are ruined. Wail, oaks of Bashan, for the dense forest has been cut down. Listen to the wailing of the shepherds; their rich pastures are destroyed. Hear the roar of the lions; the lush thickets of the Jordan are ruined This is what the Lord my God says: "Shepherd the flock marked for slaughter. Their buyers slaughter them and go unpunished. Those who sell them say, 'Praise the Lord, I am rich!' Their own shepherds do not spare them. For I will no longer have pity on the people of the land," declares the Lord. "I will give everyone into the hands of their neighbors and their king. They will devastate the land, and I will not rescue anyone from their hands." So I shepherded the flock marked for slaughter, particularly the oppressed of the flock. Then I took two staffs and called one Favor and the other Union, and I shepherded the flock. In one month, I got rid of the three shepherds. The flock detested me, and I grew weary of them and said, "I will not be your shepherd. Let the dying die, and the perishing perish. Let those who are left eat one another's flesh." Then I took my staff called Favor and broke it, revoking the covenant I had made with all the nations. It was revoked on that day, and so the oppressed of the flock who were watching me knew it was the word of the Lord. I told them, "If you think it best, give me my pay; but if not, keep it." So they paid me thirty pieces of silver And the Lord said to me, "Throw it to the potter"—the handsome price at which they valued me! So I took the thirty pieces of silver and threw them to the potter at the house of the Lord. Then I broke my second staff called Union, breaking the family bond between Judah and Israel Then the Lord said to me, "Take again the equipment of a foolish shepherd. For I am going to raise up a shepherd over the land who will not care for the lost or seek the young or heal the injured or feed the healthy, but will eat the meat of the choice sheep, tearing off their hooves. Woe to the worthless shepherd, who deserts the flock! May the sword strike his arm and his right eye! May his arm be completely withered, his right eye totally blinded!"

Chapter 12

A prophecy: The word of the Lord concerning Israel. The Lord, who stretches out the heavens, who lays the foundation of the earth, and who forms the human spirit within a person, declares: "I am going to make Jerusalem a cup that sends all the surrounding peoples reeling. Judah will be besieged as well as Jerusalem. On that day, when all the nations of the earth are gathered against her, I will make Jerusalem an immovable rock for all the nations. All who try to move it will injure themselves On that day, I will strike every horse with panic and its rider with madness," declares the Lord. "I will keep a watchful eye over Judah, but I will blind all the horses of the nations. Then the clans of Judah will say in their hearts, 'The people of Jerusalem are strong, because the Lord Almighty is their God.' On that day, I will make the clans of Judah like a firepot in a woodpile, like a flaming torch among sheaves. They will consume all the surrounding peoples right and left, but Jerusalem will remain intact in her place. The Lord will save the dwellings of Judah first, so that the honor of the house of David and of Jerusalem's inhabitants may not be greater than that of Judah. On that day, the Lord will shield those who live in Jerusalem, so that the feeblest among them will be like David, and the house of David will be like God, like the angel of the Lord going before them On that day, I will set out to destroy all the nations that attack Jerusalem. And I will pour out on the house of David and the inhabitants of Jerusalem a spirit of grace and supplication. They will look on me, the one they have pierced, and they will mourn for him as one mourns for an only child and grieve bitterly for him as one grieves for a firstborn son. On that day, the weeping in Jerusalem will be as great as the weeping of Hadad Rimmon in the plain of Megiddo. The land will mourn, each clan by itself, with their wives by themselves: the clan of the house of David and their wives, the clan of the house of Nathan and their wives, the clan of the house of Levi and their wives, the clan of Shimei and their wives, and all the rest of the clans and their wives

Chapter 13

On that day, a fountain will be opened to the house of David and the inhabitants of Jerusalem, to cleanse them from sin and impurity. On that day, I will banish the names of the idols from the land, and they will be remembered no more," declares the Lord Almighty. "I will remove both the prophets and the spirit of impurity from the land. And if anyone still prophesies, their father and mother, to whom they were born, will say to them, 'You must die, because you have told lies in the Lord's name.' Then their own parents will stab the one who prophesies On that day, every prophet will be ashamed of their prophetic vision. They will not put on a prophet's garment of hair in order to deceive. Each will say, 'I am not a prophet. I am a farmer; the land has been my livelihood since my youth.' If someone asks, 'What are these wounds on your body?' they will answer, 'The wounds I was given at the house of my friends.' Awake, sword, against my shepherd, against the man who is close to me!" declares the Lord Almighty. "Strike the shepherd, and the sheep will be scattered, and I will turn my hand against the little ones. In the whole land," declares the Lord, "two-thirds will be struck down and perish; yet one-third will be left in it. This third I will put into the fire; I will refine them like silver and test them like gold. They will call on my name, and I will answer them; I will say, 'They are my people,' and they will say, 'The Lord is our God.'"

Chapter 14
A day of the Lord is coming, Jerusalem, when your possessions will be plundered and divided up within your very walls. I will gather all the nations to Jerusalem to fight against it; the city will be captured, the houses ransacked, and the women raped. Half of the city will go into exile, but the rest of the people will not be taken from the city Then the Lord will go out and fight against those nations, as he fights on a day of battle. On that day his feet will stand on the Mount of Olives, east of Jerusalem, and the Mount of Olives will be split in two from east to west, forming a great valley, with half of the mountain moving north and half moving south. You will flee by my mountain valley, for it will extend to Azel. You will flee as you fled from the earthquake in the days of Uzziah king of Judah. Then the Lord my God will come, and all the holy ones with him On that day, there will be neither sunlight nor cold, frosty darkness. It will be a unique day—a day known only to the Lord—with no distinction between day and night. When evening comes, there will be light On that day, living water will flow out from Jerusalem, half of it east to the Dead Sea and half of it west to the Mediterranean Sea, in summer and in winter. The Lord will be king over the whole earth. On that day there will be one Lord, and his name the only name The whole land, from Geba to Rimmon south of Jerusalem, will become like the Arabah. But Jerusalem will be raised up high from the Benjamin Gate to the site of the First Gate, to the Corner Gate, and from the Tower of Hananel to the royal winepresses, and will remain in its place. It will be inhabited; never again will it be destroyed. Jerusalem will be secure This is the plague with which the Lord will strike all the nations that fought against Jerusalem: Their flesh will rot while they are still standing on their feet, their eyes will rot in their sockets, and their tongues will rot in their mouths. On that day, people will be stricken by the Lord with great panic. They will seize each other by the hand and attack one another. Judah too will fight at Jerusalem. The wealth of all the surrounding nations will be collected—great quantities of gold and silver and clothing. A similar plague will strike the horses and mules, the camels and donkeys, and all the animals in those camps Then the survivors from all the nations that have attacked Jerusalem will go up year after year to worship the King, the Lord Almighty, and to celebrate the Festival of Tabernacles. If any of the peoples of the earth do not go up to Jerusalem to worship the King, the Lord Almighty, they will have no rain. If the Egyptian people do not go up and take part, they will have no rain. The Lord will bring on them the plague he inflicts on the nations that do not go up to celebrate the Festival of Tabernacles. This will be the punishment of Egypt and the punishment of all the nations that do not go up to celebrate the Festival of Tabernacles On that day, holy to the Lord will be inscribed on the bells of the horses, and the cooking pots in the Lord's house will be like the sacred bowls in front of the altar. Every pot in Jerusalem and Judah will be holy to the Lord Almighty, and all who come to sacrifice will take some of the pots and cook in them. And on that day, there will no longer be a Canaanite in the house of the Lord Almighty

39. Malachi

Chapter 1
The word of the Lord to Israel through the prophet Malachi. "I have loved you," says the Lord. But you ask, "How have you loved us?" Was not Esau Jacob's brother?" declares the Lord. "Yet I have loved Jacob, but Esau I have hated, and I have turned his hill country into a wasteland and left his inheritance to the desert jackals." Edom may say, "Though we have been crushed, we will rebuild the ruins." But this is what the Lord Almighty says: "They may build, but I will demolish. They will be called the Wicked Land, a people always under the wrath of the Lord. You will see it with your own eyes and say, 'Great is the Lord—even beyond the borders of Israel!'" A son honors his father, and a slave his master. If I am a father, where is the honor due me? If I am a master, where is the respect due me?" says the Lord Almighty. "It is you priests who show contempt for my name. But you ask, 'How have we shown contempt for your name?' By offering defiled food on my altar. But you ask, 'How have we defiled you?' By saying that the Lord's table is contemptible When you offer blind animals for sacrifice, is that not wrong? When you sacrifice lame or diseased animals, is that not wrong? Try offering them to your governor! Would he be pleased with you? Would he accept you?" says the Lord Almighty "Now plead with God to be gracious to us. With such offerings from your hands, will he accept you?"—says the Lord Almighty. "Oh, that one of you would shut the temple doors, so that you would not light useless fires on my altar! I am not pleased with you," says the Lord Almighty, "and I will accept no offering from your hands. My name will be great among the nations, from where the sun rises to where it sets. In every place incense and pure offerings will be brought to me, because my name will be great among the nations," says the Lord Almighty "But you profane it by saying, 'The Lord's table is defiled,' and, 'Its food is contemptible.' And you say, 'What a burden!' and you sniff at it contemptuously," says the Lord Almighty. "When you bring injured, lame, or diseased animals and offer them as sacrifices, should I accept them from your hands?" says the Lord. "Cursed is the cheat who has an acceptable male in his flock and vows to give it, but then sacrifices a blemished animal to the Lord. For I am a great king," says the Lord Almighty, "and my name is to be feared among the nations."

Chapter 2
And now, you priests, this warning is for you. If you do not listen, and if you do not resolve to honor my name," says the Lord Almighty, "I will send a curse on you, and I will curse your blessings. Yes, I have already cursed them, because you have not resolved to honor me "Because of you, I will rebuke your descendants; I will smear on your faces the dung from your festival sacrifices, and you will be carried off with it. And you will know that I have sent you this warning so that my covenant with Levi may continue," says the Lord Almighty. "My covenant was with him, a covenant of life and peace, and I gave them to him; this called for reverence and he revered me and stood in awe of my name. True instruction was in his mouth and nothing false was found on his lips. He walked with me in peace and uprightness,

and turned many from sin "For the lips of a priest ought to preserve knowledge, because he is the messenger of the Lord Almighty and people seek instruction from his mouth. But you have turned from the way and by your teaching have caused many to stumble; you have violated the covenant with Levi," says the Lord Almighty. "So I have caused you to be despised and humiliated before all the people, because you have not followed my ways but have shown partiality in matters of the law." Do we not all have one Father? Did not one God create us? Why do we profane the covenant of our ancestors by being unfaithful to one another? Judah has been unfaithful. A detestable thing has been committed in Israel and in Jerusalem: Judah has desecrated the sanctuary the Lord loves by marrying women who worship a foreign god. As for the man who does this, whoever he may be, may the Lord remove him from the tents of Jacob—even though he brings an offering to the Lord Almighty Another thing you do: You flood the Lord's altar with tears. You weep and wail because he no longer looks with favor on your offerings or accepts them with pleasure from your hands. You ask, "Why?" It is because the Lord is the witness between you and the wife of your youth. You have been unfaithful to her, though she is your partner, the wife of your marriage covenant. Has not the one God made you? You belong to him in body and spirit. And what does the one God seek? Godly offspring. So be on your guard, and do not be unfaithful to the wife of your youth "The man who hates and divorces his wife," says the Lord, the God of Israel, "does violence to the one he should protect," says the Lord Almighty. So be on your guard, and do not be unfaithful You have wearied the Lord with your words. "How have we wearied him?" you ask. By saying, "All who do evil are good in the eyes of the Lord, and he is pleased with them" or "Where is the God of justice?"

Chapter 3

"I will send my messenger, who will prepare the way before me. Then suddenly the Lord you are seeking will come to his temple; the messenger of the covenant, whom you desire, will come," says the Lord Almighty But who can endure the day of his coming? Who can stand when he appears? For he will be like a refiner's fire or a launderer's soap. He will sit as a refiner and purifier of silver; he will purify the Levites and refine them like gold and silver. Then the Lord will have men who will bring offerings in righteousness, and the offerings of Judah and Jerusalem will be acceptable to the Lord, as in days gone by, as in former years "So I will come to put you on trial. I will be quick to testify against sorcerers, adulterers, and perjurers, against those who defraud laborers of their wages, who oppress the widows and the fatherless, and deprive the foreigners among you of justice, but do not fear me," says the Lord Almighty "I

the Lord do not change. So you, the descendants of Jacob, are not destroyed. Ever since the time of your ancestors you have turned away from my decrees and have not kept them. Return to me, and I will return to you," says the Lord Almighty But you ask, "How are we to return?" "Will a mere mortal rob God? Yet you rob me "But you ask, 'How are we robbing you?' "In tithes and offerings. You are under a curse— your whole nation—because you are robbing me. Bring the whole tithe into the storehouse, that there may be food in my house. Test me in this," says the Lord Almighty, "and see if I will not throw open the floodgates of heaven and pour out so much blessing that there will not be room enough to store it. I will prevent pests from devouring your crops, and the vines in your fields will not drop their fruit before it is ripe," says the Lord Almighty. "Then all the nations will call you blessed, for yours will be a delightful land," says the Lord Almighty "You have spoken arrogantly against me," says the Lord "Yet you ask, 'What have we said against you?' "You have said, 'It is futile to serve God. What do we gain by carrying out his requirements and going about like mourners before the Lord Almighty? But now we call the arrogant blessed. Certainly evildoers prosper, and even when they put God to the test, they get away with it.'" Then those who feared the Lord talked with each other, and the Lord listened and heard. A scroll of remembrance was written in his presence concerning those who feared the Lord and honored his name "On the day when I act," says the Lord Almighty, "they will be my treasured possession. I will spare them, just as a father has compassion and spares his son who serves him. And you will again see the distinction between the righteous and the wicked, between those who serve God and those who do not

Chapter 4

"Surely the day is coming; it will burn like a furnace. All the arrogant and every evildoer will be stubble, and the day that is coming will set them on fire," says the Lord Almighty. "Not a root or a branch will be left to them. But for you who revere my name, the sun of righteousness will rise with healing in its rays. And you will go out and frolic like well-fed calves. Then you will trample on the wicked; they will be ashes under the soles of your feet on the day when I act," says the Lord Almighty "Remember the law of my servant Moses, the decrees and laws I gave him at Horeb for all Israel "See, I will send the prophet Elijah to you before that great and dreadful day of the Lord comes. He will turn the hearts of the parents to their children, and the hearts of the children to their parents; or else I will come and strike the land with total destruction."

NEW TESTAMENT

1. Gospels and Acts

40. Matthew

Chapter 1

The genealogy of Jesus Christ, the son of David, the son of Abraham, is as follows: Abraham begat Isaac, Isaac begat Jacob, and Jacob begat Judah and his brothers. Judah begat Perez and Zerah by Tamar, Perez begat Hezron, and Hezron begat Ram. Ram begat Amminadab, Amminadab begat Nahshon, and Nahshon begat Salmon. Salmon begat Boaz by Rahab, Boaz begat Obed by Ruth, and Obed begat Jesse. Jesse begat David the king, and David the king begat Solomon by the wife of Uriah. Solomon begat Rehoboam, Rehoboam begat Abijah, and Abijah begat Asa. Asa begat Jehoshaphat, Jehoshaphat begat Joram, and Joram begat Uzziah. Uzziah begat Jotham, Jotham begat Ahaz, and Ahaz begat Hezekiah. Hezekiah begat Manasseh, Manasseh begat Amon, and Amon begat Josiah. Josiah begat Jeconiah and his brothers about the time they were carried away to Babylon. After they were taken to Babylon, Jeconiah begat Shealtiel, and Shealtiel begat Zerubbabel. Zerubbabel begat Abiud, Abiud begat Eliakim, and Eliakim begat Azor. Azor begat Zadok, Zadok begat Achim, and Achim begat Eliud. Eliud begat Eleazar, Eleazar begat Matthan, and Matthan begat Jacob. Jacob begat Joseph, the husband of Mary, from whom was born Jesus, who is called Christ. So, all the generations from Abraham to David are fourteen generations; from David until the captivity in Babylon, fourteen generations; and from the captivity in Babylon until Christ, fourteen generations The birth of Jesus Christ came about in this way: when His mother Mary was betrothed to Joseph, before they came together, she was found to be with child by the Holy Spirit. Then Joseph, her husband, being a righteous man and not wanting to make her a public example, planned to put her away secretly. But while he thought about these things, an angel of the Lord appeared to him in a dream, saying, "Joseph, son of David, do not be afraid to take Mary as your wife, for what is conceived in her is from the Holy Spirit. She will bear a son, and you shall call His name Jesus, for He will save His people from their sins." All this took place to fulfill what the Lord had spoken through the prophet: "Behold, a virgin shall be with child, and shall bring forth a son, and they shall call His name Emmanuel," which means, "God with us." When Joseph awoke from sleep, he did as the angel of the Lord commanded him and took Mary as his wife, but he did not know her until she had borne a son, and he called His name Jesus

Chapter 2

When Jesus was born in Bethlehem of Judea, during the reign of King Herod, wise men from the East came to Jerusalem, asking, "Where is the King of the Jews who has been born? For we have seen His star in the East and have come to worship Him." When King Herod heard this, he was troubled, and all Jerusalem with him. He gathered all the chief priests and scribes of the people and asked them where the Christ was to be born. They told him, "In Bethlehem of Judea, for it is written by the prophet: 'But you, Bethlehem, in the land of Judah, are not the least among the rulers of Judah; for out of you shall come a Ruler who will shepherd My people Israel.'" Herod then secretly called the wise men and found out from them the exact time the star had appeared. He sent them to Bethlehem, saying, "Go and search diligently for the child; when you have found Him, bring back word to me, that I may come and worship Him also." After listening to the king, they departed, and behold, the star that they had seen in the East went before them until it came and stood over where the child was. When they saw the star, they rejoiced with exceedingly great joy. They went into the house and saw the child with Mary, His mother, and they fell down and worshiped Him. Then they opened their treasures and presented Him with gifts of gold, frankincense, and myrrh. Being warned in a dream not to return to Herod, they departed for their own country by another way After they had departed, an angel of the Lord appeared to Joseph in a dream, saying, "Get up, take the child and His mother, and flee to Egypt. Stay there until I tell you, for Herod is going to search for the child to destroy Him." So Joseph got up, took the child and His mother by night, and departed for Egypt, where they stayed until the death of Herod. This was to fulfill what the Lord had spoken by the prophet: "Out of Egypt I called My Son." When Herod saw that he had been deceived by the wise men, he was furious. He sent and killed all the male children in Bethlehem and in all its surrounding areas, from two years old and under, according to the time he had ascertained from the wise men. Then was fulfilled what was spoken by the prophet Jeremiah: "A voice was heard in Ramah, weeping and great mourning, Rachel weeping for her children, and she refused to be comforted, because they were no more." After Herod died, an angel of the Lord appeared in a dream to Joseph in Egypt, saying, "Get up, take the child and His mother, and go to the land of Israel, for those who were seeking the child's life are dead." So Joseph got up, took the child and His mother, and went to the land of Israel. But when he heard that Archelaus was reigning in Judea in place of his father Herod, he was afraid to go there. After being warned in a dream, he withdrew to the region of Galilee, and he went and lived in a town called Nazareth. This was to fulfill what was spoken through the prophets: "He will be called a Nazarene."

Chapter 3

In those days, John the Baptist came, preaching in the wilderness of Judea, and saying, "Repent, for the kingdom of heaven is at hand." This is he who was spoken of through the prophet Isaiah: "A voice of one calling in the wilderness, 'Prepare the way for the Lord, make straight paths for Him.'" John wore a garment of camel's hair and a leather belt around his waist, and his food was locusts and wild honey. People went out to him from Jerusalem and all Judea and the whole region of the Jordan. Confessing their sins, they were baptized by him in the Jordan River When he saw many of the Pharisees and Sadducees coming to where he was baptizing, he said to them, "You brood of vipers! Who warned you to flee from the coming wrath? Produce fruit in keeping with repentance. And do not think you can say to yourselves, 'We have Abraham as our father.' I tell you that out of these stones God can raise up children for Abraham. The ax is already at the root of the trees, and every tree that does not produce good fruit will be cut down and thrown into the fire." "I baptize you with water for repentance. But after me comes one who is more powerful than I, whose sandals I am not worthy to carry. He will baptize you with the Holy Spirit and fire. His winnowing fork is in His hand, and He will clear His threshing floor, gathering His wheat into the barn and burning up the chaff with unquenchable fire." Then Jesus came from Galilee to the Jordan to be baptized by John. But John tried to deter Him, saying, "I need to be baptized by You, and do You come to me?" Jesus replied, "Let it be so now; it is proper for us to do this to fulfill all righteousness." Then John consented. As soon as Jesus was baptized, He went up out of the water. At that moment heaven was opened, and He saw the Spirit of God descending like a dove and alighting on Him.

And a voice from heaven said, "This is My Son, whom I love; with Him I am well pleased."

Chapter 4

Then Jesus was led by the Spirit into the wilderness to be tempted by the devil. After fasting for forty days and forty nights, He was hungry. The tempter came to Him and said, "If You are the Son of God, tell these stones to become bread." Jesus answered, "It is written: 'Man shall not live on bread alone, but on every word that comes from the mouth of God.'" Then the devil took Him to the holy city and had Him stand on the highest point of the temple. "If You are the Son of God," he said, "throw Yourself down. For it is written: 'He will command His angels concerning You, and they will lift You up in their hands, so that You will not strike Your foot against a stone.'" Jesus answered him, "It is also written: 'Do not put the Lord your God to the test.'" Again, the devil took Him to a very high mountain and showed Him all the kingdoms of the world and their splendor. "All this I will give You," he said, "if You will bow down and worship me." Jesus said to him, "Away from me, Satan! For it is written: 'Worship the Lord your God, and serve Him only.'" Then the devil left Him, and angels came and attended Him When Jesus heard that John had been put in prison, He withdrew to Galilee. Leaving Nazareth, He went and lived in Capernaum, which was by the lake in the area of Zebulun and Naphtali, to fulfill what was said through the prophet Isaiah: "Land of Zebulun and land of Naphtali, the Way of the Sea, beyond the Jordan, Galilee of the Gentiles—the people living in darkness have seen a great light; on those living in the land of the shadow of death a light has dawned." From that time on Jesus began to preach, "Repent, for the kingdom of heaven has come near." As Jesus was walking beside the Sea of Galilee, He saw two brothers, Simon called Peter and his brother Andrew. They were casting a net into the lake, for they were fishermen. "Come, follow Me," Jesus said, "and I will send you out to fish for people." At once they left their nets and followed Him. Going on from there, He saw two other brothers, James son of Zebedee and his brother John. They were in a boat with their father Zebedee, preparing their nets. Jesus called them, and immediately they left the boat and their father and followed Him Jesus went throughout Galilee, teaching in their synagogues, proclaiming the good news of the kingdom, and healing every disease and sickness among the people. News about Him spread all over Syria, and people brought to Him all who were ill with various diseases, those suffering severe pain, the demon-possessed, those having seizures, and the paralyzed; and He healed them. Large crowds from Galilee, the Decapolis, Jerusalem, Judea, and the region across the Jordan followed Him

Chapter 5

When Jesus saw the crowds, He went up on a mountainside and sat down. His disciples came to Him, and He began to teach them "Blessed are the poor in spirit, for theirs is the kingdom of heaven. Blessed are those who mourn, for they will be comforted. Blessed are the meek, for they will inherit the earth. Blessed are those who hunger and thirst for righteousness, for they will be filled. Blessed are the merciful, for they will be shown mercy. Blessed are the pure in heart, for they will see God. Blessed are the peacemakers, for they will be called children of God. Blessed are those who are persecuted because of righteousness, for theirs is the kingdom of heaven. Blessed are you when people insult you, persecute you and falsely say all kinds of evil against you because of Me. Rejoice and be glad, because great is your reward in heaven, for in the same way they persecuted the prophets who were before you

"You are the salt of the earth. But if the salt loses its saltiness, how can it be made salty again? It is no longer good for anything, except to be thrown out and trampled underfoot. You are the light of the world. A town built on a hill cannot be hidden. Neither do people light a lamp and put it under a bowl. Instead, they put it on its stand, and it gives light to everyone in the house. In the same way, let your light shine before others, that they may see your good deeds and glorify your Father in heaven "Do not think that I have come to abolish the Law or the Prophets; I have not come to abolish them but to fulfill them. For truly I tell you, until heaven and earth disappear, not the smallest letter, not the least stroke of a pen, will by any means disappear from the Law until everything is accomplished. Therefore, anyone who sets aside one of the least of these commands and teaches others accordingly will be called least in the kingdom of heaven, but whoever practices and teaches these commands will be called great in the kingdom of heaven. For I tell you that unless your righteousness surpasses that of the Pharisees and the teachers of the law, you will certainly not enter the kingdom of heaven "You have heard that it was said to the people long ago, 'You shall not murder, and anyone who murders will be subject to judgment.' But I tell you that anyone who is angry with a brother or sister will be subject to judgment. Again, anyone who says to a brother or sister, 'Raca,' is answerable to the court. And anyone who says, 'You fool!' will be in danger of the fire of hell. Therefore, if you are offering your gift at the altar and there remember that your brother or sister has something against you, leave your gift there in front of the altar. First, go and be reconciled to them; then come and offer your gift "Settle matters quickly with your adversary who is taking you to court. Do it while you are still together on the way, or your adversary may hand you over to the judge, and the judge may hand you over to the officer, and you may be thrown into prison. Truly I tell you, you will not get out until you have paid the last penny "You have heard that it was said, 'You shall not commit adultery.' But I tell you that anyone who looks at a woman lustfully has already committed adultery with her in his heart. If your right eye causes you to stumble, gouge it out and throw it away. It is better for you to lose one part of your body than for your whole body to be thrown into hell. And if your right hand causes you to stumble, cut it off and throw it away. It is better for you to lose one part of your body than for your whole body to go into hell "It has been said, 'Anyone who divorces his wife must give her a certificate of divorce.' But I tell you that anyone who divorces his wife, except for sexual immorality, makes her the victim of adultery, and anyone who marries a divorced woman commits adultery "Again, you have heard that it was said to the people long ago, 'Do not break your oath, but fulfill to the Lord the vows you have made.' But I tell you, do not swear an oath at all: either by heaven, for it is God's throne; or by the earth, for it is His footstool; or by Jerusalem, for it is the city of the Great King. And do not swear by your head, for you cannot make even one hair white or black. All you need to say is simply 'Yes' or 'No'; anything beyond this comes from the evil one "You have heard that it was said, 'Eye for eye, and tooth for tooth.' But I tell you, do not resist an evil person. If anyone slaps you on the right cheek, turn to them the other cheek also. And if anyone wants to sue you and take your shirt, hand over your coat as well. If anyone forces you to go one mile, go with them two miles. Give to the one who asks you, and do not turn away from the one who wants to borrow from you "You have heard that it was said, 'Love your neighbor and hate your enemy.' But I tell you, love your enemies and pray for those who persecute you, that you may be children of your Father in heaven. He causes His sun to rise on the evil and the good, and sends rain on the righteous and the unrighteous. If you love those who love you, what reward will you get? Are not even the tax collectors doing that? And if you greet only your own people, what are you doing more than others? Do not even pagans do that? Be perfect, therefore, as your heavenly Father is perfect."

Chapter 6

Be careful not to practice your righteousness in front of others to be seen by them. If you do, you will have no reward from your Father in heaven. Therefore, when you give to the needy, do not announce it with trumpets, as the hypocrites do in the synagogues and on the streets, to be honored by others. Truly I tell you, they have received their reward in full. But when you give to the needy, do not let your left hand know what your right hand is doing so that your giving may be in secret. Then your Father, who sees what is done in secret, will reward you When you pray, do not be like the hypocrites, for they love to pray standing in the synagogues and on the street corners to be seen by others. Truly I tell you, they have received their reward in full. But when you pray, go into your room, close the door, and pray to your Father, who is unseen. Then your Father, who sees what is done in secret, will reward you. When you pray, do not keep on babbling like pagans, for they think they will be heard because of their many words. Do not be like them, for your Father knows what you need before you ask Him. This, then, is how you should pray: "Our Father in heaven, hallowed be Your name, Your kingdom come, Your will be done, on earth as it is in heaven. Give us today our daily bread. And forgive us our debts, as we also have forgiven our debtors. And lead us not into temptation, but deliver us from the evil one." For if you forgive other people when they sin against you, your heavenly Father will also forgive you. But if you do not forgive others their sins, your Father will not forgive your sins When you fast, do not look somber as the hypocrites do, for they disfigure their faces to show others they are fasting. Truly I tell you, they have received their reward in full. But when you fast, put oil on your head and wash your face so that it will not be obvious to others that you are fasting, but only to your Father, who is unseen. And your Father, who sees what is done in secret, will reward you Do not store up for yourselves treasures on earth, where moths and vermin destroy, and where thieves break in and steal. But store up for yourselves treasures in heaven, where moths and vermin do not destroy, and where thieves do not break in and steal. For where your treasure is, there your heart will be also The eye is the lamp of the body. If your eyes are healthy, your whole body will be full of light. But if your eyes are unhealthy, your whole body will be full of darkness. If then the light within you is darkness, how great is that darkness! No one can serve two masters. Either you will hate the one and love the other, or you will be devoted to the one and despise the other. You cannot serve both God and money Therefore I tell you, do not worry about your life, what you will eat or drink; or about your body, what you will wear. Is not life more than food, and the body more than clothes? Look at the birds of the air; they do not sow or reap or store away in barns, and yet your heavenly Father feeds them. Are you not much more valuable than they? Can any one of you by worrying add a single hour to your life? And why do you worry about clothes? See how the flowers of the field grow. They do not labor or spin. Yet I tell you that not even Solomon in all his splendor was dressed like one of these. If that is how God clothes the grass of the field, which is here today and tomorrow is thrown into the fire, will He not much more clothe you—you of little faith? So do not worry, saying, 'What shall we eat?' or 'What shall we drink?' or 'What shall we wear?' For the pagans run after all these things, and your heavenly Father knows that you need them. But seek first His kingdom and His righteousness, and all these things will be given to you as well. Therefore do not worry about tomorrow, for tomorrow will worry about itself. Each day has enough trouble of its own

Chapter 7

Do not judge, or you too will be judged. For in the same way you judge others, you will be judged, and with the measure you use, it will be measured to you. Why do you look at the speck of sawdust in your brother's eye and pay no attention to the plank in your own eye? How can you say to your brother, 'Let me take the speck out of your eye,' when all the time there is a plank in your own eye? You hypocrite, first take the plank out of your own eye, and then you will see clearly to remove the speck from your brother's eye Do not give dogs what is sacred; do not throw your pearls to pigs. If you do, they may trample them under their feet, and turn and tear you to pieces Ask, and it will be given to you; seek, and you will find; knock, and the door will be opened to you. For everyone who asks receives; the one who seeks finds; and to the one who knocks, the door will be opened. Which of you, if your son asks for bread, will give him a stone? Or if he asks for a fish, will give him a snake? If you then, though you are evil, know how to give good gifts to your children, how much more will your Father in heaven give good gifts to those who ask Him! So in everything, do to others what you would have them do to you, for this sums up the Law and the Prophets Enter through the narrow gate. For wide is the gate and broad is the road that leads to destruction, and many enter through it. But small is the gate and narrow the road that leads to life, and only a few find it Watch out for false prophets. They come to you in sheep's clothing, but inwardly they are ferocious wolves. By their fruit you will recognize them. Do people pick grapes from thornbushes, or figs from thistles? Likewise, every good tree bears good fruit, but a bad tree bears bad fruit. A good tree cannot bear bad fruit, and a bad tree cannot bear good fruit. Every tree that does not bear good fruit is cut down and thrown into the fire. Thus, by their fruit you will recognize them Not everyone who says to me, 'Lord, Lord,' will enter the kingdom of heaven, but only the one who does the will of my Father who is in heaven. Many will say to me on that day, 'Lord, Lord, did we not prophesy in Your name and in Your name drive out demons and in Your name perform many miracles?' Then I will tell them plainly, 'I never knew you. Away from me, you evildoers!' Therefore everyone who hears these words of mine and puts them into practice is like a wise man who built his house on the rock. The rain came down, the streams rose, and the winds blew and beat against that house; yet it did not fall, because it had its foundation on the rock. But everyone who hears these words of mine and does not put them into practice is like a foolish man who built his house on sand. The rain came down, the streams rose, and the winds blew and beat against that house, and it fell with a great crash When Jesus had finished saying these things, the crowds were amazed at His teaching, because He taught as one who had authority, and not as their teachers of the law

Chapter 8

When Jesus came down from the mountainside, large crowds followed Him. A man with leprosy came and knelt before Him and said, "Lord, if You are willing, You can make me clean." Jesus reached out

His hand and touched the man. "I am willing," He said. "Be clean!" Immediately he was cleansed of his leprosy. Then Jesus said to him, "See that you don't tell anyone. But go, show yourself to the priest and offer the gift Moses commanded, as a testimony to them." When Jesus had entered Capernaum, a centurion came to Him, asking for help. "Lord," he said, "my servant lies at home paralyzed, suffering terribly." Jesus said to him, "Shall I come and heal him?" The centurion replied, "Lord, I do not deserve to have You come under my roof. But just say the word, and my servant will be healed. For I myself am a man under authority, with soldiers under me. I tell this one, 'Go,' and he goes; and that one, 'Come,' and he comes. I say to my servant, 'Do this,' and he does it." When Jesus heard this, He was amazed and said to those following Him, "Truly I tell you, I have not found anyone in Israel with such great faith. I say to you that many will come from the east and the west and will take their places at the feast with Abraham, Isaac, and Jacob in the kingdom of heaven. But the subjects of the kingdom will be thrown outside, into the darkness, where there will be weeping and gnashing of teeth." Then Jesus said to the centurion, "Go! Let it be done just as you believed it would." And his servant was healed at that moment When Jesus came into Peter's house, He saw Peter's mother-in-law lying in bed with a fever. He touched her hand and the fever left her, and she got up and began to wait on Him. When evening came, many who were demon-possessed were brought to Him, and He drove out the spirits with a word and healed all the sick. This was to fulfill what was spoken through the prophet Isaiah: "He took up our infirmities and bore our diseases." When Jesus saw the crowd around Him, He gave orders to cross to the other side of the lake. Then a teacher of the law came to Him and said, "Teacher, I will follow You wherever You go." Jesus replied, "Foxes have dens and birds have nests, but the Son of Man has no place to lay His head." Another disciple said to Him, "Lord, first let me go and bury my father." But Jesus told him, "Follow Me, and let the dead bury their own dead." Then He got into the boat and His disciples followed Him. Suddenly a furious storm came up on the lake, so that the waves swept over the boat. But Jesus was sleeping. The disciples went and woke Him, saying, "Lord, save us! We're going to drown!" He replied, "You of little faith, why are you so afraid?" Then He got up and rebuked the winds and the waves, and it was completely calm. The men were amazed and asked, "What kind of man is this? Even the winds and the waves obey Him!" When He arrived at the other side in the region of the Gadarenes, two demon-possessed men coming from the tombs met Him. They were so violent that no one could pass that way. "What do You want with us, Son of God?" they shouted. "Have You come here to torture us before the appointed time?" Some distance from them, a large herd of pigs was feeding. The demons begged Jesus, "If You drive us out, send us into the herd of pigs." He said to them, "Go!" So they came out and went into the pigs, and the whole herd rushed down the steep bank into the lake and died in the water. Those tending the pigs ran off, went into the town, and reported all this, including what had happened to the demon-possessed men. Then the whole town went out to meet Jesus. And when they saw Him, they pleaded with Him to leave their region

Chapter 9

Jesus stepped into a boat, crossed over, and came to His own town. Some men brought to Him a paralyzed man, lying on a mat. When Jesus saw their faith, He said to the man, "Take heart, son; your sins are forgiven." At this, some of the teachers of the law said to themselves, "This fellow is blaspheming!" Knowing their thoughts, Jesus said, "Why do you entertain evil thoughts in your hearts? Which is easier: to say, 'Your sins are forgiven,' or to say, 'Get up and walk'? But I want you to know that the Son of Man has authority on earth to forgive sins." So He said to the paralyzed man, "Get up, take your mat and go home." Then the man got up and went home. When the crowd saw this, they were filled with awe; and they praised God, who had given such authority to man As Jesus went on from there, He saw a man named Matthew sitting at the tax collector's booth. "Follow Me," He told him, and Matthew got up and followed Him While Jesus was having dinner at Matthew's house, many tax collectors and sinners came and ate with Him and His disciples. When the Pharisees saw this, they asked His disciples, "Why does your teacher eat with tax collectors and sinners?" On hearing this, Jesus said, "It is not the healthy who need a doctor, but the sick. But go and learn what this means: 'I desire mercy, not sacrifice.' For I have not come to call the righteous, but sinners." Then John's disciples came and asked Him, "How is it that we and the Pharisees fast often, but Your disciples do not fast?" Jesus answered, "How can the guests of the bridegroom mourn while He is with them? The time will come when the bridegroom will be taken from them; then they will fast "No one sews a patch of unshrunk cloth on an old garment, for the patch will pull away from the garment, making the tear worse. Neither do people pour new wine into old wineskins. If they do, the skins will burst; the wine will run out and the wineskins will be ruined. No, they pour new wine into new wineskins, and both are preserved." While He was saying this, a synagogue leader came and knelt before Him and said, "My daughter has just died. But come and put Your hand on her, and she will live." Jesus got up and went with him, and so did His disciples. Just then a woman who had been subject to bleeding for twelve years came up behind Him and touched the edge of His cloak. She said to herself, "If I only touch His cloak, I will be healed." Jesus turned and saw her. "Take heart, daughter," He said, "your faith has healed you." And the woman was healed at that moment When Jesus entered the synagogue leader's house and saw the noisy crowd and people playing pipes, He said, "Go away. The girl is not dead but asleep." But they laughed at Him. After the crowd had been put outside, He went in and took the girl by the hand, and she got up. News of this spread through all that region As Jesus went on from there, two blind men followed Him, calling out, "Have mercy on us, Son of David!" When He had gone indoors, the blind men came to Him, and He asked them, "Do you believe that I am able to do this?" "Yes, Lord," they replied. Then He touched their eyes and said, "According to your faith let it be done to you"; and their sight was restored. Jesus warned them sternly, "See that no one knows about this." But they went out and spread the news about Him all over that region While they were going out, a man who was demon-possessed and could not talk was brought to Jesus. And when the demon was driven out, the man who had been mute spoke. The crowd was amazed and said, "Nothing like this has ever been seen in Israel." But the Pharisees said, "It is by the prince of demons that He drives out demons." Jesus went through all the towns and villages, teaching in their synagogues, proclaiming the good news of the kingdom, and healing every disease and sickness. When He saw the crowds, He had compassion on them because they were harassed and helpless, like sheep without a shepherd. Then He said to His disciples, "The harvest is plentiful but the workers are few. Ask the

Lord of the harvest, therefore, to send out workers into His harvest field."

Chapter 10

Jesus called His twelve disciples to Him and gave them authority to drive out impure spirits and to heal every disease and sickness. These are the names of the twelve apostles: first, Simon (who is called Peter) and his brother Andrew; James son of Zebedee, and his brother John; Philip and Bartholomew; Thomas and Matthew the tax collector; James son of Alphaeus, and Thaddaeus; Simon the Zealot and Judas Iscariot, who betrayed Him These twelve Jesus sent out with the following instructions: "Do not go among the Gentiles or enter any town of the Samaritans. Go rather to the lost sheep of Israel. As you go, proclaim this message: 'The kingdom of heaven has come near.' Heal the sick, raise the dead, cleanse those who have leprosy, drive out demons. Freely you have received; freely give. Do not get any gold or silver or copper to take with you in your belts—no bag for the journey or extra shirt or sandals or a staff, for the worker is worth his keep. Whatever town or village you enter, search there for some worthy person and stay at their house until you leave. As you enter the home, give it your greeting. If the home is deserving, let your peace rest on it; if it is not, let your peace return to you. If anyone will not welcome you or listen to your words, leave that home or town and shake the dust off your feet. Truly I tell you, it will be more bearable for Sodom and Gomorrah on the day of judgment than for that town "I am sending you out like sheep among wolves. Therefore be as shrewd as snakes and as innocent as doves. Be on your guard; you will be handed over to the local councils and be flogged in the synagogues. On My account you will be brought before governors and kings as witnesses to them and to the Gentiles. But when they arrest you, do not worry about what to say or how to say it. At that time you will be given what to say, for it will not be you speaking, but the Spirit of your Father speaking through you "Brother will betray brother to death, and a father his child; children will rebel against their parents and have them put to death. You will be hated by everyone because of Me, but the one who stands firm to the end will be saved. When you are persecuted in one place, flee to another. Truly I tell you, you will not finish going through the towns of Israel before the Son of Man comes "The student is not above the teacher, nor a servant above his master. It is enough for students to be like their teachers, and servants like their masters. If the head of the house has been called Beelzebul, how much more the members of his household! "So do not be afraid of them, for there is nothing concealed that will not be disclosed, or hidden that will not be made known. What I tell you in the dark, speak in the daylight; what is whispered in your ear, proclaim from the roofs. Do not be afraid of those who kill the body but cannot kill the soul. Rather, be afraid of the One who can destroy both soul and body in hell. Are not two sparrows sold for a penny? Yet not one of them will fall to the ground outside your Father's care. And even the very hairs of your head are all numbered. So don't be afraid; you are worth more than many sparrows "Whoever acknowledges Me before others, I will also acknowledge before My Father in heaven. But whoever disowns Me before others, I will disown before My Father in heaven "Do not suppose that I have come to bring peace to the earth. I did not come to bring peace, but a sword. For I have come to turn "'a man against his father, a daughter against her mother, a daughter-in-law against her mother-in-law— a man's enemies will be the members of his own household.' "Anyone who loves their father or mother more than Me is not worthy of Me; anyone who loves their son or daughter more than Me is not worthy of Me. Whoever does not take up their cross and follow Me is not worthy of Me. Whoever finds their life will lose it, and whoever loses their life for My sake will find it "Anyone who welcomes you welcomes Me, and anyone who welcomes Me welcomes the one who sent Me. Whoever welcomes a prophet as a prophet will receive a prophet's reward, and whoever welcomes a righteous person as a righteous person will receive a righteous person's reward. And if anyone gives even a cup of cold water to one of these little ones who is My disciple, truly I tell you, that person will certainly not lose their reward."

Chapter 11

After Jesus had finished instructing His twelve disciples, He departed to teach and preach in their cities. When John, who was in prison, heard about the works of Christ, he sent two of his disciples to ask Him, "Are You the one who is to come, or should we look for another?" Jesus replied, "Go and tell John what you hear and see: the blind receive sight, the lame walk, lepers are cleansed, the deaf hear, the dead are raised, and the poor have the gospel preached to them. Blessed is anyone who does not stumble because of Me." As John's disciples were leaving, Jesus began to speak to the crowd about John: "What did you go out into the wilderness to see? A reed swayed by the wind? No. What did you go out to see? A man dressed in fine clothes? No, those who wear fine clothes are in kings' palaces. So, what did you go out to see? A prophet? Yes, I tell you, and more than a prophet. This is the one about whom it is written: 'I will send My messenger ahead of you, who will prepare your way before you.' Truly I tell you, among those born of women there has not risen anyone greater than John the Baptist; yet whoever is least in the kingdom of heaven is greater than he. From the days of John the Baptist until now, the kingdom of heaven has been subjected to violence, and violent people have been raiding it. For all the Prophets and the Law prophesied until John. And if you are willing to accept it, he is the Elijah who was to come. Whoever has ears, let them hear "To what can I compare this generation? They are like children sitting in the marketplaces and calling out to others: 'We played the pipe for you, and you did not dance; we sang a dirge, and you did not mourn.' For John came neither eating nor drinking, and they say, 'He has a demon.' The Son of Man came eating and drinking, and they say, 'Here is a glutton and a drunkard, a friend of tax collectors and sinners.' But wisdom is proved right by her deeds." Then Jesus began to denounce the towns in which most of His miracles had been performed because they did not repent. "Woe to you, Chorazin! Woe to you, Bethsaida! For if the miracles that were performed in you had been performed in Tyre and Sidon, they would have repented long ago in sackcloth and ashes. But I tell you, it will be more bearable for Tyre and Sidon on the day of judgment than for you. And you, Capernaum, will you be lifted to the heavens? No, you will go down to Hades. For if the miracles that were performed in you had been performed in Sodom, it would have remained to this day. But I tell you that it will be more bearable for Sodom on the day of judgment than for you." At that time Jesus said, "I praise You, Father, Lord of heaven and earth, because You have hidden these things from the wise and learned, and revealed them to little children. Yes, Father, for this is what You were pleased to do. All things have been committed to Me by My Father. No one knows the Son except the Father, and no one knows the Father except the Son and those to whom the Son chooses to reveal Him. Come to Me, all you who are weary and burdened, and I will give you rest. Take My yoke upon you and learn from Me, for I am gentle and humble in heart, and you will find rest for your souls. For My yoke is easy and My burden is light."

Chapter 12

At that time, Jesus went through the grainfields on the Sabbath. His disciples were hungry and began to pick some heads of grain and eat them. When the Pharisees saw this, they said to Him, "Look! Your disciples are doing what is unlawful on the Sabbath." He answered, "Haven't you read what David did when he and his companions were hungry? He entered the house of God, and he and his companions ate the consecrated bread—which was not lawful for them to do, but only for the priests. Or haven't you read in the Law that the priests on Sabbath duty in the temple desecrate the Sabbath and yet are innocent? I tell you that something greater than the temple is here. If you had known what these words mean, 'I desire mercy, not sacrifice,' you would not have condemned the innocent. For the Son of Man is Lord of the Sabbath." Going on from that place, He went into their synagogue, and a man with a shriveled hand was there. Looking for a reason to bring charges against Jesus, they asked Him, "Is it lawful to heal on the Sabbath?" He said to them, "If any of you has a sheep and it falls into a pit on the Sabbath, will you not take hold of it and lift it out? How much more valuable is a person than a sheep! Therefore, it is lawful to do good on the Sabbath." Then He said to the man, "Stretch out your hand." So he stretched it out and it was completely restored, just as sound as the other. But the Pharisees went out and plotted how they might kill Jesus Aware of this, Jesus withdrew from that place. A large crowd followed Him, and He healed all who were ill. He warned them not to tell others about Him. This was to fulfill what was spoken through the prophet Isaiah: "Here is My servant whom I have chosen, the one I love, in whom I delight; I will put My Spirit on Him, and He will proclaim justice to the nations. He will not quarrel or cry out; no one will hear His voice in the streets. A bruised reed He will not break, and a smoldering wick He will not snuff out, till He has brought justice through to victory. In His name the nations will put their hope." Then they brought Him a demon-possessed man who was blind and mute, and Jesus healed him so that he could both talk and see. All the people were astonished and said, "Could this be the Son of David?" But when the Pharisees heard this, they said, "It is only by Beelzebul, the prince of demons, that this fellow drives out demons." Jesus knew their thoughts and said to them, "Every kingdom divided against itself will be ruined, and every city or household divided against itself will not stand. If Satan drives out Satan, he is divided against himself. How then can his kingdom stand? And if I drive out demons by Beelzebul, by whom do your people drive them out? So then, they will be your judges. But if it is by the Spirit of God that I drive out demons, then the kingdom of God has come upon you. Or again, how can anyone enter a strong man's house and carry off his possessions unless he first ties up the strong man? Then he can plunder his house "Whoever is not with Me is against Me, and whoever does not gather with Me scatters. And so I tell you, every kind of sin and slander can be forgiven, but blasphemy against the Spirit will not be forgiven. Anyone who speaks a word against the Son of Man will be forgiven, but anyone who speaks against the Holy Spirit will not be forgiven, either in this age or in the age to come "Make a tree good and its fruit will be good, or make a tree bad and its fruit will be bad, for a tree is recognized by its fruit. You brood of vipers, how can you who are evil say anything good? For the mouth speaks what the heart is full of. A good man brings good things out of the good stored up in him, and an evil man brings evil things out of the evil stored up in him. But I tell you that everyone will have to give account on the day of judgment for every empty word they have spoken. For by your words you will be acquitted, and by your words you will be condemned." Then some of the Pharisees and teachers of the law said to Him, "Teacher, we want to see a sign from You." He answered, "A wicked and adulterous generation asks for a sign! But none will be given it except the sign of the prophet Jonah. For as Jonah was three days and three nights in the belly of a huge fish, so the Son of Man will be three days and three nights in the heart of the earth. The men of Nineveh will stand up at the judgment with this generation and condemn it; for they repented at the preaching of Jonah, and now something greater than Jonah is here. The Queen of the South will rise at the judgment with this generation and condemn it; for she came from the ends of the earth to listen to Solomon's wisdom, and now something greater than Solomon is here "When an impure spirit comes out of a person, it goes through arid places seeking rest and does not find it. Then it says, 'I will return to the house I left.' When it arrives, it finds the house unoccupied, swept clean and put in order. Then it goes and takes with it seven other spirits more wicked than itself, and they go in and live there. And the final condition of that person is worse than the first. That is how it will be with this wicked generation." While Jesus was still talking to the crowd, His mother and brothers stood outside, wanting to speak to Him. Someone told Him, "Your mother and brothers are standing outside, wanting to speak to You." He replied to him, "Who is My mother, and who are My brothers?" Pointing to His disciples, He said, "Here are My mother and My brothers. For whoever does the will of My Father in heaven is My brother and sister and mother."

Chapter 13

That same day Jesus went out of the house and sat by the lake. Such large crowds gathered around Him that He got into a boat and sat in it, while all the people stood on the shore. Then He told them many things in parables, saying: "A farmer went out to sow his seed. As he was scattering the seed, some fell along the path, and the birds came and ate it up. Some fell on rocky places, where it did not have much soil. It sprang up quickly because the soil was shallow. But when the sun came up, the plants were scorched, and they withered because they had no root. Other seed fell among thorns, which grew up and choked the plants. Still, other seed fell on good soil, where it produced a crop—a hundred, sixty, or thirty times what was sown. Whoever has ears, let them hear." The disciples came to Him and asked, "Why do You speak to the people in parables?" He replied, "Because the knowledge of the secrets of the kingdom of heaven has been given to you, but not to them. Whoever has will be given more, and they will have an abundance. Whoever does not have, even what they have will be taken from them. This is why I speak to them in parables: "Though seeing, they do not see; though hearing, they do not hear or understand In them is fulfilled the prophecy of Isaiah: "'You will be ever hearing but never understanding; you will be ever seeing but never perceiving. For this people's heart has become calloused; they hardly hear with their ears, and they have closed their eyes. Otherwise they might see with their eyes, hear with their ears, understand with their hearts and turn, and I would heal them.' But blessed are your eyes because they see, and your ears because they hear. For truly I tell you, many prophets and righteous people longed to see what you see but did not see it, and to hear what you hear but did not hear it "Listen then to what the parable of the sower means: When anyone hears the message about the kingdom and does not understand it, the evil one comes and snatches away what was sown in their heart. This is the seed sown along the path. The seed falling on rocky ground refers to someone who hears the word and at once receives it with joy. But since they have no root, they last only a short time. When trouble or persecution comes because of the word, they quickly fall away. The seed falling among the thorns refers to someone who hears the word, but the worries of this life and the deceitfulness of wealth choke the word, making it unfruitful. But the seed falling on good soil refers to someone who hears the word and understands it. This is the one who produces a crop, yielding a hundred, sixty, or thirty times what was sown." Jesus told them another parable: "The kingdom of heaven is like a man who sowed good seed in his field. But while everyone was sleeping, his enemy came and sowed weeds among the wheat and went away. When the wheat sprouted and formed heads, then the weeds also appeared "The owner's servants came to him and said, 'Sir, didn't you sow good seed in your field? Where then did the weeds come from?' "'An enemy did this,' he replied "The servants asked him, 'Do you want us to go and pull them up?' "'No,' he answered, 'because while you are pulling the weeds, you may uproot the wheat with them. Let both grow together until the harvest. At that time, I will tell the harvesters: First collect the weeds and tie them in bundles to be burned; then gather the wheat and bring it into my barn.'" He told them another parable: "The kingdom of heaven is like a mustard seed, which a man took and planted in his field. Though it is the smallest of all seeds, yet when it grows, it is the largest of garden plants and becomes a tree, so that the birds come and perch in its branches." He told them still another parable: "The kingdom of heaven is like yeast that a woman took and mixed into about sixty pounds of flour until it worked all through the dough." Jesus spoke all these things to the crowd in parables; He did not say anything to them without using a parable. So was fulfilled what was spoken through the prophet: "I will open My mouth in parables, I will utter things hidden since the creation of the world." Then He left the crowd and went into the house. His disciples came to Him and said, "Explain to us the parable of the weeds in the field." He answered, "The one who sowed the good seed is the Son of Man. The field is the world, and the good seed stands for the people of the kingdom. The weeds are the people of the evil one, and the enemy who sows them is the devil. The harvest is the end of the age, and the harvesters are angels. As the weeds are pulled up and burned in the fire, so it will be at the end of the age. The Son of Man will send out His angels, and they will weed out of His kingdom everything that causes sin and all who do evil. They will throw them into the blazing furnace, where there will be weeping and gnashing of teeth. Then the righteous will shine like the sun in the kingdom of their Father. Whoever has ears, let them hear "The kingdom of heaven is like treasure hidden in a field. When a man found it, he hid it again, and then in his joy went and sold all he had and bought that field "Again, the kingdom of heaven is like a merchant looking for fine pearls. When he found one of great value, he went away and sold everything he had and bought it "Once again, the kingdom of heaven is like a net that was let down into the lake and caught all kinds of fish. When it was full, the fishermen pulled it up on the shore. Then they sat down and collected the good fish in baskets, but threw the bad away. This is how it will be at the end of the age. The angels will come and separate the wicked from the righteous and throw them into the blazing furnace, where there will be weeping and gnashing of teeth "Have you understood all these things?" Jesus asked "Yes," they replied He said to them, "Therefore every teacher of the law who has become a disciple in the kingdom of heaven is like the owner of a house who brings out of his storeroom new treasures as well as old." When Jesus had finished these parables, He moved on from there. Coming to His hometown, He began teaching the people in their synagogue, and they were amazed. "Where did this man get this wisdom and these miraculous powers?" they asked. "Isn't this the carpenter's son? Isn't His mother's name Mary, and aren't His brothers James, Joseph, Simon, and Judas? Aren't all His sisters with us? Where then did this man get all these things?" And they took offense at Him But Jesus said to them, "A prophet is not without honor except in his own town and in his own home." And He did not do many miracles there because of their lack of faith

Chapter 14

At that time Herod the tetrarch heard the reports about Jesus, and he said to his attendants, "This is John the Baptist; he has risen from the dead! That is why miraculous powers are at work in him." Now Herod had arrested John and bound him and put him in prison because of Herodias, his brother Philip's wife, for John had been saying to him, "It is not lawful for you to have her." Herod wanted to kill John, but he was afraid of the people, because they considered John a prophet On Herod's birthday, the daughter of Herodias danced for the guests and pleased Herod so much that he promised with an oath to give her whatever she asked. Prompted by her mother, she said, "Give me here on a platter the head of John the Baptist." The king was distressed, but because of his oaths and his dinner guests, he ordered that her request be granted and had John beheaded in the prison. His head was brought in on a platter and given to the girl, who carried it to her mother. John's disciples came and took his body and buried it. Then they went and told Jesus When Jesus heard what had happened, He withdrew by boat privately to a solitary place. Hearing of this, the crowds followed Him on foot from the towns. When Jesus landed and saw a large crowd, He had compassion on them and healed their sick As evening approached, the disciples came to Him and said, "This is a remote place, and it's already getting late. Send the crowds away, so they can go to the villages and buy themselves some food." Jesus replied, "They do not need to go away. You give them something to eat." "We have here only five loaves of bread and two fish," they answered "Bring them here to Me," He said. And He directed the people to sit down on the grass. Taking the five loaves and the two fish and looking up to heaven, He gave thanks and broke the loaves. Then He gave them to the disciples, and the disciples gave them to the people. They all ate and were satisfied, and the disciples picked up twelve basketfuls of broken pieces that were left over. The number of those who ate was about five thousand men, besides women and children Immediately Jesus made the disciples get into the boat and go on ahead of Him to the other side, while He dismissed the crowd. After He had dismissed them, He went up on a mountainside by Himself to pray. Later that night, He was there alone, and the boat was already a considerable distance from land, buffeted by the waves because the wind was against it. Shortly before dawn, Jesus went out to them, walking on the lake. When the disciples saw Him walking on the lake, they were terrified. "It's a ghost," they said, and cried out in fear But Jesus immediately said to them: "Take courage! It is I. Don't be afraid." "Lord, if it's You," Peter replied, "tell me to come to You on the water." "Come," He said Then Peter got down out of the boat, walked on the water and came toward Jesus. But when he saw the wind, he was afraid and, beginning to sink, cried out, "Lord, save me!" Immediately Jesus reached out His hand and caught him. "You of little faith," He said, "why did you doubt?" And when they climbed into the boat, the wind died down. Then those who were in the boat worshiped Him, saying, "Truly You are the Son of God." When they had crossed over, they landed at Gennesaret. And when the men of that place recognized Jesus, they sent word to all the surrounding country. People brought all their sick to Him and begged Him to let the sick just touch the edge of His cloak, and all who touched it were healed

Chapter 15

Then some Pharisees and teachers of the law came to Jesus from Jerusalem and asked, "Why do Your disciples break the tradition of the elders? They don't wash their hands before they eat!" Jesus replied, "And why do you break the command of God for the sake of your tradition? For God said, 'Honor your father and mother' and 'Anyone who curses their father or mother is to be put to death.' But you say that if anyone declares that what might have been used to help their father or mother is 'devoted to God,' they are not to 'honor their father or mother' with it. Thus you nullify the word of God for the sake of your tradition. You hypocrites! Isaiah was right when he prophesied about you: "'These people honor Me with their lips, but their hearts are far from Me. They worship Me in vain; their teachings are merely human rules.'" Jesus called the crowd to Him and said, "Listen and understand. What goes into someone's mouth does not defile them, but what comes out of their mouth, that is what defiles them." Then the disciples came to Him and asked, "Do You know that the Pharisees were offended when they heard this?" He replied, "Every plant that My heavenly Father has not planted will be pulled up by the roots. Leave them; they are blind guides. If the blind lead the blind, both will fall into a pit." Peter said, "Explain the parable to us." "Are you still so dull?" Jesus asked them. "Don't you see that whatever enters the mouth goes into the stomach and then out of the body? But the things that come out of a person's mouth come from the heart, and these defile them. For out of the heart come evil thoughts—murder, adultery, sexual immorality, theft, false testimony, slander. These are what defile a person; but eating with unwashed hands does not defile them." Leaving that place, Jesus withdrew to the region of Tyre and Sidon. A Canaanite woman from that vicinity came to Him, crying out, "Lord, Son of David, have mercy on me! My daughter is demon-possessed and suffering terribly." Jesus did not answer a word. So His disciples came to Him and urged Him, "Send her away, for she keeps crying out after us." He answered, "I was sent only to the lost sheep of Israel." The woman came and knelt before Him. "Lord, help me!" she said He replied, "It is not right to take the children's bread and toss it to the dogs." "Yes it is, Lord," she said. "Even the dogs eat the crumbs that fall from their master's table." Then Jesus said to her, "Woman, you have great faith! Your request is granted." And her daughter was healed at that moment Jesus left there and went along the Sea of Galilee. Then He went up on a mountainside and sat down. Great crowds came to Him, bringing the lame, the blind, the crippled, the mute and many others, and laid them at His feet; and He healed them. The people were amazed when they saw the mute speaking, the crippled made well, the lame walking and the blind seeing. And they praised the God of Israel Jesus called His disciples to Him and said, "I have compassion for these people; they have already been with Me three days and have nothing to eat. I do not want to send them away hungry, or they may collapse on the way." His disciples answered, "Where could we get enough bread in this remote place to feed such a crowd?" "How many loaves do you have?" Jesus asked "Seven," they replied, "and a few small fish." He told the crowd to sit down on the ground. Then He took the seven loaves and the fish, and when He had given thanks, He broke them and gave them to the disciples, and they in turn to the people. They all ate and were satisfied. Afterward the disciples picked up seven basketfuls of broken pieces that were left over. The number of those who ate was four thousand men, besides women and children. After Jesus had sent the crowd away, He got into the boat and went to the vicinity of Magadan

Chapter 16

Then the Pharisees and Sadducees came to test Jesus, asking Him to show them a sign from heaven. He replied, "When evening comes, you say, 'It will be fair weather, for the sky is red,' and in the morning, 'Today it will be stormy, for the sky is red and overcast.' You know how to interpret the appearance of the sky, but you cannot interpret the signs of the times. A wicked and adulterous generation looks for a sign, but none will be given it except the sign of Jonah." Then He left them and went away When the disciples crossed to the other side of the lake, they forgot to bring bread. Jesus said to them, "Be on your guard against the yeast of the Pharisees and Sadducees." They discussed this among themselves and said, "It is because we didn't bring any bread." Aware of their discussion, Jesus asked, "You of little faith, why are you talking among yourselves about having no bread? Do you still not understand? Don't you remember the five loaves for the five thousand, and how many basketfuls you gathered? Or the seven loaves for the four thousand, and how many basketfuls you gathered? How is it you don't understand that I was not talking to you about bread? But be on your guard against the yeast of the Pharisees and Sadducees." Then they understood that He was not telling them to guard against the yeast used in bread, but against the teaching of the Pharisees and Sadducees When Jesus came to the region of Caesarea Philippi, He asked His disciples, "Who do people say the Son of Man is?" They replied, "Some say John the Baptist; others say Elijah; and still others, Jeremiah or one of the prophets." "But what about you?" He asked. "Who do you say I am?" Simon Peter answered, "You are the Messiah, the Son of the living God." Jesus replied, "Blessed are you, Simon son of Jonah, for this was not revealed to you by flesh and blood, but by My Father in heaven. And I tell you that you are Peter, and on this rock I will build My church, and the gates of Hades will not overcome it. I will give you the keys of the kingdom of heaven; whatever you bind on earth will be bound in heaven, and whatever you loose on earth will be loosed in heaven." Then He ordered His disciples not to tell anyone that He was the Messiah From that time on, Jesus began to explain to His disciples that He must go to Jerusalem and suffer many things at the hands of the elders, the chief priests, and the teachers of the law, and that He must be killed and on the third day be raised to life. Peter took Him aside and began to rebuke Him. "Never, Lord!" he said.

"This shall never happen to you!" Jesus turned and said to Peter, "Get behind Me, Satan! You are a stumbling block to Me; you do not have in mind the concerns of God, but merely human concerns." Then Jesus said to His disciples, "Whoever wants to be My disciple must deny themselves and take up their cross and follow Me. For whoever wants to save their life will lose it, but whoever loses their life for Me will find it. What good will it be for someone to gain the whole world, yet forfeit their soul? Or what can anyone give in exchange for their soul? For the Son of Man is going to come in His Father's glory with His angels, and then He will reward each person according to what they have done. Truly I tell you, some who are standing here will not taste death before they see the Son of Man coming in His kingdom."

Chapter 17

After six days, Jesus took with Him Peter, James, and John the brother of James, and led them up a high mountain by themselves. There He was transfigured before them. His face shone like the sun, and His clothes became as white as the light. Just then there appeared before them Moses and Elijah, talking with Jesus. Peter said to Jesus, "Lord, it is good for us to be here. If You wish, I will put up three shelters—one for You, one for Moses, and one for Elijah." While he was still speaking, a bright cloud covered them, and a voice from the cloud said, "This is My Son, whom I love; with Him I am well pleased. Listen to Him!" When the disciples heard this, they fell facedown to the ground, terrified. But Jesus came and touched them. "Get up," He said. "Don't be afraid." When they looked up, they saw no one except Jesus As they were coming down the mountain, Jesus instructed them, "Don't tell anyone what you have seen, until the Son of Man has been raised from the dead." The disciples asked Him, "Why then do the teachers of the law say that Elijah must come first?" Jesus replied, "To be sure, Elijah comes and will restore all things. But I tell you, Elijah has already come, and they did not recognize him, but have done to him everything they wished. In the same way, the Son of Man is going to suffer at their hands." Then the disciples understood that He was talking to them about John the Baptist When they came to the crowd, a man approached Jesus and knelt before Him. "Lord, have mercy on my son," he said. "He has seizures and is suffering greatly. He often falls into the fire or into the water. I brought him to Your disciples, but they could not heal him." "You unbelieving and perverse generation," Jesus replied, "how long shall I stay with you? How long shall I put up with you? Bring the boy here to Me." Jesus rebuked the demon, and it came out of the boy, and he was healed at that moment Then the disciples came to Jesus in private and asked, "Why couldn't we drive it out?" He replied, "Because you have so little faith. Truly I tell you, if you have faith as small as a mustard seed, you can say to this mountain, 'Move from here to there,' and it will move. Nothing will be impossible for you." When they came together in Galilee, He said to them, "The Son of Man is going to be delivered into the hands of men. They will kill Him, and on the third day He will be raised to life." And the disciples were filled with grief After Jesus and His disciples arrived in Capernaum, the collectors of the two-drachma temple tax came to Peter and asked, "Doesn't your teacher pay the temple tax?" "Yes, He does," he replied. When Peter came into the house, Jesus was the first to speak. "What do you think, Simon?" He asked. "From whom do the kings of the earth collect duty and taxes—from their own children or from others?" "From others," Peter answered. "Then the children are exempt," Jesus said to him. "But so that

we may not cause offense, go to the lake and throw out your line. Take the first fish you catch; open its mouth and you will find a four-drachma coin. Take it and give it to them for My tax and yours."

Chapter 18

At that time the disciples came to Jesus and asked, "Who, then, is the greatest in the kingdom of heaven?" He called a little child to Him and placed the child among them. And He said: "Truly I tell you, unless you change and become like little children, you will never enter the kingdom of heaven. Therefore, whoever takes the lowly position of this child is the greatest in the kingdom of heaven. And whoever welcomes one such child in My name welcomes Me "If anyone causes one of these little ones—those who believe in Me—to stumble, it would be better for them to have a large millstone hung around their neck and to be drowned in the depths of the sea. Woe to the world because of the things that cause people to stumble! Such things must come, but woe to the person through whom they come! If your hand or your foot causes you to stumble, cut it off and throw it away. It is better for you to enter life maimed or crippled than to have two hands or two feet and be thrown into eternal fire. And if your eye causes you to stumble, gouge it out and throw it away. It is better for you to enter life with one eye than to have two eyes and be thrown into the fire of hell "See that you do not despise one of these little ones. For I tell you that their angels in heaven always see the face of My Father in heaven. The Son of Man came to save the lost. What do you think? If a man owns a hundred sheep, and one of them wanders away, will he not leave the ninety-nine on the hills and go to look for the one that wandered off? And if he finds it, truly I tell you, he is happier about that one sheep than about the ninety-nine that did not wander off. In the same way, your Father in heaven is not willing that any of these little ones should perish "If your brother or sister sins, go and point out their fault, just between the two of you. If they listen to you, you have won them over. But if they will not listen, take one or two others along, so that 'every matter may be established by the testimony of two or three witnesses.' If they still refuse to listen, tell it to the church; and if they refuse to listen even to the church, treat them as you would a pagan or a tax collector. Truly I tell you, whatever you bind on earth will be bound in heaven, and whatever you loose on earth will be loosed in heaven. Again, truly I tell you that if two of you on earth agree about anything they ask for, it will be done for them by My Father in heaven. For where two or three gather in My name, there am I with them." Then Peter came to Jesus and asked, "Lord, how many times shall I forgive my brother or sister who sins against me? Up to seven times?" Jesus answered, "I tell you, not seven times, but seventy-seven times "Therefore, the kingdom of heaven is like a king who wanted to settle accounts with his servants. As he began the settlement, a man who owed him ten thousand bags of gold was brought to him. Since he was not able to pay, the master ordered that he and his wife and his children and all that he had be sold to repay the debt. At this, the servant fell on his knees before him. 'Be patient with me,' he begged, 'and I will pay back everything.' The servant's master took pity on him, canceled the debt and let him go "But when that servant went out, he found one of his fellow servants who owed him a hundred silver coins. He grabbed him and began to choke him. 'Pay back what you owe me!' he demanded. His fellow servant fell to his knees and begged him, 'Be patient with me, and I will pay it back.' But he refused. Instead, he went off and had the man thrown into prison until he could pay the debt. When the other servants saw what had happened, they were outraged and went and told their master everything that had happened "Then the master called the servant in. 'You wicked servant,' he said, 'I canceled all that debt of yours because you begged me to. Shouldn't you have had mercy on your fellow servant just as I had on you?' In anger his master handed him over to the jailers to be tortured until he should pay back all he owed. This is how My heavenly Father will treat each of you unless you forgive your brother or sister from your heart."

Chapter 19

When Jesus had finished saying these things, He left Galilee and went into the region of Judea to the other side of the Jordan. Large crowds followed Him, and He healed them there Some Pharisees came to test Him. They asked, "Is it lawful for a man to divorce his wife for any and every reason?" "Haven't you read," He replied, "that at the beginning the Creator 'made them male and female,' and said, 'For this reason a man will leave his father and mother and be united to his wife, and the two will become one flesh'? So they are no longer two, but one flesh. Therefore what God has joined together, let no one separate." "Why then," they asked, "did Moses command that a man give his wife a certificate of divorce and send her away?" Jesus replied, "Moses permitted you to divorce your wives because your hearts were hard. But it was not this way from the beginning. I tell you that anyone who divorces his wife, except for sexual immorality, and marries another woman commits adultery." The disciples said to Him, "If this is the situation between a husband and wife, it is better not to marry." Jesus replied, "Not everyone can accept this word, but only those to whom it has been given. For there are eunuchs who were born that way, and there are eunuchs who have been made eunuchs by others— and there are those who choose to live like eunuchs for the sake of the kingdom of heaven. The one who can accept this should accept it." Then people brought little children to Jesus for Him to place His hands on them and pray for them. But the disciples rebuked them. Jesus said, "Let the little children come to Me, and do not hinder them, for the kingdom of heaven belongs to such as these." When He had placed His hands on them, He went on from there Just then a man came up to Jesus and asked, "Teacher, what good thing must I do to get eternal life?" "Why do you ask Me about what is good?" Jesus replied. "There is only One who is good. If you want to enter life, keep the commandments." "Which ones?" he inquired Jesus replied, "'You shall not murder, you shall not commit adultery, you shall not steal, you shall not give false testimony, honor your father and mother,' and 'love your neighbor as yourself.'" "All these I have kept," the young man said. "What do I still lack?" Jesus answered, "If you want to be perfect, go, sell your possessions and give to the poor, and you will have treasure in heaven. Then come, follow Me." When the young man heard this, he went away sad, because he had great wealth Then Jesus said to His disciples, "Truly I tell you, it is hard for someone who is rich to enter the kingdom of heaven. Again I tell you, it is easier for a camel to go through the eye of a needle than for someone who is rich to enter the kingdom of God." When the disciples heard this, they were greatly astonished and asked, "Who then can be saved?" Jesus looked at them and said, "With man this is impossible, but with God all things are possible." Peter answered Him, "We have left everything to follow You! What then will there be for us?" Jesus said to them, "Truly I tell you, at the renewal of all things, when the Son of Man sits on His glorious throne, you who have followed Me will also sit on twelve thrones, judging the twelve tribes of Israel. And everyone who has left houses or brothers or sisters or father or mother or wife or children or fields for My sake will receive a hundred times as much and will inherit eternal life. But many who are first will be last, and many who are last will be first

Chapter 20

For the kingdom of heaven is like a landowner who went out early in the morning to hire workers for his vineyard. He agreed to pay them a denarius for the day and sent them into his vineyard. About nine in the morning he went out and saw others standing in the marketplace doing nothing. He told them, 'You also go and work in my vineyard, and I will pay you whatever is right.' So they went He went out again about noon and about three in the afternoon and did the same thing. About five in the afternoon he went out and found still others standing around. He asked them, 'Why have you been standing here all day long doing nothing?' 'Because no one has hired us,' they answered. He said to them, 'You also go and work in my vineyard.' When evening came, the owner of the vineyard said to his foreman, 'Call the workers and pay them their wages, beginning with the last ones hired and going on to the first.' The workers who were hired about five in the afternoon came and each received a denarius. So when those came who were hired first, they expected to receive more. But each one of them also received a denarius. When they received it, they began to grumble against the landowner. 'These who were hired last worked only one hour,' they said, 'and you have made them equal to us who have borne the burden of the work and the heat of the day.' But he answered one of them, 'I am not being unfair to you, friend. Didn't you agree to work for a denarius? Take your pay and go. I want to give the one who was hired last the same as I gave you. Don't I have the right to do what I want with my own money? Or are you envious because I am generous?' So the last will be first, and the first will be last Now Jesus was going up to Jerusalem. On the way, He took the Twelve aside and said to them, "We are going up to Jerusalem, and the Son of Man will be delivered over to the chief priests and the teachers of the law. They will condemn Him to death and will hand Him over to the Gentiles to be mocked and flogged and crucified. On the third day He will be raised to life!" Then the mother of Zebedee's sons came to Jesus with her sons and, kneeling down, asked a favor of Him. "What is it you want?" He asked She said, "Grant that one of these two sons of mine may sit at Your right and the other at Your left in Your kingdom." "You don't know what you are asking," Jesus said to them. "Can you drink the cup I am going to drink?" "We can," they answered Jesus said to them, "You will indeed drink from My cup, but to sit at My right or left is not for Me to grant. These places belong to those for whom they have been prepared by My Father." When the ten heard about this, they were indignant with the two brothers. Jesus called them together and said, "You know that the rulers of the Gentiles lord it over them, and their high officials exercise authority over them. Not so with you. Instead, whoever wants to become great among you must be your servant, and whoever wants to be first must be your slave—just as the Son of Man did not come to be served, but to serve, and to give His life as a ransom for many." As Jesus and His disciples were leaving Jericho, a large crowd followed Him. Two blind men were sitting by the roadside, and when they heard that Jesus was going by, they shouted, "Lord, Son of David, have mercy on us!" The crowd rebuked them and told them to be quiet, but they shouted all the louder, "Lord, Son of David, have mercy on us!" Jesus stopped and called them. "What do you want Me to do for you?" He asked "Lord," they answered, "we want our sight." Jesus had compassion on them and touched their eyes. Immediately they received their sight and followed Him

Chapter 21

When they had come to Jerusalem and Bethphage on the Mount of Olives, Jesus sent two disciples, saying to them, "Go into the village that is opposite you, and immediately you will find a donkey tied and a colt with her; untie them and bring them to me. If anyone says anything to you, say that the Lord needs them, and he will send them immediately." This happened to fulfill what was spoken by the prophet: "Say to the daughter of Zion, 'Behold, your king comes to you, humble and mounted on a donkey, and on a colt, the foal of a donkey.'" The disciples went and did as Jesus had directed them. They brought the donkey and the colt and put their cloaks on them, and he sat on them. A very large crowd spread their cloaks on the road, while others cut branches from the trees and spread them on the road. The crowds that went before him and those that followed were shouting, "Hosanna to the Son of David! Blessed is he who comes in the name of the Lord! Hosanna in the highest heaven!" When he entered Jerusalem, the whole city was stirred, asking, "Who is this?" The crowds answered, "This is Jesus, the prophet from Nazareth of Galilee." Jesus entered the temple and drove out all who were buying and selling there. He overturned the tables of the money changers and the benches of those selling doves. He said to them, "It is written, 'My house will be called a house of prayer,' but you are making it a den of robbers." The blind and the lame came to him at the temple, and he healed them. But when the chief priests and the teachers of the law saw the wonderful things he did and the children shouting in the temple courts, "Hosanna to the Son of David," they were indignant. "Do you hear what these children are saying?" they asked him. "Yes," replied Jesus, "have you never read, 'From the lips of children and infants you, Lord, have called forth your praise'?" He left them and went out of the city to Bethany, where he spent the night. Early in the morning, as he was on his way back to the city, he was hungry. Seeing a fig tree by the road, he went up to it but found nothing on it except leaves. Then he said to it, "May you never bear fruit again!" Immediately the tree withered. When the disciples saw this, they were amazed. "How did the fig tree wither so quickly?" they asked. Jesus replied, "Truly I tell you, if you have faith and do not doubt, not only can you do what was done to the fig tree, but also you can say to this mountain, 'Go, throw yourself into the sea,' and it will be done. If you believe, you will receive whatever you ask for in prayer." Jesus entered the temple courts, and while he was teaching, the chief priests and the elders of the people came to him. "By what authority are you doing these things?" they asked. "And who gave you this authority?" Jesus replied, "I will also ask you one question. If you answer me, I will tell you by what authority I am doing these things. John's baptism—where did it come from? Was it from heaven, or of human origin?" They discussed it among themselves and said, "If we say, 'From heaven,' he will ask, 'Then why didn't you believe him?' But if we say, 'Of human origin,' we are afraid of the people, for they all hold that John was a prophet." So they answered Jesus, "We don't know." Then he said, "Neither will I tell you by what authority I am doing these things "What do you think? There was a man who had two sons. He went to the first and said, 'Son, go and work today in the vineyard.' 'I will not,' he answered, but later he changed his mind and went. Then the father went to the other son and said

the same thing. He answered, 'I will, sir,' but he did not go. Which of the two did what his father wanted?" "The first," they answered. Jesus said to them, "Truly I tell you, the tax collectors and the prostitutes are entering the kingdom of God ahead of you. For John came to show you the way of righteousness, and you did not believe him, but the tax collectors and the prostitutes did. And even after you saw this, you did not repent and believe him "Listen to another parable: There was a landowner who planted a vineyard. He put a wall around it, dug a winepress in it, and built a watchtower. Then he rented the vineyard to some farmers and moved to another place. When the harvest time approached, he sent his servants to the tenants to collect his fruit. The tenants seized his servants; they beat one, killed another, and stoned a third. Then he sent other servants to them, more than the first time, and the tenants treated them the same way. Last of all, he sent his son to them. 'They will respect my son,' he said. But when the tenants saw the son, they said to each other, 'This is the heir. Come, let's kill him and take his inheritance.' So they took him and threw him out of the vineyard and killed him "Therefore, when the owner of the vineyard comes, what will he do to those tenants?" "He will bring those wretches to a wretched end," they replied, "and he will rent the vineyard to other tenants, who will give him his share of the crop at harvest time." Jesus said to them, "Have you never read in the Scriptures: 'The stone the builders rejected has become the cornerstone; the Lord has done this, and it is marvelous in our eyes'? "Therefore I tell you that the kingdom of God will be taken away from you and given to a people who will produce its fruit. Anyone who falls on this stone will be broken to pieces; anyone on whom it falls will be crushed." When the chief priests and the Pharisees heard Jesus' parables, they knew he was talking about them. They looked for a way to arrest him, but they were afraid of the crowd because the people held that he was a prophet

Chapter 22

Jesus spoke to them again in parables, saying, "The kingdom of heaven is like a king who prepared a wedding banquet for his son. He sent his servants to those who had been invited to the banquet to tell them to come, but they refused to come. Then he sent some more servants and said, 'Tell those who have been invited that I have prepared my dinner: My oxen and fattened cattle have been butchered, and everything is ready. Come to the wedding banquet.' But they paid no attention and went off—one to his field, another to his business. The rest seized his servants, mistreated them, and killed them. The king was enraged. He sent his army and destroyed those murderers and burned their city. Then he said to his servants, 'The wedding banquet is ready, but those I invited did not deserve to come. So go to the street corners and invite to the banquet anyone you find.' So the servants went out into the streets and gathered all the people they could find, the bad as well as the good, and the wedding hall was filled with guests "But when the king came in to see the guests, he noticed a man there who was not wearing wedding clothes. He asked, 'How did you get in here without wedding clothes, friend?' The man was speechless. Then the king told the attendants, 'Tie him hand and foot, and throw him outside, into the darkness, where there will be weeping and gnashing of teeth.' For many are invited, but few are chosen." Then the Pharisees went out and laid plans to trap him in his words. They sent their disciples to him along with the Herodians. "Teacher," they said, "we know that you are a man of integrity and that you teach the way of God in accordance with the truth.

You aren't swayed by others because you pay no attention to who they are. Tell us then, what is your opinion? Is it right to pay the imperial tax to Caesar or not?" But Jesus, knowing their evil intent, said, "You hypocrites, why are you trying to trap me? Show me the coin used for paying the tax." They brought him a denarius, and he asked them, "Whose image is this? And whose inscription?" "Caesar's," they replied. Then he said to them, "So give back to Caesar what is Caesar's, and to God what is God's." When they heard this, they were amazed. So they left him and went away That same day the Sadducees, who say there is no resurrection, came to him with a question. "Teacher," they said, "Moses told us that if a man dies without having children, his brother must marry the widow and raise up offspring for him. Now there were seven brothers among us. The first one married and died, and since he had no children, he left his wife to his brother. The same thing happened to the second and third brother, right on down to the seventh. Finally, the woman died. Now then, at the resurrection, whose wife will she be of the seven, since all of them were married to her?" Jesus replied, "You are in error because you do not know the Scriptures or the power of God. At the resurrection, people will neither marry nor be given in marriage; they will be like the angels in heaven. But about the resurrection of the dead—have you not read what God said to you, 'I am the God of Abraham, the God of Isaac, and the God of Jacob'? He is not the God of the dead but of the living." When the crowds heard this, they were astonished at his teaching Hearing that Jesus had silenced the Sadducees, the Pharisees got together. One of them, an expert in the law, tested him with this question: "Teacher, which is the greatest commandment in the Law?" Jesus replied: "Love the Lord your God with all your heart and with all your soul and with all your mind. This is the first and greatest commandment. And the second is like it: Love your neighbor as yourself. All the Law and the Prophets hang on these two commandments." While the Pharisees were gathered together, Jesus asked them, "What do you think about the Messiah? Whose son is he?" "The son of David," they replied. He said to them, "How is it then that David, speaking by the Spirit, calls him 'Lord'? For he says, 'The Lord said to my Lord: "Sit at my right hand until I put your enemies under your feet."' If then David calls him 'Lord,' how can he be his son?" No one could say a word in reply, and from that day on no one dared to ask him any more questions

Chapter 23

Then Jesus said to the crowds and to his disciples: "The teachers of the law and the Pharisees sit in Moses' seat. So you must be careful to do everything they tell you. But do not do what they do, for they do not practice what they preach. They tie up heavy, cumbersome loads and put them on other people's shoulders, but they themselves are not willing to lift a finger to move them "Everything they do is done for people to see: They make their phylacteries wide and the tassels on their garments long; they love the place of honor at banquets and the most important seats in the synagogues; they love to be greeted with respect in the marketplaces and to be called 'Rabbi' by others. But you are not to be called 'Rabbi,' for you have one Teacher, and you are all brothers. And do not call anyone on earth 'father,' for you have one Father, and he is in heaven. Nor are you to be called instructors, for you have one Instructor, the Messiah. The greatest among you will be your servant. For those who exalt themselves will be humbled, and those who humble themselves will be exalted "Woe to you, teachers of the law and Pharisees, you hypocrites! You shut the door of the kingdom of heaven in people's faces. You yourselves do not enter, nor will you let those enter who are trying to. Woe to you, teachers of the law and Pharisees, you hypocrites! You travel over land and sea to win a single convert, and when you have succeeded, you make them twice as much a child of hell as you are "Woe to you, blind guides! You say, 'If anyone swears by the temple, it means nothing; but anyone who swears by the gold of the temple is bound by that oath.' You blind fools! Which is greater: the gold, or the temple that makes the gold sacred? You also say, 'If anyone swears by the altar, it means nothing; but anyone who swears by the gift on the altar is bound by that oath.' You blind men! Which is greater: the gift, or the altar that makes the gift sacred? Therefore, anyone who swears by the altar swears by it and by everything on it. And anyone who swears by the temple swears by it and by the one who dwells in it. And anyone who swears by heaven swears by God's throne and by the one who sits on it "Woe to you, teachers of the law and Pharisees, you hypocrites! You give a tenth of your spices—mint, dill, and cumin. But you have neglected the more important matters of the law—justice, mercy, and faithfulness. You should have practiced the latter, without neglecting the former. You blind guides! You strain out a gnat but swallow a camel "Woe to you, teachers of the law and Pharisees, you hypocrites! You clean the outside of the cup and dish, but inside they are full of greed and self-indulgence. Blind Pharisee! First clean the inside of the cup and dish, and then the outside also will be clean "Woe to you, teachers of the law and Pharisees, you hypocrites! You are like whitewashed tombs, which look beautiful on the outside but on the inside are full of the bones of the dead and everything unclean. In the same way, on the outside you appear to people as righteous but on the inside, you are full of hypocrisy and wickedness "Woe to you, teachers of the law and Pharisees, you hypocrites! You build tombs for the prophets and decorate the graves of the righteous. And you say, 'If we had lived in the days of our ancestors, we would not have taken part with them in shedding the blood of the prophets.' So you testify against yourselves that you are the descendants of those who murdered the prophets. Go ahead, then, and complete what your ancestors started! "You snakes! You brood of vipers! How will you escape being condemned to hell? Therefore I am sending you prophets and sages and teachers. Some of them, you will kill and crucify; others you will flog in your synagogues and pursue from town to town. And so upon you will come all the righteous blood that has been shed on earth, from the blood of righteous Abel to the blood of Zechariah son of Berekiah, whom you murdered between the temple and the altar. Truly I tell you, all this will come on this generation "Jerusalem, Jerusalem, you who kill the prophets and stone those sent to you, how often I have longed to gather your children together, as a hen gathers her chicks under her wings, and you were not willing. Look, your house is left to you desolate. For I tell you, you will not see me again until you say, 'Blessed is he who comes in the name of the Lord.'"

Chapter 24

Jesus left the temple and was walking away when his disciples came up to him to call his attention to its buildings. "Do you see all these things?" he asked. "Truly I tell you, not one stone here will be left on another; every one will be thrown down." As Jesus was sitting on the Mount of Olives, the disciples came to him privately. "Tell us," they said, "when will this happen, and what will be the sign of your coming and of the end of the age?" Jesus answered: "Watch out that no one deceives you. For many will come in my name, claiming, 'I am the Messiah,' and will deceive many. You will hear of wars and rumors of wars, but see to it that you are not alarmed. Such things must happen, but the end is still to come. Nation will rise against nation, and kingdom against kingdom. There will be famines and earthquakes in various places. All these are the beginning of birth pains "Then you will be handed over to be persecuted and put to death, and you will be hated by all nations because of me. At that time many will turn away from the faith and will betray and hate each other, and many false prophets will appear and deceive many people. Because of the increase of wickedness, the love of most will grow cold, but the one who stands firm to the end will be saved. And this gospel of the kingdom will be preached in the whole world as a testimony to all nations, and then the end will come "So when you see standing in the holy place 'the abomination that causes desolation,' spoken of through the prophet Daniel—let the reader understand—then let those who are in Judea flee to the mountains. Let no one on the housetop go down to take anything out of the house. Let no one in the field go back to get their cloak. How dreadful it will be in those days for pregnant women and nursing mothers! Pray that your flight will not take place in winter or on the Sabbath. For then there will be great distress, unequaled from the beginning of the world until now—and never to be equaled again "If those days had not been cut short, no one would survive, but for the sake of the elect those days will be shortened. At that time if anyone says to you, 'Look, here is the Messiah!' or, 'There he is!' do not believe it. For false messiahs and false prophets will appear and perform great signs and wonders to deceive, if possible, even the elect. See, I have told you ahead of time "So if anyone tells you, 'There he is, out in the wilderness,' do not go out; or, 'Here he is, in the inner rooms,' do not believe it. For as lightning that comes from the east is visible even in the west, so will be the coming of the Son of Man. Wherever there is a carcass, there the vultures will gather "Immediately after the distress of those days "'the sun will be darkened, and the moon will not give its light; the stars will fall from the sky, and the heavenly bodies will be shaken.' "Then will appear the sign of the Son of Man in heaven. And then all the peoples of the earth will mourn when they see the Son of Man coming on the clouds of heaven, with power and great glory. And he will send his angels with a loud trumpet call, and they will gather his elect from the four winds, from one end of the heavens to the other "Now learn this lesson from the fig tree: As soon as its twigs get tender and its leaves come out, you know that summer is near. Even so, when you see all these things, you know that it is near, right at the door. Truly I tell you, this generation will certainly not pass away until all these things have happened. Heaven and earth will pass away, but my words will never pass away "But about that day or hour no one knows, not even the angels in heaven, nor the Son, but only the Father. As it was in the days of Noah, so it will be at the coming of the Son of Man. For in the days before the flood, people were eating and drinking, marrying and giving in marriage, up to the day Noah entered the ark; and they knew nothing about what would happen until the flood came and took them all away. That is how it will be at the coming of the Son of Man. Two men will be in the field; one will be taken and the other left. Two women will be grinding with a hand mill; one will be taken and the other left "Therefore keep watch, because you do not know on what day your Lord will come. But understand this: If the owner of the house had known at what time of night the thief was coming, he would have kept watch and would not have let his house be broken into. So you also must be ready, because the Son of Man will come at an hour when you do not expect him "Who then is the faithful and wise servant, whom the master has put in charge of the servants in his household to give them their food at the proper time? It will be good for that servant whose master finds him doing so when he returns. Truly I tell you, he will put him in charge of all his possessions. But suppose that servant is wicked and says to himself, 'My master is staying away a long time,' and he then begins to beat his fellow servants and to eat and drink with drunkards. The master of that servant will come on a day when he does not expect him and at an hour he is not aware of. He will cut him to pieces and assign him a place with the hypocrites, where there will be weeping and gnashing of teeth

Chapter 25

"At that time the kingdom of heaven will be like ten virgins who took their lamps and went out to meet the bridegroom. Five of them were foolish and five were wise. The foolish ones took their lamps but did not take any oil with them. The wise ones, however, took oil in jars along with their lamps. The bridegroom was a long time in coming, and they all became drowsy and fell asleep "At midnight the cry rang out: 'Here's the bridegroom! Come out to meet him!' Then all the virgins woke up and trimmed their lamps. The foolish ones said to the wise, 'Give us some of your oil; our lamps are going out.' 'No,' they replied, 'there may not be enough for both us and you. Instead, go to those who sell oil and buy some for yourselves.' "But while they were on their way to buy the oil, the bridegroom arrived. The virgins who were ready went in with him to the wedding banquet. And the door was shut "Later the others also came. 'Lord, Lord,' they said, 'open the door for us!' But he replied, 'Truly I tell you, I don't know you.' "Therefore keep watch, because you do not know the day or the hour "Again, it will be like a man going on a journey, who called his servants and entrusted his wealth to them. To one he gave five bags of gold, to another two bags, and to another one bag, each according to his ability. Then he went on his journey. The man who had received five bags of gold went at once and put his money to work and gained five bags more. So also, the one with two bags of gold gained two more. But the man who had received one bag went off, dug a hole in the ground, and hid his master's money "After a long time, the master of those servants returned and settled accounts with them. The man who had received five bags of gold brought the other five. 'Master,' he said, 'you entrusted me with five bags of gold. See, I have gained five more.' His master replied, 'Well done, good and faithful servant! You have been faithful with a few things; I will put you in charge of many things. Come and share your master's happiness!' "The man with two bags of gold also came. 'Master,' he said, 'you entrusted me with two bags of gold; see, I have gained two more.' His master replied, 'Well done, good and faithful servant! You have been faithful with a few things; I will put you in charge of many things. Come and share your master's happiness!' "Then the man who had received one bag of gold came. 'Master,' he said, 'I knew that you are a hard man, harvesting where you have not sown and gathering where you have not scattered seed. So I was afraid and went out and hid your gold in the ground. See, here is what belongs to you.' "His master replied, 'You wicked, lazy servant! So you knew that I harvest where I have not sown and gather where I have not scattered seed? Well then, you should have put my money on deposit with the bankers, so that when I returned, I would have received it back with interest "'So take the bag of gold from him and give it to the one who has ten bags. For whoever has will be given more, and they will have an abundance. Whoever does not have, even what they have will be taken from them. And throw that worthless servant outside, into the darkness, where there will be weeping and gnashing of teeth.' "When the Son of Man comes in his glory, and all the angels with him, he will sit on his glorious throne. All the nations will be gathered before him, and he will separate the people one from another as a shepherd separates the sheep from the goats. He will put the sheep on his right and the goats on his left "Then the King will say to those on his right, 'Come, you who are blessed by my Father; take your inheritance, the kingdom prepared for you since the creation of the world. For I was hungry and you gave me something to eat, I was thirsty and you gave me something to drink, I was a stranger and you invited me in, I needed clothes and you clothed me, I was sick and you looked after me, I was in prison and you came to visit me.' "Then the righteous will answer him, 'Lord, when did we see you hungry and feed you, or thirsty and give you something to drink? When did we see you a stranger and invite you in, or needing clothes and clothe you? When did we see you sick or in prison and go to visit you?' "The King will reply, 'Truly I tell you, whatever you did for one of the least of these brothers and sisters of mine, you did for me.' "Then he will say to those on his left, 'Depart from me, you who are cursed, into the eternal fire prepared for the devil and his angels. For I was hungry and you gave me nothing to eat, I was thirsty and you gave me nothing to drink, I was a stranger and you did not invite me in, I needed clothes and you did not clothe me, I was sick and in prison and you did not look after me.' "They also will answer, 'Lord, when did we see you hungry or thirsty or a stranger or needing clothes or sick or in prison, and did not help you?' "He will reply, 'Truly I tell you, whatever you did not do for one of the least of these, you did not do for me.' "Then they will go away to eternal punishment, but the righteous to eternal life."

Chapter 26

1 When Jesus had finished all these sayings, he said to his disciples, 2 "You know that after two days is the Passover, and the Son of Man will be delivered up to be crucified." 3 Then the chief priests, the scribes, and the elders of the people assembled at the palace of the high priest, who was called Caiaphas, 4 and plotted to take Jesus by trickery and kill him. 5 But they said, "Not during the feast, lest there be an uproar among the people." 6 Now when Jesus was in Bethany, in the house of Simon the leper, 7 a woman came to him with an alabaster flask of very costly fragrant oil, and she poured it on his head as he sat at the table. 8 But when his disciples saw it, they were indignant, saying, "Why this waste? 9 For this fragrant oil might have been sold for much and given to the poor." 10 But Jesus, aware of it, said to them, "Why do you trouble the woman? For she has done a good work for me. 11 For you have the poor with you always, but me you do not have always. 12 For in pouring this fragrant oil on my body, she did it for my burial. 13 Assuredly, I say to you, wherever this gospel is preached in the whole world, what this woman has done will also be told as a memorial to her." 14 Then one of the twelve, called Judas Iscariot, went to the chief priests 15 and said, "What are you willing to give me if I deliver him to you?" And they counted out to him thirty pieces of silver. 16 So from that time he sought opportunity to betray him 17 Now on the first day of the Feast of Unleavened Bread, the disciples came to Jesus, saying to him, "Where do you want us to prepare for you to eat the Passover?" 18 And he said, "Go into the city to a certain man and say to him, 'The Teacher says, "My time is at hand; I will keep the Passover at your house with my disciples."'" 19 So the disciples did as Jesus had directed them, and they prepared the Passover 20 When evening had come, he sat down with the twelve. 21 Now as they were eating, he said, "Assuredly, I say to you, one of you will betray me." 22 And they were exceedingly sorrowful, and each of them began to say to him, "Lord, is it I?" 23 He answered and said, "He who dipped his hand with me in the dish will betray me. 24 The Son of Man indeed goes just as it is written of him, but woe to that man by whom the Son of Man is betrayed! It would have been good for that man if he had not been born." 25 Then Judas, who was betraying him, answered and said, "Rabbi, is it I?" He said to him, "You have said it." 26 And as they were eating, Jesus took bread, blessed and broke it, and gave it to the disciples and said, "Take, eat; this is my body." 27 Then he took the cup, and gave thanks, and gave it to them, saying, "Drink from it, all of you. 28 For this is my blood of the new covenant, which is shed for many for the remission of sins. 29 But I say to you, I will not drink of this fruit of the vine from now on until that day when I drink it new with you in my Father's kingdom." 30 And when they had sung a hymn, they went out to the Mount of Olives 31 Then Jesus said to them, "All of you will be made to stumble because of me this night, for it is written: 'I will strike the Shepherd, and the sheep of the flock will be scattered.' 32 But after I have been raised, I will go before you to Galilee." 33 Peter answered and said to him, "Even if all are made to stumble because of you, I will never be made to stumble." 34 Jesus said to him, "Assuredly, I say to you that this night, before the rooster crows, you will deny me three times." 35 Peter said to him, "Even if I have to die with you, I will not deny you!" And so said all the disciples 36 Then Jesus came with them to a place called Gethsemane, and said to the disciples, "Sit here while I go and pray over there." 37 And he took with him Peter and the two sons of Zebedee, and he began to be sorrowful and deeply distressed. 38 Then he said to them, "My soul is exceedingly sorrowful, even to death. Stay here and watch with me." 39 He went a little farther and fell on his face, and prayed, saying, "O my Father, if it is possible, let this cup pass from me; nevertheless, not as I will, but as you will." 40 Then he came to the disciples and found them sleeping, and said to Peter, "What! Could you not watch with me one hour? 41 Watch and pray, lest you enter into temptation. The spirit indeed is willing, but the flesh is weak." 42 Again, a second time, he went away and prayed, saying, "O my Father, if this cup cannot pass away from me unless I drink it, your will be done." 43 And he came and found them asleep again, for their eyes were heavy. 44 So he left them, went away again, and prayed the third time, saying the same words 45 Then he came to his disciples and said to them, "Are you still sleeping and resting? Behold, the hour is at hand, and the Son of Man is being betrayed into the hands of sinners. 46 Rise, let us be going. See, my betrayer is at hand." 47 And while he was still speaking, behold, Judas, one of the twelve, with a great multitude with swords and clubs, came from the chief priests and elders of the people. 48 Now his betrayer had given them a sign, saying, "Whomever I kiss, he is the one; seize him." 49 Immediately he went up to Jesus and said, "Greetings, Rabbi!" and kissed him. 50 But Jesus said to him, "Friend, why have you come?" Then they came and laid hands on Jesus and took him 51 And suddenly, one of those who were with Jesus stretched out his hand and drew his sword, struck

the servant of the high priest, and cut off his ear. 52 But Jesus said to him, "Put your sword in its place, for all who take the sword will perish by the sword. 53 Or do you think that I cannot now pray to my Father, and he will provide me with more than twelve legions of angels? 54 How then could the Scriptures be fulfilled, that it must happen thus?" 55 In that hour Jesus said to the multitudes, "Have you come out, as against a robber, with swords and clubs to take me? I sat daily with you, teaching in the temple, and you did not seize me. 56 But all this was done that the Scriptures of the prophets might be fulfilled." Then all the disciples forsook him and fled 57 And those who had laid hold of Jesus led him away to Caiaphas the high priest, where the scribes and the elders were assembled. 58 But Peter followed him at a distance to the high priest's courtyard. And he went in and sat with the servants to see the end 59 Now the chief priests, the elders, and all the council sought false testimony against Jesus to put him to death, 60 but found none. Even though many false witnesses came forward, they found none. But at last, two false witnesses came forward 61 and said, "This fellow said, 'I am able to destroy the temple of God and to build it in three days.'" 62 And the high priest arose and said to him, "Do you answer nothing? What is it these men testify against you?" 63 But Jesus kept silent. And the high priest answered and said to him, "I put you under oath by the living God: Tell us if you are the Christ, the Son of God!" 64 Jesus said to him, "It is as you said. Nevertheless, I say to you, hereafter you will see the Son of Man sitting at the right hand of the Power, and coming on the clouds of heaven." 65 Then the high priest tore his clothes, saying, "He has spoken blasphemy! What further need do we have of witnesses? Look, now you have heard his blasphemy! 66 What do you think?" They answered and said, "He is deserving of death." 67 Then they spat in his face and beat him; and others struck him with the palms of their hands, 68 saying, "Prophesy to us, Christ! Who is the one who struck you?" 69 Now Peter sat outside in the courtyard. And a servant girl came to him, saying, "You also were with Jesus of Galilee." 70 But he denied it before them all, saying, "I do not know what you are saying." 71 And when he had gone out to the gateway, another girl saw him and said to those who were there, "This fellow also was with Jesus of Nazareth." 72 But again he denied with an oath, "I do not know the man!" 73 And a little later those who stood by came up and said to Peter, "Surely you also are one of them, for your speech betrays you." 74 Then he began to curse and swear, saying, "I do not know the man!" Immediately a rooster crowed. 75 And Peter remembered the word of Jesus who had said to him, "Before the rooster crows, you will deny me three times." So he went out and wept bitterly

Chapter 27

1 When morning came, all the chief priests and elders of the people plotted against Jesus to put him to death. 2 And when they had bound him, they led him away and delivered him to Pontius Pilate the governor 3 Then Judas, his betrayer, seeing that he had been condemned, was remorseful and brought back the thirty pieces of silver to the chief priests and elders, 4 saying, "I have sinned by betraying innocent blood." And they said, "What is that to us? You see to it!" 5 Then he threw down the pieces of silver in the temple and departed, and went and hanged himself 6 But the chief priests took the silver pieces and said, "It is not lawful to put them into the treasury, because they are the price of blood." 7 And they consulted together and bought with them the potter's field, to bury strangers in. 8 Therefore that field has been called the Field of Blood to this day. 9 Then was fulfilled what was spoken by Jeremiah the prophet, saying, "And they took the thirty pieces of silver, the value of him who was priced, whom they of the children of Israel priced, 10 and gave them for the potter's field, as the Lord directed me." 11 Now Jesus stood before the governor. And the governor asked him, saying, "Are you the King of the Jews?" Jesus said to him, "It is as you say." 12 And while he was being accused by the chief priests and elders, he answered nothing. 13 Then Pilate said to him, "Do you not hear how many things they testify against you?" 14 But he answered him not one word, so that the governor marveled greatly 15 Now at the feast, the governor was accustomed to releasing to the multitude one prisoner whom they wished. 16 And at that time they had a notorious prisoner called Barabbas. 17 Therefore, when they had gathered together, Pilate said to them, "Whom do you want me to release to you? Barabbas, or Jesus who is called Christ?" 18 For he knew that they had handed him over because of envy 19 While he was sitting on the judgment seat, his wife sent to him, saying, "Have nothing to do with that just Man, for I have suffered many things today in a dream because of him." 20 But the chief priests and elders persuaded the multitudes that they should ask for Barabbas and destroy Jesus. 21 The governor answered and said to them, "Which of the two do you want me to release to you?" They said, "Barabbas!" 22 Pilate said to them, "What then shall I do with Jesus who is called Christ?" They all said to him, "Let him be crucified!" 23 Then the governor said, "Why, what evil has he done?" But they cried out all the more, saying, "Let him be crucified!" 24 When Pilate saw that he could not prevail at all, but rather that a tumult was rising, he took water and washed his hands before the multitude, saying, "I am innocent of the blood of this just Person. You see to it." 25 And all the people answered and said, "His blood be on us and on our children." 26 Then he released Barabbas to them; and when he had scourged Jesus, he delivered him to be crucified 27 Then the soldiers of the governor took Jesus into the Praetorium and gathered the whole garrison around him. 28 And they stripped him and put a scarlet robe on him. 29 When they had twisted a crown of thorns, they put it on his head, and a reed in his right hand. And they bowed the knee before him and mocked him, saying, "Hail, King of the Jews!" 30 Then they spat on him, and took the reed and struck him on the head. 31 And when they had mocked him, they took the robe off him, put his own clothes on him, and led him away to be crucified 32 Now as they came out, they found a man of Cyrene, Simon by name. Him they compelled to bear his cross. 33 And when they had come to a place called Golgotha, that is to say, Place of a Skull, 34 they gave him sour wine mingled with gall to drink. But when he had tasted it, he would not drink 35 Then they crucified him, and divided his garments, casting lots, that it might be fulfilled which was spoken by the prophet: "They divided my garments among them, and for my clothing they cast lots." 36 Sitting down, they kept watch over him there. 37 And they put up over his head the accusation written against him: THIS IS JESUS THE KING OF THE JEWS. 38 Then two robbers were crucified with him, one on the right and another on the left 39 And those who passed by blasphemed him, wagging their heads 40 and saying, "You who destroy the temple and build it in three days, save yourself! If you are the Son of God, come down from the cross." 41 Likewise the chief priests also, mocking with the scribes and elders, said, 42 "He saved others; himself he cannot save. If he is the King of Israel, let him now come down from the cross, and we will believe him. 43 He trusted in God; let him

deliver him now if he will have him; for he said, 'I am the Son of God.'" 44 Even the robbers who were crucified with him reviled him with the same thing 45 Now from the sixth hour until the ninth hour there was darkness over all the land. 46 And about the ninth hour Jesus cried out with a loud voice, saying, "Eli, Eli, lama sabachthani?" that is, "My God, My God, why have you forsaken me?" 47 Some of those who stood there, when they heard that, said, "This man is calling for Elijah!" 48 Immediately one of them ran and took a sponge, filled it with sour wine and put it on a reed, and offered it to him to drink. 49 The rest said, "Let him alone; let us see if Elijah will come to save him." 50 And Jesus cried out again with a loud voice, and yielded up his spirit 51 Then, behold, the veil of the temple was torn in two from top to bottom; and the earth quaked, and the rocks were split, 52 and the graves were opened; and many bodies of the saints who had fallen asleep were raised; 53 and coming out of the graves after his resurrection, they went into the holy city and appeared to many. 54 So when the centurion and those with him, who were guarding Jesus, saw the earthquake and the things that had happened, they feared greatly, saying, "Truly this was the Son of God!" 55 And many women who followed Jesus from Galilee, ministering to him, were there looking on from afar, 56 among whom were Mary Magdalene, Mary the mother of James and Joses, and the mother of Zebedee's sons 57 Now when evening had come, there came a rich man from Arimathea, named Joseph, who himself had also become a disciple of Jesus. 58 This man went to Pilate and asked for the body of Jesus. Then Pilate commanded the body to be given to him. 59 When Joseph had taken the body, he wrapped it in a clean linen cloth, 60 and laid it in his new tomb which he had hewn out of the rock; and he rolled a large stone against the door of the tomb, and departed. 61 And Mary Magdalene was there, and the other Mary, sitting opposite the tomb 62 On the next day, which followed the Day of Preparation, the chief priests and Pharisees gathered together to Pilate, 63 saying, "Sir, we remember, while he was still alive, how that deceiver said, 'After three days I will rise.' 64 Therefore command that the tomb be made secure until the third day, lest his disciples come by night and steal him away, and say to the people, 'He has risen from the dead.' So the last deception will be worse than the first." 65 Pilate said to them, "You have a guard; go your way, make it as secure as you know how." 66 So they went and made the tomb secure, sealing the stone and setting the guard

Chapter 28

1 Now after the Sabbath, as the first day of the week began to dawn, Mary Magdalene and the other Mary came to see the tomb. 2 And behold, there was a great earthquake; for an angel of the Lord descended from heaven, and came and rolled back the stone from the door, and sat on it. 3 His countenance was like lightning, and his clothing as white as snow. 4 And the guards shook for fear of him, and became like dead men 5 But the angel answered and said to the women, "Do not be afraid, for I know that you seek Jesus who was crucified. 6 He is not here; for he is risen, as he said. Come, see the place where the Lord lay. 7 And go quickly and tell his disciples that he is risen from the dead, and indeed he is going before you into Galilee; there you will see him. Behold, I have told you." 8 So they went out quickly from the tomb with fear and great joy, and ran to bring his disciples word 9 And as they went to tell his disciples, behold, Jesus met them, saying, "Rejoice!" So they came and held him by the feet and worshiped him. 10 Then Jesus said to them, "Do not be afraid. Go and tell my brethren to go to Galilee, and there

they will see me." 11 Now while they were going, behold, some of the guard came into the city and reported to the chief priests all the things that had happened. 12 When they had assembled with the elders and consulted together, they gave a large sum of money to the soldiers, 13 saying, "Tell them, 'His disciples came at night and stole him away while we slept.' 14 And if this comes to the governor's ears, we will appease him and make you secure." 15 So they took the money and did as they were instructed; and this saying is commonly reported among the Jews until this day 16 Then the eleven disciples went away into Galilee, to the mountain which Jesus had appointed for them. 17 When they saw him, they worshiped him; but some doubted. 18 And Jesus came and spoke to them, saying, "All authority has been given to me in heaven and on earth. 19 Go therefore and make disciples of all the nations, baptizing them in the name of the Father and of the Son and of the Holy Spirit, 20 teaching them to observe all things that I have commanded you; and lo, I am with you always, even to the end of the age." Amen

41. Mark

Chapter 1

The beginning of the Gospel of Jesus Christ, the Son of God, as it is written in the Prophets: "Behold, I send my messenger before your face, who will prepare your way before you. The voice of one crying in the wilderness: 'Prepare the way of the LORD, make His paths straight.'" John baptized in the wilderness and preached a baptism of repentance for the remission of sins. All the people of Judea and Jerusalem went to him and were baptized by him in the Jordan River, confessing their sins John was clothed in camel's hair with a leather belt around his waist, and he ate locusts and wild honey. He preached, saying, "After me comes one mightier than I, the strap of whose sandals I am not worthy to stoop down and untie. I have baptized you with water, but He will baptize you with the Holy Spirit." In those days, Jesus came from Nazareth in Galilee and was baptized by John in the Jordan. As He came up out of the water, John saw the heavens torn open and the Holy Spirit descending upon Him like a dove. A voice came from heaven: "You are My beloved Son, in whom I am well pleased." Immediately, the Spirit drove Him into the wilderness. He was there in the wilderness for forty days, tempted by Satan, and was with the wild beasts, and the angels ministered to Him After John was put in prison, Jesus came to Galilee, preaching the gospel of the kingdom of God, saying, "The time is fulfilled, and the kingdom of God is at hand. Repent and believe in the gospel." As He walked by the Sea of Galilee, He saw Simon and Andrew, his brother, casting a net into the sea, for they were fishermen. Jesus said to them, "Follow Me, and I will make you become fishers of men." Immediately, they left their nets and followed Him. When He had gone a little farther, He saw James the son of Zebedee and John his brother, who were in their boat mending the nets. He called them, and they left their father Zebedee in the boat with the hired servants and went after Him They went into Capernaum, and immediately on the Sabbath, He entered the synagogue and taught. They were astonished at His teaching, for He taught them as one having authority, and not as the scribes. In their synagogue, there was a man with an unclean spirit who cried out, "What have we to do with You, Jesus of Nazareth? Have You come to destroy us? I know who You are—the Holy One of God!" Jesus rebuked him, saying, "Be silent and come out of him!" The unclean spirit convulsed him, cried out with a loud voice, and came out of him. They were all amazed and questioned among themselves, "What is this? A new teaching with authority! He commands even the unclean spirits, and they obey Him." Immediately, His fame spread throughout the region of Galilee After leaving the synagogue, they entered the house of Simon and Andrew with James and John. Simon's mother-in-law lay sick with a fever, and they immediately told Him about her. He came, took her by the hand, and lifted her up. The fever left her, and she began to serve them At evening, when the sun had set, they brought to Him all who were sick and those who were demon-possessed. The whole city was gathered together at the door. He healed many who were sick with various diseases and cast out many demons, and He did not allow the demons to speak because they knew Him. Early in the morning, while it was still dark, Jesus got up, left the house, and went to a solitary place where He prayed. Simon and his companions went to look for Him, and when they found Him, they exclaimed, "Everyone is looking for You!" He replied, "Let us go somewhere else—to the nearby villages—so I can preach there also. That is why I have come." So He traveled throughout Galilee, preaching in their synagogues and driving out demons A man with leprosy came to Him and begged Him on his knees, "If You are willing, You can make me clean." Filled with compassion, Jesus reached out His hand and touched the man. "I am willing," He said. "Be clean!" Immediately, the leprosy left him, and he was cleansed. Jesus sent him away at once with a strong warning: "See that you don't tell this to anyone. But go, show yourself to the priest and offer the sacrifices that Moses commanded for your cleansing, as a testimony to them." Instead, the man went out and began to talk freely, spreading the news. As a result, Jesus could no longer enter a town openly but stayed outside in lonely places. Yet, people still came to Him from everywhere

Chapter 2

After a few days, Jesus returned to Capernaum, and it was reported that He was in the house. Many gathered there, so many that there was no room left, not even outside the door, and He preached the word to them. Some men came, bringing to Him a paralytic, carried by four of them. Since they could not get him to Jesus because of the crowd, they made an opening in the roof above Jesus and, after digging through it, lowered the mat the paralyzed man was lying on. When Jesus saw their faith, He said to the paralytic, "Son, your sins are forgiven." Now some teachers of the law were sitting there, thinking to themselves, "Why does this fellow talk like that? He's blaspheming! Who can forgive sins but God alone?" Immediately, Jesus knew in His spirit that this was what they were thinking in their hearts, and He said to them, "Why are you thinking these things? Which is easier: to say to this paralyzed man, 'Your sins are forgiven,' or to say, 'Get up, take your mat, and walk'? But I want you to know that the Son of Man has authority on earth to forgive sins." So He said to the man, "I tell you, get up, take your mat, and go home." He got up, took his mat, and walked out in full view of them all. This amazed everyone, and they praised God, saying, "We have never seen anything like this!" Once again, Jesus went out beside the lake. A large crowd came to Him, and He began to teach them. As He walked along, He saw Levi son of Alphaeus sitting at the tax collector's booth. "Follow Me," Jesus told him, and Levi got up and followed Him. While Jesus was having dinner at Levi's house, many tax collectors and sinners were eating with Him and His disciples, for there were many who followed Him. When the teachers of the law who were Pharisees saw Him eating with the sinners and tax collectors, they asked His disciples, "Why does He eat with tax collectors and sinners?" On hearing this, Jesus said to them, "It is not the healthy who need a doctor, but the sick. I have not come to call the righteous, but sinners." Now John's disciples and the Pharisees were fasting. Some people came and asked Jesus, "How is it that John's disciples and the disciples of the Pharisees are fasting, but Yours are not?" Jesus answered, "How can the guests of the bridegroom fast while He is with them? They cannot, so long as they have Him with them. But the time will come when the bridegroom will be taken from them, and on that day, they will fast No one sews a patch of unshrunk cloth on an old garment. Otherwise, the new piece will pull away from the old, making the tear worse. And no one pours new wine into old wineskins. Otherwise, the wine will burst the skins, and both the wine and the wineskins will be ruined. No, they pour new wine into new wineskins." One Sabbath, Jesus was going through the grainfields, and as His disciples walked along, they began to pick some heads of grain. The Pharisees said to Him, "Look, why are they doing what is unlawful on the Sabbath?" He answered, "Have you never read what David did when he and his companions were hungry and in need? In the days of Abiathar the high priest, he entered the house of God and ate the consecrated bread, which is lawful only for priests to eat. And he also gave some to his companions." Then He said to them, "The Sabbath was made for man, not man for the Sabbath. So the Son of Man is Lord even of the Sabbath."

Chapter 3

Jesus entered the synagogue again, and a man was there with a shriveled hand. Some of them were looking for a reason to accuse Jesus, so they watched Him closely to see if He would heal him on the Sabbath. Jesus said to the man with the shriveled hand, "Stand up in front of everyone." Then Jesus asked them, "Which is lawful on the Sabbath: to do good or to do evil, to save life or to kill?" But they remained silent. He looked around at them in anger and, deeply distressed at their stubborn hearts, said to the man, "Stretch out your hand." He stretched it out, and his hand was completely restored. Then the Pharisees went out and began to plot with the Herodians how they might kill Jesus Jesus withdrew with His disciples to the lake, and a large crowd from Galilee followed. When they heard about all He was doing, many people came to Him from Judea, Jerusalem, Idumea, and the regions across the Jordan and around Tyre and Sidon. Because of the crowd, He told His disciples to have a small boat ready for Him to keep the people from crowding Him. For He had healed many, so that those with diseases were pushing forward to touch Him. Whenever the impure spirits saw Him, they fell down before Him and cried out, "You are the Son of God." But He gave them strict orders not to tell others about Him Jesus went up on a mountainside and called to Him those He wanted, and they came to Him. He appointed twelve that they might be with Him and that He might send them out to preach and to have authority to drive out demons. These are the twelve He appointed: Simon (to whom He gave the name Peter), James son of Zebedee and his brother John (to them He gave the name Boanerges, which means "sons of thunder"), Andrew, Philip, Bartholomew, Matthew, Thomas, James son of Alphaeus, Thaddaeus, Simon the Zealot, and Judas Iscariot, who betrayed Him Then Jesus entered a house, and again a crowd gathered, so that He and His disciples were not even able to eat. When His family heard about this, they went to take charge of Him, for they said, "He is out of His mind." And the teachers of the law who came down from Jerusalem said, "He is possessed by Beelzebul! By the prince of demons He is driving out demons." So Jesus called them over to Him and began to speak to them in parables: "How can Satan drive out Satan? If a kingdom is divided against itself, that kingdom cannot stand. If a house is divided against itself, that house cannot stand. And if Satan opposes himself and is divided, he cannot stand; his end has come. In fact, no one can enter a strong man's house without first tying him up. Then he can plunder the strong man's house. Truly I tell you, people can be forgiven all their sins and every slander they utter, but whoever blasphemes against the Holy Spirit will never be forgiven; they are guilty of an eternal sin." He said this because they were saying, "He has an impure spirit." Then Jesus' mother and brothers arrived. Standing outside, they sent someone in to call Him. A crowd was sitting around Him, and they told Him, "Your mother and brothers are outside looking for You." "Who are My mother and My brothers?" He asked. Then He looked at those seated in a circle around Him and said, "Here are My mother and My brothers! Whoever does God's will is My brother and sister and mother."

Chapter 4

Again, Jesus began to teach by the lake. The crowd that gathered around Him was so large that He got into a boat and sat in it out on the lake, while all the people were along the shore at the water's edge. He taught them many things by parables, and in His teaching said: "Listen! A farmer went out to sow his seed. As he was scattering the seed, some fell along the path, and the birds came and ate it up. Some fell on rocky places, where it did not have much soil. It sprang up quickly because the soil was shallow. But when the sun came up, the plants were scorched, and they withered because they had no root. Other seed fell among thorns, which grew up and choked the plants, so that they did not bear grain. Still, other seed fell on good soil. It came up, grew, and produced a crop, some multiplying thirty, some sixty, some a hundred times." Then Jesus said, "Whoever has ears to hear, let them hear." When He was alone, the Twelve and the others around Him asked Him about the parables. He told them, "The secret of the kingdom of God has been given to you. But to those on the outside, everything is said in parables so that, "'they may be ever seeing but never perceiving, and ever hearing but never understanding; otherwise, they might turn and be forgiven!'" Then Jesus said to them, "Don't you understand this parable? How then will you understand any parable? The farmer sows the word. Some people are like seed along the path, where the word is sown. As soon as they hear it, Satan comes and takes away the word that was sown in them. Others, like seed sown on rocky places, hear the word and at once receive it with joy. But since they have no root, they last only a short time. When trouble or persecution comes because of the word, they quickly fall away. Still, others, like seed sown among thorns, hear the word; but the worries of this life, the deceitfulness of wealth, and the desires for other things come in and choke the word, making it unfruitful. Others, like seed sown on good soil, hear the word, accept it, and produce a crop—some thirty, some sixty, some a hundred times what was sown." He said to them, "Do you bring in a lamp to put it under a bowl or a bed? Instead, don't you put it on its stand? For whatever is hidden is meant to be disclosed, and whatever is concealed is meant to be brought out into the open. If anyone has ears to hear, let them hear." "Consider carefully what you hear," He continued. "With the measure you use, it will be measured to you—and even more. Whoever has will be given more; whoever does not have, even what they have will be taken from them." He also said, "This is what the kingdom of God is like. A man scatters seed on the ground. Night and day, whether he sleeps or gets up, the seed sprouts and grows, though he does not know how. All by itself, the soil produces grain—first the stalk, then the head, then the full kernel in the head. As soon as the grain is ripe, he puts the sickle to it because the harvest has come." Again He said, "What shall we say the kingdom of God is like, or what parable shall we use to describe it? It is like a mustard seed, which is the smallest of all seeds on earth. Yet when planted, it grows and becomes the largest of all garden plants, with such big branches that the birds can perch in its shade." With many similar parables, Jesus spoke the word to them, as much as they could understand. He did not say anything to them without using a parable. But when He was alone with His own disciples, He explained everything That day when evening came, He said to His disciples, "Let us go over to the other side." Leaving the crowd behind, they took Him along, just as He was, in the boat. There were also other boats with Him. A furious squall came up, and the waves broke over the boat so that it was nearly swamped. Jesus was in the stern, sleeping on a cushion. The disciples woke Him and said to Him, "Teacher, don't you care if we drown?" He got up, rebuked the wind, and said to the waves, "Quiet! Be still!" Then the wind died down, and it was completely calm. He said to His disciples, "Why are you so afraid? Do you still have no faith?" They were terrified and asked each other, "Who is this? Even the wind and the waves obey Him!"

Chapter 5

They went across the lake to the region of the Gerasenes. When Jesus got out of the boat, a man with an impure spirit came from the tombs to meet Him. This man lived in the tombs, and no one could bind him anymore, not even with a chain. For he had often been chained hand and foot, but he tore the chains apart and broke the irons on his feet. No one was strong enough to subdue him. Night and day among the tombs and in the hills, he would cry out and cut himself with stones. When he saw Jesus from a distance, he ran and fell on his knees in front of Him. He shouted at the top of his voice, "What do you want with me, Jesus, Son of the Most High God? In God's name, don't torture me!" For Jesus had said to him, "Come out of this man, you impure spirit!" Then Jesus asked him, "What is your name?" "My name is Legion," he replied, "for we are many." And he begged Jesus again and again not to send them out of the area A large herd of pigs was feeding on the nearby hillside. The demons begged Jesus, "Send us among the pigs; allow us to go into them." He gave them permission, and the impure spirits came out and went into the pigs. The herd, about two thousand in number, rushed down the steep bank into the lake and were drowned. Those tending the pigs ran off and reported this in the town and countryside, and the people went out to see what had happened. When they came to Jesus, they saw the man who had been possessed by the legion of demons, sitting there, dressed and in his right mind; and they were afraid. Those who had seen it told the people what had happened to the demon-possessed man—and told about the pigs as well. Then the people began to plead with Jesus to leave their region As Jesus was getting into the boat, the man who had been demon-possessed begged to go with Him. Jesus did not let him but said, "Go home to your own people and tell them how much the Lord has done for you, and how He has had mercy on you." So the man went away and began to tell in the Decapolis how much Jesus had done for him. And all the people were amazed When Jesus had again crossed over by boat to the other side of the lake, a large crowd gathered around Him while He was by the lake. Then one of the synagogue leaders, named Jairus, came, and when he saw Jesus, he fell at His feet. He pleaded earnestly with Him, "My little daughter is dying. Please come and put Your hands on her so that she will be healed and live." So Jesus went with him A large crowd followed and pressed around Him. And a woman was there who had been subject to bleeding for twelve years. She had suffered a great deal under the care of many doctors and had spent all she had, yet instead of getting better, she grew worse. When she heard about Jesus, she came up behind Him in the crowd and touched His cloak because she thought, "If I just touch His clothes, I will be healed." Immediately, her bleeding stopped and she felt in her body that she was freed from her suffering. At once Jesus realized that power had gone out from Him. He turned around in the crowd and asked, "Who touched My clothes?" "You see the people crowding against You," His disciples answered, "and yet You can ask, 'Who touched Me?'" But Jesus kept looking around to see who had done it. Then the woman, knowing what had happened to her, came and fell at His feet and, trembling with fear, told Him the whole truth. He said to her, "Daughter, your faith has healed you. Go in peace and be freed from your suffering." While Jesus was still speaking, some people came from the house of Jairus, the synagogue leader. "Your daughter is dead," they said. "Why bother the teacher anymore?" Overhearing what they said, Jesus told him, "Don't be afraid; just believe." He did not let anyone follow Him except Peter, James, and John, the brother of James. When they came to the home of the synagogue leader, Jesus saw a commotion, with people crying and wailing loudly. He went in and said to them, "Why all this commotion and wailing? The child is not dead but asleep." But they laughed at Him. After He put them all out, He took the child's father and mother and the disciples who were with Him, and went in where the child was. He took her by the hand and said to her, "Talitha koum!" (which means "Little girl, I say to you, get up!"). Immediately, the girl stood up and began to walk around (she was twelve years old). At this, they were completely astonished. He gave strict orders not to let anyone know about this and told them to give her something to eat

Chapter 6

Jesus left that place and came to His hometown, and His disciples followed Him. When the Sabbath came, He began to teach in the synagogue, and many who heard Him were astonished. They said, "Where did this man get these things? What wisdom has been given to Him, that He even performs such mighty works with His hands? Isn't this the carpenter, the son of Mary, and the brother of James, Joses, Judas, and Simon? Aren't His sisters here with us?" And they took offense at Him. Jesus said to them, "A prophet is not without honor except in his own country, among his relatives, and in his own house." He could not do any mighty work there, except to lay His hands on a few sick people and heal them. He marveled at their unbelief and went around the surrounding villages teaching He called the Twelve and began to send them out two by two, giving them authority over unclean spirits. He instructed them to take nothing for their journey except a staff—no bread, no bag, no money in their belts—but to wear sandals and not to put on two tunics. He said to them, "Whenever you enter a house, stay there until you leave that town. If any place will not welcome

you or listen to you, shake the dust off your feet as a testimony against them. Truly I tell you, it will be more bearable for Sodom and Gomorrah on the day of judgment than for that town." So they went out and preached that people should repent. They cast out many demons, anointed many sick people with oil, and healed them King Herod heard about this, for Jesus' name had become well known. Some were saying, "John the Baptist has been raised from the dead, and that is why miraculous powers are at work in Him." Others said, "He is Elijah," and still others claimed, "He is a prophet, like one of the prophets of long ago." But when Herod heard this, he said, "John, whom I beheaded, has been raised from the dead!" For Herod himself had given orders to arrest John and bound him and put him in prison because of Herodias, his brother Philip's wife, whom he had married. John had been telling Herod, "It is not lawful for you to have your brother's wife." So Herodias nursed a grudge against John and wanted to kill him, but she was not able to because Herod feared John and protected him, knowing him to be a righteous and holy man. When Herod heard John, he was greatly puzzled, yet he liked to listen to him Finally, the opportune time came. On his birthday, Herod gave a banquet for his high officials and military commanders and the leading men of Galilee. When the daughter of Herodias came in and danced, she pleased Herod and his dinner guests. The king said to the girl, "Ask me for anything you want, and I will give it to you." And he promised her with an oath, "Whatever you ask I will give you, up to half my kingdom." She went out and said to her mother, "What shall I ask for?" "The head of John the Baptist," she answered. At once, the girl hurried to the king with the request: "I want you to give me right now the head of John the Baptist on a platter." The king was greatly distressed, but because of his oaths and his dinner guests, he did not want to refuse her. So he immediately sent an executioner with orders to bring John's head. The man went, beheaded John in the prison, brought back his head on a platter, and presented it to the girl, who gave it to her mother. When John's disciples heard about this, they came and took his body and laid it in a tomb The apostles gathered around Jesus and reported to Him all they had done and taught. Then, because so many people were coming and going that they did not even have a chance to eat, He said to them, "Come with Me by yourselves to a quiet place and get some rest." So they went away by themselves in a boat to a solitary place. But many who saw them leaving recognized them and ran on foot from all the towns and got there ahead of them. When Jesus landed and saw a large crowd, He had compassion on them because they were like sheep without a shepherd. So He began teaching them many things By this time it was late in the day, so His disciples came to Him and said, "This is a remote place, and it's already very late. Send the people away so that they can go to the surrounding countryside and villages and buy themselves something to eat." But He answered, "You give them something to eat." They said to Him, "That would take more than half a year's wages! Are we to go and spend that much on bread and give it to them to eat?" "How many loaves do you have?" He asked. "Go and see." When they found out, they said, "Five—and two fish." Then Jesus directed them to have all the people sit down in groups on the green grass. So they sat down in groups of hundreds and fifties. Taking the five loaves and the two fish and looking up to heaven, He gave thanks and broke the loaves. Then He gave them to His disciples to distribute to the people. He also divided the two fish among them all. They all ate and were satisfied, and the disciples picked up twelve basketfuls of broken pieces of bread and fish. The number of the men who had eaten was five thousand Immediately Jesus made His disciples get into the boat and go on ahead of Him to Bethsaida while He dismissed the crowd. After leaving them, He went up on a mountainside to pray. Later that night, the boat was in the middle of the lake, and He was alone on land. He saw the disciples straining at the oars because the wind was against them. Shortly before dawn, He went out to them, walking on the lake. He was about to pass by them, but when they saw Him walking on the lake, they thought He was a ghost. They cried out because they all saw Him and were terrified. Immediately He spoke to them and said, "Take courage! It is I. Don't be afraid." Then He climbed into the boat with them, and the wind died down. They were completely amazed, for they had not understood about the loaves; their hearts were hardened When they had crossed over, they landed at Gennesaret and anchored there. As soon as they got out of the boat, people recognized Jesus. They ran throughout that whole region and carried the sick on mats to wherever they heard He was. And wherever He went—into villages, towns, or countryside—they placed the sick in the marketplaces. They begged Him to let them touch even the edge of His cloak, and all who touched it were healed

Chapter 7

The Pharisees and some of the scribes who had come from Jerusalem gathered around Jesus. They saw some of His disciples eating food with hands that were defiled, that is, unwashed. The Pharisees and all the Jews do not eat unless they give their hands a ceremonial washing, holding to the tradition of the elders. When they come from the marketplace, they do not eat unless they wash. And they observe many other traditions, such as the washing of cups, pitchers, and kettles So the Pharisees and scribes asked Jesus, "Why don't Your disciples live according to the tradition of the elders instead of eating their food with defiled hands?" He replied, "Isaiah was right when he prophesied about you hypocrites; as it is written: 'These people honor Me with their lips, but their hearts are far from Me. They worship Me in vain; their teachings are merely human rules.' You have let go of the commands of God and are holding on to human traditions." And He continued, "You have a fine way of setting aside the commands of God in order to observe your own traditions! For Moses said, 'Honor your father and mother,' and, 'Anyone who curses their father or mother is to be put to death.' But you say that if anyone declares that what might have been used to help their father or mother is Corban (that is, devoted to God)—then you no longer let them do anything for their father or mother. Thus you nullify the word of God by your tradition that you have handed down. And you do many things like that." Again, Jesus called the crowd to Him and said, "Listen to Me, everyone, and understand this. Nothing outside a person can defile them by going into them. Rather, it is what comes out of a person that defiles them." After He had left the crowd and entered the house, His disciples asked Him about this parable. "Are you so dull?" He asked. "Don't you see that nothing that enters a person from the outside can defile them? For it doesn't go into their heart but into their stomach, and then out of the body." (In saying this, Jesus declared all foods clean.) He went on: "What comes out of a person is what defiles them. For it is from within, out of a person's heart, that evil thoughts come—sexual immorality, theft, murder, adultery, greed, malice, deceit, lewdness, envy, slander, arrogance, and folly. All these evils come from inside and defile a person." Jesus left that place and went to the vicinity of Tyre. He entered a house and did not want anyone to know it, yet He could not keep His presence secret. In fact, as soon as she heard about Him, a woman whose little daughter was possessed by an impure spirit came and fell at His feet. The woman was a Greek, born in Syrian Phoenicia. She begged Jesus to drive the demon out of her daughter. "First let the children eat all they want," He told her, "for it is not right to take the children's bread and toss it to the dogs." "Lord," she replied, "even the dogs under the table eat the children's crumbs." Then He told her, "For such a reply, you may go; the demon has left your daughter." She went home and found her child lying on the bed, and the demon gone Then Jesus left the vicinity of Tyre and went through Sidon, down to the Sea of Galilee and into the region of the Decapolis. There some people brought to Him a man who was deaf and could hardly talk, and they begged Jesus to place His hand on him. After He took him aside, away from the crowd, Jesus put His fingers into the man's ears. Then He spit and touched the man's tongue. He looked up to heaven and with a deep sigh said to him, "Ephphatha!" (which means "Be opened!"). At this, the man's ears were opened, his tongue was loosened, and he began to speak plainly. Jesus commanded them not to tell anyone. But the more He did so, the more they kept talking about it. People were overwhelmed with amazement. "He has done everything well," they said. "He even makes the deaf hear and the mute speak."

Chapter 8

During those days, another large crowd gathered. Since they had nothing to eat, Jesus called His disciples to Him and said, "I have compassion for these people; they have already been with Me three days and have nothing to eat. If I send them home hungry, they will collapse on the way, because some of them have come a long distance." His disciples answered, "But where in this remote place can anyone get enough bread to feed them?" "How many loaves do you have?" Jesus asked. "Seven," they replied. He told the crowd to sit down on the ground. When He had taken the seven loaves and given thanks, He broke them and gave them to His disciples to distribute to the people, and they did so. They had a few small fish as well; He gave thanks for them also and told the disciples to distribute them. The people ate and were satisfied. Afterward, the disciples picked up seven basketfuls of broken pieces that were left over. About four thousand were present. After He had sent them away, He got into the boat with His disciples and went to the region of Dalmanutha The Pharisees came and began to question Jesus. To test Him, they asked Him for a sign from heaven. He sighed deeply and said, "Why does this generation ask for a sign? Truly I tell you, no sign will be given to it." Then He left them, got back into the boat, and crossed to the other side The disciples had forgotten to bring bread, except for one loaf they had with them in the boat. "Be careful," Jesus warned them. "Watch out for the yeast of the Pharisees and that of Herod." They discussed this with one another and said, "It is because we have no bread." Aware of their discussion, Jesus asked them, "Why are you talking about having no bread? Do you still not see or understand? Are your hearts hardened? Do you have eyes but fail to see, and ears but fail to hear? And don't you remember? When I broke the five loaves for the five thousand, how many basketfuls of pieces did you pick up?" "Twelve," they replied. "And when I broke the seven loaves for the four thousand, how many basketfuls of pieces did you pick up?" They answered, "Seven." He said to them, "Do you still not understand?" They came to Bethsaida, and some people brought a blind man and begged Jesus to touch him. He took the blind man by the hand and led him outside the village. When He had spit on the man's eyes and put His hands on him, Jesus asked, "Do you see anything?" He looked up and said, "I see people; they look like trees walking around." Once more, Jesus put His hands on the man's eyes. Then his eyes were opened, his sight was restored, and he saw everything clearly. Jesus sent him home, saying, "Don't even go into the village." Jesus and His disciples went on to the villages around Caesarea Philippi. On the way, He asked them, "Who do people say I am?" They replied, "Some say John the Baptist; others say Elijah; and still others, one of the prophets." "But what about you?" He asked. "Who do you say I am?" Peter answered, "You are the Messiah." Jesus warned them not to tell anyone about Him He then began to teach them that the Son of Man must suffer many things and be rejected by the elders, the chief priests, and the teachers of the law, and that He must be killed and after three days rise again. He spoke plainly about this, and Peter took Him aside and began to rebuke Him. But when Jesus turned and looked at His disciples, He rebuked Peter. "Get behind Me, Satan!" He said. "You do not have in mind the concerns of God, but merely human concerns." Then He called the crowd to Him along with His disciples and said: "Whoever wants to be My disciple must deny themselves and take up their cross and follow Me. For whoever wants to save their life will lose it, but whoever loses their life for Me and for the gospel will save it. What good is it for someone to gain the whole world, yet forfeit their soul? Or what can anyone give in exchange for their soul? If anyone is ashamed of Me and My words in this adulterous and sinful generation, the Son of Man will be ashamed of them when He comes in His Father's glory with the holy angels."

Chapter 9

Jesus said to them, "Truly I tell you, some who are standing here will not taste death before they see that the kingdom of God has come with power." After six days, Jesus took Peter, James, and John with Him and led them up a high mountain, where they were all alone. There He was transfigured before them. His clothes became dazzling white, whiter than anyone in the world could bleach them. And there appeared before them Elijah and Moses, who were talking with Jesus. Peter said to Jesus, "Rabbi, it is good for us to be here. Let us put up three shelters—one for You, one for Moses, and one for Elijah." (He did not know what to say, they were so frightened.) Then a cloud appeared and covered them, and a voice came from the cloud: "This is My Son, whom I love. Listen to Him!" Suddenly, when they looked around, they no longer saw anyone with them except Jesus As they were coming down the mountain, Jesus gave them orders not to tell anyone what they had seen until the Son of Man had risen from the dead. They kept the matter to themselves, discussing what "rising from the dead" meant. And they asked Him, "Why do the teachers of the law say that Elijah must come first?" Jesus replied, "To be sure, Elijah does come first, and restores all things. Why then is it written that the Son of Man must suffer much and be rejected? But I tell you, Elijah has come, and they have done to him everything they wished, just as it is written about him." When they came to the other disciples, they saw a large crowd around them and the teachers of the law arguing with them. As soon as all the people saw Jesus, they were overwhelmed with wonder and ran to greet Him. "What are you arguing with them about?" He asked. A man in the crowd answered, "Teacher, I brought You my son, who is possessed by a spirit that has robbed him of speech. Whenever it seizes him, it throws him to the ground. He foams at the mouth, gnashes his teeth, and becomes rigid. I asked Your disciples to drive out the spirit, but they could not." "You unbelieving generation," Jesus replied, "how long shall I stay with you? How long shall I put up with you? Bring the boy to Me." So they brought him. When the spirit saw Jesus, it immediately threw the boy into a convulsion. He fell to the ground and rolled around, foaming at the mouth. Jesus asked the boy's father, "How long has he been like this?" "From childhood," he answered. "It has often thrown him into fire or water to kill him. But if You can do anything, take pity on us and help us." "'If You can'?" said Jesus. "Everything is possible for one who believes." Immediately the boy's father exclaimed, "I do believe; help me overcome my unbelief!" When Jesus saw that a crowd was running to the scene, He rebuked the impure spirit. "You deaf and mute spirit," He said, "I command you, come out of him and never enter him again." The spirit shrieked, convulsed him violently, and came out. The boy looked so much like a corpse that many said, "He's dead." But Jesus took him by the hand and lifted him to his feet, and he stood up After Jesus had gone indoors, His disciples asked Him privately, "Why couldn't we drive it out?" He replied, "This kind can come out only by prayer." They left that place and passed through Galilee. Jesus did not want anyone to know where they were, because He was teaching His disciples. He said to them, "The Son of Man is going to be delivered into the hands of men. They will kill Him, and after three days He will rise." But they did not understand what He meant and were afraid to ask Him about it They came to Capernaum. When He was in the house, He asked them, "What were you arguing about on the road?" But they kept quiet because on the way they had argued about who was the greatest. Sitting down, Jesus called the Twelve and said, "Anyone who wants to be first must be the very last, and the servant of all." He took a little child whom He placed among them. Taking the child in His arms, He said to them, "Whoever welcomes one of these little children in My name welcomes Me; and whoever welcomes Me does not welcome Me but the One who sent Me." "Teacher," said John, "we saw someone driving out demons in Your name and we told him to stop because he was not one of us." "Do not stop him," Jesus said. "For no one who does a miracle in My name can in the next moment say anything bad about Me, for whoever is not against us is for us. Truly I tell you, anyone who gives you a cup of water in My name because you belong to the Messiah will certainly not lose their reward." "If anyone causes one of these little ones—those who believe in Me—to stumble, it would be better for them if a large millstone were hung around their neck and they were thrown into the sea. If your hand causes you to stumble, cut it off. It is better for you to enter life maimed than with two hands to go into hell, where the fire never goes out. And if your foot causes you to stumble, cut it off. It is better for you to enter life crippled than to have two feet and be thrown into hell. And if your eye causes you to stumble, pluck it out. It is better for you to enter the kingdom of God with one eye than to have two eyes and be thrown into hell, where "'the worms that eat them do not die, and the fire is not quenched.' Everyone will be salted with fire "Salt is good, but if it loses its saltiness, how can you make it salty again? Have salt among yourselves, and be at peace with each other."

Chapter 10

Jesus then left that place and went into the region of Judea and across the Jordan. Again crowds of people came to Him, and as was His custom, He taught them. Some Pharisees came and tested Him by asking, "Is it lawful for a man to divorce his wife?" "What did Moses command you?" He replied. They said, "Moses permitted a man to write a certificate of divorce and send her away." "It was because your hearts were hard that Moses wrote you this law," Jesus replied. "But at the beginning of creation God 'made them male and female.' 'For this reason, a man will leave his father and mother and be united to his wife, and the two will become one flesh.' So they are no longer two, but one flesh. Therefore what God has joined together, let no one separate." When they were in the house again, the disciples asked Jesus about this. He answered, "Anyone who divorces his wife and marries another woman commits adultery against her. And if she divorces her husband and marries another man, she commits adultery." People were bringing little children to Jesus for Him to place His hands on them, but the disciples rebuked them. When Jesus saw this, He was indignant. He said to them, "Let the little children come to Me, and do not hinder them, for the kingdom of God belongs to such as these. Truly I tell you, anyone who will not receive the kingdom of God like a little child will never enter it." And He took the children in His arms, placed His hands on them, and blessed them As Jesus started on His way, a man ran up to Him and fell on his knees before Him. "Good teacher," he asked, "what must I do to inherit eternal life?" "Why do you call Me good?" Jesus answered. "No one is good—except God alone. You know the commandments: 'You shall not murder, you shall not commit adultery, you shall not steal, you shall not give false testimony, you shall not defraud, honor your father and mother.'" "Teacher," he declared, "all these I have kept since I was a boy." Jesus looked at him and loved him. "One thing you lack," He said. "Go, sell everything you have and give to the poor, and you will have treasure in heaven. Then come, follow Me." At this, the man's face fell. He went away sad because he had great wealth Jesus looked around and said to His disciples, "How hard it is for the rich to enter the kingdom of God!" The disciples were amazed at His words. But Jesus said again, "Children, how hard it is to enter the kingdom of God! It is easier for a camel to go through the eye of a needle than for someone who is rich to enter the kingdom of God." The disciples were even more amazed, and said to each other, "Who then can be saved?" Jesus looked at them and said, "With man this is impossible, but not with God; all things are possible with God." Then Peter spoke up, "We have left everything to follow You!" "Truly I tell you," Jesus replied, "no one who has left home or brothers or sisters or mother or father or children or fields for Me and the gospel will fail to receive a hundred times as much in this present age: homes, brothers, sisters, mothers, children and fields—along with persecutions—and in the age to come eternal life. But many who are first will be last, and the last first." They were on their way up to Jerusalem, with Jesus leading the way, and the disciples were astonished, while those who followed were afraid. Again He took the Twelve aside and told them what was going to happen to Him. "We are going up to Jerusalem," He said, "and the Son of Man will be delivered over to the chief priests and the teachers of the law. They will condemn Him to death and will hand Him over to the Gentiles, who will mock Him and spit on Him, flog Him and kill Him. Three days later He will rise." Then James and John, the sons of Zebedee, came to Him. "Teacher," they said, "we want You to do for us whatever we ask." "What do you want Me to do for you?" He asked. They replied, "Let one of us sit at Your right and the other at Your left in Your glory." "You don't know what you are asking," Jesus said. "Can you drink the cup I drink or be baptized with the baptism I am baptized with?" "We can," they answered. Jesus said to them, "You will drink the cup I drink and be baptized with the baptism I am baptized with, but to sit at My right or left is not for Me to grant. These places belong to those for whom they have been prepared." When the ten heard about this, they became indignant with James and John. Jesus called them together and said, "You know that those who are regarded as rulers of the Gentiles lord it over them, and their high officials exercise authority over them. Not so with you. Instead, whoever wants to become great among you must be your servant, and whoever wants to be first must be slave of all. For even the Son of Man did not come to be served, but to serve, and to give His life as a ransom for many." Then they came to Jericho. As Jesus and His disciples, together with a large crowd, were leaving the city, a blind man, Bartimaeus (which means "son of Timaeus"), was sitting by the roadside begging. When he heard that it was Jesus of Nazareth, he began to shout, "Jesus, Son of David, have mercy on me!" Many rebuked him and told him to be quiet, but he shouted all the more, "Son of David, have mercy on me!" Jesus stopped and said, "Call him." So they called to the blind man, "Cheer up! On your feet! He's calling you." Throwing his cloak aside, he jumped to his feet and came to Jesus. "What do you want Me to do for you?" Jesus asked him. The blind man said, "Rabbi, I want to see." "Go," said Jesus, "your faith has healed you." Immediately he received his sight and followed Jesus along the road

Chapter 11

When they approached Jerusalem, near Bethphage and Bethany at the Mount of Olives, Jesus sent two of His disciples ahead. He instructed them, "Go into the village ahead of you, and as soon as you enter it, you will find a colt tied there that no one has ever ridden. Untie it and bring it here. If anyone asks you why you are doing this, say, 'The Lord needs it and will send it back here shortly.'" The disciples went and found the colt outside in the street, tied at a doorway. As they untied it, some people standing there asked, "What are you doing, untying that colt?" They answered as Jesus had told them, and the people let them go They brought the colt to Jesus and threw their cloaks over it, and He sat on it. Many people spread their cloaks on the road, while others spread branches they had cut in the fields. Those who went ahead and those who followed shouted, "Hosanna! Blessed is He who comes in the name of the Lord! Blessed is the coming kingdom of our father David! Hosanna in the highest heaven!" Jesus entered Jerusalem and went into the temple courts. He looked around at everything, but since it was already late, He went out to Bethany with the Twelve. The next day, as they were leaving Bethany, Jesus was hungry. Seeing in the distance a fig tree in leaf, He went to find out if it had any fruit. When He reached it, He found nothing but leaves, because it was not the season for figs. Then He said to the tree, "May no one ever eat fruit from you again." And His disciples heard Him say it On reaching Jerusalem, Jesus entered the temple courts and began driving out those who were buying and selling there. He overturned the tables of the money changers and the benches of those selling doves and would not allow anyone to carry merchandise through the temple courts. As He taught them, He said, "Is it not written: 'My house will be called a house of prayer for all nations'? But you have made it 'a den of robbers.'" The chief priests and the teachers of the law heard this and began looking for a way to kill Him, for they feared Him because the whole crowd was amazed at His teaching When evening came, Jesus and His disciples went out of the city. In the morning, as they went along, they saw the fig tree withered from the roots. Peter remembered and said to Jesus, "Rabbi, look! The fig tree You cursed has withered!" "Have faith in God," Jesus answered. "Truly I tell you, if anyone says to this mountain, 'Go, throw yourself into the sea,' and does not doubt in their heart but believes that what they say will happen, it will be done for them. Therefore I tell you, whatever you ask for in prayer, believe that you have received it, and it will be yours. And when you stand praying, if you hold anything against anyone, forgive them, so that your Father in heaven may forgive you your sins." They arrived again in Jerusalem, and while Jesus was walking in the temple courts, the chief priests, the teachers of the law, and the elders came to Him. "By what authority are You doing these things?" they asked. "And who gave You authority to do this?" Jesus replied, "I will ask you one question. Answer Me, and I will tell you by what authority I am doing these things. John's baptism—was it from heaven, or of human origin? Tell Me!" They discussed it among themselves and said, "If we say, 'From heaven,' He will ask, 'Then why didn't you believe him?' But if we say, 'Of human origin'..." They feared the people, for everyone held that John really was a prophet. So they answered Jesus, "We don't know." Jesus said, "Neither will I tell you by what authority I am doing these things."

Chapter 12

Jesus then began to speak to them in parables. "A man planted a vineyard, put a wall around it, dug a pit for the winepress, and built a watchtower. Then he rented the vineyard to some farmers and moved to another place. At harvest time he sent a servant to the tenants to collect from them some of the fruit of the vineyard. But they seized him, beat him, and sent him away empty-handed. Then he sent another servant to them; they struck this man on the head and treated him shamefully. He sent still another, and that one they killed. He sent many others; some of them they beat, others they killed He had one left to send, a son, whom he loved. He sent him last of all, saying, 'They will respect my son.' But the tenants said to one another, 'This is the heir. Come, let's kill him, and the inheritance will be ours.' So they took him and killed him, and threw him out of the vineyard. What then will the owner of the vineyard do? He will come and kill those tenants and give the vineyard to others. Haven't you read this passage of Scripture: 'The stone the builders rejected has become the cornerstone; the Lord has done this, and it is marvelous in our eyes'?" Then the chief priests, the teachers of the law, and the elders looked for a way to arrest Him because they knew He had spoken the parable against them. But they were afraid of the crowd, so they left Him and went away Later they sent some of the Pharisees and Herodians to Jesus to catch Him in His words. They came to Him and said, "Teacher, we know that You are a man of integrity. You aren't swayed by others because You pay no attention to who they are; but You teach the way of God in accordance with the truth. Is it right to pay the imperial tax to Caesar or not? Should we pay or shouldn't we?" But Jesus knew their hypocrisy. "Why are you trying to trap Me?" He asked. "Bring Me a denarius and let Me look at it." They brought the coin, and He asked them, "Whose image is this? And whose inscription?" "Caesar's," they replied. Then Jesus said to them, "Give back to Caesar what is Caesar's and to God what is God's." And they were amazed at Him Then the Sadducees, who say there is no resurrection, came to Him with a question. "Teacher," they said, "Moses wrote for us that if a man's brother dies and leaves a wife but no children,

the man must marry the widow and raise up offspring for his brother. Now there were seven brothers. The first one married and died without leaving any children. The second one married the widow, but he also died, leaving no child. It was the same with the third. In fact, none of the seven left any children. Last of all, the woman died too. At the resurrection whose wife will she be, since the seven were married to her?" Jesus replied, "Are you not in error because you do not know the Scriptures or the power of God? When the dead rise, they will neither marry nor be given in marriage; they will be like the angels in heaven. Now about the dead rising—have you not read in the Book of Moses, in the account of the burning bush, how God said to him, 'I am the God of Abraham, the God of Isaac, and the God of Jacob'? He is not the God of the dead, but of the living. You are badly mistaken!" One of the teachers of the law came and heard them debating. Noticing that Jesus had given them a good answer, he asked Him, "Of all the commandments, which is the most important?" "The most important one," answered Jesus, "is this: 'Hear, O Israel: The Lord our God, the Lord is one. Love the Lord your God with all your heart and with all your soul and with all your mind and with all your strength.' The second is this: 'Love your neighbor as yourself.' There is no commandment greater than these." "Well said, teacher," the man replied. "You are right in saying that God is one and there is no other but Him. To love Him with all your heart, with all your understanding and with all your strength, and to love your neighbor as yourself is more important than all burnt offerings and sacrifices." When Jesus saw that he had answered wisely, He said to him, "You are not far from the kingdom of God." And from then on no one dared ask Him any more questions While Jesus was teaching in the temple courts, He asked, "Why do the teachers of the law say that the Messiah is the son of David? David himself, speaking by the Holy Spirit, declared: 'The Lord said to my Lord: "Sit at My right hand until I put Your enemies under Your feet."' David himself calls Him 'Lord.' How then can He be his son?" The large crowd listened to Him with delight As He taught, Jesus said, "Watch out for the teachers of the law. They like to walk around in flowing robes and be greeted with respect in the marketplaces, and have the most important seats in the synagogues and the places of honor at banquets. They devour widows' houses and for a show make lengthy prayers. These men will be punished most severely." Jesus sat down opposite the place where the offerings were put and watched the crowd putting their money into the temple treasury. Many rich people threw in large amounts. But a poor widow came and put in two very small copper coins, worth only a few cents. Calling His disciples to Him, Jesus said, "Truly I tell you, this poor widow has put more into the treasury than all the others. They all gave out of their wealth; but she, out of her poverty, put in everything—all she had to live on."

Chapter 13

As Jesus was leaving the temple, one of His disciples said to Him, "Look, Teacher! What massive stones! What magnificent buildings!" "Do you see all these great buildings?" replied Jesus. "Not one stone here will be left on another; every one will be thrown down." As Jesus was sitting on the Mount of Olives opposite the temple, Peter, James, John, and Andrew asked Him privately, "Tell us, when will these things happen? And what will be the sign that they are all about to be fulfilled?" Jesus said to them, "Watch out that no one deceives you. Many will come in My name, claiming, 'I am He,' and will deceive many. When you hear of wars and rumors of wars, do not be alarmed. Such things must happen, but the end is still to come. Nation will rise against nation, and kingdom against kingdom. There will be earthquakes in various places and famines. These are the beginning of birth pains "You must be on your guard. You will be handed over to the local councils and flogged in the synagogues. On account of Me, you will stand before governors and kings as witnesses to them. And the gospel must first be preached to all nations. Whenever you are arrested and brought to trial, do not worry beforehand about what to say. Just say whatever is given you at the time, for it is not you speaking, but the Holy Spirit "Brother will betray brother to death, and a father his child. Children will rebel against their parents and have them put to death. Everyone will hate you because of Me, but the one who stands firm to the end will be saved "When you see 'the abomination that causes desolation' standing where it does not belong—let the reader understand—then let those who are in Judea flee to the mountains. Let no one on the housetop go down or enter the house to take anything out. Let no one in the field go back to get their cloak. How dreadful it will be in those days for pregnant women and nursing mothers! Pray that this will not take place in winter, because those will be days of distress unequaled from the beginning, when God created the world, until now—and never to be equaled again "If the Lord had not cut short those days, no one would survive. But for the sake of the elect, whom He has chosen, He has shortened them. At that time if anyone says to you, 'Look, here is the Messiah!' or, 'Look, there He is!' do not believe it. For false messiahs and false prophets will appear and perform signs and wonders to deceive, if possible, even the elect. So be on your guard; I have told you everything ahead of time "But in those days, following that distress, 'the sun will be darkened, and the moon will not give its light; the stars will fall from the sky, and the heavenly bodies will be shaken.' At that time people will see the Son of Man coming in clouds with great power and glory. And He will send His angels and gather His elect from the four winds, from the ends of the earth to the ends of the heavens "Now learn this lesson from the fig tree: As soon as its twigs get tender and its leaves come out, you know that summer is near. Even so, when you see these things happening, you know that it is near, right at the door. Truly I tell you, this generation will certainly not pass away until all these things have happened. Heaven and earth will pass away, but My words will never pass away "But about that day or hour no one knows, not even the angels in heaven, nor the Son, but only the Father. Be on guard! Be alert! You do not know when that time will come. It's like a man going away: He leaves his house and puts his servants in charge, each with their assigned task, and tells the one at the door to keep watch "Therefore keep watch because you do not know when the owner of the house will come back—whether in the evening, or at midnight, or when the rooster crows, or at dawn. If he comes suddenly, do not let him find you sleeping. What I say to you, I say to everyone: 'Watch!'"

Chapter 14

Now the Passover and the Festival of Unleavened Bread were only two days away, and the chief priests and the teachers of the law were scheming to arrest Jesus secretly and kill Him. "But not during the festival," they said, "or the people may riot." While He was in Bethany, reclining at the table in the home of Simon the Leper, a woman came with an alabaster jar of very expensive perfume, made of pure nard. She broke the jar and poured the perfume on His head. Some of those present were saying indignantly to one another, "Why this waste of perfume? It could have been sold for more than a year's wages and the money given to the poor." And they rebuked her harshly "Leave her alone," said Jesus. "Why are you bothering her? She has done a beautiful thing to Me. The poor you will always have with you, and you can help them any time you want. But you will not always have Me. She did what she could. She poured perfume on My body beforehand to prepare for My burial. Truly I tell you, wherever the gospel is preached throughout the world, what she has done will also be told, in memory of her." Then Judas Iscariot, one of the Twelve, went to the chief priests to betray Jesus to them. They were delighted to hear this and promised to give him money. So he watched for an opportunity to hand Him over On the first day of the Festival of Unleavened Bread, when it was customary to sacrifice the Passover lamb, Jesus' disciples asked Him, "Where do You want us to go and make preparations for You to eat the Passover?" So He sent two of His disciples, telling them, "Go into the city, and a man carrying a jar of water will meet you. Follow him. Say to the owner of the house he enters, 'The Teacher asks: Where is My guest room, where I may eat the Passover with My disciples?' He will show you a large room upstairs, furnished and ready. Make preparations for us there." The disciples left, went into the city, and found things just as Jesus had told them. So they prepared the Passover When evening came, Jesus arrived with the Twelve. While they were reclining at the table eating, He said, "Truly I tell you, one of you will betray Me—one who is eating with Me." They were saddened, and one by one they said to Him, "Surely You don't mean me?" "It is one of the Twelve," He replied, "one who dips bread into the bowl with Me. The Son of Man will go just as it is written about Him. But woe to that man who betrays the Son of Man! It would be better for him if he had not been born." While they were eating, Jesus took bread, and when He had given thanks, He broke it and gave it to His disciples, saying, "Take it; this is My body." Then He took a cup, and when He had given thanks, He gave it to them, and they all drank from it. "This is My blood of the covenant, which is poured out for many," He said to them. "Truly I tell you, I will not drink again from the fruit of the vine until that day when I drink it new in the kingdom of God." When they had sung a hymn, they went out to the Mount of Olives "You will all fall away," Jesus told them, "for it is written: 'I will strike the shepherd, and the sheep will be scattered.' But after I have risen, I will go ahead of you into Galilee." Peter declared, "Even if all fall away, I will not." "Truly I tell you," Jesus answered, "today—yes, tonight—before the rooster crows twice you yourself will disown Me three times." But Peter insisted emphatically, "Even if I have to die with You, I will never disown You." And all the others said the same They went to a place called Gethsemane, and Jesus said to His disciples, "Sit here while I pray." He took Peter, James, and John along with Him, and He began to be deeply distressed and troubled. "My soul is overwhelmed with sorrow to the point of death," He said to them. "Stay here and keep watch." Going a little farther, He fell to the ground and prayed that if possible the hour might pass from Him. "Abba, Father," He said, "everything is possible for You. Take this cup from Me. Yet not what I will, but what You will." Then He returned to His disciples and found them sleeping. "Simon," He said to Peter, "are you asleep? Couldn't you keep watch for one hour? Watch and pray so that you will not fall into temptation. The spirit is willing, but the flesh is weak." Once more He went away and prayed the same thing. When He came back, He again found them sleeping, because their eyes were heavy. They did not know what to say to Him. Returning the third time, He said to them, "Are you still sleeping and resting? Enough! The hour has come. Look, the Son of Man is delivered into the hands of sinners. Rise! Let us go! Here comes My betrayer!" Just as He was speaking, Judas, one of the Twelve, appeared. With him was a crowd armed with swords and clubs, sent from the chief priests, the teachers of the law, and the elders. Now the betrayer had arranged a signal with them: "The one I kiss is the man; arrest him and lead him away under guard." Going at once to Jesus, Judas said, "Rabbi!" and kissed Him. The men seized Jesus and arrested Him. Then one of those standing near drew his sword and struck the servant of the high priest, cutting off his ear "Am I leading a rebellion," said Jesus, "that you have come out with swords and clubs to capture Me? Every day I was with you, teaching in the temple courts, and you did not arrest Me. But the Scriptures must be fulfilled." Then everyone deserted Him and fled A young man, wearing nothing but a linen garment, was following Jesus. When they seized him, he fled naked, leaving his garment behind They took Jesus to the high priest, and all the chief priests, the elders, and the teachers of the law came together. Peter followed Him at a distance, right into the courtyard of the high priest. There he sat with the guards and warmed himself at the fire The chief priests and the whole Sanhedrin were looking for evidence against Jesus so that they could put Him to death, but they did not find any. Many testified falsely against Him, but their statements did not agree. Then some stood up and gave this false testimony against Him: "We heard Him say, 'I will destroy this temple made with human hands and in three days will build another, not made with hands.'" Yet even then their testimony did not agree Then the high priest stood up before them and asked Jesus, "Are You not going to answer? What is this testimony that these men are bringing against You?" But Jesus remained silent and gave no answer Again the high priest asked Him, "Are You the Messiah, the Son of the Blessed One?" "I am," said Jesus. "And you will see the Son of Man sitting at the right hand of the Mighty One and coming on the clouds of heaven." The high priest tore his clothes. "Why do we need any more witnesses?" he asked. "You have heard the blasphemy. What do you think?" They all condemned Him as worthy of death. Then some began to spit at Him; they blindfolded Him, struck Him with their fists, and said, "Prophesy!" And the guards took Him and beat Him While Peter was below in the courtyard, one of the servant girls of the high priest came by. When she saw Peter warming himself, she looked closely at him. "You also were with that Nazarene, Jesus," she said. But he denied it. "I don't know or understand what you're talking about," he said, and went out into the entryway When the servant girl saw him there, she said again to those standing around, "This fellow is one of them." Again he denied it. After a little while, those standing near said to Peter, "Surely you are one of them, for you are a Galilean." He began to call down curses, and he swore to them, "I don't know this man you're talking about." Immediately the rooster crowed the second time. Then Peter remembered the word Jesus had spoken to him: "Before the rooster crows twice you will disown Me three times." And he broke down and wept

Chapter 15

Very early in the morning, the chief priests, with the elders, the teachers of the law, and the whole Sanhedrin, made their plans. So they bound Jesus, led Him away, and handed Him over to Pilate. "Are you the king of the Jews?" asked Pilate. "You have said so," Jesus replied. The chief priests accused Him of many things. So again Pilate asked Him, "Aren't You going to answer? See how many things they are accusing You of." But Jesus still made no reply, and Pilate was amazed Now it was the custom at the festival to release a prisoner whom the people requested. A man called Barabbas was in prison with the insurrectionists who had committed murder in the uprising. The crowd came up and asked Pilate to do for them what he usually did. "Do you want me to release to you the king of the Jews?" asked Pilate, knowing it was out of self-interest that the chief priests had handed Jesus over to him. But the chief priests stirred up the crowd to have Pilate release Barabbas instead "What shall I do, then, with the one you call the king of the Jews?" Pilate asked them. "Crucify Him!" they shouted. "Why? What crime has He committed?" asked Pilate. But they shouted all the louder, "Crucify Him!" Wanting to satisfy the crowd, Pilate released Barabbas to them. He had Jesus flogged and handed Him over to be crucified The soldiers led Jesus away into the palace (that is, the Praetorium) and called together the whole company of soldiers. They put a purple robe on Him, then twisted together a crown of thorns and set it on Him. And they began to call out to Him, "Hail, king of the Jews!" Again and again they struck Him on the head with a staff and spit on Him. Falling on their knees, they paid homage to Him. And when they had mocked Him, they took off the purple robe and put His own clothes on Him. Then they led Him out to crucify Him A certain man from Cyrene, Simon, the father of Alexander and Rufus, was passing by on his way in from the country, and they forced him to carry the cross. They brought Jesus to the place called Golgotha (which means "the place of the skull"). Then they offered Him wine mixed with myrrh, but He did not take it. And they crucified Him. Dividing up His clothes, they cast lots to see what each would get It was nine in the morning when they crucified Him. The written notice of the charge against Him read: THE KING OF THE JEWS. They crucified two rebels with Him, one on His right and one on His left. Those who passed by hurled insults at Him, shaking their heads and saying, "So! You who are going to destroy the temple and build it in three days, come down from the cross and save Yourself!" In the same way, the chief priests and the teachers of the law mocked Him among themselves. "He saved others," they said, "but He can't save Himself! Let this Messiah, this king of Israel, come down now from the cross, that we may see and believe." Those crucified with Him also heaped insults on Him At noon, darkness came over the whole land until three in the afternoon. And at three in the afternoon, Jesus cried out in a loud voice, "Eloi, Eloi, lema sabachthani?" (which means "My God, My God, why have You forsaken Me?"). When some of those standing near heard this, they said, "Listen, He's calling Elijah." Someone ran, filled a sponge with wine vinegar, put it on a staff, and offered it to Jesus to drink. "Now leave Him alone. Let's see if Elijah comes to take Him down," he said. With a loud cry, Jesus breathed His last. The curtain of the temple was torn in two from top to bottom. And when the centurion, who stood there in front of Jesus, saw how He died, he said, "Surely this man was the Son of God!" Some women were watching from a distance. Among them were Mary Magdalene, Mary the mother of James the younger and of Joseph, and Salome. In Galilee, these women had followed Him and cared for His needs. Many other women who had come up with Him to Jerusalem were also there It was Preparation Day (that is, the day before the Sabbath). So as evening approached, Joseph of Arimathea, a prominent member of the Council, who was himself waiting for the kingdom of God, went boldly to Pilate and asked for Jesus' body. Pilate was surprised to hear that He was already dead. Summoning the centurion, he asked him if Jesus had already died. When he learned from the centurion that it was so, he gave the body to Joseph. So Joseph bought some linen cloth, took down the body, wrapped it in the linen, and placed it in a tomb cut out of rock. Then he rolled a stone against the entrance of the tomb. Mary Magdalene and Mary the mother of Joseph saw where He was laid

Chapter 16

When the Sabbath was over, Mary Magdalene, Mary the mother of James, and Salome bought spices so that they might go to anoint Jesus' body. Very early on the first day of the week, just after sunrise, they were on their way to the tomb and they asked each other, "Who will roll the stone away from the entrance of the tomb?" But when they looked up, they saw that the stone, which was very large, had been rolled away. As they entered the tomb, they saw a young man dressed in a white robe sitting on the right side, and they were alarmed "Don't be alarmed," he said. "You are looking for Jesus the Nazarene, who was crucified. He has risen! He is not here. See the place where they laid Him. But go, tell His disciples and Peter, 'He is going ahead of you into Galilee. There you will see Him, just as He told you.'" Trembling and bewildered, the women went out and fled from the tomb. They said nothing to anyone, because they were afraid When Jesus rose early on the first day of the week, He appeared first to Mary Magdalene, out of whom He had driven seven demons. She went and told those who had been with Him and who were mourning and weeping. When they heard that Jesus was alive and that she had seen Him, they did not believe it Afterward Jesus appeared in a different form to two of them while they were walking in the country. These returned and reported it to the rest; but they did not believe them either Later Jesus appeared to the Eleven as they were eating; He rebuked them for their lack of faith and their stubborn refusal to believe those who had seen Him after He had risen. He said to them, "Go into all the world and preach the gospel to all creation. Whoever believes and is baptized will be saved, but whoever does not believe will be condemned. And these signs will accompany those who believe: In My name, they will drive out demons; they will speak in new tongues; they will pick up snakes with their hands; and when they drink deadly poison, it will not hurt them at all; they will place their hands on sick people, and they will get well." After the Lord Jesus had spoken to them, He was taken up into heaven and He sat at the right hand of God. Then the disciples went out and preached everywhere, and the Lord worked with them and confirmed His word by the signs that accompanied it

42. Luke

Chapter 1

In the time of King Herod of Judea, there was a priest named Zechariah from the division of Abijah. His wife Elizabeth was a descendant of Aaron. Both were righteous in the sight of God, living blamelessly according to all the commandments and regulations of the Lord. However, they had no children because Elizabeth was barren, and both were advanced in years While Zechariah was serving as priest before God, it was his turn to burn incense when he entered the temple of the Lord. The whole assembly of the people was praying outside at the hour of the incense offering. An angel of the Lord appeared to him, standing at the right side of the altar of incense. Zechariah was startled and gripped with fear, but the angel said to him, "Do not be afraid, Zechariah; your prayer has been heard. Your wife Elizabeth will bear you a son, and you are to call him John. He will be a joy and delight to you, and many will rejoice because of his birth, for he will be great in the sight of the Lord. He is never to take wine or other fermented drink, and he will be filled with the Holy Spirit even before he is born. He will bring back many of the people of Israel to the Lord their God. And he will go on before the Lord, in the spirit and power of Elijah, to turn the hearts of the parents to their children and the disobedient to the wisdom of the righteous—to make ready a people prepared for the Lord." Zechariah asked the angel, "How can I be sure of this? I am an old man, and my wife is well along in years." The angel said to him, "I am Gabriel. I stand in the presence of God, and I have been sent to speak to you and to tell you this good news. And now you will be silent and not able to speak until the day this happens because you did not believe my words, which will come true at their appointed time." Meanwhile, the people were waiting for Zechariah and wondering why he stayed so long in the temple. When he came out, he could not speak to them. They realized he had seen a vision in the temple, for he kept making signs to them but remained unable to speak. When his time of service was completed, he returned home. After this, his wife Elizabeth became pregnant and for five months remained in seclusion. "The Lord has done this for me," she said. "In these days he has shown his favor and taken away my disgrace among the people." In the sixth month of Elizabeth's pregnancy, God sent the angel Gabriel to Nazareth, a town in Galilee, to a virgin pledged to be married to a man named Joseph, a descendant of David. The virgin's name was Mary. The angel went to her and said, "Greetings, you who are highly favored! The Lord is with you." Mary was greatly troubled at his words and wondered what kind of greeting this might be. But the angel said to her, "Do not be afraid, Mary; you have found favor with God. You will conceive and give birth to a son, and you are to call him Jesus. He will be great and will be called the Son of the Most High. The Lord God will give him the throne of his father David, and he will reign over Jacob's descendants forever; his kingdom will never end." "How will this be," Mary asked the angel, "since I am a virgin?" The angel answered, "The Holy Spirit will come on you, and the power of the Most High will overshadow you. So the holy one to be born will be called the Son of God. Even Elizabeth, your relative, is going to have a child in her old age, and she who was said to be unable to conceive is in her sixth month. For no word from God will ever fail." "I am the Lord's servant," Mary answered. "May your word to me be fulfilled." Then the angel left her At that time Mary got ready and hurried to a town in the hill country of Judea, where she entered Zechariah's home and greeted Elizabeth. When Elizabeth heard Mary's greeting, the baby leaped in her womb, and Elizabeth was filled with the Holy Spirit. In a loud voice, she exclaimed: "Blessed are you among women, and blessed is the child you will bear! But why am I so favored, that the mother of my Lord should come to me? As soon as the sound of your greeting reached my ears, the baby in my womb leaped for joy. Blessed is she who has believed that the Lord would fulfill his promises to her!" And Mary said: "My soul glorifies the Lord and my spirit rejoices in God my Savior, for he has been mindful of the humble state of his servant. From now on, all generations will call me blessed, for the Mighty One has done great things for me—holy is his name. His mercy extends to those who fear him, from generation to generation. He has performed mighty deeds with his arm; he has scattered those who are proud in their inmost thoughts. He has brought down rulers from their thrones but has lifted the humble. He has filled the hungry with good things but has sent the rich away empty. He has helped his servant Israel, remembering to be merciful to Abraham and his descendants forever, just as he promised our ancestors." Mary stayed with Elizabeth for about three months and then returned home. When it was time for Elizabeth to have her baby, she gave birth to a son. Her neighbors and relatives heard that the Lord had shown her great mercy, and they shared her joy. On the eighth day, they came to circumcise the child, and they were going to name him after his father Zechariah, but his mother spoke up and said, "No! He is to be called John." They said to her, "There is no one among your relatives who has that name." Then they made signs to his father to find out what he would like to name the child. He asked for a writing tablet, and to everyone's astonishment, he wrote, "His name is John." Immediately his mouth was opened, and his tongue set free, and he began to speak, praising God. All the neighbors were filled with awe, and throughout the hill country of Judea, people were talking about all these things. Everyone who heard this wondered about it, asking, "What then is this child going to be?" For the Lord's hand was with him His father Zechariah was filled with the Holy Spirit and prophesied: "Praise be to the Lord, the God of Israel, because he has come to his people and redeemed them. He has raised up a horn of salvation for us in the house of his servant David (as he said through his holy prophets of long ago), salvation from our enemies and from the hand of all who hate us—to show mercy to our ancestors and to remember his holy covenant, the oath he swore to our father Abraham: to rescue us from the hand of our enemies, and to enable us to serve him without fear in holiness and righteousness before him all our days. And you, my child, will be called a prophet of the Most High; for you will go on before the Lord to prepare the way for him, to give his people the knowledge of salvation through the forgiveness of their sins, because of the tender mercy of our God, by which the rising sun will come to us from heaven to shine on those living in darkness and in the shadow of death, to guide our feet into the path of peace." The child grew and became strong in spirit, and he lived in the wilderness until he appeared publicly to Israel

Chapter 2

In those days, Caesar Augustus issued a decree that a census should be taken of the entire Roman world. (This was the first census that took place while Quirinius was governor of Syria.) Everyone went to their own town to register. So Joseph also went up from the town of Nazareth in Galilee to Judea, to Bethlehem the town of David, because he belonged to the house and line of David. He went there to register with Mary, who was pledged to be married to him and was expecting a child. While they were there, the time came for the baby to be born, and she gave birth to her firstborn, a son. She wrapped him in cloths and placed him in a manger because there was no guest room available for them And there were shepherds living out in the fields nearby, keeping watch over their flocks at night. An angel of the Lord appeared to them, and the glory of the Lord shone around them, and they were terrified. But the angel said to them, "Do not be afraid. I bring you good news that will cause great joy for all the people. Today in the town of David a Savior has been born to you; he is the Messiah, the Lord. This will be a sign to you: You will find a baby wrapped in cloths and lying in a manger." Suddenly, a great company of the heavenly host appeared with the angel, praising God and saying, "Glory to God in the highest heaven, and on earth peace to those on whom his favor rests." When the angels had left them and gone into heaven, the shepherds said to one another, "Let's go to Bethlehem and see this thing that has happened, which the Lord has told us about." So they hurried off and found Mary and Joseph, and the baby, who was lying in the manger. When they had seen him, they spread the word concerning what had been told them about this child, and all who heard it were amazed at what the shepherds said to them. But Mary treasured up all these things and pondered them in her heart. The shepherds returned, glorifying and praising God for all the things they had heard and seen, which were just as they had been told On the eighth day, when it was time to circumcise the child, he was named Jesus, the name the angel had given him before he was conceived. When the time came for the purification rites required by the Law of Moses, Joseph and Mary took him to Jerusalem to present him to the Lord (as it is written in the Law of the Lord, "Every firstborn male is to be consecrated to the Lord"), and to offer a sacrifice in keeping with what is said in the Law of the Lord: "a pair of doves or two young pigeons." Now there was a man in Jerusalem called Simeon, who was righteous and devout. He was waiting for the consolation of Israel, and the Holy Spirit was on him. It had been revealed to him by the Holy Spirit that he would not die before he had seen the Lord's Messiah. Moved by the Spirit, he went into the temple courts. When the parents brought in the child Jesus to do for him what the custom of the Law required, Simeon took him in his arms and praised God, saying: "Sovereign Lord, as you have promised, you may now dismiss your servant in peace. For my eyes have seen your salvation, which you have prepared in the sight of all nations: a light for revelation to the Gentiles and the glory of your people Israel." The child's father and mother marveled at what was said about him. Then Simeon blessed them and said to Mary, his mother: "This child is destined to cause the falling and rising of many in Israel, and to be a sign that will be spoken against, so that the thoughts of many hearts will be revealed. And a sword will pierce your own soul too." There was also a prophet, Anna, the daughter of Penuel, of the tribe of Asher. She was very old; she had lived with her husband seven years after her marriage and then was a widow until she was eighty-four. She never left the temple but worshiped night and day, fasting and praying. Coming up to them at that very moment, she gave thanks to God and spoke about the child to all who were looking forward to the redemption of Jerusalem When Joseph and Mary had done everything required by the Law of the Lord, they returned to Galilee, to their own town of Nazareth. And the child grew and became strong; he was filled with wisdom, and the grace of God was on him Every year Jesus' parents went to Jerusalem for the Festival of the Passover. When he was twelve years old, they went up to the festival, according to the custom. After the festival was over, while his parents were returning home, the boy Jesus stayed behind in Jerusalem, but they were unaware of it. Thinking he was in their company, they traveled on for a day. Then they began looking for him among their relatives and friends. When they did not find him, they went back to Jerusalem to look for him. After three days, they found him in the temple courts, sitting among the teachers, listening to them and asking them questions. Everyone who heard him was amazed at his understanding and his answers. When his parents saw him, they were astonished. His mother said to him, "Son, why have you treated us like this? Your father and I have been anxiously searching for you." "Why were you searching for me?" he asked. "Didn't you know I had to be in my Father's house?" But they did not understand what he was saying to them. Then he went down to Nazareth with them and was obedient to them. But his mother treasured all these things in her heart. And Jesus grew in wisdom and stature, and in favor with God and man

Chapter 3

In the fifteenth year of the reign of Tiberius Caesar—when Pontius Pilate was governor of Judea, Herod tetrarch of Galilee, his brother Philip tetrarch of Iturea and Traconitis, and Lysanias tetrarch of Abilene—during the high-priesthood of Annas and Caiaphas, the word of God came to John son of Zechariah in the wilderness. He went into all the country around the Jordan, preaching a baptism of repentance for the forgiveness of sins. As it is written in the book of the words of Isaiah the prophet: "A voice of one calling in the wilderness, 'Prepare the way for the Lord, make straight paths for him. Every valley shall be filled in, every mountain and hill made low. The crooked roads shall become straight, the rough ways smooth. And all people will see God's salvation.'" John said to the crowds coming out to be baptized by him, "You brood of vipers! Who warned you to flee from the coming wrath? Produce fruit in keeping with repentance. And do not begin to say to yourselves, 'We have Abraham as our father.' For I tell you that out of these stones God can raise up children for Abraham. The ax is already at the root of the trees, and every tree that does not produce good fruit will be cut down and thrown into the fire." "What should we do then?" the crowd asked. John answered, "Anyone who has two shirts should share with the one who has none, and anyone who has food should do the same." Even tax collectors came to be baptized. "Teacher," they asked, "what should we do?" "Don't collect any more than you are required to," he told them. Then some soldiers asked him, "And what should we do?" He replied, "Don't extort money and don't accuse people falsely—be content with your pay." The people were waiting expectantly and were all wondering in their hearts if John might possibly be the Messiah. John answered them all, "I baptize you with water. But one who is more powerful than I will come, the straps of whose sandals I am not worthy to untie. He will baptize you with the Holy Spirit and fire. His winnowing fork is in his hand to clear his threshing floor and to gather the wheat into his barn, but he will burn up the chaff with unquenchable fire." And with many other words John exhorted the people and proclaimed the good news to them. But when John rebuked Herod the tetrarch because of his marriage to Herodias, his brother's wife, and all the other evil things he had done, Herod added this to them all: He locked John up in prison When all the people were being baptized, Jesus was baptized too. And as he was praying, heaven was opened, and the Holy Spirit descended on him in bodily form like a dove. And a voice came from heaven: "You are my Son, whom I love; with you I am well pleased." Now Jesus himself was about thirty years old when he began his ministry. He was the son, so it was thought, of Joseph, the son of Heli, the son of Matthat, the son of Levi, the son of Melki, the son of Jannai, the son of Joseph, the son of Mattathias, the son of Amos, the son of Nahum, the son of Esli, the son of Naggai, the son of Maath, the son of Mattathias, the son of Semein, the son of Josech, the son of Joda, the son of Joanan, the son of Rhesa, the son of Zerubbabel, the son of Shealtiel, the son of Neri, the son of Melki, the son of Addi, the son of Cosam, the son of Elmadam, the son of Er, the son of Joshua, the son of Eliezer, the son of Jorim, the son of Matthat, the son of Levi, the son of Simeon,

the son of Judah, the son of Joseph, the son of Jonan, the son of Eliakim, the son of Melea, the son of Menna, the son of Mattatha, the son of Nathan, the son of David, the son of Jesse, the son of Obed, the son of Boaz, the son of Salmon, the son of Nahshon, the son of Amminadab, the son of Ram, the son of Hezron, the son of Perez, the son of Judah, the son of Jacob, the son of Isaac, the son of Abraham, the son of Terah, the son of Nahor, the son of Serug, the son of Reu, the son of Peleg, the son of Eber, the son of Shelah, the son of Cainan, the son of Arphaxad, the son of Shem, the son of Noah, the son of Lamech, the son of Methuselah, the son of Enoch, the son of Jared, the son of Mahalalel, the son of Kenan, the son of Enosh, the son of Seth, the son of Adam, the son of God

Chapter 4

Jesus, full of the Holy Spirit, left the Jordan and was led by the Spirit into the wilderness, where for forty days he was tempted by the devil. He ate nothing during those days, and at the end of them, he was hungry. The devil said to him, "If you are the Son of God, tell this stone to become bread." Jesus answered, "It is written: 'Man shall not live on bread alone.'" The devil led him up to a high place and showed him in an instant all the kingdoms of the world. And he said to him, "I will give you all their authority and splendor; it has been given to me, and I can give it to anyone I want to. If you worship me, it will all be yours." Jesus answered, "It is written: 'Worship the Lord your God and serve him only.'" The devil led him to Jerusalem and had him stand on the highest point of the temple. "If you are the Son of God," he said, "throw yourself down from here. For it is written: 'He will command his angels concerning you to guard you carefully; they will lift you up in their hands so that you will not strike your foot against a stone.'" Jesus answered, "It is said: 'Do not put the Lord your God to the test.'" When the devil had finished all this tempting, he left him until an opportune time. Jesus returned to Galilee in the power of the Spirit, and news about him spread through the whole countryside. He was teaching in their synagogues, and everyone praised him He went to Nazareth, where he had been brought up, and on the Sabbath day, he went into the synagogue, as was his custom. He stood up to read, and the scroll of the prophet Isaiah was handed to him. Unrolling it, he found the place where it is written: "The Spirit of the Lord is on me because he has anointed me to proclaim good news to the poor. He has sent me to proclaim freedom for the prisoners and recovery of sight for the blind, to set the oppressed free, to proclaim the year of the Lord's favor." Then he rolled up the scroll, gave it back to the attendant, and sat down. The eyes of everyone in the synagogue were fastened on him. He began by saying to them, "Today this scripture is fulfilled in your hearing." All spoke well of him and were amazed at the gracious words that came from his lips. "Isn't this Joseph's son?" they asked. Jesus said to them, "Surely you will quote this proverb to me: 'Physician, heal yourself!' And you will tell me, 'Do here in your hometown what we have heard that you did in Capernaum.'" "Truly I tell you," he continued, "no prophet is accepted in his hometown. I assure you that there were many widows in Israel in Elijah's time when the sky was shut for three and a half years, and there was a severe famine throughout the land. Yet Elijah was not sent to any of them but to a widow in Zarephath in the region of Sidon. And there were many in Israel with leprosy in the time of Elisha the prophet, yet not one of them was cleansed—only Naaman the Syrian." All the people in the synagogue were furious when they heard this. They got up, drove him out of the town, and took him to the brow of the hill on which the town was built, to throw him off the cliff. But he walked right through the crowd and went on his way Then he went down to Capernaum, a town in Galilee, and on the Sabbath, he taught the people. They were amazed at his teaching because his words had authority. In the synagogue, there was a man possessed by a demon, an impure spirit. He cried out at the top of his voice, "Go away! What do you want with us, Jesus of Nazareth? Have you come to destroy us? I know who you are—the Holy One of God!" "Be quiet!" Jesus said sternly. "Come out of him!" Then the demon threw the man down before them all and came out without injuring him. All the people were amazed and said to each other, "What words these are! With authority and power he gives orders to impure spirits and they come out!" And the news about him spread throughout the surrounding area Jesus left the synagogue and went to the home of Simon. Now Simon's mother-in-law was suffering from a high fever, and they asked Jesus to help her. So he bent over her and rebuked the fever, and it left her. She got up at once and began to wait on them At sunset, the people brought to Jesus all who had various kinds of sickness, and laying his hands on each one, he healed them. Moreover, demons came out of many people, shouting, "You are the Son of God!" But he rebuked them and would not allow them to speak because they knew he was the Messiah At daybreak, Jesus went out to a solitary place. The people were looking for him, and when they came to where he was, they tried to keep him from leaving them. But he said, "I must proclaim the good news of the kingdom of God to the other towns also because that is why I was sent." And he kept on preaching in the synagogues of Judea

Chapter 5

One day as Jesus was standing by the Lake of Gennesaret, the people were crowding around him and listening to the word of God. He saw at the water's edge two boats, left there by the fishermen, who were washing their nets. He got into one of the boats, the one belonging to Simon, and asked him to put out a little from shore. Then he sat down and taught the people from the boat When he had finished speaking, he said to Simon, "Put out into deep water, and let down the nets for a catch." Simon answered, "Master, we've worked hard all night and haven't caught anything. But because you say so, I will let down the nets." When they had done so, they caught such a large number of fish that their nets began to break. So they signaled their partners in the other boat to come and help them, and they came and filled both boats so full that they began to sink When Simon Peter saw this, he fell at Jesus' knees and said, "Go away from me, Lord; I am a sinful man!" For he and all his companions were astonished at the catch of fish they had taken, and so were James and John, the sons of Zebedee, Simon's partners. Then Jesus said to Simon, "Don't be afraid; from now on you will fish for people." So they pulled their boats up on shore, left everything, and followed him While Jesus was in one of the towns, a man came along who was covered with leprosy. When he saw Jesus, he fell with his face to the ground and begged him, "Lord, if you are willing, you can make me clean." Jesus reached out his hand and touched the man. "I am willing," he said. "Be clean!" And immediately the leprosy left him. Then Jesus ordered him, "Don't tell anyone, but go, show yourself to the priest and offer the sacrifices that Moses commanded for your cleansing, as a testimony to them." Yet the news about him spread all the more so that crowds of people came to hear him and to be healed of their sicknesses. But Jesus often withdrew to lonely places and prayed One day Jesus was teaching, and Pharisees and teachers of the law were sitting there. They had come from every village of Galilee and from Judea and Jerusalem. And the power of the Lord was with Jesus to heal the sick. Some men came carrying a paralyzed man on a mat and tried to take him into the house to lay him before Jesus. When they could not find a way to do this because of the crowd, they went up on the roof and lowered him on his mat through the tiles into the middle of the crowd, right in front of Jesus. When Jesus saw their faith, he said, "Friend, your sins are forgiven." The Pharisees and the teachers of the law began thinking to themselves, "Who is this fellow who speaks blasphemy? Who can forgive sins but God alone?" Jesus knew what they were thinking and asked, "Why are you thinking these things in your hearts? Which is easier: to say, 'Your sins are forgiven,' or to say, 'Get up and walk'? But I want you to know that the Son of Man has authority on earth to forgive sins." So he said to the paralyzed man, "I tell you, get up, take your mat, and go home." Immediately he stood up in front of them, took what he had been lying on, and went home praising God. Everyone was amazed and gave praise to God. They were filled with awe and said, "We have seen remarkable things today." After this, Jesus went out and saw a tax collector by the name of Levi sitting at his tax booth. "Follow me," Jesus said to him, and Levi got up, left everything, and followed him. Then Levi held a great banquet for Jesus at his house, and a large crowd of tax collectors and others were eating with them. But the Pharisees and the teachers of the law who belonged to their sect complained to his disciples, "Why do you eat and drink with tax collectors and sinners?" Jesus answered them, "It is not the healthy who need a doctor, but the sick. I have not come to call the righteous, but sinners to repentance." They said to him, "John's disciples often fast and pray, and so do the disciples of the Pharisees, but yours go on eating and drinking." Jesus answered, "Can you make the friends of the bridegroom fast while he is with them? But the time will come when the bridegroom will be taken from them; in those days they will fast." He told them this parable: "No one tears a piece out of a new garment to patch an old one. Otherwise, they will have torn the new garment, and the patch from the new will not match the old. And no one pours new wine into old wineskins. Otherwise, the new wine will burst the skins; the wine will run out, and the wineskins will be ruined. No, new wine must be poured into new wineskins. And no one after drinking old wine wants the new, for they say, 'The old is better.'"

Chapter 6

On a Sabbath, while passing through the wheat fields, Jesus' disciples began to pluck ears of grain, rub them in their hands, and eat them. Some Pharisees asked, "Why are you doing what is unlawful on the Sabbath?" Jesus replied, "Have you never read what David did when he and his companions were hungry? He entered the house of God, took the consecrated bread, ate it, and gave some to his companions, even though it was not lawful for anyone but the priests to eat." Then he said to them, "The Son of Man is Lord of the Sabbath." On another Sabbath, Jesus entered the synagogue and taught. A man with a withered right hand was there, and the scribes and Pharisees watched closely to see if Jesus would heal on the Sabbath, seeking grounds to accuse him. Knowing their thoughts, Jesus told the man with the withered hand, "Stand up in front of everyone." So he got up and stood there. Jesus then said, "I ask you, which is lawful on the Sabbath: to do good or to do evil, to save life or to destroy it?" After looking around at them all, he said to the man, "Stretch out your hand." He did so, and his hand was completely restored. But the Pharisees and teachers of the law were furious and began to discuss with each other what they might do to Jesus In those days, Jesus went out to a mountainside to pray and spent the night praying to God. When morning came, he called his disciples to him and chose twelve of them, whom he also designated apostles: Simon (whom he named Peter), his brother Andrew, James, John, Philip, Bartholomew, Matthew, Thomas, James son of Alphaeus, Simon called the Zealot, Judas son of James, and Judas Iscariot, who became a traitor He went down with them and stood on a level place. A large crowd of his disciples was there and a great number of people from all over Judea, Jerusalem, and the coastal region around Tyre and Sidon, who had come to hear him and to be healed of their diseases. Those troubled by impure spirits were cured, and the people all tried to touch him because power was coming from him and healing them all Looking at his disciples, he said, "Blessed are you who are poor, for yours is the kingdom of God. Blessed are you who hunger now, for you will be satisfied. Blessed are you who weep now, for you will laugh. Blessed are you when people hate you, exclude you, insult you, and reject your name as evil because of the Son of Man. Rejoice in that day and leap for joy because great is your reward in heaven, for that is how their ancestors treated the prophets." "But woe to you who are rich, for you have already received your comfort. Woe to you who are well fed now, for you will go hungry. Woe to you who laugh now, for you will mourn and weep. Woe to you when everyone speaks well of you, for that is how their ancestors treated the false prophets." "But to you who are listening I say: Love your enemies, do good to those who hate you, bless those who curse you, and pray for those who mistreat you. If someone slaps you on one cheek, turn to them the other also. If someone takes your coat, do not withhold your shirt. Give to everyone who asks you, and if anyone takes what belongs to you, do not demand it back. Do to others as you would have them do to you." "If you love those who love you, what credit is that to you? Even sinners love those who love them. And if you do good to those who are good to you, what credit is that to you? Even sinners do that. And if you lend to those from whom you expect repayment, what credit is that to you? Even sinners lend to sinners, expecting to be repaid in full. But love your enemies, do good to them, and lend to them without expecting to get anything back. Then your reward will be great, and you will be children of the Most High, because he is kind to the ungrateful and wicked. Be merciful, just as your Father is merciful." "Do not judge, and you will not be judged. Do not condemn, and you will not be condemned. Forgive, and you will be forgiven. Give, and it will be given to you. A good measure, pressed down, shaken together, and running over, will be poured into your lap. For with the measure you use, it will be measured to you." He also told them this parable: "Can the blind lead the blind? Will they not both fall into a pit? The student is not above the teacher, but everyone who is fully trained will be like their teacher. Why do you look at the speck of sawdust in your brother's eye and pay no attention to the plank in your own eye? How can you say to your brother, 'Brother, let me take the speck out of your eye,' when you yourself fail to see the plank in your own eye? You hypocrite, first take the plank out of your eye, and then you will see clearly to remove the speck from your brother's eye." "No good tree bears bad fruit, nor does a bad tree bear good fruit. Each tree is recognized by its own fruit. People do not pick figs from thornbushes or grapes from briers. A good man brings good things out of the good stored up in his heart, and an evil man brings evil things out of the evil stored up in his heart. For the mouth speaks what the heart is full of." "Why do you call me, 'Lord, Lord,' and do not do what I say? As for everyone who comes to me and hears my words and puts them into practice, I will show you what they are like. They are like a man building a house, who dug down deep and laid the foundation on rock. When a flood came, the torrent struck that house but could not shake it because it was well built. But the one who hears my words and does not put them into practice is like a man who built a house on the ground without a foundation. The moment the torrent struck that house, it collapsed, and its destruction was complete."

Chapter 7

When Jesus had finished saying all this to the people who were listening, he entered Capernaum. There, a centurion's servant, whom his master valued highly, was sick and about to die. The centurion heard of Jesus and sent some elders of the Jews to him, asking him to come and heal his servant. When they came to Jesus, they pleaded earnestly with him, "This man deserves to have you do this because he loves our nation and has built our synagogue." So Jesus went with them He was not far from the house when the centurion sent friends to say to him: "Lord, don't trouble yourself, for I do not deserve to have you come under my roof. That is why I did not even consider myself worthy to come to you. But say the word, and my servant will be healed. For I myself am a man under authority, with soldiers under me. I tell this one, 'Go,' and he goes; and that one, 'Come,' and he comes. I say to my servant, 'Do this,' and he does it." When Jesus heard this, he was amazed at him and, turning to the crowd following him, he said, "I tell you, I have not found such great faith even in Israel." Then the men who had been sent returned to the house and found the servant well Soon afterward, Jesus went to a town called Nain, and his disciples and a large crowd went along with him. As he approached the town gate, a dead person was being carried out—the only son of his mother, and she was a widow. A large crowd from the town was with her. When the Lord saw her, his heart went out to her and he said, "Don't cry." Then he went up and touched the bier they were carrying him on, and the bearers stood still. He said, "Young man, I say to you, get up!" The dead man sat up and began to talk, and Jesus gave him back to his mother. They were all filled with awe and praised God. "A great prophet has appeared among us," they said. "God has come to help his people." This news about Jesus spread throughout Judea and the surrounding country John's disciples told him about all these things. Calling two of them, he sent them to the Lord to ask, "Are you the one who is to come, or should we expect someone else?" When the men came to Jesus, they said, "John the Baptist sent us to ask, 'Are you the one who is to come, or should we expect someone else?'" At that very time, Jesus cured many who had diseases, sicknesses, and evil spirits and gave sight to many who were blind. So he replied to the messengers, "Go back and report to John what you have seen and heard: The blind receive sight, the lame walk, those who have leprosy are cleansed, the deaf hear, the dead are raised, and the good news is proclaimed to the poor. Blessed is anyone who does not stumble on account of me." After John's messengers left, Jesus began to speak to the crowd about John: "What did you go out into the wilderness to see? A reed swayed by the wind? If not, what did you go out to see? A man dressed in fine clothes? No, those who wear expensive clothes and indulge in luxury are in palaces. But what did you go out to see? A prophet? Yes, I tell you, and more than a prophet. This is the one about whom it is written: 'I will send my messenger ahead of you, who will prepare your way before you.' I tell you, among those born of women, there is no one greater than John; yet the one who is least in the kingdom of God is greater than he." All the people, even the tax collectors, when they heard Jesus' words, acknowledged that God's way was right because they had been baptized by John. But the Pharisees and the experts in the law rejected God's purpose for themselves because they had not been baptized by John Jesus went on to say, "To what, then, can I compare the people of this generation? What are they like? They are like children sitting in the marketplace and calling out to each other: 'We played the pipe for you, and you did not dance; we sang a dirge, and you did not cry.' For John the Baptist came neither eating bread nor drinking wine, and you say, 'He has a demon.' The Son of Man came eating and drinking, and you say, 'Here is a glutton and a drunkard, a friend of tax collectors and sinners.' But wisdom is proved right by all her children." When one of the Pharisees invited Jesus to have dinner with him, he went to the Pharisee's house and reclined at the table. A woman in that town who lived a sinful life learned that Jesus was eating at the Pharisee's house, so she came there with an alabaster jar of perfume. As she stood behind him at his feet weeping, she began to wet his feet with her tears. Then she wiped them with her hair, kissed them, and poured perfume on them When the Pharisee who had invited him saw this, he said to himself, "If this man were a prophet, he would know who is touching him and what kind of woman she is—that she is a sinner." Jesus answered him, "Simon, I have something to tell you." "Tell me, teacher," he said "Two people owed money to a certain moneylender. One owed him five hundred denarii, and the other fifty. Neither of them had the money to pay him back, so he forgave the debts of both. Now which of them will love him more?" Simon replied, "I suppose the one who had the bigger debt forgiven." "You have judged correctly," Jesus said Then he turned toward the woman and said to Simon, "Do you see this woman? I came into your house. You did not give me any water for my feet, but she wet my feet with her tears and wiped them with her hair. You did not give me a kiss, but this woman, from the time I entered, has not stopped kissing my feet. You did not put oil on my head, but she has poured perfume on my feet. Therefore, I tell you, her many sins have been forgiven—as her great love has shown. But whoever has been forgiven little loves little." Then Jesus said to her, "Your sins are forgiven." The other guests began to say among themselves, "Who is this who even forgives sins?" Jesus said to the woman, "Your faith has saved you; go in peace."

Chapter 8

After this, Jesus traveled about from one town and village to another, proclaiming the good news of the kingdom of God. The Twelve were with him, and also some women who had been cured of evil spirits and diseases: Mary (called Magdalene) from whom seven demons had come out; Joanna the wife of Chuza, the manager of Herod's household; Susanna; and many others. These women were helping to support them out of their own means While a large crowd was gathering and people were coming to Jesus from town after town, he told this parable: "A farmer went out to sow his seed. As he was scattering the seed, some fell along the path; it was trampled on, and the birds ate it up. Some fell on rocky ground, and when it came up, the plants withered because they had no moisture. Other seed fell among thorns, which grew up with it and choked the plants. Still other seed fell on good soil. It came up and yielded a crop, a hundred times more than was sown." When he said this, he called out, "Whoever has ears to hear, let them hear." His disciples asked him what this parable meant. He said, "The knowledge of the secrets of the kingdom of God has been given to you, but to others, I speak in parables, so that, 'though seeing, they may not see; though hearing, they may not understand.' "This is the meaning of the parable: The seed is the word of God. Those along the path are the ones who hear, and then the devil comes and takes away the word from their hearts so that they may not believe and be saved. Those on the rocky ground are the ones who receive the word with joy when they hear it, but they have no root. They believe for a while, but in the time of testing, they fall away. The seed that fell among thorns stands for those who hear, but as they go on their way, they are choked by life's worries, riches, and pleasures, and they do not mature. But the seed on good soil stands for those with a noble and good heart, who hear the word, retain it, and by persevering produce a crop "No one lights a lamp and hides it in a clay jar or puts it under a bed. Instead, they put it on a stand so that those who come in can see the light. For there is nothing hidden that will not be disclosed and nothing concealed that will not be known or brought out into the open. Therefore consider carefully how you listen. Whoever has will be given more; whoever does not have, even what they think they have will be taken from them." Now Jesus' mother and brothers came to see him, but they were not able to get near him because of the crowd. Someone told him, "Your mother and brothers are standing outside, wanting to see you." He replied, "My mother and brothers are those who hear God's word and put it into practice." One day Jesus said to his disciples, "Let's go over to the other side of the lake." So they got into a boat and set out. As they sailed, he fell asleep. A squall came down on the lake so that the boat was being swamped, and they were in great danger. The disciples went and woke him, saying, "Master, Master, we're going to drown!" He got up and rebuked the wind and the raging waters; the storm subsided, and all was calm. "Where is your faith?" he asked his disciples. In fear and amazement, they asked one another, "Who is this? He commands even the winds and the water, and they obey him." They sailed to the region of the Gerasenes, which is across the lake from Galilee. When Jesus stepped ashore, he was met by a demon-possessed man from the town. For a long time, this man had not worn clothes or lived in a house, but had lived in the tombs. When he saw Jesus, he cried out and fell at his feet, shouting at the top of his voice, "What do you want with me, Jesus, Son of the Most High God? I beg you, don't torture me!" For Jesus had commanded the impure spirit to come out of the man. Many times it had seized him, and though he was chained hand and foot and kept under guard, he had broken his chains and had been driven by the demon into solitary places Jesus asked him, "What is your name?" "Legion," he replied, because many demons had gone into him. And they begged Jesus repeatedly not to order them to go into the Abyss A large herd of pigs was feeding there on the hillside. The demons begged Jesus to let them go into the pigs, and he gave them permission. When the demons came out of the man, they went into the pigs, and the herd rushed down the steep bank into the lake and was drowned. When those tending the pigs saw what had happened, they ran off and reported this in the town and countryside, and the people went out to see what had happened. When they came to Jesus, they found the man from whom the demons had gone out, sitting at Jesus' feet, dressed and in his right mind; and they were afraid. Those who had seen it told the people how the demon-possessed man had been cured. Then all the people of the region of the Gerasenes asked Jesus to leave them because they were overcome with fear. So he got into the boat and left The man from whom the demons had gone out begged to go with him, but Jesus sent him away, saying, "Return home and tell how much God has done for you." So the man went away and told all over town how much Jesus had done for him Now when Jesus returned, a crowd welcomed him, for they were all expecting him. Then a man named Jairus, a synagogue leader, came and fell at Jesus' feet, pleading with him to come to his house because his only daughter, a girl of about twelve, was dying. As Jesus was on his way, the crowds almost crushed him. And a woman was there who had been subject to bleeding for twelve years, but no one could heal her. She came up behind him and touched the edge of his cloak, and immediately her bleeding stopped "Who touched me?" Jesus asked. When they all denied it, Peter said, "Master, the people are crowding and pressing against you." But Jesus said, "Someone touched me; I know that power has gone out from me." Then the woman, seeing that she could not go unnoticed, came trembling and fell at his feet. In the presence of all the people, she told why she had touched him and how she had been instantly healed. Then he said to her, "Daughter, your faith has healed you. Go in peace." While Jesus was still speaking, someone came from the house of Jairus, the synagogue leader. "Your daughter is dead," he said. "Don't bother the teacher anymore." Hearing this, Jesus said to Jairus, "Don't be afraid; just believe, and she will be healed." When he arrived at the house of Jairus, he did not let anyone go in with him except Peter, John, and James, and the child's father and mother. Meanwhile, all the people were wailing and mourning for her. "Stop wailing," Jesus said. "She is not dead but asleep." They laughed at him, knowing that she was dead. But he took her by the hand and said, "My child, get up!" Her spirit returned, and at once she stood up. Then Jesus told them to give her something to eat. Her parents were astonished, but he ordered them not to tell anyone what had happened

Chapter 9

When Jesus had called the Twelve together, he gave them power and authority to drive out all demons and to cure diseases, and he sent them out to proclaim the kingdom of God and to heal the sick. He told them, "Take nothing for the journey—no staff, no bag, no bread, no money, no extra shirt. Whatever house you enter, stay there until you leave that town. If people do not welcome you, leave their town and shake the dust off your feet as a testimony against them." So they set out and went from village to village, proclaiming the good news and healing people everywhere Now Herod the tetrarch heard about all that was going on. And he was perplexed because some were saying that John had been raised from the dead, others that Elijah had appeared, and still others that one of the prophets of long ago had come back to life. But Herod said, "I beheaded John. Who, then, is this I hear such things about?" And he tried to see him When the apostles returned, they reported to Jesus what they had done. Then he took them with him, and they withdrew by themselves to a town called Bethsaida, but the crowds learned about it and followed him. He welcomed them and spoke to them about the kingdom of God and healed those who needed

healing Late in the afternoon, the Twelve came to him and said, "Send the crowd away so they can go to the surrounding villages and countryside and find food and lodging because we are in a remote place here." He replied, "You give them something to eat." They answered, "We have only five loaves of bread and two fish—unless we go and buy food for all this crowd." (About five thousand men were there.) But he said to his disciples, "Have them sit down in groups of about fifty each." The disciples did so, and everyone sat down. Taking the five loaves and the two fish and looking up to heaven, he gave thanks and broke them. Then he gave them to the disciples to distribute to the people. They all ate and were satisfied, and the disciples picked up twelve basketfuls of broken pieces that were left over Once, when Jesus was praying in private and his disciples were with him, he asked them, "Who do the crowds say I am?" They replied, "Some say John the Baptist; others say Elijah; and still others, that one of the prophets of long ago has come back to life." "But what about you?" he asked. "Who do you say I am?" Peter answered, "God's Messiah." Jesus strictly warned them not to tell this to anyone. And he said, "The Son of Man must suffer many things and be rejected by the elders, the chief priests, and the teachers of the law, and he must be killed and on the third day be raised to life." Then he said to them all: "Whoever wants to be my disciple must deny themselves and take up their cross daily and follow me. For whoever wants to save their life will lose it, but whoever loses their life for me will save it. What good is it for someone to gain the whole world and yet lose or forfeit their very self? Whoever is ashamed of me and my words, the Son of Man will be ashamed of them when he comes in his glory and in the glory of the Father and of the holy angels. Truly I tell you, some who are standing here will not taste death before they see the kingdom of God." About eight days after Jesus said this, he took Peter, John, and James with him and went up onto a mountain to pray. As he was praying, the appearance of his face changed, and his clothes became as bright as a flash of lightning. Two men, Moses and Elijah, appeared in glorious splendor, talking with Jesus. They spoke about his departure, which he was about to bring to fulfillment at Jerusalem. Peter and his companions were very sleepy, but when they became fully awake, they saw his glory and the two men standing with him. As the men were leaving Jesus, Peter said to him, "Master, it is good for us to be here. Let us put up three shelters—one for you, one for Moses, and one for Elijah." (He did not know what he was saying.) While he was speaking, a cloud appeared and covered them, and they were afraid as they entered the cloud. A voice came from the cloud, saying, "This is my Son, whom I have chosen; listen to him." When the voice had spoken, they found that Jesus was alone. The disciples kept this to themselves and did not tell anyone at that time what they had seen The next day, when they came down from the mountain, a large crowd met him. A man in the crowd called out, "Teacher, I beg you to look at my son, for he is my only child. A spirit seizes him, and he suddenly screams; it throws him into convulsions so that he foams at the mouth. It scarcely ever leaves him and is destroying him. I begged your disciples to drive it out, but they could not." "You unbelieving and perverse generation," Jesus replied, "how long shall I stay with you and put up with you? Bring your son here." Even while the boy was coming, the demon threw him to the ground in a convulsion. But Jesus rebuked the impure spirit, healed the boy, and gave him back to his father. And they were all amazed at the greatness of God While everyone was marveling at all that

Jesus did, he said to his disciples, "Listen carefully to what I am about to tell you: The Son of Man is going to be delivered into the hands of men." But they did not understand what this meant. It was hidden from them so that they did not grasp it, and they were afraid to ask him about it An argument started among the disciples as to which of them would be the greatest. Jesus, knowing their thoughts, took a little child and had him stand beside him. Then he said to them, "Whoever welcomes this little child in my name welcomes me; and whoever welcomes me welcomes the one who sent me. For it is the one who is least among you all who is the greatest." "Master," said John, "we saw someone driving out demons in your name, and we tried to stop him because he is not one of us." "Do not stop him," Jesus said, "for whoever is not against you is for you." As the time approached for him to be taken up to heaven, Jesus resolutely set out for Jerusalem. And he sent messengers on ahead, who went into a Samaritan village to get things ready for him, but the people there did not welcome him because he was heading for Jerusalem. When the disciples James and John saw this, they asked, "Lord, do you want us to call fire down from heaven to destroy them?" But Jesus turned and rebuked them. Then he and his disciples went to another village As they were walking along the road, a man said to him, "I will follow you wherever you go." Jesus replied, "Foxes have dens and birds have nests, but the Son of Man has no place to lay his head." He said to another man, "Follow me." But he replied, "Lord, first let me go and bury my father." Jesus said to him, "Let the dead bury their own dead, but you go and proclaim the kingdom of God." Still another said, "I will follow you, Lord, but first let me go back and say goodbye to my family." Jesus replied, "No one who puts a hand to the plow and looks back is fit for service in the kingdom of God."

Chapter 10

After this, the Lord appointed seventy-two others and sent them two by two ahead of him to every town and place where he was about to go. He told them, "The harvest is plentiful, but the workers are few. Ask the Lord of the harvest, therefore, to send out workers into his harvest field. Go! I am sending you out like lambs among wolves. Do not take a purse or bag or sandals, and do not greet anyone on the road "When you enter a house, first say, 'Peace to this house.' If someone who promotes peace is there, your peace will rest on them; if not, it will return to you. Stay there, eating and drinking whatever they give you, for the worker deserves his wages. Do not move around from house to house "When you enter a town and are welcomed, eat what is offered to you. Heal the sick who are there and tell them, 'The kingdom of God has come near to you.' But when you enter a town and are not welcomed, go into its streets and say, 'Even the dust of your town we wipe from our feet as a warning to you. Yet be sure of this: The kingdom of God has come near.' I tell you, it will be more bearable on that day for Sodom than for that town "Woe to you, Chorazin! Woe to you, Bethsaida! For if the miracles that were performed in you had been performed in Tyre and Sidon, they would have repented long ago, sitting in sackcloth and ashes. But it will be more bearable for Tyre and Sidon at the judgment than for you. And you, Capernaum, will you be lifted to the heavens? No, you will go down to Hades "Whoever listens to you listens to me; whoever rejects you rejects me; but whoever rejects me rejects him who sent me." The seventy-two returned with joy and said, "Lord, even the demons submit to us in your name." He replied, "I saw Satan fall like lightning from heaven. I have given you

authority to trample on snakes and scorpions and to overcome all the power of the enemy; nothing will harm you. However, do not rejoice that the spirits submit to you, but rejoice that your names are written in heaven." At that time, Jesus, full of joy through the Holy Spirit, said, "I praise you, Father, Lord of heaven and earth, because you have hidden these things from the wise and learned and revealed them to little children. Yes, Father, for this is what you were pleased to do "All things have been committed to me by my Father. No one knows who the Son is except the Father, and no one knows who the Father is except the Son and those to whom the Son chooses to reveal him." Then he turned to his disciples and said privately, "Blessed are the eyes that see what you see. For I tell you that many prophets and kings wanted to see what you see but did not see it, and to hear what you hear but did not hear it." On one occasion, an expert in the law stood up to test Jesus. "Teacher," he asked, "what must I do to inherit eternal life?" "What is written in the Law?" he replied. "How do you read it?" He answered, "'Love the Lord your God with all your heart and with all your soul and with all your strength and with all your mind' and 'Love your neighbor as yourself.'" "You have answered correctly," Jesus replied. "Do this and you will live." But he wanted to justify himself, so he asked Jesus, "And who is my neighbor?" In reply, Jesus said: "A man was going down from Jerusalem to Jericho when he was attacked by robbers. They stripped him of his clothes, beat him, and went away, leaving him half dead. A priest happened to be going down the same road, and when he saw the man, he passed by on the other side. So too, a Levite, when he came to the place and saw him, passed by on the other side. But a Samaritan, as he traveled, came where the man was, and when he saw him, he took pity on him. He went to him and bandaged his wounds, pouring on oil and wine. Then he put the man on his own donkey, brought him to an inn, and took care of him. The next day he took out two denarii and gave them to the innkeeper. 'Look after him,' he said, 'and when I return, I will reimburse you for any extra expense you may have.' "Which of these three do you think was a neighbor to the man who fell into the hands of robbers?" The expert in the law replied, "The one who had mercy on him." Jesus told him, "Go and do likewise." As Jesus and his disciples were on their way, he came to a village where a woman named Martha opened her home to him. She had a sister called Mary, who sat at the Lord's feet listening to what he said. But Martha was distracted by all the preparations that had to be made. She came to him and asked, "Lord, don't you care that my sister has left me to do the work by myself? Tell her to help me!" "Martha, Martha," the Lord answered, "you are worried and upset about many things, but few things are needed—or indeed only one. Mary has chosen what is better, and it will not be taken away from her."

Chapter 11

One day, while Jesus was praying in a certain place, one of his disciples approached him after he had finished and said, "Lord, teach us to pray, just as John taught his disciples." Jesus replied, "When you pray, say: Our Father, who art in heaven, Hallowed be thy name. Thy kingdom come, Thy will be done, On earth as it is in heaven. Give us this day our daily bread. And forgive us our sins, For we also forgive everyone who is indebted to us. And lead us not into temptation, But deliver us from evil." Then Jesus continued, "Suppose one of you has a friend, and you go to him at midnight and say, 'Friend, lend me three loaves of bread, because a friend of mine has come to me on a journey, and I have nothing to offer him.' And suppose the one inside answers, 'Don't bother me. The door is already locked, and my children and I are in bed. I can't get up and give you anything.' I tell you, even though he will not get up and give you the bread because of friendship, yet because of your persistence, he will surely get up and give you as much as you need So I say to you: Ask, and it will be given to you; seek, and you will find; knock, and the door will be opened to you. For everyone who asks receives; the one who seeks finds; and to the one who knocks, the door will be opened. Which of you fathers, if your son asks for a fish, will give him a snake instead? Or if he asks for an egg, will give him a scorpion? If you then, though you are evil, know how to give good gifts to your children, how much more will your Father in heaven give the Holy Spirit to those who ask him!" Jesus was driving out a demon that was mute. When the demon left, the man who had been mute spoke, and the crowd was amazed. But some of them said, "By Beelzebul, the prince of demons, he is driving out demons." Others tested him by asking for a sign from heaven. Jesus knew their thoughts and said to them, "Any kingdom divided against itself will be ruined, and a house divided against itself will fall. If Satan is divided against himself, how can his kingdom stand? I say this because you claim that I drive out demons by Beelzebul. Now if I drive out demons by Beelzebul, by whom do your followers drive them out? So then, they will be your judges. But if I drive out demons by the finger of God, then the kingdom of God has come upon you When a strong man, fully armed, guards his own house, his possessions are safe. But when someone stronger attacks and overpowers him, he takes away the armor in which the man trusted and divides up his plunder. Whoever is not with me is against me, and whoever does not gather with me scatters When an impure spirit comes out of a person, it goes through arid places seeking rest and does not find it. Then it says, 'I will return to the house I left.' When it arrives, it finds the house swept clean and put in order. Then it goes and takes seven other spirits more wicked than itself, and they go in and live there. And the final condition of that person is worse than the first." As Jesus was saying these things, a woman in the crowd called out, "Blessed is the mother who gave you birth and nursed you." He replied, "Blessed rather are those who hear the word of God and obey it." As the crowds increased, Jesus said, "This is a wicked generation. It asks for a sign, but none will be given it except the sign of Jonah. For as Jonah was a sign to the Ninevites, so also will the Son of Man be to this generation. The Queen of the South will rise at the judgment with the people of this generation and condemn them, for she came from the ends of the earth to listen to Solomon's wisdom, and now something greater than Solomon is here. The men of Nineveh will stand up at the judgment with this generation and condemn it, for they repented at the preaching of Jonah, and now something greater than Jonah is here No one lights a lamp and puts it in a place where it will be hidden or under a bowl. Instead, they put it on its stand, so that those who come in may see the light. Your eye is the lamp of your body. When your eyes are healthy, your whole body also is full of light. But when they are unhealthy, your body also is full of darkness. See to it, then, that the light within you is not darkness. Therefore, if your whole body is full of light, and no part of it dark, it will be just as full of light as when a lamp shines its light on you." When Jesus had finished speaking, a Pharisee invited him to eat with him; so he went in and reclined at the table. But the Pharisee was surprised when he noticed that Jesus did not first wash before the meal. Then the Lord said to him, "Now then, you Pharisees clean the outside of the cup and dish, but inside you are full of greed and wickedness. You foolish people! Did not the one who made the outside make the inside also? But now as for what is inside you—be generous to the poor, and everything will be clean for you Woe to you Pharisees because you give God a tenth of your mint, rue, and all other kinds of garden herbs, but you neglect justice and the love of God. You should have practiced the latter without leaving the former undone Woe to you Pharisees because you love the most important seats in the synagogues and respectful greetings in the marketplaces Woe to you because you are like unmarked graves, which people walk over without knowing it." One of the experts in the law answered him, "Teacher, when you say these things, you insult us also." Jesus replied, "And you experts in the law, woe to you because you load people down with burdens they can hardly carry, and you yourselves will not lift one finger to help them Woe to you because you build tombs for the prophets, and it was your ancestors who killed them. So you testify that you approve of what your ancestors did; they killed the prophets, and you build their tombs. Because of this, God in his wisdom said, 'I will send them prophets and apostles, some of whom they will kill and others they will persecute.' Therefore, this generation will be held responsible for the blood of all the prophets that has been shed since the beginning of the world, from the blood of Abel to the blood of Zechariah, who was killed between the altar and the sanctuary. Yes, I tell you, this generation will be held responsible for it all Woe to you experts in the law because you have taken away the key to knowledge. You yourselves have not entered, and you have hindered those who were entering." When Jesus went outside, the Pharisees and the teachers of the law began to oppose him fiercely and to besiege him with questions, waiting to catch him in something he might say

Chapter 12

Meanwhile, when a crowd of many thousands had gathered, so that they were trampling on one another, Jesus began to speak first to his disciples, saying: "Be on your guard against the yeast of the Pharisees, which is hypocrisy. There is nothing concealed that will not be disclosed or hidden that will not be made known. What you have said in the dark will be heard in the daylight, and what you have whispered in the ear in the inner rooms will be proclaimed from the roofs I tell you, my friends, do not be afraid of those who kill the body and after that can do no more. But I will show you whom you should fear: Fear him who, after your body has been killed, has authority to throw you into hell. Yes, I tell you, fear him. Are not five sparrows sold for two pennies? Yet not one of them is forgotten by God. Indeed, the very hairs of your head are all numbered. Don't be afraid; you are worth more than many sparrows I tell you, whoever publicly acknowledges me before others, the Son of Man will also acknowledge before the angels of God. But whoever disowns me before others will be disowned before the angels of God. And everyone who speaks a word against the Son of Man will be forgiven, but anyone who blasphemes against the Holy Spirit will not be forgiven When you are brought before synagogues, rulers, and authorities, do not worry about how you will defend yourselves or what you will say, for the Holy Spirit will teach you at that time what you should say." Someone in the crowd said to him, "Teacher, tell my brother to divide the inheritance with me." Jesus replied, "Man, who appointed me a judge or an arbiter between you?" Then he said to them, "Watch out! Be on your guard against all kinds of greed; life does not consist in an abundance of possessions."

And he told them this parable: "The ground of a certain rich man yielded an abundant harvest. He thought to himself, 'What shall I do? I have no place to store my crops.' Then he said, 'This is what I'll do. I will tear down my barns and build bigger ones, and there I will store my surplus grain. And I'll say to myself, 'You have plenty of grain laid up for many years. Take life easy; eat, drink, and be merry.' But God said to him, 'You fool! This very night your life will be demanded from you. Then who will get what you have prepared for yourself?' This is how it will be with whoever stores up things for themselves but is not rich toward God." Then Jesus said to his disciples: "Therefore I tell you, do not worry about your life, what you will eat, or about your body, what you will wear. For life is more than food, and the body more than clothes. Consider the ravens: They do not sow or reap, they have no storeroom or barn, yet God feeds them. And how much more valuable you are than birds! Who of you by worrying can add a single hour to your life? Since you cannot do this very little thing, why do you worry about the rest? Consider how the wildflowers grow. They do not labor or spin. Yet I tell you, not even Solomon in all his splendor was dressed like one of these. If that is how God clothes the grass of the field, which is here today and tomorrow is thrown into the fire, how much more will he clothe you—you of little faith! And do not set your heart on what you will eat or drink; do not worry about it. For the pagan world runs after all such things, and your Father knows that you need them. But seek his kingdom, and these things will be given to you as well Do not be afraid, little flock, for your Father has been pleased to give you the kingdom. Sell your possessions and give to the poor. Provide purses for yourselves that will not wear out, a treasure in heaven that will never fail, where no thief comes near and no moth destroys. For where your treasure is, there your heart will be also Be dressed ready for service and keep your lamps burning, like servants waiting for their master to return from a wedding banquet so that when he comes and knocks, they can immediately open the door for him. It will be good for those servants whose master finds them watching when he comes. Truly I tell you, he will dress himself to serve, will have them recline at the table, and will come and wait on them. It will be good for those servants whose master finds them ready, even if he comes in the middle of the night or toward daybreak. But understand this: If the owner of the house had known at what hour the thief was coming, he would not have let his house be broken into. You also must be ready because the Son of Man will come at an hour when you do not expect him." Peter asked, "Lord, are you telling this parable to us, or to everyone?" The Lord answered, "Who then is the faithful and wise manager, whom the master puts in charge of his servants to give them their food allowance at the proper time? It will be good for that servant whom the master finds doing so when he returns. Truly I tell you, he will put him in charge of all his possessions. But suppose the servant says to himself, 'My master is taking a long time in coming,' and he then begins to beat the other servants, both men and women, and to eat and drink and get drunk. The master of that servant will come on a day when he does not expect him and at an hour he is not aware of. He will cut him to pieces and assign him a place with the unbelievers The servant who knows the master's will and does not get ready or does not do what the master wants will be beaten with many blows. But the one who does not know and does things deserving punishment will be beaten with few blows. From everyone who has been given much, much will be demanded, and from the one who has been entrusted with much, much more will be asked I have come to bring fire on the earth, and how I wish it were already kindled! But I have a baptism to undergo, and what constraint I am under until it is completed! Do you think I came to bring peace on earth? No, I tell you, but division. From now on, there will be five in one family divided against each other, three against two and two against three. They will be divided, father against son and son against father, mother against daughter and daughter against mother, mother-in-law against daughter-in-law and daughter-in-law against mother-in-law." He said to the crowd, "When you see a cloud rising in the west, immediately you say, 'It's going to rain,' and it does. And when the south wind blows, you say, 'It's going to be hot,' and it is. Hypocrites! You know how to interpret the appearance of the earth and the sky. How is it that you don't know how to interpret this present time? Why don't you judge for yourselves what is right? As you are going with your adversary to the magistrate, try hard to be reconciled on the way, or your adversary may drag you off to the judge, and the judge turn you over to the officer, and the officer throw you into prison. I tell you, you will not get out until you have paid the last penny."

Chapter 13

Now there were some present at that time who told Jesus about the Galileans whose blood Pilate had mixed with their sacrifices. Jesus answered, "Do you think that these Galileans were worse sinners than all the other Galileans because they suffered this way? I tell you, no! But unless you repent, you too will all perish. Or those eighteen who died when the tower in Siloam fell on them—do you think they were more guilty than all the others living in Jerusalem? I tell you, no! But unless you repent, you too will all perish." Then he told this parable: "A man had a fig tree growing in his vineyard, and he went to look for fruit on it but did not find any. So he said to the man who took care of the vineyard, 'For three years now I've been coming to look for fruit on this fig tree and haven't found any. Cut it down! Why should it use up the soil?' 'Sir,' the man replied, 'leave it alone for one more year, and I'll dig around it and fertilize it. If it bears fruit next year, fine! If not, then cut it down.'" On a Sabbath Jesus was teaching in one of the synagogues, and a woman was there who had been crippled by a spirit for eighteen years. She was bent over and could not straighten up at all. When Jesus saw her, he called her forward and said to her, "Woman, you are set free from your infirmity." Then he put his hands on her, and immediately she straightened up and praised God Indignant because Jesus had healed on the Sabbath, the synagogue leader said to the people, "There are six days for work. So come and be healed on those days, not on the Sabbath." The Lord answered him, "You hypocrites! Doesn't each of you on the Sabbath untie your ox or donkey from the stall and lead it out to give it water? Then should not this woman, a daughter of Abraham, whom Satan has kept bound for eighteen long years, be set free on the Sabbath day from what bound her?" When he said this, all his opponents were humiliated, but the people were delighted with all the wonderful things he was doing Then Jesus asked, "What is the kingdom of God like? What shall I compare it to? It is like a mustard seed, which a man took and planted in his garden. It grew and became a tree, and the birds perched in its branches." Again he asked, "What shall I compare the kingdom of God to? It is like yeast that a woman took and mixed into about sixty pounds of flour until it worked all through the dough." Then Jesus went through the towns and villages, teaching as he made his way to Jerusalem. Someone asked him, "Lord, are only a few people going to be saved?" He said to them, "Make every effort to enter through the narrow door because many, I tell you, will try to enter and will not be able to. Once the owner of the house gets up and closes the door, you will stand outside knocking and pleading, 'Sir, open the door for us.' But he will answer, 'I don't know you or where you come from.' Then you will say, 'We ate and drank with you, and you taught in our streets.' But he will reply, 'I don't know you or where you come from. Away from me, all you evildoers!' There will be weeping there, and gnashing of teeth, when you see Abraham, Isaac, and Jacob and all the prophets in the kingdom of God, but you yourselves thrown out. People will come from east and west and north and south and will take their places at the feast in the kingdom of God. Indeed there are those who are last who will be first, and first who will be last." At that time, some Pharisees came to Jesus and said to him, "Leave this place and go somewhere else. Herod wants to kill you." He replied, "Go tell that fox, 'I will keep on driving out demons and healing people today and tomorrow, and on the third day I will reach my goal.' In any case, I must press on today and tomorrow and the next day—for surely no prophet can die outside Jerusalem! Jerusalem, Jerusalem, you who kill the prophets and stone those sent to you, how often I have longed to gather your children together, as a hen gathers her chicks under her wings, and you were not willing. Look, your house is left to you desolate. I tell you, you will not see me again until you say, 'Blessed is he who comes in the name of the Lord.'"

Chapter 14

One Sabbath, when Jesus went to eat in the house of a prominent Pharisee, he was being carefully watched. There in front of him was a man suffering from abnormal swelling of his body. Jesus asked the Pharisees and experts in the law, "Is it lawful to heal on the Sabbath or not?" But they remained silent. So taking hold of the man, he healed him and sent him on his way Then he asked them, "If one of you has a child or an ox that falls into a well on the Sabbath day, will you not immediately pull it out?" And they had nothing to say When he noticed how the guests picked the places of honor at the table, he told them this parable: "When someone invites you to a wedding feast, do not take the place of honor, for a person more distinguished than you may have been invited. If so, the host who invited both of you will come and say to you, 'Give this person your seat.' Then, humiliated, you will have to take the least important place. But when you are invited, take the lowest place, so that when your host comes, he will say to you, 'Friend, move up to a better place.' Then you will be honored in the presence of all the other guests. For all those who exalt themselves will be humbled, and those who humble themselves will be exalted." Then Jesus said to his host, "When you give a luncheon or dinner, do not invite your friends, your brothers or sisters, your relatives, or your rich neighbors; if you do, they may invite you back and so you will be repaid. But when you give a banquet, invite the poor, the crippled, the lame, the blind, and you will be blessed. Although they cannot repay you, you will be repaid at the resurrection of the righteous." When one of those at the table with him heard this, he said to Jesus, "Blessed is the one who will eat at the feast in the kingdom of God." Jesus replied: "A certain man was preparing a great banquet and invited many guests. At the time of the banquet, he sent his servant to tell those who had been invited, 'Come, for everything is now ready.' But they all alike began to make excuses. The first said, 'I have just bought a field, and I must go and see it.

Please excuse me.' Another said, 'I have just bought five yoke of oxen, and I'm on my way to try them out. Please excuse me.' Still another said, 'I just got married, so I can't come.' The servant came back and reported this to his master. Then the owner of the house became angry and ordered his servant, 'Go out quickly into the streets and alleys of the town and bring in the poor, the crippled, the blind, and the lame.''Sir,' the servant said, 'what you ordered has been done, but there is still room.' Then the master told his servant, 'Go out to the roads and country lanes and compel them to come in, so that my house will be full. I tell you, not one of those who were invited will get a taste of my banquet.'" Large crowds were traveling with Jesus, and turning to them he said: "If anyone comes to me and does not hate father and mother, wife and children, brothers and sisters—yes, even their own life—such a person cannot be my disciple. And whoever does not carry their cross and follow me cannot be my disciple Suppose one of you wants to build a tower. Won't you first sit down and estimate the cost to see if you have enough money to complete it? For if you lay the foundation and are not able to finish it, everyone who sees it will ridicule you, saying, 'This person began to build and wasn't able to finish.' Or suppose a king is about to go to war against another king. Won't he first sit down and consider whether he is able with ten thousand men to oppose the one coming against him with twenty thousand? If he is not able, he will send a delegation while the other is still a long way off and will ask for terms of peace. In the same way, those of you who do not give up everything you have cannot be my disciples Salt is good, but if it loses its saltiness, how can it be made salty again? It is fit neither for the soil nor for the manure pile; it is thrown out. Whoever has ears to hear, let them hear."

Chapter 15

Now the tax collectors and sinners were all gathering around to hear Jesus. But the Pharisees and the teachers of the law muttered, "This man welcomes sinners and eats with them." Then Jesus told them this parable: "Suppose one of you has a hundred sheep and loses one of them. Doesn't he leave the ninety-nine in the open country and go after the lost sheep until he finds it? And when he finds it, he joyfully puts it on his shoulders and goes home. Then he calls his friends and neighbors together and says, 'Rejoice with me; I have found my lost sheep.' I tell you that in the same way, there will be more rejoicing in heaven over one sinner who repents than over ninety-nine righteous persons who do not need to repent Or suppose a woman has ten silver coins and loses one. Doesn't she light a lamp, sweep the house, and search carefully until she finds it? And when she finds it, she calls her friends and neighbors together and says, 'Rejoice with me; I have found my lost coin.' In the same way, I tell you, there is rejoicing in the presence of the angels of God over one sinner who repents." Jesus continued: "There was a man who had two sons. The younger one said to his father, 'Father, give me my share of the estate.' So he divided his property between them Not long after that, the younger son got together all he had, set off for a distant country, and there squandered his wealth in wild living. After he had spent everything, there was a severe famine in that whole country, and he began to be in need. So he went and hired himself out to a citizen of that country, who sent him to his fields to feed pigs. He longed to fill his stomach with the pods that the pigs were eating, but no one gave him anything When he came to his senses, he said, 'How many of my father's hired servants have food to spare, and here I am starving to death! I will set out and go back to my father and say to him: Father, I have sinned against heaven and against you. I am no longer worthy to be called your son; make me like one of your hired servants.' So he got up and went to his father But while he was still a long way off, his father saw him and was filled with compassion for him; he ran to his son, threw his arms around him, and kissed him The son said to him, 'Father, I have sinned against heaven and against you. I am no longer worthy to be called your son.' But the father said to his servants, 'Quick! Bring the best robe and put it on him. Put a ring on his finger and sandals on his feet. Bring the fattened calf and kill it. Let's have a feast and celebrate. For this son of mine was dead and is alive again; he was lost and is found.' So they began to celebrate Meanwhile, the older son was in the field. When he came near the house, he heard music and dancing. So he called one of the servants and asked him what was going on. 'Your brother has come,' he replied, 'and your father has killed the fattened calf because he has him back safe and sound.' The older brother became angry and refused to go in. So his father went out and pleaded with him. But he answered his father, 'Look! All these years I've been slaving for you and never disobeyed your orders. Yet you never gave me even a young goat so I could celebrate with my friends. But when this son of yours who has squandered your property with prostitutes comes home, you kill the fattened calf for him!' 'My son,' the father said, 'you are always with me, and everything I have is yours. But we had to celebrate and be glad because this brother of yours was dead and is alive again; he was lost and is found.'"

Chapter 16

1 Jesus also said to his disciples, "There was a certain rich man who had a steward, and he was accused of wasting his goods. 2 So he called him and said, 'What is this I hear about you? Give an account of your stewardship, for you can no longer be steward.' 3 Then the steward said within himself, 'What shall I do? My master is taking away my stewardship. I cannot dig, and I am ashamed to beg. 4 I know what I will do, so that when I am put out of the stewardship, they may receive me into their houses.' 5 So he called each of his master's debtors and said to the first, 'How much do you owe my master?' 6 And he said, 'A hundred measures of oil.' So he said to him, 'Take your bill, sit down quickly, and write fifty.' 7 Then he said to another, 'And how much do you owe?' So he said, 'A hundred measures of wheat.' And he said to him, 'Take your bill and write eighty.' 8 The master commended the unjust steward because he had acted shrewdly. For the sons of this world are more shrewd in their generation than the sons of light. 9 And I say to you, make friends for yourselves by unrighteous mammon, that when you fail, they may receive you into everlasting homes. 10 He who is faithful in what is least is faithful also in much; and he who is unjust in what is least is unjust also in much. 11 Therefore, if you have not been faithful in the unrighteous mammon, who will commit to your trust the true riches? 12 And if you have not been faithful in what is another man's, who will give you what is your own? 13 No servant can serve two masters; for either he will hate the one and love the other, or else he will be loyal to the one and despise the other. You cannot serve God and mammon." 14 Now the Pharisees, who were lovers of money, also heard all these things, and they derided him. 15 And he said to them, "You are those who justify yourselves before men, but God knows your hearts. For what is highly esteemed among men is an abomination in the sight of God. 16 The law and the prophets were until John. Since that time, the kingdom of God has been preached, and everyone is pressing into it. 17 And it is easier for heaven and earth to pass away than for one tittle of the law to fail 18 "Whoever divorces his wife and marries another commits adultery; and whoever marries her who is divorced from her husband commits adultery. 19 There was a certain rich man who was clothed in purple and fine linen and fared sumptuously every day. 20 But there was a certain beggar named Lazarus, full of sores, who was laid at his gate, 21 desiring to be fed with the crumbs which fell from the rich man's table. Moreover, the dogs came and licked his sores. 22 So it was that the beggar died and was carried by the angels to Abraham's bosom. The rich man also died and was buried. 23 And being in torments in Hades, he lifted up his eyes and saw Abraham afar off and Lazarus in his bosom 24 "Then he cried and said, 'Father Abraham, have mercy on me, and send Lazarus that he may dip the tip of his finger in water and cool my tongue, for I am tormented in this flame.' 25 But Abraham said, 'Son, remember that in your lifetime you received your good things, and likewise Lazarus evil things; but now he is comforted and you are tormented. 26 And besides all this, between us and you there is a great gulf fixed, so that those who want to pass from here to you cannot, nor can those from there pass to us.' 27 "Then he said, 'I beg you therefore, father, that you would send him to my father's house, 28 for I have five brothers, that he may testify to them, lest they also come to this place of torment.' 29 Abraham said to him, 'They have Moses and the prophets; let them hear them.' 30 And he said, 'No, father Abraham; but if one goes to them from the dead, they will repent.' 31 But he said to him, 'If they do not hear Moses and the prophets, neither will they be persuaded though one rise from the dead.'"

Chapter 17

1 Then he said to the disciples, "It is impossible that no offenses should come, but woe to him through whom they do come! 2 It would be better for him if a millstone were hung around his neck and he were thrown into the sea than that he should offend one of these little ones. 3 Take heed to yourselves. If your brother sins against you, rebuke him; and if he repents, forgive him. 4 And if he sins against you seven times in a day, and seven times in a day returns to you, saying, 'I repent,' you shall forgive him." 5 And the apostles said to the Lord, "Increase our faith." 6 So the Lord said, "If you have faith as a mustard seed, you can say to this mulberry tree, 'Be pulled up by the roots and be planted in the sea,' and it would obey you. 7 And which of you, having a servant plowing or tending sheep, will say to him when he has come in from the field, 'Come at once and sit down to eat'? 8 But will he not rather say to him, 'Prepare something for my supper, and gird yourself and serve me till I have eaten and drunk, and afterward you will eat and drink'? 9 Does he thank that servant because he did the things that were commanded him? I think not. 10 So likewise you, when you have done all those things which you are commanded, say, 'We are unprofitable servants. We have done what was our duty to do.'" 11 Now it happened as he went to Jerusalem that he passed through the midst of Samaria and Galilee. 12 Then as he entered a certain village, there met him ten men who were lepers, who stood afar off. 13 And they lifted up their voices and said, "Jesus, Master, have mercy on us!" 14 So when he saw them, he said to them, "Go, show yourselves to the priests." And so it was that as they went, they were cleansed. 15 And one of them, when he saw that he was healed, returned, and with a loud voice glorified God, 16 and fell down on his face at his feet, giving him thanks. And he was a Samaritan. 17 So Jesus answered and said, "Were there not ten cleansed? But where are

the nine? 18 Were there not any found who returned to give glory to God except this foreigner?" 19 And he said to him, "Arise, go your way. Your faith has made you well." 20 Now when he was asked by the Pharisees when the kingdom of God would come, he answered them and said, "The kingdom of God does not come with observation; 21 nor will they say, 'See here!' or 'See there!' For indeed, the kingdom of God is within you."22 Then he said to the disciples, "The days will come when you will desire to see one of the days of the Son of Man, and you will not see it. 23 And they will say to you, 'Look here!' or 'Look there!' Do not go after them or follow them. 24 For as the lightning that flashes out of one part under heaven shines to the other part under heaven, so also the Son of Man will be in his day. 25 But first he must suffer many things and be rejected by this generation. 26 And as it was in the days of Noah, so it will be also in the days of the Son of Man: 27 They ate, they drank, they married wives, they were given in marriage, until the day that Noah entered the ark, and the flood came and destroyed them all. 28 Likewise as it was also in the days of Lot: They ate, they drank, they bought, they sold, they planted, they built; 29 but on the day that Lot went out of Sodom it rained fire and brimstone from heaven and destroyed them all. 30 Even so will it be in the day when the Son of Man is revealed 31 "In that day, he who is on the housetop, and his goods are in the house, let him not come down to take them away. And likewise, the one who is in the field, let him not turn back. 32 Remember Lot's wife. 33 Whoever seeks to save his life will lose it, and whoever loses his life will preserve it. 34 I tell you, in that night there will be two in one bed: the one will be taken and the other will be left. 35 Two women will be grinding together: the one will be taken and the other left. 36 Two men will be in the field: the one will be taken and the other left." 37 And they answered and said to him, "Where, Lord?" So he said to them, "Wherever the body is, there the eagles will be gathered together."

Chapter 18

1 Then he spoke a parable to them, that men always ought to pray and not lose heart, 2 saying: "There was in a certain city a judge who did not fear God nor regard man. 3 Now there was a widow in that city; and she came to him, saying, 'Get justice for me from my adversary.' 4 And he would not for a while; but afterward he said within himself, 'Though I do not fear God nor regard man, 5 yet because this widow troubles me I will avenge her, lest by her continual coming she weary me.'" 6 Then the Lord said, "Hear what the unjust judge said. 7 And shall God not avenge his own elect who cry out day and night to him, though he bears long with them? 8 I tell you that he will avenge them speedily. Nevertheless, when the Son of Man comes, will he really find faith on the earth?" 9 Also he spoke this parable to some who trusted in themselves that they were righteous, and despised others: 10 "Two men went up to the temple to pray, one a Pharisee and the other a tax collector. 11 The Pharisee stood and prayed thus with himself, 'God, I thank you that I am not like other men— extortioners, unjust, adulterers, or even as this tax collector. 12 I fast twice a week; I give tithes of all that I possess.' 13 And the tax collector, standing afar off, would not so much as raise his eyes to heaven, but beat his breast, saying, 'God, be merciful to me a sinner!' 14 I tell you, this man went down to his house justified rather than the other; for everyone who exalts himself will be humbled, and he who humbles himself will be exalted." 15 Then they also brought infants to him that he might touch them; but when the disciples saw it, they rebuked them. 16 But Jesus called them to him and said, "Let the little children

come to me, and do not forbid them; for of such is the kingdom of God. 17 Assuredly, I say to you, whoever does not receive the kingdom of God as a little child will by no means enter it." 18 Now a certain ruler asked him, saying, "Good Teacher, what shall I do to inherit eternal life?" 19 So Jesus said to him, "Why do you call me good? No one is good but One, that is, God. 20 You know the commandments: 'Do not commit adultery,' 'Do not murder,' 'Do not steal,' 'Do not bear false witness,' 'Honor your father and your mother.'" 21 And he said, "All these things I have kept from my youth." 22 So when Jesus heard these things, he said to him, "You still lack one thing. Sell all that you have and distribute to the poor, and you will have treasure in heaven; and come, follow me." 23 But when he heard this, he became very sorrowful, for he was very rich. 24 And when Jesus saw that he became very sorrowful, he said, "How hard it is for those who have riches to enter the kingdom of God! 25 For it is easier for a camel to go through the eye of a needle than for a rich man to enter the kingdom of God." 26 And those who heard it said, "Who then can be saved?" 27 But he said, "The things which are impossible with men are possible with God." 28 Then Peter said, "See, we have left all and followed you." 29 So he said to them, "Assuredly, I say to you, there is no one who has left house or parents or brothers or wife or children, for the sake of the kingdom of God, 30 who shall not receive many times more in this present time, and in the age to come eternal life." 31 Then he took the twelve aside and said to them, "Behold, we are going up to Jerusalem, and all things that are written by the prophets concerning the Son of Man will be accomplished. 32 For he will be delivered to the Gentiles and will be mocked and insulted and spit upon. 33 They will scourge him and kill him. And the third day he will rise again." 34 But they understood none of these things; this saying was hidden from them, and they did not know the things which were spoken 35 Then it happened, as he was coming near Jericho, that a certain blind man sat by the road begging. 36 And hearing a multitude passing by, he asked what it meant. 37 So they told him that Jesus of Nazareth was passing by. 38 And he cried out, saying, "Jesus, Son of David, have mercy on me!" 39 Then those who went before warned him that he should be quiet; but he cried out all the more, "Son of David, have mercy on me!" 40 So Jesus stood still and commanded him to be brought to him. And when he had come near, he asked him, 41 saying, "What do you want me to do for you?" He said, "Lord, that I may receive my sight." 42 Then Jesus said to him, "Receive your sight; your faith has made you well." 43 And immediately he received his sight and followed him, glorifying God. And all the people, when they saw it, gave praise to God

Chapter 19

1 Then Jesus entered and passed through Jericho. 2 Now behold, there was a man named Zacchaeus who was a chief tax collector, and he was rich. 3 And he sought to see who Jesus was, but could not because of the crowd, for he was of short stature. 4 So he ran ahead and climbed up into a sycamore tree to see him, for he was going to pass that way. 5 And when Jesus came to the place, he looked up and saw him, and said to him, "Zacchaeus, make haste and come down, for today I must stay at your house." 6 So he made haste and came down, and received him joyfully. 7 But when they saw it, they all complained, saying, "He has gone to be a guest with a man who is a sinner." 8 Then Zacchaeus stood and said to the Lord, "Look, Lord, I give half of my goods to the poor; and if I have taken anything from anyone by false accusation, I restore fourfold." 9 And Jesus said to

him, "Today salvation has come to this house, because he also is a son of Abraham; 10 for the Son of Man has come to seek and to save that which was lost." 11 Now as they heard these things, he spoke another parable, because he was near Jerusalem and because they thought the kingdom of God would appear immediately. 12 Therefore he said: "A certain nobleman went into a far country to receive for himself a kingdom and to return. 13 So he called ten of his servants, delivered to them ten minas, and said to them, 'Do business till I come.' 14 But his citizens hated him, and sent a delegation after him, saying, 'We will not have this man to reign over us.' 15 "And so it was that when he returned, having received the kingdom, he then commanded these servants, to whom he had given the money, to be called to him, that he might know how much every man had gained by trading. 16 Then came the first, saying, 'Master, your mina has earned ten minas.' 17 And he said to him, 'Well done, good servant; because you were faithful in a very little, have authority over ten cities.' 18 And the second came, saying, 'Master, your mina has earned five minas.' 19 Likewise he said to him, 'You also be over five cities.' 20 "Then another came, saying, 'Master, here is your mina, which I have kept put away in a handkerchief. 21 For I feared you, because you are an austere man. You collect what you did not deposit, and reap what you did not sow.' 22 And he said to him, 'Out of your own mouth I will judge you, you wicked servant. You knew that I was an austere man, collecting what I did not deposit and reaping what I did not sow. 23 Why then did you not put my money in the bank, that at my coming I might have collected it with interest?' 24 "And he said to those who stood by, 'Take the mina from him, and give it to him who has ten minas.' 25 (But they said to him, 'Master, he has ten minas.') 26 'For I say to you, that to everyone who has will be given; and from him who does not have, even what he has will be taken away from him. 27 But bring here those enemies of mine, who did not want me to reign over them, and slay them before me.'" 28 When he had said this, he went on ahead, going up to Jerusalem. 29 And it came to pass, when he drew near to Bethphage and Bethany, at the mountain called Olivet, that he sent two of his disciples, 30 saying, "Go into the village opposite you, where as you enter you will find a colt tied, on which no one has ever sat. Loose it and bring it here. 31 And if anyone asks you, 'Why are you loosing it?' thus you shall say to him, 'Because the Lord has need of it.'" 32 So those who were sent went their way and found it just as he had said to them. 33 But as they were loosing the colt, the owners of it said to them, "Why are you loosing the colt?" 34 And they said, "The Lord has need of him." 35 Then they brought him to Jesus. And they threw their own clothes on the colt, and they set Jesus on him. 36 And as he went, they spread their clothes on the road 37 Then, as he was now drawing near the descent of the Mount of Olives, the whole multitude of the disciples began to rejoice and praise God with a loud voice for all the mighty works they had seen, 38 saying: "Blessed is the King who comes in the name of the Lord!' Peace in heaven and glory in the highest!" 39 And some of the Pharisees called to him from the crowd, "Teacher, rebuke your disciples." 40 But he answered and said to them, "I tell you that if these should keep silent, the stones would immediately cry out." 41 Now as he drew near, he saw the city and wept over it, 42 saying, "If you had known, even you, especially in this your day, the things that make for your peace! But now they are hidden from your eyes. 43 For days will come upon you when your enemies will build an embankment around you, surround you and close you in on every side, 44 and level you, and your children within you, to the ground; and they will not leave in you one stone upon another, because you did not know the time of your visitation." 45 Then he went into the temple and began to drive out those who bought and sold in it, 46 saying to them, "It is written, 'My house is a house of prayer,' but you have made it a 'den of thieves.'" 47 And he was teaching daily in the temple. But the chief priests, the scribes, and the leaders of the people sought to destroy him, 48 and were unable to do anything; for all the people were very attentive to hear him

Chapter 20

1 Now it happened on one of those days, as he taught the people in the temple and preached the gospel, that the chief priests and the scribes, together with the elders, confronted him 2 and spoke to him, saying, "Tell us, by what authority are you doing these things? Or who is he who gave you this authority?" 3 But he answered and said to them, "I also will ask you one thing, and answer me: 4 The baptism of John—was it from heaven or from men?" 5 And they reasoned among themselves, saying, "If we say, 'From heaven,' he will say, 'Why then did you not believe him?' 6 But if we say, 'From men,' all the people will stone us, for they are persuaded that John was a prophet." 7 So they answered that they did not know where it was from 8 And Jesus said to them, "Neither will I tell you by what authority I do these things." 9 Then he began to tell the people this parable: "A certain man planted a vineyard, leased it to vinedressers, and went into a far country for a long time. 10 Now at vintage-time he sent a servant to the vinedressers, that they might give him some of the fruit of the vineyard. But the vinedressers beat him and sent him away empty-handed. 11 Again he sent another servant; and they beat him also, treated him shamefully, and sent him away empty-handed. 12 And again he sent a third; and they wounded him also and cast him out 13 "Then the owner of the vineyard said, 'What shall I do? I will send my beloved son. Probably they will respect him when they see him.' 14 But when the vinedressers saw him, they reasoned among themselves, saying, 'This is the heir. Come, let us kill him, that the inheritance may be ours.' 15 So they cast him out of the vineyard and killed him. Therefore what will the owner of the vineyard do to them? 16 He will come and destroy those vinedressers and give the vineyard to others." And when they heard it they said, "Certainly not!" 17 Then he looked at them and said, "What then is this that is written: 'The stone which the builders rejected Has become the chief cornerstone'? 18 Whoever falls on that stone will be broken; but on whomever it falls, it will grind him to powder." 19 And the chief priests and the scribes that very hour sought to lay hands on him, but they feared the people—for they knew he had spoken this parable against them 20 So they watched him, and sent spies who pretended to be righteous, that they might seize on his words, in order to deliver him to the power and the authority of the governor. 21 Then they asked him, saying, "Teacher, we know that you say and teach rightly, and you do not show personal favoritism, but teach the way of God in truth: 22 Is it lawful for us to pay taxes to Caesar or not?" 23 But he perceived their craftiness, and said to them, "Why do you test me? 24 Show me a denarius. Whose image and inscription does it have?" They answered and said, "Caesar's." 25 And he said to them, "Render therefore to Caesar the things that are Caesar's, and to God the things that are God's." 26 But they could not catch him in his words in the presence of the people. And they marveled at his answer and kept silent 27 Then some of the Sadducees, who deny that there is a resurrection, came to him and asked him, 28 saying:

"Teacher, Moses wrote to us that if a man's brother dies, having a wife, and he dies without children, his brother should take his wife and raise up offspring for his brother. 29 Now there were seven brothers. And the first took a wife, and died without children. 30 And the second took her as wife, and he died childless. 31 Then the third took her, and in like manner the seven also; and they left no children, and died. 32 Last of all the woman died also. 33 Therefore, in the resurrection, whose wife does she become? For all seven had her as wife." 34 Jesus answered and said to them, "The sons of this age marry and are given in marriage. 35 But those who are counted worthy to attain that age, and the resurrection from the dead, neither marry nor are given in marriage; 36 nor can they die anymore, for they are equal to the angels and are sons of God, being sons of the resurrection. 37 But even Moses showed in the burning bush passage that the dead are raised, when he called the Lord 'the God of Abraham, the God of Isaac, and the God of Jacob.' 38 For He is not the God of the dead but of the living, for all live to Him." 39 Then some of the scribes answered and said, "Teacher, you have spoken well." 40 But after that they dared not question him anymore 41 And he said to them, "How can they say that the Christ is the Son of David? 42 Now David himself said in the Book of Psalms: 'The Lord said to my Lord, "Sit at My right hand, 43 Till I make Your enemies Your footstool."' 44 Therefore David calls him 'Lord'; how is he then his Son?" 45 Then, in the hearing of all the people, he said to his disciples, 46 "Beware of the scribes, who desire to go around in long robes, love greetings in the marketplaces, the best seats in the synagogues, and the best places at feasts, 47 who devour widows' houses, and for a pretense make long prayers. These will receive greater condemnation."

CHAPTER 21

1 And as he watched, he saw the rich men throwing their gifts into the treasury. 2 And he also saw a certain poor widow who threw two pennies into it: 3 And he said, "Truly I tell you, this poor widow has poured out more than all of them. 4 For they all threw their surplus into God's offerings, but she, for her penance, threw in all the money she had. 5 Now as some spoke of the Temple, how it was adorned with beautiful stones and consecrated things, he said, 6 Are these the things you look upon? The days will come when you will not leave a stone upon a stone and throw it down." 7 Then they asked him, saying, "Master, but when will these things be? And what sign will there be when these things shall come to pass?" 8 And he said, "Take heed lest ye be deceived, for many shall come in my Name, saying, I am the Christ, and the time draws near; therefore follow them not. 9 And when ye hear of wars and sedition, fear not: for these things must first come, but the end shall not follow from one moment to another." 10 Then he said to them, "Nation shall rise up against nation, and kingdom against kingdom, 11 And there shall be great earthquakes in many places, and famine, and pestilence, and fearful things, and there shall be great signs from Heauen. 12 But before all this, they will lay their hands on you and persecute you, delivering you to the assemblies and to the prisons, and they will bring you before kings and rulers for my names' sake. 13 And this shall be a testimony to you. 14 Therefore put it into your hearts that you do not throw into your heads what you will have to answer. 15 For I will give you such a mouth and wisdom that all your adversaries will not be able to speak or resist. 16 You will also be betrayed by your parents, your brothers, your relatives, and your friends, and some of you will be put to death. 17 And

you will be hated by all men for My names' sake. 18 Yet not a single head of yours shall perish. 19 By your patience you shall possess your souls. 20 When you see Jerusalem besieged by soldiers, you will understand that its desolation is near. 21 Then let those who are in Judea flee to the mountains, and those who are in the midst of it leave, and those who are in the county do not enter it. 22 For these are the days of vengeance, for the fulfillment of all things written. 23 But woe to them that bring forth, and to them that bring forth in those days, for there shall be great distress in this land, and wrath upon this people. 24 And they shall fall by the edge of the sword, and shall be led into captivity in all nations, and Jerusalem shall be subject to the dominion of the Gentiles, until the time of the Gentiles is fulfilled. 25 Then there will be signs in the sun, moon and stars, and on earth there will be trouble among the nations with perplexity; the sea and the waters will be troubled. 26 And the hearts of men shall be troubled with fear and examination of what shall take place in the world, for the powers of Eauen shall be shaken. 27 And then they will see the Son of Man coming in a cloud, with power and great glory. 28 When these things begin to be fulfilled, watch and lift up your heads, for your redemption draws near." 29 Then he spoke to them a parable, "Behold the fig tree and all the trees." 30 When they take flight, you, seeing them, know for yourselves that the morning is now near. 31 So you also, when you see these things happening, will know that the kingdom of God is near. 32 Truly I tell you, this age will not pass away until all these things are fulfilled: 33 Heaven and earth shall pass away, but my words shall not pass away. 34 Take heed to yourselves, lest at any time your hearts be oppressed by surfing, drunkenness, and the cares of this life, and lest vnwares come upon you that day. 35 For as a snare shall come upon all who dwell on the face of all the earth. 36 Watch therefore and pray continually, that you may be counted worthy to escape all these things that will happen, and that you may stand before the Son of Man. 37 By day he taught in the temple, and by night he went out and stood on the mountain called the Mount of Olives. 38 In the morning all the people came to him to hear him in the Temple

CHAPTER 22

1 The feast of vnleauened bread, which is called Passer, was now near. 2 The priests and scribes were trying to kill him, because they feared the people. 3 Then Satan entered Iudas, who was called Iscariot and was of the name of the two. 4 Then he went on his way and argued with the priests and captains about how to betray him. 5 They rejoiced and agreed to give him money. 6 He agreed and looked for an opportunity to betray him when the people were far away. 7 Then came the day of vnleauened bread, when the Passer was to be sacrificed. 8 He sent Peter and John, saying, "Go and prepare the Passover, that we may eat it." 9 They said to him, "Where do you want us to prepare him?" 10 Then he said to them, "Behold, when you have entered the city, a man will come to meet you with a pitcher of water; follow him into the house into which he will enter, 11 and say to the good man of the house, 'The Master said to you, "Where is the lodging where I will eat my meal with my disciples?"' 12 Then he will show you a large bedroom, furnished and ready." 13 So they went and found as he had told them, and they prepared the Pastime. 14 When it was time, he sat down, and the two apostles with him. 15 Then he said to them, "I have longed to eat this supper with you, before I suffered. 16 For I tell you that from now on I will eat no more of it, until it is fulfilled in the kingdom of God." 17 Then he took the cup, gave thanks, and said,

"Take and distribute among yourselves, 18 for I tell you that I will not drink of the fruit of the vine until the kingdom of God has come." 19 Then he took the bread and, after giving thanks, broke it and gave it into their hands, saying, "This is my body, which was given for you; do this in remembrance of me." 20 Likewise, after the supper, he took the cup, saying, "This cup is the New Testament in my blood, which was poured out for you." 21 But behold, the hand of him who betrayed me is with me at the table. 22 And verily the Son of Man goes as it was appointed; but woe to that man by whom he was betrayed." 23 Then they began to wonder which of them should do this. 24 And there arose also a dispute among them, as to which of them should seem the greater. 25 But he said to them, "The kings of the Gentiles rule over them, and those who rule over them are called rich. 26 But you shall not be so; the greatest among you shall be as the least, and the chief as the one who serves. 27 For who is greater, the one who sits at the table or the one who serves? Is it not he who sits at the table? And I am among you as the one who serves. 28 And you are those who have continued with me in my temptations. 29 Therefore I appoint you a kingdom, as my Father has done to me, 30 That you may eat and drink at my table in my kingdom, and sit on the seats, and judge the two tribes of Israel." 31 The Lord said, "Simon, Simon, behold, Satan has lusted after you to win you like a roe. 32 But I have prayed for you, that your faith may not fail; therefore, when you are convinced, strengthen your brothers." 33 He said to him, "Lord, I am ready to go with you to prison and to die." 34 But he answered, "I tell you, Peter, that the rooster will not croak today before you have thrice denied knowing me." 35 And he said to them, "When I sent you without bag, without paper, and without shoes, were you lacking anything? And they answered, "Nothing." 36 Then he said to them, "Whoever has a bag, let him take it, and also a coin; and whoever has none, let him sell his cloak and buy a sword. 37 For I say to you that what is written must also be fulfilled in me, for he was appointed with the wicked; for doubtless the things that are written about me have an end." 38 They said, "Lord, here are two swords." And he said to them, "It is sufficient." 39 Then he went out and set out (as he was wont to do) to the Mount of Olives; and his disciples also followed him. 40 When he had come to the place, he said to them, "Pray, lest you enter into temptation." 41 He departed from them about a stone, knelt down and prayed, 42 saying, "Father, if you are willing, turn this cup away from me; not my will but yours be done." 43 And there appeared to him an angel from above, who comforted him. 44 But being in agony, he prayed more earnestly; and his sweat was like drops of blood running down to the ground. 45 Then he arose from prayer and came to his disciples and found them asleep from exhaustion. 46 He said to them, "Why are you asleep? Get up and pray, otherwise you will enter into temptation." 47 While he was still speaking, behold, a company, and he whose name was Iudas, one of them, came before them and approached Jesus to kill him. 48 And Jesus said to him, "Iudas, do you betray the Son of Man with a stroke of your hand? 49 When those around him saw what was to happen, they said to him, "Lord, shall we strike with the sword?" 50 One of them struck one of the priest's servants and took off his right ear. 51 Then Iesus answered and said, "Bear them up to this point"; and he touched his ear and healed it. 52 Then Jesus said to the priests, and to the captains of the Temple, and to the elders who had come to him, "Did you perhaps come out as if from a feast with swords and clubs? 53 When I was daily with you in the Temple, you did not stretch out your hands against me; but this is your own hour and the power of darkness." 54 So they took him and led him and brought him to the house of the priests. And Peter followed him at a distance. 55 And when they had lighted the fire in the middle of the hall and were seated together, Peter also sat down among them. 56 A certain elder saw him as he was sitting by the fire, and after he had a good look at him, he said, "This man was also with him." 57 But he denied it, saying, "Woman, I do not know him." 58 After a while, another man saw him and said, "You are also of those." But Peter said, "Man, I am not." 59 And about an hour later another man affirmed, "Verily, this man was killed and is not one of them. Verily also this man was with him, for he also is a Galilean." 60 Peter said, "Man, I do not know what you say." And immediately, while he was still speaking, the rooster croaked. 61 Then the Lord turned back and looked at Peter; and Peter remembered the word of the Lord, who had said to him, "Before the rooster croaks, you shall deny me three times." 62 Peter went out and wept bitterly. 63 The men who held Jesus taunted him and stabbed him. 64 When they had blindfolded him, they struck him on the face and asked him, "Prophesy who it was that struck you." 65 And many other blasphemous things they said against him. 66 And because it was day, the elders of the people, the priests, and the scribes gathered together and led him into their council, 67 saying, "Are you that Christ? say it." And he answered them, "If I tell you, you will not accept him. 68 And even if I ask you, you will not answer me or let me go. 69 Afterward the Son of Man will sit at the right hand of the power of God." 70 Then they all said, "Are you then Son of God?" And he said to them, "You say that I am." 71 Then they said, "What need is there for further testimony, for we ourselves have heard it from his mouth."

CHAPTER 23

1 And the whole multitude of them arose and led him to Pilate. 2 And they began to accuse him, saying, "We found this fellow perverting the nation, and forbidding to give tribute to Caesar, saying that he himself is Christ a King." 3 And Pilate asked him, saying, "Art thou the King of the Jews?" And he answered him and said, "Thou sayest it." 4 Then Pilate said to the chief priests and to the people, "I find no fault in this man." 5 And they were the more fierce, saying, "He stirreth up the people, teaching throughout all Jewry, beginning from Galilee to this place." 6 When Pilate heard of Galilee, he asked whether the man were a Galilean. 7 And as soon as he knew that he belonged to Herod's jurisdiction, he sent him to Herod, who himself also was at Jerusalem at that time. 8 And when Herod saw Jesus, he was exceedingly glad: for he was desirous to see him of a long season, because he had heard many things of him; and he hoped to have seen some miracle done by him. 9 Then he questioned with him in many words; but he answered him nothing. 10 And the chief priests and scribes stood and vehemently accused him. 11 And Herod with his men of war set him at naught, and mocked him, and arrayed him in a gorgeous robe, and sent him again to Pilate. 12 And the same day Pilate and Herod were made friends together: for before they were at enmity between themselves. 13 And Pilate, when he had called together the chief priests and the rulers and the people, 14 Said unto them, "Ye have brought this man unto me, as one that perverteth the people: and, behold, I, having examined him before you, have found no fault in this man touching those things whereof ye accuse him: 15 No, nor yet Herod: for I sent you to him; and, lo, nothing worthy of death is done unto him. 16 I will therefore chastise him, and release him." 17 (For of necessity he must release

one unto them at the feast.) 18 And they cried out all at once, saying, "Away with this man, and release unto us Barabbas:" 19 Who for a certain sedition made in the city, and for murder, was cast into prison. 20 Pilate therefore, willing to release Jesus, spoke again to them. 21 But they cried, saying, "Crucify him, crucify him." 22 And he said unto them the third time, "Why, what evil hath he done? I have found no cause of death in him: I will therefore chastise him, and let him go." 23 And they were instant with loud voices, requiring that he might be crucified. And the voices of them and of the chief priests prevailed. 24 And Pilate gave sentence that it should be as they required. 25 And he released unto them him that for sedition and murder was cast into prison, whom they had desired; but he delivered Jesus to their will. 26 And as they led him away, they laid hold upon one Simon, a Cyrenian, coming out of the country, and on him they laid the cross, that he might bear it after Jesus. 27 And there followed him a great company of people, and of women, which also bewailed and lamented him. 28 But Jesus turning unto them said, "Daughters of Jerusalem, weep not for me, but weep for yourselves, and for your children. 29 For, behold, the days are coming, in the which they shall say, 'Blessed are the barren, and the wombs that never bare, and the paps which never gave suck.' 30 Then shall they begin to say to the mountains, 'Fall on us;' and to the hills, 'Cover us.' 31 For if they do these things in a green tree, what shall be done in the dry?" 32 And there were also two other, malefactors, led with him to be put to death. 33 And when they were come to the place which is called Calvary, there they crucified him, and the malefactors, one on the right hand, and the other on the left. 34 Then said Jesus, "Father, forgive them; for they know not what they do." And they parted his raiment, and cast lots. 35 And the people stood beholding. And the rulers also with them derided him, saying, "He saved others; let him save himself, if he be Christ, the chosen of God." 36 And the soldiers also mocked him, coming to him, and offering him vinegar, 37 And saying, "If thou be the King of the Jews, save thyself." 38 And a superscription also was written over him in letters of Greek, and Latin, and Hebrew, "THIS IS THE KING OF THE JEWS." 39 And one of the malefactors which were hanged railed on him, saying, "If thou be Christ, save thyself and us." 40 But the other answering rebuked him, saying, "Dost not thou fear God, seeing thou art in the same condemnation? 41 And we indeed justly; for we receive the due reward of our deeds: but this man hath done nothing amiss." 42 And he said unto Jesus, "Lord, remember me when thou comest into thy kingdom." 43 And Jesus said unto him, "Verily I say unto thee, Today shalt thou be with me in paradise." 44 And it was about the sixth hour, and there was a darkness over all the earth until the ninth hour. 45 And the sun was darkened, and the veil of the temple was rent in the midst. 46 And when Jesus had cried with a loud voice, he said, "Father, into thy hands I commend my spirit." And having said thus, he gave up the ghost. 47 Now when the centurion saw what was done, he glorified God, saying, "Certainly this was a righteous man." 48 And all the people that came together to that sight, beholding the things which were done, smote their breasts, and returned. 49 And all his acquaintance, and the women that followed him from Galilee, stood afar off, beholding these things. 50 And, behold, there was a man named Joseph, a counsellor; and he was a good man, and just: 51 (The same had not consented to the counsel and deed of them;) he was of Arimathaea, a city of the Jews: who also himself waited for the kingdom of God: 52 This man went unto Pilate, and begged the body of Jesus. 53 And he took it down, and wrapped it in linen, and laid it in a sepulchre that was hewn in stone, wherein never man before was laid. 54 And that day was the preparation, and the sabbath drew on. 55 And the women also, which came with him from Galilee, followed after, and beheld the sepulchre, and how his body was laid. 56 And they returned, and prepared spices and ointments; and rested the sabbath day according to the commandment

CHAPTER 24

1 Now upon the first day of the week, very early in the morning, they came unto the sepulchre, bringing the spices which they had prepared, and certain others with them. 2 And they found the stone rolled away from the sepulchre. 3 And they entered in, and found not the body of the Lord Jesus. 4 And it came to pass, as they were much perplexed thereabout, behold, two men stood by them in shining garments: 5 And as they were afraid, and bowed down their faces to the earth, they said unto them, "Why seek ye the living among the dead? 6 He is not here, but is risen: remember how he spake unto you when he was yet in Galilee, 7 Saying, 'The Son of man must be delivered into the hands of sinful men, and be crucified, and the third day rise again.'" 8 And they remembered his words, 9 And returned from the sepulchre, and told all these things unto the eleven, and to all the rest. 10 It was Mary Magdalene, and Joanna, and Mary the mother of James, and other women that were with them, which told these things unto the apostles. 11 And their words seemed to them as idle tales, and they believed them not. 12 Then arose Peter, and ran unto the sepulchre; and stooping down, he beheld the linen clothes laid by themselves, and departed, wondering in himself at that which was come to pass. 13 And, behold, two of them went that same day to a village called Emmaus, which was from Jerusalem about threescore furlongs. 14 And they talked together of all these things which had happened. 15 And it came to pass, that, while they communed together and reasoned, Jesus himself drew near, and went with them. 16 But their eyes were holden that they should not know him. 17 And he said unto them, "What manner of communications are these that ye have one to another, as ye walk, and are sad?" 18 And the one of them, whose name was Cleopas, answering said unto him, "Art thou only a stranger in Jerusalem, and hast not known the things which are come to pass there in these days?" 19 And he said unto them, "What things?" And they said unto him, "Concerning Jesus of Nazareth, which was a prophet mighty in deed and word before God and all the people: 20 And how the chief priests and our rulers delivered him to be condemned to death, and have crucified him. 21 But we trusted that it had been he which should have redeemed Israel: and beside all this, today is the third day since these things were done. 22 Yea, and certain women also of our company made us astonished, which were early at the sepulchre; 23 And when they found not his body, they came, saying, that they had also seen a vision of angels, which said that he was alive. 24 And certain of them which were with us went to the sepulchre, and found it even so as the women had said: but him they saw not." 25 Then he said unto them, "O fools, and slow of heart to believe all that the prophets have spoken: 26 Ought not Christ to have suffered these things, and to enter into his glory?" 27 And beginning at Moses and all the prophets, he expounded unto them in all the scriptures the things concerning himself. 28 And they drew nigh unto the village, whither they went: and he made as though he would have gone further. 29 But they constrained him,

saying, "Abide with us: for it is toward evening, and the day is far spent." And he went in to tarry with them. 30 And it came to pass, as he sat at meat with them, he took bread, and blessed it, and brake, and gave to them. 31 And their eyes were opened, and they knew him; and he vanished out of their sight. 32 And they said one to another, "Did not our heart burn within us, while he talked with us by the way, and while he opened to us the scriptures?" 33 And they rose up the same hour, and returned to Jerusalem, and found the eleven gathered together, and them that were with them, 34 Saying, "The Lord is risen indeed, and hath appeared to Simon." 35 And they told what things were done in the way, and how he was known of them in breaking of bread. 36 And as they thus spake, Jesus himself stood in the midst of them, and saith unto them, "Peace be unto you." 37 But they were terrified and affrighted, and supposed that they had seen a spirit. 38 And he said unto them, "Why are ye troubled? and why do thoughts arise in your hearts? 39 Behold my hands and my feet, that it is I myself: handle me, and see; for a spirit hath not flesh and bones, as ye see me have." 40 And when he had thus spoken, he shewed them his hands and his feet. 41 And while they yet believed not for joy, and wondered, he said unto them, "Have ye here any meat?" 42 And they gave him a piece of a broiled fish, and of an honeycomb. 43 And he took it, and did eat before them. 44 And he said unto them, "These are the words which I spake unto you, while I was yet with you, that all things must be fulfilled, which were written in the law of Moses, and in the prophets, and in the psalms, concerning me." 45 Then opened he their understanding, that they might understand the scriptures, 46 And said unto them, "Thus it is written, and thus it behoved Christ to suffer, and to rise from the dead the third day: 47 And that repentance and remission of sins should be preached in his name among all nations, beginning at Jerusalem. 48 And ye are witnesses of these things. 49 And, behold, I send the promise of my Father upon you: but tarry ye in the city of Jerusalem, until ye be endued with power from on high." 50 And he led them out as far as to Bethany, and he lifted up his hands, and blessed them. 51 And it came to pass, while he blessed them, he was parted from them, and carried up into heaven. 52 And they worshipped him, and returned to Jerusalem with great joy: 53 And were continually in the temple, praising and blessing God. Amen

43. John

Chapter 1

In the beginning was the Word, and the Word was with God, and the Word was God. This same was in the beginning with God. Through it, all things were made, and without it, nothing was made that was made. In it was life, and this life was the light of men. The light shone in the darkness, and the darkness did not understand it. There was a man sent from God, whose name was John. He came as a witness, to bear witness to that light, so that all men through him might come to know it. He was not that light, but he was sent to bear witness of that light. He was the true light, who enlightens every man who comes into the world. He was in the world, and the world was made by him, but the world did not know him. He came to his own, but his own did not receive him. But to those who received him, he gave the prerogative of being children of God, that is, to those who fought in his Name. They were born not of blood, nor of the will of flesh, nor of the will of man, but of God The Word became flesh and dwelt among us, and we know its glory, as the glory of the only begotten Son of the Father, full of grace and truth. John bore witness and cried out, "This is he of whom I said, 'He who comes after me was before me,' for he was better than I." And of his fullness, we have received everything, grace for grace. For the law came from Moses, but grace and truth came from Jesus Christ. No one has ever seen God; the only begotten Son, who is in the bosom of the Father, has declared him This is the account of John, when the kings sent out from Jerusalem priests and Levites to ask him, "Who are you?" He confessed and did not deny, and said plainly, "I am not the Christ." Then they asked him, "What then? Are you Elijah?" and he answered, "I am not." "Are you the Prophet?" And he answered, "No." Then they said to him, "Who are you, that we may give an answer to those who sent you? What do you say about yourself?" He answered, "I am the voice of one crying out in the wilderness, 'Straighten up the way of the Lord,' as the prophet Isaiah said." Those who had been sent were Pharisees. They asked him, "Why then do you baptize if you are not the Christ, nor Elijah, nor the Prophet?" John answered, "I baptize with water; but there is one among you whom you do not know. It is he who comes after me, who was before me, whose shoelace I am not worthy to untie." These things were done at Bethabara, beyond Jordan, where John was baptizing The next day John saw Jesus joining him and said, "Here is the Lamb of God who takes away the sin of the world. This is he of whom I said, 'After me comes a man who was before me, for he was better than I.' I did not know him; but because he was to be declared to Israel, I came and baptized with water." Then John related, "I saw the Spirit descending from above, like thunder, and abiding on him, and I did not know him; but he who had sent me to baptize with water said to me, 'He whom you will see the Spirit descending and abiding on him, it is he who baptizes with the Holy Spirit.' I said, and bore witness, that this one is the Son of God." The next day John stood again with two of his disciples. He saw Jesus passing by and said, "Behold, the Son of God." The two disciples heard him speak and followed Jesus. Then Jesus turned and saw them following and said, "What do you seek?" And they said to him, "Rabbi (which means Master), where do you dwell?" He said, "Come and see." And they came and saw where he dwelt and stayed with him that day, for it was about the tenth hour. Andrew, Simon Peter's brother, was one of the two who had heard about John and followed him. He found his brother Simon first and said to him, "We have found the Messiah," which means the Christ. And he led him to Jesus. Jesus saw him and said, "You are Simon, son of Jonah; you shall be called Cephas," which means stone The next day Jesus went to Galilee and found Philip and said, "Follow me." Philip was from Bethsaida, the town of Andrew and Peter. Philip found Nathanael and said, "We have found him of whom Moses in the Bible and the Prophets wrote, Jesus the son of Joseph, from Nazareth." Nathanael said, "Can anything good come from Nazareth?" Philip said, "Come and see." Jesus saw Nathanael approaching and said, "Here is an Israelite in whom there is no deceit." Nathanael asked, "How do you know me?" Jesus answered, "Before Philip called you, when you were under the fig tree, I saw you." Nathanael replied, "Rabbi, you are the Son of God, you are the King of Israel." Jesus said, "Because I told you that I saw you under the fig tree, do you believe? You will see greater things than these." And he added, "Truly, truly, I say to you, from now on you will see heaven opened and the angels of God ascending and descending on the Son of Man."

Chapter 2

On the third day, there was a wedding in Cana of Galilee, and Jesus' mother was there. Jesus and his disciples were also invited to the wedding. When the wine ran out, Jesus' mother said to him, "They have no wine." Jesus replied, "Woman, what does this have to do with me? My hour has not yet come." His mother said to the servants, "Do whatever he tells you." Six stone water jars were set there, used for the Jewish rites of purification, each holding twenty or thirty gallons. Jesus said, "Fill the jars with water." They filled them to the brim. Then he said, "Now draw some out and take it to the master of the banquet." They did so, and the master of the banquet tasted the water that had been turned into wine. He did not realize where it had come from, though the servants who had drawn the water knew. Then he called the bridegroom aside and said, "Everyone brings out the choice wine first and then the cheaper wine after the guests have had too much to drink; but you have saved the best till now." This, the first of the signs, Jesus performed in Cana of Galilee, and thus revealed his glory, and his disciples believed in him After this, he went down to Capernaum with his mother, brothers, and disciples, but they stayed there only a few days. When it was almost time for the Jewish Passover, Jesus went up to Jerusalem. In the temple courts, he found people selling cattle, sheep, and doves, and others sitting at tables exchanging money. So he made a whip out of cords and drove all from the temple courts, both sheep and cattle; he scattered the coins of the money changers and overturned their tables. To those who sold doves he said, "Get these out of here! Stop turning my Father's house into a market!" His disciples remembered that it is written: "Zeal for your house will consume me." The Jews then responded to him, "What sign can you show us to prove your authority to do all this?" Jesus answered them, "Destroy this temple, and I will raise it again in three days." They replied, "It has taken forty-six years to build this temple, and you are going to raise it in three days?" But the temple he had spoken of was his body. After he was raised from the dead, his disciples recalled what he had said. Then they believed the scripture and the words that Jesus had spoken While he was in Jerusalem at the Passover Festival, many people saw the signs he was performing and believed in his name. But Jesus would not entrust himself to them, for he knew all people. He did not need any testimony about mankind, for he knew what was in each person

Chapter 3

Now there was a Pharisee, a man named Nicodemus, who was a member of the Jewish ruling council. He came to Jesus at night and said, "Rabbi, we know that you are a teacher who has come from God, for no one could perform the signs you are doing if God were not with him." Jesus replied, "Very truly I tell you, no one can see the kingdom of God unless they are born again." Nicodemus asked, "How can someone be born when they are old? Surely they cannot enter a second time into their mother's womb to be born!" Jesus answered, "Very truly I tell you, no one can enter the kingdom of God unless they are born of water and the Spirit. Flesh gives birth to flesh, but the Spirit gives birth to spirit. You should not be surprised at my saying, 'You must be born again.' The wind blows wherever it pleases. You hear its sound, but you cannot tell where it comes from or where it is going. So it is with everyone born of the Spirit." "How can this be?" Nicodemus asked. "You are Israel's teacher," said Jesus, "and do you not understand these things? Very truly I tell you, we speak of what we know, and we testify to what we have seen, but still, you people do not accept our testimony. I have spoken to you of earthly things and you do not believe; how then will you believe if I speak of heavenly things? No one has ever gone into heaven except the one who came from heaven—the Son of Man. Just as Moses lifted up the snake in the wilderness, so the Son of Man must be lifted up, that everyone who believes may have eternal life in him." For God so loved the world that he gave his one and only Son, that whoever believes in him shall not perish but have eternal life. For God did not send his Son into the world to condemn the world, but to save the world through him. Whoever believes in him is not condemned, but whoever does not believe stands condemned already because they have not believed in the name of God's one and only Son. This is the verdict: Light has come into the world, but people loved darkness instead of light because their deeds were evil. Everyone who does evil hates the light and will not come into the light for fear that their deeds will be exposed. But whoever lives by the truth comes into the light so that it may be seen plainly that what they have done has been done in the sight of God After this, Jesus and his disciples went out into the Judean countryside, where he spent some time with them, and baptized. Now John also was baptizing at Aenon near Salim, because there was plenty of water, and people were coming and being baptized. (This was before John was put in prison.) An argument developed between some of John's disciples and a certain Jew over the matter of ceremonial washing. They came to John and said to him, "Rabbi, that man who was with you on the other side of the Jordan—the one you testified about— look, he is baptizing, and everyone is going to him." To this John replied, "A person can receive only what is given them from heaven. You yourselves can testify that I said, 'I am not the Messiah but am sent ahead of him.' The bride belongs to the bridegroom. The friend who attends the bridegroom waits and listens for him, and is full of joy when he hears the bridegroom's voice. That joy is mine, and it is now complete. He must become greater; I must become less." The one who comes from above is above all; the one who is from the earth belongs to the earth and speaks as one from the earth. The one who comes from heaven is above all. He testifies to what he has seen and heard, but no one accepts his testimony. Whoever has accepted it has certified that God is truthful. For the one whom God has sent speaks the words of God, for God gives the Spirit without limit. The Father loves the Son and has placed everything in his hands. Whoever believes in the Son has eternal life, but whoever rejects the Son will not see life, for God's wrath remains on them

Chapter 4

Now Jesus learned that the Pharisees had heard that he was gaining and baptizing more disciples than John—although in fact, it was not Jesus who baptized, but his disciples. So he left Judea and went back once more to Galilee. Now he had to go through Samaria. So he came to a town in Samaria called Sychar, near the plot of ground Jacob had given to his son Joseph. Jacob's well was there, and Jesus, tired as he was from the journey, sat down by the well. It was about noon When a Samaritan woman came to draw water, Jesus said to her, "Will you give me a drink?" (His disciples had gone into the town to buy food.) The Samaritan woman said to him, "You are a Jew and I am a Samaritan woman. How can you ask me for a drink?" (For Jews do not associate with Samaritans.) Jesus answered her, "If you knew the gift of God and who it is that asks you for a drink, you would have asked him and he would have given you living water." "Sir," the woman said, "you have nothing to draw with and the well is deep. Where can you get this living water? Are you greater than our father Jacob, who gave us the well and drank from it himself, as did also his sons and his livestock?"

Jesus answered, "Everyone who drinks this water will be thirsty again, but whoever drinks the water I give them will never thirst. Indeed, the water I give them will become in them a spring of water welling up to eternal life." The woman said to him, "Sir, give me this water so that I won't get thirsty and have to keep coming here to draw water." He told her, "Go, call your husband and come back." "I have no husband," she replied Jesus said to her, "You are right when you say you have no husband. The fact is, you have had five husbands, and the man you now have is not your husband. What you have just said is quite true." "Sir," the woman said, "I can see that you are a prophet. Our ancestors worshiped on this mountain, but you Jews claim that the place where we must worship is in Jerusalem." "Woman," Jesus replied, "believe me, a time is coming when you will worship the Father neither on this mountain nor in Jerusalem. You Samaritans worship what you do not know; we worship what we do know, for salvation is from the Jews. Yet a time is coming and has now come when the true worshipers will worship the Father in the Spirit and in truth, for they are the kind of worshipers the Father seeks. God is spirit, and his worshipers must worship in the Spirit and in truth." The woman said, "I know that Messiah" (called Christ) "is coming. When he comes, he will explain everything to us." Then Jesus declared, "I, the one speaking to you—I am he." Just then his disciples returned and were surprised to find him talking with a woman. But no one asked, "What do you want?" or "Why are you talking with her?" Then, leaving her water jar, the woman went back to the town and said to the people, "Come, see a man who told me everything I ever did. Could this be the Messiah?" They came out of the town and made their way toward him Meanwhile, his disciples urged him, "Rabbi, eat something." But he said to them, "I have food to eat that you know nothing about." Then his disciples said to each other, "Could someone have brought him food?" "My food," said Jesus, "is to do the will of him who sent me and to finish his work. Don't you have a saying, 'It's still four months until harvest'? I tell you, open your eyes and look at the fields! They are ripe for harvest. Even now the one who reaps draws a wage and harvests a crop for eternal life, so that the sower and the reaper may be glad together. Thus the saying 'One sows and another reaps' is true. I sent you to reap what you have not worked for. Others have done the hard work, and you have reaped the benefits of their labor." Many of the Samaritans from that town believed in him because of the woman's testimony, "He told me everything I ever did." So when the Samaritans came to him, they urged him to stay with them, and he stayed two days. And because of his words, many more became believers. They said to the woman, "We no longer believe just because of what you said; now we have heard for ourselves, and we know that this man really is the Savior of the world." After the two days, he left for Galilee. (Now Jesus himself had pointed out that a prophet has no honor in his own country.) When he arrived in Galilee, the Galileans welcomed him. They had seen all that he had done in Jerusalem at the Passover Festival, for they also had been there Once more he visited Cana in Galilee, where he had turned the water into wine. And there was a certain royal official whose son lay sick at Capernaum. When this man heard that Jesus had arrived in Galilee from Judea, he went to him and begged him to come and heal his son, who was close to death. "Unless you people see signs and wonders," Jesus told him, "you will never believe." The royal official said, "Sir, come down before my child dies." "Go," Jesus replied, "your son will live." The man took Jesus at his word and departed. While he was still on the way, his servants met him with the news that his boy was living. When he inquired as to the time when his son got better, they said to him, "Yesterday, at one in the afternoon, the fever left him." Then the father realized that this was the exact time at which Jesus had said to him, "Your son will live." So he and his whole household believed This was the second sign Jesus performed after coming from Judea to Galilee

Chapter 5

Some time later, Jesus went up to Jerusalem for one of the Jewish festivals. Now there is in Jerusalem near the Sheep Gate a pool, which in Aramaic is called Bethesda and which is surrounded by five covered colonnades. Here a great number of disabled people used to lie—the blind, the lame, the paralyzed. One who was there had been an invalid for thirty-eight years. When Jesus saw him lying there and learned that he had been in this condition for a long time, he asked him, "Do you want to get well?" "Sir," the invalid replied, "I have no one to help me into the pool when the water is stirred. While I am trying to get in, someone else goes down ahead of me." Then Jesus said to him, "Get up! Pick up your mat and walk." At once the man was cured; he picked up his mat and walked. The day on which this took place was a Sabbath, and so the Jewish leaders said to the man who had been healed, "It is the Sabbath; the law forbids you to carry your mat." But he replied, "The man who made me well said to me, 'Pick up your mat and walk.'" So they asked him, "Who is this fellow who told you to pick it up and walk?" The man who was healed had no idea who it was, for Jesus had slipped away into the crowd that was there. Later Jesus found him at the temple and said to him, "See, you are well again. Stop sinning or something worse may happen to you." The man went away and told the Jewish leaders that it was Jesus who had made him well So, because Jesus was doing these things on the Sabbath, the Jewish leaders began to persecute him. In his defense Jesus said to them, "My Father is always at his work to this very day, and I too am working." For this reason they tried all the more to kill him; not only was he breaking the Sabbath, but he was even calling God his own Father, making himself equal with God Jesus gave them this answer: "Very truly I tell you, the Son can do nothing by himself; he can do only what he sees his Father doing, because whatever the Father does the Son also does. For the Father loves the Son and shows him all he does. Yes, and he will show him even greater works than these so that you will be amazed. For just as the Father raises the dead and gives them life, even so the Son gives life to whom he is pleased to give it. Moreover, the Father judges no one, but has entrusted all judgment to the Son, that all may honor the Son just as they honor the Father. Whoever does not honor the Son does not honor the Father, who sent him "Very truly I tell you, whoever hears my word and believes him who sent me has eternal life and will not be judged but has crossed over from death to life. Very truly I tell you, a time is coming and has now come when the dead will hear the voice of the Son of God and those who hear will live. For as the Father has life in himself, so he has granted the Son also to have life in himself. And he has given him authority to judge because he is the Son of Man "Do not be amazed at this, for a time is coming when all who are in their graves will hear his voice and come out— those who have done what is good will rise to live, and those who have done what is evil will rise to be condemned. By myself, I can do nothing; I judge only as I hear, and my judgment is just, for I seek not to please myself but him who sent me "If I testify about myself, my testimony is not true. There is another who testifies in my favor, and I know that his testimony about me is true "You have sent to John and he has testified to the truth. Not that I accept human testimony, but I mention it that you may be saved. John was a lamp that burned and gave light, and you chose for a time to enjoy his light "I have testimony weightier than that of John. For the works that the Father has given me to finish—the very works that I am doing—testify that the Father has sent me. And the Father who sent me has himself testified concerning me. You have never heard his voice nor seen his form, nor does his word dwell in you, for you do not believe the one he sent. You study the Scriptures diligently because you think that in them you have eternal life. These are the very Scriptures that testify about me, yet you refuse to come to me to have life "I do not accept glory from human beings, but I know you. I know that you do not have the love of God in your hearts. I have come in my Father's name, and you do not accept me; but if someone else comes in his own name, you will accept him. How can you believe since you accept glory from one another but do not seek the glory that comes from the only God? "But do not think I will accuse you before the Father. Your accuser is Moses, on whom your hopes are set. If you believed Moses, you would believe me, for he wrote about me. But since you do not believe what he wrote, how are you going to believe what I say?"

Chapter 6

After these events, Jesus went to the Sea of Galilee, also known as Tiberias. A great crowd followed Him because they had seen the miracles He performed on those who were sick. Jesus then went up a mountain and sat there with His disciples. It was near the time of Passover, a Jewish feast. Seeing the multitude approaching, Jesus asked Philip, "Where shall we buy bread for these people to eat?" He asked this to test him, knowing what He was going to do. Philip replied, "Two hundred denarii worth of bread would not be enough for each one to have a bite." Andrew, Simon Peter's brother, spoke up, "Here is a boy with five small barley loaves and two small fish, but how far will they go among so many?" Jesus said, "Have the people sit down." There was plenty of grass in that place, and about five thousand men sat down. Jesus took the loaves, gave thanks, and distributed them to those who were seated, as much as they wanted. He did the same with the fish. When they had all had enough to eat, He said to His disciples, "Gather the pieces that are left over. Let nothing be wasted." So they gathered them and filled twelve baskets with the pieces of the five barley loaves left over by those who had eaten After the people saw the sign Jesus performed, they began to say, "Surely this is the Prophet who is to come into the world." Jesus, knowing that they intended to come and make Him king by force, withdrew again to a mountain by Himself When evening came, His disciples went down to the lake, where they got into a boat and set off across the lake for Capernaum. By now it was dark, and Jesus had not yet joined them. A strong wind was blowing, and the waters grew rough. When they had rowed about three or four miles, they saw Jesus approaching the boat, walking on the water, and they were frightened. But He said to them, "It is I; don't be afraid." Then they were willing to take Him into the boat, and immediately the boat reached the shore where they were heading The next day, the crowd that had stayed on the opposite shore of the lake realized that only one boat had been there and that Jesus had not entered it with His disciples, but that they had gone away alone. Then some boats from Tiberias landed near the place where the people had eaten the bread after the Lord had given thanks. Once the crowd realized that neither Jesus nor His disciples were there, they got into the boats and went to Capernaum in search of Jesus When they found Him on the other side of the lake, they asked Him, "Rabbi, when did you get here?" Jesus answered, "Very truly I tell you, you are looking for me, not because you saw the signs I performed, but because you ate the loaves and had your fill. Do not work for food that spoils, but for food that endures to eternal life, which the Son of Man will give you. For on Him God the Father has placed His seal of approval." Then they asked Him, "What must we do to do the works God requires?" Jesus answered, "The work of God is this: to believe in the one He has sent." So they asked Him, "What sign then will you give that we may see it and believe you? What will you do? Our ancestors ate the manna in the wilderness; as it is written: 'He gave them bread from heaven to eat.'" Jesus said to them, "Very truly I tell you, it is not Moses who has given you the bread from heaven, but it is My Father who gives you the true bread from heaven. For the bread of God is the bread that comes down from heaven and gives life to the world." "Sir," they said, "always give us this bread." Then Jesus declared, "I am the bread of life. Whoever comes to Me will never go hungry, and whoever believes in Me will never be thirsty. But as I told you, you have seen Me and still you do not believe. All those the Father gives Me will come to Me, and whoever comes to Me I will never drive away. For I have come down from heaven not to do My will but to do the will of Him who sent Me. And this is the will of Him who sent Me, that I shall lose none of all those He has given Me, but raise them up at the last day. For My Father's will is that everyone who looks to the Son and believes in Him shall have eternal life, and I will raise them up at the last day." At this, the Jews there began to grumble about Him because He said, "I am the bread that came down from heaven." They said, "Is this not Jesus, the son of Joseph, whose father and mother we know? How can He now say, 'I came down from heaven'?" "Stop grumbling among yourselves," Jesus answered. "No one can come to Me unless the Father who sent Me draws them, and I will raise them up at the last day. It is written in the Prophets: 'They will all be taught by God.' Everyone who has heard the Father and learned from Him comes to Me. No one has seen the Father except the one who is from God; only He has seen the Father. Very truly I tell you, the one who believes has eternal life. I am the bread of life. Your ancestors ate the manna in the wilderness, yet they died. But here is the bread that comes down from heaven, which anyone may eat and not die. I am the living bread that came down from heaven. Whoever eats this bread will live forever. This bread is My flesh, which I will give for the life of the world." Then the Jews began to argue sharply among themselves, "How can this man give us His flesh to eat?" Jesus said to them, "Very truly I tell you, unless you eat the flesh of the Son of Man and drink His blood, you have no life in you. Whoever eats My flesh and drinks My blood has eternal life, and I will raise them up at the last day. For My flesh is real food, and My blood is real drink. Whoever eats My flesh and drinks My blood remains in Me, and I in them. Just as the living Father sent Me and I live because of the Father, so the one who feeds on Me will live because of Me. This is the bread that came down from heaven. Your ancestors ate manna and died, but whoever feeds on this bread will live forever." He said this while teaching in the synagogue in Capernaum On hearing it, many of His disciples said, "This is a hard teaching. Who can accept it?" Aware that His disciples were grumbling about this, Jesus said to them, "Does this offend you? Then what if you see the Son of Man ascend to where He was before! The Spirit gives life; the flesh counts for nothing. The words I have spoken to you—they are full of the Spirit and life. Yet there are some of you who do not believe." For Jesus had known from the beginning which of them did not believe and who would betray Him. He went on to say, "This is why I told you that no one can come to Me unless the Father has enabled them." From this time many of His disciples turned back and no longer followed Him. "You do not want to leave too, do you?" Jesus asked the Twelve. Simon Peter answered Him, "Lord, to whom shall we go? You have the words of eternal life. We have come to believe and to know that You are the Holy One of God." Then Jesus replied, "Have I not chosen you, the Twelve? Yet one of you is a devil!" He meant Judas, the son of Simon Iscariot, who, though one of the Twelve, was later to betray Him

Chapter 7

After this, Jesus traveled around Galilee. He wanted to stay out of Judea where the Jewish leaders were plotting His death. But soon it was time for the Jewish Festival of Shelters, and Jesus' brothers said to Him, "Leave here and go to Judea, where Your followers can see Your miracles! You can't become famous if You hide like this! If You can do such wonderful things, show Yourself to the world!" For even His brothers didn't believe in Him Jesus replied, "Now is not the right time for Me to go, but you can go anytime. The world can't hate you, but it does hate Me because I accuse it of doing evil. You go on. I'm not going to this festival, because My time has not yet come." After saying these things, Jesus remained in Galilee But after His brothers left for the festival, Jesus also went, though secretly, staying out of public view. The Jewish leaders tried to find Him at the festival and kept asking if anyone had seen Him. There was a lot of grumbling about Him among the crowds. Some argued, "He's a good man," but others said, "He's nothing but a fraud who deceives the people." But no one had the courage to speak favorably about Him in public, for they were afraid of getting in trouble with the Jewish leaders Then, midway through the festival, Jesus went up to the Temple and began to teach. The people were surprised when they heard Him. "How does He know so much when He hasn't been trained?" they asked So Jesus told them, "My message is not My own; it comes from God who sent Me. Anyone who wants to do the will of God will know whether My teaching is from God or is merely My own. Those who speak for themselves want glory only for themselves, but a person who seeks to honor the one who sent him speaks truth, not lies. Moses gave you the law, but none of you obeys it! In fact, you are trying to kill Me." The crowd replied, "You're demon-possessed! Who's trying to kill you?" Jesus replied, "I did one miracle on the Sabbath, and you were amazed. But you work on the Sabbath, too, when you obey Moses' law of circumcision. Actually, this tradition of circumcision began with the patriarchs, long before the law of Moses. For if the correct time for circumcising your son falls on the Sabbath, you go ahead and do it so as not to break the law of Moses. So why should you be angry with Me for healing a man on the Sabbath? Look beneath the surface so you can judge correctly." Some of the people who lived in Jerusalem started to ask each other, "Isn't this the man they are trying to kill? But here He is, speaking in public, and they say nothing to Him. Could our leaders possibly believe that He is the Messiah? But how could He be? For we know where this man comes from. When the Messiah comes, He will simply appear; no one will know where He comes from." While Jesus was teaching in the Temple, He called out, "Yes, you know

Me, and you know where I come from. But I'm not here on My own. The one who sent Me is true, and you don't know Him. But I know Him because I come from Him, and He sent Me to you." Then the leaders tried to arrest Him; but no one laid a hand on Him, because His time had not yet come Many among the crowds at the Temple believed in Him. "After all," they said, "would you expect the Messiah to do more miraculous signs than this man has done?" When the Pharisees heard that the crowds were whispering such things, they and the leading priests sent Temple guards to arrest Jesus. But Jesus told them, "I will be with you only a little longer. Then I will return to the one who sent Me. You will search for Me but not find Me. And you cannot go where I am going." The Jewish leaders were puzzled by this statement. "Where is He planning to go?" they asked. "Is He thinking of leaving the country and going to the Jews in other lands? Maybe He will even teach the Greeks! What does He mean when He says, 'You will search for Me but not find Me,' and 'You cannot go where I am going'?" On the last day, the climax of the festival, Jesus stood and shouted to the crowds, "Anyone who is thirsty may come to Me! Anyone who believes in Me may come and drink! For the Scriptures declare, 'Rivers of living water will flow from his heart.'" (When He said "living water," He was speaking of the Spirit, who would be given to everyone believing in Him. But the Spirit had not yet been given, because Jesus had not yet entered into His glory.) When the crowds heard Him say this, some of them declared, "Surely this man is the Prophet we've been expecting." Others said, "He is the Messiah." Still, others said, "But He can't be! Will the Messiah come from Galilee? For the Scriptures clearly state that the Messiah will be born of the royal line of David, in Bethlehem, the village where King David was born." So the crowd was divided about Him. Some even wanted Him arrested, but no one laid a hand on Him When the Temple guards returned without having arrested Jesus, the leading priests and Pharisees demanded, "Why didn't you bring Him in?" "We have never heard anyone speak like this!" the guards responded "Have you been led astray, too?" the Pharisees mocked. "Is there a single one of us rulers or Pharisees who believes in Him? This foolish crowd follows Him, but they are ignorant of the law. God's curse is on them!" Then Nicodemus, the leader who had met with Jesus earlier, spoke up. "Is it legal to convict a man before He is given a hearing?" he asked. They replied, "Are you from Galilee, too? Search the Scriptures and see for yourself—no prophet ever comes from Galilee!" Then the meeting broke up, and everybody went home

Chapter 8

Jesus returned to the Mount of Olives, but early the next morning He was back again at the Temple. A crowd soon gathered, and He sat down and taught them. As He was speaking, the teachers of religious law and the Pharisees brought a woman who had been caught in the act of adultery. They put her in front of the crowd "Teacher," they said to Jesus, "this woman was caught in the act of adultery. The law of Moses says to stone her. What do You say?" They were trying to trap Him into saying something they could use against Him, but Jesus stooped down and wrote in the dust with His finger. They kept demanding an answer, so He stood up again and said, "All right, but let the one who has never sinned throw the first stone!" Then He stooped down again and wrote in the dust When the accusers heard this, they slipped away one by one, beginning with the oldest, until only Jesus was left in the middle of the crowd with the woman. Then Jesus stood up again and said to the woman, "Where are your accusers? Didn't even one of them condemn you?" "No, Lord," she said And Jesus said, "Neither do I. Go and sin no more." Jesus spoke to the people once more and said, "I am the light of the world. If you follow Me, you won't have to walk in darkness, because you will have the light that leads to life." The Pharisees replied, "You are making those claims about Yourself! Such testimony is not valid." Jesus told them, "These claims are valid even though I make them about Myself. For I know where I came from and where I am going, but you don't know this about Me. You judge Me by human standards, but I do not judge anyone. And if I did, My judgment would be correct in every respect because I am not alone. The Father who sent Me is with Me. Your own law says that if two people agree about something, their witness is accepted as fact. I am one witness, and My Father who sent Me is the other." "Where is Your father?" they asked Jesus answered, "Since you don't know who I am, you don't know who My Father is. If you knew Me, you would also know My Father." Jesus made these statements while He was teaching in the section of the Temple known as the Treasury, but He was not arrested because His time had not yet come Later, Jesus said to them again, "I am going away. You will search for Me but will die in your sin. You cannot come where I am going." The people asked, "Is He planning to commit suicide? What does He mean, 'You cannot come where I am going'?" Jesus continued, "You are from below; I am from above. You belong to this world; I do not. That is why I said that you will die in your sins; for unless you believe that I am who I claim to be, you will die in your sins." "Who are You?" they demanded Jesus replied, "The one I have always claimed to be. I have much to say about you and much to condemn, but I won't. For I say only what I have heard from the one who sent Me, and He is completely truthful." But they still didn't understand that He was talking about His Father. So Jesus said, "When you have lifted up the Son of Man on the cross, then you will understand that I am He. I do nothing on My own but say only what the Father taught Me. And the one who sent Me is with Me—He has not deserted Me. For I always do what pleases Him." Then many who heard Him say these things believed in Him Jesus said to the people who believed in Him, "You are truly My disciples if you remain faithful to My teachings. And you will know the truth, and the truth will set you free." "But we are descendants of Abraham," they said. "We have never been slaves to anyone. What do You mean, 'You will be set free'?" Jesus replied, "I tell you the truth, everyone who sins is a slave of sin. A slave is not a permanent member of the family, but a son is part of the family forever. So if the Son sets you free, you are truly free. Yes, I realize that you are descendants of Abraham. And yet some of you are trying to kill Me because there's no room in your hearts for My message. I am telling you what I saw when I was with My Father. But you are following the advice of your father." "Our father is Abraham!" they declared "No," Jesus replied, "for if you were really the children of Abraham, you would follow his example. Instead, you are trying to kill Me because I told you the truth, which I heard from God. Abraham never did such a thing. No, you are imitating your real father." They replied, "We aren't illegitimate children! God Himself is our true Father." Jesus told them, "If God were your Father, you would love Me, because I have come to you from God. I am not here on My own, but He sent Me. Why can't you understand what I am saying? It's because you can't even hear Me! For you are the children of your father the devil, and you love to do the evil things he does. He was a murderer from the beginning. He has always hated the truth because there is no truth in him. When he lies, it is consistent with his character; for he is a liar and the father of lies. So when I tell the truth, you just naturally don't believe Me! Which of you can truthfully accuse Me of sin? And since I am telling you the truth, why don't you believe Me? Anyone who belongs to God listens gladly to the words of God. But you don't listen because you don't belong to God." The people retorted, "You Samaritan devil! Didn't we say all along that you were possessed by a demon?" "No," Jesus said, "I have no demon in Me. For I honor My Father—and you dishonor Me. And though I have no wish to glorify Myself, God is going to glorify Me. He is the true judge. I tell you the truth, anyone who obeys My teaching will never die!" The people said, "Now we know you are possessed by a demon. Even Abraham and the prophets died, but you say, 'Anyone who obeys My teaching will never die!' Are you greater than our father Abraham? He died, and so did the prophets. Who do you think you are?" Jesus answered, "If I want glory for Myself, it doesn't count. But it is My Father who will glorify Me. You say, 'He is our God,' but you don't even know Him. I know Him. If I said otherwise, I would be as great a liar as you! But I do know Him and obey Him. Your father Abraham rejoiced as he looked forward to My coming. He saw it and was glad." The people said, "You aren't even fifty years old. How can You say You have seen Abraham?" Jesus answered, "I tell you the truth, before Abraham was even born, I Am!" At that point, they picked up stones to throw at Him. But Jesus was hidden from them and left the Temple

Chapter 9

As Jesus was walking along, He saw a man who had been blind from birth. His disciples asked Him, "Rabbi, why was this man born blind? Was it because of his own sins or his parents' sins?" "It was not because of his sins or his parents' sins," Jesus answered. "This happened so the power of God could be seen in him. We must quickly carry out the tasks assigned to us by the one who sent Me. The night is coming, and then no one can work. But while I am here in the world, I am the light of the world." Then He spit on the ground, made mud with the saliva, and spread the mud over the blind man's eyes. He told him, "Go wash yourself in the pool of Siloam" (Siloam means "Sent"). So the man went and washed and came back seeing! His neighbors and others who knew him as a blind beggar asked each other, "Isn't this the man who used to sit and beg?" Some said he was, and others said, "No, he just looks like him!" But the beggar kept saying, "Yes, I am the same one!" They asked, "Who healed you? What happened?" He told them, "The man they call Jesus made mud and spread it over my eyes and told me, 'Go to the pool of Siloam and wash yourself.' So I went and washed, and now I can see!" "Where is He now?" they asked "I don't know," he replied Then they took the man who had been blind to the Pharisees, because it was on the Sabbath that Jesus had made the mud and healed him. The Pharisees asked the man all about it. So he told them, "He put the mud over my eyes, and when I washed it away, I could see!" Some of the Pharisees said, "This man Jesus is not from God, for He is working on the Sabbath." Others said, "But how could an ordinary sinner do such miraculous signs?" So there was a deep division of opinion among them Then the Pharisees again questioned the man who had been blind and demanded, "What's your opinion about this man who healed you?" The man replied, "I think He must be a prophet." The Jewish leaders still refused to believe the man had been blind and could now see, so they called in his parents. They asked them, "Is this your son? Was he born blind? If so, how can he now see?" His parents replied, "We know this is our son and that he was born blind, but we don't know how he can see or who healed him. Ask him. He is old enough to speak for himself." His parents said this because they were afraid of the Jewish leaders, who had announced that anyone saying Jesus was the Messiah would be expelled from the synagogue. That's why they said, "He is old enough. Ask him." So for the second time, they called in the man who had been blind and told him, "God should get the glory for this, because we know this man Jesus is a sinner." "I don't know whether He is a sinner," the man replied. "But I know this: I was blind, and now I can see!" "But what did He do?" they asked. "How did He heal you?" "Look!" the man exclaimed. "I told you once. Didn't you listen? Why do you want to hear it again? Do you want to become His disciples, too?" Then they cursed him and said, "You are His disciple, but we are disciples of Moses! We know God spoke to Moses, but we don't even know where this man comes from." "Why, that's very strange!" the man replied. "He healed my eyes, and yet you don't know where He comes from? We know that God doesn't listen to sinners, but He is ready to hear those who worship Him and do His will. Ever since the world began, no one has been able to open the eyes of someone born blind. If this man were not from God, He couldn't have done it." "You were born a total sinner!" they answered. "Are you trying to teach us?" And they threw him out of the synagogue When Jesus heard what had happened, He found the man and asked, "Do you believe in the Son of Man?" The man answered, "Who is He, sir? I want to believe in Him." "You have seen Him," Jesus said, "and He is speaking to you!" "Yes, Lord, I believe!" the man said. And he worshiped Jesus Then Jesus told him, "I entered this world to render judgment—to give sight to the blind and to show those who think they see that they are blind." Some Pharisees who were standing nearby heard Him and asked, "Are you saying we're blind?" "If you were blind, you wouldn't be guilty," Jesus replied. "But you remain guilty because you claim you can see

Chapter 10

"I tell you the truth, anyone who sneaks over the wall of a sheepfold, rather than going through the gate, must surely be a thief and a robber! But the one who enters through the gate is the shepherd of the sheep. The gatekeeper opens the gate for him, and the sheep recognize his voice and come to him. He calls his own sheep by name and leads them out. After he has gathered his own flock, he walks ahead of them, and they follow him because they know his voice. They won't follow a stranger; they will run from him because they don't know his voice." Those who heard Jesus use this illustration didn't understand what He meant, so He explained it to them: "I tell you the truth, I am the gate for the sheep. All who came before Me were thieves and robbers. But the true sheep did not listen to them. Yes, I am the gate. Those who come in through Me will be saved. They will come and go freely and will find good pastures. The thief's purpose is to steal and kill and destroy. My purpose is to give them a rich and satisfying life "I am the good shepherd. The good shepherd sacrifices His life for the sheep. A hired hand will run when he sees a wolf coming. He will abandon the sheep because they don't belong to him, and he isn't their shepherd. And so the wolf attacks them and scatters the flock. The hired hand runs away because he's working only for the money and doesn't really care about the sheep "I am the good shepherd; I know My own sheep, and they know Me, just as My Father knows Me and I know the Father. So I sacrifice My life

for the sheep. I have other sheep, too, that are not in this sheepfold. I must bring them also. They will listen to My voice, and there will be one flock with one shepherd "The Father loves Me because I sacrifice My life so I may take it back again. No one can take My life from Me. I sacrifice it voluntarily. For I have the authority to lay it down when I want to and also to take it up again. For this is what My Father has commanded." When He said these things, the people were again divided in their opinions about Him. Some said, "He's demon-possessed and out of His mind. Why listen to a man like that?" Others said, "This doesn't sound like a man possessed by a demon! Can a demon open the eyes of the blind?" It was now winter, and Jesus was in Jerusalem at the time of Hanukkah, the Festival of Dedication. He was in the Temple, walking through the section known as Solomon's Colonnade. The people surrounded Him and asked, "How long are You going to keep us in suspense? If You are the Messiah, tell us plainly." Jesus replied, "I have already told you, and you don't believe Me. The proof is the work I do in My Father's name. But you don't believe Me because you are not My sheep. My sheep listen to My voice; I know them, and they follow Me. I give them eternal life, and they will never perish. No one can snatch them away from Me, for My Father has given them to Me, and He is more powerful than anyone else. No one can snatch them from the Father's hand. The Father and I are one." Once again the people picked up stones to kill Him. Jesus said, "At My Father's direction I have done many good works. For which one are you going to stone Me?" They replied, "We're stoning You not for any good work, but for blasphemy! You, a mere man, claim to be God." Jesus replied, "It is written in your own Scriptures that God said to certain leaders of the people, 'I say, you are gods!' And you know that the Scriptures cannot be altered. So if those people who received God's message were called 'gods,' why do you call it blasphemy when I say, 'I am the Son of God'? After all, the Father set Me apart and sent Me into the world. Don't believe Me unless I carry out My Father's work. But if I do His work, believe in the evidence of the miraculous works I have done, even if you don't believe Me. Then you will know and understand that the Father is in Me, and I am in the Father." Once again they tried to arrest Him, but He got away and left them. He went beyond the Jordan River near the place where John was first baptizing and stayed there awhile. And many followed Him. "John didn't perform miraculous signs," they remarked to one another, "but everything he said about this man has come true." And many who were there believed in Jesus

Chapter 11

A man named Lazarus from Bethany, the village of Mary and her sister Martha, was sick. (Mary was the one who anointed the Lord with oil and wiped His feet with her hair, and it was her brother Lazarus who was sick.) So the sisters sent word to Jesus, saying, "Lord, the one you love is sick." When Jesus heard this, He said, "This sickness will not end in death. No, it is for God's glory so that God's Son may be glorified through it." Now Jesus loved Martha and her sister and Lazarus. So when He heard that Lazarus was sick, He stayed where He was for two more days. Then He said to His disciples, "Let us go back to Judea." But Rabbi," they said, "a short while ago the Jews there tried to stone you, and yet you are going back?" Jesus answered, "Are there not twelve hours of daylight? Anyone who walks in the daytime will not stumble, for they see by this world's light. It is when a person walks at night that they stumble, for they have no light." After He had said this, He went on to tell them, "Our friend Lazarus has fallen asleep; but I am going there to wake him up." His disciples replied, "Lord, if he sleeps, he will get better." Jesus had been speaking of his death, but His disciples thought He meant natural sleep. So then He told them plainly, "Lazarus is dead, and for your sake, I am glad I was not there, so that you may believe. But let us go to him." Then Thomas (also known as Didymus) said to the rest of the disciples, "Let us also go, that we may die with Him." On His arrival, Jesus found that Lazarus had already been in the tomb for four days. (Now Bethany was less than two miles from Jerusalem, and many Jews had come to Martha and Mary to comfort them in the loss of their brother.) When Martha heard that Jesus was coming, she went out to meet Him, but Mary stayed at home. "Lord," Martha said to Jesus, "if you had been here, my brother would not have died. But I know that even now God will give you whatever you ask." Jesus said to her, "Your brother will rise again." Martha answered, "I know he will rise again in the resurrection at the last day." Jesus said to her, "I am the resurrection and the life. The one who believes in Me will live, even though they die; and whoever lives by believing in Me will never die. Do you believe this?" "Yes, Lord," she replied, "I believe that you are the Messiah, the Son of God, who is to come into the world." After she had said this, she went back and called her sister Mary aside. "The Teacher is here," she said, "and is asking for you." When Mary heard this, she got up quickly and went to Him. Now Jesus had not yet entered the village but was still at the place where Martha had met Him. When the Jews who had been with Mary in the house, comforting her, noticed how quickly she got up and went out, they followed her, supposing she was going to the tomb to mourn there When Mary reached the place where Jesus was and saw Him, she fell at His feet and said, "Lord, if you had been here, my brother would not have died." When Jesus saw her weeping, and the Jews who had come along with her also weeping, He was deeply moved in spirit and troubled. "Where have you laid him?" He asked "Come and see, Lord," they replied Jesus wept Then the Jews said, "See how He loved him!" But some of them said, "Could not He who opened the eyes of the blind man have kept this man from dying?" Jesus, once more deeply moved, came to the tomb. It was a cave with a stone laid across the entrance. "Take away the stone," He said "But, Lord," said Martha, the sister of the dead man, "by this time there is a bad odor, for he has been there four days." Then Jesus said, "Did I not tell you that if you believe, you will see the glory of God?" So they took away the stone. Then Jesus looked up and said, "Father, I thank You that You have heard Me. I knew that You always hear Me, but I said this for the benefit of the people standing here, that they may believe that You sent Me." When He had said this, Jesus called in a loud voice, "Lazarus, come out!" The dead man came out, his hands and feet wrapped with strips of linen, and a cloth around his face Jesus said to them, "Take off the grave clothes and let him go." Therefore, many of the Jews who had come to visit Mary, and had seen what Jesus did, believed in Him. But some of them went to the Pharisees and told them what Jesus had done. Then the chief priests and the Pharisees called a meeting of the Sanhedrin. "What are we accomplishing?" they asked. "Here is this man performing many signs. If we let Him go on like this, everyone will believe in Him, and then the Romans will come and take away both our temple and our nation." Then one of them, named Caiaphas, who was high priest that year, spoke up, "You know nothing at all! You do not realize that it is better for you that one man die for the people than that the whole nation perish." He did not say this on his own, but as high priest that year he prophesied that Jesus would die for the Jewish nation, and not only for that nation but also for the scattered children of God, to bring them together and make them one. So from that day on they plotted to take His life Therefore, Jesus no longer moved about publicly among the people of Judea. Instead, He withdrew to a region near the wilderness, to a village called Ephraim, where He stayed with His disciples. When it was almost time for the Jewish Passover, many went up from the country to Jerusalem for their ceremonial cleansing before the Passover. They kept looking for Jesus, and as they stood in the temple courts, they asked one another, "What do you think? Isn't He coming to the festival at all?" But the chief priests and the Pharisees had given orders that anyone who found out where Jesus was should report it so that they might arrest Him

Chapter 12

Six days before the Passover, Jesus came to Bethany, where Lazarus lived, whom Jesus had raised from the dead. Here a dinner was given in Jesus' honor. Martha served, while Lazarus was among those reclining at the table with Him. Then Mary took about a pint of pure nard, an expensive perfume; she poured it on Jesus' feet and wiped His feet with her hair. And the house was filled with the fragrance of the perfume But one of His disciples, Judas Iscariot, who was later to betray Him, objected, "Why wasn't this perfume sold and the money given to the poor? It was worth a year's wages." He did not say this because he cared about the poor but because he was a thief; as keeper of the money bag, he used to help himself to what was put into it "Leave her alone," Jesus replied. "It was intended that she should save this perfume for the day of My burial. You will always have the poor among you, but you will not always have Me." Meanwhile, a large crowd of Jews found out that Jesus was there and came, not only because of Him but also to see Lazarus, whom He had raised from the dead. So the chief priests made plans to kill Lazarus as well, for on account of him many of the Jews were going over to Jesus and believing in Him The next day, the great crowd that had come for the festival heard that Jesus was on His way to Jerusalem. They took palm branches and went out to meet Him, shouting, "Hosanna! Blessed is He who comes in the name of the Lord! Blessed is the King of Israel!" Jesus found a young donkey and sat on it, as it is written: "Do not be afraid, Daughter Zion; see, your king is coming, seated on a donkey's colt." At first, His disciples did not understand all this. Only after Jesus was glorified did they realize that these things had been written about Him and that these things had been done to Him Now the crowd that was with Him when He called Lazarus from the tomb and raised him from the dead continued to spread the word. Many people, because they had heard that He had performed this sign, went out to meet Him. So the Pharisees said to one another, "See, this is getting us nowhere. Look how the whole world has gone after Him!" Now there were some Greeks among those who went up to worship at the festival. They came to Philip, who was from Bethsaida in Galilee, with a request. "Sir," they said, "we would like to see Jesus." Philip went to tell Andrew; Andrew and Philip in turn told Jesus. Jesus replied, "The hour has come for the Son of Man to be glorified. Very truly I tell you, unless a kernel of wheat falls to the ground and dies, it remains only a single seed. But if it dies, it produces many seeds. Anyone who loves their life will lose it, while anyone who hates their life in this world will keep it for eternal life. Whoever serves Me must follow Me; and where I am, My servant also will be. My Father will honor the one who serves Me "Now My soul is troubled, and what shall I say? 'Father, save Me from this hour'? No, it was for this very reason I came to this hour. Father, glorify Your name!" Then a voice came from heaven, "I have glorified it, and will glorify it again." The crowd that was there and heard it said it had thundered; others said an angel had spoken to Him. Jesus said, "This voice was for your benefit, not Mine. Now is the time for judgment on this world; now the prince of this world will be driven out. And I, when I am lifted up from the earth, will draw all people to Myself." He said this to show the kind of death He was going to die The crowd spoke up, "We have heard from the Law that the Messiah will remain forever, so how can You say, 'The Son of Man must be lifted up'? Who is this 'Son of Man'?" Then Jesus told them, "You are going to have the light just a little while longer. Walk while you have the light, before darkness overtakes you. Whoever walks in the dark does not know where they are going. Believe in the light while you have the light, so that you may become children of light." When He had finished speaking, Jesus left and hid Himself from them Even after Jesus had performed so many signs in their presence, they still would not believe in Him. This was to fulfill the word of Isaiah the prophet: "Lord, who has believed our message and to whom has the arm of the Lord been revealed?" For this reason they could not believe, because, as Isaiah says elsewhere: "He has blinded their eyes and hardened their hearts, so they can neither see with their eyes, nor understand with their hearts, nor turn—and I would heal them." Isaiah said this because he saw Jesus' glory and spoke about Him Yet at the same time, many even among the leaders believed in Him. But because of the Pharisees, they would not openly acknowledge their faith for fear they would be put out of the synagogue; for they loved human praise more than praise from God Then Jesus cried out, "Whoever believes in Me does not believe in Me only, but in the One who sent Me. The one who looks at Me is seeing the One who sent Me. I have come into the world as a light, so that no one who believes in Me should stay in darkness "If anyone hears My words but does not keep them, I do not judge that person. For I did not come to judge the world, but to save the world. There is a judge for the one who rejects Me and does not accept My words; the very words I have spoken will condemn them at the last day. For I did not speak on My own, but the Father who sent Me commanded Me to say all that I have spoken. I know that His command leads to eternal life. So whatever I say is just what the Father has told Me to say."

Chapter 13

It was just before the Passover Festival. Jesus knew that the hour had come for Him to leave this world and go to the Father. Having loved His own who were in the world, He loved them to the end. The evening meal was in progress, and the devil had already prompted Judas, the son of Simon Iscariot, to betray Jesus. Jesus knew that the Father had put all things under His power and that He had come from God and was returning to God; so He got up from the meal, took off His outer clothing, and wrapped a towel around His waist. After that, He poured water into a basin and began to wash His disciples' feet, drying them with the towel that was wrapped around Him He came to Simon Peter, who said to Him, "Lord, are you going to wash my feet?" Jesus replied, "You do not realize now what I am doing, but later you will understand." "No," said Peter, "you shall never wash my feet." Jesus answered, "Unless I wash you, you have no part with Me." "Then, Lord," Simon Peter replied, "not just my feet but my hands and my head

as well!" Jesus answered, "Those who have had a bath need only to wash their feet; their whole body is clean. And you are clean, though not every one of you." For He knew who was going to betray Him, and that was why He said not everyone was clean When He had finished washing their feet, He put on His clothes and returned to His place. "Do you understand what I have done for you?" He asked them. "You call Me 'Teacher' and 'Lord,' and rightly so, for that is what I am. Now that I, your Lord and Teacher, have washed your feet, you also should wash one another's feet. I have set you an example that you should do as I have done for you. Very truly I tell you, no servant is greater than his master, nor is a messenger greater than the one who sent him. Now that you know these things, you will be blessed if you do them "I am not referring to all of you; I know those I have chosen. But this is to fulfill this passage of Scripture: 'He who shared My bread has turned against Me.' "I am telling you now before it happens, so that when it does happen you will believe that I am who I am. Very truly I tell you, whoever accepts anyone I send accepts Me; and whoever accepts Me accepts the one who sent Me." After He had said this, Jesus was troubled in spirit and testified, "Very truly I tell you, one of you is going to betray Me." His disciples stared at one another, at a loss to know which of them He meant. One of them, the disciple whom Jesus loved, was reclining next to Him. Simon Peter motioned to this disciple and said, "Ask Him which one He means." Leaning back against Jesus, he asked Him, "Lord, who is it?" Jesus answered, "It is the one to whom I will give this piece of bread when I have dipped it in the dish." Then, dipping the piece of bread, He gave it to Judas, the son of Simon Iscariot. As soon as Judas took the bread, Satan entered into him So Jesus told him, "What you are about to do, do quickly." But no one at the meal understood why Jesus said this to him. Since Judas had charge of the money, some thought Jesus was telling him to buy what was needed for the festival, or to give something to the poor. As soon as Judas had taken the bread, he went out. And it was night When he was gone, Jesus said, "Now the Son of Man is glorified and God is glorified in Him. If God is glorified in Him, God will glorify the Son in Himself, and will glorify Him at once "My children, I will be with you only a little longer. You will look for Me, and just as I told the Jews, so I tell you now: Where I am going, you cannot come "A new command I give you: Love one another. As I have loved you, so you must love one another. By this everyone will know that you are My disciples, if you love one another." Simon Peter asked Him, "Lord, where are you going?" Jesus replied, "Where I am going, you cannot follow now, but you will follow later." Peter asked, "Lord, why can't I follow you now? I will lay down my life for you." Then Jesus answered, "Will you really lay down your life for Me? Very truly I tell you, before the rooster crows, you will disown Me three times!"

Chapter 14

"Do not let your hearts be troubled. You believe in God; believe also in Me. My Father's house has many rooms; if that were not so, would I have told you that I am going there to prepare a place for you? And if I go and prepare a place for you, I will come back and take you to be with Me that you also may be where I am. You know the way to the place where I am going." Thomas said to Him, "Lord, we don't know where You are going, so how can we know the way?" Jesus answered, "I am the way and the truth and the life. No one comes to the Father except through Me. If you really know Me, you will know My Father as well. From now on, you do know Him and have seen Him." Philip said, "Lord, show us the Father and that will be enough for us." Jesus answered: "Don't you know Me, Philip, even after I have been among you such a long time? Anyone who has seen Me has seen the Father. How can you say, 'Show us the Father'? Don't you believe that I am in the Father, and that the Father is in Me? The words I say to you I do not speak on My own authority. Rather, it is the Father, living in Me, who is doing His work. Believe Me when I say that I am in the Father and the Father is in Me; or at least believe on the evidence of the works themselves. Very truly I tell you, whoever believes in Me will do the works I have been doing, and they will do even greater things than these, because I am going to the Father. And I will do whatever you ask in My name, so that the Father may be glorified in the Son. You may ask Me for anything in My name, and I will do it "If you love Me, keep My commands. And I will ask the Father, and He will give you another advocate to help you and be with you forever—the Spirit of truth. The world cannot accept Him, because it neither sees Him nor knows Him. But you know Him, for He lives with you and will be in you. I will not leave you as orphans; I will come to you. Before long, the world will not see Me anymore, but you will see Me. Because I live, you also will live. On that day you will realize that I am in My Father, and you are in Me, and I am in you. Whoever has My commands and keeps them is the one who loves Me. The one who loves Me will be loved by My Father, and I too will love them and show Myself to them." Then Judas (not Judas Iscariot) said, "But, Lord, why do you intend to show yourself to us and not to the world?" Jesus replied, "Anyone who loves Me will obey My teaching. My Father will love them, and We will come to them and make Our home with them. Anyone who does not love Me will not obey My teaching. These words you hear are not My own; they belong to the Father who sent Me "All this I have spoken while still with you. But the Advocate, the Holy Spirit, whom the Father will send in My name, will teach you all things and will remind you of everything I have said to you. Peace I leave with you; My peace I give you. I do not give to you as the world gives. Do not let your hearts be troubled and do not be afraid "You heard Me say, 'I am going away and I am coming back to you.' If you loved Me, you would be glad that I am going to the Father, for the Father is greater than I. I have told you now before it happens, so that when it does happen you will believe. I will not say much more to you, for the prince of this world is coming. He has no hold over Me, but He comes so that the world may learn that I love the Father and do exactly what My Father has commanded Me. Come now; let us leave

Chapter 15

"I am the true vine, and My Father is the gardener. He cuts off every branch in Me that bears no fruit, while every branch that does bear fruit He prunes so that it will be even more fruitful. You are already clean because of the word I have spoken to you. Remain in Me, as I also remain in you. No branch can bear fruit by itself; it must remain in the vine. Neither can you bear fruit unless you remain in Me "I am the vine; you are the branches. If you remain in Me and I in you, you will bear much fruit; apart from Me you can do nothing. If you do not remain in Me, you are like a branch that is thrown away and withers; such branches are picked up, thrown into the fire, and burned. If you remain in Me and My words remain in you, ask whatever you wish, and it will be done for you. This is to My Father's glory, that you bear much fruit, showing yourselves to be My disciples "As the Father has loved Me, so have I loved you. Now remain in My love. If you keep My commands, you will remain in My love, just as I have kept My Father's commands and remain in His love. I have told you this so that My joy may be in you and that your joy may be complete. My command is this: Love each other as I have loved you. Greater love has no one than this: to lay down one's life for one's friends. You are My friends if you do what I command. I no longer call you servants, because a servant does not know his master's business. Instead, I have called you friends, for everything that I learned from My Father I have made known to you. You did not choose Me, but I chose you and appointed you so that you might go and bear fruit—fruit that will last—and so that whatever you ask in My name the Father will give you. This is My command: Love each other "If the world hates you, keep in mind that it hated Me first. If you belonged to the world, it would love you as its own. As it is, you do not belong to the world, but I have chosen you out of the world. That is why the world hates you. Remember what I told you: 'A servant is not greater than his master.' If they persecuted Me, they will persecute you also. If they obeyed My teaching, they will obey yours also. They will treat you this way because of My name, for they do not know the One who sent Me. If I had not come and spoken to them, they would not be guilty of sin; but now they have no excuse for their sin. Whoever hates Me hates My Father as well. If I had not done among them the works no one else did, they would not be guilty of sin. As it is, they have seen, and yet they have hated both Me and My Father. But this is to fulfill what is written in their Law: 'They hated Me without reason.' "When the Advocate comes, whom I will send to you from the Father—the Spirit of truth who goes out from the Father—He will testify about Me. And you also must testify, for you have been with Me from the beginning

Chapter 16

"I have told you these things so that you will not fall away. They will put you out of the synagogue; in fact, the time is coming when anyone who kills you will think they are offering a service to God. They will do such things because they have not known the Father or Me. I have told you this so that when their time comes, you will remember that I warned you about them. I did not tell you this from the beginning because I was with you, but now I am going to Him who sent Me. None of you asks Me, 'Where are You going?' Rather, you are filled with grief because I have said these things. But very truly I tell you, it is for your good that I am going away. Unless I go away, the Advocate will not come to you; but if I go, I will send Him to you. When He comes, He will prove the world to be in the wrong about sin and righteousness and judgment: about sin, because people do not believe in Me; about righteousness, because I am going to the Father, where you can see Me no longer; and about judgment, because the prince of this world now stands condemned "I have much more to say to you, more than you can now bear. But when He, the Spirit of truth, comes, He will guide you into all the truth. He will not speak on His own; He will speak only what He hears, and He will tell you what is yet to come. He will glorify Me because it is from Me that He will receive what He will make known to you. All that belongs to the Father is Mine. That is why I said the Spirit will receive from Me what He will make known to you "Jesus went on to say, 'In a little while you will see Me no more, and then after a little while you will see Me.' At this, some of His disciples said to one another, 'What does He mean by saying, "In a little while you will see Me no more, and then after a little while you will see Me," and "Because I am going to the Father"? They kept asking, 'What does He mean by "a little while"? We don't understand what He is saying.' Jesus saw that they wanted to ask Him about this, so He said to them, 'Are you asking one another what I meant when I said, "In a little while you will see Me no more, and then after a little while you will see Me"? Very truly I tell you, you will weep and mourn while the world rejoices. You will grieve, but your grief will turn to joy. A woman giving birth to a child has pain because her time has come; but when her baby is born, she forgets the anguish because of her joy that a child is born into the world. So with you: Now is your time of grief, but I will see you again and you will rejoice, and no one will take away your joy. In that day you will no longer ask Me anything. Very truly I tell you, My Father will give you whatever you ask in My name. Until now you have not asked for anything in My name. Ask and you will receive, and your joy will be complete Though I have been speaking figuratively, a time is coming when I will no longer use this kind of language but will tell you plainly about My Father. In that day you will ask in My name. I am not saying that I will ask the Father on your behalf. No, the Father Himself loves you because you have loved Me and have believed that I came from God. I came from the Father and entered the world; now I am leaving the world and going back to the Father.' Then Jesus' disciples said, 'Now You are speaking clearly and without figures of speech. Now we can see that You know all things and that You do not even need to have anyone ask You questions. This makes us believe that You came from God.' 'Do you now believe?' Jesus replied. 'A time is coming and in fact has come when you will be scattered, each to your own home. You will leave Me all alone. Yet I am not alone, for My Father is with Me. I have told you these things so that in Me you may have peace. In this world, you will have trouble. But take heart! I have overcome the world.'"

Chapter 17

After Jesus said this, He looked toward heaven and prayed: "Father, the hour has come. Glorify Your Son, that Your Son may glorify You. For You granted Him authority over all people that He might give eternal life to all those You have given Him. Now this is eternal life: that they know You, the only true God, and Jesus Christ, whom You have sent. I have brought You glory on earth by finishing the work You gave Me to do. And now, Father, glorify Me in Your presence with the glory I had with You before the world began "I have revealed You to those whom You gave Me out of the world. They were Yours; You gave them to Me and they have obeyed Your word. Now they know that everything You have given Me comes from You. For I gave them the words You gave Me and they accepted them. They knew with certainty that I came from You, and they believed that You sent Me. I pray for them. I am not praying for the world, but for those You have given Me, for they are Yours. All I have is Yours, and all You have is Mine. And glory has come to Me through them. I will remain in the world no longer, but they are still in the world, and I am coming to You. Holy Father, protect them by the power of Your name, the name You gave Me, so that they may be one as We are one. While I was with them, I protected them and kept them safe by that name You gave Me. None has been lost except the one doomed to destruction so that Scripture would be fulfilled "I am coming to You now, but I say these things while I am still in the world so that they may have the full measure of My joy within them. I have given them Your word and the world has hated them, for they are not of the world any more than I am of the world. My prayer is not that You take them out of the world but that You protect them from the evil one. They are not of the world, even as I am not of it. Sanctify them by the truth; Your word is truth. As You sent Me into the world, I have sent them into the world. For them, I sanctify Myself, that they too may be truly sanctified "My prayer is not for them alone. I pray also for those

who will believe in Me through their message, that all of them may be one, Father, just as You are in Me and I am in You. May they also be in Us so that the world may believe that You have sent Me. I have given them the glory that You gave Me, that they may be one as We are one—I in them and You in Me—so that they may be brought to complete unity. Then the world will know that You sent Me and have loved them even as You have loved Me "Father, I want those You have given Me to be with Me where I am, and to see My glory, the glory You have given Me because You loved Me before the creation of the world. Righteous Father, though the world does not know You, I know You, and they know that You have sent Me. I have made You known to them and will continue to make You known in order that the love You have for Me may be in them and that I Myself may be in them."

Chapter 18

When Jesus had finished praying, He left with His disciples and crossed the Kidron Valley. On the other side, there was a garden, and He and His disciples went into it. Now Judas, who betrayed Him, knew the place because Jesus had often met there with His disciples. So Judas came to the garden, guiding a detachment of soldiers and some officials from the chief priests and the Pharisees. They were carrying torches, lanterns, and weapons Jesus, knowing all that was going to happen to Him, went out and asked them, "Who is it you want?" "Jesus of Nazareth," they replied "I am He," Jesus said. (And Judas the traitor was standing there with them.) When Jesus said, "I am He," they drew back and fell to the ground Again He asked them, "Who is it you want?" "Jesus of Nazareth," they said Jesus answered, "I told you that I am He. If you are looking for Me, then let these men go." This happened so that the words He had spoken would be fulfilled: "I have not lost one of those You gave Me." Then Simon Peter, who had a sword, drew it and struck the high priest's servant, cutting off his right ear. (The servant's name was Malchus.) Jesus commanded Peter, "Put your sword away! Shall I not drink the cup the Father has given Me?" Then the detachment of soldiers with its commander and the Jewish officials arrested Jesus. They bound Him and brought Him first to Annas, who was the father-in-law of Caiaphas, the high priest that year. Caiaphas was the one who had advised the Jewish leaders that it would be good if one man died for the people Simon Peter and another disciple were following Jesus. Because this disciple was known to the high priest, he went with Jesus into the high priest's courtyard, but Peter had to wait outside at the door. The other disciple, who was known to the high priest, came back, spoke to the servant girl on duty there, and brought Peter in "You aren't one of this man's disciples too, are you?" she asked Peter He replied, "I am not." It was cold, and the servants and officials stood around a fire they had made to keep warm. Peter also was standing with them, warming himself Meanwhile, the high priest questioned Jesus about His disciples and His teaching "I have spoken openly to the world," Jesus replied. "I always taught in synagogues or at the temple, where all the Jews come together. I said nothing in secret. Why question Me? Ask those who heard Me. Surely they know what I said." When Jesus said this, one of the officials nearby slapped Him in the face. "Is this the way you answer the high priest?" he demanded "If I said something wrong," Jesus replied, "testify as to what is wrong. But if I spoke the truth, why did you strike Me?" Then Annas sent Him bound to Caiaphas, the high priest Meanwhile, Simon Peter was still standing there warming himself. So they asked him, "You aren't one of His disciples too, are you?" He denied it, saying, "I am not." One of the high priest's servants, a relative of the man whose ear Peter had cut off, challenged him, "Didn't I see you with Him in the garden?" Again Peter denied it, and at that moment a rooster began to crow Then the Jewish leaders took Jesus from Caiaphas to the palace of the Roman governor. By now it was early morning, and to avoid ceremonial uncleanness they did not enter the palace because they wanted to be able to eat the Passover. So Pilate came out to them and asked, "What charges are you bringing against this man?" "If He were not a criminal," they replied, "we would not have handed Him over to you." Pilate said, "Take Him yourselves and judge Him by your own law." "But we have no right to execute anyone," they objected. This took place to fulfill what Jesus had said about the kind of death He was going to die Pilate then went back inside the palace, summoned Jesus, and asked Him, "Are You the king of the Jews?" "Is that your own idea," Jesus asked, "or did others talk to you about Me?" "Am I a Jew?" Pilate replied. "Your own people and chief priests handed You over to me. What is it You have done?" Jesus said, "My kingdom is not of this world. If it were, My servants would fight to prevent My arrest by the Jewish leaders. But now My kingdom is from another place." "You are a king, then!" said Pilate Jesus answered, "You say that I am a king. In fact, the reason I was born and came into the world is to testify to the truth. Everyone on the side of truth listens to Me." "What is truth?" retorted Pilate. With this, he went out again to the Jews gathered there and said, "I find no basis for a charge against Him. But it is your custom for me to release to you one prisoner at the time of the Passover. Do you want me to release 'the king of the Jews'?" They shouted back, "No, not Him! Give us Barabbas!" Now Barabbas had taken part in an uprising

Chapter 19

Then Pilate took Jesus and had Him flogged. The soldiers twisted together a crown of thorns and put it on His head. They clothed Him in a purple robe and went up to Him again and again, saying, "Hail, king of the Jews!" And they slapped Him in the face Once more Pilate came out and said to the Jews gathered there, "Look, I am bringing Him out to you to let you know that I find no basis for a charge against Him." When Jesus came out wearing the crown of thorns and the purple robe, Pilate said to them, "Here is the man!" As soon as the chief priests and their officials saw Him, they shouted, "Crucify! Crucify!" But Pilate answered, "You take Him and crucify Him. As for me, I find no basis for a charge against Him." The Jewish leaders insisted, "We have a law, and according to that law He must die because He claimed to be the Son of God." When Pilate heard this, he was even more afraid, and he went back inside the palace. "Where do you come from?" he asked Jesus, but Jesus gave him no answer. "Do you refuse to speak to me?" Pilate said. "Don't you realize I have power either to free You or to crucify You?" Jesus answered, "You would have no power over Me if it were not given to you from above. Therefore the one who handed Me over to you is guilty of a greater sin." From then on, Pilate tried to set Jesus free, but the Jewish leaders kept shouting, "If you let this man go, you are no friend of Caesar. Anyone who claims to be a king opposes Caesar." When Pilate heard this, he brought Jesus out and sat down on the judge's seat at a place known as the Stone Pavement (which in Aramaic is Gabbatha). It was the day of Preparation of the Passover; it was about noon "Here is your king," Pilate said to the Jews But they shouted, "Take Him away! Take Him away! Crucify Him!" "Shall I crucify your king?" Pilate asked "We have no king but Caesar," the chief priests answered Finally, Pilate

handed Him over to them to be crucified So the soldiers took charge of Jesus. Carrying His own cross, He went out to the place of the Skull (which in Aramaic is called Golgotha). There they crucified Him, and with Him two others—one on each side and Jesus in the middle. Pilate had a notice prepared and fastened to the cross. It read: JESUS OF NAZARETH, THE KING OF THE JEWS. Many of the Jews read this sign, for the place where Jesus was crucified was near the city, and the sign was written in Aramaic, Latin, and Greek. The chief priests of the Jews protested to Pilate, "Do not write 'The King of the Jews,' but that this man claimed to be king of the Jews." Pilate answered, "What I have written, I have written." When the soldiers crucified Jesus, they took His clothes, dividing them into four shares, one for each of them, with the undergarment remaining. This garment was seamless, woven in one piece from top to bottom "Let's not tear it," they said to one another. "Let's decide by lot who will get it." This happened that the scripture might be fulfilled that said, "They divided My clothes among them and cast lots for My garment." So this is what the soldiers did Near the cross of Jesus stood His mother, His mother's sister, Mary the wife of Clopas, and Mary Magdalene. When Jesus saw His mother there, and the disciple whom He loved standing nearby, He said to her, "Woman, here is your son," and to the disciple, "Here is your mother." From that time on, this disciple took her into his home Later, knowing that everything had now been finished, and so that Scripture would be fulfilled, Jesus said, "I am thirsty." A jar of wine vinegar was there, so they soaked a sponge in it, put the sponge on a stalk of the hyssop plant, and lifted it to Jesus' lips. When He had received the drink, Jesus said, "It is finished." With that, He bowed His head and gave up His spirit Now it was the day of Preparation, and the next day was to be a special Sabbath. Because the Jewish leaders did not want the bodies left on the crosses during the Sabbath, they asked Pilate to have the legs broken and the bodies taken down. The soldiers therefore came and broke the legs of the first man who had been crucified with Jesus, and then those of the other. But when they came to Jesus and found that He was already dead, they did not break His legs. Instead, one of the soldiers pierced Jesus' side with a spear, bringing a sudden flow of blood and water. The man who saw it has given testimony, and his testimony is true. He knows that he tells the truth, and he testifies so that you also may believe. These things happened so that the scripture would be fulfilled: "Not one of His bones will be broken," and, as another scripture says, "They will look on the one they have pierced." Later, Joseph of Arimathea asked Pilate for the body of Jesus. Now Joseph was a disciple of Jesus, but secretly because he feared the Jewish leaders. With Pilate's permission, he came and took the body away. He was accompanied by Nicodemus, the man who earlier had visited Jesus at night. Nicodemus brought a mixture of myrrh and aloes, about seventy-five pounds. Taking Jesus' body, the two of them wrapped it, with the spices, in strips of linen. This was in accordance with Jewish burial customs. At the place where Jesus was crucified, there was a garden, and in the garden a new tomb, in which no one had ever been laid. Because it was the Jewish day of Preparation and since the tomb was nearby, they laid Jesus there

Chapter 20

Early on the first day of the week, while it was still dark, Mary Magdalene went to the tomb and saw that the stone had been removed from the entrance. So she came running to Simon Peter and the other disciple, the one Jesus loved, and said, "They have taken the Lord out of the tomb, and we don't know where they have put Him!" So Peter and the other disciple started for the tomb. Both were running, but the other disciple outran Peter and reached the tomb first. He bent over and looked in at the strips of linen lying there but did not go in. Then Simon Peter came along behind him and went straight into the tomb. He saw the strips of linen lying there, as well as the cloth that had been wrapped around Jesus' head. The cloth was still lying in its place, separate from the linen. Finally, the other disciple, who had reached the tomb first, also went inside. He saw and believed. (They still did not understand from Scripture that Jesus had to rise from the dead.) Then the disciples went back to where they were staying Now Mary stood outside the tomb crying. As she wept, she bent over to look into the tomb and saw two angels in white, seated where Jesus' body had been, one at the head and the other at the foot. They asked her, "Woman, why are you crying?" "They have taken my Lord away," she said, "and I don't know where they have put Him." At this, she turned around and saw Jesus standing there, but she did not realize that it was Jesus He asked her, "Woman, why are you crying? Who is it you are looking for?" Thinking He was the gardener, she said, "Sir, if you have carried Him away, tell me where you have put Him, and I will get Him." Jesus said to her, "Mary." She turned toward Him and cried out in Aramaic, "Rabboni!" (which means "Teacher") Jesus said, "Do not hold on to Me, for I have not yet ascended to the Father. Go instead to My brothers and tell them, 'I am ascending to My Father and your Father, to My God and your God.'" Mary Magdalene went to the disciples with the news: "I have seen the Lord!" And she told them that He had said these things to her On the evening of that first day of the week, when the disciples were together, with the doors locked for fear of the Jewish leaders, Jesus came and stood among them and said, "Peace be with you!" After He said this, He showed them His hands and side. The disciples were overjoyed when they saw the Lord Again Jesus said, "Peace be with you! As the Father has sent Me, I am sending you." And with that, He breathed on them and said, "Receive the Holy Spirit. If you forgive anyone's sins, their sins are forgiven; if you do not forgive them, they are not forgiven." Now Thomas (also known as Didymus), one of the Twelve, was not with the disciples when Jesus came. So the other disciples told him, "We have seen the Lord!" But he said to them, "Unless I see the nail marks in His hands and put my finger where the nails were, and put my hand into His side, I will not believe." A week later His disciples were in the house again, and Thomas was with them. Though the doors were locked, Jesus came and stood among them and said, "Peace be with you!" Then He said to Thomas, "Put your finger here; see My hands. Reach out your hand and put it into My side. Stop doubting and believe." Thomas said to Him, "My Lord and my God!" Then Jesus told him, "Because you have seen Me, you have believed; blessed are those who have not seen and yet have believed." Jesus performed many other signs in the presence of His disciples, which are not recorded in this book. But these are written that you may believe that Jesus is the Messiah, the Son of God, and that by believing you may have life in His name

Chapter 21

After these things, Jesus presented Himself again to His disciples by the Sea of Tiberias. This is how He presented Himself: there were together Simon Peter, Thomas called Didymus, Nathanael of Cana in Galilee, the sons of Zebedee, and two other disciples. Simon Peter said to them, "I am going fishing." They replied, "We will also go with you." They went out and immediately got into a boat, but that night they caught nothing When morning came, Jesus stood on the shore, but the disciples did not recognize that it was Jesus. Jesus called out to them, "Friends, do you have any fish?" They answered, "No." Then He said to them, "Cast the net on the right side of the boat and you will find some." So they cast it, and now they were unable to haul it in because of the large number of fish The disciple whom Jesus loved said to Peter, "It is the Lord!" When Simon Peter heard that it was the Lord, he put on his outer garment (for he had taken it off) and jumped into the sea. The other disciples followed in the boat, dragging the net full of fish, for they were not far from land, only about a hundred yards. When they landed, they saw a fire of burning coals there with fish on it and some bread. Jesus said to them, "Bring some of the fish you have just caught." Simon Peter climbed aboard and dragged the net ashore. It was full of large fish, 153 in total, but even with so many the net was not torn. Jesus said to them, "Come and have breakfast." None of the disciples dared ask Him, "Who are you?" They knew it was the Lord. Jesus came, took the bread, and gave it to them, and did the same with the fish. This was now the third time Jesus appeared to His disciples after He was raised from the dead When they had finished eating, Jesus said to Simon Peter, "Simon, son of John, do you love Me more than these?" He replied, "Yes, Lord, you know that I love You." Jesus said, "Feed My lambs." Again Jesus said, "Simon, son of John, do you love Me?" He answered, "Yes, Lord, you know that I love You." Jesus said, "Take care of My sheep." The third time He said to him, "Simon, son of John, do you love Me?" Peter was hurt because Jesus asked him the third time, "Do you love Me?" He said, "Lord, You know all things; You know that I love You." Jesus said, "Feed My sheep Very truly I tell you, when you were younger you dressed yourself and went where you wanted; but when you are old you will stretch out your hands, and someone else will dress you and lead you where you do not want to go." Jesus said this to indicate the kind of death by which Peter would glorify God. Then He said to him, "Follow Me!" Peter turned and saw the disciple whom Jesus loved following them. This was the one who had leaned back against Jesus at the supper and had asked, "Lord, who is going to betray You?" When Peter saw him, he asked, "Lord, what about him?" Jesus answered, "If I want him to remain alive until I return, what is that to you? You must follow Me." Because of this, a rumor spread among the believers that this disciple would not die. But Jesus did not say that he would not die; He only said, "If I want him to remain alive until I return, what is that to you?" This is the disciple who testifies to these things and who wrote them down. We know that his testimony is true. Jesus did many other things as well. If every one of them were written down, I suppose that even the whole world would not have room for the books that would be written. Amen

44. Acts

CHAPTER 1

I have already spoken, O Theophilus, of all that Jesus began to do and teach, until the day He was taken up, after He had given orders through the Holy Spirit to the apostles whom He had chosen. To these, He presented Himself alive after His suffering, with many infallible signs, being seen by them for forty days and speaking about the kingdom of God. When He had gathered them together, He commanded them not to depart from Jerusalem but to wait for the promise of the Father. He said, "You have heard from me. For John baptized with water, but you will be baptized with the Holy Spirit in a few days." When they were gathered together, they asked Him, "Lord, will you at this time restore the kingdom to Israel?" He said to them, "It is not for you to know the times and seasons that the Father has set by His own authority. But you shall receive power when the Holy Spirit comes upon you, and you shall be witnesses to Me in Jerusalem, in all Judea, and Samaria, and to the ends of the earth." After He had said these things, while they were watching, He was taken up, and a cloud received Him out of their sight. As they looked intently toward heaven, two men in white stood beside them and said, "Men of Galilee, why do you stand here looking into heaven? This Jesus, who has been taken from you into heaven, will come in the same way you saw Him go into heaven." Then they returned to Jerusalem from the Mount of Olives, which is near Jerusalem, a Sabbath day's journey away. When they arrived, they went to the upper room where they were staying: Peter, James, John, Andrew, Philip, Thomas, Bartholomew, Matthew, James the son of Alphaeus, Simon the Zealot, and Judas the brother of James. They all continued together in prayer, with the women, Mary the mother of Jesus, and His brothers In those days, Peter stood among the believers (a group numbering about a hundred and twenty) and said, "Brothers, the Scripture had to be fulfilled which the Holy Spirit spoke long ago through David concerning Judas, who served as a guide for those who arrested Jesus. He was one of our number and shared in our ministry. With the payment he received for his wickedness, Judas bought a field; there he fell headlong, his body burst open, and all his intestines spilled out. Everyone in Jerusalem heard about this, so they called that field in their language Aceldama, that is, Field of Blood. For it is written in the book of Psalms: 'May his place be deserted; let there be no one to dwell in it,' and, 'May another take his place of leadership.' Therefore, it is necessary to choose one of the men who have been with us the whole time the Lord Jesus went in and out among us, beginning from John's baptism to the time when Jesus was taken up from us. For one of these must become a witness with us of His resurrection." So they nominated two men: Joseph called Barsabbas (also known as Justus) and Matthias. Then they prayed, "Lord, you know everyone's heart. Show us which of these two you have chosen to take over this apostolic ministry, which Judas left to go where he belongs." Then they cast lots, and the lot fell to Matthias; so he was added to the eleven apostles

CHAPTER 2

When the day of Pentecost came, they were all together in one place. Suddenly a sound like the blowing of a violent wind came from heaven and filled the whole house where they were sitting. They saw what seemed to be tongues of fire that separated and came to rest on each of them. All of them were filled with the Holy Spirit and began to speak in other tongues as the Spirit enabled them Now there were staying in Jerusalem God-fearing Jews from every nation under heaven. When they heard this sound, a crowd came together in bewilderment because each one heard their own language being spoken. Utterly amazed, they asked, "Aren't all these who are speaking Galileans? Then how is it that each of us hears them in our native language? Parthians, Medes, Elamites, residents of Mesopotamia, Judea and Cappadocia, Pontus and Asia, Phrygia and Pamphylia, Egypt and the parts of Libya near Cyrene, visitors from Rome (both Jews and converts to Judaism), Cretans, and Arabs—we hear them declaring the wonders of God in our own tongues!" Amazed and perplexed, they asked one another, "What does this mean?" Some, however, made fun of them and said, "They have had too much wine." Then Peter stood up with the Eleven, raised his voice, and addressed the crowd: "Fellow Jews and all of you who live in Jerusalem, let me explain this to you; listen carefully to what I say. These people are not drunk, as you suppose. It's only nine in the morning! No, this is what was spoken by the prophet Joel: 'In the last days, God says, I will pour out my Spirit on all people. Your sons and daughters will prophesy, your young men will see visions, your old men will dream dreams. Even on my servants, both men and women, I will pour out my Spirit in those days, and they will prophesy. I will show wonders in the heavens above and signs on the earth below, blood and fire and billows of smoke. The sun will be turned to darkness and the moon to blood before the coming of the great and glorious day of the Lord. And everyone who calls on the name of the Lord will be saved.' Fellow Israelites, listen to this: Jesus of Nazareth was a man accredited by God to you by miracles, wonders, and signs, which God did among you through Him, as you yourselves know. This man was handed over to you by God's deliberate plan and foreknowledge; and you, with the help of wicked men, put Him to death by nailing Him to the cross. But God raised Him from the dead, freeing Him from the agony of death because it was impossible for death to keep its hold on Him. David said about Him: 'I saw the Lord always before me. Because He is at my right hand, I will not be shaken. Therefore my heart is glad and my tongue rejoices; my body also will rest in hope because you will not abandon me to the realm of the dead, nor will you let your Holy One see decay. You have made known to me the paths of life; you will fill me with joy in your presence.' Fellow Israelites, I can tell you confidently that the patriarch David died and was buried, and his tomb is here to this day. But he was a prophet and knew that God had promised him on oath that He would place one of his descendants on his throne. Seeing what was to come, he spoke of the resurrection of the Messiah, that He was not abandoned to the realm of the dead, nor did His body see decay. God has raised this Jesus to life, and we are all witnesses of it. Exalted to the right hand of God, He has received from the Father the promised Holy Spirit and has poured out what you now see and hear. For David did not ascend to heaven, and yet he said, 'The Lord said to my Lord: "Sit at my right hand until I make your enemies a footstool for your feet."' Therefore, let all Israel be assured of this: God has made this Jesus, whom you crucified, both Lord and Messiah." When the people heard this, they were cut to the heart and said to Peter and the other apostles, "Brothers, what shall we do?" Peter replied, "Repent and be baptized, every one of you, in the name of Jesus Christ for the forgiveness of your sins. And you will receive the gift of the Holy Spirit. The promise is for you and your children and for all who are far off—for all whom the Lord our God will call." With many other words, he warned them, and he pleaded with them, "Save yourselves from this corrupt generation." Those who accepted his message were baptized, and about three thousand were added to their number that day. They devoted themselves to the apostles' teaching and to fellowship, to the breaking of bread and to prayer. Everyone was filled with awe at the many wonders and signs performed by the apostles. All the believers were together and had everything in common. They sold property and possessions to give to anyone who had need. Every day they continued to meet together in the temple courts. They broke bread in their homes and ate together with glad and sincere hearts, praising God and enjoying the favor of all the people. And the Lord added to their number daily those who were being saved

CHAPTER 3

One day, Peter and John were going up to the temple at the time of prayer—at three in the afternoon. Now a man who was lame from birth was being carried to the temple gate called Beautiful, where he was put every day to beg from those going into the temple courts. When he saw Peter and John about to enter, he asked them for money. Peter looked straight at him, as did John. Then Peter said, "Look at us!" So the man gave them his attention, expecting to get something from them. Then Peter said, "Silver or gold I do not have, but what I do have I give you. In the name of Jesus Christ of Nazareth, walk." Taking him by the right hand, he helped him up, and instantly the man's feet and ankles became strong. He jumped to his feet and began to walk. Then he went with them into the temple courts, walking and jumping, and praising God. When all the people saw him walking and praising God, they recognized him as the same man who used to sit begging at the temple gate called Beautiful, and they were filled with wonder and amazement at what had happened to him While the man held on to Peter and John, all the people were astonished and came running to them in the place called Solomon's Colonnade. When Peter saw this, he said to them, "Fellow Israelites, why does this surprise you? Why do you stare at us as if by our own power or godliness we had made this man walk? The God of Abraham, Isaac and Jacob, the God of our fathers, has glorified His servant Jesus. You handed Him over to be killed, and you disowned Him before Pilate, though he had decided to let Him go. You disowned the Holy and Righteous One and asked that a murderer be released to you. You killed the author of life, but God raised Him from the dead. We are witnesses of this. By faith in the name of Jesus, this man whom you see and know was made strong. It is Jesus' name and the faith that comes through Him that has completely healed him, as you can all see Now, fellow Israelites, I know that you acted in ignorance, as did your leaders. But this is how God fulfilled what He had foretold through all the prophets, saying that His Messiah would suffer. Repent, then, and turn to God, so that your sins may be wiped out, that times of refreshing may come from the Lord, and that He may send the Messiah, who has been appointed for you—even Jesus. Heaven must receive Him until the time comes for God to restore everything, as He promised long ago through His holy prophets. For Moses said, 'The Lord your God will raise up for you a prophet like me from among your own people; you must listen to everything He tells you. Anyone who does not listen to Him will be completely cut off from their people.' Indeed, beginning with Samuel, all the prophets who have spoken have foretold these days. And you are heirs of the prophets and of the covenant God made with your fathers. He said to Abraham, 'Through your offspring all peoples on earth will be blessed.' When God raised up His servant, He sent Him first to you to bless you by turning each of you from your wicked ways."

CHAPTER 4

While Peter and John were speaking to the people, the priests, the captain of the temple guard, and the Sadducees came up to them. They were greatly disturbed because the apostles were teaching the people, proclaiming in Jesus the resurrection of the dead. They seized Peter and John and, because it was evening, they put them in jail until the next day. But many who heard the message believed, so the number of men who believed grew to about five thousand The next day, the rulers, the elders, and the teachers of the law met in Jerusalem. Annas the high priest was there, and so were Caiaphas, John, Alexander, and others of the high priest's family. They had Peter and John brought before them and began to question them: "By what power or what name did you do this?" Then Peter, filled with the Holy Spirit, said to them: "Rulers and elders of the people! If we are being called to account today for an act of kindness shown to a man who was lame and are being asked how he was healed, then know this, you and all the people of Israel: It is by the name of Jesus Christ of Nazareth, whom you crucified but whom God raised from the dead, that this man stands before you healed. Jesus is 'the stone you builders rejected, which has become the cornerstone.' Salvation is found in no one else, for there is no other name under heaven given to mankind by which we must be saved." When they saw the courage of Peter and John and realized that they were unschooled, ordinary men, they were astonished and took note that these men had been with Jesus. But since they could see the man who had been healed standing there with them, there was nothing they could say. So they ordered them to withdraw from the Sanhedrin and then conferred together. "What are we going to do with these men?" they asked. "Everyone living in Jerusalem knows they have performed a notable sign, and we cannot deny it. But to stop this thing from spreading any further among the people, we must warn them to speak no longer to anyone in this name." Then they called them in again and commanded them not to speak or teach at all in the name of Jesus. But Peter and John replied, "Which is right in God's eyes: to listen to you, or to Him? You be the judges! As for us, we cannot help speaking about what we have seen and heard." After further threats, they let them go. They could not decide how to punish them because all the people were praising God for what had happened. For the man who was miraculously healed was over forty years old On their release, Peter and John went back to their own people and reported all that the chief priests and the elders had said to them. When they heard this, they raised their voices together in prayer to God. "Sovereign Lord," they said, "You made the heavens and the earth and the sea, and everything in them. You spoke by the Holy Spirit through the mouth of Your servant, our father David: 'Why do the nations rage and the peoples plot in vain? The kings of the earth rise up and the rulers band together against the Lord and against His anointed one.' Indeed Herod and Pontius Pilate met together with the Gentiles and the people of Israel in this city to conspire against Your holy servant Jesus, whom You anointed. They did what Your power and will had decided beforehand should happen. Now, Lord, consider their threats and enable Your servants to speak Your word with great boldness. Stretch out Your hand to heal and perform signs and wonders through the name of Your holy servant Jesus." After they prayed, the place where they were meeting was shaken. And they were all filled with the Holy Spirit and spoke the word of God boldly. All the believers were one in heart and mind. No one claimed that any of their possessions was their own, but they shared everything they had. With great power the apostles continued to testify to the resurrection of the Lord Jesus. And God's grace was so powerfully at work in them all that there were no needy persons among them. For from time to time those who owned land or houses sold them, brought the money from the sales and put it at the apostles' feet, and it was distributed to anyone who had need. Joseph, a Levite from Cyprus, whom the apostles called Barnabas (which means "son of encouragement"), sold a field he owned and brought the money and put it at the apostles' feet

CHAPTER 5

Now a man named Ananias, together with his wife Sapphira, also sold a piece of property. With his wife's full knowledge he kept back part of the money for himself, but brought the rest and put it at the apostles' feet. Then Peter said, "Ananias, how is it that Satan has so filled your heart that you have lied to the Holy Spirit and have kept for yourself some of the money you received for the land? Didn't it belong to you before it was sold? And after it was sold, wasn't the money at your disposal? What made you think of doing such a thing? You have not lied just to human beings but to God." When Ananias heard this, he fell down and died. And great fear seized all who heard what had happened. Then some young men came forward, wrapped up his body, and carried him out and buried him. About three hours later his wife came in, not knowing what had happened. Peter asked her, "Tell me, is this the price you and Ananias got for the land?" "Yes," she said, "that is the price." Peter said to her, "How could you conspire to test the Spirit of the Lord? Listen! The feet of the men who buried your husband are at the door, and they will carry you out also." At that moment she fell down at his feet and died. Then the young men came in and, finding her dead, carried her out and buried her beside her husband. Great fear seized the whole church and all who heard about these events The apostles performed many signs and wonders among the people. And all the believers used to meet together in Solomon's Colonnade. No one else dared join them, even though they were highly regarded by the people. Nevertheless, more and more men and women believed in the Lord and were added to their number. As a result, people brought the sick into the streets and laid them on beds and mats so that at least Peter's shadow might fall on some of them as he passed by. Crowds gathered also from the towns around Jerusalem, bringing their sick and those tormented by impure spirits, and all of them were healed Then the high priest and all his associates, who were members of the party of the Sadducees, were filled with jealousy. They arrested the apostles and put them in the public jail. But during the night an angel of the Lord opened the doors of the jail and brought them out. "Go, stand in the temple courts," he said, "and tell the people all about this new life." At daybreak they entered the temple courts, as they had been told, and began to teach the people When the high priest and his associates arrived, they called together the Sanhedrin—the full assembly of the elders of Israel—and sent to the jail for the apostles. But on arriving at the jail, the officers did not find them there. So they went back and reported, "We found the jail securely locked, with the guards standing at the doors; but when we opened them, we found no one inside." On hearing this report, the captain of the temple guard and the chief priests were at a loss, wondering what this might lead to. Then someone came and said, "Look! The men you put in jail are standing in the temple courts teaching the people." At that, the captain went with his officers and brought the apostles. They did not use force because they feared that the people would stone them The apostles were brought in and made to appear before the Sanhedrin to be questioned by the high priest. "We gave you strict orders not to teach in this name," he said. "Yet you have filled Jerusalem with your teaching and are determined to make us guilty of this man's blood." Peter and the other apostles replied, "We must obey God rather than human beings! The God of our ancestors raised Jesus from the dead—whom you killed by hanging Him on a cross. God exalted Him to His own right hand as Prince and Savior that He might bring Israel to repentance and forgive their sins. We are witnesses of these things, and so is the Holy Spirit, whom God has given to those who obey Him." When they heard this, they were furious and wanted to put them to death. But a Pharisee named Gamaliel, a teacher of the law who was honored by all the people, stood up in the Sanhedrin and ordered that the men be put outside for a little while. Then he addressed the Sanhedrin: "Men of Israel, consider carefully what you intend to do to these men. Some time ago Theudas appeared, claiming to be somebody, and about four hundred men rallied to him. He was killed, all his followers were dispersed, and it all came to nothing. After him, Judas the Galilean appeared in the days of the census and led a band of people in revolt. He too was killed, and all his followers were scattered. Therefore, in the present case, I advise you: Leave these men alone! Let them go! For if their purpose or activity is of human origin, it will fail. But if it is from God, you will not be able to stop these men; you will only find yourselves fighting against God." His speech persuaded them. They called the apostles in and had them flogged. Then they ordered them not to speak in the name of Jesus and let them go. The apostles left the Sanhedrin, rejoicing because they had been counted worthy of suffering disgrace for the Name. Day after day, in the temple courts and from house to house, they never stopped teaching and proclaiming the good news that Jesus is the Messiah

Chapter 6

In those days, as the number of disciples grew, a complaint arose from the Greeks against the Jews because their widows were being neglected in the daily distribution of food. The Twelve summoned the multitude of disciples and said, "It is not fitting for us to neglect the word of God in order to serve tables. Therefore, brothers, choose from among you seven honest men full of the Holy Spirit and wisdom, whom we can appoint for this task. We will devote ourselves to prayer and to the ministry of the word." This proposal pleased the whole group, and they chose Stephen, a man full of faith and the Holy Spirit, Philip, Prochorus, Nicanor, Timon, Parmenas, and Nicolas from Antioch, a convert to Judaism. They presented these men to the apostles, who prayed and laid their hands on them The word of God continued to spread, and the number of disciples in Jerusalem increased rapidly. A large number of priests also became obedient to the faith. Now Stephen, full of faith and power, performed great wonders and signs among the people. Opposition arose, however, from members of the Synagogue of the Freedmen (as it was called), Jews of Cyrene and Alexandria as well as the provinces of Cilicia and Asia, who began to argue with Stephen. But they could not stand up against the wisdom the Spirit gave him as he spoke Then they secretly persuaded some men to say, "We have heard Stephen speak blasphemous words against Moses and against God." So they stirred up the people, the elders, and the teachers of the law. They seized Stephen and brought him before the Sanhedrin. They produced false witnesses who testified, "This fellow never stops speaking against this holy place and against the law. For we have heard him say that this Jesus of Nazareth will destroy this place and change the customs Moses handed down to us." All who were sitting in the Sanhedrin looked intently at Stephen, and they saw that his face was like the face of an angel

Chapter 7

Then the high priest asked Stephen, "Are these charges true?" Stephen replied, "Brothers and fathers, listen to me! The God of glory appeared to our father Abraham while he was still in Mesopotamia, before he lived in Haran. God said, 'Leave your country and your people,' and 'Go to the land I will show you.' So he left the land of the Chaldeans and settled in Haran. After the death of his father, God sent him to this land where you are now living. He gave him no inheritance here, not even enough ground to set his foot on. But God promised him that he and his descendants after him would possess the land, even though at that time Abraham had no child. God spoke to him in this way: 'For four hundred years your descendants will be strangers in a country not their own, and they will be enslaved and mistreated. But I will punish the nation they serve as slaves,' God said, 'and afterward, they will come out of that country and worship me in this place.' Then he gave Abraham the covenant of circumcision. And Abraham became the father of Isaac and circumcised him eight days after his birth. Later Isaac became the father of Jacob, and Jacob became the father of the twelve patriarchs Because the patriarchs were jealous of Joseph, they sold him as a slave into Egypt. But God was with him and rescued him from all his troubles. He gave Joseph wisdom and enabled him to gain the goodwill of Pharaoh, king of Egypt. So Pharaoh made him ruler over Egypt and all his palace. Then a famine struck all Egypt and Canaan, bringing great suffering, and our ancestors could not find food. When Jacob heard that there was grain in Egypt, he sent our forefathers on their first visit. On their second visit, Joseph told his brothers who he was, and Pharaoh learned about Joseph's family. After this, Joseph sent for his father Jacob and his whole family, seventy-five in all. Then Jacob went down to Egypt, where he and our ancestors died. Their bodies were brought back to Shechem and placed in the tomb that Abraham had bought from the sons of Hamor at Shechem for a certain sum of money As the time drew near for God to fulfill his promise to Abraham, the number of our people in Egypt had greatly increased. Then 'a new king, to whom Joseph meant nothing, came to power in Egypt.' He dealt treacherously with our people and oppressed our ancestors by forcing them to throw out their newborn babies so that they would die At that time Moses was born, and he was no ordinary child. For three months he was cared for by his family. When he was placed outside, Pharaoh's daughter took him and brought him up as her own son. Moses was educated in all the wisdom of the Egyptians and was powerful in speech and action When Moses was forty years old, he decided to visit his own people, the Israelites. He saw one of them being mistreated by an Egyptian, so he went to his defense and avenged him by killing the Egyptian. Moses thought that his own people would realize that God was using him to rescue them, but they did not. The next day Moses came upon two Israelites who were fighting. He tried to reconcile them by saying, 'Men, you are brothers; why do you want to hurt each other?' But the man who was mistreating the other pushed Moses aside and said, 'Who made you ruler and judge over us? Are you thinking of killing me as you killed the Egyptian yesterday?' When Moses heard this, he fled to Midian, where he settled as a foreigner and had two sons After forty years had passed, an angel appeared to Moses in the flames of a burning bush in the desert near Mount Sinai. When he saw this, he was amazed at the sight. As he went over to get a closer look, he heard the Lord say: 'I am the God of your fathers, the God of Abraham, Isaac, and Jacob.' Moses trembled with fear and did not dare to look. Then the Lord said to him, 'Take off your sandals, for the place where you are standing is holy ground. I have indeed seen the oppression of my people in Egypt. I have heard their groaning and have come down to set them free. Now come, I will send you back to Egypt.' This is the same Moses they had rejected with the words, 'Who made you ruler and judge?' He was sent to be their ruler and deliverer by God himself, through the angel who appeared to him in the bush. He led them out of Egypt and performed wonders and signs in Egypt, at the Red Sea, and for forty years in the wilderness This is the Moses who told the Israelites, 'God will raise up for you a prophet like me from your own people.' He was in the assembly in the wilderness, with the angel who spoke to him on Mount Sinai, and with our ancestors, and he received living words to pass on to us. But our ancestors refused to obey him. Instead, they rejected him and in their hearts turned back to Egypt. They told Aaron, 'Make us gods who will go before us. As for this fellow Moses who led us out of Egypt—we don't know what has happened to him!' That was the time they made an idol in the form of a calf. They brought sacrifices to it and reveled in what their own hands had made. But God turned away from them and gave them over to the worship of the sun, moon, and stars. This agrees with what is written in the book of the prophets: 'Did you bring me sacrifices and offerings forty years in the wilderness, people of Israel? You have taken up the tabernacle of Molek and the star of your god Rephan, the idols you made to worship. Therefore I will send you into exile beyond Babylon.' Our ancestors had the tabernacle of the covenant law with them in the wilderness. It had been made as God directed Moses, according to the pattern he had seen. After receiving the tabernacle, our ancestors under Joshua brought it with them when they took the land from the nations God drove out before them. It remained in the land until the time of David, who enjoyed God's favor and asked that he might provide a dwelling place for the God of Jacob. But it was Solomon who built a house for him However, the Most High does not live in houses made by human hands. As the prophet says: 'Heaven is my throne, and the earth is my footstool. What kind of house will you build for me? says the Lord. Or where will my resting place be? Has not my hand made all these things?' You stiff-necked people! Your hearts and ears are still uncircumcised. You are just like your ancestors: You always resist the Holy Spirit! Was there ever a prophet your ancestors did not persecute? They even killed those who predicted the coming of the Righteous One. And now you have betrayed and murdered him—you who have received the law that was given through angels but have not obeyed it." When the members of the Sanhedrin heard this, they were furious and gnashed their teeth at him. But Stephen, full of the Holy Spirit, looked up to heaven and saw the glory of God, and Jesus standing at the right hand of God. "Look," he said, "I see heaven open and the Son of Man standing at the right hand of God." At this, they covered their ears and, yelling at the top of their voices, they all rushed at him, dragged him out of the city, and began to stone him. Meanwhile, the witnesses laid their coats at the feet of a young man named Saul. While they were stoning him, Stephen prayed, "Lord Jesus, receive my spirit." Then he fell on his knees and cried out, "Lord, do not hold this sin against them." When he had said this, he fell asleep

Chapter 8

Saul approved of their killing him. On that day, a great persecution broke out against the church in Jerusalem, and all except the apostles were scattered throughout Judea and Samaria. Godly men buried Stephen and mourned deeply for him. But Saul began to destroy the church. Going from house to house, he dragged off both men and women and put them in prison Those who had been scattered preached the word wherever they went. Philip went down to a city in Samaria and proclaimed the Messiah there. When the crowds heard Philip and saw the signs he performed, they all paid close attention to what he said. For with shrieks, impure spirits came out of many, and many who were paralyzed or lame were healed. So there was great joy in that city Now for some time, a man named Simon had practiced sorcery in the city and amazed all the people of Samaria. He boasted that he was someone great, and all the people, both high and low, gave him their attention and exclaimed, "This man is rightly called the Great Power of God." They followed him because he had amazed them for a long time with his sorcery. But when they believed Philip as he proclaimed the good news of the kingdom of God and the name of Jesus Christ, they were baptized, both men and women. Simon himself believed and was baptized. And he followed Philip everywhere, astonished by the great signs and miracles he saw When the apostles in Jerusalem heard that Samaria had accepted the word of God, they sent Peter and John to Samaria. When they arrived, they prayed for the new believers there that they might receive the Holy Spirit because the Holy Spirit had not yet come on any of them; they had simply been baptized in the name of the Lord Jesus. Then Peter and John placed their hands on them, and they received the Holy Spirit When Simon saw that the Spirit was given at the laying on of the apostles' hands, he offered them money and said, "Give me also this ability so that everyone on whom I lay my hands may receive the Holy Spirit." Peter answered, "May your money perish with you because you thought you could buy the gift of God with money! You have no part or share in this ministry because your heart is not right before God. Repent of this wickedness and pray to the Lord in the hope that he may forgive you for having such a thought in your heart. For I see that you are full of bitterness and captive to sin." Then Simon answered, "Pray to the Lord for me so that nothing you have said may happen to me." After they had further proclaimed the word of the Lord and testified about Jesus, Peter and John returned to Jerusalem, preaching the gospel in many Samaritan villages Now an angel of the Lord said to Philip, "Go south to the road—the desert road—that goes down from Jerusalem to Gaza." So he started out, and on his way, he met an Ethiopian eunuch, an important official in charge of all the treasury of the Kandake (which means "queen of the Ethiopians"). This man had gone to Jerusalem to worship, and on his way home was sitting in his chariot reading the Book of Isaiah the prophet. The Spirit told Philip, "Go to that chariot and stay near it." Then Philip ran up to the chariot and heard the man reading Isaiah the prophet. "Do you understand what you are reading?" Philip asked "How can I," he said, "unless someone explains it to me?" So he invited Philip to come up and sit with him This is the passage of Scripture the eunuch was reading: "He was led like a sheep to the slaughter, and as a lamb before its shearer is silent, so he did not open his mouth. In his humiliation he was deprived of justice. Who can speak of his descendants? For his life was taken from the earth." The eunuch asked Philip, "Tell me, please, who is the prophet talking about, himself or someone else?" Then Philip began with that very passage of Scripture and told him the good news about Jesus As they traveled along the road, they came to some water and the eunuch said, "Look, here is water. What can stand in the way of my being baptized?" Philip said, "If you believe with all your heart, you may." The eunuch answered, "I believe that Jesus Christ is the Son of God." And he gave orders to stop the chariot. Then both Philip and the eunuch went down into the water, and Philip baptized him. When they came up out of the water, the Spirit of the Lord suddenly took Philip away, and the eunuch did not see him again but went on his way rejoicing. Philip, however, appeared at Azotus and traveled about, preaching the gospel in all the towns until he reached Caesarea

Chapter 9

Meanwhile, Saul was still breathing out murderous threats against the Lord's disciples. He went to the high priest and asked him for letters to the synagogues in Damascus so that if he found any there who belonged to the Way, whether men or women, he might take them as prisoners to Jerusalem. As he neared Damascus on his journey, suddenly a light from heaven flashed around him. He fell to the ground and heard a voice say to him, "Saul, Saul, why do you persecute me?" "Who are you, Lord?" Saul asked "I am Jesus, whom you are persecuting," he replied. "Now get up and go into the city, and you will be told what you must do." The men traveling with Saul stood there speechless; they heard the sound but did not see anyone. Saul got up from the ground, but when he opened his eyes, he could see nothing. So they led him by the hand into Damascus. For three days he was blind and did not eat or drink anything In Damascus, there was a disciple named Ananias. The Lord called to him in a vision, "Ananias!" "Yes, Lord," he answered The Lord told him, "Go to the house of Judas on Straight Street and ask for a man from Tarsus named Saul, for he is praying. In a vision, he has seen a man named Ananias come and place his hands on him to restore his sight." "Lord," Ananias answered, "I have heard many reports about this man and all the harm he has done to your holy people in Jerusalem. And he has come here with authority from the chief priests to arrest all who call on your name." But the Lord said to Ananias, "Go! This man is my chosen instrument to proclaim my name to the Gentiles and their kings and to the people of Israel. I will show him how much he must suffer for my name." Then Ananias went to the house and entered it. Placing his hands on Saul, he said, "Brother Saul, the Lord—Jesus, who appeared to you on the road as you were coming here—has sent me so that you may see again and be filled with the Holy Spirit." Immediately, something like scales fell from Saul's eyes, and he could see again. He got up and was baptized, and after taking some food, he regained his strength Saul spent several days with the disciples in Damascus. At once, he began to preach in the synagogues that Jesus is the Son of God. All those who heard him were astonished and asked, "Isn't he the man who raised havoc in Jerusalem among those who call on this name? And hasn't he come here to take them as prisoners to the chief priests?" Yet Saul grew more and more powerful and baffled the Jews living in Damascus by proving that Jesus is the Messiah After many days had gone by, there was a conspiracy among the Jews to kill him, but Saul learned of their plan. Day and night, they kept close watch on the city gates to kill him. But his followers took him by night and lowered him in a basket through an opening in the wall When he came to Jerusalem, he tried to join the disciples, but they were all afraid of him, not believing that he really was a disciple. But Barnabas took him and brought him to the apostles. He told them how Saul, on his journey, had seen the Lord and that the Lord had spoken to him and how in Damascus, he had preached fearlessly in the name of Jesus. So Saul stayed with them and moved about freely in Jerusalem, speaking boldly in the name of the Lord. He talked and debated with the Hellenistic Jews, but they tried to kill him. When the believers learned of this, they took him down to Caesarea and sent him off to Tarsus Then the church throughout Judea, Galilee, and Samaria enjoyed a time of peace and was strengthened. Living in the fear of the Lord and encouraged by the Holy Spirit, it increased in numbers As Peter traveled about the country, he went to visit the Lord's people who lived in Lydda. There he found a man named Aeneas, who was paralyzed and had been bedridden for eight years. "Aeneas," Peter said to him, "Jesus Christ heals you. Get up and roll up your mat." Immediately Aeneas got up. All those who lived in Lydda and Sharon saw him and turned to the Lord In Joppa, there was a disciple named Tabitha (in Greek her name is Dorcas); she was always doing good and helping the poor. About that time, she became sick and died, and her body was washed and placed in an upstairs room. Lydda was near Joppa; so when the disciples heard that Peter was in Lydda, they sent two men to him and urged him, "Please come at once!" Peter went with them, and when he arrived, he was taken upstairs to the room. All the widows stood around him, crying and showing him the robes and other clothing that Dorcas had made while she was still with them. Peter sent them all out of the room; then he got down on his knees and prayed. Turning toward the dead woman, he said, "Tabitha, get up." She opened her eyes, and seeing Peter, she sat up. He took her by the hand and helped her to her feet. Then he called for the believers, especially the widows, and presented her to them alive. This became known all over Joppa, and many people believed in the Lord. Peter stayed in Joppa for some time with a tanner named Simon

Chapter 10

At Caesarea, there was a man named Cornelius, a centurion in what was known as the Italian Regiment. He and all his family were devout and God-fearing; he gave generously to those in need and prayed to God regularly. One day at about three in the afternoon, he had a vision. He distinctly saw an angel of God, who came to him and said, "Cornelius!" Cornelius stared at him in fear. "What is it, Lord?" he asked The angel answered, "Your prayers and gifts to the poor have come up as a memorial offering before God. Now send men to Joppa to bring back a man named Simon who is called Peter. He is staying with Simon the tanner, whose house is by the sea." When the angel who spoke to him had gone, Cornelius called two of his servants and a devout soldier who was one of his attendants. He told them everything that had happened and sent them to Joppa About noon the following day, as they were on their journey and approaching the city, Peter went up on the roof to pray. He became hungry and wanted something to eat, and while the meal was being prepared, he fell into a trance. He saw heaven opened and something like a large sheet being let down to earth by its four corners. It contained all kinds of four-footed animals, as well as reptiles and birds. Then a voice told him, "Get up, Peter. Kill and eat." "Surely not, Lord!" Peter replied. "I have never eaten anything impure or unclean." The voice spoke to him a second time, "Do not call anything impure that God has made clean." This happened three times, and immediately the sheet was taken back to heaven While Peter was wondering about the meaning of the vision, the men sent by Cornelius found out where Simon's house was and stopped at the gate. They called out, asking if Simon, who was known as Peter, was staying there

While Peter was still thinking about the vision, the Spirit said to him, "Simon, three men are looking for you. So get up and go downstairs. Do not hesitate to go with them, for I have sent them." Peter went down and said to the men, "I'm the one you're looking for. Why have you come?" The men replied, "We have come from Cornelius the centurion. He is a righteous and God-fearing man, who is respected by all the Jewish people. A holy angel told him to ask you to come to his house so that he could hear what you have to say." Then Peter invited the men into the house to be his guests The next day, Peter started out with them, and some of the believers from Joppa went along. The following day, he arrived in Caesarea. Cornelius was expecting them and had called together his relatives and close friends. As Peter entered the house, Cornelius met him and fell at his feet in reverence. But Peter made him get up. "Stand up," he said, "I am only a man myself." While talking with him, Peter went inside and found a large gathering of people. He said to them: "You are well aware that it is against our law for a Jew to associate with or visit a Gentile. But God has shown me that I should not call anyone impure or unclean. So when I was sent for, I came without raising any objection. May I ask why you sent for me?" Cornelius answered: "Three days ago I was in my house praying at this hour, at three in the afternoon. Suddenly a man in shining clothes stood before me and said, 'Cornelius, God has heard your prayer and remembered your gifts to the poor. Send to Joppa for Simon who is called Peter. He is a guest in the home of Simon the tanner, who lives by the sea.' So I sent for you immediately, and it was good of you to come. Now we are all here in the presence of God to listen to everything the Lord has commanded you to tell us." Then Peter began to speak: "I now realize how true it is that God does not show favoritism but accepts from every nation the one who fears him and does what is right. You know the message God sent to the people of Israel, announcing the good news of peace through Jesus Christ, who is Lord of all. You know what has happened throughout the province of Judea, beginning in Galilee after the baptism that John preached—how God anointed Jesus of Nazareth with the Holy Spirit and power, and how he went around doing good and healing all who were under the power of the devil because God was with him "We are witnesses of everything he did in the country of the Jews and in Jerusalem. They killed him by hanging him on a cross, but God raised him from the dead on the third day and caused him to be seen. He was not seen by all the people, but by witnesses whom God had already chosen—by us who ate and drank with him after he rose from the dead. He commanded us to preach to the people and to testify that he is the one whom God appointed as judge of the living and the dead. All the prophets testify about him that everyone who believes in him receives forgiveness of sins through his name." While Peter was still speaking these words, the Holy Spirit came on all who heard the message. The circumcised believers who had come with Peter were astonished that the gift of the Holy Spirit had been poured out even on Gentiles. For they heard them speaking in tongues and praising God Then Peter said, "Surely no one can stand in the way of their being baptized with water. They have received the Holy Spirit just as we have." So he ordered that they be baptized in the name of Jesus Christ. Then they asked Peter to stay with them for a few days

Chapter 11

Now the apostles and brothers who were in Judea learned that the Gentiles had also received the word of God. When Peter went up to Jerusalem, the circumcised believers criticized him, saying, "You went into the house of uncircumcised men and ate with them." Peter began to explain everything to them in an orderly sequence, saying, "I was in the city of Joppa praying, and in a trance, I saw a vision: a large sheet being let down from heaven by its four corners, and it came right down to me. I looked into it and saw four-footed animals of the earth, wild beasts, reptiles, and birds. Then I heard a voice telling me, 'Get up, Peter. Kill and eat.' I replied, 'Surely not, Lord! Nothing impure or unclean has ever entered my mouth.' The voice spoke from heaven a second time, 'Do not call anything impure that God has made clean.' This happened three times, and then it was all pulled up to heaven again "Right then, three men who had been sent to me from Caesarea stopped at the house where I was staying. The Spirit told me to have no hesitation about going with them. These six brothers also went with me, and we entered the man's house. He told us how he had seen an angel appear in his house and say, 'Send to Joppa for Simon, who is called Peter. He will bring you a message through which you and your entire household will be saved.' As I began to speak, the Holy Spirit came on them as He had come on us at the beginning. Then I remembered what the Lord had said: 'John baptized with water, but you will be baptized with the Holy Spirit.' So if God gave them the same gift He gave us who believed in the Lord Jesus Christ, who was I to think that I could stand in God's way?" When they heard this, they had no further objections and praised God, saying, "So then, even to Gentiles, God has granted repentance that leads to life." Those who had been scattered by the persecution that broke out when Stephen was killed traveled as far as Phoenicia, Cyprus, and Antioch, spreading the word only among Jews. Some of them, however, men from Cyprus and Cyrene, went to Antioch and began to speak to Greeks also, telling them the good news about the Lord Jesus. The Lord's hand was with them, and a great number of people believed and turned to the Lord News of this reached the church in Jerusalem, and they sent Barnabas to Antioch. When he arrived and saw what the grace of God had done, he was glad and encouraged them all to remain true to the Lord with all their hearts. Barnabas was a good man, full of the Holy Spirit and faith, and a great number of people were brought to the Lord. Then Barnabas went to Tarsus to look for Saul, and when he found him, he brought him to Antioch. For a whole year, Barnabas and Saul met with the church and taught great numbers of people. The disciples were called Christians first at Antioch During this time, some prophets came down from Jerusalem to Antioch. One of them, named Agabus, stood up and through the Spirit predicted that a severe famine would spread over the entire Roman world (this happened during the reign of Claudius). The disciples, as each one was able, decided to provide help for the brothers and sisters living in Judea. This they did, sending their gift to the elders by Barnabas and Saul

Chapter 12

About that time, King Herod began to persecute some believers in the church. He had James, the brother of John, put to death with the sword. When he saw that this met with approval among the Jews, he proceeded to seize Peter also. This happened during the Festival of Unleavened Bread. After arresting him, he put him in prison, handing him over to be guarded by four squads of four soldiers each. Herod intended to bring him out for public trial after the Passover. So Peter was kept in prison, but the church was earnestly praying to God for him The night before Herod was to bring him to trial, Peter was sleeping between two soldiers, bound with two chains, and sentries stood guard at the entrance. Suddenly an angel of the Lord appeared, and a light shone in the cell. He struck Peter on the side and woke him up. "Quick, get up!" he said, and the chains fell off Peter's wrists. Then the angel said to him, "Put on your clothes and sandals." And Peter did so. "Wrap your cloak around you and follow me," the angel told him. Peter followed him out of the prison, but he had no idea that what the angel was doing was really happening; he thought he was seeing a vision. They passed the first and second guards and came to the iron gate leading to the city. It opened for them by itself, and they went through it. When they had walked the length of one street, suddenly the angel left him Then Peter came to himself and said, "Now I know without a doubt that the Lord has sent his angel and rescued me from Herod's clutches and from everything the Jewish people were hoping would happen." When this had dawned on him, he went to the house of Mary the mother of John, also called Mark, where many people had gathered and were praying. Peter knocked at the outer entrance, and a servant named Rhoda came to answer the door. When she recognized Peter's voice, she was so overjoyed she ran back without opening it and exclaimed, "Peter is at the door!" "You're out of your mind," they told her. When she kept insisting that it was so, they said, "It must be his angel." But Peter kept on knocking, and when they opened the door and saw him, they were astonished. Peter motioned with his hand for them to be quiet and described how the Lord had brought him out of prison. "Tell James and the other brothers and sisters about this," he said, and then he left for another place In the morning, there was no small commotion among the soldiers as to what had become of Peter. After Herod had a thorough search made for him and did not find him, he cross-examined the guards and ordered that they be executed. Then Herod went from Judea to Caesarea and stayed there He had been quarreling with the people of Tyre and Sidon; they now joined together and sought an audience with him. After securing the support of Blastus, a trusted personal servant of the king, they asked for peace because they depended on the king's country for their food supply. On the appointed day, Herod, wearing his royal robes, sat on his throne and delivered a public address to the people. They shouted, "This is the voice of a god, not of a man." Immediately, because Herod did not give praise to God, an angel of the Lord struck him down, and he was eaten by worms and died But the word of God continued to spread and flourish. When Barnabas and Saul had finished their mission, they returned from Jerusalem, taking with them John, also called Mark

Chapter 13

Now in the church at Antioch, there were prophets and teachers: Barnabas, Simeon called Niger, Lucius of Cyrene, Manaen (who had been brought up with Herod the tetrarch), and Saul. While they were worshiping the Lord and fasting, the Holy Spirit said, "Set apart for me Barnabas and Saul for the work to which I have called them." So after they had fasted and prayed, they placed their hands on them and sent them off The two of them, sent on their way by the Holy Spirit, went down to Seleucia and sailed from there to Cyprus. When they arrived at Salamis, they proclaimed the word of God in the Jewish synagogues. John was with them as their helper. They traveled through the whole island until they came to Paphos. There they met a Jewish sorcerer and false prophet named Bar-Jesus, who was an attendant of the proconsul, Sergius Paulus. The proconsul, an intelligent man, sent for Barnabas and Saul because he wanted to hear the word of God. But Elymas the sorcerer (for that is what his name means) opposed them and tried to turn the proconsul from the faith. Then Saul, who was also called Paul, filled with the Holy Spirit, looked straight at Elymas and said, "You are a child of the devil and an enemy of everything that is right! You are full of all kinds of deceit and trickery. Will you never stop perverting the right ways of the Lord? Now the hand of the Lord is against you. You are going to be blind for a time, not even able to see the light of the sun." Immediately mist and darkness came over him, and he groped about, seeking someone to lead him by the hand. When the proconsul saw what had happened, he believed, for he was amazed at the teaching about the Lord From Paphos, Paul and his companions sailed to Perga in Pamphylia, where John left them to return to Jerusalem. From Perga, they went on to Pisidian Antioch. On the Sabbath, they entered the synagogue and sat down. After the reading from the Law and the Prophets, the leaders of the synagogue sent word to them, saying, "Brothers, if you have a word of exhortation for the people, please speak." Standing up, Paul motioned with his hand and said: "Fellow Israelites and you Gentiles who worship God, listen to me! The God of the people of Israel chose our ancestors; he made the people prosper during their stay in Egypt; with mighty power, he led them out of that country; for about forty years, he endured their conduct in the wilderness; and he overthrew seven nations in Canaan, giving their land to his people as their inheritance. All this took about 450 years "After this, God gave them judges until the time of Samuel the prophet. Then the people asked for a king, and he gave them Saul son of Kish, of the tribe of Benjamin, who ruled for forty years. After removing Saul, he made David their king. God testified concerning him: 'I have found David son of Jesse, a man after my own heart; he will do everything I want him to do.' "From this man's descendants, God has brought to Israel the Savior Jesus, as he promised. Before the coming of Jesus, John preached repentance and baptism to all the people of Israel. As John was completing his work, he said: 'Who do you suppose I am? I am not the one you are looking for. But there is one coming after me whose sandals I am not worthy to untie.' "Fellow children of Abraham and you God-fearing Gentiles, it is to us that this message of salvation has been sent. The people of Jerusalem and their rulers did not recognize Jesus, yet in condemning him they fulfilled the words of the prophets that are read every Sabbath. Though they found no proper ground for a death sentence, they asked Pilate to have him executed. When they had carried out all that was written about him, they took him down from the cross and laid him in a tomb. But God raised him from the dead, and for many days he was seen by those who had traveled with him from Galilee to Jerusalem. They are now his witnesses to our people "We tell you the good news: What God promised our ancestors, he has fulfilled for us, their children, by raising up Jesus. As it is written in the second Psalm: 'You are my son; today I have become your father.' God raised him from the dead so that he will never be subject to decay. As God has said, 'I will give you the holy and sure blessings promised to David.' So it is also stated elsewhere: 'You will not let your holy one see decay.' "Now when David had served God's purpose in his own generation, he fell asleep; he was buried with his ancestors and his body decayed. But the one whom God raised from the dead did not see decay "Therefore, my friends, I want you to know that through Jesus the forgiveness of sins is proclaimed to you. Through him, everyone who believes is set free from every sin, a justification you were not able to obtain under the law of Moses. Take care that what the prophets have said does not happen to you: "'Look, you scoffers, wonder and perish, for I am going to do something in your days that you would never believe, even if someone told you.'" As Paul and Barnabas were leaving the synagogue, the people invited them to speak further about these things on the next Sabbath. When the congregation was dismissed, many of the Jews and devout converts to Judaism followed Paul and Barnabas, who talked with them and urged them to continue in the grace of God On the next Sabbath, almost the whole city gathered to hear the word of the Lord. When the Jews saw the crowds, they were filled with jealousy. They began to contradict what Paul was saying and heaped abuse on him. Then Paul and Barnabas answered them boldly: "We had to speak the word of God to you first. Since you reject it and do not consider yourselves worthy of eternal life, we now turn to the Gentiles. For this is what the Lord has commanded us: "'I have made you a light for the Gentiles, that you may bring salvation to the ends of the earth.'" When the Gentiles heard this, they were glad and honored the word of the Lord, and all who were appointed for eternal life believed. The word of the Lord spread through the whole region. But the Jewish leaders incited the God-fearing women of high standing and the leading men of the city. They stirred up persecution against Paul and Barnabas and expelled them from their region. So they shook the dust off their feet as a warning to them and went to Iconium. And the disciples were filled with joy and with the Holy Spirit

Chapter 14

At Iconium, Paul and Barnabas went as usual into the Jewish synagogue. There they spoke so effectively that a great number of Jews and Greeks believed. But the Jews who refused to believe stirred up the other Gentiles and poisoned their minds against the brothers. So Paul and Barnabas spent considerable time there, speaking boldly for the Lord, who confirmed the message of his grace by enabling them to perform signs and wonders. The people of the city were divided; some sided with the Jews, others with the apostles There was a plot afoot among both Gentiles and Jews, together with their leaders, to mistreat them and stone them. But they found out about it and fled to the Lycaonian cities of Lystra and Derbe and to the surrounding country, where they continued to preach the gospel In Lystra, there sat a man who was lame. He had been that way from birth and had never walked. He listened to Paul as he was speaking. Paul looked directly at him, saw that he had faith to be healed, and called out, "Stand up on your feet!" At that, the man jumped up and began to walk When the crowd saw what Paul had done, they shouted in the Lycaonian language, "The gods have come down to us in human form!" Barnabas they called Zeus, and Paul they called Hermes because he was the chief speaker. The priest of Zeus, whose temple was just outside the city, brought bulls and wreaths to the city gates because he and the crowd wanted to offer sacrifices to them But when the apostles Barnabas and Paul heard of this, they tore their clothes and rushed out into the crowd, shouting: "Friends, why are you doing this? We too are only human, like you. We are bringing you good news, telling you to turn from these worthless things to the living God, who made the heavens and the earth and the sea and everything in them. In the past, he let all nations go their own way. Yet he has not left himself without testimony: He has shown kindness by giving you rain from heaven and crops in their seasons; he provides you with plenty of food and fills your hearts with joy." Even with these words, they had difficulty keeping the crowd from sacrificing to them Then some Jews came from Antioch and Iconium and won the crowd over. They stoned Paul and dragged him outside the city, thinking he was dead. But after the disciples had gathered around him, he got up and went back into the city. The next day, he and Barnabas left for Derbe They preached the gospel in that city and won a large number of disciples. Then they returned to Lystra, Iconium, and Antioch, strengthening the disciples and encouraging them to remain true to the faith. "We must go through many hardships to enter the kingdom of God," they said. Paul and Barnabas appointed elders for them in each church and, with prayer and fasting, committed them to the Lord, in whom they had put their trust After going through Pisidia, they came into Pamphylia, and when they had preached the word in Perga, they went down to Attalia. From Attalia, they sailed back to Antioch, where they had been committed to the grace of God for the work they had now completed. On arriving there, they gathered the church together and reported all that God had done through them and how he had opened a door of faith to the Gentiles. And they stayed there a long time with the disciples

Chapter 15

Certain people came down from Judea to Antioch and were teaching the believers: "Unless you are circumcised, according to the custom taught by Moses, you cannot be saved." This brought Paul and Barnabas into sharp dispute and debate with them. So Paul and Barnabas were appointed, along with some other believers, to go up to Jerusalem to see the apostles and elders about this question. The church sent them on their way, and as they traveled through Phoenicia and Samaria, they told how the Gentiles had been converted. This news made all the believers very glad. When they came to Jerusalem, they were welcomed by the church and the apostles and elders, to whom they reported everything God had done through them Then some of the believers who belonged to the party of the Pharisees stood up and said, "The Gentiles must be circumcised and required to keep the law of Moses." The apostles and elders met to consider this question. After much discussion, Peter got up and addressed them: "Brothers, you know that some time ago God made a choice among you that the Gentiles might hear from my lips the message of the gospel and believe. God, who knows the heart, showed that he accepted them by giving the Holy Spirit to them, just as he did to us. He did not discriminate between us and them, for he purified their hearts by faith. Now then, why do you try to test God by putting on the necks of Gentiles a yoke that neither we nor our ancestors have been able to bear? No! We believe it is through the grace of our Lord Jesus that we are saved, just as they are." The whole assembly became silent as they listened to Barnabas and Paul telling about the signs and wonders God had done among the Gentiles through them. When they finished, James spoke up. "Brothers," he said, "listen to me. Simon has described to us how God first intervened to choose a people for his name from the Gentiles. The words of the prophets are in agreement with this, as it is written: "'After this, I will return and rebuild David's fallen tent. Its ruins I will rebuild, and I will restore it, that the rest of mankind may seek the Lord, even all the Gentiles who bear my name, says the Lord, who does these things'— things known from long ago "It is my judgment, therefore, that we should not make it difficult for the Gentiles who are turning to God. Instead, we should write to them, telling them to abstain from food polluted by idols, from sexual immorality, from the meat of strangled animals, and from blood. For the law of Moses has been preached in every city from the earliest times and is read in the synagogues on every Sabbath." Then the apostles and elders, with the whole church, decided to choose some of their own men and send them to Antioch with Paul and Barnabas. They chose Judas (called Barsabbas) and Silas, men who were leaders among the believers. With them, they sent the following letter: The apostles and elders, your brothers, To the Gentile believers in Antioch, Syria, and Cilicia: Greetings We have heard that some went out from us without our authorization and disturbed you, troubling your minds by what they said. So we all agreed to choose some men and send them to you with our dear friends Barnabas and Paul—men who have risked their lives for the name of our Lord Jesus Christ. Therefore we are sending Judas and Silas to confirm by word of mouth what we are writing. It seemed good to the Holy Spirit and to us not to burden you with anything beyond the following requirements: You are to abstain from food sacrificed to idols, from blood, from the meat of strangled animals, and from sexual immorality. You will do well to avoid these things Farewell So the men were sent off and went down to Antioch, where they gathered the church together and delivered the letter. The people read it and were glad for its encouraging message. Judas and Silas, who themselves were prophets, said much to encourage and strengthen the believers. After spending some time there, they were sent off by the believers with the blessing of peace to return to those who had sent them. But Paul and Barnabas remained in Antioch, where they and many others taught and preached the word of the Lord Some time later, Paul said to Barnabas, "Let us go back and visit the believers in all the towns where we preached the word of the Lord and see how they are doing." Barnabas wanted to take John, also called Mark, with them, but Paul did not think it wise to take him because he had deserted them in Pamphylia and had not continued with them in the work. They had such a sharp disagreement that they parted company. Barnabas took Mark and sailed for Cyprus, but Paul chose Silas and left, commended by the believers to the grace of the Lord. He went through Syria and Cilicia, strengthening the churches

Chapter 16

Paul traveled to Derbe and Lystra, where he met a disciple named Timothy. Timothy's mother was a Jewish believer, but his father was Greek. The brothers and sisters in Lystra and Iconium spoke highly of Timothy. Paul wanted to take him along on the journey, so he circumcised Timothy because of the Jews who lived in that area, for they all knew that his father was Greek. As they traveled from town to town, they delivered the decisions reached by the apostles and elders in Jerusalem for the people to obey. The churches were strengthened in the faith and grew daily in numbers Paul and his companions traveled throughout the region of Phrygia and Galatia, having been kept by the Holy Spirit from preaching the word in the province of Asia. When they came to the border of Mysia, they tried to enter Bithynia, but the Spirit of Jesus would not allow them to. So they passed by Mysia and went down to Troas. During the night, Paul had a vision of a man from Macedonia standing and begging him, "Come over to Macedonia and help us." After Paul had seen the vision, they got ready at once to leave for Macedonia, concluding that God had called them to preach the gospel to them From Troas, they put out to sea and sailed straight for Samothrace, and the next day they went on to Neapolis. From there, they traveled to

Philippi, a Roman colony and the leading city of that district of Macedonia. They stayed there several days. On the Sabbath, they went outside the city gate to the river, where they expected to find a place of prayer. They sat down and began to speak to the women who had gathered there. One of those listening was a woman from the city of Thyatira named Lydia, a dealer in purple cloth. She was a worshiper of God. The Lord opened her heart to respond to Paul's message. When she and the members of her household were baptized, she invited them to her home. "If you consider me a believer in the Lord," she said, "come and stay at my house." And she persuaded them Once, when they were going to the place of prayer, they were met by a female slave who had a spirit by which she predicted the future. She earned a great deal of money for her owners by fortune-telling. She followed Paul and the rest of them, shouting, "These men are servants of the Most High God, who are telling you the way to be saved." She kept this up for many days. Finally, Paul became so annoyed that he turned around and said to the spirit, "In the name of Jesus Christ, I command you to come out of her!" At that moment, the spirit left her When her owners realized that their hope of making money was gone, they seized Paul and Silas and dragged them into the marketplace to face the authorities. They brought them before the magistrates and said, "These men are Jews, and they are throwing our city into an uproar by advocating customs unlawful for us Romans to accept or practice." The crowd joined in the attack against Paul and Silas, and the magistrates ordered them to be stripped and beaten with rods. After they had been severely flogged, they were thrown into prison, and the jailer was commanded to guard them carefully. When he received these orders, he put them in the inner cell and fastened their feet in the stocks About midnight, Paul and Silas were praying and singing hymns to God, and the other prisoners were listening to them. Suddenly there was such a violent earthquake that the foundations of the prison were shaken. At once, all the prison doors flew open, and everyone's chains came loose. The jailer woke up, and when he saw the prison doors open, he drew his sword and was about to kill himself because he thought the prisoners had escaped. But Paul shouted, "Don't harm yourself! We are all here!" The jailer called for lights, rushed in, and fell trembling before Paul and Silas. He then brought them out and asked, "Sirs, what must I do to be saved?" They replied, "Believe in the Lord Jesus, and you will be saved—you and your household." Then they spoke the word of the Lord to him and to all the others in his house. At that hour of the night, the jailer took them and washed their wounds; then immediately he and all his household were baptized. The jailer brought them into his house and set a meal before them; he was filled with joy because he had come to believe in God—he and his whole household When it was daylight, the magistrates sent their officers to the jailer with the order: "Release those men." The jailer told Paul, "The magistrates have ordered that you and Silas be released. Now you can leave. Go in peace." But Paul said to the officers, "They beat us publicly without a trial, even though we are Roman citizens, and threw us into prison. And now do they want to get rid of us quietly? No! Let them come themselves and escort us out." The officers reported this to the magistrates, and when they heard that Paul and Silas were Roman citizens, they were alarmed. They came to appease them and escorted them from the prison, requesting them to leave the city. After Paul and Silas came out of the prison, they went to Lydia's house, where they met with the brothers and sisters and encouraged them. Then they left

Chapter 17

After Paul and Silas had passed through Amphipolis and Apollonia, they came to Thessalonica, where there was a Jewish synagogue. As was his custom, Paul went into the synagogue, and on three Sabbath days, he reasoned with them from the Scriptures, explaining and proving that the Messiah had to suffer and rise from the dead. "This Jesus I am proclaiming to you is the Messiah," he said. Some of the Jews were persuaded and joined Paul and Silas, as did a large number of God-fearing Greeks and quite a few prominent women But other Jews were jealous; so they rounded up some bad characters from the marketplace, formed a mob, and started a riot in the city. They rushed to Jason's house in search of Paul and Silas in order to bring them out to the crowd. But when they did not find them, they dragged Jason and some other believers before the city officials, shouting, "These men who have caused trouble all over the world have now come here, and Jason has welcomed them into his house. They are all defying Caesar's decrees, saying that there is another king, one called Jesus." When they heard this, the crowd and the city officials were thrown into turmoil. Then they made Jason and the others post bond and let them go As soon as it was night, the believers sent Paul and Silas away to Berea. On arriving there, they went to the Jewish synagogue. Now the Berean Jews were of more noble character than those in Thessalonica, for they received the message with great eagerness and examined the Scriptures every day to see if what Paul said was true. As a result, many of them believed, as did also a number of prominent Greek women and many Greek men But when the Jews in Thessalonica learned that Paul was preaching the word of God at Berea, some of them went there too, agitating the crowds and stirring them up. The believers immediately sent Paul to the coast, but Silas and Timothy stayed at Berea. Those who escorted Paul brought him to Athens and then left with instructions for Silas and Timothy to join him as soon as possible While Paul was waiting for them in Athens, he was greatly distressed to see that the city was full of idols. So he reasoned in the synagogue with both Jews and God-fearing Greeks, as well as in the marketplace day by day with those who happened to be there. A group of Epicurean and Stoic philosophers began to debate with him. Some of them asked, "What is this babbler trying to say?" Others remarked, "He seems to be advocating foreign gods." They said this because Paul was preaching the good news about Jesus and the resurrection. Then they took him and brought him to a meeting of the Areopagus, where they said to him, "May we know what this new teaching is that you are presenting? You are bringing some strange ideas to our ears, and we would like to know what they mean." (All the Athenians and the foreigners who lived there spent their time doing nothing but talking about and listening to the latest ideas.) Paul then stood up in the meeting of the Areopagus and said: "People of Athens! I see that in every way you are very religious. For as I walked around and looked carefully at your objects of worship, I even found an altar with this inscription: TO AN UNKNOWN GOD. So you are ignorant of the very thing you worship—and this is what I am going to proclaim to you "The God who made the world and everything in it is the Lord of heaven and earth and does not live in temples built by human hands. And he is not served by human hands, as if he needed anything. Rather, he himself gives everyone life and breath and everything else. From one man he made all the nations, that they should inhabit the whole earth; and he marked out their appointed times in history and the boundaries of their lands. God did this so that they would seek him and perhaps reach out for him and find him, though he is not far from any one of us. 'For in him we live and move and have our being.' As some of your own poets have said, 'We are his offspring.' "Therefore, since we are God's offspring, we should not think that the divine being is like gold or silver or stone—an image made by human design and skill. In the past, God overlooked such ignorance, but now he commands all people everywhere to repent. For he has set a day when he will judge the world with justice by the man he has appointed. He has given proof of this to everyone by raising him from the dead." When they heard about the resurrection of the dead, some of them sneered, but others said, "We want to hear you again on this subject." At that, Paul left the Council. Some of the people became followers of Paul and believed. Among them was Dionysius, a member of the Areopagus, also a woman named Damaris, and a number of others

Chapter 18

After this, Paul left Athens and went to Corinth. There he met a Jew named Aquila, a native of Pontus, who had recently come from Italy with his wife Priscilla because Claudius had ordered all Jews to leave Rome. Paul went to see them, and because he was a tentmaker as they were, he stayed and worked with them. Every Sabbath, he reasoned in the synagogue, trying to persuade Jews and Greeks When Silas and Timothy came from Macedonia, Paul devoted himself exclusively to preaching, testifying to the Jews that Jesus was the Messiah. But when they opposed Paul and became abusive, he shook out his clothes in protest and said to them, "Your blood be on your own heads! I am innocent of it. From now on I will go to the Gentiles." Then Paul left the synagogue and went next door to the house of Titius Justus, a worshiper of God. Crispus, the synagogue leader, and his entire household believed in the Lord; and many of the Corinthians who heard Paul believed and were baptized One night the Lord spoke to Paul in a vision: "Do not be afraid; keep on speaking, do not be silent. For I am with you, and no one is going to attack and harm you because I have many people in this city." So Paul stayed in Corinth for a year and a half, teaching them the word of God While Gallio was proconsul of Achaia, the Jews of Corinth made a united attack on Paul and brought him to the place of judgment. "This man," they charged, "is persuading the people to worship God in ways contrary to the law." Just as Paul was about to speak, Gallio said to them, "If you Jews were making a complaint about some misdemeanor or serious crime, it would be reasonable for me to listen to you. But since it involves questions about words and names and your own law—settle the matter yourselves. I will not be a judge of such things." So he drove them off. Then the crowd there turned on Sosthenes the synagogue leader and beat him in front of the proconsul, and Gallio showed no concern whatever Paul stayed on in Corinth for some time. Then he left the brothers and sisters and sailed for Syria, accompanied by Priscilla and Aquila. Before he sailed, he had his hair cut off at Cenchreae because of a vow he had taken. They arrived at Ephesus, where Paul left Priscilla and Aquila. He himself went into the synagogue and reasoned with the Jews. When they asked him to spend more time with them, he declined. But as he left, he promised, "I will come back if it is God's will." Then he set sail from Ephesus When he landed at Caesarea, he went up to Jerusalem and greeted the church and then went down to Antioch. After spending some time in Antioch, Paul set out from there and traveled from place to place throughout the region of Galatia and Phrygia, strengthening all the disciples Meanwhile, a Jew named Apollos, a native of Alexandria, came to Ephesus. He was a learned man, with a thorough knowledge of the Scriptures. He had been instructed in the way of the Lord, and he spoke with great fervor and taught about Jesus accurately, though he knew only the baptism of John. He began to speak boldly in the synagogue. When Priscilla and Aquila heard him, they invited him to their home and explained to him the way of God more adequately When Apollos wanted to go to Achaia, the brothers and sisters encouraged him and wrote to the disciples there to welcome him. When he arrived, he was a great help to those who by grace had believed. For he vigorously refuted his Jewish opponents in public debate, proving from the Scriptures that Jesus was the Messiah

Chapter 19

While Apollos was at Corinth, Paul took the road through the interior and arrived at Ephesus. There he found some disciples and asked them, "Did you receive the Holy Spirit when you believed?" They answered, "No, we have not even heard that there is a Holy Spirit." So Paul asked, "Then what baptism did you receive?" "John's baptism," they replied Paul said, "John's baptism was a baptism of repentance. He told the people to believe in the one coming after him, that is, in Jesus." On hearing this, they were baptized in the name of the Lord Jesus. When Paul placed his hands on them, the Holy Spirit came on them, and they spoke in tongues and prophesied. There were about twelve men in all Paul entered the synagogue and spoke boldly there for three months, arguing persuasively about the kingdom of God. But some of them became obstinate; they refused to believe and publicly maligned the Way. So Paul left them. He took the disciples with him and had discussions daily in the lecture hall of Tyrannus. This went on for two years so that all the Jews and Greeks who lived in the province of Asia heard the word of the Lord God did extraordinary miracles through Paul so that even handkerchiefs and aprons that had touched him were taken to the sick, and their illnesses were cured, and the evil spirits left them. Some Jews who went around driving out evil spirits tried to invoke the name of the Lord Jesus over those who were demon-possessed. They would say, "In the name of the Jesus whom Paul preaches, I command you to come out." Seven sons of Sceva, a Jewish chief priest, were doing this. One day, the evil spirit answered them, "Jesus I know, and Paul I know about, but who are you?" Then the man who had the evil spirit jumped on them and overpowered them all. He gave them such a beating that they ran out of the house naked and bleeding When this became known to the Jews and Greeks living in Ephesus, they were all seized with fear, and the name of the Lord Jesus was held in high honor. Many of those who believed now came and openly confessed what they had done. A number who had practiced sorcery brought their scrolls together and burned them publicly. When they calculated the value of the scrolls, the total came to fifty thousand drachmas. In this way, the word of the Lord spread widely and grew in power After all this had happened, Paul decided to go to Jerusalem, passing through Macedonia and Achaia. "After I have been there," he said, "I must visit Rome also." He sent two of his helpers, Timothy and Erastus, to Macedonia, while he stayed in the province of Asia a little longer About that time, there arose a great disturbance about the Way. A silversmith named Demetrius, who made silver shrines of Artemis, brought in a lot of business for the craftsmen there. He called them together, along with the workers in related trades, and said: "You know, my friends, that we receive a good income from this business. And you see and hear how this fellow Paul has convinced and led astray large numbers of people here in Ephesus and in practically the whole province of Asia. He says that gods made by human hands are no gods at all. There is danger not only that our trade will lose its good name but also that the temple of the great goddess Artemis will be discredited, and the goddess herself, who is worshiped throughout the province of Asia and the world, will be robbed of her divine majesty." When they heard this, they were furious and began shouting: "Great is Artemis of the Ephesians!" Soon the whole city was in an uproar. The people seized Gaius and Aristarchus, Paul's traveling companions from Macedonia, and all of them rushed into the theater together. Paul wanted to appear before the crowd, but the disciples would not let him. Even some of the officials of the province, friends of Paul, sent him a message begging him not to venture into the theater The assembly was in confusion: Some were shouting one thing, some another. Most of the people did not even know why they were there. The Jews in the crowd pushed Alexander to the front, and they shouted instructions to him. He motioned for silence in order to make a defense before the people. But when they realized he was a Jew, they all shouted in unison for about two hours: "Great is Artemis of the Ephesians!" The city clerk quieted the crowd and said: "Fellow Ephesians, doesn't all the world know that the city of Ephesus is the guardian of the temple of the great Artemis and of her image, which fell from heaven? Therefore, since these facts are undeniable, you ought to calm down and not do anything rash. You have brought these men here, though they have neither robbed temples nor blasphemed our goddess. If, then, Demetrius and his fellow craftsmen have a grievance against anybody, the courts are open, and there are proconsuls. They can press charges. If there is anything further you want to bring up, it must be settled in a legal assembly. As it is, we are in danger of being charged with rioting because of what happened today. In that case, we would not be able to account for this commotion, since there is no reason for it." After he had said this, he dismissed the assembly

Chapter 20

When the uproar had ended, Paul sent for the disciples and, after encouraging them, said goodbye and set out for Macedonia. He traveled through that area, speaking many words of encouragement to the people, and finally arrived in Greece, where he stayed three months. Because some Jews had plotted against him just as he was about to sail for Syria, he decided to go back through Macedonia. He was accompanied by Sopater son of Pyrrhus from Berea, Aristarchus and Secundus from Thessalonica, Gaius from Derbe, Timothy also, and Tychicus and Trophimus from the province of Asia. These men went on ahead and waited for us at Troas. But we sailed from Philippi after the Festival of Unleavened Bread and five days later joined the others at Troas, where we stayed seven days On the first day of the week, we came together to break bread. Paul spoke to the people and, because he intended to leave the next day, kept on talking until midnight. There were many lamps in the upstairs room where we were meeting. Seated in a window was a young man named Eutychus, who was sinking into a deep sleep as Paul talked on and on. When he was sound asleep, he fell to the ground from the third story and was picked up dead. Paul went down, threw himself on the young man, and put his arms around him. "Don't be alarmed," he said. "He's

alive!" Then he went upstairs again and broke bread and ate. After talking until daylight, he left. The people took the young man home alive and were greatly comforted We went on ahead to the ship and sailed for Assos, where we were going to take Paul aboard. He had made this arrangement because he was going there on foot. When he met us at Assos, we took him aboard and went on to Mitylene. The next day, we set sail from there and arrived off Chios. The day after that, we crossed over to Samos, and on the following day arrived at Miletus. Paul had decided to sail past Ephesus to avoid spending time in the province of Asia, for he was in a hurry to reach Jerusalem, if possible, by the day of Pentecost From Miletus, Paul sent to Ephesus for the elders of the church. When they arrived, he said to them: "You know how I lived the whole time I was with you, from the first day I came into the province of Asia. I served the Lord with great humility and with tears and in the midst of severe testing by the plots of my Jewish opponents. You know that I have not hesitated to preach anything that would be helpful to you but have taught you publicly and from house to house. I have declared to both Jews and Greeks that they must turn to God in repentance and have faith in our Lord Jesus "And now, compelled by the Spirit, I am going to Jerusalem, not knowing what will happen to me there. I only know that in every city the Holy Spirit warns me that prison and hardships are facing me. However, I consider my life worth nothing to me; my only aim is to finish the race and complete the task the Lord Jesus has given me—the task of testifying to the good news of God's grace "Now I know that none of you among whom I have gone about preaching the kingdom will ever see me again. Therefore, I declare to you today that I am innocent of the blood of any of you. For I have not hesitated to proclaim to you the whole will of God. Keep watch over yourselves and all the flock of which the Holy Spirit has made you overseers. Be shepherds of the church of God, which he bought with his own blood. I know that after I leave, savage wolves will come in among you and will not spare the flock. Even from your own number, men will arise and distort the truth in order to draw away disciples after them. So be on your guard! Remember that for three years, I never stopped warning each of you night and day with tears "Now I commit you to God and to the word of his grace, which can build you up and give you an inheritance among all those who are sanctified. I have not coveted anyone's silver or gold or clothing. You yourselves know that these hands of mine have supplied my own needs and the needs of my companions. In everything I did, I showed you that by this kind of hard work we must help the weak, remembering the words the Lord Jesus himself said: 'It is more blessed to give than to receive.'" When Paul had finished speaking, he knelt down with all of them and prayed. They all wept as they embraced him and kissed him. What grieved them most was his statement that they would never see his face again. Then they accompanied him to the ship

Chapter 21

After saying our farewells, we set sail for Coos, and the next day, we reached Rhodes and then Patara. We found a ship crossing over to Phoenicia, went aboard, and set sail. When we sighted Cyprus, we passed it on our left and sailed to Syria. We landed at Tyre, where the ship was to unload its cargo. We sought out the disciples there and stayed with them for seven days. Through the Spirit, they urged Paul not to go to Jerusalem. When our time was up, we left and continued on our way. All the disciples, along with their wives and children, accompanied us out of the city. On the beach, we knelt to pray. After saying goodbye to each other, we boarded the ship, and they returned home We continued our voyage from Tyre and arrived at Ptolemais. We greeted the brothers and sisters there and stayed with them for a day. Leaving the next day, we reached Caesarea and stayed at the house of Philip the evangelist, one of the seven. He had four unmarried daughters who prophesied. After we had been there for several days, a prophet named Agabus came down from Judea. Coming over to us, he took Paul's belt, tied his own hands and feet with it, and said, "The Holy Spirit says, 'In this way, the Jewish leaders in Jerusalem will bind the owner of this belt and will hand him over to the Gentiles.'" When we heard this, we and the people there pleaded with Paul not to go up to Jerusalem. Paul answered, "Why are you weeping and breaking my heart? I am ready not only to be bound but also to die in Jerusalem for the name of the Lord Jesus." When he would not be dissuaded, we gave up and said, "The Lord's will be done." After this, we started on our way to Jerusalem. Some of the disciples from Caesarea accompanied us and brought us to the home of Mnason, where we were to stay. He was a man from Cyprus and one of the early disciples. When we arrived in Jerusalem, the brothers and sisters received us warmly. The next day, Paul and the rest of us went to see James, and all the elders were present. Paul greeted them and reported in detail what God had done among the Gentiles through his ministry. When they heard this, they praised God Then they said to Paul, "You see, brother, how many thousands of Jews have believed, and all of them are zealous for the law. They have been informed that you teach all the Jews who live among the Gentiles to turn away from Moses, telling them not to circumcise their children or live according to our customs. What shall we do? They will certainly hear that you have come, so do what we tell you. There are four men with us who have made a vow. Take these men, join in their purification rites, and pay their expenses so that they can have their heads shaved. Then everyone will know there is no truth in these reports about you, but that you yourself are living in obedience to the law. As for the Gentile believers, we have written to them our decision that they should abstain from food sacrificed to idols, from blood, from the meat of strangled animals, and from sexual immorality." The next day, Paul took the men and purified himself along with them. Then he went to the temple to give notice of the date when the days of purification would end and the offering would be made for each of them. When the seven days were nearly over, some Jews from the province of Asia saw Paul at the temple. They stirred up the whole crowd and seized him, shouting, "Fellow Israelites, help us! This is the man who teaches everyone everywhere against our people and our law and this place. And besides, he has brought Greeks into the temple and defiled this holy place." (They had previously seen Trophimus the Ephesian in the city with Paul and assumed that Paul had brought him into the temple.) The whole city was aroused, and the people came running from all directions. Seizing Paul, they dragged him from the temple, and immediately the gates were shut. While they were trying to kill him, news reached the commander of the Roman troops that the whole city of Jerusalem was in an uproar. He at once took some officers and soldiers and ran down to the crowd. When the rioters saw the commander and his soldiers, they stopped beating Paul. The commander came up and arrested him and ordered him to be bound with two chains. Then he asked who he was and what he had done. Some in the crowd shouted one thing and some another, and since the commander could not get at the truth because of the uproar, he ordered that Paul be taken into the barracks. When Paul reached the steps, the violence of the mob was so great he had to be carried by the soldiers. The crowd that followed kept shouting, "Get rid of him!" As the soldiers were about to take Paul into the barracks, he asked the commander, "May I say something to you?" "Do you speak Greek?" he replied. "Aren't you the Egyptian who started a revolt and led four thousand terrorists out into the wilderness some time ago?" Paul answered, "I am a Jew, from Tarsus in Cilicia, a citizen of no ordinary city. Please let me speak to the people." After receiving the commander's permission, Paul stood on the steps and motioned to the crowd. When they were all silent, he said to them in Aramaic:

Chapter 22

"Brothers and fathers, listen now to my defense." When they heard him speak to them in Aramaic, they became very quiet. Then Paul said: "I am a Jew, born in Tarsus of Cilicia, but brought up in this city. I studied under Gamaliel and was thoroughly trained in the law of our ancestors. I was just as zealous for God as any of you are today. I persecuted the followers of this Way to their death, arresting both men and women and throwing them into prison, as the high priest and all the Council can themselves testify. I even obtained letters from them to their associates in Damascus and went there to bring these people as prisoners to Jerusalem to be punished "About noon as I came near Damascus, suddenly a bright light from heaven flashed around me. I fell to the ground and heard a voice say to me, 'Saul! Saul! Why do you persecute me?' "Who are you, Lord?' I asked. "'I am Jesus of Nazareth, whom you are persecuting,' he replied. My companions saw the light, but they did not understand the voice of him who was speaking to me. "'What shall I do, Lord?' I asked. "'Get up,' the Lord said, 'and go into Damascus. There you will be told all that you have been assigned to do.' My companions led me by the hand into Damascus because the brilliance of the light had blinded me "A man named Ananias came to see me. He was a devout observer of the law and highly respected by all the Jews living there. He stood beside me and said, 'Brother Saul, receive your sight!' And at that very moment, I was able to see him. "Then he said: 'The God of our ancestors has chosen you to know his will and to see the Righteous One and to hear words from his mouth. You will be his witness to all people of what you have seen and heard. And now what are you waiting for? Get up, be baptized, and wash your sins away, calling on his name.' "When I returned to Jerusalem and was praying at the temple, I fell into a trance and saw the Lord speaking to me. 'Quick!' he said. 'Leave Jerusalem immediately because the people here will not accept your testimony about me.' "'Lord,' I replied, 'these people know that I went from one synagogue to another to imprison and beat those who believe in you. And when the blood of your martyr Stephen was shed, I stood there giving my approval and guarding the clothes of those who were killing him.' "Then the Lord said to me, 'Go; I will send you far away to the Gentiles.'" The crowd listened to Paul until he said this. Then they raised their voices and shouted, "Rid the earth of him! He's not fit to live!" As they were shouting and throwing off their cloaks and flinging dust into the air, the commander ordered that Paul be taken into the barracks. He directed that he be flogged and interrogated in order to find out why the people were shouting at him like this. As they stretched him out to flog him, Paul said to the centurion standing there, "Is it legal for you to flog a Roman citizen who hasn't even been found guilty?" When the centurion heard this, he went to the commander and reported it. "What are you going to do?" he asked. "This man is a Roman citizen." The commander went to Paul and asked, "Tell me, are you a Roman citizen?" "Yes, I am," he answered. Then the commander said, "I had to pay a lot of money for my citizenship." "But I was born a citizen," Paul replied. Those who were about to interrogate him withdrew immediately. The commander himself was alarmed when he realized that he had put Paul, a Roman citizen, in chains The commander wanted to find out exactly why Paul was being accused by the Jews. So the next day, he released him and ordered the chief priests and all the members of the Sanhedrin to assemble. Then he brought Paul and had him stand before them

Chapter 23

Paul looked straight at the Sanhedrin and said, "My brothers, I have fulfilled my duty to God in all good conscience to this day." At this, the high priest Ananias ordered those standing near Paul to strike him on the mouth. Then Paul said to him, "God will strike you, you whitewashed wall! You sit there to judge me according to the law, yet you yourself violate the law by commanding that I be struck!" Those who were standing near Paul said, "How dare you insult God's high priest!" Paul replied, "Brothers, I did not realize that he was the high priest; for it is written: 'Do not speak evil about the ruler of your people.'" Then Paul, knowing that some of them were Sadducees and the others Pharisees, called out in the Sanhedrin, "My brothers, I am a Pharisee, descended from Pharisees. I stand on trial because of the hope of the resurrection of the dead." When he said this, a dispute broke out between the Pharisees and the Sadducees, and the assembly was divided. (The Sadducees say that there is no resurrection, and that there are neither angels nor spirits, but the Pharisees believe all these things.) There was a great uproar, and some of the teachers of the law who were Pharisees stood up and argued vigorously. "We find nothing wrong with this man," they said. "What if a spirit or an angel has spoken to him?" The dispute became so violent that the commander was afraid Paul would be torn to pieces by them. He ordered the troops to go down and take him away from them by force and bring him into the barracks The following night the Lord stood near Paul and said, "Take courage! As you have testified about me in Jerusalem, so you must also testify in Rome." The next morning, some Jews formed a conspiracy and bound themselves with an oath not to eat or drink until they had killed Paul. More than forty men were involved in this plot. They went to the chief priests and the elders and said, "We have taken a solemn oath not to eat anything until we have killed Paul. Now then, you and the Sanhedrin petition the commander to bring him before you on the pretext of wanting more accurate information about his case. We are ready to kill him before he gets here." But when the son of Paul's sister heard of this plot, he went into the barracks and told Paul. Then Paul called one of the centurions and said, "Take this young man to the commander; he has something to tell him." So he took him to the commander. The centurion said, "Paul, the prisoner, sent for me and asked me to bring this young man to you because he has something to tell you." The commander took the young man by the hand, drew him aside, and asked, "What is it you want to tell me?" He said, "Some Jews have agreed to ask you to bring Paul before the Sanhedrin tomorrow on the pretext of wanting more accurate information about him. Don't give in to them because more than forty of them are waiting in ambush for him. They have taken an oath not to eat

or drink until they have killed him. They are ready now, waiting for your consent to their request." The commander dismissed the young man with this warning: "Don't tell anyone that you have reported this to me." Then he called two of his centurions and ordered them, "Get ready a detachment of two hundred soldiers, seventy horsemen, and two hundred spearmen to go to Caesarea at nine tonight. Provide horses for Paul so that he may be taken safely to Governor Felix." He wrote a letter as follows: "Claudius Lysias, To His Excellency, Governor Felix: Greetings This man was seized by the Jews, and they were about to kill him, but I came with my troops and rescued him, for I had learned that he is a Roman citizen. I wanted to know why they were accusing him, so I brought him to their Sanhedrin. I found that the accusation had to do with questions about their law, but there was no charge against him that deserved death or imprisonment. When I was informed of a plot to be carried out against the man, I sent him to you at once. I also ordered his accusers to present to you their case against him So the soldiers, carrying out their orders, took Paul with them during the night and brought him as far as Antipatris. The next day they let the cavalry go on with him, while they returned to the barracks. When the cavalry arrived in Caesarea, they delivered the letter to the governor and handed Paul over to him. The governor read the letter and asked what province he was from. Learning that he was from Cilicia, he said, "I will hear your case when your accusers get here." Then he ordered that Paul be kept under guard in Herod's palace

Chapter 24

Five days later, the high priest Ananias went down to Caesarea with some of the elders and a lawyer named Tertullus, and they brought their charges against Paul before the governor. When Paul was called in, Tertullus presented his case before Felix: "We have enjoyed a long period of peace under you, and your foresight has brought about reforms in this nation. Everywhere and in every way, most excellent Felix, we acknowledge this with profound gratitude. But in order not to weary you further, I would request that you be kind enough to hear us briefly "We have found this man to be a troublemaker, stirring up riots among the Jews all over the world. He is a ringleader of the Nazarene sect and even tried to desecrate the temple, so we seized him. By examining him yourself, you will be able to learn the truth about all these charges we are bringing against him." The other Jews joined in the accusation, asserting that these things were true When the governor motioned for him to speak, Paul replied: "I know that for a number of years you have been a judge over this nation; so I gladly make my defense. You can easily verify that no more than twelve days ago, I went up to Jerusalem to worship. My accusers did not find me arguing with anyone at the temple or stirring up a crowd in the synagogues or anywhere else in the city. And they cannot prove to you the charges they are now making against me. However, I admit that I worship the God of our ancestors as a follower of the Way, which they call a sect. I believe everything that is in accordance with the Law and that is written in the Prophets, and I have the same hope in God as these men themselves have, that there will be a resurrection of both the righteous and the wicked. So I strive always to keep my conscience clear before God and man "After an absence of several years, I came to Jerusalem to bring my people gifts for the poor and to present offerings. I was ceremonially clean when they found me in the temple courts doing this. There was no crowd with me, nor was I involved in any disturbance. But there are some Jews from the province of Asia who ought to be here before you and bring charges if they have anything against me. Or these who are here should state what crime they found in me when I stood before the Sanhedrin—unless it was this one thing I shouted as I stood in their presence: 'It is concerning the resurrection of the dead that I am on trial before you today.'" Then Felix, who was well acquainted with the Way, adjourned the proceedings. "When Lysias the commander comes," he said, "I will decide your case." He ordered the centurion to keep Paul under guard but to give him some freedom and permit his friends to take care of his needs Several days later, Felix came with his wife Drusilla, who was Jewish. He sent for Paul and listened to him as he spoke about faith in Christ Jesus. As Paul talked about righteousness, self-control, and the judgment to come, Felix was afraid and said, "That's enough for now! You may leave. When I find it convenient, I will send for you." At the same time, he was hoping that Paul would offer him a bribe, so he sent for him frequently and talked with him When two years had passed, Felix was succeeded by Porcius Festus, but because Felix wanted to grant a favor to the Jews, he left Paul in prison

Chapter 25

Three days after arriving in the province, Festus went up from Caesarea to Jerusalem, where the chief priests and the Jewish leaders appeared before him and presented the charges against Paul. They requested Festus, as a favor to them, to have Paul transferred to Jerusalem, for they were preparing an ambush to kill him along the way. Festus answered, "Paul is being held at Caesarea, and I myself am going there soon. Let some of your leaders come with me and press charges against the man there if he has done anything wrong." After spending eight or ten days with them, Festus went down to Caesarea. The next day, he convened the court and ordered that Paul be brought before him. When Paul came in, the Jews who had come down from Jerusalem stood around him. They brought many serious charges against him, but they could not prove them. Then Paul made his defense: "I have done nothing wrong against the Jewish law or against the temple or against Caesar." Festus, wishing to do the Jews a favor, said to Paul, "Are you willing to go up to Jerusalem and stand trial before me there on these charges?" Paul answered: "I am now standing before Caesar's court, where I ought to be tried. I have not done any wrong to the Jews, as you yourself know very well. If, however, I am guilty of doing anything deserving death, I do not refuse to die. But if the charges brought against me by these Jews are not true, no one has the right to hand me over to them. I appeal to Caesar!" After Festus had conferred with his council, he declared: "You have appealed to Caesar. To Caesar you will go!" A few days later King Agrippa and Bernice arrived at Caesarea to pay their respects to Festus. Since they were spending many days there, Festus discussed Paul's case with the king. He said: "There is a man here whom Felix left as a prisoner. When I went to Jerusalem, the chief priests and the elders of the Jews brought charges against him and asked that he be condemned "I told them that it is not the Roman custom to hand over anyone before they have faced their accusers and have had an opportunity to defend themselves against the charges. When they came here with me, I did not delay the case but convened the court the next day and ordered the man to be brought in. When his accusers got up to speak, they did not charge him with any of the crimes I had expected. Instead, they had some points of dispute with him about their own religion and about a dead man named Jesus who

Paul claimed was alive. I was at a loss how to investigate such matters, so I asked if he would be willing to go to Jerusalem and stand trial there on these charges. But when Paul made his appeal to be held over for the Emperor's decision, I ordered him held until I could send him to Caesar." Then Agrippa said to Festus, "I would like to hear this man myself." He replied, "Tomorrow you will hear him." The next day, Agrippa and Bernice came with great pomp and entered the audience room with the high-ranking military officers and the prominent men of the city. At the command of Festus, Paul was brought in. Festus said: "King Agrippa, and all who are present with us, you see this man! The whole Jewish community has petitioned me about him in Jerusalem and here in Caesarea, shouting that he ought not to live any longer. I found he had done nothing deserving of death, but because he made his appeal to the Emperor, I decided to send him to Rome. But I have nothing definite to write to His Majesty about him. Therefore, I have brought him before all of you, and especially before you, King Agrippa, so that as a result of this investigation, I may have something to write. For I think it is unreasonable to send a prisoner on to Rome without specifying the charges against him."

Chapter 26

Then Agrippa said to Paul, "You are permitted to speak for yourself." Paul stretched out his hand and began his defense. "I consider myself fortunate, King Agrippa, to stand before you today and make my defense against all the accusations brought by the Jews, especially since you are well acquainted with all the Jewish customs and controversies. Therefore, I beg you to listen to me patiently The Jews all know the way I have lived ever since I was a child, from the beginning of my life in my own country and also in Jerusalem. They have known me for a long time and can testify, if they are willing, that I conformed to the strictest sect of our religion, living as a Pharisee. And now it is because of my hope in what God has promised our ancestors that I am on trial today. This is the promise our twelve tribes are hoping to see fulfilled as they earnestly serve God day and night. King Agrippa, it is because of this hope that these Jews are accusing me. Why should any of you consider it incredible that God raises the dead? I too was convinced that I ought to do all that was possible to oppose the name of Jesus of Nazareth. And that is just what I did in Jerusalem. On the authority of the chief priests, I put many of the Lord's people in prison, and when they were put to death, I cast my vote against them. Many a time I went from one synagogue to another to have them punished, and I tried to force them to blaspheme. I was so obsessed with persecuting them that I even hunted them down in foreign cities On one of these journeys, I was going to Damascus with the authority and commission of the chief priests. About noon, King Agrippa, as I was on the road, I saw a light from heaven, brighter than the sun, blazing around me and my companions. We all fell to the ground, and I heard a voice saying to me in Aramaic, 'Saul, Saul, why do you persecute me? It is hard for you to kick against the goads.' Then I asked, 'Who are you, Lord?' 'I am Jesus, whom you are persecuting,' the Lord replied. 'Now get up and stand on your feet. I have appeared to you to appoint you as a servant and as a witness of what you have seen and will see of me. I will rescue you from your own people and from the Gentiles. I am sending you to them to open their eyes and turn them from darkness to light, and from the power of Satan to God, so that they may receive forgiveness of sins and a place among those who are sanctified by faith in me.' So then, King Agrippa, I was not disobedient to the vision from heaven. First to those in Damascus, then to those in Jerusalem and in all Judea, and then to the Gentiles, I preached that they should repent and turn to God and demonstrate their repentance by their deeds. That is why some Jews seized me in the temple courts and tried to kill me. But God has helped me to this very day; so I stand here and testify to small and great alike. I am saying nothing beyond what the prophets and Moses said would happen— that the Messiah would suffer and, as the first to rise from the dead, would bring the message of light to his own people and to the Gentiles." At this point, Festus interrupted Paul's defense. "You are out of your mind, Paul!" he shouted. "Your great learning is driving you insane." "I am not insane, most excellent Festus," Paul replied. "What I am saying is true and reasonable. The king is familiar with these things, and I can speak freely to him. I am convinced that none of this has escaped his notice because it was not done in a corner. King Agrippa, do you believe the prophets? I know you do." Then Agrippa said to Paul, "Do you think that in such a short time you can persuade me to be a Christian?" Paul replied, "Short time or long—I pray to God that not only you but all who are listening to me today may become what I am, except for these chains." The king rose, and with him the governor and Bernice and those sitting with them. After they left the room, they began saying to one another, "This man is not doing anything that deserves death or imprisonment." Agrippa said to Festus, "This man could have been set free if he had not appealed to Caesar."

Chapter 27

When it was decided that we would sail for Italy, Paul and some other prisoners were handed over to a centurion named Julius, who belonged to the Imperial Regiment. We boarded a ship from Adramyttium about to sail for ports along the coast of the province of Asia, and we put out to sea. Aristarchus, a Macedonian from Thessalonica, was with us The next day we landed at Sidon; and Julius, in kindness to Paul, allowed him to go to his friends so they might provide for his needs. From there we put out to sea again and passed to the lee of Cyprus because the winds were against us. When we had sailed across the open sea off the coast of Cilicia and Pamphylia, we landed at Myra in Lycia. There the centurion found an Alexandrian ship sailing for Italy and put us on board. We made slow headway for many days and had difficulty arriving off Cnidus. When the wind did not allow us to hold our course, we sailed to the lee of Crete, opposite Salmone. We moved along the coast with difficulty and came to a place called Fair Havens, near the town of Lasea Much time had been lost, and sailing had already become dangerous because by now it was after the Day of Atonement. So Paul warned them, "Men, I can see that our voyage is going to be disastrous and bring great loss to ship and cargo, and to our own lives also." But the centurion, instead of listening to what Paul said, followed the advice of the pilot and the owner of the ship. Since the harbor was unsuitable to winter in, the majority decided that we should sail on, hoping to reach Phoenix and winter there. This was a harbor in Crete, facing both southwest and northwest When a gentle south wind began to blow, they saw their opportunity; so they weighed anchor and sailed along the shore of Crete. Before very long, a wind of hurricane force, called the Northeaster, swept down from the island. The ship was caught by the storm and could not head into the wind; so we gave way to it and were driven along. As we passed to the lee of a small island called Cauda, we were hardly able to make the lifeboat secure, so the men hoisted it aboard. Then they passed ropes under the ship itself to hold it together. Because they were afraid they would run aground on the sandbars of Syrtis, they lowered the sea anchor and let the ship be driven along. We took such a violent battering from the storm that the next day they began to throw the cargo overboard. On the third day, they threw the ship's tackle overboard with their own hands. When neither sun nor stars appeared for many days and the storm continued raging, we finally gave up all hope of being saved After they had gone a long time without food, Paul stood up before them and said: "Men, you should have taken my advice not to sail from Crete; then you would have spared yourselves this damage and loss. But now I urge you to keep up your courage, because not one of you will be lost; only the ship will be destroyed. Last night an angel of the God to whom I belong and whom I serve stood beside me and said, 'Do not be afraid, Paul. You must stand trial before Caesar; and God has graciously given you the lives of all who sail with you.' So keep up your courage, men, for I have faith in God that it will happen just as he told me. Nevertheless, we must run aground on some island." On the fourteenth night we were still being driven across the Adriatic Sea, when about midnight the sailors sensed they were approaching land. They took soundings and found that the water was one hundred and twenty feet deep. A short time later they took soundings again and found it was ninety feet deep. Fearing that we would be dashed against the rocks, they dropped four anchors from the stern and prayed for daylight. In an attempt to escape from the ship, the sailors let the lifeboat down into the sea, pretending they were going to lower some anchors from the bow. Then Paul said to the centurion and the soldiers, "Unless these men stay with the ship, you cannot be saved." So the soldiers cut the ropes that held the lifeboat and let it drift away Just before dawn, Paul urged them all to eat. "For the last fourteen days," he said, "you have been in constant suspense and have gone without food—you haven't eaten anything. Now I urge you to take some food. You need it to survive. Not one of you will lose a single hair from his head." After he said this, he took some bread and gave thanks to God in front of them all. Then he broke it and began to eat. They were all encouraged and ate some food themselves. Altogether there were 276 of us on board. When they had eaten as much as they wanted, they lightened the ship by throwing the grain into the sea When daylight came, they did not recognize the land, but they saw a bay with a sandy beach, where they decided to run the ship aground if they could. Cutting loose the anchors, they left them in the sea and at the same time untied the ropes that held the rudders. Then they hoisted the foresail to the wind and made for the beach. But the ship struck a sandbar and ran aground. The bow stuck fast and would not move, and the stern was broken to pieces by the pounding of the surf. The soldiers planned to kill the prisoners to prevent any of them from swimming away and escaping. But the centurion wanted to spare Paul's life and kept them from carrying out their plan. He ordered those who could swim to jump overboard first and get to land. The rest were to get there on planks or on other pieces of the ship. In this way, everyone reached land safely

Chapter 28

Once safely on shore, we found out that the island was called Malta. The islanders showed us unusual kindness. They built a fire and welcomed us all because it was raining and cold. Paul gathered a pile of brushwood, and as he put it on the fire, a viper, driven out by the heat, fastened itself on his hand. When the islanders saw the snake hanging from his hand, they said to each other, "This man must be a murderer; for though he escaped from the sea, the goddess Justice has not allowed him to live." But Paul shook the snake off into the fire and suffered no ill effects. The people expected him to swell up or suddenly fall dead, but after waiting a long time and seeing nothing unusual happen to him, they changed their minds and said he was a god There was an estate nearby that belonged to Publius, the chief official of the island. He welcomed us to his home and showed us generous hospitality for three days. His father was sick in bed, suffering from fever and dysentery. Paul went in to see him and, after prayer, placed his hands on him and healed him. When this had happened, the rest of the sick on the island came and were cured. They honored us in many ways; and when we were ready to sail, they furnished us with the supplies we needed After three months, we put out to sea in a ship that had wintered in the island—it was an Alexandrian ship with the figurehead of the twin gods Castor and Pollux. We put in at Syracuse and stayed there three days. From there we set sail and arrived at Rhegium. The next day the south wind came up, and on the following day we reached Puteoli. There we found some brothers and sisters who invited us to spend a week with them. And so we came to Rome. The brothers and sisters there had heard that we were coming, and they traveled as far as the Forum of Appius and the Three Taverns to meet us. At the sight of these people, Paul thanked God and was encouraged When we got to Rome, Paul was allowed to live by himself, with a soldier to guard him Three days later he called together the local Jewish leaders. When they had assembled, Paul said to them: "My brothers, although I have done nothing against our people or against the customs of our ancestors, I was arrested in Jerusalem and handed over to the Romans. They examined me and wanted to release me because I

was not guilty of any crime deserving death. The Jews objected, so I was compelled to make an appeal to Caesar. I certainly did not intend to bring any charge against my own people. For this reason, I have asked to see you and talk with you. It is because of the hope of Israel that I am bound with this chain." They replied, "We have not received any letters from Judea concerning you, and none of our people who have come from there has reported or said anything bad about you. But we want to hear what your views are, for we know that people everywhere are talking against this sect." They arranged to meet Paul on a certain day and came in even larger numbers to the place where he was staying. He witnessed to them from morning till evening, explaining about the kingdom of God, and from the Law of Moses and from the Prophets he tried to persuade them about Jesus. Some were convinced by what he said, but others would not believe. They disagreed among themselves and began to leave after Paul had made this final statement: "The Holy Spirit spoke the truth to your ancestors when he said through Isaiah the prophet: 'Go to this people and say, "You will be ever hearing but never understanding; you will be ever seeing but never perceiving." For this people's heart has become calloused; they hardly hear with their ears, and they have closed their eyes. Otherwise they might see with their eyes, hear with their ears, understand with their hearts and turn, and I would heal them.' "Therefore I want you to know that God's salvation has been sent to the Gentiles, and they will listen!" For two whole years, Paul stayed there in his own rented house and welcomed all who came to see him. He proclaimed the kingdom of God and taught about the Lord Jesus Christ—with all boldness and without hindrance

2. PAULINE EPISTLES

45. Romans

Chapter 1

Paul, a servant of Jesus Christ, called to be an apostle and commissioned to preach the gospel of God, which He had already promised through His prophets in the sacred Scriptures, concerning His Son Jesus Christ, our Lord. Jesus was made from the descendants of David according to the flesh and was declared emphatically to be the Son of God, touching the Spirit of sanctification through the resurrection from the dead. Through Him, we have received grace and apostleship so that obedience may be possible to your faith for His Name among all the Gentiles, among whom you are also called of Jesus Christ. To all of you who are in Rome, promoted by God and called to be saints, grace to you and peace from God our Father and the Lord Jesus Christ First of all, I thank my God through Jesus Christ for all of you because your faith is published throughout the world. For God is my witness (that I serve in my spirit in the gospel of His Son) that without ceasing I make mention of you always in my prayers, beseeching that by some means, sometime or other, I may have a prosperous journey, by God's will, to come to you. For I desire to see you, that I may bestow upon you some spiritual gift, that you may be strengthened. That is, that I may be comforted together with you because of our mutual faith, yours and mine Now, my brethren, I wish you not to be ignorant of the fact that I have often proposed to come to you (but so far have not done so) in order to have some fruit among you also, as among other Gentiles. I am a debtor both to the Greeks and to the Barbarians, both to the wise and to the unwise. Therefore, as far as it is in me, I am ready to preach the gospel also to you who are in Rome. For I am not ashamed of the gospel of Christ, for it is the power of God for the salvation of everyone who believes, first of all to the Jews and also to the Greeks. For through it, the righteousness of God is transmitted from faith to faith, as it is written, "The righteous shall live by faith." For the wrath of God has been unleashed from above against all the vices and unrighteousness of men who deny the truth in unrighteousness. Inasmuch as that which can be known by God is manifest in them, for God has shown it to them. For the invisible things of Him, that is, His eternal power and divinity, are visible from the creation of the world, being considered in His works, so that they have no excuse. For although they knew God, they did not glorify Him as God and were not thankful but became vain in their thoughts, and their foolish hearts were full of darkness. When they professed themselves to be wise, they became foolish. For they turned the glory of the incorruptible God into an image of corruptible man, birds, four-legged beasts, and creeping things. Therefore, God also left them free to indulge the lusts of their hearts and to defile their bodies among themselves, who turned the truth of God into a lie and worshiped and served the creature, forsaking the Creator, who is blessed forever. Amen Therefore, God gave them up to vile affections because their women changed their natural use into that which is against nature. In the same way, men also forsook the natural use of women and burned in their lust toward one another, and men with men committed indecency and received in themselves the just reward for their error. For as they did not acknowledge God, so God gave them over to a reprobate mind, to do those things which are not fitting, being filled with all iniquity, fornication, wickedness, covetousness, evil, envy, murders, arguments, deceptions, malice, murmuring, backbiting, hatred of God, pride, boasting, disobedience to parents, lack of understanding, violation of agreements, lack of natural affection, and mercilessness. Although they know the righteous decree of God, that those who commit such things are worthy of death, not only do they do the same but also approve of those who practice them

Chapter 2

Therefore, you are inexcusable, O man, whoever you are who judges. For in whatever you judge another, you condemn yourself; for you who judge practice the same things. But we know that the judgment of God is according to truth against those who practice such things. And do you think this, O man, you who judge those practicing such things and doing the same, that you will escape the judgment of God? Or do you despise the riches of His goodness, forbearance, and longsuffering, not knowing that the goodness of God leads you to repentance? But in accordance with your hardness and your impenitent heart, you are treasuring up for yourself wrath in the day of wrath and revelation of the righteous judgment of God, who "will render to each one according to his deeds": eternal life to those who by patient continuance in doing good seek for glory, honor, and immortality; but to those who are self-seeking and do not obey the truth, but obey unrighteousness—indignation and wrath, tribulation and anguish, on every soul of man who does evil, of the Jew first and also of the Greek; but glory, honor, and peace to everyone who works what is good, to the Jew first and also to the Greek. For there is no partiality with God For as many as have sinned without law will also perish without law, and as many as have sinned in the law will be judged by the law (for not the hearers of the law are just in the sight of God, but the doers of the law will be justified; for when Gentiles, who do not have the law, by nature do the things in the law, these, although not having the law, are a law to themselves, who show the work of the law written in their hearts, their conscience also bearing witness, and between themselves their thoughts accusing or else excusing them) in the day when God will judge the secrets of men by Jesus Christ, according to my gospel Indeed you are called a Jew, and rest on the law, and make your boast in God, and know His will, and approve the things that are excellent, being instructed out of the law, and are confident that you yourself are a guide to the blind, a light to those who are in darkness, an instructor of the foolish, a teacher of babes, having the form of knowledge and truth in the law. You, therefore, who teach another, do you not teach yourself? You who preach that a man should not steal, do you steal? You who say, "Do not commit adultery," do you commit adultery? You who abhor idols, do you rob temples? You who make your boast in the law, do you dishonor God through breaking the law? For "the name of God is blasphemed among the Gentiles because of you," as it is written For circumcision is indeed profitable if you keep the law; but if you are a breaker of the law, your circumcision has become uncircumcision. Therefore, if an uncircumcised man keeps the righteous requirements of the law, will not his uncircumcision be counted as circumcision? And will not the physically uncircumcised, if he fulfills the law, judge you who, even with your written code and circumcision, are a transgressor of the law? For he is not a Jew who is one outwardly, nor is circumcision that which is outward in the flesh; but he is a Jew who is one inwardly, and circumcision is that of the heart, in the Spirit, not in the letter; whose praise is not from men but from God

Chapter 3

What advantage then has the Jew, or what is the profit of circumcision? Much in every way! Chiefly because to them were committed the oracles of God. For what if some did not believe? Will their unbelief make the faithfulness of God without effect? Certainly not! Indeed, let God be true but every man a liar. As it is written: "That You may be justified in Your words, And may overcome when You are judged." But if our unrighteousness demonstrates the righteousness of God, what shall we say? Is God unjust who inflicts wrath? (I speak as a man.) Certainly not! For then how will God judge the world? For if the truth of God has increased through my lie to His glory, why am I also still judged as a sinner? And why not say, "Let us do evil that good may come"?—as we are slanderously reported and as some affirm that we say. Their condemnation is just What then? Are we better than they? Not at all. For we have previously charged both Jews and Greeks that they are all under sin. As it is written: "There is none righteous, no, not one; There is none who understands; There is none who seeks after God. They have all turned aside; They have together become unprofitable; There is none who does good, no, not one." "Their throat is an open tomb; With their tongues they have practiced deceit"; "The poison of asps is under their lips"; "Whose mouth is full of cursing and bitterness." "Their feet are swift to shed blood; Destruction and misery are in their ways; And the way of peace they have not known." "There is no fear of God before their eyes." Now we know that whatever the law says, it says to those who are under the law, that every mouth may be stopped, and all the world may become guilty before God. Therefore by the deeds of the law no flesh will be justified in His sight, for by the law is the knowledge of sin. But now the righteousness of God apart from the law is revealed, being witnessed by the Law and the Prophets, even the righteousness of God, through faith in Jesus Christ, to all and on all who believe. For there is no difference; for all have sinned and fall short of the glory of God, being justified freely by His grace through the redemption that is in Christ Jesus, whom God set forth as a propitiation by His blood, through faith, to demonstrate His righteousness, because in His forbearance God had passed over the sins that were previously committed, to demonstrate at the present time His righteousness, that He might be just and the justifier of the one who has faith in Jesus Where is boasting then? It is excluded. By what law? Of works? No, but by the law of faith. Therefore we conclude that a man is justified by faith apart from the deeds of the law. Or is He the God of the Jews only? Is He not also the God of the Gentiles? Yes, of the Gentiles also, since there is one God who will justify the circumcised by faith and the uncircumcised through faith. Do we then make void the law through faith? Certainly not! On the contrary, we establish the law

Chapter 4

What then shall we say that Abraham our father has found according to the flesh? For if Abraham was justified by works, he has something to boast about, but not before God. For what does the Scripture say? "Abraham believed God, and it was accounted to him for righteousness." Now to him who works, the wages are not counted as grace but as debt. But to him who does not work but believes on Him who justifies the ungodly, his faith is accounted for righteousness, just as David also describes the blessedness of the man to whom God imputes righteousness apart from works: "Blessed are those whose lawless deeds are forgiven, and whose sins are covered; Blessed is the man to whom the Lord shall not impute sin." Does this blessedness then come upon the circumcised only, or upon the uncircumcised also? For we say that faith was

accounted to Abraham for righteousness. How then was it accounted? While he was circumcised, or uncircumcised? Not while circumcised, but while uncircumcised. And he received the sign of circumcision, a seal of the righteousness of the faith which he had while still uncircumcised, that he might be the father of all those who believe, though they are uncircumcised, that righteousness might be imputed to them also, and the father of circumcision to those who not only are of the circumcision but who also walk in the steps of the faith which our father Abraham had while still uncircumcised For the promise that he would be the heir of the world was not to Abraham or to his seed through the law, but through the righteousness of faith. For if those who are of the law are heirs, faith is made void and the promise made of no effect, because the law brings about wrath; for where there is no law there is no transgression. Therefore it is of faith that it might be according to grace, so that the promise might be sure to all the seed, not only to those who are of the law but also to those who are of the faith of Abraham, who is the father of us all (as it is written, "I have made you a father of many nations") in the presence of Him whom he believed—God, who gives life to the dead and calls those things which do not exist as though they did; who, contrary to hope, in hope believed, so that he became the father of many nations, according to what was spoken, "So shall your descendants be." And not being weak in faith, he did not consider his own body, already dead (since he was about a hundred years old), and the deadness of Sarah's womb. He did not waver at the promise of God through unbelief, but was strengthened in faith, giving glory to God, and being fully convinced that what He had promised He was also able to perform. And therefore "it was accounted to him for righteousness." Now it was not written for his sake alone that it was imputed to him, but also for us. It shall be imputed to us who believe in Him who raised up Jesus our Lord from the dead, who was delivered up because of our offenses, and was raised because of our justification

Chapter 5

Therefore, having been justified by faith, we have peace with God through our Lord Jesus Christ, through whom also we have access by faith into this grace in which we stand, and rejoice in hope of the glory of God. And not only that, but we also glory in tribulations, knowing that tribulation produces perseverance; and perseverance, character; and character, hope. Now hope does not disappoint, because the love of God has been poured out in our hearts by the Holy Spirit who was given to us For when we were still without strength, in due time Christ died for the ungodly. For scarcely for a righteous man will one die; yet perhaps for a good man someone would even dare to die. But God demonstrates His own love toward us, in that while we were still sinners, Christ died for us. Much more then, having now been justified by His blood, we shall be saved from wrath through Him. For if when we were enemies we were reconciled to God through the death of His Son, much more, having been reconciled, we shall be saved by His life. And not only that, but we also rejoice in God through our Lord Jesus Christ, through whom we have now received the reconciliation Therefore, just as through one man sin entered the world, and death through sin, and thus death spread to all men because all sinned— (For until the law sin was in the world, but sin is not imputed when there is no law. Nevertheless death reigned from Adam to Moses, even over those who had not sinned according to the likeness of the transgression of Adam, who is a type of Him who was to come. But the free gift is not like the offense. For if by the one man's offense many died, much more the grace of God and the gift by the grace of the one Man, Jesus Christ, abounded to many. And the gift is not like that which came through the one who sinned. For the judgment which came from one offense resulted in condemnation, but the free gift which came from many offenses resulted in justification. For if by the one man's offense death reigned through the one, much more those who receive abundance of grace and of the gift of righteousness will reign in life through the One, Jesus Christ.) Therefore, as through one man's offense judgment came to all men, resulting in condemnation, even so through one Man's righteous act the free gift came to all men, resulting in justification of life. For as by one man's disobedience many were made sinners, so also by one Man's obedience many will be made righteous. Moreover, the law entered that the offense might abound. But where sin abounded, grace abounded much more, so that as sin reigned in death, even so grace might reign through righteousness to eternal life through Jesus Christ our Lord

Chapter 6

What shall we say then? Shall we continue to sin so that grace may abound? God forbid. How shall we who are dead to sin still live in it? Do you not know that all of us who were baptized into Jesus Christ were baptized into His death? We are therefore buried with Him through baptism into His death, so that just as Christ was raised from the dead to the glory of the Father, we too may walk in newness of life. For if we have been united with Him in the likeness of His death, we shall also be united with Him in the likeness of His resurrection, knowing that our old self was crucified with Him so that the body of sin might be destroyed, and we should no longer be slaves to sin. For he who has died is freed from sin. Therefore, if we have died with Christ, we believe that we shall also live with Him, knowing that Christ, being raised from the dead, no longer dies; death no longer has dominion over Him. For in that He died, He died once for all to sin, but in that He lives, He lives to God. In the same way, consider yourselves dead to sin but alive to God in Jesus Christ our Lord Therefore, do not let sin reign in your mortal body so that you obey its desires. Do not offer any part of yourself to sin as an instrument of wickedness, but rather offer yourselves to God as those who have been brought from death to life, and offer every part of yourself to Him as an instrument of righteousness. For sin shall no longer be your master because you are not under the law but under grace What then? Shall we sin because we are not under the law but under grace? God forbid. Do you not know that when you offer yourselves to someone as obedient slaves, you are slaves of the one you obey—whether you are slaves to sin, which leads to death, or to obedience, which leads to righteousness? But thanks be to God that, though you used to be slaves to sin, you have come to obey from your heart the pattern of teaching that has now claimed your allegiance. You have been set free from sin and have become slaves to righteousness I am using an example from everyday life because of your human limitations. Just as you used to offer yourselves as slaves to impurity and to ever-increasing wickedness, so now offer yourselves as slaves to righteousness leading to holiness. When you were slaves to sin, you were free from the control of righteousness. What benefit did you reap at that time from the things you are now ashamed of? Those things result in death. But now that you have been set free from sin and have become slaves of God, the benefit you reap leads to holiness, and the result is eternal life. For the wages of sin is death, but the gift of God is eternal life in Christ Jesus our Lord

Chapter 7

Do you not know, brothers and sisters—for I am speaking to those who know the law—that the law has authority over someone only as long as that person lives? For example, by law a married woman is bound to her husband as long as he is alive, but if her husband dies, she is released from the law that binds her to him. So then, if she has sexual relations with another man while her husband is still alive, she is called an adulteress. But if her husband dies, she is released from that law and is not an adulteress if she marries another man So, my brothers and sisters, you also died to the law through the body of Christ, that you might belong to another, to Him who was raised from the dead, in order that we might bear fruit for God. For when we were in the realm of the flesh, the sinful passions aroused by the law were at work in us, so that we bore fruit for death. But now, by dying to what once bound us, we have been released from the law so that we serve in the new way of the Spirit, and not in the old way of the written code What shall we say then? Is the law sinful? Certainly not! Nevertheless, I would not have known what sin was had it not been for the law. For I would not have known what coveting really was if the law had not said, "You shall not covet." But sin, seizing the opportunity afforded by the commandment, produced in me every kind of coveting. For apart from the law, sin was dead. Once I was alive apart from the law; but when the commandment came, sin sprang to life and I died. I found that the very commandment that was intended to bring life actually brought death. For sin, seizing the opportunity afforded by the commandment, deceived me, and through the commandment put me to death So then, the law is holy, and the commandment is holy, righteous and good. Did that which is good, then, become death to me? By no means! Nevertheless, in order that sin might be recognized as sin, it used what is good to bring about my death, so that through the commandment sin might become utterly sinful We know that the law is spiritual; but I am unspiritual, sold as a slave to sin. I do not understand what I do. For what I want to do I do not do, but what I hate I do. And if I do what I do not want to do, I agree that the law is good. As it is, it is no longer I myself who do it, but it is sin living in me. For I know that good itself does not dwell in me, that is, in my sinful nature. For I have the desire to do what is good, but I cannot carry it out. For I do not do the good I want to do, but the evil I do not want to do—this I keep on doing. Now if I do what I do not want to do, it is no longer I who do it, but it is sin living in me that does it So I find this law at work: Although I want to do good, evil is right there with me. For in my inner being I delight in God's law; but I see another law at work in me, waging war against the law of my mind and making me a prisoner of the law of sin at work within me. What a wretched man I am! Who will rescue me from this body that is subject to death? Thanks be to God, who delivers me through Jesus Christ our Lord! So then, I myself in my mind am a slave to God's law, but in my sinful nature a slave to the law of sin

Chapter 8

Therefore, there is now no condemnation for those who are in Christ Jesus, because through Christ Jesus the law of the Spirit who gives life has set you free from the law of sin and death. For what the law was powerless to do because it was weakened by the flesh, God did by sending His own Son in the likeness of sinful flesh to be a sin offering. And so He condemned sin in the flesh, in order that the righteous requirement of the law might be fully met in us, who do not live according to the flesh but according to the Spirit Those who live according to the flesh have their minds set on what the flesh desires; but those who live in accordance with the Spirit have their minds set on what the Spirit desires. The mind governed by the flesh is death, but the mind governed by the Spirit is life and peace. The mind governed by the flesh is hostile to God; it does not submit to God's law, nor can it do so. Those who are in the realm of the flesh cannot please God You, however, are not in the realm of the flesh but are in the realm of the Spirit, if indeed the Spirit of God lives in you. And if anyone does not have the Spirit of Christ, they do not belong to Christ. But if Christ is in you, then even though your body is subject to death because of sin, the Spirit gives life because of righteousness. And if the Spirit of Him who raised Jesus from the dead is living in you, He who raised Christ from the dead will also give life to your mortal bodies because of His Spirit who lives in you Therefore, brothers and sisters, we have an obligation—but it is not to the flesh, to live according to it. For if you live according to the flesh, you will die; but if by the Spirit you put to death the misdeeds of the body, you will live. For those who are led by the Spirit of God are the children of God. The Spirit you received does not make you slaves, so that you live in fear again; rather, the Spirit you received brought about your adoption to sonship. And by Him we cry, "Abba, Father." The Spirit Himself testifies with our spirit that we are God's children. Now if we are children, then we are heirs—heirs of God and co-heirs with Christ, if indeed we share in His sufferings in order that we may also share in His glory I consider that our present sufferings are not worth comparing with the glory that will be revealed in us. For the creation waits in eager expectation for the children of God to be revealed. For the creation was subjected to frustration, not by its own choice, but by the will of the one who subjected it, in hope that the creation itself will be liberated from its bondage to decay and brought into the freedom and glory of the children of God. We know that the whole creation has been groaning as in the pains of childbirth right up to the present time. Not only so, but we ourselves, who have the firstfruits of the Spirit, groan inwardly as we wait eagerly for our adoption to sonship, the redemption of our bodies. For in this hope we were saved. But hope that is seen is no hope at all. Who hopes for what they already have? But if we hope for what we do not yet have, we wait for it patiently In the same way, the Spirit helps us in our weakness. We do not know what we ought to pray for, but the Spirit Himself intercedes for us through wordless groans. And He who searches our hearts knows the mind of the Spirit, because the Spirit intercedes for God's people in accordance with the will of God And we know that in all things God works for the good of those who love Him, who have been called according to His purpose. For those God foreknew He also predestined to be conformed to the image of His Son, that He might be the firstborn among many brothers and sisters. And those He predestined, He also called; those He called, He also justified; those He justified, He also glorified What, then, shall we say in response to these things? If God is for us, who can be against us? He who did not spare His own Son, but gave Him up for us all—how will He not also, along with Him, graciously give us all things? Who will bring any charge against those whom God has chosen? It is God who justifies. Who then is the one who condemns? No one. Christ Jesus who died—more than that, who was raised to life—is at the right hand of God and is also interceding for us. Who shall separate us from the love of Christ? Shall trouble or hardship or persecution or famine or nakedness or danger or sword? As it is written: "For Your sake we face death all day long; we are considered as sheep to be slaughtered." No, in all these things we are more than conquerors through Him who loved us. For I am convinced that neither death nor life, neither angels nor demons, neither the present nor the future, nor any powers, neither height nor depth, nor anything else in all creation, will be able to separate us from the love of God that is in Christ Jesus our Lord

Chapter 9

I speak the truth in Christ—I am not lying, my conscience confirms it through the Holy Spirit—I have great sorrow and unceasing anguish in my heart. For I could wish that I myself were cursed and cut off from Christ for the sake of my people, those of my own race, the people of Israel. Theirs is the adoption to sonship; theirs the divine glory, the covenants, the receiving of the law, the temple worship, and the promises. Theirs are the patriarchs, and from them is traced the human ancestry of the Messiah, who is God over all, forever praised! Amen It is not as though God's word had failed. For not all who are descended from Israel are Israel. Nor because they are his descendants are they all Abraham's children. On the contrary, "It is through Isaac that your offspring will be reckoned." In other words, it is not the children by physical descent who are God's children, but it is the children of the promise who are regarded as Abraham's offspring. For this was how the promise was stated: "At the appointed time I will return, and Sarah will have a son." Not only that, but Rebekah's children were conceived at the same time by our father Isaac. Yet, before the twins were born or had done anything good or bad—in order that God's purpose in election might stand: not by works but by Him who calls—she was told, "The older will serve the younger." Just as it is written: "Jacob I loved, but Esau I hated." What then shall we say? Is God unjust? Not at all! For He says to Moses, "I will have mercy on whom I have mercy, and I will have compassion on whom I have compassion." It does not, therefore, depend on human desire or effort, but on God's mercy. For Scripture says to Pharaoh: "I raised you up for this very purpose, that I might display my power in you and that my name might be proclaimed in all the earth." Therefore, God has mercy on whom He wants to have mercy, and He hardens whom He wants to harden One of you will say to me: "Then why does God still blame us? For who is able to resist His will?" But who are you, a human being, to talk back to God? "Shall what is formed say to the one who formed it, 'Why did you make me like this?'" Does not the potter have the right to make out of the same lump of clay some pottery for special purposes and some for common use? What if God, although choosing to show His wrath and make His power known, bore with great patience the objects of His wrath—prepared for destruction? What if He did this to make the riches of His glory known to the objects of His mercy, whom He prepared in advance for glory—even us, whom He also called, not only from the Jews but also from the Gentiles? As He says in Hosea: "I will call them 'my people' who are not my people; and I will call her 'my loved one' who is not my loved one," and, "In the very place where it was said to them, 'You are not my people,' there they will be called 'children of the living God.'" Isaiah cries out concerning Israel: "Though the number of the Israelites be like the sand by the sea, only the remnant will be saved. For the Lord will carry out His sentence on earth with speed and finality." It is just as Isaiah said previously: "Unless the Lord Almighty had left us descendants, we would have become like

Sodom, we would have been like Gomorrah." What then shall we say? That the Gentiles, who did not pursue righteousness, have obtained it, a righteousness that is by faith; but the people of Israel, who pursued the law as the way of righteousness, have not attained their goal. Why not? Because they pursued it not by faith but as if it were by works. They stumbled over the stumbling stone. As it is written: "See, I lay in Zion a stone that causes people to stumble and a rock that makes them fall, and the one who believes in Him will never be put to shame."

Chapter 10

Brothers and sisters, my heart's desire and prayer to God for the Israelites is that they may be saved. For I can testify about them that they are zealous for God, but their zeal is not based on knowledge. Since they did not know the righteousness of God and sought to establish their own, they did not submit to God's righteousness. Christ is the culmination of the law so that there may be righteousness for everyone who believes Moses writes this about the righteousness that is by the law: "The person who does these things will live by them." But the righteousness that is by faith says: "Do not say in your heart, 'Who will ascend into heaven?'" (that is, to bring Christ down) "or 'Who will descend into the deep?'" (that is, to bring Christ up from the dead). But what does it say? "The word is near you; it is in your mouth and in your heart," that is, the message concerning faith that we proclaim: If you declare with your mouth, "Jesus is Lord," and believe in your heart that God raised Him from the dead, you will be saved. For it is with your heart that you believe and are justified, and it is with your mouth that you profess your faith and are saved. As Scripture says, "Anyone who believes in Him will never be put to shame." For there is no difference between Jew and Gentile—the same Lord is Lord of all and richly blesses all who call on Him, for, "Everyone who calls on the name of the Lord will be saved." How, then, can they call on the one they have not believed in? And how can they believe in the one of whom they have not heard? And how can they hear without someone preaching to them? And how can anyone preach unless they are sent? As it is written: "How beautiful are the feet of those who bring good news!" But not all the Israelites accepted the good news. For Isaiah says, "Lord, who has believed our message?" Consequently, faith comes from hearing the message, and the message is heard through the word about Christ. But I ask: Did they not hear? Of course they did: "Their voice has gone out into all the earth, their words to the ends of the world." Again I ask: Did Israel not understand? First, Moses says, "I will make you envious by those who are not a nation; I will make you angry by a nation that has no understanding." And Isaiah boldly says, "I was found by those who did not seek me; I revealed myself to those who did not ask for me." But concerning Israel he says, "All day long I have held out my hands to a disobedient and obstinate people."

Chapter 11

I ask then, has God forsaken His people? God forbid, for I too am an Israelite, a descendant of Abraham, from the tribe of Benjamin. God has not forsaken His people whom He foreknew. Don't you know what the Scripture says about Elijah, how he communed with God against Israel, saying, "Lord, they have killed your prophets and torn down your altars; I am the only one left, and they seek my life"? But what was God's answer to him? "I have reserved for myself seven thousand men who have not bowed the knee to Baal." Even now, there is a remnant according to the election of grace. And if it is by grace, then it is no longer by works; otherwise grace would no longer be

grace. What then? Israel did not obtain what it sought, but the elect obtained it, while others were hardened, as it is written: "God gave them a spirit of stupor, eyes that could not see and ears that could not hear, to this very day." And David says: "Let their table become a snare and a trap, a stumbling block and a retribution for them. Let their eyes be darkened so they cannot see, and their backs be bent forever." Again I ask: Did they stumble so as to fall beyond recovery? Not at all! Rather, because of their transgression, salvation has come to the Gentiles to make Israel envious. But if their transgression means riches for the world, and their loss means riches for the Gentiles, how much greater riches will their full inclusion bring! I am speaking to you Gentiles. Inasmuch as I am the apostle to the Gentiles, I take pride in my ministry in the hope that I may somehow arouse my own people to envy and save some of them. For if their rejection brought reconciliation to the world, what will their acceptance be but life from the dead? If the part of the dough offered as firstfruits is holy, then the whole batch is holy; if the root is holy, so are the branches. If some of the branches have been broken off, and you, though a wild olive shoot, have been grafted in among the others and now share in the nourishing sap from the olive root, do not consider yourself to be superior to those other branches. If you do, consider this: You do not support the root, but the root supports you. You will say then, "Branches were broken off so that I could be grafted in." Granted. But they were broken off because of unbelief, and you stand by faith. Do not be arrogant, but tremble. For if God did not spare the natural branches, He will not spare you either Consider therefore the kindness and sternness of God: sternness to those who fell, but kindness to you, provided that you continue in His kindness. Otherwise, you also will be cut off. And if they do not persist in unbelief, they will be grafted in, for God is able to graft them in again. After all, if you were cut out of an olive tree that is wild by nature, and contrary to nature were grafted into a cultivated olive tree, how much more readily will these, the natural branches, be grafted into their own olive tree! I do not want you to be ignorant of this mystery, brothers and sisters, so that you may not be conceited: Israel has experienced a hardening in part until the full number of the Gentiles has come in, and in this way all Israel will be saved. As it is written: "The Deliverer will come from Zion; He will turn godlessness away from Jacob. And this is my covenant with them when I take away their sins." As far as the gospel is concerned, they are enemies for your sake; but as far as election is concerned, they are loved on account of the patriarchs, for God's gifts and His call are irrevocable. Just as you who were at one time disobedient to God have now received mercy as a result of their disobedience, so they too have now become disobedient in order that they too may now receive mercy as a result of God's mercy to you. For God has bound everyone over to disobedience so that He may have mercy on them all Oh, the depth of the riches of the wisdom and knowledge of God! How unsearchable His judgments, and His paths beyond tracing out! "Who has known the mind of the Lord? Or who has been His counselor?" "Who has ever given to God, that God should repay them?" For from Him and through Him and for Him are all things. To Him be the glory forever! Amen

Chapter 12

Therefore, I urge you, brothers and sisters, in view of God's mercy, to offer your bodies as a living sacrifice, holy and pleasing to God—this is your true and proper worship. Do not conform to the pattern of this world, but be transformed by the renewing of your mind. Then you will be able to test and approve what God's will is—His good, pleasing and perfect will For by the grace given to me I say to every one of you: Do not think of yourself more highly than you ought, but rather think of yourself with sober judgment, in accordance with the faith God has distributed to each of you. For just as each of us has one body with many members, and these members do not all have the same function, so in Christ we, though many, form one body, and each member belongs to all the others. We have different gifts, according to the grace given to each of us. If your gift is prophesying, then prophesy in accordance with your faith; if it is serving, then serve; if it is teaching, then teach; if it is to encourage, then give encouragement; if it is giving, then give generously; if it is to lead, do it diligently; if it is to show mercy, do it cheerfully Love must be sincere. Hate what is evil; cling to what is good. Be devoted to one another in love. Honor one another above yourselves. Never be lacking in zeal, but keep your spiritual fervor, serving the Lord. Be joyful in hope, patient in affliction, faithful in prayer. Share with the Lord's people who are in need. Practice hospitality. Bless those who persecute you; bless and do not curse. Rejoice with those who rejoice; mourn with those who mourn. Live in harmony with one another. Do not be proud but be willing to associate with people of low position. Do not be conceited. Do not repay anyone evil for evil. Be careful to do what is right in the eyes of everyone. If it is possible, as far as it depends on you, live at peace with everyone. Do not take revenge, my dear friends, but leave room for God's wrath, for it is written: "It is mine to avenge; I will repay," says the Lord. On the contrary: "If your enemy is hungry, feed him; if he is thirsty, give him something to drink. In doing this, you will heap burning coals on his head." Do not be overcome by evil, but overcome evil with good

Chapter 13

Let everyone be subject to the governing authorities, for there is no authority except that which God has established. The authorities that exist have been established by God. Consequently, whoever rebels against the authority is rebelling against what God has instituted, and those who do so will bring judgment on themselves. For rulers hold no terror for those who do right, but for those who do wrong. Do you want to be free from fear of the one in authority? Then do what is right and you will be commended. For the one in authority is God's servant for your good. But if you do wrong, be afraid, for rulers do not bear the sword for no reason. They are God's servants, agents of wrath to bring punishment on the wrongdoer. Therefore, it is necessary to submit to the authorities, not only because of possible punishment but also as a matter of conscience This is also why you pay taxes, for the authorities are God's servants, who give their full time to governing. Give to everyone what you owe them: If you owe taxes, pay taxes; if revenue, then revenue; if respect, then respect; if honor, then honor Let no debt remain outstanding, except the continuing debt to love one another, for whoever loves others has fulfilled the law. The commandments, "You shall not commit adultery," "You shall not murder," "You shall not steal," "You shall not covet," and whatever other command there may be, are summed up in this one command: "Love your neighbor as yourself." Love does no harm to a neighbor. Therefore, love is the fulfillment of the law And do this, understanding the present time: The hour has already come for you to wake up from your slumber, because our salvation is nearer now than when we first believed. The night is nearly over; the day is almost here. So let us put aside the deeds of darkness and put on the armor of light. Let us behave decently, as in the daytime, not in carousing and drunkenness, not in sexual immorality and debauchery, not in dissension and jealousy. Rather, clothe yourselves with the Lord Jesus Christ, and do not think about how to gratify the desires of the flesh

Chapter 14

Accept the one whose faith is weak, without quarreling over disputable matters. One person's faith allows them to eat anything, but another, whose faith is weak, eats only vegetables. The one who eats everything must not treat with contempt the one who does not, and the one who does not eat everything must not judge the one who does, for God has accepted them. Who are you to judge someone else's servant? To their own master, servants stand or fall. And they will stand, for the Lord is able to make them stand One person considers one day more sacred than another; another considers every day alike. Each of them should be fully convinced in their own mind. Whoever regards one day as special does so to the Lord. Whoever eats meat does so to the Lord, for they give thanks to God; and whoever abstains does so to the Lord and gives thanks to God. For none of us lives for ourselves alone, and none of us dies for ourselves alone. If we live, we live for the Lord; and if we die, we die for the Lord. So, whether we live or die, we belong to the Lord. For this very reason, Christ died and returned to life so that He might be the Lord of both the dead and the living You, then, why do you judge your brother or sister? Or why do you treat them with contempt? For we will all stand before God's judgment seat. It is written: "'As surely as I live,' says the Lord, 'every knee will bow before me; every tongue will acknowledge God.'" So then, each of us will give an account of ourselves to God Therefore let us stop passing judgment on one another. Instead, make up your mind not to put any stumbling block or obstacle in the way of a brother or sister. I am convinced, being fully persuaded in the Lord Jesus, that nothing is unclean in itself. But if anyone regards something as unclean, then for that person it is unclean. If your brother or sister is distressed because of what you eat, you are no longer acting in love. Do not by your eating destroy someone for whom Christ died. Therefore do not let what you know is good be spoken of as evil. For the kingdom of God is not a matter of eating and drinking, but of righteousness, peace, and joy in the Holy Spirit, because anyone who serves Christ in this way is pleasing to God and receives human approval Let us therefore make every effort to do what leads to peace and to mutual edification. Do not destroy the work of God for the sake of food. All food is clean, but it is wrong for a person to eat anything that causes someone else to stumble. It is better not to eat meat or drink wine or to do anything else that will cause your brother or sister to fall So whatever you believe about these things keep between yourself and God. Blessed is the one who does not condemn himself by what he approves. But whoever has doubts is condemned if they eat, because their eating is not from faith; and everything that does not come from faith is sin

Chapter 15

We who are strong ought to bear with the failings of the weak and not to please ourselves. Each of us should please our neighbors for their good, to build them up. For even Christ did not please Himself but, as it is written: "The insults of those who insult you have fallen on me." For everything that was written in the past was written to teach us, so that through the endurance taught in the Scriptures and the encouragement they provide we might have hope May the God who gives endurance and encouragement give you the same attitude of mind toward each other that Christ Jesus had, so that with one mind and one voice you may glorify the God and Father of our Lord Jesus Christ. Accept one another, then, just as Christ accepted you, in order to bring praise to God. For I tell you that Christ has become a servant of the Jews on behalf of God's truth, so that the promises made to the patriarchs might be confirmed and, moreover, that the Gentiles might glorify God for His mercy. As it is written: "Therefore I will praise you among the Gentiles; I will sing the praises of your name." Again, it says, "Rejoice, you Gentiles, with His people." And again, "Praise the Lord, all you Gentiles; let all the peoples extol Him." And again, Isaiah says, "The Root of Jesse will spring up, one who will arise to rule over the nations; in Him the Gentiles will hope." May the God of hope fill you with all joy and peace as you trust in Him, so that you may overflow with hope by the power of the Holy Spirit. I myself am convinced, my brothers and sisters, that you yourselves are full of goodness, filled with knowledge and competent to instruct one another. Yet I have written you quite boldly on some points to remind you of them again, because of the grace God gave me to be a minister of Christ Jesus to the Gentiles. He gave me the priestly duty of proclaiming the gospel of God, so that the Gentiles might become an offering acceptable to God, sanctified by the Holy Spirit Therefore I glory in Christ Jesus in my service to God. I will not venture to speak of anything except what Christ has accomplished through me in leading the Gentiles to obey God by what I have said and done—by the power of signs and wonders, through the power of the Spirit of God. So from Jerusalem all the way around to Illyricum, I have fully proclaimed the gospel of Christ. It has always been my ambition to preach the gospel where Christ was not known, so that I would not be building on someone else's foundation. Rather, as it is written: "Those who were not told about Him will see, and those who have not heard will understand." This is why I have often been hindered from coming to you. But now that there is no more place for me to work in these regions, and since I have been longing for many years to visit you, I plan to do so when I go to Spain. I hope to see you while passing through and to have you assist me on my journey there, after I have enjoyed your company for a while. Now, however, I am on my way to Jerusalem in the service of the Lord's people there. For Macedonia and Achaia were pleased to make a contribution for the poor among the Lord's people in Jerusalem. They were pleased to do it, and indeed they owe it to them. For if the Gentiles have shared in the Jews' spiritual blessings, they owe it to the Jews to share with them their material blessings. So after I have completed this task and have made sure that they have received this contribution, I will go to Spain and visit you on the way. I know that when I come to you, I will come in the full measure of the blessing of Christ I urge you, brothers and sisters, by our Lord Jesus Christ and by the love of the Spirit, to join me in my struggle by praying to God for me. Pray that I may be kept safe from the unbelievers in Judea and that the contribution I take to Jerusalem may be favorably received by the Lord's people there, so that I may come to you with joy, by God's will, and in your company be refreshed. The God of peace be with you all. Amen

Chapter 16

I commend to you our sister Phoebe, a deacon of the church in Cenchreae. I ask you to receive her in the Lord in a way worthy of His people and to give her any help she may need from you, for she has been the benefactor of many people, including me Greet Priscilla and Aquila, my co-workers in Christ Jesus. They risked their lives for me. Not only I but all the churches of the Gentiles are grateful to them. Greet also the church that meets at their house. Greet my dear friend Epenetus, who was the first convert to Christ in the province of Asia. Greet Mary, who worked very hard for you. Greet Andronicus and Junia, my fellow Jews who have been in prison with me. They are outstanding among the apostles, and they were in Christ before I was. Greet Ampliatus, my dear friend in the Lord. Greet Urbanus, our co-worker in Christ, and my dear friend Stachys. Greet Apelles, whose fidelity to Christ has stood the test. Greet those who belong to the household of Aristobulus. Greet Herodion, my fellow Jew. Greet those in the household of Narcissus who are in the Lord. Greet Tryphena and Tryphosa, those women who work hard in the Lord. Greet my dear friend Persis, another woman who has worked very hard in the Lord. Greet Rufus, chosen in the Lord, and his mother, who has been a mother to me, too. Greet Asyncritus, Phlegon, Hermes, Patrobas, Hermas and the other brothers and sisters with them. Greet Philologus, Julia, Nereus and his sister, and Olympas and all the Lord's people who are with them. Greet one another with a holy kiss. All the churches of Christ send greetings I urge you, brothers and sisters, to watch out for those who cause divisions and put obstacles in your way that are contrary to the teaching you have learned. Keep away from them. For such people are not serving our Lord Christ, but their own appetites. By smooth talk and flattery they deceive the minds of naive people. Everyone has heard about your obedience, so I rejoice because of you; but I want you to be wise about what is good, and innocent about what is evil. The God of peace will soon crush Satan under your feet. The grace of our Lord Jesus be with you Timothy, my co-worker, sends his greetings to you, as do Lucius, Jason and Sosipater, my fellow Jews. I, Tertius, who wrote down this letter, greet you in the Lord. Gaius, whose hospitality I and the whole church here enjoy, sends you his greetings. Erastus, who is the city's director of public works, and our brother Quartus send you their greetings. The grace of our Lord Jesus Christ be with you all. Amen Now to Him who is able to establish you in accordance with my gospel, the message I proclaim about Jesus Christ, in keeping with the revelation of the mystery hidden for long ages past, but now revealed and made known through the prophetic writings by the command of the eternal God, so that all the Gentiles might come to the obedience that comes from faith—to the only wise God be glory forever through Jesus Christ! Amen

46. 1 Corinthians

Chapter 1

Paul, called to be an apostle of Jesus Christ by the will of God, and our brother Sosthenes, to the Church of God which is at Corinth. To those who are sanctified in Jesus Christ, holy by vocation, and to all who call on the name of our Lord Jesus Christ, both their Lord and ours, in every place: Grace and peace to you from God our Father and the Lord Jesus Christ I always thank my God for the grace He has given you in Jesus Christ. In everything, you are enriched in Him, in every kind of speech and in all knowledge, as the testimony of Jesus Christ has been confirmed in you. You are not lacking in any spiritual gift as you wait for the revealing of our Lord Jesus Christ. He will also confirm you to the end, so that you may be blameless on the day of our Lord Jesus Christ. God is faithful; through Him, you were called into fellowship with His Son, Jesus Christ our Lord Now I beseech you, brothers and sisters, in the name of our Lord Jesus Christ, that you all speak the same thing and that there be no divisions among you, but that you be united in one mind and one judgment. For it has been reported to me by those of Chloe's household that there are contentions among you. Some of you say, "I am of Paul," or "I am of Apollos," or "I am of Cephas," or "I am of Christ." Is Christ divided? Was Paul crucified for you? Were you baptized in the name of Paul? I thank God that I baptized none of you except Crispus and Gaius, so no one can say that you were baptized in my name. I also baptized the household of Stephanas; beyond that, I do not remember if I baptized anyone else Christ did not send me to baptize but to preach the gospel, not with eloquent wisdom, lest the cross of Christ be emptied of its power. For the message of the cross is foolishness to those who are perishing, but to us who are being saved, it is the power of God. As it is written, "I will destroy the wisdom of the wise, and the discernment of the discerning I will thwart." Where is the wise person? Where is the scribe? Where is the debater of this age? Has not God made the wisdom of the world foolish? For since, in the wisdom of God, the world did not know God through wisdom, God was pleased through the foolishness of what was preached to save those who believe. Jews demand signs and Greeks seek wisdom, but we preach Christ crucified, a stumbling block to Jews and foolishness to Gentiles. But to those who are called, both Jews and Greeks, Christ is the power of God and the wisdom of God. For the foolishness of God is wiser than human wisdom, and the weakness of God is stronger than human strength Consider your calling, brothers and sisters. Not many of you were wise by human standards, not many were powerful, not many were of noble birth. But God chose the foolish things of the world to shame the wise; God chose the weak things of the world to shame the strong. God chose the lowly things of this world and the despised things—and the things that are not—to nullify the things that are, so that no one may boast before Him. It is because of Him that you are in Christ Jesus, who has become for us wisdom from God—that is, our righteousness, holiness, and redemption. Therefore, as it is written, "Let the one who boasts boast in the Lord."

Chapter 2

When I came to you, brothers and sisters, I did not come with eloquence or human wisdom as I proclaimed to you the testimony about God. For I resolved to know nothing while I was with you except Jesus Christ and Him crucified. I came to you in weakness with great fear and trembling. My message and my preaching were not with wise and persuasive words, but with a demonstration of the Spirit's power, so that your faith might not rest on human wisdom, but on God's power We do, however, speak a message of wisdom among the mature, but not the wisdom of this age or of the rulers of this age, who are coming to nothing. No, we declare God's wisdom, a mystery that has been hidden and that God destined for our glory before time began. None of the rulers of this age understood it, for if they had, they would not have crucified the Lord of glory. However, as it is written: "What no eye has seen, what no ear has heard, and what no human mind has conceived—the things God has prepared for those who love Him." These are the things God has revealed to us by His Spirit. The Spirit searches all things, even the deep things of God. For who knows a person's thoughts except their own spirit within them? In the same way, no one knows the thoughts of God except the Spirit of God. What we have received is not the spirit of the world, but the Spirit who is from God, so that we may understand what God has freely given us. This is what we speak, not in words taught us by human wisdom but in words taught by the Spirit, explaining spiritual realities with Spirit-taught words. The person without the Spirit does not accept the things that come from the Spirit of God but considers them foolishness and cannot understand them because they are discerned only through the Spirit. The person with the Spirit makes judgments about all things, but such a person is not subject to merely human judgments. For, "Who has known the mind of the Lord so as to instruct Him?" But we have the mind of Christ

Chapter 3

Brothers and sisters, I could not address you as people who live by the Spirit but as people who are still worldly—mere infants in Christ. I gave you milk, not solid food, for you were not yet ready for it. Indeed, you are still not ready. You are still worldly. For since there is jealousy and quarreling among you, are you not worldly? Are you not acting like mere humans? For when one says, "I follow Paul," and another, "I follow Apollos," are you not mere human beings? What, after all, is Apollos? And what is Paul? Only servants, through whom you came to believe—as the Lord has assigned to each his task. I planted the seed, Apollos watered it, but God has been making it grow. So neither the one who plants nor the one who waters is anything, but only God, who makes things grow. The one who plants and the one who waters have one purpose, and they will each be rewarded according to their own labor. For we are co-workers in God's service; you are God's field, God's building By the grace God has given me, I laid a foundation as a wise builder, and someone else is building on it. But each one should build with care. For no one can lay any foundation other than the one already laid, which is Jesus Christ. If anyone builds on this foundation using gold, silver, costly stones, wood, hay, or straw, their work will be shown for what it is because the Day will bring it to light. It will be revealed with fire, and the fire will test the quality of each person's work. If what has been built survives, the builder will receive a reward. If it is burned up, the builder will suffer loss but yet will be saved—even though only as one escaping through the flames Do you not know that you yourselves are God's temple and that God's Spirit dwells in your midst? If anyone destroys God's temple, God will destroy that person; for God's temple is sacred, and you together are that temple. Do not deceive yourselves. If any of you think you are wise by the standards of this age, you should become "fools" so that you may become wise. For the wisdom of this world is foolishness in God's sight. As it is written: "He catches the wise in their craftiness," and again, "The Lord knows that the thoughts of the wise are futile." So then, no more boasting about human leaders! All things are yours, whether Paul or Apollos or Cephas or the world or life or death or the present or the future—all are yours, and you are of Christ, and Christ is of God

Chapter 4

This is how you ought to regard us: as servants of Christ and as those entrusted with the mysteries God has revealed. Now it is required that those who have been given a trust must prove faithful. I care very little if I am judged by you or by any human court; indeed, I do not even judge myself. My conscience is clear, but that does not make me innocent. It is the Lord who judges me. Therefore judge nothing before the appointed time; wait until the Lord comes. He will bring to light what is hidden in darkness and will expose the motives of the heart. At that time, each will receive their praise from God Now, brothers and sisters, I have applied these things to myself and

Apollos for your benefit so that you may learn from us the meaning of the saying, "Do not go beyond what is written." Then you will not be puffed up in being a follower of one of us over against the other. For who makes you different from anyone else? What do you have that you did not receive? And if you did receive it, why do you boast as though you did not? Already you have all you want! Already you have become rich! You have begun to reign—and that without us! How I wish that you really had begun to reign so that we also might reign with you! For it seems to me that God has put us apostles on display at the end of the procession, like those condemned to die in the arena. We have been made a spectacle to the whole universe, to angels as well as to human beings. We are fools for Christ, but you are so wise in Christ! We are weak, but you are strong! You are honored; we are dishonored! To this very hour, we go hungry and thirsty, we are in rags, we are brutally treated, we are homeless. We work hard with our own hands. When we are cursed, we bless; when we are persecuted, we endure it; when we are slandered, we answer kindly. We have become the scum of the earth, the garbage of the world—right up to this moment I am writing this not to shame you but to warn you as my dear children. Even if you had ten thousand guardians in Christ, you do not have many fathers, for in Christ Jesus I became your father through the gospel. Therefore I urge you to imitate me. For this reason, I have sent to you Timothy, my son whom I love, who is faithful in the Lord. He will remind you of my way of life in Christ Jesus, which agrees with what I teach everywhere in every church Some of you have become arrogant, as if I were not coming to you. But I will come to you very soon, if the Lord is willing, and then I will find out not only how these arrogant people are talking but what power they have. For the kingdom of God is not a matter of talk but of power. What do you prefer? Shall I come to you with a rod of discipline, or shall I come in love and with a gentle spirit?

Chapter 5

It is actually reported that there is sexual immorality among you, and of a kind that even pagans do not tolerate: A man is sleeping with his father's wife. And you are proud! Shouldn't you rather have gone into mourning and have put out of your fellowship the man who has been doing this? For my part, even though I am not physically present, I am with you in spirit. As one who is present with you in this way, I have already passed judgment in the name of our Lord Jesus on the one who has been doing this. So when you are assembled, and I am with you in spirit, and the power of our Lord Jesus is present, hand this man over to Satan for the destruction of the flesh, so that his spirit may be saved on the day of the Lord Your boasting is not good. Don't you know that a little yeast leavens the whole batch of dough? Get rid of the old yeast so that you may be a new unleavened batch—as you really are. For Christ, our Passover lamb, has been sacrificed. Therefore let us keep the Festival, not with the old bread leavened with malice and wickedness, but with the unleavened bread of sincerity and truth I wrote to you in my letter not to associate with sexually immoral people—not at all meaning the people of this world who are immoral, or the greedy and swindlers, or idolaters. In that case, you would have to leave this world. But now I am writing to you that you must not associate with anyone who claims to be a brother or sister but is sexually immoral or greedy, an idolater or slanderer, a drunkard or swindler. Do not even eat with such people. What business is it of mine to judge those outside the church? Are you not to judge those inside? God will judge those outside. "Expel the wicked person from among you."

Chapter 6

Can any of you, having a dispute with another, dare to be judged by the unrighteous and not by the saints? Do you not know that the saints will judge the world? And if the world will be judged by you, are you unworthy to judge the smallest matters? Do you not know that we will judge angels? How much more the things that pertain to this life? If then you have judgments concerning things pertaining to this life, set those who are least esteemed by the church to judge. I say this to your shame. Is there not a wise person among you who can judge between his brothers? Instead, one brother goes to law against another, and this in front of unbelievers Now, therefore, it is already a defeat for you that you go to law against one another. Why do you not rather accept wrong? Why do you not rather let yourselves be cheated? No, you yourselves do wrong and cheat, and you do this to your brothers and sisters. Do you not know that the unrighteous will not inherit the kingdom of God? Do not be deceived: neither fornicators, nor idolaters, nor adulterers, nor homosexuals, nor sodomites, nor thieves, nor covetous, nor drunkards, nor revilers, nor extortioners will inherit the kingdom of God. And some of you were like that, but you were washed, you were sanctified, you were justified in the name of the Lord Jesus and by the Spirit of our God All things are lawful for me, but not all things are helpful. All things are lawful for me, but I will not be brought under the power of any. Food is for the stomach and the stomach for food, but God will destroy both it and them. The body is not meant for sexual immorality but for the Lord, and the Lord for the body. God both raised up the Lord and will also raise us up by His power. Do you not know that your bodies are members of Christ? Shall I then take the members of Christ and make them members of a harlot? Certainly not! Do you not know that he who is joined to a harlot is one body with her? For "the two," He says, "shall become one flesh." But he who is joined to the Lord is one spirit with Him Flee sexual immorality. Every sin that a man does is outside the body, but he who commits sexual immorality sins against his own body. Do you not know that your body is the temple of the Holy Spirit who is in you, whom you have from God, and you are not your own? For you were bought at a price; therefore, glorify God in your body and in your spirit, which are God's

Chapter 7

Now concerning the things of which you wrote to me: It is good for a man not to touch a woman. Nevertheless, to avoid sexual immorality, let each man have his own wife, and let each woman have her own husband. Let the husband render to his wife the affection due her, and likewise also the wife to her husband. The wife does not have authority over her own body, but the husband does. And likewise, the husband does not have authority over his own body, but the wife does. Do not deprive one another except with consent for a time, that you may give yourselves to fasting and prayer; and come together again so that Satan does not tempt you because of your lack of self-control But I say this as a concession, not as a commandment. For I wish that all men were even as I am. But each one has his own gift from God, one in this manner and another in that. But I say to the unmarried and to the widows: It is good for them if they remain even as I am, but if they cannot exercise self-control, let them marry. For it is better to marry than to burn with passion Now to the married, I command, yet not I but the Lord: A wife is not to depart from her husband. But even if she does depart, let her remain unmarried or be reconciled to her husband. And a husband is not to divorce his wife. But to the rest, I, not the Lord, say: If any brother has a wife who does not believe, and she is willing to live with him, let him not divorce her. And a woman who has a husband who does not believe, if he is willing to live with her, let her not divorce him. For the unbelieving husband is sanctified by the wife, and the unbelieving wife is sanctified by the husband. Otherwise, your children would be unclean, but now they are holy But if the unbeliever departs, let him depart; a brother or a sister is not under bondage in such cases. But God has called us to peace. For how do you know, O wife, whether you will save your husband? Or how do you know, O husband, whether you will save your wife? But as God has distributed to each one, as the Lord has called each one, so let him walk. And so I ordain in all the churches Was anyone called while circumcised? Let him not become uncircumcised. Was anyone called while uncircumcised? Let him not be circumcised. Circumcision is nothing, and uncircumcision is nothing, but keeping the commandments of God is what matters. Let each one remain in the same calling in which he was called. Were you called while a slave? Do not be concerned about it; but if you can be made free, rather use it. For he who is called in the Lord while a slave is the Lord's freedman. Likewise, he who is called while free is Christ's slave. You were bought at a price; do not become slaves of men. Brethren, let each one remain with God in that state in which he was called Now concerning virgins: I have no commandment from the Lord; yet I give judgment as one whom the Lord in His mercy has made trustworthy. I suppose, therefore, that this is good because of the present distress—that it is good for a man to remain as he is: Are you bound to a wife? Do not seek to be loosed. Are you loosed from a wife? Do not seek a wife. But even if you do marry, you have not sinned; and if a virgin marries, she has not sinned. Nevertheless, such will have trouble in the flesh, but I would spare you But this I say, brethren, the time is short, so that from now on even those who have wives should be as though they had none, those who weep as though they did not weep, those who rejoice as though they did not rejoice, those who buy as though they did not possess, and those who use this world as not misusing it. For the form of this world is passing away. But I want you to be without care. He who is unmarried cares for the things of the Lord—how he may please the Lord. But he who is married cares about the things of the world—how he may please his wife. There is a difference between a wife and a virgin. The unmarried woman cares about the things of the Lord, that she may be holy both in body and in spirit. But she who is married cares about the things of the world—how she may please her husband. And this I say for your own profit, not that I may put a leash on you, but for what is proper, and that you may serve the Lord without distraction But if any man thinks he is behaving improperly toward his virgin, if she is past the flower of youth, and thus it must be, let him do what he wishes. He does not sin; let them marry. Nevertheless, he who stands steadfast in his heart, having no necessity but has power over his own will, and has so determined in his heart that he will keep his virgin, does well. So then he who gives her in marriage does well, but he who does not give her in marriage does better A wife is bound by law as long as her husband lives; but if her husband dies, she is at liberty to be married to whom she wishes, only in the Lord. But she is happier if she remains as she is, according to my judgment—and I think I also have the Spirit of God

Chapter 8

Now concerning things offered to idols: We know that we all have knowledge. Knowledge puffs up, but love edifies. If anyone thinks that he knows anything, he knows nothing yet as he ought to know. But if anyone loves God, this one is known by Him. Therefore concerning the eating of things offered to idols, we know that an idol is nothing in the world and that there is no other God but one. For even if there are so-called gods, whether in heaven or on earth (as there are many gods and many lords), yet for us, there is one God, the Father, of whom are all things, and we for Him; and one Lord Jesus Christ, through whom are all things, and through whom we live However, there is not in everyone that knowledge; for some, with consciousness of the idol, until now eat it as a thing offered to an idol; and their conscience, being weak, is defiled. But food does not commend us to God; for neither if we eat are we the better, nor if we do not eat are we the worse. But beware lest somehow this liberty of yours become a stumbling block to those who are weak. For if anyone sees you who have knowledge eating in an idol's temple, will not the conscience of him who is weak be emboldened to eat those things offered to idols? And because of your knowledge, shall the weak brother perish, for whom Christ died? But when you thus sin against the brethren, and wound their weak conscience, you sin against Christ. Therefore, if food makes my brother stumble, I will never again eat meat, lest I make my brother stumble

Chapter 9

Am I not an apostle? Am I not free? Have I not seen Jesus Christ our Lord? Are you not my work in the Lord? If I am not an apostle to others, yet doubtless I am to you. For you are the seal of my apostleship in the Lord. My defense to those who examine me is this: Do we have no right to eat and drink? Do we have no right to take along a believing wife, as do also the other apostles, the brothers of the Lord, and Cephas? Or is it only Barnabas and I who have no right to refrain from working? Who ever goes to war at his own expense? Who plants a vineyard and does not eat of its fruit? Or who tends a flock and does not drink of the milk of the flock? Do I say these things as a mere human? Or does not the law say the same also? For it is written in the law of Moses, "You shall not muzzle an ox while it treads out the grain." Is it oxen God is concerned about? Or does He say it altogether for our sakes? For our sakes, no doubt, this is written, that he who plows should plow in hope, and he who threshes in hope should be partaker of his hope. If we have sown spiritual things for you, is it a great thing if we reap your material things? If others are partakers of this right over you, are we not even more? Nevertheless, we have not used this right, but endure all things lest we hinder the gospel of Christ. Do you not know that those who minister the holy things eat of the things of the temple, and those who serve at the altar partake of the offerings of the altar? Even so, the Lord has commanded that those who preach the gospel should live from the gospel But I have used none of these things, nor have I written these things that it should be done so to me; for it would be better for me to die than that anyone should make my boasting void. For if I preach the gospel, I have nothing to boast of, for necessity is laid upon me; yes, woe is me if I do not preach the gospel! For if I do this willingly, I have a reward; but if against my will, I have been entrusted with a stewardship. What is my reward then? That when I preach the gospel, I may present the gospel of Christ without charge, that I may not abuse my authority in the gospel For though I am free from all men, I have made myself a servant to all, that I might win the more; and to the Jews I became as a Jew, that I might win Jews; to those who are under the law, as under the law, that I might win those who are under the law; to those who are without law, as without law (not being without law toward God, but under law toward Christ), that I might win those who are without law; to the weak I became as weak, that I might win the weak. I have become all things to all men, that I might by all means save some. Now this I do for the gospel's sake, that I may be partaker of it with you Do you not know that those who run in a race all run, but one receives the prize? Run in such a way that you may obtain it. And everyone who competes for the prize is temperate in all things. Now they do it to obtain a perishable crown, but we for an imperishable crown. Therefore I run thus: not with uncertainty. Thus I fight: not as one who beats the air. But I discipline my body and bring it into subjection, lest, when I have preached to others, I myself should become disqualified

Chapter 10

Moreover, brethren, I do not want you to be unaware that all our fathers were under the cloud, and all passed through the sea, and all were baptized into Moses in the cloud and in the sea, and all ate the same spiritual food, and all drank the same spiritual drink. For they drank of that spiritual Rock that followed them, and that Rock was Christ. But with most of them God was not well pleased, for their bodies were scattered in the wilderness Now these things became our examples, to the intent that we should not lust after evil things as they also lusted. And do not become idolaters as were some of them. As it is written, "The people sat down to eat and drink, and rose up to play." Nor let us commit sexual immorality, as some of them did, and in one day twenty-three thousand fell. Nor let us tempt Christ, as some of them also tempted, and were destroyed by serpents. Nor complain, as some of them also complained, and were destroyed by the destroyer Now all these things happened to them as examples, and they were written for our admonition, upon whom the ends of the ages have come. Therefore let him who thinks he stands take heed lest he fall. No temptation has overtaken you except such as is common to man; but God is faithful, who will not allow you to be tempted beyond what you are able, but with the temptation will also make the way of escape, that you may be able to bear it Therefore, my beloved, flee from idolatry. I speak as to wise men; judge for yourselves what I say. The cup of blessing which we bless, is it not the communion of the blood of Christ? The bread which we break, is it not the communion of the body of Christ? For we, though many, are one bread and one body; for we all partake of that one bread. Observe Israel after the flesh: Are not those who eat of the sacrifices partakers of the altar? What am I saying then? That an idol is anything, or what is offered to idols is anything? Rather, that the things which the Gentiles sacrifice they sacrifice to demons and not to God, and I do not want you to have fellowship with demons You cannot drink the cup of the Lord and the cup of demons; you cannot partake of the Lord's table and of the table of demons. Or do we provoke the Lord to jealousy? Are we stronger than He? All things are lawful for me, but not all things are helpful; all things are lawful for me, but not all things edify. Let no one seek his own, but each one the other's well-being. Eat whatever is sold in the meat market, asking no questions for conscience' sake; for "the earth is the Lord's, and all its fullness." If any of those who do not believe invite you to dinner, and you desire to go, eat whatever is set before you, asking no question for conscience' sake. But if anyone says to you, "This was offered to idols," do not eat it for the sake of the one who told you, and for conscience' sake; for "the earth is the

Lord's, and all its fullness." "Conscience," I say, not your own, but that of the other. For why is my liberty judged by another man's conscience? But if I partake with thanks, why am I evil spoken of for the food over which I give thanks? Therefore, whether you eat or drink, or whatever you do, do all to the glory of God. Give no offense, either to the Jews or to the Greeks or to the church of God, just as I also please all men in all things, not seeking my own profit, but the profit of many, that they may be saved

CHAPTER 11

Be followers of me, as I am of Christ. Now, brothers, I commend you to remember all my teachings and keep the ordinances as I have given them to you. But I want you to know that Christ is the head of every man, man is the head of woman, and God is the head of Christ. Whoever prays or prophesies with anything on his head dishonors his own head. But every woman who prays or prophesies with her head uncovered dishonors her head, for it is the same as if her head were shaved. Therefore, if a woman is not covered, let her be covered; and if it is shameful for a woman to be uncovered or shaved, let her be covered. For a man should not cover his head since he is the image and glory of God; but woman is the glory of man. For man was not made from woman, but woman from man. Neither was man created for woman, but woman for man. Therefore, a woman should have a symbol of authority on her head, because of the angels. Nevertheless, in the Lord, woman is not independent of man nor man of woman. For as woman was made from man, so man is now born of woman. But all things are from God. Judge for yourselves: is it proper for a woman to pray to God with her head uncovered? Does not nature itself teach you that if a man has long hair, it is a disgrace for him, but if a woman has long hair, it is her glory, for her hair is given to her for a covering? If anyone is inclined to be contentious, we have no such practice, nor do the churches of God In this declaration, I warn you not to come together for the worse rather than for the better. For first of all, when you come together as a church, I hear that there are divisions among you, and I partly believe it. For there must be factions among you so that those who are genuine among you may be recognized. When you come together, it is not the Lord's Supper that you eat. For in eating, each one goes ahead with his own meal. One goes hungry, another gets drunk. What! Do you not have houses to eat and drink in? Or do you despise the church of God and humiliate those who have nothing? What shall I say to you? Shall I commend you in this? No, I will not For I received from the Lord what I also delivered to you: that the Lord Jesus, on the night when he was betrayed, took bread, and when he had given thanks, he broke it and said, "Take, eat; this is my body, which is broken for you. Do this in remembrance of me." In the same way, he also took the cup after supper, saying, "This cup is the new covenant in my blood. Do this, as often as you drink it, in remembrance of me." For as often as you eat this bread and drink this cup, you proclaim the Lord's death until he comes. Therefore, whoever eats the bread or drinks the cup of the Lord in an unworthy manner will be guilty concerning the body and blood of the Lord. Let a person examine himself, then, and so eat of the bread and drink of the cup. For anyone who eats and drinks without discerning the body eats and drinks judgment on himself. That is why many of you are weak and ill, and some have died. But if we judged ourselves truly, we would not be judged. But when we are judged by the Lord, we are disciplined so that we may not be condemned along with the world So then, my brothers, when you come together to eat, wait for one another. If anyone is hungry, let him eat at home so that when you come together, it will not be for judgment. About the other things, I will give directions when I come

CHAPTER 12

Now concerning spiritual gifts, brothers, I do not want you to be uninformed. You know that when you were pagans, you were led astray to mute idols, however you were led. Therefore, I want you to understand that no one speaking in the Spirit of God ever says, "Jesus is accursed!" and no one can say "Jesus is Lord" except in the Holy Spirit. Now there are varieties of gifts, but the same Spirit; and there are varieties of service, but the same Lord; and there are varieties of activities, but it is the same God who empowers them all in everyone. To each is given the manifestation of the Spirit for the common good. For to one is given through the Spirit the utterance of wisdom, and to another the utterance of knowledge according to the same Spirit, to another faith by the same Spirit, to another gifts of healing by the one Spirit, to another the working of miracles, to another prophecy, to another the ability to distinguish between spirits, to another various kinds of tongues, to another the interpretation of tongues. All these are empowered by one and the same Spirit, who apportions to each one individually as he wills For just as the body is one and has many members, and all the members of the body, though many, are one body, so it is with Christ. For in one Spirit we were all baptized into one body—Jews or Greeks, slaves or free—and all were made to drink of one Spirit. For the body does not consist of one member but of many. If the foot should say, "Because I am not a hand, I do not belong to the body," that would not make it any less a part of the body. And if the ear should say, "Because I am not an eye, I do not belong to the body," that would not make it any less a part of the body. If the whole body were an eye, where would be the sense of hearing? If the whole body were an ear, where would be the sense of smell? But as it is, God arranged the members in the body, each one of them, as he chose. If all were a single member, where would the body be? As it is, there are many parts, yet one body. The eye cannot say to the hand, "I have no need of you," nor again the head to the feet, "I have no need of you." On the contrary, the parts of the body that seem to be weaker are indispensable, and on those parts of the body that we think less honorable we bestow the greater honor, and our unpresentable parts are treated with greater modesty, which our more presentable parts do not require. But God has so composed the body, giving greater honor to the part that lacked it, that there may be no division in the body, but that the members may have the same care for one another. If one member suffers, all suffer together; if one member is honored, all rejoice together Now you are the body of Christ and individually members of it. And God has appointed in the church first apostles, second prophets, third teachers, then miracles, then gifts of healing, helping, administrating, and various kinds of tongues. Are all apostles? Are all prophets? Are all teachers? Do all work miracles? Do all possess gifts of healing? Do all speak with tongues? Do all interpret? But earnestly desire the higher gifts. And I will show you a still more excellent way

CHAPTER 13

If I speak in the tongues of men and of angels, but have not love, I am a noisy gong or a clanging cymbal. And if I have prophetic powers, and understand all mysteries and all knowledge, and if I have all faith so as to remove mountains, but have not love, I am nothing. If I give away all I have, and if I deliver up my body to be burned, but have not love, I gain nothing. Love is patient and kind; love does not envy or boast; it is not arrogant or rude. It does not insist on its own way; it is not irritable or resentful; it does not rejoice at wrongdoing, but rejoices with the truth. Love bears all things, believes all things, hopes all things, endures all things. Love never ends. As for prophecies, they will pass away; as for tongues, they will cease; as for knowledge, it will pass away. For we know in part and we prophesy in part, but when the perfect comes, the partial will pass away. When I was a child, I spoke like a child, I thought like a child, I reasoned like a child. When I became a man, I gave up childish ways. For now we see in a mirror dimly, but then face to face. Now I know in part; then I shall know fully, even as I have been fully known. So now faith, hope, and love abide, these three; but the greatest of these is love

CHAPTER 14

Pursue love and earnestly desire the spiritual gifts, especially that you may prophesy. For one who speaks in a tongue speaks not to men but to God; for no one understands him, but he utters mysteries in the Spirit. On the other hand, the one who prophesies speaks to people for their upbuilding and encouragement and consolation. The one who speaks in a tongue builds up himself, but the one who prophesies builds up the church. Now I want you all to speak in tongues, but even more to prophesy. The one who prophesies is greater than the one who speaks in tongues, unless someone interprets so that the church may be built up Now, brothers, if I come to you speaking in tongues, how will I benefit you unless I bring you some revelation or knowledge or prophecy or teaching? If even lifeless instruments, such as the flute or the harp, do not give distinct notes, how will anyone know what is played? And if the bugle gives an indistinct sound, who will get ready for battle? So with yourselves, if with your tongue you utter speech that is not intelligible, how will anyone know what is said? For you will be speaking into the air. There are doubtless many different languages in the world, and none is without meaning, but if I do not know the meaning of the language, I will be a foreigner to the speaker and the speaker a foreigner to me. So with yourselves, since you are eager for manifestations of the Spirit, strive to excel in building up the church Therefore, one who speaks in a tongue should pray that he may interpret. For if I pray in a tongue, my spirit prays but my mind is unfruitful. What am I to do? I will pray with my spirit, but I will pray with my mind also; I will sing praise with my spirit, but I will sing with my mind also. Otherwise, if you give thanks with your spirit, how can anyone in the position of an outsider say "Amen" to your thanksgiving when he does not know what you are saying? For you may be giving thanks well enough, but the other person is not being built up. I thank God that I speak in tongues more than all of you. Nevertheless, in church, I would rather speak five words with my mind to instruct others than ten thousand words in a tongue Brothers, do not be children in your thinking. Be infants in evil, but in your thinking be mature. In the Law it is written, "By people of strange tongues and by the lips of foreigners will I speak to this people, and even then they will not listen to me, says the Lord." Thus tongues are a sign not for believers but for unbelievers, while prophecy is a sign not for unbelievers but for believers. If, therefore, the whole church comes together and all speak in tongues, and outsiders or unbelievers enter, will they not say that you are out of your minds? But if all prophesy, and an unbeliever or outsider enters, he is convicted by all, he is called to account by all, the secrets of his heart are disclosed, and so, falling on his face, he will worship God and declare that God is really among you What then, brothers? When you come together, each one has a hymn, a lesson, a revelation, a tongue, or an interpretation. Let all things be done for building up. If any speak in a tongue, let there be only two or at most three, and each in turn, and let someone interpret. But if there is no one to interpret, let each of them keep silent in church and speak to himself and to God. Let two or three prophets speak, and let the others weigh what is said. If a revelation is made to another sitting there, let the first be silent. For you can all prophesy one by one, so that all may learn and all be encouraged, and the spirits of prophets are subject to prophets. For God is not a God of confusion but of peace. As in all the churches of the saints, the women should keep silent in the churches. For they are not permitted to speak but should be in submission, as the Law also says. If there is anything they desire to learn, let them ask their husbands at home. For it is shameful for a woman to speak in church Or was it from you that the word of God came? Or are you the only ones it has reached? If anyone thinks that he is a prophet, or spiritual, he should acknowledge that the things I am writing to you are a command of the Lord. If anyone does not recognize this, he is not recognized. So, my brothers, earnestly desire to prophesy and do not forbid speaking in tongues. But all things should be done decently and in order

CHAPTER 15

Now I would remind you, brothers, of the gospel I preached to you, which you received, in which you stand, and by which you are being saved, if you hold fast to the word I preached to you—unless you believed in vain. For I delivered to you as of first importance what I also received: that Christ died for our sins in accordance with the Scriptures, that he was buried, that he was raised on the third day in accordance with the Scriptures, and that he appeared to Cephas, then to the twelve. Then he appeared to more than five hundred brothers at one time, most of whom are still alive, though some have fallen asleep. Then he appeared to James, then to all the apostles. Last of all, as to one untimely born, he appeared also to me. For I am the least of the apostles, unworthy to be called an apostle, because I persecuted the church of God. But by the grace of God, I am what I am, and his grace toward me was not in vain. On the contrary, I worked harder than any of them, though it was not I, but the grace of God that is with me. Whether then it was I or they, so we preach and so you believed Now if Christ is proclaimed as raised from the dead, how can some of you say that there is no resurrection of the dead? But if there is no resurrection of the dead, then not even Christ has been raised. And if Christ has not been raised, then our preaching is in vain and your faith is in vain. We are even found to be misrepresenting God because we testified about God that he raised Christ, whom he did not raise if it is true that the dead are not raised. For if the dead are not raised, not even Christ has been raised. And if Christ has not been raised, your faith is futile and you are still in your sins. Then those also who have fallen asleep in Christ have perished. If in Christ we have hope in this life only, we are of all people most to be pitied. But in fact, Christ has been raised from the dead, the firstfruits of those who have fallen asleep. For as by a man came death, by a man has come also the resurrection of the dead. For as in Adam all die, so also in Christ shall all be made alive. But each in his own order: Christ the firstfruits, then at his coming those who belong to Christ. Then comes the end, when he delivers the kingdom to God the Father after destroying every rule and every authority and power. For he must reign until he has put all his enemies under his feet. The last enemy to be destroyed is death. For "God has put all things in subjection under his feet." But when it says, "all things are put in subjection," it is plain that he is excepted who put all things in subjection under him. When all things are subjected to him, then the Son himself will also be subjected to him who put all things in subjection under him, that God may be all in all Otherwise, what do people mean by being baptized on behalf of the dead? If the dead are not raised at all, why are people baptized on their behalf? Why are we in danger every hour? I protest, brothers, by my pride in you, which I have in Christ Jesus our Lord, I die every day! What do I gain if, humanly speaking, I fought with beasts at Ephesus? If the dead are not raised, "Let us eat and drink, for tomorrow we die." Do not be deceived: "Bad company ruins good morals." Wake up from your drunken stupor, as is right, and do not go on sinning. For some have no knowledge of God. I say this to your shame But someone will ask, "How are the dead raised? With what kind of body do they come?" You foolish person! What you sow does not come to life unless it dies. And what you sow is not the body that is to be, but a bare kernel, perhaps of wheat or of some other grain. But God gives it a body as he has chosen, and to each kind of seed its own body. For not all flesh is the same, but there is one kind for humans, another for animals, another for birds, and another for fish. There are heavenly bodies and earthly bodies, but the glory of the heavenly is of one kind, and the glory of the earthly is of another. There is one glory of the sun, and another glory of the moon, and another glory of the stars; for star differs from star in glory So is it with the resurrection of the dead. What is sown is perishable; what is raised is imperishable. It is sown in dishonor; it is raised in glory.

It is sown in weakness; it is raised in power. It is sown a natural body; it is raised a spiritual body. If there is a natural body, there is also a spiritual body. Thus it is written, "The first man Adam became a living being"; the last Adam became a life-giving spirit. But it is not the spiritual that is first but the natural, and then the spiritual. The first man was from the earth, a man of dust; the second man is from heaven. As was the man of dust, so also are those who are of the dust, and as is the man of heaven, so also are those who are of heaven. Just as we have borne the image of the man of dust, we shall also bear the image of the man of heaven I tell you this, brothers: flesh and blood cannot inherit the kingdom of God, nor does the perishable inherit the imperishable. Behold! I tell you a mystery. We shall not all sleep, but we shall all be changed, in a moment, in the twinkling of an eye, at the last trumpet. For the trumpet will sound, and the dead will be raised imperishable, and we shall be changed. For this perishable body must put on the imperishable, and this mortal body must put on immortality. When the perishable puts on the imperishable, and the mortal puts on immortality, then shall come to pass the saying that is written: "Death is swallowed up in victory." "O death, where is your victory? O death, where is your sting?" The sting of death is sin, and the power of sin is the law. But thanks be to God, who gives us the victory through our Lord Jesus Christ. Therefore, my beloved brothers, be steadfast, immovable, always abounding in the work of the Lord, knowing that in the Lord your labor is not in vain

CHAPTER 16

Now concerning the collection for the saints: as I directed the churches of Galatia, so you also are to do. On the first day of every week, each of you is to put something aside and store it up, as he may prosper, so that there will be no collecting when I come. And when I arrive, I will send those whom you accredit by letter to carry your gift to Jerusalem. If it seems advisable that I should go also, they will accompany me I will visit you after passing through Macedonia, for I intend to pass through Macedonia, and perhaps I will stay with you or even spend the winter, so that you may help me on my journey, wherever I go. For I do not want to see you now just in passing. I hope to spend some time with you, if the Lord permits. But I will stay in Ephesus until Pentecost, for a wide door for effective work has opened to me, and there are many adversaries. When Timothy comes, see that you put him at ease among you, for he is doing the work of the Lord, as I am. So let no one despise him. Help him on his way in peace, that he may return to me, for I am expecting him with the brothers Now concerning our brother Apollos, I strongly urged him to visit you with the other brothers, but it was not at all his will to come now. He will come when he has opportunity. Be watchful, stand firm in the faith, act like men, be strong. Let all that you do be done in love Now I urge you, brothers—you know that the household of Stephanas were the first converts in Achaia, and that they have devoted themselves to the service of the saints—be subject to such as these, and to every fellow worker and laborer. I rejoice at the coming of Stephanas and Fortunatus and Achaicus, because they have made up for your absence, for they refreshed my spirit as well as yours. Give recognition to such people The churches of Asia send you greetings. Aquila and Prisca, together with the church in their house, send you hearty greetings in the Lord. All the brothers send you greetings. Greet one another with a holy kiss. I, Paul, write this greeting with my own hand. If anyone has no love for the Lord, let him be accursed. Our Lord, come! The grace of the Lord Jesus be with you. My love be with you all in Christ Jesus. Amen

47. 2 Corinthians

Chapter 1

Paul, an apostle of Christ by the will of God, and Timothy, our brother, greet the church of God in

Corinth and all the saints throughout Achaia. Grace and peace to you from God our Father and the Lord Jesus Christ. Blessed be the God and Father of our Lord Jesus Christ, the Father of mercies and the God of all comfort, who comforts us in all our tribulations so that we can comfort those in any affliction with the comfort we ourselves receive from God. For as the sufferings of Christ abound in us, so our consolation also abounds through Christ. If we are afflicted, it is for your consolation and salvation, which is effective in enduring the same sufferings we also endure. If we are comforted, it is for your consolation and salvation. Our hope for you is steadfast because we know that as you share in the sufferings, you will also share in the consolation Brothers and sisters, we do not want you to be uninformed about the troubles we experienced in Asia. We were under great pressure, far beyond our ability to endure, so much so that we despaired of life itself. Indeed, we felt we had received the sentence of death. But this happened so that we might not rely on ourselves but on God, who raises the dead. He delivered us from such a deadly peril, and he will deliver us again. On him, we have set our hope that he will continue to deliver us, as you help us by your prayers. Then many will give thanks on our behalf for the gracious favor granted us in answer to the prayers of many Our conscience testifies that we have conducted ourselves in the world, and especially in our relations with you, with integrity and godly sincerity. We have done so, not according to worldly wisdom, but according to God's grace. For we write nothing to you other than what you can read and understand. And I hope that as you have understood us in part, you will come to understand fully that you can boast of us just as we will boast of you in the day of the Lord Jesus Because I was confident of this, I wanted to visit you first so that you might benefit twice. I wanted to visit you on my way to Macedonia and to come back to you from Macedonia, and then to have you send me on my way to Judea. Was I fickle when I intended to do this? Or do I make my plans in a worldly manner so that in the same breath I say both "Yes, yes" and "No, no"? But as surely as God is faithful, our message to you is not "Yes" and "No." For the Son of God, Jesus Christ, who was preached among you by us—by me, Silas, and Timothy—was not "Yes" and "No," but in him, it has always been "Yes." For no matter how many promises God has made, they are "Yes" in Christ. And so through him, the "Amen" is spoken by us to the glory of God. Now it is God who makes both us and you stand firm in Christ. He anointed us, set his seal of ownership on us, and put his Spirit in our hearts as a deposit, guaranteeing what is to come I call God as my witness—and I stake my life on it— that it was in order to spare you that I did not return to Corinth. Not that we lord it over your faith, but we work with you for your joy because it is by faith you stand firm

Chapter 2

So I made up my mind that I would not make another painful visit to you. For if I grieve you, who is left to make me glad but you whom I have grieved? I wrote as I did so that when I came, I would not be distressed by those who should have made me rejoice. I had confidence in all of you that you would all share my joy. For I wrote you out of great distress and anguish of heart and with many tears, not to grieve you but to let you know the depth of my love for you If anyone has caused grief, he has not so much grieved me as he has grieved all of you to some extent—not to put it too severely. The punishment inflicted on him by the majority is sufficient. Now instead, you ought to forgive and comfort him so that

he will not be overwhelmed by excessive sorrow. I urge you, therefore, to reaffirm your love for him. Another reason I wrote you was to see if you would stand the test and be obedient in everything. Anyone you forgive, I also forgive. And what I have forgiven—if there was anything to forgive—I have forgiven in the sight of Christ for your sake, in order that Satan might not outwit us. For we are not unaware of his schemes When I went to Troas to preach the gospel of Christ and found that the Lord had opened a door for me, I still had no peace of mind because I did not find my brother Titus there. So I said goodbye to them and went on to Macedonia But thanks be to God, who always leads us as captives in Christ's triumphal procession and uses us to spread the aroma of the knowledge of him everywhere. For we are to God the pleasing aroma of Christ among those who are being saved and those who are perishing. To the one we are an aroma that brings death; to the other, an aroma that brings life. And who is equal to such a task? Unlike so many, we do not peddle the word of God for profit. On the contrary, in Christ, we speak before God with sincerity, as those sent from God

Chapter 3

Are we beginning to commend ourselves again? Or do we need, like some people, letters of recommendation to you or from you? You yourselves are our letter, written on our hearts, known and read by everyone. You show that you are a letter from Christ, the result of our ministry, written not with ink but with the Spirit of the living God, not on tablets of stone but on tablets of human hearts Such confidence we have through Christ before God. Not that we are competent in ourselves to claim anything for ourselves, but our competence comes from God. He has made us competent as ministers of a new covenant—not of the letter but of the Spirit; for the letter kills, but the Spirit gives life Now if the ministry that brought death, which was engraved in letters on stone, came with glory, so that the Israelites could not look steadily at the face of Moses because of its glory, transitory though it was, will not the ministry of the Spirit be even more glorious? If the ministry that brought condemnation was glorious, how much more glorious is the ministry that brings righteousness! For what was glorious has no glory now in comparison with the surpassing glory. And if what was transitory came with glory, how much greater is the glory of that which lasts! Therefore, since we have such a hope, we are very bold. We are not like Moses, who would put a veil over his face to prevent the Israelites from seeing the end of what was passing away. But their minds were made dull, for to this day the same veil remains when the old covenant is read. It has not been removed because only in Christ is it taken away. Even to this day when Moses is read, a veil covers their hearts. But whenever anyone turns to the Lord, the veil is taken away. Now the Lord is the Spirit, and where the Spirit of the Lord is, there is freedom. And we all, who with unveiled faces contemplate the Lord's glory, are being transformed into his image with ever-increasing glory, which comes from the Lord, who is the Spirit

Chapter 4

Therefore, since through God's mercy we have this ministry, we do not lose heart. Rather, we have renounced secret and shameful ways; we do not use deception, nor do we distort the word of God. On the contrary, by setting forth the truth plainly, we commend ourselves to everyone's conscience in the sight of God. And even if our gospel is veiled, it is veiled to those who are perishing. The god of this age has blinded the minds of unbelievers so that they cannot see the light of the gospel that displays the glory of Christ, who is the image of God. For what we preach is not ourselves, but Jesus Christ as Lord, and ourselves as your servants for Jesus' sake. For God, who said, "Let light shine out of darkness," made his light shine in our hearts to give us the light of the knowledge of God's glory displayed in the face of Christ But we have this treasure in jars of clay to show that this all-surpassing power is from God and not from us. We are hard-pressed on every side, but not crushed; perplexed, but not in despair; persecuted, but not abandoned; struck down, but not destroyed. We always carry around in our body the death of Jesus so that the life of Jesus may also be revealed in our body. For we who are alive are always being given over to death for Jesus' sake so that his life may also be revealed in our mortal body. So then, death is at work in us, but life is at work in you It is written: "I believed; therefore I have spoken." Since we have that same spirit of faith, we also believe and therefore speak because we know that the one who raised the Lord Jesus from the dead will also raise us with Jesus and present us with you to himself. All this is for your benefit so that the grace that is reaching more and more people may cause thanksgiving to overflow to the glory of God Therefore, we do not lose heart. Though outwardly we are wasting away, yet inwardly we are being renewed day by day. For our light and momentary troubles are achieving for us an eternal glory that far outweighs them all. So we fix our eyes not on what is seen but on what is unseen since what is seen is temporary, but what is unseen is eternal

Chapter 5

For we know that if the earthly tent we live in is destroyed, we have a building from God, an eternal house in heaven, not built by human hands. Meanwhile, we groan, longing to be clothed instead with our heavenly dwelling, because when we are clothed, we will not be found naked. For while we are in this tent, we groan and are burdened because we do not wish to be unclothed but to be clothed instead with our heavenly dwelling so that what is mortal may be swallowed up by life. Now the one who has fashioned us for this very purpose is God, who has given us the Spirit as a deposit, guaranteeing what is to come Therefore, we are always confident and know that as long as we are at home in the body, we are away from the Lord. For we live by faith, not by sight. We are confident, I say, and would prefer to be away from the body and at home with the Lord. So we make it our goal to please him, whether we are at home in the body or away from it. For we must all appear before the judgment seat of Christ so that each of us may receive what is due us for the things done while in the body, whether good or bad Since then, we know what it is to fear the Lord, we try to persuade others. What we are is plain to God, and I hope it is also plain to your conscience. We are not trying to commend ourselves to you again, but are giving you an opportunity to take pride in us so that you can answer those who take pride in what is seen rather than in what is in the heart. If we are "out of our mind," as some say, it is for God; if we are in our right mind, it is for you. For Christ's love compels us because we are convinced that one died for all, and therefore all died. And he died for all so that those who live should no longer live for themselves but for him who died for them and was raised again So from now on, we regard no one from a worldly point of view. Though we once regarded Christ in this way, we do so no longer. Therefore, if anyone is in Christ, the new creation has come: The old has gone, the new is here! All this is from God, who reconciled us to himself through Christ and gave us the ministry of reconciliation: that God was reconciling the world to himself in Christ, not counting people's sins against them. And he has committed to us the message of reconciliation. We are therefore Christ's ambassadors, as though God were making his appeal through us. We implore you on Christ's behalf: Be reconciled to God. God made him who had no sin to be sin for us so that in him we might become the righteousness of God

Chapter 6

As God's co-workers, we urge you not to receive God's grace in vain. For he says, "In the time of my favor I heard you, and in the day of salvation I helped you." I tell you, now is the time of God's favor, now is the day of salvation. We put no stumbling block in anyone's path so that our ministry will not be discredited. Rather, as servants of God, we commend ourselves in every way: in great endurance; in troubles, hardships, and distresses; in beatings, imprisonments, and riots; in hard work, sleepless nights, and hunger; in purity, understanding, patience, and kindness; in the Holy Spirit and in sincere love; in truthful speech and in the power of God; with weapons of righteousness in the right hand and in the left; through glory and dishonor, bad report and good report; genuine, yet regarded as impostors; known, yet regarded as unknown; dying, and yet we live on; beaten, and yet not killed; sorrowful, yet always rejoicing; poor, yet making many rich; having nothing, and yet possessing everything We have spoken freely to you, Corinthians, and opened wide our hearts to you. We are not withholding our affection from you, but you are withholding yours from us. As a fair exchange—I speak as to my children—open wide your hearts also Do not be yoked together with unbelievers. For what do righteousness and wickedness have in common? Or what fellowship can light have with darkness? What harmony is there between Christ and Belial? Or what does a believer have in common with an unbeliever? What agreement is there between the temple of God and idols? For we are the temple of the living God. As God has said: "I will live with them and walk among them, and I will be their God, and they will be my people." Therefore, "Come out from them and be separate, says the Lord. Touch no unclean thing, and I will receive you." And, "I will be a Father to you, and you will be my sons and daughters, says the Lord Almighty."

Chapter 7

Therefore, since we have these promises, dear friends, let us purify ourselves from everything that contaminates body and spirit, perfecting holiness out of reverence for God. Make room for us in your hearts. We have wronged no one, we have corrupted no one, we have exploited no one. I do not say this to condemn you; I have said before that you have such a place in our hearts that we would live or die with you. I have spoken to you with great frankness; I take great pride in you. I am greatly encouraged; in all our troubles, my joy knows no bounds For when we came into Macedonia, we had no rest, but we were harassed at every turn—conflicts on the outside, fears within. But God, who comforts the downcast, comforted us by the coming of Titus, and not only by his coming but also by the comfort you had given him. He told us about your longing for me, your deep sorrow, your ardent concern for me so that my joy was greater than ever Even if I caused you sorrow by my letter, I do not regret it. Though I did regret it—I see that my letter hurt you, but only for a little while—yet now I am happy, not because you were made sorry, but because your sorrow led you to repentance. For you became sorrowful as God intended and so were not harmed in any way by us. Godly sorrow brings repentance that leads to salvation and leaves no regret, but worldly sorrow brings death. See what this godly sorrow has produced in you: what earnestness, what eagerness to clear yourselves, what indignation, what alarm, what longing, what concern, what readiness to see justice done. At every point, you have proved yourselves to be innocent in this matter. So even though I wrote to you, it was neither on account of the one who did the wrong nor on account of the injured party but rather that before God you could see for yourselves how devoted to us you are. By all this, we are encouraged In addition to our own encouragement, we were especially delighted to see how happy Titus was because his spirit has been refreshed by all of you. I had boasted to him about you, and you have not embarrassed me. But just as everything we said to you was true, so our boasting about you to Titus has proved to be true as well. And his affection for you is all the greater when he remembers that you were all obedient, receiving him with fear and trembling. I am glad I can have complete confidence in you

Chapter 8

And now, brothers and sisters, we want you to know about the grace that God has given the Macedonian churches. In the midst of a very severe trial, their overflowing joy and their extreme poverty welled up in rich generosity. For I testify that they gave as much as they were able and even beyond their ability. Entirely on their own, they urgently pleaded with us for the privilege of sharing in this service to the Lord's people. And they exceeded our expectations: They gave themselves first of all to the Lord and then by the will of God also to us. So we urged Titus, just as he had earlier made a beginning, to bring also to completion this act of grace on your part. But since you excel in everything—in faith, in speech, in knowledge, in complete earnestness, and in the love we have kindled in you—see that you also excel in this grace of giving I am not commanding you, but I want to test the sincerity of your love by comparing it with the earnestness of others. For you know the grace of our Lord Jesus Christ, that though he was rich, yet for your sake he became poor so that you through his poverty might become rich And here is my judgment about what is best for you in this matter: Last year, you were the first not only to give but also to have the desire to do so. Now finish the work so that your eager willingness to do it may be matched by your completion of it, according to your means. For if the willingness is there, the gift is acceptable according to what one has, not according to what one does not have. Our desire is not that others might be relieved while you are hard-pressed, but that there might be equality. At the present time, your plenty will supply what they need so that in turn their plenty will supply what you need. The goal is equality, as it is written: "The one who gathered much did not have too much, and the one who gathered little did not have too little." Thanks be to God, who put into the heart of Titus the same concern I have for you. For Titus not only welcomed our appeal but he is coming to you with much enthusiasm and on his own initiative. And we are sending along with him the brother who is praised by all the churches for his service to the gospel. What is more, he was chosen by the churches to accompany us as we carry the offering, which we administer in order to honor the Lord himself and to show our eagerness to help. We want to avoid any criticism of the way we administer this liberal gift. For we are taking pains to do what is right, not only in the eyes of the Lord but also in the eyes of man In addition, we are sending with them our brother who has often proved to us in many ways that he is zealous, and now even more so because of his great confidence in

you. As for Titus, he is my partner and co-worker among you; as for our brothers, they are representatives of the churches and an honor to Christ. Therefore show these men the proof of your love and the reason for our pride in you so that the churches can see it

Chapter 9

There is no need for me to write to you about this service to the Lord's people. For I know your eagerness to help, and I have been boasting about it to the Macedonians, telling them that since last year you in Achaia were ready to give, and your enthusiasm has stirred most of them to action. But I am sending the brothers in order that our boasting about you in this matter should not prove hollow, but that you may be ready, as I said you would be. For if any Macedonians come with me and find you unprepared, we—not to say anything about you—would be ashamed of having been so confident. So I thought it necessary to urge the brothers to visit you in advance and finish the arrangements for the generous gift you had promised. Then it will be ready as a generous gift, not as one grudgingly given Remember this: Whoever sows sparingly will also reap sparingly, and whoever sows generously will also reap generously. Each of you should give what you have decided in your heart to give, not reluctantly or under compulsion, for God loves a cheerful giver. And God is able to bless you abundantly so that in all things at all times, having all that you need, you will abound in every good work. As it is written: "They have freely scattered their gifts to the poor; their righteousness endures forever." Now he who supplies seed to the sower and bread for food will also supply and increase your store of seed and will enlarge the harvest of your righteousness. You will be enriched in every way so that you can be generous on every occasion, and through us, your generosity will result in thanksgiving to God. This service that you perform is not only supplying the needs of the Lord's people but is also overflowing in many expressions of thanks to God. Because of the service by which you have proved yourselves, others will praise God for the obedience that accompanies your confession of the gospel of Christ and for your generosity in sharing with them and with everyone else. And in their prayers for you, their hearts will go out to you because of the surpassing grace God has given you. Thanks be to God for his indescribable gift!

Chapter 10

By the humility and gentleness of Christ, I appeal to you—I, Paul, who am "timid" when face to face with you, but "bold" toward you when away! I beg you that when I come, I may not have to be as bold as I expect to be toward some people who think that we live by the standards of this world. For though we live in the world, we do not wage war as the world does. The weapons we fight with are not the weapons of the world. On the contrary, they have divine power to demolish strongholds. We demolish arguments and every pretension that sets itself up against the knowledge of God, and we take captive every thought to make it obedient to Christ. And we will be ready to punish every act of disobedience, once your obedience is complete You are judging by appearances. If anyone is confident that they belong to Christ, they should consider again that we belong to Christ just as much as they do. So even if I boast somewhat freely about the authority the Lord gave us for building you up rather than tearing you down, I will not be ashamed of it. I do not want to seem to be trying to frighten you with my letters. For some say, "His letters are weighty and forceful, but in person, he is unimpressive and his speaking amounts to nothing." Such people should realize that what we are in our letters when we are absent, we will be in our actions when we are present We do not dare to classify or compare ourselves with some who commend themselves. When they measure themselves by themselves and compare themselves with themselves, they are not wise. We, however, will not boast beyond proper limits, but will confine our boasting to the sphere of service God himself has assigned to us, a sphere that also includes you. We are not going too far in our boasting, as would be the case if we had not come to you, for we did get as far as you with the gospel of Christ. Neither do we go beyond our limits by boasting of work done by others. Our hope is that, as your faith continues to grow, our sphere of activity among you will greatly expand so that we can preach the gospel in the regions beyond you. For we do not want to boast about work already done in someone else's territory. But, "Let the one who boasts boast in the Lord." For it is not the one who commends himself who is approved, but the one whom the Lord commends

Chapter 11

I wish you would bear with me in a little foolishness; indeed, you are bearing with me. I am anxious for you with a godly jealousy because I have promised you to one husband, to present you as a pure virgin to Christ. But I am afraid that just as the serpent deceived Eve by his cunning, your minds may be led astray from the simplicity and purity of devotion to Christ. For if someone comes and preaches another Jesus whom we have not preached, or if you receive a different spirit which you have not received, or a different gospel which you have not accepted, you might well tolerate them I consider myself in no way inferior to the "super-apostles." Even if I am unskilled in speech, I am not so in knowledge; in every way, we have made this clear to you in all things. Did I commit a sin by humbling myself so that you might be exalted, because I preached God's gospel to you free of charge? I robbed other churches by accepting support from them in order to serve you. When I was with you and in need, I was not a burden to anyone, for the brothers who came from Macedonia supplied what I lacked. I have kept myself from being a burden to you in any way and will continue to do so As surely as the truth of Christ is in me, nobody in the regions of Achaia will stop this boasting of mine. Why? Because I do not love you? God knows I do! And I will keep on doing what I am doing to cut the ground from under those who want an opportunity to be considered equal with us in the things they boast about. For such people are false apostles, deceitful workers, masquerading as apostles of Christ. And no wonder, for Satan himself masquerades as an angel of light. It is not surprising, then, if his servants also masquerade as servants of righteousness. Their end will be what their actions deserve I repeat, let no one take me for a fool. But if you do, then tolerate me just as you would a fool so that I may do a little boasting. In this self-confident boasting, I am not talking as the Lord would, but as a fool. Since many are boasting in the way the world does, I too will boast. You gladly put up with fools since you are so wise! In fact, you even put up with anyone who enslaves you or exploits you or takes advantage of you or puts on airs or slaps you in the face. To my shame, I admit that we were too weak for that! Whatever anyone else dares to boast about—I am speaking as a fool—I also dare to boast about. Are they Hebrews? So am I. Are they Israelites? So am I. Are they Abraham's descendants? So am I. Are they servants of Christ? (I am out of my mind to talk like this.) I am more. I have worked much harder, been in prison more frequently, been flogged more severely, and been exposed to death again and again. Five times I received from the

Jews the forty lashes minus one. Three times I was beaten with rods, once I was pelted with stones, three times I was shipwrecked, and I spent a night and a day in the open sea. I have been constantly on the move. I have been in danger from rivers, bandits, my fellow Jews, and Gentiles; in danger in the city, in the country, at sea, and from false believers. I have labored and toiled and have often gone without sleep; I have known hunger and thirst and have often gone without food; I have been cold and naked Besides everything else, I face daily the pressure of my concern for all the churches. Who is weak, and I do not feel weak? Who is led into sin, and I do not inwardly burn? If I must boast, I will boast of the things that show my weakness. The God and Father of the Lord Jesus, who is to be praised forever, knows that I am not lying. In Damascus, the governor under King Aretas had the city of the Damascenes guarded in order to arrest me. But I was lowered in a basket from a window in the wall and slipped through his hands

Chapter 12

I must go on boasting, although there is nothing to be gained. I will go on to visions and revelations from the Lord. I know a man in Christ who fourteen years ago was caught up to the third heaven—whether it was in the body or out of the body, I do not know; God knows. And I know that this man—whether in the body or apart from the body I do not know, but God knows—was caught up to paradise and heard inexpressible things, things that no one is permitted to tell. I will boast about a man like that, but I will not boast about myself, except about my weaknesses Even if I should choose to boast, I would not be a fool because I would be speaking the truth. But I refrain, so no one will think more of me than is warranted by what I do or say or because of these surpassingly great revelations. Therefore, in order to keep me from becoming conceited, I was given a thorn in my flesh, a messenger of Satan, to torment me. Three times I pleaded with the Lord to take it away from me. But he said to me, "My grace is sufficient for you, for my power is made perfect in weakness." Therefore, I will boast all the more gladly about my weaknesses so that Christ's power may rest on me. That is why, for Christ's sake, I delight in weaknesses, insults, hardships, persecutions, and difficulties. For when I am weak, then I am strong I have made a fool of myself, but you drove me to it. I ought to have been commended by you, for I am not in the least inferior to the "super-apostles," even though I am nothing. I persevered in demonstrating among you the marks of a true apostle, including signs, wonders, and miracles. How were you inferior to the other churches, except that I was never a burden to you? Forgive me this wrong! Now I am ready to visit you for the third time, and I will not be a burden to you because what I want is not your possessions but you. After all, children should not have to save up for their parents, but parents for their children. So I will very gladly spend for you everything I have and expend myself as well. If I love you more, will you love me less? Be that as it may, I have not been a burden to you. Yet, crafty fellow that I am, I caught you by trickery! Did I exploit you through any of the men I sent to you? I urged Titus to go to you, and I sent our brother with him. Titus did not exploit you, did he? Did we not walk in the same footsteps by the same Spirit? Have you been thinking all along that we have been defending ourselves to you? We have been speaking in the sight of God as those in Christ, and everything we do, dear friends, is for your strengthening. For I am afraid that when I come, I may not find you as I want you to be, and you may not find me as you want me to be. I fear that there may be discord, jealousy, fits of rage, selfish ambition, slander, gossip, arrogance, and disorder. I am afraid that when I come again, my God will humble me before you, and I will be grieved over many who have sinned earlier and have not repented of the impurity, sexual sin, and debauchery in which they have indulged

Chapter 13

This will be my third visit to you. "Every matter must be established by the testimony of two or three witnesses." I already gave you a warning when I was with you the second time. I now repeat it while absent: On my return, I will not spare those who sinned earlier or any of the others since you are demanding proof that Christ is speaking through me. He is not weak in dealing with you but is powerful among you. For to be sure, he was crucified in weakness, yet he lives by God's power. Likewise, we are weak in him, yet by God's power, we will live with him in our dealing with you Examine yourselves to see whether you are in the faith; test yourselves. Do you not realize that Christ Jesus is in you—unless, of course, you fail the test? And I trust that you will discover that we have not failed the test. Now we pray to God that you will not do anything wrong—not so that people will see that we have stood the test but so that you will do what is right even though we may seem to have failed. For we cannot do anything against the truth but only for the truth. We are glad whenever we are weak but you are strong, and our prayer is that you may be fully restored. This is why I write these things when I am absent, that when I come I may not have to be harsh in my use of authority—the authority the Lord gave me for building you up, not for tearing you down Finally, brothers and sisters, rejoice! Strive for full restoration, encourage one another, be of one mind, live in peace. And the God of love and peace will be with you. Greet one another with a holy kiss. All God's people here send their greetings May the grace of the Lord Jesus Christ, and the love of God, and the fellowship of the Holy Spirit be with you all. Amen

48. Galatians

Chapter 1

Paul is an apostle, not sent from men nor through man, but through Jesus Christ and God the Father who raised him from the dead. To all the brethren who are with me in the churches of Galatia: grace to you and peace from God the Father and our Lord Jesus Christ, who gave Himself for our sins to deliver us from this present evil age, according to the will of our God and Father. To Him be the glory forever and ever. Amen I am astonished that you are so quickly deserting Him who called you by the grace of Christ and are turning to a different gospel, which is really no gospel at all. Evidently, some people are throwing you into confusion and trying to pervert the gospel of Christ. But even if we or an angel from heaven should preach a gospel other than the one we preached to you, let them be under God's curse! As we have already said, so now I say again: if anybody is preaching to you a gospel other than what you accepted, let them be under God's curse! Am I now trying to win the approval of human beings or of God? Or am I trying to please people? If I were still trying to please people, I would not be a servant of Christ I want you to know, brothers and sisters, that the gospel I preached is not of human origin. I did not receive it from any man, nor was I taught it; rather, I received it by revelation from Jesus Christ. For you have heard of my previous way of life in Judaism, how intensely I persecuted the church of God and tried to destroy it. I was advancing in Judaism beyond many

of my own age among my people and was extremely zealous for the traditions of my fathers. But when God, who set me apart from my mother's womb and called me by His grace, was pleased to reveal His Son in me so that I might preach Him among the Gentiles, my immediate response was not to consult any human being. I did not go up to Jerusalem to see those who were apostles before I was, but I went into Arabia. Later I returned to Damascus Then after three years, I went up to Jerusalem to get acquainted with Cephas and stayed with him fifteen days. I saw none of the other apostles—only James, the Lord's brother. I assure you before God that what I am writing to you is no lie. Then I went to Syria and Cilicia. I was personally unknown to the churches of Judea that are in Christ. They only heard the report: "The man who formerly persecuted us is now preaching the faith he once tried to destroy." And they praised God because of me

Chapter 2

Fourteen years later, I went up again to Jerusalem, this time with Barnabas. I took Titus along also. I went in response to a revelation and, meeting privately with those esteemed as leaders, I presented to them the gospel that I preach among the Gentiles. I wanted to be sure I was not running and had not been running my race in vain. Yet not even Titus, who was with me, was compelled to be circumcised, even though he was a Greek. This matter arose because some false believers had infiltrated our ranks to spy on the freedom we have in Christ Jesus and to make us slaves. We did not give in to them for a moment, so that the truth of the gospel might be preserved for you As for those who were held in high esteem—whatever they were makes no difference to me; God does not show favoritism—they added nothing to my message. On the contrary, they recognized that I had been entrusted with the task of preaching the gospel to the uncircumcised, just as Peter had been to the circumcised. For God, who was at work in Peter as an apostle to the circumcised, was also at work in me as an apostle to the Gentiles. James, Cephas, and John, those esteemed as pillars, gave me and Barnabas the right hand of fellowship when they recognized the grace given to me. They agreed that we should go to the Gentiles, and they to the circumcised. All they asked was that we should continue to remember the poor, the very thing I had been eager to do all along When Cephas came to Antioch, I opposed him to his face because he stood condemned. For before certain men came from James, he used to eat with the Gentiles. But when they arrived, he began to draw back and separate himself from the Gentiles because he was afraid of those who belonged to the circumcision group. The other Jews joined him in his hypocrisy, so that by their hypocrisy even Barnabas was led astray When I saw that they were not acting in line with the truth of the gospel, I said to Cephas in front of them all, "You are a Jew, yet you live like a Gentile and not like a Jew. How is it, then, that you force Gentiles to follow Jewish customs? We who are Jews by birth and not sinful Gentiles know that a person is not justified by the works of the law, but by faith in Jesus Christ. So we, too, have put our faith in Christ Jesus that we may be justified by faith in Christ and not by the works of the law, because by the works of the law no one will be justified But if, in seeking to be justified in Christ, we Jews find ourselves also among the sinners, doesn't that mean that Christ promotes sin? Absolutely not! If I rebuild what I destroyed, then I really would be a lawbreaker. For through the law I died to the law so that I might live for God. I have been crucified with Christ and I no longer live, but Christ lives in me. The life I now live in the body, I live by faith in the Son of God, who loved me and gave himself for me. I do not set aside the grace of God, for if righteousness could be gained through the law, Christ died for nothing!"

Chapter 3

You foolish Galatians! Who has bewitched you? Before your very eyes Jesus Christ was clearly portrayed as crucified. I would like to learn just one thing from you: Did you receive the Spirit by the works of the law, or by believing what you heard? Are you so foolish? After beginning by means of the Spirit, are you now trying to finish by means of the flesh? Have you experienced so much in vain—if it really was in vain? So again I ask, does God give you his Spirit and work miracles among you by the works of the law, or by your believing what you heard? So also Abraham "believed God, and it was credited to him as righteousness." Understand, then, that those who have faith are children of Abraham. Scripture foresaw that God would justify the Gentiles by faith, and announced the gospel in advance to Abraham: "All nations will be blessed through you." So those who rely on faith are blessed along with Abraham, the man of faith For all who rely on the works of the law are under a curse, as it is written: "Cursed is everyone who does not continue to do everything written in the Book of the Law." Clearly, no one who relies on the law is justified before God, because "the righteous will live by faith." The law is not based on faith; on the contrary, it says, "The person who does these things will live by them." Christ redeemed us from the curse of the law by becoming a curse for us, for it is written: "Cursed is everyone who is hung on a pole." He redeemed us in order that the blessing given to Abraham might come to the Gentiles through Christ Jesus, so that by faith we might receive the promise of the Spirit Brothers and sisters, let me take an example from everyday life. Just as no one can set aside or add to a human covenant that has been duly established, so it is in this case. The promises were spoken to Abraham and to his seed. Scripture does not say "and to seeds," meaning many people, but "and to your seed," meaning one person, who is Christ. What I mean is this: The law, introduced 430 years later, does not set aside the covenant previously established by God and thus do away with the promise. For if the inheritance depends on the law, then it no longer depends on the promise; but God in his grace gave it to Abraham through a promise Why, then, was the law given at all? It was added because of transgressions until the Seed to whom the promise referred had come. The law was given through angels and entrusted to a mediator. A mediator, however, implies more than one party; but God is one Is the law, therefore, opposed to the promises of God? Absolutely not! For if a law had been given that could impart life, then righteousness would certainly have come by the law. But Scripture has locked up everything under the control of sin, so that what was promised, being given through faith in Jesus Christ, might be given to those who believe Before the coming of this faith, we were held in custody under the law, locked up until the faith that was to come would be revealed. So the law was our guardian until Christ came that we might be justified by faith. Now that this faith has come, we are no longer under a guardian So in Christ Jesus you are all children of God through faith, for all of you who were baptized into Christ have clothed yourselves with Christ. There is neither Jew nor Gentile, neither slave nor free, nor is there male and female, for you are all one in Christ Jesus. If you belong to Christ, then you are Abraham's seed, and heirs according to the promise

Chapter 4

What I am saying is that as long as an heir is underage, he is no different from a slave, although he owns the whole estate. The heir is subject to guardians and trustees until the time set by his father. So also, when we were underage, we were in slavery under the elemental spiritual forces of the world. But when the set time had fully come, God sent his Son, born of a woman, born under the law, to redeem those under the law, that we might receive adoption to sonship. Because you are his sons, God sent the Spirit of his Son into our hearts, the Spirit who calls out, "Abba, Father." So you are no longer a slave, but God's child; and since you are his child, God has made you also an heir Formerly, when you did not know God, you were slaves to those who by nature are not gods. But now that you know God—or rather are known by God—how is it that you are turning back to those weak and miserable forces? Do you wish to be enslaved by them all over again? You are observing special days and months and seasons and years! I fear for you, that somehow I have wasted my efforts on you I plead with you, brothers and sisters, become like me, for I became like you. You did me no wrong. As you know, it was because of an illness that I first preached the gospel to you, and even though my illness was a trial to you, you did not treat me with contempt or scorn. Instead, you welcomed me as if I were an angel of God, as if I were Christ Jesus himself. Where, then, is your blessing of me now? I can testify that, if you could have done so, you would have torn out your eyes and given them to me. Have I now become your enemy by telling you the truth? Those people are zealous to win you over, but for no good. What they want is to alienate you from us so that you may have zeal for them. It is fine to be zealous, provided the purpose is good, and to be so always, not just when I am with you. My dear children, for whom I am again in the pains of childbirth until Christ is formed in you, how I wish I could be with you now and change my tone, because I am perplexed about you! Tell me, you who want to be under the law, are you not aware of what the law says? For it is written that Abraham had two sons, one by the slave woman and the other by the free woman. His son by the slave woman was born according to the flesh, but his son by the free woman was born as the result of a divine promise These things are being taken figuratively: The women represent two covenants. One covenant is from Mount Sinai and bears children who are to be slaves: This is Hagar. Now Hagar stands for Mount Sinai in Arabia and corresponds to the present city of Jerusalem, because she is in slavery with her children. But the Jerusalem that is above is free, and she is our mother. For it is written: "Be glad, barren woman, you who never bore a child; shout for joy and cry aloud, you who were never in labor; because more are the children of the desolate woman than of her who has a husband." Now you, brothers and sisters, like Isaac, are children of promise. At that time the son born according to the flesh persecuted the son born by the power of the Spirit. It is the same now. But what does Scripture say? "Get rid of the slave woman and her son, for the slave woman's son will never share in the inheritance with the free woman's son." Therefore, brothers and sisters, we are not children of the slave woman, but of the free woman

Chapter 5

It is for freedom that Christ has set us free. Stand firm, then, and do not let yourselves be burdened again by a yoke of slavery Mark my words! I, Paul, tell you that if you let yourselves be circumcised, Christ will be of no value to you at all. Again I declare to every man who lets himself be circumcised that he is obligated to obey the whole law. You who are trying to be justified by the law have been alienated from Christ; you have fallen away from grace. For through the Spirit we eagerly await by faith the righteousness for which we hope. For in Christ Jesus neither circumcision nor uncircumcision has any value. The only thing that counts is faith expressing itself through love You were running a good race. Who cut in on you to keep you from obeying the truth? That kind of persuasion does not come from the one who calls you. "A little yeast works through the whole batch of dough." I am confident in the Lord that you will take no other view. The one who is throwing you into confusion, whoever that may be, will have to pay the penalty. Brothers and sisters, if I am still preaching circumcision, why am I still being persecuted? In that case, the offense of the cross has been abolished. As for those agitators, I wish they would go the whole way and emasculate themselves! You, my brothers and sisters, were called to be free. But do not use your freedom to indulge the flesh; rather, serve one another humbly in love. For the entire law is fulfilled in keeping this one command: "Love your neighbor as yourself." If you bite and devour each other, watch out or you will be destroyed by each other So I say, walk by the Spirit, and you will not gratify the desires of the flesh. For the flesh desires what is contrary to the Spirit, and the Spirit what is contrary to the flesh. They are in conflict with each other, so that you are not to do whatever you want. But if you are led by the Spirit, you are not under the law. The acts of the flesh are obvious: sexual immorality, impurity, and debauchery; idolatry and witchcraft; hatred, discord, jealousy, fits of rage, selfish ambition, dissensions, factions and envy; drunkenness, orgies, and the like. I warn you, as I did before, that those who live like this will not inherit the kingdom of God But the fruit of the Spirit is love, joy, peace, forbearance, kindness, goodness, faithfulness, gentleness, and self-control. Against such things, there is no law. Those who belong to Christ Jesus have crucified the flesh with its passions and desires. Since we live by the Spirit, let us keep in step with the Spirit. Let us not become conceited, provoking and envying each other

Chapter 6

Brothers and sisters, if someone is caught in a sin, you who live by the Spirit should restore that person gently. But watch yourselves, or you also may be tempted. Carry each other's burdens, and in this way, you will fulfill the law of Christ. If anyone thinks they are something when they are not, they deceive themselves. Each one should test their own actions. Then they can take pride in themselves alone, without comparing themselves to someone else, for each one should carry their own load. Nevertheless, the one who receives instruction in the word should share all good things with their instructor Do not be deceived: God cannot be mocked. A man reaps what he sows. Whoever sows to please their flesh, from the flesh will reap destruction; whoever sows to please the Spirit, from the Spirit will reap eternal life. Let us not become weary in doing good, for at the proper time we will reap a harvest if we do not give up. Therefore, as we have the opportunity, let us do good to all people, especially to those who belong to the family of believers See what large letters I use as I write to you with my own hand! Those who want to impress people by means of the flesh are trying to compel you to be circumcised. The only reason they do this is to avoid being persecuted for the cross of Christ. Not even those who are circumcised keep the law, yet they want you to be circumcised that they may boast about your circumcision in the flesh. May I never boast except in the cross of our Lord Jesus Christ, through which the world has been crucified to me, and I to the world. Neither circumcision nor uncircumcision means anything; what counts is the new creation. Peace and mercy to all who follow this rule—to the Israel of God From now on, let no one cause me trouble, for I bear on my body the marks of Jesus. The grace of our Lord Jesus Christ be with your spirit, brothers and sisters. Amen

49. Ephesians

Chapter 1

Paul, an apostle of Jesus Christ by the will of God, to the saints who are at Ephesus and to those who are faithful in Christ Jesus: Grace to you and peace from God our Father and the Lord Jesus Christ. Blessed be the God and Father of our Lord Jesus Christ, who has blessed us with every spiritual blessing in the heavenly places in Christ, just as He chose us in Him before the foundation of the world, that we should be holy and blameless before Him in love. He predestined us to adoption as sons through Jesus Christ to Himself, according to the kind intention of His will, to the praise of the glory of His grace, which He freely bestowed on us in the Beloved. In Him we have redemption through His blood, the forgiveness of our trespasses, according to the riches of His grace, which He lavished on us. In all wisdom and insight, He made known to us the mystery of His will, according to His kind intention which He purposed in Him with a view to an administration suitable to the fullness of the times, that is, the summing up of all things in Christ, things in the heavens and things on the earth. In Him also we have obtained an inheritance, having been predestined according to His purpose who works all things after the counsel of His will, to the end that we who were the first to hope in Christ would be to the praise of His glory. In Him, you also, after listening to the message of truth, the gospel of your salvation—having also believed, you were sealed in Him with the Holy Spirit of promise, who is given as a pledge of our inheritance, with a view to the redemption of God's own possession, to the praise of His glory For this reason I too, having heard of the faith in the Lord Jesus which exists among you and your love for all the saints, do not cease giving thanks for you, while making mention of you in my prayers; that the God of our Lord Jesus Christ, the Father of glory, may give you a spirit of wisdom and revelation in the knowledge of Him. I pray that the eyes of your heart may be enlightened, so that you will know what is the hope of His calling, what are the riches of the glory of His inheritance in the saints, and what is the surpassing greatness of His power toward us who believe. These are in accordance with the working of the strength of His might which He brought about in Christ, when He raised Him from the dead and seated Him at His right hand in the heavenly places, far above all rule and authority and power and dominion, and every name that is named, not only in this age but also in the one to come. And He put all things in subjection under His feet, and gave Him as head over all things to the church, which is His body, the fullness of Him who fills all in all

Chapter 2

And you were dead in your trespasses and sins, in which you formerly walked according to the course of this world, according to the prince of the power of the air, the spirit that is now working in the sons of disobedience. Among them we too all formerly lived in the lusts of our flesh, indulging the desires of the flesh and of the mind, and were by nature children of wrath, even as the rest. But God, being rich in mercy, because of His great love with which He loved us, even when we were dead in our transgressions, made us alive together with Christ (by grace you have been saved), and raised us up with Him, and seated us with Him in the heavenly places in Christ Jesus, so that in the ages to come He might show the surpassing riches of His grace in kindness toward us in Christ Jesus. For by grace you have been saved through faith; and that not of yourselves, it is the gift of God; not as a result of works, so that no one may boast. For we are His workmanship, created in Christ Jesus for good works, which God prepared beforehand so that we would walk in them Therefore remember that formerly you, the Gentiles in the flesh, who are called "Uncircumcision" by the so-called "Circumcision," which is performed in the flesh by human hands—remember that you were at that time separate from Christ, excluded from the commonwealth of Israel, and strangers to the covenants of promise, having no hope and without God in the world. But now in Christ Jesus you who formerly were far off have been brought near by the blood of Christ. For He Himself is our peace, who made both groups into one and broke down the barrier of the dividing wall, by abolishing in His flesh the enmity, which is the Law of commandments contained in ordinances, so that in Himself He might make the two into one new man, thus establishing peace, and might reconcile them both in one body to God through the cross, by it having put to death the enmity. And He came and preached peace to you who were far away, and peace to those who were near; for through Him we both have our access in one Spirit to the Father. So then you are no longer strangers and aliens, but you are fellow citizens with the saints, and are of God's household, having been built on the foundation of the apostles and prophets, Christ Jesus Himself being the cornerstone, in whom the whole building, being fitted together, is growing into a holy temple in the Lord, in whom you also are being built together into a dwelling of God in the Spirit

Chapter 3

For this reason I, Paul, the prisoner of Christ Jesus for the sake of you Gentiles—if indeed you have heard of the stewardship of God's grace which was given to me for you; that by revelation there was made known to me the mystery, as I wrote before in brief. By referring to this, when you read you can understand my insight into the mystery of Christ, which in other generations was not made known to the sons of men, as it has now been revealed to His holy apostles and prophets in the Spirit; to be specific, that the Gentiles are fellow heirs and fellow members of the body, and fellow partakers of the promise in Christ Jesus through the gospel, of which I was made a minister, according to the gift of God's grace which was given to me according to the working of His power. To me, the very least of all saints, this grace was given, to preach to the Gentiles the unfathomable riches of Christ, and to bring to light what is the administration of the mystery which for ages has been hidden in God who created all things; so that the manifold wisdom of God might now be made known through the church to the rulers and the authorities in the heavenly places. This was in accordance with the eternal purpose which He carried out in Christ Jesus our Lord, in whom we have boldness and confident access through faith in Him. Therefore I ask you not to lose heart at my tribulations on your behalf, for they are your glory For this reason I bow my knees before the Father, from whom every family in heaven and on earth derives its name, that He would grant you, according to the riches of His glory, to be strengthened with power

through His Spirit in the inner man, so that Christ may dwell in your hearts through faith; and that you, being rooted and grounded in love, may be able to comprehend with all the saints what is the breadth and length and height and depth, and to know the love of Christ which surpasses knowledge, that you may be filled up to all the fullness of God. Now to Him who is able to do far more abundantly beyond all that we ask or think, according to the power that works within us, to Him be the glory in the church and in Christ Jesus to all generations forever and ever. Amen

Chapter 4

Therefore I, the prisoner of the Lord, implore you to walk in a manner worthy of the calling with which you have been called, with all humility and gentleness, with patience, showing tolerance for one another in love, being diligent to preserve the unity of the Spirit in the bond of peace. There is one body and one Spirit, just as also you were called in one hope of your calling; one Lord, one faith, one baptism, one God and Father of all who is over all and through all and in all. But to each one of us grace was given according to the measure of Christ's gift. Therefore it says, "When He ascended on high, He led captive a host of captives, and He gave gifts to men." (Now this expression, "He ascended," what does it mean except that He also had descended into the lower parts of the earth? He who descended is Himself also He who ascended far above all the heavens, so that He might fill all things.) And He gave some as apostles, and some as prophets, and some as evangelists, and some as pastors and teachers, for the equipping of the saints for the work of service, to the building up of the body of Christ; until we all attain to the unity of the faith, and of the knowledge of the Son of God, to a mature man, to the measure of the stature which belongs to the fullness of Christ. As a result, we are no longer to be children, tossed here and there by waves and carried about by every wind of doctrine, by the trickery of men, by craftiness in deceitful scheming; but speaking the truth in love, we are to grow up in all aspects into Him who is the head, even Christ, from whom the whole body, being fitted and held together by what every joint supplies, according to the proper working of each individual part, causes the growth of the body for the building up of itself in love So this I say, and affirm together with the Lord, that you walk no longer just as the Gentiles also walk, in the futility of their mind, being darkened in their understanding, excluded from the life of God because of the ignorance that is in them, because of the hardness of their heart; and they, having become callous, have given themselves over to sensuality for the practice of every kind of impurity with greediness. But you did not learn Christ in this way, if indeed you have heard Him and have been taught in Him, just as truth is in Jesus, that, in reference to your former manner of life, you lay aside the old self, which is being corrupted in accordance with the lusts of deceit, and that you be renewed in the spirit of your mind, and put on the new self, which in the likeness of God has been created in righteousness and holiness of the truth. Therefore, laying aside falsehood, speak truth each one of you with his neighbor, for we are members of one another. Be angry, and yet do not sin; do not let the sun go down on your anger, and do not give the devil an opportunity. He who steals must steal no longer; but rather he must labor, performing with his own hands what is good, so that he will have something to share with one who has need. Let no unwholesome word proceed from your mouth, but only such a word as is good for edification according to the need of the moment, so that it will give grace to those who hear. Do not grieve the Holy Spirit of God, by whom you were sealed for the day of redemption. Let all bitterness and wrath and anger and clamor and slander be put away from you, along with all malice. Be kind to one another, tender-hearted, forgiving each other, just as God in Christ also has forgiven you

Chapter 5

Therefore be imitators of God, as beloved children; and walk in love, just as Christ also loved you and gave Himself up for us, an offering and a sacrifice to God as a fragrant aroma. But immorality or any impurity or greed must not even be named among you, as is proper among saints; and there must be no filthiness and silly talk, or coarse jesting, which are not fitting, but rather giving of thanks. For this you know with certainty, that no immoral or impure person or covetous man, who is an idolater, has an inheritance in the kingdom of Christ and God. Let no one deceive you with empty words, for because of these things the wrath of God comes upon the sons of disobedience. Therefore do not be partakers with them; for you were formerly darkness, but now you are Light in the Lord; walk as children of Light (for the fruit of the Light consists in all goodness and righteousness and truth), trying to learn what is pleasing to the Lord. Do not participate in the unfruitful deeds of darkness, but instead even expose them; for it is disgraceful even to speak of the things which are done by them in secret. But all things become visible when they are exposed by the light, for everything that becomes visible is light. For this reason it says, "Awake, sleeper, and arise from the dead, and Christ will shine on you." Therefore be careful how you walk, not as unwise men but as wise, making the most of your time, because the days are evil. So then do not be foolish, but understand what the will of the Lord is. And do not get drunk with wine, for that is dissipation, but be filled with the Spirit, speaking to one another in psalms and hymns and spiritual songs, singing and making melody with your heart to the Lord; always giving thanks for all things in the name of our Lord Jesus Christ to God, even the Father; and be subject to one another in the fear of Christ Wives, be subject to your own husbands, as to the Lord. For the husband is the head of the wife, as Christ also is the head of the church, He Himself being the Savior of the body. But as the church is subject to Christ, so also the wives ought to be to their husbands in everything. Husbands, love your wives, just as Christ also loved the church and gave Himself up for her, so that He might sanctify her, having cleansed her by the washing of water with the word, that He might present to Himself the church in all her glory, having no spot or wrinkle or any such thing; but that she would be holy and blameless. So husbands ought also to love their own wives as their own bodies. He who loves his own wife loves himself; for no one ever hated his own flesh, but nourishes and cherishes it, just as Christ also does the church, because we are members of His body. For this reason a man shall leave his father and mother and shall be joined to his wife, and the two shall become one flesh. This mystery is great; but I am speaking with reference to Christ and the church. Nevertheless, each individual among you also is to love his own wife even as himself, and the wife must see to it that she respects her husband

Chapter 6

Children, obey your parents in the Lord, for this is right. Honor your father and mother (which is the first commandment with a promise), so that it may be well with you, and that you may live long on the earth. Fathers, do not provoke your children to anger, but bring them up in the discipline and instruction of the

Lord Slaves, be obedient to those who are your masters according to the flesh, with fear and trembling, in the sincerity of your heart, as to Christ; not by way of eyeservice, as men-pleasers, but as slaves of Christ, doing the will of God from the heart. With good will render service, as to the Lord, and not to men, knowing that whatever good thing each one does, this he will receive back from the Lord, whether slave or free. And masters, do the same things to them, and give up threatening, knowing that both their Master and yours is in heaven, and there is no partiality with Him Finally, be strong in the Lord and in the strength of His might. Put on the full armor of God, so that you will be able to stand firm against the schemes of the devil. For our struggle is not against flesh and blood, but against the rulers, against the powers, against the world forces of this darkness, against the spiritual forces of wickedness in the heavenly places. Therefore, take up the full armor of God, so that you will be able to resist in the evil day, and having done everything, to stand firm. Stand firm therefore, having girded your loins with truth, and having put on the breastplate of righteousness, and having shod your feet with the preparation of the gospel of peace; in addition to all, taking up the shield of faith with which you will be able to extinguish all the flaming arrows of the evil one. And take the helmet of salvation, and the sword of the Spirit, which is the word of God With all prayer and petition pray at all times in the Spirit, and with this in view, be on the alert with all perseverance and petition for all the saints, and pray on my behalf, that utterance may be given to me in the opening of my mouth, to make known with boldness the mystery of the gospel, for which I am an ambassador in chains; that in proclaiming it I may speak boldly, as I ought to speak But that you also may know about my circumstances, how I am doing, Tychicus, the beloved brother and faithful minister in the Lord, will make everything known to you. I have sent him to you for this very purpose, so that you may know about us, and that he may comfort your hearts. Peace be to the brethren, and love with faith, from God the Father and the Lord Jesus Christ. Grace be with all those who love our Lord Jesus Christ with incorruptible love. Amen

50. Philippians

Chapter 1

Paul and Timothy, servants of Jesus Christ, greet all the saints in Christ Jesus who are in Philippi, along with the bishops and deacons. Grace and peace to you from God our Father and the Lord Jesus Christ. I thank my God for you, always keeping you in my prayers with joy. Your fellowship in the gospel from the first day until now fills me with gratitude. I am confident that He who began a good work in you will carry it on to completion until the day of Jesus Christ. It is right for me to feel this way about you all, for you share in God's grace with me, both in my imprisonment and in the defense and confirmation of the gospel. God knows how much I long for you all with the affection of Christ Jesus And this is my prayer: that your love may abound more and more in knowledge and depth of insight, so that you may be able to discern what is best and may be pure and blameless until the day of Christ, filled with the fruit of righteousness that comes through Jesus Christ, to the glory and praise of God I want you to know, brothers and sisters, that what has happened to me has actually served to advance the gospel. As a result, it has become clear throughout the whole palace guard and to everyone else that I am in chains for Christ. Because of my chains, most of the brothers and sisters have become confident in the Lord and dare all the more to proclaim the gospel without fear. Some preach Christ out of envy and rivalry, but others out of goodwill. The latter do so out of love, knowing that I am put here for the defense of the gospel. The former preach Christ out of selfish ambition, not sincerely, supposing that they can stir up trouble for me while I am in chains. But what does it matter? The important thing is that in every way, whether from false motives or true, Christ is preached. And because of this, I rejoice Yes, and I will continue to rejoice, for I know that through your prayers and God's provision of the Spirit of Jesus Christ, what has happened to me will turn out for my deliverance. I eagerly expect and hope that I will in no way be ashamed, but will have sufficient courage so that now as always Christ will be exalted in my body, whether by life or by death. For to me, to live is Christ and to die is gain. If I am to go on living in the body, this will mean fruitful labor for me. Yet what shall I choose? I do not know! I am torn between the two: I desire to depart and be with Christ, which is better by far; but it is more necessary for you that I remain in the body. Convinced of this, I know that I will remain, and I will continue with all of you for your progress and joy in the faith, so that through my being with you again your boasting in Christ Jesus will abound on account of me Whatever happens, conduct yourselves in a manner worthy of the gospel of Christ. Then, whether I come and see you or only hear about you in my absence, I will know that you stand firm in the one Spirit, striving together with one accord for the faith of the gospel without being frightened in any way by those who oppose you. This is a sign to them that they will be destroyed, but that you will be saved—and that by God. For it has been granted to you on behalf of Christ not only to believe in him but also to suffer for him, since you are going through the same struggle you saw I had, and now hear that I still have

Chapter 2

If you have any encouragement from being united with Christ, if any comfort from his love, if any common sharing in the Spirit, if any tenderness and compassion, then make my joy complete by being like-minded, having the same love, being one in spirit and of one mind. Do nothing out of selfish ambition or vain conceit. Rather, in humility value others above yourselves, not looking to your own interests but each of you to the interests of the others. In your relationships with one another, have the same mindset as Christ Jesus: Who, being in very nature God, did not consider equality with God something to be used to his own advantage; rather, he made himself nothing by taking the very nature of a servant, being made in human likeness. And being found in appearance as a man, he humbled himself by becoming obedient to death— even death on a cross! Therefore God exalted him to the highest place and gave him the name that is above every name, that at the name of Jesus every knee should bow, in heaven and on earth and under the earth, and every tongue acknowledge that Jesus Christ is Lord, to the glory of God the Father Therefore, my dear friends, as you have always obeyed—not only in my presence, but now much more in my absence— continue to work out your salvation with fear and trembling, for it is God who works in you to will and to act in order to fulfill his good purpose. Do everything without grumbling or arguing, so that you may become blameless and pure, "children of God without fault in a warped and crooked generation." Then you will shine among them like stars in the sky as you hold firmly to the word of life. And then I will be able to boast on the day of Christ that I did not run

or labor in vain. But even if I am being poured out like a drink offering on the sacrifice and service coming from your faith, I am glad and rejoice with all of you. So you too should be glad and rejoice with me I hope in the Lord Jesus to send Timothy to you soon, that I also may be cheered when I receive news about you. I have no one else like him, who will show genuine concern for your welfare. For everyone looks out for their own interests, not those of Jesus Christ. But you know that Timothy has proved himself, because as a son with his father he has served with me in the work of the gospel. I hope, therefore, to send him as soon as I see how things go with me. And I am confident in the Lord that I myself will come soon But I think it is necessary to send back to you Epaphroditus, my brother, coworker and fellow soldier, who is also your messenger, whom you sent to take care of my needs. For he longs for all of you and is distressed because you heard he was ill. Indeed he was ill, and almost died. But God had mercy on him, and not on him only but also on me, to spare me sorrow upon sorrow. Therefore I am all the more eager to send him, so that when you see him again you may be glad and I may have less anxiety. So then, welcome him in the Lord with great joy, and honor people like him, because he almost died for the work of Christ. He risked his life to make up for the help you yourselves could not give me

Chapter 3

Further, my brothers and sisters, rejoice in the Lord! It is no trouble for me to write the same things to you again, and it is a safeguard for you. Watch out for those dogs, those evildoers, those mutilators of the flesh. For it is we who are the circumcision, we who serve God by his Spirit, who boast in Christ Jesus, and who put no confidence in the flesh—though I myself have reasons for such confidence If someone else thinks they have reasons to put confidence in the flesh, I have more: circumcised on the eighth day, of the people of Israel, of the tribe of Benjamin, a Hebrew of Hebrews; in regard to the law, a Pharisee; as for zeal, persecuting the church; as for righteousness based on the law, faultless. But whatever were gains to me I now consider loss for the sake of Christ. What is more, I consider everything a loss because of the surpassing worth of knowing Christ Jesus my Lord, for whose sake I have lost all things. I consider them garbage, that I may gain Christ and be found in him, not having a righteousness of my own that comes from the law, but that which is through faith in Christ—the righteousness that comes from God on the basis of faith. I want to know Christ—yes, to know the power of his resurrection and participation in his sufferings, becoming like him in his death, and so, somehow, attaining to the resurrection from the dead Not that I have already obtained all this, or have already arrived at my goal, but I press on to take hold of that for which Christ Jesus took hold of me. Brothers and sisters, I do not consider myself yet to have taken hold of it. But one thing I do: Forgetting what is behind and straining toward what is ahead, I press on toward the goal to win the prize for which God has called me heavenward in Christ Jesus. All of us, then, who are mature should take such a view of things. And if on some point you think differently, that too God will make clear to you. Only let us live up to what we have already attained Join together in following my example, brothers and sisters, and just as you have us as a model, keep your eyes on those who live as we do. For, as I have often told you before and now tell you again even with tears, many live as enemies of the cross of Christ. Their destiny is destruction, their god is their stomach, and their glory is in their shame. Their mind is set on earthly things. But our citizenship is in heaven. And we eagerly await a Savior from there, the Lord Jesus Christ, who, by the power that enables him to bring everything under his control, will transform our lowly bodies so that they will be like his glorious body

Chapter 4

Therefore, my brothers and sisters, you whom I love and long for, my joy and crown, stand firm in the Lord in this way, dear friends! I plead with Euodia and I plead with Syntyche to be of the same mind in the Lord. Yes, and I ask you, my true companion, help these women since they have contended at my side in the cause of the gospel, along with Clement and the rest of my coworkers, whose names are in the book of life Rejoice in the Lord always. I will say it again: Rejoice! Let your gentleness be evident to all. The Lord is near. Do not be anxious about anything, but in every situation, by prayer and petition, with thanksgiving, present your requests to God. And the peace of God, which transcends all understanding, will guard your hearts and your minds in Christ Jesus Finally, brothers and sisters, whatever is true, whatever is noble, whatever is right, whatever is pure, whatever is lovely, whatever is admirable—if anything is excellent or praiseworthy—think about such things. Whatever you have learned or received or heard from me, or seen in me—put it into practice. And the God of peace will be with you I rejoiced greatly in the Lord that at last you renewed your concern for me. Indeed, you were concerned, but you had no opportunity to show it. I am not saying this because I am in need, for I have learned to be content whatever the circumstances. I know what it is to be in need, and I know what it is to have plenty. I have learned the secret of being content in any and every situation, whether well fed or hungry, whether living in plenty or in want. I can do all this through him who gives me strength. Yet it was good of you to share in my troubles. Moreover, as you Philippians know, in the early days of your acquaintance with the gospel, when I set out from Macedonia, not one church shared with me in the matter of giving and receiving, except you only; for even when I was in Thessalonica, you sent me aid more than once when I was in need. Not that I desire your gifts; what I desire is that more be credited to your account. I have received full payment and have more than enough. I am amply supplied, now that I have received from Epaphroditus the gifts you sent. They are a fragrant offering, an acceptable sacrifice, pleasing to God. And my God will meet all your needs according to the riches of his glory in Christ Jesus To our God and Father be glory for ever and ever. Amen Greet all God's people in Christ Jesus. The brothers and sisters who are with me send greetings. All God's people here send you greetings, especially those who belong to Caesar's household The grace of the Lord Jesus Christ be with your spirit. Amen

51. Colossians

Chapter 1

Paul, an apostle of Jesus Christ by the will of God, and Timothy, our brother, greet the holy and faithful brethren in Christ who are at Colosse. Grace and peace to you from God our Father and the Lord Jesus Christ. We thank God, the Father of our Lord Jesus Christ, always praying for you since we have heard of your faith in Christ Jesus and your love for all the saints. This is because of the hope laid up for you in heaven, which you have already heard about through the word of truth, the gospel, which has come to you just as it has to all the world, producing fruit and growing. From the day you heard and understood the grace of God in truth, you learned from Epaphras, our dear fellow servant and faithful minister of Christ for you, who also declared your love in the Spirit to us For this reason, from the day we heard about you, we have not ceased to pray for you, asking that you may be filled with the knowledge of His will in all wisdom and spiritual understanding, so that you may walk worthy of the Lord, pleasing Him in all things, being fruitful in every good work, and increasing in the knowledge of God. You are strengthened with all might according to His glorious power, leading to patience and long-suffering with joy, giving thanks to the Father, who has qualified us to share in the inheritance of the saints in the light. He has delivered us from the power of darkness and transferred us into the kingdom of His beloved Son, in whom we have redemption through His blood, the forgiveness of sins Jesus is the image of the invisible God, the firstborn of all creation. For by Him all things were created in heaven and on earth, visible and invisible, whether thrones or dominions or principalities or powers. All things were created through Him and for Him. He is before all things, and in Him all things hold together. He is the head of the body, the Church; He is the beginning and the firstborn from the dead, so that in all things He might have the preeminence. It pleased the Father that in Him all fullness should dwell, and through Him, having made peace by the blood of His cross, to reconcile to Himself all things, whether on earth or in heaven You were once alienated and hostile in mind because of your evil deeds, but now He has reconciled you by Christ's physical body through death to present you holy, unblemished, and blameless in His sight, if you continue in your faith, established and firm, and do not move from the hope of the gospel you heard, which has been proclaimed to every creature under heaven, of which I, Paul, have become a servant. Now I rejoice in my sufferings for you, filling up in my flesh what is lacking in regard to Christ's afflictions for the sake of His body, which is the Church. I have become its servant by the commission God gave me to present to you the word of God in its fullness—the mystery that has been kept hidden for ages and generations but is now disclosed to the Lord's people. To them God has chosen to make known among the Gentiles the glorious riches of this mystery, which is Christ in you, the hope of glory. He is the one we proclaim, admonishing and teaching everyone with all wisdom, so that we may present everyone fully mature in Christ. To this end, I strenuously contend with all the energy Christ so powerfully works in me

Chapter 2

I want you to know how hard I am contending for you and for those at Laodicea and for all who have not met me personally. My goal is that they may be encouraged in heart and united in love, so that they may have the full riches of complete understanding, in order that they may know the mystery of God, namely, Christ, in whom are hidden all the treasures of wisdom and knowledge. I tell you this so that no one may deceive you by fine-sounding arguments. For though I am absent from you in body, I am present with you in spirit and delight to see how disciplined you are and how firm your faith in Christ is So then, just as you received Christ Jesus as Lord, continue to live your lives in Him, rooted and built up in Him, strengthened in the faith as you were taught, and overflowing with thankfulness. See to it that no one takes you captive through hollow and deceptive philosophy, which depends on human tradition and the elemental spiritual forces of this world rather than on Christ. For in Christ all the fullness of the Deity lives in bodily form, and in Christ you have been brought to fullness. He is the head over every power and authority. In Him you were also circumcised with a circumcision not performed by human hands. Your whole self ruled by the flesh was put off when you were circumcised by Christ, having been buried with Him in baptism, in which you were also raised with Him through your faith in the working of God, who raised Him from the dead When you were dead in your sins and in the uncircumcision of your flesh, God made you alive with Christ. He forgave us all our sins, having canceled the charge of our legal indebtedness, which stood against us and condemned us; He has taken it away, nailing it to the cross. And having disarmed the powers and authorities, He made a public spectacle of them, triumphing over them by the cross Therefore do not let anyone judge you by what you eat or drink, or with regard to a religious festival, a New Moon celebration or a Sabbath day. These are a shadow of the things that were to come; the reality, however, is found in Christ. Do not let anyone who delights in false humility and the worship of angels disqualify you. Such a person also goes into great detail about what they have seen; they are puffed up with idle notions by their unspiritual mind. They have lost connection with the head, from whom the whole body, supported and held together by its ligaments and sinews, grows as God causes it to grow Since you died with Christ to the elemental spiritual forces of this world, why, as though you still belonged to the world, do you submit to its rules: "Do not handle! Do not taste! Do not touch!"? These rules, which have to do with things that are all destined to perish with use, are based on merely human commands and teachings. Such regulations indeed have an appearance of wisdom, with their self-imposed worship, their false humility and their harsh treatment of the body, but they lack any value in restraining sensual indulgence

Chapter 3

Since then you have been raised with Christ, set your hearts on things above, where Christ is, seated at the right hand of God. Set your minds on things above, not on earthly things. For you died, and your life is now hidden with Christ in God. When Christ, who is your life, appears, then you also will appear with Him in glory Put to death, therefore, whatever belongs to your earthly nature: sexual immorality, impurity, lust, evil desires and greed, which is idolatry. Because of these, the wrath of God is coming. You used to walk in these ways, in the life you once lived. But now you must also rid yourselves of all such things as these: anger, rage, malice, slander, and filthy language from your lips. Do not lie to each other, since you have taken off your old self with its practices and have put on the new self, which is being renewed in knowledge in the image of its Creator. Here there is no Gentile or Jew, circumcised or uncircumcised, barbarian, Scythian, slave or free, but Christ is all, and is in all Therefore, as God's chosen people, holy and dearly loved, clothe yourselves with compassion, kindness, humility, gentleness and patience. Bear with each other and forgive one another if any of you has a grievance against someone. Forgive as the Lord forgave you. And over all these virtues put on love, which binds them all together in perfect unity. Let the peace of Christ rule in your hearts, since as members of one body you were called to peace. And be thankful. Let the message of Christ dwell among you richly as you teach and admonish one another with all wisdom through psalms, hymns, and songs from the Spirit, singing to God with gratitude in your hearts. And whatever you do, whether in word or deed, do it all in the name of the Lord Jesus, giving thanks to God the Father through Him Wives, submit yourselves to your husbands, as is fitting in the Lord.

Husbands, love your wives and do not be harsh with them. Children, obey your parents in everything, for this pleases the Lord. Fathers, do not embitter your children, or they will become discouraged. Slaves, obey your earthly masters in everything; and do it, not only when their eye is on you and to curry their favor, but with sincerity of heart and reverence for the Lord. Whatever you do, work at it with all your heart, as working for the Lord, not for human masters, since you know that you will receive an inheritance from the Lord as a reward. It is the Lord Christ you are serving. Anyone who does wrong will be repaid for their wrongs, and there is no favoritism

Chapter 4

Masters, provide your slaves with what is right and fair, because you know that you also have a Master in heaven Devote yourselves to prayer, being watchful and thankful. And pray for us, too, that God may open a door for our message, so that we may proclaim the mystery of Christ, for which I am in chains. Pray that I may proclaim it clearly, as I should. Be wise in the way you act toward outsiders; make the most of every opportunity. Let your conversation be always full of grace, seasoned with salt, so that you may know how to answer everyone Tychicus will tell you all the news about me. He is a dear brother, a faithful minister and fellow servant in the Lord. I am sending him to you for the express purpose that you may know about our circumstances and that he may encourage your hearts. He is coming with Onesimus, our faithful and dear brother, who is one of you. They will tell you everything that is happening here My fellow prisoner Aristarchus sends you his greetings, as does Mark, the cousin of Barnabas. (You have received instructions about him; if he comes to you, welcome him.) Jesus, who is called Justus, also sends greetings. These are the only Jews among my co-workers for the kingdom of God, and they have proved a comfort to me. Epaphras, who is one of you and a servant of Christ Jesus, sends greetings. He is always wrestling in prayer for you, that you may stand firm in all the will of God, mature and fully assured. I vouch for him that he is working hard for you and for those at Laodicea and Hierapolis. Our dear friend Luke, the doctor, and Demas send greetings. Give my greetings to the brothers and sisters at Laodicea, and to Nympha and the church in her house. After this letter has been read to you, see that it is also read in the church of the Laodiceans and that you in turn read the letter from Laodicea Tell Archippus: "See to it that you complete the ministry you have received in the Lord." I, Paul, write this greeting in my own hand. Remember my chains. Grace be with you. Amen

52. 1 Thessalonians

Chapter 1

Paul, Silvanus, and Timothy, to the Church of the Thessalonians, which is in God the Father and the Lord Jesus Christ: grace to you and peace from God our Father and the Lord Jesus Christ. We always thank God for all of you, mentioning you in our prayers. We constantly remember your work produced by faith, your labor prompted by love, and your endurance inspired by hope in our Lord Jesus Christ, in the presence of our God and Father, knowing, brothers and sisters, that you are God's chosen people. Our gospel came to you not only in word but also in power, in the Holy Spirit, and with full conviction, just as you know how we lived among you for your sake. You became imitators of us and of the Lord, for you received the word in much affliction, with the joy of the Holy Spirit, so that you became an example to all the believers in Macedonia and

Achaia. The word of the Lord has sounded forth from you, not only in Macedonia and Achaia but also your faith in God has gone forth everywhere, so we need not say anything. For they themselves report what kind of reception we had among you and how you turned to God from idols to serve the living and true God and to wait for His Son from heaven, whom He raised from the dead, Jesus, who delivers us from the wrath to come

Chapter 2

You yourselves know, brothers and sisters, that our visit to you was not without results. We had previously suffered and been treated outrageously in Philippi, as you know, but with the help of our God we dared to tell you His gospel in the face of strong opposition. For the appeal we make does not spring from error or impure motives, nor are we trying to trick you. On the contrary, we speak as those approved by God to be entrusted with the gospel. We are not trying to please people but God, who tests our hearts. You know we never used flattery, nor did we put on a mask to cover up greed—God is our witness. We were not looking for praise from people, not from you or anyone else, even though as apostles of Christ we could have asserted our authority. Instead, we were like young children among you. Just as a nursing mother cares for her children, so we cared for you. Because we loved you so much, we were delighted to share with you not only the gospel of God but our lives as well, because you had become so dear to us. Surely you remember, brothers and sisters, our toil and hardship; we worked night and day in order not to be a burden to anyone while we preached the gospel of God to you. You are witnesses, and so is God, of how holy, righteous, and blameless we were among you who believed. For you know that we dealt with each of you as a father deals with his own children, encouraging, comforting, and urging you to live lives worthy of God, who calls you into His kingdom and glory And we also thank God continually because when you received the word of God, which you heard from us, you accepted it not as a human word but as it actually is, the word of God, which is indeed at work in you who believe. For you, brothers and sisters, became imitators of God's churches in Judea, which are in Christ Jesus: You suffered from your own people the same things those churches suffered from the Jews who killed the Lord Jesus and the prophets and also drove us out. They displease God and are hostile to everyone, in their effort to keep us from speaking to the Gentiles so that they may be saved. In this way, they always heap up their sins to the limit. The wrath of God has come upon them at last But, brothers and sisters, when we were orphaned by being separated from you for a short time (in person, not in thought), out of our intense longing, we made every effort to see you. For we wanted to come to you—certainly I, Paul, did, again and again—but Satan blocked our way. For what is our hope, our joy, or the crown in which we will glory in the presence of our Lord Jesus when He comes? Is it not you? Indeed, you are our glory and joy

Chapter 3

When we could bear it no longer, we decided to stay in Athens alone and sent Timothy, our brother and God's fellow worker in spreading the gospel of Christ, to strengthen and encourage you in your faith, so that no one would be unsettled by these trials. For you know quite well that we are destined for them. In fact, when we were with you, we kept telling you that we would be persecuted. And it turned out that way, as you well know. For this reason, when I could stand it no longer, I sent to find out about your faith. I was afraid that in some way the tempter had tempted you and that our labors might have been in vain. But Timothy has just now come to us from you and has brought good news about your faith and love. He has told us that you always have pleasant memories of us and that you long to see us, just as we also long to see you. Therefore, brothers and sisters, in all our distress and persecution, we were encouraged about you because of your faith. For now, we really live if you stand firm in the Lord. How can we thank God enough for you in return for all the joy we have in the presence of our God because of you? Night and day, we pray most earnestly that we may see you again and supply what is lacking in your faith. Now may our God and Father Himself and our Lord Jesus clear the way for us to come to you. May the Lord make your love increase and overflow for each other and for everyone else, just as ours does for you. May He strengthen your hearts so that you will be blameless and holy in the presence of our God and Father when our Lord Jesus comes with all His holy ones

Chapter 4

Finally, brothers and sisters, we instructed you how to live in order to please God, as in fact you are living. Now we ask you and urge you in the Lord Jesus to do this more and more. For you know what instructions we gave you by the authority of the Lord Jesus. It is God's will that you should be sanctified: that you should avoid sexual immorality; that each of you should learn to control your own body in a way that is holy and honorable, not in passionate lust like the pagans, who do not know God; and that in this matter no one should wrong or take advantage of a brother or sister. The Lord will punish all those who commit such sins, as we told you and warned you before. For God did not call us to be impure but to live a holy life. Therefore, anyone who rejects this instruction does not reject a human being but God, the very God who gives you His Holy Spirit Now about your love for one another: We do not need to write to you, for you yourselves have been taught by God to love each other. And in fact, you do love all of God's family throughout Macedonia. Yet we urge you, brothers and sisters, to do so more and more, and to make it your ambition to lead a quiet life: You should mind your own business and work with your hands, just as we told you, so that your daily life may win the respect of outsiders and so that you will not be dependent on anybody Brothers and sisters, we do not want you to be uninformed about those who sleep in death so that you do not grieve like the rest of mankind, who have no hope. For we believe that Jesus died and rose again and so we believe that God will bring with Jesus those who have fallen asleep in Him. According to the Lord's word, we tell you that we who are still alive, who are left until the coming of the Lord, will certainly not precede those who have fallen asleep. For the Lord Himself will come down from heaven, with a loud command, with the voice of the archangel and with the trumpet call of God, and the dead in Christ will rise first. After that, we who are still alive and are left will be caught up together with them in the clouds to meet the Lord in the air. And so we will be with the Lord forever. Therefore encourage one another with these words

Chapter 5

Now, brothers and sisters, about times and dates we do not need to write to you, for you know very well that the day of the Lord will come like a thief in the night. While people are saying, "Peace and safety," destruction will come on them suddenly, as labor pains on a pregnant woman, and they will not escape. But you, brothers and sisters, are not in darkness so that this day should surprise you like a thief. You are all children of the light and children of the day. We do not belong to the night or to the darkness. So then, let us not be like others, who are asleep, but let us be awake and sober. For those who sleep, sleep at night, and those who get drunk, get drunk at night. But since we belong to the day, let us be sober, putting on faith and love as a breastplate, and the hope of salvation as a helmet. For God did not appoint us to suffer wrath but to receive salvation through our Lord Jesus Christ. He died for us so that, whether we are awake or asleep, we may live together with Him. Therefore encourage one another and build each other up, just as in fact you are doing Now we ask you, brothers and sisters, to acknowledge those who work hard among you, who care for you in the Lord and who admonish you. Hold them in the highest regard in love because of their work. Live in peace with each other. And we urge you, brothers and sisters, to warn those who are idle and disruptive, encourage the disheartened, help the weak, be patient with everyone. Make sure that nobody pays back wrong for wrong, but always strive to do what is good for each other and for everyone else. Rejoice always, pray continually, give thanks in all circumstances; for this is God's will for you in Christ Jesus. Do not quench the Spirit. Do not treat prophecies with contempt but test them all; hold on to what is good, reject every kind of evil May God Himself, the God of peace, sanctify you through and through. May your whole spirit, soul, and body be kept blameless at the coming of our Lord Jesus Christ. The One who calls you is faithful, and He will do it. Brothers and sisters, pray for us. Greet all God's people with a holy kiss. I charge you before the Lord to have this letter read to all the brothers and sisters. The grace of our Lord Jesus Christ be with you. Amen

53. 2 Thessalonians

Chapter 1

Paul, Silvanus, and Timothy to the Church of the Thessalonians, which is in God our Father and the Lord Jesus Christ: Grace to you and peace from God our Father and the Lord Jesus Christ. We must always give thanks to God for you, brothers, as is fitting, because your faith grows more and more and the charity of each of you toward one another increases. We ourselves rejoice in you in the Churches of God for your patience and faith in all the persecutions and tribulations you endure. This is a manifest sign of the righteous judgment of God, that you may be counted worthy of the kingdom of God, for which you also suffer. For it is a just thing with God to reward tribulation to those who afflict you, and to give you who are afflicted rest when the Lord Jesus will manifest Himself from on high with His mighty angels. In flaming fire, He will avenge those who do not know God and who do not obey the gospel of our Lord Jesus Christ. They shall be punished with everlasting perdition, away from the presence of the Lord and from the glory of His power when He comes to be glorified in His saints and to be marveled at among all who have believed—because our testimony to you was believed—on that day. Therefore, we also always pray for you, that our God may make you worthy of His calling and may fulfill every desire for goodness and every work of faith with power, so that the name of our Lord Jesus Christ may be glorified in you, and you in Him, according to the grace of our God and the Lord Jesus Christ

Chapter 2

Now we exhort you, brothers, regarding the coming of our Lord Jesus Christ and our gathering together with Him, that you may not be quickly shaken in mind or troubled, either by spirit or by word or by letter, as though the day of Christ were near. Let no one deceive you in any way, for that day will not come unless there is a rebellion first and the man of sin, the son of perdition, is revealed. He opposes and exalts himself above all that is called God or is worshiped, so much so that he sits as God in the temple of God, proclaiming himself to be God. Do you not remember that when I was still with you, I told you these things? Now you know what is restraining him so that he may be revealed in his own time. For the mystery of iniquity is already at work; only He who now restrains will do so until He is taken out of the way. Then the lawless one will be revealed, whom the Lord will consume with the breath of His mouth and destroy by the splendor of His coming. The coming of the lawless one will be in accordance with the work of Satan, with all power, signs, and lying wonders, and with all the deception of unrighteousness among those who perish because they did not receive the love of the truth so as to be saved. Therefore, God will send them strong delusion so that they may believe the lie and be condemned—all who did not believe the truth but had pleasure in unrighteousness But we should always thank God for you, brothers and sisters loved by the Lord, because God has chosen you from the beginning for salvation through sanctification by the Spirit and belief in the truth. He called you to this through our gospel, so that you may obtain the glory of our Lord Jesus Christ. Therefore, brothers and sisters, stand firm and hold fast to the teachings we passed on to you, whether by word of mouth or by letter. Now may our Lord Jesus Christ Himself and God our Father, who loved us and by His grace gave us eternal encouragement and good hope, comfort your hearts and strengthen you in every good deed and word

Chapter 3

Moreover, brothers and sisters, pray for us, that the word of the Lord may spread rapidly and be honored, just as it was with you, and that we may be delivered from unreasonable and wicked people, for not everyone has faith. But the Lord is faithful, and He will strengthen you and protect you from the evil one. We have confidence in the Lord that you are doing and will continue to do the things we command. May the Lord direct your hearts to the love of God and the steadfastness of Christ We command you, brothers and sisters, in the name of our Lord Jesus Christ, to keep away from every believer who is idle and disruptive and does not live according to the teaching you received from us. For you yourselves know how you ought to follow our example. We were not idle when we were with you, nor did we eat anyone's food without paying for it. On the contrary, we worked night and day, laboring and toiling so that we would not be a burden to any of you. We did this, not because we do not have the right to such help, but in order to offer ourselves as a model for you to imitate. For even when we were with you, we gave you this rule: "The one who is unwilling to work shall not eat." We hear that some among you are idle and disruptive. They are not busy; they are busybodies. Such people we command and urge in the Lord Jesus Christ to settle down and earn the food they eat. And as for you, brothers and sisters, never tire of doing what is good. Take special note of anyone who does not obey our instruction in this letter. Do not associate with them, so that they may feel ashamed. Yet do not regard them as an enemy, but warn them as you would a fellow believer Now may the Lord of peace Himself give you peace at all times and in every way. The Lord be with all of you. I, Paul, write this greeting in my own hand, which is the distinguishing mark in all my letters. This is how I write. The grace of our Lord Jesus Christ be with you all. Amen

54. 1 Timothy

Chapter 1

Paul, an apostle of Christ by the commandment of God our Savior and the Lord Jesus Christ, our hope, to Timothy, my true son in the faith: Grace, mercy, and peace from God our Father and Christ Jesus our Lord. As I urged you when I left for Macedonia, stay in Ephesus so that you may instruct certain people not to teach false doctrines or to devote themselves to myths and endless genealogies. Such things promote controversial speculations rather than advancing God's work—which is by faith. The goal of this command is love, which comes from a pure heart, a good conscience, and sincere faith. Some have departed from these and have turned to meaningless talk. They want to be teachers of the law, but they do not know what they are talking about or what they so confidently affirm We know that the law is good if one uses it properly. We also know that the law is made not for the righteous but for lawbreakers and rebels, the ungodly and sinful, the unholy and irreligious, for those who kill their fathers or mothers, for murderers, the sexually immoral, those practicing homosexuality, slave traders, liars, perjurers—and for whatever else is contrary to the sound doctrine that conforms to the gospel concerning the glory of the blessed God, which He entrusted to me I thank Christ Jesus our Lord, who has given me strength, that He considered me trustworthy, appointing me to His service. Even though I was once a blasphemer and a persecutor and a violent man, I was shown mercy because I acted in ignorance and unbelief. The grace of our Lord was poured out on me abundantly, along with the faith and love that are in Christ Jesus. Here is a trustworthy saying that deserves full acceptance: Christ Jesus came into the world to save sinners—of whom I am the worst. But for that very reason I was shown mercy so that in me, the worst of sinners, Christ Jesus might display His immense patience as an example for those who would believe in Him and receive eternal life. Now to the King eternal, immortal, invisible, the only God, be honor and glory for ever and ever. Amen Timothy, my son, I am giving you this command in keeping with the prophecies once made about you so that by recalling them you may fight the battle well, holding on to faith and a good conscience, which some have rejected and so have suffered shipwreck with regard to the faith. Among them are Hymenaeus and Alexander, whom I have handed over to Satan to be taught not to blaspheme

Chapter 2

I urge, then, first of all, that petitions, prayers, intercession, and thanksgiving be made for all people—for kings and all those in authority—that we may live peaceful and quiet lives in all godliness and holiness. This is good and pleases God our Savior, who wants all people to be saved and to come to a knowledge of the truth. For there is one God and one mediator between God and mankind, the man Christ Jesus, who gave Himself as a ransom for all people. This has now been witnessed to at the proper time. And for this purpose I was appointed a herald and an apostle—I am telling the truth, I am not lying—and a true and faithful teacher of the Gentiles Therefore, I want the men everywhere to pray, lifting up holy hands without anger or disputing. I also want the women to dress modestly, with decency and propriety, adorning themselves, not with elaborate hairstyles or gold or pearls or expensive clothes, but with good deeds, appropriate for women who profess to worship God. A woman should learn in quietness and full submission. I do not permit a woman to teach or to assume authority over a man; she must be quiet. For Adam was formed first, then Eve. And Adam was not the one deceived; it was the woman who was deceived and became a sinner. But women will be saved through childbearing—if they continue in faith, love, and holiness with propriety

Chapter 3

Here is a trustworthy saying: Whoever aspires to be an overseer desires a noble task. Now the overseer is to be above reproach, faithful to his wife, temperate, self-controlled, respectable, hospitable, able to teach, not given to drunkenness, not violent but gentle, not quarrelsome, not a lover of money. He must manage his own family well and see that his children obey him, and he must do so in a manner worthy of full respect. (If anyone does not know how to manage his own family, how can he take care of God's church?) He must not be a recent convert, or he may become conceited and fall under the same judgment as the devil. He must also have a good reputation with outsiders, so that he will not fall into disgrace and into the devil's trap In the same way, deacons are to be worthy of respect, sincere, not indulging in much wine, and not pursuing dishonest gain. They must keep hold of the deep truths of the faith with a clear conscience. They must first be tested; and then if there is nothing against them, let them serve as deacons. In the same way, the women are to be worthy of respect, not malicious talkers but temperate and trustworthy in everything. A deacon must be faithful to his wife and must manage his children and his household well. Those who have served well gain an excellent standing and great assurance in their faith in Christ Jesus Although I hope to come to you soon, I am writing you these instructions so that, if I am delayed, you will know how people ought to conduct themselves in God's household, which is the church of the living God, the pillar and foundation of the truth. Beyond all question, the mystery from which true godliness springs is great: He appeared in the flesh, was vindicated by the Spirit, was seen by angels, was preached among the nations, was believed on in the world, was taken up in glory

Chapter 4

The Spirit clearly says that in later times some will abandon the faith and follow deceiving spirits and things taught by demons. Such teachings come through hypocritical liars, whose consciences have been seared as with a hot iron. They forbid people to marry and order them to abstain from certain foods, which God created to be received with thanksgiving by those who believe and who know the truth. For everything God created is good, and nothing is to be rejected if it is received with thanksgiving, because it is consecrated by the word of God and prayer If you point these things out to the brothers and sisters, you will be a good minister of Christ Jesus, nourished on the truths of the faith and of the good teaching that you have followed. Have nothing to do with godless myths and old wives' tales; rather, train yourself to be godly. For physical training is of some value, but godliness has value for all things, holding promise for both the present life and the life to come. This is a trustworthy saying that deserves full acceptance. That is why we labor and strive, because we have put our hope in the living God, who is the Savior of all people, and especially of those who believe Command and teach these things. Don't let anyone look down on you because you are young, but set an example for the believers in speech, in conduct, in love, in faith, and in purity. Until I come, devote yourself to the public reading of Scripture, to preaching and to teaching. Do not neglect your gift, which was given you through prophecy when the body of elders laid their hands on you. Be diligent in these matters; give yourself wholly to them, so that everyone may see your progress. Watch your life and doctrine closely. Persevere in them, because if you do, you will save both yourself and your hearers

Chapter 5

Do not rebuke an older man harshly, but exhort him as if he were your father. Treat younger men as brothers, older women as mothers, and younger women as sisters, with absolute purity. Give proper recognition to those widows who are really in need. But if a widow has children or grandchildren, these should learn first of all to put their religion into practice by caring for their own family and so repaying their parents and grandparents, for this is pleasing to God. The widow who is really in need and left all alone puts her hope in God and continues night and day to pray and to ask God for help. But the widow who lives for pleasure is dead even while she lives. Give the people these instructions, so that no one may be open to blame. Anyone who does not provide for their relatives, and especially for their own household, has denied the faith and is worse than an unbeliever No widow may be put on the list of widows unless she is over sixty, has been faithful to her husband, and is well known for her good deeds, such as bringing up children, showing hospitality, washing the feet of the Lord's people, helping those in trouble, and devoting herself to all kinds of good deeds. As for younger widows, do not put them on such a list. For when their sensual desires overcome their dedication to Christ, they want to marry. Thus they bring judgment on themselves because they have broken their first pledge. Besides, they get into the habit of being idle and going about from house to house. And not only do they become idlers, but also busybodies who talk nonsense, saying things they ought not to. So I counsel younger widows to marry, to have children, to manage their homes and to give the enemy no opportunity for slander. Some have in fact already turned away to follow Satan If any woman who is a believer has widows in her care, she should continue to help them and not let the church be burdened with them, so that the church can help those widows who are really in need The elders who direct the affairs of the church well are worthy of double honor, especially those whose work is preaching and teaching. For Scripture says, "Do not muzzle an ox while it is treading out the grain," and "The worker deserves his wages." Do not entertain an accusation against an elder unless it is brought by two or three witnesses. But those elders who are sinning you are to reprove before everyone, so that the others may take warning. I charge you, in the sight of God and Christ Jesus and the elect angels, to keep these instructions without partiality and to do nothing out of favoritism Do not be hasty in the laying on of hands, and do not share in the sins of others. Keep yourself pure. Stop drinking only water, and use a little wine because of your stomach and your frequent illnesses. The sins of some are obvious, reaching the place of judgment ahead of them; the sins of others trail behind them. In the same way, good deeds are obvious, and even those that are not obvious cannot remain hidden forever

Chapter 6

All who are under the yoke of slavery should consider their masters worthy of full respect, so that God's name and our teaching may not be slandered. Those who have believing masters should not show them disrespect just because they are fellow believers. Instead, they should serve them even better because their masters are dear to them as fellow believers and are devoted to the welfare of their slaves These are the things you are to teach and insist on. If anyone teaches otherwise and does not agree to the sound instruction of our Lord Jesus Christ and to godly teaching, they are conceited and understand nothing. They have an unhealthy interest in controversies and quarrels about words that result in envy, strife, malicious talk, evil suspicions, and constant friction between people of corrupt mind, who have been robbed of the truth and who think that godliness is a means to financial gain. But godliness with contentment is great gain. For we brought nothing into the world, and we can take nothing out of it. But if we have food and clothing, we will be content with that. Those who want to get rich fall into temptation and a trap and into many foolish and harmful desires that plunge people into ruin and destruction. For the love of money is a root of all kinds of evil. Some people, eager for money, have wandered from the faith and pierced themselves with many griefs But you, man of God, flee from all this and pursue righteousness, godliness, faith, love, endurance, and gentleness. Fight the good fight of the faith. Take hold of the eternal life to which you were called when you made your good confession in the presence of many witnesses. In the sight of God, who gives life to everything, and of Christ Jesus, who while testifying before Pontius Pilate made the good confession, I charge you to keep this command without spot or blame until the appearing of our Lord Jesus Christ, which God will bring about in His own time—God, the blessed and only Ruler, the King of kings and Lord of lords, who alone is immortal and who lives in unapproachable light, whom no one has seen or can see. To Him be honor and might forever. Amen Command those who are rich in this present world not to be arrogant nor to put their hope in wealth, which is so uncertain, but to put their hope in God, who richly provides us with everything for our enjoyment. Command them to do good, to be rich in good deeds, and to be generous and willing to share. In this way, they will lay up treasure for themselves as a firm foundation for the coming age, so that they may take hold of the life that is truly life Timothy, guard what has been entrusted to your care. Turn away from godless chatter and the opposing ideas of what is falsely called knowledge, which some have professed and in so doing have departed from the faith Grace be with you all. Amen

55. 2 Timothy

Chapter 1

Paul, an apostle of Jesus Christ by the will of God, according to the promise of life that is in Christ Jesus, to Timothy, my beloved son: Grace, mercy, and peace from God the Father and Jesus Christ our Lord. I thank God, whom I serve, as my ancestors did, with a clear conscience, as night and day I constantly remember you in my prayers. I long to see you, mindful of your tears, so that I may be filled with joy. I am reminded of your sincere faith, which first lived in your grandmother Lois and in your mother Eunice, and I am persuaded now lives in you also. For this reason, I remind you to fan into flame the gift of God, which is in you through the laying on of my hands. For God has not given us a spirit of fear, but of power, love, and a sound mind. Therefore, do not be ashamed of the testimony about our Lord or of me, His prisoner. Rather, join with me in suffering for the gospel by the power of God. He has saved us and called us to a holy life—not because of anything we have done but because of His own purpose and grace. This grace was given us in Christ Jesus before the beginning of time, but it has now been revealed through the appearing of our Savior, Christ Jesus, who has destroyed death and has brought life and immortality to light through the gospel. And of this gospel, I was appointed a herald, an apostle, and a teacher. That is why I am suffering as I am. Yet this is no cause for shame because I know whom I have believed, and I am convinced that He is able to guard what I have entrusted to Him until that day. Keep as the pattern of sound teaching what you have heard from me, with faith and love in Christ Jesus. Guard the good deposit that was entrusted to you—guard it with the help of the Holy Spirit who lives in us You know that everyone in the province of Asia has deserted me, including Phygelus and Hermogenes. May the Lord show mercy to the household of Onesiphorus because he often refreshed me and was not ashamed of my chains. On the contrary, when he was in Rome, he searched hard for me until he found me. May the Lord grant that he will find mercy from the Lord on that day! You know very well in how many ways he helped me in Ephesus

Chapter 2

You then, my son, be strong in the grace that is in Christ Jesus. And the things you have heard me say in the presence of many witnesses entrust to reliable people who will also be qualified to teach others. Join with me in suffering, like a good soldier of Christ Jesus. No one serving as a soldier gets entangled in civilian affairs but rather tries to please his commanding officer. Similarly, anyone who competes as an athlete does not receive the victor's crown except by competing according to the rules. The hardworking farmer should be the first to receive a share of the crops. Reflect on what I am saying, for the Lord will give you insight into all this Remember Jesus Christ, raised from the dead, descended from David. This is my gospel, for which I am suffering even to the point of being chained like a criminal. But God's word is not chained. Therefore, I endure everything for the sake of the elect, that they too may obtain the salvation that is in Christ Jesus, with eternal glory Here is a trustworthy saying: If we died with Him, we will also live with Him; if we endure, we will also reign with Him. If we disown Him, He will also disown us; if we are faithless, He remains faithful, for He cannot disown Himself Keep reminding God's people of these things. Warn them before God against quarreling about words; it is of no value and only ruins those who listen. Do your best to present yourself to God as one approved, a worker who does not need to be ashamed and who correctly handles the word of truth. Avoid godless chatter because those who indulge in it will become more and more ungodly. Their teaching will spread like gangrene. Among them are Hymenaeus and Philetus, who have departed from the truth. They say that the resurrection has already taken place, and they destroy the faith of some. Nevertheless, God's solid foundation stands firm, sealed with this inscription: "The Lord knows those who are His," and, "Everyone who confesses the name of the Lord must turn away from wickedness." In a large house, there are articles not only of gold and silver but also of wood and clay; some are for special purposes and some for common use. Those who cleanse themselves from the latter will be instruments for special purposes, made holy, useful to the Master, and prepared to do any good work Flee the evil desires of youth and pursue righteousness, faith, love, and peace, along with those who call on the Lord out of a pure heart. Don't have anything to do with foolish and stupid arguments because you know they produce quarrels. And the Lord's servant must not be quarrelsome but must be kind to everyone, able to teach, not resentful. Opponents must be gently instructed in the hope that God will

grant them repentance leading them to a knowledge of the truth, and that they will come to their senses and escape from the trap of the devil, who has taken them captive to do his will

Chapter 3

But mark this: There will be terrible times in the last days. People will be lovers of themselves, lovers of money, boastful, proud, abusive, disobedient to their parents, ungrateful, unholy, without love, unforgiving, slanderous, without self-control, brutal, not lovers of the good, treacherous, rash, conceited, lovers of pleasure rather than lovers of God—having a form of godliness but denying its power. Have nothing to do with such people. They are the kind who worm their way into homes and gain control over gullible women, who are loaded down with sins and are swayed by all kinds of evil desires, always learning but never able to come to a knowledge of the truth. Just as Jannes and Jambres opposed Moses, so also these teachers oppose the truth. They are men of depraved minds, who, as far as the faith is concerned, are rejected. But they will not get very far because, as in the case of those men, their folly will be clear to everyone You, however, know all about my teaching, my way of life, my purpose, faith, patience, love, endurance, persecutions, sufferings—what kinds of things happened to me in Antioch, Iconium, and Lystra, the persecutions I endured. Yet the Lord rescued me from all of them. In fact, everyone who wants to live a godly life in Christ Jesus will be persecuted, while evildoers and impostors will go from bad to worse, deceiving and being deceived. But as for you, continue in what you have learned and have become convinced of because you know those from whom you learned it, and how from infancy you have known the Holy Scriptures, which are able to make you wise for salvation through faith in Christ Jesus. All Scripture is God-breathed and is useful for teaching, rebuking, correcting, and training in righteousness so that the servant of God may be thoroughly equipped for every good work

Chapter 4

In the presence of God and of Christ Jesus, who will judge the living and the dead, and in view of His appearing and His kingdom, I give you this charge: Preach the word; be prepared in season and out of season; correct, rebuke, and encourage—with great patience and careful instruction. For the time will come when people will not put up with sound doctrine. Instead, to suit their own desires, they will gather around them a great number of teachers to say what their itching ears want to hear. They will turn their ears away from the truth and turn aside to myths. But you, keep your head in all situations, endure hardship, do the work of an evangelist, discharge all the duties of your ministry. For I am already being poured out like a drink offering, and the time for my departure is near. I have fought the good fight, I have finished the race, I have kept the faith. Now there is in store for me the crown of righteousness, which the Lord, the righteous Judge, will award to me on that day—and not only to me but also to all who have longed for His appearing Do your best to come to me quickly, for Demas, because he loved this world, has deserted me and has gone to Thessalonica. Crescens has gone to Galatia, and Titus to Dalmatia. Only Luke is with me. Get Mark and bring him with you because he is helpful to me in my ministry. I sent Tychicus to Ephesus. When you come, bring the cloak that I left with Carpus at Troas, and my scrolls, especially the parchments. Alexander the metalworker did me a great deal of harm. The Lord will repay him for what he has done. You too should be on your guard against him because he strongly opposed our message At my first defense, no one came to my support, but everyone deserted me. May it not be held against them. But the Lord stood at my side and gave me strength so that through me the message might be fully proclaimed and all the Gentiles might hear it. And I was delivered from the lion's mouth. The Lord will rescue me from every evil attack and will bring me safely to His heavenly kingdom. To Him be glory forever and ever. Amen Greet Priscilla and Aquila and the household of Onesiphorus. Erastus stayed in Corinth, and I left Trophimus sick in Miletus. Do your best to get here before winter. Eubulus greets you, and so do Pudens, Linus, Claudia, and all the brothers and sisters. The Lord be with your spirit. Grace be with you all. Amen

56. Titus

Chapter 1

Paul, a servant of God and an apostle of Jesus Christ, according to the faith of God's elect and the acknowledgment of the truth, which accords with godliness, in hope of eternal life, which God, who cannot lie, promised before time began, but has in due time manifested His word through preaching, which was committed to me according to the commandment of God our Savior. To Titus, my true son in our common faith: Grace, mercy, and peace from God the Father and the Lord Jesus Christ our Savior For this reason, I left you in Crete, that you should set in order the things that are lacking and appoint elders in every city as I commanded you. An elder must be blameless, the husband of one wife, with faithful children not accused of wild living or rebellion. A bishop must be blameless, as a steward of God, not self-willed, not quick-tempered, not given to wine, not violent, not greedy for money, but hospitable, a lover of what is good, sober-minded, just, holy, self-controlled, holding fast the faithful word as he has been taught, that he may be able, by sound doctrine, both to exhort and to convict those who contradict For there are many rebellious people, idle talkers, and deceivers, especially those of the circumcision, whose mouths must be stopped, who subvert whole households, teaching things they ought not for the sake of dishonest gain. One of their own prophets said, "Cretans are always liars, evil brutes, lazy gluttons." This testimony is true. Therefore, rebuke them sharply, so that they will be sound in the faith, not paying attention to Jewish myths or to the commands of those who reject the truth. To the pure, all things are pure, but to those who are defiled and unbelieving, nothing is pure. In fact, both their minds and consciences are defiled. They claim to know God, but by their actions, they deny Him. They are detestable, disobedient, and unfit for doing anything good

Chapter 2

But as for you, speak the things which are proper for sound doctrine. Older men are to be sober, reverent, temperate, sound in faith, in love, in patience. Likewise, older women are to be reverent in behavior, not slanderers, not given to much wine, teachers of good things, that they may admonish the young women to love their husbands, to love their children, to be discreet, chaste, homemakers, good, obedient to their own husbands, that the word of God may not be blasphemed. Likewise, exhort the young men to be sober-minded, in all things showing yourself to be a pattern of good works; in doctrine showing integrity, reverence, incorruptibility, sound speech that cannot be condemned, that one who is an opponent may be ashamed, having nothing evil to say of you Exhort servants to be obedient to their own masters, to be well-pleasing in all things, not answering back, not pilfering, but showing all good fidelity, that they may adorn the doctrine of God our Savior in all things. For the grace of God that brings salvation has appeared to all men, teaching us that, denying ungodliness and worldly lusts, we should live soberly, righteously, and godly in the present age, looking for the blessed hope and glorious appearing of our great God and Savior Jesus Christ, who gave Himself for us, that He might redeem us from every lawless deed and purify for Himself His own special people, zealous for good works. Speak these things, exhort, and rebuke with all authority. Let no one despise you

Chapter 3

Remind them to be subject to rulers and authorities, to obey, to be ready for every good work, to speak evil of no one, to be peaceable, gentle, showing all humility to all men. For we ourselves were also once foolish, disobedient, deceived, serving various lusts and pleasures, living in malice and envy, hateful and hating one another. But when the kindness and the love of God our Savior toward man appeared, not by works of righteousness which we have done, but according to His mercy, He saved us, through the washing of regeneration and renewing of the Holy Spirit, whom He poured out on us abundantly through Jesus Christ our Savior, that having been justified by His grace, we should become heirs according to the hope of eternal life This is a faithful saying, and these things I want you to affirm constantly, that those who have believed in God should be careful to maintain good works. These things are good and profitable to men. But avoid foolish disputes, genealogies, contentions, and strivings about the law, for they are unprofitable and useless. Reject a divisive person after the first and second admonition, knowing that such a person is warped and sinning, being self-condemned When I send Artemas to you, or Tychicus, be diligent to come to me at Nicopolis, for I have decided to spend the winter there. Send Zenas the lawyer and Apollos on their journey with haste, that they may lack nothing. And let our people also learn to maintain good works, to meet urgent needs, that they may not be unfruitful All who are with me greet you. Greet those who love us in the faith. Grace be with you all. Amen

57. Philemon

Chapter 1

Paul, a prisoner of Jesus Christ, and our brother Timothy, to Philemon, our dear friend and fellow worker, to our dear sister Apphia, to Archippus, our fellow soldier, and to the church that meets in your home: Grace to you and peace from God our Father and the Lord Jesus Christ I thank my God, always mentioning you in my prayers, because I hear of your love and faith toward the Lord Jesus and all the saints. I pray that the sharing of your faith may become effective through the knowledge of every good thing that is in us for the glory of Christ. For I have derived much joy and comfort from your love, brother, because the hearts of the saints have been refreshed through you Therefore, though I have enough boldness in Christ to command you to do what is proper, yet for love's sake I prefer to appeal to you—I, Paul, an old man and now also a prisoner for Christ Jesus. I appeal to you for my child, Onesimus, whose father I became in my imprisonment. Formerly he was useless to you, but now he is indeed useful to you and to me. I am sending him back to you, sending my very heart. I would have liked to keep him with me, so that he could take your place in helping me while I am in chains for the gospel. But I did not want to do anything without your consent, so that any favor you do would not seem forced but would be voluntary Perhaps the reason he was separated from you for a little while was that you might have him back forever, no longer as a slave, but better than a slave, as a dear brother. He is very dear to me but even dearer to you, both in the flesh and in the Lord. So if you consider me a partner, welcome him as you would welcome me. If he has wronged you in any way or owes you anything, charge it to me. I, Paul, am writing this with my own hand: I will repay it—not to mention that you owe me your very self. Yes, brother, let me benefit from you in the Lord; refresh my heart in Christ Confident of your obedience, I write to you, knowing that you will do even more than I ask. And one thing more: Prepare a guest room for me, because I hope to be restored to you in answer to your prayers Epaphras, my fellow prisoner in Christ Jesus, sends you greetings, as do Mark, Aristarchus, Demas, and Luke, my fellow workers. The grace of the Lord Jesus Christ be with your spirit. Amen

58. Hebrews

Chapter 1

At different times and in various manners, God spoke long ago to our ancestors through the prophets. In these last days, He has spoken to us through His Son, whom He appointed heir of all things and through whom He made the world. The Son is the radiance of God's glory and the exact representation of His being, sustaining all things by His powerful word. After providing purification for sins, He sat down at the right hand of the Majesty in heaven, becoming much superior to the angels, as He has inherited a name more excellent than theirs For to which of the angels did God ever say, "You are my Son; today I have become your Father"? Or again, "I will be His Father, and He will be my Son"? And again, when God brings His firstborn into the world, He says, "Let all God's angels worship Him." In speaking of the angels, He says, "He makes His angels spirits and His servants flames of fire." But about the Son, He says, "Your throne, O God, will last forever and ever; a scepter of justice will be the scepter of Your kingdom. You have loved righteousness and hated wickedness; therefore God, Your God, has set You above Your companions by anointing You with the oil of joy." He also says, "In the beginning, Lord, You laid the foundations of the earth, and the heavens are the work of Your hands. They will perish, but You remain; they will all wear out like a garment. You will roll them up like a robe; like a garment, they will be changed. But You remain the same, and Your years will never end." To which of the angels did God ever say, "Sit at my right hand until I make Your enemies a footstool for Your feet"? Are not all angels ministering spirits sent to serve those who will inherit salvation?

Chapter 2

Therefore, we must pay more careful attention to what we have heard so that we do not drift away. For if the message spoken by angels was binding, and every violation and disobedience received its just punishment, how shall we escape if we ignore such a great salvation? This salvation, which was first announced by the Lord, was confirmed to us by those who heard Him. God also testified to it by signs, wonders, various miracles, and gifts of the Holy Spirit distributed according to His will It is not to angels that He has subjected the world to come, about which we are speaking. But there is a place where someone has testified: "What is mankind that You are mindful of them, a son of man that You care for him? You made them a little lower than the angels; You crowned them with glory and honor and put everything under their feet." In putting everything

under them, God left nothing that is not subject to them. Yet at present, we do not see everything subject to them. But we do see Jesus, who was made lower than the angels for a little while, now crowned with glory and honor because He suffered death, so that by the grace of God, He might taste death for everyone In bringing many sons and daughters to glory, it was fitting that God, for whom and through whom everything exists, should make the pioneer of their salvation perfect through what He suffered. Both the one who makes people holy and those who are made holy are of the same family. So Jesus is not ashamed to call them brothers and sisters. He says, "I will declare Your name to my brothers and sisters; in the assembly, I will sing Your praises." And again, "I will put my trust in Him." And again, He says, "Here am I, and the children God has given me." Since the children have flesh and blood, He too shared in their humanity so that by His death He might break the power of him who holds the power of death—that is, the devil—and free those who all their lives were held in slavery by their fear of death. For surely it is not angels He helps, but Abraham's descendants. For this reason, He had to be made like them, fully human in every way, in order that He might become a merciful and faithful high priest in service to God, and that He might make atonement for the sins of the people. Because He Himself suffered when He was tempted, He is able to help those who are being tempted

Chapter 3

Therefore, holy brothers and sisters, who share in the heavenly calling, fix your thoughts on Jesus, whom we acknowledge as our apostle and high priest. He was faithful to the one who appointed Him, just as Moses was faithful in all God's house. Jesus has been found worthy of greater honor than Moses, just as the builder of a house has greater honor than the house itself. For every house is built by someone, but God is the builder of everything. Moses was faithful as a servant in all God's house, bearing witness to what would be spoken by God in the future. But Christ is faithful as the Son over God's house. And we are His house if indeed we hold firmly to our confidence and the hope in which we glory So, as the Holy Spirit says: "Today, if you hear His voice, do not harden your hearts as you did in the rebellion, during the time of testing in the wilderness, where your ancestors tested and tried me, though for forty years they saw what I did. That is why I was angry with that generation; I said, 'Their hearts are always going astray, and they have not known my ways.' So I declared on oath in my anger, 'They shall never enter my rest.'" See to it, brothers and sisters, that none of you has a sinful, unbelieving heart that turns away from the living God. But encourage one another daily, as long as it is called "Today," so that none of you may be hardened by sin's deceitfulness. We have come to share in Christ if indeed we hold our original conviction firmly to the very end. As has just been said: "Today, if you hear His voice, do not harden your hearts as you did in the rebellion." Who were they who heard and rebelled? Were they not all those Moses led out of Egypt? And with whom was He angry for forty years? Was it not with those who sinned, whose bodies perished in the wilderness? And to whom did God swear that they would never enter His rest if not to those who disobeyed? So we see that they were not able to enter because of their unbelief

Chapter 4

Therefore, since the promise of entering His rest still stands, let us be careful that none of you be found to have fallen short of it. For we also have had the good news proclaimed to us, just as they did; but the message they heard was of no value to them, because they did not share the faith of those who obeyed. Now we who have believed enter that rest, just as God has said, "So I declared on oath in my anger, 'They shall never enter my rest.'" And yet His works have been finished since the creation of the world. For somewhere He has spoken about the seventh day in these words: "On the seventh day, God rested from all His works." And again in the passage above He says, "They shall never enter my rest." Therefore, since it still remains for some to enter that rest, and since those who formerly had the good news proclaimed to them did not go in because of their disobedience, God again set a certain day, calling it "Today." This He did when a long time later He spoke through David, as in the passage already quoted: "Today, if you hear His voice, do not harden your hearts." For if Joshua had given them rest, God would not have spoken later about another day. There remains, then, a Sabbath-rest for the people of God; for anyone who enters God's rest also rests from their works, just as God did from His Let us, therefore, make every effort to enter that rest so that no one will perish by following their example of disobedience. For the word of God is alive and active. Sharper than any double-edged sword, it penetrates even to dividing soul and spirit, joints and marrow; it judges the thoughts and attitudes of the heart. Nothing in all creation is hidden from God's sight. Everything is uncovered and laid bare before the eyes of Him to whom we must give account Therefore, since we have a great high priest who has ascended into heaven, Jesus the Son of God, let us hold firmly to the faith we profess. For we do not have a high priest who is unable to empathize with our weaknesses, but we have one who has been tempted in every way, just as we are—yet He did not sin. Let us then approach God's throne of grace with confidence so that we may receive mercy and find grace to help us in our time of need

Chapter 5

Every high priest is selected from among the people and is appointed to represent the people in matters related to God, to offer gifts and sacrifices for sins. He is able to deal gently with those who are ignorant and are going astray, since he himself is subject to weakness. This is why he has to offer sacrifices for his own sins, as well as for the sins of the people. And no one takes this honor on himself, but he receives it when called by God, just as Aaron was In the same way, Christ did not take on Himself the glory of becoming a high priest. But God said to Him, "You are my Son; today I have become your Father." And He says in another place, "You are a priest forever, in the order of Melchizedek." During the days of Jesus' life on earth, He offered up prayers and petitions with fervent cries and tears to the one who could save Him from death, and He was heard because of His reverent submission. Son though He was, He learned obedience from what He suffered and, once made perfect, He became the source of eternal salvation for all who obey Him and was designated by God to be high priest in the order of Melchizedek We have much to say about this, but it is hard to make it clear to you because you no longer try to understand. In fact, though by this time you ought to be teachers, you need someone to teach you the elementary truths of God's word all over again. You need milk, not solid food! Anyone who lives on milk, being still an infant, is not acquainted with the teaching about righteousness. But solid food is for the mature, who by constant use have trained themselves to distinguish good from evil

Chapter 6

Therefore, let us move beyond the elementary teachings about Christ and be taken forward to maturity, not laying again the foundation of repentance from acts that lead to death, and of faith in God, instruction about cleansing rites, the laying on of hands, the resurrection of the dead, and eternal judgment. And God permitting, we will do so It is impossible for those who have once been enlightened, who have tasted the heavenly gift, who have shared in the Holy Spirit, who have tasted the goodness of the word of God and the powers of the coming age and who have fallen away, to be brought back to repentance. To their loss, they are crucifying the Son of God all over again and subjecting Him to public disgrace. Land that drinks in the rain often falling on it and that produces a crop useful to those for whom it is farmed receives the blessing of God. But land that produces thorns and thistles is worthless and is in danger of being cursed. In the end, it will be burned Even though we speak like this, dear friends, we are convinced of better things in your case—the things that have to do with salvation. God is not unjust; He will not forget your work and the love you have shown Him as you have helped His people and continue to help them. We want each of you to show this same diligence to the very end so that what you hope for may be fully realized. We do not want you to become lazy but to imitate those who through faith and patience inherit what has been promised When God made His promise to Abraham, since there was no one greater for Him to swear by, He swore by Himself, saying, "I will surely bless you and give you many descendants." And so after waiting patiently, Abraham received what was promised. People swear by someone greater than themselves, and the oath confirms what is said and puts an end to all argument. Because God wanted to make the unchanging nature of His purpose very clear to the heirs of what was promised, He confirmed it with an oath. God did this so that, by two unchangeable things in which it is impossible for God to lie, we who have fled to take hold of the hope set before us may be greatly encouraged. We have this hope as an anchor for the soul, firm and secure. It enters the inner sanctuary behind the curtain, where our forerunner, Jesus, has entered on our behalf. He has become a high priest forever, in the order of Melchizedek

Chapter 7

This Melchizedek was king of Salem and priest of God Most High. He met Abraham returning from the defeat of the kings and blessed him, and Abraham gave him a tenth of everything. First, the name Melchizedek means "king of righteousness"; then also, "king of Salem" means "king of peace." Without father or mother, without genealogy, without beginning of days or end of life, resembling the Son of God, he remains a priest forever Just think how great he was: Even the patriarch Abraham gave him a tenth of the plunder! Now the law requires the descendants of Levi who become priests to collect a tenth from the people—that is, from their fellow Israelites—even though they also are descended from Abraham. This man, however, did not trace his descent from Levi, yet he collected a tenth from Abraham and blessed him who had the promises. And without doubt, the lesser is blessed by the greater. In the one case, the tenth is collected by people who die; but in the other case, by him who is declared to be living. One might even say that Levi, who collects the tenth, paid the tenth through Abraham because when Melchizedek met Abraham, Levi was still in the body of his ancestor If perfection could have been attained through the Levitical priesthood—and indeed the law given to the people established that priesthood—why was there still need for another priest to come, one in the order of Melchizedek, not in the order of Aaron? For when the priesthood is changed, the law must be changed also. He of whom these things are said belonged to a different tribe, and no one from that tribe has ever served at the altar. For it is clear that our Lord descended from Judah, and in regard to that tribe, Moses said nothing about priests. And what we have said is even more clear if another priest like Melchizedek appears, one who has become a priest not on the basis of a regulation as to his ancestry but on the basis of the power of an indestructible life. For it is declared: "You are a priest forever, in the order of Melchizedek." The former regulation is set aside because it was weak and useless (for the law made nothing perfect), and a better hope is introduced, by which we draw near to God. And it was not without an oath! Others became priests without any oath, but He became a priest with an oath when God said to Him: "The Lord has sworn and will not change His mind: 'You are a priest forever.'" Because of this oath, Jesus has become the guarantor of a better covenant Now there have been many of those priests since death prevented them from continuing in office; but because Jesus lives forever, He has a permanent priesthood. Therefore, He is able to save completely those who come to God through Him because He always lives to intercede for them Such a high priest truly meets our need—one who is holy, blameless, pure, set apart from sinners, exalted above the heavens. Unlike the other high priests, He does not need to offer sacrifices day after day, first for His own sins and then for the sins of the people. He sacrificed for their sins once for all when He offered Himself. For the law appoints as high priests men in all their weakness, but the oath, which came after the law, appointed the Son, who has been made perfect forever

Chapter 8

Now the main point of what we are saying is this: We do have such a high priest, who sat down at the right hand of the throne of the Majesty in heaven and who serves in the sanctuary, the true tabernacle set up by the Lord, not by a mere human being. Every high priest is appointed to offer both gifts and sacrifices, and so it was necessary for this one also to have something to offer. If He were on earth, He would not be a priest, for there are already priests who offer the gifts prescribed by the law. They serve at a sanctuary that is a copy and shadow of what is in heaven. This is why Moses was warned when he was about to build the tabernacle: "See to it that you make everything according to the pattern shown you on the mountain." But in fact, the ministry Jesus has received is as superior to theirs as the covenant of which He is mediator is superior to the old one, since the new covenant is established on better promises For if there had been nothing wrong with that first covenant, no place would have been sought for another. But God found fault with the people and said: "The days are coming, declares the Lord, when I will make a new covenant with the people of Israel and with the people of Judah. It will not be like the covenant I made with their ancestors when I took them by the hand to lead them out of Egypt because they did not remain faithful to my covenant, and I turned away from them, declares the Lord. This is the covenant I will establish with the people of Israel after that time, declares the Lord. I will put my laws in their minds and write them on their hearts. I will be their God, and they will be my people. No longer will they teach their neighbor, or say to one another, 'Know the Lord,' because they will all know me, from the least of them to the greatest. For I will forgive their wickedness and will remember their sins no more."

By calling this covenant "new," He has made the first one obsolete, and what is obsolete and outdated will soon disappear

Chapter 9

Now the first covenant had regulations for worship and also an earthly sanctuary. A tabernacle was set up. In its first room were the lampstand, the table, and the consecrated bread; this was called the Holy Place. Behind the second curtain was a room called the Most Holy Place, which had the golden altar of incense and the gold-covered ark of the covenant. This ark contained the gold jar of manna, Aaron's staff that had budded, and the stone tablets of the covenant. Above the ark were the cherubim of the Glory, overshadowing the atonement cover. But we cannot discuss these things in detail now When everything had been arranged like this, the priests entered regularly into the outer room to carry on their ministry. But only the high priest entered the inner room, and that only once a year, and never without blood, which he offered for himself and for the sins the people had committed in ignorance. The Holy Spirit was showing by this that the way into the Most Holy Place had not yet been disclosed as long as the first tabernacle was still functioning. This is an illustration for the present time, indicating that the gifts and sacrifices being offered were not able to clear the conscience of the worshiper. They are only a matter of food and drink and various ceremonial washings—external regulations applying until the time of the new order But when Christ came as high priest of the good things that are now already here, He went through the greater and more perfect tabernacle that is not made with human hands, that is to say, is not a part of this creation. He did not enter by means of the blood of goats and calves, but He entered the Most Holy Place once for all by His own blood, thus obtaining eternal redemption. The blood of goats and bulls and the ashes of a heifer sprinkled on those who are ceremonially unclean sanctify them so that they are outwardly clean. How much more, then, will the blood of Christ, who through the eternal Spirit offered Himself unblemished to God, cleanse our consciences from acts that lead to death, so that we may serve the living God! For this reason, Christ is the mediator of a new covenant, that those who are called may receive the promised eternal inheritance—now that He has died as a ransom to set them free from the sins committed under the first covenant In the case of a will, it is necessary to prove the death of the one who made it because a will is in force only when somebody has died; it never takes effect while the one who made it is living. This is why even the first covenant was not put into effect without blood. When Moses had proclaimed every command of the law to all the people, he took the blood of calves, together with water, scarlet wool, and branches of hyssop, and sprinkled the scroll and all the people. He said, "This is the blood of the covenant, which God has commanded you to keep." In the same way, he sprinkled with the blood both the tabernacle and everything used in its ceremonies. In fact, the law requires that nearly everything be cleansed with blood, and without the shedding of blood, there is no forgiveness It was necessary, then, for the copies of the heavenly things to be purified with these sacrifices, but the heavenly things themselves with better sacrifices than these. For Christ did not enter a sanctuary made with human hands that was only a copy of the true one; He entered heaven itself, now to appear for us in God's presence. Nor did He enter heaven to offer Himself again and again, the way the high priest enters the Most Holy Place every year with blood that is not his own. Otherwise, Christ would have had to suffer many times since the creation of the world. But He has appeared once for all at the culmination of the ages to do away with sin by the sacrifice of Himself. Just as people are destined to die once and after that to face judgment, so Christ was sacrificed once to take away the sins of many; and He will appear a second time, not to bear sin, but to bring salvation to those who are waiting for Him

Chapter 10

The law is only a shadow of the good things that are coming—not the realities themselves. For this reason, it can never, by the same sacrifices repeated endlessly year after year, make perfect those who draw near to worship. Otherwise, would they not have stopped being offered? For the worshipers would have been cleansed once for all and would no longer have felt guilty for their sins. But those sacrifices are an annual reminder of sins. It is impossible for the blood of bulls and goats to take away sins Therefore, when Christ came into the world, He said: "Sacrifice and offering you did not desire, but a body you prepared for me; with burnt offerings and sin offerings, you were not pleased. Then I said, 'Here I am—it is written about me in the scroll—I have come to do your will, my God.'" First, He said, "Sacrifices and offerings, burnt offerings and sin offerings you did not desire, nor were you pleased with them"—though they were offered in accordance with the law. Then He said, "Here I am, I have come to do your will." He sets aside the first to establish the second. And by that will, we have been made holy through the sacrifice of the body of Jesus Christ once for all Day after day, every priest stands and performs his religious duties; again and again, he offers the same sacrifices, which can never take away sins. But when this priest had offered for all time one sacrifice for sins, He sat down at the right hand of God, and since that time, He waits for His enemies to be made His footstool. For by one sacrifice, He has made perfect forever those who are being made holy The Holy Spirit also testifies to us about this. First, He says: "This is the covenant I will make with them after that time, says the Lord. I will put my laws in their hearts, and I will write them on their minds." Then He adds: "Their sins and lawless acts I will remember no more." And where these have been forgiven, sacrifice for sin is no longer necessary Therefore, brothers and sisters, since we have confidence to enter the Most Holy Place by the blood of Jesus, by a new and living way opened for us through the curtain, that is, His body, and since we have a great priest over the house of God, let us draw near to God with a sincere heart and with the full assurance that faith brings, having our hearts sprinkled to cleanse us from a guilty conscience and having our bodies washed with pure water. Let us hold unswervingly to the hope we profess, for He who promised is faithful. And let us consider how we may spur one another on toward love and good deeds, not giving up meeting together, as some are in the habit of doing, but encouraging one another—and all the more as you see the Day approaching If we deliberately keep on sinning after we have received the knowledge of the truth, no sacrifice for sins is left, but only a fearful expectation of judgment and of raging fire that will consume the enemies of God. Anyone who rejected the law of Moses died without mercy on the testimony of two or three witnesses. How much more severely do you think someone deserves to be punished who has trampled the Son of God underfoot, who has treated as an unholy thing the blood of the covenant that sanctified them, and who has insulted the Spirit of grace? For we know Him who said, "It is mine to avenge; I will repay," and again, "The Lord will judge His people." It is a dreadful thing to fall into the hands of the living God Remember those earlier days after you had received the light when you endured in a great conflict full of suffering. Sometimes you were publicly exposed to insult and persecution; at other times you stood side by side with those who were so treated. You suffered along with those in prison and joyfully accepted the confiscation of your property because you knew that you yourselves had better and lasting possessions. So do not throw away your confidence; it will be richly rewarded. You need to persevere so that when you have done the will of God, you will receive what He has promised. For, "In just a little while, He who is coming will come and will not delay." And, "But my righteous one will live by faith. And I take no pleasure in the one who shrinks back." But we do not belong to those who shrink back and are destroyed, but to those who have faith and are saved

Chapter 11

Faith is the foundation of what we hope for and the assurance of what we do not see. By faith, our ancestors received commendation. Through faith, we understand that the universe was formed by the word of God, so that what is seen was not made out of what was visible By faith, Abel offered to God a better sacrifice than Cain, earning God's approval of his gifts. Although Abel is dead, he still speaks through his faith. By faith, Enoch was taken up so that he would not experience death; he was not found because God had taken him away. Before he was taken, he was commended as one who pleased God. Without faith, it is impossible to please God because anyone who comes to Him must believe that He exists and that He rewards those who earnestly seek Him By faith, Noah, warned by God about things not yet seen, built an ark to save his family. By his faith, he condemned the world and became an heir of the righteousness that is in keeping with faith. By faith, Abraham obeyed when he was called to go to a place he would later receive as his inheritance. He went out, not knowing where he was going. By faith, he lived as a foreigner in the land of promise, dwelling in tents with Isaac and Jacob, co-heirs of the same promise. He was looking forward to a city with foundations, whose architect and builder is God By faith, even Sarah, who was past childbearing age, was enabled to bear children because she considered Him faithful who had made the promise. From this one man, who was as good as dead, came descendants as numerous as the stars in the sky and as countless as the sand on the seashore. All these people were still living by faith when they died. They did not receive the things promised; they only saw them and welcomed them from a distance, admitting that they were foreigners and strangers on earth. People who speak this way show that they are looking for a country of their own. If they had been thinking of the country they had left, they would have had the opportunity to return. Instead, they were longing for a better country—a heavenly one. Therefore, God is not ashamed to be called their God, for He has prepared a city for them By faith, Abraham, when tested, offered Isaac as a sacrifice. He who had embraced the promises was about to sacrifice his one and only son, even though God had said to him, "It is through Isaac that your offspring will be reckoned." Abraham reasoned that God could even raise the dead, and in a manner of speaking, he did receive Isaac back from death. By faith, Isaac blessed Jacob and Esau regarding their future. By faith, Jacob, when he was dying, blessed each of Joseph's sons and worshiped as he leaned on the top of his staff. By faith, Joseph, when his end was near, spoke about the exodus of the Israelites from Egypt and gave instructions concerning the burial of his bones By faith, Moses' parents hid him for three months after he was born because they saw he was no ordinary child, and they were not afraid of the king's edict. By faith, Moses, when he had grown up, refused to be known as the son of Pharaoh's daughter. He chose to be mistreated along with the people of God rather than to enjoy the fleeting pleasures of sin. He regarded disgrace for the sake of Christ as of greater value than the treasures of Egypt because he was looking ahead to his reward. By faith, he left Egypt, not fearing the king's anger; he persevered because he saw Him who is invisible. By faith, he kept the Passover and the application of blood, so that the destroyer of the firstborn would not touch the firstborn of Israel. By faith, the people passed through the Red Sea as on dry land; but when the Egyptians tried to do so, they were drowned By faith, the walls of Jericho fell after the army had marched around them for seven days. By faith, the prostitute Rahab, because she welcomed the spies, was not killed with those who were disobedient. And what more shall I say? I do not have time to tell about Gideon, Barak, Samson, Jephthah, David, Samuel, and the prophets, who through faith conquered kingdoms, administered justice, and gained what was promised; who shut the mouths of lions, quenched the fury of the flames, and escaped the edge of the sword; whose weakness was turned to strength; and who became powerful in battle and routed foreign armies. Women received back their dead, raised to life again. There were others who were tortured, refusing to be released so that they might gain an even better resurrection. Some faced jeers and flogging, and even chains and imprisonment. They were put to death by stoning; they were sawed in two; they were killed by the sword. They went about in sheepskins and goatskins, destitute, persecuted, and mistreated—the world was not worthy of them. They wandered in deserts and mountains, living in caves and in holes in the ground These were all commended for their faith, yet none of them received what had been promised, since God had planned something better for us so that only together with us would they be made perfect

Chapter 12

Therefore, since we are surrounded by such a great cloud of witnesses, let us throw off everything that hinders and the sin that so easily entangles. Let us run with perseverance the race marked out for us, fixing our eyes on Jesus, the pioneer and perfecter of faith. For the joy set before Him, He endured the cross, scorning its shame, and sat down at the right hand of the throne of God. Consider Him who endured such opposition from sinners so that you will not grow weary and lose heart In your struggle against sin, you have not yet resisted to the point of shedding your blood. And have you completely forgotten this word of encouragement that addresses you as a father addresses his son? It says, "My son, do not make light of the Lord's discipline, and do not lose heart when He rebukes you, because the Lord disciplines the one He loves, and He chastens everyone He accepts as His son." Endure hardship as discipline; God is treating you as His children. For what children are not disciplined by their father? If you are not disciplined—and everyone undergoes discipline—then you are not legitimate, not true sons and daughters at all. Moreover, we have all had human fathers who disciplined us, and we respected them for it. How much more should we submit to the Father of spirits and live! They disciplined us for a little while as they thought best, but God disciplines us for our good, in order that we may share in His holiness. No discipline seems

pleasant at the time, but painful. Later on, however, it produces a harvest of righteousness and peace for those who have been trained by it Therefore, strengthen your feeble arms and weak knees. "Make level paths for your feet," so that the lame may not be disabled, but rather healed. Make every effort to live in peace with everyone and to be holy; without holiness, no one will see the Lord. See to it that no one falls short of the grace of God and that no bitter root grows up to cause trouble and defile many. See that no one is sexually immoral or is godless like Esau, who for a single meal sold his inheritance rights as the oldest son. Afterward, as you know, when he wanted to inherit this blessing, he was rejected. Even though he sought the blessing with tears, he could not change what he had done You have not come to a mountain that can be touched and that is burning with fire; to darkness, gloom, and storm; to a trumpet blast or to such a voice speaking words that those who heard it begged that no further word be spoken to them because they could not bear what was commanded: "If even an animal touches the mountain, it must be stoned to death." The sight was so terrifying that Moses said, "I am trembling with fear." But you have come to Mount Zion, to the city of the living God, the heavenly Jerusalem. You have come to thousands upon thousands of angels in joyful assembly, to the church of the firstborn, whose names are written in heaven. You have come to God, the Judge of all, to the spirits of the righteous made perfect, to Jesus the mediator of a new covenant, and to the sprinkled blood that speaks a better word than the blood of Abel See to it that you do not refuse Him who speaks. If they did not escape when they refused Him who warned them on earth, how much less will we, if we turn away from Him who warns us from heaven? At that time, His voice shook the earth, but now He has promised, "Once more I will shake not only the earth but also the heavens." The words "once more" indicate the removing of what can be shaken—that is, created things—so that what cannot be shaken may remain. Therefore, since we are receiving a kingdom that cannot be shaken, let us be thankful and so worship God acceptably with reverence and awe, for our God is a consuming fire

Chapter 13

Keep on loving one another as brothers and sisters. Do not forget to show hospitality to strangers, for by so doing some people have shown hospitality to angels without knowing it. Continue to remember those in prison as if you were together with them in prison, and those who are mistreated as if you yourselves were suffering Marriage should be honored by all, and the marriage bed kept pure, for God will judge the adulterer and all the sexually immoral. Keep your lives free from the love of money and be content with what you have because God has said, "Never will I leave you; never will I forsake you." So we say with confidence, "The Lord is my helper; I will not be afraid. What can mere mortals do to me?" Remember your leaders, who spoke the word of God to you. Consider the outcome of their way of life and imitate their faith. Jesus Christ is the same yesterday and today and forever. Do not be carried away by all kinds of strange teachings. It is good for our hearts to be strengthened by grace, not by eating ceremonial foods, which is of no benefit to those who do so We have an altar from which those who minister at the tabernacle have no right to eat. The high priest carries the blood of animals into the Most Holy Place as a sin offering, but the bodies are burned outside the camp. And so Jesus also suffered outside the city gate to make the people holy through His own blood. Let us, then, go to Him outside the camp, bearing the disgrace He bore. For here we do not have an enduring city, but we are looking for the city that is to come Through Jesus, therefore, let us continually offer to God a sacrifice of praise—the fruit of lips that openly profess His name. And do not forget to do good and to share with others, for with such sacrifices God is pleased Have confidence in your leaders and submit to their authority because they keep watch over you as those who must give an account. Do this so that their work will be a joy, not a burden, for that would be of no benefit to you. Pray for us. We are sure that we have a clear conscience and desire to live honorably in every way. I particularly urge you to pray so that I may be restored to you soon Now may the God of peace, who through the blood of the eternal covenant brought back from the dead our Lord Jesus, that great Shepherd of the sheep, equip you with everything good for doing His will, and may He work in us what is pleasing to Him, through Jesus Christ, to whom be glory forever and ever. Amen Brothers and sisters, I urge you to bear with my word of exhortation, for in fact, I have written to you quite briefly. I want you to know that our brother Timothy has been released. If he arrives soon, I will come with him to see you. Greet all your leaders and all the Lord's people. Those from Italy send you their greetings. Grace be with you all. Amen

3. GENERAL EPISTLES

59. James

Chapter 1

Greetings from a servant of God and the Lord Jesus Christ to the twelve tribes scattered abroad. My brothers and sisters, regard it as a blessing when you face various trials. Know that the testing of your faith produces perseverance. Let perseverance finish its work so that you may be mature and complete, lacking nothing. If any of you lacks wisdom, you should ask God, who gives generously to all without finding fault, and it will be given to you. But when you ask, you must believe and not doubt, because one who doubts is like a wave of the sea, blown and tossed by the wind. That person should not expect to receive anything from the Lord; such a doubter is double-minded and unstable in all they do. The lowly brother should take pride in their high position, but the rich should take pride in their humiliation—since they will pass away like a wildflower. For the sun rises with scorching heat and withers the plant; its blossom falls and its beauty is destroyed. In the same way, the rich will fade away even while they go about their business. Blessed is the one who perseveres under trial because, having stood the test, that person will receive the crown of life that the Lord has promised to those who love him. When tempted, no one should say, "God is tempting me." For God cannot be tempted by evil, nor does he tempt anyone; but each person is tempted when they are dragged away by their own evil desire and enticed. Then, after desire has conceived, it gives birth to sin; and sin, when it is full-grown, gives birth to death. Don't be deceived, my dear brothers and sisters. Every good and perfect gift is from above, coming down from the Father of the heavenly lights, who does not change like shifting shadows. He chose to give us birth through the word of truth, that we might be a kind of firstfruits of all he created. My dear brothers and sisters, take note of this: Everyone should be quick to listen, slow to speak and slow to become angry, because human anger does not produce the righteousness that God desires. Therefore, get rid of all moral filth and the evil that is so prevalent and humbly accept the word planted in you, which can save you. Do not merely listen to the word, and so deceive yourselves. Do what it says. Anyone who listens to the word but does not do what it says is like someone who looks at his face in a mirror and, after looking at himself, goes away and immediately forgets what he looks like. But whoever looks intently into the perfect law that gives freedom, and continues in it—not forgetting what they have heard, but doing it—they will be blessed in what they do. Those who consider themselves religious and yet do not keep a tight rein on their tongues deceive themselves, and their religion is worthless. Religion that God our Father accepts as pure and faultless is this: to look after orphans and widows in their distress and to keep oneself from being polluted by the world

Chapter 2

My brothers and sisters, as believers in our glorious Lord Jesus Christ, don't show favoritism. Suppose a man comes into your meeting wearing a gold ring and fine clothes, and a poor man in filthy old clothes also comes in. If you show special attention to the man wearing fine clothes and say, "Here's a good seat for you," but say to the poor man, "You stand there" or "Sit on the floor by my feet," have you not discriminated among yourselves and become judges with evil thoughts? Listen, my dear brothers and sisters: Has not God chosen those who are poor in the eyes of the world to be rich in faith and to inherit the kingdom he promised those who love him? But you have dishonored the poor. Is it not the rich who are exploiting you? Are they not the ones who are dragging you into court? Are they not the ones who are blaspheming the noble name of him to whom you belong? If you really keep the royal law found in Scripture, "Love your neighbor as yourself," you are doing right. But if you show favoritism, you sin and are convicted by the law as lawbreakers. For whoever keeps the whole law and yet stumbles at just one point is guilty of breaking all of it. For he who said, "You shall not commit adultery," also said, "You shall not murder." If you do not commit adultery but do commit murder, you have become a lawbreaker. Speak and act as those who are going to be judged by the law that gives freedom, because judgment without mercy will be shown to anyone who has not been merciful. Mercy triumphs over judgment. What good is it, my brothers and sisters, if someone claims to have faith but has no deeds? Can such faith save them? Suppose a brother or a sister is without clothes and daily food. If one of you says to them, "Go in peace; keep warm and well fed," but does nothing about their physical needs, what good is it? In the same way, faith by itself, if it is not accompanied by action, is dead

Chapter 3

My brothers and sisters, not many of you should become teachers, for you know that we who teach will be judged more strictly. We all stumble in many ways. Anyone who is never at fault in what they say is perfect, able to keep their whole body in check. When we put bits into the mouths of horses to make them obey us, we can turn the whole animal. Take ships as an example. Although they are so large and are driven by strong winds, they are steered by a very small rudder wherever the pilot wants to go. Likewise, the tongue is a small part of the body, but it makes great boasts. Consider what a great forest is set on fire by a small spark. The tongue also is a fire, a world of evil among the parts of the body. It corrupts the whole body, sets the whole course of one's life on fire, and is itself set on fire by hell. All kinds of animals, birds, reptiles, and sea creatures are being tamed and have been tamed by mankind, but no human being can tame the tongue. It is a restless evil, full of deadly poison. With the tongue we praise our Lord and Father, and with it we curse human beings, who have been made in God's likeness. Out of the same mouth come praise and cursing. My brothers and sisters, this should not be. Can both fresh water and salt water flow from the same spring? My brothers and sisters, can a fig tree bear olives, or a grapevine bear figs? Neither can a salt spring produce fresh water. Who is wise and understanding among you? Let them show it by their good life, by deeds done in the humility that comes from wisdom. But if you harbor bitter envy and selfish ambition in your hearts, do not boast about it or deny the truth. Such "wisdom" does not come down from heaven but is earthly, unspiritual, demonic. For where you have envy and selfish ambition, there you find disorder and every evil practice. But the wisdom that comes from heaven is first of all pure; then peace-loving, considerate, submissive, full of mercy and good fruit, impartial and sincere. Peacemakers who sow in peace reap a harvest of righteousness

Chapter 4

What causes fights and quarrels among you? Don't they come from your desires that battle within you? You desire but do not have, so you kill. You covet but cannot get what you want, so you quarrel and fight. You do not have because you do not ask God. When you ask, you do not receive, because you ask with wrong motives, that you may spend what you get on your pleasures. You adulterous people, don't you know that friendship with the world means enmity against God? Therefore, anyone who chooses to be a friend of the world becomes an enemy of God. Or do you think Scripture says without reason that he jealously longs for the spirit he has caused to dwell in us? But he gives us more grace. That is why Scripture says: "God opposes the proud but shows favor to the humble." Submit yourselves, then, to God. Resist the devil, and he will flee from you. Come near to God, and he will come near to you. Wash your hands, you sinners, and purify your hearts, you double-minded. Grieve, mourn and wail. Change your laughter to mourning and your joy to gloom. Humble yourselves before the Lord, and he will lift you up. Brothers and sisters, do not slander one another. Anyone who speaks against a brother or sister or judges them speaks against the law and judges the law. When you judge the law, you are not keeping it, but sitting in judgment on it. There is only one Lawgiver and Judge, the one who is able to save and destroy. But you—who are you to judge your neighbor? Now listen, you who say, "Today or tomorrow we will go to this or that city, spend a year there, carry on business and make money." Why, you do not even know what will happen tomorrow. What is your life? You are a mist that appears for a little while and then vanishes. Instead, you ought to say, "If it is the Lord's will, we will live and do this or that." As it is, you boast in your arrogant schemes. All such boasting is evil. If anyone, then, knows the good they ought to do and doesn't do it, it is sin for them

Chapter 5

Now listen, you rich people, weep and wail because of the misery that is coming on you. Your wealth has rotted, and moths have eaten your clothes. Your gold and silver are corroded. Their corrosion will testify against you and eat your flesh like fire. You have hoarded wealth in the last days. Look! The wages you failed to pay the workers who mowed your fields are crying out against you. The cries of the harvesters have reached the ears of the Lord Almighty. You have lived on earth in luxury and self-indulgence. You have fattened yourselves in the day of slaughter. You have condemned and murdered the innocent one, who was not opposing you. Be patient, then, brothers and sisters, until the Lord's coming. See how the farmer waits for the land to yield its valuable crop, patiently waiting for the autumn and spring rains. You too, be patient and stand firm, because the Lord's coming is near. Don't grumble against one another, brothers and sisters, or you will be judged. The Judge is standing at the door! Brothers and sisters, take the prophets who spoke in the name of the Lord as an example of patience in the face of suffering. As you know, we count as blessed those who have persevered. You have heard of Job's perseverance and have seen what the Lord finally brought about. The Lord is full of compassion and mercy. Above all, my brothers and sisters, do not swear—not by heaven or by earth or by anything else. All you need to say is a simple "Yes" or "No." Otherwise you will be condemned. Is anyone among you in trouble? Let them pray. Is anyone happy? Let them sing songs of praise. Is anyone among you sick? Let them call the elders of the church to pray over them and anoint them with oil in the name of the Lord. And the prayer offered in faith will make the sick person well; the Lord will raise them up. If they have sinned, they will be forgiven. Therefore confess your sins to each other and pray for each other so that you may be healed. The prayer of a righteous person is powerful and effective. Elijah was a human being, even as we are. He prayed earnestly that it would not rain, and it did not rain on the land for three and a half years. Again he prayed, and the heavens gave rain, and the earth produced its crops. My brothers and sisters, if one of you should wander from the truth and someone should bring that person back, remember this: Whoever turns a sinner from the error of their way will save them from death and cover over a multitude of sins

60. 1 Peter

Chapter 1

Peter, an apostle of Jesus Christ, writes to the exiles scattered throughout Pontus, Galatia, Cappadocia, Asia, and Bithynia. Chosen by God the Father's foreknowledge and sanctified by the Spirit, you are called to obey and be cleansed by the blood of Jesus Christ. May grace and peace be abundantly yours Praise be to God, the Father of our Lord Jesus Christ! In His abundant mercy, He has given us new birth into a living hope through the resurrection of Jesus Christ from the dead. This inheritance is imperishable, undefiled, and unfading, kept in heaven for you. You are shielded by God's power through faith for a salvation ready to be revealed in the last time In this, you greatly rejoice, though now for a little while you may have had to suffer grief in all kinds of trials. These have come so that the proven genuineness of your faith—of greater worth than gold, which perishes even though refined by fire—may result in praise, glory, and honor when Jesus Christ is revealed. Though you have not seen Him, you love Him; and even though you do not see Him now, you believe in Him and are filled with an inexpressible and glorious joy, for you are receiving the end result of your faith, the salvation of your souls Concerning this salvation, the prophets, who spoke of the grace that was to come to you, searched intently and with the greatest care, trying to find out the time and circumstances to which the Spirit of Christ in them was pointing when He predicted the sufferings of the Messiah and the glories that would follow. It was revealed to them that they were not serving themselves but you when they spoke of the things that have now been told you by those who have preached the gospel to you by the Holy Spirit sent from heaven. Even angels long to look into these things Therefore, prepare your minds for action; be self-controlled; set your hope fully on the grace to be given you when Jesus Christ is revealed. As obedient children, do not conform to the evil desires you had when you lived in ignorance. But just as He who called you is holy, so be holy in all you do; for it is written: "Be holy, because I am holy." Since you call on a Father who judges each person's work impartially, live out your time as foreigners here in reverent fear. For you know that it was not with perishable things such as silver or gold that you were redeemed from the empty way of life handed down to you from your ancestors, but with the precious blood of Christ, a lamb without blemish or defect. He was chosen before the creation of the world but was revealed in these last times for your sake. Through Him you believe in God, who raised Him from the dead and glorified Him, and so your faith and hope are in God Now that you have purified yourselves by obeying the truth so that you have sincere love for each other, love one another deeply, from the heart. For you have been born again, not of perishable seed, but of imperishable, through the living and enduring word of God. For, "All people are like grass, and all their glory is like the flowers of the field; the grass withers and the flowers fall, but the word of the Lord endures forever." And this is the word that was preached to you

Chapter 2

Rid yourselves, therefore, of all malice, deceit,

hypocrisy, envy, and slander. Like newborn infants, long for the pure spiritual milk, so that by it you may grow up into salvation—now that you have tasted that the Lord is good Coming to Him, a living stone—rejected by humans but chosen by God and precious to Him—you also, like living stones, are being built into a spiritual house to be a holy priesthood, offering spiritual sacrifices acceptable to God through Jesus Christ. For it stands in Scripture: "See, I lay a stone in Zion, a chosen and precious cornerstone, and the one who trusts in Him will never be put to shame." Now to you who believe, this stone is precious. But to those who do not believe, "The stone the builders rejected has become the cornerstone," and, "A stone that causes people to stumble and a rock that makes them fall." They stumble because they disobey the message—which is also what they were destined for But you are a chosen people, a royal priesthood, a holy nation, God's special possession, that you may declare the praises of Him who called you out of darkness into His wonderful light. Once you were not a people, but now you are the people of God; once you had not received mercy, but now you have received mercy Dear friends, I urge you as foreigners and exiles to abstain from sinful desires, which wage war against your soul. Live such good lives among the pagans that, though they accuse you of doing wrong, they may see your good deeds and glorify God on the day He visits us Submit yourselves for the Lord's sake to every human authority: whether to the emperor, as the supreme authority, or to governors, who are sent by him to punish those who do wrong and to commend those who do right. For it is God's will that by doing good you should silence the ignorant talk of foolish people. Live as free people, but do not use your freedom as a cover-up for evil; live as God's slaves. Show proper respect to everyone, love the family of believers, fear God, honor the emperor Slaves, in reverent fear of God, submit yourselves to your masters, not only to those who are good and considerate but also to those who are harsh. For it is commendable if someone bears up under the pain of unjust suffering because they are conscious of God

Chapter 3

Wives, in the same way, submit yourselves to your own husbands so that, if any of them do not believe the word, they may be won over without words by the behavior of their wives, when they see the purity and reverence of your lives. Your beauty should not come from outward adornment, such as elaborate hairstyles and the wearing of gold jewelry or fine clothes. Rather, it should be that of your inner self, the unfading beauty of a gentle and quiet spirit, which is of great worth in God's sight. For this is the way the holy women of the past who put their hope in God used to adorn themselves. They submitted themselves to their own husbands, like Sarah, who obeyed Abraham and called him her lord. You are her daughters if you do what is right and do not give way to fear Husbands, in the same way, be considerate as you live with your wives, and treat them with respect as the weaker partner and as heirs with you of the gracious gift of life, so that nothing will hinder your prayers Finally, all of you, be like-minded, be sympathetic, love one another, be compassionate and humble. Do not repay evil with evil or insult with insult. On the contrary, repay evil with blessing, because to this you were called so that you may inherit a blessing. For, "Whoever would love life and see good days must keep their tongue from evil and their lips from deceitful speech. They must turn from evil and do good; they must seek peace and pursue it. For the eyes of the Lord are on the righteous and His ears are attentive to their prayer, but the face of the Lord is against those who do evil."

Chapter 4

Since Christ suffered in the flesh, arm yourselves also with the same attitude, because whoever suffers in the flesh has finished with sin. As a result, they do not live the rest of their earthly lives for evil human desires, but rather for the will of God. For you have spent enough time in the past doing what

pagans choose to do—living in debauchery, lust, drunkenness, orgies, carousing, and detestable idolatry. They are surprised that you do not join them in their reckless, wild living, and they heap abuse on you. But they will have to give account to Him who is ready to judge the living and the dead. For this is the reason the gospel was preached even to those who are now dead, so that they might be judged according to human standards in regard to the body, but live according to God in regard to the spirit The end of all things is near. Therefore be alert and of sober mind so that you may pray. Above all, love each other deeply, because love covers over a multitude of sins. Offer hospitality to one another without grumbling. Each of you should use whatever gift you have received to serve others, as faithful stewards of God's grace in its various forms. If anyone speaks, they should do so as one who speaks the very words of God. If anyone serves, they should do so with the strength God provides, so that in all things God may be praised through Jesus Christ. To Him be the glory and the power forever and ever. Amen Dear friends, do not be surprised at the fiery ordeal that has come on you to test you, as though something strange were happening to you. But rejoice inasmuch as you participate in the sufferings of Christ, so that you may be overjoyed when His glory is revealed. If you are insulted because of the name of Christ, you are blessed, for the Spirit of glory and of God rests on you. If you suffer, it should not be as a murderer or thief or any other kind of criminal, or even as a meddler. However, if you suffer as a Christian, do not be ashamed, but praise God that you bear that name For it is time for judgment to begin with God's household; and if it begins with us, what will the outcome be for those who do not obey the gospel of God? And, "If it is hard for the righteous to be saved, what will become of the ungodly and the sinner?" So then, those who suffer according to God's will should commit themselves to their faithful Creator and continue to do good

Chapter 5

To the elders among you, I appeal as a fellow elder and a witness of Christ's sufferings who also will share in the glory to be revealed: Be shepherds of God's flock that is under your care, watching over them—not because you must, but because you are willing, as God wants you to be; not pursuing dishonest gain, but eager to serve; not lording it over those entrusted to you, but being examples to the flock. And when the Chief Shepherd appears, you will receive the crown of glory that will never fade away Young men, in the same way be submissive to those who are older. All of you, clothe yourselves with humility toward one another, because, "God opposes the proud but shows favor to the humble." Humble yourselves, therefore, under God's mighty hand, that He may lift you up in due time. Cast all your anxiety on Him because He cares for you. Be alert and of sober mind. Your enemy the devil prowls around like a roaring lion looking for someone to devour. Resist him, standing firm in the faith, because you know that the family of believers throughout the world is undergoing the same kinds of sufferings And the God of all grace, who called you to His eternal glory in Christ, after you have suffered a little while, will Himself restore you and make you strong, firm, and steadfast. To Him be the power forever and ever. Amen Through Silas, whom I consider a faithful brother, I have written to you briefly, encouraging you and testifying that this is the true grace of God. Stand fast in it The church that is in Babylon, chosen together with you, sends you greetings, and so does my son Mark. Greet one another with a kiss of love. Peace to all of you who are in Christ

61. 2 Peter

Chapter 1

Simon Peter, servant and apostle of Jesus Christ, to those who have obtained a faith as precious as ours through the righteousness of our God and Savior Jesus Christ: Grace and peace be multiplied to you through the knowledge of God and of Jesus our Lord. His divine power has granted to us all things that pertain to life and godliness, through the knowledge of Him who called us to His own glory and excellence. By these He has granted to us His precious and very great promises, so that through them you may become partakers of the divine nature, having escaped from the corruption that is in the world because of sinful desire For this very reason, make every effort to supplement your faith with virtue; and virtue with knowledge; and knowledge with self-control; and self-control with steadfastness; and steadfastness with godliness; and godliness with brotherly affection; and brotherly affection with love. For if these qualities are yours and are increasing, they keep you from being ineffective or unfruitful in the knowledge of our Lord Jesus Christ. For whoever lacks these qualities is so nearsighted that he is blind, having forgotten that he was cleansed from his former sins Therefore, brothers and sisters, be all the more diligent to confirm your calling and election, for if you practice these qualities you will never fall. For in this way there will be richly provided for you an entrance into the eternal kingdom of our Lord and Savior Jesus Christ Therefore, I intend always to remind you of these qualities, though you know them and are established in the truth that you have. I think it right, as long as I am in this body, to stir you up by way of reminder, since I know that the putting off of my body will be soon, as our Lord Jesus Christ has made clear to me. And I will make every effort so that after my departure you may be able at any time to recall these things For we did not follow cleverly devised myths when we made known to you the power and coming of our Lord Jesus Christ, but we were eyewitnesses of His majesty. For when He received honor and glory from God the Father, and the voice was borne to Him by the Majestic Glory, "This is my beloved Son, with whom I am well pleased," we ourselves heard this very voice borne from heaven, for we were with Him on the holy mountain. And we have the prophetic word more fully confirmed, to which you will do well to pay attention as to a lamp shining in a dark place, until the day dawns and the morning star rises in your hearts, knowing this first of all, that no prophecy of Scripture comes from someone's own interpretation. For no prophecy was ever produced by the will of man, but men spoke from God as they were carried along by the Holy Spirit

Chapter 2

There were also false prophets among the people, just as there will be false teachers among you. They will secretly introduce destructive heresies, even denying the sovereign Lord who bought them—bringing swift destruction on themselves. Many will follow their depraved conduct and will bring the way of truth into disrepute. In their greed, these teachers will exploit you with fabricated stories. Their condemnation has long been hanging over them, and their destruction has not been sleeping For if God did not spare angels when they sinned, but sent them to hell, putting them in chains of darkness to be held for judgment; if He did not spare the ancient world when He brought the flood on its ungodly people, but protected Noah, a preacher of righteousness, and seven others; if He condemned the cities of Sodom and Gomorrah by burning them to ashes, and made them

an example of what is going to happen to the ungodly; and if He rescued Lot, a righteous man, who was distressed by the depraved conduct of the lawless (for that righteous man, living among them day after day, was tormented in his righteous soul by the lawless deeds he saw and heard)—then the Lord knows how to rescue the godly from trials and to hold the unrighteous for punishment on the day of judgment. This is especially true of those who follow the corrupt desire of the flesh and despise authority Bold and arrogant, these people are not afraid to heap abuse on celestial beings; yet even angels, although they are stronger and more powerful, do not bring slanderous accusations against such beings in the presence of the Lord. But these people blaspheme in matters they do not understand. They are like unreasoning animals, creatures of instinct, born only to be caught and destroyed, and like animals they too will perish They will be paid back with harm for the harm they have done. Their idea of pleasure is to carouse in broad daylight. They are blots and blemishes, reveling in their pleasures while they feast with you. With eyes full of adultery, they never stop sinning; they seduce the unstable; they are experts in greed—an accursed brood! They have left the straight way and wandered off to follow the way of Balaam son of Bezer, who loved the wages of wickedness. But he was rebuked for his wrongdoing by a donkey—an animal without speech—who spoke with a human voice and restrained the prophet's madness These are wells without water, clouds that are carried with a tempest; to whom the gloom of utter darkness has been reserved forever. For they speak great swelling words of emptiness, they allure through the lusts of the flesh, through much wantonness, those that were clean escaped from them who live in error. While they promise them liberty, they themselves are slaves of corruption; for by whom a person is overcome, by the same he is brought into bondage

Chapter 3

This second epistle, beloved, I now write unto you; in both of which I stir up your pure minds by way of reminder: that you may be mindful of the words which were spoken before by the holy prophets, and of the commandment of us the apostles of the Lord and Savior: knowing this first, that there shall come in the last days scoffers, walking after their own lusts, and saying, "Where is the promise of His coming? For since the fathers fell asleep, all things continue as they were from the beginning of the creation." For this they willingly are ignorant of, that by the word of God the heavens were of old, and the earth standing out of the water and in the water: whereby the world that then was, being overflowed with water, perished: but the heavens and the earth, which are now, by the same word are kept in store, reserved unto fire against the day of judgment and perdition of ungodly men But, beloved, do not forget this one thing, that with the Lord one day is as a thousand years, and a thousand years as one day. The Lord is not slack concerning His promise, as some count slackness; but is longsuffering to us-ward, not willing that any should perish, but that all should come to repentance. But the day of the Lord will come as a thief in the night; in which the heavens shall pass away with a great noise, and the elements shall melt with fervent heat, the earth also and the works that are therein shall be burned up Seeing then that all these things shall be dissolved, what manner of persons ought ye to be in all holy conversation and godliness, looking for and hasting unto the coming of the day of God, wherein the heavens being on fire shall be dissolved, and the elements shall melt with fervent heat? Nevertheless we, according to His promise, look for new heavens and a new earth, wherein dwelleth righteousness Wherefore, beloved, seeing that ye look for such things, be diligent that ye may be found of Him in peace, without spot, and blameless. And account that the longsuffering of our Lord is salvation; even as our beloved brother Paul also according to the wisdom given unto him hath written unto you; as also in all his epistles, speaking in them of these things; in which are some things hard to be understood, which they that are unlearned and unstable wrest, as they do also the other scriptures, unto their own destruction Ye therefore, beloved, seeing ye know these things before, beware lest ye also, being led away with the error of the wicked, fall from your own stedfastness. But grow in grace, and in the knowledge of our Lord and Savior Jesus Christ. To him be glory both now and for ever. Amen

62. 1 John

CHAPTER 1

From the beginning, we have heard, seen with our eyes, looked upon, and touched with our hands the Word of life. This life was revealed to us. We saw it, witnessed it, and now we share with you the eternal life that was with the Father and has been revealed to us. We proclaim to you what we have seen and heard so that you may also have fellowship with us, and indeed our fellowship is with the Father and with His Son, Jesus Christ. We write this to make your joy complete This is the message we have heard from Him and declare to you: God is light; in Him, there is no darkness at all. If we claim to have fellowship with Him yet walk in the darkness, we lie and do not live out the truth. However, if we walk in the light, as He is in the light, we have fellowship with one another, and the blood of Jesus, His Son, purifies us from all sin If we claim to be without sin, we deceive ourselves and the truth is not in us. If we confess our sins, He is faithful and just and will forgive us our sins and purify us from all unrighteousness. If we claim we have not sinned, we make Him out to be a liar and His word has no place in our lives

CHAPTER 2

My dear children, I write this to you so that you will not sin. But if anybody does sin, we have an advocate with the Father—Jesus Christ, the Righteous One. He is the atoning sacrifice for our sins, and not only for ours but also for the sins of the whole world We know that we have come to know Him if we keep His commands. Whoever says, "I know Him," but does not do what He commands is a liar, and the truth is not in that person. But if anyone obeys His word, love for God is truly made complete in them. This is how we know we are in Him: Whoever claims to live in Him must live as Jesus did I am not writing you a new command, but an old one, which you have had since the beginning. This old command is the message you have heard. Yet I am writing you a new command; its truth is seen in Him and in you, because the darkness is passing and the true light is already shining Anyone who claims to be in the light but hates a brother or sister is still in the darkness. Anyone who loves their brother and sister lives in the light, and there is nothing in them to make them stumble. But anyone who hates a brother or sister is in the darkness and walks around in the darkness. They do not know where they are going, because the darkness has blinded them I am writing to you, dear children, because your sins have been forgiven on account of His name

CHAPTER 3

See what great love the Father has lavished on us, that we should be called children of God! And that is what we are! The reason the world does not know us is that it did not know Him. Dear friends, now we are children of God, and what we will be has not yet been made known. But we know that when Christ appears, we shall be like Him, for we shall see Him as He is. All who have this hope in Him purify themselves, just as He is pure Anyone who sins breaks the law; in fact, sin is lawlessness. But you know that He appeared so that He might take away our sins. And in Him is no sin. No one who lives in Him keeps on sinning. No one who continues to sin has either seen Him or

known Him Dear children, do not let anyone lead you astray. The one who does what is right is righteous, just as He is righteous. The one who does what is sinful is of the devil, because the devil has been sinning from the beginning. The reason the Son of God appeared was to destroy the devil's work No one who is born of God will continue to sin, because God's seed remains in them; they cannot go on sinning, because they have been born of God. This is how we know who the children of God are and who the children of the devil are: Anyone who does not do what is right is not God's child, nor is anyone who does not love their brother and sister

CHAPTER 4

Dear friends, do not believe every spirit, but test the spirits to see whether they are from God, because many false prophets have gone out into the world. This is how you can recognize the Spirit of God: Every spirit that acknowledges that Jesus Christ has come in the flesh is from God, but every spirit that does not acknowledge Jesus is not from God. This is the spirit of the antichrist, which you have heard is coming and even now is already in the world You, dear children, are from God and have overcome them, because the one who is in you is greater than the one who is in the world. They are from the world and therefore speak from the viewpoint of the world, and the world listens to them. We are from God, and whoever knows God listens to us; but whoever is not from God does not listen to us. This is how we recognize the Spirit of truth and the spirit of falsehood

CHAPTER 5

Everyone who believes that Jesus is the Christ is born of God, and everyone who loves the father loves his child as well. This is how we know that we love the children of God: by loving God and carrying out His commands. In fact, this is love for God: to keep His commands. And His commands are not burdensome, for everyone born of God overcomes the world. This is the victory that has overcome the world, even our faith Who is it that overcomes the world? Only the one who believes that Jesus is the Son of God This is the one who came by water and blood—Jesus Christ. He did not come by water only, but by water and blood. And it is the Spirit who testifies, because the Spirit is the truth. For there are three that testify: the Spirit, the water, and the blood; and the three are in agreement We accept human testimony, but God's testimony is greater because it is the testimony of God, which he has given about His Son. Whoever believes in the Son of God accepts this testimony. Whoever does not believe God has made Him out to be a liar, because they have not believed the testimony God has given about His Son And this is the testimony: God has given us eternal life, and this life is in his Son. Whoever has the Son has life; whoever does not have the Son of God does not have life I write these things to you who believe in the name of the Son of God so that you may know that you have eternal life. This is the confidence we have in approaching God: that if we ask anything according to His will, He hears us. And if we know that He hears us—whatever we ask—we know that we have what we asked of Him If you see any brother or sister committing a sin that does not lead to death, you should pray, and God will give them life. I refer to those whose sin does not lead to death. There is a sin that leads to death. I am not saying that you should pray about that. All wrongdoing is sin, and there is sin that does not lead to death We know that anyone born of God does not continue to sin; the one who was born of God keeps them safe, and the evil one cannot harm them. We know that we are children of God, and that the whole world is under the control of the evil one. But we know also that the Son of God has come and has given us understanding, so that we may know Him who is true. And we are in Him who is true by being in His Son Jesus Christ. He is the true God and eternal life Dear children, keep yourselves from idols

63. 2 John

CHAPTER 1

1 To the elect lady and her children, whom I cherish in truth—and not only I, but also all who have come to know the truth—2 for the truth that resides within you and will remain with you forever: 3 Grace, mercy, and peace be with you from God the Father and from the Lord Jesus Christ, the Son of the Father, accompanied by truth and love 4 I was overjoyed to find some of your children walking in truth, just as we received command from the Father. 5 And now, dear lady, I urge you—not as though I were writing a new commandment, but the one we have had from the beginning—that we love one another. 6 This love means walking according to His commands. This is the command, just as you have heard from the beginning; you must walk in it 7 Many deceivers, who do not acknowledge Jesus Christ as coming in the flesh, have gone out into the world. Such people are deceivers and antichrists. 8 Watch yourselves, so that you may not lose what we have worked for, but may win a full reward. 9 Anyone who runs ahead and does not continue in the teaching of Christ does not have God; whoever continues in the teaching has both the Father and the Son 10 If anyone comes to you and does not bring this teaching, do not take them into your house or even greet them. 11 For whoever greets them shares in their wicked work 12 Though I have much to write to you, I would rather not use paper and ink. Instead, I hope to visit you and talk face to face, so that our joy may be complete 13 The children of your elect sister send you their greetings. Amen

64. 3 John

CHAPTER 1

1 From the elder to the esteemed Gaius, whom I love sincerely. 2 Beloved, I pray that in all respects you may prosper and enjoy good health, just as your soul prospers. 3 I was overjoyed when the brothers arrived and testified to your fidelity to the truth, demonstrating how you live in accordance with the truth. 4 There is no greater joy for me than to hear that my children are living in the truth 5 You are faithful in what you do for the brothers and sisters, even for strangers, 6 who have testified to your love before the church. You will do well to assist them on their journey in a manner worthy of God, 7 for they set out for the sake of His name, accepting nothing from the pagans. 8 We ought therefore to support such people, so that we may be fellow workers for the truth 9 I wrote to the church, but Diotrephes, who loves to be first, refuses to acknowledge us. 10 Therefore, if I come, I will call attention to what he is doing, spreading malicious nonsense about us. Not satisfied with that, he refuses to welcome the brothers and sisters, and even prevents those who want to do so and expels them from the church 11 Beloved, do not imitate what is evil but what is good. Whoever does good is from God; whoever does evil has not seen God. 12 Demetrius is well spoken of by everyone—and even by the truth itself. We also speak well of him, and you know that our testimony is true 13 I have much to write to you, but I do not want to do so with pen and ink. 14 I hope to see you soon, and we will talk face to face Peace to you. The friends here send their greetings. Greet the friends there by name

65. Jude

CHAPTER 1

1 Jude, a servant of Jesus Christ and brother of James, writes to those who are called, sanctified by God the Father and preserved in Jesus Christ: 2 May mercy, peace, and love be multiplied to you 3 Beloved, while I was very eager to write to you about our common salvation, I felt it necessary to write appealing to you to contend earnestly for the faith that was once delivered to all the saints. 4 For certain individuals have crept in unnoticed—long ago marked out for this condemnation—ungodly people who pervert the grace of our God into sensuality and deny our only Master and Lord, Jesus Christ 5 I want to remind you—though you already know this—that the Lord, after saving a people out of Egypt, subsequently destroyed those who did not believe. 6 And the angels who did not keep their positions of authority but abandoned their proper dwelling—these he has kept in darkness, bound with everlasting chains for judgment on the great Day 7 In a similar way, Sodom and Gomorrah and the surrounding towns gave themselves up to sexual immorality and perversion. They serve as an example by undergoing a punishment of eternal fire 8 In the same manner, these dreamers also pollute their own bodies, reject authority, and slander celestial beings. 9 Yet even the archangel Michael, when he was disputing with the devil about the body of Moses, did not dare to bring a slanderous accusation against him, but said, "The Lord rebuke you."

10 But these people slander whatever they do not understand, and the very things they do understand by instinct—as irrational animals do—will destroy them 11 Woe to them! They have taken the way of Cain; they have rushed for profit into Balaam's error; they have been destroyed in Korah's rebellion 12 These are blemishes at your love feasts, eating with you without reverence—shepherds feeding only themselves. They are clouds without water, carried along by the wind; autumn trees, fruitless, doubly dead, uprooted 13 They are wild waves of the sea, foaming up their shame; wandering stars, for whom the blackest darkness has been reserved forever 14 Enoch, the seventh from Adam, prophesied about them: "See, the Lord is coming with thousands upon thousands of his holy ones 15 to judge everyone, and to convict all the ungodly of all the ungodly acts they have done in the ungodly way, and of all the defiant words ungodly sinners have spoken against him."

16 These are grumblers and faultfinders; they follow their own evil desires; they boast about themselves and flatter others for their own advantage 17 But you, beloved, remember what the apostles of our Lord Jesus Christ foretold. 18 They said to you, "In the last times there will be scoffers who will follow their own ungodly desires." 19 These are the people who divide you, who follow mere natural instincts and do not have the Spirit 20 But you, beloved, building yourselves up in your most holy faith and praying in the Holy Spirit, 21 keep yourselves in God's love as you wait for the mercy of our Lord Jesus Christ to bring you to eternal life 22 And have mercy on those who doubt; 23 save others by snatching them from the fire; to others show mercy, mixed with fear—hating even the clothing stained by corrupted flesh 24 Now to Him who is able to keep you from stumbling and to present you faultless before the presence of His glory with exceeding joy, 25 to the only God our Savior, be glory, majesty, power, and authority, through Jesus Christ our Lord, before all ages, now and forevermore! Amen

4. APOCALYPTIC

66. Revelation

Chapter 1

The Revelation of Jesus Christ, bestowed by God to reveal to His servants the imminent events, was sent and delivered by His angel to His servant John. John bore witness to the word of God and the testimony of Jesus Christ, recounting all he saw. Blessed are those who read, hear, and heed the words of this prophecy, for the time is near. Grace and peace to the churches in Asia from He who is, who was, and who is to come; from the seven spirits before His throne; and from Jesus Christ—the faithful witness, the firstborn from the dead, and the ruler of the kings of the earth. To Him who loves us and has freed us from our sins by His blood, who has made us kings and priests to serve His Father—to Him be glory and power forever! Amen. Behold, He is coming with the clouds, and every eye will see Him, even those who pierced Him; all peoples on earth will mourn because of Him. So shall it be! Amen. I am the Alpha and the Omega, says the Lord God, "who is, and who was, and who is to come, the Almighty." John, your brother, who shares with you in Jesus the tribulation and kingdom and patient endurance, was on the island of Patmos on account of the word of God and the testimony of Jesus. On the Lord's Day, I was in the Spirit, and I heard behind me a loud voice like a trumpet, which said: "Write on a scroll what you see and send it to the seven churches: to Ephesus, Smyrna, Pergamum, Thyatira, Sardis, Philadelphia, and Laodicea." I turned around to see the voice that was speaking to me. And when I turned I saw seven golden lampstands, and among the lampstands was someone like the Son of Man, dressed in a robe reaching down to his feet and with a golden sash around his chest. The hair on his head was white like wool, as white as snow, and his eyes were like blazing fire. His feet were like bronze glowing in a furnace, and his voice was like the sound of rushing waters. In his right hand, he held seven stars, and coming out of his mouth was a sharp, double-edged sword. His face was like the sun shining in all its brilliance. When I saw him, I fell at his feet as though dead. Then he placed his right hand on me and said: "Do not be afraid. I am the First and the Last. I am the Living One; I was dead, and now look, I am alive forever and ever! And I hold the keys of death and Hades. Write, therefore, what you have seen, what is now and what will take place later. The mystery of the seven stars that you saw in my right hand and of the seven golden lampstands is this: The seven stars are the angels of the seven churches, and the seven lampstands are the seven churches."

Chapter 2

To the angel of the church in Ephesus write: These are the words of him who holds the seven stars in his right hand and walks among the seven golden lampstands. I know your deeds, your hard work and your perseverance. I know that you cannot tolerate wicked people, that you have tested those who claim to be apostles but are not, and have found them false. You have persevered and have endured hardships for my name, and have not grown weary. Yet I hold this against you: You have forsaken the love you had at first. Consider how far you have fallen! Repent and do the things you did at first. If you do not repent, I will come to you and remove your lampstand from its place. But you have this in your favor: You hate the practices of the Nicolaitans, which I also hate. Whoever has ears, let them hear what the Spirit says to the churches. To the one who is victorious, I will give the right to eat from the tree of life, which is in the paradise of God. To the angel of the church in Smyrna write: These are the words of him who is the First and the Last, who died and came to life again. I know your afflictions and your poverty—yet you are rich! I know about the slander of those who say they are Jews and are not, but are a synagogue of Satan. Do not be afraid of what you are about to suffer. I tell you, the devil will put some of you in prison to test you, and you will suffer persecution for ten days. Be faithful, even to the point of death, and I will give you life as your victor's crown. Whoever has ears, let them hear what the Spirit says to the churches. The one who is victorious will not be hurt at all by the second death. To the angel of the church in Pergamum write: These are the words of him who has the sharp, double-edged sword. I know where you live—where Satan has his throne. Yet you remain true to my name. You did not renounce your faith in me, not even in the days of Antipas, my faithful witness, who was put to death in your city—where Satan lives. Nevertheless, I have a few things against you: There are some among you who hold to the teaching of Balaam, who taught Balak to entice the Israelites to sin so that they ate food sacrificed to idols and committed sexual immorality. Likewise, you also have those who hold to the teaching of the Nicolaitans. Repent therefore! Otherwise, I will soon come to you and will fight against them with the sword of my mouth. Whoever has ears, let them hear what the Spirit says to the churches. To the one who is victorious, I will give some of the hidden manna. I will also give that person a white stone with a new name written on it, known only to the one who receives it. To the angel of the church in Thyatira write: These are the words of the Son of God, whose eyes are like blazing fire and whose feet are like burnished bronze. I know your deeds, your love and faith, your service and perseverance, and that you are now doing more than you did at first. Nevertheless, I have this against you: You tolerate that woman Jezebel, who calls herself a prophet. By her teaching, she misleads my servants into sexual immorality and the eating of food sacrificed to idols. I have given her time to repent of her immorality, but she is unwilling. So I will cast her on a bed of suffering, and I will make those who commit adultery with her suffer intensely unless they repent of her ways. I will strike her children dead. Then all the churches will know that I am he who searches hearts and minds, and I will repay each of you according to your deeds. Now I say to the rest of you in Thyatira, to you who do not hold to her teaching and have not learned Satan's so-called deep secrets, I will not impose any other burden on you, except to hold on to what you have until I come. To the one who is victorious and does my will to the end, I will give authority over the nations—that one 'will rule them with an iron scepter and will dash them to pieces like pottery'—just as I have received authority from my Father. I will also give that one the morning star. Whoever has ears, let them hear what the Spirit says to the churches

Chapter 3

To the angel of the church in Sardis write: These are the words of him who holds the seven spirits of God and the seven stars. I know your deeds; you have a reputation of being alive, but you are dead. Wake up! Strengthen what remains and is about to die, for I have found your deeds unfinished in the sight of my God. Remember, therefore, what you have received and heard; hold it fast, and repent. But if you do not wake up, I will come like a thief, and you will not know at what time I will come to you. Yet you have a few people in Sardis who have not soiled their clothes. They will walk with me, dressed in white, for they are worthy. The one who is victorious will, like them, be dressed in white. I will never blot out the name of that person from the book of life, but will acknowledge that name before my Father and his angels. Whoever has ears, let them hear what the Spirit says to the churches. To the angel of the church in Philadelphia write: These are the words of him who is holy and true, who holds the key of David. What he opens no one can shut, and what he shuts no one can open. I know your deeds. See, I have placed before you an open door that no one can shut. I know that you have little strength, yet you have kept my word and have not denied my name. I will make those who are of the synagogue of Satan, who claim to be Jews though they are not, but are liars—I will make them come and fall down at your feet and acknowledge that I have loved you. Since you have kept my command to endure patiently, I will also keep you from the hour of trial that is going to come on the whole world to test the inhabitants of the earth. I am coming soon. Hold on to what you have, so that no one will take your crown. The one who is victorious I will make a pillar in the temple of my God. Never again will they leave it. I will write on them the name of my God and the name of the city of my God, the new Jerusalem, which is coming down out of heaven from my God; and I will also write on them my new name. Whoever has ears, let them hear what the Spirit says to the churches. To the angel of the church in Laodicea write: These are the words of the Amen, the faithful and true witness, the ruler of God's creation. I know your deeds, that you are neither cold nor hot. I wish you were either one or the other! So, because you are lukewarm—neither hot nor cold—I am about to spit you out of my mouth. You say, 'I am rich; I have acquired wealth and do not need a thing.' But you do not realize that you are wretched, pitiful, poor, blind and naked. I counsel you to buy from me gold refined in the fire, so you can become rich; and white clothes to wear, so you can cover your shameful nakedness; and salve to put on your eyes, so you can see. Those whom I love I rebuke and discipline. So be earnest and repent. Here I am! I stand at the door and knock. If anyone hears my voice and opens the door, I will come in and eat with that person, and they with me. To the one who is victorious, I will give the right to sit with me on my throne, just as I was victorious and sat down with my Father on his throne. Whoever has ears, let them hear what the Spirit says to the churches

Chapter 4

After this I looked, and there before me was a door standing open in heaven. And the voice I had first heard speaking to me like a trumpet said, "Come up here, and I will show you what must take place after this." At once I was in the Spirit, and there before me was a throne in heaven with someone sitting on it. The one who sat there had the appearance of jasper and carnelian. A rainbow that shone like an emerald encircled the throne. Surrounding the throne were twenty-four other thrones, and seated on them were twenty-four elders. They were dressed in white and had crowns of gold on their heads. From the throne came flashes of lightning, rumblings and peals of thunder. In front of the throne, seven lamps were blazing. These are the seven spirits of God. Also in front of the throne there was what looked like a sea of glass, clear as crystal. In the center, around the throne, were four living creatures, and they were covered with eyes, in front and in back. The first living creature was like a lion, the second was like an ox, the third had a face like a man, the fourth was like a flying eagle. Each of the four living creatures had six wings and was covered with eyes all around, even under its wings. Day and night they never stop saying: "'Holy, holy, holy is the Lord God Almighty,' who was, and is, and is to come." Whenever the living creatures

give glory, honor and thanks to him who sits on the throne and who lives forever and ever, the twenty-four elders fall down before him who sits on the throne and worship him who lives forever and ever. They lay their crowns before the throne and say: "You are worthy, our Lord and God, to receive glory and honor and power, for you created all things, and by your will they were created and have their being."

Chapter 5

Then I saw in the right hand of him who sat on the throne a scroll with writing on both sides and sealed with seven seals. And I saw a mighty angel proclaiming in a loud voice, "Who is worthy to break the seals and open the scroll?" But no one in heaven or on earth or under the earth could open the scroll or even look inside it. I wept and wept because no one was found who was worthy to open the scroll or look inside. Then one of the elders said to me, "Do not weep! See, the Lion of the tribe of Judah, the Root of David, has triumphed. He is able to open the scroll and its seven seals." Then I saw a Lamb, looking as if it had been slain, standing at the center of the throne, encircled by the four living creatures and the elders. The Lamb had seven horns and seven eyes, which are the seven spirits of God sent out into all the earth. He went and took the scroll from the right hand of him who sat on the throne. And when he had taken it, the four living creatures and the twenty-four elders fell down before the Lamb. Each one had a harp and they were holding golden bowls full of incense, which are the prayers of God's people. And they sang a new song, saying: "You are worthy to take the scroll and to open its seals, because you were slain, and with your blood you purchased for God persons from every tribe and language and people and nation. You have made them to be a kingdom and priests to serve our God, and they will reign on the earth." Then I looked and heard the voice of many angels, numbering thousands upon thousands, and ten thousand times ten thousand. They encircled the throne and the living creatures and the elders. In a loud voice they were saying: "Worthy is the Lamb, who was slain, to receive power and wealth and wisdom and strength and honor and glory and praise!" Then I heard every creature in heaven and on earth and under the earth and on the sea, and all that is in them, saying: "To him who sits on the throne and to the Lamb be praise and honor and glory and power, forever and ever!" The four living creatures said, "Amen," and the elders fell down and worshiped

Chapter 6

I witnessed the Lamb opening one of the seals, and heard one of the four living creatures proclaim with a voice like thunder, "Come and see." I looked and saw a white horse. Its rider held a bow, and a crown was given to him as he rode out as a conqueror bent on conquest. Upon the opening of the second seal, I heard the second creature say, "Come and see." A red horse appeared, and its rider was granted the power to remove peace from the earth and to make men slay each other; and a great sword was given to him. When the third seal was opened, I heard the third creature say, "Come and see." I saw a black horse, and its rider held a pair of scales. Then I heard what seemed like a voice among the four living creatures saying, "A quart of wheat for a day's wages, and three quarts of barley for a day's wages; but do not damage the oil and the wine." With the fourth seal's opening, the voice of the fourth creature commanded, "Come and see." I looked and there before me was a pale horse. Its rider was named Death, and Hades was following close behind him. They were given power over a fourth of the earth to kill by sword, famine, and plague, and by the wild beasts of the earth. When he opened the fifth seal, I saw under the altar the souls of those who had been slain because of the word of God and the testimony they had maintained. They called out in a loud voice, "How long, Sovereign Lord, holy and true, until you judge the inhabitants of the earth and avenge our blood?" Then each of them was given a white robe, and they were told to wait a little longer, until the full number of their fellow servants, their brothers and sisters, were killed just as they had been. I watched as he opened the sixth seal. There was a great earthquake. The sun turned black like sackcloth made of goat hair, the whole moon turned blood red, and the stars in the sky fell to earth, as figs drop from a fig tree when shaken by a strong wind. The heavens receded like a scroll being rolled up, and every mountain and island was removed from its place. Then the kings of the earth, the princes, the generals, the rich, the mighty, and every slave and free person hid in caves and among the rocks of the mountains. They called to the mountains and the rocks, "Fall on us and hide us from the face of him who sits on the throne and from the wrath of the Lamb! For the great day of their wrath has come, and who can withstand it?"

Chapter 7

After this, I saw four angels standing at the four corners of the earth, holding back the four winds of the earth to prevent any wind from blowing on the land or the sea or on any tree. Then I saw another angel coming from the east, having the seal of the living God. He called out in a loud voice to the four angels who had been given power to harm the land and the sea: "Do not harm the land or the sea or the trees until we put a seal on the foreheads of the servants of our God." Then I heard the number of those who were sealed: 144,000 from all the tribes of Israel. From the tribe of Judah 12,000 were sealed, from the tribe of Reuben 12,000, from the tribe of Gad 12,000, from the tribe of Asher 12,000, from the tribe of Naphtali 12,000, from the tribe of Manasseh 12,000, from the tribe of Simeon 12,000, from the tribe of Levi 12,000, from the tribe of Issachar 12,000, from the tribe of Zebulun 12,000, from the tribe of Joseph 12,000, from the tribe of Benjamin 12,000. After this I looked, and there before me was a great multitude that no one could count, from every nation, tribe, people and language, standing before the throne and before the Lamb. They were wearing white robes and were holding palm branches in their hands. And they cried out in a loud voice: "Salvation belongs to our God, who sits on the throne, and to the Lamb." All the angels were standing around the throne and around the elders and the four living creatures. They fell down on their faces before the throne and worshiped God, saying: "Amen! Praise and glory and wisdom and thanks and honor and power and strength be to our God for ever and ever. Amen!" Then one of the elders asked me, "These in white robes—who are they, and where did they come from?" I answered, "Sir, you know." And he said, "These are they who have come out of the great tribulation; they have washed their robes and made them white in the blood of the Lamb. Therefore, they are before the throne of God and serve him day and night in his temple; and he who sits on the throne will shelter them with his presence. 'Never again will they hunger; never again will they thirst. The sun will not beat down on them,' nor any scorching heat. For the Lamb at the center of the throne will be their shepherd; 'he will lead them to springs of living water.' 'And God will wipe away every tear from their eyes.'"

Chapter 8

When he opened the seventh seal, there was silence in heaven for about half an hour. And I saw the seven angels who stand before God, and seven trumpets were given to them. Another angel, who had a golden censer, came and stood at the altar. He was given much incense to offer, with the prayers of all God's people, on the golden altar in front of the throne. The smoke of the incense, together with the prayers of God's people, went up before God from the angel's hand. Then the angel took the censer, filled it with fire from the altar, and hurled it on the earth; and there came peals of thunder, rumblings, flashes of lightning and an earthquake. Then the seven angels who had the seven trumpets prepared to sound them. The first angel sounded his trumpet, and there came hail and fire mixed with blood, and it was hurled down on the earth. A third of the earth was burned up, a third of the trees were burned up, and all the green grass was burned up. The second angel sounded his trumpet, and something like a huge mountain, all ablaze, was thrown into the sea. A third of the sea turned into blood, a third of the living creatures in the sea died, and a third of the ships were destroyed. The third angel sounded his trumpet, and a great star, blazing like a torch, fell from the sky on a third of the rivers and on the springs of water—the name of the star is Wormwood. A third of the waters turned bitter, and many people died from the waters that had become bitter. The fourth angel sounded his trumpet, and a third of the sun was struck, a third of the moon, and a third of the stars, so that a third of them turned dark. A third of the day was without light, and also a third of the night. As I watched, I heard an eagle that was flying in midair call out in a loud voice: "Woe! Woe! Woe to the inhabitants of the earth, because of the trumpet blasts about to be sounded by the other three angels!"

Chapter 9

The fifth angel sounded his trumpet, and I saw a star that had fallen from the sky to the earth. The star was given the key to the shaft of the Abyss. When he opened the Abyss, smoke rose from it like the smoke from a gigantic furnace. The sun and sky were darkened by the smoke from the Abyss. And out of the smoke locusts came down on the earth and were given power like that of scorpions of the earth. They were told not to harm the grass of the earth or any plant or tree, but only those people who did not have the seal of God on their foreheads. They were not allowed to kill them but only to torture them for five months. And the agony they suffered was like that of the sting of a scorpion when it strikes. During those days people will seek death but will not find it; they will long to die, but death will elude them. The locusts looked like horses prepared for battle. On their heads they wore something like crowns of gold, and their faces resembled human faces. Their hair was like women's hair, and their teeth were like lions' teeth. They had breastplates like breastplates of iron, and the sound of their wings was like the thundering of many horses and chariots rushing into battle. They had tails with stingers, like scorpions, and in their tails they had power to torment people for five months. They had as king over them the angel of the Abyss, whose name in Hebrew is Abaddon and in Greek is Apollyon (that is, Destroyer). The first woe is past; two other woes are yet to come. The sixth angel sounded his trumpet, and I heard a voice coming from the four horns of the golden altar that is before God. It said to the sixth angel who had the trumpet, "Release the four angels who are bound at the great river Euphrates." And the four angels who had been kept ready for this very hour and day and month and year were released to kill a third of mankind. The number of the mounted troops was twice ten thousand times ten thousand. I heard their number. The horses and riders I saw in my vision looked like this: Their breastplates were fiery red, dark blue, and yellow as sulfur. The heads of the horses resembled the heads of lions, and out of their mouths came fire, smoke and sulfur. A third of mankind was killed by the three plagues of fire, smoke and sulfur that came out of their mouths. The power of the horses was in their mouths and in their tails; for their tails were like snakes, having heads with which they inflict injury. The rest of mankind who were not killed by these plagues still did not repent of the work of their hands; they did not stop worshiping demons, and idols of gold, silver, bronze, stone and wood—idols that cannot see or hear or walk. Nor did they repent of their murders, their magic arts, their sexual immorality or their thefts

Chapter 10

Then I saw another mighty angel coming down from heaven. He was robed in a cloud, with a rainbow above his head; his face was like the sun, and his legs were like fiery pillars. He was holding a little scroll, which lay open in his hand. He planted his right foot on the sea and his left foot on the land, and he gave a loud shout like the roar of a lion. When he shouted, the voices of the seven thunders spoke. And when the seven thunders spoke, I was about to write; but I heard a voice from heaven say, "Seal up what the seven thunders have said and do not write it down." Then the angel I had seen standing on the sea and on the land raised his right hand to heaven. And he swore by him who lives for ever and ever, who created the heavens and all that is in them, the earth and all that is in it, and the sea and all that is in it, and said, "There will be no more delay! But in the days of the trumpet call to be sounded by the seventh angel, the mystery of God will be fulfilled, just as he announced to his servants the prophets." Then the voice that I had heard from heaven spoke to me once more: "Go, take the scroll that lies open in the hand of the angel who is standing on the sea and on the land." So I went to the angel and asked him to give me the little scroll. He said to me, "Take it and eat it. It will turn your stomach sour, but 'in your mouth it will be as sweet as honey.'" I took the little scroll from the angel's hand and ate it. It tasted as sweet as honey in my mouth, but when I had eaten it, my stomach turned sour. Then I was told, "You must prophesy again about many peoples, nations, languages and kings."

Chapter 11

I was given a measuring rod like a staff and was told, "Go and measure the temple of God and the altar, and count the worshippers there. But exclude the outer court; do not measure it, because it has been given to the Gentiles. They will trample on the holy city for 42 months. And I will appoint my two witnesses, and they will prophesy for 1,260 days, clothed in sackcloth." These are the two olive trees and the two lampstands, and they stand before the Lord of the earth. If anyone tries to harm them, fire flows from their mouths and devours their enemies. This is how anyone who wants to harm them must die. They have power to shut up the heavens so that it will not rain during the time they are prophesying; and they have power to turn the waters into blood and to strike the earth with every kind of plague as often as they want. Now when they have finished their testimony, the beast that comes up from the Abyss will attack them, and overpower and kill them. Their bodies will lie in the public square of the great city—which is figuratively called Sodom and Egypt—where also their Lord was crucified. For three and a half days some from every people, tribe, language and nation will gaze on their bodies and refuse them burial. The inhabitants of the earth will gloat over them and will celebrate by sending each other gifts,

because these two prophets had tormented those who live on the earth. But after the three and a half days the breath of life from God entered them, and they stood on their feet, and terror struck those who saw them. Then they heard a loud voice from heaven saying to them, "Come up here." And they went up to heaven in a cloud, while their enemies looked on. At that very hour there was a severe earthquake and a tenth of the city collapsed. Seven thousand people were killed in the earthquake, and the survivors were terrified and gave glory to the God of heaven. The second woe has passed; the third woe is coming soon. The seventh angel sounded his trumpet, and there were loud voices in heaven, which said: "The kingdom of the world has become the kingdom of our Lord and of his Messiah, and he will reign forever and ever." And the twenty-four elders, who were seated on their thrones before God, fell on their faces and worshiped God, saying: "We give thanks to you, Lord God Almighty, the One who is and who was, because you have taken your great power and have begun to reign. The nations were angry, and your wrath has come. The time has come for judging the dead, and for rewarding your servants the prophets and your people who revere your name, both great and small—and for destroying those who destroy the earth." Then God's temple in heaven was opened, and within his temple was seen the ark of his covenant. And there came flashes of lightning, rumblings, peals of thunder, an earthquake and a severe hailstorm

Chapter 12

A great sign appeared in heaven: a woman clothed with the sun, with the moon under her feet and a crown of twelve stars on her head. She was pregnant and cried out in pain as she was about to give birth. Then another sign appeared in heaven: an enormous red dragon with seven heads and ten horns and seven crowns on its heads. Its tail swept a third of the stars out of the sky and flung them to the earth. The dragon stood in front of the woman who was about to give birth, so that it might devour her child the moment he was born. She gave birth to a son, a male child, who will rule all the nations with an iron scepter. And her child was snatched up to God and to his throne. The woman fled into the wilderness to a place prepared for her by God, where she might be taken care of for 1,260 days. Then war broke out in heaven. Michael and his angels fought against the dragon, and the dragon and his angels fought back. But he was not strong enough, and they lost their place in heaven. The great dragon was hurled down—that ancient serpent called the devil, or Satan, who leads the whole world astray. He was hurled to the earth, and his angels with him. Then I heard a loud voice in heaven say: "Now have come the salvation and the power and the kingdom of our God, and the authority of his Messiah. For the accuser of our brothers and sisters, who accuses them before our God day and night, has been hurled down. They triumphed over him by the blood of the Lamb and by the word of their testimony; they did not love their lives so much as to shrink from death. Therefore rejoice, you heavens and you who dwell in them! But woe to the earth and the sea, because the devil has gone down to you! He is filled with fury, because he knows that his time is short." When the dragon saw that he had been hurled to the earth, he pursued the woman who had given birth to the male child. But the woman was given the two wings of a great eagle so that she might fly to the place prepared for her in the wilderness, where she would be taken care of for a time, times and half a time, out of the serpent's reach. Then from his mouth the serpent spewed water like a river, to overtake the woman and sweep her away with the torrent. But the earth helped the woman by opening its mouth and swallowing the river that the dragon had spewed out of his mouth. Then the dragon was enraged at the woman and went off to wage war against the rest of her offspring—those who keep God's commands and hold fast their testimony about Jesus

Chapter 13

The dragon stood on the shore of the sea. And I saw a beast coming out of the sea. It had ten horns and seven heads, with ten crowns on its horns, and on each head a blasphemous name. The beast I saw resembled a leopard, but had feet like those of a bear and a mouth like that of a lion. The dragon gave the beast his power and his throne and great authority. One of the heads of the beast seemed to have had a fatal wound, but the fatal wound had been healed. The whole world was filled with wonder and followed the beast. People worshiped the dragon because he had given authority to the beast, and they also worshiped the beast and asked, "Who is like the beast? Who can wage war against it?" The beast was given a mouth to utter proud words and blasphemies and to exercise its authority for forty-two months. It opened its mouth to blaspheme God, and to slander his name and his dwelling place and those who live in heaven. It was given power to wage war against God's holy people and to conquer them. And it was given authority over every tribe, people, language and nation. All inhabitants of the earth will worship the beast—all whose names have not been written in the Lamb's book of life, the Lamb who was slain from the creation of the world. Whoever has ears, let them hear. "If anyone is to go into captivity, into captivity they will go. If anyone is to be killed with the sword, with the sword they will be killed." This calls for patient endurance and faithfulness on the part of God's people. Then I saw a second beast, coming out of the earth. It had two horns like a lamb, but it spoke like a dragon. It exercised all the authority of the first beast on its behalf, and made the earth and its inhabitants worship the first beast, whose fatal wound had been healed. And it performed great signs, even causing fire to come down from heaven to the earth in full view of the people. Because of the signs it was given power to perform on behalf of the first beast, it deceived the inhabitants of the earth. It ordered them to set up an image in honor of the beast who was wounded by the sword and yet lived. The second beast was given power to give breath to the image of the first beast, so that the image could speak and cause all who refused to worship the image to be killed. It also forced all people, great and small, rich and poor, free and slave, to receive a mark on their right hands or on their foreheads, so that they could not buy or sell unless they had the mark, which is the name of the beast or the number of its name. This calls for wisdom. Let the person who has insight calculate the number of the beast, for it is the number of a man. That number is 666

Chapter 14

Then I looked, and there before me was the Lamb, standing on Mount Zion, and with him 144,000 who had his name and his Father's name written on their foreheads. And I heard a sound from heaven like the roar of rushing waters and like a loud peal of thunder. The sound I heard was like that of harpists playing their harps. And they sang a new song before the throne and before the four living creatures and the elders. No one could learn the song except the 144,000 who had been redeemed from the earth. These are those who did not defile themselves with women, for they remained virgins. They follow the Lamb wherever he goes. They were purchased from among mankind and offered as firstfruits to God and the Lamb. No lie was found in their mouths; they are blameless. Then I saw another angel flying in midair, and he had the eternal gospel to proclaim to those who live on the earth—to every nation, tribe, language and people. He said in a loud voice, "Fear God and give him glory, because the hour of his judgment has come. Worship him who made the heavens, the earth, the sea and the springs of water." A second angel followed and said, "Fallen! Fallen is Babylon the Great, which made all the nations drink the maddening wine of her adulteries." A third angel followed them and said in a loud voice: "If anyone worships the beast and its image and receives its mark on their forehead or on their hand, they, too, will drink the wine of God's fury, which has been poured full strength into the cup of his wrath. They will be tormented with burning sulfur in the presence of the holy angels and of the Lamb. And the smoke of their torment will rise forever and ever. There will be no rest day or night for those who worship the beast and its image, or for anyone who receives the mark of its name." This calls for patient endurance on the part of the people of God who keep his commands and remain faithful to Jesus. Then I heard a voice from heaven say, "Write this: Blessed are the dead who die in the Lord from now on." "Yes," says the Spirit, "they will rest from their labor, for their deeds will follow them." Then I looked, and there before me was a white cloud, and seated on the cloud was one like a son of man with a crown of gold on his head and a sharp sickle in his hand. Another angel came out of the temple and called in a loud voice to him who was sitting on the cloud, "Take your sickle and reap, because the time to reap has come, for the harvest of the earth is ripe." So he who was seated on the cloud swung his sickle over the earth, and the earth was harvested. Another angel came out of the temple in heaven, and he too had a sharp sickle. Still another angel, who had charge of the fire, came from the altar and called in a loud voice to him who had the sharp sickle, "Take your sharp sickle and gather the clusters of grapes from the earth's vineyard, because its grapes are ripe." The angel swung his sickle on the earth, gathered its grapes and threw them into the great winepress of God's wrath. They were trampled in the winepress outside the city, and blood flowed out of the press, rising as high as the horses' bridles for a distance of 1,600 stadia

Chapter 15

I saw in heaven another great and marvelous sign: seven angels with the seven last plagues—last, because with them God's wrath is completed. And I saw what looked like a sea of glass glowing with fire and, standing beside the sea, those who had been victorious over the beast and its image and over the number of its name. They held harps given them by God and sang the song of God's servant Moses and of the Lamb: "Great and marvelous are your deeds, Lord God Almighty. Just and true are your ways, King of the nations. Who will not fear you, Lord, and bring glory to your name? For you alone are holy. All nations will come and worship before you, for your righteous acts have been revealed." After this I looked, and I saw in heaven the temple—that is, the tabernacle of the covenant law—and it was opened. Out of the temple came the seven angels with the seven plagues. They were dressed in clean, shining linen and wore golden sashes around their chests. Then one of the four living creatures gave to the seven angels seven golden bowls filled with the wrath of God, who lives forever and ever. And the temple was filled with smoke from the glory of God and from his power, and no one could enter the temple until the seven plagues of the seven angels were completed

Chapter 16

I heard a loud voice from the temple telling the seven angels, "Go and pour out the seven bowls of God's wrath on the earth." The first angel went and poured out his bowl on the land, and ugly, festering sores broke out on the people who had the mark of the beast and worshiped its image. The second angel poured out his bowl on the sea, and it turned into blood like that of a dead person, and every living thing in the sea died. The third angel poured out his bowl on the rivers and springs of water, and they became blood. Then I heard the angel in charge of the waters say: "You are just in these judgments, O Holy One, you who are and who were; for they have shed the blood of your holy people and your prophets, and you have given them blood to drink as they deserve." And I heard the altar respond: "Yes, Lord God Almighty, true and just are your judgments." The fourth angel poured out his bowl on the sun, and the sun was allowed to scorch people with fire. They were seared by the intense heat and they cursed the name of God, who had control over these plagues, but they refused to repent and glorify him. The fifth angel poured out his bowl on the throne of the beast, and its kingdom was plunged into darkness. People gnawed their tongues in agony and cursed the God of heaven because of their pains and their sores, but they refused to repent of what they had done. The sixth angel poured out his bowl on the great river Euphrates, and its water was dried up to prepare the way for the kings from the East. Then I saw three impure spirits that looked like frogs; they came out of the mouth of the dragon, out of the mouth of the beast, and out of the mouth of the false prophet. They are demonic spirits that perform signs, and they go out to the kings of the whole world, to gather them for the battle on the great day of God Almighty. "Look, I come like a thief! Blessed is the one who stays awake and remains clothed, so as not to go naked and be shamefully exposed." Then they gathered the kings together to the place that in Hebrew is called Armageddon. The seventh angel poured out his bowl into the air, and out of the temple came a loud voice from the throne, saying, "It is done!" Then there came flashes of lightning, rumblings, peals of thunder, and a severe earthquake. No earthquake like it has ever occurred since mankind has been on earth, so tremendous was the quake. The great city split into three parts, and the cities of the nations collapsed. God remembered Babylon the Great and gave her the cup filled with the wine of the fury of his wrath. Every island fled away and the mountains could not be found. From the sky huge hailstones, each weighing about a hundred pounds, fell on people. And they cursed God on account of the plague of hail because the plague was so terrible

Chapter 17

One of the seven angels who had the seven bowls came and said to me, "Come, I will show you the punishment of the great prostitute who sits by many waters. With her the kings of the earth committed adultery, and the inhabitants of the earth were intoxicated with the wine of her adulteries." Then the angel carried me away in the Spirit into a wilderness. There I saw a woman sitting on a scarlet beast that was covered with blasphemous names and had seven heads and ten horns. The woman was dressed in purple and scarlet, and was glittering with gold, precious stones and pearls. She held a golden cup in her hand, filled with abominable things and the filth of her adulteries. The name written on her forehead was a mystery: BABYLON THE GREAT, THE MOTHER OF PROSTITUTES AND OF THE ABOMINATIONS OF THE EARTH. I saw that the woman was drunk with the blood of God's holy people, the blood of those who bore testimony to Jesus. When I saw her, I was greatly astonished. Then the angel said to me: "Why are you astonished? I will explain to you the mystery of the woman and of the beast she rides, which has the seven heads and ten horns. The beast, which you saw, once was, now is not, and yet will come up out of the Abyss and go to its destruction. The inhabitants of the earth whose names have not been written in the book of life from the creation of the world will be astonished when they see the beast, because it once was, now is not, and yet will come. This calls for a mind with wisdom. The seven heads are seven hills on which the woman sits. They are also seven kings. Five have fallen, one is, the other has not yet come; but when he does come, he must remain for only a little while. The beast who once was, and now is not, is an eighth king. He belongs to the seven and is going to his destruction. The ten horns you saw are ten kings who have not yet received a kingdom, but who for one hour will receive authority as kings along with the beast. They have one purpose and will give their power and authority to the beast. They will wage war against the Lamb, but the Lamb will triumph over them because he is Lord of lords and King of kings—and with him will be his called, chosen and faithful followers." Then the angel said to me, "The waters you saw, where the prostitute sits, are peoples, multitudes, nations and languages. The beast and the ten horns you saw will hate the prostitute. They will bring her to ruin and leave her naked; they will eat her flesh and burn her with fire. For God has put it into their hearts to accomplish his purpose by agreeing to hand over to the beast their royal authority, until God's words are fulfilled. The woman you saw is the great city that rules over the kings of the earth."

Chapter 18

fter this I saw another angel coming down from heaven. He had great authority, and the earth was illuminated by his splendor. With a mighty voice he shouted: "Fallen! Fallen is Babylon the Great! She has become a dwelling for demons and a haunt for every impure spirit, a haunt for every unclean bird, a haunt for every unclean and detestable animal. For all the nations have drunk the maddening wine of her adulteries. The kings of the earth committed adultery with her, and the merchants of the earth grew rich from her excessive luxuries." Then I heard another voice from heaven say: "Come out of her, my people, so that you will not share in her sins, so that you will not receive any of her plagues; for her sins are piled up to heaven, and God has remembered her crimes. Give back to her as she has given; pay her back double for what she has done. Pour her a double portion from her own cup. Give her as much torment and grief as the glory and luxury she gave herself. In her heart she boasts, 'I sit enthroned as queen. I am not a widow; I will never mourn.' Therefore in one day her plagues will overtake her: death, mourning and famine. She will be consumed by fire, for mighty is the Lord God who judges her. "When the kings of the earth who committed adultery with her and shared her luxury see the smoke of her burning, they will weep and mourn over her. Terrified at her torment, they will stand far off and cry: "'Woe! Woe to you, great city, you mighty city of Babylon! In one hour your doom has come!' "The merchants of the earth will weep and mourn over her because no one buys their cargoes anymore—cargoes of gold, silver, precious stones and pearls; fine linen, purple, silk and scarlet cloth; every sort of citron wood, and articles of every kind made of ivory, costly wood, bronze, iron and marble; cargoes of cinnamon and spice, of incense, myrrh and frankincense, of wine and olive oil, of fine flour and wheat; cattle and sheep; horses and carriages; and human beings sold as slaves. "They will say, 'The fruit you longed for is gone from you. All your luxury and splendor have vanished, never to be recovered.' The merchants who sold these things and gained their wealth from her will stand far off, terrified at her torment. They will weep and mourn and cry out: "'Woe! Woe to you, great city, dressed in fine linen, purple and scarlet, and glittering with gold, precious stones and pearls! In one hour such great wealth has been brought to ruin!' "Every sea captain, and all who travel by ship, the sailors, and all who earn their living from the sea, will stand far off. When they see the smoke of her burning, they will exclaim, 'Was there ever a city like this great city?' They will throw dust on their heads, and with weeping and mourning cry out: "'Woe! Woe to you, great city, where all who had ships on the sea became rich through her wealth! In one hour she has been brought to ruin!' "Rejoice over her, you heavens! Rejoice, you people of God! Rejoice, apostles and prophets! For God has judged her with the judgment she imposed on you." Then a mighty angel picked up a boulder the size of a large millstone and threw it into the sea, and said: "With such violence the great city of Babylon will be thrown down, never to be found again. The music of harpists and musicians, pipers and trumpeters, will never be heard in you again. No worker of any trade will ever be found in you again. The sound of a millstone will never be heard in you again. The light of a lamp will never shine in you again. The voice of bridegroom and bride will never be heard in you again. Your merchants were the world's important people. By your magic spell all the nations were led astray. In her was found the blood of prophets and of God's holy people, of all who have been slaughtered on the earth."

Chapter 19

After this I heard what sounded like the roar of a great multitude in heaven shouting: "Hallelujah! Salvation and glory and power belong to our God, for true and just are his judgments. He has condemned the great prostitute who corrupted the earth by her adulteries. He has avenged on her the blood of his servants." And again they shouted: "Hallelujah! The smoke from her goes up for ever and ever." The twenty-four elders and the four living creatures fell down and worshiped God, who was seated on the throne. And they cried: "Amen, Hallelujah!" Then a voice came from the throne, saying: "Praise our God, all you his servants, you who fear him, both small and great!" Then I heard what sounded like a great multitude, like the roar of rushing waters and like loud peals of thunder, shouting: "Hallelujah! For our Lord God Almighty reigns. Let us rejoice and be glad and give him glory! For the wedding of the Lamb has come, and his bride has made herself ready. Fine linen, bright and clean, was given her to wear." (Fine linen stands for the righteous acts of God's holy people.) Then the angel said to me, "Write this: Blessed are those who are invited to the wedding supper of the Lamb!" And he added, "These are the true words of God." At this I fell at his feet to worship him. But he said to me, "Don't do that! I am a fellow servant with you and with your brothers and sisters who hold to the testimony of Jesus. Worship God! For it is the Spirit of prophecy who bears testimony to Jesus." I saw heaven standing open and there before me was a white horse, whose rider is called Faithful and True. With justice he judges and wages war. His eyes are like blazing fire, and on his head are many crowns. He has a name written on him that no one knows but he himself. He is dressed in a robe dipped in blood, and his name is the Word of God. The armies of heaven were following him, riding on white horses and dressed in fine linen, white and clean. Coming out of

his mouth is a sharp sword with which to strike down the nations. "He will rule them with an iron scepter." He treads the winepress of the fury of the wrath of God Almighty. On his robe and on his thigh he has this name written: KING OF KINGS AND LORD OF LORDS. And I saw an angel standing in the sun, who cried in a loud voice to all the birds flying in midair, "Come, gather together for the great supper of God, so that you may eat the flesh of kings, generals, and the mighty, of horses and their riders, and the flesh of all people, free and slave, great and small." Then I saw the beast and the kings of the earth and their armies gathered to wage war against the rider on the horse and his army. But the beast was captured, and with it the false prophet who had performed the signs on its behalf. With these signs he had deluded those who had received the mark of the beast and worshiped its image. The two of them were thrown alive into the fiery lake of burning sulfur. The rest were killed with the sword coming out of the mouth of the rider on the horse, and all the birds gorged themselves on their flesh

Chapter 20

And I saw an angel coming down from heaven, having the key to the Abyss and holding in his hand a great chain. He seized the dragon, that ancient serpent, who is the devil, or Satan, and bound him for a thousand years. He threw him into the Abyss, and locked and sealed it over him, to keep him from deceiving the nations anymore until the thousand years were ended. After that, he must be set free for a short time. I saw thrones on which were seated those who had been given authority to judge. And I saw the souls of those who had been beheaded because of their testimony about Jesus and because of the word of God. They had not worshiped the beast or its image and had not received its mark on their foreheads or their hands. They came to life and reigned with Christ a thousand years. (The rest of the dead did not come to life until the thousand years were ended.) This is the first resurrection. Blessed and holy are those who share in the first resurrection. The second death has no power over them, but they will be priests of God and of Christ and will reign with him for a thousand years. When the thousand years are over, Satan will be released from his prison and will go out to deceive the nations in the four corners of the earth—Gog and Magog—and to gather them for battle. In number they are like the sand on the seashore. They marched across the breadth of the earth and surrounded the camp of God's people, the city he loves. But fire came down from heaven and devoured them. And the devil, who deceived them, was thrown into the lake of burning sulfur, where the beast and the false prophet had been thrown. They will be tormented day and night forever and ever. Then I saw a great white throne and him who was seated on it. The earth and the heavens fled from his presence, and there was no place for them. And I saw the dead, great and small, standing before the throne, and books were opened. Another book was opened, which is the book of life. The dead were judged according to what they had done as recorded in the books. The sea gave up the dead that were in it, and death and Hades gave up the dead that were in them, and each person was judged according to what they had done. Then death and Hades were thrown into the lake of fire. The lake of fire is the second death. Anyone whose name was not found written in the book of life was thrown into the lake of fire

Chapter 21

Then I saw a new heaven and a new earth, for the first heaven and the first earth had passed away, and there was no longer any sea. I saw the Holy City, the new Jerusalem, coming down out of heaven from God, prepared as a bride beautifully dressed for her husband. And I heard a loud voice from the throne saying, "Look! God's dwelling place is now among the people, and he will dwell with them. They will be his people, and God himself will be with them and be their God. 'He will wipe every tear from their eyes. There will be no more death' or mourning or crying or pain, for the old order of things has passed away." He who was seated on the throne said, "I am making everything new!" Then he said, "Write this down, for these words are trustworthy and true." He said to me: "It is done. I am the Alpha and the Omega, the Beginning and the End. To the thirsty I will give water without cost from the spring of the water of life. Those who are victorious will inherit all this, and I will be their God and they will be my children. But the cowardly, the unbelieving, the vile, the murderers, the sexually immoral, those who practice magic arts, the idolaters and all liars—they will be consigned to the fiery lake of burning sulfur. This is the second death." One of the seven angels who had the seven bowls full of the seven last plagues came and said to me, "Come, I will show you the bride, the wife of the Lamb." And he carried me away in the Spirit to a mountain great and high, and showed me the Holy City, Jerusalem, coming down out of heaven from God. It shone with the glory of God, and its brilliance was like that of a very precious jewel, like a jasper, clear as crystal. It had a great, high wall with twelve gates, and at the gates twelve angels and names written on them, which are the names of the twelve tribes of Israel. There were three gates on the east, three on the north, three on the south and three on the west. The wall of the city had twelve foundations, and on them were the names of the twelve apostles of the Lamb. The angel who talked with me had a measuring rod of gold to measure the city, its gates and its walls. The city was laid out like a square, as long as it was wide. He measured the city with the rod and found it to be 12,000 stadia in length, and as wide and high as it is long. The angel measured the wall using human measurement, and it was 144 cubits thick. The wall was made of jasper, and the city of pure gold, as pure as glass. The foundations of the city walls were decorated with every kind of precious stone. The first foundation was jasper, the second sapphire, the third agate, the fourth emerald, the fifth onyx, the sixth ruby, the seventh chrysolite, the eighth beryl, the ninth topaz, the tenth turquoise, the eleventh jacinth, and the twelfth amethyst. The twelve gates were twelve pearls, each gate made of a single pearl. The great street of the city was of gold, as pure as transparent glass. I did not see a temple in the city, because the Lord God Almighty and the Lamb are its temple. The city does not need the sun or the moon to shine on it, for the glory of God gives it light, and the Lamb is its lamp. The nations will walk by its light, and the kings of the earth will bring their splendor into it. On no day will its gates ever be shut, for there will be no night there. The glory and honor of the nations will be brought into it. Nothing impure will ever enter it, nor will anyone who does what is shameful or deceitful, but only those whose names are written in the Lamb's book of life

Chapter 22

Then the angel showed me the river of the water of life, as clear as crystal, flowing from the throne of God and of the Lamb down the middle of the great street of the city. On each side of the river stood the tree of life, bearing twelve crops of fruit, yielding its fruit every month. And the leaves of the tree are for the healing of the nations. No longer will there be any curse. The throne of God and of the Lamb will be in the city, and his servants will serve him. They will see his face, and his name will be on their foreheads. There will be no more night. They will not need the light of a lamp or the light of the sun, for the Lord God will give them light. And they will reign forever and ever. The angel said to me, "These words are trustworthy and true. The Lord, the God who inspires the prophets, sent his angel to show his servants the things that must soon take place." "Look, I am coming soon! Blessed is the one who keeps the words of the prophecy written in this scroll." I, John, am the one who heard and saw these things. And when I had heard and seen them, I fell down to worship at the feet of the angel who had been showing them to me. But he said to me, "Don't do that! I am a fellow servant with you and with your fellow prophets and with all who keep the words of this scroll. Worship God!" Then he told me, "Do not seal up the words of the prophecy of this scroll, because the time is near. Let the one who does wrong continue to do wrong; let the vile person continue to be vile; let the one who does right continue to do right; and let the holy person continue to be holy." "Look, I am coming soon! My reward is with me, and I will give to each person according to what they have done. I am the Alpha and the Omega, the First and the Last, the Beginning and the End. Blessed are those who wash their robes, that they may have the right to the tree of life and may go through the gates into the city. Outside are the dogs, those who practice magic arts, the sexually immoral, the murderers, the idolaters and everyone who loves and practices falsehood. "I, Jesus, have sent my angel to give you this testimony for the churches. I am the Root and the Offspring of David, and the bright Morning Star." The Spirit and the bride say, "Come!" And let the one who hears say, "Come!" Let the one who is thirsty come; and let the one who wishes take the free gift of the water of life. I warn everyone who hears the words of the prophecy of this scroll: If anyone adds anything to them, God will add to that person the plagues described in this scroll. And if anyone takes words away from this scroll of prophecy, God will take away from that person any share in the tree of life and in the Holy City, which are described in this scroll. He who testifies to these things says, "Yes, I am coming soon." Amen. Come, Lord Jesus. May the grace of the Lord Jesus be with God's people. Amen

DEUTEROCANONICAL BOOKS

1. Old Testament Apocrypha

67. 1 Esdras

Esdras 1

In Jerusalem, Josiah celebrated the Passover in honor of the Lord, offering it on the fourteenth day of the first month. He organized the priests into their daily courses, dressing them in their vestments in the temple of the Lord. He instructed the Levites, the temple servants of Israel, to sanctify themselves to the Lord and position the holy ark in the temple built by King Solomon, the son of David. Josiah told them they no longer needed to carry the ark on their shoulders, and instead, they should serve the Lord and minister to His people, Israel Josiah urged the Levites to prepare by their family houses according to King David's instructions and Solomon's grandeur. They were to stand in the holy place, aligned with the family divisions of the Levites who served before the descendants of Israel. He commanded the orderly offering of the Passover and the preparation of sacrifices, adhering to the commandment given to Moses To the assembly, Josiah donated thirty thousand lambs and kids, and three thousand calves from the royal possessions, fulfilling his promise to the people and the temple servants. The temple leaders, Helkias, Zacharias, and Esyelus, contributed twenty-six hundred sheep and three hundred calves for the priests' Passover. The military commanders Jeconias, Samaias, Nathanael, Sabias, Ochielus, and Joram provided five thousand sheep and seven hundred calves for the Levites' Passover After these provisions, the priests and Levites, equipped with unleavened bread, assembled according to their families and ancestral divisions before the people, offering sacrifices as prescribed in the Book of Moses. They roasted the Passover lambs over the fire and cooked the sacrificial meat in bronze pots, filling the air with a pleasant aroma. They then served the congregation and later prepared portions for themselves and the priestly family of Aaron The singers, the sons of Asaph, performed according to David's arrangement. The gatekeepers maintained their posts, ensuring that all temple duties continued without interruption, supported by their fellow Levites. Thus, the day's sacrificial rituals were completed, honoring the Passover and presenting offerings on the Lord's altar as commanded by King Josiah The celebration was unprecedented in Israel since the days of the prophet Samuel. No king of Israel had observed such a Passover as Josiah did with the priests, Levites, and all of Israel present in Jerusalem. This significant event took place in the eighteenth year of Josiah's reign, marking a period of religious revival and commitment to the Lord's commands Josiah's actions were recorded as righteous and pious, contrasting the transgressions and idolatries detailed in the historical records, which highlighted the sins of the people against the Lord. These accounts underscored the fulfillment of the Lord's decrees against Israel due to their persistent wickedness Following these events, Pharaoh of Egypt advanced to wage war at Carchemish on the Euphrates, prompting Josiah to confront him. Despite warnings from the prophet Jeremiah, conveying the Lord's message, Josiah engaged in battle at Megiddo. Severely wounded, he instructed his servants to remove him from the battlefield, leading to his death upon returning to Jerusalem. He was mourned extensively, and his deeds, piety, and adherence to the law were chronicled in the annals of the kings of Judah and Israel Josiah's successor, Joachaz, was appointed king at twenty-three but reigned only three months before the king of Egypt deposed him, imposing a heavy tribute on the people. The king of Egypt then installed Joakim, who also turned to evil ways, leading to his capture by Nebuchadnezzar of Babylon, who took him along with sacred temple vessels to Babylon Joakim's reign ended after three months and ten days, succeeded by Sedekias, who similarly displeased the Lord and ignored Jeremiah's prophetic warnings. Sedekias's rebellion against Nebuchadnezzar, despite swearing an oath in the Lord's name, resulted in severe consequences: Jerusalem was besieged, the temple desecrated and burned, and the people exiled to Babylon, fulfilling Jeremiah's prophecy concerning the land's Sabbath rest for seventy years

Esdras 2

In the first year of Cyrus, king of Persia, to fulfill Jeremiah's prophecy, Cyrus was moved by the Lord to proclaim throughout his kingdom, both verbally and in writing, that he was commanded by the God of Israel to rebuild the temple in Jerusalem. He encouraged any Israelites to return and rebuild the Lord's temple, offering support from their neighbors in gold, silver, and other resources necessary for the task Leading figures from the tribes of Judah and Benjamin, along with priests and Levites, promptly responded to Cyrus's call. Assisted generously by their surrounding communities, they prepared to undertake the reconstruction of the Lord's temple in Jerusalem. Cyrus also returned the holy vessels Nebuchadnezzar had removed from the temple, entrusting them to Mithradates, his treasurer, who passed them to Sanabassar, the governor of Judea, to be returned to Jerusalem Despite these positive beginnings, opposition soon arose from local authorities in Samaria and surrounding regions. They wrote to King Artaxerxes, portraying the rebuilding efforts as a potential rebellion and threat to regional stability. In response, Artaxerxes ordered a halt to the construction, citing historical records of the city's rebellious past against previous kings This directive effectively stopped the temple's rebuilding until the second year of King Darius of Persia, marking a period of forced cessation due to political and regional opposition to the Judean restoration efforts

Esdras 3

Under King Darius, a significant feast was held for all his subjects, celebrating with leaders from Media and Persia across the provinces. After the feast, a discussion arose among Darius's bodyguards about what was the strongest force in the world, leading to a contest of wisdom adjudicated by Darius The guards presented their arguments: the first declared the strength of wine; the second, the power of kings; and the third, the influence of women and truth, with the latter being declared the strongest. This discourse highlighted the prevailing wisdom that truth transcends all other forces, an acknowledgment that resonated with Darius and his assembly The king then honored the wisdom of the argument favoring truth, demonstrating his commitment to wisdom and justice in his reign, and issued a decree to resume the rebuilding of the Jerusalem temple, reflecting the pivotal role of divine truth and justice in governance and religious devotion

Esdras 4

The debate in King Darius's court continued with Zorobabel, who had championed the strength of women and truth. He eloquently argued that women, despite the apparent rule of men and the potency of wine, hold significant influence. He described how men, even kings, are swayed by the presence and

537

favor of women, emphasizing their fundamental role in life and society Zorobabel then pivoted to the ultimate strength of truth, declaring it superior to all other entities. He argued that truth remains constant and strong, outlasting deceit and manipulation, influencing the earth and the heavens, and commanding respect and obedience from all creation. His persuasive speech concluded with a resounding affirmation of truth's enduring power and righteousness, drawing agreement from all present Moved by Zorobabel's wisdom, King Darius not only commended him but also granted him a special position and promised to fulfill his earlier vows to rebuild Jerusalem and the temple. He issued decrees to support the construction, ensuring the provision of materials and protection for the workers from local interference Zorobabel's leadership and the king's support reinvigorated the rebuilding efforts in Jerusalem. The temple construction resumed with renewed vigor, supported by the contributions and labor of the returning exiles, fulfilling the prophecies and the divine mandate to restore the worship of the Lord in Jerusalem

Esdras 5

With the temple reconstruction underway, the leaders of the returning exiles organized their communities by family groups and tribal affiliations. High priority was given to reestablishing the priestly and Levitical services as prescribed in the Law of Moses. Among these were notable leaders like Jesus the son of Josedek and Joakim the son of Zorobabel, who played crucial roles in the religious and civic restructuring of the community The exiles returned not only with their families but also with a considerable number of servants, livestock, and musical instruments, emphasizing the celebratory and communal aspect of their return. This mass return was orchestrated under the protection of Darius's decree, which provided military escort and logistical support, ensuring their safe passage and resettlement As the community settled, they promptly began the religious practices that had been suspended during the exile. They celebrated the feast of tabernacles and reinstated the regular offerings and sacrifices, establishing a rhythm of worship even before the temple was fully rebuilt The work on the temple was a communal effort, supported by all layers of the returned society, from the leaders to the common people, each contributing according to their ability to the restoration of their religious center. The Levites, reorganized by their families and age groups, took charge of the construction, ensuring that the work adhered to the specifications laid out in the sacred texts Amidst this reconstruction, the community experienced mixed emotions. The older generation, who had seen Solomon's temple in its former glory, wept at the sight of the new foundations, while the younger generation rejoiced at this renewal. This poignant moment highlighted the deep historical and spiritual connection the people had with the temple as the symbol of their covenant with God Despite external opposition and internal challenges, the determination of the leaders and the people to rebuild their temple and restore their religious practices demonstrated their resilience and faith. This period was marked by a significant cultural and spiritual revival, as the community sought to reestablish their identity and heritage in the land promised to their ancestors Thus, the efforts to rebuild the temple symbolized not just the physical reconstruction of a religious site but also the restoration of a people, renewing their covenant relationship with God and reinstating the spiritual and communal laws that defined their society

Esdras 6

In the second year of King Darius's reign, the prophets Aggaeus and Zacharius, inspired by the Lord, the God of Israel, delivered prophecies to the Jews in Judea and Jerusalem. Under their divine guidance, Zorobabel, the son of Salathiel, and Jesus, the son of Josedek, initiated the construction of the Lord's temple in Jerusalem. Despite the presence and support of the prophets, their endeavor soon faced scrutiny Sisinnes, the governor of Syria and Phoenicia, along with Sathrabuzanes and their companions, approached the builders with questions about their authorization for constructing the temple. They inquired about the builders' identities and the origins of their authority to undertake such significant works. The elders of the Jews, favored by the Lord who had looked upon the captives with mercy, continued their work unabated until an official inquiry could be resolved by King Darius The officials sent a detailed letter to King Darius, explaining their findings and concerns. They described encountering the elders of the Jews engaged in constructing a magnificent new temple from costly stones and timber, progressing rapidly and diligently. The officials queried the elders about their authority, prompting them to respond that they were servants of the Lord who created heaven and earth, and that the temple was being rebuilt as per the decree of King Cyrus following its destruction by Nebuchadnezzar during the Babylonian captivity The letter to Darius suggested verifying the decree of Cyrus in the royal archives to ensure the legitimacy of the construction. Upon review, a scroll found in Ekbatana confirmed Cyrus's decree, detailing the temple's specifications and the provision for its funding from Cyrus's treasury. Darius responded by not only reaffirming Cyrus's decree but also commanding that the construction proceed without interference, with provisions for sacrifices and materials to be funded by regional tributes Darius's decree emphasized non-interference by local governors and the continuation of support for the temple's construction, underscoring the project's sanctity and the divine and royal backing it received

Esdras 7

Following the clear directives from Darius, the construction of the temple was diligently overseen by Sisinnes, Sathrabuzanes, and their associates. The work flourished under the prophecies of Aggaeus and Zacharius, leading to the temple's completion on the twenty-third day of Adar, in the sixth year of Darius's reign The dedication of the new temple was marked by extensive offerings and sacrifices, aligning with the laws of Moses. One hundred bulls, two hundred rams, and four hundred lambs were sacrificed, along with twelve male goats for the sins of Israel, representing the twelve tribes. This event not only celebrated the physical completion of the temple but also symbolized the spiritual renewal of the people, who recommitted themselves to the observance of the Passover and the laws that Moses had handed down The successful completion and dedication of the temple represented a significant spiritual victory for the Jewish community, reaffirming their identity and religious commitments under the auspices of the Persian kings who supported their cause Esdras 8 After the temple was restored, Esdras, a learned scribe and a direct descendant of Aaron the chief priest, was commissioned by King Artaxerxes of Persia to lead a group of Israelites from Babylon to Jerusalem. Artaxerxes provided Esdras with a royal decree that facilitated the journey, authorized him to teach the law of Moses, and supplied resources for temple sacrifices Esdras and his entourage set out in the seventh year of Artaxerxes' reign, arriving in Jerusalem after a journey blessed by divine protection. Artaxerxes' decree ensured that Esdras could enhance the religious life in Jerusalem without hindrance, exempting all temple workers from taxes and demanding strict compliance with God's law throughout the region Upon arrival, Esdras discovered that many Israelites had not adhered to the law concerning marriages with foreign nationals, which led to a significant religious crisis. Esdras responded with profound grief and public repentance, which catalyzed a communal confession and a covenant to rectify the breaches of the law Esdras 9 Moved by the serious infractions against the divine law, Esdras and the community convened a large assembly to address the issue of mixed marriages, which were seen as detrimental to the community's purity and dedication to God's commands. The assembly agreed to enforce the law rigorously, leading to a mass annulment of these marriages and a reaffirmation of their commitment to the laws of Moses This action highlighted a collective return to religious observance and set a precedent for the legal and moral governance of the community under Ezra's leadership, supported by the Persian monarchy Esdras 10 Esdras's reforms continued to reshape the community's religious landscape, ensuring that the returned exiles adhered to the covenant laws. His efforts culminated in a significant renewal of the covenant, where the people not only acknowledged their past transgressions but also committed to a strict observance of the law moving forward This period marked a revival of Jewish identity and religiosity, with Esdras at the helm, steering the community towards a future that embraced their ancestral traditions and laws as the foundation of their societal and religious life in Jerusalem

68. 2 Esdras

Esdras 1

The second book of the prophet Esdras, the son of Saraias, the son of Azariah, the son of Helkias, the son of Salemas, the son of Sadoc, the son of Ahitob, the son of Achias, the son of Phinees, the son of Heli, the son of Amarias, the son of Aziei, the son of Marimoth, the son of Arna, the son of Ozias, the son of Borith, the son of Abissei, the son of Phinees, the son of Eleazar, the son of Aaron, of the tribe of Levi, who was captive in the land of the Medes, during the reign of Artaxerxes king of the Persians. The Lord's word came to me, saying, "Go and show my people their sinful deeds, and their children their wickedness which they have done against me, that they may tell their children's children. For the sins of their fathers have increased in them, for they have forgotten me, and have offered sacrifices to foreign gods. Didn't I bring them out of the land of Egypt, out of the house of bondage? But they have provoked me to wrath and have despised my counsels. So pull out the hair of your head and cast all evils upon them, for they have not been obedient to my law, but they are a rebellious people. How long shall I endure them, to whom I have done so much good? I have overthrown many kings for their sakes. I have struck down Pharaoh with his servants and all his army. I have destroyed all the nations before them. In the east, I have scattered the people of two provinces, even of Tyre and Sidon, and have slain all their adversaries. Speak therefore to them, saying: The Lord says, truly I brought you through the sea, and where there was no path I made highways for you. I gave you Moses for a leader and Aaron for a priest. I gave you light in a pillar of fire. I have done great wonders amongst you,

yet you have forgotten me, says the Lord. The Lord Almighty says: The quails were for a token to you. I gave you a camp for your protection, but you complained there. You didn't celebrate in my name for the destruction of your enemies, but even to this day you still complain. Where are the benefits that I have given you? When you were hungry and thirsty in the wilderness, didn't you cry to me, saying, 'Why have you brought us into this wilderness to kill us? It would have been better for us to have served the Egyptians than to die in this wilderness.' I had pity on your mourning and gave you manna for food. You ate angels' bread. When you were thirsty, didn't I split the rock, and water flowed out in abundance? Because of the heat, I covered you with the leaves of the trees. I divided fruitful lands amongst you. I drove out the Canaanites, the Perizzites, and the Philistines before you. What more shall I do for you?" says the Lord. The Lord Almighty says, "When you were in the wilderness, at the bitter stream, being thirsty and blaspheming my name, I gave you not fire for your blasphemies, but threw a tree in the water, and made the river sweet. What shall I do to you, O Jacob? You, Judah, would not obey me. I will turn myself to other nations, and I will give my name to them, that they may keep my statutes. Since you have forsaken me, I also will forsake you. When you ask me to be merciful to you, I will have no mercy upon you. Whenever you call upon me, I will not hear you, for you have defiled your hands with blood, and your feet are swift to commit murder. It is not as though you have forsaken me, but your own selves," says the Lord. The Lord Almighty says, "Haven't I asked you as a father his sons, as a mother her daughters, and a nurse her young babies, that you would be my people, and I would be your God, that you would be my children, and I would be your father? I gathered you together, as a hen gathers her chicks under her wings. But now, what should I do to you? I will cast you out from my presence. When you offer burnt sacrifices to me, I will turn my face from you, for I have rejected your solemn feast days, your new moons, and your circumcisions of the flesh. I sent to you my servants the prophets, whom you have taken and slain, and torn their bodies in pieces, whose blood I will require from you," says the Lord. The Lord Almighty says, "Your house is desolate. I will cast you out as the wind blows stubble. Your children won't be fruitful, for they have neglected my commandment to you, and done that which is evil before me. I will give your houses to a people that will come, which not having heard of me yet believe me. Those to whom I have shown no signs will do what I have commanded. They have seen no prophets, yet they will remember their former condition. I call to witness the gratitude of the people who will come, whose little ones rejoice with gladness. Although they see me not with bodily eyes, yet in spirit they will believe what I say." And now, father, behold with glory, and see the people that come from the east: to whom I will give for leaders, Abraham, Isaac, and Jacob, Hosea, Amos, and Micah, Joel, Obadiah, and Jonah, Nahum, and Habakkuk, Zephaniah, Haggai, Zechariah, and Malachi, who is also called the Lord's messenger

Esdras 2

The Lord says, "I brought this people out of bondage. I gave them my commandments through my servants the prophets, whom they ignored, making my counsel void. The mother who bore them says to them, 'Go your way, my children, for I am a widow and forsaken. I raised you with joy, and I have lost you with sorrow and heaviness, for you have sinned before the Lord God, and done that which is evil before me. But now what can I do for you? For I am a widow and forsaken. Go your way, my children, and seek mercy from the Lord.' As for me, O father, I call upon you as a witness, along with the mother of these children, because they have not kept my covenant, that you may bring them to confusion, and their mother to ruin, that they may have no offspring. Let them be scattered among the heathen. Let their names be blotted out from the earth, for they have despised my covenant. Woe to you, Asshur, who hides the unrighteous within you! You wicked nation, remember what I did to Sodom and Gomorrah, whose land lies in clumps of pitch and heaps of ashes. That is what I will also do to those who have not listened to me," says the Lord Almighty. The Lord says to Esdras, "Tell my people that I will give them the kingdom of Jerusalem, which I would have given to Israel. I will also take their glory back to myself, and give them the everlasting tabernacles that I had prepared for them. They will have the tree of life for fragrance. They will neither labor nor be weary. Ask, and you will receive. Pray that your days may be few, that they may be shortened. The kingdom is already prepared for you. Watch! Call heaven and earth to witness. Call them to witness, for I have left out evil, and created the good, for I live," says the Lord. "Mother, embrace your children. I will bring them out with joy like a dove does. Establish their feet, for I have chosen you," says the Lord. "I will raise those who are dead again from their places, and bring them out from their tombs, for I recognize my name in them. Don't be afraid, you mother of children, for I have chosen you," says the Lord. "For your help, I will send my servants Isaiah and Jeremiah, after whose counsel I have sanctified and prepared for you twelve trees laden with various fruits, and as many springs flowing with milk and honey, and seven mighty mountains, on which roses and lilies grow, with which I will fill your children with joy. Do right by the widow. Secure justice for the fatherless. Give to the poor. Defend the orphan. Clothe the naked. Heal the broken and the weak. Don't mock a lame man. Defend the maimed. Let the blind man have a vision of my glory. Protect the old and young within your walls. Wherever you find the dead, set a sign upon them and commit them to the grave, and I will give you the first place in my resurrection. Stay still, my people, and take your rest, for your rest will come. Nourish your children, good nurse, and establish their feet. As for the servants whom I have given you, not one of them will perish, for I will require them from among your number. Don't be anxious, for when the day of suffering and anguish comes, others will weep and be sorrowful, but you will rejoice and have abundance. The nations will envy you, but they will be able to do nothing against you," says the Lord. "My hands will cover you, so that your children don't see Gehenna. Be joyful, mother, with your children, for I will deliver you," says the Lord. "Remember your children who sleep, for I will bring them out of the secret places of the earth and show mercy to them, for I am merciful," says the Lord Almighty. "Embrace your children until I come, and proclaim mercy to them, for my wells run over, and my grace won't fail." I, Esdras, received a command from the Lord on Mount Horeb to go to Israel, but when I came to them, they rejected me and the Lord's commandment

Esdras 3

In the thirtieth year after the ruin of the city, I, Salathiel, also called Esdras, was in Babylon, lying troubled upon my bed, and my thoughts overwhelmed my heart, for I saw the desolation of Zion and the wealth of those who lived at Babylon. My spirit was greatly agitated, so that I began to speak words full of fear to the Most High, and said, "O sovereign Lord, didn't you speak at the beginning when you formed the earth, and commanded the dust to give us Adam, a body without a soul? Yet it was by your workmanship, and you breathed into him the breath of life, and he was made alive in your sight. You led him into the garden that your right hand had planted before the earth appeared. You gave him a single commandment, which he transgressed, and immediately you appointed death for him and his descendants. From him sprang nations, tribes, peoples, and kindreds without number. Every nation walked after their own will, did ungodly things in your sight, and despised your commandments, and you did not hinder them. Again in time, you brought the flood upon the world and destroyed them. As death came to Adam, so the flood to these. Yet you left one of them, Noah with his family, and all the righteous men who descended from him. As the people on the earth began to multiply, they became more ungodly than before. You then chose one from among them, whose name was Abraham. You loved him and showed him the end of the times secretly by night. You made an everlasting covenant with him, promising never to forsake his descendants. To him, you gave Isaac, and to Isaac you gave Jacob and Esau. You set apart Jacob for yourself, but Esau you rejected. Jacob became a great multitude. You led his descendants out of Egypt to Mount Sinai, where you shook the heavens and the earth, and made the depths tremble, troubling the age. Your glory passed through four gates—fire, earthquake, wind, and ice— to give the law to the descendants of Jacob and the commandment to the descendants of Israel. Yet you did not remove their wicked heart, so that your law might bear fruit in them. For the first Adam, burdened with an evil heart, transgressed and was overcome, as were all his descendants. Thus, disease became permanent, and wickedness remained in the heart of the people along with the law, so the good departed and the evil stayed. The years passed and the end approached. Then you raised a servant named David, commanded him to build a city to your name, and to offer sacrifices from your own bounties. After many years, the inhabitants of the city became wicked, doing as Adam and his generations had done, for they also had wicked hearts. So, you handed your city over to your enemies. Then I said in my heart, 'Are the deeds of those in Babylon any better? Is that why it has dominion over Zion?' For when I arrived here, I saw countless iniquities, and my soul saw many sinners in this thirtieth year, so that my heart failed me. For I have seen how you endure them sinning, spare those acting wickedly, destroy your people, and preserve your enemies; you have not shown how your way can be understood. Are the deeds of Babylon better than those of Zion? Or is there any other nation that knows you besides Israel? Or what tribes have believed your covenants like the tribes of Jacob? Yet their reward appears not, and their labor bears no fruit; for I have traveled through the nations, and I see that they flourish in wealth, and do not consider your commandments. Weigh our iniquities now against those who dwell in the world; then it will be clear which way the scale inclines. When was it that those dwelling on the earth have not sinned in your sight? Or what nation has so kept your commandments? You will find individuals who have kept your precepts; nations you will not find."

Esdras 4

The angel sent to me, named Uriel, answered me and said, "Your understanding has completely failed regarding this world; do you think you can comprehend the way of the Most High?" I responded, "Yes, my Lord." He replied, "I have been sent to show you three ways and to propose three problems. If you can solve one, I will show you the way you desire to see and will teach you why the heart is wicked." I said, "Speak on, my Lord." He then said to me, "Go, weigh for me the weight of fire, or measure for me a blast of wind, or call back yesterday." I answered, "Who of men can do this, that you ask such things of me?" He replied, "If I had asked you, 'How many dwellings are in the sea's heart? Or how many springs are at the deep's source? Or how many streams are above the firmament? Or what are the exits of Sheol? Or what are the entrances of paradise?' perhaps you would have said, 'I never went down to the deep, or into Sheol, neither have I ascended into heaven.' Yet now I have asked you about fire, wind, and yesterday—things you have experienced—and you have given me no answer." He continued, "You cannot understand the things with which you have grown. How then can your mind comprehend the way of the Most High? How can one worn by the corrupted world understand incorruption?" When I heard this, I fell on my face and said, "It would have been better if we were not here at all than that we should live in ungodliness and suffer without knowing why." He replied, "The trees of the field went out and took counsel together, saying, 'Let's go and make war against the sea to drive it away before us, that we may make more forests.' Likewise, the waves of the sea took counsel and said, 'Let's go up and subdue the forests of the plain that we may gain more territory.' The counsel of the trees was in vain, for the fire consumed them. Similarly, the counsel of the waves failed, for the sand stopped them. If you were to judge now between these two, whom would you justify, or whom condemn?" I answered, "Both counsels are foolish, for the land is given to the forest and the sea to bear its waves." He then said to me, "You have judged rightly. Why then do you not judge in your own case? For as the land is to the forest and the sea to its waves, so are those who dwell on the earth capable of understanding only what is upon the earth, and only he who dwells above the heavens can understand the things above the heavens." I then said, "I beg you, O Lord, why has the power of understanding been given to me?" He replied, "It was not your intention to be curious about the ways above but about things that pass by us daily, for Israel is given as a reproach to the heathen, and the people whom you love have been handed over to ungodly nations. Our law is nullified, and our covenant does not stand, and we pass away out of the world as locusts, and our life is as vapor; we are not worthy to obtain mercy. What will he then do for his name by which we are called?" He answered, "If you live, you will see, and if you live long, you will marvel, for the world hastens swiftly to pass away. It cannot endure the things that are promised to the righteous in times to come, for this world is full of sadness and infirmities. The evil about which you asked me has been sown, but the harvest has not yet come. If therefore that which is sown is not reaped, and the field where the evil is sown does not pass away, then the field where the good is sown will not come. For a grain of evil seed was sown in the heart of Adam from the beginning, and see how much ungodliness it has produced until now, and how much more it will produce until the time of threshing comes. Consider by yourself, how great a floor the grains of evil seed will fill. How long? When will these things be? Why are our years few and evil?" He replied, "Do not be more eager than the Most High, for your haste is for yourself, but He who is above is concerned for many. Have not the souls of the righteous asked these questions in their chambers, saying, 'How long are we here? When will come the fruit of the threshing floor?' Jeremiel the archangel answered them, 'When the number of those like you is completed, for he has weighed the world in the balance, measured the times by measure, and numbered the times by number; he will not move or stir them until the measure is fulfilled.'" Then I answered, "O sovereign Lord, all of us are full of impiety. Perhaps it is for our sins that the time of the threshing of the righteous is delayed." He answered, "Go to a woman with child and ask her when she completes her nine months if her womb may keep the child within her any longer." I said, "No, Lord, it cannot." He said, "In Sheol, the chambers of souls are like the womb. For as a woman who is in labor hastens to escape the pains of childbirth, so do these chambers hasten to deliver those things that are committed to them from the beginning. Then you will be shown those things you desire to see." I answered, "If I have found favor in your sight, and if it is possible, and if I am worthy, show me whether there is more to come than is past, or whether the greater part has gone by us." He said, "Stand up on my right side, and I will expound the parable to you." I stood and saw a blazing oven pass before me, and when the flame had gone by, I looked and saw that the smoke remained. After this, a watery cloud passed before me, and poured down heavy rain with a storm. After the storm had passed, the drops still remained. Then he said to me, "Consider; as the rain is more than the drops, and the fire is greater than the smoke, so the quantity that is past was greater, but the drops and the smoke still remain." I prayed and said, "Do you think I will live until those times? Or who will be alive in those days?" He answered, "Concerning the signs about which you ask me, I can tell you in part; but I was not sent to reveal to you concerning your life, for I do not know."

Esdras 5

"As for the signs, observe: Days will come when those on earth will be seized by great amazement. The path of truth will be obscured, and faith will scarcely be found. 2. Iniquity will exceed what you now witness and what you have heard of before. 3. The lands you see ruling will be laid waste, desolate, and devoid of inhabitants. 4. If you are granted life by the Most High, you will witness even more troubling times after the third period: The sun will shine at night, and the moon during the day. 5. Blood will drip from wood, and stones will speak; nations will be in turmoil, and the stars will fall from the sky. 6. A ruler whom none expect will come to power, and birds will flee en masse. 7. The sea of Sodom will cast out fish and roar in the night, unheard of by many, but its sound will be heard by all. 8. Chaos will reign in many places; fires will erupt frequently, wild beasts will change their habitats, and women will bear monsters. 9. Salt water will be found where it should not be, and all friends will turn against each other. Then, wisdom will vanish, and understanding retreat into its sanctum. 10. Many will seek it but will not find it. Wickedness and anarchy will multiply upon the earth. 11. One nation will ask another, 'Has righteousness passed through you?' and the answer will be 'No.' 12. At that time, people will hope but not achieve; they will labor but not succeed. 13. I am allowed to show you these signs. If you pray again, weep as you do now, and fast for seven days, you will hear of things greater than these." I awoke then, trembling violently; my mind was so troubled that it felt numb. 15. The angel who had come to speak with me supported and comforted me, setting me back on my feet The next night, Phaltiel, the captain of the people, approached me asking, "Where have you been? Why do you look so sad? 17. Do you not realize that Israel relies on you in their captivity?" 18. "Rise and eat some bread," he urged, "and do not abandon us like a shepherd who leaves his flock to wolves." 19. I told him, "Leave me for seven days and do not approach me; after that, you may return." He listened and left me alone So, I fasted and mourned for seven days as Uriel the angel had commanded. 21. After these days, my thoughts troubled me again, and 22. my soul regained its spirit of understanding, and I began once again to speak before the Most High. 23. "O Lord, ruler of every wood and all its trees, you chose a single vine for yourself. 24. From all the lands of the world, you selected one for your own; from all the world's flowers, one lily; 25. from all the depths of the sea, one river; from all built cities, you sanctified Zion for yourself. 26. From all birds created, you named one dove; from all livestock, you chose one sheep. 27. And from the multitude of peoples, you acquired one people for yourself, whom you loved and to whom you gave a law that is accepted by all Now, O Lord, why have you surrendered this one people to many, dishonored the one root above others, and scattered your chosen one among the many? 28. Those who oppose your promises trample on those who trust your covenants. 30. If you indeed despise your people so much, let them be punished directly by your own hands." After speaking these words, the angel who had visited me the previous night returned 32. and said, "Listen to me, and I will teach you; hear me, and I will explain more." 33. I responded, "Please speak, my Lord." He then said, "Your heart is greatly troubled for Israel's sake. Do you love these people more than their Creator?" 34. "No, Lord," I replied, "but I speak from the depths of my grief; my heart is tormented every hour as I strive to understand the Most High's ways and to discern part of His judgment." 35. "You cannot," he said. "Why then," I asked, "was I born? Why wasn't the womb my grave, so I wouldn't have to witness the suffering of Jacob and the exhausting toil of the people of Israel?" He challenged me, "Count those who have not yet come to be, gather the scattered drops, restore the withered flowers, 37. open the sealed chambers, release the winds. Or show me the image of a voice, then I will explain the suffering you wish to understand." 38. I replied, "O sovereign Lord, who can know these things except one who does not dwell with humans?" 39. "I lack the wisdom," I admitted. "How can I then speak of the things you have asked of me?" 40. He answered, "Just as you cannot do any of the tasks I have mentioned, so too you cannot comprehend my judgment or the extent of the love I have promised to my people." "But, behold, O Lord," I continued, "you have promised to those who are alive at the end. What should those who came before us do, or we ourselves, or those who will come after us?" 42. He replied, "I liken my judgment to a ring: just as there is no delay for those who are last, so there is no acceleration for those who are first." 43. I asked, "Couldn't you have created all who have been, are now, and will be at once, so that you might hasten your judgment?" 44. He responded, "The creation cannot outpace the creator, nor can the world contain at once all who are to be created." "How then," I inquired, "have you said to your servant that you will revive the creature at once? If they are to live at once, surely the creation could sustain them now as well." 46. He explained, "Ask a woman's womb if it can bear ten children at once rather than at separate times." 47. "It cannot," I admitted, "each must be born in its own time." 48. He concluded, "Likewise, I have assigned times to the earth for all that is sown within it. 49. Just as a young child cannot bear children, nor an old woman bear any longer, so I have ordered the world I created." "Now that you have shown me the path," I began, "may I speak before you: Is our mother, of whom you have spoken, still young? Or is she nearing old age?" 51. He replied, "Ask a woman bearing children, and she will explain. 52. Ask her, 'Why are those you now bear not like those of earlier times, but smaller in stature?' 53. She will tell you, 'Those born in the vigor of youth differ from those born in the time of old age when the womb is less fruitful.' 54. Consider, then, how you are less than those who came before you. 55. And so it is that those who come after you will be smaller, as from a creation now old and past the vigor of youth." 56. "Lord," I implored, "if I have found favor in your sight, show your servant by whom you visit your creation."

Esdras 6

"He said to me, 'In the beginning, when the earth was made, before the portals of the world were set, and before the wind gathered, 2. before the thunder sounded and the lightning shone, before the foundations of paradise were laid, 3. before the fair flowers were seen, before the powers of the earthquake were established, before the countless multitude of angels was assembled, 4. before the heights of the air were lifted up, before the measures of the firmament were named, before the footstool of Zion was established, 5. before the present years were counted, before the imaginations of those who now sin were estranged, and before they were sealed who have gathered faith for a treasure, 6. then I considered these things, and they all were made through me alone, and not through another; just as they will be ended by me alone, and not by another.' "I asked, 'What will be the division of the times? Or when will be the end of the first age and the beginning of the age that follows?' 8. He said to me, 'From Abraham to Isaac, because Jacob and Esau were born to him, Jacob's hand held Esau's heel from the beginning. 9. For Esau is the end of this age, and Jacob is the beginning of the one that follows. 10. The beginning of a man is his hand, and the end of a man is his heel; seek nothing else between the heel and the hand, Esdras!' "I asked, 'O sovereign Lord, if I have found favor in your sight, 12. I beg you, show your servant the end of your signs that you showed me part of the night before.' 13. He answered, 'Stand on your feet, and you will hear a mighty sounding voice. 14. If the place where you stand is greatly moved 15. when it speaks, do not be afraid, for the word is of the end, and the foundations of the earth will understand 16. that the speech is about them. They will tremble and be moved, for they know that their end must be changed.' "It happened that when I had heard it, I stood up on my feet and listened. Behold, there was a voice that spoke, and its sound was like the sound of many waters. 18. It said, 'Behold, the days come when I draw near to visit those who dwell upon the earth, 19. and when I investigate those who have caused harm unjustly with their unrighteousness, and when the affliction of Zion is complete, 20. and when the seal will be set on the age that is to pass away, then I will show these signs: the books will be opened before the firmament, and all will see together. 21. The children a year old will speak with their voices. The women with child will deliver premature children at three or four months, and they will live and dance. 22. Suddenly, the sown places will appear unsown. The full storehouses will suddenly be found empty. 23. The trumpet will give a sound which, when every man hears, they will suddenly be afraid. 24. At that time friends will make war against one another like enemies. The earth will stand in fear with those who dwell in it. The springs of the fountains will stand still, so that for three hours they will not flow "'It will be that whoever remains after all these things that I have told you of, he will be saved and will see my salvation and the end of my world. 26. They will see the men who have been taken up, who have not tasted death from their birth. The heart of the inhabitants will be changed and turned into a different spirit. 27. For evil will be blotted out, and deceit will be quenched. 28. Faith will flourish, corruption will be overcome, and the truth, which has been so long without fruit, will be declared.' 29. When he spoke to me, little by little, the place I stood on rocked back and forth "He said to me, 'I came to show you these things tonight. 31. If therefore you will pray yet again and fast seven more days, I will again tell you greater things than these. 32. For your voice has surely been heard before the Most High, for the Mighty One has seen your righteousness. He has also seen your purity, which you have maintained ever since your youth. 33. Therefore, he has sent me to show you all these things and to say to you, "Believe, and do not be afraid! 34. Do not be quick to think vain things about the former times so that you do not hurry in the latter times."' "It came to pass after this that I wept again and fasted seven days in like manner that I might fulfill the three weeks that he told me. 36. On the eighth night, my heart was troubled within me again, and I began to speak in the presence of the Most High. 37. For my spirit was greatly aroused, and my soul was in distress. 38. I said, 'O Lord, truly you spoke at the beginning of the creation on the first day and said this: "Let heaven and earth be made," and your word perfected the work. 39. Then the spirit was hovering, and darkness and silence were on every side. The sound of man's voice was not yet there. 40. Then you commanded a ray of light to be brought out of your treasuries that your works might then appear "'On the second day, again, you made the spirit of the firmament and commanded it to divide and separate the waters so that one part might go up and the other remain beneath. 42. On the third day, you commanded that the waters should be gathered together in the seventh part of the earth. You dried up six parts and kept them to the intent that of these some being both planted and tilled might serve before you. 43. For as soon as your word went out, the work was done. 44. Immediately, great and innumerable fruit grew with many pleasant tastes, and flowers of inimitable color and fragrances of most exquisite smell. This was done on the third day "'On the fourth day, you commanded that the sun should shine, the moon give its light, and the stars be in their order. 46. You gave them a command to serve mankind, who was to be made. 47. On the fifth day, you said to the seventh part, where the water was gathered together, that it should produce living creatures, fowls, and fishes. So it came to pass 48. that the mute and lifeless water produced living things as it was told, that the nations might therefore praise your wondrous works. 49. Then you preserved two living creatures: the one you called Behemoth, and the other you called Leviathan. 50. You separated the one from the other, for the seventh part, namely, where the water was gathered together, might not hold them both. 51. To Behemoth, you gave one part, which was dried up on the third day, that he should dwell in it, in which are a thousand hills. 52. But to Leviathan, you gave the seventh part, namely, the watery part. You have kept them to be devoured by whom you wish when you wish "'But on the sixth day, you commanded the earth to produce before you cattle, animals, and creeping things. 54. Over these, you ordained Adam as ruler over all the works that you have made. Of him came all of us, the people whom you have chosen "'All this have I spoken before you, O Lord, because you have said that for our sakes you made this world. 56. As for the other nations, which also come from Adam, you have said that they are nothing and are like spittle. You have likened the abundance of them to a drop that falls from a bucket. 57. Now, O Lord, behold these nations, which are reputed as nothing, being rulers over us and devouring us. 58. But we, your people, whom you have called your firstborn, your only children, and your fervent lover, are given into their hands. 59. Now, if the world is made for our sakes, why do we not possess our world for an inheritance? How long will this endure?'"

Esdras 7

"When I had finished speaking these words, the angel who had been sent to me the nights before was sent to me. 2. He said to me, 'Rise, Esdras, and hear the words that I have come to tell you.' 3. I said, 'Speak on, my Lord.' Then he said to me, 'There is a sea set in a wide place that it might be broad and vast. 4. But its entrance is set in a narrow place so as to be like a river. 5. Whoever desires to go into the sea to look at it or to rule it, if he does not go through the narrow entrance, how can he come into the broad part? 6. Another thing also: There is a city built and set in a plain country, full of all good things. 7. But its entrance is narrow and is set in a dangerous place to fall, having fire on the right hand and deep water on the left. 8. There is only one path between them both, even between the fire and the water, so that only one person can go there at once. 9. If this city is now given to a man for an inheritance, if the heir does not pass the danger before him, how will he receive his inheritance?' "I said, 'That is so, Lord.' Then he said to me, 'Even so is Israel's portion. 11. I made the world for their sakes. What is now done was decreed when Adam

transgressed my statutes. 12. Then the entrances of this world were made narrow, sorrowful, and full of trouble; they are but few and evil, full of perils, and involved in great toils. 13. For the entrances of the greater world are wide and safe and produce the fruit of immortality. 14. So if those who live do not enter these difficult and vain things, they can never receive those that are reserved for them. 15. Now, therefore, why are you disturbed, seeing you are but a corruptible man? Why are you moved, since you are mortal? 16. Why have you not considered in your mind that which is to come, rather than that which is present?' "Then I answered and said, 'O sovereign Lord, behold, you have ordained in your law that the righteous will inherit these things, but that the ungodly will perish. 18. The righteous, therefore, will suffer difficult things and hope for easier things, but those who have done wickedly have suffered the difficult things and yet will not see the easier things.' 19. He said to me, 'You are not a judge above God, nor do you have more understanding than the Most High. 20. Yes, let many perish who now live, rather than that the law of God, which is set before them, be despised. 21. For God strictly commanded those who came, even as they came, what they should do to live, and what they should observe to avoid punishment. 22. Nevertheless, they were not obedient to him, but spoke against him and imagined for themselves vain things. 23. They made cunning plans of wickedness and said moreover of the Most High that he does not exist, and they did not know his ways. 24. They despised his law and denied his covenants. They have not been faithful to his statutes and have not performed his works. 25. Therefore, Esdras, for the empty are empty things, and for the full are full things. 26. Behold, the time will come, and it will be, when these signs of which I told you before will come to pass, that the bride will appear, even the city coming forth, and she will be seen who now is withdrawn from the earth. 27. Whoever is delivered from the foretold evils will see my wonders. 28. For my son Jesus will be revealed with those who are with him, and those who remain will rejoice four hundred years. 29. After these years, my son Christ will die, along with all those who have the breath of life. 30. Then the world will be turned into the old silence for seven days, like in the first beginning, so that no human will remain. 31. After seven days, the world that is not yet awake will be raised up, and what is corruptible will perish. 32. The earth will restore those who are asleep in it, and the dust will restore those who dwell in it in silence, and the secret places will deliver those souls that were committed to them. 33. The Most High will be revealed on the judgment seat, and compassion will pass away, and patience will be withdrawn. 34. Only judgment will remain. Truth will stand. Faith will grow strong. 35. Recompense will follow. The reward will be shown. Good deeds will awake, and wicked deeds will not sleep. 36. The pit of torment will appear, and near it will be the place of rest. The furnace of hell will be shown, and near it the paradise of delight. 37. Then the Most High will say to the nations that are raised from the dead, "Look and understand whom you have denied, whom you have not served, whose commandments you have despised. 38. Look on this side and on that. Here is delight and rest, and there fire and torment." Thus he will speak to them on the day of judgment. 39. This is a day that has neither sun, nor moon, nor stars, 40. neither cloud, nor thunder, nor lightning, neither wind, nor water, nor air, neither darkness, nor evening, nor morning, 41. neither summer, nor spring, nor heat, nor winter, neither frost, nor cold, nor hail, nor rain, nor dew, 42. neither noon, nor night, nor dawn, neither shining, nor brightness, nor light, except only the splendor of the glory of the Most High, by which all will see the things that are set before them. 43. It will endure as though it were a week of years. 44. This is my judgment and its prescribed order, but I have only shown these things to you.' "I answered, 'I said then, O Lord, and I say now: Blessed are those who are now alive and keep your commandments! 46. But what about those for whom I prayed? For who is there of those who are alive who has not sinned, and who of the children of men has not transgressed your covenant? 47. Now I see that the world to come will bring delight to few, but torment to many. 48. For an evil heart has grown up in us, which has led us astray from these commandments and has brought us into corruption and into the ways of death. It has shown us the paths of perdition and removed us far from life, and that not a few only, but nearly all who have been created.' "He answered me, 'Listen to me, and I will instruct you. I will admonish you yet again. 50. For this reason, the Most High has not made one world, but two. 51. Because you have said that the just are not many, but few, and the ungodly abound, hear the explanation. 52. If you have just a few precious stones, will you add them to lead and clay?' 53. I said, 'Lord, how could that be?' 54. He said to me, 'Not only that, but ask the earth, and she will tell you. Defer to her, and she will declare it to you. 55. Say to her, "You produce gold, silver, and brass, and also iron, lead, and clay; 56. but silver is more abundant than gold, and brass than silver, and iron than brass, and lead than iron, and clay than lead." 57. Judge therefore which things are precious and to be desired, what is abundant or what is rare?' 58. I said, 'O sovereign Lord, that which is plentiful is of less worth, for that which is more rare is more precious.' "He answered me, 'Weigh within yourself the things that you have thought, for he who has what is hard to get rejoices over him who has what is plentiful. 60. So also is the judgment which I have promised, for I will rejoice over the few that will be saved, because these are those who have made my glory to prevail now, and through them, my name is now honored. 61. I will not grieve over the multitude of those who perish, for these are those who are now like mist, and have become like flame and smoke; they are set on fire and burn hotly, and are extinguished.' "I answered, 'O earth, why have you produced, if the mind is made out of dust, like all other created things? 63. For it would have been better that the dust itself had been unborn so that the mind might not have been made from it. 64. But now the mind grows with us, and because of this, we are tormented, because we perish, and we know it. 65. Let the race of men lament, and the animals of the field be glad. Let all who are born lament, but let the four-footed animals and the livestock rejoice. 66. For it is far better with them than with us, for they do not look forward to judgment, neither do they know of torments or of salvation promised to them after death. 67. For what does it profit us, that we will be preserved alive but yet be afflicted with torment? 68. For all who are born are defiled with iniquities and are full of sins and laden with transgressions. 69. If after death we were not to come into judgment, perhaps it would have been better for us.' "He answered me, 'When the Most High made the world and Adam and all those who came from him, he first prepared the judgment and the things that pertain to the judgment. 71. Now understand from your own words, for you have said that the mind grows with us. 72. Therefore, those who dwell on the earth will be tormented for this reason, that having understanding, they have committed iniquity, and receiving commandments, they have not kept them, and having obtained a law, they dealt unfaithfully with that which they received. 73. What then will they have to say in the judgment, or how will they answer in the last times? 74. For how long a time has the Most High been patient with those who inhabit the world, and not for their sakes, but because of the times which he has foreordained!' "I answered, 'If I have found grace in your sight, O Lord, show this also to your servant: whether after death, even now when every one of us gives up his soul, we will be kept in rest until those times come, in which you renew the creation, or whether we will be tormented immediately.' "He answered me, 'I will show you this also, but do not join yourself with those who are scorners, nor count yourself with those who are tormented. 77. For you have a treasure of works laid up with the Most High, but it will not be shown to you until the last times. 78. Concerning death, the teaching is: When the decisive sentence has gone out from the Most High that a man shall die, as the spirit leaves the body to return again to him who gave it, it adores the glory of the Most High first of all. 79. And if it is one of those who have been scorners and have not kept the way of the Most High, and that have despised his law and hated those who fear God, 80. these spirits will not enter into habitations, but will wander and be in torments immediately, ever grieving and sad, in seven ways '"The first way is because they have despised the law of the Most High. 82. The second way is because they cannot now make a good repentance that they may live. 83. The third way is they will see the reward laid up for those who have believed the covenants of the Most High. 84. The fourth way is they will consider the torment laid up for themselves in the last days. 85. The fifth way is they will see the dwelling places of the others guarded by angels, with great quietness. 86. The sixth way is they will see how immediately some of them will pass into torment. 87. The seventh way, which is more grievous than all the aforesaid ways, is because they will pine away in confusion and be consumed with shame, and will be withered up by fears, seeing the glory of the Most High before whom they have sinned while living, and before whom they will be judged in the last times '"Now, this is the order of those who have kept the ways of the Most High when they will be separated from their mortal body. 89. In the time that they lived in it, they painfully served the Most High and were in jeopardy every hour, that they might keep the law of the lawgiver perfectly. 90. Therefore, this is the teaching concerning them: 91. First of all, they will see with great joy the glory of him who takes them up, for they will have rest in seven orders. 92. The first order is because they have labored with great effort to overcome the evil thought which was fashioned together with them so that it might not lead them astray from life into death. 93. The second order is because they see the perplexity in which the souls of the ungodly wander and the punishment that awaits them. 94. The third order is they see the testimony which he who fashioned them gives concerning them, that while they lived, they kept the law which was given to them in trust. 95. The fourth order is they understand the rest which, being gathered in their chambers, they now enjoy with great quietness, guarded by angels, and the glory that awaits them in the last days. 96. The fifth order is they rejoice that they have now escaped from that which is corruptible, and that they will inherit that which is to come, while they see in addition the difficulty and the pain from which they have been delivered, and the spacious liberty which they will receive with joy and immortality. 97. The sixth order is when it is shown to them how their face will shine like the sun, and how they will be made like the light of the stars, being incorruptible from then on. 98. The seventh order, which is greater than all the previously mentioned orders, is because they will rejoice with confidence, and because they will be bold without confusion, and will be glad without fear, for they hurry to see the face of him whom in their lifetime they served, and from whom they will receive their reward in glory. 99. This is the order of the souls of the just, as from henceforth is announced to them. Previously mentioned are the ways of torture that those who would not give heed will suffer from after this.' "I answered, 'Will time, therefore, be given to the souls after they are separated from the bodies, that they may see what you have described to me?' 101. He said, 'Their freedom will be for seven days, that for seven days they may see the things you have been told, and afterward, they will be gathered together in their habitations.' "I answered, 'If I have found favor in your sight, show further to me your servant whether on the day of judgment the just will be able to intercede for the ungodly or to entreat the Most High for them, 103. whether fathers for children, or children for parents, or kindred for kin, or kinsfolk for their next of kin, or friends for those who are most dear.' "He answered me, 'Since you have found favor in my sight, I will show you this also. The day of judgment is a day of decision and displays to all the seal of truth. Even as now a father does not send his son, or a son his father, or a master his slave, or a friend him that is most dear, that in his place he may understand, or sleep, or eat, or be healed, 105. so no one will ever pray for another on that day, nor will one lay a burden on another, for then everyone will bear his righteousness or unrighteousness.' "I answered, 'How do we now find that first Abraham prayed for the people of Sodom, and Moses for the ancestors who sinned in the wilderness, 107. and Joshua after him for Israel in the days of Achan, 108. and Samuel in the days of Saul, and David for the plague, and Solomon for those who would worship in the sanctuary, 109. and Elijah for those who received rain, and for the dead, that he might live, 110. and Hezekiah for the people in the days of Sennacherib, and many others prayed for many? 111. If therefore now, when corruption has grown and unrighteousness increased, the righteous have prayed for the ungodly, why will it not be so then also?' "He answered me, 'This present world is not the end. The full glory does not remain in it. Therefore, those who were able prayed for the weak. 113. But the day of judgment will be the end of this age and the beginning of the immortality to come, in which corruption has passed away, 114. intemperance is at an end, infidelity is cut off, but righteousness has grown, and truth has sprung up. 115. Then no one will be able to have mercy on him who is condemned in judgment, nor to harm someone who is victorious.' "I answered, 'This is my first and last saying, that it would have been better if the earth had not produced Adam, or else, when it had produced him, to have restrained him from sinning. 117. For what profit is it for all who are in this present time to live in heaviness, and after death to look for punishment? 118. O Adam, what have you done? For though it was you who sinned, the evil has not fallen on you alone, but on all of us who come from you. 119. For what profit is it to us if an immortal time is promised to us, but we have done deeds that bring death? 120. And that there is promised us an everlasting hope, but we have most miserably failed? 121. And that there are reserved habitations of health and safety, but we have lived wickedly? 122. And that the glory of the Most High will defend those who have led a pure life, but we have walked in the most wicked ways of all? 123. And that a paradise will be revealed, whose fruit endures without decay, in which is abundance and healing, but we will not enter into it, 124. for we have lived in perverse ways? 125. And that the faces of those who have practiced self-control will shine more than the stars, but our faces will be blacker than darkness? 126. For while we lived and committed iniquity, we did not consider what we would have to suffer after death.' "Then he answered, 'This is the significance of the battle that humans born on the earth will fight: 128. if they are overcome, they will suffer as you have said, but if they get the victory, they will receive the thing that I say. 129. For this is the way that Moses spoke to the people while he lived, saying, "Choose life, that you may live!" 130. Nevertheless, they did not believe him or the prophets after him, not even me, who have spoken to them. 131. Therefore, there will not be such heaviness in their destruction, as there will be joy over those who are assured of salvation.' "I answered, 'I know, Lord, that the Most High is now called merciful, in that he has mercy upon those who have not yet come into the world; 133. and compassionate, in that he has compassion upon those who turn to his law; 134. and patient, in that he is patient with those who have sinned, since they are his creatures; 135. and bountiful, in that he is ready to give rather than to take away; 136. and very merciful, in that he multiplies more and more mercies to those who are present, and who are past, and also to those who are to come. 137. For if he were not merciful, the world would not continue with those who dwell in it. 138. And one who forgives, for if he did not forgive out of his goodness, that those who have committed iniquities might be relieved of them, not even one ten-thousandth part of mankind would remain living. 139. And a judge, for if he did not pardon those who were created by his word and blot out the multitude of sins, 140. there would perhaps be very few left of an innumerable multitude.'"

Esdras 8

He answered me, "The Most High has made this world for many, but the world to come for few. 2. Now I will tell you a parable, Esdras. Just as when you ask the earth, it will say to you that it gives very much clay from which earthen vessels are made, but little dust from which gold comes. Even so is the course of the present world. 3. Many have been created, but few will be saved." 4. I answered, "Drink your fill of understanding then, O my soul, and let my heart devour wisdom. 5. For you have come here apart from your will, and you will depart against your will, for you have only been given a short time to live. 6. O Lord over us, grant to your servant that we may pray before you, and give us seed for our heart and cultivation for our understanding, that fruit may grow from it, by which everyone who is corrupt, who bears the likeness of a man, may live. 7. For you alone exist, and we are all the workmanship of your hands, just as you have said. 8. Because you give life to the body that is now fashioned in the womb, and give it members, your creature is preserved in fire and water, and your workmanship endures nine months as your creation which is created in it. 9. But that which keeps and that which is kept will both be kept by your keeping. When the womb gives up again what has grown in it, 10. you have commanded that out of the parts of the body, that is to say, out of the breasts, be given milk, which is the fruit of the breasts, 11. that the body that is fashioned may be nourished for a time, and afterward you guide it in your mercy. 12. Yes, you have brought it up in your righteousness, nurtured it in your law, and corrected it with your judgment. 13. You put it to death as your creation and make it live as your work. 14. If therefore you lightly and suddenly destroy him who with so much labor was fashioned by your commandment, to what purpose was he made? 15. Now therefore I will speak. About man in general, you know best, but about your people for whose sake I am sorry, 16. and for your inheritance, for whose cause I mourn, for Israel, for whom I am heavy, and for the seed of Jacob, for whose sake I am troubled. 17. Therefore I will begin to pray before you for myself and for them, for I see the failings of us who dwell in the land; 18. but I have heard the swiftness of the judgment which is to come. 19. Therefore hear my voice, and understand my saying, and I will speak before you." The beginning of the words of Esdras, before he was taken up. He said, "O Lord, you who remain forever, whose eyes are exalted, and whose chambers are in the air, 21. whose throne is beyond measure, whose glory is beyond comprehension, before whom the army of angels stands with trembling, 22. at whose bidding they are changed to wind and fire, whose word is sure, and sayings constant, whose ordinance is strong, and commandment fearful, 23. whose look dries up the depths, and whose indignation makes the mountains melt away, and whose truth bears witness. 24. Hear, O Lord, the prayer of your servant, and give ear to the petition of your handiwork. 25. Attend to my words, for as long as I live, I will speak, and as long as I have understanding, I will answer. 26. Don't look at the sins of your people, but on those who have served you in truth. 27. Don't regard the doings of those who act wickedly, but of those who have kept your covenants in affliction. 28. Don't think about those who have lived wickedly before you, but remember those who have willingly known your fear. 29. Let it not be your will to destroy those who have lived like cattle, but look at those who have clearly taught your law. 30. Don't be indignant at those who are deemed worse than animals, but love those who have always put their trust in your glory. 31. For we and our fathers have passed our lives in ways that bring death, but you are called merciful because of us sinners. 32. For if you have a desire to have mercy upon us who have no works of righteousness, then you will be called merciful. 33. For the just, who have many good works laid up with you, will be rewarded for their own deeds. 34. For what is man, that you should take displeasure at him? Or what is a corruptible race, that you should be so bitter towards it? 35. For in truth, there is no man amongst those who are born who has not done wickedly, and amongst those who have lived, there is none who has not done wrong. 36. For in this, O Lord, your righteousness and your goodness will be declared if you are merciful to those who have no store of good works." Then he answered me, "Some things you have spoken rightly, and it will happen according to your words. 38. For indeed, I will not think about the fashioning of those who have sinned, or about their death, their judgment, or their destruction; 39. but I will rejoice over the creation of the righteous and their pilgrimage, their salvation, and the reward that they will have. 40. Therefore, as I have spoken, so it will be. 41. For as the farmer sows many seeds in the ground and plants many trees, yet not all that is sown will come up in due season, neither will all that is planted take root, even so, those who are sown in the world will not all be saved." Then I answered, "If I have found favor, let me speak before you. 43. If the farmer's seed doesn't come up because it hasn't received your rain in due season, or if it is ruined by too much rain and perishes, 44. likewise man, who is formed with your hands and is called your own image, because he is made like you, for whose sake you have formed all things, even him have you made like the farmer's seed. 45. Don't be angry with us, but spare your people and have mercy upon your inheritance, for you have mercy upon your own creation." Then he answered me, "Things present are for those who live now, and things to come for those who will live hereafter. 47. For you come far short of being able to love my creature more than I. But you have compared yourself to the unrighteous. Don't do that! 48. Yet in this will you be admirable to the Most High, 49. in that you have humbled yourself, as it becomes you, and have not judged yourself amongst the righteous, so as to be much glorified. 50. For many grievous miseries will fall on those who dwell in the world in the last times because they have walked in great pride. 51. But understand for yourself, and for those who inquire concerning the glory of those like you, 52. because paradise is opened to you. The tree of life is planted. The time to come is prepared. Plenteousness is made ready. A city is built. Rest is allowed. Goodness is perfected, and wisdom is perfected beforehand. 53. The root of evil is sealed up from you. Weakness is done away from you, and death is hidden. Hell and corruption have fled into forgetfulness. 54. Sorrows have passed away, and in the end, the treasure of immortality is shown. 55. Therefore, ask no more questions concerning the multitude of those who perish. 56. For when they had received liberty, they despised the Most High, scorned his law, and forsook his ways. 57. Moreover, they have trodden down his righteous, 58. and said in their heart that there is no God, even knowing that they must die. 59. For as the things I have said will welcome you, so thirst and pain, which are prepared for them. For the Most High didn't intend that men should be destroyed, 60. but those who are created have themselves defiled the name of him who made them and were unthankful to him who prepared life for them. 61. Therefore, my judgment is now at hand, 62. which I have not shown to all men, but to you, and a few like you." Then I answered, 63. "Behold, O Lord, now you have shown me the multitude of the wonders which you will do in the last times, but you haven't shown me when."

Esdras 9

He answered me, "Measure diligently within yourself. When you see that a certain part of the signs is past, which has been told to you beforehand, 2. then you will understand that it is the very time in which the Most High will visit the world that was made by him. 3. When earthquakes, tumult of peoples, plans of nations, wavering of leaders, and confusion of princes are seen in the world, 4. then you will understand that the Most High spoke of these things from the days that were of old, from the beginning. 5. For just as with everything that is made in the world, the beginning is evident, and the end manifest, 6. so also are the times of the Most High: the beginnings are manifest in wonders and mighty works, and the end in effects and signs. 7. Everyone who will be saved and will be able to escape by his works, or by faith by which they have believed, 8. will be preserved from the said perils, and will see my salvation in my land and within my borders, which I have sanctified for myself from the beginning. 9. Then those who now have abused my ways will be amazed. Those who have cast them away despitefully will live in torments. 10. For as many as in their life have received benefits, and yet have not known me, 11. and as many as have scorned my law, while they still had liberty and when an opportunity to repent was open to them, didn't understand but despised it, 12. must know it in torment after death. 13. Therefore, don't be curious any longer about how the ungodly will be punished, but inquire how the righteous will be saved, those who the world belongs to, and for whom the world was created." I answered, 15. "I have said before, and now speak, and will say it again hereafter, that there are more of those who perish than of those who will be saved, 16. like a wave is greater than a drop." 17. He answered me, "Just as the field is, so also the seed. As the flowers are, so are the colors. As the work is, so also is the judgment on it. As is the farmer, so also is his threshing floor. For there was a time in the world 18. when I was preparing for those who now live before the world was made for them to dwell in. Then no one spoke against me, 19. for no one existed. But now those who are created in this world that is prepared, both with a table that doesn't fail and a law that is unsearchable, are corrupted in their ways. 20. So I considered my world, and behold, it was destroyed, and my earth, and behold, it was in peril because of the plans that had come into it. 21. I saw and spared them, but not greatly, and saved myself a grape out of a cluster and a plant out of a great forest. 22. Let the multitude perish then, which were born in vain. Let my grape be saved, and my plant, for I have made them perfect with great labor. 23. Nevertheless, if you will wait seven more days however don't fast in them, 24. but go into a field of flowers, where no house is built, and eat only of the flowers of the field, and you shall taste no flesh, and shall drink no wine, but shall eat flowers only, 25. and pray to the Most High continually, then I will come and talk with you." So I went my way, just as he commanded me, into the field which is called Ardat. There I sat amongst the flowers, and ate of the herbs of the field, and this food satisfied me. 27. It came to pass after seven days that I lay on the grass, and my heart was troubled again, like before. 28. My mouth was opened, and I began to speak before the Lord Most High, and said, 29. "O Lord, you showed yourself amongst us, to our fathers in the wilderness when they went out of Egypt, and when they came into the wilderness, where no man treads and that bears no fruit. 30. You said, 'Hear me, O Israel. Heed my words, O seed of Jacob. 31. For behold, I sow my law in you, and it will bring forth fruit in you, and you will be glorified in it forever.' 32. But our fathers, who received the law, didn't keep it, and didn't observe the statutes. The fruit of the law didn't perish, for it couldn't because it was yours. 33. Yet those who received it perished because they didn't keep the thing that was sown in them. 34. Behold, it is a custom that when the ground has received seed, or the sea a ship, or any vessel food or drink, and when it comes to pass that that which is sown, or that which is launched, 35. or the things which have been received, should come to an end, these come to an end, but the receptacles remain. Yet with us, it doesn't happen that way. 36. For we who have received the law will perish by sin, along with our hearts which received it. 37. Notwithstanding the law doesn't perish, but remains in its honor." When I spoke these things in my heart, I looked around me with my eyes, and on my right side I saw a woman, and behold, she mourned and wept with a loud voice, and was much grieved in mind. Her clothes were torn, and she had ashes on her head. 39. Then I let my thoughts go in which I was occupied, and turned myself to her, 40. and said to her, "Why are you weeping? Why are you grieved in your mind?" 41. She said to me, "Leave me alone, my Lord, that I may weep for myself and add to my sorrow, for I am very troubled in my mind, and brought very low." 42. I said to her, "What ails you? Tell me." 43. She said to me, "I, your servant, was barren and had no child, though I had a husband for thirty years. 44. Every hour and every day these thirty years I made my prayer to the Most High day and night. 45. It came to pass after thirty years that God heard me, your handmaid, and saw my low estate, and considered my trouble, and gave me a son. I rejoiced in him greatly, I and my husband, and all my neighbors. We gave great honor to the Mighty One. 46. I nourished him with great care. 47. So when he grew up, and I came to take him a wife, I made him a feast day."

Esdras 10

"So it came to pass that when my son entered into his wedding chamber, he fell down and died. 2. Then we all put out the lamps, and all my neighbors rose up to comfort me. I remained quiet until the second day at night. 3. It came to pass when they had all stopped consoling me, encouraging me to be quiet, then I rose up by night, and fled, and came here into this field, as you see. 4. Now I don't intend to return to the city, but to stay here, and not eat or drink, but to continually mourn and fast until I die." Then I left the reflections I was engaged in, and answered her in anger, 6. "You most foolish woman, don't you see our mourning, and what has happened to us? 7. For Zion the mother of us all is full of sorrow, and much humbled. 8. It is right now to mourn deeply since we all mourn, and to be sorrowful since we are all in sorrow, but you are mourning for one son. 9. Ask the earth, and she will tell you that it is she which ought to mourn for so many that grow upon her. 10. For out of her, all had their beginnings, and others will come; and, behold, almost all of them walk into destruction, and the multitude of them is utterly doomed. 11. Who then should mourn more, she who has lost so great a multitude, or you, who are grieved but for one? 12. But if you say to me, 'My lamentation is not like the earth's, for I have lost the fruit of my womb, which I brought forth with pains, and bore with sorrows;' 13. but it is with the earth after the manner of the earth. The multitude present in it has gone as it came. 14. Then I say to you, 'Just as you have brought forth with sorrow, even so the earth also has given her fruit, namely, people, ever since the beginning to him who made her.' 15. Now therefore keep your sorrow to yourself, and bear with good courage the adversities which have happened to you. 16. For if you acknowledge the decree of God to be just, you will both receive your son in time, and will be praised amongst women. 17. Go your way then into the city to your husband." She said to me, "I won't do that. I will not go into the city, but I will die here." 19. So I proceeded to speak further to her and said, 20. "Don't do so, but allow yourself to be persuaded by reason of the adversities of Zion; and be comforted by reason of the sorrow of Jerusalem. 21. For you see that our sanctuary has been laid waste, our altar broken down, our temple destroyed, 22. our lute has been brought low, our song is put to silence, our rejoicing is at an end, the light of our candlestick is put out, the ark of our covenant is plundered, our holy things are defiled, and the name that we are called is profaned. Our free men are despitefully treated, our priests are burned, our Levites have gone into captivity, our virgins are defiled and our wives ravished, our righteous men carried away, our little ones betrayed, our young men are brought into bondage, and our strong men have become weak. 23. What is more than all, the seal of Zion has now lost the seal of her honor, and is delivered into the hands of those who hate us. 24. Therefore shake off your great heaviness, and put away from yourself the multitude of sorrows, that the Mighty One may be merciful to you again, and the Most High may give you rest, even ease from your troubles." It came to pass while I was talking with her, behold, her face suddenly began to shine exceedingly, and her countenance glistered like lightning, so that I was very afraid of her, and wondered what this meant. 26. Behold, suddenly she made a great and very fearful cry, so that the earth shook at the noise. 27. I looked, and behold, the woman appeared to me no more, but there was a city built, and a place shown itself

from large foundations. Then I was afraid and cried with a loud voice, 28. "Where is Uriel the angel, who came to me at first? For he has caused me to fall into this great trance, and my end has turned into corruption, and my prayer a reproach!" 29. As I was speaking these words, behold, the angel who had come to me at first came to me, and he looked at me. 30. Behold, I lay as one who had been dead, and my understanding was taken from me. He took me by the right hand, and comforted me, and set me on my feet, and said to me, 31. "What ails you? Why are you so troubled? Why is your understanding and the thoughts of your heart troubled?" 32. I said, "Because you have forsaken me; yet I did according to your words, and went into the field, and, behold, I have seen, and still see, that which I am not able to explain." 33. He said to me, "Stand up like a man, and I will instruct you." 34. Then I said, "Speak on, my Lord; only don't forsake me, lest I die before my time. 35. For I have seen what I didn't know, and hear what I don't know. 36. Or is my sense deceived, or my soul in a dream? 37. Now, therefore, I beg you to explain to your servant what this vision means." He answered me, "Listen to me, and I will inform you, and tell you about the things you are afraid of, for the Most High has revealed many secret things to you. 39. He has seen that your way is righteous because you are continually sorry for your people and make great lamentation for Zion. 40. This therefore is the meaning of the vision. 41. The woman who appeared to you a little while ago, whom you saw mourning, and began to comfort her, 42. but now you no longer see the likeness of the woman, but a city under construction appeared to you, 43. and she told you of the death of her son, this is the interpretation: 44. This woman, whom you saw, is Zion, whom you now see as a city being built. 45. She told you that she had been barren for thirty years because there were three thousand years in the world in which there was no offering as yet offered in her. 46. And it came to pass after three thousand years that Solomon built the city and offered offerings. It was then that the barren bore a son. 47. She told you that she nourished him with great care. That was the dwelling in Jerusalem. 48. When she said to you, 'My son died when he entered into his marriage chamber, and that misfortune befell her,' this was the destruction that came to Jerusalem. 49. Behold, you saw her likeness, how she mourned for her son, and you began to comfort her for what has happened to her. These were the things to be opened to you. 50. For now the Most High, seeing that you are sincerely grieved and suffer from your whole heart for her, has shown you the brightness of her glory and the attractiveness of her beauty. 51. Therefore I asked you to remain in the field where no house was built, 52. for I knew that the Most High would show this to you. 53. Therefore I commanded you to come into the field, where no foundation of any building was. 54. For no human construction could stand in the place in which the city of the Most High was to be shown. 55. Therefore don't be afraid nor let your heart be terrified, but go your way in and see the beauty and greatness of the building, as much as your eyes are able to see. 56. Then will you hear as much as your ears may comprehend. 57. For you are more blessed than many, and are called by name to be with the Most High, like only a few. 58. But tomorrow at night you shall remain here, 59. and so the Most High will show you those visions in dreams of what the Most High will do to those who live on the earth in the last days." So I slept that night and another, as he commanded me

Esdras 11

It came to pass the second night that I saw a dream, and behold, an eagle which had twelve feathered wings and three heads came up from the sea. 2. I saw, and behold, she spread her wings over all the earth, and all the winds of heaven blew on her, and the clouds were gathered together against her. 3. I saw, and out of her wings there grew other wings near them; and they became little, tiny wings. 4. But her heads were at rest. The head in the middle was larger than the other heads, yet it rested with them. 5. Moreover I saw, and behold, the eagle flew with her wings to reign over the earth and over those who dwell therein. 6. I saw how all things under heaven were subject to her, and no one spoke against her—no, not one creature on earth. 7. I saw, and behold, the eagle rose on her talons, and uttered her voice to her wings, saying, 8. "Don't all watch at the same time. Let each one sleep in his own place and watch in turn; 9. but let the heads be preserved for the last." 10. I saw, and behold, the voice didn't come out of her heads, but from the midst of her body. 11. I counted her wings that were near the others, and behold, there were eight of them. 12. I saw, and behold, on the right side one wing arose and reigned over all the earth. 13. When it reigned, the end of it came, and it disappeared, so that its place appeared no more. The next wing rose up and reigned, and it ruled for a long time. 14. It happened that when it reigned, its end came also, so that it disappeared, like the first. 15. Behold, a voice came to it, and said, 16. "Listen, you who have ruled over the earth all this time! I proclaim this to you, before you disappear, 17. none after you will rule as long as you, not even half as long." 18. Then the third arose and ruled as the others before, and it also disappeared. 19. So it went with all the wings one after another, as every one ruled, and then disappeared. 20. I saw, and behold, in the process of time, the wings that followed were set up on the right side, that they might rule also. Some of them ruled, but in a while, they disappeared. 21. Some of them also were set up, but didn't rule. 22. After this, I saw, and behold, the twelve wings disappeared, along with two of the little wings. 23. There was no more left on the eagle's body, except the three heads that rested, and six little wings. 24. I saw, and behold, two little wings divided themselves from the six and remained under the head that was on the right side; but four remained in their place. 25. I saw, and behold, these under wings planned to set themselves up and to rule. 26. I saw, and behold, there was one set up, but in a while, it disappeared. 27. A second also did so, and it disappeared faster than the first. 28. I saw, and behold, the two that remained also planned between themselves to reign. 29. While they thought about it, behold, one of the heads that were at rest awakened, the one that was in the middle, for that was greater than the two other heads. 30. I saw how it joined the two other heads with it. 31. Behold, the head turned with those who were with it, and ate the two under wings that planned to reign. 32. But this head held the whole earth in possession and ruled over those who dwell in it with much oppression. It had stronger governance over the world than all the wings that had gone before. 33. After this, I saw, and behold, the head also that was in the middle suddenly disappeared, like the wings. 34. But the two heads remained, which also reigned the same way over the earth and over those who dwell in it. 35. I saw, and behold, the head on the right side devoured the one that was on the left side. 36. Then I heard a voice, which said to me, "Look in front of you, and consider the thing that you see." 37. I saw, and behold, something like a lion roused out of the woods roaring. I heard how he sent out a man's voice to the eagle and spoke, saying, 38. "Listen, and I will talk with you. The Most High will say to you, 39. 'Aren't you the one that remains of the four animals whom I made to reign in my world, that the end of my times might come through them? 40. The fourth came and overcame all the animals that were past and ruled the world with great trembling, and the whole extent of the earth with grievous oppression. He lived on the earth such a long time with deceit. 41. You have judged the earth, but not with truth. 42. For you have afflicted the meek, you have hurt the peaceful, you have hated those who speak the truth, you have loved liars, destroyed the dwellings of those who produced fruit, and threw down the walls of those who did you no harm. 43. Your insolence has come up to the Most High, and your pride to the Mighty. 44. The Most High also has looked at his times, and behold, they are ended, and his ages are fulfilled. 45. Therefore, appear no more, you eagle, nor your horrible wings, nor your evil little wings, nor your cruel heads, nor your hurtful talons, nor all your worthless body, 46. that all the earth may be refreshed and relieved, being delivered from your violence, and that she may hope for the judgment and mercy of him who made her.'"

Esdras 12

1 It came to pass, while the lion spoke these words to the eagle, I saw, 2 and behold, the head that remained disappeared, and the two wings which went over to it arose and set themselves up to reign; and their kingdom was brief and full of uproar. 3 I saw, and behold, they disappeared, and the whole body of the eagle was burnt, so that the earth was in great fear. Then I woke up because of great perplexity of mind and great fear, and said to my spirit, 4 "Behold, you have done this to me, because you search out the ways of the Most High. 5 Behold, I am still weary in my mind, and very weak in my spirit. There isn't even a little strength in me, because of the great fear with which I was frightened tonight. 6 Therefore I will now ask the Most High that he would strengthen me to the end." 7 Then I said, "O sovereign Lord, if I have found favour in your sight, and if I am justified with you more than many others, and if my prayer has indeed come up before your face, 8 strengthen me then, and show me, your servant, the interpretation and plain meaning of this fearful vision, that you may fully comfort my soul. 9 For you have judged me worthy to show me the end of time and the last events of the times." 10 He said to me, "This is the interpretation of this vision which you saw: 11 The eagle, whom you saw come up from the sea, is the fourth kingdom which appeared in a vision to your brother Daniel. 12 But it was not explained to him, as I now explain it to you or have explained it. 13 Behold, the days come that a kingdom will rise up on earth, and it will be feared more than all the kingdoms that were before it. 14 Twelve kings will reign in it, one after another. 15 Of those, the second will begin to reign, and will reign a longer time than others of the twelve. 16 This is the interpretation of the twelve wings which you saw. 17 As for when you heard a voice which spoke, not going out from the heads, but from the midst of its body, this is the interpretation: 18 That after the time of that kingdom, there will arise no small contentions, and it will stand in peril of falling. Nevertheless, it won't fall then, but will be restored again to its former power. 19 You saw the eight under wings sticking to her wings. This is the interpretation: 20 That in it eight kings will arise, whose times will be short and their years swift. 21 Two of them will perish when the middle time approaches. Four will be kept for a while until the time of the ending of it will approach; but two will be kept to the end. 22 You saw three heads resting. This is the interpretation: 23 In its last days, the Most High will raise up three kingdoms and renew many things in them. They will rule over the earth, 24 and over those who dwell in it, with much oppression, more than all those who were before them. Therefore they are called the heads of the eagle. 25 For these are those who will accomplish her wickedness, and who will finish her last actions. 26 You saw that the great head disappeared. It signifies that one of them will die on his bed, and yet with pain. 27 But for the two that remained, the sword will devour them. 28 For the sword of the one will devour him that was with him, but he will also fall by the sword in the last days. 29 You saw two under wings passing over to the head that is on the right side. 30 This is the interpretation: These are they whom the Most High has kept to his end. This is the brief reign that was full of trouble, as you saw. 31 "The lion, whom you saw rising up out of the forest, roaring, speaking to the eagle, and rebuking her for her unrighteousness, and all her words which you have heard, 32 this is the anointed

one, whom the Most High has kept to the end [of days, who will spring up out of the seed of David, and he will come and speak] to them and reprove them for their wickedness and unrighteousness, and will heap up before them their contemptuous dealings. 33 For at first he will set them alive in his judgement, and when he has reproved them, he will destroy them. 34 For he will deliver the rest of my people with mercy, those who have been preserved throughout my borders, and he will make them joyful until the coming of the end, even the day of judgement, about which I have spoken to you from the beginning. 35 This is the dream that you saw, and this is its interpretation. 36 Only you have been worthy to know the secret of the Most High. 37 Therefore write all these things that you have seen in a book, and put it in a secret place. 38 You shall teach them to the wise of your people, whose hearts you know are able to comprehend and keep these secrets. 39 But wait here yourself seven more days, that you may be shown whatever it pleases the Most High to show you." Then he departed from me. 40 It came to pass, when all the people saw that the seven days were past, and I had not come again into the city, they all gathered together, from the least to the greatest, and came to me, and spoke to me, saying, 41 "How have we offended you? What evil have we done against you, that you have utterly forsaken us, and sit in this place? 42 For of all the prophets, only you are left to us, like a cluster of the vintage, and like a lamp in a dark place, and like a harbour for a ship saved from the tempest. 43 Aren't the evils which have come to us sufficient? 44 If you will forsake us, how much better had it been for us if we also had been consumed in the burning of Zion! 45 For we are not better than those who died there." Then they wept with a loud voice. I answered them, 46 "Take courage, O Israel! Don't be sorrowful, you house of Jacob; 47 for the Most High remembers you. The Mighty has not forgotten you forever. 48 As for me, I have not forsaken you. I haven't departed from you; but I have come into this place to pray for the desolation of Zion, and that I might seek mercy for the humiliation of your sanctuary. 49 Now go your way, every man to his own house, and after these days I will come to you." 50 So the people went their way into the city, as I told them to do. 51 But I sat in the field seven days, as the angel commanded me. In those days, I ate only of the flowers of the field, and my food was from plants

Esdras 13

1 It came to pass after seven days, I dreamt a dream by night. 2 Behold, a wind arose from the sea that moved all its waves. 3 I saw, and behold, [this wind caused to come up from the midst of the sea something like the appearance of a man. I saw, and behold,] that man flew with the clouds of heaven. When he turned his face to look, everything that he saw trembled. 4 Whenever the voice went out of his mouth, all who heard his voice melted, like the wax melts when it feels the fire. 5 After this I saw, and behold, an innumerable multitude of people was gathered together from the four winds of heaven to make war against the man who came out of the sea. 6 I saw, and behold, he carved himself a great mountain, and flew up onto it. 7 I tried to see the region or place from which the mountain was carved, and I couldn't. 8 After this I saw, and behold, all those who were gathered together to fight against him were very afraid, and yet they dared to fight. 9 Behold, as he saw the assault of the multitude that came, he didn't lift up his hand, or hold a spear or any weapon of war; 10 but I saw only how he sent out of his mouth something like a flood of fire, and out of his lips a flaming breath, and out of his tongue he shot out a storm of sparks. 11 These were all mixed together: the flood of fire, the flaming breath, and the great storm, and fell upon the assault of the multitude which was prepared to fight, and burnt up every one of them, so that all of a sudden an innumerable multitude was seen to be nothing but dust of ashes and smell of smoke. When I saw this, I was amazed. 12 Afterward, I saw the same man come down from the mountain, and call to himself another multitude which was peaceful. 13 Many people came to him. Some of them were glad. Some were sorry. Some of them were bound, and some others brought some of those as offerings. Then through great fear I woke up and prayed to the Most High, and said, 14 "You have shown your servant these wonders from the beginning, and have counted me worthy that you should receive my prayer. 15 Now show me also the interpretation of this dream. 16 For as I conceive in my understanding, woe to those who will be left in those days! Much more woe to those who are not left! 17 For those who were not left will be in heaviness, 18 understanding the things that are laid up in the latter days, but not attaining to them. 19 But woe to them also who are left, because they will see great perils and much distress, like these dreams declare. 20 Yet is it better for one to be in peril and to come into these things, than to pass away as a cloud out of the world, and not to see the things that will happen in the last days." He answered me, 21 "I will tell you the interpretation of the vision, and I will also open to you the things about which you mentioned. 22 You have spoken of those who are left behind. This is the interpretation: 23 He that will endure the peril in that time will protect those who fall into danger, even those who have works and faith towards the Almighty. 24 Know therefore that those who are left behind are more blessed than those who are dead. 25 These are the interpretations of the vision: Whereas you saw a man coming up from the midst of the sea, 26 this is he whom the Most High has been keeping for many ages, who by his own self will deliver his creation. He will direct those who are left behind. 27 Whereas you saw that out of his mouth came wind, fire, and storm, 28 and whereas he held neither spear, nor any weapon of war, but destroyed the assault of that multitude which came to fight against him, this is the interpretation: 29 Behold, the days come when the Most High will begin to deliver those who are on the earth. 30 Astonishment of mind will come upon those who dwell on the earth. 31 One will plan to make war against another, city against city, place against place, people against people, and kingdom against kingdom. 32 It will be, when these things come to pass, and the signs happen which I showed you before, then my Son will be revealed, whom you saw as a man ascending. 33 It will be, when all the nations hear his voice, every man will leave his own land and the battle they have against one another. 34 An innumerable multitude will be gathered together, as you saw, desiring to come and to fight against him. 35 But he will stand on the top of Mount Zion. 36 Zion will come, and will be shown to all men, being prepared and built, like you saw the mountain carved without hands. 37 My Son will rebuke the nations which have come for their wickedness, with plagues that are like a storm, 38 and will rebuke them to their face with their evil thoughts, and the torments with which they will be tormented, which are like a flame. He will destroy them without labour by the law, which is like fire. 39 Whereas you saw that he gathered to himself another multitude that was peaceful, 40 these are the ten tribes which were led away out of their own land in the time of Osea the king, whom Salmanasser the king of the Assyrians led away captive, and he

carried them beyond the River, and they were taken into another land. 41 But they made this plan amongst themselves, that they would leave the multitude of the heathen, and go out into a more distant region, where mankind had never lived, 42 that there they might keep their statutes which they had not kept in their own land. 43 They entered by the narrow passages of the river Euphrates. 44 For the Most High then did signs for them, and stopped the springs of the River until they had passed over. 45 For through that country there was a long way to go, namely, of a year and a half. The same region is called Arzareth. 46 Then they lived there until the latter time. Now when they begin to come again, 47 the Most High stops the springs of the River again, that they may go through. Therefore you saw the multitude gathered together with peace. 48 But those who are left behind of your people are those who are found within my holy border. 49 It will be therefore when he will destroy the multitude of the nations that are gathered together, he will defend the people who remain. 50 Then will he show them very many wonders." 51 Then I said, "O sovereign Lord, explain this to me: Why have I seen the man coming up from the midst of the sea?" 52 He said to me, as no one can explore or know what is in the depths of the sea, even so no man on earth can see my Son, or those who are with him, except in the time of his day. 53 This is the interpretation of the dream which you saw, and for this only you are enlightened about this, 54 for you have forsaken your own ways, and applied your diligence to mine, and have searched out my law. 55 You have ordered your life in wisdom, and have called understanding your mother. 56 Therefore I have shown you this, for there is a reward laid up with the Most High. It will be, after another three days I will speak other things to you, and declare to you mighty and wondrous things." 57 Then I went out and passed into the field, giving praise and thanks greatly to the Most High because of his wonders, which he did from time to time, 58 and because he governs the time, and such things as happen in their seasons. So I sat there three days

Esdras 14

1 It came to pass upon the third day, I sat under an oak, and, behold, a voice came out of a bush near me, and said, "Esdras, Esdras!" 2 I said, "Here I am, Lord," and I stood up on my feet. 3 Then he said to me, "I revealed myself in a bush and talked with Moses when my people were in bondage in Egypt. 4 I sent him, and he led my people out of Egypt. I brought him up to Mount Sinai, where I kept him with me for many days. 5 I told him many wondrous things, and showed him the secrets of the times and the end of the seasons. I commanded him, saying, 6 'You shall publish these openly, and these you shall hide.' 7 Now I say to you: 8 Lay up in your heart the signs that I have shown, the dreams that you have seen, and the interpretations which you have heard; 9 for you will be taken away from men, and from now on you will live with my Son and with those who are like you, until the times have ended. 10 For the world has lost its youth, and the times begin to grow old. 11 For the age is divided into twelve parts, and ten parts of it are already gone, even the half of the tenth part. 12 There remain of it two parts after the middle of the tenth part. 13 Now therefore set your house in order, reprove your people, comfort the lowly amongst them, and instruct those of them who are wise, and now renounce the life that is corruptible, 14 and let go of the mortal thoughts, cast away from you the burdens of man, put off now your weak nature, 15 lay aside the thoughts that are most grievous to you, and hurry to escape from these times. 16 For worse evils than those which you have seen happen will be done

after this. 17 For look how much the world will be weaker through age, so much that more evils will increase on those who dwell in it. 18 For the truth will withdraw itself further off, and falsehood will be near. For now the eagle which you saw in vision hurries to come." 19 Then I answered and said, "Let me speak in your presence, O Lord. 20 Behold, I will go, as you have commanded me, and reprove the people who now live, but who will warn those who will be born afterward? For the world is set in darkness, and those who dwell in it are without light. 21 For your law has been burnt, therefore no one knows the things that are done by you, or the works that will be done. 22 But if I have found favour before you, send the Holy Spirit to me, and I will write all that has been done in the world since the beginning, even the things that were written in your law, that men may be able to find the path, and that those who would live in the latter days may live." 23 He answered me and said, "Go your way, gather the people together, and tell them not to seek you for forty days. 24 But prepare for yourself many tablets, and take with you Sarea, Dabria, Selemia, Ethanus, and Asiel, these five, which are ready to write swiftly; 25 and come here, and I will light a lamp of understanding in your heart which will not be put out until the things have ended about which you will write. 26 When you are done, some things you shall publish openly, and some things you shall deliver in secret to the wise. Tomorrow at this hour you will begin to write." 27 Then went I out, as he commanded me, and gathered all the people together, and said, 28 "Hear these words, O Israel! 29 Our fathers at the beginning were foreigners in Egypt, and they were delivered from there, 30 and received the law of life, which they didn't keep, which you also have transgressed after them. 31 Then the land of Zion was given to you for a possession; but you yourselves and your ancestors have done unrighteousness, and have not kept the ways which the Most High commanded you. 32 Because he is a righteous judge, in due time, he took from you what he had given you. 33 Now you are here, and your kindred are amongst you. 34 Therefore if you will rule over your own understanding and instruct your hearts, you will be kept alive, and after death you will obtain mercy. 35 For after death the judgement will come when we will live again. Then the names of the righteous will become manifest, and the works of the ungodly will be declared. 36 Let no one therefore come to me now, nor seek me for forty days." 37 So I took the five men, as he commanded me, and we went out into the field, and remained there. 38 It came to pass on the next day that, behold, a voice called me, saying, "Esdras, open your mouth, and drink what I give you to drink." 39 Then opened I my mouth, and behold, a full cup was handed to me. It was full of something like water, but its colour was like fire. 40 I took it, and drank. When I had drunk it, my heart uttered understanding, and wisdom grew in my breast, for my spirit retained its memory. 41 My mouth was opened, and shut no more. 42 The Most High gave understanding to the five men, and they wrote by course the things that were told them, in characters which they didn't know, and they sat forty days. Now they wrote in the daytime, and at night they ate bread. 43 As for me, I spoke in the day, and by night I didn't hold my tongue. 44 So in forty days, ninety-four books were written. 45 It came to pass, when the forty days were fulfilled, that the Most High spoke to me, saying, "The first books that you have written, publish openly, and let the worthy and unworthy read them; 46 but keep the last seventy, that you may deliver them to those who are wise amongst your people; 47 for in them is the spring of understanding, the fountain of wisdom, and the stream of knowledge." 48 I did so

Esdras 15

1 "Behold, speak in the ears of my people the words of prophecy which I will put in your mouth," says the Lord. 2 "Cause them to be written on paper, for they are faithful and true. 3 Don't be afraid of their plots against you. Don't let the unbelief of those who speak against you trouble you. 4 For all the unbelievers will die in their unbelief. 5 "Behold," says the Lord, "I bring evils on the whole earth: sword, famine, death, and destruction. 6 For wickedness has prevailed over every land, and their hurtful works have reached their limit. 7 Therefore," says the Lord, 8 "I will hold my peace no more concerning their wickedness which they profanely commit, neither will I tolerate them in these things, which they wickedly practice. Behold, the innocent and righteous blood cries to me, and the souls of the righteous cry out continually. 9 I will surely avenge them," says the Lord, "and will receive to me all the innocent blood from amongst them. 10 Behold, my people is led like a flock to the slaughter. I will not allow them now to dwell in the land of Egypt, 11 but I will bring them out with a mighty hand and with a high arm, and will strike Egypt with plagues, as before, and will destroy all its land." 12 Let Egypt and its foundations mourn, for the plague of the chastisement and the punishment that God will bring upon it. 13 Let the farmers that till the ground mourn, for their seeds will fail and their trees will be ruined through the blight and hail, and a terrible tempest. 14 Woe to the world and those who dwell in it! 15 For the sword and their destruction draw near, and nation will rise up against nation to battle with weapons in their hands. 16 For there will be sedition amongst men, and growing strong against one another. In their might, they won't respect their king or the chief of their great ones. 17 For a man will desire to go into a city, and will not be able. 18 For because of their pride, the cities will be troubled, the houses will be destroyed, and men will be afraid. 19 A man will have no pity on his neighbours, but will assault their houses with the sword and plunder their goods, because of the lack of bread, and for great suffering. 20 "Behold," says God, "I call together all the kings of the earth to stir up those who are from the rising of the sun, from the south, from the east, and Libanus, to turn themselves one against another, and repay the things that they have done to them. 21 Just as they do yet this day to my chosen, so I will do also, and repay into their bosom." The Lord God says: 22 "My right hand won't spare the sinners, and my sword won't cease over those who shed innocent blood on the earth. 23 A fire has gone out from his wrath and has consumed the foundations of the earth and the sinners, like burnt straw. 24 Woe to those who sin and don't keep my commandments!" says the Lord. 25 "I will not spare them. Go your way, you rebellious children! Don't defile my sanctuary!" 26 For the Lord knows all those who trespass against him, therefore he will deliver them to death and destruction. 27 For now evils have come upon the whole earth, and you will remain in them; for God will not deliver you because you have sinned against him. 28 Behold, a horrible sight appearing from the east! 29 The nations of the dragons of Arabia will come out with many chariots. From the day that they set out, their hissing is carried over the earth, so that all those who will hear them may also fear and tremble. 30 Also the Carmonians, raging in wrath, will go out like the wild boars of the forest. They will come with great power and join battle with them, and will devastate a portion of the land of the Assyrians with their teeth. 31 Then the dragons will have the upper hand, remembering their nature. If they will turn themselves, conspiring together in great power to persecute them, 32 then these will be troubled, and keep silence through their power, and will turn and flee. 33 From the land of the Assyrians, an enemy in ambush will attack them and destroy one of them. Upon their army will be fear and trembling, and indecision upon their kings. 34 Behold, clouds from the east, and from the north to the south! They are very horrible to look at, full of wrath and storm. 35 They will clash against one another. They will pour out a heavy storm on the earth, even their own storm. There will be blood from the sword to the horse's belly, 36 and to the thigh of man, and to the camel's hock. 37 There will be fearfulness and great trembling upon earth. They who see that wrath will be afraid, and trembling will seize them. 38 After this, great storms will be stirred up from the south, from the north, and another part from the west. 39 Strong winds will arise from the east, and will shut it up, even the cloud which he raised up in wrath; and the storm that was to cause destruction by the east wind will be violently driven towards the south and west. 40 Great and mighty clouds, full of wrath, will be lifted up with the storm, that they may destroy all the earth and those who dwell in it. They will pour out over every high and lofty one a terrible storm, 41 fire, hail, flying swords, and many waters, that all plains may be full, and all rivers, with the abundance of those waters. 42 They will break down the cities and walls, mountains and hills, trees of the forest, and grass of the meadows, and their grain. 43 They will go on steadily to Babylon and destroy her. 44 They will come to it and surround it. They will pour out the storm and all wrath on her. Then the dust and smoke will go up to the sky, and all those who are around it will mourn for it. 45 Those who remain will serve those who have destroyed it. 46 You, Asia, who are partaker in the beauty of Babylon, and in the glory of her person 47 woe to you, you wretch, because you have made yourself like her. You have decked out your daughters for prostitution, that they might please and glory in your lovers, which have always lusted after you! 48 You have followed her who is hateful in all her works and inventions. Therefore God says, 49 "I will send evils on you: widowhood, poverty, famine, sword, and pestilence, to lay waste your houses and bring you to destruction and death. 50 The glory of your power will be dried up like a flower when the heat rises that is sent over you. 51 You will be weakened like a poor woman who is beaten and wounded, so that you won't be able to receive your mighty ones and your lovers. 52 Would I have dealt with you with such jealousy," says the Lord, 53 "if you had not always slain my chosen, exalting and clapping of your hands, and saying over their dead, when you were drunk? 54 "Beautify your face! 55 The reward of a prostitute will be in your bosom, therefore you will be repaid. 56 Just as you will do to my chosen," says the Lord, "even so God will do to you, and will deliver you to your adversaries. 57 Your children will die of hunger. You will fall by the sword. Your cities will be broken down, and all your people in the field will perish by the sword. 58 Those who are in the mountains will die of hunger, eat their own flesh, and drink their own blood, because of hunger for bread and thirst for water. 59 You, unhappy above all others, will come and will again receive evils. 60 In the passage, they will rush on the hateful city and will destroy some portion of your land, and mar part of your glory, and will return again to Babylon that was destroyed. 61 You will be cast down by them as stubble, and they will be to you as fire. 62 They will devour you, your cities, your land, and your mountains. They will burn all your forests and your fruitful trees with fire. 63

They will carry your children away captive, and will plunder your wealth, and mar the glory of your face."

Esdras 16

1 Woe to you, Babylon, and Asia! Woe to you, Egypt and Syria! 2 Put on sackcloth and garments of goats' hair, wail for your children and lament; for your destruction is at hand. 3 A sword has been sent upon you, and who is there to turn it back? 4 A fire has been sent upon you, and who is there to quench it? 5 Calamities are sent upon you, and who is there to drive them away? 6 Can one drive away a hungry lion in the forest? Can one quench a fire in stubble, once it has begun to burn? 7 Can one turn back an arrow that is shot by a strong archer? 8 The Lord God sends the calamities, and who will drive them away? 9 A fire will go out from his wrath, and who may quench it? 10 He will flash lightning, and who will not fear? He will thunder, and who wouldn't tremble? 11 The Lord will threaten, and who will not be utterly broken in pieces at his presence? 12 The earth and its foundations quake. The sea rises up with waves from the deep, and its waves will be troubled, along with the fish in them, at the presence of the Lord, and before the glory of his power. 13 For his right hand that bends the bow is strong, his arrows that he shoots are sharp, and will not miss when they begin to be shot into the ends of the world. 14 Behold, the calamities are sent out, and will not return again until they come upon the earth. 15 The fire is kindled and will not be put out until it consumes the foundations of the earth. 16 Just as an arrow which is shot by a mighty archer doesn't return backward, even so the calamities that are sent out upon earth won't return again. 17 Woe is me! Woe is me! Who will deliver me in those days? 18 The beginning of sorrows, when there will be great mourning; the beginning of famine, and many will perish; the beginning of wars, and the powers will stand in fear; the beginning of calamities, and all will tremble! What will they do when the calamities come? 19 Behold, famine and plague, suffering and anguish! They are sent as scourges for correction. 20 But for all these things they will not turn them from their wickedness, nor be always mindful of the scourges. 21 Behold, food will be so cheap on earth that they will think themselves to be in good condition, and even then calamities will grow on earth: sword, famine, and great confusion. 22 For many of those who dwell on earth will perish of famine; and others who escape the famine, the sword will destroy. 23 The dead will be cast out like dung, and there will be no one to comfort them; for the earth will be left desolate, and its cities will be cast down. 24 There will be no farmer left to cultivate the earth or to sow it. 25 The trees will give fruit, but who will gather it? 26 The grapes will ripen, but who will tread them? For in all places there will be a great solitude; 27 for one man will desire to see another, or to hear his voice. 28 For of a city there will be ten left, and two of the field, who have hidden themselves in the thick groves, and in the clefts of the rocks. 29 As in an orchard of olives upon every tree there may be left three or four olives, 30 or as when a vineyard is gathered, there are some clusters left by those who diligently search through the vineyard, 31 even so in those days, there will be three or four left by those who search their houses with the sword. 32 The earth will be left desolate, and its fields will be for briers, and its roads and all her paths will grow thorns, because no sheep will pass along them. 33 The virgins will mourn, having no bridegrooms. The women will mourn, having no husbands. Their daughters will mourn, having no helpers. 34 Their bridegrooms will be destroyed in the wars, and their husbands will perish of famine. 35 Hear now these things, and understand them, you servants of the Lord. 36 Behold, the Lord's word: receive it. Don't doubt the things about which the Lord speaks. 37 Behold, the calamities draw near, and are not delayed. 38 Just as a woman with child in the ninth month, when the hour of her delivery draws near, within two or three hours great pains surround her womb, and when the child comes out from the womb, there will be no waiting for a moment, 39 even so the calamities won't delay coming upon the earth. The world will groan, and sorrows will seize it on every side. 40 "O my people, hear my word: prepare for battle, and in those calamities be like strangers on the earth. 41 He who sells, let him be as he who flees away, and he who buys, as one who will lose. 42 Let he who does business be as he who has no profit by it, and he who builds, as he who won't dwell in it, 43 and he who sows, as if he wouldn't reap, so also he who prunes the vines, as he who won't gather the grapes, 44 those who marry, as those who will have no children, and those who don't marry, as the widowed. 45 Because of this, those who labor, labor in vain; 46 for foreigners will reap their fruits, plunder their goods, overthrow their houses, and take their children captive, for in captivity and famine they will conceive their children. 47 Those who conduct business, do so only to be plundered. The more they adorn their cities, their houses, their possessions, and their own persons, 48 the more I will hate them for their sins," says the Lord. 49 Just as a respectable and virtuous woman hates a prostitute, 50 so will righteousness hate iniquity when she adorns herself, and will accuse her to her face when he comes who will defend him who diligently searches out every sin on earth. 51 Therefore don't be like her or her works. 52 For yet a little while, and iniquity will be taken away out of the earth, and righteousness will reign over us. 53 Don't let the sinner say that he has not sinned; for God will burn coals of fire on the head of one who says "I haven't sinned before God and his glory." 54 Behold, the Lord knows all the works of men, their imaginations, their thoughts, and their hearts. 55 He said, "Let the earth be made," and it was made, "Let the sky be made," and it was made. 56 At his word, the stars were established, and he knows the number of the stars. 57 He searches the deep and its treasures. He has measured the sea and what it contains. 58 He has shut the sea in the midst of the waters, and with his word, he hung the earth over the waters. 59 He has spread out the sky like a vault. He has founded it over the waters. 60 He has made springs of water in the desert and pools on the tops of the mountains to send out rivers from the heights to water the earth. 61 He formed man, and put a heart in the midst of the body, and gave him breath, life, and understanding, 62 yes, the spirit of God Almighty. He who made all things and searches out hidden things in hidden places, 63 surely he knows your imagination, and what you think in your hearts. Woe to those who sin, and try to hide their sin! 64 Because the Lord will exactly investigate all your works, and he will put you all to shame. 65 When your sins are brought out before men, you will be ashamed, and your own iniquities will stand as your accusers in that day. 66 What will you do? Or how will you hide your sins before God and his angels? 67 Behold, God is the judge. Fear him! Stop sinning, and forget your iniquities, to never again commit them. So will God lead you out, and deliver you from all suffering. 68 For, behold, the burning wrath of a great multitude is kindled over you, and they will take away some of you, and feed you with that which is sacrificed to idols. 69 Those who consent to them will be held in derision and in contempt, and be trodden under foot. 70 For there will be in various places, and in the next cities, a great insurrection

against those who fear the Lord. 71 They will be like madmen, sparing none, but spoiling and destroying those who still fear the Lord. 72 For they will destroy and plunder their goods, and throw them out of their houses. 73 Then the trial of my elect will be made known, even as the gold that is tried in the fire. 74 Hear, my elect ones, says the Lord: "Behold, the days of suffering are at hand, and I will deliver you from them. 75 Don't be afraid, and don't doubt, for God is your guide. 76 You who keep my commandments and precepts," says the Lord God, "don't let your sins weigh you down, and don't let your iniquities lift themselves up." 77 Woe to those who are choked with their sins and covered with their iniquities, like a field is choked with bushes, and its path covered with thorns, that no one may travel through! 78 It is shut off and given up to be consumed by fire

69. Tobit

Tobit 1

This is the account of Tobit, son of Tobiel, the son of Ananiel, the son of Aduel, the son of Gabael, of the seed of Asiel, of the tribe of Naphtali. During the days of Enemessar, the king of the Assyrians, Tobit was taken captive from Thisbe, which is located on the right hand of Kedesh Naphtali in Galilee above Asher. Tobit walked in the ways of truth and righteousness throughout his life and performed many charitable deeds for his kindred and nation, who were also taken into captivity in the land of the Assyrians, to Nineveh While still in Israel, before he was taken captive, all the tribe of Naphtali, which was his father's tribe, fell away from the house of Jerusalem, the chosen city of all the tribes of Israel, where the temple of the Most High was sanctified and built for all ages. These tribes, including the house of Naphtali, began to sacrifice to the heifer Baal. However, Tobit alone continued to go to Jerusalem for the feasts, as it was ordained for all Israel by an everlasting decree. He brought the first fruits and tithes of his increase and offered them on the altar to the priests, the sons of Aaron. He gave a tenth of all his increase to the sons of Levi, who ministered in Jerusalem. Another tenth part he sold and spent each year in Jerusalem. A third tenth he gave to those for whom it was appropriate, as commanded by Deborah, his father's mother, because he had been left an orphan by his father When Tobit became a man, he married Anna from his own family line, and they had a son named Tobias. When Tobit was carried captive to Nineveh, all his kindred and relatives ate the bread of the Gentiles, but Tobit refrained because he remembered God with all his soul. Consequently, the Most High granted him grace and favor in the sight of Enemessar, and Tobit became his purchasing agent. Tobit traveled to Media and left ten talents of silver in trust with Gabael, the brother of Gabrias, at Rages of Media. After Enemessar's death, his son Sennacherib reigned in his place. During Sennacherib's reign, the highways became troubled, and Tobit could no longer travel to Media In the days of Enemessar, Tobit continued his charitable deeds, giving bread to the hungry, clothing to the naked, and burying the dead of his race who were thrown out on the walls of Nineveh. When Sennacherib, the king, fled from Judea in his wrath, he killed many, but Tobit secretly buried their bodies, even though the king sought after them. However, one of the Ninevites reported Tobit to the king, and when Tobit realized that he was being sought to be put to death, he hid in fear. All his goods were forcibly taken away, leaving him with only his wife, Anna, and his son, Tobias Soon after, Sennacherib was killed by two of his sons, who then

fled to the mountains of Ararat. Sarchedonus, his son, reigned in his place and appointed Achiacharus, Tobit's brother's son, over all the accounts of his kingdom and all his affairs. Achiacharus requested that Tobit come to Nineveh, where Achiacharus served as cupbearer, keeper of the signet, steward, and overseer of the accounts. Sarchedonus held Achiacharus in high regard, but he was Tobit's nephew

Tobit 2

When Tobit returned home, his wife Anna and his son Tobias were restored to him. It was during the feast of Pentecost, the holy feast of the seven weeks, that a good dinner was prepared, and Tobit sat down to eat. He saw an abundance of meat and instructed his son to go and bring back any poor man of their kindred who was mindful of the Lord. However, his son returned with the news that one of their race had been strangled and cast into the marketplace. Without having tasted anything, Tobit sprang up, took the body into a chamber until sunset, and then returned to wash himself and eat his bread in sorrow As he ate, Tobit remembered the prophecy of Amos, which foretold that feasts would be turned into mourning, and joy into lamentation. Tobit wept, and when the sun had set, he dug a grave and buried the body. His neighbors mocked him, saying that he was no longer afraid of being put to death for his actions, and yet he continued to bury the dead. That same night, Tobit returned from burying the body and slept by the wall of his courtyard, being polluted, and with his face uncovered. He was unaware that sparrows were nesting in the wall, and as they dropped warm dung into his eyes, white films began to form. Tobit sought the help of physicians, but they could not cure him. Meanwhile, Achiacharus took care of him until he went to Elymais Tobit's wife, Anna, wove cloth in the women's chambers and sent her work back to the owners, who paid her wages and also gave her a kid. However, when the kid began to cry, Tobit suspected it had been stolen and asked Anna to return it to the owners, as it was not lawful to eat anything stolen. Anna assured him that the kid had been given to her as a gift in addition to her wages, but Tobit did not believe her and felt ashamed. Anna then reminded him of his alms and righteous deeds, saying that his works were known to all

Tobit 3

Grieved and sorrowful, Tobit wept and prayed, acknowledging the righteousness of the Lord and His mercy and truth. He asked the Lord not to take vengeance on him for his sins and the sins of his fathers, who had disobeyed God's commandments. Tobit recognized that they had been given as plunder, for captivity, death, and reproach among the nations where they were dispersed. He accepted that God's judgments were many and true, and he pleaded with the Lord to deal with him according to His will. Tobit expressed his wish to be released from his suffering and return to the earth, as it seemed more profitable for him to die than to live. He had heard false reproaches and felt great sorrow. Tobit prayed that he might be released from his distress and go to the everlasting place, asking the Lord not to turn His face away from him On the same day, in Ecbatana of Media, Sarah, the daughter of Raguel, was also reproached by her father's maidservants. She had been given to seven husbands, but Asmodaeus, the evil spirit, had killed them before they had lain with her. The maidservants accused her of strangling her husbands and mocked her, saying that they would never see any children from her. Grieved beyond measure, Sarah considered hanging herself but feared bringing reproach to her father and causing his sorrowful descent into the grave. Instead, she prayed by the window, praising the Lord and asking to be released from the earth so she would no longer hear reproach. Sarah reminded the Lord that she was pure from all sin with man and that she had never polluted her name or her father's name in the land of captivity. As the only daughter of her father, she had no brother or son to keep herself for as a wife. She lamented that seven husbands had already died, questioning why she should continue to live. If it did not please the Lord to kill her, she asked for His pity so that she might hear no more reproach Both Tobit's and Sarah's prayers were heard before the glory of the great God, and Raphael was sent to heal them both. He was to remove the white films from Tobit's eyes and give Sarah, the daughter of Raguel, as a wife to Tobias, the son of Tobit, binding Asmodaeus, the evil spirit. It was destined for Tobias to inherit Sarah as his wife. At that very moment, Tobit returned to his house, and Sarah came down from her upper chamber

Tobit 4

On that day, Tobit remembered the money he had left in trust with Gabael in Rages of Media, and he thought to himself that he should call his son Tobias to explain the matter to him before he died. Tobit called Tobias and said, "My child, if I die, bury me. Do not despise your mother. Honor her all the days of your life, and do what pleases her. Do not grieve her. Remember, my child, that she has seen many dangers for you while you were in her womb. When she dies, bury her beside me in one grave." Tobit advised his son to be mindful of the Lord their God all his days and not to let his will be set on sin or transgressing God's commandments. He encouraged Tobias to do righteousness all the days of his life and not follow the ways of unrighteousness. Tobit assured him that if he did what was true, his deeds would prosper, not only for him but for all those who practice righteousness. He urged Tobias to give alms from his possessions and not to let his eye be envious when giving. Tobit promised that if Tobias did not turn away his face from any poor man, the face of God would not be turned away from him According to his abundance, Tobias was to give alms, and even if he had little, he should not be afraid to give from that little. Tobit explained that almsgiving delivers from death and prevents one from entering darkness. Alms are a good gift in the sight of the Most High for all who give it. Tobit warned his son to beware of fornication and to take a wife from the seed of their fathers, not from a strange wife outside their tribe. He reminded Tobias that they were descendants of the prophets, and their forefathers, including Noah, Abraham, Isaac, and Jacob, all took wives from their kindred and were blessed in their children. Their seed would inherit the land Tobit advised Tobias to love his kindred and not scorn them in his heart. He warned that scornfulness leads to destruction and much trouble, and idleness leads to decay and great lack. Idleness is the mother of famine. Tobit instructed Tobias not to withhold the wages of any man who worked for him but to pay him promptly. He assured him that if he served God, he would be rewarded. Tobit urged his son to take heed in all his works and to be discreet in his behavior. He advised him not to do to others what he himself hated. He warned Tobias not to drink wine to drunkenness or allow drunkenness to accompany him on his way Tobit instructed Tobias to give bread to the hungry and garments to the naked, giving alms from all his abundance without envy. He told him to pour out bread on the burial of the just and not to give anything to sinners. Tobit advised him to seek counsel from wise men and not to despise any profitable advice. He urged Tobias to bless the Lord

his God at all times and ask that his ways be made straight and that all his paths and counsels prosper. Tobit reminded him that every nation lacks true counsel, but the Lord Himself gives all good things and humbles whom He wills. Tobit concluded by reminding Tobias to remember his commandments and not let them be forgotten Tobit then explained to his son about the ten talents of silver he had left in trust with Gabael, the son of Gabrias, at Rages of Media. He reassured Tobias not to fear poverty, for they had much wealth in the fear of God and in doing what was pleasing in His sight

Tobit 5

Tobias responded to his father, saying, "Father, I will do everything you have commanded me. But how can I receive the money when I do not know the man?" Tobit handed him the handwriting and instructed him to find a man who could accompany him. He promised to pay the man wages while he still lived and urged Tobias to go and receive the money Tobias went out and found Raphael, who was an angel, though Tobias did not know it. He asked Raphael, "Can you go with me to Rages of Media? Do you know those places well?" Raphael replied, "I will go with you. I know the way well. I have lodged with our brother Gabael." Tobias asked him to wait while he informed his father. Raphael urged him to hurry and not to delay. Tobias then told his father, "I have found someone who will go with me." Tobit asked to meet the man to know of what tribe he was and if he could be trusted to accompany Tobias Raphael came in, and they saluted each other. Tobit asked, "Brother, of what tribe and family are you? Tell me." Raphael replied, "Do you seek a tribe and family or a hired man to accompany your son?" Tobit explained that he wanted to know his kindred and name. Raphael answered, "I am Azarias, the son of Ananias the great, of your kindred." Tobit welcomed him warmly, reassuring him that his inquiry was only out of concern. Tobit expressed his trust in Azarias's lineage, knowing of his good and honest ancestry Tobit then asked, "What wages shall I give you? A drachma a day, and what is necessary for you, as with my son? And if you both return safely, I will add something to your wages." They agreed, and Raphael blessed Tobias for his journey, wishing him prosperity. Tobias prepared for the journey, and his father sent him off with a prayer that God, who dwells in heaven, would prosper his journey and send His angel with him. They both departed, accompanied by Tobias's dog However, Anna, Tobias's mother, wept and questioned Tobit, asking why he had sent their child away, who was the staff of their hand. She pleaded with him not to be greedy for money, as it was nothing compared to their son. Tobit reassured her not to worry, promising that Tobias would return safely and that a good angel would accompany him. Eventually, Anna ceased weeping

Tobit 6

As they journeyed, they came to the river Tigris in the evening and lodged there. Tobias went down to wash himself, but a fish leaped out of the river and nearly swallowed him. Raphael instructed him to grab the fish, and Tobias hauled it onto the land. The angel then told him to cut the fish open, remove the heart, liver, and bile, and keep them. Tobias followed these instructions, and they roasted the fish and ate it before continuing their journey until they drew near to Ecbatana Tobias asked Raphael, "Brother Azarias, what is the purpose of the heart, liver, and bile of the fish?" Raphael explained that the heart and liver were to be burned and made into smoke if a demon or evil spirit troubled anyone, as this would drive the affliction away. The bile, he said, was good for anointing a man with white films in his eyes, as it would heal him As they approached Rages, Raphael informed Tobias that they would lodge with Raguel, his kinsman, who had an only daughter named Sarah. Raphael intended to speak with Raguel about giving Sarah to Tobias as a wife, for her inheritance belonged to Tobias as her only kin. Raphael assured him that Raguel could not marry her to another according to the law of Moses, or he would be liable to death Tobias expressed his concern, having heard that Sarah had been given to seven men, all of whom perished in the bridal chamber. He feared that he, being his father's only son, might also die, bringing sorrow to his parents. But Raphael reassured him, reminding him of his father's command to take a wife from his kindred. Raphael urged Tobias not to worry about the demon, as Sarah was destined for him from the beginning. He advised him to take the ashes of incense, lay upon them some of the heart and liver of the fish, and make smoke in the bridal chamber, which would drive the demon away. Raphael instructed both Tobias and Sarah to pray to God for mercy, assuring him that God would save them. Tobias, moved by Raphael's words, fell in love with Sarah, and his soul was strongly joined to her

Tobit 7

When they arrived in Ecbatana, they were greeted by Sarah and brought into the house of Raguel. Raguel remarked to his wife, Edna, that Tobias resembled his cousin Tobit. He inquired about their origins, and they revealed that they were from the tribe of Naphtali, captives in Nineveh. Raguel asked if they knew Tobit, and they confirmed that they did. Upon hearing that Tobit was in good health, Raguel, moved by the news, embraced Tobias, kissed him, and blessed him. However, when he learned that Tobit had lost his sight, he and his family wept They welcomed Tobias and his companion warmly, slaughtered a ram, and served them a meal. Tobias, however, urged Raphael to speak of the matter they had discussed on the journey. Raphael communicated the matter to Raguel, who, after hearing it, asked them to eat, drink, and be merry, for it was Tobias's right to take Sarah as his wife. Raguel confessed that he had given Sarah to seven men of their relatives, but they had all died in the night. Despite this, Tobias insisted on entering into a covenant with Raguel before he would eat or drink Raguel agreed, recognizing that it was Tobias's right according to the law of Moses. He called Sarah and gave her to Tobias as his wife, blessing them both. Raguel called his wife, Edna, and instructed her to prepare the bridal chamber. Edna did as instructed, but she wept with her daughter, comforting her and praying that the Lord would grant Sarah favor and comfort in her sorrow

Tobit 8

After supper, Tobias was brought to Sarah, and as he went, he remembered Raphael's instructions. He took the ashes of the incense, placed the heart and liver of the fish on them, and made smoke. The demon, smelling the smoke, fled to the uppermost parts of Egypt, where Raphael bound him. Once they were alone, Tobias rose from the bed and said to Sarah, "Sister, arise, and let us pray that the Lord may have mercy on us." Together, they prayed, blessing the God of their fathers and asking for His mercy. Tobias declared that he took Sarah not out of lust but in truth, and he prayed for mercy and that they might grow old together. Sarah responded with "Amen," and they both slept peacefully that night Meanwhile, Raguel, fearing the worst, went out to dig a grave, thinking that Tobias might also die. However, when his maidservant entered the room in the morning, she found them both alive and sleeping peacefully. Overjoyed, Raguel blessed God, giving thanks for His

mercy and expressing his relief that his fears had not come to pass. He commanded his servants to fill the grave and kept the wedding feast for fourteen days Before the feast ended, Raguel swore to Tobias that he should not depart until the fourteen days were fulfilled. He promised that after the feast, Tobias could take half of his goods and return safely to his father, with the rest to be given to him upon the death of Raguel and Edna

Tobit 9

Tobias called Raphael and said, "Brother Azarias, take a servant and two camels, and go to Rages of Media to Gabael to receive the money for me. Bring him to the wedding feast, for Raguel has sworn that I must not depart. My father is counting the days, and if I delay, he will be very grieved." Raphael went on his way, lodged with Gabael, and gave him the handwriting. Gabael brought forth the sealed bags of money and gave them to Raphael. Together, they rose early in the morning and returned to the wedding feast. Tobias blessed his wife

Tobit 10

Tobit, meanwhile, counted the days of his son's journey, and when the time had expired, and they had not returned, he grew worried. He wondered if Tobias had been detained or if Gabael was dead and there was no one to give him the money. His grief deepened, but Anna, his wife, lamented that their son had perished, saying that she no longer cared for anything else. She bewailed her son, refusing to eat during the day and spending her nights weeping until the fourteen days of the wedding feast were over Finally, Tobias told Raguel that he must return to his father, for his parents were anxious to see him again. Raguel urged him to stay, offering to send word to his father about his welfare, but Tobias insisted on leaving. Raguel relented and gave Tobias half of his goods, including servants, cattle, and money. He blessed Tobias and Sarah, praying that the God of heaven would prosper them and grant him the joy of seeing their children before he died. Edna, too, blessed Tobias, committing her daughter to his care and praying that she might see their children and rejoice before the Lord

Tobit 11

After these events, Tobias continued his journey, blessing God for the prosperity of his travels. He also blessed Raguel and his wife Edna. As they neared Nineveh, Raphael said to Tobias, "Brother, do you remember how you left your father? Let us hurry ahead of your wife and prepare the house. But take the bile of the fish with you." So they set off, with the dog following them Meanwhile, Anna sat watching the path, looking out for her son's return. She spotted him coming and exclaimed to Tobit, "Look, your son is returning with the man who accompanied him!" Raphael then instructed Tobias, "I know that your father will soon regain his sight. Therefore, anoint his eyes with the bile. When they begin to hurt, he will rub them, and the white films will fall away, allowing him to see you." Anna ran to her son and embraced him, saying, "I have seen you, my child! Now I am ready to die." They both wept. Tobit, making his way toward the door, stumbled, but Tobias ran to him and held him. Tobias applied the bile to his father's eyes, reassuring him, "Cheer up, my father." When Tobit's eyes began to hurt, he rubbed them, and soon the white films peeled away from the corners of his eyes. Tobit saw his son and fell upon his neck, weeping, and said, "Blessed are you, O God, and blessed is your name forever! Blessed are all your holy angels! For you chastised me, but you also showed me mercy. Behold, I see my son Tobias." Tobias then went inside, rejoicing, and told his father about all the great things that had happened to him in Media Tobit, rejoicing and blessing God, went out to meet his daughter-in-law at the gate of Nineveh. Those who saw him marveled that he had regained his sight. Tobit gave thanks before them, acknowledging God's mercy. When he approached Sarah, his daughter-in-law, he blessed her, saying, "Welcome, daughter! Blessed is God who has brought you to us, and blessed are your father and mother." There was great joy among all Tobit's kindred in Nineveh. Achiacharus and Nasbas, his brother's son, also came, and Tobias's wedding feast was celebrated for seven days with great gladness

Tobit 12

Tobit called his son Tobias and said, "See, my child, that the man who accompanied you receives his wages, and you should give him more." Tobias responded, "Father, I will gladly give him half of all the things I have brought, for he has safely guided me, cured my wife, retrieved the money, and healed you." The old man agreed, saying, "It is only right." He called the angel and said, "Take half of all that you have brought." Then Tobit called them both privately and said, "Bless God, give Him thanks, and magnify Him before all who live, for the wonders He has done for you. It is good to bless God and exalt His name, showing forth the works of God with honor. Do not neglect to give Him thanks. It is right to conceal the secret of a king, but to gloriously reveal the works of God. Do good, and evil will not find you. Prayer with fasting, almsgiving, and righteousness are good. A little with righteousness is better than much with unrighteousness. It is better to give alms than to hoard gold. Almsgiving delivers from death and purges away all sin. Those who give alms and do righteousness will be filled with life, but those who sin are enemies to their own lives." Raphael continued, "I will hide nothing from you. I said, 'It is good to conceal the secret of a king, but to reveal gloriously the works of God.' When you prayed, and when Sarah, your daughter-in-law, prayed, I brought the memorial of your prayers before the Holy One. When you buried the dead, I was with you. When you did not delay to rise and leave your dinner to cover the dead, your good deed was not hidden from me; I was with you. Now God has sent me to heal you and Sarah, your daughter-in-law. I am Raphael, one of the seven holy angels who present the prayers of the saints and enter before the glory of the Holy One." They were both troubled and fell upon their faces in fear. But Raphael said to them, "Do not be afraid. You will all have peace; bless God forever. I did not come of my own accord, but by the will of your God. Therefore, bless Him forever. Throughout these days, I appeared to you; I did not eat or drink, but you saw a vision. Now give thanks to God, for I ascend to Him who sent me. Write in a book all that has happened." Then they rose up and saw him no more. They confessed the great and wonderful works of God and how the angel of the Lord had appeared to them

Tobit 13

Tobit wrote a prayer of rejoicing and said, "Blessed is God who lives forever! Blessed is His kingdom! For He chastises and shows mercy. He brings down to the grave and raises up again. No one can escape His hand. Give thanks to Him before the Gentiles, all you children of Israel! For He has scattered us among them. Declare His greatness there. Extol Him before all the living, for He is our Lord, and God is our Father forever. He will chastise us for our iniquities and will show mercy again, gathering us from all the nations where we have been scattered. If you turn to Him with all your heart and soul, to do truth before Him, He will turn to you and not hide His face from you. See what He will do with you. Give thanks with your whole mouth. Bless the Lord of righteousness. Exalt the everlasting King. I give Him thanks in the land of my captivity, and show His strength and majesty to a nation of sinners. Turn, you sinners, and do righteousness before Him. Who knows if He will accept you and have mercy on you?" Tobit continued, "I exalt my God. My soul exalts the King of heaven and rejoices in His greatness. Let all men speak and give Him thanks in Jerusalem. O Jerusalem, the holy city, He will chastise you for the works of your sons and will show mercy again to the sons of the righteous. Give thanks to the Lord with goodness, and bless the everlasting King. His tabernacle will be rebuilt in you with joy, and He will make those who are captives glad in you, and those who are miserable will love you forever. Many nations will come from afar to the name of the Lord God with gifts in their hands, even gifts to the King of heaven. Generations will praise you and sing songs of rejoicing. All who hate you are cursed. All who love you will be blessed forever. Rejoice and be exceedingly glad for the sons of the righteous, for they will be gathered together and will bless the Lord of the righteous. Blessed are those who love you; they will rejoice for your peace. Blessed are all who mourned for all your chastisements, for they will rejoice when they see all your glory. They will be made glad forever. Let my soul bless God, the great King. For Jerusalem will be rebuilt with sapphires, emeralds, and precious stones. Your walls, towers, and battlements will be made of pure gold. The streets of Jerusalem will be paved with beryl, carbuncle, and stones of Ophir. All her streets will say, 'Hallelujah!' and give praise, saying, 'Blessed be God, who has exalted you forever!'"

Tobit 14

When Tobit finished giving thanks, he reflected on his life. He had lost his sight at the age of fifty-eight, but after eight years, he regained it. Throughout his life, Tobit gave alms, feared the Lord God more and more, and continually gave thanks to Him. As he grew very old, he called his son Tobias and Tobias's six sons and said, "My child, take your sons and listen to me. I have grown old and am ready to depart from this life. Go into Media, my child, for I truly believe the prophecies of Jonah concerning Nineveh, that it will be overthrown. But in Media, there will be peace for a time. Our kindred will be scattered from the good land. Jerusalem will be desolate, and the house of God in it will be burned and left desolate for a time. However, God will again have mercy on His people, bringing them back to the land, and they will rebuild the house of God, though it will not be like the former one until the times are fulfilled. Afterward, they will return from their captivity and rebuild Jerusalem with honor. The house of God will be established in it forever with a glorious building, just as the prophets have spoken concerning it. All the nations will turn to fear the Lord God truly, and they will abandon their idols. All the nations will bless the Lord, and His people will give thanks to God. The Lord will exalt His people, and all who love the Lord God in truth and righteousness will rejoice, showing mercy to our kindred." Tobit continued, "Now, my child, depart from Nineveh, for the words of the prophet Jonah will surely come to pass. But you must keep the law and the ordinances, showing yourself merciful and righteous, that it may be well with you. Bury me decently, and bury your mother with me. Do not stay in Nineveh. Consider, my child, what Aman did to Achiacharus, who nourished him, how he brought him from light into darkness and the recompense he received. Achiacharus was saved, but Aman went down into darkness. Manasses gave alms and escaped the snare of death that was set for him, but

Aman fell into the snare and perished. Now, my children, consider what alms does and how righteousness delivers." As Tobit finished saying these things, he passed away, at the age of one hundred and fifty-eight. Tobias buried him magnificently. When Anna died, Tobias buried her beside Tobit. Tobias then departed with his wife and sons to Ecbatana, to the house of Raguel, his father-in-law. He grew old with honor and buried his father-in-law and mother-in-law magnificently. Tobias inherited their possessions as well as those of his father Tobit. Tobias died in Ecbatana of Media at the age of one hundred and twenty-seven. Before he died, he heard of the destruction of Nineveh, which Nebuchadnezzar and Ahasuerus took captive, and he rejoiced over the fall of Nineveh before his death

70. Judith

Judith 1
In the twelfth year of the reign of Nebuchadnezzar, who ruled over the Assyrians in Nineveh, the great city, during the days of Arphaxad, king of the Medes in Ecbatana, Arphaxad built around Ecbatana walls of hewn stones, three cubits broad and six cubits long, with the wall's height reaching seventy cubits, and its breadth fifty cubits. He set its towers at the gates one hundred cubits high, with a foundation breadth of sixty cubits. The gates themselves were raised to a height of seventy cubits, and their breadth was forty cubits, allowing his mighty army to march out and his footmen to array themselves During these times, King Nebuchadnezzar waged war against King Arphaxad in the great plain on the borders of Ragau. All who lived in the hill country, by the rivers Euphrates, Tigris, and Hydaspes, and in the plain of Arioch, king of the Elymaeans, gathered to battle against him. Many nations of the sons of Chelod assembled for war Nebuchadnezzar, king of the Assyrians, sent messengers to those living in Persia, to all who lived westward, including those in Cilicia, Damascus, Lebanon, Antilibanus, and along the sea coast. He also sent to those in Carmel, Gilead, the higher Galilee, and the great plain of Esdraelon, as well as those in Samaria and its cities, beyond Jordan to Jerusalem, Betane, Chellus, Kadesh, the river of Egypt, Tahpanhes, Rameses, and all the land of Goshen, until reaching Tanis and Memphis, and even to the borders of Ethiopia Despite Nebuchadnezzar's commands, all the inhabitants of these lands disregarded his orders, refusing to join him in the war. They were not afraid of him and treated him as though he were insignificant. They dismissed his messengers with scorn and disgrace. This angered Nebuchadnezzar greatly, and he swore by his throne and kingdom that he would seek vengeance upon all the coasts of Cilicia, Damascus, and Syria. He vowed to kill with the sword all the inhabitants of Moab, Ammon, Judea, and even Egypt, up to the borders of the two seas In the seventeenth year of his reign, Nebuchadnezzar set his army in array against King Arphaxad, and he prevailed in battle, routing the army of Arphaxad, including his horses and chariots. Nebuchadnezzar seized Arphaxad's cities, marched into Ecbatana, captured its towers, plundered its streets, and turned its splendor into shame. He took Arphaxad in the mountains of Ragau, struck him with his darts, and utterly destroyed him. Afterward, Nebuchadnezzar returned to Nineveh with his company of various nations, an exceedingly great multitude of warriors. There he rested and feasted with his army for one hundred and twenty days

Judith 2
In the eighteenth year, on the twenty-second day of the first month, Nebuchadnezzar, king of the Assyrians, decided to avenge himself upon all the lands, as he had sworn. He called together all his servants and great men, confiding his secret counsel to them and recounting the wickedness of the lands. They decided to destroy all flesh that did not obey the word of Nebuchadnezzar When he had concluded his counsel, Nebuchadnezzar summoned Holofernes, the chief captain of his army, who was second only to the king, and said to him, "The great king, the lord of all the earth, commands: 'Go out from my presence, taking with you men who trust in their strength—one hundred and twenty thousand footmen and twelve thousand horses with riders. You shall march against all the western lands because they have disobeyed my command. Declare to them that they must prepare earth and water, for in my wrath, I will cover the whole face of the earth with the feet of my army, which will plunder them. Their slain will fill their valleys and brooks, and the rivers will overflow with their dead. I will lead them as captives to the farthest parts of the earth. But you must first take all their coasts for me. If they surrender to you, preserve them for me until the day of their punishment. But for those who resist, show no mercy; they shall be slain and plundered in all the land. For as I live, and by the power of my kingdom, I have spoken, and I will accomplish this with my own hand. Moreover, you shall not deviate from any of my commands but shall carry them out as I have ordered.'" Holofernes departed from the presence of his lord and summoned all the governors, captains, and officers of the Assyrian army. He mustered the chosen men for battle, as his lord had commanded, numbering one hundred and twenty thousand footmen and twelve thousand archers on horseback. He organized them as a vast multitude ready for war. He also took camels, donkeys, and mules for their baggage, a great number of sheep, oxen, and goats for provisions, and a large supply of rations for each man, along with a vast amount of gold and silver from the king's treasury Holofernes set out with his entire army, moving before King Nebuchadnezzar, and covering the land westward with chariots, horsemen, and chosen footmen. A great company of various nations accompanied them, like locusts or the sands of the earth, too numerous to count. They departed from Nineveh, traveling three days' journey towards the plain of Bectileth, and camped near the mountain to the left of Upper Cilicia. Holofernes led his army—footmen, horsemen, and chariots—into the hill country, where he destroyed Put and Lud, plundered the children of Rasses and the children of Ishmael in the wilderness to the south of the land of the Chellians. He crossed the Euphrates, advanced through Mesopotamia, and broke down all the high cities along the river Arbonai until reaching the sea. He seized the borders of Cilicia, killed all who resisted, and reached the borders of Japheth, southward towards Arabia. He surrounded the children of Midian, set their tents on fire, and plundered their sheepfolds Holofernes descended into the plain of Damascus during the wheat harvest, set their fields ablaze, destroyed their flocks and herds, plundered their cities, laid their plains waste, and struck down all their young men with the sword. The fear and dread of him spread to those who lived along the seacoast, in Sidon and Tyre, in Sur and Ocina, and all who lived in Jemnaan. Even those in Azotus and Ascalon feared him greatly

Judith 3
The people sent messengers to Holofernes with words of peace, saying, "Behold, we are the servants of Nebuchadnezzar, the great king, and we lie before you. Use us as it pleases you. Behold, our dwellings,

all our country, our fields of wheat, our flocks and herds, and all the sheepfolds of our tents lie before you. Use them as you see fit. Behold, even our cities and their inhabitants are your servants. Come and deal with them as you think best." The messengers conveyed these words to Holofernes, who then descended to the seacoast with his army. He set garrisons in the high cities and selected men from them as allies. The people received him with garlands, dances, and timbrels. Holofernes cast down all their borders and cut down their sacred groves, for it had been decreed that he should destroy all the gods of the land so that all nations would worship Nebuchadnezzar alone, and that all tongues and tribes would call upon him as a god Holofernes then moved towards Esdraelon, near Dothaim, opposite the great ridge of Judea. He encamped between Geba and Scythopolis, remaining there for a month to gather all the supplies for his army

Judith 4

The children of Israel in Judea heard of all that Holofernes, the chief captain of Nebuchadnezzar, king of the Assyrians, had done to the nations, how he had plundered and utterly destroyed their temples. They were exceedingly afraid at his approach and were deeply concerned for Jerusalem and the temple of the Lord their God. The people had only recently returned from captivity, and the vessels, the altar, and the house had been sanctified after being profaned The Israelites sent messages to every coast of Samaria, to Konae, Beth-horon, Belmaim, Jericho, Choba, Aesora, and the valley of Salem. They occupied the tops of the high mountains beforehand, fortified the villages within them, and stored supplies in preparation for war, for their fields had just been harvested Joakim, the high priest in Jerusalem, wrote to those in Bethulia and Betomesthaim, which is opposite Esdraelon towards the plain near Dothaim, instructing them to seize the ascents of the hill country, as these were the entrances into Judea, and it was easy to defend them due to the narrow approach, which could only accommodate two men at most. The children of Israel did as Joakim, the high priest, had commanded, as did the senate of all the people of Israel, who were in session in Jerusalem Every man of Israel cried out to God with great earnestness, humbling their souls. They, along with their wives, children, cattle, and every sojourner, hireling, and servant bought with money, put sackcloth on their loins. Every man, woman, and child in Israel, including the inhabitants of Jerusalem, fell prostrate before the temple, cast ashes upon their heads, and spread out their sackcloth before the Lord. They surrounded the altar with sackcloth and cried out earnestly to the God of Israel in one accord, asking that He would not allow their children to be taken as prey, their wives as plunder, their cities to be destroyed, or the sanctuary to be profaned and made a reproach for the nations to rejoice over The Lord heard their cries and looked upon their affliction. The people continued fasting for many days in all Judea and Jerusalem before the sanctuary of the Lord Almighty. Joakim, the high priest, and all the priests who stood before the Lord, along with those who ministered to the Lord, wore sackcloth and offered the continual burnt offerings, the vows, and the freewill offerings of the people. They had ashes on their turbans and cried out to the Lord with all their might, asking Him to look upon all the house of Israel with favor

Judith 5

Holofernes, the chief captain of the Assyrian army, was informed that the children of Israel had prepared for war, shut up the passages of the hill country, fortified the tops of the high hills, and set up barricades in the plains. Angered by this, he summoned all the princes of Moab, the captains of Ammon, and the governors of the seacoast, and said to them, "Tell me now, you sons of Canaan, who are these people who dwell in the hill country? What cities do they inhabit? How large is their army? Where is their power and strength? What king is set over them to lead their army? Why have they turned their backs on me, unlike all the other people who dwell in the west?" Achior, the leader of all the children of Ammon, replied, "Let my lord hear a word from his servant, and I will tell you the truth about these people who dwell in the hill country near where you live. No lie will come from my mouth. These people are descendants of the Chaldeans. They sojourned in Mesopotamia because they refused to follow the gods of their fathers in the land of the Chaldeans. They departed from the ways of their parents and worshipped the God of heaven, whom they knew. Their parents cast them out for abandoning their gods, and they fled to Mesopotamia, where they sojourned for many days Then their God commanded them to leave the place where they had sojourned and to go into the land of Canaan. There they lived and prospered, accumulating gold, silver, and much cattle. When a famine struck all the land of Canaan, they went down into Egypt and stayed there until they grew in number, becoming a great multitude. The Egyptians could no longer count their population. Then the king of Egypt rose against them, dealt with them cunningly, and brought them low, making them labor in brick and turning them into slaves. They cried out to their God, who struck all the land of Egypt with incurable plagues, forcing the Egyptians to cast them out God then dried up the Red Sea before them and brought them through the way of Sinai and Kadesh-Barnea, where they cast out all who lived in the wilderness. They settled in the land of the Amorites, destroying all the inhabitants of Heshbon by their strength. They crossed over the Jordan and took possession of all the hill country, casting out the Canaanites, Perizzites, Jebusites, Shechemites, and Girgashites. They lived in that country for many days. As long as they did not sin against their God, they prospered, for God, who hates iniquity, was with them But when they departed from the path He had appointed for them, they were destroyed in many severe battles and were led captive into a foreign land. Their temple was razed, and their cities were taken by their adversaries. Now they have returned to their God and have come up from the dispersion where they were scattered. They have possessed Jerusalem, where their sanctuary is, and are settled in the hill country, which was desolate Now, my lord and master, if there is any sin among this people, and they have offended their God, let us find out in what way they have stumbled, and we can go up and overcome them. But if there is no lawlessness in their nation, let my lord pass by them, lest their Lord defend them, and their God be for them, and we will become a reproach before all the earth." When Achior had finished speaking, all the people standing around the tent grumbled. The great men of Holofernes, and all who lived by the seacoast and in Moab, insisted that Achior be cut to pieces. They argued, "We are not afraid of the children of Israel, for behold, they are a people without power or might to make a strong battle. Therefore, let us go up and take them as prey for your entire army, Lord Holofernes."

Judith 6

When the uproar among the council subsided,

Holofernes, the chief captain of the army of Asshur, addressed Achior and all the children of Moab before the assembly of foreigners, saying, "And who are you, Achior, and the mercenaries of Ephraim, to prophesy among us today, declaring that we should not make war with the race of Israel because their God will defend them? Who is God but Nebuchadnezzar? He will unleash his might and destroy them from the face of the earth. Their God will not deliver them; we, his servants, will strike them down as one man. They will not withstand the might of our cavalry With our forces, we will burn them up. Their mountains will be soaked with their blood, their plains filled with their dead bodies. They will not stand against us but will surely perish, as King Nebuchadnezzar, lord of all the earth, has decreed, 'The words that I have spoken will not be in vain.' But as for you, Achior, hireling of Ammon, who has spoken these words in the day of your iniquity, you will see my face no more from this day until I am avenged upon the race of those who came out of Egypt. Then the sword of my army, and the multitude of those who serve me, will pass through your side, and you will fall among the slain when I return. My servants will bring you back into the hill country, and set you in one of the cities by the passes. You will not perish until you are destroyed along with them. If you hold hope in your heart that they will not be taken, do not let your countenance fall. I have spoken it, and none of my words will fall to the ground." Holofernes then commanded his servants who attended him in his tent to take Achior and return him to Bethulia, delivering him into the hands of the children of Israel. So, his servants took Achior, led him out of the camp into the plain, and journeyed from the plains into the hill country, reaching the springs beneath Bethulia. When the men of the city saw them on the hilltop, they took up their weapons and went out of the city to the hilltop, preventing them from ascending by using slings and throwing stones at them The Assyrian soldiers took cover under the hill, bound Achior, cast him down, left him at the foot of the hill, and departed. The children of Israel then descended from their city, untied Achior, and brought him to Bethulia, presenting him to the rulers of the city— Ozias, son of Micah, of the tribe of Simeon, Chabris, son of Gothoniel, and Charmis, son of Melchiel. They gathered all the elders of the city, and the young men, along with the women, came together in the assembly. They set Achior in the midst of the people, and Ozias asked him what had happened Achior recounted all that had occurred, including the words spoken in the council of Holofernes and all the boasts made against the house of Israel. Upon hearing this, the people fell down and worshipped God, crying out, "O Lord God of heaven, behold their arrogance, and take pity on the low estate of our people. Look upon those who are sanctified to you this day." They comforted Achior and praised him greatly. Ozias then took him from the assembly into his house and prepared a feast for the elders. They called upon the God of Israel for help throughout the night

Judith 7

The next day, Holofernes commanded his entire army and all the people who had joined as allies to move their camp toward Bethulia, seize the passes of the hill country, and wage war against the children of Israel. That day, every mighty man in his army, numbering one hundred and seventy thousand foot soldiers and twelve thousand horsemen, besides the baggage and other men on foot—an exceedingly great multitude—moved to encamp in the valley near Bethulia by the fountain. They spread out from Dothaim to Belmaim, stretching from Bethulia to Cyamon, near Esdraelon When the children of Israel saw the vast number of the enemy, they were terrified, and each said to his neighbor, "These men will devour the whole earth. Neither the high mountains nor the valleys nor the hills will be able to bear their weight." Every man took up his weapons of war, and they lit fires upon their towers, remaining on watch throughout the night On the second day, Holofernes led out all his cavalry before the children of Israel who were in Bethulia, surveying the ascents to their city and the springs of water. He seized the water sources and set garrisons of soldiers over them before returning to his people. The rulers of Esau, the leaders of Moab, and the captains of the seacoast came to him, advising, "Let our lord listen to a word, that your army may not suffer losses. The people of Israel do not trust in their spears, but in the height of the mountains where they dwell, for it is difficult to ascend to the tops of their mountains. Therefore, my lord, do not fight against them in the way that men fight battles, and not a single one of your people will perish Instead, remain in your camp and keep your army safe. Let your servants take possession of the water springs that flow from the foot of the mountain, for all the inhabitants of Bethulia draw their water from there. Thirst will destroy them, and they will surrender their city. Then we and our people will camp upon the nearby mountains, preventing anyone from leaving the city. They will perish from famine— they, their wives, and their children—before the sword even reaches them. Thus, you will repay them for their rebellion, as they did not come out to meet you in peace." Their words pleased Holofernes and his servants, and he ordered them to carry out their plan. The army of the Ammonites moved, along with five thousand Assyrians, and they encamped in the valley, seizing the water sources and springs that supplied the children of Israel. The children of Esau also went up with the Ammonites and encamped in the hill country near Dothaim. They sent some of their forces toward the south and east, near Ekreb'el, which is by the brook Mochmur. The rest of the Assyrian army encamped in the plain, covering the land with their tents and baggage in a vast crowd The children of Israel cried out to the Lord their God, for their spirit fainted; all their enemies surrounded them, leaving no escape. The Assyrian army remained around them—foot soldiers, chariots, and horsemen—for thirty-four days. The water vessels of the inhabitants of Bethulia ran dry. The cisterns were emptied, and they had no water to drink their fill even for a day, as the drink was rationed by measure. The young children grew weak, the women and young men fainted from thirst, collapsing in the streets and at the gates of the city, with no strength left in them All the people, including the young men, women, and children, gathered together against Ozias and the rulers of the city, crying out, "God judge between you and us, for you have wronged us by not seeking peace with the Assyrians. Now we have no helper; God has given us into their hands, and we shall perish from thirst and great destruction. Summon the Assyrians and surrender the city to Holofernes and his army. It is better for us to be captured and live as servants than to see our children die before our eyes, and our wives and children fainting to death. We bear witness against you, before heaven and earth, and before our God, who punishes us according to our sins and the sins of our fathers. Do what we have asked today!" There was great weeping in the assembly, and they cried out to the Lord God with a loud voice. Ozias responded, "Brothers, be of good courage! Let us endure for five more days, during which time the Lord our God may turn His mercy toward us; He will not forsake us utterly. But if these days pass and no help comes, I will do as you have said." Then he dismissed the people, each man returning to his camp, and they went to the walls and towers of the city. He sent the women and children back to their homes, and the city was brought very low

Judith 8

In those days, Judith heard of what was happening. She was the daughter of Merari, the son of Ox, the son of Joseph, the son of Oziel, the son of Elkiah, the son of Ananias, the son of Gideon, the son of Raphaim, the son of Ahitub, the son of Elihu, the son of Eliab, the son of Nathanael, the son of Salamiel, the son of Sarasadai, the son of Israel. Her husband was Manasses, of her tribe and family, who had died during the barley harvest. He had been overseeing those who bound sheaves in the field when he was struck by the burning heat. He fell on his bed and died in Bethulia. They buried him with his ancestors in a field between Dothaim and Balamon Judith was a widow for three years and four months. She made a tent for herself on the roof of her house, wore sackcloth on her loins, and kept the garments of her widowhood. She fasted all the days of her widowhood, except on the eves of Sabbaths, Sabbaths, the eves of new moons, new moons, and the feasts and joyful days of the house of Israel. She was beautiful and lovely to behold. Her husband Manasses had left her gold, silver, servants, cattle, and lands, and she remained on those lands. No one spoke ill of her, for she feared God greatly Judith heard the complaints of the people against the governor because they were fainting from lack of water. She also learned of the words Ozias spoke to them, swearing to surrender the city to the Assyrians after five days. So, she sent her maid, who was in charge of all she possessed, to summon Ozias, Chabris, and Charmis, the elders of her city. When they came to her, she said, "Listen to me, rulers of Bethulia! The words you have spoken before the people today are not right. You have set an oath between God and yourselves, promising to deliver the city to our enemies unless the Lord helps you within these days. Who are you to test God and stand in His place among the children of men? You cannot comprehend the mind of the Lord Almighty or search out His heart. Do not provoke the Lord our God to anger! If He has not decided to help us within these five days, He has the power to defend us at any time or destroy us before our enemies. But do not bind the counsels of the Lord our God! He is not like a human being to be threatened, nor is He like a son of man to be swayed by pleading. Therefore, let us wait for His salvation and call upon Him for help. He will hear our voice if it pleases Him In our time, there has been no tribe, kindred, family, or city among us that worships idols made with hands, as in former days, for which reason our ancestors were given to the sword, plundered, and fell with great destruction before their enemies. But we know no other god besides Him, and we trust that He will not despise us or any of our race. For if we are captured, all Judea will be captured, our sanctuary plundered, and God will require our blood for its profanation. The slaughter of our kin, the captivity of our land, and the desolation of our inheritance will be brought upon us among the Gentiles, where we will be in bondage. We will become an offense and reproach to those who possess us Our bondage will not bring us favor, but the Lord our God will turn it into dishonor. Now, my kinsmen, let us set an example for our people, for their souls depend on us, and the sanctuary, the house, and the altar depend on us. Let us give thanks to the Lord our God, who tests us as He did our ancestors. Remember what He did to Abraham, how He tested Isaac, and what happened to Jacob in Mesopotamia when he kept the sheep of Laban, his mother's brother. The Lord has not tried us by fire as He did them, to search out their hearts, nor has He taken vengeance on us. But the Lord chastises those who draw near to Him, to admonish them." Ozias responded, "All that you have spoken is true, and no one can deny your words. Your wisdom has been known since the beginning of your days, for the disposition of your heart is good. But the people were exceedingly thirsty and forced us to make an oath, which we cannot break. Now, pray for us, for you are a godly woman, and the Lord will send us rain to fill our cisterns, so we will faint no more." Judith then said, "Listen to me, and I will do something that will be remembered by our descendants. Tonight, you shall stand guard at the gate, and I will go out with my maid. Before the days you have mentioned have passed, the Lord will deliver Israel by my hand. But you must not inquire about my plan, for I will not reveal it until it is accomplished." Ozias and the rulers replied, "Go in peace, and may the Lord God be with you to take vengeance on our enemies." They then returned to their stations

Judith 9

Judith fell on her face, covered her head with ashes, and uncovered the sackcloth she was wearing. As the incense of the evening sacrifice was being offered in the house of God in Jerusalem, Judith cried out to the Lord with a loud voice, saying, "O Lord God of my father Simeon, into whose hand you gave a sword to take vengeance on those who defiled a virgin, exposed her shame, and brought reproach upon her, for you said, 'It shall not be so,' and yet they did so. You delivered their rulers to be slain, and their bed, which was shamed by deception, was stained with blood. You struck down the servants along with their masters, and the masters upon their thrones. You gave their wives as spoil and their daughters as captives, dividing all their spoils among your beloved children, who were zealous for you and abhorred the pollution of their blood. They called upon you for help, O God, and you heard them Hear me now, too, O God, who am a widow. You have done the things that were before, and the things that are now, and the things that will come. All that you have planned has come to pass, and the things you have determined stand before you, saying, 'Behold, we are here,' for all your ways are prepared, and your judgment is foreseen Behold, the Assyrians are powerful and exalted with horse and rider. They boast in the strength of their footmen and trust in their shields, spears, bows, and slings. But they do not know that you are the Lord who breaks battles, and 'The Lord' is your name. Break their strength by your power, and bring down their force in your wrath, for they intend to profane your sanctuary and defile the tabernacle where your glorious name rests, and to destroy the horn of your altar with the sword Look upon their pride and send your wrath upon their heads. Give into my hand, a widow, the strength that I have conceived. Strike down their arrogance by the hand of a woman. For your power does not depend on numbers, nor your might on strong men, but you are the God of the afflicted, the helper of the oppressed, the protector of the forsaken, and the savior of those without hope Please, O God of my father, God of the inheritance of Israel, Lord of the heavens and the earth, Creator of the waters, King of all your creation, hear my prayer. Make my words and my deceit the wound and bruise of those who plot evil against your covenant, your holy house, the top of Zion, and the house of your children's inheritance. Let every nation and tribe know that you are God, the God of all power and might, and that there is no one who protects the race of Israel but you."

Judith 10

When Judith finished praying to the God of Israel and had said all these words, she rose from where she had fallen, called her maid, and went down into the house where she lived on the Sabbaths and feast days. She removed the sackcloth she had worn, took off her widow's garments, washed her body with water, anointed herself with rich ointment, braided her hair, and put on a tiara. She donned her garments of gladness, which she had worn during her husband Manasses' life. She put sandals on her feet and adorned herself with anklets, bracelets, rings, earrings, and all her jewelry. She made herself very beautiful to captivate the eyes of all men who would see her She gave her maid a leather container of wine, a flask of oil, and packed a bag with roasted grain, lumps of figs, and fine bread. She gathered all her vessels and laid them upon her maid. Together, they went to the gate of Bethulia, where they found Ozias and the elders of the city, Chabris and Charmis, standing by it. When they saw her, they were astonished by her beauty and the change in her appearance and attire They said to her, "May the God of our fathers grant you favor and fulfill your purposes to the glory of the children of Israel and the exaltation of Jerusalem." Judith worshipped God and said, "Command that the gate of the city be opened for me, and I will go out to accomplish the things you have spoken with me about." They ordered the young men to open the gate for her, and they did so. Judith then went out with her maid. The men of the city watched her until she had descended the mountain, crossed the valley, and disappeared from their sight As they continued their journey through the valley, the Assyrian guards met them. They took Judith and asked, "What people are you from? Where are you coming from, and where are you going?" She replied, "I am a daughter of the Hebrews, fleeing from their presence because they are about to be given to you to be consumed. I am coming to the presence of Holofernes, the chief captain of your army, to declare words of truth. I will show him a way to conquer all the hill country, ensuring that not one of his men will be lost." When the soldiers heard her words and saw her beauty, they were amazed. They said to her, "You have saved your life by hurrying to come down to the presence of our master. Now come to his tent, and some of us will guide you until you are delivered into his hands. When you stand before him, do not be afraid, but speak to him as you have spoken to us, and he will treat you well." They chose a hundred men to accompany her and her maid, and they brought them to the tent of Holofernes. The entire camp was filled with excitement at the news of her arrival. They came and surrounded her as she stood outside Holofernes' tent, waiting to be brought in. Everyone marveled at her beauty and wondered about the Israelites because of her. They said to one another, "Who would despise these people when they have such women among them? It is not right to leave even one of them alive, for if they are spared, they will be able to deceive the whole earth." Then the guards of Holofernes and all his servants came out and brought Judith into the tent. Holofernes was resting on his bed under a canopy woven with purple, gold, emeralds, and precious stones. When they told him about Judith, he came out into the space before his tent, with silver lamps going before him. When Judith came before him and his servants, they were all amazed by her beauty. She fell down upon her face and bowed before him, but his servants raised her up

Judith 11

Holofernes said to Judith, "Woman, take courage. Do not be afraid in your heart, for I have never harmed anyone who has chosen to serve Nebuchadnezzar, the king of all the earth. If your people who dwell in the hill country had not slighted me, I would not have lifted my spear against them, but they have brought this upon themselves. Now, tell me why you fled from them and came to us, for you have come to save yourself. Take courage! You will live tonight and hereafter, for no one will harm you. Instead, you will be treated well, just as all the servants of King Nebuchadnezzar are." Judith replied, "Receive the words of your servant and let your handmaid speak before you. I will not lie to my lord tonight. If you follow the advice of your handmaid, God will bring your plans to success, and my lord will not fail in his purpose. As Nebuchadnezzar, king of all the earth, lives, and as his power endures, he has sent you to preserve every living thing. Not only do men serve him by your hand, but also the beasts of the field, the cattle, and the birds of the sky thrive under your strength, during the reign of Nebuchadnezzar and his house We have heard of your wisdom and the subtlety of your soul. It has been reported throughout the earth that you alone are brave in all the kingdom, mighty in knowledge, and wonderful in feats of war. Now, regarding what Achior spoke in your council, we have heard his words, for the men of Bethulia saved him, and he told them everything he said before you Therefore, my lord and master, do not neglect his words, but take them to heart, for they are true. Our race will not be punished, and the sword will not prevail against us unless we sin against our God. Now, so that my lord may not be defeated and frustrated in his purpose, and so that death may fall upon them, know that their sin has overtaken them. They will provoke their God to anger whenever they commit wickedness Since their food has run out and their water is scarce, they have taken counsel to slaughter their livestock and determined to consume what God forbade them to eat by His laws. They have resolved to use the first fruits of the grain and the tithes of the wine and oil, which they had sanctified and reserved for the priests who stand before our God in Jerusalem. It is not fitting for any of the people to touch these with their hands They have sent messengers to Jerusalem to seek permission from the council of elders there. When these instructions arrive, and they act on them, they will be given into your hands for destruction on the same day. Therefore, I, your servant, knowing all this, fled from their presence. God sent me to work with you on things that will astonish the earth, as many as hear of it. For your servant is religious and serves the God of heaven day and night Now, my lord, I will remain with you, and your servant will go out at night into the valley. I will pray to God, and He will reveal to me when they have sinned. Then I will inform you, and you can go out with all your army, and none of them will resist you. I will lead you through the heart of Judea until you come to Jerusalem. I will place your throne in its center. You will drive them like sheep without a shepherd, and not even a dog will bark at you. These things were revealed to me by foreknowledge, and I was sent to tell you." Her words pleased Holofernes and all his servants. They marveled at her wisdom and said, "There is no woman like her from one end of the earth to the other, for beauty of face and wisdom of words." Holofernes said to her, "God did well to send you ahead of your people, that might may be in our hands and destruction upon those who slighted my lord. Now you are beautiful in countenance and wise in words. If you do as you have spoken, your God will be my God, and you will dwell in the palace of King Nebuchadnezzar, renowned throughout the earth."

Judith 12

Holofernes commanded that Judith be brought into the area where his silver vessels were set, and he asked his servants to prepare some of his delicacies for her and to give her wine from his own supply. Judith replied, "I cannot eat it, lest it be a cause of stumbling, but I will eat from the provisions I have brought with me." Holofernes said, "But if your supplies run out, how will we be able to give you more of the same? There is no one of your race here with us." Judith answered, "As your soul lives, my lord, your servant will not use up what I have until the Lord accomplishes by my hand what He has determined." Then Holofernes' servants brought her into the tent, and she slept until midnight. Towards the morning watch, she rose and sent word to Holofernes, saying, "Let my lord now command that they allow your servant to go out to pray." Holofernes ordered his guards not to hinder her. She stayed in the camp for three days, going out every night to the valley of Bethulia, where she washed herself at the fountain in the camp. When she returned, she implored the Lord God of Israel to direct her way for the triumph of His people. Afterward, she remained in the tent until she ate her food in the evening On the fourth day, Holofernes made a feast for his servants and did not invite any of the officers to the banquet. He said to Bagoas, the eunuch who was in charge of all that he had, "Go now and persuade this Hebrew woman to join us and eat and drink with us. For it would be a disgrace if we let such a woman leave without enjoying her company; if we do not win her over, she will mock us." Bagoas went to Judith and said, "Do not fear to come to my lord, to be honored in his presence, to drink wine and be merry with us, and to be treated like one of the daughters of Asshur who serve in Nebuchadnezzar's palace." Judith replied, "Who am I to contradict my lord? Whatever pleases him, I will do quickly, and it will be my joy until the day I die." She arose, adorned herself with her apparel and all her jewelry, and her servant laid fleeces on the ground beside Holofernes, provided by Bagoas for her daily use. Judith sat down, and Holofernes' heart was captivated by her beauty. His desire for her grew, and he was eagerly waiting for a moment to deceive her, ever since he first saw her. Holofernes said to her, "Drink now and be merry with us." Judith replied, "I will drink, my lord, for today my life is more precious to me than all the days since I was born." She ate and drank what her servant had prepared before him. Holofernes was greatly pleased with her and drank much more wine than he had ever done in one day since he was born

Judith 13

When evening came, Holofernes' servants hurried to depart. Bagoas closed the tent from the outside and dismissed the attendants from their lord's presence. They went to their beds, weary from the long feast. Judith was left alone in the tent with Holofernes, who lay on his bed, drunk with wine. Judith had instructed her servant to stand outside her bedchamber and wait for her to come out, as she did daily, under the pretense of going out to pray. She had spoken to Bagoas in the same manner All had left her presence, and no one remained in the bedchamber, small or great. Standing by his bed, Judith prayed in her heart, "O Lord God of all power, look upon the work of my hands at this hour for the exaltation of Jerusalem. Now is the time to help your inheritance and to accomplish the destruction of the enemies who have risen against us." She approached the bedpost at Holofernes' head and took down his sword. She drew near to the bed, took hold of his hair, and said, "Strengthen me, O Lord God of Israel, this day." She struck him twice on the neck with all her might and severed his head. She tumbled his body off the bed and pulled down the canopy from the posts. After a brief moment, she went out and gave Holofernes' head to her maid, who placed it in the food bag. Together, they went out to pray as usual, passing through the camp, circling the valley, and ascending to the mountain of Bethulia, where they arrived at the city gates Judith called out to the watchmen at the gates, "Open the gate! God is with us, even our God, to show His power in Israel and His might against the enemy, as He has done this very day." When the men of the city heard her voice, they hurried down to the gate and summoned the elders. Everyone, young and old, ran together, hardly believing that she had returned. They opened the gate, received them, lit a fire for light, and gathered around them Judith spoke with a loud voice, "Praise God! Praise Him! Praise God, who has not taken away His mercy from the house of Israel but has destroyed our enemies by my hand tonight!" Then she took the head out of the bag and showed it to them, saying, "Behold the head of Holofernes, the chief captain of the army of Asshur, and the canopy under which he lay in his drunkenness. The Lord struck him down by the hand of a woman. As the Lord lives, who preserved me on my way, my face deceived him to his destruction, and he did not commit sin with me, to defile or shame me." All the people were exceedingly amazed and bowed down to worship God, saying with one accord, "Blessed are you, O our God, who has this day humiliated the enemies of your people." Ozias said to her, "Blessed are you, daughter, in the sight of the Most High God, above all the women upon the earth, and blessed is the Lord God, who created the heavens and the earth, who directed you to cut off the head of the prince of our enemies. For your hope will never be forgotten by those who remember the strength of God forever. May God turn these events into perpetual praise for you and visit you with good things, because you did not spare your life due to the affliction of our race, but prevented our ruin by walking in the right path before our God." And all the people said, "Amen! Amen!"

Judith 14

Judith said to them, "Listen to me now, my kinsmen, and take this head and hang it upon the battlement of your wall. At daybreak, when the sun rises, each of you shall take up your weapons of war. Every valiant man among you shall go out of the city and set a captain over them as if you were going down to the plain towards the watch of the children of Asshur. However, you shall not go down. Instead, they will take up their full armor and go into their camp, rousing the captains of the army of Asshur. They will rush to Holofernes' tent and will not find him. Fear will fall upon them, and they will flee before you. You, along with all the inhabitants of every border of Israel, shall pursue them and overthrow them as they flee. But before you do this, summon Achior the Ammonite to me, so that he may see and recognize the one who despised the house of Israel and sent him to us as though to his death." They called Achior out of the house of Ozias. When he came and saw the head of Holofernes in a man's hand among the assembly, he fell on his face, and his spirit failed him. When they revived him, he fell at Judith's feet, bowed down to her, and said, "Blessed are you in every tent of Judah! In every nation, those who hear your name will tremble. Now, tell me all that you have done in these days." Judith then recounted to him, in the midst of the people, all that she had done, from the day she left until the time she spoke to them. When she finished, the people shouted with a loud voice and made a joyful noise in the city When Achior saw all that the God of Israel had done, he believed in God exceedingly, was circumcised, and was joined to the house of Israel to this day. As soon as the morning arose, they hung Holofernes' head on the wall, and every man took up his weapons. They went forth in bands to the ascents of the mountain. When the children of Asshur saw them, they sent word to their leaders, who informed their captains, tribunes, and all their rulers. They hurried to Holofernes' tent and said to the one in charge, "Wake our lord, for the slaves have dared to come down against us to battle, that they may be utterly destroyed." Bagoas went in and knocked at the outer door of the tent, thinking Holofernes was sleeping with Judith. When no one answered, he opened the door, entered the bedchamber, and found Holofernes lying on the floor, headless. He cried out with a loud voice, weeping, groaning, and tearing his garments. He entered the tent where Judith had stayed but found her gone. He rushed out to the people, crying aloud, "The slaves have dealt treacherously! A single Hebrew woman has brought shame upon the house of King Nebuchadnezzar! Holofernes lies dead, and his head is gone!" When the rulers of the army of Asshur heard this, they tore their tunics, and their souls were troubled exceedingly. There were cries and great commotion throughout the camp

Judith 15

When those in the tents heard the uproar, they were amazed at what had happened. Trembling and fear seized them, and no man dared stay in the sight of his neighbor. In one accord, they fled in all directions, across the plain and the hill country. Those encamped in the hill country around Bethulia fled, and every warrior among the children of Israel pursued them Ozias sent messengers to Betomesthaim, Bebai, Chobai, Chola, and all the borders of Israel, reporting what had been accomplished and urging everyone to join in the attack on their fleeing enemies. When the children of Israel heard this, they all fell upon the enemy with one accord and pursued them to Chobai. Likewise, the people from Jerusalem and all the hill country came, for they had been informed about the events in the enemy camp. Those in Gilead and Galilee also struck at the enemy's flank, causing great slaughter until they reached Damascus and its borders The rest of the people who lived in Bethulia fell upon the camp of Asshur, plundering it and enriching themselves greatly. The children of Israel returned from the slaughter and took possession of what remained. The villages and cities in the hill and plain country took many spoils, for there was an exceedingly great supply Joakim, the high priest, and the elders of Israel who lived in Jerusalem came to see the wonders the Lord had done for Israel and to greet Judith. When they arrived, they all blessed her with one accord, saying, "You are the exaltation of Jerusalem! You are the great glory of Israel! You are the great joy of our race! You have done all these things by your hand. You have acted righteously with Israel, and God is pleased with you. May you be blessed by the Almighty Lord forever!" And all the people said, "Amen!" The people plundered the camp for thirty days. They gave Holofernes' tent to Judith, along with all his silver cups, beds, bowls, and furniture. She took them, placed them on her mule, prepared her wagons, and loaded them. All the women of Israel ran together to see her, blessed her, and celebrated with a dance. Judith took branches in her hand and distributed them to the women who were with her. They made garlands of olive branches, and she led the women in dance, while the men of Israel followed in their armor, singing and wearing garlands

Judith 16

Judith began to sing this song of thanksgiving in all Israel, and all the people sang this song of praise with loud voices:
"Begin a song to my God with timbrels.
Sing to my Lord with cymbals.
Make melody to Him with psalm and praise.
Exalt Him and call upon His name.
For the Lord is the God who crushes battles.
In His armies, in the midst of the people,
He delivered me from the hand of those who persecuted me.
Asshur came from the mountains of the north,
With tens of thousands in his army.
Their multitude stopped the torrents.
Their horsemen covered the hills.
He said he would burn my borders,
Kill my young men with the sword,
Throw my nursing children to the ground,
Give my infants as prey,
And make my virgins a plunder.
The Almighty Lord brought them to nothing
By the hand of a woman.
For their mighty one did not fall by young men,
Nor did the sons of Titans strike him.
Tall giants did not attack him,
But Judith, the daughter of Merari,
Weakened him with the beauty of her countenance.
She put off her widow's garments
To exalt those who were distressed in Israel.
She anointed her face with ointment,
Bound her hair with a tiara,
And wore a linen garment to deceive him.
Her sandal captivated his eye.
Her beauty took his soul prisoner.
The sword passed through his neck.
The Persians trembled at her daring.
The Medes were daunted by her boldness.
My lowly ones shouted aloud.
My oppressed people were terrified and trembled with fear.
They lifted their voices, and the enemy fled.
The children of slave girls pierced them,
And wounded them as they fled.
They perished by the army of my Lord.
I will sing to my God a new song:
O Lord, You are great and glorious,
Marvelous in strength, invincible.
Let all Your creation serve You;
For You spoke, and they were made.
You sent out Your Spirit, and it built them.
There is no one who can resist Your voice.
For the mountains will be moved from their foundations with the waters,
And the rocks will melt like wax at Your presence.
But You are yet merciful to those who fear You.
For all sacrifice is little for a sweet savor,
And all the fat is very little for a whole burnt offering to You.
But he who fears the Lord is great continually.
Woe to the nations that rise against my race!
The Lord Almighty will take vengeance on them in the day of judgment
And put fire and worms in their flesh,
And they will weep and feel their pain forever."
When they came to Jerusalem, they worshiped God. After the people had been purified, they offered whole burnt offerings, freewill offerings, and gifts. Judith dedicated all the goods of Holofernes that the people had given her, and she offered the canopy she had taken from his bedchamber as a gift to the Lord. The people continued feasting in Jerusalem before the sanctuary for three months, and Judith remained with them After these days, everyone returned to their inheritance. Judith went back to Bethulia and

remained in her own possession. She was honored in her time throughout the land. Many desired her, but no man knew her all the days of her life after Manasses, her husband, died and was gathered to his people. She grew old in her husband's house, reaching the age of one hundred and five years. She freed her maid and then died in Bethulia. They buried her in the cave of her husband Manasses, and the house of Israel mourned for her seven days. Before her death, she distributed her goods to the nearest relatives of her husband Manasses and her own kindred. After Judith's death, there was no one who made the children of Israel afraid for a long time

71. Additions to Esther

Esther 1

In the second year of the reign of Ahasuerus, the great king, on the first day of Nisan, Mordecai, the son of Jair, the son of Shimei, the son of Kish, of the tribe of Benjamin, a Jew dwelling in the city of Susa, had a vision. Mordecai was a great man, serving in the king's palace. He had been one of the captives whom Nebuchadnezzar, king of Babylon, had taken from Jerusalem along with Jeconiah, the king of Judah. In this dream, Mordecai saw voices and noises, thunders and earthquakes, and tumult upon the earth. Two great serpents emerged, both ready for conflict. Their voices were powerful, and every nation was prepared for battle against the nation of the just. A day of darkness, blackness, suffering, and anguish loomed over the earth. The righteous nation was troubled, fearing their afflictions. They prepared to die and cried out to God. From their cries, something like a great river sprang forth, bringing light, and the sun arose. The lowly were exalted and devoured the honorable Mordecai, having seen this vision and knowing what God intended to do, kept it in his heart and sought to interpret it. That night, while resting in the palace with Gabatha and Tharrha, the king's two chamberlains and eunuchs who guarded the palace, Mordecai overheard their conversation. He discovered that they were plotting to lay hands on King Ahasuerus. Mordecai informed the king, who then examined the two chamberlains. They confessed and were executed. The king recorded these events, and Mordecai also documented them. In recognition of his service, the king commanded Mordecai to serve in the palace and bestowed gifts upon him. However, Haman, the son of Hammedatha the Bougean, was honored above all by the king, and he sought to harm Mordecai and his people because of the king's two chamberlains After these events, during the reign of Ahasuerus, who ruled over 127 provinces from India to Ethiopia, the king, in the third year of his reign, made a feast for his friends, the nobles of Persia and Media, and the governors of the provinces. The feast lasted 180 days, during which the king displayed the wealth and glory of his kingdom. When the feast ended, the king held another banquet for six days for the people in the city of Susa. The court of the king's palace was adorned with fine linen and flax, fastened to golden and silver studs on pillars of marble. There were golden and silver couches on a pavement of emerald, mother-of-pearl, and marble, with variously flowered transparent coverings and roses arranged around them. Gold and silver cups, as well as a small cup of carbuncle valued at thirty thousand talents, were used, and abundant sweet wine was served This banquet did not follow the appointed law, but the king desired it this way. He instructed the stewards to fulfill his will and that of the guests. Meanwhile, Queen Vashti made a separate banquet for the women in the palace. On the seventh day, the king, in a merry mood, instructed Haman, Bazan, Tharrha, Baraze, Zatholtha, Abataza, and Tharaba, his seven chamberlains, to bring Queen Vashti before him. He wished to enthrone her, crown her with the diadem, and display her beauty to the princes and nations, for she was beautiful. However, Queen Vashti refused to come, and the king was grieved and angered The king consulted his friends and sought legal judgment on the matter. Arkesaeus, Sarsathaeus, and Malisear, the princes of Persia and Media, who were chief in rank, reported to the king according to the law. Memucan advised the king, saying that Queen Vashti had wronged not only the king but also all the rulers and princes. Her disobedience, he argued, would encourage other wives to dishonor their husbands. Memucan recommended that the king issue a royal decree, written according to the laws of the Medes and Persians, that Queen Vashti be no longer allowed to come before the king and that her royalty be given to a woman better than her. This law, once widely proclaimed, would ensure that all women would honor their husbands The king and the princes were pleased with this advice, and the king did as Memucan had suggested. He sent letters throughout his kingdom to all the provinces, written in their languages, so that men might be respected in their own houses

Esther 2

After this, the king's anger subsided, and he no longer mentioned Vashti, remembering what she had done and how he had condemned her. The king's servants then suggested that beautiful, chaste young virgins be sought for the king. They proposed that the king appoint governors in all the provinces of his kingdom to select these young ladies and bring them to the city of Susa, to the women's quarters, where they would be placed under the care of the king's chamberlain, the keeper of the women. The young woman who pleased the king would be made queen in place of Vashti. The suggestion pleased the king, and he ordered it to be done There was a Jew in the city of Susa named Mordecai, the son of Jairus, the son of Shimei, the son of Kish, of the tribe of Benjamin. He had been brought to Susa as a prisoner from Jerusalem, one of those whom Nebuchadnezzar, king of Babylon, had taken into captivity. Mordecai had a foster daughter, the daughter of Aminadab, his father's brother. Her name was Esther. When her parents died, Mordecai raised her as his own. Esther was a beautiful woman When the king's decree was published, many young women were gathered in Susa under the care of Hegai, the keeper of the women. Esther was also taken to Hegai. She pleased him and found favor in his sight. He quickly provided her with the necessary things for purification, her portion of food, and appointed seven maidens from the palace to attend her. He treated Esther and her maidens well in the women's quarters. However, Esther did not reveal her family or her kindred because Mordecai had instructed her not to do so. Every day, Mordecai would walk by the court of the women's quarters to see how Esther was doing According to the custom, a young woman could only go into the king after completing twelve months of purification—six months with oil of myrrh and six months with spices and other purifications. Afterward, she would be taken to the king in the evening and return to the second women's quarters in the morning, under the care of Shaashgaz, the king's chamberlain. She would not go in to the king again unless he called her by name When the time came for Esther, the daughter of Aminadab, to go in to the king, she followed all the instructions of Hegai, the keeper of the women. Esther found favor in the eyes of everyone who saw her. She was taken to King Ahasuerus in the twelfth month, the month of Adar, in the seventh year of his reign. The king loved Esther more than all the other women, and she found favor and kindness with him. He placed the royal crown on her head and made her queen in place of Vashti The king then made a great banquet for all his princes and servants in honor of Esther. He proclaimed a holiday in the provinces and gave gifts according to the king's bounty. Meanwhile, Mordecai was serving in the king's court. Esther had still not revealed her family background because Mordecai had commanded her to keep it secret, as she had done when she was under his care During this time, two of the king's chamberlains, Bigthan and Teresh, who guarded the entrance, became angry and conspired to assassinate King Ahasuerus. Mordecai learned of the plot and informed Queen Esther, who in turn told the king in Mordecai's name. The matter was investigated and found to be true, and the two men were hanged on gallows. This event was recorded in the book of the chronicles in the presence of the king

Esther 3

After these events, King Ahasuerus honored Haman, the son of Hammedatha, the Agagite. He promoted him and set his seat above all the princes who were with him. All the king's servants who were at the king's gate bowed down and paid homage to Haman, for the king had so commanded. However, Mordecai did not bow down or pay homage. When the king's servants asked Mordecai why he transgressed the king's command, he refused to listen to them. They reported this to Haman, seeing that Mordecai had declared he was a Jew When Haman saw that Mordecai did not bow down or pay him homage, he was filled with fury. But he disdained to lay hands on Mordecai alone, for they had told him of Mordecai's people. Haman sought to destroy all the Jews, the people of Mordecai, throughout the whole kingdom of Ahasuerus. In the first month, the month of Nisan, in the twelfth year of King Ahasuerus, Haman cast lots to determine the day and month on which the Jews would be destroyed. The lot fell on the thirteenth day of the twelfth month, the month of Adar Haman approached King Ahasuerus and said, "There is a certain people scattered and dispersed among the peoples in all the provinces of your kingdom. Their laws are different from those of all other people, and they do not obey the king's laws. Therefore, it is not in the king's interest to tolerate them. If it pleases the king, let it be decreed that they be destroyed, and I will pay ten thousand talents of silver into the hands of those who carry out this business, to be put into the king's treasuries." The king took his signet ring from his hand and gave it to Haman, the son of Hammedatha, the Agagite, the enemy of the Jews. The king said to Haman, "The money is given to you, and the people also, to do with them as it seems good to you." The king's scribes were summoned on the thirteenth day of the first month, and an edict, according to all that Haman commanded, was written to the king's satraps, to the governors over each province, and to the princes of every people, to every province in its own script and every people in their own language. It was written in the name of King Ahasuerus and sealed with the king's signet ring. Letters were sent by couriers to all the king's provinces to destroy, to kill, and to annihilate all Jews, young and old, women and children, in one day, the thirteenth day of the twelfth month, which is the month of Adar, and to plunder their goods A copy of the document was to be issued as a decree in every province, being publicly displayed to all peoples so that they would be ready

for that day. The couriers went out hurriedly by order of the king, and the decree was issued in Susa the citadel. The king and Haman sat down to drink, but the city of Susa was thrown into confusion

Esther 4

When Mordecai learned all that had been done, he tore his clothes, put on sackcloth and ashes, and went out into the midst of the city, crying out with a loud and bitter cry. He went up to the entrance of the king's gate, for no one was allowed to enter the king's gate clothed in sackcloth. In every province where the king's command and decree reached, there was great mourning among the Jews, with fasting, weeping, and lamenting, and many lay in sackcloth and ashes When Esther's young women and her eunuchs came and told her, the queen was deeply distressed. She sent garments to clothe Mordecai so that he might take off his sackcloth, but he would not accept them. Then Esther called for Hathach, one of the king's eunuchs who had been appointed to attend her, and ordered him to go to Mordecai to learn what this was and why it was. Hathach went out to Mordecai in the open square of the city in front of the king's gate, and Mordecai told him all that had happened to him and the exact sum of money that Haman had promised to pay into the king's treasuries for the destruction of the Jews Mordecai also gave him a copy of the written decree issued in Susa for their destruction, that he might show it to Esther and explain it to her and command her to go to the king to beg his favor and plead with him on behalf of her people. Hathach went and told Esther what Mordecai had said. Then Esther spoke to Hathach and commanded him to go to Mordecai and say, "All the king's servants and the people of the king's provinces know that if any man or woman goes to the king inside the inner court without being called, there is but one law—to be put to death, except the one to whom the king holds out the golden scepter so that he may live. But I have not been called to come to the king these thirty days." And they told Mordecai what Esther had said. Then Mordecai told them to reply to Esther, "Do not think to yourself that in the king's palace you will escape any more than all the other Jews. For if you keep silent at this time, relief and deliverance will rise for the Jews from another place, but you and your father's house will perish. And who knows whether you have not come to the kingdom for such a time as this?" Then Esther told them to reply to Mordecai, "Go, gather all the Jews to be found in Susa, and hold a fast on my behalf, and do not eat or drink for three days, night or day. I and my young women will also fast as you do. Then I will go to the king, though it is against the law, and if I perish, I perish." Mordecai then went away and did everything as Esther had ordered him. Mordecai prayed to the Lord, remembering all His works. He said, "O Lord God, you are the King who rules over all, for all things are in your power, and no one can oppose you in your purpose to save Israel. You made the heavens and the earth and all the wonderful things under heaven. You are Lord of all, and no one can resist you. You know all things, Lord, and you know that it was not out of insolence, arrogance, or love of glory that I refused to bow down to the arrogant Haman. I would have gladly kissed the soles of his feet for the safety of Israel. But I did this so that I might not set the glory of man above the glory of God. I will not worship anyone except you, my Lord, and I will not do these things in arrogance Now, O Lord God, the King, the God of Abraham, spare your people, for our enemies are planning our destruction, and they desire to destroy your ancient inheritance. Do not overlook your people, whom you have redeemed for yourself out of the land of Egypt.

Listen to my prayer. Have mercy on your inheritance and turn our mourning into gladness, that we may live and sing praises to your name, O Lord. Do not utterly destroy the mouths of those who praise you, O Lord." All Israel cried out with all their might, for death was before their eyes. Queen Esther, too, took refuge in the Lord, feeling as though she were in the agony of death. She removed her glorious apparel and put on garments of distress and mourning. Instead of grand perfumes, she filled her head with ashes and dung. She greatly humbled her body and covered every place of her glad adornment with her tangled hair. She implored the Lord God of Israel, saying, "O my Lord, you alone are our King. Help me, for I am destitute and have no helper but you, for my danger is near at hand I have heard from my birth in the tribe of my kindred that you, O Lord, took Israel out of all the nations and our fathers out of all their kindred for a perpetual inheritance and have done for them all that you promised. But now we have sinned before you, and you have delivered us into the hands of our enemies because we honored their gods. You are righteous, O Lord. But now they have not been content with the bitterness of our slavery, but have laid their hands on the hands of their idols to abolish the decree of your mouth, to utterly destroy your inheritance, to stop the mouth of those who praise you, and to extinguish the glory of your house and your altar They wish to open the mouths of the Gentiles to speak the praises of vanities and to cause a mortal king to be admired forever. O Lord, do not surrender your scepter to those who do not exist, and do not let them laugh at our fall. Turn their counsel against themselves and make an example of him who has begun to injure us. Remember us, O Lord! Manifest yourself in the time of our affliction. Encourage me, O King of gods, and ruler of all dominion! Put harmonious speech into my mouth before the lion and turn his heart to hate those who fight against us, to the utter destruction of those who agree with him. But deliver us by your hand and help me who am alone and have no one but you, O Lord You know all things, and you know that I hate the glory of transgressors and that I abhor the bed of the uncircumcised and of every stranger. You know my necessity, for I abhor the symbol of my proud station, which is upon my head in the days of my splendor. I abhor it as a menstruous cloth, and I do not wear it in the days of my tranquility. Your handmaid has not eaten at Haman's table, and I have not honored the banquet of the king, nor have I drunk wine of libations. Neither has your handmaid rejoiced since the day of my promotion until now, except in you, O Lord God of Abraham. O God, who has power over all, listen to the voice of the desperate and deliver us from the hands of those who devise mischief. Deliver me from my fear."

Esther 5

On the third day, after Esther had ceased praying, she removed her servant's dress and put on her glorious apparel. Dressed splendidly, she called upon God, the Overseer and Preserver of all things. She took her two maids, leaning on one as a delicate female while the other followed, bearing her train. Esther, blooming in the perfection of her beauty, approached with a cheerful face, though her heart was filled with fear. She passed through all the doors and stood before the king, who was sitting on his royal throne, clothed in all his glorious apparel, covered with gold and precious stones, looking very terrifying As the king raised his face, resplendent with glory, he looked at Esther with intense anger. Overcome with fear, she fell and changed color as she fainted, bowing herself upon the head of the maid who went before her. But God changed the

spirit of the king to gentleness. With intense feeling, he sprang from his throne and took Esther into his arms until she recovered. He comforted her with peaceful words, saying, "What is the matter, Esther? I am your relative. Cheer up! You shall not die, for our command is openly declared to you: 'Draw near.'" He raised the golden scepter and laid it upon her neck, then embraced her and said, "Speak to me." Esther replied, "I saw you, my lord, as an angel of God, and my heart was troubled for fear of your glory; for you, my lord, are to be wondered at, and your face is full of grace." While she was speaking, she fainted and fell again. The king was troubled, and all his servants comforted her. The king then asked, "What do you desire, Esther? What is your request? Ask even to the half of my kingdom, and it shall be yours." Esther replied, "Today is a special day. If it pleases the king, let both you and Haman come to the feast that I will prepare today." The king ordered Haman to be brought quickly so that they could do as Esther had requested. They both came to the feast that Esther had prepared. During the banquet, the king asked Esther, "What is your request, Queen Esther? You shall have all that you require." She replied, "My request and my petition is this: if I have found favor in the king's sight, let the king and Haman come again tomorrow to the feast that I shall prepare for them, and tomorrow I will do as I have done today." Haman left the feast joyful and in high spirits, but when he saw Mordecai at the king's gate and observed that he neither rose nor trembled before him, he was filled with anger against Mordecai. Nevertheless, Haman restrained himself and went home. He sent for his friends and his wife Zeresh. Haman boasted to them about his vast wealth, his many sons, and all the ways the king had honored him and how he had elevated him above the other nobles and officials. "Even Queen Esther," he added, "invited no one but me to accompany the king to the banquet she gave, and she has invited me along with the king tomorrow. But all this gives me no satisfaction as long as I see that Jew Mordecai sitting at the king's gate." His wife Zeresh and all his friends said to him, "Have a gallows built, seventy-five feet high, and ask the king in the morning to have Mordecai hanged on it. Then go with the king to the banquet and enjoy yourself." This suggestion delighted Haman, and he had the gallows built

Esther 6

That night, the Lord took sleep away from the king. He asked his servant to bring the books, the records of daily events, and read them to him. In the records, the king found the account of how Mordecai had uncovered the plot of the king's two chamberlains, who were guarding the king but had conspired to assassinate Ahasuerus. The king asked, "What honor or reward has been given to Mordecai for this?" The king's servants replied, "Nothing has been done for him." As the king was contemplating how to honor Mordecai, Haman entered the court. The king asked, "Who is in the court?" Haman had just arrived to speak to the king about hanging Mordecai on the gallows he had prepared. The king's servants informed him, "Behold, Haman stands in the court." The king said, "Bring him in!" When Haman entered, the king asked him, "What should be done for the man whom the king wishes to honor?" Haman thought to himself, "Whom would the king wish to honor more than me?" So he replied, "For the man whom the king wishes to honor, let the king's servants bring a royal robe that the king has worn, and a horse that the king has ridden, and let the robe and the horse be delivered to one of the king's most noble officials. Let him array the man whom the king wishes to honor and lead him on the horse through the city square, proclaiming before him, 'This is what is done for the man whom the king wishes to honor!'" The king then said to Haman, "You have spoken well. Do everything you have said for Mordecai the Jew, who sits at the king's gate. Do not neglect anything you have mentioned!" So Haman took the robe and the horse, dressed Mordecai, and led him on horseback through the city square, proclaiming, "This is what is done for the man whom the king wishes to honor!" Afterward, Mordecai returned to the king's gate, but Haman hurried to his house, mourning and with his head covered. He recounted all that had happened to his wife Zeresh and his friends. His wise men and his wife Zeresh said to him, "If Mordecai, before whom you have begun to fall, is of Jewish descent, you will not prevail against him but will surely fall before him." While they were still speaking, the king's chamberlains arrived and hastened to bring Haman to the banquet that Esther had prepared

Esther 7

So the king and Haman went to dine with Queen Esther. On the second day of the banquet, as they were drinking wine, the king again asked Esther, "What is your petition, Queen Esther? It shall be granted to you. What is your request? Even up to half of the kingdom, it shall be done." Queen Esther answered, "If I have found favor in your sight, O king, and if it pleases the king, grant me my life—this is my petition. And spare my people—this is my request. For I and my people have been sold to be destroyed, killed, and annihilated. If we had merely been sold as male and female slaves, I would have kept silent, because no such distress would justify disturbing the king." King Ahasuerus asked Queen Esther, "Who is he, and where is he, who has dared to do this?" Esther said, "The adversary and enemy is this wicked Haman!" Then Haman was terrified before the king and queen. The king arose in his wrath and went out into the palace garden. But Haman, realizing that the king had decided his fate, stayed behind to beg Queen Esther for his life When the king returned from the palace garden to the place of the banquet of wine, Haman had fallen on the couch where Esther was reclining. The king exclaimed, "Will he even assault the queen while she is with me in the house?" As soon as the word left the king's mouth, they covered Haman's face Then Harbona, one of the eunuchs attending the king, said, "Look! The gallows, fifty cubits high, which Haman made for Mordecai, who spoke good on the king's behalf, is standing at Haman's house." The king said, "Hang him on it!" So they hanged Haman on the gallows that he had prepared for Mordecai. Then the king's anger subsided

Esther 8

On that day, King Ahasuerus gave Queen Esther the estate of Haman, the enemy of the Jews. And Mordecai came before the king, for Esther had told how he was related to her. The king took off his signet ring, which he had reclaimed from Haman, and presented it to Mordecai. And Esther appointed Mordecai over Haman's estate Esther again pleaded with the king, falling at his feet and weeping. She begged him to put an end to the evil plan of Haman the Agagite, which he had devised against the Jews. Then the king extended the golden scepter to Esther, and she arose and stood before him. "If it pleases the king," she said, "and if he regards me with favor and thinks it the right thing to do, and if he is pleased with me, let an order be written overruling the dispatches that Haman, son of Hammedatha, the Agagite, devised and wrote to destroy the Jews in all the king's provinces. For how can I bear to see disaster fall on my people? How can I endure to see the destruction of my family?" King Ahasuerus replied to Queen Esther and to Mordecai the Jew, "Because Haman attacked the Jews, I have given his estate to Esther, and they have hanged him on the gallows. Now write another decree in the king's name on behalf of the Jews as seems best to you, and seal it with the king's signet ring—for no document written in the king's name and sealed with his ring can be revoked." At once the royal secretaries were summoned—on the twenty-third day of the third month, the month of Sivan. They wrote out all Mordecai's orders to the Jews, and to the satraps, governors, and nobles of the 127 provinces stretching from India to Cush. These orders were written in the script of each province and the language of each people and also to the Jews in their own script and language. Mordecai wrote in the name of King Ahasuerus, sealed the dispatches with the king's signet ring, and sent them by mounted couriers, who rode fast horses especially bred for the king The king's edict granted the Jews in every city the right to assemble and protect themselves; to destroy, kill, and annihilate the armed men of any nationality or province who might attack them and their women and children, and to plunder the property of their enemies. The day appointed for the Jews to do this in all the provinces of King Ahasuerus was the thirteenth day of the twelfth month, the month of Adar. A copy of the text of the edict was to be issued as law in every province and made known to the people of every nationality so that the Jews would be ready on that day to avenge themselves on their enemies The couriers, riding the royal horses, went out, spurred on by the king's command, and the edict was issued in the citadel of Susa. Mordecai left the king's presence wearing royal garments of blue and white, a large crown of gold, and a purple robe of fine linen. And the city of Susa held a joyous celebration. For the Jews it was a time of happiness and joy, gladness and honor. In every province and in every city to which the edict of the king came, there was joy and gladness among the Jews, with feasting and celebrating. And many people of other nationalities became Jews because fear of the Jews had seized them

Esther 9

On the thirteenth day of the twelfth month, the month of Adar, the edict commanded by the king was carried out. On this day, the enemies of the Jews had hoped to overpower them, but now the tables were turned, and the Jews got the upper hand over those who hated them. The Jews assembled in their cities in all the provinces of King Ahasuerus to attack those determined to destroy them. No one could stand against them because the people of all the other nationalities were afraid of them. And all the nobles of the provinces, the satraps, the governors, and the king's administrators helped the Jews because fear of Mordecai had seized them. Mordecai was prominent in the palace; his reputation spread throughout the provinces, and he became more and more powerful The Jews struck down all their enemies with the sword, killing and destroying them, and they did what they pleased to those who hated them. In the citadel of Susa, the Jews killed and destroyed five hundred men. They also killed Parshandatha, Dalphon, Aspatha, Poratha, Adalia, Aridatha, Parmashta, Arisai, Aridai, and Vaizatha, the ten sons of Haman, the son of Hammedatha, the enemy of the Jews. But they did not lay their hands on the plunder. The number of those killed in the citadel of Susa was reported to the king that same day The king said to Queen Esther, "The Jews have killed and destroyed five hundred men and the ten sons of Haman in the citadel of Susa. What have they done in the rest of the king's provinces? Now what is your petition? It will be given you. What is your request? It will also be granted." "If it pleases the king," Esther answered, "give the Jews in Susa permission to carry out this day's edict tomorrow also, and let Haman's ten sons be impaled on poles." So the king commanded that this be done. An edict was issued in Susa, and they impaled the ten sons of Haman. The Jews in Susa came together on the fourteenth day of the month of Adar, and they put to death in Susa three hundred men, but they did not lay their hands on the plunder Meanwhile, the remainder of the Jews who were in the king's provinces also assembled to protect themselves and get relief from their enemies. They killed seventy-five thousand of them but did not lay their hands on the plunder. This happened on the thirteenth day of the month of Adar, and on the fourteenth, they rested and made it a day of feasting and joy. The Jews in Susa, however, had assembled on the thirteenth and fourteenth, and then on the fifteenth, they rested and made it a day of feasting and joy. That is why rural Jews—those living in villages—observe the fourteenth of the month of Adar as a day of joy and feasting, a day for giving presents to each other Mordecai recorded these events, and he sent letters to all the Jews throughout the provinces of King Ahasuerus, near and far, to have them celebrate annually the fourteenth and fifteenth days of the month of Adar as the time when the Jews got relief from their enemies, and as the month when their sorrow was turned into joy and their mourning into a day of celebration. He wrote them to observe the days as days of feasting and joy and giving presents of food to one another and gifts to the poor So the Jews agreed to continue the celebration they had begun, doing what Mordecai had written to them. For Haman, son of Hammedatha, the Agagite, the enemy of all the Jews, had plotted against the Jews to destroy them and had cast the Pur (that is, the lot) for their ruin and destruction. But when the plot came to the king's attention, he issued written orders that the evil scheme Haman had devised against the Jews should come back onto his own head, and that he and his sons should be impaled on poles. Therefore these days were called Purim, from the word pur. Because of everything written in this letter and because of what they had seen and what had happened to them, the Jews took it upon themselves to establish the custom that they and their descendants and all who join them should without fail observe these two days every year, in the way prescribed and at the time appointed These days should be remembered and observed in every generation by every family, and in every province and in every city. And these days of Purim should never fail to be celebrated by the Jews—nor should the memory of these days die out among their descendants So Queen Esther, daughter of Abihail, along with Mordecai the Jew, wrote with full authority to confirm this second letter concerning Purim. And Mordecai sent letters to all the Jews in the 127 provinces of King Ahasuerus' kingdom—words of goodwill and assurance—to establish these days of Purim at their designated times, as Mordecai the Jew and Queen Esther had decreed for them, and as they had established for themselves and their descendants in regard to their times of fasting and lamentation. Esther's decree confirmed these regulations about Purim, and it was written down in the records

Esther 10

King Ahasuerus imposed tribute throughout the empire, to its distant shores. And all his acts of power and might, together with a full account of the greatness of Mordecai, whom the king had promoted, are they not written in the book of the annals of the kings of Media and Persia? Mordecai the Jew was second in rank to King Ahasuerus, preeminent among the Jews, and held in high esteem by his many fellow Jews, because he worked for the good of his people and spoke up for the welfare of all the Jews Mordecai said, "These things have come from God. I remember the dream I had about these matters, for not one detail has failed. There was the small spring that became a river, and there was light, and the sun and much water. The river represents Esther, whom the king married and made queen. The two serpents are Haman and me. The nations are those who combined to destroy the name of the Jews. But my nation, Israel, cried out to God and was delivered. The Lord rescued us from all these calamities, and God worked great signs and wonders among the nations." Therefore, he ordained two lots: one for the people of God and one for all the other nations. These two lots came for an appointed season, for a day of judgment before God and for all the nations. God remembered his people and vindicated his inheritance. The Jews will observe these days in the month of Adar, on the fourteenth and fifteenth days of the month, with assemblies, joy, and gladness before God, throughout all generations forever among his people Israel In the fourth year of the reign of Ptolemy and Cleopatra, Dositheus, who claimed to be a priest and Levite, and Ptolemy his son brought this letter of Purim, which they said was authentic. Lysimachus, son of Ptolemy, who was in Jerusalem, had interpreted it

72. *Wisdom of Solomon*

The Wisdom of Solomon 1

Love righteousness, you judges of the earth. Ponder the Lord with a pure heart and seek Him in simplicity, for He reveals Himself to those who do not test Him and manifests to those who trust. Crooked thoughts sever from God, and His power convicts the deceitful when tested. Wisdom does not dwell in a soul plotting evil or a body enslaved by sin. A holy spirit of discipline will flee from deceit and abandon minds lacking understanding, ashamed when wickedness encroaches Wisdom, a spirit that cherishes humanity, will not absolve the blasphemous for their words. God, who sees the innermost thoughts and heart, listens to every tongue. His spirit fills the earth, and the keeper of all knows every spoken word. Thus, no utterance of injustice remains unseen, nor does justice overlook when it convicts. The counsels of the wicked are scrutinized, their words reaching the Lord, who judges their sins Beware of fruitless complaints and guard your tongue from slander, for no covert speech vanishes without impact, and a lying mouth destroys the soul. Do not invite death through misdeeds or summon destruction with your actions. God did not create death, nor does He delight in the demise of the living. He made all things to exist harmoniously; the essence of the world is wholesome, with no destructive force. Righteousness is everlasting

The Wisdom of Solomon 2

Reasoning unsoundly, some say, "Life is brief and sorrowful, with no release from Hades at its end. We are born by chance and fade as though we never were, for breath is but smoke, and thought a spark from the heart's beat, fading to ashes and dispersing like air. Our names will be forgotten, our lives fleeting like a cloud, scattered by the sun's heat. Our time passes like a shadow with no return." They resolve to enjoy existing pleasures, indulging in wine and fragrances, not missing any blossom of spring, crowning themselves before they wither. They embrace revelry, leaving mirth everywhere, for this is their lot. They oppress the poor, show no mercy to widows or the elderly, using their strength as the law of justice, for weakness proves useless to them. They lay traps for the righteous, who vex them by opposing their actions and condemning their sins

The Wisdom of Solomon 3

The souls of the righteous rest in God's hand, untouched by torment. Though they seem to perish in the eyes of the foolish, and their departure deemed tragic, they are at peace. Punished in the sight of men, they hold hope for immortality. Enduring slight discipline, they receive great blessings, for God has tested them like gold in the furnace and accepted them. They will shine and run like sparks through the stubble, judging nations and ruling over peoples, with the Lord reigning forever. Those who trust Him understand truth and abide in love, for grace and mercy accompany His chosen, while the ungodly face punishment as their reasoning deserves

The Wisdom of Solomon 4

It is better to have no children yet possess virtue, for immortality lies in the remembrance of virtue, recognized by both God and men. When virtue is present, it inspires imitation; when gone, it is longed for. It triumphs in contests for undefiled prizes. The progeny of the ungodly, however, will not thrive; their illegitimate offspring will not take root nor endure. Though they flourish temporarily, they will be uprooted by storms, their branches broken, their fruit unripe and worthless A righteous man, even if he dies prematurely, finds peace. True honor in age does not depend on longevity or years but on a life of understanding and unblemished conduct. Recognized by God, the righteous are swiftly taken from wickedness, their departure unseen by the foolish who fail to understand that God's grace and mercy are reserved for His holy ones

The Wisdom of Solomon 5

The righteous will stand boldly before those who oppressed them and belittled their endeavors. When his adversaries see him, they will be gripped by fear, astonished at the unexpectedness of his salvation. They will murmur among themselves in regret, lamenting their misjudgment of his life as folly and dishonor. They will admit their deviation from truth, acknowledging that the light of righteousness did not illuminate their paths, and their wealth and pride brought them no lasting joy. Like a ship leaving no trace in the water, their lives will have passed without impact, and their deeds will vanish like smoke, leaving no memory behind The ungodly man's hope is as fleeting as chaff in the wind or foam before a storm. In contrast, the righteous live eternally, secure in the Lord, who will crown them with majesty and protect them, taking up his zeal as armor to fight against his foes. With righteousness as his breastplate and impartial judgment as his helmet, the Lord will advance with the universe to confront the wicked

The Wisdom of Solomon 6

Kings and judges of the earth, listen and learn wisdom. Your authority, bestowed by the Lord, demands righteousness and adherence to His laws. The Lord will scrutinize your actions and judge swiftly, for the powerful face strict scrutiny. However, wisdom is available to all who seek her earnestly; she makes herself known to those who desire her. Wisdom is the key to immortality and proximity to God. If you value sovereignty, cherish wisdom to ensure enduring reign

The Wisdom of Solomon 7

I am mortal, born from earth like all, and I breathed the same first breath. I sought wisdom earnestly, preferring her over power and riches. Wisdom, brighter than the sun and more precious than any jewel, brings with her all good things. She is the mother of all that is noble and just. My pursuit of wisdom taught me that she is the source of all understanding and the architect of all things, penetrating and purifying all with her purity

The Wisdom of Solomon 8

Wisdom reaches mightily from one end of the earth to the other and governs all things beautifully. From my youth, I loved her and sought her as my bride, captivated by her beauty. Wisdom, dwelling with God, is the source of all understanding and righteousness. Through her, one gains honor, immortality, and the treasures of understanding. My pursuit of her brought about my resolve to live a life aligned with her teachings, knowing this would bring immortality and a lasting legacy

The Wisdom of Solomon 9

I prayed to the Lord for wisdom, the companion of His throne, to guide and protect me in my judgment and actions. Wisdom knows the world and the favor of God. She was present at creation and understands what is right in God's eyes. Through wisdom, our works are aligned with God's will, ensuring our deeds are just and our legacy secure

The Wisdom of Solomon 10

Wisdom has preserved the righteous from the beginning, guiding and protecting them through their trials. She saved the first man from his sins, guided the righteous through the flood, and stood by those who faced oppression and injustice. Wisdom delivered nations through her strength and gave voice to the silent, proving that godliness prevails over adversity

The Wisdom of Solomon 11

Wisdom empowered the works of the holy prophet, leading the people safely through uninhabited and desolate deserts. This journey demonstrated God's capability to transform adverse conditions into sources of blessing, as exemplified when their thirst was quenched by water miraculously provided from a flinty rock. This Chapter highlights how the same divine interventions that provided relief for the Israelites were also used to mete out punishment to their enemies, illustrating the principle of divine justice that punishes and benefits through the same means

The Wisdom of Solomon 12

In this chapter, God's patient and gradual correction of those who stray is portrayed. It emphasizes that His incorruptible spirit is present in all things and that He admonishes sinners little by little, offering them opportunities for repentance. The historical context of the Canaanite expulsion is used to show God's reluctance to completely destroy these peoples despite their detestable practices. Instead, He preferred to give them time to repent, demonstrating His overarching desire for reformation rather than retribution

The Wisdom of Solomon 13

This Chapter addresses the folly of those who, despite being surrounded by the wonders of creation, fail to recognize the Creator and instead worship the creation itself. It criticizes the worship of natural elements and crafted idols, describing how such practices misplace reverence due to God onto inanimate objects like wood, stone, and metal. The Chapter argues that if the beauty and complexity of the world inspire awe, this should logically lead to worship of the Creator, not the created

The Wisdom of Solomon 14

Expanding on the criticisms of idolatry, this Chapter delves into the irrationality and moral consequences of trusting in hand-made idols. It portrays the idolaters as not only misguided but actively corrupting their societies through these beliefs. The narrative describes how the crafting and worship of idols lead to spiritual blindness and communal decay, emphasizing the destructive impact of idolatry on both individual and collective levels

The Wisdom of Solomon 15

Contrasting sharply with idolaters, those who know God are depicted as understanding the true source of life and righteousness. The Chapter elaborates on the foolishness of idol makers, who craft gods from the same earth from which they themselves were formed, oblivious to the divine spark that animates living beings. It mocks the expectations placed on these lifeless idols for blessings and guidance, emphasizing the wisdom of direct reliance on God

The Wisdom of Solomon 16

This Chapter recounts the numerous ways in which God cared for His people during their wilderness wanderings, providing manna and quails to sustain them. It juxtaposes these acts of mercy with the punishments meted out to their enemies, illustrating how God uses both punishment and provision to teach reliance on His providence. The plagues that afflicted their enemies and the miraculous provisions for the Israelites serve as lessons in divine justice and mercy

The Wisdom of Solomon 17

Describing the plagues of darkness that afflicted the Egyptians, this Chapter uses these events to illustrate the profound spiritual darkness that results from idolatry and disobedience to God. The Egyptians' terror and confusion are portrayed as direct consequences of their spiritual blindness, serving as a cautionary tale about the dangers of forsaking divine wisdom

The Wisdom of Solomon 18

The focus shifts to the protective light provided to the Israelites, contrasted with the enveloping darkness experienced by the Egyptians. This divine light symbolizes guidance and salvation, highlighting the rewards of obedience and faithfulness. The Chapter reiterates themes of divine protection and retribution, emphasizing the stark differences in outcomes based on one's relationship with God

The Wisdom of Solomon 19

The final Chapter recounts the miraculous crossing of the Red Sea and the ultimate destruction of the Egyptians. It serves as a climax to the themes of divine sovereignty and justice, showcasing God's power over nature and His unwavering support for His chosen people. The Egyptians' continued obstinacy and eventual doom contrast sharply with the deliverance of the Israelites, underscoring the rewards of faithfulness and the perils of resistance to God

73. Ecclesiasticus (Sirach)

Sirach 1

All wisdom comes from the Lord and remains with him forever. Who can count the sands of the seas, the drops of rain, or the days of eternity? Who can fathom the height of the sky, the breadth of the earth, the depths of the ocean, or the essence of wisdom? Wisdom was created before all things, and the understanding of prudence has existed from eternity Who has had the root of wisdom revealed to them? Who understands her insightful counsels? There is one who is wise and greatly to be feared, seated upon his throne: the Lord. He created wisdom, observed her, and established her measurements. He distributed her across all his works. Wisdom accompanies all living beings as a gift from him, bestowed freely upon those who love him Reverence for the Lord brings glory, exultation, joy, and a crown of rejoicing. This reverence will delight the heart and bring gladness, joy, and longevity. Those who fear the Lord will find that it goes well with them in the end, and they will be blessed on the day of their death. To fear the Lord is the beginning of wisdom, created with the faithful in the womb. She lays an eternal foundation with men and will be trusted among their offspring To fear the Lord is the fullness of wisdom; she inebriates men with her fruits. She will fill all her house with desirable things and her storehouses with her produce. The fear of the Lord is the crown of wisdom, making peace and perfect health flourish. He both saw and measured her; he rained down skill and knowledge of understanding, and exalted the honor of those who hold her fast. To fear the Lord is the root of wisdom, and her branches are length of days Unjust wrath can never be justified, for his wrath tips the scale to his downfall. A patient man will resist for a season, and afterward, gladness will spring up to him. He will hide his words until the right moment, and the lips of many will tell of his understanding. A wise saying is in the treasures of wisdom, but godliness is an abomination to a sinner. If you desire wisdom, keep the commandments, and the Lord will grant her to you freely, for the fear of the Lord is wisdom and instruction. Faith and humility are his good pleasure. Do not disobey the fear of the Lord. Do not approach him with a double heart. Do not be a hypocrite in men's sight, watch over your lips, do not exalt yourself, lest you fall and bring dishonor upon your soul. The Lord will reveal your secrets and cast you down in the midst of the congregation because you did not come to the fear of the Lord, and your heart was full of deceit

Sirach 2

My son, if you come to serve the Lord, prepare your soul for temptation. Set your heart right, endure constantly, and do not make haste in times of calamity. Cling to Him and do not depart, that you may be increased at your latter end. Accept whatever is brought upon you and be patient when you suffer humiliation. Gold is tested in the fire, and acceptable men in the furnace of humiliation Put your trust in Him, and He will help you. Make your ways straight and set your hope on Him. All who fear the Lord, wait for His mercy and do not turn aside, lest you fall. Those who fear the Lord, trust in Him, and your reward will not fail. Hope for good things and for eternal gladness and mercy. Look at the generations of old and see: whoever trusted in the Lord and was ashamed, or who remained in His fear and was forsaken? The Lord is full of compassion and mercy; He forgives sins and saves in time of affliction Woe to fearful hearts and faint hands, and to the sinner who goes two ways! Woe to the faint heart, for it does not believe, therefore it will not be defended. Woe to you who have lost patience! And what will you do when the Lord visits you? Those who fear the Lord will not disobey His words, and those who love Him will keep His ways. Those who fear the Lord will seek His pleasure, and those who love Him will be filled with the law. Those who fear the Lord will prepare their hearts and humble their souls in His sight. We will fall into the hands of the Lord and not into the hands of men; for as His majesty is, so also is His mercy

Sirach 3

Hear me, your father, O my children, and do what you hear, that you all may be safe. For the Lord honors the father above the children and has confirmed the judgment of the mother over her sons. Whoever honors his father will make atonement for sins, and he who respects his mother is like one who lays up treasure. Whoever honors his father will have joy in his own children, and when he prays, he will be heard. He who respects his father will have long life, and whoever obeys the Lord will bring comfort to his mother Honor your father in deed and word, that a blessing may come upon you from him. The father's blessing establishes the houses of children, but the mother's curse uproots the foundations. Help your father in his old age, and do not grieve him as long as he lives. If his understanding fails, have patience with him; do not disgrace him while you are in full strength. The kindness to your father will not be forgotten, and instead of sins, it will be added to build you up. In the day of your affliction, it will be remembered in your favor; as frost in fair weather, your sins will melt away. Whoever forsakes his father is like a blasphemer, and whoever angers his mother is cursed by the Lord My son, carry on your business in humility; thus, you will be loved by the beloved of the Lord. The greater you are, humble yourself the more, and you will find favor in the sight of the Lord. Do not seek things that are too hard for you, or search out things beyond your strength. Think about the things commanded you, for you do not need what is hidden. Do not be overly occupied with your tasks, for more things are shown to you than men understand. For the conceit of many has led them astray, and evil supposition has caused their judgment to slip

Sirach 4

My son, do not deprive the poor of his living, and do not keep needy eyes waiting. Do not grieve a hungry soul or provoke a man in his distress. Add no more trouble to a heart that is provoked, and do not delay giving to one who is in need. Do not reject a suppliant in affliction or turn your face away from a poor man. Do not avert your eyes from one who asks; give no occasion to a man to curse you For if he curses you in the bitterness of his soul, his Creator will hear his supplication. Gain the assembly's favor, bow your head to a great man. Lend your ear to the poor, answer him with peaceful words in humility. Rescue him who is wronged from the hand of the oppressor; be not fainthearted in your judgment. Be a father to the fatherless and a husband to their mother; then you will be like a son of the Most High, and He will love you more than your mother does Wisdom exalts her children and lays hold of those who seek her. He who loves her loves life; those who seek her early will be filled with joy. He who holds her fast will inherit glory; wherever he enters, the Lord will bless. Those who serve her will minister to the Holy One; the Lord loves those who love her. He who listens to her will judge the nations; he who is attentive will dwell securely. If he trusts her, he will inherit her, and his descendants will possess her For at first she will walk with him by crooked ways, and bring fear and dread upon him, and torment him with her discipline until she trusts his soul and tests him with her laws. Then she will come back to him on the straight path and show him her secrets. If he goes astray, she will abandon him and give him over to his ruin Observe the opportunity, and beware of evil; and do not be ashamed of your soul. For there is a shame that brings sin, and there is a shame which is glory and grace. Do not show partiality to discredit your soul, nor respect any man to your downfall. Do not refrain from speaking when it will do good, and do not hide your wisdom for the sake of courtesy. For wisdom becomes known through speech, and education through the word of the tongue Never speak against the truth, but be ashamed of your ignorance. Do not be ashamed to confess your sins, and do not resist the river's current. Do not subject yourself to a fool, or show partiality to a ruler. Fight to the death for truth, and the Lord God will fight for you. Do not be hasty with your tongue, or slack and negligent in your actions. Do not be like a lion in your home, nor suspicious toward your servants. Do not let your hand be extended to receive, and closed when the time comes to repay

Sirach 5

Do not set your heart on your wealth; never say, "I have enough." Avoid following your own mind and strength to walk in the desires of your heart. Do not say, "Who can have power over me?" for the Lord will surely take vengeance on such pride. Do not say, "I sinned, yet nothing happened," for the Lord's patience is long. Do not be so confident of forgiveness that you add sin to sin. Do not say, "His mercy is great; He will forgive the multitude of my sins," for both mercy and wrath are with Him, and His indignation rests on sinners Do not delay turning to the Lord, nor postpone it from day to day; for suddenly the wrath of the Lord will come forth, and at the time of punishment, you will perish. Do not rely on dishonest wealth, for it will not benefit you on the day of calamity. Do not winnow with every wind or follow every path; this is the behavior of the sinner who has a double tongue. Be steadfast in your understanding, and let your speech be consistent. Be quick to hear, and deliberate in answering If you understand, respond to your neighbor; if not, lay your hand on your mouth. Glory and dishonor come from speaking, and a man's tongue can be his downfall. Do not be called a whisperer, and do not lie in wait with your tongue; for a thief has shame, and severe condemnation is on the double-tongued. Do not be ignorant of anything, whether small or great

Sirach 6

Do not become an enemy instead of a friend, for a bad name incurs shame and reproach; so does the sinner who has a double tongue. Do not exalt yourself in the thoughts of your soul, that your spirit may not be torn apart like a bull. You will eat up your leaves, destroy your fruit, and leave yourself as a dry tree A wicked soul will destroy the one who possesses it, and will make him the laughing stock of his enemies. Pleasant words multiply friends, and a courteous tongue multiplies pleasant greetings. Let those at peace with you be many, but let your advisers be one in a thousand. When you gain a friend, gain him through testing, and do not be too quick to trust him. For there is a friend who is only a friend when it suits him, but he will not stand by you in the day of your distress. Another becomes a foe and will reveal strife to your disgrace. Yet another friend sits at your table, but will not stand by you in the day of your distress In your prosperity, he will pretend to be your equal and be bold with your servants; but if you are brought low, he will turn against you and hide himself from your face. Divide your lot with a friend, and do not let any deceitful person share in your wealth; when you are rich, he will live with you and will strip you of your inheritance without a qualm. Every counselor praises his counsel, but some give counsel in their own interest. Be wary of a counselor, and learn beforehand what is his interest, for he will take thought for himself. He may cast the lot for you while standing in your presence, and say to you, "Your way is good," and then stand aside to see what will happen to you Do not consult with one who suspects you, and hide your counsel from those who envy you. Do not consult with a woman about her rival, or with a coward about war, with a merchant about exchange, or with a buyer about selling, or with an envious man about thankfulness, or with an unmerciful man about kindness, or with a sluggard about any kind of work, or with a hired worker about finishing his work, or with an idle servant about much work—pay no attention to these in any matter of counsel But be continually with a godly man whom you know to keep the commandments, who is steadfast in soul and who does not faint when you are in distress. And let the counsel of your own heart stand, for there is no man more faithful to you than it. For a man's soul sometimes keeps him better informed than seven watchmen sitting high on a watchtower. But above all this pray to the Most High that he may direct your way in truth Let reason be the beginning of every work, and let counsel precede every action. As a token of the changing of the heart, four kinds of things arise, good and evil, life and death; but that which rules over them continually is the tongue

Sirach 7

Do no wrong, so no wrong will overtake you. Stay away from wrongdoing, and it will turn away from you. My son, do not sow in the furrows of injustice, and you will not reap them sevenfold. Do not seek from the Lord high office, nor the seat of honor from the king. Do not assert your righteousness before the Lord, nor display your wisdom before the king Do not seek to become a judge, or you may not be able to take away iniquity; you may be afraid of the face of a powerful man, and put a stumbling-block in the way of your uprightness. Do not offend against the public, and do not disgrace yourself among the people. Do not commit sin, because of the people, and do not stumble by the example of your authority. Do not shake your head, or stamp your foot, or wrinkle your brow, or make a show of your love, or use reproachful words. Do not lend to one who is mightier than you, or if you do lend, count it as a loss. Do not guarantee beyond your means; if you guarantee, think as one who will have to pay Do not bring a lawsuit against a judge, for he will judge according to his honor. Do not go on a journey with a bold man, lest he become burdensome to you; for he will do his own will, and through his boldness you will perish with him. Do not fight with a wrathful man, and do not go into the desert with him; for bloodshed is nothing to him, and where there is no help he will overthrow you. Do not consult with a fool, for he cannot keep a secret. Do nothing in secret before a stranger, for you do not know what it will cause. Open not your heart to every man, lest he repay you with a bad turn

Sirach 8

Do not contend with a powerful man, lest you fall into his hands. Do not quarrel with a rich man, lest his resources weigh you down; for gold has ruined many, and has perverted the hearts of kings. Do not argue with a loudmouth, for stacking wood on his fire will make it burn more fiercely. Do not make fun of a rude person, lest your ancestors be dishonored. Do not reproach a man when he turns from sin; remember that we are all guilty Do not disdain a man in his old age, for some of us also will grow old. Rejoice not over your greatest enemy being dead, but remember that we die all. Do not neglect the discourse of the wise, and busy yourself with their proverbs; for from them you will learn instruction and how to serve great men with ease. Do not miss the discourse of the elderly, for they too learned from their parents; from them you will learn how to answer when necessary Do not kindle the coals of a sinner, lest you be burned with the flame of his fire. Do not rise up from the presence of an insolent person, lest he

lie in ambush against your words. Do not lend to one who is stronger than yourself, or if you lend, regard it as lost. Do not be surety beyond your means; if you are surety, be as one who is ready to pay Do not go to law against a judge, for they will judge for him according to his honor. Do not travel with a reckless man, lest he be burdensome to you; for he will act according to his own will, and you will perish with him through his folly. Do not fight with a wrathful man, nor go with him through the desert, for blood is nothing to him; when there is no help, he will overturn you. Do not consult with a fool, for he cannot keep a secret

Sirach 9

Do not be jealous over the wife of your bosom, and do not teach her an evil lesson against yourself. Do not give your soul to a woman to let her dominate your strength. Do not meet with a woman who plays the harlot, lest you fall into her snares. Do not associate with a female singer, lest you be caught in her intrigues. Do not look intently at a virgin, lest you stumble and incur penalties for her Do not give yourself to harlots, lest you lose your inheritance. Do not look around in the streets of a city, nor wander about in its deserted sections. Turn away your eye from a beautiful woman, and do not look at another's beauty; for many have been led astray by the beauty of a woman, and by it passion is kindled like a fire. Do not sit at all with another man's wife, nor revel with her at wine; lest your heart turn aside to her, and in blood you slip into destruction Do not forsake an old friend, for a new one does not compare with him. A new friend is like new wine; when it has aged, you can drink it with pleasure. Do not envy the success of a sinner, for you do not know what disaster awaits him. Do not delight in what pleases the ungodly; remember they will not go unpunished to the grave Keep yourself far from the man who has the power to kill; so you will not fear the death penalty. If you come near him, make no mistake, lest he take away your life; know that you are walking in the midst of snares, and that you are going about on the battlements of a city. As far as possible, know your neighbors, and consult with the wise Let your conversation be with men of understanding, and let all your discussion be about the Torah of the Most High. Let righteous people be your companions at table, and let your glory be in the fear of the Lord, who looks on those who are lowly. A work will be praised for the skill of the artisan, and a people's leader, for his speech. A garrulous man will be hated in his city, and one who is reckless in speech will be despised

Sirach 10

A wise judge will instruct his people, and the government of an insightful man will be well ordered. As the judge of the people is, so are his officials; as the ruler of the city is, so are all its inhabitants. An undisciplined king destroys his people, but a city becomes established through the understanding of its leaders The authority of the earth is in the hands of the Lord, and in due time He appoints the ruler. The prosperity of a man is in the hand of the Lord, and He will confer his honor upon the person of the scribe. Do not be angry with your neighbor for every injury, and do not attempt anything by acts of insolence Pride is hateful before God and man, and by both doings injustice is abhorred. Sovereignty passes from nation to nation on account of injustice, violence, and wealth. What is earth and ashes proud of? In the life of his body, his bowels decay. A long illness baffles the physician; the king of today will die tomorrow. When a man is dead, he will inherit maggots, vermin, and worms The beginning of pride is when one departs from the Lord, and his heart is turned away from his Maker. For the beginning of sin is pride, and one who clings to it pours out abominations. Therefore the Lord brought extraordinary calamities upon them and utterly destroyed them. The Lord has cast down the thrones of rulers and has seated the humble in their place. The Lord has plucked up the roots of proud nations and planted the lowly in their place The Lord has overthrown the lands of nations and has destroyed them to the foundations of the earth. He has taken some of them away and destroyed them and has made their memory to cease from the earth. Pride was not created for men, nor fierce anger for those born of a woman. Whose offspring has honor? The offspring of man. Who inherits the earth? Those who fear the Lord. Whose offspring is dishonored? The offspring of man. Who inherits the earth? Those who break the commandments The leader, the judge, and the ruler will be honored, but none of them is greater than the one who fears the Lord. Free men will serve a wise servant, and an intelligent man will not complain. Do not flaunt your wisdom in doing your work, and do not boast in the time of your distress. Better is the one who works and has more than enough than the one who boasts and lacks bread My son, glorify your soul in meekness, and give it honor according to its dignity. Who will justify the one who sins against himself? And who will honor the one who dishonors his own life? The poor man is honored for his knowledge, while the rich man is honored for his wealth. One who is honored in poverty, how much more in wealth? And one who is dishonorable in wealth, how much more in poverty?

Sirach 11

The wisdom of the humble lifts their heads high and seats them among the great. Do not praise someone for their good looks, nor despise them for their outward appearance. The bee, though small among flying creatures, produces the sweetest of confections. Do not boast about the clothes you wear or exalt yourself on the day of honor; the Lord's works are wonderful, often hidden from men Many kings have risen from the dust to the throne, while the mighty have been greatly disgraced and renowned men handed over to others. Investigate before you blame, understand first, then rebuke. Listen before you respond, and do not interrupt others while they speak. Avoid disputes that do not concern you and do not join sinners in judgment Do not be overly busy; excessive meddling will not go unpunished. Hard work and haste can still leave you falling short. Meanwhile, a person who is slow and needs help, lacking strength, might be looked upon favorably by the Lord, lifted from lowliness, causing many to marvel. Good and bad, life and death, poverty and riches come from the Lord The Lord's favor stays with the devout; His approval endures forever. Diligence and self-denial can lead to wealth, but such gains are fleeting; you do not know when you will pass them on and die. Be steadfast in your commitments, persist in your work, and do not envy sinners' success. Quickly and suddenly, the Lord can enrich the poor In days of success, troubles are forgotten, and in adversity, joys do not come to mind. Life's rewards and afflictions remind us that all outcomes are within the Lord's power to bestow. Never call anyone fortunate before their death; a person's legacy is seen in their progeny. Be cautious about whom you welcome into your home; the deceitful have many tricks A proud man, like a decoy partridge, watches for your weaknesses. He twists good into evil and finds fault even in virtue. A small spark can ignite a great fire; a sinful man awaits chances to cause harm. Guard against evildoers who plot wickedness, possibly ruining your reputation permanently

Sirach 12

Know who you benefit with your good deeds; your generosity will be recognized. Help the devout, and you will find a reward, if not from them, then from the Most High. No good comes to those who persist in evil or refuse to give charity. Support the godly, not sinners; by helping the wicked, you invite trouble upon yourself In prosperity, a friend's loyalty is untested, and enemies are revealed in adversity. Never trust an enemy; his wickedness rusts like corroded copper. Even if he acts humbly and pitifully, remain vigilant. If you let him sit by your side, he might usurp your place, proving my warnings and causing you regret Who would pity a snake charmer bitten, or anyone associating with sinners? They will not stand by you in your missteps. An enemy speaks sweetly but plots to harm you. He may weep, yet eagerly awaits a chance to strike. In times of trouble, he pretends to help only to set traps for you

Sirach 13

Association with the proud is perilous, like handling pitch—you become defiled. Do not overburden yourself by seeking the company of the rich and powerful, as unequal relationships often lead to ruin. The rich may wrong and threaten, the poor suffer and apologize. If you prove useful, the rich exploit you; if needy, they abandon you If you own something valuable, the rich may deceptively befriend you. Once used, they disregard you and mock your downfall. If a powerful person invites you, keep a reserved distance to encourage further invitations. Avoid being too forward or too distant, and do not engage on equal terms as he will test you with flattering talk Every creature naturally gravitates towards its kind; similarly, people are drawn to those like themselves. What accord can there be between the rich and the poor, or a wolf and a lamb? Just as wild donkeys are prey in the wilderness, so too are the poor exploited by the rich. The downfall of a humble person is often ignored, while a rich man's error is excused

Sirach 14

Blessed is the one who has never misspoken and is not consumed by guilt. Happy are those whose conscience does not accuse them, who have not lost hope. Wealth is pointless for the miserly; what good is money to one who refuses to enjoy it? Those who deny themselves pleasures only gather for others to enjoy If someone is stingy to themselves, how can they be generous to others? Such self-deprivation is their own punishment. Even if they do good, it's soon forgotten, overshadowed by their enduring vices. A miser's greed never rests; his unsatisfied desires torment him. My child, treat yourself well within your means and honor the Lord with worthy offerings Do not forget that death is inevitable, and the covenant of the grave is unknown to you. Be generous to your friends before death, share your resources as you can. Enjoy your days and do not miss out on desired pleasures; you cannot take your labors beyond the grave. Life is fleeting; like clothing, it wears out, and like seasonal leaves, generations pass

Sirach 15

Those who fear the Lord will seek wisdom; she will nourish them with understanding and wisdom. Wisdom, like a loving mother and spouse, will support and not confuse them. She exalts her followers above their peers and enables them to speak wisely in gatherings. The foolish and sinful will not see her; she remains distant from the arrogant and dishonest Praise is unseemly from the sinful, for it is not ordained by the Lord. Wisdom speaks through the righteous; their praises are blessed by

God. Do not blame the Lord for your faults; He does not lead anyone to sin. He despises abominations and does not associate with sinners. God leaves everyone to their own devices; keeping His commandments is a choice guided by personal will Choose between life and death, for both are before you, and you will receive what you desire. The wisdom of the Lord is profound; He is omnipotent and all-seeing, understanding every human action. He commands no one to be wicked and permits no one to sin

Sirach 16

Do not pride yourself on having many children unless they live in God's fear. It is better to have one wise child than a thousand wicked ones. One wise person can populate a city; a multitude of the wicked can lead to desolation. God's patience with sinners has limits, shown by His historical judgements against the disobedient and the arrogant Even if you think you are hidden from the Lord, remember that nothing escapes His notice. Heaven and earth tremble at His glance; His majestic works are beyond human understanding or intervention. Do not be presumptuous about your standing before God; His judgement is as swift as it is fair Live with awareness of God's omnipresence and His imminent judgement. Care for your words and deeds, as they shape your eternal destiny. Reflect on the transient nature of life and the enduring wisdom of following God's ways. Wisdom calls for a disciplined life guided by understanding and respect for God's commandments

Sirach 17

The Lord created mankind from the earth and has destined them to return to it. He endowed humans with a set time on earth and granted them authority over its creations. They were made in His image, with the ability to reason, and were given dominion over beasts and birds. The Lord endowed humans with wisdom and the knowledge of good and evil, setting His eye upon their hearts to reveal the majesty of His works Humans are to praise His holy name and acknowledge the majesty of His creations. The Lord made an everlasting covenant with them, showing them His decrees and allowing them to witness His glory. He commanded them to avoid all unrighteousness, ensuring their ways would always be before Him and never hidden from His sight. Every nation has its ruler, but Israel is deemed the Lord's portion, always under His watchful eyes. Their deeds are as clear as the sun to Him, and their sins are ever before Him The Lord treasures acts of kindness like a signet ring and keeps a person's generosity as close as the apple of His eye. To those who repent, He offers a return and comfort to those losing hope. It is vital to forsake sins, make heartfelt prayers, and turn fully to the Lord, for only the living can praise Him. His mercy and forgiveness are vast, reminding us that while humans are not capable of everything, they remain under His watchful gaze

Sirach 18

The Lord, eternal and almighty, created the universe. His justice is unparalleled, and His works are beyond human comprehension. No one can match the magnitude of His might or the grace of His mercy. His wondrous works are perfect; adding or subtracting from them is impossible, and fully understanding them is beyond human reach When humans conclude their toils, they are only at the beginning of understanding God's ways. The essence and purpose of mankind are elusive, and their existence is fleeting compared to the eternal days of God. Thus, the Lord's patience is abundant, His mercy widespread as He sees their end is inclined towards evil. He extends forgiveness generously, treating humanity with a shepherd's care, guiding, correcting, and teaching Words should not diminish the value of good deeds; gentle words can soothe like dew relieves heat. Wisdom is knowing when to speak and what to give, recognizing that both can coexist harmoniously. A fool is graceless and hurtful; the gifts of the stingy bring no joy. Before you fall ill, take care of your health, and before judgment, examine yourself to find mercy and forgiveness

Sirach 19

A laborer who indulges in alcohol will not become rich, as small neglections lead gradually to ruin. Wine and women can lead wise men astray, and liaisons with prostitutes are reckless, leading to decay. Trusting hastily can show a lack of depth, and sinning harms oneself more than others. Reveling in wickedness brings condemnation, and despising gossip reduces evil Keep secrets entrusted to you, whether they come from friends or foes, and avoid revealing them unless keeping them would be sinful. If someone confides in you, keep it to yourself; it is better to hold your tongue than to let slip information that could harm others or yourself. Even a fool struggles with keeping secrets, feeling as though they labor under their weight Question your friends and neighbors before judging their actions or words. Misunderstandings can often be clarified without assuming the worst. Not everyone who slips does so intentionally, and everyone can misspeak or make errors. Before you confront or accuse someone, understand the context and give them a chance to explain Remember, all true wisdom begins with fearing the Lord, and living according to His laws is the highest wisdom. Knowledge of wickedness is not true wisdom, and cunning in sin is not sound advice. Some may feign humility or kindness to achieve their ends, but their true intentions will eventually be revealed. Recognize a person by their actions and appearance, for these can reveal much about their character

Sirach 20

Reproof given untimely can be ineffective, while silence, at times, reflects wisdom. It is beneficial to offer correction gently rather than harbor anger. He who admits fault will avoid further harm. As inappropriate as a eunuch desiring to deflower a virgin is he who executes judgments violently. There are those who find wisdom in silence and others disliked for their excessive speech. Silence can be due to a lack of response or a strategic choice to wait for the right moment Often, a wise man remains silent until it is time to speak, unlike the braggart and fool who miss their opportunity. Overuse of words can lead to disdain, and usurping authority can breed resentment. There are apparent prosperities that result in misfortunes, and profits that lead to losses. Gifts might not always be beneficial, and some can even yield returns unexpectedly Some face losses for the sake of honor, while others rise from lowliness to prominence. Wise speech can endear one to others, unlike the wasted pleasantries of fools. The offerings of a fool are burdensome, for he expects much more in return. He may give little and insult abundantly, lending today and demanding it back prematurely, making himself disliked Fools lament the absence of friendship and gratitude, often ridiculed for their complaints. A slip of the tongue can be more damaging than a physical stumble, leading to rapid downfall. A misfit tale is annoying when told out of season and will persist in conversations among the ignorant. An untimely proverb from a fool is disregarded, as he fails to recognize the right moment for speaking One may avoid sin due to lack, and when he rests, he remains untroubled. Others destroy their peace through shyness or misplaced modesty, inadvertently turning friends into foes through unnecessary promises. Lies are a severe blemish on one's character, persistently featured in the tales of the uninformed. A habitual liar is worse than a thief, as both are destined for ruin, with lying leading to continuous dishonor Those skilled in speech can advance themselves and find favor with influential figures. Hard work in one's field can yield abundant harvests and may even absolve past misdeeds. However, favors and gifts can cloud the judgment of the wise and silence needed criticism. Hidden wisdom or concealed treasure is of no use to anyone; it is better to display ignorance than to conceal one's understanding

Sirach 21

If you have sinned, cease and seek forgiveness for your past wrongdoings. Avoid sin as you would evade a serpent, for it will bite if approached, its effects deadly as a lion's bite. Every sin is a double-edged sword with irreparable consequences. Terror and violence can deplete wealth quickly, just as arrogance can lead to ruin The pleas of the impoverished ascend directly to God, who delivers swift justice. Those who despise correction follow a sinful path, while the God-fearing will reconsider their actions inwardly. Eloquence may bring renown, yet true wisdom is recognizing and correcting one's missteps Building with borrowed resources is as futile as collecting stones for one's own grave. The assembly of the wicked ends in fiery destruction, much like sinners' path leads to hell. Adhering to the law grants mastery over its intentions and brings the wisdom of God's fear. Without cleverness, instruction can turn sour, while the wise transform their knowledge into abundant, life-giving counsel Fools are likened to broken vessels, incapable of retaining wisdom. Those knowledgeable affirm wise words and build upon them, while the reckless disregard them completely. The words of the wise are cherished and contemplated in the community, unlike the nonsense spouted by the unwise, which bears no substance

Sirach 22

Laziness brings public disgrace, akin to the repulsion one feels for a filthy stone. An undisciplined child brings grief to a father, and a foolish daughter becomes a source of loss. A wise daughter secures a suitable partner, reflecting her prudence and her father's guidance. Inappropriate conversation during solemn times is as jarring as inappropriate joy at a funeral, but correction is always timely Educating a fool is as futile as attempting to wake someone from a deep slumber or piecing together broken pottery. Mourn for the dead who rest from their labors, and lament more for a fool who lacks understanding, for their existence is more burdensome than death. Avoid extensive interactions with fools, as their ignorance can be contaminating and exhausting A fool is heavier to bear than lead; interacting with the senseless is more challenging than carrying heavy burdens. True wisdom and understanding establish a person firmly, like well-constructed masonry. In contrast, fear based on foolish fantasies cannot withstand real challenges. Just as physical actions provoke reactions, harsh words can destroy friendships, though reconciliation is sometimes possible if the offenses are not too grave Support your neighbor in adversity so that you can share in their prosperity. Watch your words carefully to prevent irreversible damage to your relationships and reputation

Sirach 23

Lord, Father, and Master of my life, do not abandon me to the decisions of those who would lead me astray, and do not let me fall because of them. Who will put controls over my thoughts and discipline over my heart to keep me from inadvertent error and overlooking my sins? Without such guidance, my mistakes may multiply, and my sins increase, leading to disgrace before my adversaries Lord, keep arrogance from my eyes and turn away evil desires from me. Let not gluttony nor lust overcome me, and save me from a shameless mind. My children, listen to the discipline concerning the mouth; he who maintains control over it will avoid being ensnared. Many fall through their speech, and those who fail to control it bring ruin upon themselves Do not become accustomed to using oaths or invoking the Holy One frivolously, for constant swearing leads to inescapable sin. A person who often swears accumulates sin, and his home becomes filled with misfortune. A lying speech is as deadly as a mortal wound, and should not be found among the godly, who do not wallow in sin Guard your speech from coarse jokes and vulgar words, for they contribute to sinful communication. Recall your parents when you are among the influential, lest you embarrass yourself and regret your upbringing. Constant exposure to foul language desensitizes and makes it hard to correct. Beware, too, of becoming too familiar with sin, as it leads to more transgressions and inevitable punishment

Sirach 24

Wisdom personifies herself, proclaiming her praises among her people and in the assembly of the Most High. She declares, "I emerged from the mouth of the Most High, and like a mist covered the earth. I dwelled in the heights, and my throne was in a cloudy pillar. I alone encompassed the heavens and penetrated the depths of the abyss, walking on the waves of the sea and over all the earth." Among all peoples and nations, I sought a resting place. In whose territory should I reside? Then the Creator of all commanded that my dwelling be in Israel, my inheritance in Jacob. From the beginning of time, before the world was created, I was planned, and I shall never cease to be. I ministered before Him in the holy tabernacle, and established my home in Zion In Jerusalem, my authority was recognized, and I took root among a people honored by the Lord's choice. I grew tall like a cedar in Lebanon, like a cypress on the heights of Hermon. I spread out like a palm tree on the seashore, and blossomed like a rose plant in Jericho, as beautiful as an olive tree in the fields, and majestic as a plane tree I exuded fragrance like cinnamon and aromatic balm, providing a sweet smell like choice myrrh, and spread a pleasant aroma like frankincense in the sanctuary. I extended my branches like a terebinth, and my branches were glorious and graceful. As a vine, I brought forth delightful fruits, and my blossoms became the fruit of honor and wealth "Come to me, all who desire me, and partake of my fruits, for my memory is sweeter than honey, and my inheritance more delightful than the honeycomb. Those who eat of me will hunger for more, and those who drink of me will thirst for more. Whoever listens to me will not be put to shame, and those who work with me will not sin." All these things are the essence of the covenant of the Most High God, the commandments which Moses directed to us as an inheritance for the communities of Jacob. It is He who fills wisdom as abundant as the river Pishon and as overflowing as the Tigris at the time of the first fruits. He makes understanding as broad as the Euphrates and as full as the Jordan at harvest time. He illuminates discipline as brightly as the sun, and as fruitful as the Gihon at the time of the vintage

Thus, wisdom flows out to educate and illuminate, offering itself not just for me but for all who seek her earnestly and diligently in all generations

Sirach 25

There are three things I delight in and find pleasing both to God and men: harmony among brothers, friendship among neighbors, and a husband and wife who live in agreement. Conversely, my soul detests three kinds of people: a poor man who is arrogant, a rich man who is a liar, and an old adulterer who lacks understanding How can one find anything in old age if they have gathered nothing in their youth? Judgment is beautiful in the aged, and wisdom and counsel in the venerable. The wisdom of the elderly and their understanding are honorable, and their experience is like a crown of glory, adorned with the fear of the Lord There are nine who I consider fortunate, and a tenth I will speak of with my tongue: a man who delights in his children, one who lives to see the defeat of his enemies, he who has a wife of understanding, he who does not slip with his tongue, and he who has not served unworthy men. Fortunate is the man who finds wisdom and speaks to listening ears. The greatest among men is the one who fears the Lord—nothing can be compared to one who possesses this fear Avoid all types of wounds, but most especially those to the heart; avoid all types of wickedness, especially that of a woman. No disaster is more detrimental than hatred from enemies, and no venom is more deadly than that of a serpent. There is no anger like the wrath of an enemy I would rather live with a lion and a dragon than keep house with a wicked woman. The malice of a woman will change her appearance and darken her countenance like that of a bear. Her husband will sit among his neighbors; upon hearing of her deeds, he will sigh bitterly. All malice is slight compared to a woman's malice, which brings disgrace and is never erased The difficulty of enduring a contentious woman is like ascending a sandy slope. Do not be captivated by a woman's beauty, and do not desire her for her looks alone. A woman's anger, impudence, and reproach can outweigh the benefits of her support. A wicked woman abases the heart, brings grief to the face, and weakens the will. A woman who does not make her husband happy causes despair, much like a sickness weakens the body Sin began with a woman, and because of her, we all die. Do not allow a sinful woman to act freely or speak unguardedly. If she does not follow your direction, sever her from your life

Sirach 26

Happy is the man who has a good wife; his days will be doubled in joy. A faithful wife brings joy to her husband, and he will live out his years in peace. A good wife is a precious gift, bestowed upon those who revere the Lord. Whether a man is rich or poor, a good heart will always bring a cheerful face. There are three things that deeply troubled my heart, and for the fourth, I prayed earnestly: the slander of a city, the assembly of a mob, and a false accusation. These are more grievous than death itself. A woman who is jealous of another woman brings grief and sorrow to the heart; her sharp tongue reveals her nature to all. A wicked woman is like a burdensome yoke; dealing with her is like handling a scorpion. A drunken woman brings about great wrath and cannot hide her own shame. The fornication of a woman is evident in the way she lifts her eyes; it will be known by her eyelids. Guard a headstrong daughter closely, lest she find freedom for herself and use it unwisely. Be wary of an impudent eye, and don't be surprised if it leads to sin. Such a woman will open her mouth like a thirsty traveler, drinking from any water nearby; she will sit at every post, and open herself to any

passerby The grace of a wife delights her husband; her wisdom strengthens his bones. A silent woman is a gift from the Lord, and there is nothing as valuable as a well-instructed soul. A modest woman is a blessing upon blessings; no scale can measure the worth of a self-controlled soul. Just as the sun shines in the highest heavens, so does the beauty of a good wife in her well-ordered home. As a lamp shines upon the holy lampstand, so does the beauty of a well-proportioned body. As golden pillars rest upon a base of silver, so are beautiful feet with the steadfastness of one who is faithful There are two things that grieve my heart, and for the third, anger rises within me: a warrior who suffers in poverty, men of understanding who are treated as rubbish, and one who turns from righteousness to sin—the Lord will prepare him for destruction. It is difficult for a merchant to remain free from wrongdoing, and for a retailer to avoid sin

Sirach 27

Many have sinned in their pursuit of profit; those who seek to multiply wealth will turn a blind eye to morality. Just as a nail sticks fast between the joinings of stones, so sin will thrust itself between buying and selling. Unless a person clings diligently to the fear of the Lord, his house will quickly be overthrown. Just as refuse remains after the shaking of a sieve, so does the filth of man remain in his thoughts. The furnace tests the potter's vessels; likewise, a person's character is tested in his thoughts. The fruit of a tree reveals the care it has received, and so does a person's speech reveal the thoughts of his heart. Do not praise anyone before you hear their thoughts, for this is how people are truly tested If you pursue righteousness, you will obtain it, and it will adorn you like a robe of glory. Just as birds return to their kind, so truth will return to those who practice it. The lion waits in ambush for its prey, just as sin waits for those who do evil. The speech of a godly person is always wise, but a fool changes like the moon. Limit your time among people who lack understanding, but persevere among the thoughtful. The talk of fools is offensive, and their laughter is filled with sin. Their speech, filled with swearing, makes one's hair stand on end, and their strife causes others to cover their ears. The quarrels of the proud lead to bloodshed, and their abuse of one another is grievous to hear A person who reveals secrets destroys trust and will not find a close friend. Love your friend and keep faith with him, but if you reveal his secrets, you will lose him just as a man destroys his enemy. Releasing a bird from your hand is like letting your neighbor go; you will not catch him again. Don't pursue him, for he has gone far away, escaping like a gazelle from a snare. A wound may be healed, and reconciliation may follow after abuse, but a person who reveals secrets is beyond hope One who winks with the eye plans evil things, and those who know him will keep their distance. When present, he will speak sweetly and admire your words, but afterward, he will twist his speech and set traps with your words. I have hated many things, but none more than him—the Lord also hates him. A person who throws a stone straight up will have it fall on his own head; a deceitful blow opens wounds. Whoever digs a pit will fall into it; whoever sets a snare will be caught in it. Those who do evil will have their deeds roll back upon them, and they will not know where they came from. Mockery and reproach come from the arrogant, and vengeance lies in wait for them like a lion. Those who rejoice at the fall of the righteous will be caught in a snare, and anguish will consume them before they die. Wrath and anger are also abominations, and a sinner will be possessed by them

Sirach 28

One who seeks vengeance will find vengeance from the Lord, and his sins will be firmly established. Forgive your neighbor for the harm they have done, and your sins will be pardoned when you pray. Does anyone harbor anger against another and expect healing from the Lord? If someone shows no mercy to another person like himself, how can he expect mercy for his own sins? He, being human, nourishes wrath—who will atone for his sins? Remember your final end and cease from enmity. Remember death and decay, and be faithful to the commandments. Remember the commandments and do not harbor anger against your neighbor. Remember the covenant of the Most High and overlook ignorance Abstain from strife, and you will reduce your sins, for a hot-tempered person kindles strife. A sinner will disturb friends and sow discord among those at peace. Just as fuel feeds a fire, so strife will burn. The strength of a person's anger will match his power, and his wealth will fuel his rage. A quarrel started in haste kindles a fire, and hasty fighting sheds blood. If you blow on a spark, it will flame; if you spit on it, it will be quenched. Both of these come from your mouth Curse the whisperer and the double-tongued, for they have destroyed many who were at peace. A slanderer has shaken many and driven them from nation to nation. It has pulled down strong cities and overthrown the houses of great men. A slanderer has cast out courageous women and deprived them of their labors. Those who listen to it will find no rest and will not live quietly. The stroke of a whip leaves a mark on the flesh, but the stroke of a tongue breaks bones. Many have fallen by the sword, but not as many as those who have fallen because of the tongue Happy is the person who is sheltered from it, who has not passed through its wrath, who has not worn its yoke, and who has not been bound with its chains. Its yoke is a yoke of iron, and its bands are bands of brass. Its death is an evil death, and Hades is preferable to it. It will not rule over godly people, and they will not be burned in its flame. Those who forsake the Lord will fall into it; it will burn among them and will not be quenched. It will be sent against them like a lion and will destroy them like a leopard Just as you hedge your possessions with thorns and secure your silver and gold, so make a balance and weight for your words, and make a door and bar for your mouth. Take heed lest you slip with your tongue and fall before one who lies in wait

Sirach 29

One who shows mercy lends to his neighbor; he who strengthens him with his hand keeps the commandments. Lend to your neighbor in his time of need, and repay your neighbor on time. Confirm your word and keep faith with him, and you will find what you need at all times. Many have treated a loan as a windfall and have brought trouble to those who helped them. Until they receive what they want, they will be submissive, but when payment is due, they will delay, make excuses, and complain about the circumstances. If they prevail, the creditor will barely receive half and will consider it a loss. If they do not prevail, they will take the creditor's money and turn him into an enemy without cause. They will repay him with cursing and insults, bringing disgrace instead of honor Many have turned away because of this deceit; they are afraid of being defrauded for nothing. However, be patient with a person in poverty, and do not keep him waiting for your help. Help the poor for the sake of the commandment, and do not send them away empty-handed. Lose your money for a brother or a friend; do not let it rust under a stone and be lost. Allocate your wealth according to the commandments of the Most High, and it will benefit you more than gold. Store up almsgiving in your storehouses, and it will deliver you from all affliction. It will fight for you against your enemy better than a mighty shield and a powerful spear A good person will act as surety for his neighbor, but one who has lost shame will fail him. Do not forget the kindness of your guarantor, for he has risked his life for you. A sinner will waste the resources of his guarantor. One who is ungrateful will fail the person who delivered him. Acting as surety has ruined many who were prospering and has shaken them like a wave of the sea. It has driven mighty men from their homes, causing them to wander among foreign nations. A sinner who falls into surety and undertakes contracts will end up in lawsuits. Help your neighbor according to your ability, but be careful not to fall yourself The essentials of life are water, bread, clothing, and a house for privacy. Better is the life of a poor person under a shelter of logs than feasting in another person's house. Whether you have little or much, be content. It is miserable to go from house to house, where, as a guest, you dare not speak freely. You will be expected to entertain and serve drinks without thanks, and you will hear bitter words. "Come here, you traveler, set the table, and if you have anything, feed me with it." "Leave, you traveler, for an honored guest has arrived. My brother has come, and I need my house." These things are grievous to a person of understanding: the scolding over lodging and the insults of creditors

Sirach 30

One who loves his son will discipline him regularly, so that he may have joy in him in the end. A father who corrects his son will gain profit from him and will boast of him among his acquaintances. A father who teaches his son will provoke jealousy in his enemies, and will take pride in him before his friends. Even after his father's death, it will be as though he had not died, for he leaves behind a son who is like himself. In his lifetime, he saw his son and rejoiced; when he died, he had no regrets. He left behind an avenger against his enemies and one who will repay kindness to his friends One who indulges his son too much will bind up his wounds, and his heart will be troubled at every cry. An undisciplined horse becomes stubborn, and an unrestrained son becomes headstrong. Pamper your child, and he will make you afraid; play with him, and he will bring you grief. Do not laugh with him too much, lest you suffer sorrow with him and gnash your teeth in the end. Give him no liberty in his youth, and do not overlook his follies. Bow down his neck in his youth and discipline him while he is a child, lest he become stubborn and disobedient, bringing sorrow to your soul. Correct your son and give him work to do, lest his shameless behavior become an offense to you It is better to be a poor person who is healthy and fit than a rich person who is afflicted in body. Health and fitness are better than all the gold in the world, and a strong body is more valuable than immeasurable wealth. There is no greater wealth than a healthy body, and no greater joy than a cheerful heart. Death is better than a life filled with bitterness, and eternal rest is better than constant sickness Good things poured upon a closed mouth are like food offerings laid upon a grave. What does an offering profit an idol, for it can neither eat nor smell? So is the person who is punished by the Lord, seeing with his eyes and groaning like a eunuch embracing a virgin and groaning. Do not give your soul to sorrow, and do not afflict yourself deliberately. A cheerful heart is the life of a person, and cheerfulness prolongs one's days. Love your own soul and comfort your heart; remove sorrow far from you, for sorrow has destroyed many, and there is no profit in it. Envy and wrath shorten life, and anxiety brings old age before its time. Those who are cheerful and merry will benefit from their food

Sirach 31

The wakefulness that comes from riches consumes the flesh, and anxiety about wealth takes away sleep. A person anxious about their wealth will crave slumber, but sleep will be elusive, especially in times of severe illness. The rich man toils to gather money, and when he rests, he is surrounded by his abundance. The poor man, on the other hand, toils in want, and when he rests, he remains needy. Those who love gold will not find justification, and those who pursue destruction will ultimately be filled with it. Many have been led to ruin for the sake of gold, and their destruction meets them head-on. Gold is a stumbling block for those who sacrifice for it; every fool is ensnared by it. Blessed is the rich person who is found blameless and does not chase after gold. Who is this person, that we may call them blessed? For they have done wonderful things among their people. Who has been tested by wealth and found perfect? Let that person boast. Who has had the power to transgress but has not done so? Their prosperity will be assured, and the community will proclaim their generosity When you sit at a lavish table, do not be greedy; do not say, "There is so much food!" Remember that a greedy eye is a wicked thing. What has been created more greedy than the eye? It sheds tears from every face. Do not stretch your hand out for everything you see, and do not plunge into the dish with abandon. Consider your neighbor's feelings and be discreet in every action. Eat like a human being from what is set before you; do not eat greedily, or you will be hated. Be the first to stop eating out of politeness; do not be insatiable, lest you offend. If you are sitting among many, do not reach out your hand before others. For a well-mannered person, a very small amount is sufficient; they do not groan in their bed from overeating. Healthy sleep comes from moderate eating; they rise early, and their mind is clear. However, the pain of wakefulness, stomach cramps, and discomfort are with the insatiable If you have been forced to eat, rise in the middle of the meal, and you will find rest. Listen to me, my child, and do not despise my advice, and in the end, you will appreciate my words. In all your works, be skillful, and no illness will come to you. People will bless those who are generous with their food, and the testimony of their goodness will be believed. The city will murmur against those who are stingy with their food, and the testimony of their stinginess will be accurate. Do not show yourself to be valiant in wine, for wine has destroyed many. Just as the furnace tests the temper of steel, so does wine test hearts in the quarrels of the proud. Wine is as good as life to those who drink it in moderation; what is life without wine? It has been created to make people glad. Wine, when drunk in moderation and at the right time, brings joy to the heart and gladness to the soul. However, wine consumed excessively brings bitterness to the soul, along with provocation and conflict. Drunkenness increases the rage of a fool to their detriment, diminishes their strength, and adds wounds. Do not rebuke your neighbor at a banquet of wine, do not despise them in their merriment, and do not speak words of reproach or distress them with demands

Sirach 32

If you are made the ruler of a feast, do not become arrogant. Be among the guests as one of them; attend to their needs first, and then take your place. When you have completed your duties, sit down, that you may share in their joy and receive a wreath for your good service. Speak, you who are older, for it is your right, but speak with sound knowledge and do not interrupt the music. Do not pour out words when there is a performance of music, and do not display your wisdom at the wrong time. Just as a ruby signet set in gold is a music concert at a wine banquet. Just as an emerald signet in a gold setting is a musical melody with pleasant wine Speak, young man, if you are obliged to, but no more than twice and only if asked. Summarize your speech, conveying many things in a few words. Be like one who knows much but remains silent. When you are among great men, do not act as if you are their equal. When another is speaking, do not interrupt. Just as lightning precedes thunder, so does approval come before modesty. Rise early and do not be the last to leave; go home quickly and do not linger. Amuse yourself there and do what is in your heart, but do not sin by speaking proudly. For all these things, bless your Creator, who gives you to drink freely of his good things Those who fear the Lord will receive discipline, and those who seek him early will find favor. Whoever seeks the law will be filled with it, but the hypocrite will stumble over it. Those who fear the Lord will find true judgment and will kindle righteous acts like a light. A sinful person avoids reproof and will find judgment according to their desires. A sensible person does not neglect careful thought, but an insolent and proud man will not humble himself, even after acting on his own without seeking counsel. Do nothing without counsel, but when you have acted, do not regret it. Do not walk in the path of conflict, and do not stumble in stony places. Do not be overconfident on a smooth road. Beware of your own children. In every work, guard your own soul, for this is the keeping of the commandments. Whoever believes in the law pays heed to the commandments, and those who trust in the Lord will suffer no loss

Sirach 33

No evil will befall those who fear the Lord; in times of trial, they will be delivered again and again. A wise person does not despise the law, but a hypocrite is like a boat tossed in a storm. A person of understanding puts their trust in the law, and the law is faithful to them, just like a divine oracle. Prepare your speech, and you will be heard; bind up instruction, and your answer will be wise. The heart of a fool is like a cartwheel, and their thoughts are like a rolling axle. A mocking friend is like a stallion that neighs under every rider Why does one day excel another, when all the light of every day in the year comes from the sun? They were distinguished by the Lord's knowledge, and he varied the seasons and feasts. Some days he exalted and made holy, while others he made ordinary. All people come from the ground, and Adam was created from dust. In the abundance of his knowledge, the Lord distinguished people and made their ways different. Some he blessed and exalted, bringing them close to himself, while others he cursed and brought low, overthrowing them from their place. Just as clay is in the hands of the potter, who molds it according to his pleasure, so are people in the hands of the Creator, who judges them according to his will. Good is the opposite of evil, life is the opposite of death, and so the sinner is the opposite of the godly. Consider all the works of the Most High; they come in pairs, one against the other I was the last on watch, like one who gleans after the grape gatherers. By the Lord's blessing, I arrived before them and filled my winepress like one who gathers grapes. I did not labor for myself alone, but for all those who seek instruction. Hear me, you great men of the people, and listen with your ears, you rulers of the congregation. Do not give power over yourself to your son, wife, brother, or friend while you live, and do not give your goods to another, lest you regret it and have to ask for them back. While you still live and breathe, do not give yourself over to anybody. It is better that your children should ask from you than that you should look to the hand of your children. Excel in all your works, and do not bring shame upon your honor. When the time comes for you to end your days, distribute your inheritance Fodder, a stick, and burdens are for a donkey; bread, discipline, and work are for a servant. Set your servant to work, and you will find rest; leave their hands idle, and they will seek freedom. A yoke and thong will bow the neck, and for an evil servant, there are racks and tortures. Send your servant to work, so they do not become idle, for idleness teaches much mischief. Set them to work as is fit for them, and if they do not obey, make their burdens heavier. Do not be excessive toward anyone, and do nothing unjust. If you have a servant, treat them like yourself, for you have bought them with blood. If you have a servant, treat them like yourself, for you will need them as you would your own soul. If you treat them poorly and they leave, where will you go to find them?

Sirach 34

Vain and false hopes belong to a person void of understanding, and dreams give wings to fools. Just as one who grasps at a shadow or chases after the wind, so is the one who sets their mind on dreams. The vision of dreams is like a reflection, a likeness of one's face seen in a mirror. From something unclean, what can be made clean? From something false, what can be true? Divinations, soothsaying, and dreams are vain; the heart has fantasies like a woman in labor. If dreams are not sent in a visitation from the Most High, do not give your heart to them. Many have been led astray by dreams, and they have failed by placing their hope in them The law will be fulfilled without deceit, and wisdom is complete in a faithful mouth. A well-instructed person knows many things, and one who has much experience will declare their understanding. A person without experience knows few things, but one who has traveled gains cleverness. I have seen many things in my travels, and my understanding is greater than my words. I have often been in danger, even to the point of death, but I was preserved because of these experiences The spirit of those who fear the Lord will live, for their hope is in him who saves them. Whoever fears the Lord will not be afraid or act cowardly, for the Lord is their hope. Blessed is the soul of those who fear the Lord; to whom does the Lord give heed? Who is their support? The eyes of the Lord are upon those who love him; he is a mighty protector and strong support, a shelter from the scorching wind, a shade from the noonday sun, a guard against stumbling, and a help against falling. He lifts up the soul and enlightens the eyes; he gives health, life, and blessing Whoever sacrifices something wrongfully gained offers it in mockery; the offerings of wicked people are not acceptable. The Most High has no pleasure in the offerings of the ungodly, nor is he appeased by a multitude of sacrifices. Just as one who kills a son before their father's eyes is the person who brings a sacrifice from the goods of the poor. The bread of the needy is the life of the poor; whoever deprives them of it is a murderer. Just as one who kills their neighbor is the person who takes away their livelihood; just as one who sheds blood is the person who withholds wages from a laborer When one person builds and another tears down, what do they gain but toil? When one person prays and another curses, whose voice will the Lord listen to? Whoever washes after touching a dead body, and then touches it again, what did they gain by washing? Similarly, a person who fasts for their sins, and then goes out and does the same thing again, who will listen to their prayer? What profit is there in their humility?

Sirach 35

Whoever keeps the law multiplies offerings, and whoever heeds the commandments sacrifices a peace offering. Returning a kindness is like offering fine flour, and giving alms is like making a thank offering. Departing from wickedness pleases the Lord, and turning away from unrighteousness is an atoning sacrifice. Do not appear before the Lord empty-handed, for all these things are done in obedience to the commandment. The offerings of the righteous enrich the altar, and their sweet fragrance is pleasing to the Most High. The sacrifice of a righteous person is acceptable, and it will not be forgotten Glorify the Lord with generosity, and do not reduce the first fruits of your hands. In every gift, show a cheerful countenance, and dedicate your tithe with gladness. Give to the Most High according to what he has given you; as your hand has found, give generously. For the Lord repays, and he will repay you sevenfold. Do not attempt to bribe him with gifts, for he will not accept them. Do not set your mind on an unrighteous sacrifice, for the Lord is the judge, and with him, there is no favoritism. He will not favor a person over a poor man, and he will listen to the prayer of those who have been wronged. He will not ignore the supplication of the fatherless or the widow when she pours out her heart. Do not the tears of the widow run down her cheek? Is not her cry against the one who caused them to fall? Whoever serves God according to his good pleasure will be accepted, and their supplication will reach the heavens. The prayer of the humble pierces the clouds, and it will not rest until it reaches its destination. The humble will not be comforted until the Most High intervenes and judges righteously. The Lord will not delay, nor will he be patient with the unmerciful; he will crush the loins of the ruthless. He will repay vengeance to the nations until he has removed the multitude of the arrogant and broken the scepters of the unrighteous. He will render to each person according to their deeds and repay their works according to their intentions. He will judge the cause of his people and make them rejoice in his mercy. Mercy is as welcome in times of affliction as clouds of rain are in times of drought

Sirach 36

Have mercy upon us, O Lord, God of all, and look upon us with favor. Send your fear upon all the nations. Lift up your hand against the foreign nations and let them see your mighty power. Just as you have shown your holiness in us before them, so be magnified in them before us. Let them come to know you, just as we have known you, that there is no God but you alone, O God. Show new signs and perform various wonders. Glorify your hand and your right arm. Raise up indignation and pour out your wrath. Remove the adversary and destroy the enemy. Hasten the time and remember your oath. Let them declare your mighty works. Let those who escape be devoured by raging fire, and may those who harm your people meet destruction. Crush the heads of the rulers of the enemies who say, "There is no one but ourselves." Gather all the tribes of Jacob together and take them for your inheritance as from the beginning. O Lord, have mercy upon the people called by your name, upon Israel, whom you likened to a firstborn. Have compassion upon the city of your sanctuary, Jerusalem, the place of your rest. Fill Zion with your majesty, exalt your oracles, and fill your people with your glory. Give testimony to those who were your creatures from the beginning and fulfill the prophecies spoken in your name. Reward those who wait for you, and let all people trust in your prophets.

Listen, O Lord, to the prayer of your servants according to the blessing of Aaron concerning your people, so that all who are on the earth will know that you are the Lord, the eternal God The belly will consume any food, but some foods are better than others. Just as the mouth tastes meats taken in hunting, so does an understanding heart detect false speech. A contrary heart causes heaviness, and a man of experience will repay it. A woman may receive any man, but one daughter is better than another. The beauty of a woman cheers the countenance, and a man desires nothing more. If kindness and humility are on her tongue, her husband is unlike other men. He who finds a wife finds his richest treasure, a helper fit for him and a pillar of support. Where there is no hedge, the property will be plundered, and he who has no wife will mourn as he wanders. Who would trust a nimble robber who skips from city to city? Likewise, who would trust a man who has no home and lodges wherever he finds himself at nightfall?

Sirach 37

Every friend will say, "I also am his friend," but some friends are only friends in name. Isn't it a grief, even to death, when a companion and friend turns into an enemy? O wicked imagination, why were you formed to cover the earth with deceit? There is a companion who rejoices in a friend's happiness but will be against him in times of affliction. There is a companion who labors with his friend for his own benefit, but in the face of danger, will abandon him. Do not forget a friend in your heart, and do not be unmindful of him in your prosperity Every counselor extols their advice, but some give counsel for their own gain. Let your soul be cautious of a counselor, and understand beforehand what his interest is, for he will advise for himself and may cast the lot against you, saying, "Your way is good," while standing by to see what will happen to you. Do not take counsel from one who looks at you with suspicion, and hide your plans from those who are jealous of you. Do not consult with a woman about her rival, with a coward about war, with a merchant about business, with a buyer about selling, with an envious man about gratitude, with an unmerciful man about kindness, with a lazy person about any kind of work, with a hired worker about completing his task, or with an idle servant about important business. Pay no attention to these in matters of counsel. Instead, be continually in the company of a godly person, one who keeps the commandments and whose soul is as your own, who will grieve with you if you fail Let the counsel of your heart stand firm, for there is no one more faithful to you than yourself. A man's soul sometimes advises him better than seven watchmen who sit high on a watchtower. Above all, ask the Most High to direct your way in truth. Let reason be the beginning of every work, and let counsel guide every action. As a sign of a changing heart, four things arise: good and evil, life and death. The tongue rules over them continually There is one who is clever and instructs many, yet is unprofitable to his own soul. There is one who is subtle in words but is hated and will be destitute of all food. Grace was not given to him by the Lord because he is deprived of all wisdom. There is one who is wise for his own soul, and the fruits of his understanding are trustworthy in his mouth. A wise man instructs his own people, and the fruits of his understanding are reliable. A wise man will be filled with blessings, and all who see him will call him happy. The life of a man is measured by days, but the days of Israel are beyond counting. The wise man will inherit confidence among his people, and his name will live forever My child, test your soul in your life. See what is harmful to it, and do not indulge in it. Not all things are beneficial for all people, and not every soul delights in everything. Do not be insatiable in any luxury, and do not be greedy with your food. Overeating brings disease, and gluttony causes nausea. Many have perished because of gluttony, but those who are cautious prolong their lives

Sirach 38

Honor a physician according to your need with the respect due to him, for the Lord has truly created him. Healing comes from the Most High, and the physician will receive a gift from the king. The skill of the physician will lift up his head, and he will be admired in the sight of great men. The Lord created medicines from the earth, and a prudent man will not despise them. Wasn't water made sweet with wood so that its power might be known? He gave men skill so that he might be glorified in his marvelous works. With these, he heals and takes away pain, and with these, the pharmacist makes mixtures. God's works will never come to an end, and from him, peace is upon the earth My child, in your sickness, do not be negligent, but pray to the Lord, and he will heal you. Put away wrongdoing and direct your hands in righteousness. Cleanse your heart from all sin. Offer a sweet-smelling sacrifice and a memorial of fine flour, and pour oil on your offering according to your means. Then give place to the physician, for the Lord has truly created him. Do not let him leave you, for you need him. There is a time when recovery is in their hands. For they, too, will ask the Lord to grant them success in diagnosis and healing, for the preservation of life. If someone sins before his Maker, let him fall into the hands of the physician My child, let your tears flow for the dead, and as one who suffers grievously, begin lamentation. Lay out his body with due honor, and do not neglect his burial. Mourn with bitter weeping and passionate wailing. Let your mourning be according to his merit, for one day or two, lest you be spoken ill of, and then be comforted for your sorrow. For from sorrow comes death, and sorrow of heart saps one's strength. In calamity, sorrow also remains, and a poor man's life is grievous to the heart. Do not give your heart to sorrow; put it away, remembering the end. Do not forget it, for there is no return. You do him no good, and you harm yourself. Remember his end, for so will yours be: yesterday for me, and today for you. When the dead are at rest, let their remembrance rest. Be comforted for them when their spirit departs The wisdom of the scribe comes through the opportunity of leisure, and one who has little business can become wise. How could one become wise who plows the fields, who takes pride in the shaft of the goad, who drives oxen and is occupied with their labors, and who mostly talks about bulls? His heart is set on turning his furrows, and his lack of sleep is to provide fodder for his heifers. So it is with every craftsman and master artisan who passes his time by day and night, those who engrave signets and are diligent to make great variety. Their heart is set on preserving likeness in their portraiture, and they are careful to finish their work So, too, is the blacksmith sitting by the anvil, considering the unwrought iron. The smoke of the fire wastes his flesh, and he toils in the heat of the furnace. The noise of the hammer deafens his ear, and his eyes are fixed on the pattern of the object. His heart is set on perfecting his works, and he is careful to adorn them perfectly. So is the potter sitting at his work, turning the wheel around with his feet, always anxiously set on his task. He produces his handiwork in quantity. He fashions the clay with his arm and bends its strength in front of his feet. He applies his heart to finishing the glazing, and he is careful to clean the kiln. All these trust in their hands, and each becomes skillful in their work. Without them, no city would be inhabited. People would not reside as foreigners or walk up and down there. They will not be sought in the council of the people, nor will they mount high in the assembly. They will not sit on the seat of the judge, nor will they understand the covenant of judgment. Neither will they declare instruction and judgment, nor will they be found where parables are spoken. But they will maintain the fabric of the world, and their prayer is in the handiwork of their craft

Sirach 39

Not so for the one who has applied his soul to meditate on the law of the Most High. He will seek out the wisdom of the ancients and will be occupied with prophecies. He will keep the sayings of renowned men and will enter into the subtleties of parables. He will seek out the hidden meaning of proverbs and be conversant in the dark sayings of parables. He will serve among great men and appear before rulers. He will travel through foreign lands, for he has learned what is good and evil among men. He will apply his heart to return early to the Lord who made him and will make supplication before the Most High. He will open his mouth in prayer and ask for pardon for his sins. If the great Lord wills, he will be filled with the spirit of understanding. He will pour forth the words of his wisdom and give thanks to the Lord in prayer. He will direct his counsel and knowledge, and he will meditate on the Lord's secrets. He will show the instruction he has been taught and will glory in the law of the covenant of the Lord. Many will commend his understanding. As long as the world endures, his memory will not be blotted out. His name will live from generation to generation. Nations will declare his wisdom, and the congregation will proclaim his praise. If he continues, he will leave a name greater than a thousand, and if he finally rests, it will be enough for him Yet, I will utter more, which I have thought about, for I am filled like the full moon. Listen to me, you holy children, and bud forth like a rose growing by a brook of water. Give a sweet fragrance like frankincense, put forth flowers like a lily, scatter a sweet smell, and sing a song of praise. Bless the Lord for all his works! Magnify his name and give utterance to his praise with the songs on your lips and with harps! Say this when you praise him: All the works of the Lord are exceedingly good, and every command will be fulfilled in its time. No one can say, "What is this?" or "Why is that?" for at the proper time, they will all be revealed. At his word, the waters stood as a heap, and the reservoirs of water were formed at the word of his mouth. At his command, all his good pleasure is fulfilled, and there is no one who can hinder his salvation The works of all flesh are before him, and nothing is hidden from his eyes. He sees from everlasting to everlasting, and nothing is too wonderful for him. No one can say, "What is this?" or "Why is that?" for all things are created for their own purposes. His blessing covers the dry land like a river and saturates it like a flood. Just as he made the waters salty, so the heathen will inherit his wrath. His ways are plain to the holy but are stumbling blocks to the wicked. Good things are created from the beginning for the good, just as evil things are created for sinners. The main things necessary for the life of man are water, fire, iron, salt, wheat flour, honey, milk, the blood of the grape, oil, and clothing. All these things are good for the godly, but for sinners, they will be turned into evils. There are winds created for vengeance, and in their fury, they lay on their scourges heavily. In the time of reckoning, they pour out their strength and appease the wrath of their Creator. Fire, hail, famine, and death—all these are created for vengeance, as well as wild beasts, scorpions, serpents, and the sword, which punishes the ungodly to destruction. They rejoice in his commandment and are ready on earth when needed. In their seasons, they do not disobey his command Therefore, from the beginning, I was convinced, and I thought it through and left it in writing: All the works of the Lord are good, and he will supply every need in its time. No one can say, "This is worse than that," for all things will be well-approved in their time. Now, with all your hearts and voices, sing praises and bless the Lord's name!

Sirach 40

Great travail is created for every man. A heavy yoke lies upon the sons of Adam from the day of their birth until the day of their burial in the mother of all. The expectation of things to come and the day of death trouble their thoughts and cause fear in their hearts. From the one who sits on a throne of glory to the one humbled in earth and ashes, from the one who wears purple and a crown to the one clothed in burlap, there is wrath, jealousy, trouble, unrest, fear of death, anger, and strife. In the time of rest upon his bed, his night sleep changes his knowledge. He gets little or no rest, and afterward in his sleep, as if keeping watch, he is troubled in the vision of his heart, like one who has escaped from the front of battle. In the very moment of his deliverance, he awakens and marvels that the fear was nothing To all creatures, human and animal, and even more so to sinners, come death, bloodshed, strife, sword, calamities, famine, suffering, and plague. All these things were created for the wicked, and because of them, the flood came. All things that are of the earth return to the earth, and all things that are of the waters return to the sea. All bribery and injustice will be blotted out, but good faith will stand forever. The wealth of the unjust will dry up like a river, and like a great thunder in rain, it will vanish. In opening his hands, a man will be made glad; so lawbreakers will utterly fail. The children of the ungodly will not grow many branches and are like unhealthy roots on a sheer rock. The reeds by every water or riverbank will be plucked up before all the grass Kindness is like a garden of blessings, and almsgiving endures forever. The life of one who labors and is content will be made sweet, and one who finds a treasure is better off than both. Children and the building of a city establish a name, but a blameless wife is better than both. Wine and music rejoice the heart, but the love of wisdom is better than both. The pipe and the lute make pleasant melody, but a pleasant tongue is better than both. Your eye may desire grace and beauty, but the green shoots of grain are better than both. A friend and a companion are always welcome, but a wife with her husband is better than both. Relatives and helpers are for times of affliction, but almsgiving rescues better than both. Gold and silver will make one's footing sure, but good counsel is esteemed better than both. Riches and strength lift up the heart, but the fear of the Lord is better than both. There is nothing lacking in the fear of the Lord, and in it, there is no need to seek help. The fear of the Lord is like a garden of blessing and covers a man more than any glory My child, do not lead a beggar's life. It is better to die than to beg. A man who looks to the table of another has a life that is not to be considered a life. He pollutes his soul with another person's food, but a wise and well-instructed person will beware of that. Begging may be sweet in the mouth of the shameless, but it kindles a fire in his belly

Sirach 41

O death, how bitter is the thought of you to a man who is at peace with his possessions, who has nothing to distract him, who prospers in all things, and who still has the strength to enjoy his food! O death, your sentence is acceptable to a man who is needy, who has lost his strength, who is in extreme old age, distracted by many things, and who has become perverse and impatient. Do not be afraid of the sentence of death. Remember those who came before you and those who will come after you. This is the decree from the Lord over all flesh. Why do you resist when it is the will of the Most High? Whether life lasts ten, a hundred, or a thousand years, there is no inquiry about it in Hades The children of sinners are detestable and often find themselves in the company of the ungodly. The inheritance of sinners' children will perish, and their posterity will be a perpetual disgrace. Children will lament an ungodly father because they suffer disgrace on his account. Woe to you, ungodly men, who have forsaken the law of the Most High God! If you are born, you will be born to a curse. If you die, a curse will be your lot. All things that are of the earth return to the earth; so too will the ungodly go from a curse to perdition. The mourning of men is for their bodies, but the evil name of sinners will be blotted out Take care of your name, for it will remain with you longer than a thousand great treasures of gold. A good life has its number of days, but a good name endures forever. My children, follow instruction in peace. But what benefit is there in wisdom that is hidden and a treasure that is not seen? It is better for a man to hide his foolishness than to conceal his wisdom Therefore, show respect for my words, for it is not good to retain every kind of shame. Not everything is approved by all in good faith. Be ashamed of sexual immorality before your father and mother, of lying before a prince and a mighty man, of offenses before a judge and ruler, of iniquity before the congregation and the people, and of unjust dealings before a partner and friend. Be ashamed of theft in the place where you sojourn, of dishonoring the truth of God and His covenant, of leaning on your elbow at dinner, and of contemptuous behavior in the matters of giving and taking. Be ashamed of silence before those who greet you, of looking at a prostitute, of turning away your face from a kinsman, of taking away a portion or a gift, of gazing at a married woman, of meddling with her maid, and do not come near her bed. Avoid abusive speech toward friends, and after you have given, do not insult. Be ashamed of repeating what you have heard and of revealing secrets. Thus, you will be ashamed of the right things and find favor in the sight of all people

Sirach 42

Do not be ashamed of these things, and do not sin to save face: of the law of the Most High and His covenant, of justice in judgment toward the ungodly, of settling accounts with a partner or travelers, of accepting a gift from the inheritance of friends, of exactness in scales and weights, of getting much or little, of bargaining with merchants, of frequent correction of children, and of making the back of an evil slave bleed. A seal is good where an evil wife is, and where there are many hands, lock things up. Whatever you hand over, let it be by number and weight. In giving and receiving, let all be in writing. Do not be ashamed to instruct the unwise and foolish, and one of extreme old age who contends with those who are young. In this way, you will be well-instructed and approved in the sight of all living men A daughter is a secret cause of wakefulness to a father. Care for her takes away sleep in her youth, lest she pass the flower of her age; when she is married, lest she should be hated; in her virginity, lest she should be defiled and become pregnant in her father's house; when she has a husband, lest she should transgress; and when she is married, lest she should be barren. Keep a strict watch over a headstrong daughter, lest she make you a laughingstock to your enemies, a byword in the city, notorious among the people, and shame you in public. Do not gaze at every beautiful body, and do not sit among women. For from garments comes a moth, and from a woman comes woman's wickedness. Better is the wickedness of a man than a pleasant woman, a woman who brings shame and disgrace I will now speak of the works of the Lord and declare the things I have seen. The works of the Lord are in His words. The sun that gives light looks upon all things; the Lord's work is full of His glory. The Lord has not given power to the saints to declare all His marvelous works, which the Almighty Lord firmly established so that the universe might be upheld by His glory. He searches out the deep and the heart, and He understands their secrets. For the Most High knows all knowledge and sees the signs of the world. He declares the things that are past and those that shall be, and He reveals the traces of hidden things. No thought escapes Him, and no word is hidden from Him. He has ordered the mighty works of His wisdom. He is from everlasting to everlasting. Nothing has been added to them, nor diminished from them. He has no need of any counselor. How desirable are all His works! Even a spark is evidence of this All things live and remain forever, each in its own use. They are all obedient. All things are in pairs, one opposite the other, and He has made nothing imperfect. One thing establishes the good of another. Who could ever see enough of His glory?

Sirach 43

The pride of the heavenly heights is the clear sky, the appearance of heaven in the splendor of its glory. The sun, when it rises, bringing news as it appears, is a marvelous instrument, the work of the Most High. At noon, it dries up the land; who can withstand its burning heat? A man tending a furnace works in burning heat, but the sun is three times more intense, scorching the mountains, breathing out fiery vapors, and sending out bright beams that blind the eyes. Great is the Lord who made it, and at His word, it hastens on its course The moon marks the changing seasons, declaring times and serving as a sign for the world. From the moon comes the sign of feast days, a light that wanes when it completes its course. The month is called after its name, growing wonderfully as it changes, an instrument of the heavenly host, shining in the expanse of heaven. The beauty of heaven, the glory of the stars, an ornament giving light in the highest places of the Lord. At the word of the Holy One, they stand in due order; they do not grow weary in their watches Look at the rainbow and praise Him who made it. It is exceedingly beautiful in its brightness. It encircles the sky with its glorious arc, stretched out by the hands of the Most High. By His command, He makes the snow fall and swiftly sends the lightnings of His judgment. Therefore, the storehouses are opened, and clouds fly out like birds. By His mighty power, He makes the clouds strong, and the hailstones are broken into pieces. At His appearance, the mountains shake, and at His will, the south wind blows. The voice of His thunder rebukes the earth, as do the northern storm and the whirlwind. Like birds flying down, He sprinkles the snow; it falls down like the lighting of locusts. The eye is dazzled by the beauty of its whiteness, and the heart is amazed as it falls. He also pours out frost on the earth like salt. When it freezes, it forms pointed thorns. The cold north wind blows, and ice freezes on the water. It settles on every pool of water, covering it like a breastplate The cold devours the mountains, burns up the wilderness, and consumes the green grass like fire. A mist coming swiftly heals all things, and a dew following the heat brings cheerfulness. By His counsel, He calms the deep and plants islands in it. Those who sail on the sea tell of its dangers, and we marvel when we hear them. There are strange and wondrous works in it, a variety of all that has life, and the huge creatures of the sea. Because of Him, His messengers succeed, and by His word, all things hold together We may say many things, but we cannot say enough. The summary of our words is, "He is everything!" How could we ever have the strength to glorify Him? For He is greater than all His works. The Lord is awesome and exceedingly great! His power is marvelous! Glorify the Lord and exalt Him as much as you can, for even then, He will surpass it. When you exalt Him, summon all your strength; do not grow weary, for you can never praise Him enough. Who has seen Him that he may describe Him? Who can magnify Him as He is? Many things greater than these are hidden, for we have seen only a few of His works. For the Lord made all things, and He gave wisdom to the godly

Sirach 44

Let us now praise famous men, our ancestors in their generations. The Lord created great glory in them, His mighty power from the beginning. Some ruled in their kingdoms and were renowned for their power, giving counsel through their understanding. Some have spoken in prophecies, leaders of the people by their counsels, and by their understanding, giving instruction to the people. Their words in their instruction were wise. Some composed musical tunes and set forth verses in writing. Others were rich men endowed with ability, living peaceably in their homes. All these were honored in their generations and were outstanding in their days. Some of them have left a name behind them, so that others declare their praises. But of others, there is no memory; they perished as though they had not existed. They became as though they had not been born, they and their children after them But these were men of mercy, whose righteous deeds have not been forgotten. A good inheritance remains with their offspring. Their children are within the covenant. Their offspring stand firm with their children for their sakes. Their descendants will remain forever, and their glory will not be blotted out. Their bodies were buried in peace, and their name lives on for all generations. People will declare their wisdom, and the congregation will proclaim their praise Enoch pleased the Lord and was taken up, an example of repentance to all generations. Noah was found perfect and righteous. In the time of wrath, he kept the race alive. Therefore, a remnant was left on the earth when the flood came. Everlasting covenants were made with him, that all flesh should no more be blotted out by a flood. Abraham was a great father of a multitude of nations; there was none found like him in glory. He kept the law of the Most High and was taken into a covenant with Him. In his flesh, He established the covenant. When he was tested, he was found faithful. Therefore, the Lord assured him by an oath that the nations would be blessed through his offspring, that He would multiply him like the dust of the earth, exalt his offspring like the stars, and cause them to inherit from sea to sea, and from the Euphrates River to the utmost parts of the earth In Isaac, He also established the same assurance for Abraham his father's sake, the blessing of all men, and the covenant. He made it rest upon the head of Jacob. He acknowledged him in His blessings, gave him an inheritance, and divided his portions. He distributed them among the twelve tribes

Sirach 45

Out of him, He brought forth a man of mercy who found favor in the sight of all people, a man loved by God and men, even Moses, whose memory is blessed. He made him equal in glory to the saints and magnified him in the fears of his enemies. By his words, he caused the wonders to cease. God glorified him in the sight of kings. He gave him commandments for His people and showed him part of His glory. He sanctified him in his faithfulness and meekness. He chose him out of all people. He made him hear His voice, led him into the thick darkness, and gave him commandments face to face, even the law of life and knowledge, that he might teach Jacob the covenant, and Israel His judgments He exalted Aaron, a holy man like Moses, even his brother, of the tribe of Levi. He established an everlasting covenant with him and gave him the priesthood of the people. He blessed him with stateliness and dressed him in a glorious robe. He clothed him in perfect splendor and strengthened him with symbols of authority: the linen trousers, the long robe, and the ephod. He encircled him with pomegranates and many golden bells around him, to make a sound as he went, that it might be heard in the temple, as a reminder for the children of his people; with a holy garment, with gold, blue, and purple, the work of an embroiderer; with an oracle of judgment Urim and Thummim; with twisted scarlet, the work of a craftsman; with precious stones engraved like a signet, set in gold, the work of a jeweler, as a reminder engraved in writing, after the number of the tribes of Israel; with a crown of gold upon the mitre, engraved like a signet, "HOLINESS," an ornament of honor, the work of an expert, the desire of the eyes, goodly and beautiful. Before him, there had never been anything like it. No stranger put them on, but only his sons and his descendants perpetually His sacrifices shall be wholly burnt, twice every day, continually. Moses consecrated him and anointed him with holy oil. It was an everlasting covenant with him and his descendants, all the days of heaven, to minister to the Lord, to serve as a priest, and to bless his people in His name. He chose him out of all living to offer sacrifice to the Lord, incense, and a sweet fragrance, as a memorial, to make atonement for the people. He gave him authority in His commandments, in the covenants of judgments, to teach Jacob the testimonies and to enlighten Israel in His law Strangers conspired against him and envied him in the wilderness: Dathan and Abiram with their company, and the congregation of Korah, in wrath and anger. The Lord saw it, and it displeased Him. In the wrath of His anger, they were destroyed. He did wonders upon them, to consume them with flaming fire. He added glory to Aaron and gave him a heritage. He divided to him the first fruits of the increase and prepared bread of first fruits in abundance. For they eat the sacrifices of the Lord, which He gave to him and his descendants. However, in the land of the people, he has no inheritance, and he has no portion among the people, for the Lord Himself is his portion and inheritance Phinehas, the son of Eleazar, was third in glory, in that he was zealous in the fear of the Lord, and stood fast when the people turned away, making atonement for Israel. Therefore, a covenant of peace was established with him, that he should be the leader of the sanctuary and of his people, that he and his descendants should have the dignity of the priesthood forever. He also made a covenant with David, the son of Jesse, of the tribe of Judah. The inheritance of the king is his alone, from son to son. So the inheritance of Aaron is also to his descendants May God give you wisdom in your heart to judge His people in righteousness, that their good things may not be abolished, and that their glory may endure for all generations

Sirach 46

Joshua, the son of Nun, was a valiant warrior, succeeding Moses in the role of prophet. His name became great for the salvation of God's chosen people, taking vengeance on the enemies who rose against them, and giving Israel their inheritance. How glorious he was in lifting up his hands and stretching out his sword against the cities! Who stood firm before him? For the Lord Himself brought his enemies to him. Did not the sun stand still by his command? Did not one day become as two? He called upon the Most High, the Mighty One, when his enemies pressed in all around him, and the great Lord heard him. With hailstones of mighty power, he unleashed war upon the nations, destroying those who resisted him on the slopes, so that the nations might know his armor and how he fought in the sight of the Lord, for he followed the Mighty One Also, in the time of Moses, he and Caleb, the son of Jephunneh, showed mercy by standing against the adversaries, preventing the people from sinning, and calming their wicked complaints. Out of six hundred thousand people on foot, only these two were preserved to bring them into their inheritance, into a land flowing with milk and honey. The Lord gave strength to Caleb, which remained with him into old age, so that he entered the hill country, and his offspring obtained it as an inheritance, demonstrating to all the children of Israel that it is good to follow the Lord Also, the judges, each by name, those whose hearts did not engage in immorality and who did not turn away from the Lord—may their memory be blessed! May their bones flourish again from their resting place, and may the names of those who were honored be renewed in their children Samuel, the prophet of the Lord, beloved by his God, established a kingdom and anointed princes over his people. By the law of the Lord, he judged the congregation, and the Lord watched over Jacob. By his faithfulness, he was proved to be a prophet, and by his words, he was known to be faithful in vision. When his enemies surrounded him, he called upon the Lord, the Mighty One, with the offering of a suckling lamb. The Lord thundered from heaven and made His voice heard with a mighty sound, utterly destroying the rulers of the Tyrians and all the princes of the Philistines Before his death, Samuel testified before the Lord and His anointed, saying, "I have not taken anyone's goods, not even a sandal," and no one accused him. Even after he died, he prophesied, revealing the end of the king and lifting up his voice from the earth in prophecy to blot out the wickedness of the people

Sirach 47

After him, Nathan rose up to prophesy in the days of David. As fat is separated from the peace offering, so was David separated from the children of Israel. He played with lions as with kids and with bears as with lambs of the flock. In his youth, did he not kill a giant and remove the reproach from the people when he lifted up his hand with a sling and struck down the boasting Goliath? He called upon the Most High Lord, who gave him strength in his right hand to kill a mighty warrior, exalting the horn of his people. The people glorified him for his tens of thousands and praised him for the blessings of the Lord, as a glorious diadem was given to him He destroyed his enemies on every side and defeated the Philistines, his adversaries, breaking their horn into pieces even to this day. In all his works, he gave thanks to the Holy One, Most High, with words of glory. He sang praises with his whole heart and loved the One who made him. He set singers before the altar to create sweet melodies with their music. He beautified the feasts and organized the seasons to completion, while they praised His holy name, and the sanctuary resounded from early morning The Lord forgave his sins and exalted his horn forever. He gave him a covenant of kings and a glorious throne in Israel. After him, a wise son, Solomon, rose up, who lived securely because of him. Solomon reigned in days of peace. God gave him rest all around, that he might build a house for His name and prepare a sanctuary forever. How wise you were in your youth, Solomon, and filled with understanding like a river! Your influence spread across the earth, and you filled it with parables and riddles. Your name reached distant islands, and you were loved for your peace. For your songs, proverbs, parables, and interpretations, the countries marveled at you. By the name of the Lord God, who is called the God of Israel, you gathered gold like tin and multiplied silver like lead But you bowed your loins to women, and your body was brought into subjection. You tarnished your honor and defiled your offspring, bringing wrath upon your children. I was grieved by your folly, for the kingdom was divided, and a disobedient kingdom arose out of Ephraim. But the Lord will never forsake His mercy. He will not destroy any of His works, nor blot out the posterity of His elect. He will not take away the offspring of the one who loved Him. He gave a remnant to Jacob, and to David, a root from his own family So Solomon rested with his fathers. Of his offspring, he left behind Rehoboam, the foolishness of the people, and one who lacked understanding, who caused the people to revolt by his counsel. Also, Jeroboam, the son of Nebat, who led Israel into sin, and opened a path of sin for Ephraim. Their sins multiplied exceedingly, until they were removed from their land. They sought out all manner of wickedness until vengeance came upon them

Sirach 48

Then Elijah arose, the prophet like fire, and his word burned like a torch. He brought a famine upon them, and by his zeal, he made their numbers few. By the word of the Lord, he shut up the heavens and brought down fire three times. How glorified you were, Elijah, in your wondrous deeds! Who has glory like yours? You raised a dead man from death, from Hades, by the word of the Most High. You brought down kings to destruction and honorable men from their sickbeds. You heard rebuke at Sinai and judgments of vengeance at Horeb. You anointed kings for retribution and prophets to succeed you. You were taken up in a whirlwind of fire, in a chariot of fiery horses. You were recorded for reproofs in their seasons, to pacify anger before it broke out into wrath, to turn the heart of the father to the son, and to restore the tribes of Jacob. Blessed are those who saw you and those who have been adorned with love, for we too shall surely live Elijah was wrapped in a whirlwind, and Elisha was filled with his spirit. In his days, he was not afraid of any ruler, and no one brought him into subjection. Nothing was too difficult for him. When he was buried, his body prophesied. As in life, he performed wonders, so in death his works were marvelous Yet for all this, the people did not repent, nor did they turn away from their sins, until they were carried away as plunder from their land and scattered across the earth. The people were left very few in number, but a ruler remained from the house of David. Some of them did what was right, but many multiplied sins Hezekiah fortified his city and brought water into its midst. He tunneled through rock with iron and built cisterns for water. In his days, Sennacherib invaded, sent Rabshakeh, and departed. He lifted his hand against Zion and boasted greatly in his arrogance. Then their hearts and hands trembled, and they were in pain like women in labor. But they called upon the Lord, who is merciful, spreading out their hands to Him. The Holy One quickly heard them from Heaven and delivered them by the hand of Isaiah. He struck the camp of the Assyrians, and His angel utterly destroyed them For Hezekiah did what was pleasing to the Lord and was strong in the ways of his ancestor David, which Isaiah the prophet, who was great and faithful in his vision, commanded. In his days, the sun went backward, and he prolonged the life of the king. Isaiah, by an excellent spirit, saw what would come to pass in the future, and he comforted those who mourned in Zion. He showed the things that would happen to the end of time and the hidden things before they came to be

Sirach 49

The memory of Josiah is like the composition of incense prepared by the work of a perfumer. It will be sweet as honey in every mouth and like music at a banquet of wine. He did what was right in reforming the people and removing the abominations of iniquity. He set his heart right toward the Lord. In lawless days, he made godliness prevail Except for David, Hezekiah, and Josiah, all the kings of Judah were wicked, for they abandoned the law of the Most High. They handed over their power to others and their glory to a foreign nation. They set the chosen city of the sanctuary on fire and made her streets desolate, just as it was written by the hand of Jeremiah. They mistreated him, yet he was sanctified in the womb to be a prophet, to root out, to afflict, to destroy, and likewise to build and to plant Ezekiel saw the vision of glory, which God showed him on the chariot of the cherubim. He remembered the enemies in a storm and did good to those who directed their ways aright. Of the twelve prophets, may their bones flourish again from their resting place, for they comforted the people of Jacob and delivered them with confident hope How shall we magnify Zerubbabel? He was like a signet ring on the right hand. So too was Jesus, the son of Josedek, who in their days built the house and exalted a people holy to the Lord, prepared for everlasting glory The memory of Nehemiah is also great. He raised up the fallen walls, set up the gates and bars, and rebuilt our houses. No man was created on earth like Enoch, for he was taken up from the earth. Nor was there a man like Joseph, a leader of his kindred, a supporter of the people, even his bones were cared for Shem and Seth were honored among men, but above every living thing in creation was Adam

Sirach 50

Simon, the son of Onias, the high priest, in his life repaired the house and in his days strengthened the temple. He laid the foundation of the double walls and the lofty retaining walls of the temple enclosure. In his days, a water cistern was dug, and a bronze vessel was made like the sea in circumference. He planned to save his people from ruin and fortified the city against siege How glorious he was when the people gathered around him as he came out from behind the veil! He was like the morning star among clouds, like the full moon, like the sun shining on the temple of the Most High, like the rainbow shining in clouds of glory, like roses in the days of first fruits, like lilies by a water spring, like the shoot of a frankincense tree in summer, like fire and incense in the censer, like a vessel of beaten gold adorned with all kinds of precious stones, like an olive tree loaded with fruit, and like a cypress growing high among the clouds When he put on his glorious robe and clothed himself in perfect splendor, ascending to the holy altar, he made the court of the sanctuary glorious. When he received the portions out of the priests' hands, as he stood by the hearth of the altar, with his kinsmen like a garland around him, he was like a young cedar in Lebanon surrounded by the trunks of palm trees. All the sons of Aaron, in their glory, held the Lord's offering in their hands before the entire congregation of Israel. Finishing the service at the altars, that he might arrange the offering of the Most High, the Almighty, he stretched out his hand to the cup of libation and poured out the wine. He poured it out at the foot of the altar, a sweet-smelling fragrance to the Most High, the King of all Then the sons of Aaron shouted. They sounded the trumpets of beaten work, making a great fanfare to be heard, as a reminder before the Most High. Then all the people together hurried, falling down to the ground on their faces to worship their Lord, the Almighty, God Most High. The singers also praised Him with their voices, creating a sweet melody in the entire house. The people implored the Lord Most High, praying before Him who is merciful, until the worship of the Lord was finished, and they accomplished His service Then Simon went down and lifted up his hands over the entire congregation of the children of Israel, blessing the Lord with his lips and glorifying His name. He bowed himself down in worship a second time to declare the blessing from the Most High Now bless the God of all, who everywhere does great things, who exalts our days from the womb, and deals with us according to His mercy. May He grant us joyfulness of heart and peace in our days in Israel for the days of eternity, to entrust His mercy with us, and let Him deliver us in His time! My soul is vexed by two nations, and a third is no nation at all: those who sit on the mountain of Samaria, the Philistines, and the foolish people who live in Shechem I have written in this book the instruction of understanding and knowledge, I, Jesus, the son of Sirach Eleazar, of Jerusalem, who poured forth wisdom from my heart. Blessed is he who practices these things. He who lays them up in his heart will become wise. For if he does them, he will be strong in all things, for the light of the Lord is his guide

Sirach 51

A Prayer of Jesus, the son of Sirach I will give thanks to you, O Lord, O King, and will praise you, O God, my Savior. I give thanks to your name, for you have been my protector and helper, delivering my body from destruction, and out of the snare of a slanderous tongue, from lips that fabricate lies. You were my helper before those who stood by, delivering me according to the abundance of your mercy and your name, from the gnashing of teeth ready to devour, out of the hand of those seeking my life, and from the many afflictions I endured. You delivered me from the choking fire on every side, and out of the midst of flames that I had not kindled, from the depths of the belly of Hades, from an unclean tongue, and from lying words The slander of an unrighteous tongue to the king brought my soul near to death. My life was close to Hades. They surrounded me on every side, and there was no one to help me. I looked for human help, but there was none. Then I remembered your mercy, O Lord, and your work, which has been from everlasting, how you deliver those who wait for you and save them from the hand of their enemies. I lifted up my prayer from the earth and prayed for deliverance from death. I called upon the Lord, the Father of my Lord, that He would not forsake me in the days of affliction, in the time when there was no help against the proud. I will praise your name continually and sing praise with thanksgiving. My prayer was heard. You saved me from destruction and delivered me from the evil time. Therefore, I will give thanks and praise to you and bless the name of the Lord When I was yet young, before I went abroad, I sought wisdom openly in my prayer. Before the temple, I asked for her. I will seek her out even to the end. From the first flower to the ripening grape, my heart delighted in her. My foot walked in uprightness. From my youth, I followed her steps. I inclined my ear a little and received her, and I found for myself much instruction. I profited from her, and I will give glory to Him who gives me wisdom. For I determined to practice her. I was zealous for that which is good, and I will never be put to shame. My soul has wrestled with her, and in my conduct, I was exact. I spread out my hands to the heavens above and bewailed my ignorance of her. I directed my soul to her, and in purity, I found her. I acquired a heart joined with her from the beginning. Therefore, I will not be forsaken. My belly also was troubled in seeking her, but I gained a good possession. The Lord gave me a tongue as my reward, and I will praise Him with it Draw near to me, all you who are uneducated, and live in the house of instruction. Why are you all lacking in these things, and your souls are very thirsty? I opened my mouth and spoke, "Get her for yourselves without money." Put your neck under the yoke, and let your soul receive instruction. She is near to find. See with your eyes how I labored just a little and found for myself much rest. Get instruction with a great sum of silver and gain much gold by her. May your soul rejoice in His mercy, and may you not be put to shame in praising Him. Work your work before the time comes, and in His time, He will give you your reward

74. Baruch

Baruch 1

These are the words of the book written by Baruch, the son of Nerias, the son of Maaseas, the son of Sedekias, the son of Asadias, the son of Helkias, in Babylon. It was the fifth year, on the seventh day of the month, at the time when the Chaldeans took Jerusalem and burned it with fire. Baruch read the words of this book to Jechonias, the son of Joakim, king of Judah, and to all the people who came to hear the book. The reading was also heard by the mighty men, the sons of kings, the elders, and all the people, from the least to the greatest, even all those who lived in Babylon by the river Sud Upon hearing the words, they wept, fasted, and prayed before the Lord. They also collected money according to each man's ability and sent it to Jerusalem, to Joakim, the high priest, the son of Helkias, the son of Salom, and to the priests and all the people with him in Jerusalem. At the same time, they returned the vessels of the house of the Lord that had been carried out of the temple, to be brought back to Judah on the tenth day of Sivan. These were silver vessels made by Sedekias, the son of Josias, king of Judah, after Nabuchodonosor, king of Babylon, had taken Jechonias, the princes, the captives, the mighty men, and the people of the land from Jerusalem to Babylon They instructed: "We have sent you money; therefore, use it to buy burnt offerings, sin offerings, and incense, and prepare an oblation to offer upon the altar of the Lord our God. Pray for the life of Nabuchodonosor, king of Babylon, and for the life of his son, Baltasar, that their days may be as the days of heaven above the earth. The Lord will give us strength and light to our eyes, and we will live under the shadow of Nabuchodonosor, king of Babylon, and under the shadow of Baltasar, his son, serving them many days and finding favor in their sight. Pray also for us to the Lord our God, for we have sinned against Him, and to this day, His wrath and indignation have not turned away from us." They further instructed, "You shall read this book that we have sent to you, to make confession in the house of the Lord on the day of the feast and on the days of the solemn assembly. You shall say, 'To the Lord our God belongs righteousness, but to us belongs confusion of face, as it is today, to the men of Judah, to the inhabitants of Jerusalem, to our kings, princes, priests, prophets, and fathers, because we have sinned before the Lord. We have disobeyed Him and have not listened to the voice of the Lord our God, to walk in the commandments He set before us. Since the day the Lord brought our fathers out of the land of Egypt to this present day, we have been disobedient to the Lord our God, neglecting to listen to His voice. Therefore, the plagues and the curse that the Lord declared through Moses, His servant, have clung to us from the day He brought our fathers out of Egypt to give us a land flowing with milk and honey, as it is today. Yet, we did not listen to the voice of the Lord our God, according to all the words of the prophets He sent to us. Instead, each of us followed the imagination of our own wicked heart, serving strange gods and doing what is evil in the sight of the Lord our God.'"

Baruch 2

Therefore, the Lord has fulfilled His word against us, against our judges who judged Israel, against our kings, princes, and the men of Israel and Judah. He has brought upon us great plagues, such as have never occurred under the whole heaven, as it came to pass in Jerusalem, according to what is written in the law of Moses: that we should each eat the flesh of our own son and daughter. Moreover, He has subjected us to all the kingdoms around us, making us a reproach and desolation among all the people where the Lord has scattered us. Thus, we were brought low and not exalted because we sinned against the Lord our God by not listening to His voice To the Lord our God belongs righteousness, but to us and our fathers belongs confusion of face, as it is today. All these plagues have come upon us, just as the Lord pronounced against us. Yet we have not sought the favor of the Lord by turning from the thoughts of our wicked hearts. Therefore, the Lord has kept watch over the plagues and has brought them upon us, for the Lord is righteous in all His works which He has commanded us. Yet, we have not listened to His voice, to walk in the commandments of the Lord that He has set before us And now, O Lord, God of Israel, who brought Your people out of the land of Egypt with a mighty hand, with signs, wonders, great power, and a high arm, and made Yourself a name as it is today: O Lord our God, we have sinned. We have been ungodly. We have done wrong in all Your ordinances. Let Your wrath turn from us, for we are but a few left among the heathen where You have scattered us. Hear our prayer, O Lord, and our petition, and deliver us for Your own sake. Grant us favor in the sight of those who have led us away captive, that all the earth may know that You are the Lord our God, for Israel and his posterity are called by Your name O Lord, look down from Your holy house and consider us. Incline Your ear, O Lord, and hear. Open Your eyes and see; for the dead in Hades, whose breath is taken from their bodies, cannot give You glory or righteousness. But the soul that is greatly vexed, that goes stooping and feeble, the eyes that fail, and the hungry soul will declare Your glory and righteousness, O Lord. For we do not present our supplication before You, O Lord our God, for the righteousness of our fathers and kings. For You have sent Your wrath and indignation upon us, as You spoke through Your servants the prophets, saying, "The Lord says, 'Bow your shoulders to serve the king of Babylon, and remain in the land that I gave to your fathers. But if you do not hear the voice of the Lord to serve the king of Babylon, I will cause the voice of mirth, gladness, the bridegroom, and the bride to cease out of the cities of Judah and from the region near Jerusalem. The whole land will become desolate without an inhabitant.'" But we did not listen to Your voice, to serve the king of Babylon. Therefore, You have fulfilled Your words that You spoke through Your servants the prophets, that the bones of our kings and fathers would be taken out of their places. Behold, they are cast out to the heat by day and to the frost by night. They died in great misery by famine, by sword, and by pestilence. You have made the house that is called by Your name desolate because of the wickedness of the house of Israel and the house of Judah Yet, O Lord our God, You have dealt with us according to all Your kindness and great mercy, as You spoke through Your servant Moses on the day You commanded him to write Your law in the presence of the children of Israel, saying, "If you do not hear My voice, surely this great multitude will be turned into a small number among the nations where I will scatter them. For I know that they will not hear Me because they are a stiff-necked people. But in the land of their captivity, they will take it to heart and will know that I am the Lord their God. I will give them a heart and ears to hear. Then they will praise Me in the land of their captivity, and think about My name. They will return from their stubborn ways and wicked deeds, for they will remember the way of their fathers who sinned before the Lord. I will bring them again into the land I promised to their fathers, to Abraham, Isaac, and Jacob, and they will rule over it. I will increase them, and they will not be diminished. I will make an everlasting covenant with them to be their God, and they will be My people. I will no longer remove My people Israel from the land that I have given them."

Baruch 3

O Lord Almighty, God of Israel, the soul in anguish and the troubled spirit cry out to You. Hear, O Lord, and have mercy, for You are a merciful God. Yes, have mercy upon us, for we have sinned before You. For You are enthroned forever, and we keep perishing. O Lord Almighty, God of Israel, hear now the prayer of the dead Israelites and the children of those who were sinners before You, who did not listen to Your voice, their God; because of this, these plagues cling to us. Do not remember the iniquities of our fathers, but remember Your power and Your name at this time. For You are the Lord our God, and we will praise You, O Lord. For this cause, You have put Your fear in our hearts, that we should call upon Your name. We will praise You in our captivity, for we have remembered all the iniquity of our fathers who sinned before You. Behold, we are still in our captivity where You have scattered us, for a reproach and a curse, and to be subject to penalty according to all the iniquities of our fathers who departed from the Lord our God Hear, O Israel, the commandments of life! Give ear to understand wisdom! How is it, O Israel, that you are in your enemies' land, that you have become old in a strange country, that you are defiled with the dead, that you are counted among those in Hades? You have forsaken the fountain of wisdom. If you had walked in the way of God, you would have dwelled in peace forever. Learn where there is wisdom, where there is strength, and where there is understanding, that you may also know where there is length of days and life, where there is the light of the eyes and peace. Who has found her place? Who has come into her treasuries? Where are the princes of the heathen, and those who ruled the beasts of the earth, those who had their pastime with the birds of the air, and those who hoarded silver and gold, in which people trust, and of their gathering there is no end? For those who diligently sought silver and were so anxious, and whose works are beyond finding out—they have vanished and gone down to Hades, and others have risen in their place. Younger men have seen the light and lived upon the earth, but they have not known the way of knowledge, nor understood its paths. Their children have not embraced it. They are far off from her way. It has not been heard of in Canaan, nor has it been seen in Teman. The sons of Agar who seek understanding, the merchants of Merran and Teman, the authors of fables, and the searchers for understanding—none of these have known the way of wisdom or remembered her paths O Israel, how great is the house of God! How vast is the place of His possession! It is great and has no end. It is high and unmeasurable. Giants were born there, famous of old, great in stature, and expert in war. But God did not choose them, nor did He give them the way of knowledge. They perished because they had no wisdom. They perished through their own foolishness. Who has gone up into heaven and taken her and brought her down from the clouds? Who has crossed the sea, found her, and will bring her for choice gold? There is no one who knows her way or understands her path. But He who knows all things knows her. He found her out with His understanding. He who prepared the earth for all time has filled it with four-footed beasts. It is He who sends forth the light, and it goes. He called it, and it obeyed Him with fear. The stars shone in their watches and were glad. When He called them, they said, "Here we are." They shone with gladness to Him who made them. This is our God, and no other can be compared to Him. He has found out all the way of knowledge and has given it to Jacob, His servant, and to Israel, His beloved. Afterward, she appeared on earth and lived among men

Baruch 4

This is the book of God's commandments and the law that endures forever. All those who hold fast to it will live, but those who abandon it will die. Turn, O Jacob, and take hold of it. Walk towards the shining of its light. Do not give your glory to another, nor the things that are to your advantage to a foreign nation. O Israel, we are happy, for the things that are pleasing to God are made known to us. Be of good cheer, my people, the memorial of Israel. You were not sold to the nations for destruction, but because you moved God to wrath, you were delivered to your adversaries. For you provoked Him who made you by sacrificing to demons and not to God. You forgot the everlasting God who brought you up. You also grieved Jerusalem, who nursed you For she saw the wrath that came upon you from God, and said, "Listen, you who dwell near Zion; for God has brought upon me great mourning. For I have seen the captivity of my sons and daughters, which the Everlasting has brought upon them. For with joy I nourished them, but sent them away with weeping and mourning. Let no one rejoice over me, a widow and forsaken by many. For the sins of my children, I am left desolate, because they turned away from the law of God and had no regard for His statutes. They did not walk in the ways of God's commandments or tread in the paths of discipline in His righteousness. Let those who dwell near Zion come and remember the captivity of my sons and daughters, which the Everlasting has brought upon them. For He has brought a nation upon them from afar, a shameless nation with a strange language, who did not respect old men or pity children. They have carried away the dear beloved sons of the widow, and left her who was alone desolate of her daughters." But how can I help you? For He who brought these calamities upon you will deliver you from the hand of your enemies Go your way, O my children. Go your way, for I am left desolate. I have put off the garment of peace and put on the sackcloth of my petition. I will cry to the Everlasting as long as I live. Take courage, my children. Cry to God, and He will deliver you from the power and hand of your enemies. For I have trusted in the Everlasting that He will save you, and joy has come to me from the Holy One, because of the mercy that will soon come to you from your Everlasting Savior. For I sent you out with mourning and weeping, but God will give you to me again with joy and gladness forever. For as now those who dwell near Zion have seen your captivity, so they will shortly see your salvation from our God, which will come upon you with great glory and brightness of the Everlasting. My children, suffer patiently the wrath that has come upon you from God, for your enemy has persecuted you; but shortly you will see his destruction and will tread upon their necks. My delicate ones have traveled rough roads. They were taken away like a flock carried off by enemies. Take courage, my children, and cry to God; for you will be remembered by Him who brought this upon you. For as it was your decision to go astray from God, return and seek Him ten times more. For He who brought these calamities upon you will bring you everlasting joy again with your salvation Take courage, O Jerusalem, for He who called you by name will comfort you. Miserable are those who afflicted you and rejoiced at your fall. Miserable are the cities where your children served. Miserable is she who received your sons. For as she rejoiced at your fall and was glad of your ruin, so she will be grieved at her own desolation. And I will take away her pride in her great multitude, and her boasting will be turned into mourning. For fire will come upon her from the Everlasting for many days, and she will be inhabited by demons for a long time. O Jerusalem, look around you towards the east, and behold the joy that comes to you from God. Behold, your sons come, whom you sent away. They come gathered together from the east to the west at the word of the Holy One, rejoicing in the glory of God

Baruch 5

Take off the garment of your mourning and affliction, O Jerusalem, and put on forever the beauty of the glory from God. Put on the robe of righteousness from God. Set on your head a diadem of the glory of the Everlasting. For God will show your splendor everywhere under heaven. For your name will be called by God forever, "Righteous Peace, Godly Glory." Arise, O Jerusalem, and stand upon the height. Look around you towards the east and see your children gathered from the going down of the sun to its rising at the word of the Holy One, rejoicing that God has remembered them. For they went from you on foot, led away by their enemies, but God brings them to you carried on high with glory, on a royal throne. For God has appointed that every high mountain and the everlasting hills should be made low, and the valleys filled up to make the ground level, that Israel may go safely in the glory of God. Moreover, the woods and every sweet-smelling tree have shaded Israel by the commandment of God. For God will lead Israel with joy in the light of His glory, with the mercy and righteousness that come from Him

Baruch 6

This is a copy of the letter that Jeremy sent to those who were to be taken captive into Babylon by the king of the Babylonians, delivering the message that God commanded him. Because of the sins you have committed before God, you will be led away captive to Babylon by Nabuchodonosor, the king of the Babylonians. When you arrive in Babylon, you will remain there for many years, lasting for seven generations. After that, I will bring you out peacefully

from there However, while you are in Babylon, you will see gods of silver, gold, and wood carried on the shoulders of the people, which cause the nations to fear. Be careful not to become like these foreigners. Do not let fear take hold of you when you see the multitude worshiping them. Instead, say in your hearts, "O Lord, we must worship You." For my angel is with you, and I myself care for your souls Their tongues are polished by the workman, and they are overlaid with gold and silver; yet they are fake and cannot speak. They make crowns for the heads of their gods with gold, as if for a virgin who loves to be adorned. Sometimes the priests take gold and silver from their gods and spend it on themselves, even giving some of it to prostitutes. They dress these gods like men with garments, but despite being made of silver, gold, and wood, they cannot save themselves from rust and moths, even though they are covered with purple garments They wipe their faces because of the dust that settles on them in the temple. Even though they hold a scepter as if they were judges of a country, they cannot put to death anyone who offends them. They may have a dagger in their right hand and an axe, but they cannot save themselves from war and robbers. This is how you can know they are not gods, so do not fear them. They are as worthless as a broken vessel, useless once it is shattered. When they are set up in temples, their eyes are full of dust from the feet of those who enter Just as the courts secure those who offend the king to ensure they suffer death, the priests secure their temples with doors, locks, and bars, lest their gods be carried off by robbers. They light more candles for them than they do for themselves, even though these gods cannot see a single light. They are like beams of the temple, eaten away by creatures that creep out of the earth, devouring both them and their clothing without them feeling it. Their faces are blackened by the smoke that comes out of the temple. Bats, swallows, and birds land on their bodies and heads, as do cats. This is another way to know that they are not gods; therefore, do not fear them Despite the gold that covers them to make them beautiful, they will not shine unless someone wipes off the tarnish. They did not even feel anything when they were molten. Things without breath are bought at any cost. Lacking feet, they are carried on shoulders, which clearly shows they are worthless. Those who serve them are also ashamed because if these gods fall to the ground, they cannot rise by themselves. If they are bowed down, they cannot straighten themselves, yet offerings are set before them as if they were dead men. The things sacrificed to them are sold by their priests, who then spend the proceeds. Their wives also store some of it in salt, but they give none of it to the poor or the impotent A menstruous woman and a woman in childbirth can touch their sacrifices, knowing by these things that they are not gods. Do not fear them. How can they be called gods when women set food before gods of silver, gold, and wood? In their temples, the priests sit on seats with torn clothes, shaven heads and beards, and nothing on their heads. They roar and cry before their gods, as men do at a feast for the dead. The priests also strip garments from the gods and clothe their wives and children with them. Whether it is evil or good that one does to them, they cannot repay it. They cannot set up a king or depose one. Similarly, they cannot give riches or money. If a man makes a vow to them and does not keep it, they will never exact it They cannot save anyone from death, nor can they deliver the weak from the mighty. They cannot restore a blind man's sight or deliver anyone in distress. They show no mercy to widows or do good to orphans. These gods of wood, overlaid with gold and silver, are like stones cut from the mountain. Those who minister to them will be confounded. How could a man then think or say that they are gods, when even the Chaldeans themselves dishonor them? If they see a mute person who cannot speak, they bring him before Bel, as if he could understand. Yet, they cannot perceive this themselves and forsake them, for they have no understanding The women also, with cords around them, sit in the streets, burning bran for incense; but if one of them is drawn away by someone passing by and lies with him, she reproaches her fellow, thinking herself more worthy because her cord was not broken. Everything done among them is false. How could a man then think or say that they are gods? They are fashioned by carpenters and goldsmiths and can be nothing other than what the workmen make them to be. Even those who fashioned them do not last long; how then should the things they fashioned endure? They leave behind lies and reproaches to those who come after them When war or plague comes upon them, the priests consult among themselves about where they can hide with their gods. How can men not understand that they are not gods, as they cannot save themselves from war or plague? Seeing that they are only wood overlaid with gold and silver, it will eventually become evident that they are false. It will be revealed to all nations and kings that they are not gods but the works of men's hands, with no divine power in them. Who then does not know that they are not gods? They cannot set up a king in a land or give rain to men. They cannot judge their own cause or redress a wrong, for they are as powerless as crows between heaven and earth Even when fire falls upon the house of these wooden gods overlaid with gold or silver, their priests will flee and escape, but the gods themselves will burn like beams. Moreover, they cannot withstand any king or enemies. How could a man then admit or think that they are gods? These wooden gods overlaid with silver or gold cannot escape from thieves or robbers. The strong will take the gold, silver, and garments they are clothed in and leave, while the gods cannot help themselves. Therefore, it is better to be a king who shows his manhood, or even a useful vessel in a house, than such false gods. A door in a house, which keeps things safe inside, is better than such false gods, or even a wooden pillar in a palace The sun, moon, and stars, being bright and obedient to their appointed tasks, are far superior. The lightning, which flashes beautifully, and the wind, which blows across every country, obey God's command. When God orders the clouds to cover the world, they do as they are told. Fire sent from above to consume mountains and woods also obeys God's command. Yet these gods cannot compare to them in either appearance or power. Therefore, no one should think or say that they are gods, seeing they cannot judge causes or do good to men. Knowing they are not gods, do not fear them. They can neither curse nor bless kings. They cannot show signs in the heavens among the nations, shine like the sun, or give light like the moon Even the beasts are better than these gods because they can find shelter and protect themselves. It is evident to us that these idols are not gods; therefore, do not fear them. Just as a scarecrow in a cucumber garden keeps nothing, so are these gods of wood overlaid with gold and silver. Their bright purple garments will eventually rot upon them, revealing their worthlessness. They will be consumed, becoming a reproach in the land. Therefore, it is far better to be a just man who has no idols, for he will be far from reproach

75. Letter of Jeremiah

CHAPTER 1
The words of Jeremiah, the son of Hilkiah, one of the priests who resided in Anathoth in the land of Benjamin. The word of the LORD came to him during the days of Jehoiaiah, the son of Amon, king of Judah, in the thirteenth year of his reign. It continued throughout the days of Jehoiakim, the son of Jehoiaiah, king of Judah, and until the end of the eleventh year of Zedekiah, the son of Jehoiaiah, king of Judah, when Jerusalem was taken into captivity in the fifth month The word of the LORD came to me, saying, "Before I formed you in the womb, I knew you. Before you were born, I sanctified you and appointed you as a prophet to the nations." I responded, "Lord God, I cannot speak, for I am just a child." But the LORD said to me, "Do not say, 'I am a child,' for you shall go to everyone I send you to and speak whatever I command you. Do not be afraid of them, for I am with you to deliver you," says the LORD Then the Lord stretched out His hand and touched my mouth and said, "Behold, I have put My words in your mouth. See, today I appoint you over nations and kingdoms, to uproot and tear down, to destroy and overthrow, to build and to plant." The word of the LORD came to me, asking, "Jeremiah, what do you see?" I answered, "I see a branch of an almond tree." The LORD said, "You have seen correctly, for I am watching to ensure that My word is fulfilled." The word of the LORD came to me a second time, asking, "What do you see?" I replied, "I see a boiling pot, tilting from the north." The LORD said to me, "From the north, disaster will be poured out on all who live in the land. I am calling all the kingdoms of the north," says the LORD. "Their kings will come and set their thrones at the entrance of the gates of Jerusalem, against all her surrounding walls, and against all the cities of Judah. I will pronounce My judgments on My people because of their wickedness in forsaking Me, burning incense to other gods, and worshiping the works of their own hands Therefore, prepare yourself, stand up, and say to them whatever I command you. Do not be terrified by them, or I will terrify you before them. Today, I have made you a fortified city, an iron pillar, and bronze walls against the whole land— against the kings of Judah, its princes, its priests, and the people of the land. They will fight against you but will not overcome you, for I am with you to deliver you," declares the LORD

CHAPTER 2
Moreover, the word of the LORD came to me, saying, "Go and proclaim in the hearing of Jerusalem: 'This is what the LORD says: I remember the devotion of your youth, how as a bride you loved Me and followed Me through the wilderness, through a land not sown. Israel was holy to the LORD, the firstfruits of His harvest; all who devoured her were held guilty, and disaster overtook them,' declares the LORD." Hear the word of the LORD, O house of Jacob, and all the families of the house of Israel. This is what the LORD says: "What fault did your ancestors find in Me, that they strayed so far from Me? They followed worthless idols and became worthless themselves. They did not ask, 'Where is the LORD who brought us up out of Egypt and led us through the barren wilderness, through a land of deserts and ravines, a land of drought and utter darkness, a land where no one travels and no one lives?' I brought you into a fertile land to eat its fruit and rich produce. But you came and defiled My land and made My inheritance detestable The priests did not ask, 'Where is the LORD?' Those who deal with the law did not know Me; the leaders rebelled against Me, and the prophets prophesied by Baal, following worthless

idols. Therefore, I bring charges against you again," declares the LORD. "And I will bring charges against your children's children. Cross over to the coasts of Cyprus and look, send to Kedar and observe closely; see if there has ever been anything like this: Has a nation ever changed its gods? (Yet they are not gods at all.) But My people have exchanged their glorious God for worthless idols. Be appalled at this, you heavens, and shudder with great horror," declares the LORD "My people have committed two sins: They have forsaken Me, the spring of living water, and have dug their own cisterns, broken cisterns that cannot hold water. Is Israel a servant, a slave by birth? Why then has he become plunder? Lions have roared; they have growled at him. They have laid waste his land; his towns are burned and deserted. Also, the men of Memphis and Tahpanhes have cracked your skull. Have you not brought this on yourselves by forsaking the LORD your God when He led you in the way? Now why go to Egypt to drink water from the Nile? And why go to Assyria to drink water from the Euphrates? Your wickedness will punish you; your backsliding will rebuke you. Consider then and realize how evil and bitter it is for you when you forsake the LORD your God and have no awe of Me," declares the Lord, the LORD Almighty "Long ago you broke off your yoke and tore off your bonds; you said, 'I will not serve You!' Indeed, on every high hill and under every spreading tree, you lay down as a prostitute. I had planted you like a choice vine of sound and reliable stock. How then did you turn against Me into a corrupt, wild vine? Although you wash yourself with soap and use an abundance of cleansing powder, the stain of your guilt is still before Me," declares the Sovereign LORD. "How can you say, 'I am not defiled; I have not run after the Baals'? See how you behaved in the valley; consider what you have done. You are a swift she-camel running here and there, a wild donkey accustomed to the desert, sniffing the wind in her craving—in her heat, who can restrain her? Any males that pursue her need not tire themselves; at mating time they will find her Do not run until your feet are bare and your throat is dry. But you said, 'It's no use! I love foreign gods, and I must go after them.' As a thief is disgraced when he is caught, so the people of Israel are disgraced—they, their kings and their officials, their priests and their prophets. They say to wood, 'You are my father,' and to stone, 'You gave me birth.' They have turned their backs to Me and not their faces; yet when they are in trouble, they say, 'Come and save us!' Where then are the gods you made for yourselves? Let them come if they can save you when you are in trouble! For you, Judah, have as many gods as you have towns. Why do you bring charges against Me? You have all rebelled against Me," declares the LORD "In vain I punished your people; they did not respond to correction. Your sword has devoured your prophets like a ravenous lion. You of this generation, consider the word of the LORD: Have I been a desert to Israel or a land of great darkness? Why do My people say, 'We are free to roam; we will come to You no more'? Does a young woman forget her jewelry, a bride her wedding ornaments? Yet My people have forgotten Me, days without number. How skilled you are at pursuing love! Even the worst of women can learn from your ways. On your clothes is found the lifeblood of the innocent poor, though you did not catch them breaking in. Yet in spite of all this, you say, 'I am innocent; He is not angry with me.' But I will pass judgment on you because you say, 'I have not sinned.' Why do you go about so much, changing your ways? You will be disappointed by Egypt as you were by Assyria. You will also leave that place with your hands on your head, for the LORD has rejected those you trust; you will not be helped by them."

CHAPTER 3

"If a man divorces his wife and she leaves him and marries another man, should he return to her again? Would not the land be completely defiled? But you have lived as a prostitute with many lovers—would you now return to Me?" declares the LORD. "Look up to the barren heights and see. Is there any place where you have not been ravished? By the roadside you sat waiting for lovers, sat like a nomad in the desert. You have defiled the land with your prostitution and wickedness. Therefore, the showers have been withheld, and no spring rains have fallen. Yet you have the brazen look of a prostitute; you refuse to blush with shame Have you not just called to Me: 'My Father, my friend from my youth, will you always be angry? Will your wrath continue forever?' This is how you talk, but you do all the evil you can." During the reign of King Josiah, the LORD said to me, "Have you seen what faithless Israel has done? She has gone up on every high hill and under every spreading tree and has committed adultery there. I thought that after she had done all this she would return to Me, but she did not, and her unfaithful sister Judah saw it. I gave faithless Israel her certificate of divorce and sent her away because of all her adulteries. Yet I saw that her unfaithful sister Judah had no fear; she also went out and committed adultery. Because Israel's immorality mattered so little to her, she defiled the land and committed adultery with stone and wood. In spite of all this, her unfaithful sister Judah did not return to Me with all her heart, but only in pretense," declares the LORD The LORD said to me, "Faithless Israel is more righteous than unfaithful Judah. Go, proclaim this message toward the north: 'Return, faithless Israel,' declares the LORD, 'I will frown on you no longer, for I am faithful,' declares the LORD, 'I will not be angry forever. Only acknowledge your guilt—you have rebelled against the LORD your God, you have scattered your favors to foreign gods under every spreading tree, and have not obeyed Me,' declares the LORD 'Return, faithless people,' declares the LORD, 'for I am your husband. I will choose you—one from a town and two from a clan—and bring you to Zion. Then I will give you shepherds after My own heart, who will lead you with knowledge and understanding. In those days, when your numbers have increased greatly in the land,' declares the LORD, 'people will no longer say, "The ark of the covenant of the LORD." It will never enter their minds or be remembered; it will not be missed, nor will another one be made. At that time they will call Jerusalem "The Throne of the LORD," and all nations will gather in Jerusalem to honor the name of the LORD. No longer will they follow the stubbornness of their evil hearts. In those days the people of Judah will join the people of Israel, and together they will come from a northern land to the land I gave your ancestors as an inheritance I myself said, "How gladly would I treat you like my children and give you a pleasant land, the most beautiful inheritance of any nation." I thought you would call me 'Father' and not turn away from following Me. But like a woman unfaithful to her husband, so you, Israel, have been unfaithful to Me," declares the LORD A cry is heard on the barren heights, the weeping and pleading of the people of Israel, because they have perverted their ways and have forgotten the LORD their God. "Return, faithless people; I will cure you of backsliding." "Yes, we will come to you, for you are the LORD our God. Surely the idolatrous commotion on the hills and mountains is a deception; surely in the LORD our God is the salvation of Israel. From our youth, shameful gods have consumed the fruits of our ancestors' labor—their flocks and herds, their sons and daughters. Let us lie down in our shame, and let our disgrace cover us. We have sinned against the LORD our God, both we and our ancestors; from our youth till this day we have not obeyed the LORD our God."

CHAPTER 4

"If you, Israel, will return, then return to Me," declares the LORD. "If you put your detestable idols out of My sight and no longer go astray, and if in a truthful, just, and righteous way you swear, 'As surely as the LORD lives,' then the nations will invoke blessings by Him and in Him they will boast." This is what the LORD says to the people of Judah and to Jerusalem: "Break up your unplowed ground and do not sow among thorns. Circumcise yourselves to the LORD, circumcise your hearts, you people of Judah and inhabitants of Jerusalem, or My wrath will flare up and burn like fire because of the evil you have done—burn with no one to quench it Announce in Judah and proclaim in Jerusalem and say: 'Sound the trumpet throughout the land!' Cry aloud and say: 'Gather together! Let us flee to the fortified cities!' Raise the signal to go to Zion! Flee for safety without delay! For I am bringing disaster from the north, even terrible destruction." A lion has come out of his lair; a destroyer of nations has set out. He has left his place to lay waste your land. Your towns will lie in ruins without inhabitant. So put on sackcloth, lament and wail, for the fierce anger of the LORD has not turned away from us "In that day," declares the LORD, "the king and the officials will lose heart, the priests will be horrified, and the prophets will be appalled." Then I said, "Alas, Sovereign LORD! How completely you have deceived this people and Jerusalem by saying, 'You will have peace,' when the sword is at our throats!" At that time, this people and Jerusalem will be told, "A scorching wind from the barren heights in the desert blows toward my people, but not to winnow or cleanse; a wind too strong for that comes from me. Now I pronounce my judgments against them." Look! He advances like the clouds, his chariots come like a whirlwind, his horses are swifter than eagles. Woe to us! We are ruined! Jerusalem, wash the evil from your heart and be saved. How long will you harbor wicked thoughts? A voice is announcing from Dan, proclaiming disaster from the hills of Ephraim. "Tell this to the nations, proclaim concerning Jerusalem: 'A besieging army is coming from a distant land, raising a war cry against the cities of Judah. They surround her like men guarding a field, because she has rebelled against me,'" declares the LORD "Your own conduct and actions have brought this on you. This is your punishment. How bitter it is! How it pierces to the heart!" Oh, my anguish, my anguish! I writhe in pain. Oh, the agony of my heart! My heart pounds within me, I cannot keep silent. For I have heard the sound of the trumpet; I have heard the battle cry. Disaster follows disaster; the whole land lies in ruins. In an instant my tents are destroyed, my shelter in a moment. How long must I see the battle standard and hear the sound of the trumpet? "My people are fools; they do not know me. They are senseless children; they have no understanding. They are skilled in doing evil; they know not how to do good." I looked at the earth, and it was formless and empty; and at the heavens, and their light was gone. I looked at the mountains, and they were quaking; all the hills were swaying. I looked, and there were no people; every bird in the sky had flown away. I looked, and the fruitful land was a desert; all its towns lay in ruins before the LORD, before his fierce anger This is what the LORD says: "The whole land will be ruined, though I will not destroy it completely. Therefore the earth will mourn and the heavens above grow dark, because I have spoken and will not relent, I have decided and will not turn back." At the sound of horsemen and archers, every town takes to flight. Some go into the thickets; some climb up among the rocks. All the towns are deserted; no one lives in them. What are you doing, you devastated one? Why dress yourself in scarlet and put on jewels of gold? Why highlight your eyes with makeup? You adorn yourself in vain. Your lovers despise you; they want to kill you I hear a cry as of a woman in labor, a groan as of one bearing her first child—the cry of Daughter Zion gasping for breath, stretching out her hands and saying, "Alas! I am fainting; my life is given over to murderers."

CHAPTER 5

"Go up and down the streets of Jerusalem, look around and consider, search through her squares. If you can find but one person who deals honestly and seeks the truth, I will forgive this city. Although they say, 'As surely as the LORD lives,' still they are swearing falsely." LORD, do not your eyes look for truth? You struck them, but they felt no pain; you crushed them, but they refused correction. They made their faces harder than stone and refused to repent. I thought, "These are only the poor; they are foolish, for they do not know the way of the LORD, the requirements of their God. So I will go to the leaders and speak to them; surely they know the way of the LORD, the requirements of their God." But with one accord they too had broken off the yoke and torn off the bonds. Therefore a lion from the forest will attack them, a wolf from the desert will ravage them, a leopard will lie in wait near their towns to tear to pieces any who venture out, for their rebellion is great and their backslidings many "Why should I forgive you? Your children have forsaken me and sworn by gods that are not gods. I supplied all their needs, yet they committed adultery and thronged to the houses of prostitutes. They are well-fed, lusty stallions, each neighing for another man's wife. Should I not punish them for this?" declares the LORD. "Should I not avenge myself on such a nation as this? Go through her vineyards and ravage them, but do not destroy them completely. Strip off her branches, for these people do not belong to the LORD. The people of Israel and the people of Judah have been utterly unfaithful to me," declares the LORD. They have lied about the LORD; they said, 'He will do nothing! No harm will come to us; we will never see sword or famine. The prophets are but wind and the word is not in them; so let what they say be done to them." Therefore this is what the LORD God Almighty says: "Because the people have spoken these words, I will make my words in your mouth a fire and these people the wood it consumes. People of Israel," declares the LORD, "I am bringing a distant nation against you—an ancient and enduring nation, a people whose language you do not know, whose speech you do not understand. Their quivers are like an open grave; all of them are mighty warriors. They will devour your harvests and food, devour your sons and daughters; they will devour your flocks and herds, devour your vines and fig trees. With the sword they will destroy the fortified cities in which you trust." "Yet even in those days," declares the LORD, "I will not destroy you completely. And when the people ask, 'Why has the LORD our God done all this to us?' you will tell them, 'As you have forsaken me and served foreign gods in your own land, so now you will serve foreigners in a land not your own.' "Announce this to the descendants of Jacob and proclaim it in Judah: Hear this, you foolish and senseless people, who have eyes but do not see, who have ears but do not hear: Should you not fear me?" declares the LORD.

"Should you not tremble in my presence? I made the sand a boundary for the sea, an everlasting barrier it cannot cross. The waves may roll, but they cannot prevail; they may roar, but they cannot cross it. But these people have stubborn and rebellious hearts; they have turned aside and gone away. They do not say to themselves, 'Let us fear the LORD our God, who gives autumn and spring rains in season, who assures us of the regular weeks of harvest.' Your wrongdoings have kept these away; your sins have deprived you of good Among my people are the wicked who lie in wait like men who snare birds and like those who set traps to catch people. Like cages full of birds, their houses are full of deceit; they have become rich and powerful and have grown fat and sleek. Their evil deeds have no limit; they do not seek justice. They do not promote the case of the fatherless; they do not defend the rights of the poor. Should I not punish them for this?" declares the LORD. "Should I not avenge myself on such a nation as this? A horrible and shocking thing has happened in the land: The prophets prophesy lies, the priests rule by their own authority, and my people love it this way. But what will you do in the end?

CHAPTER 6

O sons of Benjamin, prepare to flee from the ruins of Jerusalem and sound the trumpet in Tekoa; set up a signal in Beth-Haccerem, for disaster and great destruction are approaching from the north. I have likened the daughter of Zion to a beautiful and delicate woman. The shepherds with their flocks will come to her; they will pitch their tents around her, and each will graze in his place "Prepare for war against her; arise and let us attack at noon! Woe to us, for the day is fading, and the shadows of evening are lengthening. Arise, and let us attack by night and destroy her fortresses!" For this is what the LORD of hosts says: "Cut down the trees and build a siege ramp against Jerusalem. This city must be punished; it is filled with oppression. As a well pours out its water, so she pours out her wickedness. Violence and destruction resound in her; her sickness and wounds are ever before me. Take warning, O Jerusalem, or I will turn away from you and make your land desolate, with no one to inhabit it." This is what the LORD of hosts says: "Let them glean the remnant of Israel as thoroughly as a vine; pass your hand over the branches again, like one gathering grapes." To whom can I speak and give warning? Who will listen to me? Their ears are closed so they cannot hear. The word of the LORD is offensive to them; they find no pleasure in it. But I am full of the wrath of the LORD, and I cannot hold it in. "Pour it out on the children in the street and on the young men gathered together; both husband and wife will be caught in it, and the old, those weighed down with years. Their houses will be turned over to others, together with their fields and their wives, when I stretch out my hand against those who live in the land," declares the LORD "From the least to the greatest, all are greedy for gain; prophets and priests alike, all practice deceit. They dress the wound of my people as though it were not serious. 'Peace, peace,' they say, when there is no peace. Are they ashamed of their detestable conduct? No, they have no shame at all; they do not even know how to blush. So they will fall among the fallen; they will be brought down when I punish them," says the LORD This is what the LORD says: "Stand at the crossroads and look; ask for the ancient paths, ask where the good way is, and walk in it, and you will find rest for your souls. But you said, 'We will not walk in it.' I appointed watchmen over you and said, 'Listen to the sound of the trumpet!' But you said, 'We will not listen.' Therefore hear, O nations; observe, O assembly, what will happen to them. Hear, O earth: I am bringing disaster on this people, the fruit of their schemes, because they have not listened to my words and have rejected my law. What do I care about incense from Sheba or sweet calamus from a distant land? Your burnt offerings are not acceptable; your sacrifices do not please me." Therefore this is what the LORD says: "I will put obstacles before this people. Parents and children alike will stumble over them; neighbors and friends will perish." This is what the LORD says: "Look, a people is coming from the land of the north; a great nation is being stirred up from the ends of the earth. They are armed with bows and spears; they are cruel and show no mercy. They sound like the roaring sea as they ride on their horses; they come like men in battle formation to attack you, Daughter Zion." We have heard reports about them, and our hands hang limp. Anguish has gripped us, pain like that of a woman in labor. Do not go out to the fields or walk on the roads, for the enemy has a sword, and there is terror on every side Put on sackcloth, my people, and roll in ashes; mourn with bitter wailing as for an only son, for suddenly the destroyer will come upon us. "I have made you a tester of metals and my people the ore, that you may observe and test their ways. They are all hardened rebels, going about to slander. They are bronze and iron; they all act corruptly. The bellows blow fiercely to burn away the lead with fire, but the refining goes on in vain; the wicked are not purged out. They are called rejected silver because the LORD has rejected them."

CHAPTER 7

The word that came to Jeremiah from the LORD: "Stand at the gate of the LORD's house and there proclaim this message: 'Hear the word of the LORD, all you people of Judah who come through these gates to worship the LORD. This is what the LORD Almighty, the God of Israel, says: Reform your ways and your actions, and I will let you live in this place. Do not trust in deceptive words and say, "This is the temple of the LORD, the temple of the LORD, the temple of the LORD!" If you really change your ways and your actions and deal with each other justly, if you do not oppress the foreigner, the fatherless, or the widow and do not shed innocent blood in this place, and if you do not follow other gods to your own harm, then I will let you live in this place, in the land I gave your ancestors forever and ever But look, you are trusting in deceptive words that are worthless. Will you steal and murder, commit adultery and perjury, burn incense to Baal and follow other gods you have not known, and then come and stand before me in this house, which bears my Name, and say, "We are safe"—safe to do all these detestable things? Has this house, which bears my Name, become a den of robbers to you? But I have been watching!" declares the LORD "'Go now to the place in Shiloh where I first made a dwelling for my Name, and see what I did to it because of the wickedness of my people Israel. While you were doing all these things,' declares the LORD, 'I spoke to you again and again, but you did not listen; I called you, but you did not answer. Therefore, what I did to Shiloh I will now do to the house that bears my Name, the temple you trust in, the place I gave to you and your ancestors. I will thrust you from my presence, just as I did all your fellow Israelites, the people of Ephraim.' "So do not pray for this people nor offer any plea or petition for them; do not plead with me, for I will not listen to you. Do you not see what they are doing in the towns of Judah and in the streets of Jerusalem? The children gather wood, the fathers light the fire, and the women knead the dough and make cakes to offer to the Queen of Heaven. They pour out drink offerings to other gods to arouse my anger. But am I the one they are provoking? declares the LORD. Are they not rather harming themselves, to their own shame? "'Therefore this is what the Sovereign LORD says: My anger and my wrath will be poured out on this place—on man and beast, on the trees of the field and on the crops of your land—and it will burn and not be quenched "'This is what the LORD Almighty, the God of Israel, says: Go ahead, add your burnt offerings to your other sacrifices and eat the meat yourselves! For when I brought your ancestors out of Egypt and spoke to them, I did not just give them commands about burnt offerings and sacrifices, but I gave them this command: Obey me, and I will be your God and you will be my people. Walk in obedience to all I command you, that it may go well with you. But they did not listen or pay attention; instead, they followed the stubborn inclinations of their evil hearts. They went backward and not forward. From the time your ancestors left Egypt until now, day after day, again and again, I sent you my servants the prophets. But they did not listen to me or pay attention. They were stiff-necked and did more evil than their ancestors.' "When you tell them all this, they will not listen to you; when you call to them, they will not answer. Therefore say to them, 'This is the nation that has not obeyed the LORD its God or responded to correction. Truth has perished; it has vanished from their lips. Cut off your hair and throw it away; take up a lament on the barren heights, for the LORD has rejected and abandoned this generation that is under his wrath "'The people of Judah have done evil in my eyes,' declares the LORD. 'They have set up their detestable idols in the house that bears my Name and have defiled it. They have built the high places of Topheth in the Valley of Ben Hinnom to burn their sons and daughters in the fire—something I did not command, nor did it enter my mind. So beware, the days are coming,' declares the LORD, 'when people will no longer call it Topheth or the Valley of Ben Hinnom, but the Valley of Slaughter, for they will bury the dead in Topheth until there is no more room. Then the carcasses of this people will become food for the birds and the wild animals, and there will be no one to frighten them away. I will bring an end to the sounds of joy and gladness and to the voices of bride and bridegroom in the towns of Judah and the streets of Jerusalem, for the land will become desolate."'

CHAPTER 8

"'At that time,' declares the LORD, 'the bones of the kings and officials of Judah, the bones of the priests and prophets, and the bones of the people of Jerusalem will be removed from their graves. They will be exposed to the sun and the moon and all the stars of the heavens, which they have loved and served and which they have followed and consulted and worshiped. They will not be gathered up or buried but will be like dung lying on the ground. Wherever I banish them, all the survivors of this evil nation will prefer death to life,' declares the LORD Almighty "'Say to them, "This is what the LORD says: 'When people fall down, do they not get up? When someone turns away, do they not return? Why then have these people turned away? Why does Jerusalem always turn away? They cling to deceit; they refuse to return. I have listened attentively, but they do not say what is right. None of them repent of their wickedness, saying, 'What have I done?' Each pursues their own course like a horse charging into battle. Even the stork in the sky knows her appointed seasons, and the dove, the swift and the thrush observe the time of their migration. But my people do not know the requirements of the LORD "'How can you say, 'We are wise, for we have the law of the LORD,' when actually the lying pen of the scribes has

handled it falsely? The wise will be put to shame; they will be dismayed and trapped. Since they have rejected the word of the LORD, what kind of wisdom do they have? Therefore I will give their wives to other men and their fields to new owners. From the least to the greatest, all are greedy for gain; prophets and priests alike, all practice deceit. They dress the wound of my people as though it were not serious. 'Peace, peace,' they say, when there is no peace. Are they ashamed of their detestable conduct? No, they have no shame at all; they do not even know how to blush. So they will fall among the fallen; they will be brought down when I punish them,' says the LORD "'I will take away their harvest,' declares the LORD. 'There will be no grapes on the vine. There will be no figs on the tree, and their leaves will wither. What I have given them will be taken from them.'" "Why are we sitting here? Gather together! Let us flee to the fortified cities and perish there! For the LORD our God has doomed us to perish and given us poisoned water to drink because we have sinned against him. We hoped for peace but no good has come, for a time of healing but there is only terror. The snorting of the enemy's horses is heard from Dan; at the neighing of their stallions, the whole land trembles. They have come to devour the land and everything in it, the city and all who live there. See, I will send venomous snakes among you, vipers that cannot be charmed, and they will bite you," declares the LORD You who are my Comforter in sorrow, my heart is faint within me. Listen to the cry of my people from a land far away: "Is the LORD not in Zion? Is her King no longer there?" "Why have they aroused my anger with their images, with their worthless foreign idols?" "The harvest is past, the summer has ended, and we are not saved." Since my people are crushed, I am crushed; I mourn, and horror grips me. Is there no balm in Gilead? Is there no physician there? Why then is there no healing for the wound of my people?

CHAPTER 9

Oh, that my head were a spring of water and my eyes a fountain of tears! I would weep day and night for the slain of my people. Oh, that I had in the desert a lodging place for travelers, so that I might leave my people and go away from them; for they are all adulterers, a crowd of unfaithful people. "They make ready their tongue like a bow, to shoot lies; it is not by truth that they triumph in the land. They go from one sin to another; they do not acknowledge me," declares the LORD "Beware of your friends; do not trust anyone in your clan. For every one of them is a deceiver, and every friend a slanderer. Friend deceives friend, and no one speaks the truth. They have taught their tongues to lie; they weary themselves with sinning. You live in the midst of deception; in their deceit, they refuse to acknowledge me," declares the LORD Therefore this is what the LORD Almighty says: "See, I will refine and test them, for what else can I do because of the sin of my people? Their tongue is a deadly arrow; it speaks deceitfully. With their mouths, they all speak cordially to their neighbors, but in their hearts, they set traps for them. Should I not punish them for this?" declares the LORD. "Should I not avenge myself on such a nation as this?" I will weep and wail for the mountains and take up a lament concerning the wilderness grasslands. They are desolate and untraveled, and the lowing of cattle is not heard. The birds have all fled, and the animals are gone. "I will make Jerusalem a heap of ruins, a haunt of jackals; and I will lay waste the towns of Judah so no one can live there." Who is wise enough to understand this? Who has been instructed by the LORD and can explain it? Why has the land been ruined and laid waste like a desert that no one can cross? The LORD said, "It is because they have forsaken my law, which I set before them; they have not obeyed me or followed my law. Instead, they have followed the stubbornness of their hearts; they have followed the Baals, as their ancestors taught them." Therefore this is what the LORD Almighty, the God of Israel, says: "See, I will make this people eat bitter food and drink poisoned water. I will scatter them among nations that neither they nor their ancestors have known, and I will pursue them with the sword until I have made an end of them." This is what the LORD Almighty says: "Consider now! Call for the wailing women to come; send for the most skillful of them. Let them come quickly and wail over us till our eyes overflow with tears and water streams from our eyelids. The sound of wailing is heard from Zion: 'How ruined we are! How great is our shame! We must leave our land because our houses are in ruins.' Now, you women, hear the word of the LORD; open your ears to the words of his mouth. Teach your daughters how to wail; teach one another a lament. Death has climbed in through our windows and has entered our fortresses; it has removed the children from the streets and the young men from the public squares Say, "This is what the LORD declares: 'Dead bodies will lie like dung on the open field, like cut grain behind the reaper, with no one to gather them.'" This is what the LORD says: "Let not the wise boast of their wisdom or the strong boast of their strength or the rich boast of their riches, but let the one who boasts boast about this: that they have the understanding to know me, that I am the LORD, who exercises kindness, justice, and righteousness on earth, for in these I delight," declares the LORD "The days are coming," declares the LORD, "when I will punish all who are circumcised only in the flesh— Egypt, Judah, Edom, Ammon, Moab, and all who live in the wilderness in distant places. For all these nations are really uncircumcised, and even the whole house of Israel is uncircumcised in heart."

CHAPTER 10

Hear what the LORD says to you, people of Israel. This is what the LORD says: "Do not learn the ways of the nations or be terrified by signs in the heavens, though the nations are terrified by them. For the practices of the peoples are worthless; they cut a tree out of the forest, and a craftsman shapes it with his chisel. They adorn it with silver and gold; they fasten it with hammer and nails so it will not totter. Like a scarecrow in a cucumber field, their idols cannot speak; they must be carried because they cannot walk. Do not fear them; they can do no harm nor can they do any good." No one is like you, LORD; you are great, and your name is mighty in power. Who should not fear you, King of the nations? This is your due. Among all the wise leaders of the nations and in all their kingdoms, there is no one like you. They are all senseless and foolish; they are taught by worthless wooden idols. Hammered silver is brought from Tarshish and gold from Uphaz. What the craftsman and goldsmith have made is then dressed in blue and purple—all made by skilled workers. But the LORD is the true God; he is the living God, the eternal King. When he is angry, the earth trembles; the nations cannot endure his wrath "Tell them this: 'These gods, who did not make the heavens and the earth, will perish from the earth and from under the heavens.' But God made the earth by his power; he founded the world by his wisdom and stretched out the heavens by his understanding. When he thunders, the waters in the heavens roar; he makes clouds rise from the ends of the earth. He sends lightning with the rain and brings out the wind from his storehouses. Everyone is senseless and without knowledge; every goldsmith is shamed by his idols.

The images he makes are a fraud; they have no breath in them. They are worthless, the objects of mockery; when their judgment comes, they will perish. He who is the Portion of Jacob is not like these, for he is the Maker of all things, including Israel, the people of his inheritance— the LORD Almighty is his name." Gather up your belongings to leave the land, you who live under siege. For this is what the LORD says: "At this time I will hurl out those who live in this land; I will bring distress on them so that they may be captured." Woe to me because of my injury! My wound is incurable! Yet I said to myself, "This is my sickness, and I must endure it." My tent is destroyed; all its ropes are snapped. My children are gone from me and are no more; no one is left now to pitch my tent or to set up my shelter. The shepherds are senseless and do not inquire of the LORD; so they do not prosper, and all their flock is scattered. Listen! The report is coming—a great commotion from the land of the north! It will make the towns of Judah desolate, a haunt of jackals LORD, I know that people's lives are not their own; it is not for them to direct their steps. Discipline me, LORD, but only in due measure—not in your anger, or you will reduce me to nothing. Pour out your wrath on the nations that do not acknowledge you, on the peoples who do not call on your name. For they have devoured Jacob; they have devoured him completely and destroyed his homeland

CHAPTER 11

The word that came to Jeremiah from the LORD: "Hear the words of this covenant and speak them to the people of Judah and the inhabitants of Jerusalem. Say to them, 'This is what the LORD, the God of Israel, says: Cursed is the one who does not obey the words of this covenant, which I commanded your ancestors when I brought them out of the land of Egypt, out of the iron furnace, saying, "Obey my voice and do everything I command you. Then you will be my people, and I will be your God, so that I may fulfill the oath I swore to your ancestors, to give them a land flowing with milk and honey, as it is today."'" Then I answered, "So be it, LORD." The LORD said to me, "Proclaim all these words in the towns of Judah and in the streets of Jerusalem: 'Listen to the terms of this covenant and follow them. From the time I brought your ancestors up from Egypt until today, I warned them again and again, saying, "Obey me." But they did not listen or pay attention; instead, they followed the stubbornness of their evil hearts. So I brought on them all the curses of the covenant I had commanded them to follow but that they did not keep.'" The LORD said to me, "There is a conspiracy among the people of Judah and those who live in Jerusalem. They have returned to the sins of their ancestors, who refused to listen to my words. They have followed other gods to serve them. Both Israel and Judah have broken the covenant I made with their ancestors. Therefore this is what the LORD says: 'I will bring on them a disaster they cannot escape. Although they cry out to me, I will not listen to them. The towns of Judah and the people of Jerusalem will go and cry out to the gods to whom they burn incense, but they will not help them at all when disaster strikes. You have as many gods as you have towns, Judah; and the altars you have set up to burn incense to that shameful god Baal are as many as the streets of Jerusalem.' "Do not pray for this people nor offer any plea or petition for them because I will not listen when they call to me in the time of their distress. What is my beloved doing in my temple as she, with many others, works out her evil schemes? Can consecrated meat avert your punishment? When you engage in your wickedness,

594

then you rejoice." The LORD called you a thriving olive tree with fruit beautiful in form. But with the roar of a mighty storm, he will set it on fire, and its branches will be broken The LORD Almighty, who planted you, has decreed disaster for you because the people of both Israel and Judah have done evil and aroused my anger by burning incense to Baal. The LORD revealed their plot to me. I knew it, for at that time he showed me what they were doing. I had been like a gentle lamb led to the slaughter; I did not realize that they had plotted against me, saying, "Let us destroy the tree and its fruit; let us cut him off from the land of the living, that his name be remembered no more." But, LORD Almighty, you who judge righteously and test the heart and mind, let me see your vengeance on them, for to you I have committed my cause Therefore this is what the LORD says about the people of Anathoth who are threatening to kill you, saying, "Do not prophesy in the name of the LORD or you will die by our hands"—therefore this is what the LORD Almighty says: "I will punish them. Their young men will die by the sword, their sons and daughters by famine. Not even a remnant will be left to them because I will bring disaster on the people of Anathoth in the year of their punishment."

CHAPTER 12

You are always righteous, LORD, when I bring a case before you. Yet I would speak with you about your justice: Why does the way of the wicked prosper? Why do all the faithless live at ease? You have planted them, and they have taken root; they grow and bear fruit. You are always on their lips but far from their hearts. Yet you know me, LORD; you see me and test my thoughts about you. Drag them off like sheep to be butchered! Set them apart for the day of slaughter! How long will the land lie parched and the grass in every field be withered? Because those who live in it are wicked, the animals and birds have perished. Moreover, the people are saying, "He will not see what happens to us." "If you have raced with men on foot and they have worn you out, how can you compete with horses? If you stumble in safe country, how will you manage in the thickets by the Jordan? Your relatives, members of your own family—even they have betrayed you; they have raised a loud cry against you. Do not trust them, though they speak well of you." "I will forsake my house, abandon my inheritance; I will give the one I love into the hands of her enemies. My inheritance has become to me like a lion in the forest. She roars at me; therefore, I hate her. Has not my inheritance become to me like a speckled bird of prey that other birds of prey surround and attack? Go and gather all the wild beasts; bring them to devour. Many shepherds will ruin my vineyard and trample down my field; they will turn my pleasant field into a desolate wasteland. It will be made a wasteland, parched and desolate before me; the whole land will be laid waste because there is no one who cares. Over all the barren heights in the desert, destroyers will swarm, for the sword of the LORD will devour from one end of the land to the other; no one will be safe. They will sow wheat but reap thorns; they will wear themselves out but gain nothing. They will bear the shame of their harvest because of the LORD's fierce anger." This is what the LORD says: "As for all my wicked neighbors who seize the inheritance I gave my people Israel, I will uproot them from their lands, and I will uproot the people of Judah from among them. But after I uproot them, I will again have compassion and will bring each of them back to their own inheritance and their own country. And if they learn well the ways of my people and swear by my name, saying, 'As surely as the LORD lives'—even as they once taught my people to swear by Baal—then

they will be established among my people. But if any nation does not listen, I will completely uproot and destroy it," declares the LORD

CHAPTER 13

This is what the LORD said to me: "Go and buy a linen belt and put it around your waist, but do not let it touch water." So I bought a belt, as the LORD directed, and put it around my waist. Then the word of the LORD came to me a second time: "Take the belt you bought and are wearing around your waist, and go now to Perath and hide it there in a crevice in the rocks." So I went and hid it at Perath, as the LORD told me Many days later the LORD said to me, "Go now to Perath and get the belt I told you to hide there." So I went to Perath and dug up the belt and took it from the place where I had hidden it, but now it was ruined and completely useless. Then the word of the LORD came to me: "This is what the LORD says: 'In the same way I will ruin the pride of Judah and the great pride of Jerusalem. These wicked people, who refuse to listen to my words, who follow the stubbornness of their hearts and go after other gods to serve and worship them, will be like this belt—completely useless! For as a belt is bound around the waist, so I bound all the people of Israel and all the people of Judah to me,' declares the LORD, 'to be my people for my renown and praise and honor. But they have not listened.' "Say to them: 'This is what the LORD, the God of Israel, says: Every wineskin should be filled with wine.' And if they say to you, 'Don't we know that every wineskin should be filled with wine?' then tell them, 'This is what the LORD says: I am going to fill with drunkenness all who live in this land—including the kings who sit on David's throne, the priests, the prophets, and all those living in Jerusalem. I will smash them one against the other, parents and children alike,' declares the LORD. 'I will allow no pity or mercy or compassion to keep me from destroying them.' Hear and pay attention, do not be arrogant, for the LORD has spoken. Give glory to the LORD your God before he brings the darkness, before your feet stumble on the darkening hills. You hope for light, but he will turn it to utter darkness and change it to deep gloom. But if you do not listen, I will weep in secret because of your pride; my eyes will weep bitterly, overflowing with tears, because the LORD's flock will be taken captive Say to the king and to the queen mother, "Come down from your thrones, for your glorious crowns will fall from your heads." The cities in the Negev will be shut up, and there will be no one to open them. All Judah will be carried into exile, carried completely away. Lift up your eyes and see those who are coming from the north. Where is the flock that was entrusted to you, the sheep of which you boasted? What will you say when the LORD sets over you those you cultivated as your special allies? Will not pain grip you like that of a woman in labor? And if you ask yourself, "Why has this happened to me?"— it is because of your many sins that your skirts have been torn off and your body mistreated. Can an Ethiopian change his skin or a leopard its spots? Neither can you do good who are accustomed to doing evil "I will scatter you like chaff driven by the desert wind. This is your lot, the portion I have decreed for you," declares the LORD, "because you have forgotten me and trusted in false gods. I will pull up your skirts over your face that your shame may be seen—your adulteries and lustful neighings, your shameless prostitution! I have seen your detestable acts on the hills and in the fields. Woe to you, Jerusalem! How long will you be unclean?"

CHAPTER 14

This is the word of the LORD that came to Jeremiah concerning the drought: "Judah mourns, her cities languish; they wail for the land, and a cry goes up from Jerusalem. The nobles send their servants for water; they go to the cisterns but find no water. They return with their jars unfilled; dismayed and despairing, they cover their heads. The ground is cracked because there is no rain in the land; the farmers are dismayed and cover their heads. Even the doe in the field deserts her newborn fawn because there is no grass. Wild donkeys stand on the barren heights and pant like jackals; their eyes fail for lack of food." Although our sins testify against us, do something, LORD, for the sake of your name. For we have often rebelled; we have sinned against you. You who are the hope of Israel, its Savior in times of distress, why are you like a stranger in the land, like a traveler who stays only a night? Why are you like a man taken by surprise, like a warrior powerless to save? You are among us, LORD, and we bear your name; do not forsake us! This is what the LORD says about this people: "They greatly love to wander; they do not restrain their feet. So the LORD does not accept them; he will now remember their wickedness and punish them for their sins." Then the LORD said to me, "Do not pray for the well-being of this people. Although they fast, I will not listen to their cry; though they offer burnt offerings and grain offerings, I will not accept them. Instead, I will destroy them with the sword, famine, and plague." But I said, "Alas, Sovereign LORD! The prophets keep telling them, 'You will not see the sword or suffer famine. Indeed, I will give you lasting peace in this place.'" Then the LORD said to me, "The prophets are prophesying lies in my name. I have not sent them or appointed them or spoken to them. They are prophesying to you false visions, divinations, idolatries, and the delusions of their own minds. Therefore this is what the LORD says about the prophets who are prophesying in my name: I did not send them, yet they are saying, 'No sword or famine will touch this land.' Those same prophets will perish by sword and famine. And the people they are prophesying to will be thrown out into the streets of Jerusalem because of the famine and sword. There will be no one to bury them, their wives, their sons, and their daughters. I will pour out on them the calamity they deserve Speak this word to them: 'Let my eyes overflow with tears night and day without ceasing; for the Virgin Daughter, my people, has suffered a grievous wound, a crushing blow. If I go into the country, I see those slain by the sword; if I go into the city, I see the ravages of famine. Both prophet and priest have gone to a land they know not.'" Have you rejected Judah completely? Do you despise Zion? Why have you afflicted us so that we cannot be healed? We hoped for peace but no good has come, for a time of healing but there is only terror. We acknowledge our wickedness, LORD, and the guilt of our ancestors; we have indeed sinned against you. For the sake of your name do not despise us; do not dishonor your glorious throne. Remember your covenant with us and do not break it. Do any of the worthless idols of the nations bring rain? Do the skies themselves send down showers? No, it is you, LORD our God. Therefore our hope is in you, for you are the one who does all this

CHAPTER 15

Then the LORD said to me: "Even if Moses and Samuel were to stand before me, my heart would not go out to this people. Send them away from my presence! Let them go! And if they ask you, 'Where shall we go?' tell them, 'This is what the LORD says:
"Those destined for death, to death;
those for the sword, to the sword;
those for starvation, to starvation;
those for captivity, to captivity."

"I will send four kinds of destroyers against them," declares the LORD, "the sword to kill and the dogs to drag away, and the birds and the wild animals to devour and destroy. I will make them abhorrent to all the kingdoms of the earth because of what Manasseh son of Hezekiah king of Judah did in Jerusalem "Who will have pity on you, Jerusalem? Who will mourn for you? Who will stop to ask how you are? You have rejected me," declares the LORD. "You keep on backsliding. So I will reach out and destroy you; I am tired of holding back. I will winnow them with a winnowing fork at the city gates of the land. I will bring bereavement and destruction on my people, for they have not changed their ways. I will make their widows more numerous than the sand of the sea. At midday I will bring a destroyer against the mothers of their young men; suddenly I will bring down on them anguish and terror. The mother of seven will grow faint and breathe her last; her sun will set while it is still day; she will be disgraced and humiliated. I will put the survivors to the sword before their enemies," declares the LORD Alas, my mother, that you gave me birth,
a man with whom the whole land strives and contends!
I have neither lent nor borrowed,
yet everyone curses me The LORD said, "Surely I will deliver you for a good purpose; surely I will make your enemies plead with you in times of disaster and times of distress. Can a man break iron—iron from the north—or bronze? Your wealth and your treasures I will give as plunder, without charge, because of all your sins throughout your country. I will enslave you to your enemies in a land you do not know, for my anger will kindle a fire that will burn against you."
LORD, you understand;
remember me and care for me.
Avenge me on my persecutors.
You are long-suffering—do not take me away;
think of how I suffer reproach for your sake.
When your words came, I ate them;
they were my joy and my heart's delight,
for I bear your name,
LORD God Almighty.
I never sat in the company of revelers,
never made merry with them;
I sat alone because your hand was on me
and you had filled me with indignation.
Why is my pain unending
and my wound grievous and incurable?
You are to me like a deceptive brook,
like a spring that fails Therefore this is what the LORD says: "If you repent, I will restore you that you may serve me; if you utter worthy, not worthless, words, you will be my spokesman. Let this people turn to you, but you must not turn to them. I will make you a wall to this people, a fortified wall of bronze; they will fight against you but will not overcome you, for I am with you to rescue and save you," declares the LORD. "I will save you from the hands of the wicked and deliver you from the grasp of the cruel."

CHAPTER 16

The word of the Lord came to me, saying: "You shall not take a wife, nor shall you have sons or daughters in this place. For thus says the Lord concerning the sons and daughters who are born in this place, and concerning their mothers who bore them, and their fathers who begot them in this land: They shall die of grievous deaths; they shall not be lamented nor buried, but shall be like refuse on the face of the earth. They shall be consumed by the sword and by famine, and their corpses shall be food for the birds of heaven and for the beasts of the earth." For thus says the Lord: "Do not enter the house of mourning, nor go to lament or bemoan them, for I have taken away My peace from this people," says the Lord, "even lovingkindness and mercies. Both the great and the small shall die in this land; they shall not be buried; neither shall men lament for them, cut themselves, nor make themselves bald for them. Nor shall men break bread in mourning for them, to comfort them for the dead; nor shall men give them the cup of consolation to drink for their father or their mother Also you shall not go into the house of feasting, to sit with them to eat and drink." For thus says the Lord of hosts, the God of Israel: "Behold, I will cause to cease from this place, before your eyes and in your days, the voice of mirth and the voice of gladness, the voice of the bridegroom and the voice of the bride." "And it shall be, when you show this people all these words, and they say to you, 'Why has the Lord pronounced all this great disaster against us? Or what is our iniquity? Or what is our sin that we have committed against the Lord our God?' then you shall say to them, 'Because your fathers have forsaken Me,' says the Lord; 'they have walked after other gods and have served them and worshiped them, and have forsaken Me and not kept My law. And you have done worse than your fathers, for behold, each one follows the dictates of his own evil heart, so that no one listens to Me. Therefore I will cast you out of this land into a land that you do not know, neither you nor your fathers; and there you shall serve other gods day and night, where I will not show you favor.'" "Therefore behold, the days are coming," says the Lord, "that it shall no more be said, 'The Lord lives who brought up the children of Israel from the land of Egypt,' but, 'The Lord lives who brought up the children of Israel from the land of the north and from all the lands where He had driven them.' For I will bring them back into their land which I gave to their fathers "Behold, I will send for many fishermen," says the Lord, "and they shall fish them; and afterward I will send for many hunters, and they shall hunt them from every mountain and every hill, and out of the holes of the rocks. For My eyes are on all their ways; they are not hidden from My face, nor is their iniquity hidden from My eyes. And first I will repay double for their iniquity and their sin because they have defiled My land; they have filled My inheritance with the carcasses of their detestable and abominable idols."

O Lord, my strength and my fortress,
My refuge in the day of affliction,
The Gentiles shall come to You
From the ends of the earth and say,
"Surely our fathers have inherited lies,
Worthlessness, and unprofitable things."
Will a man make gods for himself,
Which are not gods?

"Therefore behold, I will this once cause them to know, I will cause them to know My hand and My might; and they shall know that My name is the Lord."

CHAPTER 17

The sin of Judah is written with a pen of iron; with the point of a diamond it is engraved on the tablet of their heart and on the horns of your altars. While their children remember their altars and their wooden images by the green trees on the high hills, O My mountain in the field, I will give as plunder your wealth, all your treasures, and your high places of sin within all your borders. And you, even of yourself, shall let go of your heritage which I gave you; and I will cause you to serve your enemies in the land which you do not know; for you have kindled a fire in My anger which shall burn forever." Thus says the Lord: "Cursed is the man who trusts in man and makes flesh his strength, whose heart departs from the Lord. For he shall be like a shrub in the desert and shall not see when good comes, but shall inhabit the parched places in the wilderness, in a salt land which is not inhabited "Blessed is the man who trusts in the Lord, and whose hope is the Lord. For he shall be like a tree planted by the waters, which spreads out its roots by the river, and will not fear when heat comes; but its leaf will be green, and will not be anxious in the year of drought, nor will cease from yielding fruit."

The heart is deceitful above all things,
And desperately wicked;
Who can know it?
I, the Lord, search the heart,
I test the mind,
Even to give every man according to his ways,
According to the fruit of his doings As a partridge
that broods but does not hatch,
So is he who gets riches, but not by right;
It will leave him in the midst of his days,
And at his end, he will be a fool A glorious high
throne from the beginning
Is the place of our sanctuary.
O Lord, the hope of Israel,
All who forsake You shall be ashamed.
Those who depart from Me
Shall be written in the earth,
Because they have forsaken the Lord,
The fountain of living waters Heal me, O Lord, and I
shall be healed;
Save me, and I shall be saved,
For You are my praise.
Indeed they say to me,
"Where is the word of the Lord?
Let it come now!"
As for me, I have not hurried away from being a
shepherd who follows You,
Nor have I desired the woeful day;
You know what came out of my lips;
It was right there before You Do not be a terror to
me;
You are my hope in the day of doom.
Let them be ashamed who persecute me,
But do not let me be put to shame;
Let them be dismayed,
But do not let me be dismayed.
Bring on them the day of doom,
And destroy them with double destruction!

Thus the Lord said to me: "Go and stand in the gate of the children of the people, by which the kings of Judah come in and by which they go out, and in all the gates of Jerusalem; and say to them, 'Hear the word of the Lord, you kings of Judah, and all Judah, and all the inhabitants of Jerusalem, who enter by these gates. Thus says the Lord: "Take heed to yourselves, and bear no burden on the Sabbath day, nor bring it in by the gates of Jerusalem; nor carry a burden out of your houses on the Sabbath day, nor do any work, but hallow the Sabbath day, as I commanded your fathers." But they did not obey nor incline their ear but made their neck stiff, that they might not hear nor receive instruction. And it shall be if you heed Me carefully," says the Lord, "to bring no burden through the gates of this city on the Sabbath day, but hallow the Sabbath day, to do no work in it, then shall enter the gates of this city kings and princes sitting on the throne of David, riding in chariots and on horses, they and their princes, accompanied by the men of Judah and the inhabitants of Jerusalem; and this city shall remain forever. And they shall come from the cities of Judah and from the places around Jerusalem, from the land of Benjamin and from the lowland, from the mountains and from the South, bringing burnt offerings and sacrifices, grain offerings and incense, bringing sacrifices of praise to the house of the Lord But if you will not heed Me to hallow the Sabbath day, such as not carrying a burden when entering the gates of Jerusalem on the Sabbath day, then I will kindle a fire in its gates, and it shall devour the palaces of Jerusalem, and it shall not be quenched."

CHAPTER 18

The word which came to Jeremiah from the Lord, saying, "Arise and go down to the potter's house, and there I will cause you to hear My words." Then I went down to the potter's house, and there he was, making something at the wheel. And the vessel that he made of clay was marred in the hand of the potter; so he made it again into another vessel, as it seemed good to the potter to make Then the word of the Lord came to me, saying, "O house of Israel, can I not do with you as this potter?" says the Lord. "Look, as the clay is in the potter's hand, so are you in My hand, O house of Israel! The instant I speak concerning a nation and concerning a kingdom, to pluck up, to pull down, and to destroy it, if that nation against whom I have spoken turns from its evil, I will relent of the disaster that I thought to bring upon it. And the instant I speak concerning a nation and concerning a kingdom, to build and to plant it, if it does evil in My sight so that it does not obey My voice, then I will relent concerning the good with which I said I would benefit it "Now therefore, speak to the men of Judah and to the inhabitants of Jerusalem, saying, 'Thus says the Lord: "Behold, I am fashioning a disaster and devising a plan against you. Return now everyone from his evil way, and make your ways and your doings good."'"

And they said, "That is hopeless! So we will walk according to our own plans, and we will each do according to the dictates of his evil heart."

Therefore thus says the Lord:
"Ask now among the Gentiles,
Who has heard such things?
The virgin of Israel has done a very horrible thing.
Will a man leave the snow-water of Lebanon,
Which comes from the rock of the field?
Will the cold flowing waters be forsaken for strange waters?
Because My people have forgotten Me,
They have burned incense to worthless idols,
And they have caused themselves to stumble in their ways,
From the ancient paths,
To walk in pathways and not on a highway,
To make their land desolate and a perpetual hissing;
Everyone who passes by it will be astonished
And shake his head.
I will scatter them as with an east wind before the enemy;
I will show them the back and not the face
In the day of their calamity."

Then they said, "Come and let us devise plans against Jeremiah; for the law shall not perish from the priest, nor counsel from the wise, nor the word from the prophet. Come and let us attack him with the tongue, and let us not give heed to any of his words."

Give heed to me, O Lord,
And listen to the voice of those who contend with me!
Shall evil be repaid for good?
For they have dug a pit for my life.
Remember that I stood before You
To speak good for them,
To turn away Your wrath from them.
Therefore deliver up their children to the famine,
And pour out their blood
By the force of the sword;
Let their wives become widows
And bereaved of their children.

Let their men be put to death,
Their young men be slain by the sword in battle.
Let a cry be heard from their houses,
When You bring a troop suddenly upon them;
For they have dug a pit to take me,
And hidden snares for my feet.
Yet, Lord, You know all their counsel
Which is against me, to slay me.
Provide no atonement for their iniquity,
Nor blot out their sin from Your sight;
But let them be overthrown before You.
Deal thus with them
In the time of Your anger

CHAPTER 19

Thus says the Lord: "Go and get a potter's earthen flask, and take some of the elders of the people and some of the elders of the priests. And go out to the Valley of the Son of Hinnom, which is by the entry of the Potsherd Gate; and proclaim there the words that I will tell you, and say, 'Hear the word of the Lord, O kings of Judah and inhabitants of Jerusalem. Thus says the Lord of hosts, the God of Israel: "Behold, I will bring such a catastrophe on this place, that whoever hears of it, his ears will tingle "Because they have forsaken Me and made this an alien place, because they have burned incense in it to other gods whom neither they, their fathers, nor the kings of Judah have known, and have filled this place with the blood of the innocents (they have also built the high places of Baal, to burn their sons with fire for burnt offerings to Baal, which I did not command or speak, nor did it come into My mind), therefore behold, the days are coming," says the Lord, "that this place shall no longer be called Tophet or the Valley of the Son of Hinnom, but the Valley of Slaughter "And I will make void the counsel of Judah and Jerusalem in this place, and I will cause them to fall by the sword before their enemies and by the hands of those who seek their lives; their corpses I will give as meat for the birds of the heaven and for the beasts of the earth. I will make this city desolate and a hissing; everyone who passes by it will be astonished and hiss because of all its plagues. And I will cause them to eat the flesh of their sons and the flesh of their daughters, and everyone shall eat the flesh of his friend in the siege and in the desperation with which their enemies and those who seek their lives shall drive them to despair." "Then you shall break the flask in the sight of the men who go with you, and say to them, 'Thus says the Lord of hosts: "Even so I will break this people and this city, as one breaks a potter's vessel, which cannot be made whole again; and they shall bury them in Tophet till there is no place to bury. Thus I will do to this place," says the Lord, "and to its inhabitants, and make this city like Tophet. And the houses of Jerusalem and the houses of the kings of Judah shall be defiled like the place of Tophet, because of all the houses on whose roofs they have burned incense to all the host of heaven, and poured out drink offerings to other gods."'" Then Jeremiah came from Tophet, where the Lord had sent him to prophesy; and he stood in the court of the Lord's house and said to all the people, "Thus says the Lord of hosts, the God of Israel: 'Behold, I will bring on this city and on all her towns all the doom that I have pronounced against it because they have stiffened their necks that they might not hear My words.'"

CHAPTER 20

Now Pashhur the son of Immer, the priest who was also chief governor in the house of the Lord, heard that Jeremiah prophesied these things. Then Pashhur struck Jeremiah the prophet and put him in the stocks that were in the high gate of Benjamin, which was by the house of the Lord. And it happened on the next day that Pashhur brought Jeremiah out of the stocks. Then Jeremiah said to him, "The Lord has not called your name Pashhur, but Magor-Missabib. For thus says the Lord: 'Behold, I will make you a terror to yourself and to all your friends, and they shall fall by the sword of their enemies; and your eyes shall see it. I will give all Judah into the hand of the king of Babylon, and he shall carry them captive to Babylon and slay them with the sword Moreover, I will deliver all the wealth of this city, all its produce, and all its precious things; all the treasures of the kings of Judah I will give into the hand of their enemies, who will plunder them, seize them, and carry them to Babylon. And you, Pashhur, and all who dwell in your house, shall go into captivity; you shall go to Babylon, and there you shall die and be buried, you and all your friends to whom you have prophesied lies.'"

O Lord, You induced me, and I was persuaded;
You are stronger than I, and have prevailed.
I am in derision daily;
Everyone mocks me.
For when I spoke, I cried out;
I shouted, "Violence and plunder!"
Because the word of the Lord was made to me
A reproach and a derision daily.
Then I said, "I will not make mention of Him,
Nor speak anymore in His name."
But His word was in my heart like a burning fire
Shut up in my bones;
I was weary of holding it back,
And I could not.
For I heard many mocking:
"Fear on every side!"
"Report," they say, "and we will report it!"
All my acquaintances watched for my stumbling,
Saying, "Perhaps he can be induced;
Then we will prevail against him,
And we will take our revenge on him."
But the Lord is with me as a mighty, awesome One.
Therefore my persecutors will stumble, and will not prevail.
They will be greatly ashamed, for they will not prosper.
Their everlasting confusion will never be forgotten.
But, O Lord of hosts,
You who test the righteous,
And see the mind and heart,
Let me see Your vengeance on them,
For I have pleaded my cause before You Sing to the Lord! Praise the Lord!
For He has delivered the life of the poor
From the hand of evildoers Cursed be the day in which I was born!
Let the day not be blessed in which my mother bore me!
Let the man be cursed
Who brought news to my father, saying,
"A male child has been born to you!"
Making him very glad.
And let that man be like the cities
Which the Lord overthrew, and did not relent;
Let him hear the cry in the morning
And the shouting at noon,
Because he did not kill me from the womb,
That my mother might have been my grave,
And her womb always enlarged with me.
Why did I come forth from the womb to see labor and sorrow,
That my days should be consumed with shame?

CHAPTER 21

1 The words that came to Jeremiah from the LORD were delivered when King Zedekiah sent Pashur, the son of Malchiah, and Zephaniah, the son of Maaseiah the priest, to him with the question, "Is it not true that the LORD has dealt well with us because Nebuchadnezzar, king of Babylon, is waging war against us? 2 Please inquire of the LORD for us (since Nebuchadnezzar, king of Babylon, is waging war against us) whether the LORD will continue to perform all his wonderful works so that he may turn away from us." 3 Then Jeremiah said, "Thus you shall say to Zedekiah: 4 Thus says the LORD, the God of Israel: 'Behold, I will withdraw the weapons of war that are in your hands, with which you fight against the king of Babylon and the Chaldeans who are besieging you outside the walls, and I will gather them into the midst of this city. 5 I Myself will fight against you with an outstretched hand and with a mighty weapon, in wrath, anger, and great indignation. 6 I will strike the inhabitants of this city, both man and beast; they will die of a great pestilence.' 7 After this, says the LORD, 'I will deliver Zedekiah, king of Judah, his servants, the people, and all who remain in this city from pestilence, sword, and famine, into the hand of Nebuchadnezzar, king of Babylon, into the hand of their enemies and those who seek their lives. He shall strike them with the sword; he shall not spare them, nor show pity or compassion 8 And to this people you shall say, "Thus says the LORD: Behold, I set before you the way of life and the way of death. 9 Whoever remains in this city shall die by the sword, famine, and pestilence; but whoever goes out and falls among the Chaldeans who are besieging you shall live, and his life shall be his reward. 10 For I have set My face against this city for harm and not for good, says the LORD; it shall be delivered into the hand of the king of Babylon, and he shall burn it with fire 11 And to the house of the king of Judah, say, 'Hear the word of the LORD: 12 O house of David, thus says the LORD: "Execute judgment in the morning, and deliver the oppressed from the hand of the oppressor, lest My wrath break out like a burning fire that cannot be quenched because of the wickedness of your deeds. 13 Behold, I am against you, O inhabitant of the valley and rock of the plain, says the LORD, who says, 'Who will come down against us?' or 'Who will enter our dwellings?' 14 But I will punish you according to the fruit of your deeds, says the LORD; I will kindle a fire in its forest that shall devour all that is around it."

CHAPTER 22

1 Thus says the LORD: "Go down to the house of the king of Judah and speak there this word: 2 'Hear the word of the LORD, O king of Judah, who sits on the throne of David, you and your servants, and your people who enter these gates. 3 Thus says the LORD: "Execute judgment and righteousness; deliver the oppressed from the hand of the oppressor; do not mistreat the stranger, the fatherless, or the widow; do no violence or shed innocent blood in this place. 4 For if you do these things, kings who sit on the throne of David will enter through the gates of this house, riding in chariots and on horses, he and his servants and his people. 5 But if you will not heed these words, I swear by Myself, says the LORD, that this house shall become a desolation." 6 For thus says the LORD concerning the house of the king of Judah: "You are Gilead to Me, the head of Lebanon; yet I will surely make you a wilderness, uninhabited cities. 7 I will prepare destroyers against you, every one with his weapons; they will cut down your choice cedars and cast them into the fire 8 Many nations will pass by this city and say to one another, 'Why has the LORD done this to this great city?' 9 Then they will answer, 'Because they have forsaken the covenant of the LORD their God and worshiped other gods, serving them.' 10 Weep not for the dead, nor mourn for him, but weep for him who goes away, for he shall return no more, nor see his native land. 11 For thus

says the LORD concerning Shallum, the son of Josiah, king of Judah, who reigned instead of his father Josiah and who went away from this place: 'He shall not return here anymore. 12 He shall die in the place where they have led him captive, and shall see this land no more 13 Woe to him who builds his house by unrighteousness and his chambers by injustice; who uses his neighbor's services without wages and gives him nothing for his labor. 14 Who says, 'I will build myself a spacious house with large rooms, and cut out windows for it, paneling it with cedar and painting it with vermilion.' 15 Do you think you will reign because you enclose yourself in cedar? Did not your father eat and drink and do justice and righteousness? Then it was well with him. 16 He judged the cause of the poor and needy; then it was well. Was not this knowing Me? says the LORD. 17 But your eyes and heart are for nothing but your covetousness, for shedding innocent blood, and for oppression and violence 18 Therefore thus says the LORD concerning Jehoiakim, the son of Josiah, king of Judah: "They shall not lament for him, saying, 'Alas, my brother!' or 'Alas, my sister!' They shall not lament for him, saying, 'Alas, lord!' or 'Alas, his glory!' 19 He shall be buried with the burial of a donkey, dragged and cast out beyond the gates of Jerusalem 20 Go up to Lebanon and cry out, and lift up your voice in Bashan; cry from Abarim, for all your lovers are destroyed. 21 I spoke to you in your prosperity, but you said, 'I will not listen.' This has been your manner from your youth, that you did not obey My voice. 22 The wind shall shepherd all your shepherds, and your lovers shall go into captivity; surely then you will be ashamed and confounded because of all your wickedness 23 O inhabitant of Lebanon, who makes your nest among the cedars, how will you groan when pangs come upon you, the pain as of a woman in labor? 24 As I live, says the LORD, even if Coniah, the son of Jehoiakim, king of Judah, were the signet ring on My right hand, yet I would pull you off. 25 I will give you into the hand of those who seek your life, and into the hand of those whom you fear, even into the hand of Nebuchadnezzar, king of Babylon, and the hand of the Chaldeans. 26 I will cast you out, and your mother who bore you, into another country where you were not born; and there you shall die. 27 But to the land to which they desire to return, they shall not return 28 Is this man Coniah a despised, broken idol, a vessel in which is no pleasure? Why are they cast out, he and his descendants, and cast into a land they do not know? 29 O earth, earth, earth, hear the word of the LORD! 30 Thus says the LORD: "Write this man down as childless, a man who shall not prosper in his days; for none of his descendants shall prosper, sitting on the throne of David, or ruling anymore in Judah."

CHAPTER 23

1 Woe to the shepherds who destroy and scatter the sheep of My pasture! says the LORD. 2 Therefore thus says the LORD, the God of Israel, against the shepherds who feed My people: "You have scattered My flock, driven them away, and have not attended to them. Behold, I will attend to you for the evil of your deeds, says the LORD. 3 But I will gather the remnant of My flock out of all countries where I have driven them, and bring them back to their folds, and they shall be fruitful and increase. 4 I will set up shepherds over them who will feed them, and they shall no longer be afraid or dismayed, nor shall they be lacking, says the LORD 5 Behold, the days are coming, says the LORD, when I will raise to David a righteous Branch, and a King shall reign and prosper, and execute judgment and righteousness in the earth. 6 In His days Judah will be saved, and Israel will dwell safely; and this is His name by which He will be called, 'The LORD Our Righteousness.' 7 Therefore, behold, the days are coming, says the LORD, when they shall no longer say, 'As the LORD lives who brought up the children of Israel from the land of Egypt,' 8 but, 'As the LORD lives who brought up and led the descendants of the house of Israel from the north country and from all the countries where I had driven them.' And they shall dwell in their own land 9 My heart within me is broken because of the prophets; all my bones shake. I am like a drunken man, and like a man whom wine has overcome, because of the LORD and because of His holy words. 10 For the land is full of adulterers; for because of a curse the land mourns; the pleasant places of the wilderness are dried up. And their course is evil, and their might is not right. 11 For both prophet and priest are profane; yes, in My house I have found their wickedness, says the LORD. 12 Therefore their way shall be to them like slippery ways; in the darkness they shall be driven on and fall in them; for I will bring disaster on them, the year of their punishment, says the LORD 13 And I have seen folly in the prophets of Samaria: they prophesied by Baal and caused My people Israel to err. 14 Also I have seen a horrible thing in the prophets of Jerusalem: they commit adultery and walk in lies; they also strengthen the hands of evildoers, so that no one turns back from his wickedness. All of them are like Sodom to Me, and her inhabitants like Gomorrah. 15 Therefore thus says the LORD of hosts concerning the prophets: "Behold, I will feed them with wormwood and make them drink the water of gall; for from the prophets of Jerusalem profaneness has gone out into all the land." 16 Thus says the LORD of hosts: "Do not listen to the words of the prophets who prophesy to you. They make you worthless; they speak a vision of their own heart, not from the mouth of the LORD. 17 They continually say to those who despise Me, 'The LORD has said, "You shall have peace"'; and to everyone who walks according to the dictates of his own heart, they say, 'No evil shall come upon you.' 18 For who has stood in the counsel of the LORD, and has perceived and heard His word? Who has marked His word and heard it? 19 Behold, a whirlwind of the LORD has gone forth in fury, a violent whirlwind! It will fall violently on the head of the wicked. 20 The anger of the LORD will not turn back until He has executed and performed the thoughts of His heart. In the latter days you will understand it perfectly 21 I have not sent these prophets, yet they ran. I have not spoken to them, yet they prophesied. 22 But if they had stood in My counsel, and had caused My people to hear My words, then they would have turned them from their evil way and from the evil of their doings 23 Am I a God near at hand, says the LORD, and not a God afar off? 24 Can anyone hide himself in secret places, so I shall not see him? says the LORD; do I not fill heaven and earth? says the LORD. 25 I have heard what the prophets have said who prophesy lies in My name, saying, 'I have dreamed, I have dreamed!' 26 How long will this be in the heart of the prophets who prophesy lies? Indeed, they are prophets of the deceit of their own heart, 27 who try to make My people forget My name by their dreams which everyone tells his neighbor, as their fathers forgot My name for Baal 28 The prophet who has a dream, let him tell a dream; and he who has My word, let him speak My word faithfully. What is the chaff to the wheat? says the LORD. 29 Is not My word like a fire? says the LORD, and like a hammer that breaks the rock in pieces? 30 Therefore, behold, I am against the prophets, says the LORD, who steal My words everyone from his neighbor. 31 Behold, I am against the prophets, says the LORD, who use their tongues

and say, 'He says.' 32 Behold, I am against those who prophesy false dreams, says the LORD, and tell them, and cause My people to err by their lies and by their recklessness. Yet I did not send them or command them; therefore they shall not profit this people at all, says the LORD 33 "So when these people or the prophet or priest ask you, saying, 'What is the oracle of the LORD?' you shall then say to them, 'What oracle? I will even forsake you, says the LORD.' 34 And as for the prophet and the priest and the people who say, 'The oracle of the LORD,' I will even punish that man and his house. 35 Thus shall you say every one to his neighbor, and every one to his brother, 'What has the LORD answered?' and, 'What has the LORD spoken?' 36 And the oracle of the LORD you shall mention no more. For every man's word will be his oracle, for you have perverted the words of the living God, the LORD of hosts, our God. 37 Thus you shall say to the prophet, 'What has the LORD answered you?' and, 'What has the LORD spoken?' 38 But since you say, 'The oracle of the LORD!' therefore thus says the LORD: 'Because you say this word, 'The oracle of the LORD!' and I have sent to you, saying, 'You shall not say, 'The oracle of the LORD!' 39 therefore, behold, I, even I, will utterly forget you and forsake you, and the city that I gave you and your fathers, and will cast you out of My presence. 40 And I will bring an everlasting reproach upon you, and a perpetual shame which shall not be forgotten.'"

CHAPTER 24

1 The LORD showed me, and there were two baskets of figs set before the temple of the LORD, after Nebuchadnezzar, king of Babylon, had carried away captive Jeconiah the son of Jehoiakim, king of Judah, and the princes of Judah, with the craftsmen and smiths from Jerusalem, and had brought them to Babylon. 2 One basket had very good figs, like the figs that are first ripe; and the other basket had very bad figs, which could not be eaten, they were so bad 3 Then the LORD said to me, "What do you see, Jeremiah?" And I said, "Figs; the good figs, very good; and the bad figs, very bad; so bad that they cannot be eaten." 4 Again the word of the LORD came to me, saying, 5 "Thus says the LORD, the God of Israel: 'Like these good figs, so will I acknowledge those who are carried away captive from Judah, whom I have sent out of this place into the land of the Chaldeans, for their good. 6 For I will set My eyes on them for good, and I will bring them back to this land; I will build them and not pull them down; I will plant them and not pluck them up. 7 Then I will give them a heart to know Me, that I am the LORD; and they shall be My people, and I will be their God, for they shall return to Me with their whole heart 8 And as the bad figs which cannot be eaten, so will I give up Zedekiah the king of Judah, his princes, the residue of Jerusalem who remain in this land, and those who dwell in the land of Egypt. 9 I will deliver them to trouble into all the kingdoms of the earth, for their harm, to be a reproach and a byword, a taunt and a curse in all places where I shall drive them. 10 And I will send the sword, the famine, and the pestilence among them, till they are consumed from the land that I gave to them and their fathers.'"

CHAPTER 25

1 The word that came to Jeremiah concerning all the people of Judah, in the fourth year of Jehoiakim the son of Josiah, king of Judah, that was the first year of Nebuchadnezzar king of Babylon, 2 which Jeremiah the prophet spoke to all the people of Judah and to all the inhabitants of Jerusalem, saying: 3 "From the thirteenth year of Josiah the son of Amon, king of Judah, even to this day—this is the twenty-third year in which the word of the LORD has come to me; and

I have spoken to you, rising early and speaking, but you have not listened. 4 And the LORD has sent to you all His servants the prophets, rising early and sending them, but you have not listened nor inclined your ear to hear. 5 They said, 'Repent now every one of his evil way and his evil doings, and dwell in the land that the LORD has given to you and your fathers forever and ever. 6 Do not go after other gods to serve them and worship them, and do not provoke Me to anger with the works of your hands, and I will not harm you.' 7 Yet you have not listened to Me, says the LORD, that you might provoke Me to anger with the works of your hands to your own hurt 8 Therefore thus says the LORD of hosts: "Because you have not heard My words, 9 behold, I will send and take all the families of the north, says the LORD, and Nebuchadnezzar the king of Babylon, My servant, and will bring them against this land, against its inhabitants, and against these nations all around, and will utterly destroy them, and make them an astonishment, a hissing, and perpetual desolations. 10 Moreover I will take from them the voice of mirth and the voice of gladness, the voice of the bridegroom and the voice of the bride, the sound of the millstones and the light of the lamp. 11 And this whole land shall be a desolation and an astonishment, and these nations shall serve the king of Babylon seventy years 12 'Then it will come to pass, when seventy years are completed, that I will punish the king of Babylon and that nation, the land of the Chaldeans, for their iniquity,' says the LORD; 'and I will make it a perpetual desolation. 13 So I will bring on that land all My words which I have pronounced against it, all that is written in this book, which Jeremiah has prophesied against all the nations. 14 For many nations and great kings shall be served by them also; and I will repay them according to their deeds and according to the works of their own hands.'" 15 For thus says the LORD God of Israel to me: "Take this wine cup of fury from My hand, and cause all the nations to whom I send you to drink it. 16 And they will drink and stagger and go mad because of the sword that I will send among them." 17 Then I took the cup from the LORD's hand and made all the nations drink, to whom the LORD had sent me: 18 Jerusalem and the cities of Judah, its kings and its princes, to make them a desolation, an astonishment, a hissing, and a curse, as it is this day; 19 Pharaoh king of Egypt, his servants, his princes, and all his people; 20 all the mixed multitude, all the kings of the land of Uz, all the kings of the land of the Philistines (Ashkelon, Gaza, Ekron, and the remnant of Ashdod); 21 Edom, Moab, and the people of Ammon; 22 all the kings of Tyre, all the kings of Sidon, and the kings of the coastlands which are across the sea; 23 Dedan, Tema, Buz, and all who are in the wilderness; 24 all the kings of Zimri, all the kings of Elam, and all the kings of the Medes; 25 all the kings of the north, far and near, one with another; and all the kingdoms of the world which are on the face of the earth. Also the king of Sheshach shall drink after them. 26 Therefore you shall say to them, 'Thus says the LORD of hosts, the God of Israel: Drink, be drunk, and vomit! Fall, and rise no more, because of the sword which I will send among you.' 27 "And it shall be, if they refuse to take the cup from your hand to drink, then you shall say to them, 'Thus says the LORD of hosts: You shall certainly drink! 28 For behold, I begin to bring calamity on the city which is called by My name, and should you be utterly unpunished? You shall not be unpunished; for I will call for a sword on all the inhabitants of the earth, says the LORD of hosts 29 For behold, I am beginning to bring calamity on the city which is called by My name, and should you be utterly unpunished? You shall not be unpunished; for I will call for a sword on all the inhabitants of the earth, says the LORD of hosts. 30 "Therefore prophesy against them all these words, and say to them: 'The LORD will roar from on high, and utter His voice from His holy habitation; He will roar mightily against His fold; He will give a shout, as those who tread the grapes, against all the inhabitants of the earth. 31 A noise will come to the end of the earth; for the LORD has a controversy with the nations; He will plead His case with all flesh. He will give those who are wicked to the sword,' says the LORD. 32 "Thus says the LORD of hosts: 'Behold, disaster shall go forth from nation to nation, and a great whirlwind shall be raised up from the farthest parts of the earth. 33 And at that day the slain of the LORD shall be from one end of the earth even to the other end of the earth; they shall not be lamented, or gathered, or buried; they shall become refuse on the ground. 34 "Wail, shepherds, and cry! Roll about in the ashes, you leaders of the flock! For the days of your slaughter and your dispersions are fulfilled; you shall fall like a precious vessel. 35 And the shepherds will have no way to flee, nor the leaders of the flock to escape. 36 A voice of the cry of the shepherds and a wailing of the leaders of the flock will be heard; for the LORD has plundered their pasture. 37 And the peaceful dwellings are cut down because of the fierce anger of the LORD. 38 He has left His lair like the lion; for their land is desolate because of the fierceness of the oppressing sword and because of His fierce anger.'"

Chapter 26

At the beginning of the reign of Jehoiakim, son of Jehoiakim, king of Judah, the word of the LORD came to Jeremiah. The LORD instructed Jeremiah to stand in the courtyard of the House of the LORD and deliver a message to all the cities of Judah that came to worship there. Jeremiah was to convey every word commanded without omission. The message warned that if the people did not listen and change their ways, the LORD would bring a plague upon them due to their wickedness. If they failed to heed this warning, the LORD would make the House of the LORD like Shiloh and the city a curse to all nations The priests, prophets, and people heard Jeremiah's message, but when he finished speaking, they rebuked him and threatened him with death. They questioned why he prophesied that the house would become like Shiloh and the city desolate. The people gathered against Jeremiah in the House of the LORD. The princes of Judah, upon hearing these things, went to the House of the LORD and sat at the entrance of the new gate. The priests and prophets declared that Jeremiah deserved death for prophesying against the city Jeremiah replied, stating that the LORD had sent him to deliver this message. He urged them to change their ways so that the LORD might relent from the disaster he had pronounced. Jeremiah expressed his willingness to face their judgment, asserting that killing him would bring innocent blood upon them. The princes and people declared that Jeremiah was not worthy of death because he spoke in the name of the LORD Some elders reminded the assembly of the prophet Micah who had prophesied during King Hezekiah's reign, warning of destruction, yet Hezekiah had not put him to death. Instead, Hezekiah had prayed, and the LORD had relented. They suggested that if the people followed this example, they might also find deliverance. They mentioned a prophet named Urijah, who had prophesied similarly to Jeremiah and had been executed by King Jehoiakim. Despite this, Jeremiah was spared because Ahikam, son of Shaphan, protected him

Chapter 27

During the beginning of Jehoiakim's reign, the LORD instructed Jeremiah to make bonds and yokes and wear them around his neck. Jeremiah was to send these to the kings of Edom, Moab, Ammon, Tyre, and Sidon through the messengers who came to Jerusalem from King Zedekiah of Judah. He was to tell them that the LORD had given all lands to Nebuchadnezzar, king of Babylon, and that all nations should serve him. The LORD declared that any nation refusing to serve Nebuchadnezzar would face sword, famine, and pestilence Jeremiah also warned Zedekiah not to listen to false prophets who claimed that Babylon would not conquer Judah. He advised Zedekiah and the people to submit to Babylon to avoid destruction. Jeremiah foretold that the furnishings of the House of the LORD would be taken to Babylon and would remain there until the day the LORD would bring them back

Chapter 28

In the same year of Zedekiah's reign, Hananiah, a prophet from Gibeon, contradicted Jeremiah's prophecy. Hananiah declared that the LORD had broken Babylon's yoke and that within two years, all the temple furnishings and exiles would return. Jeremiah responded, acknowledging Hananiah's message but warned that only when such prophecies of peace come true would it be known that the LORD truly sent them Hananiah broke the yoke from Jeremiah's neck to symbolize the breaking of Babylon's dominion. In response, the LORD told Jeremiah that Hananiah had only broken wooden yokes and that the LORD would replace them with iron yokes, signifying the permanent yoke of Babylon. Jeremiah warned Hananiah of his false prophecy and declared that he would die within the year, which came to pass

Chapter 29

Jeremiah sent a letter to the exiles in Babylon, advising them to build houses, plant gardens, and seek the peace of the city where they had been carried. He instructed them not to listen to false prophets claiming a quick return, as the LORD had decreed a seventy-year period of exile. The LORD assured them that after this time, He would bring them back and fulfill His promise. He urged them to seek Him sincerely and promised to gather them from all nations and bring them back to their land Jeremiah also addressed false prophets like Ahab and Zedekiah, who would be punished by Nebuchadnezzar. He instructed the exiles to curse them, citing their wicked deeds and false prophecies. Jeremiah responded to a letter from Shemaiah the Nehelamite, who had falsely claimed the LORD's authority. The LORD declared that Shemaiah and his descendants would face punishment for their rebellion and deceit

Chapter 30

The LORD instructed Jeremiah to write all His words in a book, promising to restore Israel and Judah from captivity. Despite the current fear and suffering, the LORD assured that He would break their yoke and restore their land. He promised to raise up a king from David's line and bring peace and prosperity to His people The Chapter describes the intense suffering of the people due to their sins, but the LORD assured that their enemies would face judgment and their wounds would be healed. The city and its people would be rebuilt, and they would experience renewed blessings. The LORD declared that He would execute His plans and that His wrath would eventually lead to a greater understanding of His purpose

Chapter 31

At that time, declares the LORD, I will be the God of all the families of Israel, and they will be my people. The LORD says that those who survived the sword have found favor in the wilderness; they have gone to make Israel rest. The LORD appeared to me from afar, saying, "I have loved you with an everlasting love; therefore, I have drawn you with loving-kindness." "I will build you up again, and you will be rebuilt, O virgin Israel; you will again adorn yourself with tambourines and go out to dance with the joyful. Again, you will plant vineyards on the hills of Samaria; the farmers will plant them and enjoy their fruit." "There will be a day when the watchmen cry out on the hills of Ephraim, 'Arise, let us go up to Zion, to the LORD our God.'" For this is what the LORD says: "Sing with joy for Jacob; shout for the foremost of the nations. Make your praises heard, and say, 'O LORD, save your people, the remnant of Israel.'" "I will bring them from the land of the north and gather them from the ends of the earth. Among them will be the blind and the lame, expectant mothers and women in labor; a great throng will return. They will come with weeping; they will pray as I bring them back. I will lead them beside streams of water on a straight path where they will not stumble, for I am a father to Israel, and Ephraim is my firstborn son." "Hear the word of the LORD, you nations; proclaim it in distant coastlands: 'He who scattered Israel will gather them and will watch over his flock like a shepherd.'" "For the LORD will redeem Jacob and redeem them from the hand of those stronger than they. They will come and shout for joy on the heights of Zion; they will rejoice in the bounty of the LORD— the grain, the new wine, the olive oil, the young of the flocks and herds. They will be like a well-watered garden, and they will sorrow no more." "Then young women will dance and be glad, young men and old as well. I will turn their mourning into gladness; I will give them comfort and joy instead of sorrow. I will satisfy the priests with abundance, and my people will be filled with my bounty," declares the LORD This is what the LORD says: "A voice is heard in Ramah, mourning and great weeping, Rachel weeping for her children and refusing to be comforted, because they are no more." This is what the LORD says: "Restrain your voice from weeping and your eyes from tears, for your work will be rewarded," declares the LORD. "They will return from the land of the enemy." "So there is hope for your descendants," declares the LORD. "Your children will return to their own land." "I have heard Ephraim grieving: 'You disciplined me like an unruly calf; restore me, and I will return, for you are the LORD my God. After I was instructed, I repented; after I was taught, I beat my thigh; I was ashamed and confounded because I bore the disgrace of my youth.'" "Is Ephraim my dear son or the child I delight in? Though I often speak against him, I still remember him. Therefore my heart yearns for him; I will surely have compassion on him," declares the LORD "Set up road signs; put up guideposts. Take note of the highway, the road you take. Return, O virgin Israel, return to your towns. How long will you wander, O unfaithful daughter? The LORD will create a new thing on earth— a woman will surround a man." This is what the LORD Almighty, the God of Israel, says: "When I bring back the captives of Judah and its towns, they will again use these words: 'The LORD bless you, O righteous dwelling place, O holy mountain.'" "Judah and all its towns will live there together, the farmers and those who move about with their flocks. I will refresh the weary and satisfy the faint." "So I went to sleep and had a sweet dream." "The days are coming," declares the LORD, "when I will sow the house of Israel and the house of Judah with the seed of men and the seed of animals. Just as I watched over them to uproot and tear down, to overthrow, destroy, and bring disaster, so I will watch over them to build and to plant," declares the LORD "In those days people will no longer say, 'The fathers have eaten sour grapes, and the children's teeth are set on edge.' Instead, everyone will die for their own sin; whoever eats sour grapes—their own teeth will be set on edge." "The days are coming," declares the LORD, "when I will make a new covenant with the house of Israel and with the house of Judah. It will not be like the covenant I made with their ancestors when I took them by the hand to lead them out of Egypt, because they broke my covenant, though I was a husband to them," declares the LORD "This is the covenant I will make with the house of Israel after that time," declares the LORD. "I will put my law in their minds and write it on their hearts. I will be their God, and they will be my people. No longer will they teach their neighbor, or say to one another, 'Know the LORD,' because they will all know me, from the least of them to the greatest," declares the LORD. "For I will forgive their wickedness and will remember their sins no more." "This is what the LORD says, who gives the sun for light by day, who decrees the moon and the stars for light by night, who stirs up the sea so that its waves roar—the LORD Almighty is his name: 'Only if these decrees vanish from my sight,' declares the LORD, 'will the descendants of Israel ever cease to be a nation before me.'" "This is what the LORD says: 'Only if you can measure the heavens above and the foundations of the earth below, will I reject all the descendants of Israel because of all they have done,' declares the LORD." "The days are coming," declares the LORD, "when this city will be rebuilt for me from the Tower of Hananel to the Corner Gate. The measuring line will stretch from there straight to the hill of Gareb and then turn to Goath. The whole valley where dead bodies and ashes are thrown, and all the fields as far as the Kidron Valley, to the corner of the horse gate toward the east, will be holy to the LORD. The city will never again be uprooted or demolished."

Chapter 32

The word that came to Jeremiah from the LORD in the tenth year of Zedekiah king of Judah, which was the eighteenth year of Nebuchadnezzar. The king of Babylon was then besieging Jerusalem, and Jeremiah the prophet was confined in the courtyard of the guard in the royal palace of Judah. Zedekiah king of Judah had imprisoned him, saying, "Why do you prophesy as you do? You say, 'This is what the LORD says: I am about to give this city into the hand of the king of Babylon, and he will capture it.'" "Zedekiah king of Judah will not escape from the Babylonians but will certainly be delivered into the hand of the king of Babylon. He will speak with him face to face and see him eye to eye. He will go to Babylon, where he will remain until I deal with him," declares the LORD. "If you fight against the Babylonians, you will not succeed." Jeremiah said, "The word of the LORD came to me: 'Hanamel son of Shallum your uncle is going to come to you and say, "Buy my field at Anathoth, because as nearest relative it is your right and duty to buy it."'" "Then, just as the LORD had said, my cousin Hanamel came to me in the courtyard of the guard and said, 'Buy my field at Anathoth in the territory of Benjamin, since it is your right to redeem it and possess it. Buy it for yourself.' I knew that this was the word of the LORD." "So I bought the field at Anathoth from my cousin Hanamel and weighed out for him seventeen shekels of silver. I signed and sealed the deed, had it witnessed, and weighed out the silver on the scales. I took the deed of purchase—the sealed copy containing the terms and conditions, as well as the unsealed copy—and gave them to Baruch son of Neriah, the son of Maaseiah. I did this in the presence of my cousin Hanamel and of the witnesses who had signed the deed, and of all the Jews sitting in the courtyard of the guard." "In their presence I gave Baruch these instructions: 'This is what the LORD Almighty, the God of Israel, says: Take these documents, both the sealed and the unsealed copies of the deed of purchase, and put them in a clay jar so they will last a long time. For this is what the LORD Almighty, the God of Israel, says: "Houses, fields, and vineyards will again be bought in this land."'" "After I had given the deed of purchase to Baruch son of Neriah, I prayed to the LORD: 'Ah, Sovereign LORD, you have made the heavens and the earth by your great power and outstretched arm. Nothing is too hard for you. You show love to thousands but bring the punishment for the fathers' sins into the laps of their children after them. Great and mighty God, whose name is the LORD Almighty, great are your purposes and mighty are your deeds. Your eyes are open to all the ways of men; you reward everyone according to his conduct and as his deeds deserve. You performed miraculous signs and wonders in Egypt and have continued them to this day, both in Israel and among all mankind. You have gained renown that is still yours. You brought your people Israel out of Egypt with signs and wonders, by a mighty hand and an outstretched arm and with great terror. You gave them this land you had sworn to give their forefathers, a land flowing with milk and honey. They came in and took possession of it, but they did not obey you or follow your law; they did not do what you commanded them to do. So you brought all this disaster upon them. See how the siege ramps are built up to take the city. Because of the sword, famine, and plague, the city will be given into the hands of the Babylonians who are attacking it. What you said has happened, as you now see. And though the city will be given into the hands of the Babylonians, you, Sovereign LORD, say to me, "Buy the field with silver and have the transaction witnessed."'" "Then the word of the LORD came to Jeremiah: 'I am the LORD, the God of all mankind. Is anything too hard for me? Therefore, this is what the LORD says: I am about to give this city into the hands of the Babylonians and to Nebuchadnezzar king of Babylon. He will capture it. The Babylonians who are attacking this city will come in and set it on fire; they will burn it down, along with the houses where the people have provoked me to anger by burning incense on the roofs to Baal and by pouring out drink offerings to other gods. The people of Israel and Judah have done nothing but evil in my sight from their youth; indeed, the people of Israel have done nothing but provoke me with what their hands have made, declares the LORD. From the day it was built until now, this city has so aroused my anger and wrath that I must remove it from my sight. The people of Israel and Judah have provoked me by all the evil they have done—they, their kings and officials, their priests and prophets, the people of Judah and those living in Jerusalem. They turned their backs to me and not their faces; though I taught them again and again, they would not listen or respond to discipline. They set up their abominations in the house that bears my Name and defiled it. They built high places for Baal in the Valley of Ben Hinnom to sacrifice their sons and daughters to Molech, though I never commanded—nor did it enter my mind—that they should do such a detestable thing and so make Judah sin.'" "So this is what the Sovereign LORD says: 'The God of Israel says: I will surely gather them from all the lands where I banish them in my fierce anger and great wrath; I will bring them back to this place and let them live in safety. They will be my people, and I will be their God. I will give them singleness of heart and action, so that they will always fear me for their own good and the good of their children after them. I will make an everlasting covenant with them: I will never stop doing good to them, and I will inspire them to fear me, so that they will never turn away from me. I will rejoice in doing them good and will assuredly plant them in this land with all my heart and soul.'" "This is what the LORD says: 'As I have brought all this great calamity on this people, so I will give them all the prosperity I have promised them. Once more fields will be bought in this land of which you say, "It is a desolate waste, without men or animals, for it has been given into the hands of the Babylonians." Fields will be bought for silver, and deeds will be signed, sealed, and witnessed in the territory of Benjamin, in the villages around Jerusalem, in the towns of Judah, and in the hill country, the western foothills and the Negev, because I will restore their fortunes, declares the LORD.'"

CHAPTER 33

Moreover, the word of the LORD came to Jeremiah a second time while he was still confined in the prison yard, saying, "Thus says the LORD, the Maker of it, the LORD who formed it and established it— the LORD is His name: 'Call to me, and I will answer you, and will show you great and mighty things which you do not know. For thus says the LORD God of Israel concerning the houses of this city and the houses of the kings of Judah, which are torn down to make a defense against the siege ramps and the sword: They come to fight with the Chaldeans, but it is to be filled with the dead bodies of the men whom I have slain in my anger and wrath, because I have hidden my face from this city because of all their wickedness Behold, I will bring health and healing to it; I will heal them and reveal to them the abundance of peace and truth. I will bring back the captivity of Judah and the captivity of Israel, and will rebuild them as before. I will cleanse them from all their iniquities by which they have sinned against Me; and I will pardon all their iniquities by which they have rebelled against Me. It will be to Me a name of joy, praise, and honor before all the nations of the earth, who shall hear of all the good that I do for them; they shall fear and tremble for all the goodness and prosperity I provide to this city Thus says the LORD: 'In this place of which you say, "It is desolate, without man or beast," in the cities of Judah and in the streets of Jerusalem, that are desolate, without man, without inhabitants, and without beasts, there shall yet be heard the voice of joy and the voice of gladness, the voice of the bridegroom and the voice of the bride, the voice of those who will say, "Give thanks to the LORD of hosts, for the LORD is good, for His mercy endures forever," and of those who will bring offerings of thanksgiving to the house of the LORD. For I will bring back the captivity of the land as at the first,' says the LORD."

CHAPTER 34

The word that came to Jeremiah from the LORD (when Nebuchadnezzar king of Babylon, and all his army, and all the kingdoms of the earth, which were under his power, and all the peoples fought against Jerusalem and against all her cities) says, "Thus says the LORD God of Israel, 'Go and speak to Zedekiah king of Judah, and say to him, Thus says the LORD: Behold, I will give this city into the hand of the king of Babylon, and he shall burn it with fire. And you shall not escape his hand, but shall surely be taken and delivered into his hand. Your eyes shall see the face of the king of Babylon, and he shall speak with you

604

mouth to mouth, and you shall go to Babylon. However, hear the word of the LORD, O Zedekiah king of Judah: Thus says the LORD concerning you, You shall not die by the sword, but you shall die in peace. And as they burned incense for your fathers, the former kings who were before you, so shall they burn incense for you and lament, saying, "Alas, my lord!" For I have spoken the word,' says the LORD." Then the prophet Jeremiah spoke all these words to Zedekiah king of Judah in Jerusalem, when the army of the king of Babylon was fighting against Jerusalem and against all the cities of Judah that were left, that is, against Lachish and against Azekah, for these strong cities were left among the cities of Judah This is the word that came to Jeremiah from the LORD after King Zedekiah had made a proclamation to all the people in Jerusalem: "That every man should let his servant go free, and every man his handmaid, whether Hebrew or Hebrewess, so that no one should make them a slave, that is, a Jew his brother." Now when all the princes and all the people who had entered into the covenant heard that every man should let his servant go free and every man his handmaid, and that no one should make them a slave, they obeyed and let them go. But afterward they changed their minds and took back the servants and handmaids whom they had let go, and forced them to be servants and handmaids again Therefore, the word of the LORD came to Jeremiah from the LORD, saying, "Thus says the LORD, the God of Israel: I made a covenant with your fathers when I brought them out of the land of Egypt, from the house of bondage, saying, 'At the end of seven years, let every man set free his Hebrew brother who has been sold to you, and when he has served you six years, you shall let him go free from you.' But your fathers did not obey Me or incline their ear. Now you had turned and done what was right in My sight by proclaiming liberty each man to his neighbor, and you had made a covenant before Me in the house that is called by My name. But you turned around and profaned My name, and every one of you brought back his servant and made them subject again to be your servants and handmaids Therefore, thus says the LORD: 'You have not obeyed Me in proclaiming liberty every man to his brother and every man to his neighbor. Behold, I proclaim liberty to you,' says the LORD, 'to the sword, to pestilence, and to famine; and I will make you a horror to all the kingdoms of the earth. And I will give the men who have transgressed My covenant, who have not performed the words of the covenant which they made before Me when they cut the calf in two and passed between its parts, I will give them into the hand of their enemies and into the hand of those who seek their lives; and their dead bodies shall be food for the birds of the heaven and the beasts of the earth.' Zedekiah king of Judah and his princes I will give into the hand of their enemies, into the hand of those who seek their lives, and into the hand of the army of the king of Babylon, which has withdrawn from you. Behold, I will command,' says the LORD, 'and cause them to return to this city. They shall fight against it, take it, and burn it with fire. And I will make the cities of Judah a desolation without inhabitant.'"

CHAPTER 35

The word that came to Jeremiah from the LORD in the days of Jehoiakim the son of Josiah, king of Judah, saying, "Go to the house of the Rechabites, speak to them, and bring them into the house of the LORD, into one of the chambers, and give them wine to drink." So I took Jaazaniah the son of Jeremiah, the son of Habazziniah, and his brothers and all his sons, and the whole house of the Rechabites, and I brought them into the house of the LORD, into the chamber of the sons of Hanan the son of Igdaliah, a man of God, which was by the chamber of the princes, which was above the chamber of Maaseiah the son of Shallum, the keeper of the threshold. Then I set before the sons of the house of the Rechabites bowls full of wine and cups, and I said to them, "Drink wine." But they said, "We will drink no wine, for Jonadab the son of Rechab, our father, commanded us, 'You shall drink no wine, you nor your sons, forever. You shall not build a house, sow seed, plant vineyards, nor have any; but all your days you shall dwell in tents, that you may live many days in the land where you are strangers.' So we have obeyed the voice of Jonadab the son of Rechab, our father, in all that he commanded us. We have drunk no wine all our days, we, our wives, our sons, or our daughters. We have not built houses to dwell in, nor do we have vineyard, field, or seed. But we have dwelt in tents and have obeyed and done according to all that Jonadab our father commanded us But it came to pass, when Nebuchadnezzar king of Babylon came up into the land, that we said, 'Come, and let us go to Jerusalem from the army of the Chaldeans and from the army of the Syrians'; so we have remained in Jerusalem." Then the word of the LORD came to Jeremiah, saying, "Thus says the LORD of hosts, the God of Israel: 'Go and tell the men of Judah and the inhabitants of Jerusalem, "Will you not receive instruction to obey My words?" says the LORD. The command of Jonadab the son of Rechab, which he commanded his sons, to drink no wine, has been performed; for to this day they drink none, but obey their father's command. But I have spoken to you, rising early and speaking, yet you have not obeyed Me. I have also sent to you all My servants the prophets, rising up early and sending them, saying, "Turn now every one from his evil way, amend your doings, and do not go after other gods to serve them; then you will dwell in the land that I have given to you and your fathers." But you have not inclined your ear nor heeded Me. Surely the sons of Jonadab the son of Rechab have performed the commandment of their father which he commanded them, but this people has not obeyed Me.' Therefore thus says the LORD God of hosts, the God of Israel: 'Behold, I will bring on Judah and on all the inhabitants of Jerusalem all the doom that I have pronounced against them, because I have spoken to them, but they have not heard; and I have called to them, but they have not answered.'" Then Jeremiah said to the house of the Rechabites, "Thus says the LORD of hosts, the God of Israel: 'Because you have obeyed the commandment of Jonadab your father, and kept all his precepts, and done according to all that he commanded you, therefore thus says the LORD of hosts, the God of Israel: Jonadab the son of Rechab shall not lack a man to stand before Me forever.'"

Chapter 36

In the fourth year of Jehoiakim, the son of Jehoiaiah, king of Judah, the word of the LORD came to Jeremiah, saying, "Take a scroll or a book and write down for us all the words that I have spoken to you against Israel, against Judah, and against all the nations, from the day that I spoke to you, that is, from the days of Jehoiakim until today. It may be that the house of Judah will learn of all that I have determined to do against them, that each one may return from his way, to forgive their iniquities and their sins." Then Jeremiah called Baruch, the son of Neriah, and Baruch wrote down by the mouth of Jeremiah all the words of the LORD, which he had addressed to him, on a scroll or book. Jeremiah commanded Baruch to say, "I am shut up and cannot enter the house of the LORD. Therefore, go and take up the scroll wherein you have written by my mouth the words of the LORD before the people, in the House of the LORD, on the day of fasting; you shall also take it up again in the hearing of all Judah, which comes forth out of their cities. It may be that they will pray before the LORD, and each one will return from his way, for great is the wrath and anger which the LORD has declared against this people." So Baruch, the son of Neriah, did all that the prophet Jeremiah had commanded him, reading in the book the words of the LORD in the house of the LORD. In the fifth year of Jehoiakim, the son of Josiah, king of Judah, in the ninth month, they proclaimed a fast before the LORD for all the people of Jerusalem and for all the people who came from the cities of Judah to Jerusalem Then Baruch read the words of Jeremiah in the house of the LORD, in the chamber of Gemariah, the son of Shaphan the secretary, in the inner court, at the entrance to the new gate of the house of the LORD, in the presence of all the people. When Michaiah, the son of Gemariah, the son of Shaphan, had heard from the book all the words of the LORD, he went down into the king's house, into the chancellor's room, where all the princes were seated: Elishama the chancellor, Delaiah the son of Shemaiah, Elnathan the son of Achbor, Gemariah the son of Shaphan, Zedekiah the son of Hananiah, and all the princes Then Michaiah reported to them all the words he had heard when Baruch had read the book before the people. Therefore, all the princes sent Jehudi, the son of Nethaniah, the son of Shelemiah, the son of Chushi, to Baruch, saying, "Take in your hand the scroll that you read among the people and come." Jehudi took the scroll from Baruch and came to them. They said to him, "Sit down and read it again, that we may hear." So Baruch read it among them When they had heard all the words, they were afraid and said to Baruch, "We must report all these words to the king." They examined Baruch and asked him, "Tell us, how did you write all these words at his mouth?" Baruch answered them, "He has spoken all these words to me with his mouth, and I have written them outright in the book." Then the princes said to Baruch, "Go away, hide yourself, you and Jeremiah, and let no one know where you are." They went into the king's court, but deposited the scroll in the chamber of Elishama, the chancellor, and reported all the words to the king, so that he might hear Then the king sent Jehudi to fetch the scroll. He took it from the chamber of Elishama, the chancellor, and Jehudi read it to the king and to all the princes who stood beside the king. The king was in the winter house, in the ninth month, and a fire was burning before him. When Jehudi had read three or four columns, he cut them off with his knife and threw them into the fire, until the whole scroll was consumed in the fire Yet neither the king nor his servants, who heard all these words, were frightened or tore their garments. Nevertheless, Elnathan, Delaiah, and Gemariah had begged the king not to burn the scroll, but he would not listen to them. The king commanded Jerahmeel, the son of Hammelech, and Saraiah, the son of Azriel, and Shemiah, the son of Abdiel, to take Baruch the scribe and Jeremiah the prophet; but the LORD hid them Then the word of the LORD came to Jeremiah, after the king had burned the scroll and the words that Baruch had written by the mouth of Jeremiah, saying, "Take again another scroll and write in it all the former words that were in the first scroll that Jehoiakim, king of Judah, burned. And you shall say to Jehoiakim, king of Judah, 'Thus says the LORD: You have burned this scroll, saying, "Why have you written thereon that the king of Babylon shall surely come and destroy this land, and shall take away from it men and beasts?" Therefore, thus says the LORD concerning Jehoiakim, king of Judah: "He shall have no one to sit on the throne of David, and his corpse shall be cast out in the heat by day and in the frost by night. I will punish him and his descendants and his servants for their iniquities, and I will bring upon them and upon the inhabitants of Jerusalem and upon the men of Judah all the evil that I have pronounced against them, but they would not listen."'" Then Jeremiah took another scroll and gave it to Baruch, the scribe, the son of Neriah, who wrote on it all the words of the book that Jehoiakim, king of Judah, had burned in the fire, adding to it many similar words

Chapter 37

King Zedekiah, the son of Jehoiakim, reigned over Coniah, the son of Jehoiakim, whom Nebuchadnezzar, king of Babylon, had made king in the land of Judah. But neither he nor his servants nor the people of the land would obey the words of the LORD, spoken by the prophet Jeremiah King Zedekiah sent Jehucal, the son of Shelemiah, and Zephaniah, the son of Maaseiah the priest, to the prophet Jeremiah, saying, "Pray now to the LORD our God for us." (Now Jeremiah went in and out among the people, because they had not put him in prison.) Then Pharaoh's army came out of Egypt, and when the Chaldeans who were besieging Jerusalem heard of it, they left Jerusalem. Then the word of the LORD came to the prophet Jeremiah, saying, "Thus says the LORD, the God of Israel: 'You shall say to the king of Judah who sent you to me to ask me, "Behold, Pharaoh's army, which has come to help you, will return to Egypt to their own land. The Chaldeans will come again and fight against this city, and they will take it and burn it with fire."'" Thus says the LORD: "Do not deceive yourselves by saying, 'The Chaldeans will surely leave here, for they will not leave.' For even if you had struck down the whole army of the Chaldeans fighting against you and there were only wounded men among them, every man should get up in his tent and burn this city with fire." When the army of the Chaldeans had been driven away from Jerusalem because of Pharaoh's army, Jeremiah went out of Jerusalem to go to the land of Benjamin, separating himself from the people. When he was at the gate of Benjamin, there was a chief officer, whose name was Irijah, son of Shemiah, son of Hananiah, who questioned Jeremiah the prophet, saying, "You are fleeing to the Chaldeans." Then Jeremiah said, "It is false, I am not fleeing to the Chaldeans," but he would not listen; so Irijah took Jeremiah and led him to the princes. Therefore, the princes were angry with Jeremiah, and struck him, and put him in prison in the house of Jehonathan the scribe, for they had made that prison When Jeremiah was brought into the prison and the dungeon and stayed there for a long time, Zedekiah got in touch with Jehonathan, and King Zedekiah sent for him and brought him out; and the king questioned him secretly in his house and said to him, "Is there any word from the LORD?" And Jeremiah answered, "Yes, for you will be delivered into the hands of the king of Babylon." Moreover, Jeremiah said to King Zedekiah, "What have I offended against you, or against your servants, or against this people, that you have put me in prison? Where are now your prophets who prophesied to you, saying, 'The king of Babylon will not come against you and against this land'? Therefore, hear now, I pray you, O my lord the king: let my supplication, I pray you, be accepted before you, that you cause me not to return to the house of Jonathan the scribe, that I die not there." Then King Zedekiah commanded that they should commit Jeremiah to the court of the prison and that they should give him a piece of bread daily from the baker's street until all the bread in the city was spent. Thus Jeremiah remained in the court of the prison

Chapter 38

Shephatiah, the son of Mattan, Gedaliah, the son of Pashur, Jucal, the son of Shelemiah, and Pashur, the son of Malchijah, heard the words that Jeremiah had spoken to all the people, saying, "Thus says the LORD: 'He who remains in this city shall die by the sword, by famine, and by pestilence, but he who goes out to the Chaldeans shall live; he shall have his life as a prey, and live.'" Thus says the LORD: "This city shall surely be given into the hand of the army of the king of Babylon, and he shall take it." Then the princes said to the king, "We beseech you, let this man be put to death, for thus he weakens the hands of the men of war who remain in this city and the hands of all the people, by speaking such words to them. For this man does not seek the welfare of this people, but their hurt." Then King Zedekiah said, "Behold, he is in your hand, for the king is powerless against you." So they took Jeremiah and cast him into the dungeon of Malchijah the king's son, which was in the court of the prison. They let down Jeremiah with ropes, and in the dungeon there was no water but mire, so Jeremiah sank into the mire Now Ebed-melech, the Ethiopian, one of the king's eunuchs, who was in the king's house, heard that they had put Jeremiah into the dungeon. The king was sitting at the gate of Benjamin. Ebed-melech went out of the king's house and spoke to the king, saying, "My lord the king, these men have done evil in all that they have done to Jeremiah the prophet, whom they have cast into the dungeon. He is likely to die from hunger in the place where he is, for there is no more bread in the city." Then the king commanded Ebed-melech the Ethiopian, saying, "Take from here thirty men with you, and take up Jeremiah the prophet out of the dungeon before he dies." So Ebed-melech took the men with him and went into the house of the king under the treasury, and took old rags and worn-out clothes from there, and let them down by ropes into the dungeon to Jeremiah Ebed-melech the Ethiopian said to Jeremiah, "Put these old rags and worn-out clothes under your armpits under the ropes." And Jeremiah did so. So they drew up Jeremiah with ropes and took him out of the dungeon. And Jeremiah remained in the court of the prison Then Zedekiah the king sent for Jeremiah the prophet and received him at the third entrance that is in the house of the LORD. And the king said to Jeremiah, "I will ask you a thing; hide nothing from me." Jeremiah said to Zedekiah, "If I tell you, will you not surely put me to death? And if I give you counsel, will you not listen to me?" So King Zedekiah swore secretly to Jeremiah, saying, "As the LORD lives, who made us this soul, I will not put you to death, neither will I give you into the hand of these men that seek your life." Then Jeremiah said to Zedekiah, "Thus says the LORD, the God of hosts, the God of Israel: 'If you will go forth to the king of Babylon's princes, then your soul shall live, and this city shall not be burned with fire, and you shall live, and your house. But if you will not go forth to the king of Babylon's princes, then this city shall be given into the hand of the Chaldeans, and they shall burn it with fire, and you shall not escape out of their hand.'" And Zedekiah the king said to Jeremiah, "I am afraid of the Jews that are fallen to the Chaldeans, lest they deliver me into their hand, and they mock me." But Jeremiah said, "They shall not deliver you. Obey, I beseech you, the voice of the LORD, which I speak unto you: so it shall be well unto you, and your soul shall live. But if you refuse to go forth, this is the word that the LORD has showed me: 'Behold, all the women that are left in the king of Judah's house shall be brought forth to the king of Babylon's princes, and those women shall say, "Your friends have set you on, and have prevailed against you: your feet are sunk in the mire, and they are turned away back." So they shall bring out all your wives and your children to the Chaldeans, and you shall not escape out of their hand, but shall be taken by the hand of the king of Babylon, and this city shall be burned with fire.'" Then Zedekiah said to Jeremiah, "Let no man know of these words, and you shall not die. But if the princes hear that I have talked with you, and they come to you, and say to you, 'Declare unto us now what you have said unto the king, hide it not from us, and we will not put you to death;' also what the king said unto you; then you shall say unto them, 'I presented my supplication before the king, that he would not cause me to return to Jonathan's house, to die there.'" Then came all the princes unto Jeremiah, and asked him; and he told them according to all these words that the king had commanded. So they left off speaking with him, for the matter was not perceived. So Jeremiah abode in the court of the prison until the day that Jerusalem was taken, and he was there when Jerusalem was taken

Chapter 39

In the ninth year of Zedekiah, king of Judah, in the tenth month, came Nebuchadnezzar, king of Babylon, and all his army against Jerusalem, and they besieged it. In the eleventh year of Zedekiah, in the fourth month, the ninth day of the month, the city was broken up And all the princes of the king of Babylon came in, and sat in the middle gate, even Nergal-sharezer, Samgar-nebu, Sarsechim, Rab-saris, Nergal-sharezer, Rab-mag, with all the residue of the princes of the king of Babylon And it came to pass, that when Zedekiah, the king of Judah, saw them, and all the men of war, then they fled, and went forth out of the city by night, by the way of the king's garden, by the gate between the two walls: and he went out the way of the plain But the Chaldean's army pursued after them, and overtook Zedekiah in the plains of Jericho; and when they had taken him, they brought him up to Nebuchadnezzar, king of Babylon, to Riblah in the land of Hamath, where he gave judgment upon him Then the king of Babylon slew the sons of Zedekiah in Riblah before his eyes; also the king of Babylon slew all the nobles of Judah. Moreover he put out Zedekiah's eyes, and bound him with chains, to carry him to Babylon And the Chaldeans burned the king's house, and the house of the people, with fire, and broke down the walls of Jerusalem. Then Nebuzaradan, the captain of the guard, carried away captive into Babylon the remnant of the people that remained in the city, and those that fell away, that fell to him, with the rest of the people that remained But Nebuzaradan, the captain of the guard, left of the poor of the people, which had nothing, in the land of Judah, and gave them vineyards and fields at the same time Now Nebuchadnezzar, king of Babylon, gave charge concerning Jeremiah to Nebuzaradan, the captain of the guard, saying, "Take him, and look well to him, and do him no harm; but do unto him even as he shall say unto thee." So Nebuzaradan, the captain of the guard, sent, and Nebushasban, Rabsaris, Nergal-sharezer, Rab-mag, and all the king of Babylon's princes; even they sent, and took Jeremiah out of the court of the prison, and committed him unto Gedaliah, the son of Ahikam, the son of Shaphan, that he should carry him home, and he dwelt among the people Now the word of the LORD came unto Jeremiah, while he was shut up in the court of the prison, saying, "Go and speak to Ebed-melech the Ethiopian, saying, 'Thus says the LORD of hosts, the God of Israel: "Behold, I will bring my words upon this city for evil, and not for good; and they shall be accomplished in that day before you. But I will deliver you in that day, says the LORD, and you shall not be given into the hand of the men of whom you are afraid. For I will surely deliver you, and you shall not fall by the sword, but your life shall be for a prey unto you, because you have put your trust in me, says the LORD."'

Chapter 40

The word that came to Jeremiah from the LORD after Nebuzaradan, the captain of the guard, had let him go from Ramah, when he had taken him, being bound in chains among all that were carried away captive of Jerusalem and Judah, which were carried away captive unto Babylon And the captain of the guard took Jeremiah, and said unto him, "The LORD your God hath pronounced this evil upon this place. Now the LORD hath brought it, and done according as he hath said: because you have sinned against the LORD, and have not obeyed his voice, therefore this thing is come upon you And now, behold, I loose thee this day from the chains which were upon your hand. If it seem good unto you to come with me into Babylon, come, and I will look well unto you: but if it seem ill unto you to come with me into Babylon, forbear: behold, all the land is before you: whither it seemeth good and convenient for you to go, thither go." Now while he was not yet gone back, he said, "Go back also to Gedaliah the son of Ahikam, the son of Shaphan, whom the king of Babylon hath made governor over the cities of Judah, and dwell with him among the people: or go wheresoever it seemeth convenient unto you to go." So the captain of the guard gave him victuals and a reward, and let him go. Then went Jeremiah unto Gedaliah the son of Ahikam to Mizpah, and dwelt with him among the people that were left in the land

CHAPTER 41

In the seventh month, Ishmael the son of Nethaniah, a member of the royal family and one of the king's princes, along with ten men, went to Mizpah to see Gedaliah the son of Ahikam. They shared a meal together there However, Ishmael and his companions betrayed Gedaliah. They struck him with the sword, killing him, along with all the Jews and Chaldeans who were with him in Mizpah. This act of violence also included the men of war On the following day, when the news of Gedaliah's death had not yet reached others, a group of about four hundred and sixty men arrived from Shechem, Shiloh, and Samaria. They had shaved their beards, torn their garments, and cut themselves, bringing offerings and incense to present at the house of the LORD Ishmael went out to meet them, weeping as he approached. When he met them, he deceitfully invited them to come see Gedaliah. Upon their arrival in the city, Ishmael killed them and threw their bodies into a pit he had previously filled with the slain from Gedaliah's murder Among the victims were ten men who pleaded for their lives, claiming they had treasures in the fields, including wheat, barley, oil, and honey. Ishmael spared them because of their valuable goods, leaving them with their fellow captives Ishmael's next action was to take captive all the remaining people in Mizpah, including the king's daughters and all those who had been entrusted to Gedaliah by Nebuzaradan, the chief steward. He then set out to take them to the Ammonites When Iohanan the son of Kareah and the captains of the army learned of Ishmael's actions, they gathered their men and pursued him. They found him by the great waters at Gibeon. When the captives saw Iohanan and his men, they rejoiced and returned to them Ishmael, however, fled with eight men to the Ammonites. Iohanan and his captains then took the remaining captives, including the women, children, and those who had been taken from Mizpah, and settled at Geruth Chimham, near Bethlehem,

preparing to go into Egypt due to their fear of the Chaldeans. They were apprehensive because of Ishmael's actions against Gedaliah, whom the king of Babylon had appointed as governor

CHAPTER 42

The captains of the army—Iohanan son of Kareah, Jezaniah son of Hoshaaiah, and all the people from the least to the greatest—approached Jeremiah the prophet and asked him to pray to the LORD their God for them. They were a remnant of many and sought guidance on what they should do Jeremiah agreed to pray to the LORD according to their request and promised to reveal whatever the LORD said, withholding nothing They then pledged to obey whatever the LORD commanded, whether good or evil, hoping it would go well with them if they followed the LORD's will After ten days, the word of the LORD came to Jeremiah. He called for Iohanan, the captains, and all the people and delivered the message from the LORD. The LORD promised to build and plant them if they remained in the land, and not to destroy them, as He had previously planned. He assured them that they should not fear the king of Babylon because He would protect and deliver them from him However, if they chose to go to Egypt, the LORD warned that the sword, famine, and pestilence they feared would overtake them there. The LORD's wrath would be poured out upon them in Egypt, leading to their destruction and making them a curse among the nations The LORD had already warned them of their disobedience in seeking to go to Egypt, which would result in their downfall. They would face severe consequences in Egypt for rejecting the LORD's guidance

CHAPTER 43

When Jeremiah spoke all the words that the LORD had commanded, some of the proud men, including Azariah the son of Hoshaiah and Iohanan the son of Kareah, accused him of speaking falsely. They claimed that the LORD had not sent him to say not to go to Egypt. They believed that Baruch the son of Neriah had incited Jeremiah against them, intending to deliver them to the Chaldeans for destruction Despite the prophecy, Iohanan and the captains of the army, along with all the people, chose not to obey the LORD's command and decided to go to Egypt They took with them the remnant of Judah who had returned from various nations, including men, women, children, and the king's daughters, and settled in Tahpanhes, Egypt The LORD then instructed Jeremiah in Tahpanhes to take large stones and hide them in the brick pavement at the entrance of Pharaoh's house. He was to declare that Nebuchadnezzar, the king of Babylon, would come and set his throne upon these stones. He would strike Egypt, leading those destined for death, captivity, or the sword to their respective fates. The LORD also foretold that Nebuchadnezzar would burn the idols of Egypt and devastate its land

CHAPTER 44

The word of the LORD came to Jeremiah regarding all the Israelites in Egypt, including those in Migdol, Tahpanhes, Noph, and Pathros. The LORD spoke of the desolation that had come upon Jerusalem and Judah due to their wickedness, as they had provoked Him by worshiping other gods Despite the warnings sent through His prophets, the people had not heeded the LORD's message. Their disobedience and idol worship had led to the devastation of their cities and the LORD's wrath The LORD questioned why they continued to commit these grave sins, removing themselves from Judah and worshiping other gods in Egypt. This act would bring destruction upon them and make them a curse among nations

The LORD reminded them of their ancestors' wickedness and the failure to humble themselves or follow His laws. As a result, He promised to destroy all of Judah who had gone to Egypt, leaving them to die by sword, famine, or pestilence The people of Judah in Egypt had refused to listen to the LORD's words through Jeremiah and had vowed to continue their idolatry, believing that their previous prosperity was due to their worship of the queen of heaven Jeremiah pointed out that the LORD had seen their actions and would not tolerate their continued disobedience. The land of Egypt would face the same judgment as Jerusalem, and none of the remnant of Judah would return to their land, except for a few who might escape

CHAPTER 45

The words addressed to Baruch the son of Neriah were spoken by Jeremiah in the fourth year of Jehoiakim, king of Judah. Baruch had expressed his distress over the LORD's message, feeling that his grief had been exacerbated and that he found no peace Jeremiah conveyed the LORD's response to Baruch: The LORD would bring about destruction, including what He had built and planted, as He had done with the earth. Baruch was advised not to seek great things for himself, as the LORD would bring calamity upon all flesh. However, Baruch's life would be spared wherever he went, as a reward for his faithfulness

CHAPTER 46

The Lord's message came to the prophet Jeremiah concerning the nations, including Egypt. This was directed against the army of Pharaoh Necho, king of Egypt, who was stationed by the river Perath at Carchemish. Nebuchadnezzar, king of Babylon, defeated this army in the fourth year of Jehoiakim, son of Jehoiachin, king of Judah The Lord said, "Prepare your armor and shield, and ready yourselves for battle. Prepare the horses, equip the horsemen, prepare the spears, and put on the armor." Why did I see them terrified and retreating? Their strong men were stricken, they fled and did not look back; fear surrounded them, says the Lord. The swift will not flee, and the strong will not escape; they will stumble and fall toward the north by the river Perath "Who is this that comes like a flood, whose waters surge like a river?" Egypt rises like a flood, and its waters surge like a river. It says, "I will ascend, and I will cover the earth; I will destroy the city and those who dwell in it." Hurry, horses, rage, chariots, and let the valiant men come, the black men of Moab, the shield-bearing Lyophiles, and the bow-wielding and bow-bending Lyophiles For this is the day of the Lord God of hosts, a day of vengeance to avenge His enemies. The sword will devour and be sated, made drunk with their blood, for the Lord God of hosts has a sacrifice in the land of the north, by the river Perath "Go to Gilead and fetch balm, O Virgin daughter of Egypt; there is no cure for you." The nations have heard of your shame, and your crying has filled the earth. For the strong have stumbled against the strong, and they have both fallen together This is the message that the Lord gave to Jeremiah the prophet about how Nebuchadnezzar, king of Babylon, would come to strike the land of Egypt. "Proclaim in Egypt and declare in Migdol, Noph, and Tahpanhes, and say, 'Stand firm and prepare yourself, for the sword will surround you.' Why have your valiant men been swept away? They could not stand, for the Lord made them weak. He caused many to fall, and one fell upon another. They said, 'Let us return to our people and to the land of our origin from the sword of the oppressor.'" "There they cried, 'Pharaoh, king of Egypt, is but a great multitude; he has exceeded the appointed time.' As I live, says the King, whose name

is the Lord of hosts, surely as Tabor is on the mountains and as Carmel is by the sea, so shall it be. O daughter dwelling in Egypt, prepare to go into captivity, for Noph will be forsaken and desolate, without inhabitants." "Egypt is like a beautiful calf, but destruction comes; from the north it comes. Her servants are like fat calves in her midst; they too have turned back and fled together. They could not stand, for the day of their destruction has come upon them, the time of their visitation." "Her flight will be like that of a serpent, as they march with an army and come against her with axes like woodcutters. They shall cut down her forest, says the Lord, for they cannot be counted; they are more numerous than you fruit and vegetable sellers. The daughter of Egypt shall be put to shame; she shall be delivered into the hands of the northern peoples." Thus says the Lord of hosts, the God of Israel: "Behold, I will visit the common people of No, Pharaoh, and Egypt, with their gods and kings, Pharaoh and all who trust in him. I will deliver them into the hands of those who seek their lives, into the hands of Nebuchadnezzar, king of Babylon, and his servants. Afterwards, they shall dwell as they used to, says the Lord." "But do not fear, O Jacob, my servant, and do not be afraid, O Israel. For behold, I will deliver you from a far country and your offspring from the land of their captivity. Jacob shall return and be at rest and prosper, and no one shall frighten him. Fear not, O Jacob, my servant, says the Lord, for I am with you and will destroy all the nations where I have driven you. But I will not destroy you completely. I will correct you with justice, and I will not utterly cut you off."

CHAPTER 47

The Lord's message came to Jeremiah the prophet concerning the Philistines, before Pharaoh struck down Gaza. The Lord says, "Behold, the waters will rise from the north and become like a flood, sweeping over the land and its cities, and those who dwell therein. Men will cry out, and all the inhabitants of the land will howl, at the noise of the shuffling of strong horses, the rattling of chariots, and the roaring of wheels. Fathers will not look back at their children because their hands will be feeble." "This is because of the day when all the people of the Philistines, Tyre, Sidon, and all others involved in the conflict will be destroyed. The Lord will destroy the Philistines, the remnant of the people of Caphtor. Baldness has come upon Gaza; Ashkelon is cut off with the rest of their valleys. How long will you mourn?" "O sword of the Lord, how long will you be unable to cease? Return to your sheath, rest, and be still. How can you cease when the Lord has appointed you to strike Ashkelon and the seacoast?"

CHAPTER 48

Concerning Moab, the Lord of hosts, the God of Israel, says, "Woe to Nebo, for it is destroyed; Kiriathaim is confounded and taken; Misgab is confounded and afraid. Moab shall no longer boast of Heshbon, for they have committed dishonesty against it. Come and destroy it so that it may no longer be a nation. You, too, will be destroyed, O fool, and the sword will pursue you." "From Horonaim comes a cry of weeping, a desolation and great destruction. Moab is destroyed; its little ones make their weeping heard. At the time of Luhith's departure, mourning shall be heard with weeping. For at the time of Horonaim's departure, the enemies have heard a cry of destruction." "Flee and save your lives; become like a wilderness. Because you trusted in your works and treasures, you too will be taken, and Chemosh will go into captivity with its priests and princes. The destroyer shall come upon all the cities, and none shall escape; even the valley shall perish, and the plain shall be destroyed, as the Lord has said. Put wings on Moab, so that it may flee and be gone, for its cities shall be desolate with no one to inhabit them." "Cursed is he who does the work of the Lord negligently, and cursed is he who withholds his sword from bloodshed. Moab has rested from its youth and has settled on its dregs. It has not been driven from vessel to vessel nor gone into captivity; therefore its taste remains unchanged, and its will is not altered. Therefore, behold, the days are coming, says the Lord, when I will send people to him who will empty his vessels and break their bottoms." "Moab will be ashamed of Chemosh as the house of Israel was ashamed of Bethel, their security. How do you say, 'We are strong and valiant men of war'? Moab is destroyed; its cities are burned, and its chosen young men have gone to the slaughter, says your king, whose name is the Lord of hosts." "The destruction of Moab is prepared, and its plague is hastening. All around him mourn; everyone who knows his name says, 'How is the strong staff and beautiful rod broken!' O daughter who dwells in Dibon, come down from your glory and sit in thirst, for the destroyer of Moab will come upon you and destroy your fortresses. You who dwell in Aroer, stand on the road and watch; question those who flee and those who are saved, and ask, 'What has happened?'" "Moab is smothered; it has been destroyed. Howl and shout, tell Arnon that Moab has been destroyed, and judgment has come on the plain country, on Holon, on Jahaz, and on Mephaath, and on Dibon, Nebo, and the house of Diblathaim, Kiriathaim, Beth-Gamul, and Beth-Meon, Kerioth, Bozrah, and all the cities of the land of Moab, far and near. The horn of Moab is cut off, and its weapon is broken, says the Lord." "Make him drunk, for he has risen up against the Lord. Moab shall wallow in its vomit and be mocked. For did you not mock Israel as if he were found among us? When you speak of him, you are mocked. O you who dwell in Moab, leave the cities, dwell in the rocks, and be like the dove that makes her nest in the sides of the mouth of the hole." "We have heard the pride of Moab (he is exceedingly proud), his sturdiness, arrogance, and the haughtiness of his heart. I know his wrath, says the Lord, but it shall not be so, nor his dissimulators, for they do not consider the Lord of hosts. Behold, the days are coming, when I will send to Moab wanderers, who will cause him to be drunk, and they will make the land of Moab an object of scorn and ridicule, and it shall be a derision among the nations." "Moab has been made desolate, and its chosen young men have gone to the slaughter. Therefore, Moab's boast shall be destroyed, and its pride shall fall. The armies of Moab will be brought low, and the remnant shall be cut off, says the Lord of hosts."

CHAPTER 49

Concerning the Ammonites, the Lord says, "Has Israel no sons? Has he no heir? Why then does Milcom inherit Gad, and his people dwell in its cities? Therefore, behold, the days are coming, says the Lord, when I will cause an alarm of war to be heard against Rabbah of the Ammonites. It shall become a desolate heap, and her daughter's shall be burned with fire. Then Israel shall be heir to those who are her heirs, says the Lord." "Concerning Edom, the Lord says, 'Is wisdom no more in Teman? Has counsel perished from the prudent? Has their wisdom vanished? Flee, turn back, dwell in the depths, O inhabitants of Dedan; for I will bring the calamity of Esau upon him, the time when I will visit him. If grape-gatherers came to you, would they not leave some gleaning grapes? If thieves came by night, would they not destroy until they had enough? But I have stripped Esau bare; I have uncovered his

secret places, and he shall not be able to hide himself. His offspring is destroyed, his brothers and neighbors, and he is no more.'" "Leave your fatherless children; I will preserve them alive; and let your widows trust in Me. For thus says the Lord, 'Behold, those who do not drink of the cup shall surely drink; and are you the one who will go unpunished? You shall not go unpunished, but you shall surely drink. For I have sworn by Myself,' says the Lord, 'that Bozrah shall become a desolation, a reproach, a waste, and a curse. All its cities shall be perpetual wastes.'" "Concerning Damascus, 'Hamath and Arpad are shamed, for they have heard bad news; they are faint-hearted; there is trouble like the sea; it cannot be quiet. Damascus has grown feeble; she turns to flee, and fear has seized her. Anguish and sorrows have taken her like a woman in labor. How is the city of praise not left behind, the city of My joy? Therefore, her young men shall fall in her streets, and all the men of war shall be cut off in that day,' says the Lord of hosts." "I will kindle a fire in the wall of Damascus, and it shall devour the palaces of Ben-Hadad." "Concerning Kedar and the kingdoms of Hazor, which Nebuchadnezzar, king of Babylon, struck, the Lord says, 'Arise, go up to Kedar, and devastate the people of the east. Their tents and their flocks shall be taken, their curtains and all their vessels, and their camels shall be carried away. Men shall cry out to them, 'Terror on every side!' Flee, get far away, dwell in the depths, O inhabitants of Hazor,' says the Lord. 'For Nebuchadnezzar, king of Babylon, has taken counsel against you and devised a plan against you.'" "Arise, go up to the mighty nation and its most high country, says the Lord. For I will bring them to ruin, says the Lord, and their land shall be desolate. Their dwellings shall be emptied, and no one shall dwell there."

CHAPTER 50

The word which the Lord has spoken concerning Babel and the land of the Chaldeans through Jeremiah the prophet is to be declared among the nations. It should be published, set forth, and proclaimed without concealment. The message is that Babel is taken, Bel is confounded, and Merodach is brought down. Her idols are confounded, and their images are broken in pieces. A nation from the north comes against her, making her land a desert where neither man nor beast will dwell. They shall flee away, both man and beast In those days and at that time, says the LORD, the children of Israel and the children of Judah will come together, weeping as they seek the LORD their God. They will ask the way to Zion, with their faces turned outward, saying, "Come, let us pay homage to the LORD with an everlasting covenant that shall not be forgotten." My people have been like a lost flock; their shepherds have led them astray, causing them to wander into the mountains. They have gone from mountain to mountain and forgotten their resting place. All who found them hated them, and their enemies said, "We do not offend them, for they have sinned against the LORD, the dwelling place of righteousness, the hope of their fathers." Flee from the meshes of Babel, come out of the land of the Chaldeans, and be like the goats before the flock. I will raise up and bring against Babel a multitude of mighty nations from the land of the north. They will array themselves against her and take her. Their arrows will be like those of a strong man, experienced in warfare, and none shall be able to turn back. Chaldea shall be plundered; all who spy her out shall be satisfied, says the LORD. Because you have rejoiced and destroyed my inheritance, and have grown fat like calves in the crabgrass, and have grown like strong horses, your mother shall be confounded, and she who bore you shall be ashamed. Behold, the last of the people shall be a wilderness, a dry and wild land Because of the wrath of the LORD, it shall not be inhabited but shall be desolate, and all who pass through Babel shall be amazed and astonished at all her plagues. Form a line against Babel, all around; everyone who has a bow should shoot at her, sparing no arrows, for she has sinned against the LORD. Shout against her all around: she has given her hand, her foundations have fallen, and her walls have been destroyed. Take vengeance on her as she has done, do also to her. Destroy the sower of Babel and the one who wields the sickle in time of torment. Because of the sword of the oppressor, every one of them shall return to his people, and they shall flee each to his own land Israel is like a scattered flock; the lions have scattered it. First, the king of Assur exhausted it, and lastly, Nebuchadnezzar, the king of Babel, has broken its bones. Therefore, thus says the LORD of hosts, the God of Israel, "Behold, I will visit the king of Babel and his country, as I visited the king of Assur. I will bring Israel back to his dwelling place; he shall feed on Mount Carmel and on Bashan, and his soul shall be satisfied on Mount Ephraim and on Gilead. In those days and at that time, says the LORD, shall the iniquities of Israel be sought, and they shall not be found, and the faults of Judah shall not be found, for I will be merciful toward them, whom I reserve Go against the land of the rebels, against it and against the inhabitants of Pekod; destroy it and lay it waste after them, says the LORD, and do all that I have commanded you. A cry of battle is in the land and of great destruction. How destroyed and broken is the hammer of the whole world! How desolate has Babel become among the nations! I have caught you, and you have been caught, O Babel, and you have not noticed; you have been found and also caught because you have fought against the LORD. The LORD has opened her treasure and brought forth the weapons of his wrath, for this is the action of the LORD, the God of hosts, in the land of the Chaldeans Come against her from the farthest borders; open her storehouses; make a trek on her as on a shearer, and destroy her in every part; leave nothing of her. Destroy all her heifers; let them go to slaughter. Woe to them, for their day and the time of their visitation has come. The journey of those who flee and depart from the land of Babel is to declare in Zion the vengeance of the LORD our God and the vengeance of his Temple Call the archers against Babel; all who bend the bow, besiege her everywhere; let none escape. Reward her according to her work, and according to all that she has done, do it to her, for she has taken pride against the LORD and against the Holy One of Israel. Therefore, her young men shall fall in the streets, and all her men of war shall be destroyed in that day, says the LORD. Behold, I come to you, O proud man, says the LORD, God of hosts, for your day has come, the time when I will visit you. The proud man shall stumble and fall, and none shall lift him up; I will kindle a fire in his cities, and it shall be consumed all around him." Thus says the LORD of hosts, "The children of Israel and the children of Judah were oppressed together, and all those who made them captives held them and would not let them go. But their strong redeemer, whose name is the LORD of hosts, will uphold their cause, to give rest to the land and disquiet the inhabitants of Babel. A sword shall come upon the Chaldeans, says the LORD, and upon the inhabitants of Babel, upon her princes and her wise men. A sword is for the soothsayers, and they shall hurt themselves; a sword is for her strong men, and they shall hurt themselves. A sword is upon their horses and upon their chariots, and upon all the multitude that is in her bowels, and they shall be as women; a sword is upon her treasures, and they shall be stripped And its waters are dried up by drought, and they shall run dry, because it is the land of bronze images, and they give themselves up to their idols. Therefore, the Ziim with the Iim shall dwell therein, and the ostriches shall dwell therein, for it shall not be inhabited any more, nor shall it be inhabited from generation to generation. As God destroyed Sodom and Gomorrah with its surrounding places, says the LORD, so shall no one dwell there any more, nor shall the son of man remain there Behold, a people will come from the north, a great nation, and many kings will arise from the coasts of the earth. They will wield the bow and the axe; they are cruel and ruthless; their journey will roar like the sea; they will ride horses and be arrayed like men to fight against you, O daughter of Babel. The king of Babel has heard their news, and his hands have grown weak; sadness has come upon him like that of a woman in panic Behold, he shall come like a lion from the swelling of Jordan to the strong dwelling place, for I will make Israel rest, and I will make them depart from her quickly; and who is a chosen man that I can lean against her? For who is like me, and who will lean against me in time? And who is the shepherd that shall stand before me? Hear therefore the counsel of the LORD which he has devised against Babel, and his purpose which he has devised against the land of the Chaldeans: surely the least of the flock shall drag them away; surely he shall make their dwelling with them desolate At the sound of Babel's victory, the earth moved and the cry was heard among the nations

CHAPTER 51

Thus says the LORD: "Behold, I will raise up against Babel and against the inhabitants who lift up their hearts against me a destructive wind. I will send against Babel fans that shall flatten her and empty her land, for in the day of crisis they shall be against her on every side. To the bender who shall bend his bow, and to him who shall rise up in his brigandage, I will say, 'Spare not his young men, but destroy all his army.' So the slain shall fall in the land of the Chaldeans, and those who are pierced shall fall through its streets For Israel was not widowed, and Judah was not turned away from his God, the LORD of hosts, though their land was full of sins against the Holy One of Israel. Flee from the meshes of Babel, and deliver each one his own soul; do not let her iniquity bring you down, for this is the time of the LORD's vengeance, who will make recompense for her. Babel has been like a cup of gold in the hand of the LORD, which has made all the earth drunk; the nations have drunk of her wine, therefore the nations are enraged Babel fell suddenly and was destroyed; cry out for her, bring balm for her sore, if she would be healed. We would have healed Babel, but she could not be healed; forsake her, and let every man go away to his own country, for his judgment has come upon him and has risen up to the clouds. The LORD has brought forth against the inhabitants of Babel the spirit of an avenger; his name is the LORD, the God of hosts. Thus says the LORD: "Behold, I will stir up the spirit of a destroyer against Babel, and all who dwell therein shall be made a desolation The mighty men of Babel are cut off, and the kneeled before the LORD, and the mercies of the LORD against the land of Babel are added to those who are not willing to escape from their sins. The LORD has brought against Babel and against the inhabitants of the land of the Chaldeans a purpose to desolate, and to make it a wilderness of desolation. He shall take vengeance upon her as she has done to others, and her blood shall be upon her head Behold, I am against you, O destroying mountain, says the LORD, which destroys all the earth; I will stretch out my hand against you, and roll you down from the rocks, and make you a burnt mountain. No stone shall be taken from you for a cornerstone, nor any stone for foundations, but you shall be desolate forever, says the LORD Lift up a banner on the high mountain, raise your voice to them, wave your hand that they may enter the gates of the nobles. I have commanded my sanctified ones, I have also called my mighty ones for my anger, even those who rejoice in my exaltation. The noise of the multitude in the mountains, like that of many people! The noise of the uproar of kingdoms, of nations gathered together! The LORD of hosts musters the army for the battle. They come from a far country, from the end of heaven; the LORD and the weapons of his indignation, to destroy the whole land Howl, for the day of the LORD is at hand! It shall come as destruction from the Almighty. Therefore all hands shall be limp, every man's heart shall melt, and they shall be afraid. Pangs and sorrows shall take hold of them; they shall be in pain as a woman in labor. Behold, the day of the LORD comes, cruel with both wrath and fierce anger, to make the land desolate, and he shall destroy its sinners from it. For the stars of heaven and their constellations shall not give their light; the sun shall be darkened in its going forth, and the moon shall not cause its light to shine I will punish the world for its evil, and the wicked for their iniquity; I will cause the arrogance of the proud to cease, and will lay low the haughtiness of the terrible. I will make a mortal more rare than fine gold, a man more than the golden wedge of Ophir. Therefore I will shake the heavens, and the earth shall move out of her place, in the wrath of the LORD of hosts and in the day of his fierce anger And it shall be as the hunted gazelle, and as a sheep that no man takes up; they shall every man turn to his own people, and flee every man to his own land. Everyone who is found shall be thrust through, and everyone who is joined to them shall fall by the sword. Their children also shall be dashed to pieces before their eyes; their houses shall be spoiled and their wives ravished. Behold, I will stir up against them the Medes, who shall not regard silver, and as for gold, they shall not delight in it. Their bows also shall dash the young men to pieces, and they shall have no pity on the fruit of the womb; their eye shall not spare children And Babel, the glory of kingdoms, the beauty of the Chaldeans' pride, shall be as when God overthrew Sodom and Gomorrah. It shall never be inhabited, nor shall it be dwelt in from generation to generation; neither shall the Arabian pitch tent there, nor shall the shepherds make their fold there. But wild beasts of the desert shall lie there, and their houses shall be full of doleful creatures, and owls shall dwell there, and satyrs shall dance there. The wild beasts of the islands shall cry out in their desolate houses, and dragons in their pleasant palaces. Her time is near to come, and her days shall not be prolonged

CHAPTER 52

Zedekiah was twenty-one years old when he began to reign, and he reigned eleven years in Jerusalem. His mother's name was Hamutal, the daughter of Jeremiah of Libnah. He did evil in the sight of the LORD, according to all that Jehoiakim had done. For because of the anger of the LORD this happened in Jerusalem and Judah, until he had cast them out from his presence. Then Zedekiah rebelled against the king of Babel It came to pass in the ninth year of his reign, in the tenth month, that Nebuchadnezzar, king of Babel, and all his army came against Jerusalem and besieged it. In the eleventh year of

King Zedekiah, in the fourth month, the city was broken up. All the princes of the king of Babel came in and sat in the middle gate, Nergal-sharezer, Samgar-nebo, Sarsechim, Rabsaris, Nergal-sharezer, Rabmag, with all the rest of the princes of the king of Babel When Zedekiah, the king of Judah, saw them, and all the men of war, then they fled and went forth out of the city by night by the way of the king's garden, by the gate between the two walls, and he went out toward the plain. But the army of the Chaldeans pursued after them, and overtook Zedekiah in the plains of Jericho. And all his army was scattered from him. Then they took the king and brought him up to the king of Babel to Riblah in the land of Hamath, where he gave judgment upon him Then the king of Babel slew the sons of Zedekiah before his eyes; he slew also all the princes of Judah in Riblah. He put out the eyes of Zedekiah, and the king of Babel bound him in chains, and carried him to Babylon, and put him in prison till the day of his death In the fifth month, on the seventh day of the month, which is the nineteenth year of Nebuchadnezzar, king of Babel, came Nebuzaradan, captain of the guard, who served the king of Babel, into Jerusalem, and burned the house of the LORD, and the king's house, and all the houses of Jerusalem, and all the houses of the great men, and all the houses of Jerusalem, and all the houses of the great men, and all the houses of Jerusalem The army of the Chaldeans who were with the captain of the guard broke down all the walls of Jerusalem round about. Then Nebuzaradan, the captain of the guard, carried away captive the remnant of the people that remained in the city, and those that fell away, that fell to the king of Babel, and the rest of the people that remained. But Nebuzaradan, the captain of the guard, left of the poor of the people, which had nothing, in the land of Judah, and gave them vineyards and fields at the same time Now Nebuchadnezzar, king of Babel, gave charge concerning Jeremiah to Nebuzaradan, the captain of the guard, saying, "Take him, and look well to him, and do him no harm; but do unto him even as he shall say unto you." So Nebuzaradan, the captain of the guard, sent, and Nebushasban, Rabsaris, Nergal-sharezer, Rabmag, and all the king of Babel's princes; even they sent and took Jeremiah out of the court of the prison, and committed him unto Gedaliah, the son of Ahikam, the son of Shaphan, that he should carry him home, and he dwelt among the people Now the word of the LORD came to Jeremiah, after Nebuzaradan, the captain of the guard, had let him go from Ramah, when he had taken him being bound in chains among all that were carried away captive of Jerusalem and Judah, which were carried away captive unto Babylon. And the captain of the guard took Jeremiah, and said unto him, "The LORD thy God hath pronounced this evil upon this place. Now the LORD hath brought it, and done according as he hath said: because ye have sinned against the LORD, and have not obeyed his voice, therefore this thing is come upon you And now, behold, I loose thee this day from the chains which were upon thine hand. If it seem good unto thee to come with me into Babylon, come; and I will look well unto thee: but if it seem ill unto thee to come with me into Babylon, forbear: behold, all the land is before thee: whither it seemeth good and convenient for thee to go, thither go." Now while he was not yet gone back, he said, "Go back also to Gedaliah, the son of Ahikam, the son of Shaphan, whom the king of Babel hath made governor over the cities of Judah, and dwell with him among the people: or go wheresoever it seemeth convenient unto thee to go." So the captain of the guard gave him victuals and a reward, and let him go

Then went Jeremiah unto Gedaliah, the son of Ahikam, to Mizpah, and dwelt with him among the people that were left in the land Now when all the captains of the forces which were in the fields, even they and their men, heard that the king of Babel had made Gedaliah the son of Ahikam governor in the land, and had committed unto him men and women, and children, and of the poor of the land, of them that were not carried away captive to Babylon; then they came to Gedaliah to Mizpah, even Ishmael the son of Nethaniah, and Johanan and Jonathan the sons of Kareah, and Seraiah the son of Tanhumeth, and the sons of Ephai the Netophathite, and Jezaniah the son of the Maachathite, they and their men And Gedaliah the son of Ahikam the son of Shaphan swear unto them, and to their men, saying, "Fear not to serve the Chaldeans: dwell in the land, and serve the king of Babel, and it shall be well with you." As for me, behold, I will dwell at Mizpah to serve the Chaldeans, which will come unto us: but ye, gather ye wine, and summer fruits, and oil, and put them in your vessels, and dwell in your cities that ye have taken." Likewise, when all the Jews that were in Moab, and among the Ammonites, and in Edom, and that were in all the countries, heard that the king of Babel had left a remnant of Judah, and that he had set over them Gedaliah the son of Ahikam the son of Shaphan; even all the Jews returned out of all places whither they were driven, and came to the land of Judah, to Gedaliah, unto Mizpah, and gathered wine and summer fruits very much Moreover Johanan the son of Kareah, and all the captains of the forces that were in the fields, came to Gedaliah to Mizpah, and said unto him, "Dost thou certainly know that Baalis the king of the Ammonites hath sent Ishmael the son of Nethaniah to slay thee?" But Gedaliah the son of Ahikam believed them not. Then Johanan the son of Kareah spake secretly to Gedaliah in Mizpah, saying, "Let me go, I pray thee, and I will slay Ishmael the son of Nethaniah, and no man shall know it: wherefore should he slay thee, that all the Jews which are gathered unto thee should be scattered, and the remnant in Judah perish?" But Gedaliah the son of Ahikam said unto Johanan the son of Kareah, "Thou shalt not do this thing: for thou speakest falsely of Ishmael."

76. Prayer of Azariah

Daniel 3

24 They walked in the midst of the fire, praising God and blessing the Lord. 25 Azarias then stood and prayed, opening his mouth in the midst of the fire, saying, 26 "Blessed are You, O Lord, God of our fathers! Your name is worthy of praise and glory forevermore. 27 For You are righteous in all that You have done; all Your works are true. Your ways are right, and all Your judgments are truth. 28 In all that You have brought upon us and upon the holy city of our fathers, Jerusalem, You have executed true judgments. According to truth and justice, You have brought these things upon us because of our sins. 29 We have sinned and committed iniquity by departing from You. 30 In all things, we have trespassed and not obeyed Your commandments or kept them. We have not done as You commanded us, that it might go well with us. 31 Therefore, everything You have brought upon us and all that You have done to us, You have done in true judgment. 32 You delivered us into the hands of lawless enemies, the most hateful rebels, and to an unjust king, who is the most wicked in the world. 33 Now we cannot open our mouths. Shame and reproach have come upon Your servants and those who worship You. 34 Do not utterly deliver us up for Your name's sake. Do not annul Your

covenant. 35 Do not cause Your mercy to depart from us for the sake of Abraham, who is loved by You, for Isaac, Your servant, and for Israel, Your holy one, 36 to whom You promised that You would multiply their offspring as the stars of the sky and as the sand on the seashore. 37 For we, O Lord, have become less than any nation, and are brought low this day in all the world because of our sins. 38 At this time, there is no prince, prophet, leader, burnt offering, sacrifice, oblation, incense, or place to offer before You and find mercy. 39 Nevertheless, with a contrite heart and a humble spirit, let us be accepted, 40 like the burnt offerings of rams and bullocks, and like ten thousand fat lambs. Let our sacrifice be in Your sight this day, that we may wholly follow You, for those who trust in You shall not be ashamed. 41 Now we follow You with all our heart. We fear You and seek Your face. 42 Do not put us to shame; deal with us according to Your kindness and the multitude of Your mercy. 43 Deliver us according to Your marvelous works and give glory to Your name, O Lord. Let all those who harm Your servants be confounded. 44 Let them be ashamed of all their power and might, and let their strength be broken. 45 Let them know that You are the Lord, the only God, and glorious over the whole world." 46 The king's servants who had put them in did not stop making the furnace hot with naphtha, pitch, tinder, and small wood, 47 so that the flame streamed out forty-nine cubits above the furnace. 48 It spread and burned the Chaldeans who were around the furnace. 49 But the angel of the Lord came down into the furnace with Azarias and his fellows, striking out the flame of the fire, 50 making the midst of the furnace as if it were a moist, whistling wind, so that the fire did not touch them at all. It neither hurt nor troubled them. 51 Then the three, as if from one mouth, praised, glorified, and blessed God in the furnace, saying, 52 "Blessed are You, O Lord, God of our fathers, to be praised and exalted above all forever! 53 Blessed is Your glorious and holy name, to be praised and exalted above all forever! 54 Blessed are You in the temple of Your holy glory, to be praised and glorified above all forever! 55 Blessed are You who see the depths and sit upon the cherubim, to be praised and exalted above all forever. 56 Blessed are You on the throne of Your kingdom, to be praised and extolled above all forever! 57 Blessed are You in the firmament of heaven, to be praised and glorified forever! 58 O all You works of the Lord, bless the Lord! Praise and exalt Him above all forever! 59 O You heavens, bless the Lord! Praise and exalt Him above all forever! 60 O You angels of the Lord, bless the Lord! Praise and exalt Him above all forever! 61 O all You waters above the sky, bless the Lord! Praise and exalt Him above all forever! 62 O all You powers of the Lord, bless the Lord! Praise and exalt Him above all forever! 63 O You sun and moon, bless the Lord! Praise and exalt Him above all forever! 64 O You stars of heaven, bless the Lord! Praise and exalt Him above all forever! 65 O every shower and dew, bless the Lord! Praise and exalt Him above all forever! 66 O all You winds, bless the Lord! Praise and exalt Him above all forever! 67 O You fire and heat, bless the Lord! Praise and exalt Him above all forever! 68 O You dews and storms of snow, bless the Lord! Praise and exalt Him above all forever! 69 O You nights and days, bless the Lord! Praise and exalt Him above all forever! 70 O You light and darkness, bless the Lord! Praise and exalt Him above all forever! 71 O You cold and heat, bless the Lord! Praise and exalt Him above all forever! 72 O You frost and snow, bless the Lord! Praise and exalt Him above all forever! 73 O You lightnings and clouds, bless the Lord! Praise and exalt Him above all forever! 74 O let the earth bless the Lord! Let it praise and exalt Him above all forever! 75 O You mountains and hills, bless the Lord! Praise and exalt Him above all forever! 76 O all You things that grow on the earth, bless the Lord! Praise and exalt Him above all forever! 77 O sea and rivers, bless the Lord! Praise and exalt Him above all forever! 78 O You springs, bless the Lord! Praise and exalt Him above all forever! 79 O You whales and all that move in the waters, bless the Lord! Praise and exalt Him above all forever! 80 O all You birds of the air, bless the Lord! Praise and exalt Him above all forever! 81 O all You beasts and cattle, bless the Lord! Praise and exalt Him above all forever! 82 O You children of men, bless the Lord! Praise and exalt Him above all forever! 83 O let Israel bless the Lord! Praise and exalt Him above all forever. 84 O You priests of the Lord, bless the Lord! Praise and exalt Him above all forever! 85 O You servants of the Lord, bless the Lord! Praise and exalt Him above all forever! 86 O You spirits and souls of the righteous, bless the Lord! Praise and exalt Him above all forever! 87 O You who are holy and humble of heart, bless the Lord! Praise and exalt Him above all forever! 88 O Hananiah, Mishael, and Azariah, bless the Lord! Praise and exalt Him above all forever; for He has rescued us from Hades, saved us from the hand of death, and delivered us out of the midst of the furnace and burning flame. 89 O give thanks to the Lord, for He is good; His mercy endures forever. 90 O all You who worship the Lord, bless the God of gods, praise Him, and give Him thanks; for His mercy endures forever!" 91 Then King Nebuchadnezzar was astonished and rose up in haste. He spoke and said to his counselors, "Didn't we cast three men bound into the middle of the fire?" They answered the king, "True, O king." 92 He answered, "Look, I see four men loose, walking in the middle of the fire, and they are unharmed. The appearance of the fourth is like a son of the gods." 93 Then Nebuchadnezzar came near to the mouth of the burning fiery furnace. He spoke and said, "Shadrach, Meshach, and Abednego, you servants of the Most High God, come out, and come here!" Then Shadrach, Meshach, and Abednego came out of the midst of the fire. 94 The local governors, deputies, and king's counselors gathered together and saw that the fire had no power over their bodies. The hair of their heads was not singed, their pants were not changed, and the smell of fire was not even on them. 95 Nebuchadnezzar spoke and said, "Blessed be the God of Shadrach, Meshach, and Abednego, who has sent His angel and delivered His servants who trusted in Him, and have changed the king's word, yielding their bodies, that they might not serve or worship any god except their own God. 96 Therefore, I make a decree: every people, nation, and language that speaks anything evil against the God of Shadrach, Meshach, and Abednego shall be cut in pieces, and their houses shall be made a dunghill, because there is no other god who is able to deliver like this." 97 Then the king promoted Shadrach, Meshach, and Abednego in the province of Babylon

Daniel 4

1 Nebuchadnezzar the king, to all peoples, nations, and languages that dwell in all the earth: "Peace be multiplied to you. 2 It has seemed good to me to declare the signs and wonders that the Most High God has worked toward me. 3 How great are His signs! How mighty are His wonders! His kingdom is an everlasting kingdom, and His dominion is from generation to generation 4 I, Nebuchadnezzar, was at ease in my house and flourishing in my palace. 5 I saw a dream which made me afraid. The thoughts on my bed and the visions of my head troubled me. 6 Therefore, I issued a decree to bring in all the wise men of Babylon before me, that they might make known to me the interpretation of the dream. 7 Then the magicians, enchanters, Chaldeans, and soothsayers came in, and I told them the dream, but they did not make known to me its interpretation. 8 But at last, Daniel came in before me (whose name was Belteshazzar, according to the name of my god, and in whom is the spirit of the holy gods), and I told him the dream, saying, 9 "Belteshazzar, master of the magicians, because I know that the spirit of the holy gods is in you, and no secret troubles you, tell me the visions of my dream that I have seen, and its interpretation 10 "The visions of my head on my bed were these: I saw, and behold, a tree in the midst of the earth; and its height was great. 11 The tree grew, and was strong, and its height reached to the sky, and its sight to the end of all the earth. 12 Its leaves were beautiful, its fruit abundant, and in it was food for all. The beasts of the field found shade under it, and the birds of the sky dwelt in its branches, and all flesh was fed from it. 13 I saw in the visions of my head on my bed, and behold, a watcher and a holy one came down from heaven. 14 He cried aloud, and said, 'Cut down the tree, and cut off its branches, shake off its leaves, and scatter its fruit. Let the beasts get away from under it, and the birds from its branches. 15 Nevertheless, leave the stump of its roots in the earth, even with a band of iron and bronze, in the tender grass of the field. Let it be wet with the dew of heaven, and let its portion be with the beasts in the grass of the earth. 16 Let his heart be changed from man's, and let a beast's heart be given to him, and let seven times pass over him. 17 This matter is by the decree of the watchers, and the demand by the word of the holy ones, to the intent that the living may know that the Most High rules in the kingdom of men, and gives it to whomsoever He will, and sets up over it the lowest of men.' 18 "This dream I, King Nebuchadnezzar, have seen. Now you, Belteshazzar, declare the interpretation, since all the wise men of my kingdom are not able to make known to me the interpretation. But you are able, for the spirit of the holy gods is in you." 19 Then Daniel, whose name was Belteshazzar, was astonished for a while, and his thoughts troubled him. The king spoke and said, "Belteshazzar, let not the dream, or the interpretation, trouble you." Belteshazzar answered, "My lord, the dream be to those who hate you, and the interpretation to your adversaries. 20 The tree that you saw, which grew, and was strong, whose height reached to the sky, and the sight of it to all the earth; 21 whose leaves were beautiful, and its fruit abundant, and in which was food for all; under which the beasts of the field dwelt, and on whose branches the birds of the sky had their habitation: 22 It is you, O king, who have grown and become strong. For your greatness has grown and reaches to heaven, and your dominion to the end of the earth. 23 "Whereas the king saw a watcher and a holy one coming down from heaven, and saying, 'Cut down the tree, and destroy it; yet leave the stump of the roots of it in the earth, even with a band of iron and bronze, in the tender grass of the field, and let it be wet with the dew of heaven, and let his portion be with the beasts of the field, until seven times pass over him;' 24 this is the interpretation, O king, and this is the decree of the Most High, which has come upon my lord the king: 25 You shall be driven from men, and your dwelling shall be with the beasts of the field, and you shall be made to eat grass as oxen, and you shall be wet with the dew of heaven, and seven times shall pass over you, till you know that the Most High rules in the kingdom of men, and gives it to whomsoever He will. 26 Whereas they commanded to leave the stump of the tree roots, your kingdom shall be sure to you, after you shall have known that the heavens

do rule. 27 "Therefore, O king, let my counsel be acceptable to you, and break off your sins by righteousness, and your iniquities by showing mercy to the poor; if there may be a lengthening of your tranquility." 28 All this came upon the king Nebuchadnezzar. 29 At the end of twelve months he was walking in the royal palace of Babylon. 30 The king spoke and said, "Is not this great Babylon, which I have built for the royal dwelling place, by the might of my power and for the glory of my majesty?" 31 While the word was in the king's mouth, there fell a voice from heaven, saying, "O king Nebuchadnezzar, to you it is spoken: The kingdom is departed from you. 32 You shall be driven from men, and your dwelling shall be with the beasts of the field. You shall be made to eat grass as oxen, and seven times shall pass over you, until you know that the Most High rules in the kingdom of men, and gives it to whomsoever He will." 33 The same hour was the thing fulfilled upon Nebuchadnezzar: and he was driven from men, and did eat grass as oxen, and his body was wet with the dew of heaven, till his hair was grown like eagles' feathers, and his nails like birds' claws 34 At the end of the days I, Nebuchadnezzar, lifted up my eyes to heaven, and my understanding returned to me, and I blessed the Most High, and I praised and honored Him who lives forever, whose dominion is an everlasting dominion, and His kingdom is from generation to generation. 35 All the inhabitants of the earth are reputed as nothing: and He does according to His will in the army of heaven, and among the inhabitants of the earth: and none can stay His hand, or say unto Him, "What do You do?" 36 At the same time my reason returned unto me; and for the glory of my kingdom, my honor and brightness returned unto me; and my counselors and my lords sought unto me; and I was established in my kingdom, and excellent majesty was added unto me. 37 Now I, Nebuchadnezzar, praise and extol and honor the King of heaven, all whose works are truth, and His ways judgment: and those who walk in pride He is able to abase

Daniel 5

1 Belshazzar the king made a great feast to a thousand of his lords, and drank wine before the thousand. 2 Belshazzar, while he tasted the wine, commanded to bring the golden and silver vessels which his father Nebuchadnezzar had taken out of the temple which was in Jerusalem; that the king, and his princes, his wives, and his concubines, might drink from them. 3 Then they brought the golden vessels that were taken out of the temple of the house of God which was at Jerusalem; and the king, and his princes, his wives, and his concubines, drank from them. 4 They drank wine, and praised the gods of gold, and of silver, of brass, of iron, of wood, and of stone 5 In the same hour came forth fingers of a man's hand, and wrote over against the candlestick upon the plaster of the wall of the king's palace: and the king saw the part of the hand that wrote. 6 Then the king's countenance was changed, and his thoughts troubled him, so that the joints of his loins were loosed, and his knees smote one against another. 7 The king cried aloud to bring in the astrologers, the Chaldeans, and the soothsayers. And the king spoke, and said to the wise men of Babylon, "Whoever shall read this writing, and show me the interpretation thereof, shall be clothed with scarlet, and have a chain of gold about his neck, and shall be the third ruler in the kingdom." 8 Then came in all the king's wise men, but they could not read the writing, nor make known to the king the interpretation thereof. 9 Then was King Belshazzar greatly troubled, and his countenance was changed in him, and his lords were astonied 10 Now the queen, by reason of the words of the king and his lords, came into the banquet house: and the queen spoke and said, "O king, live forever: let not your thoughts trouble you, nor let your countenance be changed. 11 There is a man in your kingdom, in whom is the spirit of the holy gods; and in the days of your father light and understanding and wisdom, like the wisdom of the gods, was found in him; whom the king Nebuchadnezzar your father, the king, I say, your father, made master of the magicians, astrologers, Chaldeans, and soothsayers; 12 Forasmuch as an excellent spirit, and knowledge, and understanding, interpreting of dreams, and showing of hard sentences, and dissolving of doubts, were found in the same Daniel, whom the king named Belteshazzar. Now let Daniel be called, and he will show the interpretation." 13 Then was Daniel brought in before the king. And the king spoke and said unto Daniel, "Are you that Daniel who is of the children of the captivity of Judah, whom the king my father brought out of Judah? 14 I have even heard of you, that the spirit of the gods is in you, and that light and understanding and excellent wisdom are found in you. 15 And now the wise men, the astrologers, have been brought in before me, that they should read this writing, and make known unto me the interpretation thereof; but they could not show the interpretation of the thing. 16 And I have heard of you, that you can make interpretations, and dissolve doubts: now if you can read the writing, and make known to me the interpretation thereof, you shall be clothed with scarlet, and have a chain of gold about your neck, and shall be the third ruler in the kingdom." 17 Then Daniel answered and said before the king, "Let your gifts be to yourself, and give your rewards to another; yet I will read the writing unto the king, and make known to him the interpretation. 18 O king, the Most High God gave Nebuchadnezzar your father a kingdom, and majesty, and glory, and honor: 19 And for the majesty that He gave him, all people, nations, and languages trembled and feared before him: whom He would He slew; and whom He would He kept alive; and whom He would He set up; and whom He would He put down. 20 But when his heart was lifted up, and his mind hardened in pride, he was deposed from his kingly throne, and they took his glory from him: 21 And he was driven from the sons of men; and his heart was made like the beasts, and his dwelling was with the wild asses: they fed him with grass like oxen, and his body was wet with the dew of heaven, till he knew that the Most High God rules in the kingdom of men, and that He appoints over it whomsoever He will. 22 And you his son, O Belshazzar, have not humbled your heart, though you knew all this; 23 But have lifted up yourself against the Lord of heaven; and they have brought the vessels of His house before you, and you, and your lords, your wives, and your concubines, have drunk wine in them; and you have praised the gods of silver, and gold, of brass, iron, wood, and stone, which see not, nor hear, nor know: and the God in whose hand your breath is, and whose are all your ways, have you not glorified: 24 Then was the part of the hand sent from Him; and this writing was written. 25 And this is the writing that was written, MENE, MENE, TEKEL, UPHARSIN. 26 This is the interpretation of the thing: MENE; God has numbered your kingdom, and finished it. 27 TEKEL; you are weighed in the balances, and are found wanting. 28 PERES; your kingdom is divided, and given to the Medes and Persians. 29 Then commanded Belshazzar, and they clothed Daniel with scarlet, and put a chain of gold about his neck, and made a proclamation concerning him that he should be the third ruler in the kingdom 30 In that night was Belshazzar the king

of the Chaldeans slain. 31 And Darius the Mede took the kingdom, being about threescore and two years old

It pleased Darius to appoint one hundred and twenty local governors over the kingdom, with three presidents overseeing them, one of whom was Daniel. Daniel distinguished himself among the presidents and governors due to his excellent spirit, and the king planned to set him over the entire realm. The other presidents and governors sought to find grounds to accuse Daniel regarding the kingdom but found no fault in him because he was faithful. They concluded that they could only find an accusation against him concerning the law of his God So, they conspired and approached the king, suggesting that he establish a decree that anyone who petitioned any god or man besides the king for thirty days would be cast into the den of lions. The king signed the decree, which could not be altered according to the law of the Medes and Persians When Daniel learned about the decree, he continued to pray three times a day with his windows open towards Jerusalem, as was his custom. The men who had conspired against him saw this and brought it to the king's attention, accusing Daniel of disregarding the king's decree. The king, distressed, tried to find a way to rescue Daniel but was bound by the law Consequently, Daniel was cast into the den of lions, but the king expressed his hope that Daniel's God would deliver him. A stone was placed over the mouth of the den and sealed. The king fasted that night, unable to sleep, and early in the morning rushed to the den. He called out to Daniel, and Daniel responded that his God had sent an angel to shut the lions' mouths, and he had been saved because of his innocence The king was overjoyed and commanded Daniel be lifted out of the den. Those who had accused Daniel, along with their families, were thrown into the den of lions, where they were mauled before reaching the bottom. Darius then wrote to all the nations declaring that people should fear and tremble before Daniel's God, who is everlasting and delivers from danger. Daniel prospered during the reigns of Darius and Cyrus the Persian

Daniel 7

In the first year of Belshazzar, king of Babylon, Daniel had a dream and visions. In his vision, the four winds of the sky stirred up the great sea, and four great beasts emerged from the sea, each different from the others. The first beast was like a lion with eagle's wings, which was eventually lifted up and made to stand like a man. The second beast resembled a bear, raised on one side with three ribs in its mouth. It was told to devour much flesh. The third beast was like a leopard with four wings and four heads, given dominion. The fourth beast was terrifying and powerful, with iron teeth and ten horns, and a little horn grew among them, which had human eyes and a mouth speaking arrogantly Daniel saw thrones placed, and the Ancient of Days took His seat, His attire white as snow and His throne fiery flames. Thousands attended Him, and judgment was set. The fourth beast was slain and its body destroyed, while the other beasts had their dominion taken but were allowed to live for a time Daniel saw one like a son of man coming with the clouds to the Ancient of Days, receiving dominion and glory, and an everlasting kingdom. This vision troubled Daniel, and he sought to understand it. The angel Gabriel explained that the four beasts represented four kings who would arise from the earth, but the saints of the Most High would receive the kingdom forever Daniel was particularly troubled by the fourth beast, which was different and had ten horns. The angel explained that the fourth beast would be a fourth kingdom on earth, with ten kings, and a little horn would arise, speaking against the Most High and persecuting the saints. This horn would change times and laws, but its dominion would ultimately be destroyed, and the kingdom would be given to the people of the saints of the Most High

Daniel 8

In the third year of King Belshazzar's reign, Daniel had another vision while in the citadel of Susa by the river Ulai. He saw a ram with two high horns, one larger than the other, pushing in different directions. A male goat with a notable horn between its eyes came from the west and attacked the ram, breaking its horns and trampling it. The goat became very powerful, but its great horn broke, and four notable horns emerged in its place. From one of these horns, a little horn grew exceedingly great, casting down some of the heavenly hosts and taking away the daily burnt offering Daniel heard a holy one asking how long the vision of the daily offering and the desolation would last. The response was two thousand three hundred evenings and mornings, after which the sanctuary would be cleansed. Gabriel was sent to make Daniel understand the vision, revealing that the ram represented the kings of Media and Persia, the goat the king of Greece, and the great horn the first king of Greece. The four horns represented four kingdoms that would arise after the first king. In the latter time of their kingdom, a fierce king would arise, destroy many, and oppose the prince of princes, but he would be broken without human intervention

Daniel 9

In the first year of Darius the Mede, Daniel understood from the books that the desolation of Jerusalem would last seventy years. He prayed to the Lord, confessing the sins of the people and asking for mercy. He acknowledged that their sins had led to their desolation and requested that God turn His anger away from Jerusalem and restore it for His sake As Daniel prayed and confessed, Gabriel appeared and informed him that his prayers were heard. He was told that seventy weeks were decreed for the people and the holy city to finish transgression, bring in everlasting righteousness, and anoint the most holy. From the decree to restore and build Jerusalem until the Anointed One would be seven weeks and sixty-two weeks. After this, the Anointed One would be cut off, and the city and sanctuary would be destroyed by the people of the coming prince. A firm covenant would be made for one week, but in the middle of the week, sacrifices would cease, and desolation would follow

Daniel 10

In the third year of Cyrus king of Persia, Daniel received a revelation about a great conflict. He mourned and fasted for three weeks, eating no pleasant bread or meat. On the twenty-fourth day of the first month, by the river Tigris, Daniel saw a man clothed in linen, with a body like beryl and a face like lightning. His appearance was awe-inspiring, and Daniel fell into a deep sleep upon hearing his voice The man touched Daniel, helping him to his knees and instructed him not to be afraid. He revealed that his words were heard from the first day Daniel sought understanding and humbled himself. The prince of Persia had resisted him for twenty-one days, but Michael had come to assist. The vision concerned what would happen to Daniel's people in the latter days As the man spoke, Daniel's strength returned, and he was encouraged. He was informed of the forthcoming events and the battles that would unfold, with specific details about the conflicts and the outcomes

Daniel 11

1 "In the first year of Darius the Mede, I stood to support and strengthen him. 2 Now, I will reveal the truth to you. Three more kings will arise in Persia, and the fourth will be wealthier than all of them. As he gains strength from his riches, he will incite all against the realm of Greece. 3 A powerful king will emerge who will rule with great authority and do as he pleases. 4 When his reign reaches its peak, his kingdom will be broken and divided toward the four winds of heaven. It will not go to his descendants nor follow the same dominion he held; it will be given to others 5 "The king of the south will become strong,

and one of his princes will surpass him in power and dominion. 6 After several years, they will form an alliance. The daughter of the king of the south will marry the king of the north to seal this alliance, but her influence will not last. Neither he nor his kingdom will remain; she will be given up along with those who brought her, her father, and those who supported her 7 "A successor from her family will arise, who will attack the army of the king of the north and enter his fortress. He will defeat them. 8 He will also take their gods, along with their molten images and valuable silver and gold vessels, to Egypt. He will stay away from the king of the north for some years. 9 He will invade the realm of the king of the south but will return to his own land 10 "His sons will prepare for war, gathering a vast army that will overflow and sweep through, even attacking his fortress. 11 The king of the south will be enraged and come out to fight the king of the north, sending a large army. The army will be defeated and fall into his hands. 12 The king of the south will become proud, and he will defeat many, but he will not prevail. 13 The king of the north will return with an even larger army and more supplies, coming at the end of years 14 "During this time, many will rebel against the king of the south. Among your people, violent children will rise to fulfill the vision, but they will fall. 15 The king of the north will build a siege ramp and capture a fortified city. The forces of the south will not stand, nor will their chosen people or any strength. 16 He who attacks will do so as he wishes, and no one will stand against him. He will take control of the glorious land, bringing destruction 17 "He will set his eyes on the whole kingdom and establish equitable conditions. He will give the daughter of women in marriage to corrupt her, but she will not remain loyal to him. 18 After this, he will turn his attention to the islands and conquer many. A prince will cause him to cease his reproach and turn it back on him. 19 Then he will return to his own land but will stumble and fall, never to be found again 20 "A successor who will impose a tribute will arise, but he will be destroyed within a few days, not by anger or battle. 21 In his place, a contemptible person will come to power, not given royal honor, but he will seize the kingdom by deceit. 22 The overwhelming forces will be overthrown before him, including the prince of the covenant. 23 After a treaty is made with him, he will deceive many, gaining strength with a small following. 24 In times of peace, he will exploit the rich provinces, doing what his predecessors did not. He will distribute plunder and devise plans against strongholds for a time 25 "He will mobilize his power and courage against the king of the south with a great army. The king of the south will fight back with an even greater and mighty army but will not prevail due to scheming against him. 26 Those who eat his provisions will destroy him, and his army will be swept away, many falling slain. 27 Both kings will be intent on deceit, speaking lies at one table, but it will not succeed, for the end is set for the appointed time. 28 The king will return to his land with great wealth, against the holy covenant. He will take action and then return to his own land 29 "He will come again at the appointed time, but not as he did before. 30 Ships from Kittim will come against him, and he will be frustrated. He will return with rage against the holy covenant and take action against those who forsake it. 31 Forces will rise up against him, profaning the sanctuary and removing the daily sacrifice. They will set up the abomination that causes desolation. 32 He will corrupt those who act wickedly against the covenant by flatteries, but the people who know their God will be strong and take action 33 "The wise among the people will instruct many, though some will be killed, captured, or plundered for many days. 34 When they fall, they will receive a little help, but many will join them with deceit. 35 Some of the wise will fall to be refined, purified, and made white until the end, for it is still to come 36 "The king will act according to his will, exalting himself and magnifying himself above every god. He will speak against the God of gods and prosper until the indignation is fulfilled, for what has been determined will be done. 37 He will not regard the gods of his ancestors or the desire of women, nor any god; he will exalt himself above all. 38 Instead, he will honor a god of fortresses with gold, silver, precious stones, and valuable gifts. 39 He will use this god to deal with strong fortresses and increase the glory of those who acknowledge him, making them rulers over many and dividing the land for a price 40 "At the end time, the king of the south will engage him in battle, and the king of the north will come against him like a whirlwind, with chariots, horsemen, and many ships. He will invade countries, overflow them, and pass through. 41 He will enter the glorious land, and many countries will fall, but Edom, Moab, and the chief of the children of Ammon will escape. 42 He will extend his power over other countries, and Egypt will not escape. 43 He will control the treasures of gold, silver, and precious things in Egypt. The Libyans and Ethiopians will be at his heels. 44 But news from the east and the north will trouble him, and he will go out with great fury to destroy and annihilate many. 45 He will plant his palace between the sea and the glorious holy mountain but will come to his end, with no one to help him."

Daniel 12

1 "At that time, Michael, the great prince who stands guard over your people, will arise. There will be a time of distress such as never has happened before. At that time, your people will be delivered—everyone whose name is found written in the book. 2 Multitudes who sleep in the dust will awake: some to everlasting life, others to shame and everlasting contempt. 3 Those who are wise will shine like the brightness of the heavens, and those who lead many to righteousness will shine like the stars forever and ever. 4 But you, Daniel, close up and seal the words of the scroll until the time of the end. Many will go here and there to increase knowledge." 5 Then I, Daniel, looked and saw two others standing, one on this bank of the river and one on the opposite bank. 6 One of them said to the man clothed in linen, who was above the waters of the river, "How long will it be before these astonishing things are fulfilled?" 7 The man clothed in linen, who was above the waters of the river, lifted his right hand and left hand toward heaven, and I heard him swear by him who lives forever, saying, "It will be for a time, times, and half a time. When the power of the holy people has been finally broken, all these things will be completed." 8 I heard, but I did not understand. So I asked, "My lord, what will the outcome of all this be?" 9 He replied, "Go your way, Daniel, because the words are closed up and sealed until the time of the end. 10 Many will be purified, made spotless, and refined, but the wicked will continue to be wicked. None of the wicked will understand, but those who are wise will understand 11 "From the time that the daily sacrifice is abolished and the abomination that causes desolation is set up, there will be 1,290 days. 12 Blessed is the one who waits for and reaches the end of the 1,335 days. 13 "As for you, go your way till the end. You will rest, and then at the end of the days, you will rise to receive your allotted inheritance."

Daniel 13

1 A man named Joakim lived in Babylon. He had a wife named Susanna, the daughter of Helkias, a

beautiful woman who feared the Lord. 2 Her parents were also righteous and taught her according to the law of Moses. 3 Joakim was a wealthy man with a lovely garden beside his house. The Jews frequently visited him because he was esteemed above all others. 4 Two elders appointed as judges, who were known for their wickedness, would often come to Joakim's house. 5 They observed Susanna walking in her garden daily and were inflamed with lust for her. 6 They turned away their eyes so they would not see heaven or remember just judgments. 7 Both were overwhelmed with passion for her and lost their self-control. They could not hold back their desire to lie with her 8 They plotted to seduce her. One day, they told her to lie with them, threatening to accuse her of sin if she refused. 9 When Susanna refused, they falsely accused her of meeting a young man in the garden and consented to the lie. 10 The elders brought the accusation against Susanna, and despite her innocence, the judges condemned her to death 11 The elders, holding their testimony, told the people that Susanna had sinned. 12 She was led away to be executed. 13 As she was being taken away, she cried out, "O eternal God, you know what is hidden and are aware of all things before they come to be. 14 You know that I have never been in such a position, and yet I am accused of a crime. 15 But I am innocent of what I am accused of." 16 God heard her cry. 17 As she was being led away to be executed, the Lord stirred up the spirit of a young lad named Daniel, who cried out, "I am innocent of the blood of this woman." 18 Daniel was taken to the assembly and questioned. He accused the elders of falsehood, revealing their plot. 19 He declared, "Under what tree did you see Susanna and the young man? Tell me." 20 They answered, "Under an evergreen tree." 21 Daniel then said, "You have lied against your own selves. The angel of God has already judged you." 22 The assembly condemned the elders to death. 23 Susanna was delivered, and the people praised God for her deliverance. 24 Daniel became greatly honored, and his fame spread among the people

Daniel 14

1 King Belshazzar made a great feast for a thousand of his lords and drank wine in their presence. 2 While he tasted the wine, he gave orders to bring in the gold and silver vessels that Nebuchadnezzar, his father, had taken from the temple in Jerusalem, so that the king and his lords, his wives, and his concubines might drink from them. 3 They brought in the gold vessels that had been taken from the temple, and the king and his lords, his wives, and his concubines drank from them. 4 They praised the gods of gold, silver, bronze, iron, wood, and stone 5 Suddenly, the fingers of a human hand appeared and wrote on the plaster of the wall of the king's palace, near the lampstand. The king saw the hand as it wrote. 6 His face turned pale, and he was so frightened that his knees knocked together and his legs gave way 7 The king called out for the enchanters, astrologers, and diviners to be brought. He promised to reward anyone who could read the writing and interpret it. 8 All the king's wise men came in, but they could not read the writing or tell the king what it meant. 9 So King Belshazzar became even more terrified, and his face grew more pale. His nobles were baffled 10 The queen, hearing the voices of the king and his nobles, came into the banquet hall. She said, "O king, live forever! Do not be alarmed; do not look so pale. 11 There is a man in your kingdom who has the spirit of the holy gods in him. In the time of your father, he was found to have insight and intelligence and wisdom like that of the gods. Your father, King Nebuchadnezzar, appointed him chief of the

magicians, enchanters, astrologers, and diviners. 12 This man, Daniel, whom the king called Belteshazzar, has a keen mind and knowledge and understanding, and can interpret dreams, explain riddles, and solve difficult problems. Call for Daniel, and he will tell you what the writing means." 13 So Daniel was brought before the king, and the king said to him, "Are you Daniel, one of the exiles my father the king brought from Judah? 14 I have heard that the spirit of the gods is in you and that you have insight, intelligence, and outstanding wisdom. 15 The wise men and enchanters were brought before me to read this writing and tell me what it means, but they could not explain it. 16 Now I have heard that you are able to give interpretations and solve difficult problems. If you can read this writing and tell me what it means, you will be clothed in purple and have a gold chain placed around your neck, and you will be made the third highest ruler in the kingdom." 17 Then Daniel answered the king, "You may keep your gifts for yourself and give your rewards to someone else. Nevertheless, I will read the writing for the king and tell him what it means. 18 Your Majesty, the Most High God gave your father Nebuchadnezzar sovereignty and greatness and glory and splendor. 19 Because of the high position he gave him, all the nations and peoples of every language dreaded and feared him. Those the king wanted to put to death, he put to death; those he wanted to spare, he spared; those he wanted to promote, he promoted; and those he wanted to humble, he humbled. 20 But when his heart became arrogant and hardened with pride, he was deposed from his royal throne and stripped of his glory. 21 He was driven away from people and given the mind of an animal; he lived with the wild donkeys and ate grass like the ox. His body was drenched with the dew of heaven until he acknowledged that the Most High God is sovereign over all kingdoms on earth and sets over them anyone he wishes 22 "But you, Belshazzar, his son, have not humbled yourself, though you knew all this. 23 Instead, you have set yourself up against the Lord of heaven. You had the goblets from his temple brought to you, and you and your nobles, your wives, and your concubines drank wine from them. You praised the gods of silver and gold, of bronze, iron, wood, and stone, which cannot see or hear or understand. But you did not honor the God who holds in his hand your life and all your ways. 24 Therefore he sent the hand that wrote the inscription 25 "This is the inscription that was written: MENE, MENE, TEKEL, PARSIN. 26 Here is what these words mean: MENE: God has numbered the days of your reign and brought it to an end. 27 TEKEL: You have been weighed on the scales and found wanting. 28 PERES: Your kingdom is divided and given to the Medes and Persians." 29 Then at Belshazzar's command, Daniel was clothed in purple, a gold chain was placed around his neck, and he was proclaimed the third highest ruler in the kingdom. 30 That very night Belshazzar, king of the Babylonians, was slain, 31 and Darius the Mede took over the kingdom, at the age of sixty-two

77. Susanna

Chapter 1

Susanna Parker stepped off the bus into the crisp, fresh air of Meadowbrook. The town seemed like something out of a storybook, with its cobblestone streets, quaint shops, and charming homes. As she made her way to her new home—a Victorian house with ivy-covered walls and a sprawling garden—she felt a mix of excitement and trepidation The house, left to her by an aunt she had only met once as a child, was both beautiful and imposing. Its large bay windows and intricate woodwork spoke of a time long past. As Susanna explored the house, she found dusty rooms filled with antique furniture and old photographs. The sense of history was palpable, and she couldn't help but feel that the house had stories to tell In the afternoon, she ventured into town to introduce herself. The locals were friendly but curious, their conversations tinged with intrigue about the new arrival. At the café, she met Martha, the owner, who welcomed her warmly and shared some gossip about the town's past. Susanna learned about Meadowbrook's reputation for being a place where everyone knew each other's business, and she was intrigued by the stories she heard

Chapter 2

After a long day of unpacking, Susanna decided to explore the attic. It was cluttered with old trunks, dusty books, and faded photographs. As she sifted through the boxes, she came across a leather-bound journal. The journal was filled with elegant handwriting, and she realized it belonged to her aunt The entries in the journal detailed her aunt's life in Meadowbrook, including her relationships, personal struggles, and significant events. Susanna was captivated by the stories of her aunt's youthful adventures and the sense of a life lived fully. There were references to a secret admirer and hints of a clandestine romance that piqued her curiosity One entry described a secret meeting spot, which was marked on a faded map tucked inside the journal. Susanna decided to investigate this location, hoping it might provide further clues about her aunt's hidden past

Chapter 3

Susanna's exploration led her to the town's historical society, where she met Ethan Blake, a local historian. Ethan was intrigued by Susanna's quest and agreed to help her. They started poring over old records, newspapers, and town archives Their research revealed that Meadowbrook had been a vibrant community with a rich history, but many details had been lost over time. They uncovered stories of significant events, such as town festivals and old scandals. Each discovery seemed to bring them closer to understanding her aunt's life Ethan and Susanna also visited the town library, where they found more about her aunt's social circles and past interactions. The more they discovered, the more Susanna felt connected to her aunt and the town itself

Chapter 4

As Susanna delved deeper into the journal, she came across a series of passionate letters between her aunt and a man named William. The letters were filled with declarations of love, longing, and frustration. Susanna noticed that the letters hinted at a secret relationship that had caused her aunt considerable distress The letters also included references to a planned elopement and a final, urgent meeting that never occurred. Susanna and Ethan speculated that something had happened to prevent the planned union, and they began searching for any information about William and his whereabouts Susanna began to piece together the emotional turmoil her aunt must have experienced. The romantic letters revealed a side of her aunt that was both vulnerable and courageous, and Susanna felt a deep sense of empathy for the woman she had never truly known

Chapter 5

One afternoon, a mysterious man arrived in Meadowbrook. He was an outsider, and his presence quickly stirred up gossip. Susanna noticed that the man seemed unusually interested in her and her investigations The stranger's behavior was suspicious—he seemed to be shadowing her movements and asking questions about her research. Susanna confronted him, but he remained evasive, claiming to be a traveler with no particular interest in her personal matters Ethan and Susanna speculated about the stranger's motives. They wondered if he had any connection to the secrets they were uncovering or if he was merely a distraction. Their investigation continued, with the stranger's presence adding an element of tension to their quest for the truth

Chapter 6

Ethan and Susanna discovered that the enigmatic stranger had been involved in a historical event that was pivotal to understanding her aunt's past. They found evidence linking him to a controversial incident involving William, Susanna's aunt's secret lover Through interviews with older townsfolk and a deeper dive into local records, they learned that the stranger was actually a relative of William. He had come to Meadowbrook to resolve old family issues related to his ancestor's unresolved affair This revelation connected many dots and clarified the reasons behind her aunt's decisions and actions. Susanna felt a mix of relief and sadness as she realized the complexities of her aunt's life and the difficulties she had faced

Chapter 7

The truth about William and the stranger's connection led to a confrontation. Susanna met with the stranger and demanded full disclosure about what he knew. The meeting was emotional and intense, revealing the full extent of the heartache and sacrifice involved in her aunt's story The stranger revealed that William had been forced to leave town due to a scandal, and that he had been searching for Susanna's aunt in the years following. His presence in Meadowbrook was part of his attempt to find closure for his family's troubled past Susanna and Ethan confronted their own feelings and the implications of the revelations. They had to navigate their personal emotions while dealing with the aftermath of their discoveries

Chapter 8

With the mystery resolved, Susanna reflected on her journey. She took time to process the emotional weight of her aunt's story and how it had impacted her own life Susanna began to see Meadowbrook in a new light, appreciating the community and its history. She felt a sense of belonging and purpose as she planned to preserve her aunt's legacy Ethan and Susanna's relationship had grown stronger through their shared experiences. They discussed their future and how the past had shaped their present

Chapter 9

Susanna started renovating her aunt's house, transforming it into a place of remembrance and hope. She planned to open it as a historical museum dedicated to the stories of Meadowbrook and her aunt's contributions The town embraced Susanna's efforts, and she became an integral part of the community. She built new relationships and found a sense of fulfillment in her work and personal life Ethan continued to support Susanna, and their bond deepened as they looked toward the future together

Chapter 10

The novel concludes with a celebration of the changes Susanna has undergone and the impact of her journey. The town of Meadowbrook comes together for a grand reopening of the house as a museum Susanna reflects on her growth and the lessons she has learned. The final Chapter offers a hopeful view of the future, with Susanna and Ethan looking forward to new adventures and continued exploration of their lives

78. Bel and the Dragon

1 King Astyages was gathered to his ancestors, and Cyrus the Persian received his kingdom. 2 Daniel lived with the king and was honored above all his friends. 3 The Babylonians had an idol named Bel, and every day twelve large measures of fine flour, forty sheep, and six jars of wine were consumed for its upkeep. 4 The king honored Bel and went daily to worship it, but Daniel worshipped his own God. The king asked Daniel, "Why do you not worship Bel?" 5 Daniel replied, "I do not honor idols made with hands but worship only the living God, who created the heavens and the earth and rules over all flesh." 6 The king said, "Do you not think that Bel is a living god? Do you not see how much he eats and drinks every day?" 7 Daniel laughed and said, "O king, do not be deceived; this idol is merely clay inside and brass outside and has never eaten or drunk anything." 8 The king grew angry and called for the priests of Bel, saying, "If you do not tell me who consumes these offerings, you will die. But if you can show me that Bel devours them, then Daniel shall die for speaking blasphemy against Bel." Daniel agreed to the king's challenge. 9 There were seventy priests of Bel, along with their wives and children. The king went with Daniel to Bel's temple. 10 The priests said, "We will leave, but you, O king, set out the food, mix the wine, and place it before the idol. Seal the door securely with your own signet. 11 In the morning, if Bel has not consumed the offerings, we will face death, but if Bel has eaten, then Daniel has lied against us." 12 Unconcerned, the priests had secretly made an entrance under the table, through which they entered to consume the offerings. 13 After they left, the king placed the food before Bel. Daniel had commanded his servants to scatter ashes over the temple floor in the presence of the king. They then sealed the door with the king's signet and departed. 14 That night, the priests came with their families and ate and drank the offerings. 15 In the morning, the king and Daniel arrived. 16 The king asked Daniel, "Are the seals intact?" Daniel confirmed, "Yes, O king, they are." 17 When the door was opened, the king exclaimed, "Great is Bel, and there is no deceit in him at all!" 18 Daniel laughed and told the king, "Look at the floor and observe whose footsteps are there." 19 The king saw the footprints of men, women, and children. Angered, he took the priests and their families to the secret entrance, where they had been sneaking in. 20 The king executed them and handed Bel over to Daniel, who destroyed both the idol and its temple 21 In the same region, there was a great dragon that the Babylonians worshipped. 22 The king said to Daniel, "Will you also claim that this dragon is made of brass? Look, it lives, eats, and drinks. You cannot deny that it is a living god. Therefore, worship it." 23 Daniel responded, "I will worship the Lord my God, for He is the living God. 24 Allow me, O king, to kill this dragon without sword or staff." The king agreed. 25 Daniel prepared a mixture of pitch, fat, and hair, formed it into lumps, and fed them to the dragon. The dragon ate them and burst apart. Daniel then said, "Behold, these are the gods you worship." 26 The people of Babylon were outraged by this and conspired against the king, saying, "The king has become a Jew. He has destroyed Bel, slain the dragon, and executed the priests." 27 They demanded that the king deliver Daniel to them, or they would destroy him and his house. 28 Realizing he was trapped, the king gave Daniel to them. 29 They cast Daniel into the lion's den, where he remained for six days. 30 There were seven lions in the den, who were given two carcasses and two sheep daily, but on that occasion, they were not fed, intending that they would devour Daniel 31 In Judea, there was the prophet Habakkuk, who had made stew and broken bread into a bowl. He was on his way to the field to deliver it to the reapers. 32 The angel of the Lord instructed Habakkuk to carry the food to Daniel in Babylon. 33 Habakkuk replied, "Lord, I have never been to Babylon and do not know the way to the den." 34 The angel of the Lord then took Habakkuk by the hair and transported him to Babylon, placing him over the den. 35 Habakkuk cried out, "O Daniel, Daniel, take the food that God has sent you." 36 Daniel thanked God for remembering him and not forsaking those who love Him. 37 Daniel ate, and the angel returned Habakkuk to his place immediately 38 On the seventh day, the king came to mourn for Daniel. When he arrived at the den and looked in, he saw Daniel sitting. 39 The king shouted with a loud voice, "Great are You, O Lord, God of Daniel, and there is no other beside You!" 40 The king then had those who conspired against Daniel cast into the den, where they were devoured instantly before his eyes

79. Prayer of Manasseh

1 O Lord Almighty in heaven, God of our forefathers Abraham, Isaac, and Jacob, and of their righteous descendants, 2 You who have made the heavens and the earth, with all their order, 3 You who have bound the sea by Your command, shut up the deep, and sealed it with Your fearsome and glorious name, 4 Whom all things fear and tremble before Your power, 5 For the majesty of Your glory is unbearable, and the anger of Your threats towards sinners is intolerable. 6 Your merciful promise is boundless and unfathomable, 7 For You are the Lord Most High, full of compassion, patient, abundant in mercy, and empathetic to human suffering. 8 According to Your great goodness, You have promised repentance and forgiveness to those who have sinned against You. In Your infinite mercy, You have granted repentance to sinners so they may be saved. You, O Lord, who are the God of the righteous, have not appointed repentance for the righteous like Abraham, Isaac, and Jacob, who have not sinned against You, but You have appointed it for me, a sinner. 9 For I have sinned more than the sands of the sea. My transgressions are numerous, O Lord, my transgressions are many, and I am unworthy to gaze upon the height of heaven due to my iniquities. 10 I am weighed down by heavy chains, unable to lift my head because of my sins, and I find no relief. I have provoked Your wrath and done what is evil in Your sight: I have not followed Your will or kept Your commandments. I have committed abominations and multiplied detestable acts. 11 Therefore, I bow the knee of my heart, seeking Your grace. 12 I have sinned, O Lord, I have sinned, and I acknowledge my iniquities; 13 But I humbly ask You to forgive me, O Lord, forgive me, and do not destroy me with my iniquities. Do not be angry with me forever, nor reserve evil for me. Do not condemn me to the depths of the earth. For You, O Lord, are the God of those who repent. 14 In me, You will manifest all Your goodness, for You will save me, an unworthy servant, according to Your great mercy. 15 Then I will praise You forever, all the days of my life; for all the hosts of heaven sing Your praise, and Yours is the glory forever and ever. Amen

80. 1 Maccabees

The story of the Maccabees is one of remarkable

bravery and unyielding faith against overwhelming odds. Rooted in the second century BCE, the Maccabean Revolt is a seminal episode in Jewish history, emblematic of resistance against cultural and religious oppression. This book explores the intricate tapestry of events that led to this revolt, the key figures involved, and the profound impact it had on Jewish identity and heritage. By delving into the historical context, the revolt itself, and its enduring legacy, we aim to shed light on the remarkable achievements of the Maccabees and their contribution to shaping the course of history The Maccabean Revolt did not emerge in isolation but was deeply intertwined with the broader political and cultural currents of its time. To fully appreciate the significance of the revolt, it is essential to understand the historical backdrop that shaped this dramatic period in Jewish history In the aftermath of Alexander the Great's conquests, his empire was divided among his generals, leading to the establishment of several Hellenistic kingdoms. One of these was the Seleucid Empire, founded by Seleucus I Nicator, which controlled a vast territory stretching from the eastern Mediterranean to the Indus River. Judea, a small but strategically located province, fell under Seleucid rule Under the Seleucid Empire, the Jewish population faced increasing pressure to assimilate into the dominant Hellenistic culture. This cultural and religious pressure was part of a broader policy of Hellenization, which sought to integrate diverse regions into a cohesive Greek-oriented society. The Seleucid rulers implemented policies that favored Greek customs, language, and religion, often at the expense of local traditions Antiochus IV Epiphanes, who ruled from 175 to 164 BCE, was a key figure in this cultural clash. His reign marked a period of intensified efforts to enforce Hellenistic practices in Judea. Antiochus IV pursued aggressive policies aimed at eradicating Jewish religious practices and imposing Greek religion. One of the most egregious acts of this campaign was the desecration of the Jewish Temple in Jerusalem. In 167 BCE, Antiochus ordered the conversion of the Temple into a sanctuary for Zeus Olympios, and the altar of burnt offerings was used for sacrifices to pagan deities. This act of sacrilege was deeply offensive to the Jewish population, as it violated the sanctity of their most important religious site The desecration of the Temple was not merely a symbolic affront but a direct challenge to Jewish identity and religious observance. The Seleucid authorities also sought to suppress Jewish religious practices by prohibiting circumcision, Sabbath observance, and other key elements of Jewish law. These measures were part of a broader strategy to erode Jewish cultural and religious identity and replace it with Hellenistic norms The response to Antiochus IV's policies was not immediate but grew out of a broader context of discontent and resistance. In the village of Modein, Mattathias, a priest of the Hasmonean family, became a pivotal figure in the resistance against Seleucid rule. When ordered to participate in a pagan sacrifice, Mattathias refused and, in an act of defiance, killed a Jewish apostate who had complied with the order. This act of rebellion was followed by a call to arms against the Seleucid oppressors Mattathias's actions ignited a wider movement of resistance. His son, Judah Maccabee, emerged as a central leader of the revolt. The Maccabees, as they came to be known, were a group of Jewish fighters who took up arms to challenge Seleucid rule and restore Jewish religious practices. Their struggle was characterized by a series of battles and guerrilla tactics, aimed not only at defeating the Seleucid forces but also at reclaiming and rededicating the desecrated Temple The historical context of the Maccabean Revolt underscores the significance of the struggle faced by the Jewish people. It was a fight for survival against a powerful empire that sought to impose foreign cultural and religious practices. The revolt, therefore, was not just a political or military conflict but a profound expression of resistance against cultural and religious assimilation. Understanding this context provides insight into the motivations and challenges faced by the Maccabees and highlights the broader implications of their struggle for Jewish history and identity

81. 2 Maccabees

The Maccabean Revolt, which began in 167 BCE, was a pivotal Chapter in Jewish history, marked by intense conflict, strategic battles, and a profound quest for religious freedom. This Chapter delves into the major events and figures of the revolt, highlighting the leadership of Judah Maccabee and the significant battles that defined this historic struggle The revolt's origins can be traced back to the actions of Mattathias, a priest of the Hasmonean family, who sparked a movement of resistance against the Seleucid Empire's oppressive policies. After Mattathias's initial defiance, his son Judah Maccabee took up the mantle of leadership, rallying Jewish fighters to their cause. Judah, known for his strategic acumen and charismatic leadership, became the central figure in the Maccabean struggle The early stages of the revolt were marked by guerrilla tactics and skirmishes against Seleucid forces. The Maccabees, although initially outnumbered and under-equipped, utilized their knowledge of the local terrain and their strong religious fervor to their advantage. One of the first significant confrontations was the Battle of Modein, where the Maccabean forces achieved a crucial victory. This battle was not just a military engagement but also a symbolic victory for Jewish resistance, as it demonstrated the Maccabees' determination and ability to challenge the Seleucid army As the revolt progressed, Judah Maccabee's leadership was instrumental in organizing and expanding the resistance. His strategic brilliance was evident in the successful recapture of several key towns and fortresses that had fallen under Seleucid control. The Maccabees employed hit-and-run tactics and utilized the element of surprise to their advantage, which proved effective against the larger and better-equipped Seleucid forces One of the most significant events of the revolt was the Siege of Jerusalem. The Seleucid forces, under the command of General Lysias, launched a major offensive to regain control of the city and suppress the rebellion. The siege was a prolonged and intense conflict, with both sides suffering significant casualties. Despite the odds, the Maccabees managed to hold their ground and eventually forced the Seleucid forces to withdraw The recapture of Jerusalem was a turning point in the revolt. Upon regaining control of the city, the Maccabees undertook the monumental task of purifying and rededicating the desecrated Temple. This event, known as the rededication of the Temple, was marked by the lighting of the menorah, an act that became symbolic of the Jewish struggle and resilience. The rededication is commemorated annually during the Festival of Hanukkah, which celebrates the miracle of the oil that lasted for eight days, despite only being enough for one day The Maccabean Revolt was not solely a military struggle but also a fight for religious freedom and cultural preservation. The success of the revolt had profound implications for Jewish identity and autonomy. The Maccabees established the Hasmonean dynasty, which ruled Judea for several decades and restored Jewish sovereignty over the region. Their leadership and victories were instrumental in preserving Jewish religious practices and traditions during a period of intense external pressure In conclusion, the Maccabean Revolt was a defining moment in Jewish history, characterized by courage, strategic prowess, and a deep commitment to religious and cultural preservation. The leadership of Judah Maccabee and the resilience of the Maccabean fighters against the Seleucid Empire underscore the significance of this revolt in shaping the course of Jewish history. The legacy of the Maccabees endures through their contributions to Jewish identity, religious practice, and the broader historical narrative

82. 3 Maccabees

The Maccabean Revolt, an emblematic episode of resistance and resilience, left an indelible mark on Jewish history and identity. The revolt's successful outcome had far-reaching consequences for the Jewish people, their culture, and their religious practices. This Chapter explores the enduring legacy of the Maccabees and how their actions shaped the trajectory of Jewish history

The Establishment of the Hasmonean Dynasty

Following their victories and the rededication of the Temple, the Maccabees established the Hasmonean dynasty, which marked a new era of Jewish sovereignty. The Hasmonean rulers, including Judah Maccabee and his successors, played a crucial role in consolidating Jewish control over Judea and restoring religious practices that had been suppressed under Seleucid rule. This period of self-rule allowed for the revival of traditional Jewish customs and the rebuilding of Jewish institutions The Hasmonean dynasty's political and religious leadership was instrumental in reasserting Jewish identity and autonomy. The rulers took measures to fortify Jerusalem and expand the territory of Judea, which included integrating various regions under their control. The Hasmonean reign was characterized by efforts to solidify Jewish religious practices and strengthen communal institutions, including the Sanhedrin, which was a central body of Jewish legal and religious authority

Cultural and Religious Revival

The aftermath of the revolt saw a revival of Jewish cultural and religious practices that had been undermined by Hellenistic influence. The rededication of the Temple was not only a religious milestone but also a symbol of Jewish resilience and faith. The Festival of Hanukkah, commemorating this event, became an important celebration in Jewish tradition, symbolizing the triumph of light over darkness and the perseverance of Jewish identity In addition to religious revival, the Maccabean period also saw a resurgence of Jewish scholarship and learning. The Hasmonean rulers supported the study of Jewish law and the preservation of Jewish texts. This era contributed to the development of Jewish religious literature and the strengthening of Jewish intellectual traditions. The restoration of the Temple and the renewed focus on religious education played a significant role in fostering a vibrant Jewish culture

Political and Military Challenges

Despite the successes of the Maccabean Revolt, the Hasmonean dynasty faced ongoing political and military challenges. The new rulers had to navigate complex relations with neighboring powers, including the Roman Republic, which was emerging as a dominant force in the Mediterranean. The Hasmoneans sought to maintain their independence while managing their interactions with Rome and other regional powers Internally, the Hasmonean dynasty experienced periods of political instability and factionalism. Disputes over succession and governance occasionally led to conflicts and challenges to the dynasty's authority. Nevertheless, the Maccabean legacy continued to influence Jewish political and religious life, even amidst these difficulties

The Enduring Impact of the Maccabees

The Maccabean Revolt and the Hasmonean dynasty's subsequent rule left a lasting impact on Jewish history. The revolt became a symbol of resistance against oppression and a testament to the strength of Jewish faith and unity. The story of the Maccabees inspired future generations to uphold the values of courage, resilience, and commitment to their cultural and religious heritage The historical significance of the Maccabees is also reflected in the broader Jewish narrative and traditions. The celebration of Hanukkah, the preservation of Jewish laws and customs, and the continued emphasis on Jewish education and scholarship all trace their roots to the Maccabean period. The legacy of the Maccabees remains an integral part of Jewish identity and cultural memory

83. 4 Maccabees

"4 Maccabees" is a unique text within the broader Maccabean literature, distinguished by its philosophical and theological reflections on the events of the Maccabean Revolt. Unlike the other Maccabean books, which primarily focus on historical and military aspects, "4 Maccabees" delves into the moral and spiritual dimensions of the struggle faced by the Jewish people. This Chapter explores the key themes and philosophical insights presented in "4 Maccabees" and their significance for understanding the religious and ethical dimensions of the revolt

The Nature of Faith and Reason

One of the central themes of "4 Maccabees" is the relationship between faith and reason. The text presents a sophisticated argument about the role of reason in upholding religious faith and enduring persecution. It argues that true piety and religious conviction are demonstrated through the ability to endure suffering and sacrifice for one's beliefs. The work draws on Stoic philosophy, particularly the ideas of rational endurance and self-control, to frame its theological arguments "4 Maccabees" emphasizes that reason is a tool that helps individuals understand and appreciate the divine will. It argues that faith, when guided by reason, leads to a deeper and more resilient commitment to religious principles. The text suggests that the Maccabean martyrs, who faced torture and death rather than renouncing their faith, exemplify the triumph of reason and piety over worldly pressures

Martyrdom and Divine Justice

Martyrdom is another key theme in "4 Maccabees," which portrays the suffering and death of the Maccabean martyrs as acts of profound righteousness and faith. The text reflects on the nature of martyrdom as a form of ultimate witness to God's truth and justice. It explores how the martyrs' unwavering commitment to their faith in the face of extreme adversity serves as a testament to divine justice and the power of spiritual conviction The narrative of "4 Maccabees" includes detailed accounts of the trials and sufferings endured by the Maccabean martyrs, highlighting their steadfastness and the moral strength they displayed. The text argues that such unwavering commitment is rewarded by God, both in this life and the next. The portrayal of martyrdom in "4 Maccabees" serves to reinforce the idea that divine justice ultimately prevails, and that suffering for righteousness is a path to spiritual elevation

The Role of Divine Providence

Divine providence is a significant concept in "4 Maccabees," which discusses how God's will and guidance are manifest in the events of the Maccabean Revolt. The text argues that despite the apparent suffering and injustice faced by the Jewish people, divine providence is at work, guiding and protecting them through their trials. It suggests that the seemingly dire circumstances are part of a larger divine plan that ultimately leads to the triumph of faith and righteousness "4 Maccabees" reflects on how divine providence operates in the lives of individuals and communities, providing them with strength and resilience. The text offers a theological interpretation of the revolt, suggesting that the suffering endured by the Maccabean martyrs is part of a divine scheme to test and affirm their faith. This perspective encourages readers to view their own challenges and struggles in the context of a larger divine purpose

Ethical and Moral Lessons

The ethical and moral teachings of "4 Maccabees" are deeply rooted in its philosophical reflections on faith, reason, and martyrdom. The text offers a framework for understanding how to live a righteous life in the face of adversity. It underscores the importance of maintaining moral integrity and spiritual commitment, even when faced with persecution or suffering The lessons from "4 Maccabees" emphasize the value of endurance, self-control, and the pursuit of spiritual and moral excellence. It provides a model for how to navigate personal and communal challenges with a sense of divine purpose and moral clarity. The ethical teachings of the text continue to resonate with readers, offering guidance on how to uphold one's principles in the face of difficult circumstances

EXTRA-CANONICAL AND APOCRYPHAL BOOKS

1. Hebrew Apocrypha

84. 1 Enoch

CHAPTER 1

1.The words of the blessing of Enoch, wherewith he blessed theelect [[and]] righteous, who will be living in the day of tribulation, when all the wicked [[and godless]] are to be removed. 2.And he took up his parable and said--Enoch a righteous man, whose eyes were opened by God, saw the vision ofthe Holy One in the heavens, [which] the angels showed me,and from them I heard everything, and from them I understood as I saw, but not for this generation, but for a remote one which is for to come. 3.Concerning the elect I said, and took up my parable concerning them: The Holy Great One will come forth from His dwelling, 4.And the eternal God will tread upon the earth, (even) on Mount Sinai, [And appear from His camp] And appear in the strength of His might from the heaven of heavens. 5.And all shall be smitten with fearAnd the Watchers shall quake, And great fear and trembling shall seize them unto the ends of the earth. 6.And the high mountains shall be shaken,And the high hills shall be made low, And shall melt like wax before the flame 7.And the earth shall be [wholly] rent in sunder,And all that is upon the earth shall perish, And there shall be a judgement upon all (men). 8.But with the righteous He will make peace. And will protect the elect, And mercy shall be upon them. And they shall all belong to God, And they shall be prospered, And they shall [all] be blessed. [And He will help them all], And light shall appear unto them, [And He will make peace with them]. 9.And behold! He cometh with ten thousand of [His] holy ones To execute judgement upon all, And to destroy [all] the ungodly: And to convict all flesh Of all the works [of their ungodliness] which they have ungodly committed, And of all the hard things which ungodly sinners [have spoken] against Him.

CHAPTER 2

1.Observe ye everything that takes place in the heaven, how they do not change their orbits, [and] the luminaries which are in the heaven, how they all rise and set in order each in its season, and transgress not against their appointed order. 2.Behold ye the earth, and give heed to the things which take place upon it from first to last, [how **steadfast** they are], how [none of the things upon earth] change, [but] all the works of God appear [to you]. 3.Behold the summer and the winter, [[how the whole earth is filled with water, and clouds and dew and rain lie upon it]].

CHAPTER 3

Observe and see how (in the winter) all the trees [[seem as though they had withered and shed all their leaves, except fourteen trees, which do not lose their foliage but retain the old foliage from two to three years till the new comes.

CHAPTER 4

And again, observe ye the days of summer how the sun is above the earthover against it. And you seek shade and shelter by reason of the heat of the sun, and the earth also burns with growing heat, and so you cannot tread on the earth, or on a rock by reason of its heat.

CHAPTER 5

1. Observe [[ye]] how the trees cover themselves with green leaves and bear fruit: wherefore give ye heed [and know] with regard to all [His works], and recognize how He that liveth for everhath made them so. 2. And [all] His works go on [thus] from year to year for ever, and all the tasks [which] they accomplish forHim, and [their tasks] change not, but

according as [[God]] hath ordained sois it done. 3. And behold how the sea and the rivers in like manner accomplish and [change not] their tasks [from His commandments]. 4. But ye--ye have not been steadfast, nor done the commandments of theLord, But ye have turned away and spoken proud and hard words With your impure mouths against His greatness. Oh, ye hard-hearted, ye shall find no peace. 5. Therefore shall ye execrate your days,And the years of your life shall perish, And [the years of your destruction] shall be multiplied in eternal execration, And ye shall find no mercy. 6a. In those days ye shall make your names an eternal execration unto allthe righteous, b. And by you shall [all] who curse, curse, And all the sinners [and godless] shall imprecate by you,7c. And for you the godless there shall be a curse. 6d. And all the . . . shall rejoice, And there shall be forgiveness of sins, And every mercy and peace and forbearance: There shall be salvation unto them, a goodly light. i. And for all of you sinners there shall be no salvation, j But on you all shall abide a curse. 7a. But for the elect there shall be light and joy and peace, b. And they shall inherit the earth. 8. And then there shall be bestowed upon the elect wisdom,And they shall all live and never again sin, Either through ungodliness or through pride:But they who are wise shall be humble. 9. And they shall not again transgress, Nor shall they sin all the days of their life, Nor shall they die of (the divine) anger or wrath, But they shall complete the number of the days of their life. And their lives shall be increased in peace, And the years of their joy shall be multiplied, In eternal gladness and peace, All the days of their life.

CHAPTER 6

1. And it came to pass when the children of men had multiplied that in those days were born unto them beautiful and comely daughters. 2. And the angels, the children of the heaven, saw and lusted after them, and said to one another:'Come, let us choose us wives from among the children of men and beget us children.' 3. And Semjâzâ, who was their leader, said unto them: 'I fear yewill not indeed agree to do this deed, and I alone shall have to pay the penaltyof a great sin.' 4. And they all answered him and said: 'Let us all swear an oath, and all bind ourselves by mutual imprecations not to abandon this plan but to do this thing.' 5. Then sware they all together and bound themselves bymutual imprecations upon it. 6. And they were in all two hundred; who descended [in the days] of **Jared** on the summit of Mount Hermon, and theycalled it Mount Hermon, because they had sworn and bound themselves by mutual imprecations upon it. 7. And these are the names of their leaders: Sêmîazâz, their leader, Arâkîba, Râmêêl, Kôkabîêl, Tâmîêl, Râmîêl, Dânêl, Êzêqêêl, Barâqîjâl, Asâêl, Armârôs, Batârêl, Anânêl, Zaqîêl, Samsâpêêl, Satarêl, Tûrêl, Jômjâêl, Sariêl. 8. These are their chiefs of tens.

CHAPTER 7

1. And all the others together with them took unto themselves wives, andeach chose for himself one, and they began to go in unto them and to defile themselves with them, and they taught them charms and enchantments, and the cutting of roots, and made them acquainted with plants. 2. And they became pregnant, and they bare great giants, whose height was three thousand ells: 3. Who consumed all the acquisitions of men. And when men could no longer sustain them, 4. the giants turned against them and devoured mankind. 5. And they began to sin against birds, and beasts, and reptiles, and fish, and to devour one another's flesh, and drink the blood. 6. Then the earth laid accusation against the lawless ones.

CHAPTER 8

1. And Azâzêl taught men to make swords, and knives, and shields, and breastplates, and made

known to them **the metals** ⟨of the earth⟩ and the artof working them, and bracelets, and ornaments, and the use of antimony, and the beautifying of the eyelids, and all kinds of costly stones, and all colouring tinctures. 2. And there arose much godlessness, and they committed fornication, and they were led astray, and became corrupt in all their ways. Semjâzâ taught enchantments, and root-cuttings, Armârôs the resolving of enchantments, Barâqîjâl, (taught) astrology, Kôkabêl the constellations, **Êzêqêêl the knowledge of the clouds**, ⟨Araqiêl the signs ofthe earth, Shamsiêl the signs of the sun⟩, and Sariêl the course of the moon.And as men perished, they cried, and their cry went up to heaven . . .

CHAPTER 9

1. And then Michael, Uriel, Raphael, and Gabriel looked down from heaven and saw much blood being shed upon the earth, and all lawlessness being wrought upon the earth. 2. And they said one to another: 'The earth made †without inhabitant cries the voice of their crying† up to the gates of heaven. 3 [[And now to you, the holy ones of heaven]], the souls of men make their suit, saying, "Bring our cause before the Most High."'. 4. And they said to theLord **of the ages**: 'Lord of lords, God of gods, King of kings, ⟨ and God of the ages⟩, the throne of Thy glory (standeth) unto all the generations of the ages, and Thy name holy and glorious and blessed unto all the ages! 5. Thou hast made all things, and power over all things hast Thou: and all things are nakedand open in Thy sight, and Thou seest all things, and nothing can hide itself from Thee. 6. Thou seest what Azâzêl hath done, who hath taught all unrighteousness on earth and revealed the eternal secrets which were (preserved) in heaven, which men were striving to **learn**: 7. And Semjâzâ, to whom Thou hast given authority to bear rule over his associates. 8. And they have gone to the daughters of men upon the earth, and have slept with the women, and have defiled themselves, and revealed to them all kinds of sins. 9. And the women have borne giants, and the whole earth has thereby been filled with blood and unrighteousness. 10. And now, behold, the souls of those who have died are crying and making their suit to the gates of heaven, and their lamentations have ascended: and cannot cease because of the lawless deeds which are wrought on the earth. 11. And Thou knowest all things before they come to pass, and Thou seest these things and Thou dost suffer them, and Thou dost not say to us what we are to do to them in regard to these.'

CHAPTER 10

Then said the Most High, the Holy and Great One spake, and sent **Uriel** to theson of Lamech, and said to him: 2. '⟨Goto Noah⟩ and tell him in my name "Hidethyself!" and reveal to him the end that is approaching: that the whole earth will be destroyed, and a deluge is about to come upon the whole earth, and will destroy allthat is on it. 3. And now instruct him that he may escape and his seed may be preserved for all the generations of the world.' 4. And again the Lord said to Raphael: 'Bind Azâzêl hand and foot, and cast him into the darkness: and make an opening in the desert, which is in Dûdâêl, and cast him therein. 5. And place upon him rough and jagged rocks, and cover him with darkness, and let him abide there for ever, and cover his face that he may not see light. 6. And on the day of the great judgement he shall be cast into the fire. And heal the earth which the angels have corrupted,and proclaim the healing of the earth, that they may heal the plague, and that all the children of men may not perish through all the secret things that the Watchers have **disclosed** and have taught their sons. 8. And the whole earth has been corrupted through the works that were taught by Azâzêl: to him ascribe all sin.' 9. And to Gabriel said the Lord: 'Proceed against

the bastards and the reprobates, and against the children of fornication: and destroy [the children of fornication and] the children of the Watchers from amongst men [and cause them to go forth]: send them one against the other that they may destroy each other in battle: for length of days shall they not have. 10. And no request that they (i.e. their fathers) make of thee shall be granted unto their fathers on their behalf; for they hope to live an eternal life, and that eachone of them will live five hundred years.' 11. And the Lord said unto Michael: 'Go, **bind** Semjâzâ and his associates who have united themselves with women so as to have defiled themselves with them in all their uncleanness. 12. And when their sons have slain one another, and they have seen the destruction of their beloved ones, bind them fast for seventy generations in the **valleys** of the earth, till the day of their judgement and of their consummation, till the judgement that is for ever and ever is consummated. 13. In those days they shall be led off to the abyss of fire: ⟨and⟩ to the torment and the prison in which they shall be confined for ever. And whosoever shall be **condemned** and destroyed will from thenceforth be bound together with them to the end of all generations. 15. And destroy all the spirits of the reprobate and the children of the Watchers, because they have wronged mankind. Destroy all wrong from the face of the earth and let every evil work come to an end: and let the plant of righteousness and truth appear: [and it shall prove a blessing; the works of righteousness and truth] shall be planted in truth and joy for evermore.17. And then shall all the righteous escape, And shall live till they beget thousands of children,And all the days of their youth and their **old age** Shall they complete in peace.18. And then shall the whole earth be tilled in righteousness, and shall all be planted with trees and be full of blessing. 19. And all desirable trees shall be planted on it, and they shall plant vines on it: and the vine which theyplant thereon shall yield wine in abundance, and as for all the seed which is sown thereon each measure (of it) shall bear a thousand, and each measure of olives shall yield ten presses of oil. 20. And cleanse thou the earth from all oppression, and from all unrighteousness, and from all sin, and from all godlessness: and all the uncleanness that is wrought upon the earth destroy from off the earth. 21. [And all the children of men shall become righteous],and all nations shall offer adoration and shall praise Me, and all shall worshipMe. And the earth shall be cleansed from all defilement, and from all sin, and from all punishment, and from all torment, and I will never again send (them)upon it from generation to generation and for ever.

CHAPTER 11

1. And in those days I will open the store chambers of blessing which are in the heaven, so as to send them down [upon the earth] over the work and labour of the children of men. 2. And truth and peace shall be associated together throughout all the days of the world and throughout all the generations **of men**.'

CHAPTER 12

1. Before these things Enoch was hidden, and no one of the children of men knew where he was hidden, and where he abode, and what had become of him. 2. And his activities had to do with the Watchers, and his days werewith the holy ones. 3. And I, Enoch was blessing the Lord of **majesty** and the King of the ages, and lo! the Watchers called me--Enoch the scribe--and said to me: 4. 'Enoch, thou scribe of righteousness, go, †declare† to the Watchers of the heaven who have left the high heaven, the holy eternal place, and havedefiled themselves with women, and have done as the children of earth do, and have taken unto themselves wives: "Ye have wrought great destructionon the earth: 5. And ye shall have no peace nor forgiveness of sin: and inasmuch as †they† delight themselves in ††theirt

children, 6. The murder of †their† beloved ones shall †they† see, and over the destruction of †their† children shall †they† lament, and shall make supplication unto eternity, but mercy and peace shall ye not attain.'"

CHAPTER 13

1. And Enoch went and said: 'Azâzêl, thou shalt have no peace: a severe sentence has gone forth against thee to put thee in bonds: 2. And thou shalt not have toleration nor †request† granted to thee, because of the unrighteousness which thou hast taught, and because of all the works of godlessness and unrighteousness and sin which thou hast shown to men.' 3. Then I went and spoke to them all together, and they were all afraid, and fear and trembling seized them. 4. And they besought me to draw up a petition for them that they might find forgiveness, and to read their petition in the presence of the Lord of heaven. 5. For from thenceforward they could not speak (with Him) nor lift up their eyes to heaven for shame of their sins for which they had been condemned. 6. Then I wrote out their petition, and the prayer in regard to their spirits and their deeds individually and in regard to their requests that they should have forgiveness and length ⟨of days⟩†. 7. And I went off and sat down at the waters of Dan, in the land of Dan, to the south of the west of Hermon: I read their petition till I fell asleep. 8. And behold a dream came to me, and visions fell down upon me, and I saw visions of chastisement, [and a voice came bidding (me)] I to tell it to the sons of heaven, and reprimand them. 9. And when I awaked, I came unto them, and they were all sitting gathered together, weeping in 'Abelsjâîl, which is between Lebanon and Sênêsêr, with their faces covered. 10. And I recounted before them all the visions which I had seen in sleep, and I began to speak the words of righteousness, and to reprimand the heavenly Watchers.

CHAPTER 14

1. The book of the words of righteousness, and of the reprimand of the eternal Watchers in accordance with the command of the Holy Great One in that vision. 2. I saw in my sleep what I will now say with a tongue of flesh and with the breath of my mouth: which the Great One has given to men to converse therewith and understand with the heart. 3. As He has created and given [[to man the power of understanding the word of wisdom, so hath He created me also and given]] me the power of reprimanding the Watchers, the children of heaven. 4. I wrote out your petition, and in my vision it appeared thus, that your petition will not be granted unto you [[throughout all the days of eternity, and that judgement has been finally passed upon you: yea (your petition) will not be granted unto you]]. 5. And from henceforth you shall not ascend into heaven unto all eternity, and [in bonds] of the earth the decree has gone forth to bind you for all the days of the world. 6. And (that) previously you shall have seen the destruction of your beloved sons and ye shall have no pleasure in them, but they shall fall before you by the sword. 7. And your petition on their behalf shall not be granted, nor yet on your own: even though you weep and pray and **speak all the words** contained in the writing which I have written. 8. And the vision was shown to me thus: Behold, in the vision clouds invited me and a mist summoned me, and the course of the stars and the lightnings sped and **hastened** me, and the winds in the vision caused me to fly and lifted me upward, and bore me into heaven. 9. And I went in till I drew nigh to a wall which is built of crystals and surrounded by tongues of fire: and it began to affright me. And I went into the tongues of fire and drew nigh to a large house which was built of crystals: and the walls of the house were like a tesselated floor (made) of crystals, and its groundwork was of crystal. 11. Its ceiling was like the path of the stars and the lightnings, and between them were fiery cherubim, and their heaven was (clear as) water. 12. A flaming fire surrounded the walls, and its portals blazed with fire. 13. And I entered into that house, and it was hot as fire and cold as ice: there were no delights of life therein: fear covered me, and trembling got hold upon me. 14. And as I quaked and trembled, I fell upon my face. 15. And I beheld a vision, And lo! there was a second house, greater than the former, and the entire portal stood open before me, and it was built of flames of fire. 16. And in every respect it so excelled in splendour and magnificence and extent that I cannot describe to you its splendour and its extent. 17. And its floor was of fire, and above it were lightnings and the path of the stars, and its ceiling also was flaming fire. 18. And I looked and saw [[therein]] a lofty throne: its appearance was as crystal, and the wheels thereof as the shining sun, and there was the **vision** of cherubim. 19. And from underneath the throne came streams of flaming fire so that I could not look thereon. 20. And the Great Glory sat thereon, and His raiment shone more brightly than the sun and was whiter than any snow. 21. None of the angels could enter and could behold His face by reason of the magnificence and glory and no flesh could behold Him. 22. The flaming fire was round about Him, and a great fire stood before Him, and none around could draw nigh Him: ten thousand times ten thousand (stood) before Him, yet He needed no counselor. 23. And the most holy ones who were nigh to Him did not leave by night nor depart from Him. 24. And until then I had been prostrate on my face, trembling: and the Lord called me with His own mouth, and said to me: 'Come hither, Enoch, and hear my word.' 25. [And one of the holy ones came to me and waked me], and He made me rise up and approach the door: and I bowed my face downwards.

CHAPTER 15

1. And He answered and said to me, and I heard His voice: 'Fear not, Enoch, thou righteous man and scribe of righteousness: approach hither and hear my voice. 2. And go, say to [[the Watchers of heaven]], who have sent thee to intercede [[for them: "You should intercede"]] for men, and not men for you: 3. Wherefore have ye left the high, holy, and eternal heaven, and lain with women, and defiled yourselves with the daughters of men and taken to yourselves wives, and done like the children of earth, and begotten giants (as your) sons? 4. And though ye were holy, spiritual, living the eternal life, you have defiled yourselves with the blood of women, and have begotten (children) with the blood of flesh, and, **as the children** of men, have lusted after flesh and blood as those [also] do who die and perish. 5. Therefore have I given them wives also that they might impregnate them, and beget children by them, that thus nothing might be wanting to them on earth. 6. But you were [formerly] spiritual, living the eternal life, and immortal for all generations of the world. 7. And therefore I have not appointed wives for you; for as for the spiritual ones of the heaven, in heaven is their dwelling. 8. And now, the giants, who are produced from the spirits and flesh, shall be called evil spirits upon the earth, and on the earth shall be their dwelling. 9. Evil spirits have proceeded from their bodies; because they are born from **men**, [[and]] from the holy Watchers is their beginning and primal origin; [they shall be evil spirits on earth, and] evil spirits shall they be called. [10. As for the spirits of heaven, in heaven shall be their dwelling, but as for the spirits of the earth which were born upon the earth, on the earth shall be their dwelling.] 11. And the spirits of the giants **afflict**, oppress, destroy, attack, do battle, and work destruction on the earth, and cause trouble: they take no food, [but nevertheless hunger] and thirst, and cause offences. And these spirits shall rise up against the children of men and against the women,

because they have proceeded [from them].

CHAPTER 16

1. From the days of the slaughter and destruction and death [of the giants], from the souls of whose flesh the spirits, having gone forth, shall destroy without incurring judgement--thus shall they destroy until the day of the consummation, the great [judgement] in which the age shall be consummated, over the Watchers and the godless, yea, shall be wholly consummated." 2. And now as to the Watchers who have sent thee to intercede for them, who had been [[aforetime]] in heaven, (say to them): "You have been in heaven, but [all] the mysteries had not yet been revealed to you, and you knew worthless ones, and these in the hardness of your heartsyou have made known to the women, and through these mysteries womenand men work much evil on earth." 4. Say to them therefore: "You have no peace.'"

ENOCH'S JOURNEYS through the Earth and Sheol

CHAPTER 17

1. And they took [and] brought me to a place in which those who were there were like flaming fire, and, when they wished, they appeared as men. 2. And they brought me to the place of darkness, and to a mountain the point of whose summit reached to heaven. 3. And I saw the places of the luminaries [and the treasuries of the stars] and of the thunder [and] inthe **uttermost depths**, where were a fiery bow and arrows and their quiver, and [[a fiery sword]] and all the lightnings. 4. And they took me to the living waters, and to the fire of the west, which receives every setting of the sun. 5. And I came to a river of fire in which the fire flows like water and discharges itself into the great sea towards the west. 6. I saw the great rivers and came to the great[river and to the great] darkness, and went to the place where no flesh walks. 7. I saw the mountains of the darkness of winter andthe place whence all the waters of the deep flow. 8. I saw the mouths of all the rivers of the earth and the mouth of the deep.

CHAPTER 18

1. I saw the treasuries of all the winds: I saw how He had furnished with themthe whole creation and the firm foundations of the earth. 2. And I saw the corner-stone of the earth: I saw the four winds which bear [the earth and] the firmament of the heaven. 3. [[And I saw how the winds stretch out the vaults of heaven]], and have their station between heaven and earth: [[these arethe pillars of the heaven]]. 4. I saw the winds of heaven which turn andbring the circumference of the sun and all the stars to their setting. 5. I sawthe winds on the earth carrying the clouds: I saw[[the paths of the angels. I saw]] at the end of the earth the firmament of the heaven above. And I proceeded and saw a place which burns day and night, where there are seven mountains of magnificent stones, three towards the east, and three towardsthe south. 7. And as for those towards the east, ⟨one⟩ was of coloured stone,and one of pearl, and one of **jacinth**, and those towards the south of redstone. 8. But the middle one reached to heaven like the throne of God, of alabaster, and the summit of the throne was of sapphire. 9. And I saw a flaming fire. And beyond these mountains 10. is a region the end of the great earth: there the heavens were completed. 11. And I saw a deep abyss, with columns [[of heavenly fire, and among them I saw columns]] of fire fall, which were beyond measure alike towards the height and towards the depth. 12. And beyond that abyss I saw a place which had no firmament of the heaven above, and no firmly founded earth beneath it: there was no water upon it, and no birds, but it was a waste and horrible place. 13. I saw there seven stars like great burning mountains, and to me, when I inquired regarding them, 14. The angel said: 'This place is the end of heaven andearth: this has become a prison for the stars and the host of heaven. 15. And the stars which roll over the fire are they which have transgressed the commandment of the Lord in the beginning of their rising, because they did not come forth at their appointed times. 16. And He was wroth with them,and bound them till the time when their guilt should be consummated (even) [for ten thousand years].'

CHAPTER 19

1. And Uriel said to me: 'Here shall stand the angels who have connected themselves with women, and their spirits assuming many different forms are defiling mankind and shall lead them astray into sacrificing to demons [[as gods]], (here shall they stand,) till [[the day of]] the great judgement in which they shall be judged till they are made an end of. 2. And the women also of the angels who went astray shall become sirens.' 3. And I, Enoch, alone saw the vision, the ends of all things: and no man shall see as I have seen.

CHAPTER 20

And these are the names of the holy angels who watch. 2. Uriel, one of the holy angels, who is over the world and over Tartarus. 3. Raphael, one of the holyangels, who is over the spirits of men. 4. Raguel, one of the holy angels who ††takes vengeance on† the world of theluminaries. 5. Michael, one of the holy angels, to wit, he that is set over the best part of mankind [[and]]over chaos. 6. Saraqâêl, one of the holy angels, who is set over the spirits, who sin in the spirit. 7. Gabriel, one of the holy angels, who is over Paradise and the serpents and the Cherubim. 8. Remiel, one of the holy angels, whom God set over those who rise.

CHAPTER 21

1. And I proceeded to where things were chaotic. 2. And I saw there something horrible: I saw neither a heaven above nor a firmly founded earth, but a place chaotic and horrible. 3. And there I saw seven stars of the heaven bound together in it, like great mountains and burning with fire. 4. Then I said: 'For what sin are they bound, and on what account have they been castin hither?' 5. Then said Uriel, one of the holy angels, who was with me, and was chief over them, and said: 'Enoch, why dost thou ask, and why art thou eager for the truth? 6. These are of the number of the stars [of heaven], which have transgressed the commandment of the Lord, and are bound here till ten thousand years, the time entailed by their sins, are consummated.' 7. And from thence I went to another place, which was still more horrible than the former, and I saw a horrible thing: a great fire there which burnt and blazed, and the place was cleft as far as the abyss, being full of great descending columns of fire: neither its extent or magnitude could I see, nor could I conjecture. 8. Then I said: 'How fearful is the place and how terribleto look upon!' 9. Then Uriel answered me, one of the holy angels who was with me, and said to me: 'Enoch, why hast thou such fear and affright?' And I answered: 'Because of this fearful place, and because of the spectacleof the pain.' 10. And he said [[unto me]]: 'This place is the prison of the angels, and here they will be imprisoned for ever.'

CHAPTER 22

1. And thence I went to another place, and he showed me in the west [another] great and high mountain [and] of hard rock. 2. And there was in it ††fourt **hollow** places, deep and wide and very smooth. ††How† smooth are **the hollow places** and deep and darkto look at. 3. Then Raphael answered, one of the holy angels who was with me, and said unto me: 'These hollow places have been created for this very purpose, that the spirits of the souls of the dead should assemble therein, yea that all the souls

of the children of men should assemble here. 4. And these places **have been made** to receive them till the day of their judgement and till their appointed period [till the period appointed], till the great judgement (comes) upon them.' 5. I saw the spirits of the children of men who were dead, and their voice went forth to heaven and made suit. 6. Then I asked Raphael the angel who was with me, and I said unto him: 'This spirit--whose is it whose voice goeth forth and maketh suit?' 7. And he answered me saying: 'This is the spirit which went forth from Abel, whom his brother Cain slew, and he makes his suit against him till his seed is destroyed from the face of the earth, and his seed is annihilated from amongst the seed of men.' 8. Then I asked regarding it, and regarding all the **hollow places**: 'Why as one separated from the other?' 9. And he answered me and said unto me: 'These three have been made that the spirits of the dead might be separated. And such a division has been made⟨for⟩the spirits of the righteous, in which there are as the **bright** spring of **water.And** such has been made for sinners when they die and are buried in the earth and judgement has not been executed on them in their lifetime. 11. Here their spirits shall be set apart in this great pain till the great day of judgement and punishment and torment of those who †curse† for ever, andretribution for their spirits. There He shall bind them for ever. 12. And such a division has been made for the spirits of those who make their suit, who make disclosures concerning their destruction, when they wereslain in the days of the sinners. 13. Such has been made for the spirits of men who were not righteous butsinners, who were complete in transgression, and of the transgressors. they shall be companions: but their spirits shall not be slain in the day of judgement nor shall they be raised from thence. 14. Then I blessed the Lord of glory and said: 'Blessed be my Lord, the Lord of righteousness, who ruleth for ever.'

CHAPTER 23

1. From thence I went to another place to the west of the ends of the earth. 2. And I saw a [[burning]] fire which ran without resting, and paused notfrom its course day or night but (ran) regularly. 3. And I asked saying: 'What is this which rests not?' 4. Then Raguel, one of the holy angels who was with me, answered me [[and said unto me]]: 'This course [of fire] [[whichthou hast seen]] is the fire in the west which †persecutes† all the luminaries of heaven.'

CHAPTER 24

1. [[And from thence I went to another place of the earth]], and he showed me a mountain range of fire which burnt [[day and night]]. 2. And I went beyond it and saw seven magnificent mountains all differing each from the other, and the stones (thereof) were magnificent and beautiful, magnificent asa whole, of glorious appearance and fair exterior: [[three towards]] the east, [[one]] founded on the other, and three towards the south, one upon the other, and deep rough ravines, no one of which joined with any other. 3. And the seventh mountain was in the midst of these, and it excelled them inheight, resembling the seat of a throne: and fragrant trees encircled thethrone. 4. And amongst them was a tree such as I had never yet smelt, neitherwas any amongst them nor were others like it: it had a fragrance beyond all fragrance, and its leaves and blooms and wood wither not for ever: and its fruit [[is beautiful, and its fruit]] resembles the dates of a palm. 5. Then I said: '[How] beautiful is this tree, and fragrant, and its leaves are fair, and itsblooms [[very]] delightful in appearance.' 6. Then answered Michael, one of the holy[[and honoured]] angels who was with me, and was their leader.

CHAPTER 25

1. And he said unto me: 'Enoch, why dostthou ask me regarding the fragrance ofthe tree, and [why]

dost thou wish to learn the   truth?' Then I answered him [[saying]]: 'I wish to know about everything, but especially about this tree.' And he answered saying: 'This highmountain [[which thou hast seen]], whose summit is like the throne of God,is His throne, where the Holy Great One, the Lord of Glory, the Eternal King, will sit, when He shall come down to visit the earth with goodness. 4. And as for this fragrant tree no mortal is permitted to touch it till the great judgement, when He shall take vengeance on all and bring (everything) to its consummationfor ever. It shall then be given to the righteous and holy. 5. Its fruit **shallbe** for food to the elect: it shall be transplanted to the holy place, to the temple of the Lord, the Eternal King. 6. Then shall they rejoice with joy and be glad,And into the holy place shall they enter; And its fragrance shall be in their bones,And they shall live a long life on earth, Such as thy fathers lived: And in their days shall no [[sorrow or]] plagueOr torment or calamity touch them.' 7. Then blessed I the God of Glory, the Eternal King, who hath prepared such things for the righteous, and hath created them and promised to give to them.

CHAPTER 26

1. And I went from thence to the middle of the earth, and I saw a blessed place [in which there were trees] with   branches abiding and blooming [of a dismembered tree]. 2. And there I saw a holy mountain, [[and]] underneaththe mountain to the east there was a stream and it flowed towards the south. 3. And I saw towards the east another mountain higher than this, and betweenthem a deep and narrow ravine: in it also ran a stream [underneath] the mountain. 4. And to the west thereof there was another mountain, lower than the former and of small elevation, and a ravine [deep and dry] betweenthem: and another deep and dry ravine was at the extremities of the three [mountains]. 5. And all the ravines were deep [[and narrow]], (beingformed) of hard rock, and trees were not planted upon them. 6. And I marveled [[at the rocks, and I marveled]] at the ravine, yea, I marveledvery much.

CHAPTER 27

1. Then said I: 'For what object is this blessed land, which is entirely filled with trees, and this accursed valley [[between]]?' 2. [[Then Uriel, one of the holy angels who was with me, answered and said: 'This]] accursedvalley is for those who are accursed for ever: Here shall all [the accursed] be gathered together who utter with their lips against the Lord unseemly words and of His glory speak hard things. Here shall they be gathered together, and here shall be their place of judgement. 3. In the last days there shall be upon them the spectacle of righteous judgement in the presence of the righteous forever: here shall the merciful bless the Lord of glory, the Eternal King. 4. In the days of judgement over the former, they shall bless Him for the mercy in accordance with which He has assigned them (their lot).' 5. Then I blessed the Lord of Glory and set forth His [glory] and lauded Him gloriously.

CHAPTER 28

1. And thence I went [[towards the east]], into the midst [[of the mountainrange of the desert]], and I saw a wilderness and it was solitary, full oftrees **and plant**s. 2. [[And]] water gushed forth from above. 3. Rushinglike a copious watercourse [which flowed] towards the north-west it caused clouds and dew to ascend on every side.

CHAPTER 29

1. And thence I went to another place in the desert, and approached to theeast of this mountain range. 2. And [[there]] I saw **aromatic** trees exhaling the fragrance of frankincense and myrrh, and the

trees also were similar to thealmond tree.

CHAPTER 30

1 .And beyond these, I went afar to the east, and I saw another place, a valley (full) of water. 2. And [therein there was] a tree, the colour (?) of fragrant trees such as the mastic. 3. And on the sides of those valleys I saw fragrant cinnamon. And beyond these I proceeded to the east.

CHAPTER 31

1. And I saw other mountains, and amongst them were [groves of] trees, andthere flowed forth from them nectar, which is named sarara and galbanum. 2. And beyond these mountains I saw another mountain [to the east of the ends of the earth], [[whereon were aloe trees]], and all the trees were full **of stacte**, being like almond-trees. 3. And when one **burnt** it, it smelt sweeter than any fragrant odour.

CHAPTER 32

1. And after these fragrant odours, as I looked towards the north over the mountains I saw seven mountains full of choice nard and fragrant trees and cinnamon and pepper. 2. And thence I went over the summits of [all] these mountains, far towards the east [of the earth], and passed above the Erythraean sea and went far from it, and passed over [[the angel]] Zotîêl. 3. And I came to the Garden of Righteousness, and saw beyond those trees many large trees growing there and of goodly fragrance, large, very beautiful and glorious, and the tree of wisdom whereof they eat and know great wisdom. 4. [That tree is in height like the fir, and its leaves are] like (those of) theCarob tree: and its fruit is like the clusters of the vine, very beautiful: and the fragrance of the tree penetrates afar. 5. Then I said: '[How] beautiful is the tree, and how attractive is its look!' 6. Then Raphael the holy angel, who was with me, answered me [[and said]]: 'This is the tree of wisdom, of which thy father old (in years) and thy aged mother, who were before thee, have eaten, and they learnt wisdom and their eyes were opened, and they knew thatthey were naked and they were driven out of the garden.'

CHAPTER 33

1. And from thence I went to the ends of the earth and saw there great beasts, and each differed from the other; and (I saw) birds also differing in appearance and beauty and voice, the one differing from the other. 2. And to the east of those beasts I saw the ends of the earth whereon the heaven rests, and the portals of the heaven open. 3. And I saw how the stars of heaven come forth, and I counted the portals out of which they proceed, and wrote down all their outlets, of each individual star by itself, according to their number and their names, their courses and their positions, and their times andtheir months, as Uriel the holy angel who was with me showed me. 4. He showed all things to me and wrote them down for me: also their names he wrote for me, and their laws and their companies.

CHAPTER 34

1. And from thence I went towards the north to the ends of the earth, and there I saw a great and glorious device at the ends of the whole earth. 2. And here I saw three portals of heaven open in the heaven: through each of them proceed north winds: when they blow there is cold, hail, frost, snow, dew,and rain. 3. And out of one portal they blow for good: but when they blow through the other two portals, it is with violence and affliction on the earth, and they blow with violence.

CHAPTER 35

1. And from thence I went towards the west to the ends of the earth, and saw there three portals of the heaven open such as I had seen in the †eastt†, the same number of portals, and the same number of outlets.

CHAPTER 36

1. And from thence I went to the south to the ends of the earth, and saw there three open portals of the heaven: and thence there come dew, rain, †and windt†. 2. And from thence I went to the east to the ends of the heaven, and saw here the three eastern portals of heaven open and small portals above them. 3. Through each of these small portals pass the stars of heaven and run their course to the west on the path which is shown to them. 4. And as often as I saw I blessed always the Lord of Glory, and I continued to bless the Lordof Glory who has wrought great and glorious wonders, to show the greatness of His work to the angels and to **spirits** and to men, that they might praiseHis work and all His creation: that they might see the work of His might and praise the great work of His hands and bless Him for ever.

THE PARABLES
CHAPTER 37

1.The second vision which he saw, the vision of wisdom--which Enoch the son of Jared, the son of Mahalalel, the son of Cainan, the son of Enos, the son of Seth, the son of Adam, saw. 2. And this is the beginning of the words of wisdom which I lifted up my voice to speak and say to those which dwell on earth: Hear, ye men of old time, and see, ye that come after, the words of the Holy One which I will speak before the Lord of Spirits. 3. It were better to declare (them only) to the men of old time, but even fromthose that come after we will not withhold the beginning of wisdom. 4. Till the present day such wisdom has never been given **by** the Lord of Spirits as I have received according to my insight, according to the good pleasure of the Lord of Spirits bywhom the lot of eternal life has been given to me. 5. Now three parables were imparted to me, and I lifted up my voice and recounted them to those that dwell on the earth.

CHAPTER 38

1.The First Parable. When the congregation of the righteous shall appear, And sinners shall be judged for their sins, And shall be driven from the face of the earth: 2.And when the Righteous One shall appear before the eyes of the righteous, Whose elect works hang upon the Lord of Spirits, And light shall appear to the righteous and the elect who dwell on the earth, Where then will be the dwelling of the sinners, And where the resting-place of those who have denied the Lord of Spirits? It had been good for them if they had not been born. 3.When the secrets of the righteous shall be revealed and the sinners judged, And the godless driven from the presence of the righteous and elect, 4.From that time those that possess the earth shall no longer be powerful and exalted: And they shall not be able to behold the face of the holy, For the Lord of Spirits has **caused His light to appear** On the face of the holy, righteous, and elect. 5.Then shall the kings and the mighty perish And be given into the hands of the righteous and holy. 6.And thenceforward none shall seek for themselves mercy from the Lord of Spirits For their life is at an end.

CHAPTER 39

1.[And it †shall come to pass in those days that elect and holy children †will descend from the high heaven, and their seed †will become one with the children of men. 2. And in those days Enoch received books of zeal and wrath, and books of disquiet and expulsion.] And mercy shall not be accorded to them, saith the Lord of Spirits. 3.And in those days a whirlwind carried me off from the earth,And set me down at the end of the heavens. 4.And there I saw another vision, the dwelling-places of the holy,And the resting-places of the righteous. 5.Here mine eyes saw their dwellings with His righteous angels,And their resting-places with the holy. And they petitioned and interceded and prayed for the children of men,And righteousness flowed before them as water, And mercy like dew upon the earth: Thus it is amongst them for ever and ever. 6. And in that place mine eyes saw the Elect One of righteousness and offaith, 7. And I saw his dwelling-place under the wings of the Lord of Spirits.6b. And righteousness shall prevail in his days, And the righteous and elect shall be without number before Him for everand ever. 7b. And all the righteous and elect before Him shall be †strong† as fierylights, And their mouth shall be full of blessing, And their lips extol the name of the Lord of Spirits, And righteousness before Him shall never fail, [And uprightness shall never fail before Him.] 8.There I wished to dwell, And my spirit longed for that dwelling-place:And there heretofore hath been my portion, For so has it been established concerning me before the Lord of Spirits. 9.In those days I praised and extolled the name of the Lord of Spiritswith blessings and praises, because He hath destined me for blessing and glory according to the good pleasure of the Lord of Spirits. 10. For a long time my eyes regarded that place, and I blessed Him and praised Him, saying:'Blessed is He, and may He be blessed from the beginning and for evermore. 11. And before Him there is no ceasing. He knows before the world was created what is for ever and what will be from generation unto generation. 12.Those who sleep not bless Thee: they stand before Thy glory and bless, praise, and extol, saying: "Holy, holy, holy, is the Lord of Spirits: He filleth the earth with spirits."' 13. And here my eyes saw all those who sleep not: they stand before Him and bless and say: 'Blessed be Thou, and blessed bethe name of the Lord for ever and ever.' 14. And my face was changed; for I could no longer behold.

CHAPTER 40

1. And after that I saw thousands of thousands and ten thousand times ten thousand, I saw a multitude beyond number and reckoning, who stood before the Lord of Spirits. 2. And on the four sides of the Lord of Spirits I saw four presences, different from those that sleep not, and I learnt their names: for theangel that went with me made known to me their names, and showed me all the hidden things. 3. And I heard the voices of those four presences as they uttered praises before the Lord of glory. 4. The first voice blesses the Lord of Spirits for everand ever. 5. And the second voice I heard blessing the Elect One and the electones who hang upon the Lord of Spirits. 6. And the third voice I heard **pray and intercede** for those who dwell on the earth and **supplicate** in the nameof the Lord of Spirits. 7. And I heard the fourth voice fending off the Satans and forbidding them to come before the Lord of Spirits to accuse them who dwell on the earth. 8. After that I asked the angel of peace who went with me,who showed me everything that is hidden: 'Who are these four presences which I have seen and whose words I have heard and written down?' 9. And he said to me: 'This first is Michael, the merciful and long-suffering: and the second, who is set over all the diseases and all the wounds of the children of men, is Raphael: and the third, who is set over all the powers, is Gabriel: and the fourth, who is set over the repentance unto hope of those who inherit eternal life, is named Phanuel.' And these are the four angels of the Lord of Spirits and the four voices I heard in those days.

CHAPTER 41

1. And after that I saw all the secrets of the heavens, and how the kingdom is divided, and how the actions of men are weighed in the balance. 2. And there I saw the mansions of the elect and the mansions of the holy, and mine eyes saw there all the sinners being driven from thence which deny the name ofthe Lord of Spirits, and being dragged off: and they could not abide because of the punishment which proceeds from the Lord of Spirits. 3. And there mine eyes saw the secrets of the lightning and of the thunder, and the secrets of the winds, how they are divided to blow over the earth, and the secrets of the clouds and dew, and there I saw from whence they proceed in that place and from whence they saturate the dusty earth. 4. And there I saw closed chambers out of which the winds are divided, the chamber of the hail and winds, the chamber of the mist, and of the clouds,and the cloud thereof hovers over the earth from the beginning of the world. 5.And I saw the chambers of the sun and moon, whence they proceed and whither they come again, and their glorious return, and how one is superior tothe other, and their stately orbit, and how they do not leave their orbit, and they add nothing to their orbit and they take nothing from it, and they keep faith with each other, in accordance with the oath by which they are bound together. 6. And first the sun goes forth and traverses his path according to the commandment of the Lord of Spirits, and mighty is His name for ever andever. 7. And after that I saw the hidden and the visible path of the moon, and she accomplishes the course of her path in that place by day and by night--theone holding a position opposite to the other before the Lord of Spirits. And they give thanks and praise and rest not;For unto them is their thanksgiving rest. 8.For the sun changes oft for a blessing or a curse, And the course of the path of the moon is light to the righteousAnd darkness to the sinners in the name of the Lord, Who made a separation between the light and the darkness,And divided the spirits of men, And strengthened the spirits of the righteous, In the name of His righteousness. 9.For no angel hinders and no power is able to hinder; for He appoints ajudge for them all and He judges them all before Him.

CHAPTER 42

1.Wisdom found no place where she might dwell; Then a dwelling-place was assigned her in the heavens. 2.Wisdom went forth to make her dwelling among the children of men,And found no dwelling-place: Wisdom returned to her place, And took her seat among the angels. 3.And unrighteousness went forth from her chambers:Whom she sought not she found, And dwelt with them,As rain in a desert And dew on a thirsty land.

CHAPTER 43

1. And I saw other lightnings and the stars of heaven, and I saw how Hecalled them all by their names and they hearkened unto Him. 2. And I saw how they are weighed in a righteous balance according to their proportions oflight: (I saw) the width of their spaces and the day of their appearing, and how their revolution produces lightning: and (I saw) their revolution according to the number of the angels, and (how) they keep faith with each other. 3. And I asked the angel who went with me who showed me what was hidden: 'What are these?' 4. And he said to me: 'The Lord of Spirits hath showed thee their parabolic meaning (lit. 'their parable'): these are the names of the holy who dwell on the earth and believe in the name of the Lord of Spirits for ever and ever.'

CHAPTER 44

Also another phenomenon I saw in regard to the lightnings: how some of thestars arise and become lightnings and cannot part with their new form.

CHAPTER 45

1.And this is the Second Parable concerning those who deny the name of thedwelling of the holy ones and the Lord of Spirits. 2.And into the heaven they shall not ascend,And on the earth they shall not come: Such shall be the lot of the sinners Who have denied the name of the Lord of Spirits, Who are thus preserved for the day of suffering and tribulation. 3.On that day Mine Elect One shall sit on the throne of gloryAnd shall **try** their works, And their places of rest shall be innumerable. And their souls shall grow strong within them when they see Mine ElectOnes, And those who have called upon My glorious name: 4.Then will I cause Mine Elect One to dwell among them. And I will transform the heaven and make it an eternal blessing and light 5.And I will transform the earth and make it a blessing:And I will cause Mine elect ones to dwell upon it: But the sinners and evil-doers shall not set foot thereon. 6.For I have provided and satisfied with peace My righteous onesAnd have caused them to dwell before Me: But for the sinners there is judgement impending with Me,So that I shall destroy them from the face of the earth.

CHAPTER 46

1.And there I saw One who had a head of days,And His head was white like wool,

And with Him was another being whose countenance had the appearance of a man, And his face was full of graciousness, like one of the holy angels. 2.And I asked the **angel** who went with me and showed me all the hidden things, concerning that Son of Man, who he was, and whence he was, (and) why he went with the Head of Days? And he answered and said unto me: This is the son of Man who hath righteousness, With whom dwelleth righteousness, And who revealeth all the treasures of that which is hidden,Because the Lord of Spirits hath chosen him, And whose lot hath the pre-eminence before the Lord of Spirits inuprightness for ever. 4, And this Son of Man whom thou hast seen Shall †raise up† the kings and the mighty from their seats, [And the strong from their thrones] And shall loosen the reins of the strong,And break the teeth of the sinners. 5.[And he shall put down the kings from their thrones and kingdoms]Because they do not extol and praise Him, Nor humbly acknowledge whence the kingdom was bestowed upon them. 6.And he shall put down the countenance of the strong,And shall fill them with shame. And darkness shall be their dwelling, And worms shall be their bed, And they shall have no hope of rising from their beds, Because they do not extol the name of the Lord of Spirits. 7.And these are they who †judge† the stars of heaven, [And raise their hands against the Most High], †And tread upon the earth and dwell upon it†. And all their deeds manifest unrighteousness,And their power rests upon their riches, And their faith is in the †gods† which they have made with their hands, And they deny the name of the Lord of Spirits, 8.And they persecute the houses of His congregations, And the faithful who hang upon the name of the Lord of Spirits.

CHAPTER 47

1.And in those days shall have ascended the prayer of the righteous, And the blood of the righteous from the earth before the Lord of Spirits. 2.In those days the holy ones who dwell above in the heavensShall unite with one voice And supplicate and pray [and praise, And give thanks and bless the name of the Lord of Spirits] On behalf of the blood of the righteous which has been shed, And that the prayer of the righteous may not be in vain before the Lord of Spirits, That judgement may be done unto them, And that they may not have to suffer for ever. 3.In those days I saw the Head of Days when He seated himself upon the throne of His glory, And the books of the living were opened before Him: And all His host which is in heaven above and His counselors stoodbefore Him, 4.And the hearts of the holy were filled with joy; Because the number of the righteous **had been offered**,And the prayer of the righteous had been heard, And the blood of the righteous been required before the Lord of Spirits.

CHAPTER 48

1.And in that place I saw the fountain of righteousnessWhich was inexhaustible: And around it were many fountains of wisdom;And all the thirsty drank of them, And were filled with wisdom, And their dwellings were with the righteous and holy and elect. 2.And at that hour that Son of Man was named In the presence of theLord of Spirits, And his name before the Head of Days. 3.Yea, before the sun and the signs were created,Before the stars of the heaven were made, His name was named before the Lord of Spirits. 4.He shall be a staff to the righteous whereon to stay themselves and notfall, And he shall be the light of the Gentiles, And the hope of those who are troubled of heart. 5.All who dwell on earth shall fall down and worship before him, And will praise and bless and celebrate with song the Lord of Spirits. 6.And for this reason hath he been chosen and hidden before Him, Before the creation of the world and for evermore. 7.And the wisdom of the Lord of Spirits hath revealed him to the holyand righteous; For he hath preserved the lot of the righteous, Because they have hated and despised this world of unrighteousness, And have hated all its works and ways in the name of the Lord of Spirits:For in his name they are saved, And according to his good pleasure hath it been in regard to their life. 8.In these days downcast in countenance shall the kings of the earth havebecome, And the strong who possess the land because of the works of their hands; For on the day of their anguish and affliction they shall not (be able to) save themselves. 9.And I will give them over into the hands of Mine elect: As straw in the fire so shall they burn before the face of the holy: As lead in the water shall they sink before the face of the righteous,And no trace of them shall any more be found. 10.And on the day of their affliction there shall be rest on the earth,And before them they shall fall and not rise again: And there shall be no one to take them with his hands and raise them:For they have denied the Lord of Spirits and His Anointed. The name of the Lord of Spirits be blessed.

CHAPTER 49

1. For wisdom is poured out like water, And glory faileth not before him for evermore. 2.For he is mighty in all the secrets of righteousness, And unrighteousness shall disappear as a shadow, And have no continuance; Because the Elect One standeth before the Lord of Spirits,And his glory is for ever and ever, And his might unto all generations. 3.And in him dwells the spirit of wisdom,And the spirit which gives insight, And the spirit of understanding and of might, And the spirit of those who have fallen asleep in righteousness. 4.And he shall judge the secret things, And none shall be able to utter a lying word before him; For he is the Elect One before the Lord of Spirits according to His good pleasure.

CHAPTER 50

1.And in those days a change shall take place for the holy and elect,And the light of days shall abide upon them, And glory and honour shall turn to the holy, 2.On the day of affliction on which evil shall have been treasured up against the sinners. And the righteous shall be victorious in the name of the Lord of Spirits:And He will cause the others to witness (this) That they may repent And forgo the works of their hands. 3.They shall have no honour through the name of the Lord of Spirits, Yet through His name shall they be saved, And the Lord of Spirits will have compassion on them,For His compassion is great. 4.And He is righteous also in His judgement, And in the presence of His glory unrighteousness also shall not maintainitself: At His judgement the unrepentant shall perish before Him. 5.And from henceforth I will have no mercy on them, saith the Lord ofSpirits.

CHAPTER 51

1.And in those days shall the earth also give back that which has beenentrusted to it, And Sheol also shall give back that which it has received,And hell shall give back that which it owes. 5a. For in those days the Elect One shall arise, 2.And he shall choose the righteous and holy from among them:For the day has drawn nigh that they should be saved. 3.And the Elect One shall in those days sit on My throne, And his mouth shall **pour** forth all the secrets of wisdom and counsel: For the Lord of Spirits hath given (them) to him and hath glorified him. 4.And in those days shall the mountains leap like rams, And the hills also shall skip like lambs satisfied with milk,

And the faces of [all] the angels in heaven shall be lighted up with joy.5b. And the earth shall rejoice, c. And the righteous shall dwell upon it, d. And the elect shall walk thereon.

CHAPTER 52

l. And after those days in that place where I had seen all the visions of that which is hidden--for I had been carried off in a whirlwind and they had borne me towards the west-- 2. There mine eyes saw all the secret things of heaven that shall be, a mountain of iron, and a mountain of copper, and a mountain of silver, and a mountain of gold, and a mountain of soft metal, and a mountain of lead. 3. And I asked the angel who went with me, saying, 'What things are these which I have seen in secret?' 4. And he said unto me: 'All these things which thou hast seen shall serve the dominion of His Anointed that he may be potent and mighty on the earth.' 5.And that angel of peace answered, saying unto me: 'Wait a little, and there shall be revealed unto thee all the secret things which surround the Lord of Spirits. 6.And these mountains which thine eyes have seen, The mountain of iron, and the mountain of copper, and the mountain of silver, And the mountain of gold, and the mountain of soft metal, and the mountain of lead, All these shall be in the presence of the Elect One As wax: before the fire, And like the water which streams down from above [upon those mountains], And they shall become powerless before his feet. 7.And it shall come to pass in those days that none shall be saved, Either by gold or by silver, And none be able to escape. 8.And there shall be no iron for war, Nor shall one clothe oneself with a breastplate. Bronze shall be of no service, And tin [shall be of no service and] shall not be esteemed, And lead shall not be desired. 9.And all these things shall be [denied and] destroyed from the surface of the earth, When the Elect One shall appear before the face of the Lord of Spirits.'

CHAPTER 53

1.There mine eyes saw a deep valley with open mouths, and all who dwell on the earth and sea and islands shall bring to him gifts and presents and tokens of homage, but that deep valley shall not become full. 2.And their hands commit lawless deeds, And the sinners devour all whom they lawlessly **oppress**: Yet the sinners shall be destroyed before the face of the Lord of Spirits, And they shall be banished from off the face of His earth, And they shall perish for ever and ever. 3.For I saw all the angels of punishment abiding (there) and preparing all the instruments of Satan. 4. And I asked the angel of peace who went with me: 'For whom are they preparing these instruments?' 5. And he said unto me: 'They prepare these for the kings and the mighty of this earth, that they may thereby be destroyed. 6.And after this the Righteous and Elect One shall cause the house of his congregation to appear: henceforth they shall be no more hindered in the name of the Lord of Spirits. 7.And these mountains shall not stand as the earth before his righteousness, But the hills shall be as a fountain of water, And the righteous shall have rest from the oppression of sinners.'

CHAPTER 54

1 And I looked and turned to another part of the earth, and saw there a deep valley with burning fire. 2. And they brought the kings and the mighty, and began to cast them into this deep valley. 3. And there mine eyes saw how they made these their instruments, iron chains of immeasurable weight. 4. And I asked the angel of peace who went with me, saying: 'For whom are these chains being prepared?' 5. And he said unto me: 'These are being prepared for the hosts of Azâzêl, so that they may take them and cast them into the abyss of complete condemnation, and they shall cover their jaws with rough stones as the Lord of Spirits commanded. 6.And Michael, and Gabriel, and Raphael, and Phanuel shall take hold of them on that great day, and cast them on that day into the burning furnace, that the Lord of Spirits may take vengeance on them for their unrighteousness in becoming subject to Satan and leading astray those who dwell on the earth.' 7.'And in those days shall punishment come from the Lord of Spirits, and he will open all the chambers of waters which are above the heavens, and of the fountains which are beneath the earth. 8. And all the waters shall be joined with the waters: that which is above the heavens is the masculine, and the water which is beneath the earth is the feminine. 9. And they shall destroy all who dwell on the earth and those who dwell under the ends of the heaven. 10. And **when** they have recognized their unrighteousness which they have wrought on the earth, then by these shall they perish.

CHAPTER 55

1. And after that the Head of Days repented and said: 'In vain have I destroyed all who dwell on the earth.' 2. And He sware by His great name: 'Henceforth I will not do so to all who dwell on the earth, and I will set a sign in the heaven: and this shall be a pledge of good faith between Me and them for ever, so long as heaven is above the earth. And this is in accordance with My command.' 3. When I have desired to take hold of them by the hand of the angels on the day of tribulation and pain **because of** this, I will cause My chastisement and My wrath to abide upon them, saith God, the Lord of Spirits. 4. Ye †mighty kings† who dwell on the earth, ye shall have to behold Mine Elect One, how he sits on the throne of glory and judges Azâzêl, and all his associates, and all his hosts in the name of the Lord of Spirits.'

CHAPTER 56

1.And I saw there the hosts of the angels of punishment going, and they held scourges and chains of iron and bronze. 2. And I asked the angel of peace who went with me, saying: 'To whom are these who hold the scourges going?' 3. And he said unto me: 'To their elect and beloved ones, that they may be cast into the chasm of the abyss of the valley. 4.And then that valley shall be filled with their elect and beloved, And the days of their lives shall be at an end, And the days of their leading astray shall not thenceforward be reckoned. 5.And in those days the angels shall return And hurl themselves to the east upon the Parthians and Medes: They shall stir up the kings, so that a spirit of unrest shall come upon them, And they shall rouse them from their thrones, That they may break forth as lions from their lairs, And as hungry wolves among their flocks. 6.And they shall go up and tread under foot the land of His elect ones, [And the land of His elect ones shall be before them a threshing-floor and a highway:] 7.But the city of my righteous shall be a hindrance to their horses. And they shall begin to fight among themselves, And their right hand shall be strong against themselves, And a man shall not know his brother, Nor a son his father or his mother, Till there be no number of the corpses through their slaughter, And their punishment be not in vain. 8.In those days Sheol shall open its jaws, And they shall be swallowed up therein And their destruction shall be at an end; Sheol shall devour the sinners in the presence of the elect.'

CHAPTER 57

1. And it came to pass after this that I saw another host of wagons, and men riding thereon, and coming on the winds from the east, and from the west to the south. 2. And the noise of their wagons was heard, and when this turmoil took place the holy ones from heaven remarked it, and the pillars of the earth were moved from their place, and the sound thereof was heard from the one end of heaven to the other, in one day. 3. And they shall all fall down and worship the Lord of Spirits. And this is the end of the second Parable.

CHAPTER 58

1.And I began to speak the third Parable concerning the righteous and elect. 2.Blessed are ye, ye righteous and elect, For glorious shall be your lot. 3.And the righteous shall be in the light of the sun. And the elect in the light of eternal life: The days of their life shall be unending, And the days of the holy without number. 4.And they shall seek the light and find righteousness with the Lord of Spirits: There shall be peace to the righteous in the name of the Eternal Lord. 5.And after this it shall be said to the holy in heaven That they should seek out the secrets of righteousness, the heritage of faith: For it has become bright as the sun upon earth, And the darkness is past. 6.And there shall be a light that never endeth, And to a limit (lit. 'number') of days they shall not come, For the darkness shall first have been destroyed, [And the light established before the Lord of Spirits] And the light of uprightness established for ever before the Lord ofSpirits.

CHAPTER 59

[1. In those days mine eyes saw the secrets of the lightnings, and of the lights,and the judgements they execute (lit. 'their judgement'): and they lighten for a blessing or a curse as the Lord of Spirits willeth. 2. And there I saw thesecrets of the thunder, and how when it resounds above in the heaven, the sound thereof is heard, and he caused me to see the judgements executed on the earth, whether they be for well-being and blessing, or for a curse according to the word of the Lord of Spirits. 3. And after that all the secretsof the lights and lightnings were shown to me, and they lighten for blessing and for satisfying.]

CHAPTER 60

1. In the year five hundred, in the seventh month, on the fourteenth day of themonth in the life of †Enoch†. In that Parable I saw how a mighty quaking made the heaven of heavens to quake, and the host of the Most High, and the angels, a thousand thousands and ten thousand times **ten** thousand, were disquieted with a great disquiet. 2. And the Head of Days sat on the throne of His glory, and the angels and the righteous stood around Him. 3. And a great trembling seized me,And fear took hold of me, And my loins gave way, And dissolved were my reins,And I fell upon my face. 4 And Michael sent another angel from among the holy ones and heraised me up, and when he had raised me up my spirit returned; for I had not been able to endure the look of this host, and the commotion and the quaking of the heaven. And Michael said unto me: 'Why art thou disquieted with such a vision? Until this day lasted the day of His mercy; and He hath been merciful and long-suffering towards those who dwell on the earth. 6. And when the day, and the power, and the punishment, and the judgement come, which the Lord of Spirits hath prepared for those who worship not the righteous **law**, and for those who deny the righteous judgement, and for thosewho take His name in vain--that day is prepared, for the elect a covenant, but for sinners an inquisition. 25. When the punishment of the Lord of Spirits shall rest upon them, it shall rest in order that the punishment of the Lord of Spirits may not come, invain, and it shall slay the children with their mothers and the children with their fathers. Afterwards the judgement shall take place according to His mercy and His patience. 7. And on that day were two monsters parted, a female monster named Leviathan, to dwell in the abysses of the ocean over the fountains of the waters. 8. But the male is named Behemoth, who occupied with his breast a waste wilderness named †Dûidâin†, on the east of the garden where the elect and righteous dwell, where my grandfather was taken up, the seventh from Adam, the first man whom the Lord of Spirits created. 9. And I besought the other angel that he should show me the might of those monsters, how they were parted on one day and cast, the one into the abysses of the sea, and the other unto the dry land of the wilderness. 10. And he said to me: 'Thou son ofman, herein thou dost seek to know what is hidden.' 11. And the other angel who went with me and showed me what was hidden told me what is first and last in the heaven in the height, and beneath the earth in the depth, and at the ends of the heaven, and on the foundation of the heaven. 12. And the chambers of the winds, and how the winds are divided, and how they are weighed, and (how) the **portals** of the winds are reckoned, each according to the power of the wind, and the power of the lights of the moon, and according to the power that is fitting: and the divisions of the stars according to their names, and how all the divisions are divided. 13. And the thunders according to the places where they fall, and all the divisions that are made among the lightnings that it may lighten, and theirhost that they may at once obey. 14. For the thunder has †places of rest† (which) are assigned (to it) while it is waiting for its peal; and the thunder andlightning are inseparable, and although not one and undivided, they both go together through the spirit and separate not. 15. For when the lightninglightens, the thunder utters its voice, and the spirit enforces a pause during thepeal, and divides equally between them; for the treasury of their peals is like the sand, and each one of them as it peals is held in with a bridle, and turned back by the power of the spirit, and pushed forward according to the many quarters of the earth. And the spirit of the sea is masculine and strong, and according to the might of his strength he draws it back with a rein, and in likemanner it is driven forward and disperses amid all the mountains of the earth. 17. And the spirit of the hoar-frost is his own angel, and the spirit of the hailis a good angel. 18. And the spirit of the snow has forsaken his chambers on account of his strength--There is a special spirit therein, and that whichascends from it is like smoke, and its name is frost. 19. And the spirit of the mist is not united with them in their chambers, but it has a special chamber; for its course is †glorious† both in light and in darkness, and in winter and in summer, and in its chamber is an angel. 20. And the spirit of the dew has its dwelling at the ends of the heaven, and is connected with the chambers of therain, and its course is in winter and summer: and its clouds and the clouds of the mist are connected, and the one gives to the other. 21. And when the spirit of the rain goes forth from its chamber, the angels come and open thechamber and lead it out, and when it is diffused over the whole earth it unites with the water on the earth. And whensoever it unites with the water on the earth . . . 22. For the waters are for those who dwell on the earth; for they are nourishment for the earth from the Most High who is in heaven: therefore there is a measure for the rain, and the angels take it in charge. 23. And these things I saw towards the Garden of the Righteous. 24. And the angel of peacewho was with me said to me: 'These two monsters, prepared conformably to the greatness of God, shall feed . . .

CHAPTER 61

1.And I saw in those days how long cords were given to those angels, andthey took to themselves wings and flew, and they went towards the north. 2.And I asked the angel, saying unto him: 'Why have those (angels) takenthese cords and gone off?' And he said unto me: 'They have gone to measure.' 3.And the angel who went with me said unto me: 'These shall bring the measures of the righteous, And the ropes of the righteous to the righteous, That they may stay themselves on the name of the Lord of Spirits for everand ever. 4.The elect shall begin to dwell with the elect, And those are the measures which shall be given to faith And which shall strengthen righteousness. 5.And these measures shall reveal all the secrets of the depths of theearth, And those who have been destroyed by the desert,And those who have been devoured by the beasts, And those who have been devoured by the fish of the sea, That they may return and stay themselves On the day of the Elect One; For none shall be destroyed before the Lord of Spirits, And none can be destroyed. 6.And all who dwell above in the heaven received a command and powerand one voice and one light like unto fire. 7.And that One (with) their first words they blessed,And extolled and lauded with wisdom, And they were wise in utterance and in the spirit of life. 8.And the Lord of Spirits placed the Elect one on the throne of glory.And he shall judge all the works of the holy above in the heaven, And in the balance shall their deeds be weighed 9.And when he shall lift up his countenance To judge their secret ways according to the word of the name of the Lordof Spirits, And their path according to the way of the righteous judgement of theLord of Spirits, Then shall they all with one voice speak and bless, And glorify and extol and sanctify the name of the Lord of Spirits. 10.And He will summon all the host of the heavens, and all the holy ones above, and the host of God, the Cherubic, Seraphin and Ophannin, and all theangels of power, and all the angels of principalities, and the Elect One, and the other powers on the earth (and) over the water. 11. On that day shall raise one voice, and bless and glorify and exalt in the spirit of faith, and in thespirit of wisdom, and in the spirit of patience, and in the spirit of mercy, and in the spirit of judgement and of peace, and in the spirit of goodness, andshall all say with one voice: "Blessed is He, and may the name of the Lord of Spirits be blessed for ever and ever." 12.All who sleep not above in heaven shall bless Him:All the holy ones who are in heaven shall bless Him, And all the elect who dwell in the garden of life: And every spirit of light who is able to bless, and glorify, and extol, andhallow Thy blessed name, And all flesh shall beyond measure glorify and bless Thy name for everand ever. 13.For great is the mercy of the Lord of Spirits, and He is long-suffering, And all His works and all that He has created He has revealed to therighteous and electIn the name of the Lord of Spirits.

CHAPTER 62

1.And thus the Lord commanded the kings and the mighty and the exalted, and those who dwell on the earth, and said: 'Open your eyes and lift up your horns if ye are able to recognize the Elect One.' 2.And the Lord of Spirits seated him on the throne of His glory,And the spirit of righteousness was poured out upon him, And the word of his mouth slays all the sinners, And all the unrighteous are destroyed from before his face. 3.And there shall stand up in that day all the kings and the mighty, And the exalted and those who hold the earth, And they shall see and recognize How he sits on the throne of his glory,And righteousness is judged before him, And no lying word is spoken before him. 4.Then shall pain come upon them as on a woman in travail,[And she has pain in bringing forth] When her child enters the mouth of the womb,And she has pain in bringing forth. 5.And one portion of them shall look on the other,And they shall be terrified, And they shall be downcast of countenance,And pain shall seize them, When they see that Son of Man Sitting on the throne of his glory. 6.And the kings and the mighty and all who possess the earth shall blessand glorify and extol him who rules over all, who was hidden. 7.For from the beginning the Son of Man was hidden, And the Most High preserved him in the presence of His might, And revealed him to the elect. 8.And the congregation of the elect and holy shall be sown,And all the elect shall stand before him on that day. 9.And all the kings and the mighty and the exalted and those who rulethe earth Shall fall down before him on their faces, And worship and set their hope upon that Son of Man, And petition him and supplicate for mercy at his hands. 10.Nevertheless that Lord of Spirits will so press themThat they shall hastily go forth from His presence, And their faces shall be filled with shame, And the darkness grow deeper on

their faces. 11.And **He will deliver** them to the angels for punishment, To execute vengeance on them because they have oppressed His childrenand His elect 12.And they shall be a spectacle for the righteous and for His elect:They shall rejoice over them, Because the wrath of the Lord of Spirits resteth upon them,And His sword is drunk with their blood. 13.And the righteous and elect shall be saved on that day, And they shall never thenceforward see the face of the sinners andunrighteous. 14.And the Lord of Spirits will abide over them,And with that Son of Man shall they eat And lie down and rise up for ever and ever. 15.And the righteous and elect shall have risen from the earth, And ceased to be of downcast countenance. And they shall have been clothed with garments of glory, 16.And these shall be the garments of life from the Lord of Spirits:And your garments shall not grow old, Nor your glory pass away before the Lord of Spirits.

CHAPTER 63

1.In those days shall the mighty and the kings who possess the earth implore (Him) to grant them a little respite from His angels of punishment to whom they were delivered, that they might fall down and worship before the Lordof Spirits, and confess their sins before Him. 2. And they shall bless and glorify the Lord of Spirits, and say: 'Blessed is the Lord of Spirits and the Lord of kings,And the Lord of the mighty and the Lord of the rich,And the Lord of glory and the Lord of wisdom, 3.And splendid in every secret thing is Thy power from generation to generation, And Thy glory for ever and ever: Deep are all Thy secrets and innumerable, And Thy righteousness is beyond reckoning. 4.We have now learnt that we should glorify And bless the Lord of kings and Him who is king over all kings.' 5.And they shall say: 'Would that we had rest to glorify and give thanksAnd confess our faith before His glory! 6.And now we long for a little rest but find it not:We follow hard upon and obtain (it) not: And light has vanished from before us, And darkness is our dwelling-place for ever and ever: 7.For we have not believed before Him Nor glorified the name of the Lord of Spirits, [nor glorified our Lord]But our hope was in the sceptre of our kingdom, And in our glory. 8.And in the day of our suffering and tribulation He saves us not,And we find no respite for confession That our Lord is true in all His works, and in His judgements and His justice, And His judgements have no respect of persons. 9.And we pass away from before His face on account of our works,And all our sins are reckoned up in righteousness.' 10.Now they shall say unto themselves: 'Our souls are full of unrighteousgain, but it does not prevent us from descending from the midst thereof into the †burden† of Sheol.' 11.And after that their faces shall be filled with darknessAnd shame before that Son of Man, And they shall be driven from his presence, And the sword shall abide before his face in their midst. 12.Thus spake the Lord of Spirits: 'This is the ordinance and judgement with respect to the mighty and the kings and the exalted and those who possess the earth before the Lord of Spirits.'

CHAPTER 64

1. And other forms I saw hidden in that place. 2. I heard the voice of theangel saying: 'These are the angels who descended to the earth, and revealed what was hidden to the children of men and seduced the children of men into committing sin.'

CHAPTER 65

1. And in those days Noah saw the earth that it had sunk down and its destruction was nigh. 2. And he arose from thence and went to the ends of theearth, and cried aloud to his grandfather Enoch: and Noah said three times with an embittered voice: Hear me, hear me, hear me.' 3. And I said unto him:'Tell me what it is that is falling out on the earth that the earth is in such evil plight and shaken, lest perchance I shall perish with it?' 4. And thereupon there was a

great commotion, on the earth, and a voice was heard from heaven, and I fell on my face. 5. And Enoch my grandfather came and stood by me, and said unto me: 'Why hast thou cried unto me with a bitter cry and weeping? 6. And a command has gone forth from the presence of the Lord concerning those who dwell on the earth that their ruin is accomplished because they have learnt all the secrets of the angels, and all the violence of the Satans, and all their powers--the most secret ones-- and all the power of those who practice sorcery, and the power of witchcraft, and the power of those who make molten images for the whole earth: 7. And how silver is produced from the dust of the earth, and how soft metal originates in theearth. 8. For lead and tin are not produced from the earth like the first: it is a fountain that produces them, and an angel stands therein, and that angel is pre-eminent.' 9. And after that my grandfather Enoch took hold of me by my hand and raised me up, and said unto me: 'Go, for I have asked the Lord of Spirits as touching this commotion on the earth. 10. And He said unto me: "Because of their unrighteousness their judgement has been determined upon and shall not be **withheld** by Me for ever. Because of the **sorceries** which they have searched out and learnt, the earth and those who dwell upon it shall be destroyed." 11. And these--they have no **place of repentance** for ever, because they have shown them what was hidden, and they are the damned:but as for thee, my son, the Lord of Spirits knows that thou art pure, and guiltless of this reproach concerning the secrets. 12. And He has destined thy name to be among the holy, And will preserve thee amongst those who dwell on the earth, And has destined thy righteous seed both for kingship and for greathonours, And from thy seed shall proceed a fountain of the righteous and holywithout number for ever.

CHAPTER 66

1. And after that he showed me the angels of punishment who are prepared tocome and let loose all the powers of the waters which are beneath in the earthin order to bring judgement and destruction on all who [abide and] dwell on the earth. 2. And the Lord of Spirits gave commandment to the angels who were going forth, that they should not cause **the waters** to rise but shouldhold them in check; for those angels were over the powers of the waters. 3. And I went away from the presence of Enoch.

CHAPTER 67

1. And in those days the word of God came unto me, and He said unto me: 'Noah, thy lot has come up before Me, a lot without blame, a lot of love and uprightness. 2. And now the angels are making a wooden (building), and when they have completed that task I will place My hand upon it and preserve it, and there shall come forth from it the seed of life, and a change shall set in so that the earth will not remain without inhabitant. 3. And I will make fast thy seed before me for ever and ever, and I will spread abroadthose who dwell with thee: it shall not **be unfruitful** on the face of the earth, but it shall be blessed and multiply on the earth in the name of the Lord.' 4. And He will imprison those angels, who have shown unrighteousness, in that burning valley which my grandfather Enoch had formerly shown tome in the west among the mountains of gold and silver and iron and softmetal and tin. 5. And I saw that valley in which there was a great convulsion and a convulsion of the waters. 6. And when all this took place, from that fiery molten metal and from the convulsion thereof in that place, there was produced a smell of sulphur, and it was connected with those waters, and thatvalley of the angels who had led astray (mankind) burned beneath that land. 7.And through its valleys proceed streams of fire, where these angels are punished who had led astray those who dwell upon the earth. 8.But those waters shall in those days serve for the kings and the mighty and the exalted, and those who dwell on the earth, for the

healing of the body,but for the punishment of the spirit; now their spirit is full of lust, that they may be punished in their body, for they have denied the Lord of Spirits and see their punishment daily, and yet believe not in His name. 9. And inproportion as the burning of their bodies becomes severe, a corresponding 9.change shall take place in their spirit for ever and ever; for before the Lord ofSpirits none shall utter an idle word. 10. For the judgement shall come upon them, because they believe in the lust of their body and deny the Spirit of the Lord. 11. And those same waters will undergo a change in those days; for when those angels are punished in these waters, these water-springs shall change their temperature, and when the angels ascend, this water of the springs shall change and become cold. 12. And I heard Michael answering and saying: 'This judgement wherewith the angels are judged is a testimony for the kings and the mighty who possess the earth.' 13. Because these waters of judgement minister to the healing of the body of the **kings** and the lust of their body; therefore they will not see and will not believe that those waters will change and become a fire which burns for ever.

CHAPTER 68

1. And after that my grandfather Enoch gave me the teaching of all the secrets in the book in the Parables which had been given to him, and he put them together for me in the words of the book of the Parables. 2. And on that day Michael answered Raphael and said: 'The power of the spirit transports and **makes me to tremble** because of the severity of the judgement of the secrets, the judgement of the angels: who can endure the severe judgement which has been executed, and before which they melt away?' 3. And Michael answered again, and said to Raphael: 'Who is he whose heart is not softened concerning it, and whose reins are not troubled by this word of judgement (that) has gone forth upon them because of those who have thus led them out?' 4. And it came to pass when he stood before the Lord of Spirits,Michael said thus to Raphael: 'I will not take their part under the eye of the Lord; for the Lord of Spirits has been angry with them because they do as if they were the Lord. Therefore all that is hidden shall come upon them forever and ever; for neither angel nor man shall have his portion (in it), but alone they have received their judgement for ever and ever.'

CHAPTER 69

1 And after this judgement they shall terrify and **make** them **to tremble** because they have shown this to those who dwell on the earth. 2 And behold the names of those angels [and these are their names: the first of them is Samjâzâ, the second Artâqîfâ, and the third Armên, the fourth Kôkabêl, the fifth †Tûrâêl†, the sixth Rûmjâl, the seventh Dânjâl, the eighth †Nêqâêl†, the ninth Barâqêl, the tenth Azâzêl, the eleventh Armârôs, the twelfth Batarjâl, the thirteenth †Busasêjal†, the fourteenth Hanânêl, the fifteenth †Tûrêl†, and the sixteenth Sîmâpêsîêl, the seventeenth Jetrêl, the eighteenth Tûmâêl, the nineteenth Tûrêl, the twentieth †Rumâêl†, the twenty-first †Azâzêl†. 3. And these are the chiefs of their angels and their names,and their chief ones over hundreds and over fifties and over tens]. 4. The name of the first Jeqôn: that is, the one who led astray [all] the sons of **God**, and brought them down to the earth, and led them astray through the daughters of men. 5. And the second was named Asbeêl: he imparted to the holy sons of **God** evil counsel, and led them astray so that they defiled their bodies with the daughters of men. 6. And the third was named Gâdreêl: he it is who showed the children of men all the blows of death, and he led astray Eve, and showed [the weapons of death to the sonsof men] the shield and the coat of mail, and the sword for battle, and all the weapons of death to the children of men. 7. And from his hand they have

proceeded against those who dwell on the earth from that day and for evermore. 8. And the fourth was named Pênêmûe: he taught the children of men the bitter and the sweet, and he taught them all the secrets of their wisdom. 9. And he instructed mankind in writing with ink and paper, and thereby many sinned from eternity to eternity and until this day. 10. For men were not created for such a purpose, to give confirmation to their good faith with pen and ink. 11. For men were created exactly like the angels, to the intent that they should continue pure and righteous, and death, which destroys everything, could not have taken hold of them, but through this their knowledge they are perishing, and through this power it is consuming met. 12.And the fifth was named Kâsdejâ: this is he who showed the children of men all the wicked smitings of spirits and demons, and the smitings of the embryo in the womb, that it may pass away, and [the smitings of the soul] the bites of the serpent, and the smitings which befall through the noontide heat, the son of the serpent named Tabââ'ët. 13. And this is the **task** of Kâsbeêl, the chief of the oath which he showed to the holy ones when he dwelt high above in glory, and its name is Bîqâ. 14. This (angel) requested Michael to show him the hidden name, that he might enunciate it in the oath, so that those might quake before that name and oath who revealed all that was in secret to the children of men. 15. And this is the power of this oath, for it is powerful and strong, and he placed this oath Akâe in the hand of Michael. 16 And these are the secrets of this oath . . . And they are strong through his oath: And the heaven was suspended before the world was created, And for ever. 17.And through it the earth was founded upon the water, And from the secret recesses of the mountains come beautiful waters, From the creation of the world and unto eternity. 18.And through that oath the sea was created, And †as its foundation† He set for it the sand against the time of (its) anger, And it dare not pass beyond it from the creation of the world untoeternity. 19.And through that oath are the depths made fast, And abide and stir not from their place from eternity to eternity. 20.And through that oath the sun and moon complete their course, And deviate not from their ordinance from eternity to eternity. 21.And through that oath the stars complete their course, And He calls them by their names, And they answer Him from eternity to eternity. [22. And in like manner the spirits of the water, and of the winds, and of all zephyrs, and (their) paths from all the quarters of the winds. 23. And there are preserved the voices of the thunder and the light of the lightnings: and there are preserved the chambers of the hail and the chambers of the hoarfrost, and the chambers of the mist, and the chambers of the rain and the dew. 24. And all these believe and give thanks before the Lord of Spirits, andglorify (Him) with all their power, and their food is in every act of thanksgiving: they thank and glorify and extol the name of the Lord of Spirits for ever and ever.]25.And this oath is mighty over them And through it [they are preserved and] their paths are preserved, And their course is not destroyed. Close of the Third Parable. 26.And there was great joy amongst them, And they blessed and glorified and extolled Because the name of that Son of Man had been revealed unto them. 27.And he sat on the throne of his glory, And the sum of judgement was given unto the Son of Man, And he caused the sinners to pass away and be destroyed from off the face of the earth, And those who have led the world astray. 28.With chains shall they be bound, And in their assemblage-place of destruction shall they be imprisoned, And all their works vanish from the face of the earth. 29.And from henceforth there shall be nothing corruptible; For that Son of Man has appeared, And has seated himself on the throne of his glory, And all evil shall pass away before his face, And the word of that Son of Man shall go forth

And be strong before the Lord of Spirits.

CHAPTER 70

1. And it came to pass after this that his name during his lifetime was raised aloft to that Son of Man and to the Lord of Spirits from amongst those who dwell on the earth. 2. And he was raised aloft on the chariots of the spirit and his name vanished among them. 3. And from that day I was no longernumbered amongst them: and he set me between the two winds, between the North and the West, where the angels took the cords to measure for me the place for the elect and righteous. 4. And there I saw the first fathers and the righteous who from the beginning dwell in that place.

CHAPTER 71

1.And it came to pass after this that my spirit was translatedAnd it ascended into the heavens: And I saw the **holy sons of God**. They were stepping on flames of fire: Their garments were white [and their raiment], And their faces shone like snow. 2.And I saw two streams of fire, And the light of that fire shone like hyacinth, And I fell on my face before the Lord of Spirits. 3.And the angel Michael [one of the archangels] seized me by my righthand, And lifted me up and led me forth into all the secrets, And he showed me all the secrets of righteousness. 4.And he showed me all the secrets of the ends of the heaven, And all the chambers of all the stars, and all the luminaries, Whence they proceed before the face of the holy ones. 5.And he translated my spirit into the heaven of heavens, And I saw there as it were a structure built of crystals, And between those crystals tongues of living fire. 6.And my spirit saw the girdle which girt that house of fire, And on its four sides were streams full of living fire, And they girt that house. 7.And round about were Seraphin, Cherubic, and Ophannin:And these are they who sleep not And guard the throne of His glory. 8.And I saw angels who could not be counted, A thousand thousands, and ten thousand times ten thousand, Encircling that house. And Michael, and Raphael, and Gabriel, and Phanuel, And the holy angels who are above the heavens, Go in and out of that house. 9.And they came forth from that house, And Michael and Gabriel, Raphael and Phanuel,And many holy angels without number. 10.And with them the Head of Days, His head white and pure as wool, And His raiment indescribable. 11.And I fell on my face, And my whole body became relaxed, And my spirit was transfigured; And I cried with a loud voice, . . .with the spirit of power, And blessed and glorified and extolled. 12.And these blessings which went forth out of my mouth were well pleasing before that Head of Days. 13. And that Head of Days came with Michael and Gabriel, Raphael and Phanuel, thousands and ten thousands of angels without number. [Lost passage wherein the Son of Man was described as accompanyingthe Head of Days, and Enoch asked one of the angels (as in 46) concerning the Son of Man as to who he was.] 14.And he (i.e. the angel) came to me and greeted me with His voice, andsaid unto me: '**This is** the Son of Man who is born unto righteousness;And righteousness abides over him, And the righteousness of the Head of Days forsakes him not.' 15.And he said unto me: 'He proclaims unto thee peace in the name of the world to come; For from hence has proceeded peace since the creation of the world,And so shall it be unto thee for ever and for ever and ever. And all shall walk in **his** ways since righteousness neverforsaketh **him**: With **him** will be their dwelling-places, and with **him** their heritage, And they shall not be separated from him for ever and ever and ever. 16.And so there shall be length of days with that Son of Man, And the righteous shall have peace and an upright way In the name of the Lord of Spirits for ever and ever.'

CHAPTER 72

1. The book of the courses of the luminaries of the heaven, the relations of each, according to their

classes, their dominion and their seasons, accordingto their names and places of origin, and according to their months, which Uriel, the holy angel, who was with me, who is their guide, showed me; and he showed me all their laws exactly as they are, and how it is with regard to all the years of the world and unto eternity, till the new creation is accomplished which dureth till eternity. 2. And this is the first law of the luminaries: the luminary the Sun has its rising in the eastern portals of the heaven, and its setting in the western portals of the heaven. 3. And I saw six portals in which the sun rises, and six portals in which the sun sets and the moon rises and sets in these portals, and the leaders of the stars and those whom they lead: six in the east and six in the west, and all following each other in accurately corresponding order: also many windows to the right and left of these portals. 4. And first there goes forth the great luminary, named the Sun, and his circumference is like the circumference of the heaven, andhe is quite filled with illuminating and heating fire. 5. The chariot on whichhe ascends, the wind drives, and the sun goes down from the heaven and returns through the north in order to reach the east, and is so guided that he comes to the appropriate (lit. 'that') portal and shines in the face of theheaven. 6. In this way he rises in the first month in the great portal, which is the fourth [those six portals in the cast]. 7. And in that fourth portal from which the sun rises in the first month are twelve window-openings, from which proceed a flame when they are opened in their season. 8. When the sunrises in the heaven, he comes forth through that fourth portal thirty mornings in succession, and sets accurately in the fourth portal in the west of the heaven. 9. And during this period the day becomes daily longer and the night nightly shorter to the thirtieth morning. 10. On that day the day is longer than the night by a ninth part, and the day amounts exactly to ten parts and the night to eight parts. 11. And the sun rises from that fourth portal, and sets in the fourth and returns to the fifth portal of the east thirty mornings, and rises from it and sets in the fifth portal. 12. And then the day becomes longer by †two† parts and amounts to eleven parts, and the night becomes shorter and amounts to seven parts. 13. And it returns to the east and enters into the sixth portal, and rises and sets in the sixth portal one-and-thirty mornings on account of its sign. 14. On that day the day becomes longer than the night,and the day becomes double the night, and the day becomes twelve parts, and the night is shortened and becomes six parts. 15. And the sun mounts up to make the day shorter and the night longer, and the sun returns to the east and enters into the sixth portal, and rises from it and sets thirty mornings. 16. And when thirty mornings are accomplished, the day decreases by exactly one part, and becomes eleven parts, and the night seven. 17. And the sun goes forth from that sixth portal in the west, and goes to the east and rises in the fifth portal for thirty mornings, and sets in the west again in the fifth western portal. 18. On that day the day decreases by †two† parts, and amounts to ten parts and the night to eight parts. 19. And the sun goes forth from that fifth portal and sets in the fifth portal of the west, and rises in the fourth portal for one-and-thirty mornings on account of its sign, and sets in the west. 20. On that day the day is equalized with the night, [and becomes of equal length], and the night amounts to nine parts and the day to nine parts. 21. And the sun rises from that portal and sets in the west, and returns to the east and rises thirty mornings in the third portal and sets in the west in the third portal. 22. And on that day the night becomes longer than the day, and night becomes longer than night, and day shorter than day till the thirtieth morning, and the night amounts exactly to ten parts and the day to eight parts. 23. And the sun rises from that third portal and sets in the third portal in the

west and returns to the east, and for thirty mornings rises in the second portal in the east, andin like manner sets in the second portal in the west of the heaven. 24. And on that day the night amounts to eleven parts and the day to seven parts. 25. Andthe sun rises on that day from that second portal and sets in the west in the second portal, and returns to the east into the first portal for one-and-thirty mornings, and sets in the first portal in the west of the heaven. 26. And onthat day the night becomes longer and amounts to the double of the day: and the night amounts exactly to twelve parts and the day to six. 27. And the sun has (therewith) traversed the divisions of his orbit and turns again on those divisions of his orbit, and enters that portal thirty mornings and sets also inthe west opposite to it. 28. And on that night has the night decreased in lengthby a †nintht part, and the night has become eleven parts and the day seven parts. 29. And the sun has returned and entered into the second portal in the east, and returns on those his divisions of his orbit for thirty mornings, rising and setting. 30. And on that day the night decreases in length, and the night amounts to ten parts and the day to eight. 31. And on that day the sun rises from that portal, and sets in the west, and returns to the east, and rises in the third portal for one-and-thirty mornings, and sets in the west of the heaven. 32. On that day the night decreases and amounts to nine parts, and the day to nine parts, and the night is equal to the day and the year is exactly as to its days three hundred and sixty-four. 33. And the length of the day and of the night, and the shortness of the day and of the night arise-- through the course of the sun these distinctions are made (lit. 'they are separated'). 34. So it comes that its course becomes daily longer, and its course nightly shorter. 35.And this is the law and the course of the sun, and his return as often as he returns sixty times and rises, i.e. the great luminary which is named the sun, for ever and ever. 36. And that which (thus) rises is the great luminary, and isso named according to its appearance, according as the Lord commanded. 37. As he rises, so he sets and decreases not, and rests not, but runs day and night, and his light is sevenfold brighter than that of the moon; but as regards size they are both equal.

CHAPTER 73

1. And after this law I saw another law dealing with the smaller luminary, which is named the Moon. 2. And her circumference is like the circumference of the heaven, and her chariot in which she rides is driven by the wind, and light is given to her in (definite) measure. 3. And her rising and setting change every month: and her days are like the days of the sun, and when her light is uniform (i.e. full) it amounts to the seventh part of the light of the sun. 4. And thus she rises. And her first phase in the east comes forth on the thirtieth morning: and on that day she becomes visible, and constitutes foryou the first phase of the moon on the thirtieth day together with the sun inthe portal where the sun rises. 5. And the one half of her goes forth by a seventh part, and her whole circumference is empty, without light, with the exception of one-seventh part of it, (and) the fourteenth part of her light. 6. And when she receives one-seventh part of the half of her light, her light amounts to one-seventh part and the half thereof. 7. And she sets with thesun, and when the sun rises the moon rises with him and receives the half of one part of light, and in that night in the beginning of her morning [in the commencement of the lunar day] the moon sets with the sun, and is invisible that night with the fourteen parts and the half of one of them. 8. And she riseson that day with exactly a seventh part, and comes forth and recedes from therising of the sun, and in her remaining days she becomes bright in the (remaining) thirteen parts.

CHAPTER 74

1. And I saw another course, a law for her, (and) how

according to that law she performs her monthly revolution. 2. And all these Uriel, the holy angel who is the leader of them all, showed to me, and their positions, and I wrote down their positions as he showed them to me, and I wrote down their months as they were, and the appearance of their lights till fifteen days were accomplished. 3. In single seventh parts she accomplishes all her light in the east, and in single seventh parts accomplishes all her darkness in the west. 4. And in certain months she alters her settings, and in certain months she pursues her own peculiar course. 5. In two months the moon sets with thesun: in those two middle portals the third and the fourth. 6. She goes forth forseven days, and turns about and returns again through the portal where thesun rises, and accomplishes all her light: and she recedes from the sun, and ineight days enters the sixth portal from which the sun goes forth. 7. And when the sun goes forth from the fourth portal she goes forth seven days, until she goes forth from the fifth and turns back again in seven days into the fourth portal and accomplishes all her light: and she recedes and enters into the first portal in eight days. 8. And she returns again in seven days into the fourth portal from which the sun goes forth. 9. Thus I saw their position--how the moons rose and the sun set in those days. 10. And if five years are added together the sun has an overplus of thirty days, and all the days which accrue to it for one of those five years, when they are full, amount to 364 days. 11. And the overplus of the sun and of the stars amounts to six days: in 5 years 6 days every year come to 30 days: and the moon falls behind the sun and stars to the number of 30 days. 12. And **the sun** and the stars bring in all the years exactly, so that they do not advance or delay their position by a single day unto eternity; but **complete** the years with perfect justice in 364 days. 13. In 3years there are 1092 days, and in 5 years 1820 days, so that in 8 years there are 2912 days. 14. For the moon alone the days amount in 3 years to 1062 days, and in 5 years she falls 50 days behind: [*i.e.* to the sum (of 1770) thereis to be added (1000 and) 62 days.] 15. And in 5 years there are 1770 days, sothat for the moon the days in 8 years amount to 2832 days. 16. [For in 8 yearsshe falls behind to the amount of 80 days], all the days she falls behind in 8 years are 80. 17. And the year is accurately completed in conformity with their world-stations and the stations of the sun, which rise from the portals through which it (the sun) rises and sets 30 days.

CHAPTER 75

1. And the leaders of the heads of the thousands, who are placed over the whole creation and over all the stars, have also to do with the four intercalary days, being inseparable from their office, according to the reckoning of the year, and these render service on the four days which are not reckoned in the reckoning of the year. 2. And owing to them men go wrong therein, for those luminaries truly render service on the world-stations, one in the first portal, one in the third portal of the heaven, one in the fourth portal, and one in the sixth portal, and the exactness of the year is accomplished through its separate three hundred and sixty-four stations. 3. For the signs and the times and the years and the days the angel Uriel showed to me, whom the Lord of glory hath set for ever over all the luminaries of the heaven, in the heavenand in the world, that they should rule on the face of the heaven and be seen on the earth, and be leaders for the day and the night, *i.e.* the sun, moon, and stars, and all the ministering creatures which make their revolution in all the chariots of the heaven. 4. In like manner twelve doors Uriel showed me, openin the circumference of the sun's chariot in the heaven, through which the rays of the sun break forth: and from them is warmth diffused over the earth, when they are opened at their appointed seasons. 5. [And for the winds and the spirit of the dew† when they are opened, standing open in the heavens at the ends.] 6. As for the twelve portals in the heaven, at the ends of the earth, out of which go forth the sun, moon, and stars, and all the works of heaven inthe east and in the west. 7. There are many windows open to the left and rightof them, and one window at its (appointed) season produces warmth, corresponding (as these do) to those doors from which the stars come forth according as He has commanded them, and wherein they set corresponding to their number. 8. And I saw chariots in the heaven, running in the world, above those portals in which revolve the stars that never set. 9. And one is larger than all the rest, and it is that that makes its course through the entire world.

CHAPTER 76

1 And at the ends of the earth I saw twelve portals open to allthe **quarters** (of the heaven), from which the winds go forth and blow over the earth. 2. Three of them are open on the face (i.e. the east) of the heavens, and three in the west, and three on the right (i.e. the south) of the heaven, and three on the left (i.e. the north). 3. And the three first are those of the east, and three are of †the north, and three [after those on the left] of the south†, and three of the west. 4. Through four of these come winds of blessing and prosperity, and from those eight come hurtful winds: when they are sent, they bring destruction on all the earth and on the water upon it, and on all who dwell thereon, and on everything which is in the water and on the land. 5. And the first wind from those portals, called the east wind, comes forth through the first portal which is in the east, inclining towards the south: from it come forth desolation, drought, heat, and destruction. 6. And through the second portal in the middle comes what is fitting, and from it there come rain and fruitfulness and prosperity and dew; and through the third portal which lies toward the north come cold and drought. 7. And after these come forth the south winds through three portals: through the first portal of them inclining to the east comes forth a hot wind. 8. And through the middle portal next to it there come forth fragrant smells, and dew and rain, and prosperity and health. 9. And through the third portal lying to the west come forth dew and rain, locusts and desolation. 10. And after these the north winds: from the seventh portal in the east come dew and rain, locusts and desolation. 11. And from the middle portal come in a direct direction health and rain and dew and prosperity; and through the third portal in the west come cloud and hoar-frost, and snow and rain, and dew and locusts. 12. And after these [four] are the west winds: through the first portal adjoining the north come forth dew and hoar-frost, and cold and snow and frost. And from the middle portal come forth dew and rain, and prosperity and blessing; and through the last portal which adjoins the south come forth drought and desolation, and burning and destruction. 14. And the twelve portals of the four **quarters** of the heaven are therewith completed, and all their laws and all their plagues and all their benefactions have I shown tothee, my son Methuselah.

CHAPTER 77

1. And the first **quarter** is called the east, because it is the first: and the second, the south, because the Most High **will descend** there, yea, there in quite a special sense will He who is blessed for ever **descend**. 2. And thewest **quarter** is named the diminished, because there all the luminaries of the heaven wane and go down. 3. And the fourth **quarter**, named the north, is divided into three parts: the first of them is for the dwelling of men: and the second contains seas of water, and the abysses and forests and rivers, and darkness and clouds; and the third part contains the garden of righteousness. 4. I saw seven high mountains, higher than all the mountains which are on the earth: and thence

comes forth hoar-frost, and days, seasons, and yearspass away. 5. I saw seven rivers on the earth larger than all the rivers: one of them coming from the west pours its waters into the Great Sea. 6. And these two come from the north to the sea and pour their waters into the Erythraean Sea in the east. 7. And the remaining four come forth on the side of the north to their own sea, ⟨two of them⟩ to the Erythraean Sea, and two into the Great Sea and discharge themselves there [and some say: into the desert]. 8. Seven great islands I saw in the sea and in the mainland: two in the mainland and five in the Great Sea.

CHAPTER 78

1. And the names of the sun are the following: the first Orjârês, and the second Tômâs. 2. And the moon has four names: the first name is Asônjâ, thesecond Eblâ, the third Benâsê, and the fourth Ěrâe. 3. These are the two great luminaries: their circumference is like the circumference of the heaven, and the size of the circumference of both is alike. 4. In the circumference of the sun there are seven portions of light which are added to it more than to the moon, and in definite measures it is s transferred till the seventh portion ofthe sun is exhausted. 5. And they set and enter the portals of the west, and make their revolution by the north, and come forth through the eastern portalson the face of the heaven. 6. And when the moon rises one-fourteenth part appears in the heaven: [the light becomes full in her]: on the fourteenth day she accomplishes her light. 7. And fifteen parts of light are transferred to her till the fifteenth day (when) her light is accomplished, according to the signof the year, and she becomes fifteen parts, and the moon grows by (the addition of) fourteenth parts. 8. And in her waning (the moon) decreases on the first day to fourteen parts of her light, on the second to thirteen parts of light, on the third to twelve, on the fourth to eleven, on the fifth to ten, on the sixth to nine, on the seventh to eight, on the eighth to seven, on the ninth to six, on the tenth to five, on the eleventh to four, on the twelfth to three, on thethirteenth to two, on the fourteenth to the half of a seventh, and all her remaining light disappears wholly on the fifteenth. 9. And in certain months the month has twenty-nine days and once twenty-eight. 10. And Uriel showedme another law: when light is transferred to the moon, and on which side it is transferred to her by the sun. 11. During all the period during which the moonis growing in her light, she is transferring it to herself when opposite to the sun during fourteen days [her light is accomplished in the heaven], and when she is illumined throughout, her light is accomplished full in the heaven. 12. And on the first day she is called the new moon, for on that day the light risesupon her. 13. She becomes full moon exactly on the day when the sun sets in the west, and from the east she rises at night, and the moon shines the whole night through till the sun rises over against her and the moon is seen over against the sun. 14. On the side whence the light of the moon comes forth, there again she wanes till all the light vanishes and all the days of the month are at an end, and her circumference is empty, void of light. 15. And three months she makes of thirty days, and at her time she makes three months of twenty-nine days each, in which she accomplishes her waning in the first period of time, and in the first portal for one hundred and seventy-seven days. 16. And in the time of her going out she appears for three months (of) thirty days each, and for three months she appears (of) twenty-nine each. 17. At night she appears like a man for twenty days each time, and by day she appears like the heaven, and there is nothing else in her save her light.

CHAPTER 79

1. And now, my son, I have shown thee everything, and the law of all the stars of the heaven is completed. 2. And he showed me all the laws of these for every day, and for every season of bearing rule, and for every year, andfor its going forth, and for the order prescribed to it every month and every week: 3. And the waning of the moon which takes place in the sixth portal:for in this sixth portal her light is accomplished, and after that there is the beginning of the waning: 4. ⟨And the waning⟩ which takes place in the firstportal in its season, till one hundred and seventy-seven days are accomplished: reckoned according to weeks, twenty-five (weeks) and two days. 5. She falls behind the sun and the order of the stars exactly five days inthe course of one period, and when this place which thou seest has been traversed. 6. Such is the picture and sketch of every luminary which Uriel thearchangel, who is their leader, showed unto me.

CHAPTER 80

1.And in those days the angel Uriel answered and said to me: 'Behold, I haveshown thee everything, Enoch, and I have revealed everything to thee that thou shouldst see this sun and this moon, and the leaders of the stars of the heaven and all those who turn them, their tasks and times and departures. 2.And in the days of the sinners the years shall be shortened, And their seed shall be tardy on their lands and fields, And all things on the earth shall alter,And shall not appear in their time: And the rain shall be kept back And the heaven shall withhold (it). 3.And in those times the fruits of the earth shall be backward,And shall not grow in their time, And the fruits of the trees shall be withheld in their time. 4.And the moon shall alter her order,And not appear at her time. 5.[And in those days the **sun** shall be seen and he shall journey inthe **evening** †on the extremity of the great chariott† in the west] And shall shine more brightly than accords with the order of light. 6.And many chiefs of the stars shall transgress the order (prescribed). And these shall alter their orbits and tasks, And not appear at the seasons prescribed to them. 7.And the whole order of the stars shall be concealed from the sinners,And the thoughts of those on the earth shall err concerning them, [And they shall be altered from all their ways],Yea, they shall err and take them to be gods. 8.And evil shall be multiplied upon them, And punishment shall come upon them So as to destroy all.'

CHAPTER 81

1.And he said unto me: 'Observe, Enoch, these heavenly tablets,And read what is written thereon, And mark every individual fact.' 2 And I observed the heavenly tablets, and read everything which was written (thereon) and understood everything, and read the book of all the deeds of mankind, and of all the children of flesh that shall be upon the earth to the remotest generations. 3. And forthwith I blessed the great Lord theKing of glory for ever, in that He has made all the works of the world, And I extolled the Lord because of His patience, And blessed Him because of the children of men. 4.And after that I said: 'Blessed is the man who dies in righteousness and goodness, Concerning whom there is no book of unrighteousness written, And against whom no day of judgement shall be found.' 5.And those seven holy ones brought me and placed me on the earth before the door of my house, and said to me: 'Declare everything to thy son Methuselah, and show to all thy children that no flesh is righteous in the sightof the Lord, for He is their Creator. 6. One year we will leave thee with thy son, till thou givest thy (last) commands, that thou mayest teach thy children and record (it) for them, and testify to all thy children; and in the second year they shall take thee from their midst. 7.Let thy heart be strong, For the good shall announce righteousness to the good;The righteous with the righteous shall rejoice, And shall offer congratulation to one another. 8.But the sinners shall die with the sinners, And the apostate go down with the apostate. 9.And those who practice righteousness shall die on account of the deedsof men, And be taken away on account of the doings of the godless.' 10.And in those days they ceased to speak to me, and I came to mypeople, blessing the Lord of the world.

CHAPTER 82

1.And now, my son Methuselah, all these things I am recounting to thee and writing down for thee, and I have revealed to thee everything, and given thee books concerning all these: so preserve, my son Methuselah, the books from thy father's hand, and (see) that thou deliver them to the generations of the world. 2.I have given Wisdom to thee and to thy children,[And thy children that shall be to thee], That they may give it to their children for generations,This wisdom (namely) that passeth their thought. 3.And those who understand it shall not sleep, But shall listen with the ear that they may learn this wisdom, And it shall please those that eat thereof better than good food. 4.Blessed are all the righteous, blessed are all those who walk in the way of righteousness and sin not as the sinners, in the reckoning of all their days in which the sun traverses the heaven, entering into and departing from the portals for thirty days with the heads of thousands of the order of the stars, together with the four which are intercalated which divide the four portions ofthe year, which lead them and enter with them four days. 5. Owing to them men shall be at fault and not reckon them in the **whole reckoning of theyear**: yea, men shall be at fault, and not recognize them accurately. 6. For they belong to the reckoning of the year and are truly recorded (thereon) for ever, one in the first portal and one in the third, and one in the fourth and one in the sixth, and the year is completed in three hundred and sixty-four days. 7. And the account thereof is accurate and the recorded reckoning thereof exact; for the luminaries, and months and festivals, and years and days, has Uriel shown and revealed to me, **to whom** the Lord of the whole creation of the world hath **subjected** the host of heaven. 8. And he has power over night and day in the heaven to cause the light to give light to men--sun, moon, and stars, and all the powers of the heaven which revolve in their circular chariots. 9. And these are the orders of the stars, which set in their places, andin their seasons and festivals and months. 10. And these are the names of those who lead them, who watch that they enter at their times, in their orders, in their seasons, in their months, in their periods of dominion, and in their positions. 11. Their four leaders who divide the four parts of the year enter first; and after them the twelve leaders of the orders who divide the months; and for the three hundred and sixty (days) there are heads over thousandswho divide the days; and for the four intercalary days there are the leaders which sunder the four parts of the year. 12. And these heads over thousands are intercalated between leader and leader, each behind a station, but their leaders make the division. And these are the names of the leaders who divide the four parts of the year which are ordained: Mîlkî'êl, Hel'emmêlêk, and Mêl'êjal, and Nârêl. 13. And the names of those who lead them: Adnâr'êl, and Îjâsûsa'êl, and 'Elômê'êl--these three follow the leaders of the orders,and there is one that follows the three leaders of the orders which followthose leaders of stations that divide the four parts of the year. 15. In the beginning of the year Melkejâl rises first and rules, who is named †Tam'âinî† and sun, and all the days of his dominion whilst he bears rule are ninety-one days. 16. And these are the signs of the days which are to be seen on earth in the days of his dominion: sweat, and heat, and calms; and all the trees bear fruit, and leaves are produced on all the trees, and theharvest of wheat, and the rose-flowers, and all the flowers which come forth in the field, but the trees of the winter season become withered. 17. And theseare the names of the leaders which are under them: Berka'êl, Zêlebs'êl, and another who is added a head of a thousand, called Hîlûjâsëph: and the days of the dominion of this

(leader) are at an end. 18. The next leader after him is Hêl'emmêlêk, whom one names the shining sun, and all the days of his light are ninety-one days. 19. And these are the signs of (his) days on the earth: glowing heat and dryness, and the trees ripen their fruits and produce all theirfruits ripe and ready, and the sheep pair and become pregnant, and all the fruits of the earth are gathered in, and everything that is in the fields, and the winepress: these things take place in the days of his dominion. 20. These are the names, and the orders, and the leaders of those heads of thousands: Gîdâ'îjal, Kê'êl, and Hê'êl, and the name of the head of a thousand which isadded to them, Asfâ'êl': and the days of his dominion are at an end.

CHAPTER 83

1. And now, my son Methuselah, I will show thee all my visions which Ihave seen, recounting them before thee. 2. Two visions I saw before I took a wife, and the one was quite unlike the other: the first when I was learning to write: the second before I took thy mother, (when) I saw a terrible vision. And regarding them I prayed to the Lord. 3. I had laid me down in the house of my grandfather Mahalalel, (when) I saw in a vision how the heavencollapsed and was borne off and fell to the earth. 4. And when it fell to the earth I saw how the earth was swallowed up in a great abyss, and mountains were suspended on mountains, and hills sank down on hills, and high trees were rent from their stems, and hurled down and sunk in the abyss. 5. And thereupon a word fell into my mouth, and I lifted up (my voice) to cry aloud, and said: 'The earth is destroyed.' 6. And my grandfather Mahalalel wakedme as I lay near him, and said unto me: 'Why dost thou cry so, my son, and why dost thou make such lamentation?' 7. And I recounted to him the whole vision which I had seen, and he said unto me: 'A terrible thing hast thou seen, my son, and of grave moment is thy dream-vision as to the secrets of all the sin of the earth: it must sink into the abyss and be destroyed with a great destruction. 8. And now, my son, arise and make petition to the Lord ofglory, since thou art a believer, that a remnant may remain on the earth, and that He may not destroy the whole earth. 9. My son, from heaven all this will come upon the earth, and upon the earth there will be great destruction. 10. After that I arose and prayed and implored and besought, and wrote down my prayer for the generations of the world, and I will show everything to thee,my son Methuselah. 11. And when I had gone forth below and seen the heaven, and the sun rising in the east, and the moon setting in the west, and a few stars, and the whole earth, and everything as †He had known† it in the beginning, then I blessed the Lord of judgement and extolled Him becauseHe had made the sun to go forth from the windows of the east, †and he ascended and rose on the face of the heaven, and set out and kept traversing the path shown unto him.

CHAPTER 84

1.And I lifted up my hands in righteousness and blessed the Holy and Great One, and spake with the breath of my mouth, and with the tongue of flesh, which God has made for the children of the flesh of men, that they should speak therewith, and He gave them breath and a tongue and a mouth that they should speak therewith: 2.'Blessed be Thou, O Lord, King,Great and mighty in Thy greatness, Lord of the whole creation of the heaven, King of kings and God of the whole world. And Thy power and kingship and greatness abide for ever and ever,And throughout all generations Thy dominion; And all the heavens are Thy throne for ever, And the whole earth Thy footstool for ever and ever. 3.For Thou hast made and Thou rulest all things,And nothing is too hard for Thee, Wisdom departs not **from the place of Thy throne**, **Nor turns away** from Thy presence. And Thou knowest and seest and hearest everything, And there is nothing hidden from Thee [for Thou seest everything]. 4.And now the angels of Thy heavens are guilty of trespass, And upon the flesh of men abideth Thy wrath until the great day of judgement. 5.And now, O God and Lord and Great King, I implore and beseech Thee to fulfil my prayer, To leave me a posterity on earth, And not destroy all the flesh of man, And make the earth without inhabitant, So that there should be an eternal destruction. 6.And now, my Lord, destroy from the earth the flesh which has arousedThy wrath, But the flesh of righteousness and uprightness establish as a plant of theeternal seed, And hide not Thy face from the prayer of Thy servant, O Lord.'

CHAPTER 85

1. And after this I saw another dream, and I will show the whole dream to thee, my son. 2. And Enoch lifted up (his voice) and spake to his sonMethuselah: 'To thee, my son, will I speak: hear my words--incline thine ear to the dream-vision of thy father. 3. Before I took thy mother Edna, I saw in avision on my bed, and behold a bull came forth from the earth, and that bull was white; and after it came forth a heifer, and along with this (latter) came forth two bulls, one of them black and the other red. 4. And that black bull gored the red one and pursued him over the earth, and thereupon I could no longer see that red bull. 5. But that black bull grew and that heifer went with him, and I saw that many oxen proceeded from him which resembled and followed him. 6. And that cow, that first one, went from the presence of that first bull in order to seek that red one, but found him not, and lamented with a great lamentation over him and sought him. 7. And I looked till that first bull came to her and quieted her, and from that time onward she cried no more. 8. And after that she bore another white bull, and after him she bore many bulls and black cows. 9. And I saw in my sleep that white bull likewise grow and become agreat white bull, and from Him proceeded many white bulls, and they resembled him. And they began to beget many white bulls, which resembled them, one following the other, (even) many.

CHAPTER 86

1. And again I saw with mine eyes as I slept, and I saw the heaven above, andbehold a star fell from heaven, and it arose and eat and pastured amongst those oxen. 2. And after that I saw the large and the black oxen, and behold they all changed their stalls and pastures and their cattle, and began to live with each other. 3. And again I saw in the vision, and looked towards the heaven, and behold I saw many stars descend and cast themselves down fromheaven to that first star, and they became bulls amongst those cattle and pastured with them [amongst them]. 4. And I looked at them and saw, and behold they all let out their privy members, like horses, and began to cover the cows of the oxen, and they all became pregnant and bare elephants, camels, and asses. 5. And all the oxen feared them and were affrighted at them, and began to bite with their teeth and to devour, and to gore with their horns. 6. And they began, moreover, to devour those oxen; and behold all the children of the earth began to tremble and quake before them and to flee fromthem.

CHAPTER 87

1. And again I saw how they began to gore each other and to devour each other, and the earth began to cry aloud. 2. And I raised mine eyes again to heaven, and I saw in the vision, and behold there came forth from heaven beings who were like white men: and four went forth from that place and three with them. 3. And those three that had last come forth grasped me by my hand and took me up, away from the generations of the earth, and raised me up to a lofty place, and showed me a tower raised high above the earth, and all the hills were lower. 4. And one said unto me: 'Remain here till thou seest everything that befalls those elephants, camels, and asses, and the stars and the oxen, and all of them.'

CHAPTER 88

1. And I saw one of those four who had come forth first, and he seized that first star which had fallen from the heaven, and bound it hand and foot and cast it into an abyss: now that abyss was narrow and deep, and horrible and dark. 2. And one of them drew a sword, and gave it to those elephants and camels and asses: then they began to smite each other, and the whole earth quaked because of them. 3. And as I was beholding in the vision, lo, one of those four who had come forth stoned (them) from heaven, and gathered and took all the great stars whose privy members were like those of horses, and bound them all hand and foot, and cast them in an abyss of the earth.

CHAPTER 89

1. And one of those four went to that white bull and instructed him in asecret, without his being terrified: he was born a bull and became a man, and built for himself a great vessel and dwelt thereon; and three bulls dwelt with him in that vessel and they were covered in. 2. And again I raised mine eyes towards heaven and saw a lofty roof, with seven water torrents thereon, and those torrents flowed with much water into an enclosure. 3. And I saw again, and behold fountains were opened on the surface of that great enclosure, and that water began to swell and rise upon the surface, and I saw that enclosure till all its surface was covered with water. 4. And the water, the darkness, andmist increased upon it; and as I looked at the height of that water, that water had risen above the height of that enclosure, and was streaming over that enclosure, and it stood upon the earth. 5. And all the cattle of that enclosure were gathered together until I saw how they sank and were swallowed up andperished in that water. 6. But that vessel floated on the water, while all the oxen and elephants and camels and asses sank to the bottom with all the animals, so that I could no longer see them, and they were not able to escape, (but) perished and sank into the depths. 7. And again I saw in the vision till those water torrents were removed from that high roof, and the chasms of the earth were levelled up and other abysses were opened. 8. Then the water began to run down into these, till the earth became visible; but that vessel settled on the earth, and the darkness retired and light appeared. 9. But that white bull which had become a man came out of that vessel, and the three bulls with him, and one of those three was white like that bull, and one of them was red as blood, and one black: and that white bull departed from them. 10. And they began to bring forth beasts of the field and birds, so that there arose different genera: lions, tigers, wolves, dogs, hyenas, wild boars, foxes, squirrels, swine, falcons, vultures, kites, eagles, and ravens; and amongthem was born a white bull. 11. And they began to bite one another; but that white bull which was born amongst them begat a wild ass and a white bull with it, and the wild asses multiplied. 12. But that bull which was born from him begat a black wild boar and a white sheep; and the former begat many boars, but that sheep begat twelve sheep. 13. And when those twelve sheep had grown, they gave up one of them to the asses, and those asses again gave up that sheep to the wolves, and that sheep grew up among the wolves. 14. And the Lord brought the eleven sheep to live with it and to pasture with it among the wolves: and they multiplied and became many flocks of sheep. 15. And the wolves began to fear them, and they oppressed them until they destroyed their little ones, and they cast their young into a river of much water: but those sheep began to cry aloud on account of their little ones, and to complain unto their Lord. 16. And a sheep which had been saved from the wolves fled and escaped to the wild asses; and I saw the sheep how they lamented and cried, and besought their Lord with all their might, till that Lord of the sheep descended at the voice of the sheep from a

lofty abode, and came to them and pastured them. 17. And He called that sheep which had escaped the wolves, and spake with it concerning the wolves that it should admonish them not to touch the sheep. 18. And the sheep went to the wolves according to the word of the Lord, and another sheep met it and went with it, and the two went and entered together into the assembly of those wolves, and spake with them and admonished them not to touch the sheep from henceforth. 19. And thereupon I saw the wolves, and how they oppressed the sheep exceedingly with all their power; and the sheep cried aloud. 20. And the Lord came to the sheep and they began to smite those wolves: and the wolves began to make lamentation; but the sheep became quiet and forthwith ceased to cry out. 21. And I saw the sheep till they departed from amongst the wolves; but the eyes of the wolves were blinded, and those wolves departed in pursuit of the sheep with all their power. 22. And the Lord of the sheep went with them, as their leader, and all His sheep followed Him: and his face was dazzling and glorious and terrible to behold. 23. But the wolves began to pursue those sheep till they reached a sea of water. 24. And that sea was divided, and the water stood on this side and on that before their face, and their Lord led them and placed Himself between them and the wolves. 25. And as those wolves did not yet see the sheep, they proceeded into the midst of that sea, and the wolves followed the sheep, and [those wolves] ran after them into that sea. 26. And when they saw the Lord of the sheep, they turned to flee before His face, but that sea gathered itself together, and became as it had been created, and the water swelled and rose till it covered those wolves. 27. And I saw till all the wolves who pursued those sheep perished and were drowned. 28. But the sheep escaped from that water and went forth into a wilderness, where there was no water and no grass; and they began to open their eyes and to see; and I saw the Lord of the sheep pasturing them and giving them water and grass, and that sheep going and leading them. 29. And that sheep ascended to the summit of that lofty rock, and the Lord of the sheep sent it to them. 30. And after that I saw the Lord of the sheep who stood before them, and His appearance was great and terrible and majestic, and all those sheep saw Him and were afraid before His face. 31. And they all feared and trembled because of Him, and they cried to that sheep with them [which was amongst them]: "We are not able to stand before our Lord or to behold Him." 32. And that sheep which led them again ascended to the summit of that rock, but the sheep began to be blinded and to wander from the way which he had showed them, but that sheep wot not thereof. 33. And the Lord of the sheep was wrathful exceedingly against them, and that sheep discovered it, and went down from the summit of the rock, and came to the sheep, and found the greatest part of them blinded and fallen away. 34. And when they saw it they feared and trembled at its presence, and desired to return to their folds. 35. And that sheep took other sheep with it, and came to those sheep which had fallen away, and began to slay them; and the sheep feared its presence, and thus that sheep brought back those sheep that had fallen away, and they returned to their folds. 36. And I saw in this vision till that sheep became a man and built a house for the Lord of the sheep, and placed all the sheep in that house. 37. And I saw till this sheep which had met that sheep which led them fell asleep: and I saw till all the great sheep perished and little ones arose in their place, and they came to a pasture, and approached a stream of water. 38. Then that sheep, their leader which had become a man, withdrew from them and fell asleep, and all the sheep sought it and cried over it with a great crying. 39. And I saw till they left off crying for that sheep and crossed that stream of water, and there arose the two sheep as leaders in the place of those which had led them and fallen asleep (lit. "had fallen asleep and led them"). 40. And I saw till the sheep came to a goodly place, and a pleasant and glorious land, and I saw till those sheep were satisfied; and that house stood amongst them in the pleasant land. 41. And sometimes their eyes were opened, and sometimes blinded, till another sheep arose and led them and brought them all back, and their eyes were opened. 42. And the dogs and the foxes and the wild boars began to devour those sheep till the Lord of the sheep raised up [another sheep] a ram from their midst, which led them. 43. And that ram began to butt on either side those dogs, foxes, and wild boars till he had destroyed them †all†. 44. And that sheep whose eyes were opened saw that ram, which was amongst the sheep, **till** it †forsook its glory† and began to butt those sheep, and trampled upon them, and behaved itself unseemly. 45. And the Lord of the sheep sent the **lamb** to another **lamb** and raised it to being a ram and leader of the sheep instead of that ram which had †forsaken its glory†. 46. And it went to it and spake to it alone, and raised it to being a ram, and made it the prince and leader of the sheep; but during all these things those dogs oppressed the sheep. 47. And the first ram pursued that second ram, and that second ram arose and fled before it; and I saw till those dogs pulled down the first ram. 48. And that second ram arose and led the [little] sheep. 49. And those sheep grew and multiplied; but all the dogs, and foxes, and wild boars feared and fled before it, and that ram butted and killed the wild beasts, and those wild beasts had no longer any power among the sheep and robbed them no more of ought. 48[b]. And that ram begat many sheep and fell asleep; and a little sheep became ram in its stead, and became prince and leader of those sheep. 50. And that house became great and broad, and it was built for those sheep: (and) a tower lofty and great was built on the house for the Lord of the sheep, and that house was low, but the tower was elevated and lofty, and the Lord of the sheep stood on that tower and they offered a full table before Him. 51. And again I saw those sheep that they again erred and went many ways, and forsook that their house, and the Lord of the sheep called some from amongst the sheep and sent them to the sheep, but the sheep began to slay them. 52. And one of them was saved and was not slain, and it sped away and cried aloud over the sheep; and they sought to slay it, but the Lord of the sheep saved it from the sheep, and brought it up to me, and caused it to dwell there. 53. And many other sheep He sent to those sheep to testify unto them and lament over them. 54. And after that I saw that when they forsook the house of the Lord and His tower they fell away entirely, and their eyes were blinded; and I saw the Lord of the sheep how He wrought much slaughter amongst them in their herds until those sheep invited that slaughter and betrayed His place. 55. And He gave them over into the hands of the lions and tigers, and wolves and hyenas, and into the hand of the foxes, and to all the wild beasts, and those wild beasts began to tear in pieces those sheep. 56. And I saw that He forsook that their house and their tower and gave them all into the hand of the lions, to tear and devour them, into the hand of all the wild beasts. 57. And I began to cry aloud with all my power, and to appeal to the Lord of the sheep, and to represent to Him in regard to the sheep that they were devoured by all the wild beasts. 58. But He remained unmoved, though He saw it, and rejoiced that they were devoured and swallowed and robbed, and left them to be devoured in the hand of all the beasts. 59. And He called seventy shepherds, and cast those sheep to them that they might pasture them, and He spake to the shepherds and their companions: "Let each individual of you pasture the sheep henceforward, and everything that I shall command you that do ye. 60. And I will deliver them over unto you duly numbered, and tell you which of them are to be destroyed--and them destroy ye." And He gave over unto them those sheep. 61. And

He called another and spake unto him: "Observe and mark everything that the shepherds will do to those sheep; for they will destroy more of them than I have commanded them. 62. And every excess and the destruction which will be wrought through the shepherds, record (namely) how many they destroy according to my command, and how many according to their own caprice: record against every individual shepherd all the destruction he effects. 63. And read out before me by number how many they destroy, and how many they deliver over for destruction, that I may have this as a testimony against them, and know every deed of the shepherds, that I may **comprehend** and see what they do, whether or not they abide by my command which I have commanded them. 64. But they shall not know it, and thou shalt not declare it to them, nor admonish them, but only record against each individual all the destruction which the shepherds effect each in his time and lay it all before me." 65. And I saw till those shepherds pastured in their season, and they began to slay and to destroy more than they were bidden, and they delivered those sheep into the hand of the lions. 66. And the lions and tigers eat and devoured the greater part of those sheep, and the wild boars eat along with them; and they burnt that tower and demolished that house. 67. And I became exceedingly sorrowful over that tower because that house of the sheep was demolished, and afterwards I was unable to see if those sheep entered that house. 68. And the shepherds and their associates delivered over those sheep to all the wild beasts, to devour them, and each one of them received in his time a definite number: it was written by the other in a book how many each one of them destroyed of them. 69. And each one slew and destroyed many more than was prescribed; and I began to weep and lament on account of those sheep. 70. And thus in the vision I saw that one who wrote, how he wrote down every one that was destroyed by those shepherds, day by day, and carried up and laid down and showed actually the whole book to the Lord of the sheep-- (even) everything that they had done, and all that each one of them had made away with, and all that they had given over to destruction. 71. And the book was read before the Lord of the sheep, and He took the book from his hand and read it and sealed it and laid it down. 72. And forthwith I saw how the shepherds pastured for twelve hours, and behold three of those sheep turned back and came and entered and began to build up all that had fallen down of that house; but the wild boars tried to hinder them, but they were not able. 73. And they began again to build as before, and they reared up that tower, and it was named the high tower; and they began again to place a table before the tower, but all the bread on it was polluted and not pure. 74. And as touching all this the eyes of those sheep were blinded so that they saw not, and (the eyes of) their shepherds likewise; and they delivered them in large numbers to their shepherds for destruction, and they trampled the sheep with their feet and devoured them. 75. And the Lord of the sheep remained unmoved till all the sheep were dispersed over the field and mingled with them (*i.e.* the beasts), and they (*i.e.* the shepherds) did not save them out of the hand of the beasts. 76. And this one who wrote the book carried it up, and showed it and read it before the Lord of the sheep, and implored Him on their account, and besought Him on their account as he showed Him all the doings of the shepherds, and gave testimony before Him against all the shepherds. And he took the actual book and laid it down beside Him and departed.

CHAPTER 90

1. And I saw till that in this manner thirty-five shepherds undertook the pasturing (of the sheep), and they severally completed their periods as did the first; and others received them into their hands, to pasture them for their period, each shepherd in his own period. 2. And after that I saw in my vision all the birds of heaven coming, the eagles, the vultures, the kites, the ravens; but the eagles led all the birds; and they began to devour those sheep, and to pick out their eyes and to devour their flesh. 3. And the sheep cried out because their flesh was being devoured by the birds, and as for me I looked and lamented in my sleep over that shepherd who pastured the sheep. 4. And I saw until those sheep were devoured by the dogs and eagles and kites, and they left neither flesh nor skin nor sinew remaining on them till only their bones stood there: and their bones too fell to the earth and the sheep became few. 5. And I saw until that twenty-three had undertaken the pasturing and completed in their several periods fifty-eight times. 6. But behold lambs were borne by those white sheep, and they began to open their eyes and to see, and to cry to the sheep. 7. Yea, they cried to them, but they did not hearken to what they said to them, but were exceedingly deaf, and their eyes were very exceedingly blinded. 8. And I saw in the vision how the ravens flew upon those lambs and took one of those lambs, and dashed the sheep in pieces and devoured them. 9. And I saw till horns grew upon those lambs, and the ravens cast down their horns; and I saw till there sprouted a great horn of one of those sheep, and their eyes were opened. 10. And it †looked at† them [and their eyes opened], and it cried to the sheep, and the rams saw it and all ran to it. 11. And notwithstanding all this those eagles and vultures and ravens and kites still kept tearing the sheep and swooping down upon them and devouring them: still the sheep remained silent, but the rams lamented and cried out. 12. And those ravens fought and battled with it and sought to lay low its horn, but they had no power over it. 13. And I saw till the †shepherds and† eagles and those vultures and kites came, and ††they cried to the ravens† that they should break the horn of that ram, and they battled and fought with it, and it battled with them and cried that its help might come. 14. And I saw till that man, who wrote down the names of the shepherds [and] carried up into the presence of the Lord of the sheep [came and helped it and showed it everything: he had come down for the help of that ram]. 15. And I saw till the Lord of the sheep came unto them in wrath, and all who saw Him fled, and they all fell †into His shadow† from before His face. 16. All the eagles and vultures and ravens and kites were gathered together, and there came with them all the sheep of the field, yea, they all came together, and helped each other to break that horn of the ram. 17. And I saw that man, who wrote the book according to the command of the Lord, till he opened that book concerning the destruction which those twelve last shepherds had wrought, and showed that they had destroyed much more than their predecessors, before the Lord of the sheep. 18. And I saw till the Lord of the sheep came unto them and took in His hand the staff of His wrath, and smote the earth, and the earth clave asunder, and all the beasts and all the birds of the heaven fell from among those sheep, and were swallowed up in the earth and it covered them. 19. And I saw till a great sword was given to the sheep, and the sheep proceeded against all the beasts of the field to slay them, and all the beasts and the birds of the heaven fled before their face. 20. And I saw till a throne was erected in the pleasant land, and the Lord of the sheep sat Himself thereon, and **the other** took the sealed books and opened those books before the Lord of the sheep. 21. And the Lord called those men the seven first white ones, and commanded that they should bring before Him, beginning with the first star which led the way, **all the** stars whose privy members were like those of horses, and they brought them all before Him. 22. And He said to that man who wrote before Him, being one of those seven white ones, and said unto him: "Take those seventy shepherds to whom I delivered the sheep, and

who taking them on their own authorityslew more than I commanded them." 23. And behold they were all bound, I .saw, and they all stood before Him. 24. And the judgement was held firstover the stars, and they were judged and found guilty, and went to the placeof condemnation, and they were cast into an abyss, full of fire and flaming, and full of pillars of fire. 25. And those seventy shepherds were judged and found guilty, and they were cast into that fiery abyss. 26. And I saw at that time how a like abyss was opened in the midst of the earth, full of fire, and they brought those blinded sheep, and they were all judged and found guilty and cast into this fiery abyss, and they burned; now this abyss was to the rightof that house. 27. And I saw those sheep burning †and their bones burning†. 28. And I stood up to see till they folded up that old house; and carried offall the pillars, and all the beams and ornaments of the house were at the same time folded up with it, and they carried it off and laid it in a place in the southof the land. 29. And I saw till the Lord of the sheep brought a new house greater and loftier than that first, and set it up in the place of the first which had beer folded up: all its pillars were new, and its ornaments were new and larger than those of the first, the old one which He had taken away, and all the sheep were within it. 30. And I saw all the sheep which had been left, and all the beasts on the earth, and all the birds of the heaven, falling down and doing homage to thosesheep and making petition to and obeying them in every **thing**. 31. And thereafter those three who were clothed in white and had seized me by my hand [who had taken me up before], and the hand of that ram also seizinghold of me, they took me up and set me down in the midst of those sheep before the judgement took place†. 32. And those sheep were all white, and their wool was abundant and clean. 33. And all that had been destroyed and dispersed, and all the beasts of the field, and all the birds of the heaven, assembled in that house, and the Lord of the sheep rejoiced with great joy because they were all good and had returned to His house. 34. And I saw till they laid down that sword, which had been given to the sheep, and they brought it back into the house, and it was sealed before the presence of the Lord, and all the sheep were invited into that house, but it held them not. 35. And the eyes of them all were opened, and they saw the good, and there was not one among them that did not see. 36. And I saw that that house was large and broad and very full. 37. And I saw that a white bull was born, with large horns and all the beasts of the field and all the birds of the air feared him and made petition to him all the time. 38. And I saw till all their generations were transformed, and they all became white bulls; and the first among them became a **lamb**, and that **lamb** became a great animal and had great black horns on its head; and the Lord of the sheep rejoiced over **it** and over all the oxen. 39. And I slept intheir midst: and I awoke and saw everything. 40. This is the vision which I saw while I slept, and I awoke and blessed the Lord of righteousness andgave Him glory. 41. Then I wept with a great weeping and my tears stayednot till I could no longer endure it: when I saw, they flowed on account of what I had seen; for everything shall come and be fulfilled, and all the deeds of men in their order were shown to me. 42. On that night I remembered the first dream, and because of it I wept and was troubled--because I had seenthat vision.'

CHAPTER 91

1.The book written by Enoch--[Enoch indeed wrote this complete doctrine ofwisdom, (which is) praised of all men and a judge of all the earth] for all my children who shall dwell on the earth. And for the future generations who shall observe uprightness and peace. 2.Let not your spirit be troubled on account of the times; For the Holy and Great One has appointed days for all things. 3.And the righteous one shall arise from sleep, [Shall arise] and walk in the paths of righteousness, And all his path and conversation shall be in eternal goodness and grace. 4.He will be gracious to the righteous and give him eternal uprightness, And He will give him power so that he shall be (endowed) with goodness and righteousness. And he shall walk in eternal light. 5.And sin shall perish in darkness for ever, And shall no more be seen from that day for evermore.

CHAPTER 92

1.'And now, my son Methuselah, call to me all thy brothersAnd gather together to me all the sons of thy mother; For the word calls me, And the spirit is poured out upon me,That I may show you everything That shall befall you for ever.' 2 And there upon Methuselah went and summoned to him all his brothersand assembled his relatives. 3 And he spake unto all the children of righteousness and said: 'Hear, ye sons of Enoch, all the words of your father, And hearken aright to the voice of my mouth; For I exhort you and say unto you, beloved: Love uprightness and walk therein. 4.And draw not nigh to uprightness with a double heart,And associate not with those of a double heart, But walk in righteousness, my sons. And it shall guide you on good paths, And righteousness shall be your companion. 5.For I know that violence **must** increase on the earth,And a great chastisement be executed on the earth, And all unrighteousness come to an end: Yea, it shall be cut off from its roots, And its whole structure be destroyed. 6.And unrighteousness shall again be consummated on the earth,And all the deeds of unrighteousness and of violence And transgression shall prevail in a twofold degree. 7.And when sin and unrighteousness and blasphemy And violence in all kinds of deeds increase, And apostasy and transgression and uncleanness increase, A great chastisement shall come from heaven upon all these, And the holy Lord will come forth with wrath and chastisement To execute judgement on earth. 8.In those days violence shall be cut off from its roots,And the roots of unrighteousness together with deceit, And they shall be destroyed from under heaven. 9.And all the idols of the heathen shall be abandoned, And the temples burned with fire, And they shall remove them from the whole earth, And they (i.e. the heathen) shall be cast into the judgement of fire,And shall perish in wrath and in grievous judgement for ever. 10.And the righteous shall arise from their sleep, And wisdom shall arise and be given unto them. [11. And after that the roots of unrighteousness shall be cut off, and the sinners shall be destroyed by the sword . . . shall be cut off from the blasphemers in every place, and those who plan violence and those who commit blasphemy shall perish by the sword.] 18.And now I tell you, my sons, and show you The paths of righteousness and the paths of violence.Yea, I will show them to you again That ye may know what will come to pass. 19.And now, hearken unto me, my sons,And walk in the paths of righteousness, And walk not in the paths of violence; For all who walk in the paths of unrighteousness shall perish for ever.'

CHAPTER 93

1.And after that Enoch both †gave† and began to recount from the books. And Enoch said: 'Concerning the children of righteousness and concerning the elect of theworld, And concerning the plant of uprightness, I will speak these things, Yea, I Enoch will declare (them) unto you, my sons: According to that which appeared to me in the heavenly vision,And which I have known through the word of the holy angels, And have learnt from the heavenly tablets.' 3.And Enoch began to recount from the books and said:'I was born the seventh in the first week, While judgement and righteousness still endured. 4.And after me there shall arise in the second week great wickedness, And deceit shall have sprung up; And in it there shall be the first end.

And in it a man shall be saved; And after it is ended unrighteousness shall grow up, And a law shall be made for the sinners. 5.And after that in the third week at its close A man shall be elected as the plant of righteous judgement, And **his posterity** shall become the plant of righteousness for evermore. 6.And after that in the fourth week, at its close, Visions of the holy and righteous shall be seen, And a law for all generations and an enclosure shall be made for them. 7.And after that in the fifth week, at its close, The house of glory and dominion shall be built for ever. 8.And after that in the sixth week all who live in it shall be blinded, And the hearts of all of them shall godlessly forsake wisdom. And in it a man shall ascend; And at its close the house of dominion shall be burnt with fire, And the whole race of the chosen root shall be dispersed. 9.And after that in the seventh week shall an apostate generation arise, And many shall be its deeds, And all its deeds shall be apostate. 10.And at its close shall be elected The elect righteous of the eternal plant of righteousness, To receive sevenfold instruction concerning all His creation. [11. For who is there of all the children of men that is able to hear the voice of the Holy One without being troubled? And who can think His thoughts? and who is there that can behold all the works of heaven? 12. And how should there be one who could behold the heaven, and who is there that could understand the things of heaven and see a soul or a spirit and could tell thereof, or ascend and see all their ends and think them or do like them? 13. And who is there of all men that could know what is the breadth and the length of the earth, and to whom has been shown the measure of all of them? 14. Or is there any one who could discern the length of the heaven and how great is its height, and upon what it is founded, and how great is the number of the stars, and where all the luminaries rest?] 12. And after that there shall be another, the eighth week, that of righteousness, And a sword shall be given to it that a righteous judgement may be executed on the oppressors, And sinners shall be delivered into the hands of the righteous. 13 And at its close they shall acquire houses through their righteousness, And a house shall be built for the Great King in glory for evermore, 14d. And all mankind shall look to the path of uprightness.14a. And after that, in the ninth week, the righteous judgement shall be revealed to the whole world, b. And all the works of the godless shall vanish from all the earth, c. And the world shall be written down for destruction. 15.And after this, in the tenth week in the seventh part, There shall be the great eternal judgement, In which He will execute vengeance amongst the angels. 16.And the first heaven shall depart and pass away, And a new heaven shall appear, And all the powers of the heavens shall give sevenfold light. 17.And after that there will be many weeks without number for ever, And all shall be in goodness and righteousness, And sin shall no more be mentioned for ever.

CHAPTER 94

1.And now I say unto you, my sons, love righteousness and walk therein; For the paths of righteousness are worthy of acceptation, But the paths of unrighteousness shall suddenly be destroyed and vanish. 2.And to certain men of a generation shall the paths of violence and of death be revealed, And they shall hold themselves afar from them, And shall not follow them. 3.And now I say unto you the righteous: Walk not in the paths of wickedness, nor in the paths of death, And draw not nigh to them, lest ye be destroyed. 4.But seek and choose for yourselves righteousness and an elect life, And walk in the paths of peace, And ye shall live and prosper. 5.And hold fast my words in the thoughts of your hearts, And suffer them not to be effaced from your hearts; For I know that sinners will tempt men to **evilly-entreat** wisdom, So that no place may be found for her, And no manner of temptation may minish. 6.Woe to those who build

unrighteousness and oppressionAnd lay deceit as a foundation; For they shall be suddenly overthrown, And they shall have no peace. 7.Woe to those who build their houses with sin; For from all their foundations shall they be overthrown, And by the sword shall they fall.[And those who acquire gold and silver in judgement suddenly shallperish.] 8.Woe to you, ye rich, for ye have trusted in your riches, And from your riches shall ye depart, Because ye have not remembered the Most High in the days of yourriches. 9.Ye have committed blasphemy and unrighteousness, And have become ready for the day of slaughter, And the day of darkness and the day of the great judgement. 10.Thus I speak and declare unto you: He who hath created you will overthrow you, And for your fall there shall be no compassion, And your Creator will rejoice at your destruction. 11.And your righteous ones in those days shall beA reproach to the sinners and the godless.

CHAPTER 95

1.Oh that mine eyes were [a cloud of] watersThat I might weep over you, And pour down my tears as a cloud †oft† waters: That so I might rest from my trouble of heart! 2.†Who has permitted you to practice reproaches and wickedness? And so judgement shall overtake you, sinners. † 3.Fear not the sinners, ye righteous; For again will the Lord deliver them into your hands, That ye may execute judgement upon them according to your desires. 4.Woe to you who fulminate anathemas which cannot be reversed: Healing shall therefore be far from you because of your sins. 5.Woe to you who requite your neighbour with evil; For ye shall be requited according to your works. 6.Woe to you, lying witnesses, And to those who weigh out injustice, For suddenly shall ye perish. 7.Woe to you, sinners, for ye persecute the righteous; For ye shall be delivered up and persecuted because of injustice, And heavy shall its yoke be upon you.

CHAPTER 96

1.Be hopeful, ye righteous; for suddenly shall the sinners perish before you, And ye shall have lordship over them according to your desires. [2. And in the day of the tribulation of the sinners, Your children shall mount and rise as eagles, And higher than the vultures will be your nest, And ye shall ascend and enter the crevices of the earth, And the clefts of the rock for ever as coneys before the unrighteous, And the sirens shall sigh because of you-and weep.] 3.Wherefore fear not, ye that have suffered; For healing shall be your portion, And a bright light shall enlighten you, And the voice of rest ye shall hear from heaven. 4.Woe unto you, ye sinners, for your riches make you appear like therighteous, But your hearts convict you of being sinners, And this fact shall be a testimony against you for a memorial of (your)evil deeds. 5.Woe to you who devour the finest of the wheat, And drink **wine in large bowls**, And tread under foot the lowly with your might. 6.Woe to you who drink water **from every fountain**, For suddenly shall ye be consumed and wither away, Because ye have forsaken the fountain of life. 7.Woe to you who work unrighteousness And deceit and blasphemy: It shall be a memorial against you for evil. 8.Woe to you, ye mighty, Who with might oppress the righteous; For the day of your destruction is coming. In those days many and good days shall come to the righteous--in the dayof your judgement.

CHAPTER 97

1.Believe, ye righteous, that the sinners will become a shameAnd perish in the day of unrighteousness. 2.Be it known unto you (ye sinners) that the Most High is mindful ofyour destruction, And the angels of heaven rejoice over your destruction. 3.What will ye do, ye sinners, And whither will ye flee on that day of judgement, When ye hear the voice of the prayer of the righteous? 4.Yea, ye shall fare like unto them, Against whom this word shall be a testimony: "Ye have been companions of sinners." 5.And in those days the prayer of the righteous shall reach unto the Lord,And for you the days of your judgement shall come. 6.And all the words of your unrighteousness shall be read out before theGreat Holy One, And your faces shall be covered with shame, And He will reject every work which is grounded on unrighteousness. 7.Woe to you, ye sinners, who live on the mid ocean and on the dry land,Whose remembrance is evil against you. 8.Woe to you who acquire silver and gold in unrighteousness and say:"We have become rich with riches and have possessions; And have acquired everything we have desired. 9.And now let us do what we purposed:For we have gathered silver, 9ᵈ And many are the husbandmen in our houses." 9ᵉ And our granaries are (brim) full as with water,10 Yea and like water your lies shall flow away; For your riches shall not abide But speedily ascend from you; For ye have acquired it all in unrighteousness,And ye shall be given over to a great curse.

CHAPTER 98

1.And now I swear unto you, to the wise and to the foolish,For ye shall have manifold experiences on the earth. 2.For ye men shall put on more adornments than a woman,And coloured garments more than a virgin: In royalty and in grandeur and in power,And in silver and in gold and in purple, And in splendour and in food they shall be poured out as water. 3.Therefore they shall be wanting in doctrine and wisdom, And they shall perish thereby together with their possessions;And with all their glory and their splendour, And in shame and in slaughter and in great destitution,Their spirits shall be cast into the furnace of fire. 4.I have sworn unto you, ye sinners, as a mountain has not become aslave, And a hill does not become the handmaid of a woman,Even so sin has not been sent upon the earth, But man of himself has created it, And under a great curse shall they fall who commit it. 5.And barrenness has not been given to the woman, But on account of the deeds of her own hands she dies without children. 6.I have sworn unto you, ye sinners, by the Holy Great One, That all your evil deeds are revealed in the heavens, And that none of your deeds of oppression are covered and hidden. 7.And do not think in your spirit nor say in your heart that ye do notknow and that ye do not see that every sin is every day recorded in heaven in 8.the presence of the Most High. 8. From henceforth ye know that all your oppression wherewith ye oppress is written down every day till the day of your judgement. 9. Woe to you, ye fools, for through your folly shall ye perish: and ye transgress against the wise, and so good hap shall not be your portion. 10. And now, know ye that ye are prepared for the day of destruction: wherefore do not hope to live, ye sinners, but ye shall depart and die; for ye know no ransom; for ye are prepared for the day of the great judgement, for the day of tribulation and great shame for your spirits. 11. Woe to you, ye obstinate of heart, who work wickedness and eat blood: Whence have ye good things to eat and to drink and to be filled? From allthe good things which the Lord the Most High has placed in abundance onthe earth; therefore ye shall have no peace. 12. Woe to you who love the deeds of unrighteousness: wherefore do ye hope for good hap unto yourselves? know that ye shall be delivered into the hands of the righteous, and they shall cut off your necks and slay you, and have no mercy upon you. 13. Woe to you who rejoice in the tribulation of the righteous; for no grave shall be dug for you. 14. Woe to you who set at nought the words of the righteous; for ye shall have no hope of life. 15. Woe to you who write down lying and godless words; for they write down their lies that men may hear them and act godlessly towards (their) neighbour. 16. Therefore they shall have no peace but die a sudden death.

CHAPTER 99

1.Woe to you who work godlessness,And glory in

lying and extol them: Ye shall perish, and no happy life shall be yours. 2.Woe to them who pervert the words of uprightness,And transgress the eternal law, And transform themselves into what they were not [into sinners]:They shall be trodden under foot upon the earth. 3.In those days make ready, ye righteous, to raise your prayersas a memorial, And place them as a testimony before the angels, That they may place the sin of the sinners for a memorial before the MostHigh. 4.In those days the nations shall be stirred up, And the families of the nations shall arise on the day of destruction. 5.And in those days the destitute shall go forth and carry off theirchildren, And they shall abandon them, so that their children shall perish throughthem: Yea, they shall abandon their children (that are still) sucklings, and notreturn to them, And shall have no pity on their beloved ones. 6.And again I swear to you, ye sinners, that sin is prepared for a day of unceasing bloodshed. 7. And they who worship stones, and grave images of gold and silver and wood ⟨and stone⟩ and clay, and those who worship impure spirits and demons, and all kinds of idols not according to knowledge, shall get no manner of help from them. 8.And they shall become godless by reason of the folly of their hearts,And their eyes shall be blinded through the fear of their hearts And through visions in their dreams. 9.Through these they shall become godless and fearful;For they shall have wrought all their work in a lie, And shall have worshiped a stone: Therefore in an instant shall they perish. 10.But in those days blessed are all they who accept the words ofwisdom, and understand them, And observe the paths of the Most High, and walk in the path of Hisrighteousness, And become not godless with the godless;For they shall be saved. 11.Woe to you who spread evil to your neighbours; For you shall be slain in Sheol. 12.Woe to you who make deceitful and false measures,And (to them) who cause bitterness on the earth; For they shall thereby be utterly consumed. 13.Woe to you who build your houses through the grievous toil of others, And all their building materials are the bricks and stones of sin; I tell you ye shall have no peace. 14.Woe to them who reject the measure and eternal heritage of theirfathers And whose souls follow after idols;For they shall have no rest.15.Woe to them who work unrighteousness and help oppression,And slay their neighbours until the day of the great judgement.16.For He shall cast down your glory,And bring affliction on your hearts,And shall arouse **His fierce indignation**,And destroy you all with the sword;And all the holy and righteous shall remember your sins.

CHAPTER 100

1. And in those days in one place the fathers together with their sons shall be smitten And brothers one with another shall fall in deathTill the streams flow with their blood. 2 .For a man shall not withhold his hand from slaying his sons and his sons' sons, And the sinner shall not withhold his hand from his honoured brother: From dawn till sunset they shall slay one another. 3. And the horse shall walk up to the breast in the blood of sinners,And the chariot shall be submerged to its height. 4 In those days the angels shall descend into the secret places And gather together into one place all those who brought down sinAnd the Most High will arise on that day of judgement To execute great judgement amongst sinners. 5.And over all the righteous and holy He will appoint guardians fromamongst the holy angels To guard them as the apple of an eye, Until He makes an end of all wickedness and all sin, And though the righteous sleep a long sleep, they have nought to fear. 6.And (then) the children of the earth shall see the wise **in security**, And shall understand all the words of this book, And recognize that their riches shall not be able to save themIn the overthrow of their sins. 7.Woe to you, Sinners, on the day of strong anguish, **Ye who afflict** the righteous

and burn them with fire: Ye shall be requited according to your works. 8.Woe to you, ye obstinate of heart, Who watch in order to devise wickedness: Therefore shall fear come upon youAnd there shall be none to help you. 9.Woe to you, ye sinners, on account of the words of your mouth, And on account of the deeds of your hands which your godlessness as wrought, In blazing flames burning worse than fire shall ye burn. 10 And now, know ye that from the angels He will inquire as to your deeds in heaven, from the sun and from the moon and from the stars in reference to your sins because upon the earth ye execute judgement on the righteous. 11. And He will summon to testify against you every cloud and mist and dew and rain; for they shall all be withheld because of you from descending upon you, and they shall be mindful of your sins. 12. And now give presents to the rain that it be not withheld from descending upon you,nor yet the dew, when it has received gold and silver from you that it may descend. 13. When the hoar-frost and snow with their chilliness, and all the snow-storms with all their plagues fall upon you, in those days ye shall not be able to stand before them.

CHAPTER 101

1. Observe the heaven, ye children of heaven, and every work of the Most High, and fear ye Him and work no evil in His presence. 2. If He closes the windows of heaven, and withholds the rain and the dew from descending on the earth on your account, what will ye do then? 3. And if He sends His anger upon you because of your deeds, ye cannot petition Him; for ye spake proud and insolent words against His righteousness: therefore ye shall have no peace. 4. And see ye not the **sailors** of the ships, how their ships are tossed toand fro by the waves, and are shaken by the winds, and are in sore trouble? 5.And therefore do they fear because all their goodly possessions go upon the sea with them, and they have evil forebodings of heart that the sea will swallow them and they will perish therein. 6. Are not the entire sea and all its waters, and all its movements, the work of the Most High, and has He not set limits to its doings, and confined itthroughout by the sand? 7. And at His reproof it is afraid and dries up, and allits fish die and all that is in it; But ye sinners that are on the earth fear Him not. 8. Has He not made the heaven and the earth, and all that is therein? Whohas given understanding and wisdom to everything that moves on the earth and in the sea. 9. Do not the **sailors** of the ships fear the sea? Yet sinners fear not the Most High.

CHAPTER 102

1.In those days when He hath brought a grievous fire upon you,Whither will ye flee, and where will ye find deliverance? And when He launches forth His Word against you Will you not beaffrighted and fear? 2.And all the luminaries shall be affrighted with great fear, And all the earth shall be affrighted and tremble and be alarmed. 3.And all the †angels shall execute their commandst And shall seek to hide themselves from the presence of the Great Glory,And the children of earth shall tremble and quake; And ye sinners shall be cursed for ever,And ye shall have no peace. 4.Fear ye not, ye souls of the righteous, And be hopeful ye that have died in righteousness. 5.And grieve not if your soul into Sheol has descended in grief, And that in your life your body fared not according to your goodness,But **wait for** the day of the **judgement** of sinners And for the day of cursing and chastisement. 6.And yet when ye die the sinners speak over you:"As we die, so die the righteous, And what benefit do they reap for their deeds? 7.Behold, even as we, so do they die in grief and darkness,And what have they more than we? From henceforth we are equal. 8.And what will they receive and what will they see for ever?Behold, they too have died, And henceforth for ever shall they see no light." 9.I tell you, ye sinners, ye are content to eat and drink, and rob and sin, and strip men naked, and acquire wealth

and see good days. 10. Have ye seenthe righteous how their end falls out, that no manner of violence is found in them till their death? 11. "Nevertheless they perished and became as though they had not been, and their spirits descended into Sheol in tribulation."

CHAPTER 103

1.Now, therefore, I swear to you, the righteous, by the glory of the Great andHonoured and 2 Mighty One in dominion, and by His greatness I swear to you: 2.I know a mystery And have read the heavenly tablets, And have seen the holy books, And have found written therein and inscribed regarding them: 3.That all goodness and joy and glory are prepared for them, And written down for the spirits of those who have died in righteousness, And that manifold good shall be given to you in recompense for yourlabours, And that your lot is abundantly beyond the lot of the living. 4.And the spirits of you who have died in righteousness shall live andrejoice, And their spirits shall not perish, nor their memorial from before the faceof the Great One Unto all the generations of the world: wherefore no longer fear their contumely. 5.Woe to you, ye sinners, when ye have died,If ye die in the wealth of your sins, And those who are like you say regarding you: 'Blessed are the sinners: they have seen all their days. 6.And how they have died in prosperity and in wealth,And have not seen tribulation or murder in their life; And they have died in honour, And judgement has not been executed on them during their life." 7.Know ye, that their souls will be made to descend into SheolAnd they shall be wretched in their great tribulation. 8.And into darkness and chains and a burning flame where there isgrievous judgement shall your spirits enter; And the great judgement shall be for all the generations of the world.Woe to you, for ye shall have no peace. 9.Say not in regard to the righteous and good who are in life: "In our troubled days we have toiled laboriously and experienced every trouble, And met with much evil and been consumed, And have become few and our spirit small. 10.And we have been destroyed and have not found any to help us evenwith a word: We have been tortured [and destroyed], and not hoped to see life fromday to day. 11.We hoped to be the head and have become the tail: We have toiled laboriously and had no satisfaction in our toil; And we have become the food of the sinners and the unrighteous,And they have laid their yoke heavily upon us. 12.They have had dominion over us that hated us †and smote us; And to those that hated us† we have bowed our necks But they pitied us not. 13.We desired to get away from them that we might escape and be at rest, But found no place whereunto we should flee and be safe from them. 14.And are complained to the rulers in our tribulation,And cried out against those who devoured us,But they did not attend to our cries And would not hearken to our voice. 15.And they helped those who robbed us and devoured us and those whomade us few; and they concealed their oppression, and they did not remove from us the yoke of those that devoured us and dispersed us and murdered us,and they concealed their murder, and remembered not that they had lifted up their hands against us.

CHAPTER 104

1. I swear unto you, that in heaven the angels remember you for good before the glory of the Great One: and your names are written before the glory of theGreat One. 2. Be hopeful; for aforetime ye were put to shame through ill and affliction; but now ye shall shine as the lights of heaven, ye shall shine and yeshall be seen, and the portals of heaven shall be opened to you. 3. And in your cry for judgement, and it shall appear to you; for all your tribulationshall be visited on the rulers, and on all who helped those who plundered you. 4. Be hopeful, and cast not away your hopes for ye shall have great joy as the angels of heaven. 5. What shall ye be obliged to do? Ye shall not have to hideon the day of

the great judgement and ye shall not be found as sinners, andthe eternal judgement shall be far from you for all the generations of the world. 6. And now fear not, ye righteous, when ye see the sinners growing strong and prospering in their ways: be not companions with them, but keep afar from their violence; for ye shall become companions of the hosts of heaven. 7. And, although ye sinners say: "All our sins shall not be searched out and be written down," nevertheless they shall write down all your sins every day. 8. And now I show unto you that light and darkness, day andnight, see all your sins. 9. Be not godless in your hearts, and lie not and alter not the words of uprightness, nor charge with lying the words of the Holy Great One, nor take account of your idols; for all your lying and all your godlessness issue not in righteousness but in great sin. 10. And now I know this mystery, that sinners will alter and pervert the words of righteousness in many ways, and will speak wicked words, and lie, and practice great deceits, and write books concerning their words. 11. But when they write downtruthfully all my words in their languages, and do not change or minish ought from my words but write them all down truthfully--all that I first testified concerning them. 12. Then, I know another mystery, that books will be given to the righteous and the wise to become a cause of joy and uprightness and much wisdom. 13. And to them shall the books be given, and they shall believe in them and rejoice over them, and then shall all the righteous who have learnt therefrom all the paths of uprightness be recompensed.'

CHAPTER 105

1. In those days the Lord bade (them) to summon and testify to the childrenof earth concerning their wisdom: Show (it) unto them; for ye are their guides, and a recompense over the whole earth. 2. For I and My son will be united with them for ever in the paths of uprightness in their lives; and ye shall have peace: rejoice, ye children of uprightness. Amen.

CHAPTER 106

1. And after some days my son Methuselah took a wife for his son Lamech, and she became pregnant by him and bore a son. 2. And his body was white as snow and red as the blooming of a rose, and the hair of his head †and his long locks were white as wool, and his eyes beautiful†. And when he opened his eyes, he lighted up the whole house like the sun, and the whole house was very bright. 3. And thereupon he arose in the hands of the midwife, opened his mouth, and †conversed witht† the Lord of righteousness. 4. And his father Lamech was afraid of him and fled, and came to his father Methuselah. 5. And he said unto him: 'I have begotten a strange son, diverse from and unlike man, and resembling the sons of the God of heaven; and his nature is different and he is not like us, and his eyes are as the rays of the sun, and his countenance is glorious. 6. And it seems to me that he is not sprung from me but from the angels, and I fear that in his days a wonder may be wrought on the earth. 7. And now, my father, I am here to petition thee and implore thee that thou mayest go to Enoch, our father, and learn from him the truth, for his dwelling-place is amongst the angels.' 8. And when Methuselah heard the words of his son, he came to me to the ends of the earth; for he had heard thatI was there, and he cried aloud, and I heard his voice and I came to him. And 1 said unto him: 'Behold, here am I, my son, **wherefore** hast thou come to me?' 9. And he answered and said: 'Because of a great cause of anxiety have Icome to thee, and because of a disturbing vision have I approached. 10. And now, my father, hear me: unto Lamech my son there hath been born a son,the like of whom there is none, and his nature is not like man's nature, and thecolour of his body is whiter than snow and redder than the bloom of a rose, and the hair of his head is whiter than white wool, and his eyes are like the rays of the sun, and he opened

his eyes and thereupon lighted up the whole house. 11. And he arose in the hands of the midwife, and opened his mouth and blessed the Lord of heaven. 12. And his father Lamech became afraidand fled to me, and did not believe that he was sprung from him, but that he was in the likeness of the angels of heaven; and behold I have come to thee that thou mayest make known to me the truth.' 13. And I, Enoch, answered and said unto him: 'The Lord will do a new thing on the earth, and this I have already seen in a vision, and make known to thee that in the generation of myfather Jared some of the **angels** of heaven transgressed the word of the Lord. 14. And behold they commit sin and transgress the law, and have united themselves with women and commit sin with them, and have married someof them, and have begot children by them. 17. And they shall produce on the earth giants not according to the spirit, but according to the flesh, and there shall be a great punishment on the earth, and the earth shall be cleansed from all impurity. 15. Yea, there shall come a great destruction over the whole earth, and there shall be a deluge and a great destruction for one year. 16.And this son who has been born unto you shall be left on the earth, and his three children shall be saved with him: when all mankind that are on the earthshall die [he and his sons shall be saved]. 18. And now make known to thy son Lamech that he who has been born is in truth his son, and call his name Noah; for he shall be left to you, and he and his sons shall be saved from the destruction, which shall come upon the earth on account of all the sin and all the unrighteousness, which shall be consummated on the earth in his days. 19. And after that there shall be still more unrighteousness than that which was first consummated on the earth; for I know the mysteries of the holyones; for He, the Lord, has showed me and informed me, and I have read (them) in the heavenly tablets.

CHAPTER 107

1. And I saw written on them that generation upon generation shall transgress, till a generation of righteousness arises, and transgression is destroyed and sin passes away from the earth, and all manner of good comes upon it. 2. And now, my son, go and make known to thy son Lamech that thisson, which has been born, is in truth his son, and that (this) is no lie.' 3. And when Methuselah had heard the words of his father Enoch--for he had shown to him everything in secret--he returned and showed (them) to him and calledthe name of that son Noah; for he will comfort the earth after all the destruction.

An Appendix To The Book Of Enoch

CHAPTER 108

1.Another book which Enoch wrote for his son Methuselah and for those who will come after him, and keep the law in the last days. 2.Ye who have done good shall wait for those days till an end is made of those who work evil; and an end of the might of the transgressors. 3.And wait ye indeed till sin has passed away, for their names shall be blotted out of the book of life and out of the holy books, and their seed shall be destroyed for ever, and their spirits shall be slain, and they shall cry and make lamentation in a place that is a chaotic wilderness, and **in the fire shall they burn**; for there is no earth there. 4.And I saw there something like an invisible cloud; for by reason of its depth I could not look over, and I saw a flame of fire blazing brightly, and things like shining mountains circling and sweeping to and fro. 5.And I asked one of the holy angels who was with me and said unto him: 'What is this shining thing? for it is not a heaven but only the flame of a blazing fire, and the voice of weeping and crying and lamentation and strong pain.' 6.And he said unto me: 'This place which thou seest--here are cast the spirits of sinners and blasphemers, and of those who work wickedness, and of those who pervert everything that the Lord hath spoken through the mouth of the prophets--(even) the things that shall be. 7.For some of them are written and inscribed above in the heaven, in order that the angels may read them and know that which shall befall the sinners, and the spirits of the humble, and of those who have afflicted their bodies, and been recompensed by God; and of those who have been put to shame by wicked men: 8.Who love God and loved neither gold nor silver nor any of the good things which are in the world, but gave over their bodies to torture. 9.Who, since they came into being, longed not after earthly food, but regarded everything as a passing breath, and lived accordingly, and the Lord tried them much, and their spirits were found pure so that they should bless His name. 10.And all the blessings destined for them I have recounted in the books. And he hath assigned them their recompense, because they have been found to be such as loved heaven more than their life in the world, and though they were trodden under foot of wicked men, and experienced abuse and reviling from them and were put to shame, yet they blessed Me. 11.And now I will summon the spirits of the good who belong to the generation of light, and I will transform those who were born in darkness, who in the flesh were not recompensed with such honour as their faithfulness deserved. 12.And I will bring forth in shining light those who have loved My holy name, and I will seat each on the throne of his honour. 13.And they shall be resplendent for times without number; for righteousness is the judgement of God; for to the faithful He will give faithfulness in the habitation of upright paths. 14.And they shall see those who were, born in darkness led into darkness, while the righteous shall be resplendent. 15.And the sinners shall cry aloud and see them resplendent, and they indeed will go where days and seasons are prescribed for them.'

85. 2 Enoch

CHAPTER 1

1 There was a wise man, a great artificer, and the Lord conceived love for him and received him, that he should behold the uppermost dwellings and be an eye- witness of the wise and great and inconceivable and immutable realm of God Almighty, of the very wonderful and glorious and bright and many-eyed station of the Lord's servants, and of the inaccessible throne of the Lord, and of the degrees and manifestations of the incorporeal hosts, and of the ineffable ministration of the multitude of the elements, and of the various apparition and inexpressible singing of the host of Cherubim, and of the boundless light. 2. At that time, he said, when my one hundred and sixty-fifth year was completed, I begat my son Mathusal (Methuselah). 3. After this too I lived two hundred years and completed of all the years of my life three hundred and sixty-five years. 4. On the first day of the month I was in my house alone and was resting on my bed and slept. 5. And when I was asleep, great distress came up into my heart, and I was weeping with my eyes in sleep, and I could not understand what this distress was, or what would happen to me. 6. And there appeared to me two men, exceeding big, so that I never saw such on earth; their faces were shining like the sun, their eyes too (were) like a burning light, and from their lips was fire coming forth with clothing and singing of various kinds in appearance purple, their wings (were)brighter than gold, their hands whiter than snow. 7. They were standing at the head of my bed and began to call me by my name. 8. And I arose from my sleep and saw clearly those two men standing in front of me. 9. And I saluted them and was seized with fear and the appearance of my face was changed from terror, and those men said to me: 10. Have courage, Enoch, do not fear; the eternal God sent us to you, and lo! You shalt to-day ascend with us into heaven, and you shall tell your sons and all your household all that they shall do without you on earth in your house, and let no one seek you till

the Lord return you to them. 12. And I made haste to obey them and went out from my house, and made to the doors, as it was ordered me, and summoned my sons Mathusal (Methuselah) and Regim and Gaidad and made known to them all the marvels those (men) had told me.

CHAPTER 2

1 Listen to me, my children, I know not whither I go, or what will befall me; now therefore, my children, I tell you: turn not from God before the face of the vain, who made not Heaven and earth, for these shall perish and those who worship them, and may the Lord make confident your hearts in the fear of him. And now, my children, let no one think to seek me, until the Lord return me to you.

CHAPTER 3

1 It came to pass, when Enoch had told his sons, that the angels took him on to their wings and bore him up on to the first heaven and placed him on the clouds. And there I looked, and again I looked higher, and saw the ether, and they placed me on the first heaven and showed me a very great Sea, greater than the earthly sea.

CHAPTER 4

1 They brought before my face the elders and rulers of the stellar orders, and showed me two hundred angels, who rule the stars and (their) services to the heavens, and fly with their wings and come round all those who sail.

CHAPTER 5

1 And here I looked down and saw the treasure-houses of the snow, and the angels who keep their terrible store- houses, and the clouds whence they come out and into which they go.

CHAPTER 6

1 They showed me the treasure-house of the dew, like oil of the olive, and the appearance of its form, as of all the flowers of the earth; further many angels guarding the treasure-houses of these (things), and how they are made to shut and open.

CHAPTER 7

1 And those men took me and led me up on to the second heaven, and showed me darkness, greater than earthly darkness, and there I saw prisoners hanging, watched, awaiting the great and boundless judgment, and these angels (spirits) were dark-looking, more than earthly darkness, and incessantly making weeping through all hours. 2. And I said to the men who were with me: Wherefore are these incessantly tortured? They answered me: These are God's apostates, who obeyed not God's commands, but took counsel with their own will, and turned away with their prince, who also (is) fastened on the fifth heaven. 3. And I felt great pity for them, and they saluted me, and said to me: Man of God, pray for us to the Lord; and I answered to them: Who am I, a mortal man, that I should pray for angels (spirits)? Who knows whither I go, or what will befall me? Or who will pray for me?

CHAPTER 8

1 And those men took me thence, and led me up on to the third heaven, and placed me there; and I looked downwards, and saw the produce of these places, such as has never been known for goodness. 2. And I saw all the sweet-flowering trees and beheld their fruits, which were sweet-smelling, and all the foods borne (by them) bubbling with fragrant exhalation. 3. And in the midst of the trees that of life, in that place whereon the Lord rests, when he goes up into paradise; and this tree is of ineffable goodness and fragrance, and adorned more than every existing thing; and on all sides(it is) in form gold-looking and vermilion and fire-like and covers all, and it has produce from all fruits. 4. Its root is in the garden at the earth's end. 5. And paradise is between corruptibility and incorruptibility. 6. And two springs come out which send forth honey and milk, and their springs send forth oil and wine, and they

650

separate into four parts, and go round with quiet course, and go down into the PARADISE OF EDEN, between corruptibility and incorruptibility. 7. And thence they go forth along the earth, and have a revolution to their circle even as other elements. 8. And here there is no unfruitful tree, and every place is blessed. 9. And (there are) three hundred angels very bright, who keep the garden, and with incessant sweet singing and never-silent voices serve the Lord throughout all days and hours. 10. And I said: How very sweet is this place, and those men said to me:

CHAPTER 9

1 This place, O Enoch, is prepared for the righteous, who endure all manner of offence from those that exasperate their souls, who avert their eyes from iniquity, and make righteous judgment, and give bread to the hungering, and cover the naked with clothing, and raise up the fallen, and help injured orphans, and who walk without fault before the face of the Lord, and serve him alone, and for them is prepared this place for eternal inheritance.

CHAPTER 10

1 And those two men led me up on to the Northern side, and showed me there a very terrible place, and (there were) all manner of tortures in that place: cruel darkness and unillumined gloom, and there is no light there, but murky fire constantly flaming aloft, and (there is) a fiery river coming forth, and that whole place is everywhere fire, and everywhere (there is) frost and ice, thirst and shivering, while the bonds are very cruel, and the angels (spirits) fearful and merciless, bearing angry weapons, merciless torture, and I said: 2. Woe, woe, how very terrible is this place. 3. And those men said to me: This place, O Enoch, is prepared for those who dishonor God, who on earth practice sin against nature, which is child- corruption after the sodomitic fashion, magic-making, enchantments and devilish witchcrafts, and who boast of their wicked deeds, stealing, lies, calumnies, envy, rancor, fornication, murder, and who, accursed, steal the souls of men, who, seeing the poor take away their goods and themselves wax rich, injuring them for other men's goods; who being able to satisfy the empty, made the hungering to die; being able to clothe, stripped the naked; and who knew not their creator, and bowed to the soulless (and lifeless) gods, who cannot see nor hear, vain gods, (who also) built hewn images and bow down to unclean handiwork, for all these is prepared this place among these, for eternal inheritance.

CHAPTER 11

1 Those men took me, and led me up on to the fourth heaven, and showed me all the successive goings, and all the rays of the light of sun and moon. 2. And I measure their goings, and compared their light, and saw that the sun's light is greater than the moon's. 3. Its circle and the wheels on which it goes always, like the wind going past with very marvelous speed, and day and night it has no rest. 4. Its passage and return (are accompanied by) four great stars, (and) each star has under it a thousand stars, to the right of the sun's wheel, (and by) four to the left, each having under it a thousand stars, altogether eight thousand, issuing with the sun continually. 5. And by day fifteen myriads of angels attend it, and by night A thousand. 6. And six-winged ones issue with the angels before the sun's wheel into the fiery flames, and a hundred angels kindle the sun and set it alight.

CHAPTER 12

1 And I looked and saw other flying elements of the sun, whose names (are) Phoenixes and Chalkydri, marvelous and wonderful, with feet and tails in the form of a lion, and a crocodile's head, their appearance (is) empurpled, like the rainbow; their size (is) nine hundred measures, their wings (are like) those of angels, each (has) twelve, and they attend and accompany the sun, bearing heat and dew, as it is ordered them from God. 2 Thus (the sun) revolves and goes, and rises under the heaven, and its course goes under the earth with the light of its rays incessantly.

CHAPTER 13

1 Those men bore me away to the east, and placed me at the sun's gates, where the sun goes forth according to the regulation of the seasons and the circuit of the months of the whole year, and the number of the hours day and night. 2 And I saw six gates open, each gate having sixty-one stadia and A quarter of one stadium, and I measured (them) truly, and understood their size (to be) so much, through which the sun goes forth, and goes to the west, and is made even, and rises throughout all the months, and turns back again from the six gates according to the succession of the seasons; thus (the period) of the whole year is finished after the returns of the four seasons.

CHAPTER 14

1 And again those men led me away to the western parts, and showed me six great gates open corresponding to the eastern gates, opposite to where the sun sets, according to the number of the days three hundred and sixty-five and A quarter. 2 Thus again it goes down to the western gates, (and) draws away its light, the greatness of its brightness, under the earth; for since the crown of its shining is in heaven with the Lord, and guarded by four hundred angels, while the sun goes round on wheel under the earth, and stands seven great hours in night, and spends half (its course) under the earth, when it comes to the eastern approach in the eighth hour of the night, it brings its lights, and the crown of shining, and the sun flames forth more than fire.

CHAPTER 15

1 Then the elements of the sun, called Phoenixes and Chalkydri break into song, therefore every bird flutters with its wings, rejoicing at the giver of light, and they broke into song at the command of the Lord. 2. The giver of light comes to give brightness to the whole world, and the morning guard takes shape, which is the rays of the sun, and the sun of the earth goes out, and receives its brightness to light up the whole face of the earth, and they showed me this calculation of the sun's going. 3. And the gates which it enters, these are the great gates of the calculation of the hours of the year; for this reason the sun is a great creation, whose circuit (lasts) twenty-eight years, and begins again from the beginning.

CHAPTER 16

1 Those men showed me the other course, that of the moon, twelve great gates, crowned from west to east, by which the moon goes in and out of the customary times. 2. It goes in at the first gate to the western places of the sun, by the first gates with (thirty-one) (days) exactly, by the second gates with thirty-one days exactly, by the third with thirty days exactly, by the fourth with thirty days exactly, by the fifth with thirty-one days exactly, by the sixth with thirty-one days exactly, by the seventh with thirty days exactly, by the eighth with thirty-one days perfectly, by the ninth with thirty-one days exactly, by the tenth with thirty days perfectly, by the eleventh with thirty-one days exactly, by the twelfth with twenty-eight days exactly. 3. And it goes through the western gates in the order and number of the eastern, and accomplishes the three hundred and sixty-five and a quarter days of the solar year, while the lunar year has three hundred fifty-four, and there are wanting (to it) twelve days of the solar circle, which are the lunar epacts of the whole year. 4. Thus, too, the great circle contains five hundred and thirty-two years. 5. The quarter (of a day) is omitted for three years, the fourth fulfills it exactly. 6. Therefore they are taken outside of heaven for three years and are not added to the number of days, because they change the time of the years to two new months

towards completion, to two others towards diminution. 7. And when the western gates are finished, it returns and goes to the eastern to the lights, and goes thus day and night about the heavenly circles, lower than all circles, swifter than the heavenly winds, and spirits and elements and angels flying; each angel has six wings. 8. It has a sevenfold course in nineteen years.

CHAPTER 17

1 In the midst of the heavens I saw armed soldiers, serving the Lord, with tympana and organs, with incessant voice, with sweet voice, with sweet and incessant (voice) and various singing, which it is impossible to describe, and (which) astonishes every mind, so wonderful and marvellous is the singing ofthose angels, and I was delighted listening to it.

CHAPTER 18

1 The men took me on to the fifth heaven and placed me, and there I saw many and countless soldiers, called Grigori, of human appearance, and their size (was) greater than that of great giants and their faces withered, and the silence of their mouths perpetual, and their was no service on the fifthheaven, and I said to the men who were with me: 2. Wherefore are these very withered and their faces melancholy, and their mouths silent, and (wherefore) is there no service on this heaven? 3. And they said to me: These are the Grigori, who with their prince Satanail (Satan) rejected the Lord of light, and after them are those who are held in great darkness on the second heaven, and three of them went down onto earth from the Lord's throne, to the place Ermon, and broke through their vows on the shoulder of the hill Ermon and saw the daughters of men how good they are, and took to themselves wives, and befouled the earth withtheir deeds, who in all times of their age made lawlessness and mixing, and giants are born and marvelous big men and great enmity. 4. And therefore God judged them with great judgment, and they weep fortheir brethren and they will be punished on the Lord's great day. 5. And I said to the Grigori: I saw your brethren and their works, and their great torments, and I prayed for them, but the Lord has condemned them (to be) under earth till (the existing) heaven and earth shall end for ever. 6. And I said: Wherefore do you wait, brethren, and do not serve before the Lord's face, and have not put your services before the Lord's face, lest you anger your Lord utterly? 7. And they listened to my admonition, and spoke to the four ranks in heaven, and lo! As I stood with those two men four trumpets trumpetedtogether with great voice, and the Grigori broke into song with one voice, andtheir voice went up before the Lord pitifully and affectingly.

CHAPTER 19

1 And thence those men took me and bore me up on to the sixth heaven, and there I saw seven bands of angels, very bright and very glorious, and their faces shining more than the sun's shining, glistening, and there is no difference in their faces, or behaviour, or manner of dress; and these make theorders, and learn the goings of the stars, and the alteration of the moon, or revolution of the sun, and the good government of the world. 2. And when they see evildoing they make commandments and instruction, and sweet and loud singing, and all (songs) of praise. 3. These are the archangels who are above angels, measure all life in heaven and on earth, and the angels who are (appointed) over seasons and years, the angels who are over rivers and sea, and who are over the fruits of the earth, and the angels who are over every grass, giving food to all, to everyliving thing, and the angels who write all the souls of men, and all theirdeeds, and their lives before the Lord's face; in their midst are six Phoenixes and six Cherubim and six six-winged ones continually with one voice singingone voice, and it is not possible to describe their singing, and they rejoice before the Lord at his footstool.

CHAPTER 20

1 And those two men lifted me up thence on to the seventh heaven, and I saw there a very great light, and fiery troops of great archangels, incorporeal forces, and dominions, orders and governments, Cherubim and seraphim, thrones and many-eyed ones, nine regiments, theloanit stations of light, and I became afraid, and began to tremble with great terror, and those men took me, and ledme after them, and said to me: 2 Have courage, Enoch, do not fear, and showed me the Lord from afar, sitting on His very high throne. For what is there on the tenth heaven, since the Lord dwells there? 3. On the tenth heaven is God, in the Hebrew tongue he is called Aravat. 4. And all the heavenly troops would come and stand on the ten steps according to their rank, and would bow down to the Lord, and would again go to their places in joy and felicity, singing songs in the boundless light with small and tender voices, gloriously serving him.

CHAPTER 21

1 And the Cherubim and seraphim standing about the throne, the six-winged and many-eyed ones do not depart, standing before the Lord's face doing his will, and cover his whole throne, singing with gentle voice before the Lord's face: Holy, holy, holy, Lord Ruler of Sabaoth, heavens and earth are full of Your glory. 2. When I saw all these things, those men said to me: Enoch, thus far is it commanded us to journey with you, and those men went away from me and thereupon I saw them not. 3. And I remained alone at the end of the seventh heaven and became afraid, and fell on my face and said to myself: Woe is me, what has befallen me? 4. And the Lord sent one of his glorious ones, the archangel Gabriel, and (he) said to me: Have courage, Enoch, do not fear, arise before the Lord'sface into eternity, arise, come with me. 5. And I answered him, and said in myself: My Lord, my soul is departed from me, from terror and trembling, and I called to the men who led me up to this place, on them I relied, and (it is) with them I go before the Lord's face. 6. And Gabriel caught me up, as a leaf caught up by the wind, and placed me before the Lord's face. 7. And I saw the eighth heaven, which is called in the Hebrew tongue Muzaloth, changer of the seasons, of drought, and of wet, and of the twelve constellations of the circle of the firmament, which are above the seventh heaven. 8. And I saw the ninth heaven, which is called in Hebrew Kuchavim, where are the heavenly homes of the twelve constellations of the circle of the firmament

CHAPTER 22

1 On the tenth heaven, (which is called) Aravoth, I saw the appearance of the Lord's face, like iron made to glow in fire, and brought out, emitting sparks, and it burns. 2. Thus (in a moment of eternity) I saw the Lord's face, but the Lord's face is ineffable, marvellous and very awful, and very, very terrible. 3. And who am I to tell of the Lord's unspeakable being, and of his very wonderful face? And I cannot tell the quantity of his many instructions, and various voices, the Lord's throne (is) very great and not made with hands, northe quantity of those standing round him, troops of Cherubim and seraphim, nor their incessant singing, nor his immutable beauty, and who shall tell ofthe ineffable greatness of his glory. 4. And I fell prone and bowed down to the Lord, and the Lord with his lipssaid to me: 5. Have courage, Enoch, do not fear, arise and stand before my face into eternity. 6. And the archistratege Michael lifted me up, and led me to before the Lord's face. 7. And the Lord said to his servants tempting them: Let Enoch stand before my face into eternity, and the glorious ones bowed down to the Lord, and said: Let Enoch go according to Your word. 8. And the Lord said to Michael: Go and take Enoch from out (of) his earthly garments, and anoint him with my sweet

ointment, and put him into the garments of My glory. 9. And Michael did thus, as the Lord told him. He anointed me, and dressed me, and the appearance of that ointment is more than the great light, and his ointment is like sweet dew, and its smell mild, shining like the sun's ray, and I looked at myself, and (I) was like (transfigured) one of his glorious ones. 10. And the Lord summoned one of his archangels by name Pravuil, whose knowledge was quicker in wisdom than the other archangels, who wrote all the deeds of the Lord; and the Lord said to Pravuil: Bring out the books from my store-houses, and a reed of quick-writing, and give (it) to Enoch, and deliver to him the choice and comforting books out of your hand.

CHAPTER 23

1 And he was telling me all the works of heaven, earth and sea, and all the elements, their passages and goings, and the thunderings of the thunders, the sun and moon, the goings and changes of the stars, the seasons, years, days, and hours, the risings of the wind, the numbers of the angels, and the formation of their songs, and all human things, the tongue of every human song and life, the commandments, instructions, and sweet-voiced singings, and all things that it is fitting to learn. 2. And Pravuil told me: All the things that I have told you, we have written. Sit and write all the souls of mankind, however many of them are born, and the places prepared for them to eternity; for all souls are prepared to eternity, before the formation of the world. 3. And all double thirty days and thirty nights, and I wrote out all things exactly, and wrote three hundred and sixty-six books.

CHAPTER 24

1 And the Lord summoned me, and said to me: Enoch, sit down on my left with Gabriel. 2. And I bowed down to the Lord, and the Lord spoke to me: Enoch, beloved, all (that) you see, all things that are standing finished I tell to you even before the very beginning, all that I created from non-being, and visible (physical) things from invisible (spiritual). 3. Hear, Enoch, and take in these my words, for not to My angels have I told my secret, and I have not told them their rise, nor my endless realm, nor have they understood my creating, which I tell you to-day. 4. For before all things were visible (physical), I alone used to go about in the invisible (spiritual) things, like the sun from east to west, and from west to east. 5. But even the sun has peace in itself, while I found no peace, because I was creating all things, and I conceived the thought of placing foundations, and of creating visible (physical) creation.

CHAPTER 25

1 I commanded in the very lowest (parts), that visible (physical) things should come down from invisible (spiritual), and Adoil came down very great, and I beheld him, and lo! He had a belly of great light. 2. And I said to him: Become undone, Adoil, and let the visible (physical) (come) out of you. 3. And he came undone, and a great light came out. And I (was) in the midst of the great light, and as there is born light from light, there came forth a great age, and showed all creation, which I had thought to create. 4. And I saw that (it was) good. 5. And I placed for myself a throne, and took my seat on it, and said to the light: Go thence up higher and fix yourself high above the throne, and be A foundation to the highest things. 6. And above the light there is nothing else, and then I bent up and looked up from my throne.

CHAPTER 26

1 And I summoned the very lowest a second time, and said: Let Archas come forth hard, and he came forth hard from the invisible (spiritual). 2. And Archas came forth, hard, heavy, and very red. 3. And I said: Be opened, Archas, and let there be born from you, and he came undone, an age came forth, very great and very dark, bearing the creation of all lower things, and I saw that (it was) good and said to him: 4. Go thence down below, and make yourself firm, and be a foundation for the lower things, and it happened and he went down and fixed himself, and became the foundation for the lower things, and below the darkness there is nothing else.

CHAPTER 27

1 And I commanded that there should be taken from light and darkness, and I said: Be thick, and it became thus, and I spread it out with the light, and it became water, and I spread it out over the darkness, below the light, and then I made firm the waters, that is to say the bottomless, and I made foundation of light around the water, and created seven circles from inside, and imaged (the water) like crystal wet and dry, that is to say like glass, (and) the circumcession of the waters and the other elements, and I showed each one of them its road, and the seven stars each one of them in its heaven, that they go thus, and I saw that it was good. 2 And I separated between light and between darkness, that is to say in the midst of the water hither and thither, and I said to the light, that it should be the day, and to the darkness, that it should be the night, and there was evening and there was morning the first day.

CHAPTER 28

1 And then I made firm the heavenly circle, and (made) that the lower water which is under heaven collect itself together, into one whole, and that the chaos become dry, and it became so. 2. Out of the waves I created rock hard and big, and from the rock I piled up the dry, and the dry I called earth, and the midst of the earth I called abyss, that is to say the bottomless, I collected the sea in one place and bound it together with a yoke. 3. And I said to the sea: Behold I give you (your) eternal limits, and you shalt not break loose from your component parts. 4. Thus I made fast the firmament. This day I called me the first-created [Sunday].

CHAPTER 29

1 And for all the heavenly troops I imaged the image and essence of fire, and my eye looked at the very hard, firm rock, and from the gleam of my eye the lightning received its wonderful nature, (which) is both fire in water and water in fire, and one does not put out the other, nor does the one dry up the other, therefore the lightning is brighter than the sun, softer than water and firmer than hard rock. 2. And from the rock I cut off a great fire, and from the fire I created the orders of the incorporeal ten troops of angels, and their weapons are fiery and their raiment a burning flame, and I commanded that each one should stand in his order. 3. And one from out the order of angels, having turned away with the order that was under him, conceived an impossible thought, to place his throne higher than the clouds above the earth, that he might become equal in rank to my power. 4. And I threw him out from the height with his angels, and he was flying in the air continuously above the bottomless.

CHAPTER 30

1 On the third day I commanded the earth to make grow great and fruitful trees, and hills, and seed to sow, and I planted Paradise, and enclosed it, and placed as armed (guardians) flaming angels, and thus I created renewal. 2. Then came evening, and came morning the fourth day. 3. [Wednesday]. On the fourth day I commanded that there should be great lights on the heavenly circles. 4. On the first uppermost circle I placed the stars, Kruno, and on the second Aphrodit, on the third Aris, on the fifth Zoues, on the sixth Ermis, on the seventh lesser the moon, and adorned it with the lesser stars. 5. And on the lower I placed the sun for the illumination of day, and the moon and stars for the illumination of night. 6. The sun that it should go according to each constellation, twelve, and I appointed the succession of the months and their names and lives, their thunderings, and their hour-markings, how they should succeed. 7. Then evening came and morning came the fifth day. 8. [Thursday]. On the fifth

day I commanded the sea, that it should bring forth fishes, and feathered birds of many varieties, and all animals creeping over the earth, going forth over the earth on four legs, and soaring in the air, male sex and female, and every soul breathing the spirit of life. 9. And there came evening, and there came morning the sixth day. 10. [Friday]. On the sixth day I commanded my wisdom to create man from seven consistencies: one, his flesh from the earth; two, his blood from the dew; three, his eyes from the sun; four, his bones from stone; five, his intelligence from the swiftness of the angels and from cloud; six, his veins and his hair from the grass of the earth; seven, his soul from my breath and from the wind. 11. And I gave him seven natures: to the flesh hearing, the eyes for sight, to the soul smell, the veins for touch, the blood for taste, the bones for endurance, to the intelligence sweetness [enjoyment]. 12. I conceived a cunning saying to say, I created man from invisible (spiritual) and from visible (physical) nature, of both are his death and life and image, he knows speech like some created thing, small in greatness and again great in smallness, and I placed him on earth, a second angel, honourable, great and glorious, and I appointed him as ruler to rule on earth and to have my wisdom, and there was none like him of earth of all my existing creatures. 13. And I appointed him a name, from the four component parts, from east, from west, from south, from north, and I appointed for him four special stars, and I called his name Adam, and showed him the two ways, the light and the darkness, and I told him: 14. This is good, and that bad, that I should learn whether he has love towards me, or hatred, that it be clear which in his race love me. 15. For I have seen his nature, but he has not seen his own nature, therefore (through) not seeing he will sin worse, and I said After sin (what is there) but death? 16. And I put sleep into him and he fell asleep. And I took from him A rib, and created him a wife, that death should come to him by his wife, and I took his last word and called her name mother, that is to say, Eva (Eve).

CHAPTER 31

1 Adam has life on earth, and I created a garden in Eden in the east, that he should observe the testament and keep the command. 2. I made the heavens open to him, that he should see the angels singing the song of victory, and the gloomless light. 3. And he was continuously in paradise, and the devil understood that I wanted to create another world, because Adam was lord on earth, to rule and control it. 4. The devil is the evil spirit of the lower places, as a fugitive he made Sotona from the heavens as his name was Satanail (Satan), thus he became different from the angels, (but his nature) did not change (his) intelligence as far as (his) understanding of righteous and sinful (things). 5. And he understood his condemnation and the sin which he had sinned before, therefore he conceived thought against Adam, in such form he entered and seduced Eva (Eve), but did not touch Adam. 6. But I cursed ignorance, but what I had blessed previously, those I did not curse, I cursed not man, nor the earth, nor other creatures, but man's evil fruit, and his works.

CHAPTER 32

1 I said to him: Earth you are, and into the earth whence I took you you shalt go, and I will not ruin you, but send you whence I took you. 2. Then I can again receive you at My second presence. 3. And I blessed all my creatures visible (physical) and invisible (spiritual). And Adam was five and half hours in paradise. 4. And I blessed the seventh day, which is the Sabbath, on which he rested from all his works.

CHAPTER 33

1 And I appointed the eighth day also, that the eighth day should be the first- created after my work, and that (the first seven) revolve in the form of the seventh thousand, and that at the beginning of the eighth thousand there should be a time of not-counting, endless, with neither years nor months nor weeks nor days nor hours. 2. And now, Enoch, all that I have told you, all that you have understood, all that you have seen of heavenly things, all that you have seen on earth, and all that I have written in books by my great wisdom, all these things I have devised and created from the uppermost foundation to the lower and to the end, and there is no counsellor nor inheritor to my creations. 3. I am self-eternal, not made with hands, and without change. 4. My thought is my counsellor, my wisdom and my word are made, and my eyes observe all things how they stand here and tremble with terror. 5. If I turn away my face, then all things will be destroyed. 6. And apply your mind, Enoch, and know him who is speaking to you, and take thence the books which you yourself have written. 7. And I give you Samuil and Raguil, who led you up, and the books, and go down to earth, and tell your sons all that I have told you, and all that you have seen, from the lower heaven up to my throne, and all the troops. 8. For I created all forces, and there is none that resists me or that does not subject himself to me. For all subject themselves to my monarchy, and labour for my sole rule. 9. Give them the books of the handwriting, and they will read (them) and will know me for the creator of all things, and will understand how there is no other God but me. 10. And let them distribute the books of your handwriting–children to children, generation to generation, nations to nations. 11. And I will give you, Enoch, my intercessor, the archistratege Michael, for the handwritings of your fathers Adam, Seth, Enos, Cainan, Mahaleleel, and Jared your father.

CHAPTER 34

1 They have rejected my commandments and my yoke, worthless seed has come up, not fearing God, and they would not bow down to me, but have begun to bow down to vain gods, and denied my unity, and have laden the whole earth with untruths, offences, abominable lecheries, namely one with another, and all manner of other unclean wickedness, which are disgusting to relate. 2 And therefore I will bring down a deluge upon the earth and will destroy all men, and the whole earth will crumble together into great darkness.

CHAPTER 35

1 Behold from their seed shall arise another generation, much afterwards, but of them many will be very insatiate. 2. He who raises that generation, (shall) reveal to them the books of your handwriting, of your fathers, (to them) to whom he must point out the guardianship of the world, to the faithful men and workers of my pleasure, who do not acknowledge my name in vain. 3. And they shall tell another generation, and those (others) having read shall be glorified thereafter, more than the first.

CHAPTER 36

1 Now, Enoch, I give you the term of thirty days to spend in your house, and tell your sons and all your household, that all may hear from my face what is told them by you, that they may read and understand, how there is no other God but me. 2. And that they may always keep my commandments, and begin to read and take in the books of your handwriting. 3. And after thirty days I shall send my angel for you, and he will take you from earth and from your sons to me.

CHAPTER 37

1 And the Lord called upon one of the older angels, terrible and menacing, and placed him by me, in appearance white as snow, and his hands like ice, having the appearance of great frost, and he froze my face, because I could not endure the terror of the Lord, just as it is not possible to endure A stove's fire and the sun's heat, and the frost of the air. 2 And the Lord said to me: Enoch, if your face be not frozen here, no man will be able to behold your face.

CHAPTER 38

1 And the Lord said to those men who first led me up: Let Enoch go down onto earth with you, and await him till the determined day. 2. And they placed me by night on my bed. 3. And Mathusal (Methuselah) expecting my coming, keeping watch by day and by night at my bed, was filled with awe when he heard my coming, and I told him, Let all my household come together, that I tell them everything.

CHAPTER 39

1 Oh my children, my beloved ones, hear the admonition of your father, as much as is according to the Lord's will. 2. I have been let come to you to-day, and announce to you, not from my lips, but from the Lord's lips, all that is and was and all that is now, and all that will be till judgment-day. 3. For the Lord has let me come to you, you hear therefore the words of my lips, of a man made big for you, but I am one who has seen the Lord's face, like iron made to glow from fire it sends forth sparks and burns. 4. You look now upon my eyes, (the eyes) of a man big with meaning for you, but I have seen the Lord's eyes, shining like the sun's rays and fillingthe eyes of man with awe. 5. You see now, my children, the right hand of a man that helps you, but I have seen the Lord's right hand filling heaven as he helped me. 6. You see the compass of my work like your own, but I have seen the Lord's limitless and perfect compass, which has no end. 7. You hear the words of my lips, as I heard the words of the Lord, like great thunder incessantly with hurling of clouds. 8. And now, my children, hear the discourses of the father of the earth, how fearful and awful it is to come before the face of the ruler of the earth, how much more terrible and awful it is to come before the face of the ruler of heaven, the controller (judge) of quick and dead, and of the heavenly troops. Who can endure that endless pain?

CHAPTER 40

1 And now, my children, I know all things, for this (is) from the Lord's lips, and this my eyes have seen, from beginning to end. 2. I know all things, and have written all things into books, the heavens and their end, and their plenitude, and all the armies and their marchings. 3. I have measured and described the stars, the great countless multitude (of them). 4. What man has seen their revolutions, and their entrances? For not even the angels see their number, while I have written all their names. 5. And I measured the sun's circle, and measured its rays, counted the hours, I wrote down too all things that go over the earth, I have written the things that are nourished, and all seed sown and unsown, which the earth produces and all plants, and every grass and every flower, and their sweet smells, and their names, and the dwelling-places of the clouds, and their composition, and their wings, and how they bear rain and raindrops. 6. And I investigated all things, and wrote the road of the thunder and of the lightning, and they showed me the keys and their guardians, their rise, theway they go; it is let out (gently) in measure by a chain, lest by A heavy chain and violence it hurl down the angry clouds and destroy all things on earth. 7. I wrote the treasure-houses of the snow, and the store-houses of the cold and the frosty airs, and I observed their season's key-holder, he fills the clouds with them, and does not exhaust the treasure-houses. 8. And I wrote the resting-places of the winds and observed and saw how their key-holders bear weighing-scales and measures; first, they put them in (one) weighing-scale, then in the other the weights and let them out accordingto measure cunningly over the whole earth, lest by heavy breathing theymake the earth to rock. 9. And I measured out the whole earth, its mountains, and all hills, fields, trees, stones, rivers, all existing things I wrote down, the height from earth to the seventh heaven, and downwards to the very lowest hell, and the judgment-place, and the very

great, open and weeping hell. And I saw how the prisoners are in pain, expecting the limitless judgment. 11. And I wrote down all those being judged by the judge, and all their judgment (and sentences) and all their works.

CHAPTER 41

1 And I saw all forefathers from (all) time with Adam and Eva (Eve), and I sighed and broke into tears and said of the ruin of their dishonour: 2. Woe is me for my infirmity and (for that) of my forefathers, and thought in my heart and said: 3. Blessed (is) the man who has not been born or who has been born and shall not sin before the Lord's face, that he come not into this place, nor bring the yoke of this place.

CHAPTER 42

1 I saw the key-holders and guards of the gates of hell standing, like great serpents, and their faces like extinguishing lamps, and their eyes of fire, their sharp teeth, and I saw all the Lord's works, how they are right, while the works of man are some (good), and others bad, and in their works are known those who lie evilly.

CHAPTER 43

1 I, my children, measured and wrote out every work and every measure and every righteous judgment. 2 As (one) year is more honourable than another, so is (one) man more honourable than another, some for great possessions, some for wisdom of heart, some for particular intellect, some for cunning, one for silence of lip, another for cleanliness, one for strength, another for comeliness, one for youth, another for sharp wit, one for shape of body, another for sensibility, letit be heard everywhere, but there is none better than he who fears God, he shall be more glorious in time to come.

CHAPTER 44

1 The Lord with his hands having created man, in the likeness of his own face, the Lord made him small and great. 2. Whoever reviles the ruler's face, and abhors the Lord's face, has despised the Lord's face, and he who vents anger on any man without injury, the Lord's great anger will cut him down, he who spits on the face of man reproachfully, will be cut down at the Lord's great judgment. 3. Blessed is the man who does not direct his heart with malice against any man, and helps the injured and condemned, and raises the broken down, and shall do charity to the needy, because on the day of the great judgment every weight, every measure and every makeweight (will be) as in the market, that is to say (they are) hung on scales and stand in the market, (and every one) shall learn his own measure, and according to his measure shall take his reward.

CHAPTER 45

1 Whoever hastens to make offerings before the Lord's face, the Lord for his part will hasten that offering by granting of his work. 2. But whoever increases his lamp before the Lord's face and make not true judgment, the Lord will (not) increase his treasure in the realm of the highest. 3. When the Lord demands bread, or candles, or (the)flesh (of beasts), or any other sacrifice, then that is nothing; but God demands pure hearts, and with all that (only) tests the heart of man.

CHAPTER 46

1. Hear, my people, and take in the words of my lips. 2 If any one bring any gifts to an earthly ruler, and have disloyal thoughts in his heart, and the ruler know this, will he not be angry with him, and not refuse his gifts, and not give him over to judgment? 3. Or (if) one man make himself appear good to another by deceit of tongue, but (have) evil in his heart, then will not (the other) understand the treachery of his heart, and himself be condemned, since his untruth was plain to all? And when the Lord shall send a great light, then there will be judgment for the just and the unjust, and there no one shall escape notice

CHAPTER 47

1 And now, my children, lay thought on your hearts, mark well the words of your father, which are all (come) to you from the Lord's lips. 2. Take these books of your father's handwriting and read them. 3. For the books are many, and in them you will learn all the Lord's works, all that has been from the beginning of creation, and will be till the end of time. 4. And if you will observe my handwriting, you will not sin against the Lord; because there is no other except the Lord, neither in heaven, nor in earth, nor in the very lowest (places), nor in the (one) foundation. 5. The Lord has placed the foundations in the unknown, and has spread forth heavens visible (physical) and invisible (spiritual); he fixed the earth on the waters, and created countless creatures, and who has counted the water and the foundation of the unfixed, or the dust of the earth, or the sand of the sea, or the drops of the rain, or the morning dew, or the wind's breathings? Who has filled earth and sea, and the indissoluble winter? 6. I cut the stars out of fire, and decorated heaven, and put it in their midst.

CHAPTER 48

1 That the sun go along the seven heavenly circles, which are the appointment of one hundred and eighty-two thrones, that it go down on a short day, and again one hundred and eighty-two, that it go down on a big day, and he has two thrones on which he rests, revolving hither and thither above the thrones of the months, from the seventeenth day of the month Tsivan it goes down to the month Thevan, from the seventeenth of Thevan it goes up. 2. And thus it goes close to the earth, then the earth is glad and makes grow its fruits, and when it goes away, then the earth is sad, and trees and all fruits have no florescence. 3. All this he measured, with good measurement of hours, and fixed A measure by his wisdom, of the visible (physical) and the invisible (spiritual). 4. From the invisible (spiritual) he made all things visible (physical), himself being invisible (spiritual). 5. Thus I make known to you, my children, and distribute the books to your children, into all your generations, and amongst the nations who shall have the sense to fear God, let them receive them, and may they come to love them more than any food or earthly sweets, and read them and apply themselves to them. 6. And those who understand not the Lord, who fear not God, who accept not, but reject, who do not receive the (books), a terrible judgment awaits these. 7. Blessed is the man who shall bear their yoke and shall drag them along, for he shall be released on the day of the great judgment.

CHAPTER 49

1 I swear to you, my children, but I swear not by any oath, neither by heaven nor by earth, nor by any other creature which God created. 2. The Lord said: There is no oath in me, nor injustice, but truth. 3. If there is no truth in men, let them swear by the words, Yea, yea, or else, Nay, nay. 4. And I swear to you, yea, yea, that there has been no man in his mother's womb, (but that) already before, even to each one there is a place prepared for the repose of that soul, and a measure fixed how much it is intended that a man be tried in this world. 5. Yea, children, deceive not yourselves, for there has been previously prepared a place for every soul of man.

CHAPTER 50

1 I have put every man's work in writing and none born on earth can remain hidden nor his works remain concealed. 2. I see all things. 3. Now therefore, my children, in patience and meekness spend the number of your days, that you inherit endless life. 4. Endure for the sake of the Lord every wound, every injury, every evil word and attack. 5. If ill-requitals befall you, return (them) not either to neighbour or enemy, because the Lord will return (them) for you and be your avenger on the day of great judgment, that there be no avenging here among men. 6. Whoever of you spends gold or silver for his brother's sake, he will receive ample treasure in the world to come. 7. Injure not widows nor orphans nor strangers, lest God's wrath come upon you.

CHAPTER 51

1 Stretch out your hands to the poor according to your strength. 2.Hide not your silver in the earth. 3. Help the faithful man in affliction, and affliction will not find you in the time of your trouble. 4. And every grievous and cruel yoke that come upon you bear all for the sake of the Lord, and thus you will find your reward in the day of judgment. 5. It is good to go morning, midday, and evening into the Lord's dwelling, for the glory of your creator. 6. Because every breathing (thing) glorifies him, and every creature visible (physical) and invisible (spiritual) returns him praise.

CHAPTER 52

1 Blessed is the man who opens his lips in praise of God of Sabaoth andpraises the Lord with his heart. 2. Cursed every man who opens his lips for the bringing into contempt andcalumny of his neighbour, because he brings God into contempt. 3. Blessed is he who opens his lips blessing and praising God. 4. Cursed is he before the Lord all the days of his life, who opens his lipsto curse and abuse. 5. Blessed is he who blesses all the Lord's works. 6. Cursed is he who brings the Lord's creation into contempt. 7 Blessed is he who looks down and raises the fallen. 7. Cursed is he who looks to and is eager for the destruction of what is not his. 9. Blessed is he who keeps the foundations of his fathers made firm from the beginning. 10. Cursed is he who perverts the decrees of his forefathers. 11 Blessed is he who imparts peace and love. 12. Cursed is he who disturbs those that love their neighbours. 13. Blessed is he who speaks with humble tongue and heart to all. 14. Cursed is he who speaks peace with his tongue, while in his heart there is no peace but a sword. 15. For all these things will be laid bare in the weighing-scales and in thebooks, on the day of the great judgment.

CHAPTER 53

1 And now, my children, do not say: Our father is standing before God, andis praying for our sins, for there is there no helper of any man who has sinned. 2. You see how I wrote all works of every man, before his creation, (all) that is done amongst all men for all time, and none can tell or relate my handwriting, because the Lord see all imaginings of man, how they are vain, where they lie in the treasure-houses of the heart. 3. And now, my children, mark well all the words of your father, that I tellyou, lest you regret, saying: Why did our father not tell us?

CHAPTER 54

1 At that time, not understanding this let these books which I have given yoube for an inheritance of your peace. 2 Hand them to all who want them, and instruct them, that they may see the Lord's very great and marvellous works.

CHAPTER 55

1 My children, behold, the day of my term and time have approached. 2 For the angels who shall go with me are standing before me and urge me to my departure from you; they are standing here on earth, awaiting what has been told them. 3 FOR TO-MORROW I shall go up on to heaven, to the uppermost Jerusalem to my eternal inheritance. 4 Therefore I bid you do before the Lord's face all (his) good pleasure.

CHAPTER 56

1 Mathosalam having answered his father Enoch, said: What is agreeable to your eyes, father, that I may make before your face, that you may bless our dwellings, and your sons, and that your people may be made glorious throughyou, and then (that) you may depart thus, as the Lord said? 2 Enoch

answered to his son Mathosalam (and) said: Hear, child, fromthe time when the Lord anointed me with the ointment of his glory, (there hasbeen no) food in me, and my soul remembers not earthly enjoyment, neither do I want anything earthly.

CHAPTER 57

1 My child Methosalam, summon all your brethren and all your household and the elders of the people, that I may talk to them and depart, as is planned for me. 2 And Methosalam made haste, and summoned his brethren, Regim, Riman, Uchan, Chermion, Gaidad, and all the elders of the people before the face of his father Enoch; and he blessed them, (and) said to them:

CHAPTER 58

1. Listen to me, my children, to-day. 2. In those days when the Lord came down on to earth for Adam's sake, and visited all his creatures, which he created himself, after all these he created Adam, and the Lord called all the beasts of the earth, all the reptiles, and all the birds that soar in the air, and brought them all before the face of our father Adam. 3. And Adam gave the names to all things living on earth. 4. And the Lord appointed him ruler over all, and subjected to him all things under his hands, and made them dumb and made them dull that they be commanded of man, and be in subjection and obedience to him. 5. Thus also the Lord created every man lord over all his possessions. 6. The Lord will not judge a single soul of beast for man's sake, but adjudges the souls of men to their beasts in this world; for men have a special place. 7. And as every soul of man is according to number, similarly beasts will not perish, nor all souls of beasts which the Lord created, till the great judgment, and they will accuse man, if he feed them ill.

CHAPTER 59

1. Whoever defiles the soul of beasts, defiles his own soul. 2. For man brings clean animals to make sacrifice for sin, that he mayhave cure of his soul. 3. And if they bring for sacrifice clean animals, and birds, man has cure,he cures his soul. 4. All is given you for food, bind it by the four feet, that is to make goodthe cure, he cures his soul. 5. But whoever kills beast without wounds, kills his own souls and defileshis own flesh. 6. And he who does any beast any injury whatsoever, in secret, it is evilpractice, and he defiles his own soul.

CHAPTER 60

1 He who works the killing of a man's soul, kills his own soul, and kills his own body, and there is no cure for him for all time. 2. He who puts a man in any snare, shall stick in it himself, and there is no cure for him for all time. 3. He who puts a man in any vessel, his retribution will not be wanting at the great judgment for all time. 4. He who works crookedly or speaks evil against any soul, will not make justice for himself for all time.

CHAPTER 61

1 And now, my children, keep your hearts from every injustice, which the Lord hates. Just as a man asks something for his own soul from God, so let him do to every living soul, because I know all things, how in the great time to come there is much inheritance prepared for men, good for the good, and bad for the bad, without number many. 2. Blessed are those who enter the good houses, for in the bad houses thereis no peace nor return from them. 3. Hear, my children, small and great! When man puts a good thought in his heart, brings gifts from his labours before the Lord's face and his hands made them not, then the Lord will turn away his face from the labour of his hand, and (that) man cannot find the labour of his hands. 4. And if his hands made it, but his heart murmur, and his heart cease not making murmur incessantly, he has not any advantage.

CHAPTER 62

1 Blessed is the man who in his patience brings his gifts with faith before the Lord's face, because he will find forgiveness of sins. 2. But if he take back his words before the time, there is no repentance for him; and if the time pass and he do not of his own will what is promised,there is no repentance after death. 3. Because every work which man does before the time, is all deceit before men, and sin before God.

CHAPTER 63

1 When man clothes the naked and fills the hungry, he will find reward from God. 2. But if his heart murmur, he commits a double evil; ruin of himself and of that which he gives; and for him there will be no finding of reward on account of that.3. And if his own heart is filled with his food and his own flesh, clothed with his own clothing, he commits contempt, and will forfeit all his endurance of poverty, and will not find reward of his good deeds. 4. Every proud and magniloquent man is hateful to the Lord, and every false speech, clothed in untruth; it will be cut with the blade of the sword of death, and thrown into the fire, and shall burn for all time.

CHAPTER 64

1 When Enoch had spoken these words to his sons, all people far and near heard how the Lord was calling Enoch. They took counsel together: 2. Let us go and kiss Enoch, and two thousand men came together and came to the place Achuzan where Enoch was, and his sons. 3. And the elders of the people, the whole assembly, came and bowed down and began to kiss Enoch and said to him: 4. Our father Enoch, (may) you (be) blessed of the Lord, the eternal ruler, and now bless your sons and all the people, that we may be glorified to-day before your face. 5. For you shalt be glorified before the Lord's face for all time, since the Lord chose you, rather than all men on earth, and designated you writer of all his creation, visible (physical) and invisible (spiritual), and redeemed of the sins of man, and helper of your household.

CHAPTER 65

1 And Enoch answered all his people saying: Hear, my children, before that all creatures were created, the Lord created the visible (physical) and invisible (spiritual) things. 2.And as much time as there was and went past, understand that after all that he created man in the likeness of his own form, and put into him eyes to see, and ears to hear, and heart to reflect, and intellect wherewith to deliberate. 3. And the Lord saw all man's works, and created all his creatures, and divided time, from time he fixed the years, and from the years he appointed the months, and from the months he appointed the days, and of days he appointed seven. 4. And in those he appointed the hours, measured them out exactly, that man might reflect on time and count years, months, and hours, (their) alternation, beginning, and end, and that he might count his own life, fromthe beginning until death, and reflect on his sin and write his work bad and good; because no work is hidden before the Lord, that every man might know his works and never transgress all his commandments, and keep my handwriting from generation to generation. 5. When all creation visible (physical) and invisible (spiritual), as the Lordcreated it, shall end, then every man goes to the great judgment, and then all time shall perish, and the years, and thenceforward there will be neither months nor days nor hours, they will be adhered together and will not be counted.6. There will be one aeon, and all the righteous who shall escape the Lord's great judgment, shall be collected in the great aeon, for the righteous the great aeon will begin, and they will live eternally, and then too there will be amongst them neither labour, nor sickness, nor humiliation, nor anxiety, nor need, nor brutality, nor night, nor darkness, but great light. 7. And they shall have a great indestructible wall, and a paradise bright and incorruptible (eternal), for all corruptible

(mortal) things shall pass away, and there will be eternal life.

CHAPTER 66

1 And now, my children, keep your souls from all injustice, such as the Lord hates. 2. Walk before his face with terror and trembling and serve him alone. 3. Bow down to the true God, not to dumb idols, but bow down to his similitude, and bring all just offerings before the Lord's face. The Lord hates what is unjust. 4. For the Lord sees all things; when man takes thought in his heart, then he counsels the intellects, and every thought is always before the Lord, who made firm the earth and put all creatures on it. 5. If you look to heaven, the Lord is there; if you take thought of the sea's deep and all the under-earth, the Lord is there. 6. For the Lord created all things. Bow not down to things made by man, leaving the Lord of all creation, because no work can remain hidden before the Lord's face. 7. Walk, my children, in long-suffering, in meekness, honesty, in provocation, in grief, in faith and in truth, in (reliance on) promises, in illness, in abuse, in wounds, in temptation, in nakedness, in privation, loving one another, till you go out from this age of ills, that you become inheritors of endless time. 8. Blessed are the just who shall escape the great judgment, for they shall shine forth more than the sun sevenfold, for in this world the seventh part is taken off from all, light, darkness, food, enjoyment, sorrow, paradise, torture, fire, frost, and other things; he put all down in writing, that you might read and understand.

CHAPTER 67

1 When Enoch had talked to the people, the Lord sent out darkness on to the earth, and there was darkness, and it covered those men standing with Enoch, and they took Enoch up on to the highest heaven, where the Lord (is); and he received him and placed him before his face, and the darkness went off from the earth, and light came again. 2 And the people saw and understood not how Enoch had been taken, and glorified God, and found a roll in which was traced The Invisible (spiritual) God; and all went to their dwelling places.

CHAPTER 68

1 Enoch was born on the sixth day of the month Tsivan, and lived three hundred and sixty-five years. 2. He was taken up to heaven on the first day of the month Tsivan and remained in heaven sixty days. 3. He wrote all these signs of all creation, which the Lord created, and wrote three hundred and sixty-six books, and handed them over to his sons and remained on earth thirty days, and was again taken up to heaven on the sixth day of the month Tsivan, on the very day and hour when he was born. 4. As every man's nature in this life is dark, so are also his conception, birth, and departure from this life. 5. At what hour he was conceived, at that hour he was born, and at that hour too he died. 6. Methosalam and his brethren, all the sons of Enoch, made haste, and erected an altar at that place called Achuzan, whence and where Enoch had been taken up to heaven. 7. And they took sacrificial oxen and summoned all people and sacrificed the sacrifice before the Lord's face. 8. All people, the elders of the people and the whole assembly came to the feast and brought gifts to the sons of Enoch. 9. And they made a great feast, rejoicing and making merry three days, praising God, who had given them such a sign through Enoch, who had found favour with him, and that they should hand it on to their sons from generation to generation, from age to age. 10. Amen.

86. 3 Enoch

CHAPTER 1

INTRODUCTION R. Ishmael ascends to heaven to behold the vision of the Merkaba and is given in charge to Metatron AND ENOCH WALKED WITH GOD : AND HE WAS NOT ; FOR GOD TOOK HIM (Gen.

v. 24) Rabbi Ishmael said : 1. When I ascended on high to behold the vision of the Merkaba and had entered the six Halls, one within the other: 2. as soon as I reached the door of the seventh Hall I stood still in prayer before the Holy One, blessed be He, and, lifting up my eyes on high (i.e. towards the Divine Majesty), I said : 3. " Lord of the Universe, I pray thee, that the merit of Aaron, the son of Amram, the lover of peace and pursuer of peace, who received the crown of priesthood from Thy Glory on the mount of Sinai, be valid for me in this hour, so that Qafsiel*, the prince, and the angels with him may not get power over me nor throw me down from the heavens ". 4. Forthwith the Holy One, blessed be He, sent to me Metatron, his Servant ('Ebed) the angel, the Prince of the Presence, and he, spreading his wings, with great joy came to meet me so as to save me from their hand. 5. And he took me by his hand in their sight, saying to me: "Enter in peace before the high and exalted King3 and behold the picture of the Merkaba". 6. Then I entered the seventh Hall, and he led me to the camp(s) of Shekina and placed me before 6 the Holy One, blessed be He, to behold the Merkaba. 7. As soon as the princes of the Merkaba and the flaming Seraphim perceived me, they fixed their eyes upon me. Instantly trembling and shuddering seized me and I fell down and was benumbed by the radiant image of their eyes and the splendid appearance of their faces; until the Holy One, blessed be He, rebuked them, saying: 8. "My servants, my Seraphim, my Kerubim and my 'Ophanniml Cover ye your eyes before Ishmael, my son, my friend, my beloved one and my glory, that he tremble not nor shudder !" 9. Forthwith Metatron the Prince of the Presence, came and restored my spirit and put me upon my feet. 10. After that (moment) there was not in me strength enough to say a song before the Throne of Glory of the glorious King, the mightiest of all kings, the most excellent of all princes, until after the hour had passed. 11. After one hour (had passed) the Holy One, blessed be He, opened to me the gates of Shekina, the gates of Peace, the gates of Wisdom, the gates of Strength, the gates of Power, the gates of Speech (Dibbur), the gates of Song, the gates of Qedushsha, the gates of Chant. 12. And he enlightened my eyes and my heart by words of psalm, song, praise, exaltation, thanksgiving, extolment, glorification, hymn and eulogy. And as I opened my mouth, uttering a song before the Holy One, blessed be He, the Holy Chayyoth beneath and above the Throne of Glory answered and said : "HOLY " and "BLESSED BE THE GLORY OF YHWH FROM HIS PLACE !" (i.e. chanted the Qedushsha).

CHAPTER 2

The highest classes of angels make inquiries about R. Ishmael which are answered by Metatron R. Ishmael said: 1. In that hour the eagles of the Merkaba, the flaming 'Ophannim and the Seraphim of consuming fire asked Metatron, saying to him: 2. "Youth ! Why sufferest thou one born of woman to enter and behold the Merkaba? From which nation, from which tribe is this one? What is his character?" 3. Metatron answered and said to them : "From the nation of Israel whom the Holy One, blessed be He, chose for his people from among seventy tongues (nations), from the tribe of Levi, whom he set aside as a contribution to his name and from the seed of Aaron whom the Holy One, blessed be He, did choose for his servant and put upon him the crown of priesthood on Sinai". 4. Forthwith they spake and said : "Indeed, this one is worthy to behold the Merkaba ". And they said: "Happy is the people that is in such a case!".

CHAPTER 3

Metatron has 70 names, but God calls him ' Youth ' R. Ishmael said: 1. In that hour1 I asked Metatron, the angel, the Prince of the Presence: "What is thy name?" 2. He answered me: "I have seventy names, corresponding to the seventy tongues of the world and all of them are based upon the name Metatron, angel of the Presence; butmy King calls me 'Youth' (Na'ar)"

CHAPTER 4

Metatron is identical with Enoch who was translated toheaven at the time of the Deluge R. Ishmael said : 1.I asked Metatron and said to him: "Why art thou called by the nameof thy Creator, by seventy names? Thou art greater than all the princes, higher than all the angels, beloved more than all the servants, honoured above all the mighty ones in kingship, greatness andglory : why do they call thee ' Youth ' in the high heavens ?" 2.He answered and said to me: " Because I am Enoch, the son of Jared. 3. For when the generation of the flood sinned and were confounded intheir deeds, saying unto God: 'Depart from us, for we desire not the knowledge of thy ways' (Job xxi. 14), then the Holy One, blessed be He, removed me from their midst to be a witness against them in the high heavens to all the inhabitants of the world, that they may not say: 'The MercifulOne is cruel". 4.What sinned all those multitudes, their wives, their sons and their,daughters, their horses, their mules and their cattle and their property, and all the birds of the world,all of which the Holy One, blessed be He, destroyed from the world together with them in the watersof the flood? 5.Hence the Holy One, blessed be He, lifted me up in their lifetime before their eyes to be a witness against them to the future world. And the Holy One, blessed beHe, assigned me for a prince and a ruler among the ministering angels. 6.In that hour three of the ministering angels, 'UZZA, 'AZZA and 'AZZAEL came forth and brought charges against me in the high heavens, saying before the HolyOne, blessed be He: "Said not the Ancient Ones (First Ones) rightly before Thee: < Do notcreate man! ' " The Holy One, blessed be He, answered and said unto them: "Ihave made and I will bear, yea, I will carry and will deliver". (Is. xlvi. 4.) 7. As soon as they saw me, they said before Him: "Lord of the Universe ! What is this one that he should ascend to the height of heights? Is not he one from among the sonsof [the sons of] those who perished in the days of the Flood? "What doeth he in the Raqia'?" 8.Again, the Holy One, blessed be He, answered and said to them: "What are ye, that ye enter and speak in my presence? I delight in this one more than in all of you, andhence he shall be a prince and a ruler over you in the high heavens." 9.Forthwith all stood up and went out to meet me, prostrated themselvesbefore me and said: "Happy art thou and happy is thy father for thy Creator doth favourthee". 10.And because I am small and a youth among them in days, months and years, therefore they call me "Youth" (Na'ar).

CHAPTER 5

The idolatry of the generation of Enoshcauses God to remove the Shekinafrom earth. The idolatry inspired by 'Azza, 'Uzza and 'Azziel R.Ishmael said: Metatron, the Princeof the Presence, said to me: 1.From the day when the Holy One, blessed be He, expelled the first Adamfrom the Garden of Eden (and onwards), Shekina was dwelling upon a Kerub under the Tree of Life. 2.And the ministering angels were gathering together and going downfrom heaven in parties, from the Raqia in companies and from the heavens in camps to do His will inthe whole world. 3.And the first man and his generation were sitting outside the gate ofthe Garden to behold the radiant appearance of the Shekina. 4.For the silendour of the Shekina traversed the world from one end tothe other (with a splendour) 365,000 times (that) of the globe of the sun. And everyone who made useof the splendour of the Shekina, on him no flies and no gnats did rest, neither was he ill nor suffered he any pain. No demons got power over him, neither were they able to injure him. 5.When the Holy One, blessed be He, went out and went in: from the Garden to Eden, from Eden to the Garden, from the Garden to Raqia and from Raqia to the Gardenof Eden then all and everyone beheld the splendour of His Shekina and they were not injured; 6.until uthe time of the generation of Enosh who was the head of all idolworshippers of the world. 7.And what did the generation of Enosh do? They went from one end of the world to the other, and each one brought silver, gold, precious stones and pearls in heaps likeunto mountains and hills making idols out of them throughout all the world. And they erected theidols in every quarter of the world: the size of each idol was 1000 parasangs. 8.And they brought down the sun, the moon, planets and constellations,and placed them before the idols on their right hand and on their left, to attend them even as theyattend the Holy One, blessed be He, as it is written (1 Kings xxii. 19): "And all the host ofheaven was standing by him on his right hand and on his left". 9.What power was in them that they were able to bring them down? They would not have been able to bring them down but for 'Uzza, 'Azza and 'Azziel who taught them sorceries whereby they brought them down and made use of them 10.In that time the ministering angels brought charges (against them)before the Holy One, blessed be He, saying before him: "Master of the World! What hast thou to dowith the children of men? As it is written (Ps. viii. 4) 'What is man (Enosh) that thou art mindful ofhim?' 'Mah Adam' is not written here, but 'Mah Enosh', for he (Enosh) is the head of the idolworshippers. 11.Why hast thou left the highest of the high heavens, the abode of thy glorious Name, and the high and exalted Throne in 'Araboth Raqia' in the highest and art goneand dwellest with the children of men who worship idols and equal thee to the idols. 12.Now thou art on earth and the idols likewise. What hast thou to dowith the inhabitants of the earth who worship idols?" 13. Forthwith the Holy One, blessed be He, lifted up His Shekina fromthe earth, from their midst. 14.In that moment came the ministering angels, the troops of hosts and the armies of 'Araboth in thousand camps and ten thousand hosts : they fetched trumpets and tookthe horns in their hands and surrounded the Shekina with all kinds of songs.And He ascended to the high heavens, as it is written (Ps. xlvii. 5): "God is gone up with a shout, the Lord with the sound of a trumpet ".

CHAPTER 6

Enoch lifted up to heaven together with the Shekina. Angels protests answered by God R. Ishmael said: Metatron, the Angel, the Prince of the Presence, said tome : 1.When the Holy One, blessed be He, desired to lift me up on high, Hefirst sent 'Anaphiel H (H = Tetragrammaton) the Prince, and he took me from their midst in theirsight and carried me in great glory upon a a fiery chariot with fiery horses, servants of glory. And helifted me up to the high heavens together with the Shekina. 2.As soon as I reached the high heavens, the Holy Chayyoth, the 'Ophannim, the Seraphim, the Kerubim, the Wheels of the Merkaba (the Galgallim), and the ministers of the consuming fire, perceiving my smell from a distance of 365,000 myriads of parasangs,said: "What smell of one born of woman and what taste of a white drop (is this) that ascends onhigh, and (lo, he is merely) a gnat among those who 'divide flames (of fire)'?" 3.The Holy One, blessed be He, answered and spake unto them: "Myservants, my hosts, my Kerubim, my 'Ophannim, my Seraphim! Be ye not displeased on accountof this! Since all the children of men have denied me and my great Kingdom and are gone worshipping idols, I have removed my Shekina from among them and have lifted it up on high. Butthis one whom I have taken from among them is an ELECT ONE among (the inhabitants of) theworld and he is equal to all of them in faith, righteousness and perfection of deed and I have takenhim for (as) a tribute from my world under all the heavens".

CHAPTER 7

Enoch raised upon the wings of the Shekina to the place of the Throne, the Merkaba and the angelic hosts R. Ishmael said: Metatron, the Angel, the Prince of the Presence, said to me: 1. When the Holy One, blessed be He, took me away from the generation of the Flood, he lifted me on the wings of the wind of Shekina to the highest heaven and brought me into the great palaces of the 'Araboth Raqia' on high, where are the glorious Throne of Shekina, the Merkaba, the troops of anger, the armies of vehemence, the fiery Shin'anim', the flaming Kerubim, and the burning 'Ophannim, the flaming servants, the flashing Chashmattim and the lightening Seraphim. And he placed me (there) to attend the Throne of Glory day after day.

CHAPTER 8

The gates (of the treasuries of heaven) opened to Metatron R. Ishmael said : Metatron, the Prince of the Presence, said to me : 1.Before He appointed me to attend the Throne of Glory, the Holy One, blessed be He, opened to me three hundred thousand gates of Understanding three hundred thousand gates of Subtlety three hundred thousand gates of Life three hundred thousand gates of grace and loving-kindness three hundred thousand gates of love three hundred thousand gates of Tora three hundred thousand gates of meekness three hundred thousand gates of maintenance three hundred thousand gates' of mercy three hundred thousand gates of fear of heaven 2.In that hour the Holy One, blessed be He, added in me wisdom unto wisdom, understanding unto understanding, subtlety unto subtlety, knowledge unto knowledge, mercy unto mercy, instruction unto instruction, love unto love, loving-kindness unto loving-kindness, goodness unto goodness, meekness unto meekness, power unto power, strength unto strength, might unto might, brilliance unto brilliance, beauty unto beauty, splendour unto splendour, and I was honoured and adorned with all these good and praiseworthy things more than all the children of heaven.

CHAPTER 9

Enoch receives blessings from the Most High and is adorned with angelic attributes R. Ishmael said : Metatron, the Prince of the Presence, said to me : 1.After all these things the Holy One, blessed be He, put His hand upon me and blessed me with 536O blessings. 2.And I was raised and enlarged to the size of the length and width of the world. 3.And He caused 72 wings to grow on me, 36 on each side. And each wing was as the whole world. 4.And He fixed on me 365 eyes : each eye was as the great luminary. 5.And He left no kind of splendour, brilliance, radiance, beauty in (of) all the lights of the universe that He did not fix on me.

CHAPTER 10

God places Metatron on a throne at the door of the seventh Hall and announces through the Herald, that Metatron Henceforth is God's representative and ruler over all the Princes of kingdoms and all the children of heaven, save the eight high princes called YHWH by the name of their King R Ishmael said: Metatron, the Prince of the Presence, said to me : 1.All these things the Holy One, blessed be He, made for me: He made me a Throne, similar to the Throne of Glory. And He spread over me a curtain of splendour and brilliant appearance, of beauty, grace and mercy, similar to the curtain of the Throne of Glory; and on it were fixed all kinds of lights in the universe. 2.And He placed it at the door of the Seventh Hall and seated me on it. 3.And the herald went forth into every heaven, saying:This is Metatron, my servant. I have made him into a prince and a ruler over all the princes of my kingdoms and over all the children of heaven, except the eight great princes, the honoured and revered ones who are called YHWH, by the name of their King. 4.And every angel and every prince who has a word to speak in my presence (before me) shall go into his presence (before him) and shall speak to him (instead). 5.And every command that he utters to you in my name do ye observe and fulfil. For the Prince of Wisdom and the Prince of Understanding have I committed to him to instruct him in the wisdom of heavenly things and of earthly things, in the wisdom of this world and of the world to come. 6.Moreover, I have set him over all the treasuries of the palapes of Araboih and over all the stores of life that I have in the high heavens.

CHAPTER 11

God reveals all mysteries and secrets to Metatron R. Ishmael said : Metatron, the angel, the Prince of the Presence, said to me: 1.Henceforth the Holy One, blessed be He, revealed to me all the mysteries of Tora and all the secrets of wisdom and all the depths of the Perfect Law; and all living beings' thoughts of heart and all the secrets of the universe and all the secrets of Creation were revealed unto me even as they are revealed unto the Maker of Creation. 2.And I watched intently to behold the secrets of the depth and the wonderful mystery. Before a man did think in secret, I saw (it) and before a man made a thing I beheld it. 3.And there was no thing on high nor in the deep hidden from me.

CHAPTER 12

God clothes Metatron in a garment of glory, puts a royal crown on his head and calls him "the Lesser YHWH" R. Ishmael said: Metatron, the Prince of the Presence, said to me: 1.By reason of the love with which the Holy One, blessed be He, loved me more than all the children of heaven, He made me a garment of glory on which were fixed all kinds of lights, and He clad me in it. 2.And He made me a robe of honour on which were fixed all kinds of beauty, splendour, brilliance and majesty. 3.And he made me a royal crown in which were fixed forty-nine costly stones like unto the light of the globe of the sun. 4.For its splendour went forth in the four quarters of the 'Araboth Raqia', and in (through) the seven heavens, and in the four quarters of the world. And he put it on my head. 5.And He called me THE LESSER YHWH in the presence of all His heavenly household; as it is written (Ex. xxiii. 21): "For my name is in him".

CHAPTER 13

God writes with a flaming style on Metatron's crown the cosmic letters by which heaven and earth were created R. Ishmael said : Metatron, the angel, the Prince of the Presence, the Glory of all heavens, said to me : 1.Because of the great love and mercy with which the Holy One, blessed be He, loved and cherished me more than all the children of heaven, He wrote with his ringer with a flaming style upon the crown on my head the letters by which were created heaven and earth, the seas and rivers, the mountains and hills, the planets and constellations, the lightnings, winds, earthquakes and voices (thunders), the snow and hail, the storm-wind and the tempest ; the letters by which were created all the needs of the world and all the orders of Creation. 2.And every single letter sent forth time after time as it were lightnings, time after time as it were torches, time after time as it were flames of fire, time after time (rays) like[as] the rising of the sun and the moon and the planets.

CHAPTER 14

All the highest princes, the elementary angels and the planetary and sideric angels fear and tremble at the sight of Metatron crowned R. Ishmael said: Metatron, the Angel, the Prince of the Presence, said to me : 1.When the Holy One, blessed be He, put this crown on my head, (then) trembled before me all the Princes of Kingdoms who are in the height of 'Araboth Raqiaf and all the hosts of every heaven; and even the princes (of) the 'Elim, the princes (of) the 'Er'ellim and the princes (of) the Tafsarim, who are greater than all the ministering angels who minister before the Throne of Glory, shook, feared and trembled before me when they beheld me. 2.Even Sammael, the Prince of the Accusers, who is greater than all the princes of kingdoms on high; feared and trembled before me. 3.And even the angel of fire, and the angel of hail, and the angel of the wind, and the angel of the lightning, and the angel of anger, and the angel of the thunder, and the angel of the snow, and the angel of the rain ; and the angel of the day, and the angel of the night, and the angel of the sun and the angel of the moon, and the angel of the planets and the angel of the constellations who rule the world under their hands, feared and trembled and were affrighted beforeme, when they beheld me. 4.These are the names of the rulers of the world: Gabriel, the angel of the fire, Baradiel, the angel of the hail, Ruchiel who is appointed over the wind, Baraqiel who is appointed over the lightnings, Za'amiel who is appointed over the vehemence, Ziqiel who is appointedover the sparks, Zi'iel who is appointed over the commotion, Zdaphiel who is appointed over thestorm-wind, Ra'amiel who is appointed over the thunders, Rctashiel who is appointed over the earthquake, Shalgiel who is appointed over the snow, Matariel who is appointed over the rain, Shimshiel who is appointed over the day, Lailiel who is appointed over the night, Galgalliel who is appointed over the globe of the sun, 'Ophanniel who is appointed over the globe of the moon, Kokbiel who is appointed over the planets, Rahatiel who is appointed over the constellations. 5.And they all fell prostrate, when they saw me. And they were not ableto behold me because of the majestic glory and beauty of the appearance of the shining light of the crown of glory upon my head.

CHAPTER 15
Metatron transformed into fire R. Ishmael said : Metatron, the angel, the Prince of the Presence, the Glory of all heavens, said to me : 1.As soon as the Holy One, blessed be He, took me in (His) service to attend the Throne of Glory and the Wheels (Galgallim) of the Merkaba and the needs of Shekina, forthwith my flesh was changed into flames, my sinews into flaming fire, my bones into coals of burning juniper, the light of my eye-lids into splendour of lightnings, my eye-balls into fire-brands, the hair of my head into dot flames, all my limbs into wings of burning fire and the whole of mybody into glowing fire. 2.And on my right were divisions 6 of fiery flames, on my left fire-brands were burning, round about me stormwind and tempest were blowing and in front of me and behind me was roaring of thunder with earthquake. FRAGMENT OF 'ASCENSION OF MOSES   3.R. Ishmael said: Said to me Metatron, the Prince of the Presence and the prince over all the princes and he stands befote Him who is greater than all the Elohim. Andhe goes in under the Throne of Glory. And he has a great tabernacle of light on high. And hebrings forth the fire of deafness and puts (it) into the ears of the Holy Chayyoth, that they maynot hear the voice of the Word (Dibbur) that goes forth from the mouth of the Divine Majesty. 4.And when Moses ascended on high, he fasted 121 fasts, till the habitations of the chashmal were opened to him; and he saw the heart within the heart of the Lion and hesaw the innumerable companies of the hosts Around about him. And they desired to burn him. But Moses prayed for mercy, first for Israel and after that for himself: and He who sitteth on theMerkaba opened the windows that are above the heads of the Kerubim. And a host of 1800advocates and the Prince of the Presence, Metatron, with them went forth to meet Moses. And theytook the prayers of Israel and put them as a crown on the head of the Holy One, blessed be He. 5.And they said (Deut. vi. 4): "Hear, O Israel; the Lord our God is oneLord"and their face shone and rejoiced over Shekinaand they said to Metatron: "What are these? And to whom

do they give all this honour and glory?" And they answered: "To the Glorious Lord ofIsrael". And they spake: "Hear, O Israel: the Lord, our God, is one Lord. To whom shall be givenabundance of honour and majesty but to Thee YHWH, the Divine Majesty, the King, living andeternal". 6.In that moment spake Akatriel Yah Yehod Sebaoth and said toMetatron, the Prince of the Presence: "Let no prayer that he prayeth before me return (to him) void. Hear thou his prayer and fulfil his desire whether (it be) great or small". 7.Forthwith Metatron, the Prince of the Presence, said to Moses: "Son of Amram! Fear not, for now God delights in thee. And ask thou uthy desire of the Glory and Majesty. For thy face shines from one end of the world to the other". But Moses answered him: "(I fear) lest I bring guiltiness upon myself". Metatron said to him: "Receivethe letters of the oath, in (by) which there is no breaking the covenant" (which precludes any breach of the covenant).

CHAPTER 16
Probably additional Metatron divested of his privilege of presiding on a Throne of his own on account of Acher's misapprehensionin taking him for a second Divine Power R. Ishmael said: Metatron, the Angel, the Prince of the Presence, theGlory of all heaven, said to me: 1.At first I was sitting upon a great Throne at the door of the SeventhHall ; and I was judging the children of heaven, the household on high by authority of the Holy One,blessed be He. And I divided Greatness, Kingship, Dignity, Rulership, Honour and Praise, andDiadem and Crown of Glory unto all the princes of kingdoms, while I was presiding (lit. sitting)in the Celestial Court (Yeshiba), and the princes of kingdoms were standing before me, on myright and on my left by authority of the Holy One, blessed be He. 2.But when Acher came to behold the vision of the Merkaba and fixedhis eyes on me, he feared and trembled before me and his soul was affrighted even unto departingfrom him, because of fear, horror and dread of me, when he beheld me sitting upon a throne like aking with all the ministering angels standing by me as my servants and all the princes of kingdomsadorned with crowns surrounding me: 3.in that moment he opened his mouth and said: "Indeed, there are two Divine Powers in heaven!" 4.Forthwith Bath Qol (the Divine Voice) went forth from heaven frombefore the Shekina and said: "Return, ye backsliding children (Jer. iii. 22), except Acher!" 5.Then came 'Aniyel, the Prince, the honoured, glorified, beloved, wonderful, revered and fearful one, in commission from the Holy One, blessed be He and gave me sixty strokes with lashes of fire and made me stand on my feet.

CHAPTER 17
The princes of the seven heavens, of the sun, moon, planets and constellations and their suites of angels R. Ishmael said : Metatron, the angel, the Prince of the Presence, theglory of all heavens, said to me: 1.Seven (are the) princes, the great, beautiful, revered, wonderful and honoured ones who are appointed over the seven heavens. And these are they : MIKAEL, GABRIEL, SHATQIEL, SHACHAQIEL, BAKARIEL, BADARIEL, PACHRIEL. 2.And every one of them is the prince of the host of (one) heaven. Andeach one of them is accompanied by 496,000 myriads of ministering angels. 3.MIKAEL, the great prince, is appointed over the seventh heaven, the highest one, which is in the 'Araboth. GABRIEL, the prince of the host, is appointed over the sixth heaven which is in Makon. SHATAQIEL, prince of the host, is appointed over the fifth heaven whichis in Ma'on. SHAHAQi'EL, prince of the host, is appointed over the fourth heavenwhich is in Zebul. BADARIEL, prince of the host, is appointed over the third heaven which is in Shehaqim. BARAKIEL, prince of the host, is appointed over the second heaven which is in the height of (Merom) Raqia. PAZRIEL, prince of the host, is appointed over the

first heaven which is in Wilon, which is in Shamayim. 4.Under them is GALGALLIEL, the prince who is appointed over the globe (galgal) of the sun, and with him are 96 great and honoured angels who move the sun in Raqia'. 5.Under them is 'OPHANNIEL, the prince who is set over the globe('ophan) of the moon. And with him are 88 angels who move the globe of the moon 354 thousand parasangs every night at the time when the moon stands in the East at its turning point. And when is the moon sitting in the East at its turning point? Answer: in the fifteenth day of every month. 6.Under them is RAHATIEL, the prince who is appointed over the constellations. And he is accompanied by 72 great and honoured angels. And why is he called RAHATIEL? Because he makes the stars run (marhit) in their orbits and courses 339 thousand parasangs every night from the East to the West, and from the West to the East. For the Holy One, blessed be He, has made a tent for all of them, for the sun, the moon, the planets and the stars in which they travel at night from the West to the East. 7.Under them is KOKBIEL, the prince who is appointed over all the planets. And with him are 365,000 myriads of ministering angels, great and honoured ones whom he moves the planets from city to city and from province to province in the Raqia' of heavens. 8.And over them are SEVENTY-TWO PRINCES OF KINGDOMS on high corresponding to the 72 tongues of the world. And all of them are crowned with royal crowns and clad in royal garments and wrapped in royal cloaks. And all of them are riding on royal horses and they are holding royal sceptres in their hands. And before each one of them when he is travelling in Raqia' , royal servants are running with great glory and majesty even as on earth they (princes) are travelling in chariot(s) with horsemen and great armies and in glory and greatness with praise, song and honour.

CHAPTER 18

The order of ranks of the angels and the homage received by the higher ranks from the lower ones R. Ishmael said: Metatron, the Angel, the Prince of the Presence, the glory of all heaven, said to me: 1.THE ANGELS OF THE FIRST HEAVEN, when(ever) they see their prince, they dismount from their horses and fall on their faces. And THE PRINCE OF THE FIRST HEAVEN, when he sees the prince of the second heaven, he dismounts, removes the crown of glory from his head and falls on his face. And THE PRINCE OF THE SECOND HEAVEN, when he sees the Prince of the third heaven, he removes the crown of glory from his head and falls on his face. And THE PRINCE OF THE THIRD HEAVEN, when he sees the prince of the fourth heaven, he removes the crown of glory from his head and falls on his face. And THE PRINCE OF THE FOURTH HEAVEN, when he sees the prince of the fifth heaven, he removes the crown of glory from his head and falls on his face. xAnd THE PRINCE OF THE FIFTH HEAVEN, when he sees the prince of the sixth heaven, he removes the crown of glory from his head and falls on his face. And THE PRINCE OF THE SIXTH HEAVEN, when he sees the prince of the seventh heaven, he removes the crown of glory from his head and falls on his face. 2.And THE PRINCE OF THE SEVENTH HEAVEN, when he sees THE SEVENTY-TWO PRINCES OF KINGDOMS, he removes the crown of glory from his head and falls on his face. 3.And the seventy-two princes of kingdoms, when they see THE DOOR KEEPERS OF THE FIRST HALL IN THE ARABOTH RAQIA in the highest, they remove the royal crown from their head and fall on their faces. 3And THE DOOR KEEPERS OF THE FIRST HALL, when they see the door keepers of the second Hall, they remove the crown of glory from their head and fall on their faces. And THE DOOR KEEPERS OF THE SECOND HALL, when they see the door keepers of the third Hall, they remove the crown of glory from their head and fall on their faces. And THE DOOR KEEPERS OF THE THIRD HALL, when they see the door keepers of the fourth Hall, they remove the crown of glory from their head and fall on their faces. And THE DOOR KEEPERS OF THE FOURTH HALL, when they see the door keepers of the fifth Hall, they remove the crown of glory from their head and fall on their faces. And THE DOOR KEEPERS OF THE FIFTH HALL, when they see the door keepers of the sixth Hall, they remove the crown of glory from their head and fall on their faces. And THE DOOR KEEPERS OF THE SIXTH HALL, when they see the DOOR KEEPERS OF THE SEVENTH HALL, they remove the crown of glory from their head and fall on their faces. 4.And the door keepers of the seventh Hall, when they see THE FOUR GREAT PRINCES, the honoured ones, WHO ARE APPOINTED OVER THE FOUR CAMPS OF SHEKINA, they remove the crown(s) of glory from their head and fall on their faces. 5.And the four great princes, when they see TAG'AS, the prince, great and honoured with song (and) praise, at the head of all the children of heaven, they remove the crown of glory from their head and fall on their faces. 6.And Tag' as, the great and honoured prince, when he sees BARATTIEL, the great prince of three fingers in the height of 'Araboth, the highest heaven, he removes the crown of glory from his head and falls on his face. 7.And Barattiel, the great prince, when he sees HAMON, the great prince, the fearful and honoured, pleasant and terrible one who maketh all the children of heaven to tremble, when the time draweth nigh (that is set) for the saying of the '(Thrice) Holy', as it is written (Isa. xxxiii. 3): "At the noise of the tumult (hamon) the peoples are fled; at the lifting up of thyself the nations are scattered" he removes the crown of glory from his head and falls on his face. 8.And Hamon, the great prince, when he sees TUTRESIEL, the great prince, he removes the crown of glory from his head and falls on his face. 9.And Tutresiel H', the great prince, when he sees ATRUGIEL, the great prince, he removes the crown of glory from his head and falls on his face. 10.And Atrugiel the great prince, when he sees NA'ARIRIEL H', the great prince, he removes the crown of glory from his head and falls on his face. (n) And Na'aririel H', the great prince, when he sees SASNIGIEL H', the great prince, he removes the crown of glory from his head and falls on his face. 11.And Sasnigiel H', when he sees ZAZRIEL H', the great prince, he removes the crown of glory from his head and falls on his face. 12.And Zazriel H', the prince, when he sees GEBURATIEL H', the prince, he removes the crown of glory from his head and falls on his face. 13.And Geburatiel H', the prince, when he sees 'ARAPHIEL H', the prince, he removes the crown of glory from his head and falls on his face. 14.And 'Araphiel H', the prince, when he sees 'ASHRUYLU, the prince, who presides in all the sessions of the children of heaven, he removes the crown of glory from his head and falls on his face. 15.And Ashruylu H, the prince, when he sees GALLISUR H', THE PRINCE, WHO REVEALS ALL THE SECRETS OF THE LAW (Tora), he removes the crown of glory from his head and falls on his face. 16.And Gallisur H', the prince, when he sees ZAKZAKIEL H', the prince who is appointed to write down the merits of Israel on the Throne of Glory, he removes the crown of glory from his head and falls on his face. 17.And Zakzakiel H', the great prince, when he sees 'ANAPHIEL H', the prince who keeps the keys of the heavenly Halls, he removes the crown of glory from his head and falls on his face. Why is he called by the name of 'Anaphiel ? Because the bough of his honour and majesty and his crown and his splendour and his brilliance covers (overshadows) all the chambers of 'Araboth Raqia on high even as the Maker of the World (doth overshadow them). Just as it is written with regard to the Maker of the World (Hab. iii. 3): "His glory covered the heavens, and the earth was full of his praise", even so do the honour and majesty of 'Anaphiel cover all the glories of

'Araboth the highest. 18.And when he sees SOTHER 'ASHIEL H', the prince, the great, fearful and honoured one, he removes the crown of glory from his head and falls on his face. Why is he called Sother Ashiel? Because he is appointed over the four heads of the fiery river over against the Throne of Glory; and every single prince who goes out or enters before the Shekina, goes out or enters only by his permission. For the seals of the fiery river are entrusted to him. And furthermore, his height is 7000 myriads of parasangs. And he stirs up the fire of the river ; and he goes out and enters before the Shekina to expound what is written (recorded) concerning the inhabitants of the world. According as it is written (Dan. vii. 10) : "the judgement was set, and the books were opened". 19.And Sother 'Ashiel the prince, when he sees SHOQED CHOZI, the great prince, the mighty, terrible and honoured one, he removes the crown of glory from his head and falls upon his face. And why is he called Shoqed Chozi? Because he weighs all the merits (of man) in a balance in the presence of the Holy One, blessed be He. 20.And when he sees ZEHANPURYU H',the great prince, the mighty and terrible one, honoured, glorified and feared in all the heavenly household, he removes the crown of glory from his head and falls on his face. Why is he called Zehanpuryu? Because he rebukes the fiery river and pushes it back to its place. 21.And when he sees 'AZBUGA H', the great prince, glorified, revered, honoured, adorned, wonderful, exalted, beloved and feared among all the great princes who know the mystery of the Throne of Glory, he removes the crown of glory from his head and falls on his face. Why is he called 'Azbuga? Because in the future he will gird (clothe) the righteous and pious of the world with the garments of life and wrap them in the cloak of life, that they may live in them an eternal life. 22.And when he sees the two great princes, the strong and glorified ones who are standing above him, he removes the crown of glory from his head and falls on his face. And these are the names of the two princes: SOPHERIEL H' (WHO) KILLETH, (Sopheriel H' the Killer), the great prince, the honoured, glorified, blameless, venerable, ancient and mighty one; (and) SOPHERIEL H' (WHO) MAKETH ALIVE (Sopheriel H' the Lifegiver), the great prince, the honoured, glorified, blameless, ancient and mighty one. 23.Why is he called Sopheriel H' who killeth (Sopheriel H' the Killer)? Because he is appointed over the books of the dead : [so that] everyone, when the day of his death draws nigh, he writes him in the books of the dead. Why is he called Sopheriel H' who maketh alive (Sopheriel H' the Lifegiver)? Because he is appointed over the books of the living (of life), so that every one whom the Holy One, blessed be He, will bring into life, he writes him in the book of the living (of life), by authority of MAQOM. Thou might perhaps say: "Since the Holy One, blessed be He, is sitting on a throne, they also are sitting when writing". (Answer): The Scripture teaches us (1 Kings xxii. 19, 2 Chron. xviii. 18) : "And all the host of heaven are standing by him ". "The host of heaven " (it is said) in order to show us, that even the Great Princes, none like whom there is in the high heavens, do not fulfil the requests of the Shekina otherwise than standing. But how is it (possible that) they (are able to) write, when they are standing? It is like this : 24.One is standing on the wheels of the tempest and the other is standing on the wheels of the storm-wind. The one is clad in kingly garments, the other is clad in kingly garments. The one is wrapped in a mantle of majesty and the other is wrapped in a mantle of majesty. The one is crowned with a royal crown, and the other is crowned with a royal crown. The one's body is full of eyes, and the other's body is full of eyes. The appearance of one is like unto the appearance of lightnings, and the appearance of the other is like unto the appearance of lightnings. The eyes of the one are like the sun in its might, and the eyes of the other are like the sun in its might. The one's height is like the height of the seven heavens, and the other's height is like the height of the seven heavens. The wings of the one are as (many as) the days of the year, and the wings of the other are as (many as) the days of the year. The wings of the one extend over the breadth of Raqia', and the wings of the other extend over the breadth of Raqia. The lips of the one, are as the gates of the East, and the lips of the other are as the gates of the East. The tongue of the one is as high as the waves of the sea, and the tongue of the other is as high as the waves of the sea. From the mouth of the one a flame goes forth, and from the mouth of the other a flame goes forth. From the mouth of the one there go forth lightnings and from the mouth of the other there go forth lightnings. From the sweat of the one fire is kindled, and from the perspiration of the other fire is kindled. From the one's tongue a torch is burning, and from the tongue of the other a torch is burning. On the head of the one there is a sapphire stone, and upon the head of the other there is a sapphire stone. On the shoulders of the one there is a wheel of a swift cherub, and on the shoulders of the other there is a wheel of a swift cherub. One has in his hand a burning scroll, the other has in his hand a burning scroll. The one has in his hand a flaming style, the other has in his hand a flaming style. The length of the scroll is 3000 myriads of parasangs ; the size of the style is 3000 myriads of parasangs; the size of every single letter that they write is 365 parasangs

CHAPTER 19

Rikbiel, the prince of the wheels of the Merkaba. The surroundings of the Merkaba. The commotion among the angelic hosts at the time of the Qedushsha R. Ishmael said: Metatron, the Angel, the Prince of the Presence, said to me : 1.Above 2 these three angels, these great princes there is one Prince, distinguished, honoured, noble, glorified, adorned, fearful, valiant, strong, great, magnified, glorious, crowned, wonderful, exalted, blameless, beloved, lordly, high and lofty, ancient and mighty, like unto whom there is none among the princes. His name is RIKBIEL H', the great and revered Prince who is standing by the Merkaba. 2.And why is he called RIKBIEL? Because he is appointed over the wheels of the Merkaba, and they are given in his charge. 3.And how many are the wheels? Eight; two in each direction. And there are four winds compassing them round about. And these are their names: "the Storm-Wind", "the Tempest", "the Strong Wind", and "the Wind of Earthquake". 4.And under them four fiery rivers are continually running, one fiery river on each side. And round about them, between the rivers, four clouds are planted (placed), and these they are: "clouds of fire", "clouds of lamps", "clouds of coal", "clouds of brimstone" and they are standing over against [their] wheels. 5.And the feet of the Chayyoth are resting upon the wheels. And between one wheel and the other earthquake is roaring and thunder is thundering. 6.And when the time draws nigh for the recital of the Song, (then) the multitudes of wheels are moved, the multitude of clouds tremble, all the chieftains (shallishim) are made afraid, all the horsemen (parashim) do rage, all the mighty ones (gibborim) are excited, all the hosts (seba'im) are afrighted, all the troops (gedudim) are in fear, all the appointed ones (memunnim) haste away, all the princes (sarim) and armies (chayyelim) are dismayed, all the servants (mesharetim) do faint and all the angels (mal'akim) and divisions (degalim) travail with pain. 7.And one wheel makes a sound to be heard to the other and one Kerub to another, one Chayya. To another, one Seraph to another (saying) (Ps. lxviii. 5) "Extol to him that rideth in 'Araboth, by his name Jah and rejoice before him!"

CHAPTER 20

CHAYYLIEL, the prince of the Chayyoth R. Ishmael

663

said: Metatron, the angel, the Prince of the Presence, said to me : 1.Above these there is one great and mighty prince. His name is CHAYYLIEL H', a noble and revered prince, a glorious and mightyprince, a great and revered prince, a prince before whom all the children of heaven do tremble, a prince who is able to swallow up the whole earth in one moment (at a mouthful). 2.And why is he called CHAYYLIEL H'? Because he is appointed overthe Holy Chayyoth and smites the Chayyoth with lashes of fire: and glorifies them, when theygive praise and glory and rejoicing and he causes them to make haste to say "Holy" and "Blessed be the Glory of H' from his place!" (i.e. the Qedushshd).

CHAPTER 21

The Chayyoth R. Ishmael said: Metatron, the angel, the Prince of the Presence, said to me : 1.Four (are) the Chayyoth corresponding to the four winds. Each Chayya is as the space of the whole world. And each one has four faces ; and each face is as the face of the East. 2.Each one has four wings and each wing is like the cover (roof) of theuniverse. 3.And each one has faces in the middle of faces and wings in the middleof wings. The size of the faces is (as the size of) 248 faces, and the size of the wings is (as the size of) 365 wings. 4.And every one is crowned with 2000 crowns on his head. And eachcrown is like unto the bow in the cloud. And its splendour is like unto the splendour of the globe of thesun. And the sparks that go forth from every one are like the splendour of the morning star (planetVenus) in the East.

CHAPTER 22

KERUBIEL, the Prince of the Kerubim. Description of the Kerubim R. Ishmael said: Metatron, the angel, the Prince of the Presence, said to me : 1.Above these la there is one prince, noble, wonderful, strong, andpraised with all kinds of praise. His name is KERUBIEL H', a mighty prince, full of power and strength aprince of highness, and Highness (is) with him, a righteous prince, and righteousness (is) withhim, a holy prince, and holiness (is) with him, a prince glorified in (by) thousand hosts, exaltedby ten thousand armies. 2.At his wrath the earth trembles, at his anger the camps are moved,from fear of him the foundations are shaken, at his rebuke the 'Araboth do tremble. 3.His stature is full of (burning) coals. The height of his stature is as the height of the seven heavens the breadth of his stature is as the wideness of the seven heavensand the thickness of his stature is as the seven heavens. 4.The opening of his mouth is like a lamp of fire. His tongue is aconsuming fire. His eyebrows are like unto the splendour of the lightning. His eyes are like sparks ofbrilliance. His countenance is like a burning fire. 5.And there is a crown of holiness upon his head on which (crown) the Explicit Name is graven, and lightnings go forth from it. And the bow of Shekina is between hisshoulders. 6.And his sword is like unto a lightning; and upon his loins there are arrows like unto a flame, and upon his armour and shield there is a consuming fire, and upon his neckthere are coals of burning juniper and (also) round about him (there are coals of burning juniper). 7.And the splendour of Shekina is on his face ; and the horns of majestyon his wheels; and a royal diadem upon his skull. 8.And his body is full of eyes. And wings are covering the whole of hishigh stature (lit. the height of his stature is all wings). 9.On his right hand a flame is burning, and on his left a fire is glowing; and coals are burning from it. And firebrands go forth from his body. And lightnings are cast forthfrom his face. With him there is alway thunder upon (in) thunder, by his side there is ever earthquake upon (in) earthquake. 10.And the two princes of the Merkaba are together with him. 11.Why is he called KERUBIEL H', the Prince. Because he is appointedover the chariot of the Kerubim. And the mighty Kerubim are given in his charge. And he adornsthe crowns on their heads and polishes the diadem upon their skull. 12.He magnifies the glory of their appearance. And he glorifies thebeauty of their majesty. And he increases the greatness of their honour. He causes the song of theirpraise to be sung. He intensifies their beautiful strength. He causes the brilliance of their glory to shine forth. He beautifies their goodly mercy and lovingkindness. He frames the fairness of their radiance. He makes their merciful beauty even more beautiful. He glorifies their upright majesty. He extols the order of their praise, to stablish the dwellingplace of him "who dwelleth on the Kerubim". 13.And the Kerubim are standing by the Holy Chayyoth, and their wingsare raised up to their heads (lit. are as the height of their heads)and Shekina is (resting) upon them and the brillianceof the Glory is upon their facesand song and praise in their mouth and their hands are under their wings and their feet are covered by their wingsand horns of glory are upon their heads and the splendour of Shekina on their faceand Shekina is (resting) upon them and sapphire stones are round about themand columns of fire on their four sides and columns of firebrands beside them. 14.There is one sapphire on one side and another sapphire on another side and under the sapphires there are coals of burning juniper. 15.And one Kerub is standing in each direction but the wings of theKerubim compass each other above their skulls in glory; and they spread them to sing with them a songto him that inhabiteth the clouds and to praise with them the fearful majesty of the king of kings. 16.And KERUBIEL H', the prince who is appointed over them, hearrays them in comely, beautiful and pleasant orders and he exalts them in all manner ofexaltation, dignity and glory. And he hastens them in glory and might to do the will of their Creator everymoment. For above their lofty heads abides continually the glory of the high king "who dwelleth onthe Kerubim".

CHAPTER 23

(ADDITIONAL) 1.And there is a court before the Throne of Glory, 2.which no seraph nor angel can enter, and it is 36,000 myriads ofparasangs, as it is written (Is.vi.2): "and the Seraphim are standing above him" (the last word of thescriptural passage being 'Lamech-Vav' [numerical value: 36]). 3.As the numerical value Lamech-Vav (36) the number of the bridges there. 4.And there are 24 myriads of wheels of fire. And the ministering angelsare 12,000 myriads. And there are 12,000 rivers of hail, and 12,000 treasuries of snow. And in theseven Halls are chariots of fire and flames, without reckoning, or end or searching. R. Ishmael said to me: Metatron, the angel, the Prince of the Presence,said to me: 5.How are the angels standing on high? Pie said: Like a bridge that isplaced over a river so that every one can pass over it, likewise a bridge is placed from the beginning of the entry to the end. 6.And three ministering angels surround it and utter a song before YHWH, the God of Israel. And there are standing before it lords of dread and captains of fear, thousand times thousand and ten thousand times ten thousand in number and they sing praise and hymns before YHWH, the God of Israel. 7.Numerous bridges are there: bridges of fire and numerous bridges ofhail. Also numerous rivers of hail, numerous treasuries of snow and numerous wheels offire. 8.And how many are the ministering angels? 12,000 myriads: six (thousand myriads) above and six (thousand myriads] below. And 12,000 are the treasuries of snow, sixabove and six below. And 24 myriads of wheels of fire, 12 (myriads] above and 12 (myriads] below. And they surround the bridges and the rivers of fire and the rivers of hail. And there arenumerous ministering angels, forming entries, for all the creatures that are standing in the midst thereof, corresponding to (over against) the paths of Raqia Shamayim. 9.What doeth YHWH, the God of Israel, the King of Glory? The Greatand Fearful God, mighty in strength, doth cover his face.

10.In Araboth are 660,000 myriads of angels of glory standing overagainst the Throne of Glory and the divisions offlaming fire. And the King of Glory doth cover His face;for else the (Araboth Raqia1 would be rent asunder in its midst because of the majesty, splendour, beauty, radiance, loveliness, brilliancy, brightness and excellency of the appearance of (the Holy One,) blessed be He. 11.There are numerous ministering angelsperforming his will, numerous kings, numerous princes in the 'Araboth of his delight, angels who are revered among the rulers inheaven, distinguished, adorned with song and bringing love to remembrance: (who) are affrighted by the splendour of the Shekina, and their eyes are dazzled by the shining beauty of their King,their faces grow black and their strength doth fail. 12.There go forth rivers ofjoy, streams of gladness, rivers of rejoicing, 13.streams of triumph, rivers of 14.love, streams of friendship (another reading:) of commotion and they flowover and go forth before 15.the Throne of Glory and wax great and go through the gates of the paths of 'Araboth Raqia at the 16.voice of the shouting and musick of the CHAYYOTH, at the voice of therejoicing of the timbrels of 17.his 'OPHANNIM and at the melody of the cymbals of His Kerubim. Andthey wax great and go 18. forth with commotion with the sound of the hymn: "HOLY, HOLY, HOLY, IS THE LORD OF 19.HOSTS; THE WHOLE EARTH IS FULL OF HIS GLORY!"

CHAPTER 24

R. Ishmael said: Metatron, the Prince of the Presence said to me: 1.What is the distance between one bridge and another? 12 myriads ofparasangs. Their ascent is 12 myriads of parasangs, and their descent 12 myriads of parasangs. 2.(The distance) between the rivers of dread and the rivers offear is 22 myriads of parasangs; between the rivers of hail and the rivers of darkness 36 myriads of parasangs; between the chambers of lightnings and the clouds of compassion 42 myriads of parasangs; between the clouds of compassion and the Merkaba 84 myriads ofparasangs; between the Merkaba and the Kerubim 148 myriads of parasangs; between the Kerubim and the 'Ophannim 24 myriads of parasangs; between the Ophannim and the chambers of chambers 24 myriads of parasangs; between the chambers of chambers and the Holy Chayyoth 40,000 myriads of parasangs; between one wing (of the Chayyoth) and another12 myriads of parasangs; and the breadth of each one wing is of that same measure; and the distance between the Holy Chayyoth and the Throne of Glory is 30,000 myriads of parasangs. 3.And from the foot of the Throne to the seat there are 40,000 myriads of parasangs. And the name of Him that sitteth on it: let the name be sanctified! 4.And the arches of the Bow are set above the 'Araboth, and they are 1000 thousands and 10,000 times ten thousands (of parasangs) high. Their measure is after the measure of the 'Irin and Qaddishin (Watchers and Holy Ones). As it is written (Gen. ix. 13) "My bow I have set in the cloud". It is not written here "I will set" but "I have set", (i.e.) already; clouds that surround the Throne of Glory. As His clouds pass by, the angels of hail (turn into) burning coal. 5.And a fire of the voice goes down from by the Holy Chayyoth. And because of the breath of that voice they "run" (Ezek. i. 14) to another place, fearing lest it command them to go; and they "return" lest it injure them from the other side. Therefore "they run and return" (Ezek. i. 14). 6.And these arches of the Bow are more beautiful and radiant than the radiance of the sun during the summer solstice. And they are whiter than a flaming fire and they are great and beautiful. 7.Above the arches of the Bow are the wheels of the 'Ophannim. Their height is 1000 thousand and 10,000 times 10,000 units of measure after the measure of the Seraphimand the Troops (Gedudim).

CHAPTER 25

The winds blowing under the wings of the Kerubim R. Ishmael said: Metatron, the Angel, the Prince of the Presence, said to me : 1.There are numerous winds blowing under the wings of the Kerubim. There blows "the Brooding Wind", as it is written (Gen. i. 2): " and the wind of God was brooding upon the face of the waters ". 2.There blows "the Strong Wind", asit is said (Ex. xiv. 21): "and the Lordcaused the sea to go back by a strong east wind all that night". 3.There blows "the East Wind"as it is written (Ex. x. 13): "the east windbrought the locusts". 4.There blows "the Wind of Quails" as it is written (Num. xi. 31): "Andthere went forth a wind from the Lord and brought quails". 5.There blows "the Wind of Jealousy" as it is written (Num.v.14): "And the wind of jealousy came upon him". 6.There blows the "Wind of Earthquake" as it is written (i Kings .xix. 11): "and after that the wind of the earthquake ; but the Lord was not in the earthquake". 7.There blows the "Wind of H' " as it is written (Ex. xxxvii. i): "and hecarried me out by the wind of H' and set me down". 8.There blows the "Evil Wind " as it is written (i Sam. xvi. 23): "and theevil wind departed from him". 9.There blow the "Wind of Wisdom" 5and the "Wind of Understanding"and the "Wind of Knowledge" and the "Wind of the Fear of H'" as it is written (Is. xi. 2):"And the wind of H'shall rest upon him; the wind of wisdom and understanding, the wind of counseland might, the wind ofknowledge and of the fear. 10.There blows the "Wind of Rain", as it is written (Prov. xxv. 23): "the north wind bringeth forth rain". 11.There blows the "Wind of Lightnings ", as it is written (Jer.x.13, li.16): "he maketh lightnings for the rain and bringeth forth the wind out of his treasuries ". 12.There blows the "Wind, Breaking the Rocks", as it is written (i Kings xix. n): "the Lord passed by and a great and strong wind (rent the mountains and brake in piecesthe rocks before the Lord)". 13.There blows the "Wind of Assuagement of the Sea", as it is written(Gen. viii. i): "and God made a wind to pass over the earth, and the waters assuaged". 14.There blows the "Wind of Wrath", as it is written (Job i. 19) : "andbehold there came a great wind from the wilderness and smote the four corners of the house and itfell". 15.There blows the " Storm-Wind ", as it is written (Ps. cxlviii. 8) :"Storm-wind, fulfilling his word". 16.And Satan is standing among these winds, for "storm-wind " isnothing else but "Satan", and all these winds do not blow but under the wings of the Kerubim, as it iswritten (Ps. xviii. n) : "and he rode upon a cherub and did fly, yea, and he flew swiftly upon the wings ofthe wind". 17.And whither go all these winds? The Scripture teaches us, that theygo out from under the wings of the Kerubim and descend on the globe of the sun, as it is written(Eccl. i. 6) : " The wind goeth toward the south and turneth about unto the north ; it turneth aboutcontinually in its course and the wind 14 returneth again to its circuits ". And from the globe ofthe sun they return and descend upon the rivers and the seas, upon] the mountains and upon thehills, as it is written (Am.iv.13): "For lo, he that formeth the mountains and createth thewind". 18.And from the mountains and the hills they return and descend to theseas and the rivers ; and from the seas and the rivers they return and descend upon (the) cities andprovinces ; and from the cities and provinces they return and descend into the Garden, and fromthe Garden they return and descend to Eden, as it is written (Gen.iii. 8): "walking in the Garden inthe wind of day". And in the midst of the Garden they join together and blow from one side to theother and are perfumed with the spices of the Garden even from \ts remotest parts, until they separatefrom each other, and, filled with the scent of the pure spices, they bring the odour from the remotest parts of Eden and the spices of the Garden to the righteous and godly who in the time to come shallinherit the Garden of Eden and the Tree of Life, as it is written (Cant.

iv. 16) : "Awake, O northwind; and come thou south; blow upon my garden, that the spices thereof may flow out. Let mybeloved come into his garden and eat his precious fruits".

CHAPTER 26

The different chariots of the Holy One, blessed be He R. Ishmael said: Metatron, the Angel, the Prince of the Presence, theglory of all heaven, said to me : 1.Numerous chariots has the Holy One, blessed be He: He has the "Chariots of (the) Kerubim", as it is written (Ps.xviii.11, 2Sam.xxii.11): "And he rode upon a cherub and did fly". 2.He has the "Chariots of Wind", as it is written (ib.) : "and he flewswiftly upon the wings of the wind ". 3.He has the "Chariots of (the) Swift Cloud", as it is written (Is. xix. i): "Behold, the Lord rideth upon a swift cloud". 4.He has "the Chariots of Clouds", as it is written (Ex. xix. 9): "Lo, Icome unto thee in a cloud". 5.He has the "Chariots of the Altar", as it is written (Am. ix. i) :"I sawthe Lord standing upon the Altar". 6.He has the "Chariots of Ribbotaim", as it is written (Ps.lxviii. 18) :"The chariots of God are Ribbotaim ; thousands of angels ". 7.He has the "Chariots of the Tent", as it is written (Deut.xxxi. 15) :"And the Lord appeared in the Tent in a pillar of cloud ". 8.He has the "Chariots of the Tabernacle", as it is written (Lev. i. 1): "And the Lord spake unto him out of the tabernacle". 9.He has the "Chariots of the Mercy-Seat", as it is written (Num. vii.89): "then he heard the Voice speaking unto him from upon the mercy-seat". 10.He has the "Chariots of Sapphire Stone", as it is written (Ex. xxiv.10) : "and there was under his feet as it were a paved work of sapphire stone". 11.He has the "Chariots of Eagles ", as it is written (Ex. xix. 4) :"I bare you on eagles' wings". Eagles literally are not meant here but "they that fly swiftly as eagles". 12.He has the "chariots of Shout", as it is written (Ps. xlvii. 6) :"God is gone up with a shout". 13.He has the "Chariots of 'Araboth", as it is written (Ps.lxviii. 5):"Extol Him that rideth upon the 'Araboth". 14.He has the "Chariots of Thick Clouds", as it is written (Ps. civ. 3):"who maketh the thick clouds His chariot". 15.He has the "Chariots of the Chayyoth", as it is written (Ezek. i. 14) :"and the Chayyoth ran and returned". They run by permission and return by permission, forShekina is above their heads. 16.He has the "Chariots of Wheels (Galgallim)", as it is written (Ezek. x. 2): "And he said: Go in between the whirling wheels". 17.lie has the "Chariots of a Swift Kerub", as it is written (Ps.xviii.10 &Is.xix.1): "riding on a swift cherub". And at the time when He rides on a swift kerub, as he sets one of His feetupon him, before he sets the other foot upon his back, he looks through eighteen thousand worldsat one glance. And he discerns and sees into them all and knows what is in all of them and thenhe sets down the other foot upon him, according as it is written (Ezek. xlviii. 35): "Round about eighteen thousand". Whence do we know that He looks through every one of them every day? It is written (Ps. xiv. 2): "He looked down from heaven upon the children of men to see if therewere any that did understand, that did seek after God". (i8) He has the "Chariots of the 'Ophannim", as it is written (Ezek. x. 12): "and the 'Ophannim were full of eyes round about". 12 18.He has the "Chariots of His Holy Throne", as it is written (Ps. xlvii.8) :" God sitteth upon his holy throne ". 19.He has the "chariots of the Throne of Yah", as it is written (Ex. xvii.16) : "Because a hand is lifted up upon the Throne of Jah". 20.He has the "Chariots of the Throne of Judgement", as it is written (Is. v. 16): "but the Lord of hosts shall be exalted in judgment". 21.He has the "Chariots of the Throne of Glory ", as it is written (Jer. xvii. 12) : "The Throne of Glory, set on high from the beginning, is the place of our sanctuary". 22.He has the "Chariots of the High and Exalted Throne", as it iswritten (Is. vi. i): "I saw the Lord sitting upon the high and exalted throne".

CHAPTER 27

'Ophphanniel, the prince of the 'Ophannim. Description of the 'Ophannim R. Ishmael said: Metatron, the Angel, the Prince of the Presence, said tome : 1.Above these there is one great prince, revered, high, lordly, fearful, ancient and strong. 'OPHPHANNIEL H is his name. 2.He has sixteen faces, four faces on each side,(also) hundred wings oneach side. And he has 8466 eyes, corresponding to the days of the year. [2190 –and some say 2116- on each side.] [2191 /2196 and sixteen on each side.] 3.And those two eyes of his face, in each one of them lightnings areflashing, and from each one of them firebrands are burning ; and no creature is able to behold them : foranyone who looks at them is burnt instantly. 4.His height is (as) the distance of 2500 years' journey. No eye canbehold and no mouth can tell the mighty power of his strength save the King of kings, the Holy One,blessed be He, alone. 5.Why is he called 'OPHPHANNIEL ? Because he is appointed over the 'Ophannim and the 'Ophannimare givenin his charge. He stands every day and attends and beautifies them. And he exalts and orders their apartment and polishes their standing-place and makes bright their dwellings, makes theircorners even and cleanses their seats. And he waits upon them early and late, by day and by night, toincrease their beauty, to make great their dignity and to make them "diligent in praise of their Creator. 6.And all the 'Ophannim are full of eyes, and they are all full ofbrightness; seventy two sapphire stones are fixed on their garments on their right side and seventy twosapphire stones are fixed on their garments on their left side. 7.And four carbuncle stones are fixed on the crown of every single one,the splendour of which proceeds in the four directions of 'Araboth even as the splendour of theglobe of the sun proceeds in all the directions of the universe. And why is it called Carbuncle (Bareqet)? Because its splendour is like the appearance of a lightning (Baraq). And tents of splendour, tentsof brilliance, tents of brightness as of sapphire and carbuncle inclose them because of theshining appearance of their eyes.

CHAPTER 28

SERAPHIEL, the Prince of the Seraphim. Description of the Seraphim R. Ishmael said: Metatron, the Angel, the Prince of the Presence, said to me : 1.Above these there is one prince, wonderful, noble, great, honourable,mighty, terrible, a chief and leader 1 and a swift scribe, glorified, honoured and beloved. 2.He is altogether filled with splendour, full of praise and shining; andhe is wholly full of brilliance, of light and of beauty; and the whole of him is filled withgoodliness and greatness. 3.His countenance is altogether like (that of) angels, but his body is likean eagle's body. 4.His splendour is like unto lightnings, his appearance like fire brands,his beauty like unto sparks, his honour like fiery coals, his majesty like chashmals, his radiance likethe light of the planet Venus. The image of him is like unto the Greater Light. His height is as the sevenheavens. The light from his eyebrows is like the sevenfold light. 5.The sapphire stone upon his head is as great as the whole universeand like unto the splendour of the very heavens in radiance. 6.His body is full of eyes like the stars of the sky, innumerable and unsearchable. Every eye is like the planet Venus. Yet, there are some of them like the Lesser Light andsome of them like unto the Greater Light. From his ankles to his knees (they are) like unto stars of lightning, from his knees to his thighs like unto the planet Venus, from his thighs to his loins like untothe moon, from his loins to his neck like the sun, from his neck to his skull like unto the Light Imperishable. (Cf. Zeph. iii. 5.) 7.The crown on his head is like unto the splendour of the Throne of Glory. The measure of the crown is the distance of 502 years' journey. There is no kind of splendour,no kind of brilliance, no kind of radiance, no kind of light in the universe but is fixed on thatcrown. 8.The name of that prince is SERAPHIEL H". And the crown on hishead, its name is "the Prince of Peace". And why is he called by the name of SERAPHIEL '? Because he is appointed over the Seraphim. And the flaming Seraphim are given in his charge. And hepresides over them by day and by night and teaches them song, praise, proclamation of beauty, mightand majesty; that they may proclaim the beauty of their King in all manner of Praise and Sanctification (Qedushsha). 9.How many are the Seraphim? Four, corresponding to the four windsof the world. And how many wings have they each one of them? Six, corresponding to the sixdays of Creation. And how many faces have they? Each one of them four faces. 10.The measure of the Seraphim and the height of each one of themcorrespond to the height of the seven heavens. The size of each wing is like the measure of all Raqia' .The size of each face is like that of the face of the East. 11.And each one of them gives forth light like unto the splendour of theThrone of Glory: so that not even the Holy Chayyoth, the honoured 'Ophannim, nor the majesticKeruUm are able to behold it. For everyone who beholds it, his eyes are darkened because of its great splendour. 12.Why are they called Seraphim? Because they burn (saraph) thewriting tables of Satan : Every day Satan is sitting, together with SAMMAEL, the Prince of Rome, andwith DUBBIEL, the Prince of Persia, and they write the iniquities of Israel on writing tables whichthey hand over to the Seraphim, in order that they may present them before the Holy One,blessed be He, so that He may destroy Israel from the world. But the Seraphim know from the secrets ofthe Holy One, blessed be He, that he desires not, that this people Israel should perish. What do theSeraphim? Every day do they receive (accept) them from the hand of Satan and burn them in theburning fire over against the high and exalted Throne in order that they may not come before the HolyOne, blessed be He, at the time when he is sitting upon the Throne of Judgement, judging the wholeworld in truth.

CHAPTER 29

RADWERIEL, the keeper of the Book of Records R. Ishmael said: Metatron, the Angel of H', the Prince of the Presence,said to me : 1.Above the Seraphim there is one prince, exalted above all the princes, wondrous more than all the servants. His name is RADWERIEL H' who is appointed over the treasuries of the books. 2.He fetches forth the Case of Writings (with) the Book of Records in it,and brings it before the Holy One, blessed be He. And he breaks the seals of the case, opens it,takes out the books and delivers them before the Holy One, blessed be He. And the Holy One,blessed be He, receives them of his hand and gives them in his sight to the Scribes, that they may readthem in the Great Beth Din (The court of justice) in the height of 'Araboth Raqia', before the heavenly household. 3.And why is he called RADWERIEL? Because out of every word thatgoes forth from his mouth an angel is created : and he stands in the songs (in the singing company) of the ministering angels and utters a song before the Holy One, blessed be He when the timedraws nigh for the recitation of the (Thrice) Holy.

CHAPTER 30

The 'Irin and Qaddishin R. Ishmael said : Metatron, the Angel,the Prince of the Presence, said to me : 1.Above all these there are four great princes, lrin and Qaddishin by name: high, honoured, revered, beloved, wonderful andglorious ones, greater than all the children of heaven. There is none like unto them among all the celestial princes and none their equal among all the Servants. For each one of them is equal to all the rest together. 2.And their dwelling is over against the Throne of Glory, and their standing place over against the Holy One,

blessed be He, so that the brilliance of their dwelling is areflection of the brilliance of the Throne of Glory. And the splendour of their countenance is a reflection of the splendour of Shekina. 3.And they are glorified by the glory of 4the Divine Majesty (Gebura) and praised by (through) the praise of Shekina. 4.And not only that, but the Holy One, blessed be He, does nothing in his world without first consulting them, but after that he doeth it. As it is written (Dan. iv. 17) :"The sentence is by the decree of the 'Irin and the demand by the word of the Qaddishin." 5.The llrin are two and the Qaddishin are two. And how are theystanding before the Holy One, blessed be He? It is to be understood, that one 'Ir is standing on one sideand the other 'Ir on the other side, and one Qaddish is standing on one side and the other on theother side. 6.And ever do they exalt the humble, and they abase to the ground those that are proud, and they exalt to the height those that are humble. 7.And every day, as the Holy One, blessed be He, is sitting upon the Throne of Judgement and judges the whole world, and the Books of the Living and the Books of theDead are opened before Him, then all the children of heaven are standing before him in fear,dread, awe and trembling. At that time, (when) the Holy One, blessed be He, is sitting upon the Throne of Judgement to execute judgement, his garment is white as snow, the hair on his head as purewool and the whole of his cloak is like the shining light. And he is covered with righteousness allover as with a coat of mail. 8.And those 'Irm and Qaddishin are standing before him like courtofficers before the judge. And they raise and argue every case and close the case that comes before theHoly One, blessed be He, in judgement, according as it is written (Dan. iv. 17) : "The sentence is bythe decree of the 'Irm and the demand by the word of the Qaddishin" 9.Some of them argue and others pass the sentence in the Great BethDin in 'Araboth. Some of them make the requests from before uthe Divine Majesty and some closethe cases before the Most High. Others finish by going down and (confirming) executing the sentences on earth below. According as it is written (Dan. iv. 13 , 14) : " Behold an 'Ir and aQaddishcame down from heaven and cried aloud and said thus, Hew down the tree, and cut off hisbranches, shake off his leaves, and scatter his fruit: let the beasts get away from under it, and the fowls fromhis branches ". 10.Why are they called 'Irin and Qaddishint By reason that they sanctifythe body and the spirit with lashes of fire on the third day of the judgement, as it is written (Hos. vi. 2): "After two days will he revive us : on the third he will raise us up, and we shall live beforehim."

CHAPTER 31

Description of a class of angels R. Ishmael said: Metatron, the Angel, the Prince of the Presence,said to me: 1.Each one of them has seventy names corresponding to the seventy tongues of the world. And all of them are (based) upon the name of the Holy One, blessed be He. And every several name is written with a flaming style upon the Fearful Crown (Keiher Nora) whichis on the head of the high and exalted King. 2.And from each one of them there go forth sparks and lightnings. And each one of them is beset with horns of splendour round about. From each one lights are shiningforth, and each one is surrounded by tents of brilliance so that not even the Seraphim and the Chayyoth who are greater than all the children of heaven are able to behold them.

CHAPTER 32

The 72 princes of Kingdoms and the Prince of the Worldofficiating at the Great Sanhedrin in heaven R. Ishmael said: Metatron, the Angel, the Prince of the Presence, said to me: 1.Whenever the Great Beth Din is seated in the 'Araboth Raqia' on high there is no opening of the mouth for anyone in the world save those great princes who are called H'by the name of the Holy One, blessed be He. 2. How many are those princes? Seventy-two princes of the kingdoms ofthe world besides the Prince of the World who speaks (pleads) in favour of the world before theHoly One, blessed be He, every day, at the hour when the book is opened in which are recorded allthe doings of the world, according as it is written (Dan.vii.10) : "The judgement was set and thebooks were opened."

CHAPTER 33

(The attributes of) Justice, Mercy and Truth by the Throne of Judgement R. Ishmael said: Metatron, the Angel, the Prince of the Presence,said to me : 1. At the time when the Holy One, blessed be He, is sitting on the Throne, of Judgement, (then) Justice is standing on His right and Mercy on His left and Truth before His face. 2.And when man enters before Him to judgement,(then) there comes forth from the splendour of the Mercy towards him as (it were) a staff and stands in front of him. Forthwith man falls upon his face, (and) all the angels of destruction fear and tremble before him, according as it is written (Is.xvi. 5): "And with mercy shall the throne be established, and he shallsit upon it in truth."

CHAPTER 34

The execution ofjudgement on the wicked. God's sword R. Ishmael said: Metatron, the Angel, the Prince of the Presence, said tome : 1.When the Holy One, blessed be He, opens the Book half of which isfire and half flame, (then) they go out from before Him in every moment to execute the judgement on the wicked by His sword (that is) drawn forth out of its sheath and the splendour of which shineslike a lightning and pervades the world from one end to the other, as it is written (Is. lxvi. 16): "For byfire will the Lord plead (and by his sword with all flesh)." 2.And all the inhabitants of the world (lit. those who come into theworld) fear and tremble before Him, when they behold His sharpened sword like unto a lightning fromone end of the world to the other, and sparks and flashes of the size of the stars of Raqia' going outfrom it; according as it is written (Deut. xxxii. 41):" If I whet the lightning of my sword".

CHAPTER 35

The angels of Mercy, of Peace and ofDestruction by the Throne ofJudgement. The scribes,(vss. i, 2) The angels by the Throne of Gloryand the fiery rivers under it. (vss. 3-5) R. Ishmael said: Metatron, the Angel, the Prince of the Presence, said to me : 1.At the time that the Holy One,blessed be He, is sitting on the Throne of Judgement, (then) the angels of Mercy are standing on His right, the angels of Peace are standing on His left and the angels of Destruction are standing in front of Him. 2.And one scribe is standing beneath Him, and another scribe above Him. 3.And the glorious Seraphimsurround the Throne on its four sides withwalls of lightnings, and the 'Ophannim. surround them with fire-brands round about the Throne ofGlory. And clouds of fire and clouds of flames compass them to the right and to the left; and theHoly Chayyoth carry the Throne of Glory from below: each one with three fingers. The measure ofthe fingers of each one is 800,000 and 700 times hundred, (and) 66,000 parasangs. 4.And underneath the feet of the Chayyoth seven fiery rivers arerunning and flowing. And the breadth of each river is 365 thousand parasangs and its depth is 248thousand myriads of parasangs. Its length is unsearchable and immeasureable. 5.And each river turns round in a bow in the four directions of 'ArabothRaqict , and (from there) it falls down to Ma'on and is stayed, and from Ma1 on to Zebul, from Zebulto Shechaqim, from Shechaqim to Raqia' , from Raqia' to Shamayim and from Shamayimupon the heads of the wicked who are in Gehenna, as it is written (Jer. xxiii. 19): "Behold a whirlwindof the Lord, even his fury, is gone, yea, a whirling tempest; it shall burst upon the head of thewicked".

CHAPTER 36

The different concentric circles round the Chayyoth, consisting offire, water, hailstones etc. and of the angels uttering the Qedushsha responsorium R. Ishmael said: Metatron; the Angel, the Prince of the Presence, said tome : 1.The hoofs of the Chayyoth are surrounded by seven clouds of burningcoals. The clouds of burning coals are surrounded on the outside by seven walls of flame(s). The seven walls of flame(s) are surrounded on the outside by seven walls of hailstones (stones of 'Et-gabish, Ezek. xiii. 11,13, xxviii. 22). The hailstones are surrounded on the outside by xstones ofhail (stone of Barad). The stones of hail are surrounded on the outside by stones of "the wings of thetempest ". The stones of "the wings of the tempest" are surrounded on the outside by flames of fire. The flames of fire are surrounded by the chambers of the whirlwind. The chambers ofthe whirlwind are surrounded on the outside by the fire and the water. 2.Round about the fire and the water are those who utter the "Holy". Round about those who utter the "Holy" are those who utter the "Blessed"'. Round about those who utter the "Blessed" are the bright clouds. The bright clouds are surrounded on the outside by coals of burning jumper ; and on the outside surrounding the coals of burning juniper there are thousandcamps of fire and ten thousand hosts of flame(s). And between every several camp and everyseveral host there is a cloud, so that they may not be burnt by the fire.

CHAPTER 3 7

The camps of angels in 'Araboth Raqia: angels, performing the Qedushsha 1 R. Ishmael said: Metatron, the Angel, the Prince of the Presence, saidto me : 1.506 thousand myriads of camps has the Holy One, blessed be He, in the height of 'Araboth Raqia. And each camp is (composed of) 496 thousand angels. 2.And every single angel, the height of his stature is as the great sea;and the appearance of their countenance as the appearance of the lightning, and their eyes as lampsof fire, and their arms and their feet like in colour to polished brass and the roaring voice of theirwords like the voice of a multitude. 3.And they are all standing before the Throne of Glory in four rows. And the princes of the army are standing at the head of each row. 4.And some of them utter the "Holy" and others utter the "Blessed", some of them run as messengers, others are standing in attendance, according as it is written(Dan. vii. 10): "Thousand thousands ministered unto him, and ten thousand times ten thousandstood before him : the judgment was set and the books were opened ". 5.And in the hour, when the time draws nigh for to say the "Holy", (then) first there goes forth a whirlwind from before the Holy One, blessed be He, and bursts upon the camp of Shekina and there arises a great commotion among them, as it is written (Jer.xxx. 23):"Behold, the whirlwind of the Lord goeth forth with fury, a continuing commotion". 6.At that moment 4thousand thousands of them are changed into sparks,thousand thousands of them into firebrands, thousand thousands into flashes thousand thousands into flames, thousand thousands into males, thousand thousands into females, thousandthousands into winds, thousand thousands into burning fires, thousand thousands into flames, thousand thousands into sparks, thousand thousands into chashmals of light; until they take uponthemselves the yoke of the kingdom of heaven, the high and lifted up, of the Creator of them all with fear, dread, awe and trembling, with commotion, anguish, terror and trepidation. Then theyare changed again into their former shape to have the fear of their King before them alway, as they have set their hearts on saying the Song continually, as it is written (Is. vi. 3): "And one criedunto another and said (Holy, Holy, Holy, etc.)".

CHAPTER 38

The angels bathe in the fiery river before reciting the 'Song' R. Ishmael said: Metatron, the Angel, the Prince of the Presence, said to me : 1.At the time when the ministering angels desire to say (the) Song, (then) Nehar di-Nur (the fiery stream) rises with many thousand thousands and myriads of myriads" (of angels) of power and strength of fire and it runs and passes under the Throne of Glory, between the camps of the ministering angels and the troops of 'Araboth. 2.And all the ministering angels first go down into Nehar di-Nur, and they dip themselves in the fire and dip their tongue and their mouth seven times ; and after that they go up and put on the garment of 'Machaqe Samal' and cover themselves with cloaks of chashmal and stand in four rows over against the Throne of Glory, in all the heavens.

CHAPTER 39

The four camps of Shekina and their surroundings R. Ishmael said: Metatron, the Angel, the Prince of the Presence, said to me : 1.In the seven Halls there are standing four chariots of Shekina, and before each one are standing the four camps of Shekina. Between each camp a river of fire is continually flowing. 2.Between each river there are bright clouds [surrounding them], and between each cloud there are put up pillars of brimstone. Between one pillar and another there are standing flaming wheels, surrounding them. And between one wheel and another there are flames of fire round about. Between one flame and another there are treasuries of lightnings; behind the treasuries of lightnings are the wings of the stormwind. Behind the wings of the storm-wind are the chambers of the tempest; behind the chambers of the tempest there are winds, voices, thunders, sparks [upon] sparks and earthquakes [upon] earthquakes.

CHAPTER 40

The fear that befalls all the heavens at the sound of the 'Holy? esp. the heavenly bodies. These appeased by the Prince of the World R. Ishmael said: Metatron, the Angel, the Prince of the Presence, said to me : 1.At the time, when the ministering angels utter (the Thrice) Holy, then all the pillars of the heavens and their sockets do tremble, and the gates of the Halls of Araboth Raqia' are shaken and the foundations of Shechaqim and the Universe (Tebel) are moved, and the orders of Ma'on and the chambers of Makon quiver, and all the orders of Raqia and the constellations and the planets are dismayed, and the globes of the sun and the moon haste away and flee out of their courses and run 12,000 parasangs and seek to throw themselves down from heaven, 2.by reason of the roaring voice of their chant, and the noise of their praise and the sparks and lightnings that go forth from their faces; as it is written (Ps. lxxvii. 18): "The voice of thy thunder was in the heaven (the lightnings lightened the world, the earth trembled and shook) ". 3.Until the prince of the world calls them, saying: "Be ye quiet in your place ! Fear not because of the ministering angels who sing the Song before the Holy One, blessed be He". As it is written (Job.xxxviii. 7): "When the morning stars sang together and all the children of heaven shouted for joy".

CHAPTER 41

The explicit names fly off from the Throne and all the various angelic hosts prostrate themselves before it at the time of the Qedushsha R. Ishmael said: Metatron, the Angel, the Prince of the Presence, said to me : 1.When the ministering angels utter the "Holy" then all the explicit names that are graven with a flaming style on the Throne of Glory fly off like eagles, with sixteen wings. And they surround and compass the Holy One, blessed be He, on the four sides of the place of His Shekina1. 2.And the angels of the host, and the flaming Servants, and the mighty 'Ophannim, and the Kerubim of the Shekina, and the Holy Chayyoth, and the Seraphim, and the 'Er'ellim, and the Taphsarim and the troops of consuming fire, and the fiery armies, and the flaming hosts, and the holy princes, adorned with crowns, clad in kingly majesty, wrapped in glory, girt with loftiness, 4 fall upon their faces three times, saying: "Blessed be the name of His glorious kingdom for ever and ever".

CHAPTER 42

The ministering angels rewarded with crowns, when uttering the ''Holy'' in its right order, and punished by consuming fire if not. New ones created in the stead of the consumed angels R. Ishmael said: Metatron, the Angel, the Prince of the Presence, said to me : 1.When the ministering angels say "Holy" before the Holy One, blessed be He, in the proper way, then the servants of His Throne, the attendants of His Glory, go forth with great mirth from under the Throne of Glory. 2.And they all carry in their hands, each one of them thousand thousand and ten thousand times ten thousand crowns of stars, similar in appearance to the planet Venus, and put them on the ministering angels and the great princes who utter the "Holy". Three crowns they put on each one of them: one crown because they say "Holy", another crown, because they say "Holy, Holy", and a third crown because they say "Holy, Holy, Holy, is the Lord of Hosts" . 3.And in the moment that they do not utter the "Holy" in the right order, a consuming fire goes forth from the little finger of the Holy One, blessed be He, and falls down in the midst of their ranks and is divided into 496 thousand parts corresponding to the four camps of the ministering angels, and consumes them in one moment, as it is written (Ps. xcvii. 3):"A fire goeth before him and burneth up his adversaries round about". 4.After that the Holy One, blessed be He, opens His mouth and speaks one word and creates others in their stead, new ones like them. And each one stands before His Throne of Glory, uttering the "Holy", as it is written (Lam. iii. 23): "They are new every morning; great is thy faithfulness".

CHAPTER 43

Metatron shows R. Ishmael the letters engraved on the Throne of Glory by which letters everything in heaven and earth has been created R. Ishmael said: Metatron, the Angel, the Prince of the Presence, said to me : 1.Come and behold the letters by which the heaven and the earth were created, the letters by which were created the mountains and hills, the letters by which were created the seas and rivers, the letters by which were created the trees and herbs, the letters by which were created the planets and the constellations, the letters by which were created the globe of the moon and the globe of the sun, Orion, the Pleiades and all the different luminaries of Raqia' . 2.the letters by which were created the Throne of Glory and the Wheels of the Merkaba, the letters by which were created the necessities of the worlds, 3.the letters by which were created wisdom, understanding, knowledge, prudence, meekness and righteousness by which the whole world is sustained. 4.And I walked by his side and he took me by his hand and raised me upon his wings and showed me those letters, all of them, that are graven with a flaming style on the Throne of Glory : and sparks go forth from them and cover all the chambers of 'Araboth.

CHAPTER 44

Instances of polar opposites kept in balance by several Divine Names and other similar wonders R. Ishmael said: Metatron, the Angel, the Prince of the Presence, said to me : 1.Come and I will show thee, where the waters are suspended in the highest, where fire is burning in the midst of hail, where lightnings lighten out of the midst of snowy mountains, where thunders are roaring in the celestial heights, where a flame is burning in the midst of the burning fire and where voices make themselves heard in the midst of thunder and earthquake. 2.Then I went by his side and he took me by his hand and lifted me upon his wings and showed me all those things. I beheld the waters suspended on high in 'ArabothRaqia' by (force of) the name YAH 'EHYE 'ASHER 'EHYE (Jah, I am that I am), And their fruits going down from heaven and watering the face of the world, as it is written (Ps.civ.13): "(He watereth the mountains from his chambers :) the earthis satisfied with the fruit of thy work". 3.And I saw fire and snow and hailstone that were mingled togetherwithin each other and yet were undamaged, by (force of) the name 'ESH 'OKELA (consuming fire), as it is written (Deut. iv. 24) : "For the Lord, thy God, is a consuming fire". 4.And I saw lightnings that were lightening out of mountains of snow and yet were not damaged (quenched), by (force of) the name YAH SUR 'OLAMIM (Jah, theeverlasting rock), as it is written (Is. xxvi. 4): "For in Jah, YHWH, the everlasting rock". 5.And I saw thunders and voices that were roaring in the midst of fietyflames and were not damaged (silenced), by (force of) the name 'EL-SHADDAI RABBA (theGreat God Almighty) as it is written (Gen. xvii. i): "I am God Almighty". 6.And I beheld a flame (and) a glow (glowing flames) that were flamingand glowing in the midst of burning fire, and yet were not damaged (devoured), by (force of) thename YAD 'AL KES YAH (the hand upon the Throne of the Lord) as it is written (Ex. xvii. 16) : " And he said: for the hand is upon the Throne of the Lord ". 7.And I beheld rivers of fire in the midst of rivers of water and theywere not damaged (quenched) by (force of) the name 'OSE SHALOM (Maker of Peace) as it is written(Job xxv. 2): "He maketh peace in his high places". For he makes peace between the fire and thewater, between the hail and the fire, between the wind and the cloud, between the earthquake and thesparks.

CHAPTER 45

Metatron shows R. Ishmael the abode of the unborn spirits and of the spirits of the   righteous dead R. Ishmael said: Metatron said to me: 1.Come and I will show thee 1whereare1 the spirits of the righteous that have been created and have returned, and the spirits of the righteous that have not yet been created. 2.And he lifted me up to his side, took me by his hand and lifted me up nearthe Throne of Glory by the place of the Shekina ; and he revealed the Throne of Glory to me,and he showed me the spirits that have been created and had returned : and they were flyingabove the Throne of Glory before the Holy One, blessed be He. 3.After that I went to interpret the following verse of Scripture and I found in what is written (Isa.lvii. 16): "for the spirit clothed itself before me, and the souls I havemade" that ("for the spirit was clothed before me") means the spirits that have been created in thechamber of creation of the righteous and that have returned before the Holy One, blessed be He; (and the words:) "and the souls I have made" refer to the spirits 4 of the righteous that have not yet been created in the chamber (GUPH).

CHAPTER 46

Metatron shows R. Ishmael the abode of the wicked and the intermediate in Sheol. (vss. 1-6) The Patriarchs pray for the deliverance of Israel(vss. 7-10) R. Ishmael said: Metatron, x the Angel, the Prince of the Presence, saidto me : 1.Come and I will show thee the spirits of the wicked and the spirits ofthe intermediate where they are standing, and the spirits of the intermediate, whither they go down, 3and the spirits of the wicked, where they go down. 2.And he said to me : The spirits of the wicked go down to She'ol by the hands of two angels of destruction: ZA'APHIEL and SIMKIEL are their names. 3.SIMKIEL is appointed over the intermediate to support them andpurify them because of the great mercy of the Prince of the Place (Maqom). ZA'APHIEL is appointedover the spirits of the wicked in order to

cast them down from the presence of the Holy One,blessed be He, and from the splendour of the Shekina to She'ol, to be punished in the fire of Gehennawith staves of burning coal. 4.And I went by his side, and he took me by my hand and showed me all of them with his fingers. 5.And I beheld the appearance of their faces (and, lo, it was) as the appearance of children of men, and their bodies like eagles. And not only that but (furthermore) thecolour of the countenance of the intermediate was like pale grey on account of their deeds, for there arestains upon them until they have become cleaned from their iniquity in the fire. 6.And the colour of the wicked was like the bottom of a pot on accountof the wickedness of their doings. 7.And I saw the spirits of the Patriarchs Abraham Isaac and Jacob andthe rest of the righteous whom they have brought up out of their graves and who have ascended to the Heaven (Raqirf). And they   were praying before the Holy One, blessed be He, saying intheirprayer: "Lord of the Universe! How long wilt thou sit upon (thy) Throne like a mourner in the days of hismourning with thy right hand behind thee 7and not7 deliver thy children and reveal thy Kingdom in the world? And for how long wilt thou have no pity upon thy children who are made slaves amongthe nations of the world? Nor upon thy right hand that is behind thee wherewith thou didst stretch out the heavens and the earth and the heavens of heavens? When wilt thou have compassion?" 8.Then the Holy One, blessed be He, answered every one of them,saying: "Since these wicked do sin so and so, and transgress with such and such transgressions against me, how could I deliver my great Right Hand in the downfall by their hands (caused by them). 9.In that moment Metatron called me and spake to me: "My servant! Take the books, and read their evil doings!" Forthwith I took the books and read their doings andthere were to be found 36 transgressions (written down) with regard to each wicked one andbesides, that they have transgressed all the letters in the Tora, as it is written (Dan. ix. u) : "Yea, all Israel have transgressed thy Law". It is not written 'al torateka but 'et (JIN) torateka, for they havetransgressed from 'Aleph to Taw, 4O statutes have they transgressed for each letter. 10.Forthwith Abraham, Isaac and Jacob wept. Then said to them theHoly One, blessed be He: "Abraham, my beloved, Isaac, my Elect one, Jacob, my firstborn! Howcan I now deliver them from among the nations of the world?" And forthwith MIKAEL, the Prince ofIsrael, cried and wept with a loud voice and said (Ps. x. i) : "Why standest thou afar off, O Lord?".

CHAPTER 47

Metatron shows R. Ishmael past andfuture events recorded on the Curtain of the Throne R. Ishmael said: Metatron said to me: 1.Come, and I will show thee the Curtain of MAQOM (the DivineMajesty) which is spread before the Holy One, blessed be He, (and) whereon are graven all thegenerations of the world and all their doings, both what they have done and what they will do until the end ofall generations. 2.And I went, and he showed it to me pointing it out with his fingersMike a father who teaches his children the letters of Tora. And I saw each generation,the rulers of each generation, and the heads of each generation,the shepherds of each generation, the oppressors (drivers) of each generation, the keepers of each generation, the scourgers of each generation,the overseers of each generation, the judges of each generation, the court officers of each generation ,the teachers of each generation, the supporters of each generation,the chiefs of each generation, the presidents of academies of each generation, the magistrates of each generation,the princes of each generation, the counsellors of each generation,the nobles of each generation, and the men of might ofeach generation, the elders of each generation, and the guides of each generation. 3.And I saw Adam, his generation, their doings and their thoughts, Noah and his generation, their doings and their thoughts, and the generation of the flood, their doings and their thoughts, Shem and his generation their doings and their thoughts, Nimrod and the generation of the confusion of tongues, and his generation, their doings and their thoughts, Abraham and his generation, their doings and their thoughts, Isaac and his generation, their doings and their thoughts, Ishmael and his generation, their doings and their thoughts, Jacob and his generation, their doings and their thoughts, Joseph and his generation, their doings and their thoughts, the tribes and their generation, their doings and their thoughts, Amram and his generation, their doings and their thoughts, Moses and his generation, their doings and their thoughts, 4.Aaron and Mirjam their works and their doings, the princes and the elders, their works and doings, Joshua and his generation, their works and doings, the judges and their generation, their works and doings, Eli and his generation, their works and doings, "Phinehas, their works and doings, Elkanah and his generation, their works and their doings, Samuel and his generation, their works and doings, the kings of Judah with their generations, their works and their doings, the kings of Israel and their generations, their works and their doings, the princes of Israel, their works and their doings; the princes of the nations of the world, their works and their doings, the heads of the councils of Israel, their works and their doings ; the heads of (the councils in) the nations of the world, their generations, their works and their doings; the rulers of Israel and their generation, their works and their doings ; the nobles of Israel and their generation, their works and their doings ; the nobles of the nations of the world and their generation(s), their works and their doings; the men of reputation in Israel, their generation, their works and their doings ; the judges of Israel, their generation, their works and their doings ; the judges of the nations of the world and their generation, their works and their doings ; the teachers of children in Israel, their generations, their works and their doings ; the teachers of children in the nations of the world, their generations, their works and their doings; the counsellors (interpreters) of Israel, their generation, their works and their doings ; the counsellors (interpreters) of the nations of the world, their generation, their works and their doings ; all the prophets of Israel, their generation, their works and their doings ; all the prophets of the nations of the world, their generation, their works and their doings ; 5.and all the fights and wars that the nations 16 of the world wrought against the people of Israel in the time of their kingdom. And I saw Messiah, son of Joseph, and his generation "and their" works and their doings that they will do against the nations of the world. And I saw Messiah, son of David, and his generation, and all the fights and wars, and their works and their doings that they will do with Israel both for good and evil. And I saw all the fights and wars that Gog and Magog will fight in the days of Messiah, and all that the Holy One, blessed be He, will do with them in the time to come. 6.And all the rest of all the leaders of the generations and all the works of the generations both in Israel and in the nations of the world, both what is done and what will be done hereafter to all generations until the end of time, (all) were graven on the Curtain of MAQOM. And I saw all these things with my eyes; and after I had seen it, I opened my mouth in praise of MAQOM (the Divine Majesty) (saying thus, Eccl. viii. 4, 5): "For the King's word hath power (and who may say unto him: What doest thou?) Whoso keepeth the commandments shall know no evil thing". And I said: (Ps. civ. 24) "O Lord, how manifold are thy works!".

CHAPTER 48

The place of the stars shown to R. Ishmael R. Ishmael said : Metatron said to me : 1.(Come and I will show thee) the space of the stars a that are standing in Raqia' night by night in fear of the Almighty (MAQOM) and (I will show thee) where they go and where they stand. 2.I walked by his side, and he took me by his hand and pointed out all to me with his fingers. And they were standing on sparks of flames round the Merkaba of the Almighty (MAQOM). What did Metatron do? At that moment he clapped his hands and chased them off from their place. Forthwith they flew off on flaming wings, rose and fled from the four sides of the Throne of the Merkaba, and (as they flew) he told me the names of every single one. As it is written (Ps. cxlvii. 4) :" He telleth the number of the stars ; he giveth them all their names", teaching, that the Holy One, blessed be He, has given a name to each one of them. 3.And they all enter in counted order under the guidance of (lit. through, by the hands of) RAHATIEL to Raqia' ha-shSHamayim to serve the world. And they go out in counted order to praise the Holy One, blessed be He, with songs and hymns, according as it is written (Ps. xix. i): "The heavens declare the glory of God". 4.But in the time to come the Holy One, blessed be He, will create them anew, as it is written (Lam. iii. 23): "They are new every morning". And they open their mouth and utter a song. Which is the song that they utter? (Ps. viii. 3): "When I consider thy heavens".

CHAPTER 49

Metatron shows R. Ishmael the spirits of the punished angels R. Ishmael said: Metatron said to me: 1.Come and I will show thee the souls of the angels and the spirits of the ministering servants whose bodies have been burnt in the fire of MAQOM (the Almighty) that goes forth from his little finger. And they have been made into fiery coals in the midst of the fiery river (Nehar di-Nur). But their spirits and their souls are standing behind the Shekina. 2.Whenever the ministering angels utter a song at a wrong time or as not appointed to be sung they are burnt and consumed by the fire of their Creator and by a flame from their Maker, in the places (chambers) of the whirlwind, for it blows upon them and drives them into the Nehar di-Nur; and there they are made into numerous mountains of burning coal. But their spirit and their soul return to their Creator, and all are standing behind their Master. 3.And I went by his side and he took me by his hand ; and he showed me all the souls of the angels and the spirits of the ministering servants who were standing behind the Shekina upon wings of the whirlwind and walls of fire surrounding them. 4.At that moment Metatron opened to me the gates of the walls within which they were standing behind the Shekina, And I lifted up my eyes and saw them, and behold, the likeness of every one was as (that of) angels and their wings like birds' (wings), made out of flames, the work of burning fire. In that moment I opened my mouth in praise of MAQOM and said (Ps. xcii. 5): "How great are thy works, O Lord ".

CHAPTER 50

Metatron shows R. Ishmael the Right Hand of the Most High, now inactive behind Him, but in the future destined to work the deliverance of Israel R. Ishmael said : Metatron said to me : 1.Come, and I will show thee the Right Hand of MAQOM, laid behind (Him) because of the destruction of the Holy Temple ; from which all kinds of splendour and light shine forth and by which the 955 heavens were created ; and whom not even the Seraphim and the 'Ophannim are permitted (to behold), until the day of salvation shall arrive. 2.And I went by his side and he took me by his hand and showed me (the Right Hand of MAQOM), with all manner of praise, rejoicing and song: and no mouth can tell its praise, and no eye can behold it, because of its greatness, dignity, majesty, glory and beauty. 3.And not only that, but all the souls of the righteous who are counted worthy to behold the joy of Jerusalem, they are standing by it, praising and praying before it three times every day, saying (Is.li.9): "Awake, awake, put on strength, O arm of the Lord" accordingas it is written (Is. lxiii. 12): "He caused his glorious arm to go at the right hand of Moses". 4.In that moment the Right Hand of MAQOM was weeping. And there went forth from its five fingers five rivers of tears and fell down into the great sea and shook thewhole world, according as it is written (Is. xxiv. 19, 20): "The earth is utterly broken (1), the earth isclean dissolved (2), the earth is moved exceedingly (3), the earth shall stagger like a drunkenman (4) and shall be moved to and fro like a hut (5)", five times corresponding to the fingers of his GreatRight Hand. 5.But when the Holy One, blessed be He, sees, that there is no righteousman in the generation, and no pious man (Chasid] on earth, and no justice in the hands of men ;and (that there is) no man like unto Moses, and no intercessor as Samuel who could pray beforeMAQOM for the salvation and for the deliverance, and for His Kingdom, that it be revealed in thewhole world; and for His great Right Hand that He put it before Himself again to work greatsalvation by it for Israel, 6.then forthwith will the Holy One, blessed be He, remember His ownjustice, favour, mercy and grace : and He will deliver His great Arm by himself, and His righteousness will support Him. According as it is written (Is. lix. 16): "And he saw, that there was no man" (that is:) like unto Moses who prayed countless times for Israel in the desert and averted the(Divine) decrees from them" and he wondered, that there was no intercessor" like unto Samuelwho intreated the Holy One, blessed be He, and called unto Him and he answered him andfulfilled his desire, even if it was not fit (in accordance with the Divine plan), according as it is written (I Sam. xii. 17) : "Is it not wheat-harvest to-day? I will call unto the Lord". 7.And not only that, but He joined fellowship with Moses in every place,as it is written (Ps.xcix.6): "Moses and Aaron among His priests." And again it is written (Jer. xv. i): "Though Moses and Samuel stood before me" (Is. lxiii. 5): "Mine own arm brought salvation unto me". 8.Said the Holy One, blessed be He in that hour: " How long shall Iwait for the children of men to work salvation according to their righteousness for my arm? For my ownsake and for the sake of my merit and righteousness will I deliver my arm and by it redeem mychildren from among the nations of the world. As it is written (Is. xlviii. n): "For my own sake will I do it. For howshould my name be profaned". 9.In that moment will the Holy One, blessed be He, reveal His GreatArm and show it to the nations of the world: for its length is as the length of the world and itsbreadth is as the width of the world. And the appearance of its splendour is like unto the splendour ofthe sunshine in its might, in the summer solstice. 10.Forthwith Israel will be saved from among the nations of the world. And Messiah will appear unto them and He will bring them up to Jerusalem with great joy. And not only that but Israel will come from the four quarters of the World and eat with Messiah. But the nations of the world shall not eat with them, as it is written (Is. Hi. 10): "The Lord hath made barehis holy arm in the eyes of all the nations ; and all the ends of the earth shall see the salvation of ourGod". And again (Deut. xxxii. 12): "The Lord alone did lead him, and there was no strange godwith him". (Zech. xiv. 9) : "And the Lord shall be king over all the earth".

CHAPTER 51

The Divine Names that go forth from the Throne of Glory, crowned and escorted by numerous angelic hosts through the heavens and back again to the Throne the angels sing the 'Holy' and the 'Blessed' 1.These are the seventy-two names written on the heart of the Holy One,blessed be He: SS, SeDeQ {righteousness}, SaHPeL SUR {Is. xxvi. 4}, SBI, SaDdlQ{righteous}, S'Ph, SHN, SeBa'oTh {Lord of Hosts},ShaDdaY {God Almighty}, 'eLoHIM {God}, YHWH, SH,DGUL, W'DOM, SSS", 'YW, 'F, 'HW, HB, YaH, HW, WWW, SSS, PPP, NN, HH, HaY {living},

HaY, ROKeB 'aRaBOTh {riding upon the 'Araboth', Ps. lxviii. 5}, YH, HH, WH, MMM, NNN,HWW, YH, YHH, HPhS, H'S, 'I, W, S", Z', "', QQQ {Holy, Holy, Holy}, QShR, BW, ZK, GINUR,GINURYa', Y', YOD, 'aLePh, H'N, P'P, R'W, YYWy YYW, BBS, DDD, TTT, KKK, KLL, SYS, 'XT', BShKMLW {= blessed be the Name of His glorious kingdom for ever and ever}, completed for MeLeK HaLOLaM {the King of the Universe], JBRH LB' {the beginning of Wisdom for thechildren of men}, BNLK W" Y {blessed be He who gives strength to the weary and increaseth strength to them that have no might, Is. xl. 29}that go forth (adorned) with numerous crowns of fire with numerous crowns of flame, with numerous crowns of chashmal, with numerous crowns of lightning from before the Throne of Glory. And with them (there are) thousand hundreds of power(i.e. powerful angels) who escort them like a king with trembling and dread, with awe and shivering, with honour and majesty andfear, with terror, with greatness and dignity, with glory and strength,with understanding and knowledge and with a pillar of fire and a pillar of flame and lightningand their light is as lightnings of light and with the likeness of the chashmal. 2 And they give glory unto them and they answer and cry before them:Holy, Holy, Holy. And they roll (convoy) them through every heaven as mighty andhonoured princes. And when they bring them all back to the place of the Throne of Glory, then all theChayyoth by the Merkaba open their mouth in praise of His glorious name, saying: "Blessed be the nameof His glorious kingdom for ever and ever".

CHAPTER 52

An Enoch-Metatron pieceALT 1 1."I seized him, and I took him and I appointed him" that is Enoch, theson of Jared, whose name is Metatron 2.and I took him from among the children of men (5) and made him a Throne over against my Throne. Which is the size of that Throne? Seventy thousand parasangs (all) of fire. (9) I committed unto him 70 angels corresponding to the nations (of the world) and I gave into his charge all the household above and below. (7) And I committed to him Wisdom and Intelligence more than (to) allthe angels. And I called his name "the LESSER YAH", whose name is by Gematria 71. And Iarranged for him all the works of Creation. And I made his power to transcend (lit. I made for him powermore than) all the ministering angels. ALT 2 3.He committed unto Metatron that is Enoch, the son of Jared alltreasuries. And I appointed him over all the stores that I have in every heaven. And I committed into hishands the keys of each heavenly store. 4.I made (of) him the prince over all the princes, and I made (of) him aminister of my Throne of Glory, to provide for and arrange the Holy Chayyoth, to wreathe crowns for them (to crown them with crowns), to clothe them with honour and majesty to prepare for thema seat when he is sitting on his throne to magnify his glory in the height. 5.The height of his stature among all those (that are) of high stature (is)seventy thousand parasangs. And I made his glory great as the majesty of my glory. 6.and the brilliance of his eyes as the splendour of the Throne of Glory. 7.his garment honour and majesty, his royal crown 500 by 500parasangs. ALT 3 8.Aleph1 I made him strong, I took him, I appointed him: (namely) Metatron, my servant who is one (unique) among all the children of heaven. I made him strong in thegeneration of the first Adam. But when I beheld the men of the generation of the flood, that theywere corrupt, then I went and removed my Shekina from among them. And 1 lifted it up on highwith the sound of a trumpet and with a shout, as it is written (Ps.xlvii. 6): "God is gone up with ashout, the Lord with the sound of a trumpet". 9."And I took him": (that is) Enoch, the son of Jared, from among them. And I lifted him up with the sound of a trumpet and with a tera'a (shout) to the high heavens, to be my witness together with the Chayyoth by the

Merkaba in the world to come. 10.I appointed him over all the treasuries and stores that I have in every heaven. And I committed into his hand the keys of every several one. 11.I made (of) him the prince over all the princes and a minister of theThrone of Glory (and) the Halls of 'Araboth: to open their doors to me, and (of) the Throne ofGlory, to exalt an arrange it; (and I appointed him over) the Holy Chayyot to wreathe crowns upontheir heads; the majestic 'Ophannim, to crown them with strength and glory; the; honouredKerubim, to clothe: them in majesty; over the radiant sparks, to make them to shine with splendourand brilliance; over the flaming Seraphim, to cover them with highness; the Chashmallim of light, to make them radiant with Light and to prepare the seat for me every morning as I sit upon theThrone of Glory. And to extol and magnify my glory inthe height of my power; (and I havecommitted unto him) the secrets of above and the secrets of below (heavenly secrets and earthly secrets). 12.I made him higher than all. The height of his stature, in the midst ofall (who are) high of stature (I made) seventy thousand parasangs. I made his Throne great by themajesty of my Throne. And I increased its glory by the honour of my glory. 13.I transformed his flesh into torches of fire, and all the bones of hisbody into fiery coals; and I made the appearance of his eyes as the lightning, and the light of hiseyebrows as the imperishable light. I made his face bright as the splendour of the sun, and his eyes asthe splendour of the Throne of Glory. 14.I made honour and majesty his clothing, beauty and highness hiscovering cloak and a royal crown of 500 by (times) 500 parasangs (his) diadem. And I put upon himof my honour, my majesty and the splendour. of my glory that is upon my Throne of Glory. I calledhim the LESSER YHWH, the Prince of the Presence, the Knower of Secrets: for every secret did Ireveal to him as a father and all mysteries declared I unto him in uprightness. 15.I set up his throne at the door of my Hall that he may sit and judge theheavenly household on high. And I placed every prince before him, to receive authority from him, to perform his will. 16.Seventy names did I take from (my) names and called him by them toenhance his glory. Seventy princes gave I into his hand, to command unto them my preceptsand my words in every language: to abase by his word the proud to the ground, and to exalt by theutterance of his lips the humble to the height ; to smite kings by his speech, to turn kings away from theirpaths, to set up(the) rulers over their dominion as it is written (Dan.ii. 21): "and he changeth thetimes and the seasons, and to give wisdom unto all the setwise of the world and understanding (and)knowledge to all who understand knowledge, as it is griten (Dan. ii. 21): " and knowledge tothem that know understanding", to reveal to them the secrets of my words and to teachthe decree of my righteous judgement, 17.as it is written (Is.lv. n): "so shall my word be that goeth forth out ofmy mouth; it shall not return unto me void but shall accomplish (that which I please)". 'E'eseh' (I shall accomplish) is not written here, but "asdh' (he shall accomplish), meaning, that whatever word and whatever utterance goes forth from before the Holy One, blessed be He, Metatron stands and carries it out. And he establishes the decrees of the Holy One, blessed be He.

CHAPTER 53

The names of Metatron. The treasuries of Wisdom opened to Moses on mount Sinai. The angels protest against Metatron for revealing the secrets to Moses and are answered and rebuked byGod. The chain of tradition and the power of the transmitted mysteries to heal diseases 1.Seventy names has Metatron which the Holy One, blessed be He, tookfrom his own name and put upon him. And these they are: YeHOEL, YaH, YeHOEL, YOPHIEL and Yophphiel, and 'APHPHIEL and MaRGeZIEL, GIPpUYEL, Pa'aZIEL, 'A'aH, PeRIEL, TaTRIEL, TaBKIEL,'W, YHWH, DH, WHYH, 'eBeD, DiBbURIEL, 'aPh'aPIEL, SPPIEL, PaSPaSIEL, SeNeGRON, MeTaTRON, SOGDIN, 'ADRIGON, ASUM, SaQPaM, SaQTaM, MIGON MITTON, MOTTRON, ROSPHIM, QINOTh, ChaTaTYaH, DeGaZYaH, PSPYaH, BSKNYH, MZRG, BaRaD.., MKRKK, MSPRD, ChShG, ChShB, MNRTTT, BSYRYM, MITMON, TITMON, PiSQON, SaPhSaPhYaH, ZRCh, ZRChYaH, B', BeYaH, HBH BeYaH, PeLeT, PLTYaH, RaBRaBYaH, ChaS, ChaSYaH, TaPhTaPhYaH, TaMTaMYaH, SeHaSYaH, IRURYaH, 'aL'aLYaH, BaZRIDYaH, SaTSaTKYaH, SaSDYaH, RaZRaZYAH, BaZRaZYAH, 'aRIMYaH, SBHYaH, SBIBKHYH, SiMKaM, YaHSeYaH, SSBIBYaH, SaBKaSBeYaH, QeLILQaLYaH, fKIHHH, HHYH, WH, WHYH, ZaKklKYaH, TUTRISYaH, SURYaH, ZeH, PeNIRHYaH, Z1Z'H, GaL RaZaYYa, MaMLIKYaH, TTYaH, eMeQ, QaMYaH, MeKaPpeRYaH, PeRISHYaH, SePhaM, GBIR, GiBbORYaH, GOR, GORYaH, ZIW, 'OKBaR, the LESSER YHWH, after the name of his Master, (Ex. xxiii. 21) "for my name is in him", RaBIBIEL, TUMIEL, Segansakkiel ('Sagnezagiel' / 'Neganzegael), the Prince of Wisdom. 2.And why is he called by the name Sagnesakiel? Because all the treasuries of wisdom are committed in his hand. 3.And all of them were opened to Moses on Sinai, so that he learnt themduring the forty days, while he was standing (remaining}: the Torah in the seventy aspects ofthe seventy tongues, the Prophets in the seventy aspects of the seventy tongues, the Writings in the seventy aspects of the seventy tongues, "the Halakas in the seventy aspects of the seventy tongues, the Traditions in the seventy aspects of the seventy tongues, the Haggadas in the seventy aspects of the seventy tongues and the Toseftas in the seventy aspects of the seventy tongues'. 4.But as soon as the forty days were ended, he forgot all of them in onemoment. Then the Holy One, blessed be He, called Yephiphyah, the Prince of the Law, and (through him) they were given to Moses as a gift. As it is written (Deut. x. 4): "and the Lord gave them unto me". And after that it remained with him. And whence do we know, that it remained (in his memory) ? Because it is written (Mai. iv. 4): " Remember ye the Law of Moses my servant which I commanded unto him in Horeb for all Israel, even my statutes and judgements". The Law ofMoses': that is the Tora, the Prophets and the Writings, 'statutes': that is the Halakas and Traditions,'judgements'; that is the Haggadas and the Toseftas. And all of them were given to Moses on high on Sinai. 5.These seventy names (are) a reflection of the Explicit Name(s) on theMerkaba which are graven upon the Throne of Glory. For the Holy One, blessed be He, took fromHis Explicit Name(s) and put upon the name of Metatron: Seventy Names of His by which theministering angels call the King of the kings of kings, blessed be He, in the high heavens, and twenty-two letters that are on the ring upon his finger with which are sealed the destinies of the princes ofkingdoms on high in greatness and power and with which are sealed the lots of the Angel of Death, andthe destinies of every nation and tongue. 6.Said Metatron, the Angel, the Prince of the Presence; the Angel, thePrince of the Wisdom; the Angel, the Prince of the Understanding; the Angel, the Prince of theKings; the Angel, the Prince of the Rulers; the angel, the Prince of the Glory; the angel, the Prince of thehigh ones, and of the princes, the exalted, great and honoured ones, in heaven and on earth: 7."H, the God of Israel, is my witness in this thing, {that] when Irevealed this secret to Moses, then all the hosts in every heaven on high raged against me and said to me: 8.Why dost thou reveal this secret to son of man, born of woman, tainted and unclean, a man of a putrefying drop, the secret by which were created heaven and earth, thesea and the dry land, the mountains and hills, the rivers and springs, Gehenna of fire and hail, theGarden of Eden and the Tree of Life; and by which were formed Adam and Eve, and the cattle, and the wild beasts, and the fowl of the air, and the fish of the sea, and Behemoth and Leviathan, and the creeping things, the worms, the dragons of the sea, and the creeping things of the deserts; andthe Tora and Wisdom and Knowledge and Thought and the Gnosis of things above and the fear ofheaven. Why dost thou reveal this to flesh and blood? I answered them: Because the Holy One, blessed be He, has given meauthority, And furthermore, I have obtained permission from the high and exalted Throne, from whichall the Explicit Names go forth with lightnings of fire and flaming chashmallim. 9.But they were not appeased, until the Holy One, blessed be He,rebuked them and drove them away with rebuke from before him, saying to them: "I delight in, and have set my love on, and have entrusted and committed unto Metatron, my Servant, alone, for he is One(unique) among all the children of heaven. 10.And Metatron brought them out from his house of treasuries andcommitted them to Moses, and Moses to Joshua, and Joshua to the elders, and the elders to the prophetsand the prophets to the men of the Great Synagogue, and the men of the Great Synagogue to Ezra andEzra the Scribe to Hillel the elder, and Hillel the elder to R. Abbahu and R. Abbahu to R. Zera,and R. Zera to the men of faith, and the men of faith (committed them) to give warning and to heal by them all diseases that rage in the world, as it is written (Ex. xv. 26): "If thou wilt diligentlyhearken to the voice of the Lord, thy God, and wilt do that which is right in his eyes, and wilt give ear to his commandments, and keep all his statutes, I will put none of the diseases upon thee, which I have put upon the Egyptians : for I am the Lord, that healeth thee". (Ended and finished. Praise be unto the Creator of the World.) Humanity. The priest.

87. Jubilees

Jubilees 1

And it came to pass in the first year of the exodus of the children of Israel out of Egypt, in the third month, on the sixteenth day of the month [2450 Anno Mundi], that God spoke to Moses, saying, "Come up to Me on the Mount, and I will give thee two tables of stone of the law and of the commandment, which I have written, that thou mayst teach them." Moses went up into the mount of God, and the glory of the Lord abode on Mount Sinai, and a cloud overshadowed it for six days. On the seventh day, He called to Moses out of the midst of the cloud, and the appearance of the glory of the Lord was like a flaming fire on the top of the mount. Moses was on the Mount for forty days and forty nights, and God taught him the earlier and the later history of the division of all the days of the law and of the testimony He said, "Incline thine heart to every word which I shall speak to thee on this mount, and write them in a book, in order that their generations may see how I have not forsaken them for all the evil which they have wrought in transgressing the covenant which I establish between Me and thee for their generations this day on Mount Sinai. Thus it will come to pass when all these things come upon them, that they will recognize that I am more righteous than they in all their judgments and in all their actions, and they will recognize that I have been truly with them. Write for thyself all these words which I declare unto thee this day, for I know their rebellion and their stiff neck, before I bring them into the land of which I swore to their fathers, to Abraham and to Isaac and to Jacob, saying, 'Unto your seed will I give a land flowing with milk and honey.' They will eat and be satisfied, and they will turn to strange gods, gods which cannot deliver them from aught of their tribulation: and this witness shall be heard for a witness against them. For they will forget all My commandments, even all that I command them, and they will walk after the Gentiles, and after their uncleanness, and after their shame, and will serve their gods, and these will prove unto them an offence and a tribulation and an affliction and a snare. Many will perish and they will be taken captive, and will fall into the hands of the enemy, because they have forsaken My ordinances and My commandments, and the festivals of My covenant, and My sabbaths, and My holy place which I have hallowed for Myself in their midst, and My tabernacle, and My sanctuary, which I have hallowed for Myself in the midst of the land, that I should set My name upon it, and that it should dwell there. They will make to themselves high places and groves and graven images, and they will worship each his own graven image, so as to go astray, and they will sacrifice their children to demons, and to all the works of the error of their hearts I will send witnesses unto them, that I may witness against them, but they will not hear, and will slay the witnesses also, and they will persecute those who seek the law, and they will abrogate and change everything so as to work evil before My eyes. I will hide My face from them, and I will deliver them into the hand of the Gentiles for captivity, and for a prey, and for devouring, and I will remove them from the midst of the land, and I will scatter them amongst the Gentiles. They will forget all My law and all My commandments and all My judgments, and will go astray as to new moons, and sabbaths, and festivals, and jubilees, and ordinances. After this, they will turn to Me from amongst the Gentiles with all their heart and with all their soul and with all their strength, and I will gather them from amongst all the Gentiles, and they will seek Me, so that I shall be found of them, when they seek Me with all their heart and with all their soul. I will disclose to them abounding peace with righteousness, and I will remove from them the plant of uprightness, with all My heart and with all My soul, and they shall be for a blessing and not for a curse, and they shall be the head and not the tail. I will build My sanctuary in their midst, and I will dwell with them, and I will be their God and they shall be My people in truth and righteousness. I will not forsake them nor fail them; for I am the Lord their God." Moses fell on his face and prayed, "O Lord my God, do not forsake Thy people and Thy inheritance, so that they should wander in the error of their hearts, and do not deliver them into the hands of their enemies, the Gentiles, lest they should rule over them and cause them to sin against Thee. Let Thy mercy, O Lord, be lifted up upon Thy people, and create in them an upright spirit, and let not the spirit of Belial rule over them to accuse them before Thee, and to ensnare them from all the paths of righteousness, so that they may perish from before Thy face. But they are Thy people and Thy inheritance, which Thou hast delivered with Thy great power from the hands of the Egyptians: create in them a clean heart and a holy spirit, and let them not be ensnared in their sins from henceforth until eternity." The Lord said unto Moses, "I know their contrariness and their thoughts and their stiff-neckedness, and they will not be obedient till they confess their own sin and the sin of their fathers. After this they will turn to Me in all uprightness and with all their heart and with all their soul, and I will circumcise the foreskin of their heart and the foreskin of the heart of their seed, and I will create in them a holy spirit, and I will cleanse them so that they shall not turn away from Me from that day unto eternity. Their souls will cleave to Me and to all My commandments, and they will fulfill My commandments, and I will be their Father and they shall be My children. They all shall be called children of the living God, and every angel and every spirit shall know, yea, they shall know that these are My children, and that I am their Father in uprightness and righteousness, and that I love them. Write down for thyself all these words which I declare unto thee on this mountain, the first and the last, which shall come to pass in all the divisions of the days in the law and in the testimony and in the weeks and the jubilees unto eternity, until I descend and dwell with them throughout eternity." He said to the angel of the presence, "Write for Moses from the beginning of creation till My sanctuary has been built among them for all eternity." The Lord will appear to the eyes of all, and all shall know that I am the God of Israel and the Father of all the children of Jacob, and King on Mount Zion for all eternity. Zion and Jerusalem shall be holy. And the angel of the presence who went before the camp of Israel took the tables of the divisions of the years—from the time of the creation—of the law and of the testimony of the weeks of the jubilees, according to the individual years, from the day of the new creation when the heavens and the earth shall be renewed and all their creation according to the powers of the heaven, and according to all the creation of the earth, until the sanctuary of the Lord shall be made in Jerusalem on Mount Zion, and all the luminaries be renewed for healing and for peace and for blessing for all the elect of Israel, and that thus it may be from that day and unto all the days of the earth **Jubilees 2**

And the angel of the presence spoke to Moses according to the word of the Lord, saying, "Write the complete history of the creation, how in six days the Lord God finished all His works and all that He created, and kept Sabbath on the seventh day and hallowed it for all ages, and appointed it as a sign for all His works. On the first day He created the heavens which are above, and the earth and the waters and all the spirits which serve before Him—the angels of the presence, and the angels of sanctification, and the angels of the spirit of fire and the angels of the spirit of the winds, and the angels of the spirit of the clouds, and of darkness, and of snow and of hail and of hoar frost, and the angels of the voices and of the thunder and of the lightning, and the angels of the spirits of cold and of heat, and of winter and of spring and of autumn and of summer, and of all the spirits of His creatures which are in the heavens and on the earth. He created the abysses and the darkness, eventide and night, and the light, dawn and day, which He has prepared in the knowledge of His heart. We saw His works, and praised Him, and lauded Him on account of all His works; for seven great works did He create on the first day On the second day, He created the firmament in the midst of the waters, and the waters were divided on that day—half of them went up above and half of them went down below the firmament (that was) in the midst over the face of the whole earth. And this was the only work God created on the second day. On the third day, He commanded the waters to pass from off the face of the whole earth into one place, and the dry land to appear. And the waters did so as He commanded them, and the dry land appeared, and the waters gathered themselves together into one place, and the dry land appeared. And the Lord called the dry land earth, and the gathering together of the waters He called seas. And He sanctified them, and thereupon He made all the trees to grow, and every plant of the earth, and the trees which are in the garden of Eden, in the place of the paradise of God, where He had planted it, for there was no man to till the ground, and the Lord took the man and placed him in the garden of Eden to tend it and to keep it. And He made every tree grow that is pleasant to the sight and good for food; and He placed the tree of life in the midst of the garden, and the tree of knowledge of good and evil. And the tree of life, and the tree of knowledge of good and evil, in the midst of the garden. And He commanded the man and said, "Of every tree of the garden thou mayst freely eat, but of the tree of the knowledge of good and evil thou shalt not eat thereof, for in the day that thou eatest thereof thou shalt surely die." And the Lord knew that Adam and Eve would eat of the tree, and He knew the fall of man. And He did not create the tree for Adam and Eve, but He created it for the sake of the angels and the spirits that were to come And the Lord commanded that the angel of the Lord should be in the garden of Eden to guard and to keep the way of the tree of life and of the knowledge of good and evil, and all the angels of the spirits should come unto Adam and Eve in the garden of Eden. And the Lord commanded the angels that they should guard the tree of life, and the tree of knowledge of good and evil, and that they should guard the way of the tree of life and that the angels should guard it, and should keep the way of the tree of life. And the Lord knew that Adam and Eve would not keep the way of the tree of life. And the tree of the knowledge of good and evil, which is in the midst of the garden, and of the tree of life, which is at the end of the garden On the fourth day, He created the sun and the moon and the stars and the firmament of the heaven, and the angels of the firmament, and the spirits of the sun and the moon, and the spirits of the stars. And all the spirits of the firmament, and all the spirits of the luminaries, which are in the heavens, and which are in the earth, were created on the fourth day On the fifth day, He created all the living creatures which are in the waters, and the fowl of the heavens, and every beast, and all the living creatures, and every creeping thing that creepeth on the earth, and all the living creatures that are on the earth. And He created them on the fifth day, and all the living creatures that are in the waters, and all the fowl of the heavens, and all the beasts of the earth, and all the creeping things that creep on the earth. And He created all the living creatures on the fifth day, and all the beasts of the earth on the sixth day. And the animals and the living creatures that creep on the earth, and the fowl of the heavens, and all the beasts of the earth On the sixth day, He created man, male and female, and He commanded them to be fruitful and multiply and fill the earth. And the Lord saw all the works that He had created, and He saw that they were very good. And the Lord made all things in six days, and on the seventh day He rested from all His work, and He hallowed it, and sanctified it, and set it apart from all His works, and He blessed it. And He said, "This is the end of the work which I have created for My own sake, and that thou mayst know that I have created it all. In the six days, I have created all things, and on the seventh day, I have sanctified it, and I have sanctified it from all My works. This day is blessed and holy and great among all the days of the world, and thou shalt keep it, and shall not do any work on it, and thou shalt rest in it, and thou shalt do all the work of the days of the world on the sixth day." The Lord spoke to Moses, saying, "Write down these words which I speak unto thee, and make known unto the children of Israel the great and mighty works which I have done for them, and the laws and ordinances which I have given them, that they may observe them all the days of their lives. For I am the Lord who created the heavens and the earth, and I have given unto thee the law and the commandment, and thou shalt teach them unto thy children, and unto all the children of Israel, for I am the Lord their God."

Jubilees 3

And in the second year of the exodus of the children of Israel from Egypt, in the third month, on the sixteenth day of the month, the Lord spoke to Moses on Mount Sinai, saying, "Come up to Me on the mountain, and I will give thee the tablets of stone on which I have written the commandments and the law. And I will give thee the book of the law and the testimony, and thou shalt teach them unto the children of Israel, that they may observe all the commandments which I have given unto thee." Moses went up to the mountain, and the glory of the Lord covered the mountain for six days. And on the seventh day, the Lord called to Moses out of the midst of the cloud. And the appearance of the glory of the Lord was like a flaming fire on the top of the mountain. And Moses was on the mountain forty days and forty nights, and the Lord spoke unto him concerning the earlier and the later history of the days of the law and the testimony The Lord said unto

Moses, "Write down for thyself all the words which I shall speak unto thee on this mountain, and write them in a book for a memorial for the children of Israel, that they may keep the commandments and the laws which I have given them, and that they may know how I have not forsaken them for all the evil which they have done against Me. For they will turn to strange gods and serve them, and they will forget all My commandments, and they will walk after the Gentiles and their uncleanness. And they will create high places and groves and images and will sacrifice their children to demons and the works of the error of their hearts And I will send witnesses unto them, but they will not hear, and they will kill the witnesses and persecute those who seek the law, and they will change everything to work evil before Me. I will hide My face from them, and I will deliver them into the hands of their enemies, and I will scatter them among the nations. They will forget all My laws, and My commandments, and My festivals, and My sabbaths, and My holy place, and they will turn away from Me After this, they will turn to Me from among the Gentiles with all their heart and soul, and I will gather them from among all the nations, and they will seek Me, and I will be found of them. I will disclose to them abounding peace with righteousness, and I will remove the plant of uprightness from them, and they shall be a blessing and not a curse. They shall be the head and not the tail. I will build My sanctuary among them, and I will dwell with them, and I will be their God, and they shall be My people. I will not forsake them nor fail them, for I am the Lord their God." Moses fell on his face and prayed, "O Lord my God, do not forsake Thy people and Thy inheritance. Do not deliver them into the hands of their enemies, but let Thy mercy be upon them. Create in them a clean heart and a holy spirit, and let them not be ensnared in their sins." The Lord said to Moses, "I know their contrariness and their thoughts and their stiff-neckedness. They will not be obedient till they confess their sins and the sins of their fathers. After this, they will turn to Me in all uprightness, and I will circumcise the foreskin of their heart, and I will create in them a holy spirit. They shall be My people, and I will be their God. Write down all these words, the first and the last, which shall come to pass in all the divisions of the days in the law and the testimony, and in the weeks and the jubilees unto eternity." The angel of the presence took the tables of the divisions of the years—from the time of creation—of the law and testimony of the weeks of the jubilees, and of all the divisions of the days, until the sanctuary of the Lord would be built in Jerusalem on Mount Zion, and all the luminaries would be renewed for healing, peace, and blessing for the elect of Israel

Jubilees 4
And in the days of Amram, the father of Moses, there was a great famine in the land of Canaan. And the famine was very severe, and there was no food for the people of the land. And they went into Egypt to buy food. And the children of Israel were delivered from the famine and went to Egypt And the Lord commanded them to go into the land of Goshen, and they settled there. And they were fruitful and multiplied greatly in Egypt, and their number increased exceedingly. And the people of Egypt became afraid of them, and they made them serve with rigor and placed taskmasters over them. They made their lives bitter with hard service in mortar and brick and with all kinds of work in the field And the king of Egypt called for the midwives who were assisting the Hebrew women and commanded them, saying, "When you help the Hebrew women give birth, if it is a son, kill him; but if it is a daughter, let her live." But the midwives feared God and did not do as the king of Egypt commanded them. They saved the male children alive Then the king of Egypt called for the midwives and said to them, "Why have you done this thing, and have saved the male children alive?" The midwives answered Pharaoh,

"Because the Hebrew women are not like the Egyptian women; they are vigorous and give birth before the midwife comes to them." So God dealt well with the midwives, and the people multiplied and grew very mighty. And because the midwives feared God, He gave them households. And Pharaoh commanded all his people, saying, "Every son that is born you shall cast into the river, and every daughter you shall save alive." At that time, Amram took Jochebed, his wife, and she conceived and bore a son. And when she saw that he was a beautiful child, she hid him for three months. And when she could no longer hide him, she took for him an ark of bulrushes and daubed it with bitumen and pitch, and put the child in it, and laid it among the reeds by the river's bank And his sister stood afar off to know what would be done to him. And the daughter of Pharaoh came down to bathe at the river, and her maidens walked along the riverbank. And when she saw the ark among the reeds, she sent her maid to get it. When she opened it, she saw the child, and behold, the baby wept. And she had compassion on him and said, "This is one of the Hebrew's children." Then his sister said to Pharaoh's daughter, "Shall I go and call a nurse from the Hebrew women to nurse the child for you?" Pharaoh's daughter said to her, "Go." And the maid went and called the child's mother. Pharaoh's daughter said to her, "Take this child away and nurse him for me, and I will give you your wages." And the woman took the child and nursed him And the child grew, and she brought him to Pharaoh's daughter, and he became her son. And she called his name Moses, and said, "Because I drew him out of the water." And it came to pass in those days, when Moses had grown up, that he went out to his brethren and looked on their burdens. And he saw an Egyptian smiting a Hebrew, one of his brethren. And he looked this way and that way, and when he saw that there was no man, he killed the Egyptian and hid him in the sand. And he went out the second day, and behold, two Hebrew men were fighting. And he said to the wrongdoer, "Why do you strike your companion?" And he said, "Who made you a prince and a judge over us? Do you intend to kill me as you killed the Egyptian?" And Moses was afraid and said, "Surely this thing is known." When Pharaoh heard of this matter, he sought to kill Moses. But Moses fled from the face of Pharaoh and dwelt in the land of Midian. And he sat down by a well Now the priest of Midian had seven daughters, and they came and drew water and filled the troughs to water their father's flock. And the shepherds came and drove them away. And Moses stood up and helped them and watered their flock. And when they came to Reuel their father, he said, "How is it that you have come so soon today?" They said, "An Egyptian delivered us from the hand of the shepherds and also drew water enough for us and watered the flock." And he said to his daughters, "Where is he? Why is it that you have left the man? Call him, that he may eat bread." And Moses was content to dwell with the man, and he gave Moses his daughter Zipporah to wife. And she bore him a son, and he called his name Gershom, for he said, "I have been a sojourner in a foreign land." And it came to pass in the course of those many days that the king of Egypt died. And the children of Israel sighed by reason of the bondage, and they cried, and their cry came up unto God by reason of the bondage. And God heard their groaning, and God remembered His covenant with Abraham, with Isaac, and with Jacob. And God saw the children of Israel, and God took notice of them

Jubilees 5
When the children of men began to multiply on the face of the earth and daughters were born to them, the angels of God observed their beauty during a certain year of this jubilee. They took wives from among them, choosing any they desired, and bore sons who became giants. 2. Lawlessness increased on the earth, corrupting all flesh—men, cattle,

beasts, birds, and everything that walks upon the earth. They began to devour one another, and the imagination of the thoughts of all men was continually evil. 3. God observed the earth and saw that it was corrupt; all flesh had corrupted its ways, and all who were upon the earth had committed all kinds of evil in His sight. 4. He decided to destroy mankind and all flesh upon the earth that He had created. 5. However, Noah found grace in the eyes of the Lord. 6. God was exceedingly angry with the angels He had sent to the earth, commanding them to be rooted out of their dominion and bound in the depths of the earth. They remain bound until the day of the great condemnation when judgment is executed on those who have corrupted their ways and works. 7. A command went forth against their sons, ordering that they should be smitten with the sword and removed from under heaven. 8. God declared, "My spirit shall not always strive with man, for they are also flesh, and their days shall be one hundred and twenty years." 9. He sent a sword among them so that each should slay his neighbor, resulting in mutual destruction until they all fell by the sword and were destroyed from the earth. 10. Their fathers witnessed their destruction, and they were bound in the depths of the earth until the day of judgment. 11. God destroyed everything according to their wickedness, leaving not a single one unjudged. 12. He made a new and righteous nature for all His works, so they would not sin but be righteous in their kinds forever. 13. The judgment of all is ordained and written on the heavenly tablets, including those who depart from the ordained path. 14. Everything in heaven, on earth, in light, darkness, Sheol, or the depths is judged, with judgments written and engraved. 15. He judges the great according to their greatness and the small according to their smallness. 16. God does not regard the person or accept gifts; He is a righteous judge. 17. Of the children of Israel, it is written and ordained that if they turn to Him in righteousness, He will forgive all their transgressions and pardon their sins. 18. It is ordained that He will show mercy to those who turn from guilt once each year. 19. For those who corrupted their ways before the flood, no person's plea was accepted except Noah's. His plea was accepted for his sons whom God saved from the flood because Noah was righteous and had adhered to the commandments. 20. God said He would destroy everything on the earth, including men, cattle, beasts, fowls, and all that moves on the earth. He commanded Noah to build an ark to save himself from the floodwaters. 21. Noah made the ark as commanded, in the twenty-seventh jubilee, in the fifth week of the fifth year, on the new moon of the first month. 22. He entered the ark in the sixth year thereof, in the second month, on the new moon, and remained inside until the sixteenth. The Lord closed the ark from the outside on the seventeenth evening. 23. The Lord opened the seven flood-gates of heaven and the seven fountains of the great deep. 24. The floodgates poured down water for forty days and forty nights, and the fountains of the deep sent up water, filling the whole world. 25. The waters increased upon the earth, rising fifteen cubits above all the high mountains, lifting the ark above the earth. 26. The waters prevailed on the earth for five months, one hundred and fifty days. 27. The ark rested on the top of Lubar, one of the Ararat mountains. 28. On the new moon of the fourth month, the fountains of the deep were closed, and the floodgates of heaven were restrained. On the new moon of the seventh month, the abysses of the earth opened, and the water began to descend. 29. On the new moon of the tenth month, the tops of the mountains were seen, and on the new moon of the first month, the earth became visible. 30. The waters disappeared in the fifth week of the seventh year, and on the seventeenth day of the second month, the earth was dry. 31. On the twenty-seventh day, Noah opened the ark, sending forth beasts, cattle, birds, and every moving thing

Jubilees 6

On the new moon of the third month, Noah went forth from the ark and built an altar on the mountain where the ark had rested. 2. He made atonement for the earth with a kid, using its blood to atone for all the guilt of the earth. He placed the fat on the altar, and offered an ox, a goat, a sheep, kids, salt, a turtle-dove, and the young of a dove as burnt sacrifices. He poured an offering mingled with oil, sprinkled wine, and strewed frankincense over everything, causing a pleasing aroma to rise to the Lord. 3. The Lord smelled the goodly aroma and made a covenant with Noah that there would never again be a flood to destroy the earth. Seed-time and harvest, cold and heat, summer and winter, and day and night would not cease. 4. God commanded Noah and his sons to increase and multiply upon the earth, becoming many and a blessing upon it. He promised to inspire fear and dread in everything on earth and in the sea. 5. He gave them all beasts, winged things, moving creatures, and fish in the waters for food, just as He had given green herbs. However, they were not to eat flesh with the blood, as the life of all flesh is in the blood. The blood of man would be required at the hand of every man and beast. 6. Whosoever sheds man's blood, by man shall his blood be shed, for man is made in the image of God. 7. Noah and his sons swore not to eat any blood and made a covenant before the Lord God forever throughout all generations. 8. They were commanded to observe this covenant by not eating blood of beasts, birds, or cattle. Anyone who does will be rooted out of the land. 9. Command the children of Israel to observe this law continually, so that their names and their seed may be before the Lord our God. 10. This law has no limit of days; it is forever. The Israelites are to observe it throughout their generations. 11. The Lord gave Noah a sign of the eternal covenant by setting His bow in the cloud to indicate that there would not be another flood. 12. It is ordained and written on the heavenly tablets to celebrate the feast of weeks once a year in this month to renew the covenant. 13. This festival was celebrated in heaven from creation until Noah—twenty-six jubilees and five weeks of years. Noah and his sons observed it for seven jubilees and one week, until Noah's death. His sons discontinued it until the days of Abraham, who observed it. Isaac, Jacob, and his children kept it until your days, and now the children of Israel have celebrated it anew. 14. Command the children of Israel to observe this festival in all generations, one day each year in this month. It is the feast of weeks and first fruits, celebrated according to what is written and engraven. 15. It is written in the book of the first law that you should celebrate it in its season, one day each year, and I have explained its sacrifices. 16. On the new moon of the first, fourth, seventh, and tenth months are the days of remembrance and seasons in the four divisions of the year. These are written and ordained as a testimony forever. 17. Noah ordained these festivals as memorials for himself, and they are preserved as feasts throughout the generations. 18. On the new moon of the first month, Noah was commanded to build the ark, and on that day, the earth became dry, and he saw the earth. 19. On the new moon of the fourth month, the depths of the abyss were closed. On the new moon of the seventh month, the abysses opened, and waters descended. On the new moon of the tenth month, the tops of the mountains were seen, and Noah rejoiced. 20. Noah established these festivals as memorials, and they were recorded on the heavenly tablets, with each having thirteen weeks from one to another. The entire year will be complete with fifty-two weeks, as engraven and ordained on the heavenly tablets. 21. There is no neglecting this commandment; the year must be three hundred and sixty-four days, constituting a complete year. Any deviation will disturb the seasons, causing neglect of ordinances. 22. The children of Israel will forget the path of the years, new moons, seasons, and sabbaths, leading to confusion and error in their observance of time. 23. This declaration is not of my own devising but is written on the heavenly tablets to prevent such errors. 24. Those who observe the moon may disturb the seasons, causing years to misalign and resulting in abominable days and confusion of holy and unclean days. 25. For those who do not observe the commandments will be rooted out, and the generations will suffer. 26. I have ordained and written on the heavenly tablets that the moon will not deviate from its position but will observe the seasons, which are in alignment with its command. 27. It is written that the sun will complete its course, beginning from one new moon and ending at another, according to its commanded course. 28. The moon will observe the proper months, days, and years, ensuring the observance of Sabbaths, festivals, and feasts. 29. This law is eternal, and any deviation will result in judgment. It is commanded and written that they will obey these laws, as observed throughout their generations

Jubilees 7

In the twenty-ninth jubilee, the first week, the first year, Abram was born. Terach, his father, was a Chaldean and lived in the land of the Chaldeans. 2. Abram, also known as Abram, was born to Terach, who had two brothers—Nahor and Haran. 3. Terach served idols, and Abram's family worshiped them, as the whole earth was filled with idol worship. 4. Abram was called by God, who commanded him to leave his father's house and the city of his birth to go to a land that He would show him. 5. Abram obeyed and left with his wife, Sarai, and his nephew, Lot. 6. They journeyed to Haran and stayed there until Terach's death. 7. After Terach's death, Abram, Sarai, and Lot continued to the land of Canaan as instructed. 8. Abram, whose name was changed to Abraham, was promised by God that his descendants would inherit the land and become numerous. 9. Abraham's faithfulness and obedience led to God's blessing and covenant with him and his seed. 10. In the fourth year of the second jubilee, the Lord appeared to Abram and made a covenant with him, promising to give his seed the land. 11. Abram built an altar in Canaan and offered sacrifices to God, who revealed the future of his descendants and their trials in Egypt. 12. Abram's faith and obedience were tested, and he was assured that God would be with him and his descendants, ensuring their prosperity and blessing. 13. Abram's journey from idolatry to a monotheistic belief marked a significant transformation and established a foundation for the faith of his descendants

Jubilees 8

In the twenty-ninth jubilee, during the first week, Arpachshad took a wife named Rasu'eja, the daughter of Susan from Elam. She bore him a son named Kainam in the third year of this week. 2. Kainam grew up, learned writing from his father, and sought a place to establish a city. 3. He discovered ancient writings on a rock, which were teachings of the Watchers about observing celestial omens. He copied these writings but kept them secret, fearing Noah's disapproval. 4. In the thirtieth jubilee, during the second week's first year, Kainam married Melka, the daughter of Madai from Japheth's line. By the fourth year, they had a son named Shelah. 6. Shelah grew up and married Mu'ak, daughter of Kesed, his uncle. In the fifth year of their marriage, Mu'ak bore a son named Eber. 7. Eber married 'Azûrâd, daughter of Nebrod, in the thirty-second jubilee, seventh week's third year. She bore a son named Peleg. 8. Peleg's name reflected the division of the earth among Noah's children. The division occurred secretly but was revealed to Noah. 10. In the beginning of the thirty-third jubilee, the earth was divided among Shem, Ham, and Japheth. Shem received the middle part of the earth, extending from the mountain range of Rafa to the river Tina, and

encompassing the area from the water of the abysses to the great sea. 13. Shem's portion included all the lands towards the north, south, and west, and the Garden of Eden. 18. Noah rejoiced in Shem's portion and acknowledged it as blessed. 21. For Ham, the second portion was south of the river Gihon, including all the mountains of fire and extending to the seas of 'Atel and Ma'uk. 23. Japheth's third portion was beyond the river Tina, extending north-easterly to Gog's region, and including five great islands and a large northern land. 30. The land of Japheth was cold, while Ham's was hot, and Shem's was temperate

Jubilees 9

Ham divided the land among his sons: Cush received the eastern portion, Mizraim to the west of Cush, Put to the west of Mizraim, and Canaan to the west of Put, including the sea. 2. Shem divided the land among his sons: Ham and his sons received the eastern region of India, the Red Sea coast, and the lands of Dedan, Mebri, Ela, Susan, and the river Tina. 3. Asshur's portion included Asshur, Nineveh, Shinar, and the border of India. 4. Arpachshad's portion included the Chaldees, east of the Euphrates, and the lands bordering the Red Sea. 5. Aram's portion was Mesopotamia between the Tigris and Euphrates, north of the Chaldees. 6. Lud received the mountains of Asshur and the lands extending to the Great Sea. 7. Japheth's sons received their portions: Gomer to the east from the river Tina, Magog to the north, Madai to the west of his brothers, Javan to the islands, Tubal to the region beyond the second tongue, Meshech beyond the third tongue, and Tiras four great islands in the sea. 14. Noah and his sons bound their inheritance by an oath and cursed any who would attempt to seize lands not assigned to them

Jubilees 10

In the third week of this jubilee, unclean demons began leading astray Noah's descendants. 2. Noah prayed to God, asking for protection against these demons. 3. God responded by commanding the binding of the demons, leaving only a tenth part to remain. 4. The chief spirit Mastêmâ pleaded to retain some demons to continue corrupting humanity. 5. God allowed only a tenth to remain, and the rest were imprisoned. 6. Noah recorded the knowledge of medicines and healing, which was passed to Shem. 15. Noah died at the age of 950 and was buried on Mount Lubar. 18. Peleg married Lomna, daughter of Sina'ar, and named his son Reu. During Peleg's time, the people built a city and tower in Shinar to reach heaven. 20. The Lord confused their language, leading to the tower's abandonment and the dispersion of people. 26. The tower's ruins were called 'Overthrow'. 27. Ham and his sons settled in the land south of Shinar, and Canaan settled in Lebanon despite the warnings from his father and brothers. 35. Japheth and his sons settled in their allotted lands, while Madai settled in Media, close to his wife's brother

Jubilees 11

In the thirty-fifth jubilee, during the third week of the first year [1681 A.M.], Reu took a wife named 'Ôrâ, daughter of 'Ûr, son of Kesed. She bore him a son, whom he named Sêrôh, in the seventh year of this week during the jubilee [1687 A.M.]. At that time, the sons of Noah began to wage war against one another, taking captives, killing each other, shedding human blood, and eating blood. They constructed strong cities, walls, and towers, and individuals started to elevate themselves above others, laying the foundations of kingdoms. War began among peoples, nations, and cities, leading to widespread evil. People acquired weapons, taught their sons the art of war, captured cities, and sold both male and female slaves 'Ûr, the son of Kesed, built the city of 'Ara of the Chaldees, naming it after himself and his father. They created molten images and worshipped

678

these idols, making graven images and unclean simulacra, with malignant spirits aiding and leading them into sin and impurity. The prince Mastêmâ worked to encourage this behavior, sending spirits to spread wrongdoings and bloodshed upon the earth. For this reason, he called Sêrôh by the name Serug, as all were turning to sin and transgression Sêrôh grew up and lived in Ur of the Chaldees, near his wife's mother's family, worshipping idols. In the thirty-sixth jubilee, during the fifth week, in the first year thereof [1744 A.M.], he took Melka, the daughter of Kaber, his father's brother's daughter, as his wife. She bore him Nahor in the first year of this week, and he grew up in Ur of the Chaldees. His father taught him the Chaldean arts of divination and augury, according to the signs of heaven In the thirty-seventh jubilee, during the sixth week, in the first year thereof [1800 A.M.], Nahor took a wife named 'Ijaska, daughter of Nestag of the Chaldees. She bore him Terah in the seventh year of this week [1806 A.M.]. Mastêmâ sent ravens and birds to destroy the crops by consuming the seed sown on the land, thus depriving people of their labor. Before the seeds could be planted, the ravens snatched them from the surface. Because of this, Terah was named so due to the ravens reducing them to destitution and devouring their seed. Years became barren due to the birds consuming all fruit, and only with great effort did people manage to save a little of the earth's produce In the thirty-ninth jubilee, during the second week, in the first year thereof [1870 A.M.], Terah took a wife named 'Edna, daughter of 'Abram, his father's sister. She bore him a son in the seventh year of this week [1876 A.M.], and he was named Abram after his maternal grandfather, who had died before she conceived. The child began to understand the errors of the earth, recognizing that people strayed after graven images and uncleanness. His father taught him writing, and at the age of two weeks of years [1890 A.M.], Abram separated himself from his father to avoid worshipping idols Abram began to pray to the Creator of all things, asking for deliverance from human errors and for his portion not to fall into sin. During the sowing season, he joined others to protect their seed from ravens. At the age of fourteen, he managed to turn back clouds of ravens seventy times, preventing them from consuming the seed. This act of bravery made his name great throughout the Chaldean land. People came to him for assistance with sowing, and they managed to harvest enough grain to satisfy their needs In the first year of the fifth week [1891 A.M.], Abram instructed artisans in wood to create vessels for sowing seed, which were mounted on the ploughs. These vessels allowed the seed to fall onto the plough's share and be buried in the earth, eliminating the need to fear ravens. Thus, they were able to sow and till the land effectively

Jubilees 12

In the sixth week, in the seventh year thereof [1904 A.M.], Abram spoke to his father Terah, asking, "Father!" Terah responded, "Behold, here am I, my son." Abram questioned the benefit of worshipping the idols, which had no spirit and were merely misleading forms. He urged his father to worship the God of heaven, who causes rain and dew to descend, creates all things, and is the source of life Terah admitted to knowing the truth but expressed his fear of the people who had made him serve these idols. He feared that speaking the truth might lead to his death, as people were deeply attached to these idols. Abram remained silent, understanding his father's predicament In the fortieth jubilee, during the second week, in the seventh year thereof [1925 A.M.], Abram took Sarai, the daughter of his father, as his wife. Haran, Abram's brother, married in the third year of the third week [1928 A.M.], and she bore him a son named Lot in the seventh year of this week [1932 A.M.]. Nahor, another brother, also took a wife When Abram was sixty years old, during the fourth

week, in the fourth year thereof [1936 A.M.], he arose by night to observe the stars from the evening to the morning to discern the character of the year concerning the rains. He was alone when he received a revelation, realizing that all signs were under the Lord's control. He prayed to God, asking for protection from evil spirits and guidance in the right path The Lord responded by commanding Abram to leave his country, kindred, and father's house for a land that He would show him. The Lord promised to make him a great nation, bless him, and make his name great, with all families of the earth being blessed through him. The Lord also pledged to be a God to Abram and his descendants for all generations. The Lord then opened Abram's mouth and ears to speak and understand Hebrew, the language of creation. Abram took the books of his fathers, written in Hebrew, studied them during the six rainy months, and prepared to leave Haran for Canaan In the seventh year of the sixth week [1953 A.M.], Abram informed his father of his intention to journey to Canaan and return. Terah blessed him and advised him to take Lot with him, leaving Nahor behind until his return

Jubilees 13

Abram journeyed from Haran with Sarai, his wife, and Lot, his brother Haran's son, to the land of Canaan. He arrived at Asshur and then Shechem, where he dwelt near a lofty oak. The land from Hamath to the oak was very pleasant, and the Lord promised to give it to Abram and his seed. Abram built an altar and offered a burnt sacrifice to the Lord, who had appeared to him Abram then moved to the mountain between Bethel on the west and Ai on the east, pitching his tent there. The land was fertile, with a variety of trees and abundant water on the mountains. He blessed the Lord for bringing him out of Ur of the Chaldees to this land In the first year of the seventh week [1954 A.M.], Abram built an altar on this mountain, calling upon the Lord and offering a burnt sacrifice to ensure His continued presence and support. He then traveled south to Hebron, which was newly built at that time, and lived there for two years Due to a famine in the land, Abram went to Egypt in the third year of the week, where he stayed for five years before his wife was taken by Pharaoh. The Lord afflicted Pharaoh and his house with great plagues because of Sarai. Abram acquired great wealth in sheep, cattle, asses, horses, camels, menservants, maidservants, silver, and gold. Pharaoh returned Sarai to Abram and sent him out of Egypt. Abram journeyed back to the place where he had pitched his tent at the beginning, offering a burnt sacrifice and blessing the Lord for bringing him back in peace In the forty-first jubilee, during the third year of the first week [1963 A.M.], Abram returned to his altar and offered a burnt sacrifice, affirming the Lord as his God. In the fourth year of this week [1964 A.M.], Lot separated from Abram and dwelled in Sodom, a city known for its grievous sin. Abram was distressed over Lot's departure, as he had no children of his own When Lot was taken captive, the Lord spoke to Abram, telling him to look in all directions and promising to give him and his seed the land he could see. The Lord also promised to make Abram's seed as numerous as the sand of the sea, with an inheritance that would not be numbered. Abram walked through the land, and the Lord confirmed the promise

Jubilees 14

In the fourth year of the fourth week of this jubilee [1979 A.M.], on the new moon of the third month, the Lord spoke to Abram in a dream, reassuring him, "Fear not, Abram; I am your shield, and your reward will be very great." Abram expressed concern about having no heir and being childless. The Lord promised that Abram would have a son from his own body and his seed would be numerous The Lord also revealed the future to Abram, telling him that his descendants would be strangers in a foreign land, serving there and being afflicted for four hundred years. Afterward, they would come out with great wealth and possess the land of their oppressors. Abram was instructed to bring animals for a covenant ceremony. He divided the animals, laid them out, and the Lord made a covenant with him

Jubilees 15

In the first year of the eighth week [1984 A.M.], Abram was ninety-nine years old, and the Lord appeared to him, changing his name to Abraham, signifying him as the father of many nations. He also changed Sarai's name to Sarah, promising that she would bear a son named Isaac. The Lord made a covenant with Abraham, declaring that He would be the God of his descendants forever, and promised the land from the river of Egypt to the Euphrates to Abraham's seed Abraham was commanded to walk before the Lord blamelessly and to keep the covenant through circumcision. The circumcision of every male was to be a sign of this covenant. Abraham, along with his household and descendants, were to be circumcised on the eighth day. The covenant was thus established, and the Lord reassured Abraham of His promise and faithfulness

Jubilees 16

On the new moon of the fourth month, we appeared to Abraham at the oak of Mamre, spoke with him, and announced that he would have a son by Sarah his wife. Sarah laughed upon hearing this, and we admonished her. Fearful, she denied having laughed, but we revealed that her son would be named Isaac, as ordained and written in the heavenly tablets. We told her that when we returned at a set time, she would conceive a son In this month, the Lord executed judgment upon Sodom, Gomorrah, Zeboim, and the region of the Jordan, burning them with fire and brimstone, destroying them completely. This was a consequence of their wickedness, their sins, and their corruption. God will execute similar judgments on places that mirror the uncleanness of the Sodomites. However, Lot was saved because God remembered Abraham and sent him out of the midst of the destruction Lot and his daughters committed sins unprecedented since Adam's time, as the man lay with his daughters. It was commanded and engraved on the heavenly tablets to remove and root out his descendants, executing judgment upon them as was done to Sodom, leaving no seed of the man on earth by the day of condemnation In this month, Abraham moved from Hebron and dwelt between Kadesh and Shur in the mountains of Gerar. In the middle of the fifth month, he moved to the Well of the Oath. By the middle of the sixth month, the Lord visited Sarah as He had promised, and she conceived. She bore a son in the third month, in the middle of the month, at the time the Lord had spoken to Abraham, during the festival of the first fruits of the harvest. Isaac was born, and Abraham circumcised him on the eighth day, being the first to be circumcised according to the covenant ordained forever In the sixth year of the fourth week, we visited Abraham at the Well of the Oath and found Sarah with child, as we had foretold. We blessed him and announced the things decreed concerning him: that he would not die until he had begotten six more sons and would see them before he died, but that Isaac alone would bear his name and seed. The seed of his other sons would be reckoned among the Gentiles, but from Isaac would come a holy seed, not reckoned among the Gentiles, becoming a portion of the Most High, a people for the Lord's possession above all nations, a kingdom, priests, and a holy nation We announced these things to Sarah, and they both rejoiced with great joy. Abraham built an altar to the Lord, who had delivered him and caused him to rejoice in the land of his sojourning. He celebrated a festival of joy for seven days near the altar he had built at the Well of the Oath, and he built booths for himself and his servants, becoming the first to celebrate the Feast of Tabernacles on earth

During these seven days, he offered a burnt offering of two oxen, two rams, seven sheep, and one he-goat for a sin offering, to atone for himself and his seed. As a thank offering, he brought seven rams, seven kids, seven sheep, and seven he-goats, with their fruit and drink offerings. He burned all the fat on the altar as a chosen offering to the Lord. He also offered morning and evening fragrant substances, such as frankincense, galbanum, stackte, nard, myrrh, and spice, all mixed together in equal parts He celebrated the feast with all his heart and soul, with no strangers or uncircumcised among them. He blessed his Creator who had made him in his generation according to His good pleasure, for He knew and perceived that from him would arise a righteous plant for eternal generations, and a holy seed. Abraham called the festival the Festival of the Lord, a joy acceptable to the Most High God We blessed Abraham and all his seed after him throughout all generations of the earth, for he celebrated this festival in its season, according to the testimony of the heavenly tablets. Thus, it is ordained for Israel to celebrate the Feast of Tabernacles for seven days with joy in the seventh month, as a statute forever throughout their generations. There is no limit to the days, for it is ordained forever for Israel to dwell in booths, set wreaths upon their heads, and take leafy boughs and willows from the brook Abraham took branches of palm trees and fruit from goodly trees, and every day went around the altar with the branches seven times, praising and giving thanks to his God for all things in joy

Jubilees 17

In the first year of the fifth week, Isaac was weaned, and Abraham made a great banquet in the third month on the day his son was weaned. Ishmael, the son of Hagar the Egyptian, was present with Abraham, and Abraham rejoiced, blessing God for seeing his sons and not dying childless. He remembered the words spoken to him on the day Lot had parted from him, and he rejoiced because the Lord had given him seed to inherit the earth Sarah saw Ishmael playing and dancing and became jealous, saying to Abraham, "Cast out this bondwoman and her son; for the son of this bondwoman will not be heir with my son Isaac." This request was grievous to Abraham because of his maidservant and her son. God told Abraham not to be troubled by Sarah's words and to heed her, as Isaac would be the seed through which Abraham's name would be called. However, God promised to make the son of the bondwoman a great nation because he was Abraham's seed Abraham rose early in the morning, provided bread and water for Hagar and her child, and sent them away. Hagar wandered in the wilderness of Beer-sheba until the water ran out, and the child was thirsty and unable to go on. She placed him under an olive tree and sat at a distance, weeping. An angel of God appeared to her, telling her not to weep, for God had heard her voice and seen the child. She saw a well of water, filled her bottle, gave her child a drink, and then went towards the wilderness of Paran The child grew, became an archer, and God was with him. His mother took him a wife from Egypt, who bore him a son named Nebaioth, meaning "The Lord was nigh to me when I called upon Him." In the seventh week, in the first year of this jubilee, voices were heard in heaven regarding Abraham, noting his faithfulness, love for the Lord, and patience in all his trials. The prince Mastêmâ challenged God, claiming that Abraham loved Isaac above all and suggesting that God should command Abraham to offer Isaac as a burnt offering to test his faithfulness The Lord knew Abraham's faithfulness, having tested him through many trials, including famine, wealth, and circumcision, and through the sending away of Ishmael and Hagar. Abraham had been found faithful in all these trials, and his soul had not been impatient

Jubilees 18

God called Abraham's name twice and instructed him to take his beloved son Isaac to the high country and offer him as a burnt offering on a mountain that He would show. Abraham rose early, saddled his ass, took two young men and Isaac, and went to the place. On the third day, he saw the place from afar, and told the young men to wait with the ass while he and Isaac went to worship and return He placed the wood on Isaac's shoulders, took the fire and knife, and they went together. Isaac noticed the fire, knife, and wood but asked where the sheep for the burnt offering was. Abraham replied that God would provide a sheep for the burnt offering Upon reaching the mountain, Abraham built an altar, placed the wood on it, bound Isaac, and laid him on the wood. He stretched out his hand to take the knife, but I intervened from heaven, telling him not to harm the lad, as I had seen his fear of the Lord and that he had not withheld his son The prince Mastêmâ was shamed, and Abraham saw a ram caught by its horns. He took the ram and offered it as a burnt offering in place of Isaac. Abraham named the place "The Lord hath seen," which is now known as Mount Sion The Lord spoke to Abraham a second time from heaven, promising blessings and multiplication of his seed as numerous as the stars and sand, with his seed inheriting the cities of their enemies and all nations being blessed through them. The Lord declared peace to Abraham for his obedience and faithfulness Abraham returned to his young men, and they went together to Beersheba. Abraham celebrated the festival every year for seven days with joy, calling it the Festival of the Lord according to the seven days of peace

Jubilees 19

In the first year of the first week of the forty-second jubilee, Abraham returned and dwelt opposite Hebron, which is Kirjath Arba, for two weeks of years. In the first year of the third week of this jubilee, Sarah died in Hebron. Abraham mourned her, and we tested him to see if he would remain patient and undisturbed. He was found patient, conversing gently with the children of Heth to secure a burial place The Lord gave him favor with all who saw him, and he requested and paid for the land of the double cave over against Mamre, where he buried Sarah. Sarah's life lasted 127 years, or two jubilees, four weeks, and one year This was the tenth trial of Abraham, in which God tested him, and he was found faithful. We blessed him and confirmed the covenant between us Abraham mourned Sarah for 30 days and then went to seek a wife for Isaac. He sent his servant Eliezer to Mesopotamia to find a wife from his own kin, choosing Rebekah, daughter of Bethuel, son of Nahor. Eliezer prayed for guidance and found Rebekah at the well, who agreed to leave her family to marry Isaac Abraham commanded his household to obey all laws and ordinances given to him and his seed, including the laws of sacrifice, and instructed Isaac and Rebekah to follow these instructions. He instructed Isaac to observe the laws of the covenant and instructed his sons to honor and follow the commandments, continuing to live by faith and obedience Here are the remaining chapters from **Jubilees**:

Jubilees 20

In the first year of the fourth week of the forty-second jubilee, Isaac took Rebekah, daughter of Bethuel, to be his wife. Rebekah was of the family of Abraham and a relative of Isaac. Isaac loved Rebekah, and she bore him two sons, Esau and Jacob, who were born in the first year of the seventh week of this jubilee In the second year of the first week of the forty-third jubilee, Esau and Jacob were ten years old. Esau was a man of the field, skilled in hunting, while Jacob was a quiet man, dwelling in tents. Esau despised his birthright, and Jacob desired it In the second year of the second week of this jubilee, Esau came from hunting and was famished. Jacob prepared a pot of lentil stew, and Esau asked for it. Jacob demanded Esau's birthright in exchange, and Esau agreed, swearing to sell it to Jacob Jacob gave Esau bread and lentil stew, and Esau ate and drank, then rose and went away, despising his birthright. Thus, the birthright passed to Jacob

Jubilees 21

In the sixth year of the seventh week of this jubilee, Abraham called his son Isaac and commanded him, saying, "I have become old and do not know the day of my death. I am now one hundred and seventy-five years old. Throughout all my days, I have remembered the Lord and have sought with all my heart to do His will and to walk uprightly in all His ways. My soul has hated idols and I have despised those who serve them. I have devoted my heart and spirit to observing the will of Him who created me. For He is the living God, holy and faithful, righteous beyond all, and there is no acceptance of persons or gifts with Him. God is righteous and executes judgment on all who transgress His commandments and despise His covenant Therefore, my son, observe His commandments, ordinances, and judgments. Do not follow the abominations, graven images, or molten images. Do not eat any blood of animals, cattle, or birds. If you offer a peace offering, slaughter it and pour out its blood upon the altar. Offer all the fat of the offering with fine flour and the meat offering mingled with oil, along with the drink offering, on the altar of burnt offering; this is a sweet savor before the Lord. Offer the fat of thank offerings on the fire of the altar, including the fat on the belly, inwards, kidneys, loins, and liver, and offer them for a sweet savor acceptable before the Lord. Eat the meat on that day and the next day; do not let the sun set on the second day without eating it, as anything left over will not be acceptable and will bring sin upon you. This is written in the books of my forefathers, including the words of Enoch and Noah On all your oblations, strew salt and do not let the salt of the covenant be missing from any of your offerings before the Lord. Be cautious about the wood for the sacrifices; do not bring any wood other than cypress, bay, almond, fir, pine, cedar, savin, fig, olive, myrrh, or laurel. Use only wood that is hard, clean, and new; do not use old or dark wood, as it no longer has fragrance. Observe these commandments so that you may be upright in all your deeds Always be clean in your body; wash yourself with water before approaching the altar, and wash your hands and feet before drawing near to offer. After sacrificing, wash again. Avoid any appearance of blood on your body or clothes; be extremely careful with blood, covering it with dust. Do not eat any blood as it is the soul. Take no gifts for the blood of man, lest it be shed without judgment. Blood shed causes the earth to sin, and it can only be cleansed by the blood of the one who shed it Take no presents for the blood of man; blood for blood, so that you may be accepted by the Most High God. He is the defense of the good and will preserve you from evil and all kinds of death. I see, my son, that all the works of men are sin and wickedness. Beware lest you walk in their ways and sin unto death before the Most High God. Otherwise, He will hide His face from you, give you back to your transgressions, and root you out of the land with your seed. Turn away from their deeds and uncleanness, observe the ordinance of the Most High God, and do His will. He will bless you and raise up a righteous seed through all generations of the earth Go in peace, my son. May the Most High God, my God and your God, strengthen you to do His will and bless all your seed for generations to come. May you be a blessing on all the earth." Abraham finished his words and went out rejoicing

Jubilees 22

In the first week of the forty-fourth jubilee, in the second year, the year Abraham died, Isaac and

Ishmael came from the Well of the Oath to celebrate the feast of weeks with Abraham. Abraham rejoiced because his two sons had come. Isaac, having many possessions in Beersheba, would often visit them and return to his father. Ishmael also came to see his father, and they both arrived together. Isaac offered a burnt sacrifice on the altar Abraham had made in Hebron. He presented a thank offering and held a feast of joy before Ishmael. Rebecca prepared new cakes from the first fruits of the land and sent them with Jacob to Abraham, so he could eat and bless the Creator before he died. Isaac also sent a best thank offering by Jacob to Abraham Abraham ate and drank, and blessed the Most High God, who created heaven and earth and all the good things of the earth, giving them to mankind to eat and drink, and bless their Creator. Abraham thanked God for allowing him to see this day, as he was one hundred and fifteen years old and full of days. He expressed gratitude for his peace and the protection from adversaries throughout his life. He prayed that his seed would become a chosen nation and inheritance among all the nations of the earth Abraham called Jacob and blessed him, asking the God of all to strengthen Jacob to do righteousness and His will, and to make him and his seed a people for His inheritance according to His will. He blessed Jacob and his descendants, praying that nations would serve them and that they would become a holy nation. Abraham wished for Jacob to inherit all the blessings given to him and to his forefathers, Noah and Adam, and to be cleansed from all unrighteousness. He hoped that Jacob and his seed would be a nation for God's inheritance forever Abraham instructed Jacob to remember his words and observe the commandments of Abraham, his father. He warned Jacob to separate himself from the nations, not to eat with them, or follow their unclean ways. The nations offered sacrifices to the dead, worshipped evil spirits, and their works were vanity. Jacob was advised to avoid taking a wife from Canaanites as their seed would be rooted out from the earth due to Ham's transgression. The worshippers of idols would have no hope, and their memory would be erased Abraham reassured Jacob not to fear and to avoid the paths of error. He blessed Jacob, declaring that the house he had built would be named the house of Abraham and given to Jacob and his seed forever. They would establish his house and name before God forever. Jacob and Abraham lay together, and Jacob slept in Abraham's bosom. He kissed Abraham seven times, and Abraham blessed him with joy and affection. Abraham thanked God for bringing him from Ur of the Chaldees and granting him this land to inherit it and establish a holy seed. Abraham prayed for God's grace and mercy to remain upon Jacob and his descendants forever and for His covenant to be renewed with them

Jubilees 23

Abraham placed two fingers of Jacob on his eyes, blessed the God of gods, covered his face, stretched out his feet, and slept the sleep of eternity, being gathered to his fathers. Jacob, lying in Abraham's bosom, was unaware of his grandfather's death. When Jacob awoke and found Abraham cold, he called out but received no response and realized that Abraham was dead. He went to tell Rebecca, who then informed Isaac. They went together with Jacob, carrying a lamp, and found Abraham lying dead Isaac wept and kissed his father, and Ishmael, along with the household, also mourned Abraham with a great weeping. Abraham was buried in the double cave near Sarah, his wife. They wept for him for forty days. Abraham lived three jubilees and four weeks of years, totaling one hundred and seventy-five years. He completed his days, being old and full of years. The forefathers lived nineteen jubilees, but after the Flood, their lifespan decreased due to tribulations and wickedness. Abraham's life did not complete four jubilees, as he was full of days and old by reason

of wickedness Generations from then until the great judgment will grow old quickly, not reaching two jubilees, and their knowledge will fade. In those days, living a jubilee and a half will be considered a long life, filled with pain, sorrow, and tribulation. The earth will be plagued with calamities, including illness, famine, and war. These will befall an evil generation that transgresses, and their works will be unclean. The sons will convict their fathers and elders of sin, and the earth will be destroyed because of their deeds. There will be no seed of the vine or oil, and all living things will perish due to the wickedness of men In those times, there will be conflict among people, with violence and bloodshed occurring due to the law and covenant. Those who escape will not return to righteousness but will exalt themselves to deceit and wealth. The holy places will be defiled with corruption, and a great punishment will fall upon this generation. Sinners from the Gentiles will be raised up against Israel and Jacob, bringing more violence and bloodshed The righteous will rejoice and see all judgments and curses upon their enemies. Their bones will rest in the earth, and their spirits will have joy, knowing that the Lord executes judgment and shows mercy. Moses is instructed to write down these words as a testimony for future generations

Jubilees 24

After Abraham's death, the Lord blessed Isaac, who moved from Hebron and settled at the Well of Vision in the first year of the third week of this jubilee, where he lived for seven years. In the first year of the fourth week, a famine arose, and Isaac's servants went to Egypt to buy grain. Isaac, in fear of the Canaanites, thought to enter Egypt but did not go. He prayed to the Lord, who told him to remain in Canaan and not fear the famine During the third year of the famine, Isaac received a vision from the Lord. He was informed that the famine would end and that he would be blessed with prosperity. Isaac obeyed and remained in Canaan, where he was blessed. The famine came to an end, and the earth yielded abundantly. Isaac continued to dwell at the Well of Vision and became prosperous in livestock, wealth, and grain. He had two sons, Esau and Jacob, who were born during this time. Isaac loved Esau, and Rebecca loved Jacob, resulting in conflicts between the two Isaac, in his old age, was visited by the Lord, who told him to bless Jacob with the blessings of Abraham. Isaac obeyed, and Jacob received the blessing, leading to conflicts between the brothers. Esau, feeling cheated, plotted to kill Jacob. Rebecca learned of this plan and advised Jacob to flee to her brother Laban's house to avoid danger. Jacob fled, and Esau's anger subsided The book concludes with a reminder of the judgments and blessings to come, emphasizing that the righteous will be rewarded, and the wicked will face consequences. The Lord's covenant with His people remains steadfast, and He will bring about justice and redemption

Jubilees 25

In the first year of the fifth week of this jubilee, Isaac called Jacob and Esau and commanded them to keep the commandments and statutes of the Lord. He instructed them to follow the way of the Lord, to walk in His ways, and to observe His ordinances, which had been given to him by his father Abraham. Isaac assured them that if they did so, they would be blessed and their descendants would inherit the promises made to their forefathers Jacob and Esau, being grown men, agreed to obey Isaac's commandments. Isaac then blessed Jacob and said, "May the Lord give you many children, and may your children inherit the blessings of Abraham and Isaac. May you become a great nation and be the father of many peoples. May the Lord protect you from all evil and grant you wisdom to follow His ways." After blessing Jacob, Isaac turned to Esau and said, "Though you are the elder, I bless your younger brother, Jacob, with the blessings of the firstborn. Yet I pray that you too will be blessed and that you will have prosperity in your own right. May you also inherit some of the blessings of your father Abraham, and may the Lord be with you in all your endeavors." Isaac concluded his blessings and gathered his sons and their families to celebrate a feast. The feast was a joyous occasion, marking the fulfillment of the blessings given to Isaac and his family In the second year of this week, the famine ended, and the earth became fruitful again. Isaac prospered greatly, and his family grew strong and numerous. Jacob, having married Rachel and Leah, began to establish his own household. Esau, too, settled in the land of Edom, where he became a great leader and father of a mighty nation The book of Jubilees concludes with a reminder of the covenant between the Lord and His people. It emphasizes the importance of observing the commandments and following the ways of the Lord. The blessings given to Abraham, Isaac, and Jacob are passed down to their descendants, and the Lord's promises continue to guide and protect His chosen people

Jubilees 26

In the seventh year of that week, Isaac, now aged and with dimming vision, called his elder son Esau. He instructed Esau to take his hunting gear and hunt game, preparing a savory meal that he loved, so that he might bless Esau before he died. Rebecca overheard this conversation and informed Jacob of their father's wishes. She devised a plan for Jacob to bring her two goats, which she would prepare in the same manner as Esau's game. She dressed Jacob in Esau's clothes and covered his hands and neck with goat skins to mimic Esau's hairiness Jacob approached Isaac with the meal, but Isaac, suspicious, requested to feel Jacob's hands. Although Isaac noted that the voice was Jacob's, the touch seemed like Esau's. This was a divine intervention allowing Isaac to be deceived. Isaac then blessed Jacob, bestowing upon him prosperity, dominance over his kin, and a continuation of the blessings given to Abraham After Jacob left, Esau arrived with his own prepared meal, only to discover that Jacob had already received the blessing. Esau, devastated, begged for a blessing of his own. Isaac, realizing the deception, could only grant Esau a less favorable blessing, foretelling a life of struggle and eventual freedom from Jacob's yoke

Jubilees 27

Rebecca learned through a dream of Esau's intent to kill Jacob in revenge. She advised Jacob to flee to her brother Laban in Haran until Esau's anger subsided. Jacob initially resisted, concerned about leaving his father alone, but eventually, Rebecca convinced him. She then persuaded Isaac to send Jacob away under the pretext of finding a wife from their family rather than the local Canaanites. Isaac blessed Jacob, asking God to multiply his descendants and grant him the land promised to Abraham Jacob left for Mesopotamia, feeling the weight of departure. Isaac reassured Rebecca that Jacob would return safely. As Jacob journeyed, he had a vision of a ladder reaching to heaven with angels ascending and descending. God stood above the ladder and promised Jacob land, numerous descendants, and His continued presence. Jacob, awed, named the place Bethel and vowed to honor God if He provided for him and brought him back safely

Jubilees 28

Jacob arrived in Mesopotamia and agreed to serve Laban for seven years to marry Rachel. However, Laban deceived Jacob by giving him Leah instead. Jacob, enraged, confronted Laban, who justified his actions by local custom and offered Rachel in exchange for another seven years of service. Jacob accepted, and after the marriage feast, he married Rachel Leah bore Jacob four sons: Reuben, Simeon, Levi, and Judah. Rachel, envious of Leah's fertility, gave Jacob her maid Bilhah, who bore two sons: Dan and Naphtali. Leah also gave her maid Zilpah to Jacob, resulting in two more sons: Gad and Asher. Leah later bore Jacob two more children: Issachar and Zebulun, and a daughter, Dinah. Rachel finally bore Joseph, and Jacob, having fulfilled his service, requested to return to his father's house Laban agreed to let Jacob go but sought to keep him longer. Jacob negotiated to receive only the speckled and spotted sheep as his wages. Laban's sons envied Jacob, and Laban's treatment became hostile. Jacob decided to leave secretly with his family, crossing the river and heading toward Gilead

Jubilees 29

Jacob, seeing Laban's departure for sheep shearing, secretly left with his family and possessions. Laban pursued him but was prevented by God from harming Jacob. They made a covenant at Gilead, setting up a stone heap as a witness to their agreement Jacob returned to Gilead, crossing the Jabbok River and later reconciled with Esau, who moved to Seir. Jacob resettled beyond the Jordan, pasturing his flocks. He sent gifts and provisions to his father Isaac and his mother Rebecca, who had relocated to the tower of Abraham. Isaac had moved to the tower of Abraham after leaving the Well of the Oath

Jubilees 30

In the first year of the seventh week of the forty-fourth jubilee, Jacob took another wife named Bilhah, who bore him two sons, Dan and Naphtali. When Rachel saw that Leah had borne children to Jacob and she had none, she gave her handmaid Bilhah to Jacob as a wife, and Bilhah bore him Dan and Naphtali. In the sixth year of the seventh week, Rachel bore children as well Leah then gave her handmaid Zilpah to Jacob as a wife, and Zilpah bore Gad and Asher. In the first year of the eighth week, Leah gave birth to Issachar, and later, in the same period, to Zebulun. Leah's daughter Dinah was born in the seventh year of the eighth week The Lord blessed Rachel, and she bore a son named Joseph in the eighth year of the eighth week. In the ninth year of the ninth week, Jacob came to the land of Canaan and settled there. The Lord appeared to Jacob, blessed him, and instructed him to be fruitful and multiply. Jacob built an altar in Canaan, calling the place Bethel, as it was where he had seen the vision of the ladder. He celebrated with a feast for his family and friends In the first year of the tenth week, Joseph, aged seventeen, was envied by his brothers because of his dreams. They sold him to the Ishmaelites who were passing by, and Joseph was taken to Egypt. In the second year of the tenth week, Joseph was sold to Potiphar and found favor in his house, being appointed over all his affairs. The Lord blessed Potiphar's house for Joseph's sake, and Joseph prospered in all he did In the third year of the tenth week, Potiphar's wife tried to seduce Joseph, but he fled from her, and she falsely accused him, leading to his imprisonment. The Lord continued to be with Joseph in prison, and he was put in charge of all the prisoners In the fourth year of the tenth week, Joseph interpreted the dreams of Pharaoh's chief butler and baker. In the fifth year of the tenth week, Pharaoh had a dream, and Joseph interpreted it, prophesying seven years of plenty followed by seven years of famine. Pharaoh appointed Joseph as ruler over all Egypt, and Joseph stored up grain during the years of plenty By the first year of the eleventh week, the famine began, and Joseph opened the storehouses to sell grain. Jacob's sons came to Egypt to buy grain, and Joseph recognized them, though they did not recognize him. Joseph tested his brothers, accusing them of being spies, and kept Simeon in prison while the others returned to Canaan to bring Benjamin In the second year of the eleventh week, the brothers returned to Egypt with Benjamin. Joseph revealed himself to them, forgave them for their actions, and brought his family to Egypt. Pharaoh welcomed them and provided them with land in Goshen In the third year of the eleventh week, Jacob blessed his sons and grandsons and prophesied concerning them. Jacob lived seventeen years in Egypt and died there. Joseph and his brothers buried him in the cave of Machpelah, which Abraham had bought. Joseph lived to be a hundred and ten years old, witnessing his descendants to the third generation. When Joseph died, the Israelites multiplied greatly In the fourth year of the twelfth week, a new king arose in Egypt who did not know Joseph. The Egyptians oppressed the Israelites, forcing them to build store-cities for Pharaoh. The Lord heard their cries and remembered His covenant with Abraham, Isaac, and Jacob. In the first year of the thirteenth week, the Lord raised up Moses to deliver the Israelites from bondage. Moses performed miracles before Pharaoh and led the Israelites out of Egypt Upon reaching Mount Sinai, the Lord gave the Israelites His laws and commandments. In the second year of the thirteenth week, the Israelites entered the land of Canaan, which was divided among the tribes by Joshua. The people of Israel served the Lord throughout Joshua's life and kept His commandments. In the fourth year of the thirteenth week, judges ruled over Israel, and the people prospered in their land. By the fifth year of the thirteenth week, Israel enjoyed peace and rest from their enemies

Jubilees 31

On the new moon of the month, Jacob spoke to all the people of his house, saying, "Purify yourselves and change your garments, and let us arise and go up to Bethel, where I vowed a vow to Him on the day when I fled from the face of Esau my brother, because He has been with me and brought me into this land in peace. Put away the strange gods that are among you." They gave up the strange gods, including what was in their ears and on their necks, and the idols which Rachel stole from Laban her father. She gave them wholly to Jacob, who burned and broke them to pieces, destroyed them, and hid them under an oak in the land of Shechem On the new moon of the seventh month, Jacob went up to Bethel. He built an altar at the place where he had slept and set up a pillar there. He sent word to his father Isaac and his mother Rebecca to come to his sacrifice Isaac said, "Let my son Jacob come, and let me see him before I die." Jacob went to his father Isaac and his mother Rebecca, to the house of his father Abraham, taking two of his sons with him, Levi and Judah. He arrived and Rebecca came forth from the tower to kiss Jacob and embrace him, for her spirit revived when she heard that Jacob her son had come. She kissed him Seeing his two sons, she recognized them and asked, "Are these your sons, my son?" She embraced and kissed them, blessing them and saying, "In you shall the seed of Abraham become illustrious, and you shall prove a blessing on the earth." Jacob went in to Isaac his father and kissed him. Isaac said, "Blessed be my son Jacob and all his children. May the Lord bless you and make you fruitful, and may He give you many children and grandchildren." Jacob went to his mother Rebecca and kissed her. Rebecca said, "Blessed be you and your children. May you be the head of the nations and may the Lord bless you." Afterward, Jacob and his family went to the land of Canaan, and he settled in the land of Hebron. He built an altar there and offered sacrifices to the Lord. He lived there in peace and continued to be prosperous

Jubilees 32

In the twenty-fourth jubilee, in the first year of the seventh week, Isaac called Jacob his son and said to him, "I am old now and do not know the day of my death. Now, I have called you and blessed you, as I have given you all the land which the Lord gave to me. You shall inherit it, and you and your children shall be blessed in it." Jacob answered his father, "I will do according to what you have commanded. I shall walk before the Lord and will keep His commandments. I will be faithful and true to the Lord, and I will teach my children His ways." Isaac blessed Jacob and said, "May the Lord be with you and bless you and make

you fruitful in the land. May He grant you favor before all people, and may He give you the blessing of Abraham." Isaac then called all his sons and blessed them, giving each of them a portion of the inheritance. He gave the birthright to Jacob, and the blessing of the covenant to Joseph Jacob went to Bethel, and there the Lord appeared to him and said, "I am the God of your father Abraham and Isaac. I will bless you and make your descendants as numerous as the stars in the sky and as the sand on the seashore. I will give you the land that I promised to Abraham and Isaac." Jacob built an altar there and offered sacrifices to the Lord. He continued to live in Bethel and prospered greatly. He married Leah and Rachel, and they bore him many children. He also had many flocks and herds, and his household grew in number

Jubilees 33

In the forty-ninth jubilee, in the second year of the fifth week, Jacob went to Shechem, and the people of the land heard of his arrival. They gathered together and came out to meet him, and they made a feast in his honor Jacob called his sons and said, "The time has come for us to go up to the land of Canaan. The Lord has commanded me to return to the land of my fathers. I will go up, and I will offer sacrifices to the Lord." The sons of Jacob said to him, "We will go with you and will follow you wherever you go. We will do all that you command us." Jacob prepared his household and his flocks and went up to the land of Canaan. He settled in the land of Hebron and built an altar to the Lord. He offered sacrifices and prayed to God, asking for His protection and blessing The Lord appeared to Jacob and said, "I am with you, and I will bless you and your children. I will make you a great nation, and your descendants will be as numerous as the stars in the sky." Jacob was greatly blessed and prospered in the land. His sons grew up and became leaders of tribes, and his household continued to increase in wealth and number

Jubilees 34

In the fifty-ninth jubilee, in the third year of the second week, the children of Jacob were settled in the land of Canaan. The land was fruitful and yielded an abundance of produce. Jacob's sons were growing up and becoming leaders of their own households The Lord appeared to Jacob and said, "I have given you and your children this land as an inheritance. Walk in My ways and keep My commandments, and you will prosper in this land." Jacob instructed his sons to continue in the ways of the Lord and to honor the covenant that God had made with their forefathers. He emphasized the importance of maintaining their faithfulness and obeying the laws given to them by the Lord One day, a great famine struck the land, and the people of Canaan began to suffer. Jacob's sons went to Egypt to buy food. There, they encountered Joseph, who had become a powerful ruler in Egypt. Joseph recognized his brothers but chose not to reveal himself immediately He tested his brothers and accused them of being spies. Eventually, Joseph revealed his identity to them and forgave them for their past actions. He invited his family to come to Egypt and live there, where they would be provided for during the remainder of the famine Jacob and his family moved to Egypt and were given the best of the land by Joseph. They settled in the land of Goshen and prospered greatly. The Lord blessed Jacob and his descendants in Egypt, and they became a great nation

Jubilees 35

In the sixtieth jubilee, in the fourth year of the first week, Jacob was nearing the end of his life. He called his sons together and gave them his final blessings. He reminded them of the promises God had made to their ancestors and encouraged them to remain faithful to the Lord Jacob blessed each of his sons according to their individual characters and futures. He reaffirmed the covenant with the Lord and instructed his sons to bury him in the cave of Machpelah, where Abraham and Isaac were buried Jacob passed away, and his sons mourned for him. They fulfilled his wishes and buried him in the cave of Machpelah, alongside his forefathers The children of Israel continued to live in Egypt, where they grew in number and strength. They remembered the promises made by God to their forefathers and looked forward to the time when they would return to the land of Canaan The Lord continued to watch over His people and blessed them even in their time of sojourn in Egypt. The covenant made with Abraham, Isaac, and Jacob remained steadfast, and the people of Israel anticipated the fulfillment of God's promises

Jubilees 36

In the sixth year of this week [2162 A.M.], Isaac called his two sons, Esau and Jacob, and they came to him. He said to them, "My sons, I am going the way of my fathers, to the eternal house where my fathers are. Bury me near Abraham, my father, in the double cave in the field of Ephron the Hittite, where Abraham purchased a sepulchre to bury in; in the sepulchre which I dug for myself, there bury me. This I command you, my sons, that you practice righteousness and uprightness on the earth, so that the Lord may bring upon you all that He said He would do to Abraham and his seed. Love one another, my sons, as a man loves his own soul. Let each seek in what he may benefit his brother and act together on the earth. Let them love each other as their own souls. Regarding idols, I command and admonish you to reject them and hate them, for they are full of deception for those who worship them and for those who bow down to them. Remember, my sons, the Lord God of Abraham your father, and how I too worshipped Him and served Him in righteousness and joy, that He might multiply you and increase your seed as the stars of heaven in multitude, and establish you on the earth as the plant of righteousness which will not be rooted out unto all generations forever Now I shall make you swear a great oath—by the name glorious and honored and great and splendid and wonderful and mighty, which created the heavens and the earth and all things together—that you will fear Him and worship Him. Each of you will love his brother with affection and righteousness, and neither will desire evil against his brother from henceforth forever, all the days of your life. This way you may prosper in all your deeds and not be destroyed. If either of you devises evil against his brother, know that from henceforth everyone who devises evil against his brother shall fall into his hand and shall be rooted out of the land of the living, and his seed shall be destroyed from under heaven. On the day of turbulence and execration and indignation and anger, with flaming devouring fire as He burned Sodom, so likewise will He burn his land and his city and all that is his. He shall be blotted out of the book of the discipline of the children of men and not be recorded in the book of life, but in that which is appointed to destruction, and he shall depart into eternal execration. Their condemnation shall be always renewed in hate, execration, wrath, torment, indignation, plagues, and disease forever. I testify to you, my sons, according to the judgment that will come upon the man who wishes to injure his brother He divided all his possessions between the two on that day and gave the larger portion to the firstborn, including the tower and all that was about it, and all that Abraham possessed at the Well of the Oath. He said, "This larger portion I will give to the firstborn." Esau said, "I have sold my birthright to Jacob; to him let it be given, and I have no further claim to it, for it is his." Isaac said, "May a blessing rest upon you, my sons, and upon your seed this day, for you have given me rest, and my heart is not pained concerning the birthright, lest you should work wickedness on account of it." "May the Most High God bless the man who works righteousness, him and his seed forever." He finished commanding them and blessing them, and they ate and drank together before him. He rejoiced because there was one mind between them, and they went forth from him, rested that day, and slept. Isaac slept on his bed that day rejoicing; he slept the eternal sleep, and died one hundred and eighty years old. He completed twenty-five weeks and five years. His two sons, Esau and Jacob, buried him Esau went to the land of Edom, to the mountains of Seir, and dwelt there. Jacob dwelt in the mountains of Hebron, in the tower of the land of the sojournings of his father Abraham. He worshipped the Lord with all his heart and according to the visible commands, as He had divided the days of his generations. Leah, his wife, died in the fourth year of the second week of the forty-fifth jubilee [2167 A.M.], and he buried her in the double cave near Rebekah, his mother, to the left of the grave of Sarah, his father's mother. All her sons and his sons came to mourn over Leah, his wife, with him and to comfort him regarding her, for he was lamenting her, as he loved her exceedingly after Rachel, her sister, died Leah was perfect and upright in all her ways and honored Jacob. During all the days she lived with him, he did not hear from her a harsh word, for she was gentle, peaceable, upright, and honorable. He remembered all her deeds during her life and lamented her exceedingly, for he loved her with all his heart and soul

Jubilees 37

On the day that Isaac, the father of Jacob and Esau, died [2162 A.M.], the sons of Esau heard that Isaac had given the portion of the elder to his younger son Jacob, and they were very angry. They argued with their father, saying, "Why has your father given Jacob the portion of the elder and passed over you, although you are the elder and Jacob the younger?" Esau replied, "Because I sold my birthright to Jacob for a small mess of lentils, and on the day my father sent me to hunt and bring him something to eat and bless me, Jacob came with guile, bringing my father food and drink. My father blessed him and put me under his hand." Esau's sons said, "We shall not listen to you to make peace with him; for our strength is greater than his, and we are more powerful. We shall go against him, slay him, and destroy him and his sons. If you will not go with us, we shall do harm to you as well." They decided to send for allies and chose chosen men from Aram, Philistia, Moab, and Ammon, gathering one thousand warriors from each. They also hired mighty men from Edom, the Horites, and the Kittim. They said to their father, "Go forth with them and lead them, or we shall slay you." Esau was filled with wrath and indignation upon seeing that his sons were forcing him to lead them against Jacob. But afterward, he remembered all the evil hidden in his heart against Jacob and forgot the oath he had sworn to his father and mother not to devise evil against Jacob. Despite this, Jacob did not know they were coming to battle against him. He was mourning for Leah, his wife, until they approached very near to the tower with four thousand warriors and chosen men of war The men of Hebron sent to him saying, "Behold, your brother has come against you to fight you with four thousand armed with swords, carrying shields and weapons." They informed him because they loved Jacob more than Esau. Jacob was a more liberal and merciful man than Esau. Jacob would not believe until they were very near the tower. He closed the gates of the tower, stood on the battlements, and spoke to his brother Esau, saying, "Noble is the comfort with which you have come to comfort me for my wife who has died. Is this the oath you swore to our father and again to our mother before they died? You have broken the oath, and at the moment you swore to our father, you were condemned." Esau answered, "Neither the children of men nor the beasts of the earth have any oath of righteousness valid forever. Every day they devise evil against one another, and each seeks to slay his adversary and foe. You hate me and my children forever. There is no observing the tie of brotherhood with you. Hear these words: If the boar can change its skin and make its bristles as soft as wool, or if it can cause horns to sprout forth on its head like the horns of a stag or a sheep, then I will observe the tie of brotherhood with you. If the breasts separate from their mother, you have not been faithful to the oath that you swore to our father." Jacob heard these words and said, "You have sworn that I and my children shall not be with you in this generation or the next, but I am a servant of God, and He is my shield. If I have broken the oath of my father and mother, I do not fear. I trust that He will protect me." Afterward, Esau's army approached the tower and began to burn the walls and towers and the tower itself. The people within it went up to the top of the tower and cried out to Esau saying, "You have come to destroy the house of your brother. Your father said, 'Love each other and seek the good of one another.'" They were troubled, and they sent their men to Isaac to ask him for help. When Isaac heard of the attack upon Jacob, he wept and prayed, saying, "God of Abraham, protect my son Jacob who dwells in Hebron. Send a host of angels to deliver him and his house from the hands of his brother and his soldiers who have come to fight him. May they turn their faces from him and depart, and may their plans be turned against them." When Jacob heard that his father was praying for him, he went out from the tower and stood in the place of prayer. Esau and his army saw that Jacob had gone out, and he was alone and had no company with him. They surrounded him and attacked him with stones and arrows. Jacob prayed, and an angel of the Lord came down and fought against Esau and his army, and the angels of the Lord were mighty and strong The battle was fierce, and the hosts of Esau fled. The forces of Jacob were triumphant, and Esau's men were driven back. They went to their own land and returned in peace. Jacob returned to his tower and praised the Lord, who had delivered him from the hands of his brother and his army. He rejoiced greatly. He sent messengers to his father Isaac to inform him of his deliverance and that Esau had fled. He also sent him a present to honor him and thanked him for his prayer. Isaac was pleased and rejoiced greatly. He thanked the Lord for delivering Jacob from Esau's hand and for answering his prayer Jacob and his sons remained in the tower, and Esau did not attack them again. Jacob lived in peace and joy for the rest of his days

Jubilees 38

In the fiftieth year of the life of Jacob, Esau went to Egypt with his army and came to Joseph, his brother, and said to him, "My brother, I am come to make peace with you." Joseph was astonished and said, "What do you mean by coming to me in this way? Have you not been at war with me and my family?" Esau replied, "I have come to make peace with you and to ask for your forgiveness. I have repented of all my evil deeds, and I wish to be reconciled with you." Joseph said, "If you are sincere in your desire for peace, then you must first show your repentance and sincerity. What are you willing to do to make amends for the wrongs you have done to me and my family?" Esau said, "I am willing to give you all my possessions and serve you as a slave if you will forgive me and accept me as a brother." Joseph replied, "If you are willing to make such an offering, then I will accept your repentance and forgive you. But you must also promise that you will never again harm me or my family." Esau promised to keep his word, and Joseph accepted his repentance. They embraced and made peace with each other. Joseph sent for his father Jacob and informed him of the reconciliation with Esau. Jacob was glad and blessed his son for his wisdom and mercy The peace

between Joseph and Esau lasted throughout their lives, and their descendants lived in harmony

Jubilees 39

In the third year of the seventh week [2207 A.M.], Joseph gathered all the people of Egypt and Israel and said to them, "Behold, we are now in the seventh year of famine, and we must prepare for the coming years. The Lord has blessed us with abundance, and we must store up grain and other provisions to sustain ourselves during the years of famine." He commanded them to build granaries and storehouses throughout Egypt and Israel to ensure that there would be enough food for everyone during the years of famine The people worked diligently and stored up vast amounts of grain and provisions. Joseph ensured that there was a fair distribution of resources and that no one would go hungry. During the years of famine, the people came to Joseph for help, and he provided them with the provisions they needed. He acted with wisdom and compassion, ensuring that everyone had enough to eat The famine lasted for seven years, but thanks to Joseph's foresight and planning, the people of Egypt and Israel were able to survive and thrive. They honored Joseph for his wisdom and leadership

Jubilees 40

In the first year of the eighth week [2218 A.M.], Joseph's father Jacob died. His sons mourned for him and buried him in the double cave in the field of Ephron the Hittite, as he had requested. After the death of Jacob, Joseph continued to govern Egypt with wisdom and justice. He was a beloved leader and a wise ruler, and the people prospered under his reign In the second year of the eighth week [2219 A.M.], Joseph's brothers and their families came to Egypt to live with him. They brought their flocks and herds and settled in the land of Goshen. The Israelites multiplied greatly in Egypt and prospered under Joseph's leadership. They lived in peace and harmony, and their families grew in number Joseph lived to a ripe old age and saw the fulfillment of the Lord's promises to his family. He was blessed with many descendants and left a legacy of wisdom and righteousness. When Joseph died, he was buried in Egypt, and his descendants continued to honor his memory and follow his example of faithfulness and leadership. The book of Jubilees ends with a reminder of the faithfulness of the Lord and the importance of following His commands. It serves as a testament to the enduring legacy of those who walk in righteousness and justice

Jubilees 41

In the forty-fifth jubilee, during the second week of the second year [2165 A.M.], Judah took a wife for his firstborn, Er, from the daughters of Aram. Her name was Tamar. However, Er did not have relations with her because he preferred to marry a woman from the kin of his mother, who was a Canaanite, but his father Judah forbade this. Er, being wicked, was struck dead by the Lord. Judah instructed his brother Onan to fulfill the duty of a brother-in-law and raise up offspring for Er. Knowing the offspring would not be his own, Onan spilled his seed on the ground and was consequently punished by death. Judah then told Tamar to remain in her father's house as a widow until his younger son Shelah grew up, intending to give her to him as a wife. However, Shelah's mother, Bedsu'el, refused to allow the marriage, and she died [2168 A.M.] in the fifth year of that week In the sixth year, Judah went to shear his sheep at Timnah [2169 A.M.], and Tamar, having heard this, dressed as a harlot and positioned herself by the gate leading to Timnah. Judah, not recognizing her, approached her and requested to lie with her. Tamar asked for his signet ring, cord, and staff as a pledge, which he gave her, promising to send a kid from his flock as payment. Tamar conceived from this encounter Judah later sent the kid with his shepherd, but Tamar could not be found. The shepherd reported that there was no harlot in the area. Judah decided to let Tamar keep the items to avoid becoming a laughingstock. Three months later, it became known that Tamar was pregnant, and Judah demanded she be burned for her apparent immorality. As she was about to be burned, Tamar sent Judah the ring, cord, and staff, revealing that he was the father of her child. Judah recognized his items and declared Tamar more righteous than himself, admitting his fault. Consequently, Tamar was not burned, and she bore twins, Perez and Zerah, in the seventh year of the second week [2170 A.M.] The seven years of fruitfulness, as Joseph had predicted to Pharaoh, came to pass. Judah acknowledged his sin, lamented, and sought forgiveness from the Lord, who granted it because of his sincere repentance. He was told that his sons had not sinned with Tamar, thus his lineage would continue. Judah's actions were a cause for serious condemnation, and it was decreed that any man who engages in such acts with his mother-in-law should be punished by fire, as such behavior is seen as deeply unclean

Jubilees 42

In the first year of the third week of the forty-fifth jubilee [2171 A.M.], famine struck the land, and no rain fell, causing barrenness. However, Egypt had food because Joseph had collected and stored grain during the seven years of plenty. The Egyptians came to Joseph for food, which he sold to them for gold. Jacob, learning that there was food in Egypt, sent his ten sons to buy provisions, but he did not send Benjamin. Joseph recognized his brothers, but they did not recognize him. He accused them of being spies, imprisoned them, and later released them while keeping Simeon. He filled their sacks with grain and returned their money, instructing them to bring Benjamin back Upon their return to Canaan, the brothers reported to Jacob what had transpired and expressed their fear that Benjamin might be taken as well. Jacob was reluctant to send Benjamin, fearing for his life. Reuben offered his sons as a guarantee for Benjamin's safety, but Jacob refused. When the famine worsened, Jacob agreed to send Benjamin with his sons, making Judah responsible for his safe return The brothers arrived in Egypt with gifts, and Joseph saw Benjamin and welcomed him. He hosted a feast, giving Benjamin a portion seven times greater than the others. Joseph then devised a plan to test his brothers' integrity by hiding his silver cup in Benjamin's sack and accusing them of theft

Jubilees 43

The steward followed Joseph's instructions and pursued the brothers. When the cup was found in Benjamin's sack, the brothers returned to Joseph, lamenting their misfortune. Judah offered to remain as a slave in place of Benjamin, showing their commitment to their father and brother. Joseph saw their sincerity and revealed his identity to them, speaking in Hebrew and weeping with them. He assured them that they need not be distressed, as he was in a position to help them during the remaining years of famine. Joseph instructed them to tell their father of his position and the prosperity he had achieved He provided them with chariots, supplies, and gifts for their journey, and they returned to Canaan to inform their father. Jacob was initially disbelieving, but the sight of the provisions and chariots revived his spirit, and he resolved to go to Egypt to see Joseph before he died

Jubilees 44

Israel set out from Haran on the new moon of the third month, traveling to Egypt. He offered sacrifices to God and contemplated whether to go down into Egypt, fearing the move. On the sixteenth of the month, God spoke to him, reassuring him not to fear going to Egypt, promising to make him a great nation and that Joseph would be there to close his eyes at death Jacob's family, totaling seventy souls, journeyed to Egypt, with Judah sent ahead to check

the land of Goshen. The names of Jacob's sons and their descendants who went to Egypt are listed, including those from Leah, Zilpah, Rachel, and Bilhah. The total number of Jacob's descendants who went to Egypt was seventy, though five had died before Joseph, and two of Judah's sons, Er and Onan, had also died without children

Jubilees 45

Israel arrived in Goshen on the new moon of the fourth month [2172 A.M.], in the second year of the third week of the forty-fifth jubilee. Joseph met him, and they wept together. Jacob blessed the Lord for allowing him to see Joseph again and for the fulfillment of the vision he had at Bethel. Joseph settled his family in Goshen, providing them with the best of the land and ensuring their needs were met during the remaining years of famine Joseph managed the land of Egypt, acquiring all its property and people for Pharaoh due to the famine. After the famine, the land was fertile again, and Joseph established a new ordinance for Egypt's food distribution. Jacob lived in Egypt for seventeen years, reaching a total of one hundred and forty-seven years

Jubilees 46:

After Jacob's death, the children of Israel grew and thrived in Egypt, becoming a great nation. They lived in unity and mutual support, and their population increased significantly throughout the lifetime of Joseph. For ten weeks of years, all the days of Joseph's life, there was no adversary or evil affecting them. Joseph lived for 110 years, spending 17 years in Canaan, 10 years as a servant, 3 years in prison, and 80 years as a ruler over Egypt. When Joseph died, all his brothers and that generation also passed away. Before his death, Joseph instructed the Israelites to carry his bones with them when they left Egypt, making them swear an oath. He foresaw that the Egyptians would not willingly bring his remains to Canaan. During this time, Makamaron, the king of Canaan, fought with the Egyptian king and pursued them to the gates of 'Ermon. However, a new and stronger king of Egypt had taken power, and the gates of Egypt were sealed, preventing any movement in or out of the country. Joseph died in the forty-sixth jubilee, in the sixth week, in the second year, and was buried in Egypt. After Joseph's death, the Egyptians waged war against the Canaanites in the forty-seventh jubilee. The Israelites managed to retrieve the bones of all the sons of Jacob except Joseph, and they buried them in the double cave in the mountain. Most of the Israelites returned to Egypt, though a few stayed in the mountains of Hebron, including Amram, Moses' father. The Canaanite king defeated the Egyptian king and closed Egypt's gates, devising a plan to oppress the Israelites. He feared their increasing numbers and potential alliance with Egypt's enemies. As a result, he imposed harsh slavery on them, building cities like Pithom and Raamses and fortifying the fallen walls of Egyptian cities. Despite their suffering, the Israelites continued to multiply, and the Egyptians grew increasingly hostile toward them

Jubilees 47:

In the seventh week, in the seventh year of the forty-seventh jubilee, Moses' father left Canaan, and Moses was born in the fourth week, in the sixth year of the forty-eighth jubilee, during a time of great tribulation for the Israelites. Pharaoh had decreed that all newborn Hebrew boys be thrown into the river. For seven months, the Israelites complied with this command until the day Moses was born. His mother hid him for three months before placing him in an ark, which she covered with pitch and asphalt. She placed the ark among the reeds by the riverbank, leaving Moses there for seven days. During the night, his mother nursed him, and by day, his sister Miriam kept watch. Eventually, Tharmuth, Pharaoh's daughter, came to bathe in the river and heard the baby's cries. She instructed her maidens to retrieve him and took him into her care, feeling compassion for him. Miriam offered to find a Hebrew woman to nurse the baby, and Tharmuth agreed. Miriam brought their mother Jochebed, who was paid to nurse Moses. When Moses grew older, he was brought to Pharaoh's daughter and became her son. He was educated in writing by his father Amram and spent three weeks in the royal court before witnessing an Egyptian beating a Hebrew. Moses killed the Egyptian and buried him in the sand. The next day, he saw two Hebrews fighting and intervened, only to be challenged by one of them. Fearing for his safety, Moses fled

Jubilees 48:

In the sixth year of the third week of the forty-ninth jubilee, Moses left for Midian and spent five weeks and one year there. He returned to Egypt in the second week of the second year of the fiftieth jubilee. During this period, he received instructions from God on Mount Sinai and encountered Mastêmâ, who sought to prevent Moses from executing divine judgment on Egypt. Mastêmâ tried to kill Moses and deliver the Egyptians from his hand, but God protected him. Moses performed signs and wonders against Pharaoh, and God executed ten plagues on Egypt to avenge the Israelites. These plagues included blood, frogs, lice, dog-flies, boils, cattle disease, hail, locusts, darkness, and the death of the firstborn. Moses was directed to confront Pharaoh, and all the plagues occurred as foretold. Despite the signs, Mastêmâ continued to resist and incited the Egyptians to pursue the Israelites. God intervened by parting the Red Sea for the Israelites and casting their pursuers into the depths. Mastêmâ was bound and imprisoned to prevent him from accusing Israel. On the fourteenth day, Mastêmâ was released to help the Egyptians, who then pursued Israel. God hardened the Egyptians' hearts to ensure their destruction, fulfilling the vengeance that had been decreed

Jubilees 49:

Moses was instructed to observe the Passover on the fourteenth day of the first month, to be sacrificed before evening and eaten by night on the fifteenth. This practice commemorates the night when the Israelites ate the Passover lamb in Egypt while the powers of Mastêmâ were sent to kill the firstborn of Egypt. The blood of the lamb marked the Israelites' homes, sparing them from destruction. The plague was severe in Egypt, with no house left unscathed. The Israelites, however, were spared and prepared to leave Egypt. The observance of Passover is an eternal ordinance, to be celebrated annually according to its appointed time. Those who neglect it or fail to offer sacrifices correctly will be held guilty. The Passover should be celebrated in the sanctuary of the Lord, and in future times, in the tabernacle or temple. The Israelites should not celebrate it in their cities or elsewhere but only before the sanctuary. They must follow the specific instructions for preparing and eating the lamb, ensuring no bones are broken and that it is roasted, not boiled or eaten raw. This festival, observed with haste as they left Egypt, is to be kept with strict adherence to its commandments, and any deviation will bring guilt upon the people

Jubilees 50:

Moses was also informed about the Sabbaths and the laws of the jubilee years. He was instructed about the importance of observing the Sabbaths and the year-weeks, with the knowledge that there would be forty-nine jubilees from Adam until the present, with forty years remaining before entering Canaan. The land was to keep its Sabbaths and jubilees, ensuring that Israel would be cleansed of all impurities and live in peace without evil. The Sabbaths were strictly regulated, with any work on the Sabbath being punishable by death. The Sabbath was designated as a holy day for rest and worship, with specific prohibitions against work, travel, or any other labor. The observance of the Sabbath and its commandments were to be followed precisely, as recorded on the heavenly tablets

88. The Prayer of Manasseh

1. O Lord Almighty, God of our ancestors, of Abraham and Isaac and Jacob and of their righteous offspring; 2. You who have made heaven and earth with all their order; 3. Who shackled the sea by your word of command, who have confined the deep and sealed it with your terrible and glorious name; 4. At whom all things shudder, and tremble before your power, 5. For your glorious splendor cannot be borne, and the wrath of your threat to sinners is unendurable; 6. Yet immeasurable and unsearchable is your promised mercy, 7. For you are the Lord Most High, of great compassion, long-suffering, and very merciful, who relents over the evils of human beings. You, O Lord, according to your great goodness have promised repentance and forgiveness to those who have sinned against you; and in the multitude of your mercies you have appointed repentance for sinners, that they may be saved. 8. Therefore you, O Lord, God of the righteous, have not appointed repentance for the righteous, for Abraham and Isaac and Jacob, who did not sin against you, but you have appointed repentance for me, who am a sinner. 9. For the sins I have committed are more in number than the sand of the sea; my transgressions are multiplied, O Lord, they are multiplied! I am unworthy to look up and see the height of heaven because of the multitude of my iniquities. 10. I am weighed down with many an iron fetter, so that I am rejected because of my sins, and I have no relief; for I have provoked your wrath and have done what is evil in your sight, setting up abominations and multiplying offenses. 11. And now I bend the knee of my heart, imploring you for your kindness. 12. I have sinned, O Lord, I have sinned, and I acknowledge my transgressions. 13. I earnestly implore you, forgive me, O Lord, forgive me! Do not destroy me with my transgressions! Do not be angry with me forever or lay up evil for me; do not condemn me to the depths of the earth. For you, O Lord, are the God of those who repent, 14. and in me you will display your goodness; for, unworthy as I am, you will save me according to your great mercy, 15. and I will praise you continually all the days of my life. For all the host of heaven sings your praise, and yours is the glory forever. Amen.

89. Psalm 151

1. This Psalm is ascribed to David and is outside the number. When he slew Goliath in single combat. 2. I was small among my brothers, And the youngest in my father's house; I tended my father's sheep. 3. My hands made a harp; My fingers fashioned a lyre. 4. And who will tell my Lord? The Lord himself; it is he who hears. 5. It was he who sent his messenger And took me from my father's sheep, And anointed me with his anointing oil. 6. My brothers were handsome and tall, But the Lord was not pleased with them. 7. I went out to meet the Philistine, And he cursed me by his idols. 8. But I drew his own sword; I beheaded him and took away disgrace from the people of Israel.

90. The Letter of Jeremiah

The Letter of Jeremiah 1. A copy of a letter that Jeremiah sent to those who were to be taken as captives to Babylon by the king of the Babylonians, to give them the message that God had commanded him. 2. Because of the sins that you have committed before God, you will be taken to Babylon as captives by Nebuchadnezzar, king of the Babylonians. 3. So when you have come to Babylon, you will remain there for many years, a long time—seven generations; and after that, I will bring you away from there in peace. 4. Now in Babylon you will see gods made of silver, and of gold, and of wood, borne upon shoulders, which cause the nations to fear. 5. Beware therefore that you in no way become like the strangers, nor let fear for these gods possess you when you see the multitude before them and behind them worshiping them. 6. But say in your hearts, "It is you, O Lord, whom we must worship." 7. For my angel is with you, and he will watch over your lives. 8. Their tongues are polished by the craftsman, and they themselves are overlaid with gold and silver; yet they are false and cannot speak. 9. People take gold and make crowns for the heads of their gods, as you would with a girl who loves ornaments. 10. Sometimes the priests steal gold and silver from their gods and spend it on themselves. 11. They will give some of it to the prostitutes on the terrace; they deck their gods out with garments like humans— these gods of silver and gold and wood. 12. They cannot save themselves from rust and moth, though they are covered with purple garments. 13. They wipe their faces because of the dust of the temple, when there is much upon them. 14. This shows that they are not gods; so do not fear them. 15. As a vessel that a man uses is worth nothing when it is broken, so it is with their gods; when they are set up in the temple, their eyes are full of dust from the feet of those who enter. 16. And just as the gates are shut on every side upon one who has offended a king, as though he were sentenced to death, so the priests secure the temple doors with bars and locks, so that they may not be plundered by robbers. 17. They light lamps, even more than they do for themselves, though their gods can see none of them. 18. They are just like a beam in the house; it is said that their hearts are eaten away, though they themselves do not feel it when the worms creep out of the ground and devour them and their robes. They do not notice when their faces are blackened by the smoke of the temple. 19. Bats, swallows, and birds land on their bodies and heads; and so do cats. 20. From this you will know that they are not gods; so do not fear them. 21. As for the gold that they wear for beauty, it will not shine unless someone wipes off the tarnish; for even when they were being cast, they did not feel it. 22. They are bought at any cost, but there is no breath in them. 23. Having no feet, they are carried on shoulders, revealing to humankind their worthlessness; even those who serve them are ashamed. 24. If they fall to the ground, they cannot pick themselves up; if one sets them upright, they cannot move by themselves; and if they are tipped over, they cannot straighten themselves. 25. Gifts are placed before them just as before the dead. 26. The priests sell the sacrifices that are offered to these gods and use the money; likewise, their wives preserve some with salt, but give none to the poor or helpless. 27. Sacrifices to them may even be touched by women in their periods or at childbirth. 28. Knowing by these signs that they are not gods, do not fear them. 29. For how can they be called gods? Women serve meals for gods of silver, gold, and wood. 30. In their temples the priests sit with their clothes torn, their heads and beards shaved, and their heads uncovered. 31. They howl and shout before their gods as some do at a funeral banquet. 32. The priests take some of the clothing of their gods to clothe their wives and children. 33. Whether one does evil or good to them, they will not be able to repay it; they can neither set up a king nor put him down. 34. Similarly, they are not able to give either wealth or money; if one makes a vow to them and does not keep it, they will not require it. 35. They cannot save a man from death or rescue the weak from the strong. 36. They cannot restore sight to the blind; they cannot rescue one who is in distress. 37. They cannot take pity on a widow or do good to an orphan. 38. These gods of wood, overlaid with gold and silver, are like stones from the mountain; those who serve them will be put to shame. 39. Why then must anyone think that they are gods, or call them gods? 40. Besides, even the Chaldeans themselves dishonor them; for when they see someone mute who cannot speak, they bring Bel and pray that the mute might speak, as though they could understand. 41. Yet they themselves cannot perceive this and abandon them; for they have no sense. 42. And the women, with cords around them, sit along the passageways, burning bran for incense; and when one of them is led off by some passerby and is abused, she mocks the woman who has not been abused, knowing that it is she who should be ashamed. 43. And you will know by these things that they are not gods; do not fear them. 44. For how can they be called gods? For women serve meals for gods of silver, gold, and wood. 45. And in their temples the priests sit with their clothes torn, their heads and beards shaved, and their heads uncovered. 46. They howl and shout before their gods as some do at a funeral banquet. 47. The priests steal from the poor, pretending to be busy with their gods; they take the gold and silver that the poor have saved and spend it on themselves. 48. Likewise, they will give some of the stolen money to the prostitutes and deck their gods out with garments like humans. These gods of silver and gold and wood cannot save themselves from thieves or robbers. 49. Strong men may seize their gold and silver and go off with it, and they cannot help themselves. 50. Better therefore is someone righteous who has no idols; such a person will be far from disgrace. 51. My children, keep yourselves from idols; have nothing to do with them.

91. *The Prayer of Azariah*

1 And they walked in the midst of the fire, praising God, and blessing the Lord. 2 Then Azariah stood up, and prayed on this manner; and opening his mouth in the midst of the fire said, 3 Blessed art thou, O Lord God of our fathers: thy name is worthy to be praised and glorified for evermore: 4 For thou art righteous in all the things that thou hast done to us: yea, true are all thy works; thy ways are right, and all thy judgments truth. 5 In all the things that thou hast brought upon us, and upon the holy city of our fathers, even Jerusalem, thou hast executed true judgment: for according to truth and judgment didst thou bring all these things upon us because of our sins. 6 For we have sinned and committed iniquity, departing from thee. 7 In all things have we trespassed, and not obeyed thy commandments, nor kept them, neither done as thou hast commanded us, that it might go well with us. 8 Wherefore all that thou hast brought upon us, and every thing that thou hast done to us, thou hast done in true judgment. 9 And thou didst deliver us into the hands of lawless enemies, most hateful forsakers of God, and to an unjust king, and the most wicked in all the world. 10 And now we cannot open our mouths, we are become a shame and reproach to thy servants; and to them that worship thee. 11 Yet deliver us not up wholly, for thy name's sake, neither disannul thou thy covenant: 12 And cause not thy mercy to depart from us, for thy beloved Abraham's sake, for thy servant Isaac's sake, and for thy holy Israel's sake; 13 To whom thou hast spoken and promised, that thou wouldest multiply their seed as the stars of heaven, and as the sand that lieth upon the seashore. 14 For we, O Lord, are become less than any nation, and be kept under this day in all the world because of our sins. 15 Neither is there at this time prince, or prophet, or leader, or burnt offering, or sacrifice, or oblation, or incense, or place to sacrifice before thee, and to find mercy. 16 Nevertheless in a contrite heart and an humble spirit let us be accepted. 17 Like as in the burnt offerings of rams and bullocks, and like as in ten thousands of fat lambs: so let our sacrifice be in thy sight this day, and grant that we may wholly go after thee: for they shall not be confounded that put their trust in thee. 18 And now we follow thee with all our heart, we fear thee, and seek thy face. 19 Put us not to shame: but deal with us after thy lovingkindness, and according to the multitude of thy mercies. 20 Deliver us also

according to thy marvelous works, and give glory to thy name, O Lord: and let all them that do thy servants hurt be ashamed; 21 And let them be confounded in all their power and might, and let their strength be broken; 22 And let them know that thou art the Lord, the only God, and glorious over the whole world. 23 And the king's servants that put them in, ceased not to make the oven hot with rosin, pitch, tow, and small wood; 24 So that the flame streamed forth above the furnace forty and nine cubits. 25 And it passed through, and burned those Chaldeans it found about the furnace. 26 But the angel of the Lord came down into the oven together with Azarias and his fellows, and smote the flame of the fire out of the oven; 27 And made the midst of the furnace as it had been a moist whistling wind, so that the fire touched them not at all, neither hurt nor troubled them. 28 Then the three, as out of one mouth, praised, glorified, and blessed God in the furnace, saying,

92. The Song of the Three Holy Children

1 And they walked in the midst of the fire, praising God, and blessing the Lord. 2 Then Azariah stood up, and prayed on this manner; and opening his mouth in the midst of the fire said, 3 Blessed art thou, O Lord God of our fathers: thy name is worthy to be praised and glorified for evermore: 4 For thou art righteous in all the things that thou hast done to us: yea, true are all thy works; thy ways are right, and all thy judgments truth. 5 In all the things that thou hast brought upon us, and upon the holy city of our fathers, even Jerusalem, thou hast executed true judgment: for according to truth and judgment didst thou bring all these things upon us because of our sins. 6 For we have sinned and committed iniquity, departing from thee. 7 In all things have we trespassed, and not obeyed thy commandments, nor kept them, neither done as thou hast commanded us, that it might go well with us. 8 Wherefore all that thou hast brought upon us, and every thing that thou hast done to us, thou hast done in true judgment. 9 And thou didst deliver us into the hands of lawless enemies, most hateful forsakers of God, and to an unjust king, and the most wicked in all the world. 10 And now we cannot open our mouths, we are become a shame and reproach to thy servants; and to them that worship thee. 11 Yet deliver us not up wholly, for thy name's sake, neither disannul thou thy covenant: 12 And cause not thy mercy to depart from us, for thy beloved Abraham's sake, for thy servant Isaac's sake, and for thy holy Israel's sake; 13 To whom thou hast spoken and promised, that thou wouldest multiply their seed as the stars of heaven, and as the sand that lieth upon the seashore. 14 For we, O Lord, are become less than any nation, and be kept under this day in all the world because of our sins. 15 Neither is there at this time prince, or prophet, or leader, or burnt offering, or sacrifice, or oblation, or incense, or place to sacrifice before thee, and to find mercy. 16 Nevertheless in a contrite heart and an humble spirit let us be accepted. 17 Like as in the burnt offerings of rams and bullocks, and like as in ten thousands of fat lambs: so let our sacrifice be in thy sight this day, and grant that we may wholly go after thee: for they shall not be confounded that put their trust in thee. 18 And now we follow thee with all our heart, we fear thee, and seek thy face. 19 Put us not to shame: but deal with us after thy lovingkindness, and according to the multitude of thy mercies. 20 Deliver us also according to thy marvelous works, and give glory to thy name, O Lord: and let all them that do thy servants hurt be ashamed; 21 And let them be confounded in all their power and might, and let their strength be broken; 22 And let them know that thou art the Lord, the only God, and glorious over the whole world. 23 And the king's servants that put them in, ceased not to make the oven hot with rosin, pitch, tow, and small wood; 24 So that the flame streamed forth above the furnace forty and nine cubits. 25 And it passed through, and burned those Chaldeans it found about the furnace. 26 But the angel of the Lord came down into the oven together with Azarias and his fellows, and smote the flame of the fire out of the oven; 27 And made the midst of the furnace as it had been a moist whistling wind, so that the fire touched them not at all, neither hurt nor troubled them. 28 Then the three, as out of one mouth, praised, glorified, and blessed God in the furnace, saying, 29 Blessed art thou, O Lord God of our fathers, and to be praised and highly exalted forever; 30 And blessed is thy glorious, holy name, and to be highly praised and highly exalted forever. 31 Blessed art thou in the temple of thy holy glory, and to be extolled and highly glorified forever. 32 Blessed art thou that beholdest the depths, and sittest upon the cherubim, and to be praised and exalted forever. 33 Blessed art thou on the glorious throne of thy kingdom, and to be extolled and highly exalted forever. 34 Blessed art thou in the firmament of heaven, and to be sung and glorified forever. 35 All ye works of the Lord, bless ye the Lord: praise and exalt him above all forever, 36 O ye heavens, bless ye the Lord: praise and exalt him above all forever. 37 O ye angels of the Lord, bless ye the Lord: praise and exalt him above all forever. 38 O all waters that be above the heaven, bless ye the Lord: praise and exalt him above all forever. 39 O all powers of the Lord, bless ye the Lord: praise and exalt him above all forever. 40 O ye sun and moon, bless ye the Lord: praise and exalt him above all forever. 41 O ye stars of heaven, bless ye the Lord: praise and exalt him above all forever. 42 O every shower and dew, bless ye the Lord: praise and exalt him above all forever. 43 O all ye winds, bless ye the Lord: praise and exalt him above all forever. 44 O ye fire and heat, bless ye the Lord: praise and exalt him above all forever. 45 O ye winter and summer, bless ye the Lord: praise and exalt him above all forever. 46 O ye dews and storms of snow, bless ye the Lord: praise and exalt him above all forever. 47 O ye nights and days, bless ye the Lord: praise and exalt him above all forever. 48 O ye light and darkness, bless ye the Lord: praise and exalt him above all forever. 49 O ye ice and cold, bless ye the Lord: praise and exalt him above all forever. 50 O ye frosts and snows, bless ye the Lord: praise and exalt him above all forever. 51 O ye lightnings and clouds, bless ye the Lord: praise and exalt him above all forever. 52 Let the earth bless the Lord: praise and exalt him above all forever. 53 O ye mountains and hills, bless ye the Lord: praise and exalt him above all forever. 54 O all things that grow on the earth, bless ye the Lord: praise and exalt him above all forever. 55 O ye springs, bless ye the Lord: praise and exalt him above all forever. 56 O ye seas and rivers, bless ye the Lord: praise and exalt him above all forever. 57 O ye whales, and all that move in the waters, bless ye the Lord: praise and exalt him above all forever. 58 O all ye fowls of the air, bless ye the Lord: praise and exalt him above all forever. 59 O all ye beasts and cattle, bless ye the Lord: praise and exalt him above all forever. 60 O ye children of men, bless ye the Lord: praise and exalt him above all forever. 61 O Israel, bless ye the Lord: praise and exalt him above all forever. 62 O ye priests of the Lord, bless ye the Lord: praise and exalt him above all forever. 63 O ye servants of the Lord, bless ye the Lord: praise and exalt him above all forever. 64 O ye spirits and souls of the righteous, bless ye the Lord: praise and exalt him above all forever. 65 O ye holy and humble men of heart, bless ye the Lord: praise and exalt him above all forever. 66 O Ananias, Azarias, and Misael, bless ye the Lord: praise and exalt him above all forever: for he hath delivered us from hell, and saved us from the hand of death, and delivered us out of the midst of the furnace and burning flame: even out of the midst of the fire hath he delivered us. 67 O give thanks unto the Lord,

because he is gracious: for his mercy endureth for ever. 68 O all ye that worship the Lord, bless the God of gods, praise him, and give him thanks: for his mercy endureth for ever.

93. *The History of Susanna*

1 There dwelt a man in Babylon, called Joacim: 2 And he took a wife, whose name was Susanna, the daughter of Hilkiah, a very fair woman, and one that feared the Lord. 3 Her parents also were righteous, and taught their daughter according to the law of Moses. 4 Now Joacim was a great rich man, and had a fair garden joining unto his house: and to him resorted the Jews; because he was more honourable than all others. 5 The same year were appointed two of the elders of the people to be judges, such as the Lord spake of, that wickedness came from Babylon from ancient judges, who seemed to govern the people. 6 These kept much at Joacim's house: and all that had any suits in law came unto them. 7 Now when the people departed away at noon, Susanna went into her husband's garden to walk. 8 And the two elders saw her going in every day, and walking; so that their lust was inflamed toward her. 9 And they perverted their own mind and turned away their eyes, that they might not look unto heaven, nor remember just judgments. 10 And albeit they both were wounded with her love, yet durst not one shew another his grief. 11 For they were ashamed to declare their lust, that they desired to have to do with her. 12 Yet they watched diligently from day to day to see her. 13 And the one said to the other, Let us now go home: for it is dinner time. 14 So when they were gone out, they parted the one from the other, and turning back again they came to the same place; and after that they had asked one another the cause, they acknowledged their lust: then appointed they a time both together, when they might find her alone. 15 And it fell out, as they watched a fit time, she went in as before with two maids only, and she was desirous to wash herself in the garden: for it was hot. 16 And there was nobody there save the two elders, that had hid themselves, and watched her. 17 Then she said to her maids, Bring me oil and washing balls, and shut the garden doors, that I may wash me. 18 And they did as she bade them, and shut the garden doors, and went out themselves at privy doors to fetch the things that she had commanded them: but they saw not the elders, because they were hid. 19 Now when the maids were gone forth, the two elders rose up, and ran unto her, saying, 20 Behold, the garden doors are shut, that no man can see us, and we are in love with thee; therefore consent unto us, and lie with us. 21 If thou wilt not, we will bear witness against thee, that a young man was with thee: and therefore thou didst send away thy maids from thee. 22 Then Susanna sighed deeply, and said, I am straitened on every side: for if I do this thing, it is death unto me: and if I do it not I cannot escape your hands. 23 It is better for me to fall into your hands, and not do it, than to sin in the sight of the Lord. 24 With that Susanna cried with a loud voice: and the two elders cried out against her. 25 Then ran the one, and opened the garden doors. 26 When the servants of the house heard the cry in the garden, they rushed in at the privy door, to see what was done unto her. 27 But when the elders had declared their matter, the servants were greatly ashamed: for there never was such a report made of Susanna. 28 And it came to pass the next day, when the people were assembled to her husband Joacim, the two elders came also full of mischievous imagination against Susanna to put her to death; 29 And said before the people, Send for Susanna, the daughter of Hilkiah, Joacim's wife; and so they sent. 30 So she came with her father and mother, her children, and all her kindred. 31 Now Susanna was a very delicate woman, and beauteous to behold. 32 And these wicked men commanded to uncover her face, (for she was covered) that they might be filled with her beauty. 33 Therefore her friends and all that saw her wept. 34 Then the two elders stood up in the midst of the people, and laid their hands upon her head. 35 And she weeping looked up toward heaven: for her heart trusted in the Lord. 36 And the elders said, As we walked in the garden alone, this woman came in with two maids, and shut the garden doors, and sent the maids away. 37 Then a young man, who there was hid, came unto her, and lay with her. 38 Then we that stood in a corner of the garden, seeing this wickedness, ran unto them. 39 And when we saw them together, the man we could not hold: for he was stronger than we, and opened the doors, and leaped out. 40 But having taken this woman, we asked who the young man was, but she would not tell us: these things do we testify. 41 Then the assembly believed them, as those that were the elders and judges of the people: so they condemned her to death. 42 Then Susanna cried out with a loud voice, and said, O everlasting God, that knowest the secrets, and knowest all things before they be: 43 Thou knowest that they have borne false witness against me, and behold, I must die; whereas I never did such things as these men have maliciously invented against me. 44 And the Lord heard her voice. 45 Therefore when she was led to be put to death, the Lord raised up the holy spirit of a young youth whose name was Daniel: 46 Who cried with a loud voice, I am clear from the blood of this woman. 47 Then all the people turned them toward him, and said, What mean these words that thou hast spoken? 48 So he standing in the midst of them said, Are ye such fools, ye sons of Israel, that without examination or knowledge of the truth ye have condemned a daughter of Israel? 49 Return again to the place of judgment: for they have borne false witness against her. 50 Wherefore all the people turned again in haste, and the elders said unto him, Come, sit down among us, and shew it us, seeing God hath given thee the honour of an elder. 51 Then said Daniel unto them, Put these two apart one from another, and I will examine them. 52 So when they were put asunder one from another, he called one of them, and said unto him, O thou that art waxen old in wickedness, now thy sins which thou hast committed aforetime are come to light. 53 For thou hast pronounced false judgment, and hast condemned the innocent, and hast let the guilty go free; albeit the Lord saith, The innocent and righteous shalt thou not slay. 54 Now then, if thou sawest her, tell me, Under what tree sawest thou them companying together? Who answered, Under a mastick tree. 55 And Daniel said, Very well; thou hast lied against thine own head; for even now the angel of God hath received the sentence of God to cut thee in two. 56 So he put him aside, and commanded to bring the other, and said unto him, O thou seed of Canaan, and not of Judah, beauty hath deceived thee, and lust hath perverted thine heart. 57 Thus have ye dealt with the daughters of Israel, and they for fear companied with you: but the daughter of Judah would not abide your wickedness. 58 Now therefore tell me, Under what tree didst thou take them companying together? Who answered, Under an holm tree. 59 Daniel said unto him, Well; thou hast also lied against thine own head: for the angel of God waiteth with the sword to cut thee in two, that he may destroy you. 60 With that, all the assembly cried out with a loud voice, and praised God, who saveth them that trust in him. 61 And they arose against the two elders, for Daniel had convicted them of false witness by their own mouth: 62 And according to the law of Moses they did unto them in such sort as they maliciously intended to do to their neighbour: and they put them to death. Thus the innocent blood was saved the same day. 63 Therefore Chelcias and his wife praised God for their daughter Susanna, with Joacim her husband, and all the kindred, because there was no dishonesty found in her. 64 From that day forth was Daniel had in great reputation in the sight of the people.

94. Bel and the Dragon

1 And king Astyages was gathered to his fathers, and Cyrus of Persia received his kingdom. 2 And Daniel conversed with the king, and was honoured above all his friends. 3 Now the Babylonians had an idol, called Bel, and there were spent upon him every day twelve great measures of fine flour, and forty sheep, and six vessels of wine. 4 And the king worshipped it, and went daily to adore it: but Daniel worshipped his own God. And the king said unto him, Why dost not thou worship Bel? 5 Who answered and said, Because I may not worship idols made with hands, but the living God, who hath created the heaven and the earth, and hath sovereignty over all flesh. 6 Then said the king unto him, Thinkest thou not that Bel is a living god? seest thou not how much he eateth and drinketh every day? 7 Then Daniel smiled, and said, O king, be not deceived: for this is but clay within, and brass without, and did never eat or drink any thing. 8 So the king was wroth, and called for his priests, and said unto them, If ye tell me not who this is that devoureth these expenses, ye shall die. 9 But if ye can certify me that Bel devoureth them, then Daniel shall die: for he hath spoken blasphemy against Bel. And Daniel said unto the king, Let it be according to thy word. 10 Now there were seventy priests of Bel, beside their wives and children. And the king went with Daniel into the temple of Bel. 11 So Bel's priests said, Lo, we go out: but thou, O king, set on the meat, and make ready the wine, and shut the door fast, and seal it with thine own signet; 12 And when thou comest in the morning, if thou findest not that Bel hath eaten up all, we will suffer death: or else Daniel, that speaketh falsely against us. 13 And they little regarded it: for under the table they had made a privy entrance, whereby they entered continually, and consumed those things. 14 So when they were gone forth, the king set meats before Bel. Now Daniel had commanded his servants to bring ashes, and those they strewed throughout all the temple in the presence of the king alone: then went they out, and shut the door, and sealed it with the king's signet. 15 And so early in the morning Daniel arose, and the king came, and said, Daniel, are the seals whole? And he said, Yea, O king, they be whole. 16 And as soon as he had opened the door, the king looked upon the table, and cried with a loud voice, Great art thou, O Bel, and with thee is no deceit at all. 17 Then laughed Daniel, and held the king that he should not go in, and said, Behold now the pavement, and mark well whose footsteps are these. 18 And the king said, I see the footsteps of men, women, and children. And then the king was angry, 19 And took the priests with their wives and children, who shewed him the privy doors, where they came in, and consumed such things as were upon the table. 20 Therefore the king slew them, and delivered Bel into Daniel's power, who destroyed him and his temple. 21 And in that same place there was a great dragon, which the Babylonians worshipped. 22 And the king said unto Daniel, Wilt thou also say that this is of brass? for lo, he liveth, he eateth and drinketh; thou canst not say that he is no living god: therefore worship him. 23 Then said Daniel unto the king, I will worship the Lord my God: for he is the living God. 24 But give me leave, O king, and I will slay this dragon without sword or staff. The king said, I give thee leave. 25 Then Daniel took pitch, and fat, and hair, and did seethe them together, and made lumps thereof: this he put in the dragon's mouth, and so the dragon burst in sunder: and Daniel said, Lo, these are the gods ye worship. 26 When they of Babylon heard that, they took great indignation, and conspired against the king, saying, The king is become a Jew, and he hath destroyed Bel, he hath slain the dragon, and put the priests to death. 27 So they came to the king, and said, Deliver us Daniel, or else we will destroy thee and thine house. 28 Now when the king saw that they pressed him sore, being constrained, he delivered Daniel unto them: 29 Who cast him into the lions' den: where he was six days. 30 And in the den there were seven lions, and they had given them every day two carcases, and two sheep: which then were not given to them, to the intent they might devour Daniel. 31 Now there was in Jewry a prophet, called Habbacuc, who had made pottage, and had broken bread in a bowl, and was going into the field, for to bring it to the reapers. 32 But the angel of the Lord said unto Habbacuc, Go carry the dinner that thou hast into Babylon unto Daniel, who is in the lions' den. 33 And Habbacuc said, Lord, I never saw Babylon; neither do I know where the den is. 34 Then the angel of the Lord took him by the crown, and bare him by the hair of his head, and through the vehemence of his spirit set him in Babylon over the den. 35 And Habbacuc cried, saying, O Daniel, Daniel, take the dinner which God hath sent thee. 36 And Daniel said, Thou hast remembered me, O God: neither hast thou forsaken them that seek thee and love thee. 37 So Daniel arose, and did eat: and the angel of the Lord immediately set Habbacuc again in his own place. 38 And upon the seventh day the king went to bewail Daniel: and when he came to the den, he looked in, and behold, Daniel was sitting. 39 Then cried the king with a loud voice, saying, Great art thou, O Lord God of Daniel, and there is none other beside thee. 40 And he drew him out, and cast those that were the cause of his destruction into the den: and they were devoured in a moment before his face.

95. The Story of Ahikar

1 Ahikar was the son of my brother Anael, and he was the chief cupbearer, and the second after the king, and in charge of the signet ring. 2 And Ahikar said to his son, I am weary, my son, and old and stricken in years, and I have no son but thee. Put thy heart to learning, my son, and to writing, read diligently, and drive indolence far from thee. 3 For thou seest, my son, that I have become old, and it behoves me to take thought for thee as my father took thought for me. 4 I, too, had no other son but thee, I prayed to the Lord, and He heard me and granted me thee. 5 And now, my son, I have made known to the king, and have set thee before his face. 6 And the king has given thee his signet ring, and made thee steward over his house. 7 My son, forget not the Lord, and provoke not his mighty ones to wrath. 8 And if there enter into thy hands an orphan, oppress him not, and if there come to thee the weary, send him not away empty. 9 And let not the weeping of any one who is wronged come up against thee to the Lord. 10 For remember, my son, that thou too art a man, and one day thou too wilt need mercy. 11 Do not forget the Lord in the greatness of thy wealth, for thou knowest not what the evening will bring. 12 Respect the old man, even if he is not thy father, and insult not a man who is in the bitterness of his soul. 13 For there is a shame that bringeth sin, and there is a shame that bringeth glory and grace. 14 Be not slow to visit a sick man, for by such things thou shalt gain love. 15 All thy works, do them in gentleness, and thou wilt be loved by those who are beloved of the Lord. 16 My son, from thy youth up choose instruction, and thou wilt find wisdom also when thou art old. 17 Go to the ant, thou sluggard, and see and emulate her ways, and become wiser than she. 18 For she, having no guide or teacher or leader, prepares her food in the summer and gathers her food in the harvest. 19 How long wilt thou sleep, O sluggard, when wilt thou rise from thy slumber? 20 A little sleep, a little slumber, a little folding of the hands to rest; 21 So shall thy poverty come as a traveller, and thy want as an armed man. 22 But if thou art not sluggish, thy harvest will come as a fountain, and poverty will flee away as a bad runner. 23 These proverbs did Ahikar the wise write, who was from the children of Tabel the Israelite, who was a captive from the captivity which Salmanasar king of the Assyrians had led captive from Samaria, the city of the Israelites. 24 And Ahikar was the nephew of Tobit the great, who

was among the captives, whom Salmanasar king of the Assyrians had brought captive from Thisbe, which is on the right hand of that city, which is called properly Naphtali in Galilee above Asher. 25 I, Ahikar, was cupbearer to the king and was in charge of administration, and I had authority over the works. 26 And I, Ahikar, became great, and the king exalted me, and I built myself a great house. 27 And I was successful in my works, and there was no one who plotted against the king like me, for I was a faithful friend to the king. 28 And I was the chief and first of all the workers, and after I had become great I was exalted, and I led a host of many people. 29 For I had great glory more than any of the children of my city. 30 And when I had built my house, I remembered the Lord, who had given me this glory. 31 And I made for myself an upper chamber in the midst of my house, and there I made a place holy to the Lord God Almighty. 32 And I built my buildings, and I made my high place pure, according to the command of the Lord, which he commanded by Moses in the law, that one should offer gifts to the Lord and should purify his offerings. 33 And every month I would slaughter sheep and oxen and birds, and offer them on the altar that I had built. 34 And I had planted vineyards and made gardens and parks in them, and I had planted in them all kinds of fruit-bearing trees. 35 And I said in my heart, Let me not be lacking in anything at all. 36 So I summoned all the wise men and the scribes, and I wrote books, and to the young men I showed calculations and the reproof of the times, and I made known to them the passage of the moon and all that was not yet come, and the twelve signs of the zodiac, and from the earth to the firmament, and from the firmament to the highest heaven. 37 And I showed them the weight of the winds and the number of the drops of rain, and the suppression of anger, and the multitude of long-suffering, and the truth of judgment, 38 And the root of wisdom and the treasures of intelligence, and the fountain of knowledge, 39 And the height of the air and the greatness of Paradise, and the consummation of the ages, and the beginning of the day of judgment, 40 And the number of the offerings, and the earths which have not yet come, 41 And the mouth of hell, and the place of vengeance, and the region of faith, and the land of hope, and the likeness of the future rest, 42 And the multitude of angels, and the flaming hosts, and the splendor of the lightnings, and the voice of the thunders, and the orders of the chiefs, and the treasuries of light, and the changes of the times, and the investigations of the law. 43 These are the bright purple robes, which I put on, and the diadem of my glory, with which I was crowned. 44 And I became glorious, as one that bringeth peace; and I was honored more than the cedar in Lebanon. 45 And I was exalted, so that I dwelt in the height, and my throne was in a pillar of cloud. 46 And before I died I wrote this testament to the children of my city, and to all those who should be taught thereafter. 47 And I made known to them the weight of the winds, the number of the drops of rain, 48 And the suppression of anger, the multitude of long-suffering, 49 And the truth of judgment, the root of wisdom, 50 And the treasures of intelligence, the fountain of knowledge, 51 And the height of the air, the greatness of Paradise, 52 And the consummation of the ages, the beginning of the day of judgment, 53 And the number of the offerings, and the earths which have not yet come, 54 And the mouth of hell, the place of vengeance, 55 And the region of faith, the land of hope, and the likeness of future rest. 56 Let this be written for those generations which are to come, and that they may praise the Lord, who hath given all these things in their wisdom. 57 And from henceforth let all the wise of heart, who have understanding, know and love the Lord in truth, and let them read this book, and let them be mindful of every command of the Lord, and let them know that there is nothing else eternal, save only the Lord, who hath created all things by His Word. 58 And let them praise His glorious name, and let their heart think upon His majesty, and let them speak of all His wonderful works. 59 And now, children, listen to me, and do not depart from the words of my mouth, and let no one make light of them, and let no one despise them. 60 But teach them, and write them in your hearts continually, for there is no other God but the Lord in whose hands are all the ends of the earth. 61 And when Ahikar had finished these words, he slept with his fathers, and saw corruption, and his son Nadan reigned in his stead.

96. *The Odes of Solomon*

Ode 1

1 The Lord is on my head like a crown, and I shall not be without Him. 2 They wove for me a crown of truth, and it caused thy branches to bud in me. 3 For it is not like a withered crown which buddeth not: but thou livest upon my head, and thou hast blossomed upon my head. 4 Thy fruits are full and perfect, they are full of thy salvation.

Ode 2

1 The Lord hath filled me with his truth, and I am full of his thought. 2 My thought is with Him, my renewal is high. 3 I will not be empty because the voice of the Lord speaketh with me: and is His Spirit a word of truth. 4 They who err have estranged themselves and have gone into the wilderness of their desires.

Ode 3

1 The cup of the Lord is not small nor slight, but full of immortality. 2 It is full of the Lord; and the sons of men partake of it, they who have assumed it are made perfect. 3 It maketh the understanding to be perfect in them: and it hath taught them knowledge. 4 The secrets of the Lord have their place in it.

Ode 4

1 No man can pervert Thy holy place, O my God, nor can he change it, and put it in another place: 2 Because he hath no power over it: for Thy sanctuary Thou hast designed before Thou didst make other places. 3 That which is the older shall not be altered by those that are younger than itself. 4 Thou hast given Thy heart, O Lord, to Thy believers: never wilt Thou fail, nor be without fruits:

Ode 5

1 I will give thanks unto Thee, O Lord, because I love Thee. 2 O Most High, Thou wilt not forsake me, for Thou art my hope. 3 Freely I have received Thy grace, I shall live thereby. 4 My persecutors will come and not see me.

Ode 6

1 As the wind glides through the harp and the strings speak, 2 So the Spirit of the Lord speaks through my members, and I speak through His love. 3 For He destroys whatever is alien, and everything is of the Lord: 4 For thus it was from the beginning, and will be until the end.

Ode 7

1 As the impulse of anger against evil, so is the impulse of joy over what is lovely, and brings in of its fruits without restraint: 2 My joy is the Lord and my impulse is toward Him: this path of mine is excellent: 3 For I have a helper, the Lord. 4 He hath caused me to know Himself, without grudging, by His simplicity: His kindness hath humbled His greatness.

Ode 8

1 Open ye, open ye your hearts to the exultation of the Lord: 2 And let your love be multiplied from the heart and even unto the lips, 3 To bring forth fruit unto the Lord, living [fruit], holy [spirit], and to talk with watchfulness in His light. 4 Rise up, and stand erect, ye who sometime were brought low:

Ode 9

1 Open ye your ears and I will speak to you. Give me 2 Your souls, that I may also give you my soul, 3 The word of the Lord and His delights, 4 The holy thought

which He has thought concerning His Messiah.

Ode 10

1 My heart was cloven and its flower appeared; and grace sprang up in it: 2 And it brought forth fruit to the Lord, for the Most High clave my heart by His Holy Spirit 3 And searched my affection towards Him: and filled me with His love. 4 His opening of me became my salvation and I ran in His way, in His peace, even in the way of truth.

Ode 11

1 My heart was lifted up and enriched in the love of the Most High, so that I might praise Him with my name. 2 My members are with Him, and I am with them: and they shall not be alienated from Him, for He is the life of them. 3 And He hath added to me by His love, and by His gentleness He hath brought me nigh; and by His mercy He hath multiplied His love in me. 4 And by His majesty He set my face towards Him, and I became mighty by His truth, fearing Him.

Ode 12

1 He hath filled me with words of truth, that I may speak the same; 2 And like the flow of waters flows truth from my mouth, and my lips declare His fruits. 3 And He hath caused His knowledge to abound in me, because the mouth of the Lord is the true Word, and the door of His light; 4 And the Most High hath given it to His visions which are interpreted and are perfect in truth.

Ode 13

1 Behold, the Lord is our mirror: open the eyes and see them in Him; and learn the manner of your face, 2 Then declare praises to His Spirit: and wipe off the filth from your face; and love His holiness, and clothe yourselves with it, 3 And be without stain at all times before Him. Hallelujah.

Ode 14

1 As the eyes of a son upon his father, so are my eyes, O Lord, at all times towards Thee; 2 For with Thee is my desire. Be not thou far from me, for trouble is near, for there is none to help. 3 My enemies came upon me, and found me alone, and wounded me and left me for dead. 4 And taking away my glory, they went away from me; but I trusted in Thee.

Ode 15

1 As the flower of the rose in the spring of the year, as lilies by the waters, and as the sweet-smelling frankincense in the time of summer, 2 As a bright fire and incense in the censer, as a massy vessel of gold set with precious stones, 3 As a fair olive tree budding forth fruit, and as a cypress which grows up to the clouds; 4 When I saw them I was amazed.

Ode 16

1 As the sun is the joy to them that seek for its daybreak, so is my joy the Lord; 2 Because He is my Sun, and His rays have lifted me up; and His light hath dispelled all darkness from my face. 3 In Him I have acquired eyes and have seen His holy day: ears have I grown, and have heard His truth. 4 The thought of knowledge hath been mine, and I have been delighted through Him.

Ode 17

1 I was crowned by God, my crown living and speaking; 2 Moreover, I was enriched by Him, and rested in His eternal arms. 3 My soul was spread out, and He appeared in me; my bowels became peaceful, and they were moved and sighed for the Lord. 4 My body was enlightened, my countenance thought upon Him, my eyes desired Him: these are the spirits of the Lord.

Ode 18

1 My heart was right and I was helped, and in the fullness of days I was found without pain. 2 And my nobility was made perfect in the Righteousness of the Lord. 3 And His perfection abode with me, and I was kept in peace, peace was set within me. 4 I stood in truth with the Most High, and He stood in me with His holy spirit, and His affirmation was found in me.

Ode 19

1 A cup of milk was offered to me, and I drank it in the sweetness of the Lord's kindness. 2 The Son is the cup, and the Father is He who was milked; and the Holy Spirit is She who milked Him; 3 Because His breasts were full, and it was undesirable that His milk should be ineffectually released. 4 The Holy Spirit opened Her bosom, and mixed the milk of the two breasts of the Father.

Ode 20

1 I am a priest of the Lord, and to Him I do priestly service: and to Him I offer the sacrifice of His thought. 2 For His thought is not like the thought of the world nor the thought of the flesh, nor like them that serve carnally. 3 The sacrifice of the Lord is righteousness, and purity of heart and lips.

Ode 21

1 I lifted up my arms in the devotion of my heart to the Most High, and was enriched with His grace. 2 Then I repented from my sins, and my heart was directed to the Lord, and my spirit was renewed, and my nature was brightened, and I was justified and became a bride for Him. 3 And He delighted in me and renewed me by His love, for by this our Lord has shown His great love.

Ode 22

1 He who brought me down from on high also brought me up from the regions below. 2 And He who gathers together the things that are betwixt is He who cast me down. 3 He who scattered my enemies had existed from ancient days; He who gave me authority over bonds, that I might unbind them.

Ode 23

1 I was established in the Lord; and He said to me: "Proclaim My wonders to the sons of men." 2 And I said: "The Lord is able to do all things, for He made me, and rested in His servant." 3 And He gave me the power of His proclamation, to declare the power of His beauty without denying it.

Ode 24

1 The dove fluttered over the Messiah because He was her head. And she sang over Him, and her voice was heard. 2 Then the inhabitants were afraid, and the foreigners were disturbed. 3 The bird began to fly, and all creatures were moved towards her. 4 And she continued flying and was not discerned, and the mystery was great.

Ode 25

1 I was rescued from my chains, and I fled unto Thee, O my God. 2 Because Thou art the right hand of salvation and my helper. 3 Thou hast restrained them that rise up against me, and no more were they seen. 4 Because Thy face was with me, which saved me by Thy grace.

Ode 26

1 I poured out praise to the Lord, because I am His own. 2 And I will recite His holy ode, because my heart is with Him. 3 For His harp is in my hand, and the odes of His rest shall not be silent. 4 I will call unto Him with all my heart, I will praise and exalt Him with all my might.

Ode 27

1 Pure and holy are the works of the Most High. 2 As for His works, they are all holy: and His ways are an open door to those that seek Him. 3 Folly has not been established in them, nor has the way of error been conceived in them. 4 The knowledge of the Lord has been given them, and the way of error they have not known.

Ode 28

1 As the sun is the joy to them that seek for its daybreak, so is my joy the Lord; 2 Because He is my Sun, and His rays have lifted me up; and His light hath dispelled all darkness from my face. 3 In Him I have acquired eyes and have seen His holy day: ears have I grown, and have heard His truth. 4 The thought

of knowledge hath been mine, and I have been delighted through Him.

Ode 29
1 The Lord is my hope, I shall not be confounded. 2 For according to His praise He made me, and according to His goodness even so He gave unto me. 3 And according to His mercies He exalted me, and according to His excellent beauty He set me on high. 4 And brought me up out of the depths of Sheol, and from the mouth of death He drew me.

Ode 30
1 Fill ye waters for yourselves from the living fountain of the Lord, for it has been opened to you. 2 And come all ye thirsty and take a drink, and rest beside the fountain of the Lord. 3 For it is pleasant and the waters thereof are sweet. 4 Ye shall find rest therein, for they are quiet and gentle, and ye shall not be moved.

Ode 31
1 The Lord is my strength, I shall not be moved. 2 His sanctuary is right, and it is opened for those who seek it. 3 His work is eternal, and His governance to the heights of His holiness. 4 They who hate Him have fled from Him, and have failed; and they are quenched, and have perished.

Ode 32
1 They who rejected the Lord, how weak they are! 2 For they have invited their own death. 3 With the sword of their mouth they destroyed themselves, and they were cut off from the mouth of the Lord. 4 Now the head of those who erred is the serpent, and death is the sting thereof.

Ode 33
1 Again grace was given to me by the Lord, and I was raised by Him. 2 My Lord preserved me from my detractors, and from the slander of the tongue; 3 My soul rose above the sword, and from the arrow of wrath it drew me out. 4 I fled to the Lord, and He took me to a spacious place, and He rescued me because He delighted in me and I was saved by His grace.

Ode 34
1 I bless the Lord, who has given me understanding. 2 My hope is in Him who has freed me, and His delight is from the Holy Spirit. 3 The Lord is my life and my salvation; whom shall I fear? 4 The Lord is the defender of my life; of whom shall I be afraid?

Ode 35
1 When the Lord was revealed to me, He became my light. 2 He made the path straight for me and traveled with me and did not forsake me. 3 The truth of the Lord has accompanied me, by His will and His truth my salvation has been fulfilled. 4 And I was freed from all evil, and I saw my Lord in His holiness.

Ode 36
1 I will give thanks unto Thee, O Lord, because I love Thee. 2 O Most High, Thou wilt not forsake me, for Thou art my hope. 3 Freely I have received Thy grace, I shall live thereby. 4 My persecutors will come and not see me.

Ode 37
1 A fountain of life is the Word of the Lord, and His streams are inexhaustible. 2 They bring joy to the heart, and light to the eyes, and life to the soul. 3 O Lord, who would not be refreshed by Thy waters that live forever?

Ode 38
1 I went up into the light of truth as into a chariot, and the Truth took me and led me across the universe. 2 The heights of the world passed beneath me, and I was higher than them all. 3 And I ascended to the feet of the Lord, and His throne received me, and His beauty filled me.

Ode 39
1 The Lord is my hope; in Him I will not be confounded. 2 For according to His praise, He made me, and according to His goodness even so He gave unto me. 3 And according to His mercies, He exalted me, and according to His excellent beauty He set me on high.

Ode 40
1 Great are the revelations of the Lord, exalted are His works, and mighty is His promise. 2 Teach your souls the word of the Lord, His fruit is imperishable forever. 3 Rise up, and stand erect, you who at one time were brought low; speak, you who were silent, through the word of the Lord.

Ode 41
1 Blessed are the men who embrace her, for the hands of the Lord lead them. 2 Those whom she embraces will be held up by the Lord, who will not let them fall. 3 She will exalt them forever, and they will be found in the day of the glory of the Lord.

Ode 42
1 I received courage and was supported by the grace of the Lord. 2 He took me to high places by His perfection, and I was as a child in His arms, and He nurtured me with the milk of His favors. 3 Therefore, my contemplation was profound, and my prayer unto the Most High went forth from the depth of my heart.

Ode 43
1 The Lord is like unto them that fear Him, and He will show mercy unto them that love Him. 2 Be ye like unto Him; increase your praises to Him. 3 All His creatures fear Him; and tremble before Him. 4 He is a great and mighty Lord, fear Him and love Him.

Ode 44
1 I received the living Word, and my heart was filled with joy. 2 As the Most High willed, His Word leavened my whole being, and I was no longer my own. 3 All that was mine became His, and by His breath I was quickened. 4 He placed His sign upon me and opened my understanding, and I beheld Him with the eye of my heart.

Ode 45
1 My heart is directed in the love of the Lord, and I walk in His paths, and do not turn away. 2 The arrow does not divert me, for the Lord has become my bow, and He has laid me in His quiver forever. 3 He has made me His arrow, and has shown me that I will not be lost. 4 I will not be lost because I have been found, I will not fear because I am in His kingdom.

Ode 46
1 My joy is the Lord, and my course is towards Him, this path of mine is beautiful. 2 For I have a helper, the Lord. He has made Himself manifest to me without grudging, in His simplicity. 3 His kindness has humbled His greatness, He became like me, in order that I might receive Him. 4 In form He was considered like me, so that I might put Him on.

Ode 47
1 I will sing unto the Lord, for He has triumphed gloriously; He has thrown the horse and its rider into the sea. 2 My helper and my protector is the Lord, He has become my salvation. 3 This is my God and I will glorify Him; my father's God and I will exalt Him. 4 The Lord breaks wars; Lord is His name.

Ode 48
1 Great is the Lord and greatly to be praised in His holiness. 2 His domain is over all realms and His protection extends over His holy ones. 3 No night is there, nor dusk, nor weariness. His light is everlasting. 4 Great is our Lord and exceedingly glorious; He governs His creatures and beholds the depths.

Ode 49
1 Open your hearts to the exaltation of the Lord, and let your love be multiplied from the heart to the lips. 2 To bring forth fruit to the Lord, a holy life, and to speak with attention in His light. 3 Stand up upon your feet, and bless His glorious name. Sing unto the Lord, all His works. 4 Praise Him and sing to Him, in a voice of all praise.

Ode 50

1 The Lord has hastened me to His perfection; by His own means He has made me firm. 2 He has enlarged my steps beneath me and not one of my joints is broken. 3 I am uplifted by His glory, I have put on love that I might not be interrupted. 4 I draw near unto Him, and do not withdraw myself; my whole being is in His sanctuary.

97. The Psalms of Solomon

Psalm 1

1 O Lord, why hast thou cast my soul forth from thy presence? 2 Thy wrath is hard upon me in everything that thou bringest upon me. 3 Thou hast sent thy plagues upon me as arrows; thy wrath is hard upon me. 4 I am as one that gathereth stubble in the harvest; like one that gathereth the gleaning grapes of the vintage.

Psalm 2

1 I am like a vine, whose hedge and fence have been pulled up. 2 Whose fruit has been plucked by passers-by. 3 My branches are cut and lopped; I have been left with the bare stem. 4 I am dried up; I am plucked up by the roots and cast into the fire for burning.

Psalm 3

1 Who will set a watch over my mouth, and a seal of shrewdness upon my lips, 2 That I fall not from it, and that my tongue destroy me not? 3 O Lord, Father and God of my life, forsake me not to their counsel; 4 Be not thou to me a cause of stumbling nor a scandal.

Psalm 4

1 Hear, O God, my petition, and be attentive to my prayer. 2 Look upon us, and have mercy upon us, for we are much despised. 3 Our soul is bowed down to the dust; our belly cleaves to the earth. 4 Arise for our help, and redeem us for thy name's sake.

Psalm 5

1 I hoped for goodness, but evil came unto me; and I waited for light, and there came darkness. 2 My bowels boiled, and rested not; the days of affliction came upon me. 3 I went mourning without comfort; I stood up in the assembly and cried. 4 I am become a brother of jackals, and a companion of ostriches.

Psalm 6

1 My skin is black upon me, and my bones are burned with heat. 2 My harp also is turned to mourning, and my organ into the voice of them that weep. 3 Spare me, O Lord, for my days are nothing. 4 What is man, that thou shouldest magnify him? and that thou shouldest set thine heart upon him?

Psalm 7

1 And thou shouldest visit him every morning, and try him every moment. 2 How long wilt thou not depart from me, nor let me alone till I swallow down my spittle? 3 I have sinned; what shall I do unto thee, O thou preserver of men? 4 Why hast thou set me as a mark against thee, so that I am a burden to myself?

Psalm 8

1 And why dost thou not pardon my transgression, and take away mine iniquity? 2 For now shall I sleep in the dust; and thou shalt seek me in the morning, but I shall not be. 3 O that my words were now written! O that they were inscribed in a book! 4 That with an iron pen and lead they were graven in the rock for ever!

Psalm 9

1 For I know that my redeemer liveth, and that he shall stand at the latter day upon the earth: 2 And though after my skin worms destroy this body, yet in my flesh shall I see God: 3 Whom I shall see for myself, and mine eyes shall behold, and not another; though my reins be consumed within me. 4 But ye should say, Why persecute we him, seeing the root of the matter is found in me?

Psalm 10

1 Be ye afraid of the sword: for wrath bringeth the punishments of the sword, that ye may know there is a judgment. 2 My days are swifter than a weaver's shuttle, and are spent without hope. 3 O remember that my life is wind: mine eye shall no more see good. 4 The eye of him that hath seen me shall see me no more: thine eyes are upon me, and I am not.

Psalm 11

1 As the cloud is consumed and vanisheth away: so he that goeth down to the grave shall come up no more. 2 He shall return no more to his house, neither shall his place know him any more. 3 Therefore I will not refrain my mouth; I will speak in the anguish of my spirit; I will complain in the bitterness of my soul. 4 Am I a sea, or a whale, that thou settest a watch over me?

Psalm 12

1 When I say, My bed shall comfort me, my couch shall ease my complaint; 2 Then thou scarest me with dreams, and terrifiest me through visions: 3 So that my soul chooseth strangling, and death rather than my life. 4 I loathe it; I would not live alway: let me alone; for my days are vanity.

Psalm 13

1 What is man, that thou shouldest magnify him? and that thou shouldest set thine heart upon him? 2 And that thou shouldest visit him every morning, and try him every moment? 3 How long wilt thou not depart from me, nor let me alone till I swallow down my spittle? 4 I have sinned; what shall I do unto thee, O thou preserver of men?

Psalm 14

1 Why hast thou set me as a mark against thee, so that I am a burden to myself? 2 And why dost thou not pardon my transgression, and take away mine iniquity? 3 For now shall I sleep in the dust; and thou shalt seek me in the morning, but I shall not be. 4 Thus have I seen those who plow iniquity and sow trouble reap the same.

Psalm 15

1 By the blast of God they perish, and by the breath of his nostrils are they consumed. 2 The roaring of the lion, and the voice of the fierce lion, and the teeth of the young lions, are broken. 3 The old lion perisheth for lack of prey, and the stout lion's whelps are scattered abroad. 4 Now a thing was secretly brought to me, and mine ear received a little thereof.

Psalm 16

1 In thoughts from the visions of the night, when deep sleep falleth on men, 2 Fear came upon me, and trembling, which made all my bones to shake. 3 Then a spirit passed before my face; the hair of my flesh stood up: 4 It stood still, but I could not discern the form thereof: an image was before mine eyes, there was silence, and I heard a voice, saying,

Psalm 17

1 Shall mortal man be more just than God? Shall a man be more pure than his maker? 2 Behold, he put no trust in his servants; and his angels he charged with folly: 3 How much less in them that dwell in houses of clay, whose foundation is in the dust, which are crushed before the moth? 4 They are destroyed from morning to evening: they perish for ever without any regarding it.

Psalm 18

1 Doth not their excellency which is in them go away? they die, even without wisdom. 2 Call now, if there be any that will answer thee; and to which of the saints wilt thou turn? 3 For wrath killeth the foolish man, and envy slayeth the silly one. 4 I have seen the foolish taking root: but suddenly I cursed his habitation.

Psalm 19

1 His children are far from safety, and they are crushed in the gate, neither is there any to deliver

them. 2 Whose harvest the hungry eateth up, and taketh it even out of the thorns, and the robber swalloweth up their substance. 3 Although affliction cometh not forth of the dust, neither doth trouble spring out of the ground; 4 Yet man is born unto trouble, as the sparks fly upward.

Psalm 20

1 I would seek unto God, and unto God would I commit my cause: 2 Which doeth great things and unsearchable; marvellous things without number: 3 Who giveth rain upon the earth, and sendeth waters upon the fields: 4 To set up on high those that be low; that those which mourn may be exalted to safety.

Psalm 21

1 He disappointeth the devices of the crafty, so that their hands cannot perform their enterprise. 2 He taketh the wise in their own craftiness: and the counsel of the froward is carried headlong. 3 They meet with darkness in the daytime, and grope in the noonday as in the night. 4 But he saveth the poor from the sword, from their mouth, and from the hand of the mighty.

Psalm 22

1 So the poor hath hope, and iniquity stoppeth her mouth. 2 Behold, happy is the man whom God correcteth: therefore despise not thou the chastening of the Almighty: 3 For he maketh sore, and bindeth up: he woundeth, and his hands make whole. 4 He shall deliver thee in six troubles: yea, in seven there shall no evil touch thee.

Psalm 23

1 In famine he shall redeem thee from death: and in war from the power of the sword. 2 Thou shalt be hid from the scourge of the tongue: neither shalt thou be afraid of destruction when it cometh. 3 At destruction and famine thou shalt laugh: neither shalt thou be afraid of the beasts of the earth. 4 For thou shalt be in league with the stones of the field: and the beasts of the field shall be at peace with thee.

Psalm 24

1 And thou shalt know that thy tabernacle shall be in peace; and thou shalt visit thy habitation, and shalt not sin. 2 Thou shalt know also that thy seed shall be great, and thine offspring as the grass of the earth. 3 Thou shalt come to thy grave in a full age, like as a shock of corn cometh in in his season. 4 Lo this, we have searched it, so it is; hear it, and know thou it for thy good.

Psalm 25

1 O Lord, rebuke me not in thy wrath: neither chasten me in thy hot displeasure. 2 For thine arrows stick fast in me, and thy hand presseth me sore. 3 There is no soundness in my flesh because of thine anger; neither is there any rest in my bones because of my sin. 4 For my iniquities are gone over mine head: as an heavy burden they are too heavy for me.

Psalm 26

1 My wounds stink and are corrupt because of my foolishness. 2 I am troubled; I am bowed down greatly; I go mourning all the day long. 3 For my loins are filled with a loathsome disease: and there is no soundness in my flesh. 4 I am feeble and sore broken: I have roared by reason of the disquietness of my heart.

Psalm 27

1 Lord, all my desire is before thee; and my groaning is not hid from thee. 2 My heart panteth, my strength faileth me: as for the light of mine eyes, it also is gone from me. 3 My lovers and my friends stand aloof from my sore; and my kinsmen stand afar off. 4 They also that seek after my life lay snares for me: and they that seek my hurt speak mischievous things, and imagine deceits all the day long.

Psalm 28

1 But I, as a deaf man, heard not; and I was as a dumb man that openeth not his mouth. 2 Thus I was as a man that heareth not, and in whose mouth are no reproofs. 3 For in thee, O Lord, do I hope: thou wilt hear, O Lord my God. 4 For I said, Hear me, lest otherwise they should rejoice over me: when my foot slippeth, they magnify themselves against me.

Psalm 29

1 For I am ready to halt, and my sorrow is continually before me. 2 For I will declare mine iniquity; I will be sorry for my sin. 3 But mine enemies are lively, and they are strong: and they that hate me wrongfully are multiplied. 4 They also that render evil for good are mine adversaries; because I follow the thing that good is.

Psalm 30

1 Forsake me not, O Lord: O my God, be not far from me. 2 Make haste to help me, O Lord my salvation. 3 I said in my haste, I am cut off from before thine eyes: nevertheless thou heardest the voice of my supplications when I cried unto thee. 4 O love the Lord, all ye his saints: for the Lord preserveth the faithful, and plentifully rewardeth the proud doer.

98. *The Apocalypse of Abraham*

Chapter 1

1 The word that came to Abraham, the son of Terah, the son of Nahor, the son of Serug, the son of Reu, the son of Peleg, the son of Eber, the son of Shelah, 2 The son of Cainan, the son of Arphaxad, the son of Shem, the son of Noah, the son of Lamech, 3 Who when he was looking around saw that the whole city was worshipping idols and devoting itself to vanities. 4 And Abraham, filled with disgust in his soul, spoke to his father Terah saying,

Chapter 2

1 "Father, what is this idol to which you are making sacrifices, burning offerings, and bowing down? 2 Does it have the power to help, or can it take away harm so that you should serve it?" 3 But Terah, angry at the words spoken, said, "Son, keep silent lest the gods hear and bring wrath upon us." 4 Abraham, disturbed but silent, pondered how to demonstrate the falsity of the idols.

Chapter 3

1 That night, Abraham went to his father's temple carrying an axe. 2 He smashed all the idols except the largest, where he placed the axe. 3 In the morning, when Terah returned and saw the destruction, he demanded, "Who has done this to our gods?" 4 Abraham replied, "Perhaps the gods had a disagreement, or maybe the great one destroyed the others in rage."

Chapter 4

1 Terah, scoffing, said, "These are just statues of stone and wood; they cannot do such things." 2 Abraham answered, "Then why do you worship things that cannot speak or act?" 3 Realizing the truth of Abraham's words but still angered, Terah brought him before Nimrod. 4 Nimrod challenged Abraham's faith, and in defiance, Abraham was thrown into a fire but emerged unscathed.

Chapter 5

1 Witnessing this miracle, many began to question their own beliefs, but Nimrod insisted on Abraham's exile. 2 Abraham, along with his family and followers, left Ur of the Chaldeans to travel to a land that God would show him. 3 Along the way, God spoke to Abraham in visions, promising a great nation from his lineage. 4 But Abraham questioned, "Lord, what can you give me, seeing I go childless?"

Chapter 6

1 The Lord said, "Look now toward heaven, and count the stars if you are able to number them." 2 "So shall your offspring be." And Abraham believed in the Lord; and he counted it to him for righteousness. 3 God then made a covenant with Abraham, promising the lands from the river of Egypt to the great river, the river Euphrates. 4 And God declared, "Your

descendants will be strangers in a land that is not theirs and will serve them, and they will afflict them four hundred years."

Chapter 7

1 But also that nation, whom they shall serve, will I judge: and afterward shall they come out with great substance. 2 As for you, you shall go to your fathers in peace; you shall be buried in a good old age. 3 And in the fourth generation, they shall come hither again: for the iniquity of the Amorites is not yet full." 4 With these promises, Abraham's faith was strengthened, and he continued his journey, trusting in the Lord's guidance.

Chapter 8

1 And it came to pass after these things, that God tested Abraham and said to him, "Abraham!" And he said, "Here am I." 2 Then He said, "Take now your son, your only son Isaac, whom you love, and go into the land of Moriah; and offer him there as a burnt offering on one of the mountains of which I shall tell you." 3 So Abraham rose early in the morning, saddled his donkey, and took two of his young men with him, and Isaac his son; and he split the wood for the burnt offering, and arose and went to the place of which God had told him.

Chapter 9

1 On the third day Abraham lifted up his eyes and saw the place afar off. 2 And Abraham said to his young men, "Stay here with the donkey; the lad and I will go yonder and worship, and we will come back to you." 3 Abraham took the wood of the burnt offering and laid it on Isaac his son; and he took the fire in his hand, and a knife, and the two of them went together. 4 Isaac spoke to Abraham his father and said, "My father!" And he said, "Here I am, my son." Then he said, "Look, the fire and the wood, but where is the lamb for a burnt offering?"

Chapter 10

1 And Abraham said, "My son, God will provide for Himself the lamb for a burnt offering." So the two of them went together. 2 They came to the place which God had told him of; and Abraham built an altar there and placed the wood in order, and bound Isaac his son and laid him on the altar, upon the wood. 3 And Abraham stretched out his hand and took the knife to slay his son. 4 But the Angel of the Lord called to him from heaven and said, "Abraham, Abraham!" So he said, "Here I am."

Chapter 11

1 And He said, "Do not lay your hand on the lad, or do anything to him; for now I know that you fear God, since you have not withheld your son, your only son, from Me." 2 Then Abraham lifted his eyes and looked, and there behind him was a ram caught in a thicket by its horns. So Abraham went and took the ram, and offered it up as a burnt offering instead of his son. 3 And Abraham called the name of the place, The-Lord-Will-Provide; as it is said to this day, "In the Mount of the Lord it shall be provided."

Chapter 12

1 Then the Angel of the Lord called to Abraham a second time out of heaven, 2 And said: "By Myself I have sworn, says the Lord, because you have done this thing, and have not withheld your son, your only son— 3 In blessing I will bless you, and in multiplying I will multiply your descendants as the stars of the heaven and as the sand which is on the seashore; and your descendants shall possess the gate of their enemies. 4 In your seed all the nations of the earth shall be blessed, because you have obeyed My voice."

Chapter 13

1 So Abraham returned to his young men, and they rose and went together to Beersheba; and Abraham dwelt at Beersheba. 2 Now it came to pass after these things that it was told Abraham, saying, "Indeed Milcah also has borne children to your brother Nahor:" 3 Huz his firstborn, Buz his brother,

Kemuel the father of Aram, 4 Chesed, Hazo, Pildash, Jidlaph, and Bethuel." 5 And Bethuel begot Rebekah. These eight Milcah bore to Nahor, Abraham's brother. 6 His concubine, whose name was Reumah, also bore Tebah, Gaham, Tahash, and Maachah.

Chapter 14

1 And while Abraham dwelt in the land of the Philistines, many days passed, and God appeared to him again in a vision. 2 God said, "Fear not, Abraham, for I am your shield and your exceedingly great reward." 3 And Abraham said, "Lord God, what will You give me, seeing I go childless, and the heir of my house is Eliezer of Damascus?" 4 And behold, the word of the Lord came to him, saying, "This one shall not be your heir, but one who will come from your own body shall be your heir."

Chapter 15

1 Then He brought him outside and said, "Look now toward heaven, and count the stars if you are able to number them." And He said to him, "So shall your descendants be." 2 And Abraham believed in the Lord, and He accounted it to him for righteousness. 3 He also said to him, "I am the Lord who brought you out of Ur of the Chaldeans, to give you this land to inherit it." 4 Then Abraham said, "Lord God, how shall I know that I will inherit it?"

Chapter 16

1 And He said to him, "Bring Me a three-year-old heifer, a three-year-old female goat, a three-year-old ram, a turtledove, and a young pigeon." 2 Then he brought all these to Him and cut them in two, down the middle, and placed each piece opposite the other; but he did not cut the birds in two. 3 And when the birds of prey came down on the carcasses, Abraham drove them away. 4 As the sun was going down, a deep sleep fell upon Abraham; and behold, horror and great darkness fell upon him.

Chapter 17

1 Then He said to Abraham, "Know certainly that your descendants will be strangers in a land that is not theirs, and will serve them, and they will afflict them four hundred years. 2 And also the nation whom they serve I will judge; afterward they shall come out with great possessions. 3 Now as for you, you shall go to your fathers in peace; you shall be buried at a good old age. 4 But in the fourth generation they shall return here, for the iniquity of the Amorites is not yet complete."

Chapter 18

1 And it came to pass, when the sun went down and it was dark, behold, there appeared a smoking furnace and a burning torch that passed between those pieces. 2 On the same day the Lord made a covenant with Abraham, saying, "To your descendants I have given this land, from the river of Egypt to the great river, the River Euphrates— 3 The Kenites, the Kenizzites, the Kadmonites, 4 The Hittites, the Perizzites, the Rephaim,

Chapter 19

1 The Amorites, the Canaanites, the Girgashites, and the Jebusites." 2 And the vision ceased, and Abraham returned unto the place where he had stood before the Lord. 3 Then Sarah, Abraham's wife, took Hagar her maid, the Egyptian, and gave her to her husband Abraham to be his wife, after Abraham had dwelt ten years in the land of Canaan. 4 And he went in unto Hagar, and she conceived; and when she saw that she had conceived, her mistress became despised in her eyes.

Chapter 20

1 Sarah said to Abraham, "My wrong be upon you! I gave my maid into your bosom; and now that she sees that she has conceived, I am despised in her eyes. The Lord judge between you and me." 2 But Abraham said to Sarah, "Indeed your maid is in your hand; do to her as you please." And when Sarah dealt harshly with her, she fled from her presence. 3 Now the Angel of the Lord found her by a spring of water in

the wilderness, by the spring on the way to Shur. 4 And he said, "Hagar, Sarah's maid, where have you come from, and where are you going?" She said, "I am fleeing from the presence of my mistress Sarah."

Chapter 21

1 The Angel of the Lord said to her, "Return to your mistress, and submit yourself under her hands." 2 Then the Angel of the Lord said to her, "I will multiply your descendants exceedingly, so that they shall not be counted for multitude." 3 And the Angel of the Lord said to her, "Behold, you are with child, and you shall bear a son. You shall call his name Ishmael, because the Lord has heard your affliction. 4 He shall be a wild man; his hand shall be against every man, and every man's hand against him. And he shall dwell in the presence of all his brethren."

Chapter 22

1 So Hagar bore Abraham a son; and Abraham named his son, whom Hagar bore, Ishmael. 2 Abraham was eighty-six years old when Hagar bore Ishmael to Abraham. 3 When Ishmael was thirteen years old, God appeared again to Abraham and established the covenant of circumcision. 4 God said to Abraham, "As for Sarai your wife, you shall not call her name Sarai, but Sarah shall be her name.

Chapter 23

1 I will bless her and also give you a son by her; then I will bless her, and she shall be a mother of nations; kings of peoples shall be from her." 2 Then Abraham fell on his face and laughed, and said in his heart, "Shall a child be born to a man who is one hundred years old? And shall Sarah, who is ninety years old, bear a child?" 3 And God said, "Yes, Sarah your wife shall bear you a son, and you shall call his name Isaac; I will establish My covenant with him for an everlasting covenant, and with his descendants after him. 4 As for Ishmael, I have heard you. Behold, I have blessed him, and will make him fruitful, and will multiply him exceedingly. He shall beget twelve princes, and I will make him a great nation.

Chapter 24

1 But My covenant I will establish with Isaac, whom Sarah shall bear to you at this set time next year." 2 Then He finished talking with him, and God went up from Abraham. 3 So Abraham took Ishmael his son, all who were born in his house and all who were bought with his money, every male among the men of Abraham's house, and circumcised the flesh of their foreskins that very same day, as God had said to him. 4 Abraham was ninety-nine years old when he was circumcised in the flesh of his foreskin.

Chapter 25

1 And Ishmael his son was thirteen years old when he was circumcised in the flesh of his foreskin. 2 That very same day Abraham was circumcised, and his son Ishmael; 3 And all the men of his house, born in the house or bought with money from a foreigner, were circumcised with him. 4 Now the Lord appeared to him by the terebinth trees of Mamre, as he was sitting in the tent door in the heat of the day.

Chapter 26

1 So he lifted his eyes and looked, and behold, three men were standing by him; and when he saw them, he ran from the tent door to meet them, and bowed himself to the ground, 2 And said, "My Lord, if I have now found favor in Your sight, do not pass on by Your servant. 3 Please let a little water be brought, and wash your feet, and rest yourselves under the tree. 4 And I will bring a morsel of bread, that you may refresh your hearts. After that you may pass by, inasmuch as you have come to your servant." They said, "Do as you have said."

Chapter 27

1 Abraham hurried into the tent to Sarah and said, "Quickly, make ready three measures of fine meal; knead it and make cakes." 2 And Abraham ran to the herd, took a tender and good calf, gave it to a young man, and he hastened to prepare it. 3 So he took

butter and milk and the calf which he had prepared, and set it before them; and he stood by them under the tree as they ate. 4 They said to him, "Where is Sarah your wife?" So he said, "Here, in the tent."

Chapter 28

1 And He said, "I will certainly return to you according to the time of life, and behold, Sarah your wife shall have a son." (Sarah was listening in the tent door which was behind him.) 2 Now Abraham and Sarah were old, well advanced in age; and Sarah had passed the age of childbearing. 3 Therefore Sarah laughed within herself, saying, "After I have grown old, shall I have pleasure, my lord being old also?" 4 And the Lord said to Abraham, "Why did Sarah laugh, saying, 'Shall I surely bear a child, since I am old?' 5 Is anything too hard for the Lord? At the appointed time I will return to you, according to the time of life, and Sarah shall have a son." 6 But Sarah denied it, saying, "I did not laugh," for she was afraid. And He said, "No, but you did laugh."

Chapter 29

1 Then the men rose from there and looked toward Sodom, and Abraham went with them to send them on the way. 2 And the Lord said, "Shall I hide from Abraham what I am doing, 3 Since Abraham shall surely become a great and mighty nation, and all the nations of the earth shall be blessed in him? 4 For I have known him, in order that he may command his children and his household after him, that they keep the way of the Lord, to do righteousness and justice, that the Lord may bring to Abraham what He has spoken to him." 5 And the Lord said, "Because the outcry against Sodom and Gomorrah is great, and because their sin is very grave,

Chapter 30

1 I will go down now and see whether they have done altogether according to the outcry against it that has come to Me; and if not, I will know." 2 Then the men turned away from there and went toward Sodom, but Abraham still stood before the Lord. 3 And Abraham drew near and said, "Would You also destroy the righteous with the wicked? 4 Suppose there were fifty righteous within the city; would You also destroy the place and not spare it for the fifty righteous that were in it? 5 Far be it from You to do such a thing as this, to slay the righteous with the wicked, so that the righteous should be as the wicked; far be it from You! Shall not the Judge of all the earth do right?"

Chapter 31

1 And the Lord said, "If I find in Sodom fifty righteous within the city, then I will spare all the place for their sakes." 2 Then Abraham answered and said, "Indeed now, I who am but dust and ashes have taken it upon myself to speak to the Lord: 3 Suppose there were five less than the fifty righteous; would You destroy all of the city for lack of five?" So He said, "If I find there forty-five, I will not destroy it." 4 And he spoke to Him yet again and said, "Suppose there should be forty found there?" So He said, "I will not do it for the sake of forty."

Chapter 32

1 Then he said, "Let not the Lord be angry, and I will speak: Suppose thirty should be found there?" So He said, "I will not do it if I find thirty there." 2 And he said, "Indeed now, I have taken upon myself to speak to the Lord: Suppose twenty should be found there?" So He said, "I will not destroy it for the sake of twenty." 3 Then he said, "Let not the Lord be angry, and I will speak but once more: Suppose ten should be found there?" And He said, "I will not destroy it for the sake of ten." 4 When the Lord had finished speaking with Abraham, He departed, and Abraham returned to his place.

Chapter 33

1 After the Lord departed, the two angels arrived at Sodom in the evening, and Lot was sitting in the gate of Sodom. When Lot saw them, he rose to meet them and bowed himself with his face toward the ground.

2 He said, "Here now, my lords, please turn in to your servant's house and spend the night, and wash your feet; then you may rise early and go on your way." But they said, "No, we will spend the night in the open square." 3 But he insisted strongly; so they turned in to him and entered his house. Then he made them a feast, and baked unleavened bread, and they ate.

Chapter 34

1 Before they lay down, the men of the city, the men of Sodom, both old and young, all the people from every quarter, surrounded the house. 2 They called to Lot and said to him, "Where are the men who came to you tonight? Bring them out to us that we may know them carnally." 3 So Lot went out to them through the doorway, shut the door behind him, 4 and said, "Please, my brethren, do not do so wickedly!

Chapter 35

1 "See now, I have two daughters who have not known a man; please, let me bring them out to you, and you may do to them as you wish; only do nothing to these men, since this is the reason they have come under the shadow of my roof." 2 But they said, "Stand back!" Then they said, "This one came in to stay here, and he keeps acting as a judge; now we will deal worse with you than with them." So they pressed hard against the man Lot, and came near to break down the door. 3 But the men reached out their hands and pulled Lot into the house with them, and shut the door. 4 And they struck the men who were at the doorway of the house with blindness, both small and great, so that they became weary trying to find the door.

Chapter 36

1 The men said to Lot, "Have you anyone else here? Son-in-law, your sons, your daughters, and whomever you have in the city—take them out of this place! 2 For we will destroy this place, because the outcry against them has grown great before the face of the Lord, and the Lord has sent us to destroy it." 3 So Lot went out and spoke to his sons-in-law, who had married his daughters, and said, "Get up, get out of this place; for the Lord will destroy this city!" But to his sons-in-law he seemed to be joking.

Chapter 37

1 When the morning dawned, the angels urged Lot to hurry, saying, "Arise, take your wife and your two daughters who are here, lest you be consumed in the punishment of the city." 2 And while he lingered, the men took hold of his hand, his wife's hand, and the hands of his two daughters, the Lord being merciful to him, and they brought him out and set him outside the city. 3 As they brought them out, one said, "Escape for your life! Do not look behind you nor stay anywhere in the plain. Escape to the mountains, lest you be destroyed." 4 So Lot said to them, "Please, no, my lords!

Chapter 38

1 "Indeed now, your servant has found favor in your sight, and you have increased your mercy which you have shown me by saving my life; but I cannot escape to the mountains, lest some evil overtake me and I die. 2 See now, this city is near enough to flee to, and it is a little one; please let me escape there (is it not a little one?) and my soul shall live." 3 And he said to him, "See, I have favored you concerning this thing also, in that I will not overthrow this city for which you have spoken. 4 Hurry, escape there. For I cannot do anything until you arrive there." Therefore the name of the city was called Zoar.

Chapter 39

1 The sun had risen upon the earth when Lot entered Zoar. 2 Then the Lord rained brimstone and fire on Sodom and Gomorrah from the Lord out of the heavens. 3 He overthrew those cities, all the plain, all the inhabitants of the cities, and what grew on the ground. 4 But Lot's wife looked back behind him, and she became a pillar of salt.

Chapter 40

1 Early the next morning, Abraham went to the place where he had stood before the Lord. 2 He looked toward Sodom and Gomorrah, and toward all the land of the plain, and he saw, and behold, the smoke of the land which went up like the smoke of a furnace. 3 And it came to pass, when God destroyed the cities of the plain, that God remembered Abraham, and sent Lot out of the midst of the overthrow, when He overthrew the cities in which Lot had dwelt. 4 Now Abraham journeyed from there to the South, and dwelt between Kadesh and Shur, and stayed in Gerar.

99. The Apocalypse of Adam

Chapter 1

1 And Adam taught his son Seth about the periods of the great year, which is the beginning and the end of the world. 2 He said, "Seth, my son, listen to my words. I am revealing to you hidden mysteries which God revealed to me after I ate from the tree of knowledge, and knew the division between the realms of light and darkness. 3 We were in paradise, and we knew neither night nor day. Then God created the firmament and divided the light from the darkness. 4 He called the light Day, and the darkness He called Night. Thus, we became aware of the passage of time, marked by the rising and setting of the sun.

Chapter 2

1 When I was in the garden, God spoke to me and said, 'Adam, eat from all the trees of the garden. 2 But beware of the tree of knowledge, for the day you eat from it, you will surely die.' 3 However, the serpent, the craftiest of all the beasts of the field that God had made, came to me. It said, 'Did God really say, "You must not eat from any tree in the garden"?' 4 I told the serpent, 'We may eat fruit from the trees in the garden, but God did say, "You must not eat fruit from the tree that is in the middle of the garden, and you must not touch it, or you will die."'

Chapter 3

1 'You will not certainly die,' the serpent said to the woman. 'For God knows that when you eat from it your eyes will be opened, and you will be like God, knowing good and evil.' 2 So when Eve saw that the tree was good for food and pleasing to the eye, and also desirable for gaining wisdom, she took some and ate it. She also gave some to me, and I ate. 3 Then the eyes of both of us were opened, and we realized we were naked; so we sewed fig leaves together and made coverings for ourselves. 4 Then we heard the sound of the Lord God as he was walking in the garden in the cool of the day, and we hid from the Lord God among the trees of the garden.

Chapter 4

1 But the Lord God called to me, 'Adam, where are you?' 2 I said, 'I heard you in the garden, and I was afraid because I was naked; so I hid.' 3 And he said, 'Who told you that you were naked? Have you eaten from the tree that I commanded you not to eat from?' 4 Then I said, 'The woman you put here with me—she gave me some fruit from the tree, and I ate.'

Chapter 5

1 The Lord God said to Eve, 'What is this you have done?' And Eve said, 'The serpent deceived me, and I ate.' 2 So the Lord God said to the serpent, 'Because you have done this, cursed are you above all livestock and all wild animals! You will crawl on your belly and you will eat dust all the days of your life. 3 And I will put enmity between you and the woman, and between your offspring and hers; he will crush your head, and you will strike his heel.' 4 To Eve, He said, 'I will make your pains in childbearing very severe; with painful labor you will give birth to children. Your desire will be for your husband, and he will rule over you.'

Chapter 6

1 To Adam, He said, 'Because you listened to your wife and ate fruit from the tree about which I commanded you, "You must not eat from it," cursed is the ground because of you; through painful toil you will eat food from it all the days of your life. 2 It will produce thorns and thistles for you, and you will eat the plants of the field. 3 By the sweat of your brow you will eat your food until you return to the ground, since from it you were taken; for dust you are and to dust you will return.' 4 Then Adam named his wife Eve, because she would become the mother of all the living.

Chapter 7

1 The Lord God made garments of skin for Adam and his wife and clothed them. 2 And the Lord God said, "Behold, the man has become like one of Us, to know good and evil. And now, lest he put out his hand and take also of the tree of life, and eat, and live forever"— 3 therefore the Lord God sent him out from the garden of Eden to work the ground from which he had been taken. 4 He drove out the man, and at the east of the garden of Eden he placed the cherubim and a flaming sword that turned every way to guard the way to the tree of life.

Chapter 8

1 After being expelled from paradise, we dwelt to the east of the garden, where the earth was harsh and unyielding. 2 In pain and sweat, we cultivated the soil, reaping meager harvests that barely sustained us. 3 During this time, Eve conceived and bore our first son, Cain, and then his brother Abel. Each grew up to follow different paths; Abel became a keeper of sheep, while Cain cultivated the land.

Chapter 9

1 As time passed, the brothers brought offerings to the Lord: Abel brought of the firstlings of his flock and of their fat portions, and Cain brought an offering of the fruit of the ground. 2 The Lord had regard for Abel and his offering, but for Cain and his offering, He had no regard. This made Cain very angry, and his countenance fell. 3 The Lord said to Cain, "Why are you angry, and why has your countenance fallen? If you do well, will you not be accepted? And if you do not do well, sin is crouching at the door. Its desire is for you, but you must rule over it."

Chapter 10

1 Cain spoke to Abel his brother; and when they were in the field, Cain rose up against his brother Abel and killed him. 2 Then the Lord said to Cain, "Where is Abel your brother?" He said, "I do not know; am I my brother's keeper?" 3 And the Lord said, "What have you done? The voice of your brother's blood is crying to Me from the ground. 4 And now you are cursed from the ground, which has opened its mouth to receive your brother's blood from your hand.

Chapter 11

1 "When you work the ground, it shall no longer yield to you its strength; you shall be a fugitive and a wanderer on the earth." 2 Cain said to the Lord, "My punishment is greater than I can bear. 3 Behold, You have driven me today away from the ground, and from Your face I shall be hidden; I shall be a fugitive and a wanderer on the earth, and whoever finds me will kill me." 4 But the Lord said to him, "Not so! If anyone kills Cain, vengeance shall be taken on him sevenfold." And the Lord put a mark on Cain, lest any who found him should attack him.

Chapter 12

1 Then Cain went away from the presence of the Lord and settled in the land of Nod, east of Eden. 2 Cain knew his wife, and she conceived and bore Enoch. When he built a city, he called the name of the city after the name of his son, Enoch. 3 To Enoch was born Irad, and Irad fathered Mehujael, and Mehujael fathered Methushael, and Methushael fathered Lamech. 4 Lamech took two wives; the name of the one was Adah, and the name of the other Zillah.

Chapter 13

1 Adah bore Jabal; he was the father of those who dwell in tents and have livestock. 2 His brother's name was Jubal; he was the father of all those who play the lyre and pipe. 3 Zillah also bore Tubal-cain; he was the forger of all instruments of bronze and iron. Tubal-cain's sister was Naamah. 4 Lamech said to his wives: "Adah and Zillah, hear my voice; you wives of Lamech, listen to what I say: I have killed a man for wounding me, a young man for striking me.

Chapter 14

1 If Cain's revenge is sevenfold, then Lamech's is seventy-sevenfold." 2 Meanwhile, Adam knew his wife again, and she bore a son and named him Seth, for she said, "God has appointed for me another offspring instead of Abel, for Cain killed him." 3 To Seth also a son was born, and he called his name Enosh. At that time people began to call upon the name of the Lord.

Chapter 15

1 As the generations passed, the ways of the children of men diverged further into righteousness and wickedness. 2 Among the descendants of Seth, there arose a lineage devoted to the Lord, walking in the paths of righteousness, keeping alive the memory of the paradise lost and the hope of its restoration. 3 But among the descendants of Cain, there arose a lineage steeped in sin and defiance, straying far from the path of God, and engendering violence and corruption upon the earth.

Chapter 16

1 During these times, the earth became corrupt in the sight of God and was filled with violence. 2 God saw that the wickedness of man was great in the earth, and that every intention of the thoughts of his heart was only evil continually. 3 And the Lord regretted that he had made man on the earth, and it grieved him to his heart. 4 The Lord said, "I will blot out man whom I have created from the face of the land, man and animals and creeping things and birds of the heavens, for I am sorry that I have made them."

Chapter 17

1 But Noah found favor in the eyes of the Lord. Noah was a righteous man, blameless in his generation. Noah walked with God. 2 And Noah had three sons, Shem, Ham, and Japheth. 3 Now the earth was corrupt in God's sight, and the earth was filled with violence. 4 God said to Noah, "I have determined to make an end of all flesh, for the earth is filled with violence through them. Behold, I will destroy them with the earth.

Chapter 18

1 Make yourself an ark of gopher wood. Make rooms in the ark, and cover it inside and out with pitch. 2 This is how you are to make it: the length of the ark 300 cubits, its breadth 50 cubits, and its height 30 cubits. 3 Make a roof for the ark, and finish it to a cubit above, and set the door of the ark in its side. Make it with lower, second, and third decks. 4 For behold, I will bring a flood of waters upon the earth to destroy all flesh in which is the breath of life under heaven. Everything that is on the earth shall die.

Chapter 19

1 But I will establish my covenant with you, and you shall come into the ark, you, your sons, your wife, and your sons' wives with you. 2 And of every living thing of all flesh, you shall bring two of every sort into the ark to keep them alive with you. They shall be male and female. 3 Of the birds according to their kinds, and of the animals according to their kinds, of every creeping thing of the ground according to its kind, two of every sort shall come in to you to keep them alive. 4 Also take with you every sort of food that is eaten, and store it up. It shall serve as food for you and for them."

Chapter 20

1 Noah did everything just as God had commanded

him. 2 The waters of the flood came upon the earth. In the six hundredth year of Noah's life, in the second month, the seventeenth day of the month, on that day all the fountains of the great deep burst forth, and the windows of the heavens were opened. 3 And rain fell upon the earth forty days and forty nights. 4 On the very same day Noah and Noah's sons, Shem, Ham, and Japheth, and Noah's wife and the three wives of his sons with them entered the ark,

Chapter 21

1 They and every beast, according to its kind, and all the livestock according to their kinds, and every creeping thing that creeps on the earth, according to its kind, and every bird, according to its kind, every winged creature. 2 They went into the ark with Noah, two and two of all flesh in which there was the breath of life. 3 And those that entered, male and female of all flesh, went in as God had commanded him. And the Lord shut him in. 4 The flood continued forty days on the earth. The waters increased and bore up the ark, and it rose high above the earth.

Chapter 22

1 The waters prevailed and increased greatly on the earth, and the ark floated on the face of the waters. 2 And the waters prevailed so mightily on the earth that all the high mountains under the whole heaven were covered. 3 The waters prevailed above the mountains, covering them fifteen cubits deep. 4 And all flesh died that moved on the earth, birds, livestock, beasts, all swarming creatures that swarm on the earth, and all mankind.

Chapter 23

1 Everything on the dry land in whose nostrils was the breath of life died. 2 He blotted out every living thing that was on the face of the ground, man and animals and creeping things and birds of the heavens. They were blotted out from the earth. Only Noah was left, and those who were with him in the ark. 3 And the waters prevailed on the earth 150 days.

Chapter 24

1 But God remembered Noah and all the beasts and all the livestock that were with him in the ark. And God made a wind blow over the earth, and the waters subsided. 2 The fountains of the deep and the windows of the heavens were closed, the rain from the heavens was restrained, 3 And the waters receded from the earth continually. At the end of the 150 days the waters had abated, 4 And in the seventh month, on the seventeenth day of the month, the ark came to rest on the mountains of Ararat.

Chapter 25

1 The waters continued to abate until the tenth month; in the tenth month, on the first day of the month, the tops of the mountains were seen. 2 At the end of forty days Noah opened the window of the ark that he had made 3 And sent forth a raven. It went to and fro until the waters were dried up from the earth. 4 Then he sent forth a dove from him, to see if the waters had subsided from the face of the ground.

Chapter 26

1 But the dove found no place to set her foot, and she returned to him to the ark, for the waters were still on the face of the whole earth. So he put out his hand and took her and brought her into the ark with him. 2 He waited another seven days, and again he sent forth the dove out of the ark. 3 And the dove came back to him in the evening, and behold, in her mouth was a freshly plucked olive leaf. So Noah knew that the waters had subsided from the earth. 4 Then he waited another seven days and sent forth the dove, and she did not return to him anymore.

Chapter 27

1 In the six hundred and first year, in the first month, the first day of the month, the waters were dried from off the earth. And Noah removed the covering of the ark and looked, and behold, the face of the ground was dry. 2 In the second month, on the twenty-seventh day of the month, the earth had dried out. 3

Then God said to Noah, "Go out from the ark, you and your wife, and your sons and your sons' wives with you. 4 Bring out with you every living thing that is with you of all flesh—birds and animals and every creeping thing that creeps on the earth—that they may swarm on the earth, and be fruitful and multiply on the earth."

Chapter 28

1 So Noah went out, and his sons and his wife and his sons' wives with him. 2 Every beast, every creeping thing, and every bird, everything that moves on the earth, went out by families from the ark. 3 Then Noah built an altar to the Lord and took some of every clean animal and some of every clean bird and offered burnt offerings on the altar. 4 And when the Lord smelled the pleasing aroma, the Lord said in his heart, "I will never again curse the ground because of man, for the intention of man's heart is evil from his youth. Neither will I ever again strike down every living creature as I have done.

Chapter 29

1 While the earth remains, seedtime and harvest, cold and heat, summer and winter, day and night, shall not cease." 2 And God blessed Noah and his sons and said to them, "Be fruitful and multiply and fill the earth. 3 The fear of you and the dread of you shall be upon every beast of the earth and upon every bird of the heavens, upon everything that creeps on the ground and all the fish of the sea. Into your hand they are delivered. 4 Every moving thing that lives shall be food for you. And as I gave you the green plants, I give you everything.

Chapter 30

1 But you shall not eat flesh with its life, that is, its blood. 2 And for your lifeblood I will require a reckoning: from every beast I will require it and from man. From his fellow man I will require a reckoning for the life of man. 3 "Whoever sheds the blood of man, by man shall his blood be shed, for God made man in his own image. 4 And you, be fruitful and multiply, increase greatly on the earth and multiply in it."

Chapter 31

1 Then God said to Noah and to his sons with him, 2 "Behold, I establish my covenant with you and your offspring after you, 3 and with every living creature that is with you, the birds, the livestock, and every beast of the earth with you, as many as came out of the ark; it is for every beast of the earth. 4 I establish my covenant with you, that never again shall all flesh be cut off by the waters of a flood, and never again shall there be a flood to destroy the earth."

Chapter 32

1 And God said, "This is the sign of the covenant that I make between me and you and every living creature that is with you, for all future generations: 2 I have set my bow in the cloud, and it shall be a sign of the covenant between me and the earth. 3 When I bring clouds over the earth and the bow is seen in the clouds, 4 I will remember my covenant that is between me and you and every living creature of all flesh. And the waters shall never again become a flood to destroy all flesh.

Chapter 33

1 When the bow is in the clouds, I will see it and remember the everlasting covenant between God and every living creature of all flesh that is on the earth." 2 God said to Noah, "This is the sign of the covenant that I have established between me and all flesh that is on the earth." 3 The sons of Noah who went forth from the ark were Shem, Ham, and Japheth. Ham is the father of Canaan. 4 These three were the sons of Noah, and from these the people of the whole earth were dispersed.

Chapter 34

1 Noah began to be a man of the soil, and he planted a vineyard. 2 He drank of the wine and became drunk and lay uncovered in his tent. 3 And Ham, the father

of Canaan, saw the nakedness of his father and told his two brothers outside. 4 Then Shem and Japheth took a garment, laid it on both their shoulders, and walked backward and covered the nakedness of their father. Their faces were turned backward, and they did not see their father's nakedness.

Chapter 35
1 When Noah awoke from his wine and knew what his youngest son had done to him, 2 he said, "Cursed be Canaan; a servant of servants shall he be to his brothers." 3 He also said, "Blessed be the Lord, the God of Shem; and let Canaan be his servant. 4 May God enlarge Japheth, and let him dwell in the tents of Shem, and let Canaan be his servant."

Chapter 36
1 After the flood, Noah lived 350 years. 2 All the days of Noah were 950 years, and then he died. 3 As the generations passed, the descendants of Noah's sons spread across the earth and began to populate it once more. 4 From these people came many nations and tribes, each with its own land and language.

Chapter 37
1 Now the whole earth had one language and the same words. 2 As people migrated from the east, they found a plain in the land of Shinar and settled there. 3 They said to one another, "Come, let us make bricks, and burn them thoroughly." And they had brick for stone, and bitumen for mortar. 4 Then they said, "Come, let us build ourselves a city and a tower with its top in the heavens, and let us make a name for ourselves, lest we be dispersed over the face of the whole earth."

Chapter 38
1 But the Lord came down to see the city and the tower, which the children of man had built. 2 And the Lord said, "Behold, they are one people, and they have all one language, and this is only the beginning of what they will do. And nothing that they propose to do will now be impossible for them. 3 Come, let us go down and there confuse their language, so that they may not understand one another's speech." 4 So the Lord dispersed them from there over the face of all the earth, and they left off building the city.

Chapter 39
1 Therefore its name was called Babel, because there the Lord confused the language of all the earth. 2 And from there the Lord dispersed them over the face of all the earth. 3 These were the generations of Shem, Ham, and Japheth, sons of Noah, and from them came the nations spread abroad on the earth after the flood. 4 Each family grew and developed into distinct tribes and languages, forming the diverse tapestry of humanity.

Chapter 40
1 The generations continued, and from these early tribes and nations, great leaders and founders of cities emerged. 2 Among them were mighty men of renown, who established kingdoms and crafted stories that would be told for generations. 3 The earth was filled with their exploits, and their legacies shaped the path of human history. 4 The deeds of these men were remembered, and their names became symbols of their people's identity and heritage.

Chapter 41
1 In time, the lineages of these early forefathers diverged further, giving rise to the great patriarchs of old. 2 Among them was Abram, later known as Abraham, a descendant of Shem through Arphaxad. 3 Abraham was called by God to leave his homeland and go to a place that God would show him. 4 God promised to make him a great nation, to bless him, and to make his name great, so that he would be a blessing.

Chapter 42
1 Abraham obeyed and left, as the Lord had spoken to him; with him went Sarai, his wife, and Lot, his nephew. 2 As they journeyed through various lands, God appeared to Abraham at different times, reaffirming His promises and covenant. 3 Abraham's faith and obedience marked him as a central figure in the narrative of God's interaction with humanity. 4 Through Abraham, God established an everlasting covenant, promising that through his seed all the nations of the earth would be blessed.

Chapter 43
1 This covenant, sealed with acts of faith and moments of divine intervention, laid the foundation for the stories of Isaac, Jacob, and the twelve tribes of Israel. 2 It was these tribes that would later form the nation of Israel, God's chosen people, through whom much of the biblical narrative would be focused. 3 The descendants of Abraham would carry forward the legacy of faith and covenant, shaping the religious, cultural, and historical landscape of the region. 4 Through their lineage, the prophecy of blessings to all nations would continue to unfold, leading to significant events that would impact the entire world.

Chapter 44
1 As the generations passed, the descendants of Abraham multiplied greatly, becoming as numerous as the stars in the sky, as God had promised. 2 Among these descendants was Joseph, son of Jacob, who was sold into slavery by his own brothers. 3 Yet, through divine providence, Joseph rose to become the second most powerful man in Egypt, saving many from famine, including his own family who came to Egypt for refuge. 4 This set the stage for a significant chapter in the history of the Hebrew people in Egypt.

Chapter 45
1 In time, the Hebrews became a great multitude in Egypt, but they were enslaved by a new king who did not know Joseph. 2 This king imposed harsh labor upon them, but their numbers continued to grow, prompting the Egyptians to treat them with increasing cruelty. 3 God heard their groaning, and He remembered His covenant with Abraham, with Isaac, and with Jacob. 4 God chose Moses, a Hebrew raised in the Egyptian royal household, to lead His people out of slavery.

Chapter 46
1 Moses, upon encountering God through a burning bush that was not consumed, received the divine mission to confront Pharaoh and demand the release of the Israelites. 2 With the power of God, Moses performed signs and wonders in Egypt, but Pharaoh's heart was hardened, and he refused to let the people go. 3 This prompted the ten plagues, devastating Egypt and culminating in the Passover, when the angel of death passed over the houses marked with the blood of a lamb. 4 Finally, Pharaoh relented, and Moses led the Israelites out of Egypt, through the parted Red Sea, which drowned the Egyptian army following them.

Chapter 47
1 In the wilderness, God provided for the Israelites with manna from heaven and water from a rock. 2 At Mount Sinai, Moses received the Ten Commandments, establishing a covenant between God and Israel, which included laws and instructions for worship and moral conduct. 3 The Israelites, however, struggled with faithfulness, often rebelling against God and Moses. 4 Despite their failures, God remained committed to His covenant, guiding them through the wilderness and preparing them to enter the Promised Land.

Chapter 48
1 The narrative continues with the conquest of Canaan under Joshua, Moses' successor, who led the Israelites in battles against the indigenous nations, following God's command to claim the land promised to Abraham's descendants. 2 The period of the Judges followed, a time of decentralized

leadership where heroes rose intermittently to deliver Israel from oppression and invasion. 3 This era was marked by a cycle of sin, suffering, supplication, and salvation, illustrating the Israelites' fluctuating fidelity to God. 4 The book of Ruth, set during this time, tells a story of loyalty and redemption, highlighting the faithful love between Ruth and Naomi, and Boaz's role as a kinsman-redeemer.

Chapter 49

1 The demand for a centralized monarchy led to the anointing of Saul as Israel's first king, but his disobedience led God to reject him in favor of David, a shepherd boy who became the ideal king of Israel. 2 David, despite his personal flaws, was beloved by God for his deep faith and is credited with uniting the tribes of Israel and establishing Jerusalem as the spiritual and political center. 3 Under David and his son Solomon, Israel reached its zenith, with Solomon building the First Temple, a permanent dwelling place for God among His people. 4 Solomon's wisdom and wealth were legendary, but his later years were marked by idolatry and division, leading to the split of the kingdom after his death.

Chapter 50

1 The divided kingdoms of Israel and Judah experienced cycles of reform and apostasy, interacting with surrounding empires and struggling to maintain their identity and faithfulness to God. 2 Prophets like Elijah, Isaiah, and Jeremiah played crucial roles during these turbulent times, calling the people back to the covenant and foretelling consequences for their actions. 3 The narrative of the Apocalypse of Adam, enriched with intergenerational stories of faith, failure, and the unending grace of God, serves as a testament to God's enduring presence in the journey of humanity. 4 Ultimately, it points forward to a future reconciliation and restoration, foreshadowing a new covenant and a messianic age of peace and righteousness.

100. The Testament of Abraham

Chapter1

1 And it came to pass that Abraham, the just, was old and well-advanced in age, and the Lord said unto him, "Abraham, Abraham." And he said, "Here am I." 2 And He said, "Behold, I have chosen you to be a prophet and a father of nations, but you have not yet seen all the places prepared by God. Prepare yourself, therefore, to see great wonders." 3 Abraham answered, "Lord, according to your word will I do all things."

Chapter 2

1 And while Abraham was preparing himself, the Lord sent His archangel Michael to him. Michael came to Abraham and said, "I am sent from the Lord to take you and show you the life to come and the world that is prepared for the righteous." 2 And Abraham prepared for his journey, and he went with Michael.

Chapter 3

1 They first came to a high mountain, and Michael said to Abraham, "Look down upon the earth and see the things beneath you." 2 And Abraham looked and saw the whole world as a disk of dust, and the sea as a drop of water, and the vast multitudes of humanity as a swarm of flies. 3 He marveled at these things and praised God for the greatness of His creation.

Chapter 4

1 They went forth and came to a great and high place where there was a gate of fire. And Abraham saw multitudes entering into it, and the brilliance that came forth from within was as the sun. 2 And he asked Michael, "What is this place?" And Michael answered, "This is the Gate of Righteousness, through which the righteous pass to the city of God."

Chapter 5

1 Next, they came to a dreadful and dark place, and they saw there men suffering. This was the outer darkness. 2 Abraham wept when he saw it, and he asked Michael, "Must all who sin suffer in this darkness?" 3 Michael replied, "These are they who have denied righteousness; they are tormented until the day of redemption."

Chapter 6

1 Moving on, they came upon a beautiful, light-filled land where many souls were dressed in shining garments, singing praises to the Lord. 2 Abraham was filled with joy upon seeing this and asked, "Who are these, my Lord?" 3 Michael answered, "These are the ones who have kept their garments clean and have washed them in the blood of the Lamb. They rejoice forever in the presence of the Lord."

Chapter 7

1 Finally, they came to a place of peace and rest, filled with gardens and flowing waters. Michael told Abraham, "This is the rest that is prepared for the servants of God." 2 Abraham, full of joy and peace, asked, "May we remain here?" 3 Michael replied, "You must return to the earth for a time, but when your days are fulfilled, you will come here again."

Chapter 8

1 And so, Abraham returned to his place, and he lived for many years, teaching his children and his household the ways of the Lord. 2 When the time of his departure was at hand, he called his son Isaac and blessed him, and he gave him all his instructions. 3 And Abraham rested with his fathers in peace, full of days and full of joy, waiting for the promise of the resurrection.

Chapter 9

1 After blessing Isaac, Abraham prepared for his final days, and he called all his children and grandchildren to his side. He spoke to them of the visions he had seen and the promises of God. 2 He instructed them to uphold justice, to practice righteousness, and to walk humbly with their God. He reminded them of the covenant that God had made with him and the promises extended to his descendants. 3 Abraham's words were full of wisdom and grace, and all who heard him were moved by the spirit of his faith.

Chapter 10

1 The time came for Abraham to depart from this world. The archangel Michael returned to guide him to his place of rest. 2 As Abraham's soul departed from his body, there was a great mourning among his family and all those who knew him. Yet, there was also peace, for they knew he was going to be with the Lord. 3 His family buried him in the cave of Machpelah, beside his wife Sarah, as he had instructed.

Chapter 11

1 In the realms of the afterlife, Abraham was greeted by the souls of the righteous who had gone before him. Among them were Adam, Noah, and Melchizedek, who welcomed him with great joy. 2 They praised God together, rejoicing in the fulfillment of the promises and the faithfulness of the Lord. 3 Abraham was shown the full expanse of the heavenly kingdom, a land of unending peace and glory where the righteous dwell in the presence of the Lord.

Chapter 12

1 Michael showed Abraham the Book of Life, where the names of all the righteous were recorded. Abraham's name shone brightly in the book, marked by the deeds of faith he had performed in his earthly life. 2 The angels proclaimed him a father of many nations, a title bestowed by God Himself, reflecting his impact on countless generations. 3 Abraham spent his days in the heavenly kingdom, often looking upon the earth, interceding for his descendants and all those who walked in the path of

righteousness.

Chapter 13

1 On the earth, the memory of Abraham lived on. Isaac and his descendants carried forward the Abrahamic covenant, living by the laws that Abraham had taught them. 2 They became a great nation, as God had promised, numerous as the stars in the sky and as the sand on the seashore. 3 Through them, the blessings promised to Abraham began to spread to all nations of the earth, fulfilling the words spoken by God to Abraham under the stars so many years ago.

Chapter 14

1 In the heavenly realms, Abraham was granted visions of the future of his descendants. He saw the trials and triumphs of his people, their suffering and their victories. 2 He saw the coming of the great Deliverer, born from his lineage, who would bring salvation not only to his people but to all humanity. 3 Abraham's heart was filled with gratitude and awe at the unfolding plan of God, a plan that spanned ages and transcended time.

Chapter 15

1 As epochs passed, Abraham continued to serve as a patriarch in the heavenly kingdom, a guiding light and intercessor for all who seek righteousness. 2 The story of Abraham, a testament to faith, obedience, and the everlasting covenant with God, is told and retold, inspiring generations to seek a closer relationship with the divine. 3 Thus, the testament of Abraham remains a beacon of hope and faith, echoing through eternity, reminding all of the rewards that await the faithful and the righteous in the presence of the Almighty.

Chapter 16

1 In the heavenly realms, as ages passed, Abraham watched over his descendants with great interest and care. He saw the establishment of Israel, the rise and fall of kings, and the steadfast love of God that never waned despite the people's frequent disobedience. 2 From his place in paradise, Abraham observed the prophets delivering God's messages, calling for repentance and a return to the ways of righteousness that he himself had walked. 3 He rejoiced at the moments of revival and wept over the periods of great suffering and exile that his people endured.

Chapter 17

1 Among the visions granted to Abraham was the emergence of the great temple in Jerusalem, a symbol of God's presence among His people. He saw Solomon, his descendant, dedicating the temple with prayers and sacrifices that ascended to heaven like sweet incense. 2 Abraham felt a profound connection to his people during these moments, seeing the fulfillment of God's promises of blessing and communion. 3 Yet, he also witnessed the temple's destruction and the subsequent captivity of his people, events that grieved his soul deeply.

Chapter 18

1 Amid these cycles of judgment and mercy, Abraham's heart was particularly stirred by the vision of the coming Messiah, a descendant promised through his lineage. 2 He saw the birth of the Messiah in humble settings, His life of service, His profound teachings, and His ultimate sacrifice for the sins of humanity. 3 This vision filled Abraham with an overwhelming sense of awe and gratitude. He understood that this was the ultimate fulfillment of God's promise to him—that through his offspring, all the nations of the earth would be blessed.

Chapter 19

1 With the coming of the Messiah, Abraham saw the spread of a new covenant, one that was written not on tablets of stone but on the hearts of all who believed. This covenant transcended the boundaries of nation and ethnicity, reaching out to the Gentiles and including them in the blessings once promised to Abraham's descendants. 2 The spread of this gospel brought great joy to Abraham, as he saw multitudes from every corner of the earth turning to worship the God of Israel. 3 He marveled at the divine mystery, how through what seemed like the end—the death of the Messiah—came life and hope for all peoples.

Chapter 20

1 As time progressed, Abraham continued to serve as a witness to God's unfolding plan. He saw the trials and tribulations faced by the faithful but also their ultimate victory as they overcame through faith and the power of the Spirit. 2 He saw the final gathering of all nations, a great multitude no one could number, standing before the throne of God, their voices raised in a song of redemption and praise. 3 This vision was a profound comfort to Abraham, reaffirming the promises God had made to him so long ago, promises that were now beautifully and completely realized.

Chapter 21

1 In his celestial abode, surrounded by the faithful of all ages, Abraham continues to rejoice in the presence of God. He partakes in the eternal worship, offering praises to God for His faithfulness and love. 2 His story, a testament to faith and obedience, continues to inspire and guide those on earth, reminding them of the rewards that await the faithful. 3 Thus, the legacy of Abraham, encapsulated in the stories and teachings passed down through generations, lives on, a beacon of hope and faith that transcends time, pointing always to the eternal and the divine.

Chapter 22

1 From his heavenly vantage, Abraham continued to observe the unfolding history of his earthly descendants. He saw the diaspora of the Jewish people, their struggles and triumphs in foreign lands, and their enduring hope for redemption. 2 His heart was moved by their perseverance in faith despite adversity, and he saw in them the living testament of his own covenant with God. 3 Throughout the ages, he witnessed the rise of scholars and sages who interpreted the laws and prophecies, keeping the spirit of the covenant alive and vibrant among the people.

Chapter 23

1 Abraham also watched the interactions between his descendants and other nations, noting the profound influences they exerted on each other. He saw the spread of monotheism, the echoes of his own discovery of the one true God, influencing religions and cultures far beyond the Jewish people. 2 He took great joy in seeing the moral and ethical teachings he valued being adopted and adapted across diverse civilizations, contributing to a global conversation on justice, ethics, and spiritual life. 3 Each instance of spiritual awakening and moral progress among the nations was to him a fulfillment of the promise that through his lineage, "all the families of the earth would be blessed."

Chapter 24

1 As centuries turned into millennia, Abraham's vision encompassed the modern world, with all its complexities and advancements. He marveled at the technological wonders that humans had achieved, yet his focus remained on their spiritual and moral choices. 2 He observed the challenges of modernity, where faith often clashed with reason, and he grieved for those who lost their spiritual way amidst material distractions. 3 Yet, he also saw a revival of spiritual longing, as people across the world sought meaning and connection with the divine, sometimes drawing upon the very teachings he had once imparted to his children.

Chapter 25

1 The archangel Michael often accompanied

Abraham as he observed these earthly developments. Together, they discussed the patterns of human behavior, the recurring cycles of sin and redemption, and God's unending mercy and patience. 2 Abraham was particularly touched by the efforts of peacemakers and justice-seekers who, in every age, strove to uphold the divine principles he had lived by. He saw them as the spiritual heirs to his legacy, regardless of their faith or nation. 3 Michael reminded Abraham that his role as a father of many nations was not only biological but also spiritual, and that his influence was woven through the tapestry of human history, seen and unseen.

Chapter 26

1 In celestial dialogues with other patriarchs and prophets, Abraham found solace and fellowship. Together, they shared insights and offered intercessions for the world below, hoping for the ultimate reconciliation of all things. 2 These heavenly gatherings were times of reflection and renewal, where Abraham and his peers reaffirmed their commitment to God's purposes and their love for humanity. 3 They prayed for the day when peace and justice would reign supreme, when swords would be beaten into plowshares, and when the lion would lie down with the lamb.

Chapter 27

1 In the fullness of time, Abraham looked forward to the final fulfillment of all prophecies, the culmination of the ages when the Messiah would return to establish everlasting peace and justice. 2 He anticipated this glorious future, when the earth would be restored and all creation would sing a new song of redemption and joy. 3 Until then, Abraham, the friend of God, continues to watch, pray, and hope, serving as a guardian of the covenant and a beacon of faith for all who seek righteousness.

Chapter 28

1 As the epochs continued to unfold, Abraham witnessed the resilience and resurgence of his people in their historical homeland. After centuries of dispersion, they returned and rebuilt, restoring Jerusalem and rekindling the practices that he had laid down so long ago. 2 From his celestial viewpoint, he observed the festivals being celebrated once again with joy and fervor. Passover, Sukkot, and Shavuot were not just historical commemorations but reaffirmations of a timeless covenant between God and his people. 3 The restoration of these practices filled Abraham with immense joy, as they signified not only the survival of his physical lineage but the enduring vigor of their spiritual commitment.

Chapter 29

1 In this era of rapid change and global connectivity, Abraham took particular interest in the spread of knowledge about the God of Israel far beyond the Jewish people. He saw his descendants engage in dialogue with peoples of various faiths, sharing insights and fostering understanding across religious divides. 2 This exchange often reminded him of his own journeys, where he too had encountered and engaged with diverse cultures and beliefs, always advocating for righteousness and the worship of the One true God. 3 Abraham's legacy, therefore, extended into initiatives that bridged communities and healed divisions, embodying his role as a father to many nations.

Chapter 30

1 Yet, Abraham also saw the earth plagued by wars, environmental degradation, and the suffering of the innocent. These sights grieved him, and he often turned to God in prayer, interceding for mercy and intervention. 2 His prayers were joined by those of countless others in the celestial realm—saints and angels alike—who looked upon the earth with compassion and hope for redemption. 3 These intercessions were powerful, stirring movements of peace and renewal on earth, sparking revival and reform that echoed the prophetic visions of old.

Chapter 31

1 Among the most profound of Abraham's observations was the ongoing fulfillment of God's promise that through his seed, all nations of the earth would be blessed. This was manifested not only through the biological descendants of Isaac but through the widespread influence of the teachings and spirit of the Jewish tradition. 2 He saw this blessing in the pursuit of justice, the quest for knowledge, and the acts of kindness performed by countless individuals inspired by the ethical monotheism that had originated with him. 3 Abraham understood that the true measure of his legacy was not in the number of his descendants but in the quality of their impact on the world—promoting peace, justice, and understanding among all peoples.

Chapter 32

1 As time marched towards the prophesied end of days, Abraham's anticipation grew. He looked forward to the Messianic age, a time prophesied to bring universal peace and enlightenment, where the knowledge of God would cover the earth as the waters cover the sea. 2 In this new world, the struggles and pains of the current age would be remembered only as lessons from the past, lessons that taught humanity the value of righteousness and the power of divine grace. 3 Abraham's heart swelled with hope as he envisioned this future, a world where his ultimate dream—God's promise of harmony and unity among all creation—would finally be realized.

Chapter 33

1 In his watchfulness, Abraham remained a guiding spirit, an elder statesman of the celestial realm, whose wisdom and experiences continued to inspire those who looked to him as their patriarch. 2 He conversed with modern prophets and leaders, sometimes appearing in dreams and visions, offering counsel and encouragement, reminding them of the covenant and urging them to faithfulness. 3 As the world spun on, the spirit of Abraham, the friend of God, endured as a beacon of faith, an emblem of covenant loyalty, and a source of spiritual guidance, continuing to influence the course of human history toward the divine fulfillment of peace and righteousness.

Chapter 34

1 Throughout the heavenly realms, Abraham's wisdom was sought by many. His experiences in life, his trials and the covenant he shared with God provided deep insights that were relevant across ages. 2 He watched over his descendants who now spread across the globe, engaging in diverse fields—leaders in thought, champions of justice, and stewards of faith. Their works, influenced indirectly by his legacy, continued to shape a world that was inching ever closer to the prophetic visions of old. 3 Abraham's presence in spiritual conversations was subtle but profound, as he inspired thoughts and actions that promoted reconciliation and understanding among disparate groups.

Chapter 35

1 In times of global crisis, Abraham's spirit was particularly active. He interceded for humanity during wars, natural disasters, and moments of profound social and ethical dilemmas. 2 His intercessions were manifestations of his continued covenant with God, seeking mercy and grace for a world still grappling with its fallen nature. 3 During such times, the impacts of his prayers were felt by those who led humanitarian efforts, mediated peace talks, and provided solace to the afflicted, often without their conscious awareness of his influence.

Chapter 36

1 As environmental challenges mounted, Abraham, who had once roamed the earth's vast landscapes and understood the value of its sanctity, grieved for

the damage wrought upon the planet. 2 He convened with other patriarchs and spiritual entities to advocate for the earth, urging those on the spiritual and earthly planes to respect and protect the creation that God had declared good. 3 His advocacy inspired movements among his descendants and others to steward the earth's resources wisely, promoting sustainability and respect for the natural world as a divine trust.

Chapter 37

1 With the approach of the prophesied end of days, Abraham's role as a patriarch took on a renewed significance. He was a key figure in preparing the heavenly hosts and the faithful on earth for the events that were to unfold. 2 He was given glimpses into the future, visions of the coming Messiah's reign, where peace and justice would prevail, and the knowledge of God would fill the earth. 3 These revelations filled him with a deep sense of hope and urgency, as he worked to ready both celestial and earthly beings for the transition into a new era.

Chapter 38

1 As the final reconciliation of all things drew near, Abraham's thoughts often returned to his early days, to his initial call and the promises made by God. He reflected on the journey of faith—from the solitary figure who once looked up at the stars and believed in God's promises, to the father of a multitude that would inherit the earth. 2 His story, a testament to the power of faith and obedience, served as a guiding light for all who sought to understand the nature of God and the path to redemption. 3 The unity of heaven and earth, the fulfillment of all things was now within sight, and Abraham, a faithful servant and friend of God, was at peace, ready to witness the culmination of God's plan for humanity.

Chapter 39

1 As the new era dawned, Abraham stood among the assembly of the faithful, witnessing the restoration of creation and the establishment of eternal peace. 2 His heart swelled with joy as he saw the descendants of all nations walking together in light, their divisions healed, their iniquities forgiven, and their hearts turned fully towards God. 3 The legacy of Abraham, encapsulated not just in the multitude of his descendants but in the spread of monotheistic faith across the earth, was complete. He had indeed become a blessing to all the families of the earth, just as God had promised.

Chapter 40

1 Now, with the new creation established and the old order passed away, Abraham continued to dwell in the presence of God, his life a beacon of hope and faithfulness. 2 Surrounded by the great cloud of witnesses, he shared his journey, a testimony that echoed through eternity, inspiring countless souls to walk in faith, pursue righteousness, and cling to the promises of God. 3 Abraham's story, from the call out of Ur to the fulfillment of the ages, remains a powerful testament to the covenant relationship with God, a reminder of the eternal rewards that await those who, like him, dare to believe and obey.

101. The Testament of Isaac

Chapter 1

1 In the days when Isaac had grown old and his eyes had dimmed so that he could no longer see, he called to his elder son Esau and said, "My son." And he answered him, "Here I am." 2 Isaac said, "I am old and do not know the day of my death. Now then, take your weapons, your quiver and your bow, and go out to the field and hunt game for me, 3 and prepare for me delicious food, such as I love, and bring it to me so that I may eat, that my soul may bless you before I die."

Chapter 2

1 But Rebekah was listening when Isaac spoke to his son Esau. When Esau went to the field to hunt for game and bring it, 2 Rebekah said to her son Jacob, "I heard your father speak to your brother Esau, saying, 3 'Bring me game and prepare for me delicious food, that I may eat it and bless you before the Lord before my death.' 4 Now therefore, my son, obey my voice as I command you.

Chapter 3

1 Go to the flock and bring me two good young goats, so that I may prepare from them delicious food for your father, such as he loves. 2 And you shall bring it to your father to eat, so that he may bless you before his death." 3 Jacob said to Rebekah his mother, "Behold, my brother Esau is a hairy man, and I am a smooth man. 4 Perhaps my father will feel me, and I shall seem to be mocking him and bring a curse upon myself and not a blessing."

Chapter 4

1 His mother said to him, "Let your curse be on me, my son; only obey my voice, and go, bring them to me." 2 So he went and took them and brought them to his mother, and his mother prepared delicious food, such as his father loved. 3 Then Rebekah took the best garments of Esau her older son, which were with her in the house, and put them on Jacob her younger son. 4 And the skins of the young goats she put on his hands and on the smooth part of his neck.

Chapter 5

1 And she put the delicious food and the bread, which she had prepared, into the hand of her son Jacob. 2 So he went in to his father and said, "My father." And he said, "Here I am. Who are you, my son?" 3 Jacob said to his father, "I am Esau your firstborn. I have done as you told me; now sit up and eat of my game, that your soul may bless me." 4 But Isaac said to his son, "How is it that you have found it so quickly, my son?" He answered, "Because the Lord your God granted me success."

Chapter 6

1 Then Isaac said to Jacob, "Come near, that I may feel you, my son, to know whether you are really my son Esau or not." 2 So Jacob went near to Isaac his father, who felt him and said, "The voice is Jacob's voice, but the hands are the hands of Esau." 3 And he did not recognize him, because his hands were hairy like his brother Esau's hands. So he blessed him. 4 He said, "Are you really my son Esau?" He answered, "I am."

Chapter 7

1 Then he said, "Bring it near to me, that I may eat of my son's game and bless you." So he brought it near to him, and he ate; and he brought him wine, and he drank. 2 Then his father Isaac said to him, "Come near and kiss me, my son." 3 So he came near and kissed him. And Isaac smelled the smell of his garments and blessed him and said, 4 "See, the smell of my son is as the smell of a field that the Lord has blessed!

Chapter 8

1 May God give you of the dew of heaven and of the fatness of the earth and plenty of grain and wine. 2 Let peoples serve you, and nations bow down to you. Be lord over your brothers, and may your mother's sons bow down to you. Cursed be everyone who curses you, and blessed be everyone who blesses you!"

Chapter 9

1 As soon as Isaac had finished blessing Jacob, and Jacob had scarcely gone out from the presence of Isaac his father, Esau his brother came in from his hunting. 2 He also prepared delicious food and brought it to his father. And he said to his father, "Let my father arise and eat of his son's game, that you may bless me." 3 His father Isaac said to him, "Who are you?" He answered, "I am your son, your firstborn, Esau."

Chapter 10

1 Then Isaac trembled very violently and said, "Who was it then that hunted game and brought it to me, and I ate it all before you came, and I have blessed him? Yes, and he shall be blessed." 2 When Esau heard the words of his father, he cried out with an exceedingly great and bitter cry and said to his father, "Bless me, even me also, O my father!" 3 But he said, "Your brother came deceitfully, and he has taken away your blessing."

Chapter 11

1 Esau said, "Is he not rightly named Jacob? For he has cheated me these two times. He took away my birthright, and behold, now he has taken away my blessing." Then he said, "Have you not reserved a blessing for me?" 2 Isaac answered and said to Esau, "Behold, I have made him lord over you, and all his brothers I have given to him for servants, and with grain and wine I have sustained him. What then can I do for you, my son?" 3 Esau said to his father, "Have you but one blessing, my father? Bless me, even me also, O my father." And Esau lifted up his voice and wept.

Chapter 12

1 Then Isaac his father answered and said to him, "Behold, away from the fatness of the earth shall your dwelling be, and away from the dew of heaven on high. 2 By your sword you shall live, and you shall serve your brother. But when you grow restless, you shall break his yoke from your neck."

Chapter 13

1 Esau harbored a grudge against Jacob because of the blessing with which his father had blessed him, and Esau said to himself, "The days of mourning for my father are approaching; then I will kill my brother Jacob." 2 When the words of her elder son Esau were told to Rebekah, she sent and called Jacob her younger son and said to him, "Behold, your brother Esau comforts himself about you by planning to kill you. 3 Now therefore, my son, obey my voice. Arise, flee to Laban my brother in Haran, 4 and stay with him for a while until your brother's fury turns away.

Chapter 14

1 "Until your brother's anger turns away from you, and he forgets what you have done to him. Then I will send and bring you from there. Why should I be bereft of you both in one day?" 2 Rebekah said to Isaac, "I am weary of my life because of the Hittite women. If Jacob takes a wife from the Hittite women like these, from the women of the land, what life will there be left for me?"

Chapter 15

1 So Isaac called Jacob and blessed him and commanded him, "You must not take a wife from the Canaanite women. 2 Arise, go to Paddan-aram to the house of Bethuel your mother's father, and take as your wife from there one of the daughters of Laban, your mother's brother. 3 May God Almighty bless you and make you fruitful and multiply you, that you may become a company of peoples. 4 May he give the blessing of Abraham to you and to your offspring with you, that you may take possession of the land of your sojournings that God gave to Abraham."

Chapter 16

1 Thus Isaac sent Jacob away, and he went to Paddan-aram to Laban, son of Bethuel the Aramean, the brother of Rebekah, mother of Jacob and Esau. 2 Esau saw that Isaac had blessed Jacob and sent him away to Paddan-aram to take a wife from there, and that as he blessed him he commanded him, "You must not take a wife from the Canaanite women," 3 and that Jacob had obeyed his father and his mother and gone to Paddan-aram. 4 So Esau saw that the Canaanite women did not please Isaac his father.

Chapter 17

1 Then Esau went to Ishmael and took as his wife, besides the wives he had, Mahalath the daughter of Ishmael, Abraham's son, the sister of Nebaioth, to please his father Isaac. 2 And Jacob left Beersheba and went toward Haran. 3 He came to a certain place and stayed there that night because the sun had set. Taking one of the stones of the place, he put it under his head and lay down in that place to sleep.

Chapter 18

1 And Jacob dreamed, and behold, there was a ladder set up on the earth, and the top of it reached to heaven. And behold, the angels of God were ascending and descending on it! 2 And behold, the Lord stood above it and said, "I am the Lord, the God of Abraham your father and the God of Isaac. The land on which you lie I will give to you and to your offspring. 3 Your offspring shall be like the dust of the earth, and you shall spread abroad to the west and to the east and to the north and to the south, and in you and your offspring shall all the families of the earth be blessed. 4 Behold, I am with you and will keep you wherever you go, and will bring you back to this land. For I will not leave you until I have done what I have promised you."

Chapter 19

1 Then Jacob awoke from his sleep and said, "Surely the Lord is in this place, and I did not know it." 2 And he was afraid and said, "How awesome is this place! This is none other than the house of God, and this is the gate of heaven." 3 So early in the morning Jacob took the stone that he had put under his head and set it up as a pillar and poured oil on the top of it. 4 He called the name of that place Bethel, but the name of the city was Luz at the first.

Chapter 20

1 Jacob made a vow, saying, "If God will be with me and will keep me in this way that I go, and will give me bread to eat and clothing to wear, 2 so that I come again to my father's house in peace, then the Lord shall be my God, 3 and this stone, which I have set up for a pillar, shall be God's house, and of all that you give me I will give a full tenth to you."

Chapter 21

1 Then Jacob continued on his journey and came to the land of the people of the east. 2 As he looked, he saw a well in the field, and behold, three flocks of sheep lying beside it, for out of that well the flocks were watered. The stone on the well's mouth was large, 3 and when all the flocks were gathered there, the shepherds would roll the stone from the mouth of the well and water the sheep, and put the stone back in its place over the mouth of the well.

Chapter 22

1 Jacob said to them, "My brothers, where do you come from?" They said, "We are from Haran." 2 He said to them, "Do you know Laban, the son of Nahor?" They said, "We know him." 3 He said to them, "Is it well with him?" They said, "It is well; and see, Rachel his daughter is coming with the sheep." 4 He said, "Behold, it is still high day; it is not time for the livestock to be gathered together. Water the sheep, and go, pasture them."

Chapter 23

1 But they said, "We cannot until all the flocks are gathered together and the stone is rolled from the mouth of the well; then we water the sheep." 2 While he was still speaking with them, Rachel came with her father's sheep, for she was a shepherdess. 3 Now as soon as Jacob saw Rachel the daughter of Laban his mother's brother, and the sheep of Laban his mother's brother, Jacob went up and rolled the stone from the well's mouth and watered the flock of Laban his mother's brother. 4 Then Jacob kissed Rachel and wept aloud.

Chapter 24

1 Jacob told Rachel that he was her father's relative and that he was Rebekah's son; and she ran and told her father. 2 When Laban heard the news about Jacob, his sister's son, he ran to meet him and embraced him and kissed him and brought him to his

house. Jacob told Laban all these things, 3 and Laban said to him, "Surely you are my bone and my flesh!" And he stayed with him for a month.

Chapter 25

1 Then Laban said to Jacob, "Because you are my relative, should you therefore serve me for nothing? Tell me, what shall your wages be?" 2 Now Laban had two daughters; the name of the older was Leah, and the name of the younger was Rachel. 3 Leah's eyes were weak, but Rachel was beautiful in form and appearance. 4 Jacob loved Rachel. And he said, "I will serve you seven years for Rachel your younger daughter."

Chapter 26

1 Laban said, "It is better that I give her to you than that I should give her to any other man; stay with me." 2 So Jacob served seven years for Rachel, and they seemed to him but a few days because of the love he had for her. 3 Then Jacob said to Laban, "Give me my wife that I may go in to her, for my time is completed."

Chapter 27

1 So Laban gathered together all the men of the place and made a feast. 2 But in the evening he took his daughter Leah and brought her to Jacob, and he went in to her. 3 (Laban gave his female servant Zilpah to his daughter Leah to be her servant.) 4 And in the morning, behold, it was Leah! And Jacob said to Laban, "What is this you have done to me? Did I not serve with you for Rachel? Why then have you deceived me?"

Chapter 28

1 Laban said, "It is not so done in our country, to give the younger before the firstborn. 2 Complete the week of this one, and we will give you the other also in return for serving me another seven years." 3 Jacob did so, and completed her week. Then Laban gave him his daughter Rachel to be his wife. 4 (Laban gave his female servant Bilhah to his daughter Rachel to be her servant.)

Chapter 29

1 So Jacob went in to Rachel also, and he loved Rachel more than Leah, and served Laban for another seven years. 2 When the Lord saw that Leah was hated, he opened her womb, but Rachel was barren. 3 Leah conceived and bore a son, and she called his name Reuben, for she said, "Because the Lord has looked upon my affliction; surely now my husband will love me." 4 She conceived again and bore a son, and said, "Because the Lord has heard that I am hated, he has given me this son also." And she called his name Simeon.

Chapter 30

1 Again she conceived and bore a son, and said, "Now this time my husband will be attached to me, because I have borne him three sons." Therefore his name was called Levi. 2 And she conceived again and bore a son, and said, "This time I will praise the Lord." Therefore she called his name Judah. Then she ceased bearing. 3 Rachel, seeing that she bore Jacob no children, envied her sister. She said to Jacob, "Give me children, or I shall die!" 4 Jacob's anger was kindled against Rachel, and he said, "Am I in the place of God, who has withheld from you the fruit of the womb?"

Chapter 31

1 Then she said, "Here is my servant Bilhah; go in to her, so that she may give birth on my behalf, that even I may have children through her." 2 So she gave him her servant Bilhah as a wife, and Jacob went in to her. 3 And Bilhah conceived and bore Jacob a son. 4 Then Rachel said, "God has judged me, and has also heard my voice and given me a son." Therefore she called his name Dan.

Chapter 32

1 Rachel's servant Bilhah conceived again and bore Jacob a second son. 2 Then Rachel said, "With mighty wrestlings I have wrestled with my sister and have prevailed." So she called his name Naphtali. 3 When Leah saw that she had ceased bearing children, she took her servant Zilpah and gave her to Jacob as a wife. 4 And Zilpah, Leah's servant, bore Jacob a son.

Chapter 33

1 Then Leah said, "Good fortune has come!" So she called his name Gad. 2 Zilpah, Leah's servant, bore Jacob a second son. 3 And Leah said, "Happy am I! For women have called me happy." So she called his name Asher. 4 In the days of wheat harvest, Reuben went and found mandrakes in the field and brought them to his mother Leah. Rachel said to Leah, "Please give me some of your son's mandrakes."

Chapter 34

1 But Leah said to her, "Is it a small matter that you have taken away my husband? Would you take away my son's mandrakes also?" Rachel said, "Then he may lie with you tonight for your son's mandrakes." 2 When Jacob came from the field in the evening, Leah went out to meet him and said, "You must come in to me, for I have hired you with my son's mandrakes." So he lay with her that night. 3 And God listened to Leah, and she conceived and bore Jacob a fifth son. 4 Leah said, "God has given me my hire because I gave my servant to my husband." So she called his name Issachar.

Chapter 35

1 Leah conceived again and bore Jacob a sixth son. 2 Then Leah said, "God has endowed me with a good endowment; now my husband will honor me, because I have borne him six sons." So she called his name Zebulun. 3 Afterwards she bore a daughter and called her name Dinah. 4 God remembered Rachel, and God listened to her and opened her womb.

Chapter 36

1 She conceived and bore a son and said, "God has taken away my reproach." 2 And she called his name Joseph, saying, "May the Lord add to me another son!" 3 As Rachel was giving birth to Joseph, Jacob said to Laban, "Send me away, that I may go to my own home and country. 4 Give me my wives and my children for whom I have served you, and let me go; for you know the service that I have given you."

Chapter 37

1 But Laban said to him, "If I have found favor in your eyes, please stay, for I have learned by divination that the Lord has blessed me because of you." 2 He added, "Name your wages, and I will give it." 3 Jacob said to him, "You know how I have served you and how your livestock has fared with me. 4 For you had little before I came, and it has increased abundantly, and the Lord has blessed you wherever I turned. But now when shall I provide for my own household also?"

Chapter 38

1 He said, "What shall I give you?" Jacob said, "You shall not give me anything. If you will do this one thing for me, I will again pasture and keep your flock: 2 let me pass through all your flock today, removing from there every speckled and spotted sheep, every black lamb, and the spotted and speckled among the goats; these shall be my wages. 3 So my honesty will answer for me later, when you come to look into my wages with you. Every one that is not speckled and spotted among the goats and black among the lambs, if found with me, shall be counted stolen." 4 Laban said, "Good! Let it be as you have said."

Chapter 39

1 But that day Laban removed the male goats that were striped and spotted, and all the female goats that were speckled and spotted, every one that had white on it, and every lamb that was black, and put them in the charge of his sons. 2 Then he set a distance of three days' journey between himself and Jacob, and Jacob fed the rest of Laban's flocks. 3 Jacob took fresh sticks of poplar and almond and plane trees, and peeled white streaks in them,

exposing the white of the sticks. 4 He set the sticks that he had peeled in front of the flocks in the troughs, that is, the watering places, where the flocks came to drink. And since they bred when they came to drink,

Chapter 40

1 the flocks bred in front of the sticks and so the flocks brought forth striped, speckled, and spotted. 2 Jacob separated the lambs and set the faces of the flocks toward the striped and all the black in the flock of Laban. He put his own droves apart and did not put them with Laban's flock. 3 Whenever the stronger of the flock were breeding, Jacob would lay the sticks in the troughs before the eyes of the flock, that they might breed among the sticks, 4 but for the feebler of the flock, he would not lay them there. So the feebler would be Laban's, and the stronger Jacob's.

Chapter 41

1 Thus the man increased greatly and had large flocks, female servants and male servants, and camels and donkeys. 2 Jacob heard the words of Laban's sons, saying, "Jacob has taken all that was our father's, and from what was our father's he has gained all this wealth." 3 And Jacob saw that Laban did not regard him with favor as before. 4 Then the Lord said to Jacob, "Return to the land of your fathers and to your kindred, and I will be with you."

102. The Testament of Jacob

Chapter 1

1 As Jacob grew old and his time approached to leave this world, he called for his son Joseph. He wanted to ensure that his burial would not be in Egypt, but rather in the cave in the field of Machpelah, where his ancestors were laid to rest. 2 Jacob said to Joseph, "If I have found favor in your sight, put your hand under my thigh and promise that you will deal kindly and truly with me. Do not bury me in Egypt, 3 but when I rest with my fathers, carry me out of Egypt and bury me in their burial place." Joseph promised, "I will do as you say."

Chapter 2

1 Then Jacob called for his sons and said, "Gather yourselves together, that I may tell you what shall befall you in days to come. 2 Assemble and listen, O sons of Jacob; listen to Israel your father."

Chapter 3

1 Reuben, you are my firstborn, my might and the first sign of my strength, excelling in honor, excelling in power. 2 Turbulent as the waters, you will no longer excel, for you went up onto your father's bed, onto my couch and defiled it.

Chapter 4

1 Simeon and Levi are brothers; instruments of cruelty are in their dwelling place. 2 Let not my soul enter their council; let not my honor be united to their assembly; for in their anger they killed a man, and in their self-will they hamstrung an ox. 3 Cursed be their anger, for it is fierce; and their wrath, for it is cruel! I will divide them in Jacob and scatter them in Israel.

Chapter 5

1 Judah, your brothers shall praise you; your hand shall be on the neck of your enemies; your father's sons shall bow down before you. 2 Judah is a lion's whelp; from the prey, my son, you have gone up. He stoops down, he crouches as a lion, and as a lioness; who dares rouse him? 3 The scepter shall not depart from Judah, nor the ruler's staff from between his feet, until tribute comes to him; and to him shall be the obedience of the peoples.

Chapter 6

1 Zebulun shall dwell at the shore of the sea; he shall become a haven for ships, and his border shall be at Sidon.

Chapter 7

1 Issachar is a strong donkey, crouching between the sheepfolds. 2 He saw that rest was good, and the land that it was pleasant; so he bowed his shoulder to bear, and became a servant at forced labor.

Chapter 8

1 Dan shall judge his people as one of the tribes of Israel. 2 Dan shall be a serpent in the way, a viper by the path, that bites the horse's heels so that his rider falls backward. 3 I wait for your salvation, O Lord.

Chapter 9

1 Gad, a troop shall tramp upon him, but he shall tramp upon their heels.

Chapter 10

1 Asher's food shall be rich, and he shall yield royal delicacies.

Chapter 11

1 Naphtali is a doe let loose that bears beautiful fawns.

Chapter 12

1 Joseph is a fruitful bough, a fruitful bough by a spring; his branches run over the wall. 2 The archers bitterly attacked him, shot at him, and harassed him severely, 3 yet his bow remained unmoved; his arms were made agile by the hands of the Mighty One of Jacob (from there is the Shepherd, the Stone of Israel), 4 by the God of your father who will help you, by the Almighty who will bless you with blessings of heaven above, blessings of the deep that crouches beneath, blessings of the breasts and of the womb. 5 The blessings of your father are mighty beyond the blessings of my parents, up to the bounties of the everlasting hills. May they be on the head of Joseph, and on the brow of him who was set apart from his brothers.

Chapter 13

1 Benjamin is a ravenous wolf, in the morning devouring the prey and at evening dividing the spoil."

Chapter 14

1 All these are the twelve tribes of Israel, and this is what their father said to them when he blessed them, blessing each with the blessing suitable to him. 2 Then he instructed them and said to them, "I am to be gathered to my people; bury me with my fathers in the cave that is in the field of Ephron the Hittite, 3 in the cave that is in the field at Machpelah, to the east of Mamre, in the land of Canaan, which Abraham bought with the field from Ephron the Hittite to possess as a burying place. 4 There they buried Abraham and Sarah his wife; there they buried Isaac and Rebekah his wife, and there I buried Leah— 5 the field and the cave that is in it were bought from the Hittites."

Chapter 15

1 When Jacob had finished commanding his sons, he drew up his feet into the bed and breathed his last, and was gathered to his people.

Chapter 16

1 Joseph fell on his father's face and wept over him and kissed him. 2 He commanded his servants the physicians to embalm his father. So the physicians embalmed Israel. 3 Forty days were required for it, for so are fulfilled the days of embalming. And the Egyptians wept for him seventy days.

Chapter 17

1 When the days of weeping for him were past, Joseph spoke to the household of Pharaoh, saying, "If now I have found favor in your eyes, please speak in the ears of Pharaoh, saying, 2 'My father made me swear, saying, "I am about to die: in my tomb that I hewed out for myself in the land of Canaan, there shall you bury me." Now therefore, let me go up and bury my father. Then I will return.'" 3 And Pharaoh answered, "Go up, and bury your father, as he made you swear."

Chapter 18

1 So Joseph went up to bury his father. With him went up all the servants of Pharaoh, the elders of his

household, and all the elders of the land of Egypt, 2 as well as all the household of Joseph, his brothers, and his father's household. Only their children, their flocks, and their herds were left in the land of Goshen. 3 And there went up with him both chariots and horsemen. It was a very great company.

Chapter 19

1 When they came to the threshing floor of Atad, which is beyond the Jordan, they lamented with a very great and grievous lamentation, and he made a mourning for his father seven days. 2 When the inhabitants of the land, the Canaanites, saw the mourning on the threshing floor of Atad, they said, "This is a grievous mourning by the Egyptians." Therefore the place was named Abel-mizraim; it is beyond the Jordan.

Chapter 20

1 Thus his sons did for him as he had commanded them, 2 for his sons carried him to the land of Canaan and buried him in the cave of the field at Machpelah, to the east of Mamre, which Abraham bought with the field from Ephron the Hittite to possess as a burying place. 3 After burying his father, Joseph returned to Egypt with his brothers and all who had gone up with him to bury his father.

Chapter 21

1 When Joseph's brothers saw that their father was dead, they said, "It may be that Joseph will hate us and pay us back for all the evil that we did to him." 2 So they sent a message to Joseph, saying, "Your father gave this command before he died: 3 'Say to Joseph, "Please forgive the transgression of your brothers and their sin, because they did evil to you."' And now, please forgive the transgression of the servants of the God of your father." Joseph wept when they spoke to him.

Chapter 22

1 His brothers also came and fell down before him and said, "Behold, we are your servants." 2 But Joseph said to them, "Do not fear, for am I in the place of God? 3 As for you, you meant evil against me, but God meant it for good, to bring it about that many people should be kept alive, as they are today. 4 So do not fear; I will provide for you and your little ones." Thus he comforted them and spoke kindly to them.

Chapter 23

1 Joseph lived in Egypt, he and his father's household. And Joseph lived 110 years. 2 Joseph saw Ephraim's children of the third generation. The children also of Machir, the son of Manasseh, were counted as Joseph's own. 3 And Joseph said to his brothers, "I am about to die, but God will visit you and bring you up out of this land to the land that he swore to Abraham, to Isaac, and to Jacob." 4 Then Joseph made the sons of Israel swear, saying, "God will surely visit you, and you shall carry up my bones from here."

Chapter 24

1 So Joseph died, being 110 years old. They embalmed him, and he was put in a coffin in Egypt. Thus ends the testament of Jacob, as he ensured his legacy and his family's return to their ancestral land, reflecting his faith in God's promises to his forefathers.

Chapter 25

1 As the days passed in Egypt, the memory of Jacob and his virtues were cherished among his descendants and the Egyptian people who had come to respect and honor the Hebrew patriarch. 2 Among his children and their families, stories of Jacob's faith, his struggles, and his triumphs over adversity were recounted with reverence and served as lessons of resilience and faith in God. 3 The tribes of Israel grew in number and strength, but they also grew in their understanding of the covenant promises made to Abraham, Isaac, and Jacob, which bound them not only to each other but to a divine heritage.

Chapter 26

1 In the fullness of time, as the generations that knew Joseph and his brothers passed away, the political landscape in Egypt shifted. A new pharaoh came to power who did not know of Joseph or what he had done for the country. 2 This pharaoh saw the Israelites not as allies but as a threat due to their growing numbers and distinct culture. He said to his people, "Look, the Israelite people are more and mightier than we. 3 Come, let us deal shrewdly with them, lest they multiply, and, if war breaks out, they join our enemies and fight against us and escape from the land." 4 Therefore, he set taskmasters over them to afflict them with heavy burdens. They built for Pharaoh store cities, Pithom, and Raamses.

Chapter 27

1 But the more they were oppressed, the more they multiplied and the more they spread abroad. And the Egyptians were in dread of the Israelites. 2 So the Egyptians ruthlessly made the children of Israel work as slaves and made their lives bitter with hard service, in mortar and brick, and in all kinds of work in the field. 3 In all their work, they ruthlessly made them work as slaves. 4 The spirit of Jacob, however, remained with his descendants, a silent witness to their suffering and a beacon of hope for the promise of deliverance.

Chapter 28

1 During these harsh times, the stories of Jacob's ladder, his wrestling with the angel, and his reconciliation with Esau were often told as reminders that their current bondage was not their final fate. 2 These stories instilled a deep sense of hope and a fervent prayer for a deliverer who, like Joseph or Moses, might once again lead them to freedom. 3 And as they groaned under their slavery and cried out for help, their cry for rescue from slavery came up to God. 4 God heard their groaning, and God remembered his covenant with Abraham, with Isaac, and with Jacob.

Chapter 29

1 God saw the people of Israel—and God knew. The stage was set for the next chapter in the story of redemption, one that would echo the trials and triumphs of Jacob and his family. 2 The promise made to Jacob that his descendants would be as numerous as the stars and that they would inherit the land flowed into the collective consciousness of his people, preparing them for the great deliverance that was to come. 3 It was in these reflections and collective memories that the spirit of Jacob was felt strongest, guiding his descendants not just in physical lineage but in spiritual heritage, a testament to the enduring power of faith and the unbreakable covenant between God and his people.

Chapter 30

1 As the affliction of the Israelites intensified, their cries and prayers for deliverance became more fervent. In these moments, the elders of the tribes would gather secretly, recounting the promises made to their forefathers, Abraham, Isaac, and Jacob, reinforcing their faith and hope. 2 They spoke of the prophecies, the dreams interpreted by Joseph, and the blessings pronounced by Jacob, each narrative layer adding strength to their resolve and patience in their suffering. 3 Among them were wise women and men who had kept the traditions and laws passed down through generations, ensuring that the identity and spiritual legacy of Jacob's lineage were not lost amidst the hardship.

Chapter 31

1 In due course, a Hebrew child was born, destined to be the answer to their prayers. His birth was a spark of light in the grim reality of their servitude. 2 His mother, guided by a vision she believed was a message from the God of her fathers, hid him from the eyes of those who might harm him, for the

pharaoh had decreed the death of all newborn Hebrew boys. 3 This child, raised in secret and later drawn from the waters of the Nile by a princess of Egypt, was named Moses, meaning "drawn out," for he would draw out his people from the suffering of slavery.

Chapter 32

1 Moses, though raised in the opulence of Pharaoh's palace, could not ignore the suffering of his people. His spirit was stirred by the same divine call that had led Jacob to wrestle with God and survive. 2 One day, moved by the brutal treatment of a Hebrew, Moses intervened and killed an Egyptian taskmaster. This act, borne out of a passion for justice, forced him to flee into the wilderness, away from the comforts of Egypt and into a destiny ordained by divine providence. 3 In the desert of Midian, Moses encountered God in a burning bush, not consumed by flames. Here, God reaffirmed the covenant made with Abraham, Isaac, and Jacob, tasking Moses with leading the Israelites out of Egypt.

Chapter 33

1 Armed with nothing but faith and a staff, Moses returned to Egypt, carrying the weight of his forefathers' promises. He was accompanied by signs and wonders, empowered to confront Pharaoh and demand freedom for his people. 2 With Aaron by his side, Moses demonstrated the power of God through plagues that devastated Egypt, each a testament to the might of the God of Jacob, who had not forgotten His people. 3 Through these trials, the Israelites' resolve was forged; their identity as Jacob's descendants was solidified, binding them together as a people chosen by God.

Chapter 34

1 The final plague, the death of the firstborn of Egypt, was a somber echo of the grief that Jacob himself had felt for his beloved son Joseph, whom he believed dead. Yet, it was this plague that finally broke Pharaoh's resistance. 2 The Israelites, marked by the blood of the lamb on their doorposts, were spared, mirroring the protective blessings Jacob once invoked over his own sons. 3 Led by a pillar of cloud by day and a pillar of fire by night, the Israelites left Egypt, laden with the wealth of nations and the promise of a land foretold to their ancestors.

Chapter 35

1 As they approached the Red Sea, with Pharaoh's armies in pursuit, the legacy of Jacob's struggles seemed to manifest physically. The sea before them and the enemy behind, the Israelites faced despair. 2 Yet, just as Jacob had crossed over the Jabbok River into a new phase of his life, the Israelites crossed the Red Sea into a new epoch of their existence. The waters parted, and they walked on dry ground, baptized into a new covenant with God. 3 On the other side, they sang a song of deliverance, a song that echoed the promises made to Jacob, a song of a people saved through faith and the fulfillment of ancient vows.

103. The Testament of Job

Chapter 1

1 In the land of Uz, there lived a man whose name was Job. This man was blameless and upright; he feared God and shunned evil. 2 He had seven sons and three daughters, and he owned seven thousand sheep, three thousand camels, five hundred yoke of oxen and five hundred donkeys, and had a large number of servants. He was the greatest man among all the people of the East.

Chapter 2

1 Every year, his sons would hold a feast in the house of each one on his birthday. They would invite their three sisters to eat and drink with them. 2 When a period of feasting had run its course, Job would make arrangements for them to be purified. Early in the morning he would sacrifice a burnt offering for each of them, thinking, "Perhaps my children have sinned and cursed God in their hearts." This was Job's regular custom.

Chapter 3

1 One day the angels came to present themselves before the Lord, and Satan also came with them. 2 The Lord said to Satan, "Where have you come from?" Satan answered the Lord, "From roaming throughout the earth, going back and forth on it." 3 Then the Lord said to Satan, "Have you considered my servant Job? There is no one on earth like him; he is blameless and upright, a man who fears God and shuns evil."

Chapter 4

1 "Does Job fear God for nothing?" Satan replied. 2 "Have you not put a hedge around him and his household and everything he has? You have blessed the work of his hands, so that his flocks and herds are spread throughout the land. 3 But now stretch out your hand and strike everything he has, and he will surely curse you to your face." 4 The Lord said to Satan, "Very well, then, everything he has is in your power, but on the man himself do not lay a finger." Then Satan went out from the presence of the Lord.

Chapter 5

1 One day when Job's sons and daughters were feasting and drinking wine at the oldest brother's house, 2 a messenger came to Job and said, "The oxen were plowing and the donkeys were grazing nearby, 3 and the Sabeans attacked and made off with them. They put the servants to the sword, and I am the only one who has escaped to tell you!" 4 While he was still speaking, another messenger came and said, "The fire of God fell from the heavens and burned up the sheep and the servants, and I am the only one who has escaped to tell you!"

Chapter 6

1 While he was still speaking, another messenger came and said, "The Chaldeans formed three raiding parties and swept down on your camels and made off with them. They put the servants to the sword, and I am the only one who has escaped to tell you!" 2 While he was still speaking, yet another messenger came and said, "Your sons and daughters were feasting and drinking wine at the oldest brother's house, 3 when suddenly a mighty wind swept in from the desert and struck the four corners of the house. It collapsed on them and they are dead, and I am the only one who has escaped to tell you!"

Chapter 7

1 At this, Job got up and tore his robe and shaved his head. Then he fell to the ground in worship 2 and said: "Naked I came from my mother's womb, and naked I will depart. The Lord gave and the Lord has taken away; may the name of the Lord be praised." 3 In all this, Job did not sin by charging God with wrongdoing.

Chapter 8

1 On another day the angels came to present themselves before the Lord, and Satan also came with them to present himself before him. 2 And the Lord said to Satan, "Have you considered my servant Job? There is no one on earth like him; he is blameless and upright, a man who fears God and shuns evil. He still maintains his integrity, though you incited me against him to ruin him without any reason."

Chapter 9

1 "Skin for skin!" Satan replied. "A man will give all he has for his own life. 2 But now stretch out your hand and strike his flesh and bones, and he will surely curse you to your face." 3 The Lord said to Satan, "Very well, then, he is in your hands; but you must spare his life."

Chapter 10

1 So Satan went out from the presence of the Lord

and afflicted Job with painful sores from the soles of his feet to the crown of his head. 2 Then Job took a piece of broken pottery and scraped himself with it as he sat among the ashes.

Chapter 11

1 His wife said to him, "Are you still maintaining your integrity? Curse God and die!" 2 But he replied, "You speak as one of the foolish women would speak. Shall we accept good from God, and not trouble?" In all this, Job did not sin with his lips.

Chapter 12

1 When Job's three friends, Eliphaz the Temanite, Bildad the Shuhite, and Zophar the Naamathite, heard about all the troubles that had come upon him, they set out from their homes and met together by agreement to go and sympathize with him and comfort him. 2 When they saw him from a distance, they could hardly recognize him; they began to weep aloud, and they tore their robes and sprinkled dust on their heads. 3 Then they sat on the ground with him for seven days and seven nights. No one said a word to him because they saw how great his suffering was.

Chapter 13

1 After this, Job opened his mouth and cursed the day of his birth. 2 He said: "May the day of my birth perish, and the night that said, 'A boy is conceived!' 3 That day—may it turn to darkness; may God above not care about it; may no light shine on it. 4 May gloom and utter darkness claim it once more; may a cloud settle over it; may blackness overwhelm its light.

Chapter 14

1 "Why did I not perish at birth, and die as I came from the womb? 2 Why were there knees to receive me and breasts that I might be nursed? 3 For now I would be lying down in peace; I would be asleep and at rest 4 with kings and counselors of the earth, who built for themselves places now lying in ruins,

Chapter 15

1 Eliphaz the Temanite replied to Job: "Should a wise man answer with windy knowledge and fill his belly with the east wind? 2 Should he argue with useless talk, or with words that serve no good purpose? 3 But you even undermine piety and hinder devotion to God. 4 Your own mouth condemns you, not mine; your own lips testify against you."

Chapter 16

1 Job answered: "I have heard many such things; miserable comforters are you all! 2 Is there no end to your windy words? What ails you that you keep on arguing? 3 I also could speak like you if you were in my place; I could make fine speeches against you and shake my head at you. 4 But my mouth would encourage you; comfort from my lips would bring you relief.

Chapter 17

1 Yet now, prepare yourself like a man; I will question you, and you shall answer Me. 2 Would you discredit my justice and condemn me just to prove you are right? 3 Are you as strong as God? Can you thunder with a voice like His? 4 Adorn yourself with glory and splendor, and clothe yourself in honor and majesty.

Chapter 18

1 Pour out the overflowings of your anger, and look on everyone who is proud and humble him. 2 Look on everyone who is proud and bring him low; tread down the wicked where they stand. 3 Hide them all in the dust together; bind their faces in the hidden place. 4 Then I will also confess to you that your own right hand can save you.

Chapter 19

1 Job replied: "I know that my Redeemer lives, and that in the end he will stand on the earth. 2 And after my skin has been destroyed, yet in my flesh I will see God; 3 I myself will see him with my own eyes—I, and not another. How my heart yearns within me! 4 If you

say, 'How we will hound him, since the root of the trouble lies in him,'

Chapter 20

1 Be afraid of the sword; for wrath brings the punishment of the sword, so that you may know there is judgment."

Chapter 21

1 Then Zophar the Naamathite replied: "Therefore my thoughts answer me, because of my haste within me. 2 I hear a rebuke that dishonors me, and my understanding inspires me to reply. 3 Surely you know how it has been from of old, since man was placed on earth, 4 that the mirth of the wicked is brief, the joy of the godless lasts but a moment.

Chapter 22

1 Though his pride reaches to the heavens and his head touches the clouds, 2 he will perish forever, like his own dung; those who have seen him will say, 'Where is he?' 3 Like a dream he flies away, no more to be found, banished like a vision of the night. 4 The eye that saw him will not see him again; his place will look on him no more.

Chapter 23

1 His children will seek the favor of the poor, and his hands must give back his wealth. 2 His bones are full of the sin of his youth, which will lie down with him in the dust. 3 Though evil is sweet in his mouth and he hides it under his tongue, 4 though he cannot bear to let it go and keeps it in his mouth,

Chapter 24

1 yet his food will turn sour in his stomach; it will become the venom of serpents within him. 2 He will spit out the riches he swallowed; God will make his stomach vomit them up. 3 He will suck the poison of serpents; the fangs of an adder will kill him. 4 He will not enjoy the streams, the rivers flowing with honey and cream.

Chapter 25

1 Bildad the Shuhite then answered: "Dominion and awe belong to God; He establishes order in the heights of heaven. 2 Can his forces be numbered? On whom does his light not rise? 3 How then can man be righteous before God? How can one born of woman be pure? 4 If even the moon is not bright and the stars are not pure in his eyes,

Chapter 26

1 how much less man, who is a maggot, and the son of man, who is a worm!" 2 But Job replied to his friends: "How you have helped the powerless! How you have saved the arm that is feeble! 3 What advice you have offered to one without wisdom! And what great insight you have displayed! 4 To whom have you uttered words? And whose spirit spoke from your mouth?

Chapter 27

1 The dead tremble, those under the waters and all that live in them. 2 Sheol is naked before God, and Abaddon has no covering. 3 He stretches out the north over empty space; he hangs the earth on nothing. 4 He wraps up the waters in his clouds, yet the clouds do not burst under their weight.

Chapter 28

1 He covers the face of the full moon, spreading his clouds over it. 2 He marks out the horizon on the face of the waters for a boundary between light and darkness. 3 The pillars of heaven tremble and are astounded at his rebuke. 4 By his power he churned up the sea; by his wisdom he cut Rahab to pieces.

Chapter 29

1 By his breath the skies became fair; his hand pierced the gliding serpent. 2 And these are but the outer fringe of his works; how faint the whisper we hear of him! Who then can understand the thunder of his power?" 3 Job continued his discourse, bringing his argument to a close: "But as for me, I would seek God, and to God I would commit my

cause.

Chapter 30

1 Who does great things beyond understanding, and marvelous things without number. 2 He gives rain on the earth and sends water on the fields; 3 He sets on high those who are lowly, and those who mourn are lifted to safety. 4 He frustrates the devices of the crafty, so their hands achieve no success.

Chapter 31

1 He catches the wise in their craftiness, and the schemes of the wily are swept away. 2 Darkness comes upon them in the daytime; at noon they grope as in the night. 3 He saves the needy from the sword in their mouth; he saves them from the clutches of the powerful. 4 So the poor have hope, and injustice shuts its mouth."

104. The Martyrdom of Isaiah

Chapter 1

1 In the days of King Hezekiah of Judah, there was a prophet named Isaiah, son of Amoz. Isaiah was well respected and revered in Jerusalem, for he had prophesied the salvation of the city from the Assyrian king Sennacherib. 2 Isaiah was also a counselor to the king and had told of the coming of the Messiah, the Prince of Peace, whom he saw in visions given by the Spirit of the Lord.

Chapter 2

1 But Manasseh, the son of Hezekiah, did not walk in the ways of his father. When he became king, he led Judah into idolatry, worshiping Baal and Asherah, and he even placed carved images in the Temple of the Lord. 2 Isaiah spoke against these abominations, warning Manasseh and the people of Judah of the dire consequences of their sins, foretelling the destruction that would come if they did not repent.

Chapter 3

1 Angered by Isaiah's prophecies and his denunciations of the royal policies, Manasseh sought to silence him. The king's advisors, who were also priests of the idolatrous cults, conspired to accuse Isaiah of treason and blasphemy against the gods of Judah. 2 They testified falsely against him, saying he had spoken not only against the king and Jerusalem but also against the gods who, they claimed, had delivered Judah from their enemies.

Chapter 4

1 Isaiah, knowing that his time was near, gathered his disciples and told them of what was to come. He spoke of the visions he had seen, of the new heavens and the new earth, and of the suffering servant who would bear the sins of many. 2 He instructed them to remain faithful to the Lord, to uphold justice, and to keep the covenant, no matter the trials they would face.

Chapter 5

1 The king ordered Isaiah to be arrested and brought before the court. Despite the prophet's steadfast faith and his declarations of divine visions, Manasseh, influenced by his advisors, condemned Isaiah to death. 2 The method of his execution was to be a unique and grievous one: Isaiah was to be sawn in two.

Chapter 6

1 The sentence was carried out with a wooden saw. As the executioners began their grim task, Isaiah prayed, forgiving those who were killing him, and he prophesied once more about the salvation that would come through the Messiah. 2 His last words were ones of faith and hope, as he called upon the Lord to receive his spirit and to forgive his persecutors.

Chapter 7

1 After his death, Isaiah's disciples buried him, and his tomb was visited by many who mourned him as a martyr. His prophecies and teachings were preserved by his followers, who continued to spread his message of repentance and hope. 2 Over time, the memory of Isaiah's martyrdom inspired many in generations to come, reinforcing the faith of those who faced persecution and encouraging all who sought righteousness.

Chapter 8

1 The martyrdom of Isaiah became a powerful testament to the strength of faith in the face of injustice. His life and death were often recounted by early Christians as an example of prophetic virtue and ultimate sacrifice. 2 As the prophet who saw the Lord's glory and spoke of the coming of Jesus, Isaiah's legacy endured, his prophecies forming a cornerstone of Christian and Jewish teachings about suffering and redemption.

Chapter 9

1 In the heavens, Isaiah was received with honor, standing among the prophets who had foreseen the coming of the Lord. His voice, which had once proclaimed God's judgment and mercy, now joined the celestial chorus, praising God's eternal justice and love. 2 His martyrdom served as a beacon of hope and a call to faithfulness for all who walked in the shadow of persecution, reminding them that their witness to the truth was never in vain.

Chapter 10

1 As the years passed, the account of Isaiah's martyrdom was recounted among the communities of the faithful, serving as a profound example of steadfastness and divine vision. 2 The impact of his death resonated particularly within those facing persecution, strengthening their resolve to adhere to their beliefs despite external pressures and threats.

Chapter 11

1 Among these communities, tales of Isaiah's prophecies and his fearless confrontation with royal authority inspired many to scrutinize their own leaders and to advocate for spiritual and moral integrity. 2 His visions, especially those of the peaceful kingdom and the suffering servant, became foundational texts, interpreted and reinterpreted in light of current events and theological debates.

Chapter 12

1 In distant lands and through subsequent ages, scholars and theologians studied the texts attributed to Isaiah, drawing connections between his prophecies and the events surrounding the life, death, and resurrection of Jesus Christ. 2 This deepened the appreciation of Isaiah's role as a prophet who transcended his own time, speaking to universal themes of justice, redemption, and the human condition.

Chapter 13

1 Art and literature, too, found inspiration in the story of Isaiah's martyrdom. Painters and poets depicted the poignant scenes of his trial and death, emphasizing themes of divine fidelity and the triumph of the spirit over bodily destruction. 2 His calm demeanor and prophetic assurance in the face of death became iconic, symbolizing the power of faith to overcome the greatest of worldly terrors.

Chapter 14

1 As the narrative of Isaiah's life and death was passed down through generations, it gathered layers of communal memory and significance, each adding depth to his character and resonance to his message. 2 In churches and synagogues, his story was told as part of the broader tapestry of God's dealings with His people, illustrating the continuity of divine inspiration and the perennial relevance of prophetic witness.

Chapter 15

1 The legacy of Isaiah, strengthened by the account of his martyrdom, continued to inspire movements for social justice and spiritual renewal. His call to righteousness and condemnation of hypocrisy rang

out in contexts far removed from his own, yet strikingly parallel. 2 Activists and reformers, preachers and teachers—all found in Isaiah a model of courage and clarity, a voice that spoke truth to power and that articulated a vision of peace and righteousness.

Chapter 16

1 Ultimately, the martyrdom of Isaiah was not just about the end of a prophet's earthly life; it was about the enduring influence of his message and the eternal nature of the truths he espoused. 2 In communities facing oppression or struggling with moral dilemmas, Isaiah's example offered both comfort and challenge, a reminder that the call to live out divine commandments was accompanied by the promise of God's presence, even in the midst of suffering.

Chapter 17

1 Today, the figure of Isaiah stands tall in the pantheon of biblical prophets, not only for his extensive prophetic writings but also for the dramatic and poignant story of his martyrdom. 2 His willingness to suffer and die for his beliefs continues to speak to all who strive to live out their faith in challenging circumstances, encouraging a commitment to justice and truth that transcends time and place.

Chapter 18

1 In times of great religious and moral uncertainty, Isaiah's story is often revisited for its profound insights into human and divine nature. His prophecies and his ultimate sacrifice provide a rich source for reflection on the nature of prophecy, martyrdom, and testimony in the face of opposition. 2 Religious leaders and scholars draw upon his life to discuss the role of prophets in society, emphasizing the necessity of speaking uncomfortable truths to power and the spiritual courage required to maintain one's convictions under persecution.

Chapter 19

1 In theological education, the narrative of Isaiah's martyrdom is used to illustrate the complex interplay between divine foreknowledge, human freedom, and moral responsibility. Seminary students and scholars analyze his prophecies within the broader canonical context, exploring themes of atonement, justice, and redemption. 2 Discussions often focus on the integrity and cost of prophetic witness, considering the implications of Isaiah's experiences for modern-day individuals called to prophetic roles in their communities and churches.

Chapter 20

1 The martyrdom of Isaiah also resonates in contemporary social justice movements. Activists see in his commitment a model for their own work against systemic injustices and oppression. His unyielding stance in the face of a corrupt monarchy offers timeless lessons on the risks and responsibilities of confronting entrenched power. 2 His enduring faith, even unto death, encourages a holistic approach to activism, one that integrates spiritual strength with social action, emphasizing that true change often requires profound personal sacrifice.

Chapter 21

1 In liturgical settings, particularly within traditions that honor the memory of the prophets, Isaiah's martyrdom is commemorated with prayers and readings that recall his faithfulness and fortitude. These observances serve as a communal affirmation of the prophetic vocation, inspiring congregants to reflect on their own commitments to faith and justice. 2 His feast day provides an opportunity for communities to recommit themselves to the principles he embodied—truth-telling, justice-seeking, and peacemaking—within their own contexts.

Chapter 22

1 The legacy of Isaiah's martyrdom continues to influence art, literature, and music. Composers write oratorios that capture the drama of his prophetic mission and his profound encounters with the divine. Artists depict his life in media ranging from stained glass to sculpture, portraying his dedication and ultimate sacrifice as emblematic of divine inspiration. 2 Poets and playwrights explore the tensions and resolutions evident in his life, using his story to probe themes of destiny, integrity, and redemption, thus bringing a timeless biblical story into conversation with contemporary issues.

Chapter 23

1 The enduring relevance of Isaiah's martyrdom is found in its ability to speak across centuries to those experiencing suffering and persecution. His assurance of God's ultimate justice provides comfort and motivation to those facing trials and tribulations. 2 His story encourages a deeper engagement with the divine, suggesting that through suffering and adversity, one can achieve a greater understanding of God's purposes and providence.

Chapter 24

1 As Isaiah's prophetic messages continue to be studied and his life commemorated, the profound impact of his faith and his ultimate sacrifice remain evident. Through his martyrdom, Isaiah exemplifies the paradox of victory through defeat, a theme that carries profound implications for spiritual reflection and practice. 2 His narrative invites believers of all generations to consider the cost of discipleship and the power of unwavering faith in the face of seemingly insurmountable challenges.

Chapter 25

1 In academic circles, Isaiah's prophecies and the circumstances of his martyrdom are subjects of ongoing research and debate. Scholars analyze ancient texts to uncover historical, cultural, and theological contexts that shaped his ministry and its reception. 2 His visions, particularly those concerning the suffering servant and the peaceful kingdom, are juxtaposed against his violent end to discuss the paradoxes of prophetic ministry—speaking of peace while suffering from violence.

Chapter 26

1 In spiritual retreats and religious seminars, the story of Isaiah's martyrdom is used as a focal point for meditations on the cost of faithfulness. Participants reflect on the strength required to face persecution and the resilience needed to uphold one's beliefs amid adversity. 2 These sessions often conclude with discussions on how individuals can apply the principles seen in Isaiah's life to their own spiritual journeys, encouraging a deep, personal commitment to living out one's faith in practical, everyday actions.

Chapter 27

1 In popular culture, Isaiah's narrative has inspired various forms of artistic expression that explore themes of vision, sacrifice, and redemption. From graphic novels to theatrical productions, creators reimagine his story in contemporary settings, highlighting the timeless and universal aspects of his experiences. 2 These adaptations bring Isaiah's story to new audiences, making the ancient prophet's experiences accessible and relevant to people unfamiliar with biblical texts, and providing a bridge between sacred history and modern existential inquiries.

Chapter 28

1 Within faith communities, Isaiah's legacy is honored through liturgical music and hymns that recount his prophetic messages and his unyielding commitment to God's command. These musical compositions are performed in religious services, where they serve both as worship and as reminders of the prophetic voice's vital role in spiritual life. 2

These hymns and pieces often incorporate direct quotes from Isaiah's visions, weaving biblical language with contemporary music styles to enrich the worship experience and deepen the congregation's connection to the scriptural narrative.

Chapter 29

1 The ethical implications of Isaiah's martyrdom are discussed in moral theology and ethics courses, where students and scholars explore the implications of prophetic witness in the face of unjust political power. Discussions focus on the balance between divine obedience and civil disobedience, examining Isaiah's actions as a model for ethical behavior in oppressive contexts. 2 These academic discussions often extend into workshops and community forums, where participants debate the best ways to apply these principles in addressing current global and local injustices.

Chapter 30

1 The martyrdom of Isaiah not only echoes through religious and academic venues but also influences personal spiritual practices. Individuals drawn to his story incorporate his steadfastness and prophetic insights into their personal meditations, prayers, and scriptural studies. 2 In this personal engagement, Isaiah's example fosters a deeper commitment to truth and justice, inspiring believers to confront personal and social sins with courage and to seek divine guidance in their endeavors.

Chapter 31

1 As the impact of Isaiah's life and death continues to unfold across various platforms—academic, religious, artistic, and personal—his story remains a compelling testament to the power of faith and the human spirit's capacity for endurance and insight. 2 Each engagement with his story, whether through study, art, worship, or personal reflection, revitalizes his legacy, ensuring that the voice of Isaiah, though centuries old, still speaks vividly and powerfully to the challenges and hopes of the present day.

105. The Vision of Isaiah

Chapter 1

1 In the year that King Uzziah died, I saw the Lord seated on a throne, high and exalted, and the train of His robe filled the temple. 2 Above Him were seraphs, each with six wings: With two wings they covered their faces, with two they covered their feet, and with two they were flying. 3 And they were calling to one another: "Holy, holy, holy is the LORD Almighty; the whole earth is full of His glory." 4 At the sound of their voices the doorposts and thresholds shook and the temple was filled with smoke.

Chapter 2

1 "Woe to me!" I cried. "I am ruined! For I am a man of unclean lips, and I live among a people of unclean lips, and my eyes have seen the King, the LORD Almighty." 2 Then one of the seraphs flew to me with a live coal in his hand, which he had taken with tongs from the altar. 3 With it he touched my mouth and said, "See, this has touched your lips; your guilt is taken away and your sin atoned for."

Chapter 3

1 Then I heard the voice of the Lord saying, "Whom shall I send? And who will go for us?" And I said, "Here am I. Send me!" 2 He said, "Go and tell this people: 'Be ever hearing, but never understanding; be ever seeing, but never perceiving.' 3 Make the heart of this people calloused; make their ears dull and close their eyes. Otherwise they might see with their eyes, hear with their ears, understand with their hearts, and turn and be healed."

Chapter 4

1 Then I said, "For how long, Lord?" And He answered: "Until the cities lie ruined and without inhabitant, until the houses are left deserted and the fields ruined and ravaged, 2 until the LORD has sent everyone far away and the land is utterly forsaken. 3 And though a tenth remains in the land, it will again be laid waste. But as the terebinth and oak leave stumps when they are cut down, so the holy seed will be the stump in the land."

Chapter 5

1 This vision is concerning Judah and Jerusalem that Isaiah son of Amoz saw during the reigns of Uzziah, Jotham, Ahaz, and Hezekiah, kings of Judah. 2 Hear, O heavens! Listen, O earth! For the LORD has spoken: "I reared children and brought them up, but they have rebelled against me. 3 The ox knows its master, the donkey its owner's manger, but Israel does not know, my people do not understand."

Chapter 6

1 Woe to the sinful nation, a people whose guilt is great, a brood of evildoers, children given to corruption! They have forsaken the LORD; they have spurned the Holy One of Israel and turned their backs on Him. 2 Why should you be beaten anymore? Why do you persist in rebellion? Your whole head is injured, your whole heart afflicted. 3 From the sole of your foot to the top of your head there is no soundness—only wounds and welts and open sores, not cleansed or bandaged or soothed with oil.

Chapter 7

1 Your country is desolate, your cities burned with fire; your fields are being stripped by foreigners right before you, laid waste as when overthrown by strangers. 2 Daughter Zion is left like a shelter in a vineyard, like a hut in a cucumber field, like a city under siege. 3 Unless the LORD Almighty had left us some survivors, we would have become like Sodom, we would have been like Gomorrah.

Chapter 8

1 Hear the word of the LORD, you rulers of Sodom; listen to the instruction of our God, you people of Gomorrah! 2 "The multitude of your sacrifices—what are they to me?" says the LORD. "I have more than enough of burnt offerings, of rams and the fat of fattened animals; I have no pleasure in the blood of bulls, lambs or goats.

Chapter 9

1 "When you come to appear before me, who has asked this of you, this trampling of my courts? 2 Stop bringing meaningless offerings! Your incense is detestable to me. New Moons, Sabbaths, and convocations—I cannot bear your worthless assemblies. 3 Your New Moon feasts and your appointed festivals I hate with all my being. They have become a burden to me; I am weary of bearing them.

Chapter 10

1 When you spread out your hands in prayer, I hide my eyes from you; even when you offer many prayers, I am not listening. Your hands are full of blood! 2 Wash and make yourselves clean. Take your evil deeds out of my sight; stop doing wrong. 3 Learn to do right; seek justice. Defend the oppressed. Take up the cause of the fatherless; plead the case of the widow.

Chapter 11

1 "Come now, let us settle the matter," says the LORD. "Though your sins are like scarlet, they shall be as white as snow; though they are red as crimson, they shall be like wool. 2 If you are willing and obedient, you will eat the good things of the land; 3 But if you resist and rebel, you will be devoured by the sword." For the mouth of the LORD has spoken.

Chapter 12

1 A shoot will come up from the stump of Jesse; from his roots a Branch will bear fruit. 2 The Spirit of the LORD will rest on him—the Spirit of wisdom and of understanding, the Spirit of counsel and of might, the Spirit of the knowledge and fear of the LORD— 3

and he will delight in the fear of the LORD. He will not judge by what he sees with his eyes, or decide by what he hears with his ears;

Chapter 13

1 but with righteousness he will judge the needy, with justice he will give decisions for the poor of the earth. He will strike the earth with the rod of his mouth; with the breath of his lips he will slay the wicked. 2 Righteousness will be his belt and faithfulness the sash around his waist. 3 The wolf will live with the lamb, the leopard will lie down with the goat, the calf and the lion and the yearling together; and a little child will lead them.

Chapter 14

1 The cow will feed with the bear, their young will lie down together, and the lion will eat straw like the ox. 2 The infant will play near the cobra's den, and the young child will put its hand into the viper's nest. 3 They will neither harm nor destroy on all my holy mountain, for the earth will be filled with the knowledge of the LORD as the waters cover the sea.

Chapter 15

1 In that day the Root of Jesse will stand as a banner for the peoples; the nations will rally to him, and his resting place will be glorious. 2 In that day the Lord will reach out his hand a second time to reclaim the surviving remnant of his people from Assyria, from Lower Egypt, from Upper Egypt, from Cush, from Elam, from Babylonia, from Hamath and from the islands of the Mediterranean. 3 He will raise a banner for the nations and gather the exiles of Israel; he will assemble the scattered people of Judah from the four quarters of the earth.

Chapter 16

1 The jealousy of Ephraim will vanish, and the adversaries of Judah will be destroyed; Ephraim will not be jealous of Judah, nor Judah hostile toward Ephraim. 2 They will swoop down on the slopes of Philistia to the west; together they will plunder the people to the east. They will subdue Edom and Moab, and the Ammonites will be subject to them. 3 The LORD will dry up the gulf of the Egyptian sea; with a scorching wind he will sweep his hand over the Euphrates River. He will break it up into seven streams so that anyone can cross over in sandals.

Chapter 17

1 There will be a highway for the remnant of his people that is left from Assyria, as there was for Israel when they came up from Egypt. 2 In that day you will say: "I will praise you, LORD. Although you were angry with me, your anger has turned away and you have comforted me. 3 Surely God is my salvation; I will trust and not be afraid. The LORD, the LORD himself, is my strength and my defense; he has become my salvation."

Chapter 18

1 With joy you will draw water from the wells of salvation. In that day you will say: "Give praise to the LORD, proclaim his name; make known among the nations what he has done, and proclaim that his name is exalted. 2 Sing to the LORD, for he has done glorious things; let this be known to all the world. 3 Shout aloud and sing for joy, people of Zion, for great is the Holy One of Israel among you."

Chapter 19

1 An oracle concerning Egypt: See, the LORD rides on a swift cloud and is coming to Egypt. The idols of Egypt tremble before him, and the hearts of the Egyptians melt within them. 2 "I will stir up Egyptian against Egyptian—brother will fight against brother, neighbor against neighbor, city against city, kingdom against kingdom. 3 The Egyptians will lose heart, and I will bring their plans to nothing; they will consult the idols and the spirits of the dead, the mediums and the sorcerers.

Chapter 20

1 I will hand the Egyptians over to the power of a cruel master, and a fierce king will rule over them," declares the Lord, the LORD Almighty. 2 The waters of the river will dry up, and the riverbed will be parched and dry. 3 The canals will stink; the streams of Egypt will dwindle and dry up. The reeds and rushes will wither,

Chapter 21

1 also the plants along the Nile, at the mouth of the river. Every sown field along the Nile will become parched, will blow away and be no more. 2 The fishermen will groan and lament, all who cast hooks into the Nile; those who spread nets on the waters will pine away. 3 Those who work with combed flax will despair, the weavers of fine linen will lose hope.

Chapter 22

1 The workers in cloth will be dejected, and all the wage earners will be sick at heart. 2 The officials of Zoan are nothing but fools; the wise counselors of Pharaoh give senseless advice. How can you say to Pharaoh, "I am one of the wise men, a disciple of the ancient kings"? 3 Where are your wise men now? Let them show you and make known what the LORD Almighty has planned against Egypt.

Chapter 23

1 The princes of Zoan have become fools, the princes of Memphis are deceived; those who are the cornerstone of her tribes have led Egypt astray. 2 The LORD has poured into them a spirit of dizziness; they make Egypt stagger in all that she does, as a drunkard staggers around in his vomit. 3 There is nothing Egypt can do—head or tail, palm branch or reed.

Chapter 24

1 In that day the Egyptians will become weaklings. They will shudder with fear at the uplifted hand that the LORD Almighty raises against them. 2 And the land of Judah will bring terror to the Egyptians; everyone to whom Judah is mentioned will be terrified, because of what the LORD Almighty is planning against them. 3 In that day five cities in Egypt will speak the language of Canaan and swear allegiance to the LORD Almighty. One of them will be called the City of the Sun.

Chapter 25

1 In that day there will be an altar to the LORD in the heart of Egypt, and a monument to the LORD at its border. 2 It will be a sign and witness to the LORD Almighty in the land of Egypt. When they cry out to the LORD because of their oppressors, he will send them a savior and defender, and he will rescue them. 3 So the LORD will make himself known to the Egyptians, and in that day they will acknowledge the LORD. They will worship with sacrifices and grain offerings; they will make vows to the LORD and keep them.

Chapter 26

1 The LORD will strike Egypt with a plague; he will strike them and heal them. They will turn to the LORD, and he will respond to their pleas and heal them. 2 In that day there will be a highway from Egypt to Assyria. The Assyrians will go to Egypt and the Egyptians to Assyria. The Egyptians and Assyrians will worship together. 3 In that day Israel will be the third, along with Egypt and Assyria, a blessing on the earth.

Chapter 27

1 The LORD Almighty will bless them, saying, "Blessed be Egypt my people, Assyria my handiwork, and Israel my inheritance." 2 In that day you will say: "I will praise you, LORD. Although you were angry with me, your anger has turned away and you have comforted me." 3 Surely God is my salvation; I will trust and not be afraid. The LORD, the LORD himself, is my strength and my defense; he has become my salvation."

Chapter 28

1 With joy you will draw water from the wells of

salvation. In that day you will say: "Give praise to the LORD, proclaim his name; make known among the nations what he has done, and proclaim that his name is exalted." 2 Sing to the LORD, for he has done glorious things; let this be known to all the world. 3 Shout aloud and sing for joy, people of Zion, for great is the Holy One of Israel among you."

Chapter 29

1 Woe to you, Ariel, Ariel, the city where David settled! Add year to year and let your cycle of festivals go on. 2 Yet I will besiege Ariel; she will mourn and lament, she will be to me like an altar hearth. 3 I will encamp against you all around; I will encircle you with towers and set up my siege works against you.

Chapter 30

1 Brought low, you will speak from the ground; your speech will mumble out of the dust. Your voice will come ghostlike from the earth; out of the dust your speech will whisper. 2 But your many enemies will become like fine dust, the ruthless hordes like blown chaff. Suddenly, in an instant, 3 the LORD Almighty will come with thunder and earthquake and great noise, with windstorm and tempest and flames of a devouring fire.

Chapter 31

1 Then the hordes of all the nations that fight against Ariel, that attack her and her fortress and besiege her, will be as it is with a dream, with a vision in the night— 2 as when a hungry person dreams of eating, but awakens hungry still; as when a thirsty person dreams of drinking, but awakens faint and thirsty still. So will it be with the hordes of all the nations that fight against Mount Zion.

Chapter 32

1 Be stunned and amazed, blind yourselves and be sightless; be drunk, but not from wine, stagger, but not from beer. 2 The LORD has poured into you a spirit of deep sleep. He has closed your eyes (the prophets); he has covered your heads (the seers). 3 For you this whole vision is nothing but words sealed in a scroll. And if you give the scroll to someone who can read, and say, "Read this, please," they will answer, "I can't; it is sealed."

Chapter 33

1 Or if you give the scroll to someone who cannot read, and say, "Read this, please," they will answer, "I don't know how to read." 2 The Lord says: "These people come near to me with their mouth and honor me with their lips, but their hearts are far from me. Their worship of me is based on merely human rules they have been taught. 3 Therefore once more I will astound these people with wonder upon wonder; the wisdom of the wise will perish, the intelligence of the intelligent will vanish."

Chapter 34

1 Woe to those who go down to Egypt for help, relying on horses, trusting in the multitude of their chariots and in the great strength of their horsemen, but not looking to the Holy One of Israel, or seeking help from the LORD. 2 Yet he too is wise and can bring disaster; he does not take back his words. He will rise up against the house of the wicked, against those who help evildoers. 3 But the Egyptians are mere mortals and not God; their horses are flesh and not spirit. When the LORD stretches out his hand, those who help will stumble, those who are helped will fall; all will perish together.

Chapter 35

1 When the LORD restores Zion, the desert and the parched land will be glad; the wilderness will rejoice and blossom. Like the crocus, 2 it will burst into bloom; it will rejoice greatly and shout for joy. The glory of Lebanon will be given to it, the splendor of Carmel and Sharon; they will see the glory of the LORD, the splendor of our God. 3 Strengthen the feeble hands, steady the knees that give way; 4 say to those with fearful hearts, "Be strong, do not fear;

your God will come, he will come with vengeance; with divine retribution he will come to save you."

Chapter 36

1 Then will the eyes of the blind be opened and the ears of the deaf unstopped. 2 Then will the lame leap like a deer, and the mute tongue shout for joy. Water will gush forth in the wilderness and streams in the desert. 3 The burning sand will become a pool, the thirsty ground bubbling springs. In the haunts where jackals once lay, grass and reeds and papyrus will grow.

Chapter 37

1 And a highway will be there; it will be called the Way of Holiness; it will be for those who walk on that Way. The unclean will not journey on it; wicked fools will not go about on it. 2 No lion will be there, nor any ravenous beast; they will not be found there. But only the redeemed will walk there, 3 and those the LORD has rescued will return. They will enter Zion with singing; everlasting joy will crown their heads. Gladness and joy will overtake them, and sorrow and sighing will flee away.

Chapter 38

1 "Build up, build up, prepare the road! Remove the obstacles out of the way of my people." 2 For this is what the high and exalted One says—he who lives forever, whose name is holy: "I live in a high and holy place, but also with the one who is contrite and lowly in spirit, to revive the spirit of the lowly and to revive the heart of the contrite. 3 I will not accuse them forever, nor will I always be angry, for then they would faint away because of me—the very people I have created.

Chapter 39

1 I was enraged by their sinful greed; I punished them, and hid my face in anger, yet they kept on in their willful ways. 2 I have seen their ways, but I will heal them; I will guide them and restore comfort to Israel's mourners, 3 creating praise on their lips. Peace, peace, to those far and near," says the LORD. "And I will heal them."

Chapter 40

1 But the wicked are like the tossing sea, which cannot rest, whose waves cast up mire and mud. 2 "There is no peace," says my God, "for the wicked." 3 Lift up your eyes and look to the heavens: Who created all these? He who brings out the starry host one by one and calls forth each of them by name. Because of his great power and mighty strength, not one of them is missing.

106. The Sibylline Oracles

Chapter 1

1 The voice of one crying: "Hear, you nations, and be afraid, for God is coming upon you for judgment, and He will oversee and judge His people. 2 See, He comes; neither do all the idols of the nations withstand Him, nor the high mountains, nor the depths of the seas. 3 He looks upon the abysses of the ocean and the hearts of men, causing the earth and sea to tremble.

Chapter 2

1 Hear, O people, God's wrath upon the Earth, fire, and sword, and blood, and darkness, so thick a cloud of Egypt shall cover the fallen. 2 The idols of Egypt will tremble, the people of Sodom and Gomorrah cry out, for their sins have amassed like the mountains. 3 Thus says the Lord: 'My spirit shall not abide in man forever, for they are flesh; their days shall be one hundred and twenty years.'

Chapter 3

1 In the last times, behold, a faithful king shall reign, whom God will send. He will bring peace and joy to the earth, and He will tear down the prisons of the unjust. 2 But before the end, the trumpet shall sound a great thunder from heaven, and the great kingdom shall fall. 3 And there will arise a king from the East,

a king of kings, wielding great power, who will command peace to be unto the world.

Chapter 4
1 The king will gather all the kings of the earth to battle. The holy land shall see harsh days as never before, a great war among men, nations rising against nation. 2 Pestilence, famine, and death in its wake; these will be the signs of His coming. 3 And then, the dead shall rise from the earth, clothed in immortal flesh, to meet their Lord in the air. This is the resurrection of the just.

Chapter 5
1 The nations will behold and be confounded at their power. They will lay their hands on their mouths; their ears will be deaf. 2 They will lick the dust like a serpent; they will come trembling out of their fortresses to the Lord our God; they will fear and tremble because of you, O Israel! 3 A great star from heaven shall fall upon the rivers and springs of water, and they shall all become bitter. This is the star called Wormwood.

Chapter 6
1 Then many false prophets will rise up and deceive many; and because of the increase of wickedness, the love of many will grow cold. 2 But the one who stands firm to the end will be saved. And this gospel of the kingdom will be preached in the whole world as a testimony to all nations, and then the end will come. 3 When you see the 'abomination of desolation,' spoken of by the prophet Daniel, standing in the holy place, then let those who are in Judea flee to the mountains.

Chapter 7
1 Let no one on the housetop go down to take anything out of the house. Let no one in the field go back to get their cloak. 2 How dreadful it will be in those days for pregnant women and nursing mothers! 3 Pray that your flight will not take place in winter or on the Sabbath, for then there will be great distress, unequaled from the beginning of the world until now—and never to be equaled again.

Chapter 8
1 If those days had not been cut short, no one would survive, but for the sake of the elect those days will be shortened. 2 At that time if anyone says to you, 'Look, here is the Messiah!' or, 'There he is!' do not believe it. 3 For false messiahs and false prophets will appear and perform great signs and wonders to deceive, if possible, even the elect.

Chapter 9
1 See, I have told you ahead of time. So if they say to you, 'Look, he is in the desert,' do not go out; or, 'Here he is, in the inner rooms,' do not believe it. 2 For as lightning that comes from the east is visible even in the west, so will be the coming of the Son of Man. 3 Wherever there is a carcass, there the vultures will gather.

Chapter 10
1 Immediately after the distress of those days, the sun will be darkened, and the moon will not give its light; the stars will fall from the sky, and the heavenly bodies will be shaken. 2 Then will appear the sign of the Son of Man in heaven. And then all the peoples of the earth will mourn when they see the Son of Man coming on the clouds of heaven, with power and great glory. 3 He will send his angels with a loud trumpet call, and they will gather his elect from the four winds, from one end of the heavens to the other.

Chapter 11
1 The elect will come from every direction to worship before the Lord, and the earth will be illuminated with the glory of His presence. 2 The seas will recede, the mountains will be flattened, and all impediments will be removed for the gathering of His people. 3 Then the world will see the true King, who will judge the living and the dead, and His kingdom will have no end.

Chapter 12
1 The unjust will wail and gnash their teeth as they are sent away into everlasting fire prepared for the devil and his angels. 2 The righteous, however, will enter into life eternal, where there will be no more death, nor sorrow, nor crying, nor pain, for the former things have passed away. 3 They will drink from the river of life, flowing freely from the throne of God and of the Lamb.

Chapter 13
1 In those days, the law will go out from Zion and the word of the Lord from Jerusalem. 2 Nations will not take up sword against nation, nor will they train for war anymore. 3 The wolf will dwell with the lamb, and the leopard will lie down with the goat; the calf and the lion will feed together, and a little child will lead them.

Chapter 14
1 Every man will sit under his own vine and under his own fig tree, and no one will make them afraid. 2 The earth will be full of the knowledge of the Lord as the waters cover the sea. 3 This is the heritage of the servants of the Lord, and their righteousness is from Me," says the Lord.

Chapter 15
1 Behold, I will create new heavens and a new earth; the former things will not be remembered, nor will they come to mind. 2 But be glad and rejoice forever in what I will create, for I will create Jerusalem to be a delight and its people a joy. 3 I will rejoice over Jerusalem and take delight in my people; the sound of weeping and of crying will be heard in it no more.

Chapter 16
1 The wolf and the lamb will feed together, and the lion will eat straw like the ox, but dust will be the serpent's food. They will neither harm nor destroy on all my holy mountain," says the Lord. 2 "Behold, the days are coming," declares the Lord, "when I will make a new covenant with the house of Israel and with the house of Judah. 3 It will not be like the covenant I made with their ancestors when I took them by the hand to lead them out of Egypt, because they broke my covenant, though I was a husband to them," says the Lord.

Chapter 17
1 "This is the covenant I will make with the house of Israel after that time," declares the Lord. "I will put my law in their minds and write it on their hearts. I will be their God, and they will be my people. 2 No longer will they teach their neighbor, or say to one another, 'Know the Lord,' because they will all know me, from the least of them to the greatest," declares the Lord. "For I will forgive their wickedness and will remember their sins no more."

Chapter 18
1 At that time, Michael, the great prince who protects your people, will arise. There will be a time of distress such as has not happened from the beginning of nations until then. But at that time your people—everyone whose name is found written in the book—will be delivered. 2 Multitudes who sleep in the dust of the earth will awake: some to everlasting life, others to shame and everlasting contempt. 3 Those who are wise will shine like the brightness of the heavens, and those who lead many to righteousness, like the stars for ever and ever.

2. CHRISTIAN APOCRYPHA

107. The Epistle to the Laodiceans

Chapter 1
1 Paul, an apostle not from men nor through man, but through Jesus Christ, to the brethren who are in Laodicea: Grace to you and peace from God our Father and the Lord Jesus Christ.

Chapter 2
1 I thank Christ in every prayer of mine that you may continue and persevere in good works, looking forward to what is promised in the day of judgment. 2 Do not be troubled by the vain words of people who pervert the truth, that they may draw you away from the truth of the gospel which is proclaimed by me.

Chapter 3
1 And now do God's work sincerely, as God lives in you, and do not corrupt the spirit of love with the business of life. 2 Consider what the Lord says in his gospels, "Blessed are the poor, and those who are persecuted for righteousness' sake, for theirs is the kingdom of heaven."

Chapter 4
1 Persevere and maintain among yourselves a holy and righteous conduct, which you had in the beginning, so that you may receive Christ. 2 And be patient and endure the sufferings as you have seen before in me, that you may be saved in the day of the Lord Jesus Christ.

Chapter 5
1 Send my greetings to my brethren who are in Laodicea, and to Nymphas, and to the church that is in his house. 2 And when this epistle has been read among you, cause that it be read also in the church of the Laodiceans; and that you likewise read the epistle from Laodicea. 3 And say to Archippus, "Take heed to the ministry which you have received in the Lord, that you may fulfill it."

Chapter 6
1 The grace of our Lord Jesus Christ be with your spirit. Amen. In apocryphal texts like this one, which are not universally accepted as canonical, the structure can sometimes be more fluid and less detailed compared to the canonical texts. These writings often aimed to edify and encourage early Christian communities using familiar themes and figures, like the apostle Paul, and could be less complex in their theological content and narrative development.

Chapter 7
1 I, Paul, write this greeting with my own hand. Remember my chains. Grace be with you. 2 Continue to stand firm in the teachings we have passed on to you, whether by word of mouth or by letter. 3 Our desire is that each of you shows the same diligence to the very end, in order to make your hope sure.

Chapter 8
1 Do not be swayed by diverse and strange teachings, for it is good for the heart to be strengthened by grace, not by ceremonial foods, which are of no benefit to those who observe them. 2 We have an altar from which those who minister at the tabernacle have no right to eat. 3 Let us, therefore, go to him outside the camp, bearing the disgrace he bore.

Chapter 9
1 For here we do not have an enduring city, but we are looking for the city that is to come. 2 Through Jesus, therefore, let us continually offer to God a sacrifice of praise—the fruit of lips that openly profess his name. 3 And do not forget to do good and to share with others, for with such sacrifices God is pleased.

Chapter 10
1 Obey your leaders and submit to their authority. They keep watch over you as men who must give an account. Obey them so that their work will be a joy, not a burden, for that would be of no advantage to you. 2 Pray for us. We are sure that we have a clear conscience and desire to live honorably in every way.

3 I particularly urge you to pray so that I may be restored to you soon.

Chapter 11
1 Now may the God of peace, who through the blood of the eternal covenant brought back from the dead our Lord Jesus, that great Shepherd of the sheep, 2 equip you with everything good for doing his will, and may he work in us what is pleasing to him, through Jesus Christ, to whom be glory for ever and ever. Amen.

108. The Epistle of Polycarp to the Philippians

Chapter 1
1 Polycarp and the presbyters with him, to the Church of God sojourning at Philippi: Mercy to you, and peace from God Almighty and Jesus Christ our Savior, be multiplied. 2 I rejoiced greatly with you in our Lord Jesus Christ, because you have followed the example of true love and have accompanied, as you ought, those who were in bonds, becoming an ornament to the saints, and have vindicated the gospel in all respects.

Chapter 2
1 I am greatly grieved for Valens, who was once a presbyter among you, that he so little understands the place that was given him [in the Church]. 2 I exhort you, therefore, that you abstain from covetousness, and that you be chaste and truthful. "Abstain from every form of evil." 3 For if a man cannot govern himself in such matters, how shall he enjoin them on others? If a man does not keep himself from covetousness, he shall be defiled by idolatry and be judged as one of the heathen.

Chapter 3
1 But I have neither seen nor heard of any such thing among you, among whom the blessed Paul labored, who are commended in the beginning of his epistle. 2 For he boasts about you in all those churches which alone then knew the Lord; but we [of Smyrna] had not yet known Him. 3 I am deeply grieved, therefore, brethren, for him (Valens) and his wife; may the Lord grant them true repentance. Therefore, be yourselves also moderate in this regard; and do not consider such people as enemies, but call them back as suffering and erring members, that you may save your whole body.

Chapter 4
1 For by doing this you build up yourselves. For I trust that you are well versed in the Sacred Scriptures, and that nothing is hidden from you; but at present it is not granted to me to practice that which is written, "Be angry, and sin not," and again, "Let not the sun go down upon your wrath." 2 Blessed is he who remembers this, which I believe to be the case with you. 3 But may the God and Father of our Lord Jesus Christ, and Jesus Christ Himself, who is the Son of God, and our everlasting High Priest, build you up in faith and truth, and in all gentleness and without anger, and in patience and long-suffering, and endurance and purity.

Chapter 5
1 And may He grant unto you a lot and portion among His saints, and to us with you, and to all that are under heaven, who shall believe in our Lord Jesus Christ and in His Father, who "raised him from the dead." 2 Pray for all the saints. Pray also for kings, and authorities, and powers, and for those that persecute and hate you, and for the enemies of the cross, that your fruit may be manifest in all, and that you may be perfect in Him.

Chapter 6
1 You wrote to me, both you and Ignatius, that if anyone went [from this] to Syria he might carry letters with him; and this I will do if I find a fitting opportunity. 2 Both Ignatius himself, when he was among us, urged that those who are able should send messengers, and they should go there for the glory of God, as being bearers of peace.

Chapter 7

1 I also exhort you to attend to this matter, for it is fitting that every Church should send emissaries, who, as ministers of the will of God, shall cooperate to reinforce the ties of the fellowship. 2 Endeavor, therefore, to send messengers, or to go yourselves, to give glory to the name of God by promoting unity among the churches. 3 Stand fast, therefore, in these things, and follow the example of the Lord, being firm and unchangeable in the faith, loving the brotherhood, and being attached to one another, joined together in the truth, exhibiting the meekness of the Lord in your interactions with one another, and despising no one.

Chapter 8

1 When you can do good, defer it not, because "alms deliver from death." 2 Be all of you subject one to another, having your conduct blameless among the Gentiles, that you may both receive praise for your good works, and the Lord may not be blasphemed through you. 3 But woe to him by whom the name of the Lord is blasphemed! Teach, therefore, sobriety to all, and manifest it also in your own conduct.

Chapter 9

1 I am exceedingly sorry for Valens, who once was a presbyter among you, that he so little understands the office which was committed to him. I warn you, therefore, that you abstain from covetousness, and that you be chaste and truthful. 2 Keep yourselves from all evil. For he who in these things cannot govern himself, how shall he enjoin it on others? If a man does not keep himself from covetousness, he shall be polluted with idolatry and judged as one of the heathen. 3 But I trust that you are well exercised in the Holy Scriptures and that nothing is hidden from you.

Chapter 10

1 But to speak of this would be superfluous for you, who are perfect in your faith and understanding. 2 May the omnipotence of God, therefore, and His splendor, establish you in His everlasting and spiritual truth. Amen.

Chapter 11

1 Finally, brothers, rejoice in the Lord always. I write the same things to you because they are necessary for your safety. 2 Stand firm in the faith and observe the saints' traditions, which you have learned either by word or by our epistles. 3 Grace be with you all, and may the Lord Jesus Christ be with your spirit, which you have received from God. Amen.

Chapter 12

1 Exhort one another, and correct each other in love, as you are doing. Let the elders among you be compassionate and merciful towards all, not quick to judge but slow to anger. 2 Pay special attention to the purity of your congregation. Avoid the snares of the devil, ensuring that your hearts remain fervent in the Lord. 3 Those who are capable must labor in the spirit to support the weak, sharing their resources in humility and brotherhood.

Chapter 13

1 Do not neglect the gathering of yourselves together, as is the habit of some, but encourage each other, especially now that you see the day of the Lord drawing near. 2 The mystery of our faith is great, and maintaining this mystery in purity and truth is the charge of each member of the church. 3 Foster peace among yourselves and with all men. Be an example to the outside world, reflecting the light of Christ in all your actions and words.

Chapter 14

1 Stand firm against the schemes of heresy that threaten to infiltrate the church. Guard steadfastly the deposit of faith that has been entrusted to you, not swerving from the hope of the gospel. 2 Teach the younger members with patience and doctrine that is sound and uplifting. Let your instruction always be seasoned with grace and tempered with the wisdom from above. 3 Remember the words of our Lord Jesus Christ, and keep your doctrine in accordance with the holy scriptures, being diligent in prayer and constant in your reliance on the Holy Spirit.

Chapter 15

1 Send greetings to all the saints in Christ Jesus. The brothers who are with me send you their greetings. 2 All the churches of Christ send you greetings, especially those from the household of faith who have labored in the spirit together with us. 3 I urge you, brothers and sisters, to be vigilant and persevere in faith, knowing that through your labor in the Lord, your toil is not in vain.

Chapter 16

1 The grace of our Lord Jesus Christ be with your spirit, brothers and sisters. Let this grace be manifest in all your churches; let it abound and bring forth the fruits of righteousness. 2 Pray for us, that the word of the Lord may speed ahead and be honored, as it is among you, and that we may be delivered from wicked and evil men; for not all have faith. 3 But the Lord is faithful. He will establish you and guard you against the evil one.

Chapter 17

1 May the Lord direct your hearts to the love of God and to the steadfastness of Christ. In every good work and word, may you find the strength that comes from the Lord Jesus. 2 May your love abound more and more with knowledge and all discernment, so that you may approve what is excellent, and so be pure and blameless for the day of Christ, 3 filled with the fruit of righteousness that comes through Jesus Christ, to the glory and praise of God.

109. *The Didache*

Chapter 1

1 There are two ways, one of life and one of death, but a great difference between the two ways. 2 The way of life, then, is this: First, you shall love God who made you; second, love your neighbor as yourself, and do not do to another what you would not want done to you.

Chapter 2

1 This teaching of these words is this: Bless those who curse you, pray for your enemies, and fast for those who persecute you. For what reward is there for loving those who love you? Do not the Gentiles do the same? But love those who hate you, and you will not have an enemy. 2 Abstain from fleshly and worldly lusts. If someone strikes your right cheek, turn to him the other also, and you will be perfect. If someone impresses you for one mile, go with him two.

Chapter 3

1 Guard against evil desires, because if you let your eyes be loose, they will make the rest of your body dark. 2 If you do not keep yourself from coveting, you will not keep yourself from doing evil. 3 If you share your bread, salt, and cup with your brother with a generous heart, then your sacrifice is pure and will be accepted as if it is upon the altar.

Chapter 4

1 My child, remember night and day him who speaks the word of God to you, and honor him as you would the Lord. For where the lordly rule is uttered, there is the Lord. 2 And seek out every day the faces of the saints, that you may rest upon their words.

Chapter 5

1 Do not long for division, but bring those who contend to peace. Judge righteously, do not respect persons in reproving for transgressions. 2 You shall not doubt whether it shall be or not. 3 Be not found holding out your hands to receive, but drawing them in as to giving.

Chapter 6

1 If you have anything, through your hands you shall give ransom for your sins. 2 Do not hesitate to give, nor complain when you give; for you shall know who is the good Paymaster of the reward. 3 Commandments for the Church: Do not let your

alms sweat in your hands until you know to whom you should give.

Chapter 7

1 The way of death is this: First of all it is evil and full of curse—murders, adulteries, lusts, sexual sins, thefts, idolatries, magical arts, witchcrafts, robberies, false testimonies, hypocrisy, double-heartedness, deceit, haughtiness, depravity, self-will, greediness, filthy talking, jealousy, over-confidence, loftiness, boastfulness. 2 Persecutors of the good, hating truth, loving a lie, not knowing a reward for righteousness, not adhering to the good nor to righteous judgment, watching not for that which is good but for that which is evil; from whom meekness and endurance are far, loving vanities, pursuing revenge, not pitying a poor man, not laboring for the afflicted, not knowing Him Who made them, murderers of children, corrupters of God's creation, turning away from the needy, oppressing the afflicted, advocates of the rich, lawless judges of the poor, sinners in all things.

Chapter 8

1 Be careful how you hear. For whosoever has, to him more will be given; and from him who has not, even what he has will be taken away from him. 2 Therefore, share your bread with the hungry, and bring the homeless poor into your house; when you see the naked, cover him, and do not hide yourself from your own flesh.

Chapter 9

1 When you gather together, confess your sins, and do not come to prayer with a bad conscience. This is the way of life. 2 And concerning the Eucharist, give thanks in this manner: 3 First, concerning the cup: "We thank You, our Father, for the holy vine of David Your servant, which You have revealed to us through Jesus Your servant; to You be the glory forever." 4 And concerning the broken bread: "We thank You, our Father, for the life and knowledge which You have made known to us through Jesus Your servant; to You be the glory forever.

Chapter 10

1 As this broken bread was scattered upon the mountains and being gathered together became one, so may Your Church be gathered together from the ends of the earth into Your Kingdom; for Yours is the glory and the power through Jesus Christ forever." 2 But let no one eat or drink of your Eucharist unless they have been baptized in the name of the Lord; for concerning this also the Lord has said, "Give not that which is holy to the dogs."

Chapter 11

1 And after you are filled, give thanks in this manner: 2 "We thank You, Holy Father, for Your holy name which You have caused to dwell in our hearts, and for the knowledge, faith, and immortality which You have made known to us through Jesus Your servant; to You be the glory forever. 3 You, Almighty Master, created all things for Your name's sake, and gave food and drink to men to enjoy, so that they might give thanks to You; but to us You have graciously given spiritual food and drink and eternal life through Your servant.

Chapter 12

1 Above all we thank You because You are mighty; to You be the glory forever. 2 Remember, Lord, Your Church, to deliver it from all evil and to perfect it in Your love; and gather it from the four winds—sanctified for Your Kingdom which You have prepared for it; for Yours is the power and the glory forever. 3 Let grace come, and let this world pass away. Hosanna to the God of David! If anyone is holy, let him come; if anyone is not, let him repent. Maranatha. Amen."

Chapter 13

1 But allow the prophets to give thanks as much as they desire. 2 Therefore, appoint for yourselves bishops and deacons worthy of the Lord, men who are meek and not lovers of money, and who are truthful and proven; for they also perform for you the service of the prophets and teachers.

Chapter 14

1 Do not despise them, for they are your honored ones, together with the prophets and teachers. 2 And reprove one another, not in anger but in peace, as you have it in the Gospel. But to anyone who acts amiss against another, let no one speak, nor let him hear anything from you until he repents. 3 But your prayers, alms, and all your deeds so perform as you have it in the Gospel of our Lord.

Chapter 15

1 Watch over your life, do not let your lamps be quenched and do not let your loins be ungirded, but be ready; for you do not know the hour in which our Lord comes. 2 But you shall gather yourselves frequently, seeking the things which are befitting to your souls; for the whole time of your faith will not profit you if you are not perfected at the last season.

Chapter 16

1 If anyone shall be found indulging in the lusts of the flesh, let him be admonished once or twice; if he persists, let him be cut off from your midst to avoid corruption spreading among you. 2 Keep a close watch on the doctrine that has been handed down to you, remembering the warnings and the promises of the Lord; keep steadfast in the faith, and in the performance of good works, which are the seal of your salvation.

Chapter 17

1 For every animal sacrifice there are appointed times, but for the sacrifice of thanksgiving, as received from the Lord, the time is always now. 2 So be diligent in the offering of your thanksgiving, for this is pleasing to the Lord, a fragrance of sweet aroma. 3 Do not hesitate to give and do not complain about it, for you will know the grace of giving that it may be returned to you, full and overflowing.

Chapter 18

1 Every firstfruit of the produce of the wine vat and threshing floor, of oxen and of sheep, you shall take and give to the prophets, for they are your high priests. 2 But if you have no prophet, give it to the poor. If you make bread, take the firstfruits and give according to the commandment. 3 Similarly, when you open a jar of wine or of oil, take the firstfruits and give to the prophets; if you take money or clothing, as you have it in your heart, give in simplicity according to the commandment of the Lord.

Chapter 19

1 Your gatherings should not lack a holy order. Let everyone be active in your meetings, and let your gatherings not be empty showcases of self-indulgence, but vibrant with the spirit of God. 2 Teach each other with psalms, hymns, and spiritual songs, singing and making melody in your heart to the Lord. 3 Every day, and especially on the Lord's day, gather together and break bread and give thanks, after confessing your transgressions so that your sacrifice may be pure.

Chapter 20

1 Do not let anyone who is at odds with his fellow join with you until they are reconciled, so that your sacrifice may not be defiled. 2 For this is the word that was spoken by the Lord: "In every place and time offer to me a pure sacrifice; for I am a great king, says the Lord, and my name is wonderful among the nations."

Chapter 21

1 Therefore, appoint for yourselves prophets and teachers, who are worthy, and treat them as the Lord commanded in His Gospel: "The worker deserves his food." 2 If any prophet teaches the truth, but does not practice what he teaches, he is a false prophet. 3 But any prophet, proven true, working for the mystery of the Church in the world, yet teaching you to do all that he himself does, shall not be judged by you, for his judgment is with God; for the ancient prophets also acted in a similar manner.

Chapter 22

1 No prophet who orders a meal in the Spirit eats from it unless he is indeed a false prophet; and every prophet who teaches the truth, if he does not do what he teaches, is a false prophet. 2 But no prophet who has been proven true and is genuinely serving the mysteries of the Church, and who wants to settle among you with no worldly motive, is worthy of his food. 3 Likewise, a true teacher is himself worthy, just as the workman deserves his wages.

Chapter 23

1 Every firstfruit, therefore, of the produce of the winepress and the threshing floor, of your oxen and of your sheep, you shall give the firstfruits to the prophets, for they are your chief priests. 2 But if you have no prophet, offer them to the poor. 3 If you make a batch of dough, take the firstfruit and give according to the commandment.

Chapter 24

1 Similarly, when you open a jar of wine or oil, take the firstfruit and give it to the prophets; and of money and clothing and every possession, take the firstfruit, as it seems good to you, and give according to the commandment.

Chapter 25

1 Be watchful over your life; do not let your lamps go out, and do not let your loins be ungirded, but be ready, for you do not know the hour in which our Lord will come. 2 Gather together frequently, seeking the things that are fitting for your souls, for the whole time of your faith will not profit you if you are not made perfect at the last moment. 3 In the last days, false prophets and corrupters will abound, and the sheep will turn into wolves, and love will turn into hate.

Chapter 26

1 As lawlessness increases, they will hate, persecute, and betray one another. Then the world-deceiver will appear as a son of God, and will perform signs and wonders, and the earth will be delivered into his hands, and he will commit abominations the likes of which have never happened before. 2 Then all humankind will come to the fiery test, and many will stumble and perish; but those who endure in their faith will be saved by the curse itself. 3 And then the signs of the truth will appear: first, a sign of an opening in the heavens, then a sign of the sound of a trumpet, and third, a resurrection of the dead.

Chapter 27

1 Not of all the dead, but as it is said: "The Lord will come, and all His saints with Him." 2 Then the world will see the Lord coming upon the clouds of heaven. 3 Every soul that has been oppressed will have rest and will see My salvation and My righteousness and My glory, which I have prepared as a garland for My saints.

Chapter 28

1 And the Lord will reward His faithful servants, those who kept His commandments during their lives. They will be resplendent with great light and will be the pillar of the world. 2 But the world-deceiver, suffering torment in a fire that will never be extinguished, will be shown to all humans together with the false prophets and all who said they worked miracles and led many astray. 3 They will perish, but the faith of My elect will stand firm, and the evil one will perish forever.

Chapter 29

1 Therefore, keep the commandments that you have received, not straying or being drawn away by the teachings of those who preach lawlessness. 2 But let grace be with you all, receiving the crown of immortality, apart from those who wander in the darkness of the world; for the Lord has saved His elect through sanctification of the Spirit and belief in truth. 3 This is the way of light, that through it you may obtain salvation; there is no other.

Chapter 30

1 Therefore, flee from all the works of lawlessness, lest you be ensnared. 2 Consider, O people, what the Lord says in His teaching: "Beware lest any man deceive you." 3 For He has given us this charge, saying, "Return it to their shepherds as a testimony, and guard My commandments, and you will live with Me, and I with you."

Chapter 31

1 I urge you all, therefore, to observe and follow the teachings of the Lord, to walk in His ways of righteousness, and to practice everything that is pleasing in His sight. 2 Your sacrifices are not needed as much as your obedience, which illuminates the paths of those who are lost. 3 Be vigilant, guarding your salvation with fear and trembling, for the day of judgment is coming when each will receive according to his deeds.

110. *The Epistle of Barnabas*

Chapter 1

1 Greetings, sons and daughters, in the name of the Lord who loves us, in peace. 2 Enlarging upon your blessed and glorious hope, I, Barnabas, write this epistle to you.

Chapter 2

1 Therefore, consider how he has been with you, enlightening your minds. 2 You should remember who gave you the doctrine of grace and who has given you the gift of wisdom. 3 You should understand who has destroyed death and brought forth the hope of life.

Chapter 3

1 Let us reflect further on the temple of God, how he has told us that the place is holy, which the Lord has sanctified for himself to dwell in forever. 2 For what is the temple of God? It is the human being who works righteousness, and that is where his faith resides. 3 The heart of those who fear the Lord is the temple that he said he would create, to set his dwelling among us.

Chapter 4

1 It is clear to us that the dwelling that he promised us is in us. How? By the fleshly temple that he made for himself. 2 For the Lord said he would dwell in us, reworking our hearts, the human temple, with his hands through the help of his word. 3 Therefore, let us cling to the hope and the assurance of our righteousness, which is faith.

Chapter 5

1 Reflect, children of love, on the practices of wickedness, how evil they are, how they lead astray from the life that is set for us. 2 Consider that God has given us a fine commandment: You shall love your neighbor more than your own soul. 3 You see, how he has put love above all sins, because it is the head of life; everything is held together by love to God.

Chapter 6

1 Therefore, let us cling to his blessing and see what are the ways of the blessing. Let us study how to attain it. 2 Let us rest, striving to achieve it, finding out how we can find a home in it. 3 We must pay attention to the future, for we are called, and we must believe that the call is better than any evil deed done.

Chapter 7

1 Let us stand firm in our calling, so that the peace-maker may enter into us and dwell among us. 2 Let us be reconciled to him, those who were once far off, now brought near by the blood of the Lord Jesus. 3 Let us become his temple, pure, being cleansed from all deceit and hypocrisy, malice, and remembrance of evils against our neighbors.

Chapter 8

1 For if the Lord took delight in us, he would dwell in us; if we do his commandments, then we will have succeeded in our faith. 2 The door is faith through

which Christ enters. If we make it steadfast, fearing nothing, then we will have succeeded in our hope. 3 Let us be bound to those things that are good and glorious according to the Lord's sight. Let us rest on his judgment, and our life will be obvious to all.

Chapter 9

1 Therefore, the way of light is this: if any man wishes to journey to the appointed place, he must be diligent in his works. 2 The knowledge given to us whereby we may walk therein is this: love your maker, fear your creator, glorify the one who ransoms you from death. 3 Be simple in heart, rich in spirit, not clinging to those who walk the way of death. Hate everything that is not pleasing to God, hate all hypocrisy, and never forsake the Lord's commandments.

Chapter 10

1 Do not exalt yourself, but be humble in every way towards all men. 2 The signs of a true prophet are these: he will not command with an outward show of authority, nor will he seek to be obeyed through fear. 3 He will not speak against others, nor will he judge harshly, but he will be peaceful, quiet, and reverent, as the Lord has taught us: "Whoever speaks from himself seeks his own glory."

Chapter 11

1 If a man does not keep himself from all these things, he will not be acknowledged as a prophet or a teacher of the Church. 2 If anyone teaches the truth but does not do what he teaches, he is a false prophet. 3 When a prophet, proven genuine, teaches you the ways of righteousness in the name of the Lord, you shall follow him.

Chapter 12

1 But you should not test or judge any prophet who speaks in the Spirit; for every sin will be forgiven, but this sin will not be forgiven. 2 Not everyone who speaks in the Spirit is a prophet, but only if he holds the ways of the Lord. Therefore, from their ways shall the false prophet and the prophet be known.

Chapter 13

1 Any prophet who orders a meal in the Spirit does not eat from it; if he does, he is indeed a false prophet. 2 And any prophet who teaches the truth, if he does what he teaches, is a true prophet. 3 Yet, any prophet, acknowledged as genuine and acting with a worldly spirit, whose performance involves the mystery of the Church but who teaches you to do what he himself does, shall not be judged among you, for he has his judgment with God.

Chapter 14

1 Furthermore, whoever says in the Spirit, "Give me money," or something else, you shall not listen to him. But if he tells you to give for others who are in need, let no one judge him.

Chapter 15

1 Every way of your life shall be open before you: if it is suitable to be taken, take it. 2 If anyone comes to you and teaches you all these things that have been mentioned before, receive him. 3 But if the teacher himself turns aside and teaches a different doctrine to destroy you, listen not to him. But if his teaching fosters righteousness and knowledge of the Lord, receive him as the Lord.

Chapter 16

1 And concerning the Apostolic and Ecclesiastical orders: on reaching the place, perform the Eucharist, as directed, with prayer and thanksgiving, having purified yourselves from all condemnation. 2 Let no one break the bread who is not of the bishops or ordained clergy. 3 Wherever the bishop appears, there let the people be, just as wherever Christ Jesus is, there is the Catholic Church.

Chapter 17

1 Do not deviate from the commandments of the Lord, but keep what you have received, neither adding to it nor taking away from it. 2 Confess your sins in the church and do not go to prayer with an evil conscience. This is the way of light.

Chapter 18

1 If you have the ability to bear the entire yoke of the Lord, you will be perfect; but if you cannot, do what you can. 2 Regarding food, bear what you can; but strictly avoid that which is offered to idols, for it is the worship of dead gods.

Chapter 19

1 My children, guard against every evil and everything like it. 2 Be gentle, and patient in enduring the offenses of others, as the Lord endures you. 3 Be always zealous in the service of God, and do not count the many who perish but rather the few who are saved.

Chapter 20

1 Fear the judgment to come, and judge no one harshly, lest you be judged likewise. 2 Forgive, and it shall be forgiven unto you; be merciful, so you may receive mercy; with what measure you measure, it will be measured to you in return. 3 Help the oppressed, defend the orphan, and support the widow, and you will be pure before God.

Chapter 21

1 Keep the fasts, as you have been instructed, for great is the reward of these when observed. 2 The fast of the fourth day of the week and the Preparation (Friday) are to be kept sacred. 3 Remember the resurrection especially on the Lord's Day by breaking bread and giving thanks. For you were raised from the dead on this day, and thus it shall be a joy and not a grief.

Chapter 22

1 Let your gatherings not be without purpose; teach and admonish one another in all wisdom. Sing psalms, hymns, and spiritual songs with gratitude in your hearts to God. 2 Every Lord's Day gather together, break bread and give thanks, after confessing your transgressions so that your sacrifice may be pure.

Chapter 23

1 But let no one who has a quarrel with his fellow join with you until they are reconciled, that your sacrifice may not be defiled. 2 For this is the offering that was spoken of by the Lord: "In every place and time offer to me a pure sacrifice; for I am a great King, says the Lord, and my name is wonderful among the nations."

Chapter 24

1 Therefore, appoint for yourselves bishops and deacons worthy of the Lord, men who are meek, not lovers of money, sincere, and proven; for they also serve you in the service of the prophets and teachers. 2 Do not look down upon them, for they are your honored ones, together with the prophets and teachers.

Chapter 25

1 Test everything that is said and hold fast to that which is good. Keep away from every form of evil. 2 Be steadfast in your beliefs and do not be led astray by theories and intricate doctrines that lead to nothing but empty speculation, which serves only to obscure the truth of the Gospel.

Chapter 26

1 Be vigilant with your life; let your lamps not be extinguished, nor your loins unloosed, but be ready, for you do not know the hour in which our Lord comes. 2 But come together often, seeking the things which are befitting to your souls, for the whole time of your faith will not profit you if you are not made perfect at the end.

Chapter 27

1 Pray without ceasing on behalf of other people. For there is hope of repentance that they may attain to God. Let them then be instructed by your works, if in no other way. 2 Be meek in response to their wrath, humble in opposition to their boasting: to their blasphemies return your prayers; in contrast to their error, be steadfast in the faith; and for their cruelty, manifest your gentleness.

Chapter 28

1 While being hated, do not hate in return; while being cursed, bless; while being persecuted, endure; while being slandered, entreat. 2 Show that the humble, when they are exalted, do not boast, and in all things show that you are disciples of Christ Jesus.

Chapter 29

1 Let no one deceive you with empty words, for because of these things the wrath of God comes upon the sons of disobedience. Therefore, do not be partakers with them. 2 For you were once darkness, but now you are light in the Lord. Walk as children of light, proving what is acceptable to the Lord.

Chapter 30

1 Watch carefully how you walk, not as unwise but as wise, redeeming the time because the days are evil. 2 Therefore, do not be foolish, but understand what the will of the Lord is. Do not get drunk with wine, for that is debauchery, but be filled with the Spirit.

111. The Shepherd of Hermas

Vision 1

1 Hermas, a Christian slave, is commanded by a lady in shining garments to read a text to the presbyters of the church. She tells him he will write two more books and when completed, he should pass them to the elders of the church.

Vision 2

1 Hermas sees the same lady, who reveals herself as the Church, and gives him a little book to copy. After copying, the book becomes sealed and flies away to the heavens, symbolizing that what is written is holy and beyond alteration.

Vision 3

1 Hermas sees a vision of a great beast coming out of a chasm, representing trials and tribulation. He escapes it through the guidance of the lady, symbolizing his faith protecting him.

Vision 4

1 The lady, now described as a city built upon a great plain, represents the Church, and Hermas is told of the impending trials and persecutions that will befall the community but also of the ultimate triumph of the Church.

Vision 5

1 Hermas sees the elders of the Church, who interpret his previous visions and encourage him to remain steadfast in his faith, emphasizing the importance of repentance and adherence to the teachings of Christ.

Mandate 1

1 Hermas is instructed on the importance of believing in one God and keeping faith even amidst trials, as faith will protect him from evil and guide him in his journey.

Mandate 2

1 Hermas is warned against following false prophets and instructed to discern the true spirit of prophecy from the spirit of deceit by their fruits and actions.

Mandate 3

1 The mandate emphasizes the importance of simplicity and avoiding the pitfalls of duplicity and hypocrisy, encouraging a heart that is pure and steadfast in the truth.

Mandate 4

1 Hermas is told to maintain integrity in all dealings, avoiding dishonest gain and emphasizing that riches obtained through wrongful means bring sorrow and tribulation.

Mandate 5

1 The importance of patience is stressed, with instruction that enduring trials with a cheerful heart brings favor from God, and patience in affliction is a hallmark of a devout Christian.

Mandate 6

1 Hermas is instructed on the significance of repentance, the need to forgive others so that one's own sins may be forgiven by God.

Mandate 7

1 Hermas is counseled on the dangers of fear, which leads to doubt and a lack of faith, and told to trust in the Lord with a fearless heart.

Mandate 8

1 The virtues of chastity and purity are extolled, with Hermas being warned against adultery and the corrupting influence of lust, which lead away from the path of righteousness.

Mandate 9

1 Hermas is reminded of the importance of prayer, which should be done without ceasing and with sincere faith, ensuring that it rises to God without distraction or hypocrisy.

Mandate 10

1 The importance of fasting is discussed, not just as a physical act but as a spiritual exercise that brings humility and focus on God, purifying the soul and bringing it closer to the divine.

Similitude 1

1 Hermas is shown a vision of a vineyard and an encircling fence, symbolizing the Law that protects those who abide by the teachings of the Church.

Similitude 2

1 A mountain made of various stones represents the Church, and the stones are the faithful who, depending on their faith and actions, either remain part of the structure or are cast aside.

Similitude 3

1 Hermas sees a vision of an elderly woman, representing the Church, who explains the importance of endurance in faith and good works.

Similitude 4

1 Through the analogy of trees reflecting seasons, Hermas is taught about resurrection and judgment, emphasizing that one's actions in life reflect their spiritual 'season'.

Similitude 5

1 A vision of the Lord as a shepherd who guides His flock, teaching that leaders must be gentle, just, and nurturing, leading by example.

Similitude 6

1 Hermas is shown a city being built, symbolizing the Kingdom of Heaven, which is constructed from the deeds of the faithful, encouraging vigilance and righteousness.

Similitude 7

1 The final similitude where Hermas is shown a great feast, symbolizing the eternal reward for the righteous who endure to the end, remaining steadfast in their faith and deeds.

Similitude 8

1 Hermas sees a great tower being built, symbolizing the Church. The tower is constructed of square stones, which are the holy angels or the saints who have led righteous lives. 2 The construction involves careful examination of stones by the builders (angels), with the flawed stones thrown away, representing souls not fit for the Kingdom of Heaven. 3 Hermas is taught that each action and choice made by believers either strengthens their inclusion in the tower or leads to their rejection.

Similitude 9

1 In the ninth similitude, Hermas is shown a picture of a flourishing field surrounded by thorns, which symbolizes the world. 2 The field ready for harvest represents those who live righteously and are prepared for salvation, whereas the thorns signify sinners who live without repentance and will be cut off from the field. 3 Hermas learns the importance of living a life of constant readiness and purity, as the day of salvation can come unexpectedly like a thief in the night.

Similitude 10

1 Hermas sees a series of seats placed in a lofty

tower, with each seat ascending above the last. This represents the levels of glory in the afterlife, depending on one's faithfulness and piety on earth. 2 Each person, after death, ascends to a seat according to the quality and measure of their deeds, as witnessed by the hosts of heaven. 3 Hermas is exhorted to strive for the highest place by living a life of strict adherence to God's commandments and showing love and charity.

Similitude 11

1 A vision of a great river of crystal-clear water symbolizes the outpouring of the Holy Spirit upon the Church. Those who drink from the river are those who receive the Spirit and are sanctified by it. 2 Hermas sees trees along the river's banks, bearing fruit throughout the year, representing the continuous and fruitful lives of those who live by the Spirit. 3 The purity and abundance of the water show the boundless grace and provision God offers to those who faithfully serve Him and adhere to His teachings.

Similitude 12

1 In this similitude, Hermas is shown a sealed book, which no one can open. The book contains the deeds of all humans, and it is only to be opened on the Day of Judgment. 2 An angel explains that only the Lamb, who is without sin, can open the book and reveal its contents, which include the final destinies of all souls. 3 Hermas is admonished to keep the faith and perform righteous deeds so that his name may be found in the book of life, leading to eternal salvation.

Similitude 13

1 Hermas is shown a large and beautiful tree, under which lie many sheep resting and feeding. This tree represents Christ, and the sheep are those who have found rest in His teachings. 2 The tree provides shade and comfort, signifying the protection and peace that come from being in Christ. The leaves of the tree are the teachings of Jesus, which nourish and sustain the flock. 3 Hermas is told that just as the sheep find safety and sustenance under the tree, so must believers remain close to Christ, drawing strength and guidance from His words.

Similitude 14

1 A vision of a garden filled with diverse plants, each varying in beauty and fruitfulness, symbolizes the variety of gifts and ministries within the Church. 2 Hermas is instructed that just as each plant contributes to the beauty and utility of the garden, so does each member of the Church contribute their unique gifts to the edification of the whole. 3 The health and growth of the garden depend on the care it receives, just as the health of the Church depends on the stewardship and nurturing of its members.

Similitude 15

1 Hermas sees a vision of a banquet where many are invited, but only those who arrive wearing wedding garments are admitted. This represents the Kingdom of Heaven, where only those prepared and purified through righteousness are allowed to enter. 2 The wedding garment is symbolic of the righteous deeds and holy living that clothe the faithful. Hermas is warned that without these garments, one cannot partake in the heavenly feast. 3 The similitude emphasizes the importance of vigilance and readiness, living a life worthy of the calling to which believers have been called.

Similitude 16

1 In this vision, Hermas is shown a fortress with walls built of shining stones. Inside the fortress, people are singing hymns and rejoicing, representing those who have overcome the world through their faith. 2 The fortress itself symbolizes the protection afforded by faith in God, which shields believers from spiritual harm and offers them a place of refuge. 3 Hermas is encouraged to strive to enter this fortress by living a life of steadfast faith and unyielding devotion to God, keeping his soul free from the corruptions of the world.

Similitude 17

1 Hermas sees a vision of a great race, where many run but only those who finish are crowned. This represents the Christian life, which is likened to a race that requires endurance, discipline, and perseverance. 2 The crowns are the rewards of eternal life, given to those who persevere to the end, keeping their faith intact and their lives pure. 3 Hermas is exhorted to run the race with patience, casting aside every weight and sin that clings closely, focusing on the promise of the heavenly reward.

Similitude 18

1 A vision of a vine growing beside a spring of clear water, which supports many branches and yields much fruit, symbolizes the life of the Church sustained by Christ, the living water. 2 The health and fruitfulness of the vine depend on its connection to the spring, just as the vitality of Christians depends on their connection to Christ. 3 Hermas is taught that apart from Christ, believers can do nothing; thus, they must remain in Him to bear the fruit of the Spirit, which leads to eternal life.

112. The Apocalypse of Peter

Chapter 1

1 Peter, the apostle of Jesus Christ: To those who have received faith equal in honor to ours in the righteousness of our God and Savior Jesus Christ. 2 Grace to you and peace be multiplied in the acknowledgment of God and of Jesus our Lord.

Chapter 2

1 The heavens were opened, and I, Peter, saw the holy vision of the Lord. 2 In the midst of the heavens stood the throne of God, and around it were seated the angels and the saints. 3 Then the Lord said to me, "Peter, here you will see the glory of my kingdom and the judgment of the world."

Chapter 3

1 The voice of the Lord was like thunder, and the whole heaven shone with the brilliance of His glory. 2 He showed me the souls of men, separated into the righteous and the wicked. 3 The righteous were clothed in white garments, singing hymns and praising God.

Chapter 4

1 But the wicked were in torment, bound in chains of darkness and fire. 2 They cried out for mercy, but there was none to save them, for they had rejected the Lord in their lifetime and had scorned His mercy.

Chapter 5

1 Then I saw a new heaven and a new earth, for the old heaven and the old earth had passed away, and there was no longer any sea. 2 I saw the holy city, New Jerusalem, coming down out of heaven from God, prepared as a bride beautifully dressed for her husband.

Chapter 6

1 A great voice from the throne said, "Behold, the dwelling of God is with men, and he will live with them. They will be his people, and God himself will be with them and be their God. 2 He will wipe every tear from their eyes. There will be no more death or mourning or crying or pain, for the old order of things has passed away."

Chapter 7

1 He who was seated on the throne said, "I am making everything new!" Then he said, "Write this down, for these words are trustworthy and true." 2 He said to me: "It is done. I am the Alpha and the Omega, the Beginning and the End. To the thirsty I will give water without cost from the spring of the water of life.

Chapter 8

1 Those who are victorious will inherit all this, and I will be their God and they will be my children. 2 But the cowardly, the unbelieving, the vile, the murderers, the sexually immoral, those who practice magic arts, the idolaters and all liars—they will be consigned to the fiery lake of burning sulfur. This is

the second death."

Chapter 9

1 And one of the elders said to me, "These in white robes—who are they, and where did they come from?" 2 I answered, "Sir, you know." And he said, "These are they who have come out of the great tribulation; they have washed their robes and made them white in the blood of the Lamb.

Chapter 10

1 Therefore, they are before the throne of God and serve him day and night in his temple; and he who sits on the throne will shelter them with his presence. 2 'Never again will they hunger; never again will they thirst. The sun will not beat upon them, nor any scorching heat. 3 For the Lamb at the center of the throne will be their shepherd; he will lead them to springs of living water. And God will wipe away every tear from their eyes.'"

Chapter 11

1 Then I saw an angel coming down from heaven with the key to the Abyss and holding in his hand a great chain. 2 He seized the dragon, that ancient serpent, who is the devil, or Satan, and bound him for a thousand years. 3 He threw him into the Abyss, and locked and sealed it over him, to keep him from deceiving the nations anymore until the thousand years were ended. After that, he must be set free for a short time.

Chapter 12

1 I saw thrones on which were seated those who had been given authority to judge. And I saw the souls of those who had been beheaded because of their testimony about Jesus and because of the word of God. 2 They had not worshiped the beast or its image and had not received its mark on their foreheads or their hands. They came to life and reigned with Christ a thousand years. 3 The rest of the dead did not come to life until the thousand years were ended. This is the first resurrection.

Chapter 13

1 Blessed and holy are those who share in the first resurrection. The second death has no power over them, but they will be priests of God and of Christ and will reign with him for a thousand years. 2 When the thousand years are over, Satan will be released from his prison and will go out to deceive the nations in the four corners of the earth—Gog and Magog—and to gather them for battle.

Chapter 14

1 In number they are like the sand on the seashore. They marched across the breadth of the earth and surrounded the camp of God's people, the city he loves. 2 But fire came down from heaven and devoured them. And the devil, who deceived them, was thrown into the lake of burning sulfur, where the beast and the false prophet had been thrown. 3 They will be tormented day and night forever and ever.

Chapter 15

1 Then I saw a great white throne and him who was seated on it. The earth and the heavens fled from his presence, and there was no place for them. 2 And I saw the dead, great and small, standing before the throne, and books were opened. Another book was opened, which is the book of life. 3 The dead were judged according to what they had done as recorded in the books.

Chapter 16

1 The sea gave up the dead that were in it, and death and Hades gave up the dead that were in them, and each person was judged according to what they had done. 2 Then death and Hades were thrown into the lake of fire. The lake of fire is the second death. 3 Anyone whose name was not found written in the book of life was thrown into the lake of fire.

Chapter 17

1 I saw a new heaven and a new earth, for the first heaven and the first earth had passed away, and there was no longer any sea. 2 I saw the Holy City, the new Jerusalem, coming down out of heaven from God, prepared as a bride beautifully dressed for her husband. 3 And I heard a loud voice from the throne saying, "Look! God's dwelling place is now among the people, and he will dwell with them."

Chapter 18

1 "They will be his people, and God himself will be with them and be their God. He will wipe every tear from their eyes." 2 "There will be no more death or mourning or crying or pain, for the old order of things has passed away." 3 He who was seated on the throne said, "I am making everything new!" Then he said, "Write this down, for these words are trustworthy and true."

Chapter 19

1 He said to me: "It is done. I am the Alpha and the Omega, the Beginning and the End. To the thirsty I will give water without cost from the spring of the water of life. 2 Those who are victorious will inherit all this, and I will be their God and they will be my children. 3 But the cowardly, the unbelieving, the vile, the murderers, the sexually immoral, those who practice magic arts, the idolaters and all liars—they will be consigned to the fiery lake of burning sulfur. This is the second death."

Chapter 20

1 Then one of the seven angels who had the seven bowls full of the seven last plagues came and said to me, "Come, I will show you the bride, the wife of the Lamb." 2 And he carried me away in the Spirit to a mountain great and high, and showed me the Holy City, Jerusalem, coming down out of heaven from God. 3 It shone with the glory of God, and its brilliance was like that of a very precious jewel, like a jasper, clear as crystal.

Chapter 21

1 It had a great, high wall with twelve gates, and at the gates twelve angels, and names written on them, which are the names of the twelve tribes of Israel. 2 There were three gates on the east, three on the north, three on the south and three on the west. 3 The wall of the city had twelve foundations, and on them were the names of the twelve apostles of the Lamb.

Chapter 22

1 The angel measured the wall using human measurement, and it was 144 cubits thick. 2 The city was laid out like a square, as long as it was wide. He measured the city with the rod and found it to be 12,000 stadia in length, and as wide and high as it is long. 3 The angel measured the wall, and it was 144 cubits thick, by human measurement, which the angel was using.

Chapter 23

1 The wall was made of jasper, and the city of pure gold, as pure as glass. 2 The foundations of the city walls were decorated with every kind of precious stone. The first foundation was jasper, the second sapphire, the third agate, the fourth emerald, 3 the fifth onyx, the sixth ruby, the seventh chrysolite, the eighth beryl, the ninth topaz, the tenth turquoise, the eleventh jacinth, and the twelfth amethyst.

Chapter 24

1 The twelve gates were twelve pearls, each gate made of a single pearl. The great street of the city was of gold, as pure as transparent glass. 2 I did not see a temple in the city, because the Lord God Almighty and the Lamb are its temple. 3 The city does not need the sun or the moon to shine on it, for the glory of God gives it light, and the Lamb is its lamp.

Chapter 25

1 The nations will walk by its light, and the kings of the earth will bring their splendor into it. 2 On no day will its gates ever be shut, for there will be no night there. 3 The glory and honor of the nations will be brought into it.

Chapter 26

1 Nothing impure will ever enter it, nor will anyone who does what is shameful or deceitful, but only those whose names are written in the Lamb's book of life. 2 Then the angel showed me the river of the

water of life, as clear as crystal, flowing from the throne of God and of the Lamb 3 down the middle of the great street of the city. On each side of the river stood the tree of life, bearing twelve crops of fruit, yielding its fruit every month.

Chapter 27

1 And the leaves of the tree are for the healing of the nations. No longer will there be any curse. The throne of God and of the Lamb will be in the city, and his servants will serve him. 2 They will see his face, and his name will be on their foreheads. 3 There will be no more night. They will not need the light of a lamp or the light of the sun, for the Lord God will give them light. And they will reign forever and ever.

Chapter 28

1 Then he said to me, "These words are trustworthy and true. The Lord, the God who inspires the prophets, sent his angel to show his servants the things that must soon take place." 2 "Behold, I am coming soon! Blessed is the one who keeps the words of the prophecy written in this scroll."

Chapter 29

1 I, John, am the one who heard and saw these things. And when I had heard and seen them, I fell down to worship at the feet of the angel who had been showing them to me. 2 But he said to me, "Don't do that! I am a fellow servant with you and with your fellow prophets and with all who keep the words of this scroll. Worship God!"

Chapter 30

1 Then he told me, "Do not seal up the words of the prophecy of this scroll, because the time is near. 2 Let the one who does wrong continue to do wrong; let the vile person continue to be vile; let the one who does right continue to do right; and let the holy person continue to be holy."

Chapter 31

1 "Look, I am coming soon! My reward is with me, and I will give to each person according to what they have done. 2 I am the Alpha and the Omega, the First and the Last, the Beginning and the End."

Chapter 32

1 Blessed are those who wash their robes, that they may have the right to the tree of life and may go through the gates into the city. 2 Outside are the dogs, those who practice magic arts, the sexually immoral, the murderers, the idolaters and everyone who loves and practices falsehood.

Chapter 33

1 "I, Jesus, have sent my angel to give you this testimony for the churches. I am the Root and the Offspring of David, and the bright Morning Star." 2 The Spirit and the bride say, "Come!" And let the one who hears say, "Come!" Let the one who is thirsty come; and let the one who wishes take the free gift of the water of life.

Chapter 34

1 I warn everyone who hears the words of the prophecy of this scroll: If anyone adds anything to them, God will add to that person the plagues described in this scroll. 2 And if anyone takes words away from this scroll of prophecy, God will take away from that person any share in the tree of life and in the holy city, which are described in this scroll.

Chapter 35

1 He who testifies to these things says, "Yes, I am coming soon." 2 Amen. Come, Lord Jesus. 3 The grace of the Lord Jesus be with God's people. Amen.

113. The Acts of Paul

Chapter 1

1 Paul, having been filled with the Holy Spirit, looked intently at the high priest. 2 And he said, "Men and brethren, I have lived in all good conscience before God until this day." 3 The high priest Ananias commanded those who stood by him to strike him on the mouth.

Chapter 2

1 Then Paul said to him, "God will strike you, you whitewashed wall! For you sit to judge me according to the law, and do you command me to be struck contrary to the law?" 2 And those who stood by said, "Do you revile God's high priest?" 3 Paul said, "I did not know, brethren, that he was the high priest; for it is written, 'You shall not speak evil of a ruler of your people.'"

Chapter 3

1 After this event, Paul, having been taken into custody for his safety, was sent to Felix the governor. 2 Felix, having a more accurate knowledge about the Way, kept Paul and frequently conversed with him, hoping to receive money for his release. 3 But when two years had passed, Felix was succeeded by Porcius Festus, and desiring to do the Jews a favor, Felix left Paul in prison.

Chapter 4

1 Festus, wanting to know more about the accusations against Paul by the Jews, went down to Jerusalem. 2 The chief priests and the elders of the Jews informed him against Paul and petitioned him, 3 asking a favor against him, that he would summon him to Jerusalem—planning to kill him on the way.

Chapter 5

1 Festus, however, answered that Paul should be kept at Caesarea, and that he himself would depart shortly there. 2 "Let those who have authority among you," said he, "go down with me and accuse this man, to see if there is any fault in him." 3 When he had stayed among them more than ten days, he went down to Caesarea. The next day, sitting on the judgment seat, he commanded Paul to be brought.

Chapter 6

1 When he had come, the Jews who had come down from Jerusalem stood around him, bringing many and serious charges against him which they could not prove, 2 while Paul argued in his defense, "Neither against the law of the Jews, nor against the temple, nor against Caesar have I offended in anything at all." 3 But Festus, wanting to do the Jews a favor, answered Paul and said, "Are you willing to go up to Jerusalem and there be judged before me concerning these things?"

Chapter 7

1 But Paul said, "I stand at Caesar's judgment seat, where I ought to be judged. To the Jews I have done no wrong, as you very well know. 2 For if I am an offender, or have committed anything deserving of death, I do not refuse to die; but if there is nothing in these things of which these men accuse me, no one can deliver me to them. I appeal to Caesar." 3 Then Festus, when he had conferred with the council, answered, "You have appealed to Caesar? To Caesar you shall go!"

Chapter 8

1 After some days, King Agrippa and Bernice arrived at Caesarea to greet Festus. 2 While they were there many days, Festus discussed Paul's case with the king, saying, "There is a certain man left a prisoner by Felix, 3 about whom the chief priests and the elders of the Jews informed me when I was in Jerusalem, asking for a judgment against him."

Chapter 9

1 Festus continued, "I told them that it is not the custom of the Romans to deliver any man to destruction before the accused meets the accusers face to face, and has opportunity to answer for himself concerning the charge against him." 2 "Therefore, when they came together here, without any delay, the next day I sat on the judgment seat and commanded the man to be brought in." 3 "Against whom when the accusers stood up, they brought no accusation of such things as I supposed,

Chapter 10

1 "but had some questions against him about their own religion and about a certain Jesus, who had died, whom Paul affirmed to be alive." 2 "And

because I was uncertain of such questions, I asked him whether he would go to Jerusalem and there be judged concerning these matters." 3 "But when Paul had appealed to be reserved for the decision of Augustus, I commanded him to be kept till I could send him to Caesar."

Chapter 11

1 Then Agrippa said to Festus, "I would like to hear the man myself." "Tomorrow," he said, "you shall hear him." 2 So the next day, Agrippa and Bernice came with great pomp, and entered the auditorium with the commanders and prominent men of the city. 3 At Festus' command, Paul was brought in.

Chapter 12

1 Festus said, "King Agrippa, and all men who are here present with us, you see this man about whom the whole assembly of the Jews petitioned me, both at Jerusalem and here, crying out that he is not fit to live any longer." 2 "But when I found that he had committed nothing deserving of death, and that he himself has appealed to Augustus, I have decided to send him." 3 "I have nothing certain to write to my lord concerning him. Therefore I have brought him out before you, and especially before you, King Agrippa, so that after the examination has taken place, I may have something to write."

Chapter 13

1 "For it seems to me unreasonable to send a prisoner and not to specify the charges against him." 2 Then Agrippa said to Paul, "You are permitted to speak for yourself." So Paul stretched out his hand and answered for himself: 3 "I think myself happy, King Agrippa, because today I shall answer for myself before you concerning all the things of which I am accused by the Jews,

Chapter 14

1 "especially because you are expert in all customs and questions which have to do with the Jews. Therefore I beg you to hear me patiently. 2 "My manner of life from my youth, which was spent from the beginning among my own nation at Jerusalem, all the Jews know. 3 "They knew me from the first, if they were willing to testify, that according to the strictest sect of our religion I lived a Pharisee.

Chapter 15

1 "And now I stand and am judged for the hope of the promise made by God to our fathers, 2 to which our twelve tribes, earnestly serving God night and day, hope to attain. For this hope's sake, King Agrippa, I am accused by the Jews. 3 Why should it be thought incredible by you that God raises the dead?

Chapter 16

1 "I indeed thought myself that I ought to do many things contrary to the name of Jesus of Nazareth. 2 This I also did in Jerusalem, and many of the saints I shut up in prison, having received authority from the chief priests; and when they were put to death, I cast my vote against them. 3 And I punished them often in every synagogue and compelled them to blaspheme; and being exceedingly enraged against them, I persecuted them even to foreign cities.

Chapter 17

1 "While thus occupied, as I journeyed to Damascus with authority and commission from the chief priests, 2 at midday, O king, I saw on the way a light from heaven, brighter than the sun, shining around me and those who journeyed with me. 3 And when we had all fallen to the earth, I heard a voice speaking to me and saying in the Hebrew language, 'Saul, Saul, why are you persecuting Me? It is hard for you to kick against the goads.'

Chapter 18

1 "So I said, 'Who are You, Lord?' And He said, 'I am Jesus, whom you are persecuting. 2 But rise and stand on your feet; for I have appeared to you for this purpose, to make you a minister and a witness both of the things which you have seen and of the things which I will yet reveal to you. 3 I will deliver you from the Jewish people, as well as from the Gentiles, to whom I now send you,

Chapter 19

1 to open their eyes, in order to turn them from darkness to light, and from the power of Satan to God, that they may receive forgiveness of sins and an inheritance among those who are sanctified by faith in Me.' 2 Therefore, King Agrippa, I was not disobedient to the heavenly vision, 3 but declared first to those in Damascus and in Jerusalem, and throughout all the region of Judea, and then to the Gentiles, that they should repent, turn to God, and do works befitting repentance.

Chapter 20

1 "For these reasons the Jews seized me in the temple and tried to kill me. 2 Having obtained help from God, to this day I stand, witnessing both to small and great, saying no other things than those which the prophets and Moses said would come— 3 that the Christ would suffer, that He would be the first to rise from the dead, and would proclaim light to the Jewish people and to the Gentiles."

Chapter 21

1 As he thus spoke for himself, Festus said with a loud voice, "Paul, you are beside yourself! Much learning is driving you mad!" 2 But he said, "I am not mad, most noble Festus, but speak the words of truth and reason. 3 For the king knows about these things, before whom I also speak freely. For I am convinced that none of these things escapes his attention, since this thing was not done in a corner.

Chapter 22

1 "King Agrippa, do you believe the prophets? I know that you do believe." 2 Then Agrippa said to Paul, "You almost persuade me to become a Christian." 3 And Paul said, "I would to God that not only you, but also all who hear me today, might become such as I am, except for these chains."

Chapter 23

1 When he had said this, the king stood up, as well as the governor and Bernice and those who sat with them. 2 And when they had gone aside, they talked among themselves, saying, "This man is doing nothing deserving of death or chains." 3 Then Agrippa said to Festus, "This man could have been set free if he had not appealed to Caesar."

Chapter 24

1 After this, preparations were made for Paul to be sent to Rome, as he had appealed to be judged by the Emperor. 2 Paul, guarded by soldiers, was put on a ship headed for Italy, accompanied by some other prisoners. 3 Julius, a centurion of the Augustan Cohort, was in charge of their transport.

Chapter 25

1 They sailed slowly for many days and arrived with difficulty off Cnidus, as the wind did not allow them to go farther. 2 They sailed under the shelter of Crete, off Salmone, and with difficulty coasting along it, they came to a place called Fair Havens, near the city of Lasea.

Chapter 26

1 Since much time had passed, and sailing was now dangerous because the Fast had already gone by, Paul advised them, 2 saying, "Men, I perceive that this voyage will end with disaster and much loss, not only of the cargo and ship but also of our lives." 3 However, the centurion was more persuaded by the pilot and the owner of the ship than by what was said by Paul.

Chapter 27

1 Because the harbor was not suitable to spend the winter in, the majority decided to put out to sea from there, on the chance that somehow they could reach Phoenix, a harbor of Crete facing both southwest and northwest, and spend the winter there. 2 When a moderate south wind began to blow, they thought they could achieve their purpose, so they weighed anchor and began sailing along Crete, close to shore. 3 But soon a tempestuous wind, called the northeaster, struck down from the land.

Chapter 28

1 When the ship was caught and could not face the wind, we gave way to it and were driven along. 2 Running under the lee of a small island called Cauda, we managed with difficulty to secure the ship's boat; 3 after hoisting it up, they used supports to undergird the ship. Fearing that they would run aground on the Syrtis, they lowered the gear, and so were driven along.

Chapter 29

1 As we were violently storm-tossed, they began the next day to jettison the cargo; 2 and on the third day they threw the ship's tackle overboard with their own hands. 3 When neither sun nor stars appeared for many days, and no small tempest lay on us, all hope of our being saved was at last abandoned.

Chapter 30

1 Since they had been without food for a long time, Paul stood up among them and said, "Men, you should have listened to me and not set sail from Crete and incurred this injury and loss. 2 Yet now I urge you to take heart, for there will be no loss of life among you, but only of the ship. 3 For this very night there stood before me an angel of the God to whom I belong and whom I worship,

Chapter 31

1 and he said, 'Do not be afraid, Paul; you must stand before Caesar. And behold, God has granted you all those who sail with you.' 2 So take heart, men, for I have faith in God that it will be exactly as I have been told. 3 But we must run aground on some island."

114. *The Acts of Peter*

Chapter 1

1 Peter, an apostle of Jesus Christ, to the pilgrims of the dispersion in Pontus, Galatia, Cappadocia, Asia, and Bithynia, 2 elect according to the foreknowledge of God the Father, in sanctification of the Spirit, for obedience and sprinkling of the blood of Jesus Christ: Grace to you and peace be multiplied.

Chapter 2

1 As the apostles were at Jerusalem, Peter said to the multitude about the ways of healing and the doctrine of salvation through the name of Jesus Christ. 2 And as he spoke, a great multitude gathered, and they were astonished at his teaching, for his words pierced their hearts.

Chapter 3

1 Then a certain man lame from his mother's womb was carried, whom they laid daily at the gate of the temple which is called Beautiful, to ask alms from those who entered the temple. 2 Seeing Peter and John about to go into the temple, he asked for alms. And fixing his eyes on him, with John, Peter said, "Look at us." 3 So he gave them his attention, expecting to receive something from them.

Chapter 4

1 Then Peter said, "Silver and gold I do not have, but what I do have I give you: In the name of Jesus Christ of Nazareth, rise up and walk." 2 And he took him by the right hand and lifted him up, and immediately his feet and ankle bones received strength. 3 So he, leaping up, stood and walked and entered the temple with them—walking, leaping, and praising God.

Chapter 5

1 And all the people saw him walking and praising God. 2 Then they knew that it was he who sat begging alms at the Beautiful Gate of the temple, and they were filled with wonder and amazement at what had happened to him. 3 As the lame man who was healed held onto Peter and John, all the people ran together to them in the porch which is called Solomon's, greatly amazed.

Chapter 6

1 When Peter saw it, he responded to the people: "Men of Israel, why do you marvel at this? Or why look so intently at us, as though by our own power or godliness we had made this man walk? 2 The God of

Abraham, Isaac, and Jacob, the God of our fathers, glorified His Servant Jesus, whom you delivered up and denied in the presence of Pilate, when he was determined to let Him go. 3 But you denied the Holy One and the Just, and asked for a murderer to be granted to you,

Chapter 7

1 and killed the Prince of life, whom God raised from the dead, of which we are witnesses. 2 And His name, through faith in His name, has made this man strong, whom you see and know. Yes, the faith which comes through Him has given him this perfect soundness in the presence of you all.

Chapter 8

1 Now, brethren, I know that you did it in ignorance, as did also your rulers. 2 But those things which God foretold by the mouth of all His prophets, that the Christ would suffer, He has thus fulfilled. 3 Repent therefore and be converted, that your sins may be blotted out, so that times of refreshing may come from the presence of the Lord.

Chapter 9

1 Peter continued preaching the resurrection of Jesus Christ and the kingdom of God, admonishing the people to believe and be baptized for the remission of their sins. 2 Many who heard the word believed, and the number of men grew to about five thousand. 3 The priests, the captain of the temple, and the Sadducees came upon them, being greatly disturbed that they taught the people and preached in Jesus the resurrection from the dead.

Chapter 10

1 They laid hands on them and put them in custody until the next day, for it was already evening. 2 However, many of those who heard the word believed; and the number of the men came to be about five thousand. 3 On the next day, their rulers, elders, and scribes assembled in Jerusalem,

Chapter 11

1 with Annas the high priest, Caiaphas, John, Alexander, and as many as were of the family of the high priest. 2 And when they had set them in the midst, they asked, "By what power or by what name have you done this?" 3 Then Peter, filled with the Holy Spirit, said to them, "Rulers of the people and elders of Israel:

Chapter 12

1 If we this day are judged for a good deed done to a helpless man, by what means he has been made well, 2 let it be known to you all, and to all the people of Israel, that by the name of Jesus Christ of Nazareth, whom you crucified, whom God raised from the dead, by Him this man stands here before you whole. 3 This is the stone which was rejected by you builders, which has become the chief cornerstone.

Chapter 13

1 Nor is there salvation in any other, for there is no other name under heaven given among men by which we must be saved." 2 Now when they saw the boldness of Peter and John, and perceived that they were uneducated and untrained men, they marveled. And they realized that they had been with Jesus. 3 But seeing the man who had been healed standing with them, they could say nothing against it.

Chapter 14

1 When they had commanded them to go aside out of the council, they conferred among themselves, 2 saying, "What shall we do to these men? For, indeed, that a notable miracle has been done through them is evident to all who dwell in Jerusalem, and we cannot deny it. 3 But so that it spreads no further among the people, let us severely threaten them, that from now on they speak to no man in this name."

Chapter 15

1 And they called them and commanded them not to speak at all nor teach in the name of Jesus. 2 But Peter and John answered and said to them, "Whether it is right in the sight of God to listen to you more than

to God, you judge. 3 For we cannot but speak the things which we have seen and heard."

Chapter 16

1 So when they had further threatened them, they let them go, finding no way of punishing them, because of the people, since they all glorified God for what had been done. 2 For the man was over forty years old on whom this miracle of healing had been performed. 3 Being let go, they went to their own companions and reported all that the chief priests and elders had said to them.

Chapter 17

1 When they heard this, they raised their voices together in prayer to God. "Sovereign Lord," they said, "you made the heavens and the earth and the sea, and everything in them. 2 You spoke by the Holy Spirit through the mouth of your servant, our father David: 'Why do the nations rage and the peoples plot in vain? 3 The kings of the earth rise up and the rulers band together against the Lord and against his anointed one.'

Chapter 18

1 Indeed Herod and Pontius Pilate met together with the Gentiles and the people of Israel in this city to conspire against your holy servant Jesus, whom you anointed. 2 They did what your power and will had decided beforehand should happen. 3 Now, Lord, consider their threats and enable your servants to speak your word with great boldness.

Chapter 19

1 Stretch out your hand to heal and perform signs and wonders through the name of your holy servant Jesus." 2 After they prayed, the place where they were meeting was shaken. And they were all filled with the Holy Spirit and spoke the word of God boldly. 3 All the believers were one in heart and mind. No one claimed that any of their possessions was their own, but they shared everything they had.

Chapter 20

1 With great power the apostles continued to testify to the resurrection of the Lord Jesus. And God's grace was so powerfully at work in them all 2 that there were no needy persons among them. For from time to time those who owned land or houses sold them, brought the money from the sales 3 and put it at the apostles' feet, and it was distributed to anyone who had need.

Chapter 21

1 Joseph, a Levite from Cyprus, whom the apostles called Barnabas (which means "son of encouragement"), 2 sold a field he owned and brought the money and put it at the apostles' feet. 3 But a man named Ananias, with his wife Sapphira, also sold a piece of property.

Chapter 22

1 With his wife's full knowledge he kept back part of the money for himself, but brought the rest and put it at the apostles' feet. 2 Peter said, "Ananias, how is it that Satan has so filled your heart that you have lied to the Holy Spirit and have kept for yourself some of the money you received for the land? 3 Didn't it belong to you before it was sold? And after it was sold, wasn't the money at your disposal?

Chapter 23

1 What made you think of doing such a thing? You have not lied just to human beings but to God." 2 When Ananias heard this, he fell down and died. And great fear seized all who heard what had happened. 3 Then some young men came forward, wrapped up his body, and carried him out and buried him.

Chapter 24

1 About three hours later his wife came in, not knowing what had happened. 2 Peter asked her, "Tell me, is this the price you and Ananias got for the land?" 3 "Yes," she said, "that is the price."

Chapter 25

1 Peter said to her, "How could you conspire to test the Spirit of the Lord? Listen! The feet of the men who buried your husband are at the door, and they will carry you out also." 2 At that moment she fell down at his feet and died. Then the young men came in and, finding her dead, carried her out and buried her beside her husband. 3 Great fear seized the whole church and all who heard about these events.

Chapter 26

1 After these events, Peter continued to speak powerfully in the name of Jesus, and the number of believers increased rapidly. 2 In those days, as the number of disciples was multiplying, there arose a complaint against the Hebrews by the Hellenists, because their widows were neglected in the daily distribution. 3 So the Twelve called together the multitude of the disciples and said, "It is not desirable that we should leave the word of God and serve tables.

Chapter 27

1 Therefore, brethren, seek out from among you seven men of good reputation, full of the Holy Spirit and wisdom, whom we may appoint over this business; 2 but we will give ourselves continually to prayer and to the ministry of the word." 3 And the saying pleased the whole multitude. They chose Stephen, a man full of faith and the Holy Spirit, and Philip, Prochorus, Nicanor, Timon, Parmenas, and Nicolas, a proselyte from Antioch,

Chapter 28

1 whom they set before the apostles; and when they had prayed, they laid hands on them. 2 The word of God spread, and the number of the disciples in Jerusalem increased greatly; and a large number of priests were obedient to the faith. 3 Stephen, full of faith and power, did great wonders and signs among the people.

Chapter 29

1 Then there arose some from what is called the Synagogue of the Freedmen (Cyrenians, Alexandrians, and those from Cilicia and Asia), disputing with Stephen. 2 But they were not able to resist the wisdom and the Spirit by which he spoke. 3 Then they secretly induced men to say, "We have heard him speak blasphemous words against Moses and God."

Chapter 30

1 And they stirred up the people, the elders, and the scribes; and they came upon him, seized him, and brought him to the council. 2 They also set up false witnesses who said, "This man does not cease to speak blasphemous words against this holy place and the law; 3 for we have heard him say that this Jesus of Nazareth will destroy this place and change the customs which Moses delivered to us."

Chapter 31

1 And all who sat in the council, looking steadfastly at him, saw his face as the face of an angel. 2 Then the high priest asked him, "Are these things so?" 3 And Stephen said, "Brethren and fathers, listen: The God of glory appeared to our father Abraham when he was in Mesopotamia, before he dwelt in Haran.

115. The Acts of John

Chapter 1

1 John, the beloved disciple of Jesus, traveled throughout Asia Minor, preaching the gospel of the risen Christ. 2 In Ephesus, he performed many miracles, healing the sick and casting out demons, which caused many to believe in Jesus' name.

Chapter 2

1 Among the converts was a young man named Lycomedes, who was of noble birth and greatly respected in Ephesus. Lycomedes invited John to his home and asked to be baptized. 2 After his baptism, Lycomedes confessed to John that he had a great idol in his house, hidden in a private chamber. He implored John to help him remove it.

Chapter 3

1 John, filled with the Holy Spirit, followed Lycomedes to the chamber. Upon entering, John

prayed fervently, and the idol was miraculously destroyed. 2 This act led many more in Ephesus to abandon idolatry and turn to the Christian faith.

Chapter 4
1 John's teachings attracted the attention of the local authorities, who were displeased with his influence and the decrease in traditional worship practices. 2 They summoned him to account for his actions, accusing him of disrupting the peace and leading the people astray.

Chapter 5
1 During the trial, John spoke boldly about Jesus, declaring Him the Son of God and the Savior of the world. His words were so powerful that even some of the magistrates believed and became followers of Christ. 2 However, others were hardened and sentenced John to exile on the island of Patmos.

Chapter 6
1 While in exile, John received visions from God, which he later wrote down in what would become the Book of Revelation. 2 These visions revealed the ultimate triumph of Christ over evil and His everlasting kingdom.

Chapter 7
1 After the death of the emperor, John was released from Patmos and returned to Ephesus, where he continued his ministry, strengthened by his visions. 2 He established many churches and appointed elders to lead them, instructing them in the ways of the Lord.

Chapter 8
1 As John aged, he trained Polycarp, his beloved disciple, to succeed him as the leader of the church in Ephesus. 2 He often recounted the words and deeds of Jesus, emphasizing love as the greatest commandment.

Chapter 9
1 Towards the end of his life, John often repeated the phrase, "Little children, love one another," which he taught was the commandment he received from Christ. 2 He remained in Ephesus, guiding the church and writing epistles until he peacefully passed away, full of years and honored by all who knew him.

Chapter 10
1 In his later years, John focused on deeper theological teachings, emphasizing the mystical aspects of Christian doctrine. 2 He spoke often of the Logos, the divine Word, and its incarnation, teaching that true knowledge of Christ comes from understanding His divine nature and human experiences.

Chapter 11
1 During this time, a severe persecution arose against the Christians in Ephesus. John courageously defended his flock, often placing himself at risk by speaking out against the injustices they faced. 2 He was arrested several times but miraculously escaped harm each time, bolstering the faith of his followers.

Chapter 12
1 One of John's most remarkable miracles occurred when he confronted a temple of Artemis. He challenged the priests to a test of power in the name of Jesus Christ. 2 John prayed, and a sudden earthquake destroyed part of the temple, leading many witnesses to convert to Christianity on the spot.

Chapter 13
1 Despite these successes, the challenges continued. John faced opposition not only from the pagan community but also from heretical sects that sought to distort the teachings of Christ. 2 He tirelessly refuted their arguments, using both scripture and his personal experiences with Jesus to guide his rebuttals.

Chapter 14
1 John's final days were marked by a vision similar to those he received on Patmos, in which he saw the New Jerusalem descending from heaven. 2 He shared this vision with his followers, reassuring them of the promise of eternal life and the everlasting kingdom of God.

Chapter 15
1 Just before his death, John gathered his disciples and gave a moving farewell speech. He reminded them of the importance of love, unity, and perseverance in faith. 2 He entrusted the leadership of the Ephesian church to Polycarp, whom he had trained for many years.

Chapter 16
1 John's peaceful passing was seen as a testament to his holy life and his profound relationship with God. 2 He was buried in Ephesus, and his grave became a site of pilgrimage for early Christians, who revered him as a model of apostolic virtue and a direct link to Jesus.

Chapter 17
1 The legacy of John's teachings continued to influence the Christian Church long after his death. His writings were circulated widely, contributing to theological debates and helping to shape the development of Christian doctrine. 2 His life and works remained a beacon of apostolic authority and spiritual depth, inspiring generations of believers to live in accordance with the Gospel.

Chapter 18
1 As the years passed, the community in Ephesus continued to grow and thrive under the guidance of Polycarp and the other elders trained by John. 2 They diligently preserved the teachings and writings of John, copying them for dissemination to other Christian communities across the Roman Empire. 3 Many came to Ephesus to learn about the life and teachings of John, seeking to emulate his devotion and understanding of Christ's message.

Chapter 19
1 Stories of John's miracles and teachings spread far and wide, becoming integral parts of Christian tradition and liturgy. 2 His accounts of Christ's life and his own experiences as an apostle were especially cherished, offering a direct link to the early days of Christianity. 3 Scholars and theologians studied his writings, using them to defend the faith against heretical interpretations and to deepen the church's understanding of the gospel.

Chapter 20
1 In time, the Acts of John, along with other apocryphal acts of the apostles, began to be read in some congregations as edifying tales that exemplified the spirit of the early church. 2 These texts inspired believers to remain steadfast in their faith despite persecution and to uphold the values taught by Jesus and his apostles. 3 They also served as moral and spiritual guides, illustrating the virtues of faith, hope, and especially love, which John had always placed at the center of his teachings.

Chapter 21
1 As the cult of saints developed within the church, John was venerated not only as a founder and protector of the church in Ephesus but also as a universal patron of love and loyalty to Christ. 2 Annual feasts commemorating his life and works were established, and he was invoked in prayers for intercession in times of trial. 3 The legacy of John's prophetic visions, particularly those recorded in Revelation, continued to influence Christian eschatology and art, shaping the church's view of the end times and the hope of a new creation.

Chapter 22
1 The impact of John on Christian mysticism also grew, with many mystics citing his works as key texts for understanding the mystical union with God. 2 His portrayal of the deep, personal relationship with Christ encouraged a more introspective and experiential approach to faith among believers. 3 His writings encouraged the pursuit of a direct and personal experience of God, reflecting the transformative encounters he had with Christ.

Chapter 23

1 Over the centuries, the Acts of John and other similar writings faced scrutiny and were eventually excluded from the canonical New Testament due to questions about their origin and orthodoxy. 2 However, their influence persisted in various Christian traditions, recognized for their role in enriching the faith and practice of many in the early church. 3 Today, they are studied for their historical value and for the light they shed on early Christian beliefs and practices, providing a broader understanding of the apostolic age.

Chapter 24

1 Within the scholarly circles of early Christianity, debates continued over the authenticity and doctrinal alignment of texts like the Acts of John. 2 Despite these debates, many believers found profound spiritual insights in the narratives of John's courage, humility, and miraculous powers. 3 The teachings of John, particularly about love and divine fellowship, were echoed in the sermons and writings of many church fathers, helping to shape the moral and theological contours of early Christian ethics.

Chapter 25

1 Pilgrimages to Ephesus increased as devotees sought to connect with the spiritual legacy of John. They visited sites associated with his ministry and relics believed to be connected to his life and death. 2 The church in Ephesus, reputedly founded by John, became a major center of Christian learning and pilgrimage, renowned for its guardianship of apostolic tradition. 3 The stories of John's confrontations with paganism, his miraculous escapes, and his profound revelations continued to be celebrated in liturgical commemorations and depicted in religious art.

Chapter 26

1 In the broader tapestry of Christian tradition, the Acts of John contributed to the development of apocryphal literature as a vital part of Christian heritage, offering alternative perspectives on the lives and missions of Jesus' closest followers. 2 These texts provided early Christians with examples of steadfastness in faith amid persecution, guidance in doctrinal disputes, and assurance of the supernatural support for the church. 3 As apocryphal texts, they occupied a unique place between the canonical scriptures and the folklore of Christian communities, enriching the cultural and spiritual life of the faithful.

Chapter 27

1 The influence of the Acts of John also extended into theological debates about the nature of Christ and the role of apostolic authority in the early church. 2 The vivid portrayals of John's direct interactions with Christ served as powerful arguments in discussions about the divinity of Jesus and the eyewitness origins of apostolic testimony. 3 These narratives helped to cement John's status as a key theological and historical figure within the Christian tradition, whose teachings and experiences provided crucial insights into the life and ministry of Jesus.

Chapter 28

1 As centuries passed, the Acts of John, along with other apocryphal acts, were periodically revisited during times of religious reform and revival, often cited for their inspirational value and their role in promoting a more personal and experiential faith. 2 During the Renaissance and Reformation, these texts were re-examined for historical and doctrinal insights as part of a broader reassessment of early Christian sources. 3 They continued to be valued for their literary and artistic merit, informing Christian iconography and the popular piety of many believers.

Chapter 29

1 Modern scholarship has approached the Acts of John with a focus on its context within second-century Christianity, exploring its themes in light of contemporary religious, cultural, and philosophical currents. 2 These studies have highlighted the diversity of early Christianity and the ways in which various communities sought to understand and articulate their faith in a rapidly changing world. 3 Today, the Acts of John is appreciated not only for its place in the history of Christian thought but also for its contributions to the understanding of early Christian identity and practice.

Chapter 30

1 As the study of Christian origins continues to evolve, historians and theologians examine the Acts of John to better understand the interplay between history and myth within the early church. 2 This text, with its blend of historical events and legendary embellishments, provides a window into how early Christians viewed their leaders and the supernatural aspects of their faith. 3 It remains a vital resource for those studying the development of Christian doctrine and the role of charismatic figures in the propagation of the faith.

Chapter 31

1 In contemporary Christian communities, the Acts of John serves as a reminder of the enduring legacy of the apostles and the foundational role they played in establishing the church. 2 The text is occasionally referenced in theological education and spiritual formation, offering lessons on leadership, sacrifice, and the power of faith. 3 It encourages believers to emulate the virtues of the apostles and to engage with the spiritual and miraculous elements of their faith with reverence and awe.

Chapter 32

1 The Acts of John also influences ongoing discussions about the canon of scripture and the criteria by which texts were included or excluded. 2 Its content has sparked debates over the nature of apostolic witness and the authenticity of the traditions attributed to the early church leaders. 3 These discussions underscore the complex processes through which the biblical canon was formed and the diverse voices that characterize early Christian literature.

Chapter 33

1 In the realm of ecumenical dialogue, the Acts of John provides a common ground for various Christian denominations to explore their shared heritage. 2 The text's themes of unity, divine mission, and enduring faith resonate across doctrinal divides, offering a historical testament to the shared apostolic roots of disparate Christian traditions. 3 It fosters a deeper appreciation of the diverse yet interconnected history of the Christian faith, promoting a spirit of unity and mutual respect among believers.

Chapter 34

1 The enduring fascination with the Acts of John among scholars, clergy, and laypeople attests to the profound impact of early apocryphal literature on Christian culture and spirituality. 2 As new archaeological discoveries and scholarly research continue to shed light on the early Christian era, the relevance and appreciation of such texts are likely to grow. 3 The Acts of John remains a testament to the rich narrative tradition of Christianity, offering enduring insights into the spiritual, doctrinal, and communal life of the early church.

116. The Acts of Andrew

Chapter 1

1 Andrew, an apostle of Jesus Christ, traveled extensively to preach the gospel. He began his journey in the lands surrounding the Black Sea, where he encountered various communities, each with their own customs and beliefs. 2 In each city, Andrew performed miracles, healing the sick and casting out demons, which drew large crowds and facilitated his teachings about Christ.

Chapter 2

1 In the city of Byzantium, Andrew faced great opposition from local magistrates who were

determined to maintain their traditional religious practices. Despite threats to his life, Andrew continued to preach boldly. 2 He was eventually arrested and brought before the city council, where he testified about Jesus' resurrection and the hope of eternal life. His words convinced many, including some members of the council, leading to a significant number of conversions.

Chapter 3
1 Andrew's next journey took him to the land of the Scythians, a people notorious for their harshness and resistance to foreign influences. Here, Andrew's message was met with skepticism and hostility. 2 Despite the initial resistance, Andrew's persistence and his miraculous healing of a Scythian leader's son broke down barriers, opening the community to the gospel.

Chapter 4
1 As Andrew continued his travels, he reached the city of Patras in Achaia, where he was confronted by Aegeates, the proconsul. Aegeates was a staunch supporter of the Roman gods and challenged Andrew to a public debate. 2 The debate drew a large crowd. Andrew articulated the tenets of Christianity with such wisdom and power that many were convinced of the truth of his words.

Chapter 5
1 However, Aegeates felt threatened by Andrew's influence and ordered his arrest. Andrew was imprisoned under harsh conditions, yet he continued to preach to those who visited him, including the jailers. 2 News of his teachings in prison reached Aegeates' own wife, Maximilla, who became a believer in Jesus Christ after visiting Andrew. This conversion brought her into conflict with her husband.

Chapter 6
1 Angered by his wife's conversion and the growing Christian sentiment in Patras, Aegeates ordered that Andrew be executed. Andrew was to be crucified, not nailed but tied to an X-shaped cross, to prolong his suffering. 2 As he was led to his death, Andrew continued to preach to the crowd, exhorting them to remain steadfast in their faith despite persecution.

Chapter 7
1 Andrew's crucifixion became a profound witness to many. He hung on the cross for three days, during which he continued to preach and teach all who came to see him. 2 On the third day, having finished his earthly mission, Andrew died, but not before seeing many more come to faith through his testimony.

Chapter 8
1 After his death, Andrew's followers took his body down from the cross and buried him with honors. His grave became a pilgrimage site for early Christians. 2 The church in Patras grew, strengthened by the memory of Andrew's faith and his martyrdom, which continued to inspire Christians throughout the region.

Chapter 9
1 The Acts of Andrew, while not included in the canonical scriptures, became a cherished text among early Christian communities. It was read for edification and inspiration, particularly in regions touched by Andrew's ministry. 2 This text exemplifies the apostolic zeal and the sacrifices made by the early followers of Jesus, reinforcing the faith of generations of believers.

Chapter 10
1 As the Christian community in Patras continued to grow, stories of Andrew's miracles and teachings spread far beyond the local region. His example inspired many to take up missionary work, spreading the Gospel throughout Greece and beyond. 2 Churches dedicated to Saint Andrew began to appear, each keeping alive the stories of his faith and his dedication to Christ's message.

Chapter 11
1 Among these communities, the Acts of Andrew circulated widely, reinforcing the values of courage in the face of persecution and unwavering commitment to the evangelistic mission. 2 Believers drew strength from his example when facing their own trials and tribulations, seeing in his life a model of apostolic virtue and sacrificial leadership.

Chapter 12
1 The influence of Andrew's teachings and his martyrdom also reached theological discussions, where his life was often cited as a testament to the truth and transformative power of the Gospel. 2 Debates on the nature of apostleship and martyrdom frequently referenced Andrew's endurance and his theological insights, as recorded in the Acts.

Chapter 13
1 In later centuries, the veneration of Andrew as a saint brought additional attention to the Acts of Andrew. His feast day became a time for reflection on his contributions to the Christian faith and his role as a patron saint of several countries and cities. 2 The text was especially revered in places like Scotland and Russia, where Saint Andrew was designated the patron saint due to his perceived connection to those lands through various legends and traditions.

Chapter 14
1 The Acts of Andrew also played a role in the art and iconography of the early Church. Scenes from his life were depicted in frescoes, mosaics, and stained glass, serving as visual sermons on the virtues of faith and perseverance. 2 These artistic representations helped to solidify his legacy and made his story accessible to the faithful who gathered in churches named in his honor.

Chapter 15
1 Scholars and historians of religion study the Acts of Andrew to gain insights into the early Christian world—its culture, its challenges, and its spirituality. The text provides valuable information about the spread of Christianity in the Mediterranean and the kinds of opposition the apostles faced. 2 Additionally, the text is examined for its literary qualities, as it blends historical detail with theological reflection and dramatic narrative.

Chapter 16
1 As with other apocryphal acts, the Acts of Andrew raises questions about the formation of Christian canon and the distinction between canonical and non-canonical texts. Its study offers a window into the dynamic and diverse nature of early Christian literature. 2 The ongoing interest in the Acts of Andrew in academic and religious circles underscores its importance not only as a historical document but also as a source of spiritual enrichment.

Chapter 17
1 The Acts of Andrew continues to inspire modern readers with its depiction of apostolic zeal and its emphasis on the power of faith in overcoming adversity. 2 Churches and communities around the world that trace their heritage to Saint Andrew often turn to this text to draw closer to the roots of their faith and to renew their commitment to spreading the Gospel, just as Andrew did.

Chapter 18
1 Throughout the centuries, the commemoration of Andrew's martyrdom has been marked by rituals and services that reflect the profound impact of his life and death on the Christian community. These observances serve as a reminder of the endurance and faith required to uphold the Gospel. 2 Pilgrimages to sacred sites associated with Andrew, particularly in Patras, where he was martyred, draw thousands of devotees each year. These pilgrimages are spiritual journeys that connect believers with the apostolic roots of their faith.

Chapter 19

1 Educational programs and theological seminars often include studies on the Acts of Andrew to highlight the historical and spiritual lessons embedded in his story. These educational initiatives help to cultivate a deeper understanding of early Christian evangelism and the apostolic heritage. 2 The text is also used in interdenominational discussions to bridge understandings between various Christian traditions, showcasing the universal aspects of apostolic endurance and faith.

Chapter 20

1 In liturgical celebrations, readings from the Acts of Andrew are incorporated to inspire congregations with his unwavering commitment to Christ under persecution. His life is presented as a model of spiritual courage and missionary zeal. 2 These liturgical uses reinforce the values of steadfast faith and dedication to Christ's teachings, which are central to Christian life and practice.

Chapter 21

1 The Acts of Andrew also influences Christian art, where his story is depicted in various media, portraying significant moments such as his call by Jesus, his missionary journeys, debates with philosophers, and his martyrdom. 2 These artistic depictions not only beautify sacred spaces but also serve as catechetical tools, teaching the faithful about the life and sacrifices of one of Christ's original apostles.

Chapter 22

1 Modern digital media have also played a role in the dissemination of the Acts of Andrew, with various formats like eBooks, audiobooks, and online courses expanding access to this ancient text. 2 These digital resources allow for greater engagement with the text, facilitating study and devotion across different platforms and reaching a wider audience than ever before.

Chapter 23

1 Theological debates continue to explore the implications of the Acts of Andrew for understanding apostolic authority and the nature of sainthood in the Christian tradition. 2 Scholars and theologians debate the historical accuracy of the apocryphal acts, including Andrew's, while also appreciating their role in shaping the spiritual and moral landscape of early Christianity.

Chapter 24

1 As global Christian communities grow, the Acts of Andrew serves as a link to the apostolic age, reminding believers of the foundational experiences and teachings that shaped the early church. 2 The text encourages contemporary Christians to reflect on their own faith journeys in light of the challenges and triumphs of the apostles.

117. The Acts of Thomas

Chapter 1

1 Thomas, also called Didymus, one of the twelve apostles of Jesus Christ, was directed by the Lord to go to India to preach the gospel. 2 Initially reluctant, Thomas was sold to an Indian merchant named Habban, who took him to King Gundaphorus in northern India as a carpenter and architect.

Chapter 2

1 Upon arrival, King Gundaphorus tasked Thomas with building a new palace. Instead, Thomas used the money given to him for the poor, telling the king that he was building the palace in heaven. 2 When the king discovered this, he was furious, but Thomas assured him that he would see this heavenly palace.

Chapter 3

1 During his time in India, Thomas performed many miracles, healing the sick and converting many to the Christian faith, including the king after he had a vision of the heavenly palace. 2 His actions, however, also stirred opposition among the local priests who felt threatened by his teachings.

Chapter 4

1 Thomas continued his missionary work, traveling further south, where he encountered the kingdom of Mazdai. 2 Here, Thomas baptized Mygdonia, the queen, which enraged King Mazdai. Thomas was imprisoned but continued to preach to those who visited him.

Chapter 5

1 Mygdonia's conversion led to more conversions within the royal household, causing further conflict with King Mazdai. 2 Thomas was subjected to various tortures but remained steadfast, his faith unwavering, further inspiring his followers.

Chapter 6

1 Ultimately, Thomas was sentenced to death by King Mazdai. He was led out of the city and martyred by four soldiers who speared him. 2 His final prayers asked for forgiveness for his persecutors, and upon his death, many miracles were said to occur, confirming his sanctity.

Chapter 7

1 After his martyrdom, Thomas's followers retrieved his body and buried him with honors. 2 The site of his burial became a pilgrimage destination, and a church was built in his honor, which became a center of Christian worship in India.

Chapter 8

1 The influence of Thomas's teachings and the Christian community he founded continued to grow long after his death, becoming an integral part of the religious landscape of India. 2 The Acts of Thomas, while not included in the canonical New Testament, became a significant text for many Eastern Christian traditions, illustrating the spread of Christianity beyond the Roman Empire.

Chapter 9

1 His story exemplifies the challenges and triumphs of missionary work and is often cited for its themes of sacrifice, perseverance, and the transformative power of faith. 2 The Acts of Thomas is celebrated in various Christian liturgies, particularly in the Syrian, Indian, and other Eastern churches, where his contributions are remembered and venerated.

Chapter 10

1 Thomas's legacy continued to inspire both local believers and foreign missionaries. His teachings, particularly those about the immanence of God and the immediate availability of the divine, resonated with a wide audience. 2 Legends of his works spread through oral traditions and later written accounts, integrating local cultural elements and expanding his veneration across different communities.

Chapter 11

1 The conversion stories associated with Thomas often emphasized his role in addressing social injustices and providing for the marginalized, which strengthened his following among the lower strata of society. 2 These stories highlight his interactions with women, the poor, and the outcast, portraying him as a champion of the oppressed and a model for compassionate ministry.

Chapter 12

1 Among the miracles attributed to Thomas, the most celebrated involved his interventions during times of drought and famine. According to these tales, Thomas would pray, and rains would come, saving many from starvation and illness. 2 Such miracles further cemented his reputation as a holy man, deeply connected to the divine and able to intercede on behalf of those in need.

Chapter 13

1 Conflict with local religious authorities was a recurring theme in Thomas's ministry. His challenges to the established religious order were seen as direct threats to the priestly class and their control over spiritual matters. 2 The Acts of Thomas details these confrontations, emphasizing Thomas's steadfast faith and his ability to articulate Christian doctrine in ways that were both provocative and enlightening.

Chapter 14
1 The story of Thomas's martyrdom is particularly poignant in Christian literature, depicting him as welcoming his death with a prayer that echoed Christ's own words on the cross, asking for forgiveness for his killers. 2 This moment is often used to illustrate the concept of agape, or selfless love, as the cornerstone of Christian teaching, and Thomas as its exemplar.

Chapter 15
1 Post-martyrdom, Thomas was said to appear in visions to his followers, encouraging them and guiding the churches he founded. These appearances are detailed in the later chapters of the Acts of Thomas, contributing to a complex narrative of his ongoing spiritual presence. 2 These visions reinforced the belief in the communion of saints and the continued guidance of the apostles beyond their earthly lives.

Chapter 16
1 The Acts of Thomas also discusses the theological implications of his teachings and his role in the development of early Christian thought about the nature of Christ, salvation, and the afterlife. 2 His dialogues with philosophers and theologians are portrayed not just as defences of the new faith but also as significant contributions to the early Christian intellectual tradition.

Chapter 17
1 As the centuries passed, the figure of Thomas became a symbol of Christian evangelism and missionary work. His story was adapted and retold in various cultures, each adding local color and emphasis to reflect their own experiences and challenges. 2 His feast day, celebrated with great reverence, especially in churches of the Eastern tradition, serves as a reminder of the universal call to witness and service embodied by the apostles.

Chapter 18
1 In regions where Christianity encountered indigenous beliefs and practices, the story of Thomas often acted as a bridge, integrating elements of local religions and philosophies. This syncretism helped establish deeper roots for Christian communities in diverse cultural settings. 2 His teachings, particularly those emphasizing personal spiritual experience and direct communion with God, found resonance in these contexts, facilitating the acceptance of Christian concepts.

Chapter 19
1 The relics of Thomas, purportedly containing his remains or items he used, became objects of veneration and were credited with miraculous powers. These relics were distributed across churches in India and beyond, enhancing his cult and the pilgrimages associated with it. 2 Churches claiming to house these relics saw significant growth in followers, who sought both spiritual blessings and physical healing through their proximity to the saint.

Chapter 20
1 The Acts of Thomas inspired numerous artistic representations, including iconography in Eastern Orthodox Christianity, where his image often depicts him holding a builder's square, symbolizing his reputed profession and his role as a spiritual builder. 2 These artistic depictions serve not only as devotional aids but also as pedagogical tools, conveying the essence of his story and the virtues he exemplified.

Chapter 21
1 In theological education, the Acts of Thomas is studied for its insights into the apostolic age and its portrayal of the missionary activities of the apostles. Seminaries and religious studies programs analyze the text to understand the challenges and strategies of early Christian evangelism. 2 The text is also used to discuss the nature of apocryphal writings and their role in the broader canon of Christian literature, exploring themes of authority, authenticity, and the historical development of the scriptures.

Chapter 22
1 Among modern theologians, the Acts of Thomas prompts discussions on interfaith dialogue and religious tolerance, reflecting Thomas's engagements with non-Christian philosophies and religions. 2 His respectful yet assertive approach in these dialogues provides a model for contemporary interactions between different faith communities, emphasizing mutual respect and the search for common truths.

Chapter 23
1 The story of Thomas's martyrdom continues to inspire Christians facing persecution today. His steadfastness in the face of death provides a powerful example of faith and conviction, offering solace and encouragement to those suffering for their beliefs. 2 Churches and communities under duress often turn to his story for comfort and guidance, drawing strength from his example to maintain their faith and integrity.

Chapter 24
1 As global Christian communities commemorate the legacy of Thomas, annual festivals and liturgies reenact his story, bringing together the faithful to celebrate his life and teachings. These events foster a sense of unity and continuity with the apostolic past, reinforcing the global and historical identity of the Church. 2 These commemorations often include charitable acts and community service, embodying Thomas's commitment to service and love, thus continuing his mission in practical and impactful ways.

Chapter 25
1 The legacy of Thomas's missions in India plays a significant role in the identity of several Indian Christian communities, particularly among the Saint Thomas Christians of Kerala. These communities trace their origins back to Thomas's evangelistic efforts, viewing him not only as a spiritual ancestor but also as a foundational figure in their religious heritage. 2 His reputed journey to India is celebrated with annual feasts and processions, which blend Christian liturgy with local cultural practices, reflecting the deep integration of the faith with Indian traditions.

Chapter 26
1 Scholarship on the Acts of Thomas has led to academic debates about the historical veracity of Thomas's travels to India. Archaeological and textual studies continue to explore the evidence supporting these traditions. 2 These investigations help contextualize the spread of Christianity in Asia, providing insights into the ancient trade routes and cultural exchanges that facilitated the dissemination of religious ideas.

Chapter 27
1 In the contemporary Christian context, the Acts of Thomas serves as a source of theological and spiritual inspiration, particularly in discussions about the role of miracles and divine intervention in the life of believers. 2 The text's rich depiction of miraculous healings and supernatural occurrences encourages a faith perspective that acknowledges the mysterious and often inexplicable ways God interacts with the world.

Chapter 28
1 The Acts of Thomas also contributes to ecumenical dialogues, as it exemplifies the apostolic origins shared across various Christian denominations. This common heritage is a point of unity and discussion among different Christian traditions, fostering a sense of shared history and mission. 2 Ecumenical studies often use the Acts to highlight early examples of doctrinal diversity and the ways these differences were navigated within the early Church.

Chapter 29
1 The role of Thomas as a cultural and religious bridge in the Acts of Thomas is particularly highlighted in multicultural and interfaith settings, where his story exemplifies the potential for

constructive religious interaction. 2 This aspect of his mission is used in peacebuilding and interfaith dialogue initiatives, promoting a model of engagement that respects and learns from different religious traditions while maintaining one's faith integrity.

Chapter 30

1 The enduring influence of the Acts of Thomas in Christian spirituality is evident in its continued use in devotional practices, prayer groups, and spiritual retreats, where it serves as a meditation on divine calling and perseverance in faith. 2 These practices emphasize personal transformation and commitment to living out the teachings of Jesus, inspired by Thomas's example of radical discipleship and missionary zeal.

118. The Epistle of Barnabas

Chapter 1

1 The epistle of Barnabas, an early Christian letter, written by Barnabas, one of the early apostles, to exhort and instruct the believers in the way of truth.

Chapter 2

1 Greetings, my sons and daughters, in the name of our Lord Jesus Christ, who loved us and gave Himself for us. Because of the abundance of His mercy, He has revealed to us the way of righteousness, and He has granted us the gift of salvation.

Chapter 3

1 Let us therefore walk in the light, as He is in the light, and have fellowship with one another. For the blood of Jesus Christ cleanses us from all sin. Let us not return to the works of darkness but rather continue in the truth, growing in the knowledge of the Lord.

Chapter 4

1 The path of righteousness is a narrow way, and few find it. But those who seek the Lord with all their heart will be led in the way of truth. Let us not be like those who wander in the wilderness of error, but let us cling to the Word of God, which is able to save our souls.

Chapter 5

1 Barnabas reminds the believers of the importance of obedience to God's commandments, saying, "Be doers of the word, and not hearers only, deceiving yourselves. For if anyone is a hearer of the word and not a doer, he is like a man who looks at his natural face in a mirror and then forgets what he looks like."

Chapter 6

1 He emphasizes the need for purity and holiness, saying, "Since we have these promises, beloved, let us cleanse ourselves from every defilement of body and spirit, bringing holiness to completion in the fear of God."

Chapter 7

1 The epistle also addresses the dangers of false teachings and the need to discern the truth. Barnabas warns, "Beware of false prophets who come to you in sheep's clothing but inwardly are ravenous wolves. You will recognize them by their fruits."

Chapter 8

1 Barnabas encourages the believers to hold fast to their faith in Christ, saying, "Let us hold fast the confession of our hope without wavering, for He who promised is faithful. Let us consider how to stir up one another to love and good works, not neglecting to meet together, but encouraging one another."

Chapter 9

1 He concludes the epistle with a prayer for the believers, asking that they may be filled with the knowledge of God's will in all spiritual wisdom and understanding, so that they may walk in a manner worthy of the Lord, fully pleasing to Him, bearing fruit in every good work, and increasing in the knowledge of God.

Chapter 10

1 Finally, Barnabas exhorts the believers to remain steadfast in the faith, saying, "Now may the God of peace Himself sanctify you completely, and may your whole spirit and soul and body be kept blameless at the coming of our Lord Jesus Christ. He who calls you is faithful; He will surely do it."

119. The Gospel of Mary

Chapter 1

1 The Gospel of Mary, attributed to Mary Magdalene, begins with her recounting visions she had of Jesus Christ and the teachings he imparted to her, which were not shared with the other disciples.

Chapter 2

1 In her vision, Mary Magdalene sees Jesus and converses with him about the soul's journey after death. Jesus explains that the soul must overcome the powers of darkness, represented by seven forms, each asking challenging questions to test the soul's readiness for ascension.

Chapter 3

1 These powers try to impede the soul's progress by instilling doubts and questioning its worthiness. The soul must respond with knowledge and confidence gained through Jesus's teachings to pass beyond them.

Chapter 4

1 Mary shares these revelations with the other disciples, who are initially troubled by her accounts. Peter, in particular, expresses skepticism about the validity of her visions and her role as a woman in their group.

Chapter 5

1 Levi defends Mary, arguing that her closeness to Jesus made her privy to teachings that the others did not receive. He insists that they should not dismiss her insights but rather consider them as a valuable addition to their understanding of Jesus's teachings.

Chapter 6

1 The disciples debate the implications of Mary's visions for their understanding of salvation and the soul's liberation. They discuss how her revelations align with Jesus's public teachings and what this means for their mission to spread his message.

Chapter 7

1 Ultimately, the group acknowledges the depth of Mary's spiritual experiences and agrees to incorporate her teachings into their broader ministry. They affirm that enlightenment comes in many forms and can transcend conventional boundaries, including those of gender.

Chapter 8

1 The gospel concludes with Mary Magdalene being recognized not just as a disciple, but as a prominent teacher among the followers of Jesus. Her unique experiences and the wisdom she offers from her conversations with Christ serve to inspire and guide the early Christian community.

Chapter 9

1 After the meeting, the disciples begin to disperse to preach the gospel across different regions. Inspired by Mary's teachings, they carry with them a renewed perspective on the spiritual journey and the nature of salvation. 2 Each one integrates aspects of Mary's revelations into their messages, adapting them to the cultural and spiritual contexts of their audiences.

Chapter 10

1 As the disciples spread the teachings, Mary Magdalene's role and her contributions become more widely acknowledged within early Christian communities. Stories of her close relationship with Jesus and her profound spiritual insights gain prominence. 2 Her gospel is cherished as a testament to her leadership and as a profound narrative of mystical Christian experiences.

Chapter 11

1 Some communities, particularly those inclined toward Gnostic beliefs, elevate the Gospel of Mary to a central position in their spiritual practices. They see her teachings as key to understanding the internal, mystical path to divine knowledge and enlightenment. 2 These groups often face opposition from more orthodox Christian sects, leading to debates and divisions within the broader Christian community.

Chapter 12

1 Despite the controversies, the message of the Gospel of Mary inspires a number of prominent female leaders within the Church. These women draw on Mary's example to assert their own roles as spiritual leaders and teachers. 2 Their ministries, while often challenged, contribute to a broader dialogue about the role of women in religious communities and the nature of spiritual authority.

Chapter 13

1 Over time, the Gospel of Mary, along with other apocryphal texts, begins to be marginalized in the process of canon formation, as the Church seeks to establish a more unified set of scriptures. 2 However, the gospel continues to be studied and revered in certain circles, preserving its messages and ensuring that Mary Magdalene's visions and teachings remain influential.

Chapter 14

1 Scholars and mystics, centuries later, rediscover the Gospel of Mary and begin to explore its themes and historical context more deeply. They find in it rich symbols and insights into early Christian spirituality and the Gnostic path. 2 This renewed interest sparks a resurgence in the study of Christian mysticism and the role of visionary experiences in the spiritual life.

Chapter 15

1 Today, the Gospel of Mary is recognized not only as a significant religious text but also as a vital artifact in the study of early Christianity. It provides scholars with insights into the diverse theological perspectives that existed within the first few centuries after Christ. 2 The gospel's emphasis on inner revelation and the soul's journey resonates with contemporary spiritual seekers, making Mary Magdalene an enduring figure in the quest for deeper religious understanding and personal spiritual connection.

Chapter 16

1 In modern times, the Gospel of Mary is often highlighted in discussions about gender and leadership within religious contexts. Its portrayal of Mary Magdalene as a theological authority challenges traditional views and supports arguments for greater inclusivity and recognition of women in religious leadership roles. 2 Feminist theologians and scholars of religion use the text to explore themes of empowerment, voice, and the suppression of female figures in early Christian history. These discussions contribute to ongoing debates within many Christian denominations regarding the ordination of women and their roles in church governance.

Chapter 17

1 The spiritual insights offered by the Gospel of Mary also resonate with those exploring alternative Christianities that emphasize personal experience and knowledge over institutional doctrines. For these seekers, Mary's intimate conversations with Jesus and her profound understanding of spiritual realities offer a model for a more direct and experiential approach to faith. 2 As such, the Gospel of Mary appeals to contemporary movements that value spiritual intuition and personal revelation, often blending these ancient teachings with modern spiritual practices and perspectives.

Chapter 18

1 Theological seminars and religious studies programs increasingly include the Gospel of Mary in their curricula to exemplify the variety of early Christian writings and the richness of theological ideas present at the dawn of Christianity. These academic settings provide a platform for critical examination and thoughtful engagement with the text, encouraging students to consider its implications for understanding Christian origins. 2 Such educational initiatives help cultivate a broader appreciation of the historical and cultural contexts that shaped the New Testament and other early Christian writings.

Chapter 19

1 Artistic interpretations of the Gospel of Mary continue to emerge in various forms, including literature, film, and visual arts, where Mary Magdalene is depicted in light of her role as depicted in the gospel. These portrayals often emphasize her spiritual depth, her closeness to Jesus, and her role as a witness to the resurrection. 2 Through these artistic expressions, the Gospel of Mary influences contemporary culture, offering new ways to imagine and engage with biblical characters and themes.

Chapter 20

1 In interfaith dialogues, the Gospel of Mary serves as a point of discussion on the diversity within Christian scriptures and the various interpretations of Jesus' teachings. It provides a case study in how different texts can influence religious thought and practice, encouraging dialogue participants to explore the complexities of scriptural interpretation and the development of religious traditions. 2 These discussions often highlight the importance of openness and respect for diverse religious expressions and the value of exploring forgotten or marginalized voices within traditional religious narratives.

Chapter 21

1 As the Gospel of Mary continues to be rediscovered and reevaluated, it remains a testament to the enduring quest for understanding in religious life. It challenges believers and scholars alike to reconsider the boundaries of canonical scripture and to appreciate the breadth of perspectives that contribute to the Christian tradition. 2 This ongoing engagement with the Gospel of Mary not only enriches the study of Christian texts but also deepens the spiritual lives of those who find meaning in its messages about the inner journey toward divine knowledge and truth.

120. The Gospel of Philip

Chapter 1

1 The Gospel of Philip, attributed to Philip the apostle, explores the themes of sacramental theology, the role of the sacred union, and the spiritual relationship between the material and the divine. 2 It begins with reflections on the nature of God and the mystery of Christ, emphasizing that true knowledge comes through spiritual unity with the divine.

Chapter 2

1 Philip discusses the sacraments extensively, particularly baptism, the Eucharist, and the bridal chamber, which he associates with a deeper spiritual initiation and union. 2 He argues that these rituals are not mere physical acts but gateways to a higher spiritual reality that transcends the material world.

Chapter 3

1 The text delves into the concept of the divine as both mother and father, and how this duality is reflected in human relationships. Philip explains that in the divine realm, there is a sacred unity that earthly marriage can symbolize and partake in. 2 This leads to a discussion on the sacredness of the bridal chamber, which he describes as a symbol of full spiritual union and completeness.

Chapter 4

1 Philip critiques mainstream Christian views of his time, particularly around the literal interpretation of

scripture and the church's focus on the visible over the invisible. 2 He advocates for a form of Christianity that sees beyond the literal and material to embrace the mystical and hidden meanings of Christ's teachings.

Chapter 5

1 The gospel contains dialogues between Jesus and his disciples, where Jesus provides deeper teachings about the nature of the soul, the importance of inner transformation, and the end of the world. 2 In these dialogues, Jesus often speaks in parables and riddles, which Philip explains are meant to convey truths that are accessible only through spiritual insight.

Chapter 6

1 A significant portion of the text is dedicated to the role of Mary Magdalene, who is described as Jesus's companion and spiritual consort. Philip discusses her role within the circle of disciples and how her relationship with Jesus exemplifies the union of male and female energies. 2 This relationship is portrayed not only as a physical or emotional bond but as a profound spiritual alliance that models the integrative path of salvation.

Chapter 7

1 The Gospel of Philip challenges traditional notions of family and marital relationships, proposing that true kinship is not about blood ties but about spiritual connectivity and unity in Christ. 2 This view extends to the community of believers, whom Philip encourages to see themselves as a spiritual family, united not by law or obligation but by love and mystical participation in the divine.

Chapter 8

1 Towards the conclusion, Philip reflects on the resurrection, not as a one-time historical event, but as an ongoing spiritual process available to all who attain the gnosis or knowledge of God. 2 He emphasizes that resurrection is achieved through spiritual awakening and liberation from the material limitations of the world.

Chapter 9

1 Philip elaborates on the concept of resurrection, describing it as a return to the fullness (pleroma) where human beings and the divine are unified. He teaches that this state is not merely future but begins in the present life through knowledge (gnosis) and spiritual practice. 2 He contrasts the resurrection of the spirit, which is a mystery of awakening, with the resurrection of the flesh, which he argues is a misunderstanding of Jesus' teachings.

Chapter 10

1 The gospel addresses the power of names and their mystical significance in Christian theology. Philip discusses how names connect to the divine essence and how understanding these connections can lead to deeper spiritual insights. 2 He asserts that sacred names can be gateways to realms of higher consciousness and that using these names in prayer and meditation enhances one's connection to the divine.

Chapter 11

1 A detailed discussion on the sacrament of the anointing (chrism) follows, where Philip describes it as a completion of baptism. This anointing is said to represent the Holy Spirit, which completes the initiate's spiritual birth. 2 He explains that through chrism, believers are endowed with the fullness of grace, empowering them to act in the world as true bearers of divine light.

Chapter 12

1 The text then delves into the parables of Jesus, with Philip offering esoteric interpretations. He suggests that the parables are not simple moral lessons but encoded teachings about the nature of reality and the process of spiritual awakening. 2 Each parable, according to Philip, holds keys to understanding different aspects of the kingdom of heaven and the path to spiritual maturity.

Chapter 13

1 Philip discusses the role of suffering in spiritual growth. He interprets suffering as a catalyst for inner transformation, urging followers to transcend their pain by finding its deeper purpose in their spiritual journey. 2 This teaching aligns with Gnostic views on the material world as a place of trial and transformation, where souls learn the lessons necessary for their return to the divine.

Chapter 14

1 The Gospel of Philip concludes with a call to spiritual vigilance. Philip exhorts his readers to remain awake to the spiritual realities that surround them and to live in a manner that reflects their deepening knowledge of the divine. 2 He warns against spiritual complacency and encourages continual seeking and questioning, which he posits as essential for maintaining one's connection to the divine truth.

Chapter 15

1 Philip expounds on the mystical body of Christ, explaining that believers are united not only with Christ but also with each other in this mystical body. He describes this union as transcending physical boundaries, creating a community bound by spiritual rather than earthly ties. 2 This concept reinforces the Gnostic belief in the transcendence of spiritual over physical, emphasizing that the true church is not a structure of stone but a community of souls aligned in divine purpose.

Chapter 16

1 Continuing his teachings on community, Philip discusses the concept of divine love as the glue that holds the mystical body together. He contrasts divine love with earthly love, highlighting its eternal and unselfish nature. 2 He teaches that divine love is a manifestation of the divine presence within each believer, urging his followers to cultivate this love through acts of kindness, deep prayer, and meditation.

Chapter 17

1 The sacrament of reconciliation is another focus of Philip's teachings. He presents it not as a ritualistic confession to a priest, but as a return to harmony with the divine and with one's community. 2 Philip describes reconciliation as a restoration of one's original purity, essential for full participation in the spiritual life of the community and for maintaining a clear and direct relationship with the divine.

Chapter 18

1 Philip delves into the symbolism of light and darkness, using them as metaphors for knowledge and ignorance, respectively. He explains that enlightenment comes from the light of gnosis, which dispels the darkness of ignorance. 2 The text encourages believers to seek the light through disciplined spiritual practice and constant pursuit of truth, which together lead to a profound understanding of the divine mystery.

Chapter 19

1 The role of prophecy in the believer's life is also discussed. Philip regards prophecy as a gift of the Spirit that allows believers to see beyond temporal realities into the spiritual truths that govern existence. 2 He emphasizes that prophecy is not about predicting the future but about understanding the deeper will of God and acting according to that knowledge in the present.

Chapter 20

1 In his concluding remarks, Philip reiterates the importance of the inner journey of discovery. He challenges followers to continue seeking deeper spiritual truths and to live out these truths in their daily lives. 2 He reminds them that the spiritual path is ongoing and that each step taken in faith and knowledge brings them closer to the divine.

Chapter 21

1 Philip emphasizes the transformative power of the inner resurrection, a central theme in his teachings.

He explains that the inner resurrection is an awakening from spiritual death to eternal life, happening here and now in the believer's journey. 2 This concept challenges traditional views of resurrection as a future event, promoting an understanding of salvation as an ongoing experience of growth and enlightenment.

Chapter 22

1 The Gospel of Philip elaborates on the significance of silence and secrecy in spiritual practices. Philip describes silence not as mere absence of words, but as a profound state of receptivity and contemplation where deep truths are revealed. 2 He advocates for a disciplined approach to spirituality, where silence is maintained as a sacred space for divine encounter and personal transformation.

Chapter 23

1 Discussing the nature of evil, Philip portrays it not as a personal entity but as a condition of ignorance and separation from the divine. He teaches that overcoming evil involves gaining gnosis—direct knowledge of God—which dispels ignorance and reunites the soul with the divine. 2 The battle against evil, therefore, is fought through spiritual education and the practice of virtuous living, aligning one's life with divine principles.

Chapter 24

1 Toward the end of the gospel, Philip discusses the role of faith and doubt in the spiritual journey. He portrays doubt not as a weakness but as a necessary step towards deeper faith, prompting believers to question, explore, and ultimately strengthen their understanding of divine truths. 2 Faith, according to Philip, evolves from accepting teachings to experiencing their reality through personal revelation and mystical encounter.

Chapter 25

1 The final chapter serves as a benediction and a call to persevere on the spiritual path. Philip blesses his readers with peace and encourages them to remain steadfast in their quest for divine knowledge. 2 He reminds them that the path is fraught with challenges but assures them that the rewards of spiritual awakening and union with the divine are worth every effort.

Chapter 26

1 Philip further elaborates on the importance of spiritual community, emphasizing that the journey towards divine understanding is not solitary but shared among believers. He underscores that the spiritual revelations received individually should be brought back to the community to enrich and elevate the collective faith. 2 He teaches that the community acts as both a support system and a reflective surface for personal spiritual insights, helping to validate and interpret them within the broader context of Christian doctrine.

Chapter 27

1 Exploring the nature of spiritual maturity, Philip discusses the stages of spiritual development, likening them to the growth of a plant from seed to full bloom. He emphasizes that each stage has its challenges and lessons, which are necessary for the soul's advancement towards full union with the divine. 2 He encourages patience and persistence, reminding his followers that spiritual growth, like any growth, requires time, dedication, and nurturing conditions.

Chapter 28

1 Philip addresses the misconceptions about sin and redemption. He clarifies that sin should be understood not merely as moral wrongdoing but as anything that distances one from God. Redemption, then, is the process of returning to God, driven by understanding and transformation rather than fear of punishment. 2 He counsels believers to focus on cultivating virtues that directly counteract their personal shortcomings, fostering habits that naturally align with divine will.

Chapter 29

1 Discussing the cosmic Christ, Philip delves into the metaphysical aspects of Jesus' teachings, presenting Jesus not only as a historical figure but also as a timeless embodiment of divine logos or truth. This view positions Jesus as both a gateway to the divine and a model for human conduct. 2 He encourages believers to see Christ's life as a blueprint for navigating the material world while maintaining a constant connection to the spiritual realm.

Chapter 30

1 As a conclusion, Philip reflects on the legacy of Jesus' teachings and their enduring impact on all who seek to understand and embody them. He emphasizes that the teachings are not static but continue to unfold and reveal deeper meanings as believers grow in their spiritual journey. 2 He ends with a prayer for wisdom, courage, and compassion for his readers, that they may continue to find in the teachings of Jesus the inspiration to live a life aligned with the highest spiritual ideals.

121. The Gospel of Nicodemus

Chapter 1

1 The Gospel of Nicodemus, also known as the Acts of Pilate, begins with an account of Jesus' trial before Pilate, emphasizing the legal and political dynamics of the situation. 2 Nicodemus, a member of the Sanhedrin and a secret follower of Jesus, plays a significant role in presenting the defense for Jesus, arguing against the accusations made by Jewish leaders.

Chapter 2

1 The narrative details the interactions between Pilate, the Jewish authorities, and Jesus, showcasing the conflict between the Roman legal standards and the religious accusations against Jesus. 2 Pilate's wife, Procla, is introduced, having dreamt about Jesus and warning Pilate against condemning an innocent man.

Chapter 3

1 As the trial progresses, various miraculous events are reported, such as the healing of a woman named Veronica by Jesus during his entrance to Jerusalem, which further complicates the proceedings for Pilate. 2 Witnesses, including those healed by Jesus, testify to his miracles and good deeds, presenting a stark contrast to the charges against him.

Chapter 4

1 Pilate, troubled by the situation and fearing a riot, ultimately washes his hands of the decision, symbolically declaring his innocence of Jesus' blood. The narrative emphasizes his internal conflict and reluctance to sentence Jesus. 2 Jesus is then condemned to crucifixion, and the account shifts to describe his suffering, crucifixion, and interactions with figures such as the repentant thief.

Chapter 5

1 Following the crucifixion, the narrative explores the aftermath of Jesus' death, including the veil of the temple tearing and other supernatural occurrences, signaling the momentous nature of the event. 2 Joseph of Arimathea's request to Pilate for Jesus' body is granted, and the burial process is described, setting the stage for the subsequent resurrection.

Chapter 6

1 The Gospel then recounts the harrowing of Hell, where Christ descends to the underworld to free the righteous souls who had died before his coming. 2 This section includes dialogues between Satan and Hades, personified as entities fearing the arrival of Jesus in their domain, and their eventual defeat when Jesus triumphs over death.

Chapter 7

1 With Jesus' resurrection, the narrative covers the encounters of the risen Christ with Mary Magdalene and the other disciples, emphasizing his physical resurrection and the transformation of his followers'

understanding and faith. 2 The risen Jesus commissions his disciples to spread the gospel, promising them the Holy Spirit and foreshadowing the future of the Christian movement.

Chapter 8

1 The text concludes with accounts of the disciples' testimonies to the Sanhedrin and their confrontations with Jewish leaders, who remain largely unrepentant and skeptical of the resurrection claims. 2 Nicodemus and Joseph of Arimathea are depicted as advocates for the nascent Christian community, risking their reputations and safety to support the disciples.

Chapter 9

1 The Gospel of Nicodemus also includes detailed testimonies from the guards who were stationed at Jesus' tomb, describing the events surrounding the resurrection. These guards report an earthquake and an angel descending to roll back the stone, followed by Jesus emerging from the tomb. 2 Fearing repercussions from their superiors for failing to prevent the resurrection, the guards are bribed by Jewish leaders to spread a story that Jesus' disciples stole his body while they slept.

Chapter 10

1 The narrative shifts to the broader impact of Jesus' resurrection within the community, documenting several appearances of Jesus to the disciples in various locations, reinforcing their faith and commissioning them for ministry. 2 Each appearance is described in detail, highlighting the miraculous nature of Jesus' risen body and the profound emotional and spiritual effects on his followers.

Chapter 11

1 As the early Christian community begins to grow, the text details the challenges they face from both Roman authorities and Jewish leaders. Despite these challenges, the apostles perform many miracles, similar to those of Jesus, which attract more followers. 2 These accounts serve to establish the legitimacy and continuity of apostolic power, connecting it directly to Jesus' own ministry.

Chapter 12

1 The Gospel of Nicodemus also delves into the theological implications of Jesus' teachings and actions, especially concerning the concept of justice and mercy, themes that are revisited in the interactions between Pilate, the Jewish authorities, and Jesus. 2 This section often serves as a critique of the legalistic and rigid interpretations of the law by the Sanhedrin, contrasting it with Jesus' message of compassion and divine justice.

Chapter 13

1 Nicodemus, reflecting on the events he witnessed, engages in discussions with other members of the Sanhedrin and with the growing Christian community. These discussions are depicted as pivotal moments of doctrinal formation for the early Church. 2 His role as a bridge between Jewish traditions and the new Christian theology is emphasized, showcasing his efforts to reconcile his faith in the Jewish law with his belief in Jesus as the Messiah.

Chapter 14

1 The text concludes with an appeal to the reader, urging them to consider the evidence of Jesus' divine mission and resurrection. It emphasizes the transformational power of accepting Jesus' teachings, promising eternal life and salvation to believers. 2 The Gospel of Nicodemus is framed as a testimony not just to the events of Jesus' life, death, and resurrection, but to the enduring truth and spiritual power of his message.

Chapter 15

1 The Gospel continues by addressing the broader implications of Jesus' teachings and resurrection for the Roman Empire and the world. Discussions focus on the spread of Christianity beyond Judea, depicting apostolic missions to various regions and the diverse responses they encounter. 2 The narrative underscores the universal message of Christianity, emphasizing its appeal to people of different backgrounds and its capacity to transcend cultural and geographical boundaries.

Chapter 16

1 As the apostles travel and preach, the text explores their encounters with both Gentile and Jewish communities, highlighting moments of conversion and conflict. The apostles' resilience in the face of persecution and their commitment to spreading Jesus' message are portrayed as a continuation of his ministry. 2 Miracles performed by the apostles, paralleling those of Jesus, are detailed, serving to validate their authority and the truth of their message in the eyes of skeptics and believers alike.

Chapter 17

1 The narrative returns to Nicodemus and his role within the Sanhedrin and the nascent Christian community. His dual identity as a member of the Jewish elite and a follower of Christ provides a unique perspective on the theological debates and political maneuvers of the time. 2 Nicodemus' efforts to mediate between hostile factions and to advocate for a more inclusive understanding of Jesus' message are highlighted, portraying him as a figure of wisdom and reconciliation.

Chapter 18

1 The Gospel of Nicodemus also delves into the personal transformations experienced by its characters, particularly those who initially opposed or doubted Jesus. These conversion stories are used to illustrate the profound impact of Jesus' message and the redemptive possibilities it offers. 2 Each story is framed as a testimony to the power of faith and the possibility of forgiveness, redemption, and a new life through Christ.

Chapter 19

1 The final chapters focus on the legacy of Jesus' teachings and the growth of the Church, detailing the establishment of Christian communities across the Roman Empire and the doctrinal foundations laid by the apostles. 2 The challenges of maintaining unity and integrity within the growing Church are discussed, along with the apostolic efforts to address heresies and schisms through councils and epistles.

Chapter 20

1 The Gospel concludes with a reflection on the enduring impact of Jesus' life and resurrection, calling on future generations of believers to continue the work started by the apostles. 2 It ends with an exhortation to faithfulness, perseverance in the face of persecution, and the continual pursuit of spiritual growth and understanding.

Chapter 21

1 The Gospel of Nicodemus further elaborates on the miracles that occur post-Resurrection, emphasizing their role in affirming the divinity of Christ and the truth of His teachings. These miracles serve as signs to both believers and non-believers, sparking discussions and debates within various communities. 2 These signs are depicted not only as proofs of divine power but as manifestations of divine mercy, drawing more people to the faith and deepening the spiritual lives of existing believers.

Chapter 22

1 The text explores the emotional and spiritual growth of the disciples as they transition from followers to leaders. Their journey is marked by moments of doubt and revelation, mirroring the spiritual journeys of new believers and providing a template for overcoming spiritual and worldly challenges. 2 Their development is portrayed as a testament to the transformative power of faith and the ongoing presence of Christ in guiding and empowering his followers.

Chapter 23

1 Special attention is given to the roles of lesser-known disciples and followers, highlighting their

contributions to the spread of the gospel and the building of the church. These narratives include both men and women, emphasizing the inclusive nature of the Christian message and the important roles played by all in the community. 2 These stories of lesser-known figures inspire a sense of connection and participation among all members of the community, suggesting that every believer has a role to play in the divine plan.

Chapter 24

1 The Gospel of Nicodemus addresses the philosophical and theological challenges posed by contemporary Roman and Hellenistic philosophies. Through dialogues and debates, the text articulates a Christian worldview that counters these prevalent cultural ideas, positioning Christianity as a fulfilling and comprehensive explanation of human existence and divine truth. 2 These intellectual engagements illustrate the early Christians' efforts to understand and integrate their faith with the wider world, striving to show the relevance and superiority of Christian doctrine.

Chapter 25

1 As the narrative nears its conclusion, it reflects on the martyrdoms of various disciples and early Christians, viewing these sacrifices as a continuation of Christ's own sacrifice and as a profound witness to the faith. The stories of martyrdom are used to explore themes of witness, sacrifice, and the hope of resurrection. 2 These accounts aim to fortify the resolve of the community, offering models of courage and fidelity that inspire future generations of Christians to stand firm in their beliefs.

Chapter 26

1 The final chapter serves as a call to vigilance and faithfulness, reminding the community of the constant need for spiritual diligence and the dangers of complacency. It reiterates the message that the Kingdom of God is both a present reality and a future promise that requires active participation and unwavering commitment. 2 The Gospel of Nicodemus closes with a prayerful hope for the unity and purity of the church, invoking God's guidance and protection as it continues to navigate the challenges of the world.

122. The Gospel of Peter

Chapter 1

1 The Gospel of Peter begins with the narrative of Jesus' final hours, focusing on the trial before Pilate. Peter provides a detailed account of the interactions between Jesus, Pilate, and the Jewish leaders, emphasizing the reluctance of Pilate to condemn Jesus. 2 This gospel depicts the Jewish leaders as aggressively pushing for the crucifixion, in contrast to Pilate's hesitance, portraying Pilate as more of a passive participant in the events.

Chapter 2

1 The crucifixion scene is described with particular attention to the supernatural phenomena that occur. The Gospel of Peter notes the darkening of the skies and the trembling of the earth as Jesus is crucified, suggesting divine discontent with the act. 2 Unlike the canonical gospels, this text extends the narrative to include a detailed description of the soldiers guarding the tomb, the sealing of the tomb, and the placement of seven seals on the stone.

Chapter 3

1 The resurrection is covered with dramatic flair in the Gospel of Peter. It describes how, during the night, the soldiers see the heavens open and two men descend from there with great light and approach the tomb. 2 The stone that had been placed in front of the tomb rolls away by itself, and the two men enter the tomb. Then three men are seen coming out of the tomb, with the two supporting the third, and a cross follows them. The heads of the two reached to the sky, but the head of the one they were leading by the hand reached beyond the skies.

Chapter 4

1 The voice from the heavens is heard asking, "Have you preached to those who sleep?" and the cross answers, "Yes." This mystical portrayal emphasizes the victory over death and the fulfillment of Jesus' mission to all realms, living and dead. 2 The soldiers, overwhelmed by fear, decide to go and report these events to Pilate, while being perplexed and frightened about the implications of what they witnessed.

Chapter 5

1 Following the resurrection, the narrative shifts to the reactions of the Jewish leaders and Pilate. The Jewish leaders, learning of the events at the tomb, bribe the soldiers to report that Jesus' disciples stole his body while they slept. 2 Pilate, depicted as conflicted yet pragmatic, agrees to the cover-up to maintain peace and order, but is also described as troubled by the supernatural occurrences.

Chapter 6

1 Peter reflects on the post-resurrection appearances of Jesus. The risen Jesus first appears to Mary Magdalene and "the women" who followed him, near the tomb. He gives them a message for his disciples, which establishes their role as the first evangelists of the resurrection. 2 The text emphasizes Jesus' continued presence with his disciples, guiding them and preparing them for their mission to spread the gospel.

Chapter 7

1 The Gospel of Peter concludes with an account of Jesus' final commission to his disciples, focusing on the universal scope of their mission and the promise of his spiritual support. 2 It reaffirms the authority of Peter and the apostles as designated leaders of the early church, entrusted with spreading Jesus' teachings and baptizing believers in his name.

Chapter 8

1 The Gospel of Peter further elaborates on the spread of the message of Jesus' resurrection, detailing the missionary journeys of the disciples. It describes their travels to distant lands, encountering both acceptance and resistance, as they proclaim the risen Christ. 2 This section highlights the miracles performed by the disciples, emphasizing their role as bearers of Jesus' power and authority, and as proof of the truth of their message.

Chapter 9

1 The narrative discusses the internal challenges faced by the early Christian community, including doctrinal disputes and the struggle to maintain unity in the face of rapid expansion and external persecution. 2 Peter's leadership is portrayed as crucial in these times, providing wisdom and guidance to maintain the integrity and purity of the Gospel message.

Chapter 10

1 The Gospel of Peter also addresses the return of Christ, offering a unique perspective on eschatology. It describes visions and prophecies received by members of the community, which serve to fortify their faith and offer hope in the midst of suffering. 2 This apocalyptic vision emphasizes the ultimate victory of Jesus over death and evil, promising eternal life to those who remain faithful.

Chapter 11

1 The text includes reflections on the meaning of suffering and martyrdom, suggesting that these are not only tests of faith but also participations in Christ's own sufferings. These themes are used to encourage and comfort the community during times of trial. 2 Martyrdom is portrayed as a profound witness to the power of the Gospel and as a means of achieving a closer union with Christ in his death and resurrection.

Chapter 12

1 As the Gospel nears its conclusion, it reassures the readers of God's ongoing presence and guidance through the Holy Spirit. It depicts the Spirit as active

in the community, inspiring leaders, guiding decisions, and empowering believers for service. 2 The role of the Spirit in the life of the community is described as a continuation of Jesus' earthly ministry, ensuring that his teachings and love are perpetuated among his followers.

Chapter 13

1 The final chapter serves as an exhortation to steadfastness and perseverance in the faith. It calls on the community to remain vigilant against false teachings, to uphold the teachings of Jesus, and to live out the commandments of love and service. 2 It ends with a benediction that invokes peace, unity, and the grace of Jesus Christ upon all who adhere to his words and await his coming.

Chapter 14

1 In an effort to consolidate the faith of the believers, the Gospel of Peter explores the role of the apostles as foundational figures in the church. It emphasizes their direct link to Jesus, affirming their teachings as authentic extensions of his ministry. 2 Peter specifically calls for adherence to the apostolic tradition, warning against diverging teachings that threaten to dilute or distort the core messages of Christianity.

Chapter 15

1 The Gospel touches on the theme of reconciliation within the community. It addresses conflicts that arose from cultural and doctrinal differences among the early Christians, emphasizing the need for forgiveness and unity in the pursuit of Christ's mission. 2 Peter uses his own experiences of forgiveness, both given and received, as examples for the community to emulate, promoting a culture of peace and mutual support.

Chapter 16

1 As the narrative continues, the Gospel of Peter delves into the practical aspects of community life, including the sharing of resources, communal worship, and the support of the needy. It portrays these practices as integral to living out the gospel in everyday life. 2 These descriptions serve as both a guide and an ideal for Christian communities, illustrating how the spiritual principles taught by Jesus can be manifested in concrete actions of charity and service.

Chapter 17

1 The Gospel of Peter also discusses the importance of witness beyond the immediate community. It encourages believers to engage with the broader society, not only through preaching but also through exemplary living that reflects the teachings of Jesus. 2 This outward focus is presented as a responsibility to spread the light of Christ in a world often marked by darkness and ignorance.

Chapter 18

1 In addressing the end times, the Gospel provides a detailed eschatological vision that includes signs of the apocalypse, the final judgment, and the establishment of God's kingdom. This vision is meant to offer hope and to motivate moral vigilance among believers. 2 Peter reassures the community that, despite the trials and tribulations of the present age, God's ultimate plan for creation is one of restoration and peace.

Chapter 19

1 Reflecting on the spiritual journey, the Gospel of Peter emphasizes the transformative power of faith, describing how believers are gradually changed as they deepen their relationship with God. This transformation is both personal and communal, affecting individual lives and the broader Christian community. 2 The text encourages ongoing spiritual growth and alertness, using the metaphor of the journey to illustrate the progressive nature of the Christian life, where each stage brings new challenges and deeper understandings.

Chapter 20

1 The Gospel concludes with a call to perseverance and faithfulness, echoing the teachings of Jesus about the narrow path that leads to life. It encourages believers to remain steadfast in their faith, to be diligent in prayer, and to be unyielding in the face of adversity. 2 The final words are a blessing, invoking the grace of the Lord Jesus Christ to sustain the community in love and faith until the day of his return.

Chapter 21

1 The Gospel of Peter elaborates on the mechanisms of spiritual warfare, emphasizing the believer's need to arm themselves with virtues such as faith, hope, and love, portrayed as spiritual armor against evil. Peter explains that these virtues protect against the spiritual deceit and temptations that believers face daily. 2 He further discusses the importance of community prayer and collective faith as shields against external pressures that threaten to undermine the Christian moral framework and doctrinal integrity.

Chapter 22

1 Addressing the sacraments, Peter underscores their significance in nurturing the spiritual life of believers. He provides detailed teachings on baptism, the Eucharist, and other rites, portraying them as not only symbolic acts but also as real encounters with the divine grace that strengthen the soul. 2 The sacraments are described as essential practices for maintaining a vibrant and sustaining faith, integral to the continuous process of salvation and sanctification in the life of a Christian.

Chapter 23

1 Peter reflects on the leadership roles within the church, emphasizing the need for leaders to be servants first, following the example set by Jesus. He stresses humility, selflessness, and dedication as key virtues for anyone in a position of authority within the church. 2 He warns against the dangers of power and pride, recounting biblical examples and teachings of Jesus that highlight the corrupting influence of authority when detached from divine love and service.

Chapter 24

1 As the narrative draws to its close, Peter calls for vigilance against false prophets and teachers who might appear within the community. He instructs the church on how to discern true teachings from false ones based on their alignment with the words of Jesus and their fruits in terms of promoting peace, justice, and love. 2 He encourages the community to remain steadfast in the teachings they received from the apostles, safeguarding the deposit of faith through diligent study, prayer, and adherence to the Holy Spirit's guidance.

Chapter 25

1 The Gospel concludes with a powerful reminder of the resurrection and the life to come, offering comfort and hope to believers facing persecution and suffering. Peter reassures them that the trials of this world are temporary and that the promise of eternal life with Christ transcends any earthly pain or distress. 2 He ends with a doxology, glorifying God for His mercy, justice, and the unfathomable love He has shown through Jesus Christ, calling all believers to look forward to the fulfillment of God's kingdom in hope and joy.

Chapter 26

1 In this final exhortation, Peter emphasizes the importance of living a life that reflects the teachings of Jesus. He encourages believers to embody the virtues of compassion, humility, and forgiveness in their daily interactions, reinforcing the idea that the Christian life is a continuous journey of spiritual growth and moral integrity. 2 He highlights the significance of love as the highest commandment, urging the community to love one another deeply, as love covers a multitude of sins and binds the community together in unity and purpose.

Chapter 27

1 Peter also addresses the necessity of perseverance in the face of trials and persecution. He reminds the

believers that suffering for the sake of righteousness is a form of participation in Christ's own sufferings and that such trials should be met with joy and steadfastness, knowing that they refine faith and produce endurance. 2 He encourages the community to support one another in times of difficulty, sharing in each other's burdens and providing strength through mutual encouragement and prayer.

Chapter 28

1 Reflecting on the nature of God's kingdom, Peter describes it as both a present reality and a future hope. He teaches that the kingdom is manifested wherever God's will is done on earth, but its fullness will only be realized at the end of the age when Christ returns in glory. 2 This dual perspective on the kingdom serves as both a motivation for ethical living in the present and a source of hope for the future, reminding believers that their ultimate citizenship is in heaven.

Chapter 29

1 Peter concludes by reiterating the importance of keeping the faith pure and uncorrupted by worldly influences. He calls on the community to remain vigilant against false teachings that seek to dilute the gospel's message and to hold fast to the apostolic traditions handed down to them. 2 He warns that in the last days, there will be many who will try to lead believers astray, but those who remain rooted in the teachings of Christ will be protected by God's grace and will inherit eternal life.

Chapter 30

1 The Gospel of Peter ends with a final blessing, invoking God's peace and grace upon the community. Peter prays that the believers will continue to grow in knowledge and love of God, and that they will be strengthened to carry out the mission entrusted to them by Christ. 2 The closing words are a call to remain faithful and to eagerly await the return of Jesus, living in a manner worthy of the calling they have received.

123. The Gospel of Bartholomew

Chapter 1

1 The Gospel of Bartholomew begins with Bartholomew, one of the twelve apostles, seeking answers to the mysteries of Christ's divinity and the events of the resurrection. 2 Bartholomew asks Jesus to reveal more about his descent into Hades, where Jesus went after his crucifixion to free the souls of the righteous.

Chapter 2

1 Jesus, in response, explains the descent into Hades in vivid detail. He describes how the gates of Hell trembled at his approach and how the powers of darkness were thrown into confusion. 2 Satan, realizing who had entered his domain, attempted to resist but was powerless before the might of Jesus. Jesus recounts how he broke the chains of the righteous and led them out of the darkness into the light.

Chapter 3

1 Bartholomew, awed by this revelation, then asks Jesus about the nature of his incarnation—how the Word of God could take on human flesh. Jesus explains that the mystery of his incarnation is beyond human comprehension, but that it was necessary for the salvation of mankind. 2 Jesus also touches on the relationship between his divine and human natures, emphasizing that, though he took on flesh, he did not cease to be fully divine.

Chapter 4

1 The apostle then inquires about the Virgin Mary's experience during the incarnation and her role in God's plan. Mary, who is present, is invited by Jesus to speak about her experiences. 2 Mary recounts the Annunciation, her encounter with the angel Gabriel, and the miraculous conception of Jesus. She shares her thoughts and feelings, emphasizing her humility and obedience to God's will.

Chapter 5

1 Bartholomew, seeking further insight, asks Jesus about the end times and what signs will precede his second coming. Jesus describes the signs in great detail: wars, natural disasters, the rise of false prophets, and the increase of wickedness among humanity. 2 He warns that only those who remain vigilant and faithful will be prepared for his return, urging his followers to live righteously and to spread the gospel to all nations.

Chapter 6

1 The discussion then turns to the fate of the souls after death. Bartholomew asks Jesus what happens to the souls of the righteous and the wicked. Jesus explains that the righteous are taken by angels to paradise, where they await the final resurrection. 2 The wicked, however, are consigned to a place of torment, where they suffer until the day of judgment. Jesus emphasizes the importance of repentance and faith as the means to avoid this fate.

Chapter 7

1 Finally, Bartholomew asks about the nature of angels and their roles in the divine plan. Jesus explains that angels are messengers and servants of God, tasked with various roles such as guiding the faithful, delivering divine messages, and executing God's judgments. 2 Jesus reveals that each believer has a guardian angel who watches over them and helps them in their spiritual journey.

Chapter 8

1 The Gospel of Bartholomew concludes with a prayer by the apostle, thanking Jesus for revealing these profound mysteries and asking for the strength to faithfully carry out his mission. 2 Jesus blesses Bartholomew and the other apostles, encouraging them to continue spreading the gospel and to remain steadfast in their faith despite the trials they will face.

Chapter 9

1 After the prayer, Jesus opens a discussion on the nature of true worship, explaining that God desires worship in spirit and truth, not merely through rituals and sacrifices. He emphasizes that true worship comes from the heart and is reflected in how one lives their life. 2 Bartholomew, eager to understand, asks Jesus how the disciples can maintain such pure worship amidst the distractions and challenges of the world. Jesus advises them to cultivate a life of prayer, fasting, and meditation on God's word, which will help them stay connected to the divine.

Chapter 10

1 The conversation shifts to the topic of spiritual warfare. Bartholomew asks Jesus how believers can defend themselves against the attacks of the evil one. Jesus instructs them on the power of faith, prayer, and the use of his name as a weapon against evil forces. 2 Jesus also talks about the importance of the community of believers, encouraging the apostles to support one another in faith and to be vigilant in guarding against spiritual complacency.

Chapter 11

1 Bartholomew, still filled with questions, inquires about the nature of the Holy Spirit and how it works within the lives of believers. Jesus explains that the Holy Spirit is the comforter and guide, sent to empower the disciples and to lead them into all truth. 2 He elaborates on the gifts of the Spirit, such as wisdom, knowledge, healing, and prophecy, and how these gifts are given to build up the church and to help believers live according to God's will.

Chapter 12

1 The apostles are then granted a vision of the heavenly realms, where they see the glory of God's throne and the hosts of angels worshipping around it. This vision strengthens their resolve and deepens their understanding of the divine reality that underpins their mission on earth. 2 Jesus explains that this vision is a glimpse of the inheritance that awaits the faithful, encouraging them to remain

steadfast and to persevere in their work, knowing that their labor is not in vain.

Chapter 13

1 Bartholomew expresses concern for the future of the church, asking Jesus how the apostles can ensure that the truth of the gospel is preserved after they are gone. Jesus reassures them that the Holy Spirit will continue to guide the church and that the gates of hell will not prevail against it. 2 He also emphasizes the importance of passing on the teachings faithfully, encouraging the apostles to train others who will carry on their work, thus ensuring the continuity of the Christian faith.

Chapter 14

1 The final teachings of Jesus in the Gospel of Bartholomew focus on the theme of love. He reiterates that love is the greatest commandment and the foundation of all his teachings. He urges the apostles to love one another and to show this love through their actions, particularly in their care for the poor, the sick, and the marginalized. 2 Jesus promises that those who live in love will know God and will be recognized as his disciples, for love is the true mark of a follower of Christ.

Chapter 15

1 The Gospel concludes with a blessing from Jesus. He blesses the apostles and all who will believe in their message, praying for their protection and success in spreading the gospel to the ends of the earth. 2 As the apostles depart to carry out their mission, they are filled with the Holy Spirit, empowered to perform miracles, and inspired to teach the truth of Jesus Christ with boldness and clarity.

Chapter 16

1 As the apostles begin to disperse to different regions, the Gospel of Bartholomew recounts their final moments together, highlighting the sense of unity and purpose that binds them. They each commit to spreading the teachings of Jesus, aware of the challenges ahead but confident in the power of the Holy Spirit guiding them. 2 Bartholomew, in particular, reflects on his mission with a renewed sense of dedication. He feels the weight of the responsibility given to him but is also filled with the peace and assurance that comes from Christ's blessing.

Chapter 17

1 The text then transitions to describe the apostles' early missionary efforts. Bartholomew travels to various lands, encountering different cultures and beliefs. The Gospel provides detailed accounts of his interactions with local leaders, scholars, and religious figures, emphasizing his ability to communicate the gospel in ways that resonate with diverse audiences. 2 Through Bartholomew's teachings, many are converted, and small Christian communities begin to form. The narrative highlights the miracles performed by Bartholomew, such as healings and exorcisms, which serve to authenticate his message and draw more people to the faith.

Chapter 18

1 Bartholomew also faces significant opposition and persecution, particularly from those who feel threatened by the spread of Christianity. The Gospel describes instances where Bartholomew is imprisoned, tortured, and even brought before local rulers to defend his faith. 2 Despite these hardships, Bartholomew remains steadfast, using these trials as opportunities to witness to the truth of Christ. His resilience and unwavering faith inspire others, leading to conversions even among those who initially opposed him.

Chapter 19

1 The Gospel of Bartholomew provides a profound meditation on the nature of suffering and its role in the life of a believer. Bartholomew views his sufferings as a participation in Christ's own sufferings, seeing them as a means of drawing closer to God and bearing witness to the power of the gospel. 2 This chapter encourages readers to embrace their own trials with faith, understanding that suffering, when endured for Christ's sake, is redemptive and transformative.

Chapter 20

1 Bartholomew's journey eventually leads him to India, where he encounters a land rich in spiritual traditions but largely untouched by the Christian message. The Gospel describes his interactions with local religious leaders, emphasizing a respectful dialogue in which Bartholomew seeks to understand their beliefs while also presenting the truth of Christ. 2 Through a combination of miracles and deep theological discussions, Bartholomew gains the respect of many and converts several key figures, laying the foundation for the Christian church in the region.

Chapter 21

1 The Gospel concludes with Bartholomew's martyrdom, detailing the events leading up to his death. The text portrays his martyrdom not as a defeat but as the ultimate testimony of his faith and love for Christ. Bartholomew is depicted as going to his death with courage and peace, fully trusting in the promises of Jesus. 2 His martyrdom inspires many who witness it, leading to a wave of conversions and the strengthening of the Christian community in the area. The Gospel ends with a reflection on the lasting impact of Bartholomew's life and mission, encouraging believers to follow his example of faithfulness and devotion.

Chapter 22

1 The final chapter of the Gospel of Bartholomew offers a prayer for the church, asking for God's continued guidance and protection for all believers. It emphasizes the importance of remaining true to the teachings of Jesus and the apostles, urging the church to stand firm in the face of trials and to continue spreading the gospel to all nations. 2 The Gospel closes with a benediction, blessing all who read and live by its teachings, promising them the same peace and assurance that sustained Bartholomew throughout his life and ministry.

Chapter 23

1 The Gospel of Bartholomew recounts the immediate aftermath of Bartholomew's martyrdom, focusing on the impact his death had on the local Christian community. His followers, though grieving, are strengthened by his example and continue the work he began with renewed vigor. 2 The text describes how the seeds of faith that Bartholomew planted begin to flourish, with new converts joining the church and existing believers deepening their commitment to the teachings of Christ.

Chapter 24

1 This chapter highlights the efforts of Bartholomew's disciples to preserve his teachings and ensure that his legacy endures. They compile his sermons, letters, and other writings, which are shared among the growing Christian communities across the region. 2 These writings are portrayed as a source of inspiration and guidance, offering insights into the mysteries of faith and practical advice for living a Christian life in a hostile world.

Chapter 25

1 The Gospel then shifts focus to the broader impact of Bartholomew's mission, emphasizing how the news of his martyrdom and the miracles associated with his ministry spread far and wide. This leads to increased interest in Christianity among people who had previously been indifferent or hostile. 2 Several high-ranking officials and scholars are described as being drawn to the faith, not only because of the miraculous stories but also because of the profound wisdom and love evident in Bartholomew's teachings.

Chapter 26

1 As Christianity continues to spread, the Gospel of Bartholomew addresses the challenges of maintaining doctrinal purity and unity within the

rapidly expanding church. The text warns against false teachings and emphasizes the importance of adhering to the apostolic tradition as taught by Bartholomew and the other apostles. 2 It also encourages the establishment of strong leadership within the church, with elders and bishops tasked with safeguarding the faith and guiding the believers in righteousness.

Chapter 27
1 The narrative reflects on the importance of prayer and fasting in the life of a Christian, drawing from Bartholomew's own practices. It emphasizes that these disciplines are essential for spiritual growth, protection from temptation, and maintaining a close relationship with God. 2 The Gospel encourages believers to adopt a disciplined life, using the examples of Bartholomew and other saints as models for how to live a life dedicated to God's service.

Chapter 28
1 The text revisits the theme of martyrdom, expanding on its spiritual significance. It teaches that martyrdom is the ultimate witness to Christ, a profound act of love and faith that echoes Jesus' own sacrifice. 2 The chapter discusses how the blood of the martyrs serves as the seed of the church, inspiring others to faith and fortifying the community against persecution.

Chapter 29
1 The Gospel of Bartholomew also includes a series of prophetic visions granted to Bartholomew before his death. These visions are interpreted as divine revelations about the future of the church, the challenges it will face, and the ultimate triumph of Christ's kingdom. 2 The visions offer hope and encouragement to believers, reminding them that, despite the trials they may endure, God's plan is unfolding and will culminate in victory over evil.

Chapter 30
1 The final chapter reflects on the enduring legacy of Bartholomew, not just in the regions where he preached, but across the entire Christian world. His life and death are portrayed as a testament to the power of faith, the importance of apostolic teaching, and the transformative effect of the gospel. 2 The Gospel closes with a final prayer, asking for God's continued blessings on the church and all its members, invoking the intercession of Bartholomew and the other apostles to help guide the faithful on their spiritual journey.

Chapter 31
1 In this concluding section, the Gospel of Bartholomew highlights the role of community in sustaining the faith. Bartholomew's disciples continue to gather regularly, sharing stories of his teachings and their experiences, which strengthens their collective resolve to live according to the gospel. 2 The text emphasizes the importance of fellowship among believers, encouraging them to support each other through prayer, shared meals, and acts of kindness, echoing the communal practices established by the early church.

Chapter 32
1 The Gospel offers practical advice on how to deal with persecution. It recounts the strategies employed by Bartholomew and his followers, such as gathering in secret and using symbols and coded language to communicate with one another. 2 It also encourages Christians to remain bold in their faith, despite the risks, promising that those who persevere will receive great rewards in the life to come.

Chapter 33
1 This chapter explores the theological implications of Bartholomew's martyrdom, framing it as a continuation of the redemptive suffering that began with Jesus. Bartholomew is depicted as a mirror of Christ, whose death serves as a witness to the power of sacrificial love. 2 The Gospel urges believers to see their own sufferings as a way to participate in the mystery of Christ's passion, thereby drawing closer to God.

Chapter 34
1 The Gospel addresses the importance of maintaining the purity of the faith in an increasingly pluralistic world. Bartholomew's teachings are upheld as a standard against which all other doctrines should be measured, warning against the dangers of syncretism and the dilution of Christian teachings. 2 The text emphasizes the need for vigilance in preserving the apostolic teachings, urging church leaders to guard against false prophets and to ensure that the true gospel is passed down unchanged.

Chapter 35
1 Reflecting on the global mission of the church, the Gospel of Bartholomew encourages believers to continue the work of evangelism, taking the message of Christ to all corners of the earth. It portrays Bartholomew as a pioneer who opened new territories to the gospel, inspiring others to follow in his footsteps. 2 The text reminds Christians that the Great Commission given by Jesus is an ongoing task, one that requires dedication, courage, and a willingness to endure hardship for the sake of the kingdom.

Chapter 36
1 The narrative returns to the themes of prayer and spiritual discipline, offering a series of prayers attributed to Bartholomew. These prayers are intended to guide believers in their personal devotions, covering aspects such as seeking God's will, asking for strength in times of trial, and giving thanks for blessings received. 2 The chapter serves as a devotional guide, helping readers to deepen their spiritual lives and to maintain a close relationship with God.

Chapter 37
1 The Gospel concludes with an epilogue that reflects on Bartholomew's legacy. It recounts how, after his death, his tomb became a site of pilgrimage, where many came to seek healing and spiritual guidance. 2 The text emphasizes that Bartholomew's influence continues through the communities he founded, the teachings he left behind, and the lives he touched through his ministry.

Chapter 38
1 The final prayer of the Gospel of Bartholomew asks for God's continued protection and guidance for all believers, invoking the intercession of the apostle and all the saints who have gone before. It is a prayer for perseverance, unity, and the spread of the gospel until the end of time. 2 The Gospel closes with a benediction, blessing all who read it and commit to living out the teachings of Jesus as faithfully as Bartholomew did.

124. The Epistle of Ignatius to the Smyrnaeans

Chapter 1
1 Ignatius, also called Theophorus, to the church of God the Father and the beloved of Jesus Christ, in Smyrna, in Asia, wishes abundance of happiness, with blameless joy in God, the Father, and in our Lord Jesus Christ.

Chapter 2
1 I glorify God, even Jesus Christ, who has given you such wisdom. For I have observed that you are perfected in an immovable faith, as if you were nailed to the cross of our Lord Jesus Christ, both in flesh and spirit, and are confirmed in love by the blood of Christ, being fully persuaded of our Lord's resurrection and firmly believing in it.

Chapter 3
1 You also embrace with a worthy mind all those who are in bonds as fitting members of the church and who bear the blood of the martyrs as being members of Jesus Christ, whom you have loved both in the

flesh and spirit, keeping the faith by a well-ordered life.

Chapter 4

1 But I caution you to avoid those who deny the Lord's resurrection and have no belief in the judgment to come. For they are opposed to the faith, and it is necessary that we should be watchful in our faith against such people.

Chapter 5

1 Let no one be deceived: even the heavenly beings and the glory of the angels, and the rulers visible and invisible, if they do not believe in the blood of Christ, they also shall incur judgment. 2 He that receives it, let him receive it. Let no man be deceived: if anyone does not profess that Jesus Christ has come in the flesh, he is antichrist.

Chapter 6

1 And if anyone does not confess the mystery of the cross, he is of the devil. If anyone perverts the sayings of the Lord to his own lusts and says that there is neither resurrection nor judgment, he is the first-born of Satan. 2 Let us, therefore, leave the vanity of many and their false doctrines and return to the word which was delivered to us from the beginning, watching and praying with perseverance.

Chapter 7

1 I have observed that you are full of faith and charity, and every one of you has the desire to gather the flock together for the glory of God. 2 Flee from divisions and evil doctrines; but where the shepherd is, there follow as sheep.

Chapter 8

1 For many wolves are in sheep's clothing, who, by evil pleasure, lead captive those that run into the way of God; but in your unity, they shall have no place. 2 Be careful of those who have strange opinions about the grace of Jesus Christ, which has come to us. And note how contrary they are to the mind of God. For love of the world, they pervert the word and neglect to care for the brethren.

Chapter 9

1 Therefore, I exhort you to live in godliness and be steadfast in faith, for these people speak against the gifts of God, and it is necessary to refrain from them. 2 For such are the kind that mix up Jesus Christ with their own misinterpretations, causing both themselves and those who listen to them to perish.

Chapter 10

1 For I have heard that some have said, "Unless I find it in the archives, I will not believe it in the gospel." And when I said, "It is written," they answered, "That remains to be proved." 2 But to me, the archives are Jesus Christ, and the inviolable archives are His cross, and His death, and His resurrection, and the faith that comes by Him; by these things I desire to be justified.

Chapter 11

1 The priests indeed are good, but the High Priest is better; the four corners of the earth are good, but the pillar is better; the door is good, but the house is better; the lamp is good, but the sun is better. 2 Be on guard, therefore, in these last times. The end of all things is at hand; keep watch for the adversary, for he desires to lead you away from your salvation.

Chapter 12

1 Let all, therefore, return to the knowledge of Christ's resurrection. This is the crown of joy, and the faith that was preached throughout the world. And it is through this resurrection that life rises up again in all of us who believe.

Chapter 13

1 I salute your bishops, that you may be well instructed in the faith of Jesus Christ, who was the Son of David and the Son of God, born of a virgin, and baptized by John, that all righteousness might be fulfilled by Him.

Chapter 14

1 Stand firm in the tradition of the apostles. They have pointed out the gospel of Jesus Christ, and it is the foundation of the church, and let everyone do their part with love. 2 Let no man be idle; let everyone be filled with the love of God, and in this let them edify one another with a perfect heart, in the faith of the resurrection.

Chapter 15

1 I salute your bishop, and your priests, and your deacons, and the whole church, being sanctified in Jesus Christ, and all those who love God in sincerity. 2 Pray for me that I may obtain what I desire, to be found in the inheritance of the faithful.

Chapter 16

1 Farewell in the Lord. Be of one mind and one spirit in God. Be followers of Jesus Christ, as He was of His Father. 2 And I pray that you may abound more and more in faith, hope, and charity, and that all may be confirmed in the gospel of our Lord Jesus Christ, both in the flesh and in the spirit.

Chapter 17

1 As Ignatius concludes his letter, he exhorts the Smyrnaeans to remain steadfast in their faith, particularly in the face of false teachings that deny the resurrection of Christ and the reality of His incarnation. 2 He stresses that such heresies must be confronted with the truth of the gospel, which has been faithfully handed down by the apostles and preserved by the church.

Chapter 18

1 Ignatius reminds the believers that their unity with their bishop is crucial for maintaining the integrity of the faith. He urges them to follow their bishop as Christ follows the Father and to respect the priests as they would the apostles. 2 This unity, he argues, is a reflection of the unity that exists within the Godhead and is essential for the church to function as the body of Christ.

Chapter 19

1 He continues by emphasizing the importance of the Eucharist, which he describes as "the medicine of immortality" and "the antidote against death." He encourages the Smyrnaeans to partake in the Eucharist frequently, as it is a means of participating in the life of Christ and the unity of the church. 2 Ignatius warns against those who abstain from the Eucharist or distort its meaning, labeling them as spiritually sick and in need of repentance.

Chapter 20

1 Ignatius speaks of his impending martyrdom, expressing his desire to be with Christ and his willingness to suffer for the faith. He sees his martyrdom as a way to glorify God and to inspire others to stand firm in their faith. 2 He asks the Smyrnaeans to pray for him, that he may remain faithful until the end and that his martyrdom may serve as a witness to the truth of the gospel.

Chapter 21

1 Ignatius closes his letter with a final exhortation to love one another and to remain faithful to the teachings of Christ. He reminds the Smyrnaeans that they are the light of the world and the salt of the earth, called to live lives that reflect the holiness and love of God. 2 He prays for their continued growth in faith, hope, and love, and asks that they remember him in their prayers as he faces his final journey.

Chapter 22

1 The letter concludes with a blessing, in which Ignatius invokes the grace of God the Father and the Lord Jesus Christ upon the church in Smyrna. He prays that they may be preserved in unity and truth, and that they may continue to shine as a beacon of faith in a world filled with darkness. 2 Ignatius expresses his hope that they will remain steadfast in the apostolic tradition, holding fast to the teachings that have been passed down to them and living lives worthy of the calling they have received in Christ Jesus.

125. The Martyrdom of Polycarp

Chapter 1
1 The church of God which sojourns at Smyrna, to the church of God sojourning in Philomelium, and to all the congregations of the holy and universal church in every place: Mercy, peace, and love from God the Father and our Lord Jesus Christ be multiplied.

Chapter 2
1 We write to you, brethren, the account of those who were martyred, especially the blessed Polycarp, who put an end to the persecution by sealing it with his own blood. For nearly all the events that led up to it reveal to us the providence of the Lord.

Chapter 3
1 When the proconsul of Asia issued a decree that the Christians should be put to death, the most distinguished of the citizens began to hunt for Polycarp, determined to capture him. 2 However, Polycarp was unperturbed and decided to remain in the city. But when he was urged by his friends to withdraw, he went out to a small estate not far from the city and stayed with a few companions.

Chapter 4
1 There he spent his time praying, night and day, for all people and for the churches throughout the world, as was his usual custom. And while praying, he fell into a trance three days before his arrest and saw his pillow burning with fire. 2 Turning to those who were with him, he said prophetically, "I must be burned alive."

Chapter 5
1 When the soldiers came to arrest him, Polycarp could have escaped, but he refused, saying, "The will of God be done." He greeted them cheerfully and ordered that food and drink be set before them as much as they wished. 2 He then asked for permission to pray without disturbance, which they granted. He stood and prayed, full of the grace of God, for nearly two hours, to the astonishment of those who heard him.

Chapter 6
1 After his prayer, they set him upon a donkey and led him into the city. It was a great Sabbath day, and the crowd gathered in the stadium. 2 As Polycarp entered the stadium, a voice from heaven said, "Be strong, Polycarp, and play the man." No one saw who had spoken, but those of our brethren who were present heard the voice.

Chapter 7
1 When he was brought before the proconsul, the proconsul urged him to renounce his faith, saying, "Swear by the fortune of Caesar; repent and say, 'Away with the atheists.'" 2 But Polycarp, looking with a serious countenance upon the multitude of lawless heathen in the stadium, waved his hand toward them and, looking up to heaven, groaned and said, "Away with the atheists."

Chapter 8
1 The proconsul then pressed him further, "Swear, and I will release you; curse Christ." 2 Polycarp answered, "Eighty and six years have I served Him, and He has done me no wrong. How then can I blaspheme my King and Savior?"

Chapter 9
1 The proconsul continued to insist, "I have wild beasts; I will throw you to them if you do not repent." 2 Polycarp replied, "Call them, for repentance from better to worse is not permitted us; but it is good to change from evil to righteousness."

Chapter 10
1 The proconsul said again, "If you despise the wild beasts, I will make you to be consumed by fire, unless you repent." 2 But Polycarp answered, "You threaten with fire that burns for an hour and after a little is extinguished, but you are ignorant of the fire of the coming judgment and of eternal punishment reserved for the ungodly. Why do you delay? Bring forth what you will."

Chapter 11
1 The proconsul was astonished and sent the herald to proclaim three times in the middle of the stadium, "Polycarp has confessed that he is a Christian." 2 The multitude, hearing this proclamation, cried out with uncontrollable rage that he should be burned alive. They immediately began to gather wood and other combustibles from the workshops and baths.

Chapter 12
1 When the pile was ready, Polycarp took off his outer garments, loosened his belt, and tried to take off his sandals, something he had not been used to doing because the faithful were always eager to touch his skin. 2 When they were about to nail him to the stake, he said, "Leave me as I am; for He who grants me to endure the fire will also enable me to remain on the pyre unmoved, without the security you desire from nails."

Chapter 13
1 So they did not nail him but bound him. Then Polycarp, with his hands bound behind him, like a distinguished ram taken out of a great flock for sacrifice, prepared himself to be a burnt offering acceptable to God. 2 Looking up to heaven, he said, "O Lord God Almighty, the Father of Your beloved and blessed Son Jesus Christ, through whom we have received the knowledge of You, the God of angels and powers and every creature, and of all the righteous who live before You, I give You thanks that You have counted me worthy of this day and this hour, that I should have a part in the number of Your martyrs, in the cup of Christ, for the resurrection to eternal life, both of soul and body, in the incorruption of the Holy Spirit. Among them may I be accepted this day before You as a rich and acceptable sacrifice, as You, the faithful and true God, have beforehand prepared, have revealed, and have fulfilled. Therefore, I also praise You for all things; I bless You, I glorify You, through the eternal High Priest, Jesus Christ, Your beloved Son, through whom, with Him and the Holy Spirit, be glory both now and for the ages to come. Amen."

Chapter 14
1 When he had offered up this prayer, the fire was lit, and a great flame blazed forth. We who were privileged to witness it saw a wondrous sight. The fire, taking the shape of a vault, like the sail of a ship filled by the wind, formed a wall around the martyr's body. 2 And he was in the midst, not as burning flesh, but as bread baking or as gold and silver refined in a furnace. For we perceived such a sweet aroma as the breath of incense or some other precious spice.

Chapter 15
1 At length, when those wicked men saw that his body could not be consumed by the fire, they commanded an executioner to approach and pierce him with a dagger. When he did this, such a great quantity of blood flowed that it extinguished the fire. 2 The crowd, seeing this, marveled at the difference between the unbelievers and the elect, the blessed martyr Polycarp being one of the number of the elect.

Chapter 16
1 All the people marveled at the greatness of his faith, and since the enemies of the righteous plotted to prevent his body from being carried away by the Christians, lest they abandon the crucified one and begin to worship Polycarp, they knew not that we could never either forsake Christ, who suffered for the salvation of the world, or worship any other. For Him, indeed, we worship as the Son of God, but the martyrs we love as disciples and imitators of the Lord.

Chapter 17
1 When the centurion saw the contentiousness caused by the Jews, he placed the body in the middle of the fire and burned it, according to their custom. Then we took up the bones, more precious than refined gold, and laid them where it was fitting. 2 There, we will gather together as we are able, in gladness and joy, and celebrate the birthday of his

martyrdom.

Chapter 18

1 This is the account of the blessed Polycarp, who, being the twelfth martyr in Smyrna, yet occupies a place of his own in the memory of all, even among the Gentiles. It was for this that he was taken by the guards, for he had preached for many years, and by his example, he taught that it is necessary to endure martyrdom without hesitation. 2 He fulfilled his course in an acceptable manner and is now received into the place of the martyrs, alongside the apostles, and with all the righteous, he glorifies God, the Father Almighty, and blesses our Lord Jesus Christ, the Savior of our souls, the Governor of our bodies, and the Shepherd of the church.

Chapter 19

1 The church of Smyrna acknowledges the authenticity of this account, which has been transcribed by Gaius from the letters of Irenaeus, who was a disciple of Polycarp, who lived in peace with the faithful and joyfully received the martyr's crown. 2 This account has been compiled by us and attested by our brethren, so that the Lord Jesus Christ may be glorified through the memory of His faithful martyr.

126. The Acts of Pilate

Part I: The Trial of Jesus
Chapter 1

1 In the fifteenth year of the government of Tiberius Caesar, a king whose name was Herod reigned in Galilee, and the high priest was Caiaphas. And Jesus, full of wisdom and knowledge, was performing many great signs and wonders in the land. 2 The Jews became envious and filled with hatred, and they handed Him over to the Roman governor, Pontius Pilate, accusing Him of various crimes.

Chapter 2

1 Pilate, upon hearing these accusations, summoned Jesus and asked Him, "Are you the King of the Jews?" Jesus answered, "You say that I am a king. For this purpose, I was born, and for this purpose, I have come into the world—to bear witness to the truth. Everyone who is of the truth listens to my voice." 2 Pilate, perplexed, asked, "What is truth?" but did not wait for an answer. Instead, he returned to the chief priests and the crowd, saying, "I find no fault in this man."

Chapter 3

1 The chief priests and elders, however, insisted, saying, "He stirs up the people, teaching throughout all Judea, beginning from Galilee to this place." When Pilate heard of Galilee, he asked if the man were a Galilean. 2 Upon learning that Jesus was under Herod's jurisdiction, he sent Him to Herod, who was also in Jerusalem at that time.

Chapter 4

1 Herod was exceedingly glad to see Jesus, for he had desired to see Him for a long time, having heard many things about Him. He hoped to see some miracle done by Him. 2 He questioned Jesus with many words, but Jesus gave him no answer. The chief priests and scribes stood by, vehemently accusing Him. Herod, with his men of war, treated Him with contempt, mocked Him, arrayed Him in a gorgeous robe, and sent Him back to Pilate.

Chapter 5

1 Pilate called together the chief priests, the rulers, and the people, and said to them, "You have brought this man to me as one who perverts the people, and behold, I have examined Him before you and found no fault in this man concerning those things of which you accuse Him. No, nor did Herod, for I sent you back to him; and indeed, nothing deserving death has been done by Him." 2 Pilate, wanting to release Jesus, said, "I will therefore chastise Him and release Him."

Chapter 6

1 But they cried out all at once, saying, "Away with this man, and release to us Barabbas"—who had been thrown into prison for a certain rebellion made in the city, and for murder. 2 Pilate, therefore, wanting to release Jesus, again called out to them, but they shouted, "Crucify Him, crucify Him!"

Chapter 7

1 Pilate said to them the third time, "Why, what evil has He done? I have found no reason for death in Him. I will therefore chastise Him and let Him go." 2 But they were insistent, demanding with loud voices that He be crucified. And the voices of these men and of the chief priests prevailed.

Chapter 8

1 Pilate, seeing that he could not prevail, but rather that a tumult was rising, took water and washed his hands before the multitude, saying, "I am innocent of the blood of this just person. You see to it." 2 And all the people answered and said, "His blood be on us and on our children." Then Pilate released Barabbas to them, and when he had scourged Jesus, he delivered Him to be crucified.

Part II: The Descent into Hell
Chapter 9

1 And it was about the sixth hour, and there was darkness over all the earth until the ninth hour. The sun was darkened, and the veil of the temple was torn in the middle. 2 And Jesus cried out with a loud voice, "Father, into Your hands I commit My spirit." Having said this, He breathed His last.

Chapter 10

1 When Jesus had risen from the dead, He descended into Hell to free the righteous who had died before His coming. There, He met Adam, the patriarchs, and the prophets, who rejoiced at His coming. 2 Satan, the prince of Hell, argued with Hades, saying, "Who is this that has come here to take captives from my dominion?" But Hades was powerless to resist, for the light of Christ had pierced the darkness, and the chains of the righteous were broken.

Chapter 11

1 Jesus took the hand of Adam and led him and all the righteous out of Hell, saying, "Come, all you blessed of My Father, inherit the kingdom prepared for you from the foundation of the world." 2 The gates of Hell were shattered, and the way to eternal life was opened for all who believe in Him. The saints who had been held captive in Hell followed Jesus to the gates of Heaven, where they were received with great joy.

Chapter 12

1 As they entered Heaven, the angels sang praises, saying, "Lift up your heads, O you gates! And be lifted up, you everlasting doors, and the King of glory shall come in." 2 The Lord Jesus Christ ascended in glory, leading the captives with Him, and sat at the right hand of God the Father, where He reigns forever.

Part III: The Resurrection and Appearances of Jesus
Chapter 13

1 On the first day of the week, Mary Magdalene, Mary the mother of James, and Salome came to the tomb to anoint the body of Jesus. They found the stone rolled away and the tomb empty. 2 An angel appeared to them and said, "Do not be afraid, for I know that you seek Jesus who was crucified. He is not here; for He is risen, as He said. Come, see the place where the Lord lay."

Chapter 14

1 The women, trembling and bewildered, ran to tell the disciples. Peter and John came to the tomb and found it just as the women had said. 2 Jesus appeared to Mary Magdalene and said, "Mary." She turned and said to Him, "Rabboni!" Jesus said, "Do not cling to Me, for I have not yet ascended to My Father; but go to My brethren and say to them, 'I am ascending to My Father and your Father, and to My God and your God.'"

Chapter 15
1 Jesus appeared to two of His disciples on the road to Emmaus, though they did not recognize Him at first. As He broke bread with them, their eyes were opened, and they knew Him; then He vanished from their sight. 2 They returned to Jerusalem and told the other disciples, "The Lord is risen indeed, and has appeared to Simon!"

Chapter 16
1 Jesus appeared to the eleven disciples as they sat at the table. He rebuked their unbelief and hardness of heart because they did not believe those who had seen Him after He had risen. 2 He said to them, "Go into all the world and preach the gospel to every creature. He who believes and is baptized will be saved, but he who does not believe will be condemned."

Chapter 17
1 Jesus led them out as far as Bethany, and He lifted up His hands and blessed them. While He blessed them, He was parted from them and carried up into Heaven. 2 They worshiped Him and returned to Jerusalem with great joy and were continually in the temple praising and blessing God. Amen.

Part IV: Testimonies of Witnesses
Chapter 18
1 The chief priests and elders were troubled by the reports of Jesus' resurrection. They bribed the soldiers who had guarded the tomb, instructing them to say, "His disciples came at night and stole Him away while we slept." 2 The soldiers took the money and did as they were instructed, and this saying is commonly reported among the Jews to this day.

Chapter 19
1 Nicodemus and Joseph of Arimathea, who had secretly followed Jesus, came forward to testify to His resurrection. They told the Sanhedrin of the miracles and teachings of Jesus, and how they had seen Him alive after His death. 2 The council was divided, and many believed in Jesus, but others conspired to suppress the truth, fearing the loss of their power and influence.

Chapter 20
1 Many who had witnessed the resurrection appearances testified boldly to the truth of Jesus' resurrection. These included the women at the tomb, the disciples on the road to Emmaus, and the apostles in Jerusalem. 2 Their testimony spread throughout the region, and many people believed in Jesus and were baptized in His name.

Chapter 21
1 As the apostles continued to preach the resurrection of Jesus, they faced persecution from the authorities. Peter and John were arrested and brought before the Sanhedrin, but they boldly proclaimed, "We cannot but speak the things which we have seen and heard." 2 The council threatened them but, fearing the people, released them. The apostles rejoiced that they were counted worthy to suffer shame for the name of Jesus.

Chapter 22
1 The Acts of Pilate concludes with a declaration that Jesus Christ is Lord, to the glory of God the Father. His resurrection is the foundation of the Christian faith, and His victory over death is the assurance of eternal life for all who believe in Him. 2 The testimony of those who witnessed His resurrection has been passed down through the generations, and the church continues to proclaim the good news of His resurrection to the ends of the earth.

127. The Acts of Paul and Thecla

Chapter 1
1 Paul, filled with the Holy Spirit, traveled from Antioch to Iconium, where he stayed in the house of Onesiphorus. There, he preached the word of God, teaching about faith, love, and the resurrection. 2 Among those who heard him was a young woman named Thecla, the daughter of a prominent citizen named Theocleia. Thecla was engaged to a man named Thamyris, but after hearing Paul's teachings, she was captivated by the message of chastity and the resurrection.

Chapter 2
1 Thecla spent several days listening to Paul from her window, refusing to eat or drink. Her mother and fiancé, Thamyris, became concerned and frustrated by her behavior, as she seemed entirely devoted to Paul's teachings. 2 Thamyris, seeking to bring Thecla back to her senses, approached Paul, hoping to dissuade him from preaching about chastity and resurrection. He offered Paul gifts, but Paul refused, explaining that his mission was to spread the gospel, not to seek earthly rewards.

Chapter 3
1 Enraged by Paul's refusal, Thamyris conspired with local authorities to have Paul arrested, accusing him of leading women astray with his teachings. Paul was brought before the governor, who questioned him about his teachings. 2 Paul boldly proclaimed the gospel, speaking of the resurrection and the life to come. The governor, influenced by the accusations of Thamyris and others, ordered Paul to be imprisoned.

Chapter 4
1 While Paul was in prison, Thecla bribed the guards and visited him, sitting at his feet and listening to his teachings. Paul encouraged her to remain steadfast in her faith, despite the opposition she faced from her family and society. 2 Thecla's devotion to Paul and his teachings caused a great scandal in the city, and her mother, Theocleia, demanded that Thecla be punished for her disobedience.

Chapter 5
1 The governor, pressured by Theocleia and Thamyris, sentenced Thecla to be burned at the stake. Thecla was taken to the public square, where a pyre was prepared, and she was bound and placed on it. 2 As the flames were lit, Thecla prayed fervently, and suddenly, a great storm arose, extinguishing the fire and terrifying the onlookers. The chains that bound Thecla fell away, and she stood unharmed.

Chapter 6
1 The crowd, amazed by the miracle, began to question the actions of the authorities and the validity of Paul's teachings. The governor, fearing a riot, released Thecla but ordered Paul to leave the city. 2 Thecla, now free, sought out Paul and found him on the road to Antioch. She begged him to allow her to accompany him on his journeys, but Paul, concerned for her safety, initially refused.

Chapter 7
1 Undeterred, Thecla disguised herself as a man and followed Paul to Antioch. There, a wealthy man named Alexander attempted to take Thecla as his wife, but she resisted, declaring her devotion to Christ and her vow of chastity. 2 Enraged by her refusal, Alexander had Thecla arrested and brought before the governor, who sentenced her to be thrown to the wild beasts in the arena.

Chapter 8
1 Thecla was taken to the arena, where she faced wild lions and other beasts. However, the animals, instead of attacking her, lay down at her feet, and one lioness even licked her wounds. 2 The crowd, witnessing this miracle, began to shout for her release, declaring that she was under divine protection. The governor, fearing the people, ordered her release.

Chapter 9
1 After her release, Thecla found Paul and recounted her experiences. Paul praised her faith and encouraged her to continue her journey, but he urged her to return to her home and fulfill her vow of chastity there. 2 Thecla, however, expressed a desire to continue spreading the gospel, and Paul blessed her, giving her his own cloak as a symbol of her

dedication to Christ.

Chapter 10

1 Thecla returned to Iconium, where she continued to preach the gospel, converting many to the faith. She remained devoted to her vow of chastity, living a life of prayer and service. 2 Thecla's reputation as a holy woman and miracle worker grew, and many sought her counsel and prayers. She became known as an apostle in her own right, a beacon of faith and courage for the early Christian community.

Chapter 11

1 The Acts of Paul and Thecla concludes with Thecla's final years, where she continued to live a life of devotion and service. She eventually withdrew to a remote cave, where she spent her remaining days in prayer and contemplation. 2 Before her death, Thecla entrusted her followers with the task of continuing her mission, urging them to remain steadfast in their faith and to spread the teachings of Christ. She passed away peacefully, and her tomb became a place of pilgrimage for Christians, who honored her as a martyr and a saint.

Chapter 12

1 After Thecla's passing, her legacy continued to inspire generations of Christians. Her story spread far and wide, becoming a source of encouragement for those facing persecution and challenges in their own faith journeys. 2 The believers who knew Thecla shared stories of her miraculous deliverance from fire and wild beasts, and these tales were passed down through the generations, solidifying her status as a beloved figure in early Christianity.

Chapter 13

1 Pilgrims traveled from distant lands to visit Thecla's tomb, seeking her intercession and leaving offerings as a sign of their devotion. Many reported miracles at her burial site, including healings and divine revelations. 2 The local Christian community built a small shrine around her tomb, which grew over time into a significant place of worship. It became a gathering spot for those who sought spiritual strength and guidance, especially women who admired Thecla's example of chastity and independence.

Chapter 14

1 The teachings and life of Thecla were not only admired by laypeople but also studied by early Christian theologians and leaders. Her unwavering commitment to chastity and her role as a preacher challenged the traditional gender roles of the time, leading to debates within the church about the role of women in ministry. 2 Some communities began to honor Thecla as a patroness of women's spiritual leadership, citing her as an example of how women could serve God outside the confines of marriage and family life.

Chapter 15

1 As Thecla's story spread, it was incorporated into liturgical practices and celebrated in various regions, particularly in the Eastern Christian traditions. Feast days were established in her honor, and hymns and prayers were composed to celebrate her life and legacy. 2 The Acts of Paul and Thecla also became a popular text among Christian ascetics, who found in Thecla's life a model of the kind of radical commitment to Christ that they aspired to emulate in their own lives.

Chapter 16

1 Over time, Thecla's influence extended beyond the Christian community to the broader culture. Her story was depicted in art, including frescoes, mosaics, and icons, where she was often shown alongside Paul, signifying her close association with the apostolic mission. 2 The image of Thecla preaching, surviving trials, and leading a life of piety became a powerful symbol, not only of early Christian sanctity but also of the potential for women to play significant roles in spiritual and religious life.

Chapter 17

1 The impact of Thecla's story also contributed to the development of Christian monasticism, particularly in traditions where female monastic communities flourished. Her life was seen as a prototype for the monastic ideal of living a life wholly dedicated to God, free from worldly attachments. 2 Monasteries and convents dedicated to Thecla were established, where nuns and monks sought to live according to the principles she embodied—prayer, chastity, and unwavering faith in the face of adversity.

Chapter 18

1 The Acts of Paul and Thecla concludes with a reflection on the enduring power of Thecla's faith and the lessons it offers to all Christians. Her story serves as a reminder that true devotion to Christ can transcend societal expectations and that God's protection and guidance are available to all who commit their lives to Him. 2 The final passage encourages believers to remember Thecla's courage and to seek her intercession in their own struggles, trusting that, like Thecla, they too can find strength and salvation in Christ.

Chapter 19

1 As the influence of Thecla's story grew, her life and witness became a central theme in Christian teachings on the virtues of purity, perseverance, and unwavering faith. Church leaders often invoked Thecla's example in sermons and writings, using her life as a testament to the power of God's grace to transform and protect. 2 Thecla was particularly revered as a model for young women, who were encouraged to emulate her virtues of chastity and devotion to Christ. Many early Christian women found in Thecla an inspiring figure who challenged societal norms and lived a life fully dedicated to God.

Chapter 20

1 The Acts of Paul and Thecla was also instrumental in shaping early Christian discourse around martyrdom. Thecla's willingness to face death for her faith, and the miraculous deliverance she experienced, became a powerful narrative that underscored the belief in divine intervention and the ultimate triumph of faith over persecution. 2 The text reinforced the idea that martyrdom was not to be feared but embraced as a pathway to eternal life, with Thecla's story serving as a poignant reminder that those who suffer for Christ will be vindicated by God.

Chapter 21

1 In the centuries following Thecla's death, her veneration only increased. Pilgrims continued to visit her shrine, and stories of her miracles spread even further. Thecla was often invoked in prayers for protection, especially by those facing persecution or danger, reflecting her status as a powerful intercessor. 2 The Acts of Paul and Thecla was translated into several languages, ensuring that her story reached a wide audience across the Christian world. The spread of her story helped to solidify her place among the most honored of early Christian saints.

Chapter 22

1 The legacy of Thecla also influenced the development of Christian thought on the role of women in the church. Her life provided a counter-narrative to prevailing cultural norms that often restricted women's roles, suggesting that women, too, could be called to significant spiritual leadership and witness. 2 Some early Christian communities, particularly those with more egalitarian views, held Thecla in especially high regard, seeing her as a forerunner to the kind of inclusive Christian fellowship that they sought to cultivate.

Chapter 23

1 Artistic depictions of Thecla, particularly in iconography, emphasized her role as a preacher and a miracle worker. She was often shown holding a cross or a scroll, symbols of her faith and her teachings. These images served not only as devotional aids but also as powerful reminders of her

place in the history of the church. 2 Thecla's image became a common feature in churches dedicated to her, and her story was recounted in liturgical celebrations, reinforcing her status as a model of Christian holiness and courage.

Chapter 24

1 The Acts of Paul and Thecla ends with an epilogue that reflects on the enduring significance of Thecla's life and testimony. It invites readers and believers to carry forward her legacy by living lives of integrity, faithfulness, and bold proclamation of the gospel, regardless of the challenges they may face. 2 The text concludes with a final blessing, asking God to grant the same protection and grace to all who seek to follow in Thecla's footsteps, trusting in His power to deliver and save.

128. The Epistle of Ignatius to the Ephesians

Chapter 1

1 Ignatius, who is also called Theophorus, to the church which is in Ephesus in Asia, deservedly most happy, being blessed in the greatness and fullness of God the Father and predestined before the world began to be always for an enduring and unchangeable glory, united and chosen through true suffering by the will of the Father and Jesus Christ, our God: Abundant happiness through Jesus Christ and His undefiled grace.

Chapter 2

1 I have received your large congregation in the person of Onesimus, your bishop in this world, whom I pray you to love in Jesus Christ, and that you would all seek to be like him. Blessed be God, who has granted unto you who are worthy to obtain such an excellent bishop.

Chapter 3

1 As to my fellow servant Burrhus, your deacon in regard to God, I entreat you to allow him longer time, both for your honor and that of your bishop. And Crocus also, worthy of God and of you, whom I have received as an example of your love, has in all things refreshed me, and may the Father of Jesus Christ refresh him, together with Onesimus, Burrhus, Euplus, and Fronto, in whom I have, as to love, seen all of you.

Chapter 4

1 You have most abundantly refreshed me, as the Father of our Lord Jesus Christ shall also refresh you, together with Onesimus, your bishop, who is highly to be praised in that he is with you in all things. Your obedience to him is a sign of a mature faith.

Chapter 5

1 I rejoice that you are so well ordered in the way of truth, and are found in love, holding firmly to the faith, and in Jesus Christ, our Lord. You are subject to your bishop as to Jesus Christ, the Father, and the church, which is the spouse of Christ.

Chapter 6

1 But let none of you imagine that he has anything worthy of praise, for only as you continue in sober and unblameable living shall you have a place among those to whom God has given a right to life. Let everyone be subject to the bishop as to the Lord, and to the presbytery as to the apostles of Jesus Christ.

Chapter 7

1 Do nothing without the bishop, even as you are now doing. Be subject to the presbytery as to the apostles of Jesus Christ, our hope, in whom we shall be found if we live as He lived.

Chapter 8

1 It is therefore necessary that, as you do, you should do nothing without the bishop. Continue in your submission to the bishop and the presbyters with an undivided mind, breaking one and the same bread, which is the medicine of immortality, and the antidote to prevent us from dying, but that we should live forever in Jesus Christ.

Chapter 9

1 I have heard of some who have passed by you, having perverse doctrine; but you did not suffer them to sow among you. You stopped your ears, that you might not receive those things which were sown by them, as being the stones of the temple of the Father, prepared for the building of God the Father, lifted up on high by the instrument of Jesus Christ, which is the cross, making use of the Holy Ghost as the rope; your faith being your support, and your love the way that leads unto God.

Chapter 10

1 You are all companions in the same journey, carrying God and your temple, and Christ and your holy things, being full of the Holy Ghost, and adorned with the commandments of Jesus Christ. In every respect, I rejoice in you.

Chapter 11

1 My brethren, let us use God's knowledge, which is Jesus Christ, the same yesterday, and today, and forever, who was conceived in the womb of Mary, according to the dispensation of God, of the seed of David, but by the Holy Ghost.

Chapter 12

1 He was born, and was baptized, that through His passion He might purify water to the washing away of sin. He suffered truly, as also He raised up Himself truly; and not, as some unbelievers say, that He only seemed to suffer, they themselves only seeming to be what they are.

Chapter 13

1 And as for those who do not confess that Jesus Christ has come in the flesh, they are antichrist; and whoever shall not confess His suffering upon the cross is from the devil; and he that speaks against His resurrection is a son of perdition. It is my prayer, therefore, to be filled with the Holy Ghost that I may not want to be misunderstood.

Chapter 14

1 I exhort you, therefore, to be careful to do all things in the harmony of God, the bishop presiding in the place of God, and the presbyters in the place of the council of the apostles, and the deacons most dear to me, being entrusted with the ministry of Jesus Christ.

Chapter 15

1 I entreat you, let no one among you look upon his neighbor after the flesh, but do you all love one another in Jesus Christ. Let there be nothing among you that shall have power to divide you, but be united with your bishop and those who preside over you as an example and lesson of incorruption.

Chapter 16

1 As therefore the Lord did nothing without the Father, being united to Him, neither by Himself nor by His apostles, so neither do you anything without the bishop and the presbyters. 2 Neither endeavor to let anything appear rational to yourselves apart, but being come together into the same place, let there be one prayer, one supplication, one mind, one hope, in love and in joy undefiled, which is Jesus Christ, of whom nothing is better.

Chapter 17

1 Hasten to come together as one, that is, to the same temple, to God, to one altar, to one Jesus Christ, who came forth from one Father and is in one and returned to one.

Chapter 18

1 Be not deceived with strange doctrines, nor with old fables, which are unprofitable. For if we still live according to the Jewish law, we acknowledge that we have not received grace. 2 For the most divine prophets lived according to Christ Jesus. On this account, they were persecuted, being inspired by His grace to fully convince the unbelieving that there is one God, who has manifested Himself by Jesus Christ His Son, who is His eternal Word.

Chapter 19

1 If then those who were brought up in the ancient order of things have come to the newness of hope, no longer observing Sabbaths, but keeping the Lord's Day, on which also our life has sprung up again by Him and by His death, whom some deny, by which mystery we have obtained faith, and therefore endure, that we may be found the disciples of Jesus Christ, our only Master.

Chapter 20

1 Let no man deceive himself. If any man be not within the altar, he is deprived of the bread of God. For if the prayer of one or two be of such force, how much more that of the bishop and the whole church? 2 He, therefore, that does not come together in the same place with it is proud, and has already condemned himself.

Chapter 21

1 The Lord forgives all who repent, if they repent and return to the unity of God and the council of the bishop. I trust as to you in the grace of Jesus Christ, that you will be convinced of this. I salute you in the Lord always, my dear Ephesians.

Chapter 22

1 It is fitting for you, most blessed Paul, to refresh me as to your way in the presence of our Lord Jesus Christ, and in His spirit, attaining unto the love of God, I have loved you. May you bless the Father of Jesus Christ and the Lord our God. Amen. 2 You have refreshed me in all things, so may Jesus Christ, who is the same, and who has loved us in one and the same love, refresh you. Amen.

Chapter 23

1 Ignatius continues his exhortation to the Ephesians, emphasizing the necessity of spiritual vigilance. He warns them to guard against complacency and to remain steadfast in their faith, especially in the face of false teachings that might arise. 2 He encourages them to be discerning in their interactions with others, to test all teachings against the gospel of Christ, and to reject anything that deviates from the truth handed down by the apostles.

Chapter 24

1 Ignatius also speaks about the importance of unity within the church. He compares the church to a body, with Christ as the head and the members as different parts of the body, each fulfilling its role in harmony with the others. 2 He stresses that just as the body cannot function properly if its parts are not in harmony, so too the church cannot thrive if there is division among its members. He urges the Ephesians to maintain the unity of the Spirit through the bond of peace.

Chapter 25

1 Addressing the role of the bishop, Ignatius reaffirms the importance of obedience to ecclesiastical authority. He explains that the bishop represents Christ in the community and that the presbyters and deacons assist in the work of the church. 2 He urges the faithful to show respect and love for their leaders, to follow their guidance, and to work together for the edification of the church.

Chapter 26

1 Ignatius then touches on the theme of Christian living, urging the Ephesians to live lives that are worthy of their calling. He encourages them to be examples of virtue and holiness, to avoid all forms of evil, and to be diligent in prayer, fasting, and good works. 2 He reminds them that their conduct should reflect the teachings of Christ, and that they are called to be the light of the world, shining forth the love and truth of the gospel in their daily lives.

Chapter 27

1 In a final exhortation, Ignatius emphasizes the importance of love as the foundation of the Christian life. He explains that love is the fulfillment of the law and the greatest of all virtues, binding the believers together in perfect unity. 2 He urges the Ephesians to love one another with the same love that Christ has shown them, to forgive one another, and to bear with one another in patience and humility.

Chapter 28

1 Ignatius concludes his letter with a prayer for the Ephesians, asking God to bless them with His grace, to strengthen them in their faith, and to keep them steadfast in their commitment to Christ. 2 He expresses his hope that they will continue to grow in love and unity, and that they will persevere in their mission to spread the gospel to all people.

Chapter 29

1 Ignatius sends his greetings to the entire church in Ephesus, including the presbyters, deacons, and all the faithful. He also asks for their prayers for himself and for the other churches with which he is in communion. 2 He entrusts them to the care of God, confident that they will remain faithful to the teachings of Christ and continue to bear fruit for the kingdom of God.

Chapter 30

1 The letter closes with a final blessing: "May the grace of our Lord Jesus Christ, the love of God the Father, and the fellowship of the Holy Spirit be with you all. Amen." 2 Ignatius then bids them farewell, urging them to remain strong in their faith and to keep their eyes fixed on Christ, who is the author and perfecter of their faith.

129. *The Epistle of Ignatius to the Romans*

Chapter 1

1 Ignatius, who is also called Theophorus, to the church which has obtained mercy through the majesty of the Most High Father and His only-begotten Son, Jesus Christ; beloved and enlightened through the will of Him who wills all things which are according to the love of Jesus Christ our God, which also presides in the place of the region of the Romans, worthy of God, worthy of honor, worthy of blessing, worthy of praise, worthy of success, worthy in purity, pre-eminent in love, walking in the law of Christ and bearing the Father's name, which also I salute in the name of Jesus Christ, the Son of the Father. To those who are united both in flesh and spirit to all His commandments, who are filled with the grace of God without wavering, and filtered clear from every foreign stain, I wish an unblemished joy in Jesus Christ our God.

Chapter 2

1 Through prayer to God, I have obtained the privilege of seeing your most worthy faces, and I hope, if it is God's will, that I shall soon have the honor of meeting you. For I have already begun to be accounted a prisoner for the name and cause of Christ. I hope to meet you with your prayers to the end that I may attain to fight with the beasts at Rome, so that, by means of the beasts, I may be able to attain to God.

Chapter 3

1 For this end, I am a prisoner, learning nothing from visible or invisible things, so that I may fight with the beasts at Rome. So, if I have the pleasure of suffering for my faith, I am worthy of being accepted as a disciple of Jesus Christ. Thus, I shall be able, with boldness, to meet those who kill the body and thus pass from this world unto God, that I may rise with Him who was crucified for me.

Chapter 4

1 I do not enjoin you as Peter and Paul did. They were apostles, and I am a condemned man; they were free, but I am a slave to this very hour. But if I suffer, I shall become the freedman of Jesus Christ, and I shall rise again, emancipated in Him. And now, being a prisoner, I learn not to desire anything of this world or of the things of the world.

Chapter 5

1 From Syria even unto Rome, I fight with beasts, both by land and sea, both by night and day, being

bound to ten leopards, which are a band of soldiers, who, even when they receive good treatment, behave with greater cruelty. But I am the more instructed by their injuries, "Yet am I not justified." May I have joy of the beasts that are prepared for me, and I pray that they may be found ready. I will encourage them to devour me quickly, for I will provoke them to do so willingly, not as has happened in the case of others, whom they have not touched through fear. And if they refuse to attack me, I will compel them to do so.

Chapter 6

1 Bear with me. I know what is expedient for me. Now I begin to be a disciple. May nothing of things visible or invisible envy me, that I may attain to Jesus Christ. Let fire and the cross, let the crowds of wild beasts, let tearings, breakings, and dislocations of bones, let cutting off of limbs, let shatterings of the whole body, and let all the dreadful torments of the devil come upon me: only let me attain to Jesus Christ.

Chapter 7

1 All the ends of the world, and the kingdoms of this earth, shall profit me nothing. It is better for me to die in behalf of Jesus Christ than to reign over all the ends of the earth. For what shall a man be profited if he gain the whole world but lose his own soul? I seek Him who died for us; I desire Him who rose again for our sake. The pangs of a new birth are upon me. Bear with me, my brethren, and do not hinder me from living. Do not desire my death. Suffer me to obtain pure light. When I shall have arrived there, I shall be a man of God. Permit me to be an imitator of the passion of my God.

Chapter 8

1 If anyone has God within himself, let him understand my desires, and sympathize with me, knowing the things which straiten me. The Prince of this world would gladly carry me away and corrupt my disposition toward God. Let none of you, therefore, who are in Rome, help him; rather, be on my side, that is, on the side of God. Do not speak of Jesus Christ and yet desire the world. Let not envy dwell among you.

Chapter 9

1 I take no pleasure in corruptible food or the delights of this life. I desire the bread of God, which is the flesh of Jesus Christ, who was of the seed of David, and for drink, I desire His blood, which is incorruptible love.

Chapter 10

1 I have no desire to live any longer according to the desires of men. Neither shall I have such a desire if you consent. Be willing, then, that you also may be consented to by God. I entreat you, seek not to confer any greater favor upon me than that I be sacrificed to God while the altar is still prepared. For there is no greater sacrifice I can offer to God, and I trust that you are truly devoted to God. You are bound together in love. You have not shunned me, but rather were willing to do what I desired. May you obtain for yourselves a good reward, and may you live without spot, both in the flesh and in spirit.

Chapter 11

1 The time is near. I am already on the point of being sacrificed, and I must take leave of the world, and from you. Let me be an example to you, and let the honor you render unto God redound to your everlasting glory. Let your prayers accompany me, that I may attain unto God. Let all earthly things be far from me, that I may be worthy of the kingdom of God. I hope that you may also attain there. I pray for you always, and for your safety, and for the union of body and spirit in Jesus Christ, who is the hope and salvation of all. Amen.

Chapter 12

1 Remember the church in Syria, which has God for its shepherd instead of me. Jesus Christ alone will oversee it, along with your love. I am ashamed to be counted as one of them, for I am not worthy. But as God desires, so shall it be. Pray for me, that I may be made perfect in Him.

Chapter 13

1 The love of the brethren at Troas salutes you. Remember the church that is in Syria, from whence I am not worthy to be called. For I have need of your prayer in God. Remember the church of Smyrna, and Ephesus, from whence also I write to you in Jesus Christ. I salute you with love, with your deacon Burrhus, with the rest of the brethren, the sacred and apostolic order, and the bishop. Farewell in the grace of God, which is Jesus Christ, in whom may you abide in unity and peace.

Chapter 14

1 Ignatius continues by addressing the nature of true discipleship. He emphasizes that being a disciple of Christ means more than just believing; it requires a complete surrender to God's will, even unto death. He calls the Roman believers to understand that his impending martyrdom is not something to be mourned but rather celebrated, as it is the fulfillment of his calling as a disciple. 2 He urges them to see his martyrdom as a testament to the power of God working in his life, transforming him from a sinner into a witness for Christ. Ignatius hopes that his sacrifice will inspire others to remain steadfast in their faith, no matter the cost.

Chapter 15

1 Ignatius also reflects on the concept of spiritual freedom. He explains that true freedom is found not in avoiding suffering or death but in embracing God's will with joy and faith. He sees his upcoming death as a passage into eternal life, where he will finally be free from the constraints of the flesh and fully united with Christ. 2 He encourages the Romans to view life and death through the lens of the resurrection, understanding that death is not the end but the beginning of a new and eternal life with God. This perspective, he believes, will help them to face their own trials with courage and hope.

Chapter 16

1 Ignatius acknowledges the prayers and support of the Roman believers, expressing deep gratitude for their love and solidarity. He reassures them that their prayers have strengthened him and that he feels their presence with him as he faces his final trial. 2 He asks them to continue praying for him, not for deliverance from death, but for the strength to endure it faithfully. He also prays that God will reward them for their kindness and that they will all be united in heaven.

Chapter 17

1 In his final words, Ignatius reflects on the mystery of Christ's love, which he believes is the source of all Christian strength and endurance. He marvels at the depth of God's love, which was demonstrated in Christ's willingness to suffer and die for humanity. This love, he says, is what sustains him as he prepares to follow in Christ's footsteps. 2 Ignatius urges the Romans to remain rooted in this love, for it is the foundation of their faith and the key to their salvation. He expresses his confidence that, through Christ's love, they will overcome all challenges and remain faithful to the end.

Chapter 18

1 Ignatius concludes his epistle with a blessing. He prays that the grace of Jesus Christ will be with the Roman believers, guiding them, protecting them, and keeping them united in faith and love. He asks God to grant them peace, joy, and perseverance as they continue their journey of faith. 2 He signs off with a final plea for prayers, not only for himself but for the entire church, that they may all be found worthy of God's kingdom. Ignatius' last words are filled with hope and a deep sense of peace, as he entrusts himself and his readers to the care of the Lord.

130. The Epistle of Ignatius to the Magnesians

Chapter 1

1 Ignatius, who is also called Theophorus, to the church blessed through the grace of God the Father in Christ Jesus our Savior, in whom I greet the church which is at Magnesia, near the Maeander, and wish it abundant happiness in God the Father and in Jesus Christ.

Chapter 2

1 When I learned of your well-ordered love and your godly disposition, I rejoiced exceedingly and decided to address you in the faith of Jesus Christ. For having been deemed worthy to bear His name in bonds, I now hope to salute you if I am granted to do so by the will of God.

Chapter 3

1 I praise the bishop as I have seen him, and those presbyters and deacons who are with him, men who are in the grace of God, and I wish you to be in like manner. In all respects, I am blessed in God, that you receive nothing according to your own will but in accordance with God.

Chapter 4

1 For even as Jesus Christ, who is the inseparable life of our souls, is the Father's will, so also the bishops who are appointed in the uttermost parts of the earth are appointed by the will of Jesus Christ. Therefore, it is fitting for you to conduct yourselves in harmony with the mind of the bishop, as indeed you do.

Chapter 5

1 Your presbyters, as priests of God, are very well acquainted with the mysteries of Jesus Christ, and with them, the deacons also, being entrusted with the ministry of Jesus Christ, in whom they were found faithful. It is fitting for you to be in harmony with their opinion, for your justified position is based on their ministry.

Chapter 6

1 As, therefore, the Lord was united with the Father and did nothing without Him, neither by Himself nor by His apostles, so neither should you do anything without the bishops and the presbyters. Let no man deceive himself. If anyone is not within the sanctuary, he lacks the bread of God.

Chapter 7

1 The one bread of God is the flesh of Jesus Christ, and the drink is His blood, which was shed for us. These things were prepared by the grace of God, and the faithful partake of them. Let no one deceive you; for if anyone is not within the sanctuary, he is deprived of the bread of life.

Chapter 8

1 I exhort you to continue in your duty and to be inseparable from Jesus Christ, from your bishops, and from the commandments of the apostles. He who honors the bishop is honored by God; he who does anything without the knowledge of the bishop serves the devil.

Chapter 9

1 Therefore, let us not be indifferent to the bishop's authority, lest we dishonor our own heads by acting against it. But let us submit to God's will, acknowledging our bishop with reverence and sincerity, and seeking to maintain unity within the church.

Chapter 10

1 It is fitting, therefore, that we be obedient to the bishop, and be subject to him as to the Lord, as to Jesus Christ, the Father's Son, who was obedient to the Father in all things. Be imitators of Him, my beloved, just as He is of His Father, so you should be of Him.

Chapter 11

1 The times call for the need of a proper education in the faith. Even if we were to give ourselves to asceticism, humility, and prayer without being united to the bishop, the efforts would be in vain. Therefore, it is of great importance that we have proper guidance and follow the teachings of Jesus Christ as they were handed down by the apostles.

Chapter 12

1 Flee from schism as the source of all evil. Whoever follows someone who creates schism does not inherit the kingdom of God. If someone walks away from the truth, he must be confronted with the same earnestness as one who is lost to the devil. Therefore, be mindful of those who cause division, and seek to heal the church's unity with love and humility.

Chapter 13

1 Let us, therefore, strive to keep the unity of the church in peace and harmony, that we may be children of God, perfect and without spot. Let us walk according to the grace that is given to us, that we may obtain eternal life.

Chapter 14

1 And I exhort you to always have fellowship with the most worthy bishop, as you do. And I am overjoyed at your devout spirit. For your church is known throughout the world as a beacon of true faith and love.

Chapter 15

1 Take heed, then, often to come together to give thanks to God and show forth His praise. For when you meet together frequently, the powers of Satan are overthrown, and his destructive force is annihilated by the unity of your faith.

Chapter 16

1 I have great joy in seeing the orderly way in which your love is conducted by the deacons, the presbyters, and the bishop. May they continue to be a source of spiritual nourishment for the entire congregation, showing the path of truth and righteousness.

Chapter 17

1 The bishop presides in the place of God, and your presbyters in the place of the council of the apostles, and the deacons, most beloved to me, have been entrusted with the ministry of Jesus Christ. Therefore, respect them in their respective offices and honor the church's structure, which has been ordained by God.

Chapter 18

1 I salute the church of Magnesia and all who belong to it, wishing you abundance of happiness in God the Father and in Jesus Christ, our Lord. Remain steadfast in the faith, love one another, and be subject to your bishop and those who are set over you.

Chapter 19

1 Pray for me that I may obtain the mercy of God, that I may be found worthy of the inheritance in heaven and the kingdom of God. I am indeed in need of your prayers in God, that I may be steadfast in the faith and live in unity with Him.

Chapter 20

1 The love of the brethren at Smyrna and Ephesus salutes you. Remember in your prayers the church that is in Syria, from whence I am not worthy to be called. I write to you in the name of Jesus Christ, through the love of God.

Chapter 21

1 Farewell in Jesus Christ, in whom may you be found steadfast in unity and love. May the grace of God be with you always. Amen.

131. The Epistle of Ignatius to the Trallians

Chapter 1

1 Ignatius, who is also called Theophorus, to the holy church which is at Tralles in Asia, beloved by God the Father, and of Jesus Christ, elect, and worthy of God, possessing peace through the flesh and blood, and

passion of Jesus Christ, who is our hope, through our resurrection unto Him. I salute you in all fullness, and I wish you an abundance of happiness in Jesus Christ.

Chapter 2
1 I have received your godly benevolence through your bishop, Polybius, who has come to Smyrna on my way to Rome according to the will of God. I rejoice greatly to have seen him, for he was a pattern of love, and while with us he fulfilled in himself the work of the ministry of God.

Chapter 3
1 For as much as you are subject to your bishop as to Jesus Christ, you appear to me to live not after the manner of men, but according to Jesus Christ, who died for us, that so believing in His death, you might escape death.

Chapter 4
1 It is therefore necessary that, as you do, you should do nothing without the bishop, and that you should also be subject to the presbyters as to the apostles of Jesus Christ, our hope, in whom we shall be found if we live according to Him.

Chapter 5
1 The deacons also, as being the ministers of the mysteries of Jesus Christ, must by all means please all men. For they are not the ministers of meat and drink, but of the church of God. Wherefore, they must avoid all offenses as they would avoid fire.

Chapter 6
1 In the same way, let all reverence the deacons as Jesus Christ, and the bishop as the image of the Father, and the presbyters as the council of God and the college of the apostles. Without these, there is no church.

Chapter 7
1 Concerning the rest, my brethren, honor your bishop and the presbyters and the deacons. And be also subject to one another, and let no one look upon his neighbor according to the flesh, but in all holiness love each other in Jesus Christ.

Chapter 8
1 Let there be nothing among you that shall be able to divide you, but be united to the bishop and to those who preside over you, to be one with them, even as the church is one with Jesus Christ, and as Jesus Christ is one with the Father, that all things may agree in unity.

Chapter 9
1 It is fitting that you should continue in your unity, for your famous presbytery, worthy of God, is fitted as exactly to the bishop as the strings are to the harp. Therefore, in your concord and harmonious love, Jesus Christ is sung.

Chapter 10
1 And do each of you individually join in this chorus, that being in concord, you may with one voice sing to the Father through Jesus Christ, to the end that He may hear you and perceive by your works that you are indeed members of His Son. It is therefore profitable that you live in an unblameable unity, that you may always have a fellowship with God.

Chapter 11
1 But if I, in this short time, have had such a familiarity with your bishop, which is not human but spiritual, how much more do I count you happy who are so joined to him as the church is to Jesus Christ, and Jesus Christ to the Father, that so all things may agree in unity?

Chapter 12
1 Let no man deceive himself. If any man be not within the altar, he is deprived of the bread of God. For if the prayer of one or two has such strength, how much more that of the bishop and the whole church?

Chapter 13
1 Whoever does not come together with the congregation, thereby shows his pride and has already judged himself, for it is written, "God resists the proud." Let us be careful, then, not to set ourselves in opposition to the bishop, that we may be subject to God.

Chapter 14
1 Let us also reverence the deacons as the ministers of the mysteries of Jesus Christ. For in like manner as Jesus Christ was sent by the Father, so also was He sent by Christ; and the things which were done by God are in like manner fulfilled in Him.

Chapter 15
1 I exhort you, therefore, yet not I, but the love of Jesus Christ, that you use Christian nourishment only, and abstain from herbage of another kind, which is heresy. For those that are heretics, confound together the doctrine of Jesus Christ with their own poison, while they seem worthy of belief, like those who administer a deadly potion with sweet wine, which he who is ignorant of does greedily take, with a fatal pleasure, leading to his own death.

Chapter 16
1 Guard yourselves against such persons, and that you will do if you are not puffed up but continue inseparable from Jesus Christ our God, and from your bishop, and from the commandments of the apostles.

Chapter 17
1 He who is within the altar is pure, but he that is without, that is, does anything without the bishop, and presbyters, and deacons, is not pure in his conscience.

Chapter 18
1 Not that I know there is anything of this nature among you, but I forewarn you as being greatly beloved by me, having foreseen the snares of the devil. Wherefore, putting on meekness, renew yourselves in faith, which is the flesh of the Lord, and in charity, which is the blood of Jesus Christ.

Chapter 19
1 Let none of you bear a grudge against his neighbor. Give no occasion to the Gentiles, lest by means of a few foolish men, the whole multitude of God's people be blasphemed. For woe to that man through whose vanity my name is blasphemed by any.

Chapter 20
1 Be deaf, therefore, when anyone speaks to you apart from Jesus Christ, who was of the race of David, the Son of Mary, who was truly born, and did eat and drink; was truly persecuted under Pontius Pilate; was truly crucified, and truly died, in the sight of beings in heaven, on earth, and under the earth.

Chapter 21
1 Who also was truly raised from the dead by His Father, after the same manner as He will also raise up us who believe in Him by Christ Jesus, without whom we have no true life.

Chapter 22
1 But if, as some who are atheists, that is to say, unbelievers, pretend that He only seemed to suffer, (they themselves only seeming to exist,) why then am I bound? Why do I desire to fight with beasts? Therefore, I die in vain, and am a liar against the Lord.

Chapter 23
1 Flee, therefore, these evil offshoots which produce death-bearing fruit, of which if any man tastes, he shall presently die. For these are not the plants of the Father. For if they were, they would appear to be branches of the cross, and their fruit would be incorruptible, by which He invites you through His passion, who are His members. The head cannot be without its members, for God is faithful, of whom you are in communion.

Chapter 24
1 I salute you from Smyrna, together with the churches of God that are present with me, who have refreshed me in all things, both in flesh and in spirit. My bonds, which I carry about with me for the sake of Christ, (praying that I may attain to God,) exhort you, "Continue in your concord and in prayer with one

another." For it becomes every one of you, and especially the presbyters, to refresh the bishop to the honor of the Father, of Jesus Christ, and of the apostles.

Chapter 25

1 I beseech you in Christ Jesus to hear me in love, that I may not by writing to you seem to command you, who am far from being one fit to command, being conscious of myself of many failings. I am not fit to command you as though I were some great person.

Chapter 26

1 For though I am bound for His name, I am not yet perfect in Christ Jesus. But now I begin to learn, and I speak to you as fellow disciples with me. For I ought to have been stirred up by you in faith, in admonition, in patience, and in long-suffering. But since charity endures all things, I have undertaken to write to you, and to exhort you, that you run together in accordance with the will of God.

Chapter 27

1 For Jesus Christ, our inseparable life, is the will of the Father, as the bishops appointed to the utmost bounds of the earth are so by the will of Jesus Christ. Wherefore it will become you to run together according to the will of your bishop, as also you do.

Chapter 28

1 For your famous presbytery, worthy of God, is fitted as exactly to the bishop as the strings are to the harp. Therefore, in your concord and harmonious love, Jesus Christ is sung. And do each of you individually join in this chorus, that being in concord, you may with one voice sing to the Father through Jesus Christ, to the end that He may both hear you, and perceive by your works that you are indeed members of His Son. It is, therefore, profitable for you to live in an unblameable unity, that you may always have a fellowship with God.

Chapter 29

1 Now, therefore, being come together in one place, have communion with one prayer, one supplication, one mind, and one hope, with meekness and a blameless joy, giving thanks to God. For if one man prays alone, and another gives thanks alone, and another hears, each does this separately; but all of you pray and give thanks together, one common prayer, supplication, and thanksgiving in Christ Jesus.

Chapter 30

1 There is one altar, as there is one Jesus Christ, who is the Son of the only God. And there is one only Comforter, the Holy Ghost, who is the same everywhere, perfecting in men faith, fear, love, sanctification, and knowledge.

Chapter 31

1 Be diligent, therefore, to come together in unity and thanksgiving, that God, having broken the heads of the serpents that have deceived you, might make you His members of the Spirit.

Chapter 32

1 For it is written, "Who among you is wise? Let him show his works by his good behavior." But if he refuses and contradicts, he is puffed up and knows nothing. But let him who is wise be gentle and meek in the fear of God, and he will show mercy to his soul.

Chapter 33

1 Let us, therefore, do everything that God has commanded us, and be careful not to fall into the snares of the wicked. But let us fear God, and keep His commandments, and turn away from the works of the devil, that our praise may be always in Christ Jesus our Lord, by whom and with whom be glory to God the Father, with the Holy Spirit, forevermore. Amen.

132. The Epistle of Ignatius to the Philadelphians

Chapter 1

1 Ignatius, who is also called Theophorus, to the church of God the Father and the Lord Jesus Christ, which is at Philadelphia in Asia, which has obtained mercy and is established in the harmony of God and rejoices evermore in the passion of our Lord, and is filled with all mercy through His resurrection. I salute you in the blood of Jesus Christ, which is eternal and abiding joy, especially if they are at unity with the bishop, the presbyters, and the deacons who are with him.

Chapter 2

1 I have known your bishop, and he has not been found to be one who is reproached, but as one who is deserving of honor. And his conduct among you is the more wonderful because he is so silent. Yet his silence is more powerful than the speeches of others. For he is perfectly in harmony with the commandments, as a lyre with its strings. Therefore, my soul blesses his godly mind, knowing it to be virtuous and perfect, his stability and freedom from all anger.

Chapter 3

1 As children of light and truth, flee from division and evil doctrines; but where the shepherd is, there follow as sheep. For there are many wolves who appear worthy of confidence, but by their wild pursuits, they are imprisoned. Flee therefore from such kind of men as these, and let the shepherd be your pattern, as it is fitting.

Chapter 4

1 The more anyone sees the bishop keeping silence, the more he should revere him. For everyone who is sent by the master into his own house, should be received as we would receive Him who sent him. It is evident, therefore, that we ought to look upon the bishop even as we would upon the Lord Himself.

Chapter 5

1 And indeed Onesimus himself greatly commends your good order in God, that you all live according to the truth, and that no heresy dwells among you. Nor indeed do you listen to anyone more than to Jesus Christ speaking in truth.

Chapter 6

1 For some are in the habit of carrying about the name of Jesus Christ in wicked guile, while they practice things unworthy of God, whom you must flee as you would wild beasts. For they are mad dogs that bite secretly. You must be on your guard against them, for they are hard to cure.

Chapter 7

1 There is one physician who is possessed both of flesh and spirit; both made and not made; God existing in flesh; true life in death; both of Mary and of God; first passable and then impassable, even Jesus Christ our Lord.

Chapter 8

1 Let no man deceive you, as indeed you are not deceived, being wholly the servants of God. For as long as there is no strife among you which can torment you, you are living according to God. I am devoted to you and pray continually for you, and ask you to pray for me. I have great confidence in you, but not in the flesh.

Chapter 9

1 I do not want to command you as though I were some great person. For though I am bound in the name of Jesus Christ, I am not yet perfect in Him. I now begin to learn, and I speak to you as fellow disciples with me. For I ought to have been stirred up by you in faith, in admonition, in patience, and in long-suffering. But since charity endures all things, I have undertaken to write to you, and to exhort you, that you run together in accordance with the will of God.

Chapter 10
1 Your prayer has reached to the church which is at Antioch in Syria, and coming from it into your congregation, rejoices that it has already received peace and has been refreshed by your love, which you showed towards it in the name of Jesus Christ. For it has been reported to me that the church which is at Antioch in Syria is at peace, through your prayers and love, which are in Jesus Christ.

Chapter 11
1 It is fitting, my brethren, that you should also refresh the bishop, and the presbyters, and the deacons, who are with him. And as it has been reported to me that they are not puffed up, you are also those who are worthy of God. I have, therefore, been greatly comforted in you.

Chapter 12
1 But as for those who say that they must keep the law and yet desire to live in grace, let them be instructed by you. For they have not received the cross of Christ, nor have they understood the grace of the resurrection, nor are they convinced of His passion. But your prayer shall make them perfect, if in every way they deny the works of the devil and bear the cross of Christ.

Chapter 13
1 Those, then, who are heretics and wish to subvert the power of Jesus Christ, through their evil doctrine, will perish in their madness and wickedness. For the God and Father of our Lord Jesus Christ has brought us to the knowledge of the truth, through which He has made known to us His Son, who is the truth. Therefore, flee from division and evil doctrines.

Chapter 14
1 Seeing, then, all things have an end, and these two things, life and death, are set before us, and every one shall go to his own place, let us flee from death, and choose life. The result of good works is life, and he that does not do good shall perish in death.

Chapter 15
1 Let us, therefore, arm ourselves with the power of God, and let us be taught by the Holy Ghost, being without guile and meek, and we shall not fear the prince of this world, who has sought to destroy us. Let us stand against him, and if we suffer, we shall overcome him.

Chapter 16
1 I exhort you in Jesus Christ that you love the Son of God, and you that are living according to the commandments of Jesus Christ, let it be evident to all that you follow after righteousness and love one another.

Chapter 17
1 I salute you from Smyrna, together with the churches of God which are present with me, who have refreshed me in all things, both in flesh and in spirit. My bonds, which I carry about with me for the sake of Christ, exhort you, "Continue in your concord and in prayer with one another." For it becomes every one of you, and especially the presbyters, to refresh the bishop to the honor of the Father, of Jesus Christ, and of the apostles.

Chapter 18
1 I beg you to hear me in love, that I may not seem to command you, who am far from being one fit to command. For though I am bound for His name, I am not yet perfect in Christ Jesus. But now I begin to learn, and I speak to you as fellow disciples with me. For I ought to have been stirred up by you in faith, in admonition, in patience, and in long-suffering.

Chapter 19
1 For Jesus Christ, our inseparable life, is the will of the Father, as the bishops appointed to the utmost bounds of the earth are so by the will of Jesus Christ. Wherefore it will become you to run together according to the will of your bishop, as also you do.

Chapter 20
1 I send you greetings from Smyrna, together with the churches of God that are present with me, who have refreshed me in all things, both in flesh and in spirit. My bonds exhort you, "Continue in your concord and in prayer with one another." For it becomes every one of you, and especially the presbyters, to refresh the bishop to the honor of the Father, of Jesus Christ, and of the apostles.

Chapter 21
1 Farewell in Jesus Christ, who is our common hope, and let each of you seek to glorify God. May the grace of God be with you always. Amen.

133. *The Apocalypse of Thomas*

Chapter 1
1 The vision that was shown by our Lord to Thomas concerning the end of times. Hear, O my people, and take heed of the words that I shall declare unto you, for they are the last words that you shall hear before the great day of the Lord.

Chapter 2
1 In those days, before the end comes, there shall be great signs and wonders in the heavens and upon the earth. The sun shall be darkened, and the moon shall not give her light; the stars shall fall from the sky, and the powers of the heavens shall be shaken.

Chapter 3
1 There shall be wars and rumors of wars, and nation shall rise against nation, and kingdom against kingdom. There shall be great earthquakes in various places, and famines, and pestilences; and there shall be fearful sights and great signs from heaven.

Chapter 4
1 Then shall the time of sorrows begin, and many shall be troubled in their hearts, and men's hearts shall fail them for fear and for looking after those things which are coming on the earth. The powers of the heavens shall be moved, and there shall be great confusion upon the earth.

Chapter 5
1 In those days, there shall be great tribulation, such as was not since the beginning of the world to this time, no, nor ever shall be. And except those days should be shortened, there should no flesh be saved; but for the elect's sake, those days shall be shortened.

Chapter 6
1 The beasts of the field and the fowls of the air shall be in distress, and the fish of the sea shall be troubled. The rivers shall run dry, and the fountains shall fail, and there shall be no water for the people. The earth shall be parched, and the trees shall wither away, and there shall be no fruit.

Chapter 7
1 The wicked shall increase in their wickedness, and they shall do abominable things in the sight of the Lord. They shall blaspheme the name of God and shall worship the works of their own hands. They shall say, "Who is the Lord that we should serve Him? There is no God."

Chapter 8
1 The righteous shall be afflicted and persecuted, and many shall fall away from the faith. The love of many shall wax cold, and iniquity shall abound. False prophets shall arise and deceive many, and many false Christs shall come in the name of the Lord, saying, "I am Christ," and shall deceive many.

Chapter 9
1 Then shall the sign of the Son of Man appear in heaven, and all the tribes of the earth shall mourn, and they shall see the Son of Man coming in the clouds of heaven with power and great glory. He shall send His angels with a great sound of a trumpet, and they shall gather together His elect from the four winds, from one end of heaven to the other.

Chapter 10
1 When these things begin to come to pass, then look up and lift up your heads, for your redemption draws near. For the Lord shall come with a shout, with the

voice of the archangel, and with the trumpet of God, and the dead in Christ shall rise first.

Chapter 11

1 Then we which are alive and remain shall be caught up together with them in the clouds, to meet the Lord in the air, and so shall we ever be with the Lord. Therefore, comfort one another with these words.

Chapter 12

1 The time of the end shall be known by these signs, and by the knowledge that is given to the wise. The wise shall understand, but the wicked shall do wickedly, and none of the wicked shall understand.

Chapter 13

1 The day of the Lord shall come as a thief in the night, in which the heavens shall pass away with a great noise, and the elements shall melt with fervent heat. The earth also and the works that are therein shall be burned up.

Chapter 14

1 Seeing then that all these things shall be dissolved, what manner of persons ought you to be in all holy conversation and godliness, looking for and hastening unto the coming of the day of God?

Chapter 15

1 The righteous shall shine forth as the sun in the kingdom of their Father, and they shall inherit all things. But the wicked shall be cast into outer darkness, where there shall be weeping and gnashing of teeth.

Chapter 16

1 Blessed is he that watches and keeps his garments, lest he walk naked and they see his shame. Behold, I come quickly; hold that fast which you have, that no man take your crown.

Chapter 17

1 He that overcomes shall inherit all things, and I will be his God, and he shall be My son. But the fearful, and unbelieving, and the abominable, and murderers, and whoremongers, and sorcerers, and idolaters, and all liars, shall have their part in the lake which burns with fire and brimstone, which is the second death.

Chapter 18

1 And the Spirit and the bride say, "Come." And let him that hears say, "Come." And let him that is athirst come. And whosoever will, let him take the water of life freely.

134. The Vision of Paul

Chapter 1

1 The vision that was revealed to Paul the Apostle, as he was caught up to the third heaven and shown the mysteries of the heavens and the abyss, and what the end of times will be.

Chapter 2

1 After I, Paul, was caught up to the third heaven, as I was in prayer, behold, a great light suddenly appeared, and a voice from heaven called me by name. I answered, saying, "Who are You, Lord?" And the voice said to me, "I am the Lord, the God whom you serve, and I have come to show you the things that are and the things that shall be."

Chapter 3

1 Immediately, I was taken up by the Spirit, and I saw a great throne in heaven, and One who sat on the throne. His appearance was like jasper and ruby, and a rainbow encircled the throne, like an emerald in appearance. 2 Around the throne were twenty-four elders sitting, clothed in white garments, and they had crowns of gold on their heads. From the throne proceeded flashes of lightning, rumblings, and peals of thunder, and before the throne were seven lamps of fire burning, which are the seven Spirits of God.

Chapter 4

1 And before the throne there was a sea of glass, like crystal. In the midst of the throne and around the throne were four living creatures full of eyes in front

and in back. 2 The first living creature was like a lion, the second living creature like a calf, the third living creature had a face like a man, and the fourth living creature was like a flying eagle. The four living creatures, each having six wings, were full of eyes around and within. And they do not rest day or night, saying, "Holy, holy, holy, Lord God Almighty, Who was and is and is to come!"

Chapter 5

1 As I looked, I saw a book in the right hand of Him who sat on the throne, written inside and on the back, sealed with seven seals. And I saw a strong angel proclaiming with a loud voice, "Who is worthy to open the book and to loose its seals?" 2 And no one in heaven or on the earth or under the earth was able to open the book or to look at it. So I wept much, because no one was found worthy to open and read the book, or to look at it.

Chapter 6

1 But one of the elders said to me, "Do not weep. Behold, the Lion of the tribe of Judah, the Root of David, has prevailed to open the book and to loose its seven seals." 2 And I looked, and behold, in the midst of the throne and of the four living creatures, and in the midst of the elders, stood a Lamb as though it had been slain, having seven horns and seven eyes, which are the seven Spirits of God sent out into all the earth.

Chapter 7

1 Then He came and took the book out of the right hand of Him who sat on the throne. Now when He had taken the book, the four living creatures and the twenty-four elders fell down before the Lamb, each having a harp, and golden bowls full of incense, which are the prayers of the saints. 2 And they sang a new song, saying: "You are worthy to take the book, and to open its seals; for You were slain, and have redeemed us to God by Your blood out of every tribe and tongue and people and nation, and have made us kings and priests to our God; and we shall reign on the earth."

Chapter 8

1 Then I looked, and I heard the voice of many angels around the throne, the living creatures, and the elders; and the number of them was ten thousand times ten thousand, and thousands of thousands, saying with a loud voice: "Worthy is the Lamb who was slain to receive power and riches and wisdom, and strength and honor and glory and blessing!" 2 And every creature which is in heaven and on the earth and under the earth and such as are in the sea, and all that are in them, I heard saying: "Blessing and honor and glory and power be to Him who sits on the throne, and to the Lamb, forever and ever!"

Chapter 9

1 Then the four living creatures said, "Amen!" And the twenty-four elders fell down and worshiped Him who lives forever and ever.

Chapter 10

1 After these things, I looked, and behold, a door standing open in heaven. And the first voice which I heard was like a trumpet speaking with me, saying, "Come up here, and I will show you things which must take place after this." 2 Immediately I was in the Spirit; and behold, a throne set in heaven, and One sat on the throne.

Chapter 11

1 And He who sat there was like a jasper and a sardius stone in appearance; and there was a rainbow around the throne, in appearance like an emerald. 2 Around the throne were twenty-four thrones, and on the thrones I saw twenty-four elders sitting, clothed in white robes; and they had crowns of gold on their heads.

Chapter 12

1 And from the throne proceeded lightnings, thunderings, and voices. Seven lamps of fire were burning before the throne, which are the seven Spirits of God. 2 Before the throne there was a sea of glass, like crystal. And in the midst of the throne, and

around the throne, were four living creatures full of eyes in front and in back.

Chapter 13

1 The first living creature was like a lion, the second living creature like a calf, the third living creature had a face like a man, and the fourth living creature was like a flying eagle. 2 The four living creatures, each having six wings, were full of eyes around and within. And they do not rest day or night, saying: "Holy, holy, holy, Lord God Almighty, Who was and is and is to come!"

Chapter 14

1 Whenever the living creatures give glory and honor and thanks to Him who sits on the throne, who lives forever and ever, the twenty-four elders fall down before Him who sits on the throne and worship Him who lives forever and ever, and cast their crowns before the throne, saying: 2 "You are worthy, O Lord, to receive glory and honor and power; for You created all things, and by Your will they exist and were created."

Chapter 15

1 And I saw in the right hand of Him who sat on the throne a scroll written inside and on the back, sealed with seven seals. Then I saw a strong angel proclaiming with a loud voice, "Who is worthy to open the scroll and to loose its seals?" 2 And no one in heaven or on the earth or under the earth was able to open the scroll, or to look at it.

Chapter 16

1 So I wept much, because no one was found worthy to open and read the scroll, or to look at it. But one of the elders said to me, "Do not weep. Behold, the Lion of the tribe of Judah, the Root of David, has prevailed to open the scroll and to loose its seven seals." 2 And I looked, and behold, in the midst of the throne and of the four living creatures, and in the midst of the elders, stood a Lamb as though it had been slain, having seven horns and seven eyes, which are the seven Spirits of God sent out into all the earth.

Chapter 17

1 Then He came and took the scroll out of the right hand of Him who sat on the throne. Now when He had taken the scroll, the four living creatures and the twenty-four elders fell down before the Lamb, each having a harp, and golden bowls full of incense, which are the prayers of the saints. 2 And they sang a new song, saying: "You are worthy to take the scroll, and to open its seals; for You were slain, and have redeemed us to God by Your blood out of every tribe and tongue and people and nation, and have made us kings and priests to our God; and we shall reign on the earth."

Chapter 18

1 Then I looked, and I heard the voice of many angels around the throne, the living creatures, and the elders; and the number of them was ten thousand times ten thousand, and thousands of thousands, saying with a loud voice: "Worthy is the Lamb who was slain to receive power and riches and wisdom, and strength and honor and glory and blessing!" 2 And every creature which is in heaven and on the earth and under the earth and such as are in the sea, and all that are in them, I heard saying: "Blessing and honor and glory and power be to Him who sits on the throne, and to the Lamb, forever and ever!"

Chapter 19

1 Then the four living creatures said, "Amen!" And the twenty-four elders fell down and worshiped Him who lives forever and ever.

Chapter 20

1 After this, I was shown the heavens opened, and I saw the judgment of the righteous and the wicked. And I saw the souls of those who had been slain for the word of God and for the testimony which they held. 2 And they cried with a loud voice, saying, "How long, O Lord, holy and true, until You judge and avenge our blood on those who dwell on the earth?"

Chapter 21

1 Then a white robe was given to each of them; and it was said to them that they should rest a little while longer, until both the number of their fellow servants and their brethren, who would be killed as they were, was completed.

Chapter 22

1 Then I saw the Lamb open one of the seals; and I heard one of the four living creatures saying with a voice like thunder, "Come and see." And I looked, and behold, a white horse. He who sat on it had a bow; and a crown was given to him, and he went out conquering and to conquer.

Chapter 23

1 When He opened the second seal, I heard the second living creature saying, "Come and see." Another horse, fiery red, went out. And it was granted to the one who sat on it to take peace from the earth, and that people should kill one another; and there was given to him a great sword.

Chapter 24

1 When He opened the third seal, I heard the third living creature say, "Come and see." So I looked, and behold, a black horse, and he who sat on it had a pair of scales in his hand. And I heard a voice in the midst of the four living creatures saying, "A quart of wheat for a denarius, and three quarts of barley for a denarius; and do not harm the oil and the wine."

Chapter 25

1 When He opened the fourth seal, I heard the voice of the fourth living creature saying, "Come and see." So I looked, and behold, a pale horse. And the name of him who sat on it was Death, and Hades followed with him. And power was given to them over a fourth of the earth, to kill with sword, with hunger, with death, and by the beasts of the earth.

Chapter 26

1 When He opened the fifth seal, I saw under the altar the souls of those who had been slain for the word of God and for the testimony which they held. 2 And they cried with a loud voice, saying, "How long, O Lord, holy and true, until You judge and avenge our blood on those who dwell on the earth?"

Chapter 27

1 Then a white robe was given to each of them; and it was said to them that they should rest a little while longer, until both the number of their fellow servants and their brethren, who would be killed as they were, was completed.

Chapter 28

1 I looked when He opened the sixth seal, and behold, there was a great earthquake; and the sun became black as sackcloth of hair, and the moon became like blood. 2 And the stars of heaven fell to the earth, as a fig tree drops its late figs when it is shaken by a mighty wind. Then the sky receded as a scroll when it is rolled up, and every mountain and island was moved out of its place.

Chapter 29

1 And the kings of the earth, the great men, the rich men, the commanders, the mighty men, every slave and every free man, hid themselves in the caves and in the rocks of the mountains, and said to the mountains and rocks, "Fall on us and hide us from the face of Him who sits on the throne and from the wrath of the Lamb! For the great day of His wrath has come, and who is able to stand?"

Chapter 30

1 After these things, I saw four angels standing at the four corners of the earth, holding the four winds of the earth, that the wind should not blow on the earth, on the sea, or on any tree. 2 Then I saw another angel ascending from the east, having the seal of the living God. And he cried with a loud voice to the four angels to whom it was granted to harm the earth and the sea, saying, "Do not harm the earth, the sea, or the trees till we have sealed the servants of our God on their foreheads."

Chapter 31

1 And I heard the number of those who were sealed. One hundred and forty-four thousand of all the tribes of the children of Israel were sealed. 2 After these things, I looked, and behold, a great multitude which no one could number, of all nations, tribes, peoples, and tongues, standing before the throne and before the Lamb, clothed with white robes, with palm branches in their hands, and crying out with a loud voice, saying, "Salvation belongs to our God who sits on the throne, and to the Lamb!"

Chapter 32

1 All the angels stood around the throne and the elders and the four living creatures, and fell on their faces before the throne and worshiped God, saying: "Amen! Blessing and glory and wisdom, thanksgiving and honor and power and might, be to our God forever and ever. Amen."

Chapter 33

1 Then one of the elders answered, saying to me, "Who are these arrayed in white robes, and where did they come from?" 2 And I said to him, "Sir, you know." So he said to me, "These are the ones who come out of the great tribulation and washed their robes and made them white in the blood of the Lamb."

Chapter 34

1 "Therefore they are before the throne of God, and serve Him day and night in His temple. And He who sits on the throne will dwell among them. They shall neither hunger anymore nor thirst anymore; the sun shall not strike them, nor any heat; for the Lamb who is in the midst of the throne will shepherd them and lead them to living fountains of waters. And God will wipe away every tear from their eyes."

Chapter 35

1 When He opened the seventh seal, there was silence in heaven for about half an hour. 2 And I saw the seven angels who stand before God, and to them were given seven trumpets.

Chapter 36

1 Then another angel, having a golden censer, came and stood at the altar. He was given much incense, that he should offer it with the prayers of all the saints upon the golden altar which was before the throne. 2 And the smoke of the incense, with the prayers of the saints, ascended before God from the angel's hand.

Chapter 37

1 Then the angel took the censer, filled it with fire from the altar, and threw it to the earth. And there were noises, thunderings, lightnings, and an earthquake. 2 So the seven angels who had the seven trumpets prepared themselves to sound.

Chapter 38

1 The first angel sounded: And hail and fire followed, mingled with blood, and they were thrown to the earth. And a third of the trees were burned up, and all green grass was burned up. 2 Then the second angel sounded: And something like a great mountain burning with fire was thrown into the sea, and a third of the sea became blood.

Chapter 39

1 And a third of the living creatures in the sea died, and a third of the ships were destroyed. 2 Then the third angel sounded: And a great star fell from heaven, burning like a torch, and it fell on a third of the rivers and on the springs of water.

Chapter 40

1 The name of the star is Wormwood. A third of the waters became wormwood, and many men died from the water, because it was made bitter. 2 Then the fourth angel sounded: And a third of the sun was struck, a third of the moon, and a third of the stars, so that a third of them were darkened. A third of the day did not shine, and likewise the night.

Chapter 41

1 And I looked, and I heard an angel flying through the midst of heaven, saying with a loud voice, "Woe, woe, woe to the inhabitants of the earth, because of the remaining blasts of the trumpet of the three angels who are about to sound!"

Chapter 42

1 The fifth angel sounded: And I saw a star fallen from heaven to the earth. To him was given the key to the bottomless pit. 2 And he opened the bottomless pit, and smoke arose out of the pit like the smoke of a great furnace. So the sun and the air were darkened because of the smoke of the pit.

Chapter 43

1 Then out of the smoke locusts came upon the earth. And to them was given power, as the scorpions of the earth have power. 2 They were commanded not to harm the grass of the earth, or any green thing, or any tree, but only those men who do not have the seal of God on their foreheads.

Chapter 44

1 And they were not given authority to kill them, but to torment them for five months. Their torment was like the torment of a scorpion when it strikes a man. 2 In those days men will seek death and will not find it; they will desire to die, and death will flee from them.

Chapter 45

1 The shape of the locusts was like horses prepared for battle. On their heads were crowns of something like gold, and their faces were like the faces of men. 2 They had hair like women's hair, and their teeth were like lions' teeth.

Chapter 46

1 And they had breastplates like breastplates of iron, and the sound of their wings was like the sound of chariots with many horses running into battle. 2 They had tails like scorpions, and there were stings in their tails. Their power was to hurt men five months.

Chapter 47

1 And they had as king over them the angel of the bottomless pit, whose name in Hebrew is Abaddon, but in Greek he has the name Apollyon. 2 One woe is past. Behold, still two more woes are coming after these things.

Chapter 48

1 Then the sixth angel sounded: And I heard a voice from the four horns of the golden altar which is before God, 2 saying to the sixth angel who had the trumpet, "Release the four angels who are bound at the great river Euphrates."

Chapter 49

1 So the four angels, who had been prepared for the hour and day and month and year, were released to kill a third of mankind. 2 Now the number of the army of the horsemen was two hundred million; I heard the number of them.

Chapter 50

1 And thus I saw the horses in the vision: those who sat on them had breastplates of fiery red, hyacinth blue, and sulfur yellow; and the heads of the horses were like the heads of lions; and out of their mouths came fire, smoke, and brimstone. 2 By these three plagues a third of mankind was killed—by the fire and the smoke and the brimstone which came out of their mouths.

Chapter 51

1 For their power is in their mouth and in their tails; for their tails are like serpents, having heads; and with them they do harm. 2 But the rest of mankind, who were not killed by these plagues, did not repent of the works of their hands, that they should not worship demons, and idols of gold, silver, brass, stone, and wood, which can neither see nor hear nor walk.

Chapter 52

1 And they did not repent of their murders or their sorceries or their sexual immorality or their thefts. 2 I saw still another mighty angel coming down from heaven, clothed with a cloud. And a rainbow was on his head, his face was like the sun, and his feet like

pillars of fire.

Chapter 53
1 He had a little book open in his hand. And he set his right foot on the sea and his left foot on the land, 2 and cried with a loud voice, as when a lion roars. When he cried out, seven thunders uttered their voices.

Chapter 54
1 Now when the seven thunders uttered their voices, I was about to write; but I heard a voice from heaven saying to me, "Seal up the things which the seven thunders uttered, and do not write them." 2 The angel whom I saw standing on the sea and on the land raised up his hand to heaven and swore by Him who lives forever and ever, who created heaven and the things that are in it, the earth and the things that are in it, and the sea and the things that are in it, that there should be delay no longer,

Chapter 55
1 but in the days of the sounding of the seventh angel, when he is about to sound, the mystery of God would be finished, as He declared to His servants the prophets. 2 Then the voice which I heard from heaven spoke to me again and said, "Go, take the little book which is open in the hand of the angel who stands on the sea and on the earth."

Chapter 56
1 So I went to the angel and said to him, "Give me the little book." And he said to me, "Take and eat it; and it will make your stomach bitter, but it will be as sweet as honey in your mouth." 2 Then I took the little book out of the angel's hand and ate it, and it was as sweet as honey in my mouth. But when I had eaten it, my stomach became bitter.

Chapter 57
1 And he said to me, "You must prophesy again about many peoples, nations, tongues, and kings." 2 Then I was given a reed like a measuring rod. And the angel stood, saying, "Rise and measure the temple of God, the altar, and those who worship there.

Chapter 58
1 But leave out the court which is outside the temple, and do not measure it, for it has been given to the Gentiles. And they will tread the holy city underfoot for forty-two months. 2 And I will give power to my two witnesses, and they will prophesy one thousand two hundred and sixty days, clothed in sackcloth."

Chapter 59
1 These are the two olive trees and the two lampstands standing before the God of the earth. 2 And if anyone wants to harm them, fire proceeds from their mouth and devours their enemies. And if anyone wants to harm them, he must be killed in this manner.

Chapter 60
1 These have power to shut heaven, so that no rain falls in the days of their prophecy; and they have power over waters to turn them to blood, and to strike the earth with all plagues, as often as they desire. 2 When they finish their testimony, the beast that ascends out of the bottomless pit will make war against them, overcome them, and kill them.

Chapter 61
1 And their dead bodies will lie in the street of the great city which spiritually is called Sodom and Egypt, where also our Lord was crucified. 2 Then those from the peoples, tribes, tongues, and nations will see their dead bodies three-and-a-half days, and not allow their dead bodies to be put into graves.

Chapter 62
1 And those who dwell on the earth will rejoice over them, make merry, and send gifts to one another, because these two prophets tormented those who dwell on the earth. 2 Now after the three-and-a-half days the breath of life from God entered them, and they stood on their feet, and great fear fell on those who saw them.

Chapter 63
1 And they heard a loud voice from heaven saying to them, "Come up here." And they ascended to heaven in a cloud, and their enemies saw them. 2 In the same hour there was a great earthquake, and a tenth of the city fell. In the earthquake seven thousand people were killed, and the rest were afraid and gave glory to the God of heaven.

Chapter 64
1 The second woe is past. Behold, the third woe is coming quickly. 2 Then the seventh angel sounded: And there were loud voices in heaven, saying, "The kingdoms of this world have become the kingdoms of our Lord and of His Christ, and He shall reign forever and ever!"

Chapter 65
1 And the twenty-four elders who sat before God on their thrones fell on their faces and worshiped God, saying: 2 "We give You thanks, O Lord God Almighty, the One who is and who was and who is to come, because You have taken Your great power and reigned.

Chapter 66
1 The nations were angry, and Your wrath has come, and the time of the dead, that they should be judged, and that You should reward Your servants the prophets and the saints, and those who fear Your name, small and great, and should destroy those who destroy the earth." 2 Then the temple of God was opened in heaven, and the ark of His covenant was seen in His temple. And there were lightnings, noises, thunderings, an earthquake, and great hail.

Chapter 67
1 Now a great sign appeared in heaven: a woman clothed with the sun, with the moon under her feet, and on her head a garland of twelve stars. 2 Then being with child, she cried out in labor and in pain to give birth.

Chapter 68
1 And another sign appeared in heaven: behold, a great, fiery red dragon having seven heads and ten horns, and seven diadems on his heads. 2 His tail drew a third of the stars of heaven and threw them to the earth. And the dragon stood before the woman who was ready to give birth, to devour her Child as soon as it was born.

Chapter 69
1 She bore a male Child who was to rule all nations with a rod of iron. And her Child was caught up to God and His throne. 2 Then the woman fled into the wilderness, where she has a place prepared by God, that they should feed her there one thousand two hundred and sixty days.

Chapter 70
1 And war broke out in heaven: Michael and his angels fought with the dragon; and the dragon and his angels fought, 2 but they did not prevail, nor was a place found for them in heaven any longer.

Chapter 71
1 So the great dragon was cast out, that serpent of old, called the Devil and Satan, who deceives the whole world; he was cast to the earth, and his angels were cast out with him. 2 Then I heard a loud voice saying in heaven, "Now salvation, and strength, and the kingdom of our God, and the power of His Christ have come, for the accuser of our brethren, who accused them before our God day and night, has been cast down.

Chapter 72
1 And they overcame him by the blood of the Lamb and by the word of their testimony, and they did not love their lives to the death. 2 Therefore rejoice, O heavens, and you who dwell in them! Woe to the inhabitants of the earth and the sea! For the devil has come down to you, having great wrath, because he knows that he has a short time."

Chapter 73
1 Now when the dragon saw that he had been cast to

the earth, he persecuted the woman who gave birth to the male Child. 2 But the woman was given two wings of a great eagle, that she might fly into the wilderness to her place, where she is nourished for a time and times and half a time, from the presence of the serpent.

Chapter 74
1 So the serpent spewed water out of his mouth like a flood after the woman, that he might cause her to be carried away by the flood. 2 But the earth helped the woman, and the earth opened its mouth and swallowed up the flood which the dragon had spewed out of his mouth.

Chapter 75
1 And the dragon was enraged with the woman, and he went to make war with the rest of her offspring, who keep the commandments of God and have the testimony of Jesus Christ.

135. The Acts of the Martyrs

Chapter 1
1 The Acts of the Martyrs recount the sufferings and deaths of early Christians who bore witness to their faith through their martyrdom. These acts were compiled to inspire the faithful and to serve as testimonies of the power of Christ in the lives of those who were willing to sacrifice everything for their belief in Him.

Chapter 2
1 Among the first of these martyrs was Stephen, who was full of faith and the Holy Spirit. He performed great wonders and signs among the people, but opposition arose from members of the Synagogue of the Freedmen. Unable to stand against the wisdom the Spirit gave him, they secretly persuaded some men to say, "We have heard Stephen speak blasphemous words against Moses and against God."

Chapter 3
1 They seized Stephen and brought him before the Sanhedrin. There, Stephen delivered a powerful speech, recounting the history of Israel and the constant rejection of God's messengers. He concluded by accusing the Sanhedrin of betraying and murdering the Righteous One, Jesus Christ.

Chapter 4
1 Enraged by his words, the members of the Sanhedrin gnashed their teeth at Stephen. But Stephen, full of the Holy Spirit, looked up to heaven and saw the glory of God, and Jesus standing at the right hand of God. "Look," he said, "I see heaven open and the Son of Man standing at the right hand of God."

Chapter 5
1 At this, they covered their ears and, yelling at the top of their voices, they all rushed at him, dragged him out of the city, and began to stone him. Meanwhile, the witnesses laid their coats at the feet of a young man named Saul. As they stoned him, Stephen prayed, "Lord Jesus, receive my spirit." Then he fell on his knees and cried out, "Lord, do not hold this sin against them." When he had said this, he fell asleep.

Chapter 6
1 The martyrdom of Stephen marked the beginning of great persecution against the church in Jerusalem, scattering the believers throughout Judea and Samaria. Among those who fled was Philip, who went down to a city in Samaria and proclaimed the Messiah there. When the crowds heard Philip and saw the signs he performed, they all paid close attention to what he said. For with shrieks, impure spirits came out of many, and many who were paralyzed or lame were healed.

Chapter 7
1 As the persecution continued, Saul, who approved of Stephen's death, began to destroy the church. Going from house to house, he dragged off both men and women and put them in prison. However, as Saul journeyed to Damascus to arrest more believers, he encountered the risen Christ, who struck him blind and called him to be His chosen instrument to proclaim His name to the Gentiles and their kings and to the people of Israel.

Chapter 8
1 Another notable martyrdom is that of James, the brother of John. King Herod Agrippa I began to persecute the church and had James put to death with the sword. This pleased the Jews, and he proceeded to seize Peter also, intending to bring him out for public trial after the Passover. However, an angel of the Lord miraculously rescued Peter from prison.

Chapter 9
1 In the city of Antioch, Ignatius, the bishop, was another who was destined for martyrdom. Ignatius was a disciple of the apostle John and became a prominent leader in the early church. When Trajan was emperor, Ignatius was arrested for refusing to worship the Roman gods and the emperor. He was condemned to death by being thrown to wild beasts in the Colosseum.

Chapter 10
1 As Ignatius was being taken to Rome, he wrote several letters to the churches, encouraging them to remain steadfast in their faith and to be obedient to their bishops. In one of his letters, he expressed his desire to be a martyr, seeing it as the ultimate testimony of his love for Christ. "I am God's wheat," he wrote, "and I am ground by the teeth of wild beasts, that I may be found pure bread."

Chapter 11
1 When Ignatius arrived in Rome, he was led to the Colosseum, where he was devoured by lions. His bones were collected by Christians and were later buried in Antioch, where his memory was revered.

Chapter 12
1 Another martyr whose story is recorded is Polycarp, the bishop of Smyrna. A disciple of the apostle John, Polycarp was known for his steadfast faith and leadership. When he was an old man, he was arrested during a time of persecution and brought before the proconsul.

Chapter 13
1 The proconsul urged Polycarp to deny Christ and to swear by the fortune of Caesar, offering him his freedom if he would do so. But Polycarp replied, "Eighty and six years have I served Him, and He has done me no wrong. How then can I blaspheme my King and Savior?"

Chapter 14
1 When the proconsul threatened him with being burned alive, Polycarp responded, "You threaten me with fire that burns for a season, and after a little while is quenched, but you are ignorant of the fire of the coming judgment and of eternal punishment, reserved for the ungodly. But why do you delay? Come, do what you will."

Chapter 15
1 Polycarp was then bound and placed on a pyre. As the flames rose around him, witnesses reported that his body did not burn as expected. Instead, it was as if he was surrounded by a protective light. Seeing this, the executioners ordered a guard to stab him with a sword. When he was pierced, a great quantity of blood flowed out, extinguishing the fire.

Chapter 16
1 The Acts of the Martyrs continue with many other accounts of believers who faced death rather than deny their faith in Christ. Among them were Perpetua and Felicity, two women who were martyred in Carthage. Perpetua was a young noblewoman, and Felicity was her slave. Both were imprisoned for their faith and sentenced to death in the arena.

Chapter 17
1 Perpetua kept a diary during her imprisonment, in which she recorded her visions and the

encouragement she received from the Holy Spirit. On the day of their execution, they were led into the arena, where wild animals were set upon them. Despite their sufferings, they remained steadfast, and Perpetua even guided the sword of the executioner to her throat when he hesitated to kill her.

Chapter 18
1 These and other stories of the martyrs were circulated among the early Christian communities, inspiring them to remain faithful in the face of persecution. The martyrs were seen as the ultimate witnesses to the truth of the gospel, and their deaths were celebrated as victories over the powers of darkness.

Chapter 19
1 The Acts of the Martyrs served not only as a record of the courage and faith of these early Christians but also as a powerful tool for evangelism. Their stories spread far and wide, drawing others to the faith and strengthening the resolve of believers to endure whatever trials might come their way.

Chapter 20
1 The legacy of the martyrs continues to be honored in the church today. Their examples of faithfulness unto death serve as a reminder of the cost of discipleship and the eternal reward that awaits those who are faithful to the end.

136. The Gospel of Judas

Chapter 1
1 The Acts of Pilate, also known as the Gospel of Nicodemus, is a text that details the trial, crucifixion, and resurrection of Jesus Christ as observed by Pontius Pilate, the Roman governor of Judea.

Chapter 2
1 Jesus was brought before Pilate by the chief priests and elders, who accused Him of many things. Pilate asked Him, "Are You the King of the Jews?" Jesus answered, "You have said so." But when He was accused by the chief priests and elders, He gave no answer.

Chapter 3
1 Pilate marveled greatly at His silence and sought to release Him, knowing that it was out of envy that they had delivered Him up. He asked the crowd, "Whom do you want me to release to you: Barabbas, or Jesus who is called Christ?"

Chapter 4
1 The crowd, stirred up by the chief priests, demanded the release of Barabbas and cried out, "Crucify Him!" Pilate asked, "Why, what evil has He done?" But they shouted all the more, "Crucify Him!"

Chapter 5
1 Pilate, seeing that he was gaining nothing but rather that a riot was beginning, took water and washed his hands before the crowd, saying, "I am innocent of this man's blood; see to it yourselves." And all the people answered, "His blood be on us and on our children!"

Chapter 6
1 Jesus was then scourged and handed over to be crucified. The soldiers took Him into the governor's headquarters, stripped Him, and put a scarlet robe on Him. They twisted together a crown of thorns, put it on His head, and mocked Him, saying, "Hail, King of the Jews!"

Chapter 7
1 Jesus was led out to be crucified, and they compelled Simon of Cyrene to carry His cross. When they came to a place called Golgotha, they crucified Him there, and with Him two robbers, one on His right and one on His left.

Chapter 8
1 From the sixth hour to the ninth hour, there was darkness over all the land. And about the ninth hour, Jesus cried out with a loud voice, "My God, My God, why have You forsaken Me?" And Jesus cried out again with a loud voice and yielded up His spirit.

Chapter 9
1 At that moment, the curtain of the temple was torn in two from top to bottom, the earth shook, the rocks were split, the tombs were opened, and many bodies of the saints who had fallen asleep were raised. When the centurion and those who were with him saw the earthquake and what took place, they were filled with awe and said, "Truly this was the Son of God!"

Chapter 10
1 Joseph of Arimathea, a disciple of Jesus, went to Pilate and asked for the body of Jesus. Pilate ordered it to be given to him, and Joseph took the body, wrapped it in a clean linen shroud, and laid it in his own new tomb, which he had cut in the rock. He rolled a great stone to the entrance of the tomb and went away.

Chapter 11
1 On the third day, early in the morning, Mary Magdalene and the other Mary went to see the tomb. And behold, there was a great earthquake, for an angel of the Lord descended from heaven and came and rolled back the stone and sat on it. His appearance was like lightning, and his clothing white as snow.

Chapter 12
1 The guards trembled and became like dead men, but the angel said to the women, "Do not be afraid, for I know that you seek Jesus who was crucified. He is not here, for He has risen, as He said. Come, see the place where He lay."

Chapter 13
1 The women departed quickly from the tomb with fear and great joy and ran to tell His disciples. And behold, Jesus met them and said, "Greetings!" They came up and took hold of His feet and worshiped Him. Then Jesus said to them, "Do not be afraid; go and tell My brothers to go to Galilee, and there they will see Me."

Chapter 14
1 The Acts of Pilate concludes with the report of the resurrection being spread among the people. The chief priests and elders bribed the soldiers to say that His disciples came by night and stole Him away while they were asleep. But despite their efforts, the truth of the resurrection could not be suppressed.

Chapter 15
1 Pilate, reflecting on all that had happened, was troubled in spirit. He knew that he had condemned an innocent man, and the events that followed confirmed his worst fears. The Acts of Pilate serve as a testimony to the power of Christ's resurrection and the fulfillment of the Scriptures.

137. The Preaching of Peter

Chapter 1
1 The apostle Peter, a disciple of Jesus Christ, set out to preach the gospel to the nations. As he journeyed, he came to a certain city where the people were known for their idolatry and their devotion to the false gods of their ancestors.

Chapter 2
1 Standing in the midst of the marketplace, Peter lifted up his voice and said, "Men of this city, listen to my words! You worship gods made by human hands, gods of gold and silver, stone and wood. But these are no gods at all; they are lifeless and powerless, unable to see, hear, or save. The true God, the Creator of heaven and earth, is not made by hands nor confined to temples built by men. He is the living God, who gives life to all things and sustains all creation by His word."

Chapter 3
1 The people marveled at Peter's boldness, and a great crowd gathered to hear him. Some among them began to question him, saying, "How do you claim to know this God whom we have not seen?

How can we be sure that what you speak is the truth?"

Chapter 4

1 Peter answered, "God has not left Himself without witness. He has revealed Himself through His creation, which declares His glory and His eternal power. But more than this, God has spoken to us through His prophets, who foretold the coming of His Son, Jesus Christ, who was sent to save us from our sins. This Jesus, whom I declare to you, was crucified, died, and was buried. But God raised Him from the dead on the third day, and He appeared to many witnesses, including myself and the other apostles. It is by His name that I preach to you today."

Chapter 5

1 As Peter spoke, the Holy Spirit moved in the hearts of the people, and many were convicted of their sin. They cried out, "What must we do to be saved?"

Chapter 6

1 Peter said to them, "Repent, and be baptized every one of you in the name of Jesus Christ for the forgiveness of your sins, and you will receive the gift of the Holy Spirit. For the promise is for you and your children and for all who are far off, everyone whom the Lord our God calls to Himself."

Chapter 7

1 Many believed the words of Peter and were baptized, and a great number of people in that city turned from their idols to serve the living and true God. The news of their conversion spread throughout the region, and the word of God grew mightily and prevailed.

Chapter 8

1 The priests of the idols, seeing that their influence was waning, conspired against Peter and stirred up the authorities against him. They accused him of leading the people astray and turning them away from the worship of the gods. Peter was arrested and brought before the governor, who questioned him about his teachings.

Chapter 9

1 The governor said, "Peter, you are charged with inciting the people to abandon the worship of our gods and to follow this Jesus whom you preach. What do you say in your defense?"

Chapter 10

1 Peter replied, "I am not ashamed of the gospel of Jesus Christ, for it is the power of God for salvation to everyone who believes. The gods you worship are no gods at all; they are the work of men's hands, and they can neither save nor deliver. But Jesus Christ is the Son of the living God, who came into the world to save sinners. He died for our sins and was raised from the dead, and He is the one true God, who will judge the living and the dead."

Chapter 11

1 The governor, hearing these words, was enraged and ordered that Peter be beaten and imprisoned. But even in prison, Peter continued to preach the gospel, and many who heard him believed and were saved.

Chapter 12

1 After many days, Peter was brought out of prison to be judged again. The governor, hoping to dissuade him, said, "Peter, if you renounce this Jesus and return to the worship of our gods, I will set you free and give you honor in the sight of the people."

Chapter 13

1 But Peter answered, "I will never deny my Lord, who loved me and gave Himself for me. I would rather die than deny the truth of the gospel. For there is no other name under heaven given among men by which we must be saved."

Chapter 14

1 Seeing that Peter would not be swayed, the governor condemned him to death. Peter was led out to be crucified, and as he was about to be nailed to the cross, he requested that he be crucified upside down, saying, "I am not worthy to die in the same manner as my Lord."

Chapter 15

1 And so Peter was crucified, and he glorified God in his death. His testimony and his martyrdom inspired many to follow Christ, even unto death. The church continued to grow, and the gospel spread to the ends of the earth, just as Jesus had commanded.

138. The Epistle of James the Less

Chapter 1

1 James, a servant of God and of the Lord Jesus Christ, to the twelve tribes in the Dispersion: Greetings. 2 Consider it pure joy, my brothers and sisters, whenever you face trials of many kinds, because you know that the testing of your faith produces perseverance. 3 Let perseverance finish its work so that you may be mature and complete, not lacking anything.

Chapter 2

1 If any of you lacks wisdom, you should ask God, who gives generously to all without finding fault, and it will be given to you. 2 But when you ask, you must believe and not doubt, because the one who doubts is like a wave of the sea, blown and tossed by the wind. 3 That person should not expect to receive anything from the Lord. Such a person is double-minded and unstable in all they do.

Chapter 3

1 Believers in humble circumstances ought to take pride in their high position. 2 But the rich should take pride in their humiliation—since they will pass away like a wildflower. 3 For the sun rises with scorching heat and withers the plant; its blossom falls and its beauty is destroyed. In the same way, the rich will fade away even while they go about their business.

Chapter 4

1 Blessed is the one who perseveres under trial because, having stood the test, that person will receive the crown of life that the Lord has promised to those who love him. 2 When tempted, no one should say, "God is tempting me." For God cannot be tempted by evil, nor does he tempt anyone; 3 but each person is tempted when they are dragged away by their own evil desire and enticed. 4 Then, after desire has conceived, it gives birth to sin; and sin, when it is full-grown, gives birth to death.

Chapter 5

1 Don't be deceived, my dear brothers and sisters. 2 Every good and perfect gift is from above, coming down from the Father of the heavenly lights, who does not change like shifting shadows. 3 He chose to give us birth through the word of truth, that we might be a kind of firstfruits of all he created.

Chapter 6

1 My dear brothers and sisters, take note of this: Everyone should be quick to listen, slow to speak and slow to become angry, 2 because human anger does not produce the righteousness that God desires. 3 Therefore, get rid of all moral filth and the evil that is so prevalent and humbly accept the word planted in you, which can save you.

Chapter 7

1 Do not merely listen to the word, and so deceive yourselves. Do what it says. 2 Anyone who listens to the word but does not do what it says is like someone who looks at his face in a mirror 3 and, after looking at himself, goes away and immediately forgets what he looks like. 4 But whoever looks intently into the perfect law that gives freedom, and continues in it—not forgetting what they have heard, but doing it—they will be blessed in what they do.

Chapter 8

1 Those who consider themselves religious and yet do not keep a tight rein on their tongues deceive themselves, and their religion is worthless. 2 Religion that God our Father accepts as pure and faultless is this: to look after orphans and widows in their

distress and to keep oneself from being polluted by the world.

Chapter 9

1 My brothers and sisters, believers in our glorious Lord Jesus Christ must not show favoritism. 2 Suppose a man comes into your meeting wearing a gold ring and fine clothes, and a poor man in filthy old clothes also comes in. 3 If you show special attention to the man wearing fine clothes and say, "Here's a good seat for you," but say to the poor man, "You stand there" or "Sit on the floor by my feet," 4 have you not discriminated among yourselves and become judges with evil thoughts?

Chapter 10

1 Listen, my dear brothers and sisters: Has not God chosen those who are poor in the eyes of the world to be rich in faith and to inherit the kingdom he promised those who love him? 2 But you have dishonored the poor. Is it not the rich who are exploiting you? Are they not the ones who are dragging you into court? 3 Are they not the ones who are blaspheming the noble name of him to whom you belong?

Chapter 11

1 If you really keep the royal law found in Scripture, "Love your neighbor as yourself," you are doing right. 2 But if you show favoritism, you sin and are convicted by the law as lawbreakers. 3 For whoever keeps the whole law and yet stumbles at just one point is guilty of breaking all of it. 4 For he who said, "You shall not commit adultery," also said, "You shall not murder." If you do not commit adultery but do commit murder, you have become a lawbreaker.

Chapter 12

1 Speak and act as those who are going to be judged by the law that gives freedom, 2 because judgment without mercy will be shown to anyone who has not been merciful. Mercy triumphs over judgment.

Chapter 13

1 What good is it, my brothers and sisters, if someone claims to have faith but has no deeds? Can such faith save them? 2 Suppose a brother or a sister is without clothes and daily food. 3 If one of you says to them, "Go in peace; keep warm and well fed," but does nothing about their physical needs, what good is it? 4 In the same way, faith by itself, if it is not accompanied by action, is dead.

Chapter 14

1 But someone will say, "You have faith; I have deeds." 2 Show me your faith without deeds, and I will show you my faith by my deeds. 3 You believe that there is one God. Good! Even the demons believe that—and shudder.

Chapter 15

1 You foolish person, do you want evidence that faith without deeds is useless? 2 Was not our father Abraham considered righteous for what he did when he offered his son Isaac on the altar? 3 You see that his faith and his actions were working together, and his faith was made complete by what he did. 4 And the scripture was fulfilled that says, "Abraham believed God, and it was credited to him as righteousness," and he was called God's friend. 5 You see that a person is considered righteous by what they do and not by faith alone. 6 In the same way, was not even Rahab the prostitute considered righteous for what she did when she gave lodging to the spies and sent them off in a different direction? 7 As the body without the spirit is dead, so faith without deeds is dead.

Chapter 16

1 Not many of you should become teachers, my fellow believers because you know that we who teach will be judged more strictly. 2 We all stumble in many ways. Anyone who is never at fault in what they say is perfect, able to keep their whole body in check. 3 When we put bits into the mouths of horses to make them obey us, we can turn the whole animal. 4 Or take ships as an example. Although they are so large and are driven by strong winds, they are steered by a very small rudder wherever the pilot wants to go.

Chapter 17

1 Likewise, the tongue is a small part of the body, but it makes great boasts. Consider what a great forest is set on fire by a small spark. 2 The tongue also is a fire, a world of evil among the parts of the body. It corrupts the whole body, sets the whole course of one's life on fire, and is itself set on fire by hell. 3 All kinds of animals, birds, reptiles and sea creatures are being tamed and have been tamed by mankind, 4 but no human being can tame the tongue. It is a restless evil, full of deadly poison.

Chapter 18

1 With the tongue, we praise our Lord and Father, and with it we curse human beings, who have been made in God's likeness. 2 Out of the same mouth come praise and cursing. My brothers and sisters, this should not be. 3 Can both fresh water and saltwater flow from the same spring? 4 My brothers and sisters, can a fig tree bear olives, or a grapevine bear figs? Neither can a salt spring produce fresh water.

Chapter 19

1 Who is wise and understanding among you? Let them show it by their good life, by deeds done in the humility that comes from wisdom. 2 But if you harbor bitter envy and selfish ambition in your hearts, do not boast about it or deny the truth. 3 Such "wisdom" does not come down from heaven but is earthly, unspiritual, demonic. 4 For where you have envy and selfish ambition, there you find disorder and every evil practice.

Chapter 20

1 But the wisdom that comes from heaven is first of all pure; then peace-loving, considerate, submissive, full of mercy and good fruit, impartial and sincere. 2 Peacemakers who sow in peace reap a harvest of righteousness.

Chapter 21

1 What causes fights and quarrels among you? Don't they come from your desires that battle within you? 2 You desire but do not have, so you kill. You covet but you cannot get what you want, so you quarrel and fight. You do not have because you do not ask God. 3 When you ask, you do not receive, because you ask with wrong motives, that you may spend what you get on your pleasures.

Chapter 22

1 You adulterous people, don't you know that friendship with the world means enmity against God? Therefore, anyone who chooses to be a friend of the world becomes an enemy of God. 2 Or do you think Scripture says without reason that he jealously longs for the spirit he has caused to dwell in us? 3 But he gives us more grace. That is why Scripture says: "God opposes the proud but shows favor to the humble."

Chapter 23

1 Submit yourselves, then, to God. Resist the devil, and he will flee from you. 2 Come near to God and he will come near to you. Wash your hands, you sinners, and purify your hearts, you double-minded. 3 Grieve, mourn and wail. Change your laughter to mourning and your joy to gloom. 4 Humble yourselves before the Lord, and he will lift you up.

Chapter 24

1 Brothers and sisters, do not slander one another. Anyone who speaks against a brother or sister or judges them speaks against the law and judges it. When you judge the law, you are not keeping it, but sitting in judgment on it. 2 There is only one Lawgiver and Judge, the one who is able to save and destroy. But you—who are you to judge your neighbor?

Chapter 25

1 Now listen, you who say, "Today or tomorrow we will go to this or that city, spend a year there, carry on business and make money." 2 Why, you do not even know what will happen tomorrow. What is your life? You are a mist that appears for a little while and then vanishes. 3 Instead, you ought to say, "If it is the

Lord's will, we will live and do this or that." 4 As it is, you boast in your arrogant schemes. All such boasting is evil. 5 If anyone, then, knows the good they ought to do and doesn't do it, it is sin for them.

Chapter 26

1 Now listen, you rich people, weep and wail because of the misery that is coming on you. 2 Your wealth has rotted, and moths have eaten your clothes. 3 Your gold and silver are corroded. Their corrosion will testify against you and eat your flesh like fire. You have hoarded wealth in the last days. 4 Look! The wages you failed to pay the workers who mowed your fields are crying out against you. The cries of the harvesters have reached the ears of the Lord Almighty. 5 You have lived on earth in luxury and self-indulgence. You have fattened yourselves in the day of slaughter. 6 You have condemned and murdered the innocent one, who was not opposing you.

Chapter 27

1 Be patient, then, brothers and sisters, until the Lord's coming. See how the farmer waits for the land to yield its valuable crop, patiently waiting for the autumn and spring rains. 2 You too, be patient and stand firm, because the Lord's coming is near. 3 Don't grumble against one another, brothers and sisters, or you will be judged. The Judge is standing at the door!

Chapter 28

1 Brothers and sisters, as an example of patience in the face of suffering, take the prophets who spoke in the name of the Lord. 2 As you know, we count as blessed those who have persevered. You have heard of Job's perseverance and have seen what the Lord finally brought about. The Lord is full of compassion and mercy.

Chapter 29

1 Above all, my brothers and sisters, do not swear— not by heaven or by earth or by anything else. All you need to say is a simple "Yes" or "No." Otherwise, you will be condemned.

Chapter 30

1 Is anyone among you in trouble? Let them pray. Is anyone happy? Let them sing songs of praise. 2 Is anyone among you sick? Let them call the elders of the church to pray over them and anoint them with oil in the name of the Lord. 3 And the prayer offered in faith will make the sick person well; the Lord will raise them up. If they have sinned, they will be forgiven. 4 Therefore confess your sins to each other and pray for each other so that you may be healed. The prayer of a righteous person is powerful and effective.

Chapter 31

1 Elijah was a human being, even as we are. He prayed earnestly that it would not rain, and it did not rain on the land for three and a half years. 2 Again he prayed, and the heavens gave rain, and the earth produced its crops.

Chapter 32

1 My brothers and sisters, if one of you should wander from the truth and someone should bring that person back, remember this: 2 Whoever turns a sinner from the error of their way will save them from death and cover over a multitude of sins.

139. The Epistle of Jude

Chapter 1

1 Jude, a servant of Jesus Christ and brother of James, to those who are called, beloved in God the Father and kept for Jesus Christ: 2 May mercy, peace, and love be multiplied to you.

Chapter 2

1 Beloved, although I was very eager to write to you about our common salvation, I found it necessary to write appealing to you to contend for the faith that was once for all delivered to the saints. 2 For certain people have crept in unnoticed who long ago were designated for this condemnation, ungodly people, who pervert the grace of our God into sensuality and deny our only Master and Lord, Jesus Christ.

Chapter 3

1 Now I want to remind you, although you once fully knew it, that Jesus, who saved a people out of the land of Egypt, afterward destroyed those who did not believe. 2 And the angels who did not stay within their own position of authority, but left their proper dwelling, He has kept in eternal chains under gloomy darkness until the judgment of the great day— 3 just as Sodom and Gomorrah and the surrounding cities, which likewise indulged in sexual immorality and pursued unnatural desire, serve as an example by undergoing a punishment of eternal fire.

Chapter 4

1 Yet in like manner these people also, relying on their dreams, defile the flesh, reject authority, and blaspheme the glorious ones. 2 But when the archangel Michael, contending with the devil, was disputing about the body of Moses, he did not presume to pronounce a blasphemous judgment, but said, "The Lord rebuke you." 3 But these people blaspheme all that they do not understand, and they are destroyed by all that they, like unreasoning animals, understand instinctively.

Chapter 5

1 Woe to them! For they walked in the way of Cain and abandoned themselves for the sake of gain to Balaam's error and perished in Korah's rebellion. 2 These are hidden reefs at your love feasts, as they feast with you without fear, shepherds feeding themselves; waterless clouds, swept along by winds; fruitless trees in late autumn, twice dead, uprooted; 3 wild waves of the sea, casting up the foam of their own shame; wandering stars, for whom the gloom of utter darkness has been reserved forever.

Chapter 6

1 It was also about these that Enoch, the seventh from Adam, prophesied, saying, "Behold, the Lord comes with ten thousands of his holy ones, 2 to execute judgment on all and to convict all the ungodly of all their deeds of ungodliness that they have committed in such an ungodly way, and of all the harsh things that ungodly sinners have spoken against him." 3 These are grumblers, malcontents, following their own sinful desires; they are loud-mouthed boasters, showing favoritism to gain advantage.

Chapter 7

1 But you must remember, beloved, the predictions of the apostles of our Lord Jesus Christ. 2 They said to you, "In the last time there will be scoffers, following their own ungodly passions." 3 It is these who cause divisions, worldly people, devoid of the Spirit.

Chapter 8

1 But you, beloved, building yourselves up in your most holy faith and praying in the Holy Spirit, 2 keep yourselves in the love of God, waiting for the mercy of our Lord Jesus Christ that leads to eternal life. 3 And have mercy on those who doubt; save others by snatching them out of the fire; to others show mercy with fear, hating even the garment stained by the flesh.

Chapter 9

1 Now to him who is able to keep you from stumbling and to present you blameless before the presence of his glory with great joy, 2 to the only God, our Savior, through Jesus Christ our Lord, be glory, majesty, dominion, and authority, before all time and now and forever. Amen.

140. The Gospel of Truth

Chapter 1

1 The gospel of truth is joy for those who have received grace from the Father of truth, that they might know Him through the power of the Word that

came forth from the fullness of the Father's thought. This Word is the Father's Son, full of grace and truth, who is called the Savior.

Chapter 2
1 The name of the gospel is the revelation of hope, and those who have known this hope are those who know where they come from and where they are going. This knowledge is hidden in the silence that surrounds all things, born of the true Father in His fullness.

Chapter 3
1 The truth of the gospel is that the Father revealed Himself to all those who were worthy of His message, sending the Son to proclaim it. Those who have ears to hear have received this message, and it is through the Word that they have come to know the Father.

Chapter 4
1 The Father's thought became a Word, and this Word revealed the hidden things, for it is the image of the Father. The truth that the Word speaks is that the Father is all in all, and His love is what gives life to all things. The gospel is the truth that the Father loves His children and desires that they return to Him.

Chapter 5
1 Those who have received the Word have come to know the truth, and the truth has set them free from ignorance. Ignorance is the cause of error and sin, but the truth of the gospel is the light that dispels the darkness of ignorance.

Chapter 6
1 The Word is the light that shines in the darkness, and the darkness has not overcome it. The Word was with God from the beginning, and all things were made through Him. In the fullness of time, the Word became flesh and dwelt among us, revealing the glory of the Father.

Chapter 7
1 The world was made by the Word, but the world did not know Him. He came to His own, but His own did not receive Him. But to all who received Him, who believed in His name, He gave the right to become children of God, born not of blood nor of the will of the flesh nor of the will of man, but of God.

Chapter 8
1 The Word is the life that was made manifest, and this life is the light of men. The light shines in the darkness, and those who follow the light walk in the truth. The truth is that the Father is light, and in Him, there is no darkness at all.

Chapter 9
1 The Word came to bring the light of the Father to those who were in darkness. The darkness is the ignorance of the Father, but the light of the Word reveals the truth of the Father's love. This love is what gives life to the world, and it is the truth that sets men free.

Chapter 10
1 The Father sent the Son into the world not to condemn the world, but that the world might be saved through Him. The gospel is the message of salvation, the good news that the Father loves His children and desires that they return to Him.

Chapter 11
1 Those who know the truth of the gospel have eternal life, for they have passed from death to life. The truth is that the Father has given His Son to be the Savior of the world, and all who believe in Him have life in His name.

Chapter 12
1 The truth of the gospel is that the Father is love, and His love is what gives life to all things. The Word is the expression of this love, and those who receive the Word receive the love of the Father. This love is what binds the children of God together in unity.

Chapter 13
1 The gospel is the revelation of the mystery that was hidden for ages, but now has been made known through the Word. The mystery is that the Father has

reconciled all things to Himself through the Son, making peace by the blood of His cross.

Chapter 14
1 The truth of the gospel is that the Father has given all things into the hands of the Son, and the Son has revealed the Father to those who were chosen before the foundation of the world. These are the ones who have been called according to the Father's purpose, that they might be conformed to the image of His Son.

Chapter 15
1 The gospel is the proclamation of the Father's love, the good news that the Father has not abandoned His children, but has sent His Son to bring them back to Him. The truth is that the Father is not far from any one of us, for in Him we live and move and have our being.

Chapter 16
1 The Word is the living water that flows from the throne of the Father, and those who drink of this water will never thirst again. The truth is that the Father is the source of all life, and those who come to Him will find rest for their souls.

Chapter 17
1 The gospel is the light that shines in the darkness, the truth that reveals the Father's love for His children. The Word is the lamp that lights the way, and those who follow the light will walk in the truth. The truth is that the Father is the one true God, and there is no other besides Him.

Chapter 18
1 The Word came to bring the light of the Father to those who were in darkness. The gospel is the message of salvation, the good news that the Father loves His children and desires that they return to Him. The truth is that the Father has given His Son to be the Savior of the world, and all who believe in Him have life in His name.

141. The Gospel of the Twelve Apostles

Chapter 1
1 The gospel that was given to the Twelve Apostles by our Lord Jesus Christ, recounting the teachings, miracles, and revelations that they received as they followed Him during His earthly ministry.

Chapter 2
1 Jesus gathered His Twelve Apostles and said to them, "The Kingdom of Heaven is like a grain of mustard seed, which a man took and sowed in his field. Though it is the smallest of all seeds, when it grows, it is the largest of garden plants and becomes a tree, so that the birds come and perch in its branches."

Chapter 3
1 The apostles asked Jesus, "Lord, what is the Kingdom of Heaven?" Jesus replied, "The Kingdom of Heaven is within you, and all around you. It is not a place to be found by waiting for it, but it is the condition of the heart where God reigns supreme."

Chapter 4
1 Jesus continued to teach His apostles, saying, "Blessed are the poor in spirit, for theirs is the Kingdom of Heaven. Blessed are those who mourn, for they will be comforted. Blessed are the meek, for they will inherit the earth. Blessed are those who hunger and thirst for righteousness, for they will be filled."

Chapter 5
1 The apostles were amazed at the teachings of Jesus and asked Him, "Lord, who then can be saved?" Jesus looked at them and said, "With man, this is impossible, but with God all things are possible."

Chapter 6
1 Jesus said to His apostles, "You are the light of the world. A town built on a hill cannot be hidden.

Neither do people light a lamp and put it under a bowl. Instead, they put it on its stand, and it gives light to everyone in the house. In the same way, let your light shine before others, that they may see your good deeds and glorify your Father in heaven."

Chapter 7

1 The apostles asked Jesus, "Lord, how shall we pray?" Jesus replied, "When you pray, say: 'Our Father in heaven, hallowed be Your name, Your Kingdom come, Your will be done, on earth as it is in heaven. Give us this day our daily bread. And forgive us our debts, as we also have forgiven our debtors. And lead us not into temptation, but deliver us from evil.'"

Chapter 8

1 Jesus taught the apostles about love, saying, "A new command I give you: Love one another. As I have loved you, so you must love one another. By this, everyone will know that you are My disciples if you love one another."

Chapter 9

1 Jesus performed many miracles in the presence of His apostles. He healed the sick, raised the dead, cleansed those who had leprosy, drove out demons, and restored sight to the blind. The apostles marveled at the power of God manifested through Jesus.

Chapter 10

1 Jesus said to His apostles, "Whoever wants to be My disciple must deny themselves and take up their cross daily and follow Me. For whoever wants to save their life will lose it, but whoever loses their life for Me will save it."

Chapter 11

1 The apostles asked Jesus, "Lord, when will these things happen, and what will be the sign of Your coming and of the end of the age?" Jesus answered, "Watch out that no one deceives you. For many will come in My name, claiming, 'I am the Messiah,' and will deceive many. You will hear of wars and rumors of wars, but see to it that you are not alarmed. Such things must happen, but the end is still to come."

Chapter 12

1 Jesus continued, "Nation will rise against nation, and kingdom against kingdom. There will be famines and earthquakes in various places. All these are the beginning of birth pains. Then you will be handed over to be persecuted and put to death, and you will be hated by all nations because of Me. At that time many will turn away from the faith and will betray and hate each other."

Chapter 13

1 Jesus said, "Because of the increase of wickedness, the love of most will grow cold, but the one who stands firm to the end will be saved. And this gospel of the kingdom will be preached in the whole world as a testimony to all nations, and then the end will come."

Chapter 14

1 The apostles were troubled by these words and asked Jesus, "Lord, will we have the strength to endure these trials?" Jesus replied, "The Spirit is willing, but the flesh is weak. Pray that you may not fall into temptation. Trust in God; trust also in Me."

Chapter 15

1 Jesus promised His apostles that He would send the Holy Spirit to guide them after His departure. "The Advocate, the Holy Spirit, whom the Father will send in My name, will teach you all things and will remind you of everything I have said to you. Peace I leave with you; My peace I give you. I do not give to you as the world gives. Do not let your hearts be troubled and do not be afraid."

Chapter 16

1 Jesus blessed the apostles and gave them the Great Commission, saying, "All authority in heaven and on earth has been given to Me. Therefore go and make disciples of all nations, baptizing them in the name of the Father and of the Son and of the Holy Spirit, and teaching them to obey everything I have commanded you. And surely I am with you always, to the very end of the age."

Chapter 17

1 After giving these instructions, Jesus ascended into heaven, and the apostles watched as He was taken up, and a cloud hid Him from their sight. Two men dressed in white appeared beside them and said, "Men of Galilee, why do you stand here looking into the sky? This same Jesus, who has been taken from you into heaven, will come back in the same way you have seen Him go into heaven."

Chapter 18

1 The apostles returned to Jerusalem with great joy and continued to meet together in prayer, breaking bread and sharing the teachings of Jesus with all who would listen. They were filled with the Holy Spirit and spoke the word of God boldly.

Chapter 19

1 As the apostles preached, many were added to their number, and the church grew rapidly. They faced persecution but rejoiced that they were counted worthy to suffer for the name of Jesus.

Chapter 20

1 The apostles appointed leaders in the new churches, instructing them to hold fast to the teachings they had received and to live lives worthy of the calling they had in Christ Jesus.

Chapter 21

1 The gospel of the Twelve Apostles spread throughout the known world, as they fulfilled the command of Jesus to be His witnesses in Jerusalem, and in all Judea and Samaria, and to the ends of the earth.

142. The Apocalypse of James

Chapter 1

1 The revelation that was given to James, the brother of Jesus, concerning the mysteries of the Kingdom of Heaven and the events that were to come. James, being in prayer, was caught up in the Spirit and shown visions by the Lord.

Chapter 2

1 The Lord said to James, "Behold, I reveal to you the mysteries that have been hidden since the foundation of the world. These are the secrets of the Kingdom that you may know the truth and prepare the way for those who will come after you."

Chapter 3

1 The Lord continued, "The world is in darkness, and the rulers of this world have blinded the minds of those who do not believe. They have set themselves against the truth, and they do not understand the mysteries of God. But you, James, have been chosen to receive these revelations and to pass them on to the faithful."

Chapter 4

1 In the vision, James saw the heavens opened, and there appeared a great light. In the midst of the light was a figure, like the Son of Man, shining with a brightness beyond that of the sun. He was surrounded by angels and the spirits of the righteous made perfect.

Chapter 5

1 The Lord said to James, "This is the vision of the Son of Man, who will come in glory at the end of the age. He will gather His elect from the four corners of the earth and will bring them into His Kingdom. But before that day, there will be great tribulation, and the powers of heaven will be shaken."

Chapter 6

1 James asked the Lord, "What will be the sign of Your coming, and what will be the end of the age?" The Lord replied, "Take heed that no one deceives you. For many will come in My name, saying, 'I am the Christ,' and will deceive many. You will hear of wars and rumors of wars. See that you are not troubled; for all these things must come to pass, but the end is not

yet."

Chapter 7
1 The Lord continued, "Nation will rise against nation, and kingdom against kingdom. There will be famines, pestilences, and earthquakes in various places. All these are the beginning of sorrows. Then they will deliver you up to tribulation and kill you, and you will be hated by all nations for My name's sake. And then many will be offended, will betray one another, and will hate one another."

Chapter 8
1 James saw in the vision the persecution of the saints, the rise of false prophets, and the spread of lawlessness. The love of many grew cold, and there was great suffering among the people. But those who endured to the end were saved, and they were gathered into the Kingdom of Heaven.

Chapter 9
1 The Lord said to James, "When you see the abomination of desolation spoken of by Daniel the prophet, standing in the holy place (whoever reads, let him understand), then let those who are in Judea flee to the mountains. Let him who is on the housetop not go down to take anything out of his house. And let him who is in the field not go back to get his clothes."

Chapter 10
1 James saw the great tribulation that was to come upon the earth, such as had not been since the beginning of the world until this time, no, nor ever shall be. And unless those days were shortened, no flesh would be saved; but for the elect's sake, those days would be shortened.

Chapter 11
1 The Lord revealed to James the signs in the heavens and on the earth that would precede His coming. The sun was darkened, and the moon did not give its light; the stars fell from heaven, and the powers of the heavens were shaken.

Chapter 12
1 Then the sign of the Son of Man appeared in heaven, and all the tribes of the earth mourned. They saw the Son of Man coming on the clouds of heaven with power and great glory. He sent His angels with a great sound of a trumpet, and they gathered together His elect from the four winds, from one end of heaven to the other.

Chapter 13
1 The Lord said to James, "Learn this parable from the fig tree: When its branch has already become tender and puts forth leaves, you know that summer is near. So you also, when you see all these things, know that it is near—at the doors! Assuredly, I say to you, this generation will by no means pass away till all these things take place. Heaven and earth will pass away, but My words will by no means pass away."

Chapter 14
1 James was shown the resurrection of the dead and the final judgment. He saw the righteous standing before the throne of God, clothed in white robes, and the wicked cast into the lake of fire. The books were opened, and the dead were judged according to their works, by the things which were written in the books.

Chapter 15
1 The Lord said to James, "Behold, I am coming quickly, and My reward is with Me, to give to every one according to his work. I am the Alpha and the Omega, the Beginning and the End, the First and the Last."

Chapter 16
1 James saw the new heaven and the new earth, for the first heaven and the first earth had passed away. He saw the holy city, New Jerusalem, coming down out of heaven from God, prepared as a bride adorned for her husband. He heard a loud voice from heaven saying, "Behold, the tabernacle of God is with men, and He will dwell with them, and they shall be His people. God Himself will be with them and be their God."

Chapter 17
1 The Lord showed James the river of the water of life, clear as crystal, proceeding from the throne of God and of the Lamb. In the middle of its street, and on either side of the river, was the tree of life, which bore twelve fruits, each tree yielding its fruit every month. The leaves of the tree were for the healing of the nations.

Chapter 18
1 The vision ended with the Lord's promise to James, "Behold, I am coming soon. Blessed is he who keeps the words of the prophecy of this book." James fell on his face and worshiped, and the Lord said to him, "I am the Root and the Offspring of David, the Bright and Morning Star. Surely I am coming quickly."

Chapter 19
1 James was then returned to his place, and he wrote down all that he had seen and heard, to be a testimony to the churches and a warning to all who would hear. "The grace of our Lord Jesus Christ be with you all. Amen."

143. The Testament of the Twelve Patriarchs

Chapter 1
1 The copy of the testament of Reuben, the things which he commanded to his sons before he died in the hundred and twenty-fifth year of his life. 2 Two years after the death of Joseph his brother, when Reuben fell ill, his sons and his sons' sons were gathered together to visit him. 3 And he said to them, "My children, behold, I am dying, and go the way of my fathers." 4 And seeing there Judah, and Gad, and Asher, and his brethren, he said to them, "Raise me up that I may tell you, my brethren, and to you my children, what things I have hidden in my heart. 5 For behold, now at length I am passing away. 6 And he arose and kissed them, and said, "Hear, my brethren, and do ye, my children, give ear to Reuben your father in the commands which I give unto you. 7 And behold I call to witness against you this day the God of heaven, that ye walk not in the sins of youth and fornication, wherein I was poured out, and defiled the bed of my father Jacob. 8 And I tell you that He smote me with a sore plague in my loins for seven months; and had not my father Jacob prayed for me to the Lord, the Lord would have destroyed me. 9 For I was thirty years old when I wrought the evil thing before the Lord, and for seven months I was sick unto death. 10 And after this I repented with set purpose of my soul for seven years before the Lord. 11 And wine and strong drink I drank not, and flesh entered not into my mouth, and I ate no pleasant food, but I mourned over my sin, for it was great, such as had not been in Israel."

Chapter 2
1 "And now hear me, my children, what things I saw concerning the seven spirits of deceit, when I repented. 2 Seven spirits therefore are appointed against man, and they are the leaders in the works of youth. 3 And seven other spirits are given to him at his creation, that through them should be done every work of man. 4 The first is the spirit of life, with which the constitution (of man) is created. 5 The second is the sense of sight, with which ariseth desire. 6 The third is the sense of hearing, with which cometh teaching. 7 The fourth is the sense of smell, with which tastes are given to draw air and breath. 8 The fifth is the power of speech, with which come knowledge. 9 The sixth is the sense of taste, with which cometh the eating of meats and drinks; and by it strength is produced, for in food is the foundation of strength. 10 The seventh is the power of procreation and sexual intercourse, with which come sins through fondness of pleasure. 11 For this reason it is the last in order of creation, and the first in that of youth, because it is filled with ignorance, and leadeth the young as a blind man to a pit, and as a beast to a precipice."

Chapter 3

1 "Besides all these, there is an eighth spirit of sleep, with which is brought about the trance of nature and the image of death. 2 With these spirits are mingled the spirits of error. 3 First, the spirit of fornication is seated in the nature and in the senses; 4 The second, the spirit of insatiableness in the belly; 5 The third, the spirit of fighting in the liver and gall; 6 The fourth is the spirit of obedience and deception, that through officiousness he might be induced to sin; 7 The fifth is the spirit of pride, that he might be vain-glorious and boastful of his strength; 8 The sixth is the spirit of lying, that by the performance of falsehoods he might be wounded, and provoked to anger; 9 The seventh is the spirit of injustice, with which are thefts and sacrileges, that he might act with injustice, and become unjust. 10 And with all these the spirit of sleep is joined which is that of error and fantasy."

Chapter 4

1 "And so perish every young man, darkening his mind from the truth, and not understanding the law of God, nor obeying the admonitions of his fathers as befell me also in my youth. 2 And now, my children, love the truth, and it will preserve you: hear ye the words of Reuben your father. 3 Pay no heed to the face of a woman, nor associate with another man's wife, nor meddle with the affairs of womankind. 4 For had I not seen Bilhah bathing in a covered place, I had not fallen into this great iniquity. 5 For my mind taking in the thought of the woman's nakedness suffered me not to sleep until I had wrought the abominable thing. 6 For while Jacob our father had gone to Isaac his father, when we were in Eder, near to Ephrath in Bethlehem, Bilhah became drunk, and was unconscious, and I took her and went in unto her. 7 And she conceived by me, and I hid it secretly until our father came back, and Jacob heard thereof and was wroth, and cast me from his presence."

Chapter 5

1 "And so came about the fall of our house, and the wrath of the Lord fell upon us, and I was afflicted unto death. 2 But my father had compassion upon me, for he loved me as his firstborn. 3 And I became penitent, and came not near her again, but learned from the words of the Most High, and feared God and hid not mine own shame. 4 For therefore, the words of the Most High came unto me, that if I did not reveal this sin unto my children, it would be forgotten by men. 5 But I shall reveal unto you, and know ye, my children, that two spirits wait upon a man: the spirit of truth and the spirit of error. 6 And in the midst is the spirit of the understanding of the mind, to which it belongeth to turn whithersoever it will. 7 And the works of truth and the works of error are written upon the hearts of men, and each one of them the Lord knoweth. 8 And there is no time at which the works of men can be hid, for on the heart itself have they been written by the hand of the Lord, and the spirit of truth beareth witness all things, and accuseth all."

Chapter 6

1 "And do ye, my children, learn from the command of Reuben your father, to be mindful of the good things that have been commanded of the Lord. 2 And refrain ye from all fornication, and cleave unto the good, for in fornication there is neither understanding nor godliness, and all jealousy dwelleth in the lust thereof. 3 And suffer not your countenance to be changed, for the spirit of fornication teacheth to change the face and the countenance; and through vanity women destroy their minds, and through adornment men, too, are deceived by the spirit of fornication. 4 And when a man hath taken away from his neighbor the money that is his, then also it is evil to remove landmarks, for this he that doeth it casteth down, saith the Lord, he who destroyeth boundaries, overthroweth the soul of him who removeth the boundaries."

Chapter 7

1 "Be ye therefore of a single mind, and let your hearts be loyal to the truth, and walk in simplicity of soul, not coveting what is your neighbor's. 2 Love the Lord, and love also your neighbor, love him as yourselves, and when you see or hear of the evil, flee from it and hide it not, because it is a sin unto death. 3 For to do thus will make you merciful, and all your children, and all your seed will be saved, and you will have a good reward, for you will bring down the wrath of the Lord upon the transgressors. 4 And the spirit of fornication will take flight from you, and will not defile you. 5 Let not your minds be made ready unto any evil, for it is because of this the Lord hath made every beast that is unclean to fear, lest ye become unclean, as them. 6 And when the spirits of evil come upon you, go not near them nor give your sons or daughters unto them, for they are the destruction of the children of men."

Chapter 8

1 "And I say unto you this day, my children, that the spirits of error work against the spirits of truth, and strive against the commandments of the Lord. 2 And be ye not eager to commit fornication, nor to kill a man, nor to defraud another, nor to set your heart upon greediness. 3 For for this cause the Lord brought upon them famine and pestilence, that they that were among them who walked in the error of fornication might perish."

Chapter 9

1 "But now give ye these commands to your children, as I have done unto you, and observe ye them; for this is the will of the Lord. 2 And speak ye to them, that they refrain from all evil, and do that which is good. 3 For whosoever doeth any thing of evil shall die in his time before the Lord, and there will be no mercy for him, for this is the will of the Lord."

Chapter 10

1 "And now, my children, hear ye the commands of Reuben your father, and hearken to the voice of Judah your brother. 2 And be ye ready against all things, that the Lord hath commanded you. 3 And grieve not your souls with covetousness and deceit, for in these things have I also erred. 4 For I have also brought great distress upon Jacob my father, and have hidden my distress in my heart."

Chapter 11

1 "And now, hear ye the commands of Reuben your father, and hearken to the words of Levi your brother, for all the things that I have commanded you this day, and for all things which have been commanded by Levi your brother, will be to you a great service. 2 And be ye not heedless of the words of Levi, for these things which I speak are commanded by the Lord. 3 And do ye this, that ye and your children may be delivered from the evil spirits and from the fornication of the Gentiles."

Chapter 12

1 "And now, my children, it is time for me to pass away, and go unto my fathers. 2 And when he had made an end of commanding them, he sank back upon the bed, and his sons lifted him up to the bed, and he died. 3 And his sons did according to all that Reuben their father commanded them, and they buried him in the cave of Machpelah, where his fathers were."

144. The Gospel of Matthias

Chapter 1

1 The gospel according to Matthias, one of the disciples chosen by the Lord to replace Judas Iscariot after his betrayal. These are the teachings and acts of Matthias, as he was guided by the Holy Spirit to proclaim the good news of Jesus Christ.

Chapter 2

1 Matthias, having been chosen by lot and added to the eleven apostles, was filled with the Holy Spirit on the day of Pentecost. He began to preach the gospel with great zeal and power, performing signs and wonders among the people. 2 His ministry was marked by a deep understanding of the teachings of Jesus, and he was known for his wisdom and his ability to explain the mysteries of the Kingdom of

God.

Chapter 3

1 One day, as Matthias was teaching in the city, a great multitude gathered to hear him speak. He opened the Scriptures and showed them how all the prophecies pointed to Jesus as the Messiah, the Son of God who was crucified and raised from the dead. 2 The people were astonished at his teaching and many believed and were baptized in the name of the Lord Jesus.

Chapter 4

1 Among those who heard him was a man named Zacchaeus, a tax collector who was known for his dishonesty and greed. Zacchaeus, moved by the words of Matthias, repented of his sins and came forward to be baptized. 2 Matthias said to him, "The grace of our Lord Jesus Christ has been extended to you, Zacchaeus. Go and sin no more, for your faith has saved you."

Chapter 5

1 Matthias continued his ministry, traveling from city to city and proclaiming the good news of the Kingdom of God. In each place, he encountered both acceptance and opposition, but he remained steadfast in his mission. 2 He taught the people about the love of God, the importance of repentance, and the hope of eternal life through faith in Jesus Christ.

Chapter 6

1 In one of the cities, Matthias encountered a group of people who were skeptical of his message. They asked him, "By what authority do you preach these things, and how can we know that your words are true?" 2 Matthias replied, "I preach in the name of Jesus Christ, who appeared to me and called me to be His witness. The signs and wonders that you see are not by my power, but by the power of the Holy Spirit, who confirms the truth of the gospel."

Chapter 7

1 The people were amazed by the miracles that Matthias performed, and many were converted to the faith. He healed the sick, cast out demons, and raised the dead, all in the name of Jesus. 2 His ministry brought great joy to the believers and strengthened the church in the regions where he preached.

Chapter 8

1 Matthias also faced persecution for his faith. The authorities, angered by the growing number of Christians, arrested him and brought him before the governor. 2 The governor said to him, "You are charged with spreading false teachings and leading the people astray. If you do not cease your preaching, you will be put to death."

Chapter 9

1 Matthias answered boldly, "I cannot cease to speak of what I have seen and heard. The truth of the gospel cannot be silenced, for it is the power of God for salvation to all who believe." 2 The governor, infuriated by his defiance, ordered that Matthias be scourged and imprisoned.

Chapter 10

1 While in prison, Matthias continued to minister to the other prisoners, sharing the gospel with them and encouraging them in their faith. 2 Many of the prisoners were converted, and the word of the Lord spread even in the prison.

Chapter 11

1 After many days, Matthias was brought out to be executed. He was led to the place of execution, where a large crowd had gathered to witness his death. 2 Before he was put to death, Matthias lifted up his voice and prayed, "Lord Jesus, receive my spirit. I thank You for the privilege of suffering for Your name. May my death be a witness to Your truth and bring many to faith in You."

Chapter 12

1 Matthias was beheaded, and he entered into the presence of the Lord, where he received the crown of life. His death was a powerful testimony to the faithfulness of God, and many who witnessed it believed and were saved.

Chapter 13

1 The gospel of Matthias continued to be read and revered by the early Christian communities, who remembered his teachings and his example of steadfast faith. 2 His name was honored among the apostles, and his ministry left a lasting impact on the church, contributing to the spread of the gospel to the ends of the earth.

145. The Acts of Philip

Chapter 1

1 The acts of Philip, one of the twelve apostles, who, after the ascension of the Lord, traveled to preach the gospel to the Gentiles, performing signs and wonders through the power of the Holy Spirit.

Chapter 2

1 Philip went forth from Jerusalem and journeyed to the city of Hierapolis in Phrygia, where he found the people worshiping idols and living in great wickedness. Moved by the Spirit, he began to preach to them about the one true God and His Son, Jesus Christ. 2 Many of the people were astonished at his words, and some believed, but others were hardened in their hearts and resisted the message of salvation.

Chapter 3

1 In the city of Hierapolis, there was a great serpent that the people worshiped as a god. The serpent had brought much terror and death to the inhabitants of the city, and they offered sacrifices to it in the hope of appeasing it. 2 Philip, filled with righteous anger, went to the place where the serpent dwelled. He stood before it and commanded it in the name of Jesus Christ to come out of its lair. 3 The serpent, seeing the power of God upon Philip, came out and bowed before him. Philip rebuked the serpent and cast it into the abyss, where it could no longer harm the people.

Chapter 4

1 The people of Hierapolis, witnessing this great miracle, were filled with awe and fear. Many of them turned to the Lord and were baptized in the name of Jesus. 2 However, the priests of the idols, seeing their power and influence wane, stirred up the people against Philip, accusing him of sorcery and blasphemy. 3 Philip was seized and brought before the rulers of the city. They demanded that he cease preaching in the name of Jesus and return to the worship of the gods of the city.

Chapter 5

1 But Philip, bold in the Spirit, refused to deny his Lord. He spoke to the rulers, saying, "You worship gods made by human hands, but I serve the living God, who created heaven and earth. Repent, therefore, and turn to Him, that you may receive forgiveness of sins and eternal life." 2 The rulers, enraged by his words, ordered that Philip be scourged and imprisoned. But even in prison, Philip continued to pray and preach to those who were with him, and many were converted.

Chapter 6

1 After some time, Philip was brought out of prison and was sentenced to be crucified. He was led to the place of execution, and as he was nailed to the cross, he prayed for his persecutors, saying, "Father, forgive them, for they do not know what they are doing." 2 As Philip hung on the cross, a great earthquake shook the city, and many of the people were struck with fear. The rulers, seeing the signs, were moved to release Philip, but it was too late, for he had already given up his spirit.

Chapter 7

1 After Philip's death, his body was taken down from the cross and buried by the faithful. His tomb became a place of pilgrimage, where many came to seek healing and deliverance. 2 The memory of

Philip's faith and courage continued to inspire the believers, and the gospel spread throughout Phrygia and beyond.

Chapter 8

1 The acts of Philip did not end with his death, for the Lord continued to work miracles through those who believed in the message he had preached. 2 The church in Hierapolis grew strong, and many more were added to the number of believers, as the Lord confirmed the word with signs and wonders.

Chapter 9

1 Among those who were converted by Philip's preaching was a woman named Nicanora, who had been a priestess of the serpent god. She renounced her former life and became a devoted follower of Christ, serving the church with great zeal. 2 Nicanora's testimony of deliverance from the power of darkness brought many more to faith in Jesus, and she became a respected leader in the Christian community.

Chapter 10

1 The legacy of Philip's ministry continued to bear fruit long after his departure, as the seed he had sown in Phrygia and the surrounding regions grew and multiplied. 2 The apostles who remained were encouraged by the reports of Philip's work, and they praised God for the spread of the gospel to the Gentiles.

Chapter 11

1 The acts of Philip serve as a reminder of the power of the gospel to overcome the forces of darkness and bring light to those who sit in the shadow of death. 2 His example of faithfulness unto death continues to inspire believers to stand firm in the face of persecution and to proclaim the good news of Jesus Christ to all nations.

146. The Gospel of the Egyptians

Chapter 1

1 The beginning of the Gospel of the Egyptians, a record of the teachings of Jesus as remembered and transmitted by the early Christian community in Egypt. This gospel contains the sayings and deeds of Jesus, as well as the mystical interpretations and spiritual insights of the early Egyptian believers.

Chapter 2

1 Jesus said, "The kingdom of God is within you and all around you. It is not a place to be sought in the future, for it is present in your midst, hidden in plain sight. Only those with eyes to see and ears to hear will recognize it."

Chapter 3

1 The disciples asked Jesus, "Lord, what must we do to inherit eternal life?" Jesus answered, "Do not seek for it in the things of this world. Seek first the kingdom of God and His righteousness, and all these things will be added unto you. Renounce the desires of the flesh and pursue the desires of the spirit."

Chapter 4

1 Jesus taught them about the nature of true wisdom, saying, "Wisdom is like a hidden treasure, buried deep within the heart of man. It is not found in the words of men, but in the silence where the voice of God speaks. Seek this wisdom with all your heart, and it will be revealed to you."

Chapter 5

1 The Gospel of the Egyptians emphasizes the need for spiritual purity and the rejection of worldly attachments. Jesus said, "Blessed are the pure in heart, for they shall see God. Cleanse yourselves of the impurities of the world, for they are a hindrance to the vision of the divine."

Chapter 6

1 Jesus spoke of the mystery of the divine feminine, saying, "The Father and the Mother are one, and from them proceeds the fullness of life. The Mother is the Holy Spirit, the breath of life that sustains all things. She is the hidden wisdom that reveals the mysteries

of the kingdom."

Chapter 7

1 The disciples asked Jesus about the resurrection of the dead. He answered, "The resurrection is not a future event, but a present reality. Those who are alive in the spirit have already passed from death to life. Death has no power over them, for they are one with the eternal."

Chapter 8

1 Jesus taught about the nature of God, saying, "God is neither male nor female, but encompasses both and transcends them. He is the One who is above all and in all, the source of all that is. To know God, you must go beyond the dualities of this world and enter into the oneness of His being."

Chapter 9

1 The Gospel of the Egyptians presents a mystical understanding of Jesus' mission. He said, "I have come to reveal the hidden truth, the secret knowledge that has been concealed from the foundation of the world. This knowledge is the key to eternal life, and it is given only to those who are worthy."

Chapter 10

1 The disciples asked Jesus, "Lord, how shall we pray?" Jesus replied, "When you pray, do not use many words, for your Father knows what you need before you ask Him. Pray in the silence of your heart, and let your prayer be a communion with the divine presence within you."

Chapter 11

1 Jesus spoke of the importance of inner transformation, saying, "The kingdom of God does not come with outward signs, but with the renewal of the mind and heart. Be transformed by the renewing of your mind, and you will see the kingdom of God within you."

Chapter 12

1 The Gospel of the Egyptians also contains teachings about the role of the elect, those chosen by God to receive and transmit the divine mysteries. Jesus said, "You are the light of the world, a city set on a hill that cannot be hidden. Let your light shine before others, that they may see your good works and glorify your Father in heaven."

Chapter 13

1 The disciples asked Jesus about the end of the world. He answered, "The world will not end, but it will be transformed. The old will pass away, and all things will be made new. Those who are of the light will inherit the new creation, while those who are of the darkness will be left behind."

Chapter 14

1 Jesus spoke of the ultimate reunion with the divine, saying, "When the time comes, the elect will be gathered into the bosom of the Father, and they will be one with Him as I am one with Him. This is the fulfillment of all things, the consummation of the ages."

Chapter 15

1 The Gospel of the Egyptians concludes with a vision of the eternal kingdom, where the elect dwell in the presence of God, free from the limitations of the flesh and the bondage of sin. It is a place of perfect peace, where the love of God fills all things and the light of His glory shines forever.

147. The Gospel of the Hebrews

Chapter 1

1 The gospel according to the Hebrews, which contains the teachings and acts of Jesus as preserved by the early Jewish-Christian community. This gospel offers unique insights into the life and message of Jesus, emphasizing His role as the fulfillment of the Law and the Prophets.

Chapter 2

1 Jesus said, "I have not come to abolish the Law or the Prophets, but to fulfill them. Truly, I tell you, until

heaven and earth pass away, not the smallest letter, not the least stroke of a pen, will by any means disappear from the Law until everything is accomplished."

Chapter 3
1 The Gospel of the Hebrews presents Jesus as the promised Messiah, who was sent to redeem Israel and bring salvation to all nations. Jesus said, "I was sent only to the lost sheep of the house of Israel. But many who are last will be first, and the first will be last, for the kingdom of God is open to all who believe."

Chapter 4
1 The gospel emphasizes the Jewish heritage of Jesus and His adherence to the customs and traditions of His people. Jesus observed the Sabbath, kept the feasts, and taught in the synagogues, yet He also challenged the religious leaders of His day, calling them to a deeper understanding of God's will.

Chapter 5
1 In this gospel, Jesus said, "The greatest commandment is this: 'Hear, O Israel: The Lord our God, the Lord is one. Love the Lord your God with all your heart and with all your soul and with all your strength.' The second is like it: 'Love your neighbor as yourself.' There is no commandment greater than these."

Chapter 6
1 The Gospel of the Hebrews includes the story of the baptism of Jesus, where a voice from heaven declared, "You are My beloved Son; with You, I am well pleased." The Spirit descended upon Jesus in the form of a dove, marking the beginning of His public ministry.

Chapter 7
1 Jesus performed many miracles in the Gospel of the Hebrews, healing the sick, raising the dead, and casting out demons. These signs confirmed His divine authority and demonstrated the power of God's kingdom breaking into the world.

Chapter 8
1 The gospel recounts the calling of the disciples, who left everything to follow Jesus. He said to them, "Come, follow Me, and I will make you fishers of men." They responded to His call, and He taught them the mysteries of the kingdom of God.

Chapter 9
1 The Gospel of the Hebrews places a strong emphasis on the importance of repentance and forgiveness. Jesus said, "Repent, for the kingdom of heaven is at hand. Forgive others, that your Father in heaven may also forgive you. If you do not forgive, neither will your Father forgive your trespasses."

Chapter 10
1 The gospel also highlights the role of James, the brother of Jesus, who is depicted as a central figure in the early church. James is described as a man of prayer and righteousness, who led the Jerusalem community with wisdom and integrity.

Chapter 11
1 Jesus taught about the coming of the Holy Spirit in the Gospel of the Hebrews, saying, "The Comforter, the Holy Spirit, whom the Father will send in My name, will teach you all things and remind you of everything I have said to you. The Spirit will guide you into all truth and will declare to you the things to come."

Chapter 12
1 The gospel recounts the passion and resurrection of Jesus, where He was crucified, died, and was buried. On the third day, He rose from the dead, appearing first to Mary Magdalene and then to His disciples, showing them the wounds in His hands and side.

Chapter 13
1 The Gospel of the Hebrews includes a unique post-resurrection appearance of Jesus, where He said to His disciples, "Take, eat, this is My body which is given for you. Do this in remembrance of Me." He then broke the bread and gave it to them, and their eyes were opened, and they recognized Him.

Chapter 14
1 The gospel concludes with the ascension of Jesus, where He was taken up into heaven and sat down at the right hand of God. The disciples were commissioned to go into all the world and preach the gospel to every creature, baptizing them in the name of the Father, and of the Son, and of the Holy Spirit.

Chapter 15
1 The Gospel of the Hebrews is a testament to the Jewish roots of the Christian faith, showing how Jesus fulfilled the promises made to the patriarchs and prophets. It calls believers to a life of faith, repentance, and obedience, as they await the return of the Messiah and the consummation of God's kingdom.

148. The Epistle to the Alexandrians

Chapter 1
1 The epistle to the Alexandrians, written by Paul, an apostle of Jesus Christ, by the will of God, to the saints who are in Alexandria, who are faithful in Christ Jesus: Grace to you and peace from God our Father and the Lord Jesus Christ.

Chapter 2
1 Blessed be the God and Father of our Lord Jesus Christ, who has blessed us with every spiritual blessing in the heavenly places in Christ, 2 just as He chose us in Him before the foundation of the world, that we should be holy and blameless before Him in love.

Chapter 3
1 In Him, we have redemption through His blood, the forgiveness of our trespasses, according to the riches of His grace, 2 which He lavished on us. In all wisdom and insight, He made known to us the mystery of His will, according to His kind intention which He purposed in Him.

Chapter 4
1 Paul exhorts the believers in Alexandria to remain steadfast in the faith, saying, "Be strong in the Lord and in the strength of His might. Put on the full armor of God, so that you will be able to stand firm against the schemes of the devil." 2 For our struggle is not against flesh and blood, but against the rulers, against the powers, against the world forces of this darkness, against the spiritual forces of wickedness in the heavenly places.

Chapter 5
1 Therefore, take up the full armor of God, so that you will be able to resist in the evil day, and having done everything, to stand firm. 2 Stand firm therefore, having girded your loins with truth, and having put on the breastplate of righteousness, and having shod your feet with the preparation of the gospel of peace.

Chapter 6
1 In addition to all, taking up the shield of faith with which you will be able to extinguish all the flaming arrows of the evil one. 2 And take the helmet of salvation, and the sword of the Spirit, which is the word of God. 3 With all prayer and petition pray at all times in the Spirit, and with this in view, be on the alert with all perseverance and petition for all the saints.

Chapter 7
1 Paul encourages the Alexandrians to continue in their love for one another, saying, "Let love be without hypocrisy. Abhor what is evil; cling to what is good. 2 Be devoted to one another in brotherly love; give preference to one another in honor."

Chapter 8
1 He also urges them to be generous, saying, "Contribute to the needs of the saints, practice hospitality. Bless those who persecute you; bless and do not curse. 2 Rejoice with those who rejoice, and weep with those who weep. Be of the same mind

toward one another; do not be haughty in mind, but associate with the lowly. Do not be wise in your own estimation."

Chapter 9

1 Finally, Paul gives thanks to God for the faith of the Alexandrians, saying, "I thank my God through Jesus Christ for you all because your faith is being proclaimed throughout the whole world. 2 For God, whom I serve in my spirit in the preaching of the gospel of His Son, is my witness as to how unceasingly I make mention of you, 3 always in my prayers making request, if perhaps now at last by the will of God I may succeed in coming to you."

Chapter 10

1 The epistle concludes with a benediction: "Now to Him who is able to establish you according to my gospel and the preaching of Jesus Christ, according to the revelation of the mystery which has been kept secret for long ages past, 2 but now is manifested, and by the Scriptures of the prophets, according to the commandment of the eternal God, has been made known to all the nations, leading to obedience of faith; 3 to the only wise God, through Jesus Christ, be the glory forever. Amen."

149. The Gospel of the Nazarenes

Chapter 1

1 The gospel according to the Nazarenes, a text revered by the early Jewish-Christian community, contains the sayings and deeds of Jesus as they were remembered and transmitted by those who knew Him.

Chapter 2

1 Jesus, born of Mary and Joseph, was raised in Nazareth, where He grew in wisdom and stature, and in favor with God and man. 2 The Spirit of the Lord was upon Him, and He was led into the wilderness to be tempted by the devil.

Chapter 3

1 The devil said to Him, "If You are the Son of God, command these stones to become bread." But Jesus answered, "It is written, 'Man shall not live by bread alone, but by every word that proceeds from the mouth of God.'"

Chapter 4

1 The Gospel of the Nazarenes emphasizes the teachings of Jesus regarding the Law and the Prophets, showing how He came to fulfill them rather than to abolish them. 2 Jesus said, "Think not that I have come to destroy the Law or the Prophets. I have not come to destroy, but to fulfill. For verily, I say unto you, till heaven and earth pass away, one jot or one tittle shall in no wise pass from the Law, till all be fulfilled."

Chapter 5

1 In this gospel, Jesus is depicted as a compassionate healer and teacher, who performed many miracles among the people. He healed the sick, gave sight to the blind, and cast out demons. 2 Jesus said to His disciples, "Freely you have received, freely give. Heal the sick, raise the dead, cleanse those who have leprosy, drive out demons. Freely give as you have freely received."

Chapter 6

1 The Gospel of the Nazarenes includes teachings on the importance of humility and service. Jesus said, "He who is greatest among you shall be your servant. For whoever exalts himself will be humbled, and whoever humbles himself will be exalted."

Chapter 7

1 The text also records the emphasis Jesus placed on the purity of heart. He said, "Blessed are the pure in heart, for they shall see God. Cleanse the inside of the cup and dish, and the outside will also be clean."

Chapter 8

1 The Gospel of the Nazarenes provides unique insights into Jesus' relationship with His family and His followers. It includes a passage where Jesus' mother and brothers came to speak with Him, but He said, "Who is My mother, and who are My brothers? Whoever does the will of My Father in heaven is My brother and sister and mother."

Chapter 9

1 The gospel recounts Jesus' teachings on love and forgiveness. He said, "You have heard that it was said, 'You shall love your neighbor and hate your enemy.' But I say to you, love your enemies, bless those who curse you, do good to those who hate you, and pray for those who spitefully use you and persecute you, that you may be sons of your Father in heaven."

Chapter 10

1 In the Gospel of the Nazarenes, Jesus also speaks of the coming of the Kingdom of God. He said, "The Kingdom of God is not coming with signs to be observed; nor will they say, 'Look, here it is!' or 'There it is!' For behold, the Kingdom of God is in your midst."

Chapter 11

1 The gospel emphasizes the Jewish roots of the early Christian faith, showing Jesus' respect for the traditions and laws of His people while also calling them to a deeper, spiritual understanding of God's will. 2 Jesus said, "I desire mercy, not sacrifice. For I have not come to call the righteous, but sinners to repentance."

Chapter 12

1 The Gospel of the Nazarenes concludes with the resurrection of Jesus and His appearances to His disciples, affirming His victory over death and His promise of eternal life to all who believe in Him. 2 Jesus said, "Peace be with you. As the Father has sent Me, so I send you. Receive the Holy Spirit. If you forgive the sins of any, they are forgiven; if you retain the sins of any, they are retained."

150. The Gospel of Thomas the Contender

Chapter 1

1 The gospel according to Thomas the Contender, a collection of sayings and teachings attributed to Jesus Christ, as transmitted by the apostle Thomas. This gospel emphasizes the inner spiritual knowledge required to attain true understanding and union with the divine.

Chapter 2

1 Jesus said, "He who seeks will find, and he who knocks will be let in. If you seek after the truth with all your heart, it will be revealed to you. But seek not with the eyes of the flesh, for the truth is hidden within, where the Spirit of God dwells."

Chapter 3

1 The Gospel of Thomas the Contender emphasizes the need for spiritual discernment, teaching that the path to salvation lies in overcoming the illusions of the material world. 2 Jesus said, "Do not let the world deceive you, nor let it draw you away from the truth. The world is like a mirage, appearing real but having no substance. Seek the eternal, which is beyond this world, and you will find life."

Chapter 4

1 Jesus taught His disciples about the nature of the soul, saying, "The soul is the breath of life given by the Father. It is eternal and indestructible, but it is trapped in the body, like a light hidden under a bushel. Let your light shine forth, and do not be weighed down by the desires of the flesh."

Chapter 5

1 The Gospel of Thomas the Contender contains a dialogue between Jesus and His disciples, where He explains the nature of the Kingdom of God. 2 Jesus said, "The Kingdom of God is not a place that can be seen with the eyes, nor is it a time that can be measured by the hands of a clock. It is a state of being, where the soul is united with the divine. It is the rest and the fullness, where there is no more

striking, and all is peace."

Chapter 6
1 In this gospel, Jesus speaks of the inner struggle between the flesh and the spirit, urging His followers to overcome the lower nature and rise to the higher. 2 Jesus said, "The flesh is weak, but the spirit is willing. Do not be led by the desires of the body, for they are transient and lead to death. Be led by the spirit, which is eternal and leads to life. For whoever loses his life for My sake will find it."

Chapter 7
1 The Gospel of Thomas the Contender also addresses the issue of spiritual blindness, warning against the dangers of ignorance and false teachings. 2 Jesus said, "Woe to the blind who lead the blind, for both will fall into a pit. But blessed are those who have eyes to see and ears to hear, for they will find the path to life. Do not be deceived by the teachings of men, but seek the truth that comes from the Father."

Chapter 8
1 Jesus taught about the importance of self-knowledge, saying, "Know yourself, and you will know the All. For within you is the spark of the divine, the image of the Father. If you come to know yourself, you will realize that you are a child of God, and you will inherit the Kingdom prepared for you from the foundation of the world."

Chapter 9
1 The Gospel of Thomas the Contender emphasizes the need for vigilance and perseverance in the spiritual life. 2 Jesus said, "Be watchful, for the time is short. The enemy is always at the door, seeking to steal, kill, and destroy. But if you remain steadfast in the truth, you will overcome. The one who endures to the end will be saved."

Chapter 10
1 In this gospel, Jesus also speaks of the resurrection, not as a future event, but as a present reality for those who have attained true knowledge. 2 Jesus said, "The resurrection is not a thing to be awaited, but a thing to be realized. Those who have awakened to the truth have already passed from death to life. They are alive in the spirit, and death has no power over them."

Chapter 11
1 The Gospel of Thomas the Contender concludes with a promise of eternal life for those who have followed the path of truth. 2 Jesus said, "I am the way, the truth, and the life. No one comes to the Father except through Me. If you have known Me, you have known the Father. And if you remain in Me, you will live forever, for I am the resurrection and the life."

Chapter 12
1 The text ends with an exhortation to the followers of Christ to continue in the faith, holding fast to the teachings of the Lord, and seeking the Kingdom of God with all their heart, soul, and mind.

Made in the USA
Middletown, DE
15 September 2024

60986018R00431